Award-winning trade titles are also available for packaging with *The Bedford Anthology* ___ ___ *an Literature* at significant savings. Choose from hundreds of titles from ___ ___ ___ ___, Straus and Giroux, Picador, St. Martin's Press, and other Macmillan trade publishers—at discounts of up to 50% off the regular price. To learn more, visit **bedfordstmartins.com/tradeup**, or contact your local Bedford/St. Martin's sales representative.

American Born Chinese
by Gene Luen Yang
©2006 |
ISBN 9781596431522

A Rumor of War
Philip Caputo
©1996 |
ISBN 9780805046953

The Autobiography of an Ex-Coloured Man
James Weldon Johnson
Introduction by Arna Bontemps
©1991 |
ISBN 9780809000326

Lucy
A Novel
Jamaica Kincaid
©2002 |
ISBN 9780374527358

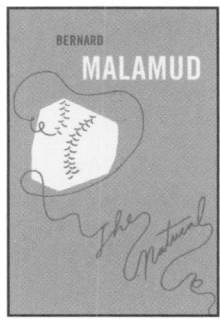

The Natural
Bernard Malamud
Introduction by Kevin Baker
©2003 |
ISBN 9780374502003

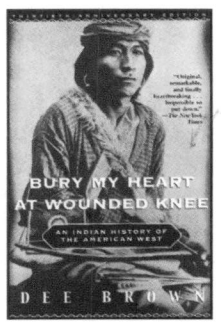

Bury My Heart at Wounded Knee
An Indian History of the American West
Dee Brown
©2007 |
ISBN 9780805086843

"Its selections are judiciously made, its introductions sound and focused on the real-world concerns of authorship in American history, its contextual material diverse, enriching, and to-the-point. I think that instructors who want for their undergraduate students a manageable anthology with an essential and diverse selection of texts, engaging biographical introductions, and contexts that ground the literature practically in the world of reading, publishing, and authorship will find *The Bedford Anthology of American Literature* a very attractive choice."

— Robert D. Habich, *Ball State University*

The Bedford Anthology of American Literature

SHORTER SEOND EDITION
Beginnings tone Present

SHORTER SECOND EDITION

The Bedford Anthology of American Literature

Beginnings to the Present

Susan Belasco
University of Nebraska, Lincoln

Linck Johnson
Colgate University

Bedford / St. Martin's
BOSTON · NEW YORK

For our students

For Bedford/St. Martin's

SENIOR EXECUTIVE EDITOR: Stephen A. Scipione
SENIOR DEVELOPMENTAL EDITOR: Maura Shea
PRODUCTION EDITOR: Kerri A. Cardone
SENIOR PRODUCTION SUPERVISOR: Dennis J. Conroy
MARKETING MANAGER: Stacey Propps
EDITORIAL ASSISTANT: Sherry Mooney
COPY EDITOR: Melissa Cook
INDEXER: Steve Csipke
PHOTO RESEARCHER: Linda Finigan
PERMISSIONS MANAGER: Kalina K. Ingham
SENIOR ART DIRECTOR: Anna Palchik
TEXT DESIGN: Judith Arisman, Arisman Design Studio, and Janis Owens, Books by Design
COVER DESIGN: Donna Lee Dennison
COVER ILLUSTRATOR: Scott McKowen, Punch & Judy Inc.
COVER ART: Authors from top left corner proceeding clockwise: Frederick Douglass, Carl Sandburg, Harriet Beecher Stowe, Sylvia Plath, Ralph Waldo Emerson, Mark Twain, Joy Harjo, Walt Whitman, Toni Morrison, Emily Dickinson, Langston Hughes, Eugene O'Neill
COMPOSITION: Cenveo® Publisher Services
PRINTING AND BINDING: Quad/Graphics

PRESIDENT, BEDFORD/ST. MARTIN'S: Denise B. Wydra
EDITOR IN CHIEF: Karen S. Henry
DIRECTOR OF MARKETING: Karen R. Soeltz
PRODUCTION DIRECTOR: Susan W. Brown
DIRECTOR OF RIGHTS AND PERMISSIONS: Hilary Newman

Library of Congress Control Number: 2012939680

Manufactured in the United States of America.

8   7   6   5   4   3
f   e   d   c   b   a

ISBN 978-0-312-67868-5 (Volume One)
ISBN 978-0-312-67869-2 (Volume Two)
ISBN 978-0-312-59713-9 (Shorter Second Edition)

Acknowledgments

Acknowledgments and copyrights appear at the back of the book on pages 2315–27, which constitute an extension of the copyright page. It is a violation of the law to reproduce these selections by any means whatsoever without the written permission of the copyright holder.

Preface

The Bedford Anthology of American Literature was originally conceived to meet the growing challenges of teaching courses in American literature from its beginnings to the present day. Our anthology was and is designed as a tool for teaching and learning, not simply as a collection of texts bound into volumes. Because we wanted to prepare a textbook for *classroom* use with students firmly in mind, we carefully considered the ways in which literature teachers today help students understand literature. The New Criticism, with its emphasis on treating literary works as self-contained, self-referential aesthetic objects, was for decades a primary departure point in the classroom. As new theories and ideas about teaching literature in its historical and cultural contexts evolved, anthologies of American literature became larger and more diverse, but otherwise they changed relatively little in terms of providing contextual information. Although close reading remains an essential departure point for teachers, we have incorporated historical and cultural information throughout the text, through illustrations, timelines, and historical commentaries. In designing a new anthology, we therefore sought to provide a textbook that would at once support the ways in which most instructors actually teach literature and offer students some fresh ways of experiencing literature.

Perhaps the most striking departure from traditional anthologies is our extensive use of visual materials, which we have further expanded in the second edition. This shorter edition includes more than five hundred carefully selected illustrations, ranging from engravings published in early travel narratives and examples of Native American arts, to paintings or photographs of contemporary scenes and a wide range of images illustrating the history of literary and print culture, including manuscript pages, broadsides, periodicals, and the covers, frontispieces, and title pages of books. We have also included a portrait or photograph of virtually every author in the anthology whenever possible, choosing a youthful image that also suggests something about his or her background, character, class, or status. Although their inclusion is in part designed to enhance the attractiveness and appeal of the volumes, the main purpose of the illustrations is pedagogical. Through our own teaching and in discussions with many other instructors, we have discovered that students increasingly respond to such visual materials, especially those that help them connect with authors and grasp the cultural, material, and social conditions in which literary works were produced. In fact, many of the selections in all volumes of this anthology were first published in illustrated books or periodicals, and such illustrations can generate fruitful discussions about both the literary work and its initial audience. In various ways, those and other illustrations raise questions about identity—the role of class, gender, race, and religion—and about self-representation and the representation of reality—questions that we believe may offer useful points of departure for a discussion of the central concerns and broader contexts of the literary texts. Thumbnails of some of the illustrations are used as visual markers in the timelines, which along with several maps, are designed to help students negotiate the long history and the complex geography covered in *The Bedford Anthology of American Literature.*

In a further effort to make the anthology more user-friendly, we have sought to achieve broad representation rather than comprehensive coverage. The expansion of the canon has generated a similar expansion of anthologies of American literature, some of which now stretch into several volumes. But we were and are concerned about the impact of that development on instructors and students alike. How, in the limited span of a semester or a quarter, can an instructor hope to cover the ever-growing list of writers and works or assign more than a relatively small number of the selections in most anthologies? And how do students respond when they find themselves skipping over large sections of an anthology? Moreover, we know from direct experience, and the comments of other instructors, that students find it awkward and unappealing to read certain kinds of works, especially novels and other extended prose narratives, in the somewhat cumbersome format of an anthology. Consequently, lengthy novels are available in a growing list of low-cost Bedford College Editions, designed to accompany the anthology. Like all teachers, we also grapple with questions about the selection, organization, and presentation of material in a course, especially in relation to a changing student population who are increasingly diverse in their backgrounds, experiences, and preparation for literary study. At the same time, the swift changes in technology have profoundly shaped and changed students' understanding of language and communication, as well as their responses to both texts and textbooks.

Enhancements to the Second Edition

The second edition of *The Bedford Anthology of American Literature* represents our continued effort to preserve the strengths of traditional anthologies while responding to changes in both the canon and in teaching methods that have emerged over the last forty years. At every stage of our work on this new edition, we have been guided by the needs of instructors, their students, and our own. We have drawn on our extensive experiences at a wide range of institutions, and we have communicated with hundreds of instructors in colleges and universities across the country about how a new edition might best meet their needs and the needs of contemporary college students. In this new edition, we have added or expanded numerous texts and deleted a few others, revised notes and introductions, and provided additional contextual and illustrative materials while retaining a rich but not unlimited range of choices to instructors facing the daunting task of creating syllabi and reading assignments of representative works from every period of American literature.

Two of the major pedagogical challenges facing teachers of the American literature survey course are engaging students in the readings and helping them understand history and context. We have, therefore, sought to bring together in an attractive format texts chosen on the basis of their literary or historical importance, their inherent interest, and their proven effectiveness in the classroom, either when studied on their own or in relation to other texts in the anthology. In addition to a core of commonly taught texts that instructors rely on, we have included rarely anthologized texts that have proven to be very successful in the classroom, on the advice of users of the first edition of *The Bedford Anthology of American Literature*. Within the anthology, we have given increased prominence to various kinds of life writings, which we view as a vital element in American literature and which we have found to be particularly attractive to students. In a further effort to stimulate student interest in and understanding of literary texts, as well as of their vital social, political, and cultural contexts, throughout the volumes we have added more illustrations that reveal the changing material conditions in which literary works were produced and provide a visually stimulating experience for students as they read and study. We have updated introductions based on current scholarship in the field and written new notes that pay special attention to unfamiliar terms, places, and people. With *The Bedford Anthology of American Literature*, Second Edition, we have thus sought to offer in reasonably compact volumes a foundation of essential texts that instructors need with a substantial amount of additional material to help them construct their own surveys of American literature. For students, our anthology offers a variety of ways to read and think about American literature and, we hope, fosters a greater understanding and appreciation of it.

Features of *The Bedford Anthology of American Literature*, in Detail

A New Shorter Edition Covers All of American Literature in One Volume.   For the first time, we are offering *The Bedford Anthology of American Literature* in one concise volume that covers all of American literature from the beginning to the present. It includes all the features of the longer volumes, but with a choice of texts better suited for single-semester or broad two-semester comprehensive survey courses.

A Representative and Diverse Collection of Literary Works.   The selection of writers and works has been shaped by the new understandings of and approaches to American literature that have emerged over the last three decades. The selections consequently reflect the rich diversity of American literature, especially in terms of gender, race, and ethnicity. At the same time, the selection of writers and texts has been guided by what is actually taught in survey courses of American literature, based on extensive analysis of syllabi and reviews by over five hundred instructors nationwide.

An Emphasis on Complete and Expanded Selections.   In choosing selections for the second edition, we have sought to include **complete texts** whenever possible. In the shorter edition, we include all of Frederick Douglass's *Narrative of the Life of Frederick Douglass.* We have included portions of extended works of nonfiction that can be effectively excerpted, including William Bradford's *Of Plimoth Plantation,* Benjamin Franklin's *Autobiography,* Elizabeth Ashbridge's *Some Account for the Fore Part of the Life of Elizabeth Ashbridge,* Olaudah Equiano's *The Interesting Narrative of the Life of Olaudah Equiano,* Henry David Thoreau's *Walden,* Booker T. Washington's *Up from Slavery,* and W.E.B. DuBois's *The Souls of Black Folk.* All poems are printed in their entirety, and we have selected sketches and stories rather than excerpts from novels, which we believe students find far more comfortable to read as separate texts.

While we hope that many instructors will find the selections from key writers fully adequate for their purposes, we understand that other instructors may well wish to supplement the anthology with longer works of fiction. In order to make such works available for packaging with the anthology or for independent purchase, Bedford / St. Martin's has published the Bedford College Editions, attractive and very affordable reprints of several of the most frequently taught American novels available in print or e-book formats.

The Unique Illustration Program integrates images with texts and the narrative of American literature. The more than five hundred illustrations throughout tell a story of American literature visually, providing important contexts for the literature, and making the authors and selections more appealing and accessible for students. For instance, a Slave Sale Broadside from 1852, listing the names, ages, and physical attributes of slaves to be sold, informs students' reading of Harriet Jacobs' *Incidents in the Life of a Slave Girl* and Frederick Douglass' *Narrative.* In the frontispiece to the first edition of *Leaves of Grass,* Whitman intentionally includes a portrait of himself dressed as a workingman, which illuminates students' understanding of his poetry. Generous captions make connections between the images and the literature.

Editorial Apparatus Designed and Written for Students.   We have sought to make the introductory materials in the anthology lively and readable, while providing other features designed to engage the interest of students and enhance their appreciation and understanding of the texts. Biographical introductions highlight important aspects of the authors' backgrounds and experiences, while charting the course of their careers as writers. Marginal quotations, most often appreciative observations by other writers, call attention to the characteristics or value of the author's work, and Web site references point to further information. Individual prose works and

Slave Sale Broadside, 1852

The abolitionists often cited the selling of slaves and the consequent breaking up of their families as a vivid illustration of the inhumanity of the system that mistreated and sought to [keep] human being[s]. (As the [title] of this [advertisement] [demon]strates, the cate[...] beg[...] sep[...]

Sale of Slaves and Stock.

The Negroes and stock listed below, are a Prime Lot, and being in the ESTATE OF THE LATE LUTHER McGOWAN, and will be sold on Monday, Sept. 22nd, 1852, at the Fair Grounds...

...kaah. Georgia, at 1:00...

...to the grounds two days previ[ous] ...may be inspected by prospective buyer[s]...

...account of the low prices listed below, they w[ill]... [be sold] [fo]r only, and must be taken into custody within two hour[s]...

No.	Name.	Age.	Remarks.	Price
1	Lunesta	27	Prime Rice Planter,	$1,275.0
2	Violet	16	Housework and Nursemaid,	900.0
3	Lizzie	30	Rice, Unsound,	300.0
4	Minda	27	Cotton, Prime Woman,	1,200.0
5	Adam	28	Cotton, Prime Young Man,	1,100.0
6	Abel	41	Rice Hand, Eyesight Poor,	675.0
7	Tanney	22	Prime Cotton Hand,	950.0
8	Flementina	39	Good Cook, Stiff Knee,	400.0
9	Lanney	34	Prime Cottom Man,	1,000.0
10	Sally	10	Handy in Kitchen,	675.
11	Maccabey	35	Prime Man, Fair Carpenter,	980
12	Dorcas Judy	25	Seamstress, Handy in House,	80
13	Happy	60	Blacksmith,	
14	Mowden	15	Prime Cotton Boy,	
15	Bills	21	Handy with Mules,	
	Theopolis	39	Rice Hand, Gets Fits,	
	Coolidge	29	Rice Hand and Blacksmith,	
		69	Infirm, Sews,	
		1	Strong Likely Boy	
		41	Prime Man, Good wi[th] [...]	
			Prime Woma[n]	

long years of [...] end slavery, not [...] vince President Linc[oln] [...] ended slavery only in are[...] efforts were finally crowned by the [...] Amendment shortly before the end of the Civil War. The abolition of slavery hardly ended injustice in the United States. On the contrary, African Americans and other minorities continued to struggle for full equality, while women, who had contributed so much to the antislavery movement, did not gain the right to vote until 1920. Nonetheless, the end of slavery was a major victory for the abolitionists, who like so many reformers and writers of the period 1830–65 had persistently sought to expose the gap between American ideals of freedom and equality and the often harsh realities of life in the United States.

COMPARATIVE TIMELINE, 1750–1830

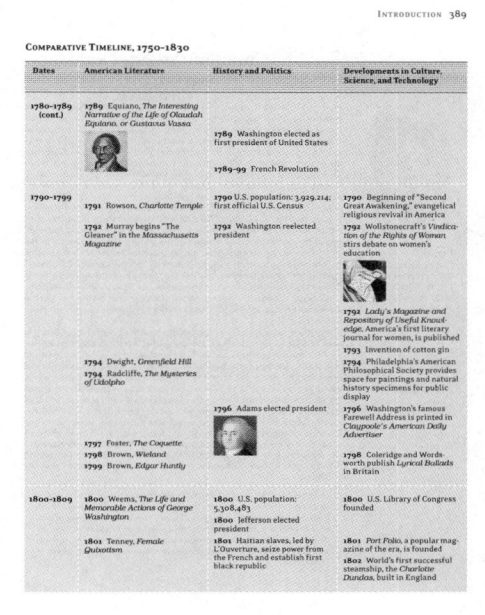

Dates	American Literature	History and Politics	Developments in Culture, Science, and Technology
1780–1789 (cont.)	1789 Equiano, *The Interesting Narrative of the Life of Olaudah Equiano, or Gustavus Vassa*	1789 Washington elected as first president of United States	
		1789–99 French Revolution	
1790–1799	1791 Rowson, *Charlotte Temple*	1790 U.S. population: 3,929,214; first official U.S. Census	1790 Beginning of "Second Great Awakening," evangelical religious revival in America
	1791 Murray begins "The Gleaner" in the *Massachusetts Magazine*	1793 Washington reelected president	1792 Wollstonecraft's *Vindication of the Rights of Woman* stirs debate on women's education
			1792 *Lady's Magazine and Repository of Useful Knowledge*, America's first literary journal for women, is published
			1793 Invention of cotton gin
	1794 Dwight, *Greenfield Hill*		1794 Philadelphia's American Philosophical Society provides space for paintings and natural history specimens for public display
	1794 Radcliffe, *The Mysteries of Udolpho*	1796 Adams elected president	1796 Washington's famous Farewell Address is printed in *Claypoole's American Daily Advertiser*
	1797 Foster, *The Coquette*		
	1798 Brown, *Wieland*		1798 Coleridge and Wordsworth publish *Lyrical Ballads* in Britain
	1799 Brown, *Edgar Huntly*		
1800–1809	1800 Weems, *The Life and Memorable Actions of George Washington*	1800 U.S. population: 5,308,483	1800 U.S. Library of Congress founded
		1800 Jefferson elected president	
	1801 Tenney, *Female Quixotism*	1801 Haitian slaves, led by L'Ouverture, seize power from the French and establish first black republic	1801 *Port Folio*, a popular magazine of the era, is founded
			1802 World's first successful steamship, the *Charlotte Dundas*, built in England

Walt Whitman

[1819–1892]

The poet familiarly known as Walt Whitman was born on May 31, 1819, on Long Island, New York, one of nine children born to a farmer, Walter Whitman Sr., and his wife, Louisa Van Velsor Whitman. In 1823 the family moved to Brooklyn, where Whitman spent his childhood, such as it was. By the age of eleven, he had left school to work as an office boy in a law firm; by fifteen, he was mostly supporting himself by working in the printing trade, perhaps initially as a compositor (a typesetter) in New York. After a devastating fire destroyed much of the publishing district in 1835, Whitman rejoined his family, which had by then moved back to Long Island. Although he taught sporadically at several schools there, Whitman was clearly not suited to the classroom. In 1838 he started his own weekly newspaper, the *Long Islander*, and by the early 1840s he had left teaching altogether. For the next several years, he worked as a printer in New York; edited a daily paper, the *Aurora*; and returned to Brooklyn, first to write for the *Long Island Star* and then to edit the *Brooklyn Daily Eagle*. Whitman was also writing, primarily prose pieces like the numerous literary and art reviews he printed in the *Eagle*, but also some poetry. Fired from the *Eagle* in 1848 for his free-soil politics – like a growing number of Democrats in the North, he strongly opposed the extension of slavery into territories gained during the Mexican War – Whitman was hired to be the first editor of the *Crescent*, a newspaper in New Orleans, where he headed along with his younger brother Jeff. By the end of the year, Whitman was again in New York, where he immersed himself in the pulsing life of that rising metropolis: riding the streets in horse-drawn buses or enjoying rambling walks around the city; attending the opera, which he loved, and going to museums; and spending time with his eclectic group of friends, who ranged from workingmen to artists. Whitman supported himself by working as a carpenter, but he increasingly devoted himself to reading, studying, and writing poetry, for which he finally gave up all other forms of labor.

In 1855, Whitman published the first edition of *Leaves of Grass*, which was thereafter the primary focus of his life and work. Whitman himself set the type for his self-published book, which he vigorously promoted by writing several anonymous reviews. He also sent a copy to Ralph Waldo Emerson, who in a congratulatory letter to Whitman exclaimed, "I greet you at the beginning of a great career, which yet must have had a long foreground somewhere, for such a start." If the Harvard-educated Emerson had then known about the unlikely foreground of *Leaves of Grass*, he would surely have been even more astonished by Whitman's remarkable poems. But few shared Emerson's appreciation of *Leaves of Grass*, which was attacked for what critics viewed as its crudeness, its vulgar language, and its scandalous subject matter. Undaunted, Whitman continued to work on the volume, adding new poems and publishing a second edition in 1856. By the beginning of the following year, he was already planning

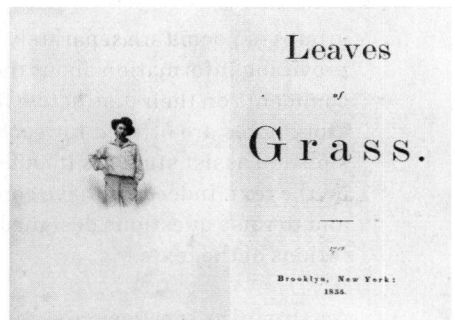

Leaves of Grass.

Brooklyn, New York:
1855.

The First Edition of *Leaves of Grass* (1855)

This portrait of Whitman was engraved from a daguerreotype made in 1854, when he was thirty-five. In contrast to the portraits of most other literary figures, who were customarily depicted in formal attire and equally formal poses, Whitman projected an image of himself as a workingman and man of the people. In an anonymous self-review of *Leaves of Grass*, Whitman described the poet portrayed in the frontispiece as "One of the roughs, his costume manly and free, his face sunburnt and bearded, his posture strong and erect."

another edition, but Whitman apparently wrote relatively few poems while he was editor of the *Brooklyn Daily Times* from March 1857 to June 1859. Freed of those editorial responsibilities, he began to expand and reconstruct *Leaves of Grass*, which a firm in Boston published in 1860. When the Civil War broke out the following year, Whitman moved to Washington, D.C., where he did volunteer work as a nurse in army hospitals and wrote the poems published as *Drum-Taps* early in 1865. Working with the wounded men made a profound impression on Whitman. In his letters to his mother and other family members, Whitman wrote frequently about the bravery of "my soldier boys," as he sometimes called them. Deeply affected by the

bedfordstmartins.com/americanlit for research links on Whitman

Pauline E. Hopkins
[1859–1930]

Pauline E. Hopkins
This photograph appeared in the supplement to the March 1904 issue of the *Colored American Magazine*.

[Pauline Hopkins] has given us a sense of her day, a clue collection, and we can use the light of it to clarify our understanding and our intuition. We can take the building blocks she does supply us and use them to fill in old gaps.
—Gwendolyn Brooks

Pauline Elizabeth Hopkins, who has been hailed as "the Dean of African American women writers," was born in Portland, Maine, in 1859. Her father died when Hopkins was a young child, and her mother married William A. Hopkins, a tailor and a veteran of the Civil War. The family moved to Boston, where Hopkins attended public schools and developed an interest in writing. When she was fifteen, Hopkins won first prize in an essay contest sponsored in part by William Wells Brown, the abolitionist, activist, and author of *Clotel* (1853), the first novel published by an African American. After her graduation from Boston Girls High School, Hopkins, her mother, and her stepfather formed a theatrical troupe, the Hopkins Colored Troubadours. In 1880, the group performed a play written by Hopkins, *Peculiar Sam; or, The Underground Railroad,* one of the earliest musical dramas in the history of black theater in the United States. An accomplished singer, Hopkins toured with the troupe for twelve years, becoming widely known as "Boston's Favorite Soprano." Early in the 1890s, however, she left the troupe and trained as a stenographer to support herself while she pursued a career in writing. Hopkins soon began to earn a reputation as a speaker, lecturing on African American history at churches and reading her fiction at women's clubs in Boston.

Within a decade, Hopkins reached the zenith of her brief but remarkable literary career. In 1900, she published her first and best-known novel, *Contending Forces; or, A Romance Illustrative of Negro Life North and South,* the saga of the injustices suffered by several generations of a black family before and after the Civil War. The epigraph to the novel, which she took from Ralph Waldo Emerson's 1844 "Address on the Emancipation in the British West Indies," expresses a central thesis in all of Hopkins's work: "The civility of no race can be perfect whilst another race is degraded." The year the novel was published, Hopkins helped found the *Colored American Magazine* in Boston. As an announcement read, the new magazine was designed to be *"Of the Race, By the Race, For the Race,"* an echo of the closing lines of Abraham Lincoln's Gettysburg Address. When Hopkins became its editor in 1903, she stated that the magazine was

intended to show that the colored people can advance on all the lines of progress known to other races, that they can be more than tillers of the soils, hewers of wood and drawers of water – that they can attain to eminence (both the men and women among them) as thinkers, writers, as doctors, as lawyers, as clergymen, as singers, musicians, artists, actors, and also as successful business men, in the conduct of enterprises of importance.

Hopkins was also the major contributor to the *Colored American Magazine.* True to her goal of illustrating the potential of African Americans and instilling pride in their achievements, Hopkins wrote two extended series of essays for the magazine, *Famous Men of the Negro Race* (1900–01) and *Famous Women of the Negro Race* (1901–02). She also published a substantial amount of fiction in the magazine, seven stories and three serialized novels: *Hagar's Daughter: A Story of Southern Caste Prejudice* (1901–02); *Winona: A Tale of Negro Life in the South and Southwest* (1902); and *Of One Blood; or, The Hidden Self* (1902–03).

Following that prolific period of creativity, Hopkins's literary career virtually ended. In 1904, the *Colored American Magazine* came under the control of Booker T. Washington, who strongly disapproved of what he considered to be Hopkins's radical politics and her commitment to the doctrine of racial uplift espoused by African American leaders such as W. E. B. Du Bois. Hopkins was consequently ousted from the editorship of the magazine, in which no more of her works appeared. Despite that painful rebuff, she published two groundbreaking historical works the following year: a pamphlet entitled *A Primer of Facts Pertaining to the Early Greatness of the African Race and the Possibility of Restoration by Its Descendants* and "The Dark Races of the Twentieth Century," a four-part series of essays on the global African community that appeared in *The Voice of the Negro.* More than a decade later, in 1916, she published a two-part essay in another African American magazine, the *New Era.* But she apparently did little other writing. Hopkins died in 1930 in a house fire at her home in Cambridge, Massachusetts, where she was working as a stenographer for the Massachusetts Institute of Technology.

Reading Hopkins's " 'As the Lord Lives, He Is One of Our Mother's Children.' " This story was one of Hopkins's final contributions to the *Colored American Magazine.* Although it was primarily literary, the magazine included a wide range of essays on the past and present experiences of African Americans, as well as articles on current social issues in the United States. Many of the stories and serialized novels published in the magazine were also strongly shaped by social activism. A major concern was lynching, most often the hanging of black men for their alleged crimes by lawless white mobs. The number of such lynchings, which were rampant in the South for five decades after the end of Reconstruction in 1876, peaked during the 1890s. In " 'As the Lord Lives, He Is One of Our Mother's Children,' " Hopkins offers a powerful indictment of that murderous manifestation of racial prejudice and the hatred of blacks in the United States, what the antilynching activist Ida B. Wells called "our country's national crime." The text is taken from the first printing in the *Colored American Magazine,* November 1903.

bedfordstmartins.com/ americanlit for research links on Hopkins

groups of poems are separately introduced in a headnote about *reading* the selections, providing information about the writing and publication of the works, as well as brief comments on their distinctive features or literary and historical significance. Explanatory notes are offered for each text, and are designed to foster reading comprehension and assist students in understanding a work, not to provide critical commentary on the text. Indeed, we have consistently sought to provide contexts for reading texts and to raise questions designed to stimulate discussion rather than to offer interpretations of the texts.

An Organization Designed for Greater Coherence and Comprehension.   The overall organization of the anthology is chronological but with a pedagogical slant. The shorter edition begins with Native American origin tales and concludes with the present. The volume is divided into six **literary periods**. Within each of those periods, we have divided selections into related groups of authors or kinds of texts. Such **chapter groupings** are designed to serve several purposes. First, they bring into close proximity within the anthology, works that might usefully be taught together thus creating fruitful juxtapositions and helping instructors create pedagogical units for syllabi. We have also sought to address a problem we have often encountered when teaching with anthologies. Students sometimes find it difficult to relate the general

American Literature
1914–1945

The Emergence
of Modern American Drama

DURING THE EARLY DECADES of the twentieth century, "Broadway," the area around Times Square in New York City, at once symbolized and dominated theater in the United States. Many of the plays performed by hundreds of touring companies originated on Broadway, where the number of theatrical productions rose from seventy during the 1900–01 season to a peak of almost three hundred during 1926–27, after which the audience for theater was eroded by the growing popularity of "talkies" in movie theaters and the onset of the Great Depression. Operettas were especially popular on Broadway, as were musical extravaganzas such as Florenz Ziegfeld's *Follies*, which he produced virtually every year from 1907 through 1927.

◀ The Great White Way

Taken around 1910, this photograph shows Broadway at night, looking south from 42nd Street. The number and intensity of lights on theater marquees and billboard advertisements along the stretch of Broadway just north and south of 42nd Street inspired the nickname the "Great White Way."

765

information provided in a period introduction to the specific selections that follow or tend to forget much of that information by the time they read selections toward the end of the period. In addition to an introduction to each period, we also offer an introduction to each group of selections within the period, focusing on the specific cultural, historical, and especially literary backgrounds students may need in order to read those selections with understanding and appreciation.

Pervasive Attention to the History of Reading and Writing in America.   A thematic thread—the history of reading and writing in America—is woven throughout both volumes. This thread aids students in understanding the context of the works and to emphasize the role literature has played in the unfolding story of culture and history in what became the United States. In the period introductions, as well as in the introductions to groups of authors and texts within each period, we emphasize developments such as the growth of literacy, the expansion of the educational system, changes in the production and distribution of books, and the emergence and increasing importance of periodicals in the literary culture of the United States. We further develop that theme in our introductions to authors, in which we indicate the ways such developments shaped their writings and literary careers, as well as in our headnotes to selections, in which we discuss the writing and initial publication of the works. The history of reading and writing is further delineated in illustrations ranging from **manuscript pages**, including the opening of Bradford's *Of Plimoth Plantation*, a poem by Emily Dickinson, and through a wide array of printed materials beginning with Columbus's 1493 letter describing the results of his first voyage to what came to be called America.

EMILY DICKINSON 1471

Since Dickinson did not task of deciphering her difficult handwriting editors have confronted the task of deciphering her difficult handwriting and interpreting other features of her manuscripts. Some of those editorial complications are illustrated by the first poem reprinted here: "These are the days when Birds come back—" (130; Fr 122). There were several manuscript versions of this poem; the manuscript reproduced here is the copy found by Lavinia. Dickinson had sent another manuscript of the poem to Susan Dickinson, probably in 1859; yet another copy was clearly sent to the editor of the newspaper *Drum Beat*, where the poem was published as "October" on March 11, 1864. It is not known, however, who sent the poem to the newspaper. The manuscript of the poem is reproduced here along with two published versions, one from the first collection of *Poems by Emily Dickinson* (1890) and the other from Johnson's 1960 edition. Comparing the various versions of the poem demonstrates some of

"American Contexts" Unify a Wide Range of Writings in Compelling Topics.   In addition to the works of the individual authors included in the anthology, brief selections from many other writers are gathered together in clusters of related works called **"American Contexts."** Those sections focus on topics ranging from **a new section, "The Salem Witchcraft Trials,"** to "'The America of the Mind': Critics, Writers, and the Representation of Reality." Such clusters are designed to extend the range and resonance of the anthology by introducing additional voices and other kinds of writing, from diaries, journals, and memoirs to editorials, critical essays, political speeches, and social

American Contexts

THE SALEM WITCHCRAFT TRIALS

THE FOLLOWING SELECTIONS from writings by Deodat Lawson, Cotton Mather, Thomas Brattle, and Samuel Sewall illuminate the most notorious episode in the history of colonial New England, the witchcraft trials that took place in Salem Village, now Danvers, Massachusetts. To understand what happened in that small community north of Boston, it is important to recall that at the time of the trials in 1692 a belief in both witches and the religious necessity of punishing them was universal throughout Europe and England, as well as in New England. Certainly, the Puritans firmly believed not only in the active presence of the devil, but also that he recruited women and men to work for him. In Hartford, Connecticut, a woman had been executed for witchcraft in 1648 and a married couple in 1651, while in Boston a woman had been hanged for witchcraft in 1656.

But those isolated episodes hardly prefigured the witchcraft hysteria of the early 1690s, a tumultuous period in the Massachusetts Bay Colony. In the aftermath of the devastation caused by King Philip's War, sporadic Indian attacks on frontier settlements continued to generate tension and anxiety. The nature of the Massachusetts Bay Colony was also changing, especially after the new colonial charter of 1691 gave freedom to all religions, opening the door to an influx of Quakers and Anglicans. These new arrivals posed a significant challenge to the very foundation of Puritan

252

society, which was further shaken by changing social and economic conditions in New England. Class divisions were intensified by the emergence of a new mercantile class, and some scholars also argue that the turmoil in Salem was in part a reflection of concerns about the growing economic and social power of women. More than three-quarters of those accused of witchcraft were women, and of those most were over forty years of age, many of them affluent widows whose independence may well have been deemed a threat to the traditional social order.

All of those factors probably contributed to the outpouring of accusations, which began in the home of Samuel Parris, the new minister of

Incidents of Witchcraft
These illustrations appeared in one of the numerous editions of Joseph Glanvill's *Saducismus Triumphatus; or, Full and Plain Evidence Concerning Witches and Apparitions*, first published in London in 1681. Fearing that the loss of belief in ghosts, spirits, and witches would intimately lead to the loss of belief in Christianity, Glanvill recounted "true" incidents of witchcraft and other supernatural activity in his popular book, which strongly influenced colonial ministers such as Increase and Cotton Mather.

---

criticism. Although individual selections within those clusters could of course be assigned separately, the "American Contexts" are designed as coherent units, most often intended to be taught as either an introduction or a coda to a larger period or grouping in the anthology. Some clusters invite discussion of distinctive genres, while others allow an opportunity to explore contested ideological issues, critical controversies, cultural developments, and responses to events like the Civil War.

"Through a Modern Lens" and "Writers on Writers" Helps Students Make Connections between Writers from the Past and the Present.   In order to bring later perspectives to bear on some of the writers and texts in the first half of this volume, we have included brief sections throughout the volume under the general rubric **"Through a Modern Lens."** These include but are not limited to N. Scott Momaday's recent celebration of Native American origin and creation stories, and a tribute by the contemporary African American poet Robert Hayden to Frederick Douglass. In addition to revealing connections across time and space, the "Through a Modern Lens" feature offers rich opportunities for discussion of a number of connected issues: the imaginative effort required to understand the attitudes, conditions, and modes of expression of earlier periods; the sometimes tense relations between later readers and writers and earlier

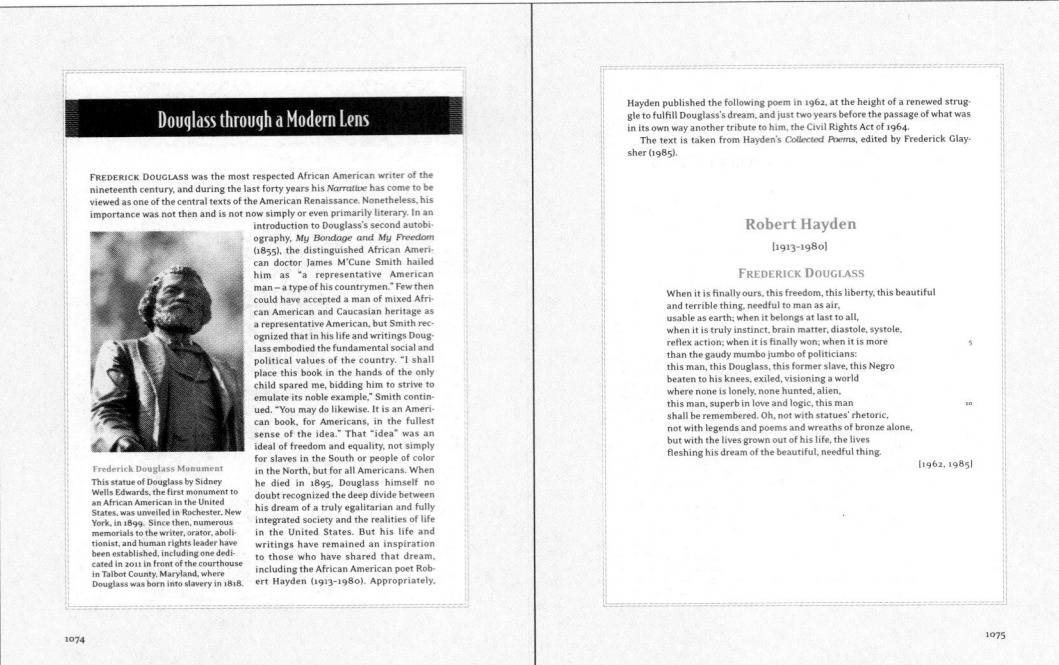

texts; and the ongoing influence of earlier authors on writers in the twentieth and twenty-first centuries, even as the works of those later writers reveal markedly different aesthetic values, literary practices, and philosophical or religious convictions. In the second half of this volume, a **new feature** is **Writers on Writers**, brief commentaries by one writer on another, such as the African American novelist Toni Morrison's observations about the work of the most famous Southern writer, William Faulkner. Like "Through a Modern Lens," this feature essentially puts writers in conversation with each other, helping students understand the complex ways that writers read, influence, and inspire one another.

A Note on Editorial Procedures

In general, we have taken the texts in the anthology from the first printings or from authoritative modern editions of early books and manuscripts. The selections from Anne Bradstreet are taken from the standard, modernized edition of her works, but as far as is practicable we have otherwise sought to reproduce the texts as they were originally written or published. We've retained their historical features in order to preserve the flavor of the authors' styles and familiarize students with changes in

English usage and the conventions of capitalization, punctuation, and spelling. Since spelling was not standardized until the late eighteenth century, we do not alter British spellings, such as *humour*; early variant spellings that can be clearly understood, such as *chearful* for *cheerful*; early past-tense forms, such as *learnt* for *learned*; or contractions that were commonly used in early texts, such as *us'd* for *used* and *tho'* for *though.* To aid students in their reading of early texts, we have provided footnotes for many terms that are now archaic or obsolete. We have altered early printer's conventions that would cause confusion, such as the long *s* in *Bleſſings*, which is printed as *Blessings.* We have silently expanded some abbreviations, including early abbreviated forms like y^e (the) and y^t (that) and abbreviations of the books of the Bible. We have also corrected obvious typographical errors, and we have altered punctuation, spelling, or other features of a text in instances where the reading comprehension of students might be significantly compromised. We cite the published sources of texts in the headnotes, and each text is followed by the year of its first printing or original composition and, when it is different, the year of publication of the edition from which the text is taken.

Options for Bringing More Classic and Contemporary American Literature to Your Course

Bedford College Editions are reprints of enduring literary works that can be affordably packaged with the anthology. They are available **in print or as Bedford E-Books to Go**, which are downloadable to e-readers. The literary works include: Susanna Rowson's *Charlotte Temple*, edited by Pattie Cowell; Nathaniel Hawthorne's *The Scarlet Letter*, edited by Susan S. Williams; Harriet Beecher Stowe's *Uncle Tom's Cabin*, edited by Stephen Railton; Herman Melville's *Benito Cereno*, edited by Wyn Kelley; Mark Twain's *Adventures of Huckleberry Finn*, edited by Gregg Camfield; Henry James's *Daisy Miller*, edited by William Merrill Decker; Kate Chopin's *The Awakening*, edited by Sharon M. Harris; Willa Cather's *My Antonia*, edited by Guy Reynolds; and Nella Larsen's *Quicksand*, edited by DoVeanna Fulton Minor. Prepared by eminent scholars and teachers, the text of each work is lightly annotated and accompanied by editorial matter that includes a chronology of the life of the author; an illustrated introduction to the contexts and major issues of the text in its time and ours; an annotated bibliography for further reading in backgrounds, criticism, and online; and a concise glossary of literary terms.

Award-Winning Contemporary Literature Available for Packaging at Significant Savings.   In addition to Bedford College Editions, *The Bedford Anthology of American Literature* can be packaged with any of a thousand titles from Farrar, Straus & Giroux, Picador, St. Martin's Press, and other Macmillan trade publishers — at discounts of up to 50 percent off the regular price. To learn more, or to package a trade book with *The Bedford Anthology of American Literature*, contact your local Bedford/St. Martin's sales representative.

To see a complete list of titles available for packaging, go to **bedfordstmartins
.com/tradeup**.

Options to Enhance Teaching and Learning American Literature

Companion Web Site at bedfordstmartins.com/americanlit.   This site is equipped
with student and instructor resources that include annotated research links (LitLinks)
for almost every author in the anthology, as well as for broader topics in American
literature; maps, including all of the maps in the book plus access to many more at
Map Central; This Year in American History, which offers a snapshot of an important
literary, historical, and cultural moment; additional critical essays directly related
to several selections in the anthology; the instructor's manual (downloadable); and
sample syllabi.

Resources for Teaching The Bedford Anthology of American Literature, Volume One by
Lisa Logan, University of Central Florida; Volume Two by Michael Soto, Trinity University. This extensive instructor's manual includes entries for every author and every
thematic cluster and offers approaches to teaching; sample syllabi with tips on planning the course; connections to other authors and texts; classroom-tested suggestions
for discussion, writing, and oral presentations; and print and multimedia resources
for further research. The instructor's manuals are available in print — a combined
volume — or as downloadable files from the companion Web site.

Background Readings for Teachers of American Literature, compiled by Venetria
Patton, Purdue University. This collection of critical essays for instructors provides
an overview of recent changes in the field of American literary studies. The readings
include important scholarship, newer critical approaches, and practical ideas from
experienced teachers. Organized by various approaches ranging from historical context to race and ethnicity and gender and sexuality, this professional resource is
relevant to a wide range of courses in American literature, from surveys to graduate
seminars.

Acknowledgments

The Bedford Anthology of American Literature is the product of the most challenging, enjoyable, and rewarding work the editors have ever undertaken. We have taken equal pleasure and satisfaction in working with and learning from others who share our deep commitment to teaching American literature. This anthology is the result of a truly collaborative effort, not only between the editors, but also among the hundreds of dedicated people who have helped shape the contents, design, and features of the anthology, including our colleagues, the staff at Bedford/St. Martin's, the authors and editors of the companion and ancillary texts, the members of our Editorial Advisory Board, and the hundreds of reviewers and survey respondents whose thoughtful comments have so enriched our understanding of the needs of instructors and their students at a wide range of institutions all across the United States.

We are delighted to thank all of those who have contributed to our work on this anthology, both directly and indirectly. From graduate school onward, we have learned from our teachers, students in our classes, and our colleagues. We would especially like to remember the late E. Hudson Long of Baylor University and the late Joseph L. Slater of Colgate University, two remarkable individuals with distinguished careers in the study and teaching of American literature. For their support and stimulating conversation, we want to thank our valued colleagues at Colgate University and the University of Nebraska, Lincoln: Peter Balakian, Michael Coyle, George Hudson, Neill Joy, Jane Pinchin, Phillip Richards, and Sarah Wider; and Grace Bauer, Stephen Behrendt, Kwakiutl Dreher, Thomas C. Gannon, Melissa Homestead, Maureen Honey, Tom Lynch, Amelia Montes, Kenneth Price, Guy Reynolds, Judy Slater, and the late Gerald Shapiro. We are also deeply and directly indebted to the authors of the two-volume *Resources for Teaching The Bedford Anthology of American Literature* for their many excellent suggestions: Lisa Logan, University of Central Florida, and Michael Soto, Trinity University. The editors of the companion volumes also provided many ideas and shared a variety of important insights. Venetria Patton, Purdue University, editor of *Background Readings for Teachers of American Literature*, offered us several excellent ideas as she compiled the essays for that volume. The editors of the novels in the Bedford College Editions series also made numerous suggestions: Gregg Camfield, University of the Pacific; Pattie Cowell, Colorado State University; William Merrill Decker, Oklahoma State University; Sharon M. Harris, University of Connecticut; Wyn Kelley, Massachusetts Institute of Technology; Stephen Railton, University of Virginia; Guy Reynolds, University of Nebraska, Lincoln; and Susan S. Williams, Ohio State University. Members of our Editorial Advisory Board have provided detailed reviews, sound advice, and helpful support on Volume One and the first half of the shorter edition: David J. Carlson, California State University, San Bernardino; Matt Cohen, University of Texas at Austin; Pattie Cowell, Colorado State University; Paul Crumbley, Utah State University; William Merrill Decker, Oklahoma State University; Heather Duda, University of Rio Grande & Rio Grande Community College; Thomas C. Gannon, University of Nebraska, Lincoln; Ivonne M. García, Kenyon College; Sharon M. Harris, University of Connecticut; Lisa Logan, University of Central Florida; Laura L. Mielke, University of Kansas; Richard Millington, Smith College; Venetria Patton,

Purdue University; Sarah Robbins, Texas Christian University; and Michael Soto, Trinity University. Members of our Editorial Advisory Board have also provided detailed reviews, sound advice, and helpful support on Volume Two and the second half of the shorter edition: Elizabeth Ammons, Tufts University; Donna Campbell, Washington State University; David Chinitz, Loyola University Chicago; Michael Coyle, Colgate University; Robert Donahoo, Sam Houston State University; Chuck Johanningsmeier, University of Nebraska, Omaha; AnaLouise Keating, Texas Woman's University; Tom Lynch, University of Nebraska, Lincoln; Beth Maxfield, Henderson State University; Paul Sorrentino, Virginia Tech; Michael Soto, Trinity University; Susan Tomlinson, University of Massachusetts, Boston; Nicole Tonkovich, University of California, San Diego; and Lara Vetter, University of North Carolina, Charlotte. Throughout the years that we have been working on *The Bedford Anthology of American Literature*, we have been helped and guided by a large number of instructors at a variety of institutions. For their suggestions on Volume One, we are thankful to Christopher Black, Oklahoma State University; Ethel L. Bonds, Virginia Western Community College; Cyrus Brock, Bevill State Community College; Sydney Bufkin, University of Texas at Austin; Teresa Coronado, University of Wisconsin-Parkside; Margaret H. Davis, Spring Hill College; Joshua Dickinson, Jefferson Community College (SUNY); Gerri Dobbins, Gaston College; Gary D. Hall, The Victoria College; John L. Hare, Montgomery College; Ghazala Hashmi, J. Sargent Reynolds Community College; Harold Hellwig, Idaho State University; William Huntting Howell, Boston University; Ann C. Hunter, Vernon College; Brian Kent, University of Vermont; Kristina L. Knotts, Westfield State College; Amber LaPiana, Washington State University; Baker Lawley, Gustavus Adolphus College; Virgil Mathes, San Juan College; Christopher McBride, Solano College; Michael Minassian, Broward College; Joelle Moen, Washington State University; Scott Alan Orme, Spokane Community College; Kenneth Poff, St. Philip's College; LuElla Putnam, Oklahoma State University; Peter P. Reed, University of Mississippi; Michael L. Schroeder, Savannah State University; Margaret Sherve, Minot State University; Bryan Sinche, University of Hartford; Vanessa Steinroetter, Washburn University; Nancy Sweet, California State University, Sacramento; James T.F. Tanner, University of North Texas; James Trout, Washington State University; Sara K. White, Keystone College; Rebecca L. Williams, Essex County College; and Martha Willoughby, Pearl River Community College. For their suggestions on Volume Two, we are thankful to Christopher Anderson, Pittsburg State University; Christopher Black, Oklahoma State University; Cyrus Brock, Bevill State Community College, Fayette; Sydney Bufkin, University of Texas at Austin; Gloria D. Bunnell, Mississippi University for Women; Sandra Gayle Dillingham, Haywood Community College; Sheilah Stokes Dobyns, Fullerton College; Ronald Gard, University of New Orleans; Susan Gilmore, Central Connecticut State University; Jesse Graves, East Tennessee State University; Darrin L. Grinder, Northwest Nazarene University; Jill Hampton, University of South Carolina, Aiken; Robin Havenick, Linn Benton Community College; Desiree Henderson, University of Texas, Arlington; Avis Hewitt, Grand Valley State University; John Hildebrand, University of Wisconsin-Eau Claire; Tamara Hollins, Cheyney University; Annie Merrill Ingram, Davidson College; Amber LaPiana, Washington State University; Priscilla Leder, Texas State University-

San Marcos; Sue-Im Lee, Temple University; Beth Maxfield, Pearl River Community College; Donna Metcalf, Benedictine University at Springfield; Joelle Moen, Washington State University; Ann H. Moser, Virginia Western Community College; Kevin Nebergall, Kirkwood Community College; Keith R. Prendergast, Pensacola Junior College; LuElla Putnam, Oklahoma State University; Deborah Renville, Kankakee Community College; Charlotte Rich, Eastern Kentucky University; Tiechera Samuell, Three Rivers Community College; Don M. Shipley, Louisiana College; Vanessa Steinroetter, Washburn University; Melissa J. Strong, Northeastern State University; Matt Theado, Gardner-Webb University; James Trout, Washington State University; Anastasia Turner, University of Alabama, Huntsville; and Kenneth Walker, University of Nevada, Reno.

Staff members of the University of Nebraska, Lincoln, and Colgate University libraries have helped us locate texts and solve bibliographic problems. For this, we are especially appreciative of Kathy Johnson and Carl Peterson. We have also benefited from the several students who served so ably as research assistants for this project: Soojin Ahn, Jaclyn Cruikshank, Amanda Gailey, Ramon Guerra, Elizabeth Lorang, Janel Simons, and Stephanie Veverka. We are also grateful to the many students in our classes in American literature who have provided ideas and inspiration throughout our teaching careers at several colleges and universities.

Working with the extraordinarily talented staff members of Bedford/St. Martin's has been an enriching educational experience as well as a constant pleasure. The first member of the editorial staff we met at Bedford/St. Martin's was executive editor Steve Scipione, and we have come to depend on his expert professional opinions and high good humor. Our untiring editor, Maura Shea, provided strong support and wise counsel on an almost daily basis for nearly four years. Joan Feinberg, co-president of Macmillan Higher Education, and Denise Wydra, president of Bedford/St. Martin's, imaginatively guided a long series of stimulating discussions about American literature in general and our anthology in particular. Karen Henry, editor in chief, has been a constant source of sound advice and soothing reassurance. Other members of the editorial staff—Karen Sikola and Sherry Mooney—have also helped in many ways, large and small. We also want to thank the members of the new media staff who have taught us much about the technical possibilities of Web sites: Harriet Wald and Melanie MacFarlane. Kerri Cardone and the other members of the production staff, Sue Brown, Elizabeth Schaaf, Dennis Conroy, and Elise Kaiser patiently made hundreds—perhaps thousands—of invaluable suggestions. We greatly respect and admire the members of the art and design staff: Donna Dennison, Anna Palchik, Linda Finigan, and Martha Friedman. We also thank Virginia Creeden for her work on permissions and Stacey Propps for teaching us about marketing plans.

Finally, our wonderful family members have offered enthusiastic encouragement and happy diversions: Max Johnson; Peggy Belasco; Bill Belasco and Teresa Morales; Janet and Steve Jenkins; Lance Johnson and Eva Vig; and Roslyn and Vincent Reilly.

We warmly dedicate *The Bedford Anthology of American Literature* to our students, who have taught us so much about teaching American literature.

Susan Belasco
Linck Johnson

About the Editors

Susan Belasco (B.A., Baylor University; Ph.D., Texas A&M University) is chair of the Department of English at the University of Nebraska, Lincoln, where she is also a professor of English and women's and gender studies. She has taught courses in writing and American literature at several institutions since 1974, including McLennan Community College (Texas); Allegheny College; California State University, Los Angeles; and the University of Tulsa. The editor of Margaret Fuller's *Summer on the Lakes*, Fanny Fern's *Ruth Hall*, and *Stowe in Her Own Time*, she is also the coeditor of three collections of essays: *Approaches to Teaching Stowe's "Uncle Tom's Cabin," Periodical Literature in Nineteenth Century America*, and *Leaves of Grass: The Sesquicentennial Essays*. The editor of "Walt Whitman's Periodical Poetry" for the *Walt Whitman Archive* (**whitmanarchive.org**), she is a past president of the Research Society for American Periodicals.

Linck Johnson (B.A., Cornell University; Ph.D., Princeton University), the Charles A. Dana Professor of English and former Director of the Division of the Arts and Humanities at Colgate University, has taught courses in writing and American literature and culture since 1974. He is the author of *Thoreau's Complex Weave: The Writing of "A Week on the Concord and Merrimack Rivers," with the Text of the First Draft*; the Historical Introduction to *A Week* in the Princeton University Press edition of the *Writings of Henry D. Thoreau*; and numerous articles and contributions to books, most recently the *Oxford Handbook of Transcendentalism*. The recipient of a National Endowment for the Humanities Fellowship at the American Antiquarian Society, he is a member of the Editorial Board of the *Collected Works of Ralph Waldo Emerson*.

Contents

Preface   *v*
About the Editors   *xx*

≡ LITERATURE TO 1750 ≡

INTRODUCTION   **2**
    America before Columbus   **3**
    Christianity, Islam, and the Lure of Asia   **4**
    Map: Native American Peoples, 1492   *5*
    Conquest and Colonization in the New World   **7**
    Map: Early European Explorations   *11*
    **The Protestant Reformation and the Puritan "Errand into the
       Wilderness"**   **14**
    Literature and Cultural Diversity in Colonial America   **18**
    Comparative Timeline   *22*

Native American Origin and Creation Stories

Introduction   29

Iroquois Confederacy   33
Origin of Folk Stories   35

Cherokee   37
How the World Was Made   39

Lakota   40
Wohpe and the Gift of the Pipe   42

Akimel O'odham (Pima)   45
The Story of the Creation   46

Hupa   48
The Boy Who Grew Up at Ta'k'imiłding   50

NATIVE AMERICAN STORIES THROUGH A MODERN
LENS   51

N. Scott Momaday (b. 1934)
The Becoming of the Native: Man in America before Columbus, 1993   52

Explorations and Early Encounters

Introduction   59

Christopher Columbus (1451–1506)   64
Letter of Columbus, Describing the Results of
    His First Voyage   67

Álvar Núñez Cabeza de Vaca (c. 1490–c. 1557)   73
from The Narrative of Cabeza de Vaca   76
    Proem   76
    Chapter 15: What befell us among the people of Malhado   77
    Chapter 16: The Christians leave the island of Malhado   78
    Chapter 19: Our separation by the Indians   80
    Chapter 20: Of our escape   81
    Chapter 21: Our cure of some of the afflicted   82

Samuel de Champlain (c. 1570–1635)   83
from The Voyages of Samuel de Champlain   85

Colonial Settlements

Introduction   91

Captain John Smith (1580–1631)   104
from The Generall Historie of Virginia, New-England, and the Summer Isles   107
   from The Third Book, Ch. II, "What happened till the first supply"   107

William Bradford (1590–1657)   116
from Of Plimoth Plantation   119
   [*From Booke* 1]   119
   from Chapter 1   120
   Chapter 9 Of their voyage, & how they passed the sea, and of their safe arrivall at Cape
      Codd   121
   Chapter 10 Showing how they sought out a place of habitation, and what befell them
      theraboute   124
   From Booke 2   129
   The remainder of Anno: 1620   129
   from Anno: 1621   134
   from Anno Domini: 1632   135

John Winthrop (1588–1649)   136
A Modell of Christian Charity   138

Anne Bradstreet (1612–1672)   150
The Prologue   153
An Epitaph on My Dear and Ever-Honoured Mother Mrs. Dorothy Dudley, Who
   Deceased December 27, 1643, and of Her Age, 61   155
To Her Father with Some Verses   155
The Author to Her Book   156
Before the Birth of One of Her Children   156
To My Dear and Loving Husband   157
A Letter to Her Husband, Absent upon Public Employment   158
Here Follows Some Verses upon the Burning of Our House July 10th, 1666.
   Copied Out of a Loose Paper   159
To My Dear Children   161

   BRADSTREET THROUGH A MODERN LENS   166

   Rose Murray
   Puritan Woman, 1971   167

Mary Rowlandson (1636?–1711)   169
The Sovereignty and Goodness of God   171

AMERICAN CONTEXTS
THE SALEM WITCHCRAFT TRIALS

Introduction   189

Deodat Lawson (?–1715?)   194
from A Brief and True Narrative   194

Cotton Mather (1663–1728)   201
from The Wonders of the Invisible World   201

Thomas Brattle (1658–1713)   206
from Letter of Thomas Brattle, 1692   207

Samuel Sewall (1652–1730)   212
from The Diary of Samuel Sewall   213

Edward Taylor (c. 1642–1729)   217
  PREPATORY MEDITATIONS   218
Prologue   219
Meditation 8 (First Series) John 6:51 I am the Living Bread   220
  MISCELLANEOUS POEMS   221
Upon Wedlock, and Death of Children   221
Upon a Spider Catching a Fly   223
Huswifery   224

William Byrd (1674–1744)   225
from The Secret Diary of William Byrd of Westover   227

Jonathan Edwards (1703–1758)   231
Personal Narrative   233
Sinners in the Hands of an Angry God   245

≡ AMERICAN LITERATURE, 1750–1830 ≡

INTRODUCTION   260
  Print Culture and the Road to Revolution   262
  Map: The Thirteen Colonies in 1775   264
  Society and Culture in the New Nation   267
  Map: The Missouri Compromise   271
  The Emergence of an American Literature   274
  Comparative Timeline   279

Writing Colonial Lives

Introduction 285

Benjamin Franklin (1706–1790) 290
from The Autobiography of Benjamin Franklin 294
  Part I 294
  Part II 311

Elizabeth Ashbridge (1713–1755) 322
from Some Account of the Fore Part of the Life of Elizabeth Ashbridge 324

John Woolman (1720–1772) 335
from The Journal of John Woolman 336
  Chapter 1 336
  from Chapter III 343

Samson Occom (1723–1792) 347
A Short Narrative of My Life 349

  OCCOM THROUGH A MODERN LENS 355

  James Ottery (b. 1953)
  The Diary of Samson Occum, 2001 356

Olaudah Equiano (1745?–1797) 359
from The Interesting Narrative of the Life of Olaudah Equiano, or Gustavus Vassa,
  the African, Written by Himself 361
  Chapter 2 361

AMERICAN CONTEXTS
"TO BEGIN THE WORLD OVER AGAIN": THE EMERGING IDEA OF "AMERICA"

Introduction 372

J. Hector St. John de Crèvecoeur (1735–1813) 374
Letters from an American Farmer 375
from Letter III, What Is an American? 375

Thomas Paine (1737–1809) 379
from Common Sense, 1776 379

John Adams (1735–1826) and Abigail Adams (1744–1818) 383
Letter from Abigail Adams to John Adams, March 31, 1776 384
Letter from John Adams to Abigail Adams, April 14, 1776 385
Letters from John Adams to Abigail Adams, July 3, 1776 386

Thomas Jefferson (1743–1826)   387
Draft of the Declaration of Independence, 1776   389
from Notes on the State of Virginia   394
Query XVII The different religions received into that state?   394
Query XVIII The *particular* customs and manners that may happen to be received in that state?   397

George Washington (1732–1799)   399
Letter to the Touro Synagogue, Newport   400

Judith Sargent Murray (1751–1820)   401
from On the Equality of the Sexes, Part 1, 1790   402

Absalom Jones (1746–1818)   406
Petition of the People of Colour   407

Tecumseh (1768–1813)   409
Speech of Tecumseh to Governor Harrison   410

Literature for a New Nation

Introduction   413

Philip Freneau (1752–1832)   421
On the Emigration to America   423
The Wild Honey Suckle   425
The Indian Burying Ground   426

Phillis Wheatley (c.1753–1784)   427
On Being Brought from Africa to America   430
To the University of Cambridge, in New England   430
To the Right Honourable William, Earl of Dartmouth, His Majesty's Principal Secretary of State for North-America, & C.   431
To S.M., a Young *African* Painter, on Seeing His Works   432
To His Excellency General Washington   434
Letter to Samson Occom   435

Washington Irving (1783–1859)   436
  THE SKETCH BOOK   438
The Author's Account of Himself   439
Rip Van Winkle   441

Catharine Maria Sedgwick (1789–1867)   454
Cacoethes Scribendi   456

William Cullen Bryant (1794–1878)   467
Thanatopsis   468
The Yellow Violet   471
To a Waterfowl   472
To Cole, the Painter, Departing for Europe   473

Jane Johnston Schoolcraft (1800–1841)   473
Mishosha, or the Magician and His Daughters   475

≡ AMERICAN LITERATURE, 1830–1865 ≡

INTRODUCTION   484
   Technology, Transportation, and the Growth of the Literary
      Marketplace   486
   Religion, Immigration, and Territorial Expansion   490
   Sectionalism and the Coming of the Civil War   495

   Map: The Compromise of 1850 and the Kansas-Nebraska Act of 1854   495

   Comparative Timeline   498

The Era of Reform

Introduction   503

AMERICAN CONTEXTS
"I WILL BE HEARD":
THE RHETORIC OF ANTEBELLUM REFORM

Introduction   512

The Cherokee Memorials   514
Memorial of the Cherokee Council, November 5, 1829   514

David Walker (1785–1830)   519
from An Appeal to the Colored Citizens of the World   520

William Lloyd Garrison (1805–1879)   522
To the Public   523

Orestes A. Brownson (1803–1876)   524
from The Laboring Classes   525

Seneca Falls Woman's Convention   527
Declaration of Sentiments   528

Sojourner Truth (1795–1883)   531
Speech to a Women's Rights Convention   531

William Apess (1798–1839)   533
An Indian's Looking-Glass for the White Man   534

Ralph Waldo Emerson (1803–1882)   539
The American Scholar   542
Self-Reliance   555
Experience   574
    EMERSON'S POETRY   590
The Rhodora: On Being Asked, Whence Is the Flower?   590
The Snow-Storm   591
Hamatreya   592
Days   593

Margaret Fuller (1810–1850)   594
from Woman in the Nineteenth Century   596

Harriet Beecher Stowe (1811–1896)   607
The Seamstress   609
The Freeman's Dream: A Parable   616
Preface to Uncle Tom's Cabin   617

Harriet Jacobs (1813–1897)   619
Letter from a Fugitive Slave   620
Incidents in the Life of a Slave Girl   624
    Preface by the Author   624
    I. Childhood   625
    VII. The Lover   627
    X. A Perilous Passage in the Slave Girl's Life   631
    XIV. Another Link to Life   635
    XVII. The Flight   637
    XXI. The Loophole of Retreat   639
    XLI. Free at Last   642

Henry David Thoreau (1817–1862)   648
Resistance to Civil Government   650
Walden   666
    from Economy   666

Where I Lived, and What I Lived For   671
The Bean-Field   681
The Village   688
Conclusion   692

Frederick Douglass (1818–1895)   700
Narrative of the Life of Frederick Douglass, an American Slave, Written
    by Himself   702

Douglass through a Modern Lens   768

Robert Hayden (1913–1980)
Frederick Douglass   769

American Facts and American Fiction

Introduction   771

Nathaniel Hawthorne (1804–1864)   779
My Kinsman, Major Molineux   782
Young Goodman Brown   796
Rappaccini's Daughter   806

Edgar Allan Poe (1809–1849)   827
The Fall of the House of Usher   829
The Tell-Tale Heart   843
The Purloined Letter   847
    Poe's Poetry   861
Sonnet – to Science   861
To Helen   862
The Raven   862
Annabel Lee   865

Fanny Fern (Sara Payson Willis Parton) (1811–1872)   866
Hints to Young Wives   869
The Tear of a Wife   870
The Sober Husband   870
Male Criticism on Ladies' Books   872
A Law More Nice Than Just   873
The "Coming" Woman   874
"Independence"   875

Herman Melville (1819–1891)   876
Bartleby, the Scrivener   879

Rebecca Harding Davis (1831–1910)   905
Life in the Iron-Mills   908

New Poetic Voices

Introduction   937

AMERICAN CONTEXTS
THE AMERICAN MUSE: POETRY AT MIDCENTURY

Lydia Sigourney (1791–1865)   945
Indian Names   946
To a Shred of Linen   947

Elizabeth Oakes Smith (1806–1893)   949
The Unattained   950
The Drowned Mariner   951

Henry Wadsworth Longfellow (1807–1882)   953
The Jewish Cemetery at Newport   954
My Lost Youth   956

John Greenleaf Whittier (1807–1892)   958
The Hunters of Men   959
The Farewell of a Virginia Slave Mother to Her Daughters Sold into Southern
   Bondage   960

Frances E.W. Harper (1825–1911)   962
The Slave Mother   963
Ethiopia   964

Rose Terry Cooke (1827–1892)   965
Here   966
Captive   966
"The Harvest Is Past"   967

Walt Whitman (1819–1892)   968
Leaves of Grass [1891–92 Edition]   971
   FROM INSCRIPTIONS   972
One's-Self I Sing   972
Thou Reader   972
Song of Myself   973
   FROM CHILDREN OF ADAM   1019
Once I Pass'd through a Populous City   1019
As Adam Early in the Morning   1020

From Calamus   1020
In Paths Untrodden   1020
City of Orgies   1021
I Saw in Louisiana a Live-Oak Growing   1021
Here the Frailest Leaves of Me   1021

From Sea-Drift   1022
Out of the Cradle Endlessly Rocking   1022

From Drum-Taps   1027
Beat! Beat! Drums!   1027
Cavalry Crossing a Ford   1027
Vigil Strange I Kept on a Field One Night   1028
A Sight in Camp in the Daybreak Gray and Dim   1028
The Wound-Dresser   1029
Reconciliation   1031

From Memories of President Lincoln   1032
When Lilacs Last in the Dooryard Bloom'd   1032

From Whispers of Heavenly Death   1039
A Noiseless Patient Spider   1039

From Songs of Parting   1039
As the Time Draws Nigh   1039

Whitman through a Modern Lens   1040

Langston Hughes (1902–1967)
Old Walt 1954   1041

Allen Ginsberg (1926–1997)
A Supermarket in California, 1956   1041

Emily Dickinson (1830–1886)   1043
130 [Fr122]   Manuscript Version of These are the days when Birds come
               back –   1045
130 [Fr122]   Indian Summer (1890 version of These are the days when Birds come
               back –)   1046
49 [Fr39]   I never lost as much but twice   1046
67 [Fr112]   Success is counted sweetest   1047
185 [Fr202]   "Faith" is a fine invention   1047
199 [Fr225]   I'm "wife" – I've finished that –   1047
214 [Fr207]   I taste a liquor never brewed –   1048
216 [Fr124]   Safe in their Alabaster Chambers – (1859 version)   1048
216 [Fr124]   Safe in their Alabaster Chambers – (1861 version)   1048
241 [Fr339]   I like a look of Agony   1049
249 [Fr269]   Wild Nights – Wild Nights!   1049
252 [Fr312]   I can wade Grief –   1050
258 [Fr320]   There's a certain Slant of light,   1050
280 [Fr340]   I felt a funeral, in my Brain   1051

288 [Fr260]   I'm Nobody! Who are you?   1051
303 [Fr409]   The Soul Selects her own Society –   1051
324 [Fr236]   Some keep the Sabbath going to Church –   1052
341 [Fr372]   After great pain, a formal feeling comes–   1052
357 [Fr615]   God is a distant – stately Lover –   1053
401 [Fr675]   What Soft – Cherubic Creatures –   1053
409 [Fr545]   They dropped like Flakes –   1054
435 [Fr620]   Much Madness is divinest Sense   1054
441 [Fr519]   This is my letter to the World   1054
444 [Fr524]   It feels a shame to be Alive –   1054
448 [Fr446]   This was a Poet – It is That   1055
465 [Fr591]   I heard a Fly buzz – when I died –   1056
501 [Fr373]   This World is not Conclusion.   1056
508 [Fr353]   I'm ceded – I've stopped being Theirs –   1057
512 [Fr360]   The Soul has Bandaged moments –   1057
605 [Fr513]   The Spider holds a Silver Ball   1058
632 [Fr598]   The Brain – is wider than the Sky –   1058
650 [Fr760]   Pain – has an Element of Blank –   1059
657 [Fr466]   I dwell in Possibility –   1059
709 [Fr788]   Publication – is the Auction   1059
712 [Fr479]   Because I could not stop for Death –   1060
754 [Fr764]   My Life had stood – a Loaded Gun –   1061
883 [Fr930]   The Poets light but Lamps –   1061
986 [Fr1096]   A Narrow Fellow in the Grass   1062
1052 [Fr800]   I never saw a Moor –   1062
1072 [Fr194]   Title divine – is mine!   1063
1078 [Fr1108]   The Bustle in a House   1063
1082 [Fr1044]   Revolution is the Pod   1063
1129 [Fr1263]   Tell all the Truth but tell it slant –   1064
1463 [Fr1489]   A Route of Evanescence   1064
1651 [Fr1715]   A Word made Flesh is seldom   1064
1732 [Fr1773]   My life closed twice before its close –   1065
1737 [Fr267]   Rearrange a "Wife's" affection!   1065
1760 [Fr1590]   Elysium is as far to   1066

LETTERS   1066

Exchange with Susan Gilbert (Dickinson), 1861   1067
To Thomas Wentworth Higginson, 7 June 1862   1068

DICKINSON THROUGH A MODERN LENS   1070

Adrienne Rich (1929-2012)
'I Am in Danger – Sir –', 1966   1071

Cathy Song (b. 1955)
A Poet in the House 2001   1072

AMERICAN CONTEXTS
"MINE EYES HAVE SEEN THE GLORY:"
THE MEANINGS OF THE CIVIL WAR

Introduction   1074

John Brown (1800–1859)   1076
John Brown's Last Speech   1077

Jefferson Davis (1808–1889)   1078
Jefferson Davis's Inaugural Address   1079

Civil War Songs   1082
Dixie's Land   1083
John Brown's Body   1084
Battle Hymn of the Republic   1085

Abraham Lincoln (1809–1865)   1086
The Gettysburg Address, 1863   1087
Second Inaugural Address, March, 1865   1088

Henry Highland Garnet (1815–1882)   1090
from A Memorial Discourse   1091

Mary Boykin Miller Chesnut (1823–1886)   1093
A Diary from Dixie, April 19-22, 1865   1094

William Cullen Bryant (1794–1878)   1096
The Death of Lincoln   1097

Walt Whitman (1819–1892)   1098
from Memoranda During the War   1098

≡ AMERICAN LITERATURE, 1865–1914 ≡

INTRODUCTION   1102

The Aftermath of the Civil War   1102

Expansion, Industrialization, and the Emergence of Modern America   1108

Map: Immigrants in the United States, 1900   *1111*

Innovation, Technology, and the Literary Marketplace   1117

Comparative Timeline   *1124*

Realism, Regionalism, and Naturalism

Introduction   1131

AMERICAN CONTEXTS
"THE AMERICA OF THE MIND":
CRITICS, WRITERS, AND THE REPRESENTATION OF
REALITY

Introduction   1140

Julian Hawthorne (1846–1934)   1142
from The American Element in Fiction   1142

Henry James (1843–1916)   1143
from The Art of Fiction   1144

Anonymous (A "Lady from Philadelphia")   1145
from The Coming American Novelist   1145

William Dean Howells (1837–1920)   1147
from Criticism and Fiction   1148

Hamlin Garland (1860–1940)   1150
from Literary Emancipation of the West   1151

Frank Norris (1870–1902)   1152
A Plea for Romantic Fiction   1152

Mark Twain (Samuel L. Clemens) (1835–1910)   1157
Jim Smiley and His Jumping Frog   1159
A True Story, Repeated Word for Word as I Heard It   1164
The Private History of a Campaign That Failed   1167
The War Prayer   1181

WRITERS ON WRITERS: ARTHUR MILLER ON MARK TWAIN   1184

Arthur Miller (1915–2005)
from Introduction to *Chapters from My Autobiography*   1184

William Dean Howells (1837–1920)   1187
Editha   1190

Ambrose Bierce (1842–1914?)   1199
Chickamauga   1203

Henry James (1843–1916)   1207
The Real Thing   1210
The Jolly Corner   1230

Sarah Orne Jewett (1849–1909)   1254
A White Heron   1256

Kate Chopin (1850–1904)   1263
At the 'Cadian Ball   1265

Charles W. Chesnutt (1858–1932)   1273
The Passing of Grandison   1275

Pauline E. Hopkins (1859–1930)   1287
"As the Lord Lives, He Is One of Our Mother's Children"   1290

Charlotte Perkins Gilman (1860–1935)   1296
The Yellow Wall-Paper   1299

Edith Wharton (1862–1937)   1311
The Quicksand   1315

Sui Sin Far (Edith Maud Eaton) (1865–1914)   1327
"Its Wavering Image"   1330

Edwin Arlington Robinson (1869–1935)   1334
Luke Havergal   1337
Richard Cory   1338
Miniver Cheevy   1338
The Mill   1339

Stephen Crane (1871–1900)   1340
The Open Boat   1342
    THE BLACK RIDERS AND OTHER LINES   1360
I   [Black riders came from the sea.]   1360
XIV   [There was crimson clash of war.]   1360
XIX   [A god in wrath]   1361
XXIV   [I saw a man pursuing the horizon;]   1361
    WAR IS KIND   1361
I   [Do not weep, maiden, for war is kind]   1361

Theodore Dreiser (1871–1945)   1362
Butcher Rogaum's Door   1365

Paul Laurence Dunbar (1872–1906)   1376
An Ante-bellum Sermon   1378

We Wear the Mask   1381
Sympathy   1381

Willa Cather (1873–1947)   1382
A Wagner Matinée   1385

Writing "American" Lives

Introduction   1393

José Martí (1853–1895)   1399
Impressions of America   1402
   I.   1402
   III.   1405

Zitkala-Ša (Gertrude Simmons Bonnin) (1876–1938)   1407
The School Days of an Indian Girl   1409

Booker T. Washington (1856–1915)   1420
Up from Slavery   1423
   Chapter XIV. The Atlanta Exposition Address   1423

W. E. B. Du Bois (1868–1963)   1431
The Souls of Black Folk   1434
   I. Of Our Spiritual Strivings   1434
   III. Of Mr. Booker T. Washington and Others   1440

Henry Adams (1838–1918)   1451
The Education of Henry Adams   1455
   Preface   1455
   Chapter XXV: The Dynamo and the Virgin (1900)   1456

Mary Antin (1881–1949)   1465
from The Promised Land   1469
   from Chapter IX: The Promised Land   1469

≡ AMERICAN LITERATURE, 1914–1945 ≡

INTRODUCTION   1482
   Art and Society in the Era of the Great War   1483
   American Culture in the 1920s   1489
   Map: The Great Migration, 1914–1930   1490
   From the Great Depression to World War II   1497
   Comparative Timeline   1504

Modernisms in American Poetry

Introduction   1511

AMERICAN CONTEXTS
"MAKE IT NEW": THEORIES OF MODERN POETRY

Introduction   1520

Harriet Monroe (1860–1936)   1522
The Motive of the Magazine   1522

Ezra Pound (1885–1972)   1523
from A Few Don'ts by an Imagiste   1524

Amy Lowell (1874–1925)   1526
The New Manner in Modern Poetry   1527

T. S. Eliot (1888–1965)   1530
from Tradition and the Individual Talent   1531

James Weldon Johnson (1871–1938)   1534
from Preface to *The Book of American Negro Poetry*   1535

Langston Hughes (1902–1967)   1536
The Negro Artist and the Racial Mountain   1537

Hart Crane (1899–1932)   1541
from Modern Poetry   1541

Robert Frost (1874–1963)   1543
The Figure a Poem Makes   1543

James Weldon Johnson (1871–1938)   1546
The Creation   1549

Amy Lowell (1874–1925)   1551
The Taxi   1553
Aubade   1554
Venus Transiens   1554
Madonna of the Evening Flowers   1555
A Decade   1555

Robert Frost (1874–1963)   1556
Mending Wall   1558

After Apple-Picking   1559
The Road Not Taken   1560
Birches   1561
Fire and Ice   1562
Nothing Gold Can Stay   1563
Stopping by Woods on a Snowy Evening   1563
Acquainted with the Night   1564
Desert Places   1564
The Gift Outright   1565

Carl Sandburg (1878–1967)   1565
Chicago   1568
A Fence   1568
Fog   1569
Grass   1569

Wallace Stevens (1879–1955)   1570
Sunday Morning   1572
Thirteen Ways of Looking at a Blackbird   1576
The Death of a Soldier   1578
Anecdote of the Jar   1578
The Snow Man   1579
Tea at the Palaz of Hoon   1579
The Emperor of Ice-Cream   1580
Of Modern Poetry   1581

Mina Loy (1882–1966)   1581
Love Songs   1584

William Carlos Williams (1883–1963)   1586
The Young Housewife   1590
Danse Russe   1590
Portrait of a Lady   1591
Willow Poem   1591
Queen-Anne's-Lace   1592
The Widow's Lament in Springtime   1592
The Great Figure   1593
To Elsie   1594
The Red Wheelbarrow   1596
This Is Just to Say   1596
A Sort of a Song   1596

Ezra Pound (1885–1972)   1597
Portrait d'une Femme   1599
A Pact   1600
The Rest   1601
In a Station of the Metro [First Version 1913]   1602

In a Station of the Metro [Final Version 1916, 1949]   1602

CATHAY   **1603**
The River-Merchant's Wife: A Letter   1603
The Jewel Stairs' Grievance   1604
Lament of the Frontier Guard   1604

H.D. (Hilda Doolittle) (1886–1961)   1605
Oread   1607
The Pool   1608
Garden   1608
Sea Rose   1609
Leda   1609
Helen   1610

Marianne Moore (1887–1972)   1611
Poetry [First Version 1919]   1614
Poetry [Final Version 1919, 1980]   1615
To Military Progress   1615
The Fish   1616
To a Snail   1617
An Egyptian Pulled Glass Bottle in
     the Shape of a Fish   1618

WRITERS ON WRITERS: ELIZABETH BISHOP ON MARIANNE MOORE   1619

Elizabeth Bishop (1911–1979)
from As We Like It   1619

Jun Fujita (1888–1963)   1621
Diminuendo   1622
Michigan Boulevard   1622
Chicago River   1623

T. S. Eliot (1888–1965)   1623
The Love Song of J. Alfred Prufrock   1626
The Waste Land   1633
Journey of the Magi   1650
Burnt Norton   1652

Claude McKay (1889–1948)   1658
The Harlem Dancer   1660
If We Must Die   1661
The Lynching   1661
America   1662
Africa   1662

Edna St. Vincent Millay (1892–1950)   1663
First Fig   1665

Second Fig   1666
[I, being born a woman and distressed]   1666
[Oh, oh, you will be sorry for that word!]   1666
Justice Denied in Massachusetts   1667

E. E. Cummings (1894–1962)   1668
[in Just-]   1672
[Buffalo Bill 's]   1672
[the Cambridge ladies who live in furnished souls]   1673
["next to of course god america i]   1673
[i sing of Olaf glad and big]   1674
[anyone lived in a pretty how town]   1675

Hart Crane (1899–1932)   1676
Voyages I–VI   1679
To Brooklyn Bridge   1682

Sterling A. Brown (1901–1989)   1684
Southern Road   1686
Strong Men   1688

Langston Hughes (1902–1967)   1690
The Negro Speaks of Rivers   1693
Mother to Son   1694
Jazzonia   1694
I, Too   1695
The Weary Blues   1696
Cross   1697
Brass Spittoons   1697
Christ in Alabama   1698
Harlem   1699

Countee Cullen (1903–1946)   1699
Yet Do I Marvel   1701
Heritage   1702

The Emergence of Modern American Drama

Introduction   1707

Susan Glaspell (1876–1948)   1714
Trifles   1717

Eugene O'Neill (1888–1953)   1726
The Emperor Jones   1731

At Home and Abroad:
American Fiction between the Wars

Introduction 1753

Gertrude Stein (1874–1946) 1761
Ada 1763
Picasso 1765

Sherwood Anderson (1876–1941) 1767
   WINESBURG, OHIO **1770**
Hands 1770
Paper Pills 1774

Katherine Anne Porter (1890–1980) 1776
Flowering Judas 1779

Zora Neale Hurston (1891–1960) 1788
The Gilded Six-Bits 1791

   WRITERS ON WRITERS: ALICE WALKER ON ZORA NEALE HURSTON 1800

   Alice Walker (b. 1944)
   from "A Cautionary Tale and a Partisan View" 1800

María Cristina Mena (1893–1965) 1802
The Vine-Leaf 1804

Jean Toomer (1894–1967) 1809
   CANE 1812
Portrait in Georgia 1812
Blood-Burning Moon 1812

F. Scott Fitzgerald (1896–1940) 1818
The Ice Palace 1821

William Faulkner (1897–1962) 1840
That Evening Sun 1843
Barn Burning 1855

   WRITERS ON WRITERS: TONI MORRISON ON WILLIAM FAULKNER 1869

   Toni Morrison (b. 1931)
   from Faulkner and Women 1869

Ernest Hemingway (1899–1961) 1871
Big Two-Hearted River 1874

John Steinbeck (1902–1968)   1887
Flight   1889

Richard Wright (1908–1960)   1902
Almos' a Man   1905

Eudora Welty (1909–2001)   1914
Lily Daw and the Three Ladies   1916

Carlos Bulosan (1911–1956)   1924
The End of the War   1927

≡ AMERICAN LITERATURE SINCE 1945 ≡

INTRODUCTION   1934
   Culture and Society in the Age of Affluence   1935
   Conflicts at Home and Abroad   1943
   Into the Twenty-First Century   1949
   Comparative Timeline   *1955*

From Modernism to Postmodernism

Introduction   1965

Theodore Roethke (1908–1963)   1977
My Papa's Waltz   1979
Cuttings   1980
Cuttings (later)   1980
Root Cellar   1980
The Waking   1981

‖ WRITERS ON WRITERS: SHERMAN ALEXIE ON THEODORE ROETHKE   1982

   Sherman Alexie (b. 1966)
   from "A Conversation: Sherman Alexie and Diane Thiel"   1982

Elizabeth Bishop (1911–1979)   1984
Sestina   1986
The Armadillo   1987
In the Waiting Room   1988
One Art   1991

Tennessee Williams (1911–1983)   1992
Portrait of a Madonna   1995

Robert Hayden (1913–1980)   2005
Middle Passage   2007

Tillie Olsen (1912?–2007)   2013
I Stand Here Ironing   2015

John Berryman (1914–1972)   2021
    THE DREAM SONGS   2023
1   [Huffy Henry hid   the day,]   2023
4   [Filling her compact & delicious body]   2024
14   [Life, friends, is boring. We must not say so.]   2024
26   [The glories of the world struck me, made me aria, once.]   2025

Ralph Ellison (1913–1994)   2025
The Invisible Man   2028

Saul Bellow (1915–2005)   2039
Looking for Mr. Green   2041

Robert Lowell (1917–1977)   2056
Memories of West Street and Lepke   2059
Skunk Hour   2061
For the Union Dead   2063

Gwendolyn Brooks (1917–2000)   2065
    A STREET IN BRONZEVILLE   2068
kitchenette building   2068
the mother   2069
a song in the front yard   2070

The Bean Eaters   2070
We Real Cool   2071
Malcolm X   2071

Hisaye Yamamoto (1921–2011)   2072
Seventeen Syllables   2074

James Baldwin (1924–1987)   2083
Notes of a Native Son   2086

Flannery O'Connor (1925–1964)   2101
A Good Man Is Hard to Find   2104

Allen Ginsberg (1926–1997)   2115
Howl   2117

John Ashbery (b. 1927)   2127
The One Thing That Can Save America   2129
My Erotic Double   2130
Paradoxes and Oxymorons   2131

Adrienne Rich (1929–2012)   2131
A Valediction Forbidding Mourning   2134
Trying to Talk with a Man   2134
Diving into the Wreck   2135

Ursula K. Le Guin (b. 1929)   2138
She Unnames Them   2140

Gary Snyder (b. 1930)   2142
Riprap   2145
Wave   2145
Axe Handles   2146

Donald Barthelme (1931–1989)   2147
The School   2149

Toni Morrison (b. 1931)   2151
Recitatif   2153

Sylvia Plath (1932–1963)   2168
Morning Song   2170
Mirror   2170
Daddy   2171
Lady Lazarus   2174

John Updike (1932–2009)   2177
A & P   2179

Amiri Baraka (LeRoi Jones) (b. 1934)   2183
Dutchman   2186

Audre Lorde (1934–1992)   2201
Coal   2203
The Woman Thing   2204
Black Mother Woman   2205

Don DeLillo (b. 1936)   2205
Videotape   2208

Michael S. Harper (b. 1938)   2211
American History   2213
Dear John, Dear Coltrane   2214
Martin's Blues   2216

Raymond Carver (1938–1988)   2216
Are These Actual Miles?   2219

Gloria Anzaldúa (1942–2004)   2224
El sonavabitche   2226

WRITERS ON WRITERS: SANDRA CISNEROS ON GLORIA ANZALDÚA   2232

Sandra Cisneros (b. 1954)
A Note to Gloria from the Bottom of the Sea   2232

Alice Walker (b. 1944)   2234
Everyday Use   2236

August Wilson (1945–2005)   2243
The Janitor   2246

Tim O'Brien (b. 1946)   2247
The Things They Carried   2250

Yusef Komunyakaa (b. 1947)   2263
The Dead at Quang Tri   2265
Tu Do Street   2266
Prisoners   2267
Facing It   2269

Leslie Marmon Silko (b. 1948)   2270
Yellow Woman   2272

Joy Harjo (b. 1951)   2279
New Orleans   2281
If You Look with the Mind of the Swirling Earth   2283
This Land Is a Poem   2283

Rita Dove (b. 1952)   2284
The House Slave   2285
Kentucky, 1833   2286
Canary   2287
History   2287

Sandra Cisneros (b. 1954)   2288
Mericans   2289

Martín Espada (b. 1957)   2292
Alabanza: In Praise of Local 100   2294

Sherman Alexie (b. 1966)   2296
What You Pawn I Will Redeem   2298

Index of Authors and Titles   2328

P. Mortier

LITERATURE TO 1750

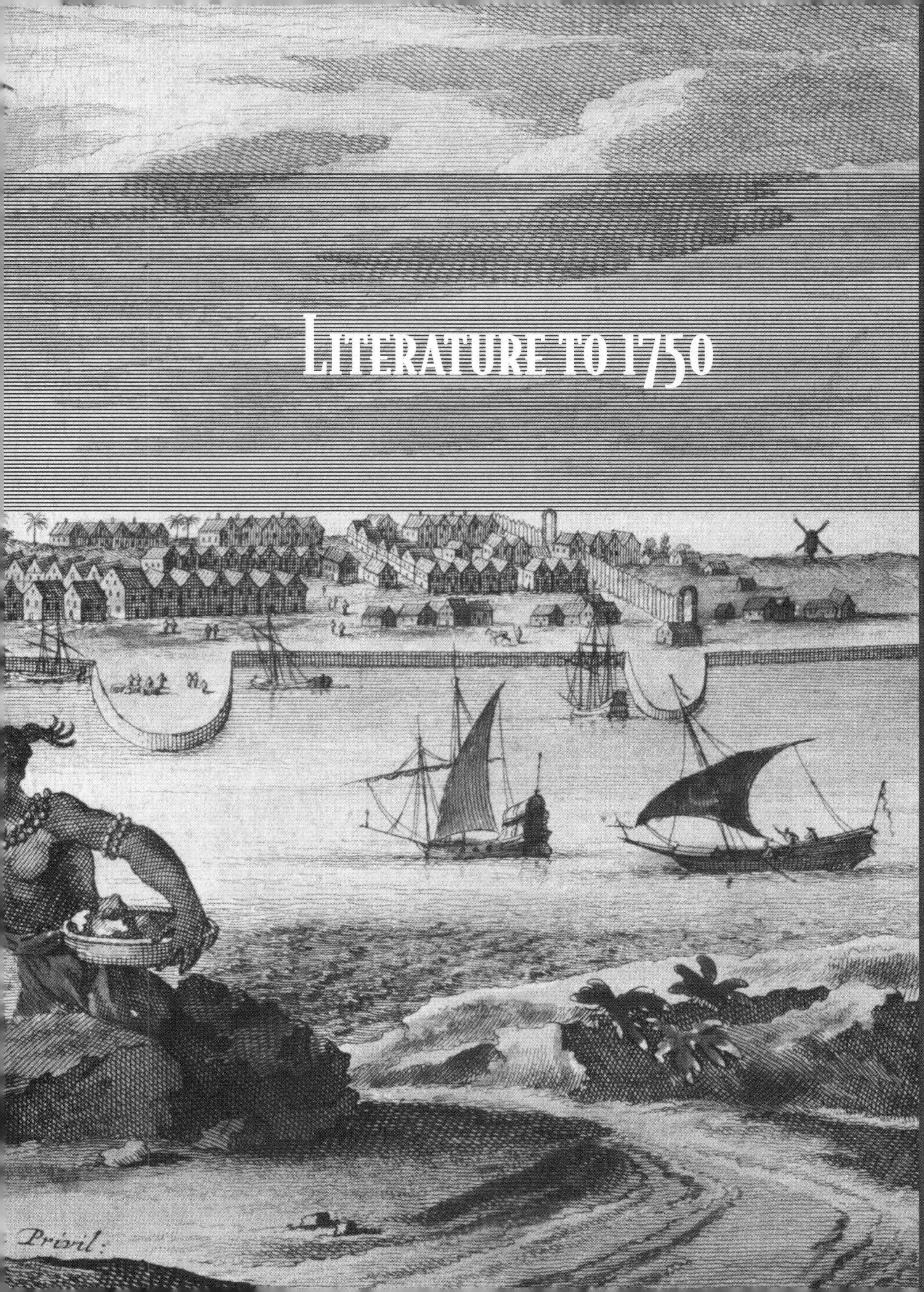

Privil:

ᴇARLY IN 1493, less than fifty years after the invention of the printing press by Johannes Gutenberg in Germany, an untitled letter addressed to Luis de Santángel, secretary of the royal court of Spain, was published in Barcelona. Written in Spanish by an Italian navigator Christopher Columbus, the letter was soon translated into Latin and other languages and disseminated throughout Europe. By the end of 1493, eleven editions of the letter had been printed, making it one of the early "bestsellers" in European publishing. The popularity of the letter is understandable since it was the first public account of the discoveries Columbus had made during his voyage in 1492, from Spain westward to what he called "the Indies." Although he was clearly disappointed that he had not reached his ultimate goal, the fabled province of Cathay on the mainland of Asia, Columbus excitedly described the lands he had touched upon and immediately claimed for the sponsors of his expedition, King Ferdinand and Queen Isabel of Spain: "There I found very many islands, filled with people innumerable, and of them all I have taken possession for their highnesses, by proclamation and with the royal standard unfurled, and no opposition was offered to me."

Those "people innumerable" were the Arawak, some of whom — the Taino — were the indigenous inhabitants of what are now the Bahamas, Cuba, and Hispaniola (Haiti and the Dominican Republic). Thinking he had reached the East Indies, however, Columbus called the inhabitants of the islands *los indios,* "the Indians," a name that would thereafter be applied indiscriminately to all the indigenous peoples of the Western Hemisphere. Those peoples were first represented to Europe by the natives Columbus described in his letter: a simple, timid, unlettered people who went naked and lived an Eden-like existence amid the beauty and bounty of the islands. For Columbus, those people were part of the bounty of the islands, at once a source of potential converts to Christianity and a boundless source of slaves.

◀ (Oᴠᴇʀʟᴇᴀғ)

New Amsterdam, or New York in America

This engraving was published around 1700, less than a century after Henry Hudson and the small crew of the Dutch exploration ship *Half Moon* sighted in 1609 what is now Manhattan Island at the mouth of the river that came to bear his name. The Dutch subsequently established a colonial settlement at the southern tip of the island, New Amsterdam, which in 1664 the English captured and renamed New York, after the Duke of York. Long before the arrival of the Europeans, however, the island had been inhabited by the Lenape Indians, who called it *Mannahatta,* or "island of many hills." Despite the prominence of Native Americans in the foreground of this fanciful scene, the Lenape population had been dramatically reduced by disease, starvation, and migration during the seventeenth century. During the same period, New York had grown into a major trading port. As indicated in this picture by the number of ships in its harbor and the expanding city in the distance, an island that had been covered by trees and teeming with wildlife was beginning to be transformed into one of the most densely populated areas in the world.

As he departed the first island, Columbus thus took several captives to provide information and evidence of his discoveries, an act that anticipated the carnage and devastation that Europeans following his lead would bring to the indigenous peoples of what soon came to be called "America."

America before Columbus

The early European explorers of the Americas had little sense of the long and complex history of what they conceived to be a "New World." For them, the history of North and South America effectively began in 1492. But recent discoveries in archaeology and anthropology have dramatically altered our sense of the early history of the Americas, demonstrating the existence of many long-established civilizations all across the continents. The New World was actually an ancient world, new only to the Europeans.

Many scholars now believe that the earliest inhabitants of North America began migrating from Siberia about 13,000 to 16,000 years ago, though recent archaeological finds suggest an even earlier date. As global climate changes ended the Ice Age and altered the position of glaciers in the Bering Strait, it became possible for populations to cross over from Asia to North America. Waves of migration took place, and groups of people subsequently pushed eastward to present-day Canada and southward along the Pacific coast to what are now the southwestern United States and Mexico. These earliest settlers of North America, called Paleo-Indians by anthropologists, were nomadic tribes who hunted large animals and gathered edible plants, berries, and nuts. When food supplies ran short, they moved on to new areas. Although population estimates vary, historians believe that roughly 100,000 people inhabited North America at the end of the Paleolithic era, between about 8000 and 6000 BCE.

Gradual alterations in climate and the extinction of many of the large animals caused changes in the living patterns of the human inhabitants. About five thousand years ago, they began to live in larger territorial groups and learned to cultivate crops for food. These Archaic Indians, as they are now usually called by anthropologists, probably grew to a population of about one million people, dispersed across the continent. As they adapted to their local environments, they began to develop distinct languages, rituals, stories, kinship systems, and trade networks. By 1500 BCE, agriculture was becoming established in the Americas. Maize or Indian corn was a staple, and two other important crops, squash and beans, were grown in abundance. As the native populations continued to expand across North and South America, the age of the Archaic Indian gave way to new phases in the history of the indigenous peoples. In North America, the sophisticated Mayan civilization flourished in Mexico while the Hohokam and Anasazi cultures emerged with highly developed towns and irrigation systems in the American Southwest. In the center of the continent, the Mississippi River valley became a densely settled area of towns and villages. In the Northeast and Southeast, an extensive network of native tribes lived in villages near rivers, lakes, and the ocean, where they could fish and hunt. By the time of Columbus's first voyage in 1492, the North and South American continents were populated by approximately 50 million people, an estimated five million of whom lived in what is today the continental United States.

From its earliest history, the complex society that developed in North America was multilingual and culturally diverse. The population was divided into roughly three hundred distinct cultural groups. Those groups spoke about two hundred languages, plus many different dialects of those languages, and embraced a wide variety of customs and systems of belief. They also developed distinctive cultural traditions, creating masterpieces of arts and crafts in a wide range of media, including stone, ceramics, wood, shell, and copper. Some groups employed petroglyphs and pictographs, images carved in or painted on rock, while others developed different methods of recording important historical and political events, exemplified by the wampum belts of the Iroquois Confederacy. In the absence of written languages, however, a crucial means of cultural transmission was the spoken word, as tribal customs, history, and traditions were passed down generation to generation through poems, songs, and stories. At the same time, cultural differences and competition among the various groups frequently led to violent clashes and tribal wars. Larger villages also dealt with a variety of internal problems. These included the environmental challenges of overcultivation of the land, overhunting, and waste disposal, as well as social issues, such as the maintenance of law and order. Indeed, the native populations that the earliest European explorers variously viewed as primitive, savage, or simple were actually composed of widely varying groups of people dealing with complex problems.

Christianity, Islam, and the Lure of Asia

European exploration of that world did not begin in earnest until the end of the fifteenth century. Much earlier, around 1000, the Vikings made a series of exploratory voyages from their colony in Greenland. Traveling in their longboats to the eastern shore of Canada, the Vikings apparently undertook fairly extensive explorations but made no significant effort to establish permanent colonies. During the following centuries, much of the attention of Europe was focused on the Middle East and Asia, not on the unknown continents to the west. Those centuries were marked by a growing struggle for global domination and control among competing cultures, especially between the Christian countries of Europe and the Islamic nations of Africa and the Middle East. Islam had become the most dynamic and powerful culture in the world, united by a common language, Arabic, and Islamic nations far outstripped Europe in technology, science, and

ARCTIC OCEAN
INUIT
ALEUT
INUIT
INUIT (ESKIMO)
DENE
TLINGIT
DOGRIB
HAIDA
TSIMSHIAN
CHIPEWYAN
INUIT
NASKAPI
CREE
MONTAGNAIS
BEOTHUK
BLACKFOOT
SALISH
NOOTKA
KOOTENAI
ASSINIBOINE
CREE
ALGONKIN
MICMAC
CROW
OJIBWA (CHIPPEWA)
ABENAKI
NEZ PERCE
PASSAMAQUODDY
CHEYENNE
LAKOTA (SIOUX)
IROQUOIS
HUPA
PAIUTE
PAWNEE
SAUK
HURON
NARRAGANSETT
POMO
SHOSHONE
IOWA
POTAWATOMI
SUSQUEHANNOCK
PEQUOT
DELAWARE
ARAPAHO
ILLINOIS
POWHATAN
UTE
SHAWNEE
TUSCARORA
YOKUT
NAVAJO
KIOWA
CHEROKEE
ATLANTIC OCEAN
HOPI
CHICKASAW
APACHE
COMANCHE
CREEK
PAPAGO/PIMA
CHOCTAW
COCHIMI
COAHUILTEC
CALUSA
LUCAYO
SEMINOLE
ZACATEC
Gulf of Mexico
CIBONEY
SUB-TAINO
TAINO
PACIFIC OCEAN
TOLTEC
NAHUATL (AZTEC)
MIXTEC
MAYA
Caribbean Sea
ZAPOTEC
MISKITO
CUNA

Native American Peoples, 1492

At the time of Columbus's first voyage in 1492, the entire Western Hemisphere was populated by diverse groups of Native Americans. This map illustrates the approximate locations of some of the larger groups in North and Central America. The linguistic and cultural diversity of Native American peoples, as well as local conflicts among different tribes, made it difficult to organize united resistance to European invaders.

warfare. By the twelfth century, Islam dominated the Iberian Peninsula, comprising Spain and Portugal, all of North Africa, and much of what was known as Asia Minor. Between the eleventh and fourteenth centuries, Europe undertook a series of religious crusades in an effort to oust Muslims from the Holy Land, but those wars ended in failure. In the thirteenth century, the Mongol Empire, under the leadership of Genghis Khan, conquered much of China and pressed into both Europe and the Islamic world. In the fourteenth century, a powerful group of Muslims, the Ottoman Turks, fought back against the Mongols and came to dominate the crucial trade routes to Asia in the eastern Mediterranean. As a consequence, Muslim merchants along those trade routes made lucrative profits and swelled their own economies at the expense of Europe.

For Europeans, the allure of Asia was intensified by a type of travel writing known as the "Wonders of the East." That genre included two of the most popular books of the Middle Ages: *The Travels of Marco Polo*, written at the end of the thirteenth century, and *Mandeville's Travels*, also known as *The*

Cliff Dwellings

Several ancient Pueblo peoples often collectively called the *Anasazi*—the Navajo word for "the Old Ones"—flourished in the high country of what is now known as the "Four Corners," where the states of Utah, Arizona, New Mexico, and Arizona meet. In a survey of the area in the early 1870s, Timothy Sullivan took this photograph of Anasazi ruins called the "White House," dwellings built in a niche fifty feet above the floor of the Canyon de Chelly in Arizona.

Book of Sir John Mandeville, written in the middle of the fourteenth century. There was apparently no such person as "Sir John Mandeville," and the account was equally fictitious. But it was evidently accepted as a factual narrative by most medieval readers, who were treated to descriptions of wonders like the riches of the great khan of Cathay, whose palace, "the most passing fair in all the world," was graced by "twenty-four pillars of gold" and whose throne "was all wrought of gold and of precious stones and great pearls." Marco Polo described similar splendors in his account of his journey along what was later called the "Silk Road," actually a series of overland trade routes from Turkey to China, and the seventeen years he claimed to have spent in the kingdom of Kublai Khan. Although his book was widely known as *Il Milione*, shorthand for "The Million Lies," it captured the imagination of Europeans. Manuscript editions in various languages ran into the hundreds, and the book became a bestseller when a printed edition appeared late in the fifteenth century, after the invention of the printing press in 1450.

At the same time that they were being dazzled by the *Travels* of Mandeville and Marco Polo, Europeans were paying exorbitant prices for silks, spices, gold, and ivory from Asia. Since the Turks continued to dominate the overland trade routes, European nations increasingly turned west in an effort to gain easier access to the riches of the East. For many Christians in

Niccolò and Maffeo Polo with Caravan
In his famous journey to the Far East in 1271, the Venetian merchant and writer Marco Polo joined his father (Niccolò) and his uncle (Maffeo), who in this illustration from a Catalonian map are shown traveling in a caravan on the overland trade route to China.

Europe, especially in Spain and Portugal, the desire to discover sea routes to the East and thus to overcome the commercial advantages enjoyed by Muslims was heightened by centuries of fighting for control of the Iberian Peninsula. In fact, *conquistadores*, or "conquerors," the term used to refer to the Spanish explorers and soldiers on expeditions to the Americas, was derived from *reconquista*, the effort to reconquer the Iberian Peninsula from the Muslim Moors from North Africa. Significantly, after almost six centuries of conflict, the Spanish Christians finally expelled the Moors in 1492, the year Columbus made his first voyage across the Atlantic.

Conquest and Colonization in the New World

Columbus's voyages were part of a broader European movement, especially by Portugal and Spain, to explore and exploit new territories. Portuguese navigators were among the first to use advances in maritime technology in order to undertake increasingly extended voyages. Bartholomeu Dias (1450-1500) rounded the tip of Africa in 1487, and Vasco da Gama (1469-1524) sailed around the Cape of Good Hope to India in 1497. While the Portuguese generally pursued southern and eastern routes, especially along the African coast, the Spanish began to push west across the Atlantic. During his four voyages from 1492 to 1504, Columbus landed on most of the major islands of the Caribbean, as well as parts of the coasts of South and Central America. He continued to believe that he had reached Asia, but Columbus recognized that the lands he encountered constituted a "New World" to Europeans. Although many of those places were densely populated by peoples with their own languages and names, Columbus renamed the inhabitants and their lands, in effect claiming both for Spain. When he landed on the first of the islands that he encountered during his first voyage in 1492, an island its Taino inhabitants called *Guanahani*, Columbus renamed it *San Salvador*, in turn naming the other islands he landed upon *Santa María de la Concepción, Fernandina, Isabella, Juana* (after Prince Don Juan, son of King Ferdinand and Queen Isabel), and finally *Española*, derived from *España*, or "Spain."

Ironically, given his zeal for naming, the lands Columbus discovered were later named for another Italian navigator working for Spain, Amerigo Vespucci (1451-1512). A merchant in Seville who sold pickles, which were eaten by mariners to prevent scurvy during extended voyages, Vespucci claimed to have made as many as five trips to the northern parts of the New World beginning in 1497. Although it is not clear that he ever set foot in North America, accounts of Vespucci's voyages were published in *Cosmographiae Introductio* (1507), a manual of geography by the German cartographer Martin Waldseemüller. Believing that Amerigo Vespucci was the discoverer of the previously unknown landmass between Europe and Asia, Waldseemüller called it "America," which swiftly became the popular name for the New World. During the following centuries, questions about the suitability of that name persisted, especially in what came to be called the United States of America, which many believed should have been named *Columbia* in honor of Columbus. In his book *English Traits* (1856), Ralph Waldo Emerson emphasized the incongruity of the fact that "broad America must wear the name of a thief," Amerigo Vespucci, "the pickle-dealer at Seville, who . . . managed in this lying world to supplant Columbus, and baptize half the earth with his own dishonest name."

Although Columbus's name was not applied to the lands he explored, his initial voyages led to Spain's domination over much of the New World. The brutal process of conquest and colonization initiated in the islands of the Caribbean swiftly spread to large portions of the Americas. Within forty years of Columbus's first voyage, Hernán Cortés (1485-1547) had conquered the Aztec and Mayan Empires of Mexico and Central America, while Francisco Pizarro (1475-1541) had conquered the Inca of Peru.

The New World

The first document known to name America was Martin Waldseemüller's famous map of the world, published in 1507. In an inset from the map, the Italian navigator Amerigo Vespucci is shown with some navigational instruments beside the continent he claimed to be a New World, "because none of those countries were known to our ancestors."

Inspired by reports of gold and other riches in areas to the north, Hernando de Soto (c. 1496–1542) and Francisco Vásquez de Coronado (c. 1510–1554) explored and claimed lands from Florida all across the southern parts of the present United States. By the middle of the sixteenth century, the Spanish had gained an extensive and fabulously rich empire, won at an enormous cost to the indigenous inhabitants of the Americas. Through the encounter with diseases for which it had no immunity, as well as by large-scale enslavement or slaughter, the native population decreased dramatically, leaving in some places only a handful of survivors of tribes whose history, names, and ancient cultures had been virtually erased.

*"And it is a great sorrow and
heartbreak to see this coastal
land which was so flourishing, now a depopulated
desert."*

Within a few years of Columbus's landing on Hispaniola, for example, its enslaved Taino population had declined so precipitously that the Spaniards began to import slaves, first from other islands and then from Africa.

The brutality of Spanish policies was exposed and publicized by a Dominican missionary, Bartolomé de Las Casas. Initially, he sought reform through oral arguments and letters to Holy Roman Emperor Charles V of Spain. Determined to exploit the power of the printed word, however, Las Casas ignored the requirement that he receive royal permission to publish a powerful exposé of Spanish policies, *The Brief Relation of the Devastation of the Indies* (1552). In that horrifying account of the atrocities committed by the Spanish, Las Casas observed that nearly two million people had been taken captive and brought from other islands to work as slaves in the gold mines of Hispaniola and San Juan (now Puerto Rico), adding, "And it is a great sorrow and heartbreak to see this coastal land which was so flourishing, now a depopulated desert." Translated into French in 1579 and into English in 1583, Las Casas's account caused a sensation throughout Europe. It also helped give rise to what came to be called the "Black Legend," the stereotype of helpless and innocent natives slaughtered by cruel and bloodthirsty Spaniards. Indeed,

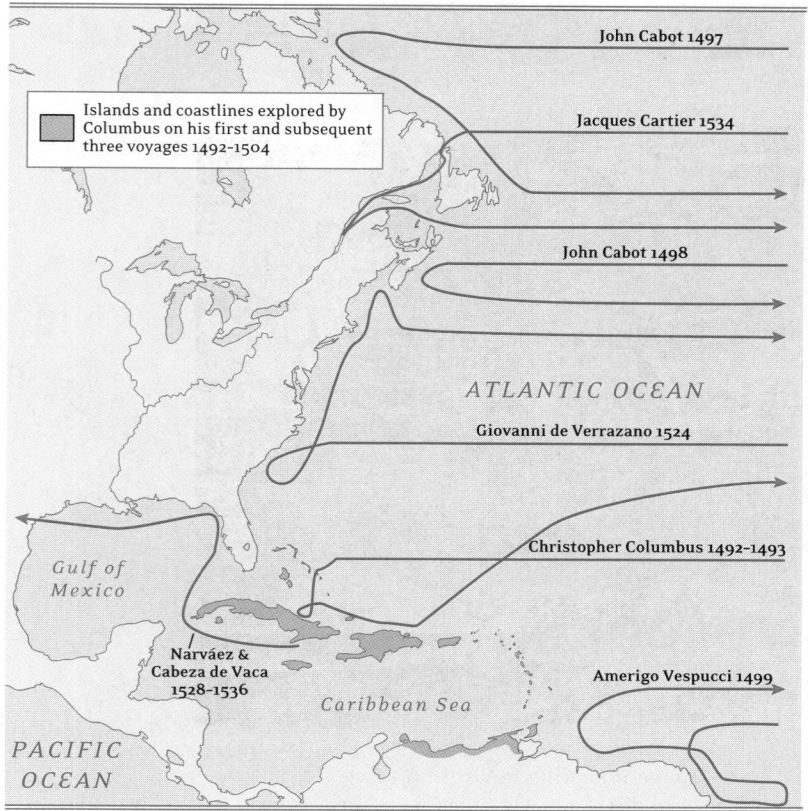

Islands and coastlines explored by Columbus on his first and subsequent three voyages 1492–1504

John Cabot 1497

Jacques Cartier 1534

John Cabot 1498

ATLANTIC OCEAN

Giovanni de Verrazano 1524

Christopher Columbus 1492–1493

Gulf of Mexico

Narváez & Cabeza de Vaca 1528–1536

Caribbean Sea

Amerigo Vespucci 1499

PACIFIC OCEAN

Early European Explorations

This map illustrates the approximate routes of some of the early European explorations of the Americas, as countries like France and England followed Spain in the effort to claim and conquer an empire in the New World.

both the French and English later seized upon the account to justify their efforts to supplant Spain in the Americas.

Inspired by Spanish gains there, other European countries began to explore the Americas in the ongoing effort to find new and shorter trade routes to Asia. When he learned of Columbus's success, John Cabot (born Giovanni Caboto in Italy about 1451) went to England and received a grant for a voyage from King Henry VII. Believing that shorter routes to Asia were possible by taking a more northerly direction, Cabot crossed the Atlantic twice, in 1497 and 1498, eventually exploring the coastline from Newfoundland and Labrador as far south as the Chesapeake Bay. The English discontinued their explorations after Cabot failed to find what was called a "Northwest Passage" to Asia, but the French continued the quest for such a northern sea route to the Pacific Ocean. Jacques Cartier (1491–1557) made three voyages to present-day Canada in 1534, 1535, and 1541. He was later followed by Samuel de Champlain (c. 1567–1635), who sailed up the St. Lawrence River in 1603. On subsequent

"Their Manner of Fishing in Virginia"
This richly detailed engraving, which appeared in Thomas Hariot's *A Briefe and True Report of the New Found Land of Virginia* (1588), was based on observations Hariot made as the scientific adviser for an expedition to Roanoke Island off the coast of present-day North Carolina in 1585.

voyages in search of the elusive Northwest Passage, Champlain charted much of Nova Scotia and present-day Massachusetts and Rhode Island. He also established French settlements, including a trading post on the St. Lawrence River—Quebec—one of the first European settlements whose name was derived from a Native American word, the Algonkian term *Kebec*, meaning "where the river narrows." Champlain fully recognized the potential wealth to be gained through the fur trade with the Indians, and the publication of his accounts of voyages and discoveries spurred French interest in establishing the colony of New France.

Meanwhile, the English once again began to turn their attention to the New World, this time with an eye to establishing settlements in America. In part, they sought to check Spanish power there, especially during the Anglo-Spanish War (1585–1604). Even before the formal outbreak of hostilities, the English navigator Sir Francis Drake (1540?-1596) had circumnavigated the globe in 1577-80, plundering Spanish ships and settlements in the Americas. The destruction of the Spanish Armada in 1588 led to the ascendancy of English sea power, fueling the country's desire for an empire in the New World. That desire was also heightened by the printing and popularity of accounts of the explorations of that world, for example Richard Hakluyt's *Divers Voyages Touching the Discoverie of America and the Ilands Adjacent unto the Same* (1582). In what is now usually called *Discourse Concerning Western Planting*, written two years later, Hakluyt outlined a new approach to colonization, proposing that the poor and discontented in the mother country should be resettled in new lands in North America, where they could gather and export the raw materials that would sustain the growing manufacturing capability of England. Under the direction of Sir Walter Raleigh, the English in 1585 attempted to establish a colony in Virginia, an area named after their "virgin" queen Elizabeth I. The colony at Roanoke Island, off the coast of present-day North Carolina, was abandoned after only ten months, and a second group of more than one hundred settlers who arrived there in 1587 disappeared, leaving hardly a trace and giving rise to the mystery of the so-called Lost Colony.

Despite the disastrous end of the colony at Roanoke Island, the English pursued their efforts to explore and colonize North America. Its beauty and seemingly limitless potential were promoted by the English historian and naturalist Thomas Hariot in his *A Briefe and True Report of the New Found Land of Virginia* (1588), which is generally considered to be the first original book about North America published in English. After cataloging the animals, plants, and other natural resources that had been discovered in the relatively small area that he and others had explored during their stay at Roanoke Island in 1585, Hariot asked, "Why may wee not then looke for in good hope from the inner parts of more and greater plentie, as well as of other things, as of those which wee have alreadie discovered?" In 1607, the English finally established a permanent colony in Virginia, Jamestown, named after Queen Elizabeth's successor, King James I. A key figure in the early survival of the colony, which was undermined by organizational problems, rampant disease, and conflicts with the tribes of the Powhatan Confederacy, was Captain John Smith. An adventurer, explorer, and a professional soldier, Smith was also a brilliant publicist who tirelessly promoted colonization in widely distributed works like *A Map of Virginia: With a Description of the Countrey* (1612). He also explored and named an area that became the next dramatic stage for English colonization, which Smith urged in yet another of his best-selling works, *A Description of New England* (1616).

> *"Why may wee not then looke for in good hope from the inner parts of more and greater plentie, as well as of other things, as of those which wee have alreadie discovered?"*

The Protestant Reformation
and the Puritan "Errand into the Wilderness"

In addition to commercial interests and the nationalistic desire to dispossess the Spanish, English colonization was driven by religious forces unleashed by the Protestant Reformation. Throughout the Middle Ages, Roman Catholicism was the sole Christian religion of Europe. During the early Renaissance, however, advancements in science and technology, the rise of the middle class, and an increasingly literate population brought significant challenges to the power and authority of the Catholic Church. In the view of growing numbers of people, the church, with its extensive hierarchy and vast wealth, had moved away from the simplicity and spirituality of the religion practiced by Christ and his disciples. Efforts to reform the church began as early as the 1380s. A central figure of that movement in England was John Wycliffe, who has been described as the "Morning Star of the Reformation." The official Bible of the Catholic Church was the Latin Vulgate (meaning common or vulgar tongue), a fourth-century translation by St. Jerome. Over the centuries, however, Latin became the language of the highly educated; common people could not understand church liturgy or read the Bible. Strongly believing that all Christians should be able to read the Bible, Wycliffe translated it from Latin into English and recruited itinerant preachers, called Lollards, to spread the scriptures in English.

Although the movement he inspired was short-lived, Wycliffe anticipated the efforts of later reformers, who also emphasized the importance of individual reading and interpretation of the Bible. Their efforts to make it available in translation to large numbers of people were powerfully aided by the development of the printing press. Martin Luther, the leader of the Protestant Reformation in Germany, hurried his translation of the New Testament through the press in 1522 and then published parts of the Old Testament as he completed them, finally printing the whole Bible in 1534. After seizing control of the holdings of the Catholic Church and establishing the Church of England, Henry VIII ordered the preparation and publication of the Great Bible (1537), the first authorized Bible in English. The Reformation in England was briefly checked when the Catholic queen, Mary Tudor, ascended the throne in 1553. The widespread religious persecutions during her five-year reign drove many Protestant clergymen to Geneva, Switzerland, where with the support of the radical reformers John Calvin and John Knox the English exiles produced the Geneva Bible (1560). The first Bible in English to add numbers to chapters and verses for easy reference, as well as interpretive marginal notes, the Geneva Bible was so popular that nearly 150 editions were published between 1560 and 1644.

During those decades, Protestantism became firmly established in England. But more radical religious reformers faced growing pressure to conform to the practices and teachings of the Church of England. Elizabeth I, who assumed the throne after the death of Queen Mary in 1558, had little sympathy for the "Puritans," those who sought further to "purify" the Church of England of the vestiges of Roman Catholicism. Her successor, James I, who ruled England from 1603 to 1625, was even more disdainful of the Puritans. In an effort to supplant the strongly anti-Catholic Geneva Bible, the favored Bible of the Puritans, James sponsored a new translation, the King James Version, which became the official Bible of the Church of England. Most Puritans remained committed to the established church, which they sought to reform from within. Others formally separated themselves from the Church of England. Following the model established by John Calvin in Geneva, such "Separatists" formed independent churches, each based on a formal covenant, or binding agreement, freely entered into by all members of the church. That drastic step was seen as an act of treason, and King James described a Separatist as "a rat to be trapped and tossed away."

Geneva Bible

The title page from the 1560 edition of the Geneva Bible depicts the Egyptians pursuing the Hebrews as they near the Red Sea. This Bible was used by both the Pilgrims and the Puritans, who conceived of themselves as the new Israelites journeying out of spiritual bondage to a promised land.

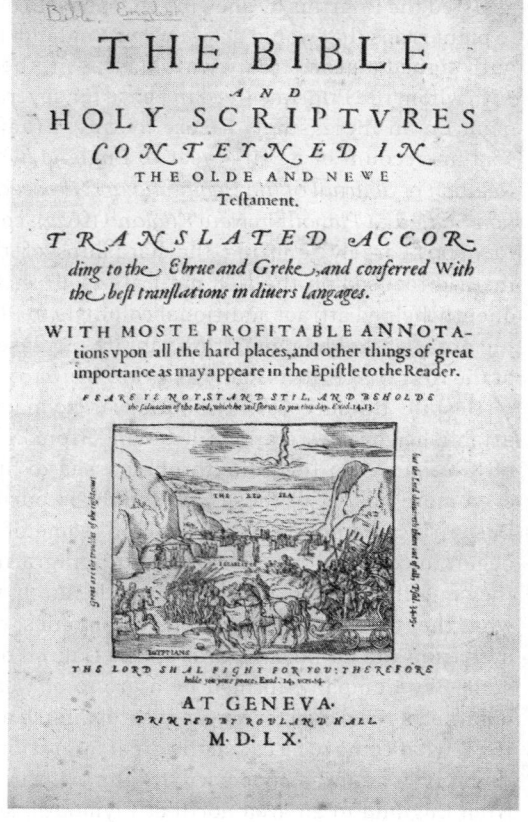

Facing growing persecution in England, a small group of Separatists that called themselves "Pilgrims" fled the country in 1608.

After living in the Netherlands for more than a decade, the Pilgrims sailed to New England on the *Mayflower* in 1620. In a moving description of their arrival on the shores of Cape Cod in November, William Bradford in his history *Of Plimoth Plantation* declared, "Besides, what could they see but a hidious & desolate wildernes, full of wild beasts & wild men." But the survival of the Pilgrims would be due in large part to the aid and security provided by those "wild men." The Pilgrims established their colony on the south shore of Massachusetts Bay, on the grounds of what they thought was an abandoned Indian village but was actually the summer home of a local tribe, the Wampanoag. After a difficult winter, during which about half of the ninety-nine "first comers" who had arrived at Plymouth aboard the *Mayflower* died of disease and malnutrition, the forlorn Pilgrims were visited by Squanto. A Patuxet Indian who had been captured as a young man and taken to England, where he learned to speak English, Squanto assisted the Pilgrims by showing them how to hunt and fish as well as how to plant crops that would grow in New England. In 1621, the colony at Plymouth signed a peace treaty with Massasoit, the chief of the Wampanoag, with whom the Pilgrims lived in peace for several decades. With the settlement on an increasingly secure footing, Bradford and Edward Winslow sent an account of its first year to England, where it was published as *A Relation or Journal of the Beginning and Proceedings of the English Plantation Settled at Plimoth in New England* (1622), commonly known as *Mourt's Relation.* Largely ignoring the hardships of the first winter, the book instead focused on the rich natural resources of New England. It consequently helped attract additional colonists to Plymouth and the surrounding area, where the population rapidly increased from the fifty survivors of the first winter to as many as 3,000 by 1640.

> "Besides, what could they see but a hidious & desolate wildernes, full of wild beasts & wild men."

Despite its success, Plymouth was soon overshadowed by a colony established by new religious dissidents from England. Following the death of King James in 1625, the throne passed to his son, Charles I, who was even more hostile to those who sought to purify the Church of England. Despairing of conditions in England, some of the beleaguered Puritans began to consider the possibility of immigrating to New England, where they might establish a truly reformed church, without the hierarchy and what they viewed as the noxious ceremonies, rituals, and trappings held over from the Catholic Church in the Church of England. The Massachusetts Bay Company, formed by a group of wealthy Puritans in London, obtained a royal charter, or grant, to establish a colony in New England. In 1630, what came to be called the great migration began, as a group of more than seven hundred people led by John Winthrop sailed on a fleet of ships from England to an area north of Plymouth, around present-day Boston.

Unlike the Pilgrims, who were forced by circumstances to leave first England and then Holland, the Puritans embarked on what the minister Samuel Danforth later described as an "errand into the wilderness," a journey as fraught with significance as the analogous journey of the ancient Israelites out of bondage in Egypt to the promised land. Indeed, the Puritans viewed themselves as God's new chosen people, whose holy task was to establish a church and community based strictly on the revealed word of God in the Bible. As many historians have emphasized, however, the Puritans were also strongly entrepreneurial and eager to capitalize on the plentiful land and rich opportunities available in the New World. Although the early years of the Massachusetts Bay Colony were difficult, the settlements grew and expanded from the coastal regions into the interior of New England. Over time, additional colonies were established, including new ones in present-day Rhode Island, Connecticut, and New Hampshire. By 1660, some 33,000 colonists were living in New England.

The growth and expansion of the colonies generated increasing conflicts with the indigenous population. The seal of the Massachusetts Bay Colony, which depicts an Indian saying, "Come Over and Help Us," suggests that a major impulse for colonization was to bring civilization and Christianity to the native peoples of New England. But their populations were increasingly decimated by the new diseases that the colonists brought with them, as well as by the Europeans' relentless incursions into tribal lands. In 1637, in the first of the many wars fought between the English

Seal of the Massachusetts Bay Colony

Designed in 1629, the seal depicts an Indian attired only in a girdle of leaves, speaking the words "Come Over and Help Us," a plea for the gifts of civilization and Christianity. In fact, most Indians neither wanted nor needed the help of the English settlers, who finally drove all but a few remnants of the native tribes out of New England.

settlers in New England and an Indian people, a military force from the Massachusetts Bay Colony attacked and burned a Pequot fort in what is now southeastern Connecticut. Between four hundred and seven hundred men, women, and children were killed, and most of the surviving Pequot were captured and divided as slaves or tributaries among the English and their Indian allies, the Mohegan and Narragansett. The Pequot War checked further Indian resistance in New England for nearly forty years. As disagreements about land boundaries increased and antagonism escalated, however, Massasoit's son Metacom led a coalition of tribes to war against the colonists in 1675. Called King Philip's War because the colonists considered Metacom as arrogant and proud as the hated King Philip of Spain, the war was devastating for both the colonists and the Indians. By the time it ended with Metacom's death in 1676, the war had claimed large numbers of casualties on both sides and caused the widespread destruction of property. Most crucially, in the aftermath of the war the power of the native tribes in New England was broken and the remaining native peoples were pushed farther and farther into the interior.

Literature and Cultural Diversity in Colonial America

As they expanded and solidified their hold on territory, the Puritans also established a vital literary culture in New England. Better educated than most other colonists, the Puritans and their New England neighbors were not simply people of the Bible. They also loved books of many kinds, which they imported and produced in growing profusion. Just as printing had earlier given enormous impetus to the early exploration and colonization of the Americas, as well as to the Protestant Reformation, print culture played an important role in the Puritan settlement of New England. Two years after the first printing press in the colonies was brought to Boston in 1638, the publication of what is commonly known as the *Bay Psalm Book* marked the beginning of the American printing industry. In the following decades, it produced Bibles, religious tracts and sermons, histories, and reprints of English books such as John Bunyan's *The Pilgrim's Progress*, among the most popular of all books written in English. Books written in New England also gained popularity. Anne Bradstreet's *The Tenth Muse* (1650), the first volume of poetry published by an English colonist, was printed in London. In 1678, a second edition was published in Boston, where two of the best-selling books in colonial America were also published: Michael Wigglesworth's *The Day of Doom* (1662) and Mary Rowlandson's *The Sovereignty and Goodness of God* (1682). The first printing of Wigglesworth's long narrative poem about Judgment Day sold out within a year and was reprinted dozens of times, while Rowlandson's account of her captivity among the Indians during King Philip's War was one of the most

The Bay Psalm Book

The first book printed in what became the United States was *The Whole Book of Psalmes Faithfully Translated into English Metre*, published in 1640 for use in churches in New England. The Puritans prohibited the use of musical instruments and other distractions from the holy scriptures, but congregations sang the psalms in a chorus of praise for God. Psalm 23 begins at the bottom of the left page, where its familiar opening verse is translated: "The Lord to mee a Shepheard is, / want therefore shall not I."

popular of all prose works published during the seventeenth century, especially in North America. By 1700, the publication of books and pamphlets was a growing business, serving more than 91,000 people in New England.

But the rapid growth of the New England colonies also led to the decline of Puritanism. Its original sense of mission and community was undermined by a variety of factors, including changing patterns of immigration and the growth of commerce and cities. In 1700, Boston was an increasingly diverse city of 7,000 inhabitants, surpassing all other settlements in the English colonies, and its population grew to 17,000 by 1750. Even as Puritanism began to wane, however, it produced what are widely regarded as two of the most significant writers in colonial American literature, Edward Taylor and Jonathan Edwards. During his long career as a minister, which lasted from the 1670s until his death in 1729, Taylor wrote hundreds of sermons and over four hundred manuscript pages of verse. Although he modestly declined to publish any of his work, the power of the printed word was exploited by other Puritan ministers, including Edwards. An influential preacher and theologian, Edwards was also one of the leaders of the "Great Awakening," an effort to revive the spirit of Puritanism in New England that lasted from roughly 1730 to 1750. Although that far-reaching religious revival was spread by itinerant preachers throughout the colonies, the Great Awakening is now perhaps best known through a single sermon, Edwards's "Sinners in the Hands of an Angry God," which was published soon after he delivered the sermon in 1741.

The emphasis on and pervasive influence of print culture in New England helps account for the central place Puritanism has assumed in the early history of American literature. Certainly, the achievements of Puritan writers have tended to overshadow other writings of the period before 1750. Nonetheless, a diverse array of histories, letters, poems, promotional tracts, and travel narratives were also produced throughout the colonies controlled by Great Britain. Partly because the printing business developed more slowly in the colonies outside of New England, most of the works in English published by settlers in or by visitors to the middle and southern colonies were printed in London. Many other works were circulated in manuscript form. The latter method was preferred by writers among the colonial gentry in southern colonies like Virginia, where the pattern of development differed radically from that followed in New England. Although the Jamestown Colony nearly succumbed to hardship, disease, and conflicts with the native peoples of the area, the successful introduction of tobacco and the cultivation of other crops spurred the development of a rapidly expanding system of slave labor and the emergence of a wealthy planter elite composed of men like William Byrd II. Educated in London, Byrd collected one of the largest and most diverse libraries in the colonies at Westover, his plantation on the James River. He also wrote a wide range of works, notably a remarkable private diary and *History of the Dividing Line*, an account of a survey conducted in 1728 of the disputed border between Virginia and North Carolina.

At the opening of that work, Byrd traced the overall development of the British colonies in North America, from the time when all English territory went under the "General Name of Virginia" to 1728, by which time that territory had been divided into twelve colonies extending from New Hampshire in the north as far south as the Carolinas. (The last of the original thirteen British colonies, Georgia, was founded in 1732 by the philanthropist James Oglethorpe as a penal colony for the resettlement of people confined in debtor prisons in England.) In contrast to most historians in New England, who piously celebrated the achievements of founders such as William Bradford and John Winthrop, Byrd satirically observed that when the first "adventurers" in Virginia finally established themselves at Jamestown "they built a church that cost no more than fifty pounds and a tavern that cost five hundred." Byrd, a firm supporter of the Church of England, was equally irreverent about the "swarm of dissenters" that had fled to Plymouth and the "Puritanical sect" that had founded the Massachusetts Bay Colony. At

Benjamin West, *William Penn's Treaty with the Indians* (1771)

West's famous painting was commissioned by Thomas Penn, who wanted a picture of his father founding the Province of Pennsylvania. Although there is no actual record of the elder Penn's meeting with Tamenend and other Lenape chiefs, which probably took place in 1682 or 1683, the legend of the "Great Treaty" and widely distributed prints of West's painting helped make the occasion a powerful symbol of friendship between European settlers and the Native Americans.

the same time, he acknowledged the achievements of those "frugal and industrious" settlers. Byrd also emphasized the vital role religion played in the establishment of the British colonies—not only in New England, but also in Maryland, established in 1634 by Sir George Calvert, "a zealous Catholic," and in Pennsylvania, founded in 1681 as a place of religious freedom by the English Quaker William Penn. "The Quakers flocked over to this country in shoals," Byrd sardonically observed, "being averse to go to Heaven the same way with the bishops [of the Church of England]."

As Byrd and many others recognized, the colonies were less a single, unified entity than a group of diverse, loosely associated provinces under the general dominion of the king of Great Britain. Moreover, those colonies together constituted only part of the rich and complex tapestry formed by the colonial experience in North America. At roughly the same time the Pilgrims and Puritans were establishing their colonies in New England, the Dutch established New Amsterdam on Manhattan Island in 1625, while in 1638 the settlements constituting New Sweden were founded farther south, primarily in the present state of Delaware. Those settlements ultimately came under control of the British, whose colonies also became increasingly less English as large numbers of immigrants were drawn from other European countries and growing numbers of slaves were forcibly transported to North America. By 1750, the thirteen British colonies had a population of nearly 1.2 million people, including large numbers of immigrants from Germany, Scotland, Ireland, and Holland, as well as nearly half a million enslaved people from Africa. In addition, those thirteen colonies occupied only a small portion of the continent of North America, vast areas of which were controlled by the French and the Spanish, as well as by Native American peoples. Although much of the original diversity of the world Columbus discovered had been destroyed since his first landing in the West Indies little more than 250 years earlier, North America had become a newly complex, multilingual, and culturally diverse land by 1750.

COMPARATIVE TIMELINE, 1450–1750

Dates	Literature of Exploration and Settlement	History and Politics	Developments in Culture, Science, and Technology
1450–1499		c. 1450 50 million native peoples occupy North and South American continents	c. 1450 Gutenberg invents first printing press with movable metal type
	1493 Columbus writes letter describing the results of his first voyage	1492 Columbus arrives in Americas 1497 Vasco da Gama sails around Cape of Good Hope to India	

COMPARATIVE TIMELINE, 1450–1750

Dates	Literature of Exploration and Settlement	History and Politics	Developments in Culture, Science, and Technology
1500–1549		1500 Native populations begin to be devastated by European diseases	
			1507 In *Cosmographiae Introductio*, Waldseemüller attributes discovery of "America" to Amerigo Vespucci
		1508 Henry VIII of England crowned	1508–12 Michelangelo creates his frescoes on the ceiling of Sistine Chapel
			1517 Martin Luther posts his Ninety-five Theses
		1519–21 Cortés conquers Aztecs in Mexico	
		1537 Pope Paul III orders missionaries to convert native peoples of New World to Christianity	
		1539 de Soto invades present-day Florida	1539 First printing press in Americas arrives in Mexico City
	1542 *The Narrative of Cabeza de Vaca*		1543 Copernicus argues in *On the Revolutions of the Heavenly Spheres* that the sun is center of universe
1550–1599	1552 Las Casas, *The Brief Relation of the Devastation of the Indies*	1558–1603 Protestant Elizabeth I reigns in England	
		1585 Raleigh reaches Roanoke Island, in what English called "Virginia"	
	1588 Hariot, *A Briefe and True Report of the New Found Land of Virginia*		
	1589 Hakluyt's *Navigations*	1585–1604 Anglo-Spanish War	
			1590 Compound microscope invented

COMPARATIVE TIMELINE, 1450–1750

Dates	Literature of Exploration and Settlement	History and Politics	Developments in Culture, Science, and Technology
1600–1609		**1603–13** Champlain explores St. Lawrence River and eventually founds Quebec	**1600** British East India Company founded
		1607 Jamestown established in present-day Virginia	**1603** Shakespeare's *Hamlet* first appears in print
		1609 John Smyth founds Baptist Church	**1609** Galileo demonstrates his first telescope
1610–1619	**1613** *Les Voyages du Sieur de Champlain* published in France	**1614** Pocahontas marries John Rolfe	**1611** King James Bible published in England
		1616–19 "Great Dying" — believed to be a combination of the plague, smallpox, cholera, measles, hepatitis, and whooping cough transmitted by Europeans — decimates Native American population	
		1619 Virginia's House of Burgesses, first European representative body in Americas, convenes	
1620–1629		**1620** *Mayflower* reaches Plymouth in present-day Massachusetts	
	1622 Bradford and Winslow's *Mourt's Relation*		**1621** First Thanksgiving celebrated at Plymouth
	1624 John Smith, *Generall Historie of Virginia, New-England, and the Summer Isles*		
			1625 Bacon, *Complete Essays*

COMPARATIVE TIMELINE, 1450–1750

Dates	Literature of Exploration and Settlement	History and Politics	Developments in Culture, Science, and Technology
1630–1639	**1630** Winthrop delivers address "A Modell of Christian Charity"; Bradford begins writing *Of Plimoth Plantation*	**1630** Great migration begins; American colonial population: 4,600 **1634** Settlers arrive in Maryland, led by Lord Baltimore **1636** After being banned from Massachusetts Bay Colony as a dissident, Roger Williams founds Rhode Island **1637** Pequot War	**1638** First printing press in colonial America arrives in Boston
1640–1649	**1640** *Bay Psalm Book*	**1640** American colonial population: 26,600 **1642** Civil war breaks out in England	**1642** Puritans close all theaters in England **1644** Descartes, *Principles of Philosophy*
1650–1659	**1650** Bradstreet, *The Tenth Muse*	**1650** American colonial population: 50,400 **1653** Oliver Cromwell becomes Lord Protector of England	
1660–1669	**1662** Wigglesworth, *The Day of Doom*	**1660** American colonial population: 75,100 **1661** Charles II restored to throne of England	**1662** Church of England publishes new edition of *Book of Common Prayer* **1663** John Eliot publishes an Algonkian translation of the Bible

COMPARATIVE TIMELINE, 1450–1750

Dates	Literature of Exploration and Settlement	History and Politics	Developments in Culture, Science, and Technology
1660–1669 (cont.)		1664 Colony of New Jersey founded 1664–65 "Great Plague" sweeps England	1665 Newton develops law of universal gravitation 1667 Milton, *Paradise Lost*
1670–1679	1673 Sewall begins writing *Diary*	1670 American colonial population: 111,900 1675–76 King Philip's War	1678 Bunyan, *The Pilgrim's Progress*
1680–1689	1682 Rowlandson, *The Sovereignty and Goodness of God* 1682–1725 Edward Taylor writes *Preparatory Meditations*	1680 American colonial population: 151,500 1681 Pennsylvania founded by William Penn 1685 James Stuart becomes King James II of England 1689 At end of Glorious Revolution, William and Mary are proclaimed rulers of England, Scotland, and Ireland	1687 Newton publishes his law of gravity
1690–1699	c. 1690 *New England Primer*	1690 American colonial population: 210,400 1692 Salem witch trials	1690 Locke, *Two Treatises of Civil Government*
1700–1709	1700 Pastorius, *Circumstantial Geographical Description of the Lately Discovered Province of Pennsylvania*	1700 American colonial population: 250,900	

COMPARATIVE TIMELINE, 1450–1750

Dates	Literature of Exploration and Settlement	History and Politics	Developments in Culture, Science, and Technology
1700–1709 (cont.)	**1702** Mather, *Magnalia Christi Americana* **1704–05** Sarah Kemble Knight travels from Boston to New York **1709–12** Byrd writes diary of daily life in Virginia	**1702** Anne Stuart takes throne of England, Scotland, and Ireland **1707** Act of Union establishes Great Britain from separate kingdoms of England, Scotland, and Ireland	**1701** Pylarini gives first small-pox inoculations **1709** First pianoforte built in Florence
1710–1719		**1710** American colonial population: 331,700 **1718** New Orleans founded by French	**1719** Defoe, *Robinson Crusoe*
1720–1729	**1728** Byrd, *History of the Dividing Line*	**1720** American colonial population: 466,200	**1721** Bach composes *Brandenburg* Concertos **1726** Swift, *Gulliver's Travels*
1730–1739		**1730** American colonial population: 629,400 **1732** James Oglethorpe obtains charter for Georgia	**1730–50** First Great Awakening **1739** Hume, *A Treatise of Human Nature*
1740–1750	**c. 1740** Jonathan Edwards writes *Personal Narrative* **1741** Jonathan Edwards, "Sinners in the Hands of an Angry God" SINNERS In the Hands of an Angry GOD.	**1740** American colonial population: 905,600 **1741** Bering explores Alaska	**1741** *American Magazine* founded by Andrew Bradford **1742** First performance of Handel's *Messiah* **1744** Benjamin Franklin publishes first novel in colonial America, Samuel Richardson's *Pamela*

Native American Origin and Creation Stories

THE ORAL LITERATURE OF Native Americans includes poems, songs, and stories, many of which existed centuries before the arrival of the earliest European explorers in the late-fifteenth and sixteenth centuries. Although the Europeans could not comprehend it, the Native American societies they encountered had long, dynamic, and complex histories. There were multiple civilizations in existence throughout the Americas. Even the more limited boundaries of what is today the continental United States

◄ Secotan Village

This engraving by Theodor de Bry was copied from a drawing by John White, an English artist who visited the village of Secotan on the coast of present-day North Carolina in 1585. White notes on the original that the building marked *A* at the lower left was a tomb where the bodies of important leaders were kept, while the fire burning at *B* was "the place of solemn prayer." In addition to the dwellings lining the central space, where men and women ate, the drawing illustrates the careful management and use of land. Men hunt deer on the outskirts of the village, whose crops include tobacco, pumpkins, and sunflowers, as well as corn in three stages of growth. White's idealized drawing depicts a world of natural abundance and social harmony, religion and peace, a world that would soon be disrupted by invaders from England.

contained enormous diversity. Native American peoples ranged from the Iroquois Confederacy of tribes in the Northeast to the Cherokee in the Southeast, from the Akimel O'odham (Pima) in the Southwest to ancient tribes like the Hupa on the West coast and several groups that came to be called the Sioux in the upper Mississippi valley and on the Great Plains. Native American peoples were divided among many tribes and bands, spoke literally hundreds of mutually unintelligible languages, and lived under a wide variety of political and social organizations. Some subsisted by hunting, fishing, and gathering nuts, seeds, and berries, while many others were farmers living in villages and towns, especially in the Northeast and Southeast. Still others lived in urban centers in the middle of the continent, where the great Mississippian culture lasted for nearly nine hundred years, as well as in the Southwest, where many tribes built complex cities and developed extensive irrigation systems for their crops.

Native American peoples were also culturally diverse in ways that were difficult for European explorers to understand or value. In contrast to Christianized Europe, a wide variety of religious and mythological beliefs flourished throughout the Americas. Although there were no written languages that Europeans could fully comprehend, Native Americans had developed various forms of writing, including Incan *quipus* (knotted cords), Mayan hieroglyphics, and the wampum belts used by the Iroquois.

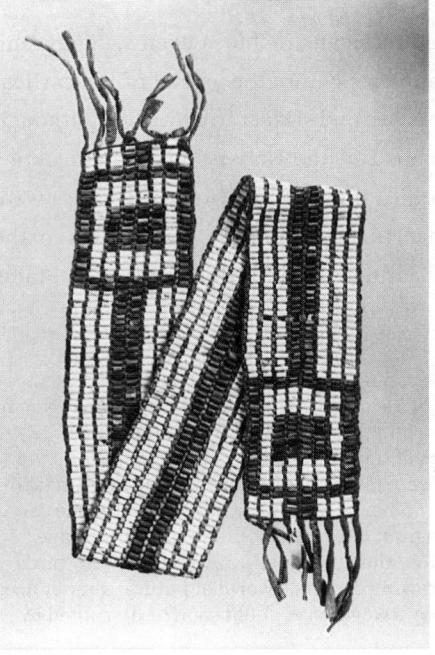

Iroquois Wampum Belt

Wampum belts, made of beads acquired through trade with coastal tribes in the Northeast, were used by the Iroquois to commemorate events, record beliefs, and seal agreements. This wampum belt represents an alliance between two peoples, symbolized by the straight path running between its two outer bands.

But the primary vehicle for the preservation of culture was spoken language, through which poems, songs, and stories were passed down from generation to generation. Storytelling was a central feature of communal life, a principal way in which Native American peoples provided entertainment, educated their young, and transmitted their traditions. European explorers and missionaries, who were emissaries of an increasingly pervasive print culture, consequently tended to view Native American societies and religions as simple and unsophisticated. They also misunderstood the names of and distinctions among various tribes and groups. For example, when the Spanish missionaries encountered tribes in the southern part of present-day Arizona, they named them the "Pima," a corruption of the tribe's word for "no," which the missionaries mistook for a proper noun. Later, the French used the word *Sioux*, their rendering of an Ojibwa word meaning enemies or "treacherous snakes," as the collective name for three large nations with different cultures and dialects. The loosely constructed group that came to be known as the Sioux called themselves names that signified allies or an alliance of friends: the Dakota, the Lakota, and the Nakota.

At the same time, some of the early explorers attempted to learn Native American languages and record the stories they heard. One of the first was Gabriel Sagard, a French missionary and early ethnographer who visited New France, as the French colony in present-day eastern Canada was called, in 1623-24. Sagard studied the Huron language and even prepared a dictionary for missionaries to use. He also transcribed and translated a version of a creation story that he learned from the Hurons, which Sagard published in an account of his journey, *Le Grand Voyage du Pays des Hurons* (1632). Sagard's book anticipated the way in which much Native American lore would be preserved. Because the societies themselves were being systematically destroyed, the primary means of preserving vestiges of their oral heritages was through transcription and translation into European languages.

In what became the United States, however, the effort at preservation did not begin in earnest until the nineteenth century, when Native Americans and their rich cultures were being erased from the landscape and memory of the nation. The texts of many ancient narratives were consequently first published at a comparatively late date, and translations of such works continue to appear in print. Both Native Americans and European Americans have participated in the effort to record the history, mythology, and narrative traditions of the Indians. Among the first Native Americans who sought to preserve oral culture in print was David Cusick, a Tuscarora who published *Sketches of the Ancient History of the Six Nations* in 1827. Another important figure who spurred the emerging interest in Native American culture and history was Henry Rowe Schoolcraft (1793-1864), a federal agent of Indian affairs for the Great Lakes region

Gabriel Sagard, *Le Grand Voyage du Pays des Hurons* (1632)

As the title page of his book indicates, Sagard offers an overview of Huron culture and a review of missionary efforts in New France. The book includes one of the earliest translations of a Native American oral story, as well as a dictionary of the Huron language.

who married the half-Ojibwa daughter of a fur trader and learned both the language and much of the lore of her tribe. His wife, Jane Johnston Schoolcraft (1800–1841), was one of the first Native Americans to write short stories based on Indian lore, while Schoolcraft himself published over twenty books about Indian history, customs, and language, notably his *Historical and Statistical Information Respecting . . . the Indian Tribes of the United States* (6 vol., 1851–57).

Throughout the late-nineteenth and twentieth centuries, hundreds of other anthropologists and historians also attempted to preserve the oral traditions of Native Americans. Versions of the same story often differed dramatically. By its very nature, an oral tradition is evolutionary and adaptive, so stories inevitably change from generation to generation. Moreover, different tellers shaped stories in various ways, while individual interpreters imposed their own cultural beliefs on the stories they transcribed and translated. Differences in language presented additional obstacles to these early interpreters, since there was no English equivalent for many of the concepts and words in Native American languages. In the Lakota story included here, "*Wohpe* and the Gift of the Pipe," for example, the term *wakan* has often been translated as "holy," especially by missionaries eager to put a Christian spin on a narrative. But the term actually has a much more complicated meaning, blending the concepts of both mystery and power. Finally, the force and meaning of many Native American poems, songs, and stories depends on oral performance, which is difficult to capture on the printed page, especially in translation. Indeed, crucial elements of oral performance—the expressions and gestures of the speaker, the rhythms and sounds of the original language, and both the physical and cultural context in which the story is told—are quite literally lost in translation into English and onto the printed page.

When making the effort to study and understand Native American oral literature, we consequently must accept the fact that the record is fragmentary and often problematic. The following stories, taken from several geographical locations, are intended as examples of the kinds of indigenous origin and creation stories that were a part of the multiple cultures in existence at the time of the first explorations of what Europeans thought of as a "new" world. The narratives presented here include accounts of the beginning of the world, the creation of natural phenomena, the history of ritual objects and sacred places, and the origin of ceremonies and cultural traditions. Each offers at least a glimpse of the richness and complexity of the earliest literature of North America.

Iroquois Confederacy

The people known as the Iroquois originally lived in a large area of present-day New York State, east of the Hudson River and south of the St. Lawrence River. At the time of the first European explorations of the area around 1600, there were approximately 20,000 people in the political union of the five tribes of the Iroquois Confederacy: the Cayuga, Mohawk, Seneca, Oneida, and Onondaga. The Tuscarora were incorporated into the league in 1722, and the confederacy became known as the Six Indian Nations or Six Nations Confederacy. The various tribes spoke dialects of what is called the Iroquoian-Northern language. The Iroquois were farmers and hunters who lived in small villages, a distinctive feature of which was the "longhouse," a large multifamily dwelling that often housed an entire clan. In fact, the Iroquois called themselves *Haudenosaunee*, or "the people of the longhouse." Their social structure was matrilineal. In addition to determining kinship and making many family decisions, women also owned property. When a couple married, the man moved into the woman's longhouse.

You don't have anything if you don't have the stories.

–Leslie Marmon Silko

*bedfordstmartins.com/
americanlit for research
links on Native American
tales and stories*

Known for their military prowess, the Iroquois were powerful and savvy warriors who used their strong political organization to their advantage. Despite their relatively small numbers, the Iroquois successfully resisted the incursions of European settlers until the Revolutionary War, when they sided with the British. American troops invaded their homeland in 1779, driving many of the Iroquois into southern Canada. In the decades following the war, they lost much of their land through deceptive treaties. Many of the Iroquois were removed to reservations in New York, from which some tribes were later relocated to Wisconsin, now the home of most of the Oneida, and to the Indian Territory, now Oklahoma, home of the modern-day Seneca-Cayuga tribe.

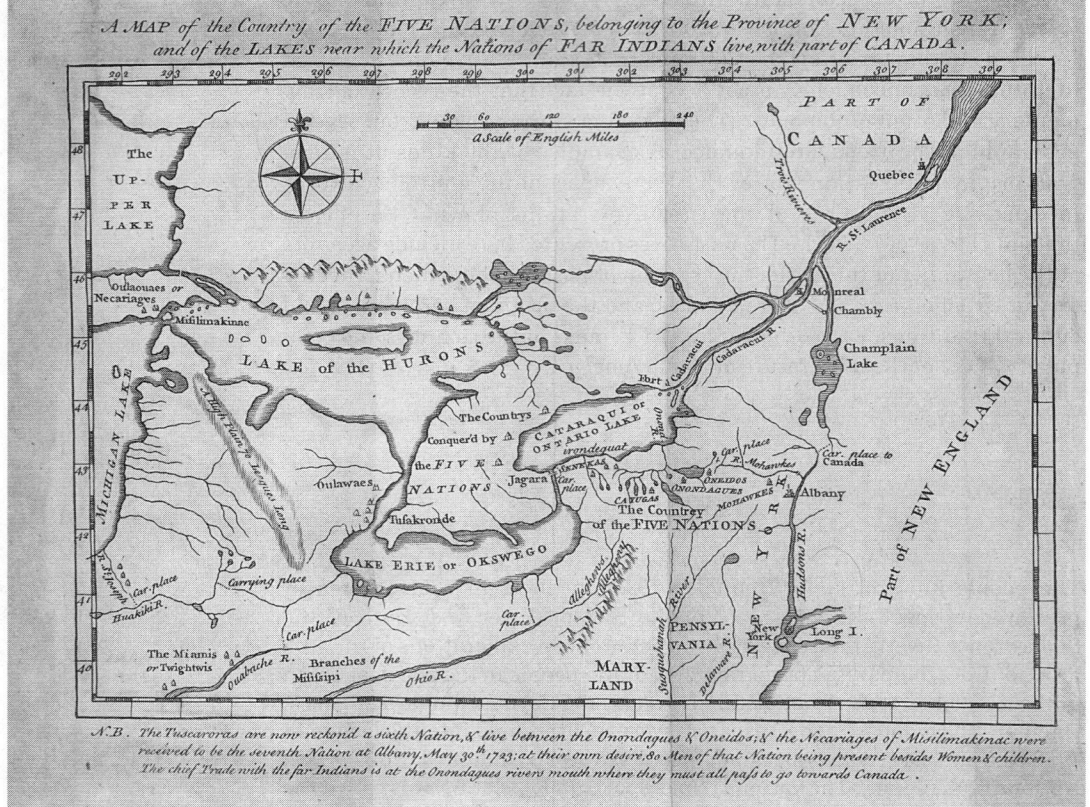

Map of the Country of the Five Nations

This map of the territories occupied by the members of the Iroquois Confederacy was included as a frontispiece to Cadwallader Colden's *The History of the Five Indian Nations* (1747). Colden was a Scottish-educated scientist and physician who moved to Philadelphia in 1710 and later relocated to New York, where he held a number of important colonial positions, including the province's first representative to the Iroquois.

Reading the "Origin of Folk Stories" (Seneca). The most populous of the original five tribes of the Iroquois Nation, the Seneca occupied an area between the Genesee River and Seneca Lake in the Finger Lakes region of present-day New York State. Like the other Iroquois tribes, the Seneca lived in villages with longhouses—dwellings for extended families—and were primarily agricultural, raising corn, squash, and beans. They also followed the political organization of the larger Iroquois Nation, holding elections to remove leaders who were proven to be corrupt or incompetent. The Seneca were fiercely protective of their homes and were skilled in warfare. One of their most famous leaders was Red Jacket (1750–1830), known for his skill as an orator, his political leadership, and his valiant efforts to maintain tribal lands and culture in the face of constant incursions by white settlers. In a speech attributed to him in 1805, Red Jacket is recorded as saying, "The Great Spirit . . . has made a great difference between his white and red children; we do not wish to destroy your religion or take it from you. We only want to enjoy our own." The oral cultures of Native American tribes depended on the telling of stories to preserve their history, religion, and traditions. There was, consequently, considerable interest in how stories originated. In the following Seneca story, which is variously known as the "Origin of Folk Stories" and "The Story-Telling Stone," an outcast orphan becomes a hero through his knowledge of the source, or origin, of stories. The text is taken from *Seneca Myths and Folk Tales* (1923), collected by Arthur C. Parker, a Seneca.

ORIGIN OF FOLK STORIES

There was once a boy who had no home. His parents were dead and his uncles would not care for him. In order to live this boy, whose name was Gaqka, or Crow, made a bower of branches for an abiding place and hunted birds and squirrels for food.

He had almost no clothing but was very ragged and dirty. When the people from the village saw him they called him Filth-Covered-One, and laughed as they passed by, holding their noses. No one thought he would ever amount to anything, which made him feel heavy-hearted. He resolved to go away from his tormentors and become a great hunter.

One night Gaqka found a canoe. He had never seen this canoe before, so he took it. Stepping in he grasped the paddle, when the canoe immediately shot into the air, and he paddled above the clouds and under the moon. For a long time he went always southward. Finally the canoe dropped into a river and then Gaqka paddled for shore.

On the other side of the river was a great cliff that had a face that looked like a man. It was at the forks of the river where this cliff stood. The boy resolved to make his home on the top of the cliff and so climbed it and built a bark cabin.

The first night he sat on the edge of the cliff he heard a voice saying, "Give me some tobacco." Looking around the boy, seeing no one, replied, "Why should I give tobacco?"

There was no answer and the boy began to fix his arrows for the next day's hunt. After a while the voice spoke again, "Give me some tobacco."

Gaqka now took out some tobacco and threw it over the cliff. The voice spoke again: "Now I will tell you a story."

Feeling greatly awed the boy listened to a story that seemed to come directly out of the rock upon which he was sitting. Finally the voice paused, for the story had ended. Then it spoke again saying, "It shall be the custom hereafter to present me with a small gift for my stories." So the boy gave the rock a few bone beads. Then the rock said, "Hereafter when I speak, announcing that I shall tell a story you must say, 'Nio,' and as I speak you must say 'Hĕⁿ´,' that I may know that you are listening. You must never fall asleep but continue to listen until I say 'Dā´neho nigagā´is.' (So thus finished is the length of my story). Then you shall give me presents and I shall be satisfied."

The next day the boy hunted and killed a great many birds. These he made into soup and roasts. He skinned the birds and saved the skins, keeping them in a bag.

That evening the boy sat on the rock again and looked westward at the sinking sun. He wondered if his friend would speak again. While waiting he chipped some new arrow-points, and made them very small so that he could use them in a blow gun. Suddenly, as he worked, he heard the voice again. "Give me some tobacco to smoke," it said. Gaqka threw a pinch of tobacco over the cliff and the voice said, "Hau'nio´´," and commenced a story. Long into the night one wonderful tale after another flowed from the rock, until it called out, "So thus finished is the length of my story." Gaqka was sorry to have the stories ended but he gave the rock an awl made from a bird's leg and a pinch of tobacco.

The next day the boy hunted far to the east and there found a village. Nobody knew who he was but he soon found many friends. There were some hunters who offered to teach him how to kill big game, and these went with him to his own camp on the high rock. At night he allowed them to listen to the stories that came forth from the rock, but it would speak only when Gaqka was present. He therefore had many friends with whom to hunt.

Now after a time Gaqka made a new suit of clothing from deer skin and desired to obtain a decorated pouch. He, therefore, went to the village and found one house where there were two daughters living with an old mother. He asked that a pouch be made and the youngest daughter spoke up and said, "It is now finished. I have been waiting for you to come for it." So she gave him a handsome pouch.

Then the old mother spoke, saying, "I now perceive that my future son-in-law has passed through the door and is here." Soon thereafter, the younger woman brought Gaqka a basket of bread and said, "My mother greatly desires that you should marry me." Gaqka looked at the girl and was satisfied, and ate the bread. The older daughter was greatly displeased and frowned in an evil manner.

That night the bride said to her husband, "We must now go away. My older sister will kill you for she is jealous." So Gaqka arose and took his bride to his own lodge. Soon the rock spoke and began to relate wonder stories of things that happened in the old days. The bride was not surprised, but said, "This standing rock, indeed, is my grandfather. I will now present you with a pouch into which you must put a trophy[1] for every tale related."

---

1. **trophy:** A token or an object used as an aid to the memory of an occasion or event.

All winter long the young couple stayed in the lodge on the great rock and heard all the wonder tales of the old days. Gaqka's bag was full of stories and he knew all the lore of former times.

As springtime came the bride said, "We must now go north to your own people and you shall become a great man." But Gaqka was sad and said, "Alas, in my own country I am an outcast and called by an unpleasant name."

The bride only laughed, saying, "Nevertheless we shall go north."

Taking their pelts and birdskins, the young couple descended the cliff and seated themselves in the canoe. "This is my canoe," said the bride. "I sent it through the air to you."

The bride seated herself in the bow of the canoe and Gaqka in the stern. Grasping a paddle he swept it through the water, but soon the canoe arose and went through the air. Meanwhile the bride was singing all kinds of songs, which Gaqka learned as he paddled.

When they reached the north, the bride said, "Now I shall remove your clothing and take all the scars from your face and body." She then caused him to pass through a hollow log, and when Gaqka emerged from the other end he was dressed in the finest clothing and was a handsome man.

Together the two walked to the village where the people came out to see them. After a while Gaqka said, "I am the boy whom you once were accustomed to call 'Cia´´dōdă'.' I have now returned." That night the people of the village gathered around and listened to the tales he told, and he instructed them to give him small presents and tobacco. He would plunge his hand in his pouch and take out a trophy, saying, "Ho ho'! So here is another one!" and then looking at his trophy would relate an ancient tale.

Everybody now thought Gaqka a great man and listened to his stories. He was the first man to find out all about the adventures of the old-time people. That is why there are so many legends now.

[1923]

Cherokee

The Cherokee originally occupied an extensive area of the Southeast, including parts of present-day North and South Carolina, Georgia, Alabama, Virginia, Tennessee, and Kentucky. When they were encountered by the Spanish explorer Hernando de Soto in the mid-sixteenth century, the Cherokee formed a large and complex nation made up of many smaller tribal units. Only rough estimates of the combined population of these units are possible, but it is thought that there were about 50,000 Cherokee in 1670. A series of smallpox epidemics introduced by European explorers decreased the Cherokee population by as much as 50 percent by the mid-1700s. The well-organized Cherokee were an agricultural people who lived in small villages with a central council house devoted to meetings and religious ceremonies. Although the social structure was matrilineal, women did not have as much power as they did in the tribes of the Iroquois Confederacy.

Sequoyah

This portrait of Sequoyah holding a copy of his alphabet of the Cherokee language, which he spent over a decade developing, appeared in *Indian Tribes of North America* (1836–44), by Thomas McKenney and James Hall.

The Cherokee spoke several dialects of Iroquoian. Theirs was an oral culture until 1821, when a written alphabet of the Cherokee language was developed by one of their leaders, Sequoyah (1776–1843). By making literacy available to the Cherokee in their own language, Sequoyah sought to combat their growing assimilation into the dominant, English-speaking culture of the United States. In 1828, the *Cherokee Phoenix* became the first newspaper in the United States published in a Native American language and English. Like other native peoples throughout the early history of the colonies and the United States, the Cherokee were pressed to give up lands to white settlers. In 1830, Congress passed the Indian Removal Act, which authorized the president to exchange lands west of the Mississippi for the lands held by eastern tribes, including the Cherokee Nation. The Cherokee, who included a population of over 17,000 in Georgia, resisted by filing a lawsuit against the state of Georgia. The Supreme Court refused to hear the case, ruling that the Cherokee had no legal standing and therefore could not sue the state. Eight years later, thousands of native peoples were forcibly removed from their lands and made to march over one thousand miles to "Indian Territory," present-day Oklahoma, a trek the Cherokee call the "Trail of Tears." Over 4,000 Cherokee died during the arduous removal. In the new territory, the Cherokee rebuilt their nation and developed a constitution, well before Oklahoma became a state in 1907.

bedfordstmartins.com/
americanlit *for research links on Native American tales and stories*

Reading "How the World Was Made" (Cherokee). The rich oral culture of the Cherokee includes a wide variety of legends, myths, and stories. The following is an account of how the natural world was made and how it might be destroyed. Unlike many other Native American creation stories, the Cherokee account does not provide explanations for the origins of animals and humans. This story was transcribed and translated by the anthropologist James Mooney (1861-1921). The text is taken from the nineteenth annual *Report of the Bureau of American Ethnology to the Secretary of the Smithsonian Institution* (1900).

HOW THE WORLD WAS MADE

The earth is a great island floating in a sea of water, and suspended at each of the four cardinal points by a cord hanging down from the sky vault, which is of solid rock. When the world grows old and worn out, the people will die and the cords will break and let the earth sink down into the ocean, and all will be water again. The Indians are afraid of this.

When all was water, the animals were above in Gălûñ´lătĭ,[1] beyond the arch; but it was very much crowded, and they were wanting more room. They wondered what was below the water, and at last Dâyuni´sĭ, "Beaver's Grandchild," the little Water-beetle, offered to go and see if it could learn. It darted in every direction over the surface of the water, but could find no firm place to rest. Then it dived to the bottom and came up with some soft mud, which began to grow and spread on every side until it became the island which we call the earth. It was afterward fastened to the sky with four cords, but no one remembers who did this.

At first the earth was flat and very soft and wet. The animals were anxious to get down, and sent out different birds to see if it was yet dry, but they found no place to alight and came back again to Gălûñ´lătĭ. At last it seemed to be time, and they sent out the Buzzard and told him to go and make ready for them. This was the Great Buzzard, the father of all the buzzards we see now. He flew all over the earth, low down near the ground, and it was still soft. When he reached the Cherokee country, he was very tired, and his wings began to flap and strike the ground, and wherever they struck the earth there was a valley, and where they turned up again there was a mountain. When the animals above saw this, they were afraid that the whole world would be mountains, so they called him back, but the Cherokee country remains full of mountains to this day.[2]

When the earth was dry and the animals came down, it was still dark, so they got the sun and set it in a track to go every day across the island from east to west, just overhead. It was too hot this way, and Tsiska´gĭlĭ´, the Red Crawfish, had his shell scorched a

---

1. **Gălûñ´lătĭ:** The Cherokee otherworld, where at one time all the animals lived.
2. **full of mountains to this day:** The Cherokee originally occupied a large area of the southern Appalachian Mountains.

bright red, so that his meat was spoiled; and the Cherokee do not eat it. The conjurers put the sun another handbreadth higher in the air, but it was still too hot. They raised it another time, and another, until it was seven handbreadths high and just under the sky arch. Then it was right, and they left it so. This is why the conjurers call the highest place Gûlkwâ´gine Di´gălûñ´lătiyûñ´, "the seventh height," because it is seven hand-breadths above the earth. Every day the sun goes along under this arch, and returns at night on the upper side to the starting place.

There is another world under this, and it is like ours in everything – animals, plants, and people – save that the seasons are different. The streams that come down from the mountains are the trails by which we reach this underworld, and the springs at their heads are the doorways by which we enter it, but to do this one must fast and go to water and have one of the underground people for a guide. We know that the seasons in the underworld are different from ours, because the water in the springs is always warmer in winter and cooler in summer than the outer air.

When the animals and plants were first made – we do not know by whom – they were told to watch and keep awake for seven nights, just as young men now fast and keep awake when they pray to their medicine. They tried to do this, and nearly all were awake through the first night, but the next night several dropped off to sleep, and the third night others were asleep, and then others, until, on the seventh night, of all the animals only the owl, the panther, and one or two more were still awake. To these were given the power to see and to go about in the dark, and to make prey of the birds and animals which must sleep at night. Of the trees only the cedar, the pine, the spruce, the holly, and the laurel were awake to the end, and to them it was given to be always green and to be greatest for medicine, but to the others it was said: "Because you have not endured to the end you shall lose your hair every winter."

Men came after the animals and plants. At first there were only a brother and sister until he struck her with a fish and told her to multiply, and so it was. In seven days a child was born to her, and thereafter every seven days another, and they increased very fast until there was danger that the world could not keep them. Then it was made that a woman should have only one child in a year, and it has been so ever since.

[1900]

Lakota

The Lakota are part of what became known as the Sioux Nation, a con-federacy of three large groups of native peoples of the same linguistic stock – the Dakota (Santee or Eastern Sioux), Lakota (Teton Sioux), and Nakota (Yankton Sioux). Those peoples are further divided into smaller tribal groups, such as the Oglala of the Lakota. When the French encoun-tered these peoples, whose own names mean allies or friends, they called them collectively the "Sioux." They originally lived south of Lake Superior in present-day northern Wisconsin and eastern Minnesota, but conflicts with the neighboring Ojibwa forced the Sioux westward during the seventeenth century. The Dakota settled in what is now southern and western Minnesota, where they retained their agricultural way of life. But the Lakota and the Nakota moved farther north and west into present-day North and South Dakota, western Nebraska, and eastern Wyoming, where they became nomadic hunters of buffalo and other large game. By 1750, there were probably 30,000 Sioux, half of them Lakota. Allies of the British in both the Revolutionary War and the War of 1812, the Sioux in 1825 signed a treaty with the United States under the terms of which they were granted possession of the "Great Sioux Reservation," a vast territory including much of present-day Minnesota, North and South Dakota, Wisconsin, Iowa, Missouri, and Wyoming.

Under the terms of a series of later treaties, however, the Sioux were steadily forced to sell or yield their lands to the federal government. They were further displaced by the Homestead Act of 1862, which offered white settlers free title to 160 acres of "public domain" land in the West. During the next thirty years, as hundreds of thousands of farms were established on the Great Plains, the Lakota struggled to survive and maintain their way of life in the Black Hills, a section of South Dakota west of the

Sitting Bull

This autographed photo of the Lakota chief holding a pipe, the sacred emblem of the Great Sioux Nation, was taken in 1884, five years before their once-vast lands were reduced to a handful of reservations with defined boundaries by an act of Congress.

Missouri River, which they were granted in perpetuity by the Fort Lara-mie Treaty of 1868. That treaty was violated when gold was discovered in the Black Hills in the 1870s, attracting thousands of white prospectors and triggering a war between the Sioux and the U.S. Army. Despite the leadership of Sitting Bull (1831-1890), a Lakota chief and medicine man, and the defeat of General George Custer at the battle of Little Bighorn in 1876, the Sioux finally bowed to the military forces of the United States and to the federal government's determination to open their lands to white settlers. As Sitting Bull said of those settlers in a speech delivered in 1877, "They claim this mother of ours, the earth, for their own and fence their neighbors away; they deface her with their buildings and their refuse. That nation is like a spring freshet that overruns its banks and destroys all who are in its path. We cannot dwell side by side." Finally, in 1889, Congress reduced the Great Sioux Reservation into five scattered reservations, the largest of which was and remains the Pine Ridge Reservation in South Dakota.

bedfordstmartins.com/
americanlit for research
links on Native American
tales and stories

Reading "*Wohpe* and the Gift of the Pipe" (Lakota).   The following Lakota story, as it was told by Finger, a holy man of the Oglala Sioux, was recorded by James R. Walker, a physician at the Pine Ridge Reserva-tion from 1896 to 1914. Other versions of this tale exist, including a later one collected in John G. Neihardt's *Black Elk Speaks* (1932), based on recordings of conversations Neihardt had in 1930 with Black Elk, an Oglala Sioux then living at Pine Ridge. A central tale to the Lakota, "*Wohpe* and the Gift of the Pipe" explains the origin and importance of what is commonly known as the peace pipe, which figured prominently in Lakota culture. Sharing the long, elaborately decorated pipe was a ritual among Lakota leaders, as well as a ceremonial way of endorsing agreements between individuals and groups. The text of the story, which was told to Walker by Finger on March 25, 1914, is taken from James R. Walker, *Lakota Belief and Ritual*, edited by Raymond J. DeMallie and Elaine A. Jahner (1980).

WOHPE AND THE GIFT OF THE PIPE

Question: You say that when *Wohpe*[1] gave the pipe to the Lakotas she was in their camp for many days. Was it she that gave the first pipe to the Lakotas?

Answer: Yes.

Question: Can you tell me how she did this?

---

1. **Wohpe**: Falling Star, the mythological White Buffalo (Calf) Woman who brings the sacred pipe to the Lakota.

Answer: Yes, but it is a long story.

Question: Will you tell it?

Answer: (The legend of the giving of the pipe to the Lakotas)

In the long ago the Lakotas were in camp and two young men lay upon a hill watching for signs. They saw a long way in the distance a lone person coming, and they ran further toward it and lay on another hill hidden so that if it were an enemy they would be able to intercept it or signal to the camp. When the person came close, they saw that it was a woman and when she came nearer that she was without clothing of any kind except that her hair was very long and fell over her body like a robe. One young man said to the other that he would go and meet the woman and embrace her and if he found her good, he would hold her in his tipi.[2] His companion cautioned him to be careful for this might be a buffalo woman who could enchant him and take him with her to her people and hold him there forever. But the young man would not be persuaded and met the woman on the hill next to where they had watched her. His companion saw him attempt to embrace her and there was a cloud closed about them so that he could not see what happened. In a short time the cloud disappeared and the woman was alone. She beckoned to the other young man and told him to come there and assured him that he would not be harmed. As she spoke in the Lakota language the young man thought she belonged to his people and went to where she stood.

When he got there, she showed him the bare bones of his companion and told him that the Crazy Buffalo had caused his companion to try to do her harm and that she had destroyed him and picked his bones bare. The young man was very much afraid and drew his bow and arrow to shoot the woman, but she told him that if he would do as she directed, no harm would come to him and he should get any girl he wished for his woman, for she was *wakan*[3] and he could not hurt her with his arrows. But if he refused to do as she should direct, or attempt to shoot her, he would be destroyed as his companion had been. Then the young man promised to do as she should bid him.

She then directed him to return to the camp and call all the council together and tell them that in a short time they would see four puffs of smoke[4] under the sun at midday. When they saw this sign they should prepare a feast, and all sit in the customary circle to have the feast served when she would enter the camp, but the men must all sit with their head bowed and look at the ground until she was in their midst. Then she would serve the feast to them and after they had feasted she would tell them what to do: that they must obey her in everything; that if they obeyed her in everything they would have their prayers to the *Wakan Tanka*[5] answered and be prosperous and happy; but that if they disobeyed her or attempted to do her any harm, they would be neglected by *Wakan Tanka* and be punished as the young man who had attempted to embrace her had been.

---

2. **tipi:** Often spelled *tepee*, a portable, conical house used by the Plains Indians, usually constructed of cottonwood poles and buffalo hides or canvas.

3. *wakan:* Powerful and spiritually mysterious.

4. **four puffs of smoke:** Four is a sacred number to the Lakota, and many other tribes, as evidenced in the four directions and the four winds.

5. *Wakan Tanka:* The Lakota "Great Spirit," or literally "Big Power."

Then she disappeared as a mist disappears so that the young man knew that she was *wakan*. He returned to the camp and told these things to the people and the council decided to do as she had instructed the young man. They made preparations for the feast and in a few days they saw four puffs of black smoke under the sun at midday, so they prepared for a feast and all dressed in their best clothing and sat in the circle ready to be served and every man bowed his head and looked toward the ground. Suddenly the women began uttering low exclamations of admiration, but all the men steadily kept their eyes toward the ground except one young man and he looked toward the entrance of the camp. He saw a puff of black smoke which blew into his eyes and a voice said, "You have disobeyed me and there will be smoke in your eyes as long as you live." From that time, that young man had very sore eyes and all the time they were as if biting smoke was in them.

Then the woman entered the circle and took the food and served it, first to the little children and then to the women and then she bade the men to look up. They did so and saw a very beautiful woman dressed in the softest deer skin which was ornamented with fringes and colors more beautiful than any woman of the Lakota had ever worked. Then she served the men with food, and when they had feasted she told them that she wished to serve them always; that they had first seen her as smoke and that they should always see her as smoke. Then she took from her pouch a pipe and willow bark and Lakota tobacco and filled the pipe with the bark and tobacco and lighted it with a coal of fire.

She smoked a few whiffs and handed the pipe to the chief and told him to smoke and hand it to another. Thus the pipe was passed until all had smoked. She then instructed the council how to gather the bark and the tobacco and prepare it, and gave the pipe into their keeping, telling them that as long as they preserved this pipe she would serve them. But she would serve them in this way. When the smoke came from the pipe she would be present and hear their prayers and take them to the *Wakan Tanka* and plead for them that their prayers should be answered.

After this she remained in this camp for many days and all the time she was there everyone was happy for she went from tipi to tipi with good words for all. When the time came for her to go, she called all the people together and bade the women to build a great fire of dried cottonwood, which they did. Then she directed all to sit in a circle about the fire and the shaman[6] to have an abundance of sweetgrass. She stood in the midst of the circle and when the fire had burned to coals she directed the shaman to place on it the sweetgrass. This made a cloud of smoke and the woman entered the smoke and disappeared. Then the shamans knew that it was *Wohpe* who had given the pipe and they appointed a custodian for it with instructions that it was to be kept sacred and used only on the most solemn and important occasions. With due ceremony they made wrappers for the pipe so that it is *wakan*. The shamans instructed the people that they could make other pipes and use them and that *Wohpe* would be in the smoke of any such pipe if smoked with proper solemnity and form.

Thus it was that the Beautiful Woman brought the pipe to the Lakotas.

[1980]

---

6. **shaman:** *Shaman* is actually a term for an East Asian medicine man. Walker may have misunderstood or mistranslated the Lakota term *wicasa wakan*, a man who acquires power through a "vision quest," a process of deep understanding of the world of the spirits.

Akimel O'odham (Pima)

The Akimel O'odham, commonly known as the Pima, are among the earliest residents of the Southwest. They are descendants of the ancient Hohokam, who as early as the second century BCE began to develop an expansive and complex civilization in what is now southern Arizona, New Mexico, and northern Mexico. Culturally similar to the natives of central Mexico, the Hohokam lived in large adobe towns, which the Spanish would call "pueblos," and built an extensive system of canals to irrigate their arid farmlands. Following a series of droughts, however, the Hohokam abandoned their majestic pueblos and moved into smaller villages along the Salt and the Gila rivers. They were an agricultural people, who developed prosperous farms and villages. When Spanish explorers encountered these dispersed peoples in the early 1600s, they renamed them the Pima and the Papago. In the eighteenth century, the Spanish were allied with the Pima against the incursions of the Apache. In the nineteenth century, Pima villages became trading posts, selling animals and food to settlers bound for southern California and those participating in the California gold rush of the late 1840s. As part of the Gadsden Purchase of 1853, however, the Pima lands in Mexico became part of the United States. The prosperity of the Pima farmers and traders ended, and the tribe was soon consigned to the Gila River Reservation, established in 1859. Today, the Pima and Papago tribes have reclaimed their original names, the Akimel O'odham (River People) and the Tohono O'odham (Desert People).

bedfordstmartins.com/ americanlit for research links on Native American tales and stories

Reading "The Story of the Creation" (Pima).   The Pima did not have a written language, and much of the record of their complex culture is lost. But some of their stories were preserved orally in tribal culture and finally transcribed by J. William Lloyd, a physician and writer. At the Pan-American Fair in Buffalo, New York, in 1901, Lloyd met Edward H. Wood, a Pima whose uncle, Thin Leather, knew many of the Pima stories and legends. Together Lloyd and Wood worked with Thin Leather in Arizona to collect and record Pima narratives. The following story begins in a way similar to that of the book of Genesis, but this Pima creation myth draws on many elements of the natural landscape of the Southwest. The text is taken from the collection put together by Lloyd and Thin Leather, *Aw-Aw-Tam Indian Nights, Being the Myths and Legends of the Pimas of Arizona* (1911).

Casa Grande

This is a drawing by J. Ross Browne of the Casa Grande, or the "Big House," an imposing four-story structure built in the fourteenth century by the Hohokam, ancestors of the Akimel O'odham (Pima). Located in present-day Coolidge, Arizona, the ruins became the first archaeological site in the United States to be protected as a national monument in 1892. The drawing of the ruins appeared as an illustration in Browne's *Adventures in Apache Country* (1869).

THE STORY OF THE CREATION

In the beginning there was no earth, no water – nothing. There was only a Person, *Juh-wert-a-Mah-kai* (*The Doctor of the Earth*).

He just floated, for there was no place for him to stand upon. There was no sun, no light, and he just floated about in the darkness, which was Darkness itself.

He wandered around in the nowhere till he thought he had wandered enough. Then he rubbed on his breast and rubbed out *moah-haht-tack*, that is perspiration, or greasy earth. This he rubbed out on the palm of his hand and held out. It tipped over three times, but the fourth time it staid straight in the middle of the air and there it remains now as the world.

The first bush he created was the greasewood bush.

And he made ants, little tiny ants, to live on that bush, on its gum which comes out of its stem.

But these little ants did not do any good, so he created white ants, and these worked and enlarged the earth; and they kept on increasing it, larger and larger, until at last it was big enough for himself to rest on.

Then he created a Person. He made him out of his eye, out of the shadow of his eyes, to assist him, to be like him, and to help him in creating trees and human beings and everything that was to be on the earth.

The name of this being was *Noo-ee* (the Buzzard).

Nooee was given all power, but he did not do the work he was created for. He did not care to help Juhwertamahkai, but let him go by himself.

And so the Doctor of the Earth himself created the mountains and everything that has seed and is good to eat. For if he had created human beings first they would have had nothing to live on.

But after making Nooee and before making the mountains and seed for food, Juhwertamahkai made the sun.

In order to make the sun he first made water, and this he placed in a hollow vessel, like an earthen dish (*hwas-hah-ah*) to harden into something like ice. And this hardened ball he placed in the sky. First he placed it in the North, but it did not work; then he placed it in the West, but it did not work; then he placed it in the South, but it did not work; then he placed it in the East and there it worked as he wanted it to.

And the moon he made in the same way and tried in the same places, with the same results.

But when he made the stars he took the water in his mouth and spurted it up into the sky. But the first night his stars did not give light enough. So he took the Doctor-stone (diamond),[1] the *tone-dum-haw-teh*, and smashed it up, and took the pieces and threw them into the sky to mix with the water in the stars, and then there was light enough.

And now Juhwertamahkai, rubbed again on his breast, and from the substance he obtained there made two little dolls, and these he laid on the earth. And they were human beings, man and woman.

And now for a time the people increased till they filled the earth. For the first parents were perfect, and there was no sickness and no death. But when the earth was full, then there was nothing to eat, so they killed and ate each other.

But Juhwertamahkai did not like the way his people acted, to kill and eat each other, and so he let the sky fall to kill them. But when the sky dropped he, himself, took a staff and broke a hole thru, thru which he and Nooee emerged and escaped, leaving behind them all the people dead.

And Juhwertamahkai, being now on the top of this fallen sky, again made a man and a woman, in the same way as before. But this man and woman became grey when old, and their children became grey still younger, and their children became grey younger still, and so on till the babies were grey in their cradles.

And Juhwertamahkai, who had made a new earth and sky, just as there had been before, did not like his people becoming grey in their cradles, so he let the sky fall on them again, and again made a hole and escaped, with Nooee, as before.

And Juhwertamahkai, on top of this second sky, again made a new heaven and a new earth, just as he had done before, and new people.

But these new people made a vice of smoking. Before human beings had never smoked till they were old, but now they smoked younger, and each generation still younger, till the infants wanted to smoke in their cradles.

And Juhwertamahkai did not like this, and let the sky fall again, and created everything new again in the same way, and this time he created the earth as it is now.

---

1. **diamond:** Probably a quartz crystal, which is prevalent in the Southwest.

But at first the whole slope of the world was westward, and tho there were peaks rising from this slope there were no true valleys, and all the water that fell ran away and there was no water for the people to drink. So Juhwertamahkai sent Nooee to fly around among the mountains, and over the earth, to cut valleys with his wings, so that the water could be caught and distributed and there might be enough for the people to drink.

Now the sun was male and the moon was female and they met once a month. And the moon became a mother and went to a mountain called *Tahs-my-et-tahn Toe-ahk* (sun striking mountain) and there was born her baby. But she had duties to attend to, to turn around and give light, so she made a place for the child by tramping down the weedy bushes and there left it. And the child, having no milk, was nourished on the earth.

And this child was the coyote, and as he grew he went out to walk and in his walk came to the house of Juhwertamahkai and Nooee, where they lived.

And when he came there Juhwertamahkai knew him and called him *Toe-hahvs*, because he was laid on the weedy bushes of that name.

But now out of the North came another powerful personage, who has two names, *See-ur-huh* and *Ee-ee-toy.*

Now Seeurhuh means older brother, and when this personage came to Juhwertamahkai, Nooee and Toehahvs he called them his younger brothers. But they claimed to have been here first, and to be older than he, and there was a dispute between them. But finally, because he insisted so strongly, and just to please him, they let him be called older brother.

[1911]

Hupa

The Hupa (or Hoopa, as the name is sometimes spelled today) and their neighbors the Yurok and the Karuk long ago established themselves in what is now northwestern California. (Tests have determined that a fire pit on the Hupa lands dates to more than seven thousand years ago.) The Hupa lived in small villages of cedar-plank houses with small round doorways on the banks of the Trinity River. They fished for the plentiful salmon in the river, gathered acorns and berries, and hunted small game. They were also skilled at crafts. Men practiced woodworking, while women fashioned distinctive bowl-shaped hats and baskets. For centuries, the Hupa were largely unknown to European explorers and settlers. Following the discovery of gold in California in 1848, however, miners and settlers moved onto Hupa lands, causing serious disruption to their way of life. In 1864, they were resettled on the Hoopa Valley Reservation, which included a large portion of their original tribal lands. The Hupa speak a dialect of the Athabascan language, which was also spoken by several Native American peoples of the Southwest and the Great Plains. The Hupa language has been extensively studied by linguists, and many of their oral narratives and stories have been transcribed and translated into English.

bedfordstmartins.com/
americanlit for research
links on Native American
tales and stories

Reading "The Boy Who Grew Up at Taʾkʾimiłding" (Hupa).   This story accounts for the origin of the World Renewal Dances, sacred ceremonies that are unique to the traditional cultures of the Yurok, Karuk, and Hupa. The dances take two forms. The purpose of the White Deerskin Dance, *xonsiť chʾidilye* or Summer World Renewal, is to inspire life and vitality for the coming year. The purpose of the Jump Dance, *xay chʾidilye* or Winter World Renewal, is to protect against disease and natural disasters. Both dances are intended to celebrate the *kʾixinay*, supernatural beings who dwell in the "Heaven" of the story and who influence the human world below. The young boy who lives in the principal village of the Hupa, *Taʾkʾimiłding*, has been chosen by the *kʾixinay* for the vital role of initiating the ceremonial dances, which are still performed in the Hoopa Valley. This version of the story is a translation by Victor Golla of a recording made in 1963 of an oral narration by Minnie Reeves (1880–1972). "Minnie Reeves's telling of this sacred story was appropriately solemn and serious," Golla observes. "Although her version was abbreviated and broken here and there by a hesitation and a groping for words, it was clear that she was reciting well-known lines and phrases — a sacred text in the most real sense." The text is taken from *Surviving through the Days: A California Indian Reader*, edited by Herbert W. Luthin (2002).

Hupa Jump Dancers

This photograph of the Hupa in the ceremonial garb worn for the Jump Dance was taken by A. W. Ericson in the 1890s. Even at a time when the policy of the federal government was to eradicate the indigenous cultures of Native American peoples, the Hupa maintained a strong sense of their cultural identity, which they have preserved to the present day.

THE BOY WHO GREW UP AT TA'K'IMIŁDING

There once was a boy who grew up at Ta'k'imiłding – born into the Big House there.

He did nothing but sing all the time. He would always be singing. He was a good boy and did what he was told, but he would stay there in the Big House at Ta'k'imiłding, singing all day long.

One day his mother went down to the river to fetch water, leaving the boy singing in the house. She dipped up some water, and was on her way back up to the house when a sound stopped her. It sounded like someone was singing inside a cloud that hovered over her house. She put her water basket down and listened. She could hear it clearly: Someone was singing there inside the hovering cloud. After a while the cloud lifted up into the air. She could still hear the singing. Eventually it vanished into the sky.

She went on back to the house. When she went inside, the boy was gone. It was clear that he had gone off inside the hovering cloud.

When her husband returned from hunting she told him what had happened. They had loved him very much, and they cried and cried.

A long time passed and there was no sign of the boy. Then, one day, many years later, the man went up the hill to hunt. After hunting for a while he got tired and decided to rest under a big tan oak. As he sat there smoking his pipe he was suddenly aware of a young man walking toward him out of the forest. Looking more closely he saw that it was the boy, now grown up. He leapt to his feet and ran to embrace his son.

"Stop there, Father! Don't come toward me," the young man said. "Don't try to touch me. I can't bear the scent of human beings anymore."

Then he continued, "The only reason I have come back is to tell people the way things should be done in the future. When I went off to Heaven in that cloud, I found them dancing there, dancing without ever stopping, dancing the whole day long.

"And that is why I have returned – why you see me now. I have come to tell you about the dances. I am here to tell you the ways they should be danced, and the places where they should happen.

"You will dance downstream through Hoopa Valley, you will finish the dance over there on Bald Hill: That is where the White Deerskin Dance is to be danced.

"Ten days after the White Deerskin Dance is finished, you will dance the Jump Dance for another ten days. There behind the Jump Dance fence I will always be looking on. I will always come back for the Jump Dance, although you won't ever see me. Because I will be looking on from there, invisible though I am, don't let anyone go back of the fence, don't even let a dog go back there.

"I will always be watching."

That is the end of the story.

[2002]

Native American Stories through a Modern Lens

As Native Americans have sought to regain their lands and to reaffirm their identities, especially during the last fifty years, their rich oral traditions have become increasingly important to writers who draw on tribal lore and memories. Indeed, some scholars have referred to the late twentieth century as the "Renaissance" of Native American literature. The writers who have participated in that rebirth are as varied as the tribes that once inhabited North America, but few figures have been as influential in the emergence of Native American literature as N. Scott Momaday. Of Kiowa, English, and Cherokee descent, Momaday was born in 1934 in Oklahoma and spent most of his childhood on Indian reservations in Arizona and New Mexico, where his parents were teachers, and where he was

Mississippian Wooden Mask

This remarkable mask, which was fashioned from red cedar and originally covered with a thin sheet of copper, dates from sometime between 1200 and 1350. It was used in rituals by Mississippian people at the largest settlement in ancient North America, Cahokia, an extensive city and ceremonial site across the Mississippi River from present-day St. Louis.

exposed to the culture and traditions of the Navajo, Apache, and Pueblo. Momaday was the first Native American to win the Pulitzer Prize for Fiction, awarded for his novel *House Made of Dawn* (1969). He has also written widely about the rituals and oral traditions of Native Americans. In the following essay, Momaday sketches a portrait of the native peoples of America before the arrival of Christopher Columbus in 1492. As he emphasizes, the "New World" that Columbus believed he had encountered was actually an ancient world, one filled with an astonishing variety of peoples and societies. But a common feature of many of those diverse cultures was and remains storytelling. Momaday explains that Native Americans "tell stories in order to affirm our being and our place in the scheme of things," demonstrating the vital importance of orality in understanding Native American cultures and literature. The text is taken from *America in 1492*, edited by Alvin M. Josephy Jr. (1993).

N. Scott Momaday

[b. 1934]

THE BECOMING OF THE NATIVE: MAN IN AMERICA BEFORE COLUMBUS

THURSDAY, 11 OCTOBER 1492
The moon, in its third quarter, rose in the east shortly before midnight. I estimate that we were making about 9 knots and had gone some 67½ miles between the beginning of night and 2 o'clock in the morning. Then, at two hours after midnight, the *Pinta* fired a cannon, my prearranged signal for the sighting of land.

FRIDAY, 12 OCTOBER 1492
At dawn we saw naked people. . . .

–The Log of Christopher Columbus

It was not until 1498, when he explored what is now Venezuela, that Columbus realized he had touched upon a continent. On his last voyage, in 1502, he reached Central America. It is almost certain that he never knew of the great landmass to the north, an expanse that reached almost to Asia and to the top of the world, or that he had found a great chain of land that linked two of the earth's seven continents. In the little time that remained to him (he died in 1506) the enormity of his discovery was virtually unknown and unimagined. Christopher Columbus, the Admiral of the Ocean Sea, went to his grave believing he had reached Asia. But his accomplishment was even greater than he dreamed. He had in fact sailed beyond the *orbis*, the circle believed to describe the limits of the earth, and beyond medieval geography. His voyage to the New World was a navigation in time; it was a passage from the Middle Ages to the Renaissance.

There are moments in history to which one can point and say, "At this hour, on this day, the history of the world was changed forever." Such a moment occurred at two o'clock on the morning of October 12, 1492, when a cannon, fired from the Spanish caravel *Pinta*, announced the sighting of land. The land sighted was probably Samana Cay in the Bahamas. It was the New World.

It is this term, "New World," with which I should like to begin this discussion, not only because it is everywhere a common designation of the Americas but also because it represents one of the great anomalies of history. The British writer J. B. Priestley,[1] after visiting the United States, commented that "New World" is a misnomer. The American Southwest seemed to him the oldest landscape he had ever seen. Indeed, the New World is ancient. Here is a quintessential irony.

For Americans in general, a real part of the irony consists of their Eurocentric understanding of history. Columbus and his Old World contemporaries knew a good deal about the past, the past that was peculiarly theirs, for it had been recorded in writing. It was informed by a continuity that could be traced back to the story of Creation in the Old Testament. Most Americans have inherited that same understanding of the past. American history, therefore, as distinct from other histories, begins in the popular mind with the European intercession in the "New World." Relatively little is known of the Americas and their peoples before Columbus, although we are learning more all the time. On the far side of 1492 in the Americas there is a prehistoric darkness in which are mysteries as profound and provocative as are those of Stonehenge and Lascaux and Afrasiab.[2]

Who were the "naked people" Columbus and his men observed at dawn on that autumn day five hundred years ago? Columbus, the first ethnographer in the New World, tells us a few things about them. They were broad in the forehead, straight and well-proportioned. They were friendly and bore gifts to their visitors. They were skilled boat-builders and boatmen. They painted their faces

---

1. **J. B. Priestley:** (1894-1984) British novelist, playwright, and essayist.
2. **Stonehenge and Lascaux and Afrasiab:** Stonehenge, a group of prehistoric stone megaliths near Wiltshire, England, dates from c. 2950 BCE. Lascaux, a cave in Dordogne, France, is decorated with Paleolithic wall paintings of animals. Afrasiab, a fortress on several hills near the ancient city of Samarkand in Uzbekistan, dates from the sixth century BCE.

and their bodies. They made clothes and hammocks out of cotton. They lived in sturdy houses. They had dogs. And they too lived their daily lives in the element of language; they traded in words and names. We do not know what name or names they conferred upon their seafaring guests, but on October 17, on the sixth day of his sojourn among them, Columbus referred to them in his log as "Indios."

In 1492 the "Indians" were widespread in North, Central, and South America. They were the only human occupants of a third of the earth's land surface. And by the year 1492 they had been in the New World for untold thousands of years.

The "Paleo-Indians," as they are known, the ancestors of modern American Indians, came from Asia and entered upon the continent of North America by means of the Bering land bridge, a wide corridor of land, now submerged, connecting Siberia and Alaska. During the last glaciation (20,000 to 14,000 years ago) the top of the world was dominated by ice. Even so, most of Asia and most of Beringia were unglaciated. From Alaska to the Great Plains of the present United States ran a kind of corridor between the Cordilleran and Laurentide ice sheets, a thoroughfare for the migration of hunters and the animals they hunted. It is known that human bands had reached the Lena River drainage in northeastern Siberia at least 18,000 years ago. Over the next 7,000 years these nomads crossed the Bering bridge and dispersed widely throughout the Americas.

This dispersal is one of the great chapters in the story of mankind. It was an explosion, a revolution on a scale scarcely to be imagined. By 1492 there were untold numbers of indigenous human societies in the New World, untold numbers of languages and dialects, architecture to rival any monument of the Old World, astronomical observatories and solar calendars, a profound knowledge of natural medicine and the healing arts, very highly developed oral traditions, dramas, ceremonies, and – above all – a spiritual comprehension of the universe, a sense of the natural and supernatural, a sense of the sacred. Here was every evidence of man's long, inexorable ascendancy to civilization.

It is appropriate that I interject here my particular point of view. I am an American Indian, and I believe that I can therefore speak to the question of America before Columbus with a certain advantage of ancestral experience, a cultural continuity that reaches far back in time. My forebears have been in North America for many thousands of years. In my blood I have a real sense of that occupation. It is worth something to me, as indeed that long, unbroken tenure is worth something to every Native American.

I am Kiowa. The Kiowas are a Plains Indian people who reside now in Oklahoma. But they are newcomers to the Southern Plains, not having ventured below the Arkansas River until the eighteenth century. In 1492 they were near the headwaters of the Yellowstone River, in what is now western Montana. Their migration to the Southern Plains is the most recent migration of all those which have described the great dispersal of native peoples, and their Plains culture is the last culture to evolve in North America.

According to their origin myth, the Kiowas entered the world through a hollow log.[3] Where was the log, I wonder. And what was at the other end? When I imagine my blood back through generations to the earliest man in America, I see in my mind's eye a procession of shamanistic figures,[4] like those strange anthropomorphic forms painted on the cliffs of Barrier Canyon, Utah, emerging from the mists. They proceed, it seems, from the source of geology itself, from timelessness into time.

When man set foot on the continent of North America he was surely an endangered species. His resources were few, as we think of them from our vantage point in the twentieth century. He was almost wholly at the mercy of the elements, and the world he inhabited was hard and unforgiving. The simple accomplishment of survival must have demanded all of his strength. But he had certain indispensable resources. He knew how to hunt. He possessed tools and weapons, however crude. He could make fire. He probably had dogs and travois, perhaps sleds. He had some sense of society, of community, of cooperation. And, alone among the creatures of the earth, he could think and speak. He had a human sense of morality, an irresistible craving for order, beauty, appropriate behavior. He was intensely spiritual.

The Kiowas provide us with a fortunate example of migration and dispersal, I believe. Although their migration from the Yellowstone to the Wichita Mountains is recent (nonetheless prehistoric in the main), it was surely preceded by countless migrations of the same kind in the same landscape, generally speaking, over a period of some thousands of years. The experience of the Kiowas, then, from earliest evidence to the present, may serve to indicate in a general way the experience of other tribes and other cultures. It may allow us to understand something about the American Indian and about the condition of his presence in America in 1492.

The hollow log of the Kiowa origin myth is a not uncommon image in comparative mythology. The story of the tree of life is found throughout the world, and in most instances it is symbolic of passage, origination, evolution. It is tempting to associate the hollow log with the passage to America, the peopling of the Americas, to find in it a metaphorical reflection of the land bridge.

We tell stories in order to affirm our being and our place in the scheme of things. When the Kiowas entered upon the Great Plains they had to tell new stories of themselves, stories that would enable them to appropriate an unknown and intimidating landscape to their experience. They were peculiarly vulnerable

---

3. **hollow log:** This is a common image in Native American narratives. For example, in "Origin of Folk Stories," the Seneca story printed on page 35, Gaqka passes through a hollow log at the urging of his wife and he is healed.

4. **shamanistic figures:** According to some worldviews, shamans are persons with special access to good and evil spirits and who have special powers of healing.

in that landscape, and they told a story of dissension, finally of a schism in the tribe, brought about by a quarrel between two great chiefs. They encountered awesome forces and features in nature, and they explained them in story too. And so they told the story of Man-Ka-Ih, the storm spirit, which speaks the Kiowa language and does the Kiowas no harm, and they told of the tree that bore the seven sisters into the sky, where they became the stars of the Big Dipper. In so doing they not only accounted for the great monolith that is Devils Tower, Wyoming (in Kiowa, Tsoai, "rock tree"), but related themselves to the stars in the process. When they came upon the Plains they were befriended by the Crows, who gave them the sun-dance fetish Tai-Me, which was from that time on their most powerful medicine, and they told a story of the coming of Tai-Me in their hour of need. Language was their element. Words, spoken words, were the manifestations of their deepest belief, of their deepest feelings, of their deepest life. When Europeans first came to America, having had writing for hundreds of years and lately the printing press, they could not conceive of the spoken word as sacred, could not understand the American Indian's profound belief in the efficacy of language.

I have told the story of the arrowmaker many times. When I was a child I heard it told more times than I can say. It was at the center of my oral tradition long before I knew what that tradition was, and that is as it should be. The story had never been written down. It had existed, perhaps hundreds of years, at the level of the human voice.

> If an arrow is well made, it will have tooth marks upon it. That is how you know. The Kiowas made fine arrows and straightened them in their teeth. Then they drew them to the bow to see that they were straight. Once there was a man and his wife. They were alone at night in their tipi. By the light of a fire the man was making arrows. After a while he caught sight of something. There was a small opening in the tipi where two hides were sewn together. Someone was there on the outside, looking in. The man went on with his work, but he said to his wife, "Someone is standing outside. Do not be afraid. Let us talk easily, as of ordinary things." He took up an arrow and straightened it in his teeth; then, as it was right for him to do, he drew it to the bow and took aim, first in this direction and then in that. And all the while he was talking, as if to his wife. But this is how he spoke: "I know that you are there on the outside, for I can feel your eyes upon me. If you are a Kiowa, you will understand what I am saying, and you will speak your name." But there was no answer, and the man went on in the same way, pointing the arrow all around. At last his aim fell upon the place where his enemy stood, and he let go of the string. The arrow went straight to the enemy's heart.

Only after I had lived with the story for many years did I understand that it is about language. The storyteller is anonymous and illiterate, but he exists in his words, and he has survived for untold generations. The arrowmaker is a man made of words, and he too is a storyteller. He achieves victory over his enemy by exerting the force of language upon the unknown. What he does is far less important than what he says. His arrows are words. His enemy (and the presence outside *is* an enemy, for the storyteller tells us so) is vanquished by the word. The story is concise, beautiful, and alive. I know of nothing in literature that is more intensely alive.

Concurrent with the evolution of an oral tradition is the rise of ceremony. The sun dance was the preeminent expression of the spiritual life of the Plains culture. And it was a whole and intricate and profound expression.

And within the symmetry of this design of language and religion there came art. Universal in the world of the American Indian is a profound aesthetic sense. From ancient rock paintings to contemporary theater, through such forms as beadwork, featherwork, leathercraft, wood carving, ceramics, ledger-book drawing, music, and dance, American Indian art has rivaled other great art of the world. In museums and galleries around the globe are treasures of that art that are scarcely to be imagined.

These various expressions of the human spirit, emblematic of the American Indian today and five hundred years ago and long before that, are informed by an equation of man and the landscape that has had to be perceived, if neither appreciated nor acknowledged, by every society that has made contact with it. The naked people Columbus saw in 1492 were the members of a society altogether worthy and well made, a people of the everlasting earth, possessed of honor and dignity and a generosity of spirit unsurpassed.

[1993]

Explorations and
Early Encounters

THE EXPLORATION AND COLONIZATION of the Americas was spurred and widely publicized by the emerging print culture of Europe. Between the time that Johannes Gutenberg invented the printing press in 1450 and Columbus's first voyage in 1492, printing was introduced throughout Europe. Printed books consequently became familiar objects to most people, especially to the growing literate population. Although exact numbers are difficult to determine, some historians believe that there were as many as thirty thousand different editions of books printed in Europe before 1500. At least half of those books were religious in nature—church

◄ *Avantures mal-heureuses du Sieur de La Salle*

This print—the title of which may be translated as "The unhappy adventures of Sir de La Salle," the famous explorer who sailed from Canada through the Great Lakes and claimed the entire Mississippi River basin for France—appeared in an account of his expeditions published in 1698. The illustration shows La Salle, priests, and others on shore as supplies are unloaded from a ship, evidently during the explorer's final expedition, an ill-fated effort to establish a French colony on the Gulf of Mexico.

histories, collections of sermons, biblical commentaries, and, of course, the Latin Bible, the first book published by Gutenberg. But many secular works were also published, ranging from books on farming and home remedies to treatises on science, especially astrology and alchemy, to editions of the Greek and Latin classics. The printing press also made books that had been popular in manuscript editions available to a far wider audience. Among the most sought after of these early printed books was *The Travels of Marco Polo*, the tales of a famous Venetian traveler who in 1298-99 had written an account of the riches and wonders of China. First published in a French translation, the book was subsequently translated into several more languages and printed in many editions, including one owned and pored over by Christopher Columbus.

Like most of those who followed his lead, Columbus exploited the power of the printed word to "discover," or bring to prominence, his "discoveries" in the "New World." Accounts of the exploration of that world served a variety of purposes for both the authors and their audiences in Europe. Navigators and explorers were eager to report their findings to the rulers or companies that sponsored them, heralding the success or (in rare cases) explaining the failure of their expeditions. Sponsors expected a good return on their investments. In many cases, they also wanted to establish an unassailable claim on new lands.

Adam and Eve in America

This celebrated engraving is the opening image in the first volume of *America*, a series of lavishly illustrated travel narratives Theodor de Bry began to publish in Frankfurt, Germany, in 1590. The engraving depicts Adam and Eve at the moment prior to the Fall, the consequences of which are illustrated by the laborers in the background. At the same time, America is symbolically represented as the Garden of Eden, an unspoiled world of peace and plenty, which captured the imagination of Europeans.

Printed accounts of explorations and discoveries consequently became a kind of official patent, a way of taking possession of territory in the Americas. On his return voyage to Spain in 1493, Columbus wrote a letter to the sovereigns of Spain, describing the inhabitants, natural beauty, and unrivaled riches of the islands he had explored off what he mistakenly thought to be the mainland of Asia. As he doubtless anticipated, the letter was swiftly published in Spain, and translations were soon printed throughout Europe. After that, a chronicle of virtually every major voyage to and investigation of the New World quickly appeared in print in Europe, where the literature of exploration became a fixed and fascinating fact of life.

During the sixteenth century, Spain remained the dominant power in the Americas. It eventually claimed territory in North, Central, and South America more than ten times the size of the Iberian Peninsula shared by Portugal and Spain. One of its few failures was an expedition in 1527 to establish a colony in present-day Florida. A leader and a survivor of this disastrous expedition, Álvar Núñez Cabeza de Vaca, spent eight years first as a captive and then as a wanderer among the Indian tribes in what is now the southwestern United States. Although he developed a growing respect for the indigenous populations and pleaded for more humane policies toward them, the adventures described in *The Narrative of Cabeza de Vaca* (1542) fueled the flames of Spanish conquest in the Americas.

Other nations also explored and began to establish colonies there. Since they did not have the means to combat the Spanish in the extensive areas under their control, the French and the English concentrated their efforts along the eastern coast of North America. Although hopes were fading of finding a Northwest Passage that would lead through the continent to China and India, the French began to recognize the region's valuable natural resources and the potential for trade with its native peoples. Under the sponsorship of Henry IV of France, Samuel de Champlain founded Quebec in 1608, the year after the English established their first permanent settlement, Jamestown, in what they called Virginia. Champlain also tirelessly promoted the vast potential of North America in a series of accounts of his adventures and explorations, including *Les Voyages du Sieur de Champlain* (1613). His books were widely read in France, generating growing enthusiasm for an empire in the New World. Indeed, by virtue of his explorations and writings, Champlain has been called "the Father of New France," a vast territory that ultimately extended from Newfoundland to Lake Superior and from Hudson Bay to the Gulf of Mexico.

In a dedicatory letter written to Marie de Médicis, the queen regent of France and widow of King Henry IV, Champlain in his *Voyages* emphasizes the importance of navigation to his country's aspirations in North America:

Les Voyages du Sieur de Champlain

This engraving from the 1619 edition of Champlain's *Voyages* shows a deer trap used by Algonkin and Montagnais tribes near the French settlement at Quebec. In contrast to many European explorers, Champlain carefully observed and described the practices of native peoples, though the stylized figures and landscape depicted here more closely resemble those in a European hunting picture than a scene from eastern Canada.

By this art we obtain a knowledge of different countries, regions, and realms. By it we attract and bring to our own land all kinds of riches; by it the idolatry of paganism is overthrown and Christianity proclaimed throughout all the regions of the earth.

Of all the most useful and excellent arts, that of navigation has always seemed to me to occupy the first place. For the more hazardous it is, and the more numerous the perils and losses by which it is attended, so much the more is it esteemed and exalted above all others, being wholly unsuited to the timid and irresolute. By this art we obtain a knowledge of different countries, regions, and realms. By it we attract and bring to our own land all kinds of riches; by it the idolatry of paganism is overthrown and Christianity proclaimed throughout all the regions of the earth. This is the art which won my love in my early years, and induced me to expose myself almost all my life to the impetuous waves of the ocean, and led me to explore the coasts of a part of America, especially of New France.

Champlain's letter reveals a good deal about both the early European explorers and the literature of exploration of the Americas. Like Champlain, the early explorers prided themselves on their courage in going where no European had gone before and gaining the first glimpse of what for them and their audience was an unknown world. Certain of their cultural superiority, they wished to enrich their own countries and to promote Christianity. Many of the early narratives of exploration were essentially imperial apologias, justifications of incursions into the Americas by soldiers and settlers carrying the flags of European nations and bearing the banner of Christianity. For the most part, European explorers were also supremely confident that they could completely understand and communicate what they heard and saw in the ancient lands they persisted in calling a New World. Even as they carefully mapped and charted that world, many of the explorers offered detailed descriptions of the plants, animals, and practices of its peoples.

But narratives that often appear to be simply factual, firsthand accounts of what the European explorers observed and experienced were complicated

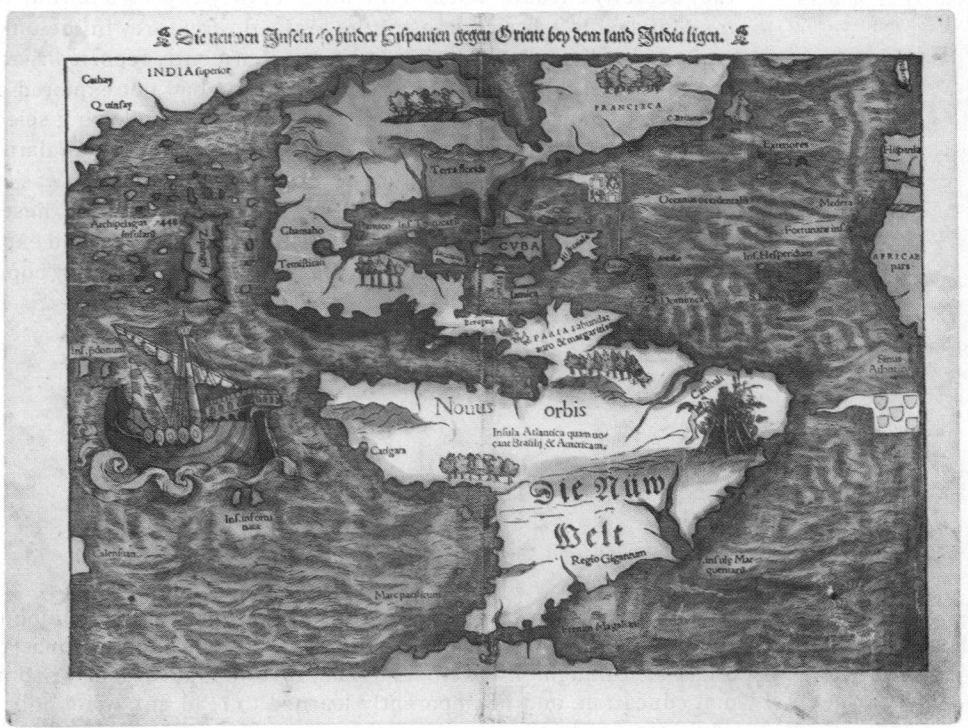

First Map of the American Continents

This woodblock-print map by German cartographer Sebastian Münster, the first separate map of the Americas and the first to show them in true continental form, originally appeared in 1540. Although he labeled the southern land mass "Novus orbis" and "die Nüw Welt" — Latin and German for "New World" — Münster also included a reference to "America." By doing so he perpetuated the name that had originated in a 1507 map by another German cartographer, Martin Waldseemüller.

by a number of factors. Lacking a vocabulary adequate to describe the unique particulars of the New World, early explorers often identified what they saw or heard in terms of what they had previously known. In his description of Hispaniola in his 1493 letter, for example, Columbus noted that he heard the song of the nightingale, or European thrush, which did not exist in the Western Hemisphere. Moreover, although European navigators and explorers cast themselves as reporters rather than writers, their accounts were influenced by literary texts ranging from ancient epics and medieval romances to popular books such as *Mandeville's Travels*, with its imaginary descriptions of the wonders of the East. In fact, the descriptions of European explorers were shaped by both what they actually encountered and the wonders they expected to find. Recalling Mandeville's descriptions of the fantastic creatures in the unknown lands of the East, Columbus in his letter confidently reported that "men are born with tails" in one of the provinces he had not explored on the island he renamed Juana, now Cuba. Indeed, as the following selections from the writings of Columbus, Cabeza de Vaca, and Champlain illustrate, in the European literature of exploration "America" was poised between imagination and reality, theory and fact. Certainly, these texts reveal some of the complex ways in which such navigators and explorers sought at once to comprehend and to make explicable a heavily populated world equal in landmass to the "world" known to Europeans before Columbus's first voyage in 1492.

Christopher Columbus

[1451–1506]

Born in the Italian seaport of Genoa in 1451, Christopher Columbus was the son of Domenico Columbo, a wool merchant, and Suzanna Fontanarossa, the daughter of a wool merchant. Columbus evidently had no formal education, and he apparently learned to read and write only as an adult. He was trained in the wool trade and may also have studied mapmaking with his brother, Bartolomeo. His first experience at sea was in 1474, when he spent a year on a ship bound for Khios, an island in the Aegean Sea. Two years later, Columbus was a member of the crew of a commercial ship that was attacked by French privateers. Few other details are known about his life until 1477, when Columbus was living in Lisbon, Portugal, where his brother was working as a mapmaker. That year, he became a merchant sailor with the Portuguese fleet and sailed to Ireland and possibly Iceland. Other voyages took him to the coast of West Africa.

Columbus was poised for a career as an explorer. In the fifteenth century, the expansion of the Muslim Ottoman Empire began to disrupt the lucrative overland trade routes from Christian Europe to India and China. Europeans were consequently determined to discover another trade route to the East. Inspired by his earlier voyages, his commitment to spreading Christianity, and a favorite book, *The Travels of Marco Polo*, with its accounts of the riches of the East, Columbus sought support for a voyage that would find a way there by sailing west across the Atlantic Ocean. By the fifteenth century, most Europeans no longer believed that the world was flat, but there was widespread disagreement about the size of the circumference of the earth. Columbus first offered his services to the rulers of Portugal. But they believed that his calculations were wrong, and their interests were, at least for the moment, focused on West Africa. Columbus then approached the courts of France and England, both of which also rejected his plan. Finally, he turned to the new monarchs of a united Spain, King Ferdinand and Queen Isabel, who granted him permission and funding for a voyage to begin in 1492. On August 3, Columbus set sail from Palos, Spain, with three ships, the *Santa María*, the *Niña*, and the *Pinta*. He reached what are now called the West Indies on October 12, 1492. Believing he had reached the East Indies, Columbus renamed each island he encountered, claiming for Spain both the lands and their natives, whom he collectively called "*los indios*," or the Indians. He also started a colony by leaving thirty-nine crew members on the island he named Hispaniola, where he assumed they would begin to Christianize the natives and establish plantations that would bring economic benefits to Spain.

Returning to Spain in 1493, Columbus reported his "discoveries" and proclaimed the great riches of the "New World." During the following five years, he undertook three additional voyages, further exploring the islands of the Caribbean as well as stretches of the coasts of Central and South America. Columbus never set foot on North America, and until the end of his life believed that the lands he explored were close to the mainland of Asia. Although he did not achieve his ultimate goal of finding a new trade route to China, Columbus gained riches for himself and paved the way for the expansion of European commerce and Christianity into these new territories for the next three hundred years.

What was a boon for Spain and later for other European nations, however, was a catastrophe for the indigenous inhabitants of the lands Columbus opened up to colonization. Ancient religious practices and cultural traditions were destroyed by colonists determined to impose European culture and spread Christianity. In addition to being exposed to diseases to which they had no immunity, the native populations were frequently subjected to enslavement or slaughter. On the island of Hispaniola, for example, the native Taino population was reduced from as many as one million in 1492 to roughly thirty thousand in 1510, only four years after Columbus died and was buried in Spain. At the request of his widow, however, his remains were later moved to Hispaniola,

bedfordstmartins.com/ **americanlit** *for research links on Columbus*

The Columbus Letter

The Latin translation of Columbus's letter published in Basel in 1494 contains the first portrait of the peoples he encountered, represented by two groups of naked "Indians." The scene focuses on the imminent exchange of gifts between the figure on the shore and the two Europeans landing on the island. Like the ship in the foreground, which bears little resemblance to the light, three-masted caravels used for exploration during the fifteenth century, the peaceful scene bears little relation to the brutal Spanish conquest of the Americas that swiftly followed Columbus's first voyage in 1492.

where they were buried by the side of the altar in the cathedral of Santa Domingo.

Reading Columbus's "Letter."

Onboard the *Niña* on his homeward passage to Spain in 1493, and in the midst of a hurricane, Columbus wrote a formal letter to Luís de Santangel, secretary to the royal court of Spain, which had supported his project to find a new trade route to China. Columbus clearly intended his letter to be read by the sovereigns who sponsored his voyage, the Spanish monarchs King Ferdinand and Queen Isabel. Although he drew heavily on the detailed journal he kept during his eight-month voyage, Columbus sought to heighten interest in his discoveries by exaggerating some of his findings, especially the "gold incalculable" to be found on the islands he had explored. Columbus also designed the letter as a public report of his voyage, discoveries, and formal claim of new territories for Spain. The letter was consequently printed in Barcelona in late March or early April 1493. A brief pamphlet printed on two leaves of folio-sized paper, the letter is considered by many scholars to be the single most important printed document in the history of the early exploration of the Americas. Copies of the pamphlet were distributed throughout Spain, and soon there were nearly two dozen editions of the letter in several European languages, some of them accompanied by fanciful illustrations of the natives Columbus had encountered. For the first time, an account of the "New World" was available for large numbers to read, and Columbus's letter fired the imaginations of Europeans and spurred further exploration of what later came to be called the Americas. The text is taken from *The Voyages of Christopher Columbus*, edited and translated from the Spanish by Cecil Jane (1930).

LETTER OF COLUMBUS,
DESCRIBING THE RESULTS OF HIS FIRST VOYAGE

Sir:

Since I know that you will be pleased at the great victory with which Our Lord has crowned my voyage, I write this to you, from which you will learn how in thirty-three days I passed from the Canary Islands to the Indies, with the fleet which the most illustrious king and queen, our sovereigns, gave to me. There I found very many islands, filled with people innumerable, and of them all I have taken possession for their highnesses, by proclamation made and with the royal standard unfurled, and no opposition was offered to me.

To the first island which I found I gave the name "San Salvador," in remembrance of the Divine Majesty, Who had marvellously bestowed all this; the Indians call it "Guanahani." To the second, I gave the name the island of "Santa Maria de Concepcion," to the third, "Fernandina," to the fourth, "Isabella," to the fifth island, "Juana," and so each received from me a new name.[1]

When I came to Juana, I followed its coast to the westward, and I found it to be so extensive that I thought that it must be the mainland, the province of Cathay.[2] And since there were neither towns nor villages on the seashore, but small hamlets only, with the people of which I could not have speech, because they all fled immediately, I went forward on the same course, thinking that I could not fail to find great cities and towns. At the end of many leagues, seeing that there was no change and that the coast was bearing me northwards, which I wished to avoid, since winter was already approaching and I

---

1. **To the first island . . . a new name:** The islands Columbus named have not been positively identified, except for *Juana*, his name for what is now Cuba.
2. **Cathay:** A province of China, which Columbus initially thought he had reached.

proposed to make from it to the south, and as, moreover, the wind was carrying me forward, I determined not to wait for a change in the weather and retraced my path as far as a remarkable harbour known to me. From that point, I sent two men inland to learn if there were a king or great cities. They travelled three days' journey, finding an infinity of small hamlets and people without number, but nothing of importance. For this reason, they returned.

I understood sufficiently from other Indians, whom I had already taken, that this land was nothing but an island, and I therefore followed its coast eastward for one hundred and seven leagues to the point where it ended. From that point, I saw another island, distant about eighteen leagues from the first, to the east, and to it I at once gave the name "Española."[3] I went there and followed its northern coast, as I had followed that of Juana, to the eastward for one hundred and eighty-eight great leagues in a straight line. This island and all the others are very fertile to a limitless degree, and this island is extremely so. In it there are many harbours on the coast of the sea, beyond comparison with others that I know in Christendom, and many rivers, good and large, which is marvellous. Its lands are high; there are in it many sierras and very lofty mountains, beyond comparison with that of Teneriffe.[4] All are most beautiful, of a thousand shapes; all are accessible and are filled with trees of a thousand kinds and tall, so that they seem to touch the sky. I am told that they never lose their foliage, and this I can believe, for I saw them as green and lovely as they are in Spain in May, and some of them were flowering, some bearing fruit, and some on another stage, according to their nature. The nightingale was singing[5] and other birds of a thousand kinds, in the month of November, there where I went. There are six or eight kinds of palm, which are a wonder to behold on account of their beautiful variety, but so are the other trees and fruits and plants. In it are marvellous pine groves; there are very wide and smiling plains, and there is honey; and there are birds of many kinds and fruits in great diversity. In the interior, there are mines of metals, and the population is without number. Española is a marvel.

The sierras and the mountains, the plains, the arable and pasture lands, are so lovely and so rich for planting and sowing, for breeding cattle of every kind, for building towns and villages. The harbours of the sea here are such as cannot be believed to exist unless they have been seen, and so with the rivers, many and great, and of good water, the majority of which contain gold. In the trees, fruits and plants, there is a great difference from those of Juana. In this island, there are many spices and great mines of gold and of other metals.

The people of this island and of all the other islands which I have found and of which I have information, all go naked, men and women, as their mothers bore them, although some of the women cover a single place with the leaf of a plant or with a net of cotton which they make for the purpose. They have no iron or steel or weapons, nor are they

---

3. "Española": Today, the island of Hispaniola includes the countries of Haiti and the Dominican Republic.
4. Teneriffe: One of the Canary Islands, an archipelago off the coast of northwestern Africa.
5. The nightingale was singing: Columbus was mistaken, since the nightingale, or European thrush, was not native to the West Indies.

fitted to use them. This is not because they are not well built and of handsome stature, but because they are very marvellously timorous. They have no other arms than spears made of canes, cut in seeding time, to the ends of which they fix a small sharpened stick. Of these they do not dare to make use, for many times it has happened that I have sent ashore two or three men to some town to have speech with them, and countless people have come out to them, and as soon as they have seen my men approaching, they have fled, a father even not waiting for his son. This is not because ill has been done to any one of them; on the contrary, at every place where I have been and have been able to have speech with them, I have given to them of that which I had, such as cloth and many other things, receiving nothing in exchange. But so they are, incurably timid. It is true that, after they have been reassured and have lost this fear, they are so guileless and so generous with all that they possess, that no one would believe it who has not seen it. They refuse nothing that they possess, if it be asked of them; on the contrary, they invite any one to share it and display as much love as if they would give their hearts. They are content with whatever trifle of whatever kind it may be that is given to them, whether it be of value or valueless. I forbade that they should be given things so worthless as fragments of broken crockery, scraps of broken glass and ends of straps, although when they were able to get them, they fancied that they possessed the best jewel in the world. So it was found that for a strap a sailor received gold to the weight of two and a half castellanos,[6] and others received much more for other things which were worth less. As for new blancas,[7] for them they would give everything which they had, although it might be two or three castellanos' weight of gold or an arroba[8] or two of spun cotton. They took even the pieces of the broken hoops of the wine barrels and, like savages, gave what they had, so that it seemed to me to be wrong and I forbade it. I gave them a thousand handsome good things, which I had brought, in order that they might conceive affection for us and, more than that, might become Christians and be inclined to the love and service of your highnesses and of the whole Castilian nation,[9] and strive to aid us and to give us of the things which they have in abundance and which are necessary to us.

They do not hold any creed nor are they idolaters; only they all believe that power and good are in the heavens and are very firmly convinced that I, with these ships and men, came from the heavens, and in this belief they everywhere received me after they had mastered their fear. This belief is not the result of ignorance, for they are, on the contrary, of a very acute intelligence and they are men who navigate all those seas, so that it is amazing how good an account they give of everything. It is because they have never seen people clothed or ships of such a kind.

As soon as I arrived in the Indies, in the first island which I found, I took by force some of the natives,[10] in order that they might learn and might give me information of that

---

6. **castellanos:** Gold coins.
7. **blancas:** Small coins worth less than a cent.
8. **arroba:** Roll of cloth.
9. **Castilian nation:** Spain.
10. **took by force some of the natives:** Columbus enslaved some natives, whom he taught Spanish so that they could serve as translators.

which there is in these parts. And so it was that they soon understood us, and we them, either by speech or signs, and they have been very serviceable. I still carry them with me, and they are always assured that I come from Heaven, for all the intercourse which they have had with me. They were the first to announce this wherever I went, and the others went running from house to house, and to the neighbouring towns, with loud cries of, "Come! Come! See the men from Heaven!" So all, men and women alike, when their minds are set at rest concerning us, came, not one, small or great, remaining behind, and they all brought something to eat and drink, which they gave with extraordinary affection.

In all the islands, they have very many canoes, which are like rowing fustas, some larger and some smaller; some are greater than a fusta of eighteen benches.[11] They are not so broad, because they are made of a single log of wood, but a fusta would not keep up with them in rowing, since their speed is a thing incredible. In these they navigate among all those islands, which are innumerable, and carry their goods. One of these canoes I have seen with seventy and eighty men in it, each one with his oar.

In all these islands, I saw no great diversity in the appearance of the people or in their manners and language. On the contrary, they all understand one another, which is a very curious thing, on account of which I hope that their highnesses will determine upon their conversion to our holy faith, towards which they are very inclined.

I have already said how I went one hundred and seven leagues in a straight line from west to east along the seashore of the island of Juana, and as a result of this voyage I can say that this island is larger than England and Scotland together, for, beyond these one hundred and seven leagues, there remain to the westward two provinces to which I have not gone. One of these provinces they call "Avan," and there people are born with tails. These provinces cannot have a length of less than fifty or sixty leagues, as I could understand from those Indians whom I have and who know all the islands.

The other island, Española, has a circumference greater than all Spain from Collioure by the seacoast to Fuenterabia in Vizcaya, for I voyaged along one side for one hundred and eighty-eight great leagues in a straight line from west to east.[12] It is a land to be desired and, when seen, never to be left. I have taken possession of all for their highnesses, and all are more richly endowed than I know how or am able to say, and I hold all for their highnesses, so that they may dispose of them as they do of the kingdoms of Castile and as absolutely. But especially, in this Española, in the situation most convenient and in the best position for the mines of gold and for all trade as well with the mainland here as with that there, belonging to the Grand Khan,[13] where will be great trade and profit, I have taken possession of a large town, to which I gave the name "Villa

---

11. **a fusta of eighteen benches:** To facilitate trade among the islands, the natives built large canoes made of a single log, with benches for rowers and space at either end for passengers and cargo.

12. **from west to east:** In equating the circuit of the island to the distance around the Spanish peninsula from Collioure on the Gulf of Lyons to Fuenterabia on the Bay of Biscay, Columbus greatly exaggerated the size of Hispaniola.

13. **Grand Khan:** The name given to the leader of the Mongolian Empire in China.

de Navidad," and in it I have made fortifications and a fort, which will now by this time be entirely completed. In it I have left enough men for such a purpose with arms and artillery and provisions for more than a year, and a fusta, and one, a master of all sea-craft, to build others, and I have established great friendship with the king of that land, so much so, that he was proud to call me "brother" and to treat me as such. And even were he to change his attitude to one of hostility towards these men, he and his do not know what arms are. They go naked, as I have already said, and they are the most timorous people in the world, so that the men whom I have left there alone would suffice to destroy all that land, and the island is without danger for their persons, if they know how to govern themselves.

In all these islands, it seems to me that all men are content with one woman, and to their chief or king they give as many as twenty. It appears to me that the women work more than do the men. I have not been able to learn if they hold private property; it seemed to me to be that all took a share in that which any one had, especially of eatable things.

In these islands I have so far found no human monstrosities, as many expected, but on the contrary the whole population is very well formed, nor are they negroes as in Guinea, but their hair is flowing and they are not born where there is intense force in the rays of the sun. It is true that the sun has there great power, although it is distant from the equinoctial line twenty-six degrees. In these islands, where there are high mountains, the cold was severe this winter, but they endure it, being used to it and with the help of meats which they consume with many and extremely hot spices. As I have found no monsters, so I have had no report of any, except in an island "Quaris," which is the second at the coming into the Indies,[14] and which is inhabited by a people who are regarded in all the islands as very fierce and who eat human flesh. They have many canoes with which they range through all the islands of India and pillage and take whatever they can. They are no more malformed than are the others, except that they have the custom of wearing their hair long like women, and they use bows and arrows of the same cane stems, with a small piece of wood at the end, owing to their lack of iron which they do not possess. They are ferocious among these other people who are cowardly to an excessive degree, but I make no more account of them than of the rest. These are they who have intercourse with the women of "Martinio,"[15] which is the first island met on the way from Spain to the Indies, in which there is not a man. These women engage in no feminine occupation, but use bows and arrows of cane, like those already mentioned, and they arm and protect themselves with plates of copper, of which they have much.

In another island, which they assure me is larger than Española, the people have no hair. In it there is gold incalculable, and from it and from the other islands I bring with me Indians as evidence.

---

14. **an island "Quaris" . . . at the coming into the Indies:** The captive natives evidently indicated the position of this island, which they called "Quaris." Columbus landed on the island, which he renamed Dominica, during his second voyage in 1494.

15. **"Martinio":** Martinique, as the island was later named by the French.

In conclusion, to speak only of that which has been accomplished on this voyage, which was so hasty, their highnesses can see that I will give them as much gold as they may need, if their highnesses will render me very slight assistance; moreover, I will give them spices and cotton, as much as their highnesses shall command; and mastic, as much as they shall order to be shipped and which, up to now, has been found only in Greece, in the island of Chios, and the Seignory[16] sells it for what it pleases; and aloe, as much as they shall order to be shipped; and slaves, as many as they shall order to be shipped and who will be from the idolaters.[17] I believe also that I have found rhubarb and cinnamon, and I shall find a thousand other things of value, which the people whom I have left there will have discovered, for I have not delayed at any point, so far as the wind allowed me to sail, except in the town of Navidad, in order to leave it secured and well established, and in truth I should have done much more if the ships had served me as reason demanded.[18]

This is enough. And the eternal God, Our Lord, Who gives to all those who walk in His way, triumph over things which appear to be impossible, and this was notably one. For, although men have talked or have written of these lands, all was conjectural, without suggestion of ocular evidence, but amounted only to this, that those who heard for the most part listened and judged rather by hearsay than from even a small something tangible. So that, since Our Redeemer has given the victory to our most illustrious king and queen, and to their renowned kingdoms, in so great a matter, for this all Christendom ought to feel delight and make great feasts and give solemn thanks to the Holy Trinity, with many solemn prayers for the great exaltation which they shall have in the turning of so many peoples to our holy faith, and afterwards for the temporal benefits, because not only Spain but all Christendom will have hence refreshment and gain.

This in accordance with that which has been accomplished, thus briefly.

Done in the caravel, off the Canary Islands, on the fifteenth of February, in the year one thousand four hundred and ninety-three.

At your orders.

THE ADMIRAL

After having written this,[19] and being in the sea of Castile, there came upon me so great a south-south-west wind that I was obliged to lighten ship. But I ran here to-day into this port of Lisbon, which was the greatest marvel in the world, whence I decided to write to their highnesses. In all the Indies, I have always found weather like May. There I went in thirty-three days and I should have returned in twenty-eight, save for these storms which have detained me for fourteen days, beating about in this sea. Here all the sailors say that never has there been so bad a winter nor so many ships lost.

Done on the fourth day of March.

[1493, 1930]

---

16. **Seignory:** The system of government in Genoa, Italy, where Columbus was born.

17. **idolaters:** Non-Christians. Columbus includes the discovery of a new source of slaves as one of the important outcomes of his voyage.

18. **ships . . . demanded:** The *Santa María,* Columbus's flagship, was grounded on a reef near Hispaniola and sank on December 25, 1492. His other ships, the *Pinta* and the *Niña,* were caravels, smaller vessels designed for speed and maneuverability in difficult waters.

19. **After having written this:** This note was wrapped around the letter and sealed.

Álvar Núñez Cabeza de Vaca

[c. 1490–c. 1557]

Álvar Núñez Cabeza de Vaca was born in Jerez, Spain, around 1490. His aristocratic family had been given the title Cabeza de Vaca, or "Head of a Cow," in honor of an ancestor who had helped the Spanish Christians gain an important victory over the Moors by marking an unguarded mountain pass with the skull of a cow. Very little is known about Cabeza de Vaca's life before he was appointed to serve as treasurer and second in command of a royal expedition led by Pánfilo de Narváez. The expedition of five ships and six hundred men left Spain on June 17, 1527, to establish a Spanish colony in Florida. By the time the expedition finally arrived in April 1528 in what is today known as Tampa Bay, the number of men had been reduced to three hundred by death and desertion. The conquistadores wandered for nearly six months north through Florida, where many of the men became sick with malaria and dysentery. They also encountered fierce opposition from the Apalachee, who tenaciously defended their lands against the invaders. Narváez consequently decided to retreat by building makeshift barges and sailing to Spanish settlements in Mexico. Separated from

La relacion y comentarios del gouernador Aluar nuñez cabeça de vaca

The frontispiece of the second edition of Cabeza de Vaca's report to the Spanish crown, published in Spain in 1555, bears the coat of arms of the Holy Roman Emperor Charles V (Charles I of Spain) held by the double-headed eagle of the House of Hapsburg.

Narváez, whose barge was apparently lost at sea, Cabeza de Vaca and eighty men on two of the other barges were shipwrecked on what he later described as the "Isle of Misfortune," probably Galveston Island off the coast of present-day Texas, in November 1528.

During the next eight years, Cabeza de Vaca underwent one of the most remarkable and transformative experiences in the early annals of European exploration of the Americas. By the end of the first winter, all but a handful of the Spaniards had died of disease, exposure, or starvation. In a twist of fate, the surviving conquistadores, the would-be conquerors, were taken captive by the Karankawa. Cabeza de Vaca was a slave for two years, after which he managed to escape to the mainland, where he lived for five years among a seminomadic tribe, the Coahuiltecans. He worked as a trader, bartering coral and seashells with the native inhabitants, from whom he eventually learned that three other survivors of the Spanish expedition were living on the coast. With them, Cabeza de Vaca decided to make his way to Mexico, embarking in 1535 upon what proved to be a two-thousand-mile journey on foot through territory that had never before been seen by Europeans. As the four men made their way across what is now the southwestern United States and northern Mexico, they gained a growing reputation as healers, finding a warm welcome and a growing following among the numerous tribes they encountered.

During these years of living among native peoples, Cabeza de Vaca experienced considerable change in his worldview. In his later account of the final approach to the Spanish settlements in Mexico, for example, he grimly described the devastating effects that had already been wrought by his countrymen, especially the Spanish slave hunters who captured slaves to work on the ranches, sugar plantations, and in the gold mines: "It made us extremely sad to see how fertile the land was, and very beautiful, and very full of springs and rivers, and to see every place deserted and burned, and the people so thin and ill, all of them fled and hidden." As they neared the end of their long journey, the ragged survivors of the Narváez expedition encountered a group of slave hunters, who to Cabeza de Vaca's horror sought to seize the hundreds of Pima Indians accompanying the revered healers into Mexico. After insisting that the Indians remain free, Cabeza de Vaca and his three companions went on to the nearest Spanish settlement, from which they were escorted to Mexico City in July 1536.

When he returned to Spain later that year, Cabeza de Vaca was a far different man than the zealous conquistador who had left the country nine years earlier. He soon began to write an account of his experiences in the New World, *La relacion que dio Aluar nuñez cabeça de vaca* (1542). Still deeply committed to the Catholic faith and Spanish culture, he sought to encourage further expeditions. But he also urged the adoption of more benign and just policies toward the native populations. Cabeza de Vaca later returned as the governor of an expedition to

bedfordstmartins.com/ americanlit for research links on Cabeza de Vaca

present-day Paraguay, where he came into conflict with Spanish colonists who were primarily interested in exploiting the lands they settled and the native peoples of the country. Accused of corruption, Cabeza de Vaca was arrested and returned in chains to Spain in 1545. When the dispute was finally settled in 1551, he was exiled to North Africa and forbidden ever to return to the New World. While in exile, he wrote an account of his experiences in South America, *La relacion y comentarios del gouernador Aluar nuñez cabeça de vaca* (1555). The account was published after he was allowed to return to Spain, where he died about 1557.

Reading Cabeza de Vaca's *Narrative*.   Begun as a formal report to Emperor Charles V of Spain on the disastrous royal expedition led by Pánfilo de Narváez, *La relacion que dio Aluar nuñez cabeça de vaca* was published in 1542. A second edition was published in 1555, and the book was subsequently translated into many languages. The first English translation was a partial version published in an early collection of travel literature compiled by Samuel Purchas in 1625. A complete English translation was not published until 1851.

Few accounts of the early explorations of the Americas equal the historical, anthropological, and literary significance of Cabeza de Vaca's *Narrative*. Even before the formal account was published, his reports of a vast area that no European had set foot on inspired Spanish expeditions into North America, notably the brutal march led by Francisco Vásquez de Coronado across the Southwest to the Great Plains. Although Cabeza de Vaca sought to inspire more humane treatment of the indigenous peoples, his account led directly to their further devastation by Spanish conquistadores. At the same time, his account contains the richest and most detailed descriptions of those indigenous peoples and their cultural traditions. Cabeza de Vaca's *Narrative* was also the first captivity narrative, a story of a European's forced immersion into and subsequent effort to come to terms with an alien culture. The following selections include the proem, or preface, addressed to Emperor Charles V, as well as chapters in which Cabeza de Vaca describes the experiences of the few Spanish survivors of the expedition after they were shipwrecked on an island off the coast of present-day Texas. The text is taken from *Spanish Explorers in the Southern United States, 1528–1543*, edited by Frederick W. Hodge (1907).

From THE NARRATIVE OF CABEZA DE VACA

Proem

Sacred Caesarian Catholic Majesty:

Among the many who have held sway, I think no prince can be found whose service has been attended with the ardor and emulation shown for that of your Highness[1] at this time. The inducement is evident and powerful: men do not pursue together the same career without motive, and strangers are observed to strive with those who are equally impelled by religion and loyalty.

Although ambition and love of action are common to all, as to the advantages that each may gain, there are great inequalities of fortune, the result not of conduct, but only accident, nor caused by the fault of any one, but coming in the providence of God and solely by His will. Hence to one arises deeds more signal than he thought to achieve; to another the opposite in every way occurs, so that he can show no higher proof of purpose than his effort, and at times even this is so concealed that it cannot of itself appear.

As for me, I can say in undertaking the march I made on the main by the royal authority, I firmly trusted that my conduct and services would be as evident and distinguished as were those of my ancestors and that I should not have to speak in order to be reckoned among those who for diligence and fidelity in affairs your Majesty honors. Yet, as neither my counsel nor my constancy availed to gain aught for which we set out, agreeably to your interests, for our sins, no one of the many armaments that have gone into those parts has been permitted to find itself in straits great like ours, or come to an end alike forlorn and fatal. To me, one only duty remains, to present a relation of what was seen and heard in the ten years I wandered lost and in privation through many and remote lands. Not merely a statement of positions and distances, animals and vegetation, but of the diverse customs of the many and very barbarous people with whom I talked and dwelt, as well as all other matters I could hear of and discern, that in some way I may avail your Highness. My hope of going out from among those nations was always small, still my care and diligence were none the less to keep in particular remembrance everything, that if at any time God our Lord should will to bring me where I now am, it might testify to my exertion in the royal behalf.

As the narrative is in my opinion of no trivial value to those who in your name go to subdue those countries and bring them to a knowledge of the true faith and true Lord, and under the imperial dominion, I have written this with much exactness; and although in it may be read things very novel and for some persons difficult to believe, nevertheless they may without hesitation credit me as strictly faithful. Better than to exaggerate, I have lessened in all things, and it is sufficient to say the relation is offered to your Majesty for truth. I beg it may be received in the name of homage, since it is the most that one could bring who returned thence naked.

---

1. **your Highness:** Emperor Charles V (1500–1558), grandson of and successor to Ferdinand and Isabel, monarchs of Spain.

Chapter 15
What befell us among the people of Malhado

On an island of which I have spoken, they wished to make us physicians without examination or inquiring for diplomas. They cure by blowing upon the sick, and with that breath and the imposing of hands they cast out infirmity. They ordered that we also should do this, and be of use to them in some way. We laughed at what they did, telling them it was folly, that we knew not how to heal. In consequence, they withheld food from us until we should practise what they required. Seeing our persistence, an Indian told me I knew not what I uttered, in saying that what he knew availed nothing; for stones and other matters growing about in the fields have virtue, and that passing a pebble along the stomach would take away pain and restore health, and certainly then we who were extraordinary men must possess power and efficacy over all other things. At last, finding ourselves in great want we were constrained to obey; but without fear lest we should be blamed for any failure or success.

Their custom is, on finding themselves sick to send for a physician, and after he has applied the cure, they give him not only all they have, but seek among their relatives for more to give. The practitioner scarifies over the seat of pain, and then sucks about the wound. They make cauteries with fire, a remedy among them in high repute, which I have tried on myself and found benefit from it. They afterwards blow on the spot, and having finished, the patient considers that he is relieved.

Our method was to bless the sick, breathing upon them, and recite a Pater-noster and an Ave-Maria,[2] praying with all earnestness to God our Lord that he would give health and influence them to make us some good return. In his clemency he willed that all those for whom we supplicated, should tell the others that they were sound and in health, directly after we made the sign of the blessed cross over them. For this the Indians treated us kindly; they deprived themselves of food that they might give to us, and presented us with skins and some trifles.

So protracted was the hunger we there experienced, that many times I was three days without eating. The natives also endured as much; and it appeared to me a thing impossible that life could be so prolonged, although afterwards I found myself in greater hunger and necessity, which I shall speak of farther on.

The Indians who had Alonzo del Castillo, Andrés Dorantes, and the others that remained alive, were of a different tongue and ancestry from these, and went to the opposite shore of the main to eat oysters, where they staid until the first day of April, when they returned. The distance is two leagues in the widest part. The island is half a league in breadth and five leagues in length.

The inhabitants of all this region go naked. The women alone have any part of their persons covered, and it is with a wool that grows on trees.[3] The damsels dress themselves in deer-skin. The people are generous to each other of what they possess. They have no chief. All that are of a lineage keep together. They speak two languages; those of

---

2. **Pater-noster and an Ave-Maria:** The recitation of two prayers important in the Catholic religion, the Lord's Prayer and the Hail Mary.
3. **a wool that grows on trees:** Spanish moss.

one are called Capoques, those of the other, Han. They have a custom when they meet, or from time to time when they visit, of remaining half an hour before they speak, weeping; and, this over, he that is visited first rises and gives the other all he has, which is received, and after a little while he carries it away, and often goes without saying a word. They have other strange customs; but I have told the principal of them, and the most remarkable, that I may pass on and further relate what befell us.

Chapter 16
The Christians leave the island of Malhado

After Dorantes and Castillo returned to the island, they brought together the Christians, who were somewhat separated, and found them in all to be fourteen. As I have said, I was opposite on the main, where my Indians had taken me, and where so great sickness had come upon me, that if anything before had given me hopes of life, this were enough to have entirely bereft me of them.

When the Christians heard of my condition, they gave an Indian the cloak of marten skins we had taken from the cacique,[4] as before related, to pass them over to where I was that they might visit me. Twelve of them crossed; for two were so feeble that their comrades could not venture to bring them. The names of those who came were Alonzo del Castillo, Andrés Dorantes, Diego Dorantes, Valdevieso, Estrada, Tostado, Chaves, Gutierrez, Asturiano a clergyman, Diego de Huelva, Estevanico the black, and Benitez; and when they reached the main land, they found another, who was one of our company, named Francisco de Leon. The thirteen together followed along the coast. So soon as they had come over, my Indians informed me of it, and that Hieronymo de Alvaniz and Lope de Oviedo remained on the island. But sickness prevented me from going with my companions or even seeing them.

I was obliged to remain with the people belonging to the island more than a year, and because of the hard work they put upon me and the harsh treatment, I resolved to flee from them and go to those of Charruco, who inhabit the forests and country of the main, the life I led being insupportable. Besides much other labor, I had to get out roots from below the water, and from among the cane where they grew in the ground. From this employment I had my fingers so worn that did a straw but touch them they would bleed. Many of the canes are broken, so they often tore my flesh, and I had to go in the midst of them with only the clothing on I have mentioned.

Accordingly, I put myself to contriving how I might get over to the other Indians, among whom matters turned somewhat more favorably for me. I set to trafficking, and strove to make my employment profitable in the ways I could best contrive, and by that means I got food and good treatment. The Indians would beg me to go from one quarter to another for things of which they have need; for in consequence of incessant hostilities, they cannot traverse the country, nor make many exchanges. With my merchandise and trade I went into the interior as far as I pleased, and travelled along the coast forty or fifty leagues. The principal wares were cones and other pieces of sea-snail, conchs

---

4. **cacique:** A native chief.

used for cutting, and fruit like a bean of the highest value among them, which they use as a medicine and employ in their dances and festivities. Among other matters were sea-beads. Such were what I carried into the interior; and in barter I got and brought back skins, ochre with which they rub and color the face, hard canes of which to make arrows, sinews, cement and flint for the heads, and tassels of the hair of deer that by dyeing they make red. This occupation suited me well; for the travel allowed me liberty to go where I wished, I was not obliged to work, and was not a slave. Wherever I went I received fair treatment, and the Indians gave me to eat out of regard to my commodities. My leading object, while journeying in this business, was to find out the way by which I should go forward, and I became well known. The inhabitants were pleased when they saw me, and I had brought them what they wanted; and those who did not know me sought and desired the acquaintance, for my reputation. The hardships that I underwent in this were long to tell, as well of peril and privation as of storms and cold. Oftentimes they overtook me alone and in the wilderness; but I came forth from them all by the great mercy of God our Lord. Because of them I avoided pursuing the business in winter, a season in which the natives themselves retire to their huts and ranches, torpid and incapable of exertion.

I was in this country nearly six years, alone among the Indians, and naked like them. The reason why I remained so long, was that I might take with me the Christian, Lope de Oviedo, from the island; Alaniz, his companion, who had been left with him by Alonzo del Castillo, and by Andrés Dorantes, and the rest, died soon after their departure; and to get the survivor out from there, I went over to the island every year, and entreated him that we should go, in the best way we could contrive, in quest of Christians. He put me off every year, saying in the next coming we would start. At last I got him off, crossing him over the bay, and over four rivers in the coast, as he could not swim. In this way we went on with some Indians, until coming to a bay a league in width, and everywhere deep. From the appearance we supposed it to be that which is called Espiritu Sancto. We met some Indians on the other side of it, coming to visit ours, who told us that beyond them were three men like us, and gave their names. We asked for the others, and were told that they were all dead of cold and hunger; that the Indians farther on, of whom they were, for their diversion had killed Diego Dorantes, Valdevieso, and Diego de Huelva, because they left one house for another; and that other Indians, their neighbors with whom Captain Dorantes now was, had in consequence of a dream, killed Esquivel and Mendez. We asked how the living were situated, and they answered that they were very ill used, the boys and some of the Indian men being very idle, out of cruelty gave them many kicks, cuffs, and blows with sticks; that such was the life they led.

We desired to be informed of the country ahead, and of the subsistence: they said there was nothing to eat, and that it was thin of people, who suffered of cold, having no skins or other things to cover them. They told us also if we wished to see those three Christians, two days from that time the Indians who had them would come to eat walnuts a league from there on the margin of that river; and that we might know what they told us of the ill usage to be true, they slapped my companion and beat him with a stick, and I was not left without my portion. Many times they threw lumps of mud at us, and every day they put their arrows to our hearts, saying that they were inclined to kill us in the way that they had destroyed our friends. Lope Oviedo, my comrade, in fear said that he wished to go back with the women of those who had crossed the bay with us, the men having remained some distance behind. I contended strongly against his returning, and urged my objections; but in no way could I keep him. So he went back, and I remained alone with those savages. They are called Quevenes, and those with whom he returned, Deaguanes.

Chapter 19
Our separation by the Indians

When the six months were over, I had to spend with the Christians to put in execution the plan we had concerted, the Indians went after prickly pears, the place at which they grew being thirty leagues off; and when we approached the point of flight, those among whom we were, quarrelled about a woman. After striking with fists, beating with sticks and bruising heads in great anger, each took his lodge and went his way, whence it became necessary that the Christians should also separate, and in no way could we come together until another year.

In this time I passed a hard life, caused as much by hunger as ill usage. Three times I was obliged to run from my masters, and each time they went in pursuit and endeavored to slay me; but God our Lord in his mercy chose to protect and preserve me; and when the season of prickly pears returned, we again came together in the same place. After we had arranged our escape, and appointed a time, that very day the Indians separated and all went back. I told my comrades I would wait for them among the prickly-pear plants until the moon should be full. This day was the first of September, and the first of the moon; and I said that if in this time they did not come as we had agreed, I would leave and go alone. So we parted, each going with his Indians. I remained with mine until the thirteenth day of the moon, having determined to flee to others when it should be full.

At this time Andrés Dorantes arrived with Estevanico and informed me that they had left Castillo with other Indians near by, called Lanegados; that they had encountered great obstacles and wandered about lost; that the next day the Indians, among whom we were, would move to where Castillo was, and were going to unite with those who held him and become friends, having been at war until then, and that in this way we should recover Castillo.

We had thirst all the time we ate the pears, which we quenched with their juice. We caught it in a hole made in the earth, and when it was full we drank until satisfied. It is sweet, and the color of must. In this manner they collect it for lack of vessels. There are many kinds of prickly pears, among them some very good, although they all appeared to me to be so, hunger never having given me leisure to choose, nor to reflect upon which were the best.

Nearly all these people drink rain-water, which lies about in spots. Although there are rivers, as the Indians never have fixed habitations, there are no familiar or known places for getting water. Throughout the country are extensive and beautiful plains with good pasturage; and I think it would be a very fruitful region were it worked and inhabited by civilized men. We nowhere saw mountains.

These Indians told us that there was another people next in advance of us, called Camones, living towards the coast, and that they had killed the people who came in the boat of Peñalosa and Tellez, who arrived so feeble that even while being slain they could offer no resistance, and were all destroyed. We were shown their clothes and arms, and were told that the boat lay there stranded. This, the fifth boat, had remained till then unaccounted for. We have already stated how the boat of the Governor had been carried out to sea, and that of the comptroller and the friars had been cast away on the coast, of which Esquevel narrated the fate of the men. We have once told how the two boats in which Castillo, I, and Dorantes came, foundered near the Island of Malhado.

Chapter 20
Of our escape

The second day after we had moved, we commended ourselves to God and set forth with speed, trusting, for all the lateness of the season and that the prickly pears were about ending, with the mast which remained in the woods [field], we might still be enabled to travel over a large territory. Hurrying on that day in great dread lest the Indians should overtake us, we saw some smokes, and going in the direction of them we arrived there after vespers, and found an Indian. He ran as he discovered us coming, not being willing to wait for us. We sent the negro[5] after him, when he stopped, seeing him alone. The negro told him we were seeking the people who made those fires. He answered that their houses were near by, and he would guide us to them. So we followed him. He ran to make known our approach, and at sunset we saw the houses. Before our arrival, at the distance of two crossbow shots from them, we found four Indians, who waited for us and received us well. We said in the language of the Mariames, that we were coming to look for them. They were evidently pleased with our company, and took us to their dwellings. Dorantes and the negro were lodged in the house of a physician,[6] Castillo and myself in that of another.

These people speak a different language, and are called Avavares. They are the same that carried bows to those with whom we formerly lived, going to traffic with them, and although they are of a different nation and tongue, they understand the other language. They arrived that day with their lodges, at the place where we found them. The community directly brought us a great many prickly pears, having heard of us before, of our cures, and of the wonders our Lord worked by us, which, although there had been no others, were adequate to open ways for us through a country poor like this, to afford us people where oftentimes there are none, and to lead us through immediate dangers, not permitting us to be killed, sustaining us under great want, and putting into those nations the heart of kindness, as we shall relate hereafter.

---

5. **the negro:** Estevánico, the Moorish slave of one of the other Spanish survivors Andrés Dorantes.
6. **physician:** Medicine man.

Chapter 21
Our cure of some of the afflicted

That same night of our arrival, some Indians came to Castillo and told him that they had great pain in the head, begging him to cure them. After he made over them the sign of the cross, and commended them to God, they instantly said that all the pain had left, and went to their houses bringing us prickly pears, with a piece of venison, a thing to us little known. As the report of Castillo's performances spread, many came to us that night sick, that we should heal them, each bringing a piece of venison, until the quantity became so great we knew not where to dispose of it. We gave many thanks to God, for every day went on increasing his compassion and his gifts. After the sick were attended to, they began to dance and sing, making themselves festive, until sunrise; and because of our arrival, the rejoicing was continued for three days.

When these were ended, we asked the Indians about the country farther on, the people we should find in it, and of the subsistence there. They answered us, that throughout all the region prickly-pear plants abounded; but the fruit was now gathered and all the people had gone back to their houses. They said the country was very cold, and there were few skins. Reflecting on this, and that it was already winter, we resolved to pass the season with these Indians.

Five days after our arrival, all the Indians went off, taking us with them to gather more prickly pears, where there were other peoples speaking different tongues. After walking five days in great hunger, since on the way was no manner of fruit, we came to a river and put up our houses. We then went to seek the product of certain trees, which is like peas. As there are no paths in the country, I was detained some time. The others returned, and coming to look for them in the dark I got lost. Thank God I found a burning tree, and in the warmth of it I passed the cold of that night. In the morning, loading myself with sticks, and taking two brands with me, I returned to seek them. In this manner I wandered five days, ever with my fire and load; for if the wood had failed me where none could be found, as many parts are without any, though I might have sought sticks elsewhere, there would have been no fire to kindle them. This was all the protection I had against cold, while walking naked as I was born. Going to the low woods near the rivers, I prepared myself for the night, stopping in them before sunset. I made a hole in the ground and threw in fuel which the trees abundantly afforded, collected in good quantity from those that were fallen and dry. About the hole I made four fires, in the form of a cross, which I watched and made up from time to time. I also gathered some bundles of the coarse straw that there abounds, with which I covered myself in the hole. In this way I was sheltered at night from cold. On one occasion while I slept, the fire fell upon the straw, when it began to blaze so rapidly that notwithstanding the haste I made to get out of it, I carried some marks on my hair of the danger to which I was exposed. All this while I tasted not a mouthful, nor did I find anything I could eat. My feet were bare and bled a good deal. Through the mercy of God, the wind did not blow from the north in all this time, otherwise I should have died.

At the end of the fifth day I arrived on the margin of a river, where I found the Indians, who with the Christians, had considered me dead, supposing that I had been stung by a viper. All were rejoiced to see me, and most so were my companions. They said that up to that time they had struggled with great hunger, which was the cause of their not having sought me. At night, all gave me of their prickly pears, and the next morning we set out for a place where they were in large quantity, with which we satisfied our great craving, the Christians rendering thanks to our Lord that He had ever given us His aid.

[1542/1555, 1907]

Samuel de Champlain

[c. 1570–1635]

The son of ship captain Antoine de Champlain and his wife, Marguerite Le Roy, Samuel de Champlain was born in Brouage, then a seaport and center of the salt industry in southwestern France. Little is known about Champlain's early life except that he was raised a Catholic and probably educated by a parish priest. Historians are not even certain of the year of his birth, which is variously given as 1567 or 1570. When he was about twenty, Champlain joined the army and fought in France's ongoing foreign wars with Spain and domestic conflicts with the Protestant French Huguenots. When the Peace of Vervins was signed between France and Spain in 1598, Champlain left the army and began to pursue navigation and exploration as a career.

Champlain's opportunity came in 1599, when he undertook the first of a series of voyages with an uncle who was the captain of the *Saint-Julian.*

Samuel de Champlain

In the only authentic portrait of him, Champlain is the central figure in this etching based on his own drawing of the 1609 battle between French soldiers, their Algonkin and Montagnais allies, and the Iroquois on the shore of what came to be named Lake Champlain. The etching was published in the 1613 edition of the explorer's *Voyages.*

The ship was chartered by the Spanish government for transporting troops and supplies to its colonies in the Americas, from which it brought back treasures to Spain. During these early voyages, Champlain traveled first to Spain, where he learned to speak Spanish, and then to the West Indies and Central America. As he would throughout his life, Champlain kept a detailed journal of his observations and experiences during these voyages. When he returned to France, he wrote his first travel account, *Bref Discours des Choses plus Remarquables que Sammeul Champlain de Brouage*, which he presented in manuscript to Henry IV, the king of France. Illustrated with sixty maps and pictures that Champlain drew, the book provided a detailed description of the lands and native peoples he encountered. Although the manuscript was evidently circulated at court, it was not published until 1858, when an English translation appeared as *Narrative of a Voyage to the West Indies and Mexico in the Years 1599-1602*.

In 1603, Champlain sailed again, this time to North America, where he became a leader in the establishment of New France. For the next thirty years, Champlain made nearly a dozen voyages across the Atlantic, charting the coast of New England, exploring the possibility of a Northwest Passage, mapping thousands of miles of territory, claiming lands for France, and establishing its first permanent settlement, Quebec. According to his biographers, Champlain was successful for several reasons. He learned from the mistakes of earlier French explorers, refusing, for example, to waste time searching for gold and other treasure. Committed to Christianizing the native peoples, he encouraged many Catholic missionaries to come to Canada. The resourceful Champlain was also adept at forging alliances with various native tribes, alliances that provided security for French business ventures and settlements. Finally, Champlain adapted to the cold climate of the northern parts of North America, where the French based their colonial economy on agriculture, fishing, and the fur trade.

Throughout his years of shuttling back and forth across the Atlantic, Champlain publicized himself and New France by writing several books that were widely read in France. He published *Des Sauvages, ou, Voyage de Samuel Champlain, de Brouage, fait en la France nouvell*, in Paris in 1603. During a visit to France in 1610, two years after he founded Quebec, Champlain married the twelve-year-old Hélène Boullé. Because of her young age, she remained with her parents until 1620, when she came to live with Champlain in Quebec. Lonely and ill-suited to colonial life, she returned permanently to France in 1624. Champlain, however, vigorously promoted colonization, notably in *Les Voyages du Sieur de Champlain*, which detailed accounts of his experiences and observations in New France. The first volume was published in 1613, a second volume appeared in 1619, and the final volume of the *Voyages* was published in 1632. Appropriately, the final volume included an appendix, *Traitté de la Marine, et du Devoir d'un bon Marinier*, in which Champlain described the qualities and characteristics of a good mariner. He died in Quebec on December 25, 1635.

Champlain, the first governor of Canada, . . . had already gone to war against the Iroquois in their forest forts, and penetrated to the Great Lakes and wintered there, before a Pilgrim had heard of New England.

—Henry David Thoreau

Reading Champlain's *Voyages.*   Although he described himself simply as a mariner or a navigator, Champlain was also a draftsman and a skilled writer. His books are filled with his own navigational charts, maps, and illustrations of native peoples and their practices, along with Champlain's descriptions of the landscape, flora, and fauna of North America, as well as of his exploits in what became New France. Seeking to contrast the actions of the French to the brutal policies of the Spanish in the Americas, Champlain placed particular emphasis on the friendly relations he established with some of the native tribes in the areas along the St. Lawrence River. During 1608-09, Champlain formed an alliance with the Algonkin, Montagnais, and Huron against the Mohawk, the keepers of the eastern door of the powerful Iroquois Confederacy. In exchange for access to remote regions and assistance with the fur trade, the three tribes asked for French help in their ongoing conflicts with the Mohawk. In the following selection, Champlain describes the first battle between the French soldiers, their Indian allies, and the Mohawk on the shore of what he named Lake Champlain. Some historians have questioned the accuracy of Champlain's account of the nature of Iroquois warfare, but the outcome and consequences of the battle are not in dispute. The Mohawk were defeated, and the French-Indian alliance provided Champlain time to develop and secure a small settlement, Quebec, effectively the beginning of New France. But the Iroquois consequently allied themselves with the Dutch and later with the English, first disrupting French trade and finally helping to bring an end to French dominion in North America. The text is taken from Charles P. Otis's translation of *Les Voyages du Sieur de Champlain* (1613), in *Voyages of Samuel de Champlain, 1604-1618*, edited by W. L. Grant (1907).

bedfordstmartins.com/
americanlit *for research*
links on Champlain

From THE VOYAGES OF SAMUEL DE CHAMPLAIN

We set out on the next day, continuing our course in the river as far as the entrance of the lake.[1] There are many pretty islands here, low, and containing very fine woods and meadows, with abundance of fowl and such animals of the chase as stags, fallow-deer, fawns, roe-bucks, bears, and others, which go from the main land to these islands. We captured a large number of these animals. There are also many beavers, not only in this river, but also in numerous other little ones that flow into it. These regions, although they are pleasant, are not inhabited by any savages, on account of their wars; but they withdraw as far as possible from the rivers into the interior, in order not to be suddenly surprised.

The next day we entered the lake, which is of great extent, say eighty or a hundred leagues long,[2] where I saw four fine islands, ten, twelve, and fifteen leagues long, which

---

1. **We set out . . . entrance of the lake:** They entered the lake from what Champlain called "the River of the Iroquois," now the Richelieu River, which flows northward out of Lake Champlain and empties into the St. Lawrence River near Montreal.

2. **eighty or a hundred leagues long:** That is, 240 to 300 miles long. Lake Champlain is actually about 110 miles long and 12 miles across at its widest point.

were formerly inhabited by the savages, like the River of the Iroquois; but they have been abandoned since the wars of the savages with one another prevail. There are also many rivers falling into the lake, bordered by many fine trees of the same kinds as those we have in France, with many vines finer than any I have seen in any other place; also many chestnut-trees on the border of this lake, which I had not seen before. There is also a great abundance of fish, of many varieties; among others, one called by the savages of the country *Chaousarou*,[3] which varies in length, the largest being, as the people told me, eight or ten feet long. I saw some five feet long, which were as large as my thigh; the head being as big as my two fists, with a snout two feet and a half long, and a double row of very sharp and dangerous teeth. Its body is, in shape, much like that of a pike; but it is armed with scales so strong that a poniard[4] could not pierce them. Its color is silver-gray. The extremity of its snout is like that of swine. This fish makes war upon all others in the lakes and rivers. It also possesses remarkable dexterity, as these people informed me, which is exhibited in the following manner. When it wants to capture birds, it swims in among the rushes, or reeds, which are found on the banks of the lake in several places, where it puts its snout out of water and keeps perfectly still: so that, when the birds come and light on its snout, supposing it to be only the stump of a tree, it adroitly closes it, which it had kept ajar, and pulls the birds by the feet down under water. The savages gave me the head of one of them, of which they make great account, saying that, when they have the headache, they bleed themselves with the teeth of this fish on the spot where they suffer pain, when it suddenly passes away.

Continuing our course over this lake on the western side, I noticed, while observing the country, some very high mountains on the eastern side,[5] on the top of which there was snow. I made inquiry of the savages whether these localities were inhabited, when they told me that the Iroquois dwelt there, and that there were beautiful valleys in these places, with plains productive in grain, such as I had eaten in this country, together with many kinds of fruit without limit. They said also that the lake extended near mountains, some twenty-five leagues distant from us, as I judge. I saw, on the south, other mountains, no less high than the first, but without any snow. The savages told me that these mountains were thickly settled, and that it was there we were to find their enemies; but that it was necessary to pass a fall in order to go there (which I afterwards saw), when we should enter another lake,[6] nine or ten leagues long. After reaching the end of the lake, we should have to go, they said, two leagues by land, and pass through a river flowing

3. *Chaousarou*: The word is not French but probably an Algonkian term for a long-nose gar, a large fish that even today can reach a length of six feet and weigh fifty pounds.
4. poniard: A small, slim dagger.
5. mountains on the eastern side: The mountains to the east of Lake Champlain are known today as the Green Mountains of Vermont; the mountains to the south and west of the lake are the Adirondack Mountains of New York.
6. pass a fall . . . another lake: The waterfall is at present-day Ticonderoga. Lake George is on the other side of the falls, directly south of Lake Champlain.

into the sea on the Norumbegue coast, near that of Florida,[7] whither it took them only two days to go by canoe, as I have since ascertained from some prisoners we captured, who gave me minute information in regard to all they had personal knowledge of, through some Algonquin interpreters, who understood the Iroquois language.

Now, as we began to approach within two or three days' journey of the abode of their enemies, we advanced only at night, resting during the day. But they did not fail to practise constantly their accustomed superstitions, in order to ascertain what was to be the result of their undertaking; and they often asked me if I had had a dream, and seen their enemies, to which I replied in the negative. Yet I did not cease to encourage them, and inspire in them hope. When night came, we set out on the journey until the next day, when we withdrew into the interior of the forest, and spent the rest of the day there. About ten or eleven o'clock, after taking a little walk about our encampment, I retired. While sleeping, I dreamed that I saw our enemies, the Iroquois, drowning in the lake near a mountain, within sight. When I expressed a wish to help them, our allies, the savages, told me we must let them all die, and that they were of no importance. When I awoke, they did not fail to ask me, as usual, if I had had a dream. I told them that I had, in fact, had a dream. This, upon being related, gave them so much confidence that they did not doubt any longer that good was to happen to them.

When it was evening, we embarked in our canoes to continue our course; and, as we advanced very quietly and without making any noise, we met on the 29th of the month the Iroquois, about ten o'clock at evening, at the extremity of a cape which extends into the lake on the western bank.[8] They had come to fight. We both began to utter loud cries, all getting their arms in readiness. We withdrew out on the water, and the Iroquois went on shore, where they drew up all their canoes close to each other and began to fell trees with poor axes, which they acquire in war sometimes, using also others of stone. Thus they barricaded themselves very well.

Our forces also passed the entire night, their canoes being drawn up close to each other, and fastened to poles, so that they might not get separated, and that they might be all in readiness to fight, if occasion required. We were out upon the water, within arrow range of their barricades. When they were armed and in array, they dispatched two canoes by themselves to the enemy to inquire if they wished to fight, to which the latter replied that they wanted nothing else: but they said that, at present, there was not much light, and that it would be necessary to wait for daylight, so as to be able to recognize each other; and that, as soon as the sun rose, they would offer us battle. This

---

7. **river . . . Florida:** In this garbled geographical account, probably the result of his inability fully to understand his Indian guides, Champlain refers to "Norumbegue," the Algonkian name for the coastal area where the Penobscot River flows into the Atlantic Ocean in present-day Maine, far to the north of Florida. The river he describes, separated by less than two leagues, or six miles, from Lake George, is actually the Hudson River, which flows south and empties into the Atlantic Ocean between Manhattan Island and New Jersey.

8. **cape . . . on the western bank:** Crown Point, on what is today the New York side of southern Lake Champlain, where the French later built an important fortress, Fort St. Frédéric. It was captured by the British during the French and Indian War, also known as the Seven Years' War (1756-63), which ended French dominion in North America.

was agreed to by our side. Meanwhile, the entire night was spent in dancing and singing, on both sides, with endless insults and other talk; as, how little courage we had, how
feeble a resistance we should make against their arms, and that, when day came, we
should realize it to our ruin. Ours also were not slow in retorting, telling them they
would see such execution of arms as never before, together with an abundance of such
talk as is not unusual in the siege of a town. After this singing, dancing, and bandying
words on both sides to the fill, when day came, my companions and myself continued
under cover, for fear that the enemy would see us. We arranged our arms in the best
manner possible, being, however, separated, each in one of the canoes of the savage
Montagnais.[9] After arming ourselves with light armor, we each took an arquebuse,[10]
and went on shore. I saw the enemy go out of their barricade, nearly two hundred in
number, stout and rugged in appearance. They came at a slow pace towards us, with a
dignity and assurance which greatly amused me, having three chiefs at their head. Our
men also advanced in the same order, telling me that those who had three large plumes
were the chiefs, and that they had only these three, and that they could be distinguished
by these plumes, which were much larger than those of their companions, and that I
should do what I could to kill them. I promised to do all in my power, and said that I was
very sorry they could not understand me, so that I might give order and shape to their
mode of attacking their enemies, and then we should, without doubt, defeat them all;
but that this could not now be obviated, and that I should be very glad to show them my
courage and good-will when we should engage in the fight.

As soon as we had landed, they began to run for some two hundred paces towards
their enemies, who stood firmly, not having as yet noticed my companions, who went
into the woods with some savages. Our men began to call me with loud cries; and, in
order to give me a passage-way, they opened in two parts, and put me at their head,
where I marched some twenty paces in advance of the rest, until I was within about
thirty paces of the enemy, who at once noticed me, and, halting, gazed at me, as I did
also at them. When I saw them making a move to fire at us, I rested my musket against
my cheek, and aimed directly at one of the three chiefs. With the same shot, two fell to
the ground; and one of their men was so wounded that he died some time after. I had
loaded my musket with four balls. When our side saw this shot so favorable for them,
they began to raise such loud cries that one could not have heard it thunder. Meanwhile, the arrows flew on both sides. The Iroquois were greatly astonished that two
men had been so quickly killed, although they were equipped with armor woven from
cotton thread, and with wood which was proof against their arrows. This caused great
alarm among them. As I was loading again, one of my companions fired a shot from the
woods, which astonished them anew to such a degree that, seeing their chiefs dead,
they lost courage, and took to flight, abandoning their camp and fort, and fleeing into

---

9. **Montagnais:** "Mountain people," the French name for the Algonkian-speaking peoples who lived in the
rugged terrain along the gulf of the St. Lawrence River near present-day Labrador, Canada.
10. **arquebuse:** An early firearm developed by the Spanish conquistadores in the mid-fifteenth century. It
was loaded through the long muzzle and fired by a slow-burning fuse, lit in advance of a battle from a spark
made by rubbing together flint and steel. When ready to fire, the shooter would blow on the fuse and pull a
trigger, which ignited the gunpowder in the base of the barrel of the gun.

the woods, whither I pursued them, killing still more of them. Our savages also killed several of them, and took ten or twelve prisoners. The remainder escaped with the wounded. Fifteen or sixteen were wounded on our side with arrow-shots; but they were soon healed.

After gaining the victory, our men amused themselves by taking a great quantity of Indian corn and some meal from their enemies, also their armor, which they had left behind that they might run better. After feasting sumptuously, dancing and singing, we returned three hours after, with the prisoners. The spot where this attack took place is in latitude 43° and some minutes, and the lake was called Lake Champlain.

[1613, 1907]

Colonial Settlements

IN THE UNITED STATES, the settlement of America has most often been represented by a single scene, the landing of the Pilgrims at Plymouth Rock. Images of the peaceful gathering of the Pilgrims and their Wampanoag neighbors at the "First Thanksgiving" the following year have tended to mask a more complex and darker reality. Indeed, the settlement of North America was characterized by ongoing conflict, not only between European settlers and Native American peoples, but also among

◄ Enrico Causini, *Landing of the Pilgrims, 1620* (1825)

This sandstone relief in the rotunda of the U.S. Capitol, the meeting place of the Senate and House of Representatives, suggests the central place the Pilgrims later assumed in U.S. history. As the Pilgrim father steps ashore at Plymouth Rock, he is greeted by an Indian offering an ear of corn, the staple crop of Native American societies throughout North America. In fact, the Pilgrims settled on the grounds of a village used in the summer by a group of Wampanoag, a tribe whose aid was crucial to the survival of Plymouth Plantation. The wave of English immigration that followed the settlement ultimately led, however, to the dispossession or destruction of Indian peoples throughout New England.

European countries, especially Spain, France, and England. Seeking to break Spain's monopoly in the Americas, a group of French Huguenots (Protestant Lutherans) sought to establish a settlement in Florida as early as 1562. But the effort ended when the settlers at the colony on St. John's River and the survivors of a French fleet sent to aid them were massacred by Spanish forces in 1564. To safeguard Florida, Spain established a fort at Saint Augustine, the first permanent European settlement in what is now the United States. The French consequently turned their attention northward, to Canada, where they established a settlement at Port Royal, in present-day Nova Scotia, in 1605, and a fur-trading post at Quebec in 1608.

John Smith's Map of Virginia

This map, which appeared in Smith's *Generall Historie of Virginia, New-England, and the Summer Isles* (1624), illustrates the Chesapeake Bay and Potomac River, among other geographical features, and includes a vignette of a council presided over by the powerful leader of the Powhatan Confederacy.

In an effort to compete with France and Spain by exploiting the resources of North America, the English concentrated their efforts in the area between Canada and Florida, an extensive territory they called "Virginia."

Despite the failure of their first settlements at Roanoke Island, off the coast of present-day North Carolina, English efforts at colonization were sustained by glowing printed accounts of the beauty and potential of the newly explored lands. Thomas Hariot's *A Briefe and True Report of the New Found Land of Virginia*, first published as a pamphlet in 1588, was swiftly reprinted by Richard Hakluyt in his popular compilation *The Principall Navigations, Voiages and Discoveries of the English Nation* (1589) and then circulated throughout Europe in lavishly illustrated editions in English and three other languages, published in 1590 by Theodor de Bry in Frankfurt, Germany. Another avid proponent of colonization who recognized the power of print was Captain John Smith. Smith was one of the leaders and the most vigorous promoter of the first permanent English colony in North America, at Jamestown, Virginia, which he helped establish in 1607. Knowing that advertisements were crucial to the success of the colony, Smith wrote a series of books designed to encourage the English colonization of North America, including his *A Map of Virginia: With a Description of the Countrey* (1612) and *A Description of New England* (1616). But his most famous work was *The Generall Historie of Virginia, New-England, and the Summer Isles* (1624), in which Smith at once promoted colonization and laid the foundations for one of the most enduring myths of North America, his dramatic rescue by the Indian "princess" Pocahontas.

That famous and possibly fictional event has also tended to mask a darker reality. Smith's heroic adventures and the rosy pictures painted in promotional tracts and travel narratives bore little relation to actualities in the Jamestown Colony. During the early decades of the colony, life there was made almost unendurable by rampant disease, the shortage of food and other supplies, and the tense relations between the colonists and the native peoples of the powerful Powhatan Confederacy. Although the successful cultivation of tobacco established the economic viability of the colony, the consequent expansion into native lands displaced Indians and triggered a devastating attack on the scattered English settlements in 1622. The cultivation of tobacco also demanded massive amounts of physical labor, which was initially provided by indentured servants from England. The grim conditions under which they lived and worked were vividly described by a young man named Richard Frethorne, who arrived in Virginia as an indentured servant in 1623. In a letter he wrote to his parents in England, Frethorne described his lack of clothing, desperate hunger, and constant fear that he would die of disease or be killed by the Indians. Listing the names of twenty people who had already perished at his small settlement, where there were only "32 to fight against 3000 if they should come," Frethorne pleaded with his parents to send aid so that he might "be redeemed out of Egypt."

Powhatan's Mantle

Made from the hides of seven deer and from thousands of shells gathered by the Algonkin peoples living in the rich area around the Chesapeake Bay, this seven-foot-long ceremonial mantle belonged to Wahunsonacock, chief of the Powhatan Confederacy and called Powhatan by the English.

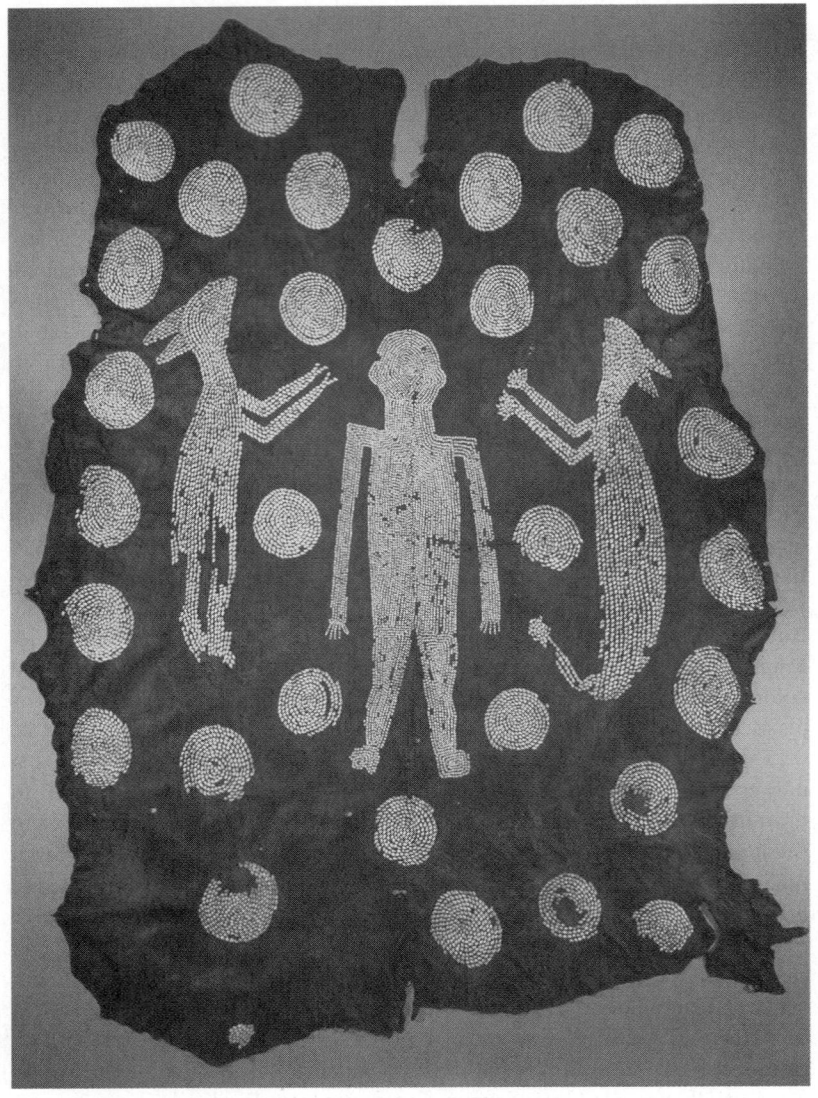

Even as Jamestown struggled for survival, other English settlers established colonies in what came to be called New England. In contrast to indentured workers such as Frethorne, the earliest settlers of New England conceived of their flight from England as a reenactment of the biblical Exodus, a journey out of spiritual bondage to a new promised land. Whereas the settlement at Jamestown was primarily a commercial venture, religion played a central role in the founding of New England. During the Protestant Reformation, reformers in England sought to restore what they viewed as the ancient purity and simplicity of the church as established by Christ and his disciples in the first century, and furthermore to "purify" the religious practices and rituals of the Church of England, which they believed had not gone far enough in ridding itself of the vestiges of Roman Catholicism. The Puritans, as they came to be called, sought reform from within the Church of England. The Pilgrims were Separatists, or Puritans who formally separated themselves from the established church in order to form their own independent church, an act of treason in England. The Pilgrims consequently left the country, settling for a time in Holland before deciding to try their fortunes in North America, where 102 colonists landed on present-day Cape Cod, Massachusetts, in November 1620. Meanwhile, the Puritans were facing mounting intolerance in England. The idea of the great migration, the resettlement of large numbers of Puritan immigrants from the Old to the New World, was born in 1629, when a wealthy group of men organized the Massachusetts Bay Company and obtained a royal charter to establish a colony in New England. The following year, seven hundred adults and children led by John Winthrop embarked from England on a fleet of ships that arrived at present-day Salem, Massachusetts, in July 1630.

Believing they had been assigned a special place in God's plan of human history, both the Pilgrims and the Puritans kept detailed records of the founding of New England. The earliest history of Plymouth was based on journals kept by two of the leaders of the colony, William Bradford and Edward Winslow, whose accounts were published as *A Relation or Journal of the Beginning and Proceeding of the English Plantation Settled at Plimoth in New England* (1622). Usually called *Mourt's Relation* because the preface was signed by "G. Mourt," the book was designed to promote the settlement at Plymouth. Drawing on his journal and his contributions to *Mourt's Relation*, Bradford in 1630 began to write *Of Plimoth Plantation*, a formal history of the Pilgrims from the establishment of their Separatist Church through their years in Holland to their arrival and the early years of their settlement at Plymouth. Bradford's book was not published until the nineteenth century, but many historians were familiar with the manuscript, which became an important source for early accounts of the founding of New England.

The Puritans were equally eager to promote their colony and to preserve its history in writing. In March of 1631, Thomas Dudley (1574-1653), then the deputy governor and later the governor of the Massachusetts Bay Colony, wrote to an English friend from his new home in Boston:

> For the satisfaction of your Honor, and some friends, and for the use of such as shall hereafter intend to increase our plantation in New England, I have in the throng of domestic, and not altogether free from public business, thought fit to commit to memory our present condition, and what hath

befallen us since our arrival here; which I will do shortly, after my usual manner, and must do rudely, having yet no table, nor other room to write in, than by the fireside upon my knee, in this sharp winter; to which my family must have leave to resort, though they break good manners, and make me sometimes forget what I would say, and say what I would not.

Even as he sought to persuade others in England to come to the new colony by offering an account of his experiences, Dudley was beset by many of the difficulties of writing in the primitive settlement of Boston. Despite such obstacles, however, writing played an integral part in the settlement of New England. At about the same time Bradford began to write his history of Plymouth in 1630, for example, John Winthrop began a journal in which he carefully recorded the history of the Massachusetts Bay Colony. Published posthumously as *A Journal of the Transactions and Occurrences in the settlement of Massachusetts and the Other New-England Colonies, from the year 1630 to 1644* (1790), Winthrop's account later appeared and is now best known as *The History of New England.*

In contrast to Bradford's small band of Pilgrims, the larger and more affluent group of Puritans had substantial resources for establishing a colony. Among the provisions they transported to North America were books, which were vital elements of the cultural and religious life of colonists in New England. The key book was the Bible, which the Puritans viewed as the revealed word of God and consequently as the ultimate source of authority in all human affairs, from domestic arrangements to the structure of civil and religious institutions. In "A Modell of Christian Charity," an address he delivered either on the eve of or during the voyage to New England, Winthrop described the venture as an effort to establish "a Citty upon a hill," a model Christian community based on the letter and the spirit of the Bible. The Puritans also brought along books offering practical aid in building the new colony, including handbooks on law and medicine, as well as technical books on carpentry and farming. Finally, just as they constructed their dwellings and laid out their fields along English lines, the Puritans transplanted European culture to New England, bringing with them dictionaries, encyclopedias, books on logic and rhetoric, and the works of Greek and Latin writers. Indeed, the Puritans were shaped not only by the Protestant Reformation but also by the humanistic values of the Renaissance.

Although they initially depended on books brought or imported from England, the Puritans soon began to publish their own. In 1638, the first printing press arrived in the Massachusetts Bay Colony, and Stephen Daye established the Glover Press in Cambridge. The first book printed in the English colonies was *The Whole Book of Psalmes Faithfully Translated into English Metre* (1640), popularly called *The Bay Psalm Book.* Of the more than two hundred books, pamphlets, and broadsides published in Massachusetts Bay Colony during the next sixty years, one of the most unusual was John

New England Primer

First published in Boston around 1690, the *New England Primer* was probably the single most successful production of the press in colonial North America. As this copy printed in 1750 indicates, the book continued to instruct children in reading, writing, and religion even after Puritanism began to wane in New England.

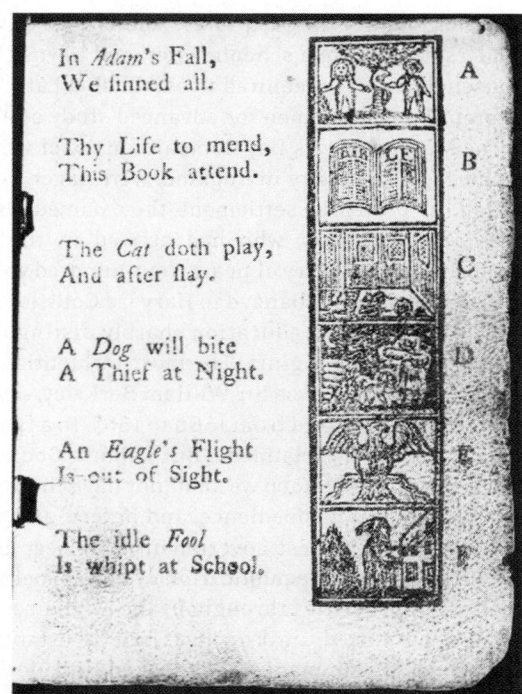

In *Adam*'s Fall,
We finned all.

Thy Life to mend,
This Book attend.

The *Cat* doth play,
And after flay.

A *Dog* will bite
A Thief at Night.

An *Eagle*'s Flight
Is out of Sight.

The idle *Fool*
Is whipt at School.

Eliot's translation of the Bible into an Algonkian language, published in 1663 as part of a broader missionary effort to Christianize the Indians. But the most familiar product of the Puritan press was the *New England Primer*, first published around 1690. During the following 150 years, more than three million copies were printed for use at home and in schools, where the so-called Little Bible of New England was used to teach spelling and reading, as well as to instill moral and religious values.

Education was a central concern of the Puritans. Like other Protestants, they placed great emphasis on the ability of individuals to read and interpret the Bible. Literacy rates had consequently been relatively high among the Puritans in England, even for women and girls, and the rates remained high among those who came to New England. Girls were generally taught to read and write at "dame schools," often run by women in private homes. The colonists also began to establish schools modeled on the grammar schools in England, in which the curriculum for young boys included religious training, instruction in mathematics and rhetoric, and the study of Latin and Greek. Gradually, laws were passed requiring the education of all children. In 1647, for example, the General Court, or legislature, of the Massachusetts Bay Colony passed an act designed to promote universal literacy and thus prevent "that old deluder Satan" from keeping "men from the knowledge of the Scriptures." Under the act, every town of fifty house-holders had to hire a schoolmaster, and towns of more than one hundred householders were required to establish a Latin grammar school capable of preparing young men for advanced study at a university. The founders of the Massachusetts Bay Company, many of whom had been educated at Cambridge University in England, were eager to establish a similar insti-tution in the early settlement they named Cambridge. In 1638, John Harvard, a minister who had arrived in the colony the year before, bequeathed his library of nearly four hundred volumes to New College, the name of which was changed to Harvard College.

The emphasis on education sharply distinguished the Massachusetts Bay Colony from Virginia. The most influential figure in the early devel-opment of Virginia was Sir William Berkeley, royal governor of the colony from 1642 to 1652 and from 1660 to 1667. In a famous diatribe, the author-itarian Berkeley exclaimed: "But I thank God, there are no free schools nor printing, and I hope we shall not have these hundred years; for learn-ing has brought disobedience, and heresy, and sects into this world, and libels against the best government. God keep us from both!" Insofar as "printing" meant the publication of newspapers, Berkeley's hostility was shared by authorities throughout the English colonies, where no newspa-per was permitted until one was briefly established in Boston in 1690. Certainly, Puritan magistrates shared Berkeley's intolerance of political and religious dissent, restricting the right to vote to men who were church members and banishing dissidents like Roger Williams (1603-1683), an English Protestant theologian who founded Rhode Island. In contrast to Berkeley, however, the Puritans viewed education as a means of promoting religious orthodoxy and social stability. They also believed that literature could serve similar ends. Although Harvard College was established to train men for the ministry, it also emphasized a broad education in the arts and sciences, includ-ing languages and literature. In a sermon delivered in 1677, the influential Puritan minister Increase Mather thus told the leg-islators of the Massachusetts Bay Colony that they must sup-port schools and the college to ensure that there would be "able instruments raised up for the propagating of Truth in succeed-ing Generations," adding, "And some have well and truly observed, that the Interest of Religion and good Literature, have risen and fallen together."

"And some have well and truly observed, that the Interest of Religion and good Literature, have risen and fallen together."

The premium placed on both literacy and literature in New England helps account for the prominence of Puritan writers in the early literary history of what became the United States. Poetry was especially valued by the Puritans, who avidly read English religious poets such as George Herbert and who also wrote a great deal of poetry. The first bestseller pub-lished in the colonies was a long narrative poem by a Puritan minister,

Michael Wigglesworth's *The Day of Doom*, "A Poetical Account of the Great and Last Judgment" (1662). The 224 ballad stanzas of the poem were read, recited, and frequently memorized by children and adults alike, revealing the powerful intersection of literature and religion among the Puritans. Although Wigglesworth is no longer well known, two other Puritan poets have assumed central places in early American literature. The first is Anne Bradstreet, who came to New England in 1630 along with her father and husband, both of whom later served as governors of the Massachusetts Bay Colony. A collection of Bradstreet's poems, *The Tenth Muse Lately Sprung up in America*, was published in London in 1650, and a second edition was later published in Boston. Her poetry was also widely read and admired at the time, in sharp contrast to the work of the other most important Puritan poet, Edward Taylor. A minister living in the isolated frontier community of Westfield, Massachusetts, Taylor wrote a staggering amount of poetry, including funeral elegies, religious meditations, and a history of Christianity. But almost none of his work was published or even circulated beyond a small group of family and friends. In fact, Taylor's work was unknown until the 1930s, when his manuscripts were discovered and some of his poems were finally published, revealing him as one of the preeminent writers among the Puritans of New England.

The habits of personal reflection and spiritual meditation that found expression in the poetry of Bradstreet and Taylor also generated significant works in prose. Those who believed they had experienced God's grace and were consequently among the elect were required to give a public account of their conversion experience. Many also recorded those

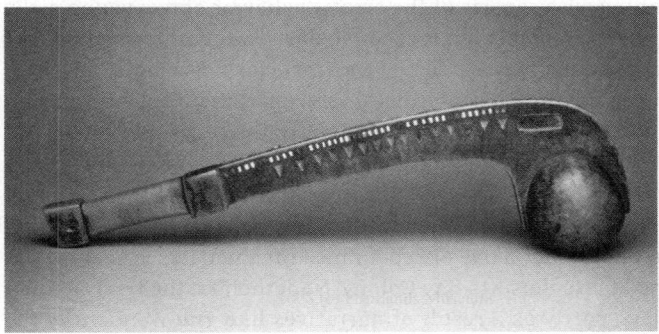

Wampanoag War Club

This seventeenth-century war club was carved from the ball root of a maple tree and inlaid with triangular pieces of horn and wampum, small beads made from shell. Long thought to have belonged to "King Philip," the name the English settlers gave to the Wampanoag chief Metacomet, the weapon was most likely manufactured by a Native American and may well have been used in King Philip's War.

experiences in diaries or wrote more formal spiritual autobiographies. The conditions and conflicts arising from the settlement of New England also spawned another kind of life writing, the captivity narrative. Despite their professed intention of spreading the light of the Gospels in what they viewed as the "wilderness," the Puritans and other European settlers more often spread disease and destruction among the native inhabitants of New England. The growing number of English settlers and their inexorable expansion into tribal lands resulted in a series of wars with the Indians. During one of the earliest and bloodiest of those conflicts, King Philip's War of 1675-76, Mary Rowlandson was taken prisoner during an attack by Narragansett, Nipmuc, and Wampanoag Indians on her settlement in Lancaster, Massachusetts. Following her release, she wrote *The Sovereignty and Goodness of God . . . Being a Narrative of the Captivity and Restoration of Mrs. Mary Rowlandson*, which was published in both Boston and London in 1682. The widespread popularity of the book, which was a major bestseller, led to the publication of many similar narratives during the following decades, as the wars between the New England colonists and the Indians became part of the larger struggle between England and France for control of North America. Indeed, the captivity narrative became and remained one of the most popular literary genres of the colonial period.

The sense of vulnerability produced by ongoing conflicts with the Indians contributed to fears of and a series of narratives about witchcraft in New England. During the seventeenth century, accusations of witchcraft were far more common in England, France, and Germany than in New England. But the most famous of all witchcraft trials took place at Salem in 1692. Beginning with reports of the erratic behavior of two young girls, and the charge of witchcraft against an enslaved woman from the West Indies, the accusations spread, fueled by fear, class divisions, and religious differences. In the view of some historians, the accusations also revealed anxieties about the increasing power of women, especially affluent widows, in the colony. Eventually, 160 people (most of them women) were accused and many of those were incarcerated. Five people died in jail, while twenty others—thirteen women and seven men—were executed. Less than five years later, a day of repentance for the trials was observed throughout the Massachusetts Bay Colony. Nonetheless, the trials gained lasting notoriety, partly as a result of narratives like *The Wonders of the Invisible World* (1692), in which the prominent Puritan minister Cotton Mather described a "horrible plot against the country by witchcraft," culminating in Satan's unleashing of an "army of devils" upon Salem.

Even as the Puritans were undergoing the convulsions of the witch trials, a new group of religious dissidents, the Society of Friends (Quakers), was seeking refuge in North America. Like the Puritans, the Quakers sought to return to what they viewed as the simplicity of early

Christianity. But the Quakers rejected the Puritan doctrines of original sin, predestination, and election, the salvation of only a few chosen by God. Instead, the Quakers believed that every individual was imbued by God with an "Inner Light" of spiritual understanding and was therefore potentially among the saved. Pacifists who refused to serve in the army or to pay taxes in support of the Anglican Church, the Quakers were widely persecuted in England. In 1680, however, a wealthy convert to the Society of Friends, William Penn, received a huge land grant in North America to pay off a debt owed to his late father by the king of England. Just as John Winthrop had earlier described the Puritan commonwealth as a "Citty upon a hill," Penn called his new colony of Pennsylvania a "holy experiment" and an "example to all Nations." In an effort to establish his experiment in religious and political freedom upon a just and secure foundation, Penn established friendly relations with the native population of the area by signing a treaty of friendship with the Delaware Confederacy in 1682. Penn also tirelessly promoted his colony, publishing tracts in English, Dutch, and German. Pennsylvania immediately began to attract thousands of Quakers from England and equal numbers of Protestants of various sects from other European countries, especially Germany. Like earlier settlers from the Netherlands and Sweden, whose colonies in North America had come under English rule, the new settlers contributed to the growing body of colonial literature written in languages other than English. For example, the leader of the first wave of German immigrants, Francis Daniel Pastorious, soon wrote *Positive Information from America* (1684), the first of a series of works he sent to Germany for publication.

The settlement of Pennsylvania added yet another element to the growing diversity, both ethnic and religious, of the English colonies in North America. As diaries and journals written around the turn of the eighteenth century illustrate, the experiences and physical circumstances of people living in different colonies were equally diverse. Sarah Kemble Knight's celebrated journal of her journey from Boston through Connecticut to New York in 1704-05 offers a fascinating account of the hardships of early travel and the social mores of the provincial world of rural New England. Only a small number of the numerous slaves that had been imported into the region worked on the family farms that predominated in New England, and farmers there had little in common with wealthy southern planters like William Byrd II. Certainly, his diary illustrates the radically different path development had taken in Virginia. Although there were class and racial divisions throughout the colonies, nowhere else was the social structure as hierarchical and rigid as in Virginia, where by the end of the eighteenth century the initial reliance on indentured servants had been replaced by an expanding system of slavery. The exploitation of slave labor led to the emergence of a small gentry class with the kind of privileged and

English Tobacconist Advertisement

In this early advertisement three gentlemen planters relax with drinks and their pipes under the shade of a tree while three slaves work in a tobacco field, an illustration of the transition from indentured servitude to slave labor in Virginia.

increasingly opulent lifestyle described by Byrd, who ultimately owned a vast estate of nearly 180,000 acres in Virginia.

A century after the establishment of the first permanent English settlement at Jamestown, the various colonies had thus developed distinctly different cultural institutions, social structures, and systems of government. There were, consequently, few widely shared colonial experiences, even within the relatively narrow boundaries of the English colonies in North America. A major exception was the Great Awakening, a religious revival that swept through the colonies from the 1730s to roughly 1750. Beginning among Presbyterians in Pennsylvania and New Jersey, the revival spread among various sects, first in the North and later to the South. The Great Awakening was closely associated with developments in England, especially the rise of Methodism within the Church of England. A major figure in the North American revival was George Whitefield, an

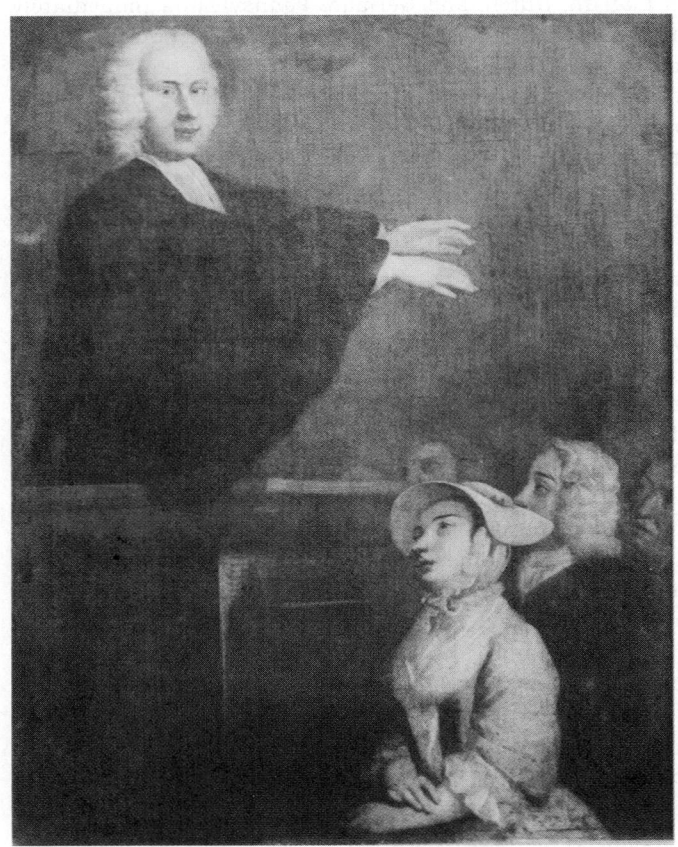

John Wollaston, *George Whitefield* (c. 1742)

In this oil portrait Wollaston emphasized Whitefield's cross-eyed appearance, which some people viewed as a sign of divine favor, and the power of his celebrated oratory, as evidenced by the mesmerized woman in the front row, who is bathed in the same spiritual light that falls upon the famous preacher's face and hands.

itinerant Methodist preacher from England who toured the colonies during 1739-42. Exploiting his formidable oratorical abilities and the growing resources of print culture, including handbills and newspaper advertising, Whitefield drew huge crowds. His mesmerizing sermons on the terrors of hell and the pressing need for conversion also sparked local revivals, first in the middle colonies and then in New England.

There, the groundwork had already been laid by another famous revivalist, Jonathan Edwards. In fact, Whitefield's evangelical style had originally been inspired by Edwards's vivid account of revivals that spread through the Connecticut Valley during the 1730s, *A Faithful Narrative of the Surprising Work of God*, which was first published in London in 1737 and then in Boston in 1738. The foremost theologian of the colonial period, Edwards also wrote a series of massive religious treatises, as well as the most famous of all Puritan spiritual autobiographies, his *Personal Narrative*. But he gained renown and is now probably best known for his sermons, especially "Sinners in the Hands of an Angry God," delivered during the height of the Great Awakening in 1741. Although many Puritan ministers opposed the movement, which they viewed as a dangerous manifestation of religious "enthusiasm," or irrational emotionalism, Edwards and other young ministers viewed the Great Awakening as a vital means of reviving the spiritual piety of the founders of the Massachusetts Bay Colony and restoring the central role the church had assumed in early New England.

In fact, as Edwards and many others recognized, the changing economy, growth of cities, and increasingly diverse population of New England had already loosened the grip of Puritanism, which continued to wane in the decades between the Great Awakening and the Revolution. Nonetheless, it remained a vital force. In reaction to what they viewed as a rising tide of rationalism and secularism, during the 1790s theological descendants of Jonathan Edwards launched a powerful counterattack, now known as the Second Great Awakening. That long-lasting revival sharply altered the course of society and culture in what by then had become the United States. Puritanism also continued to exert a strong pull, not only on those who affirmed its fundamental beliefs but also on those who questioned or rejected its religious doctrines, including philosophers, theologians, and writers as diverse as Ralph Waldo Emerson, Emily Dickinson, and Nathaniel Hawthorne. Indeed, of all the -*isms* that have shaped American culture and society, Puritanism in its varied manifestations has been among the most enduring, at once deeply coloring the American mind and profoundly shaping the contours of life in the United States.

Captain John Smith

[1580-1631]

The legendary Captain John Smith was born in Willoughby, England, in 1580. The son of a successful farmer, Smith apparently attended schools in neighboring towns until he was fifteen. Although his father wanted him to return to the farm, Smith longed for a life of adventure. In what was apparently something of a compromise between father and son, Smith was apprenticed to a merchant. When his father died in 1596, however, Smith left his apprenticeship and began a career as a soldier, going first to the Netherlands, which Protestant England was supporting in its fight for independence from Catholic Spain. For the next several years, Smith traveled widely as a soldier of fortune, visiting France, Scotland, Italy, and Greece. Eventually, he joined the Imperial Army of Austria, which was at war with the Turks. After being promoted to the rank of captain, Smith was wounded in a battle and captured by the Turks in 1602. In a later account of his adventures, Smith claimed that he was consequently sold as a slave and sent to Constantinople, where he managed to kill his master and make a daring escape. He then traveled extensively throughout Europe and finally arrived in northern Africa. A distinguished and decorated soldier, Smith returned to England in 1605.

Still eager for new adventures, Smith worked with the Virginia Company, chartered by James I of England and formed by a group of investors seeking to establish a new colony in North America. Smith invested some of his own money in the venture and joined a company of one hundred colonists that embarked on three ships in December 1606. When the group reached Virginia in April 1607, Smith learned that he had been selected by the company to serve as one of the seven council members of the new colony at Jamestown. That fall, he was also appointed supply officer and set about procuring food from the native population, a confederacy of tribes led by the emperor Powhatan. The powerful chief was determined to stop the encroachment of the English settlers. In an ambush on a small party of colonists late in 1607, Smith's companions were killed and he was captured and brought before Powhatan. According

Simon de Passe, *Captain John Smith* (1616)

This portrait of Smith in his armor, hand on his sword, portrays him as the very image of the Renaissance soldier, explorer, and adventurer. It was engraved after his final return to England, where he spent the rest of his life writing about his experiences in North America.

to the memorable story Smith told later in his life, he was ordered to be executed but saved at the last minute by Powhatan's daughter Pocahontas. But he did not mention Pocahontas in an account of his experiences written soon after his safe return to the colony, a letter published in London as *A True Relation of Such Occurrences and Accidents of Note as Hath Happened in Virginia* (1608). Smith also sent off to London a map of the area and information he had gathered from other colonists, which were later published as *A Map of Virginia: With a Description of the Countrey* (1612). In the meantime, conditions were becoming increasingly difficult at Jamestown, where Smith was elected president of the governing council in 1608. Many of the colonists were unprepared for either the hard work of settlement or the hostility of the native population, and disease and the lack of food contributed to their low morale. As a result of the strict discipline and labor policies instituted by Smith, the situation in the colony began to improve. Nonetheless, he became increasingly unpopular. After being badly burned in a gunpowder explosion, he was forced to sail to England for treatment in 1609.

Although Smith wanted to return, reports of his unpopular leadership made it impossible, and he never again set foot in Virginia. He consequently turned his attention elsewhere: to New England. In 1614, Smith sailed there in order to conduct a survey for the establishment of a new colony. On his return voyage in 1615, he was captured by pirates. During his captivity, he wrote *A Description of New England* (1616), a book that encouraged others to establish settlements there, notably the Pilgrims, to whom Smith offered his services as a guide on their voyage in 1620. But the Pilgrims did not consider Smith to be sufficiently religious, and he never again participated in a colonial settlement. Instead, the former soldier, explorer, and adventurer spent his remaining years in England, devoting himself to writing. During the final decade of his life, he published *New England's Trials* (1620, 1622), his *Generall Historie of Virginia, New-England, and the Summer Isles* (1624), and an autobiography, *The True Travels, Adventures, and Observations of Captaine John Smith, In Europe, Asia, Africa, and America* (1630). Smith did not live to complete his final work. *Advertisements for the Unexperienced Planters in New England, or Anywhere*, another attempt to promote successful colonial settlement in North America, was published shortly after his death in 1631.

This bushy-bearded, high-foreheaded, trusting man,
Who could turn his hand to anything at a pinch,
Bragging, canny, impatient, durable
And fallen in love with the country at first sight.
For that is something which happens or does not.
It did to him.
–Stephen Vincent Benét

Reading Smith's *Generall Historie of Virginia*.   The most famous of Smith's books, *The Generall Historie of Virginia, New-England, and the Summer Isles*, is among the first histories of the English colonies in North America. In April 1621, members of the Virginia Company in London proposed publishing a history of its colony in Jamestown that would generate interest among English readers and consequently encourage additional settlers to immigrate. At the time, Jamestown was beginning to thrive, largely because of the export of tobacco, which had turned the struggling colony into an increasingly profitable venture. In the following year, the always uneasy relations between the colony and the native population once again broke down, and nearly four hundred colonists were killed in an attack on settlements around Jamestown. Although Smith wanted to return to Virginia to assist in the preservation of the colony, his request was turned down by the Virginia Company. Nor is it clear that the company had Smith in mind as the author of its history of Virginia. In an effort to gain support for his return to the colony, however, Smith completed much of the first book of his *Generall Historie* by September 1622, when he published a prospectus in order to raise funds for its publication. The Duchess of Richmond and Lenox agreed to serve as his patron, and Smith dedicated the book to her when *The Generall Historie* was first published in 1624. Six more editions appeared between 1626 and 1632.

The *Generall Historie* is divided into six books, which include a detailed account of the Virginia Colony, as well as briefer histories of the exploration and English settlement of New England and the Summer Isles, also known as the Bermuda Islands. The main character in the book is Smith, who refers to himself in the third person. Much of his lengthy account was based on personal experiences and observations, but Smith also made liberal use of published sources, including material he had earlier gathered together in his *A Map of Virginia: With a Description of the Countrey* (1612). In fact, Smith probably viewed himself, and is viewed by most scholars, as the compiler or editor rather than the sole author of *The Generall Historie*. Certainly, the book is a miscellany, combining personal history, accounts written by others, editorial commentary on actions and events, adventure stories, digressions on the flora and fauna, and descriptions of the native peoples of North America. Smith's most original contribution is the third

Captain John Smith, *The Generall Historie of Virginia* (1624)

The title page of Smith's history was illustrated by engravings of several of his exploits and adventures, including his rescue by Pocahontas. The caption reads: "King Powhatan commands C. Smith to be slayne, his daughter Pokahantas beggs his life [.] his thankfulness and how he subjected 39 of their kings. reade ye history."

book of *The Generall Historie*, in which he narrates the events in Virginia from 1607 through 1609, especially his account of the strained relations between the English colonists and the confederacy of Indian tribes ruled by Powhatan. That part of *The Generall Historie* is, in turn, probably most famous for Smith's account of being saved from execution by Powhatan's daughter Pocahontas. Whether the incident actually took place and, if so, whether Smith either exaggerated its significance or simply misunderstood its meaning have been matters of dispute ever since he published his history and gave rise to one of the most enduring myths of early America. With only minor adjustments, the text of the following selections is taken from *The Generall Historie* from *The Complete Works of Captain John Smith*, edited by Philip L. Barbour (1986).

bedfordstmartins.com/ americanlit *for research links on Smith*

From THE GENERALL HISTORIE OF VIRGINIA, NEW-ENGLAND, AND THE SUMMER ISLES

From The Third Book

CHAPTER II
WHAT HAPPENED TILL THE FIRST SUPPLY

Being thus left to our fortunes, it fortuned that within ten dayes scarce ten amongst us could either goe, or well stand, such extreame weaknes and sicknes oppressed us. And thereat none need marvel, if they consider the cause and reason, which was this; whilest the ships stayed, our allowance was somewhat bettered, by a daily proportion of Bisket, which the sailers would pilfer to sell, give, or exchange with us, for money, Saxefras,[1] furres, or love. But when they departed, there remained neither taverne, beere-house, nor place of reliefe, but the common Kettell.[2] Had we beene as free from all sinnes as gluttony, and drunkennesse, we might have beene canonized for Saints. But our President would never have beene admitted, for ingrossing to his private,[3] Oatmeale, Sacke, Oyle, Aquavitae,[4] Beefe, Egges, or what not, but the Kettell; that indeed he allowed equally to be distributed, and that was halfe a pint of wheat, and as much barley boyled with water for a man a day, and this having fryed some 26. weekes in the ships hold, contained as many wormes as graines; so that we might truely call it rather so much bran than corne,[5] our drinke was water, our lodgings Castles in the ayre: with this lodging and diet, our extreame toile in bearing and planting Pallisadoes,[6] so strained and bruised us, and our continuall labour in the extremitie of the heat had so weakened us,

---

1. **Saxefras:** Leaves from the sassafras tree were used to make tea and medicines.
2. **common Kettell:** Shared resources.
3. **ingrossing to his private:** The president of the colony, Edward Maria Wingfield (c. 1560–1613), took many of the common supplies for his own use.
4. **Aquavitae:** Brandy.
5. **corne:** Grain.
6. **Pallisadoes:** Rows of fences made of wooden stakes, used for defense.

as were cause sufficient to have made us as miserable in our native Countrey, or any other place in the world. From May, to September, those that escaped, lived upon Sturgeon, and Sea-crabs, fiftie in this time we buried, the rest seeing the Presidents projects to escape these miseries in our Pinnace[7] by flight (who all this time had neither felt want nor sicknes) so moved our dead spirits, as we deposed him; and established Ratcliffe in his place, (Gosnoll being dead) Kendall deposed, Smith newly recovered, Martin and Ratcliffe was by his care preserved and relieved, and the most of the souldiers recovered, with the skilfull diligence of Master Thomas Wotton our Chirurgian[8] generall. But now was all our provision spent, the Sturgeon gone, all helps abandoned, each houre expecting the fury of the Salvages;[9] when God the patron of all good indevours, in that desperate extremitie so changed the hearts of the Salvages, that they brought such plenty of their fruits, and provision, as no man wanted.

And now where some affirmed it was ill done of the Councell to send forth men so badly provided, this incontradictable reason will shew them plainely they are too ill advised to nourish such ill conceits; first, the fault of our going was our owne, what could be thought fitting or necessary we had, but what we should find, or want, or where we should be, we were all ignorant, and supposing to make our passage in two moneths, with victuall[10] to live, and the advantage of the spring to worke; we were at Sea five moneths, where we both spent our victuall and lost the opportunitie of the time, and season to plant, by the unskilfull presumption of our ignorant transporters, that understood not at all, what they undertooke.

Such actions have ever since the worlds beginning beene subject to such accidents, and every thing of worth is found full of difficulties, but nothing so difficult as to establish a Common-wealth so farre remote from men and meanes, and where mens mindes are so untoward as neither doe well themselves, nor suffer others. But to proceed.

The new President and Martin, being little beloved, of weake judgement in dangers, and lesse industrie in peace, committed the managing of all things abroad to Captaine Smith: who by his owne example, good words, and faire promises, set some to mow, others to binde thatch, some to build houses, others to thatch them, himselfe always bearing the greatest taske for his owne share, so that in short time, he provided most of them lodgings, neglecting any for himselfe. This done, seeing the Salvages superfluitie beginne to decrease (with some of his workemen) shipped himselfe in the Shallop[11] to search the Country for trade. The want of the language, knowledge to mannage his boat without sailes, the want of a sufficient power, (knowing the multitude of the Salvages) apparell for his men, and other necessaries, were infinite impediments, yet no discouragement. Being but six or seven in company he went downe the river to Kecoughtan,[12] where at first they scorned him, as a famished man, and would in derision offer him a handfull of Corne, a peece of bread, for their swords and muskets, and such like

---

7. **Pinnace:** A small sailboat.
8. **Chirurgian:** Surgeon.
9. **Salvages:** Savages, the name given to Indians.
10. **victuall:** Food or provisions.
11. **Shallop:** A light sailboat primarily used for fishing.
12. **Kecoughtan:** Tribal village near the mouth of the James River.

proportions also for their apparell. But seeing by trade and courtesie there was nothing to be had, he made bold to try such conclusions as necessitie inforced, though contrary to his Commission: Let fly his muskets, ran his boat on shore, whereat they all fled into the woods. So marching towards their houses, they might see great heapes of corne: much adoe he had to restraine his hungry souldiers from present taking of it, expecting as it happened that the Salvages would assault them, as not long after they did with a most hydeous noyse. Sixtie or seaventie of them, some blacke, some red, some white, some party-coloured, came in a square order,[13] singing and dauncing out of the woods, with their *Okee* (which was an Idoll made of skinnes, stuffed with mosse, all painted and hung with chaines and copper) borne before them: and in this manner being well armed, with Clubs, Targets, Bowes and Arrowes, they charged the English, that so kindly received them with their muskets loaden with Pistoll shot, that downe fell their God, and divers[14] lay sprauling on the ground; the rest fled againe to the woods, and ere long sent one of their *Quiyoughkasoucks*[15] to offer peace, and redeeme their *Okee*. Smith told them, if onely six of them would come unarmed and loade his boat, he would not only be their friend, but restore them their *Okee*, and give them Beads, Copper, and Hatchets besides: which on both sides was to their contents performed: and then they brought him Venison, Turkies, wild fowle, bread, and what they had, singing and dauncing in signe of friendship till they departed. In his returne he discovered the Towne and Country of Warraskoyack.[16]

> Thus God unboundlesse by his power,
> Made them thus kind, would us devour.

Smith perceiving (notwithstanding their late miserie) not any regarded but from hand to mouth (the company being well recovered) caused the Pinnace to be provided with things fitting to get provision for the yeare following; but in the interim he made 3. or 4. journies and discovered the people of Chickahamania:[17] yet what he carefully provided the rest carelesly spent. Wingfield and Kendall living in disgrace, seeing all things at randome in the absence of Smith, the companies dislike of their Presidents weaknes, and their small love to Martins never mending sicknes, strengthened themselves with the sailers, and other confederates to regaine their former credit and authority, or at least such meanes abord the Pinnace, (being fitted to saile as Smith had appointed for trade) to alter her course and to goe for England. Smith unexpectedly returning had the plot discovered to him, much trouble he had to prevent it, till with store of sakre[18] and musket shot he forced them stay or sinke in the river, which action cost the life of captaine Kendall. These brawles are so disgustfull, as some will say they were better forgotten, yet all men of good judgement will conclude, it were better their

---

13. **square order**: In a military formation.
14. **divers**: Several or many.
15. ***Quiyoughkasoucks***: Priests or gods.
16. **Warraskoyack**: Tribal village on the Pagan River.
17. **the people of Chickahamania**: The Chickahominy tribe lived in villages along the Chickahominy River, near Jamestown.
18. **sakre**: Shot for a small cannon.

basenes should be manifest to the world, then the busines beare the scorne and shame of their excused disorders. The President and captaine Archer not long after intended also to have abandoned the country, which project also was curbed, and suppressed by Smith. The Spaniard never more greedily desired gold then he victuall, nor his souldiers more to abandon the Country, then he to keepe it. But finding plentie of Corne in the river of Chickahamania where hundreds of Salvages in divers places stood with baskets expecting his coming. And now the winter approaching, the rivers became so covered with swans, geese, duckes, and cranes, that we daily feasted with good bread, Virginia peas, pumpions, and putchamins,[19] fish, fowle, and diverse sorts of wild beasts as fat as we could eate them: so that none of our Tuftaffaty humorists[20] desired to goe for England. But our Comaedies never endured long without a Tragedie; some idle exceptions being muttered against Captaine Smith, for not discovering the head of Chickahamania river, and taxed by the Councell, to be too slow in so worthy an attempt. The next voyage hee proceeded so farre that with much labour by cutting of trees in sunder he made his passage, but when his Barge could passe no farther, he left her in a broad bay out of danger of shot, commanding none should goe a shore till his returne: himselfe with two English and two Salvages went up higher in a Canowe, but hee was not long absent, but his men went a shore, whose want of government, gave both occasion and opportunity to the Salvages to surprise one George Cassen, whom they slew, and much failed not to have cut of the boat and all the rest. Smith little dreaming of that accident, being got to the marshes at the rivers head, twentie myles in the desert, had his two men slaine (as is supposed) sleeping by the Canowe, whilst himselfe by fowling sought them victuall, who finding he was beset with 200. Salvages, two of them hee slew, still defending himselfe with the aid of a Salvage his guide, whom he bound to his arme with his garters, and used him as a buckler,[21] yet he was shot in his thigh a little, and had many arrowes that stucke in his cloathes but no great hurt, till at last they tooke him prisoner. When this newes came to James towne, much was their sorrow for his losse, fewe expecting what ensued. Sixe or seven weekes those Barbarians kept him prisoner, many strange triumphes and conjurations they made of him, yet hee so demeaned himselfe amongst them, as he not onely diverted them from surprising the Fort, but procured his owne libertie, and got himselfe and his company such estimation amongst them, that those Salvages admired him more than their owne *Quiyouckosucks.*[22] The manner how they used and delivered him, is as followeth.

    The Salvages having drawne from George Cassen whether Captaine Smith was gone, prosecuting that oportunity they followed him with 300. bowmen, conducted by the King of Pamaunkee,[23] who in divisions searching the turnings of the river, found Robinson and Emry by the fire side, those they shot full of arrowes and slew. Then finding the Captaine, as is said, that used the Salvage that was his guide as his sheld (three

---

19. **putchamins:** Persimmons.
20. **Tuftaffaty humorists:** Obstinate colonists, dressed in inappropriately ornate clothes.
21. **buckler:** A shield.
22. ***Quiyouckosucks*:** Alternate spelling for the term for priests or gods; see note 15.
23. **King of Pamaunkee:** Powhatan's half brother, Opechancanough.

of them being slaine and divers other so gauld[24]) all the rest would not come neere him. Thinking thus to have returned to his boat, regarding them, as he marched, more than his way, slipped up to the middle in an oasie[25] creeke and his Salvage with him, yet durst they not come to him till being neere dead with cold, he threw away his armes. Then according to their composition[26] they drew him forth and led him to the fire, where his men were slaine. Diligently they chafed his benummed limbs. He demanding for their Captaine, they shewed him Opechankanough, King of Pamaunkee, to whom he gave a round Ivory double compass Dyall.[27] Much they marvailed at the playing of the Fly and Needle, which they could see so plainely, and yet not touch it, because of the glasse that covered them. But when he demonstrated by that Globe-like Jewell, the roundnesse of the earth, and skies, the spheare of the Sunne, Moone, and Starres, and how the Sunne did chase the night round about the world continually; the greatnesse of the Land and Sea, the diversitie of Nations, varietie of complexions, and how we were to them Antipodes, and many other such like matters, they all stood as amazed with admiration. Notwithstanding, within an houre after they tyed him to a tree, and as many as could stand about him prepared to shoot him, but the King holding up the Compass in his hand, they all laid downe their Bowes and Arrowes, and in a triumphant manner led him to Orapaks,[28] where he was after their manner kindly feasted, and well used.

Their order in conducting him was thus; Drawing themselves all in file, the King in the middest had all their Peeces and Swords borne before him. Captaine Smith was led after him by three great Salvages, holding him fast by each arme: and on each side six went in file with their Arrowes nocked. But arriving at the Towne (which was but onely thirtie or fortie hunting houses made of Mats, which they remove as they please, as we our tents) all the women and children staring to behold him, the souldiers first all in file performed the forme of a Bissone[29] so well as could be; and on each flanke, officers as Serjeants to see them keepe their order. A good time they continued this exercise, and then cast themselves in a ring, dauncing in such severall Postures, and singing and yelling out such hellish notes and screeches; being strangely painted, every one his quiver of Arrowes, and at his backe a club; on his arme a Fox or an Otters skinne, or some such matter for his vambrace;[30] their heads and shoulders painted red, with Oyle and *Pocones*[31] mingled together, which Scarlet-like colour made an exceeding handsome shew; his Bow in his hand, and the skinne of a Bird with her wings abroad dryed, tyed on his head, a peece of copper, a white shell, a long feather, with a small rattle growing at the tayles of their snakes tyed to it, or some such like toy. All this while Smith and the King stood in the middest guarded, as before is said, and after three dances they all departed. Smith they conducted to a long house, where thirtie or fortie tall fellowes did

---

24. **gauld:** Galled or harassed in warfare, especially by arrows or shot.
25. **oasie:** Boggy.
26. **composition:** Early term for an agreement or prior arrangement.
27. **Dyall:** Dial.
28. **Orapaks:** A temporary hunting village.
29. **Bissone:** Alternate spelling for *besom*, a broom-like shape.
30. **vambrace:** A piece of armor for the forearm.
31. **Oyle and *Pocones*:** Red dye made from a vegetable root, mixed with oil.

guard him, and ere long more bread and venison was brought him then would have served twentie men, I thinke his stomacke at that time was not very good; what he left they put in baskets and tyed over his head. About midnight they set the meate againe before him, all this time not one of them would eate a bit with him, till the next morning they brought him as much more, and then did they eate all the old, and reserved the new as they had done the other, which made him thinke they would fat him to eat him. Yet in this desperate estate to defend him from the cold, one Maocassater brought him his gowne, in requitall of some beads and toyes Smith had given him at his first arrivall in Virginia.

Two dayes after a man would have slaine him (but that the guard prevented it) for the death of his sonne, to whom they conducted him to recover[32] the poore man then breathing his last. Smith told them that at James towne he had a water would doe it, if they would let him fetch it, but they would not permit that; but made all the preparations they could to assault James towne, craving his advice, and for recompence he should have life, libertie, land, and women. In part of a Table booke[33] he writ his minde to them at the Fort, what was intended, how they should follow that direction to affright the messengers, and without fayle send him such things as he writ for. And an Inventory with them. The difficultie and danger, he told the Salvages, of the Mines, great gunnes, and other Engins exceedingly affrighted them, yet according to his request they went to James towne, in as bitter weather as could be of frost and snow, and within three dayes returned with an answer.

But when they came to James towne, seeing men sally out as he had told them they would, they fled; yet in the night they came againe to the same place where he had told them they should receive an answer, and such things as he had promised them, which they found accordingly, and with which they returned with no small expedition, to the wonder of them all that heard it, that he could either divine, or the paper could speake: then they led him to the Youghtanunds, the Mattapanients, the Payankatanks, the Nantaughtacunds, and Onawmanients[34] upon the rivers of Rapahanock, and Patawomek, over all those rivers, and backe againe by divers other severall Nations, to the Kings habitation at Pamaunkee, where they entertained him with most strange and fearefull Conjurations;[35]

> As if neare led to hell,
> Amongst the Devils to dwell.

Not long after, early in a morning a great fire was made in a long house,[36] and a mat spread on the one side, as on the other, on the one they caused him to sit, and all the

---

32. **recover:** Revive or restore to life.
33. **Table booke:** A small notebook.
34. **Youghtanunds . . . Onawmanients:** Several tribes in the confederacy ruled by Powhatan.
35. **Conjurations:** Invoking of spirits. The following lines are from Martin Fotherby's *Atheomastix* (1622), a collection of translations of ancient writers such as Seneca, Solon, Lucretius, and Euripides. Smith frequently quotes from Fotherby (1549?-1619) in *The Generall Historie*.
36. **long house:** Communal dwelling house.

guard went out of the house, and presently came skipping in a great grim fellow, all painted over with coale, mingled with oyle; and many Snakes and Wesels skins stuffed with mosse, and all their tayles tyed together, so as they met on the crowne of his head in a tassell; and round about the tassell was as a Coronet of feathers, the skins hanging round about his head, backe, and shoulders, and in a manner covered his face; with a hellish voyce and a rattle in his hand. With most strange gestures and passions he began his invocation, and environed the fire with a circle of meale; which done, three more such like devils came rushing in with the like antique[37] tricks, painted halfe blacke, halfe red: but all their eyes were painted white, and some red streaks like Mutchato's,[38] along their cheekes: round about him those fiends daunced a pretty while, and then came in three more as ugly as the rest; with red eyes, and white streaks over their blacke faces, at last they all sat downe right against him; three of them on the one hand of the chiefe Priest, and three on the other. Then all with their rattles began a song, which ended, the chiefe Priest layd downe five wheat cornes: then strayning his armes and hands with such violence that he sweat, and his veynes swelled, he began a short Oration: at the conclusion they all gave a short groane; and then layd down three graines more. After that, began their song againe, and then another Oration, ever laying downe so many cornes as before, till they had twice incirculed the fire; that done, they tooke a bunch of little stickes prepared for that purpose, continuing still their devotion, and at the end of every song and Oration, they layd downe a sticke betwixt the divisions of Corne. Till night, neither he nor they did either eate or drinke, and then they feasted merrily, with the best provisions they could make. Three dayes they used this Ceremony; the meaning whereof they told him, was to know if he intended them well or no. The circle of meale signified their Country, the circles of corne the bounds of the Sea, and the stickes his Country. They imagined the world to be flat and round, like a trencher,[39] and they in the middest. After this they brought him a bagge of gunpowder, which they carefully preserved till the next spring, to plant as they did their corne; because they would be acquainted with the nature of that seede. Opitchapam[40] the Kings brother invited him to his house, where, with as many platters of bread, fowle, and wild beasts, as did environ him, he bid him wellcome; but not any of them would eate a bit with him, but put up all the remainder in Baskets. At his returne to Opechancanoughs, all the Kings women, and their children, flocked about him for their parts, as a due by Custome, to be merry with such fragments.

> But his waking mind in hydeous dreames did oft see wondrous shapes,
> Of bodies strange, and huge in growth, and of stupendious makes.[41]

At last they brought him to Meronocomoco,[42] where was Powhatan their Emperor. Here more then two hundred of those grim Courtiers stood wondering at him, as he had

---

37. **antique:** Variant spelling for *antic*, or grotesque.
38. **Mutchato's:** Moustaches.
39. **trencher:** A wooden plate or platter.
40. **Opitchapam:** Powhatan's half brother; see note 23.
41. **But . . . makes:** Lines from *Atheomastix*; see note 35.
42. **Meronocomoco:** Powhatan's village, north of Jamestown.

beene a monster; till Powhatan and his trayne had put themselves in their greatest braveries.[43] Before a fire upon a seat like a bedsted, he sat covered with a great robe, made of
Rarowcun[44] skinnes, and all the tayles hanging by. On either hand did sit a young wench
of 16 or 18 yeares, and along on each side the house, two rowes of men, and behind them
as many women, with all their heads and shoulders painted red; many of their heads
bedecked with the white downe of Birds; but every one with something: and a great
chayne of white beads about their necks. At his entrance before the King, all the people
gave a great shout. The Queene of Appamatuck[45] was appointed to bring him water to
wash his hands, and another brought him a bunch of feathers, in stead of a Towell to dry
them: having feasted him after their best barbarous manner they could, a long consultation was held, but the conclusion was, two great stones were brought before Powhatan:
then as many as could layd hands on him, dragged him to them, and thereon laid his
head, and being ready with their clubs, to beate out his braines, Pocahontas the Kings
dearest daughter, when no intreaty could prevaile, got his head in her armes, and laid
her owne upon his to save him from death: whereat the Emperour was contented he
should live to make him hatchets, and her bells, beads, and copper; for they thought him
as well of all occupations as themselves. For the King himselfe will make his owne robes,
shooes, bowes, arrowes, pots; plant, hunt, or doe any thing so well as the rest.

> They say he bore a pleasant shew,
> But sure his heart was sad.
> For who can pleasant be, and rest,
> That lives in feare and dread:
> And having life suspected, doth
> It still suspected lead.[46]

Two dayes after, Powhatan having disguised himselfe in the most fearefullest manner he could, caused Captaine Smith to be brought forth to a great house in the woods,
and there upon a mat by the fire to be left alone. Not long after from behinde a mat that
divided the house, was made the most dolefullest noyse he ever heard; then Powhatan
more like a devill then a man with some two hundred more as blacke as himselfe, came
unto him and told him now they were friends, and presently he should goe to James
towne, to send him two great gunnes, and a gryndstone, for which he would give him the
Country of Capahowosick, and for ever esteeme him as his sonne Nantaquoud. So to
James towne with 12 guides Powhatan sent him. That night they quarterd in the woods,
he still expecting (as he had done all this long time of his imprisonment) every houre to
be put to one death or other: for all their feasting. But almightie God (by his divine providence) had mollified the hearts of those sterne Barbarians with compassion. The next
morning betimes they came to the Fort, where Smith having used the Salvages with
what kindnesse he could, he shewed Rawhunt, Powhatans trusty servant two

---

43. **braveries:** Finery or fine clothes.
44. **Rarowcun:** Early spelling for *raccoon.*
45. **Queene of Appamatuck:** Opossunoquonuske was the leader of the Appamatuck, who lived in a small
village west of Jamestown.
46. **They . . . lead:** Lines from *Atheomastix;* see note 35.

demi-Culverings[47] and a millstone to carry Powhatan: they found them somewhat too heavie; but when they did see him discharge them, being loaded with stones, among the boughs of a great tree loaded with Isickles, the ice and branches came so tumbling downe, that the poore Salvages ran away halfe dead with feare. But at last we regained some conference with them, and gave them such toyes, and sent to Powhatan, his women, and children such presents, as gave them in generall full content. Now in James Towne they were all in combustion, the strongest preparing once more to run away with the Pinnace; which with the hazzard of his life, with Sakre falcon[48] and musket shot, Smith forced now the third time to stay or sinke. Some no better then they should be, had plotted with the President, the next day to have put him to death by the Leviticall law,[49] for the lives of Robinson and Emry, pretending the fault was his that had led them to their ends: but he quickly tooke such order with such Lawyers, that he layd them by the heeles till he sent some of them prisoners for England. Now ever once in foure or five dayes, Pocahontas with her attendants, brought him so much provision, that saved many of their lives, that else for all this had starved with hunger.

> Thus from numbe death our good God sent reliefe,
> The sweete asswager of all other griefe.[50]

His relation of the plenty he had seene, especially at Werawocomoco, and of the state and bountie of Powhatan, (which till that time was unknowne) so revived their dead spirits (especially the love of Pocahontas) as all mens feare was abandoned. Thus you may see what difficulties still crossed any good indevour: and the good successe of the businesse being thus oft brought to the very period of destruction; yet you see by what strange means God hath still delivered it. As for the insufficiency of them admitted in Commission, that error could not be prevented by the Electors; there being no other choise, and all strangers to each others education, qualities, or disposition. And if any deeme it a shame to our Nation to have any mention made of those inormities, let them peruse the Histories of the Spanyards Discoveries and Plantations, where they may see how many mutinies, disorders, and dissentions have accompanied them, and crossed their attempts: which being knowne to be particular mens offences; doth take away the generall scorne and contempt, which malice, presumption, covetousnesse, or ignorance might produce; to the scandall and reproach of those, whose actions and valiant resolutions deserve a more worthy respect.

Now whether it had beene better for Captaine Smith, to have concluded with any of those severall projects, to have abandoned the Countrey, with some ten or twelve of them, who were called the better sort, and have left Master Hunt our Preacher, Master Anthony Gosnoll, a most honest, worthy, and industrious Gentleman, Master Thomas Wotton, and some 27 others of his Countrymen to the fury of the Salvages, famine, and

---

47. **demi-Culverings:** Small cannons.
48. **Sakre falcon:** A small cannon, named after the saker falcon, a Middle Eastern bird of prey.
49. **Leviticall law:** That is, the law of retribution as laid down in the Old Testament — for example, Leviticus 24:21: "and he that killeth a man, he shall be put to death."
50. **Thus . . . griefe:** The first line is Smith's, while the second is from *Atheomastix;* see note 35.

all manner of mischiefes, and inconveniences, (for they were but fortie in all to keepe possession of this large Country;) or starve himselfe with them for company, for want of lodging: or but adventuring abroad to make them provision, or by his opposition to preserve the action, and save all their lives; I leave to the censure of all honest men to consider. But

> We men imagine in our Jolitie,
> That 'tis all one, or good or bad to be.
> But then anone wee alter this againe,
> If happily wee feele the sence of paine;
> For then we're turn'd into a mourning vaine.[51]

Written by Thomas Studley, the first Cape Merchant in Virginia, Robert Fenton, Edward Harrington, and J. S.[52]

[1624, 1986]

---

51. **We ... vaine:** Lines from *Atheomastix*; see note 35.
52. **Written by ... and J. S.:** *J. S.* is John Smith, but little is known about the other authors or their possible contributions to this portion of *The Generall Historie.* They may have provided notes to Smith, or he may have invoked their names in order to affirm the authenticity of his account.

William Bradford

[1590-1657]

William Bradford was born in March 1590 in Austerfield, a town in Yorkshire, northern England. His parents, William and Alice Hanson Bradford, were prosperous farmers. When Bradford was only a year old, his father died, and his mother soon remarried. Raised by his grandfather and uncles, Bradford was educated at a local grammar school and trained to be a farmer. When he was twelve or thirteen, however, he became absorbed in reading the Bible and was deeply moved by the preaching of Richard Clyfton, an Anglican priest in a nearby parish who was seeking to reform, or "purify," the Church of England. Finally deciding that such efforts were futile, Clyfton organized a Separatist congregation that met at the home of William Brewster in Scrooby, a town in Nottinghamshire. The formation of such an independent church constituted a formal secession from the Church of England, a treasonous act according to the laws of England. Nonetheless, over the strenuous opposition of his family, Bradford in 1606 left home to join the church in Scrooby.

From then until his death forty-one years later, Bradford devoted himself to the interests and welfare of the "Pilgrims," as he called members of the devout group of Separatists. But their pilgrimage was not simply spiritual; it also became an arduous physical journey in quest of a place where they could establish a church and worship God according to what Bradford later described as "the simplicity of the gospel." As the new congregation grew to be more openly defiant of the laws of church and state, the Scrooby group determined that they could avoid persecution and survive only if they left England. They consequently fled to the Netherlands, where Bradford joined them in 1609. The only occupations open to English immigrants there were handicrafts, so Bradford learned the weaving trade. In 1611, when he was twenty-one, Bradford came into an inheritance of land in England, but he did not return home. Instead, he immediately sold the property, using the proceeds to buy a loom and a house, as well as to make a contribution toward the purchase of a church building for the Separatists. Two years later, he married Dorothy May, the daughter of an English Separatist; the couple's only child, John, was born in 1618. By then, the Pilgrims were already planning yet another removal, this time from Europe to North America. Leaving behind their young son, whom they never saw again, Bradford and his wife embarked aboard the *Mayflower* for the voyage to the northern part of the Virginia Territory, near the mouth of the Hudson River, where the Separatists had obtained a land grant from the English government. But high seas prevented the ship from reaching its intended destination and after a sixty-five-day voyage it anchored instead off Cape Cod, in November 1620. While Bradford and others were exploring the coastline, Dorothy Bradford either fell or jumped overboard and drowned in Provincetown Harbor. Despite the tragic loss and possible suicide of his "dearest consort," the first of many Pilgrims who perished that winter, Bradford and the other Separatists determined to settle on the mainland at a place called "Plimoth" (later spelled *Plymouth*), the name the harbor had been given by Captain John Smith on a map included in his *Description of New England* (1616).

Bradford swiftly became the central figure in the new colony, both as its civic leader and as the primary author of its fame. Along with forty others, he signed the Mayflower Compact, establishing the basis for government in Plymouth. In 1621, he was elected governor, an office in which Bradford served for all but five of the remaining years of his life. He married a widow, Alice Carpenter, in 1623; the couple had three children. In an effort to preserve the security of the colony by establishing peaceful relations with the Indians, Bradford negotiated a long-lasting treaty with Massasoit, the chief of the Wampanoag. Bradford also became the major historian of and spokesperson for the colony. His first publication, a compilation of passages from his diary and that of Edward Winslow, was *A Relation or Journal of the Beginning and Proceedings of the English Plantation Settled at Plimoth in New England* (1622), commonly known as *Mourt's Relation.* Bradford began to write his most famous work, *Of Plimoth Plantation,* in 1630, later adding sections that carried the history of the colony up to 1647. During the last ten years of his life, the largely self-educated first historian of New England also wrote poetry, letters, and a series of five *Dialogues* designed to provide guidance for the second generation of Pilgrims, who were increasingly straying from the mission of the original settlers of Plymouth.

Shortly before his death, Bradford wrote a poem in which he movingly and with characteristic modesty offered an assessment of his life:

William Bradford

No likeness of Bradford was made during his lifetime, but he and the Pilgrims were later the subject of numerous works in every medium, including this statue Cyrus E. Dallin was commissioned to design as part of Plymouth's tercentenary celebration in 1921.

> From my years young in days of youth,
> God did make known to me this truth,
> And call'd me from my native place
> For to enjoy the means of grace.
> In wilderness he did me guide,
> And in strange lands for me provide,
> In fears and wants, through weal and woe,
> A Pilgrim passed I to and fro.

Bradford, the simple Pilgrim who in American history and myth would later take his place as the most revered of the "Pilgrim Fathers," died at his home in Plymouth on May 9, 1657.

Reading Bradford's *Of Plimoth Plantation.*   Bradford wrote his famous history over a period of twenty years. He wrote the first ten chapters in 1630, at the beginning of the great migration, during which thousands of Puritans immigrated to New England. Concerned that his own small colony would be overshadowed by the larger and more powerful group in the Massachusetts Bay Colony, Bradford clearly sought to affirm the vital role of the Pilgrims in both the English Reformation and the settlement of New England. Just as he and other Protestant reformers sought to simplify forms of worship and strip churches of ornamentation, Bradford in a prefatory note observed that he would offer his account in a plain style, with singular regard "unto the simple truth in all things." For him, that regard for "simple truth" meant accurately recording and seeking to interpret the meaning of events dictated by God, the true author of all history. Beginning with an account of the origin of the Pilgrim Church during the Reformation in England, Bradford in 1630 described the persecutions the Separatists endured, their consequent departure to and difficult years in Holland, their decision to remove to New England, and their voyage aboard the *Mayflower*, ending with their arrival at Cape Cod and their choice of a place of settlement at Plymouth. According to a note he added in 1646, Bradford wrote most of the remainder of the book intermittently during the intervening years; he added a few sections as late as 1650.

Bradford did not prepare his account for publication; indeed, the book existed only in manuscript for two hundred years. But portions of his account were known to readers of other early histories. Nathaniel Morton paraphrased much of it in *New England's Memoriall* (1669), and the manuscript was also consulted by historians such as William Hubbard, who made substantial use of it in his *History of New England*, written in 1683, and Cotton Mather, who depended on it for his *Magnalia Christi Americana* (1702). In the eighteenth century, the manuscript passed through many hands before it was mysteriously lost during the American Revolution. It later emerged in England, in the library of the Bishop of London. *Of Plimoth Plantation* was published in its entirety in 1856 under the direction of Charles Deane, an editor of publications for the Massachusetts

bedfordstmartins.com/
americanlit *for research*
links on Bradford

Bradford's Manuscript

As the precise layout and careful handwriting of this detail from the first page of Bradford's manuscript suggest, he evidently began to write his history in 1630 with an eye to publication. But he continued to add to it for nearly twenty years, and the complete manuscript was not published until 1856.

Historical Society. Regarded as one of the most important and valuable documents in early American history, the manuscript was finally returned to the United States in 1897, following forty years of negotiations involving a complex cast of characters, including American historians, politicians, and ambassadors, as well as British bishops, prime ministers, and even Queen Victoria. On May 26, 1897, the manuscript was placed in the state house of Massachusetts, an occasion marked by elaborate ceremonies in Boston and extensively reported in newspapers throughout the United States. The text of the following selections is taken from *Of Plimoth Plantation*, an exact transcription of the manuscript published in Boston by order of the Commonwealth of Massachusetts in 1898. For the most part, we have retained Bradford's original capitalization, punctuation, paragraphing, and spelling. But we have added the terminal *e* to his spelling of common words such as *here*, *there*, and *where*; and we have adjusted his spelling in a few instances where a now-archaic spelling obscures the meaning of a passage. We have regularized his inconsistent chapter headings and expanded his abbreviations, including y^e (*the*) and y^t (*that*), which Bradford used throughout his manuscript.

From OF PLIMOTH PLANTATION

[*From* Booke 1]

And first of the occasion and inducements thereunto; the which that I may truly unfould, I must begine at the very roote & rise of the same. The which I shall endevor to manefest in a plaine stile, with singuler regard unto the simple truth in all things, at least as near as my slender judgmente can attaine the same.

From *Chapter 1*

It is well knowne unto the godly and judicious, how ever since the first breaking out of the lighte of the gospell in our Honourable Nation of England, (which was the first of nations whom the Lord adorned there with, afffter that grosse darknes of popery which had covered & overspred the Christian world,) what warrs & oppossissions ever since, Satan hath raised, maintained, and continued against the Saints,[1] from time to time, in one sorte or other. Some times by bloody death and cruell torments; other whiles imprisonments, banishments, & other hard usages; as being loath his kingdom should goe downe, the truth prevaile, and the churches of God reverte to their anciente puritie, and recover their primative order, libertie, & bewtie. . . .

But that I may come more near my intendmente; when as by the travell & diligence of some godly & zealous preachers, & Gods blessing on their labours, as in other places of the land, so in the North parts,[2] many became inlightened by the word of God, and had their ignorance & sins discovered unto them, and begane by his grace to reforme their lives, and make conscience of their wayes, the worke of God was no sooner manifest in them, but presently they were both scoffed and scorned by the prophane multitude, and the ministers urged with the yoak of subscription,[3] or else must be silenced; and the poore people were so vexed with apparators, & pursuants, & the comissarie courts,[4] as truly their affliction was not smale; which, notwithstanding, they bore sundrie years with much patience, till they were occasioned (by the continuance & encrease of these troubls, and other means which the Lord raised up in those days) to see further into things by the light of the word of God. How not only these base and beggerly ceremonies were unlawfull, but also that the lordly & tiranous power of the prelats ought not to be submitted unto; which thus, contrary to the freedome of the gospell, would load & burden mens consciences, and by their compulsive power make a prophane mixture of persons & things in the worship of God. . . .

So many therfore of these proffessors[5] as saw the evill of these things, in these parts, and whose harts the Lord had touched with heavenly zeale for his trueth, they shooke off this yoake of antichristian bondage, and as the Lords free people, joyned them selves (by a covenant of the Lord[6]) into a church estate, in the felowship of the gospell, to walke in all his wayes, made known, or to be made known unto them, according to their best endeavours, whatsoever it should cost them, the Lord assisting them. And that it cost them something this ensewing historie will declare. . . .

But after these things they could not long continue in any peaceable condition, but were hunted & persecuted on every side, so as their former afflictions were but as

---

1. **Saints:** Bradford uses the term in its biblical sense, to refer to church members or God's chosen people, not to the canonized saints of the Roman Catholic Church.

2. **North parts:** Northern England and Scotland.

3. **yoak of subscription:** Compelled to subscribe to the laws of the Church of England.

4. **apparators, & pursuants, & the comissarie courts:** The various offices and officials of the Church of England.

5. **proffessors:** That is, those who professed what Bradford viewed as true Christianity.

6. **a covenant of the Lord:** An agreement entered into by all members of a congregation to act in accordance with the laws of the church.

flea-bitings in comparison of these which now came upon them. For some were taken & clapt up in prison, others had their houses besett & watcht night and day, & hardly escaped their hands; and the most were faine to flie & leave their howses & habitations, and the means of their livelehood. Yet these & many other sharper things which affterward befell them, were no other then they looked for, and therfore were the better prepared to bear them by the assistance of Gods grace & spirite. Yet seeing them selves thus molested, and that there was no hope of their continuance there, by a joynte consente they resolved to goe into the Low-Countries, where they heard was freedome of Religion for all men; as also how sundrie[7] from London, & other parts of the land, had been exiled and persecuted for the same cause, & were gone thither, and lived at Amsterdam, & in other places of the land. So affter they had continued togeither aboute a year, and kept their meetings every Saboth in one place or other, exercising the worship of God amongst them selves, notwithstanding all the dilligence & malice of their adverssaries, they seeing they could no longer continue in that condition, they resolved to get over into Holland as they could; which was in the year 1607. & 1608. . . .

CHAPTER 9

OF THEIR VOYAGE, & HOW THEY PASSED THE SEA, AND
OF THEIR SAFE ARRIVALL AT CAPE CODD

September 6. These troubls being blowne over, and now all being compacte togeather in one shipe,[8] here they put to sea againe with a prosperus winde, which continued diverce days together, which was some incouragmente unto them; yet according to the usuall maner many were afflicted with sea-sicknes. And I may not omite there a spetiall worke of Gods providence. There was a proud & very profane yonge man, one of the sea-men, of a lustie,[9] able body, which made him the more hauty; he would allway be contemning the poore people in their sickness, & cursing them dayly with grievous execrations, and did not let[10] to tell them, that he hoped to help to cast halfe of them over board before they came to their jurneys end, and to make mery with what they had; and if he were by any gently reproved, he would curse and swear most bitterly. But it pleased God before they came halfe seas over, to smite this yong man with a grievous disease, of which he dyed in a desperate maner, and so was him selfe the first that was throwne overbord. Thus his curses light on his owne head; and it was an astonishmente to all his fellows, for they noted it to be the just hand of God upon him.

After they had injoyed faire winds and weather for a season, they were incountred many times with crosse winds, and mette with many feirce stormes, with which the shipe was shroudly[11] shaken, and her upper works made very leakie; and one of the maine beames in the midd ships was bowed & craked, which put them in some fear

---

7. **sundrie:** Early spelling of *sundry*, meaning several or various.
8. **togeather in one shipe:** The original plan called for two ships to sail from England, the *Speedwell* and the *Mayflower*. The *Speedwell*, a smaller boat that brought Bradford and the other members of the Separatist community from the Netherlands to England, proved to be unseaworthy. During the delay, some decided not to go to North America; 102 people eventually sailed on the *Mayflower*.
9. **lustie:** Healthy and strong.
10. **let:** Hesitate.
11. **shroudly:** Early form of *shrewdly*, meaning wickedly.

that the shipe could not be able to performe the voyage. So some of the cheefe of the company, perceiveing the mariners to feare the suffisiencie of the shipe, as appeared by their mutterings, they entred into serious consulltation with the master & other officers of the ship, to consider in time of the danger; and rather to returne than to cast them selves into a desperate & inevitable perill. And truly there was great distraction & differance of opinion amongst the mariners them selves; faine[12] would they doe what could be done for their wages sake, (being now halfe the seas over,) and on the other hand they were loath to hazard their lives too desperatly. But in examening of all opinions, the master & others affirmed they knew the ship to be stronge & firme under water; and for the buckling of the maine beame, there was a great iron scrue the passengers brought out of Holland, which would raise the beame into his place; the which being done, the carpenter & master affirmed that with a post put under it, set firme in the lower deck, & otherways bounde, he would make it sufficiente. And as for the decks & uper workes they would calke them as well as they could, and though with the workeing of the ship they would not longe keepe stanch,[13] yet there would otherwise be no great danger, if they did not overpress her with sails. So they commited them selves to the will of God, & resolved to proseede. In sundrie of these stormes the winds were so feirce, & the seas so high, as they could not beare a knote of saile, but were forced to hull,[14] for diverce days togither. And in one of them, as they thus lay at hull, in a mighty storme, a lustie yonge man (called John Howland) coming upon some occasion above the grattings, was, with a seele[15] of the shipe throwne into [the] sea; but it pleased God that he caught hould of the top-saile halliards, which hunge over board, & rane out at length; yet he held his hould (though he was sundrie fadomes under water) till he was hald up by the same rope to the brime of the water, and then with a boat hooke & other means got into the shipe againe, & his life saved; and though he was something ill with it, yet he lived many years after, and became a profitable member both in church & comõne wealthe. In all this voyage there died but one of the passengers, which was William Butten, a youth, servant to Samuell Fuller, when they drew near the coast. But to omite other things, (that I may be breefe,) after longe beating at sea they fell with that land which is called Cape Cod; the which being made & certainly knowne to be it, they were not a litle joyfull. After some deliberation had amongst them selves & with the master of the ship, they tacked aboute and resolved to stande for the southward (the wind & weather being faire) to finde some place aboute Hudsons river for their habitation. But after they had sailed that course aboute halfe the day, they fell amongst deangerous shoals and roring breakers, and they were so farr intangled there with as they conceived them selves in great danger; & the wind shrinking upon them withall, they resolved to bear up againe for the Cape, and thought them selves hapy to gett out of those dangers before night overtooke them, as by Gods providence they did. And the next day they gott into the Cape-harbor where

---

12. **faine:** Early spelling of *fain*, meaning obliged or compelled.
13. **stanch:** Watertight.
14. **hull:** Drift with the direction of the wind using short sails.
15. **seele:** Roll or pitch.

they ridd in saftie.[16] A word or too by the way of this cape; it was thus first named by Capten Gosnole & his company,[17] Anno:[18] 1602, and after by Capten Smith was called Cape James; but it retains the former name amongst seamen. Also that pointe which first shewed those dangerous shoals unto them, they called Pointe Care, & Tuckers Terrour; but the French & Dutch to this day call it Malabarr, by reason of those peril-ous shoals, and the losses they have suffered there.[19]

Being thus arived in a good harbor and brought safe to land, they fell upon their knees & blessed the God of heaven, who had brought them over the vast & furious ocean, and delivered them from all the periles & miseries therof, againe to set their feete on the firme and stable earth, their proper elemente. And no marvell if they were thus joyfull, seeing wise Seneca was so affected with sailing a few miles on the coast of his owne Italy; as he affirmed, that he had rather remaine twentie years on his way by land, than pass by sea to any place in a short time; so tedious & dreadfull was the same unto him.[20]

But here I cannot but stay and make a pause, and stand half amased at this poore peoples presente condition; and so I thinke will the reader too, when he well considers the same. Being thus passed the vast ocean, and a sea of troubles before in their prepa-ration (as may be remembred by that which wente before), they had now no freinds to wellcome them, nor inns to entertaine or refresh their weatherbeaten bodys, no houses or much less townes to repaire too, to seeke for succoure. It is recorded in scripture as a mercie to the apostle & his shipwraked company, that the barbarians shewed them no smale kindnes[21] in refreshing them, but these savage barbarians, when they mette with them (as after will appeare) were readier to fill their sids full of arrows than otherwise. And for the season it was winter, and they that know the winters of that cuntrie know them to be sharp & violent, & subjecte to cruell & feirce stormes, deangerous to travill to known places, much more to serch an unknown coast. Besides, what could they see but a hidious & desolate wildernes, full of wild beasts & wild men? and what multituds there might be of them they knew not. Nether could they, as it were, goe up to the top of Pisgah,[22] to vew from this wildernes a more goodly cuntrie to feed their hopes; for which way soever they turnd their eyes (save upward to the heavens) they could have litle sol-ace or content in respecte of any outward objects. For summer being done, all things

---

16. **And the next day . . . saftie:** According to the Julian, or Old Style, calendar, they anchored in what is now Provincetown Harbor on November 11, 1620. In the Gregorian, or New Style, calendar — which was not adopted in England until 1752 — the date was November 21, 1620.
17. **named by Capten Gosnole & his company:** Because they took much of that fish there. [Bradford's note]
18. **Anno:** In the year of (Latin).
19. **Malabarr . . . suffered there:** The Malabar Coast of southwest India was then well known for intense mon-soon storms and perilous sandbars, as well as for conflicts among competing Europeans for access to the fer-tile rice lands.
20. **wise Seneca . . . unto him:** Epistle 53. [Bradford's note] Bradford is loosely quoting from the *Moral Epistles to Lucilius*, a central ethical work of the ancient world, by the Roman philosopher Seneca (4? BCE–65 CE).
21. **kindnes:** Acts 28. [Bradford's note] Bradford contrasts the experiences of the Pilgrims with those of the apostle Paul and his men, who were shipwrecked on the island of Malta: "And the barbarous people showed us no little kindness: for they kindled a fire, and received us every one, because of the present rain, and because of the cold" (Acts 28:2).
22. **Pisgah:** The mountain from which God showed Moses the promised land (Deuteronomy 34:1–4).

stand upon them with a wetherbeaten face; and the whole countrie, full of woods & thickets, represented a wild & savage heiw. If they looked behind them, there was the mighty ocean which they had passed, and was now as a maine barr & goulfe to seperate them from all the civill parts of the world. If it be said they had a ship to sucour them, it is trew; but what heard they daly from the master & company? but that with speede they should looke out a place with their shallop,[23] where they would be at some near distance; for the season was shuch as he would not stirr from thence till a safe harbor was discovered by them where they would be, and he might goe without danger; and that victells[24] consumed apace, but he must & would keepe sufficient for them selves & their returne. Yea, it was muttered by some, that if they gott not a place in time, they would turne them & their goods ashore & leave them. Let it also be considred what weake hopes of supply & succoure they left behinde them, that might bear up their minds in this sad condition and trialls they were under; and they could not but be very smale. It is true, indeed, the affections & love of their brethren at Leyden was cordiall & entire towards them, but they had litle power to help them, or them selves; and how the case stode betweene them & the marchants at their coming away, hath allready been declared. What could now sustaine them but the spirite of God & his grace? May not & ought not the children of these fathers rightly say: *Our faithers were Englishmen which came over this great ocean, and were ready to perish in this willderness; but they cried unto the Lord, and he heard their voyce, and looked on their adversitie, &c.*[25] *Let them therfore praise the Lord, because he is good, & his mercies endure for ever. Yea, let them which have been redeemed of the Lord, shew how he hath delivered them from the hand of the oppressour. When they wandered in the deserte willdernes out of the way, and found no citie to dwell in, both hungrie, & thirstie, their sowle was overwhelmed in them. Let them confess before the Lord his loving kindnes, and his wonderfull works before the sons of men.*[26]

CHAPTER 10

SHOWING HOW THEY SOUGHT OUT A PLACE OF HABITATION, AND
WHAT BEFELL THEM THERABOUTE

Being thus arrived at Cap-Cod the 11. of November, and necessitie calling them to looke out a place for habitation, (as well as the masters & mariners importunitie,) they having brought a large shalop with them out of England, stowed in quarters in the ship, they now gott her out & sett their carpenters to worke to trime her up; but being much bruised & shatered in the shipe with foule weather, they saw she would be longe in mending. Wherupon a few of them tendered them selves to goe by land and discovere those nearest places, whilst the shallop was in mending; and the rather because as they wente into that

---

23. **shallop:** Light sailboat used primarily for coastal fishing.
24. **victells:** Food (victuals).
25. ***Our faithers . . . adversitie, &c.:*** Deuteronomy 26:5, 7. [Bradford's note] Bradford refers to the plight of the Israelites before Moses led them to the promised land: "And the Egyptians evil entreated us, and afflicted us, and laid upon us hard bondage: And when we cried unto the LORD God of our fathers, the LORD heard our voice, and looked on our affliction, and our labor, and our oppression: And the LORD brought us forth out of Egypt with a mighty hand, and with an outstretched arm, and with great terribleness, and with signs, and with wonders" (Deuteronomy 26:6-8).
26. ***Yea, let them . . . sons of men:*** Psalms 107:1-5, 8. [Bradford's note]

harbor there seemed to be an opening some 2. or 3 leagues of, which the master judged to be a river. It was conceived there might be some danger in the attempte, yet seeing them resolute, they were permited to goe, being 16. of them well armed, under the conduct of Captain Standish,[27] having such instructions given them as was thought meete. They sett forth the 15. of November: and when they had marched aboute the space of a mile by the sea side, they espied 5. or 6. persons with a dogg coming towards them, who were salvages; but they fled from them, & ran up into the woods, and the English followed them, partly to see if they could speake with them, and partly to discover if there might not be more of them lying in ambush. But the Indeans seeing them selves thus followed, they againe forsooke the woods, & ran away on the sands as hard as they could, so as they could not come near them, but followed them by the tracte of their feet sundrie miles, and saw that they had come the same way. So, night coming on, they made their randevous & set out their sentinels, and rested in quiete *that night*, and the next morning followed their tracte till they had headed a great creake, & so left the sands, & turned an other way into the woods. But they still followed them by guess, hopeing to find their dwellings; but they soone lost both them & them selves, falling into shuch thickets as were ready to tear their cloaths & armore in peeces, but were most distresed for wante of drinke. But at length they found water & refreshed them selves, being the first New-England water they drunke of, and was now in their great thirste as pleasante unto them as wine or beer had been in for-times. Afterwards they directed their course to come to the other shore, for they knew it was a necke of land they were to crosse over, and so at length gott to the sea-side, and marched to this supposed river, & by the way found a pond[28] of clear fresh water, and shortly after a good quantitie of clear ground where the Indeans had formerly set corne, and some of their graves. And proceeding furder they saw new-stubble where corne had been set the same year, also they found where lately a house had been, where some planks and a great ketle was remaining, and heaps of sand newly padled with their hands, which they, digging up, found in them diverce faire Indean baskets filled with corne, and some in eares, faire and good, of diverce collours, which seemed to them a very goodly sight, (haveing never seen any such before). This was near the place of that supposed river they came to seeck; unto which they wente and found it to open it selfe into 2. armes with a high cliffe of sand in the enterance,[29] but more like to be creeks of salte water than any fresh, for ought they saw; and that there was good harborige for their shalope; leaving it further to be discovered by their shalop when she was ready. So their time limeted them being expired, they returned to the ship, lest they should be in fear of their saftie; and tooke with them parte of the corne, and buried up the rest, and so like the men from Eshcoll carried with them of the fruits of the land, & showed their breethren;[30] of which, & their returne, they were marvelusly glad, and their harts incouraged.

---

27. **Captain Standish:** Miles Standish (1584?-1656), an English soldier who had fought in the Netherlands, was engaged to handle military affairs for the colonists.

28. **pond:** The spring-fed pond is in present-day Truro, Massachusetts.

29. **enterance:** The Pamet River is a narrow saltwater river or creek that runs across Cape Cod, nearly dividing the peninsula.

30. **men from Eshcoll . . . breethren:** In the Old Testament account, Moses sent a group of men to investigate the promised land, where they found grapes, pomegranates, and figs near a brook, called Eshcol (Numbers 13:23-7).

After this, the shalop being got ready, they set out again for the better discovery of this place, & the master of the ship desired to goe him selfe, so there went some 30. men, but found it to be no harbor for ships but only for boats; there was allso found 2. of their houses covered with matts, & sundrie of their implements in them, but the people were rune away & could not be seen; also there was found more of their corne, & of their beans of various collours. The corne & beans they brought away, purposing to give them full satisfaction when they should meete with any of them (as about some 6. months afterward they did, to their good contente). And here is to be noted a spetiall providence of God, and a great mercie to this poore people, that here they gott seed to plant them corne the next year, or else they might have starved, for they had none, nor any likelyhood to get any till the season had beene past (as the sequell did manyfest). Neither is it likely they had had this, if the first voyage had not been made, for the ground was now all covered with snow, & hard frozen. But the Lord is never wanting unto his in their greatest needs; let his holy name have all the praise.

The month of November being spente in these affairs, & much foule weather falling in, the 6. *of December.* they sente out their shallop againe with 10. of their principall men, & some sea men, upon further discovery, intending to circulate that deepe bay of Cap-codd. The weather was very cold, & it frose so hard as the sprea of the sea lighting on their coats, they were as if they had been glased; yet *that night* betimes they gott downe into the botome of the bay, and as they drue nere the shore they saw some 10. or 12. Indeans very busie aboute some thing. They landed aboute a league or 2. from them, and had much a doe to put a shore any where, it lay so full of flats.[31] Being landed, it grew late, and they made them selves a barricade with loggs & bowes as well as they could in the time, & set out their sentenill & betooke them to rest, and saw the smoake of the fire the savages made that night. When *morning* was come they devided their company, some to coaste along the shore in the boate, and the rest marched throw the woods to see the land, if any fit place might be for their dwelling. They came allso to the place where they saw the Indans the night before, & found they had been cuting up a great fish like a grampus,[32] being some 2. inches thike of fate like a hogg, some peeces where of they had left by the way; and the shallop found 2. more of these fishes dead on the sands, a thing usuall after storms in that place, by reason of the great flats of sand that lye off. So they ranged up and doune all that day, but found no people, nor any place they liked. When the sune grue low, they hasted out of the woods to meete with their shallop, to whom they made signes to come to them into a *creek*[33] hardby, the which they did at highwater; of which they were very glad, for they had not seen each other all that day, since the morning. So they made them a barricado (as usually they did every night) with loggs, stakes, & thike pine bowes, the height of a man, leaving it open to leeward, partly to shelter them from the could & wind (making their fire in the midle, & lying round aboute it), and partly to defend them from any sudden assaults of the savages, if they should surround them. So being very weary, they betooke them to rest. But aboute *midnight*, they

---

31. **flats:** Expanse of low, level ground; they landed on a beach near present-day Eastham, Massachusetts.
32. **grampus:** A large fish the size of a dolphin (*Grampus griseus*).
33. **creek:** The Herring River in present-day Eastham, Massachusetts.

heard a hideous & great crie, and their sentinell called, "Arme, arme"; so they bestired them & stood to their armes, & shote of a cupple of moskets, and then the noys seased. They concluded it was a companie of wolves, or such like willd beasts; for one of the sea men tould them he had often heard shuch a noyse in New-found land. So they rested till about 5. of the clock in the *morning*; for the tide, & their purpose to goe from thence, made them be stiring betimes. So after praier they prepared for breakfast, and it being day dawning, it was thought best to be carring things downe to the boate. But some said it was not best to carrie the armes downe, others said they would be the readier, for they had lapped them up in their coats from the dew. But some 3. or 4. would not cary theirs till they wente them selves, yet as it fell out, the water being not high enough, they layed them downe on the banke side, & came up to breakfast. But presently, all on the sudain, they heard a great & strange crie, which they knew to be the same voyces they heard in the night, though they varied their notes, & one of their company being abroad came runing in, & cried, "Men, Indeans, Indeans"; and withall, their arowes came flying amongst them. Their men ran with all speed to recover their armes, as by the good providence of God they did. In the mean time, of those that were there ready, two muskets were discharged at them, & 2. more stood ready in the enterance of there randevoue, but were comanded not to shoote till they could take full aime at them; & the other 2. charged againe with all speed, for there were only 4. had armes there, & defended the baricado which was first assalted. The crie of the Indeans was dreadfull, espetially when they saw their men run out of the randevoue towourds the shallop, to recover their armes, the Indeans wheeling aboute upon them. But some running out with coats of malle[34] on, & cutlasses in their hands, they soone got their armes, & let flye amongs them, and quickly stopped their violence. Yet there was a lustie man, and no less valiante, stood behind a tree within halfe a musket shot, and let his arrows flie at them. He was seen shoot 3. arrowes, which were all avoyded. He stood 3. shot of a musket, till one taking full aime at him, and made the barke or splinters of the tree fly about his ears, after which he gave an extraordinary shriek, and away they wente all of them. They left some to keep the shalop, and followed them aboute a quarter of a mille, and shouted once or twise, and shot of 2. or 3. peces, & so returned. This they did, that they might conceive that they were not affrade of them or any way discouraged. Thus it pleased God to vanquish their enimies, and give them deliverance; and by his spetiall providence so to dispose that not any one of them were either hurte, or hitt, though their arrows came close by them, & on every side them, and sundry of their coats, which hunge up in the barricado, were shot throw & throw. Aterwards they gave God sollamne thanks & praise for their deliverance, & gathered up a bundle of their arrows, & sente them into England afterward by the master of the ship, and called that place the first encounter. From hence they departed, & costed all along, but discerned no place likely for harbor; & therfore hasted to a place that their pilot, (one Mr. Coppin who had bine in the cuntrie before) did assure them was a good harbor, which he had been in, and they

---

34. **coats of malle:** Coats of mail, flexible armor made of metal rings or plates.

might fetch it before night; of which they were glad, for it begane to be foule weather. After some houres sailing, it begane to snow & raine, & about the midle of the afternoone, the wind increased, & the sea became very rough, and they broake their rudder, & it was as much as 2. men could doe to steere her with a cupple of oares. But their pilot bade them be of good cheere, for he saw the harbor; but the storme increasing, & night drawing on, they bore what saile they could to gett in, while they could see. But here with they broake their mast in 3. peeces, & their saill fell over bord, in a very grown sea, so as they had likely to have been cast away; yet by Gods mercie they recovered them selves, & having the floud[35] with them, struck into the harbore. But when it came too, the pilot was deceived in the place, and said, the Lord be mercifull unto them, for his eyes never saw that place before; & he & the master mate would have run her ashore, in a cove full of breakers, before the winde. But a lusty seaman which steered, bade those which rowed, if they were men, about with her, or else they were all cast away; the which they did with speed. So he bid them be of good cheere & row lustly, for there was a faire sound before them, & he doubted not but they should find one place or other where they might ride in saftie. And though it was *very darke*, and rained sore, yet in the end they gott under the lee[36] of a smalle iland, and remained there all that night in saftie. But they knew not this to be an iland till morning, but were devided in their minds; some would keepe the boate for fear they might be amongst the Indians; others were so weake and cold, they could not endure, but got a shore, & with much adoe got fire, (all things being so wett,) and the rest were glad to come to them; for after midnight the wind shifted to the north-west, & it frose hard. But though this had been a day & night of much trouble & danger unto them, yet God gave them a *morning* of comforte & refreshing (as usually he doth to his children), for the next day was a faire sunshinig day, and they found them sellvs to be on an iland secure from the Indeans, where they might drie their stufe, fixe their peeces,[37] & rest them selves, and gave God thanks for his mercies, in their manifould deliverances. And this being the *last day of the weeke*, they prepared there to keepe the *Sabath*. On *Munday* they sounded the harbor, and founde it fitt for shipping; and marched into the land, & found diverse cornfeilds, & litle runing brooks, a place (as they supposed) fitt for situation;[38] at least it was the best they could find, and the season, & their presente necessitie, made them glad to accepte of it. So they returned to their shipp againe with this news to the rest of their people, which did much comforte their harts.

On the 15. of *December*: they wayed anchor to goe to the place they had discovered, & came within 2. leagues of it, but were faine to bear up againe; but the 16. *day* the winde came faire, and they arrived safe in this harbor. And after wards tooke better view of the place, and resolved where to pitch their dwelling; and the 25. *day* begane to erecte the first house for common use to receive them and their goods.

---

35. **floud:** Short for flood tide, a powerful, incoming tide.
36. **lee:** Sheltered side, away from the wind.
37. **peeces:** Firearms.
38. **a place . . . fitt for situation:** Near Plymouth, Massachusetts, where the Pilgrims landed on November 11/21, 1620. See note 21.

From Booke 2

The rest of this History (if God give me life, & opportunitie) I shall, for brevitis sake, handle by way of *annalls*, noteing only the heads of principall things, and passages as they fell in order of time, and may seeme to be profitable to know, or to make use of. And this may be as the 2. Booke.

THE REMAINDER OF ANNO: 1620

I shall a litle returne backe and begine with a combination[39] made by them before they came ashore, being the first foundation of their govermente in this place; occasioned partly by the discontented & mutinous speeches that some of the strangers[40] amongst them had let fall from them in the ship—That when they came a shore they would use their owne libertie; for none had power to comand them, the patente they had being for Virginia, and not for New-england, which belonged to an other Goverment, with which the Virginia Company had nothing to doe. And partly that such an acte by them done (this their condition considered) might be as firme as any patent, and in some respects more sure.

The forme was as followeth.[41]

In the name of God, Amen. We whose names are underwriten, the loyall subjects of our dread soveraigne Lord, King James, by the grace of God, of Great Britaine, France, & Ireland king, defender of the faith, &c., haveing undertaken, for the glorie of God, and advance-mente of the Christian faith, and honour of our king & countrie, a voyage to plant the first colonie in the Northerne parts of Virginia, doe by these presents solemnly & mutualy in the presence of God, and one of another, covenant & combine our selves togeather into a civill body politick, for our better ordering & preservation & furtherance of the ends aforesaid; and by vertue hearof to enacte, constitute, and frame such just & equall lawes, ordinances, acts, constitutions, & offices, from time to time, as shall be thought most meete & conve-nient for the generall good of the Colonie, unto which we promise all due submission and obedience. In witnes wherof we have hereunder subscribed our names at Cap-Codd the 11. of November, in the year of the raigne of our soveraigne lord, King James, of England, France, & Ireland the eighteenth, and of Scotland the fiftie fourth. Anno Domini[42] 1620.

After this they chose, or rather confirmed, Mr. John Carver[43] (a man godly & well approved amongst them) their Governour for that year. And after they had provided a place for their goods, or comone store, (which were long in unlading for want of boats, foulnes of winter weather, and sicknes of diverce,) and begune some small cottages for

---

39. **combination:** An agreement for union or joining together.
40. **strangers:** Those who did not follow the religious beliefs of the Pilgrims.
41. **The forme was as followeth:** The original document of the Mayflower Compact is lost. Bradford clearly used the first printing of the compact (which was published in 1622), copying it into his manuscript with a few minor alterations.
42. **Anno Domini:** Full form of AD, literally "in the year of the Lord" (Latin), which in this textbook is expressed as CE, for "contemporary era."
43. **Carver:** John Carver (1575?-1621). Along with Bradford and William Brewster (1567-1644), Carver pro-posed the immigration to America. He served as governor of the colony until his death, five months after the landing at Plymouth.

their habitation, as time would admitte, they mette and consulted of lawes & orders, both for their civill & military Govermente, as the necessitie of their condition did require, still adding therunto as urgent occasion in severall times, and as cases did require.

In these hard & difficulte beginings they found some discontents & murmurings arise amongst some, and mutinous speeches & carriages in other; but they were soone quelled & overcome by the wisdome, patience, and just & equall carrage of things by the Governour and better part, which clave[44] faithfully togeather in the maine. But that which was most sadd & lamentable was, that in 2. or 3. moneths time halfe of their company dyed, espetialy in Jan: & February, being the depth of winter, and wanting houses & other comforts; being infected with the scurvie & other diseases, which this long voyage & their inacomodate condition had brought upon them; so as there dyed some times 2. or 3. of a day, in the foresaid time; that of 100. & odd persons, scarce 50. remained. And of these in the time of most distres, there was but 6. or 7. sound persons, who, to their great comendations be it spoken, spared no pains, night nor day, but with abundance of toyle and hazard of their owne health, fetched them woode, made them fires, drest them meat, made their beds, washed their lothsome cloaths, cloathed & uncloathed them; in a word, did all the homly & necessarie offices for them which dainty & quesie stomacks cannot endure to hear named; and all this willingly & cheerfully, without any grudging in the least, shewing herein their true love unto their freinds & bretheren. A rare example & worthy to be remembred. Two of these 7. were Mr. William Brewster, their reverend Elder, & Myles Standish, their Captein & military comander, unto whom my selfe, & many others, were much beholden in our low & sicke condition. And yet the Lord so upheld these persons, as in this generall calamity they were not at all infected either with sicknes, or lameness. And what I have said of these, I may say of many others who dyed in this generall vissitation, & others yet living, that whilst they had health, yea, or any strength continuing, they were not wanting to any that had need of them. And I doubt not but their recompence is with the Lord.

But I may not here pass by an other remarkable passage not to be forgotten. As this calamitie fell among the passengers that were to be left here to plant, and were hasted a shore and made to drinke water, that the sea-men might have the more beer, and one[45] in his sicknes desiring but a small cann of beer, it was answered, that if he were their owne father he should have none, the disease begane to fall amongst them also, so as allmost halfe of their company dyed before they went away, and many of their officers and lustyest men, as the boatson,[46] gunner, 3. quarter-maisters,[47] the cooke, & others. At which the master was something strucken and sent to the sick a shore and tould the Governour he should send for beer for them that had need of it, though he drunke water homward bound. But now amongst his company there was farr another kind of carriage in this miserie than amongst the passengers; for they that before had been boone companions in drinking & joyllity in the time of their health & wellfare, begane now to

---

44. **clave:** Past tense of *cleave*, to become strongly attached to others.
45. **one:** Which was this author him selfe. [Bradford's note]
46. **boatson:** Ship's officer (a boatswain) in charge of equipment and the crew.
47. **quarter-maisters:** Ship's officers (quartermasters) responsible for providing quarters, rations, and other supplies.

deserte one another in this calamitie, saing they would not hasard there lives for them, they should be infected by coming to help them in their cabins, and so, after they came to dye by it, would doe litle or nothing for them, but if they dyed let them dye. But such of the passengers as were yet abord shewed them what mercy they could, which made some of their harts relente, as the boatson (& some others), who was a prowd yonge man, and would often curse & scofe at the passengers; but when he grew weak, they had compassion on him and helped him; then he confessed he did not deserve it at their hands, he had abused them in word & deed. O! saith he, you, I now see, shew your love like Christians indeed one to another, but we let one another lye & dye like doggs. Another lay cursing his wife, saing if it had not ben for her he had never come this unlucky voyage, and anone cursing his felows, saing he had done this & that, for some of them, he had spente so much, & so much, amongst them, and they were now weary of him, and did not help him, having need. Another gave his companion all he had, if he died, to help him in his weaknes; he went and got a litle spise & made him a mess of meat once or twise, and because he dyed not so soone as he expected, he went amongst his fellows, & swore the rogue would cousen[48] him, he would see him choaked before he made him any more meate; and yet the pore fellow dyed before morning.

All this while the Indians came skulking about them, and would sometimes show them selves aloofe of, but when any aproached near them, they would run away. And once they stoale away their tools where they had been at worke, & were gone to dinner. But about the 16. *of March* a certaine Indian came bouldly amongst them, and spoke to them in broken English, which they could well understand, but marvelled at it. At length they understood by discourse with him, that he was not of these parts, but belonged to the eastrene parts, where some English-ships came to fhish, with whom he was aquainted, & could name sundrie of them by their names, amongst whom he had gott his language. He became proftable to them in aquainting them with many things concerning the state of the country in the east-parts where he lived, which was afterwards profitable unto them; as also of the people here, of their names, number, & strength; of their situation & distance from this place, and who was cheefe amongst them. His name was *Samaset*;[49] he tould them also of another Indian whose name was *Squanto*,[50] a native of this place, who had been in England & could speake better English than him selfe. Being, after some time of entertainmente & gifts, dismist, a while after he came againe, & 5. more with him, & they brought againe all the tooles that were stolen away before, and made way for the coming of their great Sachem, called *Massasoyt*;[51] who, about 4. or 5. *days after*, came with the cheefe of his freinds & other attendance, with the aforesaid

---

48. cousen: An alternative spelling for *cozen*, meaning to cheat or defraud.
49. **Samaset**: A member of the Abenaki tribe of southeastern Maine, Samaset or Samoset (d. 1653?) had learned English from fishermen. He was the first Indian to make contact with the Pilgrims.
50. **Squanto**: A Patuxet who traveled to England with Captain John Smith (1580–1631), Squanto was later kidnapped and nearly sold as a slave. During his years away, his entire tribe died of disease; the Pilgrims settled on land the tribe had once occupied.
51. **Massasoyt**: A chief of the Wampanoag tribe, Massasoyt or Massasoit (1590?–1661) signed a peace treaty with the Pilgrims on March 22, 1621. The treaty was kept until the 1660s, when tensions between the colonists and the Indians erupted into a series of conflicts that culminated in King Philip's War (1675–76).

Squanto. With whom, after frendly entertainment, & some gifts given him, they made a peace with him (which hath now continued this 24. years) in these terms.

1. That neither he nor any of his, should injurie or doe hurte to any of their people.

2. That if any of his did any hurte to any of theirs, he should send the offender, that they might punish him.

3. That if any thing were taken away from any of theirs, he should cause it to be restored; and they should doe the like to his.

4. If any did unjustly warr against him, they would aide him; if any did warr against them, he should aide them.

5. He should send to his neighbours confederats, to certifie them of this, that they might not wrong them, but might be likewise comprised in the conditions of peace.

6. That when their men came to them, they should leave their bows & arrows behind them.

After these things he returned to his place called *Sowams,* some 40. mile from this place, but *Squanto* continued with them, and was their interpreter, and was a spetiall instrument sent of God for their good beyond their expectation. He directed them how to set their corne, where to take fish, and to procure other comodities, and was also their pilott to bring them to unknowne places for their profitt, and never left them till he dyed. He was a *native of this place,* & scarce any left alive besids him selfe. He was caried away with diverce others by one *Hunt,* a master of a ship, who thought to sell them for slaves in Spaine; but he got away for England, and was entertained by a marchante in London, & imployed to New-foundland & other parts, & lastly brought hither into these parts by one Mr. *Dermer,* a gentle-man imployed by Sr. Ferdinando Gorges & others, for discovery, & other designes in these parts. Of whom I shall say some thing, because it is mentioned in a booke set forth Anno: 1622. by the Presidente & Counsell for New-England,[52] that he made the peace betweene the salvages of these parts & the English; of which this plantation, as it is intimated, had the benefite. But what a peace it was, may apeare by what befell him & his men.

This Mr. Dermer was here the same year that these people came, as apears by a relation written by him, & given me by a freind, bearing date June 30. Anno: 1620. And they came in November: following, so there was but 4. months differance. In which relation to his honored freind, he hath these passages of this very place.

> I will first begine (saith he) with that place from whence *Squanto* or *Tisquantem,* was taken away; which in Captain *Smiths mape*[53] is called *Plimoth:* and I would that Plimoth had the like comodities. I would that the first plantation might here be seated, if there come to the number of 50. persons, or upward. Otherwise at Charlton,[54] because there the savages are less to be feared. The *Pocanawkits,*[55] which live to the *west* of *Plimoth,* bear an inveterate

---

52. **in a booke . . . New-England:** Page 17. [Bradford's note] Bradford refers to *A Briefe Relation of the Discovery and Plantation of New England* (1622), published by Sir Fernando Gorges (1566?–1647?), an English promoter of exploration and colonization.

53. **Captain *Smiths mape*:** Smith included a map in his *A Description of New England* (1616).

54. **Charlton:** The name on Smith's map of a place near the mouth of the Charles River, in present-day Boston.

55. ***Pocanawkits*:** Another name for the Wampanoag.

malice to the English, and are of more streingth than all the savages from thence to Penobscote. Their desire of revenge was occasioned by an English man, who having many of them on bord, made a great slaughter with their murderers[56] & smale shot, when as (they say) they offered no injurie on their parts. Whether they were English or no, it may be douted; yet they beleeve they were, for the Frenche have so possest them; for which cause *Squanto* cannot deney but they would have kiled me when I was at *Namasket*, had he not entreated hard for me. The soyle of the borders of this great bay, may be compared to most of the plantations which I have seene in Virginia. The land is of diverce sorts; for *Patuxite* is a hardy but strong soyle, *Nawsel* & *Saughtughtett* are for the most part a blakish & deep mould, much like that where groweth the best Tobaco in Virginia. In the botume of that great bay is store of Codd & basse, or mulett, etc.

But above all he comends *Pacanawkite* for the richest soyle, and much open ground fitt for English graine, &c.

Massachussets is about 9. leagues[57] from *Plimoth*, & situate in the midst betweene both, is full of ilands & peninsules very fertill for the most parte.

With sundrie shuch relations which I forbear to transcribe, being now better knowne than they were to him.

He was taken prisoner by the Indeans at *Manamoiak* (a place not farr from hence, now well knowne). He gave them what they demanded for his liberty, but when they had gott what they desired, they kept him still & indevored to kill his men; but he was freed by seasing on some of them, and kept them bound till they gave him a canoe's load of corne. Of which, see Purch: lib. 9. fol. 1778.[58] But this was Anno: 1619.

After the writing of the former relation he came to the Isle of *Capawack*[59] (which lyes south of this place in the way to Virginia), and the foresaid *Squanto* with him, where he going a shore amongst the Indans to trade, as he used to doe, was betrayed & assaulted by them, & *all his men slaine, but one that kept the boat*; but him selfe gott abord very sore wounded, & they had cut off his head upon the cudy[60] of his boat, had not the man reskued him with a sword. And so they got away, & made shift to gett into Virginia, where he dyed; whether of his wounds or the diseases of the cuntrie, or both togeather, is uncertaine. By all which it may appeare how farr these people were from peace, and with what danger this plantation was begune, save as the powerfull hand of the Lord did protect them. These things were partly the reason why they kept aloofe & were so long before they came to the English. An other reason (as after them selvs made known) was how aboute 3. *years before*, a French-ship was cast away at *Cap-Codd*, but the men gott ashore, & saved their lives, and much of their victails, & other goods; but after the Indeans heard of it, they geathered togeather from these parts, and never left watching & dogging

---

56. **murderers:** Ship's guns.
57. **leagues:** A league, an early measure of distance, was about three miles.
58. **see Purch . . . 1778:** Samuel Purchas (1577?–1626), an English clergyman, was the author of a four-volume compilation of travel literature, *Hakluytus Posthumus, or Purchas His Pilgrims* (1625). Using Latin abbreviations, Bradford refers to volume four, chapter nine, page 1778.
59. **Isle of *Capawack*:** Now called Martha's Vineyard.
60. **cudy:** Now spelled *cuddy*, a small room or compartment on a boat.

them till they got advantage, and *kild them all but* 3. *or* 4. which they kept, & sent from one Sachem to another, to make sporte with, and used them worse than slaves; (of which the foresaid Mr. Dermer redeemed 2. of them;) and they conceived this ship was now come to revenge it.

Also, (as after was made knowne,) before they came to the English to make freind-ship, they gott all the *Powachs*[61] of the cuntrie, for 3. days togeather, in a horid and divel-lish maner to curse & execrate them with their cunjurations, which asembly & service they held in a darke & dismale swampe.

But to returne. The spring now approaching, it pleased God the mortalitie begane to cease amongst them, and the sick and lame recovered apace, which put as it were new life into them; though they had borne their sadd affliction with much patience & con-tentednes, as I thinke any people could doe. But it was the Lord which upheld them, and had beforehand prepared them; many having long borne the yoake, yea from their youth.[62] Many other smaler maters I omite, sundrie of them having been allready pub-lished in a Jurnall made by one of the company; and some other passages of jurneys and relations allredy published, to which I referr those that are willing to know them more perticulerly. And being now come to the 25. of March I shall begine the year 1621.

From *ANNO: 1621*

They begane now to gather in the small harvest they had, and to fitte up their houses and dwellings against winter, being all well recovered in health & strenght, and had all things in good plenty; for as some were thus imployed in affairs abroad, others were excersised in fishing, aboute codd, & bass, & other fish, of which they tooke good store, of which every family had their portion. All the summer there was no wante. And now begane to come in store of fowle, as winter aproached, of which this place did abound when they came first (but afterward decreased by degrees). And besids water fowle, there was great store of wild Turkies, of which they tooke many, besids venison, &c. Besids they had aboute a peck a meale a weeke to a person, or now since harvest, Indean corne to that proportion. Which made many afterwards write so largly of their plenty here to their freinds in England, which were not fained, but true reports.[63]

---

61. **Powachs**: Medicine men.
62. **borne the yoake . . . youth**: See note 10.
63. **true reports**: In a letter to a friend in England dated December 11, 1621, and later printed in *Mourt's Relation*, Edward Winslow offered a more expansive account of the events of the autumn of 1621, later to be celebrated as the "First Thanksgiving":

> Our harvest being gotten in, our governour sent foure men on fowling, that so we might after a spe-ciall manner rejoyce together, after we had gathered the fruits of our labours; they foure in one day killed as much fowle, as with a little helpe beside, served the Company almost a weeke, at which time amongst other Recreations, we exercised our Armes, many of the Indians coming amongst us, and amongst the rest their greatest king Massasoyt, with some ninetie men, whom for three dayes we entertained and feasted, and they went out and killed five Deere, which they brought to the Plantation and bestowed on our Governour, and upon the Captaine and others. And although it be not always so plentifull, as it was at this time with us, yet by the goodness of God, we are so farre from want, that we often wish you partakers of our plentie.

From *ANNO DOMINI: 1632*

Also the people of the plantation begane to grow in their owtward estats, by reason of the flowing of many people into the cuntrie, espetially into the Bay of the Massachusets; by which means corne & cattle rose to a great prise, by which many were much inriched, and commodities grue plentifull; and yet in other regards this benefite turned to their hurte, and this accession of strength to their weaknes. For now as their stocks increased, and the increse vendible,[64] there was no longer any holding them togeather, but now they must of necessitie goe to their great lots; they could not other wise keep their cattle; and having oxen growne, they must have land for plowing & tillage. And no man now thought he could live, except he had catle and a great deale of ground to keep them; all striving to increase their stocks. By which means they were scatered all over the bay, quickly, and the towne, in which they lived compactly till now, was left very thin, and in a short time allmost desolate. And if this had been all, it had been less, though too much; but the church must also be devided, and those that had lived so long togeather in Christian & comfortable fellowship must now part and suffer many divissions. First, those that lived on their lots on the other side of the bay (called Duxberie) they could not long bring their wives & children to the publick worship & church meetings here, but with such burthen, as, growing to some competente number, they sued to be dismissed and become a body of them selves; and so they were dismiste (about this time), though very unwillingly. But to touch this sadd matter, and handle things together that fell out afterward. To prevent any further scatering from this place, and weakning of the same, it was thought best to give out some good farms to spetiall persons, that would promise to live at Plimoth, and likely to be helpfull to the church or comonewelth, and so tye the lands to Plimoth as farmes for the same; and there they might keepe their cattle & tillage by some servants, and retaine their dwellings here. And so some spetiall lands were granted at a place generall, called Greens Harbor, where no allotments had been in the former divission, a plase very weell meadowed, and fitt to keep & rear cattle, good store. But alass! this remedy proved worse then the disease; for within a few years those that had thus gott footing their rente them selves away, partly by force, and partly wearing the rest with importunitie and pleas of necessitie, so as they must either suffer them to goe, or live in continuall opposition and contention. And others still, as they conceived them selves straitened, or to want accommodation, break away under one pretence or other, thinking their owne conceived necessitie, and the example of others, a warrente sufficente for them. And this, I fear, will be the ruine of New-England, at least of the churches of God there, & will provock the Lords displeasure against them.

[1630-50, 1898]

---

64. **vendible:** Saleable.

John Winthrop

[1588-1649]

John Winthrop was born on January 22, 1588, to Adam and Anne Browne Winthrop, wealthy landowners near Groton, in Suffolk County, England. The only son in a privileged, upper-class family, Winthrop was well educated by private tutors and spent two years at Cambridge University. But he was unhappy and unpopular there, partly because his piety and newly formed Puritan beliefs alienated him from other students. Returning to Groton before receiving a degree, Winthrop in 1605 married Mary Forth, with whom he had six children. After she died in 1615, Winthrop married Thomasine Clopton, who died in childbirth before they had been married a year. In 1618, he married his third wife, Margaret Tyndal, by all accounts a remarkable woman to whom Winthrop was deeply devoted and happily married until her death in 1647. In addition to becoming the stepmother to his surviving children, she bore eight children, four of whom survived infancy. From the time he left Cambridge, Winthrop was trained to take over management of the family's ancestral estate. He also studied law to gain skills that would aid him after he succeeded his father as lord of the manor at Groton. During the 1620s, however, Puritans faced growing pressure and persecution in England. Despairing of the future there, Winthrop believed that "God will bring some heavye Affliction upon this lande," as he warned in "Arguments for the Plantation of New England," a tract published in 1629. Winthrop therefore joined with other like-minded investors to form the Massachusetts Bay Company, a trading company designed to establish a colony in New England based on Puritan religious principles.

Anonymous, *John Winthrop* (c. 1640)

This anonymous portrait, painted around 1640, suggests Winthrop's dignity and authority. The fact that his portrait was painted, as well as his elaborate neck ruff, also indicates the wealth and social status of the first governor of the Massachusetts Bay Colony.

Winthrop devoted the remaining twenty years of his life to the interests and welfare of the Massachusetts Bay Colony. Elected as governor in October 1629, Winthrop, his wife and children, and seven hundred other colonists sailed for New England in a fleet of eleven ships in the spring and summer of 1630. Either immediately before or during the voyage, he wrote and delivered "A Modell of Christian Charity," an address in which Winthrop affirmed the religious principles and social ideals of the new colony. He also began a journal that he would keep for the rest of his life, a crucial account of the founding of the colony later published and now best known as *The History of New England from 1630 to 1649.* Certainly, he was in a strong position to provide that account, since Winthrop was elected more than a dozen times as governor or deputy governor of the Massachusetts Bay Colony. He was consequently also at the center of debates over the proper balance between the authority of the governors and the liberties of the governed. Winthrop was firmly committed to the concept of centralized authority, both civil and religious, which he believed was established by the will of God, and he was sometimes accused of over-stepping the bounds of his own authority. At the same time, Winthrop remained equally committed to the vision of a harmonious, selfless community he had envisaged in "A Modell of Christian Charity." Indeed, his social idealism and skillful political leadership were crucial to the initial survival and early success of the Massachusetts Bay Colony. Winthrop died in Boston, the city he helped found, on March 26, 1649.

bedfordstmartins.com/ **americanlit** *for research links on Winthrop*

Reading Winthrop's "A Modell of Christian Charity."   It was long thought that Winthrop delivered his famous address to the assembled passengers aboard the *Arabella*, the flagship of the fleet that sailed to North America in 1630 to found the Massachusetts Bay Colony. But recent scholarship indicates that he may have delivered it in the port of Southampton on the eve of the Puritans' departure from England. As governor of their new colony, Winthrop carefully laid out the religious and social principles that would form the foundation of the Puritan commonwealth, which would be based on the letter and spirit of the Bible. He thus offered an outline of the "covenant," or agreement, the Puritans had entered into with their God, who they believed had given them a divine commission to establish a colony dedicated to his worship and governed by his word. The contractual language and precise style of the address clearly reveal Winthrop's training as a lawyer. But the address served other ends as well. Speaking to those who were leaving the comforts and security of their homes in England for the hardships and uncertainty of life in New England, Winthrop sought to articulate the larger meaning and broader significance of their errand into the "wilderness" of the New World. Woven throughout his address are frequent allusions to the Bible, especially to the Old Testament accounts of the journey of the Israelites out of bondage in Egypt to the promised land, a drama that was being reenacted by God's new chosen people, the Puritans. The original manuscript of "A Modell of Christian Charity" is lost, but a copy of the address was discovered among Winthrop's papers by one of his descendants and first published by the Massachusetts Historical Society in 1838. The following text of the address, which retains the original capitalization, punctuation, and spelling, is taken from the standard edition published in *Old South Leaflets*, Number 217, edited by Samuel E. Morison (1916).

A MODELL OF CHRISTIAN CHARITY

Christian Charitie

I.

A MODELL HEREOF

God Almightie in his most holy and wise providence, hath soe disposed of the Condition of mankinde, as in all times some must be rich, some poore, some highe and eminent in power and dignitie; others meane and in subjection.

THE REASON HEREOF

First, to hold conformity with the rest of his workes, being delighted to shewe forthe the glory of his wisdome in the variety and difference of the Creatures; and the glory of his power, in ordering all these differences for the preservation and good of the whole; and the glory of his greatnes, that as it is the glory of princes to have many officers, soe this great King will have many Stewards, counting himselfe more honoured in dispenceing his guifts to man by man, then if hee did it by his owne immediate hands.

Secondly, That he might have the more occasion to manifest the work of his Spirit: first upon the wicked in moderateing and restraineing them, soe that the riche and mighty should not eate upp the poore, nor the poore and dispised rise upp against their superiors and shake off their yoake; 2ly in the regenerate, in exerciseing his graces in them, as in the greate ones, theire love, mercy, gentlenes, temperance etc.; in the poore and inferior sorte, theire faithe patience, obedience etc.

Thirdly, that every man might have need of other, and from hence they might be all knitt more nearly together in the Bonds of brotherly affection. From hence it appeares plainely that noe man is made more honourable than another or more wealthy etc., out of any perticuler and singuler respect to himselfe, but for the glory of his Creator and the common good of the Creature, Man. Therefore God still reserves the propperty of these gifts to himself as [in] Ezekiel: 16. 17. He there calls wealthe his gold and his silver.[1] [In] Proverbs: 3. 9. he claims theire service as his due, honor the Lord with thy riches etc.[2] All men being thus (by divine providence) ranked into two sortes, riche and poore;

---

1. **He there calls . . . silver:** "Thou hast also taken thy fair jewels of my gold and of my silver, which I had given thee, and madest to thyself images of men, and didst commit whoredom with them" (Ezekiel 16:17). Winthrop probably used the Geneva Bible, a translation by William Whittingham, the brother-in-law of John Calvin, which went through over 140 editions between 1566 and 1640. This English translation was popular with the Puritans for what many saw as its Calvinist leanings and anti-Catholic stance, especially in the marginal notes that accompanied many texts. James I, king of England, disapproved of the Geneva Bible and commissioned the King James Version of the Bible, published in 1611. With the exception of the marginal notes, however, the two versions were very similar. Biblical quotations in the notes here are taken from the King James Version, which eventually superseded the Geneva Bible.

2. **he claims . . . with thy riches etc.:** "Honour the LORD with thy substance, and with the first fruits of all thine increase: So shall thy barns be filled with plenty, and thy presses shall burst out with new wine" (Proverbs 3:9-10).

under the first are comprehended all such as are able to live comfortably by theire owne meanes duely improved; and all others are poore according to the former distribution.

There are two rules whereby wee are to walke one towards another: JUSTICE and MERCY. These are allwayes distinguished in theire Act and in their object, yet may they both concurre in the same subject in eache respect; as sometimes there may be an occasion of shewing mercy to a rich man in some sudden danger of distresse, and alsoe doeing of meere justice to a poor man in regard of some perticuler contract, etc.

There is likewise a double Lawe by which wee are regulated in our conversation one towards another in both the former respects: the lawe of nature and the lawe of grace, or the morrall lawe or the lawe of the gospell, to omitt the rule of justice as not propperly belonging to this purpose otherwise then it may fall into consideration in some perticuler Cases. By the first of these lawes man as he was enabled soe withall [is] commanded to love his neighbour as himself.[3] Upon this ground stands all the precepts of the morrall lawe, which concernes our dealings with men. To apply this to the works of mercy, this lawe requires two things. First, that every man afford his help to another in every want or distresse. Secondly, that hee performed this out of the same affection which makes him carefull of his owne goods, according to that of our Savior. Matthew: "Whatsoever ye would that men should doe to you."[4] This was practised by Abraham and Lott in entertaining the Angells and the old man of Gibea.[5]

The lawe of Grace or the Gospell hath some differance from the former, as in these respects. First the lawe of nature was given to man in the estate of innocency; this of the gospell in the estate of regeneracy.[6] 2ly, the former propounds one man to another, as the same flesh and image of god; this as a brother in Christ allsoe, and in the Communion of the same spirit and soe teacheth us to put a difference betweene Christians and others. *Doe good to all, especially to the houshold of faith;* upon this ground the Israelites were to putt a difference betweene the brethren of such as were strangers though not of Canaanites.[7] 3ly. The Lawe of nature could give noe rules for dealing with enemies, for all are to be considered as friends in the state of innocency, but the Gospell commands love to an enemy. Proofe. If thine Enemie hunger, feed him; Love your Enemies, doe good to them that hate you. Matthew: 5. 44.

This lawe of the Gospell propoundes likewise a difference of seasons and occasions. There is a time when a christian must sell all and give to the poore, as they did in the

---

3. **commanded . . . as himself:** "Thou shalt love thy neighbour as thyself" (Matthew 19:19).

4. **"Whatsoever . . . you":** "Therefore all things whatsoever ye would that men should do to you, do ye even so to them: for this is the law and the prophets" (Matthew 7:12).

5. **This was practised . . . Gibea:** Winthrop's examples of selfless help to others include Abraham's welcome of three angels (Genesis 18:1–2); Abraham's nephew Lot's defense of two angels against a mob (Genesis 19:1–14); and an old man of Gibea who offered shelter to a stranger (Judges 19:16–21).

6. **in the estate of regeneracy:** Winthrop develops a central set of Puritan beliefs: that human beings were innocent when they were first created and living in the Garden of Eden; that after Adam and Eve sinned they were cast out of the garden and human beings thereafter lived in an unregenerate state; and that the sacrifice of Jesus Christ offered the possibility of regeneracy and salvation to those who believe.

7. **Canaanites:** Canaan was the promised land of the Israelites.

Apostles times.[8] There is a time allsoe when a christian (though they give not all yet) must give beyond their abillity, as they of Macedonia, Corinthians: 2, 6. Likewise community of perills calls for extraordinary liberality, and soe doth community in some speciall service for the Churche. Lastly, when there is noe other meanes whereby our Christian brother may be relieved in his distresse, wee must help him beyond our ability, rather then tempt God in putting him upon help by miraculous or extraordinary meanes.

This duty of mercy is exercised in the kinds, *Giveing, lending* and *forgiving*. –

Quest. What rule shall a man observe in giveing in respect of the measure?

Ans. If the time and occasion be ordinary he is to give out of his abundance. Let him lay aside as God hath blessed him. If the time and occasion be extraordinary, he must be ruled by them; taking this withall, that then a man cannot likely doe too much, especially if he may leave himselfe and his family under probable meanes of comfortable subsistence.

Objection. A man must lay upp for posterity, the fathers lay upp for posterity and children and he "is worse than an infidell" that "provideth not for his owne."

Ans. For the first, it is plaine that it being spoken by way of Comparison, it must be meant of the ordinary and usuall course of fathers and cannot extend to times and occasions extraordinary. For the other place, the Apostle speakes against such as walked inordinately, and it is without question, that he is worse then an Infidell who throughe his owne sloathe and voluptuousnes shall neglect to provide for his family.

Objection. "The wise mans Eies are in his head" saith Salomon, "and foreseeth the plague;"[9] therefore wee must forecast and lay upp against evill times when hee or his may stand in need of all he can gather.

Ans. This very Argument Salomon useth to persuade to liberallity, Ecclesiastes: "Cast thy bread upon the waters," and "for thou knowest not what evill may come upon the land."[10] Luke 16: "Make you friends of the riches of iniquity;"[11] you will ask how this shall be? very well. For first he that gives to the poore, lends to the lord and he will repay him even in this life an hundred fold to him or his – The righteous is ever mercifull and lendeth and his seed enjoyeth the blessing; and besides wee know what advan-

---

8. **Apostles times:** "Now when Jesus heard these things, he said unto him, 'Yet lackest thou one thing: sell all that thou hast, and distribute unto the poor, and thou shalt have treasure in heaven: and come, follow me'" (Luke 18:22).

9. **"The wise . . . plague":** "The wise man's eyes are in his head; but the fool walketh in darkness" (Ecclesiastes 2:14). Salomon, a variant of Solomon (c. 970–930 BCE), was the son of David and king of Israel, renowned for his wisdom.

10. **"Cast . . . land":** "Cast thy bread upon the waters: for thou shalt find it after many days. Give a portion to seven, and also to eight; for thou knowest not what evil shall be upon the earth" (Ecclesiastes 11:1–2).

11. **"Make . . . iniquity":** In Luke's account, Christ gives numerous examples of the responsibilities of discipleship, including his parable of the dishonest steward who reduces by half the bills of debtors to his master so that the steward will be welcome in their homes: "'And I say unto you, Make to yourselves friends of the mammon of unrighteousness; that, when ye fail, they may receive you into everlasting habitations'" (Luke 16:9).

tage it will be to us in the day of account when many such witnesses shall stand forth for Us to witnesse the improvement of our Tallent.[12] And I would knowe of those whoe pleade soe much for laying up for time to come, whether they hold that to be Gospell, Matthew 6. 19. "Lay not upp for yourselves Treasures upon Earth," etc.[13] If they acknowledge it, what extent will they allowe it? if onely to those primitive times, lett them consider the reason whereupon our Saviour groundes it. The first is that they are subject to the moathe, the rust, the Theife. Secondly, They will steale away the hearte; where the treasure is there will the heart be allsoe. The reasons are of like force at all times. Therefore the exhortation must be generall and perpetuall, with allwayes in respect of the love and affection to riches and in regard of the things themselves when any speciall service for the churche or perticuler Distresse of our brother Doe call for the use of them; otherwise it is not onely lawfull but necessary to lay upp as Joseph did[14] to have ready uppon such occasions, as the Lord (whose stewards wee are of them) shall call for them from us. Christ gives us an Instance of the first, when hee sent his disciples for the Ass, and bidds them answer the owner thus, the Lord hath need of him.[15] Soe when the Tabernacle was to be builte he sends to his people to call for their silver and gold, etc.; and yeildes them noe other reason but that it was for his worke. When Elisha comes to the widow of Sareptah and findes her prepareing to make ready her pittance for herselfe and family, he bids her first provide for him, he challengeth first god's parte which shee must first give before shee must serve her owne family.[16] All these teach us that the Lord lookes that when hee is pleased to call for his right in any thing wee have, our owne Interest wee have must stand aside till his turne be served. For the other, wee need looke noe further then to that of John I: "He whoe hath this worlds goodes and seeth his brother to neede and shutts upp his compassion from him, how dwelleth the love of God in him," which comes punctually to this Conclusion: if thy brother be in want and thou canst help him, thou needst not make doubt, what thou shouldst doe, if thou lovest God thou must help him.

Quest. What rule must wee observe in lending?

Ans. Thou must observe whether thy brother hath present or probable, or possible means of repayeing thee, if there be none of these, thou must give him according to his necessity, rather then lend him as he requires. If he hath present meanes of repayeing thee, thou art to looke at him not as an Act of mercy, but by way of Commerce, wherein thou arte to walk by the rule of Justice; but if his meanes of repayeing thee be onely probable or possible, then is hee an object of thy mercy, thou must lend him, though there be danger of loseing it, Deuteronomy: 15. 7. "If any of thy brethren be poore," etc.,

---

12. **Tallent:** A talent was a unit of currency used by the ancient Greeks and Romans.
13. **"Lay not . . ." etc.:** "'Lay not up for yourselves treasures upon earth, where moth and rust doth corrupt, and where thieves break through and steal: But lay up for yourselves treasures in heaven, where neither moth nor rust doth corrupt, and where thieves do not break through nor steal: For where your treasure is, there will your heart be also'" (Matthew 6:19-21).
14. **lay upp as Joseph did:** The son of Jacob and Rachel, Joseph stored food for seven years to prepare for a famine (Genesis 41:46-57).
15. **Christ . . . need of him:** The story is in Matthew 21:1-7.
16. **When Elisha . . . family:** 1 Kings 17:10-24.

"thou shalt lend him sufficient."[17] That men might not shift off this duty by the apparant hazzard, he tells them that though the yeare of Jubile[18] were at hand (when he must remitt it, if hee were not able to repay it before) yet he must lend him and that chearefully: "It may not greive thee to give him" saith hee; and because some might object, "why soe I should soone impovishe myself and my family," he adds "with all thy Worke,"[19] etc; for our Saviour, Matthew: 5. 42. "From him that would borrow of thee turne not away."

Quest. What rule must we observe in forgiveing?

Ans. Whether thou didst lend by way of Commerce or in mercy, if he have noething to pay thee, must forgive, (except in cause where thou hast a surety or a lawfull pleadge) Deuteronomy 15. 2. Every seaventh yeare the Creditor was to quitt that which he lent to his brother if he were poore as appears – ver[se]: 8: "Save when there shall be no poore with thee." In all these and like Cases, Christ was a generall rule, Matthew 7. 22. "Whatsoever ye would that men should doe to you, doe yee the same to them allsoe."

Quest. What rule must wee observe and walke by in cause of Community of perill?

Ans. The same as before, but with more enlargement towards others and lesse respect towards our selves and our owne right. Hence it was that in the primitive Churche they sold all, had all things in Common, neither did any man say that which he possessed was his owne. Likewise in theire returne out of the Captivity, because the worke was greate for the restoreing of the church and the danger of enemies was Common to all, Nehemiah exhortes the Jews to liberallity and readiness in remitting theire debts to theire brethren, and disposing liberally of his owne to such as wanted, and stande not upon his owne due, which hee might have demanded of them.[20] Thus did some of our forefathers in times of persecution in England, and soe did many of the faithful of other Churches, whereof wee keepe an honorable remembrance of them; and it is to be observed that both in Scriptures and latter stories of the churches that such as have beene most bountifull to the poore saintes, especially in these extraordinary times and occasions, God hath left them highly commended to posterity, as Zacheus, Cornelius, Dorcas, Bishop Hooper, the Cuttler of Brussells and divers others.[21] Observe againe that the Scripture gives noe causion to restraine any from being over liberall this way; but all men to the liberall and cherefull practise hereof by the sweetest promises; as to instance one for

---

17. **"If any . . . sufficient"**: "'If there be among you a poor man of one of thy brethren within any of thy gates in thy land, which the Lord thy God giveth thee, thou shalt not harden thine heart, nor shut thine hand from thy poor brother: But thou shalt open thine hand wide unto him, and shalt surely lend him sufficient for his need, *in that* which he wanteth'" (Deuteronomy 15:7-8).

18. **yeare of Jubile**: According to Judaic law, every seventh year is a sabbatical year, a period of time devoted wholly to religion, with no work. The Jubilee year is celebrated once every fifty years, at the conclusion of seven sabbatical-year sequences.

19. **"It may not greive . . . Worke"**: "'Beware that there be not a thought in thy wicked heart, saying, "The seventh year, the year of release, is at hand"; and thine eye be evil against thy poor brother, and thou givest him nought; and he cry unto the LORD against thee, and it be sin unto thee. Thou shalt surely give him, and thine heart shall not be grieved when thou givest unto him: because that for this thing the LORD thy God shall bless thee in all thy works, and in all that thou puttest thine hand unto'" (Deuteronomy 15:9-10).

20. **Nehemiah . . . demanded of them**: The Old Testament book of Nehemiah tells the story of the Hebrew leader who introduced religious reforms and supervised the rebuilding of the walls of Jerusalem (c. 444 BCE).

21. **as Zacheus . . . and divers others**: A list of Christian martyrs.

many, Isaiah 58. 6: "Is not this the fast I have chosen to loose the bonds of wickednes, to take off the heavy burdens, to lett the oppressed goe free and to breake every yoake, to deale thy bread to the hungry and to bring the poore that wander into thy house, when thou seest the naked to cover them. And then shall thy light breake forth as the morneing, and thy healthe shall growe speedily, thy righteousness shall goe before god, and the glory of the Lord shall embrace thee; then thou shalt call and the Lord shall Answer thee" etc. [Verse] 10: "If thou power out thy soule to the hungry, then shall thy light spring out in darknes, and the lord shall guide thee continually, and satisfie thy soule in draught, and make fatt thy bones, thou shalt be like a watered Garden, and they shalt be of thee that shall build the old wast places" etc. On the contrary, most heavy cursses are layed upon such as are straightened towards the Lord and his people, Judges 5. [23]: "Cursse ye Meroshe because ye came not to help the Lord," etc. Proverbs [21. 13] "Hee whoe shutteth his eares from hearing the cry of the poore, he shall cry and shall not be heard." Matthew 25: "Goe ye carssed into everlasting fire" etc. "I was hungry and ye fedd mee not." 2 Corinthians 9. 6: "He that soweth spareingly shall reape spareingly."

Haveing already sett forth the practice of mercy according to the rule of god's lawe, it will be usefull to lay open the groundes of it allsoe, being the other parte of the Commandment, and that is the affection from which this exercise of mercy must arise. The Apostle tells us that this love is the fullfilling of the lawe,[22] not that it is enough to love our brother and soe noe further; but in regard of the excellency of his partes gieveing any motion to the other as the Soule to the body and the power it hath to sett all the faculties on worke in the outward exercise of this duty. As when wee bid one make the clocke strike, he doth not lay hand on the hammer, which is the immediate instrument of the sound, but setts on worke the first mover or maine wheele, knoweing that will certainly produce the sound which hee intends. Soe the way to drawe men to workes of mercy, is not by force of Argument from the goodnes or necessity of the worke; for though this course may enforce a rationall minde to some present Act of mercy, as is frequent in experience, yet it cannot worke such a habit in a soule, as shall make it prompt upon all occasions to produce the same effect, but by frameing these affections of love in the hearte which will as natively bring forthe the other, as any cause doth produce effect.

The deffinition which the Scripture gives us of love is this: "Love is the bond of perfection."[23] First, it is a bond or ligament. 2ly it makes the worke perfect. There is noe body but consists of partes and that which knitts these partes together, gives the body its perfection, because it makes eache parte soe contiguous to others as thereby they doe mutually participate with each other, both in strengthe and infirmity, in pleasure and paine. To instance in the most perfect of all bodies: Christ and his church make one body. The severall partes of this body, considered aparte before they were united, were as disproportionate and as much disordering as soe many contrary qualities or

The middle (handwritten marginal note)

---

22. **The Apostle . . . lawe:** The Apostle Paul wrote, "Love worketh no ill to his neighbour: therefore love is the fulfilling of the law" (Romans 13:10).
23. **"Love is the bond of perfection":** See Colossians 3:14: "And above all these things put on charity, which is the bond of perfectness."

elements, but when Christ comes and by his spirit and love knitts all these partes to himselfe and each to other, it is become the most perfect and best proportioned body in the world. Ephesians 4. 16: "Christ, by whome all the body being knitt together by every joint for the furniture thereof, according to the effectuall power which is in the measure of every perfection of partes," "a glorious body without spott or wrinkle," the ligaments hereof being Christ, or his love, for Christ is love (1 John 4. 8). Soe this definition is right: "Love is the bond of perfection."

From hence we may frame these conclusions. 1. First of all, true Christians are of one body in Christ, 1 Corinthians 12. 12, 27: "Ye are the body of Christ and members of their parte." 2ly. The ligaments of this body which knitt together are love. 3ly. Noe body can be perfect which wants its propper ligament. 4ly. All the partes of this body being thus united are made soe contiguous in a speciall relation as they must needes partake of each other's strength and infirmity; joy and sorrowe, weale and woe. 1 Corinthians: 12. 26: "If one member suffers, all suffer with it, if one be in honor, all rejoyce with it." 5ly. This sensibleness and sympathy of each other's conditions will necessarily infuse into each parte a native desire and endeavour to strengthen, defend, preserve and comfort the other.

To insist a little on this Conclusion being the product of all the former, the truthe hereof will appear both by precept and patterne. 1 John 3. 10: "Yee ought to lay downe your lives for the brethren." Galatians 6. 2: "beare ye one another's burthens and soe fulfill the lawe of Christ." For patterns wee have that first of our Saviour whoe out of his good will in obedience to his father, becomeing a parte of this body, and being knitt with it in the bond of love, found such a native sensiblenes of our infirmities and sorrowes as hee willingly yielded himselfe to deathe to ease the infirmities of the rest of his body, and soe heald their sorrowes. From the like sympathy of partes did the Apostles and many thousands of the Saintes lay downe theire lives for Christ. Againe, the like wee may see in the members of this body among themselves. Romans 9. Paule could have beene contented to have beene separated from Christ, that the Jewes might not be cutt off from the body. It is very observable what hee professeth of his affectionate partaking with every member: "whoe is weake" saith hee "and I am not weake? whoe is offended and I burne not;"[24] and againe, 2 Corinthians: 7. 13. "therefore wee are comforted because yee were comforted." Of Epaphroditus he speaketh, Philippians 2. 30. that he regarded not his owne life to do him service.[25] Soe Phebe and others are called the servants of the churche.[26] Now it is apparent that they served not for wages, or by constrainte, but out of love. The like wee shall finde in the histories of the churche in all ages, the sweete sympathie of affections which was in the members of this body one towardes another, theire chearfullness in serveing and suffering together, how liberall they were without repineing; harbourers without grudgeing and helpfull without reproaching; and all

---

24. **"whoe is weake . . . and I burne not;":** 2 Corinthians 11:19.

25. **Of Epaphroditus . . . service:** In his letter to the Philippians, written from a Roman prison, Paul tells them that he is sending Epaphroditus to serve as their minister in his absence (Philippians 2:25-30).

26. **Soe Phebe . . . churche:** "I commend unto you Phebe our sister, which is a servant of the church which is at Cenchrea" (Romans 16:1).

from hence, because they had fervent love amongst them, which onely make the practise of mercy constant and easie.

The next consideration is how this love comes to be wrought. Adam in his first estate was a perfect modell of mankinde in all their generations, and in him this love was perfected in regard of the habit. But Adam rent himselfe from his Creator, rent all his posterity allsoe one from another; whence it comes that every man is borne with this principle in him, to love and seeke himselfe onely, and thus a man continueth till Christ comes and takes possession of the soule and infuseth another principle, love to God and our brother. And this latter haveing continuall supply from Christ, as the head and roote by which he is united, gets the predomineing in the soule, soe by little and little expells the former. 1 John 4. 7. "love cometh of god and every one that loveth is borne of god," soe that this love is the fruite of the new birthe, and none can have it but the new Creature. Now when this quallity is thus formed in the soules of men, it workes like the Spirit upon the drie bones. Ezekiel 37: "bone came to bone." It gathers together the scattered bones, or perfect old man Adam, and knitts them into one body againe in Christ, whereby a man is become againe a living soule.

The third Consideration is concerning the exercise of this love which is twofold, inward or outward. The outward hath beene handled in the former preface of this discourse. For unfolding the other wee must take in our way that maxime of philosophy *Simile simili gaudet*, or like will to like; for as it is things which are turned with disaffection to eache other, the ground of it is from a dissimilitude ariseing from the contrary or different nature of the things themselves; for the ground of love is an apprehension of some resemblance in things loved to that which affects it. This is the cause why the Lord loves the creature, soe farre as it hathe any of his Image in it; he loves his elect because they are like himselfe, he beholds them in his beloved sonne. Soe a mother loves her childe, because shee throughly conceives a resemblance of herselfe in it. Thus it is betweene the members of Christ. Eache discernes, by the worke of the Spirit, his owne Image and resemblance in another, and therefore cannot but love him as he loves himself. Now when the soule, which is of a sociable nature, findes any thing like to it selfe, it is like Adam when Eve was brought to him. She must have it one with herselfe. This is flesh of my flesh (saith the soule) and bone of my bone. Shee conceives a greate delighte in it, therefore shee desires neareness and familiarity with it. Shee hath a greate propensity to doe it good and receives such content in it, as fearing the miscarriage of her beloved, shee bestowes it in the inmost closett of her heart. Shee will not endure that it shall want any good which shee can give it. If by occasion shee be withdrawne from the company of it, shee is still looking towards the place where shee left her beloved. If shee hearde it groane, shee is with it presently. If shee finde it sadd and disconsolate, shee sighes and moanes with it. Shee hath noe such joy as to see her beloved merry and thriving. If shee see it wronged, shee canot heare it without passion. Shee setts noe boundes to her affections, nor hath any thought of reward. Shee findes recompense enough in the exercise of her love towards it. Wee may see this Acted to life in Jonathan and David.[27]

---

27. **Jonathan and David:** The account is in 1 Samuel 19–20.

Jonathan a valiant man endued with the spirit of Christ, soe soone as he discovers the same spirit in David had presently his hearte knitt to him by this linement of love, soe that it is said he loved him as his owne soule. He takes soe great pleasure in him, that hee stripps himselfe to adorne his beloved. His fathers kingdome was not soe precious to him as his beloved David. David shall have it with all his hearte, himself desires noe more but that hee may be neare to him to rejoyce in his good. Hee chooseth to converse with him in the wildernesse even to the hazzard of his owne life, rather then with the greate Courtiers in his fathers Pallace. When hee sees danger towards him, hee spares neither rare paines nor perill to direct it. When Injury was offered his beloved David, hee would not beare it, though from his owne father; and when they must parte for a season onely, they thought theire heartes would have broake for sorrowe, had not theire affections found vent by aboundance of teares. Other instances might be brought to showe the nature of this affection, as of Ruthe and Naomi,[28] and many others; but this truthe is cleared enough.

If any shall object that it is not possible that love should be bred or upheld without hope of requitall, it is graunted; but that is not our cause; for this love is allwayes under reward. It never gives, but it allwayes receives with advantage; first, in regard that among the members of the same body, love and affection are reciprocall in a most equall and sweete kinde of Commerce. 2ly, in regard of the pleasure and content that the exercise of love carries with it, as wee may see in the naturall body. The mouth is at all the paines to receive and mince the foode which serves for the nourishment of all the other partes of the body, yet it hath noe cause to complaine; for first the other partes send backe by severall passages a due proportion of the same nourishment, in a better forme for the strengthening and comforting the mouthe. 2ly the labour of the mouthe is accompanied with such pleasure and content as farre exceedes the paines it takes. Soe is it in all the labour of love among christians. The partie loving, reapes love againe, as was showed before, which the soule covetts more then all the wealthe in the world. 3ly. Nothing yeildes more pleasure and content to the soule then when it findes that which it may love fervently, for to love and live beloved is the soules paradise, both here and in heaven. In the State of Wedlock there be many comfortes to beare out the troubles of that Condition; but let such as have tryed the most, say if there be any sweetnes in that Condition comparable to the exercise of mutuall love.

From former Considerations arise these Conclusions.

1. First, This love among Christians is a reall thing, not Imaginarie.

2ly. This love is as absolutely necessary to the being of the body of Christ, as the sinews and other ligaments of a naturall body are to the being of that body.

3ly. This love is a divine, spirituall nature free, active, strong, couragious, permanent; under valueing all things beneathe its propper object; and of all the graces, this makes us nearer to resemble the virtues of our heavenly father.

---

28. **Ruthe and Naomi:** After the death of her husband and her two sons, Naomi entreats her daughters-in-law, Orpah and Ruth, to return to their own people, where they will be better off, and to their own gods. Orpah reluctantly does so, but Ruth insists on staying with Naomi, saying: "'whither thou goest, I will go; and where thou lodgest, I will lodge: thy people shall be my people, and thy God my God'" (Ruth 1:1–22).

4thly It rests in the love and welfare of its beloved. For the full and certaine knowledge of these truthes concerning the nature, use, and excellency of this grace, that which the holy ghost hath left recorded, 1 Corinthians 13, may give full satisfaction, which is needful for every true member of this lovely body of the Lord Jesus, to worke upon theire heartes by prayer, meditation, continuall exercise at least of the speciall [influence] of this grace, till Christ be formed in them and they in him, all in eache other, knitt together by this bond of love.

II. The End

It rests now to make some application of this discourse by the present designe, which gave the occasion of writeing of it. Herein are 4 things to be propounded: first the persons, 2ly the worke, 3ly the end, 4thly the meanes.

1. For the persons. Wee are a Company professing our selves fellow members of Christ, in which respect onely though wee were absent from each other many miles, and had our imployments as farre distant, yet wee ought to account ourselves knitt together by this bond of love, and live in the excercise of it, if wee would have comforte of our being in Christ. This was notorious in the practise of the Christians in former times; as is testified of the Waldenses,[29] from the mouth of one of the adversaries *Æneas sylvius*[30] "mutuo [ament] penè antequam norunt," they use to love any of theire owne religion even before they were acquainted with them.

2nly for the worke wee have in hand. It is by a mutuall consent, through a speciall overvaluing providence and a more then an ordinary approbation of the Churches of Christ, to seeke out a place of Cohabitation and Consorteshipp under a due forme of Government both civill and ecclesiasticall. In such cases as this, the care of the publique must oversway all private respects, by which, not only conscience, but meare civill pollicy, dothe binde us. For it is a true rule that particular Estates cannott subsist in the ruine of the publique.

3ly The end is to improve our lives to doe more service to the Lord; the comforte and encrease of the body of Christe whereof wee are members; that ourselves and posterity may be the better preserved from the Common corruptions of this evill world, to serve the Lord and worke out our Salvation under the power and purity of his holy ordinances.

4ly for the meanes whereby this must bee effected. They are 2fold, a Conformity with the worke and end wee aime at. These wee see are extraordinary, therefore wee must not content our selves with usuall ordinary meanes. Whatsoever wee did or ought to have done when wee lived in England, the same must wee doe, and more allsoe, where wee goe. That which the most in theire Churches maineteine as a truthe in profession onely, wee must bring into familiar and constant practise, as in this duty of love. Wee must love brotherly without dissimulation; wee must love one another with a pure hearte fervently. Wee must beare one anothers burthens. We must not looke onely on our owne

---

29. **Waldenses:** Members of a twelfth-century Protestant group organized by a French religious reformer, Peter Valdes.
30. *Æneas sylvius:* Aeneas Sylvius Piccolomini (1405-1464) became Pope Pius II in 1458.

things, but allsoe on the things of our brethren, neither must wee thinke that the lord will beare with such faileings at our hands as hee dothe from those among whome wee have lived; and that for 3 Reasons.

1. In regard of the more neare bond of marriage betweene him and us, wherein hee hath taken us to be his after a most strickt and peculiar manner, which will make him the more Jealous of our love and obedience. Soe he tells the people of Israell, you onely have I knowne of all the families of the Earthe, therefore will I punish you for your Transgressions. 2ly, because the lord will be sanctified in them that come neare him. Wee know that there were many that corrupted the service of the Lord, some setting upp Altars before his owne, others offering both strange fire and strange Sacrifices allsoe; yet there came noe fire from heaven or other sudden judgement upon them, as did upon Nadab and Abihu,[31] whoe yet wee may thinke did not sinne presumptuously. 3ly When God gives a speciall commission he lookes to have it stricktly observed in every Article. When hee gave Saule a Commission to destroy Amaleck, Hee indented with him upon certaine Articles, and because hee failed in one of the least, and that upon a faire pretence, it lost him the kingdome which should have beene his reward if hee had observed his Commission.[32]

Thus stands the cause betweene God and us. We are entered into Covenant with him for this worke.[33] Wee have taken out a Commission, the Lord hath given us leave to drawe our own Articles. Wee have professed to enterprise these Actions, upon these and those ends, wee have hereupon besought him of favour and blessing. Now if the Lord shall please to heare us, and bring us in peace to the place wee desire, then hath hee ratified this Covenant and sealed our Commission, [and] will expect a strict performance of the Articles contained in it; but if wee shall neglect the observation of these Articles which are the ends wee have propounded, and, dissembling with our God, shall fall to embrace this present world and prosecute our carnall intentions, seeking great things for our selves and our posterity, the Lord will surely breake out in wrathe against us; be revenged of such a perjured people and make us knowe the price of the breache of such a covenant.

Now the onely way to avoyde this shipwracke, and to provide for our posterity, is to followe the counsell of Micah,[34] to doe justly, to love mercy, to walke humbly with our

---

31. **Nadab and Abihu:** See Leviticus 10:1-2: "And Nadab and Abihu, the sons of Aaron, took either of them his censer, and put fire therein, and put incense thereon, and offered strange fire before the Lord, which he commanded them not. And there went out fire from the Lord, and devoured them, and they died before the Lord."

32. **When hee gave Saule ... Commission:** The story of Saul's failure to follow God's command is found in 1 Samuel 15:1-34.

33. **Covenant with him for this worke:** A covenant is a legal agreement or contract. The Puritans believed that the covenant promises of the Old Testament did not simply apply to ancient Israel but to any society that followed God's laws and commands.

34. **counsell of Micah:** The Old Testament prophet Micah called upon Israel to repent its sins, warning of the wrath of God and the destruction of Jerusalem. But he also prophesied the glorious future of the city as the center of pure worship: "And many nations shall come, and say, 'Come, and let us go up to the mountain of the LORD, and to the house of the God of Jacob; and he will teach us his ways, and we will walk in his paths': for the law shall go forth of Zion, and the word of God from Jerusalem" (Micah 4:2).

God. For this end, wee must be knitt together in this work as one man. Wee must entertaine each other in brotherly Affection, wee must be willing to abridge our selves of our superfluities, for the supply of others necessities. Wee must uphold a familiar Commerce together in all meekenes, gentlenes, patience and liberality. Wee must delight in eache other, make other's conditions our owne, rejoyce together, mourne together, labour and suffer together, allwayes haveing before our eyes our Commission and Community in the worke, our Community as members of the same body. Soe shall wee keepe the unitie of the spirit in the bond of peace. The Lord will be our God, and delight to dwell among Us as his owne people, and will command a blessing upon us in all our wayes, soe that wee shall see much more of his wisdome, power, goodnes and truthe, then formerly wee have been acquainted with. Wee shall finde that the God of Israell is among us, when tenn of us shall be able to resist a thousand of our enemies; when hee shall make us a prayse and glory that men shall say of succeeding plantations, "the lord make it like that of NEW ENGLAND." For wee must Consider that wee shall be as a Citty upon a hill.[35] The eies of all people are uppon Us, soe that if wee shall deale falsely with our god in this worke wee have undertaken, and soe cause him to withdrawe his present help from us, wee shall be made a story and a by-word through the world. Wee shall open the mouthes of enemies to speake evill of the wayes of god, and all professours for God's sake. Wee shall shame the faces of many of god's worthy servants, and cause theire prayers to be turned into Cursses upon us till wee be consumed out of the good land whither wee are a goeing.

And to shutt upp this discourse with that exhortation of Moses, that faithfull servant of the Lord, in his last farewell to Israell, Deuteronomy 30. Beloved, there is now sett before us life and good, Death and evill, in that wee are Commanded this day to love the Lord our God, and to love one another, to walke in his wayes and to keepe his Commandements and his Ordinance and his lawes, and the articles of our Covenant with him, that wee may live and be multiplied, and that the Lord our God may blesse us in the land whither wee goe to possesse it. But if our heartes shall turne away, soe that wee will not obey, but shall be seduced, and worshipp other Gods, our pleasures and proffitts, and serve them; it is propounded unto us this day, wee shall surely perishe out of the good Land whither wee passe over this vast sea to possesse it.

> Therefore lett us choose life,
> that wee and our seede
> may live by obeyeing his
> voyce and cleaveing to him,
> for hee is our life and
> our prosperity.

[1630, 1916]

---

35. **a Citty upon a hill:** See Matthew 5:14: "'Ye are the light of the world. A city that is set on an hill cannot be hid.'"

Anne Bradstreet

[c. 1612–1672]

Anne Bradstreet was born in Northampton, England, probably in 1612, the second child of Dorothy Yorke and Thomas Dudley, an estate manager of a wealthy Puritan landowner, the Earl of Lincoln. Given access to the earl's extensive library, Bradstreet was encouraged to read and write by her father, who occasionally wrote poetry. Bradstreet also received an education beyond that of most young girls of her day. Although little is known about the details of her training, the numerous allusions in her later poems indicate that she had read widely — not simply in the Bible and religious works, but also in history, literature, and natural science. In 1628, when she was about sixteen, she married Simon Bradstreet (1603–1697), a Puritan associate of her father and a graduate of Cambridge University. After Simon Bradstreet and her father became involved with the Massachusetts Bay Company, the young couple and her parents sailed to North America in 1630 aboard the *Arabella*, the flagship of the Puritan migration led by John Winthrop.

The stormy seventy-six-day voyage and the primitive conditions in New England took a physical and psychological toll on the emigrants, many of whom had lived a life of comfort and relative luxury in England. Lady Arabella Johnson, after whom the *Arabella* was named, died a few weeks after arrival; her husband, Isaac Johnson, the wealthiest and one of the most revered of the Puritans, succumbed to disease only a few months later, before he was thirty years old. Although she was frail and often ill, Bradstreet survived the initial hardships, as well as the births of eight children, a frequent cause of death for women in the seventeenth century. Her life in the colony was made all the more difficult by the family's frequent moves — from the first primitive settlement in Charlestown to Cambridge to the more distant Ipswich and finally, in 1647, to the even more isolated village of Andover — as well as by the public duties of her beloved husband, Simon. An able and highly regarded administrator, Simon Bradstreet was often away from home on the business of the colony, for which he served as a magistrate and later as governor.

> To have written poems, the first good poems in America, while rearing eight children, lying frequently sick, keeping house at the edge of wilderness, was to have managed a poet's range and extension within confines as severe as any American poet has confronted.
>
> —Adrienne Rich

Although little is known about why or exactly when Bradstreet began to write poetry, many scholars believe that she initially composed her poems primarily as a diversion from the rigors and tedium of colonial life. Bradstreet apparently had no idea of publishing her poems, which were written for her own enjoyment and circulated only among her admiring family and friends. Probably without her knowledge, her brother-in-law, the Reverend John Woodbridge, took Bradstreet's manuscript with him to England, where it was published in 1650 as *The Tenth Muse Lately Sprung up in America*. Bradstreet's name did not appear on the title page of the volume, whose author was simply identified as "a Gentlewoman in those parts." In fact, it was the first book of poetry published by any person — man or woman — living in the English colonies in North America. When Bradstreet learned of its publication, she began to work on a second edition, in which she planned to correct errors, revise earlier poems, and add some of her later work. Publication of that volume was evidently considered in 1666, when Bradstreet is thought to have written a poetic prologue to the new edition, "The Author to Her Book." But the volume was not published, and Bradstreet continued to write poems, including some verses on the devastating fire that destroyed her house in Andover in 1666. Having spent most of her sixty years struggling to make a home for herself and her family in the "wilderness" of New England, Bradstreet died six years later, in 1672.

By then, she had produced one of the most important bodies of poetry written by a colonist in seventeenth-century America. Although writing was not considered an appropriate activity for a woman in the colonies, Bradstreet was well known as a poet in her own day and her fellow colonists were clearly proud of her achievement. A second edition of her poetry was published in Boston as *Several Poems Compiled with Great Variety of*

Title Page of Anne Bradstreet's *The Tenth Muse* (1650)

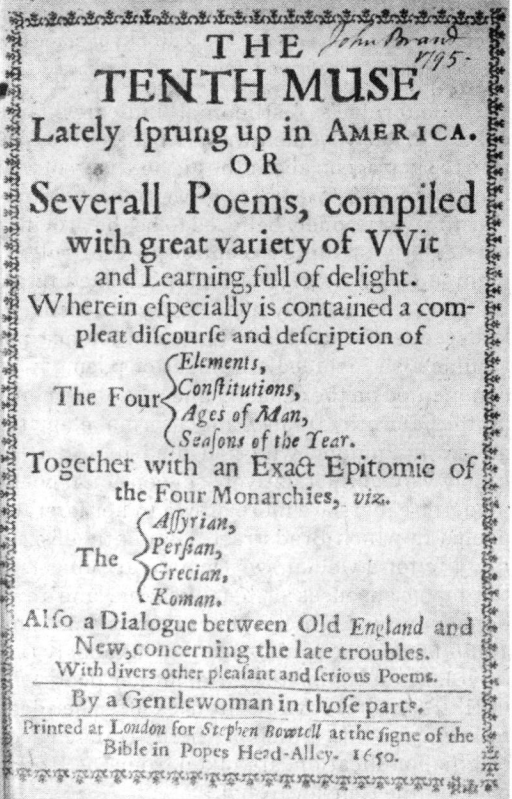

THE
TENTH MUSE
Lately sprung up in AMERICA.
OR
Severall Poems, compiled
with great variety of VVit
and Learning, full of delight.
Wherein especially is contained a com-
pleat discourse and description of

The Four { Elements,
Constitutions,
Ages of Man,
Seasons of the Year.

Together with an Exact Epitomie of
the Four Monarchies, viz.

The { Assyrian,
Persian,
Grecian,
Roman.

Also a Dialogue between Old *England* and
New, concerning the late troubles.
With divers other pleasant and serious Poems.

By a Gentlewoman in those parts.

Printed at *London* for *Stephen Bowtell* at the signe of the
Bible in Popes Head-Alley. 1650.

**bedfordstmartins.com/
americanlit** *for research
links on Bradstreet*

Wit and Learning in 1678. In his *Magnalia Christi Americana* (1702), the Puritan clergyman and historian Cotton Mather commemorated her as "Ann Bradstreet, the Daughter of our Governour Dudley, and the Consort of our Governour Bradstreet, whose Poems, divers times Printed, have afforded a grateful Entertainment unto the Ingenious, and a Monument for her Memory beyond the Stateliest *Marbles*."

Reading Bradstreet's Poetry. When he oversaw the publication in London of *The Tenth Muse Lately Sprung up in America* (1650), Bradstreet's brother-in-law John Woodbridge wrote a preface to the volume in which he anticipated that some readers might

> question whether it be a woman's work, and ask, is it possible? If any do, take this as an answer from him that dares avow it; it is the work of a woman, honored, and esteemed where she lives, for her gracious demeanor, her eminent parts, her pious conversation, her courteous disposition, her exact diligence in her place, and discreet managing of her family occasions, and more than so, these poems are the fruit but of some few hours, curtailed from her sleep and other refreshments.

As Woodbridge's testimonial indicates, and as many scholars have observed, early women writers confronted formidable obstacles. In addition to skepticism about the authenticity of their work, women faced questions about the propriety of writing at a time when both literature and learning were widely believed to be the provinces of men. Bradstreet was a particularly striking exception to that rule, since *The Tenth Muse* was dominated by a series of ambitious meditative and philosophical poems that revealed not only her artistry but also her wide reading and detailed knowledge of world history, natural science, mythology, and the Bible. The volume also included a number of poems in which Bradstreet implicitly commented on the capacity and role of women, including an epitaph to her mother, Dorothy Dudley, and a formal elegy to Elizabeth I, the celebrated queen of England who had died in 1603. Bradstreet's contemporaries highly valued the relatively conventional poems of *The Tenth Muse*. Most modern readers are more drawn to her later work, especially the personal poems in which Bradstreet poignantly describes the difficulties of colonial life for a woman, writing about subjects like her fears of childbirth, the many absences of her husband, and the burning of the Bradstreet home in 1666. Eighteen of her later poems, along with the poetry from *The Tenth Muse*, were published posthumously in Bradstreet's *Several Poems* (1678). But a complete edition of her poetry and prose was not published until 1867, almost two centuries after her death in 1672. The texts of the following poems, which are here arranged according to the dates of their original publication, are taken from *The Works of Anne Bradstreet*, edited by Jeannine Hensley (1967).

THE PROLOGUE

1

To sing of wars, of captains, and of kings,
Of cities founded, commonwealths begun,
For my mean[1] pen are too superior things:
Or how they all, or each their dates have run
Let poets and historians set these forth,   5
My obscure lines shall not so dim their worth.

2

But when my wond'ring eyes and envious heart
Great Bartas' sugared lines[2] do but read o'er,
Fool I do grudge the Muses[3] did not part
'Twixt him and me that overfluent store;   10
A Bartas can do what a Bartas will
But simple I according to my skill.

3

From schoolboy's tongue no rhet'ric we expect,
Nor yet a sweet consort[4] from broken strings,
Nor perfect beauty where's a main defect: 15
My foolish, broken, blemished Muse so sings,
And this to mend, alas, no art is able,
'Cause nature made it so irreparable.

4

Nor can I, like that fluent sweet tongued Greek,[5]
Who lisped at first, in future times speak plain.   20
By art he gladly found what he did seek,
A full requital of his striving pain.

---

1. **mean:** Humble or lowly.
2. **Great Bartas' sugared lines:** Guillaume du Bartas (1544-1590), French poet whose epic poems based on the Bible were translated into ornate heroic couplets by the English poet Joshua Sylvester (1563-1618) as *The Divine Weeks of the World's Birth* (1604).
3. **Muses:** The nine goddesses who preside over the arts and sciences in Greek mythology.
4. **consort:** Harmony.
5. **sweet tongued Greek:** Demosthenes, an Athenian orator known for putting stones in his mouth in order to practice precise enunciation.

Art can do much, but this maxim's most sure:
A weak or wounded brain admits no cure.

5

I am obnoxious to each carping tongue   25
Who says my hand a needle better fits,
A poet's pen all scorn I should thus wrong,
For such despite they cast on female wits:
If what I do prove well, it won't advance,
They'll say it's stol'n, or else it was by chance.   30

6

But sure the antique Greeks were far more mild
Else of our sex, why feigned they those nine
And poesy made Calliope's own child;[6]
So 'mongst the rest they placed the arts divine:
But this weak knot they will full soon untie,   35
The Greeks did nought, but play the fools and lie.

7

Let Greeks be Greeks, and women what they are
Men have precedency and still excel,
It is but vain unjustly to wage war;
Men can do best, and women know it well.   40
Preeminence in all and each is yours;
Yet grant some small acknowledgement of ours.

8

And oh ye high flown quills[7] that soar the skies,
And ever with your prey still catch your praise,
If e'er you deign these lowly lines your eyes,   45
Give thyme or parsley wreath, I ask no bays;[8]
This mean and unrefined ore of mine
Will make your glist'ring gold but more to shine.

[1650, 1967]

---

6. **Calliope's own child:** In Greek mythology, Calliope was the Muse of epic poetry.
7. **quills:** Figuratively poets, who wrote with quill pens made from feathers.
8. **bays:** In ancient times, bay or laurel leaves were used to make triumphal crowns for victors.

AN EPITAPH ON MY DEAR AND EVER-HONOURED MOTHER MRS. DOROTHY DUDLEY, WHO DECEASED DECEMBER 27, 1643, AND OF HER AGE, 61

Here lies,
A worthy matron of unspotted life,
A loving mother and obedient wife,
A friendly neighbor, pitiful to poor,
Whom oft she fed and clothed with her store;   5
To servants wisely awful,[1] but yet kind,
And as they did, so they reward did find.
A true instructor of her family,
The which she ordered with dexterity.
The public meetings ever did frequent,   10
And in her closet[2] constant hours she spent;
Religious in all her words and ways,
Preparing still for death, till end of days:
Of all her children, children lived to see,
Then dying, left a blessed memory.   15

[1650, 1967]

---

1. **awful:** Early term for inspiring reverence, wonder, or fear.
2. **closet:** Early term for a small, private room used for study or prayer.

TO HER FATHER WITH SOME VERSES

Most truly honoured, and as truly dear,
If worth in me or ought I do appear,
Who can of right better demand the same
Than may your worthy self from whom it came?
The principal[1] might yield a greater sum,   5
Yet handled ill, amounts but to this crumb;
My stock's[2] so small I know not how to pay,
My bond[3] remains in force unto this day;
Yet for part payment take this simple mite,
Where nothing's to be had, kings loose their right.   10
Such is my debt I may not say forgive,
But as I can, I'll pay it while I live;
Such is my bond, none can discharge but I,
Yet paying is not paid until I die.

[1678, 1967]

---

1. **principal:** A sum of money on which interest is paid.
2. **stock's:** *Stock* here refers to money or capital.
3. **bond:** A certificate promising to repay borrowed money at a fixed rate of interest and at a certain time.

THE AUTHOR TO HER BOOK

Thou ill-formed offspring[1] of my feeble brain,
Who after birth didst by my side remain,
Till snatched from thence by friends, less wise than true,
Who thee abroad, exposed to public view,
Made thee in rags, halting to th' press to trudge,   5
Where errors were not lessened (all may judge).
At thy return my blushing was not small,
My rambling brat (in print) should mother call,
I cast thee by as one unfit for light,
Thy visage was so irksome in my sight;   10
Yet being mine own, at length affection would
Thy blemishes amend, if so I could:
I washed thy face, but more defects I saw,
And rubbing off a spot still made a flaw.
I stretched thy joints to make thee even feet,[2]   15
Yet still thou run'st more hobbling than is meet;
In better dress to trim thee was my mind,
But nought save homespun cloth i' th' house I find.
In this array 'mongst vulgars[3] mayst thou roam.
In critic's hands beware thou dost not come,   20
And take thy way where yet thou art not known;
If for thy father asked, say thou hadst none;
And for thy mother, she alas is poor,
Which caused her thus to send thee out of door.

                                                    [1678, 1967]

---

1. **offspring:** Her poems. Probably without her knowledge, Bradstreet's brother-in-law had arranged for the publication of a volume of her poems as *The Tenth Muse* (1650). She may have written this poem in 1666, when the publication of a second edition of her book was a possibility.
2. **feet:** In prosody, a poetic foot is a group of syllables forming a metrical unit.
3. **vulgars:** Common or ordinary people.

BEFORE THE BIRTH OF ONE
OF HER CHILDREN

All things within this fading world hath end,
Adversity doth still our joys attend;
No ties so strong, no friends so dear and sweet,
But with death's parting blow is sure to meet.
The sentence past is most irrevocable,   5
A common thing, yet oh, inevitable.
How soon, my Dear, death may my steps attend,

How soon't may be thy lot to lose thy friend,
We both are ignorant, yet love bids me
These farewell lines to recommend to thee,   10
That when that knot's untied that made us one,
I may seem thine, who in effect am none.
And if I see not half my days that's due,
What nature would, God grant to yours and you;
The many faults that well you know I have   15
Let be interred in my oblivious grave;
If any worth or virtue were in me,
Let that live freshly in thy memory
And when thou feel'st no grief, as I no harms,
Yet love thy dead, who long lay in thine arms.   20
And when thy loss shall be repaid with gains
Look to my little babes, my dear remains.
And if thou love thyself, or loved'st me,
These O protect from step-dame's injury.[1]
And if chance to thine eyes shall bring this verse,   25
With some sad sighs honour my absent hearse;
And kiss this paper for thy love's dear sake,
Who with salt tears this last farewell did take.
                                              [1678, 1967]

---

1. **step-dame's injury:** A stepmother's unkind action.

TO MY DEAR AND LOVING HUSBAND

If ever two were one, then surely we.
If ever man were loved by wife, then thee;
If ever wife was happy in a man,
Compare with me, ye women, if you can.
I prize thy love more than whole mines of gold   5
Or all the riches that the East doth hold.
My love is such that rivers cannot quench,
Nor ought but love from thee, give recompense.
Thy love is such I can no way repay,
The heavens reward thee manifold,[1] I pray.   10
Then while we live, in love let's so persevere
That when we live no more, we may live ever.
                                              [1678, 1967]

---

1. **manifold:** In many and various ways.

A LETTER TO HER HUSBAND, ABSENT UPON PUBLIC EMPLOYMENT

My head, my heart, mine eyes, my life, nay, more,
My joy, my magazine[1] of earthly store,
If two be one, as surely thou and I,
How stayest thou there, whilst I at Ipswich[2] lie?
So many steps, head from the heart to sever,   5
If but a neck, soon should we be together.
I, like the Earth this season, mourn in black,
My Sun is gone so far in's zodiac,[3]
Whom whilst I 'joyed, nor storms, nor frost I felt,
His warmth such frigid colds did cause to melt.   10
My chilled limbs now numbed lie forlorn;
Return, return, sweet Sol, from Capricorn;[4]
In this dead time, alas, what can I more
Than view those fruits which through thy heat I bore?
Which sweet contentment yield me for a space,   15
True living pictures of their father's face.
O strange effect! now thou art southward gone,
I weary grow the tedious day so long;
But when thou northward to me shalt return,
I wish my Sun may never set, but burn   20
Within the Cancer[5] of my glowing breast,
The welcome house of him my dearest guest.
Where ever, ever stay, and go not thence,
Till nature's sad decree shall call thee hence;
Flesh of thy flesh, bone of thy bone,[6]   25
I here, thou there, yet both but one.

[1678, 1967]

---

1. **magazine:** An early term for a storehouse.
2. **Ipswich:** A town north of Boston, Massachusetts, where the Bradstreets lived from 1647 until the poet's death in 1672.
3. **zodiac:** Circuit or circle. In astrology, a belt of the heavens on either side of the path of the sun, which includes all the positions of the sun, moon, and principal planets, divided into twelve equal divisions or signs (Aries, Taurus, etc.).
4. **Return . . . from Capricorn:** *Sol* is the sun, which enters Capricorn, the tenth sign of the zodiac, near the end of December.
5. **Cancer:** The fourth sign of the zodiac, entered by the sun near the end of June.
6. **Flesh . . . bone:** See Genesis 2:23: "And Adam said, 'This *is* now bone of my bones, and flesh of my flesh: she shall be called Woman, because she was taken out of Man.'"

HERE FOLLOWS SOME VERSES UPON THE BURNING OF OUR HOUSE JULY 10TH, 1666. COPIED OUT OF A LOOSE PAPER

In silent night when rest I took
For sorrow near I did not look
I wakened was with thund'ring noise
And piteous shrieks of dreadful voice.
That fearful sound of "Fire!" and "Fire!"   5
Let no man know is my desire.
I, starting up, the light did spy,
And to my God my heart did cry
To strengthen me in my distress
And not to leave me succorless.   10
Then, coming out, beheld a space
The flame consume my dwelling place.
And when I could no longer look,
I blest His name that gave and took,[1]
That laid my goods now in the dust.   15
Yea, so it was, and so 'twas just.
It was His own, it was not mine,
Far be it that I should repine;
He might of all justly bereft
But yet sufficient for us left.   20
When by the ruins oft I past
My sorrowing eyes aside did cast,
And here and there the places spy
Where oft I sat and long did lie:
Here stood that trunk, and there that chest,   25
There lay that store I counted best.
My pleasant things in ashes lie,
And them behold no more shall I.
Under thy roof no guest shall sit,
Nor at thy table eat a bit.   30
No pleasant tale shall e'er be told,
Nor things recounted done of old.
No candle e'er shall shine in thee,
Nor bridegroom's voice e'er heard shall be.
In silence ever shall thou lie,   35

---

1. **that gave and took:** See Job 1:21: "Naked came I out of my mother's womb, and naked shall I return thither; the Lord gave, and the Lord hath taken away; blessed be the name of the Lord."

Adieu, Adieu, all's vanity.[2]
Then straight I 'gin my heart to chide,
And did thy wealth on earth abide?
Didst fix thy hope on mold'ring dust?
The arm of flesh didst make thy trust?   40
Raise up thy thoughts above the sky
That dunghill mists away may fly.
Thou hast an house on high erect,
Framed by that mighty Architect,
With glory richly furnished,   45
Stands permanent though this be fled.
It's purchased and paid for too
By Him who hath enough to do.
A price so vast as is unknown
Yet by His gift is made thine own;   50
There's wealth enough, I need no more,
Farewell, my pelf,[3] farewell my store.
The world no longer let me love,
My hope and treasure lies above.

[1867, 1972]

---

2. **all's vanity:** Worthless or futile; see Ecclesiastes 1:2: "Vanity of vanities, saith the Preacher, vanity of vanities; all *is* vanity."
3. **pelf:** Property that is gained in a dishonorable way.

Reading Bradstreet's "To My Dear Children."   Many of Bradstreet's best poems were deeply rooted in her experiences in New England. But she offered the fullest and most direct account of her life in the following memoir, written in the form of a letter to her children. Beginning with her own childhood, Bradstreet charted and meditated upon what she characterized as God's "dealings" with her. Writing in "sickness and weakness," she placed special emphasis on earlier periods of lingering illness, including a bout of smallpox when she was sixteen. For her, such afflictions represented God's effort to curb her vanity and humble her pride, sins that threatened her spiritual well-being. She thus exhorted her children, or perhaps simply reminded herself, "If at any time you are chastened of God, take it as thankfully and joyfully as in greatest mercies." Even as she described her spiritual doubts and struggles, Bradstreet thus reaffirmed the central tenet of Puritanism: God's absolute sway in human affairs. The letter survived in a manuscript copy in the handwriting of her son, the Reverend Simon Bradstreet, who noted that it was a "true copy of a Book left by my honored & dear mother to her children & found among some papers after her death." The text, which was first published in 1867, is taken from *The Works of Anne Bradstreet*, edited by Jeannine Hensley (1967).

TO MY DEAR CHILDREN

> This book by any yet unread,
> I leave for you when I am dead,
> That being gone, here you may find
> What was your living mother's mind.
> Make use of what I leave in love,
> And God shall bless you from above.
>
> A. B.[1]

My dear children,

I, knowing by experience that the exhortations of parents take most effect when the speakers leave to speak,[2] and those especially sink deepest which are spoke latest, and being ignorant whether on my death bed I shall have opportunity to speak to any of you, much less to all, thought it the best, whilst I was able, to compose some short matters (for what else to call them I know not) and bequeath to you, that when I am no more with you, yet I may be daily in your remembrance (although that is the least in my aim in what I now do), but that you may gain some spiritual advantage by my experience. I have not studied in this you read to show my skill, but to declare the truth, not to set forth myself, but the glory of God. If I had minded the former, it had been perhaps better pleasing to you, but seeing the last is the best, let it be best pleasing to you.

The method I will observe shall be this: I will begin with God's dealing with me from my childhood to this day.

In my young years, about 6 or 7 as I take it, I began to make conscience of my ways, and what I knew was sinful, as lying, disobedience to parents, etc., I avoided it. If at any time I was overtaken with the like evils, it was as a great trouble, and I could not be at rest 'till by prayer I had confessed it unto God. I was also troubled at the neglect of private duties though too often tardy that way. I also found much comfort in reading the

---

1. **This book . . . A. B.:** Bradstreet wrote her letter in a manuscript notebook she left for her children to read after her death.
2. **when the speakers leave to speak:** That is, when speakers stop speaking.

Scriptures, especially those places I thought most concerned my condition, and as I grew to have more understanding, so the more solace I took in them.

In a long fit of sickness which I had on my bed I often communed with my heart and made my supplication to the most High who set me free from that affliction.

But as I grew up to be about 14 or 15, I found my heart more carnal,[3] and sitting loose from God, vanity and the follies of youth take hold of me.

About 16, the Lord laid His hand sore upon me and smote me with the smallpox.[4] When I was in my affliction, I besought the Lord and confessed my pride and vanity, and He was entreated of me and again restored me. But I rendered not to Him according to the benefit received.

After a short time I changed my condition and was married, and came into this country, where I found a new world and new manners, at which my heart rose. But after I was convinced it was the way of God, I submitted to it and joined to the church at Boston.

After some time I fell into a lingering sickness like a consumption together with a lameness, which correction I saw the Lord sent to humble and try me and do me good, and it was not altogether ineffectual.

It pleased God to keep me a long time without a child, which was a great grief to me and cost me many prayers and tears before I obtained one, and after him gave me many more of whom I now take the care, that as I have brought you into the world, and with great pains, weakness, cares, and fears brought you to this, I now travail in birth[5] again of you till Christ be formed in you.

Among all my experiences of God's gracious dealings with me, I have constantly observed this, that He hath never suffered me long to sit loose from Him, but by one affliction or other hath made me look home, and search what was amiss; so usually thus it hath been with me that I have no sooner felt my heart out of order, but I have expected correction for it, which most commonly hath been upon my own person in sickness, weakness, pains, sometimes on my soul, in doubts and fears of God's displeasure and my sincerity towards Him; sometimes He hath smote a child with a sickness, sometimes chastened by losses in estate, and these times (through His great mercy) have been the times of my greatest getting and advantage; yea, I have found them the times when the Lord hath manifested the most love to me. Then have I gone to searching and have said with David, "Lord, search me and try me, see what ways of wickedness are in me, and lead me in the way everlasting,"[6] and seldom or never but I have found either some sin I lay under which God would have reformed, or some duty neglected which He would have

---

3. **my heart more carnal:** Occupied with material or nonspiritual matters.
4. **smallpox:** An acute, contagious, and often fatal disease characterized by the formation of deep pustules on the skin that usually leave permanent scars.
5. **travail in birth:** Do the work of childbirth.
6. **"Lord . . . everlasting":** Psalms 139:23-24.

performed, and by His help I have laid vows and bonds upon my soul to perform His righteous commands.

If at any time you are chastened of God, take it as thankfully and joyfully as in greatest mercies, for if ye be His, ye shall reap the greatest benefit by it. It hath been no small support to me in times of darkness when the Almighty hath hid His face from me that yet I have had abundance of sweetness and refreshment after affliction and more circumspection in my walking after I have been afflicted. I have been with God like an untoward child, that no longer than the rod has been on my back (or at least in sight) but I have been apt to forget Him and myself, too. Before I was afflicted, I went astray, but now I keep Thy statutes.[7]

I have had great experience of God's hearing my prayers and returning comfortable answers to me, either in granting the thing I prayed for, or else in satisfying my mind without it, and I have been confident it hath been from Him, because I have found my heart through His goodness enlarged in thankfulness to Him.

I have often been perplexed that I have not found that constant joy in my pilgrimage and refreshing which I supposed most of the servants of God have, although He hath not left me altogether without the witness of His holy spirit, who hath oft given me His word and set to His seal that it shall be well with me. I have sometimes tasted of that hidden manna that the world knows not, and have set up my Ebenezer, and have resolved with myself that against such a promise, such tastes of sweetness, the gates of hell shall never prevail;[8] yet have I many times sinkings and droopings, and not enjoyed that felicity that sometimes I have done. But when I have been in darkness and seen no light, yet have I desired to stay myself upon the Lord, and when I have been in sickness and pain, I have thought if the Lord would but lift up the light of His countenance upon me, although He ground me to powder, it would be but light to me;[9] yea, oft have I thought were I in hell itself and could there find the love of God toward me, it would be a heaven. And could I have been in heaven without the love of God, it would have been a hell to me, for in truth it is the absence and presence of God that makes heaven or hell.

Many times hath Satan troubled me concerning the verity of the Scriptures, many times by atheism how I could know whether there was a God; I never saw any miracles to

---

7. **I . . . statutes:** Cf. Psalms 119:8: "I will keep thy statutes: O forsake me not utterly."

8. **I have sometimes tasted . . . prevail:** Bradstreet blends references to three biblical passages: "To him that overcometh will I give to eat of the hidden manna" (Revelations 2:17); the Old Testament passage in which Samuel erects a stone and names it Ebenezer ("Stone of Help") to commemorate God's aid in the Israelites' victory over the Philistines (1 Samuel 7:12); and Christ's words to his disciple Peter, "And I say also unto thee, That thou art Peter, and upon this rock I will build my church; and the gates of hell shall not prevail against it" (Matthew 16:18).

9. **I have thought . . . light to me:** Bradstreet refers and alludes to several biblical passages: "LORD, lift thou up the light of thy countenance upon us" (Psalms 4:6); "And whosoever shall fall [that is, stumble] on this stone shall be broken: but on whomsoever it shall fall, it will grind him to powder" (Matthew 21:44); and perhaps Christ's words to the people in the temple, "I am the light of the world: he that follows me shall not walk in darkness, but shall have the light of life" (John 8:12).

confirm me, and those which I read of, how did I know but they were feigned? That there is a God my reason would soon tell me by the wondrous works that I see, the vast frame of the heaven and the earth, the order of all things, night and day, summer and winter, spring and autumn, the daily providing for this great household upon the earth, the preserving and directing of all to its proper end. The consideration of these things would with amazement certainly resolve me that there is an Eternal Being. But how should I know He is such a God as I worship in Trinity, and such a Saviour as I rely upon? Though this hath thousands of times been suggested to me, yet God hath helped me over. I have argued thus with myself. That there is a God, I see. If ever this God hath revealed himself, it must be in His word, and this must be it or none. Have I not found that operation by it that no human invention can work upon the soul, hath not judgments befallen divers who have scorned and contemned it, hath it not been preserved through all ages maugre[10] all the heathen tyrants and all of the enemies who have opposed it? Is there any story but that which shows the beginnings of times, and how the world came to be as we see? Do we not know the prophecies in it fulfilled which could not have been so long foretold by any but God Himself?

When I have got over this block, then have I another put in my way, that admit this be the true God whom we worship, and that be his word, yet why may not the Popish religion[11] be the right? They have the same God, the same Christ, the same word. They only enterpret it one way, we another.

This hath sometimes stuck with me, and more it would, but the vain fooleries that are in their religion together with their lying miracles and cruel persecutions of the saints, which admit were they as they term them, yet not so to be dealt withal.

The consideration of these things and many the like would soon turn me to my own religion again.

But some new troubles I have had since the world has been filled with blasphemy and sectaries,[12] and some who have been accounted sincere Christians have been carried away with them, that sometimes I have said, "Is there faith upon the earth?" and I have not known what to think; but then I have remembered the works of Christ that so it must be, and if it were possible, the very elect should be deceived. "Behold," saith our Saviour, "I have told you before."[13] That hath stayed my heart, and I can now say, "Return, O my Soul, to thy rest, upon this rock Christ Jesus will I build my faith, and if I perish, I perish";[14] but I know all the Powers of Hell shall never prevail against it. I know whom I

---

10. **maugre:** An early term meaning "in spite of."
11. **Popish religion:** Roman Catholicism.
12. **sectaries:** Heretics or those who belong to a narrow religious group or sect.
13. **"Behold . . . before":** A reference to one of Christ's several warnings against false prophets (Matthew 24:25–26).
14. **"Return . . . I perish":** Bradstreet blends references to three biblical passages: "Return, O my Soul, to thy rest" (Psalms 16:17); "That thou art Peter, and upon this rock I will build my church" (Matthew 16:18); and Esther's words before risking her life by approaching the king of Persia without being summoned, "I also and my maidens will fast likewise; and so will I go in to the king, which is not according to the law: and if I perish, I perish" (Esther 4:16).

have trusted, and whom I have believed, and that He is able to keep that I have committed to His charge.

Now to the King, immortal, eternal and invisible, the only wise God, be honour, and glory for ever and ever, Amen.[15]

This was written in much sickness and weakness, and is very weakly and imperfectly done, but if you can pick any benefit out of it, it is the mark which I aimed at.

[?, 1967]

---

15. **Now to the King ... Amen:** See Philippians 4:20.

Bradstreet through a Modern Lens

ANNE BRADSTREET'S POETRY has been read and admired for three and a half centuries. The seventeenth-century poets Nathaniel Ward, John Rogers, and John Norton all wrote poems in tribute to Bradstreet. Rogers probably compiled the second edition of her work, *Select Poems* (1676), published six years after her death and later reprinted in 1758. Nineteenth-century readers were also familiar with Bradstreet. In his introduction to *The Works of Anne Bradstreet* (1867), John

Anne Bradstreet

Relatively few portraits of women were painted in the colonies during the seventeenth century, and no likeness of Bradstreet was made during her lifetime. Here, she is imagined by the contemporary artist Ladonna Gulley Warwick in her painting *Anne Bradstreet, The Tenth Muse Lately Sprung Up in America*. Warwick and her grandson, whose likeness appears in the lower right-hand corner of the painting, are descendants of Bradstreet's sister, Mercy.

Harvard Ellis described her poems as "quaint and curious," adding that "they constitute a singular and valuable relic of the earliest literature of the country." Twentieth-century admirers have discovered a far wider range of value and resonance in Bradstreet's life and writings. In the most sustained poetic tribute, *Homage to Mistress Bradstreet* (1948), John Berryman imagined her life as a series of rebellions, initially against the grim conditions in the New World and finally against illness, personal loss, and the onset of old age. Feminist critics have discovered in Bradstreet's poetry a different pattern of resistance, one aligned against the patriarchal structures of Puritan society. Certainly, her work has assumed a central place in the tradition of women's literature, in which Bradstreet is sometimes compared to Emily Dickinson, another poet determined to make time for her work amidst the demands of everyday life. In the following poem, written when she was a college student, Rose Murray imagines the conditions of that life and suggests what writing poetry may have meant to Bradstreet. The text of the poem is taken from the online anthology *The Best Fiction and Poetry from California State University, Northridge*, where Murray published under the name Rose Shade.

Rose Murray

PURITAN WOMAN

I am obnoxious to each carping tongue
Who says my hand a needle better fits.[1]
Anne Bradstreet

There in Massachusetts
We built our "city upon a hill"[2]

---

1. **I am ... fits:** The epigraph is from stanza five of Bradstreet's "The Prologue," reprinted on page 153.
2. **"city ... hill":** Along with her parents and her husband, Bradstreet sailed to New England in 1630 aboard the *Arabella*, the flagship of the Puritan migration led by John Winthrop. Either on the eve of its departure from England or during the voyage, Winthrop delivered his address "A Modell of Christian Charity," reprinted on page 138. In it, Winthrop famously declares that the Puritan settlement would "be as a Citty upon a hill," a reference to Matthew 5:14: "'Ye are the light of the world. A city that is set on an hill cannot be hid.'"

For all the world to see
And find example in –
But that first winter   5
There was just the land,
Lying before us
Like a vast unfinished garment –
And my cold hands holding needle
Were only female   10
And busy with the work of babes.
The men would slash and shape the earth,
And style to God's design
The stuff of law and state;
I had small garments of my own   15
To fashion. So in the chill
Of winter nights by candle –
When the children were in bed –
Why did my hand, shaped only
For the shaft of spinning wheel   20
Or bar of cradle,
Dare to grasp a pen?
Perhaps it was the bare house,
The wolf's howl, the Indians,
The memory of those months of shifting sea[3] –   25
And Simon gone away for days;[4]
Perhaps the words, dancing into shape
In neat and airy couplets,[5]
Imposed design on savage vastness
And hemmed up the ragged edge of newness   30
With thread from across the seas.
So between the cradle
And the oven, with fresh brown
Bread baking and infants babbling,
I wrote, and Simon understood.   35

[1971]

---

3. **months of shifting sea:** The stormy voyage of the *Arabella* lasted two and a half months.
4. **Simon gone away for days:** Bradstreet's husband, Simon, was frequently away from home on public business.
5. **couplets:** Many of Bradstreet's poems were written in couplets, units of two rhymed lines of verse.

Mary Rowlandson

[1636?–1711]

Mary Rowlandson was born about 1636 in England, the fifth child of John and Joan White, devout Puritans who moved their family to Massachusetts in 1639. Granted a sixty-acre tract of land near Salem, John White steadily increased his holdings there before seeking additional land by moving his family to Lancaster, about thirty miles west of Boston. In 1656, Mary married the town's minister, Joseph Rowlandson, with whom she had four children, one of whom died in infancy.

Mary Rowlandson would have died in the almost total obscurity reserved for most women of her time had it not been for King Philip's War, the most traumatic event in her life and in the early life of the English colonies in New England. In *Of Plimoth Plantation*, William Bradford describes the peace treaty entered into between the Pilgrims and Massasoit, the great leader of the Wampanoag people. That treaty lasted for more than fifty years, but relations between the Indians and the colonists became increasingly strained. Even as the Indian population declined, primarily as a result of European diseases, immigration to New England steadily increased until 1649, when the triumph of parliamentary forces in the English civil war led to the establishment of a Puritan commonwealth in England. After the collapse of the commonwealth and the restoration of Charles II to the throne in 1660, however, Anglicanism once again became the official Church of England. As a result, large numbers of Puritans were once again prompted to leave the country to seek greater religious freedom and economic opportunity in New England. During the decade 1660–70, the combined population of Plymouth and the Massachusetts Bay Colony rose from roughly 20,000 to 35,000, and it continued to increase dramatically. Colonial authorities consequently sought to assert greater authority over the Indians, pressuring them to cede increasingly large tracts of land. In a desperate effort to stem the rising tide of English expansion, Massasoit's son, Metacomet – called King Philip by the colonists – finally led a coalition of tribes to war in 1675. The year-long war was fought with unprecedented ferocity on both sides. About 5,000 Indians and as many as half that number of English colonists were killed during the bitter conflict. In terms of the number of casualties relative to the total populations of the combatants, it was the bloodiest war in American history, claiming the lives of roughly 40 percent of the Indians and more than 5 percent of the colonists.

Many of the colonists were killed during raids on frontier towns in Massachusetts, as Metacomet sought to reverse the westward advance of the English. In February 1676, a combined force of Narragansett, Nipmuc, and Wampanoag attacked Lancaster, where Mary Rowlandson and her three children were taken captive. Her youngest child soon died, and she was separated from her other children during most of the three months she lived among her captors. She was finally ransomed and reunited with her husband and children in Boston, from where the family moved to

Weathersfield, Connecticut, in 1677. Rowlandson apparently wrote the account of her captivity before her husband died in 1678, but it was not published until 1682. By then, she had married Captain Samuel Talcott of Weathersfield, where Rowlandson lived until her death in 1711, thirty-five years after the events recorded in *The Sovereignty and Goodness of God.*

Reading Rowlandson's *The Sovereignty and Goodness of God.* No copy of the first edition of Rowlandson's narrative has survived, but three additional editions were published in 1682, two of them in Boston and another in London. As the title page of the "corrected and amended" second edition indicates, the full title of the narrative was *The Sovereignty & Goodness of God, Together, with the Faithfulness of His Promises Displayed; Being a Narrative of the Captivity and Restoration of Mrs. Mary Rowlandson.* (The London edition, designed to appeal to a more diverse and cosmopolitan

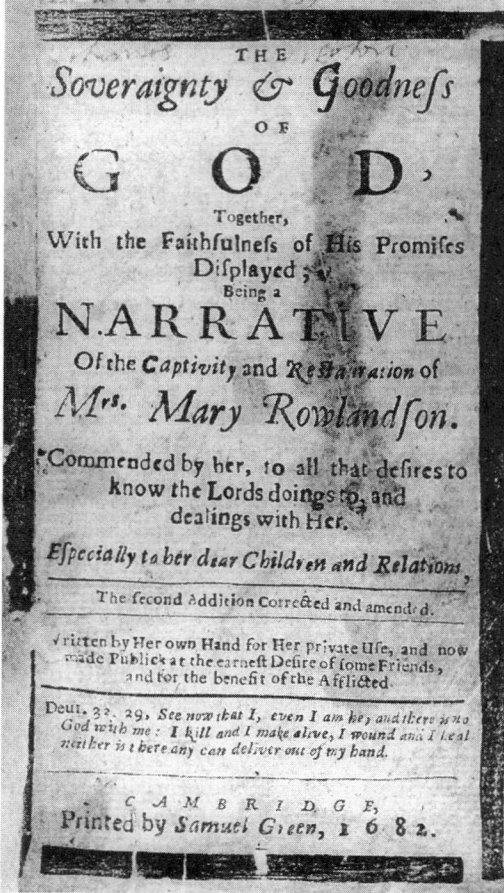

Frontispiece of the Second Edition of *The Sovereignty and Goodness of God* (1682)

audience, was simply entitled *A True History of the Captivity and Restoration of Mary Rowlandson, A Minister's Wife in New England.*) With the sole exception of Anne Bradstreet's *The Tenth Muse*, which was published in London eighteen years before a second edition of her poetry appeared in Boston in 1678, Rowlandson's account was one of the first books written by a woman to be published in the English colonies in North America. In an effort to justify what many in New England might have viewed as her immodest usurpation of male prerogative, a note on the title page explains that Rowlandson wrote the account for her "private Use," allowing it to be "made public at the earnest Desire of some Friends, and for the Benefit of the afflicted." Moreover, all of the 1682 editions included an anonymous preface, probably written by the distinguished Puritan minister Increase Mather, which also emphasizes that friends had pressed Rowlandson to allow the work to come into "public view," since it was unfitting that "such works of God should be hid from present and future generations."

Certainly, the narrative proved to have a powerful appeal for both Rowlandson's contemporaries and later generations of readers. The 1682 editions published in Boston sold more than a thousand copies, or roughly one for every hundred people in the New England colonies, where it was both widely read and frequently read aloud. Indeed, as one of the first and most compelling of the so-called captivity narratives, *The Sovereignty and Goodness of God* was the most popular book published in North America in the seventeenth century. Since those first editions of the book, more than forty others have been published, usually as either *A True History of the Captivity and Restoration of Mrs. Mary Rowlandson* or *A Narrative of the Captivity and Restoration of Mrs. Mary Rowlandson.* Although its popularity has waned during the last few decades, Rowlandson's account has become the subject of serious scholarly study. It also continues to engage the attention of readers drawn to the text for other reasons. For example, a new edition recently published as *The Captive* offers Rowlandson's story as an example of faith and endurance "to Christians of the present age." The text printed below is taken from *Narratives of the Indian Wars*, edited by Charles H. Lincoln (1913), which follows the text of the second edition published in 1682.

bedfordstmartins.com/ americanlit for research links on Rowlandson

From THE SOVEREIGNTY AND GOODNESS OF GOD

On the tenth of February 1675, Came the Indians with great numbers upon Lancaster:[1] Their first coming was about Sun-rising; hearing the noise of some Guns, we looked out; several Houses were burning, and the Smoke ascending to Heaven. There were five persons taken in one house, the Father, and the Mother and a sucking Child, they knockt on the head; the other two they took and carried away alive. There were two others, who

---

1. **On the tenth of February . . . Lancaster:** February 20, 1676; Lancaster, Massachusetts, was then an isolated frontier settlement about thirty miles west of Boston.

being out of their Garison[2] upon some occasion were set upon; one was knockt on the head, the other escaped: Another there was who running along was shot and wounded, and fell down; he begged of them his life, promising them Money (as they told me) but they would not hearken to him but knockt him in head, and stript him naked, and split open his Bowels. Another seeing many of the Indians about his Barn, ventured and went out, but was quickly shot down. There were three others belonging to the same Garison who were killed; the Indians getting up upon the roof of the Barn, had advantage to shoot down upon them over their Fortification. Thus these murtherous wretches went on, burning, and destroying before them.

At length they came and beset our own house, and quickly it was the dolefullest day that ever mine eyes saw. The House stood upon the edge of a hill; some of the Indians got behind the hill, others into the Barn, and others behind any thing that could shelter them; from all which places they shot against the House, so that the Bullets seemed to fly like hail; and quickly they wounded one man among us, then another, and then a third, About two hours (according to my observation, in that amazing time) they had been about the house before they prevailed to fire it (which they did with Flax and Hemp, which they brought out of the Barn, and there being no defence about the House, only two Flankers[3] at two opposite corners and one of them not finished) they fired it once and one ventured out and quenched it, but they quickly fired it again, and that took. Now is the dreadfull hour come, that I have often heard of (in time of War, as it was the case of others) but now mine eyes see it. Some in our house were fighting for their lives, others wallowing in their blood, the House on fire over our heads, and the bloody Heathen ready to knock us on the head, if we stirred out. Now might we hear Mothers and Children crying out for themselves, and one another, Lord, What shall we do? Then I took my Children (and one of my sisters, hers) to go forth and leave the house: but as soon as we came to the dore and appeared, the Indians shot so thick that the bulletts rattled against the House, as if one had taken an handfull of stones and threw them, so that we were fain to give back. We had six stout Dogs belonging to our Garrison, but none of them would stir, though another time, if any Indian had come to the door, they were ready to fly upon him and tear him down. The Lord hereby would make us the more to acknowledge his hand, and to see that our help is always in him. But out we must go, the fire increasing, and coming along behind us, roaring, and the Indians gaping before us with their Guns, Spears and Hatchets to devour us. No sooner were we out of the House, but my Brother in Law (being before wounded, in defending the house, in or near the throat) fell down dead, wherat the Indians scornfully shouted, and hallowed, and were presently upon him, stripping off his cloaths, the bulletts flying thick, one went through my side, and the same (as would seem) through the bowels and hand of my dear Child in my arms. One of my elder Sisters Children, named William, had then his Leg broken, which the Indians perceiving, they knockt him on head. Thus were we butchered by those merciless Heathen, standing amazed, with the blood running down to our heels. My eldest Sister being yet in the House, and seeing those wofull sights, the

---

2. **Garison:** Building erected for the defense of the settlement, usually spelled "garrison."
3. **Flankers:** Projecting fortifications designed to guard a position.

Infidels hauling Mothers one way, and Children another, and some wallowing in their blood: and her elder Son telling her that her Son William was dead, and my self was wounded, she said, And, Lord, let me dy with them; which was no sooner said, but she was struck with a Bullet, and fell down dead over the threshold. I hope she is reaping the fruit of her good labours, being faithfull to the service of God in her place. In her younger years she lay under much trouble upon spiritual accounts, till it pleased God to make that precious Scripture take hold of her heart, 2 Corinthians 12. 9. *And he said unto me, my Grace is sufficient for thee.* More then twenty years after I have heard her tell how sweet and comfortable that place was to her. But to return: The Indians laid hold of us, pulling me one way, and the Children another, and said, Come go along with us; I told them they would kill me: they answered, If I were willing to go along with them, they would not hurt me.

Oh the dolefull sight that now was to behold at this House! *Come, behold the works of the Lord, what dissolations he has made in the Earth.*[4] Of thirty seven persons who were in this one House, none escaped either present death, or a bitter captivity, save only one, who might say as he, Job 1. 15, *And I only am escaped alone to tell the News.* There were twelve killed, some shot, some stab'd with their Spears, some knock'd down with their Hatchets. When we are in prosperity, Oh the little that we think of such dreadfull sights, and to see our dear Friends, and Relations ly bleeding out their heart-blood upon the ground. There was one who was chopt into the head with a Hatchet, and stript naked, and yet was crawling up and down. It is a solemn sight to see so many Christians lying in their blood, some here, and some there, like a company of Sheep torn by Wolves, All of them stript naked by a company of hell-hounds, roaring, singing, ranting and insulting, as if they would have torn our very hearts out; yet the Lord by his Almighty power preserved a number of us from death, for there were twenty-four of us taken alive and carried Captive.

I had often before this said, that if the Indians should come, I should chuse rather to be killed by them then taken alive but when it came to the tryal my mind changed; their glittering weapons so daunted my spirit, that I chose rather to go along with those (as I may say) ravenous Beasts, then that moment to end my dayes; and that I may the better declare what happened to me during that grievous Captivity, I shall particularly speak of the severall Removes[5] we had up and down the Wilderness.

The first Remove

Now away we must go with those Barbarous Creatures, with our bodies wounded and bleeding, and our hearts no less than our bodies. About a mile we went that night, up upon a hill within sight of the Town, where they intended to lodge. There was hard by a vacant house (deserted by the English before, for fear of the Indians). I asked them whither I might not lodge in the house that night to which they answered, what will you love English men still? this was the dolefullest night that ever my eyes saw. Oh the

---

4. *Come, behold . . . in the Earth:* Psalms 46:8.
5. **Removes:** Changes in location.

roaring, and singing and danceing, and yelling of those black creatures in the night, which made the place a lively resemblance of hell. And as miserable was the wast that was there made, of Horses, Cattle, Sheep, Swine, Calves, Lambs, Roasting Pigs, and Fowl (which they had plundered in the Town) some roasting, some lying and burning, and some boyling to feed our merciless Enemies; who were joyful enough though we were disconsolate. To add to the dolefulness of the former day, and the dismalness of the present night: my thoughts ran upon my losses and sad bereaved condition. All was gone, my Husband gone (at least separated from me, he being in the Bay; and to add to my grief, the Indians told me they would kill him as he came homeward) my Children gone, my Relations and Friends gone, our House and home and all our comforts within door, and without, all was gone, (except my life) and I knew not but the next moment that might go too. There remained nothing to me but one poor wounded Babe, and it seemed at present worse than death that it was in such a pitiful condition, bespeaking Compassion, and I had no refreshing for it, nor suitable things to revive it. Little do many think what is the savageness and bruitishness of this barbarous Enemy, I[6] even those that seem to profess more than others among them, when the English have fallen into their hands.

Those seven that were killed at Lancaster the summer before upon a Sabbath day, and the one that was afterward killed upon a week day, were slain and mangled in a barbarous manner, by one-ey'd John, and Marlborough's Praying Indians,[7] which Capt. Mosely brought to Boston, as the Indians told me.

The second Remove

But now, the next morning, I must turn my back upon the Town, and travel with them into the vast and desolate Wilderness, I knew not whither. It is not my tongue, or pen can express the sorrows of my heart, and bitterness of my spirit, that I had at this departure: but God was with me, in a wonderfull manner, carrying me along, and bearing up my spirit, that it did not quite fail. One of the Indians carried my poor wounded Babe upon a horse, it went moaning all along, I shall dy, I shall dy. I went on foot after it, with sorrow that cannot be exprest. At length I took it off the horse, and carried it in my armes till my strength failed, and I fell down with it: Then they set me upon a horse with my wounded Child in my lap, and there being no furniture upon the horse back, as we were going down a steep hill, we both fell over the horses head, at which they like inhumane creatures laught, and rejoyced to see it, though I thought we should there have ended our dayes, as overcome with so many difficulties. But the Lord renewed my strength still, and carried me along, that I might see more of his Power; yea, so much that I could never have thought of, had I not experienced it.

After this it quickly began to snow, and when night came on, they stopt: and now down I must sit in the snow, by a little fire, and a few boughs behind me, with my sick

---

6. I: Early form of *ay* or *aye*, meaning yes.
7. **Marlborough's Praying Indians:** A group of Christianized Indians who lived in a settlement in Marlborough, Massachusetts, was accused of involvement in the attack on Lancaster, but the charges were disproved in court.

Child in my lap; and calling much for water, being now (through the wound) fallen into a violent Fever. My own wound also growing so stiff, that I could scarce sit down or rise up; yet so it must be, that I must sit all this cold winter night upon the cold snowy ground, with my sick Child in my armes, looking that every hour would be the last of its life; and having no Christian friend near me, either to comfort or help me. Oh, I may see the wonderfull power of God, that my Spirit did not utterly sink under my affliction: still the Lord upheld me with his gracious and mercifull Spirit, and we were both alive to see the light of the next morning.

The third Remove

The morning being come, they prepared to go on their way. One of the Indians got up upon a horse, and they set me up behind him, with my poor sick Babe in my lap. A very wearisome and tedious day I had of it; what with my own wound, and my Childs being so exceeding sick, and in a lamentable condition with her wound. It may be easily judged what a poor feeble condition we were in, there being not the least crumb of refreshing that came within either of our mouths, from Wednesday night to Saturday night, except only a little cold water. This day in the afternoon, about an hour by Sun, we came to the place where they intended, *viz.*[8] an Indian Town, called Wenimesset, Norward of Quabaug. When we were come, Oh the number of Pagans (now merciless enemies) that there came about me, that I may say as David, Psalms 27. 13, *I had fainted, unless I had believed,* etc. The next day was the Sabbath: I then remembered how careless I had been of Gods holy time, how many Sabbaths I had lost and mispent, and how evily I had walked in Gods sight; which lay so close unto my spirit, that it was easie for me to see how righteous it was with God to cut off the thread of my life, and cast me out of his presence for ever. Yet the Lord still shewed mercy to me, and upheld me; and as he wounded me with one hand, so he healed me with the other. This day there came to me one Robbert Pepper (a man belonging to Roxbury) who was taken in Captain Beers his Fight,[9] and had been now a considerable time with the Indians; and up with them almost as far as Albany, to see king Philip, as he told me, and was now very lately come into these parts. Hearing, I say, that I was in this Indian Town, he obtained leave to come and see me. He told me, he himself was wounded in the leg at Captain Beers his Fight; and was not able some time to go, but as they carried him, and as he took Oaken leaves and laid to his wound, and through the blessing of God he was able to travel again. Then I took Oaken leaves and laid to my side, and with the blessing of God it cured me also; yet before the cure was wrought, I may say, as it is in Psalms 38. 5, 6. *My wounds stink and are corrupt, I am troubled, I am bowed down greatly, I go mourning all the day long.* I sat much alone with a poor wounded Child in my lap, which moaned night and day, having nothing to revive the body, or cheer the spirits of her, but in stead of that, sometimes one Indian would come and tell me one hour, that your Master will knock your Child in

---

8. *viz.:* In other words (abbreviation of the Latin *videlicet*).
9. **taken in Captain Beers his Fight:** Captain Beers was killed, along with most of his men, at a battle in Northfield, Massachusetts, in September 1675. Those who were not killed were held in captivity.

the head, and then a second, and then a third, your Master will quickly knock your Child in the head.

This was the comfort I had from them, miserable comforters are ye all, as he said.[10] Thus nine dayes I sat upon my knees, with my Babe in my lap, till my flesh was raw again; my Child being even ready to depart this sorrowfull world, they bade me carry it out to another Wigwam (I suppose because they would not be troubled with such spectacles) Whither I went with a very heavy heart, and down I sat with the picture of death in my lap. About two houres in the night, my sweet Babe like a Lambe departed this life, on Feb. 18, 1675. It being about six yeares, and five months old. It was nine dayes from the first wounding, in this miserable condition, without any refreshing of one nature or other, except a little cold water. I cannot, but take notice, how at another time I could not bear to be in the room where any dead person was, but now the case is changed; I must and could ly down by my dead Babe, side by side all the night after. I have thought since of the wonderfull goodness of God to me, in preserving me in the use of my reason and senses, in that distressed time, that I did not use wicked and violent means to end my own miserable life. In the morning, when they understood that my child was dead they sent for me home to my Masters Wigwam: (by my Master in this writing, must be understood Quanopin, who was a Saggamore, and married King Phillips wives Sister;[11] not that he first took me, but I was sold to him by another Narrhaganset Indian, who took me when first I came out of the Garison). I went to take up my dead child in my arms to carry it with me, but they bid me let it alone: there was no resisting, but goe I must and leave it. When I had been at my masters wigwam, I took the first opportunity I could get, to go look after my dead child: when I came I askt them what they had done with it? then they told me it was upon the hill: then they went and shewed me where it was, where I saw the ground was newly digged, and there they told me they had buried it: There I left that Child in the Wilderness, and must commit it, and my self also in this Wilderness-condition, to him who is above all. God having taken away this dear Child, I went to see my daughter Mary, who was at this same Indian Town, at a Wigwam not very far off, though we had little liberty or opportunity to see one another. She was about ten years old, and taken from the door at first by a Praying Ind and afterward sold for a gun. When I came in sight, she would fall a weeping; at which they were provoked, and would not let me come near her, but bade me be gone; which was a heart-cutting word to me. I had one Child dead, another in the Wilderness, I knew not where, the third they would not let me come near to: *Me* (as he said) *have ye bereaved of my Children, Joseph is not, and Simeon is not, and ye will take Benjamin also, all these things are against me.*[12] I could not sit still in this condition, but kept walking from one place to another. And as I was going along, my heart was even overwhelm'd with the

---

10. miserable comforters . . . he said: Job 16:2.

11. Quanopin . . . married King Phillips wives Sister: Rowlandson became the servant of Quinnapin's wife Weetamoo, the older daughter of Corbitant, the sachem, or chief, of the Pocasset. Trained to succeed her father as sachem, Weetamoo was an accomplished hunter and a skilled diplomat who first married the sachem of the Wampanoag and, after he died, later married Quinnapin, the sachem of the Narragansett.

12. *Me . . . against me*: Jacobs's lamentation for his children is in Genesis 42:16.

thoughts of my condition, and that I should have Children, and a Nation which I knew not ruled over them. Whereupon I earnestly entreated the Lord, that he would consider my low estate, and shew me a token for good, and if it were his blessed will, some sign and hope of some relief. And indeed quickly the Lord answered, in some measure, my poor prayers: for as I was going up and down mourning and lamenting my condition, my Son came to me, and asked me how I did; I had not seen him before, since the destruction of the Town, and I knew not where he was, till I was informed by himself, that he was amongst a smaller percel of Indians, whose place was about six miles off; with tears in his eyes, he asked me whether his Sister Sarah was dead; and told me he had seen his Sister Mary; and prayed me, that I would not be troubled in reference to himself. The occasion of his coming to see me at this time, was this: There was, as I said, about six miles from us, a smal Plantation of Indians, where it seems he had been during his Captivity: and at this time, there were some Forces of the Indians gathered out of our company, and some also from them (among whom was my Sons master) to go to assault and burn Medfield: In this time of the absence of his master, his dame brought him to see me. I took this to be some gracious answer to my earnest and unfeigned desire. The next day, *viz.* to this, the Indians returned from Medfield,[13] all the company, for those that belonged to the other small company, came thorough the Town that now we were at. But before they came to us, Oh! the outragious roaring and hooping that there was: They began their din about a mile before they came to us. By their noise and hooping they signified how many they had destroyed (which was at that time twenty three.) Those that were with us at home, were gathered together as soon as they heard the hooping, and every time that the other went over their number, these at home gave a shout, that the very Earth rung again: And thus they continued till those that had been upon the expedition were come up to the Sagamores Wigwam; and then, Oh, the hideous insulting and triumphing that there was over some Englishmens scalps that they had taken (as their manner is) and brought with them. I cannot but take notice of the wonderfull mercy of God to me in those afflictions, in sending me a Bible. One of the Indians that came from Medfield fight, had brought some plunder, came to me, and asked me, if I would have a Bible, he had got one in his Basket. I was glad of it, and asked him, whether he thought the Indians would let me read? he answered, yes: So I took the Bible, and in that melancholy time, it came into my mind to read first the 28. Chap. of Deuteronomy, which I did, and when I had read it, my dark heart wrought on this manner, That there was no mercy for me, that the blessings were gone, and the curses come in their room, and that I had lost my opportunity. But the Lord helped me still to go on reading till I came to Chap. 30 the seven first verses, where I found, There was mercy promised again, if we would return to him by repentance; and though we were scatered from one end of the Earth to the other, yet the Lord would gather us together, and turn all those curses upon our Enemies. I do not desire to live to forget this Scripture, and what comfort it was to me.

---

13. **Medfield:** The attack on Medfield, where fifty houses were burned, took place on February 21, 1675 (March 3, 1676), eleven days after the attack on Lancaster.

Now the Indians began to talk of removing from this place, some one way, and some another. There were now besides my self nine English Captives in this place (all of them Children, except one Woman). I got an opportunity to go and take my leave of them; they being to go one way, and I another, I asked them whether they were earnest with God for deliverance, they told me, they did as they were able, and it was some comfort to me, that the Lord stirred up Children to look to him. The Woman *viz.* Goodwife Joslin told me, she should never see me again, and that she could find in her heart to run away; I wisht her not to run away by any means, for we were near thirty miles from any English Town, and she very big with Child, and had but one week to reckon; and another Child in her Arms, two years old, and bad Rivers there were to go over, and we were feeble, with our poor and course entertainment. I had my Bible with me, I pulled it out, and asked her whether she would read; we opened the Bible and lighted on Psalms 27, in which Psalm we especially took notice of that, *ver. ult.,*[14] *Wait on the Lord, Be of good courage, and he shall strengthen thine Heart, wait I say on the Lord.*

The fourth Remove

And now I must part with that little Company I had. Here I parted from my Daughter Mary, (whom I never saw again till I saw her in Dorchester, returned from Captivity), and from four little Cousins and Neighbours, some of which I never saw afterward: the Lord only knows the end of them. Amongst them also was that poor Woman before mentioned, who came to a sad end, as some of the company told me in my travel: She having much grief upon her Spirit, about her miserable condition, being so near her time, she would be often asking the Indians to let her go home; they not being willing to that, and yet vexed with her importunity, gathered a great company together about her, and stript her naked, and set her in the midst of them; and when they had sung and danced about her (in their hellish manner) as long as they pleased, they knockt her on head, and the child in her arms with her: when they had done that, they made a fire and put them both into it, and told the other Children that were with them, that if they attempted to go home, they would serve them in like manner: The Children said, she did not shed one tear, but prayed all the while. But to return to my own Journey; we travelled about half a day or little more, and came to a desolate place in the Wilderness, where there were no Wigwams or Inhabitants before; we came about the middle of the afternoon to this place, cold and wet, and snowy, and hungry, and weary, and no refreshing, for man, but the cold ground to sit on, and our poor Indian cheer.

Heart-aking thoughts here I had about my poor Children, who were scattered up and down among the wild beasts of the forrest: My head was light and dissey (either through hunger or hard lodging, or trouble or altogether) my knees feeble, my body raw by sitting double night and day, that I cannot express to man the affliction that lay upon my Spirit, but the Lord helped me at that time to express it to himself. I opened my Bible to read,

---

14. *ver. ult.*: Abbreviation for "last verse" (Latin), that is, Psalms 27:14.

and the Lord brought that precious Scripture to me, Jeremiah 31. 16. *Thus saith the Lord, refrain thy voice from weeping, and thine eyes from tears, for thy work shall be rewarded, and they shall come again from the land of the Enemy.* This was a sweet Cordial to me, when I was ready to faint, many and many a time have I sat down, and weept sweetly over this Scripture. At this place we continued about four dayes.

The twelfth Remove

It was upon a Sabbath-day-morning, that they prepared for their Travel. This morning I asked my master whither he would sell me to my Husband; he answered me *Nux*,[15] which did much rejoyce my spirit. My mistriss, before we went, was gone to the burial of a Papoos, and returning, she found me sitting and reading in my Bible; she snatched it hastily out of my hand, and threw it out of doors; I ran out and catcht it up, and put it into my pocket, and never let her see it afterward. Then they packed up their things to be gone, and gave me my load: I complained it was too heavy, whereupon she gave me a slap in the face, and bade me go; I lifted up my heart to God, hoping the Redemption was not far off: and the rather because their insolency grew worse and worse.

But the thoughts of my going homeward (for so we bent our course) much cheared my Spirit, and made my burden seem light, and almost nothing at all. But (to my amazment and great perplexity) the scale was soon turned: for when we had gone a little way, on a sudden my mistriss gives out, she would go no further, but turn back again, and said, I must go back again with her, and she called her *Sannup*, and would have had him gone back also, but he would not, but said, He would go on, and come to us again in three dayes. My Spirit was upon this, I confess, very impatient, and almost outragious. I thought I could as well have dyed as went back: I cannot declare the trouble that I was in about it; but yet back again I must go. As soon as I had an opportunity, I took my Bible to read, and that quieting Scripture came to my hand, Psalms 46. 10. *Be still, and know that I am God.* Which stilled my spirit for the present: But a sore time of tryal, I concluded, I had to go through, My master being gone, who seemed to me the best friend that I had of an Indian, both in cold and hunger, and quickly so it proved. Down I sat, with my heart as full as it could hold, and yet so hungry that I could not sit neither: but going out to see what I could find, and walking among the Trees, I found six Acorns, and two Ches-nuts, which were some refreshment to me. Towards Night I gathered me some sticks for my own comfort, that I might not ly a-cold: but when we came to ly down they bade me go out, and ly some-where-else, for they had company (they said) come in more than their own: I told them, I could not tell where to go, they bade me go look; I told them, if I went to another Wigwam they would be angry, and send me home again. Then one of the Company drew his sword, and told me he would run me thorough if I did not go presently. Then was I fain to stoop to this rude fellow, and to go out in the night, I knew not whither. Mine eyes have seen that fellow afterwards walking up and down

---

15. *Nux*: Yes.

Boston, under the appearance of a Friend-Indian, and severall others of the like Cut. I went to one Wigwam, and they told me they had no room. Then I went to another, and they said the same; at last an old Indian bade me come to him, and his Squaw gave me some Ground-nuts; she gave me also something to lay under my head, and a good fire we had: and through the good providence of God, I had a comfortable lodging that night. In the morning, another Indian bade me come at night, and he would give me six Ground-nuts, which I did. We were at this place and time about two miles from Connecticut River. We went in the morning to gather Ground-nuts, to the River, and went back again that night. I went with a good load at my back (for they when they went, though but a little way, would carry all their trumpery with them) I told them the skin was off my back, but I had no other comforting answer from them than this, That it would be no matter if my head were off too.

The twentieth Remove

It was their usual manner to remove, when they had done any mischief, lest they should be found out: and so they did at this time. We went about three or four miles, and there they built a great Wigwam, big enough to hold an hundred Indians, which they did in preparation to a great day of Dancing. They would say now amongst themselves, that the Governour would be so angry for his loss at Sudbury, that he would send no more about the Captives, which made me grieve and tremble. My Sister being not far from the place where we now were, and hearing that I was here, desired her master to let her come and see me, and he was willing to it, and would go with her: but she being ready before him, told him she would go before, and was come within a Mile or two of the place; Then he overtook her, and began to rant as if he had been mad; and made her go back again in the Rain; so that I never saw her till I saw her in Charlestown. But the Lord requited many of their ill doings, for this Indian her Master, was hanged afterward at Boston. The Indians now began to come from all quarters, against their merry dancing day. Among some of them came one Goodwife Kettle: I told her my heart was so heavy that it was ready to break: so is mine too said she, but yet said, I hope we shall hear some good news shortly. I could hear how earnestly my Sister desired to see me, and I as earnestly desired to see her: and yet neither of us could get an opportunity. My Daughter was also now about a mile off, and I had not seen her in nine or ten weeks, as I had not seen my Sister since our first taking. I earnestly desired them to let me go and see them: yea, I intreated, begged, and perswaded them, but to let me see my Daughter; and yet so hard hearted were they, that they would not suffer it. They made use of their tyrannical power whilst they had it: but through the Lords wonderfull mercy, their time was now but short.

On a Sabbath day, the Sun being about an hour high in the afternoon, came Mr. John Hoar[16] (the Council permitting him, and his own foreward spirit inclining him) together with the two forementioned Indians, Tom and Peter, with their third Letter from the

---

16. **Mr. John Hoar:** John Hoar (c. 1616–1704), a lawyer from Concord, Massachusetts, represented Rowlandson's husband at the council of the Sagamore Indians.

Council. When they came near, I was abroad: though I saw them not, they presently called me in, and bade me sit down and not stir. Then they catched up their Guns, and away they ran, as if an Enemy had been at hand; and the Guns went off apace. I manifested some great trouble, and they asked me what was the matter? I told them, I thought they had killed the English-man (for they had in the mean time informed me that an English-man was come) they said, No; They shot over his Horse and under, and before his Horse; and they pusht him this way and that way, at their pleasure: shewing what they could do: Then they let them come to their Wigwams. I begged of them to let me see the English-man, but they would not. But there was I fain to sit their pleasure. When they had talked their fill with him, they suffered me to go to him. We asked each other of our welfare, and how my Husband did, and all my Friends? He told me they were all well, and would be glad to see me. Amongst other things which my Husband sent me, there came a pound of Tobacco: which I sold for nine shillings in Money: for many of the Indians for want of Tobacco, smoaked Hemlock, and Ground-Ivy. It was a great mistake in any, who thought I sent for Tobacco: for through the favour of God, that desire was overcome. I now asked them, whither I should go home with Mr. Hoar? They answered No, one and another of them: and it being night, we lay down with that answer; in the morning, Mr Hoar invited the Saggamores to Dinner; but when we went to get it ready, we found that they had stollen the greatest part of the Provision Mr. Hoar had brought, out of his Bags, in the night. And we may see the wonderfull power of God, in that one passage, in that when there was such a great number of the Indians together, and so greedy of a little good food; and no English there, but Mr. Hoar and my self: that there they did not knock us in the head, and take what we had: there being not only some Provision, but also Tradingcloth, a part of the twenty pounds agreed upon: But instead of doing us any mischief, they seemed to be ashamed of the fact, and said, it were some Matchit Indian[17] that did it. Oh, that we could believe that there is no thing too hard for God! God shewed his Power over the Heathen in this, as he did over the hungry Lyons when Daniel was cast into the Den.[18] Mr. Hoar called them betime to Dinner, but they ate very little, they being so busie in dressing themselves, and getting ready for their Dance: which was carried on by eight of them, four Men and four Squaws: My master and mistress being two. He was dressed in his Holland shirt, with great Laces sewed at the tail of it, he had his silver Buttons, his white Stockins, his Garters were hung round with Shillings, and he had Girdles of Wampom upon his head and shoulders. She had a Kersey Coat,[19] and covered with Girdles of Wampom from the Loins upward: her armes from her elbows to her hands were covered with Bracelets; there were handfulls of Necklaces about her neck, and severall sorts of Jewels in her ears. She had fine red Stokins, and white Shoos, her hair powdered and face painted Red, that was alwayes before Black. And all the Dancers were after the same manner. There were two other

---

17. **Matchit Indian:** That is, a bad Indian.
18. **when Daniel was cast into the Den:** God sent an angel to deliver the prophet Daniel from harm when he was cast into the lion's den (Daniel 6:1–29).
19. **Kersey Coat:** A coat of coarse, ribbed wool.

singing and knocking on a Kettle for their musick. They keept hopping up and down one after another, with a Kettle of water in the midst, standing warm upon some Embers, to drink of when they were dry. They held on till it was almost night, throwing out Wampom to the standers by. At night I asked them again, if I should go home? They all as one said No, except my Husband would come for me. When we were lain down, my Master went out of the Wigwam, and by and by sent in an Indian called James the Printer, who told Mr. Hoar, that my Master would let me go home to morrow, if he would let him have one pint of Liquors. Then Mr. Hoar called his own Indians, Tom and Peter, and bid them go and see whither he would promise it before them three: and if he would, he should have it; which he did, and he had it. Then Philip smeling the business cal'd me to him, and asked me what I would give him, to tell me some good news, and speak a good word for me. I told him, I could not tell what to give him, I would any thing I had, and asked him what he would have? He said, two Coats and twenty shillings in Mony, and half a bushel of seed Corn, and some Tobacco. I thanked him for his love: but I knew the good news as well as the crafty Fox. My Master after he had had his drink, quickly came ranting into the Wigwam again, and called for Mr. Hoar, drinking to him, and saying, He was a good man: and then again he would say, Hang him Rogue: Being almost drunk, he would drink to him, and yet presently say he should be hanged. Then he called for me. I trembled to hear him, yet I was fain to go to him, and he drank to me, shewing no incivility. He was the first Indian I saw drunk all the while that I was amongst them. At last his Squaw ran out, and he after her, round the Wigwam, with his mony jingling at his knees: But she escaped him: But having an old Squaw he ran to her: and so through the Lords mercy, we were no more troubled that night. Yet I had not a comfortable nights rest: for I think I can say, I did not sleep for three nights together. The night before the Letter came from the Council, I could not rest, I was so full of feares and troubles, God many times leaving us most in the dark, when deliverance is nearest: yea, at this time I could not rest night nor day. The next night I was overjoyed, Mr. Hoar being come, and that with such good tidings. The third night I was even swallowed up with the thoughts of things, *viz.* that ever I should go home again; and that I must go, leaving my Children behind me in the Wilderness; so that sleep was now almost departed from mine eyes.

On Tuesday morning they called their General Court (as they call it) to consult and determine, whether I should go home or no: And they all as one man did seemingly consent to it, that I should go home; except Philip, who would not come among them.

But before I go any further, I would take leave to mention a few remarkable passages of providence, which I took special notice of in my afflicted time.

1. Of the fair opportunity lost in the long March, a little after the Fort-fight, when our English Army was so numerous, and in pursuit of the Enemy, and so near as to take several and destroy them: and the Enemy in such distress for food, that our men might track them by their rooting in the earth for Ground-nuts, whilest they were flying for their lives. I say, that then our Army should want Provision, and be forced to leave their pursuit and return homeward: and the very next week the Enemy came upon our Town, like Bears bereft of their whelps, or so many ravenous Wolves, rending us and our Lambs to death. But what shall I say? God seemed to leave his People to themselves, and order all things for his own holy ends. *Shal there be evil in the City and the Lord hath*

not done it? They are not grieved for the affliction of Joseph, therefore shal they go Captive, with the first that go Captive.[20] It is the Lords doing, and it should be marvelous in our eyes.

2. I cannot but remember how the Indians derided the slowness, and dulness of the English Army, in its setting out. For after the desolations at Lancaster and Medfield, as I went along with them, they asked me when I thought the English Army would come after them? I told them I could not tell: It may be they will come in May, said they. Thus did they scoffe at us, as if the English would be a quarter of a year getting ready.

3. Which also I have hinted before, when the English Army with new supplies were sent forth to pursue after the enemy, and they understanding it, fled before them till they came to Baquaug River, where they forthwith went over safely: that that River should be impassable to the English. I can but admire to see the wonderfull providence of God in preserving the heathen for farther affliction to our poor Countrey. They could go in great numbers over, but the English must stop: God had an over-ruling hand in all those things.

4. It was thought, if their Corn were cut down, they would starve and dy with hunger: and all their Corn that could be found, was destroyed, and they driven from that little they had in store, into the Woods in the midst of Winter; and yet how to admiration did the Lord preserve them for his holy ends, and the destruction of many still amongst the English! strangely did the Lord provide for them; that I did not see (all the time I was among them) one Man, Woman, or Child, die with hunger.

Though many times they would eat that, that a Hog or a Dog would hardly touch; yet by that God strengthned them to be a scourge to his People.

The chief and commonest food was Ground-nuts: They eat also Nuts and Acorns, Harty-choaks,[21] Lilly roots, Ground-beans, and several other weeds and roots, that I know not.

They would pick up old bones, and cut them to pieces at the joynts, and if they were full of wormes and magots, they would scald them over the fire to make the vermine come out, and then boile them, and drink up the Liquor, and then beat the great ends of them in a Morter, and so eat them. They would eat Horses guts, and ears, and all sorts of wild Birds which they could catch: also Bear, Vennison, Beaver, Tortois, Frogs, Squirrels, Dogs, Skunks, Rattle-snakes; yea, the very Bark of Trees; besides all sorts of creatures, and provision which they plundered from the English. I can but stand in admiration to see the wonderful power of God, in providing for such a vast number of our Enemies in the Wilderness, where there was nothing to be seen, but from hand to mouth. Many times in a morning, the generality of them would eat up all they had, and yet have some forther supply against they wanted. It is said, Psalms 81. 13, 14. *Oh, that my People had hearkned to me, and Israel had walked in my wayes, I should soon have subdued their Enemies, and turned my hand against their Adversaries.* But now our perverse and evil

---

20. **Shal there be evil . . . Captive**: Amos 3:6 and 6:6–7.
21. **Harty-choaks**: Artichokes.

carriages in the sight of the Lord, have so offended him, that instead of turning his hand against them, the Lord feeds and nourishes them up to be a scourge to the whole Land.

5. Another thing that I would observe is, the strange providence of God, in turning things about when the Indians was at the highest, and the English at the lowest. I was with the Enemy eleven weeks and five dayes, and not one Week passed without the fury of the Enemy, and some desolation by fire and sword upon one place or other. They mourned (with their black faces) for their own lossess, yet triumphed and rejoyced in their inhumane, and many times devilish cruelty to the English. They would boast much of their Victories; saying, that in two hours time they had destroyed such a Captain, and his Company at such a place; and such a Captain and his Company in such a place; and such a Captain and his Company in such a place: and boast how many Towns they had destroyed, and then scoffe, and say, They had done them a good turn, to send them to Heaven so soon. Again, they would say, This Summer that they would knock all the Rogues in the head, or drive them into the Sea, or make them flie the Countrey: thinking surely, Agag-like, *The bitterness of Death is past.*[22] Now the Heathen begins to think all is their own, and the poor Christians hopes to fail (as to man) and now their eyes are more to God, and their hearts sigh heaven-ward: and to say in good earnest, *Help Lord, or we perish:* When the Lord had brought his people to this, that they saw no help in any thing but himself: then he takes the quarrel into his own hand: and though they had made a pit, in their own imaginations, as deep as hell for the Christians that Summer, yet the Lord hurll'd them selves into it. And the Lord had not so many wayes before to preserve them, but now he hath as many to destroy them.

But to return again to my going home, where we may see a remarkable change of Providence: At first they were all against it, except my Husband would come for me; but afterwards they assented to it, and seemed much to rejoyce in it; some askt me to send them some Bread, others some Tobacco, others shaking me by the hand, offering me a Hood and Scarfe to ride in; not one moving hand or tongue against it. Thus hath the Lord answered my poor desire, and the many earnest requests of others put up unto God for me. In my travels an Indian came to me, and told me, if I were willing, he and his Squaw would run away, and go home along with me: I told him No: I was not willing to run away, but desired to wait Gods time, that I might go home quietly, and without fear. And now God hath granted me my desire. O the wonderfull power of God that I have seen, and the experience that I have had: I have been in the midst of those roaring Lyons, and Salvage Bears, that feared neither God, nor Man, nor the Devil, by night and day, alone and in company: sleeping all sorts together, and yet not one of them ever offered me the least abuse of unchastity to me, in word or action. Though some are ready to say, I speak it for my own credit; But I speak it in the presence of God, and to his Glory. Gods Power is as great now, and as sufficient to save, as when he preserved Daniel in the Lions Den; or the three Children in the fiery Furnace.[23] I may well say as his Psalms 107. 12, *Oh give thanks*

---

22. ***The bitterness of Death is past***: 1 Samuel 15:32. Agag, the king of Amalek, was defeated by Saul and later slain by Samuel.

23. **the three Children in the fiery Furnace**: Daniel's friends Shadrach, Meshach, and Abednego, who were cast into a fiery furnace for refusing to worship false gods, were delivered from death by God (Daniel 3:13–30).

unto the Lord for he is good, for his mercy endureth for ever. Let the Redeemed of the Lord say so, whom he hath redeemed from the hand of the Enemy, especially that I should come away in the midst of so many hundreds of Enemies quietly and peacably, and not a Dog moving his tongue. So I took my leave of them, and in coming along my heart melted into tears, more then all the while I was with them, and I was almost swallowed up with the thoughts that ever I should go home again. About the Sun going down, Mr. Hoar, and my self, and the two Indians came to Lancaster, and a solemn sight it was to me. There had I lived many comfortable years amongst my Relations and Neighbours, and now not one Christian to be seen, nor one house left standing. We went on to a Farm house that was yet standing, where we lay all night: and a comfortable lodging we had, though nothing but straw to ly on. The Lord preserved us in safety that night, and raised us up again in the morning, and carried us along, that before noon, we came to Concord. Now was I full of joy, and yet not without sorrow: joy to see such a lovely sight, so many Christians together, and some of them my Neighbors: There I met with my Brother, and my Brother in Law, who asked me, if I knew where his Wife was? Poor heart! he had helped to bury her, and knew it not; she being shot down by the house was partly burnt: so that those who were at Boston at the desolation of the Town, and came back afterward, and buried the dead, did not know her. Yet I was not without sorrow, to think how many were looking and longing, and my own Children amongst the rest, to enjoy that deliverance that I had now received, and I did not know whither ever I should see them again. Being recruited with food and raiment[24] we went to Boston that day, where I met with my dear Husband, but the thoughts of our dear Children, one being dead, and the other we could not tell where, abated our comfort each to other. I was not before so much hem'd in with the merciless and cruel Heathen, but now as much with pittiful, tender-hearted and compassionate Christians. In that poor, and destressed, and beggerly condition I was received in, I was kindly entertained in severall Houses: so much love I received from several (some of whom I knew, and others I knew not) that I am not capable to declare it. But the Lord knows them all by name: The Lord reward them seven fold into their bosoms of his spirituals, for their temporals.[25] The twenty pounds the price of my redemption was raised by some Boston Gentlemen, and Mrs. Usher, whose bounty and religious charity, I would not forget to make mention of. Then Mr. Thomas Shepard of Charlstown received us into his House, where we continued eleven weeks; and a Father and Mother they were to us. And many more tender-hearted Friends we met with in that place. We were now in the midst of love, yet not without much and frequent heaviness of heart for our poor Children, and other Relations, who were still in affliction. The week following, after my coming in, the Governour and Council sent forth to the Indians again; and that not without success; for they brought in my Sister, and Good-wife Kettle: Their not knowing where our Children were, was a sore tryal to us still, and yet we were not without secret hopes that we should see them again. That which was dead lay heavier upon my spirit, than those which were alive and amongst the Heathen; thinking how it suffered with its wounds, and I was no

---

24. **recruited with food and raiment:** That is, refreshed with food and clothing.
25. **temporals:** Worldly possessions.

way able to relieve it; and how it was buried by the Heathen in the Wilderness from among all Christians. We were hurried up and down in our thoughts, sometime we should hear a report that they were gone this way, and sometimes that; and that they were come in, in this place or that: We kept enquiring and listning to hear concerning them, but no certain news as yet. About this time the Council had ordered a day of publick Thanks-giving: though I thought I had still cause of mourning, and being unsettled in our minds, we thought we would ride toward the Eastward, to see if we could hear any thing concerning our Children. And as we were riding along (God is the wise disposer of all things) between Ipswich and Rowly we met with Mr. William Hubbard, who told us that our Son Joseph was come in to Major Waldrens, and another with him, which was my Sisters Son. I asked him how he knew it? He said, the Major himself told him so. So along we went till we came to Newbury; and their Minister being absent, they desired my Husband to Preach the Thanks giving for them; but he was not willing to stay there that night, but would go over to Salisbury, to hear further, and come again in the morning; which he did, and Preached there that day. At night, when he had done, one came and told him that his Daughter was come in at Providence: Here was mercy on both hands: Now hath God fulfiled that precious Scripture which was such a comfort to me in my distressed condition. When my heart was ready to sink into the Earth (my Children being gone I could not tell whither) and my knees trembled under me, And I was walking through the valley of the shadow of Death: Then the Lord brought, and now has fulfilled that reviving word unto me: *Thus saith the Lord, Refrain thy voice from weeping, and thine eyes from tears, for thy Work shall be rewarded, saith the Lord, and they shall come again from the Land of the Enemy.*[26] Now we were between them, the one on the East, and the other on the West: Our Son being nearest, we went to him first, to Portsmouth, where we met with him, and with the Major also: who told us he had done what he could, but could not redeem him under seven pounds; which the good People thereabouts were pleased to pay. The Lord reward the Major, and all the rest, though unknown to me, for their labour of Love. My Sisters Son was redeemed for four pounds, which the Council gave order for the payment of. Having now received one of our Children, we hastened toward the other; going back through Newbury, my Husband preached there on the Sabbath-day: for which they rewarded him many fold.

On Munday we came to Charlstown, where we heard that the Governour of Road-Island had sent over for our Daughter, to take care of her, being now within his Jurisdiction: which should not pass without our acknowledgments. But she being nearer Rehoboth than Road-Island, Mr. Newman went over, and took care of her, and brought her to his own House. And the goodness of God was admirable to us in our low estate, in that he raised up passionate[27] Friends on every side to us, when we had nothing to recompance any for their love. The Indians were now gone that way, that it was apprehended dangerous to go to her: But the Carts which carried Provision to the English Army, being guarded, brought her with them to Dorchester, where we received

---

26. *Thus . . . the Land of the Enemy:* Jeremiah 31:16.
27. **passionate:** Compassionate.

her safe: blessed be the Lord for it, For great is his Power, and he can do whatsoever see-meth him good. Her coming in was after this manner: She was travelling one day with the Indians, with her basket at her back; the company of Indians were got before her, and gone out of sight, all except one Squaw; she followed the Squaw till night, and then both of them lay down, having nothing over them but the heavens, and under them but the earth. Thus she travelled three dayes together, not knowing whither she was going: having nothing to eat or drink but water, and green Hirtle-berries. At last they came into Providence, where she was kindly entertained by several of that Town. The Indians often said, that I should never have her under twenty pounds: But now the Lord hath brought her in upon free-cost, and given her to me the second time. The Lord make us a blessing indeed, each to others. Now have I seen that Scripture also fulfilled, Deuteronomy 30: 4, 7. *If any of thine be driven out to the outmost parts of heaven, from thence will the Lord thy God gather thee, and from thence will he fetch thee. And the Lord thy God will put all these curses upon thine enemies, and on them which hate thee, which persecuted thee.* Thus hath the Lord brought me and mine out of that horrible pit, and hath set us in the midst of tender-hearted and compassionate Christians. It is the desire of my soul, that we may walk worthy of the mercies received, and which we are receiving.

Our Family being now gathered together (those of us that were living) the South Church in Boston hired an House for us: Then we removed from Mr. Shepards, those cordial Friends, and went to Boston, where we continued about three quarters of a year: Still the Lord went along with us, and provided graciously for us. I thought it somewhat strange to set up House-keeping with bare walls; but as Solomon sayes, *Money answers all things;*[28] and that we had through the benevolence of Christian-friends, some in this Town, and some in that, and others: And some from England, that in a little time we might look, and see the House furnished with love. The Lord hath been exceeding good to us in our low estate, in that when we had neither house nor home, nor other necessar-ies; the Lord so moved the hearts of these and those towards us, that we wanted neither food, nor raiment for our selves or ours, Proverbs 18. 24. *There is a Friend which sticketh closer than a Brother.* And how many such Friends have we found, and now living amongst? And truly such a Friend have we found him to be unto us, in whose house we lived, *viz.* Mr. James Whitcomb, a Friend unto us near hand, and afar off.

I can remember the time, when I used to sleep quietly without workings in my thoughts, whole nights together, but now it is other wayes with me. When all are fast about me, and no eye open, but his who ever waketh, my thoughts are upon things past, upon the awfull dispensation of the Lord towards us; upon his wonderfull power and might, in carrying of us through so many difficulties, in returning us in safety, and suffering none to hurt us. I remember in the night season, how the other day I was in the midst of thousands of enemies, and nothing but death before me: It is then hard work to per-swade my self, that ever I should be satisfied with bread again. But now we are fed with the finest of the Wheat, and, as I may say, With honey out of the rock: In stead of the

---

28. *Money answers all things*:   Ecclesiastes 10:19.

Husk, we have the fatted Calf: The thoughts of these things in the particulars of them, and of the love and goodness of God towards us, make it true of me, what David said of himself, Psalms 6. 6. *I watered my Couch with my tears.* Oh! the wonderfull power of God that mine eyes have seen, affording matter enough for my thoughts to run in, that when others are sleeping mine eyes are weeping.

I have seen the extreme vanity of this World: One hour I have been in health, and wealth, wanting nothing: But the next hour in sickness and wounds, and death, having nothing but sorrow and affliction.

Before I knew what affliction meant, I was ready sometimes to wish for it. When I lived in prosperity, having the comforts of the World about me, my relations by me, my Heart chearfull, and taking little care for any thing; and yet seeing many, whom I preferred before my self, under many tryals and afflictions, in sickness, weakness, poverty, losses, crosses, and cares of the World, I should be sometimes jealous least I should have my portion in this life, and that Scripture would come to my mind, Hebrews 12. 6. *For whom the Lord loveth he chasteneth and scourgeth every Son whom he receiveth.* But now I see the Lord had his time to scourge and chasten me. The portion of some is to have their afflictions by drops, now one drop and then another; but the dregs of the Cup, the Wine of astonishment, like a sweeping rain that leaveth no food, did the Lord prepare to be my portion. Affliction I wanted, and affliction I had, full measure (I thought) pressed down and running over; yet I see, when God calls a Person to any thing, and through never so many difficulties, yet he is fully able to carry them through and make them see, and say they have been gainers thereby. And I hope I can say in some measure, as David did, *It is good for me that I have been afflicted.* The Lord hath shewed me the vanity of these outward things. That they are the Vanity of vanities, and vexation of spirit; that they are but a shadow, a blast, a bubble, and things of no continuance. That we must rely on God himself, and our whole dependance must be upon him. If trouble from smaller matters begin to arise in me, I have something at hand to check my self with, and say, why am I troubled? It was but the other day that if I had had the world, I would have given it for my freedom, or to have been a Servant to a Christian. I have learned to look beyond present and smaller troubles, and to be quieted under them, as Moses said, Exodus 14. 13. *Stand still and see the salvation of the Lord.*

[1682, 1913]

American Contexts

THE SALEM WITCHCRAFT TRIALS

THE FOLLOWING SELECTIONS from writings by Deodat Lawson, Cotton Mather, Thomas Brattle, and Samuel Sewall illuminate the most notorious episode in the history of colonial New England, the witchcraft trials that took place in Salem Village, now Danvers, Massachusetts. To understand what happened in that small community north of Boston, it is important to recall that at the time of the trials in 1692 a belief in both witches and the religious necessity of punishing them was universal throughout Europe and England, as well as in New England. Certainly, the Puritans firmly believed not only in the active presence of the devil, but also that he recruited women and men to work for him. In Hartford, Connecticut, a woman had been executed for witchcraft in 1648 and a married couple in 1651, while in Boston a woman had been hanged for witchcraft in 1656.

But those isolated episodes hardly prefigured the witchcraft hysteria of the early 1690s, a tumultuous period in the Massachusetts Bay Colony. In the aftermath of the devastation caused by King Philip's War, sporadic Indian attacks on frontier settlements continued to generate tension and anxiety. The nature of the Massachusetts Bay Colony was also changing, especially after the new colonial charter of 1691 gave freedom to all religions, opening the door to an influx of Quakers and Anglicans. These new arrivals posed a significant challenge to the very foundation of Puritan society, which was further shaken by changing social and economic conditions in New England. Class divisions were intensified by the emergence of a new mercantile class, and some scholars also argue that the turmoil in Salem was in part a reflection of concerns about the growing economic and social power of women. More than three-quarters of those accused of witchcraft were women, and of those most were over forty years of age, many of them affluent widows whose independence may well have been deemed a threat to the traditional social order.

All of those factors probably contributed to the outpouring of accusations, which began in the home of Samuel Parris, the new minister of

Incidents of Witchcraft

These illustrations appeared in one of the numerous editions of Joseph Glanvill's *Saducismus Triumphatus; or, Full and Plain Evidence Concerning Witches and Apparitions*, first published in London in 1681. Fearing that the loss of belief in ghosts, spirits, and witches would ultimately lead to the loss of belief in Christianity, Glanvill recounted "true" incidents of witchcraft and other supernatural activity in his popular book, which strongly influenced colonial ministers such as Increase and Cotton Mather.

Salem Village, in late January 1692. During the long winter evenings, nine-year-old Betty Parris, her eleven-year-old cousin, Abigail Williams, and several of their friends read popular books about fortune-telling and may have been entertained by stories told by John Indian and his wife, Tituba, slaves Parris had brought with him from his plantation in Barbados. What happened next is not entirely clear, but Betty and Abigail, soon followed by five of their friends, began to exhibit strange symptoms and bizarre behavior, and a doctor declared that the afflicted girls were victims of witchcraft. On February 29th, a group of parents filed complaints of witchcraft against Tituba and two other women, Sarah Good and Sarah Osborne. At the examination conducted by the Salem magistrates, the girls told of being attacked by specters in the shapes of the accused. Tituba was pressured to confess, and the girls soon claimed that spectral forms of other women were tormenting them. After a visit to Salem Village in late March and early April, its former minister, Deodat Lawson, published *A Brief and True Narrative* (1692), a lurid account of events that convinced many that Satan and his minions were raging in Salem.

In late May the colonial governor, William Phips, appointed a special Court of Oyer and Terminer, literally a court to "hear and determine" the allegations of witchcraft in Salem Village. The nine judges included the

Cotton Mather, *The Wonders of the Invisible World*

In his famous, or infamous, book, Mather offered a detailed justification of the witchcraft trials and subsequent executions in Salem.

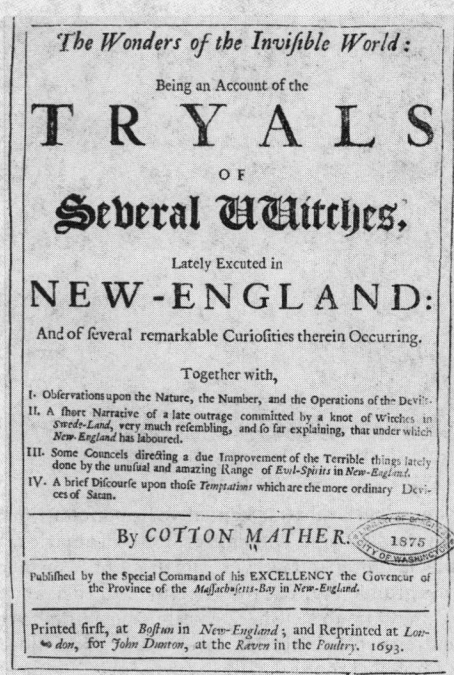

The Wonders of the Invisible World:

Being an Account of the

TRYALS

OF

Several Witches,

Lately Executed in

NEW-ENGLAND:

And of several remarkable Curiosities therein Occurring.

Together with,

I. Observations upon the Nature, the Number, and the Operations of the Devils.

II. A short Narrative of a late outrage committed by a knot of Witches in *Swede-Land*, very much resembling, and so far explaining, that under which *New-England* has laboured.

III. Some Councels directing a due Improvement of the Terrible things lately done by the unusual and amazing Range of *Evil-Spirits* in *New-England*.

IV. A brief Discourse upon those *Temptations* which are the more ordinary Devices of Satan.

By COTTON MATHER.

Published by the Special Command of his EXCELLENCY the Governour of the Province of the *Massachusetts-Bay* in *New-England*.

Printed first, at *Boston* in *New-England*; and Reprinted at *London*, for *John Dunton*, at the *Raven* in the *Poultry*. 1693.

conservative Lieutenant Governor William Stoughton, who was determined to eradicate witchcraft; John Hathorne, the great-great grandfather
of Nathaniel Hawthorne; and the prominent Boston merchant Samuel
Sewall, whose diary offers glimpses into the events in Salem Village.
Although ministers such as Cotton Mather cautioned against too great a
reliance on the kind of spectral evidence offered by the afflicted girls, the
court convicted people primarily on the basis of such testimony. The first
execution took place on June 19th, and by the end of September, nineteen
men and women had been hanged on Gallows Hill, a man had been pressed

Trial of George Jacobs Sr., August 5, 1692

The memory of the Salem trials was kept alive by popular works such as this painting, created in
1855 by Thomkins H. Matteson. The figures in the dramatic tableaux include two of Jacobs's principal accusers: his daughter-in-law, who was thought to be mentally unstable and is being
restrained; and his granddaughter, the kneeling figure near the center of the picture, who apparently testified against him to save her own life. She points to the elderly Jacobs, whose arms are
raised in supplication, while in the left foreground a boy and a girl are having "fits," or nervous
convulsions, presumably brought on by Jacobs's invisible spectral presence. Jacobs was convicted
and hanged two weeks later, on August 19, 1692.

to death for refusing to enter a plea, and nearly 200 people were in prison and awaiting trial for witchcraft. Of all of the executions, the most troubling to many was the hanging of a former minister of the village, the Reverend George Burroughs, who was convicted of being the ringleader of the "witches" in Salem. His final speech, in which he steadfastly declared his innocence, was so moving that Cotton Mather felt obliged to reassure the assembled crowd that Burroughs had been fairly convicted and "that Satan's power shall this day receive its death-blow in New England." Mather also stoutly defended the trials in his famous account *The Wonders of the Invisible World*, which was rushed into print in October 1692.

But by then the tide had begun to turn. As the witchcraft hysteria spread, more and more prominent people were accused, and many religious and secular leaders concluded that matters were out of control. In early October the prominent minister Increase Mather (Cotton Mather's father) circulated the manuscript of a book in which he cast strong doubt on the validity of spectral evidence; and in a letter circulated in manuscript at about the same time the liberal merchant Thomas Brattle offered a vigorous critique of every aspect of the proceedings of the Court of Oyer and Terminer, which Governor Phips dissolved on October 29, 1692. He turned the cases over to a Superior Court, which excluded spectral evidence, and the last witch trial was held the following January. Governor Phips ended the proceedings entirely and pardoned five condemned "witches" as well as all of the remaining accused in May 1693. In 1697 the colony observed a day of atonement for the trials, which were the last of such trials in New England.

In contrast, trials and executions for witchcraft continued throughout the eighteenth century in Europe. Despite the relatively limited scope of the proceedings in Salem, the trials deeply colored later views of Puritanism. At the conclusion of his October 1692 letter, Thomas Brattle declared: "I am afraid that ages will not wear off that reproach and those stains which these things leave behind them upon our land." So it proved. Indeed, the witchcraft trials assumed a prominent place in New England history and North American mythology, especially through innumerable nineteenth-century graphic works, paintings, and publications exploring the colonial origins of the United States. The episode has also lived on in the nation's literary imagination, perhaps most famously in works such as Nathaniel Hawthorne's short stories and Arthur Miller's *The Crucible* (1953), which is still among the most frequently performed plays in the United States.

Deodat Lawson

[?-1715?]

> Few facts are known about Deodat Lawson, a Puritan minister whose name first appears in New England historical documents in 1676. Lawson served as a minister in Salem Village from 1685 to 1688 and then lived in Boston. He was succeeded by Samuel Parris, whose daughter Betty fell ill in January and became one of several young women who were regarded as "afflicted," that is, as victims of witchcraft. At Parris's invitation, Lawson returned to Salem Village on March 19, 1692, to observe the situation for himself and to preach a sermon, "Christ's Fidelity the Only Shield against Satan's Malignity." He soon wrote *A Brief and True Narrative of Some Remarkable Passages Relating to Sundry Persons Afflicted by Witchcraft, at Salem Village Which Happened from the Nineteenth of March, to the Fifth of April, 1692.* Lawson's narrative, published as a ten-page pamphlet in Boston, provides a firsthand account of many of the initial accusations that led to the arrests, trials, and convictions of 1692. His detailed account is often credited with helping to persuade the general public that witchcraft was indeed responsible for the disturbances in Salem Village. We have silently expanded abbreviations and corrected the spelling of proper names in the following selections from the *Narrative*, the text of which is taken from *Narratives of the Witchcraft Cases, 1648–1706*, edited by George Lincoln Burr (1914).

From A Brief and True Narrative

The Bookseller to the Reader.[1]

The Ensuing Narrative, being a Collection of some Remarkables, in an Affair now upon the Stage, made by a Credible Eye-witness, is now offered unto the Reader, only as a Tast, of more that may follow in Gods Time. If the Prayers of Good People may obtain this Favour of God, That the Misterious Assaults from Hell now made upon so many of our Friends may be thoroughly Detected and Defeated, we suppose the Curious will be Entertained with as rare an History as perhaps an Age has had; whereof this Narrative is but a Forerunner.

Benjamin Harris.

On the Nineteenth day of March last I went to Salem Village,[2] and lodged at Nathaniel Ingersols near to the Minister Mr. Parris's house, and presently after I came into my Lodging Captain Walcotts Daughter Mary came to Lieutenant Ingersolls and spake to

---

1. **The Bookseller to the Reader:** This brief introduction was written by the well-known editor and publisher Benjamin Harris (1673–1716).
2. **Salem Village:** The village was a township with its own meeting house and minister, separate from the larger town of Salem, the earliest settlement of the Massachusetts Bay Colony.

me, but, suddenly after as she stood by the door, was bitten, so that she cried out of her Wrist, and looking on it with a Candle, we saw apparently the marks of Teeth both upper and lower set, on each side of her wrist.

In the beginning of the Evening, I went to give Mr. Parris a visit. When I was there, his Kins-woman, Abigail Williams, (about 12 years of age,) had a grievous fit; she was at first hurryed with Violence to and fro in the room, (though Mrs. Ingersoll endeavoured to hold her,) sometimes makeing as if she would fly, stretching up her arms as high as she could, and crying "Whish, Whish, Whish!" several times; Presently after she said there was Goodwife Nurse[3] and said, "Do you not see her? Why there she stands!" And the said Goodwife Nurse offered her The Book,[4] but she was resolved she would not take it, saying Often, "I wont, I wont, I wont, take it, I do not know what Book it is: I am sure it is none of Gods Book, it is the Divels Book, for ought I know." After that, she run to the Fire, and begun to throw Fire Brands, about the house; and run against the Back, as if she would run up Chimney, and, as they said, she had attempted to go into the Fire in other Fits.

On Lords Day, the Twentieth of March, there were sundry of the afflicted Persons at Meeting, as, Mrs. Pope, and Goodwife Bibber, Abigail Williams, Mary Walcott, Mary Lewes, and Docter Griggs' Maid.[5] There was also at Meeting, Goodwife Corey[6] (who was after-ward Examined on suspicion of being a Witch:) They had several Sore Fits, in the time of Publick Worship, which did something interrupt me in my First Prayer; being so unusual. After Psalm was Sung, Abigail Williams said to me, "Now stand up, and Name your Text": And after it was read, she said, "It is a long Text." In the beginning of Sermon, Mrs. Pope, a Woman afflicted, said to me, "Now there is enough of that." And in the afternoon, Abigail Williams upon my referring to my Doctrine said to me, "I know no Doctrine you had, If you did name one, I have forgot it."[7]

In Sermon time when Goodwife Corey was present in the Meetinghouse Abigail Williams called out, "Look where Goodwife Corey sits on the Beam suckling her Yellow bird betwixt her fingers"! Anne Putnam another Girle afflicted said there was a Yellow-bird sat on my hat as it hung on the Pin in the Pulpit: but those that were by, restrained her from speaking loud about it.

On Monday the 21st of March, The Magistrates of Salem appointed to come to Examination of Goodwife Corey. And about twelve of the Clock, they went into the Meeting-House, which was Thronged with Spectators: Mr. Noyes[8] began with a very pertinent and pathetic Prayer; and Goodwife Corey being called to answer to what was

---

3. **Goodwife Nurse:** Rebecca Towne Nurse, an elderly and respected member of the community, was accused by several young girls of witchcraft and formally tried on June 29, 1692. She was convicted and hanged on July 19.

4. **The Book:** A book in which witches were believed to sign agreements or covenants with the Devil.

5. **Doctor Griggs' Maid:** Dr. William Griggs, who served as the village physician, was probably the first to pronounce the young women "bewitched."

6. **Goodwife Corey:** Martha Corey was later convicted of witchcraft and hanged on September 22, 1692. Her husband, Giles, was pressed to death by large rocks in a failed effort to force him to enter a plea, which was required by law in order to try him for witchcraft.

7. **"I . . . forgot it":** Lawson offers Williams's inattention to the sermon as an example of the effect of witchcraft on the young women.

8. **Mr. Noyes:** Reverend Nicholas Noyes of the neighboring town of Salem served as the official minister at the trials and later at the hangings of the convicted.

Alledged against her, she desired to go to Prayer, which was much wondred at, in the presence of so many hundred people: The Magistrates told her, they would not admit it; they came not there to hear her Pray, but to Examine her, in what was Alledged against her. The Worshipful Mr. Hathorne[9] asked her, Why she Afflicted those Children? she said, she did not Afflict them. He asked her, who did then? she said, "I do not know; How should I know?" The Number of the Afflicted Persons were about that time Ten, viz.[10] Four Married Women, Mrs. Pope, Mrs. Putnam, Goodwife Bibber, and an Ancient Woman, named Goodall, three Maids, Mary Walcott, Mercy Lewes, at Thomas Putnam's and a Maid at Dr. Griggs's, there were three Girls from 9 to 12 Years of Age, each of them, or thereabouts, viz. Elizabeth Parris, Abigail Williams and Ann Putnam; these were most of them at Goodwife Corey's Examination, and did vehemently accuse her in the Assembly of afflicting them, by Biting, Pinching, Strangling, etc. And that they did in their Fit see her Likeness coming to them, and bringing a Book to them, she said, she had no Book; they affirmed, she had a Yellow-Bird, that used to suck betwixt her Fingers, and being asked about it, if she had any Familiar Spirit, that attended her, she said, She had no Familiarity with any such thing. She was a Gospel Woman: which Title she called her self by; and the Afflicted Persons told her, ah! She was, A Gospel Witch. Ann Putnam did there affirm, that one day when Lieutenant Fuller was at Prayer at her Fathers House, she saw the shape of Goodwife Corey and she thought Goodwife Nurse Praying at the same time to the Devil, she was not sure it was Goodwife Nurse she thought it was; but very sure she saw the Shape of Goodwife Corey. The said Corey said, they were poor, distracted Children, and no heed to be given to what they said. Mr. Hathorne and Mr. Noyes replyed, it was the judgment of all that were present, they were Bewitched, and only she, the Accused Person said, they were Distracted. It was observed several times, that if she did but bite her Under lip in time of Examination the persons afflicted were bitten on their armes and wrists and produced the Marks before the Magistrates, Ministers and others. And being watched for that, if she did but Pinch her Fingers, or Graspe one hand hard in another, they were Pinched and produced the Marks before the Magistrates, and Spectators. After that, it was observed, that if she did but lean her Breast against the Seat, in the Meeting House, (being the Barr at which she stood,) they were afflicted. Particularly Mrs. Pope complained of grievous torment in her Bowels as if they were torn out. She vehemently accused said Corey as the instrument, and first threw her Muff at her; but that flying not home, she got off her Shoe, and hit Goodwife Corey on the head with it. After these postures were watched, if said Corey did but stir her feet, they were afflicted in their Feet, and stamped fearfully. The afflicted persons asked her why she did not go to the company of Witches which were before the Meeting house mustering? Did she not hear the Drum beat? They accused her of having Familiarity with the Devil, in the time of Examination, in the shape of a Black man whispering in her ear; they affirmed, that her Yellow-Bird sucked betwixt her

---

9. **Mr. Hathorne:** John Hathorne, a merchant in Salem, served as a judge at the witchcraft trials. He was the great-great grandfather of Nathaniel Hawthorne, who set many of his most famous works in Puritan New England.

10. **viz.:** Abbreviation for *videlict*, meaning "namely" or "in other words" (Latin).

Fingers in the Assembly; and order being given to see if there were any sign, the Girl that saw it said, it was too late now; she had removed a Pin, and put it on her head; which was found there sticking upright.

They told her, she had Covenanted with the Devil for ten years, six of them were gone, and four more to come. She was required by the Magistrates to answer that Question in the Catechism, "How many persons be there in the God-Head?" she answered it but oddly, yet was there no great thing to be gathered from it; she denied all that was charged upon her, and said, They could not prove a Witch; she was that Afternoon Committed to Salem-Prison; and after she was in Custody, she did not so appear to them, and afflict them as before.

. . .

On Thursday the Twenty fourth of march, (being in course the Lecture Day,[11] at the Village,) Goodwife Nurse was brought before the Magistrates Mr. Hathorne and Mr. Corwin,[12] about Ten of [the] Clock, in the Fore Noon, to be Examined in the Meeting House; the Reverend Mr. Hale begun with Prayer, and the Warrant being read, she was required to give answer, Why she aflicted those persons? she pleaded her owne innocency with earnestness. Thomas Putnam's Wife, Abigail Williams and Thomas Putnam's daughter accused her that she appeared to them, and afflicted them in their fitts: but some of the other said, that they had seen her, but knew not that ever she had hurt them; amongst which was Mary Walcott, who was presently after she had so declared bitten, and cryed out of her in the meeting-house; producing the Marks of teeth on her wrist. It was so disposed, that I had not leisure to attend the whole time of Examination, but both Magistrates and Ministers told me, that the things alledged by the afflicted, and defences made by her, were much after the same manner, as the former was. And her Motions did produce like effects as to Biteing, Pinching, Bruising, Tormenting, at their Breasts, by her Leaning, and when, bended Back, were as if their Backs was broken. The afflicted persons said, the Black Man[13] whispered to her in the Assembly, and therefore she could not hear what the Magistrates said unto her. They said also that she did then ride by the Meeting-house, behind the Black Man. Thomas Putnam's wife had a grievous Fit, in the time of Examination, to the very great Impairing of her strength, and wasting of her spirits, insomuch as she could hardly move hand, or foot, when she was carried out. Others also were there grievously afflicted, so that there was once such an hideous scrietch and noise, (which I heard as I walked, at a little distance from the Meeting house,) as did amaze me, and some that were within told me the whole assembly was struck with consternation, and they were afraid, that those that sate next to them, were under the influence of Witchcraft. This woman also was that day committed to Salem Prison. The Magistrates and Ministers also did informe me, that they

---

11. **Lecture Day:** In Puritan New England, Thursdays were set aside for lectures, moral review, and spiritual renovation.
12. **Mr. Corwin:** Jonathan Corwin was the high sheriff of Essex County, whose signature sanctioned the arrest of the accused and the execution of those convicted of witchcraft in Salem Village.
13. **Black Man:** Another term for the Devil.

apprehended a child of Sarah Good[14] and Examined it, being between 4 and 5 years of Age. And as to matter of Fact, they did Unanimously affirm, that when this Child did but cast its eye upon the afflicted persons, they were tormented, and they held her Head, and yet so many as her eye could fix upon were afflicted. Which they did several times make careful observation of: the afflicted complained, they had often been Bitten by this child, and produced the marks of a small set of teeth, accordingly, this was also committed to Salem Prison; the child looked hail, and well as other Children. I saw it at Lieutenant Ingersolls. After the commitment of Goodwife Nurse, Thomas Putnam's wife was much better, and had no violent fits at all from that 24th of March to the 5th of April. Some others also said they had not seen her so frequently appear to them, to hurt them.

On the 25th of March, (as Capt. Stephen Sewall,[15] of Salem, did afterwards inform me) Elizabeth Parris had sore Fits, at his house, which much troubled himself, and his wife, so as he told me they were almost discouraged. She related, that the great Black Man came to her, and told her, if she would be ruled by him, she should have whatsoever she desired, and go to a Golden City. She relating this to Mrs. Sewall, she told the child, it was the Divel, and he was a Lyar from the Beginning, and bid her tell him so, if he came again: which she did accordingly, at the next coming to her, in her fits.

On the 26th of March, Mr. Hathorne, Mr. Corwin, and Mr. Higginson[16] were at the Prison-Keepers House, to Examine the Child,[17] and it told them there, it had a little Snake that used to Suck on the lowest Joynt of it[s] Fore-Finger; and when they inquired where, pointing to other places, it told them, not there, but there, pointing on the Lowest point of Fore-Finger; where they Observed a deep Red Spot, about the Bigness of a Flea-bite, they asked who gave it that Snake? whether the great Black man, it said no, its Mother gave it.

The 31 of March there was a Publick Fast kept at Salem on account of these Afflicted Persons. And Abigail Williams said, that the Witches had a Sacrament that day at an house in the Village, and that they had Red Bread and Red Drink. The first of April, Mercy Lewis, Thomas Putnam's Maid, in her fitt, said, they did eat Red Bread like Mans Flesh, and would have had her eat some: but she would not; but turned away her head, and Spit at them, and said, "I will not Eat, I will not Drink, it is Blood," etc. She said, "That is not the Bread of Life, that is not the Water of Life; Christ gives the Bread of Life, I will have none of it!" This first of April also Marcy Lewis aforesaid saw in her fitt a White man and was with him in a Glorious Place, which had no Candles nor Sun, yet was full of Light and Brightness; where was a great Multitude in White glittering Robes, and they Sung the Song in the fifth of Revelation the Ninth verse, and the 110 Psalm, and the

---

14. **Sarah Good:** Good and her second husband, William, were an impoverished couple who lived mostly by begging in Salem Village. Accused of witchcraft, she was convicted and hanged on July 19, 1692. Their daughter Dorcas, who was not yet five years old, was the youngest person to be imprisoned during the witchcraft trials.
15. **Sewall:** Captain Stephen Sewall was the brother of Samuel Sewall, later a judge in the Salem trials. When Reverend Samuel Parris first thought that his daughter Elizabeth was one of the afflicted girls, he sent her to the home of Stephen Sewall in Salem.
16. **Mr. Higginson:** Reverend John Higginson, the senior minister of the church in Salem.
17. **Child:** Dorcas Good; see note 14.

149 Psalm; and said with her self, "How long shall I stay here? let me be along with you": She was loth to leave this place, and grieved that she could tarry no longer. This White man hath appeared several times to some of them, and given them notice how long it should be before they had another Fit, which was sometimes a day, or day and half, or more or less: it hath fallen out accordingly.

The third of April, the Lords-Day, being Sacrament-day, at the Village, upon Mr. Parris's naming his Text, John 6, 70, *One of them is a Devil*, the said Goodwife Cloyse went immediately out of the Meeting-House, and flung the door after her violently, to the amazement of the Congregation.[18] She was afterward seen by some in their Fits, who said, "O Goodwife Cloyse, I did not think to see you here!" (and being at their Red bread and drink) said to her, "Is this a time to receive the Sacrament, you ran-away on the Lords-Day, and I scorned to receive it in the Meeting-House, and, Is this a time to receive it? I wonder at you!" This is the summ of what I either saw my self, or did receive Information from persons of undoubted Reputation and Credit.

Remarks of things more than ordinary about the Afflicted Persons.

1. They are in their Fits tempted to be Witches, are shewed the List of the Names of others, and are tortured, because they will not yield to Subscribe, or meddle with, or touch the Book, and are promised to have present Relief if they would do it.

2. They did in the Assembly mutually Cure each other, even with a Touch of their Hand, when Strangled, and otherwise Tortured; and would endeavour to get to their Afflicted, to Relieve them.

3. They did also foretel when anothers Fit was a-coming, and would say, "Look to her! she will have a Fit presently," which fell out accordingly, as many can bear witness, that heard and saw it.

4. That at the same time, when the Accused Person was present, the Afflicted Persons saw her Likeness in other places of the Meeting-House, suckling her Familiar, sometimes in one place and posture, and sometimes in another.

5. That their Motions in their Fits are Preternatural, both as to the manner, which is so strange as a well person could not Screw their Body into; and as to the violence also it is preternatural, being much beyond the Ordinary force of the same person when they are in their right mind.

6. The eyes of some of them in their fits are exceeding fast closed, and if you ask a question they can give no answer, and I do believe they cannot hear at that time, yet do they plainly converse with the Appearances, as if they did discourse with real persons.

7. They are utterly pressed against any persons Praying with them, and told by the appearances, they shall not go to Prayer, so Thomas Putnam's wife was told, I should not

---

18. **Goodwife Cloyse . . . Congregation:** Sarah Cloyse was the sister of Rebecca Nurse. When the minister announced that the text of his sermon was a biblical text about Judas, "Have not I chosen you twelve, and one of you is a Devil," she left the church and reportedly slammed the door behind her, though others said that the wind blew it shut. As indicated in the following passage, some of the young girls "in their Fits" later said that they could see Cloyse's specter in communion with the Devil. She was subsequently arrested and imprisoned, but the trials ended before she could be indicted for witchcraft.

Pray; but she said, I should: and after I had done, reasoned with the Appearance, "Did not I say he should go to Prayer?"

8. The forementioned Mary Walcott being a little better at ease, the Afflicted persons said, she had signed the book; and that was the reason she was better. Told me by Edward Putnam.

Remarks concerning the Accused.

1. For introduction to the discovery of those that afflicted them, It is reported Mr. Parris's Indian Man and Woman made a Cake of Rye Meal, and the Childrens water, baked it in the Ashes, and gave it to a Dogge, since which they have discovered, and seen particular persons hurting of them.

2. In Time of Examination, they seemed little affected, though all the Spectators were much grieved to see it.

3. Natural Actions in them produced Preternatural actions in the Afflicted, so that they are their own Image without any Poppits of Wax or otherwise.[19]

4. That they are accused to have a Company about 23 or 24 and they did Muster in Armes, as it seemed to the Afflicted Persons.

5. Since they were confined, the Persons have not been so much Afflicted with their appearing to them, Biteing or Pinching of them, etc.

6. They are reported by the Afflicted Persons to keep dayes of Fast and dayes of Thanksgiving, and Sacraments; Satan endeavours to Transforme himself to an Angel of Light, and to make his Kingdom and Administrations to resemble those of our Lord Jesus Christ.

7. Satan Rages Principally amongst the Visible Subjects of Christ's Kingdom and makes use (at least in appearance) of some of them to Afflict others; that Christ's Kingdom may be divided against it self, and so be weakened.

8. Several things used in England at Tryal of Witches, to the Number of 14 or 15, which are wont to pass instead of or in Concurrence with Witnesses, at least 6 or 7 of them are found in these accused: see Keebles Statutes.[20]

9. Some of the most solid Afflicted Persons do affirme the same things concerning seeing the accused out of their Fitts as well as in them.

10. The Witches had a Fast, and told one of the Afflicted Girles, she must not Eat, because it was Fast Day, she said, she would: they told her they would Choake her then; which when she did eat, was endeavoured.

[1692, 1914]

---

19. **Natural Actions . . . otherwise:** That is, these witches have only to act in order to produce the same action in their victim, unlike witches who could inflict pain only by torturing wax puppets or dolls made in the likeness of their victims.

20. **Keebles Statutes:** Lawson refers to a section on witchcraft in a collection of English statutes, *An Assistance to Justices of the Peace* (London, 1683), by Joseph Keeble or Keble (1632–1710).

Cotton Mather

[1663–1728]

The eldest son of the eminent Puritan minister Increase Mather, Cotton Mather became one of the most active and influential religious figures of his era. As a minister of the Second Church in Boston and in his hundreds of published writings, Mather sought to revive the spirit of the early colonial founders and to preserve the Puritan theocracy of the Massachusetts Bay Colony. Like the founders of the colony, Mather viewed the Puritans as analogous to the ancient Israelites, whose mission was to establish proper worship in a new land promised them by God. Mather celebrated the process by which the "wilderness" of New England was transformed into an ideal Christian society in his most important book, *Magnalia Christi Americana* (1702), the title of which may be translated as "A history of the wonderful works of Christ in America." But in the minds of many Mather is most closely associated with the witchcraft trials in Salem. Although he did not participate in the trials directly and urged caution in the use of "spectral" evidence, Mather clearly believed that the Devil was at the bottom of the events in Salem Village. In the face of growing unease about the trials, he wrote *The Wonders of the Invisible World*, a vigorous defense of the proceedings rushed into print in October 1692, though the title page bears the date 1693. As he emphasized in the first of the following selections from that work, Mather conceived of the events in Salem as one more chapter in the ongoing struggle for the possession of New England between the Puritans, "a People of God," and the Devil, who in Salem "is now making one Attempt more upon us; an Attempt more Difficult, more Surprizing, more snarl'd with unintelligible Circumstances than any that we have hitherto Encountered." The text is taken from Volume One of *The Witchcraft Delusion in New England*, edited by Samuel G. Drake (1866).

Peter Pelham, *Cottonus Matherus* (1728)

Mather's renown was so great that the *Boston Gazette* began running announcements of the forthcoming publication of this print portrait only six days after his death in 1728.

From THE WONDERS OF THE INVISIBLE WORLD

The *New-Englanders* are a People of God settled in those, which were once the *Devil's* Territories; and it may easily be supposed that the *Devil* was exceedingly disturbed, when he perceived such a People here accomplishing the Promise of old made unto our

Blessed Jesus, *That He should have the Utmost parts of the Earth for his Possession.*[1] There was not a greater Uproar among the *Ephesians,*[2] when the Gospel was first brought among them, than there was among, *The Powers of the Air* (after whom those *Ephesians* walked) when first the *Silver Trumpets* of the Gospel here made the *Joyful Sound.* The Devil thus Irritated, immediately try'd all sorts of Methods to overturn this poor Plantation: and so much of the Church, as was *Fled into this Wilderness,* immediately found, *The Serpent cast out of his Mouth a Flood for the carrying of it away.* I believe, that never were more *Satanical Devices* used for the Unsetling of any People under the Sun, than what have been Employ'd for the Extirpation of the *Vine* which God has here *Planted, Casting out the Heathen, and preparing a Room before it, and causing it to take deep Root, and fill the Land, so that it sent its Boughs unto the* Atlantic *Sea* Eastward, *and its Branches unto the* Connecticut *River* Westward, *and the Hills were covered with the shadow thereof.* But, All those Attempts of Hell, have hitherto been Abortive, many an *Ebenezer*[3] has been Erected unto the Praise of God, by his Poor People here; and, *Having obtained Help from God, we continue to this Day.* Wherefore the Devil is now making one Attempt more upon us; an Attempt more Difficult, more Surprizing, more snarl'd with unintelligible Circumstances than any that we have hitherto Encountred; an Attempt so *Critical,* that if we get well through, we shall soon Enjoy *Halcyon* Days with all the *Vultures* of Hell *Trodden under our Feet.*[4] He has wanted his *Incarnate Legions* to Persecute us, as the People of God have in the other Hemisphere been Persecuted: he has therefore drawn forth his more *Spiritual* ones to make an Attacque upon us. We have been advised by some Credible Christians yet alive, that a Malefactor, accused of *Witchcraft* as well as *Murder,* and Executed in this place more than Forty Years ago, did then give Notice of, *An Horrible* PLOT *against the Country* by WITCHCRAFT, *and a Foundation of* WITCHCRAFT *then laid, which if it were not seasonably discovered, would prbably Blow up, and pull down all the Churches in the Country.*[5] And we have now with Horror seen the *Discovery* of such a *Witchcraft!* An Army of *Devils* is horribly broke in upon the place which is the *Center,* and after a sort, the *First-born* of our *English* Settlements: and the Houses of the Good People there are fill'd with the doleful Shrieks of their Children and Servants, Tormented by Invisible Hands, with Tortures altogether preternatural. After the Mischiefs there Endeavoured, and since in part Conquered, the terrible Plague, of *Evil Angels,* hath made its Progress into some

---

1. *He . . . for his Possession*: Mather refers to the Lord's promise to his Son in Psalms 2:8: "Ask of me, and I shall give thee the heathen for thine inheritance, and the uttermost parts of the earth for thy possession."

2. **Uproar among the *Ephesians***: Many of the people of Ephesus, a Greek port on the southwestern coast of present-day Turkey, were fanatical followers of Diana, the Greek goddess of the hunt. When the disciple Paul sought to convert the Ephesians to Christianity, he was met with fierce opposition (Acts 19:22–41).

3. *Ebenezer*: Literally "stone of help" (Hebrew). According to the Old Testament, Samuel set up a commemorative stone to honor God's help to Israel in a battle with the Philistines (1 Samuel 7:12).

4. **if we get well through . . . *Trodden under our Feet***: That is, if the Puritans overcome the challenge posed by the Devil and destroy the witches in their midst, they will enjoy "Halcyon Days," suggestive of spiritual calm and tranquility.

5. *An Horrible* PLOT *. . . Country*: The specific incident to which Mather refers is not known, but accusations of witchcraft and alleged incidents involving witches were common in seventeenth-century New England, as well as in England and Europe.

other places, where other Persons have been in like manner Diabolically handled. These our poor Afflicted Neighbours, quickly after they become *Infected* and *Infested* with these *Daemons*, arrive to a Capacity of Discerning those which they conceive the *Shapes* of their Troublers; and notwithstanding the Great and Just Suspicion, that the *Daemons* might Impose the *Shapes* of Innocent Persons in their *Spectral Exhibitions* upon the Sufferers, (which may perhaps prove no small part of the *Witch-Plot* in the issue) yet many of the Persons thus Represented, being Examined, several of them have been Convicted of a very Damnable *Witchcraft*: yea, more than One *Twenty* have *Confessed*, that they have Signed unto a *Book*, which the Devil show'd them, and Engaged in his Hellish Design of *Bewitching*, and *Ruining* our Land. *We* know not, at least *I* know not, how far the *Delusions* of Satan may be Interwoven into some Circumstances of the *Confessions;* but one would think, all the Rules of Understanding Humane Affayrs are at an end, if after so many most Voluntary Harmonious *Confessions*, made by Intelligent Persons of all Ages, in sundry Towns, at several Times, we must not Believe the *main strokes* wherein those *Confessions* all agree: especially when we have a thousand preternatural Things every day before our eyes, wherein the *Confessors* do acknowledge their Concernment, and give Demonstration of their being so Concerned. If the Devils now can strike the minds of men with any *Poisons* of so fine a Composition and Operation, that Scores of Innocent People shall Unite, in *Confessions* of a Crime, which we see actually committed, it is a thing prodigious, beyond the Wonders of the former Ages, and it threatens no less than a sort of a Dissolution upon the World. Now, by these *Confessions* 'tis Agreed, *That* the Devil has made a dreadful Knot of *Witches* in the Country, and by the help of *Witches* has dreadfully increased that Knot: *That* these *Witches* have driven a Trade of Commissioning their *Confederate Spirits*, to do all sorts of Mischiefs to the Neighbours, whereupon there have ensued such Mischievous consequences upon the Bodies and Estates of the Neighbourhood, as could not otherwise be accounted for: yea, *That* at prodigious *Witch-Meetings*, the Wretches have proceeded so far, as to Concert and Consult the Methods of Rooting out the Christian Religion from this Country, and setting up instead of it, perhaps a more gross *Diabolism*, than ever the World saw before. And yet it will be a thing little short of *Miracle*, if in so *spread* a Business as this, the Devil should not get in some of his Juggles,[6] to confound the Discovery of all the rest.

. . .

But I shall no longer detain my Reader, from his expected Entertainment, in a brief account of the Tryals which have passed upon some of the Malefactors lately Executed at *Salem*, for the *Witchcrafts* whereof they stood Convicted. For my own part, I was not present at any of them; nor ever had I any Personal prejudice at the Persons thus brought upon the Stage; much less at the Surviving Relations of those Persons, with and for whom I would be as hearty a Mourner as any Man living in the World: *The Lord Comfort them!* But having received a Command so to do, I can do no other than shortly

---

6. **Juggles:** Early term for tricks.

relate the chief *Matters of Fact*,[7] which occur'd in the Tryals of some that were Executed, in an Abridgment Collected out of the *Court-Papers*, on this occasion put into my hands. You are to take the *Truth*, just as it was; and the Truth will hurt no good Man. There might have been more of these, if my Book would not thereby have swollen too big; and if some other worthy hands did not perhaps intend something further in these *Collections;* for which cause I have only singled out Four or Five, which may serve to illustrate the way of Dealing, wherein *Witchcrafts* use to be concerned; and I report matters not as an *Advocate*, but as an *Historian.*

. . .

V. *The Trial of* MARTHA CARRIER, *at the Court of Oyer and Terminer, held by Adjournment at Salem, August* 2, 1692.[8]

I. Martha Carrier was Indicted for the bewitching of certain Persons, according to the Form usual in such Cases, pleading *Not Guilty*, to her Indictment; there were first brought in a considerable number of the bewitched Persons; who not only made the Court sensible of an horrid Witchcraft committed upon them, but also deposed, That it was *Martha Carrier*, or her Shape, that grievously tormented them, by Biting, Pricking, Pinching and Choaking of them. It was further deposed, That while this *Carrier* was on her Examination, before the Magistrates, the Poor People were so tortured that every one expected their Death upon the very spot, but that upon the binding of *Carrier* they were eased. Moreover the Look of *Carrier* then laid the Afflicted People for dead; and her Touch, if her Eye at the same time were off them, raised them again: Which Things were also now seen upon her Tryal. And it was testified, That upon the mention of some having their Necks twisted almost round, by the Shape of this *Carrier*, she replyed, *Its no matter though their Necks had been twisted quite off.*

II. Before the Trial of this Prisoner, several of her own Children had frankly and fully confessed, not only that they were Witches themselves, but that this their Mother had made them so. This Confession they made with great Shews of Repentance, and with much Demonstration of Truth. They related Place, Time, Occasion; they gave an account of Journeys, Meetings and Mischiefs by them performed, and were very credible in what they said. Nevertheless, this Evidence was not produced against the Prisoner at the Bar, inasmuch as there was other Evidence enough to proceed upon.

III. *Benjamin Abbot* gave in his Testimony, That last *March* was a twelvemonth,[9] this *Carrier* was very angry with him, upon laying out some Land, near her Husband's: Her

---

7. **Command . . . *Matters of Fact*:** According to Mather, he was asked to look into the witch trials by Sir William Phips, the first royal governor of Massachusetts.

8. ***The Trial . . . August* 2, 1692:** Imprisoned with four of her five children, Martha Carrier denied the charges of witchcraft, some of which were made by her young children, and sharply criticized the magistrates and the trial procedures. Carrier, who lived in considerable poverty with her children and husband, Thomas, in nearby Andover, was unpopular for her independent spirit and the widespread belief that she was somehow responsible for an epidemic of smallpox that killed several people. Many scholars believe that those negative feelings contributed to the charges leveled against her. She was convicted of witchcraft by the Court of Oyer and Terminer — a term originating in English law meaning "to hear and determine" — and hanged on August 19, 1692.

9. **That last *March* was a twelvemonth:** That is, a year ago last March.

Expressions in this Anger, were, *That she would stick as close to* Abbot *as the Bark stuck to the Tree; and that he should repent of it afore seven Years came to an End, so as Doctor* Prescot *should never cure him.* These Words were heard by others besides *Abbot* himself; who also heard her say, *She would hold his Nose as close to the Grindstone as ever it was held since his Name was* Abbot. Presently after this, he was taken with a Swelling in his Foot, and then with a Pain in his Side, and exceedingly tormented. It bred into a Sore, which was launced by Doctor *Prescot*, and several Gallons of Corruption ran out of it. For six Weeks it continued very bad, and then another Sore bred in the Groin, which was also lanced by Doctor *Prescot.* Another Sore then bred in his Groin, which was likewise cut, and put him to very great Misery: He was brought unto Death's Door, and so remained until *Carrier* was taken, and carried away by the Constable, from which very Day he began to mend, and so grew better every Day, and is well ever since.

Sarah Abbot also, his Wife, testified, That her Husband was not only all this while Afflicted in his Body, but also that strange extraordinary and unaccountable Calamities befel his Cattel; their Death being such as they could guess at no Natural Reason for.

IV. *Allin Toothaker* testify'd, That *Richard*, the son of *Martha Carrier*, having some difference with him, pull'd him down by the Hair of the Head. When he Rose again, he was going to strike at *Richard Carrier;* but fell down flat on his Back to the ground, and had not power to stir hand or foot, until he told *Carrier* he yielded; and then he saw the shape of *Martha Carrier*, go off his breast.

This *Toothaker*, had Received a wound in the *Wars;* and he now testify'd, that *Martha Carrier* told him, *He should never be Cured.* Just afore the Apprehending of *Carrier*, he could thrust a knitting Needle into his wound, four inches deep; but presently after her being siezed, he was thoroughly healed.

He further testify'd, that when *Carrier* and he sometimes were at variance, she would clap her hands at him, and say, *He should get nothing by it;* whereupon he several times lost his Cattle, by strange Deaths, whereof no natural causes could be given.

V. *John Rogger* also testifyed, That upon the threatning words of this malicious *Carrier*, his Cattle would be strangely bewitched; as was more particularly then described.

VI. *Samuel Preston* testify'd, that about two years ago, having some difference with *Martha Carrier*, he lost a *Cow* in a strange Preternatural unusual manner; and about a month after this, the said *Carrier*, having again some difference with him, she told him; *He had lately lost a Cow, and it should not be long before he lost another;* which accordingly came to pass; for he had a thriving and well-kept *Cow*, which without any known cause quickly fell down and dy'd.

VII. *Phebe Chandler* testify'd, that about a Fortnight before the apprehension of *Martha Carrier*, on a Lordsday, while the Psalm was singing in the *Church*, this *Carrier* then took her by the shoulder and shaking her, asked her, *where she lived:* she made her no Answer, although as *Carrier*, who lived next door to her Fathers House, could not in reason but know who she was. Quickly after this, as she was at several times crossing the Fields, she heard a voice, that she took to be *Martha Carriers*, and it seem'd as if it was over her head. The voice told her, *she should within two or three days be poisoned.* Accordingly, within such a little time, one half of her right hand, became greatly swollen, and very painful; as also part of her Face; whereof she can give no account how it came.

It continued very bad for some dayes; and several times since, she has had a great pain in her breast; and been so siezed on her leggs, that she has hardly been able to go. She added, that lately, going well to the House of God, *Richard*, the son of *Martha Carrier*, look'd very earnestly upon her, and immediately her hand, which had formerly been poisoned, as is abovesaid, began to pain her greatly, and she had a strange Burning at her stomach; but was then struck deaf, so that she could not hear any of the prayer, or singing, till the two or three last words of the Psalm.

VIII. One *Foster*, who confessed her own share in the Witchcraft for which the Prisoner stood indicted, affirm'd, that she had seen the prisoner at some of their *Witch-meetings*, and that it was this *Carrier*, who perswaded her to be a Witch. She confessed, that the Devil carry'd them on a pole, to a Witch-meeting; but the pole broke, and she hanging about *Carriers* neck, they both fell down, and she then received an hurt by the Fall, whereof she was not at this very time recovered.

IX. One *Lacy*, who likewise confessed her share in this Witchcraft, now testify'd, that she and the prisoner were once Bodily present at a *Witch-meeting* in *Salem Village;* and that she knew the prisoner to be a Witch, and to have been at a Diabolical sacrament, and that the prisoner was the undoing of her, and her Children, by enticing them into the snare of the Devil.

X. Another *Lacy*, who also confessed her share in this Witchcraft, now testify'd, that the prisoner was at the *Witch-meeting*, in *Salem Village*, where they had Bread and Wine Administred unto them.

XI. In the time of this prisoner's Trial, one *Susanna Sheldon*, in open Court had her hands Unaccountably ty'd together with a Wheel-band, so fast that without cutting, it could not be loosed: It was done by a *Spectre;* and the Sufferer affirm'd, it was the *Prisoners.*

Memorandum. This Rampant Hag, *Martha Carrier*, was the person, of whom the Confessions of the Witches, and of her own Children among the rest, agreed, That the Devil had promised her, she should be *Queen of Hell.*

[1693, 1866]

Thomas Brattle

[1658–1713]

The son of a wealthy family, Thomas Brattle was raised in Boston and graduated from Harvard College in 1676. After traveling abroad, he returned to Boston where he became a successful merchant and was appointed treasurer of Harvard. Liberal in politics and religion, Brattle was part of a new generation of colonists who sought to loosen the rigid strictures of Puritan worship, an effort that led him to found the Brattle Street Church in 1699. Brattle was also an amateur astronomer, whose work on lunar and solar eclipses was posthumously recognized by the prestigious Royal Society of London for Improving Natural Knowledge. But he is best known for a pamphlet written in the form of a letter to an unknown minister on October 8, 1692. In the "Letter," which was not published in his day but evidently was circulated in manuscript, Brattle offered a sweeping critique of the "Salem proceedings," from the initial arrest and examination of the accused through the evidence and testimony given at their trials to their executions, at which many of the convicted professed their innocence. Clearly outraged by the events in Salem, Brattle adopted a somber tone and methodical approach to expose the unreliability of the afflicted young girls; the delusions of those who confessed to being witches; and the manifold errors made by judges in the trials, which Brattle feared would leave a lasting stain on New England. We have silently expanded abbreviations in the following selection from Brattle's letter, the text of which is taken from *Narratives of the Witchcraft Cases, 1648-1706* edited by George Lincoln Burr (1914).

From LETTER OF THOMAS BRATTLE, 1692

October 8, 1692.

Reverend Sir,[1]

Your's I received the other day, and am very ready to serve you to my uttmost. . . .

I am very open to communicate my thoughts unto you, and in plain terms to tell you what my opinion is of the Salem proceedings.

First, as to the method which the Salem Justices do take in their examinations, it is truly this: A warrant being issued out to apprehend the persons that are charged and complained of by the afflicted children, (as they are called); said persons are brought before the Justices, (the afflicted being present.) The Justices ask the apprehended why they afflict those poor children; to which the apprehended answer, they do not afflict them. The Justices order the apprehended to look upon the said children, which accordingly they do; and at the time of that look, (I dare not say by that look, as the Salem Gentlemen do) the afflicted are cast into a fitt. The apprehended are then blinded, and ordered to touch the afflicted; and at that touch, tho' not by the touch, (as above) the afflicted ordinarily do come out of their fitts. The afflicted persons then declare and affirm, that the apprehended have afflicted them; upon which the apprehended persons, tho' of never so good repute, are forthwith committed to prison, on suspicion for witchcraft. . . .

I cannot but condemn this method of the Justices, of making this touch of the hand a rule to discover witchcraft; because I am fully persuaded that it is sorcery, and a superstitious method, and that which we have no rule for, either from reason or religion. The Salem Justices, at least some of them, do assert, that the cure of the afflicted persons is a natural effect of this touch; and they are so well instructed in the Cartesian

---

1. **Reverend Sir:** The recipient of this letter has not been identified.

philosophy, and in the doctrine of *effluvia*,[2] that they undertake to give a demonstration how this touch does cure the afflicted persons; and the account they give of it is this; that by this touch, the venemous and malignant particles, that were ejected from the eye, do, by this means, return to the body whence they came, and so leave the afflicted persons pure and whole. I must confesse to you, that I am no small admirer of the Cartesian philosophy; but yet I have not so learned it. Certainly this is a strain that it will by no means allow of.

I would fain know of these Salem Gentlemen, but as yet could never know, how it comes about, that if these apprehended persons are witches, and, by a look of the eye, do cast the afflicted into their fitts by poisoning them, how it comes about, I say, that, by a look of their eye, they do not cast others into fitts, and poison others by their looks; and in particular, tender, fearfull women, who often are beheld by them, and as likely as any in the whole world to receive an ill impression from them. This Salem philosophy, some men may call the new philosophy; but I think it rather deserves the name of Salem superstition and sorcery, and it is not fitt to be named in a land of such light as New-England is. . . .

Secondly, with respect to the confessours, (as they are improperly called,) or such as confesse themselves to be witches, (the second thing you inquire into in your letter), there are now about fifty of them in Prison; many of which I have again and again seen and heard; and I cannot but tell you, that my faith is strong concerning them, that they are deluded, imposed upon, and under the influence of some evill spirit; and therefore unfitt to be evidences either against themselves, or any one else. I now speak of one sort of them, and of others afterward.

These confessours, (as they are called,) do very often contradict themselves, as inconsistently as is usual for any crazed, distempered person to do. This the Salem Gentlemen do see and take notice of; and even the Judges themselves have, at some times, taken these confessours in flat lyes, or contradictions, even in the Courts; By reason of which, one would have thought, that the Judges would have frowned upon the said confessours, discarded them, and not minded one tittle of any thing that they said; but instead thereof, (as sure as we are men,) the Judges vindicate these confessours, and salve their contradictions, by proclaiming, that the Devill takes away their memory, and imposes upon their brain. If this reflects any where, I am very sorry for it: I can but assure you, that, upon the word of an honest man, it is truth, and that I can bring you many credible persons to witnesse it, who have been eye and ear wittnesses to these things.

These confessours then, at least some of them, even in the Judges' own account, are under the influence of the Devill; and the brain of these Confessours is imposed upon

---

2. **Cartesian philosophy . . .** *effluvia:* Brattle refers to a theory of René Descartes (1596–1650), a French writer and logician who became a central figure in the development of Western philosophy and the scientific revolution. In Descartes's view, the universe is composed of two kinds of matter, dense bodies and empty space, the latter of which is filled with *effluvia*, or invisible particles. As Brattle explains in the remainder of this passage, the Salem judges argued that the toxic particles that passed from the eyes of the witches to their victims returned to the witches through their touch, thus curing their victims.

by the Devill, even in the Judges' account. But now, if, in the Judges' account, these confessours are under the influence of the Devill, and their brains are affected and imposed upon by the Devill, so that they are not their own men, why then should these Judges, or any other men, make such account of, and set so much by, the words of these Confessours, as they do? In short, I argue thus:

If the Devill does actually take away the memory of them at some times, certainly the Devill, at other times, may very reasonably be thought to affect their fancyes, and to represent false ideas to their imagination. But now, if it be thus granted, that the Devill is able to represent false ideas (to speak vulgarly) to the imaginations of the confessours, what man of sense will regard the confessions, or any of the words, of these confessours?

The great cry of many of our neighbours now is, What, will you not believe the confessours? Will you not believe men and women who confesse that they have signed to the Devill's book? that they were baptized by the Devill; and that they were at the mock-sacrament once and again? What! will you not believe that this is witchcraft, and that such and such men are witches, altho' the confessours do own and assert it?

Thus, I say, many of our good neighbours do argue; but methinks they might soon be convinced that there is nothing at all in all these their arguings, if they would but duly consider of the premises.

In the mean time, I think we must rest satisfyed in it, and be thankfull to God for it, that all men are not thus bereft of their senses; but that we have here and there considerate and thinking men, who will not thus be imposed upon, and abused, by the subtle endeavours of the crafty one.

In the next place, I proceed to the form of their inditements, and the Trials thereupon.

The Inditement runs for sorcery and witchcraft, acted upon the body of such an one, (say Mary Warren[3]), at such a particular time, (say April 14, '92,) and at divers other times before and after, whereby the said Mary Warren is wasted and consumed, pined, etc.

Now for the proof of the said sorcery and witchcraft, the prisoner at the bar pleading not guilty.

1. The afflicted persons are brought into Court; and after much patience and pains taken with them, do take their oaths, that the prisoner at the bar did afflict them: And here I think it very observable, that often, when the afflicted do mean and intend only the appearance and shape of such an one, (say Goodman Proctour[4]) yet they positively swear that Goodman Proctour did afflict them; and they have been allowed so to do; as tho' there was no real difference between Goodman Proctour and the shape of Goodman Proctour. This, methinks, may readily prove a stumbling block to the Jury, lead them into a very fundamental errour, and occasion innocent blood, yea the innocentest blood imaginable, to be in great danger. Whom it belongs unto, to be eyes unto the blind, and

---

3. **Mary Warren:** A servant of John and Elizabeth Proctor, Warren first accused others of witchcraft and was then herself accused and arrested.
4. **Goodman Proctour:** John Proctor (1632–1692), who was accused of witchcraft by Mary Warren and others, was tried, convicted, and hanged on August 19, 1692.

to remove such stumbling blocks, I know full well; and yet you, and every one else, do know as well as I who do not.[5]

2. The confessours do declare what they know of the said prisoner; and some of the confessours are allowed to give their oaths; a thing which I believe was never heard of in this world; that such as confesse themselves to be witches, to have renounced God and Christ, and all that is sacred, should yet be allowed and ordered to swear by the name of the great God! This indeed seemeth to me to be a grosse taking of God's name in vain. I know the Salem Gentlemen do say, that there is hopes that the said Confessours have repented; I shall only say, that if they have repented, it is well for themselves; but if they have not, it is very ill for you know who. But then,

3. Whoever can be an evidence against the prisoner at the bar is ordered to come into Court; and here it scarce ever fails but that evidences, of one nature and another, are brought in, tho', I think, all of them altogether aliene to the matter of inditement; for they none of them do respect witchcraft upon the bodyes of the afflicted, which is the alone matter of charge in the inditement.

4. They are searched by a Jury; and as to some of them, the Jury brought in, that [on] such or such a place there was a preternatural excrescence.[6] And I wonder what person there is, whether man or woman, of whom it cannot be said but that, in some part of their body or other, there is a preternatural excrescence. The term is a very general and inclusive term.

. . .

The Salem Gentlemen will by no means allow, that any are brought in guilty, and condemned, by virtue of spectre Evidence,[7] (as it is called,) i. e. the evidence of these afflicted persons, who are said to have spectral eyes; but whether it is not purely by virtue of these spectre evidences, that these persons are found guilty, (considering what before has been said,) I leave you, and any man of sense, to judge and determine. When any man is indited for murthering the person of A. B. and all the direct evidence be, that the said man pistolled the shadow of the said A. B. tho' there be never so many evidences that the said person murthered C. D., E. F. and ten more persons, yet all this will not amount to a legal proof, that he murthered A. B.; and upon that inditement, the person cannot be legally brought in guilty of the said inditement; it must be upon this supposition, that the evidence of a man's pistolling the shadow of A. B. is a legal evidence to prove that the said man did murther the person of A. B. Now no man will be so much out of his witts as to make this a legal evidence; and yet this seems to be our case; and how to apply it is very easy and obvious.

As to the late executions,[8] I shall only tell you, that in the opinion of many unprejudiced, considerate and considerable spectatours, some of the condemned went out of

---

5. **who do not:** In other words, the judges presiding at the trials.
6. **preternatural excrescence:** Many believed that a mark on the body that looked like a third nipple was a Devil's teat through which witches and other demons could suck blood.
7. **spectre Evidence:** By the time Brattle wrote his letter, many others were also concerned that innocent people were being convicted on the basis of spectral evidence, or evidence based on specters or apparitions.
8. **late executions:** Brattle evidently had in mind and may have been present for the executions of John Proctor, George Willard, George Jacobs, Martha Carrier, and the Reverend George Burroughs on August 19, 1692.

the world not only with as great protestations, but also with as good shews of innocency, as men could do.

They protested their innocency as in the presence of the great God, whom forthwith they were to appear before: they wished, and declared their wish, that their blood might be the last innocent blood shed upon that account. With great affection they intreated Mr. Cotton Mather to pray with them: they prayed that God would discover what witch-crafts were among us; they forgave their accusers; they spake without reflection on Jury and Judges, for bringing them in guilty, and condemning them: they prayed earnestly for pardon for all other sins, and for an interest in the pretious blood of our dear Redeemer; and seemed to be very sincere, upright, and sensible of their circumstances on all accounts; especially Proctor and Willard, whose whole management of them-selves, from the Goal to the Gallows, and whilst at the Gallows, was very affecting and melting to the hearts of some considerable Spectatours, whom I could mention to you:— but they are executed, and so I leave them.

. . .

The chief Judge[9] is very zealous in these proceedings, and says, he is very clear as to all that hath as yet been acted by this Court, and, as far as ever I could perceive, is very impatient in hearing any thing that looks another way. I very highly honour and rever-ence the wisdome and integrity of the said Judge, and hope that this matter shall not diminish my veneration for his honour; however, I cannot but say, my great fear is, that wisdome and counsell are withheld from his honour as to this matter, which yet I look upon not so much as a Judgment to his honour as to this poor land.

But altho' the Chief Judge, and some of the other Judges, be very zealous in these pro-ceedings, yet this you may take for a truth, that there are several about the Bay, men for understanding, Judgment, and Piety, inferiour to few, (if any,) in New England that do utterly condemn the said proceedings, and do freely deliver their Judgment in the case to be this, *viz.*[10] that these methods will utterly ruine and undoe poor New England.

. . .

What will be the issue of these troubles, God only knows; I am afraid that ages will not wear off that reproach and those stains which these things will leave behind them upon our land. I pray God pity us, Humble us, Forgive us, and appear mercifully for us in this our mount of distress: Herewith I conclude, and subscribe myself,

Reverend Sir, your real friend and humble servant,

T. B.

[1692, 1914]

---

9. **chief Judge:** The conservative William Stoughton, who was determined to rid the colony of witches, never apologized for his role in the Salem trials.
10. *viz.*: In other words (abbreviation of the Latin *videlicet*).

Samuel Sewall

[1652–1730]

Born into a prominent Puritan merchant family in England, Samuel Sewall was brought by his parents to the Massachusetts Bay Colony in 1661. An industrious young man with a quick intelligence, Sewall earned two degrees from Harvard College. Late in his career there, at the end of 1673, he began a diary that he kept with rare interruptions until a few months before his death in 1730. Although he was a devout Puritan, Sewall's diary devotes less attention to his private spiritual life than to his activities as a businessman and public servant of the Massachusetts Bay Colony. From 1691 to 1725, Sewall served as a member of the Governor's Council, and he played a prominent role in the trials at Salem. On May 27, 1692, Sewall was appointed to the Commission of Oyer and Terminer, a special judicial group assigned "to enquire of, hear and determine all manner of crimes and offenses" involving witchcraft at Salem. Although he kept his diary throughout the proceedings, Sewall reveals little about his personal response to the unfolding events and displays no remorse for the executions that resulted. But of the nine judges he was the only one publicly to recant his part in the trials, in a confession of sin read in December

The Repentance of Samuel Sewall

In this mural in the State House of Massachusetts, painted by Albert Hester in 1942, Sewall stands with his head bowed as a minister reads the confession of sin Sewall prepared for Fast Day, set aside by the legislature as a day of repentance for the witchcraft trials and executions in Salem. The mural is one of five paintings that depict important events in the early history of the state, under the theme "Milestones on the Road to Freedom in Massachusetts."

1696, and each year afterwards he spent a day fasting and praying for forgiveness. Sewall also argued for more humane treatment of Native Americans and wrote an early antislavery tract, *The Selling of Joseph* (1700). The text of the following selections from the diary, which was first published between 1878 and 1882, is taken from *The Diary of Samuel Sewall*, edited by M. Halsey Thomas (1973).

From THE DIARY OF SAMUEL SEWALL

April 11th 1692. Went to Salem, where, in the Meeting-house, the persons accused of Witchcraft were examined;[1] was a very great Assembly; 'twas awfull to see how the afflicted persons were agitated. Mr. Noyes pray'd at the beginning, and Mr. Higginson concluded. [*In the margin*], Vae, Vae, Vae,[2] Witchcraft.

* * * * * * *

July 20th 1692. Fast at the house of Capt. Alden,[3] upon his account. Mr. Willard pray'd. I read a Sermon out of Dr. Preston, 1st and 2d Uses of God's Alsufficiency. Capt. Scottow pray'd, Mr. Allen came in and pray'd, Mr. Cotton Mather, then Capt. Hill. Sung the first part 103. Psalms,[4] concluded about 5. aclock. Brave Shower of Rain while Capt. Scottow was praying, after much Drought. Cous. Daniel Gookin sups with us, and bespeaks my marrying of him to morrow.

July 27, 1692. A plentifull Rain falls after great Drought.

July 30, 1692. Mrs. Cary[5] makes her escape out of Cambridge-Prison, who was Committed for Witchcraft.

* * * * * * *

Augt. 19th 1692. This day [*in the margin*, Dolefull! Witchcraft] George Burrough, John Willard, John Procter, Martha Carrier and George Jacobs were executed at Salem, a very

---

1. **Went to Salem . . . examined:** This is Sewall's first reference to the trials at Salem.
2. **Vae, Vae, Vae:** Woe, Woe, Woe (Latin).
3. **Fast . . . Capt. Alden:** Sewall took part in a fast, a ritual abstention from food and drink, at the home of Captain John Alden (c. 1626–1701/2), the son of Priscilla and John Alden of Plymouth. Alden was accused of witchcraft, imprisoned for fifteen weeks, and later escaped with the help of friends.
4. **103. Psalms:** Psalms 103, which begins: "Bless the Lord, O my soul; and all that is within me, bless his holy name."
5. **Mrs. Cary:** Elizabeth Cary was tried for witchcraft, committed to prison in Cambridge, and escaped to New York.

great number of Spectators being present. Mr. Cotton Mather was there, Mr. Sims, Hale, Noyes, Chiever, &c. All of them said they were innocent, Carrier and all. Mr. Mather says they all died by a Righteous Sentence. Mr. Burrough by his Speech, Prayer, protestation of his Innocence, did much move unthinking persons, which occasions their speaking hardly concerning his being executed.

Augt. 25. Fast at the old [*First*] Church, respecting the Witchcraft, Drought, &c.

*   *   *   *   *   *   *

Monday, Sept. 19, 1692. About noon, at Salem, Giles Corey was press'd to death for standing Mute;[6] much pains was used with him two days, one after another, by the Court and Capt. Gardner of Nantucket who had been of his acquaintance: but all in vain.

Sept. 20. Now I hear from Salem that about 18 years agoe, he was suspected to have stampd and press'd a man to death, but was cleared. Twas not remembred till Anne Putnam was told of it by said Corey's Spectre the Sabbath-day night before Execution.

*   *   *   *   *   *   *

Sept. 21. A petition is sent to Town in behalf of Dorcas Hoar, who now confesses: Accordingly an order is sent to the Sherriff to forbear her Execution, notwithstanding her being in the Warrant to die to morrow. This is the first condemned person who has confess'd.[7]

*   *   *   *   *   *   *

Thorsday, Sept. 22, 1692. William Stoughton, Esqr., John Hathorne, Esqr., Mr. Cotton Mather, and Capt. John Higginson, with my Brother St., were at our house, speaking about publishing some Trials of the Witches.[8]

*   *   *   *   *   *   *

---

6. **Giles Corey . . . Mute:** Corey was pressed to death under heavy stones in an effort to force him to enter a plea, which according to the law at the time was required before he could be tried for witchcraft.
7. **confess'd:** Under the terms of the court at Salem, a confession of witchcraft ensured immunity from execution.
8. **Trials of the Witches:** *The Wonders of the Invisible World,* Mather's defense of the trials, was rushed into print in October 1692. Those who discussed the publication of the work included the conservative chief justice of the court at Salem, William Stoughton; Judge John Hathorne; and Sewall's brother Stephen, who lived in Salem.

Satterday, Oct. 15th Went to Cambridge and visited Mr. Danforth, and discoursed with Him about the Witchcraft; thinks there cannot be a procedure in the Court except there be some better consent of Ministers and People. Told me of the woman's coming into his house last Sabbath-day sennight at Even.[9]

*   *   *   *   *   *   *

Oct. 26, 1692. A Bill is sent in about calling a Fast, and Convocation of Ministers, that may be led in the right way as to the Witchcrafts. The season and manner of doing it, is such, that Court of Oyer and Terminer count themselves thereby dismissed. 29 Nos. and 33 yeas to the Bill. Capt. Bradstreet and Lieut. True, William Huchins and several other interested persons there, in the affirmative.[10]

Oct. 27th. Mr. Cotton Mather preaches from James, 1.4.[11]

Oct. 28th Lieut. Governour coming over the Cause[wa]y is, by reason of the high Tide, so wet, that is fain to go to bed till sends for dry cloaths to Dorchester; In the Afternoon, as had done several times before, desired to have the advice of the Governour and Council as to the sitting of the Court of Oyer and Terminer next week; said should move it no more; great silence, as if should say do not go.

Oct. 29. Mr. Russel asked whether the Court of Oyer and Terminer should sit, expressing some fear of Inconvenience by its fall. Governour said it must fall.[12]

*   *   *   *   *   *   *

Nov. 22, 1692. I prayd that God would pardon all my Sinfull Wanderings, and direct me for the future. That God would bless the Assembly in their debates, and that would chuse and

---

9. **Mr. Danforth . . . at Even:** Thomas Danforth (1622–1699), a wealthy and influential landowner, was one of the judges in the Salem trials. The woman visitor who came to his house "at Even"—that is, in the evening—is not identified.

10. **A Bill . . . affirmative:** Those who voted for the bill included Captain Dudley Bradstreet, a son of the former governor Simon Bradstreet and the poet Anne Bradstreet. As a magistrate in Andover, Massachusetts, Dudley Bradstreet had granted warrants against and subsequently committed forty people accused of witchcraft to prison. After he turned against such proceedings and refused to sit in judgment of any others, he and his wife were accused of witchcraft and were forced to flee to Boston.

11. **James, 1.4:** Mather preached his sermon on the final verse of the following passage: "James, a servant of God and of the Lord Jesus Christ, to the twelve tribes which are scattered abroad, greeting. My brethren, count it all joy when ye fall into divers temptations; Knowing this, that the trying of your faith worketh patience. But let patience have her perfect work, that ye may be perfect and entire, wanting nothing" (James 1 : 1–4).

12. **Governour said it must fall:** Governor William Phips dissolved the Court of Oyer and Terminer on October 29, 1692.

assist our Judges, &c., and save New England as to Enemies and Witchcrafts, and vindicate the late Judges, consisting with his Justice and Holiness, &c., with Fasting. . . .

*   *   *   *   *   *   *

Jany. 15. [1697]. . . . Copy of the Bill I put up on the Fast day;[13] giving it to Mr. Willard as he pass'd by, and standing up at the reading of it, and bowing when finished; in the Afternoon.

Samuel Sewall, sensible of the reiterated strokes of God upon himself and family; and being sensible, that as to the Guilt contracted, upon the opening of the late Commission of Oyer and Terminer at Salem (to which the order for this Day relates) he is, upon many accounts, more concerned than any that he knows of, Desires to take the Blame and Shame of it, Asking pardon of Men, And especially desiring prayers that God, who has an Unlimited Authority, would pardon that Sin and all other his Sins; personal and Relative: And according to his infinite Benignity, and Soveraignty, Not Visit the Sin of him, or of any other, upon himself or any of his, nor upon the Land: But that He would powerfully defend him against all Temptations to Sin, for the future; and vouchsafe him the Efficacious, Saving Conduct of his Word and Spirit.

[1692–1697, 1973]

---

13. **Copy of the Bill . . . Fast day:** Sewall publicly recanted his role in the witch trials and had this confession of his sins read aloud at church on the day set aside by the colony for fasting and repentance for the trials at Salem.

Edward Taylor

[c. 1642–1729]

Edward Taylor was born into a Puritan family in Leicestershire, England, probably in 1642, the year in which a civil war erupted that culminated in the execution of King Charles I and the establishment of a Puritan commonwealth in that country in 1650.

Very little is known about Taylor's childhood and early education, but he clearly studied languages and the Bible. Some historians believe that he may also have received formal training in those subjects at Cambridge University. After the restoration of King Charles II to the throne of England in 1660, however, conditions there became increasingly dangerous and difficult for Puritans like Taylor. Parliament swiftly passed the Act of Uniformity (1662), which required all teachers and ministers to sign an oath of allegiance to the Church of England. When he refused to sign the oath, Taylor lost his teaching position. Along with a growing number of other religious dissidents in England, he consequently decided to immigrate to New England.

Gravestone of Edward Taylor

No likeness of Taylor was made during his lifetime, much of which he spent in the small community of Westfield, Massachusetts, where he was the minister for nearly sixty years and where he was buried in 1729. His elaborately carved gravestone, which is typical of those erected by the Puritans throughout New England, is crowned by the representation of a winged figure, a hopeful symbol of resurrection.

There, Taylor fulfilled his cherished desire to become a Puritan minister. Arriving in Boston in 1668, at the age of twenty-six, he carried letters of introduction to such important men as the eminent Puritan minister Increase Mather. Taylor was soon admitted as an advanced student to Harvard College. Although he wrote some elegies and other poems as a student, he devoted himself to his studies, which included Hebrew, Latin, and Greek, as well as logic and church history. After his graduation in 1671, Taylor accepted a position as minister of a congregation in Westfield, Massachusetts, then a frontier town a hundred miles west of Boston. His ministry was successful, and Taylor was encouraged by the small congregation to organize it into a formal church. About this time, he met Elizabeth Fitch, with whom he began a courtship that involved the exchange of poems. Married in early November 1674, the couple had eight children, five of whom died in childhood, before Elizabeth herself died in 1689. Three years later, Taylor married Ruth Wyllys, with whom he had six additional children. Taylor died on June 24, 1729, having devoted nearly sixty years of his long life to the spiritual and temporal needs of his small congregation in Westfield.

Although he felt intellectually isolated there, Taylor read widely and created an impressive body of work. Immediately after settling in Westfield, he began to gather a library, often laboriously copying out by hand books he could not obtain by other means. In addition to his pastoral duties, he also wrote constantly. Scholars estimate that he preached about three thousand sermons, usually two a week, of which fewer than one hundred have survived. He also kept a journal and composed more than forty thousand lines of verse, poems ranging from private meditations and funeral elegies to a history of Christianity. For Taylor, writing poetry was at once a creative and a religious act, an integral part of his devotional life. For the most part, he imitated the poetic style of George Herbert, John Donne, and other seventeenth-century British writers called the "metaphysical poets." Like their verse, Taylor's poems are often complex and ornate, characterized by verbal dexterity, elaborate imagery, and extended metaphors. Family members were probably familiar with some of Taylor's poems, a few of which he also sent to friends in Boston. Aside from parts of those poems, however, none of Taylor's poetry was published during his lifetime. Moreover, at the time of his death in 1729, Taylor specifically requested that descendants keep his manuscripts private. His work consequently languished in obscurity until the manuscripts were discovered in an archive at Yale University by the scholar Thomas H. Johnson, who published the first edition of Taylor's poems in 1939. Since then, he has come to be recognized as a major colonial poet, one whose work illuminates both the intellectual and spiritual passion of Puritanism in New England.

bedfordstmartins.com/
americanlit *for research links on Taylor*

Reading Taylor's *Preparatory Meditations.*   This is perhaps the single most celebrated and important group of Taylor's poems, the full title of which is *Preparatory Meditations before my Approach to the Lord's Supper. Chiefly upon the Doctrine preached on the Day of Administration.* As that title indicates, Taylor wrote each of the poems in preparation for administering Communion, or the Lord's Supper. Taylor administered Communion roughly once a month, and 217 of his *Preparatory Meditations* survive, dating from 1682 to 1725. Although they rejected the Catholic doctrine of transubstantiation, or the transformation of bread and wine into the body and blood of Christ, Puritans believed that God's elect experienced a spiritual union with Christ at the Lord's Supper. As Taylor put it in one of a series of sermons on the Lord's Supper, the sacrament of Communion was "the marriage feast of the King's son," in which God "celebrates the espousals made between His own and only begotten Son, and heir of all things, and the souls of His elect." The sacrament, consequently, required devout preparation from the elect, including prayer, meditation, and self-examination. In contrast to his Communion-day sermon, which Taylor usually delivered upon the same biblical text, his poetic meditation on that text, or doctrine, was a private act of devotion addressed directly to God. The texts of the following selections from *Preparatory Meditations* are taken from *The Poems of Edward Taylor*, edited by Donald E. Stanford (1960).

PROLOGUE

Lord, Can a Crumb of Dust the Earth outweigh,
   Outmatch all mountains, nay the Chrystall Sky?
Imbosom in't designs that shall Display
   And trace into the Boundless Deity?
   Yea hand a Pen whose moysture doth guild ore   5
   Eternall Glory with a glorious glore.[1]

If it its Pen had of an Angels Quill,[2]
   And Sharpend on a Pretious Stone ground tite,
And dipt in Liquid Gold, and mov'de by Skill
   In Christall leaves should golden Letters write   10
   It would but blot and blur yea jag, and jar
   Unless thou mak'st the Pen, and Scribener.

I am this Crumb of Dust which is design'd
   To make my Pen unto thy Praise alone,
And my dull Phancy[3] I would gladly grinde   15
   Unto an Edge on Zions Pretious Stone.[4]
   And Write in Liquid Gold upon thy Name
   My Letters till thy glory forth doth flame.

Let not th'attempts breake down my Dust I pray
   Nor laugh thou them to scorn but pardon give.   20
Inspire this Crumb of Dust till it display
   Thy Glory through't: and then thy dust shall live.
   Its failings then thou'lt overlook I trust,
   They being Slips slipt from thy Crumb of Dust.

Thy Crumb of Dust breaths two words from its breast,   25
   That thou wilt guide its pen to write aright
To Prove thou art, and that thou art the best
   And shew thy Properties to shine most bright.
   And then thy Works will shine as flowers on Stems
   Or as in Jewellary Shops, do jems.   30

[c. 1682, 1960]

---

1. **glore:** Scottish dialect spelling of *glory*.
2. **Quill:** A writing instrument made by slitting the end of the shaft of a wing or tail feather of a large bird. The end is then dipped into ink and used as a pen.
3. **Phancy:** Fancy, the term frequently used in the seventeenth century for the imagination.
4. **Zions Pretious Stone:** In Christian thought, Zion is the heavenly city, the streets of which are paved with precious stones: "And the foundations of the wall of the city were garnished with all manner of precious stones. The first foundation was jasper; the second, sapphire; the third, a chalcedony; the fourth, an emerald" (Revelations 21:19).

MEDITATION 8 (FIRST SERIES)
JOHN 6:51 I AM THE LIVING BREAD[1]

I kening through Astronomy Divine
   The Worlds bright Battlement, wherein I spy
A Golden Path my Pensill cannot line,
   From that bright Throne unto my Threshold ly.
   And while my puzzled thoughts about it pore   5
   I finde the Bread of Life in't at my doore.

When that this Bird of Paradise[2] put in
   This Wicker Cage (my Corps) to tweedle praise
Had peckt the Fruite forbad: and so did fling
   Away its Food; and lost its golden dayes;   10
   It fell into Celestiall Famine sore:
   And never could attain a morsell more.

Alas! alas! Poore Bird, what wilt thou doe?
   The Creatures field no food for Souls e're gave.
And if thou knock at Angells dores they show   15
   An Empty Barrell: they no soul bread have.
   Alas! Poore Bird, the Worlds White Loafe is done.
   And cannot yield thee here the smallest Crumb.

In this sad state, Gods Tender Bowells[3] run
   Out streams of Grace: And he to end all strife   20
The Purest Wheate in Heaven, his deare-dear Son
   Grinds, and kneads up into this Bread of Life.
   Which Bread of Life from Heaven down came and stands
   Disht on thy Table up by Angells Hands.

Did God mould up this Bread in Heaven, and bake,   25
   Which from his Table came, and to thine goeth?
Doth he bespeake thee thus, This Soule Bread take.
   Come Eate thy fill of this thy Gods White Loafe?
   Its Food too fine for Angells, yet come, take
   And Eate thy fill. Its Heavens Sugar Cake.   30

---

1. **I am the Living Bread:** The text for this meditation is from John 6:22–59, which includes the account of Jesus Christ establishing the ritual of the Lord's Supper, the sacrament of Communion: "'I am the living bread which came down from heaven: if any man eat of this bread, he shall live for ever: and the bread that I will give is my flesh, which I will give for the life of the world'" (John 6:51).
2. **Bird of Paradise:** A beautiful tropical bird, here representing the soul encaged within the body.
3. **Bowells:** The deep interior of the body, including the heart, considered the seat of tender and compassionate emotions.

What Grace is this knead in this Loafe? This thing
    Souls are but petty things it to admire.
Yee Angells, help: This fill would to the brim
    Heav'ns whelm'd-down[4] Chrystall meele Bowle, yea and higher.
    This Bread of Life dropt in thy mouth, doth Cry.   35
    Eate, Eate me, Soul, and thou shalt never dy.

                                 [June 8, 1684, 1960]

---

4. **welm'd-down:** Turned upside down.

Reading Taylor's Miscellaneous Poems.   From the time he was in college to the end of his life, Taylor wrote a wide range of miscellaneous poems. Some of them were occasioned by specific events, including the deaths of his first wife and several of his children, while others were more abstract meditations on religious issues like the struggle between the terrors of death and the triumphant faith in Resurrection. Still other poems reveal Taylor's richly imaginative response to the mundane particulars of his immediate material world, which he uses to develop sustained and often surprising analogies or parallels to spiritual mysteries, for example the operation of God's saving grace on the souls of the elect. In such poems, Taylor reveals his mastery of a device earlier exploited by English poets such as John Donne and George Herbert, the "metaphysical conceit," which the English critic Dr. Samuel Johnson famously defined as "a combination of dissimilar images, or the discovery of occult resemblances in things apparently unlike." The texts of the following poems are taken from *Poems of Edward Taylor*, edited by Donald E. Stanford (1960).

UPON WEDLOCK, AND DEATH OF CHILDREN

    A Curious Knot[1] God made in Paradise,
        And drew it out inamled[2] neatly Fresh.
    It was the True-Love Knot, more sweet than spice
        And set with all the flowres of Graces dress.
        Its Weddens Knot,[3] that ne're can be unti'de.   5
        No Alexanders Sword[4] can it divide.

    The slips[5] here planted, gay and glorious grow:
        Unless an Hellish breath do sindge their Plumes.

---

1. **Knot:** A flower bed, sometimes called a flower-knot, laid out in an intricate design.
2. **inamled:** Enameled, or polished.
3. **Weddens Knot:** The wedding ceremony in which a couple is joined in matrimony.
4. **Alexanders Sword:** Ancient legends said that whoever could untie the Gordian knot, a complicated knot tied by Gordius, father of King Midas, would rule Asia. Alexander the Great (356-323 BCE) simply cut the knot in two with his sword and then conquered much of the ancient world.
5. **slips:** Cuttings taken from a plant for planting or grafting.

Here Primrose, Cowslips, Roses, Lilies blow
   With Violets and Pinkes that voide perfumes.   10
   Whose beautious leaves ore laid with Hony Dew.
   And Chanting birds Cherp out sweet Musick true.

When in this Knot I planted was, my Stock
   Soon knotted, and a manly flower out brake.[6]
And after it my branch again did knot   15
   Brought out another Flowre[7] its sweet breathd mate.
   One knot gave one tother the tothers place.
   Whence Checkling smiles fought in each others face.

But oh! a glorious hand from glory came
   Guarded with Angells, soon did Crop this flowre   20
Which almost tore the root up of the same
   At that unlookt for, Dolesome, darksome houre.
   In Pray're to Christ perfum'de it did ascend,
   And Angells bright did it to heaven tend.

But pausing on't, this sweet perfum'd my thought,   25
   Christ would in Glory have a Flowre, Choice, Prime,
And having Choice, chose this my branch forth brought.
   Lord take't. I thanke thee, thou takst ought of mine,
   It is my pledg in glory, part of mee
   Is now in it, Lord, glorifi'de with thee.   30

But praying ore my branch, my branch did sprout
   And bore another manly flower,[8] and gay
And after that another, sweet brake out,
   The which the former hand soon got away.[9]
   But oh! the tortures, Vomit, screechings, groans,   35
   And six weeks Fever would pierce hearts like stones.

Griefe o're doth flow: and nature fault would finde
   Were not thy Will, my Spell Charm, Joy, and Gem:
That as I said, I say, take, Lord, they're thine.
   I piecemeale pass to Glory bright in them.   40
   I joy, may I sweet Flowers for Glory breed,
   Whether thou getst them green, or lets them seed.

                              [c. 1682, 1960]

---

6. **a manly flower out brake:** Samuel Taylor, his first son, born on August 27, 1675.
7. **another Flowre:** A daughter, Elizabeth Taylor, was born on December 27, 1677; but she died a year later (see line 20).
8. **bore another manly flower:** Another son, James Taylor, was born on October 12, 1678.
9. **And after that another . . . got away:** A second daughter, Abigail Taylor, was born on August 6, 1681; as did the first daughter, she died a year later.

UPON A SPIDER CATCHING A FLY

Thou sorrow, venom Elfe.
  Is this thy play,
To spin a web out of thyselfe
    To Catch a Fly?
      For Why?   5

I saw a pettish[1] wasp
  Fall foule therein.
Whom yet thy Whorle pins[2] did not clasp
    Lest he should fiing
      His sting.   10

But as affraid, remote
  Didst stand hereat
And with thy little fingers stroke
    And gently tap
      His back.   15

Thus gently him didst treate
  Lest he should pet,
And in a froppish,[3] waspish heate
    Should greatly fret
      Thy net.   20

Whereas the silly Fly,
  Caught by its leg
Thou by the throate tookst hastily
    And 'hinde the head
      Bite Dead.   25

This goes to pot, that not
  Nature doth call.[4]
Strive not above what strength hath got
    Lest in the brawle
      Thou fall.   30

This Frey[5] seems thus to us.
  Hells Spider gets

---

1. **pettish:** Peevish or ill-humored.
2. **Whorle pins:** Small flywheels fixed on the side of a spinning wheel to regulate speed.
3. **froppish:** Fretful or peevish.
4. **This goes to pot, that not / Nature doth call:** That is, those who do not call upon "Nature," or natural reason, "go to pot."
5. **Frey:** Fray, a battle or fight.

His intrails spun to whip Cords thus
   And wove to nets
      And sets.   35

To tangle Adams race
   In's stratigems
To their Destructions, spoil'd, made base
   By venom things
      Damn'd Sins.   40

But mighty, Gracious Lord
   Communicate
Thy Grace to breake the Cord, afford
   Us Glorys Gate
      And State.   45

We'l Nightingaile sing like
   When pearcht on high
In Glories Cage, thy glory, bright,
   And thankfully,
      For joy.   50

                                             [?, 1960]

Huswifery[1]

Make me, O Lord, thy Spining Wheele compleate.[2]
   Thy Holy Worde my Distaff make for mee.
Make mine Affections thy Swift Flyers neate
   And make my Soule thy holy Spoole to bee.
My Conversation make to be thy Reele   5
And reele the yarn thereon spun of thy Wheele.

Make me thy Loome then, knit therein this Twine:
And make thy Holy Spirit, Lord, winde quills:[3]

---

1. **Huswifery:** A collective term for household duties, usually performed by the wife, or housewife. In this poem, the emphasis is on the process of making cloth, in preparation for making clothes.
2. **Spining Wheele compleate:** The spinning wheel, which produces thread from raw wool or flax, operates by using a distaff, which holds the flax or wool in place; flyers, which regulate the spinning; a spool, which captures and twists the yarn; and a reel, upon which the thread is wound.
3. **quills:** Spindles or bobbins on which thread is wound.

Then weave the Web thyselfe. The yarn is fine.
Thine Ordinances make my Fulling Mills.[4]   10
Then dy the same in Heavenly Colours Choice,
All pinkt with Varnisht Flowers of Paradise.

Then cloath therewith mine Understanding, Will,
    Affections, Judgment, Conscience, Memory
My Words, and Actions, that their shine may fill   15
    My wayes with glory and thee glorify.
Then mine apparell shall display before yee
That I am Cloathd in Holy robes for glory.

[?, 1960]

---

4. **Fulling Mills:** A mill in which cloth is "fulled," or cleaned, by being beaten with wooden mallets and cleansed with soap or "fuller's earth," an absorbent, claylike substance.

William Byrd

[1674–1744]

William Byrd II was born on March 28, 1674, in Henrico County, Virginia. His parents were William Byrd I, a wealthy planter and merchant who had come to Virginia in the 1660s at the invitation of an uncle whose estate he later inherited; and Mary Horsmanden, whose Royalist parents had come to Virginia after the establishment of the Puritan Commonwealth in England in 1649. In preparation for his future role as a prominent member of the social and political elite, when he was seven years old Byrd was sent to England, where he received a classical education at the Felsted Grammar School in Essex. He later learned the international tobacco trade from his father's business agents in London, where Byrd immersed himself in fashionable society; studied law and was admitted to the bar; and was inducted into the Royal Society in 1696. Returning to Virginia, he was elected to the House of Burgesses and soon sent back to London as the official representative of the governor and, later, of the Virginia Council. After his father's death in 1704, Byrd once again returned to Virginia, where he had inherited extensive landholdings, including Westover, a tobacco plantation on the James River. He soon married Lucy Parke, the daughter of another wealthy landowner, with whom he had two sons who died in infancy and two daughters. Although their relationship was tempestuous, Byrd was deeply grieved when his wife died of smallpox in 1715. Eight years later, he married Maria Taylor, with whom he had four more children, three daughters and a son. Active in public affairs, in 1709 Byrd was appointed to the Virginia Council, on which he served for the rest of his life, and he once again served as Virginia's official agent in London from 1715 to 1720 and 1721 to 1726.

William Byrd

This anonymous portrait was painted sometime between 1715 and 1725, when Byrd was in his forties. In the portrait, he assumes the pose of and is portrayed as the very embodiment of the colonial English gentleman, gesturing toward a natural background that may have represented Westover, his extensive plantation in Virginia.

Despite those achievements, his most enduring legacy proved to be literary, not political or diplomatic. Fluent in several languages, Byrd collected one of the largest and most diverse libraries in the North American colonies at Westover. He published some satirical poems under the pseudonym "Mr. Burrard," and the death of his first wife prompted him to write a pamphlet in which he argued for inoculation against smallpox, *A Discourse Concerning the Plague*, which was published anonymously in London in 1721. But most of his extensive writings, which were circulated in manuscript among family and friends in Virginia and England, were not published until the nineteenth or twentieth century. Perhaps his most famous work is *The History of the Dividing Line*, the account of a commission he and others undertook in 1728 to survey the disputed boundary between Virginia and North Carolina. That expedition also inspired *The Secret History of the Dividing Line*, a more candid and satirical account in which Byrd casts himself as picaresque hero Colonel Steddy. His other writings include the narrative of a trip he took in 1733, *A Journey to the Land of Eden*, a promotional tract designed to attract immigrants to the lands that he owned west of the James River, where he set out the new towns of Petersburg and Richmond. When Byrd died at Westover on August 26, 1744, he left a vast estate of nearly 180,000 acres in Virginia. The family fortune was squandered by his son, William Byrd III, a gambler and speculator who was forced to sell off his father's beloved library of more than three thousand books, as well as most of the estate and its hundreds of slaves, before committing suicide at Westover in 1777.

Reading *The Secret Diary of William Byrd of Westover.*   Many of Byrd's writings were based on his extensive diaries, which he began to keep in 1709. He wrote the diaries in a code devised by William Mason, a London secretary and author of *La Plume Volante; or, The Art of Short-Hand Improv'd* (1707). When the diaries were finally transcribed and published in the twentieth century, they were recognized as a major source of information about the plantation and slave-labor system that emerged during the century following the establishment of Jamestown. At the same time, Byrd faithfully and with remarkable candor recorded details of his private life, ranging from his daily regimen and reading in several languages to arguments with his wife and his unchecked sexual appetite. But scholars have suggested that the diaries are not simply a revealing record of his activities, attitudes, and behavior, but also a sustained effort to fashion and maintain his identity as an English gentleman amid the material and cultural conditions of provincial Virginia. The text of the following diary entries written during 1712, when Byrd turned thirty-eight, is taken from *The Secret Diary of William Byrd of Westover, 1709-1712,* edited by Louis B. Wright and Marion Tinling (1941).

From THE SECRET DIARY OF WILLIAM BYRD OF WESTOVER

January, 1712

1. I lay abed till 9 o'clock this morning to bring my wife into temper again and rogered her[1] by way of reconciliation. I read nothing because Mr. Mumford was here, nor did I say my prayers, for the same reason. However I ate boiled milk for breakfast, and after my wife tempted me to eat some pancakes with her. Mr. Mumford and I went to shoot with our bows and arrows but shot nothing, and afterwards we played at billiards till dinner, and when we came we found Ben Harrison there, who dined with us. I ate some partridge for dinner. In the afternoon we played at billiards again and I won two bits. I had a letter from Colonel Duke by H-l[2] the bricklayer who came to offer his services to work for me. Mr. Mumford went away in the evening and John Bannister with him to see his mother. I took a walk about the plantation and at night we drank some mead of my wife's making which was very good. I gave the people some cider and a dram to the negroes. I read some Latin in Terence[3] and had good health, good thoughts, and good humor, thank God Almighty. I said my prayers.

16. I rose about 7 o'clock and read a chapter in Hebrew and some Greek in Lucian.[4] I said my prayers and ate boiled milk for breakfast. I danced my dance.[5] My wife was

---

1. **rogered her:** That is, had sexual intercourse with her. As his diary illustrates, Byrd had a tempestuous relationship with his first wife, Lucy Parke (d. 1719), who later died of smallpox when Byrd was working as a colonial agent in London.
2. **H-l:** Because Byrd wrote his diary in shorthand, he often did not include vowels in names, making them difficult or impossible to transcribe.
3. **Latin in Terence:** African-born Roman writer (185-159 BCE) of comedies, which Byrd was reading in Latin.
4. **some Greek in Lucian:** A Greek satirist (c. 120-180) famous for his parodies of ancient myths.
5. **I danced my dance:** Most scholars believe that Byrd refers to performing exercises or calisthenics.

something better and rode out because it was very fine weather and not cold. We killed a beef this morning that came yesterday from Burkland where they were all well, thank God. I settled some accounts till dinner and then I ate some hash of beef. In the afternoon my wife shaved me and then I walked out to see my people plant trees and I was angry with John for mistaking Mr. G-r-l's directions. Then I showed him again and helped him plant several trees. Then I took a walk till night. When I came in my [wife] persuaded me me [sic] to eat skim milk for supper. Then I read some Latin in Terence. I said my prayers and had good thoughts, good humor, and good health, thank God Almighty. I dreamed a coffin was brought into my house and thrown into the hall.

18. I rose about 7 o'clock and read a chapter in Hebrew and some Greek in Lucian. I said my prayers and ate boiled milk for breakfast. I danced my dance. The weather was clear and cold but the wind was northeast. I settled several accounts and then read some Latin in Terence till dinner, and then I ate some boiled beef but I was displeased with my wife for giving the child marrow against my opinion. In the afternoon I read a little more Latin and then went to see my people plant peach trees and afterwards took a great walk about the plantation and found everything in order, for which I praised God. I was entertained with seeing a hawk which had taken a small bird pursued by another hawk, so that he was forced to let go his prey. My walk lasted till the evening and at night I read some Latin in Terence. I said my prayers and had good health, good thoughts, and good humor, thank God Almighty. . . .

February, 1712

5. I rose about 8 o'clock, my wife kept me so long in bed where I rogered her. I read nothing because I put my matters in order. I neglected to say my prayers but ate boiled milk for breakfast. My wife caused several of the people[6] to be whipped for their laziness. I settled accounts and put several matters in order till dinner. I ate some boiled beef. In the afternoon I ordered my sloop to go to Colonel Eppes' for some poplar trees for the Governor and then I went to visit Mrs. Harrison that I found in a small way. She entertained me with apples and bad wine and I stayed with her till evening and then I took a walk about my plantation. When I returned I learned Peter Poythress had been here. At night I read some Latin. I said my prayers and had good health, good thoughts, and good humor, thank God Almighty. I rogered my wife again.

March, 1712

2. I rose about 7 o'clock and read a chapter in Hebrew but no Greek because Mr. G-r-l was here and I wished to talk with him. I ate boiled milk for breakfast and danced my dance. I reprimanded him for drawing so many notes on me. However I told him if he would let me know his debts I would pay them provided he would let a mulatto of mine

---

6. **people:** Although many of the Byrds' servants were slaves brought from Africa, some were white indentured servants from Europe who also labored under difficult and often inhumane conditions.

that is his apprentice come to work at Falling Creek the last two years of his service, which he agreed. I had a terrible quarrel with my wife concerning Jenny that I took away from her when she was beating her with the tongs. She lifted up her hands to strike me but forbore to do it. She gave me abundance of bad words and endeavored to strangle herself, but I believe in jest only. However after acting a mad woman a long time she was passive again. I ate some roast beef for dinner. In the afternoon Mr. G-r-l went away and I took a walk about the plantation. At night we drank some cider by way of reconciliation and I read nothing. I said my prayers and had good health, good thoughts, and good humor, thank God Almighty. I sent Tom to Williamsburg with some fish to the Governor and my sister Custis. My daughter was indisposed with a small fever.

23. I rose about 6 o'clock and read two chapters in Hebrew and some Greek in the Greek Testament.[7] I said my prayers and ate boiled milk for breakfast. I danced my dance. The sloop came from Appomattox with 60 hogsheads of tobacco. Shockoe Billy came from the Falls and bore a letter from Tom Turpin which let me know all was well there. He desired me to provide myself with another overseer because I found fault with some of his management and I wrote him word I would do as he desired. I ate some roast shoat for dinner. My wife had a little fever this morning but it soon went off again. About 2 o'clock Tom Randolph came and was wet with a gust that happened about that time and soon after came Tom from Williamsburg and told me the Doctor was gone to Rappahannock with Mrs. Russell and would not be home before this night. Mr. Randolph and I took a walk about the plantation. At night came G-r-l and told me all was well at Falling Creek. We drank a bottle of cider. I said a short prayer and had good health, good thoughts, and good humor, thank God Almighty. It thundered and rained this evening. My wife [took] another dose of bark.[8]

April, 1712

4. I rose about 7 o'clock and read a chapter in Hebrew and some Greek in Lucian. I said my prayers and ate boiled milk for breakfast. I wrote two letters to the quarters and one to Williamsburg and sent the last by my sister Custis who would go, notwithstanding it was like to rain. About 11 o'clock Mr. Salle went away likewise. I settled several accounts and wrote in my journal till dinner and then I ate some fish. In the afternoon I rogered my wife again. The weather was very bad and it rained almost all day so that my poor sister was terribly wet except she called at some house. My wife and I took a nap after dinner and after our roger. I settled several accounts and read some news. It rained till night so that I could not walk. At night came the master of a ship lately come from Lisbon. We gave him some supper and I ate some broiled turkey with him. He told me he would let me have eight dozen of bottles of Lisbon wine. I said my prayers and had good health, good thoughts, and good humor, thank God Almighty.

---

7. **Greek Testament:** The New Testament of the Bible, published in Greek.
8. **bark:** Quinine, made from the bark of the cinchona tree ground into powder, was taken as a medicine to reduce fever.

May, 1712

22. I rose about 6 o'clock and read two chapters in Hebrew and some Greek in Lucian. I said my prayers and ate boiled milk for breakfast. I danced my dance. It rained a little this morning. My wife caused Prue[9] to be whipped violently notwithstanding I desired not, which provoked me to have Anaka[10] whipped likewise who had deserved it much more, on which my wife flew into such a passion that she hoped she would be revenged of me. I was moved very much at this but only thanked her for the present lest I should say things foolish in my passion. I wrote more accounts to go to England. My wife was sorry for what she had said and came to ask my pardon and I forgave her in my heart but seemed to resent, that she might be the more sorry for her folly. She ate no dinner nor appeared the whole day. I ate some bacon for dinner. In the afternoon I wrote two more accounts till the evening and then took a walk in the garden. I said my prayers and was reconciled to my wife and gave her a flourish in token of it. I had good health, good thoughts, but was a little out of humor, for which God forgive me.

25. I rose about 8 o'clock and read two chapters in Hebrew and no Greek. I said my prayers and ate boiled milk for breakfast. I danced my dance. The weather was very clear and cold. About 11 o'clock we went to church where Mr. Anderson gave us a good sermon. The two Mrs. Thomsons were come up to see Mrs. Eppes and I invited them to come and see us. I took three of the masters of ships home with us to dinner and I ate some dried beef. In the afternoon the masters went away very early and we went to take a walk in the evening. At night we drank a bottle and the women went upstairs by themselves. I said my prayers and was out of humor that my wife did not come to bed soon. I had good health, good humor, and good health [*sic*], thank God Almighty.

27. I rose about 5 o'clock and read a chapter in Hebrew and some Greek. I said my prayers and ate milk and hominy for breakfast. I danced my dance. The weather was cloudy and hot. My wife was pretty well, thank God. About 9 o'clock Mr. Mumford and Tom Randolph went away. I read some English and then a sermon in Tillotson till dinner and then I ate some roast mutton for dinner. In the afternoon I took a nap and then read some news. My wife and Mrs. Dunn went out in the coach and I read some Latin till the evening and then I took a walk about the plantation and in the orchard where there was abundance of fruit. I said my prayers and had good health, good thoughts, and good humor, thank God Almighty. Negro Sue was brought to bed of a boy.

September, 1712

29. I rose about 7 o'clock and went again into the river against my ague.[11] I read a chapter in Hebrew and some Greek in Lucian. I said my prayers and ate boiled milk for breakfast. I danced my dance. I continued very well, thank God. The weather was cold, the wind northeast. My wife was pretty well. About 11 o'clock I was a little fevered and

---

9. **Prue:** A servant; her race and status are not known.
10. **Anaka:** An enslaved African woman.
11. **ague:** A bout of fever and shivering, often associated with malaria, which was then common in the southern colonies.

my head ached a little; however I would not give way to it. I had not much stomach to dinner; however I ate some broiled beef. In the afternoon I put several things in order in the library and at night Mr. Catesby came and told me he had seen a bear. I took Tom L-s-n and went with a gun and Mr. Catesby shot him. It was only a cub and he sat on a tree to eat grapes. I was better with this diversion and we were merry in the evening. I said my prayers and had good health, good thoughts, and good humor, thank God Almighty.

[1712, 1941]

Jonathan Edwards

[1703-1758]

Jonathan Edwards was born in East Windsor, Connecticut, on October 5, 1703. He was one of eleven children but the only son of Esther Stoddard, the daughter of an influential minister, and Timothy Edwards, the minister of the congregation of East Windsor. Edwards was tutored at home by his father and mother, learning Latin, Greek, and Hebrew. At age thirteen, he went to the Yale Collegiate School at Wethersfield, about ten miles from his home. He was a good student who clearly flourished at the school. At the same time, Edwards was deeply religious and pursued many solitary interests, including a fascination with nature. In his *Personal Narrative*—which along with some letters to his father constitute most of the information available about his early life—Edwards describes an illness at college and his ongoing concern with the state of his soul: "[God] brought me nigh to the grave, and shook me over the pit of hell." In the aftermath of his illness, Edwards eventually found a new inner peace and what he describes in his *Narrative* as a "delightful" conviction of the absolute sovereignty of God, a conviction that he held throughout his life.

Joseph Badger, *Jonathan Edwards* (1720)

Painted when he was only seventeen and in his final year at Yale College, this portrait reveals the gravity that Edwards would later display as one of the greatest preachers in the history of New England.

Given his background, education, and profound piety, Edwards was virtually destined to become a famous Puritan minister. From an early age, he was also distinguished by his remarkable intellect and wide-ranging interests. He spent his final year of college at Yale in New Haven, where in addition to pursuing his theological studies Edwards wrote "Of Insects," one of the earliest of a series of essays that included "Of Atoms," "Of Light

Rays," and "Of the Rainbow." Like his other scientific and philosophical writings, those essays revealed his abiding interest in natural phenomena and his rigorous study of the "new" sciences, especially the optical and astronomical theories of Isaac Newton. After he graduated first in his class in 1720, Edwards remained at Yale in order to prepare for the ministry. Licensed to preach in 1722, he accepted a position in a small Presbyterian church in New York City, where Edwards continued his habits of meditation and solitary reflection during long walks on the banks of the Hudson River. In a diary he kept during those years, Edwards prays: "Lord, grant that I may hence learn to withdraw my thoughts, affections, desires and expectations, entirely from the world, and may fix them on the heavenly state, where reigns heavenly, sweet, calm and delightful love without alloy."

Edwards, however, became deeply involved in the religious affairs and theological conflicts of this world. In May of 1724, Yale offered him the position of tutor, which meant that he was, in effect, the president of the college. Edwards remained there until he was ordained as a minister in 1727. He then became an assistant pastor in the church led by his grandfather Solomon Stoddard, sometimes called "Pope" Stoddard in derisive recognition of the influence he wielded from his powerful pulpit in the affluent commercial town of Northampton, Massachusetts. That year, Edwards also married Sarah Pierpont, with whom he eventually had eleven children. After his grandfather's death in 1729, Edwards succeeded him as pastor of the church in Northampton, from which his renown soon spread throughout New England. A sermon he delivered in Boston, "God Glorified," was published amid great acclaim in 1731. He began to publish his sermons regularly, and a collection of them appeared as *Discourses on Various Important Subjects* in 1738. Edwards was quickly becoming a foremost Puritan writer. But he gained his greatest fame as one of the leaders of the Great Awakening, a religious revival that flared up locally in 1734-35 and then swept across the colonies in the early 1740s. Answering critics who viewed the first revival as an uncontrolled manifestation of religious "enthusiasm," or mere emotionalism, Edwards published *A Faithful Narrative of the Surprising Works of God in the Conversion of Many Hundred Souls in Northampton and Neighboring Towns* (1736). During the second and far-more-intense wave of revivals, Edwards delivered his most famous sermon, "Sinners in the Hands of an Angry God," which was published soon after he delivered it in 1741. Two years later, he published his fullest defense of the Great Awakening, *Some Thoughts Concerning the Present Revival of Religion in New-England, and the Way in Which It Ought to Be Acknowledged and Prompted* (1743).

In the aftermath of the Great Awakening, Edwards was increasingly at odds with his congregation in Northampton. Although there were numerous sources of tension, the major point of contention was the requirement for participation in the sacrament of Communion, or the Lord's Supper. In an earlier period, Communion was administered only to full church members — that is, those who had experienced and given a public account of their conversion. As the number of full church members declined, however, the strict requirement was relaxed by ministers like Solomon Stoddard, who argued that Communion should be open to all members of the congregation, whether or not they had given evidence of their conversion. Edwards initially followed that practice, but in his *Treatise Concerning Religious Affections* (1746) he argued for a return to the earlier requirement. His effort to impose that rule ultimately led to his dismissal from his church in Northampton, where Edwards vigorously defended his position in his "Farewell Sermon," delivered in June 1750. Undaunted by "the People's Publick Rejection of their Minister," as he described it in the full title of the published version of the sermon, Edwards became a missionary to the Housatonic River Indians in Stockbridge, Massachusetts. There, he composed a number of works, including two of his most important theological treatises, *Freedom of Will* (1754) and *The Great Christian Doctrine of Original Sin Defended* (1758). In 1757, he was appointed president of Princeton College, but he died a few months after his induction, on February 16, 1758.

bedfordstmartins.com/ americanlit for research links on Edwards

Reading Edwards's *Personal Narrative.*   In his autobiography, Edwards offers few details concerning the outward aspects of his life or his personal relationships. Instead, his is a spiritual autobiography, designed as a record of his religious doubts, struggles, and triumphs. Since the latest date he refers to in the narrative is 1739, Edwards evidently wrote it later, probably around 1740. Although we do not know why he wrote the account, it may well have been inspired by his involvement in the wave of religious revivals known collectively as the Great Awakening. Even though he was a strong supporter of the movement, Edwards was concerned about the possibility that some of those who were swept up in the spirit of the revivals might confuse mere emotional excess as a sign of a true conversion experience. Edwards may consequently have written his dispassionate account as a kind of spiritual guide for others, an effort to help them distinguish between false or misleading signs and true evidences of the operation of God's grace within their souls. The narrative apparently circulated in manuscript, but it did not appear in print until seven years after Edwards's death, when Samuel Hopkins published it as "An Account of His Conversion, Experiences, and Religious Exercises" in *The Life and Character of the Late Rev. Mr. Jonathan Edwards* (1765). The following text is taken from the Yale University Press *Works of Jonathan Edwards*, Vol. 16, edited by George S. Claghorn (1998).

PERSONAL NARRATIVE

I had a variety of concerns and exercises about my soul from my childhood; but had two more remarkable seasons of awakening,[1] before I met with that change, by which I was brought to those new dispositions, and that new sense of things, that I have since had.

---

1. **awakening:** Spiritual awakening.

The first time was when I was a boy, some years before I went to college, at a time of remarkable awakening in my father's congregation. I was then very much affected for many months, and concerned about the things of religion, and my soul's salvation; and was abundant in duties. I used to pray five times a day in secret, and to spend much time in religious talk with other boys; and used to meet with them to pray together. I experienced I know not what kind of delight in religion. My mind was much engaged in it, and had much self-righteous pleasure; and it was my delight to abound in religious duties. I, with some of my schoolmates joined together, and built a booth in a swamp, in a very secret and retired place, for a place of prayer. And besides, I had particular secret places of my own in the woods, where I used to retire by myself; and used to be from time to time much affected. My affections seemed to be lively and easily moved, and I seemed to be in my element, when engaged in religious duties. And I am ready to think, many are deceived with such affections, and such a kind of delight, as I then had in religion, and mistake it for grace.

But in process of time, my convictions and affections wore off; and I entirely lost all those affections and delights, and left off secret prayer, at least as to any constant performance of it; and returned like a dog to his vomit,[2] and went on in ways of sin.

Indeed, I was at some times very uneasy, especially towards the latter part of the time of my being at college. Till it pleased God, in my last year at college, at a time when I was in the midst of many uneasy thoughts about the state of my soul, to seize me with a pleurisy;[3] in which he brought me nigh to the grave, and shook me over the pit of hell.

But yet, it was not long after my recovery, before I fell again into my old ways of sin. But God would not suffer me to go on with any quietness; but I had great and violent inward struggles: till after many conflicts with wicked inclinations, and repeated resolutions, and bonds that I laid myself under by a kind of vows to God, I was brought wholly to break off all former wicked ways, and all ways of known outward sin; and to apply myself to seek my salvation, and practice the duties of religion: but without that kind of affection and delight, that I had formerly experienced. My concern now wrought more by inward struggles and conflicts, and self-reflections. I made seeking my salvation the main business of my life. But yet it seems to me, I sought after a miserable manner: which has made me sometimes since to question, whether ever it issued in that which was saving; being ready to doubt, whether such miserable seeking was ever succeeded. But yet I was brought to seek salvation, in a manner that I never was before. I felt a spirit to part with all things in the world, for an interest in Christ. My concern continued and prevailed, with many exercising things and inward struggles; but yet it never seemed to be proper to express my concern that I had, by the name of terror.

From my childhood up, my mind had been wont to be full of objections against the doctrine of God's sovereignty, in choosing whom he would to eternal life, and rejecting whom he pleased; leaving them eternally to perish, and be everlastingly tormented in

---

2. **returned like a dog to his vomit:** See Proverbs 26:11: "As a dog returneth to his vomit, so a fool returneth to his folly."
3. **pleurisy:** An upper-respiratory illness that makes it difficult and painful to breathe.

hell. It used to appear like a horrible doctrine to me. But I remember the time very well, when I seemed to be convinced, and fully satisfied, as to this sovereignty of God, and his justice in thus eternally disposing of men, according to his sovereign pleasure. But never could give an account, how, or by what means, I was thus convinced; not in the least imagining, in the time of it, nor a long time after, that there was any extraordinary influence of God's Spirit in it: but only that now I saw further, and my reason apprehended the justice and reasonableness of it. However, my mind rested in it; and it put an end to all those cavils and objections, that had till then abode with me, all the preceding part of my life. And there has been a wonderful alteration in my mind, with respect to the doctrine of God's sovereignty, from that day to this; so that I scarce ever have found so much as the rising of an objection against God's sovereignty, in the most absolute sense, in showing mercy on whom he will show mercy, and hardening and eternally damning whom he will.[4] God's absolute sovereignty, and justice, with respect to salvation and damnation, is what my mind seems to rest assured of, as much as of anything that I see with my eyes; at least it is so at times. But I have oftentimes since that first conviction, had quite another kind of sense of God's sovereignty, than I had then. I have often since, not only had a conviction, but a *delightful* conviction. The doctrine of God's sovereignty has very often appeared, an exceeding pleasant, bright and sweet doctrine to me: and absolute sovereignty is what I love to ascribe to God. But my first conviction was not with this.

The first that I remember that ever I found anything of that sort of inward, sweet delight in God and divine things, that I have lived much in since, was on reading those words, I Timothy 1:17, "Now unto the King eternal, immortal, invisible, the only wise God, be honor and glory forever and ever, Amen." As I read the words, there came into my soul, and was as it were diffused through it, a sense of the glory of the divine being; a new sense, quite different from anything I ever experienced before. Never any words of Scripture seemed to me as these words did. I thought with myself, how excellent a Being that was; and how happy I should be, if I might enjoy that God, and be wrapt up to God in heaven, and be as it were swallowed up in him. I kept saying, and as it were singing over these words of Scripture to myself; and went to prayer, to pray to God that I might enjoy him; and prayed in a manner quite different from what I used to do; with a new sort of affection. But it never came into my thought, that there was anything spiritual, or of a saving nature in this.

From about that time, I began to have a new kind of apprehensions and ideas of Christ, and the work of redemption, and the glorious way of salvation by him. I had an inward, sweet sense of these things, that at times came into my heart; and my soul was led away in pleasant views and contemplations of them. And my mind was greatly engaged, to spend my time in reading and meditating on Christ; and the beauty and excellency of his person, and the lovely way of salvation, by free grace in him. I found no books so delightful to me, as those that treated of these subjects. Those words

---

4. **in showing mercy . . . and eternally damning whom he will:** See Romans 9:18: "Therefore hath he mercy on whom he will have mercy, and whom he will he hardeneth."

(Canticles 2:1)[5] used to be abundantly with me: "I am the rose of Sharon, the lily of the valleys." The words seemed to me, sweetly to represent, the loveliness and beauty of Jesus Christ. And the whole book of Canticles used to be pleasant to me; and I used to be much in reading it, about that time. And found, from time to time, an inward sweetness, that used, as it were, to carry me away in my contemplations; in what I know not how to express otherwise, than by a calm, sweet abstraction of soul from all the concerns o[f] this world; and a kind of vision, or fixed ideas and imaginations, of being alone in the mountains, or some solitary wilderness, far from all mankind, sweetly conversing with Christ, and wrapt and swallowed up in God. The sense I had of divine things, would often of a sudden as it were, kindle up a sweet burning in my heart; an ardor of my soul, that I know not how to express.

Not long after I first began to experience these things, I gave an account to my father, of some things that had passed in my mind. I was pretty much affected by the discourse we had together. And when the discourse was ended, I walked abroad alone, in a solitary place in my father's pasture, for contemplation. And as I was walking there, and looked up on the sky and clouds; there came into my mind, a sweet sense of the glorious majesty and grace of God, that I know not how to express. I seemed to see them both in a sweet conjunction: majesty and meekness joined together: it was a sweet and gentle, and holy majesty; and also a majestic meekness; an awful sweetness; a high, and great, and holy gentleness.

After this my sense of divine things gradually increased, and became more and more lively, and had more of that inward sweetness. The appearance of everything was altered: there seemed to be, as it were, a calm, sweet cast, or appearance of divine glory, in almost everything. God's excellency, his wisdom, his purity and love, seemed to appear in everything; in the sun, moon and stars; in the clouds, and blue sky; in the grass, flowers, trees; in the water, and all nature; which used greatly to fix my mind. I often used to sit and view the moon, for a long time; and so in the daytime, spent much time in viewing the clouds and sky, to behold the sweet glory of God in these things: in the meantime, singing forth with a low voice, my contemplations of the Creator and Redeemer. And scarce anything, among all the works of nature, was so sweet to me as thunder and lightning. Formerly, nothing had been so terrible to me. I used to be a person uncommonly terrified with thunder: and it used to strike me with terror, when I saw a thunderstorm rising. But now, on the contrary, it rejoiced me. I felt God at the first appearance of a thunderstorm. And used to take the opportunity at such times, to fix myself to view the clouds, and see the lightnings play, and hear the majestic and awful voice of God's thunder: which often times was exceeding entertaining, leading me to sweet contemplations of my great and glorious God. And while I viewed, used to spend my time, as it always seemed natural to me, to sing or chant forth my meditations; to speak my thoughts in soliloquies, and speak with a singing voice.

---

5. **Canticles 2:1:** Canticles is another name for the Song of Solomon, a collection of love poems in the Old Testament. In the Christian tradition, it has been interpreted as an allegory of the love of Christ for his bride the church, or of the individual's experience of divine love.

I felt then a great satisfaction as to my good estate.[6] But that did not content me. I had vehement longings of soul after God and Christ, and after more holiness; wherewith my heart seemed to be full, and ready to break: which often brought to my mind, the words of the Psalmist, Psalms 119:28, "My soul breaketh for the longing it hath." I often felt a mourning and lamenting in my heart, that I had not turned to God sooner, that I might have had more time to grow in grace. My mind was greatly fixed on divine things; I was almost perpetually in the contemplation of them. Spent most of my time in thinking of divine things, year after year. And used to spend abundance of my time, in walking alone in the woods, and solitary places, for meditation, soliloquy and prayer, and converse with God. And it was always my manner, at such times, to sing forth my contemplations. And was almost constantly in ejaculatory prayer, wherever I was. Prayer seemed to be natural to me; as the breath, by which the inward burnings of my heart had vent.

The delights which I now felt in things of religion, were of an exceeding different kind, from those forementioned, that I had when I was a boy. They were totally of another kind; and what I then had no more notion or idea of, than one born blind has of pleasant and beautiful colors. They were of a more inward, pure, soul-animating and refreshing nature. Those former delights, never reached the heart; and did not arise from any sight of the divine excellency of the things of God; or any taste of the soul-satisfying, and life-giving good, there is in them.

My sense of divine things seemed gradually to increase, till I went to preach at New York;[7] which was about a year and a half after they began. While I was there, I felt them, very sensibly, in a much higher degree, than I had done before. My longings after God and holiness, were much increased. Pure and humble, holy and heavenly Christianity, appeared exceeding amiable to me. I felt in me a burning desire to be in everything a complete Christian; and conformed to the blessed image of Christ: and that I might live in all things, according to the pure, sweet and blessed rules of the gospel. I had an eager thirsting after progress in these things. My longings after it, put me upon pursuing and pressing after them. It was my continual strife day and night, and constant inquiry, how I should be more holy, and live more holily, and more becoming a child of God, and disciple of Christ. I sought an increase of grace and holiness, and that I might live an holy life, with vastly more earnestness, than ever I sought grace, before I had it. I used to be continually examining myself, and studying and contriving for likely ways and means, how I should live holily, with far greater diligence and earnestness, than ever I pursued anything in my life: but with too great a dependence on my own strength; which afterwards proved a great damage to me. My experience had not then taught me, as it has done since, my extreme feebleness and impotence, every manner of way; and the innumerable and bottomless depths of secret corruption and deceit, that there was in my heart. However, I went on with my eager pursuit after more holiness; and sweet conformity to Christ.

The heaven I desired was a heaven of holiness; to be with God, and to spend my eternity in divine love, and holy communion with Christ. My mind was very much taken up

---

6. **estate:** Condition of life or spiritual condition.
7. **till I went to preach at New York:** Edwards was an assistant minister in a Presbyterian church in New York City from August 1722 through April 1723.

with contemplations on heaven, and the enjoyments of those there; and living there in perfect holiness, humility and love. And it used at that time to appear a great part of the happiness of heaven, that there the saints could express their love to Christ. It appeared to me a great clog and hindrance and burden to me, that what I felt within, I could not express to God, and give vent to, as I desired. The inward ardor of my soul, seemed to be hindered and pent up, and could not freely flame out as it would. I used often to think, how in heaven, this sweet principle should freely and fully vent and express itself. Heaven appeared to me exceeding delightful as a world of love. It appeared to me, that all happiness consisted in living in pure, humble, heavenly, divine love.

I remember the thoughts I used then to have of holiness. I remember I then said sometimes to myself, I do certainly know that I love holiness, such as the gospel pre-scribes. It appeared to me, there was nothing in it but what was ravishingly lovely. It appeared to me, to be the highest beauty and amiableness, above all other beauties: that it was a divine beauty; far purer than anything here upon earth; and that everything else, was like mire, filth and defilement, in comparison of it.

Holiness, as I then wrote down some of my contemplations on it, appeared to me to be of a sweet, pleasant, charming, serene, calm nature. It seemed to me, it brought an inex-pressible purity, brightness, peacefulness and ravishment to the soul: and that it made the soul like a field or garden of God, with all manner of pleasant flowers; that is all pleasant, delightful and undisturbed; enjoying a sweet calm, and the gently vivifying beams of the sun. The soul of a true Christian, as I then wrote my meditations, appeared like such a little white flower, as we see in the spring of the year; low and humble on the ground, opening its bosom, to receive the pleasant beams of the sun's glory; rejoicing as it were, in a calm rapture; diffusing around a sweet fragrancy; standing peacefully and lovingly, in the midst of other flowers round about; all in like manner opening their bosoms, to drink in the light of the sun.

There was no part of creature-holiness, that I then, and at other times, had so great a sense of the loveliness of, as humility, brokenness of heart and poverty of spirit: and there was nothing that I had such a spirit to long for. My heart as it were panted after this, to lie low before GOD, and in the dust; that I might be nothing, and that God might be all; that I might become as a little child.[8]

While I was there at New York, I sometimes was much affected with reflections on my past life, considering how late it was, before I began to be truly religious; and how wick-edly I had lived till then: and once so as to weep abundantly, and for a considerable time together.

On January 12, 1722/3,[9] I made a solemn dedication of myself to God, and wrote it down; giving up myself, and all that I had to God; to be for the future in no respect my own; to act as one that had no right to himself, in any respect. And solemnly vowed to

---

8. **that I might become as a little child:** See Mark 10:15: "'Verily I say unto you, Whosoever shall not receive the kingdom of God as a little child, he shall not enter therein.'"

9. **January 12, 1722/3:** The year was 1722 in the Julian — or Old Style — calendar, in which the year begins on March 25 instead of January 1, and 1723 in the Gregorian — or New Style — calendar, which was not adopted in England until 1752.

take God for my whole portion and felicity; looking on nothing else as any part of my happiness, nor acting as if it were: and his law for the constant rule of my obedience; engaging to fight with all my might, against the world, the flesh and the devil, to the end of my life. But have reason to be infinitely humbled, when I consider, how much I have failed of answering my obligation.

I had then abundance of sweet religious conversation in the family where I lived, with Mr. John Smith, and his pious mother. My heart was knit in affection to those, in whom were appearances of true piety; and I could bear the thoughts of no other companions, but such as were holy, and the disciples of the blessed Jesus.

I had great longings for the advancement of Christ's kingdom in the world. My secret prayer used to be in great part taken up in praying for it. If I heard the least hint of anything that happened in any part of the world, that appeared to me, in some respect or other, to have a favorable aspect on the interest of Christ's kingdom, my soul eagerly catched at it; and it would much animate and refresh me. I used to be earnest to read public news-letters, mainly for that end; to see if I could not find some news favorable to the interest of religion in the world.

I very frequently used to retire into a solitary place, on the banks of Hudson's River, at some distance from the city, for contemplation on divine things, and secret converse with God; and had many sweet hours there. Sometimes Mr. Smith and I walked there together, to converse of the things of God; and our conversation used much to turn on the advancement of Christ's kingdom in the world, and the glorious things that God would accomplish for his church in the latter days.

I had then, and at other times, the greatest delight in the holy Scriptures, of any book whatsoever. Oftentimes in reading it, every word seemed to touch my heart. I felt an harmony between something in my heart, and those sweet and powerful words. I seemed often to see so much light, exhibited by every sentence, and such a refreshing ravishing food communicated, that I could not get along in reading. Used oftentimes to dwell long on one sentence, to see the wonders contained in it; and yet almost every sentence seemed to be full of wonders.

I came away from New York in the month of April 1723, and had a most bitter parting with Madam Smith and her son. My heart seemed to sink within me, at leaving the family and city, where I had enjoyed so many sweet and pleasant days. I went from New York to Wethersfield by water.[10] As I sailed away, I kept sight of the city as long as I could; and when I was out of sight of it, it would affect me much to look that way, with a kind of melancholy mixed with sweetness. However, that night after this sorrowful parting, I was greatly comforted in God at Westchester, where we went ashore to lodge: and had a pleasant time of it all the voyage to Saybrook. It was sweet to me to think of meeting dear Christians in heaven, where we should never part more. At Saybrook we went ashore to lodge on Saturday, and there kept sabbath; where I had a sweet and refreshing season, walking alone in the fields.

---

10. **from New York ... by water:** Edwards sailed home on the Long Island Sound and the Connecticut River, stopping along the way at Westchester, New York, and Saybrook, Connecticut.

After I came home to Windsor, remained much in a like frame of my mind, as I had been in at New York; but only sometimes felt my heart ready to sink, with the thoughts of my friends at New York. And my refuge and support was in contemplations on the heavenly state; as I find in my diary of May 1, 1723. It was my comfort to think of that state, where there is fullness of joy; where reigns heavenly, sweet, calm and delightful love, without alloy; where there are continually the dearest expressions of this love; where is the enjoyment of the persons loved, without ever parting; where these persons that appear so lovely in this world, will really be inexpressibly more lovely, and full of love to us. And how sweetly will the mutual lovers join together to sing the praises of God and the Lamb! How full will it fill us with joy, to think, that this enjoyment, these sweet exercises will never cease or come to an end; but will last to all eternity!

Continued much in the same frame in the general, that I had been in at New York, till I went to New Haven, to live there as Tutor of the College; having one special season of uncommon sweetness: particularly once at Bolton, in a journey from Boston, walking out alone in the fields. After I went to New Haven, I sunk in religion; my mind being diverted from my eager and violent pursuits after holiness, by some affairs that greatly perplexed and distracted my mind.

In September 1725, was taken ill at New Haven; and endeavoring to go home to Windsor, was so ill at the North Village, that I could go no further: where I lay sick for about a quarter of a year. And in this sickness, God was pleased to visit me again with the sweet influences of his spirit. My mind was greatly engaged there on divine, pleasant contemplations, and longings of soul. I observed that those who watched with me, would often be looking out for the morning, and seemed to wish for it. Which brought to my mind those words of the Psalmist, which my soul with sweetness made its own language, "My soul waiteth for the Lord more than they that watch for the morning: I say, more than they that watch for the morning" [Psalms 130:6]. And when the light of the morning came, and the beams of the sun came in at the windows, it refreshed my soul from one morning to another. It seemed to me to be some image of the sweet light of God's glory.

I remember, about that time, I used greatly to long for the conversion of some that I was concerned with. It seemed to me, I could gladly honor them, and with delight be a servant to them, and lie at their feet, if they were but truly holy.

But sometime after this, I was again greatly diverted in my mind, with some temporal concerns, that exceedingly took up my thoughts, greatly to the wounding of my soul: and went on through various exercises, that it would be tedious to relate, that gave me much more experience of my own heart, than ever I had before.

Since I came to this town,[11] I have often had sweet complacency in God in views of his glorious perfections, and the excellency of Jesus Christ. God has appeared to me, a glorious and lovely being, chiefly on the account of his holiness. The holiness of God has always appeared to me the most lovely of all his attributes. The doctrines of God's

---

11. **Since I came to this town:** Northampton, Massachusetts, where Edwards took a position as assistant pastor in 1727.

absolute sovereignty, and free grace, in showing mercy to whom he would show mercy; and man's absolute dependence on the operations of God's Holy Spirit, have very often appeared to me as sweet and glorious doctrines. These doctrines have been much my delight. God's sovereignty has ever appeared to me, as great part of his glory. It has often been sweet to me to go to God, and adore him as a sovereign God, and ask sovereign mercy of him.

I have loved the doctrines of the gospel: they have been to my soul like green pastures. The gospel has seemed to me to be the richest treasure; the treasure that I have most desired, and longed that it might dwell richly in me. The way of salvation by Christ, has appeared in a general way, glorious and excellent, and most pleasant and beautiful. It has often seemed to me, that it would in a great measure spoil heaven, to receive it in any other way. That text has often been affecting and delightful to me, Isaiah 32:2, "A man shall be an hiding place from the wind, and a covert from the tempest," etc.

It has often appeared sweet to me, to be united to Christ; to have him for my head, and to be a member of his body: and also to have Christ for my teacher and prophet. I very often think with sweetness and longings and pantings of soul, of being a little child, taking hold of Christ, to be led by him through the wilderness of this world. That text, Matthew 18 at the beginning, has often been sweet to me, "Except ye be converted, and become as little children" etc. I love to think of coming to Christ, to receive salvation of him, poor in spirit, and quite empty of self; humbly exalting him alone; cut entirely off from my own root, and to grow into, and out of Christ: to have God in Christ to be all in all; and to live by faith on the Son of God, a life of humble, unfeigned confidence in him. That Scripture has often been sweet to me, Psalms 115:1, "Not unto us, O Lord, not unto us, but unto thy name give glory, for thy mercy, and for thy truth's sake." And those words of Christ, Luke 10:21, "In that hour Jesus rejoiced in spirit, and said, I thank thee, O Father, Lord of heaven and earth, that thou hast hid these things from the wise and prudent, and hast revealed them unto babes: even so Father, for so it seemed good in thy sight." That sovereignty of God that Christ rejoiced in, seemed to me to be worthy to be rejoiced in; and that rejoicing of Christ, seemed to me to show the excellency of Christ, and the spirit that he was of.

Sometimes only mentioning a single word, causes my heart to burn within me: or only seeing the name of Christ, or the name of some attribute of God. And God has appeared glorious to me, on account of the Trinity. It has made me have exalting thoughts of God, that he subsists in three persons; Father, Son, and Holy Ghost.

The sweetest joys and delights I have experienced, have not been those that have arisen from a hope of my own good estate; but in a direct view of the glorious things of the gospel. When I enjoy this sweetness, it seems to carry me above the thoughts of my own safe estate. It seems at such times a loss that I cannot bear, to take off my eye from the glorious, pleasant object I behold without me, to turn my eye in upon myself, and my own good estate.

My heart has been much on the advancement of Christ's kingdom in the world. The histories of the past advancement of Christ's kingdom, have been sweet to me. When I have read histories of past ages, the pleasantest thing in all my reading has been, to read of the kingdom of Christ being promoted. And when I have expected in my reading, to come to any such thing, I have lotted[12] upon it all the way as I read. And my mind has been much entertained and delighted, with the Scripture promises and prophecies, of the future glorious advancement of Christ's kingdom on earth.

I have sometimes had a sense of the excellent fullness of Christ, and his meetness and suitableness as a savior; whereby he has appeared to me, far above all, the chief of ten thousands.[13] And his blood and atonement has appeared sweet, and his righteousness sweet; which is always accompanied with an ardency of spirit, and inward strugglings and breathings and groanings, that cannot be uttered, to be emptied of myself, and swallowed up in Christ.

Once, as I rid out into the woods for my health, *anno*[14] 1737; and having lit from my horse in a retired place, as my manner commonly has been, to walk for divine contemplation and prayer; I had a view, that for me was extraordinary, of the glory of the Son of God; as mediator between God and man; and his wonderful, great, full, pure and sweet grace and love, and meek and gentle condescension. This grace, that appeared to me so calm and sweet, appeared great above the heavens. The person of Christ appeared ineffably excellent, with an excellency great enough to swallow up all thought and conception. Which continued, as near as I can judge, about an hour; which kept me, the bigger part of the time, in a flood of tears, and weeping aloud. I felt withal, an ardency of soul to be, what I know not otherwise how to express, than to be emptied and annihilated; to lie in the dust, and to be full of Christ alone; to love him with a holy and pure love; to trust in him; to live upon him; to serve and follow him, and to be totally wrapt up in the fullness of Christ; and to be perfectly sanctified and made pure, with a divine and heavenly purity. I have several other times, had views very much of the same nature, and that have had the same effects.

I have many times had a sense of the glory of the third person in the Trinity, in his office of Sanctifier; in his holy operations communicating divine light and life to the soul. God in the communications of his Holy Spirit, has appeared as an infinite fountain of divine glory and sweetness; being full and sufficient to fill and satisfy the soul: pouring forth itself in sweet communications, like the sun in its glory, sweetly and pleasantly diffusing light and life.

I have sometimes had an affecting sense of the excellency of the word of God, as a word of life; as the light of life; a sweet, excellent, life-giving word: accompanied with a thirsting after that word, that it might dwell richly in my heart.

I have often since I lived in this town, had very affecting views of my own sinfulness and vileness; very frequently so as to hold me in a kind of loud weeping, sometimes for a considerable time together: so that I have often been forced to shut myself up. I have had a vastly greater sense of my own wickedness, and the badness of my heart, since my conversion, than ever I had before. It has often appeared to me, that if God should mark iniquity against me, I should appear the very worst of all mankind; of all that have been

---

12. **lotted:** Relied.
13. **the chief of ten thousands:** See the Song of Solomon 5:10: "My beloved is white and ruddy, the chiefest among ten thousand."
14. ***anno*:** In the year of (Latin).

since the beginning of the world to this time: and that I should have by far the lowest place in hell. When others that have come to talk with me about their soul concerns, have expressed the sense they have had of their own wickedness, by saying that it seemed to them, that they were as bad as the devil himself; I thought their expressions seemed exceeding faint and feeble, to represent my wickedness. I thought I should wonder, that they should content themselves with such expressions as these, if I had any reason to imagine, that their sin bore any proportion to mine. It seemed to me, I should wonder at myself, if I should express my wickedness in such feeble terms as they did.

My wickedness, as I am in myself, has long appeared to me perfectly ineffable, and infinitely swallowing up all thought and imagination; like an infinite deluge, or infinite mountains over my head. I know not how to express better, what my sins appear to me to be, than by heaping infinite upon infinite, and multiplying infinite by infinite. I go about very often, for this many years, with these expressions in my mind, and in my mouth, "Infinite upon infinite. Infinite upon infinite!" When I look into my heart, and take a view of my wickedness, it looks like an abyss infinitely deeper than hell. And it appears to me, that were it not for free grace, exalted and raised up to the infinite height of all the fullness and glory of the great Jehovah,[15] and the arm of his power and grace stretched forth, in all the majesty of his power, and in all the glory of his sovereignty; I should appear sunk down in my sins infinitely below hell itself, far beyond sight of everything, but the piercing eye of God's grace, that can pierce even down to such a depth, and to the bottom of such an abyss.

And yet, I ben't in the least inclined to think, that I have a greater conviction of sin than ordinary. It seems to me, my conviction of sin is exceeding small, and faint. It appears to me enough to amaze me, that I have no more sense of my sin. I know certainly, that I have very little sense of my sinfulness. That my sins appear to me so great, don't seem to me to be, because I have so much more conviction of sin than other Christians, but because I am so much worse, and have so much more wickedness to be convinced of. When I have had these turns of weeping and crying for my sins, I thought I knew in the time of it, that my repentance was nothing to my sin.

I have greatly longed of late, for a broken heart, and to lie low before God. And when I ask for humility of God, I can't bear the thoughts of being no more humble, than other Christians. It seems to me, that though their degrees of humility may be suitable for them; yet it would be a vile self-exaltation in me, not to be the lowest in humility of all mankind. Others speak of their longing to be humbled to the dust. Though that may be a proper expression for them, I always think for myself, that I ought to be humbled down below hell. 'Tis an expression that it has long been natural for me to use in prayer to God. I ought to lie infinitely low before God.

It is affecting to me to think, how ignorant I was, when I was a young Christian, of the bottomless, infinite depths of wickedness, pride, hypocrisy and deceit left in my heart.

I have vastly a greater sense, of my universal, exceeding dependence on God's grace and strength, and mere good pleasure, of late, than I used formerly to have; and have

---

15. **Jehovah**: A form of the Hebrew name for God.

experienced more of an abhorrence of my own righteousness. The thought of any comfort or joy, arising in me, on any consideration, or reflection on my own amiableness, or any of my performances or experiences, or any goodness of heart or life, is nauseous and detestable to me. And yet I am greatly afflicted with a proud and self-righteous spirit; much more sensibly, than I used to be formerly. I see that serpent rising and putting forth its head, continually, everywhere, all around me.

Though it seems to me, that in some respects I was a far better Christian, for two or three years after my first conversion, than I am now; and lived in a more constant delight and pleasure: yet of late years, I have had a more full and constant sense of the absolute sovereignty of God, and a delight in that sovereignty; and have had more of a sense of the glory of Christ, as a mediator, as revealed in the gospel. On one Saturday night in particular, had a particular discovery of the excellency of the gospel of Christ, above all other doctrines; so that I could not but say to myself; "This is my chosen light, my chosen doctrine": and of Christ, "This is my chosen prophet." It appeared to me to be sweet beyond all expression, to follow Christ, and to be taught and enlightened and instructed by him; to learn of him; and live to him.

Another Saturday night, January 1738/9,[16] had such a sense, how sweet and blessed a thing it was, to walk in the way of duty, to do that which was right and meet to be done, and agreeable to the holy mind of God; that it caused me to break forth into a kind of a loud weeping, which held me some time; so that I was forced to shut myself up, and fasten the doors. I could not but as it were cry out, "How happy are they which do that which is right in the sight of God! They are blessed indeed, they are the happy ones!" I had at the same time, a very affecting sense, how meet and suitable it was that God should govern the world, and order all things according to his own pleasure; and I rejoiced in it, that God reigned, and that his will was done.

[c. after 1739, 1998]

---

16. January 1738/9: See note 9.

Reading Edwards's *Sinners in the Hands of an Angry God.*   Edwards delivered this sermon in Enfield, Connecticut, on Sunday, July 8, 1741. Perhaps his most famous—or infamous—work, it has tended to cast Edwards as a preacher of "fire and brimstone," a phrase used in the sermon. According to one of his early biographers, however, Edwards delivered the sermon in a quiet, unexpressive voice, reading slowly from his prepared text. As he read the sermon, many in the crowd began to moan and cry. One member of the audience, the Reverend Stephen William, recorded in his diary that "the shrieks & crys were piercing & Amazing." The sermon was swiftly published in Boston, giving added impetus to what Edwards in an earlier work had called the "Surprising Work of God," now known as the Great Awakening, the religious revivals that spread throughout the American colonies during the 1730s and 1740s. The text is taken from the Yale University Press *Works of Jonathan Edwards*, Vol. 22, edited by Harry S. Stout and Nathan O. Hatch (2003).

First Printing of
Edwards's Most Famous
Sermon

SINNERS

In the Hands of an

Angry GOD.

A SERMON

Preached at *Enfield, July* 8th 1 7 4 1.

At a Time of great Awakenings ; and attended with
remarkable Impreſſions on many of the Hearers.

By *Jonathan Edwards*, A.M.

Paſtor of the Church of CHRIST in *Northampton*.

Amos ix. 2, 3. *Though they dig into Hell, thence ſhall mine Hand
take them ; though they climb up to Heaven, thence will I bring
them down. And though they hide themſelves in the Top of
Carmel, I will ſearch and take them out thence ; and though
they be hid from my Sight in the Bottom of the Sea, thence I will
command the Serpent, and he ſhall bite them.*

B O S T O N : Printed and Sold by S. KNEELAND
and T. GREEN. in Queen-Street over againſt the
Priſon, 1 7 4 1.

SINNERS IN THE HANDS OF AN ANGRY GOD

DEUTERONOMY 32:35.

Their foot shall slide in due time.[1]

In this verse is threatened the vengeance of God on the wicked unbelieving Israelites, that
were God's visible people, and lived under means of grace;[2] and that, notwithstanding

---

1. *Their foot . . . in due time*: The complete verse from Deuteronomy reads: "To me belongeth vengeance, and
recompence; their foot shall slide in due time: for the day of their calamity is at hand, and the things that
shall come upon them make haste."
2. **means of grace**: For the Israelites, the "means of grace" were the Ten Commandments, given to them by
God. For the Puritans, the principal statement of Protestant beliefs and practices was the Westminster
Confession of Faith, a creed completed in 1646 by an assembly of ministers, delegates of Parliament, and representatives of Scotland. In the Westminster Confession, "God's covenant with man" is outlined in chapter 7
as "the preaching of the Word, and the administration of the sacraments of Baptism and the Lord's Supper."

all God's wonderful works that he had wrought towards that people, yet remained, as is expressed, v. 28, "void of counsel,"[3] having no understanding in them; and that, under all the cultivations of heaven, brought forth bitter and poisonous fruit;[4] as in the two verses next preceding the text.

The expression that I have chosen for my text, "Their foot shall slide in due time," seems to imply the following things, relating to the punishment and destruction that these wicked Israelites were exposed to.

1. That they were *always* exposed to destruction, as one that stands or walks in slippery places is always exposed to fall. This is implied in the manner of their destruction's coming upon them, being represented by their foot's sliding. The same is expressed, Psalms 73:18, "Surely thou didst set them in slippery places: thou castedst them down into destruction."

2. It implies that they were always exposed to *sudden* unexpected destruction. As he that walks in slippery places is every moment liable to fall; he can't foresee one moment whether he shall stand or fall the next; and when he does fall, he falls at once, without warning. Which is also expressed in that, Psalms 73:18-19, "Surely thou didst set them in slippery places: thou castedst them down into destruction. How are they brought into desolation as in a moment!"

3. Another thing implied is that they are liable to fall *of themselves*, without being thrown down by the hand of another. As he that stands or walks on slippery ground, needs nothing but his own weight to throw him down.

4. That the reason why they are not fallen already, and don't fall now, is only that God's appointed time is not come. For it is said, that when that due time, or appointed time comes, "their foot shall slide." Then they shall be left to fall as they are inclined by their own weight. God won't hold them up in these slippery places any longer, but will let them go; and then, at that very instant, they shall fall into destruction; as he that stands in such slippery declining ground on the edge of a pit that he can't stand alone, when he is let go he immediately falls and is lost.

The observation from the words that I would now insist upon is this:

[Doctrine]

THERE IS NOTHING THAT KEEPS WICKED MEN, AT ANY ONE MOMENT,
OUT OF HELL, BUT THE MERE PLEASURE OF GOD.

By "the mere pleasure of God," I mean his sovereign pleasure, his arbitrary will, restrained by no obligation, hindered by no manner of difficulty, any more than if nothing else but

---

3. **"void of counsel"**: "For they are a nation void of counsel, neither is there any understanding in them" (Deuteronomy 32:28).

4. **poisonous fruit**: "For their vine is of the vine of Sodom, and of the fields of Gomorrah: their grapes are grapes of gall, their clusters are bitter: Their wine is the poison of dragons, and the cruel venom of asps" (Deuteronomy 32:32-33). For the evil and immoral behavior of their citizens, the cities of Sodom and Gomorrah were destroyed by God (Genesis 19:24-26).

God's mere will had in the least degree, or in any respect whatsoever, any hand in the preservation of wicked men one moment.

The truth of this observation may appear by the following considerations.

I. There is no want of *power* in God to cast wicked men into hell at any moment. Men's hands can't be strong when God rises up: the strongest have no power to resist him, nor can any deliver out of his hands.

He is not only able to cast wicked men into hell, but he can most *easily* do it. Sometimes an earthly prince meets with a great deal of difficulty to subdue a rebel, that has found means to fortify himself, and has made himself strong by the numbers of his followers. But it is not so with God. There is no fortress that is any defense from the power of God. Though hand join in hand, and vast multitudes of God's enemies combine and associate themselves, they are easily broken in pieces: they are as great heaps of light chaff[5] before the whirlwind; or large quantities of dry stubble before devouring flames. We find it easy to tread on and crush a worm that we see crawling on the earth; so 'tis easy for us to cut or singe a slender thread that anything hangs by; thus easy is it for God when he pleases to cast his enemies down to hell. What are we, that we should think to stand before him, at whose rebuke the earth trembles, and before whom the rocks are thrown down?

II. They *deserve* to be cast into hell; so that divine justice never stands in the way, it makes no objection against God's using his power at any moment to destroy them. Yea, on the contrary, justice calls aloud for an infinite punishment of their sins. Divine justice says of the tree that brings forth such grapes of Sodom, "Cut it down; why cumbreth[6] it the ground" (Luke 13:7). The sword of divine justice is every moment brandished over their heads, and 'tis nothing but the hand of arbitrary mercy, and God's mere will, that holds it back.

III. They are *already* under a sentence of condemnation to hell. They don't only justly deserve to be cast down thither; but the sentence of the law of God, that eternal and immutable rule of righteousness that God has fixed between him and mankind, is gone out against them, and stands against them; so that they are bound over already to hell. John 3:18, "He that believeth not is condemned already." So that every unconverted man properly belongs to hell; that is his place; from thence he is. John 8:23, "Ye are from beneath." And thither he is bound; 'tis the place that justice, and God's Word, and the sentence of his unchangeable law assigns to him.

IV. They are now the objects of that very *same* anger and wrath of God that is expressed in the torments of hell: and the reason why they don't go down to hell at each moment, is not because God, in whose power they are, is not then very angry with them; as angry as he is with many of those miserable creatures that he is now tormenting in hell, and do there feel and bear the fierceness of his wrath. Yea, God is a great deal more angry with great numbers that are now on earth, yea, doubtless with many that are now

---

5. **chaff:** Husks of corn or other grains, separated by winnowing or threshing.
6. **cumbreth:** Obstruct.

in this congregation, that it may be are at ease and quiet, than he is with many of those that are now in the flames of hell.

So that it is not because God is unmindful of their wickedness, and don't resent it, that he don't let loose his hand and cut them off. God is not altogether such an one as themselves, though they may imagine him to be so. The wrath of God burns against them, their damnation don't slumber, the pit is prepared, the fire is made ready, the furnace is now hot, ready to receive them, the flames do now rage and glow. The glittering sword is whet, and held over them, and the pit hath opened her mouth under them.

V. The *devil* stands ready to fall upon them and seize them as his own, at what moment God shall permit him. They belong to him; he has their souls in his possession, and under his dominion. The Scripture represents them as his "goods" (Luke 11:21). The devils watch them; they are ever by them, at their right hand; they stand waiting for them, like greedy hungry lions that see their prey, and expect to have it, but are for the present kept back; if God should withdraw his hand, by which they are restrained, they would in one moment fly upon their poor souls. The old serpent is gaping for them; hell opens its mouth wide to receive them; and if God should permit it, they would be hastily swallowed up and lost.

VI. There are in the souls of wicked men those hellish *principles* reigning, that would presently kindle and flame out into hell fire, if it were not for God's restraints. There is laid in the very nature of carnal men a foundation for the torments of hell: there are those corrupt principles, in reigning power in them, and in full possession of them, that are seeds of hell fire. These principles are active and powerful, and exceeding violent in their nature, and if it were not for the restraining hand of God upon them, they would soon break out, they would flame out after the same manner as the same corruptions, the same enmity does in the hearts of damned souls, and would beget the same torments in 'em as they do in them. The souls of the wicked are in Scripture compared to the troubled sea (Isaiah 57:20). For the present God restrains their wickedness by his mighty power, as he does the raging waves of the troubled sea, saying, "Hitherto shalt thou come, and no further" [Job 38:11]; but if God should withdraw that restraining power, it would soon carry all afore it. Sin is the ruin and misery of the soul; it is destructive in its nature; and if God should leave it without restraint, there would need nothing else to make the soul perfectly miserable. The corruption of the heart of man is a thing that is immoderate and boundless in its fury; and while wicked men live here, it is like fire pent up by God's restraints, whenas if it were let loose it would set on fire the course of nature; and as the heart is now a sink of sin, so, if sin was not restrained, it would immediately turn the soul into a fiery oven, or a furnace of fire and brimstone.

VII. It is no security to wicked men for one moment, that there are no *visible means of death* at hand. 'Tis no security to a natural man,[7] that he is now in health, and that he don't see which way he should now immediately go out of the world by any accident, and that there is no visible danger in any respect in his circumstances. The manifold and

---

7. **a natural man:** That is, an unredeemed person living in a state of nature rather than in a state of grace.

continual experience of the world in all ages, shows that this is no evidence that a man is not on the very brink of eternity, and that the next step won't be into another world. The unseen, unthought of ways and means of persons going suddenly out of the world are innumerable and inconceivable. Unconverted men walk over the pit of hell on a rotten covering, and there are innumerable places in this covering so weak that they won't bear their weight, and these places are not seen. The arrows of death fly unseen at noonday;[8] the sharpest sight can't discern them. God has so many different unsearchable ways of taking wicked men out of the world and sending 'em to hell, that there is nothing to make it appear that God had need to be at the expense of a miracle, or go out of the ordinary course of his providence, to destroy any wicked man, at any moment. All the means that there are of sinners going out of the world, are so in God's hands, and so universally absolutely subject to his power and determination, that it don't depend at all less on the mere will of God, whether sinners shall at any moment go to hell, than if means were never made use of, or at all concerned in the case.

VIII. Natural men's *prudence* and *care* to preserve their own *lives*, or the care of others to preserve them, don't secure 'em a moment. This divine providence and universal experience does also bear testimony to. There is this clear evidence that men's own wisdom is no security to them from death: that if it were otherwise we should see some difference between the wise and politic men of the world, and others, with regard to their liableness to early and unexpected death; but how is it in fact? Ecclesiastes 2:16, "How dieth the wise man? as the fool."

IX. All wicked men's *pains* and *contrivance* they use to escape *hell*, while they continue to reject Christ, and so remain wicked men, don't secure 'em from hell one moment. Almost every natural man that hears of hell, flatters himself that he shall escape it; he depends upon himself for his own security; he flatters himself in what he has done, in what he is now doing, or what he intends to do; everyone lays out matters in his own mind how he shall avoid damnation, and flatters himself that he contrives well for himself, and that his schemes won't fail. They hear indeed that there are but few saved, and that the bigger part of men that have died heretofore are gone to hell; but each one imagines that he lays out matters better for his own escape than others have done: he don't intend to come to that place of torment; he says within himself, that he intends to take care that shall be effectual, and to order matters so for himself as not to fail.

But the foolish children of men do miserably delude themselves in their own schemes, and in their confidence in their own strength and wisdom; they trust to nothing but a shadow. The bigger part of those that heretofore have lived under the same means of grace, and are now dead, are undoubtedly gone to hell: and it was not because they were not as wise as those that are now alive; it was not because they did not lay out matters as well for themselves to secure their own escape. If it were so, that we could come to speak with them, and could inquire of them, one by one, whether they expected when alive, and

---

8. **The arrows . . . noonday:** See Psalms 91:5-6: "Thou shalt not be afraid for the terror by night; nor for the arrow that flieth by day; / Nor for the pestilence that walketh in darkness; nor for the destruction that wasteth at noonday."

when they used to hear about hell, ever to be the subjects of that misery, we doubtless should hear one and another reply, "No, I never intended to come here; I had laid out matters otherwise in my mind; I thought I should contrive well for myself; I thought my scheme good; I intended to take effectual care; but it came upon me unexpected; I did not look for it at that time, and in that manner; it came as a thief; death outwitted me; God's wrath was too quick for me; O my cursed foolishness! I was flattering myself, and pleasing myself with vain dreams of what I would do hereafter, and when I was saying, 'Peace and safety,' then sudden destruction came upon me" [I Thessalonians 5:3].

X. God has laid himself under *no obligation* by any promise to keep any natural man out of hell one moment. God certainly has made no promises either of eternal life, or of any deliverance or preservation from eternal death, but what are contained in the covenant of grace,[9] the promises that are given in Christ, in whom all the promises are yea and amen. But surely they have no interest in the promises of the covenant of grace that are not the children of the covenant, and that don't believe in any of the promises of the covenant, and have no interest in the *Mediator*[10] of the covenant.

So that whatever some have imagined and pretended about promises made to natural men's earnest seeking and knocking, 'tis plain and manifest that whatever pains a natural man takes in religion, whatever prayers he makes, till he believes in Christ, God is under no manner of obligation to keep him a *moment* from eternal destruction.

So that thus it is, that natural men are held in the hand of God over the pit of hell; they have deserved the fiery pit, and are already sentenced to it; and God is dreadfully provoked, his anger is as great towards them as to those that are actually suffering the executions of the fierceness of his wrath in hell, and they have done nothing in the least to appease or abate that anger, neither is God in the least bound by any promise to hold 'em up one moment; the devil is waiting for them, hell is gaping for them, the flames gather and flash about them, and would fain lay hold on them, and swallow them up; the fire pent up in their own hearts is struggling to break out; and they have no interest in any mediator, there are no means within reach that can be any security to them. In short, they have no refuge, nothing to take hold of, all that preserves them every moment is the mere arbitrary will, and uncovenanted unobliged forbearance of an incensed God.

Application

The *Use* may be of *Awakening* to unconverted persons in this congregation. This that you have heard is the case of everyone of you that are out of Christ. That world of misery, that lake of burning brimstone is extended abroad under you. *There* is the dreadful pit of the glowing flames of the wrath of God; there is hell's wide gaping mouth open; and you

---

9. **covenant of grace:** In Christian theology, God created a new covenant by sending his son, Jesus Christ, to intercede for fallen humankind. In this covenant of grace, those who believe in Jesus may be saved.
10. ***Mediator:*** In the covenant of grace, Jesus Christ is the mediator between God and human beings.

have nothing to stand upon, nor anything to take hold of: there is nothing between you and hell but the air; 'tis only the power and mere pleasure of God that holds you up.

You probably are not sensible of this; you find you are kept out of hell, but don't see the hand of God in it, but look at other things, as the good state of your bodily constitution, your care of your own life, and the means you use for your own preservation. But indeed these things are nothing; if God should withdraw his hand, they would avail no more to keep you from falling, than the thin air to hold up a person that is suspended in it.

Your wickedness makes you as it were heavy as lead, and to tend downwards with great weight and pressure towards hell; and if God should let you go, you would immediately sink and swiftly descend and plunge into the bottomless gulf, and your healthy constitution, and your own care and prudence, and best contrivance, and all your righteousness, would have no more influence to uphold you and keep you out of hell, than a spider's web would have to stop a falling rock. Were it not that so is the sovereign pleasure of God, the earth would not bear you one moment; for you are a burden to it; the creation groans with you; the creature is made subject to the bondage of your corruption, not willingly; the sun don't willingly shine upon you to give you light to serve sin and Satan; the earth don't willingly yield her increase to satisfy your lusts; nor is it willingly a stage for your wickedness to be acted upon; the air don't willingly serve you for breath to maintain the flame of life in your vitals, while you spend your life in the service of God's enemies. God's creatures are good, and were made for men to serve God with, and don't willingly subserve to any other purpose, and groan when they are abused to purposes so directly contrary to their nature and end. And the world would spew you out, were it not for the sovereign hand of him who hath subjected it in hope. There are the black clouds of God's wrath now hanging directly over your heads, full of the dreadful storm, and big with thunder; and were it not for the restraining hand of God it would immediately burst forth upon you. The sovereign pleasure of God for the present stays his rough wind; otherwise it would come with fury, and your destruction would come like a whirlwind, and you would be like the chaff of the summer threshing floor.

The wrath of God is like great waters that are dammed for the present; they increase more and more, and rise higher and higher, till an outlet is given, and the longer the stream is stopped, the more rapid and mighty is its course, when once it is let loose. 'Tis true, that judgment against your evil works has not been executed hitherto; the floods of God's vengeance have been withheld; but your guilt in the meantime is constantly increasing, and you are every day treasuring up more wrath; the waters are continually rising and waxing more and more mighty; and there is nothing but the mere pleasure of God that holds the waters back that are unwilling to be stopped, and press hard to go forward; if God should only withdraw his hand from the floodgate, it would immediately fly open, and the fiery floods of the fierceness and wrath of God would rush forth with inconceivable fury, and would come upon you with omnipotent power; and if your strength were ten thousand times greater than it is, yea, ten thousand times greater than the strength of the stoutest, sturdiest devil in hell, it would be nothing to withstand or endure it.

The bow of God's wrath is bent, and the arrow made ready on the string, and Justice bends the arrow at your heart, and strains the bow, and it is nothing but the mere pleasure of God, and that of an angry God, without any promise or obligation at all, that keeps the arrow one moment from being made drunk with your blood.

Thus are all you that never passed under a great change of heart, by the mighty power of the Spirit of God upon your souls; all that were never born again, and made new creatures, and raised from being dead in sin, to a state of new, and before altogether unexperienced light and life (however you may have reformed your life in many things, and may have had religious affections, and may keep up a form of religion in your families and closets,[11] and in the house of God, and may be strict in it), you are thus in the hands of an angry God; 'tis nothing but his mere pleasure that keeps you from being this moment swallowed up in everlasting destruction.

However unconvinced you may now be of the truth of what you hear, by and by you will be fully convinced of it. Those that are gone from being in the like circumstances with you, see that it was so with them; for destruction came suddenly upon most of them, when they expected nothing of it, and while they were saying, "Peace and safety": now they see, that those things that they depended on for peace and safety, were nothing but thin air and empty shadows.

The God that holds you over the pit of hell, much as one holds a spider, or some loathsome insect, over the fire, abhors you, and is dreadfully provoked; his wrath towards you burns like fire; he looks upon you as worthy of nothing else, but to be cast into the fire; he is of purer eyes than to bear to have you in his sight; you are ten thousand times so abominable in his eyes as the most hateful venomous serpent is in ours. You have offended him infinitely more than ever a stubborn rebel did his prince: and yet 'tis nothing but his hand that holds you from falling into the fire every moment; 'tis to be ascribed to nothing else, that you did not go to hell the last night; that you was suffered to awake again in this world, after you closed your eyes to sleep: and there is no other reason to be given why you have not dropped into hell since you arose in the morning, but that God's hand has held you up; there is no other reason to be given why you han't gone to hell since you have sat here in the house of God, provoking his pure eyes by your sinful wicked manner of attending his solemn worship: yea, there is nothing else that is to be given as a reason why you don't this very moment drop down into hell.

O sinner! Consider the fearful danger you are in: 'tis a great furnace of wrath, a wide and bottomless pit, full of the fire of wrath, that you are held over in the hand of that God, whose wrath is provoked and incensed as much against you as against many of the damned in hell; you hang by a slender thread, with the flames of divine wrath flashing about it, and ready every moment to singe it, and burn it asunder; and you have no interest in any mediator, and nothing to lay hold of to save yourself, nothing to keep off the flames of wrath, nothing of your own, nothing that you ever have done, nothing that you can do, to induce God to spare you one moment.

---

11. **closets:** Private rooms used for study or prayer.

And consider here more particularly several things concerning that wrath that you are in such danger of.

First. Whose wrath it is: it is the wrath of the infinite God. If it were only the wrath of man, though it were of the most potent prince, it would be comparatively little to be regarded. The wrath of kings is very much dreaded, especially of absolute monarchs, that have the possessions and lives of their subjects wholly in their power, to be disposed of at their mere will. Proverbs 20:2, "The fear of a king is as the roaring of a lion: whoso provoketh him to anger, sinneth against his own soul." The subject that very much enrages an arbitrary prince, is liable to suffer the most extreme torments, that human art can invent or human power can inflict. But the greatest earthly potentates, in their greatest majesty and strength, and when clothed in their greatest terrors, are but feeble despicable worms of the dust, in comparison of the great and almighty Creator and King of heaven and earth: it is but little that they can do, when most enraged, and when they have exerted the utmost of their fury. All the kings of the earth before God are as grasshoppers, they are nothing and less than nothing: both their love and their hatred is to be despised. The wrath of the great King of kings is as much more terrible than their's, as his majesty is greater. Luke 12:4-5, "And I say unto you my friends, Be not afraid of them that kill the body, and after that have no more that they can do. But I will forewarn you whom ye shall fear: Fear him which after he hath killed hath power to cast into hell; yea, I say unto you, fear him."

Second. 'Tis the *fierceness* of his wrath that you are exposed to. We often read of the *fury* of God; as in Isaiah 59:18, "According to their deeds, accordingly he will repay fury to his adversaries." So Isaiah 66:15, "For, behold, the Lord will come with fire, and with chariots like a whirlwind, to render his anger with fury, and his rebukes with flames of fire." And so in many other places. So we read of God's *fierceness*. Revelations 19:15, there we read of "the winepress of the fierceness and wrath of almighty God." The words are exceeding terrible: if it had only been said, "the wrath of God," the words would have implied that which is infinitely dreadful; but 'tis not only said so, but "the fierceness and wrath of God": the fury of God! the fierceness of Jehovah![12] Oh how dreadful must that be! Who can utter or conceive what such expressions carry in them! But it is not only said so, but "the fierceness and wrath of *almighty God*." As though there would be a very great manifestation of his almighty power, in what the fierceness of his wrath should inflict, as though omnipotence should be as it were enraged, and exerted, as men are wont to exert their strength in the fierceness of their wrath. Oh! then what will be the consequence! What will become of the poor worm that shall suffer it! Whose hands can be strong? and whose heart endure? To what a dreadful, inexpressible, inconceivable depth of misery must the poor creature be sunk, who shall be the subject of this!

Consider this, you that are here present, that yet remain in an unregenerate state. That God will execute the fierceness of his anger, implies that he will inflict wrath without any pity: when God beholds the ineffable extremity of your case, and sees your torment to be so vastly disproportioned to your strength, and sees how your poor soul is

---

12. **Jehovah:** A form of the Hebrew name for God.

crushed and sinks down, as it were into an infinite gloom, he will have no compassion upon you, he will not forbear the executions of his wrath, or in the least lighten his hand; there shall be no moderation or mercy, nor will God then at all stay his rough wind; he will have no regard to your welfare, nor be at all careful lest you should suffer too much, in any other sense than only that you shall not suffer beyond what strict justice requires: nothing shall be withheld, because it's so hard for you to bear. Ezekiel 8:18, "Therefore will I also deal in fury: mine eye shall not spare, neither will I have pity; and though they cry in mine ears with a loud voice, yet I will not hear them." Now God stands ready to pity you; this is a day of mercy; you may cry now with some encouragement of obtaining mercy: but when once the day of mercy is past, your most lamentable and dolorous cries and shrieks will be in vain; you will be wholly lost and thrown away of God as to any regard to your welfare; God will have no other use to put you to but only to suffer misery; you shall be continued in being to no other end; for you will be a vessel of wrath fitted to destruction; and there will be no other use of this vessel but only to be filled full of wrath: God will be so far from pitying you when you cry to him, that 'tis said he will only laugh and mock (Proverbs 1:25-32).

How awful are those words, Isaiah 63:3, which are the words of the great God, "I will tread them in mine anger, and will trample them in my fury, and their blood shall be sprinkled upon my garments, and I will stain all my raiment." 'Tis perhaps impossible to conceive of words that carry in them greater manifestations of these three things, viz.[13] contempt, and hatred, and fierceness of indignation. If you cry to God to pity you, he will be so far from pitying you in your doleful case, or showing you the least regard or favor, that instead of that he'll only tread you under foot: and though he will know that you can't bear the weight of omnipotence treading upon you, yet he won't regard that, but he will crush you under his feet without mercy; he'll crush out your blood, and make it fly, and it shall be sprinkled on his garments, so as to stain all his raiment. He will not only hate you, but he will have you in the utmost contempt; no place shall be thought fit for you, but under his feet, to be trodden down as the mire of the streets.

Third. The misery you are exposed to is that which God will inflict to that end, that he might *show* what that *wrath* of Jehovah is. God hath had it on his heart to show to angels and men, both how excellent his love is, and also how terrible his wrath is. Sometimes earthly kings have a mind to show how terrible *their* wrath is, by the extreme punishments they would execute on those that provoke 'em. Nebuchadnezzar, that mighty and haughty monarch of the Chaldean empire, was willing to show *his* wrath, when enraged with Shadrach, Meshach, and Abednego;[14] and accordingly gave order that the burning fiery furnace should be het seven times hotter than it was before; doubtless it was raised to the utmost degree of fierceness that human art could raise it: but the great God is also willing to show *his wrath*, and magnify his awful majesty and mighty power in the extreme sufferings of his enemies. Romans 9:22, "What if God, willing to show *his* wrath, and to make his

---

13. **viz.:** Namely (abbreviation of the Latin word *videlicet*).
14. **Shadrach, Meshach, and Abednego:** The story of their deliverance from the fiery furnace is recounted in Daniel 3:1-30.

power known, endured with much longsuffering the vessels of wrath fitted to destruction?" And seeing this is his design, and what he has determined, to show how terrible the unmixed, unrestrained wrath, the fury and fierceness of Jehovah is, he will do it to effect. There will be something accomplished and brought to pass, that will be dreadful with a witness. When the great and angry God hath risen up and executed his awful vengeance on the poor sinner; and the wretch is actually suffering the infinite weight and power of his indignation, then will God call upon the whole universe to behold that awful majesty, and mighty power that is to be seen in it. Isaiah 33:12-14. "And the people shall be as the burning of lime: as thorns cut up shall they be burnt in the fire. Hear, ye that are far off, what I have done; and ye that are near, acknowledge my might. The sinners in Zion are afraid; fearfulness hath surprised the hypocrites. Who among us shall dwell with the devouring fire? who among us shall dwell with everlasting burnings?"

Thus it will be with you that are in an unconverted state, if you continue in it; the infinite might, and majesty and terribleness of the omnipotent God shall be magnified upon you, in the ineffable strength of your torments: you shall be tormented in the presence of the holy angels, and in the presence of the Lamb; and when you shall be in this state of suffering, the glorious inhabitants of heaven shall go forth and look on the awful spectacle, that they may see what the wrath and fierceness of the Almighty is, and when they have seen it, they will fall down and adore that great power and majesty. Isaiah 66:23-24, "And it shall come to pass, that from one new moon to another, and from one sabbath to another, shall all flesh come to worship before me, saith the Lord. And they shall go forth, and look upon the carcasses of the men that have transgressed against me: for their worm shall not die, neither shall their fire be quenched; and they shall be an abhorring unto all flesh."

Fourth. 'Tis *everlasting* wrath. It would be dreadful to suffer this fierceness and wrath of almighty God one moment; but you must suffer it to all eternity: there will be no end to this exquisite horrible misery. When you look forward, you shall see a long forever, a boundless duration before you, which will swallow up your thoughts, and amaze your soul; and you will absolutely despair of ever having any deliverance, any end, any mitigation, any rest at all; you will know certainly that you must wear out long ages, millions of millions of ages, in wrestling and conflicting with this almighty merciless vengeance; and then when you have so done, when so many ages have actually been spent by you in this manner, you will know that all is but a point to what remains. So that your punishment will indeed be infinite. Oh who can express what the state of a soul in such circumstances is! All that we can possibly say about it, gives but a very feeble faint representation of it; 'tis inexpressible and inconceivable: for "who knows the power of God's anger?" [Psalms 90:11].

How dreadful is the state of those that are daily and hourly in danger of this great wrath, and infinite misery! But this is the dismal case of every soul in this congregation, that has not been born again, however moral and strict, sober and religious they may otherwise be. Oh that you would consider it, whether you be young or old. There is reason to think, that there are many in this congregation now hearing this discourse, that will actually be the subjects of this very misery to all eternity. We know not who they are, or in what seats they sit, or what thoughts they now have: it may be they are now at ease, and hear all these things without much disturbance, and are now flattering them-selves that they are not the persons, promising themselves that they shall escape. If we knew that there was one person, and but one, in the whole congregation that was to be the subject of this misery, what an awful thing would it be to think of! If we knew who it was, what an awful sight would it be to see such a person! How might all the rest of the congregation lift up a lamentable and bitter cry over him! But alas! instead of one, how many is it likely will remember this discourse in hell? And it would be a wonder if some that are now present, should not be in hell in a very short time, before this year is out. And it would be no wonder if some person that now sits here in some seat of this meet-ing house in health, and quiet and secure, should be there before tomorrow morning. Those of you that finally continue in a natural condition, that shall keep out of hell lon-gest, will be there in a little time! your damnation don't slumber; it will come swiftly, and in all probability very suddenly upon many of you. You have reason to wonder, that you are not already in hell. 'Tis doubtless the case of some that heretofore you have seen and known, that never deserved hell more than you, and that heretofore appeared as likely to have been now alive as you: their case is past all hope; they are crying in extreme misery and perfect despair; but here you are in the land of the living, and in the house of God, and have an opportunity to obtain salvation. What would not those poor damned, hopeless souls give for one day's such opportunity as you now enjoy!

And now you have an extraordinary opportunity, a day wherein Christ has flung the door of mercy wide open, and stands in the door calling and crying with a loud voice to poor sinners; a day wherein many are flocking to him, and pressing into the kingdom of God; many are daily coming from the east, west, north and south; many that were very lately in the same miserable condition that you are in, are in now an happy state, with their hearts filled with love to him that has loved them and washed them from their sins in his own blood, and rejoicing in hope of the glory of God. How awful is it to be left behind at such a day! To see so many others feasting, while you are pining and perish-ing! To see so many rejoicing and singing for joy of heart, while you have cause to mourn for sorrow of heart, and howl for vexation of spirit! How can you rest one moment in such a condition? Are not your souls as precious as the souls of the people at Suffield,[15] where they are flocking from day to day to Christ?

Are there not many here that have lived *long* in the world, that are not to this day born again, and so are aliens from the commonwealth of Israel, and have done nothing ever since they have lived, but treasure up wrath against the day of wrath? Oh sirs, your case in an especial manner is extremely dangerous; your guilt and hardness of heart is extremely great. Don't you see how generally persons of your years are passed over and left, in the present remarkable and wonderful dispensation of God's mercy? You had need to consider yourselves, and wake thoroughly out of sleep; you cannot bear the fierceness and wrath of the infinite God.

And you that are *young men*, and *young women*, will you neglect this precious season that you now enjoy, when so many others of your age are renouncing all youthful

---

15. **Suffield:** The next neighbor town. [Edwards's note]

vanities, and flocking to Christ? You especially have now an extraordinary opportunity; but if you neglect it, it will soon be with you as it is with those persons that spent away all the precious days of youth in sin, and are now come to such a dreadful pass in blindness and hardness.

And you *children* that are unconverted, don't you know that you are going down to hell, to bear the dreadful wrath of that God that is now angry with you every day, and every night? Will you be content to be the children of the devil, when so many other children in the land are converted, and are become the holy and happy children of the King of kings?

And let everyone that is yet out of Christ, and hanging over the pit of hell, whether they be old men and women, or middle aged, or young people, or little children, now hearken to the loud calls of God's Word and providence. This acceptable year of the Lord, that is a day of such great favor to some, will doubtless be a day of as remarkable vengeance to others. Men's hearts harden, and their guilt increases apace at such a day as this, if they neglect their souls: and never was there so great danger of such persons being given up to hardness of heart, and blindness of mind. God seems now to be hastily gathering in his elect in all parts of the land; and probably the bigger part of adult persons that ever shall be saved, will be brought in now in a little time, and that it will be as it was on that great outpouring of the Spirit upon the Jews in the apostles' days, the election will obtain, and the rest will be blinded. If this should be the case with you, you will eternally curse this day, and will curse the day that ever you was born, to see such a season of the pouring out of God's Spirit; and will wish that you had died and gone to hell before you had seen it. Now undoubtedly it is, as it was in the days of John the Baptist, the ax is in an extraordinary manner laid at the root of the trees, that every tree that brings not forth good fruit, may be hewn down, and cast into the fire.

Therefore let everyone that is out of Christ, now awake and fly from the wrath to come. The wrath of almighty God is now undoubtedly hanging over great part of this congregation: let everyone fly out of Sodom. Haste and escape for your lives, look not behind you, escape to the mountain, lest you be consumed [Genesis 19:17].

[1741, 2003]

UNDER ✦ MY ✦ WINGS ✦ ✦ ✦

A VIEW of NEW ORLEANS TAKEN F

EVERY THING PROSPER

American Literature

1750–1830

M THE PLANTATION OF MARIGNY

ERHAPS THE MOST FAMILIAR and celebrated event of the period 1750–1830 is the signing of the Declaration of Independence. As symbolically charged as that occasion was, the story of the Declaration also reveals the crucial roles that writing, reading, and printing played in the colonies and later in the new nation. Early in 1776, the Second Continental Congress appointed a committee of five delegates to draft a declaration. The committee, in turn, assigned the task to its youngest member, Thomas Jefferson, already renowned for his powerful writing style. Jefferson later stated that he "used neither book nor pamphlet" as he wrote the Declaration, which he intended "to be an expression of the American mind." But the document was also a concentrated expression of the political ideas of the Enlightenment, ideas that had been developed by a broad range of thinkers and writers in America and Europe. Indeed, the justification for declaring independence was firmly based on some of the fundamental tenets of Enlightenment thought: that the natural world, human nature, and social institutions are governed by universal laws; that all men are created equal and are endowed with certain natural rights; and that governments exist only by the consent of the governed, who are justified in rebelling if their natural rights are violated, as most colonists believed their rights had been violated by Parliament and King George III.

Jefferson's draft of the Declaration was slightly revised by John Adams, Benjamin Franklin, and other members of the committee before being presented to the Second Continental Congress. Following its formal approval by the congress on July 4, 1776, the Declaration was "engrossed," the term for the preparation of the final, handwritten copy of an official document. A common misconception about the Declaration is that the handwritten parchment document was signed on July 4. In fact, the engrossed copy was not ready until August 2, when John Hancock, the president of the congress, led the way by famously signing his name in very large handwriting. Fifty-six representatives eventually signed the document, though not all of them were present at the ceremony on

◄ (OVERLEAF)

John L. Boquete de Woiseri, *View of New Orleans from the Plantation of the Marigny*

The largest real-estate transaction in American history was completed on December 20, 1803, with the official transfer of the Louisiana Purchase territory of 827,987 square miles of land from France to the United States. Although many of the French inhabitants of New Orleans opposed the sale, the local artist Boquete de Woiseri commemorated the event with an optimistic painting in which a huge American eagle spreads its protective wings over the rooftops of the city, bearing in its beak a banner that reads: "Under My Wings Every Thing Prospers."

The Declaration of Independence Read to a Crowd

Printed copies of the Declaration were distributed
throughout the colonies,
where they were published
in newspapers and read
aloud in public spaces.
This illustration from an
early history of England
shows a man on horseback
reading the Declaration to
a cheering crowd. The
notice posted on the wall
reads "America Indepen-
dant, 1776."

August 2, and some of them signed it much later. When the Declaration
was originally approved on July 4, however, a copy was simply delivered to
a Philadelphia printer, John Dunlap. He immediately prepared a "broadside," a single printed sheet that was sent to the British government and
distributed throughout the thirteen colonies. During the following week,
the Declaration was read aloud to enthusiastic crowds in Philadelphia and
Boston, as well as to General George Washington's troops in New York.
But most colonists read the text, which was printed in twenty-four newspapers, beginning on July 6 with the *Pennsylvania Evening Post*. The Declaration was also printed in German, in Philadelphia's *Pennsylvanischer
Staatsbote*. The printed version—published and widely distributed well
before the official handwritten document was signed—was the means by
which both the colonists and the British government learned that the
American Revolution was at hand.

Print Culture and the Road to Revolution

Colonial printers and newspapers did not simply spread the news of separation from Great Britain. They were also deeply involved in the political events leading up to the Declaration of Independence. Changes in print culture between 1750 and 1776 were crucial to the development of both colonial solidarity and a growing sense of national identity that culminated in the American Revolution. In the middle of the eighteenth century, there was little unity or unanimity among the colonies, each of which had developed its own assemblies and forms of government. When in 1754 Franklin offered his "plan of union" (the Albany Plan), under which all of the colonies would have been united for defense against Indian attacks, it was rejected by both the British government and the individual colonies. They were further divided by differing economies and patterns of immigration. Although English settlers lived throughout the colonies, even that group was divided by religious differences among the Congregationalists of Puritan descent in New England; Anglicans (Church of England) and Quakers, primarily in the middle colonies or the South; and Catholics in Maryland. At the same time, there were large numbers of settlers from other countries: Scotch-Irish Presbyterians, who spoke English but were hostile to English settlers and especially to the British government that had forced them out of northern Ireland; people of Dutch descent, primarily in or near New York City; and immigrants from Germany, the majority of them in Pennsylvania. Most of the Indians had been driven out of the thirteen colonies, but there were still remnants of the Iroquois Confederacy in western New York and Pennsylvania, as well as significant numbers of Cherokee, Creek, Choctaw, and Chickasaw on the frontiers of Georgia and North Carolina. There were also more than half a million people from Africa in the colonies, 90 percent of them slaves in the South.

Such ethnic, racial, religious, and linguistic diversity led to deep divisions within and among the colonies, which were connected by rudimentary postal services and transportation systems. Such conditions also posed formidable obstacles to the development of print culture in colonial America. There was a thriving manuscript culture, especially but not exclusively among women writers, who circulated poems and stories in letters and kept handwritten commonplace books. But the publishing trade was still in its infancy in the colonies. The technology of printing had not developed significantly since the perfection of moveable type in the middle of the fifteenth century, and presses were little different from the first one introduced into Massachusetts Bay Colony in 1639. Colonial print shops were small operations, generally consisting of a single room with a hand-cranked press on which printers and their apprentices could produce only about 800 to 1,000 finished sheets in a day. Most of the colonies had weekly newspapers, but they were designed to serve a particular region. Of the twenty or so newspapers in the colonies in 1750, four were in Boston; three were in New York City; and three were in Philadelphia, one of which was published in German. The magazine developed only gradually in the eighteenth century, and few American magazines were successful until after the Revolutionary War. While many printers operated book shops and newspapers advertised a variety of titles, books were expensive and were regarded as a luxury by most colonists. Moreover, only those living in cities along the coast had ready access to significant numbers of books, most of which were imported from England.

Nonetheless, by 1750 a more vital and widespread print culture began to emerge in the colonies. Few figures were as central to that process as Benjamin Franklin, who in writing his own epitaph called himself simply "B. Franklin Printer." In fact, as some of his biographers have suggested, Franklin's printing business was the first media conglomerate. After establishing his business in Philadelphia, Franklin acquired the *Pennsylvania Gazette*, which he transformed into one of the most successful newspapers in the colonies. In addition to his own popular annual, *Poor Richard's Almanack*, his publishing house produced a steady stream of pamphlets, broadsides, and books, including Bibles. Most of the books that Franklin printed were British, including his edition of Samuel Richardson's *Pamela* (1744), the first novel published in colonial America. But novels were widely viewed with suspicion in the colonies, where the few who wrote books generally devoted themselves to religious themes and experiences. Among the most notable examples of such works were Phillis Wheatley's *Poems on Various Subjects, Religious and Moral* (1773), the first book of poetry published by an African American; and Quaker spiritual autobiographies such as *Some Account of the Fore Part of the Life of Elizabeth Ashbridge*, probably written in the 1750s and published in England in 1774; and *The Journal of John Woolman*, published the same year in Philadelphia. In 1771, Franklin himself began to write a very different kind of personal narrative, his *Autobiography*. But he did not return to work on the book until 1784, explaining that the "Affairs of the Revolution occasion'd the Interruption."

Indeed, from the early 1760s through the Revolutionary War, editors, printers, and most writers were increasingly preoccupied by political issues, especially the growing conflicts between the colonies and the government of Great Britain. Under the terms of the treaty that ended the French and Indian War, also known as the Seven Years' War (1756-63), France ceded to Great Britain its claim to all territories in Canada and east of the Mississippi River. Seeking ways to pay its large postwar debt, as well as to support its army in North America, the British Parliament in 1764 passed the American Revenue Act, the first of a series of bills designed to raise money in the colonies. The acts generated heated opposition among colonists, who denounced them as "taxation without representation."

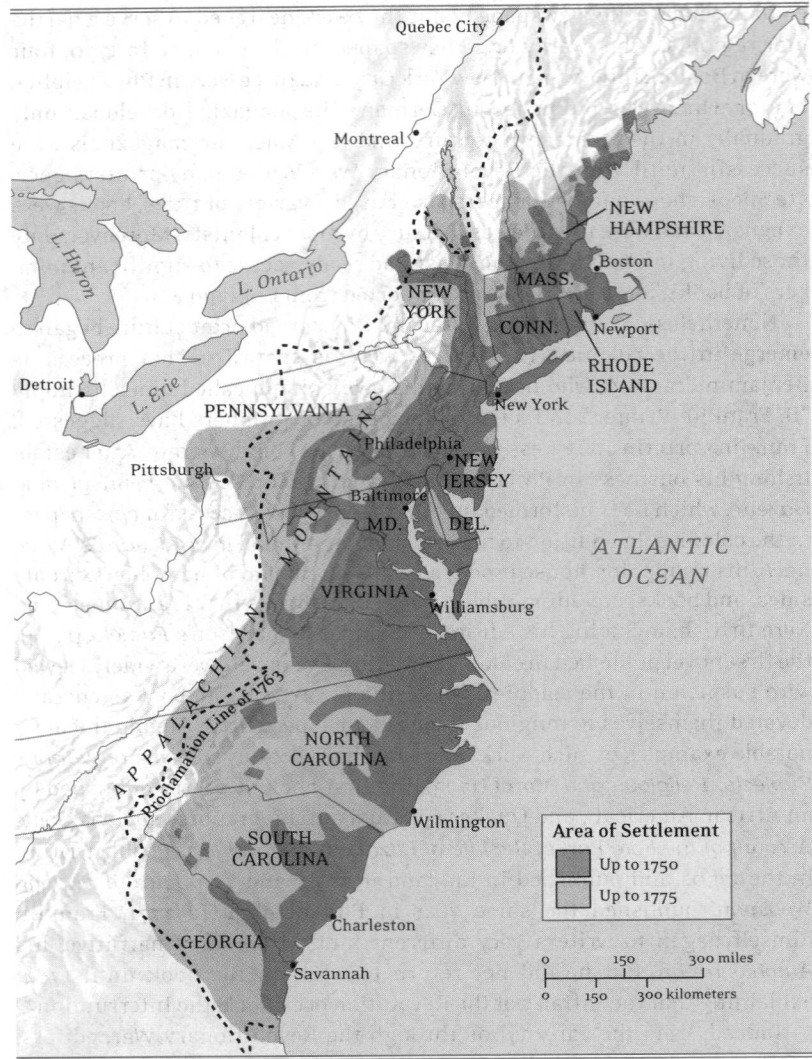

The Thirteen Colonies in 1775

This map of the colonies on the eve of independence includes the "proclamation line" of 1763, a royal decree prohibiting settlement in lands west of the Appalachian Mountains, which were reserved as hunting grounds for Native Americans. By 1775, colonial settlers had already expanded into the prohibited area. Within another fifty years, as a result of the treaty that ended the Revolutionary War in 1783, the Louisiana Purchase of 1803, and a treaty with Spain in 1819, the boundaries of the United States would extend from Canada to the tip of Florida and from the Atlantic coast to the Rocky Mountains.

Join, or Die.

Benjamin Franklin's famous illustration, the first American political cartoon, was published as part of his editorial on "the present disunited state of the British Colonies" in the *Pennsylvania Gazette* on May 9, 1754. Based on the popular superstition that a snake would come back to life if its severed parts were placed together before sunset, the cartoon was designed to generate support for Franklin's plan to unite the colonies for defense against attacks by the French and the Indians. The cartoon was reprinted in virtually all of the colonial newspapers, and played a crucial role in uniting the colonies against Great Britain.

Resistance grew even stronger following the passage in 1765 of the Stamp Act, which imposed a special tax on broadsides, pamphlets, books, newspapers, and legal documents of all types. The passage of the act was a galvanizing event for American printers, who along with other influential groups — like lawyers — had a strong economic stake in opposing the tax. The tax would mean the end to many newspapers and make it almost impossible to begin new ventures. Divided by geography, a limited transportation system, and their different political affiliations, the printers of the twenty-six newspapers in the colonies were united in their opposition to the Stamp Act. As a representative of Pennsylvania, the former printer Benjamin Franklin testified against the act before Parliament. Its repeal in 1766 demonstrated the growing power of the colonial press.

During the turbulent decade that followed, the press assumed an increasingly central role in the political life of the colonies. Many intellectuals absorbed Enlightenment political ideas directly through books imported from Europe, notably works by the English philosopher John Locke, whose *Treatises of Civil Government* strongly shaped the ideas to

Colonial Response to the Stamp Act

The Stamp Act generated strong opposition, especially in colonial newspapers, as illustrated by this response in William Bradford's "expiring" *Pennsylvania Gazette* on October 31, 1765. The skull and crossbones served as "An Emblem of the Effects of the Stamp," both for individual newspapers and "Liberty of the Press."

The TIMES are Dreadful, Dismal, Doleful, Dolorous, and DOLLAR-LESS.

An Emblem of the Effects of the STAMP. O! the fatal Stamp

Thursday, October 31, 1765.　　NUMB. 1195.

THE

PENNSYLVANIA JOURNAL;

AND

WEEKLY ADVERTISER.

EXPIRING: In Hopes of a Resurrection to LIFE again.

I AM sorry to be obliged to acquaint my Readers, that as The STAMP-ACT, is fear'd to be obligatory upon us after the *First of November* ensuing, (the *fatal To-morrow*) the Publisher of this Paper unable to bear the Burthen, has thought it expedient to stop awhile, in order to deliberate, whether any Methods can be found to elude the Chains forged for us, and escape the insupportable Slavery, which it is hoped, from the last Representations now made against that Act, may be effected. Mean while, I must earnestly Request every Individual of my Subscribers, many of whom have been long behind Hand, that they would immediately Discharge their respective Arrears that I may be able, not only to support myself during the Interval, but be better prepared to proceed again with this Paper, whenever an opening for that Purpose appears, which I hope will be soon.　　WILLIAM BRADFORD

which Jefferson finally gave such eloquent expression in the Declaration of Independence. Long before that document was written, however, Locke's ideas were widely disseminated in almanacs, newspapers, and pamphlets. The importance colonial Americans placed on rudimentary education and the ability to read created a growing audience for such works, which made information about social and political developments available even to common people living on isolated farms or in villages distant from urban centers. Almanacs, which one printer claimed were "read by Multitudes who read nothing else," were especially influential. So were the growing number of newspapers, which helped generate unity among the colonies through the sharing and copying of news, unquestioned aspects of periodical publication in the era before copyright laws.

The text that most powerfully strengthened that unity, as well as the resolve of the colonies to declare their independence from Great Britain, was also written by a newspaper editor, Thomas Paine, whose pamphlet *Common Sense* appeared in January 1776. At a time when few copies of individual books were printed — usually no more than two thousand — Paine's pamphlet sold half a million copies, becoming the first bestseller written in colonial America. A few months before it appeared, Benjamin Franklin said that he had never heard an expression in support of independence "from any person, drunk or sober." Following the publication of *Common Sense*, the logic of separation from Great Britain seemed irresistibly clear to most colonists, including the delegates to the Second Continental Congress, who

"The Revolution was in the Minds of the People."

Thomas Paine,
***Common Sense* (1776)**

The influence of Paine's modest pamphlet is well illustrated by its impact on one of its first readers, George Washington. Even after he accepted command of the Continental army in June 1775, Washington firmly declared that he would not prosecute the war in order to gain independence. Two weeks after *Common Sense* was published in January 1776, however, Washington observed that "the sound doctrine and unanswerable reasoning contained in the pamphlet . . . will not leave numbers at a loss to decide upon the propriety of separation" from Great Britain.

voted in favor of independence six months later, on July 2. If the Declaration of Independence, approved two days afterward, laid the foundation for the United States, the site had first been cleared and prepared by a decade of agitation in colonial newspapers, as well as in anti-British broadsides and political tracts culminating in *Common Sense.* As John Adams later recalled in a letter to Thomas Jefferson, "the Revolution was in the Minds of the People" before the first shots were fired.

Society and Culture in the New Nation

The Declaration of Independence and the long war that ensued established an independent country. But the new nation was forged and the foundations of a national culture were laid during the period of consolidation and rapid expansion in the decades following the Revolution. In 1775, there were roughly 2.5 million inhabitants of the thirteen colonies, who were squeezed into a relatively narrow corridor of land between the Atlantic Ocean and the Appalachian Mountains. As part of the peace treaty that formally ended the Revolutionary War in 1783, Britain ceded to the United States all of the land east of the Mississippi River between Canada and the Spanish claim in Florida. In 1790, the year of the first census, the population of the country was nearly 4 million. Although Native Americans were not counted in the census, it nonetheless revealed the remarkable diversity of the new nation. Only 48 percent of its inhabitants were of English descent. People of African descent, the overwhelming majority of them slaves, constituted the second largest group (19 percent); and a provision in the Constitution provided that the importation of slaves could not be prohibited until 1808. The next largest groups were Scots or Scotch-Irish (12 percent) and Germans (10 percent), followed by smaller numbers of the French, Irish, Welsh, Dutch, and Swedes.

Between 1790 and 1830, both the population and the size of the country grew dramatically. In 1803, a vast territory was acquired through the Louisiana Purchase, which extended the nation's boundaries to the Rocky

View from Bushongo Tavern 5 Miles from York Town on the Baltimore Road
This engraving, which is attributed to James Trenchard and appeared in the frontispiece of the July 1788 issue of the *Columbian Magazine*, depicts the log cabins, farms, and dirt roads of what was then the frontier in south central Pennsylvania.

William Clark's Journal

The fullest record of the Lewis and Clark expedition is contained in the journals kept by its two coleaders, whom one historian has called "the writingest explorers of their time." This page from Clark's journal contains a drawing and a detailed description of what he identified as the "large Black & White *Pheasant*," now commonly known as the spruce grouse, which "is peculiar to that portion of the Rocky Mountains watered by the Columbian River."

Mountains. From 1804 to 1806, an expedition led by Meriwether Lewis and William Clark explored the territory along the Missouri River and across the Rocky Mountains to the mouth of the Columbia River in present-day Washington. Although the journals of Lewis and Clark were not published until 1814, government documents, newspaper reports, and an account written by a member of the expedition – Patrick Gass's *Journal* (1807) – offered the American public their first glimpses of the vast potential of the immense area west of the Mississippi River. In 1807, Thomas Jefferson prophetically referred to "our country, from the Mississippi to the Pacific." By 1810, the nation's population exceeded 7 million people, an increasing number of whom were pressing westward, driving Native Americans from lands coveted by the white settlers.

During the following decade, the expanding country survived two crises. The seizure of ships and the impressments of thousands of American sailors by the British navy culminated in the War of 1812. The three-year war ended in a stalemate. Nonetheless, it drew Americans together and fueled nationalism – indeed, it served as a kind of second

American Revolution. In an 1819 treaty, Spain ceded Florida and its claim to territory in the northwest to the United States. But growing divisions over slavery generated a bitter sectional crisis that was resolved in 1820 by the Missouri Compromise, under the terms of which Missouri entered the Union as a slave state but slavery was excluded from all the Louisiana Purchase territory to the north and west of it. By 1830, there were twenty-four states (twelve free and twelve slave) with a total population approaching 13 million, including nearly 2 million slaves in the South.

Most slaves were prohibited by law or other restrictions from learning to read and write, but the burgeoning white population was increasingly literate. At the time of the Revolution, adult literacy rates for white men and women were generally higher in the colonies than in western Europe, ranging from 50 to 60 percent in the southern colonies to as high as 90 percent in New England. But the rates for recent immigrants from Scotland, Ireland, and other European countries were much lower. Literacy rates also varied widely according to class, religion, and locale, since they were higher in urban than in rural areas. Following the Revolution, however, the belief that the survival of republican values and institutions depended on an informed citizenry led most states to mandate publicly funded education. That nationalistic educational philosophy also promoted the growth of libraries, providing at least some Americans with increased access to books and periodicals. Two kinds of libraries existed: social or membership libraries, established by specific groups or organizations, and commercial circulating libraries, which charged fees for the loan of books. The number of books available for loan in either kind of library was generally small (three thousand was the median number in the first decade of the nineteenth century) and access to them was often limited to white men. At the same time, there was a growing emphasis on the need to educate women. Despite their important role in the war effort, women made few political gains during the Revolution. In the following years, however, the emerging ideal of "republican mothers," who would nurture and help instill civic virtues in the rising generation of Americans, led to the establishment of institutions like the Young Ladies' Academy, founded in 1786. "I expect to see our young women forming a new era in female history," Judith Sargent Murray proclaimed in 1798. Her vision proved to be far too optimistic, but the modest educational and social advances women made helped prepare the way for their increasing participation in the cultural life of the new nation.

> "I expect to see our young women forming a new era in female history."

The most immediate beneficiaries of rising literacy rates and the expanding population were newspapers. Following the Revolutionary War, during which the printing business was severely disrupted by

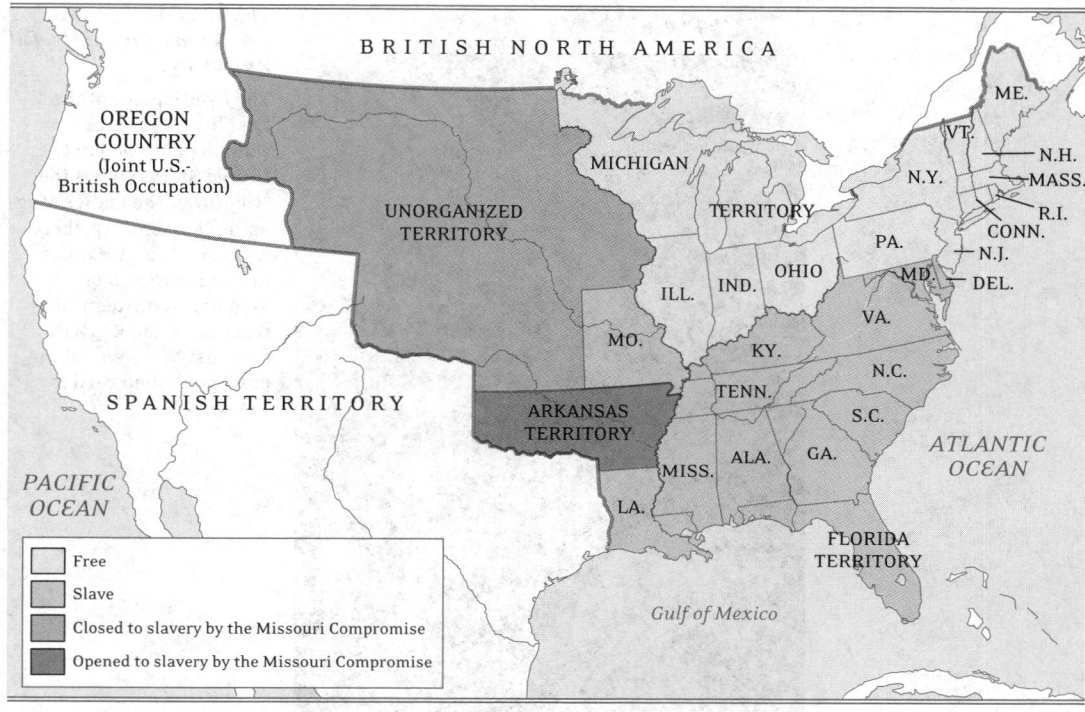

The Missouri Compromise
This map reveals the remarkable expansion of the nation between the end of the Revolution and the Missouri Compromise in 1820. Under the terms of the Compromise, Maine was admitted as a free state and Missouri as a slave state, thus retaining the precarious balance between free and slave states.

shortages of paper and other basic supplies, newspapers swiftly rebounded. The newspaper in which the Declaration of Independence was first printed, the weekly *Philadelphia Evening Post* became the first daily in the United States on May 30, 1783. As in the decade before the war, politics remained a central preoccupation of newspapers in the years leading up to the ratification of the Constitution in 1788 and the election of George Washington as the first president in 1789. The debate over the Constitution was largely conducted in print, notably in the letters to newspapers written by Alexander Hamilton, John Jay, and James Madison in favor of ratification, which were collected and published as *The Federalist* (1788), better known as the *Federalist Papers*. Despite the title of Washington's famous Farewell Address — issued on the occasion of his

FRONTISPIECE.

Thackara & Vallance sculp.

Publish'd at Philad.ᵃ Dec.ʳ 1.ˢᵗ 1792.

The Lady's Magazine and Repository of Useful Knowledge

The frontispiece of the first literary journal for women published in the United States shows the "Genius of the Ladies Magazine" presenting Liberty with a copy of *A Vindication of the Rights of Woman*, an influential treatise by the English feminist Mary Wollstonecraft published earlier in 1792.

retirement from the presidency — it was not delivered as a speech but was instead printed in *Claypoole's American Daily Advertiser* on September 17, 1796. That year, newspapers also played a central role in the country's first contested presidential election, in which John Adams narrowly defeated Thomas Jefferson. Certainly, newspapers revealed the growing political divisions in the United States. By 1800, there were more than two hundred newspapers in the country, almost all of them firmly allied with either the Federalists, who favored a strong federal government and advocated the development of industries and trade, or the Jeffersonian Republicans, who opposed centralized government and advocated a primarily agrarian society.

Although book production lagged behind the strong growth of newspapers, it slowly increased during the decades following the Revolution. The war and its heroes provided ready materials for American writers such as Mercy Otis Warren, a poet and dramatist who published a three-volume history of the American Revolution in 1805, and Mason Weems, whose two enormously popular biographies of George Washington (1800 and 1806) included the famous and undoubtedly fictitious account of his refusal to lie about chopping down a cherry tree. American publishers also reprinted books by two of the "Founding Fathers," Jefferson's *Notes on the State of Virginia* and an early edition of Franklin's *Autobiography*, both of which had originally been published in Paris and London.

But the books read by many common people were often limited to almanacs and the Bible, still found in most homes in America. The fervor generated by the series of religious revivals known as the Great Awakening of 1720-50 waned during the second half of the eighteenth century. Beginning in the 1790s, however, there was a resurgence of evangelical activity known as the "Second Great Awakening." The movement was in large part a reaction against Deism, the "rational" religion of the Enlightenment that rejected orthodox Christian doctrines such as miracles, revelation, and the divinity of Jesus. The Second Great Awakening had a profound impact on all aspects of life in the new nation, including its print culture, as the evangelicals began to spread their message not only through preaching but also by distributing Christian books designed to offer moral and religious instruction to the American masses.

At the same time, the emphasis on secular instruction created a strong market for basic schoolbooks. Noah Webster published the first volume of his *Grammatical Institute of the English Language*, the *Speller* (later called *The American Spelling Book*) in 1783. Since there was then no federal copyright law, which was not passed by Congress until 1790, under the new Constitution, Webster was obliged to travel around the country to secure a copyright for the book in each of the states. The first American "speller," the book was reprinted throughout the nineteenth century and ultimately sold an estimated 100 million copies. The royalties on such books allowed him to work on his most cherished project, *An American Dictionary of the English Language* (1828), which the patriotic Webster in his preface hoped would result in "the continued increase of the wealth, the learning, the moral and religious elevation of character, and the glory of my country."

"... the continued increase of the wealth, the learning, the moral and religious elevation of character, and the glory of my country."

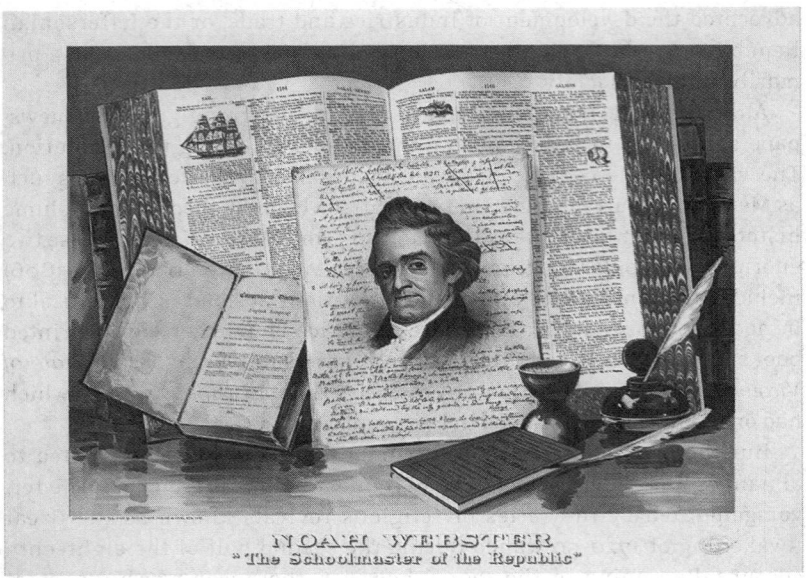

Noah Webster: "The Schoolmaster of the Republic"

This late-nineteenth-century print celebrates Webster's contributions to education and the culture of the new nation, including his *Spelling Book* and his famous *American Dictionary of the English Language* (1828).

The Emergence of an American Literature

The patriotism that inspired Webster's lexical work also spurred the development of imaginative literature, including drama. George Washington's name appeared first on the list of subscribers supporting the publication of Royall Tyler's *The Contrast* (1787), the first play written by an American to be performed by a professional acting company in the United States. Although the stage was dominated by English actors and plays, especially those of Shakespeare, there were numerous efforts to introduce drama written by and for Americans. The journalist Judith Sargent Murray also wrote plays, including *The Medium, or Virtue Triumphant* (1795), the first play written by an American to be performed at the Federal Street Theatre in Boston. A plea for women's rights, the play was not well received, so Murray followed it with *The Traveller Returned* (1796), a comedy set during the American Revolution. Other episodes in the nation's history also provided material for playwrights. The first of the so-called Indian plays, which became enormously popular in the following decades, was apparently *The Indian Princess*, a retelling of the Pocahontas story staged in New York in 1808.

Frontispiece of
The Contrast

This engraving, from the published edition of Royall Tyler's play, includes likenesses of some of the original cast members, including Thomas Signell as Jonathan (center).

Poets also explored American history, even as they predicted a bright future for the new nation. In one of her final works, Phillis Wheatley hailed the end of the Revolutionary War with "Liberty and Peace," a celebration of the glorious destiny of America. Other poets also wrote in support of the cause, including Philip Freneau, often called "the poet of the American Revolution." The growing political divisions in the country were mirrored by its poets, especially by the deep divide between Freneau, who was accused of being Jefferson's Antifederalist mouthpiece, and Federalist poets such as Joel Barlow, Timothy Dwight, and other members of a literary group at Yale College known as the "Connecticut Wits." Like the radical Freneau, however, the conservative group patriotically championed a literature based on American scenes and themes, as exemplified by Barlow's massive epic, *The Vision of Columbus* (1787), and Dwight's *Greenfield Hill* (1794), a long pastoral poem celebrating an idealized Connecticut as a utopian model for economic and social development in the United States.

As the novel became an increasingly popular form, writers also sought to produce "American" novels, though they were closely modeled on works imported from England. Taking their cue from earlier English novels like Samuel Richardson's *Pamela*, which Franklin had reprinted fifty years earlier, in the 1790s the American writers William Hill Brown, Susanna Rowson, and Hannah Webster Foster wrote novels with strong instructive lessons for women. Ironically, one of those lessons was the danger of taking ideas about life and love from novels, as the heroine does in Tabitha Gilman Tenney's *Female Quixotism* (1801). Nonetheless, in yet another reaction against eighteenth-century rationalism, such works revealed the growing emphasis on emotion and sentiment in American literature. Even more heightened emotions and far more extreme psychological states were staples of the so-called gothic romances, sensational tales of horror and the supernatural like Ann Radcliffe's *The Mysteries of Udolpho* (1794) and Matthew Gregory Lewis's *The Monk* (1796), two bestsellers imported from England. With their heavy doses of doom, gloom, magic, and mystery, such works strongly influenced the Philadelphia native Charles Brockden Brown. But he and other American novelists faced an uphill battle in their struggle against foreign competition, since the copyright law of 1790 accorded protection only to books published in the United States, not to those that were first published elsewhere. As Brown bitterly complained, cheap, pirated editions of English novels consequently swamped the limited literary marketplace in the United States.

The growth of periodical publishing provided somewhat brighter prospects for American writers. None of the magazines established before or during the Revolutionary War survived the conflict. By 1800, however, many new magazines appeared, often with patriotic titles, including the *American Magazine*, the *Columbian Magazine*, the *National Magazine*, and the *United States Magazine*. "Those institutions are the most effectual guard to public liberty which diffuse the rudiments of literature among a people," the editors of one magazine declared in 1790. Others viewed magazines and other periodicals as vital, not only to the preservation of liberty, but also to the development of American literature. Washington Irving, who would later become the first American to earn his living as a professional writer, began his career by contributing essays on New York culture and society to his brother's newspaper, the *Morning Courier*. In 1807, he and his brother started a satirical magazine, *Salmagundi*, and during the War of 1812 Irving edited yet another periodical, the *Analectic Magazine*. The resurgent nationalism of the postwar period led to the establishment of many more magazines, notably the *North American Review*, a distinguished literary journal founded in Boston in 1815. A new term, *magazinist*, began

> *"Those institutions are the most effectual guard to public liberty which diffuse the rudiments of literature among a people."*

Alexander Anderson,
Evening Amusements

This woodcut, produced around 1820, illustrates the growing popularity of reading in American homes as books became cheaper and more widely available. Although most of the books read were from England, during the following decade American authors would claim an increasing share of the literary marketplace in the United States.

to be used for those who wrote for magazines, more than one hundred of which were in circulation in 1825.

During the 1820s, conditions for American writers and for the creation of a national literature improved dramatically. The publication of *The Sketch Book of Geoffrey Crayon, Gent.* (1819–20) gained Irving international attention, which had never before been accorded to a writer from the United States. It was swiftly followed by William Cullen Bryant's celebrated first book, *Poems*, and James Fenimore Cooper's first significant novel, *The Spy*, both published in 1821. The commercial success of Cooper's novels illustrated the impact of both cultural changes and advances in the production of books, the costs of which were decreased by new methods of papermaking and typesetting, as well as the use of cloth rather than leather bindings. The small first printing of *The Spy* was quickly followed by additional printings of three thousand and then five thousand copies. Cooper's subsequent novels sold even more briskly. When *The Pioneers* was published in 1823, for example, people waited in line in New York City to buy the book, and the first edition of thirty-five hundred copies sold out by noon on the day it appeared in bookstores. Where Charles Brockden Brown had earlier complained about pirated editions of English novels in the United States, Cooper complained that his popular novels were being published in pirated editions in England.

The literary marketplace was still dominated by English works, but the critical and commercial success of writers like Irving and Cooper inspired other would-be authors in the United States. An increasing number of them were women, including Catharine Maria Sedgwick, whose first novel appeared in 1822. She also contributed numerous sketches and stories to periodicals, including annual gift books, the popularity of which provided yet another outlet for American writers. Boston, New York, and Philadelphia remained the centers of American publishing, but periodicals were also established to serve distant population centers in the Ohio Valley, especially Cincinnati, other parts of the Midwest, and the South. At the same time, a written Native American literature began to emerge in works such as those of Jane Johnston Schoolcraft (Bame-wa-wa-ge-zhik-a-quay, or The Sounds the Stars Make Rushing through the Sky). Schoolcraft's acclaimed stories based on the legends and tales of her mother's tribe, the Ojibwa, appeared in a manuscript magazine she and her husband, Henry Rowe Schoolcraft, hand copied and circulated from their remote home in the Michigan Territory to cities in the Midwest and Northeast. At about the same time, Augustus Baldwin Longstreet established the tradition of American frontier humor in a series of sketches he first published in obscure Southern newspapers and later collected as *Georgia Scenes*. Like so many other writers of the period, Longstreet looked back to an earlier time, in his case the first decades of the Republic. By the time he began to write those sketches in 1830, however, life on the former frontier was not the only thing that had changed — so had American literature. A distinctly national literature was no longer simply a patriotic hope or the distant possibility envisaged by early critics. It was increasingly a reality for publishers, readers, and writers in the United States.

COMPARATIVE TIMELINE, 1750–1830

Dates	American Literature	History and Politics	Developments in Culture, Science, and Technology
1750–1759	**1751** Jonathan Edwards's "Farewell Sermon Preached at the First Precinct in Northampton" is published	**1750** Population of thirteen colonies: 1,170,800 **1756–63** French and Indian Wars (Seven Years' War)	**1750** English astronomer Thomas Wright first proposes existence of Milky Way galaxy **1752** Franklin's famous kite experiment proves lightning is electricity **1754** New York Society Library offers books on loan for annual membership fee **1755** Samuel Johnson publishes first English dictionary **1755** "Yankee Doodle" is a popular song **1759** British Museum opens in London
1760–1769	**1765** John Dickinson, *Declaration of Rights and Grievances* **1768** Occom, *A Short Narrative of My Life* **1768** John Dickinson, "The Liberty Song"	**1760** Population of thirteen colonies: 1,593,600 **1765** Stamp Act imposes special tax on all publications and legal documents in American colonies	**1763** All thirteen colonies have printing presses

COMPARATIVE TIMELINE, 1750–1830

Dates	American Literature	History and Politics	Developments in Culture, Science, and Technology
1770–1779	**1771** Franklin begins writing his *Autobiography* **1773** Wheatley, *Poems on Various Subjects, Religious and Moral* **1774** *Journal of John Woolman* **1774** *Some Account . . . of the Life of Elizabeth Ashbridge* **1776** Paine, *Common Sense*	**1770** Population of thirteen colonies: 2,148,100 **1775** Battles of Lexington, Concord, and Bunker Hill **1776** Declaration of Independence is ratified by Second Continental Congress **1776–83** American Revolutionary War	 **1779** *United States Magazine* is founded in Philadelphia
1780–1789	**1782** Crèvecoeur, *Letters from an American Farmer* **1787** Royall Tyler, *The Contrast* **1787** Barlow, *The Vision of Columbus* **1788** *The Federalist Papers*, Hamilton, Jay, and Madison's writings in favor of ratifying the Constitution, are published **1789** Brown, *The Power of Sympathy*	**1780** U.S. population: 2,780,400 **1784** Methodist Church organized in United States **1788** U.S. Constitution ratified	**1783** *Philadelphia Evening Post* becomes America's first daily newspaper **1783** Webster publishes first volume of *Grammatical Institute of the English Language*, the *Speller* **1786** *Columbian Magazine* is founded **1786** Young Ladies' Academy of Philadelphia is established as first institution to offer formal education for women in America **1787** *American Magazine* is founded **1788** Wedgwood creates his famous medallion showing the figure of a supplicant slave, which is eventually adopted as a symbol of the abolitionist movement

COMPARATIVE TIMELINE, 1750–1830

Dates	American Literature	History and Politics	Developments in Culture, Science, and Technology
1780–1789 (cont.)	**1789** Equiano, *The Interesting Narrative of the Life of Olaudah Equiano, or Gustavus Vassa*	**1789** Washington elected as first president of United States **1789–99** French Revolution	
1790–1799	**1791** Rowson, *Charlotte Temple* **1792** Murray begins "The Gleaner" in the *Massachusetts Magazine* **1794** Dwight, *Greenfield Hill* **1794** Radcliffe, *The Mysteries of Udolpho* **1797** Foster, *The Coquette* **1798** Brown, *Wieland* **1799** Brown, *Edgar Huntly*	**1790** U.S. population: 3,929,214; first official U.S. Census **1792** Washington reelected president **1796** Adams elected president	**1790** Beginning of "Second Great Awakening," evangelical religious revival in America **1792** Wollstonecraft's *Vindication of the Rights of Woman* stirs debate on women's education **1792** *Lady's Magazine and Repository of Useful Knowledge*, America's first literary journal for women, is published **1793** Invention of cotton gin **1794** Philadelphia's American Philosophical Society provides space for paintings and natural history specimens for public display **1796** Washington's famous Farewell Address is printed in *Claypoole's American Daily Advertiser* **1798** Coleridge and Wordsworth publish *Lyrical Ballads* in Britain
1800–1809	**1800** Weems, *The Life and Memorable Actions of George Washington* **1801** Tenney, *Female Quixotism*	**1800** U.S. population: 5,308,483 **1800** Jefferson elected president **1801** Haitian slaves, led by L'Ouverture, seize power from the French and establish first black republic	**1800** U.S. Library of Congress founded **1801** *Port Folio*, a popular magazine of the era, is founded **1802** World's first successful steamship, the *Charlotte Dundas*, built in England

COMPARATIVE TIMELINE, 1750–1830

Dates	American Literature	History and Politics	Developments in Culture, Science, and Technology
1800–1809 (cont.)		1803 Louisiana Purchase 1804 Jefferson reelected president 1807 Slave trade is abolished in Great Britain 1808 Madison elected president	1805 Lewis and Clark expedition reaches Pacific Ocean 1808 Scott, *Marmion*
1810–1819	 1815 Freneau, *A Collection of Poems* 1819–20 Irving, *The Sketch Book of Geoffrey Crayon, Gent.*	1810 U.S. population: 7,239,881 1812 Madison reelected president 1812–15 War of 1812 1816 Monroe elected president 1819 United States acquires Florida from Spain	1810 Scott, *The Lady of the Lake* 1811 First steam-powered ferry begins operation between New York City and Hoboken, New Jersey 1812–15 Byron, *Childe Harold* 1813 Stereotype printing revolutionizes production of multiple copies of a text 1814 Scott, *Waverly* 1815 *North American Review* founded in Boston 1816 *Boston Recorder*, first religious newspaper, founded
1820–1830	 1821 Cooper, *The Spy* 1821 Bryant, *Poems* 1822 Sedgwick, *A New-England Tale*	1820 U.S. population: 9,638,453 1820 Monroe reelected president 1820 The Missouri Compromise excludes slavery from Louisiana Purchase territory to north and west of Missouri	1821 *Saturday Evening Post* begins publication in United States

COMPARATIVE TIMELINE, 1750–1830

Dates	American Literature	History and Politics	Developments in Culture, Science, and Technology
1820–1830 (cont.)	**1823** Cooper, *The Pioneers*	**1824** John Quincy Adams elected president	**1824** Debut of Beethoven's Symphony no. 9
			1825 Erie Canal opens, providing passage from Albany, New York, to Lake Erie
			1825–1880s Cole and other Hudson River School artists depict romanticized American landscapes
	1826 Cooper, *Last of the Mohicans*		**1826** Morey patents internal combustion engine
	1827 Sedgwick, *Hope Leslie*		**1827** *Freedom's Journal*, first African American periodical, is founded
		1828 Jackson elected president	**1828** Webster publishes *An American Dictionary of the English Language*
			1828 *Cherokee Phoenix*, first Native American newspaper, is founded
	1830 Longstreet begins to write sketches of *Georgia Scenes*		

Writing Colonial Lives

WHEN BENJAMIN FRANKLIN began writing his celebrated "autobiography" in 1771, that term was not used to identify such first-person narratives. The term was not commonly used until the early decades of the nineteenth century, and *The Autobiography of Benjamin Franklin* was not published under that title until 1868. Nonetheless, autobiography has a long history in Western culture, most often traced back to the *Confessions* of St. Augustine (354–430), the Roman Catholic bishop of Hippo in North Africa.

◀ Benjamin Franklin

The author of the *Autobiography of Benjamin Franklin*, one of the most famous self-portraits in American literature, was also frequently the subject of portraiture. This painting by George Dunlop Leslie, after the original painted in London by Mason Chamberlain in 1762, depicts Franklin as a writer and scientist. The thunderstorm raging outside the window is an allusion to his celebrated experiments with electricity. (The bells behind him are rigged to ring when lightning strikes outside.) But the books visible at the extreme left, behind the bells, and especially the manuscript and the quill pen Franklin holds were equally central to both his sense of identity and his growing fame.

As that genealogy suggests, one important source of autobiography was the Christian emphasis on self-examination, an exercise that assumed even greater importance during the Protestant Reformation of the sixteenth and seventeenth centuries. Since for most Protestants the sole promise of salvation was the operation of God's grace within the soul, individuals were encouraged to turn inward to discover signs of their ultimate spiritual destiny. The settlement of New England was powerfully fueled by the Reformation, and the Puritans produced large numbers of autobiographical writings, including journals, captivity narratives, and more-formal spiritual autobiographies such as Jonathan Edwards's *Personal Narrative*.

Franklin, who was born and raised in Puritan Boston, also emphasized the need for self-examination. But his narrative is anything but a spiritual autobiography. Despite his professed belief in God and Providence, Franklin displayed little interest in the spiritual life. In what he called a "History of my Life," Franklin turned not inward to the soul but outward to the world of men (which virtually all of the major characters in his narrative are) and events. Indeed, his *Autobiography* was very much a product of the Enlightenment. Like many Enlightenment thinkers, who viewed themselves as the "party of humanity," Franklin placed less importance on salvation or the need to prepare for the next world than on the pursuit of happiness and the need to improve conditions in this world. With his satirical wit, his distaste for religious orthodoxy and social pretense, and his focus on reason and tolerance, Franklin displayed an especially strong kinship with Voltaire and other Enlightenment writers in France. He was even more directly influenced by the major philosophers of the Enlightenment in Great Britain. Just as the Declaration revealed the impact of the political philosophy of John Locke's *Treatises of Government*, the *Autobiography* reflects the empirical philosophy of Locke's *Essay Concerning Human Understanding*. Affirming the natural goodness of human beings, Locke denied that there were innate ideas. Instead, he argued that the human mind was a tabula rasa, a blank slate inscribed by sense experience alone. Locke's views were further developed by one of the friends Franklin made in England, the Scottish philosopher David Hume. The skeptical and utilitarian Hume emphasized the limitations of human knowledge, which in his view did not extend beyond what we can observe, and the primary task of which was to provide us with a practical guide to life. A similar understanding of human nature and individual understanding is revealed in the *Autobiography*, in which Franklin charts his intellectual growth through observation and education, especially his voracious reading.

In fact, Franklin's account was probably inspired by a number of the books he mentions in his *Autobiography*. For example, he refers to *Plutarch's Lives*, which was widely available in English translations in the

John Bunyan, *The Pilgrim's Progress*

The frontispiece from this early edition shows the author asleep, as in his dream the character Christian — with his guidebook, the Bible, in hand — begins his journey from the City of Destruction to the Celestial City. Bunyan's allegory, which has been more widely read than any book in English except the Bible, remained enormously popular in America for at least two hundred years after it was first published in 1678.

eighteenth century. Those brief biographies of eminent Greek and Roman statesmen were very popular reading, especially in schools. By the time he began his autobiography, Franklin surely had a sense of his own growing importance as a historical figure as well as his role in the emerging effort to establish a new republic in America. Franklin also alludes to an even more popular book of the period, John Bunyan's *The Pilgrim's Progress* (1678), an allegorical account of the adventures of Christian, a young man who journeys from the City of Destruction to salvation in the Celestial City. In fact, Franklin's story may be read as a kind of secularized version of *The Pilgrim's Progress*, which was second only to the Bible among the books read in many homes in colonial America. Certainly, it provided a compelling narrative model to Franklin, though, as one of his recent biographers has observed, his "was the story of a very real pilgrim . . . in a very real world."

His "was the story of a very real pilgrim . . . in a very real world."

In offering an account of his triumphant progress through that world, Franklin cast himself as an exemplary figure, at once a distinct individual and a representative American. At the very time when many people in the colonies first began to think of themselves as Americans, Franklin was one of the first to develop an idea of what it meant to be one. He began his

Autobiography shortly before the Revolution, while he was in England seeking to gain greater economic and political autonomy for the colonies. Franklin wrote the later sections of the *Autobiography* after the United States had gained independence from England. The triumphant story of his own rise in the world was thus also the story of the rise of his country. Franklin had broken away from his older brother, to whom he had been indentured at an early age, and gone on to gain international fame as a scientist and statesman. At the same time, the colonies finally broke away from Great Britain, afterwards assuming an increasingly important place in the affairs of the world.

Although it has overshadowed virtually all other early American auto-biographies, Franklin's was not the only one written by a colonist during the last half of the eighteenth century. Nor did Franklin tell the whole story of life in colonial America. In contrast to his *Autobiography*, the nar-ratives by two other authors represented in this section, the Quakers Elizabeth Ashbridge and John Woolman, followed the long tradition of the spiritual autobiography. In fact, like other autobiographies written by Quakers, or members of the Society of Friends, their narratives were pub-lished posthumously only after a committee had determined that the works were of sufficient didactic and spiritual value to merit publication. Ashbridge told the story of her difficult life and struggles, from her early days in England—when she wept because she was not born a boy and therefore could not become an Anglican priest—to the spiritual crisis that finally led her to become an active member and teacher among the Quakers in North America. Through her involvement in the Society of Friends, Ashbridge gained what few women had in colonial America: the right to speak publicly and to write her own story. But perhaps the most famous of all Quaker spiritual autobiographies is *The Journal of John Woolman*. Raised in a Quaker colony near Philadelphia, Woolman traced his journey from a spiritually troubled youth to a successful businessman to his final transformation into a tireless missionary and preacher, seeking to con-vert others and to promote antislavery among members of the Society of Friends.

Other significant autobiographies of the period also contained pleas on behalf of oppressed groups. Samson Occom, a Mohegan who converted to Christianity and became a missionary among the Indians, bitterly described their harsh treatment by the European colonists of New England. Occom was thus among the first Native American writers in English to use his adopted language to expose the plight of the Indians. Another convert to Christianity, Olaudah Equiano, used an account of his torturous experiences to reveal the horrors of slavery and the slave trade. His celebrated account also helped establish a new and vital genre, the slave narrative. Describing such works as the print origins (as distin-guished from oral sources) of black literature in the United States, the eminent African American novelist Toni Morrison has observed that slave narratives also "gave fuel to the fires that abolitionists were setting everywhere." Indeed, just as Equiano's narrative was instrumental in abolishing the Atlantic slave trade, other writers would later develop the slave narrative into one of the most powerful of all weapons employed in the antislavery crusade during the decades before the Civil War.

Slave narratives also "gave fuel to the fires that abolitionists were setting everywhere."

The Washington Family

This engraving, based on a life-sized group portrait by the American painter Edward Savage, was marketed to an international audience shortly before George Washington's death in 1799. The captions in English and French identified the other figures as his wife Martha, the wealthy widow Washington had married in 1759; and her two grandchildren. Explaining the symbolism of the painting, Savage noted that Washington's "Military Character" was represented by his uniform, while the papers on which his arm rested represented his presidency. Martha Washington was shown holding "the Plan of the Federal City," the new capital named in honor of Washington. Savage added that the grandchildren were meant to represent the future of the nation, but he did not mention the figure standing in the shadows in the background. He has been identified as William Lee, a slave who served as Washington's personal servant for nearly thirty years. In his will, Washington freed William Lee, and directed that his other 123 slaves should be freed when Martha Washington died.

Even as they pursued very different ends, Ashbridge, Woolman, Occom, and Equiano offered a profoundly different image of what Franklin described as life in colonial America. Partly in an effort to attract immigrants, as well as to establish the sharp differences between his country and the countries of Europe, Franklin for the most part described a fluid, egalitarian society in which even a poor boy from a humble family could rise to fame and fortune. The other writers placed far greater emphasis on the obstacles to freedom and opportunity in the colonies. Ashbridge arrived in New York in 1732 and later made her way to Pennsylvania, where the young Franklin was already well advanced on what he later described as his smooth road to success in his adopted city of Philadelphia. Ashbridge described a different and far darker reality, a world of indentured servitude, social stratification, and religious intolerance. She also emphasized the subservient role of women, while Woolman, Occom, and Equiano exposed the bigotry and brutality faced by Native Americans and African Americans, especially the growing number of slaves in the colonies. Five years after he began his autobiography, Franklin helped prepare the Declaration of Independence, which affirmed that "all men are created equal," and that they are endowed with certain inalienable rights, including "life, liberty, and the pursuit of happiness." As the colonists set out on their path toward independence from England, however, the kind of autonomy and freedom they sought was far from the reality of many of those born in or brought to America.

Benjamin Franklin

[1706-1790]

[Franklin's Autobiography *is] a fond look back upon an earlier self, giving an intensely ambitious young man the benefit of the older man's relaxation.*

— *John Updike*

Benjamin Franklin was born in Boston on January 17, 1706, to Josiah and Abiah Folger Franklin. Josiah Franklin, a soap maker, had emigrated from England with his first wife, who died in childbirth. In addition to the five surviving children of his first marriage, Josiah and Abiah had ten children, of which Franklin was the eighth and the youngest son. His father initially intended for him to become a minister, so Franklin was sent to the Boston Latin School in preparation for study at Harvard College. For reasons that are not clear—perhaps because Franklin did not seem suited for the ministry—his father withdrew him from the Latin School and enrolled him in an academy for the practical study of writing and arithmetic. After only two years of schooling, Franklin went to work in his father's business. Later, at the age of twelve, he was apprenticed to his brother, James Franklin, who ran a printing shop. Franklin initially resisted the apprenticeship, which was one of nine years instead of the usual seven. James Franklin was also a hard taskmaster, and he and the young Franklin were frequently at odds. In 1721, James Franklin started the *New England Courant*, one of the first newspapers established in Boston. Bored with typesetting, Franklin spent all of his spare time reading. He also began to submit anonymous columns to the newspaper, adopting the persona of "Silence Dogood," an independent-minded widow of a country minister. James Franklin, who had no idea of the identity of the author of the popular "Dogood Papers," was furious when he learned that they were written by his young apprentice. From that point, the always difficult relationship between the brothers deteriorated, and Franklin decided to run away in the fall of 1723. Using the cover story that he had "got a naughty Girl with Child," Franklin booked passage on a ship to New York City and proceeded from there to Philadelphia.

During the following twenty-five years, Franklin became one of the most prominent and successful citizens of his adopted city. The year after he arrived in Philadelphia, where he found work in a printing shop, he was encouraged to start his own business by the colonial governor of Pennsylvania, Sir William Keith. Promising letters of credit, Governor Keith urged Franklin to go to England to buy equipment. When he landed there, Franklin learned that no letters had been sent. He consequently found work in a printing shop in London, where the publishing trade was far more advanced than it was in the colonies. Returning to Philadelphia two years later, in 1726, the twenty-year-old Franklin had already gained considerable experience in printing. He soon established his own business and, in 1729, he also took over a struggling newspaper. Franklin shortened its title to the *Pennsylvania Gazette* and established a lively weekly that soon became one of the most distinguished newspapers in the colonies and one of the earliest financial successes in the history of American periodicals. Building on its success, Franklin introduced his phenomenally popular annual, *Poor Richard's Almanack* (1733-58), famous for its maxims about the value of frugality and hard work. He later established the second monthly magazine in North America, the *General Magazine* (1741), and published several pamphlets, including his *Proposal for Promoting Useful Knowledge* (1743). In 1730, Franklin married Deborah Read. The couple had two children, and they took in his illegitimate son, William, later the royal governor of New Jersey. Franklin also became increasingly involved in civic affairs—he founded the first colonial subscription library, helped establish an academy that became the University of Pennsylvania, and laid the foundation for the American Philosophical Society, formed in 1743 to support "all philosophical Experiments that let Light into the Nature of Things, tend to increase the Power of Man over Matter, and multiply the Conveniencies or Pleasures of Life."

In 1748, Franklin essentially retired from business, selling the *Pennsylvania Gazette* for a considerable profit and embarking on a second career devoted to scientific investigation and public service. The publication of his *Experiments and Observations on Electricity* (1751-54) brought him international recognition, but Franklin gained even greater fame as a diplomat and statesman. As Pennsylvania's representative to the Albany

Benjamin Franklin

Robert Feke painted this earliest known portrait of Franklin around 1748, the year that the successful entrepreneur retired from business to devote himself exclusively to public service, scientific experimentation, and his many other intellectual pursuits.

Congress in the summer of 1754, his "plan of union" was among the first proposals for uniting all of the colonies under a general government. During much of the time between 1757 and 1775, Franklin was in England, serving as a colonial agent — first for Pennsylvania, and later for Georgia, New Jersey, and Massachusetts. Franklin tried to persuade the British government to allow more self-rule in the colonies, and he testified before the House of Commons for the repeal of the detested Stamp Act, one of a series of taxation measures that generated violent opposition. When Franklin returned to America in 1775, he was chosen as a delegate to the Second Continental Congress, in which he served with John Adams and Thomas Jefferson on the committee assigned to write the Declaration of Independence. The following year, he was appointed commissioner to the court of France, where Franklin helped negotiate and signed the peace treaty with Great Britain that ended the Revolutionary War in 1783. After his return to Philadelphia two years later, the tireless Franklin was elected president of the Pennsylvania Society for the Promotion of the Abolition of Slavery. He was later appointed as a delegate to the convention that framed the federal Constitution, which he signed on September 17, 1787. Throughout his four decades of public service, Franklin continued to write articles for periodicals and publish pamphlets. He also worked intermittently on his autobiography, though he was not able to complete it before his death. Franklin's last publication was an ironic letter to the *Federal Gazette*, "On the Slave Trade," published a month before he died on April 17, 1790. Nearly twenty thousand people lined the streets for his funeral procession in Philadelphia, where he was buried next to his wife in the Christ Church Burial Ground.

Reading Franklin's *Autobiography.*   What is now known as *The Autobiography of Benjamin Franklin* had a long and complex compositional history. The first part of what Franklin variously referred to as his "memoirs" and "the History of my Life" was written in the summer of 1771, while he was staying in southern England at Twyford, the summer home of his friend Jonathan Shipley (1714-1788), then the Anglican bishop of St. Asaph's in Wales. Franklin addressed this part of the narrative to his older son, William Franklin (1731-1813), who had been appointed the royal governor of New Jersey in 1762. (Sadly, there is no evidence that it was ever read by William, who was later estranged from his father when he supported the British government during the Revolution.) The second part of the manuscript was written thirteen years later, in 1784, while Franklin was living in France. The final two parts were written after his return to Philadelphia, in August 1788 and in the winter of 1789-90. The four parts of the manuscript cover his life only up until 1758, well before his greatest achievements as a diplomat and statesman. Franklin, who spent most of his early life as a printer, died before he completed or had an opportunity to prepare the manuscript for publication. His account is further complicated by the fact that Franklin did not always have copies of what he had

bedfordstmartins.com/
americanlit *for research links on Franklin*

The Private Life of the Late Benjamin Franklin

The first English edition of Franklin's *Autobiography* was a translation of the original 1791 French edition, published in Paris a year after his death.

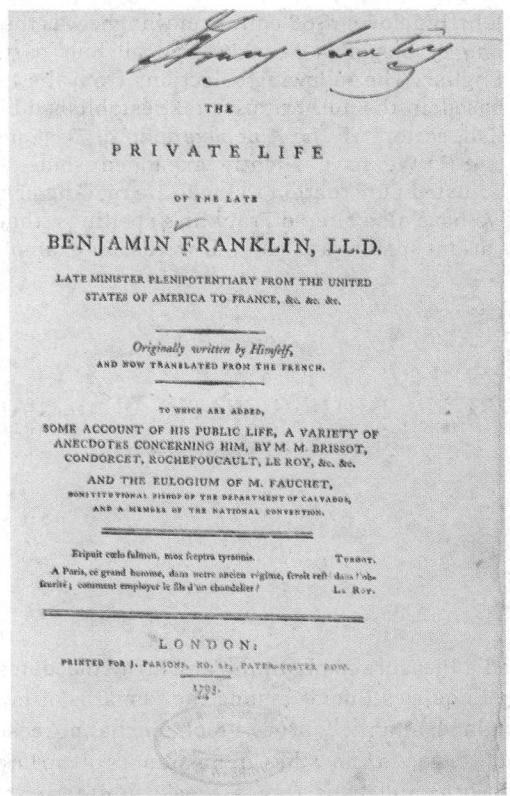

THE

PRIVATE LIFE

OF THE LATE

BENJAMIN FRANKLIN, LL.D.

LATE MINISTER PLENIPOTENTIARY FROM THE UNITED
STATES OF AMERICA TO FRANCE, &c. &c. &c.

Originally written by Himself,
AND NOW TRANSLATED FROM THE FRENCH.

TO WHICH ARE ADDED,

SOME ACCOUNT OF HIS PUBLIC LIFE, A VARIETY OF
ANECDOTES CONCERNING HIM, BY M. M. BRISSOT,
CONDORCET, ROCHEFOUCAULT, LE ROY, &c. &c.

AND THE EULOGIUM OF M. FAUCHET,
CONSTITUTIONAL BISHOP OF THE DEPARTMENT OF CALVADOS,
AND A MEMBER OF THE NATIONAL CONVENTION.

LONDON:
PRINTED FOR J. PARSONS, NO. 21, PATER-NOSTER ROW.
1793.

written earlier when he returned to work on the *Autobiography*. Moreover, he made outlines of topics he wanted to cover in the work and jotted down pages of notes without clearly indicating whether he intended to use all of those materials in the final version.

The publication history of the *Autobiography* is equally complex. At various times, Franklin shared the manuscript with friends, including his neighbor in Paris, Louis Guillaume Le Veillard. In one of the many ironies of the history of the text, what became one of the most famous of all American life writings was first published in Paris in Le Veillard's French translation of part one, *Memoires de la Vie Privée de Benjamin Franklin* (1791). In a further irony, the first edition of the autobiography published in English was actually a translation of the French edition, *The Private Life of the Late Benjamin Franklin, LL.D.*, which was published in London in 1793. Several American editions of *The Life of Dr. Benjamin Franklin* followed before his grandson and literary executor, William Temple Franklin, published a version that included the first three parts of the text in his edition of *Memoirs of the Life and Writings of Benjamin Franklin* (1818). But it was not until

John Bigelow's 1868 edition of what he was the first to call *The Autobiography of Benjamin Franklin* that all four parts of the work appeared in English. The following selections from the text of parts one and two is based on the authoritative text established by J. A. Leo Lemay and P. M. Zall, editors of *The Autobiography of Benjamin Franklin: A Genetic Text* (1981). We have silently expanded some abbreviations and slightly adjusted punctuation to facilitate reading of the text. In a few instances, we have also altered Franklin's spellings, though we have retained early variant spellings of familiar words, for example *chearfully* and *Wharff*.

From THE AUTOBIOGRAPHY OF BENJAMIN FRANKLIN

From Part One

> Twyford, at the Bishop
> of St Asaph's
> 1771.

Dear Son,

I have ever had a Pleasure in obtaining any little Anecdotes of my Ancestors. You may remember the Enquiries I made among the Remains of my Relations[1] when you were with me in England; and the Journey I took for that purpose. Now imagining it may be equally agreable to you to know the Circumstances of *my* Life, many of which you are yet unacquainted with; and expecting a Weeks uninterrupted Leisure in my present Country Retirement, I sit down to write them for you. To which I have besides some other Inducements. Having emerg'd from the Poverty & Obscurity in which I was born & bred, to a State of Affluence & some Degree of Reputation in the World, and having gone so far thro' Life with a considerable Share of Felicity, the conducing Means I made use of, which, with the Blessing of God, so well succeeded, my Posterity may like to know, as they may find some of them suitable to their own Situations, & therefore fit to be imitated. That Felicity, when I reflected on it, has induc'd me sometimes to say, that were it offer'd to my Choice, I should have no Objection to a Repetition of the same Life from its Beginning, only asking the Advantage Authors have in a second Edition to correct some Faults of the first. So would I if I might, besides correcting the Faults, change some sinister Accidents & Events of it for others more favourable, but tho' this were deny'd, I should still accept the Offer. However, since such a Repetition is not to be expected, the Thing most like living one's Life over again, seems to be a *Recollection* of that Life; and to make that Recollection as durable as possible, the putting it down in Writing. Hereby, too, I shall indulge the Inclination so natural in old Men, to be talking of themselves and

---

1. **Remains of my Relations:** Franklin and his son, William, visited surviving relatives in 1758.

their own past Actions, and I shall indulge it, without being troublesome to others who thro' respect to Age might think themselves oblig'd to give me a Hearing, since this may be read or not as any one pleases. And lastly, (I may as well confess it, since my Denial of it will be believ'd by no body) perhaps I shall a good deal gratify my own *Vanity*. Indeed I scarce ever heard or saw the introductory Words, *Without Vanity I may say*, &c. but some vain thing immediately follow'd. Most People dislike Vanity in others whatever Share they have of it themselves, but I give it fair Quarter wherever I meet with it, being persuaded that it is often productive of Good to the Possessor & to others that are within his Sphere of Action: And therefore in many Cases it would not be quite absurd if a Man were to thank God for his Vanity among the other Comforts of Life.

And now I speak of thanking God, I desire with all Humility to acknowledge, that I owe the mention'd Happiness of my past Life to his kind Providence, which led me to the Means I us'd & gave them Success. My Belief of This, induces me to *hope*, tho' I must not *presume*, that the same Goodness will still be exercis'd towards me in continuing that Happiness, or in enabling me to bear a fatal Reverso,[2] which I may experience as others have done, the Complexion of my future Fortune being known to him only: and in whose Power it is to bless to us even our Afflictions.

The Notes one of my Uncles (who had the same kind of Curiosity in collecting Family Anecdotes) once put into my Hands, furnish'd me with several Particulars, relating to our Ancestors. From those Notes I learnt that the Family had liv'd in the same Village, Ecton in Northamptonshire, for 300 Years, & how much longer he knew not, (perhaps from the Time when the Name *Franklin* that before was the Name of an Order of People, was assum'd by them for a Surname, when others took Surnames all over the Kingdom.[3]) on a Freehold of about 30 Acres, aided by the Smith's Business which had continued in the Family till his Time, the eldest Son being always bred to that Business. A Custom which he & my Father both followed as to their eldest Sons. When I search'd the Register at Ecton, I found an Account of their Births, Marriages and Burials, from the Year 1555 only, there being no Register kept in that Parish at any time preceding. By that Register I perceiv'd that I was the youngest Son of the youngest Son for 5 Generations back. My Grandfather Thomas, who was born in 1598, lived at Ecton till he grew too old to follow Business longer, when he went to live with his Son John, a Dyer at Banbury in Oxfordshire, with whom my Father serv'd an Apprenticeship. There my Grandfather died and lies buried. We saw his Gravestone in 1758. His eldest Son Thomas liv'd in the House at Ecton, and left it with the Land to his only Child, a Daughter, who with her Husband, one Fisher of Wellingborough sold it to Mr Isted, now Lord of the Manor there. My Grandfather had 4 Sons that grew up, viz.[4] Thomas, John, Benjamin and Josiah. I will give you what Account I can of them at this distance from my Papers, and if those are

---

2. **Reverso:** A backhanded stroke (a dueling term).
3. **the Name *Franklin* . . . Kingdom:** A franklin was a landowner of free but not noble birth in medieval England. Franklin evidently intended to insert a more detailed note at this point in the text about the origin of his surname. In the 1791 French edition, Louis Guillaume Le Veillard included a translation of a note Franklin had written on a separate sheet of paper.
4. **viz.:** Abbreviation for *videlicet* (Latin), meaning "namely" or "in other words."

not lost in my Absence, you will among them find many more Particulars. Thomas was bred a Smith under his Father, but being ingenious, and encourag'd in Learning (as all his Brothers like wise werre,) by an Esquire Palmer then the principal Gentleman in that Parish, he qualify'd himself for the Business of Scrivener,[5] became a considerable Man in the County Affairs, was a chief Mover of all publick Spirited Undertakings, for the County or Town of Northampton & his own Village, of which many Instances were told us at Ecton and he was much taken Notice of and patroniz'd by the then Lord Halifax. He died in 1702 Jan. 6. old Stile,[6] just 4 Years to a Day before I was born. The Account we receiv'd of his Life & Character from some old People at Ecton, I remember struck you as something extraordinary from its Similarity to what you knew of mine. Had he died on the same Day, you said one might have suppos'd a Transmigration. John was bred a Dyer, I believe of Woollens. Benjamin, was bred a Silk Dyer, serving an Apprenticeship at London. He was an ingenious Man, I remember him well, for when I was a Boy he came over to my Father in Boston, and lived in the House with us some Years. He lived to a great Age. His Grandson Samuel Franklin now lives in Boston. He left behind him two Quarto Volumes, M.S.[7] of his own Poetry, consisting of little occasional Pieces address'd to his Friends and Relations, of which the following sent to me, is a Specimen.

Sent to My Name upon a Report
of his Inclination to Martial affaires
7 July 1710

Beleeve me Ben. It is a Dangerous Trade
The Sword has Many Marr'd as well as Made
By it doe many fall Not Many Rise
Makes Many poor few Rich and fewer Wise
Fills Towns with Ruin, fields with blood beside
Tis Sloths Maintainer, And the Shield of pride
Fair Citties Rich to Day, in plenty flow
War fills with want, Tomorrow, & with woe
Ruin'd Estates, The Nurse of Vice, broke limbs & scarss
   Are the Effects of Desolating Warrs

Sent to B. F. in N. E.
15 July 1710

B   e to thy parents an Obedient Son
E   ach Day let Duty constantly be Done
N   ever give Way to sloth or lust or pride

---

5. **Scrivener:** A professional transcriber of documents.
6. **old Stile:** The Julian ("Old Style") calendar, in which the year began on March 25, did not include leap years. In 1752, England adopted the use of the Gregorian ("New Style") calendar, a more accurate astronomical calendar, which began the new year on January 1 and included an extra day every four years.
7. **Quarto Volumes, M.S.:** *M.S.* (or *ms.*) is the abbreviation for manuscript. Folio, quarto, and octavo were standard sizes of books: in a folio, the whole sheet of paper was folded once, forming two leaves; in a quarto, it was folded twice, forming four leaves; in an octavo, it was folded three times, forming eight leaves.

I   f free you'd be from Thousand Ills beside
A   bove all Ills be sure Avoide the shelfe
M   ans Danger lyes in Satan sin and selfe
I   n vertue Learning Wisdome progress Make
N   ere shrink at Suffering for thy saviours sake
F   raud and all Falshood in thy Dealings Flee
R   eligious Always in thy station be
A   dore the Maker of thy Inward part
N   ow's the Accepted time, Give him thy Heart
K   eep a Good Consceince 'tis a constant Frind
L   ike Judge and Witness This Thy Acts Attend
I   n Heart with bended knee Alone Adore
N   one but the Three in One Forevermore.

He had form'd a Shorthand of his own, which he taught me, but never practicing it I have now forgot it. I was nam'd after this Uncle, there being a particular Affection between him and my Father. He was very pious, a great Attender of Sermons of the best Preachers, which he took down in his Shorthand and had with him many Volumes of them. He was also much of a Politician, too much perhaps for his Station. There fell lately into my Hands in London a Collection he had made of all the principal Pamphlets relating to Publick Affairs from 1641 to 1717. Many of the Volumes are wanting, as appears by the Numbering, but there still remains 8 Vols. Folio, and 24 in 4to & 8vo.[8] A Dealer in old Books met with them, and knowing me by my sometimes buying of him, he brought them to me. It seems my Uncle must have left them here when he went to America, which was above 50 Years since. There are many of his Notes in the Margins.

This obscure Family of ours was early in the Reformation, and continu'd Protestants thro' the Reign of Queen Mary,[9] when they were sometimes in Danger of Trouble on Account of their Zeal against Popery. They had got an English Bible,[10] & to conceal & secure it, it was fast'ned open with Tapes under & within the Frame of a joint Stool.[11] When my Great Great Grandfather read in it to his Family, he turn'd up the Joint Stool upon his Knees, turning over the Leaves[12] then under the Tapes. One of the Children stood at the Door to give Notice if he saw the Apparitor coming, who was an Officer of the Spiritual Court.[13] In that Case the Stool was turn'd down again upon its feet, when the Bible remain'd conceal'd under it as before. This Anecdote I had from my Uncle

---

8. **4to & 8vo**: Quarto and octavo; see note 7.
9. **Queen Mary**: The daughter of Henry VIII and Catherine of Aragon, Queen Mary ruled England from 1553 to 1558. She wished to reinstate Roman Catholicism in the country and persecuted Protestants. Her reign was characterized by religious dissent, economic turmoil, and the loss of a war with France.
10. **English Bible**: The Geneva Bible (1560), first printed in England in 1575, was embraced by the Puritans, who brought it with them to the New World. It was eventually banned by the Church of England in favor of the King James Version.
11. **joint Stool**: A low, backless and armless square seat with four legs, common in the seventeenth century.
12. **Leaves**: The pages of the Bible.
13. **Apparitor . . . Spiritual Court**: An officer charged with carrying out the orders of the ecclesiastical courts in England.

Benjamin. The Family continu'd all of the Church of England till about the End of Charles the Second's Reign, when some of the Ministers that had been outed for Nonconformity, holding Conventicles in Northamptonshire, Benjamin & Josiah adher'd to them, and so continu'd all their Lives.[14] The rest of the Family remain'd with the Episcopal Church.

Josiah, my Father, married young, and carried his Wife with three Children unto New England, about 1682. The Conventicles having been forbidden by Law, & frequently disturbed, induced some considerable Men of his Acquaintance to remove to that Country, and he was prevail'd with to accompany them thither, where they expected to enjoy their Mode of Religion with Freedom. By the same Wife he had 4 Children more born there, and by a second Wife ten more, in all 17, of which I remember 13 sitting at one time at his Table, who all grew up to be Men & Women, and married; I was the youngest Son and the youngest Child but two, & was born in Boston, N. England.

My Mother the second Wife was Abiah Folger, a Daughter of Peter Folger, one of the first Settlers of New England, of whom honourable mention is made by Cotton Mather,[15] in his Church History of that Country, (entitled Magnalia Christi Americana) as a *godly learned Englishman*, if I remember the Words rightly. I have heard that he wrote sundry small occasional Pieces, but only one of them was printed which I saw now many Years since. It was written in 1675, in the homespun Verse of that Time & People, and address'd to those then concern'd in the Government there. It was in favour of Liberty of Conscience, & in behalf of the Baptists, Quakers, & other Sectaries,[16] that had been under Persecution; ascribing the Indian Wars & other Distresses, that had befallen the Country to that Persecution, as so many Judgments of God, to punish so heinous an Offence; and exhorting a Repeal of those uncharitable Laws. The whole appear'd to me as written with a good deal of Decent Plainness & manly Freedom. The six last concluding Lines I remember, tho' I have forgotten the two first of the Stanza, but the Purport of them was that his Censures proceeded from *Goodwill*, & therefore he would be known as the Author,

> because to be a Libeller, (says he)
> I hate it with my Heart.
> From Sherburne Town[17] where now I dwell,
> My Name I do put here,
> Without Offence, your real Friend,
> It is Peter Folgier.

My elder Brothers were all put Apprentices to different Trades. I was put to the Grammar School at Eight Years of Age, my Father intending to devote me as the Tithe of his Sons

---

14. **Charles the Second's Reign . . . all their Lives:** Charles II (1630-1685) was the English king from 1660 to 1685. During his reign, Nonconformists, those who refused to acknowledge the Church of England, held secret meetings, or "Conventicles," before they were outlawed in 1664.

15. **Cotton Mather:** (1663-1728) Puritan theologian and author of *Magnalia Christi Americana*, or "The Great Work of Christ in America" (1702); he actually described Folger as "an Able Godly Englishman."

16. **Sectaries:** Members of a religious or political sect.

17. **Sherburne Town:** In the Island of Nantucket. [Franklin's note]

to the Service of the Church.[18] My early Readiness in learning to read (which must have been very early, as I do not remember when I could not read) and the Opinion of all his Friends that I should certainly make a good Scholar, encourag'd him in this Purpose of his. My Uncle Benjamin too approv'd of it, and propos'd to give me all his Shorthand Volumes of Sermons I suppose as a Stock to set up with, if I would learn his Character.[19] I continu'd however at the Grammar School not quite one Year, tho' in that time I had risen gradually from the Middle of the Class of that Year to be the Head of it, and farther was remov'd into the next Class above it, in order to go with that into the third at the End of the Year. But my Father in the mean time, from a View of the Expence of a College Education which, having so large a Family, he could not well afford, and the mean Living many so educated were afterwards able to obtain, Reasons that he gave to his Friends in my Hearing, altered his first Intention, took me from the Grammar School, and sent me to a School for Writing & Arithmetic kept by a then famous Man, Mr George Brownell, very successful in his Profession generally, and that by mild encouraging Methods. Under him I acquired fair Writing pretty soon, but I fail'd in the Arithmetic, & made no Progress in it. At Ten Years old, I was taken home to assist my Father in his Business, which was that of a Tallow Chandler and Sope-Boiler.[20] A Business he was not bred to, but had assumed on his Arrival in New England & on finding his Dying Trade[21] would not maintain his Family, being in little Request. Accordingly I was employed in cutting Wick for the Candles, filling the Dipping Mold, & the Molds for cast Candles, attending the Shop, going of Errands, &c. I dislik'd the Trade and had a strong Inclination for the Sea; but my Father declar'd against it; however, living near the Water, I was much in and about it, learnt early to swim well, & to manage Boats, and when in a Boat or Canoe with other Boys I was commonly allow'd to govern, especially in any case of Difficulty; and upon other Occasions I was generally a Leader among the Boys, and sometimes led them into Scrapes, of which I will mention one Instance, as it shows an early projecting public Spirit, tho' not then justly conducted. There was a Salt Marsh that bounded part of the Mill Pond, on the Edge of which at Highwater, we us'd to stand to fish for Minews. By much Trampling, we had made it a mere Quagmire. My Proposal was to build a Wharf there fit for us to stand upon, and I show'd my Comrades a large Heap of Stones which were intended for a new House near the Marsh, and which would very well suit our Purpose. Accordingly in the Evening when the Workmen were gone, I assembled a Number of my Playfellows, and working with them diligently like so many Emmets,[22] sometimes two or three to a Stone, we brought them all away and built our little Wharff. The next Morning the Workmen were surpriz'd at Missing the Stones; which were found in our Wharff; Enquiry was made after the Removers; we were discovered & complain'd

---

18. **Tithe . . . Service of the Church:** One-tenth of one's annual income was considered the appropriate donation for the support of the church and clergy. Franklin was the tenth son, so his father intended to train him for the church.

19. **Character:** Individual shorthand notation.

20. **Tallow Chandler and Sope-Boiler:** Producer of candles and soaps (*sope* was an early spelling of *soap*).

21. **Dying Trade:** The business of dying cloth and other material.

22. **Emmets:** An early term for ants.

of; several of us were corrected by our Fathers; and tho' I pleaded the Usefulness of the Work, mine convinc'd me that nothing was useful which was not honest.

I think you may like to know something of his Person & Character. He had an excellent Constitution of Body, was of middle Stature, but well set and very strong. He was ingenious, could draw prettily, was skill'd a little in Music and had a clear pleasing Voice, so that when he play'd Psalm Tunes on his Violin & sung withal as he some times did in an Evening after the Business of the Day was over, it was extreamly agreable to hear. He had a mechanical Genius too, and on occasion was very handy in the Use of other Tradesmen's Tools. But his great Excellence lay in a sound Understanding, and solid Judgment in prudential Matters, both in private & publick Affairs. In the latter indeed he was never employed, the numerous Family he had to educate & the Straitness of his Circumstances, keeping him close to his Trade, but I remember well his being frequently visited by leading People, who consulted him for his Opinion on Affairs of the Town or of the Church he belong'd to & show'd a good deal of Respect for his Judgment and Advice. He was also much consulted by private Persons about their Affairs when any Difficulty occur'd, & frequently chosen an Arbitrator between contending Parties. At his Table he lik'd to have as often as he could, some sensible Friend or Neighbour, to converse with, and always took care to start some ingenious or useful Topic for Discourse, which might tend to improve the Minds of his Children. By this means he turn'd our Attention to what was good, just, & prudent in the Conduct of Life; and little or no Notice was ever taken of what related to the Victuals on the Table, whether it was well or ill drest, in or out of season, of good or bad flavour, preferable or inferior to this or that other thing of the kind; so that I was bro't up in such a perfect Inattention to those Matters as to be quite Indifferent what kind of Food was set before me; and so unobservant of it, that to this Day, if I am ask'd I can scarce tell, a few Hours after Dinner, what I din'd upon. This has been a Convenience to me in travelling, where my Companions have been sometimes very unhappy for want of a suitable Gratification of their more delicate because better instructed Tastes and Appetites.

My Mother had likewise an excellent Constitution. She suckled all her 10 Children. I never knew either my Father or Mother to have any Sickness but that of which they dy'd, he at 89 & she at 85 Years of age. They lie buried together at Boston, where I some Years since plac'd a Marble stone over their Grave with this Inscription

Josiah Franklin
And Abiah his Wife
Lie here interred.
They lived lovingly together in Wedlock
Fifty-five Years. —
Without an Estate or any gainful Employment,
By constant Labour and Industry,
With God's Blessing,
They maintained a large Family
Comfortably;
And brought up thirteen Children,
And seven Grandchildren

Reputably.
From this Instance, Reader,
Be encouraged to Diligence in thy Calling,
And distrust not Providence.
He was a pious & prudent Man,
She a discreet and virtuous Woman.
Their youngest Son,
In filial Regard to their Memory,
Places this Stone.
J. F. born 1655 – Died 1744. Ætat[23] 89
A. F. born 1667 – died 1752 — 85

By my rambling Digressions I perceive my self to be grown old. I us'd to write more methodically. But one does not dress for private Company as for a publick Ball. 'Tis perhaps only Negligence.

To return. I continu'd thus employ'd in my Father's Business for two Years, that is till I was 12 Years old; and my Brother John, who was bred to that Business having left my Father, married and set up for himself at Rhodeisland, there was all Appearance that I was destin'd to supply his Place and be a Tallow Chandler. But my Dislike to the Trade continuing, my Father was under Apprehensions that if he did not find one for me more agreable, I should break away and get to Sea, as his Son Josiah had done to his great Vexation. He therefore sometimes took me to walk with him, and see Joiners, Bricklayers, Turners, Braziers,[24] &c. at their Work, that he might observe my Inclination, & endeavour to fix it on some Trade or other on Land. It has ever since been a Pleasure to me to see good Workmen handle their Tools; and it has been useful to me, having learnt so much by it, as to be able to do little jobs my self in my House, when a Workman could not readily be got; & to construct little Machines for my Experiments while the Intention of making the Experiment was fresh & warm in my Mind. My Father at last fix'd upon the Cutler's Trade,[25] and my Uncle Benjamin's Son Samuel who was bred to that Business in London being about that time establish'd in Boston, I was sent to be with him some time on liking. But his Expectations of a Fee with me displeasing my Father, I was taken home again.

From a Child I was fond of Reading, and all the little Money that came into my Hands was ever laid out in Books. Pleas'd with the Pilgrim's Progress,[26] my first Collection was of John Bunyan's Works, in separate little Volumes. I afterwards sold them to enable me to buy R. Burton's Historical Collections; they were small Chapmen's Books and cheap, 40 or 50 in all. My Father's little Library consisted chiefly of Books in polemic Divinity, most of which I read, and have since often regretted, that at a time when I had such a

---

23. **Ætat:** Aged (Latin).
24. **Joiners . . . Braziers:** A list of common trades: woodworkers, bricklayers, lathe workers, and workers in brass.
25. **Cutler's Trade:** The business of making and selling utensils for eating and serving food.
26. **Pilgrim's Progress:** A tremendously popular book by the English author John Bunyan (1628–1688), *The Pilgrim's Progress* is an allegory chronicling the journey of a man named Christian from the City of Destruction to the Celestial City.

Thirst for Knowledge, more proper Books had not fallen in my Way, since it was now resolv'd I should not be a Clergyman. Plutarch's Lives[27] there was, in which I read abundantly, and I still think that time spent to great Advantage. There was also a Book of Defoe's called an Essay on Projects and another of Dr Mather's[28] call'd Essays to do Good, which perhaps gave me a Turn of Thinking that had an Influence on some of the principal future Events of my Life.

This Bookish Inclination at length determin'd my Father to make me a Printer, tho' he had already one Son, (James) of that Profession. In 1717 my Brother James return'd from England with a Press & Letters to set up his Business in Boston. I lik'd it much better than that of my Father, but still had a Hankering for the Sea. To prevent the apprehended Effect of such an Inclination, my Father was impatient to have me bound to my Brother. I stood out some time, but at last was persuaded and signed the Indentures,[29] when I was yet but 12 Years old. I was to serve as an Apprentice till I was 21 Years of Age, only I was to be allow'd Journeyman's Wages[30] during the last Year. In a little time I made great Proficiency in the Business, and became a useful Hand to my Brother. I now had Access to better Books. An Acquaintance with the Apprentices of Booksellers, enabled me sometimes to borrow a small one, which I was careful to return soon & clean. Often I sat up in my Room reading the greatest Part of the Night, when the Book was borrow'd in the Evening & to be return'd early in the Morning lest it should be miss'd or wanted. And after some time an ingenious Tradesman[31] who had a pretty Collection of Books, & who frequented our Printing House, took Notice of me, invited me to his Library, & very kindly lent me such Books as I chose to read. I now took a Fancy to Poetry, and made some little Pieces. My Brother, thinking it might turn to account encourag'd me, & put me on composing two occasional Ballads. One was called the *Light House Tragedy*, & contain'd an Account of the drowning of Capt. Worthilake with his Two Daughters; the other was a Sailor Song on the Taking of *Teach* or Blackbeard the Pirate. They were wretched Stuff, in the Grubstreet Ballad Stile,[32] and when they were printed he sent me about the Town to sell them. The first sold wonderfully, the Event being recent, having made a great Noise. This flatter'd my Vanity. But my Father discourag'd me, by ridiculing my Performances, and telling me Verse-makers were generally Beggars; so I escap'd being a Poet, most probably a very bad one. But as Prose Writing has been a great Use to me in the Course of my Life, and was a principal Means of my Advancement, I shall tell you how in such a Situation I acquir'd what little Ability I have in that Way.

---

27. **Plutarch's Lives:** Plutarch (c. 46-120), Greek biographer and author of *Parallel Lives* of the noble Greeks and Romans.
28. **Book of Defoe's . . . another of Dr Mather's:** *An Essay on Projects* (1697), by the English author Daniel Defoe (1660-1731); and Cotton Mather's *Bonifacius: An Essay upon the Good* (1710).
29. **Indentures:** Agreements binding an apprentice to a master.
30. **Journeyman's Wages:** A journeyman was no longer bound by indentures and was paid by the day.
31. **Tradesman:** Mr. Matthew Adams. [Franklin's note]
32. **Grubstreet Ballad Stile:** In the style of sensational ballads and poems written for quick profits by poor writers, many of whom lived on Grub Street in London during the eighteenth century. The ballads Franklin mentions have not been found.

There was another Bookish Lad in the Town, John Collins by Name, with whom I was intimately acquainted. We sometimes disputed, and very fond we were of Argument, & very desirous of confuting one another. Which disputacious Turn, by the way, is apt to become a very bad Habit, making People often extreamly disagreable in Company, by the Contradiction that is necessary to bring it into Practice, & thence, besides souring & spoiling the Conversation, is productive of Disgusts & perhaps Enmities where you may have occasion for Friendship. I had caught it by reading my Father's Books of Dispute about Religion. Persons of good Sense, I have since observ'd, seldom fall into it, except Lawyers, University Men, and Men of all Sorts that have been bred at Edinborough. A Question was once some how or other started between Collins & me, of the Propriety of educating the Female Sex in Learning, & their Abilities for Study. He was of Opinion that it was improper; & that they were naturally unequal to it. I took the contrary Side, perhaps a little for Dispute sake. He was naturally more eloquent, had a ready Plenty of Words, and sometimes as I thought bore me down more by his Fluency than by the Strength of his Reasons. As we parted without settling the Point, & were not to see one another again for some time, I sat down to put my Arguments in Writing, which I copied fair & sent to him. He answer'd & I reply'd. Three or four Letters of a Side had pass'd, when my Father happen'd to find my Papers, and read them. Without entring into the Discussion, he took occasion to talk to me about the Manner of my Writing, observ'd that tho' I had the Advantage of my Antagonist in correct Spelling & pointing[33] (which I ow'd to the Printing House) I fell far short in elegance of Expression, in Method and in Perspicuity, of which he convinc'd me by several Instances. I saw the Justice of his Remarks, & thence grew more attentive to the *Manner* in Writing, and determin'd to endeavour at Improvement.

About this time I met with an odd Volume of the Spectator.[34] I had never before seen any of them. I bought it, read it over and over, and was much delighted with it. I thought the Writing excellent, & wish'd if possible to imitate it. With that View, I took some of the Papers, & making short Hints of the Sentiment in each Sentence, laid them by a few Days, and then without looking at the Book, try'd to compleat the Papers again, by expressing each hinted Sentiment at length & as fully as it had been express'd before, in any suitable Words that should come to hand.

Then I compar'd my Spectator with the Original, discover'd some of my Faults & corrected them. But I found I wanted a Stock of Words or a Readiness in recollecting & using them, which I thought I should have acquir'd before that time, if I had gone on making Verses, since the continual Occasion for Words of the same Import but of different Length, to suit the Measure, or of different Sound for the Rhyme, would have laid me under a constant Necessity of searching for Variety, and also have tended to fix that Variety in my Mind, & make me Master of it. Therefore I took some of the Tales & turn'd them into Verse: And after a time, when I had pretty well forgotten the Prose, turn'd

---

33. **pointing:** Punctuation.
34. **Spectator:** A highly regarded London magazine that was concerned with reforming the manners of its readers; published between 1710 and 1712, it featured essays by Joseph Addison (1672–1719) and Richard Steele (1672–1729).

them back again. I also sometimes jumbled my Collections of Hints into Confusion, and after some Weeks, endeavour'd to reduce them into the best Order, before I began to form the full Sentences & compleat the Paper. This was to teach me Method in the Arrangement of Thoughts. By comparing my Work afterwards with the original, I discover'd many faults and amended them; but I sometimes had the Pleasure of Fancying that in certain Particulars of small Import, I had been lucky enough to improve the Method or the Language and this encourag'd me to think I might possibly in time come to be a tolerable English Writer, of which I was extreamly ambitious.

My Time for these Exercises & for Reading, was at Night after Work, or before Work began in the Morning; or on Sundays, when I contrived to be in the Printing House alone, evading as much as I could the common Attendance on publick Worship, which my Father used to exact of me when I was under his Care: – And which indeed I still thought a Duty; tho' I could not, as it seemed to me, afford the Time to practise it.

When about 16 Years of Age, I happen'd to meet with a Book written by one Tryon,[35] recommending a Vegetable Diet. I determined to go into it. My Brother being yet unmarried, did not keep House, but boarded himself & his Apprentices in another Family. My refusing to eat Flesh occasioned an Inconveniency, and I was frequently chid for my singularity. I made my self acquainted with Tryon's Manner of preparing some of his Dishes, such as Boiling Potatoes, or Rice, making Hasty Pudding, & a few others, and then propos'd to my Brother, that if he would give me Weekly half the Money he paid for my Board, I would board my self. He instantly agreed to it, and I presently found that I could save half what he paid me. This was an additional Fund for buying Books: But I had another Advantage in it. My Brother and the rest going from the Printing House to their Meals, I remain'd there alone, and dispatching presently my light Repast, (which often was no more than a Bisket or a Slice of Bread, a Handful of Raisins or a Tart from the Pastry Cook's, and a Glass of Water) had the rest of the Time till their Return, for Study, in which I made the greater Progress from that greater Clearness of Head & quicker Apprehension which usually attend Temperance in Eating & Drinking. And now it was that being on some Occasion made asham'd of my Ignorance in Figures, which I had twice fail'd in learning when at School, I took Cocker's Book of Arithmetick,[36] & went thro' the whole by my self with great Ease. I also read Seller's & Sturmy's Books of Navigation, & became acquainted with the little Geometry they contain, but never proceeded far in that Science. And I read about this Time Locke on Human Understanding and the Art of Thinking by Messrs du Port Royal.[37]

---

35. **Tryon:** Thomas Tryon (1634-1703), the author of *The Way to Health* (1691), which advocated a vegetarian diet and abstinence from tobacco and alcohol.

36. **Cocker's Book of Arithmetick:** Edward Cocker (1631-1676), an English engraver and author of *Arithmetick*. Published the year of his death, the book went through over one hundred editions during the next century.

37. **I also read . . . Messrs du Port Royal:** *An Epitome of the Art of Navigation* (1681), by John Seller (1630-1697); *The Mariner's Magazine: Or Sturmy's Mathematical and Practical Arts* (1699), by Samuel Sturmy (1633-1669); *An Essay Concerning Human Understanding* (1690), by the English philosopher John Locke (1632-1704); and *Logic: Or the Art of Thinking* (1687), by Pierre Nichol (1625?-1695) of Port Royal, a celebrated Benedictine abbey in France.

While I was intent on improving my Language, I met with an English Grammar (I think it was Greenwood's)[38] at the End of which there were two little Sketches of the Arts of Rhetoric and Logic, the latter finishing with a Specimen of a Dispute in the Socratic Method. And soon after I procur'd Xenophon's Memorable Things of Socrates,[39] wherein there are many Instances of the same Method. I was charm'd with it, adopted it, dropt my abrupt Contradiction, and positive Argumentation, and put on the humble Enquirer & Doubter. And being then, from reading Shaftsbury & Collins,[40] become a real Doubter in many Points of our Religious Doctrine, I found this Method safest for my self & very embarassing to those against whom I used it, therefore I took a Delight in it, practis'd it continually & grew very artful & expert in drawing People even of superior Knowledge into Concessions the Consequences of which they did not foresee, entangling them in Difficulties out of which they could not extricate themselves, and so obtaining Victories that neither my self nor my Cause always deserved. I continu'd this Method some few Years, but gradually left it, retaining only the Habit of expressing my self in Terms of modest Diffidence, never using when I advance any thing that may possibly be disputed, the Words, *Certainly, undoubtedly,* or any others that give the Air of Positiveness to an Opinion; but rather say, *I conceive,* or *I apprehend* a Thing to be so or so, *It appears to me,* or *I should think it so or so for such & such Reasons,* or *I imagine* it to be so, or *it is so* if *I am not mistaken.* This Habit I believe has been of great Advantage to me, when I have had occasion to inculcate my Opinions & persuade Men into Measures that I have been from time to time engag'd in promoting. And as the chief Ends of Conversation are to *inform,* or to be *informed,* to *please* or to *persuade,* I wish well meaning sensible Men would not lessen their Power of doing Good by a Positive assuming Manner that seldom fails to disgust, tends to create Opposition, and to defeat every one of those Purposes for which Speech was given us, to wit, giving or receiving Information, or Pleasure: For If you would *inform,* a positive dogmatical Manner in advancing your Sentiments, may provoke Contradiction & prevent a candid Attention. If you wish Information & Improvement from the Knowledge of others and yet at the same time express your self as firmly fix'd in your present Opinions, modest sensible Men, who do not love Disputation, will probably leave you undisturb'd in the Possession of your Error; and by such a Manner you can seldom hope to recommend your self in *pleasing* your Hearers, or to persuade those whose Concurrence you desire. Pope says, judiciously,

> *Men should be taught as if you taught them not,*
> *And things unknown propos'd as things forgot, —*

---

38. **Greenwood's:** *An Essay towards a Practical English Grammar* (1711), by James Greenwood (d. 1737).

39. **Xenophon's . . . Socrates:** The Greek historian Xenophon (434?-355 BCE) wrote a life of Socrates, which was translated by Edward Bysshe as *The Memorable Things of Socrates* (1712).

40. **Shaftsbury & Collins:** The English philosopher Anthony Ashley Cooper, third Earl of Shaftesbury (1671-1713), was the author of *Characteristics of Men, Manners, Opinions, Times* (1711); Anthony Collins (1676-1729), an English Deist, wrote *A Discourse of Free Thinking* (1713).

farther recommending it to us,

> *To speak tho' sure, with seeming Diffidence.*[41]

And he might have couple'd with this Line that which he has coupled with another, I think less properly,

> *For want of Modesty is want of Sense.*

If you ask why *less properly*, I must repeat the Lines;

> "Immodest Words admit of *no* Defence;
> "*For* Want of Modesty is Want of Sense."

Now is not *Want of Sense*, (where a Man is so unfortunate as to want it) some Apology for his *Want of Modesty?* and would not the Lines stand more justly thus?

> Immodest Words admit *but this* Defence,
> That Want of Modesty is Want of Sense.[42]

This however I should submit to better Judgments.

My Brother had in 1720 or 21, begun to print a Newspaper. It was the second that appear'd in America, & was called *The New England Courant.* The only one before it, was *the Boston News Letter.* I remember his being dissuaded by some of his Friends from the Undertaking, as not likely to succeed, one Newspaper being in their Judgment enough for America. At this time 1771 there are not less than five & twenty. He went on however with the Undertaking, and after having work'd in composing the Types & printing off the Sheets I was employ'd to carry the Papers thro' the Streets to the Customers. He had some ingenious Men among his Friends who amus'd themselves by writing little Pieces for this Paper, which gain'd it Credit, & made it more in Demand; and these Gentlemen often visited us. Hearing their Conversations, and their Accounts of the Approbation their Papers were receiv'd with, I was excited to try my Hand among them. But being still a Boy, & suspecting that my Brother would object to printing any Thing of mine in his Paper if he knew it to be mine, I contriv'd to disguise my Hand, & writing an anonymous Paper I put it in at Night under the Door of the Printing House. It was found in the Morning & communicated to his Writing Friends when they call'd in as Usual. They read it, commented on it in my Hearing, and I had the exquisite Pleasure, of finding it met with their Approbation, and that in their different Guesses at the Author none were named but Men of some Character among us for Learning & Ingenuity. I suppose now that I was rather lucky in my Judges: And that perhaps they were not really so very good ones as I then esteem'd them. Encourag'd however by this, I wrote and convey'd in the

---

41. **Men . . . *Diffidence*:** Franklin is loosely quoting from *An Essay on Criticism* (1711), by the English poet Alexander Pope (1688-1744). In the original, the lines read: "Men must be taught as if you taught them not; / And Things unknown propos'd as Things forgot;" and "And speak, tho' sure, with seeming Diffidence."
42. **Immodest . . . Sense:** Franklin is quoting not Pope but Wentworth Dillon, Earl of Roscommon (1633?-1685), the author of *Essay on Translated Verse*: "Immodest words admit of no defence, / For want of decency is want of sense."

same Way to the Press several more Papers, which were equally approv'd, and I kept my Secret till my small Fund of Sense for such Performances was pretty well exhausted, & then I discovered it;[43] when I began to be considered a little more by my Brother's Acquaintance, and in a manner that did not quite please him, as he thought, probably with reason, that it tended to make me too vain. And perhaps this might be one Occasion of the Differences that we began to have about this Time. Tho' a Brother, he considered himself as my Master, & me as his Apprentice; and accordingly expected the same Services from me as he would from another; while I thought he demean'd me too much in some he requir'd of me, who from a Brother expected more Indulgence. Our Disputes were often brought before our Father, and I fancy I was either generally in the right, or else a better Pleader, because the judgment was generally in my favour: But my Brother was passionate & had often beaten me, which I took extreamly amiss;[44] and thinking my Apprenticeship very tedious, I was continually wishing for some Opportunity of short-ening it, which at length offered in a manner unexpected.

One of the Pieces in our News-Paper, on some political Point which I have now forgot-ten, gave Offence to the Assembly. He was taken up, censur'd and imprison'd for a Month by the Speaker's Warrant, I suppose because he would not discover his Author. I too was taken up & examin'd before the Council; but tho' I did not give them any Satisfaction, they contented themselves with admonishing me, and dismiss'd me; considering me perhaps as an Apprentice who was bound to keep his Master's Secrets. During my Brother's Confinement, which I resented a good deal, notwithstanding our private Differences, I had the Management of the Paper, and I made bold to give our Rulers some Rubs in it, which my Brother took very kindly, while others began to consider me in an unfavourable Light, as a young Genius that had a Turn for Libelling & Satyr. My Brother's Discharge was accompany'd with an Order of the House, (a very odd one) *that James Franklin should no longer print the Paper called the New England Courant.* There was a Consultation held in our Printing House among his Friends what he should do in this Case. Some propos'd to evade the Order by changing the Name of the Paper; but my Brother seeing Inconveniences in that, it was finally concluded on as a better Way, to let it be printed for the future under the Name of *Benjamin Franklin.* And to avoid the Censure of the Assembly that might fall on him, as still printing it by his Apprentice, the Contrivance was, that my old Indenture should be return'd to me with a full Discharge on the Back of it, to be shown on Occasion; but to secure to him the Benefit of my Service I was to sign new Indentures for the Remainder of the Term, which were to be kept private. A very flimsy Scheme it was, but however it was immediately executed, and the Paper went on accordingly under my Name for several Months. At length a fresh Difference arising between my Brother and me, I took upon me to assert my Freedom, presuming that he would not venture to produce the new Indentures. It was not fair in me to take this Advantage, and this I therefore reckon one of the first Errata[45] of my

---

43. **discovered it:** Early usage for divulged or disclosed it.
44. **amiss:** I fancy his harsh and tyrannical Treatment of me, might be a means of impressing me with that Aversion to arbitrary Power that has stuck to me thro' my whole Life. [Franklin's note]
45. **Errata:** A printer's term for typographical errors (Latin).

Life: But the Unfairness of it weigh'd little with me, when under the Impressions of Resentment, for the Blows his Passion too often urg'd him to bestow upon me. Tho' He was otherwise not an ill-natur'd Man: Perhaps I was too saucy & provoking.

When he found I would leave him, he took care to prevent my getting Employment in any other Printing-House of the Town, by going round & speaking to every Master, who accordingly refus'd to give me Work. I then thought of going to New York as the nearest Place where there was a Printer: and I was the rather inclin'd to leave Boston, when I reflected that I had already made my self a little obnoxious, to the governing Party; & from the arbitrary Proceedings of the Assembly in my Brother's Case it was likely I might if I stay'd soon bring my self into Scrapes; and farther that my indiscrete Disputations about Religion began to make me pointed at with Horror by good People, as an Infidel or Atheist; I determin'd on the Point: but my Father now siding with my Brother, I was sensible that if I attempted to go openly, Means would be used to prevent me. My Friend Collins therefore undertook to manage a little for me. He agreed with the Captain of a New York Sloop for my Passage, under the Notion of my being a young Acquaintance of his that had got a naughty Girl with Child, whose Friends would compel me to marry her, and therefore I could not appear or come away publickly. So I sold some of my Books to raise a little Money, Was taken on board privately, and as we had a fair Wind, in three Days I found my self in New York near 300 Miles from home, a Boy of but 17, without the least Recommendation to or Knowledge of any Person in the Place, and with very little Money in my Pocket.

My Inclinations for the Sea, were by this time worne out, or I might now have gratify'd them. But having a Trade, & supposing my self a pretty good Workman, I offer'd my Service to the Printer of the Place, old Mr. W^m. Bradford. He could give me no Employment, having little to do, and Help enough already: But, says he, my Son at Philadelphia has lately lost his principal Hand, Aquila Rose, by Death. If you go thither I believe he may employ you. Philadelphia was 100 Miles farther. I set out, however, in a Boat for Amboy;[46] leaving my Chest and Things to follow me round by Sea. In crossing the Bay we met with a Squall that tore our rotten Sails to pieces, prevented our getting into the Kill,[47] and drove us upon Long Island. In our Way a drunken Dutchman, who was a Passenger too, fell over board; when he was sinking I reach'd thro' the Water to his shock Pate[48] & drew him up so that we got him in again. His Ducking sober'd him a little, & he went to sleep, taking first out of his Pocket a Book which he desir'd I would dry for him. It prov'd to be my old favourite Author Bunyan's Pilgrim's Progress in Dutch, finely printed on good Paper with copper Cuts,[49] a Dress better than I had ever seen it wear in its own Language. I have since Found that it has been translated into most of the Languages of Europe, and suppose it has been more generally read than any other Book except perhaps the Bible. Honest John was the first that I know of who

---

46. **Amboy:** Perth Amboy, on the coast of New Jersey.
47. **Kill:** Derived from *kil*, the Dutch word for a creek or stream, and frequently used to describe a strait, river, or arm of the sea in areas once claimed by the colony of New Netherland.
48. **shock Pate:** A thick head of hair.
49. **copper Cuts:** Engraved illustrations.

mix'd Narration & Dialogue, a Method of Writing very engaging to the Reader, who in the most interesting Parts finds himself as it were brought into the Company, & present at the Discourse. De foe in his Cruso,[50] his Moll Flanders, Religious Courtship, Family Instructor, & other Pieces, has imitated it with Success. And Richardson has done the same in his Pamela, &c.[51]

When we drew near the Island we found it was at a Place where there could be no Landing, there being a great Surff on the stony Beach. So we dropt Anchor & swung round towards the Shore. Some People came down to the Water Edge & hallow'd to us, as we did to them. But the Wind was so high & the Surff so loud, that we could not hear so as to understand each other. There were Canoes on the Shore, & we made Signs & hallow'd that they should fetch us, but they either did not understand us, or thought it impracticable. So they went away, and Night coming on, we had no Remedy but to wait till the Wind should abate, and in the mean time the Boatman & I concluded to sleep if we could, and so crouded into the Scuttle with the Dutchman who was still wet, and the Spray beating over the Head of our Boat, leak'd thro' to us, so that we were soon almost as wet as he. In this Manner we lay all Night with very little Rest. But the Wind abating the next Day, we made a Shift to reach Amboy before Night, having been 30 Hours on the Water without Victuals, or any Drink but a Bottle of filthy Rum: – The Water we sail'd on being salt.

In the Evening I found my self very feverish, & went ill to Bed. But having read somewhere that cold Water drank plentifully was good for a Fever, I follow'd the Prescription, sweat plentifully most of the Night, my Fever left me, and in the Morning crossing the Ferry, proceeded on my journey, on foot, having 50 Miles to Burlington,[52] where I was told I should find Boats that would carry me the rest of the Way to Philadelphia.

It rain'd very hard all the Day, I was thoroughly soak'd, and by Noon a good deal tir'd, so I stopt at a poor Inn, where I staid all Night, beginning now to wish I had never left home. I cut so miserable a Figure too, that I found by the Questions ask'd me I was suspected to be some runaway Servant, and in danger of being taken up on that Suspicion. However I proceeded the next Day, and got in the Evening to an Inn within 8 or 10 Miles of Burlington, kept by one Dr Brown.

He entred into Conversation with me while I took some Refreshment, and finding I had read a little, became very sociable and friendly. Our Acquaintance continu'd as long as he liv'd. He had been, I imagine, an itinerant Doctor, for there was no Town in England, or Country in Europe, of which he could not give a very particular Account. He had some Letters, & was ingenious, but much of an Unbeliever, & wickedly undertook some Years after to travesty the Bible in doggrel Verse as Cotton had done Virgil.[53] By this means he set many of the Facts in a very ridiculous Light, & might have hurt weak minds if his

---

50. **De foe in his Cruso:** *Robinson Crusoe* (1719), the most famous of the works Franklin mentions by Daniel Defoe (1660–1731).
51. **Richardson . . . in his Pamela, &c.:** *Pamela; or, Virtue Rewarded* (1740), one of a number of popular works by the English novelist Samuel Richardson (1689–1761).
52. **Burlington:** Burlington, New Jersey, northeast of Philadelphia.
53. **as Cotton had done Virgil:** The English poet Charles Cotton (1630–1687) published parodies of the Roman poets Virgil and Lucian.

Work had been publish'd: – but it never was. At his House I lay that Night, and the next Morning reach'd Burlington. But had the Mortification to find that the regular Boats were gone, a little before my coming, and no other expected to go till Tuesday, this being Saturday. Wherefore I return'd to an old Woman in the Town of whom I had bought Gingerbread to eat on the Water, & ask'd her Advice; she invited me to lodge at her House till a Passage by Water should offer; & being tired with my foot Travelling, I accepted the Invitation. She understanding I was a Printer, would have had me stay at that Town & follow my Business, being ignorant of the Stock necessary to begin with. She was very hospitable, gave me a Dinner of Ox Cheek with great Goodwill, accepting only of a Pot of Ale in return. And I tho't my self fix'd till Tuesday should come. However walking in the Evening by the Side of the River a Boat came by, which I found was going towards Philadelphia, with several People in her. They took me in, and as there was no Wind, we row'd all the Way; and about Midnight not having yet seen the City, some of the Company were confident we must have pass'd it, and would row no farther, the others knew not where we were, so we put towards the Shore, got into a Creek, landed near an old Fence with the Rails of which we made a Fire, the Night being cold, in October, and there we remain'd till Daylight. Then one of the Company knew the Place to be Cooper's Creek a little above Philadelphia, which we saw as soon as we got out of the Creek, and arriv'd there about 8 or 9 a Clock, on the Sunday morning, and landed at the Market street Wharff.

I have been the more particular in this Description of my Journey, & shall be so of my first Entry into that City, that you may in your Mind compare such unlikely Beginning with the Figure I have since made there. I was in my working Dress, my best Cloaths being to come round by Sea. I was dirty from my Journey; my Pockets were stuff'd out with Shirts & Stockings; I knew no Soul, nor where to look for Lodging. I was fatigu'd with Travelling, Rowing & Want of Rest. I was very hungry, and my whole Stock of Cash consisted of a Dutch Dollar and about a Shilling in Copper. The latter I gave the People of the Boat for my Passage, who at first refus'd it on Account of my Rowing; but I insisted on their taking it, a Man being sometimes more generous when he has but a little Money than when he has plenty, perhaps thro' Fear of being thought to have but little. Then I walk'd up the Street, gazing about, till near the Market House I met a Boy with Bread. I had made many a Meal on Bread, & inquiring where he got it, I went immediately to the Baker's he directed me to in second Street; and ask'd for Bisket, intending such as we had in Boston, but they it seems were not made in Philadelphia, then I ask'd for a threepenny Loaf, and was told they had none such: so not considering or knowing the Difference of Money & the greater Cheapness nor the Names of his Bread, I bad him give me three pennyworth of any sort. He gave me accordingly three great Puffy Rolls. I was surpriz'd at the Quantity, but took it, and having no Room in my Pockets, walk'd off, with a Roll under each Arm, & eating the other. Thus I went up Market Street as far as fourth Street, passing by the Door of Mr Read, my future Wife's Father, when she standing at the Door saw me, & thought I made as I certainly did a most awkward ridiculous Appearance. Then I turn'd and went down Chestnut Street and part of Walnut Street, eating my Roll all the Way, and coming round found my self again at Market street Wharff, near the Boat I came in, to which I went for a Draught of the River Water, and being fill'd with one of my Rolls, gave the other two to a Woman & her Child that came down the River in the Boat with us and were waiting to go farther. Thus refresh'd I walk'd again up the Street, which by this time had many clean dress'd People in it who were all walking the same Way; I join'd them, and thereby was led into the great Meeting House of the Quakers near the Market. I sat down among them, and after looking round a while & hearing nothing said, being very drowzy thro' Labour & want of Rest the preceding Night, I fell fast asleep, and continu'd so till the Meeting broke up, when one was kind enough to rouse me. This was therefore the first House I was in or slept in, in Philadelphia.

[1771, 1981]

From Part Two

At the time I establish'd my self in Pensylvania, there was not a good Bookseller's Shop in any of the Colonies to the Southward of Boston. In New-York & Philadelphia the Printers were indeed Stationers, they sold only Paper, &c. Almanacks, Ballads, and a few common School Books. Those who lov'd Reading were oblig'd to send for their Books from England. The Members of the Junto had each a few. We had left the Alehouse where we first met, and hired a Room to hold our Club in. I propos'd that we should all of us bring our Books to that Room, where they would not only be ready to consult in our Conferences, but become a common Benefit, each of us being at Liberty to borrow such as he wish'd to read at home. This was accordingly done, and for some time contented us. Finding the Advantage of this little Collection, I propos'd to render the Benefit from Books more common by commencing a Public Subscription Library. I drew a Sketch of the Plan and Rules that would be necessary, and got a skilful Conveyancer Mr Charles Brockden[1] to put the whole in Form of Articles of Agreement to be subscribed, by which each Subscriber engag'd to pay a certain Sum down for the first Purchase of Books and an annual Contribution for encreasing them. So few were the Readers at that time in Philadelphia, and the Majority of us so poor, that I was not able with great Industry to find more than Fifty Persons, mostly young Tradesmen, willing to pay down for this purpose Forty shillings each, & Ten Shillings per Annum. On this little Fund we began. The Books were imported. The Library was open one Day in the Week for lending them to the Subscribers, on their Promisory Notes to pay Double the Value if not duly returned. The Institution soon manifested its Utility, was imitated by other Towns and in other Provinces, the Librarys were augmented by Donations, Reading became fashionable, and our People having no publick Amusements to divert their Attention from Study became better acquainted with Books, and in a few Years were observ'd by Strangers to be better instructed & more intelligent than People of the same Rank generally are in other Countries.

When we were about to sign the above-mentioned Articles, which were to be binding on us, our Heirs, &c. for fifty Years, Mr Brockden, the Scrivener, said to us, "You are young Men, but it is scarce probable that any of you will live to see the Expiration of the Term fix'd in this Instrument." A Number of us, however, are yet living: But the Instrument was after a few Years rendered null by a Charter that incorporated & gave Perpetuity to the Company.

---

1. **Mr Charles Brockden:** (1683-1769) Lawyer who drafted legal documents for the transfer of property.

The Objections, & Reluctances I met with in Soliciting the Subscriptions, made me soon feel the Impropriety of presenting one's self as the Proposer of any useful Project that might be suppos'd to raise one's Reputation in the smallest degree above that of one's Neighbours, when one has need of their Assistance to accomplish that Project. I therefore put my self as much as I could out of sight, and stated it as a Scheme of *a Number of Friends,* who had requested me to go about and propose it to such as they thought Lovers of Reading. In this way my Affair went on more smoothly, and I ever after practis'd it on such Occasions; and from my frequent Successes, can heartily recommend it. The present little Sacrifice of your Vanity will afterwards be amply repaid. If it remains a while uncertain to whom the Merit belongs, some one more vain than yourself will be encourag'd to claim it, and then even Envy will be dispos'd to do you justice, by plucking those assum'd Feathers, & restoring them to their right Owner.

This Library afforded me the Means of Improvement by constant Study, for which I set apart an Hour or two each Day; and thus repair'd in some Degree the Loss of the Learned Education my Father once intended for me. Reading was the only Amusement I allow'd my self. I spent no time in Taverns, Games, or Frolicks of any kind. And my Industry in my Business continu'd as indefatigable as it was necessary. I was in debt for my Printinghouse, I had a young Family coming on to be educated, and I had to contend with for Business two Printers who were establish'd in the Place before me. My Circumstances however grew daily easier: my original Habits of Frugality continuing. And My Father having among his Instructions to me when a Boy, frequently repeated a Proverb of Solomon, *"Seest thou a Man diligent in his Calling, he shall stand before Kings, he shall not stand before mean Men."*[2] I from thence consider'd Industry as a Means of obtaining Wealth and Distinction, which encourag'd me; tho' I did not think that I should ever literally stand before Kings, which however has since happened. – for I have stood before five, & even had the honour of sitting down with one, the King of Denmark, to Dinner.

We have an English Proverb that says,

> He that would thrive
> Must ask his Wife;

it was lucky for me that I had one as much dispos'd to Industry & Frugality as my self. She assisted me chearfully in my Business, folding & stitching Pamphlets, tending Shop, purchasing old Linen Rags for the Paper-makers, &c &c. We kept no idle Servants, our Table was plain & simple, our Furniture of the cheapest. For instance my Breakfast was a long time Bread & Milk, (no Tea,) and I ate it out of a twopenny earthen Porringer[3] with a Pewter Spoon. But mark how Luxury will enter Families, and make a Progress, in Spite of Principle. Being Call'd one Morning to Breakfast, I found it in a China Bowl with a Spoon of Silver. They had been bought for me without my Knowledge by my Wife, and

---

2. *"Seest . . . Men"*: Proverbs 22:29.
3. **Porringer**: Early term for a basin used for soup or porridge.

had cost her the enormous Sum of three and twenty Shillings, for which she had no other Excuse or Apology to make, but that she thought *her* Husband deserv'd a Silver Spoon & China Bowl as well as any of his Neighbours. This was the first Appearance of Plate & China in our House, which afterwards in a Course of Years as our Wealth encreas'd, augmented gradually to several Hundred Pounds in Value.

I had been religiously educated as a Presbyterian; and tho' some of the Dogmas of that Persuasion, such as the Eternal Decrees of God, Election, Reprobation,[4] &c. appear'd to me unintelligible, others doubtful, & I early absented myself from the Public Assemblies of the Sect, Sunday being my Studying-Day, I never was without some religious Principles; I never doubted, for instance, the Existance of the Deity, that he made the World, & govern'd it by his Providence; that the most acceptable Service of God was the doing Good to Man; that our Souls are immortal; and that all Crime will be punished & Virtue rewarded either here or hereafter; these I esteem'd the Essentials of every Religion, and being to be found in all the Religions we had in our Country I respected them all, tho' with different degrees of Respect as I found them more or less mix'd with other Articles which without any Tendency to inspire, promote or confirm Morality, serv'd principally to divide us & make us unfriendly to one another. This Respect to all, with an Opinion that the worst had some good Effects, induc'd me to avoid all Discourse that might tend to lessen the good Opinion another might have of his own Religion; and as our Province increas'd in People and new Places of worship were continually wanted, & generally erected by voluntary Contribution, my Mite for such purpose, whatever might be the Sect, was never refused.

Tho' I seldom attended any Public Worship, I had still an Opinion of its Propriety, and of its Utility when rightly conducted, and I regularly paid my annual Subscription for the Support of the only Presbyterian Minister or Meeting we had in Philadelphia. He us'd to visit me sometimes as a Friend, and admonish me to attend his Administrations, and I was now and then prevail'd on to do so, once for five Sundays successively. Had he been, *in my Opinion*, a good Preacher perhaps I might have continued, notwithstanding the occasion I had for the Sunday's Leisure in my Course of Study: But his Discourses were chiefly either polemic Arguments, or Explications of the peculiar Doctrines of our Sect, and were all to me very dry, uninteresting and unedifying, since not a single moral Principle was inculcated or enforc'd, their Aim seeming to be rather to make us Presbyterians than good Citizens. At length he took for his Text that Verse of the 4th Chapter of Philippians, *Finally, Brethren, Whatsoever Things are true, honest, just, pure, lovely, or of good report, if there be any virtue, or any praise, think on these Things,*[5] & I imagin'd in a Sermon on such a Text, we could not miss of having some Morality: But he confin'd himself to five Points only as meant by the Apostle, viz. 1. Keeping holy the Sabbath Day. 2. Being diligent in Reading the Holy Scriptures. 3. Attending duly the Publick Worship. 4. Partaking of the Sacrament. 5. Paying a due Respect to God's Ministers. These might be all good Things, but as they were not the kind of good Things that I expected from that Text, I despaired of ever

---

4. **Reprobation:** Early term for predestined damnation.
5. *"Finally . . . Things"*: Franklin loosely quotes Philippians 4:8.

meeting with them from any other, was disgusted, and attended his Preaching no more. I had some Years before compos'd a little Liturgy or Form of Prayer for my own private Use, viz, in 1728. entitled, *Articles of Belief & Acts of Religion.* I return'd to the Use of this, and went no more to the public Assemblies. My Conduct might be blameable, but I leave it without attempting farther to excuse it, my present purpose being to relate Facts, and not to make Apologies for them.

It was about this time[6] that I conceiv'd the bold and arduous Project of arriving at moral Perfection. I wish'd to live without committing any Fault at any time; I would conquer all that either Natural Inclination, Custom, or Company might lead me into. As I knew, or thought I knew, what was right and wrong, I did not see why I might not *always* do the one and avoid the other. But I soon found I had undertaken a Task of more Difficulty than I had imagined: While my Care was employ'd in guarding against one Fault, I was often surpriz'd by another. Habit took the Advantage of Inattention. Inclination was sometimes too strong for Reason. I concluded at length, that the mere speculative Conviction that it was our Interest to be compleatly virtuous, was not sufficient to prevent our Slipping, and that the contrary Habits must be broken and good Ones acquired and established, before we can have any Dependance on a steady uniform Rectitude of Conduct. For this purpose I therefore contriv'd the following Method.

In the various Enumerations of the moral Virtues I had met with in my Reading, I found the Catalogue more or less numerous, as different Writers included more or fewer Ideas under the same Name. Temperance, for Example, was by some confin'd to Eating & Drinking, while by others it was extended to mean the moderating every other Pleasure, Appetite, Inclination or Passion, bodily or mental, even to our Avarice & Ambition. I propos'd to myself, for the sake of Clearness, to use rather more Names with fewer Ideas annex'd to each, than a few Names with more Ideas; and I included under Thirteen Names of Virtues all that at that time occurr'd to me as necessary or desirable, and annex'd to each a short Precept, which fully express'd the Extent I gave to its Meaning.

These Names of Virtues with their Precepts were

1. TEMPERANCE.
Eat not to Dulness
Drink not to Elevation.
2. SILENCE.
Speak not but what may benefit others or your self. Avoid trifling Conversation.
3. ORDER.
Let all your Things have their Places. Let each Part of your Business have its Time.
4. RESOLUTION.
Resolve to perform what you ought. Perform without fail what you resolve.
5. FRUGALITY.
Make no Expence but to do good to others or yourself: i.e. Waste nothing.
6. INDUSTRY.

---

6. **It was about this time:** Around 1730, at the time Franklin began his own business and married Deborah Read.

Lose no Time. Be always employ'd in something useful. Cut off all unnecessary Actions.

7. SINCERITY.

Use no hurtful Deceit.

Think innocently and justly; and, if you speak; speak accordingly.

8. JUSTICE.

Wrong none, by doing Injuries or omitting the Benefits that are your Duty.

9. MODERATION.

Avoid Extreams. Forbear resenting Injuries so much as you think they deserve.

10. CLEANLINESS.

Tolerate no Uncleanness in Body, Cloaths or Habitation.

11. TRANQUILITY.

Be not disturbed at Trifles, or at Accidents common or unavoidable.

12. CHASTITY.

Rarely use Venery but for Health or Offspring; Never to Dulness, Weakness, or the Injury of your own or another's Peace or Reputation.

13. HUMILITY.

Imitate Jesus and Socrates.

My intention being to acquire the *Habitude*[7] of all these Virtues, I judg'd it would be well not to distract my Attention by attempting the whole at once, but to fix it on one of them at a time, and when I should be Master of that, then to proceed to another, and so on till I should have gone thro' the thirteen. And as the previous Acquisition of some might facilitate the Acquisition of certain others, I arrang'd them with that View as they stand above. *Temperance* first, as it tends to procure that Coolness & Clearness of Head, which is so necessary where constant Vigilance was to be kept up, and Guard maintained, against the unremitting Attraction of ancient Habits, and the Force of perpetual Temptations. This being acquir'd & establish'd, *Silence* would be more easy, and my Desire being to gain Knowledge at the same time that I improv'd in Virtue, and considering that in Conversation it was obtain'd rather by the Use of the Ears than of the Tongue, & therefore wishing to break a Habit I was getting into of Prattling, Punning & Joking, which only made me acceptable to trifling Company, I gave *Silence* the second Place. This, and the next, *Order*, I expected would allow me more Time for attending to my Project and my Studies; RESOLUTION once become habitual, would keep me firm in my Endeavours to obtain all the subsequent Virtues; *Frugality* & *Industry*, by freeing me from my remaining Debt, & producing Affluence & Independance would make more easy the Practice of *Sincerity* and *Justice*, &c. &c. Conceiving then that agreeable to the Advice of Pythagoras in his Golden Verses,[8]

---

7. **Habitude**: Habitual tendency or way of behaving.
8. **Advice of Pythagoras in his Golden Verses**: Nicholas Rowe (1674–1718) translated *The Golden Verses of Pythagoras* (1732), a Greek philosopher of the sixth century BCE. Franklin indicated that the lines directing such daily self-examination should be inserted in a note; he evidently wished to include at least part of a passage beginning: "Let not the stealing God of Sleep surprize, / Nor creep in Slumbers on thy weary Eyes, / Ere ev'ry Action of the former Day, / Strictly thou dost, and righteously survey."

daily Examination would be necessary, I contriv'd the following Method for conducting that Examination.

I made a little Book in which I allotted a Page for each of the Virtues. I rul'd each Page with red Ink so as to have seven Columns, one for each Day of the Week, marking each Column with a Letter for the Day. I cross'd these Columns with thirteen red Lines, marking the Beginning of each Line with the first Letter of one of the Virtues, on which Line & in its proper Column I might mark by a little black Spot every Fault I found upon Examination, to have been committed respecting that Virtue upon that Day.

FORM OF THE PAGES

TEMPERANCE							
Eat not to Dulness. *Drink not to Elevation.*							
	S	M	T	W	T	F	S
T							
S	•	•		•		•	
O	••	•	•		•	•	•
R			•			•	
F		•			•		
I			•				
S							
J							
M							
Cl.							
T							
Ch							
H							

I determined to give a Week's strict Attention to each of the Virtues successively. Thus in the first Week my great Guard was to avoid every the least Offence against Temperance, leaving the other Virtues to their ordinary Chance, only marking every Evening the Faults of the Day. Thus if in the first Week I could keep my first Line marked T clear of Spots, I suppos'd the Habit of that Virtue so much strengthen'd and its opposite weaken'd, that I might venture extending my Attention to include the next, and for the following Week keep both Lines clear of Spots. Proceeding thus to the last, I could go thro' a Course compleat in Thirteen Weeks, and four Courses in a Year. And like him who having a Garden to weed, does not attempt to eradicate all the bad Herbs at once, which would exceed his Reach and his Strength, but works on one of the Beds at a time, & having accomplish'd the first proceeds to a second; so I should have, (I hoped) the encouraging Pleasure of seeing on my Pages the Progress I made in Virtue, by clearing successively my Lines of their Spots, till in the End by a Number of Courses, I should be happy in viewing a clean Book after a thirteen Weeks daily Examination.

This my little Book had for its Motto these Lines from *Addison's Cato*;[9]

> *Here will I hold: If there is a Pow'r above us,*
> *(And that there is, all Nature cries aloud*
> *Thro' all her Works) he must delight in Virtue,*
> *And that which he delights in must be happy.*

Another from *Cicero*.[10]

O Vitae Philosophia Dux! O Virtutum indagatrix, expultrixque vitiorum! Unus dies bene, & ex preceptis tuis actus, peccanti immortalitati est anteponendus.

Another from the Proverbs of Solomon speaking of Wisdom or Virtue;

Length of Days is in her right hand, and in her Left Hand Riches and Honours; Her Ways are Ways of Pleasantness, and all her Paths are Peace.   III, 16, 17.

And conceiving God to be the Fountain of Wisdom, I thought it right and necessary to solicit his Assistance for obtaining it; to this End I form'd the following little Prayer, which was prefix'd to my Tables of Examination; for daily Use.

O Powerful Goodness! bountiful Father! merciful Guide! Increase in me that Wisdom which discovers my truest Interests; Strengthen my Resolutions to perform what that Wisdom dictates, Accept my kind Offices to thy other Children, as the only Return in my Power for thy continual Favours to me.

I us'd also sometimes a little Prayer which I took from *Thomson's* Poems.[11] viz

> *Father of Light and Life, thou Good supreme,*
> *O teach me what is good, teach me thy self!*
> *Save me from Folly, Vanity and Vice,*
> *From every low Pursuit, and fill my Soul*
> *With Knowledge, conscious Peace, & Virtue pure,*
> *Sacred, substantial, neverfading Bliss!*

---

9. *Addison's Cato*: English author and essayist Joseph Addison (1672-1719), from his *Cato: A Tragedy* (1713), 5.1.15-18.
10. *Cicero*: Roman philosopher and orator Marcus Tullius Cicero (106-43 BCE), from his *Tusculan Disputations*. Franklin omitted several lines from the passage; the lines he quotes are translated: "O Philosophy, leader of life! O seeker of virtue, and critic of vice! From your teachings, a single day of good is preferred to an eternity of sin."
11. *Thomson's* Poems: English poet James Thomson (1700-1748); the quotation is from "Winter," lines 218-23, in *The Seasons* (1726).

The Precept of *Order* requiring that *every Part of my Business should have its allotted Time*, one Page in my little Book contain'd the following Scheme of Employment for the Twenty-four Hours of a natural Day,

The Morning Question, What Good Shall I do this Day?	5	Rise, wash, and address *Powerful Goodness*; contrive Day's Business and take the Resolution of the day; prosecute the present Study: and breakfast?
	6	
	7	
	8	
	9	Work.
	10	
	11	
	12	Read, or overlook my Accounts, and dine.
	1	
	2	Work.
	3	
	4	
	5	
Evening Question, What Good have I done to day?	6	Put Things in Their Places, Supper, Musick, or Diversion, or Conversation, Examination of the Day.
	7	
	8	
	9	
	10	Sleep –
	11	
	12	
	1	
	2	
	3	
	4	

I enter'd upon the Execution of this Plan for Self Examination, and continu'd it with occasional Intermissions for some time. I was surpriz'd to find myself so much fuller of Faults than I had imagined, but I had the Satisfaction of seeing them diminish. To avoid the Trouble of renewing now & then my little Book, which by scraping out the Marks on the Paper of old Faults to make room for new Ones in a new Course, became full of Holes: I transferr'd my Tables & Precepts to the Ivory Leaves of a Memorandum Book, on which the Lines were drawn with red Ink that made a durable Stain, and on those Lines I mark'd my Faults with a black Lead Pencil, which Marks I could easily wipe out with a wet Sponge. After a while I went thro' one Course only in a Year, and afterwards only one in several Years; till at length I omitted them entirely, being employ'd in Voyages &

Business abroad with a Multiplicity of Affairs, that interfered. But I always carried my little Book with me. My Scheme of ORDER, gave me the most Trouble, and I found, that tho' it might be practicable where a Man's Business was such as to leave him the Disposition of his Time, that of a Journey-man Printer for instance, it was not possible to be exactly observ'd by a Master, who must mix with the World, and often receive People of Business at their own Hours. *Order* too, with regard to Places for Things, Papers, &c. I found extreamly difficult to acquire. I had not been early accustomed to it, & having an exceeding good Memory, I was not so sensible of the Inconvenience attending Want of Method. This Article therefore cost me so much painful Attention & my Faults in it vex'd me so much, and I made so little Progress in Amendment, & had such frequent Relapses, that I was almost ready to give up the Attempt, and content my self with a faulty Character in that respect. Like the Man who in buying an Ax of a Smith my Neighbour, desired to have the whole of its Surface as bright as the Edge; the Smith consented to grind it bright for him if he would turn the Wheel. He turn'd while the Smith press'd the broad Face of the Ax hard & heavily on the Stone, which made the Turning of it very fatiguing. The Man came every now & then from the Wheel to see how the Work went on; and at length would take his Ax as it was without farther Grinding. No, says the Smith, Turn on, turn on; we shall have it bright by and by; as yet 'tis only speckled. Yes, says the Man; but – *I think I like a speckled Ax best.* And I believe this may have been the Case with many who having for want of some such Means as I employ'd found the Difficulty of obtaining good, & breaking bad Habits, in other Points of Vice & Virtue, have given up the Struggle, & concluded that *a speckled Ax was best.* For something that pretended to be Reason was every now and then suggesting to me, that such extream Nicety as I exacted of my self might be a kind of Foppery in Morals,[12] which if it were known would make me ridiculous; that a perfect Character might be attended with the Inconvenience of being envied and hated; and that a benevolent Man should allow a few Faults in himself, to keep his Friends in Countenance. In Truth I found myself incorrigible with respect to *Order*; and now I am grown old, and my Memory bad, I feel very sensibly the want of it. But on the whole, tho' I never arrived at the Perfection I had been so ambitious of obtaining, but fell far short of it, yet I was by the Endeavour made a better and a happier Man than I otherwise should have been, if I had not attempted it; As those who aim at perfect Writing by imitating the engraved Copies, tho' they never reach the wish'd for Excellence of those Copies, their Hand is mended by the Endeavour, and is tolerable while it continues fair & legible.

And it may be well my Posterity should be informed, that to this little Artifice, with the Blessing of God, their Ancestor ow'd the constant Felicity of his Life down to his 79th Year in which this is written. What Reverses may attend the Remainder is in the Hand of Providence: But if they arrive the Reflection on past Happiness enjoy'd ought to help his Bearing them with more Resignation. To *Temperance* he ascribes his long-continu'd Health, & what is still left to him of a good Constitution. To *Industry* and *Frugality* the early Easiness of his Circumstances, & Acquisition of his Fortune, with all

---

12. **Foppery in Morals:** That is, an affected or vain display of morality.

that Knowledge which enabled him to be an useful Citizen, and obtain'd for him some Degree of Reputation among the Learned. To *Sincerity & Justice* the Confidence of his Country, and the honourable Employs it conferr'd upon him. And to the joint Influence of the whole Mass of the Virtues, even in their imperfect State he was able to acquire them, all that Evenness of Temper, & that Chearfulness in Conversation which makes his Company still sought for, & agreable even to his younger Acquaintance. I hope therefore that some of my Descendants may follow the Example & reap the Benefit.

It will be remark'd that, tho' my Scheme was not wholly without Religion there was in it no mark of any of the distinguishing Tenets of any particular Sect. I had purposely avoided them; for being fully persuaded of the Utility and Excellency of my Method, and that it might be serviceable to People in all Religions, and intending some time or other to publish it, I would not have any thing in it that should prejudice any one of any Sect against it. I purposed writing a little Comment on each Virtue, in which I would have shown the Advantages of possessing it, & the Mischiefs attending its opposite Vice; and I should have called my Book the ART *of Virtue*, because it would have shown the *Means & Manner* of obtaining Virtue; which would have distinguish'd it from the mere Exhortation to be good, that does not instruct & indicate the Means; but is like the Apostle's Man of verbal Charity, who only, without showing to the Naked & the Hungry *how* or where they might get Cloaths or Victuals, exhorted them to be fed & clothed. *James* II, 15, 16.[13]

But it so happened that my Intention of writing & publishing this Comment was never fulfilled. I did indeed, from time to time put down short Hints of the Sentiments, Reasonings, &c. to be made use of in it; some of which I have still by me: But the necessary close Attention to private Business in the earlier part of Life, and public Business since, have occasioned my postponing it. For it being connected in my Mind with a *great and extensive Project* that required the whole Man to execute, and which an unforeseen Succession of Employs prevented my attending to, it has hitherto remain'd unfinish'd.

In this Piece it was my Design to explain and enforce this Doctrine, that vicious Actions are not hurtful because they are forbidden, but forbidden because they are hurtful, the Nature of Man alone consider'd: That it was therefore every ones Interest to be virtuous, who wish'd to be happy even in this World. And I should from this Circumstance, there being always in the World a Number of rich Merchants, Nobility, States and Princes, who have need of honest Instruments for the Management of their Affairs, and such being so rare, have endeavoured to convince young Persons, that no Qualities were so likely to make a poor Man's Fortune as those of Probity & Integrity.

My List of Virtues contain'd at first but twelve: But a Quaker Friend having kindly inform'd me that I was generally thought proud; that my Pride show'd itself frequently in Conversation; that I was not content with being in the right when discussing any Point, but was overbearing & rather insolent; of which he convinc'd me by mentioning several Instances; — I determined endeavouring to cure myself if I could of this Vice or

---

13. *James* II, 15, 16: The passage in James 2:15-16 reads: "If a brother or sister be naked, and destitute of daily food, And one of you say unto them, Depart in peace, be ye warmed and filled; notwithstanding ye give them not those things which are needful to the body; what doth it profit?"

Folly among the rest, and I added *Humility* to my List, giving an extensive Meaning to the Word. I cannot boast of much Success in acquiring the *Reality* of this Virtue; but I had a good deal with regard to the *Appearance* of it. I made it a Rule to forbear all direct Contradiction to the Sentiments of others, and all positive Assertion of my own. I even forbid myself agreable to the old Laws of our Junto, the Use of every Word or Expression in the Language that imported a fix'd Opinion; such as *certainly, undoubtedly,* &c. and I adopted instead of them, *I conceive, I apprehend,* or *I imagine* a thing to be so or so, or it so appears to me at present. When another asserted something that I thought an Error, I deny'd my self the Pleasure of contradicting him abruptly, and of showing immediately some Absurdity in his Proposition; and in answering I began by observing that in certain Cases or Circumstances his Opinion would be right, but that in the present case there *appear'd* or *seem'd* to me some Difference, &c. I soon found the Advantage of this Change in my Manners. The Conversations I engag'd in went on more pleasantly. The modest way in which I propos'd my Opinions, procur'd them a readier Reception and less Contradiction; I had less Mortification when I was found to be in the wrong, and I more easily prevail'd with others to give up their Mistakes & join with me when I happen'd to be in the right. And this Mode, which I at first put on, with some violence to natural Inclination, became at length so easy & so habitual to me, that perhaps for these Fifty Years past no one has ever heard a dogmatical Expression escape me. And to this Habit (after my Character of Integrity) I think it principally owing, that I had early so much Weight with my Fellow Citizens, when I proposed new Institutions, or Alterations in the old; and so much Influence in public Councils when I became a Member. For I was but a bad Speaker, never eloquent, subject to much Hesitation in my choice of Words, hardly correct in Language, and yet I generally carried my Points.

In reality there is perhaps no one of our natural Passions so hard to subdue as *Pride.* Disguise it, struggle with it, beat it down, stifle it, mortify it as much as one pleases, it is still alive, and will every now and then peep out and show itself. You will see it perhaps often in this History. For even if I could conceive that I had compleatly overcome it, I should probably be proud of my Humility.

Thus far written at Passy 1784

[1784, 1981]

Elizabeth Ashbridge

[1713-1755]

Elizabeth Ashbridge was born Elizabeth Sampson in Middlewich, in the county of Cheshire, England, in 1713. Most of what is known about her life is contained in her autobiography. She was raised in the Anglican Church by her parents, Thomas and Mary Sampson. Her father, a ship's surgeon, was frequently away from home, and Ashbridge was educated primarily by her devout mother. "In my very Infancy, I had an awful regard for religion & a great love for religious people, particularly the Ministers," Ashbridge later recalled, "and sometimes wept with Sorrow, that I was not a boy that I might have been one." At the age of fourteen and to the distress of her parents, she eloped with an impoverished weaver who died five months later. Thomas Sampson refused to allow his daughter to return to the family home, so Ashbridge went to live with a Quaker relative in Dublin.

Ashbridge ultimately discovered her own calling as a Quaker minister and preacher in the colonies. Agreeing to terms of indentured servitude in order to pay for her passage, she arrived in New York City in 1732. According to her later account, Ashbridge initially endured great hardship at the hands of a cruel master. But she managed to save enough money to buy herself out of her indenture and began to earn a living as a seamstress. She then entered into what Ashbridge described as yet another "cruel Servitude," her marriage to a man she identified only as Sullivan, who "fell in Love with me for my Dancing." After several years of

Quaker Meeting in Philadelphia

This undated wood engraving illustrates one of the reasons other Protestant denominations were so hostile to the Quakers — their emphasis on the equality of women, including the right of women like Elizabeth Ashbridge not only to speak in meetings but also to preach the Gospel.

spiritual struggle in her unhappy marriage, Ashbridge abandoned the Anglican Church and became increasingly devoted to the religion of the Quakers, or the Society of Friends. Despite her husband's violent objections, she became a Quaker minister in 1738. Sullivan deserted her and joined the military. He died two years later, after writing her that he had also become a Quaker. Free of her unhappy marriage, Ashbridge maintained herself by keeping a school, even as she began to earn a reputation as a Quaker preacher. In 1746, she married Aaron Ashbridge (1712-1776), a fellow Quaker, and they evidently enjoyed a happy relationship based on their mutual interests and Aaron's support of Ashbridge's calling as a preacher. While on a missionary tour of England and Ireland, she died in County Carlow, Ireland, in 1755.

Reading *Some Account of the Fore Part of the Life of Elizabeth Ashbridge.*   Ashbridge's vivid account of her eventful life and religious experiences is among the earliest autobiographies written by a woman. Just as her involvement in the Society of Friends allowed her to become a preacher, a role denied to women in virtually all other Christian denominations, the notoriety of her preaching evidently encouraged Ashbridge to write and ultimately led to the publication of her spiritual autobiography, a genre traditionally associated with men. In describing the hardships and spiritual struggles that culminated in her surrender to God and entry into the Quaker community, Ashbridge implicitly challenged both male authority and traditional conceptions of proper female behavior.

As she observes at the opening of her account, her life was "attended with many uncommon Occurrences," including her early first marriage and almost immediate widowhood, a harsh term of indentured servitude in colonial America, and the difficulties of her second marriage to a man who was unsympathetic to her efforts to find spiritual fulfillment. The autobiography ends with his death in 1740, though it is not clear when Ashbridge wrote her account. In 1774, nearly twenty years after her death, her third husband, Aaron Ashbridge, arranged for the publication of the work in England, where it appeared under the full title *Some Account of the Fore Part of the Life of Elizabeth Ashbridge, who died in Truth's service at the house of Robert Lecky at Kilnock in the County of Carlow Ireland; the 16th of 5th mo. 1755. Written by her own Hand many years ago.* The account subsequently went through several editions in the eighteenth and nineteenth centuries and was widely read by Quakers in England and the United States, where it was published in 1807. The following selection begins shortly after her second marriage, as Ashbridge begins a journey from New Jersey to visit relatives in Pennsylvania. The selection is taken from Daniel B. Shea's authoritative edition, based on early copies of Ashbridge's manuscript, which was published in *Journeys in New Worlds: Early American Women's Narratives,* edited by William L. Andrews (1990).

bedfordstmartins.com/ americanlit for research links on Ashbridge

From Some Account of the Fore Part
of the Life of Elizabeth Ashbridge

I now began to think of my Relations in Pennsylvania whom I had not yet seen; and having a great Desire that way, Got Leave of my Husband to go & also a Certificate from the Priest on Long Island in order that if I made any stay, I might be receiv'd as a Member wherever I came; Then Setting out, my husband bore me Company to the Blazing Star Ferry, saw me Safe over & then returned. On the way near a place called Maidenhead [New Jersey] I fell from my horse & I was Disabled from Traveling for some time: In the interval I abode at the house of an Honest Like Dutchman, who with his wife were very kind to me, & tho' they had much trouble going to the Doctor and waiting upon me, (for I was Several Days unable to help my self) yet would have nothing for it (which I thought Exceeding kind) but Charged me if ever I came that way again to call and Lodge there. I mention this because by and by I shall have occasion to remark this Place again.

Hence I came to Trenton [New Jersey] Ferry, where I met with no small Mortification upon hearing that my Relations were Quakers, & what was the worst of all my Aunt a Preacher. I was Sorry to hear it, for I was Exceedingly prejudiced against these People & have often wondered with what face they Could Call them Selves Christians. I Repented my Coming and had a mind to have turned back. At Last I Concluded to go & see them since I was so far on my journey, but Expected little Comfort from my Visit. But see how God brings unforeseen things to Pass, for by my going there I was brought to my Knowledge of his Truth. I went from Trenton to Philadelphia by Water, thence to my Uncle's on Horseback, where I met with very kind reception; for tho' my Uncle was dead and my Aunt married again, yet both her husband and She received me in a very kind manner.

I had not been there three Hours before I met with a Shock, & my opinion began to alter with respect to these People. For seeing a Book lying on the Table (& being much for reading) I took it up: My Aunt Observing said, "Cousin that is a Quakers' Book," for Perceiving I was not a Quaker, I suppose she thought I would not like it: I made her no answer but revolving in my mind, "what can these People write about, for I have heard that they Deny the Scriptures & have no other bible but George Fox's Journal,[1] & Deny all the holy Ordinances?" So resolved to read, but had not read two Pages before my very heart burned within me and Tears Issued from my Eyes, which I was Afraid would be seen; therefore with the Book (Saml. Crisp's Two Letters[2]) I walked into the garden, sat Down, and the piece being Small, read it through before I went in; but Some Times was forced to Stop to Vent my Tears, my heart as it were uttering these involuntary Expressions; "my God must I (if ever I come to the true knowledge of thy Truth) be of this

---

1. **George Fox's Journal:** Fox (1624–1691) was an English religious leader who founded the Society of Friends, known as the Quakers. His *Journal* (1694) recounted his spiritual experiences and became a guidebook and source of inspiration for Quakers.

2. **Saml. Crisp's Two Letters:** The book Ashbridge takes up was a famous Quaker conversion narrative, *Two Letters Written by Samuel Crisp . . . Upon his Change from a Chaplain of the Church of England, to Join with the People Called Quakers*, first published in 1722.

man's Opinion, who has sought thee as I have done & join with these People that a few hours ago I preferred the Papists before? O thou, the God of my Salvation & of my Life, who hast in an abundant manner manifested thy Long Suffering & tender Mercy, Redeeming me as from the Lowest Hell, a Monument of thy grace: Lord, my soul beseecheth thee to Direct me in the right way & keep me from Error, & then According to thy Covenant, I'll think nothing too near to Part with for thy name's Sake. If these things be so, Oh! happy People thus beloved of God."

After I came a little to my Self again I washed my face least any in the House should perceive I had been weeping. But this night got but Little Sleep, for the old Enemy began to Suggest that I was one of those that wavered & was not Steadfast in the faith, advancing several Texts of Scripture against me & them, as, in the Latter Days there should be those that would deceive the very Elect: & these were they, & that I was in danger of being deluded. Here the Subtile Serpent transformed himself so hiddenly that I verily believed this to be a timely Caution from a good Angel — so resolved to beware of the Deceiver, & for Some weeks Did not touch any of their Books.

The next Day being the first of the week I wanted to have gone to Church, which was Distant about four Miles, but being a Stranger and having nobody to go along with me, was forced to Give it out, & as most of the Family was going to Meeting, I went with them, but with a resolution not to like them, & so it was fully Suffered: for as they sat in silence I looked over the Meeting, thinking with my self, "how like fools these People sit, how much better would it be to stay at home & read the Bible or some good Book, than to come here and go to Sleep." For my Part I was very Sleepy & thought they were no better than my Self. Indeed at Length I fell a sleep, and had like to fallen Down, but this was the last time I ever fell asleep in a Meeting, Tho' often Assaulted with it.

Now I began to be lifted up with Spiritual Pride & thought my Self better than they, but thro' Mercy this did not Last Long, for in a Little time I was brought Low & saw that these were the People to whom I must join. It may seem strange that I who had Lived so long with one of this Society in Dublin, should yet be so great a Stranger to them. In answer let it be Considered that During the time I was there I never read one of their Books nor went to one Meeting, & besides I had heard such ridiculous stories of them as made me Esteem them the worst of any Society of People; but God that knew the Sincerity of my heart looked with Pity on my Weakness & soon Let me see my Error.

In a few weeks there was an afternoon's Meeting held at my Uncle's to which came that Servant of the Lord Wm. Hammans who was made then Instrumental to the Convincing me of the truth more Perfectly, & helping me over Some great Doubts: tho' I believe no one did ever sit in Greater opposition than I did when he first stood up; but I was soon brought Down for he preached the Gospel with such Power I was forced to give up & Confess it was the truth. As soon as meeting Ended I Endeavoured to get alone, for I was not fit to be seen, I being So broken; yet afterward the Restless adversary assaulted me again, on this wise. In the morning before this meeting, I had been Disputing with my Uncle about Baptism, which was the subject this good Man Dwelt upon, which was handled so Clearly as to answer all my Scruples beyond all objection: yet the Crooked Serpent alleged that the Sermon that I had heard did not proceed from divine Revelation but that my Uncle and Aunt had acquainted the Friend of me; which being Strongly

Suggested, I fell to Accusing them with it, of which they both cleared themselves, saying they had not seen him Since my Coming into these Parts until he came into the meeting. I then Concluded he was a messenger sent of God to me, & with fervent Cryes Desired I might be Directed a right and now Laid aside all Prejudice & set my heart open to receive the truth in the Love of it. And the Lord in his own good time revealed to my Soul not only the Beauty there is in truth, & how those should shine that continue faithful to it, but also the Emptiness of all shadows, which in the day were Gloryous, but now he the Son of Glory was come to put an end to them all, & to Establish Everlasting Righteousness in the room thereof, which is a work in the Soul. He likewise let me see that all I had gone through was to prepare me for this Day & that the time was near that he would require me to go forth & declare to others what he the God of Mercy had done for my Soul; at which I was Surprized & begged to be Excused for fear I should bring dishonour to the truth, and cause his Holy name to be Evil spoken of.

All the while, I never Let any know the Condition I was in, nor did I appear like a Friend, & fear'd a Discovery I now began to think of returning to my husband but found a restraint to stay where I was. I then Hired to keep School & hearing of a place for him, wrote desiring him to come to me, but Let him know nothing how it was with me. I loved to go to meetings, but did not like to be seen to go on week days, & therefore to Shun it used to go from my school through the Woods, but notwithstanding all my care the Neighbours that were not friends began to revile me, calling me Quaker, saying they supposed I intended to be a fool and turn Preacher; I then receiv'd the same censure that I (a little above a year before) had Passed on one of the handmaids of the Lord at Boston, & so weak was I, alas! I could not bear the reproach, & in order to Change their Opinions got into greater Excess in Apparel than I had freedom to Wear for some time before I came Acquainted with Friends.

In this Condition I continued till my Husband came, & then began the Tryal of my Faith. Before he reached me he heard I was turned Quaker, at which he stampt, saying, "I'd rather heard She had been dead as well as I Love her, for if so, all my comfort is gone." He then came to me & had not seen me before for four Months. I got up & met him saying, "My Dear, I am glad to see thee," at which he flew in a Passion of anger & said, "the Divel thee thee, don't thee me."[3] I used all the mild means I could to pacify him, & at Length got him fit to go & Speak to my Relations, but he was Alarmed, and as soon as we got alone said, "so I see your Quaker relations have made you one." I told him they had not, which was true, nor had I ever told him how it was with me: But he would have it that I was one, & therefore would not let me stay among them; & having found a place to his mind, hired and came Directly back to fetch me hence, & in one afternoon walked near thirty Miles to keep me from Meeting, the next Day being first Day;[4] & on the Morrow took me to the Afforesaid Place & hired Lodgings at a churchman's house; who

---

3. **"the Divel thee . . . don't thee me"**: Ashbridge's language is evidence to her husband that she is following the practices and plain speech of the Quakers, who continued to use the informal *thee* and *thou* long after those terms were displaced by *you*, originally a plural pronoun that was used in the singular to signify politeness or respect.
4. **first Day**: To avoid references to pagan deities, Quakers referred to days of the week and the months by number; first day was Sunday.

was one of the Wardens, & a bitter Enemy to Friends & used to Do all he could to irritate my Husband against them, & would tell me abundance of Ridiculous Stuff; but my Judgement was too Clearly convinced to believe it.

I still did not appear like a Friend, but they all believed I was one. When my Husband and he Used to be making their Diversion & reviling, I used to sit in Silence, but now and then an involuntary Sigh would break from me: at which he would tell my husband: "there, did not I tell you that your wife was a Quaker; & She will be a preacher." Upon which My Husband once in a Great rage came up to me, & Shaking his hand over me, said, "you had better be hanged in that Day." I then, Peter like, in a panick denied my being a Quaker, at which great horror seized upon me, which Continued near three Months: so that I again feared that by Denying the Lord that Bought me, the heavens were Shut against me; for great Darkness Surrounded, & I was again plunged into Despair. I used to Walk much alone in the Wood, where no Eye saw nor Ear heard, & there Lament my miserable Condition, & have often gone from Morning till Night and have not broke my Fast.

Thus I was brought so Low that my Life was a burden to me; the Devil seem'd to Vaunt that tho' the Sins of my youth were forgiven, yet now he was sure of Me, for that I had Committed the unpardonable Sin & Hell inevitable would be my portion, & my Torment would be greater than if I had hanged my Self at first. In this Doleful State I had none to bewail my Doleful Condition; & Even in the Night when I Could not Sleep under the painful Distress of mind, if my husband perceived me weeping he would revile me for it. At Length when he and his Friends thought themselves too weak to over Set me (tho' I feared it was all ready done) he went to the Priest at Chester [Pennsylvania] to Advise what to Do with me. This man knew I was a member of the Church, for I had Shewn him my Certificate: his advice was to take me out of Pennsylvania, and find some place where there was no Quakers; and then it would wear off. To this my Husband Agreed saying he did not Care where he went, if he Could but restore me to that Livelyness of Temper I was naturally of, & to that Church of which I was a member. I on my Part had no Spirit to oppose the Proposal, neither much cared where I was, For I seemed to have nothing to hope for, but Dayly Expected to be made a Spectacle of Divine Wrath, & was Possessed with a Thought that it would be by Thunder ere long.

The time of Removal came, & I must go. I was not Suffered to go to bid my Relations farewell; my husband was Poor & kept no horse, so I must travel on foot; we came to Wilmington [Delaware] (fifteen Miles) thence to Philadelphia by Water; here he took me to a Tavern where I soon became the Spectacle & discourse of the Company. My Husband told them, "my wife is a Quaker," & that he Designed if Possible to find out some Place where there was none. "O," thought I, "I was once in a Condition deserving that name, but now it is over with me. O! that I might from a true hope once more have an Opportunity to Confess to the truth;" tho' I was Sure of Suffering all manner of Crueltys, I would not Regard it.

These were my Concerns while he was Entertaining the Company with my Story, in which he told them that I had been a good Dancer, but now he Could get me neither to Dance nor Sing, upon which one of the Company stands up saying, "I'll go fetch my Fiddle, & we'll have a Dance," at which my husband was much pleased. The fiddle came, the sight of which put me in a sad Condition for fear if I Refused my husband would be in a great Passion: however I took up this resolution, not to Comply whatever be the Consequence. He comes to me, takes me by the hand saying, "come my Dear, shake off that Gloom, & let's have a civil Dance; you would now and then when you was a good Churchwoman, & that's better than a Stiff Quaker." I trembling desired to be Excused; but he Insisted on it, and knowing his Temper to be exceeding Cholerick, durst not say much, yet did not Consent. He then pluck'd me round the Room till Tears affected my Eyes, at Sight whereof the Musician Stopt and said, "I'll play no more, Let your wife alone," of which I was Glad.

There was also a man in Company who came from Freehold in East Jersey: he said, "I see your Wife is a Quaker, but if you will take my advice you need not go so far (for my husband's design was for Staten Island); come & live amongst us, we'll soon cure her of her Quakerism, for we want a School Master & Mistress Too" (I followed the Same Business); to which he agreed, & a happy turn it was for me, as will be seen by and by: and the Wonderfull turn of Providence, who had not yet Abandoned me, but raised a glimmering hope, affording the Answer of peace in refusing to Dance, for which I was more rejoyced than to be made Mistress of much Riches; & in floods of Tears said, "Lord, I dread to ask and yet without thy gracious Pardon I'm Miserable; I therefore fall Down before thy Throne, imploring Mercy at thine hand. O Lord once more I beseech thee, try my Obedience, & then what soever thou Commands, I will Obey, & not fear to Confess thee before men."

Thus was my Soul Engaged before God in Sincerity & he in tender Mercy heard my cries, & in me has Shewn that he Delights not in the Death of a Sinner, for he again set my mind at Liberty to praise him & I longed for an Opportunity to Confess to his Truth, which he shewed me should come, but in what manner I did not see, but believed the word that I had heard, which in a little time was fulfilled to me. My Husband as affore-said agreed to go to Freehold, & in our way thither we came to Maidenhead, where I went to see the kind Dutchman before mentioned, who made us welcome & Invited us to stay a day or Two.

While we were here, there was held a great Meeting of the Presbyterians, not only for Worship but Business also: for one of their preachers being Charged with Drunkenness, was this day to have his Trial before a great number of their Priests, &c. We went to it, of which I was afterwards glad. Here I perceived great Divisions among the People about who Should be their Shepherd: I greatly Pitied their Condition, for I now saw beyond the Men made Ministers, & What they Preached for: and which those at this Meeting might have done had not the prejudice of Education, which is very prevalent, blinded their Eyes. Some Insisted to have the old Offender restored, some to have a young man they had upon trial some weeks, a third Party was for sending for one from New England. At length stood up one & Directing himself to the Chief Speaker said "Sir, when we have been at the Expence (which will be no Small Matter) of fetching this Gentleman from New England, may be he'll not stay with us." *Answer*, "don't you know how to make him stay?" *Reply*, "no Sir." "I'll tell you then," said he (to which I gave good attention), "give him a good Salary & I'll Engage he'll Stay." "O" thought I, "these Mercenary creatures: they are all Actuated by one & the same thing, even the Love of Money, & not the regard of Souls." This (Called Reverend) Gentleman, whom these People almost adored, to my knowledge had left his flock on Long Island & moved to Philadelphia where he could get more money. I my self have heard some of them on the Island say that they almost Impoverished themselves to keep him, but not being able to Equal Philadelphia's Invitation he left them without a Shepherd. This man therefore, knowing their Ministry all proceeded from one Cause, might be purchased with the Same thing; surely these and Such like are the Shepherd that regards the fleece more than the flock, in whose mouths are Lies; saying the Lord had sent them, & that they were Christ's Ambassadors, whose Command to those he sent was, "Freely ye have receiv'd, freely give; & Blessed be his holy Name;"[5] so they do to this day.

I durst not say any Thing to my Husband of the Remarks I had made, but laid them up in my heart, & they Served to Strengthen me in my Resolution. Hence we set forward to Freehold, & Coming through Stony Brook [New Jersey] my Husband turned towards me tauntingly & Said, "Here's one of Satan's Synagogues, don't you want to be in it? O I hope to See you Cured of this New Religion." I made no answer but went on, and in a little time, we came to a large run of Water over which was no Bridge, & being Strangers knew no way to escape it, but thro' we must go: he Carried over our Clothes, which we had in Bundles. I took off my Shoes and waded over in my Stockings, which Served some what to prevent the Chill of the Water, being Very Cold & a fall of Snow in the 12 Mo.[6] My heart was Concerned in Prayer that the Lord would Sanctify all my Afflictions to me & give me Patience to bear whatsoever should be suffered to come upon me. We Walked the most part of a mile before we came to the first house, which was a sort of a Tavern. My husband Called for Some Spiritous Liquors, but I got some weakened Cider Mull'd, which when I had Drank of (the Cold being struck to my heart) made me Extremely sick, in so much that when we were a Little past the house I expected I should have Fainted, & not being able to stand, fell Down under a Fence. My husband Observing, tauntingly said, "What's the Matter now; what, are you Drunk; where is your Religion now?" He knew better & at that time I believe he Pitied me, yet was Suffered grievously to Afflict me. In a Little time I grew Better, & going on We came to another Tavern, where we Lodged: the next Day I was Indifferent well, so proceeded, and as we Journeyed a young man Driving an Empty Cart overtook us. I desired my husband to ask the young man to Let us Ride; he did, twas readily granted.

I now thought my Self well off, & took it as a great favour, for my Proud heart was humbled, & I did not regard the Looks of it, tho' the time had been that I would not have been seen in one; this Cart belonged to a man at Shrewsbury [New Jersey] & was to go thro' the place we Designed for, so we rode on (but soon had the Care of the team to our Selves from a failure in the Driver) to the place where I was Intended to be made a prey of; but see how unforeseen things are brought to Pass, by a Providential hand. Tis said and answered, "shall we do Evil that good may Come?" God forbid, yet hence good came to me. Here my husband would have had me Stay while we went to see the Team Safe at home: I Told him, no, since he had led me thro' the Country like a Vagabond, I would not

5. "Freely . . . Name": Matthew 10:8.
6. 12 Mo.: Twelfth month, or December; See note 4.

stay behind him, so went on, & Lodged that Night at the man's house who owned the Team. Next morning in our Return to Freehold, we met a man riding on full Speed, who Stopping said to my Husband, "Sir, are you a School Master?" *Answer*, "Yes." "I came to tell you," replied the Stranger, "of Two new School Houses, & want a Master in Each, & are two miles apart." How this Stranger came to hear of us, who Came but the night before, I never knew, but I was glad he was not one Called a Quaker, Least my husband might have thought it had been a Plot; and then turning to my husband I said, "my Dear, look on me with Pity; if thou has any Affections left for me, which I hope thou hast, for I am not Conscious of having Done anything to Alienate them; here is (continued I) an Opportunity to Settle us both, for I am willing to do all in my Power towards getting an Honest Livelihood."

My Expressions took place, & after a Little Pause he consented, took the young man's Directions, & made towards the place, & in our way came to the house of a Worthy Friend, Whose wife was a Preacher, tho' we did not know it. I was Surprized to see the People so kind to us that were Strangers; we had not been long in the house till we were Invited to Lodge there that night, being the Last in the Week. I said nothing but waited to hear my Master Speak; he soon Consented saying, "My wife has had a Tedious Travel & I pity her"; at which kind Expression I was Affected, for they Were now very Seldom Used to me. The friends' kindness could not proceed from my appearing in the Garb of a Quaker, for I had not yet altered my dress: The Woman of the house, after we had Concluded to Stay, fixed her Eyes upon me & Said, "I believe thou hast met with a deal of Trouble," to which I made but Little Answer. My husband, Observing they were of that sort of people he had so much Endeavoured to shun, would give us no Opportunity for any discourse that night, but the next morning I let the friend know a Little how it was with me. Meeting time came, to which I longed to go, but durst not ask my husband leave for fear of Disturbing him, till we were Settled, & then thought I, "if ever I am favoured to be in this Place, come Life or Death, I'll fight through, for my Salvation is at Stake." The Friend getting ready for Meeting, asked my husband if he would go, saying they knew who were to be his Employers, & if they were at Meeting would Speak to them. He then consented to go; then said the Woman Friend, "& wilt thou Let thy Wife go?," which he denied, making Several Objections, all which She answered so prudently that he Could not be angry, & at Last Consented; & with Joy I went, for I had not been at one for near four Months, & an Heavenly Meeting This was: I now renewed my Covenant & Saw the Word of the Lord made Good, that I should have another Opportunity to Confess his Name, for which my Spirit did rejoice in the God of my Salvation, who had brought Strange things to Pass: May I ever be preserved in Humility, never forgetting his tender Mercies to me.

Here According to my Desire we Settled; my husband got one School & I the Other, & took a Room at a Friend's house a Mile from Each School and Eight Miles from the Meeting House: before next first day we were got to our new Settlement: & now Concluded to Let my husband to see I was determined to joyn with friends. When first day Came I directed my Self to him in this manner, "My Dear, art thou willing to let me go to a Meeting?," at which he flew into a rage, saying, "No you shan't." I then Drew up my resolution & told him as a Dutyfull Wife ought, So I was ready to obey all his Lawfull

Commands, but where they Imposed upon my Conscience, I no longer Durst: For I had already done it too Long, & wronged my Self by it, & tho' he was near & I loved him as a Wife ought, yet God was nearer than all the World to me, & had made me sensible this was the way I ought to go, the which I Assured him was no Small Cross to my own will, yet had Given up My heart, & hoped that he that Called for it would Enable me the residue of my Life to keep it steadily devoted to him, whatever I Suffered for it, adding I hoped not to make him any the worse Wife for it. But all I could Say was in vain; he was Inflexible & Would not Consent.

I had now put my hand to the Plough, & resolved not to Look back, so went without Leave; but Expected to be immediately followed & forced back, but he did not: I went to one of the neighbours & got a Girl to Show me the way, then went on rejoicing & Praising God in my heart, who had thus far given me Power & another Opportunity to Confess to his Truth. Thus for some time I had to go Eight Miles on foot to Meetings, which I never thought hard; My Husband soon bought a Horse, but would not Let me ride him, neither when my Shoes were worn out would he Let me have a new Pair, thinking by that means to keep me from going to meetings, but this did not hinder me, for I have taken Strings & tyed round to keep them on.

He finding no hard Usage could alter my resolution, neither threatening to beat me, nor doing it, for he several times Struck me with sore Blows, which I Endeavoured to bear with Patience, believing the time would Come when he would see I was in the right (which he Accordingly Did), he once came up to me & took out his pen knife saying, "if you offer to go to Meeting tomorrow, with this knife I'll cripple you, for you shall not be a Quaker." I made him no Answer, but when Morning came, set out as Usual & he was not Suffered to hurt me. In Despair of recovering me himself, he now flew to the Priest for help and told him I had been a very Religious Woman in the way of the Church of England, was a member of it, & had a good Certificate from Long Island, but now was bewitched and turn'd Quaker, which almost broke his heart. He therefore Desired as he was one who had the Care of souls, he would Come and pay me a Visit and use his Endeavours to reclaim me & hoped by the Blessing of God it would be done. The Priest Consented to Come, the time was Set, which was to be that Day two Weeks, for he said he could not come Sooner. My Husband Came home extremely Pleased, & told me of it, at which I smiled Saying, "I hope to be Enabled to give him a reason for the hope that is in me," at the same time believing the Priest would never Trouble me (nor ever did).

Before his Appointed time came it was required of me in a more Publick manner to Confess to the world what I was and to give up in Prayer in a Meeting, the sight of which & the power that attended it made me Tremble, & I could not hold my Self still. I now again desired Death & would have freely given up my Natural Life a Ransom; & what made it harder to me I was not yet taken under the care of Friends, & what kept me from requesting it was for fear I might be overcome & bring a Scandal on the Society. I begged to be Excused till I was joyned to Friends & then I would give up freely, to which I receiv'd this Answer, as tho' I had heard a Distinct Voice: "I am a Covenant keeping God, and the word that I spoke to thee when I found thee In Distress, even that I would never leave thee nor forsake thee If thou would be obedient to what I should make known to thee, I will Assuredly make good: but if thou refuse, my Spirit shall not always strive; fear not, I will make way for thee through all thy difficulties, which shall be many for my name's Sake, but be thou faithfull & I will give thee a Crown of Life." I being then Sure it was God that Spoke said, "thy will O God, be done, I am in thy hand; do with me according to thy Word," & gave up. But after it was over the Enemy came in like a flood, telling me I had done what I ought not, & Should now bring Dishonour to this People. This gave me a Little Shock, but it did not at this time Last Long.

This Day as Usual I had gone on foot. My Husband (as he afterwards told me) lying on the Bed at home, these Words ran thro' him, "Lord where shall I fly to shun thee &C.,"[7] upon which he arose and seeing it Rain got his horse and Came to fetch me; and Coming just as the Meeting broke up, I got on horseback as quick as possible, least he Should hear what had happened. Nevertheless he heard of it, and as soon as we were got into the woods he began, saying, "What do you mean thus to make my Life unhappy? What, could you not be a Quaker without turning fool after this manner?" I Answered in Tears saying, "my Dear, look on me with Pity, if thou hast any. Canst thou think, that I in the Bloom of my Days, would bear all that thou knowest of & a great deal more that thou knowest not of if I did not believe it to be my Duty?" This took hold of him, & taking my hand he said, "Well, I'll E'en give you up, for I see it don't avail to Strive. If it be of God I can't over throw it, & if it be of your self it will soon fall." I saw tears stand in his Eyes, at which my heart was overcome with Joy, and I would not have Changed Conditions with a Queen.

I already began to reap the fruits of my Obedience, but my Tryal Ended not here, the time being up that the Priest was to come; but no Priest Appeared. My Husband went to fetch him, but he would not come, saying he was busy; which so Displeased my husband, that he'd never go to hear him more, & for Some time went to no place of Worship. Now the Unwearied adversary found out another Scheme, and with it wrought so Strong that I thought all I had gone through but a little to this: It came upon me in such an unexpected manner, in hearing a Woman relate a book she had read in which it was Asserted that Christ was not the son of God. As soon as She had Spoke these words, if a man had spoke I could not have more distinctly heard these words, "no more he is, it's all a fancy & the Contrivance of men," & an horrour of Great Darkness fell upon me, which Continued for three weeks.

The Exercise I was under I am not Able to Express, neither durst I let any know how it was with me. I again sought Desolate Places where I might make my moan, & have Lain whole nights, & don't know that my Eyes were Shut to Sleep. I again thought my self alone, but would not let go my Faith in him, often saying in my heart, "I'll believe till I Die," & kept a hope that he that had Delivered me out of the Paw of the Bear & out of the jaws of the Devouring Lion,[8] would in his own time Deliver me out of his temptation also; which he in Mercy Did, and let me see that this was for my good, in order to Prepare me for future Service which he had for me to Do & that it was Necessary his Ministers

---

7. **"Lord . . . &C.":** See Psalm 139:7: "Whither shall I go from thy spirit? or whither shall I flee from thy presence?"

8. **he that had Delivered . . . Devouring Lion:** Before his battle with Goliath, the champion of the Philistines, the shepherd David declared: "The Lord that delivered me out of the paw of the lion, and out of the paw of the bear, he will deliver me out of the hand of this Philistine" (1 Samuel 17:37).

should be dipt into all States, that thereby they might be able to Speak to all Conditions, for which my Soul was thankfull to him, the God of Mercies, who had at Several times redeemed me from great distress, & I found the truth of his Words, that all things should work together for good to those that Loved & feared him, which I did with my whole heart & hope ever shall while I have a being. This happened just after my first appearance, & Friends had not been to talk with me, nor did they know well what to do till I had appeared again, which was not for some time, when the Monthly Meeting appointed four Friends to give me a Visit, which I was Glad of; and gave them Such Satisfaction, that they left me well Satisfy'd. I then Joyned with Friends.

My Husband still went to no place of Worship. One day he said, "I'd go to Meeting, only I am afraid I shall hear you Clack, which I cannot bear." I used no persuasions, yet when Meeting time Came, he got the horse, took me behind him & went to Meeting: but for several months if he saw me offer to rise, he would go out, till once I got up before he was aware and then (as he afterwards said) he was ashamed to go, & from that time never did, nor hindered me from going to Meetings. And tho' he (poor man) did not take up the Cross, yet his judgement was Convinced: & sometimes in a flood of tears would say, "My Dear, I have seen the Beauty there is in the Truth, & that thou art in the Right, and I Pray God Preserve thee in it. But as for me the Cross is too heavy, I cannot Bear it." I told him, I hoped he that had given me strength Would also favour him: "O!" said he, "I can't bear the Reproach thou Doest, to be Called turncoat & to become a Laughing Stock to the World; but I'll no Longer hinder thee," which I looked on as a great favour, that my way was thus far made easy, and a little hope remained that my Prayers would be heard on his account.

In this Place he had got linked in with some, that he was afraid would make game of him, which Indeed they already Did, asking him when he Designed to Commence Preacher, for that they saw he Intended to turn Quaker, & seemed to Love his Wife better since she did than before (we were now got to a little house by our Selves which tho' Mean, & little to put in it, our Bed no better than Chaff, yet I was truly Content & did not Envy the Rich their Riches; the only Desire I had now was my own preservation, & to be Bless'd with the Reformation of my husband). These men used to Come to our house & there Provoke my husband to Sit up and Drink, some times till near day, while I have been sorrowing in a Stable. As I once sat in this Condition I heard my husband say to his Company, "I can't bear any Longer to Afflict my Poor Wife in this manner, for whatever you may think of her, I do believe she is a good Woman," upon which he came to me and said, "Come in, my Dear; God has Given thee a Deal of Patience. I'll put an End to this Practice;" and so he did, for this was the Last time they sat up at Night.

My Husband now thought that if he was in any Place where it was not known that he'd been so bitter against Friends, he Could do better than here. But I was much against his Moving; fearing it would tend to his hurt, having been for some months much Altered for the Better, & would often in a broken and Affectionate Manner condemn his bad Usage to me: I told him I hoped it had been for my Good, even to the Better Establishing me in the Truth, & therefore would not have him to be Afflicted about it, & According to the Measure of Grace received did what I could both by Example and advice for his good: & my Advice was for him to fight thro' here, fearing he would Grow Weaker and the Enemy Gain advantage over him, if he thus fled: but All I could say did not prevail against his Moving; & hearing of a place at Bordentown [New Jersey] went there, but that did not suit; he then Moved to Mount Holly [New Jersey] & there we Settled. He got a good School & So Did I.

Here we might have Done very well; we soon got our house Prettily furnished for Poor folks; I now began to think I wanted but one thing to complete my Happiness, Viz. the Reformation of my husband, which Alas! I had too much reason to Doubt; for it fell out according to my Fears, & he grew worse here, & took much to Drinking, so that it Seem'd as if my Life was to be a Continual scene of Sorrows & most Earnestly I Pray'd to Almighty God to Endue me with Patience to bear my Afflictions & submit to his Providence, which I can say in Truth I did without murmuring or ever uttering an unsavoury expression to the Best of my Knowledge; except once, my husband Coming home a little in drink (in which frame he was very fractious) & finding me at Work by a Candle, came to me, put it out & fetching me a box on the Ear said, "you don't Earn your light;" on which unkind Usage (for he had not struck me for Two Years so it went hard with me) I utter'd these Rash Expressions, "thou art a Vile Man," & was a little angry, but soon recovered & was Sorry for it; he struck me again, which I received without so much as a word in return, & that likewise Displeased him: so he went on in a Distracted like manner uttering Several Expressions that bespoke Despair, as that he now believed that he was predestinated to damnation, & he did not care how soon God would Strike him Dead, & the like. I durst say but Little; at Length in the Bitterness of my Soul, I Broke out in these Words, "Lord look Down on mine Afflictions and deliver me by some means or Other." I was answered, I Should Soon be, & so I was, but in such a manner, as I Verily thought It would have killed me. In a little time he went to Burlington where he got in Drink, & Enlisted him Self to go a Common soldier to Cuba anno 1740.

I had drank many bitter Cups — but this Seemed to Exceed them all for indeed my very Senses Seemed Shaken; I now a Thousand times blamed my Self for making Such an unadvised request, fearing I had Displeased God in it, & tho' he had Granted it, it was in Displeasure, & Suffered to be in this manner to Punish me; Tho' I can truly say I never Desired his Death, no more than my own, nay not so much. I have since had cause to believe his mind was benefitted by the Undertaking, (which hope makes up for all I have Suffered from him) being Informed he did in the army what he Could not Do at home (Viz) Suffered for the Testimony of Truth. When they Came to prepare for an Engagement, he refused to fight; for which he was whipt and brought before the General, who asked him why he Enlisted if he would not fight; "I did it," said he, "in a drunken frolick, when the Divel had the Better of me, but my judgment is convinced that I ought not, neither will I whatever I Suffer; I have but one Life, & you may take that if you Please, but I'll never take up Arms."[9] They used him with much Cruelty to make him yield but Could not, by means whereof he was So Disabled that the General sent him to the Hospital at Chelsea, where in Nine Months time he Died & I hope made a Good End, for which I prayed both night & Day, till I heard of his Death.

---

9. **"I'll never take up Arms":** Quakers are pacifists who reject the use of force to settle personal or national disputes.

Thus I thought it my duty to say what I could in his Favour, as I have been obliged to say so much of his hard usage to me, all which I hope Did me good, & altho' he was so bad, yet had Several Good Properties, & I never thought him the Worst of Men. He was one I Lov'd & had he let Religion have its Perfect work, I should have thought my Self Happy in the Lowest State of Life; & I've Cause to bless God, who Enabled me in the Station of a Wife to Do my Duty & now a Widow to Submit to his Will, always believing everything he doeth to be right. May he in all Stations of Life so Preserve me by the arm of Divine Power, that I may never forget his tender mercies to me, the Rememberance whereof doth often Bow my Soul, in Humility before his Throne, saying, "Lord, what was I; that thou should have reveal'd to me the Knowledge of thy Truth, & do so much for me, who Deserved thy Displeasure rather, But in me hast thou shewn thy Long Suffering & tender Mercy; may thou O God be Glorifyed and I abased for it is thy own Works that praise thee, and of a Truth to the humble Soul thou Makest every bitter thing Sweet. The End.

[1774, 1990]

John Woolman

[1720–1772]

John Woolman was born in Burlington County, New Jersey, on October 19, 1720, the fourth of thirteen children of Samuel and Elizabeth Burr Woolman. His parents, successful farmers, were part of a colony of Quakers who had settled in the counties near Philadelphia. Woolman was sent to a village school and, with the encouragement of his parents, developed life-long habits of reading and study. He worked on the family farm until he was twenty-one, when he left to work as a tailor's apprentice in a retail store in nearby Mount Holly. There, he gained his first direct experience of slavery, which was widespread in eighteenth-century New Jersey. When he was asked to draw up a bill of sale for a woman owned by his employer, Woolman reluctantly agreed. Afterward, however, he told his employer that he believed "slave-keeping to be a practice inconsistent with the Christian religion," as Woolman later wrote in his journal. In his late twenties, Woolman opened his own store. He also studied law so that he could prepare deeds and wills.

As his retail business grew, Woolman became increasingly concerned about the conflict between material success and the simple, spiritual life advocated by the Quakers. He consequently began to curtail his business and devote more time to the activities of the Society of Friends. After he became a Quaker minister, Woolman traveled frequently to meetings, speaking against the preoccupation with luxury and wealth, the use of force, and war. He also sought to convince his fellow Quakers to abandon slaveholding, which was then a common and accepted practice among members of the Society of Friends. Both publicly and privately, Woolman lived by his convictions, refusing to wear dyed clothes because of the poor conditions for workers in dye factories and giving up the use of sugar

John Woolman

This sketch is thought to be the only known portrait of Woolman, possibly drawn from memory by his friend Robert Smith III, also of Burlington, New Jersey.

because of the exploitation of slave labor on sugar plantations in the West Indies. In 1749, he married a longtime friend and fellow Quaker, Sarah Ellis. He later gave up his retail business altogether and supported his family by working as a tailor, occasionally as a teacher, and as a farmer. In 1752, Woolman began his journal, which would become his most important and influential work, though he also wrote numerous letters as well as essays on the slave trade and on topics such as the importance of silent worship. But he spent most of his time speaking and serving as a Quaker missionary, participating in over thirty missions throughout the colonies, including the South. While on a trip to England to participate in Quaker meetings, Woolman contracted smallpox and died in London on October 7, 1772.

Reading Woolman's *Journal*.   Inspired by the spiritual autobiography of George Fox (1624–1691), the founder of the Society of Friends whose *Journal* was published in 1694, many Quakers wrote similar accounts of their experiences. Woolman began his journal in 1752 and continued to add to it until shortly before his death in 1772. Like Fox and other Quakers, Woolman provided few details of his daily life or personal relationships. Instead, he focused on his spiritual development, tracing his progress from early doubts and struggles through the growing religious convictions that culminated in his work as a minister and missionary. The journal was first published in Philadelphia in 1774 as *A Journal of the Life, Gospel Labours, and Christian Experiences of That Faithful Minister of Jesus Christ, John Woolman, Late of Mount-Holly, in the Province of New-Jersey*. Since then, it has never been out of print, and it has been read and valued by generations of Americans for its luminous account of the development of the inner life of an individual. Its admirers have included writers such as Ralph Waldo Emerson, Walt Whitman, and the Quaker poet John Greenleaf Whittier, who published an edition of the journal in 1871. In his preface to that edition, Whittier explained that the *Journal* "has a sweetness as of violets," symbols of devotion whose purity and simplicity are mirrored in Woolman's life and writings. The text of the following selections is taken from *The Journal and Major Essays of John Woolman*, edited by Phillips P. Moulton (1971).

From THE JOURNAL OF JOHN WOOLMAN

Chapter I

1720–1742

I have often felt a motion of love to leave some hints in writing of my experience of the goodness of God, and now, in the thirty-sixth year of my age, I begin this work. I was born in Northampton, in Burlington County in West Jersey, A.D. 1720, and before I was seven years old I began to be acquainted with the operations of divine love. Through the care of my parents, I was taught to read near as soon as I was capable of it, and as I went from school one Seventh Day,[1] I remember, while my companions went to play by the way, I went forward out of sight; and sitting down, I read the twenty-second chapter of the Revelations: "He showed me a river of water, clear as crystal, proceeding out of the throne of God and the Lamb, etc." And in reading it my mind was drawn to seek after that pure habitation which I then believed God had prepared for his servants. The place where I sat and the sweetness that attended my mind remains fresh in my memory.

This and the like gracious visitations had that effect upon me, that when boys used ill language it troubled me, and through the continued mercies of God I was preserved from it. The pious instructions of my parents were often fresh in my mind when I happened amongst wicked children, and was of use to me. My parents, having a large family of children, used frequently on First Days after meeting[2] to put us to read in the Holy Scriptures or some religious books, one after another, the rest sitting by without much conversation, which I have since often thought was a good practice. From what I had read and heard, I believed there had been in past ages people who walked in uprightness before God in a degree exceeding any that I knew, or heard of, now living; and the apprehension of there being less steadiness and firmness amongst people in this age than in past ages often troubled me while I was a child.

I had a dream about the ninth year of my age as follows: I saw the moon rise near the west and run a regular course eastward, so swift that in about a quarter of an hour she reached our meridian, when there descended from her a small cloud on a direct line to the earth, which lighted on a pleasant green about twenty yards from the door of my father's house (in which I thought I stood) and was immediately turned into a beautiful green tree. The moon appeared to run on with equal swiftness and soon set in the east, at which time the sun arose at the place where it commonly does in the summer, and shining with full radiance in a serene air, it appeared as pleasant a morning as ever I saw.

All this time I stood still in the door in an awful[3] frame of mind, and I observed that as heat increased by the rising sun, it wrought so powerfully on the little green tree that the leaves gradually withered; and before noon it appeared dry and dead. There then appeared a being, small of size, full of strength and resolution, moving swift from the north, southward, called a sun worm.[4]

Another thing remarkable in my childhood was that once, going to a neighbour's house, I saw on the way a robin sitting on her nest; and as I came near she went off, but having young ones, flew about and with many cries expressed her concern for them. I stood and threw stones at her, till one striking her, she fell down dead. At first I was pleased with the exploit, but after a few minutes was seized with horror, as having in a sportive way killed an innocent creature while she was careful for her young. I beheld her lying dead and thought those young ones for which she was so careful must now

---

1. **Seventh Day:** Saturday. To avoid references to pagan deities, Quakers referred to the days of the week and the months by number.
2. **meeting:** Quakers referred to their worship services as meetings or assemblies; these were held on the first day of the week (Sunday).
3. **awful:** Full of awe and reverence.
4. **sun worm:** *Worm* was an early term for a dragon or snake, which in Woolman's dream is generated by the intense light of the midday sun.

perish for want of their dam to nourish them; and after some painful considerations on the subject, I climbed up the tree, took all the young birds and killed them, supposing that better than to leave them to pine away and die miserably, and believed in this case that Scripture proverb was fulfilled, "The tender mercies of the wicked are cruel."[5] I then went on my errand, but for some hours could think of little else but the cruelties I had committed, and was much troubled.

Thus he whose tender mercies are over all his works hath placed a principle in the human mind which incites to exercise goodness toward every living creature; and this being singly attended to, people become tender-hearted and sympathizing, but being frequently and totally rejected, the mind shuts itself up in a contrary disposition.

About the twelfth year of my age, my father being abroad, my mother reproved me for some misconduct, to which I made an undutiful reply; and the next First Day as I was with my father returning from meeting, he told me he understood I had behaved amiss to my mother and advised me to be more careful in future. I knew myself blameable, and in shame and confusion remained silent. Being thus awakened to a sense of my wickedness, I felt remorse in my mind, and getting home I retired and prayed to the Lord to forgive me, and do not remember that I ever after that spoke unhandsomely to either of my parents, however foolish in other things.

Having attained the age of sixteen years, I began to love wanton company, and though I was preserved from profane language or scandalous conduct, still I perceived a plant in me which produced much wild grapes. Yet my merciful Father forsook me not utterly, but at times through his grace I was brought seriously to consider my ways, and the sight of my backsliding affected me with sorrow. But for want of rightly attending to the reproofs of instruction, vanity was added to vanity, and repentance to repentance; upon the whole my mind was more and more alienated from the Truth, and I hastened toward destruction.[6] While I meditate on the gulf toward which I travelled and reflect on my youthful disobedience, for these things I weep; mine eye runneth down with water.

Advancing in age the number of my acquaintance increased, and thereby my way grew more difficult. Though I had heretofore found comfort in reading the Holy Scriptures and thinking on heavenly things, I was now estranged therefrom. I knew I was going from the flock of Christ and had no resolution to return; hence serious reflections were uneasy to me and youthful vanities and diversions my greatest pleasure. Running in this road I found many like myself, and we associated in that which is reverse to true friendship.

But in this swift race it pleased God to visit me with sickness, so that I doubted of recovering. And then did darkness, horror, and amazement with full force seize me, even when my pain and distress of body was very great. I thought it would have been better for me never to have had a being than to see the day which I now saw. I was filled with confusion, and in great affliction both of mind and body I lay and bewailed myself. I had not confidence to lift up my cries to God, whom I had thus offended, but in a deep sense

---

5. "The . . . cruel": Proverbs 12:10.
6. destruction: A sinful life.

of my great folly I was humbled before him, and at length that Word which is as a fire and a hammer broke and dissolved my rebellious heart. And then my cries were put up in contrition, and in the multitude of his mercies I found inward relief, and felt a close engagement that if he was pleased to restore my health, I might walk humbly before him.

After my recovery this exercise remained with me a considerable time; but by degrees giving way to youthful vanities, they gained strength, and getting with wanton young people I lost ground. The Lord had been very gracious and spoke peace to me in the time of my distress, and I now most ungratefully turned again to folly, on which account at times I felt sharp reproof but did not get low enough to cry for help. I was not so hardy as to commit things scandalous, but to exceed in vanity and promote mirth was my chief study. Still I retained a love and esteem for pious people, and their company brought an awe upon me.

My dear parents several times admonished me in the fear of the Lord, and their admonition entered into my heart and had a good effect for a season, but not getting deep enough to pray rightly, the tempter when he came found entrance. I remember once, having spent a part of the day in wantonness, as I went to bed at night there lay in a window near my bed a Bible, which I opened, and first cast my eye on the text, "We lie down in our shame, and our confusion covers us."[7] This I knew to be my case, and meeting with so unexpected a reproof, I was somewhat affected with it and went to bed under remorse of conscience, which I soon cast off again.

Thus time passed on; my heart was replenished with mirth and wantonness, while pleasing scenes of vanity were presented to my imagination till I attained the age of eighteen years, near which time I felt the judgments of God in my soul like a consuming fire, and looking over my past life the prospect was moving. I was often sad and longed to be delivered from those vanities; then again my heart was strongly inclined to them, and there was in me a sore conflict. At times I turned to folly, and then again sorrow and confusion took hold of me. In a while I resolved totally to leave off some of my vanities, but there was a secret reserve in my heart of the more refined part of them, and I was not low enough to find true peace. Thus for some months I had great trouble, there remaining in me an unsubjected will which rendered my labours fruitless, till at length through the merciful continuance of heavenly visitations I was made to bow down in spirit before the Lord.

I remember one evening I had spent some time in reading a pious author, and walking out alone I humbly prayed to the Lord for his help, that I might be delivered from all those vanities which so ensnared me. Thus being brought low, he helped me; and as I learned to bear the cross I felt refreshment to come from his presence; but not keeping in that strength which gave victory, I lost ground again, the sense of which greatly affected me; and I sought deserts and lonely places and there with tears did confess my sins to God and humbly craved help of him. And I may say with reverence he was near to me in my troubles, and in those times of humiliation opened my ear to discipline.

---

7. "We ... us": Jeremiah 3:25.

I was now led to look seriously at the means by which I was drawn from the pure Truth, and learned this: that if I would live in the life which the faithful servants of God lived in, I must not go into company as heretofore in my own will, but all the cravings of sense must be governed by a divine principle. In times of sorrow and abasement these instructions were sealed upon me, and I felt the power of Christ prevail over selfish desires, so that I was preserved in a good degree of steadiness. And being young and believing at that time that a single life was best for me, I was strengthened to keep from such company as had often been a snare to me.

I kept steady to meetings, spent First Days after noon chiefly in reading the Scriptures and other good books, and was early convinced in my mind that true religion consisted in an inward life, wherein the heart doth love and reverence God the Creator and learn to exercise true justice and goodness, not only toward all men but also toward the brute creatures; that as the mind was moved on an inward principle to love God as an invisible, incomprehensible being, on the same principle it was moved to love him in all his manifestations in the visible world; that as by his breath the flame of life was kindled in all animal and sensitive creatures, to say we love God as unseen and at the same time exercise cruelty toward the least creature moving by his life, or by life derived from him, was a contradiction in itself.

I found no narrowness respecting sects and opinions, but believed that sincere, upright-hearted people in every Society who truly loved God were accepted of him.

As I lived under the cross[8] and simply followed the openings of Truth,[9] my mind from day to day was more enlightened; my former acquaintance was left to judge of me as they would, for I found it safest for me to live in private and keep these things sealed up in my own breast.

While I silently ponder on that change wrought in me, I find no language equal to it nor any means to convey to another a clear idea of it. I looked upon the works of God in this visible creation and an awfulness covered me; my heart was tender and often contrite, and a universal love to my fellow creatures increased in me. This will be understood by such who have trodden in the same path. Some glances of real beauty may be seen in their faces who dwell in true meekness. There is a harmony in the sound of that voice to which divine love gives utterance, and some appearance of right order in their temper and conduct whose passions are fully regulated. Yet all these do not fully show forth that inward life to such who have not felt it, but this white stone and new name is known rightly to such only who have it.[10]

Now though I had been thus strengthened to bear the cross, I still found myself in great danger, having many weaknesses attending me and strong temptations to wrestle with, in the feeling whereof I frequently withdrew into private places and often with tears besought the Lord to help me, whose gracious ear was open to my cry.

---

8. **under the cross:** In accordance with the teachings of Christ.
9. **openings of Truth:** Quakers believe that, if they wait silently, God may speak directly to the faithful in moments of revelation called "openings."
10. **white stone . . . who have it:** See Revelations 2:17: "He that hath an ear, let him hear what the Spirit saith unto the churches; To him that overcometh will I give to eat of the hidden manna, and will give him a white stone, and in the stone a new name written, which no man knoweth saving he that receiveth it."

All this time I lived with my parents and wrought on the plantation,[11] and having had schooling pretty well for a planter, I used to improve in winter evenings and other leisure times. And being now in the twenty-first year of my age, a man in much business shopkeeping and baking asked me if I would hire with him to tend shop and keep books. I acquainted my father with the proposal, and after some deliberation it was agreed for me to go.

At home I had lived retired, and now having a prospect of being much in the way of company, I felt frequent and fervent cries in my heart to God, the Father of Mercies, that he would preserve me from all taint and corruption, that in this more public employ I might serve him, my gracious Redeemer, in that humility and self-denial with which I had been in a small degree exercised in a very private life.

The man who employed me furnished a shop in Mount Holly, about five miles from my father's house and six from his own, and there I lived alone and tended his shop. Shortly after my settlement here I was visited by several young people, my former acquaintance, who knew not but vanities would be as agreeable to me now as ever; and at these times I cried to the Lord in secret for wisdom and strength, for I felt myself encompassed with difficulties and had fresh occasion to bewail the follies of time past in contracting a familiarity with a libertine people. And as I had now left my father's house outwardly, I found my Heavenly Father to be merciful to me beyond what I can express.

By day I was much amongst people and had many trials to go through, but in evenings I was mostly alone and may with thankfulness acknowledge that in those times the spirit of supplication was often poured upon me, under which I was frequently exercised and felt my strength renewed.

In a few months after I came here, my master bought several Scotch menservants[12] from on board a vessel and brought them to Mount Holly to sell, one of which was taken sick and died. The latter part of his sickness he, being delirious, used to curse and swear most sorrowfully, and after he was buried I was left to sleep alone the next night in the same chamber where he died. I perceived in me a timorousness. I knew, however, I had not injured the man but assisted in taking care of him according to my capacity, and was not free to ask anyone on that occasion to sleep with me. Nature was feeble, but every trial was a fresh incitement to give myself up wholly to the service of God, for I found no helper like him in times of trouble.

After a while my former acquaintance gave over expecting me as one of their company, and I began to be known to some whose conversation was helpful to me. And now, as I had experienced the love of God through Jesus Christ to redeem me from many pollutions and to be a succour to me through a sea of conflicts, with which no person was fully acquainted, and as my heart was often enlarged in this heavenly principle, I felt a tender compassion for the youth who remained entangled in snares like those which had entangled me. From one month to another this love and tenderness increased, and my mind was more strongly engaged for the good of my fellow creatures.

---

11. **wrought on the plantation:** Worked on the family farm.
12. **menservants:** Woolman's master had bought the contracts of men whose passage to the colonies had been paid in exchange for a contracted number of years of work as indentured servants.

I went to meetings in an awful frame of mind and endeavoured to be inwardly acquainted with the language of the True Shepherd. And one day being under a strong exercise of spirit, I stood up and said some words in a meeting, but not keeping close to the divine opening,[13] I said more than was required of me; and being soon sensible of my error, I was afflicted in mind some weeks without any light or comfort, even to that degree that I could take satisfaction in nothing. I remembered God and was troubled, and in the depth of my distress he had pity upon me and sent the Comforter. I then felt forgiveness for my offense, and my mind became calm and quiet, being truly thankful to my gracious Redeemer for his mercies. And after this, feeling the spring of divine love opened and a concern to speak, I said a few words in a meeting, in which I found peace. This I believe was about six weeks from the first time, and as I was thus humbled and disciplined under the cross, my understanding became more strengthened to distinguish the language of the pure Spirit which inwardly moves upon the heart and taught [me] to wait in silence sometimes many weeks together, until I felt that rise which prepares the creature to stand like a trumpet through which the Lord speaks to his flock.

From an inward purifying, and steadfast abiding under it, springs a lively operative desire for the good of others. All faithful people are not called to the public ministry, but whoever are, are called to minister of that which they have tasted and handled spiritually. The outward modes of worship are various, but wherever men are true ministers of Jesus Christ it is from the operation of his spirit upon their hearts, first purifying them and thus giving them a feeling sense of the conditions of others. This truth was early fixed in my mind, and I was taught to watch the pure opening and to take heed lest while I was standing to speak, my own will should get uppermost and cause me to utter words from worldly wisdom and depart from the channel of the true gospel ministry.

In the management of my outward affairs I may say with thankfulness I found Truth to be my support and I was respected in my master's family, who came to live in Mount Holly within two year after my going there.

About the twenty-third year of my age, I had many fresh and heavenly openings in respect to the care and providence of the Almighty over his creatures in general, and over man as the most noble amongst those which are visible. And being clearly convinced in my judgment that to place my whole trust in God was best for me, I felt renewed engagements that in all things I might act on an inward principle of virtue and pursue worldly business no further than as Truth opened my way therein.

About the time called Christmas I observed many people from the country and dwellers in town who, resorting to the public houses, spent their time in drinking and vain sports, tending to corrupt one another, on which account I was much troubled. At one house in particular there was much disorder, and I believed it was a duty laid on me to go and speak to the master of that house. I considered I was young and that several elderly Friends in town had opportunity to see these things, and though I would gladly have been excused, yet I could not feel my mind clear.

---

13. not keeping . . . opening: When Quakers speak at meetings, they are expected to focus on the revelation from God and not comment on worldly matters.

The exercise was heavy, and as I was reading what the Almighty said to Ezekiel, respecting his duty as a watchman,[14] the matter was set home more clearly; and then with prayer and tears I besought the Lord for his assistance, who in loving-kindness gave me a resigned heart. Then at a suitable opportunity I went to the public house, and seeing the man amongst a company, I went to him and told him I wanted to speak with him; so we went aside, and there in the fear and dread of the Almighty I expressed to him what rested on my mind, which he took kindly, and afterward showed more regard to me than before. In a few years after, he died middle-aged, and I often thought that had I neglected my duty in that case it would have given me great trouble, and I was humbly thankful to my gracious Father, who had supported me herein.

My employer, having a Negro woman, sold her and directed me to write a bill of sale, the man being waiting who bought her. The thing was sudden, and though the thoughts of writing an instrument of slavery for one of my fellow creatures felt uneasy,[15] yet I remembered I was hired by the year, that it was my master who directed me to do it, and that it was an elderly man, a member of our Society, who bought her; so through weakness I gave way and wrote it, but at the executing it, I was so afflicted in my mind that I said before my master and the Friend that I believed slavekeeping to be a practice inconsistent with the Christian religion. This in some degree abated my uneasiness, yet as often as I reflected seriously upon it I thought I should have been clearer if I had desired to be excused from it as a thing against my conscience, for such it was. And some time after this a young man of our Society spake to me to write an instrument of slavery, he having lately taken a Negro into his house. I told him I was not easy to write it, for though many kept slaves in our Society, as in others, I still believed the practice was not right, and desired to be excused from writing [it]. I spoke to him in good will, and he told me that keeping slaves was not altogether agreeable to his mind, but that the slave being a gift made to his wife, he had accepted of her.

From Chapter III

1749-1756

Scrupling to do writings relative to keeping slaves having been a means of sundry small trials to me, in which I have so evidently felt my own will set aside that I think it good to mention a few of them. Tradesmen and retailers of goods, who depend on their business for a living, are naturally inclined to keep the good will of their customers; nor is it a pleasant thing for young men to be under a necessity to question the judgment or honesty of elderly men, and more especially of such who have a fair reputation. Deep-rooted customs, though wrong, are not easily altered, but it is the duty of everyone to be firm in that which they certainly know is right for them. A charitable, benevolent man, well acquainted with a Negro, may, I believe, under some certain circumstances keep him in

14. Ezekiel . . . watchman: See Ezekiel 3:17: "Son of man, I have made thee a watchman unto the house of Israel: therefore hear the word at my mouth, and give them warning from me."
15. felt uneasy: Woolman's conscience was not comfortable with writing the bill of sale for a person.

his family as a servant on no other motives than the Negro's good; but man, as man, knows not what shall be after him, nor hath he any assurance that his children will attain to that perfection in wisdom and goodness necessary in every absolute governor. Hence it is clear to me that I ought not to be the scribe where wills are drawn in which some children are made absolute masters over others during life.

About this time an ancient man of good esteem in the neighbourhood came to my house to get his will wrote. He had young Negroes, and I asking him privately how he purposed to dispose of them, he told me. I then said, "I cannot write thy will without breaking my own peace," and respectfully gave him my reasons for it. He signified that he had a choice that I should have wrote it, but as I could not consistent with my conscience, he did not desire it and so he got it wrote by some other person. And a few years after, there being great alterations in his family, he came again to get me to write his will. His Negroes were yet young, and his son, to whom he intended to give them, was since he first spoke to me, from a libertine become a sober young man; and he supposed that I would have been free on that account to write it. We had much friendly talk on the subject and then deferred it, and a few days after, he came again and directed their freedom, and so I wrote his will.

Near the time the last-mentioned friend first spoke to me, a neighbour received a bad bruise in his body and sent for me to bleed him, which being done he desired me to write his will. I took notes, and amongst other things he told me to which of his children he gave his young Negro. I considered the pain and distress he was in and knew not how it would end, so I wrote his will, save only that part concerning his slave, and carrying it to his bedside read it to him and then told him in a friendly way that I could not write any instruments by which my fellow creatures were made slaves, without bringing trouble on my own mind. I let him know that I charged nothing for what I had done and desired to be excused from doing the other part in the way he proposed. Then we had a serious conference on the subject, and at length, he agreeing to set her free, I finished his will.

Having found drawings in my mind to visit Friends on Long Island, and having got a certificate from our Monthly Meeting, I set off 12th day, 5th month, 1756. When I reached the island I lodged the first night at the house of my dear friend Richard Hallett. The next day being the first of the week, I was at their meeting, in which we had experience of the renewed manifestations of the love of Jesus Christ, to the comfort of the honest-hearted. I went that night to Flushing, and the next day in company with my beloved friend Matthew Franklin we crossed the ferry at White Stone, were at three meetings on that side the water, and then came on to the island, where I spent the remainder of the week in visiting meetings. The Lord I believe hath a people in those parts who are honestly concerned to serve him, but many I fear are too much clogged with the things of this life and do not come forward bearing the cross in such faithfulness as the Almighty calls for.

My mind was deeply engaged in this visit, both in public and private; and at several places where I was, on observing that they had slaves, I found myself under a necessity in a friendly way to labour with them on that subject, expressing as way opened the inconsistency of that practice with the purity of the Christian religion and the ill effects of it manifested amongst us.

The latter end of the week their Yearly Meeting began, at which were our Friends John Scarborough, Jane Hoskins, and Susanna Brown from Pennsylvania. The public meetings were large and measurably favoured with divine goodness.

The exercise of my mind at this meeting was chiefly on account of those who were considered as the foremost rank in the Society, and in a meeting of ministers and elders, way opened that I expressed in some measure what lay upon me; and at a time when Friends were met for transacting public business, we sitting a while silent, I felt a weight on my mind and stood up; and through the gracious regard of our Heavenly Father, strength was given fully to clear my mind of a burden which for some days had been increasing upon me.

Through the humbling dispensations of divine providence men are sometimes fitted for his service. The messages of the prophet Jeremiah were so disagreeable to the people and so reverse to the spirit they lived in that he became the object of their reproach and in the weakness of nature thought to desist from his prophetic office, but saith he: "His word was in my heart as a burning fire shut up in my bones, and I was weary with forebearing and could not stay."[16] I saw at this time that if I was honest to declare that which Truth opened in me, I could not please all men, and laboured to be content in the way of my duty, however disagreeable to my own inclination. After this I went homeward, taking Woodbridge and Plainfield in my way, in both which meetings the pure influence of divine love was manifested, in a humbling sense whereof I went home, having been out about 24 days and rode about 316 miles.

While I was out on this journey my heart was much affected with a sense of the state of the churches in our southern provinces, and believing the Lord was calling me to some further labour amongst them, I was bowed in reverence before him, with fervent desires that I might find strength to resign myself up to his heavenly will.

Until the year 1756 I continued to retail goods, besides following my trade as a tailor, about which time I grew uneasy on account of my business growing too cumbersome. I began with selling trimmings for garments and from thence proceeded to sell clothes and linens, and at length having got a considerable shop of goods, my trade increased every year and the road to large business appeared open; but I felt a stop in my mind.

Through the mercies of the Almighty I had in a good degree learned to be content with a plain way of living. I had but a small family, that on serious consideration I believed Truth did not require me to engage in much cumbrous affairs. It had been my general practice to buy and sell things really useful. Things that served chiefly to please the vain mind in people I was not easy to trade in, seldom did it, and whenever I did I found it weaken me as a Christian.

The increase of business became my burden, for though my natural inclination was toward merchandise, yet I believed Truth required me to live more free from outward cumbers, and there was now a strife in my mind between the two; and in this exercise my prayers were put up to the Lord, who graciously heard me and gave me a heart resigned to his holy will. Then I lessened my outward business, and as I had opportunity

---

16. "His . . . stay": Jeremiah 20:9.

told my customers of my intentions that they might consider what shop to turn to, and so in a while wholly laid down merchandise, following my trade as a tailor, myself only, having no apprentice. I also had a nursery of apple trees, in which I employed some of my time – hoeing, grafting, trimming, and inoculating.

In merchandise it is the custom where I lived to sell chiefly on credit, and poor people often get in debt, and when payment is expected, not having wherewith to pay, their creditors often sue for it at law. Having often observed occurrences of this kind, I found it good for me to advise poor people to take such goods as were most useful and not costly.

In the time of trading, I had an opportunity of seeing that too liberal a use of spirituous liquors and the custom of wearing too costly apparel lead some people into great inconveniences, and these two things appear to be often connected one with the other. For by not attending to that use of things which is consistent with universal righteousness, there is an increase of labour which extends beyond what our Heavenly Father intends for us. And by great labour, and often by much sweating in the heat, there is even amongst such who are not drunkards a craving of some liquors to revive the spirits: that partly by the wanton, luxurious drinking of some, and partly by the drinkings of others led to it through immoderate labour, very great quantities of rum are every year expended in our colonies, the greater part of which we should have no need did we steadily attend to pure wisdom.

Where men take pleasure in feeling their minds elevated with strong drink and so indulge their appetite as to disorder their understandings, neglect their duty as members in a family or civil society, and cast off all pretense to religion, their case is much to be pitied. And where such whose lives are for the most part regular, and whose examples have a strong influence on the minds of others, adhere to some customs which strongly draw toward the use of more strong liquor than pure wisdom directs to the use of, this also, as it hinders the spreading of the spirit of meekness and strengthens the hands of the more excessive drinkers, is a case to be lamented.

As the least degree of luxury hath some connection with evil, for those who profess to be disciples of Christ and are looked upon as leaders of the people, to have that mind in them which was also in him, and so stand separate from every wrong way, is a means of help to the weaker. As I have sometimes been much spent in the heat and taken spirits to revive me, I have found by experience that in such circumstance the mind is not so calm nor I so fitly disposed for divine meditation as when all such extremes are avoided, and have felt an increasing care to attend to that Holy Spirit which sets right bounds to our desires and leads those who faithfully follow it to apply all the gifts of divine providence to the purposes for which they were intended. Did such who have the care of great estates attend with singleness of heart to this Heavenly Instructor, which so opens and enlarges the mind that men love their neighbours as themselves, they would have wisdom given them to manage without finding occasion to employ some people in the luxuries of life or to make it necessary for others to labour too hard. But for want of steadily regarding this principle of divine love, a selfish spirit takes place in the minds of people, which is attended with darkness and manifold confusions in the world.

[1774, 1971]

Samson Occom

[1723-1792]

Samson Occom was born in 1723 near New London, Connecticut. In his autobiography, Occom later described the "wandering life" of his parents, members of the Mohegan tribe, who raised him in "Heathenism." Although they were allies of the English, by the time of Occom's birth the Mohegan were struggling with the constant encroachment of the colonists as well as the devastating effects of diseases such as smallpox and measles. During Occom's childhood, the population of the tribe dwindled to a few hundred people. At the age of sixteen, Occom heard some of the itinerant evangelists associated with the religious revival known as the Great Awakening (1735-45). These "Extraordinary Ministers," as he called them, included Eleazer Wheelock, George Whitefield, and James Davenport, who traveled throughout New England seeking to revive piety and religious fervor among the Congregationalist churches. The young Occom was deeply moved and converted to Christianity. He also began to teach himself to read and write. Eager to learn more, Occom became the first student at a college-preparatory school Wheelock established in Lebanon, Connecticut. In only four years at the school, 1743-47, Occom swiftly gained fluency in English and proficiency in Latin, Greek, and Hebrew.

Nathaniel Smibert, *An Indian Priest*

Only recently identified as Samson Occom, this portrait was painted by Smibert sometime in the period 1751-56, when Occom was a schoolmaster and preacher among the Montauk tribe on Long Island.

Although his poor health and failing eyesight prevented him from continuing his studies, Occom became a noted minister and advocate for the Indians. In 1749, he moved to eastern Long Island to become the schoolmaster of the Montauk tribe, among whom Occom taught and preached for the following decade. He married a Montauk woman, Mary Fowler, with whom he had ten children. In 1759, Occom was ordained as a minister by the Presbytery of Long Island. He then became an itinerant minister in southern New England and, in 1761, a missionary to the Oneida in central New York. By 1764, Occom and his family were living in Connecticut, assisting in raising money for Moor's Indian Charity School, which Wheelock had established in 1753 to train Indian missionaries for work among their own people. At Wheelock's request, Occom undertook a successful fund-raising campaign in England, where he preached over three hundred sermons. At the height of his fame, Occom modestly hoped that he would be rewarded with a ministry among the Mohegan. But he was not offered any position, and his understandable bitterness was reflected in his autobiography, written

I have this day received your obliging kind epistle, and am greatly satisfied with your reasons respecting negroes, and think highly reasonable what you offer in vindication of their natural rights.

— *Phillis Wheatley*

shortly after his return to New England in 1768. To his further dismay, Wheelock decided to move his school to Hanover, New Hampshire, where he used the funds Occom had raised to establish Dartmouth College.

Concerned that his people would not benefit from the new college, Occom ended his relationship with Wheelock and pursued his own plans to improve their lives. He continued to preach, and he published *A Sermon Preached at the Execution of Moses Paul* (1772), a fellow Christian Mohegan who murdered a man while drunk. An execution sermon, designed to condemn the person who was about to die and to serve as a cautionary tale for the audience, was a common and popular form. Occom's emphasis in the sermon on the need for temperance also mirrored a common concern of civil and religious leaders, who feared that excessive drinking among both Native Americans and European settlers posed a threat to the social stability of colonial America. The published sermon went through nineteen editions, and Occom also published *A Choice Collection of Spiritual Hymns* (1774). But he devoted most of his energies to a plan to establish a new settlement of Christian Indians on the lands of the Oneida tribe in central New York. The plan was finally realized in 1785, and Occom became the teacher in the new community, called Brothertown. Two years later, when the community established the first Presbyterian church organized solely by Indians, Occom became its minister. He continued to serve Brothertown and other Indian communities until his death in 1792. He is thought to be buried in an unmarked grave in an abandoned Indian cemetery in the hills above present-day Deansboro, New York.

Reading Occom's *A Short Narrative of My Life.*   Occom wrote his brief autobiography, one of the first works in English written by a Native American, shortly after he returned from a fund-raising campaign in England. He had spent three years there, working to raise money for Eleazer Wheelock, who intended to establish an Indian charity school but instead established Dartmouth College with the substantial funds Occom brought home. In part, Occom wrote his autobiography to dispel rumors spread by disgruntled fellow missionaries that he was not a Mohegan. Some also alleged that Occom had converted to Christianity solely to raise money for a school for Indians. Occom dispelled both charges in his narrative, which he wrote in a diary he kept from the 1750s to 1790. In an entry prefacing the narrative, dated September 17, 1768, he alluded to "gross Mistakes" in accounts being circulated about him, adding: "That it is against my mind to give a History of my self whilst I am alive, yet to do justice to myself and to those who may desire to know some thing concerning me, – and for the Honor of Religion I will venture to give a Short Narrative of my Life." Emphasizing his conversion to Christianity, his subsequent hunger for education, and his later work as a preacher and a teacher, Occom implicitly offers his own life as both an example of the capacity of Native Americans and an illustration of the discrimination Indian missionaries and their people suffered in colonial America. His account was possibly read by a few people at the time, but it was not published in its entirety until 1982. The following text is taken from the unedited transcription of the manuscript at Dartmouth College, which was published in *The Elders Wrote: An Anthology of Early Prose by North American Indians, 1768–1931*, edited by Bernd Peyer (1982). Occom evidently wrote the account in some haste, and we have slightly adjusted his punctuation. For example, we have omitted dashes between sentences and inserted apostrophes in some contractions, such as *Liv'd* for *Livd*.

bedfordstmartins.com/ ***americanlit*** *for research links on Occom*

A SHORT NARRATIVE OF MY LIFE

From my Birth till I received the Christian Religion

I was Born a Heathen and Brought up In Heathenism, till I was between 16 & 17 years of age, at a Place Call'd Mohegan, in New London, Connecticut, in New England. My Parents Liv'd a wandering life, for did all the Indians at Mohegan, they Chiefly Depended upon Hunting, Fishing, & Fowling for their Living and had no Connection with the English, excepting to Traffic[1] with them in their small Trifles; and they Strictly maintained and followed their Heathenish Ways, Customs & Religion, though there was Some Preaching among them. Once a Fortnight, in ye Summer Season, a Minister from New London used to come up, and the Indians to attend; not that they regarded the Christian Religion, but they had Blankets given to them every Fall of the Year and for these things they would attend and there was a Sort of School kept, when I was quite young, but I believe there never was one that ever Learnt to read any thing, – and when I was about 10 Years of age there was a man who went about among the Indian Wigwams, and wherever he Could find the Indian Children, would make them read; but the Children Used to take Care to keep out of his way; – and he used to Catch me Some times and make me Say over my Letters; and I believe I learnt Some of them. But this was Soon over too; and all this Time there was not one amongst us, that made a Profession of Christianity. Neither did we Cultivate our Land, nor kept any Sort of Creatures except Dogs, which we used in Hunting; and we Dwelt in Wigwams. These are a Sort of Tents, Covered with Matts, made of Flags.[2] And to this Time we were unaquainted with the English Tongue in general though there were a few, who understood a little of it.

---

1. **Traffic:** Early term for trade.
2. **Flags:** Long, stiff, sword-shaped leaves.

From the Time of our Reformation till I left Mr. Wheelocks

When I was 16 years of age, we heard a Strange Rumor among the English, that there were Extraordinary Ministers Preaching from Place to Place and a Strange Concern among the White People. This was in the Spring of the Year. But we Saw nothing of these things, till Some Time in the Summer, when Some Ministers began to visit us and Preach the Word of God; and the Common People all Came frequently and exhorted us to the things of God, which it pleased the Lord, as I humbly hope, to Bless and accompany with Divine Influence to the Conviction and Saving Conversion of a Number of us; amongst whom I was one that was Imprest with the things we had heard. These Preachers did not only come to us, but we frequently went to their meetings and Churches. After I was awakened[3] & converted, I went to all the meetings, I could come at; & Continued under Trouble of Mind about 6 months; at which time I began to Learn the English Letters; got me a Primer,[4] and used to go to my English Neighbours frequently for Assistance in Reading, but went to no School. And when I was 17 years of age, I had, as I trust, a Discovery of the way of Salvation through Jesus Christ, and was enabl'd to put my trust in him alone for Life & Salvation. From this Time the Distress and Burden of my mind was removed, and I found Serenity and Pleasure of Soul, in Serving God. By this time I just began to Read in the New Testament without Spelling, — and I had a Stronger Desire Still to Learn to read the Word of God, and at the Same Time had an uncommon Pity and Compassion to my Poor Brethren According to the Flesh. I used to wish I was capable of Instructing my poor Kindred. I used to think, if I Could once Learn to Read I would Instruct the poor Children in Reading, — and used frequently to talk with our Indians Concerning Religion. This continued till I was in my 19th year: by this Time I Could Read a little in the Bible. At this Time my Poor Mother was going to Lebanon, and having had Some Knowledge of Mr. Wheelock[5] and hearing he had a Number of English youth under his Tuition,[6] I had a great Inclination to go to him and be with him a week or a Fortnight, and Desired my Mother to Ask Mr. Wheelock whether he would take me a little while to Instruct me in Reading. Mother did so; and when She Came Back, She Said Mr. Wheelock wanted to See me as Soon as possible. So I went up, thinking I Should be back again in a few Days; when I got up there, he received me With kindness and Compassion and in Stead of Staying a Forthnight or 3 Weeks, I Spent 4 Years with him. After I had been with him Some Time, he began to acquaint his Friends of my being with him, and of his Intentions of Educating me, and my Circumstances. And the good People began to give Some Assistance to Mr. Wheelock, and gave me Some old and Some New Clothes. Then he represented the Case to the Honorable Commissioners at Boston, who were Commission'd by the Honorable Society in London for Propagating the gospel among the Indians in

---

3. **awakened:** To be made aware of or stirred by Christianity.
4. **Primer:** Textbook used to teach children to read.
5. **Mr. Wheelock:** Eleazer Wheelock (1711-1779), a teacher and Congregationalist minister; he later founded the Moor's Indian Charity School (1753) and Dartmouth College, established in 1769 "for the education and instruction of youth of the Indian tribes in this land in reading, writing, and all parts of learning which shall appear necessary and expedient for civilizing and Christianizing children of pagans, as well as in all liberal arts and sciences, and also of English youth and any others."
6. **Tuition:** Supervision for purposes of instruction.

New England and parts adjacent, and they allowed him 60 £ in old Tender, which was about 6 £ Sterling,[7] and they Continu'd it 2 or 3 years, I can't tell exactly. While I was at Mr. Wheelock's, I was very weakly and my Health much impaired, and at the End of 4 Years, I over Strained my Eyes to such a Degree, I Could not persue my Studies any Longer; and out of these 4 years I Lost Just about one year; – And was obliged to quit my Studies.

From the Time I left Mr. Wheelock till I went to Europe

As soon as I left Mr. Wheelock, I endeavored to find Some Employ among the Indians; went to Nahantuck, thinking they may want a School Master, but they had one; then went to Narraganset, and they were Indifferent about a School, and went back to Mohegan, and heard a number of our Indians were going to Montauk, on Long Island, and I went with them, and the Indians there were very desirous to have me keep a School amongst them, and I Consented, and went back a while to Mohegan and Some time in November I went on the Island, I think it is 17 years ago last November. I agreed to keep School with them Half a Year, and left it with them to give me what they Pleased; and they took turns to Provide Food for me. I had near 30 Scholars this winter; I had an evening School too for those that could not attend the Day School – and began to Carry on their meetings, they had a Minister, one Mr. Horton, the Scotch Society's Missionary; but he Spent, I think two thirds of his Time at Sheenecock, 30 Miles from Montauk. We met together 3 times for Divine Worship every Sabbath and once on every Wednesday evening. I (used) to read the Scriptures to them and used to expound upon Some particular Passages in my own Tongue. Visited the Sick and attended their Burials. When the half year expired, they Desired me to Continue with them, which I complied with, for another half year, when I had fulfilled that, they were urgent to have me Stay Longer, So I continued amongst them till I was Married, which was about 2 years after I went there. And Continued to Instruct them in the Same manner as I did before. After I was married a while, I found there was need of a Support more than I needed while I was Single, – and made my Case Known to Mr. Buell[8] and to Mr. Wheelock, and also the Needy Circumstances and the Desires of these Indians of my Continuing amongst them, and the Commissioners were so good as to grant £ 15 a year Sterling – And I kept on in my Service as usual, yea I had additional Service; I kept School as I did before and Carried on the Religious Meetings as often as ever, and attended the Sick and their Funerals, and did what Writings they wanted, and often Sat as a Judge to reconcile and Decide their Matters Between them, and had visitors of Indians from all Quarters; and, as our Custom is, we freely Entertain all Visitors. And was fetched often from my Tribe and from others to see into their Affairs Both Religious, Temporal, – Besides my Domestic Concerns. And it Pleased the Lord to Increase my Family fast – and Soon after I was Married, Mr. Horton left these Indians and the

7. **60 £ in old Tender . . . 6 £ Sterling:** Several different currencies, including "Old Tender," were circulated in the colonies, where the English pound sterling (£) was also widely used. Although the dollar was not introduced until after the Revolution, scholars estimate that during the period 1766-72 the value of the English pound sterling was about $4.50, or what today would be roughly equivalent to $75.
8. **Mr. Buell:** Samuel Buell (1716-1798), Presbyterian minister of the church in East Hampton, Long Island, New York. Buell preached Occom's ordination sermon in 1759.

Shenecock & after this I was (alone) and then I had the whole care of these Indians at Montauk, and visited the Shenecock Indians often. Used to set out Saturdays towards Night and come back again Mondays. I have been obliged to Set out from Home after Sun Set, and Ride 30 Miles in the Night, to Preach to these Indians. And Some Indians at Shenecock Sent their Children to my School at Montauk, I kept one of them Some Time, and had a Young Man a half year from Mohegan, a Lad from Nahantuck, who was with me almost a year; and had little or nothing for keeping them.

My Method in the School was, as Soon as the Children got together, and took their proper Seats, I Prayed with them, then began to hear them. I generally began (after some of them Could Spell and Read,) With those that were yet in their Alphabets, So around, as they were properly Seated till I got through and I obliged them to Study their Books, and to help one another. When they could not make out a hard word they Brought it to me – and I usually heard them, in the Summer Season 8 Times a Day 4 in the morning, and in ye after Noon. In the Winter Season 6 Times a Day, As Soon as they could Spell, they were obliged to Spell when ever they wanted to go out. I concluded with Prayer; I generally heard my Evening Scholars 3 Times Round, And as they go out the School, every one, that Can Spell, is obliged to Spell a Word, and to go out Leisurely one after another. I Catechised 3 or 4 Times a Week according to the Assembly's Shout or Catechism, and many Times Proposed Questions of my own, and in my own Tongue. I found Difficulty with Some Children, who were Some what Dull, most of these can soon learn to Say over their Letters, they Distinguish the Sounds by the Ear, but their Eyes can't Distinguish the Letters, and the way I took to cure them was by making an Alphabet on Small bits of paper, and glued them on Small Chips of Cedar after this manner A B & C. I put these on Letters in order on a Bench then point to one Letter and bid a Child to take notice of it, and then I order the Child to fetch me the Letter from the Bench; if he Brings the Letter, it is well, if not he must go again and again till he brings ye right Letter. When they can bring any Letters this way, then I just Jumble them together, and bid them to set them in Alphabetical order, and it is a Pleasure to them; and they soon Learn their Letters this way. I frequently Discussed or Exhorted my Scholars, in Religious matters. My Method in our Religious Meetings was this; Sabbath Morning we Assemble together about 10 o'C and begin with Singing; we generally Sung Dr. Watt's Psalms or Hymns. I distinctly read the Psalm or Hymn first, and then gave the meaning of it to them, after that Sing, then Pray, and Sing again after Prayer. Then proceed to Read from Suitable portion of Scripture, and so Just give the plain Sense of it in Familiar Discourse and apply it to them. So continued with Prayer and Singing. In the after Noon and Evening we Proceed in the Same Manner, and so in Wednesday Evening. Some Time after Mr. Horton left these Indians, there was a remarkable revival of religion among these Indians and many were hopefully converted to the Saving knowledge of God in Jesus. It is to be observed before Mr. Horton left these Indians they had Some Prejudices infused in their minds, by Some Enthusiastical Exhorters from New England, against Mr. Horton, and many of them had left him; by this means he was Discouraged, and was disposed from these Indians. And being acquainted with the Enthusiasts in New England & the make and the Disposition of the Indians I took a mild way to reclaim them. I opposed them not openly but let them go on in their way, and whenever I had an opportunity, I would read Such pages of the Scriptures, and I thought would confound their Notions, and I would come to them with all Authority, Saying "these Saith the Lord"; and by this means, the Lord was pleased to Bless my poor Endeavours, and they were reclaimed, and Brought to hear almost any of the ministers.

I am now to give an Account of my Circumstances and manner of Living. I Dwelt in a Wigwam, a Small Hut with Small Poles and Covered with Matts made of Flags, and I was oblig'd to remove twice a Year, about 2 miles Distance, by reason of the Scarcity of wood, for in one Neck of Land they Planted their Corn, and in another, they had their wood, and I was oblig'd to have my Corn carted and my Hay also, — and I got my Ground Plow'd every year, which Cost me about 12 shillings an acre; and I kept a Cow and a Horse, for which I paid 21 shillings every year York currency,[9] and went 18 miles to Mill for every Dust of meal we used in my family. I Hired or Joined with my Neighbours to go to Mill, with a Horse or ox Cart, or on Horse Back, and Some time went myself. My Family Increasing fast, and my Visitors also. I was oblig'd to contrive every way to Support my Family; I took all opportunities, to get Some thing to feed my Family Daily. I Planted my own Corn, Potatoes, and Beans; I used to be out hoeing my Corn Some times before Sun Rise and after my School is Dismist, and by this means I was able to raise my own Pork, for I was allowed to keep 5 Swine. Some mornings & Evenings I would be out with my Hook and Line to Catch fish, and in the Fall of Year and in the Spring, I used my gun, and fed my Family with Fowls. I Could more than pay for my Powder & Shot with Feathers. At other Times I Bound old Books for Easthampton People, made wooden Spoons and Ladles, Stocked Guns, & worked on Cedar to make Pails, (Piggins),[10] and Churns & C. Besides all these Difficulties I met with advers Providence, I bought a Mare, had it but a little while, and she fell into the Quick Sand and Died, After a while Bought another, I kept her about half year, and she was gone, and I never have heard of nor Seen her from that Day to this; it was Supposed Some Rogue Stole her. I got another and Died with a Distemper, and last of all I Bought a Young Mare, and kept her till She had one Colt, and She broke her Leg and Died, and Presently after the Colt[11] Died also. In the whole I Lost 5 Horse Kind; all these Losses helped to pull me down; and by this Time I got greatly in Debt, and acquainted my Circumstances to Some of my Friends, and they Represented my Case to the Commissioners of Boston, and Interceded with them for me, and they were pleased to vote 15 £ for my Help, and Soon after Sent a Letter to my good Friend at New London, acquainting him that they had Superseded their Vote; and my Friends were so good as to represent my Needy Circumstances Still to them, and they were so good at Last, as to Vote £ 15 and Sent it, for which I am very thankful; and the Reverend Mr. Buell was so kind as to write in my behalf to the gentlemen of Boston; and he told me they were much Displeased with him, and heard also once again that they blamed me for being Extravagant; I Can't Conceive how these gentlemen would have me Live. I am

9. **York currency:** In the currency issued in New York, twenty shillings also equaled a pound (£), but it was less valuable than the English £ sterling. The combined annual costs of having the ground plowed and keeping the animals was about $4.20, or what today would be roughly equivalent to $70. See note 7.
10. **Piggins:** A piggin, a small wooden pail with an upright stave for a handle, was often used as a dipper.
11. **Colt:** The manuscript reads "Cold."

ready to (forgive) their Ignorance, and I would wish they had Changed Circumstances with me but one month, that they may know, by experience what my Case really was; but I am now fully convinced, that it was not Ignorance, For I believe it can be proved to the world that these Same Gentlemen gave a young Missionary a Single man, *one Hundred Pounds* for one year, and fifty Pounds for an Interpreter, and thirty Pounds for an Introducer; so it Cost them one Hundred & Eighty Pounds in one Single Year, and they Sent too where there was no Need of a Missionary.

Now you See what difference they made between me and other missionaries; they gave me 180 Pounds for 12 years Service, which they gave for one years Services in another Mission. In my Service (I speak like a fool, but I am Constrained) I was my own Interpreter. I was both a School master and Minister to the Indians, yea I was their Ear, Eye & Hand, as Well as Mouth. I leave it with the World, as wicked as it is, to Judge, whether I ought not to have had half as much, they gave a young man Just mentioned which would have been but £ 50 a year; and if they ought to have given me that, I am not under obligations to them, I owe them nothing at all; what can be the Reason that they used me after this manner? I can't think of any thing, but this as a Poor Indian Boy Said, Who was Bound out to an English Family, and he used to Drive Plow for a young man, and he whipt and Beat him allmost every Day, and the young man found fault with him, and Complained of him to his master and the poor Boy was Called to answer for himself before his master, and he was asked, what it was he did, that he was So Complained of and beat almost every Day. He Said, he did not know, but he Supposed it was because he could not drive any better; but says he, I Drive as well as I know how; and at other Times he Beats me, because he is of a mind to beat me; but says he believes he Beats me for the most of the Time "because I am an Indian."

So I am *ready* to Say, they have used me thus, because I Can't Influence the Indians so well as other missionaries; but I can assure them I have endeavoured to teach them as well as I know how; – but I *must Say*, "I believe it is because I am a poor Indian". I Can't help that God has made me So; I did not make my self so.

[1768, 1982]

Occom through a Modern Lens

IN THE LATE EIGHTEENTH CENTURY, works by Native Americans who wrote in English were published by several printers, including Thomas and Samuel Green, descendants of a prominent family of colonial printers. The Greens printed dozens of sermons and religious books on their press in New London, Connecticut. They published Samson Occom's collection of hymns and spiritual songs, as well as his sermon on the execution of Moses Paul. Occom's works went through several editions during the eighteenth century and enjoyed considerable popularity. But Occom's autobiographical sketch existed only in manuscript until it was finally published in 1982. Since then, he has been the object of considerable attention by scholars, including James Ottery, a professor of English, a member of the Brothertown Indian Nation, and a descendant of Occom, whose name he spells *Occum.* Ottery wrote the following poem as he was contemplating the "silences" in Occom's "Diary," which Occom kept over many years and in which he wrote *A Short Narrative of My Life.* Some commentators have stressed Occom's failure to mention some of the devastating events of his life in his narrative, while scholars have emphasized its limitations as a source of ethnographic information about Native Americans. In contrast, playing off observations by non-native critics and quotations from Occom's narrative, Ottery meditates on the obstacles that confronted a Native American attempting to put his "life into words in the language / that wasn't his mother tongue." The following text, which incorporates Occom's words, is taken from the online publication of Ottery's poem (http://work.colum.edu /~jottery/IntroCW/NAC/SamsonOccum .htm).

The Reverend Mr. Samson Occom

This portrait of Occom, described in an accompanying caption as the "first Indian Minister that ever was in Europe," was published in London during or shortly after his triumphant fund-raising tour of England. Occom wrote his brief narrative of his life soon after his return to New England.

James Ottery

[b. 1953]

THE DIARY OF SAMSON OCCUM

He put his life into words: his life
as a Presbyterian preacher,[1] his life
as a preacher and teacher before that
in the Society for Propagating the Gospel in New England,
two years of his life spent raising   5
money in old England for the Indian Charity School
in Connecticut, "funds misdirected"
for the founding of a white Dartmouth College instead.
He put his life into words, in the language
that was not his mother tongue, the language   10
not learned until he was 16;
in the language that was not his
until he reached the age of 16,
he wrote of his life until then in very few words
of the language that wasn't his mother tongue —   15

> *I was born a Heathen*
> *and Brought up in Heathenism*
> *until I was between 16 & 17 Years of age,*
> *at a place call'd Mohegan . . .[2]*

He put his life into words in the language   20
that wasn't his mother tongue, the English learned
first when he was 16,
(he would begin reading Hebrew at 21,
until "after a year of study" he would stop,
because "his *eyes* would fail him"),   25
In the language that was not his mother tongue
he would write:

> *Having Seen and heard Several Representations,*
> *In England and Scotland [two words crossed out]*

---

1. **Presbyterian preacher:** Occom was ordained a Presbyterian minister in 1759.
2. *I . . . Mohegan*: The opening lines of Occom's narrative.

by . . . Some gentlemen in America, Concerning me, 30
and finding many [crossed out: misrepresentations]
gross Mistakes in their account, —I
I thought it my Duty to Give
a Short, Plain, and Honest Account of my Self
whilst I am still alive, yet to doe Justice 35
to myself and to those
who may desire [two words crossed out]
to know something concerning [word crossed out] me . . .[3]

He put his life into words and we read it
in the words of another who read enough of his life 40
to write of Mohegan "at the center of the most fervent
religious awakening in New England,"[4] and how two converted
were "Sarah Occum" and Samson her son,
how Sarah convinced a good reverend
(who would years later "misdirect" the Indian Charity School funds) 45
to teach her son the white man's language,
how she had no money to pay his lessons,
how she "probably contributed some labor" to the Rev. Wheelock
and perhaps other members of his family.

Samson Occum put his life into the words 50
of the white man because he "believed
the Indian had to conform to white ways"
in order to be saved,
conform to the ways of the white man
who slaughtered his mother's people at Mystic River,[5] 55
conform to the ways of the white man
who would crowd out the Mohegans and the rest
of the New England tribes,
conform to ways of the white man
who brought "intemperance, licentiousness and disease," 60

---

3. *Having . . . me*: The quotation is from a transcription of Occom's heavily revised introduction to his account, which is not included in the published version of *A Short Narrative of My Life*.
4. "**religious awakening in New England**": The Great Awakening, the religious revival that swept across New England during the 1730s and 1740s.
5. **slaughtered . . . at Mystic River**: In 1637, seven hundred Pequot women, children, and elderly people were killed in Mystic, Connecticut, when their fort was set ablaze by colonial troops under the command of Captain John Mason. Following the massacre, the surviving members of the tribe were sold as slaves or put under the power of other tribes, such as the Mohegan.

conform to the ways of the white man
because his ways, Samson Occum could see,
were to be the way of the New World,
conform to the ways of the white man and hope
that white men someday would be   65
better men for it.

Samson Occum put his life into the words of the white man
because he believed it was what he had to do.
But not his whole life.

In the language that's not his mother tongue: 70
he does not write much of his wife,
he does not write much of daughters and sons
he does not write much of his personal "life" —
how poverty and depression may have led to alcohol.
He does not write of these things in the white man's words: 75

        Sometimes there are not words for life
        in a language that is not your mother tongue.

            [2001]

Olaudah Equiano

[1745?-1797]

Little is known for certain about the early life of Olaudah Equiano. Recent biographical investigations indicate that he may have been born in South Carolina in 1747 and that he was later purchased by Michael Henry Pascal, an officer in the British navy, who took him to England as early as 1754. Equiano, however, tells a different story in his autobiography. According to him, he was born in an Ibo village near the Niger River in West Africa around 1745. His parents expected him to become a chief or an elder of the village, but when he was about ten years old Equiano and his sister were kidnapped by slave traders. After being separated from her, he was sold to British traders and placed aboard a slave ship bound for the Americas. Equiano was first transported to Barbados and then to Virginia, where he was purchased by a local planter in 1756. The planter soon sold Equiano to Pascal, who took him to England in 1757.

From that point on, Equiano's account is fully corroborated by historical evidence. Pascal renamed him Gustavus Vassa—after the nobleman who led the Swedish people in their struggle for independence from Denmark and later became the first Swedish king—and sent him to school in London, where Equiano learned to read and write and where he was baptized in 1759. Along with Pascal, Equiano also served in the British navy and saw action in both Canada and the Mediterranean during the Seven Years' War (also known as the French and Indian War) between England and France (1756-63). But he was denied the prize money that was usually distributed to all sailors aboard a naval ship, as well as the freedom he had been promised by Pascal, who in 1762 sold Equiano back into slavery in the West Indies. There, he was purchased by Robert King, a Quaker merchant from Philadelphia. As the assistant to King, whose trade frequently included slaves, Equiano witnessed the business of slavery first hand in both the American colonies and the West Indies. While a slave himself, he was also permitted to engage in his own modest trading business, and Equiano finally earned enough to purchase his freedom from King for £40—roughly $175, or more than $3,000 in today's currency—on July 11, 1766.

During the final three decades of his life, Equiano worked at various trades even as he increasingly devoted himself to efforts to end slavery and the slave trade. He lived mostly in London, where he sometimes worked as a hairdresser or a servant. But the curious and restless Equiano joined expeditions to the Arctic and Central America, and he made several voyages to North America. In what he viewed as a crucial turning point of his life, Equiano converted to Christianity, which further fueled his humanitarian efforts. By 1777, he was writing hostile newspaper reviews of proslavery books, and during the following decade he helped form the Sons of Africa, a group of black men who campaigned against slavery and the slave trade. As part of that campaign, Equiano wrote *The Interesting Narrative of the Life of Olaudah Equiano* (1789), which was published by subscription, and whose list of influential subscribers included the Prince of Wales. Following its

Olaudah Equiano

In this engraving, which appeared on the title page of the first edition of *The Interesting Narrative of the Life of Olaudah Equiano*, the author holds a Bible open to chapters 4-5 of Acts.

publication, Equiano frequently spoke at antislavery meetings and wrote numerous letters to newspapers in response to racist articles. As the editor of a London newspaper observed of one of those responses, "We cannot but think the letter a good argument in favour of the natural Abilities, as well as good feelings, of the Negro Race, and a solid answer in their favour." Equiano, who also spoke in favor of racial intermarriage, married an Englishwoman, Susan Cullen, in 1792. The couple had two daughters before Equiano died in London on April 31, 1797.

Reading Equiano's *Narrative.*

Equiano's famous narrative, one of the earliest autobiographical accounts written by a black person in the Anglo-American world, was first published in London in 1789. The book sold extremely well in England, Ireland, and the United States, where it was published in 1791. In the early nineteenth century, it became an international bestseller, with numerous new editions in English, Dutch, French, and Russian. Addressing members of Parliament, Equiano clearly stated his purpose in the preface to the first edition:

> My Lords and Gentlemen, Permit me, with the greatest deference and respect, to lay at your feet the following genuine narrative; the chief design of which is to excite in your august assemblies a sense of compassion for the miseries which the Slave-Trade has entailed on my unfortunate countrymen. By the horrors of that trade I was first torn away from all the tender connections that were naturally dear to my heart; but these, through the mysterious ways of Providence, I ought to regard as infinitely more than compensated by the introduction I have thence obtained to the knowledge

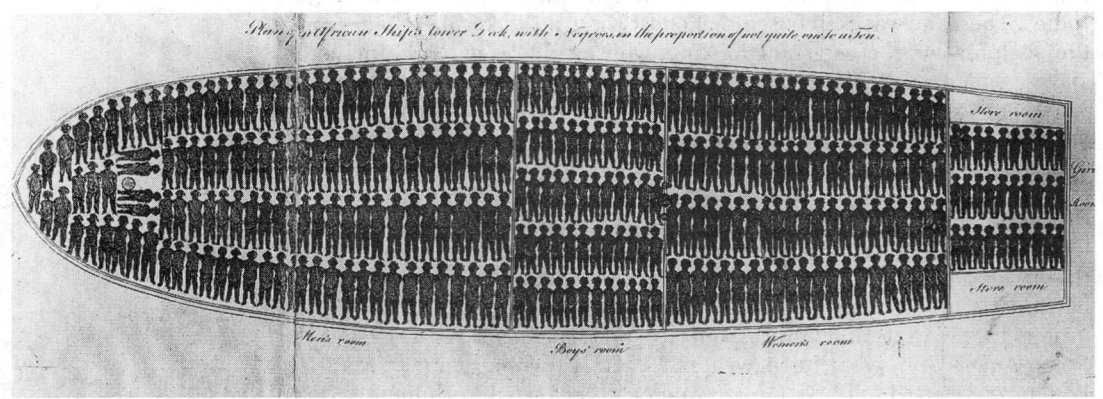

Plan of a Slave Ship

This engraving, published in 1789 by the Society for Effecting the Abolition of the Slave Trade to illustrate the brutal conditions aboard slave ships, was accompanied by the caption: "Plan of an African Ship's Lower Deck with Negroes in the Proportion of Only One to Ten."

of the Christian religion, and of a nation which, by its liberal sentiments, its humanity, the glorious freedom of its government, and its proficiency in arts and sciences, has exalted the dignity of human nature.

Questions have recently been raised about Equiano's claim that he was born in Africa, since both his baptismal record and a Royal Navy muster roll indicate that he was born in South Carolina. If he was born in the American colonies — and the evidence is not conclusive — Equiano must have based his initial account of his early life in Africa on what he had read in books and stories he had heard from other slaves. Indeed, Equiano may well have intended his account to represent the experience of the more than one million Africans who were captured and transported as slaves to the New World from 1741 to 1760. At the same time, by claiming to have been one of them, Equiano could directly and authoritatively testify to the horrors of what was called the "Middle Passage," the second leg of triangular voyages in which ships from Europe carried manufactured goods such as brandy, cloth, iron, guns, and gunpowder to Africa, traded them there for human cargoes bound for the Americas, and finally exchanged the slaves for sugar, tobacco, and other products that were shipped back to Europe. Whether it was based on his own early memories or on his later experiences of slavery and the communal memories of other slaves, the following chapter from Equiano's narrative stands as one of the most powerful of all indictments of the international slave trade, which was finally abolished by Great Britain and the United States in 1807. The text of the following chapter is taken from the first American printing of his *Narrative*, which was published in two volumes in New York City in 1791. The lengthy paragraphs of that edition have been divided into shorter units to facilitate reading.

bedfordstmartins.com/ americanlit for research links on Equiano

From THE INTERESTING NARRATIVE OF THE LIFE OF OLAUDAH EQUIANO, OR GUSTAVUS VASSA, THE AFRICAN, WRITTEN BY HIMSELF

Chapter 2

I hope the reader will not think I have trespassed on his patience in introducing myself to him with some account of the manners and customs of my country.[1] They had been implanted in me with great care, and made an impression on my mind, which time could not erase, and which all the adversity and variety of fortune I have since experienced, served only to rivet and record: for, whether the love of one's country be real or imaginary, or a lesson of reason, or an instinct of nature, I still look back with pleasure on the first scenes of my life, though that pleasure has been for the most part mingled with sorrow.

---

1. **my country:** In the first chapter, Equiano says he was born in the Ibo village of Essaka in western Africa.

I have already acquainted the reader with the time and place of my birth. My father, besides many slaves, had a numerous family, of which seven lived to grow up, including myself and sister, who was the only daughter. As I was the youngest of the sons, I became, of course, the greatest favorite with my mother, and was always with her; and she used to take particular pains to form my mind. I was trained up from my earliest years in the art of war: my daily exercise was shooting and throwing javelins, and my mother adorned me with emblems, after the manner of our greatest warriors. In this way I grew up till I had turned the age of eleven, when an end was put to my happiness in the following manner: Generally, when the grown people in the neighborhood were gone far in the fields to labor, the children assembled together in some of the neighboring premises to play; and commonly some of us used to get up a tree to look out for any assailant, or kidnapper, that might come upon us — for they sometimes took those opportunities of our parents' absence, to attack and carry off as many as they could seize. One day as I was watching at the top of a tree in our yard, I saw one of those people come into the yard of our next neighbor but one, to kidnap, there being many stout[2] young people in it. Immediately on this I gave the alarm of the rogue, and he was surrounded by the stoutest of them, who entangled him with cords, so that he could not escape, till some of the grown people came and secured him. But, alas! ere long it was my fate to be thus attacked, and to be carried off, when none of the grown people were nigh.

One day, when all our people were gone out to their works as usual, and only I and my dear sister were left to mind the house, two men and a woman got over our walls, and in a moment seized us both, and, without giving us time to cry out, or make resistance, they stopped our mouths, and ran off with us into the nearest wood. Here they tied our hands, and continued to carry us as far as they could, till night came on, when we reached a small house, where the robbers halted for refreshment, and spent the night. We were then unbound, but were unable to take any food; and, being quite overpowered by fatigue and grief, our only relief was some sleep, which allayed our misfortune for a short time. The next morning we left the house, and continued travelling all the day. For a long time we had kept the woods, but at last we came into a road which I believed I knew. I had now some hopes of being delivered; for we had advanced but a little way before I discovered some people at a distance, on which I began to cry out for their assistance; but my cries had no other effect than to make them tie me faster and stop my mouth, and then they put me into a large sack. They also stopped my sister's mouth, and tied her hands; and in this manner we proceeded till we were out of sight of these people. When we went to rest the following night, they offered us some victuals, but we refused it; and the only comfort we had was in being in one another's arms all that night, and bathing each other with our tears. But alas! we were soon deprived of even the small comfort of weeping together.

The next day proved a day of greater sorrow than I had yet experienced; for my sister and I were then separated, while we lay clasped in each other's arms. It was in vain that we besought them not to part us; she was torn from me, and immediately carried away,

---

2. **stout:** Large and strong.

while I was left in a state of distraction not to be described. I cried and grieved continually; and for several days did not eat anything but what they forced into my mouth. At length, after many days' travelling, during which I had often changed masters, I got into the hands of a chieftain, in a very pleasant country. This man had two wives and some children, and they all used me extremely well, and did all they could do to comfort me; particularly the first wife, who was something like my mother. Although I was a great many days' journey from my father's house, yet these people spoke exactly the same language with us. This first master of mine, as I may call him, was a smith,[3] and my principal employment was working his bellows, which were the same kind as I had seen in my vicinity. They were in some respects not unlike the stoves here in gentlemen's kitchens, and were covered over with leather; and in the middle of that leather a stick was fixed, and a person stood up, and worked it in the same manner as is done to pump water out of a cask with a hand pump. I believe it was gold he worked, for it was of a lovely bright yellow color, and was worn by the women on their wrists and ankles.

I was there I suppose about a month, and they at last used to trust me some little distance from the house. This liberty I used in embracing every opportunity to inquire the way to my own home; and I also sometimes, for the same purpose, went with the maidens, in the cool of the evenings, to bring pitchers of water from the springs for the use of the house. I had also remarked where the sun rose in the morning, and set in the evening, as I had travelled along; and I had observed that my father's house was towards the rising of the sun. I therefore determined to seize the first opportunity of making my escape, and to shape my course for that quarter; for I was quite oppressed and weighed down by grief after my mother and friends; and my love of liberty, ever great, was strengthened by the mortifying circumstance of not daring to eat with the free-born children, although I was mostly their companion.

While I was projecting my escape, one day an unlucky event happened, which quite disconcerted my plan, and put an end to my hopes. I used to be sometimes employed in assisting an elderly slave to cook and take care of the poultry; and one morning, while I was feeding some chickens, I happened to toss a small pebble at one of them, which hit it on the middle, and directly killed it. The old slave, having soon after missed the chicken, inquired after it; and on my relating the accident (for I told her the truth, for my mother would never suffer me to tell a lie), she flew into a violent passion, and threatened that I should suffer for it; and, my master being out, she immediately went and told her mistress what I had done. This alarmed me very much, and I expected an instant flogging, which to me was uncommonly dreadful, for I had seldom been beaten at home. I therefore resolved to fly; and accordingly I ran into a thicket that was hard by, and hid myself in the bushes. Soon afterwards my mistress and the slave returned, and, not seeing me, they searched all the house, but not finding me, and I not making answer when they called to me, they thought I had run away, and the whole neighborhood was raised in the pursuit of me.

In that part of the country, as in ours, the houses and villages were skirted with woods, or shrubberies, and the bushes were so thick that a man could readily conceal

---

3. **smith:** A metalworker; short for goldsmith.

himself in them, so as to elude the strictest search. The neighbors continued the whole day looking for me, and several times many of them came within a few yards of the place where I lay hid. I expected every moment, when I heard a rustling among the trees, to be found out, and punished by my master; but they never discovered me, though they were often so near that I even heard their conjectures as they were looking about for me; and I now learned from them that any attempts to return home would be hopeless. Most of them supposed I had fled towards home; but the distance was so great, and the way so intricate, that they thought I could never reach it, and that I should be lost in the woods. When I heard this I was seized with a violent panic, and abandoned myself to despair. Night, too, began to approach, and aggravated all my fears. I had before entertained hopes of getting home, and had determined when it should be dark to make the attempt; but I was now convinced it was fruitless, and began to consider that, if possibly I could escape all other animals, I could not those of the human kind; and that, not knowing the way, I must perish in the woods. Thus was I like the hunted deer —

> — Every leaf and every whisp'ring breath,
> Convey'd a foe, and every foe a death.[4]

I heard frequent rustlings among the leaves, and being pretty sure they were snakes, I expected every instant to be stung by them. This increased my anguish, and the horror of my situation became now quite insupportable. I at length quitted the thicket, very faint and hungry, for I had not eaten or drank anything all the day, and crept to my master's kitchen, from whence I set out at first, which was an open shed, and laid myself down in the ashes with an anxious wish for death, to relieve me from all my pains. I was scarcely awake in the morning, when the old woman slave, who was the first up, came to light the fire, and saw me in the fireplace. She was very much surprised to see me, and could scarcely believe her own eyes. She now promised to intercede for me, and went for her master, who soon after came, and, having slightly reprimanded me, ordered me to be taken care of, and not ill treated.

Soon after this, my master's only daughter, and child by his first wife, sickened and died, which affected him so much that for sometime he was almost frantic, and really would have killed himself, had he not been watched and prevented. However, in a short time afterwards he recovered, and I was again sold. I was now carried to the left of the sun's rising, through many dreary wastes and dismal woods, amidst the hideous roarings of wild beasts. The people I was sold to used to carry me very often, when I was tired, either on their shoulders or on their backs. I saw many convenient well-built sheds along the road, at proper distances, to accommodate the merchants and travellers, who lay in those buildings along with their wives, who often accompany them; and they always go well armed.

From the time I left my own nation, I always found somebody that understood me till I came to the sea coast. The languages of different nations did not totally differ, nor were they so copious as those of the Europeans, particularly the English. They were

---

4. **Every ... death:** The lines are from *Cooper's Hill* (1642), a popular work by the English poet Sir John Denham (1615–1669).

therefore easily learned; and, while I was journeying thus through Africa, I acquired two or three different tongues. In this manner I had been travelling for a considerable time, when, one evening, to my great surprise, whom should I see brought to the house where I was but my dear sister! As soon as she saw me, she gave a loud shriek, and ran into my arms—I was quite overpowered; neither of us could speak, but, for a considerable time, clung to each other in mutual embraces, unable to do anything but weep. Our meeting affected all who saw us; and, indeed, I must acknowledge, in honor of those sable destroyers of human rights, that I never met with any ill treatment, or saw any offered to their slaves, except tying them, when necessary, to keep them from running away.

When these people knew we were brother and sister, they indulged us to be together; and the man, to whom I supposed we belonged, lay with us, he in the middle, while she and I held one another by the hands across his breast all night; and thus for a while we forgot our misfortunes, in the joy of being together; but even this small comfort was soon to have an end; for scarcely had the fatal morning appeared when she was again torn from me forever! I was now more miserable, if possible, than before. The small relief which her presence gave me from pain, was gone, and the wretchedness of my situation was redoubled by my anxiety after her fate, and my apprehensions lest her sufferings should be greater than mine, when I could not be with her to alleviate them. Yes, thou dear partner of all my childish sports! thou sharer of my joys and sorrows! happy should I have ever esteemed myself to encounter every misery for you and to procure your freedom by the sacrifice of my own. Though you were early forced from my arms, your image has been always riveted in my heart, from which neither time nor fortune have been able to remove it; so that, while the thoughts of your sufferings have damped my prosperity, they have mingled with adversity and increased its bitterness. To that Heaven which protects the weak from the strong, I commit the care of your innocence and virtues, if they have not already received their full reward, and if your youth and delicacy have not long since fallen victims to the violence of the African trader, the pestilential stench of a Guinea ship, the seasoning in the European colonies, or the lash and lust of a brutal and unrelenting overseer.

I did not long remain after my sister. I was again sold, and carried through a number of places, till after travelling a considerable time, I came to a town called Tinmah, in the most beautiful country I had yet seen in Africa. It was extremely rich, and there were many rivulets which flowed through it, and supplied a large pond in the centre of the town, where the people washed. Here I saw for the first time cocoanuts, which I thought superior to any nuts I had ever tasted before; and the trees, which were loaded, were also interspersed among the houses, which had commodious shades adjoining, and were in the same manner as ours, the insides being neatly plastered and whitewashed. Here I also saw and tasted for the first time, sugar-cane. Their money consisted of little white shells, the size of the finger nail. I was sold here for one hundred and seventy-two of them, by a merchant who lived and brought me there.

I had been about two or three days at his house, when a wealthy widow, a neighbor of his, came there one evening, and brought with her an only son, a young gentleman about my own age and size. Here they saw me; and, having taken a fancy to me, I was bought of the merchant, and went home with them. Her house and premises were situated close to one of those rivulets I have mentioned, and were the finest I ever saw in Africa: they were very extensive, and she had a number of slaves to attend her. The next day I was washed and perfumed, and when meal time came, I was led into the presence of my mistress, and ate and drank before her with her son. This filled me with astonishment; and I could scarce help expressing my surprise that the young gentleman should suffer[5] me, who was bound, to eat with him who was free; and not only so, but that he would not at any time either eat or drink till I had taken first, because I was the eldest, which was agreeable to our custom. Indeed, every thing here, and all their treatment of me, made me forget that I was a slave. The language of these people resembled ours so nearly, that we understood each other perfectly. They had also the very same customs as we. There were likewise slaves daily to attend us, while my young master and I, with other boys, sported with our darts and bows and arrows, as I had been used to do at home. In this resemblance to my former happy state, I passed about two months; and I now began to think I was to be adopted into the family, and was beginning to be reconciled to my situation, and to forget by degrees my misfortunes, when all at once the delusion vanished; for, without the least previous knowledge, one morning early, while my dear master and companion was still asleep, I was awakened out of my reverie to fresh sorrow, and hurried away even amongst the uncircumcised.

Thus, at the very moment I dreamed of the greatest happiness, I found myself most miserable; and it seemed as if fortune wished to give me this taste of joy only to render the reverse more poignant. The change I now experienced was as painful as it was sudden and unexpected. It was a change indeed, from a state of bliss to a scene which is inexpressible by me, as it discovered to me an element I had never before beheld, and till then had no idea of, and wherein such instances of hardship and cruelty continually occurred, as I can never reflect on but with horror.

All the nations and people I had hitherto passed through, resembled our own in their manners, customs, and language; but I came at length to a country, the inhabitants of which differed from us in all those particulars. I was very much struck with this difference, especially when I came among a people who did not circumcise, and ate without washing their hands. They cooked also in iron pots, and had European cutlasses and cross bows, which were unknown to us, and fought with their fists among themselves. Their women were not so modest as ours, for they ate, and drank, and slept with their men. But above all, I was amazed to see no sacrifices or offerings among them. In some of those places the people ornamented themselves with scars, and likewise filed their teeth very sharp. They wanted sometimes to ornament me in the same manner, but I would not suffer them; hoping that I might some time be among a people who did not thus disfigure themselves, as I thought they did. At last I came to the banks of a large river which was covered with canoes, in which the people appeared to live with their household utensils, and provisions of all kinds. I was beyond measure astonished at this, as I had never before seen any water larger than a pond or a rivulet; and my surprise was mingled with no small fear when I was put into one of these canoes,

---

5. **suffer**: Permit or allow.

and we began to paddle and move along the river. We continued going on thus till night, and when we came to land, and made fires on the banks, each family by themselves; some dragged their canoes on shore, others stayed and cooked in theirs, and laid in them all night. Those on the land had mats, of which they made tents, some in the shape of little houses; in these we slept; and after the morning meal, we embarked again and proceeded as before. I was often very much astonished to see some of the women, as well as the men, jump into the water, dive to the bottom, come up again, and swim about.

Thus I continued to travel, sometimes by land, sometimes by water, through different countries and various nations, till, at the end of six or seven months after I had been kidnapped, I arrived at the sea coast. It would be tedious and uninteresting to relate all the incidents which befell me during this journey, and which I have not yet forgotten; of the various hands I passed through, and the manners and customs of all the different people among whom I lived — I shall therefore only observe, that in all the places where I was, the soil was exceedingly rich; the pumpkins, eadas,[6] plantains, yams, &c. &c., were in great abundance, and of incredible size. There were also vast quantities of different gums, though not used for any purpose, and everywhere a great deal of tobacco. The cotton even grew quite wild, and there was plenty of red-wood. I saw no mechanics[7] whatever in all the way, except such as I have mentioned. The chief employment in all these countries was agriculture, and both the males and females, as with us, were brought up to it, and trained in the arts of war.

The first object which saluted my eyes when I arrived on the coast, was the sea, and a slave ship, which was then riding at anchor, and waiting for its cargo. These filled me with astonishment, which was soon converted into terror, when I was carried on board. I was immediately handled, and tossed up to see if I were sound, by some of the crew; and I was now persuaded that I had gotten into a world of bad spirits, and that they were going to kill me. Their complexions, too, differing so much from ours, their long hair, and the language they spoke (which was very different from any I had ever heard), united to confirm me in this belief. Indeed, such were the horrors of my views and fears at the moment, that, if ten thousand worlds had been my own, I would have freely parted with them all to have exchanged my condition with that of the meanest slave in my own country. When I looked round the ship too, and saw a large furnance of copper boiling, and a multitude of black people of every description chained together, every one of their countenances expressing dejection and sorrow, I no longer doubted of my fate; and, quite overpowered with horror and anguish, I fell motionless on the deck and fainted. When I recovered a little, I found some black people about me, who I believed were some of those who had brought me on board, and had been receiving their pay; they talked to me in order to cheer me, but all in vain. I asked them if we were not to be eaten by those white men with horrible looks, red faces, and long hair. They told me I was not, and one of the crew brought me a small portion of spirituous liquor in a wine glass; but being

---

6. **eadas:** Also spelled *eddoes*, meaning edible roots.
7. **mechanics:** Early term for manual laborers or artisans.

afraid of him, I would not take it out of his hand. One of the blacks therefore took it from him and gave it to me, and I took a little down my palate, which, instead of reviving me, as they thought it would, threw me into the greatest consternation at the strange feeling it produced, having never tasted any such liquor before. Soon after this, the blacks who brought me on board went off, and left me abandoned to despair.

I now saw myself deprived of all chance of returning to my native country, or even the least glimpse of hope of gaining the shore, which I now considered as friendly; and I even wished for my former slavery in preference to my present situation, which was filled with horrors of every kind, still heightened by my ignorance of what I was to undergo. I was not long suffered to indulge my grief; I was soon put down under the decks, and there I received such a salutation in my nostrils as I had never experienced in my life: so that, with the loathsomeness of the stench, and crying together, I became so sick and low that I was not able to eat, nor had I the least desire to taste anything. I now wished for the last friend, death, to relieve me; but soon, to my grief, two of the white men offered me eatables; and, on my refusing to eat, one of them held me fast by the hands, and laid me across, I think, the windlass, and tied my feet, while the other flogged me severely. I had never experienced anything of this kind before, and, although not being used to the water, I naturally feared that element the first time I saw it, yet, nevertheless, could I have got over the nettings, I would have jumped over the side, but I could not; and besides, the crew used to watch us very closely who were not chained down to the decks, lest we should leap into the water; and I have seen some of these poor African prisoners most severely cut, for attempting to do so, and hourly whipped for not eating. This indeed was often the case with myself.

In a little time after, amongst the poor chained men, I found some of my own nation, which in a small degree gave ease to my mind. I inquired of these what was to be done with us? They gave me to understand, we were to be carried to these white people's country to work for them. I then was a little revived, and thought, if it were no worse than working, my situation was not so desperate; but still I feared I should be put to death, the white people looked and acted, as I thought, in so savage a manner; for I had never seen among any people such instances of brutal cruelty; and this not only shown towards us blacks, but also to some of the whites themselves. One white man in particular I saw, when we were permitted to be on deck, flogged so unmercifully with a large rope near the foremast, that he died in consequence of it; and they tossed him over the side as they would have done a brute. This made me fear these people the more; and I expected nothing less than to be treated in the same manner. I could not help expressing my fears and apprehensions to some of my countrymen; I asked them if these people had no country, but lived in this hollow place (the ship)? They told me they did not, but came from a distant one. "Then," said I, "how comes it in all our country we never heard of them?" They told me because they lived so very far off. I then asked where were their women? had they any like themselves? I was told they had. "And why," said I, "do we not see them?" They answered, because they were left behind. I asked how the vessel could go? They told me they could not tell; but that there was cloth put upon the masts by the help of the ropes I saw, and then the vessel went on; and the white men had some spell or magic they put in the water when they liked, in order to stop the vessel. I was exceedingly amazed at this account, and really thought they were spirits. I therefore wished much to be from amongst them, for I expected they would sacrifice me; but my wishes were vain – for we were so quartered that it was impossible for any of us to make our escape.

While we stayed on the coast I was mostly on deck; and one day, to my great astonishment, I saw one of these vessels coming in with the sails up. As soon as the whites saw it, they gave a great shout, at which we were amazed; and the more so, as the vessel appeared larger by approaching nearer. At last, she came to an anchor in my sight, and when the anchor was let go, I and my countrymen who saw it, were lost in astonishment to observe the vessel stop – and were now convinced it was done by magic. Soon after this the other ship got her boats out, and they came on board of us, and the people of both ships seemed very glad to see each other. Several of the strangers also shook hands with us black people, and made motions with their hands, signifying I suppose, we were to go to their country, but we did not understand them.

At last, when the ship we were in, had got in all her cargo, they made ready with many fearful noises, and we were all put under deck, so that we could not see how they managed the vessel. But this disappointment was the least of my sorrow. The stench of the hold while we were on the coast was so intolerably loathsome, that it was dangerous to remain there for any time, and some of us had been permitted to stay on the deck for the fresh air; but now that the whole ship's cargo were confined together, it became absolutely pestilential. The closeness of the place, and the heat of the climate, added to the number in the ship, which was so crowded that each had scarcely room to turn himself, almost suffocated us. This produced copious perspirations, so that the air soon became unfit for respiration, from a variety of loathsome smells, and brought on a sickness among the slaves, of which many died – thus falling victims to the improvident avarice, as I may call it, of their purchasers. This wretched situation was again aggravated by the galling of the chains, now became insupportable, and the filth of the necessary tubs,[8] into which the children often fell, and were almost suffocated. The shrieks of the women, and the groans of the dying, rendered the whole a scene of horror almost inconceivable. Happily perhaps, for myself, I was soon reduced so low here that it was thought necessary to keep me almost always on deck; and from my extreme youth I was not put in fetters. In this situation I expected every hour to share the fate of my companions, some of whom were almost daily brought upon deck at the point of death, which I began to hope would soon put an end to my miseries. Often did I think many of the inhabitants of the deep much more happy than myself. I envied them the freedom they enjoyed, and as often wished I could change my condition for theirs. Every circumstance I met with, served only to render my state more painful, and heightened my apprehensions, and my opinion of the cruelty of the whites.

One day they had taken a number of fishes; and when they had killed and satisfied themselves with as many as they thought fit, to our astonishment who were on deck, rather than give any of them to us to eat, as we expected, they tossed the remaining fish into the sea again, although we begged and prayed for some as well as we could, but in

---

8. **necessary tubs:** Latrines.

vain; and some of my countrymen, being pressed by hunger, took an opportunity, when they thought no one saw them, of trying to get a little privately; but they were discovered, and the attempt procured them some very severe floggings.

One day, when we had a smooth sea and moderate wind, two of my wearied countrymen who were chained together (I was near them at the time), preferring death to such a life of misery, somehow made through the nettings and jumped into the sea; immediately, another quite dejected fellow, who, on account of his illness, was suffered to be out of irons, also followed their example; and I believe many more would very soon have done the same, if they had not been prevented by the ship's crew, who were instantly alarmed. Those of us that were the most active, were in a moment put down under the deck; and there was such a noise and confusion amongst the people of the ship as I never heard before, to stop her, and get the boat out to go after the slaves. However, two of the wretches were drowned, but they got the other, and afterwards flogged him unmercifully, for thus attempting to prefer death to slavery. In this manner we continued to undergo more hardships than I can now relate, hardships which are inseparable from this accursed trade. Many a time we were near suffocation from the want of fresh air, which we were often without for whole days together. This, and the stench of the necessary tubs, carried off many.

During our passage, I first saw flying fishes, which surprised me very much; they used frequently to fly across the ship, and many of them fell on the deck. I also now first saw the use of the quadrant; I had often with astonishment seen the mariners make observations with it, and I could not think what it meant. They at last took notice of my surprise; and one of them, willing to increase it, as well as to gratify my curiosity, made me one day look through it. The clouds appeared to me to be land, which disappeared as they passed along. This heightened my wonder; and I was now more persuaded than ever, that I was in another world, and that every thing about me was magic.

At last we came in sight of the island of Barbadoes,[9] at which the whites on board gave a great shout, and made many signs of joy to us. We did not know what to think of this; but as the vessel drew nearer, we plainly saw the harbor, and other ships of different kinds and sizes, and we soon anchored amongst them, off Bridgetown. Many merchants and planters now came on board, though it was in the evening. They put us in separate parcels,[10] and examined us attentively. They also made us jump, and pointed to the land, signifying we were to go there. We thought by this, we should be eaten by these ugly men, as they appeared to us; and, when soon after we were all put down under the deck again, there was much dread and trembling among us, and nothing but bitter cries to be heard all the night from these apprehensions, insomuch, that at last the white people got some old slaves from the land to pacify us. They told us we were not to be eaten, but to work, and were soon to go on land, where we should see many of our country people. This report eased us much. And sure enough, soon after we were landed, there came to us Africans of all languages.

---

9. **Barbadoes:** Now spelled *Barbados*, this island in the West Indies was colonized by the English in 1625 and later became a major exporter of sugar, produced on plantations worked by slaves.
10. **parcels:** Divisions or groups.

We were conducted immediately to the merchant's yard, where we were all pent up together, like so many sheep in a fold, without regard to sex or age. As every object was new to me, everything I saw filled me with surprise. What struck me first, was, that the houses were built with bricks and stories, and in every other respect different from those I had seen in Africa; but I was still more astonished on seeing people on horseback. I did not know what this could mean; and, indeed, I thought these people were full of nothing but magical arts. While I was in this astonishment, one of my fellow prisoners spoke to a countryman of his, about the horses, who said they were the same kind they had in their country. I understood them, though they were from a distant part of Africa; and I thought it odd I had not seen any horses there; but afterwards, when I came to converse with different Africans, I found they had many horses amongst them, and much larger than those I then saw.

We were not many days in the merchant's custody, before we were sold after their usual manner, which is this: On a signal given (as the beat of a drum), the buyers rush at once into the yard where the slaves are confined, and make choice of that parcel they like best. The noise and clamor with which this is attended, and the eagerness visible in the countenances of the buyers, serve not a little to increase the apprehension of terrified Africans, who may well be supposed to consider them as the ministers of that destruction to which they think themselves devoted. In this manner, without scruple, are relations and friends separated, most of them never to see each other again.

I remember, in the vessel in which I was brought over, in the men's apartment, there were several brothers, who, in the sale, were sold in different lots; and it was very moving on this occasion, to see and hear their cries at parting. O, ye nominal Christians! might not an African ask you—Learned you this from your God, who says unto you, Do unto all men as you would men should do unto you?[11] Is it not enough that we are torn from our country and friends, to toil for your luxury and lust of gain? Must every tender feeling be likewise sacrificed to your avarice? Are the dearest friends and relations, now rendered more dear by their separation from their kindred, still to be parted from each other, and thus prevented from cheering the gloom of slavery, with the small comfort of being together, and mingling their sufferings and sorrows? Why are parents to lose their children, brothers their sisters, or husbands their wives? Surely, this is a new refinement in cruelty, which, while it has no advantage to atone for it, thus aggravates distress, and adds fresh horrors even to the wretchedness of slavery.

[1789, 1791]

---

11. **Do . . . unto you:** A paraphrase of Christ's injunction in the Sermon on the Mount: "And as ye would that men should do to you, do ye also to them likewise" (Luke 6:31).

American Contexts

"To Begin the World Over Again": The Emerging Idea of "America"

bedfordstmartins.com/
americanlit for research
links on the authors in this
section

THE DISAFFECTION with British policies that led to the American Revolution developed for more than a decade before what Ralph Waldo Emerson later called "the shot heard round the world" was fired at the battles of Concord and Lexington in April 1775. Following the French and Indian War, also known as the Seven Years' War (1756-63), which ended France's empire in North America, the colonists viewed themselves as British patriots who had fought to preserve liberty and individual rights, including the right to property. Rather than being recognized for their sacrifices during the war, they were treated as subjects by Parliament. During the following twelve years, deep divisions arose between Britain and the American colonies, especially over issues of taxation. Many of those living in the colonies consequently began to think of themselves as "Americans," a people with a distinct identity whose liberty and property were threatened by a series of repressive laws passed by Parliament. Although as many as a third of the colonists actively opposed or were hostile to the Revolution, by 1775 thousands of others were so determined to defend their rights that they were ready to take up arms against the British army. The aspirations and hopes of those colonists were perhaps most eloquently expressed by Thomas Paine, an Englishman who had only recently immigrated to America. Two years after he arrived in Philadelphia in 1774, Paine published *Common*

Sense (1776), a fifty-page pamphlet in which he powerfully affirmed the necessity for American independence from Britain. In the conclusion of his best-selling treatise, Paine reminds the colonists of the extraordinary moment in which they live: "We have it in our power to begin the world over again. A situation, similar to the present, hath not happened since the days of Noah until now. The birthday of a new world is at hand, and a race of men perhaps as numerous as all Europe contains, are to receive their portion of freedom from the event of a few months."

Paine was echoing a common sentiment in the colonies. In fact, from the beginning of English colonization of North America, it was viewed by many as a place for new beginnings, new opportunities, and new experiments of all kinds — political, religious, social, and cultural. The selection from *Common Sense* and the other documents in the following section reveal the ways in which a wide variety of speakers and writers conceived of "America" in the years before and after the Revolution. In various ways, they also addressed the famous question raised in the first of these documents, a selection from *Letters from an American Farmer*, in which

Frontispiece of the *Massachusetts Magazine* (1790)

This allegorical engraving celebrated the triumph of the Enlightenment ideals of liberty and equality in America. Two female figures radiating light, one of them holding a staff with a liberty cap, stand next to a globe on a pedestal. The items at their feet include keys, discarded shackles, and a book open to "The Rights of Men." In the background, a man in armor and a haggard woman, representing war and discord, flee into the darkness.

J. Hector St. John de Crèvecoeur asks: "What then is the American, this new man?" Responses to that question, and to broader questions about the country's emerging political and social values, include writings by three of the so-called Founding Fathers, John Adams, Thomas Jefferson, and George Washington. The selections also include appeals by those who sought to extend individual rights and liberty to marginalized or oppressed groups in the new country. Writing to her husband, John Adams—who was then serving on the committee to draft the Declaration of Independence—Abigail Adams urged him to "Remember the Ladies, and be more generous and favourable to them than your ancestors." Adams's concern with the role of women in the new republic was later amplified by the early American feminist Judith Sargent Murray in her essay "On the Equality of the Sexes." In a petition to the president and Congress, the former slave Absalom Jones asked that the rights guaranteed by the Declaration of Independence and the Bill of Rights be extended to black men. At the same time, the Shawnee warrior Tecumseh strongly protested the forced sale of tribal lands and the brutal treatment of the Indians by the government, asking the territorial governor and future president William Henry Harrison: "How can we have confidence in the white people?" Indeed, the questions that emerged as the new nation formed were far-reaching. How would the country govern and protect itself? How could the existing colonies become a single entity, the United States of America? What were the rights of citizenship? To whom would those rights be extended? How would those who had refused to be what they described as "slaves" to Great Britain deal with the institution of slavery in their own country? And how would they deal with the native inhabitants of that country? What, finally, did "America" mean; and what did it mean to be an "American"?

J. Hector St. John de Crèvecoeur

[1735–1813]

Born in France in 1735, Michel-Guillaume-Jean de Crèvecoeur left his native country when he was nineteen, moving to England, then to Canada, and finally to New York in 1759. He changed his name to J. Hector St. John de Crèvecoeur and traveled widely in the colonies as a surveyor and trader until 1769, when the newly married Crèvecoeur bought a farm in Orange County, New York. He lived there until the beginning of the Revolution, when his staunch support of British rule in the colonies forced him to leave his family and sail for England. In the preface to the first edition of

Letters from an American Farmer (1782), which he had begun to write in New Jersey and sold to the English bookseller Thomas Davies, Crèvecoeur explains: "The following Letters are the genuine production of the American Farmer whose name they bear. They were privately written to gratify the curiosity of a friend; and are made public, because they contain much authentic information, little known on this side the Atlantic: they cannot therefore fail of being highly interesting to the people of England, at a time when everybody's attention is directed toward the affairs of America." Appearing near the end of the Revolutionary War, the book was an immediate success; so was the expanded edition Crèvecoeur translated and published in France in 1783 (dated 1784). That year, Crèvecoeur returned as a French diplomat to the United States, where he discovered that his wife was dead and their farm in ruins. He later returned for good to France, where in 1787 Crèvecoeur published yet another expanded edition of his famous book, which for many in the Old World of Europe served as a major source of both information about and imaginary visions of the "new world" of America. The text of the following selection is taken from a reprint published in 1904 of the first London edition, which appeared under the full title *Letters from an American Farmer; Describing Certain Provincial Situations, Manners, and Customs, Not Generally Known; and Conveying Some Idea of the Late and Present Circumstances of the British Colonies in North America* (1782).

J. Hector St. John de Crèvecoeur

This portrait is an anonymous copy of a miniature painted by the French artist Joseph Vallière in 1786, when Crèvecoeur was back in France. Attired in a powdered wig and the formal clothing of a French diplomat, Crèvecoeur bears little resemblance to the image he projects in his celebrated book, *Letters from an American Farmer.*

LETTERS FROM AN AMERICAN FARMER

From Letter III. What Is an American?

I wish I could be acquainted with the feelings and thoughts which must agitate the heart and present themselves to the mind of an enlightened Englishman, when he first lands on this continent. He must greatly rejoice that he lived at a time to see this fair country discovered and settled; he must necessarily feel a share of national pride, when he views the chain of settlements which embellishes these extended shores. When he says to himself, this is the work of my countrymen, who, when convulsed by factions, afflicted by a variety of miseries and wants, restless and impatient, took refuge here. They brought along with them their national genius, to which they principally owe what liberty they enjoy, and what substance they possess. Here he sees the industry of his native country displayed in a new manner, and traces in their works the embrios of all the arts, sciences, and ingenuity which flourish in Europe. Here he beholds fair cities, substantial villages, extensive fields, an immense country filled with decent houses, good roads, orchards, meadows, and bridges, where an hundred years ago all was wild, woody and uncultivated! What a train of pleasing ideas this fair spectacle must suggest; it is a prospect which must inspire a good citizen with the most heartfelt pleasure. The difficulty consists in the manner of viewing so extensive a scene. He is arrived on a new continent; a modern society offers itself to his contemplation, different from what he had hitherto seen. It is not composed, as in Europe, of great lords who possess every thing, and of a herd of people who have nothing. Here are no aristocratical families, no courts, no kings, no bishops, no ecclesiastical dominion, no invisible power giving to a few a very visible one; no great manufacturers employing thousands, no great refinements of luxury. The rich and the poor are not so far removed from each other as they are in Europe. Some few towns excepted, we are all tillers of the earth, from Nova Scotia to West Florida. We are a people of cultivators, scattered over an immense territory, communicating with each other by means of good roads, and navigable rivers, united by the silken bands of mild government, all respecting the laws, without dreading their power, because they are equitable. We are all animated with the spirit of an industry which is unfettered and unrestrained, because each person works for himself. If he travels through our rural districts he views not the hostile castle, and the haughty mansion, contrasted with the clay-built hut and miserable cabin, where cattle and men help to keep each other warm, and dwell in meanness, smoke, and indigence. A pleasing uniformity of decent competence appears throughout our habitations. The meanest of our log-houses is a dry and comfortable habitation. Lawyer or merchant are the fairest titles our towns afford; that of a farmer is the only appellation of the rural inhabitants of our country. It must take some time ere he can reconcile himself to our dictionary, which is but short in words of dignity, and names of honour. There, on a Sunday, he sees a congregation of respectable farmers and their wives, all clad in neat homespun, well mounted, or riding in their own humble wagons. There is not among them an esquire, saving the unlettered magistrate. There he sees a parson as simple as his flock, a farmer who does not riot[1] on the labour of others. We have no princes, for whom we toil, starve, and bleed: we are the most perfect society now existing in the world. Here man is free as he ought to be; nor is this pleasing equality so transitory as many others are. Many ages will not see the shores of our great lakes replenished with inland nations, nor the unknown bounds of North America entirely peopled. Who can tell how far it extends? Who can tell the millions of men whom it will feed and contain? for no European foot has as yet travelled half the extent of this mighty continent!

The next wish of this traveller will be to know whence came all these people? they are a mixture of English, Scotch, Irish, French, Dutch, Germans, and Swedes. From this promiscuous breed, that race now called Americans have arisen. The eastern provinces[2] must indeed be excepted, as being the unmixed descendents of Englishmen. I have heard many wish that they had been more intermixed also: for my part, I am no wisher, and think it much better as it has happened. They exhibit a most

---

1. **riot:** To indulge in feasting, drinking, or other sensual excesses.
2. **eastern provinces:** New England.

conspicuous figure in this great and variegated picture; they too enter for a great share in the pleasing perspective displayed in these thirteen provinces. I know it is fashionable to reflect on them, but I respect them for what they have done; for the accuracy and wisdom with which they have settled their territory; for the decency of their manners; for their early love of letters; their ancient college,[3] the first in this hemisphere; for their industry; which to me who am but a farmer, is the criterion of everything. There never was a people, situated as they are, who with so ungrateful a soil have done more in so short a time. Do you think that the monarchical ingredients which are more prevalent in other governments, have purged them from all foul stains? Their histories assert the contrary.

In this great American asylum,[4] the poor of Europe have by some means met together, and in consequence of various causes; to what purpose should they ask one another what countrymen they are? Alas, two thirds of them had no country. Can a wretch who wanders about, who works and starves, whose life is a continual scene of sore affliction or pinching penury; can that man call England or any other kingdom his country? A country that had no bread for him, whose fields procured him no harvest, who met with nothing but the frowns of the rich, the severity of the laws, with jails and punishments; who owned not a single foot of the extensive surface of this planet? No! urged by a variety of motives, here they came. Every thing has tended to regenerate them; new laws, a new mode of living, a new social system; here they are become men: in Europe they were as so many useless plants, wanting vegitative mould, and refreshing showers; they withered, and were mowed down by want, hunger, and war; but now by the power of transplantation, like all other plants they have taken root and flourished! Formerly they were not numbered in any civil lists[5] of their country, except in those of the poor; here they rank as citizens. By what invisible power has this surprising metamorphosis been performed? By that of the laws and that of their industry. The laws, the indulgent laws, protect them as they arrive, stamping on them the symbol of adoption; they receive ample rewards for their labours; these accumulated rewards procure them lands; those lands confer on them the title of freemen, and to that title every benefit is affixed which men can possibly require. This is the great operation daily performed by our laws. From whence proceed these laws? From our government. Whence the government? It is derived from the original genius and strong desire of the people ratified and confirmed by the crown.[6] This is the great chain which links us all, this is the picture which every province exhibits, Nova Scotia excepted.[7] There the crown has done all; either there were no people who had genius, or it was not much

---

3. **college:** Harvard College, founded in 1636.
4. **asylum:** Place of refuge, security, and shelter.
5. **civil lists:** Rosters of individuals employed by a government.
6. **It is derived . . . confirmed by the crown:** Crèvecoeur stresses the important role of British rule in the successful government of the colonies.
7. **Nova Scotia excepted:** A reference to the Great Expulsion of 1755, when the French Acadians in Nova Scotia were rounded up by British soldiers, put on ships, and forced to leave the colony for refusing to sign an oath of allegiance to the British government.

attended to: the consequence is, that the province is very thinly inhabited indeed; the power of the crown in conjunction with the musketos has prevented men from settling there. Yet some parts of it flourished once, and it contained a mild harmless set of people. But for the fault of a few leaders, the whole were banished. The greatest political error the crown ever committed in America, was to cut off men from a country which wanted nothing but men!

What attachment can a poor European emigrant have for a country where he had nothing? The knowledge of the language, the love of a few kindred as poor as himself, were the only cords that tied him: his country is now that which gives him land, bread, protection, and consequence: *Ubi panis ibi patria*,[8] is the motto of all emigrants. What then is the American, this new man? He is either an European, or the descendant of an European, hence that strange mixture of blood, which you will find in no other country. I could point out to you a family whose grandfather was an Englishman, whose wife was Dutch, whose son married a French woman, and whose present four sons have now four wives of different nations. *He* is an American, who leaving behind him all his ancient prejudices and manners, receives new ones from the new mode of life he has embraced, the new government he obeys, and the new rank he holds. He becomes an American by being received in the broad lap of our great *Alma Mater*.[9] Here individuals of all nations are melted into a new race of men, whose labours and posterity will one day cause great changes in the world. Americans are the western pilgrims, who are carrying along with them that great mass of arts, sciences, vigour, and industry which began long since in the east; they will finish the great circle. The Americans were once scattered all over Europe; here they are incorporated into one of the finest systems of population which has ever appeared, and which will hereafter become distinct by the power of the different climates they inhabit. The American ought therefore to love this country much better than that wherein either he or his forefathers were born. Here the rewards of his industry follow with equal steps the progress of his labour; his labour is founded on the basis of nature, *self-interest*; can it want a stronger allurement? Wives and children, who before in vain demanded of him a morsel of bread, now, fat and frolicsome, gladly help their father to clear those fields whence exuberant crops are to arise to feed and to clothe them all; without any part being claimed, either by a despotic prince, a rich abbot, or a mighty lord. Here religion demands but little of him; a small voluntary salary to the minister, and gratitude to God; can he refuse these? The American is a new man, who acts upon new principles; he must therefore entertain new ideas, and form new opinions. From involuntary idleness, servile dependence, penury, and useless labour, he has passed to toils of a very different nature, rewarded by ample subsistence. – This is an American.

[1782, 1904]

---

8. *Ubi panis ibi patria*: Where there is bread, there is my country (Latin).
9. *Alma Mater*: Bounteous mother (Latin).

Thomas Paine

[1737-1809]

Born into a poor family in England and largely self-educated, Thomas Paine immigrated to the colonies after meeting Benjamin Franklin in London in 1774. As the coeditor of the *Pennsylvania Magazine*, Paine became deeply involved in political activities that would lead to the American Revolution. Following the battles of Concord and Lexington and the occupation of Boston by the British army, he wrote the first pamphlet to advocate immediate independence from England, *Common Sense*, which was published anonymously "By an Englishman" on January 10, 1776. In his introduction, Paine affirms,

Thomas Paine

Published in London in 1793, this engraving was based on a portrait of Paine done by one of his closest English friends, the renowned painter George Romney.

> The cause of America is in a great measure the cause of all mankind. Many circumstances have, and will arise, which are not local, but universal, and through which the principles of all Lovers of Mankind are affected, and in the Event of which, their Affections are interested. The laying of a Country desolate with Fire and Sword, declaring War against the natural rights of all Mankind, and extirpating the Defenders thereof from the Face of the Earth, is the Concern of every Man to whom Nature hath given the Power of feeling; of which Class, regardless of Party Censure, is the AUTHOR.

Paine's simple style—designed, as he put it, "to make those who can scarcely read understand"—contributed to the phenomenal success of *Common Sense*. Published first in English and then in a German translation, the pamphlet sold an estimated 150,000 copies in three months, and its total sales ultimately reached half a million copies, plus extracts published in newspapers. The *Connecticut Gazette* described it as "a landflood that sweeps all before it." Certainly, Paine's words swept aside much of the lingering allegiance to King George III, paving the way for the Declaration of Independence, which was signed in Philadelphia six months after *Common Sense* was published in the same city. The text of the following selection is taken from volume one of *The Writings of Thomas Paine*, edited by Moncure Daniel Conway (1894–1896).

From COMMON SENSE

As much hath been said of the advantages of reconciliation, which, like an agreeable dream, hath passed away and left us as we were, it is but right that we should examine the contrary side of the argument, and enquire into some of the many material injuries which these Colonies sustain, and always will sustain, by being connected with and dependant on Great-Britain. To examine that connection and dependance, on the principles of nature and common sense, to see what we have to trust to, if separated, and what we are to expect, if dependant.

I have heard it asserted by some, that as America has flourished under her former connection with Great-Britain, the same connection is necessary towards her future happiness, and will always have the same effect. Nothing can be more fallacious than this kind of argument. We may as well assert that because a child has thrived upon milk, that it is never to have meat, or that the first twenty years of our lives is to become a precedent for the next twenty. But even this is admitting more than is true; for I answer roundly, that America would have flourished as much, and probably much more, had no European power taken any notice of her. The commerce by which she hath enriched herself are the necessaries of life, and will always have a market while eating is the custom of Europe.

But she has protected us, say some. That she hath engrossed us is true, and defended the Continent at our expense as well as her own, is admitted; and she would have defended Turkey from the same motive, *viz.* for the sake of trade and dominion.

Alas! we have been long led away by ancient prejudices and made large sacrifices to superstition. We have boasted the protection of Great Britain, without considering, that her motive was *interest* not *attachment*; and that she did not protect us from *our enemies* on *our account*; but from *her enemies* on *her own account*, from those who had no quarrel with us on any *other account*, and who will always be our enemies on the *same account*. Let Britain waive her pretensions to the Continent, or the Continent throw off the dependance, and we should be at peace with France and Spain, were they at war with Britain. The miseries of Hanover's last war[1] ought to warn us against connections.

It hath lately been asserted in parliament, that the Colonies have no relation to each other but through the Parent Country, *i. e.* that Pennsylvania and the Jerseys,[2] and so on for the rest, are sister Colonies by the way of England; this is certainly a very round-about way of proving relationship, but it is the nearest and only true way of proving enmity (or enemyship, if I may so call it.) France and Spain never were, nor perhaps ever will be, our enemies as *Americans*, but as our being the *subjects of Great Britain*.

But Britain is the parent country, say some. Then the more shame upon her conduct. Even brutes do not devour their young, nor savages make war upon their families; Wherefore, the assertion, if true, turns to her reproach; but it happens not to be true, or only partly so, and the phrase *parent* or *mother country* hath been jesuitically[3] adopted by the King and his parasites, with a low papistical design of gaining an unfair bias on the credulous weakness of our minds. Europe, and not England, is the parent country of America. This new World hath been the asylum for the persecuted lovers of civil and religious liberty from *every part* of Europe. Hither have they fled, not from the tender embraces of the mother, but from the cruelty of the monster; and it is so far true of England, that the same tyranny which drove the first emigrants from home, pursues their descendants still.

---

1. **Hanover's last war:** The French and Indian War, also known as the Seven Years' War (1756–63), was a result of the colonial rivalry between Great Britain and France as well as internal power struggles in Germany between the kingdoms of Prussia and Hanover. (King George III of Great Britain was a descendant of the House of Hanover.) At the conclusion of the war, which eventually involved several European countries, Great Britain emerged as the dominant colonial power in North America.
2. **Jerseys:** At the time, the colony was divided into East and West Jersey.
3. **jesuitically:** Cleverly, in the manner of the Jesuits, a Roman Catholic order of priests.

In this extensive quarter of the globe, we forget the narrow limits of three hundred and sixty miles (the extent of England) and carry our friendship on a larger scale; we claim brotherhood with every European Christian, and triumph in the generosity of the sentiment.

It is pleasant to observe by what regular gradations we surmount the force of local prejudices, as we enlarge our acquaintance with the World. A man born in any town in England divided into parishes, will naturally associate most with his fellow parishioners (because their interests in many cases will be common) and distinguish him by the name of *neighbour*; if he meet him but a few miles from home, he drops the narrow idea of a street, and salutes him by the name of *townsman*; if he travel out of the county and meet him in any other, he forgets the minor divisions of street and town, and calls him *countryman, i. e. countyman*: but if in their foreign excursions they should associate in France, or any other part of *Europe*, their local remembrance would be enlarged into that of *Englishmen*. And by a just parity of reasoning, all Europeans meeting in America, or any other quarter of the globe, are *countrymen*; for England, Holland, Germany, or Sweden, when compared with the whole, stand in the same places on the larger scale, which the divisions of street, town, and county do on the smaller ones; Distinctions too limited for Continental minds. Not one third of the inhabitants, even of this province,[4] are of English descent. Wherefore, I reprobate the phrase of Parent or Mother Country applied to England only, as being false, selfish, narrow and ungenerous.

But, admitting that we were all of English descent, what does it amount to? Nothing. Britain, being now an open enemy, extinguishes every other name and title: and to say that reconciliation is our duty, is truly farcical. The first king of England, of the present line (William the Conqueror) was a Frenchman, and half the peers of England are descendants from the same country; wherefore, by the same method of reasoning, England ought to be governed by France.

Much hath been said of the united strength of Britain and the Colonies, that in conjunction they might bid defiance to the world: But this is mere presumption; the fate of war is uncertain, neither do the expressions mean any thing; for this continent would never suffer itself to be drained of inhabitants, to support the British arms in either Asia, Africa, or Europe.

Besides, what have we to do with setting the world at defiance? Our plan is commerce, and that, well attended to, will secure us the peace and friendship of all Europe; because it is the interest of all Europe to have America a free port. Her trade will always be a protection, and her barrenness of gold and silver secure her from invaders.

I challenge the warmest advocate for reconciliation to show a single advantage that this continent can reap by being connected with Great Britain. I repeat the challenge; not a single advantage is derived. Our corn[5] will fetch its price in any market in Europe, and our imported goods must be paid for buy them where we will.

---

4. **this province:** Pennsylvania.
5. **corn:** Early term for any cereal grain.

But the injuries and disadvantages which we sustain by that connection, are without number; and our duty to mankind at large, as well as to ourselves, instruct us to renounce the alliance: because, any submission to, or dependance on, Great Britain, tends directly to involve this Continent in European wars and quarrels, and set us at variance with nations who would otherwise seek our friendship, and against whom we have neither anger nor complaint. As Europe is our market for trade, we ought to form no partial connection with any part of it. It is the true interest of America to steer clear of European contentions, which she never can do, while, by her dependance on Britain, she is made the makeweight in the scale of British politics.

Europe is too thickly planted with Kingdoms to be long at peace, and whenever a war breaks out between England and any foreign power, the trade of America goes to ruin, *because of her connection with Britain.* The next war may not turn out like the last,[6] and should it not, the advocates for reconciliation now will be wishing for separation then, because neutrality in that case would be a safer convoy than a man of war. Every thing that is right or reasonable pleads for separation. The blood of the slain, the weeping voice of nature cries, 'TIS TIME TO PART. Even the distance at which the Almighty hath placed England and America is a strong and natural proof that the authority of the one over the other, was never the design of Heaven. The time likewise at which the Continent was discovered, adds weight to the argument, and the manner in which it was peopled, encreases the force of it. The Reformation was preceded by the discovery of America: As if the Almighty graciously meant to open a sanctuary to the persecuted in future years, when home should afford neither friendship nor safety. . . .

Ye that tell us of harmony and reconciliation, can ye restore to us the time that is past? Can ye give to prostitution its former innocence? neither can ye reconcile Britain and America. The last cord now is broken, the people of England are presenting addresses against us. There are injuries which nature cannot forgive; she would cease to be nature if she did. As well can the lover forgive the ravisher of his mistress, as the Continent forgive the murders of Britain. The Almighty hath implanted in us these unextinguishable feelings for good and wise purposes. They are the Guardians of his Image in our hearts. They distinguish us from the herd of common animals. The social compact would dissolve, and justice be extirpated from the earth, or have only a casual existence were we callous to the touches of affection. The robber and the murderer would often escape unpunished, did not the injuries which our tempers sustain, provoke us into justice.

O! ye that love mankind! Ye that dare oppose not only the tyranny but the tyrant, stand forth! Every spot of the old world is overrun with oppression. Freedom hath been hunted round the Globe. Asia and Africa have long expelled her. Europe regards her like a stranger, and England hath given her warning to depart. O! receive the fugitive, and prepare in time an asylum for mankind.

[1776, 1894]

---

6. **last:** The French and Indian War; see note 1.

John Adams

[1735–1826]

and

Abigail Adams

[1744–1818]

John Adams, a Boston lawyer, married Abigail Smith in 1764, ten years before he was elected as a delegate from Massachusetts to the First Continental Congress. From the beginning of their courtship throughout his long years of public service, culminating in his term as the second president (1797–1801), the couple exchanged over eleven hundred letters, which provide fascinating insights into the emergence and early development of the United States. The couple wrote frankly to each other, debating controversial issues such as the role of women in society, the subject of one of the following exchanges. The other letters reprinted here were exchanged shortly before Adams and other representatives to the Second Continental Congress voted in favor of the Declaration of Independence and reveal their anxieties about the coming revolution, as well as their excitement

Benjamin Blyth, *Portraits of Abigail and John Adams* (1766)

These paired portraits were painted by Benjamin Blyth in 1766, two years after the couple's marriage and at the beginning of a decade in which they became increasingly involved in the movement toward independence, culminating in John Adams's role in the preparation of the Declaration of Independence in 1776.

about building a new nation. The texts of the following selections from their letters are taken from *The Adams Family: An Electronic Archive*, "The Correspondence Between John and Abigail Adams," the Massachusetts Historical Society (http://www.masshist.org/digitaladams/aea/letter/).

LETTER FROM ABIGAIL ADAMS
TO JOHN ADAMS, MARCH 31, 1776

I feel very differently at the approach of spring to what I did a month ago.[1] We knew not then whether we could plant or sow with safety, whether when we had toil'd we could reap the fruits of our own industry, whether we could rest in our own Cottages, or whether we should not be driven from the sea coasts to seek shelter in the wilderness, but now we feel as if we might sit under our own vine[2] and eat the good of the land.

I feel a gaieti de Coar[3] to which before I was a stranger. I think the Sun looks brighter, the Birds sing more melodiously, and Nature puts on a more chearfull countanance. We feel a temporary peace, and the poor fugitives are returning to their deserted habitations.

Tho we felicitate ourselves, we sympathize with those who are trembling least the Lot of Boston should be theirs. But they cannot be in similar circumstances unless pusilanimity and cowardise should take possession of them. They have time and warning given them to see the Evil and shun it. — I long to hear that you have declared an independency — and by the way in the new Code of Laws which I suppose it will be necessary for you to make I desire you would Remember the Ladies, and be more generous and favourable to them than your ancestors. Do not put such unlimited power into the hands of the Husbands. Remember all Men would be tyrants if they could. If perticuliar care and attention is not paid to the Laidies we are determined to foment a Rebelion, and will not hold ourselves bound by any Laws in which we have no voice, or Representation.

That your Sex are Naturally Tyrannical is a Truth so thoroughly established as to admit of no dispute, but such of you as wish to be happy willingly give up the harsh title of Master for the more tender and endearing one of Friend. Why then, not put it out of the power of the vicious and the Lawless to use us with cruelty and indignity with impunity. Men of Sense in all Ages abhor those customs which treat us only as the vassals[4] of your Sex. Regard us then as Beings placed by providence under your protection and in immitation of the Supreem Being make use of that power only for our happiness.

---

1. **a month ago:** During the previous month, American forces had seized Dorchester Heights, from which most of Boston was within range of their artillery. The occupying British army (along with one thousand Loyalists) consequently evacuated the city by sea on March 26, 1776.
2. **sit under our own vine:** See Micah 4:4: "But they shall sit every man under his vine and under his fig tree; and none shall make them afraid: for the mouth of the LORD of hosts hath spoken it."
3. **gaieti de Coar:** Properly *gaité de Coeur* (French), meaning cheerfulness or lightness of heart.
4. **vassals:** Persons in subordinate positions.

Letter from John Adams
to Abigail Adams, April 14, 1776

Your Description of your own Gaiety de Coeur, charms me. Thanks be to God you have just Cause to rejoice – and may the bright Prospect be obscured by no Cloud.

As to Declarations of Independency, be patient. Read our Privateering Laws, and our Commercial Laws.[1] What signifies a Word.

As to your extraordinary Code of Laws, I cannot but laugh. We have been told that our Struggle has loosened the bands of Government every where. That Children and Apprentices were disobedient – that schools and Colledges were grown turbulent – that Indians slighted their Guardians and Negroes grew insolent to their Masters.

But your Letter was the first Intimation that another Tribe more numerous and powerfull than all the rest were grown discontented. – This is rather too coarse a Compliment but you are so saucy, I wont blot it out.

Depend upon it, We know better than to repeal our Masculine systems. Altho they are in full Force, you know they are little more than Theory. We dare not exert our Power in its full Latitude. We are obliged to go fair, and softly, and in Practice you know We are the subjects. We have only the Name of Masters, and rather than give up this, which would compleatly subject Us to the Despotism of the Peticoat, I hope General Washington, and all our brave Heroes would fight. I am sure every good Politician would plot, as long as he would against Despotism, Empire, Monarchy, Aristocracy, Oligarchy, or Ochlocracy.[2] – A fine Story indeed. I begin to think the Ministry as deep as they are wicked. After stirring up Tories, Landjobbers, Trimmers,[3] Bigots, Canadians, Indians, Negroes, Hanoverians, Hessians, Russians, Irish Roman Catholicks, Scotch Renegadoes, at last they have stimulated the [ladies][4] to demand new Priviledges and threaten to rebel.

---

1. **Read . . . Commercial Laws:** Although the Second Continental Congress had not yet voted in favor of independence, it had already assumed executive and legislative powers previously exercised by King George III and the British Parliament.

2. **Despotism . . . Ochlocracy:** Governmental structures that provide ruling powers by a tyrant (despotism), an emperor (empire), a king or queen (monarchy), members of the nobility (aristocracy), a small elite group (oligarchy), or a mob (ochlocracy).

3. **Tories, Landjobbers, Trimmers:** American colonists who supported the British (Tories); persons who buy and sell land on speculation (landjobbers); and persons who change political positions as their personal interests change (trimmers).

4. **[ladies]:** Adams left a blank space at this point in his letter, possibly as a kind of visual joke to indicate that he was not sure that *ladies*, the term Abigail had used in her letter, was the appropriate word to describe those who were suddenly demanding new privileges and threatening to rebel, as he put it with comic exaggeration.

LETTERS FROM JOHN ADAMS
TO ABIGAIL ADAMS, JULY 3, 1776[1]

[1]

Yesterday the greatest Question was decided, which ever was debated in America, and a greater perhaps, never was or will be decided among Men. A Resolution was passed without one dissenting Colony "that these United Colonies, are, and of right ought to be free and independent States, and as such, they have, and of Right ought to have full Power to make War, conclude Peace, establish Commerce, and to do all the other Acts and Things, which other States may rightfully do." You will see in a few days a Declaration setting forth the Causes, which have impell'd Us to this mighty Revolution, and the Reasons which will justify it, in the Sight of God and Man. A Plan of Confederation will be taken up in a few days.

When I look back to the Year 1761, and recollect the Argument concerning Writs of Assistance, in the Superior Court, which I have hitherto considered as the Commencement of the Controversy, between Great Britain and America, and run through the whole Period from that Time to this, and recollect the series of political Events, the Chain of Causes and Effects, I am surprized at the Suddenness, as well as Greatness of this Revolution. Britain has been fill'd with Folly, and America with Wisdom, at least this is my judgment. — Time must determine. It is the Will of Heaven, that the two Countries should be sundered forever. It may be the Will of Heaven that America shall suffer Calamities still more wasting and Distresses yet more dreadfull. If this is to be the Case, it will have this good Effect, at least: it will inspire Us with many Virtues, which We have not, and correct many Errors, Follies, and Vices, which threaten to disturb, dishonour, and destroy Us. — The Furnace of Affliction produces Refinement, in States as well as Individuals. And the new Governments we are assuming, in every Part, will require a Purification from our Vices, and an Augmentation of our Virtues or they will be no Blessings. The People will have unbounded Power. And the People are extreamly addicted to Corruption and Venality, as well as the Great. I am not without Apprehensions from this Quarter. — But I must submit all my Hopes and Fears, to an overruling Providence, in which, unfashionable [as] the Faith may be, I firmly believe.

[2]

Had a Declaration of Independency been made seven Months ago, it would have been attended with many great and glorious Effects. . . . We might before this Hour, have formed Alliances with foreign States. — We should have mastered Quebec and been in Possession of Canada. . . .

But on the other Hand, the Delay of this Declaration to this Time, has many great Advantages attending it. — The Hopes of Reconciliation, which were fondly entertained

---

1. July 3, 1776: Adams wrote two letters to his wife on that day; the following selections from the letters are therefore labeled [1] and [2].

by Multitudes of honest and well meaning tho weak and mistaken People, have been gradually and at last totally extinguished. — Time has been given for the whole People, maturely to consider the great Question of Independence and to ripen their judgments, dissipate their Fears, and allure their Hopes, by discussing it in News Papers and Pamphletts, by debating it, in Assemblies, Conventions, Committees of Safety and Inspection, in Town and County Meetings, as well as in private Conversations, so that the whole People in every Colony of the 13, have now adopted it, as their own Act. — This will cement the Union, and avoid those Heats and perhaps Convulsions which might have been occasioned, by such a Declaration Six Months ago.

But the Day is past. The Second Day of July 1776,[2] will be the most memorable Epocha, in the History of America. I am apt to believe that it will be celebrated, by succeeding Generations, as the great anniversary Festival. It ought to be commemorated, as the Day of Deliverance by solemn Acts of Devotion to God Almighty. It ought to be solemnized with Pomp and Parade, with Shews, Games, Sports, Guns, Bells, Bonfires and Illuminations from one End of this Continent to the other from this Time forward forever more.

You will think me transported with Enthusiasm but I am not. — I am well aware of the Toil and Blood and Treasure, that it will cost Us to maintain this Declaration, and support and defend these States. — Yet through all the Gloom I can see the Rays of ravishing Light and Glory. I can see that the End is more than worth all the Means. And that Posterity will tryumph in that Days Transaction, even altho We should rue it, which I trust in God We shall not.

[1776]

---

2. **July 1776:** On July 2, 1776, the Second Continental Congress voted in favor of a resolution declaring independence from Great Britain. On July 4, 1776, the delegates formally approved an official document, the Declaration of Independence, making the Fourth of July the day celebrated as the inception of the United States.

Thomas Jefferson

[1743–1826]

Thomas Jefferson, the third president of the United States, was born on April 13, 1743, into a wealthy family that owned a large plantation in central Virginia. His political career began in 1769 when he was elected to the Virginia House of Burgesses, where he served for six years. In 1774, Jefferson published *A Summary View of the Rights of British America*, a pamphlet in which he argued that colonial allegiance to the British monarch was strictly voluntary. The pamphlet earned him attention beyond Virginia and propelled him into an increasingly prominent role in the movement toward independence from Great Britain. At age thirty-three, Jefferson was

Thomas Jefferson

This copy of an 1805 portrait by the Philadelphia painter Rembrandt Peale shows Jefferson at the beginning of his second term as president of the United States. Peale and his famous father, Charles Willson Peale, went to Washington to paint celebrities' portraits to hang in their museum in Philadelphia.

elected to the Second Continental Congress, which appointed him to the committee charged with drafting a declaration of independence. He later served as the wartime governor of Virginia, as a member of Congress, as the minister to France, and as secretary of state in the first administration of George Washington. Jefferson ran for president in 1796 but lost to John Adams, becoming vice president under the system then in place. In 1800, Jefferson was elected president and served for two terms, after which he retired to his home in Monticello, Virginia.

Reading Jefferson's Draft of the Declaration of Independence. On June 7, 1776, Richard Henry Lee, a delegate from Virginia to the Second Continental Congress, offered a resolution that began: "Resolved: That these United Colonies are, and of right ought to be, free and independent States, that they are absolved from all allegiance to the British Crown, and that all political connection between them and the State of Great Britain is, and ought to be, totally dissolved." Although no vote was taken on Lee's resolution, a committee of five delegates — John Adams of Massachusetts, Roger Sherman of Connecticut, Benjamin Franklin of Pennsylvania, Robert R. Livingston of New York, and Thomas Jefferson of Virginia — was charged with the preparation of a formal declaration. Jefferson wrote the first draft of the document and showed it to Adams and Franklin, who made some minor changes. The committee as a whole apparently made only a few additional changes before it reported the document to Congress. On July 1, the Congress reconvened to debate Lee's resolution, which it voted to adopt the following day, July 2, 1776. The delegates then began to debate the draft of the Declaration of Independence, which was further

Opening of Jefferson's Draft of the Declaration of Independence

Jefferson carefully preserved his original draft of the Declaration, indicating the minor revisions made by other members of the committee assigned the task of preparing the document, as well as the numerous changes made by the Second Continental Congress before it approved the amended version on July 4, 1776.

revised and amended before it was formally approved on July 4. Jefferson believed that Congress had mangled his draft, copies of which he sent to friends. He also carefully preserved the original document, indicating all of the changes that had been made in his draft, which he included in a brief account of his life begun in 1821 and published after his death as his *Autobiography* (1829). "As the sentiments of men are known not only by what they receive, but what they reject also, I will state the form of the Declaration as originally reported," Jefferson observed. "The parts struck out by Congress shall be distinguished by a black line drawn under them; and those inserted by them shall be placed in the margin, or in a concurrent column." The following text of Jefferson's draft, printed here according to his instructions, is taken from volume one of *The Writings of Thomas Jefferson*, edited by Andrew A. Lipscomb and Albert Ellery Bergh (1903).

DRAFT OF THE DECLARATION OF INDEPENDENCE

A Declaration by the Representatives of the United States of America, in *General* Congress assembled.

When, in the course of human events, it becomes necessary for one people to dissolve the political bands which have connected them with another, and to assume among the powers of the earth the separate and equal station to which the laws of nature and of nature's God entitle them, a decent respect to the opinions of mankind requires that they should declare the causes which impel them to the separation.

We hold these truths to be self evident: that all men are created equal; that they are endowed by their Creator with <u>inherent and</u> inalienable   certain rights; that among these are life, liberty, and the pursuit of happiness;[1] that to secure these rights, governments are instituted among men, deriving their just powers from the consent of the governed; that whenever any form of government becomes destructive of these ends, it is the right of the people to alter or to abolish it, and to institute new government, laying its foundation on such principles, and organizing its powers in such form, as to them shall seem most likely to effect their safety and happiness. Prudence, indeed, will dictate that governments long established should not be changed for light and transient causes; and accordingly all experience hath shown that mankind are more disposed to suffer while evils are sufferable, than to right themselves by abolishing the forms to which they are accustomed. But when a long train of abuses and usurpations, <u>begun at a distinguished period and</u> pursuing invariably the same object, evinces a design to reduce them under absolute despotism, it is their right, it is

---

1. **pursuit of happiness:** In his *Second Treatise of Government* (1690), the English philosopher John Locke (1632–1704) had originally defined the natural rights of individuals as life, liberty, and estate (that is, private property).

their duty to throw off such government, and to provide new guards for their future security. Such has been the patient sufferance of these colonies; and such is now the necessity which constrains them to <u>expunge</u> their former systems of government. The history of the present king of Great Britain[2] is a history of <u>unremitting</u> injuries and usurpations, <u>among which appears no solitary fact to contradict the uniform tenor of the rest, but all have</u> in direct object the establishment of an absolute tyranny over these states. To prove this, let facts be submitted to a candid world <u>for the truth of which we pledge a faith yet unsullied by falsehood</u>.

alter

repeated
all having

He has refused his assent to laws the most wholesome and necessary for the public good.

He has forbidden his governors to pass laws of immediate and pressing importance, unless suspended in their operation till his assent should be obtained; and, when so suspended, he has utterly neglected to attend to them.

He has refused to pass other laws for the accommodation of large districts of people, unless those people would relinquish the right of representation in the legislature, a right inestimable to them, and formidable to tyrants only.

He has called together legislative bodies at places unusual, uncomfortable, and distant from the depository of their public records, for the sole purpose of fatiguing them into compliance with his measures.

He has dissolved representative houses repeatedly <u>and continually</u> for opposing with manly firmness his invasions on the rights of the people.

He has refused for a long time after such dissolutions to cause others to be elected, whereby the legislative powers, incapable of annihilation, have returned to the people at large for their exercise, the state remaining, in the meantime, exposed to all the dangers of invasion from without and convulsions within.

He has endeavored to prevent the population of these states; for that purpose obstructing the laws for naturalization of foreigners, refusing to pass others to encourage their migrations hither, and raising the conditions of new appropriations of lands.

obstructed
by

He has <u>suffered</u> the administration of justice <u>totally to cease in some of these states</u> refusing his assent to laws for establishing judiciary powers.

He has made <u>our</u> judges dependent on his will alone for the tenure of their offices, and the amount and payment of their salaries.

He has erected a multitude of new offices, <u>by a self-assumed power</u> and sent hither swarms of new officers to harass our people and eat out their substance.

He has kept among us in times of peace standing armies <u>and ships of war</u> without the consent of our legislatures.

---

2. **the present king of Great Britain:** George III reigned from 1760 to 1820.

He has affected to render the military independent of, and superior to, the civil power.

He has combined with others to subject us to a jurisdiction foreign to our constitutions and unacknowledged by our laws, giving his assent to their acts of pretended legislation for quartering large bodies of armed troops among us; for protecting them by a mock trial from punishment for any murders which they should commit on the inhabitants of these states; for cutting off our trade with all parts of the world; for imposing taxes on us without our consent; for depriving us __ of the benefits of trial by jury; · in many cases · for transporting us beyond seas to be tried for pretended offences; for abolishing the free system of English laws in a neighboring province,[3] establishing therein an arbitrary government, and enlarging its boundaries, so as to render it at once an example and fit instrument for introducing the same absolute rule into these <u>states</u>; for taking away our charters, · colonies · abolishing our most valuable laws, and altering fundamentally the forms of our governments; for suspending our own legislatures, and declaring themselves invested with power to legislate for us in all cases whatsoever.

He has abdicated government here <u>withdrawing his governors, and declaring us out of his allegiance and protection</u>. · by declaring us out of his protection, and waging war against us. ·

He has plundered our seas, ravaged our coasts, burnt our towns, and destroyed the lives of our people.

He is at this time transporting large armies of foreign mercenaries[4] to complete the works of death, desolation and tyranny already begun with circumstances of cruelty and perfidy __ unworthy the head of a civilized nation. · scarcely paralleled in the most barbarous ages, and totally ·

He has constrained our fellow citizens taken captive on the high seas, to bear arms against their country, to become the executioners of their friends and brethren, or to fall themselves by their hands.

He has __ endeavored to bring on the inhabitants of our frontiers, the merciless Indian savages, whose known rule of warfare is an undistinguished destruction of all ages, sexes and conditions <u>of existence</u>. · excited domestic insurrection among us, and has ·

<u>He has incited treasonable insurrections of our fellow citizens, with the allurements of forfeiture and confiscation of our property.</u>

<u>He has waged cruel war against human nature itself, violating its most sacred rights of life and liberty in the persons of a distant people who never offended him, captivating and carrying them into slavery in another hemisphere, or to incur miserable death in their transportation thither. This piratical warfare, the opprobrium of INFIDEL powers, is the warfare of the CHRISTIAN king of Great Britain. Determined to keep open a market</u>

---

3. **a neighboring province:** The Quebec Act of 1774, unpopular in England and especially in the American colonies, provided special concessions to the British province of Quebec, expanding its borders, retaining the use of French civil law, and guaranteeing French Canadians the right to practice Roman Catholicism.
4. **foreign mercenaries:** George III hired troops, mainly from the Hesse-Cassel state in Germany, to help suppress the growing rebellion in the American colonies.

where MEN should be bought and sold, he has prostituted his negative for suppressing every legislative attempt to prohibit or to restrain this execrable commerce. And that this assemblage of horrors might want no fact of distinguished die, he is now exciting those very people to rise in arms among us, and to purchase that liberty of which he has deprived them, by murdering the people on whom he also obtruded them: thus paying off former crimes committed against the LIBERTIES of one people, with crimes which he urges them to commit against the LIVES of another.

In every stage of these oppressions we have petitioned for redress in the most humble terms: our repeated petitions have been answered only by repeated injuries.

free

A prince whose character is thus marked by every act which may define a tyrant is unfit to be the ruler of a _ people who mean to be free. Future ages will scarcely believe that the hardiness of one man adventured, within the short compass of twelve years only, to lay a foundation so broad and so undisguised for tyranny over a people fostered and fixed in principles of freedom.

an unwarrantable; us

Nor have we been wanting in attentions to our British brethren. We have warned them from time to time of attempts by their legislature to extend a jurisdiction over these our states. We have reminded them of the circumstances of our emigration and settlement here, no one of which could warrant so strange a pretension: that these were effected at the expense of our own blood and treasure, unassisted by the wealth or the strength of Great Britain: that in constituting indeed our several forms of government, we had adopted one common king, thereby laying a foundation for perpetual league and amity with them: but that submission to their parliament was no part of our constitution, nor ever in idea, if history may be credited: and,

have
and we have conjured them by
would inevitably

we _ appealed to their native justice and magnanimity as well as to the ties of our common kindred to disavow these usurpations which were likely to interrupt our connection and correspondence. They too have been deaf to the voice of justice and of consanguinity, and when occasions have been given them, by the regular course of their laws, of removing from their councils the disturbers of our harmony, they have, by their free election, re-established them in power. At this very time too, they are permitting their chief magistrate to send over not only soldiers of our common blood, but Scotch and foreign mercenaries to invade and destroy us. These facts have given the last stab to agonizing affection, and manly spirit bids us to renounce forever these unfeeling brethren. We must endeavor to forget our former love for them, and hold them as we hold the rest of mankind, enemies in war, in peace friends. We might have been a free and a great people together; but a communication of grandeur and of freedom, it seems, is

We must therefore
and hold them as we hold the rest of mankind, enemies in war, in peace friends.

below their dignity. Be it so, since they will have it. The road to happiness and to glory is open to us, too. We will tread it apart from them, and acquiesce in the necessity which denounces our eternal separation _!

We, therefore, the representatives of the United States of America in General Congress assembled, appealing to the supreme judge of the world for the rectitude of our intentions, do in the name, and by the authority of the good people of these colonies, solemnly publish and declare, that these united colonies are, and of right ought to be free and independent states; that they are absolved from all allegiance to the British crown, and that all political connection between them and the state of Great Britain is, and ought to be, totally dissolved; and that as free and independent states, they have full power to levy war, conclude peace, contract alliances, establish commerce, and to do all other acts and things which independent states may of right do.

And for the support of this declaration, with a firm reliance on the protection of divine providence, we mutually pledge to each other our lives, our fortunes, and our sacred honor.

We therefore the representatives of the United States of America in General Congress assembled, do in the name, and by the authority of the good people of these states reject and renounce all allegiance and subjection to the kings of Great Britain and all others who may hereafter claim by, through or under them; we utterly dissolve all political connection which may heretofore have subsisted between us and the people or parliament of Great Britain: and finally we do assert and declare these colonies to be free and independent states, and that as free and independent states, they have full power to levy war, conclude peace, contract alliances, establish commerce, and to do all other acts and things which independent states may of right do.

And for the support of this declaration we mutually pledge to each other our lives, our fortunes, and our sacred honor.

[1776, 1829, 1903]

Jefferson's *Notes on the State of Virginia.* Jefferson wrote his only full-length book in response to a series of questions he received from François Barbé-Marbois (1745–1837), then the secretary to the French legation in the newly formed United States. *Notes on the State of Virginia* includes twenty-three sections, each a response to a specific "query" raised by Barbé-Marbois. In his responses, Jefferson provides detailed observations on climate, geography, population, culture, and politics, adding his views about the future development of both his state and the United States. *Notes on the State of Virginia* was privately printed in France in 1784. Concerned that an unauthorized French translation would appear, Jefferson published the book in London in 1787; four editions were published in the United States in 1788. The sections included here, "Religion" and "Manners"—a commentary on the effects of slavery—reflect Jefferson's ongoing concern with issues of freedom and natural rights. In Virginia, Jefferson had introduced a bill in the assembly providing for complete religious freedom for all inhabitants of the state, regardless of their beliefs. As a slaveholder, however, Jefferson's views on race and slavery were far more complex and often conflicting. Suggesting that blacks "are inferior to whites in endowments of both body and mind," Jefferson elsewhere in *Notes on the State of Virginia* observes: "This unfortunate difference of colour, and perhaps of faculty, is a powerful obstacle to the emancipation of these people." At the same time, in "Manners" Jefferson emphasizes the corrosive effects of slavery on both the master and the slave, insisting that the institution posed one of the greatest threats to the stability and welfare of the United States. The text of the two sections is taken from the first London edition of *Notes on the State of Virginia* (1787), as reprinted in the Library of America edition of *Thomas Jefferson: Writings* (1984).

From NOTES ON THE STATE OF VIRGINIA

Query XVII

THE DIFFERENT RELIGIONS RECEIVED INTO THAT STATE?

The first settlers in this country were emigrants from England, of the English church, just at a point of time when it was flushed with complete victory over the religious of all other persuasions. Possessed, as they became, of the powers of making, administering, and executing the laws, they shewed equal intolerance in this country with their Presbyterian brethren, who had emigrated to the northern government. The poor Quakers were flying from persecution in England. They cast their eyes on these new countries as asylums of civil and religious freedom; but they found them free only for the reigning sect. Several acts of the Virginia assembly of 1659, 1662, and 1693, had made it penal in parents to refuse to have their children baptized; had prohibited the unlawful assembling of Quakers; had made it penal for any master of a vessel to bring a Quaker into the state; had ordered those already here, and such as should come thereafter, to be imprisoned till they should abjure the country; provided a milder punishment for their first and second return, but death for their third; had inhibited all persons from suffering their meetings in or near their houses, entertaining them individually, or disposing of books which supported their tenets. If no capital execution took place here, as did in New-England, it was not owing to the moderation of the church, or spirit of the legislature, as may be inferred from the law itself; but to historical circumstances which have not been handed down to us. The Anglicans retained full possession of the country about a century. Other opinions began then to creep in, and the great care of the government to support their own church, having begotten an equal degree of indolence in its clergy, two-thirds of the people had become dissenters at the commencement of the present revolution. The laws indeed were still oppressive on them, but the spirit of the one party had subsided into moderation, and of the other had risen to a degree of determination which commanded respect.

The present state of our laws on the subject of religion is this. The convention of May 1776, in their declaration of rights, declared it to be a truth, and a natural right, that the exercise of religion should be free; but when they proceeded to form on that declaration the ordinance of government, instead of taking up every principle declared in the bill of rights, and guarding it by legislative sanction, they passed over that which asserted our religious rights, leaving them as they found them.[1] The same convention, however, when they met as a member of the general assembly in October 1776, repealed all *acts of parliament* which had rendered criminal the maintaining any opinions in matters of religion, the forbearing to repair to church, and the exercising any mode of worship; and suspended the laws giving salaries to the clergy, which suspension was made perpetual in October 1779. Statutory oppressions in religion being thus wiped away, we remain at present under those only imposed by the common law, or by our own acts of assembly. At the common law, *heresy* was a capital offence, punishable by burning. Its definition was left to the ecclesiastical judges, before whom the conviction was, till the statute of the 1 El. c. 1.[2] circumscribed it, by declaring, that nothing should be deemed heresy, but what had been so determined by authority of the canonical scriptures, or by one of the four first general councils, or by some other council having for the grounds of their declaration the express and plain words of the scriptures. Heresy, thus circumscribed, being an offence at the common law, our act of assembly of October 1777, c. 17. gives cognizance of it to the general court, by declaring, that the jurisdiction of that court shall be general in all matters at the common law. The execution is by the writ *De haeretico comburendo*.[3] By our own act of assembly of 1705, c. 30, if a person brought up in the Christian religion denies the being of a God, or the Trinity, or asserts there are more Gods than one, or denies the Christian religion to be true, or the scriptures to be of divine authority, he is punishable on the first offence by incapacity to hold any office or employment ecclesiastical, civil, or military; on the second by disability to sue, to take any gift or legacy, to be guardian, executor, or administrator, and by three years imprisonment, without bail. A father's right to the custody of his own children being founded in law on his right of guardianship, this being taken away, they may of course be severed from him, and put, by the authority of a court, into more orthodox hands. This is a summary view of that religious slavery, under which a people have been willing to remain, who have lavished their lives and fortunes for the establishment of their civil freedom.[4] The error seems not sufficiently eradicated, that the operations of the mind, as well as the acts of the body, are subject to the coercion of the laws. But our rulers can have authority over such natural rights only as we have submitted to them. The rights of conscience we never submitted, we could not submit. We are answerable for them to our God. The legitimate powers of government extend to such acts only as

---

1. **religious rights . . . as they found them:** The Virginia Declaration of Rights, passed on May 15, 1776, includes section 16, which provides: "That religion, or the duty which we owe to our Creator, and the manner of discharging it, can be directed only by reason and conviction, not by force or violence; and therefore all men are equally entitled to the free exercise of religion, according to the dictates of conscience; and that it is the mutual duty of all to practice Christian forbearance, love, and charity toward each other."
2. **1 El. c. 1.:** During the first two years of her reign in England (1558-60), Elizabeth I, a Protestant, reinstated the Acts of Supremacy, which stipulated the primacy of the ecclesiastical laws of the Church of England (the Anglicans) and maintained the monarch as the head of the Church.
3. **De haeretico comburendo:** On the burning of a heretic (Latin).
4. **civil freedom:** Furneaux passim. [Jefferson's note] In *Letters to the Honorable Mr. Justice Blackstone* (1770), the English minister Philip Furneaux (1726-1783) argues that religious views should not incur civil penalties.

are injurious to others. But it does me no injury for my neighbour to say there are twenty gods, or no god. It neither picks my pocket nor breaks my leg. If it be said, his testimony in a court of justice cannot be relied on, reject it then, and be the stigma on him. Constraint may make him worse by making him a hypocrite, but it will never make him a truer man. It may fix him obstinately in his errors, but will not cure them. Reason and free enquiry are the only effectual agents against error. Give a loose to them, they will support the true religion, by bringing every false one to their tribunal, to the test of their investigation. They are the natural enemies of error, and of error only. Had not the Roman government permitted free enquiry, Christianity could never have been introduced. Had not free enquiry been indulged, at the aera of the reformation, the corruptions of Christianity could not have been purged away. If it be restrained now, the present corruptions will be protected, and new ones encouraged. Was the government to prescribe to us our medicine and diet, our bodies would be in such keeping as our souls are now. Thus in France the emetic was once forbidden as a medicine, and the potatoe as an article of food. Government is just as infallible too when it fixes systems in physics. Galileo was sent to the inquisition for affirming that the earth was a sphere: the government had declared it to be as flat as a trencher, and Galileo was obliged to abjure his error.[5] This error however at length prevailed, the earth became a globe, and Descartes[6] declared it was whirled round its axis by a vortex. The government in which he lived was wise enough to see that this was no question of civil jurisdiction, or we should all have been involved by authority in vortices. In fact, the vortices have been exploded, and the Newtonian principle of gravitation is now more firmly established, on the basis of reason, than it would be were the government to step in, and to make it an article of necessary faith. Reason and experiment have been indulged, and error has fled before them. It is error alone which needs the support of government. Truth can stand by itself. Subject opinion to coercion: whom will you make your inquisitors? Fallible men; men governed by bad passions, by private as well as public reasons. And why subject it to coercion? To produce uniformity. But is uniformity of opinion desireable? No more than of face and stature. Introduce the bed of Procrustes[7] then, and as there is danger that the large men may beat the small, make us all of a size, by lopping the former and stretching the latter. Difference of opinion is advantageous in religion. The several sects perform the office of a Censor morum[8] over each other. Is uniformity attainable? Millions of innocent men, women, and children, since the introduction of Christianity, have been burnt, tortured, fined, imprisoned; yet we have not advanced one inch towards uniformity. What has been the effect of coercion? To make one half the world fools, and the other half hypocrites. To support roguery[9] and error all over the earth. Let us reflect that it is inhabited by a thousand millions of people. That these profess probably a

---

5. **Galileo . . . error:** Galileo Galilei (1564–1642), an Italian scientist, was forced by the Inquisition to retract his belief in the Copernican theory that Earth is round and rotates around the sun.
6. **Descartes:** René Descartes (1596–1650), French philosopher and mathematician.
7. **bed of Procrustes:** In Greek mythology, Procrustes was a host who stretched or cut off part of the legs of his guests to make them fit his bed.
8. **Censor morum:** A critic of morals (Latin).
9. **roguery:** Dishonest acts.

thousand different systems of religion. That ours is but one of that thousand. That if there be but one right, and ours that one, we should wish to see the 999 wandering sects gathered into the fold of truth. But against such a majority we cannot effect this by force. Reason and persuasion are the only practicable instruments. To make way for these, free enquiry must be indulged; and how can we wish others to indulge it while we refuse it ourselves. But every state, says an inquisitor, has established some religion. No two, say I, have established the same. Is this a proof of the infallibility of establishments? Our sister states of Pennsylvania and New York, however, have long subsisted without any establishment at all. The experiment was new and doubtful when they made it. It has answered beyond conception. They flourish infinitely. Religion is well supported; of various kinds, indeed, but all good enough; all sufficient to preserve peace and order: or if a sect arises, whose tenets would subvert morals, good sense has fair play, and reasons and laughs it out of doors, without suffering the state to be troubled with it. They do not hang more malefactors than we do. They are not more disturbed with religious dissensions. On the contrary, their harmony is unparalleled, and can be ascribed to nothing but their unbounded tolerance, because there is no other circumstance in which they differ from every nation on earth. They have made the happy discovery, that the way to silence religious disputes, is to take no notice of them. Let us too give this experiment fair play, and get rid, while we may, of those tyrannical laws. It is true, we are as yet secured against them by the spirit of the times. I doubt whether the people of this country would suffer an execution for heresy, or a three years imprisonment for not comprehending the mysteries of the Trinity. But is the spirit of the people an infallible, a permanent reliance? Is it government? Is this the kind of protection we receive in return for the rights we give up? Besides, the spirit of the times may alter, will alter. Our rulers will become corrupt, our people careless. A single zealot may commence persecutor, and better men be his victims. It can never be too often repeated, that the time for fixing every essential right on a legal basis is while our rulers are honest, and ourselves united. From the conclusion of this war we shall be going down hill. It will not then be necessary to resort every moment to the people for support. They will be forgotten, therefore, and their rights disregarded. They will forget themselves, but in the sole faculty of making money, and will never think of uniting to effect a due respect for their rights. The shackles, therefore, which shall not be knocked off at the conclusion of this war, will remain on us long, will be made heavier and heavier, till our rights shall revive or expire in a convulsion.

Query XVIII

THE PARTICULAR *CUSTOMS AND MANNERS THAT MAY HAPPEN TO BE RECEIVED IN THAT STATE?*

It is difficult to determine on the standard by which the manners of a nation may be tried, whether *catholic*,[10] or *particular*. It is more difficult for a native to bring to that standard the manners of his own nation, familiarized to him by habit. There must doubtless be an unhappy influence on the manners of our people produced by the

---

10. *catholic*: Liberal or all-embracing.

existence of slavery among us. The whole commerce between master and slave is a perpetual exercise of the most boisterous passions, the most unremitting despotism on the one part, and degrading submissions on the other. Our children see this, and learn to imitate it; for man is an imitative animal. This quality is the germ of all education in him. From his cradle to his grave he is learning to do what he sees others do. If a parent could find no motive either in his philanthropy or his self-love, for restraining the intemperance of passion towards his slave, it should always be a sufficient one that his child is present. But generally it is not sufficient. The parent storms, the child looks on, catches the lineaments of wrath, puts on the same airs in the circle of smaller slaves, gives a loose to his worst of passions, and thus nursed, educated, and daily exercised in tyranny, cannot but be stamped by it with odious peculiarities. The man must be a prodigy who can retain his manners and morals undepraved by such circumstances. And with what execration should the statesman be loaded, who permitting one half the citizens thus to trample on the rights of the other, transforms those into despots, and these into enemies, destroys the morals of the one part, and the amor patriae[11] of the other. For if a slave can have a country in this world, it must be any other in preference to that in which he is born to live and labour for another: in which he must lock up the faculties of his nature, contribute as far as depends on his individual endeavours to the evanishment of the human race, or entail his own miserable condition on the endless generations proceeding from him. With the morals of the people, their industry also is destroyed. For in a warm climate, no man will labour for himself who can make another labour for him. This is so true, that of the proprietors of slaves a very small proportion indeed are ever seen to labour. And can the liberties of a nation be thought secure when we have removed their only firm basis, a conviction in the minds of the people that these liberties are of the gift of God? That they are not to be violated but with his wrath? Indeed I tremble for my country when I reflect that God is just: that his justice cannot sleep for ever: that considering numbers, nature and natural means only, a revolution of the wheel of fortune, an exchange of situation, is among possible events: that it may become probable by supernatural interference! The Almighty has no attribute which can take side with us in such a contest. But it is impossible to be temperate and to pursue this subject through the various considerations of policy, of morals, of history natural and civil. We must be contented to hope they will force their way into every one's mind. I think a change already perceptible, since the origin of the present revolution. The spirit of the master is abating, that of the slave rising from the dust, his condition mollifying, the way I hope preparing, under the auspices of heaven, for a total emancipation, and that this is disposed, in the order of events, to be with the consent of the masters, rather than by their extirpation.

[1787, 1984]

---

11. **amor patriae:** Love of one's country (Latin).

George Washington

[1732-1799]

The son of a Virginia planter and his wife, George Washington began his military career at age twenty-two when he served as a lieutenant colonel in the French and Indian War. After the war, Washington returned to his Virginia plantation and became increasingly resistant to British interference in colonial affairs. Serving as a delegate to the Second Continental Congress in May 1775, Washington was appointed commander in chief of the Continental army, which he led for the next six years. In 1781, with the aid of French allies, Washington oversaw the surrender of the British at Yorktown, Virginia, the battle that effectively ended the Revolutionary War. When the Constitution was ratified in 1788, Washington was unanimously elected the first president of the United States and took the oath of office on April 30, 1789. As part of a tour that he and Thomas Jefferson took to campaign for the passage of the first ten amendments to the Constitution, usually called the Bill of Rights, President Washington visited Newport, Rhode Island, on August 18, 1790. Moses Seixas (1744-1809), the warden of the Hebrew Congregation at Newport, presented Washington with a letter congratulating him on his

Touro Synagogue

Dedicated in 1763, the Jeshuat Israel Synagogue in Rhode Island (later renamed the Touro Synagogue) is the sole surviving synagogue built in colonial America. The neoclassical building was designed by Peter Harrison, the foremost architect in the colonies. A designer of churches, Harrison initially refused to work on the synagogue. But he finally agreed, becoming so engaged in what he described as "a labor of love" that he charged no fee for his services.

presidency, reminding him of Jewish persecution, and urging the ongoing commitment of the new nation to religious freedom. In his letter, Seixas wrote,

> Deprived as we heretofore have been of the invaluable rights of free citizens, we now (with a deep sense of gratitude to the Almighty disposer of all events) behold a government erected by the Majesty of the People—a Government which to bigotry gives no sanction, to persecution no assistance, but generously affording to All liberty of conscience and immunities of Citizenship, deeming every one, of whatever Nation, tongue, or language, equal parts of the great governmental machine.

In response, Washington wrote a letter in which he echoed Seixas's moving words and affirmed the freedom of all Americans to worship as they chose. The letter was frequently reprinted and became one of the most influential statements in favor of religious toleration. On the occasion of the designation of the Touro Synagogue as a National Historic Site in 1946, President Harry S Truman recalled Washington's letter by writing: "The setting apart of this historic shrine as a national monument is symbolic of our national tradition of freedom, which has inspired men and women of every creed, race, and ancestry to contribute their highest gifts to the development of our national culture." The text of the letter is taken from the transcription of the original, now on display at the B'nai B'rith Klutznick National Jewish Museum, in Washington, D.C.

LETTER TO THE TOURO SYNAGOGUE

To the Hebrew Congregation in Newport Rhode Island
Gentlemen:

While I receive with much satisfaction, your Address replete with expressions of affection and esteem, I rejoice in the opportunity of answering you, that I shall always retain, a grateful remembrance of the cordial welcome I experienced in my visit to Newport, from all classes of Citizens.

The reflection on the days of difficulty and danger which are past, is rendered the more sweet, from a consciousness that they are succeeded by days of uncommon prosperity and security. If we have wisdom to make the best use of the advantages with which we are now favored, we cannot fail, under the just administration of a good Government, to become a great and a happy people.

The Citizens of the United States of America have a right to applaud themselves for having given to mankind examples of an enlarged and liberal policy: a policy worthy of imitation. All possess alike liberty of conscience and immunities of citizenship. It is now no more that toleration is spoken of, as if it was by the indulgence of one class of people, that another enjoyed the exercise of their inherent natural rights. For happily the Government of the United States, which gives to bigotry no sanction, to persecution no assistance, requires only that they who live under its protection, should demean themselves[1] as good citizens, in giving it on all occasions their effectual support. It would be inconsistent with the frankness of my character not to avow that I am pleased with your favorable opinion of my administration, and fervent wishes for my felicity. May the Children of the Stock of Abraham, who dwell in this land, continue to merit and enjoy the good will of the other inhabitants, while every one shall sit in safety under his own vine and fig tree, and there shall be none to make him afraid.[2] May the father of all mercies scatter light and not darkness in our paths, and make us all in our several vocations useful here, and in his own due time and way everlastingly happy.

George Washington
[1790]

---

1. **demean themselves:** Conduct themselves.
2. **Children of the Stock of Abraham . . . none to make him afraid:** Abraham was the Hebrew patriarch from whom all Jews trace their descent, as described in the Old Testament (Genesis 11:27–25:10). See also Micah 4:4: "But they shall sit every man under his vine and under his fig tree; and none shall make them afraid: for the mouth of the LORD of hosts hath spoken it."

Judith Sargent Murray

[1751–1820]

Judith Sargent Murray

This portrait of "Mrs. John Stevens," as Murray was known during her marriage to her first husband, was painted when she was eighteen or nineteen years old by John Singleton Copley, the foremost artist in colonial America, who gained fame for his innovative portraits of prominent people in New England.

Born into a prominent family in Gloucester, Massachusetts, Judith Sargent Murray emerged as a prominent cultural figure during the 1790s. A prolific writer and literary nationalist, she produced poetry, plays, and a novel, *The Story of Margaretta.* But she is perhaps best known for her essays, which she published under pseudonyms in various periodicals, especially the *Massachusetts Magazine; or, Monthly Museum of Knowledge and Rational Entertainment.* Beginning in 1792, Murray wrote two series for the magazine, one entitled "The Repository" and another in which she adopted the persona of Mr. Vigillius, or "The Gleaner." She later collected her popular writings for the magazine into a three-volume collection, *The Gleaner* (1798), whose list of subscribers included luminaries such as George and Martha Washington, John Hancock, and President John Adams. In her essays, Murray commented on almost every aspect of life in the new nation—culture, politics, religion, and society. She was also an early champion of women's rights and equality. Responding to the theories of the French philosopher Jean Jacques Rousseau, who argued that women's education should be designed solely to make them subservient, useful, and pleasing to men, Murray in a letter written in 1777 exclaimed: "For those sentiments, so humiliating to our sex, avowed by Rousseau, I will never forgive him." Two years later, she wrote the first draft of her most famous essay, "On the Equality of the Sexes," in which Murray vigorously challenged the notion of male superiority, arguing that education and opportunity would transform the lives of women. A decade later she revised and expanded the essay, which was published in two parts in the *Massachusetts Magazine* (March and April 1790). The following text of part one is taken from the original printing in the magazine, where the essay was signed "Constantia."

From ON THE EQUALITY OF THE SEXES

Part 1, 1790

That minds are not alike, full well I know,
This truth each day's experience will show;
To heights surprising some great spirits soar,
With inborn strength mysterious depths explore;
Their eager gaze surveys the path of light,   5
Confest it stood to Newton's piercing sight.[1]
  Deep science, like a bashful maid retires,
And but[2] the *ardent* breast her worth inspires;
By perseverance the coy fair is won.
And Genius, led by Study, wears the crown.   10
  But some there are who wish not to improve
Who never can the path of knowledge love,
Whose souls almost with the dull body one,
With anxious care each mental pleasure shun;
Weak is the level'd, enervated mind,   15
And but while here to vegetate design'd.
The torpid spirit mingling with its clod,
Can scarcely boast its origin from God;
Stupidly dull—they move progressing on—
They eat, and drink, and all their work is done.   20
While others, emulous of sweet applause,
Industrious seek for each event a cause,
Tracing the hidden springs whence knowledge flows,
Which nature all in beauteous order shows.
  Yet cannot I their sentiments imbibe,   25

---

1. **the path of light . . . Newton's piercing sight:** Sir Isaac Newton (1642–1727), the eminent English scientist; through his famous prism experiments he was the first to prove that white light is made up of a spectrum of colors.
2. **And but:** And only.

Who this distinction to the sex ascribe,
As if a woman's form must needs enrol,
A weak, a servile, an inferiour soul;
And that the guise of man must still proclaim,
Greatness of mind, and him, to be the same: 30
Yet as the hours revolve fair proofs arise,
Which the bright wreath of growing fame supplies;
And in past times some men have *sunk* so *low,*
That female records nothing *less* can show.
But imbecility is still confin'd,   35
And by the lordly sex to us consign'd;
They rob us of the power t'improve,
And then declare we only trifles love;
Yet haste the era, when the world shall know,
That such distinctions only dwell below;   40
The soul unfetter'd, to no sex confin'd,
Was for the abodes of cloudless day design'd.
    Mean time we emulate their manly fires,
Though erudition all their thoughts inspires,
Yet nature with *equality* imparts   45
And *noble passions,* swell e'en *female hearts.*

Is it upon mature consideration we adopt the idea, that nature is thus partial in her distributions? Is it indeed a fact, that she hath yielded to one half of the human species so unquestionable a mental superiority? I know that to both sexes elevated understandings, and the reverse, are common. But, suffer me to ask, in what the minds of females are so notoriously deficient, or unequal. May not the intellectual powers be ranged under these four heads — imagination, reason, memory and judgment. The province of imagination hath long since been surrendered to us, and we have been crowned and undoubted sovereigns of the regions of fancy. Invention is perhaps the most arduous effort of the mind; this branch of imagination hath been particularly ceded to us, and we have been time out of mind invested with that creative faculty. Observe the variety of fashions (here I bar the contemptuous smile) which distinguish and adorn the female world: how continually are they changing, insomuch that they almost render the wise man's assertion problematical, and we are ready to say, *there is something new under the sun.*[3] Now what a playfulness, what an exuberance of fancy, what strength of inventine imagination, doth this continual variation discover? Again, it hath been observed, that if the turpitude of the conduct of our sex, hath been ever so enormous, so extremely ready are we, that the very first thought presents us with an apology, so plausible, as to produce our actions even in an amiable light. Another instance of our creative powers, is our talent for slander; how ingenious are we at inventive scandal? what a formidable story can

---

3. *there is something new under the sun:* A revision of Ecclesiastes 1:9: "The thing that hath been, it is that which shall be; and that which is done is that which shall be done: and there is no new thing under the sun."

we in a moment fabricate merely from the force of a prolifick imagination? how many reputations, in the fertile brain of a female, have been utterly despoiled? how industrious are we at improving a hint? suspicion[4] how easily do we convert into conviction, and conviction, embellished by the power of eloquence, stalks abroad to the surprise and confusion of unsuspecting innocence. Perhaps it will be asked if I furnish these facts as instances of excellency in our sex. Certainly not; but as proofs of a creative faculty, of a lively imagination. Assuredly great activity of mind is thereby discovered, and was this activity properly directed, what beneficial effects would follow. Is the needle and kitchen sufficient to employ the operations of a soul thus organized? I should conceive not, Nay, it is a truth that those very departments leave the intelligent principle vacant, and at liberty for speculation. Are we deficient in reason? we can only reason from what we know, and if an opportunity of acquiring knowledge hath been denied us, the inferiority of our sex cannot fairly be deduced from thence. Memory, I believe, will be allowed us in common, since everyone's experience must testify, that a loquacious old woman is as frequently met with, as a communicative man; their subjects are alike drawn from the fund of other times, and the transactions of their youth, or of maturer life, entertain, or perhaps fatigue you, in the evening of their lives.

"But our judgment is not so strong—we do not distinguish so well."—Yet it may be questioned, from what doth this superiority, in this determining faculty of the soul, proceed. May we not trace its source in the difference of education, and continued advantages? Will it be said that the judgment of a male of two years old, is more sage than that of a female's of the same age? I believe the reverse is generally observed to be true. But from that period what partiality! how is the one exalted, and the other depressed, by the contrary modes of education which are adopted! the one is taught to aspire, and the other is early confined and limitted. As their years increase, the sister must be wholly domesticated, while the brother is led by the hand through all the flowery paths of science. Grant that their mind are by nature equal, yet who shall wonder at the *apparent* superiority, if indeed custom becomes *second nature*; nay if it taketh place of nature, and that it doth the experience of each day will evince. At length arrived at womanhood, the uncultivated fair one feels a void, which the employments allotted her are by no means capable of filling. What can she do? to books she may not apply; or if she doth, *to those only of the novel kind,*[5] lest she merit the appellation of a *learned lady;* and what ideas have been affixed to this term, the observation of many can testify. Fashion, scandal,and sometimes what is still more reprehensible, are then called in to her relief; and who can say to what lengths the liberties she takes may proceed. Meantime she herself is most unhappy; she feels the want of a cultivated mind. Is she single, she in vain seeks to fill up time from sexual employments or amusements. Is she united to a person whose soul nature made equal to her own, education hath set him so far above her, that in those entertainments which are productive of such rational felicity, she is not qualified to accompany him. She experiences a mortifying consciousness of inferiority, which embitters every enjoyment. Doth the person to whom

---

4. **suspicion:** Imagine.
5. *the novel kind:* Works of fiction.

her adverse fate hath consigned her, possess a mind incapable of improvement, she is equally wretched, in being so closely connected with an individual whom she cannot but despise. Now, was she permitted the same instructors as her brother, (with an eye however to their particular departments) for the employment of a rational mind an ample field would be opened. In astronomy she might catch a glimpse of the immensity of the Deity, and thence she would form amazing conceptions of the august and supreme Intelligence. In geography she would admire Jehovah in the midst of his benevolence; thus adapting this globe to the various wants and amusements of its inhabitants. In natural philosophy she would adore the infinite majesty of heaven, clothed in condescension;[6] and as she traversed the reptile world, she would hail the goodness of a creating God. A mind, thus filled, would have little room for the trifles with which our sex are, with too much justice, accused of amusing themselves, and they would thus be rendered fit companions for those, who should one day wear them as their crown. Fashions, in their variety, would then give place to conjectures, which might perhaps conduce to the improvements of literary world; and there would be no leisure for slander or detraction. Reputation would not then be blasted, but serious speculations would occupy the lively imaginations of the sex. Unnecessary visits would only be indulged by way of relaxation, or to answer the demands of consanguinity and friendship. Females would become discreet, their judgments would be invigorated, and their partners for life being circumspectly chosen, an unhappy Hymen[7] would then be as rare, as is now the reverse.

Will it be urged that those acquirements would supersede our domestick duties? I answer that every requisite in female economy[8] is easily attained; and, with truth I can add, that when once attained, they require no further *mental attention.* Nay, while we are pursuing the needle, or the superintendency of the family, I repeat, that our minds are at full liberty for reflection; that imagination may exert itself in full vigor; and that if a just foundation is early laid, our ideas will then be worthy of rational beings. If we were industrious we might easily find time to arrange them upon paper, or should avocations press too hard for such an indulgence, the hours allotted for conversation would at least become more refined and rational. Should it still be vociferated, "Your domestick employments are sufficient" — I would calmly ask, is it reasonable, that a candidate for immortality, for the joys of heaven, an intelligent being, who is to spend an eternity in contemplating the works of the Deity, should at present be so degraded, as to be allowed no other ideas, than those which are suggested by the mechanism of a pudding, or the sewing the seams of a garment? Pity that all such censurers of female improvement do not go one step further, and deny their future existence; to be consistent they surely ought.

Yes, ye lordly, ye haughty sex, our souls are by nature *equal* to yours; the same breath of God animates, enlivens, and invigorates us; and that we are not fallen lower than yourselves, let those witness who have greatly towered above the various discouragements by

---

6. **clothed in condescension:** That is, graciously revealing itself to the creatures below.
7. **Hymen:** The god of marriage in classical mythology.
8. **female economy:** Housekeeping.

which they have been so heavily oppressed; and though I am unacquainted with the list of celebrated characters on either side, yet from the observations I have made in the contracted circle in which I have moved, I dare confidently believe, that from the commencement of time to the present day, there hath been as many females, as males, who, by the *mere force of natural powers,* have merited the crown of applause; who, *thus unassisted,* have seized the wreath of fame. I know there are who assert, that as the animal power of the one sex are superiour, of course their mental faculties also must be stronger; thus attributing strength of mind to the transient organization of this earth-born tenement. But if this reasoning is just, man must be content to yield the palm to many of the brute creation, since by not a few of his brethren of the field, he is far surpassed in bodily strength. Moreover, was this argument admitted, it would prove too much, for occular demonstration evinceth, that there are many robust masculine ladies, and effeminate gentlemen. Yet I fancy that Mr. Pope, though clogged with an enervated body, and distinguished by a diminutive stature,[9] could nevertheless lay claim to greatness of soul; and perhaps there are many other instances which might be adduced to combat so unphilosophical an opinion. Do we not often see, that when the clay built tabernacle is well nigh dissolved, when it is just ready to mingle with the parent soil, the immortal inhabitant aspires to, and even attaineth heights the most sublime, and which were before wholly unexplored. Besides, were we to grant that animal strength proved any thing, taking into consideration the accustomed impartiality of nature, we should be induced to imagine, that she had invested the female mind with superiour strength as an equivalent for the bodily powers of man. But waving this however palpable advantage, for *equality only,* we wish to contend.

[1790]

---

9. **Mr. Pope . . . diminutive stature:** The prominent English poet Alexander Pope (1688–1744) suffered from congenital scoliosis, or curvature of the spine, which made him short and stooped.

Absalom Jones

[1746–1818]

Born into slavery, Absalom Jones was eventually able to buy his freedom in 1784. Having taught himself to read with a copy of the New Testament, he became the first African American priest in the Episcopal Church, then joined the Methodist Church, and finally helped form the African Methodist Episcopal Church. Actively involved in the movement to abolish the slave trade, Jones constantly underscored the contradictions between the institution of slavery and the freedoms guaranteed by the Declaration of Independence and the Bill of Rights. Jones redoubled his efforts to protest the injustice after Congress passed the Fugitive Slave Act of 1793, which provided that runaway slaves could be arrested or seized in any state or territory and returned to their masters. In the following petition, signed by Jones and seventy-three others in 1799, he

Absalom Jones (detail)

This portrait of Jones, prominently holding a large Bible, was painted in 1810 by Raphaelle Peale, son of the celebrated Philadelphia painter Charles Willson Peale. The fact that the portrait was painted indicates the status of the sitter, a former slave who became an influential religious figure and a leader of the African American community in Philadelphia.

appeals to the president and members of Congress to consider the place of "People of Color" in the United States. In 1808, Jones also published a "Thanksgiving Sermon" to commemorate the official end of the African slave trade, which a provision in the Constitution had allowed to continue for twenty years after the document was ratified in 1788. But the fugitive slave law was never rescinded. In fact, it was significantly strengthened by a second and far more rigorous law passed as part of the Compromise of 1850, more than fifty years after Jones's "Petition." The following text is taken from the publication of the "Petition" in the appendix to *Remarks on the Slavery of Black People, Particularly To Those Who are in Legislative or Executive Stations in the General or State Governments; and also To Such Individuals as Hold Them in Bondage*, by John Parrish (Philadelphia, 1806).

PETITION OF THE PEOPLE OF COLOUR

To the President, Senate, and House of Representatives.

The Petition of the People of Colour, free men, within the City and Suburbs of Philadelphia, humbly sheweth,

That, thankful to God, our Creator, and to the Government under which we live, for the blessings and benefits granted to us in the enjoyment of our natural right to liberty, and the protection of our persons and property, from the oppression and violence which so great a number of like colour and national descent are subject to, we feel ourselves bound, from a sense of these blessings, to continue in our respective allotments, and to lead honest and peaceable lives, rendering due submission unto the laws, and exciting and encouraging each other thereto, agreeable to the uniform advice of our friends, of every denomination; yet while we feel impressed with grateful sensations for the Providential favour we ourselves enjoy, we cannot be insensible of the condition of our afflicted brethren, suffering under various circumstances, in different parts of these states; but deeply sympathizing with them, are incited by a sense of social duty, and humbly conceive ourselves authorized to address and petition you on their behalf, believing them to be objects of your representation in your public councils, in common with ourselves and every other class of citizens within the jurisdiction of the United States, according to the design of the present Constitution, formed by the General Convention, and ratified in the different states, as set forth in the preamble thereto in the following words, viz.[1] "We, the people of the United States, in order to form a more perfect union, establish justice, insure domestic tranquillity, provide for the common defence, and to secure the blessings of liberty to ourselves and posterity, do ordain, &c." We apprehend this solemn compact is violated, by a trade carried on in a clandestine manner, to the coast of Guinea,[2] and another equally wicked, practised openly by citizens of some of the southern states, upon the waters of Maryland and Delaware; men sufficiently callous to qualify them for the brutal purpose, are employed in kidnapping those of our brethren that are free, and purchasing others of such as claim a property in them: thus, those poor helpless victims, like droves of cattle, are seized, fettered, and hurried into places provided for this most horrid traffic, such as dark cellars and garrets, as is notorious at Northwest-fork, Chestertown, Eastown,[3] and divers other places. After a sufficient number is obtained, they are forced on board vessels, crouded under hatches, without the least commiseration, left to deplore the sad separation of the dearest ties in nature, husband from wife, and parents from children; thus packed together, they are transported to Georgia and other places, and there inhumanly exposed to sale. Can any commerce, trade, or transaction, so detestably shock the feeling of man, or degrade the dignity of his nature equal to this? And how increasingly is the evil aggravated, when practised in a land high in profession of the benign doctrines of our Blessed Lord, who taught his followers to do unto others as they would they should do unto them. Your petitioners desire not to enlarge, though volumes might be filled with the sufferings of this grossly abused part of the human species, seven hundred thousand of whom, it is said, are now in unconditional bondage in these states: but conscious of the rectitude of our motives in a concern so nearly affecting us, and so effectually interesting to the welfare of this country, we cannot but address you as guardians of our rights, and patrons of equal and national liberties, hoping you will view the subject in an impartial, unprejudiced light. We do not ask for an immediate emancipation of all,

---

1. **viz.:** Abbreviation for *videlicet* (Latin), meaning "namely" or "in other words."
2. **the coast of Guinea:** The major part of the transatlantic slave trade was conducted in the area of western Africa referred to as Guinea, which stretched from present-day Senegal to Angola.
3. **Northwest-fork, Chestertown, Eastown:** Towns on the eastern shore of Delaware and Maryland that were centers for the slave trade.

knowing that the degraded state of many, and their want of education, would greatly disqualify for such a change; yet, humbly desire you may exert every means in your power to undo the heavy burdens, and prepare the way for the oppressed to go free, that every yoke may be broken. The law not long since enacted by Congress, called the Fugitive Bill,[4] is in its execution found to be attended with circumstances peculiarly hard and distressing; for many of our afflicted brethren, in order to avoid the barbarities wantonly exercised upon them, or through fear of being carried off by those men-stealers, being forced to seek refuge by flight, they are then, by armed men, under colour of this law, cruelly treated, or brought back in chains to those that have no claim upon them. In the Constitution and the Fugitive Bill, no mention is made of black people, or slaves; therefore, if the Bill of Rights, or the Declaration of Congress are of any validity, we beseech, that as we are men, we may be admitted to partake of the liberties and unalienable rights therein held forth; firmly believing that the extending of justice and equity to all classes, would be a means of drawing down the blessing of Heaven upon this land, for the peace and prosperity of which, and the real happiness of every member of the community, we fervently pray. Philadelphia, 30th of December, 1799.

Absalom Jones and others, 73 subscribers.

[1799, 1806]

---

4. **Fugitive Bill:** The Fugitive Slave Act of 1793. The legislation authorized slave owners or their agents to apprehend fugitives in any state or territory, and it permitted slave hunters to give oral testimony before a judge in order to gain a certificate to take custody of runaways. As a consequence, many free blacks were enslaved without any possibility of appeal.

Tecumseh

[1768-1813]

Tecumseh, a Shawnee military leader, learned from an early age about the encroachment of white settlers. His father was killed in the Battle of Point Pleasant, following which the Shawnee were pushed farther away from their lands in southern Ohio. In the early 1800s, Tecumseh decided that uniting several tribes was the only way to gain enough power and influence to persuade the new American government to deal fairly with Indians. In 1808, he and other tribal leaders established the capital of an Indian confederacy at a site near Tippecanoe in central Indiana. Meanwhile, the United States was buying up land through treaties with various tribes. William Henry Harrison (1773-1841), then governor of the Indiana Territory and later the ninth president, had specific orders from the federal government to defend existing settlements and to gain the titles to more Indian lands to enable

Tecumseh

This engraving, probably the most authentic portrait of Tecumseh, was based on a sketch done by a French artist in a live sitting with the Shawnee leader. He is depicted in a British army uniform, indicating that he fought on the British side in the War of 1812, but his head covering marks his Indian identity.

additional settlements. Tecumseh and Harrison were on a collision course in Indiana. Through the Treaty of Fort Wayne, negotiated first in 1803 and then revised in 1809, the Indians lost nearly three million acres of land. In speeches delivered to Harrison in 1810, Tecumseh strongly objected to the treaties and protested the brutal treatment of Indians by the Americans. Oratory had a long tradition in Native American culture, and Tecumseh was, by all accounts, a powerful speaker. But the governor was unmoved by the eloquent appeals. While Tecumseh was away in the summer of 1811, recruiting more tribes to join his confederation, Harrison determined to destroy Tippecanoe. After provoking an attack by the Indians, led by Tecumseh's younger brother Tenskwatawa (the Prophet), Harrison's forces defeated them and burned Tippecanoe to the ground on November 8, 1811. During the War of 1812, Tecumseh allied himself with the British. He was killed at the Battle of the Thames River in Canada, where his forces, along with British troops, were defeated by an American army commanded by Harrison. There are many versions based on rough transcriptions of the original translations of the speeches Tecumseh delivered to Harrison in August 1810. The text of the following passages from his second speech is taken from Edward Eggleston and Lillie Eggleston Seelye, *Tecumseh and the Shawnee Prophet* (1878).

SPEECH OF TECUMSEH TO GOVERNOR HARRISON

"Brother: I wish you to listen to me well. As I think you do not clearly understand what I before said to you, I will explain it again. . . .

"Brother, since the peace was made, you have killed some of the Shawnees, Winnebagoes, Delawares, and Miamis, and you have taken our land from us, and I do not see how we can remain at peace if you continue to do so. You try to force the red people to do some injury. It is you that are pushing them on to do mischief. You endeavor to make distinctions. You wish to prevent the Indians doing as we wish them—to unite, and let them consider their lands as the common property of the whole; you take tribes aside and advise them not to come into this measure; and until our design is accomplished we do not wish to accept of your invitation to go and see the President. The reason I tell you this, you want, by your distinctions of Indian tribes in allotting to each a particular tract of land, to make them to war with each other. You never see an Indian come and endeavor to make the white people do so. You are continually driving the red people; when, at last, you will drive them into the Great Lake, where they can't either stand or walk.

"Brother, you ought to know what you are doing with the Indians. Perhaps it is by direction of the President to make those distinctions. It is a very bad thing, and we do not like it. Since my residence at Tippecanoe we have endeavored to level all distinctions—to destroy village chiefs, by whom all mischief is done. It is they who sell our lands to the Americans. Our object is to let our affairs be transacted by warriors.[1]

---

1. **warriors:** Among the Shawnee and other tribes, civil chiefs were hereditary positions that were held for life, while war chiefs were chosen on the basis of their merit and skill.

"Brother, this land that was sold and the goods that were given for it were only done by a few. The treaty was afterwards brought here, and the Weas were induced to give their consent because of their small numbers. The treaty at Fort Wayne was made through the threats of Winnemac; but in future we are prepared to punish those chiefs who may come forward to propose to sell the land. If you continue to purchase of them it will produce war among the different tribes, and at last, I do not know what will be the consequence to the white people.

"Brother, I was glad to hear your speech. You said that if we could show that the land was sold by people that had no right to sell, you would restore it. Those that did sell did not own it. It was me. These tribes set up a claim, but the tribes with me will not agree with their claim. If the land is not restored to us you will see, when we return to our homes, how it will be settled. We shall have a great council, at which all the tribes will be present, when we shall show to those who sold that they had no right to the claim that they set up; and we will see what will be done to those chiefs that did sell the land to you. I am not alone in this determination; it is the determination of all the warriors and red people that listen to me. I now wish you to listen to me. If you do not, it will appear as if you wished me to kill all the chiefs that sold you the land. I tell you so because I am authorized by all the tribes to do so. I am the head of them all; I am a warrior, and all the warriors will meet together in two or three moons from this; then I will call for those chiefs that sold you the land and shall know what to do with them. If you do not restore the land, you will have a hand in killing them.

"Brother, do not believe that I came here to get presents from you. If you offer us any, we will not take. By taking goods from you, you will hereafter say that with them you purchased another piece of land from us. . . . It has been the object of both myself and brother to prevent the lands being sold. Should you not return the land, it will occasion us to call a great council that will meet at the Huron village, where the council-fire has already been lighted, at which those who sold the lands shall be called, and shall suffer for their conduct.

"Brother, I wish you would take pity on the red people and do what I have requested. If you will not give up the land and do cross the boundary of your present settlement, it will be very hard, and produce great troubles among us. How can we have confidence in the white people? When Jesus Christ came on earth, you killed him and nailed him on a cross. You thought he was dead, but you were mistaken. You have Shakers among you, and you laugh and make light of their worship.[2] Everything I have said to you is the truth. The Great Spirit has inspired me, and I speak nothing but the truth to you. . . ."

[1810, 1878]

---

2. **Shakers . . . worship:** Shakers were members of a religious movement brought to America in 1774 by the English prophet Ann Lee (1736–1784), who had a revelation that she was the Second Coming of Christ, the vital female principle in God the Father-Mother. The group, formally known as "The United Society of Believers," established communal settlements from Maine to Indiana. Their radical religious beliefs, including the requirement of celibacy, as well as the impassioned shaking that took place during their services, generated a good deal of derision and hostility among members of more orthodox Protestant sects.

Literature
for a New Nation

FOLLOWING THE TRIUMPHANT CONCLUSION of the American Revolution in 1783, Americans faced the daunting task of establishing a new nation. The most immediate and pressing problems were political — the challenges of creating a new system of government, first under the Articles of Confederation and then under the Constitution, ratified by the states in 1788. The related effort to define and establish the nation's cultural identity was equally daunting and considerably more prolonged. As many scholars

◀ Asher Durand, *Kindred Spirits*

The emergence of American literature in the 1820s coincided with the establishment of the first coherent school of American painting, the Hudson River School, a group led by Thomas Cole and Asher Durand. Like the writers Washington Irving, James Fenimore Cooper, and William Cullen Bryant, the painters associated with the school celebrated the beauty of nature and the majesty of the American landscape, especially the scenery of the Hudson River valley and the Catskill Mountains. *Kindred Spirits* (1849), painted as a memorial to Cole shortly after his premature death in 1848, depicts him and his close friend Bryant, who has taken off his hat, probably as a gesture of reverence to the spiritual power of the unspoiled natural scene. Cole directs his (and our) attention to the most famous sites in the Catskill Mountains: Kaaterskill Cove, the dramatic gorge below the spectacular waterfall in the distance, the 260-foot Kaaterskill Falls.

have noted, the culture of the new nation was at once provincial and post-colonial, still dominated by the literature and arts of Great Britain. The position of writers was particularly complex and conflicted. Their literary models were primarily British, especially earlier eighteenth-century poets such as Alexander Pope, novelists such as Samuel Richardson, and essayists like Joseph Addison and Richard Steele, who wrote for the influential periodical the *Spectator*. Given the standards of taste shaped by their works and shared by audiences on both sides of the Atlantic, American writers felt a strong need to maintain ties with England, to which many of them still looked for acceptance and approval. At the same time, they felt an increasingly strong pull toward literary independence and the establishment of new modes of expression more appropriate to the material conditions, social values, and political institutions of the United States. The position of American writers was further complicated by a lingering assumption that culture was the province of the elite and the educated, an assumption that threatened to put literature and the arts in conflict with the values of the emerging social and political order in the new nation, based on the republican principles of liberty and equality.

The characteristics of "American" culture and the role of literature and the arts in the new nation were consequently subjects of ongoing controversy during the decades of the early national period. A major forum for such discussion and debate was the periodical press, which was growing quickly and which itself became an increasingly important element of American culture. Like newspapers, many magazines were primarily vehicles for the discussion of contemporary politics. But they revealed cultural as well as growing political divisions in the United States. One of the more successful and long-lived magazines of the period was the weekly *Port Folio* (1801–27), whose editor, John Dennie, wrote a column under the name "Oliver Oldschool." Dennie's conservatism was reflected in both his literary taste and his views on language. Noah Webster, who later compiled the first *American Dictionary of the English Language* (1828), had proclaimed in 1789: "As an independent nation, our honor requires us to have a system of our own, in language as well as government." In contrast, Dennie regularly featured articles critical of "Americanisms" in language. Similarly, although he published works by a few American writers, Dennie devoted much more space to British literature in *Port Folio*. The editors of the *North American Review* were far more interested in the development of a distinctly American literature. Its first issue in 1815 opened with what became a regular feature of the magazine, a catalog and description of "books relating to America." Later that year, in an "Essay on American Language and Literature," a contributor to the *Review* complained about the "barrenness of American literature," urging writers to cultivate a national language and exploit the "native peculiarities" of the United States.

> *"As an independent nation, our honor requires us to have a system of our own, in language as well as government."*

Frontispiece of the *Columbian Magazine*, 1789

In this allegorical illustration of the country following the Revolutionary War, America is depicted as a seated young woman who has put aside her shield to enjoy the benefits of peace and prosperity, represented by the horn of plenty at her feet. Likewise, her liberty pole and cap rest against the tree behind her. The focus here is on education and the arts, as she holds a book in her hand and listens as Apollo, with a lyre, points to the Temple of Fame and sings: "America! with Peace and Freedom blest, / Pant for true Fame, and scorn inglorious rest: / Science invites; urg'd by the Voice divine, / Exert thy self, 'till every Art be thine."

America! with Peace and Freedom blest,
Pant for true Fame, and scorn inglorious rest:
Science invites; urg'd by the Voice divine,
Exert thy self, till every Art be thine.

Since poetry was still considered the highest literary form, those who were eager to develop a national literature were consequently ever alert to the emergence of significant poetic voices in the United States. Before and after the Revolution, there was an active manuscript culture in what became the United States, where poems were often circulated in letters and commonplace books. In fact, the poetry of some women writers such as the noted educator Sarah Pierce was circulated and preserved only through such manuscript publication, often in copies made by friends. Poems also appeared in early periodicals, and a few books of poetry were published, including *The Patriot Muse* (1764), a series of poems on the French and Indian War by the New York physician Benjamin Youngs Prime. Prime wrote some popular political songs during the Revolution, which he later reviewed in a long narrative poem with the telltale title *Columbia's Glory; or, British Pride Humbled* (1791). Along with much of the other patriotic verse of the period, Prime's work has fallen into obscurity, in contrast to the poetry of Phillis Wheatley, a slave who was brought to the colonies in 1761. Educated and encouraged by her masters, Wheatley was heavily influenced by Alexander Pope and the other eighteenth-century English poets she read and studied. Her *Poems on Various Subjects, Religious and Moral* (1773), the first book of poetry published by an African American, was printed in England. During the Revolution, however, Wheatley fervently embraced the American cause and wrote a number of patriotic poems, including "To His Excellency General Washington" (1776).

Wheatley died soon after the war ended, so it is not possible to guess what direction her poetry might have taken or what role she might have played in efforts to create a distinctly American literature. She almost certainly would have confronted the difficulties all poets faced in the new nation, as exemplified by the career of Philip Freneau. Primarily known as "the poet of the American Revolution," Freneau actually wrote on a wide range of subjects—the American scene, slavery, and the condition of Indians—before, during, and especially after the Revolution. But he quickly learned that poetry was not going to provide him with a living. Although newspapers and magazines regularly published poetry, much of it was copied from British periodicals. By far the most popular books of poetry in early nineteenth-century America were written by Sir Walter Scott and another wildly popular English poet, Lord Byron. Like many other American writers of his day, Freneau supported himself and his work as a poet by earning money in other ways—in his case, by editing periodicals or serving as the master of sailing ships. Although he managed to publish several books of poetry, including a two-volume edition of his collected poems in 1815, Freneau died in poverty and obscurity in 1832.

Some early American novelists fared better than poets. The novel itself was frequently condemned by critics in the United States, where many believed that the excessive reading of fiction would encourage unrealistic expectations about life, stir violent emotions, and undermine morality. Nonetheless, novels became an increasingly popular form of entertainment. In 1789, the year of the first presidential election under the recently ratified Constitution, newspapers in Massachusetts proudly announced the publication of "THE FIRST AMERICAN NOVEL," William Hill Brown's *The Power of Sympathy*. Brown sought to disarm moralistic critics by dedicating the work to "The Young Ladies" of the United States, offering them a story intended to "expose the fatal Consequences of Seduction." Although that novel soon fell into obscurity, two other didactic and sentimental stories of the seduction, betrayal, and consequent death of a young woman became the first best-selling American novels: Susanna Rowson's *Charlotte: A Tale of Truth* (1791), first published in England and better known as *Charlotte Temple*, which went through some 150 editions in the nineteenth century; and *The Coquette; or, The History of Eliza Wharton* (1797), published anonymously by "A Lady of Massachusetts," later identified as

Title Page of the First American Edition of *Charlotte Temple*

Published in England in 1791 and the United States in 1794, Rowson's enduringly popular novel went through roughly 150 editions during the following century.

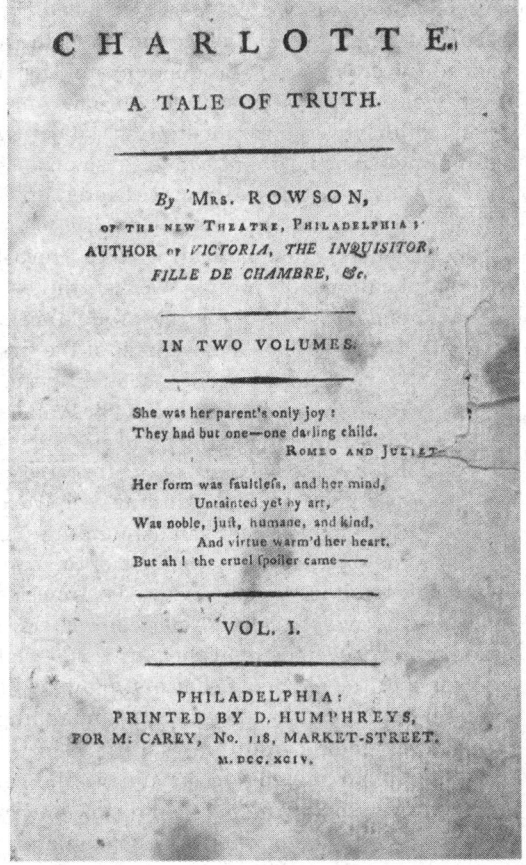

CHARLOTTE.

A TALE OF TRUTH.

By Mrs. ROWSON,
OF THE NEW THEATRE, PHILADELPHIA;
AUTHOR OF *VICTORIA, THE INQUISITOR, FILLE DE CHAMBRE, &c.*

IN TWO VOLUMES.

She was her parent's only joy :
They had but one—one darling child.
ROMEO AND JULIET.

Her form was faultless, and her mind,
Untainted yet by art,
Was noble, just, humane, and kind,
And virtue warm'd her heart.
But ah! the cruel spoiler came——

VOL. I.

PHILADELPHIA:
PRINTED BY D. HUMPHREYS,
FOR M. CAREY, No. 118, MARKET-STREET.
M. DCC. XCIV.

Hannah Webster Foster, the wife of a Massachusetts clergyman. Another significant figure in the emergence of the American novel was Charles Brockden Brown, who between 1798 and 1800 published his four major works, including *Wieland* (1798) and *Edgar Huntly* (1799). Although he essentially followed the current fashion for gothic romances, tales of mystery and psychological terror that originated in England, Brown claimed originality in his use of an American setting and indigenous material. As he observed in his preface to *Edgar Huntly*, instead of relying upon the "Gothic castles and chimeras" of English novels, Brown sought to engage the emotions and sympathies of his readers by drawing upon "incidents of Indian hostility, and the perils of the western wilderness," which he asserted were far more suitable "for a native American."

Despite such early efforts and occasional successes, American novels did not gain a wide readership until the 1820s. Only about one hundred novels by American writers were published between 1789 and 1820. One reason was the American book trade, which was still in its infancy and plagued by problems of production and distribution. Moreover, in the absence of an international copyright law, American publishers (or book-sellers, as they were still most often called) were usually more eager to reprint English books than to take a risk on an American writer. As late as 1821, the critic Alexander Everett attributed "the paucity of good books published in this country" to the failure of American book-sellers, whom he castigated for "investing their capital in repub-lications of foreign works" rather than offering "generous encouragement for the production of original compositions." The American "bestsellers" of the first two decades of the nine-teenth century were consequently almost all reprints of works by English writers, especially Sir Walter Scott. Having first gained fame with long narrative poems such as *Marmion* (1808) and *The Lady of the Lake* (1810), Scott scored even greater successes with a series of novels beginning with *Waverley* (1814). Scott's histori-cal romances were an astounding success in both England and the United States, where all of them were immediately reprinted, voraciously read, and widely reviewed in American periodicals.

As late as 1821, the critic Alexander Everett attributed "the paucity of good books published in this country" to the failure of American book-sellers, whom he castigated for "investing their capital in republications of foreign works."

Even as he overshadowed American writers, Scott offered them crucial lessons about how to exploit the native materials of their own country. In fact, some of the elements that distinguished his historical fiction – his powerful sense of place, his equally commanding sense of the past, and his keen interest in oral traditions – strongly influenced a number of Ameri-can writers who gained success during the 1820s. Taking his cue from Scott, Washington Irving pursued his own interest in the past in his first book, *A History of New York* (1809), a popular comic work in which he sati-rized both history and historians. During a trip to England a decade later, he visited Scott, who encouraged Irving to explore German Romantic lit-erature, especially the legends and tales that had been generated by the growing interest in folk culture. As a result, Irving wrote the two most famous stories in his popular collection *The Sketch Book of Geoffrey Crayon, Gent.* (1819-20): "Rip Van Winkle" and "The Legend of Sleepy Hol-low," in which he essentially naturalized German folktales and displayed his own strong sense of an American place, the Catskill Mountains of New York. Scott's historical romances exerted an even stronger influence on James Fenimore Cooper, who also capitalized on American settings and sources, especially in his historical novels *The Pioneers* (1823), *The Last of the Mohicans* (1826), and *The Prairie* (1827), the first three of his "Leather-Stocking Tales." Although he published many other works of fiction and nonfiction, that series of novels about the life and adventures of the fron-tiersman Natty Bumppo, or Leather-Stocking, earned Cooper interna-tional recognition as "the American Scott."

Prose writers also began to explore other locales and different periods of American history. Inspired by Scott, Catharine Maria Sedgwick sought to expand what she described as "the scanty stock of native American literature" by writing novels like *A New-England Tale* (1822), *Redwood* (1824), and *Hope Leslie* (1827), a historical romance set at the time of the Pequot War in seventeenth-century Connecticut. A writer for the *North American Review*, which for more than a decade had been exhorting American writers to explore "native" scenes and themes, especially commended

Christian Schussele, *Washington Irving and His Literary Friends at Sunnyside* (1863)

Painted after Irving's death in 1859, this group portrait celebrates his central role in the creation of American literature by placing him at the center of a gathering of writers who gained prominence between the 1820s and the Civil War. From left to right, they are Henry Tuckerman, Oliver Wendell Holmes, William Gilmore Simms, Fitz-Greene Halleck, Nathaniel Hawthorne, Henry Wadsworth Longfellow, Nathaniel Parker Willis, William H. Prescott, Washington Irving, James K. Paulding, Ralph Waldo Emerson, William Cullen Bryant, John Pendleton Kennedy, James Fenimore Cooper, and George Bancroft. This gathering never took place, but many of the writers represented had visited Irving at Sunnyside, his country home on the Hudson River.

(Gift of John D. Rockefeller Jr. Historic Hudson Valley. Tarrytown, New York.)

Sedgwick for her depiction of the characters, history, and landscape of New England. At the same time Cooper and Sedgwick were publishing their acclaimed novels about the early conflicts between European settlers and the Indians, Jane Johnston Schoolcraft, whose Native American name was Bame-wa-wa-ge-zhik-a-quay (The Sounds the Stars Make Rushing through the Sky), was writing stories in which she sought to preserve in English the legends and tales of her mother's tribe, the Ojibwa. Among the earliest written works of Native American literature, Schoolcraft's stories spurred interest in both Indian lore and the remote region around the Great Lakes inhabited by the Ojibwa. Indeed, regionalism became an increasingly important element in American novels, stories, and sketches, from Sedgwick's New England to Schoolcraft's "wilderness" to the southern frontier humorously depicted by Augustus Baldwin Longstreet in *Georgia Scenes*, a popular collection of sketches he began to write in 1830.

By then, the foundations of a literary culture had finally been laid in the United States. Americans even had a poet they could point to with pride, William Cullen Bryant. Just as many American prose writers followed the example of Sir Walter Scott, Bryant was strongly influenced by British Romantic poets, especially William Wordsworth. With its emphasis on the dignity of the individual, the literary value of common speech, and the vital role of nature in human life, Romanticism exerted an increasingly strong pull on American writers, whose new, democratic country was far more noted for the grandeur of its natural scenery than for the richness of its cultural traditions. At the same time, Bryant was hailed for his mastery of traditional English poetics. When his poem "Thanatopsis" was submitted to the *North American Review* in 1817, one of its editors reportedly exclaimed, "No one, on this side of the Atlantic, is capable of writing such verses!" The following year, Bryant wrote an extended essay for an influential British journal, the *Edinburgh Review*, in which he surveyed American poetry and assessed the literary situation in the United States. "The fondness for literature is fast increasing in our country," he confidently observed. "The popular English works of the day are reprinted in our country—they are dispersed all over the union—they are to be found in every body's hands—they are made the subject of every body's conversation. What should hinder our native works, if they are of equal merit, from meeting an equally favorable reception?"

"The fondness for literature is fast increasing in our country."

Certainly, the warm reception of Bryant's first book, *Poems* (1821)—as well as of the prose works by Irving, Cooper, Sedgwick, Schoolcraft, and Longstreet—indicated that there was a growing audience for such "native works" in the United States. Like earlier poets, Bryant could not earn a living as a poet. He supported himself first as a lawyer and later as the editor of the New York *Evening Post*, one of the large-circulation newspapers that were fast becoming a major force in the nation's print culture. Nonetheless, literature was also gaining a foothold in that print culture, and both Cooper and Irving demonstrated that it was possible to be professional writers in the United States. At the same time, the prose writers who emerged in the 1820s experimented with genres that later assumed a prominent place in American literature, including the sketch and short story, the potential of which would be more fully developed by writers such as Nathaniel Hawthorne and Edgar Allan Poe. In retrospect, literature from the Revolution to 1830 may appear to be simply a prelude to the "American Renaissance," the term frequently used to describe the period from 1830 to 1865. But the remarkable achievements of that later period would not have been possible without the earlier efforts of those who first struggled to create an American literature and an audience for that literature in the United States.

Philip Freneau

[1752-1832]

Philip Freneau was born in New York City on January 2, 1752, to Pierre and Agnes Watson Fresneau (the original spelling of the family name, later changed by Philip to *Freneau*). His father was descended from French Protestants, called Huguenots, thousands of whom fled religious persecution in their native country and came to the American colonies. There, the Fresneaus established a successful business in the wine trade. Freneau's mother was a member of an affluent New Jersey family, and the family made its home first in New York and then on a thousand-acre estate, named Mount Pleasant, near Monmouth County, New Jersey. Educated by tutors and then at a preparatory school, Freneau was admitted as a sophomore to the College of New Jersey (now Princeton University). His college friends included the future president James Madison and Hugh Henry Brackenridge, who became one of the first successful novelists in the new nation.

After college, Freneau taught school for a time in Maryland but appears to have had some difficulty in deciding on a direction for his life. He published a collection of his poems, *The American Village*, in 1772. But finding that it was impossible to make a living as a poet, he took a position as a secretary to a wealthy planter in the West Indies and sailed there in 1776. Although Freneau is often thought of as "the poet of the American Revolution," he spent the early years of the war in the West Indies. On a voyage home in 1778, his ship was captured by the British. After his release, he enlisted on a blockade runner and was captured again. This time, he was imprisoned aboard a British ship anchored in New York harbor, a brutal experience that inspired his poem "The British Prison Ship," published in 1781. For the next three years, Freneau lived in Philadelphia, where he wrote a series of poems in support of the American cause for the *Freeman's Journal*. Now earning a reputation as both a poet and a journalist, Freneau

Philip Freneau

Frederick Halpin engraved this portrait of Freneau expressly for a posthumous collection of his *Poems Relating to the American Revolution* (1865), the first edition of any of Freneau's writings published in the United States since 1815.

published a long narrative poem, *A Journey from Philadelphia to New York* (1787), as well as collections of his shorter poems in 1787 and 1788.

During the 1790s, Freneau spent most of his time working for the periodical press. In 1790, he joined the staff of a New York newspaper, the *Daily Advertiser*. The following year, he established his own newspaper, the *National Gazette*, in Philadelphia. Firmly connected to the Jeffersonian Republicans and bitterly opposed to Federalists such as Alexander Hamilton, Freneau was called a "rascal" by George Washington. Freneau strongly supported the French Revolution and other democratic causes, writing frequently about them for his newspaper. The *Gazette* failed in 1793, after which Freneau tried his hand at running a printing business from his home and then editing the New York *Time Piece and Literary Companion.* After 1799, Freneau retired to a farm he had inherited from his father, where he continued to publish essays and poems but lived in increasing poverty and obscurity. He died on December 18, 1832.

Reading Freneau's Poems.   Freneau began to write poetry in college, where he joined literary clubs and participated, along with many other stu-

Philip Freneau, *Poems* **(1809)**

The frontispiece and title page of this two-volume edition of Freneau's poetry emphasizes his use of American themes and his patriotic involvement in the American Revolution. From the time of the earliest European maps and settlements, the image of an Indian was frequently used as a symbol of America.

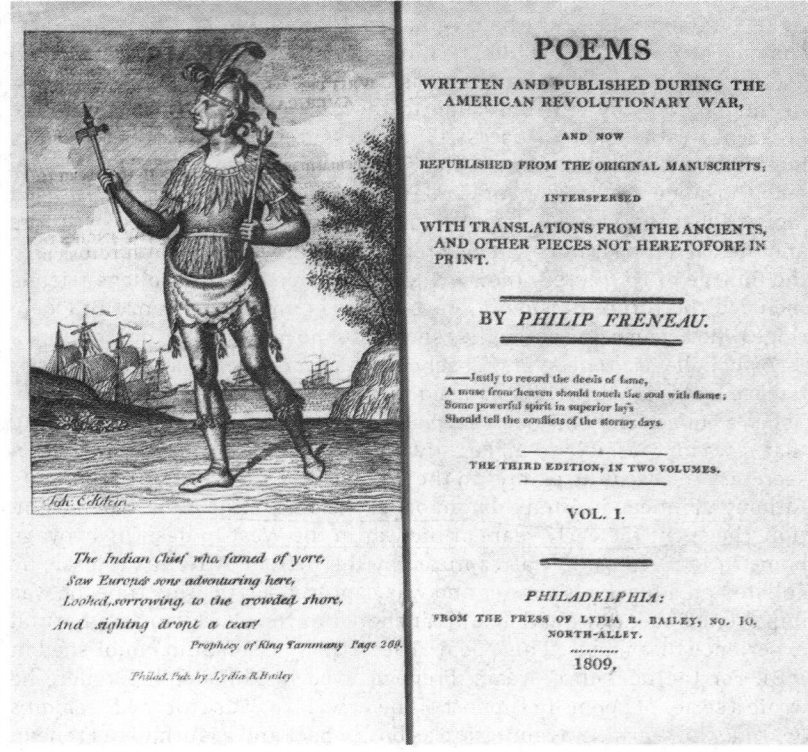

The Indian Chief who famed of yore,
Saw Europe's sons adventuring here,
Looked, sorrowing, to the crowded shore,
And sighing dropt a tear!
Prophecy of King Tammany Page 269.

Philad. Pub. by Lydia R. Bailey

POEMS
WRITTEN AND PUBLISHED DURING THE
AMERICAN REVOLUTIONARY WAR,
AND NOW
REPUBLISHED FROM THE ORIGINAL MANUSCRIPTS;
INTERSPERSED
WITH TRANSLATIONS FROM THE ANCIENTS,
AND OTHER PIECES NOT HERETOFORE IN
PRINT.

BY *PHILIP FRENEAU.*

——Justly to record the deeds of fame,
A muse from heaven should touch the soul with flame;
Some powerful spirit in superior lay's
Should tell the conflicts of the stormy days.

THE THIRD EDITION, IN TWO VOLUMES.

VOL. I.

PHILADELPHIA:
FROM THE PRESS OF LYDIA R. BAILEY, NO. 10,
NORTH-ALLEY.
1809.

dents, in the growing movement in favor of independence for the American colonies. With his friend Hugh Henry Brackenridge, Freneau wrote his best-known college poem, "The Rising Glory of America," which Brackenridge read at their graduation in 1771. Beginning with *The American Village* (1772), Freneau published several books of poetry, including a two-volume edition of his *Poems* (1809). But many of his verses first appeared in periodicals like the New York *Daily Advertiser.* Much of the poetry Freneau wrote after the Revolution was devoted to social and political commentary. Even as he participated in the increasingly heated debates between the Jeffersonian Republicans and the Federalists, however, Freneau also actively sought to establish foundations for a national literature, exploring American scenes and themes in poems such as "The Wild Honey Suckle" and "The Indian Burying Ground." In fact, "the poet of the American Revolution" is perhaps better understood as a post-Revolutionary or postcolonial poet who sought to free the new nation from the lingering cultural, political, and social influences of Great Britain. The texts of the following poems are taken from volume 2 of *The Poems of Philip Freneau* (1903), edited by F. L. Pattee.

**bedfordstmartins.com/
americanlit** *for research
links on Freneau*

ON THE EMIGRATION TO AMERICA

And Peopling the Western Country

To western woods, and lonely plains,
Palemon[1] from the crowd departs,
Where Nature's wildest genius reigns,
To tame the soil, and plant the arts —
What wonders there shall freedom show,   5
What mighty states successive grow!

From Europe's proud, despotic shores
Hither the stranger takes his way,
And in our new found world explores
A happier soil, a milder sway,   10
Where no proud despot holds him down,
No slaves insult him with a crown.

---

1. **Palemon:** The name of several literary characters that set out on journeys, such as Palamoun in "The Knight's Tale," by Geoffrey Chaucer (c. 1342–1400), and Palemon in "Autumn" of *The Seasons,* by the English poet James Thomson (1700–1748).

What charming scenes attract the eye,
On wild Ohio's savage stream!
There Nature reigns, whose works outvie   15
The boldest pattern art can frame;
There ages past have rolled away,
And forests bloomed but to decay.

From these fair plains, these rural seats,
So long concealed, so lately known,   20
The unsocial Indian far retreats,
To make some other clime his own,
When other streams, less pleasing, flow,
And darker forests round him grow.

Great Sire[2] of floods! whose varied wave   25
Through climes and countries takes its way,
To whom creating Nature gave
Ten thousand streams to swell thy sway!
No longer shall they useless prove,
Nor idly through the forests rove;   30

Nor longer shall your princely flood
From distant lakes be swelled in vain,
Nor longer through a darksome wood
Advance, unnoticed, to the main,[3]
Far other ends, the heavens decree —   35
And commerce plans new freights for thee.

While virtue warms the generous breast,
There heaven-born freedom shall reside,
Nor shall the voice of war molest,
Nor Europe's all-aspiring pride —   40
There Reason shall new laws devise,
And order from confusion rise.

Forsaking kings and regal state,
With all their pomp and fancied bliss,
The traveller owns,[4] convinced though late,   45
No realm so free, so blest as this —
The east is half to slaves consigned,
Where kings and priests enchain the mind.

---

2. **Great Sire:** "Mississippi." [Freneau's note]
3. **main:** Sea or ocean.
4. **owns:** Admits or acknowledges.

O come the time, and haste the day,
When man shall man no longer crush,   50
When Reason shall enforce her sway,
Nor these fair regions raise our blush,
Where still the African complains,
And mourns his yet unbroken chains.

Far brighter scenes a future age,   55
The muse predicts, these States will hail,
Whose genius may the world engage,
Whose deeds may over death prevail,
And happier systems bring to view,
Than all the eastern sages knew.   60

                                        [1785, 1903]

THE WILD HONEY SUCKLE

Fair flower, that dost so comely grow,
Hid in this silent, dull retreat,
Untouched thy honied blossoms blow,[1]
Unseen thy little branches greet:
 No roving foot shall crush thee here,   5
 No busy hand provoke a tear.

By Nature's self in white arrayed,
She bade thee shun the vulgar[2] eye,
And planted here the guardian shade,
And sent soft waters murmuring by;   10
 Thus quietly thy summer goes,
 Thy days declining to repose.

Smit with those charms, that must decay,
I grieve to see your future doom;
They died – nor were those flowers more gay,   15
The flowers that did in Eden bloom;
 Unpitying frosts, and Autumn's power
 Shall leave no vestige of this flower.

From morning suns and evening dews
At first thy little being came: 20

---

1. **blow:** An early term for bloom.
2. **vulgar:** An early meaning was "common" or "ordinary."

If nothing once, you nothing lose,
For when you die you are the same;
    The space between, is but an hour,
    The frail duration of a flower.

                                   [1786, 1903]

THE INDIAN BURYING GROUND

In spite of all the learned have said,
    I still my old opinion keep;
The posture, that we give the dead,
    Points out the soul's eternal sleep.

Not so the ancients of these lands —   5
    The Indian, when from life released,
Again is seated with his friends,
    And shares again the joyous feast.[1]

His imaged birds, and painted bowl,
    And venison, for a journey dressed,   10
Bespeak the nature of the soul,
    Activity, that knows no rest.

His bow, for action ready bent,
    And arrows, with a head of stone,
Can only mean that life is spent,   15
    And not the old ideas gone.

Thou, stranger, that shalt come this way,
    No fraud upon the dead commit —
Observe the swelling turf, and say
    They do not lie, but here they sit.   20

Here still a lofty rock remains,
    On which the curious eye may trace
(Now wasted, half, by wearing rains)
    The fancies of a ruder race.

Here still an aged elm aspires,   25
    Beneath whose far-projecting shade

---

1. **feast:** "The North American Indians bury their dead in a sitting posture; decorating the corpse with wampum, the images of birds, quadrupeds, &c: And (if that of a warrior) with bows, arrows, tomhawks, and other military weapons." [Freneau's note]

(And which the shepherd still admires)
   The children of the forest played!

There oft a restless Indian queen
   (Pale Shebah,[2] with her braided hair)   30
And many a barbarous form is seen
   To chide the man that lingers there.

By midnight moons, o'er moistening dews;
   In habit for the chase arrayed,
The hunter still the deer pursues,   35
   The hunter and the deer, a shade!

And long shall timorous fancy see
   The painted chief, and pointed spear,
And Reason's self shall bow the knee
   To shadows and delusions here.   40
                    [1788, 1903]

---

2. **Shebah:** *Sheba* is the biblical name of Saba in southwestern Arabia. In an Old Testament story, the queen of Sheba visited King Solomon in Jerusalem (1 Kings 10:1-13).

Phillis Wheatley

[c. 1753-1784]

Born on the west coast of Africa, Phillis Wheatley was captured by slave traders and transported on the schooner *Phillis* to Boston, where she arrived in 1761, when she was seven or eight years old. She was purchased by John Wheatley to serve as a companion for his wife, Susanna. The Wheatleys were prosperous people with a wide circle of friends and were active members of the New South Congregational Church. Their household included the Wheatley twins, Mary and Nathaniel, who were then eighteen, as well as several slaves. Although Phillis was in poor health and very young to be trained as a domestic servant, Susanna Wheatley evidently chose her because of her quick intelligence. Mary Wheatley soon began teaching her to read and write and also gave her instructions in religion and the Bible. Phillis remained legally a slave throughout her childhood, but she lived mostly as a member of the family and had considerable freedom to study. She advanced quickly, learning Latin, history, and geography, and received a good education, especially for a young girl of the time.

> *... the first decidedly American poet on this continent, Black or white, male or female.*
> — *June Jordan*

At about age twelve, Phillis began to write poetry, efforts that were strongly encouraged by the Wheatleys. Throughout her adolescence she wrote poems, and a few appeared in newspapers. Her first published poem was "On Messrs. Hussey and Coffin," based on the true story of the narrow escape of two men whose ship was wrecked during a storm. The poem appeared in the Rhode Island *Newport Mercury* on December 21, 1767. Wheatley began to keep "proposals," notes about poems she had written or that she wanted to write. Scholars have been able to piece together a publication history of her work mainly through her notes and surviving letters. In 1770, she wrote "On the Death of the Rev. Mr. George Whitefield," a memorial to a prominent British Evangelical that gained Wheatley her first important public notice. The poem was published as a broadside (a large, single sheet of paper) in Boston in 1770 and was subsequently reprinted at the end of a published sermon on the death of Whitefield by Ebenezer Pemberton, a well-known Boston clergyman. Although the publication of this broadside made her famous in New England, Wheatley was unsuccessful at publishing a collection of her poems in Boston. Taking her manuscript with her, Wheatley accompanied Nathaniel Wheatley on a trip to London, where her *Poems on Various Subjects, Religious and Moral* appeared in 1773. In England, she was not subject to the race prejudice that existed in the colonies, and she was widely acclaimed for her work, meeting a variety of people, both English and American, living in London, including Benjamin Franklin.

When she returned from London, Wheatley was emancipated by John Wheatley. But the final decade of her short life was difficult. Susanna

Phillis Wheatley, *Poems on Various Subjects* (1773)

The portrait of Wheatley on the frontispiece of her book was done by Scipio Moorhead, the artist she hailed in her poem "To S. M. a Young *African* Painter, on Seeing His Works."

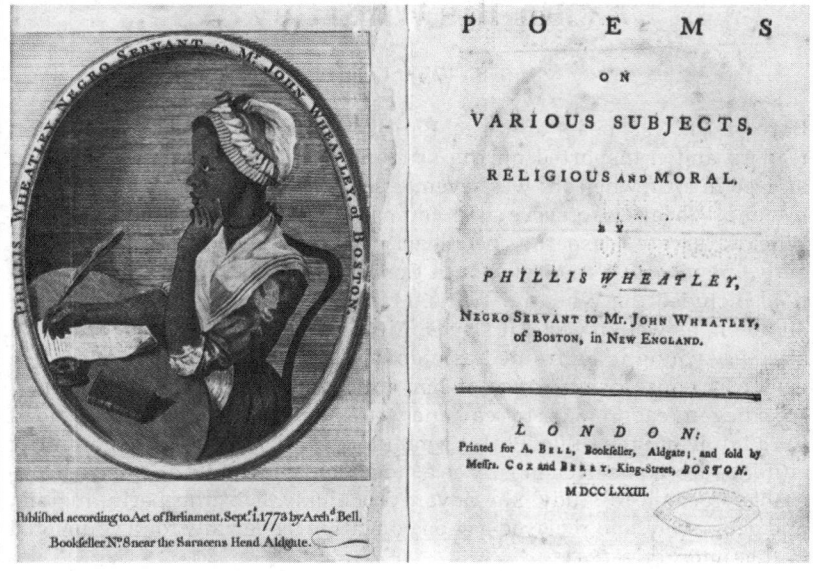

Wheatley died in 1774, and both John and Mary Wheatley died in 1778. That year, Phillis married John Peters. Little is known about him or their marriage, apart from the fact that the couple faced both financial and personal hardships, including the early death of their first two children. Wheatley's aspirations as a poet were also frequently frustrated, partly by the disruptions caused by the Revolutionary War. During the following years, there were proposals to publish a second volume of her poetry. Nothing came of those efforts, however, and Wheatley published only a few additional poems, including *Liberty and Peace*, a pamphlet that appeared shortly before her death on December 5, 1784. Her final surviving child died a short time later, and the two were buried together in a now-unknown grave in Boston.

Reading Wheatley's Poems and Letters.   Phillis Wheatley was an anomaly in the eighteenth century: a slave who had been well educated and encouraged to write. When her *Poems on Various Subjects, Religious and Moral* was published in London in 1773, the publisher offered a conventional disclaimer in a preface, explaining that the thirty-nine poems "were written for the Amusement of the Author, as they were the Products of her leisure Moments," and that she had published them only at the urging "of many of her best, and most generous Friends." In order to counter suspicions that she was not the author of the poems, however, the volume included a letter to the publisher from John Wheatley, who testified to Phillis's swift attainment of "the English language, to which she was an utter Stranger" before her arrival in Boston. The publisher also printed an "attestation" signed by eighteen influential men of the city, including the royal governor of Massachusetts, Thomas Hutchinson, who affirmed that Wheatley had "been examined by some of the best judges, and is thought qualified to write [the poems]."

From her earliest efforts to her final poems, Wheatley wrote in the style of eighteenth-century English poets who were popular on both sides of the Atlantic, especially Alexander Pope. Nonetheless, while she closely followed the poetic conventions of the period, Wheatley was also an innovator. As many scholars have noted, she was the founder not only of the African American literary tradition but also of the tradition of black women's writing in the United States. In both her poems and her letters to famous people, Wheatley's major themes are religion, politics, and the tyranny of slavery. Even before the formal Declaration of Independence, Wheatley was a fervent supporter of the American cause, which she celebrates in poems like "To His Excellency General Washington." At the same time, Wheatley recognized the contradiction between the institution of slavery in the American colonies and their struggle for "liberty," a struggle she implicitly sought to align with the cause of freedom for the slaves. The texts of the following poems and letters are taken from *The Poems of Phillis Wheatley: Revised and Enlarged Edition* (1989), edited by Julian D. Mason Jr.

*bedfordstmartins.com/
americanlit* for research
links on Wheatley

ON BEING BROUGHT FROM AFRICA TO AMERICA

'Twas mercy brought me from my *Pagan* land,
Taught my benighted soul to understand
That there's a God, that there's a *Saviour* too:
Once I redemption neither sought nor knew.
Some view our sable[1] race with scornful eye,
"Their colour is a diabolic die."
Remember, *Christians*, *Negros*, black as *Cain*,[2]
May be refin'd, and join th' angelic train.

[1773, 1989]

1. **sable:** Dark brown or black.
2. **black as Cain:** The eldest son of Adam and Eve, Cain murdered his brother Abel and was consequently cursed by God. To prevent others from killing him, "the Lord set a mark upon Cain" (Genesis 4:15), a mark that some readers of the Bible associated with blackness.

TO THE UNIVERSITY OF CAMBRIDGE,[1]
IN NEW ENGLAND

While an intrinsic ardor prompts to write,
The muses promise to assist my pen;
'Twas not long since I left my native shore
The land of errors, and *Egyptian* gloom:[2]
Father of mercy, 'twas thy gracious hand   5
Brought me in safety from those dark abodes.

Students, to you 'tis giv'n to scan the heights
Above, to traverse the ethereal space,
And mark the systems of revolving worlds.
Still more, ye sons of science ye receive   10
The blissful news by messengers from heav'n,
How *Jesus'* blood for your redemption flows.
See him with hands out-stretcht upon the cross;
Immense compassion in his bosom glows;
He hears revilers, nor resents their scorn: 15
What matchless mercy in the Son of God!
When the whole human race by sin had fall'n,
He deign'd to die that they might rise again,
And share with him in the sublimest skies,
Life without death, and glory without end.   20

1. **University of Cambridge:** Harvard College.
2. **Egyptian gloom:** A reference to the Christian belief that the unconverted live in error or wrong. Egypt (i.e., Africa) is therefore in a state of gloom, or darkness, because it has not been illuminated by the light of the Gospels.

Improve your privileges while they stay,
Ye pupils, and each hour redeem, that bears
Or good or bad report of you to heav'n.
Let sin, that baneful evil to the soul,
By you be shunn'd, nor once remit your guard;   25
Suppress the deadly serpent in its egg.
Ye blooming plants of human race devine,
An *Ethiop*[3] tells you 'tis your greatest foe;
Its transient sweetness turns to endless pain,
And in immense perdition sinks the soul.   30

[1773, 1989]

---

3. *Ethiop*: A common term in Wheatley's day for anyone from Africa.

TO THE RIGHT HONOURABLE WILLIAM, EARL OF DARTMOUTH, HIS MAJESTY'S PRINCIPAL SECRETARY OF STATE FOR NORTH-AMERICA, &C[1]

Hail, happy days, when, smiling like the morn,
Fair *Freedom* rose *New-England* to adorn:
The northern clime beneath her genial ray,
Dartmouth, congratulates thy blissful sway:
Elate with hope her race no longer mourns,   5
Each soul expands, each grateful bosom burns,
While in thine hand with pleasure we behold
The silken reins, and *Freedom's* charms unfold.
Long lost to realms beneath the northern skies
She shines supreme, while hated *faction* dies: 10
Soon as appear'd the *Goddess* long desir'd,
Sick at the view, she lanquish'd and expir'd;
Thus from the splendors of the morning light
The owl in sadness seeks the caves of night.

No more, *America*, in mournful strain   15
Of wrongs, and grievance unredress'd complain,   }
No longer shalt thou dread the iron chain,[2]
Which wanton *Tyranny* with lawless hand
Had made, and with it meant t' enslave the land.

---

1. **Earl of Dartmouth**: William Legge (1731–1801), the second Earl of Dartmouth, was appointed secretary to the American colonies in 1772. Like many others, Wheatley hoped that he would be sympathetic to colonial concerns and grievances.
2. **No more . . . chain**: The bracket-like symbol in the margin, called a brace, indicates the use here of a triplet, three rhyming lines, instead of the usual couplets, which have two rhyming lines.

Should you, my lord, while you peruse my song,   20
Wonder from whence my love of *Freedom* sprung,
Whence flow these wishes for the common good,
By feeling hearts alone best understood,
I, young in life, by seeming cruel fate
Was snatch'd from *Afric's* fancy'd happy seat: 25
What pangs excruciating must molest,
What sorrows labour in my parent's breast?
Steel'd was that soul and by no misery mov'd
That from a father seiz'd his babe belov'd:
Such, such my case. And can I then but pray   30
Others may never feel tyrannic sway?

    For favours past, great Sir, our thanks are due,
And thee we ask thy favours to renew,
Since in thy pow'r, as in thy will before,
To sooth the griefs, which thou did'st once deplore.   35
May heav'nly grace the sacred sanction give
To all thy works, and thou for ever live
Not only on the wings of fleeting *Fame*,
Though praise immortal crowns the patriot's name,
But to conduct to heav'ns refulgent fane,[3]   40
May fiery coursers sweep th' ethereal plain,
And bear thee upwards to that blest abode,
Where, like the prophet, thou shalt find thy God.

[1773, 1989]

---

3. **fane:** Early term for a temple or shrine.

To S. M.,[1] a Young *African* Painter, on Seeing His Works

To show the lab'ring bosom's deep intent,
And thought in living characters to paint,
When first thy pencil did those beauties give,
And breathing figures learnt from thee to live,

---

1. **S. M.:** Scipio Moorhead (c. 1750) was a painter tutored by Sarah Moorhead, an art teacher and the wife of his master, Reverend John Moorhead. He engraved the portrait of Wheatley that appeared opposite the title page of her *Poems on Various Subjects* (1773).

How did those prospects give my soul delight,   5
A new creation rushing on my sight?
Still, wond'rous youth! each noble path pursue,
On deathless glories fix thine ardent view:
Still may the painter's and the poet's fire
To aid thy pencil, and thy verse conspire!   10
And may the charms of each seraphic[2] theme
Conduct thy footsteps to immortal fame!
High to the blissful wonders of the skies
Elate thy soul, and raise thy wishful eyes.
Thrice happy, when exalted to survey   15
That splendid city, crown'd with endless day,
Whose twice six gates[3] on radiant hinges ring:
Celestial *Salem*[4] blooms in endless spring.

   Calm and serene thy moments glide along,
And may the muse inspire each future song!   20
Still, with the sweets of contemplation bless'd,
May peace with balmy wings your soul invest!
But when these shades of time are chas'd away,
And darkness ends in everlasting day,
On what seraphic pinions[5] shall we move,   25
And view the landscapes in the realms above?
There shall thy tongue in heav'nly murmurs flow,
And there my muse with heav'nly transport glow:
No more to tell of *Damon's*[6] tender sighs,
Or rising radiance of *Aurora's*[7] eyes,   30
For nobler themes demand a nobler strain,
And purer language on th' ethereal plain.
Cease, gentle muse! the solemn gloom of night
Now seals the fair creation from my sight.

[1773, 1989]

---

2. **seraphic:** Angelic.

3. **twice six gates:** Many early descriptions of heaven reflected the idea that it has twelve gates, corresponding to the twelve tribes of Israel.

4. ***Salem:*** Short for Jerusalem.

5. **seraphic pinions:** Angel wings.

6. ***Damon's:*** In Greek mythology, Damon offered himself as bail for his friend Pythias, who had been sentenced to death by King Dionysius I of Syracuse. When Pythias returned just in time to take his own place for execution, the king was so moved by their loyalty to each other that he released both youths.

7. ***Aurora's:*** In Roman mythology, Aurora is the goddess of the dawn.

TO HIS EXCELLENCY GENERAL WASHINGTON[1]

The following LETTER *and* VERSES, *were written by the famous* Phillis Wheatley, *the African Poetess, and presented to his Excellency Gen.* Washington.

Sir,

I have taken the freedom to address your Excellency in the enclosed poem, and entreat your acceptance, though I am not insensible of its inaccuracies. Your being appointed by the Grand Continental Congress to be Generalissimo of the armies of North America, together with the fame of your virtues, excite sensations not easy to suppress. Your generosity, therefore, I presume, will pardon the attempt. Wishing your Excellency all possible success in the great cause you are so generously engaged in. I am,

Your Excellency's most obedient humble servant,

PHILLIS WHEATLEY

Providence, Oct. 26, 1775.
His Excellency Gen. Washington.

> Celestial choir! enthron'd in realms of light,
> Columbia's[2] scenes of glorious toils I write.
> While freedom's cause her anxious breast alarms,
> She flashes dreadful in refulgent arms.
> See mother earth her offspring's fate bemoan,   5
> And nations gaze at scenes before unknown!
> See the bright beams of heaven's revolving light
> Involved in sorrows and the veil of night!
>   The goddess comes, she moves divinely fair,
> Olive and laurel binds her golden hair: 10
> Wherever shines this native of the skies,
> Unnumber'd charms and recent graces rise.
>   Muse! bow propitious while my pen relates
> How pour her armies through a thousand gates:
> As when Eolus[3] heaven's fair face deforms,   15
> Enwrapp'd in tempest and a night of storms;
> Astonish'd ocean feels the wild uproar,
> The refluent surges beat the sounding shore;
> Or thick as leaves in Autumn's golden reign,
> Such, and so many, moves the warrior's train.   20
> In bright array they seek the work of war,

---

1. **General Washington:** George Washington had been appointed commander in chief of the Continental army in June 1775. Early in 1776, Washington wrote to thank Wheatley for her letter and the poem, which were published in the *Virginia Gazette* (March 1776) and the *Pennsylvania Magazine* (April 1776).
2. **Columbia's:** America was often referred to as the land Columbus founded, or simply as *Columbia.*
3. **Eolus:** In Greek mythology, Eolus was the keeper of the winds.

Where high unfurl'd the ensign[4] waves in air.
Shall I to Washington their praise recite?
Enough thou know'st them in the fields of fight.
Thee, first in place and honours, — we demand   25
The grace and glory of thy martial band.
Fam'd for thy valour, for thy virtues more,
Hear every tongue thy guardian aid implore!
   One century scarce perform'd its destin'd round,
When Gallic powers[5] Columbia's fury found;   30
And so may you, whoever dares disgrace
The land of freedom's heaven-defended race!
Fix'd are the eyes of nations on the scales,
For in their hopes Columbia's arm prevails.
Anon Britannia droops the pensive head,   35
While round increase the rising hills of dead.
Ah! cruel blindness to Columbia's state!
Lament thy thirst of boundless power too late.
   Proceed, great chief, with virtue on thy side,
Thy ev'ry action let the goddess guide.   40
A crown, a mansion, and a throne that shine,
With gold unfading, WASHINGTON! be thine.

[1776, 1989]

---

4. **ensign:** A flag or standard.
5. **Gallic powers:** The French colonial empire in America ended with the conclusion of the French and Indian War (1754-1763).

LETTER TO SAMSON OCCOM[1]

The following is an extract of a Letter from Phillis, a Negro Girl of Mr. Wheatley's, in Boston, to the Rev. Samson Occom, which we are desired to insert as a Specimen of her Ingenuity. —It is dated 11th Feb., 1774.

Rev'd and honor'd Sir,

I have this Day received your obliging kind Epistle, and am greatly satisfied with your Reasons respecting the Negroes, and think highly reasonable what you offer in Vindication of their natural Rights: Those that invade them cannot be insensible that the divine Light is chasing away the thick Darkness which broods over the Land of Africa; and the Chaos which has reign'd so long, is converting into beautiful Order, and [r]eveals more and more clearly, the glorious Dispensation of civil and religious Liberty, which are so

---

1. **Samson Occom:** (1723-1792) Mohegan Indian minister and a longtime friend of Wheatley's (see p. 347). This letter was published in the *Connecticut Gazette;* and also in the *Universal Intelligencer* on March 11, 1774.

inseparably united, that there is little or no Enjoyment of one without the other: Otherwise, perhaps, the Israelites had been less solicitous for their Freedom from Egyptian slavery; I do not say they would have been contented without it, by no means, for in every human Breast, God has implanted a Principle, which we call Love of Freedom; it is impatient of Oppression, and pants for Deliverance; and by the Leave of our modern Egyptians I will assert, that the same Principle lives in us. God grant Deliverance in his own Way and Time, and get him honour upon all those whose Avarice impels them to countenance and help forward the Calamities of their fellow Creatures. This I desire not for their Hurt, but to convince them of the strange Absurdity of their Conduct whose Words and Actions are so diametrically opposite. How well the Cry for Liberty, and the reverse Disposition for the exercise of oppressive Power over others agree, — I humbly think it does not require the Penetration of a Philosopher to determine.

[1774, 1989]

Washington Irving

[1783–1859]

Washington Irving

This engraving was based on a portrait of Irving painted by John Wesley Jarvis in 1809, the year that the young writer achieved his first great success with the publication of his satirical *History of New York*.

Washington Irving was born in New York City on April 3, 1783, the youngest of eleven children of Sarah and William Irving. Irving's English-born mother was the granddaughter of a clergyman, and William Irving was an affluent merchant who strongly supported the cause of American independence. Born the same year that the Treaty of Paris ended the Revolution, Irving was named after its hero George Washington. As a child, Irving was part of a supportive family that would remain important to him throughout his life. He attended private schools but was not a strong student, displaying more interest in art, music, and especially English literature than in the Greek and Latin that was a staple of education for boys at the time. Since William Irving expected all of his sons to support themselves, Irving was sent to study law in 1801. The following year, his brother Peter established a newspaper, the *Morning Chronicle*, to which Irving contributed satirical pieces on New York culture and society called the "Letters of Jonathan Oldstyle, Gent.," the first of a series of pseudonyms he would adopt in his writings. Worried about his health, Irving's brothers sent him to Europe for recreation and further education in 1804, when he was twenty-one.

Returning to the United States after two years of extensive travel, Irving completed his legal studies and was admitted to the bar. But he was far more drawn to literature than to law. Along with his brother William and the writer James Kirke Paulding, Irving established a new magazine, *Salmagundi*, contributing the kind of satirical pieces in which he delighted and for which he was increasingly known. After the short-lived magazine failed in 1808, Irving wrote *A History of New York* (1809), a satire of both pedantic histories and current events, in which he adopted the persona of an elderly Dutch American antiquarian, Diedrich Knickerbocker. The book was hailed as a great comic work in both the United States and England, where its admirers included the influential writer Sir Walter Scott. Just before it was published, however, Irving suffered a devastating personal loss, the death from tuberculosis of his eighteen-year-old fiancée, Matilda Hoffman. The grief-stricken Irving would never marry. During the following years, he wrote little imaginative literature, devoting himself instead to his brothers' businesses and to editing the *Analectic Magazine*. The magazine primarily published articles and stories from foreign periodicals, but it also ran biographies of the American heroes of the War of 1812. Perhaps as a result, Irving in 1814 resigned the editorship and briefly served as a colonel in the New York State militia.

When the war ended in 1815, Irving once again went to Europe, where he lived for the next seventeen years. Initially, he worked with his brother Peter in the overseas branch of the family import business in Liverpool, England. In 1818, the business failed, taking with it much of the Irving family fortune. To earn money, Irving wrote reviews for British periodicals and served for a time as a book agent for the American bookseller Moses Thomas. He also began *The Sketch Book of Geoffrey Crayon, Gent.*, a collection of travel sketches of England in which Irving also included what would become his two most famous stories set in America, "Rip Van Winkle" and "The Legend of Sleepy Hollow." Published in installments in New York in 1819 and in book form both there and in London the following year, *The Sketch Book* was enormously popular on both sides of the Atlantic. Irving swiftly followed it with *Bracebridge Hall* (1822), another well-received collection of sketches about English country life written under the name of his persona Geoffrey Crayon. But his next book, *Tales of a Traveller* (1824), was a commercial and critical failure. Seeking both a change of scene and a new direction for his literary career, Irving accepted an invitation to become an attaché to the American legation in Madrid. There, he turned to biography and history, publishing *The Life and Voyages of Christopher Columbus* (1828) and *A Chronicle of the Conquest of Granada* (1829). Even after he returned to London as secretary of the American legation in 1829, he continued to draw upon his vivid impressions of Spain, notably in his collection of Romantic sketches and tales *The Alhambra* (1832).

After Irving returned to the United States in 1832, he primarily devoted himself to American scenes and subjects. Like many Americans at the time, he was especially fascinated by the West, which Irving explored in *A Tour on the Prairies* (1835), a narrative of his journey through what is now Arkansas and Oklahoma; *Astoria* (1836), a history of John Jacob Astor's fur-trading company in the Oregon Territory; and *The Rocky Mountains; or, Scenes, Incidents, and Adventures in the Far West* (1837). Having become the country's most celebrated author — and its first to make a living exclusively from writing — Irving in 1835 bought a country home, Sunnyside, on the banks of the Hudson River near Tarrytown, New York. With the exception of the years 1842-45, when he served with distinction as the ambassador to Spain, Irving

Irving? Thrice welcome, warm heart and fine brain . . .
— James Russell Lowell

bedfordstmartins.com/
americanlit *for research
links on Irving*

lived for the rest of his life at Sunnyside, where he enjoyed the company of his many friends and family members. Although the pace of his writing slowed, he published several additional books, including *A Book of the Hudson* (1849), and he prepared a fifteen-volume "Author's Revised Edition" of his *Works*. During the 1850s, he devoted his energies to a five-volume biography of his namesake, George Washington, which Irving completed shortly before his death at Sunnyside on November 28, 1859.

Reading Irving's *Sketch Book*.   While living in England in 1818, Irving began writing the essays, sketches, and tales for the book that gained him an international reputation, *The Sketch Book of Geoffrey Crayon, Gent.* He was encouraged by the popular English writer Sir Walter Scott, who also advised Irving to read German folktales, the primary source of his most famous story, "Rip Van Winkle." That story, ostensibly found among the papers of the antiquarian Diedrich Knickerbocker, was not typical of most of the sketches in the volume, which record the impressions and observations of Irving's other persona, Geoffrey Crayon, an American traveler in England. Irving, however, clearly recognized the appeal of "Rip Van Winkle," a humorous and satirical yet deeply resonant story set in a richly evocative American setting, the Catskill Mountains of New York State. "Rip Van Winkle" was included in the first of six installments of *The Sketch Book* published in New York between May 1819 and February 1820.

John Quidor, *The Return of Rip Van Winkle* **(1849)**

Quidor, a struggling artist who had to earn his living by painting signs, was fascinated by "Rip Van Winkle." In his dynamic rendering of the climax of the story, Quidor accurately depicts key details of the setting, especially the Dutch houses of the village against the background of the Catskill Mountains.

In the prospectus, printed at the beginning of the first installment, Irving explained:

> The following writings are published on experiment; should they please, they may be followed by others. The writer will have to contend with some disadvantages. He is unsettled in his abode, subject to interruptions, and has his share of cares and vicissitudes. He cannot, therefore, promise a regular plan, nor regular periods of publication. Should he be encouraged to proceed, much time may elapse between the appearance of his numbers; and their size must depend on the materials he has on hand. His writings will partake of the fluctuations of his own thoughts and feelings; sometimes treating of scenes before him, sometimes of others purely imaginary, and sometimes wandering back with his recollections to his native country. He will not be able to give them that tranquil attention necessary to finished composition; and as they must be transmitted across the Atlantic for publication, he must trust to others to correct the frequent errors of the press. Should his writings, however, with all their imperfections, be well received, he cannot conceal that it would be a source of the purist gratification; for though he does not aspire to those high honours that are the rewards of loftier intellects; yet it is the dearest wish of his heart to have a secure and cherished, though humble, corner in the good opinions and kind feelings of his countrymen.

As that passage suggests, Irving carefully crafted the persona of Geoffrey Crayon. By casting himself as an amateur, an idle gentleman traveler who did not take himself or his writings too seriously, Irving sought at once to disarm and appeal to an American audience still skeptical about both the claims of merely imaginative literature and the status of writing as a profession. Certainly, his "experiment" proved to be a huge success, both among Irving's "countrymen" and in England, where a full version of *The Sketch Book* was published in 1820.

The texts of the following works — two of the five Irving included in the first installment of *The Sketch Book*—are taken from the initial American publication of that installment in May 1819.

THE AUTHOR'S ACCOUNT OF HIMSELF

"I am of this mind with Homer, that as the snaile that crept out of her shel was turned eftsoones into a toad, and thereby was forced to make a stoole to sit on; so the traveller that stragleth from his owne country is in a short time transformed into so monstrous a shape, that he is faine to alter his mansion with his manners, and to live where he can, not where he would."

– Lyly's Euphues.[1]

---

1. *Lyly's Euphues*: The epigraph is from *Euphues and His England* (1580) by John Lyly (1554-1606), an English writer who developed euphuism, an elaborate prose style marked by repetition, rhetorical questions, and classical allusions.

I was always fond of visiting new scenes, and observing strange characters and manners. Even when a mere child I began my travels, and made many tours of discovery into foreign parts and unknown regions of my native city, to the frequent alarm of my parents, and the emolument of the town-crier. As I grew into boyhood, I extended the range of my observations. My holiday afternoons were spent in rambles about the surrounding country. I made myself familiar with all its places famous in history or fable. I knew every spot where a murder or robbery had been committed, or a ghost been seen. I visited the neighbouring villages, and added greatly to my stock of knowledge, by noting their habits and customs, and conversing with their sages and great men. I even journeyed one long summer's day to the summit of the most distant hill, from whence I stretched my eye over many a mile of terra incognita, and was astonished to find how vast a globe I inhabited.

This rambling propensity strengthened with my years. Books of voyages and travels became my passion, and in devouring their contents, I neglected the regular exercises of the school. How wistfully would I wander about the pier heads in fine weather, and watch the parting ships, bound to distant climes – with what longing eyes would I gaze after their lessening sails, and waft myself in imagination to the ends of the earth.

Farther reading and thinking, though they brought this vague inclination into more reasonable bounds, only served to make it more decided. I visited various parts of my own country; and had I been merely a lover of fine scenery, I should have felt little desire to seek elsewhere for its gratification: for on no country have the charms of nature been more prodigally lavished. Her mighty lakes, like oceans of liquid silver; her mountains, with their bright aerial tints; her valleys, teeming with wild fertility; her tremendous cataracts, thundering in their solitudes; her boundless plains, waving with spontaneous verdure; her broad deep rivers, rolling in solemn silence to the ocean; her trackless forests, where vegetation puts forth all its magnificence; her skies, kindling with the magic of summer clouds and glorious sunshine: – no, never need an American look beyond his own country for the sublime and beautiful of natural scenery.

But Europe held forth all the charms of storied and poetical association. There were to be seen the masterpieces of art, the refinements of highly cultivated society, the quaint peculiarities of ancient and local custom. My native country was full of youthful promise; Europe was rich in the accumulated treasures of age. Her very ruins told the history of times gone by, and every mouldering stone was a chronicle. I longed to wander over the scenes of renowned achievement – to tread, as it were, in the footsteps of antiquity – to loiter about the ruined castle – to meditate on the falling tower – to escape, in short, from the commonplace realities of the present, and lose myself among the shadowy grandeurs of the past.

I had, beside all this, an earnest desire to see the great men of the earth. We have, it is true, our great men in America: not a city but has an ample share of them. I have mingled among them in my time, and been almost withered by the shade into which they cast me; for there is nothing so baleful to a small man as the shade of a great one, particularly the great man of a city. But I was anxious to see the great men of Europe; for I had read in the works of various philosophers, that all animals degenerated in America, and man among the number.[2] A great man of Europe, therefore, thought I, must be as superior to a great man of America, as a peak of the Alps to a highland of the Hudson; and in this idea I was confirmed, by observing the comparative importance and swelling magnitude of many English travellers among us; who, I was assured, were very little people in their own country. I will visit this land of wonders, therefore, thought I, and see the gigantic race from which I am degenerated.

It has been either my good or evil lot to have my roving passion gratified. I have wandered through different countries, and witnessed many of the shifting scenes of life. I cannot say that I have studied them with the eye of a philosopher, but rather with the sauntering gaze with which humble lovers of the picturesque stroll from the window of one print shop to another; caught sometimes by the delineations of beauty, sometimes by the distortions of caricature, and sometimes by the loveliness of landscape. As it is the fashion for modern tourists to travel pencil in hand, and bring home their port folios filled with sketches, I am disposed to get up a few for the entertainment of my friends. When I look over, however, the hints and memorandums I have taken down for the purpose, my heart almost fails me to find how my idle humour has led me aside from the great objects studied by every regular traveller who would make a book. I fear I shall give equal disappointment with an unlucky landscape painter, who had travelled on the continent, but following the bent of his vagrant inclination, had sketched in nooks, and corners, and by-places. His sketch book was accordingly crowded with cottages, and landscapes, and obscure ruins; but he had neglected to paint St. Peter's, or the Coliseum; the cascade of Terni, or the bay of Naples;[3] and had not a single glacier or volcano in his whole collection.

[1819]

---

2. **man among the number:** Comte George-Louis Leclerc de Buffon (1707–1788), an influential French naturalist and scientist, had argued that people in North America would degenerate because its cold and damp climate was not conducive to physical development. Thomas Jefferson vigorously refuted Buffon, as well as critics who argued that the American environment also stunted intellectual growth, in his *Notes on the State of Virginia*, which was privately printed in Paris in 1784 and later published in London and Philadelphia.

3. **St. Peter's . . . Naples:** Irving refers to several favorite tourist destinations: St. Peter's Basilica in Rome, built in the sixteenth century; the Colosseum (as it is usually spelled), a vast amphitheater in Rome built in 75 CE; the man-made falls or cascade at Terni in Italy, built in 272 BCE; and the bay of Naples in southern Italy, upon which is located the volcano, Mount Vesuvius, and the ruins of Pompeii.

RIP VAN WINKLE

[The following Tale was found among the papers of the late Diedrich Knickerbocker, an old gentleman of New-York, who was very curious in the Dutch history of the province, and the manners of the descendants from its primitive settlers. His historical researches, however, did not lay so much among books, as among men; for the former are lamentably scanty on his favourite topics; whereas he found the old burghers, and still more, their wives, rich in that legendary lore, so invaluable to true history. Whenever, therefore, he happened upon a genuine Dutch family, snugly shut up in its low-roofed farm house, under a spreading sycamore, he looked upon it as a little clasped volume of black-letter,[1] and studied it with the zeal of a bookworm.

The result of all these researches was a history of the province, during the reign of the Dutch governors, which he published some years since. There have been various opinions as to the literary character of his work, and, to tell the truth, it is not a whit better than it should be. Its chief merit is its scrupulous accuracy, which, indeed, was a little questioned, on its first appearance, but has since been completely established; and it is now admitted into all historical collections, as a book of unquestionable authority.[2]

The old gentleman died shortly after the publication of his work, and now, that he is dead and gone, it cannot do much harm to his memory, to say, that his time might have been much better employed in weightier labours. He, however, was apt to ride his hobby his own way; and though it did now and then kick up the dust a little in the eyes of his neighbours, and grieve the spirit of some friends, for whom he felt the truest deference and affection; yet his errors and follies are remembered "more in sorrow than in anger,"[3] and it begins to be suspected, that he never intended to injure or offend. But however his memory may be appreciated by critics, it is still held dear among many folk, whose good opinion is well worth having; particularly certain biscuit bakers, who have gone so far as to imprint his likeness on their new year cakes, and have thus given him a chance for immortality, almost equal to being stamped on a Waterloo medal, or a Queen Anne's farthing.[4]]

Rip Van Winkle

A POSTHUMOUS WRITING OF DIEDRICH KNICKERBOCKER

By Woden, God of Saxons,
From whence comes Wensday, that is Wodensday,
Truth is a thing that ever I will keep
Unto thylke day in which I creep into
My sepulchre —

                                        Cartwright[5]

---

1. **clasped volume of black-letter**: In addition to using a type of font that resembled a medieval manuscript, many early printed books were fitted with clasp closures.

2. **book of unquestionable authority**: Irving's popular *A History of New York* (1809), written under the pseudonym Diedrich Knickerbocker, was a hilariously inaccurate spoof of the early history of New York, as his readers would surely have remembered.

3. **"more . . . anger"**: The quotation is from Shakespeare's *Hamlet*, 1.1.231-32. In the original text, Irving added this note: "Vide the excellent discourse of G. C. Verplanck, Esq. before the New-York Historical Society." *Vide* is the Latin term for *see*; Verplanck (1786-1870) was a well-known politician and one of Irving's friends in New York.

4. **Waterloo medal, or a Queen Anne's farthing**: Medals were given to British soldiers who had taken part in the series of battles leading up to the battle of Waterloo, where Napoleon was defeated on June 18, 1805. Queen Anne's farthings, only a small number of which were minted in 1713, were also in considerable demand by collectors in the early nineteenth century.

5. **Cartwright**: The lines are spoken by Moth, a pedantic antiquarian, in *The Ordinary*, 3.1.1050-54, by the English playwright William Cartwright (1611-1643).

Whoever has made a voyage up the Hudson, must remember the Kaatskill mountains.[6] They are a dismembered branch of the great Appalachian family, and are seen away to the west of the river, swelling up to a noble height, and lording it over the surrounding country. Every change of season, every change of weather, indeed, every hour of the day, produces some change in the magical hues and shapes of these mountains, and they are regarded by all the good wives, far and near, as perfect barometers. When the weather is fair and settled, they are clothed in blue and purple, and print their bold outlines on the clear evening sky; but some times, when the rest of the landscape is cloudless, they will gather a hood of gray vapours about their summits, which, in the last rays of the setting sun, will glow and light up like a crown of glory.

At the foot of these fairy mountains, the voyager may have descried the light smoke curling up from a village, whose shingle roofs gleam among the trees, just where the blue tints of the upland melt away into the fresh green of the nearer landscape. It is a little village of great antiquity, having been founded by some of the Dutch colonists, in the early times of the province, just about the beginning of the government of the good Peter Stuyvesant,[7] (may he rest in peace!) and there were some of the houses of the original settlers standing within a few years, with lattice windows, gable fronts surmounted with weathercocks, and built of small yellow bricks brought from Holland.

In that same village, and in one of these very houses, (which, to tell the precise truth, was sadly time worn and weather beaten,) there lived many years since, while the country was yet a province of Great Britain, a simple good natured fellow, of the name of Rip Van Winkle. He was a descendant of the Van Winkles who figured so gallantly in the chivalrous days of Peter Stuyvesant, and accompanied him to the siege of Fort Christina.[8] He inherited, however, but little of the martial character of his ancestors. I have observed that he was a simple good natured man; he was moreover a kind neighbour, and an obedient, henpecked husband. Indeed, to the latter circumstance might be owing that meekness of spirit which gained him such universal popularity; for those men are most apt to be obsequious and conciliating abroad, who are under the discipline of shrews at home. Their tempers, doubtless, are rendered pliant and malleable in the fiery furnace of domestic tribulation, and a curtain lecture[9] is worth all the sermons in the world for teaching the virtues of patience and long suffering. A termagant wife may, therefore, in some respects, be considered a tolerable blessing; and if so, Rip Van Winkle was thrice blessed.

Certain it is, that he was a great favourite among all the good wives of the village, who, as usual with the amiable sex, took his part in all family squabbles, and never

---

6. **Kaatskill mountains:** The Catskill Mountains, an extension of the Appalachian Mountains, are located in eastern New York.

7. **Peter Stuyvesant:** (1592–1672) Last governor of the Dutch province of New Netherland; he was frequently satirized by Irving in his *History of New York.*

8. **Fort Christina:** The first Swedish settlement in North America was established in 1638 at Fort Christina, near present-day Wilmington, Delaware. In 1655, the Dutch under Peter Stuyvesant took control of the fort and the land became part of New Netherland.

9. **curtain lecture:** Archaic term for a reprimand given by a wife to her husband behind lowered curtains, typically used on a four-poster bed in the seventeenth and eighteenth centuries.

failed, whenever they talked those matters over in their evening gossippings, to lay all the blame on Dame Van Winkle. The children of the village, too, would shout with joy whenever he approached. He assisted at their sports, made their playthings, taught them to fly kites and shoot marbles, and told them long stories of ghosts, witches, and Indians. Whenever he went dodging about the village, he was surrounded by a troop of them, hanging on his skirts, clambering on his back, and playing a thousand tricks on him with impunity; and not a dog would bark at him throughout the neighbourhood.

The great error in Rip's composition was an insuperable aversion to all kinds of profitable labour. It could not be for the want of assiduity or perseverance; for he would sit on a wet rock, with a rod as long and heavy as a Tartar's lance, and fish all day without a murmur, even though he should not be encouraged by a single nibble. He would carry a fowling piece on his shoulder, for hours together, trudging through woods and swamps, and up hill and down dale, to shoot a few squirrels or wild pigeons. He would never even refuse to assist a neighbour in the roughest toil, and was a foremost man at all country frolicks for husking Indian corn, or building stone fences; the women of the village, too, used to employ him to run their errands, and to do such little odd jobs as their less obliging husbands would not do for them; — in a word, Rip was ready to attend to any body's business but his own; but as to doing family duty, and keeping his farm in order, it was impossible.

In fact, he declared it was no use to work on his farm; it was the most pestilent little piece of ground in the whole country; every thing about it went wrong, and would go wrong, in spite of him. His fences were continually falling to pieces; his cow would either go astray, or get among the cabbages; weeds were sure to grow quicker in his fields than any where else; the rain always made a point of setting in just as he had some out-door work to do. So that though his patrimonial estate had dwindled away under his management, acre by acre, until there was little more left than a mere patch of Indian corn and potatoes, yet it was the worst conditioned farm in the neighbourhood.

His children, too, were as ragged and wild as if they belonged to nobody. His son Rip, an urchin begotten in his own likeness, promised to inherit the habits, with the old clothes of his father. He was generally seen trooping like a colt at his mother's heels, equipped in a pair of his father's cast-off galligaskins,[10] which he had much ado to hold up with one hand, as a fine lady does her train in bad weather.

Rip Van Winkle, however, was one of those happy mortals, of foolish, well-oiled dispositions, who take the world easy, eat white bread or brown, which ever can be got with least thought or trouble, and would rather starve on a penny than work for a pound. If left to himself, he would have whistled life away, in perfect contentment; but his wife kept continually dinning in his ears about his idleness, his carelessness, and the ruin he was bringing on his family. Morning, noon, and night, her tongue was incessantly going, and every thing he said or did was sure to produce a torrent of household eloquence. Rip had but one way of replying to all lectures of the kind, and that, by frequent use, had grown into a habit. He shrugged his shoulders, shook his head, cast up his eyes, but said

---

10. **galligaskins:** British name for loose-fitting trousers.

nothing. This, however, always provoked a fresh volley from his wife, so that he was fain to draw off his forces, and take to the outside of the house – the only side which, in truth, belongs to a henpecked husband.

Rip's sole domestic adherent was his dog Wolf, who was as much henpecked as his master; for Dame Van Winkle regarded them as companions in idleness, and even looked upon Wolf with an evil eye, as the cause of his master's so often going astray. True it is, in all points of spirit befitting an honourable dog, he was as courageous an animal as ever scoured the woods – but what courage can withstand the ever-during and all-besetting terrors of a woman's tongue? The moment Wolf entered the house, his crest fell, his tail drooped to the ground, or curled between his legs, he sneaked about with a gallows air, casting many a sidelong glance at Dame Van Winkle, and at the least flourish of a broomstick or ladle, would fly to the door with yelping precipitation.

Times grew worse and worse with Rip Van Winkle as years of matrimony rolled on; a tart temper never mellows with age, and a sharp tongue is the only edge tool that grows keener by constant use. For a long while he used to console himself, when driven from home, by frequenting a kind of perpetual club of the sages, philosophers, and other idle personages of the village, that held its sessions on a bench before a small inn, designated by a rubicund portrait of his majesty George the Third. Here they used to sit in the shade, of a long lazy summer's day, talk listlessly over village gossip, or tell endless sleepy stories about nothing. But it would have been worth any statesman's money to have heard the profound discussions that sometimes took place, when by chance an old newspaper fell into their hands, from some passing traveller. How solemnly they would listen to the contents, as drawled out by Derrick Van Bummel, the schoolmaster, a dapper learned little man, who was not to be daunted by the most gigantic word in the dictionary; and how sagely they would deliberate upon public events some months after they had taken place.

The opinions of this junto were completely controlled by Nicholas Vedder, a patriarch of the village, and landlord of the inn, at the door of which he took his seat from morning till night, just moving sufficiently to avoid the sun, and keep in the shade of a large tree; so that the neighbours could tell the hour by his movements as accurately as by a sun dial. It is true, he was rarely heard to speak, but smoked his pipe incessantly. His adherents, however, (for every great man has his adherents,) perfectly understood him, and knew how to gather his opinions. When any thing that was read or related displeased him, he was observed to smoke his pipe vehemently, and send forth short, frequent, and angry puffs; but when pleased, he would inhale the smoke slowly and tranquilly, and emit it in light and placid clouds, and sometimes taking the pipe from his mouth, and letting the fragrant vapour curl about his nose, would gravely nod his head in token of perfect approbation.

From even this strong hold the unlucky Rip was at length routed by his termagant wife, who would suddenly break in upon the tranquillity of the assemblage, call the members all to nought, nor was that august personage, Nicholas Vedder himself, sacred from the daring tongue of this terrible virago, who charged him outright with encouraging her husband in habits of idleness.

Poor Rip was at last reduced almost to despair; and his only alternative to escape from the labour of the farm and the clamour of his wife, was to take gun in hand, and stroll away into the woods. Here he would sometimes seat himself at the foot of a tree, and share the contents of his wallet[11] with Wolf, with whom he sympathised as a fellow sufferer in persecution. "Poor Wolf," he would say, "thy mistress leads thee a dogs' life of it; but never mind, my lad, while I live thou shalt never want a friend to stand by thee!" Wolf would wag his tail, look wistfully in his master's face, and if dogs can feel pity, I verily believe he reciprocated the sentiment with all his heart.

In a long ramble of the kind on a fine autumnal day, Rip had unconsciously scrambled to one of the highest parts of the Kaatskill mountains. He was after his favourite sport of squirrel shooting, and the still solitudes had echoed and re-echoed with the reports of his gun. Panting and fatigued, he threw himself, late in the afternoon, on a green knoll, covered with mountain herbage, that crowned the brow of a precipice. From an opening between the trees, he could overlook all the lower country for many a mile of rich wood-land. He saw at a distance the lordly Hudson, far, far below him, moving on its silent but majestic course, the reflection of a purple cloud, or the sail of a lagging bark, here and there sleeping on its glassy bosom, and at last losing itself in the blue highlands.

On the other side he looked down into a deep mountain glen, wild, lonely, and shagged, the bottom filled with fragments from the impending cliffs, and scarcely lighted by the reflected rays of the setting sun. For some time Rip lay musing on this scene, evening was gradually advancing, the mountains began to throw their long blue shadows over the valleys, he saw that it would be dark long before he could reach the village, and he heaved a heavy sigh when he thought of encountering the terrors of Dame Van Winkle.

As he was about to descend, he heard a voice from a distance, hallooing, "Rip Van Winkle! Rip Van Winkle!" He looked around, but could see nothing but a crow winging its solitary flight across the mountain. He thought his fancy must have deceived him, and turned again to descend, when he heard the same cry ring through the still evening air; "Rip Van Winkle! Rip Van Winkle!" – at the same time Wolf bristled up his back, and giving a low growl, skulked to his master's side, looking fearfully down into the glen. Rip now felt a vague apprehension stealing over him; he looked anxiously in the same direction, and perceived a strange figure slowly toiling up the rocks, and bending under the weight of something he carried on his back. He was surprised to see any human being in this lonely and unfrequented place, but supposing it to be some one of the neighbour-hood in need of his assistance, he hastened down to yield it.

On nearer approach, he was still more surprised at the singularity of the stranger's appearance. He was a short square built old fellow, with thick bushy hair, and a grizzled beard. His dress was of the antique Dutch fashion – a cloth jerkin[12] strapped round the waist – several pair of breeches, the outer one of ample volume, decorated with rows of buttons down the sides, and bunches at the knees. He bore on his shoulder a stout keg, that seemed full of liquor, and made signs for Rip to approach and assist him with the load. Though rather shy and distrustful of this new acquaintance, Rip complied with his usual alacrity, and mutually relieving each other, they clambered up a narrow gully, apparently the dry bed of a mountain torrent. As they ascended, Rip every now and then

---

11. **wallet:** Early term for a bag used by a traveler for holding provisions.
12. **jerkin:** A man's close-fitting jacket, usually made of leather.

heard long rolling peals, like distant thunder, that seemed to issue out of a deep ravine, or rather cleft between lofty rocks, toward which their rugged path conducted. He paused for an instant, but supposing it to be the muttering of one of those transient thunder showers which often take place in mountain heights, he proceeded. Passing through the ravine, they came to a hollow, like a small amphitheatre, surrounded by perpendicular precipices, over the brinks of which impending trees shot their branches, so that you only caught glimpses of the azure sky, and the bright evening cloud. During the whole time, Rip and his companion had laboured on in silence; for though the former marvelled greatly what could be the object of carrying a keg of liquor up this wild mountain, yet there was something strange and incomprehensible about the unknown, that inspired awe, and checked familiarity.

On entering the amphitheatre, new objects of wonder presented themselves. On a level spot in the centre was a company of odd-looking personages playing at nine-pins. They were dressed in a quaint, outlandish fashion: some wore short doublets,[13] others jerkins, with long knives in their belts, and most had enormous breeches, of similar style with that of the guide's. Their visages, too, were peculiar: one had a large head, broad face, and small piggish eyes; the face of another seemed to consist entirely of nose, and was surmounted by a white sugarloaf hat, set off with a little red cockstail. They all had beards, of various shapes and colours. There was one who seemed to be the commander. He was a stout old gentleman, with a weather-beaten countenance; he wore a laced doublet, broad belt and hanger,[14] high crowned hat and feather, red stockings, and high heeled shoes, with roses in them. The whole group reminded Rip of the figures in an old Flemish painting, in the parlour of Dominie[15] Van Schaick, the village parson, and which had been brought over from Holland at the time of the settlement.

What seemed particularly odd to Rip, was, that though these folks were evidently amusing themselves, yet they maintained the gravest faces, the most mysterious silence, and were, withal, the most melancholy party of pleasure he had ever witnessed. Nothing interrupted the stillness of the scene, but the noise of the balls, which, whenever they were rolled, echoed along the mountains like rumbling peals of thunder.

As Rip and his companion approached them, they suddenly desisted from their play, and stared at him with such fixed statue-like gaze, and such strange, uncouth, lack lustre countenances, that his heart turned within him, and his knees smote together. His companion now emptied the contents of the keg into large flagons, and made signs to him to wait upon the company. He obeyed with fear and trembling; they quaffed the liquor in profound silence, and then returned to their game.

By degrees, Rip's awe and apprehension subsided. He even ventured, when no eye was fixed upon him, to taste the beverage, which he found had much of the flavour of excellent Hollands.[16] He was naturally a thirsty soul, and was soon tempted to repeat the draught. One taste provoked another, and he reiterated his visits to the flagon so often,

---

13. **doublets:** Padded jackets, commonly worn by men from the fourteenth through the seventeenth centuries.
14. **hanger:** A short sword.
15. **Dominie:** A title for a pastor or clergyman.
16. **Hollands:** Dutch gin.

that at length his senses were overpowered, his eyes swam in his head, his head gradually declined, and he fell into a deep sleep.

On awaking, he found himself on the green knoll from whence he had first seen the old man of the glen. He rubbed his eyes – it was a bright sunny morning. The birds were hopping and twittering among the bushes, and the eagle was wheeling aloft, and breasting the pure mountain breeze. "Surely," thought Rip, "I have not slept here all night." He recalled the occurrences before he fell asleep. The strange man with the keg of liquor – the mountain ravine – the wild retreat among the rocks – the wo-begone party at nine-pins – the flagon – "Oh! that flagon! that wicked flagon!" thought Rip – "what excuse shall I make to Dame Van Winkle?"

He looked round for his gun, but in place of the clean well-oiled fowling-piece, he found an old firelock lying by him, the barrel encrusted with rust, the lock falling off, and the stock worm-eaten. He now suspected that the grave roysters of the mountain had put a trick upon him, and having dosed him with liquor, had robbed him of his gun. Wolf, too, had disappeared, but he might have strayed away after a squirrel or partridge. He whistled after him, shouted his name, but all in vain; the echoes repeated his whistle and shout, but no dog was to be seen.

He determined to revisit the scene of the last evening's gambol, and if he met with any of the party, to demand his dog and gun. As he arose to walk he found himself stiff in the joints, and wanting in his usual activity. "These mountain beds do not agree with me," thought Rip, "and if this frolick should lay me up with a fit of the rheumatism, I shall have a blessed time with Dame Van Winkle." With some difficulty he got down into the glen: he found the gully up which he and his companion had ascended the preceding evening, but to his astonishment a mountain stream was now foaming down it, leaping from rock to rock, and filling the glen with babbling murmurs. He, however, made shift to scramble up its sides, working his toilsome way through thickets of birch, sassafras, and witch hazel, and sometimes tripped up or entangled by the wild grape vines that twisted their coils and tendrils from tree to tree, and spread a kind of network in his path.

At length he reached to where the ravine had opened through the cliffs, to the amphitheatre; but no traces of such opening remained. The rocks presented a high impenetrable wall, over which the torrent came tumbling in a sheet of feathery foam, and fell into a broad deep basin, black from the shadows of the surrounding forest. Here, then, poor Rip was brought to a stand. He again called and whistled after his dog; he was only answered by the cawing of a flock of idle crows, sporting high in air about a dry tree that overhung a sunny precipice; and who, secure in their elevation, seemed to look down and scoff at the poor man's perplexities. What was to be done? the morning was passing away, and Rip felt famished for his breakfast. He grieved to give up his dog and gun; he dreaded to meet his wife; but it would not do to starve among the mountains. He shook his head, shouldered the rusty firelock, and, with a heart full of trouble and anxiety, turned his steps homeward.

As he approached the village, he met a number of people, but none that he knew, which somewhat surprised him, for he had thought himself acquainted with every one in the country round. Their dress, too, was of a different fashion from that to which he was accustomed. They all stared at him with equal marks of surprise, and whenever they cast eyes upon him, invariably stroked their chins. The constant recurrence of this gesture, induced Rip, involuntarily, to do the same, when, to his astonishment, he found his beard had grown a foot long!

He had now entered the skirts of the village. A troop of strange children ran at his heels, hooting after him, and pointing at his gray beard. The dogs, too, not one of which he recognized for his old acquaintances, barked at him as he passed. The very village seemed altered: it was larger and more populous. There were rows of houses which he had never seen before, and those which had been his familiar haunts had disappeared. Strange names were over the doors – strange faces at the windows – every thing was strange. His mind now began to misgive him, that both he and the world around him were bewitched. Surely this was his native village, which he had left but the day before. There stood the Kaatskill mountains – there ran the silver Hudson at a distance – there was every hill and dale precisely as it had always been – Rip was sorely perplexed – "That flagon last night," thought he, "has addled my poor head sadly!"

It was with some difficulty he found the way to his own house, which he approached with silent awe, expecting every moment to hear the shrill voice of Dame Van Winkle. He found the house gone to decay – the roof fallen in, the windows shattered, and the doors off the hinges. A half starved dog, that looked like Wolf, was skulking about it. Rip called him by name, but the cur snarled, showed his teeth, and passed on. This was an unkind cut indeed – "My very dog," sighed poor Rip, "has forgotten me!"

He entered the house, which, to tell the truth, Dame Van Winkle had always kept in neat order. It was empty, forlorn, and apparently abandoned. This desolateness overcame all his connubial fears – he called loudly for his wife and children – the lonely chambers rung for a moment with his voice, and then all again was silence.

He now hurried forth, and hastened to his old resort, the little village inn – but it too was gone. A large ricketty wooden building stood in its place, with great gaping windows, some of them broken, and mended with old hats and petticoats, and over the door was painted, "The Union Hotel, by Jonathan Doolittle." Instead of the great tree that used to shelter the quiet little Dutch inn of yore, there now was reared a tall naked pole, with something on top that looked like a red night cap,[17] and from it was fluttering a flag, on which was a singular assemblage of stars and stripes – all this was strange and incomprehensible. He recognised on the sign, however, the ruby face of King George, under which he had smoked so many a peaceful pipe, but even this was singularly metamorphosed. The red coat was changed for one of blue and buff,[18] a sword was stuck in the hand instead of a sceptre, the head was decorated with a cocked hat, and underneath was painted in large characters, GENERAL WASHINGTON.

There was, as usual, a crowd of folk about the door, but none that Rip recollected. The very character of the people seemed changed. There was a busy, bustling, disputatious tone about it, instead of the accustomed phlegm and drowsy tranquillity. He looked in vain for the sage Nicholas Vedder, with his broad face, double chin, and fair long pipe,

---

17. **red night cap:** A soft hat used as a republican symbol, often displayed on the top of a pole to signify liberty.
18. **blue and buff:** Colors of the uniforms of American soldiers in the Revolutionary War.

uttering clouds of tobacco smoke instead of idle speeches; or Van Bummel, the school-master, doling forth the contents of an ancient newspaper. In place of these, a lean bil-ious looking fellow, with his pockets full of handbills, was haranguing vehemently about rights of citizens—election—members of congress—liberty—Bunker's hill—heroes of seventy-six—and other words, that were a perfect Babylonish jargon[19] to the bewildered Van Winkle.

The appearance of Rip, with his long grizzled beard, his rusty fowling piece, his uncouth dress, and the army of women and children that had gathered at his heels, soon attracted the attention of the tavern politicians. They crowded around him, eyeing him from head to foot, with great curiosity. The orator bustled up to him, and drawing him partly aside, inquired "which side he voted?" Rip stared in vacant stupidity. Another short but busy little fellow pulled him by the arm, and raising on tiptoe, inquired in his ear, "whether he was Federal or Democrat."[20] Rip was equally at a loss to comprehend the question; when a knowing, self-important old gentleman, in a sharp cocked hat, made his way through the crowd, putting them to the right and left with his elbows as he passed, and planting himself before Van Winkle, with one arm akimbo, the other resting on his cane, his keen eyes and sharp hat penetrating, as it were, into his very soul, demanded, in an austere tone, "what brought him to the election with a gun on his shoulder, and a mob at his heels, and whether he meant to breed a riot in the village?" "Alas! gentlemen," cried Rip, somewhat dismayed, "I am a poor quiet man, a native of the place, and a loyal subject of the King, God bless him!"

Here a general shout burst from the bystanders—"A tory! a tory! a spy! a refugee! hustle him! away with him!" It was with great difficulty that the self-important man in the cocked hat restored order; and having assumed a tenfold austerity of brow, demanded again of the unknown culprit, what he came there for, and whom he was seeking. The poor man humbly assured them that he meant no harm; but merely came there in search of some of his neighbours, who used to keep about the tavern.

"Well—who are they?—name them."

Rip bethought himself a moment, and inquired, "where's Nicholas Vedder?"

There was a silence for a little while, when an old man replied, in a thin piping voice, "Nicholas Vedder? why he is dead and gone these eighteen years! There was a wooden tomb-stone in the church yard that used to tell all about him, but that's rotted and gone too."

"Where's Brom Dutcher?"

"Oh he went off to the army in the beginning of the war; some say he was killed at the battle of Stoney-Point—others say he was drowned in a squall, at the foot of Antony's Nose.[21] I don't know—he never came back again."

---

19. **Babylonish jargon:** Unintelligible language.

20. **Federal or Democrat:** The political parties during Washington's administrations were the Federalists, led by Alexander Hamilton, and the Democratic Republicans, led by Thomas Jefferson.

21. **Stoney-Point . . . Antony's Nose:** Stoney Point, a mountain on the Hudson River, was captured by Ameri-can troops under the command of General Anthony Wayne during the Revolution. Early in the war, the Ameri-cans built Fort Independence just south of Antony's Nose, a mountain overlooking a narrow point of the Hudson River.

"Where's Van Bummel, the schoolmaster?"

"He went off to the wars too, was a great militia general, and is now in Congress."

Rip's heart died away, at hearing of these sad changes in his home and friends, and finding himself thus alone in the world. Every answer puzzled him, too, by treating of such enormous lapses of time, and of matters which he could not understand: war – congress – Stoney-Point; – he had no courage to ask after any more friends, but cried out in despair, "does nobody here know Rip Van Winkle?"

"Oh, Rip Van Winkle!" exclaimed two or three, "Oh, to be sure! that's Rip Van Winkle yonder, leaning against the tree."

Rip looked, and beheld a precise counterpart of himself, as he went up the mountain: apparently as lazy, and certainly as ragged. The poor fellow was now completely confounded. He doubted his own identity, and whether he was himself or another man. In the midst of his bewilderment, the man in the cocked hat demanded who he was, and what was his name?

"God knows," exclaimed he, at his wit's end; "I'm not myself – I'm somebody else – that's me yonder – no – that's somebody else, got into my shoes – I was myself last night, but I fell asleep on the mountain, and they've changed my gun, and every thing's changed, and I'm changed, and I can't tell what's my name, or who I am!"

The bystanders began now to look at each other, nod, wink significantly, and tap their fingers against their foreheads. There was a whisper, also, about securing the gun, and keeping the old fellow from doing mischief. At the very suggestion of which, the self-important man in the cocked hat retired with some precipitation. At this critical moment a fresh likely woman pressed through the throng to get a peep at the gray-bearded man. She had a chubby child in her arms, which, frightened at his looks, began to cry. "Hush, Rip," cried she, "hush, you little fool, the old man won't hurt you." The name of the child, the air of the mother, the tone of her voice, all awakened a train of recollections in his mind. "What is your name, my good woman?" asked he.

"Judith Gardenier."

"And your father's name?"

"Ah, poor man, his name was Rip Van Winkle; it's twenty years since he went away from home with his gun, and never has been heard of since – his dog came home without him; but whether he shot himself, or was carried away by the Indians, nobody can tell. I was then but a little girl."

Rip had but one question more to ask; but he put it with a faltering voice:

"Where's your mother?"

"Oh, she too had died but a short time since; she broke a blood vessel in a fit of passion at a New-England pedlar."

There was a drop of comfort, at least, in this intelligence. The honest man could contain himself no longer. He caught his daughter and her child in his arms. "I am your father!" cried he – "Young Rip Van Winkle once – old Rip Van Winkle now! – Does nobody know poor Rip Van Winkle!"

All stood amazed, until an old woman, tottering out from among the crowd, put her hand to her brow, and peering under it in his face for a moment, exclaimed, "Sure enough! it is Rip Van Winkle – it is himself. Welcome home again, old neighbour – Why, where have you been these twenty long years?"

Rip's story was soon told, for the whole twenty years had been to him but as one night. The neighbours stared when they heard it; some were seen to wink at each other, and put their tongues in their cheeks; and the self-important man in the cocked hat, who, when the alarm was over, had returned to the field, screwed down the corners of his mouth, and shook his head – upon which there was a general shaking of the head throughout the assemblage.

It was determined, however, to take the opinion of old Peter Vanderdonk, who was seen slowly advancing up the road. He was a descendant of the historian of that name, who wrote one of the earliest accounts of the province.[22] Peter was the most ancient inhabitant of the village, and well versed in all the wonderful events and traditions of the neighbourhood. He recollected Rip at once, and corroborated his story in the most satisfactory manner. He assured the company that it was a fact, handed down from his ancestor the historian, that the Kaatskill mountains had always been haunted by strange beings. That it was affirmed that the great Hendrick Hudson,[23] the first discoverer of the river and country, kept a kind of vigil there every twenty years, with his crew of the Half-moon, being permitted in this way to revisit the scenes of his enterprize, and keep a guardian eye upon the river, and the great city called by his name. That his father had once seen them in their old Dutch dresses playing at nine pins in a hollow of the mountain; and that he himself had heard, one summer afternoon, the sound of their balls, like long peals of thunder.

To make a long story short, the company broke up, and returned to the more important concerns of the election. Rip's daughter took him home to live with her; she had a snug, well-furnished house, and a stout cheery farmer for a husband, whom Rip recollected for one of the urchins that used to climb upon his back. As to Rip's son and heir, who was the ditto of himself, seen leaning against the tree, he was employed to work on the farm; but evinced an hereditary disposition to attend to any thing else but his business.

Rip now resumed his old walks and habits; he soon found many of his former cronies, though all rather the worse for the wear and tear of time; and preferred making friends among the rising generation, with whom he soon grew into great favour.

Having nothing to do at home, and being arrived at that happy age when a man can do nothing with impunity, he took his place once more on the bench, at the inn door, and was reverenced as one of the patriarchs of the village, and a chronicle of the old times "before the war." It was some time before he could get into the regular track of gossip, or could be made to comprehend the strange events that had taken place during his torpor. How that there had been a revolutionary war – that the country had thrown off the yoke of old England – and that, instead of being a subject of his Majesty George the Third, he

---

22. **historian . . . province:** Adriaen van der Donk (1620-1655?), author of *Description of New Netherland* (1655).
23. **Hendrick Hudson:** Henry Hudson (1565-1611), English navigator who explored northeastern North America for the Dutch.

was now a free citizen of the United States. Rip, in fact, was no politician; the changes of states and empires made but little impression on him. But there was one species of despotism under which he had long groaned, and that was – petticoat government. Happily, that was at an end; he had got his neck out of the yoke of matrimony, and could go in and out whenever he pleased, without dreading the tyranny of Dame Van Winkle. Whenever her name was mentioned, however, he shook his head, shrugged his shoulders, and cast up his eyes; which might pass either for an expression of resignation to his fate, or joy at his deliverance.

He used to tell his story to every stranger that arrived at Mr. Doolittle's hotel. He was observed, at first, to vary on some points every time he told it, which was, doubtless, owing to his having so recently awaked. It at last settled down precisely to the tale I have related, and not a man, woman, or child in the neighbourhood, but knew it by heart. Some always pretended to doubt the reality of it, and insisted that Rip had been out of his head, and that this was one point on which he always remained flighty. The old Dutch inhabitants, however, almost universally gave it full credit. Even to this day they never hear a thunder storm of a summer afternoon, about the Kaatskill, but they say Hendrick Hudson and his crew are at their game of nine pins; and it is a common wish of all henpecked husbands in the neighbourhood, when life hangs heavy on their hands, that they might have a quieting draught out of Rip Van Winkle's flagon.

Note

The foregoing tale, one would suspect, had been suggested to Mr. Knickerbocker by a little German superstition about Charles V.[24] and the Kypphauser mountain; the subjoined note, however, which he had appended to the tale, shows that it is an absolute fact, narrated with his usual fidelity:

"The story of Rip Van Winkle may seem incredible to many, but nevertheless I give it my full belief, for I know the vicinity of our old Dutch settlements to have been very subject to marvellous events and appearances. Indeed, I have heard many stranger stories than this, in the villages along the Hudson; all of which were too well authenticated to admit of a doubt. I have even talked with Rip Van Winkle myself, who, when last I saw him, was a very venerable old man, and so perfectly rational and consistent on every other point, that I think no conscientious person could refuse to take this into the bargain; nay, I have seen a certificate on the subject taken before a country justice, and signed with a cross, in the justice's own hand writing. The story, therefore, is beyond the possibility of doubt.

D. K."

[1819]

---

24. **German superstition about Charles V.:** Irving later altered this to "The Emperor Frederick *der Rothbart*," the Holy Roman Emperor Frederick Barbarossa (1152–1190), who in legend was said to be sleeping in a mountain cave awaiting his country's rise to its former glory. Irving thus hinted at his indebtedness to German folklore but concealed his primary source for "Rip Van Winkle," the story of Peter Klaus in a collection of tales by J. C. C. N. Otmar.

Catharine Maria Sedgwick

[1789-1867]

Catharine Maria Sedgwick

This engraving was based on a portrait painted by Charles C. Ingham around 1830, by which time Sedgwick was one of the most popular and respected authors in the United States. The Irish-born Ingham moved to New York in 1816 and soon became known as the city's foremost "ladies' painter," partly because men were thought to be too busy to submit to the numerous sittings that his painstaking technique required.

Catharine Maria Sedgwick was born in Stockbridge, Massachusetts, on December 28, 1789, the sixth of seven surviving children of Theodore and Pamela Dwight Sedgwick. Her mother was descended from a distinguished Connecticut family, and her father rose from a modest background to considerable political prominence. A staunch Federalist, he served in the state legislature, as a member of Congress and the Speaker of the House of Representatives, and on the Massachusetts Supreme Court. Sedgwick received little education at home and only an adequate formal education, first at a grammar school and then a finishing school in Boston. But she was an avid reader, mostly of novels, and her father was fond of reading aloud to the family in the evening, so Sedgwick was also exposed to passages from Shakespeare's plays and other standard works of English and Continental literature. As early as 1805, Sedgwick began to divide her time between Stockbridge and the homes of her married siblings in Albany, New York, and New York City, where she spent an increasing amount of time after the death of her mother in 1807 and her father in 1813. Her substantial inheritances freed Sedgwick to travel, to read and study, and ultimately to pursue her interest in writing, which at the time promised few financial rewards.

Sedgwick's early works were inspired by both nationalistic sentiments and religious values. In 1821, she left the Calvinistic Congregational Church, in which she was raised, to join the liberal Unitarian Meeting House in New York City. Soon after that, she wrote "Mary Hollis," a tract denouncing religious intolerance that Sedgwick swiftly expanded into her first novel, *A New-England Tale* (1822). The novel was also a direct response to calls for a national literature. In a lengthy review, James Fenimore Cooper praised Sedgwick for her realistic depiction "of the multitude of local peculiarities, which form our distinctive features." Similar qualities distinguished her second novel, *Redwood* (1824), which Sedgwick dedicated to William Cullen Bryant. The popularity of that novel created strong demand for her work among the editors of periodicals and annuals like *The Atlantic Souvenir*, where the first of her more than one hundred sketches and stories appeared in 1826. Always interested in regional history, which was viewed by many critics as a major resource for American writers, Sedgwick set her next and most famous novel, *Hope Leslie* (1827), in seventeenth-century New England. In it, she sharply revised conventional histories by calling into question the Puritans' harsh treatment of Native Americans. She explored a more inspiring period of American history in *The Linwoods* (1835), a novel set during the Revolutionary War in which Sedgwick mingled fictional characters and historical figures such as General Lafayette and George Washington. Turning from American history to the more immediate religious and social concerns of her middle-class audience, Sedgwick then wrote a series of domestic fictions that were among the most widely read of all her many books: *Home: Scenes and Character Illustrating Christian Truth* (1835), *The Poor Rich Man and the Rich Poor Man* (1836), and *Live and Let Live; or, Domestic Service Illustrated* (1837).

During the final three decades of her life, Sedgwick increasingly devoted herself to charitable work and teaching, both in various Sunday schools and in her sister-in-law's Young Ladies' School. Nonetheless, she remained a literary celebrity, whose earlier works were often reprinted. She continued to write, especially works for children, but also dozens of articles, sketches, and stories for a diverse group of periodicals, from *Godey's Lady's Book* to the *United States Magazine and Democratic Review*. Although she was less engaged in reform issues than some other women writers of the period, Sedgwick was deeply involved in improving prison conditions and sympathetic to the causes of abolition and women's rights. In her final novel, *Married or Single?* (1857), Sedgwick thus supported what was then the unconventional and even radical idea that not all women must be wives and mothers. Sedgwick, who never married, at once relished her own autonomy and enjoyed a rich domestic life at the center of her siblings' growing families. She spent the last years of her life living with a niece in Boston, where Sedgwick died on July 31, 1867.

> *... in a kind and playful humour she has penetrated into all the hiding places of the heart; and she has brought them before us in pictures as simply beautiful as nature himself.*
>
> *— Lydia Maria Child*

Reading Sedgwick's "Cacoethes Scribendi."   This story was first published in *The Atlantic Souvenir*, an annual gift book established in 1826. Such annuals, designed to be given as holiday gifts, had been popular in Europe since early in the nineteenth century, but the *Souvenir* was the first to be published in the United States. In the preface to the 1826 edition, its editor explained:

> The publishers of the present volume, present to the public a work, which although on a plan by no means novel in other countries, has never yet been introduced among us. Nothing would seem more naturally to suggest itself, as one of those marks of remembrance and affection, which old custom has associated with the gaiety of Christmas, than a little volume of lighter literature, adorned with beautiful specimens of art.

By the time "Cacoethes Scribendi" appeared in the 1830 edition, the *Souvenir* had become an elaborate production, with twelve illustrations accompanying more than 350 pages of poems, sketches, and stories. Although most of the works were published anonymously, those by particularly notable writers were signed or otherwise identified. Sedgwick's story was identified as "By the Author of Hope Leslie," the title of the popular novel she had published in 1827. "Cacoethes Scribendi," a Latin phrase meaning the incurable disease of writing, suggests the satiric intent of the story, written at a time when few women wrote satire. Although by 1830 the prolific Sedgwick had become one of the most popular writers in the country, much of the satire in her story seems directed at women writers and their productions. Indeed, despite their increasing success in the literary marketplace, many women writers of the period either felt ambivalent about writing as a profession or simply felt obliged to affirm more traditional female roles, as Sedgwick may seem to do in "Cacoethes Scribendi." The text is taken from its first printing in *The Atlantic Souvenir* (1830).

bedfordstmartins.com/ americanlit *for research links on Sedgwick*

CACOETHES SCRIBENDI[1]

Glory and gain the industrious tribe provoke.
Pope[2]

The little secluded and quiet village of H. lies at no great distance from our 'literary emporium.'[3] It was never remarked or remarkable for any thing, save one mournful preeminence, to those who sojourned within its borders – it was duller even than common villages. The young men of the better class all emigrated.[4] The most daring spirits adventured on the sea. Some went to Boston; some to the south; and some to the west; and left a community of women who lived like nuns, with the advantage of more liberty and fresh air, but without the consolation and excitement of a religious vow. Literally, there was not a single young gentleman in the village – nothing in manly shape to which these desperate circumstances could give the form and quality and use of a beau.[5] Some dashing city blades, who once strayed from the turnpike to this sequestered spot, averred that the girls stared at them as if, like Miranda, they would have exclaimed –

'What is't? a spirit?
Lord, how it looks about! Believe me, sir,
It carries a brave form: – But 'tis a spirit.'[6]

A peculiar fatality hung over this devoted place. If death seized on either head of a family, he was sure to take the husband; every woman in H. was a widow or maiden;

---

1. **Cacoethes Scribendi:** A familiar Latin phrase variously translated as the incurable disease of writing, the incurable passion for writing, or an incurable itch to write. The phrase was used by several Roman authors, notably the satirist Juvenal (60-140), who famously observed: *Tenet insanabile multos scribendi cacoethes et aegro in corde senescit* (Many suffer from the incurable disease of writing, and it wastes their hearts).
2. **Glory . . . provoke:** From *The Dunciad*, 2.29, a mock epic about writers and the business of writing, by the English poet Alexander Pope (1688-1744).
3. **'Literary emporium':** Until the 1840s, Boston was the literary center of the United States.
4. **emigrated:** Common usage for people who left their birthplaces to seek fortunes elsewhere, as many of the young men in New England villages did during the early decades of the nineteenth century.
5. **beau:** Early term for a male admirer.
6. **'What . . . spirit':** Shakespeare's *The Tempest*, 1.2.411-13. The lines are spoken by Miranda, the daughter of Prospero, who has never seen any man other than her father and his servant, Caliban.

and it is a sad fact, that when the holiest office of the church was celebrated, they were compelled to borrow deacons from an adjacent village. But, incredible as it may be, there was no great diminution of happiness in consequences of the absence of the nobler sex. Mothers were occupied with their children and housewifery, and the young ladies read their books with as much interest as if they had lovers to discuss them with, and worked their frills and capes as diligently, and wore them as complacently, as if they were to be seen by manly eyes. Never were there pleasanter gatherings or parties (for that was the word even in their nomenclature) than those of the young girls of H. There was no mincing – no affectation – no hope of passing for what they were not – no envy of the pretty and fortunate – no insolent triumph over the plain and demure and neglected, – but all was good will and good humour. They were a pretty circle of girls – a garland of bright fresh flowers. Never were there more spar-kling glances, – never sweeter smiles – nor more of them. Their present was all health and cheerfulness; and their future, not the gloomy perspective of dreary singleness, for somewhere in the passage of life they were sure to be mated. Most of the young men who had abandoned their native soil, as soon as they found themselves *getting along*, loyally returned to lay their fortunes at the feet of the companions of their childhood.

The girls made occasional visits to Boston, and occasional journeys to various parts of the country, for they were all enterprising and independent, and had the characteris-tic New England avidity for seizing a 'privilege;' and in these various ways, to borrow a phrase of their good grandames, 'a door was opened for them,' and in due time they ful-filled the destiny of women.

We spoke strictly, and à la lettre,[7] when we said that in the village of H. there was not a single *beau*. But on the outskirts of the town, at a pleasant farm, embracing hill and valley, upland and meadow land; in a neat house, looking to the south, with true economy of sunshine and comfort, and overlooking the prettiest winding stream that ever sent up its sparkling beauty to the eye, and flanked on the north by a rich maple grove, beautiful in spring and summer, and glorious in autumn, and the kindest defence in winter; – on this farm and in this house dwelt a youth, to fame unknown,[8] but known and loved by every inhabitant of H., old and young, grave and gay, lively and severe. Ralph Hepburn was one of nature's favourites. He had a figure that would have adorned courts and cities; and a face that adorned human nature, for it was full of good humour, kindheartedness, spirit, and intelligence; and driving the plough or wielding the scythe, his cheek flushed with manly and profitable exercise, he looked as if he had been moulded in a poet's fancy – as farmers look in Georgics and Pasto-rals.[9] His gifts were by no means all external. He wrote verses in every album in the

---

7. **à la lettre:** Literally (French).
8. **a youth, to fame unknown:** A reference to the opening lines of the epitaph at the end of "Elegy Written in a Country Churchyard" (1751) by the English poet Thomas Gray (1716-1771): "Here rests his head upon the lap of Earth / A youth to Fortune and to Fame unknown" (ll. 117-18).
9. **Georgics and Pastorals:** Poems celebrating rural life, notably those of the Roman poet Virgil (70-19 BCE), whose pastoral *Eclogues* and *Georgics* were widely available in popular translations in the eighteenth and nineteenth centuries.

village, and very pretty album verses they were, and numerous too – for the number of albums was equivalent to the whole female population. He was admirable at pencil sketches; and once with a little paint, the refuse of a house painting, he achieved an admirable portrait of his grandmother and her cat. There was, to be sure, a striking likeness between the two figures, but he was limited to the same colours for both; and besides, it was not out of nature, for the old lady and her cat had purred together in the chimney corner, till their physiognomies bore an obvious resemblance to each other. Ralph had a talent for music too. His voice was the sweetest of all the Sunday choir, and one would have fancied, from the bright eyes that were turned on him from the long line and double lines of treble and counter singers, that Ralph Hepburn was a note book,[10] or that the girls listened with their eyes as well as their ears. Ralph did not restrict himself to psalmody.[11] He had an ear so exquisitely susceptible to the 'touches of sweet harmony,' that he discovered, by the stroke of his axe, the musical capacities of certain species of wood, and he made himself a violin of chesnut, and drew strains from it, that if they could not create a soul under the ribs of death,[12] could make the prettiest feet and the lightest hearts dance, an achievement far more to Ralph's taste than the aforesaid miracle. In short, it seemed as if nature, in her love of compensation, had showered on Ralph all the gifts that are usually diffused through a community of beaux. Yet Ralph was no prodigy; none of his talents were in excess, but all in moderate degree. No genius was ever so good humoured, so useful, so practical; and though, in his small and modest way, a Crichton,[13] he was not, like most universal geniuses, good for nothing for any particular office in life. His farm was not a pattern farm – a prize farm for an agricultural society, but in wonderful order considering – his miscellaneous pursuits. He was the delight of his grandfather for his sagacity in hunting bees – the old man's favourite, in truth his only pursuit. He was so skilled in woodcraft that the report of his gun was as certain a signal of death as the tolling of a church bell. The fish always caught at his bait. He manufactured half his farming utensils, improved upon old inventions, and struck out some new ones; tamed partridges – the most untameable of all the feathered tribe; domesticated squirrels; rivalled Scheherazade[14] herself in telling stories, strange and long – the latter quality being essential at a country fireside; and, in short, Ralph made a perpetual holiday of a life of labour.

Every girl in the village street knew when Ralph's wagon or sleigh traversed it; indeed, there was scarcely a house to which the horses did not, as if by instinct, turn up while their master greeted its fair tenants. This state of affairs had continued for two winters and two summers since Ralph came to his majority and, by the death of his father, to the sole proprietorship of the 'Hepburn farm,' – the name his patrimonial

---

10. **note book:** A book of music printed with large notes, designed to be shared by several singers.
11. **psalmody:** The singing of psalms and other sacred works.
12. **create a soul under the ribs of death:** A reference to *Comus* by the English poet John Milton (1608–1674): "I was all ear, / And took in strains that might create a soul / Under the ribs of Death" (ll. 560–62).
13. **Crichton:** Born in Scotland, James Crichton (c. 1560–1582) went to the University of St. Andrews at the age of ten and was universally recognized as a genius.
14. **Scheherazade:** The storyteller in *The Thousand and One Nights*, anonymous Arabic tales first translated into English in the eighteenth century.

acres had obtained from the singular circumstance (in our *moving* country) of their having remained in the same family for four generations. Never was the matrimonial destiny of a young lord, or heir just come to his estate, more thoroughly canvassed than young Hepburn's by mothers, aunts, daughters, and nieces. But Ralph, perhaps from sheer good heartedness, seemed reluctant to give to one the heart that diffused rays of sunshine through the whole village.

With all decent people he eschewed the doctrines of a certain erratic female lecturer on the odious monopoly of marriage,[15] yet Ralph, like a tender hearted judge, hesitated to place on a single brow the crown matrimonial which so many deserved, and which, though Ralph was far enough from a coxcomb,[16] he could not but see so many coveted.

Whether our hero perceived that his mind was becoming elated or distracted with this general favour, or that he observed a dawning of rivalry among the fair competitors, or whatever was the cause, the fact was, that he by degrees circumscribed his visits, and finally concentrated them in the family of his aunt Courland.

Mrs. Courland was a widow, and Ralph was the kindest of nephews to her, and the kindest of cousins to her children. To their mother he seemed their guardian angel. That the five lawless, daring little urchins did not drown themselves when they were swimming, nor shoot themselves when they were shooting, was, in her eyes, Ralph's merit; and then 'he was so attentive to Alice, her only daughter — a brother could not be kinder.' But who would not be kind to Alice? she was a sweet girl of seventeen, not beautiful, not handsome perhaps, — but pretty enough — with soft hazel eyes, a profusion of light brown hair, always in the neatest trim, and a mouth that could not but be lovely and loveable, for all kind and tender affections were playing about it. Though Alice was the only daughter of a doting mother, the only sister of five loving boys, the only niece of three single, fond aunts, and, last and greatest, the only cousin of our only beau, Ralph Hepburn, no girl of seventeen was ever more disinterested, unassuming, unostentatious, and unspoiled. Ralph and Alice had always lived on terms of cousinly affection — an affection of a neutral tint that they never thought of being shaded into the deep dye of a more tender passion. Ralph rendered her all cousinly offices. If he had twenty damsels to escort, not an uncommon case, he never forgot Alice. When he returned from any little excursion, he always brought some graceful offering to Alice.

He had lately paid a visit to Boston. It was at the season of the periodical inundation of annuals.[17] He brought two of the prettiest to Alice. Ah! little did she think they were to prove Pandora's box to her. Poor simple girl! she sat down to read them, as if an annual were meant to be read, and she was honestly interested and charmed. Her mother observed her delight. "What have you there, Alice?" she asked. "Oh the prettiest story,

---

15. **doctrines . . . of marriage:** In a series of lectures delivered in the late 1820s, the Scottish-born reformer Frances Wright (1795-1852) scandalized American audiences by advocating abolition, atheism, sexual freedom, and women's rights.

16. **coxcomb:** Early term for a vain or conceited man.

17. **periodical inundation of annuals:** Like the volume in which Sedgwick's story appeared, annuals were handsomely bound and illustrated collections of poetry, sketches, and stories published at the end of the year and designed to be given as holiday gifts.

mamma! – two such tried faithful lovers, and married at last! It ends beautifully: I hate love stories that don't end in marriage."

"And so do I, Alice," exclaimed Ralph, who entered at the moment, and for the first time Alice felt her cheeks tingle at his approach. He had brought a basket, containing a choice plant he had obtained for her, and she laid down the annual and went with him to the garden to see it set by his own hand.

Mrs. Courland seized upon the annual with avidity. She had imbibed a literary taste in Boston, where the best and happiest years of her life were passed. She had some literary ambition too. She read the North American Review[18] from beginning to end, and she fancied no conversation could be sensible or improving that was not about books. But she had been effectually prevented, by the necessities of a narrow income, and by the unceasing wants of five teasing boys, from indulging her literary inclinations; for Mrs. Courland, like all New England women, had been taught to consider domestic duties as the first temporal duties of her sex. She had recently seen some of the native productions with which the press is daily teeming, and which certainly have a tendency to dispel our early illusions about the craft of authorship. She had even felt some obscure intimations, within her secret soul, that she might herself become an author. The annual was destined to fix her fate. She opened it – the publisher had written the names of the authors of the anonymous pieces against their productions. Among them she found some of the familiar friends of her childhood and youth.

If, by a sudden gift of second sight, she had seen them enthroned as kings and queens, she would not have been more astonished. She turned to their pieces, and read them, as perchance no one else ever did, from beginning to end – faithfully. Not a sentence – a sentence! not a word was skipped. She paused to consider commas, colons, and dashes. All the art and magic of authorship were made level to her comprehension, and when she closed the book, she *felt a call* to become an author, and before she retired to bed she obeyed the call, as if it had been, in truth, a divinity stirring within her. In the morning she presented an article to *her* public, consisting of her own family and a few select friends. All applauded, and every voice, save one, was unanimous for publication – that one was Alice. She was a modest, prudent girl; she feared failure, and feared notoriety still more. Her mother laughed at her childish scruples. The piece was sent off, and in due time graced the pages of an annual. Mrs. Courland's fate was now decided. She had, to use her own phrase, started in the career of letters, and she was no Atalanta[19] to be seduced from her straight onward way. She was a social, sympathetic, good hearted creature too, and she could not bear to go forth in the golden field to reap alone.

She was, besides, a prudent woman, as most of her countrywomen are, and the little pecuniary equivalent for this delightful exercise of talents was not overlooked. Mrs. Courland, as we have somewhere said, had three single sisters – worthy women they were – but nobody ever dreamed of their taking to authorship. She, however, held them all in sisterly

---

18. **North American Review:** Established in Boston in 1815, this influential journal included reviews of current European and American literature as well as articles on politics, economics, and religion.

19. **Atalanta:** A huntress in Greek mythology who vowed to marry only the man who could beat her in a footrace. Hippomenes won the race by dropping three golden apples, which Atalanta stopped to retrieve.

estimation. Their talents were magnified as the talents of persons who live in a circumscribed sphere are apt to be, particularly if seen through the dilating medium of affection.

Miss Anne, the oldest, was fond of flowers, a successful cultivator, and a diligent student of the science of botany. All this taste and knowledge, Mrs. Courland thought, might be turned to excellent account; and she persuaded Miss Anne to write a little book entitled 'Familiar Dialogues on Botany.' The second sister, Miss Ruth, had a turn for education ('bachelor's wives and maid's children are always well taught'), and Miss Ruth undertook a popular treatise on that subject. Miss Sally, the youngest, was the saint of the family, and she doubted about the propriety of a literary occupation, till her scruples were overcome by the fortunate suggestion that her coup d'essai[20] should be a Saturday night book entitled 'Solemn Hours,'—and solemn hours they were to their unhappy readers. Mrs. Courland next besieged her old mother. "You know, mamma," she said, "you have such a precious fund of anecdotes of the revolution and the French war, and you talk just like the 'Annals of the Parish,'[21] and I am certain you can write a book fully as good."

"My child, you are distracted! I write a dreadful poor hand, and I never learned to spell—no girls did in my time."

"Spell! that is not of the least consequence—the printers correct the spelling."

But the honest old lady would not be tempted on the crusade, and her daughter consoled herself with the reflection that if she would not write, she was an admirable subject to be written about, and her diligent fingers worked off three distinct stories in which the old lady figured.

Mrs. Courland's ambition, of course, embraced within its widening circle her favourite nephew Ralph. She had always thought him a genius, and genius in her estimation was the philosopher's stone.[22] In his youth she had laboured to persuade his father to send him to Cambridge,[23] but the old man uniformly replied that Ralph 'was a smart lad on the farm, and steady, and by that he knew he was no genius.' As Ralph's character was developed, and talent after talent broke forth, his aunt renewed her lamentations over his ignoble destiny. That Ralph was useful, good, and happy—the most difficult and rare results achieved in life—was nothing, so long as he was but a farmer in H. Once she did half persuade him to turn painter, but his good sense and filial duty triumphed over her eloquence, and suppressed the hankerings after distinction that are innate in every human breast, from the little ragged chimneysweep that hopes to be a *boss*,[24] to the political aspirant whose bright goal is the presidential chair.

Now Mrs. Courland fancied Ralph might climb the steep of fame without quitting his farm; occasional authorship was compatible with his vocation. But alas! she could not

---

20. **coup d'essai:** A first attempt (French).

21. **'Annals of the Parish':** A common title for books that chronicled local events during the term of a pastor or parish priest. All of the titles suggested in this passage were common topics of books published in the early nineteenth century.

22. **philosopher's stone:** In the medieval science of alchemy, the elusive philosopher's stone was thought to be the substance that could turn metal into gold.

23. **Cambridge:** Harvard College in Cambridge, Massachusetts.

24. **boss:** Derived from the Dutch word *baas*, meaning "master," the term *boss* had only recently begun to be used for the person in charge of workers or an organization.

persuade Ralph to pluck the laurels that she saw ready grown to his hand. She was not offended, for she was the best natured woman in the world, but she heartily pitied him, and seldom mentioned his name without repeating that stanza of Gray's, inspired for the consolation of hopeless obscurity:

'Full many a gem of purest ray serene,' &c.[25]

Poor Alice's sorrows we have reserved to the last, for they were heaviest. 'Alice,' her mother said, 'was gifted; she was well educated, well informed; she was every thing necessary to be an author.' But Alice resisted; and, though the gentlest, most complying of all good daughters, she would have resisted to the death – she would as soon have stood in a pillory as appeared in print. Her mother, Mrs. Courland, was not an obstinate woman, and gave up in despair. But still our poor heroine was destined to be the victim of this *cacoethes scribendi*; for Mrs. Courland divided the world into two classes, or rather parts – authors and subjects for authors; the one active, the other passive. At first blush one would have thought the village of H. rather a barren field for such a reaper as Mrs. Courland, but her zeal and indefatigableness worked wonders. She converted the stern scholastic divine of H. into as much of a La Roche[26] as she could describe; a tall wrinkled bony old woman, who reminded her of Meg Merrilies,[27] sat for a witch; the school master for an Ichabod Crane;[28] a poor half witted boy was made to utter as much pathos and sentiment and wit as she could put into his lips; and a crazy vagrant was a God-send to her. Then every 'wide spreading elm,' 'blasted pine,' or 'gnarled oak,'[29] flourished on her pages. The village church and school house stood there according to their actual dimensions. One old *pilgrim* house was as prolific as haunted tower or ruined abbey. It was surveyed outside, ransacked inside, and again made habitable for the reimbodied spirits of its founders.

The most kind hearted of women, Mrs. Courland's interests came to be so at variance with the prosperity of the little community of H., that a sudden calamity, a death, a funeral, were fortunate events to her. To do her justice she felt them in a twofold capacity. She wept as a woman, and exulted as an author. The days of the calamities of authors have passed by. We have all wept over Otway and shivered at the thought of Tasso.[30] But times are changed. The lean sheaf is devouring the full one.[31] A new class

25. 'Full . . . serene,' &c.: From Gray's "Elegy Written in a Country Churchyard"; see note 8.
26. La Roche: Protestant clergyman in a story of that title by the Scottish writer Henry MacKenzie (1745–1831).
27. Meg Merrilies: A gypsy nurse in the popular novel *Guy Mannering* by the Scottish writer Sir Walter Scott (1771–1832).
28. Ichabod Crane: The hapless schoolteacher in "The Legend of Sleepy Hollow," by Washington Irving (1783–1859).
29. 'wide spreading elm' . . . 'gnarled oak': Examples of overused phrases in the popular literature of the period.
30. Otway . . . Tasso: Never able to earn a living from his writing, the English dramatist Thomas Otway (1652–1685) lived in extreme poverty and died at the age of thirty-four. The Italian poet Torquato Tasso (1544–1595) also lived a difficult life of poverty and illness.
31. The lean sheaf . . . full one: In Genesis 41:6–7, the Pharaoh has a dream that is interpreted by Jacob to mean that seven years of plenty in Egypt will be followed by seven years of famine: "And, behold, seven thin ears and blasted with the east wind sprung up after them. And the seven thin ears devoured the seven rank and full ears."

of sufferers has arisen, and there is nothing more touching in all the memoirs Mr. D'Israeli[32] has collected, than the trials of poor Alice, tragi-comic though they were. Mrs. Courland's new passion ran most naturally in the worn channel of maternal affection. Her boys were too purely boys for her art – but Alice, her sweet Alice, was preeminently lovely in the new light in which she now placed every object. Not an incident of her life but was inscribed on her mother's memory, and thence transferred to her pages, by way of precept, or example, or pathetic or ludicrous circumstance. She regretted now, for the first time, that Alice had no lover whom she might introduce among her dramatis personae.[33] Once her thoughts did glance on Ralph, but she had not quite merged the woman in the author; she knew instinctively that Alice would be particularly offended at being thus paired with Ralph. But Alice's *public life* was not limited to her mother's productions. She was the darling niece of her three aunts. She had studied botany with the eldest, and Miss Anne had recorded in her private diary all her favourite's clever remarks during their progress in the science. This diary was now a mine of gold to her, and faithfully worked up for a circulating medium. But, most trying of all to poor Alice, was the attitude in which she appeared in her aunt Sally's 'solemn hours.' Every aspiration of piety to which her young lips had given utterance was there *printed*. She felt as if she were condemned to say her prayers in the market place. Every act of kindness, every deed of charity, she had ever performed, were produced to the public. Alice would have been consoled if she had known how small that public was; but, as it was, she felt like a modest country girl when she first enters an apartment hung on every side with mirrors, when, shrinking from observation, she sees in every direction her image multiplied and often distorted; for, notwithstanding Alice's dutiful respect for her good aunts, and her consciousness of their affectionate intentions, she could not but perceive that they were unskilled painters. She grew afraid to speak or to act, and from being the most artless, frank, and, at home, social little creature in the world, she became as silent and as stiff as a statue. And, in the circle of her young associates, her natural gaiety was constantly checked by their winks and smiles, and broader allusions to her multiplied portraits; for they had instantly recognized them through the thin veil of feigned names of persons and places. They called her a blue stocking[34] too; for they had the vulgar notion that every body must be tinged that lived under the same roof with an author. Our poor victim was afraid to speak of a book – worse than that, she was afraid to touch one, and the last Waverley novel[35] actually lay in the house a month before she opened it. She avoided wearing even a blue ribbon, as fearfully as a forsaken damsel shuns the colour of green.

---

32. **Mr. D'Israeli:** Isaac D'Israeli (1766–1848), English author of popular collections of anecdotes about writers, such as *Curiosities of Literature* (1849) and *Calamities and Quarrels of Authors* (1859).
33. **dramatis personae:** Cast of characters (Latin).
34. **blue stocking:** A denigrating term commonly used in the nineteenth century to describe a woman with literary or intellectual interests.
35. **Waverley novel:** *Waverley* (1814) was the first novel by the Scottish writer Sir Walter Scott (1771–1832). The enormously popular novels he subsequently published were frequently identified as "By the Author of Waverley" and often referred to collectively as the Waverley novels.

It was during the height of this literary fever in the Courland family, that Ralph Hepburn, as has been mentioned, concentrated all his visiting there. He was of a compassionate disposition, and he knew Alice was, unless relieved by him, in solitary possession of their once social parlour, while her mother and aunts were driving their quills in their several apartments.

Oh! what a changed place was that parlour! Not the tower of Babel,[36] after the builders had forsaken it, exhibited a sadder reverse; not a Lancaster school,[37] when the boys have left it, a more striking contrast. Mrs. Courland and her sisters were all 'talking women,' and too generous to encroach on one another's rights and happiness. They had acquired the power to hear and speak simultaneously. Their parlour was the general gathering place, a sort of village exchange, where all the innocent gossips, old and young, met together. 'There are tongues in trees,'[38] and surely there seemed to be tongues in the very walls of that vocal parlour. Every thing there had a social aspect. There was something agreeable and conversable in the litter of netting and knitting work, of sewing implements, and all the signs and shows of happy female occupation.

Now, all was as orderly as a town drawing room in company hours. Not a sound was heard there save Ralph's and Alice's voices, mingling in soft and suppressed murmurs, as if afraid of breaking the chain of their aunt's ideas, or, perchance, of too rudely jarring a tenderer chain. One evening, after tea, Mrs. Courland remained with her daughter, instead of retiring, as usual, to her writing desk. "Alice, my dear," said the good mother, "I have noticed for a few days past that you look out of spirits. You will listen to nothing I say on that subject; but if you would try it, my dear, if you would only try it, you would find there is nothing so tranquillizing as the occupation of writing."

"I shall never try it, mamma."

"You are afraid of being called a blue stocking. Ah! Ralph, how are you?" Ralph entered at this moment. "Ralph, tell me honestly, do you not think it a weakness in Alice to be so afraid of blue stockings?"

"It would be a pity, aunt, to put blue stockings on such pretty feet as Alice's."

Alice blushed and smiled, and her mother said – "Nonsense, Ralph; you should bear in mind the celebrated saying of the Edinburgh wit[39] – 'no matter how blue the stockings are, if the petticoats are long enough to hide them.'"

"Hide Alice's feet! Oh aunt, worse and worse!"

"Better hide her feet, Ralph, than her talents – that is a sin for which both she and you will have to answer. Oh! you and Alice need not exchange such significant

---

36. **tower of Babel:** In Genesis 11:1–9, the townspeople of Babel attempt to build a tower to reach heaven. God thwarts the plan by causing the languages of the builders to be mutually incomprehensible.

37. **Lancaster school:** Joseph Lancaster (1778–1838), an English educator, established schools in which older students under adult supervision were responsible for monitoring and teaching the younger students. The system was widely adopted in public schools in the United States.

38. **'There . . . trees':** From Shakespeare's *As You Like It*, 2.1.15–17: "And this our life exempt from public haunt / Finds tongues in trees, books in the running brooks, / Sermons in stones, and good in every thing."

39. **Edinburgh wit:** The English writer Sydney Smith (1771–1845), the first editor and a frequent contributor to the *Edinburgh Review*, was renowned for his aphorisms and wit.

glances! You are doing yourselves and the public injustice, and you have no idea how easy writing is."

"Easy writing, but hard reading, aunt."

"That's false modesty, Ralph. If I had but your opportunities to collect materials" — Mrs. Courland did not know that in literature, as in some species of manufacture, the most exquisite productions are wrought from the smallest quantity of raw material — "There's your journey to New York, Ralph," she continued, "you might have made three capital articles out of that. The revolutionary officer would have worked up for the 'Legendary;' the mysterious lady for the 'Token;' and the man in black for the 'Remember Me;' — all founded on fact, all romantic and pathetic."[40]

"But mamma," said Alice, expressing in words what Ralph's arch smile expressed almost as plainly, "you know the officer drank too much; and the mysterious lady turned out to be a runaway milliner; and the man in black — oh! what a theme for a pathetic story! — the man in black was a widower, on his way to Newhaven, where he was to select his third wife from three *recommended* candidates."

"Pshaw! Alice: do you suppose it is necessary to tell things precisely as they are?"

"Alice is wrong, aunt, and you are right; and if she will open her writing desk for me, I will sit down this moment, and write a story — a true story — true from beginning to end; and if it moves you, my dear aunt, if it meets your approbation, my destiny is decided."

Mrs. Courland was delighted; she had slain the giant, and she saw fame and fortune smiling on her favourite. She arranged the desk for him herself; she prepared a folio sheet of paper, folded the ominous margins; and was so absorbed in her bright visions, that she did not hear a little by-talk between Ralph and Alice, nor see the tell-tale flush on their cheeks, nor notice the perturbation with which Alice walked first to one window and then to another, and finally settled herself to that best of all sedatives — hemming a ruffle. Ralph chewed off the end of his quill, mended his pen twice, though his aunt assured him 'printers did not mind the penmanship,' and had achieved a single line when Mrs. Courland's vigilant eye was averted by the entrance of her servant girl, who put a packet into her hands. She looked at the direction, cut the string, broke the seals, and took out a periodical fresh from the publisher. She opened at the first article — a strangely mingled current of maternal pride and literary triumph rushed through her heart and brightened her face. She whispered to the servant a summons to all her sisters to the parlour, and an intimation, sufficiently intelligible to them, of her joyful reason for interrupting them.

Our readers will sympathize with her, and with Alice too, when we disclose to them the secret of her joy. The article in question was a clever composition written by our devoted Alice when she was at school. One of her fond aunts had preserved it; and aunts and mother had combined in the pious fraud of giving it to the public, unknown to Alice. They were perfectly aware of her determination never to be an author. But they fancied it was the mere timidity of an unfledged bird; and that when, by their innocent artifice,

---

40. **"The revolutionary officer . . . all romantic and pathetic"**: Although *The Token* was the title of an actual annual, the passage spoofs the titles and contents of the increasingly popular literary annuals.

she found that her pinions could soar in a literary atmosphere, she would realize the sweet fluttering sensations they had experienced at their first flight. The good souls all hurried to the parlour, eager to witness the coup de théatre.[41] Miss Sally's pen stood emblematically erect in her turban; Miss Ruth, in her haste, had overset her inkstand, and the drops were trickling down her white dressing, or, as she now called it, writing gown; and Miss Anne had a wild flower in her hand, as she hoped, of an undescribed species, which, in her joyful agitation, she most unluckily picked to pieces. All bit their lips to keep impatient congratulation from bursting forth. Ralph was so intent on his writing, and Alice on her hemming, that neither noticed the irruption; and Mrs. Courland was obliged twice to speak to her daughter before she could draw her attention.

"Alice, look here – Alice, my dear."

"What is it, mamma? something new of yours?"

"No; guess again, Alice."

"Of one of my aunts, of course?"

"Neither, dear, neither. Come and look for yourself, and see if you can then tell whose it is."

Alice dutifully laid aside her work, approached and took the book. The moment her eye glanced on the fatal page, all her apathy vanished – deep crimson overspread her cheeks, brow, and neck. She burst into tears of irrepressible vexation, and threw the book into the blazing fire.

The gentle Alice! Never had she been guilty of such an ebullition of temper. Her poor dismayed aunts retreated; her mother looked at her in mute astonishment; and Ralph, struck with her emotion, started from the desk, and would have asked an explanation, but Alice exclaimed – "Don't say any thing about it, mamma – I cannot bear it now."

Mrs. Courland knew instinctively that Ralph would sympathize entirely with Alice, and quite willing to avoid an éclaircissement,[42] she said – "Some other time, Ralph, I'll tell you the whole. Show me now what you have written. How have you begun?"

Ralph handed her the paper with a novice's trembling hand.

"Oh! how very little! and so scratched and interlined! but never mind – 'c'est le premier pas qui coute.'"[43]

While making these general observations, the good mother was getting out and fixing her spectacles, and Alice and Ralph had retreated behind her. Alice rested her head on his shoulder, and Ralph's lips were not far from her ear. Whether he was soothing her ruffled spirit, or what he was doing, is not recorded. Mrs. Courland read and re-read the sentence. She dropped a tear on it. She forgot her literary aspirations for Ralph and Alice – forgot she was herself an author – forgot every thing but the mother; and rising, embraced them both as her dear children, and expressed, in her raised and moistened eye, consent to their union, which Ralph had dutifully and prettily asked in that short and true story of his love for his sweet cousin Alice.

---

41. **coup de théatre:** A dramatic or sensational turn of events, especially in a play (French).

42. **éclaircissement:** An enlightening explanation of something that has previously been obscure or inexplicable, typically someone's conduct (French).

43. **'c'est le premier pas qui coute':** It is the first step which counts (French).

In due time the village of H. was animated with the celebration of Alice's nuptials: and when her mother and aunts saw her the happy mistress of the Hepburn farm, and the happiest of wives, they relinquished, without a sigh, the hope of ever seeing her an AUTHOR.

[1830]

William Cullen Bryant

[1794-1878]

William Cullen Bryant was born on November 3, 1794, to Peter Bryant, a physician, and Sarah Snell Bryant in Cummington, Massachusetts. The family owned a large library, and Bryant was educated at home, at district schools, and later at Williams College. A precocious child, Bryant was taught to write poetry by his father. In 1807, some of his early works – imitations of the poems he read and translated from Greek and Latin – were published in a local newspaper, the Hampshire *Gazette*. The following year, the thirteen-year-old Bryant became absorbed in national politics. He wrote and (with the help of his Federalist father) published *The Embargo; or, Sketches of the Times; A Satire*, in which Bryant attacked and called for the resignation of President Thomas Jefferson. After just one year at Williams College, Bryant began to study law and was admitted to the bar in 1815. He spent the next decade working as an attorney and serving as a justice of the peace in Great Barrington, Massachusetts.

Bryant, however, was less drawn to the law than he was to literature. He began to publish poems and essays in periodicals, as well as his first book in 1821. Despite the distinction of his work, Bryant knew that he could not support himself or a family by writing poetry. Following his marriage in 1821, Bryant continued to practice law until 1825, when he moved his family to New York City. Still seeking a career in literature, he assumed the editorship of the *New York Review and Atheneum Magazine*. Although the magazine failed by the end of the year, Bryant remained in New York and joined the editorial staff of the *Evening Post*. He worked on the newspaper for the rest of his life, first as an associate editor and later as its part owner and editor in chief. Under his leadership, the *Evening Post* became one of the most respected newspapers in the country; and his frequent editorials exerted considerable political influence. Having moved well away from the conservative politics of his youth, Bryant was a strong supporter of liberal causes and initially of the Democratic Party. But his growing opposition to slavery finally prompted Bryant to help form the Republican Party, in which he was an enthusiastic supporter of Abraham Lincoln and the Union cause in the Civil War.

During his years as an editor, Bryant continued to publish poetry and became one of the most popular American poets of the first half of the nineteenth century. A second volume of his *Poems* appeared in 1832,

William Cullen Bryant

This etching was apparently based on a portrait made in the 1830s, by which time Bryant was the most famous poet in the United States.

. . . a poet who, to our mind, stands among the first in the world . . .
— Walt Whitman

bedfordstmartins.com/
americanlit *for research*
links on Bryant

followed by *The Fountain and Other Poems* (1842), *The White-Footed Deer and Other Poems* (1846), *Poems, by William Cullen Bryant* (1853), and *Thirty Poems* (1864). Drawing on his early training in Greek, Bryant published popular translations of the *Iliad* (1870) and the *Odyssey* (1872). He also published prose works, including two series of *Letters of a Traveller* (1850, 1859); a notable volume of literary criticism, *Poets and Poetry of the English Language* (1871); and a collection of his *Orations and Addresses* (1873). When he died on June 12, 1878, Bryant was widely hailed in obituaries as one of the most respected editors and revered literary figures in the United States.

Reading Bryant's Poems.   Influenced by his reading of William Wordsworth and other English Romantic poets, Bryant wrote what would become some of his best-known poems in 1814-15, including an early version of "Thanatopsis," a stoical meditation on death in which he celebrated the grandeur and endurance of nature. His father found the poem in a desk drawer, copied it, and sent it without Bryant's knowledge to the prestigious magazine of literature and politics, the *North American Review*. The publication of "Thanatopsis" in September 1817, when he was twenty-three years old, earned Bryant his first important recognition. He consequently began to contribute poems and essays on poetry to the *Review* and other periodicals in both the United States and Great Britain. In 1821, Bryant published his first book, *Poems*, which included a revised version of "Thanatopsis" and sensitive poems like "The Yellow Violet" and "To a Waterfowl," in which he found in nature both moral lessons about temporal life and reassuring signs of the presence and power of a divine being. "To Cole, The Painter, Departing for Europe" (1829), is a sonnet addressed to Bryant's close friend Thomas Cole, an important early American landscape painter and the founder of the Hudson River School of art. The texts are taken from *Poems, by William Cullen Bryant. Collected and Arranged by the Author* (1853).

THANATOPSIS[1]

> To him who in the love of Nature holds
> Communion with her visible forms, she speaks
> A various language; for his gayer hours
> She has a voice of gladness, and a smile
> And eloquence of beauty, and she glides   5
> Into his darker musings, with a mild

---

1. **Thanatopsis:** A meditation on death (Greek).

And healing sympathy, that steals away
Their sharpness, ere he is aware. When thoughts
Of the last bitter hour come like a blight
Over thy spirit, and sad images   10
Of the stern agony, and shroud, and pall,
And breathless darkness, and the narrow house,
Make thee to shudder, and grow sick at heart; —
Go forth, under the open sky, and list
To Nature's teachings, while from all around —   15
Earth and her waters, and the depths of air, —
Comes a still voice — Yet a few days, and thee
The all-beholding sun shall see no more
In all his course; nor yet in the cold ground,
Where thy pale form was laid, with many tears,   20
Nor in the embrace of ocean, shall exist
Thy image. Earth, that nourished thee, shall claim
Thy growth, to be resolved to earth again,
And, lost each human trace, surrendering up
Thine individual being, shalt thou go   25
To mix for ever with the elements,
To be a brother to the insensible rock
And to the sluggish clod, which the rude swain[2]
Turns with his share,[3] and treads upon. The oak
Shall send his roots abroad, and pierce thy mould.   30

　　Yet not to thine eternal resting-place
Shalt thou retire alone — nor couldst thou wish
Couch more magnificent. Thou shalt lie down
With patriarchs of the infant world — with kings,
The powerful of the earth — the wise, the good,   35
Fair forms, and hoary seers of ages past,
All in one mighty sepulchre. — The hills
Rock-ribbed and ancient as the sun, — the vales
Stretching in pensive quietness between;
The venerable woods — rivers that move   40
In majesty, and the complaining brooks
That make the meadows green; and, poured round all,
Old ocean's gray and melancholy waste, —
Are but the solemn decorations all
Of the great tomb of man. The golden sun,   45

---

2. **swain:** A poetic term for a country youth.
3. **share:** Short for plowshare, the main cutting blade of a plow.

The planets, all the infinite host of heaven,
Are shining on the sad abodes of death,
Through the still lapse of ages. All that tread
The globe are but a handful to the tribes
That slumber in its bosom. – Take the wings   50
Of morning – and the Barcan desert[4] pierce,
Or lose thyself in the continuous woods
Where rolls the Oregan,[5] and hears no sound,
Save his own dashings – yet – the dead are there:
And millions in those solitudes, since first   55
The flight of years began, have laid them down
In their last sleep – the dead reign there alone.
So shalt thou rest – and what if thou withdraw
Unheeded by the living, and no friend
Take note of thy departure? All that breathe   60
Will share thy destiny. The gay will laugh
When thou art gone, the solemn brood of care
Plod on, and each one as before will chase
His favourite phantom; yet all these shall leave
Their mirth and their employments, and shall come,   65
And make their bed with thee.[6] As the long train
Of ages glide away, the sons of men,
The youth in life's green spring, and he who goes
In the full strength of years, matron, and maid,
And the sweet babe, and the gray-headed man,   70
Shall one by one be gathered to thy side,
By those, who in their turn shall follow them.

    So live, that when thy summons comes to join
The innumerable caravan,[7] that moves
To that mysterious realm, where each shall take   75
His chamber in the silent halls of death,
Thou go not like the quarry-slave at night,
Scourged to his dungeon, but, sustained and soothed

---

4. **Barcan desert:** Ancient section of the Sahara Desert, south of the Mediterranean Sea in northern Africa.
5. **Oregan:** Native American name for the Columbia River.
6. **And make their bed with thee:** The first version of the poem, published in the *North American Review* in 1817, ended here. In *Poems* (1821), Bryant added the concluding passage, which he slightly revised in later editions of his work.
7. **caravan:** Historical term for a group of people, usually pilgrims, traveling together across a desert in Asia or North Africa.

By an unfaltering trust, approach thy grave,
Like one who wraps the drapery of his couch[8]   80
About him, and lies down to pleasant dreams.

[1817, 1853]

_____

8. **couch:** Early term for a bed.

THE YELLOW VIOLET

When beechen buds begin to swell,
    And woods the blue-bird's warble know,
The yellow violet's modest bell
    Peeps from the last year's leaves below.

Ere russet fields their green resume,   5
    Sweet flower, I love, in forest bare,
To meet thee, when thy faint perfume
    Alone is in the virgin air.

Of all her train, the hands of Spring
    First plant thee in the watery mould,   10
And I have seen thee blossoming
    Beside the snow-bank's edges cold.

Thy parent sun, who bade thee view
    Pale skies, and chilling moisture sip,
Has bathed thee in his own bright hue,   15
    And streaked with jet thy glowing lip.

Yet slight thy form, and low thy seat,
    And earthward bent thy gentle eye,
Unapt the passing view to meet,
    When loftier flowers are flaunting nigh.   20

Oft, in the sunless April day,
    Thy early smile has stayed my walk;
But midst the gorgeous blooms of May,
    I passed thee on thy humble stalk.

So they, who climb to wealth, forget   25
    The friends in darker fortunes tried.
I copied them — but I regret
    That I should ape the ways of pride.

And when again the genial hour
   Awakes the painted tribes of light,   30
I'll not o'erlook the modest flower
   That made the woods of April bright.

                   [1821, 1853]

TO A WATERFOWL

Whither, midst falling dew,
While glow the heavens with the last steps of day,
Far, through their rosy depths, dost thou pursue
   Thy solitary way?

Vainly the fowler's eye   5
Might mark thy distant flight to do thee wrong,
As, darkly painted on the crimson sky,
   Thy figure floats along.

Seek'st thou the plashy[1] brink
Of weedy lake, or marge of river wide,   10
Or where the rocking billows rise and sink
   On the chafed ocean side?

There is a Power whose care
Teaches thy way along that pathless coast, —
The desert and illimitable air, —   15
   Lone wandering, but not lost.

All day thy wings have fanned,
At that far height, the cold, thin atmosphere,
Yet stoop not, weary, to the welcome land,
   Though the dark night is near.   20

And soon that toil shall end;
Soon shalt thou find a summer home, and rest,
And scream among thy fellows; reeds shall bend,
   Soon, o'er thy sheltered nest.

Thou'rt gone, the abyss of heaven   25
Hath swallowed up thy form; yet, on my heart

---

1. **plashy:** A plash is a pool or a puddle.

Deeply hath sunk the lesson thou hast given,
   And shall not soon depart.

   He who, from zone to zone,
Guides through the boundless sky thy certain flight,   30
In the long way that I must tread alone,
   Will lead my steps aright.

[1818, 1853]

To Cole,[1] The Painter, Departing for Europe

A Sonnet

Thine eyes shall see the light of distant skies:
   Yet, COLE! thy heart shall bear to Europe's strand
   A living image of thy native land,
Such as on thine own glorious canvas lies;
Lone lakes — savannas[2] where the bison roves —   5
   Rocks rich with summer garlands — solemn streams —
   Skies, where the desert eagle wheels and screams —
Spring bloom and autumn blaze of boundless groves.
Fair scenes shall greet thee where thou goest — fair,
   But different — everywhere the trace of men,   10
   Paths, homes, graves, ruins, from the lowest glen
To where life shrinks from the fierce Alpine air,
   Gaze on them, till the tears shall dim thy sight,
   But keep that earlier, wilder image bright.

[1829, 1853]

---

1. **Cole:** Bryant's close friend Thomas Cole (1801–1848), the founder of the Hudson River School of art, pioneered early landscape painting in America. He traveled abroad during 1829-32. After Cole's death at age forty-seven, Bryant presented a funeral oration at the National Academy of Design in New York, in which he called Cole "not only a great artist but a great teacher; the contemplation of his works made men better."
2. **savannas:** Grassy plains.

Jane Johnston Schoolcraft

[1800–1841]

Jane Johnston Schoolcraft, whose Native American name is Bame-wa-wa-ge-zhik-a-quay (The Sounds the Stars Make Rushing through the Sky), was born near the Canadian border in present-day Sault Ste. Marie, Michigan. She was the third of eight children and the eldest daughter of an Irish fur trader, John Johnston, and Ozha-guscoday-way-quay (Woman of

Jane Johnston Schoolcraft

This is an anonymous and undated sketch of Schoolcraft as a young woman. As her attire indicates, Schoolcraft was raised and educated in the white community, but she also learned the language and lore of her mother's tribe, the Ojibwa.

By the premature death of Mrs. Schoolcraft was lost a mine of poesy.
— *Margaret Fuller*

the Green Valley), an Ojibwa chief's daughter, who took the English name *Susan* when she married Johnston. At the time of Schoolcraft's birth in 1800, the Ojibwa (also anglicized as *Chippewa, Ojibwe,* and *Ojibway*) were one of the most populous and widely distributed Indian groups in North America, inhabiting a vast area around the Great Lakes in southern Canada and the northern parts of the United States. Like her siblings, Schoolcraft learned to speak both Ojibwa and English. During her childhood, she traveled with her father to Detroit, Montreal, Quebec City, and, in 1809, to Great Britain, where he attended to the affairs of his estate in Ireland and to other business affairs in London. Schoolcraft may have attended a school during that trip and for short periods after her return in 1810, but she received most of her education at home. She was instructed by her mother in the legends and traditions of the Ojibwa, while her book-loving father taught her the classics of European literature, as well as the Bible.

In 1822, Schoolcraft met her future husband and literary collaborator, Henry Rowe Schoolcraft, a United States Indian agent who lodged with the Johnston family after he arrived in Sault Ste. Marie. A geologist who had earlier participated in and published an account of a major expedition to discover the source of the Mississippi River, Henry soon began to develop a deep interest in North American Indians. Schoolcraft taught him to speak Ojibwa and assisted him in an effort to establish a written vocabulary of the language, known to its own speakers as Anishinabe or Anishinaabemowin. After they married in 1823, the couple collaborated on a compilation of Ojibwa legends and tales. They later created a magazine to feature work on the language and lore of the tribe, the *Literary Voyager or Muzzeniegun*, an Ojibwa word for a written or printed document. Schoolcraft contributed numerous poems, in both English and Ojibwa, as well as stories based on the legends she and her husband had begun to collect. Acclaimed as the "northern Pocahontas," she was visited in her remote home by literary admirers of her work, which was used by Chandler R. Gilman in *Legends of a Log Cabin* (1835) and *Life on the Lakes* (1836). Working with her mother, Schoolcraft also gathered and authenticated much of the material her husband published in his *Algic Researches* (1839).

That book, which appeared two years before Schoolcraft's sudden death in 1841, was part of her lasting legacy. Just as she drew upon Ojibwa lore in her own stories, the legends published in *Algic Researches* inspired one of the most popular of all nineteenth-century American poems and probably the most familiar poem on Native American subjects, Henry Wadsworth Longfellow's *The Song of Hiawatha* (1855). In a graceful letter of acknowledgment written to Henry Rowe Schoolcraft, Longfellow observed, "without your books I could not have written mine." But it was equally true that *Algic Researches* and the other books on Indian history and tribal lore by Henry Rowe Schoolcraft could not have been written without the inspiration and collaboration of Jane Johnston Schoolcraft.

Reading Schoolcraft's "Mishosha, or the Magician and His Daughters."   During the winter of 1826-27, Schoolcraft and her husband, Henry Rowe Schoolcraft, produced the *Literary Voyager or Muzzeniegun.* Rather than a printed periodical, it was a weekly "manuscript magazine," handwritten copies of which were distributed to students of Indian history and culture throughout Michigan and in cities in the East, including New York City. The magazine included lists of Ojibwa words and notes on the language, as well as essays, poems, and stories. Schoolcraft wrote and published many of her pieces under her Native American name, Bame-wa-wa-ge-zhik-a-quay, or other pen names like Rosa and Leelinau. Her versions of Ojibwa legends proved to be especially attractive to readers and other writers, as a result of both the narrative appeal of the stories and the insights they offered into Native American culture. For the most part, Schoolcraft adopted the language of contemporary English and American writers, but her subject matter was strikingly original. In fact, she was among the first Native American writers to use the literary conventions of the increasingly dominant white culture to demonstrate and preserve the rich oral and cultural traditions of the native tribes of the United States. By birth and education, Schoolcraft was a product of two cultures, European and Native American, and her writings represented an early effort to bring together those frequently conflicting cultures. She consequently assumed a pioneering role in the establishment of a written Native American literature, as illustrated by the following story, based on the Ojibwa legend of two orphaned boys who are saved from an evil magician by the combined efforts of his two resourceful daughters, the elder orphan, and the powers of Nature. The first installment of the story appeared in the January 1827 issue of the *Literary Voyager.* Although production of the short-lived magazine ceased before the second installment could appear, Henry Rowe Schoolcraft published both parts in his *Algic Researches* (1839). Philip P. Mason also included both parts in his edition of the *Literary Voyager or Muzzeniegun* (1962), from which the following text of the entire story is taken.

bedfordstmartins.com /americanlit for research links on Schoolcraft

MISHOSHA,
OR THE MAGICIAN AND HIS DAUGHTERS

A Chippewa Tale or Legend

In an early age of the world, when there were fewer inhabitants in the earth than there now are, there lived an Indian, who had a wife and two children, in a remote situation. Buried in the solitude of the forest, it was not often that he saw any one, out of the circle of his own family. Such a situation seemed favorable for his pursuits; and his life passed on in uninterrupted happiness, till he discovered a wanton disposition in his wife.

This woman secretly cherished a passion for a young man whom she accidentally met in the woods, and she lost no opportunity of courting his approaches. She even planned the death of her husband, who, she justly concluded, would put her to death, should he discover her infidelity. But this design was frustrated by the alertness of the husband, who having cause to suspect her, determined to watch narrowly, to ascertain the truth, before he should come to a determination how to act. He followed her silently one day, at a distance, and hid himself behind a tree. He soon beheld a tall, handsome man approach his wife, and lead her away.

He was now convinced of her crime, and thought of killing her, the moment she returned. In the meantime he went home, and pondered on his situation. At last he came to the determination of leaving her forever, thinking that her own conscience would in the end, punish her sufficiently; and relying on her maternal feelings, to take care of the two boys, whom he determined to leave behind.

When the wife returned, she was disappointed in not finding her husband, having concerted a plan to dispatch him. When she saw that day after day passed, and he did not return she at last guessed the true cause of his absence. She then returned to her paramour, leaving the two helpless boys behind, telling them that she was going a short distance, and would return; but determined never to see them more.

The children thus abandoned, soon made way with the food that was left in the lodge, and were compelled to quit it, in search of more. The eldest boy possessed much intrepidity, as well as great tenderness for his little brother, frequently carrying him when he became weary, and gathering all the wild fruit he saw. Thus they went deeper into the forest, soon losing all traces of their former habitation, till they were completely lost in the labyrinths of the wilderness.

The elder boy fortunately had a knife, with which he made a bow and arrows, and was thus enabled to kill a few birds for himself and brother. In this way they lived some time, still pressing on, they knew not whither. At last they saw an opening through the woods, and were shortly after delighted to find themselves on the borders of a broad lake. Here the elder boy busied himself in picking the seed pods of the wild rose. In the meanwhile the younger, amused himself by shooting some arrows into the sand, one of which, happened to fall into the lake. The elder brother, not willing to lose his time in making another, waded into the water to reach it. Just as he was about to grasp the arrow, a canoe passed by him with the rapidity of lightning. An old man, sitting in the centre, seized the affrighted youth, and placed him in the canoe. In vain the boy addressed him. "My grandfather" (a term of respect for old people) "pray take my little brother also. Alone, I cannot go with you; he will starve if I leave him." The old magician (for such was his real character) laughed at him. Then giving his canoe a slap, and commanding it to go, it glided through the water with inconceivable swiftness. In a few minutes they reached the habitation of Mishosha, standing on an island in the centre of the lake. Here he lived, with his two daughters, the terror of all the surrounding country.

Leading the young man up to the lodge "Here my eldest daughter," said he, "I have brought a young man who shall become your husband." The youth saw surprise depicted in the countenance of the daughter, but she made no reply, seeming thereby to acquiesce in the commands of her father. In the evening he overheard the daughters in conversation. "There again!" said the elder daughter, "our father has brought another victim, under the pretence of giving me a husband. When will his enmity to the human race cease; or when shall we be spared witnessing such scenes of vice and wickedness, as we are daily compelled to behold."

When the old magician was asleep, the youth told the elder daughter, how he had been carried off, and compelled to leave his helpless brother on the shore. She told him to get up and take her father's canoe, and using the charm he had observed, it would carry him quickly to his brother. That he could carry him food, prepare a lodge for him, and return by morning. He did in every thing as he had been directed, and after providing for the subsistence of his brother, told him that in a short time he should come for him. Then returning to the enchanted island, resumed his place in the lodge before the magician awoke. Once during the night Mishosha awoke, and not seeing his son in law, asked his eldest daughter what had become of him. She replied that he had merely stepped out, and would be back soon. This satisfied him. In the morning, finding the young man in the lodge, his suspicions were completely lulled. "I see, my daughter, you have told me the truth."

As soon as the sun rose, Mishosha thus addressed the young man. "Come, my son, I have a mind to gather gulls eggs. I am acquainted with an island where there are great quantities; and I wish your aid in gathering them." The young man saw no reasonable excuse, and getting into the canoe, the magician gave it a slap, and bidding it go, in an instant they were at the island. They found the shore covered with gulls eggs, and the island surrounded with birds of this kind. "Go, my son," said the old man, "and gather them, while I remain in the canoe." But the young man was no sooner ashore than Mishosha pushed his canoe a little from land and exclaimed: "Listen ye gulls! you have long expected something from me. I now give you an offering. Fly down, and devour him." Then striking his canoe, left the young man to his fate.

The birds immediately came in clouds around their victim, darkening all the air with their numbers. But the youth, seizing the first that came near him, and drawing his knife, cut off its head, and immediately skinning the bird, hung the feathers as a trophy on his breast. "Thus," he exclaimed, "will I treat every one of you who approaches me. Forbear, therefore, and listen to my words. It is not for you to eat human food. You have been given by the Great Spirit as food for man. Neither is it in the power of that old magician to do you any good. Take me on your beaks and carry me to his lodge, and you shall see that I am not ungrateful."

The gulls obeyed, collecting in a cloud for him to rest upon, and quickly flew to the lodge, where they arrived before the magician. The daughters were surprised at his return, but Mishosha conducted as if nothing extraordinary had taken place.

On the following day he again addressed the youth. "Come, my son," said he, "I will take you to an island covered with the most beautiful pebbles, looking like silver. I wish you to assist me in gathering some of them. They will make handsome ornaments, and are possessed of great virtues." Entering the canoe, the magician made use of his charm, and they were carried, in a few moments, to a solitary bay in an island, where there was a smooth sandy beach. The young man went ashore as usual. "A little further, a little further," cried the old man, "upon that rock you will get some finer ones." Then pushing his canoe from land, "Come thou great king of fishes," cried he, "you have long expected an offering from me. Come, and eat the stranger I have put ashore on your island." So saying, he commanded his canoe to return, and was soon out of sight. Immediately a monstrous fish shoved his long snout from the water, moving partially on the beach, and opening wide his jaws to receive his victim.

"When" exclaimed the young man, drawing his knife, and placing himself in a threatening attitude, "when did you ever taste human food. Have a care of yourself. You were given by the Great Spirit to man, and if you, or any of your tribes, taste human flesh, you will fall sick and die. Listen not to the words of that wicked old man, but carry me back to his island, in return for which, I shall present you a piece of red cloth."

The fish complied, raising his back out of water to allow the young man to get on. Then taking his way through the lake, landed his charge safely at the island, before the return of the magician.

The daughters were still more surprised to see him thus escaped a second time, from the arts of their father. But the old man maintained his taciturnity. He could not, however, help saying to himself, "What manner of boy is this, who ever escapes from my power. His spirit shall not however save him. I will entrap him tomorrow. Ha! ha! ha!"[1]

Next day the magician addressed the young man as follows: "Come, my son," said he, "you must go with me to procure some young eagles. I wish to tame them. I have discovered an island where they are in great abundance." When they had reached the island, Mishosha led him inland until they came to the foot of a tall pine, upon which the nests were. "Now, my son," said he, "climb up this tree and bring down the birds." The young man obeyed. When he had with great difficulty got near the nest, "Now," exclaimed the magician, addressing the tree, "stretch yourself up and be very tall." The tree rose up at the command. "Listen, ye eagles," continued the old man, "you have long expected a gift from me. I now present you this boy, who has had the presumption to molest your young. Stretch forth your claws and seize him." So saying he left the young man to his fate, and returned.

But the intrepid youth drawing his knife, and cutting off the head of the first eagle that menaced him, raised his voice and exclaimed, "Thus will I deal with all who come near me. What right have you, ye ravenous birds, who were made to feed on beasts, to eat human flesh? Is it because that cowardly old canoe-man has bid you do so? He is an old woman. He can neither do you good nor harm. See, I have already

---

1. **Ha! ha! ha!:** The first installment of the story in the *Literary Voyager* ended at this point.

slain one of your number. Respect my bravery, and carry me back that I may show you how I shall treat you."

The eagles, pleased with his spirit, assented, and clustering thick around him formed a seat with their backs, and flew toward the enchanted island. As they crossed the water they passed over the magician, lying half asleep in his canoe.

The return of the young man was hailed with joy by the daughters, who now plainly saw that he was under the guidance of a strong spirit. But the ire of the old man was excited, although he kept his temper under subjection. He taxed his wits for some new mode of ridding himself of the youth, who had so successfully baffled his skill. He next invited him to go a hunting.

Taking his canoe, they proceeded to an island and built a lodge to shelter themselves during the night. In the mean while the magician caused a deep fall of snow, with a storm of wind and severe cold. According to custom, the young man pulled off his moccasins and leggings and hung them before the fire to dry. After he had gone to sleep the magician, watching his opportunity, got up, and taking one moccasin and one legging, threw them into the fire. He then went to sleep. In the morning, stretching himself as he arose and uttering an exclamation of surprise, "My son," said he, "what has become of your moccasin and legging? I believe this is the moon in which fire attracts, and I fear they have been drawn in." The young man suspected the true cause of his loss, and rightly attributed it to a design of the magician to freeze him to death on the march. But he maintained the strictest silence, and drawing his conaus[2] over his head thus communed with himself: "I have full faith in the Manito[3] who has preserved me thus far, I do not fear that he will forsake me in this cruel emergency. Great is his power, and I invoke it now that he may enable me to prevail over this wicked enemy of mankind."

He then drew on the remaining moccasin and legging, and taking a dead coal from the fireplace, invoked his spirit to give it efficacy, and blackened his foot and leg as far as the lost garment usually reached. He then got up and announced himself ready for the march. In vain Mishosha led him through snows and over morasses, hoping to see the lad sink at every moment. But in this he was disappointed, and for the first time they returned home together.

Taking courage from this success, the young man now determined to try his own power, having previously consulted with the daughters. They all agreed that the life the old man led was detestable, and that whoever would rid the world of him, would entitle himself to the thanks of the human race.

On the following day the young man thus addressed his hoary captor. "My grandfather, I have often gone with you on perilous excursions and never murmured. I must

---

2. **conaus:** This unknown word was possibly a misreading of Schoolcraft's original manuscript. The context suggests that she meant a blanketlike covering or rough cape.
3. **Manito:** Spirit of Nature.

now request that you will accompany me. I wish to visit my little brother, and to bring him home with me." They accordingly went on a visit to the main land, and found the little lad in the spot where he had been left. After taking him into the canoe, the young man again addressed the magician: "My grandfather, will you go and cut me a few of those red willows on the bank, I wish to prepare some smoking mixture." "Certainly, my son," replied the old man, "what you wish is not very hard. Ha, ha, ha! do you think me too old to get up there?" No sooner was Mishosha ashore, than the young man, placing himself in the proper position struck the canoe with his hand, and pronouncing the charm, N'CHIMAUN POLL, the canoe immediately flew through the water on its return to the island. It was evening when the two brothers arrived, and carried the canoe ashore. But the elder daughter informed the young man that unless he sat up and watched the canoe, and kept his hand upon it, such was the power of their father, it would slip off and return to him. Panigwun watched faithfully till near the dawn of day, when he could no longer resist the drowsiness which oppressed him, and fell into a short doze. In the meantime the canoe slipped off and sought its master, who soon returned in high glee. "Ha, ha, ha! my son," said he; "you thought to play me a trick. It was very clever. But you see I am too old for you."

A short time after, the young man again addressed the magician. "My grandfather, I wish to try my skill in hunting. It is said there is plenty of game on an island not far off, and I have to request that you will take me there in your canoe." They accordingly went to the island and spent the day in hunting. Night coming on they put up a temporary lodge. When the magician had sunk into a profound sleep, the young man got up, and taking one of Mishosha's leggings and moccasins from the place where they hung, threw them into the fire, thus retaliating the artifice before played upon himself. He had discovered that the foot and leg were the only vulnerable parts on the magician's body. Having committed these articles to the fire, he besought his Manito that he would raise a great storm of snow, wind, and hail, and then laid himself down beside the old man. Consternation was depicted on the countenance of the latter, when he awoke in the morning and found his moccasin and legging missing. "I believe, my grandfather," said the young man, "that this is the moon in which fire attracts, and I fear your foot and leg garments have been drawn in." Then rising and bidding the old man follow him, he began the morning's hunt, frequently turning to see how Mishosha kept up. He saw him faltering at every step, and almost benumbed with cold, but encouraged him to follow, saying, we shall soon get through and reach the shore; although he took pains, at the same time, to lead him in round-about ways, so as to let the frost take complete effect. At length the old man reached the brink of the island where the woods are succeeded by a border of smooth sand. But he could go no farther; his legs became stiff and refused motion, and he found himself fixed to the spot. But he still kept stretching out his arms and swinging his body to and fro. Every moment he found the numbness creeping higher. He felt his legs growing downward like roots, the feathers of his head turned to leaves, and in a few seconds he stood a tall and stiff sycamore, leaning toward the water.

Panigwun leaped into the canoe, and pronounced the charm, was soon transported to the island, where he related his victory to the daughters. They applauded the deed, agreed to put on mortal shapes, become wives to the two young men, and for ever quit the enchanted island. And passing immediately over to the main land, they lived lives of happiness and peace.

Bame-wa-wa-ge-zhik-a-quay
[1827, 1839, 1962]

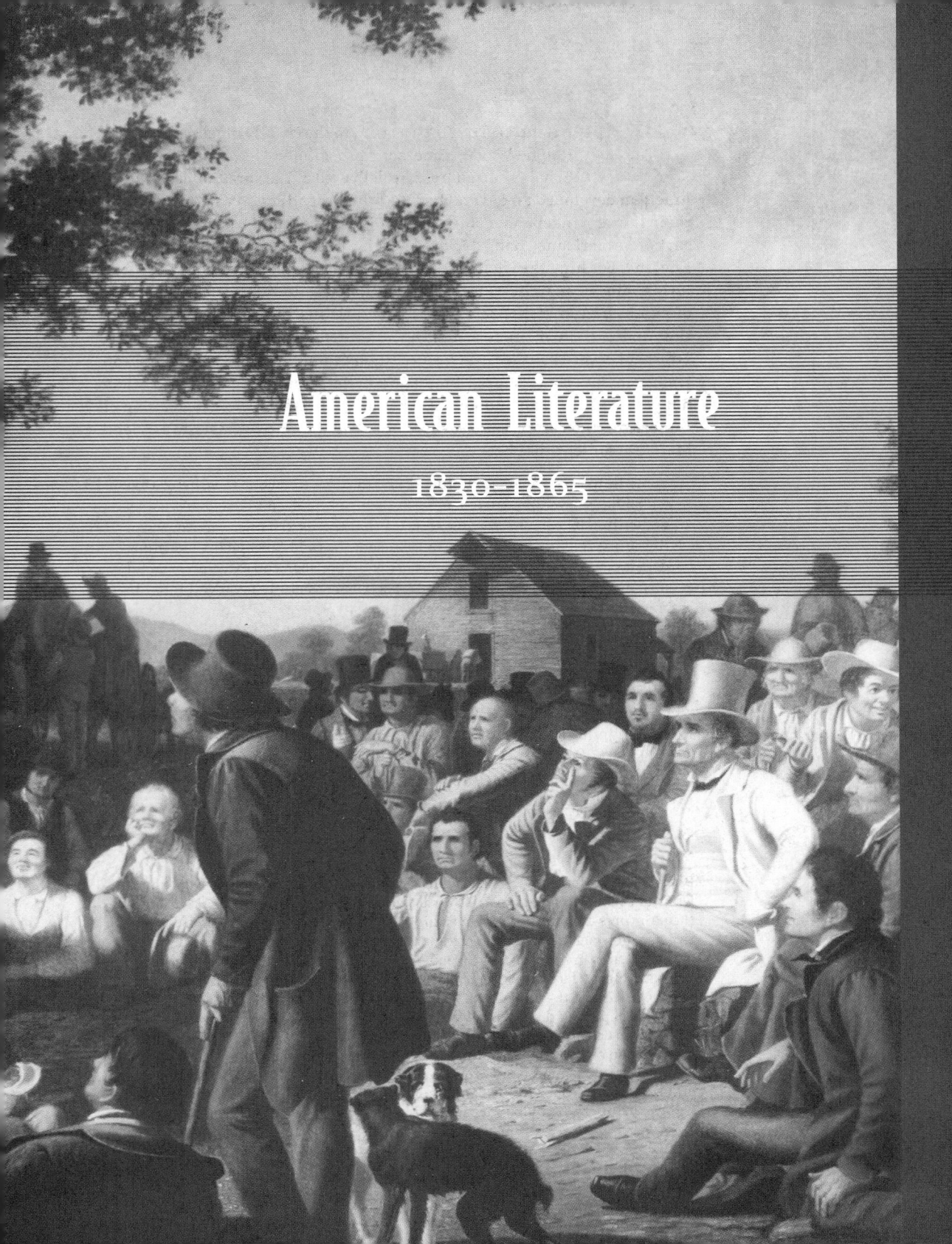

American Literature

1830–1865

"WE HAVE LISTENED TOO LONG to the courtly muses of Europe," Ralph Waldo Emerson proclaimed in "The American Scholar," an address he delivered at Harvard College in 1837. Emerson developed an old and familiar theme, calling on writers to assert their literary independence from Europe, just as more than sixty years earlier Americans had declared their political independence from England. For him, the challenge remained what it had been since the Revolution: American writers needed to develop new literary forms and modes of expression in response to the democratic institutions, material realities, and social dynamics of life in the United States. Despite the earlier efforts of revered authors such as William Cullen Bryant and Washington Irving, many critics shared Emerson's belief that American writers had not yet created a truly indigenous or "native" literature. At the opening of "American Literature," an essay published in 1846, Emerson's friend Margaret Fuller thus observed:

> Some thinkers may object to this essay, that we are about to write of that which has, as yet, no existence. For it does not follow because many books are written by persons born in America that there exists here an American literature. Books which imitate or represent the thoughts and life of Europe do not constitute an American literature. Before such can exist, an original idea must animate this nation and fresh currents of life must call into life fresh thoughts along its shores.

As difficult as it was to recognize in 1846, however, a distinctly American literature had already begun to emerge. Although nagging questions remained about what constituted an indigenous literature, some major works published during the previous decade illustrated the variety and increasing vitality of American writing. Those works also illustrated the

◄ (OVERLEAF)

George Caleb Bingham, *Stump Speaking* (1853–54)

Bingham, a professional painter widely known for his depictions of people and frontier life in Missouri, was also an active politician. In *Stump Speaking*, one of the paintings collectively known as his "election series," he portrayed a distinctive part of American electioneering, the "stump speech," so called because political candidates in frontier areas frequently stood upon the stumps of trees to address voters. Here, the speech is delivered from a makeshift platform by a politician gesturing to the crowd of men while some boys play in the foreground. In the antebellum period, the electoral franchise was extended to nearly all adult white males, who dominated the political process in the United States. But the value placed upon oratory and the numerous reform societies that sprang up during the period offered an opportunity for women, African Americans, and members of other minority groups to speak out publicly on a wide range of political and social issues during the turbulent decades before the Civil War.

ways in which European Romanticism, which exerted such a powerful force on American writers, was adapted by them to their own ends and purposes. The natural world, a major focus of many Romantic writers, took on a special, spiritual significance in Emerson's first book, *Nature* (1836). He also extended the Romantic emphasis on the importance of the individual to democratic, egalitarian ends in "Self-Reliance" and other essays in what many readers view as his two most important books, *Essays* (1841) and *Essays: Second Series* (1844). The radical and revolutionary implications of Romanticism were developed by Margaret Fuller, notably in *Woman in the Nineteenth Century*, a groundbreaking feminist analysis published in 1845. The Romantic concern for human rights and dignity gained additional resonance in such works as the *Narrative of the Life of Frederick Douglass* (1845), one of the numerous slave narratives that so enriched the literature of the United States. The nation's literature also revealed a Romantic emphasis on imagination and individual psychology, as well as on the importance of history and locale, which American writers explored in a wide range of works. One of the most popular forms was the short story, usually called the sketch or tale, which strongly appealed to the growing number of readers in the United States and which American writers brought to a new level of originality and distinction. Indeed, the short story was a primary source of the growing force and interest of American literature, as exemplified by such diverse collections as Edgar Allan Poe's *Tales of the Grotesque and Arabesque* (1840), Harriet Beecher Stowe's *The Mayflower, or Sketches of Scenes and Characters among the Descendants of the Pilgrims* (1843), and Nathaniel Hawthorne's *Twice-Told Tales* (1837) and *Mosses from an Old Manse* (1846).

The spirit of innovation that characterized many of the works published by the time Fuller's essay "American Literature" appeared in 1846 was even more apparent in the work of American writers during the following decade. Herman Melville published his first novel in 1846, and within a few years three of the most celebrated American novels appeared: Hawthorne's *The Scarlet Letter* (1850), Melville's *Moby-Dick* (1851), and Stowe's *Uncle Tom's Cabin* (1851–52). In various ways, all of those books pressed against the formal boundaries and accepted subjects of novels. They were followed in short order by other books that challenged both literary and social conventions. One was Henry Thoreau's *Walden* (1854), an experimental prose work that blended elements from a wide range of genres, including autobiography, nature writing, social criticism, and utopian tracts. Another was Walt Whitman's *Leaves of Grass* (1855), which represented a radical and self-conscious attempt to break with traditional poetic practices. Certainly, he refused to listen to "the courtly muses of Europe," whose influence on American writers Emerson had deplored in "The American Scholar." At about the same time Whitman's volume was published, the equally innovative American poet Emily Dickinson began her own remarkable career. In fact, so much important writing was produced during the early 1850s that those years have been described as the "American Renaissance," a term that with almost equal justification may be applied to the entire period from 1830 through the Civil War.

Technology, Transportation, and the Growth of the Literary Marketplace

The literary achievements of the period were spurred by a wide range of factors, from intense nationalism to major changes in the book trade in the United States. "God has predestined, mankind expects, great things from our race; and great things we feel in our souls," Melville affirmed in 1850. "We are the pioneers of the world; the advance-guard sent in through the wilderness of untried things, to break a new path in the New World that is ours." Such expansive and optimistic visions were in part a product of the nation's rapid economic growth. Although there were two severe depressions during the boom-and-bust period – in 1837 and again in 1857 – the growing prosperity of many Americans generated enormous confidence in themselves and their country. A major engine of economic growth was technology, as new inventions transformed both agriculture and industry.

"We are the pioneers of the world; the advance-guard sent in through the wilderness of untried things, to break a new path in the New World that is ours."

The production of printed materials was also radically altered by new technologies, including the introduction of cheap, machine-made paper. The development of mechanical power-presses and the lower costs of printing made it possible for an ever-larger percentage of the expanding population to afford books and periodicals. The number of readers steadily increased as a result of rising literacy rates and the significant growth in the number of schools, which were major consumers of books – as many as 40 percent of books published during the period were textbooks. Even as reading became an increasingly popular form of entertainment at home and during travel, it served as an important means of instruction and self-improvement outside the classroom, especially for groups whose educational opportunities were limited. The first four women to receive college degrees in the United States graduated from Oberlin in 1841, and only a few other colleges were open to women until after the Civil War. Economic pressures limited the formal education of most working-class Americans, including writers such as Melville and Whitman, both of whom left school to find jobs before they were twelve years old. Like many others – including former slaves such as Frederick Douglass and Harriet Jacobs, who had been denied any formal education – Melville and Whitman largely educated themselves by reading works they either purchased or withdrew from the expanding system of local libraries, yet another major market for books and periodicals in the United States.

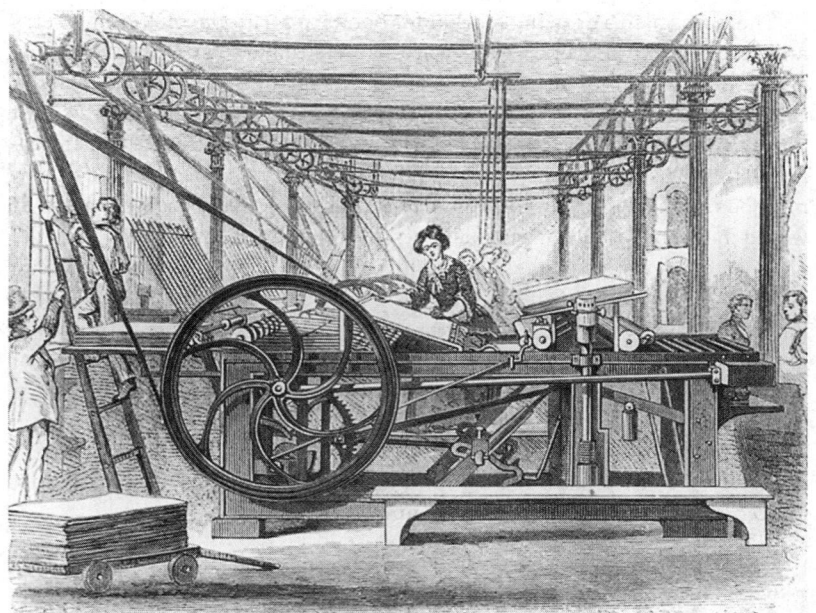

The Power-Press

An illustration from Jacob Abbott's *The Harper Establishment; Or, How the Story Books Are Made* (1855). At the time, Harper & Brothers was the largest publisher in the United States, printing a million books a year at its plant in New York City. The great pressroom contained nearly thirty power-presses, each attended by a young woman, called "the feeder." Her only job was to place fresh sheets of paper on the inclined surface in front of her, called the "apron" of the press, which mechanically printed and moved each sheet to the completed stack to her right. The sheets were then gathered, folded, placed in proper order, and stitched together to make a pamphlet or book.

The expansion of every part of the literary marketplace encouraged many aspiring writers to seek to make a career of authorship, something only a handful of American writers had managed to do before 1830. Although making a living through authorship was still a precarious pursuit, many were determined to try. By the mid-1830s, Hawthorne and Poe were regularly contributing stories and sketches to magazines, and the growing number of periodicals during the following decade spurred the efforts of other writers. Many of them were women, who claimed an increasingly large share of the market for periodical literature. After publishing a textbook in 1833, for example, Stowe soon began to write sketches and stories for religious newspapers and magazines such as *Godey's Lady's Book*.

There was also a growing market for books of all kinds, including poetry and, increasingly, novels. Novels were still viewed with suspicion by many clerical critics, who worried about the impact of romantic, unrealistic fictions on both individual readers and the morality of the country. But novels nonetheless gained increasing popularity during the period, emerging in the 1850s as the bestsellers in the United States. With the aid of new methods of production and promotion, such books sold in numbers that would have been unimaginable only decades earlier. In addition, the absence of an international copyright law made it possible for American companies to produce cheap reprints of popular British novels without having to pay royalties to the authors. Proudly describing the astonishing growth of the book trade between 1835 and 1855—when the number of books published in the United States "had advanced ten times as fast as the population"—the publisher George Palmer Putnam triumphantly added: "If we compare the *numbers* printed of each edition, the growth is still greater; for, twenty years ago who *imagined* editions of 300,000, or 75,000, or 30,000, or even the now common number of 10,000?"

The Erie Canal

This view of the village of Lockport, with its famous "Flight of Five" locks visible on the right, was published a decade after the Erie Canal opened in 1825. Running almost 400 miles across upstate New York, from Albany, on the Hudson River, to Buffalo, on Lake Erie, the canal completed a navigable route from the Atlantic Ocean to the Great Lakes and spurred both trade and the settlement of the upper Midwest.

The widespread distribution of books and periodicals was made possible by the establishment of a national postal system and a revolution in transportation, which profoundly altered virtually every aspect of life in the United States. The technological triumph and economic success of the nation's first major transportation system, the Erie Canal, triggered a canal-building boom in the Northeast and Midwest. Canals were ultimately superseded by other forms of transportation. By 1830, steamboats plied all of the major rivers in the country, as well as the Great Lakes, and railroad tracks soon began to spread out in a vast network across the nation. From 1830, when the first American-built steam locomotive went into service, to 1860, almost 35,000 miles of track were laid in the United States. That expanding system made it possible to transport cheaply both people and goods, including printed material, to even the most distant markets. It consequently led to the emergence of mass-circulation newspapers such as Horace Greeley's *New-York Tribune*, which by the 1850s was distributed throughout the country, and the establishment of magazines targeted at a national audience, including *Putnam's Monthly Magazine* and the *Atlantic Monthly*. Both of those magazines featured the work of American writers, though at the time that essentially meant writers from New England and New York. The centers of publishing in Boston, Philadelphia, and increasingly, New York City, became the major exporters of literary culture to the rest of the country, which was supplied with books, periodicals, and even lecturers from the East. Certainly the transportation revolution had a direct impact on writers like Emerson, whose extensive lecture tours took him from cities on the East Coast to towns beyond the Mississippi River. As he observed in one of his lectures,

Horace Greeley

The prominent photographer Mathew Brady made this portrait of Greeley, seated with a folded newspaper on his lap, around 1851. Under Greeley's leadership, the *New-York Tribune* became the most influential and widely distributed newspaper in the United States.

Emerson also viewed advances in transportation as a crucial means of binding together the vast and increasingly diverse country into a single, unified nation:

> Not only is distance annihilated, but when, as now, the locomotive and the steamboat, like enormous shuttles, shoot every day across the thousand various threads of national descent and employment and bind them fast in one web, an hourly assimilation goes forward, and there is no danger that local peculiarities and hostilities should be preserved.

Religion, Immigration, and Territorial Expansion

Another force that helped bind the country together was religion. Despite theological disputes among the proliferating sects of the country, most of them could gather together under the broad umbrella of Protestantism. Although Catholics, who founded Maryland in 1634, and Jews had a long history in the English colonies that became the United States, the vast majority of Americans during the first half of the nineteenth century were Protestants. Protestantism was further strengthened by the upsurge of evangelical activity in the decades before the Civil War, a period known as the Second Great Awakening, when widespread revivals led to a tremendous rise in church membership and religious sentiment in the United States. The trademark of the revivals was evangelical preaching at "camp meetings," outdoor religious gatherings that frequently drew thousands of people. But the Great Awakening was sustained by the printed as well as the spoken word. Evangelicals emphasized the importance of reading the Bible and religious tracts. Large numbers of Protestant books were published by the American Sunday-School Union and the American Tract Society, which were among the largest publishing firms in the United States. Millions of copies of their publications were distributed by members of "conversion societies," individuals or families who passed out tracts in towns and cities, and by traveling booksellers, who carried their religious wares into even the remotest rural areas, often to people who otherwise had little or no access to books. Indeed, in both their preaching and publications, the Evangelicals communicated in a language common people could readily understand. The rhetoric, symbolism, and religious themes of much of the literature of the period also revealed the impact of the Great Awakening, even on writers who questioned or subverted some of the fundamental beliefs of their more orthodox readers.

By the middle of the century, however, Protestantism faced growing challenges from both within and without. Its institutional authority was undermined by various "come-outers," religious dissenters and reformers

The Camp Meeting at Sing Sing, New York

Published in 1839, this lithograph depicts one of the many camp meetings held throughout rural America during the decades before the Civil War. In this print, tents are arranged in a rough semicircle around rows of benches facing a stage. A food tent is on the left, while men, women, and children are pictured in the foreground and background. As many as fifty ministers preached at the largest of the camp meetings, some of which attracted congregations of more than 20,000 people.

who seceded from the Protestant churches, as well as by radical abolitionists, who insisted that the support of slavery within many of those churches violated the true spirit of Christianity. In his *Narrative of the Life of Frederick Douglass*, Douglass concluded with a vigorous critique of "the *slaveholding religion* of this land," increasingly dominated by evangelical sects composed of both slaveholders in the South and those who shared their religious beliefs in the North. Conservative clergymen frequently clashed with both abolitionists and supporters of women's rights, who also appealed to the authority of Christ and the New Testament in rejecting the social dictates of American Protestantism. The rising tide of immigration posed a different kind of challenge to the religious practices, social values, and national self-image shaped by the pervasive

Protestant culture of the United States. Although most of the new immigrants were farmers and skilled laborers from Protestant countries in Europe, the single largest group—roughly two million people between 1845 and 1860—was composed of desperately poor Catholic immigrants driven to seek refuge in the United States by catastrophic crop failures and famine in Ireland.

The surge of immigration helped generate unprecedented urban and industrial growth. Viewed with distrust by American Protestants, Catholic immigrants confronted considerable hostility and various forms of discrimination. Most of the Irish immigrants were consequently crowded into slums in Boston, New York, Philadelphia, and Baltimore. Many found work in the textile mills that had been built alongside rivers in New England cities like Lowell, Massachusetts; still more, along with many other immigrants, moved on to industrial cities such as Pittsburgh or the new cities of what was then the West. Between 1830 and 1850, for example, the population of Chicago grew from fifty people to more than 100,000. By the eve of the Civil War, there were fifteen cities with populations above 50,000, and more than a million people lived in the congested metropolis of New York City. Most workers still labored on the land, and many writers of the period continued to focus their attention on nature and rural life, the realms explored in such works as Thoreau's *Walden; or, Life in the Woods.* But the city and the contours of urban life were central features in a growing number of writings, including the journalism of Lydia Maria Child, Fanny Fern, and Margaret Fuller; works of fiction such as Melville's *Bartleby, the Scrivener: A Story of Wall Street*; and the poetry of Whitman, who was, perhaps, the first genuinely urban poet in the United States. Few viewed the often-grim realities of the new urban and industrial order as unblinkingly as Rebecca Harding Davis, whose *Life in the Iron-Mills* invited Americans to confront realities they often sought to evade: the growing gap between wealth and poverty, as well as the appalling living and working conditions that many of the recent immigrants faced in the United States.

The nation's burgeoning population, which grew from under thirteen million in 1830 to over thirty-one million in 1860, also generated a growing hunger for land and increasing pressures for territorial expansion. From the time of the first arrival of European settlers, Native Americans had been forced from their lands and relentlessly driven westward, a process that culminated when Congress passed the Indian Removal Act in 1830. The law authorized the exchange of land west of the Mississippi for Indian holdings in the East, especially the rich agricultural lands of the "Five Civilized Tribes"—the Cherokee, Choctaw, Creek, Chickasaw, and Seminole—in Mississippi, Alabama, Georgia, and Florida. Although some writers and reformers protested the brutal policy, the forced removal of the Indians was supported by many white Americans.

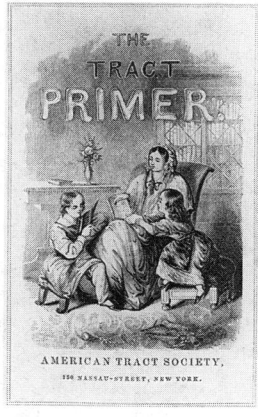

The Tract Primer
(c. 1848)

As the cover of this religious tract demonstrates, the home was widely viewed as the primary setting for the intellectual and moral instruction of children, with the mother as teacher.

End of the Poor

The full caption for this engraving in *Frank Leslie's Newspaper* read: "End of the poor – Funeral from a tenement house in Baxter Street, Five Points, New York." In the grim print, two boys drag a dog by its leg near a crowd that has gathered to watch men carry a coffin from a tenement house in the Five Points District of lower Manhattan, one of the worst slums in the United States in the mid-1850s. Five Points was notorious for crime, gangs, political corruption, poverty, and the ghastly living conditions of its tenements. But the working-class neighborhood was also in many ways the birthplace of multicultural America, a confined urban space shared by large numbers of African Americans and recent immigrants from Europe, especially the Irish, who poured into the area during the 1840s and 1850s.

But Americans were increasingly divided about the extension of slave territory. Over the protests of abolitionists and the opposition of antislavery politicians, Congress in 1844 approved the annexation of the slave state of Texas, which had been an independent republic since Anglo-American settlers had rebelled against Mexican rule in 1836. Border skirmishes along the Rio Grande in the spring of 1846 offered a pretext for the United States to declare war on Mexico. In the treaty that ended the war in 1848, Mexico relinquished all claims to Texas and ceded a vast territory to the United States. Combined with Texas, the

Crossing the Platte on the Oregon Trail
Before the completion of the transcontinental railroad in 1869, the only overland route to the new lands in the West was the Oregon Trail, which generally followed the Platte River to its headwaters, crossed the Rocky Mountains, and then split into trails leading to California or the Oregon Territory. Beginning with what was called "the great migration" of 1843, when a wagon train of one thousand settlers set off from Independence, Missouri, half a million people followed the trail, either on foot or in covered wagons. As this 1859 engraving suggests, Indian attacks were not the major threat to the settlers. They died in far greater numbers — as many as one in ten — from injuries, disease, exhaustion, and malnutrition during the arduous four- to six-month journey.

new territory added more than a million square miles to the national domain; by then, it had also been greatly expanded by the formal acquisition of a large portion of Oregon Country through an 1846 treaty with Great Britain. Even as European immigrants began to flood into eastern cities, thousands of settlers joined the great migration described in works like Francis Parkman's *The Oregon Trail* (1849), a celebration of the frontier spirit and America's westward expansion. Within a few short years, the nation had thus fulfilled what John L. O'Sullivan, the influential editor of the *United States Magazine and Democratic Review*, described in 1845 as "our manifest destiny to over spread and to possess the whole of the continent which Providence has given us for the development of the great experiment of liberty and . . . self-government entrusted to us."

> *"our manifest destiny to over spread and to possess the whole of the continent which Providence has given us for the development of the great experiment of liberty and . . . self-government entrusted to us."*

Sectionalism and the Coming of the Civil War

Ironically, what many Americans viewed as the triumphant fulfillment of their "manifest destiny" — a phrase newspapers picked up and made familiar throughout the United States — helped sow the seeds of the Civil War. The need to organize the territories gained from Mexico, which was made all the more pressing by the massive increase in westward migration triggered by the discovery of gold in California, once again raised the issue of the extension of slavery. In an effort to settle the issue once and for all, Congress forged the Compromise of 1850. Among the key provisions of the compromise, which included the admission of California as a free state but made no restriction on slavery in the other new territories, was a

The Compromise of 1850 and the Kansas-Nebraska Act of 1854

In efforts to resolve sectional divisions over the extension of slavery, Congress adopted the Compromise of 1850 and later passed the Kansas-Nebraska Act. In the former, California was admitted to the Union as a free state, while the settlers of the Utah and New Mexico Territories were allowed to vote for or against slavery. But the adoption of similar provisions for "popular sovereignty" in the Kansas and Nebraska Territories in 1854 sparked a local war between proslavery and antislavery settlers that deepened sectional divisions and served as a prelude to the Civil War.

far-more-stringent fugitive slave law. Under the revised law, a person suspected of being a runaway slave could be arrested without warrant and was denied trial by jury or the right to testify on his or her own behalf, while any person aiding a runaway was subject to a $1,000 fine and six months' imprisonment. Moreover, special commissioners were authorized to call upon the aid of all citizens to assist in the capture of runaways—in the view of many Northerners, making them complicit in slavery, which most had previously viewed as "the peculiar institution" of the South. The passage of the Fugitive Slave Act generated widespread protests in the North, where opposition was sometimes violent. Sectional divisions were deepened by the passage in 1854 of the Kansas-Nebraska Act, which incorporated the doctrine of "squatter" or "popular sovereignty"— that is, the right of the people of the territories to decide whether slavery would be prohibited—in an area where slavery had previously been excluded by the Missouri Compromise of 1820.

The Compromise of 1850 and the Kansas-Nebraska Act bitterly divided the North and South. Certainly, many works of the 1850s, frequently cited as one of the richest decades in American literary history, were shadowed by the deep divisions in the United States. That is not to say that all or even most of the writings of the period mirrored such divisions. The most popular book published in 1850 was Ik Marvel's *Reveries of a Bachelor*, in which the narrator's main concern is whether he will marry. Many of the other popular works published during the decade were novels such as Susan Warner's *The Wide, Wide World* and Maria Susanna Cummins's *The Lamplighter*, domestic fictions in which larger social and political issues generally played a minor role. But those issues were at least obliquely treated in two major novels of the period, Hawthorne's *The Scarlet Letter* and Melville's *Moby-Dick*, both of which broadly concern conflicts and divisions within a community—in the former, Puritan New England, then viewed by many as the founding place of the nation; in the latter, a whaling ship in which thirty sailors (the same number as there were states in 1850) are "federated along one keel," as Melville describes what might well have been interpreted as a symbol of the larger political union. More directly, the crisis of 1850 and especially the passage of the Fugitive Slave Act prompted Stowe to write *Uncle Tom's Cabin*, the first blockbuster novel published in the United States. In a different way, sectional divisions also shaped the most important volume of poetry published during the decade, *Leaves of Grass*, in which Whitman at once celebrated the diversity and insisted on the fundamental unity of the nation. "The United States themselves are essentially the greatest poem," he declared in the preface to the volume. "Here is not merely a nation but a teeming nation of nations."

"The United States themselves are essentially the greatest poem," he declared in the preface to the volume. "Here is not merely a nation but a teeming nation of nations."

Whitman echoed the nationalistic and patriotic sentiments that had so often been expressed during the quarter century before he published the first edition of *Leaves of Grass*, within a couple of days of July 4, 1855. By then, however, that "nation of nations" was well on its way to the Civil War, anticipated by the civil war that broke out between proslavery elements and free-soil settlers in Kansas in the spring of 1856. One of the antislavery heroes that emerged from "bleeding Kansas" was John Brown. Three years later, he led an attack on the federal arsenal at Harpers Ferry, Virginia, in an effort to generate a slave insurrection that would spread throughout the South. Before he was executed, Brown gained widespread sympathy in the North. That support deeply embittered Southerners and further hardened sectional divisions, which were starkly revealed in the election of 1860. Abraham Lincoln, who ran on a Republican platform calling for the exclusion of slavery from all new territories, carried the eighteen free states but did not gain a single electoral vote in any of the fourteen slave states. Within three months of his election, eleven Southern states seceded; on April 12, 1861, Confederate troops fired on Fort Sumter in Charleston Harbor and the war began. The American Renaissance did not abruptly end with the outbreak of the Civil War. Younger writers such as Louisa May Alcott and Elizabeth Barstow Stoddard published stories and novels during the war, which also inspired some of the finest poems written by Whitman and Dickinson, as well as a remarkable volume of verse by Melville, *Battle-Pieces and Aspects of the War* (1866). But the elegiac themes of that poetry, as well as the muted tone and realistic details of much of the other work written during the years 1861-65, marked a significant shift in both the national mood and the consciousness of writers seeking to come to terms with the devastating toll exacted by the Civil War.

COMPARATIVE TIMELINE, 1830–1865

Dates	American Literature	History and Politics	Developments in Culture, Science, and Technology
1830–1839	**1830** Second edition of David Walker's *Appeal* (1829)	**1830** U.S. population: 12,866,020	**1828–30** Steam locomotives developed; 35,000 miles of railroad track laid in the United States
	1830 Cherokee Council presents *Memorial* to U.S. Congress	**1830** Mormon Church organized and publication of the *Book of Mormon*	**1830** *Godey's Lady's Book* founded
		1830 Indian Removal Act allocates money to relocate tribes to west of Mississippi River	
		1830 Revolutions in France, Belgium, Poland	
	1831 Poe, *Poems*	**1831** Turner's slave rebellion in Virginia	**1831** Garrison founds the *Liberator*, an abolitionist newspaper
		1832 Jackson reelected president	
		1832 Black Hawk War	
	1833 Apess, "An Indian's Looking-Glass for the White Man"	**1833** Abolition of slavery in British colonies; American Anti-Slavery Society founded	**1833** *Knickerbocker* founded in New York City
	1833 Child, *Appeal on Behalf of That Class of Americans Called Africans*		**1833** First penny-press newspaper, *New York Sun*, established
			1833 First tax-supported public library (New Hampshire)
			1833 Large-scale manufacturing of eyeglasses begins
	1834 Sigourney, *Sketches and Poems*		**1834** *Southern Literary Messenger* founded
			1835 Colt invents revolver
	1836 Apess, *Eulogy on King Philip*	**1836** Van Buren elected president	
	1836 Emerson, *Nature*	**1836** Battle of the Alamo and establishment of Republic of Texas	
	1836 Holmes, *Poems*		
	1837 Hawthorne, *Twice-Told Tales*	**1837** Economic panic, severe downturn in American economy	**1837** Invention of steam-driven flatbed press for printing books
	1837 Whittier, *Poems Written during the Progress of the Abolition Question*	**1837–1901** Victoria becomes queen of Great Britain	**1837** *United States Magazine and Democratic Review* founded
			1837 Deere patents steel plow
		1838–39 "Trail of Tears": Cherokee forced from their lands by federal troops	**1838** Daguerre develops daguerreotype photographic process

COMPARATIVE TIMELINE, 1830–1865

Dates	American Literature	History and Politics	Developments in Culture, Science, and Technology
1840–1849	1840 Poe, *Tales of the Grotesque and Arabesque* 1840 Brownson, *The Laboring Classes* 1841 Catherine E. Beecher, *Treatise on Domestic Economy* 1841 Emerson, *Essays* 1842 Griswold, *The Poets and Poetry of America* 1843 Smith, *The Sinless Child and Other Poems* 1844 Emerson, *Essays; Second Series* 1845 Poe, *The Raven and Other Poems* 1845 Fuller, *Woman in the Nineteenth Century* 1845 Douglass, *Narrative of the Life of Frederick Douglass* 1846 Hawthorne, *Mosses from an Old Manse* 1849 Thoreau, "Resistance to Civil Government"	1840 U.S. population: 17,069,453 1840 Harrison elected president 1841 First wagon trains travel west on Oregon Trail 1841 Tyler becomes president after death of Harrison 1844 Polk elected president 1845–60 Roughly two million people, mostly from northern Europe (especially Ireland), immigrate to the United States 1845 United States annexes Texas, which enters Union as slave state 1846–48 United States wages war against Mexico; treaty cedes entire Southwest to United States 1846 United States acquires large portion of Oregon Country through treaty with Great Britain 1847 Brigham Young leads group of Mormons to Utah 1848 Taylor elected president 1848 Revolutions in France, the Austrian Empire, the German states, and Italian states 1848 First women's rights convention in United States held in Seneca Falls, New York 1848–49 California gold rush	1840 *Dial* established as journal of the transcendentalists 1841 *New-York Tribune* founded by Greeley 1841 *Graham's Lady's and Gentleman's Magazine* founded 1841 Barnum opens his American Museum in New York City 1841 Development of electroplate process in printing 1842 Dickens's American tour 1843 Invention of typewriter 1844 Morse invents telegraph 1844 *New York Ledger* founded 1846 Howe invents sewing machine 1847 *North Star* founded by Douglass 1848 Marx and Engels, *The Communist Manifesto*

COMPARATIVE TIMELINE, 1830–1865

Dates	American Literature	History and Politics	Developments in Culture, Science, and Technology
1850–1865	**1850** *Narrative of Sojourner Truth* **1850** Hawthorne, *The Scarlet Letter* **1850** Marvel, *Reveries of a Bachelor* **1851** Melville, *Moby-Dick* **1851** Smith, *Woman and Her Needs* **1851–52** Stowe, *Uncle Tom's Cabin* **1853** Fern, *Fern Leaves* **1854** Harper, *Poems on Miscellaneous Subjects* **1854** Thoreau, *Walden* **1855** Longfellow, *The Song of Hiawatha* **1855** Whitman, *Leaves of Grass* **1855** Melville, *Benito Cereno* **1856** Melville, *Piazza Tales* 	**1850** U.S. population: 23,191,876 **1850** Compromise of 1850 admits California to Union as a free state and enacts strict fugitive slave law **1850** Fillmore becomes president after death of Taylor **1852** Pierce elected president **1854** Kansas-Nebraska Act incorporates doctrine of popular sovereignty to decide issue of slavery; beginning of Republican Party **1856** Civil war breaks out between proslavery elements and free-soil settlers in Kansas **1856** Buchanan elected president **1857** *Dred Scott* decision declares that African Americans have no constitutional rights **1857** Economic panic, another severe downturn in American economy	**1850** *Harper's New Monthly Magazine* founded **1850** Jenny Lind, "the Swedish Nightingale," begins American tour **1851** *New York Times* is founded **1851** Powers, *The Greek Slave* (sculpture) **1853** *Putnam's Monthly Magazine* founded **1856** Bessemer invents process for manufacturing steel **1857** *Atlantic Monthly* founded by Emerson, Longfellow, and others **1857** *Harper's Weekly*, New York news and literary magazine, founded

COMPARATIVE TIMELINE, 1830–1865

Dates	American Literature	History and Politics	Developments in Culture, Science, and Technology
1850–1865 (cont.)			**1858** First transatlantic telegraph sent successfully via submarine cable
		1859 John Brown attempts to lead slave insurrection at Harpers Ferry, Virginia	**1859** Darwin, *Origin of Species*
			1859 *Anglo-African Magazine* founded
	1860–65 Dickinson writes several hundred poems	**1860** U.S. population: 31,443,321	
		1860 Lincoln elected president by carrying all eighteen free states	
	1861 Jacobs, *Incidents in the Life of a Slave Girl*	**1861** Representatives of southern states form Confederate States of America	
	1861 Cooke, *Poems*		
	1861 Davis, *Life in the Iron-Mills*	**1861** Confederate troops fire on Fort Sumter in Charleston Harbor, starting Civil War	
	1862 Stoddard, *The Morgesons*		
	1863 Alcott, *Hospital Sketches*	**1863** Emancipation Proclamation	
		1864 Lincoln reelected president	**1864** Pasteur invents pasteurization
	1865 Whitman, *Drum-Taps*	**1865** Lee surrenders at Appomattox, ending Civil War; Lincoln assassinated	**1865** Mendel discovers genetics

The Era of Reform

THE PERIOD OFTEN CALLED THE "AMERICAN RENAISSANCE," a tribute to the extraordinary richness and range of literary achievement during the decades before the Civil War, was also one of the most active periods of reform in American history. Spurred by the rapid social change and cultural ferment of the period, reformers turned their attention to virtually every aspect of life in the United States. Some focused their attention on dietary concerns and domestic relations, others worked to end slavery and

◀ **Fugitive Slave Law Convention**

This daguerreotype was taken at a Fugitive Slave Law convention in Cazenovia, New York, in August 1850. Frederick Douglass is pictured seated at the edge of the table on the right. Standing behind him is Gerrit Smith, a wealthy landowner who later helped finance John Brown's attack on Harpers Ferry. On either side of Smith, in matching attire, are the teenaged Edmonston sisters, Mary and Emily, former slaves in the District of Columbia. Two years earlier, they had been captured while attempting to escape and put up for sale at the slave pens in Alexandria, Virginia. After they were purchased for $2,250 by an agent of the New York Anti-Slavery Society, they were brought north to show the kind of people victimized by the slave trade.

other injustices, and still others sought to reform the institutions of the church and the state, including insane asylums, prisons, and schools. As diverse as the proliferating causes were, however, there were close connections among various reforms and reformers. Most activists were involved in a number of different causes, and the reformers were also united by several common assumptions and beliefs. Most were devout Protestants, who viewed social reform as a religious calling or duty. Most believed in the perfectibility – or at least the possibility of the radical improvement – of the individual and society. And virtually all reformers affirmed the power of the word, whether spoken or written.

The ability of reformers to spread that word was made possible by some of the same developments that encouraged literary production during the period. The increasing power of the periodical press led to the establishment of numerous magazines and newspapers sponsored by reform societies or devoted to a single cause. A notable example was temperance, which drew more supporters than any other reform and which enlisted scores of magazines and newspapers in its crusade against alcohol. Like many literary works of the period, the work of reform was also shaped by the popularity of lectures and the consequent development of the lyceum system, a network of local educational institutions that sponsored lecture series in which many writers and reformers found a hospitable welcome, or at least a public forum. At a time when eloquence was held in high esteem, even reformers espousing unpopular causes could hope to gain an audience through the power of their oratory, which was displayed in meetings of reform societies and in countless lectures, both at large halls in cities and in the lyceums that sprouted up in small towns and villages throughout the country. By exploiting the potent combination of print and public lectures – many of which were either reported on or printed in newspapers – reformers appealed at once to the individual consciences of their auditors and the conscience of the nation to address the many injustices in the United States.

Among the injustices that began to stir the conscience of some Americans was the treatment of Native Americans. Despite President Andrew Jackson's firm support, the Indian Removal Act passed by only a narrow margin following a prolonged and bitter debate in both houses of Congress. Its opponents included the famous frontiersman and congressman from Tennessee, David ("Davy") Crockett, who later called the act "a wicked, unjust measure." It was also opposed by missionaries such as Jeremiah Evarts, the leader of the Christian crusade against the removal of Native Americans. Even after the Indian Removal Act was signed into law in May 1830, most of the Cherokee continued to resist the policy, both in the courts of law and the court of public opinion, until they were forcibly driven from their lands during the winter of 1838–39. During the same decade, the losing battle for Native American rights was carried forward in

New England by William Apess, a Pequot of mixed Indian and Caucasian heritage. For Apess, an ordained Methodist minister, race prejudice was at odds with the preaching of Christ and the very spirit of Christianity. He also exposed the brutal treatment of Native Americans by their ostensibly "Christian" conquerors, notably in his *Eulogy on King Philip*, a lecture read in Boston in 1836.

Apess's brief career as a preacher and writer ended with the publication of that work, after which he was soon forgotten. In sharp contrast, another work published in Boston in 1836 marked the beginning of the long literary career of one of the most influential writers in American literary history, Ralph Waldo Emerson. *Nature*, Emerson's first book, became a kind of manifesto for the transcendentalists, a loosely connected group of

Robert Lindneux, *Trail of Tears*
After a decade-long struggle to retain their tribal lands in Georgia, in the winter of 1838-39 the remaining Cherokee were rounded up by federal soldiers for removal to lands west of the Mississippi. This 1942 painting portrays their long trek to "Indian Territory," present-day Oklahoma. The torturous journey, which reduced the Cherokee population by over 30 percent, came to be known as "The Path Where They Cried," or "The Trail of Tears."

writers and intellectuals living in and around Boston. Transcendentalism was an offshoot of Unitarianism, which by the 1820s became the dominant religion of eastern Massachusetts. The Unitarians rejected as "irrational" the doctrine of the Trinity—the union in one God of the Father, Son, and Holy Ghost—as well as such Puritan doctrines as predestination and the innate depravity of human beings. Instead, the Unitarians emphasized the individual's freedom of choice and capacity for good. In one of his most famous sermons, for example, the Unitarian minister William Ellery Channing celebrated what he described as the human potential to achieve "likeness to God." That conception of human capacity strongly influenced the transcendentalists, a term that was sometimes used in derision of their belief in the power of human intuition, or "inward beholding," to apprehend a "transcendent" reality that was essentially mental or spiritual in nature. Although many of them were trained as Unitarian ministers, the transcendentalists revolted against what they viewed as the cold rationality and materialism of Unitarianism. Some of them remained Unitarian ministers, seeking to infuse the church with a new spirit and to transform it into a vehicle for social reform. Others abandoned the ministry, including Emerson, who resigned from his church in Boston in 1832. Nonetheless, he remained a kind of secular minister or preacher, who once described the lyceum as his "pulpit." From that pulpit, Emerson delivered hundreds of lectures throughout the North, preaching the gospel of "self-culture," the full development of the intellectual, moral, and spiritual nature of each individual.

Although Emerson was the most prominent of the transcendentalists, the group encompassed diverse individuals and a wide range of views, especially concerning social reform. Emerson's belief that the reformation of society would ultimately be achieved only through the spiritual transformation of its individual members was shared by his young friend Henry David Thoreau. Like Emerson, Thoreau spoke out strongly against injustices like slavery and the Mexican War, notably in his famous essay "Resistance to Civil Government," now better known as "Civil Disobedience." But he rejected the associations and methods of organized reformers, suggesting that their focus on social ills blinded them to the rich resources of nature and the self. In fact, Thoreau's masterpiece, *Walden* (1854), may at least in part be understood as a kind of manual of self-reform and a challenge to those who sought to change the world through different means. He and Emerson were consequently often at odds with some of the other transcendentalists, who insisted that individual moral reform must go hand-in-hand with organized efforts to reform society. One of the earliest, most militant, and most tenacious crusaders against slavery among the transcendentalists was Theodore Parker, who attacked a wide range of social abuses from the pulpit of his church in Boston. Other members of the group turned their attention to the plight of exploited laborers in the North.

In 1840, Emerson's friend George Ripley resigned from the Unitarian ministry to establish the Brook Farm Institute of Agriculture and Education, one of the many utopian communities founded during that decade. Such experiments in communal living or "association" varied widely, but virtually all of them sought to offer models of social reorganization, harmonious communities in which individuals could escape the corrosive influences and competitive pressures of an increasingly urban and industrial society. Another of Emerson's closest friends was Margaret Fuller, a sympathetic observer of and visitor to Brook Farm. Her career illustrated the growing trend toward social activism within transcendentalism, as she became increasingly engaged in various reforms, including "woman's rights," as the feminist movement was then known. In *Woman in the Nineteenth Century* (1845), Fuller affirmed that women must develop their personal natures and their public roles, an argument that influenced many of those who emerged as leaders of the feminist movement, including Elizabeth Cady Stanton and Susan B. Anthony.

Josiah Wolcott, *Brook Farm with Rainbow*

This painting of Brook Farm suggests the hopeful nature of the utopian experiment in communal living in West Roxbury, a rural village west of Boston. Wolcott apparently completed the painting a year or two before the community was disbanded in 1846.

The crusaders for women's rights faced formidable obstacles. One was the domestic ideology of the period, often called "the cult of domesticity." On the one hand, that pervasive ideology emphasized the crucial role of women, who were widely viewed as more virtuous than men and consequently as the primary nurturers of moral values from their central position in the domestic sphere. On the other hand, the belief that women's proper place was in the home effectively barred them from careers and direct involvement in public issues. Although some women challenged such a narrow definition of their role, they encountered firm opposition and often harsh censure. The experience of the Grimké sisters, Sarah and Angelina, was instructive. Daughters of a slaveholding family from South Carolina, the sisters became devout Quakers and strong opponents of slavery. When they began to speak out publicly on the issue, first in small gatherings of women and then in larger "mixed" gatherings of men and women, the sisters were chastised in both the press and the pulpit. In a "Pastoral Letter" read from every Congregational pulpit in the state in 1837, the Congregationalist Clergy of Massachusetts called attention to what the New Testament defined as "the appropriate duties and influence of women." Asserting that the "power of woman is in her dependence," the clergy added: "When she assumes the place and tone of a man as a public reformer . . . her character becomes unnatural." Despite such opposition, the Grimkés continued to speak out against slavery and increasingly on behalf of women's rights. As Angelina Grimké observed in 1837, "The investigation of the rights of the slave has led me to a better understanding of my own." That understanding of the connections between slavery and their own oppressed condition, "the slavery of sex," led to an increase in the number of women in the feminist crusade. Their efforts to generate public discussion of the issue culminated in July 1848, when a convention was held in Seneca Falls, New York, to consider "the condition and rights of woman." That was a signal event in the history of women in the United States, largely because of the "Declaration of Sentiments" adopted at the end of the convention. At once an indictment of the "repeated injuries and usurpations on the part of man toward woman" and a call for women's full equality, that radical document gained national attention and generated strong momentum for the feminist movement during the following decade.

> *"The investigation of the rights of the slave has led me to a better understanding of my own."*

After 1850, however, women's rights and all other reforms were overshadowed by the antislavery movement. That movement had a long history in America, especially among the Quakers, who in the late eighteenth century became the first religious sect to bar slaveholders from their "Society." Beginning in the 1820s, the gentle persuasion of the Quakers began to be superseded by far more militant demands for the end of slavery, as exemplified by *An Appeal to the Colored Citizens of the World* (1829),

A Printing Press Demolished at Slavery's Bidding

The caption of this widely distributed illustration read: "The people of the free states have attacked 'the tyrant's foe, and the people's friend,' – Oct. 1835, at Utica, July 1836, at Cincinnati, O., Aug. 1837 at Alton, Ill. and finally shot E. P. Lovejoy, because he would not basely surrender 'THE LIBERTY OF THE PRESS, THE PALLADIUM OF ALL OUR LIBERTIES.'"

a fierce assault on slavery and American racism by David Walker, a free black who grew up in the South before settling in Boston. Like many other writings of the period, Walker's pamphlet revealed an important influence on antebellum reform, the religious revivalism that was such a powerful force within American Protestantism during the first half of the nineteenth century. Walker insisted that slavery must end, if necessary by a slave revolt, an affirmation of violent means that distinguished him from the most prominent of the radical abolitionists, the pacifist William Lloyd Garrison, founder and editor of the Boston *Liberator* (1831-65). That was the first newspaper to call for the immediate end of slavery, without compensation to slaveholders, and Garrison was viewed as a dangerous radical by many Americans. In fact, his views were so unpopular that Garrison was attacked by a mob in Boston in 1836, part of a wave of violence against antislavery lecturers, meetings of antislavery societies, and those seeking to distribute antislavery literature. Antislavery newspapers were also the target of violence during the decade. The first great martyr of the abolitionist movement was the Reverend Elijah P. Lovejoy, editor of the *Observer* in Alton, Illinois, where he was killed while defending his press from a proslavery mob in 1837. In response to such attacks, the abolitionists sought to link their cause with the rights of freedom of the press and freedom of speech, articles of faith among most Americans. The antislavery appeal slowly began to shape public opinion, especially after 1850, when the message began to be amplified and spread in mass-market urban dailies like Horace Greeley's *New-York Tribune*, the most influential newspaper in the United States.

As crucial as they were, newspapers were not the only means by which abolitionists exploited the growing power of the printing press. As David Walker demonstrated, books could also be used to carry the antislavery message to ever-larger numbers of people. One writer who was determined to do so was Lydia Maria Child, who risked her reputation as one of Boston's most respected authors by publishing *An Appeal on Behalf of That Class of Americans Called Africans* (1833), the first book to call for the immediate emancipation of the slaves and the end of all forms of discrimination against people of color in the United States. Among the most moving appeals for an end to slavery and racism were the so-called slave narratives, autobiographical accounts written by former slaves. "The fugitive slave literature is destined to be a powerful lever," an anonymous reviewer observed in 1849. "We see in it the easy and infallible means of abolitionizing the free States. Argument provokes argument, reason is met by sophistry. But narratives of slaves go right to the hearts of men." Of the hundreds of slave narratives published in the United States between the Revolution and the Civil War, few went so deeply into the hearts of readers in the North as *Narrative of the Life of Frederick Douglass, an American Slave, Written by Himself* (1845). The phenomenal success of his book inspired a vivid succession of similar accounts during the following few years, including *Narrative of the Life of William Wells Brown* (1848) and *Life and Adventures of Henry Bibb, Written by Himself* (1849). Such narratives also provided inspiration and material for fictional treatments of slavery, especially Stowe's *Uncle Tom's Cabin*, the best-selling novel that more than any other single work helped to generate antislavery sentiment in the North. The impact of the novel was so great that, when he met Stowe during the Civil War, Abraham Lincoln reportedly greeted her with the words, "So you're the little lady who made this big war."

Certainly, the long war of words between the abolitionists and proslavery apologists was a major source of the sectional divisions that culminated in the Civil War. On the eve of that war, Harriet Jacobs—who adopted the pseudonym "Linda Brent"—added yet another powerful appeal to Northern readers with *Incidents in the Life of a Slave Girl*, the first full-length narrative written by a former female slave in the United States. In a letter to the *Liberator*, the black abolitionist William C. Nell expressed the hope that Jacobs's account would "find its way into every family, where all, especially mothers and daughters, may learn yet about the barbarism of American slavery and the character of its victims." In fact, few read the book, which appeared only three months before the outbreak of the war in April 1861. But the abolitionists continued their crusade during the four

> *"The fugitive slave literature is destined to be a powerful lever. . . . We see in it the easy and infallible means of abolitionizing the free States. Argument provokes argument, reason is met by sophistry. But narratives of slaves go right to the hearts of men."*

Slave Sale Broadside, 1852

The abolitionists often cited the selling of slaves and the consequent breaking up of their families as a vivid illustration of the inhumanity of a system that mistreated and sought to transform human beings into brutes. (As the note at the bottom of this duotone reproduction of the broadside indicates, "Slaves will be sold separate, or in lots, as best suits the purchaser.") The struggle against such dehumanization was a major theme in many of the slave narratives and much of the antislavery fiction of the period. (Chicago Historical Society [ICHi-22003].)

Sale of Slaves and Stock.

The Negroes and Stock listed below, are a Prime Lot, and belong to the ESTATE OF THE LATE LUTHER McGOWAN, and will be sold on Monday, Sept. 22nd, 1852, at the Fair Grounds, in Savannah, Georgia, at 1:00 P. M. The Negroes will be taken to the grounds two days previous to the Sale, so that they may be inspected by prospective buyers.

On account of the low prices listed below, they will be sold for cash only, and must be taken into custody within two hours after sale.

No.	Name.	Age.	Remarks.	Price.
1	Lunesta	27	Prime Rice Planter,	$1,275.00
2	Violet	16	Housework and Nursemaid,	900.00
3	Lizzie	30	Rice, Unsound,	300.00
4	Minda	27	Cotton, Prime Woman,	1,200.00
5	Adam	28	Cotton, Prime Young Man,	1,100.00
6	Abel	41	Rice Hand, Eyesight Poor,	675.00
7	Tanney	22	Prime Cotton Hand,	950.00
8	Flementina	39	Good Cook. Stiff Knee,	400.00
9	Lanney	34	Prime Cottom Man,	1,000.00
10	Sally	10	Handy in Kitchen,	675.00
11	Maccabey	35	Prime Man, Fair Carpenter,	980.00
12	Dorcas Judy	25	Seamstress, Handy in House,	800.00
13	Happy	60	Blacksmith,	575.00
14	Mowden	15	Prime Cotton Boy,	700.00
15	Bills	21	Handy with Mules,	900.00
16	Theopolis	39	Rice Hand, Gets Fits,	575.00
17	Coolidge	29	Rice Hand and Blacksmith,	1,275.00
18	Bessie	69	Infirm, Sews,	250.00
19	Infant	1	Strong Likely Boy	400.00
20	Samson	41	Prime Man, Good with Stock,	975.00
21	Callie May	27	Prime Woman, Rice,	1,000.00
22	Honey	14	Prime Girl, Hearing Poor,	850.00
23	Angelina	16	Prime Girl, House or Field,	1,000.00
24	Virgil	21	Prime Field Hand,	1,100.00
25	Tom	40	Rice Hand, Lame Leg,	750.00
26	Noble	11	Handy Boy,	900.00
27	Judge Lesh	55	Prime Blacksmith,	800.00
28	Booster	43	Fair Mason, Unsound,	600.00
29	Big Kate	37	Housekeeper and Nurse,	950.00
30	Melie Ann	19	Housework, Smart Yellow Girl,	1,250.00
31	Deacon	26	Prime Rice Hand,	1,000.00
32	Coming	19	Prime Cotton Hand,	1,000.00
33	Mabel	47	Prime Cotton Hand,	800.00
34	Uncle Tim	60	Fair Hand with Mules,	600.00
35	Abe	27	Prime Cotton Hand,	1,000.00
36	Tennes	29	Prime Rice Hand and Coachman,	1,250.00

There will also be offered at this sale, twenty head of Horses and Mules with harness, along with thirty head of Prime Cattle. Slaves will be sold separate, or in lots, as best suits the purchaser. Sale will be held rain or shine.

long years of the conflict, which they sought to transform into a war to end slavery, not simply a struggle to preserve the Union. They helped convince President Lincoln to issue the Emancipation Proclamation, which ended slavery only in areas not controlled by Union forces, and their efforts were finally crowned by the adoption of the Thirteenth Amendment shortly before the end of the Civil War. The abolition of slavery hardly ended injustice in the United States. On the contrary, African Americans and other minorities continued to struggle for full equality, while women, who had contributed so much to the antislavery movement, did not gain the right to vote until 1920. Nonetheless, the end of slavery was a major victory for the abolitionists, who like so many reformers and writers of the period 1830-65 had persistently sought to expose the gap between American ideals of freedom and equality and the often harsh realities of life in the United States.

American Contexts

"I Will Be Heard": The Rhetoric of Antebellum Reform

IN A LETTER IN 1840, RALPH WALDO EMERSON wrote his friend the English author Thomas Carlyle that "We are a little wild here with numberless projects of social reform." As Emerson indicated, reform movements swept the nation in the decades before the Civil War. Responding to swiftly changing social, political, and economic conditions, reformers sought and called for change by exploiting every rhetorical form available to them, from speeches to newspaper articles, pamphlets, and books.

Among those who took up the pen in defense of their rights were the Cherokee. "I ask you, shall the red man live, or shall he be swept from the earth?" the Cherokee leader Elias Boudinot asked in *An Appeal to Whites*, published in 1826. "They hang upon your mercy as to a garment. Will you push them from you, or will you save them?" Those questions gained added urgency during the congressional debate over the Indian Removal Act, under the terms of which the Cherokee and other Indian nations of the East would be removed to "Indian Territory," land west of the Mississippi River in what is now Oklahoma. Many of the Cherokee were literate in English, and in 1828 Boudinot founded *The Cherokee Phoenix*, whose editorials opposing the legislation were reprinted in urban newspapers around the country. Cherokee leaders and citizens also appealed directly to Congress in a series of "memorials," or petitions, now known as the *Cherokee Memorials*.

Although such protests generated some sympathy and support for Native Americans, there was far more widespread concern with the economic exploitation of laborers, both in the institution of slavery in the South and the factory system in the North. The emergence of radical abolitionism was fueled by evangelical intensity, as both black and white Americans took up the cause. David Walker's *An Appeal to the Colored Citizens of the World* (1829) was one of the most militant attacks on the "inhuman system of slavery" by an African American. "I WILL BE HEARD," thundered William Lloyd Garrison in a fiery editorial in the first issue of his weekly antislavery newspaper, the *Liberator*, founded in 1831. Abolitionism ultimately became the dominant cause of the antebellum period, but some reformers believed that concern for the plight of slaves in the South blinded people to the condition of laborers in the North. One of the first voices raised on their behalf was that of the transcendentalist and reformer Orestes A. Brownson. Like the writings of Walker and Garrison, though for different reasons, Brownson's controversial article *The Laboring Classes* (1840) was viewed by many as a serious threat to the social order. The abolitionists were accused of fomenting slave insurrections and sectional divisions that threatened the Union. Brownson was charged with fomenting class divisions that would lead to war between the rich and the poor. Certainly, he offered one of the most radical and sweeping critiques of the "*Christian* community" in New England, which tolerated a system of labor in the mills and factories that Brownson viewed as even more oppressive than chattel slavery in the South.

bedfordstmartins.com/ americanlit for research links on the authors in this section

Women, who played an important role in the antislavery crusade, also began to press for what was called "woman's rights." But women were by no means united in their approaches to social reform. In contrast to women who argued that the division of the sexes into separate spheres of influence was crucial to both the elevation of women and the perfection of the American social experiment, women including Elizabeth Cady Stanton insisted that separate spheres were inherently unequal, since such a division of labor effectively denied women the right to earn a living, as well as their rights as citizens. That position was developed fully in the "Declaration of Sentiments," drafted by Stanton for the first "Woman's Rights Convention," as it was called, at Seneca Falls, New York, in 1848. One of the most remarkable champions of woman's rights was an illiterate former slave and itinerant preacher named Sojourner Truth, who delivered a memorable speech at a woman's rights convention in Ohio in the early summer of 1851. In her vigorous defense of the feminists from theological attacks by a group of ministers, Truth demonstrated the power of her own preaching, even as the report of her speech in an antislavery newspaper illustrated the crucial role of the press in disseminating the words of such eloquent reformers.

The Cherokee Memorials

John Ross

Of mixed Cherokee and
Scots ancestry, Ross was
educated in English and
became the most
prominent member of
the Cherokee Nation,
which he led through the
tumultuous period from
1828 until his death in
1866. As this early
portrait suggests, he also
vigorously challenged
contemporary assump-
tions about race and
Native Americans.

Thousands of years before the first Europeans came to North America,
the Cherokee occupied lands that extended roughly from present-day
North Carolina to Georgia and Alabama and also into Kentucky and
Tennessee. During their long history, the Cherokee often had defended
themselves against the incursions of other native peoples, but the most
serious challenges they faced were from British colonists who seized
their lands, and after the Revolution from the state of Georgia and the
newly formed federal government of the United States. Through a series
of treaties they were pressured to sign, the Cherokee were increasingly
displaced from their lands. In an effort to preserve some unity and
independence, they formed a constitutional government in 1828. In
response, Georgia enacted laws abolishing the Cherokee government
and asserting sovereignty over the nation and its lands. In March
1829, contesting the state's actions, the Cherokee appealed for federal
protection in one of the earliest of numerous "memorials," or petitions,
they submitted to Congress. But the newly elected president, Andrew
Jackson, supported Georgia, and later in 1829 he presented a plan to
remove the Cherokee and other Indian nations to territory west of the
Mississippi. Anticipating Jackson's initiative, the Cherokee Council
drafted the following memorial, dated November 5, 1829, and presented
it to Congress on February 15, 1830, shortly before intense debate over
the Indian Removal Act began. Though not identified, the petition's
authors probably included John Ross (1790-1866), the first elected
leader of the Cherokee Nation; and John Ridge (1802-1839), the clerk of
the Cherokee Council. Just as the Cherokee modeled their government
on the Constitution of the United States, the memorial echoes the
Declaration of Independence and suggests that the founding document
of the United States was being used to justify the destruction of the
independence of the Cherokee Nation. Despite the eloquence of the
closely argued memorial, in May 1830 the Indian Removal Act was narrowly passed and immediately signed into law by President Jackson.
During the next decade, thousands of Cherokee were subsequently
forced to leave their ancient homelands and face an uncertain future in
"Indian Territory." The text of the memorial is taken from report 311 of
the First Session of the Twenty-first Congress, 1829-31.

MEMORIAL OF THE CHEROKEE COUNCIL, NOVEMBER 5, 1829

*To the Honorable Senate and House of Representatives of
the United States of America in Congress Assembled:*

We, the representatives of the people of the Cherokee nation, in general council con-
vened, compelled by a sense of duty we owe to ourselves and nation, and confiding in
the justice of your honorable bodies, address, and make known to you the grievances

which disturb the quiet repose and harmony of our citizens, and the dangers by which we are surrounded. Extraordinary as this course may appear to you, the circumstances that have imposed upon us this duty we deem sufficient to justify the measure; and our safety as individuals, and as a nation, require that we should be heard by the immediate representatives of the people of the United States, whose humanity and magnanimity, by permission and will of Heaven, may yet preserve us from ruin and extinction.

The authorities of Georgia have recently and unexpectedly assumed a doctrine, horrid in its aspect, and fatal in its consequences to us, and utterly at variance with the laws of nations, of the United States, and the subsisting treaties between us, and the known history of said State, of this nation, and of the United States. She claims the exercise of sovereignty over this nation; and has threatened and decreed the extension of her jurisdictional limits over our people. The Executive of the United States, through the Secretary of War, in a letter to our delegation of the 18th April last, has recognized this right to be abiding in, and possessed by, the State of Georgia;[1] by the Declaration of Independence, and the treaty of peace concluded between the United States and Great Britain in 1783; and which it is urged vested in time previously, she claimed and exercised, within the limits of what constituted the "thirteen United States." It is a subject of vast importance to know whether the power of self-government abided in the Cherokee nation at the discovery of America, three hundred and thirty-seven years ago; and whether it was in any manner affected or destroyed by the charters of European potentates. It is evident from facts deducible from known history, that the Indians were found here by the white man, in the enjoyment of plenty and peace, and all the rights of soil and domain, inherited from their ancestors from time immemorial, well furnished with kings, chiefs, and warriors, the bulwarks of liberty, and the pride of their race. Great Britain established with them relationships of friendship and alliance, and at no time did she treat them as subjects, and as tenants at will, to her power. In war she fought them as a separate people, and they resisted her as a nation. In peace, she spoke the language of friendship, and they replied in the voice of independence, and frequently assisted her as allies, at their choice to fight her enemies in their own way and discipline, subject to the control of their own chiefs, and unaccountable to European officers and military law. Such was the connexion of this nation to Great Britain, to wit, that of friendship, and not allegiance, to the period of the Declaration of Independence by the United States, and during the Revolutionary contest, down to the treaty of peace between the United States and Great Britain, forty-six years ago, when she abandoned all hopes of conquest, and at the same time abandoned her Cherokee allies to the difficulties in which they had been involved, either to continue the war, or procure peace on the best terms they could, and close the scenes of carnage and blood, that had so long been witnessed and experienced by both parties. Peace was

---

1. **The Executive . . . State of Georgia:** In April 1829 the secretary of war, John Eaton, informed the Cherokee's principal chief, John Ross, that President Jackson would support Georgia's claim to sovereignty over the Cherokee Nation.

at last concluded at Hopewell, in '85,[2] under the administration of Washington, by "the Commissioners, Plenipotentiaries of the United States in Congress assembled"; and the Cherokees were received "into the favor and protection of the United States of America." It remains to be proved, under a view of all these circumstances, and the knowledge we have of history, how our right to self-government was affected and destroyed by the Declaration of Independence, which has never noticed the subject of Cherokee sovereignty; and the treaty of peace, in '83,[3] between Great Britain and the United States, to which the Cherokees were not a party; but maintained hostilities on their part of the treaty of Hopewell, afterwards concluded. If, as it is stated by the Hon. Secretary of War, that the Cherokees were mere tenants at will,[4] and only permitted to enjoy possession of the soil to pursue game; and if the States of North Carolina and Georgia were sovereigns in truth and in right over us; why did President Washington send "Commissioners Plenipotentiaries" to treat with the subjects of those states? Why did they permit the chiefs and warriors to enter into treaty, when, if they were subjects, they had grossly rebelled and revolted from their allegiance? And why did not those sovereigns make their lives pay the forfeit of their guilt, agreeable to the laws of said States? The answer must be plain — they were not subjects, but a distinct nation, and in that light viewed by Washington, and by all the people of the Union, at that period. In the first and second articles of the Hopewell treaty, and the third article of the Holston treaty,[5] the United States and the Cherokee nation were bound to a mutual exchange of prisoners taken during the war; which incontrovertibly proves the possession of sovereignty by *both* contracting parties. It ought to be remembered too, in the conclusions of the treaties to which we have referred, and most of the treaties subsisting between the United States and this nation, that the phraseology, composition, etc. was always written by the Commissioners, on the part of the United States, for obvious reasons: as the Cherokees were unacquainted with letters. Again, in the Holston treaty, eleventh article, the following remarkable evidence is contained that our nation is not under the jurisdiction of any State: "If any citizen or inhabitant of the United States, or of either of the territorial districts of the United States, shall go into any town, settlement, or territory, belonging to the Cherokees, and shall there commit any crime upon, or trespass against, the person or property of any peaceable and friendly Indian or Indians, which *if committed within the jurisdiction of any State, or within the jurisdiction*

---

2. **Hopewell, in '85:** The Treaty of Hopewell, signed on November 18, 1785, established a western boundary for white settlement in central Tennessee. The fact that the United States negotiated this treaty with the Cherokee served as the basis for their argument that they had been and were an independent, sovereign nation.

3. **treaty of peace, in '83:** The Treaty of Paris, signed on September 3, 1783, formally ended the Revolutionary War.

4. **tenants at will:** That is, the Cherokee were allowed to inhabit their ancestral lands only because individual states and the federal government willed, or allowed, them to do so.

5. **Holston treaty:** Signed on July 2, 1791, the Holston Treaty was a new agreement between the United States and the Cherokee that redrew the boundaries of the earlier Hopewell treaty. It also provided the federal government with the right to regulate trade with the Cherokee and gave Cherokee the right to punish or remove anyone who hunted or travelled on their lands without permission. The Treaty also affirmed the "perpetual peace and friendship between all the citizens of the United States of America, and all the individuals composing the whole Cherokee nation of Indians." As with the Hopewell Treaty, the terms of the new treaty were evidence that the Cherokee had consistently been treated as an independent nation by the U.S. government.

of either of the said districts, against a citizen or any white inhabitant thereof, would be punishable by the laws of such State or district, such offender or offenders shall be proceeded against in the same manner as if the offense had been committed *within the jurisdiction of the State or district* to which he or they may belong, against a citizen or white inhabitant thereof." The power of a State may be put under our national existence under its feet, and coerce us into her jurisdiction; but it would be contrary to legal right, and the plighted faith of the United States' Government. It is said by Georgia and the Honorable Secretary of War, that one sovereignty cannot exist within another, and, therefore, we must yield to the stronger power; but is not this doctrine favorable to our Government, which does not interfere with that of any other? Our sovereignty and right of enforcing legal enactments, extend no further than our territorial limits, and that of Georgia is, and has always terminated at, her limits. The constitution of the United States (article 6) contains these words: "All treaties made under the authority of the United States shall be the supreme law of the land, and the judges in every State shall be bound thereby, any thing in the laws or constitution of any State to the contrary notwithstanding." The sacredness of treaties, made under the authority of the United States, is paramount and supreme, stronger than the laws and constitution of any State. The jurisdiction, then, of our nation over its soil is settled by the laws, treaties, and constitution of the United States, and has been exercised from time out of memory.

Georgia has objected to the adoption, on our part, of a constitutional form of government, and which has in no way violated the intercourse and connexion which bind us to the United States, its constitution, and the treaties thereupon founded, and in existence between us. As a distinct nation, notwithstanding any unpleasant feelings it might have created to a neighboring State, we had a right to improve our Government, suitable to the moral, civil, and intellectual advancement of our people; and had we anticipated any notice of it, it was the voice of encouragement by an approving world. We would, also, while on this subject, refer your attention to the memorial and protest submitted before your honorable bodies, during the last session of Congress, by our delegation then at Washington.

Permit us, also, to make known to you the aggrieved and unpleasant situation under which we are placed by the claim which Georgia has set up to a large portion of our territory, under the treaty of the Indian Springs concluded with the late General M'Intosh and his party; and which was declared void, and of no effect, by a subsequent treaty between the Creek Nation and the United States, at Washington City.[6] The President of the United States, through the Secretary of War, assured our delegation, that, so far as he understood the Cherokees had rights, protection should be afforded; and, respecting the intrusions on our lands, he had been advised, "and instructions had been forwarded to the agent of the Cherokees, directing him to cause their removal; and earnestly

----

6. **Permit us . . . Washington City:** William McIntosh (1775–1825), the son of a Creek mother and a white father, signed the Treaty of Indian Springs on January 8, 1821. Under its terms, the Creek surrendered a large portion of their ancestral lands in Georgia and accepted relocation to lands west of the Mississippi. Considered by many Creek to be a traitor, McIntosh was assassinated. A delegation from the Creek National Council subsequently negotiated the Treaty of Washington in 1826, which did not require them to move farther west.

hoped, that, on this matter, all cause for future complaint would cease, and the order prove effectual." In consequence of the agent's neglecting to comply with the instructions, and a suspension of the order made by the Secretary afterwards, our border citizens are at this time placed under most unfortunate circumstances, by the intrusions of citizens of the United States, and which are almost daily increasing, in consequence of the suspension of the once contemplated "effectual order." Many of our people are experiencing all the evils of personal insult, and, in some instances, expulsion from their homes, and loss of property, from the unrestrained intruders let loose upon us, and the encouragement they are allowed to enjoy, under the last order to the agent for this nation, which amounts to a suspension of the force of treaties, and the wholesome operation of the intercourse laws[7] of the United States. The reason alleged by the War Department for this suspension is, that it had been requested so to do, until the claim the State of Georgia has made to a portion of the Cherokee country be determined; and the intruders are to remain unmolested within the border limits of this nation. We beg leave to protest against this unprecedented procedure. If the State of Georgia has a claim to any portion of our lands, and is entitled by law and justice to them, let her seek through a legal channel to establish it; and we do hope that the United States will not suffer her to take possession of them forcibly, and investigate her claim afterwards.

Arguments to effect the emigration of our people, and to escape the troubles and disquietude incident to a residence contiguous to the whites, have been urged upon us, and the arm of protection has been withheld, that we may experience still deeper and ampler proofs of the correctness of the doctrine; but we still adhere to what is right and agreeable to ourselves; and our attachment to the soil of our ancestors is too strong to be shaken. We have been invited to a retrospective view of the past history of Indians, who have melted away before the light of civilization, and the mountains of difficulties that have opposed our race in their advancement in civilized life. We have done so; and, while we deplore the fate of thousands of our complexion and kind, we rejoice that our nation stands and grows a lasting monument of God's mercy, and a durable contradiction to the misconceived opinion that the aborigines are incapable of civilization. The opposing mountains, that cast fearful shadows in the road of the Cherokee improvement, have dispersed into vernal clouds; and our people stand adorned with the flowers of achievement flourishing around them, and are encouraged to secure the attainment of all that is useful in science and Christian knowledge.

Under the fostering care of the United States we have thus prospered; and shall we expect approbation, or shall we sink under the displeasure and rebukes of our enemies?

We now look with earnest expectation to your honorable bodies for redress, and that our national existence may not be extinguished before a prompt and effectual interposition is afforded in our behalf. The faith of your Government is solemnly pledged for our protection against all illegal oppressions, so long as we remain firm to our treaties; and that we have, for a long series of years, proved to be true and loyal friends, the known history of past events abundantly proves. Your Chief Magistrate himself has borne

---

7. **intercourse laws:** The laws and regulations governing trade.

testimony of our devotedness in supporting the cause of the United States, during their late conflict with a foreign foe.[8] It is with reluctant and painful feelings that circumstances have at length compelled us to seek from you the promised protection, for the preservation of our rights and privileges. This resort to us is a last one, and nothing short of the threatening evils and dangers that beset us could have forced it upon the nation but it is a right we surely have, and in which we cannot be mistaken—that of appealing for care we have been led to the present degree of civilization, and the enjoyment of its consequent blessings. Having said thus much, with patience we shall await the final issue of your wise deliberations.

[1829, 1830]

---

8. **Your Chief Magistrate . . . foreign foe:** John Marshall (1755–1835) served as the chief justice of the Supreme Court from 1801 to 1835. Cherokee fought alongside Tennessee militia commanded by future president Andrew Jackson during the Creek War, sometimes considered part of the War of 1812.

David Walker

[1785–1830]

David Walker was born in North Carolina, the son of an enslaved father and a free mother. Sometime in the 1820s, he settled in Boston, where Walker opened a shop near the wharves and became increasingly

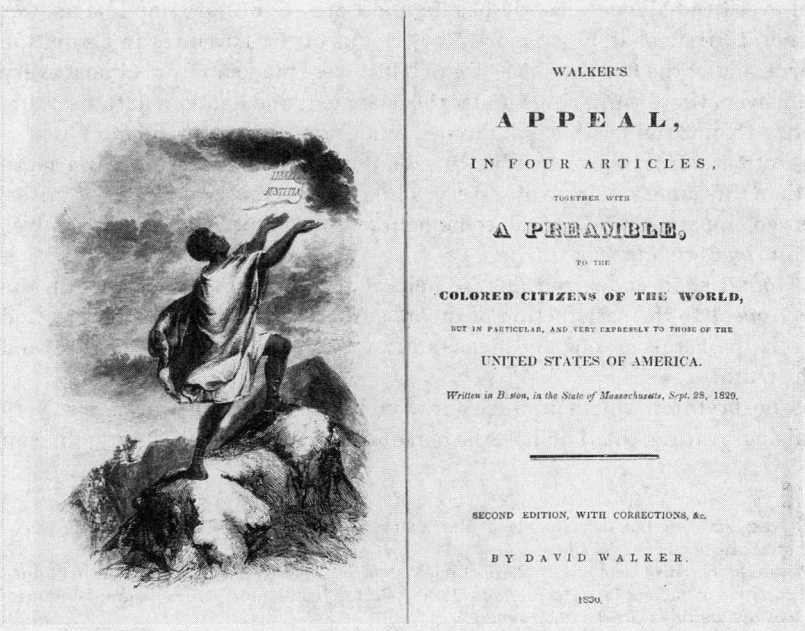

Walker's Appeal
The frontispiece of the second edition of David Walker's militant pamphlet shows an African American raising his arms to heaven, toward a banner inscribed with the words *Libertas Justitia*, Latin for "Liberty Justice."

involved in the early abolitionist movement. In addition to delivering antislavery lectures, Walker began writing articles for *Freedom's Journal*, the first African American newspaper published in the United States. Seeking to reach a larger audience, he also wrote *An Appeal to the Colored Citizens of the World*, which Walker printed at his own expense in 1829. With the help of black sailors frequenting his shop who smuggled the book into Southern ports, the *Appeal* was widely distributed, and it forever changed the antislavery movement by introducing a new urgency and militancy. The text of the following selection, the opening paragraphs of the preamble, is taken from *Walker's Appeal, in Four Articles, Together with a Preamble, to the Colored Citizens of the World, but in Particular, and Very Expressly, to Those of the United States of America* (rev. ed., 1830).

From AN APPEAL TO THE COLORED CITIZENS OF THE WORLD

My dearly beloved Brethren and Fellow Citizens.

Having travelled over a considerable portion of these United States, and having, in the course of my travels, taken the most accurate observations of things as they exist — the result of my observations has warranted the full and unshaken conviction, that we, (coloured people of these United States,) are the most degraded, wretched, and abject set of beings that ever lived since the world began; and I pray God that none like us ever may live again until time shall be no more. They tell us of the Israelites in Egypt, the Helots in Sparta, and of the Roman Slaves,[1] which last were made up from almost every nation under heaven, whose sufferings under those ancient and heathen nations, were, in comparison with ours, under this enlightened and Christian nation, no more than a cypher — or, in other words, those heathen nations of antiquity, had but little more among them than the name and form of slavery; while wretchedness and endless miseries were reserved, apparently in a phial, to be poured out upon our fathers, ourselves and our children, by *Christian* Americans!

These positions I shall endeavour, by the help of the Lord, to demonstrate in the course of this *Appeal*, to the satisfaction of the most incredulous mind — and may God Almighty, who is the Father of our Lord Jesus Christ, open your hearts to understand and believe the truth.

The *causes*, my brethren, which produce our wretchedness and miseries, are so very numerous and aggravating, that I believe the pen only of a Josephus or a Plutarch,[2] can

---

1. **Israelites . . . Slaves:** Walker refers to ancient examples of slavery, including the serfs in Sparta who were technically free but had no legal or civil rights.
2. **Josephus . . . Plutarch:** Flavius Josephus (c. 37?–100?), a Jewish priest, soldier, and historian who lived during the Roman occupation of ancient Judea (present-day Israel); Plutarch (46?–120?), Greek biographer famed for his *Parallel Lives of Illustrious Greeks and Romans*.

well enumerate and explain them. Upon subjects, then, of such incomprehensible magnitude, so impenetrable, and so notorious, I shall be obliged to omit a large class of, and content myself with giving you an exposition of a few of those, which do indeed rage to such an alarming pitch, that they cannot but be a perpetual source of terror and dismay to every reflecting mind.

I am fully aware, in making this appeal to my much afflicted and suffering brethren, that I shall not only be assailed by those whose greatest earthly desires are, to keep us in abject ignorance and wretchedness, and who are of the firm conviction that Heaven has designed us and our children to be slaves and *beasts of burden* to them and their children. I say, I do not only expect to be held up to the public as an ignorant, impudent and restless disturber of the public peace, by such avaricious creatures, as well as a mover of insubordination — and perhaps put in prison or to death, for giving a superficial exposition of our miseries, and exposing tyrants. But I am persuaded, that many of my brethren, particularly those who are ignorantly in league with slaveholders or tyrants, who acquire their daily bread by the blood and sweat of their more ignorant brethren — and not a few of those too, who are too ignorant to see an inch beyond their noses, will rise up and call me cursed — Yea, the jealous ones among us will perhaps use more abject subtlety, by affirming that this work is not worth perusing, that we are well situated, and there is no use in trying to better our condition, for we cannot. I will ask one question here. — Can our condition be any worse? — Can it be more mean and abject? If there are any changes, will they not be for the better though they may appear for the worst at first? Can they get us any lower? Where can they get us? They are afraid to treat us worse, for they know well, the day they do it they are gone. But against all accusations which may or can be preferred against me, I appeal to Heaven for my motive in writing — who knows what my object is, if possible, to awaken in the breasts of my afflicted, degraded and slumbering brethren, a spirit of inquiry and investigation respecting our miseries and wretchedness in this *Republican Land of Liberty!!!!!!*

The sources from which our miseries are derived, and on which I shall comment, I shall not combine in one, but shall put them under distinct heads and expose them in their turn; in doing which, keeping truth on my side, and not departing from the strictest rules of morality, I shall endeavour to penetrate, search out, and lay them open for your inspection. If you cannot or will not profit by them, I shall have done *my* duty to you, my country and my God.

And as the inhuman system of *slavery*, is the *source* from which most of our miseries proceed, I shall begin with that *curse to nations*, which has spread terror and devastation through so many nations of antiquity, and which is raging to such a pitch at the present day in Spain and in Portugal. It had one tug in England, in France, and in the United States of America; yet the inhabitants thereof, do not learn wisdom, and erase it entirely from their dwellings and from all with whom they have to do. The fact is, the labour of slaves comes so cheap to the avaricious usurpers, and is (as they think) of such great utility to the country where it exists, that those who are actuated by sordid avarice only, overlook the evils, which will as sure as the Lord lives, follow after the good. In fact, they are so happy to keep in ignorance and degradation, and to receive the homage and the labour of the slaves, they forget that God rules in the armies of heaven and among the inhabitants of the earth, having his ears continually open to the cries, tears and groans of his oppressed people; and being a just and holy Being will at one day appear fully in behalf of the oppressed, and arrest the progress of the avaricious oppressors; for although the destruction of the oppressors God may not effect by the oppressed, yet the Lord our God will bring other destructions upon them — for not unfrequently will he cause them to rise up one against another, to be split and divided, and to oppress each other, and sometimes to open hostilities with sword in hand. Some may ask, what is the matter with this united and happy people? — Some say it is the cause of political usurpers, tyrants, oppressors, but has not the Lord an oppressed and suffering people among them? Does the Lord condescend to hear their cries and see their tears in consequence of oppression? Will he let the oppressors rest comfortably and happy always? Will he not cause the very children of the oppressors to rise up against them, and oftimes put them to death? "God works in many ways his wonders to perform."[3]

[1829, 1830]

---

3. "God . . . perform": A paraphrase of the familiar opening lines of the hymn "Light Shining Out of Darkness" by the English poet William Cowper (1731-1800).

William Lloyd Garrison

[1805-1879]

William Lloyd Garrison

In this early portrait, the self-educated Garrison holds a copy of the anti-slavery newspaper he established and edited for more than thirty years, the *Liberator*.

William Lloyd Garrison was born in Newburyport, Massachusetts, into a poor, working-class family. At the age of thirteen, he was apprenticed to the editor of a local newspaper and became increasingly absorbed in politics. His career as an abolitionist began in 1828, when he met Benjamin Lundy (1789-1839), the editor of the *Genius of Universal Emancipation*. Lundy, a Quaker and an early pioneer in the abolition movement, established his antislavery newspaper in Mt. Pleasant, Ohio, but later moved it to Baltimore, Maryland, and then to Washington, D.C. In 1829, Garrison became Lundy's associate editor and delivered his first antislavery speech, in a Boston church. Thereafter, he lectured constantly and wrote increasingly militant antislavery articles for newspapers. With the financial support of reform-minded individuals as well as many free blacks in the North, Garrison established his own antislavery newspaper, the *Liberator*, which he edited from 1831 through 1865. The following selection "To the Public," in which Garrison outlines his antislavery position and the purpose of his newspaper, appeared in the first issue of the *Liberator*, on January 1, 1831.

TO THE PUBLIC

In the month of August, I issued proposals for publishing "THE LIBERATOR" in Washington city; but the enterprise, though hailed in different sections of the country, was palsied by public indifference. Since that time, the removal of the Genius of Universal Emancipation to the Seat of Government has rendered less imperious the establishment of a similar periodical in that quarter.

During my recent tour for the purpose of exciting the minds of the people by a series of discourses on the subject of slavery, every place that I visited gave fresh evidence of the fact, that a greater revolution in public sentiment was to be effected in the free states — *and particularly in New-England* — than at the south. I found contempt more bitter, opposition more active, detraction more relentless, prejudice more stubborn, and apathy more frozen, than among slave owners themselves. Of course, there were individual exceptions to the contrary. This state of things afflicted, but did not dishearten me. I determined, at every hazard, to lift up the standard of emancipation in the eyes of the nation, *within sight of Bunker Hill and in the birth place of liberty.* That standard is now unfurled; and long may it float, unhurt by the spoliations of time or the missiles of a desperate foe — yea, till every chain be broken, and every bondman set free! Let southern oppressors tremble — let their secret abettors tremble — let their northern apologists tremble — let all the enemies of the persecuted blacks tremble.

I deem the publication of my original Prospectus unnecessary, as it has obtained a wide circulation. The principles therein inculcated will be steadily pursued in this paper, excepting that I shall not array myself as the political partisan of any man. In defending the great cause of human rights, I wish to derive the assistance of all religions and of all parties.

Assenting to the "self-evident truth" maintained in the American Declaration of Independence, "that all men are created equal, and endowed by their Creator with certain inalienable rights — among which are life, liberty and the pursuit of happiness," I shall strenuously contend for the immediate enfranchisement of our slave population. In Parkstreet Church, on the Fourth of July, 1829, in an address on slavery, I unreflectingly assented to the popular but pernicious doctrine of gradual abolition. I seize this opportunity to make a full and unequivocal recantation, and thus publicly to ask pardon of my God, of my country, and of my brethren the poor slaves, for having uttered a sentiment so full of timidity, injustice and absurdity. A similar recantation, from my pen, was published in the Genius of Universal Emancipation at Baltimore, in September, 1829. My conscience is now satisfied.

I am aware, that many object to the severity of my language; but is there not cause for severity? I *will* be as harsh as truth, and as uncompromising as justice. On this subject, I do not wish to think, or speak, or write, with moderation. No! no! Tell a man whose house is on fire, to give a moderate alarm; tell him to moderately rescue his wife from the hand of the ravisher; tell the mother to gradually extricate her babe from the fire into which it has fallen; — but urge me not to use moderation in a cause like the present. I am in earnest — I will not equivocate — I will not excuse — I will not retreat a single inch — AND I WILL BE HEARD. The apathy of the people is enough to make every statue leap from its pedestal, and to hasten the resurrection of the dead.

It is pretended, that I am retarding the cause of emancipation by the coarseness of my invective, and the precipitancy of my measures. The *charge is not true.* On this question my influence, – humble as it is, – is felt at this moment to a considerable extent, and shall be felt in coming years – not perniciously, but beneficially – not as a curse, but as a blessing; and posterity will bear testimony that I was right. I desire to thank God, that he enables me to disregard "the fear of man which bringeth a snare," and to speak his truth in its simplicity and power. And here I close with this fresh dedication:

> Oppression! I have seen thee, face to face,
> And met thy cruel eye and cloudy brow;
> But thy soul-withering glance I fear not now –
> For dread to prouder feelings doth give place
> Of deep abhorrence! Scorning the disgrace
> Of slavish knees that at thy footstool bow,
> I also kneel – but with far other vow
> Do hail thee and thy hord of hirelings base: –
> I swear, while life-blood warms my throbbing veins,
> Still to oppose and thwart, with heart and hand,
> Thy brutalising sway – till Afric's chains
> Are burst, and Freedom rules the rescued land, –
> Trampling Oppression and his iron rod:
> *Such is the vow I take* – SO HELP ME GOD![1]

[1831]

------

1. **Oppression!** . . . SO HELP ME GOD!: A sonnet by the Scottish poet Thomas Pringle (1789-1834), the Secretary of Britain's Society for the Abolition of Slavery.

Orestes A. Brownson

[1803-1876]

Born in Stockbridge, Vermont, Orestes Augustus Brownson was raised as a Congregationalist and remained deeply religious. Turning first to Presbyterianism, he later became a Unitarian minister and an important figure in the early period of the transcendentalist movement. Increasingly uncomfortable with many Protestant tenets, Brownson converted to Roman Catholicism in 1844, after which he rejected many of his earlier associations and beliefs. During the previous decade, however, he was one of the most radical religious and social critics among the transcendentalists. From 1838 to 1842, Brownson edited the *Boston Quarterly Review.* Of all of the extended essays and reviews he wrote for the journal, none was as controversial as "The Laboring Classes," which created a furor when it was published in 1840. Indeed, in it Brownson offered an early analysis of capitalism and the class system that anticipated the work of the German socialist Karl Marx (1818-1883). The text of the following selection is

New England Textile Mill

The first factory workforce in the United States was primarily made up of
daughters from New England farm families who were recruited to work in textile
mills like those in Lowell, Massachusetts. The young women in this factory, with
their male supervisor sitting on the right, paused from their work—roughly twelve
hours a day, six days a week—to pose for this daguerreotype, made around 1850.
(Courtesy George Eastman House.)

taken from *The Laboring Classes, An Article from the* Boston Quarterly
Review, which was published as a pamphlet in 1840.

From THE LABORING CLASSES

In regard to labor two systems obtain; one that of slave labor, the other that of free labor.
Of the two, the first is, in our judgement, except so far as the feelings are concerned,
decidedly the least oppressive. If the slave has never been a free man, we think, as a general rule, his sufferings are less than those of the free laborer at wages. As to actual
freedom one has just about as much as the other. The laborer at wages has all the disadvantages of freedom and none of its blessings, while the slave, if denied the blessings, is
freed from the disadvantages. We are no advocates of slavery, we are as heartily opposed
to it as any modern abolitionist can be; but we say frankly that, if there must always be a
laboring population distinct from proprietors and employers, we regard the slave system as decidedly preferable to the system at wages. It is no pleasant thing to go days
without food, to lie idle for weeks, seeking work and finding none, to rise in the morning
with a wife and children you love, and know not where to procure them a breakfast, and
to see constantly before you no brighter prospect than the almshouse. Yet these are no
unfrequent incidents in the lives of our laboring population. Even in seasons of general

prosperity, when there was only the ordinary cry of "hard times," we have seen hundreds of people in a not very populous village, in a wealthy portion of our common country, suffering for the want of the necessaries of life, willing to work, and yet finding no work to do. Many and many is the application of a poor man for work, merely for his food, we have seen rejected. These things are little thought of, for the applicants are poor; they fill no conspicuous place in society, and they have no biographers. But their wrongs are chronicled in heaven. It is said there is no want in this country. There may be less than in some other countries. But death by actual starvation in this country is we apprehend no uncommon occurrence. The sufferings of a quiet, unassuming but useful class of females in our cities, in general sempstresses, too proud to beg or to apply to the alms-house, are not easily told. They are industrious; they do all that they can find to do; but yet the little there is for them to do, and the miserable pittance they receive for it, is hardly sufficient to keep soul and body together. And yet there is a man who employs them to make shirts, trousers, &c., and grows rich on their labors. He is one of our respectable citizens, perhaps is praised in the newspapers for his liberal donations to some charitable institution. He passes among us as a pattern of morality, and is honored as a worthy Christian. And why should he not be, since our *Christian* community is made up of such as he, and since our clergy would not dare question his piety, lest they should incur the reproach of infidelity, and lose their standing, and their salaries? Nay, since our clergy are raised up, educated, fashioned, and sustained by such as he? Not a few of our churches rest on Mammon[1] for their foundation. The basement is a trader's shop.

We pass through our manufacturing villages; most of them appear neat and flourishing. The operatives are well dressed, and we are told, well paid. They are said to be healthy, contented, and happy. This is the fair side of the picture; the side exhibited to distinguished visitors. There is a dark side, moral as well as physical. Of the common operatives, few, if any, by their wages, acquire a competence. A few of what Carlyle[2] terms not inaptly the *body-servants* are well paid, and now and then an agent or an over-seer rides in his coach. But the great mass wear out their health, spirits, and morals, without becoming one whit better off than when they commenced labor. The bills of mortality in these factory villages are not striking, we admit, for the poor girls when they can toil no longer go home to die. The average life, working life we mean, of the girls that come to Lowell,[3] for instance, from Maine, New Hampshire, and Vermont, we have been assured, is only about three years. What becomes of them then? Few of them

---

1. **Mammon:** Wealth or material gain, often personified as a deity. See Matthew 6:24: "No man can serve two masters: for either he will hate the one, and love the other; or else he will hold to the one, and despise the other. Ye cannot serve God and mammon."

2. **Carlyle:** Brownson's article was a review of *Chartism* (1839), by the British historian and social critic Thomas Carlyle (1795-1881). Carlyle argued that the working class was worse off in England than elsewhere in Europe because of the rise of the manufacturing system that exploited and oppressed laborers.

3. **Lowell:** The Boott Cotton Mills began to operate in Lowell, Massachusetts, in the 1830s. Factory "girls" who worked in the mills lived in adjacent housing.

ever marry; fewer still ever return to their native places with reputations unimpaired. "She has worked in a Factory," is almost enough to damn to infamy the most worthy and virtuous girl. We know no sadder sight on earth than one of our factory villages presents, when the bell at break of day, or at the hour of breakfast, or dinner, calls out its hundreds or thousands of operatives. We stand and look at these hard working men and women hurrying in all directions, and ask ourselves, where go the proceeds of their labors? The man who employs them, and for whom they are toiling as so many slaves, is one of our city nabobs,[4] revelling in luxury; or he is a member of our legislature, enacting laws to put money in his own pocket; or he is a member of Congress, contending for a high Tariff to tax the poor for the benefit of the rich; or in these times he is shedding crocodile tears over the deplorable condition of the poor laborer, while he docks his wages twenty-five per cent; building miniature log cabins, shouting Harrison and "hard cider."[5] And this man too would fain pass for a Christian and a republican. He shouts for liberty, stickles for equality, and is horrified at a Southern planter who keeps slaves.

One thing is certain; that of the amount actually produced by the operative, he retains a less proportion than it costs the master to feed, clothe, and lodge his slave. Wages is a cunning device of the devil, for the benefit of tender consciences, who would retain all the advantages of the slave system, without the expense, trouble, and odium of being slave-holders.

[1840]

---

4. **nabobs:** Nabob, originally the term for a governor in India under the Mogul Empire, came to stand for any person of great wealth or prominence.
5. **Harrison and "hard cider":** In the presidential campaign of 1840, William Henry Harrison's campaign staff offered free hard cider (the most popular alcoholic beverage in nineteenth-century America) to supporters of the Whig ticket of Harrison and John Tyler.

Seneca Falls Woman's Convention

[July 19-20, 1848]

On July 19-20, 1848, the first women's rights convention was held at Seneca Falls, New York. Attended by one hundred people on the first day and three hundred on the second, the convention marked the beginning of a seventy-year campaign that ended when women were finally accorded the right to vote by the ratification of the Nineteenth Amendment to the Constitution in 1920. The Seneca Falls Woman's Convention was the idea of Elizabeth Cady Stanton—an abolitionist and feminist who had moved with her husband and their children from Boston to Seneca Falls—and her close friend from Philadelphia, the Quaker reformer Lucretia Mott. Stanton, who drafted the "Declaration of Sentiments," modeled it on the

Declaration of Independence. She read the "Declaration of Sentiments" on the first day of the convention and led a section-by-section debate, finally winning approval at the end of the day, when it was signed by sixty-eight women and thirty-two men, including Frederick Douglass. But their radical demand for women's full equality generated such controversy and derision that some of those who supported the "Declaration of Sentiments" later withdrew their signatures. The following text is taken from *History of Woman Suffrage* (1881), edited by Elizabeth Cady Stanton, Susan B. Anthony, and Matilda Joslyn Gage.

DECLARATION OF SENTIMENTS

When, in the course of human events it becomes necessary for one portion of the family of man to assume among the people of the earth a position different from that which they have hitherto occupied, but one to which the laws of nature and of nature's God entitle them, a decent respect to the opinions of mankind requires that they should declare the causes that impel them to such a course.

We hold these truths to be self-evident: that all men and women are created equal; that they are endowed by their Creator with certain inalienable rights; that among these are life, liberty, and the pursuit of happiness; that to secure these rights governments are instituted, deriving their just powers from the consent of the governed. Whenever any form of government becomes destructive of these ends, it is the right of those who suffer from it to refuse allegiance to it, and to insist upon the institution of a new government, laying its foundation on such principles, and organizing its powers in such form, as to them shall seem most likely to effect their safety and happiness. Prudence indeed, will dictate that governments long established should not be changed for light and transient causes; and accordingly all experience hath shown that mankind are more disposed to suffer, while evils are sufferable, than to right themselves by abolishing the forms to which they were accustomed. But when a long train of abuses and usurpations, pursuing invariably the same object evinces a design to reduce them under absolute despotism, it is their duty to throw off such government, and to provide new guards for their future security. Such has been the patient sufferance of the women under this government, and such is now the necessity which constrains them to demand the equal station to which they are entitled.

The history of mankind is a history of repeated injuries and usurpations on the part of man toward woman, having in direct object the establishment of an absolute tyranny over her. To prove this, let facts be submitted to a candid world.

He has never permitted her to exercise her inalienable right to the elective franchise.

He has compelled her to submit to laws, in the formation of which she had no voice.

He has withheld from her rights which are given to the most ignorant and degraded men — both natives and foreigners.

Yᴱ MAY SESSION OF Yᴱ WOMAN'S RIGHTS CONVENTION—Yᴱ ORATOR OF Yᴱ DAY DENOUNCING Yᴱ LORDS OF CREATION.

A Satirical Depiction of a Woman's Rights Convention

Printed in *Harper's Weekly* in 1859, this caricature reveals that feminists were often treated with derision or hostility, especially in the popular press. Their meetings were also frequently disrupted by hecklers, like the jeering men crowded into the balconies of this hall. Despite such strong resistance, the movement gained the support of some men and a growing number of women, who as this illustration also reveals were the primary organizers of and speakers at the numerous meetings and conventions held in the wake of the 1848 convention at Seneca Falls.

Having deprived her of this first right of a citizen, the elective franchise, thereby leaving her without representation in the halls of legislation, he has oppressed her on all sides.

He has made her, if married, in the eye of the law, civilly dead.

He has taken from her all right in property, even to the wages she earns.

He has made her, morally, an irresponsible being, as she can commit many crimes with impunity, provided they be done in the presence of her husband. In the covenant of marriage, she is compelled to promise obedience to her husband, he becoming, to all intents and purposes, her master — the law giving him power to deprive her of her liberty, and to administer chastisement.

He has so framed the laws of divorce, as to what shall be the proper causes, and in case of separation, to whom the guardianship of the children shall be given, as to be wholly regardless of the happiness of women — the law, in all cases, going upon a false supposition of the supremacy of man, and giving all power into his hands.

After depriving her of all rights as a married woman, if single, and the owner of property, he has taxed her to support a government which recognizes her only when her property can be made profitable to it.

He has monopolized nearly all the profitable employments, and from those she is permitted to follow, she receives but a scanty remuneration. He closes against her all the avenues to wealth and distinction which he considers most honorable to himself. As a teacher of theology, medicine, or law, she is not known.

He has denied her the facilities for obtaining a thorough education, all colleges being closed against her.

He allows her in Church, as well as State, but a subordinate position, claiming Apostolic authority for her exclusion from the ministry, and, with some exceptions, from any public participation in the affairs of the Church.

He has created a false public sentiment by giving to the world a different code of morals for men and women, by which moral delinquencies which exclude women from society, are not only tolerated, but deemed of little account in man.

He has usurped the prerogative of Jehovah himself, claiming it as his right to assign for her a sphere of action, when that belongs to her conscience and to her God.

He has endeavored, in every way that he could, to destroy her confidence in her own powers, to lessen her self-respect, and to make her willing to lead a dependent and abject life.

Now, in view of this entire disfranchisement of one-half the people of this country, their social and religious degradation — in view of the unjust laws above mentioned, and because women do feel themselves aggrieved, oppressed, and fraudulently deprived of their most sacred rights, we insist that they have immediate admission to all the rights and privileges which belong to them as citizens of the United States.

In entering upon the great work before us, we anticipate no small amount of misconception, misrepresentation, and ridicule; but we shall use every instrumentality within our power to effect our object. We shall employ agents, circulate tracts, petition the State and National legislatures, and endeavor to enlist the pulpit and the press in our behalf. We hope this Convention will be followed by a series of Conventions embracing every part of the country.

[1848, 1881]

Sojourner Truth

[1797–1883]

Sojourner Truth, born into slavery in New York, was emancipated in 1827. Illiterate throughout her remarkable life, Truth was an ardent Christian and abolitionist. She was among the first black women to speak publicly in the United States. To a friend, Truth dictated the story of her life, which was published as *The Narrative of Sojourner Truth* in 1850. Truth sold the slim book to audiences wherever her itinerant lecturing and preaching took her. The following extemporaneous address, one of her most characteristic and famous speeches, was delivered at a women's rights convention in Akron, Ohio. The text is taken from the report of her speech in *The Anti-Slavery Bugle*, June 21, 1851.

I SELL THE SHADOW TO SUPPORT THE SUBSTANCE.
SOJOURNER TRUTH.

Sojourner Truth

A former slave in New York State, Sojourner Truth published a narrative of her life in 1850. In her bag, she often carried copies of the book to sell at her lectures. She apparently also sold visiting cards like this one, which bears the inscription: "I SELL THE SHADOW TO SUPPORT THE SUBSTANCE."

SPEECH TO A WOMEN'S RIGHTS CONVENTION

One of the most unique and interesting speeches of the Convention was made by Sojourner Truth, an emancipated slave. It is impossible to transfer it to paper, or convey any adequate idea of the effect it produced upon the audience. Those only can appreciate it who saw her powerful form, her whole-souled earnest gestures, and listened to her strong and truthful tones. She came forward to the platform and addressing the President said with great simplicity:

May I say a few words? Receiving an affirmative answer, she proceeded; I want to say a few words about this matter. I am a woman's rights. I have as much muscle as any man, and can do as much work as any man. I have plowed and reaped and husked and chopped and mowed, and can any man do more than that? I have heard much about the sexes being equal; I can carry as much as any man, and can eat as much too, if I can get it. I am as strong as any man that is now. As for intellect, all I can say is, if woman have a pint and man a quart — why can't she have her little pint full? You need not be afraid to give us our rights for fear we will take too much, — for we can't take more than our pint'll hold. The poor men seem to be all in confusion, and don't know what to do. Why children, if you have woman's rights give it to her and you will feel better. You will have your own rights, and they won't be so much trouble. I can't read, but I can hear. I have heard the bible and have learned that Eve caused man to sin. Well if woman upset the world, do give her a chance to set it right side up again. The Lady has spoken about Jesus, how he never spurned woman from him, and she was right. When Lazarus died, Mary and Martha came to him with faith and love and besought him to raise their brother. And Jesus wept — and Lazarus came forth.[1] And how came Jesus into the world? Through God who created him and woman who bore him. Man, where is your part? But the women are coming up blessed be God and a few of the men are coming up with them. But man is in a tight place, the poor slave is on him, woman is coming on him, and he is surely between a hawk and a buzzard.

[1851]

---

1. **Lazarus came forth:** Two sisters, Mary and Martha, asked Jesus to raise their brother, Lazarus, from the dead. The account of the miracle is in John 1:1-44.

William Apess

[1798-1839]

William Apess was born in Colrain, Massachusetts. According to his account in *A Son of the Forest* (1829), the first full-length autobiography published by a Native American, his paternal grandfather was a white man who married the granddaughter of King Philip, the Wampanoag tribal leader who in the seventeenth century led a losing battle against the English settlers during King Philip's War. Apess's father married an Indian woman after joining the remnants of the once-powerful Pequot tribe, which by the end of the eighteenth century was greatly diminished by disease, warfare, and ill-treatment at the hands of the English settlers and then of the government of the United States. When Apess was very young, about four, his parents separated. He was then sent to live briefly with his maternal grandparents, whom he remembered as frequently intoxicated and abusive. At about the age of five, he was put to work as an indentured servant with a series of white families. At fourteen, he escaped, joined the army, and fought in the War of 1812.

Mr. WILLIAM APES,
A NATIVE MISSIONARY OF THE PEQUOT TRIBE
OF INDIANS.

Although Apess was not raised in his native Pequot culture, he was deeply interested in the history and rights of Native Americans. An ardent Christian, he became a Methodist minister and in 1833 went to preach at Mashpee, Massachusetts, the only Indian settlement remaining in that state. There, he became involved in the settlement's struggle to retain its independence, which Apess vigorously supported in his book *Indian Nullification of the Unconstitutional Laws of Massachusetts, Relative to the Marshpee* [sic] *Tribe* (1835). Although the book was not published until after the state legislature granted the tribe's right to self-government, Apess's efforts were influential in helping the Indians to assert their rights and retain their autonomy. At a time when the Native American presence was being all but erased from the official history of the country, Apess also exhorted his white audiences to confront the brutal narrative of the conquest and displacement of the Indians by the European settlers of North America. That tragic history was the central theme of his final work, *Eulogy on King Philip*, a lecture Apess read and published in Boston in 1836. Little is known of the remaining years of his life, which ended in 1839, when he died in New York City.

bedfordstmartins.com/
americanlit *for research*
links on Apess

Reading Apess's "An Indian's Looking-Glass for the White Man." *The Experiences of Five Christian Indians of the Pequo'd Tribe* (1833), Apess's second book, is a collection of the accounts of five Pequot who were converted to Christianity. Although not much is known about the composition of the book, one of the narratives was written by his wife and another by his aunt. The first and final chapters were written and signed by Apess. In the first chapter, Apess describes his early life and conversion to Christianity. In the final chapter, reprinted here, Apess's training as a minister and preacher is evident, as he adopts a firmly Christian perspective to develop a sustained critique of the pervasive race prejudice of the period. The following text is from *On Our Own Ground: The Complete Writings of William Apess, a Pequot*, edited by Barry O'Connell (1992).

AN INDIAN'S LOOKING-GLASS
FOR THE WHITE MAN

Having a desire to place a few things before my fellow creatures who are traveling with me to the grave, and to that God who is the maker and preserver both of the white man and the Indian, whose abilities are the same and who are to be judged by one God, who will show no favor to outward appearances but will judge righteousness. Now I ask if degradation has not been heaped long enough upon the Indians? And if so, can there not be a compromise? Is it right to hold and promote prejudices? If not, why not put them all away? I mean here, among those who are civilized. It may be that many are ignorant of the situation of many of my brethren within the limits of New England. Let me for a few moments turn your attention to the reservations in the different states of New England, and, with but few exceptions, we shall find them as follows: the most mean, abject, miserable race of beings in the world—a complete place of prodigality and prostitution.

Let a gentleman and lady of integrity and respectability visit these places, and they would be surprised; as they wandered from one hut to the other they would view, with the females who are left alone, children half-starved and some almost as naked as they came into the world. And it is a fact that I have seen them as much so—while the females are left without protection, and are seduced by white men, and are finally left to be common prostitutes for them and to be destroyed by that burning, fiery curse, that has swept millions, both of red and white men, into the grave with sorrow and disgrace—rum. One reason why they are left so is because their most sensible and active men are absent at sea. Another reason is because they are made to believe they are minors and have not the abilities given them from God to take care of themselves, without it is to see to a few little articles, such as baskets and brooms. Their land is in common stock, and they have nothing to make them enterprising.

Another reason is because those men who are Agents,[1] many of them are unfaithful and care not whether the Indians live or die; they are much imposed upon by their

---

1. **Agents:** The commonwealth of Massachusetts had appointed agents to oversee the Indians of Mashpee, thus denying them the right to self-government.

neighbors, who have no principle. They would think it no crime to go upon Indian lands and cut and carry off their most valuable timber, or anything else they chose; and I doubt not but they think it clear gain. Another reason is because they have no education to take care of themselves; if they had, I would risk them to take care of their own property.

Now I will ask if the Indians are not called the most ingenious people among us. And are they not said to be men of talents? And I would ask: Could there be a more efficient way to distress and murder them by inches than the way they have taken? And there is no people in the world but who may be destroyed in the same way. Now, if these people are what they are held up in our view to be, I would take the liberty to ask why they are not brought forward and pains taken to educate them, to give them all a common education, and those of the brightest and first-rate talents put forward and held up to office. Perhaps some unholy, unprincipled men would cry out, "The skin was not good enough"; but stop, friends — I am not talking about the skin but about principles. I would ask if there cannot be as good feelings and principles under a red skin as there can be under a white. And let me ask: Is it not on the account of a bad principle that we who are red children have had to suffer so much as we have? And let me ask: Did not this bad principle proceed from the whites or their forefathers? And I would ask: Is it worthwhile to nourish it any longer? If not, then let us have a change, although some men no doubt will spout their corrupt principles against it, that are in the halls of legislation and elsewhere. But I presume this kind of talk will seem surprising and horrible. I do not see why it should so long as they (the whites) say that they think as much of us as they do of themselves.

This I have heard repeatedly, from the most respectable gentlemen and ladies — and having heard so much precept, I should now wish to see the example. And I would ask who has a better right to look for these things than the naturalist himself — the candid man would say none.

I know that many say that they are willing, perhaps the majority of the people, that we should enjoy our rights and privileges as they do. If so, I would ask, Why are not we protected in our persons and property throughout the Union? Is it not because there reigns in the breast of many who are leaders a most unrighteous, unbecoming, and impure black principle, and as corrupt and unholy as it can be — while these very same unfeeling, self-esteemed characters pretend to take the skin as a pretext to keep us from our unalienable and lawful rights? I would ask you if you would like to be disfranchised from all your rights, merely because your skin is white, and for no other crime. I'll venture to say, these very characters who hold the skin to be such a barrier in the way would be the first to cry out, "Injustice! awful injustice!"

But, reader, I acknowledge that this is a confused world, and I am not seeking for office, but merely placing before you the black inconsistency that you place before me — which is ten times blacker than any skin that you will find in the universe. And now let me exhort you to do away that principle, as it appears ten times worse in the sight of God and candid men than skins of color — more disgraceful than all the skins that Jehovah ever made. If black or red skins or any other skin of color is disgraceful to God, it appears that he has disgraced himself a great deal — for he has made fifteen colored people to one white and placed them here upon this earth.

Now let me ask you, white man, if it is a disgrace for to eat, drink, and sleep with the image of God, or sit, or walk and talk with them. Or have you the folly to think that the white man, being one in fifteen or sixteen, are the only beloved images of God? Assemble all nations together in your imagination, and then let the whites be seated among them, and then let us look for the whites, and I doubt not it would be hard finding them; for to the rest of the nations, they are still but a handful. Now suppose these skins were put together, and each skin had its national crimes written upon it — which skin do you think would have the greatest? I will ask one question more. Can you charge the Indians with robbing a nation almost of their whole continent, and murdering their women and children, and then depriving the remainder of their lawful rights, that nature and God require them to have? And to cap the climax, rob another nation to till their grounds and welter out their days under the lash with hunger and fatigue under the scorching rays of a burning sun? I should look at all the skins, and I know that when I cast my eye upon that white skin, and if I saw those crimes written upon it, I should enter my protest against it immediately and cleave to that which is more honorable. And I can tell you that I am satisfied with the manner of my creation, fully — whether others are or not.

But we will strive to penetrate more fully into the conduct of those who profess to have pure principles and who tell us to follow Jesus Christ and imitate him and have his Spirit. Let us see if they come anywhere near him and his ancient disciples. The first thing we are to look at are his precepts, of which we will mention a few. "Thou shalt love the Lord thy God with all thy heart, with all thy soul, with all thy mind, and with all thy strength. The second is like unto it. Thou shalt love thy neighbor as thyself. On these two precepts hang all the law and the prophets" (Matthew 22:37, 38, 39, 40). "By this shall all men know that they are my disciples, if ye have love one to another" (John 13:35). Our Lord left this special command with his followers, that they should love one another.

Again, John in his Epistles says, "He who loveth God loveth his brother also" (1 John 4:21). "Let us not love in word but in deed" (1 John 3:18). "Let your love be without dissimulation. See that ye love one another with a pure heart fervently" (1 Peter 1:22). "If any man say, I love God, and hateth his brother, he is a liar" (1 John 4:20). "Whosoever hateth his brother is a murderer, and no murderer hath eternal life abiding in him" [1 John 3:15]. The first thing that takes our attention is the saying of Jesus, "Thou shalt love," etc. The first question I would ask my brethren in the ministry, as well as that of the membership: What is love, or its effects? Now, if they who teach are not essentially affected with pure love, the love of God, how can they teach as they ought? Again, the holy teachers of old said, "Now if any man have not the spirit of Christ, he is none of his" (Romans 8:9). Now, my brethren in the ministry, let me ask you a few sincere questions. Did you ever hear or read of Christ teaching his disciples that they ought to despise one because his skin was different from theirs? Jesus Christ being a Jew, and those of his Apostles certainly were not whites — and did not he who completed the plan of salvation complete it for the whites as well as for the Jews, and others? And were not the whites the most degraded people on the earth at that time? And none were more so, for they sacrificed their children to dumb idols! And did not St. Paul labor more abundantly for building up a Christian nation among you than any of the Apostles? And you know as well as I that you are not indebted to a principle beneath a white skin for your religious services but to a colored one.

What then is the matter now? Is not religion the same now under a colored skin as it ever was? If so, I would ask, why is not a man of color respected? You may say, as many say, we have white men enough. But was this the spirit of Christ and his Apostles? If it had been, there would not have been one white preacher in the world — for Jesus Christ never would have imparted his grace or word to them, for he could forever have withheld it from them. But we find that Jesus Christ and his Apostles never looked at the outward appearances. Jesus in particular looked at the hearts, and his Apostles through him, being discerners of the spirit, looked at their fruit without any regard to the skin, color, or nation; as St. Paul himself speaks, "Where there is neither Greek nor Jew, circumcision nor uncircumcision, Barbarian nor Scythian, bond nor free — but Christ is all, and in all" [Colossians 3:11]. If you can find a spirit like Jesus Christ and his Apostles prevailing now in any of the white congregations, I should like to know it. I ask: Is it not the case that everybody that is not white is treated with contempt and counted as barbarians? And I ask if the word of God justifies the white man in so doing. When the prophets prophesied, of whom did they speak? When they spoke of heathens, was it not the whites and others who were counted Gentiles? And I ask if all nations with the exception of the Jews were not counted heathens. And according to the writings of some, it could not mean the Indians, for they are counted Jews.[2] And now I would ask: Why is all this distinction made among these Christian societies? I would ask: What is all this ado about missionary societies, if it be not to Christianize those who are not Christians? And what is it for? To degrade them worse, to bring them into society where they must welter out their days in disgrace merely because their skin is of a different complexion. What folly it is to try to make the state of human society worse than it is. How astonished some may be at this — but let me ask: Is it not so? Let me refer you to the churches only. And, my brethren, is there any agreement? Do brethren and sisters love one another? Do they not rather hate one another? Outward forms and ceremonies, the lusts of the flesh, the lusts of the eye, and pride of life is of more value to many professors than the love of God shed abroad in their hearts, or an attachment to his altar, to his ordinances, or to his children. But you may ask: Who are the children of God? Perhaps you may say, none but white. If so, the word of the Lord is not true.

I will refer you to St. Peter's precepts (Acts 10): "God is no respecter of persons," etc. Now if this is the case, my white brother, what better are you than God? And if no better, why do you, who profess his Gospel and to have his spirit, act so contrary to it? Let me ask why the men of a different skin are so despised. Why are not they educated and placed in your pulpits? I ask if his services well performed are not as good as if a white man performed them. I ask if a marriage or a funeral ceremony or the ordinance of the Lord's house would not be as acceptable in the sight of God as though he was white. And

---

2. **counted Jews:** Apess refers to several prevalent racial theories of the nineteenth century, among them the idea that Native Americans were descended from the ancient tribes of Israel.

if so, why is it not to you? I ask again: Why is it not as acceptable to have men to exercise their office in one place as well as in another? Perhaps you will say that if we admit you to all of these privileges you will want more. I expect that I can guess what that is — Why, say you, there would be intermarriages. How that would be I am not able to say — and if it should be, it would be nothing strange or new to me; for I can assure you that I know a great many that have intermarried, both of the whites and the Indians — and many are their sons and daughters and people, too, of the first respectability. And I could point to some in the famous city of Boston and elsewhere. You may look now at the disgraceful act in the statute law passed by the legislature of Massachusetts, and behold the fifty-pound fine levied upon any clergyman or justice of the peace that dare to encourage the laws of God and nature by a legitimate union in holy wedlock between the Indians and whites. I would ask how this looks to your lawmakers. I would ask if this corresponds with your sayings — that you think as much of the Indians as you do of the whites. I do not wonder that you blush, many of you, while you read; for many have broken the ill-fated laws made by man to hedge up the laws of God and nature. I would ask if they who have made the law have not broken it — but there is no other state in New England that has this law but Massachusetts; and I think, as many of you do not, that you have done yourselves no credit.

But as I am not looking for a wife, having one of the finest cast, as you no doubt would understand while you read her experience and travail of soul in the way to heaven, you will see that it is not my object. And if I had none, I should not want anyone to take my right from me and choose a wife for me; for I think that I or any of my brethren have a right to choose a wife for themselves as well as the whites — and as the whites have taken the liberty to choose my brethren, the Indians, hundreds and thousands of them, as partners in life, I believe the Indians have as much right to choose their partners among the whites if they wish. I would ask you if you can see anything inconsistent in your conduct and talk about the Indians. And if you do, I hope you will try to become more consistent. Now, if the Lord Jesus Christ, who is counted by all to be a Jew — and it is well known that the Jews are a colored people,[3] especially those living in the East, where Christ was born — and if he should appear among us, would he not be shut out of doors by many, very quickly? And by those too who profess religion?

By what you read, you may learn how deep your principles are. I should say they were skin-deep. I should not wonder if some of the most selfish and ignorant would spout a charge of their principles now and then at me. But I would ask: How are you to love your neighbors as yourself? Is it to cheat them? Is it to wrong them in anything? Now, to cheat them out of any of their rights is robbery. And I ask: Can you deny that you are not robbing the Indians daily, and many others? But at last you may think I am what is called a hard and uncharitable man. But not so. I believe there are many who would not hesitate to advocate our cause; and those too who are men of fame and respectability — as well as

---

3. **colored people:** Another common nineteenth-century idea was that the ancient Hebrews were people of color.

ladies of honor and virtue. There is a Webster, an Everett, and a Wirt,[4] and many others who are distinguished characters – besides a host of my fellow citizens, who advocate our cause daily. And how I congratulate such noble spirits – how they are to be prized and valued; for they are well calculated to promote the happiness of mankind. They well know that man was made for society, and not for hissing-stocks[5] and outcasts. And when such a principle as this lies within the hearts of men, how much it is like its God – and how it honors its Maker – and how it imitates the feelings of the Good Samaritan, that had his wounds bound up, who had been among thieves and robbers.

Do not get tired, ye noble-hearted – only think how many poor Indians want their wounds done up daily; the Lord will reward you, and pray you stop not till this tree of distinction shall be leveled to the earth, and the mantle of prejudice torn from every American heart – then shall peace pervade the Union.

[1833, 1992]

---

4. **a Webster, an Everett, and a Wirt:** Daniel Webster (1782–1852), a famous orator and senator from Massachusetts; Edward Everett (1794–1865), a professor of Greek at Harvard and a governor of Massachusetts; and William Wirt (1772–1834), a lawyer and politician who was once nominated for president of the United States.
5. **hissing-stocks:** An early term for *laughing-stocks*, persons subjected to mockery or ridicule.

Ralph Waldo Emerson

[1803-1882]

Ralph Waldo Emerson was born in Boston, Massachusetts, on May 25, 1803. For generations, the men in the Emerson family had served as clergymen, and his father was the pastor of the First Church of Boston. When he died in 1811, the family was nearly destitute, but Emerson's mother was determined that her sons would be educated. At the age of fourteen, Emerson enrolled in Harvard College. An undistinguished student, he graduated in 1821 and taught at a school for young women until 1825. He then entered Harvard Divinity School and was ordained as a minister in 1829. Soon after that, he became the pastor of the prominent Second Church of Boston. With such a background, and with his gift for preaching, a distinguished clerical career seemed the likely path for Emerson. But his religious convictions were deeply influenced by works of German philosophy and theology, which were becoming available to American readers in translations and filtered through English writers like Samuel Taylor Coleridge. Inspired by such Romantic idealism, Emerson increasingly came to value the moral instincts of the individual over the tenets of organized religion. His skepticism about orthodox Christianity grew, and in 1832 he resigned from his position at Second Church.

Ralph Waldo Emerson

This daguerreotype, made in 1857, shows Emerson in the formal clothing he customarily wore for lectures, a primary source of his income and the source material for nearly all of the books he published between 1840 and 1870.

Emerson then embarked on an extended tour of Europe, determined to chart a new course for his life. While there, he met a number of well-known English writers, including Coleridge, William Wordsworth, and most importantly, Thomas Carlyle, with whom he would enjoy a lifelong correspondence. When Emerson returned to the United States in 1834, he settled in Concord, Massachusetts. Unlike many of his contemporaries who had to balance the need to earn a living with their intellectual pursuits, Emerson had an independent income. In 1829, the year of his ordination, he had married Ellen Tucker, a young woman from an affluent family in New Hampshire. The shock of her death from tuberculosis sixteen months later probably contributed to Emerson's decision to leave the ministry. The settlement of her estate also left him with a legacy of $1,200 per year — at that time an income sufficient for a comfortable, though not a lavish, lifestyle. Although he apparently never got over the death of his first wife, in 1835 Emerson married Lydia Jackson, an accomplished and by all accounts remarkable person with whom he shared religious convictions, as well as a wide range of literary and philosophical interests. The couple settled into "Coolidge House," a comfortable home Emerson purchased on the outskirts of Concord. By then, all of the elements were in place for the independent scholarly life Emerson had in mind for himself. That life included reading and study, occasional preaching, and especially writing — daily entries in the journals and notebooks he would keep throughout his life; letters to an increasingly large number of correspondents in the United States and Europe; and his first book, *Nature* (1836).

Although it was published anonymously, the author of that little book was an open secret, and Emerson soon found himself at the center of a small circle of intellectuals who met regularly in Boston or Concord. Called the transcendentalists because of their embrace of idealistic or "transcendental" philosophy, the group was initially composed of Unitarian ministers but ultimately came to include writers as diverse as Emerson's friends Henry David Thoreau and Margaret Fuller. It was not, however, the publication of his first book that gained Emerson prominence. Two lectures, both delivered at Harvard, marked the beginning of his engagement with a larger audience: "The American Scholar" (1837), which Oliver Wendell Holmes called an "intellectual Declaration of Independence"; and his address to the Harvard Divinity School in 1838. That address, in which Emerson vigorously exposed what he viewed as the defects in orthodox Christianity and in the training of Unitarian ministers, generated a furious controversy in Boston. In fact, some of the conservative Unitarian clergy were so outraged, that Emerson was not invited back to speak at Harvard for thirty years. But he continued to preach occasionally, and Emerson also began to exploit a new form of communicating with audiences, both in and far beyond the confines of Boston. "A lecture is a new literature," he buoyantly observed in his journal in 1839, "which leaves aside all tradition, time, place, circumstance, & addresses an assembly as mere human beings, – no more."

The hundreds of lectures Emerson delivered during the following decades were the primary source of both his income and his books. *Essays*

(1841) was derived from his lectures, as was *Essays: Second Series* (1844). During the period in which he wrote and published those celebrated volumes, Emerson also helped to establish and edit the *Dial*, the unofficial journal of the Transcendental Club. He also wrote a good deal of poetry, which he gathered together in his *Poems*, published in 1847. From 1845 to 1846, he delivered a lecture series he would later revise and publish as *Representative Men* (1850), a collection of biographical studies of individual greatness as represented by figures ranging from Plato through Shakespeare to modern figures such as the influential German writer Johann Wolfgang von Goethe and the French military and political leader Napoleon Bonaparte. Outraged by the passage of the Fugitive Slave Act in 1850, Emerson became increasingly involved in the antislavery crusade during that decade. But he continued to spend most of his time riding what he called "the lyceum express," a reference to his tours to lyceums and lecture halls throughout the North. During those extended tours, he first delivered the lectures revised for *English Traits* (1856), based on his second trip to Europe in 1847-48, and *Conduct of Life* (1860). In the view of most scholars, those were the last of his major works, though Emerson published a collection of late essays, *Society and Solitude*, in 1870. By then, however, both his health and memory had begun to fail, and Emerson wrote little more before he died on April 27, 1882.

> *I was simmering, simmering, simmering; Emerson brought me to a boil.*
>
> *—Walt Whitman*

Reading Emerson's "The American Scholar."   Delivered at the annual meeting of the Phi Beta Kappa Society at Harvard, "The American Scholar" is probably Emerson's most famous address. It was originally published as a pamphlet entitled *An Oration, Delivered before the Phi Beta Kappa Society at Cambridge, August 31, 1837*, but Emerson later altered the title to "The American Scholar" in his collection *Nature; Addresses, and Lectures* (1849). The address initially follows a popular theme of the day, developed by many previous speakers at Harvard: It was time for the new country to cast off the influence of European models and develop its own ideas and culture. But the address also offered Emerson an occasion to celebrate individualism and to challenge the institutional structures that limit the development of the individual. His conception of the scholar as "Man Thinking," his advice about the use of books and reading, and his emphasis on the importance of "self-trust" to the individual remain among Emerson's celebrated contributions to American thought. The text is taken from the first edition of *An Oration, Delivered before the Phi Beta Kappa Society at Cambridge, August 31, 1837* (1837).

bedfordstmartins.com /americanlit for research links on Emerson

THE AMERICAN SCHOLAR

MR. PRESIDENT, AND GENTLEMEN,

I greet you on the re-commencement of our literary year. Our anniversary is one of hope, and, perhaps, not enough of labor. We do not meet for games of strength or skill, for the recitation of histories, tragedies and odes, like the ancient Greeks; for parliaments of love and poesy, like the Troubadours;[1] nor for the advancement of science, like our contemporaries in the British and European capitals. Thus far, our holiday has been simply a friendly sign of the survival of the love of letters amongst a people too busy to give to letters any more. As such, it is precious as the sign of an indestructible instinct. Perhaps the time is already come, when it ought to be, and will be something else; when the sluggard intellect of this continent will look from under its iron lids and fill the postponed expectation of the world with something better than the exertions of mechanical skill. Our day of dependence, our long apprenticeship to the learning of other lands, draws to a close. The millions that around us are rushing into life, cannot always be fed on the sere remains of foreign harvests. Events, actions arise, that must be sung, that will sing themselves. Who can doubt that poetry will revive and lead in a new age, as the star in the constellation Harp which now flames in our zenith, astronomers announce, shall one day be the pole-star for a thousand years.[2]

In the light of this hope, I accept the topic which not only usage, but the nature of our association, seem to prescribe to this day, — the AMERICAN SCHOLAR. Year by year, we come up hither to read one more chapter of his biography. Let us inquire what new lights, new events and more days have thrown on his character, his duties and his hopes.

It is one of those fables, which out of an unknown antiquity, convey an unlooked for wisdom, that the gods, in the beginning, divided Man into men, that he might be more helpful to himself; just as the hand was divided into fingers, the better to answer its end.

The old fable covers a doctrine ever new and sublime; that there is One Man, — present to all particular men only partially, or through one faculty; and that you must take the whole society to find the whole man. Man is not a farmer, or a professor, or an engineer, but he is all. Man is priest, and scholar, and statesman, and producer, and soldier. In the *divided* or social state, these functions are parcelled out to individuals, each of whom aims to do his stint of the joint work, whilst each other performs his. The fable implies that the individual to possess himself, must sometimes return from his own labor to embrace all the other laborers. But unfortunately, this original unit, this fountain of power, has been so distributed to multitudes, has been so minutely subdivided and peddled out, that it is spilled into drops, and cannot be gathered. The state of society is one in which the members have suffered amputation from the trunk, and strut about so many walking monsters, — a good finger, a neck, a stomach, an elbow, but never a man.

---

1. **Troubadours:** Courtly poets and musicians who flourished in southern France during the Middle Ages.
2. **Who can doubt . . . a thousand years:** Because of a wobble in the earth's rotation, the North Star or northern pole star changes every 26,000 years. In roughly 14,000 CE the new pole star will be Vega, the brightest star in the constellation Lyra, the Harp.

Man is thus metamorphosed into a thing, into many things. The planter, who is Man sent out into the field to gather food, is seldom cheered by any idea of the true dignity of his ministry. He sees his bushel and his cart, and nothing beyond, and sinks into the farmer, instead of Man on the farm. The tradesman scarcely ever gives an ideal worth to his work, but is ridden by the routine of his craft, and the soul is subject to dollars. The priest becomes a form; the attorney, a statute-book; the mechanic, a machine; the sailor, a rope of a ship.

In this distribution of functions, the scholar is the delegated intellect. In the right state, he is, *Man Thinking*. In the degenerate state, when the victim of society, he tends to become a mere thinker, or, still worse, the parrot of other men's thinking.

In this view of him, as Man Thinking, the whole theory of his office is contained. Him nature solicits, with all her placid, all her monitory pictures. Him the past instructs. Him the future invites. Is not, indeed, every man a student, and do not all things exist for the student's behoof? And, finally, is not the true scholar the only true master? But, as the old oracle said, "All things have two handles. Beware of the wrong one."[3] In life, too often, the scholar errs with mankind and forfeits his privilege. Let us see him in his school, and consider him in reference to the main influences he receives.

I. The first in time and the first in importance of the influences upon the mind is that of nature. Every day, the sun; and, after sunset, night and her stars. Ever the winds blow; ever the grass grows. Every day, men and women, conversing, beholding and beholden. The scholar must needs stand wistful and admiring before this great spectacle. He must settle its value in his mind. What is nature to him? There is never a beginning, there is never an end to the inexplicable continuity of this web of God, but always circular power returning into itself. Therein it resembles his own spirit, whose beginning, whose ending he never can find — so entire, so boundless. Far, too, as her splendors shine, system on system shooting like rays, upward, downward, without centre, without circumference, — in the mass and in the particle nature hastens to render account of herself to the mind. Classification begins. To the young mind, every thing is individual, stands by itself. By and by, it finds how to join two things, and see in them one nature; then three, then three thousand; and so, tyrannized over by its own unifying instinct, it goes on tying things together, diminishing anomalies, discovering roots running under ground, whereby contrary and remote things cohere, and flower out from one stem. It presently learns, that, since the dawn of history, there has been a constant accumulation and classifying of facts. But what is classification but the perceiving that these objects are not chaotic, and are not foreign, but have a law which is also a law of the human mind? The astronomer discovers that geometry, a pure abstraction of the human mind, is the measure of planetary motion. The chemist finds proportions and intelligible method throughout matter: and science is nothing but the finding of analogy, identity in the most remote parts. The ambitious soul sits down before each refractory fact; one after another, reduces all strange constitutions, all new powers, to their class and their law, and goes on forever to animate the last fibre of organization, the outskirts of nature, by insight.

---

3. **"All . . . wrong one"**: From the writings of the Greek philosopher Epictetus (c. 55-135).

Thus to him, to this school-boy under the bending dome of day, is suggested, that he and it proceed from one root; one is leaf and one is flower; relation, sympathy, stirring in every vein. And what is that Root? Is not that the soul of his soul? – A thought too bold – a dream too wild. Yet when this spiritual light shall have revealed the law of more earthly natures, – when he has learned to worship the soul, and to see that the natural philosophy that now is, is only the first gropings of its gigantic hand, he shall look forward to an ever expanding knowledge as to a becoming creator. He shall see that nature is the opposite of the soul, answering to it part for part. One is seal, and one is print. Its beauty is the beauty of his own mind. Its laws are the laws of his own mind. Nature then becomes to him the measure of his attainments. So much of nature as he is ignorant of, so much of his own mind does he not yet possess. And, in fine, the ancient precept, "Know thyself," and the modern precept, "Study nature," become at last one maxim.

II. The next great influence into the spirit of the scholar, is, the mind of the Past, – in whatever form, whether of literature, of art, of institutions, that mind is inscribed. Books are the best type of the influence of the past, and perhaps we shall get at the truth – learn the amount of this influence more conveniently – by considering their value alone.

The theory of books is noble. The scholar of the first age received into him the world around; brooded thereon; gave it the new arrangement of his own mind, and uttered it again. It came into him – life; it went out from him – truth. It came to him – short-lived actions; it went out from him – immortal thoughts. It came to him – business; it went from him – poetry. It was – dead fact; now, it is quick thought. It can stand, and it can go. It now endures, it now flies, it now inspires. Precisely in proportion to the depth of mind from which it issued, so high does it soar, so long does it sing.

Or, I might say, it depends on how far the process had gone, of transmuting life into truth. In proportion to the completeness of the distillation, so will the purity and imperishableness of the product be. But none is quite perfect. As no air-pump can by any means make a perfect vacuum, so neither can any artist entirely exclude the conventional, the local, the perishable from his book, or write a book of pure thought that shall be as efficient, in all respects, to a remote posterity, as to cotemporaries, or rather to the second age. Each age, it is found, must write its own books; or rather, each generation for the next succeeding. The books of an older period will not fit this.

Yet hence arises a grave mischief. The sacredness which attaches to the act of creation, – the act of thought, – is instantly transferred to the record. The poet chanting, was felt to be a divine man. Henceforth the chant is divine also. The writer was a just and wise spirit. Henceforward it is settled, the book is perfect; as love of the hero corrupts into worship of his statue. Instantly, the book becomes noxious. The guide is a tyrant. We sought a brother, and lo, a governor. The sluggish and perverted mind of the multitude, always slow to open to the incursions of Reason, having once so opened, having once received this book, stands upon it, and makes an outcry, if it is disparaged. Colleges are built on it. Books are written on it by thinkers, not by Man Thinking; by men of talent, that is, who start wrong, who set out from accepted dogmas, not from their own sight of principles. Meek young men grow up in libraries, believing it their duty to accept the views which Cicero, which Locke, which Bacon have given, forgetful that Cicero, Locke and Bacon[4] were only young men in libraries when they wrote these books.

Hence, instead of Man Thinking, we have the bookworm. Hence, the book-learned class, who value books, as such; not as related to nature and the human constitution, but as making a sort of Third Estate[5] with the world and the soul. Hence, the restorers of readings, the emendators, the bibliomaniacs of all degrees.

This is bad; this is worse than it seems. Books are the best of things, well used; abused, among the worst. What is the right use? What is the one end which all means go to effect? They are for nothing but to inspire. I had better never see a book than to be warped by its attraction clean out of my own orbit, and made a satellite instead of a system. The one thing in the world of value, is, the active soul, – the soul, free, sovereign, active. This every man is entitled to; this every man contains within him, although in almost all men, obstructed, and as yet unborn. The soul active sees absolute truth; and utters truth, or creates. In this action, it is genius; not the privilege of here and there a favorite, but the sound estate of every man. In its essence, it is progressive. The book, the college, the school of art, the institution of any kind, stop with some past utterance of genius. This is good, say they – let us hold by this. They pin me down. They look backward and not forward. But genius always looks forward. The eyes of man are set in his forehead, not in his hindhead. Man hopes. Genius creates. To create, – to create, – is the proof of divine presence. Whatever talents may be, if the man create not, the pure efflux of the Deity is not his: – cinders and smoke, there may be, but not yet flame. There are creative manners, there are creative actions, and creative words; manners, actions, words, that is, indicative of no custom or authority, but springing spontaneous from the mind's own sense of good and fair.

On the other part, instead of being its own seer, let it receive always from another mind its truth, though it were in torrents of light, without periods of solitude, inquest and self-recovery, and a fatal disservice is done. Genius is always sufficiently the enemy of genius by over-influence. The literature of every nation bear me witness. The English dramatic poets have Shakspearized now for two hundred years.

Undoubtedly there is a right way of reading, – so it be sternly subordinated. Man Thinking must not be subdued by his instruments. Books are for the scholar's idle times. When he can read God directly, the hour is too precious to be wasted in other men's transcripts of their readings. But when the intervals of darkness come, as come they must, – when the soul seeth not, when the sun is hid, and the stars withdraw their shining, – we repair to the lamps which were kindled by their ray to guide our steps to the East again, where the dawn is. We hear that we may speak. The Arabian proverb says, "A fig tree looking on a fig tree, becometh fruitful."

It is remarkable, the character of the pleasure we derive from the best books. They impress us ever with the conviction that one nature wrote and the same reads. We read

----

4. **Cicero, Locke and Bacon:** Marcus Tullius Cicero (106–43 BCE), a renowned Roman orator; the English philosophers John Locke (1632–1704) and Sir Francis Bacon (1561–1626).
5. **Third Estate:** Before the French Revolution in 1789, this term was used in France to describe the common people; the First Estate was the clergy, and the Second Estate was the nobility.

the verses of one of the great English poets, of Chaucer, of Marvell, of Dryden,[6] with the most modern joy, – with a pleasure, I mean, which is in great part caused by the abstraction of all *time* from their verses. There is some awe mixed with the joy of our surprise, when this poet, who lived in some past world, two or three hundred years ago, says that which lies close to my own soul, that which I also had well nigh thought and said. But for the evidence thence afforded to the philosophical doctrine of the identity of all minds, we should suppose some pre-established harmony, some foresight of souls that were to be, and some preparation of stores for their future wants, like the fact observed in insects, who lay up food before death for the young grub they shall never see.

I would not be hurried by any love of system, by any exaggeration of instincts, to underrate the Book. We all know, that as the human body can be nourished on any food, though it were boiled grass and the broth of shoes, so the human mind can be fed by any knowledge. And great and heroic men have existed, who had almost no other information than by the printed page. I only would say, that it needs a strong head to bear that diet. One must be an inventor to read well. As the proverb says, "He that would bring home the wealth of the Indies, must carry out the wealth of the Indies." There is then creative reading, as well as creative writing. When the mind is braced by labor and invention, the page of whatever book we read becomes luminous with manifold allusion. Every sentence is doubly significant, and the sense of our author is as broad as the world. We then see, what is always true, that as the seer's hour of vision is short and rare among heavy days and months, so is its record, perchance, the least part of his volume. The discerning will read in his Plato or Shakspeare, only that least part, – only the authentic utterances of the oracle, – and all the rest he rejects, were it never so many times Plato's and Shakspeare's.

Of course, there is a portion of reading quite indispensable to a wise man. History and exact science he must learn by laborious reading. Colleges, in like manner, have their indispensable office, – to teach elements. But they can only highly serve us, when they aim not to drill, but to create; when they gather from far every ray of various genius to their hospitable halls, and, by the concentrated fires, set the hearts of their youth on flame. Thought and knowledge are natures in which apparatus and pretension avail nothing. Gowns,[7] and pecuniary foundations, though of towns of gold, can never countervail the least sentence or syllable of wit. Forget this, and our American colleges will recede in their public importance whilst they grow richer every year.

III. There goes in the world a notion that the scholar should be a recluse, a valetudinarian,[8] – as unfit for any handiwork or public labor, as a penknife for an axe. The so-called "practical men" sneer at speculative men, as if, because they speculate or *see*, they could do nothing. I have heard it said that the clergy, – who are always more universally than any other class, the scholars of their day, – are addressed as women: that the rough, spontaneous conversation of men they do not hear, but only a mincing and

---

6. **Chaucer . . . Dryden:** Geoffrey Chaucer (c. 1343–1400), Andrew Marvell (1621–1678), and John Dryden (1631–1700).
7. **gowns:** Academic robes.
8. **valetudinarian:** A weak or sickly person; an invalid.

diluted speech. They are often virtually disfranchised; and, indeed, there are advocates for their celibacy. As far as this is true of the studious classes, it is not just and wise. Action is with the scholar subordinate, but it is essential. Without it, he is not yet man. Without it, thought can never ripen into truth. Whilst the world hangs before the eye as a cloud of beauty, we cannot even see its beauty. Inaction is cowardice, but there can be no scholar without the heroic mind. The preamble of thought, the transition through which it passes from the unconscious to the conscious, is action. Only so much do I know, as I have lived. Instantly we know whose words are loaded with life, and whose not.

The world, – this shadow of the soul, or *other me*, lies wide around. Its attractions are the keys which unlock my thoughts and make me acquainted with myself. I launch eagerly into this resounding tumult. I grasp the hands of those next me, and take my place in the ring to suffer and to work, taught by an instinct that so shall the dumb abyss be vocal with speech. I pierce its order; I dissipate its fear; I dispose of it within the circuit of my expanding life. So much only of life as I know by experience, so much of the wilderness have I vanquished and planted, or so far have I extended my being, my dominion. I do not see how any man can afford, for the sake of his nerves and his nap, to spare any action in which he can partake. It is pearls and rubies to his discourse. Drudgery, calamity, exasperation, want, are instructors in eloquence and wisdom. The true scholar grudges every opportunity of action past by, as a loss of power.

It is the raw material out of which the intellect moulds her splendid products. A strange process too, this, by which experience is converted into thought, as a mulberry leaf is converted into satin.[9] The manufacture goes forward at all hours.

The actions and events of our childhood and youth are now matters of calmest observation. They lie like fair pictures in the air. Not so with our recent actions, – with the business which we now have in hand. On this we are quite unable to speculate. Our affections as yet circulate through it. We no more feel or know it, than we feel the feet, or the hand, or the brain of our body. The new deed is yet a part of life, – remains for a time immersed in our unconscious life. In some contemplative hour, it detaches itself from the life like a ripe fruit, to become a thought of the mind. Instantly, it is raised, transfigured; the corruptible has put on incorruption.[10] Always now it is an object of beauty, however base its origin and neighborhood. Observe, too, the impossibility of antedating this act. In its grub state, it cannot fly, it cannot shine, – it is a dull grub. But suddenly, without observation, the selfsame thing unfurls beautiful wings, and is an angel of wisdom. So is there no fact, no event, in our private history, which shall not, sooner or later, lose its adhesive inert form, and astonish us by soaring from our body into the empyrean. Cradle and infancy, school and playground, the fear of boys, and dogs, and ferules,[11] the love of little maids and berries, and many another fact that once filled the

---

9. **satin:** The fabric made from filaments spun by silkworms, which feed on mulberry leaves.
10. **Instantly . . . incorruption:** See I Corinthians 15:52–53: "In a moment, in the twinkling of an eye, at the last trump: for the trumpet shall sound, and the dead shall be raised incorruptible, and we shall be changed. For this corruptible must put on incorruption, and this mortal must put on immortality."
11. **ferules:** Flat pieces of wood used for striking children as punishment.

whole sky, are gone already; friend and relative, profession and party, town and country, nation and world, must also soar and sing.

Of course, he who has put forth his total strength in fit actions, has the richest return of wisdom. I will not shut myself out of this globe of action and transplant an oak into a flower pot, there to hunger and pine; nor trust the revenue of some single faculty, and exhaust one vein of thought, much like those Savoyards,[12] who, getting their livelihood by carving shepherds, shepherdesses, and smoking Dutchmen, for all Europe, went out one day to the mountain to find stock, and discovered that they had whittled up the last of their pine trees. Authors we have in numbers, who have written out their vein, and who, moved by a commendable prudence, sail for Greece or Palestine, follow the trapper into the prairie, or ramble round Algiers to replenish their merchantable stock.[13]

If it were only for a vocabulary the scholar would be covetous of action. Life is our dictionary. Years are well spent in country labors; in town – in the insight into trades and manufactures; in frank intercourse with many men and women; in science; in art; to the one end of mastering in all their facts a language, by which to illustrate and embody our perceptions. I learn immediately from any speaker how much he has already lived, through the poverty or the splendor of his speech. Life lies behind us as the quarry from whence we get tiles and copestones for the masonry of to-day. This is the way to learn grammar. Colleges and books only copy the language which the field and the workyard made.

But the final value of action, like that of books, and better than books, is, that it is a resource. That great principle of Undulation in nature, that shows itself in the inspiring and expiring of the breath; in desire and satiety; in the ebb and flow of the sea, in day and night, in heat and cold, and as yet more deeply ingrained in every atom and every fluid, is known to us under the name of Polarity, – these "fits of easy transmission and reflection,"[14] as Newton called them, are the law of nature because they are the law of spirit.

The mind now thinks; now acts; and each fit reproduces the other. When the artist has exhausted his materials, when the fancy no longer paints, when thoughts are no longer apprehended, and books are a weariness, – he has always the resource *to live*. Character is higher than intellect. Thinking is the function. Living is the functionary. The stream retreats to its source. A great soul will be strong to live, as well as strong to think. Does he lack organ or medium to impart his truths? He can still fall back on this elemental force of living them. This is a total act. Thinking is a partial act. Let the grandeur of justice shine in his affairs. Let the beauty of affection cheer his lowly roof. Those "far from fame" who dwell and act with him, will feel the force of his constitution in the doings and passages of the day better than it can be measured by any public and designed display. Time shall teach him that the scholar loses no hour which the man lives. Herein he unfolds the sacred germ of his instinct screened from influence. What

---

12. **Savoyards:** Savoy is located in the French Alps.
13. **Authors . . . merchantable stock:** Emerson probably had in mind popular travel books such as Washington Irving's *A Tour on the Prairies* (1835).
14. **"fits . . . reflection":** From *Optics* (1704) by the eminent English scientist Sir Isaac Newton (1642–1727).

is lost in seemliness is gained in strength. Not out of those on whom systems of education have exhausted their culture, comes the helpful giant to destroy the old or to build the new, but out of unhandselled savage nature, out of terrible Druids and Berserkirs, come at last Alfred and Shakspear.[15]

I hear therefore with joy whatever is beginning to be said of the dignity and necessity of labor to every citizen. There is virtue yet in the hoe and the spade, for learned as well as for unlearned hands. And labor is every where welcome; always we are invited to work; only be this limitation observed, that a man shall not for the sake of wider activity sacrifice any opinion to the popular judgments and modes of action.

I have now spoken of the education of the scholar by nature, by books, and by action. It remains to say somewhat of his duties.

They are such as become Man Thinking. They may all be comprised in self-trust. The office of the scholar is to cheer, to raise, and to guide men by showing them facts amidst appearances. He plies the slow, unhonored, and unpaid task of observation. Flamsteed and Herschel,[16] in their glazed observatory, may catalogue the stars with the praise of all men, and, the results being splendid and useful, honor is sure. But he, in his private observatory, cataloguing obscure and nebulous stars of the human mind, which as yet no man has thought of as such, – watching days and months, sometimes, for a few facts; correcting still his old records; – must relinquish display and immediate fame. In the long period of his preparation, he must betray often an ignorance and shiftlessness in popular arts, incurring the disdain of the able who shoulder him aside. Long he must stammer in his speech; often forego the living for the dead. Worse yet, he must accept – how often! poverty and solitude. For the ease and pleasure of treading the old road, accepting the fashions, the education, the region of society, he takes the cross of making his own, and, of course, the self accusation, the faint heart, the frequent uncertainty and loss of time which are the nettles and tangling vines in the way of the self-relying and self-directed; and the state of virtual hostility in which he seems to stand to society, and especially to educated society. For all this loss and scorn, what offset? He is to find consolation in exercising the highest functions of human nature. He is one who raises himself from private considerations, and breathes and lives on public and illustrious thoughts. He is the world's eye. He is the world's heart. He is to resist the vulgar prosperity that retrogrades ever to barbarism, by preserving and communicating heroic sentiments, noble biographies, melodious verse, and the conclusions of history. Whatsoever oracles the human heart in all emergencies, in all solemn hours has uttered as its commentary on the world of actions, – these he shall receive and impart. And whatsoever new verdict Reason from her inviolable seat pronounces on the passing men and events of to-day, – this he shall hear and promulgate.

---

15. **out of unhandselled savage nature . . . Shakspear:** That is, out of untamed nature – as represented by the early conquerors of England, the Celts and Anglo-Saxons – come figures such as Alfred the Great (849–899), the enlightened king of the West Saxons, and the great poet and playwright Shakespeare.
16. **Flamsteed and Herschel:** The astronomers John Flamsteed (1646–1719) and William Herschel (1738–1822), who discovered the planet Uranus.

These being his functions, it becomes him to feel all confidence in himself, and to defer never to the popular cry. He and he only knows the world. The world of any moment is the merest appearance. Some great decorum, some fetish of a government, some ephemeral trade, or war, or man, is cried up by half mankind and cried down by the other half, as if all depended on this particular up or down. The odds are that the whole question is not worth the poorest thought which the scholar has lost in listening to the controversy. Let him not quit his belief that a popgun is a popgun, though the ancient and honorable of the earth affirm it to be the crack of doom. In silence, in steadiness, in severe abstraction, let him hold by himself; add observation to observation; patient of neglect, patient of reproach, and bide his own time, — happy enough if he can satisfy himself alone that this day he has seen something truly. Success treads on every right step. For the instinct is sure that prompts him to tell his brother what he thinks. He then learns that in going down into the secrets of his own mind, he has descended into the secrets of all minds. He learns that he who has mastered any law in his private thoughts, is master to that extent of all men whose language he speaks, and of all into whose language his own can be translated. The poet in utter solitude remembering his spontaneous thoughts and recording them, is found to have recorded that which men in "cities vast" find true for them also. The orator distrusts at first the fitness of his frank confessions, — his want of knowledge of the persons he addresses, — until he finds that he is the complement of his hearers; — that they drink his words because he fulfils for them their own nature; the deeper he dives into his privatest secretest presentiment, — to his wonder he finds, this is the most acceptable, most public, and universally true. The people delight in it; the better part of every man feels, This is my music: this is myself.

In self-trust, all the virtues are comprehended. Free should the scholar be, — free and brave. Free even to the definition of freedom, "without any hindrance that does not arise out of his own constitution." Brave; for fear is a thing which a scholar by his very function puts behind him. Fear always springs from ignorance. It is a shame to him if his tranquillity, amid dangerous times, arise from the presumption that like children and women, his is a protected class; or if he seek a temporary peace by the diversion of his thoughts from politics or vexed questions, hiding his head like an ostrich in the flowering bushes, peeping into microscopes, and turning rhymes, as a boy whistles to keep his courage up. So is the danger a danger still: so is the fear worse. Manlike let him turn and face it. Let him look into its eye and search its nature, inspect its origin — see the whelping of this lion, — which lies no great way back; he will then find in himself a perfect comprehension of its nature and extent; he will have made his hands meet on the other side, and can henceforth defy it, and pass on superior. The world is his who can see through its pretension. What deafness, what stone-blind custom, what overgrown error you behold, is there only by sufferance, — by your sufferance. See it to be a lie, and you have already dealt it its mortal blow.

Yes, we are the cowed, — we the trustless. It is a mischievous notion that we are come late into nature; that the world was finished a long time ago. As the world was plastic and fluid in the hands of God, so it is ever to so much of his attributes as we bring to it. To ignorance and sin, it is flint. They adapt themselves to it as they may; but in proportion as a man has anything in him divine, the firmament flows before him, and takes his signet[17] and form. Not he is great who can alter matter, but he who can alter my state of mind. They are the kings of the world who give the color of their present thought to all nature and all art, and persuade men by the cheerful serenity of their carrying the matter, that this thing which they do, is the apple which the ages have desired to pluck, now at last ripe, and inviting nations to the harvest. The great man makes the great thing. Wherever Macdonald sits, there is the head of the table.[18] Linnaeus makes botany the most alluring of studies and wins it from the farmer and the herb-woman. Davy, chemistry: and Cuvier,[19] fossils. The day is always his, who works in it with serenity and great aims. The unstable estimates of men crowd to him whose mind is filled with a truth, as the heaped waves of the Atlantic follow the moon.

For this self-trust, the reason is deeper than can be fathomed, – darker than can be enlightened. I might not carry with me the feeling of my audience in stating my own belief. But I have already shown the ground of my hope, in adverting to the doctrine that man is one. I believe man has been wronged: he has wronged himself. He has almost lost the light that can lead him back to his prerogatives. Men are become of no account. Men in history, men in the world of to-day are bugs, are spawn, and are called "the mass" and "the herd." In a century, in a millenium, one or two men; that is to say – one or two approximations to the right state of every man. All the rest behold in the hero or the poet their own green and crude being – ripened; yes, and are content to be less, so *that* may attain to its full stature. What a testimony – full of grandeur, full of pity, is borne to the demands of his own nature, by the poor clansman, the poor partisan, who rejoices in the glory of his chief. The poor and the low find some amends to their immense moral capacity, for their acquiescence in a political and social inferiority. They are content to be brushed like flies from the path of a great person, so that justice shall be done by him to that common nature which it is the dearest desire of all to see enlarged and glorified. They sun themselves in the great man's light, and feel it to be their own element. They cast the dignity of man from their downtrod selves upon the shoulders of a hero, and will perish to add one drop of blood to make that great heart beat, those giant sinews combat and conquer. He lives for us, and we live in him.

Men such as they are, very naturally seek money or power; and power because it is as good as money, – the "spoils," so called, "of office." And why not? for they aspire to the highest, and this, in their sleep-walking, they dream is highest. Wake them, and they shall quit the false good and leap to the true, and leave governments to clerks and desks. This revolution is to be wrought by the gradual domestication of the idea of Culture. The main enterprise of the world for splendor, for extent, is the upbuilding of a man.

---

17. **signet:** A seal, especially one set in a ring, or the impression made by such a seal.
18. **Wherever . . . table:** Emerson substitutes another name in an old Scottish proverb, "Where Macgregor sits, there is the head of the table."
19. **Linnaeus . . . Davy . . . Cuvier:** Carl Linnaeus or Carl von Linné (1707-1778) was the Swedish developer of taxonomy, the naming and classifying of organisms. Sir Humphry Davy (1778-1829) was an English chemist who studied the chemical effects of electricity. Georges Cuvier (1769-1832), an eminent French paleontologist, was among the most influential scientists of the early nineteenth century.

Here are the materials strown along the ground. The private life of one man shall be a more illustrious monarchy, – more formidable to its enemy, more sweet and serene in its influence to its friend, than any kingdom in history. For a man, rightly viewed, comprehendeth the particular natures of all men. Each philosopher, each bard, each actor, has only done for me, as by a delegate, what one day I can do for myself. The books which once we valued more than the apple of the eye, we have quite exhausted. What is that but saying that we have come up with the point of view which the universal mind took through the eyes of that one scribe; we have been that man, and have passed on. First, one; then, another; we drain all cisterns, and waxing greater by all these supplies, we crave a better and more abundant food. The man has never lived that can feed us ever. The human mind cannot be enshrined in a person who shall set a barrier on any one side to this unbounded, unboundable empire. It is one central fire which flaming now out of the lips of Etna, lightens the capes of Sicily; and now out of the throat of Vesuvius,[20] illuminates the towers and vineyards of Naples. It is one light which beams out of a thousand stars. It is one soul which animates all men.

But I have dwelt perhaps tediously upon this abstraction of the Scholar. I ought not to delay longer to add what I have to say, of nearer reference to the time and to this country.

Historically, there is thought to be a difference in the ideas which predominate over successive epochs, and there are data for marking the genius of the Classic, of the Romantic, and now of the Reflective or Philosophical age. With the views I have intimated of the oneness or the identity of the mind through all individuals, I do not much dwell on these differences. In fact, I believe each individual passes through all three. The boy is a Greek; the youth, romantic; the adult, reflective. I deny not, however, that a revolution in the leading idea may be distinctly enough traced.

Our age is bewailed as the age of Introversion. Must that needs be evil? We, it seems, are critical. We are embarrassed with second thoughts. We cannot enjoy any thing for hankering to know whereof the pleasure consists. We are lined with eyes. We see with our feet. The time is infected with Hamlet's unhappiness, –

"Sicklied o'er with the pale cast of thought."[21]

Is it so bad then? Sight is the last thing to be pitied. Would we be blind? Do we fear lest we should outsee nature and God, and drink truth dry? I look upon the discontent of the literary class as a mere announcement of the fact that they find themselves not in the state of mind of their fathers, and regret the coming state as untried; as a boy dreads the water before he has learned that he can swim. If there is any period one would desire to be born in, – is it not the age of Revolution; when the old and the new stand side by side, and admit of being compared; when the energies of all men are searched by fear and by hope; when the historic glories of the old, can be compensated by the rich

---

20. **Etna . . . Vesuvius:** The volcanoes Mount Etna in Sicily and Mount Vesuvius in southern Italy.
21. "Sicklied . . . thought": Shakespeare, *Hamlet*, 3.1.85.

possibilities of the new era? This time, like all times, is a very good one, if we but know what to do with it.

I read with joy some of the auspicious signs of the coming days as they glimmer already through poetry and art, through philosophy and science, through church and state.

One of these signs is the fact that the same movement which effected the elevation of what was called the lowest class in the state, assumed in literature a very marked and as benign an aspect. Instead of the sublime and beautiful, the near, the low, the common, was explored and poetised. That which had been negligently trodden under foot by those who were harnessing and provisioning themselves for long journies into far countries, is suddenly found to be richer than all foreign parts. The literature of the poor, the feelings of the child, the philosophy of the street, the meaning of household life, are the topics of the time. It is a great stride. It is a sign – is it not? of new vigor, when the extremities are made active, when currents of warm life run into the hands and the feet. I ask not for the great, the remote, the romantic; what is doing in Italy or Arabia; what is Greek art, or Provençal Minstrelsy;[22] I embrace the common, I explore and sit at the feet of the familiar, the low. Give me insight into to-day, and you may have the antique and future worlds. What would we really know the meaning of? The meal in the firkin; the milk in the pan; the ballad in the street; the news of the boat; the glance of the eye; the form and the gait of the body; – show me the ultimate reason of these matters; – show me the sublime presence of the highest spiritual cause lurking, as always it does lurk, in these suburbs and extremities of nature; let me see every trifle bristling with the polarity that ranges it instantly on an eternal law; and the shop, the plough, and the ledger, referred to the like cause by which light undulates and poets sing; – and the world lies no longer a dull miscellany and lumber room, but has form and order; there is no trifle; there is no puzzle; but one design unites and animates the farthest pinnacle and the lowest trench.

This idea has inspired the genius of Goldsmith, Burns, Cowper, and, in a newer time, of Goethe, Wordsworth, and Carlyle.[23] This idea they have differently followed and with various success. In contrast with their writing, the style of Pope, of Johnson, of Gibbon,[24] looks cold and pedantic. This writing is blood-warm. Man is surprised to find that things near are not less beautiful and wondrous than things remote. The near explains the far. The drop is a small ocean. A man is related to all nature. This perception of the worth of the vulgar, is fruitful in discoveries. Goethe, in this very thing the most modern of the moderns, has shown us, as none ever did, the genius of the ancients.

---

22. **Provençal Minstrelsy:** Music of the troubadours of Provence, in southeastern France (see note 1).

23. **Goldsmith . . . Carlyle:** The Anglo-Irish writer Oliver Goldsmith (1730-1774), the Scottish poet Robert Burns (1759-1796), and the English poet William Cowper (1731-1800) were known for their depictions of everyday life. Emerson discerns the further development of that positive tendency in the work of the German writer Johann Wolfgang von Goethe (1749-1832); the English Romantic poet William Wordsworth (1770-1850); and the Scottish essayist, historian, and social critic Thomas Carlyle (1795-1881).

24. **Pope . . . Gibbon:** Emerson refers to three English writers whose work exemplified the Neo-classical style, with its ideals of restraint, logic, and decorum: the poet Alexander Pope (1688-1744); the biographer, critic, and essayist Samuel Johnson (1709-1784), often referred to as Dr. Johnson; and the historian Edward Gibbon (1737-1794).

There is one man of genius who has done much for this philosophy of life, whose literary value has never yet been rightly estimated; — I mean Emanuel Swedenborg.[25] The most imaginative of men, yet writing with the precision of a mathematician, he endeavored to engraft a purely philosophical Ethics on the popular Christianity of his time. Such an attempt, of course, must have difficulty which no genius could surmount. But he saw and showed the connexion between nature and the affections of the soul. He pierced the emblematic or spiritual character of the visible, audible, tangible world. Especially did his shade-loving muse hover over and interpret the lower parts of nature; he showed the mysterious bond that allies moral evil to the foul material forms, and has given in epical parables a theory of insanity, of beasts, of unclean and fearful things.

Another sign of our times, also marked by an analogous political movement is, the new importance given to the single person. Every thing that tends to insulate the individual, — to surround him with barriers of natural respect, so that each man shall feel the world is his, and man shall treat with man as a sovereign state with a sovereign state; — tends to true union as well as greatness. "I learned," said the melancholy Pestalozzi,[26] "that no man in God's wide earth is either willing or able to help any other man." Help must come from the bosom alone. The scholar is that man who must take up into himself all the ability of the time, all the contributions of the past, all the hopes of the future. He must be an university of knowledges. If there be one lesson more than another which should pierce his ear, it is, The world is nothing, the man is all; in yourself is the law of all nature, and you know not yet how a globule of sap ascends; in yourself slumbers the whole of Reason; it is for you to know all, it is for you to dare all. Mr. President and Gentlemen, this confidence in the unsearched might of man, belongs by all motives, by all prophecy, by all preparation, to the American Scholar. We have listened too long to the courtly muses of Europe. The spirit of the American freeman is already suspected to be timid, imitative, tame. Public and private avarice make the air we breathe thick and fat. The scholar is decent, indolent, complaisant. See already the tragic consequence. The mind of this country taught to aim at low objects, eats upon itself. There is no work for any but the decorous and the complaisant. Young men of the fairest promise, who begin life upon our shores, inflated by the mountain winds, shined upon by all the stars of God, find the earth below not in unison with these, — but are hindered from action by the disgust which the principles on which business is managed inspire, and turn drudges, or die of disgust, — some of them suicides. What is the remedy? They did not yet see, and thousands of young men as hopeful now crowding to the barriers for the career, do not yet see, that if the single man plant himself indomitably on his instincts, and there abide, the huge world will come round to him. Patience — patience; — with the shades of all the good and great for company; and for solace, the perspective of your own infinite life; and for work, the study, and the communication of

---

25. **Emanuel Swedenborg**: Swedenborg (1688-1772) was a Swedish scientist and philosopher whose spiritual beliefs blended Christianity, mysticism, and pantheism. Emerson was strongly influenced by Swedenborg's doctrine of correspondence, the belief that there is a relationship between the natural and spiritual worlds.
26. **Pestalozzi**: Johann Heinrich Pestalozzi (1746-1827) was a Swiss educator whose ideas influenced several of the transcendentalists.

principles, the making those instincts prevalent, the conversion of the world. Is it not the chief disgrace in the world, not to be an unit; – not to be reckoned one character; – not to yield that peculiar fruit which each man was created to bear, but to be reckoned in the gross, in the hundred, or the thousand, of the party, the section, to which we belong; and our opinion predicted geographically, as the north, or the south. Not so, brothers and friends, – please God, ours shall not be so. We will walk on our own feet; we will work with our own hands; we will speak our own minds. Then shall man be no longer a name for pity, for doubt, and for sensual indulgence. The dread of man and the love of man shall be a wall of defence and a wreath of love around all. A nation of men will for the first time exist, because each believes himself inspired by the Divine Soul which also inspires all men.

[1837]

Reading Emerson's "Self-Reliance."   The second "chapter" of *Essays* (1841), "Self-Reliance" is Emerson's most confident and aggressive affirmation of the importance of self-culture to the intellectual and moral development of the individual. Written during the controversy that followed his 1838 address at the Harvard Divinity School, a critique of orthodox Christianity and the training of Unitarian ministers that had outraged conservatives, and at a time when Emerson was facing growing pressures to participate in various organized reforms, the essay is also his most sustained defense of individualism. "Trust thyself: every heart beats to that iron string," "Whoso would be a man must be a nonconformist," and "A foolish consistency is the hobgoblin of little minds" are just a few of the often-quoted assertions in his essay, admired by generations of readers and writers. The text is taken from the first edition of *Essays* (1841).

SELF-RELIANCE

Ne te quaesiveris extra.[1]

"Man is his own star, and the soul that can
Render an honest and a perfect man,
Command all light, all influence, all fate,
Nothing to him falls early or too late.
Our acts our angels are, or good or ill,
Our fatal shadows that walk by us still."
   –Epilogue to Beaumont and Fletcher's
   Honest Man's Fortune[2]

---

1. *Ne . . . extra:* From *Satire* 1.7 by Persius (34–62), a Roman satirist. "Don't seek the self outside the self."
2. *Honest Man's Fortune:* A play by the English dramatists Francis Beaumont (1586–1616) and John Fletcher (1579–1625).

> Cast the bantling on the rocks,
> Suckle him with the she-wolf's teat:
> Wintered with the hawk and fox,
> Power and speed be hands and feet.[3]

I read the other day some verses written by an eminent painter[4] which were original and not conventional. Always the soul hears an admonition in such lines, let the subject be what it may. The sentiment they instil is of more value than any thought they may contain. To believe your own thought, to believe that what is true for you in your private heart, is true for all men, — that is genius. Speak your latent conviction and it shall be the universal sense; for always the inmost becomes the outmost, — and our first thought is rendered back to us by the trumpets of the Last Judgment. Familiar as the voice of the mind is to each, the highest merit we ascribe to Moses, Plato, and Milton,[5] is that they set at naught books and traditions, and spoke not what men but what they thought. A man should learn to detect and watch that gleam of light which flashes across his mind from within, more than the lustre of the firmament of bards and sages. Yet he dismisses without notice his thought, because it is his. In every work of genius we recognise our own rejected thoughts: they come back to us with a certain alienated majesty. Great works of art have no more affecting lesson for us than this. They teach us to abide by our spontaneous impression with good humored inflexibility then most when the whole cry of voices is on the other side. Else, to-morrow a stranger will say with masterly good sense precisely what we have thought and felt all the time, and we shall be forced to take with shame our own opinion from another.

There is a time in every man's education when he arrives at the conviction that envy is ignorance; that imitation is suicide; that he must take himself for better, for worse, as his portion; that though the wide universe is full of good, no kernel of nourishing corn can come to him but through his toil bestowed on that plot of ground which is given to him to till. The power which resides in him is new in nature, and none but he knows what that is which he can do, nor does he know until he has tried. Not for nothing one face, one character, one fact makes much impression on him, and another none. It is not without preestablished harmony, this sculpture in the memory. The eye was placed where one ray should fall, that it might testify of that particular ray. Bravely let him speak the utmost syllable of his confession. We but half express ourselves, and are ashamed of that divine idea which each of us represents. It may be safely trusted as proportionate and of good issues, so it be faithfully imparted, but God will not have his work made manifest by cowards. It needs a divine man to exhibit any thing divine. A man is relieved and gay when he has put his heart into his work and done his best; but what he has said or done otherwise, shall give him no peace. It is a deliverance which

---

3. **Cast . . . feet:** The lines were written by Emerson. A bantling is a baby or an illegitimate child.
4. **eminent painter:** Washington Allston (1779–1843), who was also regarded by many of his contemporaries as an innovative poet.
5. **Moses, Plato, and Milton:** The most important prophet in Judaism; the ancient Greek philosopher and founder of the Academy in Athens; and the poet John Milton (1608–1674), generally regarded as one of the preeminent writers in English.

[Handwritten marginal note:] But what of the IMITATION of SELF? that is, Is it really possible to know ourselves apart from others? regardless —

[Handwritten note at bottom:] is it really possible to know the "SELF"? are we not just imitating notions of it (SELF)?

does not deliver. In the attempt his genius deserts him; no muse befriends; no invention, no hope.

Trust thyself: every heart vibrates to that iron string. Accept the place the divine Providence has found for you; the society of your contemporaries, the connexion of events. Great men have always done so and confided themselves childlike to the genius of their age, betraying their perception that the Eternal was stirring at their heart, working through their hands, predominating in all their being. And we are now men, and must accept in the highest mind the same transcendent destiny; and not pinched in a corner, not cowards fleeing before a revolution, but redeemers and benefactors, pious aspirants to be noble clay plastic under the Almighty effort, let us advance and advance on Chaos and the Dark.

What pretty oracles nature yields us on this text in the face and behavior of children, babes and even brutes. That divided and rebel mind, that distrust of a sentiment because our arithmetic has computed the strength and means opposed to our purpose, these have not. Their mind being whole, their eye is as yet unconquered, and when we look in their faces, we are disconcerted. Infancy conforms to nobody: all conform to it, so that one babe commonly makes four or five out of the adults who prattle and play to it. So God has armed youth and puberty and manhood no less with its own piquancy and charm, and made it enviable and gracious and its claims not to be put by, if it will stand by itself. Do not think the youth has no force because he cannot speak to you and me. Hark! in the next room, who spoke so clear and emphatic? Good Heaven! it is he! it is that very lump of bashfulness and phlegm which for weeks has done nothing but eat when you were by, that now rolls out these words like bell-strokes. It seems he knows how to speak to his contemporaries. Bashful or bold, then, he will know how to make us seniors very unnecessary.

The nonchalance of boys who are sure of a dinner, and would disdain as much as a lord to do or say aught to conciliate one, is the healthy attitude of human nature. How is a boy the master of society; independent, irresponsible, looking out from his corner on such people and facts as pass by, he tries and sentences them on their merits, in the swift summary way of boys, as good, bad, interesting, silly, eloquent, troublesome. He cumbers himself never about consequences, about interests: he gives an independent, genuine verdict. You must court him: he does not court you. But the man is, as it were, clapped into jail by his consciousness. As soon as he has once acted or spoken with éclat,[6] he is a committed person, watched by the sympathy or the hatred of hundreds whose affections must now enter into his account. There is no Lethe[7] for this. Ah, that he could pass again into his neutral, godlike independence! Who can thus lose all pledge, and having observed, observe again from the same unaffected, unbiased, unbribable, unaffrighted innocence, must always be formidable, must always engage the poet's and the man's regards. Of such an immortal youth the force would be felt. He would utter opinions on all passing affairs, which being seen to be not private but necessary, would sink like darts into the ear of men, and put them in fear.

---

6. **éclat:** Brilliance or dazzling effect (French).
7. **Lethe:** Drinking from the Lethe, a river in Greek mythology, induces forgetfulness.

These are the voices which we hear in solitude, but they grow faint and inaudible as we enter into the world. Society everywhere is in conspiracy against the manhood of every one of its members. Society is a joint-stock company in which the members agree for the better securing of his bread to each shareholder, to surrender the liberty and culture of the eater. The virtue in most request is conformity. Self-reliance is its aversion. It loves not realities and creators, but names and customs.

Whoso would be a man must be a nonconformist. He who would gather immortal palms[8] must not be hindered by the name of goodness, but must explore if it be goodness. Nothing is at last sacred but the integrity of our own mind. Absolve you to yourself, and you shall have the suffrage of the world. I remember an answer which when quite young I was prompted to make to a valued adviser who was wont to importune me with the dear old doctrines of the church. On my saying, What have I to do with the sacredness of traditions, if I live wholly from within? my friend suggested – "But these impulses may be from below, not from above." I replied, 'They do not seem to me to be such; but if I am the devil's child, I will live then from the devil.' No law can be sacred to me but that of my nature. Good and bad are but names very readily transferable to that or this; the only right is what is after my constitution, the only wrong what is against it. A man is to carry himself in the presence of all opposition as if every thing were titular and ephemeral but he. I am ashamed to think how easily we capitulate to badges and names, to large societies and dead institutions. Every decent and well-spoken individual affects and sways me more than is right. I ought to go upright and vital, and speak the rude truth in all ways. If malice and vanity wear the coat of philanthropy, shall that pass? If an angry bigot assumes this bountiful cause of Abolition, and comes to me with his last news from Barbadoes,[9] why should I not say to him, 'Go love thy infant; love thy wood-chopper: be good-natured and modest: have that grace; and never varnish your hard, uncharitable ambition with this incredible tenderness for black folk a thousand miles off. Thy love afar is spite at home.' Rough and graceless would be such greeting, but truth is handsomer than the affectation of love. Your goodness must have some edge to it – else it is none. The doctrine of hatred must be preached as the counteraction of the doctrine of love when that pules and whines. I shun father and mother and wife and brother, when my genius calls me.[10] I would write on the lintels of the door-post, *Whim*.[11] I hope it is somewhat better than whim at last, but we cannot spend the day in explanation. Expect me not to show cause why I seek or why I exclude company. Then, again, do not tell me, as a good man did to-day, of my obligation to put all poor men in good situations. Are they *my* poor? I tell thee, thou foolish philanthropist, that I grudge the dollar, the dime, the cent I give to such men as do not belong to me and to whom I do

---

8. **immortal palms:** Conquerors were crowned with palm leaves, and in the Bible a crowd covered the ground with and waved palm branches when Jesus entered Jerusalem.
9. **Barbadoes:** Barbados; Caribbean island where slavery was abolished in 1834.
10. **I shun . . . calls me:** Compare with Christ's words in Matthew: "He that loveth father or mother more than me is not worthy of me: and he that loveth son or daughter more than me is not worthy of me."
11. **I would write . . . *Whim*:** Compare with Exodus, chapter 12, where God instructs Moses to mark the side posts and upper-door posts, or lintels, of the houses of the Israelites so that they would be spared when he passed through "to smite the Egyptians."

not belong. There is a class of persons to whom by all spiritual affinity I am bought and sold; for them I will go to prison, if need be; but your miscellaneous popular charities; the education at college of fools; the building of meeting-houses to the vain end to which many now stand; alms to sots; and the thousandfold Relief Societies; – though I confess with shame I sometimes succumb and give the dollar, it is a wicked dollar which by-and-by I shall have the manhood to withhold.

Virtues are in the popular estimate rather the exception than the rule. There is the man *and* his virtues. Men do what is called a good action, as some piece of courage or charity, much as they would pay a fine in expiation of daily non-appearance on parade. Their works are done as an apology or extenuation of their living in the world, – as invalids and the insane pay a high board. Their virtues are penances. I do not wish to expiate, but to live. My life is not an apology, but a life. It is for itself and not for a spectacle. I much prefer that it should be of a lower strain, so it be genuine and equal, than that it should be glittering and unsteady. I wish it to be sound and sweet, and not to need diet and bleeding.[12] My life should be unique; it should be an alms, a battle, a conquest, a medicine. I ask primary evidence that you are a man, and refuse this appeal from the man to his actions. I know that for myself it makes no difference whether I do or forbear those actions which are reckoned excellent. I cannot consent to pay for a privilege where I have intrinsic right. Few and mean as my gifts may be, I actually am, and do not need for my own assurance or the assurance of my fellows any secondary testimony.

What I must do, is all that concerns me, not what the people think. This rule, equally arduous in actual and in intellectual life, may serve for the whole distinction between greatness and meanness. It is the harder, because you will always find those who think they know what is your duty better than you know it. It is easy in the world to live after the world's opinion; it is easy in solitude to live after our own; but the great man is he who in the midst of the crowd keeps with perfect sweetness the independence of solitude.

The objection to conforming to usages that have become dead to you, is, that it scatters your force. It loses your time and blurs the impression of your character. If you maintain a dead church, contribute to a dead Bible-Society, vote with a great party either for the Government or against it, spread your table like base housekeepers, – under all these screens, I have difficulty to detect the precise man you are. And, of course, so much force is withdrawn from your proper life. But do your thing, and I shall know you. Do your work, and you shall reinforce yourself. A man must consider what a blind-man's-buff is this game of conformity. If I know your sect, I anticipate your argument. I hear a preacher announce for his text and topic the expediency of one of the institutions of his church. Do I not know beforehand that not possibly can he say a new and spontaneous word? Do I not know that with all this ostentation of examining the grounds of the institution, he will do no such thing? Do I not know that he is pledged to himself not to look but at one side; the permitted side, not as a man, but as a parish minister? He is a retained attorney, and these airs of the bench are the emptiest affectation.

---

12. **diet and bleeding:** Bleeding was an old medical practice in which patients were "bled" in order to cleanse the body.

Well, most men have bound their eyes with one or another handkerchief, and attached themselves to some one of these communities of opinion. This conformity makes them not false in a few particulars, authors of a few lies, but false in all particulars. Their every truth is not quite true. Their two is not the real two, their four not the real four: so that every word they say chagrins us, and we know not where to begin to set them right. Meantime nature is not slow to equip us in the prison-uniform of the party to which we adhere. We come to wear one cut of face and figure, and acquire by degrees the gentlest asinine expression. There is a mortifying experience in particular which does not fail to wreak itself also in the general history; I mean, "the foolish face of praise,"[13] the forced smile which we put on in company where we do not feel at ease in answer to conversation which does not interest us. The muscles, not spontaneously moved, but moved by a low usurping wilfulness, grow tight about the outline of the face and make the most disagreeable sensation, a sensation of rebuke and warning which no brave young man will suffer twice.

For non-conformity the world whips you with its displeasure. And therefore a man must know how to estimate a sour face. The bystanders look askance on him in the public street or in the friend's parlor. If this aversation had its origin in contempt and resistance like his own, he might well go home with a sad countenance; but the sour faces of the multitude, like their sweet faces, have no deep cause, — disguise no god, but are put on and off as the wind blows, and a newspaper directs. Yet is the discontent of the multitude more formidable than that of the senate and the college. It is easy enough for a firm man who knows the world to brook the rage of the cultivated classes. Their rage is decorous and prudent, for they are timid as being very vulnerable themselves. But when to their feminine rage the indignation of the people is added, when the ignorant and the poor are aroused, when the unintelligent brute force that lies at the bottom of society is made to growl and mow,[14] it needs the habit of magnanimity and religion to treat it godlike as a trifle of no concernment.

The other terror that scares us from self-trust is our consistency; a reverence for our past act or word, because the eyes of others have no other data for computing our orbit than our past acts, and we are loath to disappoint them.

But why should you keep your head over your shoulder? Why drag about this monstrous corpse of your memory, lest you contradict somewhat you have stated in this or that public place? Suppose you should contradict yourself; what then? It seems to be a rule of wisdom never to rely on your memory alone, scarcely even in acts of pure memory, but bring the past for judgment into the thousand-eyed present, and live ever in a new day. Trust your emotion. In your metaphysics you have denied personality to the Deity: yet when the devout motions of the soul come, yield to them heart and life, though they should clothe God with shape and color. Leave your theory as Joseph his coat in the hand of the harlot, and flee.[15]

---

13. **"the . . . praise"**: Alexander Pope (1688-1744), "Epistle to Dr. Arbuthnot," line 212.
14. **mow:** To make mouths; that is, to grimace or make a wry face.
15. **Joseph . . . harlot, and flee:** In the Old Testament account, Joseph is sold into slavery by his brothers and becomes the servant of Potiphar, the captain of the guard for the Pharaoh of Egypt. Potiphar's wife tempted Joseph and grabbed his cloak. In his haste to get away from her, he left his cloak in her hands and fled (Genesis 39).

A foolish consistency is the hobgoblin of little minds, adored by little statesmen and philosophers and divines. With consistency a great soul has simply nothing to do. He may as well concern himself with his shadow on the wall. Out upon your guarded lips! Sew them up with packthread, do. Else, if you would be a man, speak what you think today in words as hard as cannon balls, and to-morrow speak what to-morrow thinks in hard words again, though it contradict every thing you said to-day. Ah, then, exclaim the aged ladies, you shall be sure to be misunderstood. Misunderstood! It is a right fool's word. Is it so bad then to be misunderstood? Pythagoras was misunderstood, and Socrates, and Jesus, and Luther, and Copernicus, and Galileo, and Newton, and every pure and wise spirit that ever took flesh. To be great is to be misunderstood.[16]

I suppose no man can violate his nature. All the sallies of his will are rounded in by the law of his being as the inequalities of Andes and Himalayas are insignificant in the curve of the sphere. Nor does it matter how you gauge and try him. A character is like an acrostic or Alexandrian stanza;—read it forward, backward, or across, it still spells the same thing. In this pleasing contrite wood-life which God allows me, let me record day by day my honest thought without prospect or retrospect, and, I cannot doubt, it will be found symmetrical, though I mean it not, and see it not. My book should smell of pines and resound with the hum of insects. The swallow over my window should interweave that thread or straw he carries in his bill into my web also. We pass for what we are. Character teaches above our wills. Men imagine that they communicate their virtue or vice only by overt actions and do not see that virtue or vice emit a breath every moment.

Fear never but you shall be consistent in whatever variety of actions, so they be each honest and natural in their hour. For of one will, the actions will be harmonious, however unlike they seem. These varieties are lost sight of when seen at a little distance, at a little height of thought. One tendency unites them all. The voyage of the best ship is a zigzag line of a hundred tacks. This is only microscopic criticism. See the line from a sufficient distance, and it straightens itself to the average tendency. Your genuine action will explain itself and will explain your other genuine actions. Your conformity explains nothing. Act singly, and what you have already done singly, will justify you now. Greatness always appeals to the future. If I can be great enough now to do right and scorn eyes, I must have done so much right before, as to defend me now. Be it how it will, do right now. Always scorn appearances, and you always may. The force of character is cumulative. All the foregone days of virtue work their health into this. What makes the majesty of the heroes of the senate and the field, which so fills the imagination? The consciousness of a train of great days and victories behind. There they all stand and shed an united light on the advancing actor. He is attended as by a visible escort of

---

16. **Pythagoras ... misunderstood:** Emerson's catalog of revolutionary thinkers and teachers includes the Greek philosopher and mathematician Pythagoras (570?-490? BCE), who founded a mystical spiritual sect; the Greek philosopher Socrates (469-399 BCE), who was tried and sentenced to death for his unconventional teachings; the German theologian Martin Luther (1483-1546), who initiated the Protestant Reformation; Nicolaus Copernicus (1473-1543), who proposed the then-controversial thesis that the earth revolved around the sun; the Italian astronomer and scientist Galileo Galilei (1564-1642), who supported Copernicus's thesis but was forced to recant his views by the Inquisition; and the English scientist Isaac Newton (1642-1727), whose discoveries and theories radically altered the ways in which people understood the universe.

angels to every man's eye. That is it which throws thunder into Chatham's voice, and dignity into Washington's port, and America into Adams's eye.[17] Honor is venerable to us because it is no ephemeris. It is always ancient virtue. We worship it to-day, because it is not of to-day. We love it and pay it homage, because it is not a trap for our love and homage, but is self-dependent, self-derived, and therefore of an old immaculate pedigree, even if shown in a young person.

I hope in these days we have heard the last of conformity and consistency. Let the words be gazetted and ridiculous henceforward. Instead of the gong for dinner, let us hear a whistle from the Spartan fife.[18] Let us bow and apologize never more. A great man is coming to eat at my house. I do not wish to please him: I wish that he should wish to please me. I will stand here for humanity, and though I would make it kind, I would make it true. Let us affront and reprimand the smooth mediocrity and squalid contentment of the times, and hurl in the face of custom, and trade, and office, the fact which is the upshot of all history, that there is a great responsible Thinker and Actor moving wherever moves a man; that a true man belongs to no other time or place, but is the centre of things. Where he is, there is nature. He measures you, and all men, and all events. You are constrained to accept his standard. Ordinarily every body in society reminds us of somewhat else or of some other person. Character, reality, reminds you of nothing else. It takes place of the whole creation. The man must be so much that he must make all circumstances indifferent, — put all means into the shade. This all great men are and do. Every true man is a cause, a country, and an age; requires infinite spaces and numbers and time fully to accomplish his thought; — and posterity seem to follow his steps as a procession. A man Caesar is born, and for ages after, we have a Roman Empire.[19] Christ is born, and millions of minds so grow and cleave to his genius, that he is confounded with virtue and the possible of man. An institution is the lengthened shadow of one man; as, the Reformation, of Luther; Quakerism, of Fox; Methodism, of Wesley; Abolition, of Clarkson. Scipio, Milton called "the height of Rome;"[20] and all history resolves itself very easily into the biography of a few stout and earnest persons.

Let a man then know his worth, and keep things under his feet. Let him not peep or steal, or skulk up and down with the air of a charity-boy, a bastard, or an interloper, in the world which exists for him. But the man in the street finding no worth in himself

---

17. **Chatham's voice . . . Adams's eye:** The English politician and renowned orator William Pitt, Earl of Chatham (1708-1778); the "port," or bearing, of George Washington (1732-1799), the first president of the United States; and probably either John Adams (1735-1826), the second president, or his son John Quincy Adams (1767-1848), the sixth president and thereafter a congressman from Massachusetts.
18. **Spartan fife:** The Spartans were ancient Greeks renowned for their rigorous education and military training.
19. **A man . . . Roman Empire:** The general and politician Julius Caesar (c. 100-44 BCE) was the central figure in the transformation of the Roman Republic into the Roman Empire.
20. **An institution . . . Rome:** In addition to the German religious reformer Martin Luther (see note 16), Emerson refers to the English dissenter George Fox (1624-1691), the founder of the Religious Society of Friends, commonly known as the Quakers; John Wesley (1703-1791), who along with his brother Charles Wesley is credited with founding the Methodist movement in England; Thomas Clarkson (1760-1846), the leading campaigner against the slave trade in the British Empire; and the Roman statesman and general Scipio Africanus (236-183 BCE), who defeated Hannibal in the final battle of the Second Punic War.

which corresponds to the force which built a tower or sculptured a marble god, feels poor when he looks on these. To him a palace, a statue, or a costly book have an alien and forbidding air, much like a gay equipage, and seem to say like that, 'Who are you, sir?' Yet they all are his, suitors for his notice, petitioners to his faculties that they will come out and take possession. The picture waits for my verdict: it is not to command me, but I am to settle its claims to praise. That popular fable of the sot who was picked up dead drunk in the street, carried to the duke's house, washed and dressed and laid in the duke's bed, and, on his waking, treated with all obsequious ceremony like the duke, and assured that he had been insane, — owes its popularity to the fact, that it symbolizes so well the state of man, who is in the world a sort of sot, but now and then wakes up, exercises his reason, and finds himself a true prince.

Our reading is mendicant and sycophantic. In history, our imagination makes fools of us, plays us false. Kingdom and lordship, power and estate are a gaudier vocabulary than private John and Edward in a small house and common day's work: but the things of life are the same to both: the sum total of both is the same. Why all this deference to Alfred, and Scanderbeg, and Gustavus?[21] Suppose they were virtuous: did they wear out virtue? As great a stake depends on your private act to-day, as followed their public and renowned steps. When private men shall act with vast views, the lustre will be transferred from the actions of kings to those of gentlemen.

The world has indeed been instructed by its kings, who have so magnetized the eyes of nations. It has been taught by this colossal symbol the mutual reverence that is due from man to man. The joyful loyalty with which men have every where suffered the king, the noble, or the great proprietor to walk among them by a law of his own, make his own scale of men and things, and reverse theirs, pay for benefits not with money but with honor, and represent the Law in his person, was the hieroglyphic by which they obscurely signified their consciousness of their own right and comeliness, the right of every man.

The magnetism which all original action exerts is explained when we inquire the reason of self-trust. Who is the Trustee? What is the aboriginal Self on which a universal reliance may be grounded? What is the nature and power of that science-baffling star, without parallax,[22] without calculable elements, which shoots a ray of beauty even into trivial and impure actions, if the least mark of independence appear? The inquiry leads us to that source, at once the essence of genius, the essence of virtue, and the essence of life, which we call Spontaneity or Instinct. We denote this primary wisdom as Intuition, whilst all later teachings are tuitions. In that deep force, the last fact behind which analysis cannot go, all things find their common origin. For the sense of being which in calm hours rises, we know not how, in the soul, is not diverse from things, from space, from light, from time, from man, but one with them, and proceedeth obviously from the same source whence their life and being also proceedeth. We first share the life by which

21. **Alfred . . . Gustavus:** Emerson refers to the national heroes of three countries: Alfred the Great (849–899) of England, Scanderbeg (1404–1468) of Albania, and Gustavus (1594–1632) of Sweden.
22. **science-baffling star, without parallax:** Parallax is the difference in the apparent position of an object viewed along different lines of sight. Here, Emerson apparently means without a position from which that metaphorical star can be observed.

things exist, and afterwards see them as appearances in nature, and forget that we have shared their cause. Here is the fountain of action and the fountain of thought. Here are the lungs of that inspiration which giveth man wisdom, of that inspiration of man which cannot be denied without impiety and atheism. We lie in the lap of immense intelligence, which makes us organs of its activity and receivers of its truth. When we discern justice, when we discern truth, we do nothing of ourselves, but allow a passage to its beams. If we ask whence this comes, if we seek to pry into the soul that causes, – all metaphysics, all philosophy is at fault. Its presence or its absence is all we can affirm. Every man discerns between the voluntary acts of his mind, and his involuntary perceptions. And to his involuntary perceptions, he knows a perfect respect is due. He may err in the expression of them, but he knows that these things are so, like day and night, not to be disputed. All my wilful actions and acquisitions are but roving; – the most trivial reverie, the faintest native emotion are domestic and divine. Thoughtless people contradict as readily the statement of perceptions as of opinions, or rather much more readily; for, they do not distinguish between perception and notion. They fancy that I choose to see this or that thing. But perception is not whimsical, but fatal. If I see a trait, my children will see it after me, and in course of time, all mankind, – although it may chance that no one has seen it before me. For my perception of it is as much a fact as the sun.

The relations of the soul to the divine spirit are so pure that it is profane to seek to interpose helps. It must be that when God speaketh, he should communicate not one thing, but all things; should fill the world with his voice; should scatter forth light, nature, time, souls, from the centre of the present thought; and new date and new create the whole. Whenever a mind is simple, and receives a divine wisdom, then old things pass away, – means, teachers, texts, temples fall; it lives now and absorbs past and future into the present hour. All things are made sacred by relation to it, – one thing as much as another. All things are dissolved to their centre by their cause, and in the universal miracle petty and particular miracles disappear. This is and must be. If, therefore, a man claims to know and speak of God, and carries you backward to the phraseology of some old mouldered nation in another country, in another world, believe him not. Is the acorn better than the oak which is its fulness and completion? Is the parent better than the child into whom he has cast his ripened being? Whence then this worship of the past? The centuries are conspirators against the sanity and majesty of the soul. Time and space are but physiological colors which the eye maketh, but the soul is light; where it is, is day; where it was, is night; and history is an impertinence and an injury, if it be anything more than a cheerful apologue or parable of my being and becoming.

Man is timid and apologetic. He is no longer upright. He dares not say 'I think,' 'I am,' but quotes some saint or sage. He is ashamed before the blade of grass or the blowing rose. These roses under my window make no reference to former roses or to better ones; they are for what they are; they exist with God to-day. There is no time to them. There is simply the rose; it is perfect in every moment of its existence. Before a leaf-bud has burst, its whole life acts; in the full-blown flower, there is no more; in the leafless root, there is no less. Its nature is satisfied, and it satisfies nature, in all moments alike. There is no time to it. But man postpones or remembers; he does not live in the present, but with reverted eye laments the past, or, heedless of the riches that surround him, stands on tiptoe to foresee the future. He cannot be happy and strong until he too lives with nature in the present, above time.

This should be plain enough. Yet see what strong intellects dare not yet hear God himself, unless he speak the phraseology of I know not what David, or Jeremiah, or Paul.[23] We shall not always set so great a price on a few texts, on a few lives. We are like children who repeat by rote the sentences of grandames and tutors, and, as they grow older, of the men of talents and character they chance to see, – painfully recollecting the exact words they spoke; afterwards, when they come into the point of view which those had who uttered these sayings, they understand them, and are willing to let the words go; for, at any time, they can use words as good, when occasion comes. So was it with us, so will it be, if we proceed. If we live truly, we shall see truly. It is as easy for the strong man to be strong, as it is for the weak to be weak. When we have new perception, we shall gladly disburthen the memory of its hoarded treasures as old rubbish. When a man lives with God, his voice shall be as sweet as the murmur of the brook and the rustle of the corn.

And now at last the highest truth on this subject remains unsaid; probably, cannot be said; for all that we say is the far off remembering of the intuition. That thought, by what I can now nearest approach to say it, is this. When good is near you, when you have life in yourself, – it is not by any known or appointed way; you shall not discern the foot-prints of any other; you shall not see the face of man; you shall not hear any name; – the way, the thought, the good shall be wholly strange and new. It shall exclude all other being. You take the way from man not to man. All persons that ever existed are its fugitive ministers. There shall be no fear in it. Fear and hope are alike beneath it. It asks nothing. There is somewhat low even in hope. We are then in vision. There is nothing that can be called gratitude nor properly joy. The soul is raised over passion. It seeth identity and eternal causation. It is a perceiving that Truth and Right are. Hence it becomes a Tranquillity out of the knowing that all things go well. Vast spaces of nature; the Atlantic Ocean, the South Sea; vast intervals of time, years, centuries, are of no account. This which I think and feel, underlay that former state of life and circumstances, as it does underlie my present, and will always all circumstance, and what is called life, and what is called death.

Life only avails, not the having lived. Power ceases in the instant of repose; it resides in the moment of transition from a past to a new state; in the shooting of the gulf; in the darting to an aim. This one fact the world hates, that the soul *becomes*; for, that forever degrades the past; turns all riches to poverty; all reputation to a shame; confounds the saint with the rogue; shoves Jesus and Judas equally aside. Why then do we prate of self-reliance? Inasmuch as the soul is present, there will be power not confident but agent. To talk of reliance, is a poor external way of speaking. Speak rather of that which relies, because it works and is. Who has more soul than I, masters me, though he should not raise his finger. Round him I must revolve by the gravitation of spirits; who has less, I rule with like facility. We fancy it rhetoric when we speak of eminent virtue. We do not

---

23. **David . . . Paul:** King David of Israel, the reputed author of many of the Psalms; the Old Testament prophet Jeremiah, whose writings are gathered in the book of Jeremiah; and the apostle Paul, author of a substantial portion of the New Testament.

yet see that virtue is Height, and that a man or a company of men plastic and permeable to principles, by the law of nature must overpower and ride all cities, nations, kings, rich men, poets, who are not.

This is the ultimate fact which we so quickly reach on this as on every topic, the resolution of all into the ever blessed ONE. Virtue is the governor, the creator, the reality. All things real are so by so much of virtue as they contain. Hardship, husbandry, hunting, whaling, war, eloquence, personal weight, are somewhat, and engage my respect as examples of the soul's presence and impure action. I see the same law working in nature for conservation and growth. The poise of a planet, the bended tree recovering itself from the strong wind, the vital resources of every vegetable and animal, are also demonstrations of the self-sufficing, and therefore self-relying soul. All history from its highest to its trivial passages is the various record of this power.

Thus all concentrates; let us not rove; let us sit at home with the cause. Let us stun and astonish the intruding rabble of men and books and institutions by a simple declaration of the divine fact. Bid them take the shoes from off their feet, for God is here within.[24] Let our simplicity judge them, and our docility to our own law demonstrate the poverty of nature and fortune beside our native riches.

But now we are a mob. Man does not stand in awe of man, nor is the soul admonished to stay at home, to put itself in communication with the internal ocean, but it goes abroad to beg a cup of water of the urns of men. We must go alone. Isolation must precede true society. I like the silent church before the service begins, better than any preaching. How far off, how cool, how chaste the persons look, begirt each one with a precinct or sanctuary. So let us always sit. Why should we assume the faults of our friend, or wife, or father, or child, because they sit around our hearth, or are said to have the same blood? All men have my blood, and I have all men's. Not for that will I adopt their petulance or folly, even to the extent of being ashamed of it. But your isolation must not be mechanical, but spiritual, that is, must be elevation. At times the whole world seems to be in conspiracy to importune you with emphatic trifles. Friend, client, child, sickness, fear, want, charity, all knock at once at thy closet door and say, 'Come out unto us.' — Do not spill thy soul; do not all descend; keep thy state; stay at home in thine own heaven; come not for a moment into their facts, into their hubbub of conflicting appearances, but let in the light of thy law on their confusion. The power men possess to annoy me, I give them by a weak curiosity. No man can come near me but through my act. "What we love that we have, but by desire we bereave ourselves of the love."[25]

If we cannot at once rise to the sanctities of obedience and faith, let us at least resist our temptations, let us enter into the state of war, and wake Thor and Woden, courage and constancy in our Saxon breasts.[26] This is to be done in our smooth times by speaking

---

24. **Bid . . . within:** Speaking from the midst of the burning bush, God tells Moses: "Draw not nigh hither: put off thy shoes from off thy feet, for the place whereon thou standest is holy ground" (Exodus 3:5).
25. **"What . . . the love":** In a notebook, Emerson attributed this otherwise-unidentified quotation to the German poet, playwright, and philosopher Friedrich von Schiller (1759-1805).
26. **wake Thor and Woden . . . Saxon breasts:** Emerson identifies the Norse gods of thunder and war as the ancestral gods of those of English ancestry, or Anglo-Saxons.

the truth. Check this lying hospitality and lying affection. Live no longer to the expectation of these deceived and deceiving people with whom we converse. Say to them, O father, O mother, O wife, O brother, O friend, I have lived with you after appearances hitherto. Henceforward I am the truth's. Be it known unto you that henceforward I obey no law less than the eternal law. I will have no covenants but proximities. I shall endeavor to nourish my parents, to support my family, to be the chaste husband of one wife, — but these relations I must fill after a new and unprecedented way. I appeal from your customs. I must be myself. I cannot break myself any longer for you, or you. If you can love me for what I am, we shall be the happier. If you cannot, I will still seek to deserve that you should. I must be myself. I will not hide my tastes or aversions. I will so trust that what is deep is holy, that I will do strongly before the sun and moon whatever inly rejoices me, and the heart appoints. If you are noble, I will love you; if you are not, I will not hurt you and myself by hypocritical attentions. If you are true, but not in the same truth with me, cleave to your companions; I will seek my own. I do this not selfishly but humbly and truly. It is alike your interest and mine and all men's, however long we have dwelt in lies, to live in truth. Does this sound harsh to-day? You will soon love what is dictated by your nature as well as mine, and if we follow the truth, it will bring us out safe at last. — But so you may give these friends pain. Yes, but I cannot sell my liberty and my power, to save their sensibility. Besides, all persons have their moments of reason when they look out into the region of absolute truth; then will they justify me and do the same thing.

The populace think that your rejection of popular standards is a rejection of all standard, and mere antinomianism;[27] and the bold sensualist will use the name of philosophy to gild his crimes. But the law of consciousness abides. There are two confessionals, in one or the other of which we must be shriven. You may fulfil your round of duties by clearing yourself in the *direct*, or, in the *reflex* way. Consider whether you have satisfied your relations to father, mother, cousin, neighbor, town, cat, and dog; whether any of these can upbraid you. But I may also neglect this reflex standard, and absolve me to myself. I have my own stern claims and perfect circle. It denies the name of duty to many offices that are called duties. But if I can discharge its debts, it enables me to dispense with the popular code. If any one imagines that this law is lax, let him keep its commandment one day.

And truly it demands something godlike in him who has cast off the common motives of humanity, and has ventured to trust himself for a task-master. High be his heart, faithful his will, clear his sight, that he may in good earnest be doctrine, society, law to himself, that a simple purpose may be to him as strong as iron necessity is to others.

If any man consider the present aspects of what is called by distinction *society*, he will see the need of these ethics. The sinew and heart of man seem to be drawn out, and we are become timorous desponding whimperers. We are afraid of truth, afraid of

---

27. **antinomianism:** The doctrine that Christians are exempt from the obligations of moral law since faith alone is necessary for salvation.

fortune, afraid of death, and afraid of each other. Our age yields no great and perfect persons. We want men and women who shall renovate life and our social state, but we see that most natures are insolvent; cannot satisfy their own wants, have an ambition out of all proportion to their practical force, and so do lean and beg day and night continually. Our housekeeping is mendicant, our arts, our occupations, our marriages, our religion we have not chosen, but society has chosen for us. We are parlor soldiers. The rugged battle of fate, where strength is born, we shun.

If our young men miscarry in their first enterprizes, they lose all heart. If the young merchant fails, men say he is *ruined.* If the finest genius studies at one of our colleges, and is not installed in an office within one year afterwards in the cities or suburbs of Boston or New York, it seems to his friends and to himself that he is right in being disheartened and in complaining the rest of his life. A sturdy lad from New Hampshire or Vermont, who in turn tries all the professions, who *teams it, farms it, peddles,* keeps a school, preaches, edits a newspaper, goes to Congress, buys a township, and so forth, in successive years, and always, like a cat, falls on his feet, is worth a hundred of these city dolls. He walks abreast with his days, and feels no shame in not 'studying a profession,' for he does not postpone his life, but lives already. He has not one chance, but a hundred chances. Let a stoic[28] arise who shall reveal the resources of man, and tell men they are not leaning willows, but can and must detach themselves; that with the exercise of self-trust, new powers shall appear; that a man is the word made flesh, born to shed healing to the nations, that he should be ashamed of our compassion, and that the moment he acts from himself, tossing the laws, the books, idolatries, and customs out of the window, — we pity him no more but thank and revere him, — and that teacher shall restore the life of man to splendor, and make his name dear to all History.

It is easy to see that a greater self-reliance, — a new respect for the divinity in man, — must work a revolution in all the offices and relations of men; in their religion; in their education; in their pursuits; their modes of living; their association; in their property; in their speculative views.

1.   In what prayers do men allow themselves! That which they call a holy office, is not so much as brave and manly. Prayer looks abroad and asks for some foreign addition to come through some foreign virtue, and loses itself in endless mazes of natural and supernatural, and mediatorial and miraculous. Prayer that craves a particular commodity — any thing less than all good, is vicious. Prayer is the contemplation of the facts of life from the highest point of view. It is the soliloquy of a beholding and jubilant soul. It is the spirit of God pronouncing his works good. But prayer as a means to effect a private end, is theft and meanness. It supposes dualism and not unity in nature and consciousness. As soon as the man is at one with God, he will not beg. He will then see prayer in all action. The prayer of the farmer kneeling in his field to weed it, the prayer of the rower kneeling with the stroke of his oar, are true prayers heard throughout

---

28. **stoic:** Adherent of a Greek school of philosophy that encouraged being attuned with one's inner self and being content with one's present state of being.

nature, though for cheap ends. Caratach, in Fletcher's *Bonduca*, when admonished to inquire the mind of the god Audate, replies,

> "His hidden meaning lie in our endeavors,
> Our valors are our best gods."[29]

Another sort of false prayers are our regrets. Discontent is the want of self-reliance: it is infirmity of will. Regret calamities, if you can thereby help the sufferer; if not, attend your own work, and already the evil begins to be repaired. Our sympathy is just as base. We come to them who weep foolishly, and sit down and cry for company, instead of imparting to them truth and health in rough electric shocks, putting them once more in communication with the soul. The secret of fortune is joy in our hands. Welcome evermore to gods and men is the self-helping man. For him all doors are flung wide. Him all tongues greet, all honors crown, all eyes follow with desire. Our love goes out to him and embraces him, because he did not need it. We solicitously and apologetically caress and celebrate him, because he held on his way and scorned our disapprobation. The gods love him because men hated him. "To the persevering mortal," said Zoroaster,[30] "the blessed Immortals are swift."

As men's prayers are a disease of the will, so are their creeds a disease of the intellect. They say with those foolish Israelites, 'Let not God speak to us, lest we die. Speak thou, speak any man with us, and we will obey.'[31] Everywhere I am bereaved of meeting God in my brother, because he has shut his own temple doors, and recites fables merely of his brother's, or his brother's brother's God. Every new mind is a new classification. If it prove a mind of uncommon activity and power, a Locke, a Lavoisier, a Hutton, a Bentham, a Spurzheim, it imposes its classification on other men, and lo! a new system.[32] In proportion always to the depth of the thought, and so to the number of the objects it touches and brings within reach of the pupil, is his complacency. But chiefly is this apparent in creeds and churches, which are also classifications of some powerful mind acting on the great elemental thought of Duty, and man's relation to the Highest. Such is Calvinism, Quakerism, Swedenborgianism.[33] The pupil takes the same delight in subordinating every thing to the new terminology that a girl does who has just learned botany, in seeing a new earth and new seasons thereby. It will happen for a time, that the pupil will feel a real debt to the teacher, — will find his intellectual power has grown by the study of his writings. This will continue until he has exhausted his master's mind. But in all unbalanced minds, the classification is idolized, passes for the end, and not for a speedily exhaustible means, so that the walls of the system blend to their eye in the

---

29. "His . . . gods": Beaumont and Fletcher's play *Bonduca* (c. 1613), lines 1294-95.
30. Zoroaster: Persian philosopher of the sixth century BCE.
31. 'Let not . . . obey': A paraphrase of what the Israelites say to Moses in Exodus 20:19.
32. If it prove . . . a new system: Emerson refers to several scientists and philosophers known for their development of systems of thinking: John Locke (1632-1704), Antoine Lavoisier (1743-1794), Charles Hutton (1737-1823), Jeremy Bentham (1748-1832), and Johann Kaspar Spurzheim (1776-1832).
33. Calvinism, Quakerism, Swedenborgianism: Religious movements founded by or based on the teachings of the French theologian John Calvin (1509-1564), the English dissenter George Fox (1624-1691), and the Swedish scientist and philosopher Emanuel Swedenborg.

remote horizon with the walls of the universe; the luminaries of heaven seem to them hung on the arch their master built. They cannot imagine how you aliens have any right to see, – how you can see; 'It must be somehow that you stole the light from us.' They do not yet perceive, that, light unsystematic, indomitable, will break into any cabin, even into theirs. Let them chirp awhile and call it their own. If they are honest and do well, presently their neat new pinfold will be too strait and low, will crack, will lean, will rot and vanish, and the immortal light, all young and joyful, million-orbed, million-colored, will beam over the universe as on the first morning.

2. It is for want of self-culture that the idol of Travelling, the idol of Italy, of England, of Egypt, remains for all educated Americans. They who made England, Italy, or Greece venerable in the imagination, did so not by rambling round creation as a moth round a lamp, but by sticking fast where they were, like an axis of the earth. In manly hours, we feel that duty is our place, and that the merrymen of circumstance should follow as they may. The soul is no traveller: the wise man stays at home with the soul, and when his necessities, his duties, on any occasion call him from his house, or into foreign lands, he is at home still, and is not gadding abroad from himself, and shall make men sensible by the expression of his countenance, that he goes the missionary of wisdom and virtue, and visits cities and men like a sovereign, and not like an interloper or a valet.

I have no churlish objection to the circumnavigation of the globe, for the purposes of art, of study, and benevolence, so that the man is first domesticated, or does not go abroad with the hope of finding somewhat greater than he knows. He who travels to be amused, or to get somewhat which he does not carry, travels away from himself, and grows old even in youth among old things. In Thebes, in Palmyra,[34] his will and mind have become old and dilapidated as they. He carries ruins to ruins.

Travelling is a fool's paradise. We owe to our first journeys the discovery that place is nothing. At home I dream that at Naples, at Rome, I can be intoxicated with beauty, and lose my sadness. I pack my trunk, embrace my friends, embark on the sea, and at last wake up in Naples, and there beside me is the stern Fact, the sad self, unrelenting, identical, that I fled from. I seek the Vatican, and the palaces. I affect to be intoxicated with sights and suggestions, but I am not intoxicated. My giant goes with me wherever I go.

3. But the rage of travelling is itself only a symptom of a deeper unsoundness affecting the whole intellectual action. The intellect is vagabond, and the universal system of education fosters restlessness. Our minds travel when our bodies are forced to stay at home. We imitate; and what is imitation but the travelling of the mind? Our houses are built with foreign taste; our shelves are garnished with foreign ornaments; our opinions, our tastes, our whole minds lean, and follow the Past and the Distant, as the eyes of a maid follow her mistress. The soul created the arts wherever they have flourished. It was in his own mind that the artist sought his model. It was an application of his own thought to the thing to be done and the conditions to be observed. And why need we copy

---

34. **Thebes . . . Palmyra:** Thebes, the capital city of ancient Egypt; Palmyra, an oasis in the Syrian desert that was a cultural center of the Greco-Roman world.

the Doric or the Gothic model?[35] Beauty, convenience, grandeur of thought, and quaint expression are as near to us as to any, and if the American artist will study with hope and love the precise thing to be done by him, considering the climate, the soil, the length of the day, the wants of the people, the habit and form of the government, he will create a house in which all these will find themselves fitted, and taste and sentiment will be satisfied also.

Insist on yourself; never imitate. Your own gift you can present every moment with the cumulative force of a whole life's cultivation; but of the adopted talent of another, you have only an extemporaneous, half possession. That which each can do best, none but his Maker can teach him. No man yet knows what it is, nor can, till that person has exhibited it. Where is the master who could have taught Shakspeare? Where is the master who could have instructed Franklin, or Washington, or Bacon, or Newton? Every great man is an unique. The Scipionism of Scipio is precisely that part he could not borrow. If any body will tell me whom the great man imitates in the original crisis when he performs a great act, I will tell him who else than himself can teach him. Shakspeare will never be made by the study of Shakspeare. Do that which is assigned thee, and thou canst not hope too much or dare too much. There is at this moment, there is for me an utterance bare and grand as that of the colossal chisel of Phidias, or trowel of the Egyptians, or the pen of Moses, or Dante,[36] but different from all these. Not possibly will the soul all rich, all eloquent, with thousand-cloven tongue, deign to repeat itself; but if I can hear what these patriarchs say, surely I can reply to them in the same pitch of voice: for the ear and the tongue are two organs of one nature. Dwell up there in the simple and noble regions of thy life, obey thy heart, and thou shalt reproduce the Foreworld again.

4. As our Religion, our Education, our Art look abroad, so does our spirit of society. All men plume themselves on the improvement of society, and no man improves.

Society never advances. It recedes as fast on one side as it gains on the other. Its progress is only apparent, like the workers of a treadmill. It undergoes continual changes: it is barbarous, it is civilized, it is christianized, it is rich, it is scientific; but this change is not amelioration. For every thing that is given, something is taken. Society acquires new arts and loses old instincts. What a contrast between the well-clad, reading, writing, thinking American, with a watch, a pencil, and a bill of exchange in his pocket, and the naked New Zealander, whose property is a club, a spear, a mat, and an undivided twentieth of a shed to sleep under. But compare the health of the two men, and you shall see that his aboriginal strength the white man has lost. If the traveller tell us truly, strike the savage with a broad axe, and in a day or two the flesh shall unite and heal as if you struck the blow into soft pitch, and the same blow shall send the white to his grave.

---

35. **Doric or the Gothic model:** Greek Revival and Gothic Revival were popular styles of architecture during the first half of the nineteenth century in the United States.

36. **Phidias . . . Dante:** Phidias, who lived during the fifth century BCE, is generally regarded as the greatest ancient Greek sculptor; the Italian poet Dante Alighieri (1265-1321) wrote one of the acknowledged masterpieces of world literature, the *Divine Comedy*.

The civilized man has built a coach, but has lost the use of his feet. He is supported on crutches, but loses so much support of muscle. He has got a fine Geneva watch, but he has lost the skill to tell the hour by the sun. A Greenwich nautical almanac he has, and so being sure of the information when he wants it, the man in the street does not know a star in the sky. The solstice he does not observe; the equinox he knows as little; and the whole bright calendar of the year is without a dial in his mind. His notebooks impair his memory; his libraries overload his wit; the insurance office increases the number of accidents; and it may be a question whether machinery does not encumber; whether we have not lost by refinement some energy, by a christianity entrenched in establishments and forms, some vigor of wild virtue. For every stoic was a stoic; but in Christendom where is the Christian?

There is no more deviation in the moral standard than in the standard of height or bulk. No greater men are now than ever were. A singular equality may be observed between the great men of the first and of the last ages; nor can all the science, art, religion and philosophy of the nineteenth century avail to educate greater men than Plutarch's heroes,[37] three or four and twenty centuries ago. Not in time is the race progressive. Phocion, Socrates, Anaxagoras, Diogenes,[38] are great men, but they leave no class. He who is really of their class will not be called by their name, but be wholly his own man, and, in his turn the founder of a sect. The arts and inventions of each period are only its costume, and do not invigorate men. The harm of the improved machinery may compensate its good. Hudson and Behring[39] accomplished so much in their fishing-boats, as to astonish Parry and Franklin,[40] whose equipment exhausted the resources of science and art. Galileo, with an opera-glass, discovered a more splendid series of facts than any one since. Columbus found the New World in an undecked boat. It is curious to see the periodical disuse and perishing of means and machinery which were introduced with loud laudation, a few years or centuries before. The great genius returns to essential man. We reckoned the improvements of the art of war among the triumphs of science, and yet Napoleon conquered Europe by the Bivouac, which consisted of falling back on naked valor, and disencumbering it of all aids. The Emperor held it impossible to make a perfect army, says Las Cases,[41] "without abolishing our arms, magazines, commissaries, and carriages, until in imitation of the Roman custom, the soldier should receive his supply of corn, grind it in his hand-mill, and bake his bread himself."

Society is a wave. The wave moves onward, but the water of which it is composed, does not. The same particle does not rise from the valley to the ridge. Its unity is only

---

37. **Plutarch's heroes:** Those celebrated in a series of biographies of famous Greeks and Romans by the Greek scholar Plutarch (46?-120?).

38. **Phocion . . . Diogenes:** Ancient Greek philosophers.

39. **Hudson and Behring:** Navigators Henry Hudson (d. 1611) and Vitus Jonassen Bering (1680-1741).

40. **Parry and Franklin:** Arctic explorers Sir William Edward Perry (1790-1855) and Sir John Franklin (1786-1847).

41. **Las Cases:** Comte Emmanuel de Las Cases (1766-1842) wrote an eight-volume biography of Napoleon, *Mémorial de Sainte-Hélène* (1823).

phenomenal. The persons who make up a nation to-day, next year die, and their experience with them.

And so the reliance on Property, including the reliance on governments which protect it, is the want of self-reliance. Men have looked away from themselves and at things so long, that they have come to esteem what they call the soul's progress, namely, the religious, learned, and civil institutions, as guards of property, and they deprecate assaults on these, because they feel them to be assaults on property. They measure their esteem of each other, by what each has, and not by what each is. But a cultivated man becomes ashamed of his property, ashamed of what he has, out of new respect for his being. Especially he hates what he has, if he see that it is accidental, – came to him by inheritance, or gift, or crime; then he feels that it is not having; it does not belong to him, has no root in him, and merely lies there, because no revolution or no robber takes it away. But that which a man is, does always by necessity acquire, and what the man acquires is permanent and living property, which does not wait the beck of rulers, or mobs, or revolutions, or fire, or storm, or bankruptcies, but perpetually renews itself wherever the man is put. "Thy lot or portion of life," said the Caliph Ali,[42] "is seeking after thee; therefore be at rest from seeking after it." Our dependence on these foreign goods leads us to our slavish respect for numbers. The political parties meet in numerous conventions; the greater the concourse, and with each new uproar of announcement, The delegation from Essex![43] The Democrats from New Hampshire! The Whigs of Maine! the young patriot feels himself stronger than before by a new thousand of eyes and arms. In like manner the reformers summon conventions, and vote and resolve in multitude. But not so, O friends! will the God deign to enter and inhabit you, but by a method precisely the reverse. It is only as a man puts off from himself all external support, and stands alone, that I see him to be strong and to prevail. He is weaker by every recruit to his banner. Is not a man better than a town? Ask nothing of men, and in the endless mutation, thou only firm column must presently appear the upholder of all that surrounds thee. He who knows that power is in the soul, that he is weak only because he has looked for good out of him and elsewhere, and so perceiving, throws himself unhesitatingly on his thought, instantly rights himself, stands in the erect position, commands his limbs, works miracles; just as a man who stands on his feet is stronger than a man who stands on his head.

So use all that is called Fortune. Most men gamble with her, and gain all, and lose all, as her wheel rolls. But do thou leave as unlawful these winnings, and deal with Cause and Effect, the chancellors of God. In the Will work and acquire, and thou hast chained the wheel of Chance, and shalt always drag her after thee. A political victory, a rise of rents, the recovery of your sick, or the return of your absent friend, or some other quite external event, raises your spirits, and you think good days are preparing for you. Do not believe it. It can never be so. Nothing can bring you peace but yourself. Nothing can bring you peace but the triumph of principles.

[1841]

---

42. **Caliph Ali:** Caliph Ali (602?-661) was the first leader of the Shiite branch of Islam.
43. **Essex:** A county in northeastern Massachusetts.

Reading Emerson's "Experience."   This essay appeared in Emerson's third book, *Essays: Second Series*, published in 1844. In a review of the volume in the *New-York Tribune*, Margaret Fuller observed,

> If only as a representative of the claims of individual culture in a nation which tends to lay such stress on artificial organization and external results, Mr. Emerson would be invaluable here. History will inscribe his name as a father of the country, for he is one who pleads her cause against herself.

Certainly, the essays in the volume were part of Emerson's ongoing critique of American culture and society. "Experience," however, was also inspired by deeply private concerns, especially Emerson's grief over the death of his beloved son Waldo at the age of five in 1842. In a striking departure from his usual practice of excluding details of his personal life from his writings, Emerson describes that loss early in "Experience." But the essay is less an autobiography than a philosophy of life or living – a kind of guide to what Emerson elsewhere called "conduct of life." Opening with images of darkness and disorientation, the essay develops on a sustained meditation on the gap between actual and ideal experience. "I know that the world I converse with in the city and in the farms is not the world I *think*," Emerson confides. In fact, most of the essay is devoted to a somber exploration of the experience of living in what Emerson characterizes as the *unreality* of the actual world. For him, that experience is illuminated and is made meaningful only by moments of "sanity and revelations," as he puts it in a final counter to the darkness and shadows evoked at the opening of the essay. However rare and fleeting, such moments open up the ultimate possibility of "the transformation of genius into practical power," Emerson's final, affirmative words in "Experience." The text is taken from the first edition of *Essays: Second Series* (1844).

EXPERIENCE

The lords of life, the lords of life, –
I saw them pass,
In their own guise,
Like and unlike,
Portly and grim,
Use and Surprise,
Surface and Dream,
Succession swift, and spectral Wrong,
Temperament without a tongue,
And the inventor of the game
Omnipresent without name; –
Some to see, some to be guessed,

> They marched from east to west:
> Little man, least of all,
> Among the legs of his guardians tall,
> Walked about with puzzled look: —
> Him by the hand dear nature took;
> Dearest nature, strong and kind,
> Whispered, 'Darling, never mind!
> Tomorrow they will wear another face,
> The founder thou! these are thy race!'[1]

Where do we find ourselves? In a series of which we do not know the extremes, and believe that it has none. We wake and find ourselves on a stair; there are stairs below us, which we seem to have ascended; there are stairs above us, many a one, which go upward and out of sight. But the Genius which, according to the old belief, stands at the door by which we enter, and gives us the lethe to drink,[2] that we may tell no tales, mixed the cup too strongly, and we cannot shake off the lethargy now at noonday. Sleep lingers all our lifetime about our eyes, as night hovers all day in the boughs of the fir-tree. All things swim and glitter. Our life is not so much threatened as our perception. Ghostlike we glide through nature, and should not know our place again. Did our birth fall in some fit of indigence and frugality in nature, that she was so sparing of her fire and so liberal of her earth, that it appears to us that we lack the affirmative principle, and though we have health and reason, yet we have no superfluity of spirit for new creation? We have enough to live and bring the year about, but not an ounce to impart or to invest. Ah that our Genius were a little more of a genius! We are like millers on the lower levels of a stream, when the factories above them have exhausted the water. We too fancy that the upper people must have raised their dams.

If any of us knew what we were doing, or where we are going, then when we think we best know! We do not know today whether we are busy or idle. In times when we thought ourselves indolent, we have afterwards discovered, that much was accomplished, and much was begun in us. All our days are so unprofitable while they pass, that 'tis wonderful where or when we ever got anything of this which we call wisdom, poetry, virtue. We never got it on any dated calendar day. Some heavenly days must have been intercalated somewhere, like those that Hermes won with dice of the Moon, that Osiris might be born.[3] It is said, all martyrdoms looked mean when they were suffered. Every ship is a romantic object, except that we sail in. Embark, and the romance quits our vessel, and hangs on every other sail in the horizon. Our life looks trivial, and we shun to record it. Men seem to have learned of the horizon the art of perpetual retreating and reference.

---

1. **The lords . . . thy race!:** The poem was written by Emerson.
2. **lethe to drink:** Drinking from the Lethe, a river in Greek mythology, induces forgetfulness.
3. **Hermes . . . born:** In *Morals*, Plutarch tells the Egyptian story of how the goddess Hermes overturned her husband's ruling that she could not bear children on any day of the year by winning five new days in the calendar from the Moon. Osiris was born on one of those days.

'Yonder uplands are rich pasturage, and my neighbor has fertile meadow, but my field,' says the querulous farmer, 'only holds the world together.' I quote another man's saying; unluckily, that other withdraws himself in the same way, and quotes me. 'Tis the trick of nature thus to degrade today; a good deal of buzz, and somewhere a result slipped magically in. Every roof is agreeable to the eye, until it is lifted; then we find tragedy and moaning women, and hard-eyed husbands, and deluges of lethe, and the men ask, 'What's the news?' as if the old were so bad. How many individuals can we count in society? how many actions? how many opinions? So much of our time is preparation, so much is routine, and so much retrospect, that the pith of each man's genius contracts itself to a very few hours. The history of literature — take the net result of Tiraboschi, Warton, or Schlegel,[4] — is a sum of very few ideas, and of very few original tales, — all the rest being variation of these. So in this great society wide lying around us, a critical analysis would find very few spontaneous actions. It is almost all custom and gross sense. There are even few opinions, and these seem organic in the speakers, and do not disturb the universal necessity.

What opium is instilled into all disaster! It shows formidable as we approach it, but there is at last no rough rasping friction, but the most slippery sliding surfaces. We fall soft on a thought. *Ate Dea* is gentle,

> "Over men's heads walking aloft,
> With tender feet treading so soft."[5]

People give and bemoan themselves, but it is not half so bad with them as they say. There are moods in which we court suffering, in the hope that here, at least, we shall find reality, sharp peaks and edges of truth. But it turns out to be scene-painting and counterfeit. The only thing grief has taught me, is to know how shallow it is. That, like all the rest, plays about the surface, and never introduces me into the reality, for contact with which, we would even pay the costly price of sons and lovers. Was it Boscovich[6] who found out that bodies never come in contact? Well, souls never touch their objects. An innavigable sea washes with silent waves between us and the things we aim at and converse with. Grief too will make us idealists. In the death of my son, now more than two years ago, I seem to have lost a beautiful estate, — no more. I cannot get it nearer to me. If tomorrow I should be informed of the bankruptcy of my principal debtors, the loss of my property would be a great inconvenience to me, perhaps, for many years; but it would leave me as it found me, — neither better nor worse. So is it with this calamity: it does not touch me: some thing which I fancied was a part of me, which could not be torn away without tearing me, nor enlarged without enriching me, falls off from me, and leaves no scar. It was caducous.[7] I grieve that grief can teach me nothing, nor carry me one step into real nature. The Indian who was laid under a curse, that the wind should not blow on him, nor

---

4. **Tiraboschi . . . Schlegel:** Literary histories by the Italian writer Girolamo Tiraboschi (1731-1794), the British writer Thomas Warton (1728-1790), and the German writer Friedrich von Schlegel (1772-1829).
5. *Ate Dea . . . treading so soft:* Roman goddess of evil, infatuation, and mischief; Homer's *The Iliad*, Book 19.
6. **Boscovich:** Ruggiero Giuseppe Boscovich (1711-1787), an Italian physicist.
7. **caducous:** Dropping off easily at an early stage or in the normal course of development of an organism.

water flow to him, nor fire burn him, is a type of us all. The dearest events are summer-rain, and we the Para coats[8] that shed every drop. Nothing is left us now but death. We look to that with a grim satisfaction, saying, there at least is reality that will not dodge us.

I take this evanescence and lubricity of all objects, which lets them slip through our fingers then when we clutch hardest, to be the most unhandsome part of our condition. Nature does not like to be observed, and likes that we should be her fools and playmates. We may have the sphere for our cricket-ball, but not a berry for our philosophy. Direct strokes she never gave us power to make; all our blows glance, all our hits are accidents. Our relations to each other are oblique and casual.

Dream delivers us to dream, and there is no end to illusion. Life is a train of moods like a string of beads, and, as we pass through them, they prove to be many-colored lenses which paint the world their own hue, and each shows only what lies in its focus. From the mountain you see the mountain. We animate what we can, and we see only what we animate. Nature and books belong to the eyes that see them. It depends on the mood of the man, whether he shall see the sunset or the fine poem. There are always sunsets, and there is always genius; but only a few hours so serene that we can relish nature or criticism. The more or less depends on structure or temperament. Temperament is the iron wire on which the beads are strung. Of what use is fortune or talent to a cold and defective nature? Who cares what sensibility or discrimination a man has at some time shown, if he falls asleep in his chair? or if he laugh and giggle? or if he apologize? or is affected with egotism? or thinks of his dollar? or cannot go by food? or has gotten a child in his boyhood? Of what use is genius, if the organ is too convex or too concave, and cannot find a focal distance within the actual horizon of human life? Of what use, if the brain is too cold or too hot, and the man does not care enough for results, to stimulate him to experiment, and hold him up in it? or if the web is too finely woven, too irritable by pleasure and pain, so that life stagnates from too much reception, without due outlet? Of what use to make heroic vows of amendment, if the same old law-breaker is to keep them? What cheer can the religious sentiment yield, when that is suspected to be secretly dependent on the seasons of the year, and the state of the blood? I knew a witty physician who found theology in the biliary duct, and used to affirm that if there was disease in the liver, the man became a Calvinist, and if that organ was sound, he became a Unitarian. Very mortifying is the reluctant experience that some unfriendly excess or imbecility neutralizes the promise of genius. We see young men who owe us a new world, so readily and lavishly they promise, but they never acquit the debt; they die young and dodge the account: or if they live, they lose themselves in the crowd.

Temperament also enters fully into the system of illusions, and shuts us in a prison of glass which we cannot see. There is an optical illusion about every person we meet. In truth, they are all creatures of given temperament, which will appear in a given character, whose boundaries they will never pass: but we look at them, they seem alive, and we presume there is impulse in them. In the moment it seems impulse; in the year,

---

8. **Para coats:** Rubber raincoats.

in the lifetime, it turns out to be a certain uniform tune which the revolving barrel of the music-box must play. Men resist the conclusion in the morning, but adopt it as the evening wears on, that temper prevails over everything of time, place, and condition, and is inconsumable in the flames of religion. Some modifications the moral sentiment avails to impose, but the individual texture holds its dominion, if not to bias the moral judgments, yet to fix the measure of activity and of enjoyment.

I thus express the law as it is read from the platform of ordinary life, but must not leave it without noticing the capital exception. For temperament is a power which no man willingly hears any one praise but himself. On the platform of physics, we cannot resist the contracting influences of so-called science. Temperament puts all divinity to rout. I know the mental proclivity of physicians. I hear the chuckle of the phrenologists.[9] Theoretic kidnappers and slave-drivers, they esteem each man the victim of another, who winds him round his finger by knowing the law of his being, and by such cheap signboards as the color of his beard, or the slope of his occiput, reads the inventory of his fortunes and character. The grossest ignorance does not disgust like this impudent knowingness. The physicians say, they are not materialists; but they are: — Spirit is matter reduced to an extreme thinness: O *so* thin! — But the definition of *spiritual* should be, *that which is its own evidence.* What notions do they attach to love! what to religion! One would not willingly pronounce these words in their hearing, and give them the occasion to profane them. I saw a gracious gentleman who adapts his conversation to the form of the head of the man he talks with! I had fancied that the value of life lay in its inscrutable possibilities; in the fact that I never know, in addressing myself to a new individual, what may befall me. I carry the keys of my castle in my hand, ready to throw them at the feet of my lord, whenever and in what disguise so ever he shall appear. I know he is in the neighborhood hidden among vagabonds. Shall I preclude my future, by taking a high seat, and kindly adapting my conversation to the shape of heads? When I come to that, the doctors shall buy me for a cent. — "But, sir, medical history; the report to the Institute; the proven facts!' — I distrust the facts and the inferences. Temperament is the veto or limitation-power in the constitution, very justly applied to restrain an opposite excess in the constitution, but absurdly offered as a bar to original equity. When virtue is in presence, all subordinate powers sleep. On its own level, or in view of nature, temperament is final. I see not, if one be once caught in this trap of so-called sciences, any escape for the man from the links of the chain of physical necessity. Given such an embryo, such a history must follow. On this platform, one lives in a sty of sensualism, and would soon come to suicide. But it is impossible that the creative power should exclude itself. Into every intelligence there is a door which is never closed, through which the creator passes. The intellect, seeker of absolute truth, or the heart, lover of absolute good, intervenes for our succor, and at one whisper of these high powers, we awake from ineffectual struggles with this nightmare. We hurl it into its own hell, and cannot again contract ourselves to so base a state.

---

9. **phrenologists:** Practitioners of phrenology, a then-popular pseudoscience based on the concept that a study of the morphology of the skull — or, in common terms, bumps on the head — revealed an individual's character.

The secret of the illusoriness is in the necessity of a succession of moods or objects. Gladly we would anchor, but the anchorage is quicksand. This onward trick of nature is too strong for us: *Pero si muove.*[10] When, at night, I look at the moon and stars, I seem stationary, and they to hurry. Our love of the real draws us to permanence, but health of body consists in circulation, and sanity of mind in variety or facility of association. We need change of objects. Dedication to one thought is quickly odious. We house with the insane, and must humor them; then conversation dies out. Once I took such delight in Montaigne, that I thought I should not need any other book; before that, in Shakspeare; then in Plutarch; then in Plotinus; at one time in Bacon; afterwards in Goethe; even in Bettine;[11] but now I turn the pages of either of them languidly, whilst I still cherish their genius. So with pictures; each will bear an emphasis of attention once, which it cannot retain, though we fain would continue to be pleased in that manner. How strongly I have felt of pictures, that when you have seen one well, you must take your leave of it; you shall never see it again. I have had good lessons from pictures, which I have since seen without emotion or remark. A deduction must be made from the opinion, which even the wise express of a new book or occurrence. Their opinion gives me tidings of their mood, and some vague guess at the new fact, but is nowise to be trusted as the lasting relation between that intellect and that thing. The child asks, 'Mamma, why don't I like the story as well as when you told it me yesterday?' Alas, child, it is even so with the oldest cherubim of knowledge. But will it answer thy question to say, Because thou wert born to a whole, and this story is a particular? The reason of the pain this discovery causes us (and we make it late in respect to works of art and intellect), is the plaint of tragedy which murmurs from it in regard to persons, to friendship and love.

That immobility and absence of elasticity which we find in the arts, we find with more pain in the artist. There is no power of expansion in men. Our friends early appear to us as representatives of certain ideas, which they never pass or exceed. They stand on the brink of the ocean of thought and power, but they never take the single step that would bring them there. A man is like a bit of Labrador spar,[12] which has no lustre as you turn it in your hand, until you come to a particular angle; then it shows deep and beautiful colors. There is no adaptation or universal applicability in men, but each has his special talent, and the mastery of successful men consists in adroitly keeping themselves where and when that turn shall be oftenest to be practised. We do what we must, and call it by the best names we can, and would fain have the praise of having intended the result which ensues. I cannot recall any form of man who is not superfluous sometimes. But is not this pitiful? Life is not worth the taking, to do tricks in.

----

10. ***Pero si muove***: "Nevertheless, it moves" (Italian); what the astronomer Galileo (1564-1642) reportedly said after he was forced by the Roman Catholic Church to deny his theory that the earth revolves around the sun.
11. **Montaigne . . . Bettine**: The French essayist Michel de Montaigne (1533-1592); the Greek biographer of famous Greeks and Romans Plutarch (46?-120?); the mystical Greek philosopher Plotinus (205?-270?); the English philosopher Sir Francis Bacon (1561-1626); the influential German writer Johann Wolfgang von Goethe (1749-1842); and Elizabeth Brentano von Arnim (1785-1859), author of *Goethe's Conversations with a Child* (1835), a book much admired by Emerson.
12. **Labrador spar**: Brilliantly colored rock solidified from lava.

Of course, it needs the whole society, to give the symmetry we seek. The parti-colored wheel must revolve very fast to appear white. Something is learned too by conversing with so much folly and defect. In fine, whoever loses, we are always of the gaining party. Divinity is behind our failures and follies also. The plays of children are nonsense, but very educative nonsense. So it is with the largest and solemnest things, with commerce, government, church, marriage, and so with the history of every man's bread, and the ways by which he is to come by it. Like a bird which alights nowhere, but hops perpetually from bough to bough, is the Power which abides in no man and in no woman, but for a moment speaks from this one, and for another moment from that one.

But what help from these fineries or pedantries? What help from thought? Life is not dialectics. We, I think, in these times, have had lessons enough of the futility of criticism. Our young people have thought and written much on labor and reform, and for all that they have written, neither the world nor themselves have got on a step. Intellectual tasting of life will not supersede muscular activity. If a man should consider the nicety of the passage of a piece of bread down his throat, he would starve. At Education-Farm,[13] the noblest theory of life sat on the noblest figures of young men and maidens, quite powerless and melancholy. It would not rake or pitch a ton of hay; it would not rub down a horse; and the men and maidens it left pale and hungry. A political orator wittily compared our party promises to western roads, which opened stately enough, with planted trees on either side, to tempt the traveller, but soon became narrow and narrower, and ended in a squirrel-track, and ran up a tree. So does culture with us; it ends in head-ache. Unspeakably sad and barren does life look to those, who a few months ago were dazzled with the splendor of the promise of the times. "There is now no longer any right course of action, nor any self-devotion left among the Iranis."[14] Objections and criticism we have had our fill of. There are objections to every course of life and action, and the practical wisdom infers an indifferency, from the omnipresence of objection. The whole frame of things preaches indifferency. Do not craze yourself with thinking, but go about your business anywhere. Life is not intellectual or critical, but sturdy. Its chief good is for well-mixed people who can enjoy what they find, without question. Nature hates peeping, and our mothers speak her very sense when they say, "Children; eat your victuals, and say no more of it." To fill the hour, — that is happiness; to fill the hour, and leave no crevice for a repentance or an approval. We live amid surfaces, and the true art of life is to skate well on them. Under the oldest mouldiest conventions, a man of native force prospers just as well as in the newest world, and that by skill of handling and treatment. He can take hold anywhere. Life itself is a mixture of power and form, and will not bear the least excess of either. To finish the moment, to find the journey's end in every step of the road, to live the greatest number of good hours, is wisdom. It is not the part of men, but of fanatics, or of mathematicians, if you will, to say, that, the shortness of life considered, it is not worth caring whether for so short a duration we were sprawling

---

13. **Education-Farm:** Brook Farm (1841–1847), the utopian community in West Roxbury, Massachusetts.
14. **"There . . . Iranis":** From a collection of Persian prophetic works translated into English, *The Desatir, or Sacred Writings of the Ancient Persian Prophets* (1818).

in want, or sitting high. Since our office is with moments, let us husband them. Five minutes of today are worth as much to me, as five minutes in the next millennium. Let us be poised, and wise, and our own, today. Let us treat the men and women well: treat them as if they were real: perhaps they are. Men live in their fancy, like drunkards whose hands are too soft and tremulous for successful labor. It is a tempest of fancies, and the only ballast I know, is a respect to the present hour. Without any shadow of doubt, amidst this vertigo of shows and politics, I settle myself ever the firmer in the creed, that we should not postpone and refer and wish, but do broad justice where we are, by whomsoever we deal with, accepting our actual companions and circumstances, however humble or odious, as the mystic officials to whom the universe has delegated its whole pleasure for us. If these are mean and malignant, their contentment, which is the last victory of justice, is a more satisfying echo to the heart, than the voice of poets and the casual sympathy of admirable persons. I think that however a thoughtful man may suffer from the defects and absurdities of his company, he cannot without affectation deny to any set of men and women, a sensibility to extraordinary merit. The coarse and frivolous have an instinct of superiority, if they have not a sympathy, and honor it in their blind capricious way with sincere homage.

The fine young people despise life, but in me, and in such as with me are free from dyspepsia, and to whom a day is a sound and solid good, it is a great excess of politeness to look scornful and to cry for company. I am grown by sympathy a little eager and sentimental, but leave me alone, and I should relish every hour and what it brought me, the pot-luck of the day, as heartily as the oldest gossip in the bar-room. I am thankful for small mercies. I compared notes with one of my friends who expects everything of the universe, and is disappointed when anything is less than the best, and I found that I begin at the other extreme, expecting nothing, and am always full of thanks for moderate goods. I accept the clangor and jangle of contrary tendencies. I find my account in sots and bores also. They give a reality to the circumjacent picture, which such a vanishing meteorous appearance can ill spare. In the morning I awake, and find the old world, wife, babes, and mother, Concord and Boston, the dear old spiritual world, and even the dear old devil not far off. If we will take the good we find, asking no questions, we shall have heaping measures. The great gifts are not got by analysis. Everything good is on the highway. The middle region of our being is the temperate zone. We may climb into the thin and cold realm of pure geometry and lifeless science, or sink into that of sensation. Between these extremes is the equator of life, of thought, of spirit, of poetry, — a narrow belt. Moreover, in popular experience, everything good is on the highway. A collector peeps into all the picture-shops of Europe, for a landscape of Poussin, a crayon-sketch of Salvator; but the Transfiguration, the Last Judgment, the Communion of St. Jerome, and what are as transcendent as these, are on the walls of the Vatican, the Uffizii, or the Louvre, where every footman may see them;[15] to say nothing of nature's

---

15. **A collector . . . see them:** Nicolas Poussin (1594-1665) was a French painter of historical scenes and events. Salvatore Rosa (1615-1673) was an Italian painter who specialized in landscapes. *The Transfiguration* by Raphael, *The Last Judgment* by Michelangelo, and *The Communion of St. Jerome* by Il Domenichino are paintings in major art museums in Rome, Florence, and Paris.

pictures in every street, of sunsets and sunrises every day, and the sculpture of the human body never absent. A collector recently bought at public auction, in London, for one hundred and fifty-seven guineas, an autograph of Shakspeare: but for nothing a school-boy can read Hamlet, and can detect secrets of highest concernment yet unpublished therein. I think I will never read any but the commonest books, – the Bible, Homer, Dante, Shakspeare, and Milton. Then we are impatient of so public a life and planet, and run hither and thither for nooks and secrets. The imagination delights in the wood-craft of Indians, trappers, and bee-hunters. We fancy that we are strangers, and not so intimately domesticated in the planet as the wild man, and the wild beast and bird. But the exclusion reaches them also; reaches the climbing, flying, gliding, feathered and four-footed man. Fox and woodchuck, hawk and snipe, and bittern, when nearly seen, have no more root in the deep world than man, and are just such superficial tenants of the globe. Then the new molecular philosophy shows astronomical interspaces betwixt atom and atom, shows that the world is all outside: it has no inside.

The mid-world is best. Nature, as we know her, is no saint. The lights of the church, the ascetics, Gentoos and Grahamites,[16] she does not distinguish by any favor. She comes eating and drinking and sinning. Her darlings, the great, the strong, the beautiful, are not children of our law, do not come out of the Sunday School, nor weigh their food, nor punctually keep the commandments. If we will be strong with her strength, we must not harbor such disconsolate consciences, borrowed too from the consciences of other nations. We must set up the strong present tense against all the rumors of wrath, past or to come. So many things are unsettled which it is of the first importance to settle, – and, pending their settlement, we will do as we do. Whilst the debate goes forward on the equity of commerce, and will not be closed for a century or two, New and Old England may keep shop. Law of copyright and international copyright is to be discussed, and, in the interim, we will sell our books for the most we can. Expediency of literature, reason of literature, lawfulness of writing down a thought, is questioned; much is to say on both sides, and, while the fight waxes hot, thou, dearest scholar, stick to thy foolish task, add a line every hour, and between whiles add a line. Right to hold land, right of property, is disputed, and the conventions convene, and before the vote is taken, dig away in your garden, and spend your earnings as a waif or godsend to all serene and beautiful purposes. Life itself is a bubble and a skepticism, and a sleep within a sleep. Grant it, and as much more as they will, – but thou, God's darling! heed thy private dream: thou wilt not be missed in the scorning and skepticism: there are enough of them: stay there in thy closet, and toil, until the rest are agreed what to do about it. Thy sickness, they say, and thy puny habit, require that thou do this or avoid that, but know that thy life is a flitting state, a tent for a night, and do thou, sick or well, finish that stint. Thou art sick, but shalt not be worse, and the universe, which holds thee dear, shall be the better.

---

16. **Gentoos and Grahamites:** *Gentoos* was an early term for Hindus, who are vegetarians; Grahamites were followers of Sylvester Graham (1794-1851), a diet reformer who later developed the graham cracker.

Human life is made up of the two elements, power and form, and the proportion must be invariably kept, if we would have it sweet and sound. Each of these elements in excess makes a mischief as hurtful as its defect. Everything runs to excess: every good quality is noxious, if unmixed, and, to carry the danger to the edge of ruin, nature causes each man's peculiarity to superabound. Here, among the farms, we adduce the scholars as examples of this treachery. They are nature's victims of expression. You who see the artist, the orator, the poet, too near, and find their life no more excellent than that of mechanics or farmers, and themselves victims of partiality, very hollow and haggard, and pronounce them failures, – not heroes, but quacks, – conclude very reasonably, that these arts are not for man, but are disease. Yet nature will not bear you out. Irresistible nature made men such, and makes legions more of such, every day. You love the boy reading in a book, gazing at a drawing, or a cast: yet what are these millions who read and behold, but incipient writers and sculptors? Add a little more of that quality which now reads and sees, and they will seize the pen and chisel. And if one remembers how innocently he began to be an artist, he perceives that nature joined with his enemy. A man is a golden impossibility. The line he must walk is a hair's breadth. The wise through excess of wisdom is made a fool.

How easily, if fate would suffer it, we might keep forever these beautiful limits, and adjust ourselves, once for all, to the perfect calculation of the kingdom of known cause and effect. In the street and in the newspapers, life appears so plain a business, that manly resolution and adherence to the multiplication-table through all weathers, will insure success. But ah! presently comes a day, or is it only a half-hour, with its angel-whispering, – which discomfits the conclusions of nations and of years! Tomorrow again, everything looks real and angular, the habitual standards are reinstated, common sense is as rare as genius, – is the basis of genius, and experience is hands and feet to every enterprise; – and yet, he who should do his business on this understanding, would be quickly bankrupt. Power keeps quite another road than the turnpikes of choice and will, namely, the subterranean and invisible tunnels and channels of life. It is ridiculous that we are diplomatists, and doctors, and considerate people: there are no dupes like these. Life is a series of surprises, and would not be worth taking or keeping, if it were not. God delights to isolate us every day, and hide from us the past and the future. We would look about us, but with grand politeness he draws down before us an impenetrable screen of purest sky, and another behind us of purest sky. 'You will not remember,' he seems to say, 'and you will not expect.' All good conversation, manners, and action, come from a spontaneity which forgets usages, and makes the moment great. Nature hates calculators; her methods are saltatory and impulsive. Man lives by pulses; our organic movements are such; and the chemical and ethereal agents are undulatory and alternate; and the mind goes antagonizing on, and never prospers but by fits. We thrive by casualties. Our chief experiences have been casual. The most attractive class of people are those who are powerful obliquely, and not by the direct stroke: men of genius, but not yet accredited: one gets the cheer of their light, without paying too great a tax. Theirs is the beauty of the bird or the morning light, and not of art. In the thought of genius there is always a surprise; and the moral sentiment is well called "the newness," for it is never other; as new to the oldest intelligence as to the young child, – "the kingdom that cometh without observation."[17] In like manner, for practical success, there must not be too much design. A man will not be observed in doing that which he can do best. There is a certain magic about his properest action, which stupefies your powers of observation, so that though it is done before you, you wist not of it. The art of life has a pudency, and will not be exposed. Every man is an impossibility, until he is born; every thing impossible, until we see a success. The ardors of piety agree at last with the coldest skepticism, – that nothing is of us or our works, – that all is of God. Nature will not spare us the smallest leaf of laurel. All writing comes by the grace of God, and all doing and having. I would gladly be moral, and keep due metes and bounds, which I dearly love, and allow the most to the will of man, but I have set my heart on honesty in this chapter, and I can see nothing at last, in success or failure, than more or less of vital force supplied from the Eternal. The results of life are uncalculated and uncalculable. The years teach much which the days never know. The persons who compose our company, converse, and come and go, and design and execute many things, and somewhat comes of it all, but an unlooked for result. The individual is always mistaken. He designed many things, and drew in other persons as coadjutors, quarrelled with some or all, blundered much, and something is done; all are a little advanced, but the individual is always mistaken. It turns out somewhat new, and very unlike what he promised himself.

The ancients, struck with this irreducibleness of the elements of human life to calculation, exalted Chance into a divinity, but that is to stay too long at the spark, – which glitters truly at one point, – but the universe is warm with the latency of the same fire. The miracle of life which will not be expounded, but will remain a miracle, introduces a new element. In the growth of the embryo, Sir Everard Home,[18] I think, noticed that the evolution was not from one central point, but co-active from three or more points. Life has no memory. That which proceeds in succession might be remembered, but that which is coexistent, or ejaculated from a deeper cause, as yet far from being conscious, knows not its own tendency. So is it with us, now skeptical, or without unity, because immersed in forms and effects all seeming to be of equal yet hostile value, and now religious, whilst in the reception of spiritual law. Bear with these distractions, with this coetaneous[19] growth of the parts: they will one day be *members*, and obey one will. On that one will, on that secret cause, they nail our attention and hope. Life is hereby melted into an expectation or a religion. Underneath the inharmonious and trivial particulars, is a musical perfection, the Ideal journeying always with us, the heaven without rent or seam. Do but observe the mode of our illumination. When I converse with a profound mind, or if at any time being alone I have good thoughts, I do not at once arrive at satisfactions, as when, being thirsty, I drink water, or go to the fire, being cold: no! but I am at first apprised of my vicinity to a new and excellent region of life. By persisting to read or to think, this region gives further sign of itself, as it were in flashes of light, in

---

17. **"the . . . observation"**: Luke 17:20.
18. **Sir Everard Home:** Scottish surgeon (1756–1832).
19. **coetaneous:** Simultaneous.

sudden discoveries of its profound beauty and repose, as if the clouds that covered it parted at intervals, and showed the approaching traveller the inland mountains, with the tranquil eternal meadows spread at their base, whereon flocks graze, and shepherds pipe and dance. But every insight from this realm of thought is felt as initial, and promises a sequel. I do not make it; I arrive there, and behold what was there already. I make! O no! I clap my hands in infantine joy and amazement, before the first opening to me of this august magnificence, old with the love and homage of innumerable ages, young with the life of life, the sunbright Mecca of the desert.[20] And what a future it opens! I feel a new heart beating with the love of the new beauty. I am ready to die out of nature, and be born again into this new yet unapproachable America I have found in the West.

> "Since neither now nor yesterday began
> These thoughts, which have been ever, nor yet can
> A man be found who their first entrance knew."[21]

If I have described life as a flux of moods, I must now add, that there is that in us which changes not, and which ranks all sensations and states of mind. The consciousness in each man is a sliding scale, which identifies him now with the First Cause, and now with the flesh of his body; life above life, in infinite degrees. The sentiment from which it sprung determines the dignity of any deed, and the question ever is, not, what you have done or forborne, but, at whose command you have done or forborne it.

Fortune, Minerva,[22] Muse, Holy Ghost, — these are quaint names, too narrow to cover this unbounded substance. The baffled intellect must still kneel before this cause, which refuses to be named, — ineffable cause, which every fine genius has essayed to represent by some emphatic symbol, as, Thales by water, Anaximenes by air, Anaxagoras[23] by (Νοῦς) thought, Zoroaster[24] by fire, Jesus and the moderns by love: and the metaphor of each has become a national religion. The Chinese Mencius[25] has not been the least successful in his generalization. "I fully understand language," he said, "and nourish well my vast-flowing vigor." — "I beg to ask what you call vast-flowing vigor?" — said his companion. "The explanation," replied Mencius, "is difficult. This vigor is supremely great, and in the highest degree unbending. Nourish it correctly, and do it no injury, and it will fill up the vacancy between heaven and earth. This vigor accords with and assists justice and reason, and leaves no hunger." — In our more correct writing, we give to this generalization the name of Being, and thereby confess that we have arrived as far as we can go. Suffice it for the joy of the universe, that we have not arrived at a wall, but at interminable oceans. Our life seems not present, so much as prospective; not for the affairs on which it is wasted, but as a hint of this vast-flowing vigor. Most of life seems to be mere advertisement of faculty: information is given us not to sell ourselves cheap; that we are

---

20. **Mecca of the desert**: A pilgrimage to Mecca, the holiest city of Islam, is obligatory for all able Muslims.
21. **"Since . . . knew"**: From *Antigone* by the ancient Greek dramatist Sophocles (496–406 BCE).
22. **Minerva**: Roman goddess of wisdom.
23. **Thales . . . Anaximenes . . . Anaxagoras**: Ancient Greek philosophers.
24. **Zoroaster**: Sixth-century BCE Persian prophet.
25. **Mencius**: Third-century BCE Confucian philosopher Meng-Tse.

very great. So, in particulars, our greatness is always in a tendency or direction, not in an action. It is for us to believe in the rule, not in the exception. The noble are thus known from the ignoble. So in accepting the leading of the sentiments, it is not what we believe concerning the immortality of the soul, or the like, but *the universal impulse to believe*, that is the material circumstance, and is the principal fact in the history of the globe. Shall we describe this cause as that which works directly? The spirit is not helpless or needful of mediate organs. It has plentiful powers and direct effects. I am explained without explaining, I am felt without acting, and where I am not. Therefore all just persons are satisfied with their own praise. They refuse to explain themselves, and are content that new actions should do them that office. They believe that we communicate without speech, and above speech, and that no right action of ours is quite unaffecting to our friends, at whatever distance; for the influence of action is not to be measured by miles. Why should I fret myself, because a circumstance has occurred, which hinders my presence where I was expected? If I am not at the meeting, my presence where I am, should be as useful to the commonwealth of friendship and wisdom, as would be my presence in that place. I exert the same quality of power in all places. Thus journeys the mighty Ideal before us; it never was known to fall into the rear. No man ever came to an experience which was satiating, but his good is tidings of a better. Onward and onward! In liberated moments, we know that a new picture of life and duty is already possible; the elements already exist in many minds around you, of a doctrine of life which shall transcend any written record we have. The new statement will comprise the skepticisms, as well as the faiths of society, and out of unbeliefs a creed shall be formed. For, skepticisms are not gratuitous or lawless, but are limitations of the affirmative statement, and the new philosophy must take them in, and make affirmations outside of them, just as much as it must include the oldest beliefs.

It is very unhappy, but too late to be helped, the discovery we have made, that we exist. That discovery is called the Fall of Man. Ever afterwards, we suspect our instruments. We have learned that we do not see directly, but mediately, and that we have no means of correcting these colored and distorting lenses which we are, or of computing the amount of their errors. Perhaps these subject-lenses have a creative power; perhaps there are no objects. Once we lived in what we saw; now, the rapaciousness of this new power, which threatens to absorb all things, engages us. Nature, art, persons, letters, religions, — objects, successively tumble in, and God is but one of its ideas. Nature and literature are subjective phenomena; every evil and every good thing is a shadow which we cast. The street is full of humiliations to the proud. As the fop contrived to dress his bailiffs in his livery, and make them wait on his guests at table, so the chagrins which the bad heart gives off as bubbles, at once take form as ladies and gentlemen in the street, shopmen or bar-keepers in hotels, and threaten or insult whatever is threatenable and unsuitable in us. 'Tis the same with our idolatries. People forget that it is the eye which makes the horizon, and the rounding mind's eye which makes this or that man a type or representative of humanity with the name of hero or saint. Jesus the "providential man," is a good man on whom many people are agreed that these optical laws shall take effect. By love on one part, and by forbearance to press objection on the other part, it is for a time settled, that we will look at him in the centre of the horizon, and ascribe to him the properties that will attach to any man so seen. But the longest love or aversion has a speedy term. The great and crescive[26] self, rooted in absolute nature, supplants all relative existence, and ruins the kingdom of mortal friendship and love. Marriage (in what is called the spiritual world) is impossible, because of the inequality between every subject and every object. The subject is the receiver of Godhead, and at every comparison must feel his being enhanced by that cryptic might. Though not in energy, yet by presence, this magazine of substance cannot be otherwise than felt: nor can any force of intellect attribute to the object the proper deity which sleeps or wakes forever in every subject. Never can love make consciousness and ascription equal in force. There will be the same gulf between every me and thee, as between the original and the picture. The universe is the bride of the soul. All private sympathy is partial. Two human beings are like globes, which can touch only in a point, and, whilst they remain in contact, all other points of each of the spheres are inert; their turn must also come, and the longer a particular union lasts, the more energy of appetency[27] the parts not in union acquire.

Life will be imaged, but cannot be divided nor doubled. Any invasion of its unity would be chaos. The soul is not twin-born, but the only begotten, and though revealing itself as child in time, child in appearance, is of a fatal and universal power, admitting no co-life. Every day, every act betrays the ill-concealed deity. We believe in ourselves, as we do not believe in others. We permit all things to ourselves, and that which we call sin in others, is experiment for us. It is an instance of our faith in ourselves, that men never speak of crime as lightly as they think: or, every man thinks a latitude safe for himself, which is nowise to be indulged to another. The act looks very differently on the inside, and on the outside; in its quality, and in its consequences. Murder in the murderer is no such ruinous thought as poets and romancers will have it; it does not unsettle him, or fright him from his ordinary notice of trifles: it is an act quite easy to be contemplated, but in its sequel, it turns out to be a horrible jangle and confounding of all relations. Especially the crimes that spring from love, seem right and fair from the actor's point of view, but, when acted, are found destructive of society. No man at last believes that he can be lost, nor that the crime in him is as black as in the felon. Because the intellect qualifies in our own case the moral judgments. For there is no crime to the intellect. That is antinomian or hypernomian,[28] and judges law as well as fact. "It is worse than a crime, it is a blunder," said Napoleon, speaking the language of the intellect. To it, the world is a problem in mathematics or the science of quantity, and it leaves out praise and blame, and all weak emotions. All stealing is comparative. If you come to absolutes, pray who does not steal? Saints are sad, because they behold sin, (even when they speculate,) from the point of view of the conscience, and not of the intellect; a confusion of thought. Sin seen from the thought, is a diminution or *less*: seen from the conscience or will, it is pravity or *bad*. The intellect names it shade, absence of light, and no essence. The conscience must feel it as essence, essential evil. This it is not: it has an objective existence, but no subjective.

---

26. **crescive:** Growing, increasing, or marked by gradual spontaneous development.
27. **appetency:** A longing, desire, or affinity.
28. **antinomian or hypernomian:** Opposed to or beyond the control of law.

Thus inevitably does the universe wear our color, and every object fall successively into the subject itself. The subject exists, the subject enlarges; all things sooner or later fall into place. As I am, so I see; use what language we will, we can never say anything but what we are; Hermes, Cadmus, Columbus, Newton, Buonaparte,[29] are the mind's ministers. Instead of feeling a poverty when we encounter a great man, let us treat the newcomer like a travelling geologist, who passes through our estate, and shows us good slate, or limestone, or anthracite, in our brush pasture. The partial action of each strong mind in one direction, is a telescope for the objects on which it is pointed. But every other part of knowledge is to be pushed to the same extravagance, ere the soul attains her due sphericity. Do you see that kitten chasing so prettily her own tail? If you could look with her eyes, you might see her surrounded with hundreds of figures performing complex dramas, with tragic and comic issues, long conversations, many characters, many ups and downs of fate, – and meantime it is only puss and her tail. How long before our masquerade will end its noise of tamborines, laughter, and shouting, and we shall find it was a solitary performance? – A subject and an object, – it takes so much to make the galvanic circuit complete, but magnitude adds nothing. What imports it whether it is Kepler[30] and the sphere; Columbus and America; a reader and his book; or puss with her tail?

It is true that all the muses and love and religion hate these developments, and will find a way to punish the chemist, who publishes in the parlor the secrets of the laboratory. And we cannot say too little of our constitutional necessity of seeing things under private aspects, or saturated with our humors. And yet is the God the native of these bleak rocks. That need makes in morals the capital virtue of self-trust. We must hold hard to this poverty, however scandalous, and by more vigorous self-recoveries, after the sallies of action, possess our axis more firmly. The life of truth is cold, and so far mournful; but it is not the slave of tears, contritions, and perturbations. It does not attempt another's work, nor adopt another's facts. It is a main lesson of wisdom to know your own from another's. I have learned that I cannot dispose of other people's facts; but I possess such a key to my own, as persuades me against all their denials, that they also have a key to theirs. A sympathetic person is placed in the dilemma of a swimmer among drowning men, who all catch at him, and if he give so much as a leg or a finger, they will drown him. They wish to be saved from the mischiefs of their vices, but not from their vices. Charity would be wasted on this poor waiting on the symptoms. A wise and hardy physician will say, *Come out of that*, as the first condition of advice.

In this our talking America, we are ruined by our good nature and listening on all sides. This compliance takes away the power of being greatly useful. A man should not be able to look other than directly and forthright. A preoccupied attention is the only answer to the importunate frivolity of other people: an attention, and to an aim which makes their wants frivolous. This is a divine answer, and leaves no appeal, and no hard thoughts. In Flaxman's drawing of the Eumenides of Aeschylus, Orestes supplicates Apollo, whilst the Furies

---

29. **Hermes . . . Buonaparte:** Hermes, multitalented Greek god of wealth, trade, and invention; Cadmus, an ancient Greek military genius and mythical inventor of the alphabet; Christopher Columbus, Italian navigator and explorer; Isaac Newton, discoverer of the law of gravity; and Napoleon Bonaparte, general who conquered much of Europe and became emperor of France.
30. **Kepler:** Johannes Kepler (1571-1630), German astronomer known for his laws of planetary motion.

sleep on the threshold.[31] The face of the god expresses a shade of regret and compassion, but calm with the conviction of the irreconcilableness of the two spheres. He is born into other politics, into the eternal and beautiful. The man at his feet asks for his interest in turmoils of the earth, into which his nature cannot enter. And the Eumenides there lying express pictorially this disparity. The god is surcharged with his divine destiny.

Illusion, Temperament, Succession, Surface, Surprise, Reality, Subjectiveness, — these are threads on the loom of time, these are the lords of life. I dare not assume to give their order, but I name them as I find them in my way. I know better than to claim any completeness for my picture. I am a fragment, and this is a fragment of me. I can very confidently announce one or another law, which throws itself into relief and form, but I am too young yet by some ages to compile a code. I gossip for my hour concerning the eternal politics. I have seen many fair pictures not in vain. A wonderful time I have lived in. I am not the novice I was fourteen, nor yet seven years ago. Let who will ask, where is the fruit? I find a private fruit sufficient. This is a fruit, — that I should not ask for a rash effect from meditations, counsels, and the hiving of truths. I should feel it pitiful to demand a result on this town and county, an overt effect on the instant month and year. The effect is deep and secular[32] as the cause. It works on periods in which mortal lifetime is lost. All I know is reception; I am and I have: but I do not get, and when I have fancied I had gotten anything, I found I did not. I worship with wonder the great Fortune. My reception has been so large, that I am not annoyed by receiving this or that superabundantly. I say to the Genius, if he will pardon the proverb, *In for a mill, in for a million.* When I receive a new gift, I do not macerate my body to make the account square, for, if I should die, I could not make the account square. The benefit overran the merit the first day, and has overran the merit ever since. The merit itself, so-called, I reckon part of the receiving.

Also, that hankering after an overt or practical effect seems to me an apostasy. In good earnest, I am willing to spare this most unnecessary deal of doing. Life wears to me a visionary face. Hardest, roughest action is visionary also. It is but a choice between soft and turbulent dreams. People disparage knowing and the intellectual life, and urge doing. I am very content with knowing, if only I could know. That is an august entertainment, and would suffice me a great while. To know a little, would be worth the expense of this world. I hear always the law of Adrastia, "that every soul which had acquired any truth, should be safe from harm until another period."[33]

I know that the world I converse with in the city and in the farms, is not the world I *think.* I observe that difference, and shall observe it. One day, I shall know the value and law of this discrepance. But I have not found that much was gained by manipular

---

31. **In Flaxman's drawing . . . sleep on the threshold:** Emerson refers to *Orestes and Apollo* (1831), a famous illustration by the English artist John Flaxman (1755-1826) of a scene in *The Eumenides* by the ancient Greek playwright Aeschylus. In it, Orestes kneels in supplication before the enthroned Apollo. The god has temporarily lulled to sleep the Eumenides, or Furies, who have been pursuing Orestes since he murdered his adulterous mother, Clytemnestra.

32. **secular:** Here used in the sense of something that exists or continues through the ages.

33. **"that every soul . . . another period":** The quotation is from the *Phaedrus* by the ancient Greek philosopher Plato (429-347 BCE). Adrastia is another name for Nemesis, the Greek goddess of fate or destiny.

attempts to realize the world of thought. Many eager persons successively make an experiment in this way, and make themselves ridiculous. They acquire democratic manners, they foam at the mouth, they hate and deny. Worse, I observe, that, in the history of mankind, there is never a solitary example of success, — taking their own tests of success. I say this polemically, or in reply to the inquiry, why not realize your world? But far be from me the despair which prejudges the law by a paltry empiricism, — since there never was a right endeavor, but it succeeded. Patience and patience, we shall win at the last. We must be very suspicious of the deceptions of the element of time. It takes a good deal of time to eat or to sleep, or to earn a hundred dollars, and a very little time to entertain a hope and an insight which becomes the light of our life. We dress our garden, eat our dinners, discuss the household with our wives, and these things make no impression, are forgotten next week; but in the solitude to which every man is always returning, he has a sanity and revelations, which in his passage into new worlds he will carry with him. Never mind the ridicule, never mind the defeat: up again, old heart! — it seems to say, — there is victory yet for all justice; and the true romance which the world exists to realize, will be the transformation of genius into practical power.

[1844]

> Reading Emerson's Poetry.   Like many of his friends and contemporaries, Emerson was deeply interested in poetry. He also affirmed the poet's central role in American life and culture. In his essay "The Poet" (1844), for example, he declared that "the poet is representative. He stands among partial men for the complete man, and apprises us not of his wealth, but of the commonwealth." Emerson himself sought and encouraged other poets to experiment. Nonetheless, his poetry was fairly conventional in form, highly intellectual in content, and constrained in feeling. The texts of "The Rhodora," "The Snow-Storm," and "Hamatreya" are taken from his first volume of poetry, *Poems* (1847). The text of "Days" is taken from its first appearance in the inaugural issue of the *Atlantic Monthly* (November 1857). Emerson later included it in his second book of poetry, *May-Day and Other Pieces* (1867).

THE RHODORA:[1]
ON BEING ASKED, WHENCE IS THE FLOWER?

In May, when sea-winds pierced our solitudes,
I found the fresh Rhodora in the woods,
Spreading its leafless blooms in a damp nook,
To please the desert and the sluggish brook.
The purple petals, fallen in the pool,   5
Made the black water with their beauty gay;
Here might the red-bird come his plumes to cool,
And court the flower that cheapens his array.

---

1. **Rhodora:** A shrub that flowers in the springtime, before its leaves appear; it is common in New England.

Rhodora! if the sages ask thee why
This charm is wasted on the earth and sky, 10
Tell them, dear, that if eyes were made for seeing,
Then Beauty is its own excuse for being:
Why thou wert there, O rival of the rose!
I never thought to ask, I never knew;
But, in my simple ignorance, suppose 15
The self-same Power that brought me there brought you.

[1839, 1847]

THE SNOW-STORM

Announced by all the trumpets of the sky,
Arrives the snow, and, driving o'er the fields,
Seems nowhere to alight: the whited air
Hides hills and woods, the river, and the heaven,
And veils the farm-house at the garden's end. 5
The sled and traveller stopped, the courier's feet
Delayed, all friends shut out, the housemates sit
Around the radiant fireplace, enclosed
In a tumultuous privacy of storm.

Come see the north wind's masonry. 10
Out of an unseen quarry evermore
Furnished with tile, the fierce artificer
Curves his white bastions with projected roof
Round every windward stake, or tree, or door.
Speeding, the myriad-handed, his wild work 15
So fanciful, so savage, nought cares he
For number or proportion. Mockingly,
On coop or kennel he hangs Parian[1] wreaths;
A swan-like form invests the hidden thorn;
Fills up the farmer's lane from wall to wall, 20
Maugre the farmer's sighs; and, at the gate,
A tapering turret overtops the work.
And when his hours are numbered, and the world
Is all his own, retiring, as he were not,
Leaves, when the sun appears, astonished Art 25
To mimic in slow structures, stone by stone,
Built in an age, the mad wind's night-work,
The frolic architecture of the snow.

[1841, 1847]

---

1. **Parian:** White marble, often used by sculptors in the nineteenth century.

HAMATREYA[1]

Minott, Lee, Willard, Hosmer, Meriam, Flint[2]
Possessed the land which rendered to their toil
Hay, corn, roots, hemp, flax, apples, wool, and wood.
Each of these landlords walked amidst his farm,
Saying, ''Tis mine, my children's, and my name's: 5
How sweet the west wind sounds in my own trees!
How graceful climb those shadows on my hill!
I fancy these pure waters and the flags[3]
Know me, as does my dog: we sympathize;
And, I affirm, my actions smack of the soil.'   10
Where are these men? Asleep beneath their grounds;
And strangers, fond as they, their furrows plough.
Earth laughs in flowers, to see her boastful boys
Earth-proud, proud of the earth which is not theirs;
Who steer the plough, but cannot steer their feet   15
Clear of the grave.
They added ridge to valley, brook to pond,
And sighed for all that bounded their domain.
'This suits me for a pasture; that's my park;
We must have clay, lime, gravel, granite-ledge,   20
And misty lowland, where to go for peat.
The land is well, — lies fairly to the south.
'Tis good, when you have crossed the sea and back,
To find the sitfast acres where you left them.'
Ah! the hot owner sees not Death, who adds   25
Him to his land, a lump of mould the more.
Hear what the Earth says: —

EARTH-SONG

'Mine and yours;
Mine, not yours.
Earth endures;   30
Stars abide —
Shine down in the old sea;
Old are the shores;

---

1. **Hamatreya:** In 1845, Emerson copied into his journal a passage from a Hindu sacred book *Vishnu Purana*, which includes stories of the origin of the universe. In the passage, the Earth sings to the god Maitreya, from which Emerson may have derived the name "Hamatreya."
2. **Minott . . . Flint:** Early settlers of Concord, Massachusetts. In a later version of this poem, Emerson revised this list to "Bulkeley, Hunt, Willard, Hosmer, Meriam, Flint," probably to include his own ancestor and early resident of Concord, the Reverend Peter Bulkeley (1583-1659).
3. **flags:** Common name for large irises that grow by watersides.

But where are old men?
I who have seen much,   35
Such have I never seen.

'The lawyer's deed
Ran sure,
In tail,[4]
To them, and to their heirs   40
Who shall succeed,
Without fail,
Forevermore.

'Here is the land,
Shaggy with wood,   45
With its old valley,
Mound, and flood.
But the heritors?
Fled like the flood's foam, —
The lawyer, and the laws,   50
And the kingdom,
Clean swept herefrom.

'They called me theirs,
Who so controlled me;
Yet every one   55
Wished to stay, and is gone.
How am I theirs,
If they cannot hold me,
But I hold them?'

When I heard the Earth-song,   60
I was no longer brave;
My avarice cooled
Like lust in the chill of the grave.

[1847]

---

4. **In tail:** A variant of *entail*, a legal term for the settlement of an estate over several generations of a family.

Days

Daughters of Time, the hypocritic Days,
Muffled and dumb, like barefoot dervishes,
And marching single in an endless file,

Bring diadems and fagots[1] in their hands.
To each they offer gifts, after his will, –   5
Bread, kingdoms, stars, or sky that holds them all.
I, in my pleached[2] garden, watched the pomp,
Forgot my morning wishes, hastily
Took a few herbs and apples, and the Day
Turned and departed silent. I, too late,   10
Under her solemn fillet saw the scorn.

[1857]

---

1. **fagots:** A bundle of sticks, used for fuel.
2. **pleached:** An arbor formed by twisting and shaping boughs of trees and shrubs.

Margaret Fuller

[1810–1850]

Margaret Fuller

This engraving of a pensive Fuller, seated with a book in her lap, was based on a portrait by Alonzo Chappel.

Margaret Fuller was born in Cambridgeport, Massachusetts, on May 23, 1810. Although her mother, Margarett Crane Fuller, had been a teacher in her local school in Canton, Massachusetts, Fuller was largely educated by her father, Timothy, a politician who was elected to the House of Representatives in 1818. Determined that his daughter would have a first-class education, Timothy Fuller began teaching her English and Latin grammar at the age of six. Greek soon followed, as well as studies in French and Italian. His precocious daughter thus enjoyed an introduction to language and cultural study rivaling that of almost any young man being prepared for a college education in the nineteenth century. At the age of fourteen, Fuller was sent to a school for women, but she had difficulty acclimating herself to the less rigorous standards of the school and found her classmates cliquish and dull. Returning home, she continued to study with her father, who encouraged her to become a writer. Her first publication was "In Defense of Brutus," an article on the often-maligned leader of the plot to assassinate Julius Caesar, which appeared in the *Boston Daily Advertiser & Patriot* in 1834.

When Timothy Fuller died suddenly in 1835, Fuller was forced to find a way of earning a living and supporting her nearly destitute family. She first opened a school for girls and young women in Boston. Fuller proved to be a popular teacher, but she found the work frustrating and decided to try to make a living as a writer. In 1838, she began an innovative series of "Conversations" for women, organizing them as discussion classes for which the participants would pay tuition. Fuller also became close friends with Ralph Waldo Emerson and other transcendentalists. Like them, she was deeply interested in German literature and philosophy. In fact, her first two books were translations of German books: *Eckermann's Conversations with Goethe* (1839) and *Correspondence of Fraulein Günderode with Bettine von Arnim* (1842). In 1840, Fuller also became the first editor of the *Dial*, the unofficial journal of the transcendentalists. Since the position did not pay a salary, however, Fuller gave it up in favor of conducting more "Conversations" and devoting herself to writing. After an ambitious trip to the Great Lakes, then the edge of the frontier in the United States, Fuller published an account of her travels, *Summer on the Lakes, in 1843* (1844).

During the following few years, Fuller moved outward from Boston to the national and then the international scene, becoming one of the best known and most influential women of her generation. In the fall of 1844, she wrote *Woman in the Nineteenth Century* (1845), a central text in the history of American feminism. After completing this book, Fuller assumed the position of literary editor for the *New-York Tribune*, through which she reached a broad national audience for the first time. Fuller wrote over 250 articles and reviews for the *Tribune*, covering a wide range of topics that included art, music, literature, and, increasingly, social reform. By the fall of 1846, when she accepted an invitation to travel to Europe with friends and to become the *Tribune*'s first woman foreign correspondent, Fuller was well prepared to cover the social upheaval that would soon begin to shake the Continent. After touring England and France, where she was entertained by some of the notable literary and cultural figures of the period, Fuller arrived in Italy at a moment when revolutionary activity was spreading across Europe. She quickly became engaged in Italian politics and wrote vivid articles for the *Tribune*, providing American readers with a fascinating, personal account of the Italian revolutions of 1848. Her personal life was as dramatic as the political events unfolding around her. When the Roman Republic was overthrown in 1849, she fled to Florence with her lover, Giovanni Angelo, Marchese d'Ossoli, and their son. Fuller decided to return with them to the United States, which was then being convulsed by the bitter controversy over the Compromise of 1850. But the possibility that she might help shape the course of events in her native country abruptly ended with her death on July 17, 1850, when the ship that was returning Fuller and her family home to New York City sank in a storm off Long Island.

Reading Fuller's Woman in the Nineteenth Century. In the July 1843 issue of the *Dial*, the literary journal that she had edited from 1840 to 1842, Fuller published an essay about the relationship between the sexes, "The Great Lawsuit: Man *versus* Men, Woman *versus* Women." With the encouragement of her friends, Fuller in 1844 decided to expand the essay into a book, *Woman in the Nineteenth Century* (1845). It was among the first books published in the United States to take up the question of the ways in which society restricts the role of women. Seeking to liberate both men and women from conventional attitudes and assumptions about gender roles, Fuller argued that women were responsible for developing their full potential. She also asserted that men, traditionally in positions of

Conviction dwells upon her lips.
—Ralph Waldo Emerson

bedfordstmartins.com /americanlit *for research links on Fuller*

power, must rethink social and political boundaries in order to facilitate the full development of members of both sexes. *Woman in the Nineteenth Century* defies easy description or brief summary, since it includes Fuller's accounts of famous women in history and myth, quasi-autobiographical passages, meditations on the importance of self-development, and extended arguments in favor of liberated, independent lives for men and women. In fact, the book's challenge to conventional literary standards mirrors Fuller's challenge to conventional thinking about the proper boundaries or roles of men and women. The text of the following selection is taken from the first American edition of *Woman in the Nineteenth Century* (1845).

From WOMAN IN THE NINETEENTH CENTURY

It should be remarked that, as the principle of liberty is better understood, and more nobly interpreted, a broader protest is made in behalf of Woman. As men become aware that few men have had a fair chance, they are inclined to say that no women have had a fair chance. The French Revolution, that strangely disguised angel, bore witness in favor of woman, but interpreted her claims no less ignorantly than those of man. Its idea of happiness did not rise beyond outward enjoyment, unobstructed by the tyranny of others. The title it gave was citoyen, citoyenne,[1] and it is not unimportant to woman that even this species of equality was awarded her. Before, she could be condemned to perish on the scaffold for treason, not as a citizen, but as a subject. The right with which this title then invested a human being, was that of bloodshed and license. The Goddess of Liberty was impure. As we read the poem addressed to her not long since, by Beranger,[2] we can scarcely refrain from tears as painful as the tears of blood that flowed when "such crimes were committed in her name."[3] Yes! man, born to purify and animate the unintelligent and the cold, can, in his madness, degrade and pollute no less the fair and the chaste. Yet truth was prophesied in the ravings of that hideous fever, caused by long ignorance and abuse. Europe is conning a valued lesson from the blood-stained page. The same tendencies, farther unfolded, will bear good fruit in this country.

Yet, by men in this country, as by the Jews, when Moses was leading them to the promised land, every thing has been done that inherited depravity could do, to hinder the promise of heaven from its fulfilment. The cross here as elsewhere, has been planted only to be blasphemed by cruelty and fraud. The name of the Prince of Peace has been profaned by all kinds of injustice toward the Gentile whom he said he came to save. But I need not

---

1. **citoyen, citoyenne**: The French masculine and feminine forms of *citizen*, the term people used to address one another when titles were abolished during the French Revolution.
2. **Beranger**: The French poet Pierre Jean de Beranger (1780–1857), who celebrated Liberty in poems such as "Ma République" ("My Republic").
3. **"such crimes . . . in her name"**: As she stood in front of the guillotine on November 8, 1783, the moderate revolutionary Marie-Jeanne Roland, known as Madame Roland, exclaimed: "O Liberté, que de crimes on commet en ton nom!" ("Oh Liberty, what crimes are committed in thy name!").

speak of what has been done towards the red man, the black man. Those deeds are the scoff of the world; and they have been accompanied by such pious words that the gentlest would not dare to intercede with "Father, forgive them, for they know not what they do."[4]

Here, as elsewhere, the gain of creation consists always in the growth of individual minds, which live and aspire, as flowers bloom and birds sing, in the midst of morasses; and in the continual development of that thought, the thought of human destiny, which is given to eternity adequately to express, and which ages of failure only seemingly impede. Only seemingly, and whatever seems to the contrary, this country is as surely destined to elucidate a great moral law, as Europe was to promote the mental culture of man.

Though the national independence be blurred by the servility of individuals, though freedom and equality have been proclaimed only to leave room for a monstrous display of slave-dealing and slave-keeping; though the free American so often feels himself free, like the Roman, only to pamper his appetites and his indolence through the misery of his fellow beings, still it is not in vain, that the verbal statement has been made, "All men are born free and equal." There it stands, a golden certainty wherewith to encourage the good, to shame the bad. The new world may be called clearly to perceive that it incurs the utmost penalty, if it reject or oppress the sorrowful brother. And, if men are deaf, the angels hear. But men cannot be deaf. It is inevitable that an external freedom, an independence of the encroachments of other men, such as has been achieved for the nation, should be so also for every member of it. That which has once been clearly conceived in the intelligence cannot fail sooner or later to be acted out. It has become a law as irrevocable as that of the Medes[5] in their ancient dominion; men will privately sin against it, but the law, as expressed by a leading mind of the age,

> *"Tutti fatti a sembianza d'un Solo,*
> *Figli tutti d'un solo riscatto,*
> *In qual'ora, in qual parte del suolo*
> *Trascorriamo quest' aura vital,*
> *Siam fratelli, siam stretti ad un patto:*
> *Maladetto colui che lo infrange,*
> *Che s'innalza sul fiacco che piange*
> *Che contrista uno spirto immortal."*[6]

> "All made in the likeness of the One,
>   All children of one ransom,
> In whatever hour, in whatever part of the soil,
>   We draw this vital air,
> We are brothers; we must be bound by one compact,
>   Accursed he who infringes it,
> Who raises himself upon the weak who weep,
>   Who saddens an immortal spirit."

---

4. "**Father . . . do**": Christ's words of forgiveness before he died on the cross, as recorded in Luke 23:34.
5. **Medes**: By the sixth century BCE, the Medes, a people who originally lived in present-day Iran, had established a vast empire that covered the area from present-day Azerbaijan to Central Asia and Afghanistan.
6. "***Tutti . . . immortal***": Manzoni. [Fuller's note] Alessandro Manzoni (1785–1873), Italian poet and novelist.

This law cannot fail of universal recognition. Accursed be he who willingly saddens an immortal spirit, doomed to infamy in later, wiser ages, doomed in future stages of his own being to deadly penance, only short of death. Accursed be he who sins in ignorance, if that ignorance be caused by sloth.

We sicken no less at the pomp than the strife of words. We feel that never were lungs so puffed with the wind of declamation, on moral and religious subjects, as now. We are tempted to implore these "word-heroes," these word-Catos,[7] word-Christs, to beware of cant[8] above all things; to remember that hypocrisy is the most hopeless as well as the meanest of crimes, and that those must surely be polluted by it, who do not reserve a part of their morality and religion for private use. Landor[9] says that he cannot have a great deal of mind who cannot afford to let the larger part of it lie fallow, and what is true of genius is not less so of virtue. The tongue is a valuable member, but should appropriate but a small part of the vital juices that are needful all over the body. We feel that the mind may "grow black and rancid in the smoke" even "of altars." We start up from the harangue to go into our closet and shut the door. There inquires the spirit, "Is this rhetoric the bloom of healthy blood or a false pigment artfully laid on?" And yet again we know where is so much smoke, must be some fire; with so much talk about virtue and freedom, must be mingled some desire for them; that it cannot be in vain that such have become the common topics of conversation among men, rather than schemes for tyranny and plunder, that the very newspapers see it best to proclaim themselves Pilgrims, Puritans, Heralds of Holiness. The king that maintains so costly a retinue cannot be a mere boast, or Carabbas fiction.[10] We have waited here long in the dust; we are tired and hungry, but the triumphal procession must appear at last.

Of all its banners, none has been more steadily upheld, and under none have more valor and willingness for real sacrifices been shown, than that of the champions of the enslaved African. And this band it is, which, partly from a natural following out of principles, partly because many women have been prominent in that cause, makes, just now, the warmest appeal in behalf of woman.

Though there has been a growing liberality on this subject, yet society at large is not so prepared for the demands of this party, but that they are and will be for some time, coldly regarded as the Jacobins[11] of their day.

"Is it not enough," cries the irritated trader, "that you have done all you could to break up the national union, and thus destroy the prosperity of our country, but now you

---

7. **word-Catos:** Marcus Porcius Cato (Cato the Elder) (234-149 BCE), a Roman statesman and orator known for his opposition to the spread of Greek culture in Rome.
8. **beware of cant:** Dr. Johnson's one piece of advice should be written on every door; "Clear your mind of cant." But Byron, to whom it was so acceptable, in clearing away the noxious vine, shook down the building. Sterling's emendation is worthy of honor: "Realize your cant, not cast it off." [Fuller's note] Fuller refers to Samuel Johnson (1709-1784), English essayist and critic; George Gordon, Lord Byron (1788-1824), English poet notorious for his rejection of religious and social conventions; and John Sterling (1806-1844), English novelist and poet.
9. **Landor:** Walter Savage Landor (1775-1864), English poet.
10. **Carabbas fiction:** The Marquess of Carabbas was the name the cat gave his master in the popular French story "Le Chat Botté" ("Puss in Boots") by Charles Perrault (1628-1703).
11. **Jacobins:** The political club that became a radical republican organization during the French Revolution.

must be trying to break up family union, to take my wife away from the cradle and the kitchen hearth to vote at polls, and preach from a pulpit? Of course, if she does such things, she cannot attend to those of her own sphere. She is happy enough as she is. She has more leisure than I have, every means of improvement, every indulgence."

"Have you asked her whether she was satisfied with these *indulgences?*"

"No, but I know she is. She is too amiable to wish what would make me unhappy, and too judicious to wish to step beyond the sphere of her sex. I will never consent to have our peace disturbed by any such discussions."

"'Consent — you?' it is not consent from you that is in question, it is assent from your wife."

"Am not I the head of my house?"

"You are not the head of your wife. God has given her a mind of her own."

"I am the head and she the heart."

"God grant you play true to one another then. I suppose I am to be grateful that you did not say she was only the hand. If the head represses no natural pulse of the heart, there can be no question as to your giving your consent. Both will be of one accord, and there needs but to present any question to get a full and true answer. There is no need of precaution, of indulgence, or consent. But our doubt is whether the heart does consent with the head, or only obeys its decrees with a passiveness that precludes the exercise of its natural powers, or a repugnance that turns sweet qualities to bitter, or a doubt that lays waste the fair occasions of life. It is to ascertain the truth, that we propose some liberating measures."

Thus vaguely are these questions proposed and discussed at present. But their being proposed at all implies much thought and suggests more. Many women are considering within themselves, what they need that they have not, and what they can have, if they find they need it. Many men are considering whether women are capable of being and having more than they are and have, *and,* whether, if so, it will be best to consent to improvement in their condition.

This morning, I open the Boston "*Daily Mail,*" and find in its "poet's corner," a translation of Schiller's "Dignity of Woman."[12] In the advertisement of a book on America, I see in the table of contents this sequence, "Republican Institutions. American Slavery. American Ladies."

I open the "*Deutsche Schnellpost,*" published in New-York, and find at the head of a column, *Juden- und Frauen-emancipation in Ungarn.* Emancipation of Jews and Women in Hungary.

The past year has seen action in the Rhode-Island legislature, to secure married women rights over their own property, where men showed that a very little examination of the subject could teach them much; an article in the Democratic Review[13] on the same subject more largely considered, written by a woman, impelled, it is said, by glaring

---

12. **"Dignity of Woman"**: A translation of "Würde der Fraue," in which the German poet, playwright, and philosopher Friedrich von Schiller (1759-1805) sharply contrasted the male and female principles.
13. **Democratic Review**: The *United States Magazine and Democratic Review*, an influential literary and political journal.

wrong to a distinguished friend having shown the defects in the existing laws, and the state of opinion from which they spring; and an answer from the revered old man, J. Q. Adams, in some respects the Phocion[14] of his time, to an address made him by some ladies. To this last I shall again advert in another place.

These symptoms of the times have come under my view quite accidentally: one who seeks, may, each month or week, collect more.

The numerous party, whose opinions are already labelled and adjusted too much to their mind to admit of any new light, strive, by lectures on some model-woman of bride-like beauty and gentleness, by writing and lending little treatises, intended to mark out with precision the limits of woman's sphere, and woman's mission, to prevent other than the rightful shepherd from climbing the wall, or the flock from using any chance to go astray.

Without enrolling ourselves at once on either side, let us look upon the subject from the best point of view which to-day offers. No better, it is to be feared, than a high house-top. A high hill-top or at least a cathedral spire, would be desirable.

It may well be an Anti-Slavery party that pleads for woman, if we consider merely that she does not hold property on equal terms with men; so that, if a husband dies without making a will, the wife, instead of taking at once his place as head of the family, inherits only a part of his fortune, often brought him by herself, as if she were a child, or ward only, not an equal partner.

We will not speak of the innumerable instances in which profligate and idle men live upon the earnings of industrious wives; or if the wives leave them, and take with them the children, to perform the double duty of mother and father, follow from place to place, and threaten to rob them of the children, if deprived of the rights of a husband, as they call them, planting themselves in their poor lodgings, frightening them into paying tribute by taking from them the children, running into debt at the expense of these otherwise so overtasked helots. Such instances count up by scores within my own memory. I have seen the husband who had stained himself by a long course of low vice, till his wife was wearied from her heroic forgiveness, by finding that his treachery made it useless, and that if she would provide bread for herself and her children, she must be separate from his ill fame. I have known this man come to instal himself in the chamber of a woman who loathed him and say she should never take food without his company. I have known these men steal their children whom they knew they had no means to maintain, take them into dissolute company, expose them to bodily danger, to frighten the poor woman, to whom, it seems, the fact that she alone had borne the pangs of their birth, and nourished their infancy, does not give an equal right to them. I do believe that this mode of kidnapping, and it is frequent enough in all classes of society, will be by the next age viewed as it is by Heaven now, and that the man who avails himself of the shelter of men's laws to steal from a mother her own children, or arrogate any superior right in them, save that of superior virtue, will bear the stigma he deserves, in common with him who steals grown men from their mother land, their hopes, and their homes.

---

14. J. Q. Adams . . . Phocion: John Quincy Adams (1767–1848), well regarded for his eloquence, was the sixth president of the United States; Phocion (402–318 BCE) was an Athenian ruler known for his integrity and powerful speeches.

I said, we will not speak of this now, yet I have spoken, for the subject makes me feel too much. I could give instances that would startle the most vulgar and callous, but I will not, for the public opinion of their own sex is already against such men, and where cases of extreme tyranny are made known, there is private action in the wife's favor. But she ought not to need this, nor, I think, can she long. Men must soon see that, on their own ground, that woman is the weaker party, she ought to have legal protection, which would make such oppression impossible. But I would not deal with "atrocious instances" except in the way of illustration, neither demand from men a partial redress in some one matter, but go to the root of the whole. If principles could be established, particulars would adjust themselves aright. Ascertain the true destiny of woman, give her legitimate hopes, and a standard within herself; marriage and all other relations would by degrees be harmonized with these.

But to return to the historical progress of this matter. Knowing that there exists in the minds of men a tone of feeling towards women as towards slaves, such as is expressed in the common phrase, "Tell that to women and children," that the infinite soul can only work through them in already ascertained limits; that the gift of reason, man's highest prerogative, is allotted to them in much lower degree; that they must be kept from mischief and melancholy by being constantly engaged in active labor, which is to be furnished and directed by those better able to think, &c., &c.; we need not multiply instances, for who can review the experience of last week without recalling words which imply, whether in jest or earnest, these views or views like these; knowing this, can we wonder that many reformers think that measures are not likely to be taken in behalf of women, unless their wishes could be publicly represented by women?

That can never be necessary, cry the other side. All men are privately influenced by women; each has his wife, sister, or female friends, and is too much biased by these relations to fail of representing their interests, and, if this is not enough, let them propose and enforce their wishes with the pen. The beauty of home would be destroyed, the delicacy of the sex be violated, the dignity of halls of legislation degraded by an attempt to introduce them there. Such duties are inconsistent with those of a mother; and then we have ludicrous pictures of ladies in hysterics at the polls, and senate chambers filled with cradles.

But if, in reply, we admit as truth that woman seems destined by nature rather for the inner circle, we must add that the arrangements of civilized life have not been, as yet, such as to secure it to her. Her circle, if the duller, is not the quieter. If kept from "excitement," she is not from drudgery. Not only the Indian squaw carries the burdens of the camp, but the favorites of Louis the Fourteenth accompany him in his journeys, and the washerwoman stands at her tub and carries home her work at all seasons, and in all states of health. Those who think the physical circumstances of woman would make a part in the affairs of national government unsuitable, are by no means those who think it impossible for the negresses to endure field work, even during pregnancy, or the sempstresses[15] to go through their killing labors.

---

15. **sempstresses:** Usually "seamstresses," women who earn their living by sewing.

As to the use of the pen, there was quite as much opposition to woman's possessing herself of that help to free agency, as there is now to her seizing on the rostrum or the desk; and she is likely to draw, from a permission to plead her cause that way, opposite inferences to what might be wished by those who now grant it.

As to the possibility of her filling with grace and dignity, any such position, we should think those who had seen the great actresses, and heard the Quaker preachers of modern times, would not doubt, that woman can express publicly the fulness of thought and creation, without losing any of the peculiar beauty of her sex. What can pollute and tarnish is to act thus from any motive except that something needs to be said or done. Women could take part in the processions, the songs, the dances of old religion; no one fancied their delicacy was impaired by appearing in public for such a cause.

As to her home, she is not likely to leave it more than she now does for balls, theatres, meetings for promoting missions, revival meetings, and others to which she flies, in hope of an animation for her existence, commensurate with what she sees enjoyed by men. Governors of ladies' fairs are no less engrossed by such a change, than the Governor of the state by his; presidents of Washingtonian societies[16] no less away from home than presidents of conventions. If men look straitly to it, they will find that, unless their lives are domestic, those of the women will not be. A house is no home unless it contain food and fire for the mind as well as for the body. The female Greek, of our day, is as much in the street as the male to cry, What news? We doubt not it was the same in Athens of old. The women, shut out from the market place, made up for it at the religious festivals. For human beings are not so constituted that they can live without expansion. If they do not get it one way, they must another, or perish.

As to men's representing women fairly at present, while we hear from men who owe to their wives not only all that is comfortable or graceful, but all that is wise in the arrangement of their lives, the frequent remark, "You cannot reason with a woman," when from those of delicacy, nobleness, and poetic culture, the contemptuous phrase "women and children," and that in no light sally of the hour, but in works intended to give a permanent statement of the best experiences, when not one man, in the million, shall I say? no, not in the hundred million, can rise above the belief that woman was made *for man*, when such traits as these are daily forced upon the attention, can we feel that man will always do justice to the interests of woman? Can we think that he takes a sufficiently discerning and religious view of her office and destiny, *ever* to do her justice, except when prompted by sentiment, accidentally or transiently, that is, for the sentiment will vary according to the relations in which he is placed. The lover, the poet, the artist, are likely to view her nobly. The father and the philosopher have some chance of liberality; the man of the world, the legislator for expediency, none.

Under these circumstances, without attaching importance, in themselves, to the changes demanded by the champions of woman, we hail them as signs of the times. We would have every arbitrary barrier thrown down. We would have every path laid open to woman as freely as to man. Were this done and a slight temporary fermentation allowed

---

16. **Washingtonian societies:** Local chapters of the Washingtonian Temperance Society, or Washingtonian Total Abstinence Society, founded in 1840.

to subside, we should see crystallizations more pure and of more various beauty. We believe the divine energy would pervade nature to a degree unknown in the history of former ages, and that no discordant collision, but a ravishing harmony of the spheres would ensue.

Yet, then and only then, will mankind be ripe for this, when inward and outward freedom for woman as much as for man shall be acknowledged as a right, not yielded as a concession. As the friend of the negro assumes that one man cannot by right, hold another in bondage, so should the friend of woman assume that man cannot, by right, lay even well-meant restrictions on women. If the negro be a soul, if the woman be a soul, appareled in flesh, to one Master only are they accountable. There is but one law for souls, and if there is to be an interpreter of it, he must come not as man, or son of man, but as son of God.

Were thought and feeling once so far elevated that man should esteem himself the brother and friend, but nowise the lord and tutor of woman, were he really bound with her in equal worship, arrangements as to function and employment would be of no consequence. What woman needs is not as a woman to act or rule, but as a nature to grow, as an intellect to discern, as a soul to live freely and unimpeded, to unfold such powers as were given her when we left our common home. If fewer talents were given her, yet if allowed the free and full employment of these, so that she may render back to the giver his own with usury, she will not complain;[17] nay I dare to say she will bless and rejoice in her earthly birth-place, her earthly lot. Let us consider what obstructions impede this good era, and what signs give reason to hope that it draws near.

I was talking on this subject with Miranda, a woman, who, if any in the world could, might speak without heat and bitterness of the position of her sex.[18] Her father was a man who cherished no sentimental reverence for woman, but a firm belief in the equality of the sexes. She was his eldest child, and came to him at an age when he needed a companion. From the time she could speak and go alone, he addressed her not as a plaything, but as a living mind. Among the few verses he ever wrote was a copy addressed to this child, when the first locks were cut from her head, and the reverence expressed on this occasion for that cherished head, he never belied. It was to him the temple of immortal intellect. He respected his child, however, too much to be an indulgent parent. He called on her for clear judgment, for courage, for honor and fidelity; in short, for such virtues as he knew. In so far as he possessed the keys to the wonders of this universe, he allowed free use of them to her, and by the incentive of a high expectation, he forbade, as far as possible, that she should let the privilege lie idle.

Thus this child was early led to feel herself a child of the spirit. She took her place easily, not only in the world of organized being, but in the world of mind. A dignified sense of self-dependence was given as all her portion, and she found it a sure anchor. Herself securely anchored, her relations with others were established with equal security. She was fortunate in a total absence of those charms which might have drawn to

---

17. **If fewer talents . . . she will not complain:** Fuller alludes to the parable of the talents (Matthew 25:14-30).
18. **Miranda . . . position of her sex:** Miranda, the name of Prospero's daughter in one of Fuller's favorite plays by Shakespeare, *The Tempest*, is a thinly veiled portrait of Fuller herself.

her bewildering flatteries, and in a strong electric nature, which repelled those who did not belong to her, and attracted those who did. With men and women her relations were noble, affectionate without passion, intellectual without coldness. The world was free to her, and she lived freely in it. Outward adversity came, and inward conflict, but that faith and self-respect had early been awakened which must always lead at last, to an outward serenity and an inward peace.

Of Miranda I had always thought as an example, that the restraints upon the sex were insuperable only to those who think them so, or who noisily strive to break them. She had taken a course of her own, and no man stood in her way. Many of her acts had been unusual, but excited no uproar. Few helped, but none checked her, and the many men, who knew her mind and her life, showed to her confidence, as to a brother, gentleness as to a sister. And not only refined, but very coarse men approved and aided one in whom they saw resolution and clearness of design. Her mind was often the leading one, always effective.

When I talked with her upon these matters, and had said very much what I have written, she smilingly replied: "and yet we must admit that I have been fortunate, and this should not be. My good father's early trust gave the first bias, and the rest followed of course. It is true that I have had less outward aid, in after years, than most women, but that is of little consequence. Religion was early awakened in my soul, a sense that what the soul is capable to ask it must attain, and that, though I might be aided and instructed by others, I must depend on myself as the only constant friend. This self dependence, which was honored in me, is deprecated as a fault in most women. They are taught to learn their rule from without, not to unfold it from within.

"This is the fault of man, who is still vain, and wishes to be more important to woman than, by right, he should be."

"Men have not shown this disposition toward you," I said.

"No! because the position I early was enabled to take was one of self-reliance. And were all women as sure of their wants as I was, the result would be the same. But they are so overloaded with precepts by guardians, who think that nothing is so much to be dreaded for a woman as originality of thought or character, that their minds are impeded by doubts till they lose their chance of fair free proportions. The difficulty is to get them to the point from which they shall naturally develope self-respect, and learn self-help.

"Once I thought that men would help to forward this state of things more than I do now. I saw so many of them wretched in the connections they had formed in weakness and vanity. They seemed so glad to esteem women whenever they could.

"The soft arms of affection," said one of the most discerning spirits, "will not suffice for me, unless on them I see the steel bracelets of strength."

But early I perceived that men never, in any extreme of despair, wished to be women. On the contrary they were ever ready to taunt one another at any sign of weakness, with,

"Art thou not like the women, who" –

The passage ends various ways, according to the occasion and rhetoric of the speaker. When they admired any woman they were inclined to speak of her as "above her sex."

Silently I observed this, and feared it argued a rooted scepticism, which for ages had been fastening on the heart, and which only an age of miracles could eradicate. Ever I have been treated with great sincerity; and I look upon it as a signal instance of this, that an intimate friend of the other sex said, in a fervent moment, that I "deserved in some star to be a man." He was much surprised when I disclosed my view of my position and hopes, when I declared my faith that the feminine side, the side of love, of beauty, of holiness, was now to have its full chance, and that, if either were better, it was better now to be a woman, for even the slightest achievement of good was furthering an especial work of our time. He smiled incredulous. "She makes the best she can of it," thought he. "Let Jews believe the pride of Jewry, but I am of the better sort, and know better."

Another used as highest praise, in speaking of a character in literature, the words "a manly woman."

So in the noble passage of Ben Jonson:

> "I meant the day-star should not brighter ride,
>   Nor shed like influence from its lucent seat;
> I meant she should be courteous, facile, sweet,
>   Free from that solemn vice of greatness, pride;
> I meant each softest virtue there should meet,
>   Fit in that softer bosom to abide,
> Only a learned and a *manly* soul,
>   I purposed her, that should with even powers,
> The rock, the spindle, and the shears control
>   Of destiny, and spin her own free hours."[19]

"Methinks," said I, "you are too fastidious in objecting to this. Jonson in using the word 'manly' only meant to heighten the picture of this, the true, the intelligent fate, with one of the deeper colors." 'And yet,' said she, 'so invariable is the use of this word where a heroic quality is to be described, and I feel so sure that persistence and courage are the most womanly no less than the most manly qualities, that I would exchange these words for others of a larger sense at the risk of marring the fine tissue of the verse. Read, 'a heavenward and instructed soul,' and I should be satisfied. Let it not be said, wherever there is energy or creative genius, 'She has a masculine mind.'

This by no means argues a willing want of generosity toward woman. Man is as generous toward her, as he knows how to be.

Wherever she has herself arisen in national or private history, and nobly shone forth in any form of excellence, men have received her, not only willingly, but with triumph. Their encomiums indeed, are always, in some sense, mortifying; they show too much surprise. Can this be you? he cries to the transfigured Cinderella; well I should never have thought it, but I am very glad. We will tell every one that you have "*surpassed your sex.*"

---

19. "**I meant . . . free hours**": The lines are from "To Lucy, Countess of Bedford," written by the English poet and playwright Ben Jonson (1572-1637) in honor of Lucy Harrington, Countess of Bedford (1581-1627), a major patron of literature and the arts.

In every-day life the feelings of the many are stained with vanity. Each wishes to be lord in a little world, to be superior at least over one; and he does not feel strong enough to retain a life-long ascendancy over a strong nature. Only a Theseus could conquer before he wed the Amazonian Queen.[20] Hercules wished rather to rest with Dejanira, and received the poisoned robe, as a fit guerdon.[21] The tale should be interpreted to all those who seek repose with the weak.

But not only is man vain and fond of power, but the same want of development, which thus affects him morally, prevents his intellectually discerning the destiny of woman. The boy wants no woman, but only a girl to play ball with him, and mark his pocket handkerchief.

Thus, in Schiller's Dignity of Woman,[22] beautiful as the poem is, there is no "grave and perfect man," but only a great boy to be softened and restrained by the influence of girls. Poets, the elder brothers of their race, have usually seen farther; but what can you expect of every-day men, if Schiller was not more prophetic as to what women must be? Even with Richter,[23] one foremost thought about a wife was that she would "cook him something good." But as this is a delicate subject, and we are in constant danger of being accused of slighting what are called "the functions," let me say in behalf of Miranda and myself, that we have high respect for those who cook something good, who create and preserve fair order in houses, and prepare therein the shining raiment for worthy inmates, worthy guests. Only these "functions" must not be a drudgery, or enforced necessity, but a part of life. Let Ulysses drive the beeves home while Penelope there piles up the fragrant loaves; they are both well employed if these be done in thought and love, willingly.[24] But Penelope is no more meant for a baker or weaver solely, than Ulysses for a cattle-herd.

The sexes should not only correspond to and appreciate, but prophesy to one another. In individual instances this happens. Two persons love in one another the future good which they aid one another to unfold. This is imperfectly or rarely done in the general life. Man has gone but little way; now he is waiting to see whether woman can keep step with him, but instead of calling out, like a good brother, "you can do it, if you only think so," or impersonally; "any one can do what he tries to do;" he often discourages with school-boy brag: "Girls can't do that; girls can't play ball." But let any one defy their taunts, break through and be brave and secure, they rend the air with shouts.

[1845]

---

20. **Theseus . . . Amazonian Queen:** According to Greek mythology, Theseus, a king of Athens, attacked a nation of women warriors called the Amazons and abducted their queen, Antiope.

21. **Hercules . . . a fit guerdon:** A guerdon is a reward or recompense. Fuller alludes to the story of Hercules, the greatest hero in Greek mythology, and his second wife, Dejanira. Fearful that her husband was growing fond of another woman, Dejanira soaked his robe in what she believed to be love potion but was actually poison that caused him excruciating pain. Seeing what she had done, Dejanira hanged herself, and Hercules ended his agony and mortal life by burning himself on a funeral pyre.

22. **Schiller's Dignity of Woman:** See note 12.

23. **Richter:** The German novelist and humorist Johann Paul Friedrich Richter (1763-1825).

24. **Let Ulysses . . . willingly:** In Homer's *Odyssey*, Penelope faithfully waits for her husband, the heroic Odysseus (Ulysses in Roman mythology), to return from the Trojan War.

Harriet Beecher Stowe

[1811–1896]

Harriet Beecher Stowe was born in Litchfield, Connecticut, in 1811. The daughter, sister, and eventually wife and mother of Protestant clergymen, she was raised in a family in which religion was an integral part of life. Education was also regarded as vital for everyone, and the young Harriet attended her sister Catherine E. Beecher's Hartford Female Seminary, one of the first schools that provided a serious education for girls. At the seminary, she met women who either were or would become famous writers, including Lydia Sigourney and Sara Willis, later widely known by her pen name, Fanny Fern. In 1832, Stowe's father, the ardent Presbyterian minister Lyman Beecher, accepted the presidency of Lane Theological Seminary and moved his family to Cincinnati, just across the Ohio River from the slaveholding state of Kentucky. In Ohio, Stowe observed fugitive slaves and became involved in antislavery activities. As a member of a local literary group, Stowe began to write short articles and stories, though her first publication was a highly successful textbook, *Primary Geography for Children* (1833). In 1836, she married Calvin Stowe, a young widower and professor at Lane Seminary. For the next fourteen years, Stowe balanced the responsibilities of caring for their young children and managing a household on a small academic salary. When she could claim some time to herself, she wrote articles and sketches for various periodicals, including *Godey's Lady's Book*, the popular magazine for women, and the *New-York Evangelist*, a religious newspaper devoted to reforms such as antislavery and temperance. Stowe also published a collection of domestic sketches and fiction, *The Mayflower, or Sketches of Scenes and Characters among the Descendents of the Pilgrims* (1843). Although it did not sell well, Stowe was gradually making a name for herself as a writer, and her steady work was supplementing the household income.

In 1850, Calvin Stowe accepted a new position as a professor at Bowdoin College in Brunswick, Maine, where the family moved from Ohio. Stowe soon agreed to become a contributor to the *National Era*, a new antislavery newspaper edited by Gamaliel Bailey. In the prospectus for the newspaper — published in Washington, D.C., where slavery was legal — Bailey explained that his purpose was "to lay before the Southern men . . . such

Harriet Beecher Stowe

The Boston firm of Southworth and Hawes, which specialized in portraits of celebrities, made this daguerreotype of Stowe in 1843. By then a rising literary star, Stowe would later gain even greater fame as the author of *Uncle Tom's Cabin*.

facts and arguments as may serve to throw further light upon the question of slavery, and its disposition." Determined to use literature as well as political articles to illustrate the evils of slavery, Bailey invited a number of popular women writers to participate in this purpose, including E.D.E.N. Southworth, Grace Greenwood, Alice and Phoebe Cary, and Stowe. After Stowe wrote several brief sketches for the *Era*, Bailey invited her to write a new story, one that might be serialized over a few weeks. Like many northerners, Stowe and her family were reeling from the passage in 1850 of the Fugitive Slave Act, which she decided to fight by writing a story about slavery. The first installment of *Uncle Tom's Cabin; or, Life among the Lowly* appeared in the *Era* on June 5, 1851. Initially planned as a three- or four-part serial, the story continued through forty-one installments, finally ending on April 1, 1852. During that period, the subscription list of the *National Era* grew from 8,000 to 28,000. The two-volume novel published shortly after the serialization concluded was even more successful. In fact, *Uncle Tom's Cabin* was the publication phenomenon of the century, selling 10,000 copies in the first week and 300,000 copies by the end of the year. It was the first blockbuster novel published in the United States, and Stowe was among the earliest of American celebrity writers.

bedfordstmartins.com /americanlit for research links on Stowe

Although nothing else she produced would or probably could have matched the success of *Uncle Tom's Cabin*, Stowe continued to write and publish. In order to counter Southern criticism that she had no firsthand knowledge of slavery, and that her novel was full of falsehoods, Stowe published a collection of articles, stories, and accounts of slavery called *The Key to Uncle Tom's Cabin* (1853). Her second antislavery novel, *Dred: A Tale of the Great Dismal Swamp*, appeared in 1856. The following year she assisted in the founding of an important new literary monthly, the *Atlantic Monthly*, one of the numerous magazines to which she contributed essays, sketches, stories, and serialized fiction during the following two decades. Although she maintained her interest in abolition, Stowe increasingly returned to the domestic subjects of her early work, especially in a series of novels set in New England: *The Minister's Wooing* (1859), *The Pearl of Orr's Island* (1862), *Oldtown Folks* (1869), and *Poganuc People* (1878), which was closely based upon her childhood in Connecticut. Although she lived for eighteen more years, until 1896, that elegiac novel effectively marked the end of her long and prolific literary career, which had made Stowe internationally famous as a writer and a revered cultural figure in the United States.

Reading Stowe's "The Seamstress."   This sketch was published in Stowe's second book, *The Mayflower, or Sketches of Scenes and Characters among the Descendents of the Pilgrims* (1843). As the title indicates, the collection primarily concerned life in New England, but Stowe wrote the stories and sketches while she was a member of a Cincinnati literary group, the Semi-Colon Club. In a preface to the book, her sister Catherine E. Beecher commented on the proliferation of sketches and tales that were being published in the 1830s, observing that "The worst stands about an equal chance with the best." To Beecher, her sister's work was among the best, and *The Mayflower* certainly established Stowe as a serious writer. In this early story advocating social reform, Stowe reveals the plight of widowed women left without the resources to make livings for themselves. The text is taken from the second edition, published as *The May Flower and Miscellaneous Writings* (1855).

A Milliner and Her Daughter

This occupational portrait of a hatmaker and her daughter was taken in Springfield, Illinois, in the 1850s. Working as a milliner or as a seamstress making dresses was one of the few "natural" and "respectable" occupations open to women, since such needle work was associated with and could be done in the home, widely regarded as "Woman's Sphere."

THE SEAMSTRESS

"Few, save the poor, feel for the poor;
   The rich know not how hard
It is to be of needful food
   And needful rest debarred.

Their paths are paths of plenteousness;
   They sleep on silk and down;
They never think how wearily
   The weary head lies down.

They never by the window sit,
   And see the gay pass by,
Yet take their weary work again,
   And with a mournful eye."

              – L. E. L.[1]

However fine and elevated, in a sentimental point of view, may have been the poetry of this gifted writer, we think we have never seen any thing from this source that *ought* to give a better opinion of her than the little ballad from which the above verses are taken.

They show that the accomplished authoress possessed, not merely a knowledge of the dreamy ideal wants of human beings, but the more pressing and homely ones, which the fastidious and poetical are often the last to appreciate. The sufferings of poverty are not confined to those of the common, squalid, every day inured to hardships, and ready, with open hand, to receive charity, let it come to them as it will. There is another class on whom

---

1. L. E. L: The epigraph was written by Letitia Elizabeth Landon (1802–1838), an English poet who signed her work L. E. L.

it presses with still heavier power—the generous, the decent, the self-respecting, who have struggled with their lot in silence, "bearing all things, hoping all things," and willing to endure all things, rather than breathe a word of complaint, or to acknowledge, even to themselves, that their own efforts will not be sufficient for their own necessities.

Pause with me a while at the door of yonder room, whose small window overlooks a little court below. It is inhabited by a widow and her daughter, dependent entirely on the labors of the needle, and those other slight and precarious resources, which are all that remain to woman when left to struggle her way through the world alone. It contains all their small earthly store, and there is scarce an article of its little stock of furniture that has not been thought of, and toiled for, and its price calculated over and over again, before every thing could be made right for its purchase. Every article is arranged with the utmost neatness and care; nor is the most costly furniture of a fashionable parlor more sedulously guarded from a scratch or a rub, than is that brightly-varnished bureau, and that neat cherry tea table and bedstead. The floor, too, boasted once a carpet; but old Time has been busy with it, picking a hole here, and making a thin place there; and though the old fellow has been followed up by the most indefatigable zeal in darning, the marks of his mischievous fingers are too plain to be mistaken. It is true, a kindly neighbor has given a bit of faded baize, which has been neatly clipped and bound, and spread down over an entirely unmanageable hole in front of the fireplace; and other places have been repaired with pieces of different colors; and yet, after all, it is evident that the poor carpet is not long for this world.

But the best face is put upon every thing. The little cupboard in the corner, that contains a few china cups, and one or two antiquated silver spoons, relics of better days, is arranged with jealous neatness, and the white muslin window curtain, albeit the muslin be old, has been carefully whitened and starched, and smoothly ironed, and put up with exact precision; and on the bureau, covered by a snowy cloth, are arranged a few books and other memorials of former times, and a faded miniature, which, though it have little about it to interest a stranger, is more precious to the poor widow than every thing besides.

Mrs. Ames is seated in her rocking chair, supported by a pillow, and busy cutting out work, while her daughter, a slender, sickly-looking girl, is sitting by the window, intent on some fine stitching.

Mrs. Ames, in former days, was the wife of a respectable merchant, and the mother of an affectionate family. But evil fortune had followed her with a steadiness that seemed like the stern decree of some adverse fate rather than the ordinary dealings of a merciful Providence. First came a heavy run of losses in business; then long and expensive sickness in the family, and the death of children. Then there was the selling of the large house and elegant furniture, to retire to a humbler style of living; and finally, the sale of all the property, with the view of quitting the shores of a native land, and commencing life again in a new one. But scarcely had the exiled family found themselves in the port of a foreign land, when the father was suddenly smitten down by the hand of death, and his lonely grave made in a land of strangers. The widow, broken-hearted and discouraged, had still a wearisome journey before her ere she could reach any whom she could consider as her friends. With her two daughters, entirely unattended, and with her finances impoverished by detention and sickness, she performed the tedious journey.

Arrived at the place of her destination, she found herself not only without immediate resources, but considerably in debt to one who had advanced money for her travelling expenses. With silent endurance she met the necessities of her situation. Her daughters, delicately reared, and hitherto carefully educated, were placed out to service, and Mrs. Ames sought for employment as a nurse. The younger child fell sick, and the hard earnings of the mother were all exhausted in the care of her; and though she recovered in part, she was declared by her physician to be the victim of a disease which would never leave her till it terminated her life.

As soon, however, as her daughter was so far restored as not to need her immediate care, Mrs. Ames resumed her laborious employment. Scarcely had she been able, in this way, to discharge the debts for her journey and to furnish the small room we have described, when the hand of disease was laid heavily on herself. Too resolute and persevering to give way to the first attacks of pain and weakness, she still continued her fatiguing employment till her system was entirely prostrated. Thus all possibility of pursuing her business was cut off, and nothing remained but what could be accomplished by her own and her daughter's dexterity at the needle. It is at this time we ask you to look in upon the mother and daughter.

Mrs. Ames is sitting up, the first time for a week, and even to-day she is scarcely fit to do so; but she remembers that the month is coming round, and her rent will soon be due; and in her feebleness she will stretch every nerve to meet her engagements with punctilious exactness.

Wearied at length with cutting out, and measuring, and drawing threads, she leans back in her chair, and her eye rests on the pale face of her daughter, who has been sitting for two hours intent on her stitching.

"Ellen, my child, your head aches; don't work so steadily."

"O, no, it don't ache *much*," said she, too conscious of looking very much tired. Poor girl! had she remained in the situation in which she was born, she would now have been skipping about, and enjoying life as other young girls of fifteen do; but now there is no choice of employments for her — no youthful companions — no visiting — no pleasant walks in the fresh air. Evening and morning, it is all the same; headache or sideache, it is all one. She must hold on the same unvarying task — a wearisome thing for a girl of fifteen.

But see! the door opens, and Mrs. Ames's face brightens as her other daughter enters. Mary has become a domestic in a neighboring family, where her faithfulness and kindness of heart have caused her to be regarded more as a daughter and a sister than as a servant. "Here, mother, is your rent money," she exclaimed; "so do put up your work and rest a while. I can get enough to pay it next time before the month comes around again."

"Dear child, I do wish you would ever think to get any thing for yourself," said Mrs. Ames. "I cannot consent to use up all your earnings, as I have done lately, and all Ellen's too; you must have a new dress this spring, and that bonnet of yours is not decent any longer."

"O, no, mother! I have made over my blue calico, and you would be surprised to see how well it looks; and my best frock, when it is washed and darned, will answer some time longer. And then Mrs. Grant has given me a ribbon, and when my bonnet is whitened and trimmed it will look very well. And so," she added, "I brought you some wine this afternoon; you know the doctor says you need wine."

"Dear child, I want to see you take some comfort of your money yourself."

"Well, I do take comfort of it, mother. It is more comfort to be able to help you than to wear all the finest dresses in the world."

Two months from this dialogue found our little family still more straitened and perplexed. Mrs. Ames had been confined all the time with sickness, and the greater part of Ellen's time and strength was occupied with attending to her.

Very little sewing could the poor girl now do, in the broken intervals that remained to her; and the wages of Mary were not only used as fast as earned, but she anticipated two months in advance.

Mrs. Ames had been better for a day or two, and had been sitting up, exerting all her strength to finish a set of shirts which had been sent in to make. "The money for them will just pay our rent," sighed she; "and if we can do a little more this week —"

"Dear mother, you are so tired," said Ellen; "do lie down, and not worry any more till I come back."

Ellen went out, and passed on till she came to the door of an elegant house, whose damask and muslin window curtains indicated a fashionable residence.

Mrs. Elmore was sitting in her splendidly-furnished parlor, and around her lay various fancy articles which two young girls were busily unrolling. "What a lovely pink scarf!" said one, throwing it over her shoulders and skipping before a mirror; while the other exclaimed, "Do look at these pocket handkerchiefs, mother! what elegant lace!"

"Well, girls," said Mrs. Elmore, "these handkerchiefs are a shameful piece of extravagance. I wonder you will insist on having such things."

"La, mamma, every body has such now; Laura Seymour has half a dozen that cost more than these, and her father is no richer than ours."

"Well," said Mrs. Elmore, "rich or not rich, it seems to make very little odds; we do not seem to have half as much money to spare as we did when we lived in the little house in Spring Street. What with new furnishing the house, and getting every thing you boys and girls say you must have, we are poorer, if any thing, than we were then."

"Ma'am, here is Mrs. Ames's girl come with some sewing," said the servant.

"Show her in," said Mrs. Elmore.

Ellen entered timidly, and handed her bundle of work to Mrs. Elmore, who forthwith proceeded to a minute scrutiny of the articles; for she prided herself on being very particular as to her sewing. But, though the work had been executed by feeble hands and aching eyes, even Mrs. Elmore could detect no fault in it.

"Well, it is very prettily done," said she. "What does your mother charge?"

Ellen handed a neatly-folded bill which she had drawn for her mother. "I must say, I think your mother's prices are very high," said Mrs. Elmore, examining her nearly empty purse; "every thing is getting so dear that one hardly knows how to live." Ellen looked at the fancy articles, and glanced around the room with an air of innocent astonishment. "Ah," said Mrs. Elmore, "I dare say it seems to you as if persons in our situation had no need of economy; but, for my part, I feel the need of it more and more every day." As she spoke she handed Ellen the three dollars, which, though it was not a quarter the price of one of the handkerchiefs, was all that she and her sick mother could claim in the world.

"There," said she; "tell your mother I like her work very much, but I do not think I can afford to employ her, if I can find any one to work cheaper."

Now, Mrs. Elmore was not a hard-hearted woman, and if Ellen had come as a beggar to solicit help for her sick mother, Mrs. Elmore would have fitted out a basket of provisions, and sent a bottle of wine, and a bundle of old clothes, and all the *et cetera* of such occasions; but the sight of *a bill* always aroused all the instinctive sharpness of her business-like education. She never had the dawning of an idea that it was her duty to pay any body any more than she could possibly help; nay, she had an indistinct notion that it was her *duty* as an economist to make every body take as little as possible. When she and her daughters lived in Spring Street, to which she had alluded, they used to spend the greater part of their time at home, and the family sewing was commonly done among themselves. But since they had moved into a large house, and set up a carriage, and addressed themselves to being genteel, the girls found that they had altogether too much to do to attend to their own sewing, much less to perform any for their father and brothers. And their mother found her hands abundantly full in overlooking her large house, in taking care of expensive furniture, and in superintending her increased train of servants. The sewing, therefore, was put out; and Mrs. Elmore *felt it a duty* to get it done the cheapest way she could. Nevertheless, Mrs. Elmore was too notable a lady, and her sons and daughters were altogether too fastidious as to the make and quality of their clothing, to admit the idea of its being done in any but the most complete and perfect manner.

Mrs. Elmore never accused herself of want of charity for the poor; but she had never considered that the best class of the poor are those who never ask charity. She did not consider that, by paying liberally those who were honestly and independently struggling for themselves; she was really doing a greater charity than by giving indiscriminately to a dozen applicants.

"Don't you think, mother, she says we charge too high for this work!" said Ellen, when she returned. "I am sure she did not know how much work we put in those shirts. She says she cannot give us any more work; she must look out for some body that will do it cheaper. I do not see how it is that people who live in such houses, and have so many beautiful things, can feel that they cannot afford to pay for what costs us so much."

"Well, child, they are more apt to feel so than people who live plainer."

"Well, I am sure," said Ellen, "we cannot afford to spend so much time as we have over these shirts for less money."

"Never mind, my dear," said the mother, soothingly; "here is a bundle of work that another lady has sent in, and if we get it done, we shall have enough for our rent, and something over to buy bread with."

It is needless to carry our readers over all the process of cutting, and fitting, and gathering, and stitching, necessary in making up six fine shirts. Suffice it to say that on Saturday evening all but one were finished, and Ellen proceeded to carry them home, promising to bring the remaining one on Tuesday morning. The lady examined the work, and gave Ellen the money; but on Tuesday, when the child came with the remaining work, she found her in great ill humor. Upon reexamining the shirts, she had discovered that in some important respects they differed from directions she meant to have given, and supposed she had given; and, accordingly, she vented her displeasure on Ellen.

"Why didn't you make these shirts as I told you?" said she, sharply.

"We did," said Ellen, mildly; "mother measured by the pattern every part, and cut them herself."

"Your mother must be a fool, then, to make such a piece of work. I wish you would just take them back and alter them over;" and the lady proceeded with the directions, of which neither Ellen nor her mother till then had had any intimation. Unused to such language, the frightened Ellen took up her work and slowly walked homeward.

"O, dear, how my head does ache!" thought she to herself; "and poor mother! she said this morning she was afraid another of her sick turns was coming on, and we have all this work to pull out and do over."

"See here, mother," said she, with a disconsolate air, as she entered the room; "Mrs. Rudd says, take out all the bosoms, and rip off all the collars, and fix them quite another way. She says they are not like the pattern she sent; but she must have forgotten, for here it is. Look, mother; it is exactly as we made them."

"Well, my child, carry back the pattern, and show her that it is so."

"Indeed, mother, she spoke so cross to me, and looked at me so, that I do not feel as if I could go back."

"I will go for you, then," said the kind Maria Stephens, who had been sitting with Mrs. Ames while Ellen was out. "I will take the pattern and shirts, and tell her the exact truth about it. I am not afraid of her." Maria Stephens was a tailoress, who rented a room on the same floor with Mrs. Ames, a cheerful, resolute, go-forward little body, and ready always to give a helping hand to a neighbor in trouble. So she took the pattern and shirts, and set out on her mission.

But poor Mrs. Ames, though she professed to take a right view of the matter, and was very earnest in showing Ellen why she ought not to distress herself about it, still felt a shivering sense of the hardness and unkindness of the world coming over her. The bitter tears would spring to her eyes, in spite of every effort to suppress them, as she sat mournfully gazing on the little faded miniature before mentioned. "When *he* was alive, I never knew what poverty or trouble was," was the thought that often passed through her mind. And how many a poor forlorn one has thought the same!

Poor Mrs. Ames was confined to her bed for most of that week. The doctor gave absolute directions that she should do nothing, and keep entirely quiet—a direction very sensible indeed in the chamber of ease and competence, but hard to be observed in poverty and want.

What pains the kind and dutiful Ellen took that week to make her mother feel easy! How often she replied to her anxious questions, "that she was quite well," or "that her head did not ache *much!*" and by various other evasive expedients the child tried to persuade herself that she was speaking the truth. And during the times her mother slept, in the day or evening, she accomplished one or two pieces of plain work, with the price of which she expected to surprise her mother.

It was towards evening when Ellen took her finished work to the elegant dwelling of Mrs. Page. "I shall get a dollar for this," said she; "enough to pay for mother's wine and medicine."

"This work is done very neatly," said Mrs. Page, "and here is some more I should like to have finished in the same way."

Ellen looked up wistfully, hoping Mrs. Page was going to pay her for the last work. But Mrs. Page was only searching a drawer for a pattern, which she put into Ellen's hands, and after explaining how she wanted her work done, dismissed her without saying a word about the expected dollar.

Poor Ellen tried two or three times, as she was going out, to turn round and ask for it; but before she could decide what to say, she found herself in the street.

Mrs. Page was an amiable, kind-hearted woman, but one who was so used to large sums of money that she did not realize how great an affair a single dollar might seem to other persons. For this reason, when Ellen had worked incessantly at the new work put into her hands, that she might get the money for all together, she again disappointed her in the payment.

"I'll send the money round to-morrow," said she, when Ellen at last found courage to ask for it. But to-morrow came, and Ellen was forgotten; and it was not till after one or two applications more that the small sum was paid.

But these sketches are already long enough, and let us hasten to close them. Mrs. Ames found liberal friends, who could appreciate and honor her integrity of principle and loveliness of character, and by their assistance she was raised to see more prosperous days; and she, and the delicate Ellen, and warm-hearted Mary were enabled to have a home and fireside of their own, and to enjoy something like the return of their former prosperity.

We have given these sketches, drawn from real life, because we think there is in general too little consideration on the part of those who give employment to those in situations like the widow here described. The giving of employment is a very important branch of charity, inasmuch as it assists that class of the poor who are the most deserving. It should be looked on in this light, and the arrangements of a family be so made that a suitable compensation can be given, and prompt and cheerful payment be made, without the dread of transgressing the rules of economy.

It is better to teach our daughters to do without expensive ornaments or fashionable elegances; better even to deny ourselves the pleasure of large donations or direct subscriptions to public charities, rather than to curtail the small stipend of her whose "candle goeth not out by night,"[2] and who labors with her needle for herself and the helpless dear ones dependent on her exertions.

[1843, 1855]

---

2. "candle . . . night": See Proverbs 31:17-18: "She perceiveth that her merchandise is good: her candle goeth not out by night. She layeth her hands to the spindle, and her hands hold the distaff."

Reading Stowe's "The Freeman's Dream: A Parable."   This brief sketch was Stowe's first significant expression of her antislavery sentiments. A "parable" designed to reveal the inhumanity of slavery, the sketch appeared in the *National Era* on August 1, 1850, at the height of the controversy over the Compromise of 1850. A key provision of the Compromise, the Fugitive Slave Act, had by then already generated months of contentious debate in the Senate, the greatest debate in congressional history. By contributing the sketch to the *Era*, which was published in Washington, D.C., Stowe perhaps sought both to shape public opinion and to fuel congressional opposition to the bill. Nonetheless, the bill passed the Senate on August 12 and the House on September 12, after which it was signed into law by President Fillmore on September 18, 1850, roughly six weeks after Stowe's sketch was published. The text is taken from the *National Era*, August 1, 1850.

THE FREEMAN'S DREAM: A PARABLE

It seemed to him that it was a fair summer evening, and he was walking calmly up and down his estate, watching the ripening grain and listening to the distant voices of his children, as they played by his door, and the song of his wife as she rocked her babe to rest, and the soul of the man grew soft within him, and he gave God thanks with a full heart.

But now there came towards him in the twilight a poor black man, worn and wasted, his clothes rent and travel-soiled, and his step crouching and fearful. He was one that had dwelt in darkness, and as one that had been long dead; and behind him stood, fearfully, a thin and trembling woman, with a wailing babe at her bosom, and a frightened child clinging to her skirts; and the man held out his hand wistfully, and begged for food and shelter, if only for one night, for the pursuer was behind him, and his soul failed him for fear.

The man was not hard, and his heart misgave him when he looked on the failing eye and toil-worn face – when he saw the worn and trembling hands stretched forth; but then he bethought him of human laws, and he feared to befriend him, and he hardened his heart, and set his face as a flint, and bade him pass on, and trouble him not.

And it was so that after he passed on, he saw that the pursuers came up with him, and the man and the woman could not escape, because they were weary and footsore, and there was no more strength in them. And the man heard their screams, and saw them bound and taken by them that would not show mercy.

And after these things the man dreamed, and it seemed to him that the sky grew dark, and the earth rocked to and fro, and the heavens flashed with strange light, and a distant rush, as of wings, was heard, and suddenly, in mid heavens, appeared the sign of the Son of Man, with his mighty angels. Upward, with countless myriads, dizzied and astounded, he seemed to be borne from the earth towards the great white throne and Him that sat thereon, before whose face the heavens and the earth fled away.

Onward, a resistless impulse impelled him towards the bar of the mighty Judge, and before him, as if written in fire, rose in a moment all the thoughts and words and deeds of his past life; and as if he had been the only son of earth to be judged, he felt himself standing alone and trembling before that all-searching Presence. Then an awful voice pierced his soul, saying – "Depart from me ye accursed! for I was an hungered, and ye gave me no meat; I was thirsty, and ye gave me no drink; I was a stranger, and ye took me not in."[1] And, terrified and subdued, the man made answer, "Lord, where?" And immediately rose before him these poor fugitive slaves, whom he had spurned from his door; and the Judge made answer – "Inasmuch as ye did it not to one of the least of these my brethren, ye did it not to me."[2] And with that, terrified and affrighted, the man awoke.

Of late, there have seemed to be many in this nation, who seem to think that there is no standard of right and wrong higher than an act of Congress, or an interpretation of

---

1. "Depart from me . . . ye took me not in": Matthew 25:43.
2. "Inasmuch . . . ye did it not to me": Matthew 25:45.

the United States Constitution. It is humiliating to think that there should be in the church of Christ men and ministers who should need to be reminded that the laws of their Master are above human laws which come in conflict with them; and that though heaven and earth pass away, His word shall not pass away.

Are not the hungry, the thirsty, the stranger, the naked, the prisoner, and every form of bleeding, suffering humanity, as much under the protection of Christ in the person of the black as the white – of the bond as the free? Has he not solemnly told us, and once for all, that every needy human being is His brother, and that neglect of his wants is neglect of Himself?

Shall any doubt if he *may* help the toil-worn, escaping fugitive, sick in heart, weary in limb, hungry and heartsore – let him rather ask, shall he dare refuse him help? To him, too, shall come a dread hour, when a lonely fugitive from life's shore, in unknown lands, he must beg for shelter and help. The only Saviour in that hour is Him who has said, "Inasmuch as ye did it not to the least of these my brethren, ye did it not to *me*!"

[1850]

Reading Stowe's Preface to *Uncle Tom's Cabin*.   In March 1852, as *Uncle Tom's Cabin* was nearing the end of its serialization in the *National Era*, Stowe signed a contract for its publication in book form by John P. Jewett. According to Jewett, his wife had closely followed the serialization and had frequently urged him to publish the book, which became the best-selling novel of its time in the United States. Already well aware of the impact that her story had made on readers of the *Era*, Stowe wrote for the book edition the following preface, in which she explained her purpose in writing the novel and her hopes for its effect on the American public. The text is taken from the first edition of *Uncle Tom's Cabin; or, Life among the Lowly* (1852).

PREFACE TO *UNCLE TOM'S CABIN*

The scenes of this story, as its title indicates, lie among a race hitherto ignored by the associations of polite and refined society; an exotic race, whose ancestors, born beneath a tropic sun, brought with them, and perpetuated to their descendants, a character so essentially unlike the hard and dominant Anglo-Saxon race,[1] as for many years to have won from it only misunderstanding and contempt.

But another and better day is dawning; every influence of literature, of poetry, and of art, in our times, is becoming more and more in unison with the great master chord of Christianity, "good-will to man." The poet, the painter, and the artist now seek out and embellish the common and gentler humanities of life, and, under the allurements of fiction, breathe a humanizing and subduing influence, favorable to the development of the great principles of Christian brotherhood.

---

1. **Anglo-Saxon race:** Stowe refers to a common notion in the nineteenth century that the descendants of the Anglo-Saxons in England were a superior race.

The hand of benevolence is everywhere stretched out, searching into abuses, righting wrongs, alleviating distresses, and bringing to the knowledge and sympathies of the world the lowly, the oppressed, and the forgotten. In this general movement, unhappy Africa is at last remembered; Africa, who began the race of civilization and human progress in the dim, gray dawn of early time, but who, for centuries, has lain bound and bleeding at the foot of civilized and Christianized humanity, imploring compassion in vain.

But the heart of the dominant race, who have been her conquerors, her hard masters, has at length been turned towards her in mercy; and it has been seen how far nobler it is in nations to protect the feeble than to oppress them. Thanks be to God, the world has at length outlived the slave-trade!

The object of these sketches is to awaken sympathy and feeling for the African race, as they exist among us; to show their wrongs and sorrows, under a system so necessarily cruel and unjust as to defeat and do away the good effects of all that can be attempted for them, by their best friends, under it. In doing this, the author can sincerely disclaim any invidious feeling towards those individuals who, often without any fault of their own, are involved in the trials and embarrassments of the legal relations of slavery. Experience has shown her that some of the noblest of minds and hearts are often thus involved; and no one knows better than they do, that what may be gathered of the evils of slavery from sketches like these is not the half that could be told of the unspeakable whole.

In the Northern States, these representations may, perhaps, be thought caricatures; in the Southern States are witnesses who know their fidelity. What personal knowledge the author has had, of the truth of incidents such as are here related, will appear in its time. It is a comfort to hope, as so many of the world's sorrows and wrongs have, from age to age, been lived down, so a time shall come when sketches similar to these shall be valuable only as memorials of what has long ceased to be. When an enlightened and Christianized community shall have, on the shores of Africa,[2] laws, language, and literature, drawn from among us, may then, the scenes from the house of bondage be to them like the remembrance of Egypt to the Israelite, — a motive of thankfulness to Him who hath redeemed them! For, while politicians contend, and men are swerved this way and that by conflicting tides of interest and passion, the great cause of human liberty is in the hands of One, of whom it is said: —

"He shall not fail nor be discouraged
    Till he have set judgment in the earth."

"He shall deliver the needy when he crieth,
    The poor, and him that hath no helper."

"He shall redeem their soul from deceit and violence,
    And precious shall their blood be in his sight."[3]

[1852]

---

2. **on the shores of Africa:** Some of those involved in the antislavery movement supported colonization, a plan to establish colonies for freed slaves in Africa.
3. **"He . . . in his sight":** Isaiah 42:4 and Psalms 72:12-14.

Harriet Jacobs

[1813–1897]

Harriet Ann Jacobs was born into slavery in Edenton, North Carolina, in 1813. Following the death of her mother in 1819, Jacobs was sold to Margaret Horniblow, who taught her to read and sew. After Horniblow's death in 1825, Jacobs became the property of Horniblow's three-year-old niece, Mary Matilda Norcom, the daughter of James Norcom, a physician. As a teenager, Jacobs was constantly subjected to sexual harassment by Norcom and blamed by his wife for his unwelcome attention to her. While embroiled in that impossible situation, Jacobs fell in love with Samuel Tredwell Sawyer, a white attorney and later U.S. congressman (1837–39). With Sawyer, Jacobs had two children: a son, Joseph, born in 1829; and a daughter, Louisa Matilda, born in 1833. Jacobs's consensual relationship with Sawyer

Harriet Jacobs

This daguerreotype, the only known portrait of Jacobs, was taken in 1894, many years after the events she recounted in *Incidents in the Life of a Slave Girl.*

infuriated Norcom, who sent Jacobs to a nearby plantation where she endured brutal treatment. Jacobs escaped from the plantation and hid, first at the home of a friend and then in the small garret of a shed attached to the house of her free grandmother, Molly Horniblow. Norcom, who never gave up trying to capture the elusive Jacobs, issued a $100 reward for her return, noting in an advertisement published on July 4, 1835, that "She speaks easily and fluently." (See p. 638.) Soon after her flight, Sawyer bought Jacobs's children from Norcom but did not free them. In 1842, after seven years of hiding in the stifling garret, Jacobs escaped to New York City and worked as a domestic servant for Nathaniel P. Willis, a successful journalist and writer. She later lived for a time in Rochester, New York, where she became friendly with Frederick Douglass and two Quaker abolitionists, Isaac and Amy Post. Fearing capture as a result of the passage of the Fugitive Slave Act, Jacobs returned to New York City in 1852 to work again as a domestic for Willis. In that year, Willis's wife, Cornelia Grinnell Willis, purchased Jacobs and her children and arranged for their emancipation.

Throughout her years of flight and hiding, Jacobs read and developed her skills as a writer. While she was living in Rochester, she worked in the antislavery reading room of Douglass's newspaper, the *North Star.* Jacobs's first publication was an anonymous "Letter from a Fugitive Slave," published

*bedfordstmartins.com/
americanlit* for research
links on Jacobs

in 1853. She subsequently published other letters and began to write the narrative of her experiences in and escape from slavery, *Incidents in the Life of a Slave Girl*, which was published with the assistance of Lydia Maria Child in 1861. Although the book received favorable reviews and was warmly welcomed by the abolitionists, the outbreak of the Civil War blunted the force of Jacobs's story and sales were disappointing. Between 1862 and 1868, Jacobs worked with the Quakers to organize schools and other institutions for newly freed slaves, first in Washington, D.C., and after the Union victory in Virginia and Georgia. While in the South, she briefly returned to her birthplace and scenes of her traumatic early experiences in North Carolina, a visit she described in a letter to Ednah Dow Cheney, secretary of the New England Freedmen's Aid Society. "I am sitting under a tree not twelve feet from where I suffered all the crushing weight of slavery," Jacobs observed; "thank God the bitter cup is drained of its last dreg." At the end of the letter, Jacobs noted that she had sent Cheney's daughter some jasmine blossoms, adding, "tell her they bear the fragrance of freedom." After returning to the North, Jacobs lived with her daughter in Cambridge, Massachusetts, and later in Washington, D.C., where she died in 1897.

Reading Jacobs's "Letter from a Fugitive Slave."   This letter, subtitled "Slaves Sold under Peculiar Circumstances," was published anonymously on June 21, 1853, in the *New-York Tribune*, an influential newspaper edited by Horace Greeley. As Jacobs indicates, the letter was prompted by the controversy over an article written by "Mrs. Tyler," that is, Julia Gardiner Tyler, wife of former president John Tyler (1841–45). Although she was born and raised in New York, after her marriage Julia Tyler had ardently embraced the views of her husband, a plantation owner from Virginia. In "To the Duchess of Sutherland and the Ladies of England," published in the *Southern Literary Messenger* in February 1853, she consequently rejected pleas by English women to women in the South to help end slavery, affirming that it was a civilizing influence and arguing that slaves lived better than the poor of London. The text of Jacobs's vigorous reply is taken from the first printing of the letter in the *New-York Tribune*, June 21, 1853.

LETTER FROM A FUGITIVE SLAVE

Slaves Sold under Peculiar Circumstances.

[We publish the subjoined communication exactly as written by the author, with the exception of corrections in punctuation and spelling, and the omission of one or two passages. – Ed.]

To the Editor of the *N.Y. Tribune.*

SIR: Having carefully read your paper for some months I became very much interested in some of the articles and comments written on Mrs. Tyler's Reply to the Ladies of England. Being a slave myself, I could not have felt otherwise. Would that I could write an article worthy of notice in your columns. As I never enjoyed the advantages of an education, therefore I could not study the arts of reading and writing, yet poor as it may be, I had rather give it from my own hand, than have it said that I employed others to do it for me. The truth can never be told so well through the second and third person as from yourself. But I am straying from the question. In that Reply to the Ladies of England, Mrs. Tyler said that slaves were never sold only under very peculiar circumstances. As Mrs. Tyler and her friend Bhains were so far used up, that he could not explain what those peculiar circumstances were, let one whose peculiar sufferings justifies her in explaining it for Mrs. Tyler.

I was born a slave, reared in the Southern hot-bed until I was the mother of two children, sold at the early age of two and four years old. I have been hunted through all of the Northern States, but no, I will not tell you of my own suffering — no, it would harrow up my soul, and defeat the object that I wish to pursue. Enough — the dregs of that bitter cup have been my bounty for many years.

And as this is the first time that I ever took my pen in hand to make such an attempt, you will not say that it is fiction, for had I the inclination I have neither the brain or talent to write it. But to this very peculiar circumstance under which slaves are sold.

My mother was held as property by a maiden lady; when she married, my younger sister was in her fourteenth year, whom they took into the family. She was as gentle as she was beautiful. Innocent and guileless child, the light of our desolate hearth! But oh, my heart bleeds to tell you of the misery and degradation she was forced to suffer in slavery. The monster who owned her had no humanity in his soul. The most sincere affection that his heart was capable of, could not make him faithful to his beautiful and wealthy bride the short time of three months, but every stratagem was used to seduce my sister. Mortified and tormented beyond endurance, this child came and threw herself on her mother's bosom, the only place where she could seek refuge from her persecutor; and yet she could not protect her child that she bore into the world. On that bosom with *bitter tears* she told her troubles, and entreated her mother to save her. And oh, Christian mothers! you that have daughters of your own, can you think of your sable sisters without offering a prayer to that God who created all in their behalf! My poor mother, naturally high-spirited, smarting under what she considered as the wrongs and outrages which her child had to bear, sought her master, entreating him to spare her child. Nothing could exceed his rage at this what he called impertinence. My mother was dragged to jail, there remained twenty-five days, with negro traders to come in as they liked to examine her, as she was offered for sale. My sister was told that she must yield, or never expect to see her mother again. There were three younger children; on no other condition could she be restored to them, without the sacrifice of one. That child gave herself up to her master's bidding, to save one that was dearer to her than life itself. And can you, Christian, find it in your heart to despise her? Ah, no! not even Mrs. Tyler;

for though we believe that the vanity of a name would lead her to bestow her hand where her heart could never go with it, yet, with all her faults and follows, she is nothing more than a *woman*. For if her domestic hearth is surrounded with slaves, ere long before this she has opened her eyes to the evils of slavery, and that the mistress as well as the slave must submit to the indignities and vices imposed on them by their lords of body and soul. But to one of those peculiar circumstances.

At fifteen, my sister held to her bosom an innocent offspring of her guilt and misery. In this way she dragged a miserable existence of two years, between the fires of her mistress's jealousy and her master's brutal passion. At seventeen, she gave birth to another helpless infant, heir to all the evils of slavery. Thus life and its sufferings was meted out to her until her twenty-first year. Sorrow and suffering had made its ravages upon her – she was less the object to be desired by the fiend who had crushed her to the earth; and as her children grew, they bore too strong a resemblance to him who desired to give them no other inheritance save Chains and Handcuffs, and in the dead hour of the night, when this young, deserted mother lay with her little ones clinging around her, little dreaming of the dark and inhuman plot that would be carried into execution before another dawn, and when the sun rose on God's beautiful earth, that broken-hearted mother was far on her way to the capitol of Virginia. That day should have refused her light to so disgraceful and inhuman an act in your boasted country of Liberty. Yet, reader, it is true, those two helpless children were the *sons* of one of your sainted Members in Congress; that agonized mother, his victim and slave. And where she now is God only knows, who has kept a record on high of all that she has suffered on earth.

And, you would exclaim, Could not the master have been more merciful to his children? God is merciful to all of his children, but it is seldom that a slaveholder has any mercy for his slave child. And you will believe it when I tell you that mother and her children were sold to make room for another sister, who was now the age of that mother when she entered the family. And this selling appeased the mistress's wrath, and satisfied her desire for *revenge* and made the path more smooth for her young rival at first. For there is a strong rivalry between a handsome mulatto girl and a jealous and *faded* mistress, and her liege lord sadly neglects those little attentions for a while that once made her happy. For the master will either neglect his wife or double his attentions, to save him from being suspected by his wife. Would you not think that Southern Women had cause to despise that Slavery which forces them to bear so much deception practiced by their *husbands?* Yet all this is true, for a slaveholder seldom takes a white mistress, for she is an expensive commodity, not submissive as he would like to have her, but more apt to be tyrannical; and when his passion seeks another object, he must leave her in quiet possession of all the gewgaws that she has sold herself for. But not so with his poor *slave victim*, that he has robbed of everything that can make life desirable; she must be torn from the little that is left to bind her to life, and sold by her *seducer* and *master*, caring not where, so that it puts him in possession of enough to purchase another victim. And such are the peculiar circumstances of American Slavery – of all the evils in God's sight the most to be abhorred.

Perhaps while I am writing this you too, dear Emily, may be on your way to the Mississippi River, for those peculiar circumstances occur every day in the midst of my poor oppressed fellow-creatures in bondage. And oh ye Christians, while your arms are extended to receive the oppressed of all nations, while you exert every power of your soul to assist them to raise funds, put weapons in their hands, tell them to return to their own country to slay every foe until they break the accursed yoke from off their necks, not buying and selling; this they never do under any circumstances. But while Americans do all this, they forget the millions of slaves they have at home, bought and sold under very peculiar circumstances.

And because one friend of the slave has dared to tell of their wrongs you would annihilate her. But in *Uncle Tom's Cabin* she has not told the half. Would that I had one spark from her store house of genius and talent I would tell you of my own sufferings — I would tell you of wrongs that Hungary has never endured, nor England ever dreamed of in this free country where all nations fly for liberty, equal rights and protection under your stripes and stars. It should be stripes and scars, for they go along with Mrs. Tyler's peculiar circumstances, of which I have told you only one.

A FUGITIVE SLAVE
[1853]

Reading Jacobs's *Incidents in the Life of a Slave Girl*.   Encouraged by her friend Amy Post, a Quaker abolitionist, as well as by the phenomenal success of Harriet Beecher Stowe's *Uncle Tom's Cabin* (1852), Jacobs apparently as early as 1853 began to write an account of her experiences in slavery and as a fugitive. Although she completed it by 1858, Jacobs could not find a publisher for the work. After first asking Stowe for help, Jacobs turned to Lydia Maria Child. Child's correspondence indicates that she worked over the manuscript fairly heavily, dividing it into chapters and making other alterations designed to make Jacobs's story "more clear and entertaining." In her introduction to the book, however, Child emphasized that she had provided only editorial assistance to Jacobs, having had "no reason for changing her lively and dramatic way of telling her own story." She also emphasized the importance of *Incidents in the Life of a Slave Girl*, which was among the first slave narratives written by a woman and the first to deal frankly with what Child called the "monstrous features" of slavery for women — their sexual harassment by white masters.

Reluctant to use her real name and in order to protect herself and her children, Jacobs published the book under the pseudonym "Linda Brent." In a letter to the *Liberator*, Jacobs's friend William C. Nell wrote that the narrative

> presents features more attractive than many of its predecessors purporting to be histories of slave life in America, because, in contrast with their mingling of fiction with fact, this record of complicated experience in the life of a young woman, a doomed victim to America's peculiar institution . . . surely needs not the charms that any pen of fiction, however gifted and graceful, could lend.

Ironically, the account later came to be viewed as a fictional slave narrative, partly because so little was known about its author and partly because portions of the story seemed so unlikely. Through the work of the scholar

Jean Fagin Yellin, we now know much more about Harriet Jacobs; we also know that the details of her story are supported by strong historical evidence.

The text is taken from the first edition of *Incidents in the Life of a Slave Girl, Written by Herself,* edited by L. Maria Child (1861). The title page included two epigraphs. The first, identified as the statement of "A Woman of North Carolina," reads: "Northerners know nothing at all about Slavery. They think it is perpetual bondage only. They have no conception of the depth of *degradation* involved in that word, Slavery; if they had, they would never cease their efforts until so horrible a system was overthrown." The second epigraph was a verse from Isaiah 32:9: "Rise up, ye women that are at ease! Hear my voice, ye careless daughters! Give ear unto my speech."

INCIDENTS IN THE LIFE OF A SLAVE GIRL

Preface by the Author

READER, be assured this narrative is no fiction. I am aware that some of my adventures may seem incredible; but they are, nevertheless, strictly true. I have not exaggerated the wrongs inflicted by Slavery; on the contrary, my descriptions fall far short of the facts. I have concealed the names of places, and given persons fictitious names. I had no motive for secrecy on my own account, but I deemed it kind and considerate towards others to pursue this course.

I wish I were more competent to the task I have undertaken. But I trust my readers will excuse deficiencies in consideration of circumstances. I was born and reared in Slavery; and I remained in a Slave State twenty-seven years. Since I have been at the North, it has been necessary for me to work diligently for my own support, and the education of my children. This has not left me much leisure to make up for the loss of early opportunities to improve myself; and it has compelled me to write these pages at irregular intervals, whenever I could snatch an hour from household duties.

When I first arrived in Philadelphia, Bishop Paine[1] advised me to publish a sketch of my life, but I told him I was altogether incompetent to such an undertaking. Though I have improved my mind somewhat since that time, I still remain of the same opinion; but I trust my motives will excuse what might otherwise seem presumptuous. I have not written my experiences in order to attract attention to myself; on the contrary, it would have been more pleasant to me to have been silent about my own history. Neither do I care to excite sympathy for my own sufferings. But I do earnestly desire to arouse the women of the North to a realizing sense of the condition of two millions of women at the South, still in bondage, suffering what I suffered, and most of them far worse. I want to add my testimony to that of abler pens to convince the people of the Free States what Slavery really is. Only by experience can any one realize how deep, and dark, and foul is that pit of abominations. May the blessing of God rest on this imperfect effort in behalf of my persecuted people!

LINDA BRENT

---

1. **Bishop Paine:** Daniel A. Payne (1811–1893), bishop of the African Methodist Episcopal Church.

I. Childhood

I was born a slave; but I never knew it till six years of happy childhood had passed away. My father was a carpenter, and considered so intelligent and skilful in his trade, that, when buildings out of the common line were to be erected, he was sent for from long distances, to be head workman. On condition of paying his mistress two hundred dollars a year, and supporting himself, he was allowed to work at his trade, and manage his own affairs. His strongest wish was to purchase his children; but, though he several times offered his hard earnings for that purpose, he never succeeded. In complexion my parents were a light shade of brownish yellow, and were termed mulattoes. They lived together in a comfortable home; and, though we were all slaves, I was so fondly shielded that I never dreamed I was a piece of merchandise, trusted to them for safe keeping, and liable to be demanded of them at any moment. I had one brother, William, who was two years younger than myself – a bright, affectionate child. I had also a great treasure in my maternal grandmother, who was a remarkable woman in many respects. She was the daughter of a planter in South Carolina, who, at his death, left her mother and his three children free, with money to go to St. Augustine, where they had relatives. It was during the Revolutionary War; and they were captured on their passage, carried back, and sold to different purchasers. Such was the story my grandmother used to tell me; but I do not remember all the particulars. She was a little girl when she was captured and sold to the keeper of a large hotel. I have often heard her tell how hard she fared during childhood. But as she grew older she evinced so much intelligence, and was so faithful, that her master and mistress could not help seeing it was for their interest to take care of such a valuable piece of property. She became an indispensable personage in the household, officiating in all capacities, from cook and wet nurse to seamstress. She was much praised for her cooking; and her nice crackers became so famous in the neighborhood that many people were desirous of obtaining them. In consequence of numerous requests of this kind, she asked permission of her mistress to bake crackers at night, after all the household work was done; and she obtained leave to do it, provided she would clothe herself and her children from the profits. Upon these terms, after working hard all day for her mistress, she began her midnight bakings, assisted by her two oldest children. The business proved profitable; and each year she laid by a little, which was saved for a fund to purchase her children. Her master died, and the property was divided among his heirs. The widow had her dower in the hotel, which she continued to keep open. My grandmother remained in her service as a slave; but her children were divided among her master's children. As she had five, Benjamin, the youngest one, was sold, in order that each heir might have an equal portion of dollars and cents. There was so little difference in our ages that he seemed more like my brother than my uncle. He was a bright, handsome lad, nearly white; for he inherited the complexion my grandmother had derived from Anglo-Saxon ancestors. Though only ten years old, seven hundred and twenty dollars were paid for him. His sale was a terrible blow to my grandmother; but she was naturally hopeful, and she went to work with renewed energy, trusting in time to be able to purchase some of her children. She had laid up three hundred dollars, which her mistress one day begged as a loan, promising to pay her soon. The reader probably knows that no promise or writing given to a slave is legally binding; for, according to Southern laws, a slave, *being* property, can *hold* no property. When my grandmother lent her hard earnings to her mistress, she trusted solely to her honor. The honor of a slave-holder to a slave!

To this good grandmother I was indebted for many comforts. My brother Willie and I often received portions of the crackers, cakes, and preserves, she made to sell; and after we ceased to be children we were indebted to her for many more important services.

Such were the unusually fortunate circumstances of my early childhood. When I was six years old, my mother died; and then, for the first time, I learned, by the talk around me, that I was a slave. My mother's mistress was the daughter of my grandmother's mistress. She was the foster sister of my mother; they were both nourished at my grandmother's breast. In fact, my mother had been weaned at three months old, that the babe of the mistress might obtain sufficient food. They played together as children; and, when they became women, my mother was a most faithful servant to her whiter foster sister. On her death-bed her mistress promised that her children should never suffer for any thing; and during her lifetime she kept her word. They all spoke kindly of my dead mother, who had been a slave merely in name, but in nature was noble and womanly. I grieved for her, and my young mind was troubled with the thought who would now take care of me and my little brother. I was told that my home was now to be with her mistress; and I found it a happy one. No toilsome or disagreeable duties were imposed upon me. My mistress was so kind to me that I was always glad to do her bidding, and proud to labor for her as much as my young years would permit. I would sit by her side for hours, sewing diligently, with a heart as free from care as that of any free-born white child. When she thought I was tired, she would send me out to run and jump; and away I bounded, to gather berries or flowers to decorate her room. Those were happy days – too happy to last. The slave child had no thought for the morrow; but there came that blight, which too surely waits on every human being born to be a chattel.

When I was nearly twelve years old, my kind mistress sickened and died. As I saw the cheek grow paler, and the eye more glassy, how earnestly I prayed in my heart that she might live! I loved her; for she had been almost like a mother to me. My prayers were not answered. She died, and they buried her in the little churchyard, where, day after day, my tears fell upon her grave.

I was sent to spend a week with my grandmother. I was now old enough to begin to think of the future; and again and again I asked myself what they would do with me. I felt sure I should never find another mistress so kind as the one who was gone. She had promised my dying mother that her children should never suffer for any thing; and when I remembered that, and recalled her many proofs of attachment to me, I could not help having some hopes that she had left me free. My friends were almost certain it would be so. They thought she would be sure to do it, on account of my mother's love and faithful service. But, alas! we all know that the memory of a faithful slave does not avail much to save her children from the auction block.

After a brief period of suspense, the will of my mistress was read, and we learned that she had bequeathed me to her sister's daughter, a child of five years old. So vanished our hopes. My mistress had taught me the precepts of God's Word: "Thou shalt love thy neighbor as thyself."[1] "Whatsoever ye would that men should do unto you, do ye even so unto them."[2] But I was her slave, and I suppose she did not recognize me as her neighbor. I would give much to blot out from my memory that one great wrong. As a child, I loved my mistress; and, looking back on the happy days I spent with her, I try to think with less bitterness of this act of injustice. While I was with her, she taught me to read and spell; and for this privilege, which so rarely falls to the lot of a slave, I bless her memory.

She possessed but few slaves; and at her death those were all distributed among her relatives. Five of them were my grandmother's children, and had shared the same milk that nourished her mother's children. Notwithstanding my grandmother's long and faithful service to her owners, not one of her children escaped the auction block. These God-breathing machines are no more, in the sight of their masters, than the cotton they plant, or the horses they tend.

VII. The Lover

Why does the slave ever love? Why allow the tendrils of the heart to twine around objects which may at any moment be wrenched away by the hand of violence? When separations come by the hand of death, the pious soul can bow in resignation, and say, "Not my will, but thine be done, O Lord!"[1] But when the ruthless hand of man strikes the blow, regardless of the misery he causes, it is hard to be submissive. I did not reason thus when I was a young girl. Youth will be youth. I loved, and I indulged the hope that the dark clouds around me would turn out a bright lining. I forgot that in the land of my birth the shadows are too dense for light to penetrate. A land

> "Where laughter is not mirth; nor thought the mind;
> Nor words a language; nor e'en men mankind.
> Where cries reply to curses, shrieks to blows,
> And each is tortured in his separate hell."[2]

There was in the neighborhood a young colored carpenter; a free born man. We had been well acquainted in childhood, and frequently met together afterwards. We became mutually attached, and he proposed to marry me. I loved him with all the ardor of a young girl's first love. But when I reflected that I was a slave, and that the laws gave no sanction to the marriage of such, my heart sank within me. My lover wanted to buy me; but I knew that Dr. Flint was too wilful and arbitrary a man to consent to that arrangement. From him, I was sure of experiencing all sorts of opposition, and I had nothing to

---

1. "Thou . . . as thyself": Mark 12:31.
2. "Whatsoever . . . unto them": Matthew 7:12.
1. "Not . . . O Lord!": See the description of Jesus in the garden of Gethsemane: "And he went a little farther, and fell on his face, and prayed, saying, O my Father, if it be possible, let this cup pass from me: nevertheless not as I will, but as thou wilt" (Matthew 26:39).
2. "Where . . . hell": From "The Lament of Tasso," by the English poet George Gordon, Lord Byron (1788–1824).

hope from my mistress. She would have been delighted to have got rid of me, but not in that way. It would have relieved her mind of a burden if she could have seen me sold to some distant state, but if I was married near home I should be just as much in her husband's power as I had previously been, – for the husband of a slave has no power to protect her. Moreover, my mistress, like many others, seemed to think that slaves had no right to any family ties of their own; that they were created merely to wait upon the family of the mistress. I once heard her abuse a young slave girl, who told her that a colored man wanted to make her his wife. "I will have you peeled and pickled, my lady," said she, "if I ever hear you mention that subject again. Do you suppose that I will have you tending *my* children with the children of that nigger?" The girl to whom she said this had a mulatto child, of course not acknowledged by its father. The poor black man who loved her would have been proud to acknowledge his helpless offspring.

Many and anxious were the thoughts I revolved in my mind. I was at a loss what to do. Above all things, I was desirous to spare my lover the insults that had cut so deeply into my own soul. I talked with my grandmother about it, and partly told her my fears. I did not dare to tell her the worst. She had long suspected all was not right, and if I confirmed her suspicions I knew a storm would rise that would prove the overthrow of all my hopes.

This love-dream had been my support through many trials; and I could not bear to run the risk of having it suddenly dissipated. There was a lady in the neighborhood, a particular friend of Dr. Flint's, who often visited the house. I had a great respect for her, and she had always manifested a friendly interest in me. Grandmother thought she would have great influence with the doctor. I went to this lady, and told her my story. I told her I was aware that my lover's being a free-born man would prove a great objection; but he wanted to buy me; and if Dr. Flint would consent to that arrangement, I felt sure he would be willing to pay any reasonable price. She knew that Mrs. Flint disliked me; therefore, I ventured to suggest that perhaps my mistress would approve of my being sold, as that would rid her of me. The lady listened with kindly sympathy, and promised to do her utmost to promote my wishes. She had an interview with the doctor, and I believe she pleaded my cause earnestly; but it was all to no purpose.

How I dreaded my master now! Every minute I expected to be summoned to his presence; but the day passed, and I heard nothing from him. The next morning, a message was brought to me: "Master wants you in his study." I found the door ajar, and I stood a moment gazing at the hateful man who claimed a right to rule me, body and soul. I entered, and tried to appear calm. I did not want him to know how my heart was bleeding. He looked fixedly at me, with an expression which seemed to say, "I have half a mind to kill you on the spot." At last he broke the silence, and that was a relief to both of us.

"So you want to be married, do you?" said he, "and to a free nigger."

"Yes, sir."

"Well, I'll soon convince you whether I am your master, or the nigger fellow you honor so highly. If you *must* have a husband, you may take up with one of my slaves."

What a situation I should be in, as the wife of one of *his* slaves, even if my heart had been interested!

I replied, "Don't you suppose, sir, that a slave can have some preference about marrying? Do you suppose that all men are alike to her?"

"Do you love this nigger?" said he, abruptly.

"Yes, sir."

"How dare you tell me so!" he exclaimed, in great wrath. After a slight pause, he added, "I supposed you thought more of yourself; that you felt above the insults of such puppies."

I replied, "If he is a puppy I am a puppy, for we are both of the negro race. It is right and honorable for us to love each other. The man you call a puppy never insulted me, sir; and he would not love me if he did not believe me to be a virtuous woman."

He sprang upon me like a tiger, and gave me a stunning blow. It was the first time he had ever struck me; and fear did not enable me to control my anger. When I had recovered a little from the effects, I exclaimed, "You have struck me for answering you honestly. How I despise you!"

There was silence for some minutes. Perhaps he was deciding what should be my punishment; or, perhaps, he wanted to give me time to reflect on what I had said, and to whom I had said it. Finally, he asked, "Do you know what you have said?"

"Yes, sir; but your treatment drove me to it."

"Do you know that I have a right to do as I like with you, — that I can kill you, if I please?"

"You have tried to kill me, and I wish you had; but you have no right to do as you like with me."

"Silence!" he exclaimed, in a thundering voice. "By heavens, girl, you forget yourself too far! Are you mad? If you are, I will soon bring you to your senses. Do you think any other master would bear what I have borne from you this morning? Many masters would have killed you on the spot. How would you like to be sent to jail for your insolence?"

"I know I have been disrespectful, sir," I replied; "but you drove me to it; I couldn't help it. As for the jail, there would be more peace for me there than there is here."

"You deserve to go there," said he, "and to be under such treatment, that you would forget the meaning of the word *peace.* It would do you good. It would take some of your high notions out of you. But I am not ready to send you there yet, notwithstanding your ingratitude for all my kindness and forbearance. You have been the plague of my life. I have wanted to make you happy, and I have been repaid with the basest ingratitude; but though you have proved yourself incapable of appreciating my kindness, I will be lenient towards you, Linda. I will give you one more chance to redeem your character. If you behave yourself and do as I require, I will forgive you and treat you as I always have done; but if you disobey me, I will punish you as I would the meanest slave on my plantation. Never let me hear that fellow's name mentioned again. If I ever know of your speaking to him, I will cowhide you both; and if I catch him lurking about my premises, I will shoot him as soon as I would a dog. Do you hear what I say? I'll teach you a lesson about marriage and free niggers! Now go, and let this be the last time I have occasion to speak to you on this subject."

Reader, did you ever hate? I hope not. I never did but once; and I trust I never shall again. Somebody has called it "the atmosphere of hell;" and I believe it is so.

For a fortnight the doctor did not speak to me. He thought to mortify me; to make me feel that I had disgraced myself by receiving the honorable addresses of a respectable colored man, in preference to the base proposals of a white man. But though his lips disdained to address me, his eyes were very loquacious. No animal ever watched its prey more narrowly than he watched me. He knew that I could write, though he had failed to make me read his letters; and he was now troubled lest I should exchange letters with another man. After a while he became weary of silence; and I was sorry for it. One morning, as he passed through the hall, to leave the house, he contrived to thrust a note into my hand. I thought I had better read it, and spare myself the vexation of having him read it to me. It expressed regret for the blow he had given me, and reminded me that I myself was wholly to blame for it. He hoped I had become convinced of the injury I was doing myself by incurring his displeasure. He wrote that he had made up his mind to go to Louisiana; that he should take several slaves with him, and intended I should be one of the number. My mistress would remain where she was; therefore I should have nothing to fear from that quarter. If I merited kindness from him, he assured me that it would be lavishly bestowed. He begged me to think over the matter, and answer the following day.

The next morning I was called to carry a pair of scissors to his room. I laid them on the table with the letter beside them. He thought it was my answer, and did not call me back. I went as usual to attend my young mistress to and from school. He met me in the street, and ordered me to stop at his office on my way back. When I entered, he showed me his letter, and asked me why I had not answered it. I replied, "I am your daughter's property, and it is in your power to send me, or take me, wherever you please." He said he was very glad to find me so willing to go, and that we should start early in the autumn. He had a large practice in the town, and I rather thought he had made up the story merely to frighten me. However that might be, I was determined that I would never go to Louisiana with him.

Summer passed away, and early in the autumn Dr. Flint's eldest son was sent to Louisiana to examine the country, with a view to emigrating. That news did not disturb me. I knew very well that I should not be sent with *him*. That I had not been taken to the plantation before this time, was owing to the fact that his son was there. He was jealous of his son; and jealousy of the overseer had kept him from punishing me by sending me into the fields to work. Is it strange that I was not proud of these protectors? As for the overseer, he was a man for whom I had less respect than I had for a bloodhound.

Young Mr. Flint did not bring back a favorable report of Louisiana, and I heard no more of that scheme. Soon after this, my lover met me at the corner of the street, and I stopped to speak to him. Looking up, I saw my master watching us from his window. I hurried home, trembling with fear. I was sent for, immediately, to go to his room. He met me with a blow. "When is mistress to be married?" said he, in a sneering tone. A shower of oaths and imprecations followed. How thankful I was that my lover was a free man! that my tyrant had no power to flog him for speaking to me in the street!

Again and again I revolved in my mind how all this would end. There was no hope that the doctor would consent to sell me on any terms. He had an iron will, and was determined to keep me, and to conquer me. My lover was an intelligent and religious man. Even if he could have obtained permission to marry me while I was a slave, the marriage would give him no power to protect me from my master. It would have made him miserable to witness the insults I should have been subjected to. And then, if we had children, I knew they must "follow the condition of the mother."[3] What a terrible blight that would be on the heart of a free, intelligent father! For *his* sake, I felt that I ought not to link his fate with my own unhappy destiny. He was going to Savannah to see about a little property left him by an uncle; and hard as it was to bring my feelings to it, I earnestly entreated him not to come back. I advised him to go to the Free States, where his tongue would not be tied, and where his intelligence would be of more avail to him. He left me, still hoping the day would come when I could be bought. With me the lamp of hope had gone out. The dream of my girlhood was over. I felt lonely and desolate.

Still I was not stripped of all. I still had my good grandmother, and my affectionate brother. When he put his arms round my neck, and looked into my eyes, as if to read there the troubles I dared not tell, I felt that I still had something to love. But even that pleasant emotion was chilled by the reflection that he might be torn from me at any moment, by some sudden freak of my master. If he had known how we loved each other, I think he would have exulted in separating us. We often planned together how we could get to the north. But, as William remarked, such things are easier said than done. My movements were very closely watched, and we had no means of getting any money to defray our expenses. As for grandmother, she was strongly opposed to her children's undertaking any such project. She had not forgotten poor Benjamin's sufferings, and she was afraid that if another child tried to escape, he would have a similar or a worse fate. To me, nothing seemed more dreadful than my present life. I said to myself, "William *must* be free. He shall go to the north, and I will follow him." Many a slave sister has formed the same plans.

X. A Perilous Passage in the
Slave Girl's Life

After my lover went away, Dr. Flint contrived a new plan. He seemed to have an idea that my fear of my mistress was his greatest obstacle. In the blandest tones, he told me that he was going to build a small house for me, in a secluded place, four miles away from the town. I shuddered; but I was constrained to listen, while he talked of his intention to give me a home of my own, and to make a lady of me. Hitherto, I had escaped my dreaded fate, by being in the midst of people. My grandmother had already had high words with my master about me. She had told him pretty plainly what she thought of his character, and there was considerable gossip in the neighborhood about our affairs, to which the open-mouthed jealousy of Mrs. Flint contributed not a little. When my master said he was going to build a house for me, and that he could do it with little trouble and expense, I was in hopes something would happen to frustrate his scheme; but I soon heard that the house was actually begun. I vowed before my Maker that I would never enter it. I had rather toil on the plantation from dawn till dark; I had rather live and die in jail, than

---

3. **"follow the condition of the mother":** By law, the legal status of the mother determined whether a child was free or a slave.

drag on, from day to day, through such a living death. I was determined that the master, whom I so hated and loathed, who had blighted the prospects of my youth, and made my life a desert, should not, after my long struggle with him, succeed at last in trampling his victim under his feet. I would do any thing, every thing, for the sake of defeating him. What *could* I do? I thought and thought, till I became desperate, and made a plunge into the abyss.

And now, reader, I come to a period in my unhappy life, which I would gladly forget if I could. The remembrance fills me with sorrow and shame. It pains me to tell you of it; but I have promised to tell you the truth and I will do it honestly, let it cost me what it may. I will not try to screen myself behind the plea of compulsion from a master; for it was not so. Neither can I plead ignorance or thoughtlessness. For years, my master had done his utmost to pollute my mind with foul images, and to destroy the pure principles inculcated by my grandmother, and the good mistress of my childhood. The influences of slavery had had the same effect on me that they had on other young girls; they had made me prematurely knowing, concerning the evil ways of the world. I knew what I did, and I did it with deliberate calculation.

But, O, ye happy women, whose purity has been sheltered from childhood, who have been free to choose the objects of your affection, whose homes are protected by law, do not judge the poor desolate slave girl too severely! If slavery had been abolished, I, also, could have married the man of my choice; I could have had a home shielded by the laws; and I should have been spared the painful task of confessing what I am now about to relate; but all my prospects had been blighted by slavery. I wanted to keep myself pure; and, under the most adverse circumstances, I tried hard to preserve my self-respect; but I was struggling alone in the powerful grasp of the demon Slavery; and the monster proved too strong for me. I felt as if I was forsaken by God and man; as if all my efforts must be frustrated; and I became reckless in my despair.

I have told you that Dr. Flint's persecutions and his wife's jealousy had given rise to some gossip in the neighborhood. Among others, it chanced that a white unmarried gentleman had obtained some knowledge of the circumstances in which I was placed. He knew my grandmother, and often spoke to me in the street. He became interested for me, and asked questions about my master, which I answered in part. He expressed a great deal of sympathy, and a wish to aid me. He constantly sought opportunities to see me, and wrote to me frequently. I was a poor slave girl, only fifteen years old.

So much attention from a superior person was, of course, flattering; for human nature is the same in all. I also felt grateful for his sympathy, and encouraged by his kind words. It seemed to me a great thing to have such a friend. By degrees, a more tender feeling crept into my heart. He was an educated and eloquent gentleman; too eloquent, alas, for the poor slave girl who trusted in him. Of course I saw whither all this was tending. I knew the impassable gulf between us; but to be an object of interest to a man who is not married, and who is not her master, is agreeable to the pride and feelings of a slave, if her miserable situation has left her any pride or sentiment. It seems less degrading to give one's self, than to submit to compulsion. There is something akin to freedom in having a lover who has no control over you, except that which he gains by kindness and attachment. A master may treat you as rudely as he pleases, and you dare not speak; moreover, the wrong does not seem so great with an unmarried man, as with one who has a wife to be made unhappy. There may be sophistry in all this; but the condition of a slave confuses all principles of morality, and, in fact, renders the practice of them impossible.

When I found that my master had actually begun to build the lonely cottage, other feelings mixed with those I have described. Revenge, and calculations of interest, were added to flattered vanity and sincere gratitude for kindness. I knew nothing would enrage Dr. Flint so much as to know that I favored another; and it was something to triumph over my tyrant even in that small way. I thought he would revenge himself by selling me, and I was sure my friend, Mr. Sands, would buy me. He was a man of more generosity and feeling than my master, and I thought my freedom could be easily obtained from him. The crisis of my fate now came so near that I was desperate. I shuddered to think of being the mother of children that should be owned by my old tyrant. I knew that as soon as a new fancy took him, his victims were sold far off to get rid of them; especially if they had children. I had seen several women sold, with his babies at the breast. He never allowed his offspring by slaves to remain long in sight of himself and his wife. Of a man who was not my master I could ask to have my children well supported; and in this case, I felt confident I should obtain the boon. I also felt quite sure that they would be made free. With all these thoughts revolving in my mind, and seeing no other way of escaping the doom I so much dreaded, I made a headlong plunge. Pity me, and pardon me, O virtuous reader! You never knew what it is to be a slave; to be entirely unprotected by law or custom; to have the laws reduce you to the condition of a chattel, entirely subject to the will of another. You never exhausted your ingenuity in avoiding the snares, and eluding the power of a hated tyrant; you never shuddered at the sound of his footsteps, and trembled within hearing of his voice. I know I did wrong. No one can feel it more sensibly than I do. The painful and humiliating memory will haunt me to my dying day. Still, in looking back, calmly, on the events of my life, I feel that the slave woman ought not to be judged by the same standard as others.

The months passed on. I had many unhappy hours. I secretly mourned over the sorrow I was bringing on my grandmother, who had so tried to shield me from harm. I knew that I was the greatest comfort of her old age, and that it was a source of pride to her that I had not degraded myself, like most of the slaves. I wanted to confess to her that I was no longer worthy of her love; but I could not utter the dreaded words.

As for Dr. Flint, I had a feeling of satisfaction and triumph in the thought of telling *him*. From time to time he told me of his intended arrangements, and I was silent. At last, he came and told me the cottage was completed, and ordered me to go to it. I told him I would never enter it. He said, "I have heard enough of such talk as that. You shall go, if you are carried by force; and you shall remain there."

I replied, "I will never go there. In a few months I shall be a mother."

He stood and looked at me in dumb amazement, and left the house without a word. I thought I should be happy in my triumph over him. But now that the truth was out, and my relatives would hear of it, I felt wretched. Humble as were their circumstances, they had pride in my good character. Now, how could I look them in the face? My self-respect was gone! I had resolved that I would be virtuous, though I was a slave. I had said, "Let the storm beat! I will brave it till I die." And now, how humiliated I felt!

I went to my grandmother. My lips moved to make confession, but the words stuck in my throat. I sat down in the shade of a tree at her door and began to sew. I think she saw something unusual was the matter with me. The mother of slaves is very watchful. She knows there is no security for her children. After they have entered their teens she lives in daily expectation of trouble. This leads to many questions. If the girl is of a sensitive nature, timidity keeps her from answering truthfully and this well-meant course has a tendency to drive her from maternal counsels. Presently, in came my mistress, like a mad woman, and accused me concerning her husband. My grandmother, whose suspicions had been previously awakened, believed what she said. She exclaimed, "O Linda! has it come to this? I had rather see you dead than to see you as you now are. You are a disgrace to your dead mother." She tore from my fingers my mother's wedding ring and her silver thimble. "Go away!" she exclaimed, "and never come to my house, again." Her reproaches fell so hot and heavy, that they left me no chance to answer. Bitter tears, such as the eyes never shed but once, were my only answer. I rose from my seat, but fell back again, sobbing. She did not speak to me; but the tears were running down her furrowed cheeks, and they scorched me like fire. She had always been so kind to me! *So* kind! How I longed to throw myself at her feet, and tell her all the truth! But she had ordered me to go, and never to come there again. After a few minutes, I mustered strength, and started to obey her. With what feelings did I now close that little gate, which I used to open with such an eager hand in my childhood! It closed upon me with a sound I never heard before.

Where could I go? I was afraid to return to my master's. I walked on recklessly, not caring where I went, or what would become of me. When I had gone four or five miles, fatigue compelled me to stop. I sat down on the stump of an old tree. The stars were shining through the boughs above me. How they mocked me, with their bright, calm light! The hours passed by, and as I sat there alone a chilliness and deadly sickness came over me. I sank on the ground. My mind was full of horrid thoughts. I prayed to die; but the prayer was not answered. At last, with great effort I roused myself, and walked some distance further, to the house of a woman who had been a friend of my mother. When I told her why I was there, she spoke soothingly to me; but I could not be comforted. I thought I could bear my shame if I could only be reconciled to my grandmother. I longed to open my heart to her. I thought if she could know the real state of the case, and all I had been bearing for years, she would perhaps judge me less harshly. My friend advised me to send for her. I did so; but days of agonizing suspense passed before she came. Had she utterly forsaken me? No. She came at last. I knelt before her, and told her the things that had poisoned my life; how long I had been persecuted; that I saw no way of escape; and in an hour of extremity I had become desperate. She listened in silence. I told her I would bear any thing and do any thing, if in time I had hopes of obtaining her forgiveness. I begged of her to pity me, for my dead mother's sake. And she did pity me. She did not say, "I forgive you;" but she looked at me lovingly, with her eyes full of tears. She laid her old hand gently on my head, and murmured, "Poor child! Poor child!"

XIV. Another Link to Life

I had not returned to my master's house since the birth of my child. The old man raved to have me thus removed from his immediate power; but his wife vowed, by all that was good and great, she would kill me if I came back; and he did not doubt her word. Sometimes he would stay away for a season. Then he would come and renew the old threadbare discourse about his forbearance and my ingratitude. He labored, most unnecessarily, to convince me that I had lowered myself. The venomous old reprobate had no need of descanting on that theme. I felt humiliated enough. My unconscious babe was the ever-present witness of my shame. I listened with silent contempt when he talked about my having forfeited *his* good opinion; but I shed bitter tears that I was no longer worthy of being respected by the good and pure. Alas! slavery still held me in its poisonous grasp. There was no chance for me to be respectable. There was no prospect of being able to lead a better life.

Sometimes, when my master found that I still refused to accept what he called his kind offers, he would threaten to sell my child. "Perhaps that will humble you," said he.

Humble *me*! Was I not already in the dust? But his threat lacerated my heart. I knew the law gave him power to fulfil it; for slaveholders have been cunning enough to enact that "the child shall follow the condition of the *mother*," not of the *father*; thus taking care that licentiousness shall not interfere with avarice. This reflection made me clasp my innocent babe all the more firmly to my heart. Horrid visions passed through my mind when I thought of his liability to fall into the slavetrader's hands. I wept over him, and said, "O my child! perhaps they will leave you in some cold cabin to die, and then throw you into a hole, as if you were a dog."

When Dr. Flint learned that I was again to be a mother, he was exasperated beyond measure. He rushed from the house, and returned with a pair of shears. I had a fine head of hair; and he often railed about my pride of arranging it nicely. He cut every hair close to my head, storming and swearing all the time. I replied to some of his abuse, and he struck me. Some months before, he had pitched me down stairs in a fit of passion; and the injury I received was so serious that I was unable to turn myself in bed for many days. He then said, "Linda, I swear by God I will never raise my hand against you again;" but I knew that he would forget his promise.

After he discovered my situation, he was like a restless spirit from the pit. He came every day; and I was subjected to such insults as no pen can describe. I would not describe them if I could; they were too low, too revolting. I tried to keep them from my grandmother's knowledge as much as I could. I knew she had enough to sadden her life, without having my troubles to bear. When she saw the doctor treat me with violence, and heard him utter oaths terrible enough to palsy a man's tongue, she could not always hold her peace. It was natural and motherlike that she should try to defend me; but it only made matters worse.

When they told me my new-born babe was a girl, my heart was heavier than it had ever been before. Slavery is terrible for men; but it is far more terrible for women. Superadded to the burden common to all, *they* have wrongs, and sufferings, and mortifications peculiarly their own.

Dr. Flint had sworn that he would make me suffer, to my last day, for this new crime against *him*, as he called it; and as long as he had me in his power he kept his word. On the fourth day after the birth of my babe, he entered my room suddenly, and commanded me to rise and bring my baby to him. The nurse who took care of me had gone out of the room to prepare some nourishment, and I was alone. There was no alternative. I rose, took up my babe, and crossed the room to where he sat. "Now stand there," said he, "till I tell you to go back!" My child bore a strong resemblance to her father, and to the deceased Mrs. Sands, her grandmother. He noticed this; and while I stood before him, trembling; with weakness, he heaped upon me and my little one every vile epithet he could think of. Even the grandmother in her grave did not escape his curses. In the midst of his vituperations I fainted at his feet. This recalled him to his senses. He took the baby from my arms, laid it on the bed, dashed cold water in my face, took me up, and shook me violently, to restore my consciousness before any one entered the room. Just then my grandmother came in, and he hurried out of the house. I suffered in consequence of this treatment; but I begged my friends to let me die, rather than send for the doctor. There was nothing I dreaded so much as his presence. My life was spared; and I was glad for the sake of my little ones. Had it not been for these ties to life, I should have been glad to be released by death, though I had lived only nineteen years.

Always it gave me a pang that my children had no lawful claim to a name. Their father offered his; but, if I had wished to accept the offer, I dared not while my master lived. Moreover, I knew it would not be accepted at their baptism. A Christian name they were at least entitled to; and we resolved to call my boy for our dear good Benjamin, who had gone far away from us.

My grandmother belonged to the church; and she was very desirous of having the children christened. I knew Dr. Flint would forbid it, and I did not venture to attempt it. But chance favored me. He was called to visit a patient out of town, and was obliged to be absent during Sunday. "Now is the time," said my grandmother; "we will take the children to church, and have them christened."

When I entered the church, recollections of my mother came over me, and I felt subdued in spirit. There she had presented me for baptism, without any reason to feel ashamed. She had been married, and had such legal rights as slavery allows to a slave. The vows had at least been sacred to *her*, and she had never violated them. I was glad she was not alive, to know under what different circumstances her grandchildren were presented for baptism. Why had my lot been so different from my mother's? *Her* master had died when she was a child; and she remained with her mistress till she married. She was never in the power of any master; and thus she escaped one class of the evils that generally fall upon slaves.

When my baby was about to be christened, the former mistress of my father stepped up to me, and proposed to give it her Christian name. To this I added the surname of my father, who had himself no legal right to it; for my grandfather on the paternal side was a white gentleman. What tangled skeins are the genealogies of slavery! I loved my father; but it mortified me to be obliged to bestow his name on my children.

When we left the church, my father's old mistress invited me to go home with her. She clasped a gold chain round my baby's neck. I thanked her for this kindness; but I did not like the emblem. I wanted no chain to be fastened on my daughter, not even if its links were of gold. How earnestly I prayed that she might never feel the weight of slavery's chain, whose iron entereth into the soul!

XVII. The Flight

Mr. Flint was hard pushed for house servants, and rather than lose me he had restrained his malice. I did my work faithfully, though not, of course, with a willing mind. They were evidently afraid I should leave them. Mr. Flint wished that I should sleep in the great house instead of the servants' quarters. His wife agreed to the proposition, but said I mustn't bring my bed into the house, because it would scatter feathers on her carpet. I knew when I went there that they would never think of such a thing as furnishing a bed of any kind for me and my little one. I therefore carried my own bed, and now I was forbidden to use it. I did as I was ordered. But now that I was certain my children were to be put in their power, in order to give them a stronger hold on me, I resolved to leave them that night. I remembered the grief this step would bring upon my dear old grandmother; and nothing less than the freedom of my children would have induced me to disregard her advice. I went about my evening work with trembling steps. Mr. Flint twice called from his chamber door to inquire why the house was not locked up. I replied that I had not done my work. "You have had time enough to do it," said he. "Take care how you answer me!"

I shut all the windows, locked all the doors, and went up to the third story, to wait till midnight. How long those hours seemed, and how fervently I prayed that God would not forsake me in this hour of utmost need! I was about to risk every thing on the throw of a die; and if I failed, O what would become of me and my poor children? They would be made to suffer for my fault.

At half past twelve I stole softly down stairs. I stopped on the second floor, thinking I heard a noise. I felt my way down into the parlor, and looked out of the window. The night was so intensely dark that I could see nothing. I raised the window very softly and jumped out. Large drops of rain were falling, and the darkness bewildered me. I dropped on my knees, and breathed a short prayer to God for guidance and protection. I groped my way to the road, and rushed towards the town with almost lightning speed. I arrived at my grandmother's house, but dared not see her. She would say, "Linda, you are killing me;" and I knew that would unnerve me. I tapped softly at the window of a room, occupied by a woman, who had lived in the house several years. I knew she was a faithful friend, and could be trusted with my secret. I tapped several times before she heard me. At last she raised the window, and I whispered, "Sally, I have run away. Let me in, quick." She opened the door softly, and said in low tones, "For God's sake, don't. Your grandmother is trying to buy you and de chillern. Mr. Sands was here last week. He tole her he was going away on business, but he wanted her to go ahead about buying you and de chillern, and he would help her all he could. Don't run away, Linda. Your grandmother is all bowed down wid trouble now."

I replied, "Sally, they are going to carry my children to the plantation to-morrow; and they will never sell them to any body so long as they have me in their power. Now, would you advise me to go back?"

"No, chile, no," answered she. "When dey finds you is gone, dey won't want de plague ob de chillern; but where is you going to hide? Dey knows ebery inch ob dis house."

I told her I had a hiding-place, and that was all it was best for her to know. I asked her to go into my room as soon as it was light, and take all my clothes out of my trunk, and pack them in hers; for I knew Mr. Flint and the constable would be there early to search my room. I feared the sight of my children would be too much for my full heart; but I could not go out into the uncertain future without one last look. I bent over the bed where lay my little Benny and baby Ellen. Poor little ones! fatherless and motherless! Memories of their father came over me. He wanted to be kind to them; but they were not all to him, as they were to my womanly heart. I knelt and prayed for the innocent little sleepers. I kissed them lightly, and turned away.

As I was about to open the street door, Sally laid her hand on my shoulder, and said, "Linda, is you gwine all alone? Let me call your uncle."

"No, Sally," I replied, "I want no one to be brought into trouble on my account."

I went forth into the darkness and rain. I ran on till I came to the house of the friend who was to conceal me.

Early the next morning Mr. Flint was at my grandmother's inquiring for me. She told him she had not seen me, and supposed I was at the plantation. He watched her face

$100 Reward

This is the advertisement that Dr. James Norcom, or "Dr. Flint," placed in the *American Beacon*, Norfolk, Virginia. The advertisement, which ran on Tuesdays, Thursdays, and Saturdays for two weeks beginning on June 30, 1835, differs in some significant ways from the poster Jacobs quotes in *Incidents*.

$100 REWARD

WILL be given for the apprehension and delivery of my Servant Girl HARRIET. She is a light mulatto, 21 years of age, about 5 feet 4 inches high, of a thick and corpulent habit, having on her head a thick covering of black hair that curls naturally, but which can be easily combed straight. She speaks easily and fluently, and has an agreeable carriage and address. Being a good seamstress, she has been accustomed to dress well, has a variety of very fine clothes, made in the prevailing fashion, and will probably appear, if abroad, tricked out in gay and fashionable finery. As this girl absconded from the plantation of my son without any known cause or provocation, it is probable she designs to transport herself to the North.

The above reward, with all reasonable charges, will be given for apprehending her, or securing her in any prison or jail within the U. States.

All persons are hereby forewarned against harboring or entertaining her, or being in any way instrumental in her escape, under the most rigorous penalties of the law.

JAMES NORCOM.

Edenton, N. C. June 30

narrowly, and said, "Don't you know any thing about her running off?" She assured him that she did not. He went on to say, "Last night she ran off without the least provocation. We had treated her very kindly. My wife liked her. She will soon be found and brought back. Are her children with you?" When told that they were, he said, "I am very glad to hear that. If they are here, she cannot be far off. If I find out that any of my niggers have had any thing to do with this damned business, I'll give 'em five hundred lashes." As he started to go to his father's, he turned round and added, persuasively, "Let her be brought back, and she shall have her children to live with her."

The tidings made the old doctor rave and storm at a furious rate. It was a busy day for them. My grandmother's house was searched from top to bottom. As my trunk was empty, they concluded I had taken my clothes with me. Before ten o'clock every vessel northward bound was thoroughly examined, and the law against harboring fugitives was read to all on board. At night a watch was set over the town. Knowing how distressed my grandmother would be, I wanted to send her a message; but it could not be done. Every one who went in or out of her house was closely watched. The doctor said he would take my children, unless she became responsible for them; which of course she willingly did. The next day was spent in searching. Before night, the following advertisement was posted at every corner, and in every public place for miles round: —

> "$300 REWARD! Ran away from the subscriber, an intelligent, bright, mulatto girl, named Linda, 21 years of age. Five feet four inches high. Dark eyes, and black hair inclined to curl; but it can be made straight. Has a decayed spot on a front tooth. She can read and write, and in all probability will try to get to the Free States. All persons are forbidden, under penalty of the law, to harbor or employ said slave. $150 will be given to whoever takes her in the state, and $300 if taken out of the state and delivered to me, or lodged in jail.
>
> DR. FLINT"

XXI. The Loophole of Retreat[1]

A small shed had been added to my grandmother's house years ago. Some boards were laid across the joists at the top, and between these boards and the roof was a very small garret, never occupied by any thing but rats and mice. It was a pent roof, covered with nothing but shingles, according to the southern custom for such buildings. The garret was only nine feet long and seven wide. The highest part was three feet high, and sloped down abruptly to the loose board floor. There was no admission for either light or air. My uncle Philip, who was a carpenter, had very skilfully made a concealed trap-door, which communicated with the storeroom. He had been doing this while I was waiting in the swamp. The storeroom opened upon a piazza. To this hole I was conveyed

---

1. **The Loophole of Retreat**: The phrase is from book 4 of *The Task* (1785), a popular poem by English poet William Cowper (1731-1800): "Tis pleasant through the loopholes of retreat / To peep at such a world."

as soon as I entered the house. The air was stifling; the darkness total. A bed had been spread on the floor. I could sleep quite comfortably on one side; but the slope was so sudden that I could not turn on the other without hitting the roof. The rats and mice ran over my bed; but I was weary, and I slept such sleep as the wretched may, when a tempest has passed over them. Morning came. I knew it only by the noises I heard; for in my small den day and night were all the same. I suffered for air even more than for light. But I was not comfortless. I heard the voices of my children. There was joy and there was sadness in the sound. It made my tears flow. How I longed to speak to them! I was eager to look on their faces; but there was no hole, no crack, through which I could peep. This continued darkness was oppressive. It seemed horrible to sit or lie in a cramped position day after day, without one gleam of light. Yet I would have chosen this, rather than my lot as a slave, though white people considered it an easy one; and it was so compared with the fate of others. I was never cruelly over-worked; I was never lacerated with the whip from head to foot; I was never so beaten and bruised that I could not turn from one side to the other; I never had my heel-strings cut to prevent my running away; I was never chained to a log and forced to drag it about, while I toiled in the fields from morning till night; I was never branded with hot iron, or torn by blood-hounds. On the contrary, I had always been kindly treated, and tenderly cared for, until I came into the hands of Dr. Flint. I had never wished for freedom till then. But though my life in slavery was comparatively devoid of hardships, God pity the woman who is compelled to lead such a life!

My food was passed up to me through the trap-door my uncle had contrived; and my grandmother, my uncle Phillip, and aunt Nancy would seize such opportunities as they could, to mount up there and chat with me at the opening. But of course this was not safe in the daytime. It must all be done in darkness. It was impossible for me to move in an erect position, but I crawled about my den for exercise. One day I hit my head against something, and found it was a gimlet.[2] My uncle had left it sticking there when he made the trap-door. I was as rejoiced as Robinson Crusoe[3] could have been at finding such a treasure. It put a lucky thought into my head. I said to myself, "Now I will have some light. Now I will see my children." I did not dare to begin my work during the day-time, for fear of attracting attention. But I groped round; and having found the side next the street, where I could frequently see my children, I stuck the gimlet in and waited for evening. I bored three rows of holes, one above another; then I bored out the interstices between. I thus succeeded in making one hole about an inch long and an inch broad. I sat by it till late into the night, to enjoy the little whiff of air that floated in. In the morning I watched for my children. The first person I saw in the street was Dr. Flint. I had a shuddering, superstitious feeling that it was a bad omen. Several familiar faces passed by. At last I heard the merry laugh of children, and presently two sweet

---

2. **gimlet**: A tool for drilling small holes.
3. **Robinson Crusoe**: In the 1719 novel of the same name by the English author Daniel Defoe (1660–1731), the title character is marooned for twenty-eight years on a desert island in the Caribbean.

little faces were looking up at me, as though they knew I was there, and were conscious of the joy they imparted. How I longed to *tell* them I was there!

My condition was now a little improved. But for weeks I was tormented by hundreds of little red insects, fine as a needle's point, that pierced through my skin, and produced an intolerable burning. The good grandmother gave me herb teas and cooling medicines, and finally I got rid of them. The heat of my den was intense, for nothing but thin shingles protected me from the scorching summer's sun. But I had my consolations. Through my peeping-hole I could watch the children, and when they were near enough, I could hear their talk. Aunt Nancy brought me all the news she could hear at Dr. Flint's. From her I learned that the doctor had written to New York to a colored woman, who had been born and raised in our neighborhood, and had breathed his contaminating atmosphere. He offered her a reward if she could find out any thing about me. I know not what was the nature of her reply; but he soon after started for New York in haste, saying to his family that he had business of importance to transact. I peeped at him as he passed on his way to the steamboat. It was a satisfaction to have miles of land and water between us, even for a little while; and it was a still greater satisfaction to know that he believed me to be in the Free States. My little den seemed less dreary than it had done. He returned, as he did from his former journey to New York, without obtaining any satisfactory information. When he passed our house next morning, Benny was standing at the gate. He had heard them say that he had gone to find me, and he called out, "Dr. Flint, did you bring my mother home? I want to see her." The doctor stamped his foot at him in a rage, and exclaimed, "Get out of the way, you little damned rascal! If you don't, I'll cut off your head."

Benny ran terrified into the house, saying, "You can't put me in jail again. I don't belong to you now." It was well that the wind carried the words away from the doctor's ear. I told my grandmother of it, when we had our next conference at the trap-door; and begged of her not to allow the children to be impertinent to the irascible old man.

Autumn came, with a pleasant abatement of heat. My eyes had become accustomed to the dim light, and by holding my book or work in a certain position near the aperture I contrived to read and sew. That was a great relief to the tedious monotony of my life. But when winter came, the cold penetrated through the thin shingle roof, and I was dreadfully chilled. The winters there are not so long, or so severe, as in northern latitudes; but the houses are not built to shelter from cold, and my little den was peculiarly comfortless. The kind grandmother brought me bed-clothes and warm drinks. Often I was obliged to lie in bed all day to keep comfortable; but with all my precautions, my shoulders and feet were frostbitten. O, those long, gloomy days, with no object for my eye to rest upon, and no thoughts to occupy my mind, except the dreary past and the uncertain future! I was thankful when there came a day sufficiently mild for me to wrap myself up and sit at the loophole to watch the passers by. Southerners have the habit of stopping and talking in the streets, and I heard many conversations not intended to meet my ears. I heard slave-hunters planning how to catch some poor fugitive. Several times I heard allusions to Dr. Flint, myself, and the history of my children, who, perhaps, were playing near the gate. One would say, "I wouldn't move my little finger to catch her, as old Flint's property." Another would say, "I'll catch *any* nigger for the reward. A man ought to have what belongs to him, if he *is* a damned brute." The opinion was often expressed that I was in the Free States. Very rarely did any one suggest that I might be in the vicinity. Had the least suspicion rested on my grandmother's house, it would have been burned to the ground. But it was the last place they thought of. Yet there was no place, where slavery existed, that could have afforded me so good a place of concealment.

Dr. Flint and his family repeatedly tried to coax and bribe my children to tell something they had heard said about me. One day the doctor took them into a shop, and offered them some bright little silver pieces and gay handkerchiefs if they would tell where their mother was. Ellen shrank away from him, and would not speak; but Benny spoke up, and said, "Dr. Flint, I don't know where my mother is. I guess she's in New York; and when you go there again, I wish you'd ask her to come home, for I want to see her; but if you put her in jail, or tell her you'll cut her head off, I'll tell her to go right back."

XLI. Free at Last[1]

Mrs. Bruce, and every member of her family, were exceedingly kind to me. I was thankful for the blessings of my lot, yet I could not always wear a cheerful countenance. I was doing harm to no one; on the contrary, I was doing all the good I could in my small way; yet I could never go out to breathe God's free air without trepidation at my heart. This seemed hard; and I could not think it was a right state of things in any civilized country.

From time to time I received news from my good old grandmother. She could not write; but she employed others to write for her. The following is an extract from one of her last letters:

"Dear Daughter: I cannot hope to see you again on earth; but I pray to God to unite us above, where pain will no more rack this feeble body of mine; where sorrow and parting from my children will be no more.[2] God has promised these things if we are faithful unto the end. My age and feeble health deprive me of going to church now; but God is with me here at home. Thank your brother for his kindness. Give much love to him, and tell him to remember the Creator in the days of his youth,[3] and strive to meet me in the Father's kingdom. Love to

---

1. **Free at Last:** The title of Jacobs's final chapter is also the title of an African American slave song that begins: "Free at last, free at last / I thank God I'm free at last." Having made her escape from the South dressed as a sailor, she found employment in the household of the writer Nathaniel P. Willis and his wife Cornelia Grinnell Willis, called Mr. and Mrs. Bruce in *Incidents.*

2. **"I pray . . . no more":** Compare Revelations 21:4: "And God shall wipe away all tears from their eyes; and there shall be no more death, neither sorrow, nor crying, neither shall there be any more pain: for the former things are passed away."

3. **"remember . . . youth":** See Ecclesiastes 12:1: "Remember now thy Creator in the days of thy youth, while the evil days come not, nor the years draw nigh, when thou shalt say, I have no pleasure in them."

Ellen and Benjamin. Don't neglect him. Tell him for me, to be a good boy. Strive, my child, to train them for God's children. May he protect and provide for you, is the prayer of your loving old mother."

These letters both cheered and saddened me. I was always glad to have tidings from the kind, faithful old friend of my unhappy youth; but her messages of love made my heart yearn to see her before she died, and I mourned over the fact that it was impossible. Some months after I returned from my flight to New England, I received a letter from her, in which she wrote, "Dr. Flint is dead. He has left a distressed family. Poor old man! I hope he made his peace with God."

I remembered how he had defrauded my grandmother of the hard earnings she had loaned; how he had tried to cheat her out of the freedom her mistress had promised her, and how he had persecuted her children; and I thought to myself that she was a better Christian than I was, if she could entirely forgive him. I cannot say, with truth, that the news of my old master's death softened my feelings towards him. There are wrongs which even the grave does not bury. The man was odious to me while he lived, and his memory is odious now.

His departure from this world did not diminish my danger. He had threatened my grandmother that his heirs should hold me in slavery after he was gone; that I never should be free so long as a child of his survived. As for Mrs. Flint, I had seen her in deeper afflictions than I supposed the loss of her husband would be, for she had buried several children; yet I never saw any signs of softening in her heart. The doctor had died in embarrassed circumstances, and had little to will to his heirs, except such property as he was unable to grasp. I was well aware what I had to expect from the family of Flints; and my fears were confirmed by a letter from the south, warning me to be on my guard, because Mrs. Flint openly declared that her daughter could not afford to lose so valuable a slave as I was.

I kept close watch of the newspapers for arrivals; out one Saturday night, being much occupied, I forgot to examine the Evening Express as usual. I went down into the parlor for it, early in the morning, and found the boy about to kindle a fire with it. I took it from him and examined the list of arrivals. Reader, if you have never been a slave, you cannot imagine the acute sensation of suffering at my heart, when I read the names of Mr. and Mrs. Dodge, at a hotel in Courtland Street. It was a third-rate hotel, and that circumstance convinced me of the truth of what I had heard, that they were short of funds and had need of my value, as *they* valued me; and that was by dollars and cents. I hastened with the paper to Mrs. Bruce. Her heart and hand were always open to every one in distress, and she always warmly sympathized with mine. It was impossible to tell how near the enemy was. He might have passed and repassed the house while we were sleeping. He might at that moment be waiting to pounce upon me if I ventured out of doors. I had never seen the husband of my young mistress, and therefore I could not distinguish him from any other stranger. A carriage was hastily ordered; and, closely veiled, I followed Mrs. Bruce, taking the baby again with me into exile. After various turnings and crossings, and returnings, the carriage stopped at the house of one of Mrs. Bruce's friends, where I was kindly received. Mrs. Bruce returned immediately, to instruct the domestics what to say if any one came to inquire for me.

It was lucky for me that the evening paper was not burned up before I had a chance to examine the list of arrivals. It was not long after Mrs. Bruce's return to her house, before several people came to inquire for me. One inquired for me, another asked for my daughter Ellen, and another said he had a letter from my grandmother, which he was requested to deliver in person.

They were told, "She *has* lived here, but she has left."

"How long ago?"

"I don't know, sir."

"Do you know where she went?"

"I do not, sir." And the door was closed.

This Mr. Dodge, who claimed me as his property, was originally a Yankee pedler in the south; then he became a merchant, and finally a slaveholder. He managed to get introduced into what was called the first society, and married Miss Emily Flint. A quarrel arose between him and her brother, and the brother cowhided him. This led to a family feud, and he proposed to remove to Virginia. Dr. Flint left him no property, and his own means had become circumscribed, while a wife and children depended upon him for support. Under these circumstances, it was very natural that he should make an effort to put me into his pocket.

I had a colored friend, a man from my native place, in whom I had the most implicit confidence. I sent for him, and told him that Mr. and Mrs. Dodge had arrived in New York. I proposed that he should call upon them to make inquiries about his friends at the south, with whom Dr. Flint's family were well acquainted. He thought there was no impropriety in his doing so, and he consented. He went to the hotel, and knocked at the door of Mr. Dodge's room, which was opened by the gentleman himself, who gruffly inquired, "What brought you here? How came you to know I was in the city?"

"Your arrival was published in the evening papers, sir; and I called to ask Mrs. Dodge about my friends at home. I didn't suppose it would give any offence."

"Where's that negro girl, that belongs to my wife?"

"What girl, sir?"

"You know well enough. I mean Linda, that ran away from Dr. Flint's plantation, some years ago. I dare say you've seen her, and know where she is."

"Yes, sir, I've seen her, and know where she is. She is out of your reach, sir."

"Tell me where she is, or bring her to me, and I will give her a chance to buy her freedom."

"I don't think it would be of any use, sir. I have heard her say she would go to the ends of the earth, rather than pay any man or woman for her freedom, because she thinks she has a right to it. Besides, she couldn't do it, if she would, for she has spent her earnings to educate her children."

This made Mr. Dodge very angry, and some high words passed between them. My friend was afraid to come where I was; but in the course of the day I received a note from him. I supposed they had not come from the south, in the winter, for a pleasure excursion; and now the nature of their business was very plain.

Mrs. Bruce came to me and entreated me to leave the city the next morning. She said her house was watched, and it was possible that some clew to me might be obtained. I refused to take her advice. She pleaded with an earnest tenderness, that ought to have moved me; but I was in a bitter, disheartened mood. I was weary of flying from pillar to post. I had been chased during half my life, and it seemed as if the chase was never to end. There I sat, in that great city, guiltless of crime, yet not daring to worship God in any of the churches. I heard the bells ringing for afternoon service, and, with contemptuous sarcasm, I said, "Will the preachers take for their text, 'Proclaim liberty to the captive, and the opening of prison doors to them that are bound'? or will they preach from the text, 'Do unto others as ye would they should do unto you'?"[4] Oppressed Poles and Hungarians could find a safe refuge in that city; John Mitchell[5] was free to proclaim in the City Hall his desire for "a plantation well stocked with slaves;" but there I sat, an oppressed American, not daring to show my face. God forgive the black and bitter thoughts I indulged on that Sabbath day! The scripture says, "Oppression makes even a wise man mad;"[6] and I was not wise.

I had been told that Mr. Dodge said his wife had never signed away her right to my children, and if he could not get me, he would take them. This it was, more than any thing else, that roused such a tempest in my soul. Benjamin was with his uncle William in California, but my innocent young daughter had come to spend a vacation with me. I thought of what I had suffered in slavery at her age, and my heart was like a tiger's when a hunter tries to seize her young.

Dear Mrs. Bruce! I seem to see the expression of her face, as she turned away discouraged by my obstinate mood. Finding her expostulations unavailing, she sent Ellen to entreat me. When ten o'clock in the evening arrived and Ellen had not returned, this watchful and unwearied friend became anxious. She came to us in a carriage, bringing a well-filled trunk for my journey — trusting that by this time I would listen to reason. I yielded to her, as I ought to have done before.

The next day, baby and I set out in a heavy snow storm, bound for New England again. I received letters from the City of Iniquity,[7] addressed to me under an assumed name. In a few days one came from Mrs. Bruce, informing me that my new master was still searching for me, and that she intended to put an end to this persecution by buying my freedom. I felt grateful for the kindness that prompted this offer, but the idea was not so pleasant to me as might have been expected. The more my mind had become enlightened, the more difficult it was for me to consider myself an article of property; and to

---

4. "Proclaim . . . unto you": Isaiah 61:1; Matthew 7:12.
5. John Mitchell: Proslavery Irish American immigrant (1815–1875) and editor of the *Citizen*, published in New York City.
6. "Oppression . . . mad": Ecclesiastes 7:7.
7. City of Iniquity: New York City, so called because it became a center of slave hunting following the passage of the Fugitive Slave Act in 1850.

pay money to those who had so grievously oppressed me seemed like taking from my sufferings the glory of triumph. I wrote to Mrs. Bruce, thanking her, but saying that being sold from one owner to another seemed too much like slavery; that such a great obligation could not be easily cancelled; and that I preferred to go to my brother in California.

Without my knowledge, Mrs. Bruce employed a gentleman in New York to enter into negotiations with Mr. Dodge. He proposed to pay three hundred dollars down, if Mr. Dodge would sell me, and enter into obligations to relinquish all claim to me or my children forever after. He who called himself my master said he scorned so small an offer for such a valuable servant. The gentleman replied, "You can do as you choose, sir. If you reject this offer you will never get any thing; for the woman has friends who will convey her and her children out of the country."

Mr. Dodge concluded that "half a loaf was better than no bread," and he agreed to the proffered terms. By the next mail I received this brief letter from Mrs. Bruce: "I am rejoiced to tell you that the money for your freedom has been paid to Mr. Dodge. Come home to-morrow. I long to see you and my sweet babe."

My brain reeled as I read these lines. A gentleman near me said, "It's true; I have seen the bill of sale." "The bill of sale!" Those words struck me like a blow. So I was *sold* at last! A human being *sold* in the free city of New York! The bill of sale is on record, and future generations will learn from it that women were articles of traffic in New York, late in the nineteenth century of the Christian religion. It may hereafter prove a useful document to antiquaries, who are seeking to measure the progress of civilization in the United States. I well know the value of that bit of paper; but much as I love freedom, I do not like to look upon it. I am deeply grateful to the generous friend who procured it, but I despise the miscreant who demanded payment for what never rightfully belonged to him or his.

I had objected to having my freedom bought, yet I must confess that when it was done I felt as if a heavy load had been lifted from my weary shoulders. When I rode home in the cars I was no longer afraid to unveil my face and look at people as they passed. I should have been glad to have met Daniel Dodge himself; to have had him seen me and known me, that he might have mourned over the untoward circumstances which compelled him to sell me for three hundred dollars.

When I reached home, the arms of my benefactress were thrown round me, and our tears mingled. As soon as she could speak, she said, "O Linda, I'm *so* glad it's all over! You wrote to me as if you thought you were going to be transferred from one owner to another. But I did not buy you for your services. I should have done just the same, if you had been going to sail for California to-morrow. I should, at least, have the satisfaction of knowing that you left me a free woman."

My heart was exceedingly full. I remembered how my poor father had tried to buy me, when I was a small child, and how he had been disappointed. I hoped his spirit was rejoicing over me now. I remembered how my good old grandmother had laid up her earnings to purchase me in later years, and how often her plans had been frustrated. How that faithful, loving old heart would leap for joy, if she could look on me and my children now that we were free! My relatives had been foiled in all their efforts, but God had raised me up a friend among strangers, who had bestowed on me the precious, long-desired boon. Friend! It is a common word often lightly used. Like other good and beautiful things, it may be tarnished by careless handling; but when I speak of Mrs. Bruce as my friend, the word is sacred.

My grandmother lived to rejoice in my freedom; but not long after, a letter came with a black seal. She had gone "where the wicked cease from troubling, and the weary are at rest."[8]

Time passed on, and a paper came to me from the south, containing an obituary notice of my uncle Phillip. It was the only case I ever knew of such an honor conferred upon a colored person. It was written by one of his friends, and contained these words: "Now that death has laid him low, they call him a good man and a useful citizen; but what are eulogies to the black man, when the world has faded from his vision? It does not require man's praise to obtain rest in God's kingdom." So they called a colored man a *citizen*! Strange words to be uttered in that region!

Reader, my story ends with freedom; not in the usual way, with marriage. I and my children are now free! We are as free from the power of slaveholders as are the white people of the north; and though that, according to my ideas, is not saying a great deal, it is a vast improvement in *my* condition. The dream of my life is not yet realized. I do not sit with my children in a home of my own. I still long for a hearthstone of my own, however humble. I wish it for my children's sake far more than for my own. But God so orders circumstances as to keep me with my friend Mrs. Bruce. Love, duty, gratitude, also bind me to her side. It is a privilege to serve her who pities my oppressed people, and who has bestowed the inestimable boon of freedom on me and my children.

It has been painful to me, in many ways, to recall the dreary years I passed in bondage. I would gladly forget them if I could. Yet the retrospection is not altogether without solace; for with those gloomy recollections come tender memories of my good old grandmother, like light, fleecy clouds floating over a dark and troubled sea.

[1861]

---

8. "where . . . at rest": Job 3:17.

Henry David Thoreau

[1817-1862]

Henry David Thoreau

This was one of three daguerreotypes of Thoreau taken by Benjamin Maxham in 1856, two years after the publication of *Walden.*

Henry David Thoreau was born on July 12, 1817, in Concord, Massachusetts. He was educated at the Concord Academy and Harvard College, from which he graduated in 1837. Returning to Concord, Thoreau confronted a problem he would grapple with throughout his life: how to earn a living without sacrificing his own freedom and autonomy. As a college graduate, Thoreau would have been expected to embark on a successful career in business, law, or one of the other professions. Instead, he accepted a teaching position in a public school in Concord. When the school committee told him that he was expected to use corporal punishment to discipline the students, Thoreau resigned. He and his older brother, John, then opened a private school in Concord.

Teaching allowed Thoreau ample time for study and, increasingly, for writing. His literary aspirations were strongly encouraged by Ralph Waldo Emerson, whose successful career as a writer and lecturer offered a powerful model to Thoreau. Partly in an effort to support such aspiring young writers, Emerson helped establish the *Dial,* a periodical in which Thoreau's earliest essays and reviews appeared. After his brother's failing health obliged them to close their school in 1841, Thoreau joined the Emerson household, where he did odd jobs and helped to edit the *Dial.* With the assistance of Nathaniel Hawthorne, who moved to Concord in 1842, Thoreau also published several pieces in periodicals in Boston and New York City. But his efforts to gain a foothold in the larger literary marketplace were unsuccessful. Consequently, after the *Dial* ceased publication in 1844, he lost the last ready outlet for his writings. When Emerson bought some land on the shore of Walden Pond, Thoreau received his permission to build a cabin on the property, where he took up residence on July 4, 1845.

The two years, two months, and two days that Thoreau lived at Walden Pond constituted the most productive and satisfying period of his often-frustrating literary career. During that period, he wrote the bulk of his first book, *A Week on the Concord and Merrimack Rivers,* and the first draft of his masterpiece, *Walden.* Unable to find a publisher for *A Week* in 1847, when he left the woods, Thoreau continued to revise the book until 1849, when he published it at his own expense. Although it received some admiring reviews, the book was a commercial failure. Of an edition of one thousand, it sold fewer than three hundred copies by 1853, when its publisher returned the unsold copies to Thoreau. "I have now a library of more than nine hundred volumes, over seven hundred of which I wrote myself," Thoreau ruefully recorded in his journal. Living with his family, he supported himself and paid off his debt to the publisher by working as a surveyor and lending a hand in his father's pencil business.

The failure of his first book did not deter Thoreau from pursuing other literary projects, especially *Walden*, which he revised and expanded before it was published in 1854. He was thereafter frequently called "the hermit of Walden Pond," which he had in fact left seven years earlier, and despite the fact that during the 1850s he lectured and published essays on a range of other subjects, including his trips to Canada, Cape Cod, and the wilderness of Maine. Thoreau also delivered two celebrated antislavery addresses: "Slavery in Massachusetts" (1854), a protest against the enforcement of the Fugitive Slave Act; and "A Plea for John Brown," an eloquent defense of the leader of the 1859 raid on the federal arsenal at Harpers Ferry, Virginia. For the most part, however, Thoreau sought to remain aloof from the heated social and political controversies of the period. He primarily devoted himself to the study of natural history, the focus of lectures like "Autumnal Tints," "The Succession of Forest Trees," and "Wild Apples," all of which he delivered in 1859-60, on the eve of the Civil War. Those lectures were small fragments of far more ambitious projects, *The Dispersion of Seeds* and *Wild Fruits*, massive manuscripts that Thoreau was not able to complete before he died from tuberculosis on May 6, 1862.

Mr. Thoreau is a keen and delicate observer of nature . . . and Nature, in return for his love, seems to adopt him as her especial child, and shows him secrets which few others are allowed to witness.

—Nathaniel Hawthorne

Reading Thoreau's "Resistance to Civil Government."   Now better known as "Civil Disobedience," the title of a revised version first published in 1866, this is Thoreau's most well-known essay. Indeed, it was an inspiration to leaders of social movements around the world during the twentieth century, notably Mohandas Gandhi and Martin Luther King Jr. But the essay was written in response to local events and to the immediate concerns of the 1840s. As early as 1842, Thoreau began to withhold his poll tax—a tax levied on all adult males in Massachusetts—first as a protest against slavery and later in opposition to the Mexican War, which broke out in the spring of 1846. That July, he was arrested and jailed for one night until one of his friends or relatives paid the tax for him. In response to those who were critical of his stand, including many of his fellow townspeople, Thoreau in January 1848 delivered a lecture on "The Rights and Duties of the Individual in Relation to the State" at the Concord Lyceum. The following year the lecture was published as "Resistance to Civil Government" in the first and only issue of *Aesthetic Papers*, a periodical edited by the reformer Elizabeth Peabody. It probably would have languished in obscurity if the revised version had not been included in a posthumously published collection, *A Yankee in Canada, with Anti-Slavery and Reform Papers* (1866). Thereafter, the essay was reprinted and translated countless times, often together with the equally famous *Walden*. The text is taken from the original printing of "Resistance to Civil Government" in *Aesthetic Papers* (1849).

bedfordstmartins.com/americanlit for research links on Thoreau

RESISTANCE TO CIVIL GOVERNMENT

I heartily accept the motto, – "That government is best which governs least;"[1] and I should like to see it acted up to more rapidly and systematically. Carried out, it finally amounts to this, which also I believe, – "That government is best which governs not at all;" and when men are prepared for it, that will be the kind of government which they will have. Government is at best but an expedient; but most governments are usually, and all governments are sometimes, inexpedient. The objections which have been brought against a standing army, and they are many and weighty, and deserve to prevail, may also at last be brought against a standing government. The standing army is only an arm of the standing government. The government itself, which is only the mode which the people have chosen to execute their will, is equally liable to be abused and perverted before the people can act through it. Witness the present Mexican War, the work of comparatively a few individuals using the standing government as their tool; for, in the outset, the people would not have consented to this measure.

This American government, – what is it but a tradition, though a recent one, endeavoring to transmit itself unimpaired to posterity, but each instant losing some of its integrity? It has not the vitality and force of a single living man; for a single man can bend it to his will. It is a sort of wooden gun to the people themselves; and, if ever they should use it in earnest as a real one against each other, it will surely split. But it is not the less necessary for this; for the people must have some complicated machinery or other and hear its din, to satisfy that idea of government which they have. Governments show thus how successfully men can be imposed on, even impose on themselves, for their own advantage. It is excellent, we must all allow; yet this government never of itself furthered any enterprise, but by the alacrity with which it got out of its way. *It* does not keep the country free. *It* does not settle the West. *It* does not educate. The character inherent in the American people has done all that has been accomplished; and it would have done somewhat more, if the government had not sometimes got in its way. For government is an expedient by which men would fain succeed in letting one another alone; and, as has been said, when it is most expedient, the governed are most let alone by it. Trade and commerce, if they were not made of India rubber, would never manage to bounce over the obstacles which legislators are continually putting in their way; and, if one were to judge these men wholly by the effects of their actions, and not partly by their intentions, they would deserve to be classed and punished with those mischievous persons who put obstructions on the railroads.

But, to speak practically and as a citizen, unlike those who call themselves no-government men,[2] I ask for, not at once no government, but *at once* a better government. Let every man make known what kind of government would command his respect, and that will be one step toward obtaining it.

---

1. **"That . . . least":** This motto was used on the masthead of the *Democratic Review*, an influential literary and political journal to which Thoreau had contributed several articles.
2. **no-government men:** Common name for the nonresistants, Christian anarchists and pacifists who called for the dissolution of what they called *human governments*, which were to be replaced by the government of God.

After all, the practical reason why, when the power is once in the hands of the people, a majority are permitted, and for a long period continue, to rule, is not because they are most likely to be in the right, nor because this seems fairest to the minority, but because they are physically the strongest. But a government in which the majority rule in all cases cannot be based on justice, even as far as men understand it. Can there not be a government in which majorities do not virtually decide right and wrong, but conscience? — in which majorities decide only those questions to which the rule of expediency is applicable? Must the citizen ever for a moment, or in the least degree, resign his conscience to the legislator? Why has every man a conscience, then? I think that we should be men first, and subjects afterward. It is not desirable to cultivate a respect for the law, so much as for the right. The only obligation which I have a right to assume, is to do at any time what I think right. It is truly enough said, that a corporation has no conscience; but a corporation of conscientious men is a corporation *with* a conscience. Law never made men a whit more just; and, by means of their respect for it, even the well-disposed are daily made the agents of injustice. A common and natural result of an undue respect for law is, that you may see a file of soldiers, colonel, captain, corporal, privates, powder-monkeys[3] and all, marching in admirable order over hill and dale to the wars, against their wills, aye, against their common sense and consciences, which makes it very steep marching indeed, and produces a palpitation of the heart. They have no doubt that it is a damnable business in which they are concerned; they are all peaceably inclined. Now, what are they? Men at all? or small moveable forts and magazines, at the service of some unscrupulous man in power? Visit the Navy Yard, and behold a marine, such a man as an American government can make, or such as it can make a man with its black arts, a mere shadow and reminiscence of humanity, a man laid out alive and standing, and already, as one may say, buried under arms with funeral accompaniments, though it may be

> "Not a drum was heard, nor a funeral note,
>   As his corse to the ramparts we hurried;
> Not a soldier discharged his farewell shot
>   O'er the grave where our hero we buried."[4]

The mass of men serve the State thus, not as men mainly, but as machines, with their bodies. They are the standing army, and the militia, jailers, constables, *posse comitatus*,[5] etc. In most cases there is no free exercise whatever of the judgment or of the moral sense; but they put themselves on a level with wood and earth and stones; and wooden men can perhaps be manufactured that will serve the purpose as well. Such command no more respect than men of straw, or a lump of dirt. They have the same sort of worth only as horses and dogs. Yet such as these even are commonly esteemed good citizens.

---

3. **powder-monkeys:** Young boys in the military whose job it was to carry gunpowder from a storehouse to the cannons.
4. "**Not . . . buried.**": Thoreau is loosely quoting the first stanza of "The Burial of Sir John Moore at Corunna" by the Irish poet Charles Wolfe (1791-1823).
5. *posse comitatus*: A body of citizens summoned by a sheriff to help keep the peace.

Others, as most legislators, politicians, lawyers, ministers, and office-holders, serve the State chiefly with their heads; and, as they rarely make any moral distinctions, they are as likely to serve the devil, without intending it, as God. A very few, as heroes, patriots, martyrs, reformers in the great sense, and *men*, serve the State with their consciences also, and so necessarily resist it for the most part; and they are commonly treated by it as enemies. A wise man will only be useful as a man, and will not submit to be "clay," and "stop a hole to keep the wind away,"[6] but leave that office to his dust at least: —

> "I am too high-born to be propertied,
> To be a secondary at control,
> Or useful serving-man and instrument
> To any sovereign state throughout the world."[7]

He who gives himself entirely to his fellow-men appears to them useless and selfish; but he who gives himself partially to them is pronounced a benefactor and philanthropist.

How does it become a man to behave toward this American government to-day? I answer that he cannot without disgrace be associated with it. I cannot for an instant recognize that political organization as *my* government which is the *slave's* government also.

All men recognize the right of revolution; that is, the right to refuse allegiance to and to resist the government, when its tyranny or its inefficiency are great and unendurable. But almost all say that such is not the case now. But such was the case, they think, in the Revolution of '75.[8] If one were to tell me that this was a bad government because it taxed certain foreign commodities brought to its ports, it is most probable that I should not make an ado about it, for I can do without them: all machines have their friction; and possibly this does enough good to counterbalance the evil. At any rate, it is a great evil to make a stir about it. But when the friction comes to have its machine, and oppression and robbery are organized, I say, let us not have such a machine any longer. In other words, when a sixth of the population of a nation which has undertaken to be the refuge of liberty are slaves, and a whole country is unjustly overrun and conquered by a foreign army, and subjected to military law, I think that it is not too soon for honest men to rebel and revolutionize. What makes this duty the more urgent is the fact, that the country so overrun is not our own, but ours is the invading army.

Paley,[9] a common authority with many on moral questions, in his chapter on the "Duty of Submission to Civil Government," resolves all civil obligation into expediency; and he proceeds to say, "that so long as the interest of the whole society requires it, that is, so long as the established government cannot be resisted or changed without public inconveniency, it is the will of God that the established government be obeyed, and no

---

6. "clay . . . away": See Shakespeare, *Hamlet*, 5.1.236-37: "Imperious Caesar, dead and turn'd to clay, / Might stop a hole to keep the wind away."
7. "I . . . world": Shakespeare, *King John*, 5.2.79-82.
8. **Revolution of '75**: The American Revolution, which began with the battles of Lexington and Concord in 1775.
9. **Paley**: William Paley (1743-1805), author of several influential books on Christianity and ethics; from his *Principles of Moral and Political Philosophy* (1785).

longer." – "This principle being admitted, the justice of every particular case of resistance is reduced to a computation of the quantity of the danger and grievance on the one side, and of the probability and expense of redressing it on the other." Of this, he says, every man shall judge for himself. But Paley appears never to have contemplated those cases to which the rule of expediency does not apply, in which a people, as well as an individual, must do justice, cost what it may. If I have unjustly wrested a plank from a drowning man, I must restore it to him though I drown myself. This, according to Paley, would be inconvenient. But he that would save his life, in such a case, shall lose it.[10] This people must cease to hold slaves, and to make war on Mexico, though it cost them their existence as a people.

In their practice, nations agree with Paley; but does any one think that Massachusetts does exactly what is right at the present crisis?

> "A drab of state, a cloth-o'-silver slut,
> To have her train borne up, and her soul trail in the dirt."[11]

Practically speaking, the opponents to a reform in Massachusetts are not a hundred thousand politicians at the South, but a hundred thousand merchants and farmers here, who are more interested in commerce and agriculture than they are in humanity, and are not prepared to do justice to the slave and to Mexico, *cost what it may.* I quarrel not with far-off foes, but with those who, near at home, co-operate with, and do the bidding of those far away, and without whom the latter would be harmless. We are accustomed to say, that the mass of men are unprepared; but improvement is slow, because the few are not materially wiser or better than the many. It is not so important that many should be as good as you, as that there be some absolute goodness somewhere; for that will leaven the whole lump. There are thousands who are *in opinion* opposed to slavery and to the war, who yet in effect do nothing to put an end to them; who, esteeming themselves children of Washington and Franklin, sit down with their hands in their pockets, and say that they know not what to do, and do nothing; who even postpone the question of freedom to the question of free-trade, and quietly read the prices-current along with the latest advices from Mexico, after dinner, and, it may be, fall asleep over them both. What is the price-current of an honest man and patriot to-day? They hesitate, and they regret, and sometimes they petition; but they do nothing in earnest and with effect. They will wait, well disposed, for others to remedy the evil, that they may no longer have it to regret. At most, they give only a cheap vote, and a feeble countenance and Godspeed, to the right, as it goes by them. There are nine hundred and ninety-nine patrons of virtue to one virtuous man; but it is easier to deal with the real possessor of a thing than with the temporary guardian of it.

All voting is a sort of gaming, like chequers or backgammon, with a slight moral tinge to it, a playing with right and wrong, with moral questions; and betting naturally

---

10. **But . . . lose it:** Compare Christ's words to his disciples, "He that findeth his life shall lose it: And he that loseth his life for my sake shall find it" (Matthew 10:38).
11. **"A . . . dirt":** Cyril Tourneur (1575?-1626), *The Revenger's Tragedy,* 4.4.72-73.

accompanies it. The character of the voters is not staked. I cast my vote, perchance, as I think right; but I am not vitally concerned that that right should prevail. I am willing to leave it to the majority. Its obligation, therefore, never exceeds that of expediency. Even voting *for the right* is *doing* nothing for it. It is only expressing to men feebly your desire that it should prevail. A wise man will not leave the right to the mercy of chance, nor wish it to prevail through the power of the majority. There is but little virtue in the action of masses of men. When the majority shall at length vote for the abolition of slavery, it will be because they are indifferent to slavery, or because there is but little slavery left to be abolished by their vote. *They* will then be the only slaves. Only *his* vote can hasten the abolition of slavery who asserts his own freedom by his vote.

I hear of a convention to be held at Baltimore, or elsewhere, for the selection of a candidate for the Presidency, made up chiefly of editors, and men who are politicians by profession; but I think, what is it to any independent, intelligent, and respectable man what decision they may come to, shall we not have the advantage of his wisdom and honesty, nevertheless? Can we not count upon some independent votes? Are there not many individuals in the country who do not attend conventions? But no: I find that the respectable man, so called, has immediately drifted from his position, and despairs of his country, when his country has more reason to despair of him. He forthwith adopts one of the candidates thus selected as the only *available* one, thus proving that he is himself *available* for any purposes of the demagogue. His vote is of no more worth than that of any unprincipled foreigner or hireling native, who may have been bought. Oh for a man who is a *man*, and, as my neighbor says, has a bone in his back which you cannot pass your hand through! Our statistics are at fault: the population has been returned too large. How many *men* are there to a square thousand miles in this country? Hardly one. Does not America offer any inducement for men to settle here? The American has dwindled into an Odd Fellow,[12] – one who may be known by the development of his organ of gregariousness, and a manifest lack of intellect and cheerful self-reliance; whose first and chief concern, on coming into the world, is to see that the alms-houses are in good repair; and, before yet he has lawfully donned the virile garb,[13] to collect a fund for the support of the widows and orphans that may be; who, in short, ventures to live only by the aid of the mutual insurance company, which has promised to bury him decently.

It is not a man's duty, as a matter of course, to devote himself to the eradication of any, even the most enormous wrong; he may still properly have other concerns to engage him; but it is his duty, at least, to wash his hands of it, and, if he gives it no thought longer, not to give it practically his support. If I devote myself to other pursuits and contemplations, I must first see, at least, that I do not pursue them sitting upon another man's shoulders. I must get off him first, that he may pursue his contemplations too. See what gross inconsistency is tolerated. I have heard some of my townsmen say, "I should like to have them order me out to help put down an insurrection of the slaves, or

---

12. **Odd Fellow:** A member of the Independent Order of Odd Fellows, a secret fraternal organization.
13. **virile garb:** The *toga virilis*, clothing a Roman boy was allowed to wear when he reached the age of fourteen as a symbol of manhood and citizenship.

to march to Mexico, – see if I would go;" and yet these very men have each, directly by their allegiance, and so indirectly, at least, by their money, furnished a substitute. The soldier is applauded who refuses to serve in an unjust war by those who do not refuse to sustain the unjust government which makes the war; is applauded by those whose own act and authority he disregards and sets at nought; as if the State were penitent to that degree that it hired one to scourge it while it sinned, but not to that degree that it left off sinning for a moment. Thus, under the name of order and civil government, we are all made at last to pay homage to and support our own meanness. After the first blush of sin, comes its indifference; and from immoral it becomes, as it were, *un*moral, and not quite unnecessary to that life which we have made.

The broadest and most prevalent error requires the most disinterested virtue to sustain it. The slight reproach to which the virtue of patriotism is commonly liable, the noble are most likely to incur. Those who, while they disapprove of the character and measures of a government, yield to it their allegiance and support, are undoubtedly its most conscientious supporters, and so frequently the most serious obstacles to reform. Some are petitioning the State to dissolve the Union,[14] to disregard the requisitions of the President. Why do they not dissolve it themselves, – the union between themselves and the State, – and refuse to pay their quota into its treasury? Do not they stand in the same relation to the State, that the State does to the Union? And have not the same reasons prevented the State from resisting the Union, which have prevented them from resisting the State?

How can a man be satisfied to entertain an opinion merely, and enjoy *it*? Is there any enjoyment in it, if his opinion is that he is aggrieved? If you are cheated out of a single dollar by your neighbor, you do not rest satisfied with knowing that you are cheated, or with saying that you are cheated, or even with petitioning him to pay you your due; but you take effectual steps at once to obtain the full amount, and see that you are never cheated again. Action from principle, – the perception and the performance of right, – changes things and relations; it is essentially revolutionary, and does not consist wholly with any thing which was. It not only divides states and churches, it divides families; aye, it divides the *individual*, separating the diabolical in him from the divine.

Unjust laws exist: shall we be content to obey them, or shall we endeavor to amend them, and obey them until we have succeeded, or shall we transgress them at once? Men generally, under such a government as this, think that they ought to wait until they have persuaded the majority to alter them. They think that, if they should resist, the remedy would be worse than the evil. But it is the fault of the government itself that the remedy *is* worse than the evil. *It* makes it worse. Why is it not more apt to anticipate and provide for reform? Why does it not cherish its wise minority? Why does it cry and resist before it is hurt? Why does it not encourage its citizens to be on the alert to point out its faults, and *do* better than it would have them? Why does it always crucify Christ, and excommunicate Copernicus and Luther, and pronounce Washington and Franklin rebels?

---

14. **Some . . . dissolve the Union:** Radical abolitionists, whose motto and official policy was "No Union with Slaveholders."

One would think, that a deliberate and practical denial of its authority was the only offence never contemplated by government; else, why has it not assigned its definite, its suitable and proportionate penalty? If a man who has no property refuses but once to earn nine shillings[15] for the State, he is put in prison for a period unlimited by any law that I know, and determined only by the discretion of those who placed him there; but if he should steal ninety times nine shillings from the State, he is soon permitted to go at large again.

If the injustice is part of the necessary friction of the machine of government, let it go, let it go: perchance it will wear smooth, — certainly the machine will wear out. If the injustice has a spring, or a pulley, or a rope, or a crank, exclusively for itself, then perhaps you may consider whether the remedy will not be worse than the evil; but if it is of such a nature that it requires you to be the agent of injustice to another, then, I say, break the law. Let your life be a counter friction to stop the machine. What I have to do is to see, at any rate, that I do not lend myself to the wrong which I condemn.

As for adopting the ways which the State has provided for remedying the evil, I know not of such ways. They take too much time, and a man's life will be gone. I have other affairs to attend to. I came into this world, not chiefly to make this a good place to live in, but to live in it, be it good or bad. A man has not every thing to do, but something; and because he cannot do *every thing*, it is not necessary that he should do *something* wrong. It is not my business to be petitioning the governor or the legislature any more than it is theirs to petition me; and, if they should not hear my petition, what should I do then? But in this case the State has provided no way: its very Constitution is the evil. This may seem to be harsh and stubborn and unconciliatory; but it is to treat with the utmost kindness and consideration the only spirit that can appreciate or deserves it. So is all change for the better, like birth and death which convulse the body.

I do not hesitate to say, that those who call themselves abolitionists should at once effectually withdraw their support, both in person and property, from the government of Massachusetts, and not wait till they constitute a majority of one, before they suffer the right to prevail through them. I think that it is enough if they have God on their side, without waiting for that other one. Moreover, any man more right than his neighbors, constitutes a majority of one already.

I meet this American government, or its representative the State government, directly, and face to face, once a year, no more, in the person of its tax-gatherer; this is the only mode in which a man situated as I am necessarily meets it; and it then says distinctly, Recognize me; and the simplest, the most effectual, and, in the present posture of affairs, the indispensablest mode of treating with it on this head, of expressing your little satisfaction with and love for it, is to deny it then. My civil neighbor, the tax-gatherer, is the very man I have to deal with, — for it is, after all, with men and not with parchment that I quarrel, — and he has voluntarily chosen to be an agent of the government. How shall he ever know well what he is and does as an officer of the government, or as a man, until he is obliged to consider whether he shall treat me, his neighbor, for whom he has respect,

---

15. **nine shillings:** The amount of the poll tax Thoreau refused to pay, about $2.25.

as a neighbor and well-disposed man, or as a maniac and disturber of the peace, and see if he can get over this obstruction to his neighborliness without a ruder and more impetuous thought or speech corresponding with his action? I know this well, that if one thousand, if one hundred, if ten men whom I could name, – if ten *honest* men only, – aye, if *one* HONEST man, in this State of Massachusetts, *ceasing to hold slaves*, were actually to withdraw from this copartnership, and be locked up in the county jail therefor, it would be the abolition of slavery in America. For it matters not how small the beginning may seem to be: what is once well done is done for ever. But we love better to talk about it: that we say is our mission. Reform keeps many scores of newspapers in its service, but not one man. If my esteemed neighbor, the State's ambassador,[16] who will devote his days to the settlement of the question of human rights in the Council Chamber, instead of being threatened with the prisons of Carolina, were to sit down the prisoner of Massachusetts, that State which is so anxious to foist the sin of slavery upon her sister, – though at present she can discover only an act of inhospitality to be the ground of a quarrel with her, – the Legislature would not wholly waive the subject the following winter.

Under a government which imprisons any unjustly, the true place for a just man is also a prison. The proper place to-day, the only place which Massachusetts has provided for her freer and less desponding spirits, is in her prisons, to be put out and locked out of the State by her own act, as they have already put themselves out by their principles. It is there that the fugitive slave, and the Mexican prisoner on parole, and the Indian come to plead the wrongs of his race, should find them; on that separate, but more free and honorable ground, where the State places those who are not *with* her but *against* her, – the only house in a slave-state in which a free man can abide with honor. If any think that their influence would be lost there, and their voices no longer afflict the ear of the State, that they would not be as an enemy within its walls, they do not know by how much truth is stronger than error, nor how much more eloquently and effectively he can combat injustice who has experienced a little in his own person. Cast your whole vote, not a strip of paper merely, but your whole influence. A minority is powerless while it conforms to the majority; it is not even a minority then; but it is irresistible when it clogs by its whole weight. If the alternative is to keep all just men in prison, or give up war and slavery, the State will not hesitate which to choose. If a thousand men were not to pay their tax-bills this year, that would not be a violent and bloody measure, as it would be to pay them, and enable the State to commit violence and shed innocent blood. This is, in fact, the definition of a peaceable revolution, if any such is possible. If the tax-gatherer, or any other public officer, asks me, as one has done, "But what shall I do?" my answer is, "If you really wish to do any thing, resign your office." When the subject has refused allegiance, and the officer has resigned his office, then the revolution is accomplished. But even suppose blood should flow. Is there not a sort of blood shed when the conscience is wounded? Through this wound a man's real manhood and immortality flow out, and he bleeds to an everlasting death. I see this blood flowing now.

---

16. **the State's ambassador:** Samuel Hoar (1778–1856), a lawyer and congressman from Concord. In 1844, he had been sent to Charleston, South Carolina, to protest the seizure of black seamen on ships from Massachusetts. He was forcibly expelled by order of the legislature of South Carolina.

I have contemplated the imprisonment of the offender, rather than the seizure of his goods,—though both will serve the same purpose,—because they who assert the purest right, and consequently are most dangerous to a corrupt State, commonly have not spent much time in accumulating property. To such the State renders comparatively small service, and a slight tax is wont to appear exorbitant, particularly if they are obliged to earn it by special labor with their hands. If there were one who lived wholly without the use of money, the State itself would hesitate to demand it of him. But the rich man—not to make any invidious comparison—is always sold to the institution which makes him rich. Absolutely speaking, the more money, the less virtue; for money comes between a man and his objects, and obtains them for him; and it was certainly no great virtue to obtain it. It puts to rest many questions which he would otherwise be taxed to answer; while the only new question which it puts is the hard but superfluous one, how to spend it. Thus his moral ground is taken from under his feet. The opportunities of living are diminished in proportion as what are called the "means" are increased. The best thing a man can do for his culture when he is rich is to endeavour to carry out those schemes which he entertained when he was poor. Christ answered the Herodians according to their condition. "Show me the tribute-money," said he;—and one took a penny out of his pocket;—If you use money which has the image of Caesar on it, and which he has made current and valuable, that is, *if you are men of the State*, and gladly enjoy the advantages of Caesar's government, then pay him back some of his own when he demands it; "Render therefore to Caesar that which is Caesar's, and to God those things which are God's,"[17]—leaving them no wiser than before as to which was which; for they did not wish to know.

When I converse with the freest of my neighbors, I perceive that, whatever they may say about the magnitude and seriousness of the question, and their regard for the public tranquillity, the long and the short of the matter is, that they cannot spare the protection of the existing government, and they dread the consequences of disobedience to it to their property and families. For my own part, I should not like to think that I ever rely on the protection of the State. But, if I deny the authority of the State when it presents its tax-bill, it will soon take and waste all my property, and so harass me and my children without end. This is hard. This makes it impossible for a man to live honestly and at the same time comfortably in outward respects. It will not be worth the while to accumulate property; that would be sure to go again. You must hire or squat somewhere, and raise but a small crop, and eat that soon. You must live within yourself, and depend upon yourself, always tucked up and ready for a start, and not have many affairs. A man may grow rich in Turkey even, if he will be in all respects a good subject of the Turkish government. Confucius said,—"If a State is governed by the principles of reason, poverty and mercy are subjects of shame; if a State is not governed by the principles of reason, riches and honors are the subjects of shame." No: until I want the protection of Massachusetts to be extended to me in some distant southern port, where my liberty is

---

17. "Show . . . God's": The account of Christ speaking to the Herodians, a political party in support of the Roman government, is in Mark 12:13-17.

endangered, or until I am bent solely on building up an estate at home by peaceful enterprise, I can afford to refuse allegiance to Massachusetts, and her right to my property and life. It costs me less in every sense to incur the penalty of disobedience to the State, than it would to obey. I should feel as if I were worth less in that case.

Some years ago, the State met me in behalf of the church,[18] and commanded me to pay a certain sum toward the support of a clergyman whose preaching my father attended, but never I myself. "Pay it," it said, "or be locked up in the jail." I declined to pay. But, unfortunately, another man saw fit to pay it. I did not see why the schoolmaster should be taxed to support the priest, and not the priest the schoolmaster; for I was not the State's schoolmaster, but I supported myself by voluntary subscription. I did not see why the lyceum should not present its tax-bill, and have the State to back its demand, as well as the church. However, at the request of the selectmen, I condescended to make some such statement as this in writing: — "Know all men by these presents, that I, Henry Thoreau, do not wish to be regarded as a member of any incorporated society which I have not joined." This I gave to the town-clerk; and he has it. The State, having thus learned that I did not wish to be regarded as a member of that church, has never made a like demand on me since; though it said that it must adhere to its original presumption that time. If I had known how to name them, I should then have signed off in detail from all the societies which I never signed on to; but I did not know where to find a complete list.

I have paid no poll-tax for six years. I was put into a jail once on this account, for one night; and, as I stood considering the walls of solid stone, two or three feet thick, the door of wood and iron, a foot thick, and the iron grating which strained the light, I could not help being struck with the foolishness of that institution which treated me as if I were mere flesh and blood and bones, to be locked up. I wondered that it should have concluded at length that this was the best use it could put me to, and had never thought to avail itself of my services in some way. I saw that, if there was a wall of stone between me and my townsmen, there was a still more difficult one to climb or break through, before they could get to be as free as I was. I did not for a moment feel confined, and the walls seemed a great waste of stone and mortar. I felt as if I alone of all my townsmen had paid my tax. They plainly did not know how to treat me, but behaved like persons who are underbred. In every threat and in every compliment there was a blunder; for they thought that my chief desire was to stand the other side of that stone wall. I could not but smile to see how industriously they locked the door on my meditations, which followed them out again without let or hinderance, and *they* were really all that was dangerous. As they could not reach me, they had resolved to punish my body; just as boys, if they cannot come at some person against whom they have a spite, will abuse his dog. I saw that the State was half-witted, that it was timid as a lone woman with her silver spoons, and that it did not know its friends from its foes, and I lost all my remaining respect for it, and pitied it.

---

18. **in behalf of the church:** At the time, members of a congregation were taxed by their church, and the money was collected by town officials. Since Thoreau's parents attended the First Parish Church (Unitarian), the church had assumed that he, too, wished to be considered a member.

Thus the State never intentionally confronts a man's sense, intellectual or moral, but only his body, his senses. It is not armed with superior wit or honesty, but with superior physical strength. I was not born to be forced. I will breathe after my own fashion. Let us see who is the strongest. What force has a multitude? They only can force me who obey a higher law than I. They force me to become like themselves. I do not hear of *men* being *forced* to live this way or that by masses of men. What sort of life were that to live? When I meet a government which says to me, "Your money or your life," why should I be in haste to give it my money? It may be in a great strait, and not know what to do: I cannot help that. It must help itself; do as I do. It is not worth the while to snivel about it. I am not responsible for the successful working of the machinery of society. I am not the son of the engineer. I perceive that, when an acorn and a chestnut fall side by side, the one does not remain inert to make way for the other, but both obey their own laws, and spring and grow and flourish as best they can, till one, perchance, overshadows and destroys the other. If a plant cannot live according to its nature, it dies; and so a man.

The night in prison was novel and interesting enough. The prisoners in their shirt-sleeves were enjoying a chat and the evening air in the door-way, when I entered. But the jailer said, "Come, boys, it is time to lock up"; and so they dispersed, and I heard the sound of their steps returning into the hollow apartments. My room-mate was introduced to me by the jailer, as "a first-rate fellow and a clever man." When the door was locked, he showed me where to hang my hat, and how he managed matters there. The rooms were whitewashed once a month; and this one, at least, was the whitest, most simply furnished, and probably the neatest apartment in the town. He naturally wanted to know where I came from, and what brought me there; and, when I had told him, I asked him in my turn how he came there, presuming him to be an honest man, of course; and, as the world goes, I believe he was. "Why," said he, "they accuse me of burning a barn; but I never did it." As near as I could discover, he had probably gone to bed in a barn when drunk, and smoked his pipe there; and so a barn was burnt. He had the reputation of being a clever man, had been there some three months waiting for his trial to come on, and would have to wait as much longer; but he was quite domesticated and contented, since he got his board for nothing, and thought that he was well treated.

He occupied one window, and I the other; and I saw, that, if one stayed there long, his principal business would be to look out the window. I had soon read all the tracts that were left there, and examined where former prisoners had broken out, and where a grate had been sawed off, and heard the history of the various occupants of that room; for I found that even here there was a history and a gossip which never circulated beyond the walls of the jail. Probably this is the only house in the town where verses are composed, which are afterward printed in a circular form, but not published. I was shown quite a long list of verses which were composed by some young men who had been detected in an attempt to escape, who avenged themselves by singing them.

I pumped my fellow-prisoner as dry as I could, for fear I should never see him again; but at length he showed me which was my bed, and left me to blow out the lamp.

It was like travelling into a far country, such as I had never expected to behold, to lie there for one night. It seemed to me that I never had heard the town-clock strike before, nor the evening sounds of the village; for we slept with the windows open, which were inside the grating. It was to see my native village in the light of the middle ages, and our Concord was turned into a Rhine stream, and visions of knights and castles passed before me. They were the voices of old burghers that I heard in the streets. I was an involuntary spectator and auditor of whatever was done and said in the kitchen of the adjacent village-inn, — a wholly new and rare experience to me. It was a closer view of my native town. I was fairly inside of it. I never had seen its institutions before. This is one of its peculiar institutions; for it is a shire town.[19] I began to comprehend what its inhabitants were about.

In the morning, our breakfasts were put through the hole in the door, in small oblong-square tin pans, made to fit, and holding a pint of chocolate, with brown bread, and an iron spoon. When they called for the vessels again, I was green enough to return what bread I had left; but my comrade seized it, and said that I should lay that up for lunch or dinner. Soon after, he was let out to work at haying in a neighboring field, whither he went every day, and would not be back till noon; so he bade me good-day, saying that he doubted if he should see me again.

When I came out of prison, — for some one interfered, and paid the tax, — I did not perceive that great changes had taken place on the common, such as he observed who went in a youth, and emerged a tottering and gray-headed man; and yet a change had to my eyes come over the scene, — the town, and State, and country, — greater than any that mere time could effect. I saw yet more distinctly the State in which I lived. I saw to what extent the people among whom I lived could be trusted as good neighbors and friends; that their friendship was for summer weather only; that they did not greatly purpose to do right; that they were a distinct race from me by their prejudices and superstitions, as the Chinamen and Malays are; that, in their sacrifices to humanity, they ran no risks, not even to their property; that, after all, they were not so noble but they treated the thief as he had treated them, and hoped, by a certain outward observance and a few prayers, and by walking in a particular straight though useless path from time to time, to save their souls. This may be to judge my neighbors harshly; for I believe that most of them are not aware that they have such an institution as the jail in their village.

It was formerly the custom in our village, when a poor debtor came out of jail, for his acquaintances to salute him, looking through their fingers, which were crossed to represent the grating of a jail window, "How do ye do?" My neighbors did not thus salute me, but first looked at me, and then at one another, as if I had returned from a long journey. I was put into jail as I was going to the shoemaker's to get a shoe which was mended. When I was let out the next morning, I proceeded to finish my errand, and, having put on my mended shoe, joined a huckleberry party, who were impatient to put themselves under my conduct; and in half an hour, — for the horse was soon tackled, — was in the midst of a huckleberry field, on one of our highest hills, two miles off; and then the State was nowhere to be seen.

This is the whole history of "My Prisons."[20]

I have never declined paying the highway tax, because I am as desirous of being a good neighbor as I am of being a bad subject; and, as for supporting schools, I am doing my part to educate my fellow-countrymen now. It is for no particular item in the tax-bill that I refuse to pay it. I simply wish to refuse allegiance to the State, to withdraw and stand aloof from it effectually. I do not care to trace the course of my dollar, if I could, till it buys a man, or a musket to shoot one with, — the dollar is innocent, — but I am concerned

---

19. **shire town:** County seat; Concord was therefore the home of the Middlesex County Jail.
20. **"My Prisons":** A reference to a popular prison memoir of that title, *Le Mie Prigioni* (1832), by the Italian poet Silvio Pellico (1788–1854).

to trace the effects of my allegiance. In fact, I quietly declare war with the State, after my fashion, though I will still make what use and get what advantage of her I can, as is usual in such cases.

If others pay the tax which is demanded of me, from a sympathy with the State, they do but what they have already done in their own case, or rather they abet injustice to a greater extent than the State requires. If they pay the tax from a mistaken interest in the individual taxed, to save his property or prevent his going to jail, it is because they have not considered wisely how far they let their private feelings interfere with the public good.

This, then, is my position at present. But one cannot be too much on his guard in such a case, lest his action be biased by obstinacy, or an undue regard for the opinions of men. Let him see that he does only what belongs to himself and to the hour.

I think sometimes, Why, this people mean well; they are only ignorant; they would do better if they knew how: why give your neighbors this pain to treat you as they are not inclined to? But I think, again, this is no reason why I should do as they do, or permit others to suffer much greater pain of a different kind. Again, I sometimes say to myself, When many millions of men, without heat, without ill-will, without personal feeling of any kind, demand of you a few shillings only, without the possibility, such is their constitution, of retracting or altering their present demand, and without the possibility, on your side, of appeal to any other millions, why expose yourself to this overwhelming brute force? You do not resist cold and hunger, the winds and the waves, thus obstinately; you quietly submit to a thousand similar necessities. You do not put your head into the fire. But just in proportion as I regard this as not wholly a brute force, but partly a human force, and consider that I have relations to those millions as to so many millions of men, and not of mere brute or inanimate things, I see that appeal is possible, first and instantaneously, from them to the Maker of them, and, secondly, from them to themselves. But, if I put my head deliberately into the fire, there is no appeal to fire or to the Maker of fire, and I have only myself to blame. If I could convince myself that I have any right to be satisfied with men as they are, and to treat them accordingly, and not according, in some respects, to my requisitions and expectations of what they and I ought to be, then, like a good Mussulman[21] and fatalist, I should endeavor to be satisfied with things as they are, and say it is the will of God. And, above all, there is this difference between resisting this and a purely brute or natural force, that I can resist this with some effect; but I cannot expect, like Orpheus,[22] to change the nature of the rocks and trees and beasts.

I do not wish to quarrel with any man or nation. I do not wish to split hairs, to make fine distinctions, or set myself up as better than my neighbors. I seek rather, I may say, even an excuse for conforming to the laws of the land. I am but too ready to conform to them. Indeed I have reason to suspect myself on this head; and each year, as the tax-gatherer comes round, I find myself disposed to review the acts and position of the general and state governments, and the spirit of the people, to discover a pretext for conformity. I believe that the State will soon be able to take all my work of this sort out

---

21. **Mussulman:** A Mohammedan, or Muslim.
22. **Orpheus:** Figure in Greek mythology whose music had magical powers over the natural world.

of my hands, and then I shall be no better a patriot than my fellow-countrymen. Seen from a lower point of view, the Constitution, with all its faults, is very good; the law and the courts are very respectable; even this State and this American government are, in many respects, very admirable and rare things, to be thankful for, such as a great many have described them; but seen from a point of view a little higher, they are what I have described them; seen from a higher still, and the highest, who shall say what they are, or that they are worth looking at or thinking of at all?

However, the government does not concern me much, and I shall bestow the fewest possible thoughts on it. It is not many moments that I live under a government, even in this world. If a man is thought-free, fancy-free, imagination-free, that which *is not* never for a long time appearing *to be* to him, unwise rulers or reformers cannot fatally interrupt him.

I know that most men think differently from myself; but those whose lives are by profession devoted to the study of these or kindred subjects, content me as little as any. Statesmen and legislators, standing so completely within the institution, never distinctly and nakedly behold it. They speak of moving society, but have no resting-place without it. They may be men of a certain experience and discrimination, and have no doubt invented ingenious and even useful systems, for which we sincerely thank them; but all their wit and usefulness lie within certain not very wide limits. They are wont to forget that the world is not governed by policy and expediency. Webster[23] never goes behind government, and so cannot speak with authority about it. His words are wisdom to those legislators who contemplate no essential reform in the existing government; but for thinkers, and those who legislate for all time, he never once glances at the subject. I know of those whose serene and wise speculations on this theme would soon reveal the limits of his mind's range and hospitality. Yet, compared with the cheap professions of most reformers, and the still cheaper wisdom and eloquence of politicians in general, his are almost the only sensible and valuable words, and we thank Heaven for him. Comparatively, he is always strong, original, and, above all, practical. Still his quality is not wisdom, but prudence. The lawyer's truth is not Truth, but consistency, or a consistent expediency. Truth is always in harmony with herself, and is not concerned chiefly to reveal the justice that may consist with wrong-doing. He well deserves to be called, as he has been called, the Defender of the Constitution. There are really no blows to be given by him but defensive ones. He is not a leader, but a follower. His leaders are the men of '87.[24] "I have never made an effort," he says, "and never propose to make an effort; I have never countenanced an effort, and never mean to countenance an effort, to disturb the arrangement as originally made, by which the various States came into the Union." Still thinking of the sanction which the Constitution gives to slavery, he says, "Because it was a part of the original compact, — let it stand." Notwithstanding his special acuteness and ability, he is unable to take a fact out of its merely political relations, and behold it as it lies absolutely to be disposed of by the intellect, — what, for instance, it behooves a man to do here in America to-day with regard to slavery, but ventures, or is

---

23. **Webster:** Daniel Webster (1782–1852), the famed senator from Massachusetts.
24. **men of '87:** Members of the Federal Constitutional Convention, held in 1787.

driven, to make some such desperate answer as the following, while professing to speak absolutely, and as a private man, — from which what new and singular code of social duties might be inferred? — "The manner," says he, "in which the governments of those States where slavery exists are to regulate it, is for their own consideration, under their responsibility to their constituents, to the general laws of propriety, humanity, and justice, and to God. Associations formed elsewhere, springing from a feeling of humanity, or any other cause, have nothing whatever to do with it. They have never received any encouragement from me, and they never will."[25]

They who know of no purer sources of truth, who have traced up its stream no higher, stand, and wisely stand, by the Bible and the Constitution, and drink at it there with reverence and humility; but they who behold where it comes trickling into this lake or that pool, gird up their loins once more, and continue their pilgrimage toward its fountainhead.

No man with a genius for legislation has appeared in America. They are rare in the history of the world. There are orators, politicians, and eloquent men, by the thousand; but the speaker has not yet opened his mouth to speak, who is capable of settling the much-vexed questions of the day. We love eloquence for its own sake, and not for any truth which it may utter, or any heroism it may inspire. Our legislators have not yet learned the comparative value of free-trade and of freedom, of union, and of rectitude, to a nation. They have no genius or talent for comparatively humble questions of taxation and finance, commerce and manufactures and agriculture. If we were left solely to the wordy wit of legislators in Congress for our guidance, uncorrected by the seasonable experience and the effectual complaints of the people, America would not long retain her rank among the nations. For eighteen hundred years, though perchance I have no right to say it, the New Testament has been written; yet where is the legislator who has wisdom and practical talent enough to avail himself of the light which it sheds on the science of legislation?

The authority of government, even such as I am willing to submit to, — for I will cheerfully obey those who know and can do better than I, and in many things even those who neither know nor can do so well, — is still an impure one: to be strictly just, it must have the sanction and consent of the governed. It can have no pure right over my person and property but what I concede to it. The progress from an absolute to a limited monarchy, from a limited monarchy to a democracy, is a progress toward a true respect for the individual. Is a democracy, such as we know it, the last improvement possible in government? Is it not possible to take a step further towards recognizing and organizing the rights of man? There will never be a really free and enlightened State, until the State comes to recognize the individual as a higher and independent power, from which all its own power and authority are derived, and treats him accordingly. I please myself with imagining a State at last which can afford to be just to all men, and to treat the individual

---

25. "I . . . will": These extracts have been inserted since the Lecture was read. [Thoreau's note] The extracts include quotations from two of Webster's speeches in the Senate: "The Admission of Texas," delivered December 22, 1845; and "Exclusion of Slavery from the Territories," delivered August 12, 1848, more than six months after Thoreau delivered his lecture at the Concord Lyceum.

with respect as a neighbor; which even would not think it inconsistent with its own repose, if a few were to live aloof from it, not meddling with it, nor embraced by it, who fulfilled all the duties of neighbors and fellow-men. A State which bore this kind of fruit, and suffered it to drop off as fast as it ripened, would prepare the way for a still more perfect and glorious State, which also I have imagined, but not yet anywhere seen.

[1849]

Reading Thoreau's *Walden*.   Thoreau built a cabin at Walden Pond in the spring of 1845, and he evidently began to plan an account of his life there soon after he settled into that ten-by-fifteen-foot dwelling that July. In February 1847, he delivered a lecture, "A History of Myself" — apparently a portion of what became the opening chapter, "Economy" — at the Concord Lyceum. By the time he left the pond in September 1847, Thoreau had completed the first draft of *Walden*, which he soon prepared for publication. When his first book, *A Week on the Concord and Merrimack Rivers*, was published in 1849, it included an announcement that *Walden* would soon be published. But the commercial failure of *A Week* delayed the publication of Thoreau's second book, which he heavily revised and greatly expanded before it was finally published as *Walden; or, Life in the Woods* in 1854. In a letter written shortly before his death in 1862, Thoreau asked his publisher to omit the subtitle in all future editions, so his most famous book is now simply and widely known as *Walden.*

   Thoreau's book has been read and appreciated in a wide variety of ways. On one level, it may be read as an inspirational manual of individual self-reform, a challenge to the organized social reformers who were so active in the decades before the Civil War. Like many other works of the period, *Walden* also represented a sweeping challenge to American materialism and ideas of progress. As the reformer and writer Lydia Maria Child admiringly observed in a contemporary review, "The life exhibited in [Thoreau's books] teaches us that this Western activity of which we are so proud, these material improvements, this commercial enterprise, this rapid accumulation of wealth, even our external associated philanthropic action, are very easily overrated." Readers have been drawn to *Walden* by Thoreau's eloquent advocacy of the simple life, with its emphasis on spiritual ends over material gains. Others have celebrated the literary artistry of the work, as displayed by Thoreau's dense and allusive prose style, as well as by the symbolic patterns and the seasonal structure of the book, in which he compressed the events of his more than two years at the pond into a narrative of a single year. Still others have been drawn to its descriptions of the natural world and emphasis on our vital connections to nature. Indeed, *Walden* has assumed a central place in the tradition of American nature writing, even as it has served as an ongoing inspiration for the environmental movement in the United States. Certainly, for many readers Thoreau's messages are even more urgent today than they were when the book was first published in 1854. The text of the following selections is taken from that first edition of *Walden; or, Life in the Woods.*

Title Page of the First Edition of *Walden* (1854)

The etching of Thoreau's cabin at Walden Pond was based on a sketch by his sister Sophia Thoreau. The epigraph is a sentence from the second chapter, "Where I Lived, and What I Lived For," where Thoreau announces: "I do not propose to write an ode to dejection, but to brag as lustily as chanticleer in the morning, standing on his roost, if only to wake my neighbors up."

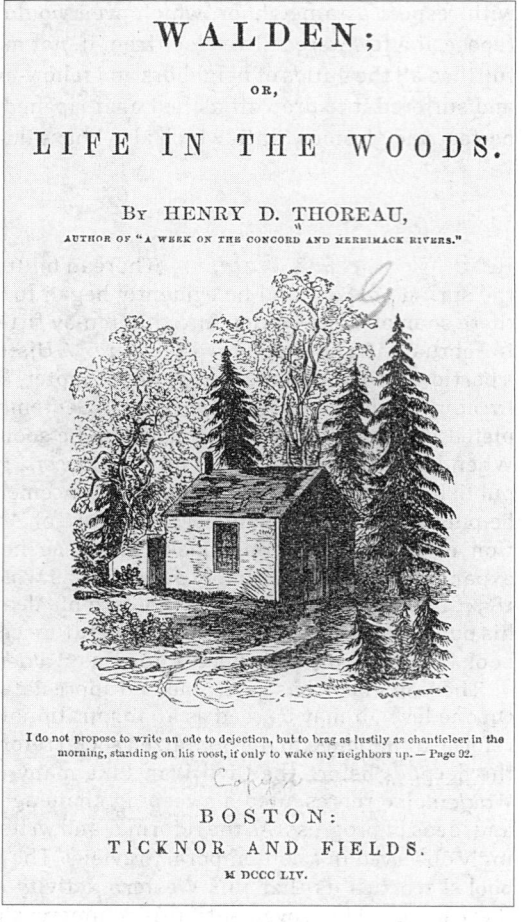

WALDEN;

OR,

LIFE IN THE WOODS.

BY HENRY D. THOREAU,

AUTHOR OF "A WEEK ON THE CONCORD AND MERRIMACK RIVERS."

I do not propose to write an ode to dejection, but to brag as lustily as chanticleer in the morning, standing on his roost, if only to wake my neighbors up. — Page 92.

BOSTON:

TICKNOR AND FIELDS.

M DCCC LIV.

WALDEN

From Economy

When I wrote the following pages, or rather the bulk of them, I lived alone, in the woods, a mile from any neighbor, in a house which I had built myself, on the shore of Walden Pond, in Concord, Massachusetts, and earned my living by the labor of my hands only. I lived there two years and two months. At present I am a sojourner in civilized life again.

I should not obtrude my affairs so much on the notice of my readers if very particular inquiries had not been made by my townsmen concerning my mode of life, which some would call impertinent, though they do not appear to me at all impertinent, but, considering the circumstances, very natural and pertinent. Some have asked what I got to eat; if I did not feel lonesome; if I was not afraid; and the like. Others have been curious to learn what portion of my income I devoted to charitable purposes; and some, who have large families, how many poor children I maintained. I will therefore ask those of my readers who feel no particular interest in me to pardon me if I undertake to answer some of these questions in this book. In most books, the *I*, or first person, is omitted; in this it will be retained; that, in respect to egotism, is the main difference. We commonly do not remember that it is, after all, always the first person that is speaking. I should not talk so much about myself if there were any body else whom I knew as well. Unfortunately, I am confined to this theme by the narrowness of my experience. Moreover, I, on my side, require of every writer, first or last, a simple and sincere account of his own life, and not merely what he has heard of other men's lives; some such account as he would send to his kindred from a distant land; for if he has lived sincerely, it must have been in a distant land to me. Perhaps these pages are more particularly addressed to poor students. As for the rest of my readers, they will accept such portions as apply to them. I trust that none will stretch the seams in putting on the coat, for it may do good service to him whom it fits.

I would fain say something, not so much concerning the Chinese and Sandwich Islanders[1] as you who read these pages, who are said to live in New England; something about your condition, especially your outward condition or circumstances in this world, in this town, what it is, whether it is necessary that it be as bad as it is, whether it cannot be improved as well as not. I have travelled a good deal in Concord; and every where, in shops, and offices, and fields, the inhabitants have appeared to me to be doing penance in a thousand remarkable ways. What I have heard of Bramins[2] sitting exposed to four fires and looking in the face of the sun; or hanging suspended, with their heads downward, over flames; or looking at the heavens over their shoulders "until it becomes impossible for them to resume their natural position, while from the twist of the neck nothing but liquids can pass into the stomach"; or dwelling, chained for life, at the foot of a tree; or measuring with their bodies, like caterpillars, the breadth of vast empires; or standing on one leg on the tops of pillars,—even these forms of conscious penance are hardly more incredible and astonishing than the scenes which I daily witness. The twelve labors of Hercules were trifling in comparison with those which my neighbors have undertaken; for they were only twelve, and had an end; but I could never see that these men slew or captured any monster or finished any labor. They have no friend Iolas to burn with a hot iron the root of the hydra's head, but as soon as one head is crushed, two spring up.[3]

I see young men, my townsmen, whose misfortune it is to have inherited farms, houses, barns, cattle, and farming tools; for these are more easily acquired than got rid of. Better if they had been born in the open pasture and suckled by a wolf,[4] that they might have seen with clearer eyes what field they were called to labor in. Who made them serfs of the soil? Why should they eat their sixty acres, when man is condemned to

---

1. **Sandwich Islanders:** Hawaiians; travel lectures were popular staples at lyceums, where Thoreau originally read portions of *Walden.*
2. **Bramins:** Usually spelled *Brahmins* or *Brahmans*; members of the highest or priestly caste of Hindus.
3. **The twelve labors . . . spring up:** The son of the Greek god Zeus and a mortal, Hercules was commanded to undertake twelve seemingly impossible tasks. His servant Iolas helped him slay the Hydra, a monster with nine heads.
4. **suckled by a wolf:** Romulus and Remus, the legendary founders of Rome, were said to have been abandoned as infants and mothered by a she-wolf.

eat only his peck of dirt? Why should they begin digging their graves as soon as they are born? They have got to live a man's life, pushing all these things before them, and get on as well as they can. How many a poor immortal soul have I met well nigh crushed and smothered under its load, creeping down the road of life, pushing before it a barn seventy-five feet by forty, its Augean stables[5] never cleansed, and one hundred acres of land, tillage, mowing, pasture, and wood-lot! The portionless, who struggle with no such unnecessary inherited encumbrances, find it labor enough to subdue and cultivate a few cubic feet of flesh.

But men labor under a mistake. The better part of the man is soon ploughed into the soil for compost. By a seeming fate, commonly called necessity, they are employed, as it says in an old book, laying up treasures which moth and rust will corrupt and thieves break through and steal.[6] It is a fool's life, as they will find when they get to the end of it, if not before. It is said that Deucalion and Pyrrha[7] created men by throwing stones over their heads behind them: —

> Inde genus durum sumus, experiensque laborum,
> Et documenta damus quâ simus origine nati.

Or, as Raleigh rhymes it in his sonorous way, —

> "From thence our kind hard-hearted is, enduring pain and care,
> Approving that our bodies of a stony nature are."

So much for a blind obedience to a blundering oracle, throwing the stones over their heads behind them, and not seeing where they fell.

Most men, even in this comparatively free country, through mere ignorance and mistake, are so occupied with the factitious cares and superfluously coarse labors of life that its finer fruits cannot be plucked by them. Their fingers, from excessive toil, are too clumsy and tremble too much for that. Actually, the laboring man has not leisure for a true integrity day by day; he cannot afford to sustain the manliest relations to men; his labor would be depreciated in the market. He has no time to be any thing but a machine. How can he remember well his ignorance — which his growth requires — who has so often to use his knowledge? We should feed and clothe him gratuitously sometimes, and recruit him with our cordials, before we judge of him. The finest qualities of our nature, like the bloom on fruits, can be preserved only by the most delicate handling. Yet we do not treat ourselves nor one another thus tenderly.

Some of you, we all know, are poor, find it hard to live, are sometimes, as it were, gasping for breath. I have no doubt that some of you who read this book are unable to

---

5. **Augean stables:** One of the twelve labors of Hercules was to clean in one day the stables of Augeas, where several thousand oxen were housed and which had not been cleaned for thirty years.
6. **old book . . . steal:** The Bible; see Matthew 6:19.
7. **Deucalion and Pyrrha:** Deucalion, the son of Prometheus, and his wife, Pyrrha, were the only survivors of the flood Zeus sent to destroy the degenerate race of mortals. Deucalion, realizing that the earth was his mother, whose bones were rocks and stones, and Pyrrha threw these over their heads to repopulate the world. The quotation that follows is from the *Metamorphoses*, 1.414-15, by the Roman poet Ovid (43 BCE–17? CE); the translation is from Sir Walter Raleigh's *History of the World* (1614).

pay for all the dinners which you have actually eaten, or for the coats and shoes which are fast wearing or are already worn out, and have come to this page to spend borrowed or stolen time, robbing your creditors of an hour. It is very evident what mean and sneaking lives many of you live, for my sight has been whetted by experience; always on the limits, trying to get into business and trying to get out of debt, a very ancient slough, called by the Latins *aes alienum*, another's brass, for some of their coins were made of brass; still living, and dying, and buried by this other's brass; always promising to pay, promising to pay, to-morrow, and dying to-day, insolvent; seeking to curry favor, to get custom, by how many modes, only not state-prison offences; lying, flattering, voting, contracting yourselves into a nutshell of civility, or dilating into an atmosphere of thin and vaporous generosity, that you may persuade your neighbor to let you make his shoes, or his hat, or his coat, or his carriage, or import his groceries for him; making yourselves sick, that you may lay up something against a sick day, something to be tucked away in an old chest, or in a stocking behind the plastering, or, more safely, in the brick bank; no matter where, no matter how much or how little.

I sometimes wonder that we can be so frivolous, I may almost say, as to attend to the gross but somewhat foreign form of servitude called Negro Slavery, there are so many keen and subtle masters that enslave both north and south. It is hard to have a southern overseer; it is worse to have a northern one; but worst of all when you are the slave-driver of yourself. Talk of a divinity in man! Look at the teamster on the highway, wending to market by day or night; does any divinity stir within him? His highest duty to fodder and water his horses! What is his destiny to him compared with the shipping interests? Does not he drive for Squire Make-a-stir? How godlike, how immortal, is he? See how he cowers and sneaks, how vaguely all the day he fears, not being immortal nor divine, but the slave and prisoner of his own opinion of himself, a fame won by his own deeds. Public opinion is a weak tyrant compared with our own private opinion. What a man thinks of himself, that it is which determines, or rather indicates, his fate. Self-emancipation even in the West Indian provinces of the fancy and imagination, — what Wilberforce[8] is there to bring that about? Think, also, of the ladies of the land weaving toilet cushions against the last day, not to betray too green an interest in their fates! As if you could kill time without injuring eternity.

The mass of men lead lives of quiet desperation. What is called resignation is confirmed desperation. From the desperate city you go into the desperate country, and have to console yourself with the bravery of minks and muskrats. A stereotyped but unconscious despair is concealed even under what are called the games and amusements of mankind. There is no play in them, for this comes after work. But it is a characteristic of wisdom not to do desperate things.

When we consider what, to use the words of the catechism, is the chief end of man,[9] and what are the true necessaries and means of life, it appears as if men had deliberately

---

8. **Wilberforce:** William Wilberforce (1759–1833), English abolitionist who led the parliamentary battle to end slavery in the British West Indies.

9. **the chief end of man:** In the words of the Shorter Catechism from the *New England Primer*, "the chief end of man . . . is to glorify God and to enjoy him forever."

chosen the common mode of living because they preferred it to any other. Yet they honestly think there is no choice left. But alert and healthy natures remember that the sun rose clear. It is never too late to give up our prejudices. No way of thinking or doing, however ancient, can be trusted without proof. What every body echoes or in silence passes by as true to-day may turn out to be falsehood to-morrow, mere smoke of opinion, which some had trusted for a cloud that would sprinkle fertilizing rain on their fields. What old people say you cannot do you try and find that you can. Old deeds for old people, and new deeds for new. Old people did not know enough once, perchance, to fetch fresh fuel to keep the fire a-going; new people put a little dry wood under a pot, and are whirled round the globe with the speed of birds, in a way to kill old people, as the phrase is. Age is no better, hardly so well, qualified for an instructor as youth, for it has not profited so much as it has lost. One may almost doubt if the wisest man has learned any thing of absolute value by living. Practically, the old have no very important advice to give the young, their own experience has been so partial, and their lives have been such miserable failures, for private reasons, as they must believe; and it may be that they have some faith left which belies that experience, and they are only less young than they were. I have lived some thirty years on this planet, and I have yet to hear the first syllable of valuable or even earnest advice from my seniors. They have told me nothing, and probably cannot tell me any thing, to the purpose. Here is life, an experiment to a great extent untried by me; but it does not avail me that they have tried it. If I have any experience which I think valuable, I am sure to reflect that this my Mentors said nothing about.

One farmer says to me, "You cannot live on vegetable food solely, for it furnishes nothing to make bones with;" and so he religiously devotes a part of his day to supplying his system with the raw material of bones; walking all the while he talks behind his oxen, which, with vegetable-made bones, jerk him and his lumbering plough along in spite of every obstacle. Some things are really necessaries of life in some circles, the most helpless and diseased, which in others are luxuries merely, and in others still are entirely unknown.

The whole ground of human life seems to some to have been gone over by their predecessors, both the heights and the valleys, and all things to have been cared for. According to Evelyn,[10] "the wise Solomon prescribed ordinances for the very distances of trees; and the Roman praetors have decided how often you may go into your neighbor's land to gather the acorns which fall on it without trespass, and what share belongs to that neighbor." Hippocrates[11] has even left directions how we should cut our nails; that is, even with the ends of the fingers, neither shorter nor longer. Undoubtedly the very tedium and ennui which presume to have exhausted the variety and the joys of life are as old as Adam. But man's capacities have never been measured; nor are we to judge of what he can do by any precedents, so little has been tried. Whatever have been thy failures hitherto, "be not afflicted, my child, for who shall assign to thee what thou hast left undone?"[12]

---

10. **According to Evelyn:** John Evelyn (1620–1706), English author and naturalist; the following quotation is from his *Sylva; or, a Discourse of Forest-Trees* (1664). "Roman praetors" were elected officials.
11. **Hippocrates:** Ancient Greek physician known as the "Father of Medicine."
12. **"be . . . undone?":** From the ancient Hindu scripture *Vishnu Purana.*

We might try our lives by a thousand simple tests; as, for instance, that the same sun which ripens my beans illumines at once a system of earths like ours. If I had remembered this it would have prevented some mistakes. This was not the light in which I hoed them. The stars are the apexes of what wonderful triangles! What distant and different beings in the various mansions of the universe are contemplating the same one at the same moment! Nature and human life are as various as our several constitutions. Who shall say what prospect life offers to another? Could a greater miracle take place than for us to look through each other's eyes for an instant? We should live in all the ages of the world in an hour; ay, in all the worlds of the ages. History, Poetry, Mythology! — I know of no reading of another's experience so startling and informing as this would be.

The greater part of what my neighbors call good I believe in my soul to be bad, and if I repent of any thing, it is very likely to be my good behavior. What demon possessed me that I behaved so well? You may say the wisest thing you can old man, — you who have lived seventy years, not without honor of a kind, — I hear an irresistible voice which invites me away from all that. One generation abandons the enterprises of another like stranded vessels.

I think that we may safely trust a good deal more than we do. We may waive just so much care of ourselves as we honestly bestow elsewhere. Nature is as well adapted to our weakness as to our strength. The incessant anxiety and strain of some is a well nigh incurable form of disease. We are made to exaggerate the importance of what work we do; and yet how much is not done by us! or, what if we had been taken sick? How vigilant we are! determined not to live by faith if we can avoid it; all the day long on the alert, at night we unwillingly say our prayers and commit ourselves to uncertainties. So thoroughly and sincerely are we compelled to live, reverencing our life, and denying the possibility of change. This is the only way, we say; but there are as many ways as there can be drawn radii from one centre. All change is a miracle to contemplate; but it is a miracle which is taking place every instant. Confucius said, "To know that we know what we know, and that we do not know what we do not know, that is true knowledge." When one man has reduced a fact of the imagination to be a fact to his understanding, I foresee that all men will at length establish their lives on that basis.

• • •

Where I Lived, and What I Lived For

At a certain season of our life we are accustomed to consider every spot as the possible site of a house. I have thus surveyed the country on every side within a dozen miles of where I live. In imagination I have bought all the farms in succession, for all were to be bought, and I knew their price. I walked over each farmer's premises, tasted his wild apples, discoursed on husbandry with him, took his farm at his price, at any price, mortgaging it to him in my mind; even put a higher price on it, — took every thing but a deed of it, — took his word for his deed, for I dearly love to talk, — cultivated it, and him too to some extent, I trust, and withdrew when I had enjoyed it long enough, leaving him to carry it on. This experience entitled me to be regarded as a sort of real-estate broker by my friends. Wherever I sat, there I might live, and the landscape radiated from me accordingly. What is a house but a *sedes*, a seat? – better if a country seat. I discovered many a site for a house not likely to be soon improved, which some might have thought too far from the village, but to my eyes the village was too far from it. Well, there I might live, I said; and there I did live, for an hour, a summer and a winter life; saw how I could let the years run off, buffet the winter through, and see the spring come in. The future inhabitants of this region, wherever they may place their houses, may be sure that they have been anticipated. An afternoon sufficed to lay out the land into orchard, woodlot, and pasture, and to decide what fine oaks or pines should be left to stand before the door, and whence each blasted tree could be seen to the best advantage; and then I let it lie, fallow perchance, for a man is rich in proportion to the number of things which he can afford to let alone.

My imagination carried me so far that I even had the refusal of several farms, – the refusal was all I wanted, – but I never got my fingers burned by actual possession. The nearest that I came to actual possession was when I bought the Hollowell place, and had begun to sort my seeds, and collected materials with which to make a wheelbarrow to carry it on or off with; but before the owner gave me a deed of it, his wife – every man has such a wife – changed her mind and wished to keep it, and he offered me ten dollars to release him. Now, to speak the truth, I had but ten cents in the world, and it surpassed my arithmetic to tell, if I was that man who had ten cents, or who had a farm, or ten dollars, or all together. However, I let him keep the ten dollars and the farm too, for I had carried it far enough; or rather, to be generous, I sold him the farm for just what I gave for it, and, as he was not a rich man, made him a present of ten dollars, and still had my ten cents, and seeds, and materials for a wheelbarrow left. I found thus that I had been a rich man without any damage to my poverty. But I retained the landscape, and I have since annually carried off what it yielded without a wheelbarrow. With respect to landscapes, –

> "I am monarch of all I *survey*,
> My right there is none to dispute."[1]

I have frequently seen a poet withdraw, having enjoyed the most valuable part of a farm, while the crusty farmer supposed that he had got a few wild apples only. Why, the owner does not know it for many years when a poet has put his farm in rhyme, the most admirable kind of invisible fence, has fairly impounded it, milked it, skimmed it, and got all the cream, and left the farmer only the skimmed milk.

The real attractions of the Hollowell farm, to me, were; its complete retirement, being about two miles from the village, half a mile from the nearest neighbor, and separated from the highway by a broad field; its bounding on the river, which the owner said protected it by its fogs from frosts in the spring, though that was nothing to me; the gray color and ruinous state of the house and barn, and the dilapidated fences, which put such an interval between me and the last occupant; the hollow and lichen-covered apple trees, gnawed by rabbits, showing what kind of neighbors I should have; but above all, the recollection I had of it from my earliest voyages up the river, when the house was

---

1. "I . . . dispute": From "Verses Supposed to Be Written by Alexander Selkirk," by the English poet William Cowper (1731-1800). Thoreau italicized the word *survey* to call attention to his pun.

concealed behind a dense grove of red maples, through which I heard the house-dog bark. I was in haste to buy it, before the proprietor finished getting out some rocks, cutting down the hollow apple trees, and grubbing up some young birches which had sprung up in the pasture, or, in short, had made any more of his improvements. To enjoy these advantages I was ready to carry it on; like Atlas, to take the world on my shoulders, — I never heard what compensation he received for that, — and do all those things which had no other motive or excuse but that I might pay for it and be unmolested in my possession of it; for I knew all the while that it would yield the most abundant crop of the kind I wanted if I could only afford to let it alone. But it turned out as I have said.

All that I could say, then, with respect to farming on a large scale, (I have always cultivated a garden,) was, that I had had my seeds ready. Many think that seeds improve with age. I have no doubt that time discriminates between the good and the bad; and when at last I shall plant, I shall be less likely to be disappointed. But I would say to my fellows, once for all, As long as possible live free and uncommitted. It makes but little difference whether you are committed to a farm or the county jail.

Old Cato,[2] whose "De Re Rusticâ" is my "Cultivator," says, and the only translation I have seen makes sheer nonsense of the passage, "When you think of getting a farm, turn it thus in your mind, not to buy greedily; nor spare your pains to look at it, and do not think it enough to go round it once. The oftener you go there the more it will please you, if it is good." I think I shall not buy greedily, but go round and round it as long as I live, and be buried in it first, that it may please me the more at last.

The present was my next experiment of this kind, which I purpose to describe more at length; for convenience, putting the experience of two years into one. As I have said, I do not propose to write an ode to dejection, but to brag as lustily as chanticleer in the morning, standing on his roost, if only to wake my neighbors up.

When first I took up my abode in the woods, that is, began to spend my nights as well as days there, which, by accident, was on Independence day, or the fourth of July, 1845, my house was not finished for winter, but was merely a defence against the rain, without plastering or chimney, the walls being of rough weather-stained boards, with wide chinks, which made it cool at night. The upright white hewn studs and freshly planed door and window casings gave it a clean and airy look, especially in the morning, when its timbers were saturated with dew, so that I fancied that by noon some sweet gum would exude from them. To my imagination it retained throughout the day more or less of this auroral character, reminding me of a certain house on a mountain which I had visited the year before. This was an airy and unplastered cabin, fit to entertain a travelling god, and where a goddess might trail her garments. The winds which passed over my dwelling were such as sweep over the ridges of mountains, bearing the broken strains, or celestial parts only, of terrestrial music. The morning wind forever blows, the poem of creation is uninterrupted; but few are the ears that hear it. Olympus is but the outside of the earth every where.

---

2. **Old Cato:** Marcus Porcius Cato, the Elder (234-149 BCE), Roman statesman; the following quotation is from his *De agri cultura*, 1.1, as translated by Thoreau.

The only house I had been the owner of before, if I except a boat, was a tent, which I used occasionally when making excursions in the summer, and this is still rolled up in my garret; but the boat, after passing from hand to hand, has gone down the stream of time. With this more substantial shelter about me, I had made some progress toward settling in the world. This frame, so slightly clad, was a sort of crystallization around me, and reacted on the builder. It was suggestive somewhat as a picture in outlines. I did not need to go out doors to take the air, for the atmosphere within had lost none of its freshness. It was not so much within doors as behind a door where I sat, even in the rainiest weather. The Harivansa[3] says, "An abode without birds is like a meat without seasoning." Such was not my abode, for I found myself suddenly neighbor to the birds; not by having imprisoned one, but having caged myself near them. I was not only nearer to some of those which commonly frequent the garden and the orchard, but to those wilder and more thrilling songsters of the forest which never, or rarely, serenade a villager, — the wood-thrush, the veery, the scarlet tanager, the field-sparrow, the whippoor-will, and many others.

I was seated by the shore of a small pond, about a mile and a half south of the village of Concord and somewhat higher than it, in the midst of an extensive wood between that town and Lincoln, and about two miles south of that our only field known to fame, Concord Battle Ground;[4] but I was so low in the woods that the opposite shore, half a mile off, like the rest, covered with wood, was my most distant horizon. For the first week, whenever I looked out on the pond it impressed me like a tarn high up on the side of a mountain, its bottom far above the surface of other lakes, and, as the sun arose, I saw it throwing off its nightly clothing of mist, and here and there, by degrees, its soft ripples or its smooth reflecting surface was revealed, while the mists, like ghosts, were stealthily withdrawing in every direction into the woods, as at the breaking up of some nocturnal conventicle. The very dew seemed to hang upon the trees later into the day than usual, as on the sides of mountains.

This small lake was of most value as a neighbor in the intervals of a gentle rain storm in August, when, both air and water being perfectly still, but the sky overcast, mid-afternoon had all the serenity of evening, and the wood-thrush sang around, and was heard from shore to shore. A lake like this is never smoother than at such a time; and the clear portion of the air above it being shallow and darkened by clouds, the water, full of light and reflections, becomes a lower heaven itself so much the more important. From a hill top near by, where the wood had been recently cut off, there was a pleasing vista southward across the pond, through a wide indentation in the hills which form the shore there, where their opposite sides sloping toward each other suggested a stream flowing out in that direction through a wooded valley, but stream there was none. That way I looked between and over the near green hills to some distant and higher ones in the horizon, tinged with blue. Indeed, by standing on tiptoe I could catch a glimpse of some of the peaks of the still bluer and more distant mountain ranges in the north-west, those true-blue coins from heaven's own mint, and also

---

3. **Harivansa:** An ancient Hindu epic.
4. **Concord Battle Ground:** Site of the second battle of the American Revolution, in April 1775.

of some portion of the village. But in other directions, even from this point, I could not see over or beyond the woods which surrounded me. It is well to have some water in your neighborhood, to give buoyancy to and float the earth. One value even of the smallest well is, that when you look into it you see that earth is not continent but insular. This is as important as that it keeps butter cool. When I looked across the pond from this peak toward the Sudbury meadows, which in time of flood I distinguished elevated perhaps by a mirage in their seething valley, like a coin in a basin, all the earth beyond the pond appeared like a thin crust insulated and floated even by this small sheet of intervening water, and I was reminded that this on which I dwelt was but *dry land.*

Though the view from my door was still more contracted, I did not feel crowded or confined in the least. There was pasture enough for my imagination. The low shrub-oak plateau to which the opposite shore arose, stretched away toward the prairies of the West and the steppes of Tartary, affording ample room for all the roving families of men. "There are none happy in the world but beings who enjoy freely a vast horizon," – said Damodara,[5] when his herds required new and larger pastures.

Both place and time were changed, and I dwelt nearer to those parts of the universe and to those eras in history which had most attracted me. Where I lived was as far off as many a region viewed nightly by astronomers. We are wont to imagine rare and delectable places in some remote and more celestial corner of the system, behind the constellation of Cassiopeia's Chair,[6] far from noise and disturbance. I discovered that my house actually had its site in such a withdrawn, but forever new and unprofaned, part of the universe. If it were worth the while to settle in those parts near to the Pleiades or the Hyades, to Aldebaran or Altair,[7] then I was really there, or at an equal remoteness from the life which I had left behind, dwindled and twinkling with as fine a ray to my nearest neighbor, and to be seen only in moonless nights by him. Such was that part of creation where I had squatted; –

> "There was a shepherd that did live,
>   And held his thoughts as high
> As were the mounts whereon his flocks
>   Did hourly feed him by."[8]

What should we think of the shepherd's life if his flocks always wandered to higher pastures than his thoughts?

Every morning was a cheerful invitation to make my life of equal simplicity, and I may say innocence, with Nature herself. I have been as sincere a worshipper of Aurora[9] as the Greeks. I got up early and bathed in the pond; that was a religious exercise, and

---

5. **Damodara:** A name for Krishna, an incarnation of Vishnu, second god of the Hindu trinity; the following quotation is from the *Harivansa.*
6. **Cassiopeia's Chair:** The five brightest stars in the constellation Cassiopeia.
7. **Pleiades . . . Altair:** Names of various stars and constellations.
8. **"There . . . by":** From an anonymous Renaissance poem reprinted in *Old Ballads* (1810).
9. **Aurora:** The Roman goddess of the dawn.

one of the best things which I did. They say that characters were engraven on the bathing tub of king Tching-thang[10] to this effect: "Renew thyself completely each day; do it again, and again, and forever again." I can understand that. Morning brings back the heroic ages. I was as much affected by the faint hum of a mosquito making its invisible and unimaginable tour through my apartment at earliest dawn, when I was sitting with door and windows open, as I could be by any trumpet that ever sang of fame. It was Homer's requiem; itself an Iliad and Odyssey in the air, singing its own wrath and wanderings. There was something cosmical about it; a standing advertisement, till forbidden,[11] of the everlasting vigor and fertility of the world. The morning, which is the most memorable season of the day, is the awakening hour. Then there is least somnolence in us; and for an hour, at least, some part of us awakes which slumbers all the rest of the day and night. Little is to be expected of that day, if it can be called a day, to which we are not awakened by our Genius, but by the mechanical nudgings of some servitor, are not awakened by our own newly-acquired force and aspirations from within, accompanied by the undulations of celestial music, instead of factory bells, and a fragrance filling the air — to a higher life than we fell asleep from; and thus the darkness bear its fruit, and prove itself to be good, no less than the light. That man who does not believe that each day contains an earlier, more sacred, and auroral hour than he has yet profaned, has despaired of life, and is pursuing a descending and darkening way. After a partial cessation of his sensuous life, the soul of man, or its organs rather, are reinvigorated each day, and his Genius tries again what noble life it can make. All memorable events, I should say, transpire in morning time and in a morning atmosphere. The Vedas[12] say, "All intelligences awake with the morning." Poetry and art, and the fairest and most memorable of the actions of men, date from such an hour. All poets and heroes, like Memnon,[13] are the children of Aurora, and emit their music at sunrise. To him whose elastic and vigorous thought keeps pace with the sun, the day is a perpetual morning. It matters not what the clocks say or the attitudes and labors of men. Morning is when I am awake and there is a dawn in me. Moral reform is the effort to throw off sleep. Why is it that men give so poor an account of their day if they have not been slumbering? They are not such poor calculators. If they had not been overcome with drowsiness they would have performed something. The millions are awake enough for physical labor; but only one in a million is awake enough for effective intellectual exertion, only one in a hundred millions to a poetic or divine life. To be awake is to be alive. I have never yet met a man who was quite awake. How could I have looked him in the face?

    We must learn to reawaken and keep ourselves awake, not by mechanical aids, but by an infinite expectation of the dawn, which does not forsake us in our soundest sleep. I know of no more encouraging fact than the unquestionable ability of man to elevate his

---

10. **Tching-thang:** Confucius (c. 551–c. 479 BCE), Chinese philosopher and teacher; the quotation is from *The Great Learning*, chapter 1.

11. **till forbidden:** The abbreviation "t f," or "till forbidden," was a printer's sign for standing advertisements in newspapers.

12. **Vedas:** Hindu scriptures; the specific source of the quotation is unknown.

13. **Memnon:** In Greek mythology, Memnon was an Ethiopian king who was killed by Achilles in the Trojan War.

life by a conscious endeavor. It is something to be able to paint a particular picture, or to carve a statue, and so to make a few objects beautiful; but it is far more glorious to carve and paint the very atmosphere and medium through which we look, which morally we can do. To affect the quality of the day, that is the highest of arts. Every man is tasked to make his life, even in its details, worthy of the contemplation of his most elevated and critical hour. If we refused, or rather used up, such paltry information as we get, the oracles would distinctly inform us how this might be done.

I went to the woods because I wished to live deliberately, to front only the essential facts of life, and see if I could not learn what it had to teach, and not, when I came to die, discover that I had not lived. I did not wish to live what was not life, living is so dear; nor did I wish to practise resignation, unless it was quite necessary. I wanted to live deep and suck out all the marrow of life, to live so sturdily and Spartan-like as to put to rout all that was not life, to cut a broad swath and shave close, to drive life into a corner, and reduce it to its lowest terms, and, if it proved to be mean, why then to get the whole and genuine meanness of it, and publish its meanness to the world; or if it were sublime, to know it by experience, and be able to give a true account of it in my next excursion. For most men, it appears to me, are in a strange uncertainty about it, whether it is of the devil or of God, and have *somewhat hastily* concluded that it is the chief end of man here to "glorify God and enjoy him forever."[14]

Still we live meanly, like ants; though the fable tells us that we were long ago changed into men; like pygmies we fight with cranes;[15] it is error upon error, and clout upon clout, and our best virtue has for its occasion a superfluous and evitable wretchedness. Our life is frittered away by detail. An honest man has hardly need to count more than his ten fingers, or in extreme cases he may add his ten toes, and lump the rest. Simplicity, simplicity, simplicity! I say, let your affairs be as two or three, and not a hundred or a thousand; instead of a million count half a dozen, and keep your accounts on your thumb nail. In the midst of this chopping sea of civilized life, such are the clouds and storms and quicksands and thousand-and-one items to be allowed for, that a man has to live, if he would not founder and go to the bottom and not make his port at all, by dead reckoning, and he must be a great calculator indeed who succeeds. Simplify, simplify. Instead of three meals a day, if it be necessary eat but one; instead of a hundred dishes, five; and reduce other things in proportion. Our life is like a German Confederacy, made up of petty states, with its boundary forever fluctuating, so that even a German cannot tell you how it is bounded at any moment. The nation itself, with all its so called internal improvements, which, by the way, are all external and superficial, is just such an unwieldy and overgrown establishment, cluttered with furniture and tripped up by its own traps, ruined by luxury and heedless expense, by want of calculation and a worthy aim, as the million households in the land; and the only cure for it as for them is in a rigid economy, a stern and more than Spartan simplicity of life and elevation of purpose. It lives too fast. Men think that it is essential that the *Nation* have commerce, and

---

14. "glorify . . . forever": See "Economy," note 9.
15. ants . . . cranes: The Greek god Zeus turned ants into men to repopulate the earth; in the opening lines of book 3 of the *Iliad*, Homer compares the Trojans to cranes fighting with pygmies.

export ice, and talk through a telegraph, and ride thirty miles an hour, without a doubt, whether *they* do or not; but whether we should live like baboons or like men, is a little uncertain. If we do not get out sleepers, and forge rails, and devote days and nights to the work, but go to tinkering upon our *lives* to improve *them*, who will build railroads? And if railroads are not built, how shall we get to heaven in season? But if we stay at home and mind our business, who will want railroads? We do not ride on the railroad; it rides upon us. Did you ever think what those sleepers[16] are that underlie the railroad? Each one is a man, an Irishman, or a Yankee man. The rails are laid on them, and they are covered with sand, and the cars run smoothly over them. They are sound sleepers, I assure you. And every few years a new lot is laid down and run over; so that, if some have the pleasure of riding on a rail, others have the misfortune to be ridden upon. And when they run over a man that is walking in his sleep, a supernumerary sleeper in the wrong position, and wake him up, they suddenly stop the cars, and make a hue and cry about it, as if this were an exception. I am glad to know that it takes a gang of men for every five miles to keep the sleepers down and level in their beds as it is, for this is a sign that they may sometime get up again.

Why should we live with such hurry and waste of life? We are determined to be starved before we are hungry. Men say that a stitch in time saves nine, and so they take a thousand stitches to-day to save nine to-morrow. As for *work*, we haven't any of any consequence. We have the Saint Vitus' dance,[17] and cannot possibly keep our heads still. If I should only give a few pulls at the parish bell-rope, as for a fire, that is, without setting the bell, there is hardly a man on his farm in the outskirts of Concord, notwithstanding that press of engagements which was his excuse so many times this morning, nor a boy, nor a woman, I might almost say, but would forsake all and follow that sound, not mainly to save property from the flames, but, if we will confess the truth, much more to see it burn, since burn it must, and we, be it known, did not set it on fire, – or to see it put out, and have a hand in it, if that is done as handsomely; yes, even if it were the parish church itself. Hardly a man takes a half hour's nap after dinner, but when he wakes he holds up his head and asks, "What's the news?" as if the rest of mankind had stood his sentinels. Some give directions to be waked every half hour, doubtless for no other purpose; and then, to pay for it, they tell what they have dreamed. After a night's sleep the news is as indispensable as the breakfast. "Pray tell me any thing new that has happened to a man any where on this globe," – and he reads it over his coffee and rolls, that a man has had his eyes gouged out this morning on the Wachito River;[18] never dreaming the while that he lives in the dark unfathomed mammoth cave of this world, and has but the rudiment of an eye himself.

For my part, I could easily do without the post-office. I think that there are very few important communications made through it. To speak critically, I never received more than one or two letters in my life – I wrote this some years ago – that were worth the

---

16. **sleepers**: Wooden ties upon which rails were laid.
17. **Saint Vitus' dance**: St. Vitus was the patron saint of those afflicted with chorea, a nervous disorder characterized by jerky, spasmodic movements.
18. **Wachito River**: The Ouachito River in southern Arkansas, then a notoriously rough part of the country.

postage. The penny-post is, commonly, an institution through which you seriously offer a man that penny for his thoughts which is so often safely offered in jest. And I am sure that I never read any memorable news in a newspaper. If we read of one man robbed, or murdered, or killed by accident, or one house burned, or one vessel wrecked, or one steamboat blown up, or one cow run over on the Western Railroad, or one mad dog killed, or one lot of grasshoppers in the winter, — we never need read of another. One is enough. If you are acquainted with the principle, what do you care for a myriad instances and applications? To a philosopher all *news*, as it is called, is gossip, and they who edit and read it are old women over their tea. Yet not a few are greedy after this gossip. There was such a rush, as I hear, the other day at one of the offices to learn the foreign news by the last arrival, that several large squares of plate glass belonging to the establishment were broken by the pressure, — news which I seriously think a ready wit might write a twelvemonth or twelve years beforehand with sufficient accuracy. As for Spain, for instance, if you know how to throw in Don Carlos and the Infanta, and Don Pedro and Seville and Granada, from time to time in the right proportions, — they may have changed the names a little since I saw the papers, — and serve up a bull-fight when other entertainments fail, it will be true to the letter, and give us as good an idea of the exact state or ruin of things in Spain as the most succinct and lucid reports under this head in the newspapers: and as for England, almost the last significant scrap of news from that quarter was the revolution of 1649;[19] and if you have learned the history of her crops for an average year, you never need attend to that thing again, unless your speculations are of a merely pecuniary character. If one may judge who rarely looks into the newspapers, nothing new does ever happen in foreign parts, a French revolution[20] not excepted.

What news! how much more important to know what that is which was never old! "Kieou-he-yu (great dignitary of the state of Wei) sent a man to Khoung-tseu to know his news. Khoung-tseu caused the messenger to be seated near him, and questioned him in these terms: What is your master doing? The messenger answered with respect: My master desires to diminish the number of his faults, but he cannot come to the end of them. The messenger being gone, the philosopher remarked: What a worthy messenger! What a worthy messenger!" The preacher, instead of vexing the ears of drowsy farmers on their day of rest at the end of the week, — for Sunday is the fit conclusion of an ill-spent week, and not the fresh and brave beginning of a new one, — with this one other draggle-tail of a sermon, should shout with thundering voice, — "Pause! Avast! Why so seeming fast, but deadly slow?"

Shams and delusions are esteemed for soundest truths, while reality is fabulous. If men would steadily observe realities only, and not allow themselves to be deluded, life, to compare it with such things as we know, would be like a fairy tale and the Arabian

---

19. **revolution of 1649:** When forces led by Oliver Cromwell overthrew the English monarchy and established the Puritan Commonwealth, which lasted until 1660.
20. **French revolution:** The Revolution of 1848, which had been widely reported in American newspapers. The revolution was swiftly quelled, leading to the establishment in 1852 of an authoritarian regime under Napoleon III.

Nights' Entertainments. If we respected only what is inevitable and has a right to be, music and poetry would resound along the streets. When we are unhurried and wise, we perceive that only great and worthy things have any permanent and absolute existence,—that petty fears and petty pleasures are but the shadow of the reality. This is always exhilarating and sublime. By closing the eyes and slumbering, and consenting to be deceived by shows, men establish and confirm their daily life of routine and habit every where, which still is built on purely illusory foundations. Children, who play life, discern its true law and relations more clearly than men, who fail to live it worthily, but who think that they are wiser by experience, that is, by failure. I have read in a Hindoo book, that "there was a king's son, who, being expelled in infancy from his native city, was brought up by a forester, and, growing up to maturity in that state, imagined himself to belong to the barbarous race with which he lived. One of his father's ministers having discovered him, revealed to him what he was, and the misconception of his character was removed, and he knew himself to be a prince. So soul," continues the Hindoo philosopher, "from the circumstances in which it is placed, mistakes its own character, until the truth is revealed to it by some holy teacher, and then it knows itself to be Brahme."[21] I perceive that we inhabitants of New England live this mean life that we do because our vision does not penetrate the surface of things. We think that that *is* which *appears* to be. If a man should walk through this town and see only the reality, where, think you, would the "Mill-dam"[22] go to? If he should give us an account of the realities he beheld there, we should not recognize the place in his description. Look at a meeting-house, or a court-house, or a jail, or a shop, or a dwelling-house, and say what that thing really is before a true gaze, and they would all go to pieces in your account of them. Men esteem truth remote, in the outskirts of the system, behind the farthest star, before Adam and after the last man. In eternity there is indeed something true and sublime. But all these times and places and occasions are now and here. God himself culminates in the present moment, and will never be more divine in the lapse of all the ages. And we are enabled to apprehend at all what is sublime and noble only by the perpetual instilling and drenching of the reality that surrounds us. The universe constantly and obediently answers to our conceptions; whether we travel fast or slow, the track is laid for us. Let us spend our lives in conceiving then. The poet or the artist never yet had so fair and noble a design but some of his posterity at least could accomplish it.

Let us spend one day as deliberately as Nature, and not be thrown off the track by every nutshell and mosquito's wing that falls on the rails. Let us rise early and fast, or break fast, gently and without perturbation; let company come and let company go, let the bells ring and the children cry,—determined to make a day of it. Why should we knock under and go with the stream? Let us not be upset and overwhelmed in that terrible rapid and whirlpool called a dinner, situated in the meridian shallows. Weather this danger and you are safe, for the rest of the way is down hill. With unrelaxed nerves, with

---

21. **a Hindoo book . . . *Brahme*"**: The source of this quotation has not been identified; in Hindu thought, Brahma is the supreme essence or spirit of the universe.
22. **"Mill-dam"**: The business and shopping center of Concord.

morning vigor, sail by it, looking another way, tied to the mast like Ulysses.[23] If the engine whistles, let it whistle till it is hoarse for its pains. If the bell rings, why should we run? We will consider what kind of music they are like. Let us settle ourselves, and work and wedge our feet downward through the mud and slush of opinion, and prejudice, and tradition, and delusion, and appearance, that alluvion which covers the globe, through Paris and London, through New York and Boston and Concord, through church and state, through poetry and philosophy and religion, till we come to a hard bottom and rocks in place, which we can call *reality*, and say, This is, and no mistake; and then begin, having a *point d'appui*,[24] below freshet and frost and fire, a place where you might found a wall or a state, or set a lamp-post safely, or perhaps a gauge, not a Nilometer,[25] but a Realometer, that future ages might know how deep a freshet of shams and appearances had gathered from time to time. If you stand right fronting and face to face to a fact, you will see the sun glimmer on both its surfaces, as if it were a cimeter, and feel its sweet edge dividing you through the heart and marrow, and so you will happily conclude your mortal career. Be it life or death, we crave only reality. If we are really dying, let us hear the rattle in our throats and feel cold in the extremities; if we are alive, let us go about our business.

Time is but the stream I go a-fishing in. I drink at it; but while I drink I see the sandy bottom and detect how shallow it is. Its thin current slides away, but eternity remains. I would drink deeper; fish in the sky, whose bottom is pebbly with stars. I cannot count one. I know not the first letter of the alphabet. I have always been regretting that I was not as wise as the day I was born. The intellect is a cleaver; it discerns and rifts its way into the secret of things. I do not wish to be any more busy with my hands than is necessary. My head is hands and feet. I feel all my best faculties concentrated in it. My instinct tells me that my head is an organ for burrowing, as some creatures use their snout and fore-paws, and with it I would mine and burrow my way through these hills. I think that the richest vein is somewhere hereabouts; so by the divining rod and thin rising vapors I judge; and here I will begin to mine.

The Bean-Field

Meanwhile my beans, the length of whose rows, added together, was seven miles already planted, were impatient to be hoed, for the earliest had grown considerably before the latest were in the ground; indeed they were not easily to be put off. What was the meaning of this so steady and self-respecting, this small Herculean labor, I knew not. I came to love my rows, my beans, though so many more than I wanted. They attached me to the earth, and so I got strength like Antaeus.[1] But why should I raise them? Only Heaven

---

23. **Ulysses:** The Roman name for Odysseus, who in Homer's *Odyssey* has himself tied to a mast so that he may hear but not succumb to the song of the Sirens.
24. *point d'appui:* Point of leverage or support; a solid footing.
25. **Nilometer:** Gauge used in ancient times to measure the rise and fall of the Nile River in Egypt.
1. **Antaeus:** Giant in Greek mythology who drew his strength from contact with his mother, the earth. He was killed in a fight with Hercules, who lifted him from the ground.

knows. This was my curious labor all summer, — to make this portion of the earth's surface, which had yielded only cinquefoil, blackberries, johnswort, and the like, before, sweet wild fruits and pleasant flowers, produce instead this pulse. What shall I learn of beans or beans of me? I cherish them, I hoe them, early and late I have an eye to them; and this is my day's work. It is a fine broad leaf to look on. My auxiliaries are the dews and rains which water this dry soil, and what fertility is in the soil itself, which for the most part is lean and effete. My enemies are worms, cool days, and most of all woodchucks. The last have nibbled for me a quarter of an acre clean. But what right had I to oust johnswort and the rest, and break up their ancient herb garden? Soon, however, the remaining beans will be too tough for them, and go forward to meet new foes.

When I was four years old, as I well remember, I was brought from Boston to this my native town, through these very woods and this field, to the pond. It is one of the oldest scenes stamped on my memory. And now to-night my flute has waked the echoes over that very water. The pines still stand here older than I; or, if some have fallen, I have cooked my supper with their stumps, and a new growth is rising all around, preparing another aspect for new infant eyes. Almost the same johnswort springs from the same perennial root in this pasture, and even I have at length helped to clothe that fabulous landscape of my infant dreams, and one of the results of my presence and influence is seen in these bean leaves, corn blades, and potato vines.

I planted about two acres and a half of upland; and as it was only about fifteen years since the land was cleared, and I myself had got out two or three cords of stumps, I did not give it any manure; but in the course of the summer it appeared by the arrow-heads which I turned up in hoeing, that an extinct nation had anciently dwelt here and planted corn and beans ere white men came to clear the land, and so, to some extent, had exhausted the soil for this very crop.

Before yet any woodchuck or squirrel had run across the road, or the sun had got above the shrub-oaks, while all the dew was on, though the farmers warned me against it, — I would advise you to do all your work if possible while the dew is on, — I began to level the ranks of haughty weeds in my bean-field and throw dust upon their heads. Early in the morning I worked barefooted, dabbling like a plastic artist in the dewy and crumbling sand, but later in the day the sun blistered my feet. There the sun lighted me to hoe beans, pacing slowly backward and forward over that yellow gravelly upland, between the long green rows, fifteen rods, the one end terminating in a shrub oak copse where I could rest in the shade, the other in a blackberry field where the green berries deepened their tints by the time I had made another bout. Removing the weeds, putting fresh soil about the bean stems, and encouraging this weed which I had sown, making the yellow soil express its summer thought in bean leaves and blossoms rather than in wormwood and piper and millet grass, making the earth say beans instead of grass, — this was my daily work. As I had little aid from horses or cattle, or hired men or boys, or improved implements of husbandry, I was much slower, and became much more intimate with my beans than usual. But labor of the hands, even when pursued to the verge of drudgery, is perhaps never the worst form of idleness. It has a constant and imperishable moral, and to the scholar it yields a classic result.

A very *agricola laboriosus*[2] was I to travellers bound westward through Lincoln and Wayland to nobody knows where; they sitting at their ease in gigs, with elbows on knees, and reins loosely hanging in festoons; I the home-staying, laborious native of the soil. But soon my homestead was out of their sight and thought. It was the only open and cultivated field for a great distance on either side of the road; so they made the most of it; and sometimes the man in the field heard more of travellers' gossip and comment than was meant for his ear: "Beans so late! peas so late!" — for I continued to plant when others had began to hoe, — the ministerial husbandman[3] had not suspected it. "Corn, my boy, for fodder; corn for fodder." "Does he *live* there?" asks the black bonnet of the gray coat; and the hard-featured farmer reins up his grateful dobbin to inquire what you are doing where he sees no manure in the furrow, and recommends a little chip dirt, or any little waste stuff, or it may be ashes or plaster. But here were two acres and a half of furrows, and only a hoe for cart and two hands to draw it, — there being an aversion to other carts and horses, — and chip dirt far away. Fellow-travellers as they rattled by compared it aloud with the fields which they had passed, so that I came to know how I stood in the agricultural world. This was one field not in Mr. Coleman's report. And, by the way, who estimates the value of the crop which Nature yields in the still wilder fields unimproved by man? The crop of *English* hay is carefully weighed, the moisture calculated, the silicates and the potash; but in all dells and pond holes in the woods and pastures and swamps grows a rich and various crop only unreaped by man. Mine was, as it were, the connecting link between wild and cultivated fields; as some states are civilized, and others half-civilized, and others savage or barbarous, so my field was, though not in a bad sense, a half-cultivated field. They were beans cheerfully returning to their wild and primitive state that I cultivated, and my hoe played the *Rans de Vaches*[4] for them.

Near at hand, upon the topmost spray of a birch, sings the brown-thrasher — or red mavis, as some love to call him — all the morning, glad of your society, that would find out another farmer's field if yours were not here. While you are planting the seed, he cries, — "Drop it, drop it, — cover it up, cover it up, — pull it up, pull it up, pull it up." But this was not corn, and so it was safe from such enemies as he. You may wonder what his rigmarole, his amateur Paganini[5] performances on one string or on twenty, have to do with your planting, and yet prefer it to leached ashes or plaster. It was a cheap sort of top dressing in which I had entire faith.

As I drew a still fresher soil about the rows with my hoe, I disturbed the ashes of unchronicled nations who in primeval years lived under these heavens, and their small

---

2. *agricola laboriosus*: Latin for hard-working farmer; the road past Walden Pond leads from Concord to the neighboring town of Lincoln and from there westward to Wayland, Massachusetts.

3. **ministerial husbandman:** The Reverend Henry Coleman (1785–1849), author of several surveys of agriculture in Massachusetts, which Thoreau refers to later in this paragraph.

4. *Rans de Vaches*: A song sung or played by Swiss herdsmen to call their cattle. The vogue of such mountain songs in the 1840s led to the publication of several collections, notably William Bradbury's *The Alpine Glee Singer* (1850).

5. **Paganini:** Nicolo Paganini (1782–1840), Italian composer and violin virtuoso acclaimed for his ability to play on one string.

implements of war and hunting were brought to the light of this modern day. They lay mingled with other natural stones, some of which bore the marks of having been burned by Indian fires, and some by the sun, and also bits of pottery and glass brought hither by the recent cultivators of the soil. When my hoe tinkled against the stones, that music echoed to the woods and the sky, and was an accompaniment to my labor which yielded an instant and immeasurable crop. It was no longer beans that I hoed, nor I that hoed beans; and I remembered with as much pity as pride, if I remembered at all, my acquaintances who had gone to the city to attend the oratorios. The night-hawk circled overhead in the sunny afternoons – for I sometimes made a day of it – like a mote in the eye, or in heaven's eye, falling from time to time with a swoop and a sound as if the heavens were rent, torn at last to very rags and tatters, and yet a seamless cope remained; small imps that fill the air and lay their eggs on the ground on bare sand or rocks on the tops of hills, where few have found them; graceful and slender like ripples caught up from the pond, as leaves are raised by the wind to float in the heavens; such kindredship is in Nature. The hawk is aerial brother of the wave which he sails over and surveys, those his perfect air-inflated wings answering to the elemental unfledged pinions of the sea. Or sometimes I watched a pair of hen-hawks circling high in the sky, alternately soaring and descending, approaching and leaving one another, as if they were the imbodiment of my own thoughts. Or I was attracted by the passage of wild pigeons from this wood to that, with a slight quivering winnowing sound and carrier haste; or from under a rotten stump my hoe turned up a sluggish portentous and outlandish spotted salamander, a trace of Egypt and the Nile, yet our contemporary. When I paused to lean on my hoe, these sounds and sights I heard and saw any where in the row, a part of the inexhaustible entertainment which the country offers.

On gala days the town fires its great guns, which echo like popguns to these woods, and some waifs of martial music occasionally penetrate thus far. To me, away there in my bean-field at the other end of the town, the big guns sounded as if a puff ball had burst; and when there was a military turnout of which I was ignorant, I have sometimes had a vague sense all the day of some sort of itching and disease in the horizon, as if some eruption would break out there soon, either scarlatina or canker-rash, until at length some more favorable puff of wind, making haste over the fields and up the Wayland road, brought me information of the "trainers."[6] It seemed by the distant hum as if somebody's bees had swarmed, and that the neighbors, according to Virgil's advice,[7] by a faint *tintinnabulum* upon the most sonorous of their domestic utensils, were endeavoring to call them down into the hive again. And when the sound died quite away, and the hum had ceased, and the most favorable breezes told no tale, I knew that they had got the last drone of them all safely into the Middlesex hive, and that now their minds were bent on the honey with which it was smeared.

---

6. **On gala days . . . "trainers":** Concord was the home of the Concord Artillery, a state militia unit known as the "trainers," who fired their guns on the gala days of April 19, the anniversary of the Concord fight of 1775, and July 4. They evidently also fired them to celebrate news of victories in the Mexican War, which Thoreau alludes to in the following paragraphs.

7. **Virgil's advice:** In book 4 of the *Georgics* by the Roman poet Virgil (70–19 BCE).

I felt proud to know that the liberties of Massachusetts and of our fatherland were in such safe keeping; and as I turned to my hoeing again I was filled with an inexpressible confidence, and pursued my labor cheerfully with a calm trust in the future.

When there were several bands of musicians, it sounded as if all the village was a vast bellows, and all the buildings expanded and collapsed alternately with a din. But sometimes it was a really noble and inspiring strain that reached these woods, and the trumpet that sings of fame, and I felt as if I could spit a Mexican with a good relish, – for why should we always stand for trifles? – and looked round for a woodchuck or a skunk to exercise my chivalry upon. These martial strains seemed as far away as Palestine, and reminded me of a march of crusaders in the horizon, with a slight tantivy and tremulous motion of the elm-tree tops which overhang the village. This was one of the *great* days; though the sky had from my clearing only the same everlastingly great look that it wears daily, and I saw no difference in it.

It was a singular experience that long acquaintance which I cultivated with beans, what with planting, and hoeing, and harvesting, and threshing, and picking over, and selling them, – the last was the hardest of all, – I might add eating, for I did taste. I was determined to know beans. When they were growing, I used to hoe from five o'clock in the morning till noon, and commonly spent the rest of the day about other affairs. Consider the intimate and curious acquaintance one makes with various kinds of weeds, – it will bear some iteration in the account, for there was no little iteration in the labor, – disturbing their delicate organizations so ruthlessly, and making such invidious distinctions with his hoe, levelling whole ranks of one species, and sedulously cultivating another. That's Roman wormwood, – that's pigweed, – that's sorrel, – that's piper-grass, – have at him, chop him up, turn his roots upward to the sun, don't let him have a fibre in the shade, if you do he'll turn himself t'other side up and be as green as a leek in two days. A long war, not with cranes, but with weeds, those Trojans who had sun and rain and dews on their side. Daily the beans saw me come to their rescue armed with a hoe, and thin the ranks of their enemies, filling up the trenches with weedy dead. Many a lusty crest-waving Hector,[8] that towered a whole foot above his crowding comrades, fell before my weapon and rolled in the dust.

Those summer days which some of my contemporaries devoted to the fine arts in Boston or Rome, and others to contemplation in India, and others to trade in London or New York, I thus, with the other farmers of New England, devoted to husbandry. Not that I wanted beans to eat, for I am by nature a Pythagorean, so far as beans are concerned, whether they mean porridge or voting,[9] and exchanged them for rice; but, perchance, as some must work in fields if only for the sake of tropes and expression, to serve a parable-maker one day. It was on the whole a rare amusement, which, continued too long, might have become a dissipation. Though I gave them no manure, and did not hoe them all once, I hoed them unusually well as far as I went, and was paid for it in the end,

---

8. **Hector:** The bravest of the Trojan warriors in Homer's *Iliad.*
9. **Pythagorean . . . voting:** The Greek philosopher Pythagoras (570?-490? BCE) refused to eat beans, which in ancient times were also often used to tally votes.

"there being in truth," as Evelyn[10] says, "no compost or laetation whatsoever comparable to this continual motion, repastination, and turning of the mould with the spade." "The earth," he adds elsewhere, "especially if fresh, has a certain magnetism in it, by which it attracts the salt, power, or virtue (call it either) which gives it life, and is the logic of all the labor and stir we keep about it, to sustain us; all dungings and other sordid temperings being but the vicars succedaneous to this improvement." Moreover, this being one of those "worn-out and exhausted lay fields which enjoy their sabbath," had perchance, as Sir Kenelm Digby[11] thinks likely, attracted "vital spirits" from the air. I harvested twelve bushels of beans.

But to be more particular, for it is complained that Mr. Coleman has reported chiefly the expensive experiments of gentlemen farmers, my outgoes were, –

For a hoe, ...	$ 0 54
Ploughing, harrowing, and furrowing, ...	7 50, Too much.
Beans for seed, ...	3 12½
Potatoes "	1 33
Peas "	0 40
Turnip seed, ...	0 06
White line for crow fence, ...	0 02
Horse cultivator and boy three hours, ...	1 00
Horse and cart to get crop, ...	0 75
In all, ...	$14 72½

My income was, (*patrem familias vendacem, non emacem esse oportet,*[12]) from

Nine bushels and twelve quarts of beans sold, ...	$16 94
Five " large potatoes, ...	2 50
Nine " small, ...	2 25
Grass, ...	1 00
Stalks, ...	0 75
In all, ...	$23 44

Leaving a pecuniary profit, as I have elsewhere said, of $ 8 71½.

This is the result of my experience in raising beans. Plant the common small white bush bean about the first of June, in rows three feet by eighteen inches apart, being careful to select fresh round and unmixed seed. First look out for worms, and supply vacancies by planting anew. Then look out for woodchucks, if it is an exposed place, for they will nibble off the earliest tender leaves almost clean as they go; and again, when the young tendrils make their appearance, they have notice of it, and will shear them off

---

10. **Evelyn:** John Evelyn (1620-1706), English diarist and writer; from his *Terra, a Philosophical Discourse of Earth* (1729).
11. **Sir Kenelm Digby:** English scientist (1603-1665); quoted in Evelyn's *Sylva, or a Discourse of Forest-Trees* (1679).
12. *patrem . . . oportet:* Cato, *De agri cultura,* 2.7: "The father of the family should have the habit of selling, not buying" (Latin).

with both buds and young pods, sitting erect like a squirrel. But above all harvest as early as possible, if you would escape frosts and have a fair and salable crop; you may save much loss by this means.

This further experience also I gained. I said to myself, I will not plant beans and corn with so much industry another summer, but such seeds, if the seed is not lost, as sincerity, truth, simplicity, faith, innocence, and the like, and see if they will not grow in this soil, even with less toil and manurance, and sustain me, for surely it has not been exhausted for these crops. Alas! I said this to myself; but now another summer is gone, and another, and another, and I am obliged to say to you, Reader, that the seeds which I planted, if indeed they *were* the seeds of those virtues, were wormeaten or had lost their vitality, and so did not come up. Commonly men will only be brave as their fathers were brave, or timid. This generation is very sure to plant corn and beans each new year precisely as the Indians did centuries ago and taught the first settlers to do, as if there were a fate in it. I saw an old man the other day, to my astonishment, making the holes with a hoe for the seventieth time at least, and not for himself to lie down in! But why should not the New Englander try new adventures, and not lay so much stress on his grain, his potato and grass crop, and his orchards,—raise other crops than these? Why concern ourselves so much about our beans for seed, and not be concerned at all about a new generation of men? We should really be fed and cheered if when we met a man we were sure to see that some of the qualities which I have named, which we all prize more than those other productions, but which are for the most part broadcast and floating in the air, had taken root and grown in him. Here comes such a subtile and ineffable quality, for instance, as truth or justice, though the slightest amount or new variety of it, along the road. Our ambassadors should be instructed to send home such seeds as these, and Congress help to distribute them over all the land.[13] We should never stand upon ceremony with sincerity. We should never cheat and insult and banish one another by our meanness, if there were present the kernel of worth and friendliness. We should not meet thus in haste. Most men I do not meet at all, for they seem not to have time; they are busy about their beans. We would not deal with a man thus plodding ever, leaning on a hoe or a spade as a staff between his work, not as a mushroom, but partially risen out of the earth, something more than erect, like swallows alighted and walking on the ground: —

> "And as he spake, his wings would now and then
> Spread, as he meant to fly, then close again,"[14]

so that we should suspect that we might be conversing with an angel. Bread may not always nourish us; but it always does us good, it even takes stiffness out of our joints, and makes us supple and buoyant, when we knew not what ailed us, to recognize any generosity in man or Nature, to share any unmixed and heroic joy.

---

13. **Congress . . . land:** It was then a popular custom for members of Congress to send free seeds to constituents who requested them.
14. **"And . . . again":** From *The Shepherd's Oracles*, by the English poet Frances Quarles (1592–1644).

Ancient poetry and mythology suggest, at least, that husbandry was once a sacred art; but it is pursued with irreverent haste and heedlessness by us, our object being to have large farms and large crops merely. We have no festival, nor procession, nor ceremony, not excepting our Cattle-shows and so called Thanksgivings, by which the farmer expresses a sense of the sacredness of his calling, or is reminded of its sacred origin. It is the premium and the feast which tempt him. He sacrifices not to Ceres and the Terrestrial Jove, but to the infernal Plutus[15] rather. By avarice and selfishness, and a grovelling habit, from which none of us is free, of regarding the soil as property, or the means of acquiring property chiefly, the landscape is deformed, husbandry is degraded with us, and the farmer leads the meanest of lives. He knows Nature but as a robber. Cato says that the profits of agriculture are particularly pious or just, (*maximeque pius quoestus*,) and according to Varro the old Romans "called the same earth Mother and Ceres, and thought that they who cultivated it led a pious and useful life, and that they alone were left of the race of King Saturn."[16]

We are wont to forget that the sun looks on our cultivated fields and on the prairies and forests without distinction. They all reflect and absorb his rays alike, and the former make but a small part of the glorious picture which he beholds in his daily course. In his view the earth is all equally cultivated like a garden. Therefore we should receive the benefit of his light and heat with a corresponding trust and magnanimity. What though I value the seed of these beans, and harvest that in the fall of the year? This broad field which I have looked at so long looks not to me as the principal cultivator, but away from me to influences more genial to it, which water and make it green. These beans have results which are not harvested by me. Do they not grow for woodchucks partly? The ear of wheat, (in Latin *spica*, obsoletely *speca*, from *spe*, hope,) should not be the only hope of the husbandman; its kernel or grain (*granum*, from *gerendo*, bearing,) is not all that it bears. How, then, can our harvest fail? Shall I not rejoice also at the abundance of the weeds whose seeds are the granary of the birds? It matters little comparatively whether the fields fill the farmer's barns. The true husbandman will cease from anxiety, as the squirrels manifest no concern whether the woods will bear chestnuts this year or not, and finish his labor with every day, relinquishing all claim to the produce of his fields, and sacrificing in his mind not only his first but his last fruits also.

The Village

After hoeing, or perhaps reading and writing, in the forenoon, I usually bathed again in the pond, swimming across one of its coves for a stint, and washed the dust of labor from my person, or smoothed out the last wrinkle which study had made, and for the afternoon was absolutely free. Every day or two I strolled to the village to hear some of the gossip which is incessantly going on there, circulating either from mouth to mouth,

---

15. **Ceres . . . Jove . . . Plutus:** In Roman mythology, Ceres was the goddess of the harvest; Jove, or Jupiter, was the ruler of heaven and earth; and Plutus was the god of wealth.
16. **"called . . . Saturn":** From the *Rerum Rusticarum* by Marcus Terentius Varro (116–27 BCE); Saturn was the Roman god of agriculture and the harvest.

or from newspaper, to newspaper, and which, taken in homoeopathic doses,[1] was really as refreshing in its way as the rustle of leaves and the peeping of frogs. As I walked in the woods to see the birds and squirrels, so I walked in the village to see the men and boys; instead of the wind among the pines I heard the carts rattle. In one direction from my house there was a colony of muskrats in the river meadows; under the grove of elms and buttonwoods in the other horizon was a village of busy men, as curious to me as if they had been prairie dogs, each sitting at the mouth of its burrow, or running over to a neighbor's to gossip. I went there frequently to observe their habits. The village appeared to me a great news room; and on one side, to support it, as once at Redding & Company's on State Street, they kept nuts and raisins, or salt and meal and other groceries. Some have such a vast appetite for the former commodity, that is, the news, and such sound digestive organs, that they can sit forever in public avenues without stirring, and let it simmer and whisper through them like the Etesian winds,[2] or as if inhaling ether, it only producing numbness and insensibility to pain, — otherwise it would often be painful to hear, — without affecting the consciousness. I hardly ever failed, when I rambled through the village, to see a row of such worthies, either sitting on a ladder sunning themselves, with their bodies inclined forward and their eyes glancing along the line this way and that, from time to time, with a voluptuous expression, or else leaning against a barn with their hands in their pockets, like caryatides, as if to prop it up. They, being commonly out of doors, heard whatever was in the wind. These are the coarsest mills, in which all gossip is first rudely digested or cracked up before it is emptied into finer and more delicate hoppers within doors. I observed that the vitals of the village were the grocery, the bar-room, the post-office, and the bank; and, as a necessary part of the machinery, they kept a bell, a big gun, and a fire-engine, at convenient places; and the houses were so arranged as to make the most of mankind, in lanes and fronting one another, so that every traveller had to run the gantlet, and every man, woman, and child might get a lick at him. Of course, those who were stationed nearest to the head of the line, where they could most see and be seen, and have the first blow at him, paid the highest prices for their places; and the few straggling inhabitants in the outskirts, where long gaps in the line began to occur, and the traveller could get over walls or turn aside into cow paths, and so escape, paid a very slight ground or window tax. Signs were hung out on all sides to allure him; some to catch him by the appetite, as the tavern and victualling cellar; some by the fancy, as the dry goods store and the jeweller's; and others by the hair or the feet or the skirts, as the barber, the shoemaker, or the tailor. Besides, there was a still more terrible standing invitation to call at every one of these houses, and company expected about these times. For the most part I escaped wonderfully from these dangers, either by proceeding at once boldly and without deliberation to the goal, as is recommended to those who run the gantlet, or by keeping my thoughts on high things, like Orpheus, who, "loudly singing the praises of the gods to his lyre,

---

1. **homoeopathic doses:** In homeopathic medicine, doctors sought to cure diseases by giving patients small doses of drugs that in healthy people produced symptoms similar to those of the disease.
2. **Etesian winds:** Winds in the Mediterranean that blow from the north every summer.

drowned the voices of the Sirens, and kept out of danger."[3] Sometimes I bolted suddenly, and nobody could tell my whereabouts, for I did not stand much about gracefulness, and never hesitated at a gap in a fence. I was even accustomed to make an irruption into some houses, where I was well entertained, and after learning the kernels and very last sieve-ful of news, what had subsided, the prospects of war and peace, and whether the world was likely to hold together much longer, I was let out through the rear avenues, and so escaped to the woods again.

It was very pleasant, when I staid late in town, to launch myself into the night, espe-cially if it was dark and tempestuous, and set sail from some bright village parlor or lecture room, with a bag of rye or Indian meal upon my shoulder, for my snug harbor in the woods, having made all tight without and withdrawn under hatches with a merry crew of thoughts, leaving only my outer man at the helm, or even tying up the helm when it was plain sailing. I had many a genial thought by the cabin fire "as I sailed." I was never cast away nor distressed in any weather, though I encountered some severe storms. It is darker in the woods, even in common nights, than most suppose. I fre-quently had to look up at the opening between the trees above the path in order to learn my route, and, where there was no cart-path, to feel with my feet the faint track which I had worn, or steer by the known relation of particular trees which I felt with my hands, passing between two pines for instance, not more than eighteen inches apart, in the midst of the woods, invariably in the darkest night. Sometimes, after coming home thus late in a dark and muggy night, when my feet felt the path which my eyes could not see, dreaming and absent-minded all the way, until I was aroused by having to raise my hand to lift the latch, I have not been able to recall a single step of my walk, and I have thought that perhaps my body would find its way home if its master should forsake it, as the hand finds its way to the mouth without assistance. Several times, when a visitor chanced to stay into evening, and it proved a dark night, I was obliged to conduct him to the cart-path in the rear of the house, and then point out to him the direction he was to pursue, and in keeping which he was to be guided rather by his feet than his eyes. One very dark night I directed thus on their way two young men who had been fishing in the pond. They lived about a mile off through the woods, and were quite used to the route. A day or two after one of them told me that they wandered about the greater part of the night, close by their own premises, and did not get home till toward morning, by which time, as there had been several heavy showers in the mean while, and the leaves were very wet, they were drenched to their skins. I have heard of many going astray even in the village streets, when the darkness was so thick that you could cut it with a knife, as the saying is. Some who live in the outskirts, having come to town a-shopping in their wagons, have been obliged to put up for the night; and gentlemen and ladies making a call have gone half a mile out of their way, feeling the sidewalk only with their feet, and not knowing when they turned. It is a surprising and memorable, as well as valuable experience, to be lost in the woods any time. Often in a snow storm, even by day, one will come out upon a well-known road and yet find it impossible to tell which way leads to

---

3. "loudly . . . danger": This is apparently Thoreau's translation or close paraphrase of a passage from the *Argonautica*, written in ancient Greek by the Alexandrian poet Apollonius Rhodius.

the village. Though he knows that he has travelled it a thousand times, he cannot recognize a feature in it, but it is as strange to him as if it were a road in Siberia. By night, of course, the perplexity is infinitely greater. In our most trivial walks, we are constantly, though unconsciously, steering like pilots by certain well-known beacons and headlands, and if we go beyond our usual course we still carry in our minds the bearing of some neighboring cape; and not till we are completely lost, or turned round, – for a man needs only to be turned round once with his eyes shut in this world to be lost, – do we appreciate the vastness and strangeness of Nature. Every man has to learn the points of compass again as often as he awakes, whether from sleep or any abstraction. Not till we are lost, in other words, not till we have lost the world, do we begin to find ourselves, and realize where we are and the infinite extent of our relations.

One afternoon, near the end of the first summer, when I went to the village to get a shoe from the cobbler's, I was seized and put into jail, because, as I have elsewhere related,[4] I did not pay a tax to, or recognize the authority of, the state which buys and sells men, women, and children, like cattle at the door of its senate-house. I had gone down to the woods for other purposes. But, wherever a man goes, men will pursue and paw him with their dirty institutions, and, if they can, constrain him to belong to their desperate odd-fellow society. It is true, I might have resisted forcibly with more or less effect, might have run "amok" against society; but I preferred that society should run "amok" against me, it being the desperate party. However, I was released the next day, obtained my mended shoe, and returned to the woods in season to get my dinner of huckleberries on Fair-Haven Hill. I was never molested by any person but those who represented the state. I had no lock nor bolt but for the desk which held my papers, not even a nail to put over my latch or windows. I never fastened my door night or day, though I was to be absent several days; not even when the next fall I spent a fortnight in the woods of Maine. And yet my house was more respected than if it had been surrounded by a file of soldiers. The tired rambler could rest and warm himself by my fire, the literary amuse himself with the few books on my table, or the curious, by opening my closet door, see what was left of my dinner, and what prospect I had of a supper. Yet, though many people of every class came this way to the pond, I suffered no serious inconvenience from these sources, and I never missed any thing but one small book, a volume of Homer, which perhaps was improperly gilded, and this I trust a soldier of our camp has found by this time. I am convinced, that if all men were to live as simply as I then did, thieving and robbery would be unknown. These take place only in communities where some have got more than is sufficient while others have not enough. The Pope's Homers[5] would soon get properly distributed. –

> "Nec bella fuerunt,
> *Faginus astabat dum scyphus ante dapes.*"[6]
> "Nor wars did men molest,
> When only beechen bowls were in request."

---

4. **as I have elsewhere related:** In "Resistance to Civil Government."
5. **Pope's Homers:** The English poet Alexander Pope (1688-1744) translated both the *Iliad* and the *Odyssey*.
6. **"Nec . . . dapes":** From the *Elegies* of the Roman poet Albius Tibullus (55?-19? BCE).

"You who govern public affairs, what need have you to employ punishments? Love virtue, and the people will be virtuous. The virtues of a superior man are like the wind; the virtues of a common man are like the grass; the grass, when the wind passes over it, bends."[7]

Conclusion

To the sick the doctors wisely recommend a change of air and scenery. Thank Heaven, here is not all the world. The buck-eye does not grow in New England, and the mocking-bird is rarely heard here. The wild-goose is more of a cosmopolite than we; he breaks his fast in Canada, takes a luncheon in the Ohio, and plumes himself for the night in a southern bayou. Even the bison, to some extent, keeps pace with the seasons, cropping the pastures of the Colorado only till a greener and sweeter grass awaits him by the Yellowstone. Yet we think that if rail-fences are pulled down, and stone-walls piled up on our farms, bounds are henceforth set to our lives and our fates decided. If you are chosen town-clerk, forsooth, you cannot go to Tierra del Fuego this summer: but you may go to the land of infernal fire nevertheless. The universe is wider than our views of it.

Yet we should oftener look over the tafferel of our craft, like curious passengers, and not make the voyage like stupid sailors picking oakum.[1] The other side of the globe is but the home of our correspondent. Our voyaging is only great-circle sailing, and the doctors prescribe for diseases of the skin merely. One hastens to Southern Africa to chase the giraffe; but surely that is not the game he would be after. How long, pray, would a man hunt giraffes if he could? Snipes and woodcocks also may afford rare sport; but I trust it would be nobler game to shoot one's self. —

> "Direct your eye right inward, and you'll find
> A thousand regions in your mind
> Yet undiscovered. Travel them, and be
> Expert in home-cosmography."[2]

What does Africa, — what does the West stand for? Is not our own interior white on the chart? black though it may prove, like the coast, when discovered. Is it the source of the Nile, or the Niger, or the Mississippi, or a North-West Passage around this continent, that we would find? Are these the problems which most concern mankind? Is Franklin the only man who is lost, that his wife should be so earnest to find him? Does Mr. Grinnell[3] know where he himself is? Be rather the Mungo Park, the Lewis and

---

7. **"You . . . bends"**: Confucius, *Analects*, 12.19.

1. **picking oakum:** Used for caulking seams in a ship, oakum was obtained by the tedious process of untwisting and picking out strands of old rope.

2. **"Direct . . . home-cosmography":** From "To My Honored Friend Sir Ed. P. Knight" by the English poet William Habbington (1605–1664). The first line in the original version of the poem read "eye sight," not "eye right," though it is not clear whether that alteration was intentional or simply a printer's error.

3. **Franklin . . . Grinnell:** John Franklin (1786–1847), English explorer lost in the Arctic while trying to find the Northwest Passage; several expeditions were sent to find him, including one funded by Henry Grinnell (1799–1874), a wealthy merchant from New York.

Clarke and Frobisher,[4] of your own streams and oceans; explore your own higher latitudes, — with shiploads of preserved meats to support you, if they be necessary; and pile the empty cans sky-high for a sign. Were preserved meats invented to preserve meat merely? Nay, be a Columbus to whole new continents and worlds within you, opening new channels, not of trade, but of thought. Every man is the lord of a realm beside which the earthly empire of the Czar is but a petty state, a hummock left by the ice. Yet some can be patriotic who have no *self*-respect, and sacrifice the greater to the less. They love the soil which makes their graves, but have no sympathy with the spirit which may still animate their clay. Patriotism is a maggot in their heads. What was the meaning of that South-Sea Exploring Expedition,[5] with all its parade and expense, but an indirect recognition of the fact, that there are continents and seas in the moral world, to which every man is an isthmus or an inlet, yet unexplored by him, but that it is easier to sail many thousand miles through cold and storm and cannibals, in a government ship with five hundred men and boys to assist one, than it is to explore the private sea, the Atlantic and Pacific Ocean of one's being alone. —

> "*Erret, et extremos alter scrutetur Iberos.*
> *Plus habet hic vitae, plus habet ille viae.*"[6]

> Let them wander and scrutinize the outlandish Australians.
> I have more of God, they more of the road.

It is not worth the while to go round the world to count the cats in Zanzibar.[7] Yet do this even till you can do better, and you may perhaps find some "Symmes' Hole"[8] by which to get at the inside at last. England and France, Spain and Portugal, Gold Coast and Slave Coast, all front on this private sea; but no bark from them has ventured out of sight of land, though it is without doubt the direct way to India. If you would learn to speak all tongues and conform to the customs of all nations, if you would travel farther than all travellers, be naturalized in all climes, and cause the Sphinx[9] to dash her head against a stone, even obey the precept of the old philosopher, and Explore thyself. Herein are demanded the eye and the nerve. Only the defeated and deserters go to the wars, cowards that run away and enlist. Start now on that farthest western way, which does not pause at the Mississippi or the Pacific, nor conduct toward a worn-out China or Japan, but leads on direct a tangent to this sphere, summer and winter, day and night, sun down, moon down, and at last earth down too.

---

4. **Mungo Park . . . Frobisher**: Mungo Park (1771–1806), Scottish explorer of Africa; Martin Frobisher (1535?–1594), English explorer and navigator who attempted to find the Northwest Passage.
5. **South-Sea Exploring Expedition**: Charles Wilkes (1798–1877) led a U.S. exploring expedition to the Antarctic and Pacific in 1838–42.
6. **"Erret . . . viae"**: From "The Old Man of Verona" by the fourth-century Latin poet Claudian.
7. **cats in Zanzibar**: One of the many subjects discussed in Charles Pickering's *The Races of Man* (1851). Zanzibar is an island off the east coast of Africa.
8. **"Symmes' Hole"**: In 1818, John Symmes published a pamphlet in which he argued that "the earth is hollow and habitable within."
9. **Sphinx**: In Greek mythology, a winged monster with a woman's head and a lion's body who killed any passersby who could not solve her riddle. When Oedipus did so, she destroyed herself by dashing her head against a rock.

It is said that Mirabeau[10] took to highway robbery "to ascertain what degree of resolution was necessary in order to place one's self in formal opposition to the most sacred laws of society." He declared that "a soldier who fights in the ranks does not require half so much courage as a foot-pad," – "that honor and religion have never stood in the way of a well-considered and a firm resolve." This was manly, as the world goes; and yet it was idle, if not desperate. A saner man would have found himself often enough "in formal opposition" to what are deemed "the most sacred laws of society," through obedience to yet more sacred laws, and so have tested his resolution without going out of his way. It is not for a man to put himself in such an attitude to society, but to maintain himself in whatever attitude he find himself through obedience to the laws of his being, which will never be one of opposition to a just government, if he should chance to meet with such.

I left the woods for as good a reason as I went there. Perhaps it seemed to me that I had several more lives to live, and could not spare any more time for that one. It is remarkable how easily and insensibly we fall into a particular route, and make a beaten track for ourselves. I had not lived there a week before my feet wore a path from my door to the pond-side; and though it is five or six years since I trod it, it is still quite distinct. It is true, I fear that others may have fallen into it, and so helped to keep it open. The surface of the earth is soft and impressible by the feet of men; and so with the paths which the mind travels. How worn and dusty, then, must be the highways of the world, how deep the ruts of tradition and conformity! I did not wish to take a cabin passage, but rather to go before the mast and on the deck of the world, for there I could best see the moonlight amid the mountains. I do not wish to go below now.

I learned this, at least, by my experiment; that if one advances confidently in the direction of his dreams, and endeavors to live the life which he has imagined, he will meet with a success unexpected in common hours. He will put some things behind, will pass an invisible boundary; new, universal, and more liberal laws will begin to establish themselves around and within him; or the old laws be expanded, and interpreted in his favor in a more liberal sense, and he will live with the license of a higher order of beings. In proportion as he simplifies his life, the laws of the universe will appear less complex, and solitude will not be solitude, nor poverty poverty, nor weakness weakness. If you have built castles in the air, your work need not be lost; that is where they should be. Now put the foundations under them.

It is a ridiculous demand which England and America make, that you shall speak so that they can understand you. Neither men nor toad-stools grow so. As if that were important, and there were not enough to understand you without them. As if Nature could support but one order of understandings, could not sustain birds as well as quadrupeds, flying as well as creeping things, and *hush* and *who*, which Bright[11] can understand, were the best English. As if there were safety in stupidity alone. I fear chiefly lest my expression may not be *extra-vagant* enough, may not wander far enough beyond the narrow limits of my daily experience, so as to be adequate to the truth of which I have

---

10. **Mirabeau:** Honoré-Gabriel Riqueti, Comte de Mirabeau (1749–1791), statesman of the French Revolution.
11. **Bright:** Common name for an ox.

been convinced. *Extra vagance!* it depends on how you are yarded. The migrating buffalo, which seeks new pastures in another latitude, is not extravagant like the cow which kicks over the pail, leaps the cow-yard fence, and runs after her calf, in milking time. I desire to speak somewhere *without* bounds; like a man in a waking moment, to men in their waking moments; for I am convinced that I cannot exaggerate enough even to lay the foundation of a true expression. Who that has heard a strain of music feared then lest he should speak extravagantly any more forever? In view of the future or possible, we should live quite laxly and undefined in front, our outlines dim and misty on that side; as our shadows reveal an insensible perspiration toward the sun. The volatile truth of our words should continually betray the inadequacy of the residual statement. Their truth is instantly *translated*; its literal monument alone remains. The words which express our faith and piety are not definite; yet they are significant and fragrant like frankincense to superior natures.

Why level downward to our dullest perception always, and praise that as common sense? The commonest sense is the sense of men asleep, which they express by snoring. Sometimes we are inclined to class those who are once-and-a-half witted with the half-witted, because we appreciate only a third part of their wit. Some would find fault with the morning-red, if they ever got up early enough. "They pretend," as I hear, "that the verses of Kabir have four different senses; illusion, spirit, intellect, and the exoteric doctrine of the Vedas";[12] but in this part of the world it is considered a ground for complaint if a man's writings admit of more than one interpretation. While England endeavors to cure the potato-rot, will not any endeavor to cure the brain-rot, which prevails so much more widely and fatally?

I do not suppose that I have attained to obscurity, but I should be proud if no more fatal fault were found with my pages on this score than was found with the Walden ice. Southern customers objected to its blue color, which is the evidence of its purity, as if it were muddy, and preferred the Cambridge ice, which is white, but tastes of weeds. The purity men love is like the mists which envelop the earth, and not like the azure ether beyond.

Some are dinning in our ears that we Americans, and moderns generally, are intellectual dwarfs compared with the ancients, or even the Elizabethan men. But what is that to the purpose? A living dog is better than a dead lion. Shall a man go and hang himself because he belongs to the race of pygmies, and not be the biggest pygmy that he can? Let every one mind his own business, and endeavor to be what he was made.

Why should we be in such desperate haste to succeed, and in such desperate enterprises? If a man does not keep pace with his companions, perhaps it is because he hears a different drummer. Let him step to the music which he hears, however measured or far away. It is not important that he should mature as soon as an apple-tree or an oak. Shall he turn his spring into summer? If the condition of things which we were made for is not yet, what were any reality which we can substitute? We will not be shipwrecked on a vain reality. Shall we with pains erect a heaven of blue glass over ourselves, though when it is done we shall be sure to gaze still at the true ethereal heaven far above, as if the former were not?

---

12. **"They . . . Vedas"**: From Garcin de Tassy, *Histoire de la Littérature Hindoui* (1839); Kabir was a fifteenth-century poet and mystic who attracted both Hindu and Muslim followers.

There was an artist in the city of Kouroo who was disposed to strive after perfection. One day it came into his mind to make a staff. Having considered that in an imperfect work time is an ingredient, but into a perfect work time does not enter, he said to himself, It shall be perfect in all respects, though I should do nothing else in my life. He proceeded instantly to the forest for wood, being resolved that it should not be made of unsuitable material; and as he searched for and rejected stick after stick, his friends gradually deserted him, for they grew old in their works and died, but he grew not older by a moment. His singleness of purpose and resolution, and his elevated piety, endowed him, without his knowledge, with perennial youth. As he made no compromise with Time, Time kept out of his way, and only sighed at a distance because he could not overcome him. Before he had found a stock in all respects suitable the city of Kouroo was a hoary ruin, and he sat on one of its mounds to peel the stick. Before he had given it the proper shape the dynasty of the Candahars was at an end, and with the point of the stick he wrote the name of the last of that race in the sand, and then resumed his work. By the time he had smoothed and pol-ished the staff Kalpa was no longer the pole-star; and ere he had put on the ferule and the head adorned with precious stone, Brahma had awoke and slumbered many times. But why do I stay to mention these things? When the finishing stroke was put to his work, it suddenly expanded before the eyes of the astonished artist into the fairest of all the cre-ations of Brahma. He had made a new system in making a staff, a world with full and fair proportions; in which, though the old cities and dynasties had passed away, fairer and more glorious ones had taken their places. And now he saw by the heap of shavings still fresh at his feet, that, for him and his work, the former lapse of time had been an illusion, and that no more time had elapsed than is required for a single scintillation from the brain of Brahma to fall on and inflame the tinder of a mortal brain. The material was pure, and his art was pure; how could the result be other than wonderful?[13]

No face which we can give to a matter will stead us so well at last as the truth. This alone wears well. For the most part, we are not where we are, but in a false position. Through an infirmity of our natures, we suppose a case, and put ourselves into it, and hence are in two cases at the same time, and it is doubly difficult to get out. In sane moments we regard only the facts, the case that is. Say what you have to say, not what you ought. Any truth is better than make-believe. Tom Hyde, the tinker, standing on the gallows, was asked if he had any thing to say. "Tell the tailors," said he, "to remember to make a knot in their thread before they take the first stitch." His companion's prayer is forgotten.

However mean your life is, meet it and live it; do not shun it and call it hard names. It is not so bad as you are. It looks poorest when you are richest. The fault-finder will find faults even in paradise. Love your life, poor as it is. You may perhaps have some pleasant, thrilling, glorious hours, even in a poor-house. The setting sun is reflected from the win-dows of the alms-house as brightly as from the rich man's abode; the snow melts before its door as early in the spring. I do not see but a quiet mind may live as contentedly there, and have as cheering thoughts, as in a palace. The town's poor seem to me often to live the

---

13. **There . . . wonderful?:** Although it sounds like a version of a story from one of the ancient Hindu texts that were so important to Thoreau, he almost certainly composed this parable. In Hindu literature, Kalpa is not "the pole-star," as he indicates, but the long period of time between the creation and destruction of the world, at the end of which it is absorbed into Brahma and then re-created.

most independent lives of any. May be they are simply great enough to receive without misgiving. Most think that they are above being supported by the town; but it oftener happens that they are not above supporting themselves by dishonest means, which should be more disreputable. Cultivate poverty like a garden herb, like sage. Do not trouble yourself much to get new things, whether clothes or friends. Turn the old; return to them. Things do not change; we change. Sell your clothes and keep your thoughts. God will see that you do not want society. If I were confined to a corner of a garret all my days, like a spider, the world would be just as large to me while I had my thoughts about me. The philosopher said: "From an army of three divisions one can take away its general, and put it in disorder; from the man the most abject and vulgar one cannot take away his thought."[14] Do not seek so anxiously to be developed, to subject yourself to many influences to be played on; it is all dissipation. Humility like darkness reveals the heavenly lights. The shadows of poverty and meanness gather around us, "and lo! creation widens to our view."[15] We are often reminded that if there were bestowed on us the wealth of Croesus,[16] our aims must still be the same, and our means essentially the same. Moreover, if you are restricted in your range by poverty, if you cannot buy books and newspapers, for instance, you are but confined to the most significant and vital experiences; you are compelled to deal with the material which yields the most sugar and the most starch. It is life near the bone where it is sweetest. You are defended from being a trifler. No man loses ever on a lower level by magnanimity on a higher. Superfluous wealth can buy superfluities only. Money is not required to buy one necessary of the soul.

I live in the angle of a leaden wall, into whose composition was poured a little alloy of bell metal. Often, in the repose of my mid-day, there reaches my ears a confused *tintinnabulum* from without. It is the noise of my contemporaries. My neighbors tell me of their adventures with famous gentlemen and ladies, what notabilities they met at the dinner-table; but I am no more interested in such things than in the contents of the Daily Times. The interest and the conversation are about costume and manners chiefly; but a goose is a goose still, dress it as you will. They tell me of California and Texas, of England and the Indies, of the Hon. Mr. — of Georgia or of Massachusetts, all transient and fleeting phenomena, till I am ready to leap from their court-yard like the Mameluke bey.[17] I delight to come to my bearings, — not walk in procession with pomp and parade, in a conspicuous place, but to walk even with the Builder of the universe, if I may, — not to live in this restless, nervous, bustling, trivial Nineteenth Century, but stand or sit thoughtfully while it goes by. What are men celebrating? They are all on a committee of arrangements, and hourly expect a speech from somebody. God is only the president of the day, and Webster is his orator.[18] I love to weigh, to settle, to gravitate toward that which

14. **"From . . . thought":** Confucius, *Analects*, 9.25.

15. **"and lo! . . . view":** From "Night and Death" by the English ecclesiastical poet Joseph White (1775-1841).

16. **wealth of Croesus:** Croesus, ruler of the ancient Greek kingdom Lydia from 560-546 BCE, was renowned for his legendary wealth.

17. **like the Mameluke bey:** The Mamelukes were an Egyptian military caste massacred in 1811, all except one officer, or "bey," who reportedly escaped their citadel by leaping from a wall onto a horse.

18. **Webster is his orator:** Daniel Webster (1782-1852), senator from Massachusetts and one of the most famous orators of the period, who abolitionists like Thoreau believed had betrayed the antislavery cause by supporting the Compromise of 1850.

most strongly and rightfully attracts me; — not hang by the beam of the scale and try to weigh less, — not suppose a case, but take the case that is; to travel the only path I can, and that on which no power can resist me. It affords me no satisfaction to commence to spring an arch before I have got a solid foundation. Let us not play at kittlybenders.[19] There is a solid bottom every where. We read that the traveller asked the boy if the swamp before him had a hard bottom. The boy replied that it had. But presently the traveller's horse sank in up to the girths, and he observed to the boy, "I thought you said that this bog had a hard bottom." "So it has," answered the latter, "but you have not got half way to it yet." So it is with the bogs and quicksands of society; but he is an old boy that knows it. Only what is thought said or done at a certain rare coincidence is good. I would not be one of those who will foolishly drive a nail into mere lath and plastering; such a deed would keep me awake nights. Give me a hammer, and let me feel for the furrowing. Do not depend on the putty. Drive a nail home and clinch it so faithfully that you can wake up in the night and think of your work with satisfaction, — a work at which you would not be ashamed to invoke the Muse. So will help you God, and so only. Every nail driven should be as another rivet in the machine of the universe, you carrying on the work.

Rather than love, than money, than fame, give me truth. I sat at a table where were rich food and wine in abundance, and obsequious attendance, but sincerity and truth were not; and I went away hungry from the inhospitable board. The hospitality was as cold as the ices. I thought that there was no need of ice to freeze them. They talked to me of the age of the wine and the fame of the vintage; but I thought of an older, a newer, and purer wine, of a more glorious vintage, which they had not got, and could not buy. The style, the house and grounds and "entertainment" pass for nothing with me. I called on the king, but he made me wait in his hall, and conducted like a man incapacitated for hospitality. There was a man in my neighborhood who lived in a hollow tree. His manners were truly regal. I should have done better had I called on him.

How long shall we sit in our porticoes practising idle and musty virtues, which any work would make impertinent? As if one were to begin the day with long-suffering, and hire a man to hoe his potatoes; and in the afternoon go forth to practise Christian meekness and charity with goodness aforethought! Consider the China pride[20] and stagnant self-complacency of mankind. This generation reclines a little to congratulate itself on being the last of an illustrious line; and in Boston and London and Paris and Rome, thinking of its long descent, it speaks of its progress in art and science and literature with satisfaction. There are the Records of the Philosophical Societies, and the public Eulogies of *Great Men*! It is the good Adam contemplating his own virtue. "Yes, we have done great deeds, and sung divine songs, which shall never die," — that is, as long as *we* can remember them. The learned societies and great men of Assyria, — where are they? What youthful philosophers and experimentalists we are! There is not one of my readers who has yet lived a whole human life. These may be but the spring months in the life of the race. If we have had the seven-years' itch, we have not seen the seventeen-year locust

---

19. **kittlybenders:** A game in which children sought to run over thin ice without breaking through it.
20. **China pride:** In Thoreau's time, the Chinese were commonly viewed as smug and arrogant.

yet in Concord. We are acquainted with a mere pellicle of the globe on which we live. Most have not delved six feet beneath the surface, nor leaped as many above it. We know not where we are. Beside, we are sound asleep nearly half our time. Yet we esteem ourselves wise, and have an established order on the surface. Truly, we are deep thinkers, we are ambitious spirits! As I stand over the insect crawling amid the pine needles on the forest floor, and endeavoring to conceal itself from my sight, and ask myself why it will cherish those humble thoughts, and hide its head from me who might, perhaps, be its benefactor, and impart to its race some cheering information, I am reminded of the greater Benefactor and Intelligence that stands over me the human insect.

There is an incessant influx of novelty into the world, and yet we tolerate incredible dulness. I need only suggest what kind of sermons are still listened to in the most enlightened countries. There are such words as joy and sorrow, but they are only the burden of a psalm, sung with a nasal twang, while we believe in the ordinary and mean. We think that we can change our clothes only. It is said that the British Empire is very large and respectable, and that the United States are a first-rate power. We do not believe that a tide rises and falls behind every man which can float the British Empire like a chip, if he should ever harbor it in his mind. Who knows what sort of seventeen-year locust will next come out of the ground? The government of the world I live in was not framed, like that of Britain, in after-dinner conversations over the wine.

The life in us is like the water in the river. It may rise this year higher than man has ever known it, and flood the parched uplands; even this may be the eventful year, which will drown out all our muskrats. It was not always dry land where we dwell. I see far inland the banks which the stream anciently washed, before science began to record its freshets. Every one has heard the story which has gone the rounds of New England, of a strong and beautiful bug which came out of the dry leaf of an old table of apple-tree wood, which had stood in a farmer's kitchen for sixty years, first in Connecticut, and afterward in Massachusetts,—from an egg deposited in the living tree many years earlier still, as appeared by counting the annual layers beyond it, which was heard gnawing out for several weeks, hatched perchance by the heat of an urn. Who does not feel his faith in a resurrection and immortality strengthened by hearing of this? Who knows what beautiful and winged life, whose egg has been buried for ages under many concentric layers of woodenness in the dead dry life of society, deposited at first in the alburnum of the green and living tree, which has been gradually converted into the semblance of its well-seasoned tomb,—heard perchance gnawing out now for years by the astonished family of man, as they sat round the festive board,—may unexpectedly come forth from amidst society's most trivial and handselled furniture, to enjoy its perfect summer life at last!

I do not say that John or Jonathan[21] will realize all this; but such is the character of that morrow which mere lapse of time can never make to dawn. The light which puts out our eyes is darkness to us. Only that day dawns to which we are awake. There is more day to dawn. The sun is but a morning star.

[1854]

---

21. **John or Jonathan:** Common names for John Bull, the Englishman, and Brother Jonathan, the American.

Frederick Douglass

[1818–1895]

Frederick Douglass, who would become internationally known as the most distinguished African American of his generation, did not know in which year he was born, who his white father was, or even much about the ancestry of his mother, a slave named Harriet Bailey. Douglass would have been proud to know that he had deep roots in the national heritage, which he so passionately proclaimed to be the shared heritage of black and white Americans. In fact, we now know that he was descended on his mother's side from a family whose history in America went back at least five generations, to the earliest settlement of the eastern shore of Maryland, where Douglass was born Frederick Bailey in February 1818.

The story of Douglass's life, which he told and retold, is a classic American success story, though it illustrates not only a triumph over poverty and obscurity but also over slavery and racism. Raised on a plantation until he was ten years old, he was then sent to work for his master's brother and sister-in-law in Baltimore, where Douglass lived for the next five years. There, the precocious boy taught himself to read, discovering books like *The Columbian Orator*, a collection of patriotic and revolutionary speeches that fueled his growing desire for freedom. After being returned to the plantation in 1833, Douglass first sought to escape in 1836, but the plan was discovered and he was returned to Baltimore. Two years later, posing as a free black sailor, he took a train to New York, where he changed his name from Bailey to Douglass and began to make a new life for himself. After he married Anna Murray, a free black woman who had aided his escape, the couple moved to New Bedford, Massachusetts. Precluded by his race from working in the shipyard as a caulker, for which he had been trained in Baltimore, Douglass took on various menial jobs until a speech he delivered at an antislavery meeting in 1839 brought him to the attention of William Lloyd Garrison, editor of the *Liberator* and president of the New England Anti-Slavery Society. As an agent of the society, Douglass traveled throughout the North for the next six years, rehearsing on the lecture platform the story he finally published in

1845 as *Narrative of the Life of Frederick Douglass, an American Slave, Written by Himself.*

Douglass would later radically revise and expand that story, first as *My Bondage and My Freedom* (1855) and later as *The Life and Times of Frederick Douglass*, different versions of which he published in 1881 and 1893. As the titles of those texts suggest, his achievements ultimately went far beyond the powerful account of the experience of slavery contained in the *Narrative*. Having revealed his true identity and consequently exposing himself to the danger of being returned to slavery, shortly after its publication Douglass sailed for Great Britain, where his lecture tour generated tremendous acclaim. After some English friends arranged for the purchase of his freedom in 1846, he returned to the United States. He settled in Rochester, New York, and established the *North Star*, later called *Frederick Douglass's Newspaper*. His growing independence and insistence that African Americans must assume a primary role in the struggle against slavery and racism led to increasing tensions with Garrison and his followers, from whom Douglass formally broke in 1851. During the following decade, he joined with political opponents of slavery; he also began to emphasize the need for armed resistance. He consequently welcomed the outbreak of the Civil War, first calling for the arming of slaves and free blacks and later urging free blacks to enlist in the Union army.

After the war, Douglass became increasingly involved in the Republican Party, through which he gained several official appointments, including U.S. marshal for the District of Columbia and consul general to Haiti. But he devoted most of his efforts to securing and defending the civil rights of African Americans. He supported the passage of the Fifteenth Amendment, which stated that the right to vote could not be denied on the basis of race, color, or previous condition of servitude. Douglass also campaigned for the enfranchisement of women. His final address, delivered on the day of his death in 1895, was to a women's rights rally in Washington, D.C. When she learned of his death the following day, his old friend Elizabeth Cady Stanton recalled the first time she had seen Douglass, at an antislavery rally in Boston. There, Stanton wrote, he had been surrounded by "the great antislavery orators of the day." But, she declared, "all the other speakers seemed tame after Frederick Douglass," who "stood there like an African prince, majestic in his wrath." Ironically, however, when that princely figure was buried, the inscription on his simple tombstone read "To the memory of Frederick Douglass, 1817–1895," perpetuating his own mistaken guess about the year of his birth.

We wish that everyone may read his book and see what a mind might have been stifled in bondage.

–Margaret Fuller

bedfordstmartins.com /americanlit *for research links on Douglass*

Reading Douglass's *Narrative of the Life of Frederick Douglass.*

Douglass wrote and published his famous narrative in 1845. In part, the account was a response to doubts about the authenticity of the story he had been telling during his years on the antislavery lecture circuit, where Douglass had been obliged to conceal key details that would have revealed his true identity. He later stated, "I was induced to write out the leading facts connected with my experience in slavery, giving names of persons, places, and dates – thus putting it in the power of any who doubted, to ascertain the truth or falsehood of my story of being a fugitive slave." As early portraits of him vividly illustrate, Douglass certainly did not fit the conventional image of a fugitive slave. To many, the mastery of language and rhetoric Douglass displayed on the lecture platform also seemed at odds with his story of laboriously teaching himself to read and write. In fact, the *Narrative* itself struck some skeptical readers as too well written to have been solely the product of his pen. Anticipating such doubts, and as was customary in slave narratives, Douglass included testimonials by two white abolitionists: a preface by William Lloyd Garrison, editor of the antislavery newspaper the *Liberator*; and a letter from Wendell Phillips, a distinguished Bostonian who had joined the antislavery crusade nearly a decade earlier. For most readers, however, their contributions were overshadowed by the compelling story Douglass told in the *Narrative*, which was both a critical and commercial success. Published in Boston in May 1845, it sold 4,500 copies by the time Douglass sailed for England in September and continued to sell briskly in both the United States and Great Britain. The text is taken from the first edition of *Narrative of the Life of Frederick Douglass, an American Slave, Written by Himself* (1845).

NARRATIVE OF THE LIFE OF FREDERICK DOUGLASS, AN AMERICAN SLAVE, WRITTEN BY HIMSELF

Preface

In the month of August, 1841, I attended an anti-slavery convention in Nantucket, at which it was my happiness to become acquainted with Frederick Douglass, the writer of the following Narrative. He was a stranger to nearly every member of that body; but, having recently made his escape from the southern prison-house of bondage, and feeling his curiosity excited to ascertain the principles and measures of the abolitionists, – of whom he had heard a somewhat vague description while he was a slave, – he was induced to give his attendance, on the occasion alluded to, though at that time a resident in New Bedford.[1]

Fortunate, most fortunate occurrence! – fortunate for the millions of his manacled brethren, yet panting for deliverance from their awful thraldom! – fortunate for the cause of negro emancipation, and of universal liberty! – fortunate for the land of his birth, which he has already done so much to save and bless! – fortunate for a large circle of friends and acquaintances whose sympathy and affection he has strongly secured

---

1. **New Bedford:** In September 1838, Douglass had escaped from slavery in Maryland and eventually settled in New Bedford, Massachusetts.

by the many sufferings he has endured by his virtuous traits of character, by his ever-abiding remembrance of those who are in bonds, as being bound with them! – fortunate for the multitudes in various parts of our republic, whose minds he has enlightened on the subject of slavery, and who have been melted to tears by his pathos, or roused to virtuous indignation by his stirring eloquence against the enslavers of men! – fortunate for himself, as it at once brought him into the field of public usefulness, "gave the world assurance of a MAN,"[2] quickened the slumbering energies of his soul, and consecrated him to the great work of breaking the rod of the oppressor, and letting the oppressed go free!

I shall never forget his first speech at the convention – the extraordinary emotion it excited in my own mind – the powerful impression it created upon a crowded auditory, completely taken by surprise – the applause which followed from the beginning to the end of his felicitous remarks. I think I never hated slavery so intensely as at that moment; certainly, my perception of the enormous outrage which is inflicted by it, on the godlike nature of its victims, was rendered far more clear than ever. There stood one, in physical proportion and stature commanding and exact – in intellect richly endowed – in natural eloquence a prodigy – in soul manifestly "created but a little lower than the angels"[3] – yet a slave, ay, a fugitive slave, – trembling for his safety, hardly daring to believe that on the American soil, a single white person could be found who would befriend him at all hazards, for the love of God and humanity! Capable of high attainments as an intellectual and moral being – needing nothing but a comparatively small amount of cultivation to make him an ornament to society and a blessing to his race – by the law of the land, by the voice of the people, by the terms of the slave code, he was only a piece of property, a beast of burden, a chattel personal, nevertheless!

A beloved friend from New Bedford prevailed on Mr. Douglass to address the convention. He came forward to the platform with a hesitancy and embarrassment, necessarily the attendants of a sensitive mind in such a novel position. After apologizing for his ignorance, and reminding the audience that slavery was a poor school for the human intellect and heart, he proceeded to narrate some of the facts in his own history as a slave, and in the course of his speech gave utterance to many noble thoughts and thrilling reflections. As soon as he had taken his seat, filled with hope and admiration, I rose, and declared that Patrick Henry, of revolutionary fame,[4] never made a speech more eloquent in the cause of liberty, than the one we had just listened to from the lips of that hunted fugitive. So I believed at that time – such is my belief now. I reminded the audience of the peril which surrounded this self-emancipated young man at the North, – even in Massachusetts, on the soil of the Pilgrim Fathers, among the descendants of revolutionary sires; and I appealed to them, whether they would ever allow him to be carried back into slavery, – law or no law, constitution or no constitution. The response was

---

2. "gave . . . MAN": Shakespeare, *Hamlet* 3.4.62.
3. "created . . . angels": Psalms 8:5 and Hebrews 2:7, 9.
4. **Patrick Henry, of revolutionary fame**: An orator and patriot who led the movement for independence in Virginia, Henry (1736-1799) is best known for the final words of a speech he delivered on March 23, 1775: "Is life so dear, or peace so sweet, as to be purchased at the price of chains and slavery? Forbid it, Almighty God! I know not what course others may take; but as for me, give me liberty, or give me death!"

unanimous and in thunder-tones – "NO!" "Will you succor and protect him as a brother-man – a resident of the old Bay State?"[5] "YES!" shouted the whole mass, with an energy so startling, that the ruthless tyrants south of Mason and Dixon's line[6] might almost have heard the mighty burst of feeling, and recognized it as the pledge of an invincible determination, on the part of those who gave it, never to betray him that wanders but to hide the outcast, and firmly to abide the consequences.

It was at once deeply impressed upon my mind, that, if Mr. Douglass could be persuaded to consecrate his time and talents to the promotion of the anti-slavery enterprise, a powerful impetus would be given to it, and a stunning blow at the same time inflicted on northern prejudice against a colored complexion. I therefore endeavored to instil hope and courage into his mind, in order that he might dare to engage in a vocation so anomalous and responsible for a person in his situation; and I was seconded in this effort by warm-hearted friends especially by the late General Agent of the Massachusetts Anti-Slavery Society, Mr. John A. Collins, whose judgment in this instance entirely coincided with my own. At first, he could give no encouragement; with unfeigned diffidence, he expressed his conviction that he was not adequate to the performance of so great a task; the path marked out was wholly an untrodden one; he was sincerely apprehensive that he should do more harm than good. After much deliberation, however, he consented to make a trial; and ever since that period, he has acted as a lecturing agent, under the auspices either of the American or the Massachusetts Anti-Slavery Society. In labors he has been most abundant; and his success in combating prejudice, in gaining proselytes, in agitating the public mind, has far surpassed the most sanguine expectations that were raised at the commencement of his brilliant career. He has borne himself with gentleness and meekness, yet with true manliness of character. As a public speaker, he excels in pathos, wit, comparison, imitation, strength of reasoning, and fluency of language. There is in him that union of head and heart, which is indispensable to an enlightenment of the heads and a winning of the hearts of others. May his strength continue to be equal to his day! May he continue to "grow in grace, and in the knowledge of God,"[7] that he may be increasingly serviceable in the cause of bleeding humanity, whether at home or abroad!

It is certainly a very remarkable fact, that one of the most efficient advocates of the slave population, now before the public, is a fugitive slave, in the person of Frederick Douglass; and that the free colored population of the United States are as ably represented by one of their own number, in the person of Charles Lenox Remond,[8] whose eloquent appeals have extorted the highest applause of multitudes on both sides of the Atlantic. Let the calumniators of the colored race despise themselves for their baseness and illiberality of spirit and henceforth cease to talk of the natural inferiority of those

---

5. **Bay State:** Nickname for Massachusetts.
6. **Mason and Dixon's line:** In the 1760s, the English surveyors Charles Mason and Jeremiah Dixon established the border between the colonies of Maryland and Pennsylvania, drawing a line that later came to represent the division between slave states and free states.
7. "**grow . . . God**":   2 Peter 3:18.
8. **Charles Lenox Remond:** Remond (1810–1873), born to free parents, was the first African American employed as a lecturer by the Massachusetts Anti-Slavery Society.

who require nothing but time and opportunity to attain to the highest point of human excellence.

It may, perhaps, be fairly questioned, whether any other portion of the population of the earth could have endured the privations, sufferings and horrors of slavery, without having become more degraded in the scale of humanity than the slaves of African descent. Nothing has been left undone to cripple their intellects, darken their minds, debase their moral nature, obliterate all traces of their relationship to mankind; and yet how wonderfully they have sustained the mighty load of a most frightful bondage, under which they have been groaning for centuries! To illustrate the effect of slavery on the white man, – to show that he has no powers of endurance, in such a condition, superior to those of his black brothers, – Daniel O'Connell,[9] the distinguished advocate of universal emancipation, and the mightiest champion of prostrate but not conquered Ireland, relates the following anecdote in a speech delivered by him in the Conciliation Hall, Dublin, before the Loyal National Repeal Association, March 31, 1845. "No matter," said Mr. O'Connell, "under what specious term it may disguise itself, slavery is still hideous. *It has a natural, an inevitable tendency to brutalize every noble faculty of man.* An American sailor, who was cast away on the shore of Africa, where he was kept in slavery for three years, was, at the expiration of that period, found to be imbruted and stultified – he had lost all reasoning power; and having forgotten his native language, could only utter some savage gibberish between Arabic and English, which nobody could understand, and which even he himself found difficulty in pronouncing. So much for the humanizing influence of THE DOMESTIC INSTITUTION!" Admitting this to have been an extraordinary case of mental deterioration, it proves at least that the white slave can sink as low in the scale of humanity as the black one.

Mr. Douglass has very properly chosen to write his own Narrative, in his own style, and according to the best of his ability, rather than to employ some one else. It is, therefore, entirely his own production; and, considering how long and dark was the career he had to run as a slave, – how few have been his opportunities to improve his mind since he broke his iron fetters, – it is, in my judgment, highly creditable to his head and heart. He who can peruse it without a tearful eye, a heaving breast, an afflicted spirit, – without being filled with an unutterable abhorrence of slavery and all its abettors, and animated with a determination to seek the immediate overthrow of that execrable system, – without trembling for the fate of this country in the hands of a righteous God, who is ever on the side of the oppressed, and whose arm is not shortened that it cannot save, – must have a flinty heart, and be qualified to act the part of a trafficker "in slaves and the souls of men." I am confident that it is essentially true in all its statements; that nothing has been set down in malice, nothing exaggerated, nothing drawn from the imagination; that it comes short of the reality, rather than overstates a single fact in regard to SLAVERY AS IT IS.[10] The experience of Frederick Douglass, as a slave, was not a

---

9. **Daniel O'Connell:** O'Connell (1775–1847) was an Irish politician who fought for Catholic emancipation and Irish independence from England.

10. **SLAVERY AS IT IS:** Probably a reference to Theodore Dwight Weld's *American Slavery As It Is* (1839), a collection of reports on the brutality of slavery gathered from southern newspapers.

peculiar one; his lot was not especially a hard one; his case may be regarded as a very fair specimen of the treatment of slaves in Maryland, in which State it is conceded that they are better fed and less cruelly treated than in Georgia, Alabama, or Louisiana. Many have suffered incomparably more, while very few on the plantations have suffered less, than himself. Yet how deplorable was his situation! what terrible chastisements were inflicted upon his person! what still more shocking outrages were perpetrated upon his mind! with all his noble powers and sublime aspirations, how like a brute was he treated, even by those professing to have the same mind in them that was in Christ Jesus! to what dreadful liabilities was he continually subjected! how destitute of friendly counsel and aid, even in his greatest extremities! how heavy was the midnight of woe which shrouded in blackness the last ray of hope, and filled the future with terror and gloom! what longings after freedom took possession of his breast, and how his misery augmented, in proportion as he grew reflective and intelligent, — thus demonstrating that a happy slave is an extinct man! how he thought, reasoned, felt, under the lash of the driver, with the chains upon his limbs! what perils he encountered in his endeavors to escape from his horrible doom! and how signal have been his deliverance and preservation in the midst of a nation of pitiless enemies!

This Narrative contains many affecting incidents, many passages of great eloquence and power; but I think the most thrilling one of them all is the description Douglass gives of his feelings, as he stood soliloquizing respecting his fate, and the chances of his one day being a freeman, on the banks of the Chesapeake Bay — viewing the receding vessels as they flew with their white wings before the breeze, and apostrophizing them as animated by the living spirit of freedom. Who can read that passage, and be insensible to its pathos and sublimity? Compressed into it is a whole Alexandrian library[11] of thought, feeling, and sentiment — all that can, all that need be urged, in the form of expostulation, entreaty, rebuke, against that crime of crimes, — making man the property of his fellow-man! O, how accursed is that system, which entombs the godlike mind of man, defaces the divine image, reduces those who by creation were crowned with glory and honor to a level with four-footed beasts, and exalts the dealer in human flesh above all that is called God! Why should its existence be prolonged one hour? Is it not evil, only evil, and that continually? What does its presence imply but the absence of all fear of God, all regard for man, on the part of the people of the United States? Heaven speed its eternal overthrow!

So profoundly ignorant of the nature of slavery are many persons, that they are stubbornly incredulous whenever they read or listen to any recital of the cruelties which are daily inflicted on its victims. They do not deny that the slaves are held as property; but that terrible fact seems to convey to their minds no idea of injustice, exposure to outrage, or savage barbarity. Tell them of cruel scourgings, of mutilations and brandings, of scenes of pollution and blood, of the banishment of all light and knowledge, and they affect to be greatly indignant at such enormous exaggerations, such wholesale

---

11. **Alexandrian library:** The library at Alexandria, Egypt, contained the greatest collection of works of any library in the ancient world.

misstatements, such abominable libels on the character of the southern planters! As if all these direful outrages were not the natural results of slavery! As if it were less cruel to reduce a human being to the condition of a thing, than to give him a severe flagellation, or to deprive him of necessary food and clothing! As if whips, chains, thumbscrews, paddles, bloodhounds, overseers, drivers, patrols, were not all indispensable to keep the slaves down, and to give protection to their ruthless oppressors! As if, when the marriage institution is abolished, concubinage, adultery, and incest, must not necessarily abound; when all the rights of humanity are annihilated, any barrier remains to protect the victim from the fury of the spoiler; when absolute power is assumed over life and liberty, it will not be wielded with destructive sway! Skeptics of this character abound in society. In some few instances, their incredulity arises from a want of reflection; but, generally, it indicates a hatred of the light, a desire to shield slavery from the assaults of its foes, a contempt of the colored race, whether bond or free. Such will try to discredit the shocking tales of slaveholding cruelty which are recorded in this truthful Narrative; but they will labor in vain. Mr. Douglass has frankly disclosed the place of his birth, the names of those who claimed ownership in his body and soul, and the names also of those who committed the crimes which he has alleged against them. His statements, therefore, may easily be disproved, if they are untrue.

In the course of his Narrative, he relates two instances of murderous cruelty, — in one of which a planter deliberately shot a slave belonging to a neighboring plantation, who had unintentionally gotten within his lordly domain in quest of fish; and in the other, an overseer blew out the brains of a slave who had fled to a stream of water to escape a bloody scourging. Mr. Douglass states that in neither of these instances was any thing done by way of legal arrest or judicial investigation. The Baltimore American, of March 17, 1845, relates a similar case of atrocity, perpetrated with similar impunity — as follows: — "*Shooting a Slave.* — We learn, upon the authority of a letter from Charles county, Maryland, received by a gentleman of this city, that a young man named Matthews, a nephew of General Matthews, and whose father, it is believed, holds an office at Washington, killed one of the slaves upon his father's farm by shooting him. The letter states that young Matthews had been left in charge of the farm; that he gave an order to the servant, which was disobeyed, when he proceeded to the house, *obtained a gun, and, returning, shot the servant.* He immediately, the letter continues, fled to his father's residence, where he still remains unmolested." — Let it never be forgotten, that no slaveholder or overseer can be convicted of any outrage perpetrated on the person of a slave, however diabolical it may be, on the testimony of colored witnesses, whether bond or free. By the slave code, they are adjudged to be as incompetent to testify against a white man, as though they were indeed a part of the brute creation. Hence, there is no legal protection in fact, whatever there may be in form, for the slave population; and any amount of cruelty may be inflicted on them with impunity. Is it possible for the human mind to conceive of a more horrible state of society?

The effect of a religious profession on the conduct of southern masters is vividly described in the following Narrative, and shown to be any thing but salutary. In the nature of the case, it must be in the highest degree pernicious. The testimony of Mr. Douglass, on this point, is sustained by a cloud of witnesses, whose veracity is unimpeachable. "A slaveholder's profession of Christianity is a palpable imposture. He is a felon of the highest grade. He is a man-stealer. It is of no importance what you put in the other scale."

Reader! are you with the man-stealers in sympathy and purpose, or on the side of their down-trodden victims? If with the former, then are you the foe of God and man. If with the latter, what are you prepared to do and dare in their behalf? Be faithful, be vigilant, be untiring in your efforts to break every yoke, and let the oppressed go free. Come what may — cost what it may — inscribe on the banner which you unfurl to the breeze, as your religious and political motto — "NO COMPROMISE WITH SLAVERY! NO UNION WITH SLAVE-HOLDERS!"

Wm. Lloyd Garrison

Boston, May 1, 1845

Letter from Wendell Phillips, Esq.

Boston, April 22, 1845

My Dear Friend:

You remember the old fable of "The Man and the Lion," where the lion complained that he should not be so misrepresented "when the lions wrote history."

I am glad the time has come when the "lions write history." We have been left long enough to gather the character of slavery from the involuntary evidence of the masters. One might, indeed, rest sufficiently satisfied with what, it is evident, must be, in general, the results of such a relation, without seeking farther to find whether they have followed in every instance. Indeed, those who stare at the half-peck of corn a week, and love to count the lashes on the slave's back, are seldom the "stuff" out of which reformers and abolitionists are to be made. I remember that, in 1838, many were waiting for the results of the West India experiment,[12] before they could come into our ranks. Those "results" have come long ago; but, alas! few of that number have come with them, as converts. A man must be disposed to judge of emancipation by other tests than whether it has increased the produce of sugar, — and to hate slavery for other reasons than because it starves men and whips women, — before he is ready to lay the first stone of his anti-slavery life.

I was glad to learn, in your story, how early the most neglected of God's children waken to a sense of their rights, and of the injustice done them. Experience is a keen teacher; and long before you had mastered your A B C, or knew where the "white sails" of the Chesapeake were bound, you began, I see, to gauge the wretchedness of the slave, not by his hunger and want, not by his lashes and toil, but by the cruel and blighting death which gathers over his soul.

---

12. **West India experiment:** Slavery was abolished in the British West Indies in 1833, leading many to ask how emancipation would affect the government and economy of the colonies.

In connection with this, there is one circumstance which makes your recollections peculiarly valuable, and renders your early insight the more remarkable. You come from that part of the country where we are told slavery appears with its fairest features. Let us hear, then, what it is at its best estate – gaze on its bright side, if it has one; and then imagination may task her powers to add dark lines to the picture, as she travels southward to that (for the colored man) Valley of the Shadow of Death,[13] where the Mississippi sweeps along.

Again, we have known you long, and can put the most entire confidence in your truth, candor, and sincerity. Every one who has heard you speak has felt, and, I am confident, every one who reads your book will feel, persuaded that you give them a fair specimen of the whole truth. No one-sided portrait, – no wholesale complaints, – but strict justice done, whenever individual kindliness has neutralized, for a moment the deadly system with which it was strangely allied. You have been with us, too, some years, and can fairly compare the twilight of rights, which your race enjoy at the North, with that "noon of night" under which they labor south of Mason and Dixon's line. Tell us whether, after all, the half-free colored man of Massachusetts is worse off than the pampered slave of the rice swamps!

In reading your life, no one can say that we have unfairly picked out some rare specimens of cruelty. We know that the bitter drops, which even you have drained from the cup, are no incidental aggravations, no individual ills, but such as must mingle always and necessarily in the lot of every slave. They are the essential ingredients, not the occasional results, of the system.

After all, I shall read your book with trembling for you. Some years ago, when you were beginning to tell me your real name and birthplace, you may remember I stopped you, and preferred to remain ignorant of all. With the exception of a vague description, so I continued, till the other day, when you read me your memoirs. I hardly knew, at the time, whether to thank you or not for the sight of them, when I reflected that it was still dangerous, in Massachusetts, for honest men to tell their names! They say the fathers, in 1776, signed the Declaration of Independence with the halter about their necks. You, too, publish your declaration of freedom with danger compassing you around. In all the broad lands which the Constitution of the United States overshadows, there is no single spot, – however narrow or desolate, – where a fugitive slave can plant himself and say, "I am safe." The whole armory of Northern Law has no shield for you. I am free to say that, in your place, I should throw the MS. into the fire.

You, perhaps, may tell your story in safety, endeared as you are to so many warm hearts by rare gifts, and a still rarer devotion of them to the service of others. But it will be owing only to your labors, and the fearless efforts of those who, trampling the laws and Constitution of the country under their feet, are determined that they will "hide the outcast," and that their hearths shall be, spite of the law, an asylum for the oppressed, if, some time or other, the humblest may stand in our streets, and bear witness in safety against the cruelties of which he has been the victim.

---

13. **Valley of the Shadow of Death:** See Psalms 23:4: "Yea, though I walk through the valley of the shadow of death, I will fear no evil: for thou art with me; thy rod and thy staff they comfort me."

Yet it is sad to think, that these very throbbing hearts which welcome your story, and form your best safeguard in telling it, are all beating contrary to the "statute in such case made and provided." Go on, my dear friend, till you, and those who, like you, have been saved, so as by fire, from the dark prison-house, shall stereotype these free, illegal pulses into statutes; and New England, cutting loose from a blood-stained Union, shall glory in being the house of refuge for the oppressed; – till we no longer merely "*hide* the outcast," or make a merit of standing idly by while he is hunted in our midst; but, consecrating anew the soil of the Pilgrims as an asylum for the oppressed, proclaim our *welcome* to the slave so loudly, that the tones shall reach every hut in the Carolinas, and make the broken-hearted bondman leap up at the thought of old Massachusetts.

God speed the day!
Till then, and ever,
Yours truly,
Wendell Phillips

Chapter I

I was born in Tuckahoe, near Hillsborough, and about twelve miles from Easton, in Talbot county, Maryland. I have no accurate knowledge of my age, never having seen any authentic record containing it. By far the larger part of the slaves know as little of their age as horses know of theirs, and it is the wish of most masters within my knowledge to keep their slaves thus ignorant. I do not remember to have ever met a slave who could tell of his birthday. They seldom come nearer to it than planting-time, harvest-time, cherry-time, spring-time, or fall-time. A want of information concerning my own was a source of unhappiness to me even during childhood. The white children could tell their ages. I could not tell why I ought to be deprived of the same privilege. I was not allowed to make any inquiries of my master concerning it. He deemed all such inquiries on the part of a slave improper and impertinent, and evidence of a restless spirit. The nearest estimate I can give makes me now between twenty-seven and twenty-eight years of age. I come to this, from hearing my master say, some time during 1835, I was about seventeen years old.

My mother was named Harriet Bailey. She was the daughter of Isaac and Betsey Bailey, both colored, and quite dark. My mother was of a darker complexion than either my grandmother or grandfather.

My father was a white man. He was admitted to be such by all I ever heard speak of my parentage. The opinion was also whispered that my master was my father; but of the correctness of this opinion, I know nothing; the means of knowing was withheld from me. My mother and I were separated when I was but an infant – before I knew her as my mother. It is a common custom, in the part of Maryland from which I ran away, to part children from their mothers at a very early age. Frequently, before the child has reached its twelfth month, its mother is taken from it, and hired out on some farm a considerable distance off, and the child is placed under the care of an old woman, too old for field labor. For what this separation is done, I do not know, unless it be to hinder the development of the child's affection toward its mother, and to blunt and destroy the natural affection of the mother for the child. This is the inevitable result.

I never saw my mother, to know her as such, more than four or five times in my life; and each of these times was very short in duration, and at night. She was hired by a Mr. Stewart, who lived about twelve miles from my home. She made her journeys to see me in the night, travelling the whole distance on foot, after the performance of her day's work. She was a field hand, and a whipping is the penalty of not being in the field at sunrise, unless a slave has special permission from his or her master to the contrary—a permission which they seldom get, and one that gives to him that gives it the proud name of being a kind master. I do not recollect of ever seeing my mother by the light of day. She was with me in the night. She would lie down with me, and get me to sleep, but long before I waked she was gone. Very little communication ever took place between us. Death soon ended what little we could have while she lived, and with it her hardships and suffering. She died when I was about seven years old, on one of my master's farms, near Lee's Mill. I was not allowed to be present during her illness, at her death, or burial. She was gone long before I knew any thing about it. Never having enjoyed, to any considerable extent, her soothing presence, her tender and watchful care, I received the tidings of her death with much the same emotions I should have probably felt at the death of a stranger.

Called thus suddenly away, she left me without the slightest intimation of who my father was. The whisper that my master was my father, may or may not be true; and, true or false, it is of but little consequence to my purpose whilst the fact remains, in all its glaring odiousness, that slaveholders have ordained, and by law established, that the children of slave women shall in all cases follow the condition of their mothers; and this is done too obviously to administer to their own lusts, and make a gratification of their wicked desires profitable as well as pleasurable; for by this cunning arrangement, the slaveholder, in cases not a few, sustains to his slaves the double relation of master and father.

I know of such cases; and it is worthy of remark that such slaves invariably suffer greater hardships, and have more to contend with, than others. They are, in the first place, a constant offence to their mistress. She is ever disposed to find fault with them; they can seldom do any thing to please her; she is never better pleased than when she sees them under the lash, especially when she suspects her husband of showing to his mulatto children favors which he withholds from his black slaves. The master is frequently compelled to sell this class of his slaves, out of deference to the feelings of his white wife; and, cruel as the deed may strike any one to be, for a man to sell his own children to human flesh-mongers, it is often the dictate of humanity for him to do so; for, unless he does this, he must not only whip them himself, but must stand by and see one white son tie up his brother, of but few shades darker complexion than himself, and ply the gory lash to his naked back; and if he lisp one word of disapproval, it is set down to his parental partiality, and only makes a bad matter worse, both for himself and the slave whom he would protect and defend.

Every year brings with it multitudes of this class of slaves. It was doubtless in consequence of a knowledge of this fact, that one great statesman of the south predicted the downfall of slavery by the inevitable laws of population. Whether this prophecy is ever fulfilled or not, it is nevertheless plain that a very different-looking class of people are springing up at the south, and are now held in slavery, from those originally brought to this country from Africa; and if their increase will do no other good, it will do away the force of the argument, that God cursed Ham,[1] and therefore American slavery is right. If the lineal descendants of Ham are alone to be scripturally enslaved, it is certain that slavery at the south must soon become unscriptural; for thousands are ushered into the world, annually, who, like myself, owe their existence to white fathers, and those fathers most frequently their own masters.

I have had two masters. My first master's name was Anthony. I do not remember his first name. He was generally called Captain Anthony — a title which, I presume, he acquired by sailing a craft on the Chesapeake Bay. He was not considered a rich slaveholder. He owned two or three farms, and about thirty slaves. His farms and slaves were under the care of an overseer. The overseer's name was Plummer. Mr. Plummer was a miserable drunkard, a profane swearer, and a savage monster. He always went armed with a cowskin and a heavy cudgel. I have known him to cut and slash the women's heads so horribly, that even master would be enraged at his cruelty, and would threaten to whip him if he did not mind himself. Master, however, was not a humane slaveholder. It required extraordinary barbarity on the part of an overseer to affect him. He was a cruel man, hardened by a long life of slaveholding. He would at times seem to take great pleasure in whipping a slave. I have often been awakened at the dawn of day by the most heart-rending shrieks of an own aunt of mine, whom he used to tie up to a joist, and whip upon her naked back till she was literally covered with blood. No words, no tears, no prayers, from his gory victim, seemed to move his iron heart from its bloody purpose. The louder she screamed, the harder he whipped; and where the blood ran fastest, there he whipped longest. He would whip her to make her scream, and whip her to make her hush; and not until overcome by fatigue, would he cease to swing the blood-clotted cowskin. I remember the first time I ever witnessed this horrible exhibition. I was quite a child, but I well remember it. I never shall forget it whilst I remember any thing. It was the first of a long series of such outrages, of which I was doomed to be a witness and a participant. It struck me with awful force. It was the blood-stained gate, the entrance to the hell of slavery, through which I was about to pass. It was a most terrible spectacle. I wish I could commit to paper the feelings with which I beheld it.

This occurrence took place very soon after I went to live with my old master, and under the following circumstances. Aunt Hester went out one night, — where or for what I do not know, — and happened to be absent when my master desired her presence. He had ordered her not to go out evenings, and warned her that she must never let him catch her in company with a young man, who was paying attention to her belonging to Colonel Lloyd. The young man's name was Ned Roberts, generally called Lloyd's Ned.

---

1. **God cursed Ham:** In chapter 9 of Genesis, Noah curses his youngest son, Ham, declaring that Ham's son Canaan shall be "a servant of servants . . . unto his brethren." Many proslavery apologists read the story as a biblical defense of slavery.

Why master was so careful of her, may be safely left to conjecture. She was a woman of noble form, and of graceful proportions, having very few equals, and fewer superiors, in personal appearance, among the colored or white women of our neighborhood.

Aunt Hester had not only disobeyed his orders in going out, but had been found in company with Lloyd's Ned; which circumstance, I found, from what he said while whipping her, was the chief offence. Had he been a man of pure morals himself, he might have been thought interested in protecting the innocence of my aunt; but those who knew him will not suspect him of any such virtue. Before he commenced whipping Aunt Hester, he took her into the kitchen, and stripped her from neck to waist, leaving her neck, shoulders, and back, entirely naked. He then told her to cross her hands, calling her at the same time a d——d b——h. After crossing her hands, he tied them with a strong rope, and led her to a stool under a large hook in the joist, put in for the purpose. He made her get upon the stool, and tied her hands to the hook. She now stood fair for his infernal purpose. Her arms were stretched up at their full length, so that she stood upon the ends of her toes. He then said to her, "Now, you d——d b——h, I'll learn you how to disobey my orders!" and after rolling up his sleeves, he commenced to lay on the heavy cowskin, and soon the warm, red blood (amid heart-rending shrieks from her, and horrid oaths from him) came dripping to the floor. I was so terrified and horror-stricken at the sight, that I hid myself in a closet, and dared not venture out till long after the bloody transaction was over. I expected it would be my turn next. It was all new to me. I had never seen any thing like it before. I had always lived with my grandmother on the outskirts of the plantation, where she was put to raise the children of the younger women. I had therefore been, until now, out of the way of the bloody scenes that often occurred on the plantation.

Chapter II

My master's family consisted of two sons, Andrew and Richard; one daughter, Lucretia, and her husband, Captain Thomas Auld. They lived in one house, upon the home plantation of Colonel Edward Lloyd. My master was Colonel Lloyd's clerk and superintendent. He was what might be called the overseer of the overseers. I spent two years of childhood on this plantation in my old master's family. It was here that I witnessed the bloody transaction recorded in the first chapter; and as I received my first impressions of slavery on this plantation, I will give some description of it, and of slavery as it there existed. The plantation is about twelve miles north of Easton, in Talbot county, and is situated on the border of Miles River. The principal products raised upon it were tobacco, corn, and wheat. These were raised in great abundance; so that, with the products of this and the other farms belonging to him, he was able to keep in almost constant employment a large sloop, in carrying them to market at Baltimore. This sloop was named Sally Lloyd, in honor of one of the colonel's daughters. My master's son-in-law, Captain Auld, was master of the vessel; she was otherwise manned by the colonel's own slaves. Their names were Peter, Isaac, Rich, and Jake. These were esteemed very highly by the other slaves, and looked upon as the privileged ones of the plantation; for it was no small affair, in the eyes of the slaves, to be allowed to see Baltimore.

Colonel Lloyd kept from three to four hundred slaves on his home plantation, and owned a large number more on the neighboring farms belonging to him. The names of the farms nearest to the home plantation were Wye Town and New Design. "Wye Town" was under the overseership of a man named Noah Willis. New Design was under the overseership of a Mr. Townsend. The overseers of these, and all the rest of the farms, numbering over twenty, received advice and direction from the managers of the home plantation. This was the great business place. It was the seat of government for the whole twenty farms. All disputes among the overseers were settled here. If a slave was convicted of any high misdemeanor, became unmanageable, or evinced a determination to run away, he was brought immediately here, severely whipped, put on board the sloop, carried to Baltimore, and sold to Austin Woolfolk, or some other slave-trader, as a warning to the slaves remaining.

Here, too, the slaves of all the other farms received their monthly allowance of food, and their yearly clothing. The men and women slaves received, as their monthly allowance of food, eight pounds of pork, or its equivalent in fish, and one bushel of corn meal. Their yearly clothing consisted of two coarse linen shirts, one pair of linen trousers, like the shirts, one jacket, one pair of trousers for winter, made of coarse negro cloth, one pair of stockings, and one pair of shoes; the whole of which could not have cost more than seven dollars. The allowance of the slave children was given to their mothers, or the old women having the care of them. The children unable to work in the field had neither shoes, stockings, jackets, nor trousers, given to them; their clothing consisted of two coarse linen shirts per year. When these failed them, they went naked until the next allowance-day. Children from seven to ten years old, of both sexes, almost naked, might be seen at all seasons of the year.

There were no beds given the slaves, unless one coarse blanket be considered such, and none but the men and women had these. This, however, is not considered a very great privation. They find less difficulty from the want of beds, than from the want of time to sleep; for when their day's work in the field is done, the most of them having their washing, mending, and cooking to do, and having few or none of the ordinary facilities for doing either of these, very many of their sleeping hours are consumed in preparing for the field the coming day; and when this is done, old and young, male and female, married and single, drop down side by side, on one common bed, — the cold, damp floor, — each covering himself or herself with their miserable blankets; and here they sleep till they are summoned to the field by the driver's horn. At the sound of this, all must rise, and be off to the field. There must be no halting; every one must be at his or her post; and woe betides them who hear not this morning summons to the field; for if they are not awakened by the sense of hearing, they are by the sense of feeling: no age nor sex finds any favor. Mr. Severe, the overseer, used to stand by the door of the quarter, armed with a large hickory stick and heavy cowskin, ready to whip any one who was so unfortunate as not to hear, or, from any other cause, was prevented from being ready to start for the field at the sound of the horn.

Mr. Severe was rightly named: he was a cruel man. I have seen him whip a woman, causing the blood to run half an hour at the time; and this, too, in the midst of her crying children, pleading for their mother's release. He seemed to take pleasure in manifesting his fiendish barbarity. Added to his cruelty, he was a profane swearer. It was enough to chill the blood and stiffen the hair of an ordinary man to hear him talk. Scarce a sentence escaped him but that was commenced or concluded by some horrid oath. The field was the place to witness his cruelty and profanity. His presence made it both the field of blood and of blasphemy. From the rising till the going down of the sun, he was cursing, raving, cutting, and slashing among the slaves of the field, in the most frightful manner. His career was short. He died very soon after I went to Colonel Lloyd's; and he died as he lived, uttering, with his dying groans, bitter curses and horrid oaths. His death was regarded by the slaves as the result of a merciful providence.

Mr. Severe's place was filled by a Mr. Hopkins. He was a very different man. He was less cruel, less profane, and made less noise, than Mr. Severe. His course was characterized by no extraordinary demonstrations of cruelty. He whipped, but seemed to take no pleasure in it. He was called by the slaves a good overseer.

The home plantation of Colonel Lloyd wore the appearance of a country village. All the mechanical operations for all the farms were performed here. The shoemaking and mending, the blacksmithing, cartwrighting, coopering, weaving, and grain-grinding, were all performed by the slaves on the home plantation. The whole place wore a business-like aspect very unlike the neighboring farms. The number of houses, too, conspired to give it advantage over the neighboring farms. It was called by the slaves the *Great House Farm*. Few privileges were esteemed higher, by the slaves of the out-farms, than that of being selected to do errands at the Great House Farm. It was associated in their minds with greatness. A representative could not be prouder of his election to a seat in the American Congress, than a slave on one of the out-farms would be of his election to do errands at the Great House Farm. They regarded it as evidence of great confidence reposed in them by their overseers; and it was on this account, as well as a constant desire to be out of the field from under the driver's lash, that they esteemed it a high privilege, one worth careful living for. He was called the smartest and most trusty fellow, who had this honor conferred upon him the most frequently. The competitors for this office sought as diligently to please their overseers, as the office-seekers in the political parties seek to please and deceive the people. The same traits of character might be seen in Colonel Lloyd's slaves, as are seen in the slaves of the political parties.

The slaves selected to go to the Great House Farm, for the monthly allowance for themselves and their fellow-slaves, were peculiarly enthusiastic. While on their way, they would make the dense old woods, for miles around, reverberate with their wild songs, revealing at once the highest joy and the deepest sadness. They would compose and sing as they went along, consulting neither time nor tune. The thought that came up, came out; — if not in the word, in the sound; — and as frequently in the one as in the other. They would sometimes sing the most pathetic sentiment in the most rapturous tone, and the most rapturous sentiment in the most pathetic tone. Into all of their songs they would manage to weave something of the Great House Farm. Especially would they do this, when leaving home. They would then sing most exultingly the following words: —

> I am going away to the Great House Farm!
> O, yea! O, yea! O!

This they would sing, as a chorus, to words which to many would seem unmeaning jargon, but which, nevertheless, were full of meaning to themselves. I have sometimes thought that the mere hearing of those songs would do more to impress some minds with the horrible character of slavery, than the reading of whole volumes of philosophy on the subject could do.

I did not, when a slave, understand the deep meaning of those rude and apparently incoherent songs. I was myself within the circle; so that I neither saw nor heard as those without might see and hear. They told a tale of woe which was then altogether beyond my feeble comprehension; they were tones loud, long, and deep; they breathed the prayer and complaint of souls boiling over with the bitterest anguish. Every tone was a testimony against slavery, and a prayer to God for deliverance from chains. The hearing of those wild notes always depressed my spirit, and filled me with ineffable sadness, I have frequently found myself in tears while hearing them. The mere recurrence to those songs, even now, afflicts me; and while I am writing these lines, an expression of feeling has already found its way down my cheek. To those songs I trace my first glimmering conception of the dehumanizing character of slavery. I can never get rid of that conception. Those songs still follow me, to deepen my hatred of slavery, and quicken my sympathies for my brethren in bonds. If any one wishes to be impressed with the soul-killing effects of slavery, let him go to Colonel Lloyd's plantation, and, on allowance-day, place himself in the deep pine woods, and there let him, in silence, analyze the sounds that shall pass through the chambers of his soul, – and if he is not thus impressed, it will only be because "there is no flesh in his obdurate heart."[1]

I have often been utterly astonished, since I came to the north, to find persons who could speak of the singing, among slaves, as evidence of their contentment and happiness. It is impossible to conceive of a greater mistake. Slaves sing most when they are most unhappy. The songs of the slave represent the sorrows of his heart; and he is relieved by them, only as an aching heart is relieved by its tears. At least, such is my experience. I have often sung to drown my sorrow, but seldom to express my happiness. Crying for joy, and singing for joy, were alike uncommon to me while in the jaws of slavery. The singing of a man cast away upon a desolate island might be as appropriately considered as evidence of contentment and happiness, as the singing of a slave; the songs of the one and of the other are prompted by the same emotion.

Chapter III

Colonel Lloyd kept a large and finely cultivated garden, which afforded almost constant employment for four men, besides the chief gardener, (Mr. M'Durmond.) This garden was probably the greatest attraction of the place. During the summer months, people came from far and near – from Baltimore, Easton, and Annapolis – to see it. It abounded in fruits of almost every description, from the hardy apple of the north to the delicate

---

1. **"there . . . obdurate heart":** From book 2, line 8 of *The Task* (1785), a popular poem by the English poet William Cowper (1731–1800).

orange of the south. This garden was not the least source of trouble on the plantation. Its excellent fruit was quite a temptation to the hungry swarms of boys, as well as the older slaves, belonging to the colonel, few of whom had the virtue or the vice to resist it. Scarcely a day passed, during the summer, but that some slave had to take the lash for stealing fruit. The colonel had to resort to all kinds of stratagems to keep his slaves out of the garden. The last and most successful one was that of tarring his fence all around; after which, if a slave was caught with any tar upon his person, it was deemed sufficient proof that he had either been into the garden, or had tried to get in. In either case, he was severely whipped by the chief gardener. This plan worked well; the slaves became as fearful of tar as of the lash. They seemed to realize the impossibility of touching *tar* without being defiled.

The colonel also kept a splendid riding equipage. His stable and carriage-house presented the appearance of some of our large city livery establishments. His horses were of the finest form and noblest blood. His carriage-house contained three splendid coaches, three or four gigs, besides dearborns and barouches of the most fashionable style.

This establishment was under the care of two slaves—old Barney and young Barney—father and son. To attend to this establishment was their sole work. But it was by no means an easy employment; for in nothing was Colonel Lloyd more particular than in the management of his horses. The slightest inattention to these was unpardonable, and was visited upon those, under whose care they were placed, with the severest punishment; no excuse could shield them, if the colonel only suspected any want of attention to his horses—a supposition which he frequently indulged, and one which, of course, made the office of old and young Barney a very trying one. They never knew when they were safe from punishment. They were frequently whipped when least deserving, and escaped whipping when most deserving it. Every thing depended upon the looks of the horses, and the state of Colonel Lloyd's own mind when his horses were brought to him for use. If a horse did not move fast enough, or hold his head high enough, it was owing to some fault of his keepers. It was painful to stand near the stable-door, and hear the various complaints against the keepers when a horse was taken out for use. "This horse has not had proper attention. He has not been sufficiently rubbed and curried, or he has not been properly fed; his food was too wet or too dry; he got it too soon or too late; he was too hot or too cold; he had too much hay, and not enough of grain; or he had too much grain, and not enough of hay; instead of old Barney's attending to the horse, he had very improperly left it to his son." To all these complaints, no matter how unjust, the slave must answer never a word. Colonel Lloyd could not brook any contradiction from a slave. When he spoke, a slave must stand, listen, and tremble; and such was literally the case. I have seen Colonel Lloyd make old Barney, a man between fifty and sixty years of age, uncover his bald head, kneel down upon the cold, damp ground, and receive upon his naked and toil-worn shoulders more than thirty lashes at the time. Colonel Lloyd had three sons—Edward, Murray, and Daniel,—and three sons-in-law, Mr. Winder, Mr. Nicholson, and Mr. Lowndes. All of these lived at the Great House Farm, and enjoyed the luxury of whipping the servants when they pleased, from old Barney down to William Wilkes, the coach-driver. I have seen Winder make one of the house-servants stand off from him a suitable distance to be touched with the end of his whip, and at every stroke raise great ridges upon his back.

To describe the wealth of Colonel Lloyd would be almost equal to describing the riches of Job.[1] He kept from ten to fifteen house-servants. He was said to own a thousand slaves, and I think this estimate quite within the truth. Colonel Lloyd owned so many that he did not know them when he saw them; nor did all the slaves of the out-farms know him. It is reported of him, that, while riding along the road one day, he met a colored man, and addressed him in the usual manner of speaking to colored people on the public highways of the south: "Well, boy, whom do you belong to?" "To Colonel Lloyd," replied the slave. "Well, does the colonel treat you well?" "No, sir," was the ready reply. "What, does he work you too hard?" "Yes, sir." "Well, don't he give you enough to eat?" "Yes, sir, he gives me enough, such as it is."

The colonel, after ascertaining where the slave belonged, rode on; the man also went on about his business, not dreaming that he had been conversing with his master. He thought, said, and heard nothing more of the matter, until two or three weeks afterwards. The poor man was then informed by his overseer that, for having found fault with his master, he was now to be sold to a Georgia trader. He was immediately chained and handcuffed; and thus, without a moment's warning, he was snatched away, and forever sundered, from his family and friends, by a hand more unrelenting than death. This is the penalty of telling the truth, of telling the simple truth, in answer to a series of plain questions.

It is partly in consequence of such facts, that slaves, when inquired of as to their condition and the character of their masters, almost universally say they are contented, and that their masters are kind. The slaveholders have been known to send in spies among their slaves, to ascertain their views and feelings in regard to their condition. The frequency of this has had the effect to establish among the slaves the maxim, that a still tongue makes a wise head. They suppress the truth rather than take the consequences of telling it, and in so doing prove themselves a part of the human family. If they have any thing to say of their masters, it is generally in their masters' favor, especially when speaking to an untried man. I have been frequently asked, when a slave, if I had a kind master, and do not remember ever to have given a negative answer; nor did I, in pursuing this course, consider myself as uttering what was absolutely false; for I always measured the kindness of my master by the standard of kindness set up among slaveholders around us. Moreover, slaves are like other people, and imbibe prejudices quite common to others. They think their own better than that of others. Many, under the influence of this prejudice, think their own masters are better than the masters of other slaves; and this, too, in some cases, when the very reverse is true. Indeed, it is not uncommon for slaves even to fall out and quarrel among themselves about the relative goodness of their masters, each contending for the superior goodness of his own over that of the others. At the very same time, they mutually execrate their masters when viewed separately. It was so on our plantation. When Colonel Lloyd's slaves met the slaves of Jacob Jepson, they seldom parted without a quarrel about their masters; Colonel Lloyd's slaves

---

1. **riches of Job:** See the description of his herds and "great household" in Job 1:3.

contending that he was the richest, and Mr. Jepson's slaves that he was the smartest, and most of a man. Colonel Lloyd's slaves would boast his ability to buy and sell Jacob Jepson. Mr. Jepson's slaves would boast his ability to whip Colonel Lloyd. These quarrels would almost always end in a fight between the parties, and those that whipped were supposed to have gained the point at issue. They seemed to think that the greatness of their masters was transferable to themselves. It was considered as being bad enough to be a slave; but to be a poor man's slave was deemed a disgrace indeed!

Chapter IV

Mr. Hopkins remained but a short time in the office of overseer. Why his career was so short, I do not know, but suppose he lacked the necessary severity to suit Colonel Lloyd. Mr. Hopkins was succeeded by Mr. Austin Gore, a man possessing, in an eminent degree, all those traits of character indispensable to what is called a first-rate overseer. Mr. Gore had served Colonel Lloyd, in the capacity of overseer, upon one of the out-farms, and had shown himself worthy of the high station of overseer upon the home or Great House Farm.

Mr. Gore was proud, ambitious, and persevering. He was artful, cruel, and obdurate. He was just the man for such a place, and it was just the place for such a man. It afforded scope for the full exercise of all his powers, and he seemed to be perfectly at home in it. He was one of those who could torture the slightest look, word, or gesture, on the part of the slave, into impudence, and would treat it accordingly. There must be no answering back to him; no explanation was allowed a slave, showing himself to have been wrongfully accused. Mr. Gore acted fully up to the maxim laid down by slaveholders, – "It is better that a dozen slaves suffer under the lash, than that the overseer should be convicted, in the presence of the slaves, of having been at fault." No matter how innocent a slave might be – it availed him nothing, when accused by Mr. Gore of any misdemeanor. To be accused was to be convicted, and to be convicted was to be punished; the one always following the other with immutable certainty. To escape punishment was to escape accusation; and few slaves had the fortune to do either, under the overseership of Mr. Gore. He was just proud enough to demand the most debasing homage of the slave, and quite servile enough to crouch, himself, at the feet of the master. He was ambitious enough to be contented with nothing short of the highest rank of overseers, and persevering enough to reach the height of his ambition. He was cruel enough to inflict the severest punishment, artful enough to descend to the lowest trickery, and obdurate enough to be insensible to the voice of a reproving conscience. He was, of all the overseers, the most dreaded by the slaves. His presence was painful; his eye flashed confusion; and seldom was his sharp, shrill voice heard, without producing horror and trembling in their ranks.

Mr. Gore was a grave man, and, though a young man, he indulged in no jokes, said no funny words, seldom smiled. His words were in perfect keeping with his looks, and his looks were in perfect keeping with his words. Overseers will sometimes indulge in a witty word, even with the slaves; not so with Mr. Gore. He spoke but to command, and commanded but to be obeyed; he dealt sparingly with his words, and bountifully with his whip, never using the former where the latter would answer as well. When he whipped, he seemed to do so from a sense of duty, and feared no consequences. He did nothing reluctantly, no matter how disagreeable; always at his post, never inconsistent. He never promised but to fulfill. He was, in a word, a man of the most inflexible firmness and stone-like coolness.

His savage barbarity was equalled only by the consummate coolness with which he committed the grossest and most savage deeds upon the slaves under his charge. Mr. Gore once undertook to whip one of Colonel Lloyd's slaves, by the name of Demby. He had given Demby but few stripes, when, to get rid of the scourging, he ran and plunged himself into a creek, and stood there at the depth of his shoulders, refusing to come out. Mr. Gore told him that he would give him three calls, and that, if he did not come out at the third call, he would shoot him. The first call was given. Demby made no response, but stood his ground. The second and third calls were given with the same result. Mr. Gore then, without consultation or deliberation with any one, not even giving Demby an additional call, raised his musket to his face, taking deadly aim at his standing victim, and in an instant poor Demby was no more. His mangled body sank out of sight, and blood and brains marked the water where he had stood.

A thrill of horror flashed through every soul upon the plantation, excepting Mr. Gore. He alone seemed cool and collected. He was asked by Colonel Lloyd and my old master, why he resorted to this extraordinary expedient. His reply was, (as well as I can remember,) that Demby had become unmanageable. He was setting a dangerous example to the other slaves,—one which, if suffered to pass without some such demonstration on his part, would finally lead to the total subversion of all rule and order upon the plantation. He argued that if one slave refused to be corrected, and escaped with his life, the other slaves would soon copy the example; the result of which would be, the freedom of the slaves, and the enslavement of the whites. Mr. Gore's defence was satisfactory. He was continued in his station as overseer upon the home plantation. His fame as an overseer went abroad. His horrid crime was not even submitted to judicial investigation. It was committed in the presence of slaves, and they of course could neither institute a suit, nor testify against him; and thus the guilty perpetrator of one of the bloodiest and most foul murders goes unwhipped of justice, and uncensured by the community in which he lives. Mr. Gore lived in St. Michael's, Talbot county, Maryland, when I left there; and if he is still alive, he very probably lives there now; and if so, he is now, as he was then, as highly esteemed and as much respected as though his guilty soul had not been stained with his brother's blood.

I speak advisedly when I say this,—that killing a slave, or any colored person, in Talbot county, Maryland, is not treated as a crime, either by the courts or the community. Mr. Thomas Lanman, of St. Michael's, killed two slaves, one of whom he killed with a hatchet, by knocking his brains out. He used to boast of the commission of the awful and bloody deed. I have heard him do so laughingly, saying, among other things, that he was the only benefactor of his country in the company, and that when others would do as much as he had done, we should be relieved of "the d—d niggers."

The wife of Mr. Giles Hick, living but a short distance from where I used to live, murdered my wife's cousin, a young girl between fifteen and sixteen years of age, mangling her person in the most horrible manner, breaking her nose and breastbone with a stick, so that the poor girl expired in a few hours afterward. She was immediately buried, but had not been in her untimely grave but a few hours before she was taken up and examined by the coroner, who decided that she had come to her death by severe beating. The offence for which this girl was thus murdered was this: – She had been set that night to mind Mrs. Hick's baby and during the night she fell asleep, and the baby cried. She, having lost her rest for several nights previous, did not hear the crying. They were both in the room with Mrs. Hicks. Mrs. Hicks, finding the girl slow to move, jumped from her bed, seized an oak stick of wood by the fireplace, and with it broke the girl's nose and breastbone, and thus ended her life. I will not say that this most horrid murder produced no sensation in the community. It did produce sensation, but not enough to bring the murderess to punishment. There was a warrant issued for her arrest, but it was never served. Thus she escaped not only punishment, but even the pain of being arraigned before a court for her horrid crime.

Whilst I am detailing bloody deeds which took place during my stay on Colonel Lloyd's plantation, I will briefly narrate another, which occurred about the same time as the murder of Demby by Mr. Gore.

Colonel Lloyd's slaves were in the habit of spending a part of their nights and Sundays in fishing for oysters, and in this way made up the deficiency of their scanty allowance. An old man belonging to Colonel Lloyd, while thus engaged, happened to get beyond the limits of Colonel Lloyd's, and on the premises of Mr. Beal Bondly. At this trespass, Mr. Bondly took offence, and with his musket came down to the shore, and blew its deadly contents into the poor old man.

Mr. Bondly came over to see Colonel Lloyd the next day, whether to pay him for his property, or to justify himself in what he had done, I know not. At any rate, this whole fiendish transaction was soon hushed up. There was very little said about it at all, and nothing done. It was a common saying, even among little white boys, that it was worth a half-cent to kill a "nigger," and a half-cent to bury one.

Chapter V

As to my own treatment while I lived on Colonel Lloyd's plantation, it was very similar to that of the other slave children. I was not old enough to work in the field, and there being little else than field work to do, I had a great deal of leisure time. The most I had to do was to drive up the cows at evening, keep the fowls out of the garden, keep the front yard clean, and run of errands for my old master's daughter, Mrs. Lucretia Auld. The most of my leisure time I spent in helping Master Daniel Lloyd in finding his birds, after he had shot them. My connection with Master Daniel was of some advantage to me. He became quite attached to me, and was a sort of protector of me. He would not allow the older boys to impose upon me, and would divide his cakes with me.

I was seldom whipped by my old master, and suffered little from any thing else than hunger and cold. I suffered much from hunger, but much more from cold. In hottest summer and coldest winter, I was kept almost naked – no shoes, no stockings, no jacket, no trousers, nothing on but a coarse tow linen shirt, reaching only to my knees. I had no bed. I must have perished with cold, but that, the coldest nights, I used to steal a bag which was used for carrying corn to the mill. I would crawl into this bag, and there sleep on the cold, damp, clay floor, with my head in and feet out. My feet have been so cracked with the frost, that the pen with which I am writing might be laid in the gashes.

We were not regularly allowanced. Our food was coarse corn meal boiled. This was called *mush.* It was put into a large wooden tray or trough, and set down upon the ground. The children were then called, like so many pigs, and like so many pigs they would come and devour the mush; some with oyster-shells, others with pieces of shingle, some with naked hands, and none with spoons. He that ate fastest got most; he that was strongest secured the best place; and few left the trough satisfied.

I was probably between seven and eight years old when I left Colonel Lloyd's plantation. I left it with joy. I shall never forget the ecstasy with which I received the intelligence that my old master (Anthony) had determined to let me go to Baltimore, to live with Mr. Hugh Auld, brother to my old master's son-in-law, Captain Thomas Auld. I received this information about three days before my departure. They were three of the happiest days I ever enjoyed. I spent the most part of all these three days in the creek, washing off the plantation scurf, and preparing myself for my departure.

The pride of appearance which this would indicate was not my own. I spent the time in washing, not so much because I wished to, but because Mrs. Lucretia had told me I must get all the dead skin off my feet and knees before I could go to Baltimore; for the people in Baltimore were very cleanly, and would laugh at me if I looked dirty. Besides, she was going to give me a pair of trousers, which I should not put on unless I got all the dirt off me. The thought of owning a pair of trousers was great indeed! It was almost a sufficient motive, not only to make me take off what would be called by pig-drovers the mange, but the skin itself. I went at it in good earnest, working for the first time with the hope of reward.

The ties that ordinarily bind children to their homes were all suspended in my case. I found no severe trial in my departure. My home was charmless; it was not home to me; on parting from it, I could not feel that I was leaving any thing which I could have enjoyed by staying. My mother was dead, my grandmother lived far off, so that I seldom saw her. I had two sisters and one brother, that lived in the same house with me; but the early separation of us from our mother had well nigh blotted the fact of our relationship from our memories. I looked for home elsewhere, and was confident of finding none which I should relish less than the one which I was leaving. If, however, I found in my new home hardship, hunger, whipping, and nakedness, I had the consolation that I should not have escaped any one of them by staying. Having already had more than a taste of them in the house of my old master, and having endured them there, I very naturally inferred my ability to endure them elsewhere, and especially at Baltimore; for I had something of the feeling about Baltimore that is expressed in the proverb, that "being hanged in England is preferable to dying a natural death in Ireland." I had the strongest desire to see Baltimore. Cousin Tom, though not fluent in speech, had inspired me with that desire by his eloquent description of the place. I could never point out any thing at the Great House, no matter how beautiful or powerful, but that he had seen something at Baltimore far exceeding, both in beauty and strength, the object which I pointed out to him. Even the Great House itself, with all its pictures, was far inferior to many buildings in Baltimore. So strong was my desire, that I thought a gratification of it would fully compensate for whatever loss of comforts I should sustain by the exchange. I left without a regret, and with the highest hopes of future happiness.

We sailed out of Miles River for Baltimore on a Saturday morning. I remember only the day of the week, for at that time I had no knowledge of the days of the month, nor the months of the year. On setting sail, I walked aft, and gave to Colonel Lloyd's plantation what I hoped would be the last look. I then placed myself in the bows of the sloop, and there spent the remainder of the day in looking ahead, interesting myself in what was in the distance rather than in things near by or behind.

In the afternoon of that day, we reached Annapolis, the capital of the State. We stopped but a few moments, so that I had no time to go on shore. It was the first large town that I had ever seen, and though it would look small compared with some of our New England factory villages, I thought it a wonderful place for its size — more imposing even than the Great House Farm!

We arrived at Baltimore early on Sunday morning, landing at Smith's Wharf, not far from Bowley's Wharf. We had on board the sloop a large flock of sheep; and after aiding in driving them to the slaughter-house of Mr. Curtis on Louden Slater's Hill, I was conducted by Rich, one of the hands belonging on board of the sloop, to my new home in Alliciana Street, near Mr. Gardner's ship-yard, on Fells Point.

Mr. and Mrs. Auld were both at home, and met me at the door with their little son Thomas, to take care of whom I had been given. And here I saw what I had never seen before; it was a white face beaming with the most kindly emotions; it was the face of my new mistress, Sophia Auld. I wish I could describe the rapture that flashed through my soul as I beheld it. It was a new and strange sight to me, brightening up my pathway with the light of happiness. Little Thomas was told, there was his Freddy, — and I was told to take care of little Thomas; and thus I entered upon the duties of my new home with the most cheering prospect ahead.

I look upon my departure from Colonel Lloyd's plantation as one of the most interesting events of my life. It is possible, and even quite probable, that but for the mere circumstance of being removed from that plantation to Baltimore, I should have to-day, instead of being here seated by my own table, in the enjoyment of freedom and the happiness of home, writing this Narrative, been confined in the galling chains of slavery. Going to live at Baltimore laid the foundation, and opened the gateway, to all my subsequent prosperity. I have ever regarded it as the first plain manifestation of that kind providence which has ever since attended me, and marked my life with so many favors. I regarded the selection of myself as being somewhat remarkable. There were a number of slave children that might have been sent from the plantation to Baltimore. There were those younger, those older, and those of the same age. I was chosen from among them all, and was the first, last, and only choice.

I may be deemed superstitious, and even egotistical, in regarding this event as a special interposition of divine Providence in my favor. But I should be false to the earliest sentiments of my soul, if I suppressed the opinion. I prefer to be true to myself, even at the hazard of incurring the ridicule of others, rather than to be false, and incur my own abhorrence. From my earliest recollection, I date the entertainment of a deep conviction that slavery would not always be able to hold me within its foul embrace; and in the darkest hours of my career in slavery, this living word of faith and spirit of hope departed not from me, but remained like ministering angels to cheer me through the gloom.[1] This good spirit was from God, and to him I offer thanksgiving and praise.

Chapter VI

My new mistress proved to be all she appeared when I first met her at the door, — a woman of the kindest heart and finest feelings. She had never had a slave under her control previously to myself, and prior to her marriage she had been dependent upon her own industry for a living. She was by trade a weaver; and by constant application to her business, she had been in a good degree preserved from the blighting and dehumanizing effects of slavery. I was utterly astonished at her goodness. I scarcely knew how to behave towards her. She was entirely unlike any other white woman I had ever seen. I could not approach her as I was accustomed to approach other white ladies. My early instruction was all out of place. The crouching servility, usually so acceptable a quality in a slave, did not answer when manifested toward her. Her favor was not gained by it; she seemed to be disturbed by it. She did not deem it impudent or unmannerly for a slave to look her in the face. The meanest slave was put fully at ease in her presence, and none left without feeling better for having seen her. Her face was made of heavenly smiles, and her voice of tranquil music.

But, alas! this kind heart had but a short time to remain such. The fatal poison of irresponsible power was already in her hands, and soon commenced its infernal work. That cheerful eye, under the influence of slavery, soon became red with rage; that voice, made all of sweet accord, changed to one of harsh and horrid discord; and that angelic face gave place to that of a demon.

Very soon after I went to live with Mr. and Mrs. Auld, she very kindly commenced to teach me the A, B, C. After I had learned this, she assisted me in learning to spell words of three or four letters. Just at this point of my progress, Mr. Auld found out what was going on, and at once forbade Mrs. Auld to instruct me further, telling her, among other things, that it was unlawful, as well as unsafe, to teach a slave to read. To use his own words, further, he said, "If you give a nigger an inch, he will take an ell. A nigger should know nothing but to obey his master — to do as he is told to do. Learning would *spoil* the best nigger in the world. Now," said he, "if you teach that nigger (speaking of myself) how to read, there would be no keeping him. It would forever unfit him to be a slave. He would at once become unmanageable, and of no value to his master. As to himself, it could do him no good, but a great deal of harm. It would make him discontented and unhappy." These words sank deep into my heart, stirred up sentiments within that lay slumbering, and called into existence an entirely new train of thought. It was a new and special revelation, explaining dark and mysterious things, with which my youthful

---

1. **ministering angels . . . gloom:** Compare the description of Christ's temptation in the wilderness in Matthew 4:11: "Then the devil leaveth him, and, behold, angels came and ministered unto him."

understanding had struggled, but struggled in vain. I now understood what had been to me a most perplexing difficulty – to wit, the white man's power to enslave the black man. It was a grand achievement, and I prized it highly. From that moment, I understood the pathway from slavery to freedom. It was just what I wanted, and I got it at a time when I the least expected it. Whilst I was saddened by the thought of losing the aid of my kind mistress, I was gladdened by the invaluable instruction which, by the merest accident, I had gained from my master. Though conscious of the difficulty of learning without a teacher, I set out with high hope, and a fixed purpose, at whatever cost of trouble, to learn how to read. The very decided manner with which he spoke, and strove to impress his wife with the evil consequences of giving me instruction, served to convince me that he was deeply sensible of the truths he was uttering. It gave me the best assurance that I might rely with the utmost confidence on the results which, he said, would flow from teaching me to read. What he most dreaded, that I most desired. What he most loved, that I most hated. That which to him was a great evil, to be carefully shunned, was to me a great good, to be diligently sought; and the argument which he so warmly urged, against my learning to read, only served to inspire me with a desire and determination to learn. In learning to read, I owe almost as much to the bitter opposition of my master, as to the kindly aid of my mistress. I acknowledge the benefit of both.

I had resided but a short time in Baltimore before I observed a marked difference, in the treatment of slaves, from that which I had witnessed in the country. A city slave is almost a freeman, compared with a slave on the plantation. He is much better fed and clothed, and enjoys privileges altogether unknown to the slave on the plantation. There is a vestige of decency, a sense of shame, that does much to curb and check those outbreaks of atrocious cruelty so commonly enacted upon the plantation. He is a desperate slaveholder, who will shock the humanity of his nonslaveholding neighbors with the cries of his lacerated slave. Few are willing to incur the odium attaching to the reputation of being a cruel master; and above all things, they would not be known as not giving a slave enough to eat. Every city slaveholder is anxious to have it known of him, that he feeds his slaves well; and it is due to them to say, that most of them do give their slaves enough to eat. There are, however, some painful exceptions to this rule. Directly opposite to us, on Philpot Street, lived Mr. Thomas Hamilton. He owned two slaves. Their names were Henrietta and Mary. Henrietta was about twenty-two years of age, Mary was about fourteen; and of all the mangled and emaciated creatures I ever looked upon, these two were the most so. His heart must be harder than stone, that could look upon these unmoved. The head, neck, and shoulders of Mary were literally cut to pieces. I have frequently felt her head and found it nearly covered with festering sores, caused by the lash of her cruel mistress. I do not know that her master ever whipped her, but I have been an eye-witness to the cruelty of Mrs. Hamilton. I used to be in Mr. Hamilton's house nearly every day. Mrs. Hamilton used to sit in a large chair in the middle of the room, with a heavy cowskin always by her side, and scarce an hour passed during the day but was marked by the blood of one of these slaves. The girls seldom passed her without her saying, "Move faster, you *black gip!*" at the same time giving them a blow with the cowskin over the head or shoulders, often drawing the blood. She would then say, "Take that, you *black gip!*" – continuing, "If you don't move faster, I'll move you!" Added to the cruel lashings to which these slaves were subjected, they were kept nearly half-starved. They seldom knew what it was to eat a full meal. I have seen Mary contending with the pigs for the offal thrown into the street. So much was Mary kicked and cut to pieces, that she was oftener called "*pecked*" than by her name.

Chapter VII

I lived in Master Hugh's family about seven years. During this time, I succeeded in learning to read and write. In accomplishing this, I was compelled to resort to various stratagems. I had no regular teacher. My mistress, who had kindly commenced to instruct me, had, in compliance with the advice and direction of her husband, not only ceased to instruct, but had set her face against my being instructed by any one else. It is due, however, to my mistress to say of her, that she did not adopt this course of treatment immediately. She at first lacked the depravity indispensable to shutting me up in mental darkness. It was at least necessary for her to have some training in the exercise of irresponsible power, to make her equal to the task of treating me as though I were a brute.

My mistress was, as I have said, a kind and tender-hearted woman; and in the simplicity of her soul she commenced, when I first went to live with her, to treat me as she supposed one human being ought to treat another. In entering upon the duties of a slaveholder, she did not seem to perceive that I sustained to her the relation of a mere chattel, and that for her to treat me as a human being was not only wrong, but dangerously so. Slavery proved as injurious to her as it did to me. When I went there, she was a pious, warm, and tender-hearted woman. There was no sorrow or suffering for which she had not a tear. She had bread for the hungry, clothes for the naked, and comfort for every mourner that came within her reach. Slavery soon proved its ability to divest her of these heavenly qualities. Under its influence, the tender heart became stone, and the lamblike disposition gave way to one of tiger-like fierceness. The first step in her downward course was in her ceasing to instruct me. She now commenced to practise her husband's precepts. She finally became even more violent in her opposition than her husband himself. She was not satisfied with simply doing as well as he had commanded; she seemed anxious to do better. Nothing seemed to make her more angry than to see me with a newspaper. She seemed to think that here lay the danger. I have had her rush at me with a face made all up of fury, and snatch from me a newspaper, in a manner that fully revealed her apprehension. She was an apt woman; and a little experience soon demonstrated, to her satisfaction, that education and slavery were incompatible with each other.

From this time I was most narrowly watched. If I was in a separate room any considerable length of time, I was sure to be suspected of having a book, and was at once called to give an account of myself. All this, however, was too late. The first step had been taken. Mistress, in teaching me the alphabet, had given me the *inch*, and no precaution could prevent me from taking the *ell*.

The plan which I adopted, and the one by which I was most successful, was that of making friends of all the little white boys whom I met in the street. As many of these as I could, I converted into teachers. With their kindly aid, obtained at different times and in different places, I finally succeeded in learning to read. When I was sent to errands, I always took my book with me, and by going one part of my errand quickly, I found time to get a lesson before my return. I used also to carry bread with me, enough of which was always in the house, and to which I was always welcome; for I was much better off in this regard than many of the poor white children in our neighborhood. This bread I used to bestow upon the hungry little urchins, who, in return, would give me that more valuable bread of knowledge. I am strongly tempted to give the names of two or three of those little boys, as a testimonial of the gratitude and affection I bear them; but prudence forbids;—not that it would injure me, but it might embarrass them; for it is almost an unpardonable offence to teach slaves to read in this Christian country. It is enough to say of the dear little fellows, that they lived on Philpot Street, very near Durgin and Bailey's ship-yard. I used to talk this matter of slavery over with them. I would sometimes say to them, I wished I could be as free as they would be when they got to be men. "You will be free as soon as you are twenty-one, *but I am a slave for life!* Have not I as good a right to be free as you have?" These words used to trouble them; they would express for me the liveliest sympathy, and console me with the hope that something would occur by which I might be free.

I was now about twelve years old, and the thought of being *a slave for life* began to bear heavily upon my heart. Just about this time, I got hold of a book entitled "The Columbian Orator."[1] Every opportunity I got, I used to read this book. Among much of other interesting matter, I found in it a dialogue between a master and his slave. The slave was represented as having run away from his master three times. The dialogue represented the conversation which took place between them, when the slave was retaken the third time. In this dialogue, the whole argument in behalf of slavery was brought forward by the master, all of which was disposed of by the slave. The slave was made to say some very smart as well as impressive things in reply to his master—things which had the desired though unexpected effect; for the conversation resulted in the voluntary emancipation of the slave on the part of the master.

In the same book, I met with one of Sheridan's mighty speeches on and in behalf of Catholic emancipation.[2] These were choice documents to me. I read them over and over again with unabated interest. They gave tongue to interesting thoughts of my own soul, which had frequently flashed through my mind, and died away for want of utterance. The moral which I gained from the dialogue was the power of truth over the conscience of even a slaveholder. What I got from Sheridan was a bold denunciation of slavery, and a powerful vindication of human rights. The reading of these documents enabled me to utter my thoughts, and to meet the arguments brought forward to sustain slavery; but while they relieved me of one difficulty, they brought on another even more painful than the one of which I was relieved. The more I read, the more I was led to abhor and detest my

---

1. **"The Columbian Orator"**: Caleb Bingham, *The Columbian Orator: Containing a Variety of Original and Selected Pieces Together with Rules Calculated to Improve Youth and Others in the Ornamental and Useful Art of Eloquence* (1797). A popular schoolbook, the collection included speeches from ancient and modern times on subjects like democracy, freedom, liberty, and virtue.

2. **Sheridan's mighty speeches . . . emancipation:** Richard Brinsley Sheridan (1751–1816) was an Irish political leader and playwright, but Douglass was actually recalling Daniel O'Connor's "Speech in the House of Commons, in Favour of the Bill for Emancipating the Roman Catholics" (1795).

enslavers. I could regard them in no other light than a band of successful robbers, who had left their homes, and gone to Africa, and stolen us from our homes, and in a strange land reduced us to slavery. I loathed them as being the meanest as well as the most wicked of men. As I read and contemplated the subject, behold! that very discontentment which Master Hugh had predicted would follow my learning to read had already come, to torment and sting my soul to unutterable anguish. As I writhed under it, I would at times feel that learning to read had been a curse rather than a blessing. It had given me a view of my wretched condition, without the remedy. It opened my eyes to the horrible pit, but to no ladder upon which to get out. In moments of agony, I envied my fellow-slaves for their stupidity. I have often wished myself a beast. I preferred the condition of the meanest reptile to my own. Any thing, no matter what, to get rid of thinking! It was this everlasting thinking of my condition that tormented me. There was no getting rid of it. It was pressed upon me by every object within sight or hearing, animate or inanimate. The silver trump of freedom had roused my soul to eternal wakefulness. Freedom now appeared, to disappear no more forever. It was heard in every sound, and seen in every thing. It was ever present to torment me with a sense of my wretched condition. I saw nothing without seeing it, I heard nothing without hearing it, and felt nothing without feeling it. It looked from every star, it smiled in every calm, breathed in every wind, and moved in every storm.

I often found myself regretting my own existence, and wishing myself dead; and but for the hope of being free, I have no doubt but that I should have killed myself, or done something for which I should have been killed. While in this state of mind, I was eager to hear any one speak of slavery. I was a ready listener. Every little while, I could hear something about the abolitionists. It was some time before I found what the word meant. It was always used in such connections as to make it an interesting word to me. If a slave ran away and succeeded in getting clear, or if a slave killed his master, set fire to a barn, or did any thing very wrong in the mind of a slaveholder, it was spoken of as the fruit of *abolition.* Hearing the word in this connection very often, I set about learning what it meant. The dictionary afforded me little or no help. I found it was "the act of abolishing;" but then I did not know what was to be abolished. Here I was perplexed. I did not dare to ask any one about its meaning, for I was satisfied that it was something they wanted me to know very little about. After a patient waiting, I got one of our city papers, containing an account of the number of petitions from the north, praying for the abolition of slavery in the District of Columbia, and of the slave trade between the States. From this time I understood the words *abolition* and *abolitionist,* and always drew near when that word was spoken, expecting to hear something of importance to myself and fellow slaves. The light broke in upon me by degrees. I went one day down on the wharf of Mr. Waters; and seeing two Irishmen unloading a scow of stone, I went, unasked, and helped them. When we had finished, one of them came to me and asked me if I were a slave. I told him I was. He asked, "Are ye a slave for life?" I told him that I was. The good Irishman seemed to be deeply affected by the statement. He said to the other that it was a pity so fine a little fellow as myself should be a slave for life. He said it was a shame to hold me. They both advised me to run away to the north; that I should find friends there, and that I should be free. I pretended not to be interested in what they said, and treated them as if I did not understand them; for I feared they might be treacherous. White men have been known to encourage slaves to escape, and then, to get the reward, catch them and return them to their masters. I was afraid that these seemingly good men might use me so; but I nevertheless remembered their advice, and from that time I resolved to run away. I looked forward to a time at which it would be safe for me to escape. I was too young to think of doing so immediately; besides, I wished to learn how to write, as I might have occasion to write my own pass. I consoled myself with the hope that I should one day find a good chance. Meanwhile, I would learn to write.

The idea as to how I might learn to write was suggested to me by being in Durgin and Bailey's ship-yard, and frequently seeing the ship carpenters, after hewing, and getting a piece of timber ready for use, write on the timber the name of that part of the ship for which it was intended. When a piece of timber was intended for the larboard side, it would be marked thus — "L." When a piece was for the starboard side, it would be marked thus — "S." A piece for the larboard side forward, would be marked thus — "L.F." When a piece was for starboard side forward, it would be marked thus — "S.F." For larboard aft, it would be marked thus — "L.A." For starboard aft, it would be marked thus — "S.A." I soon learned the names of these letters, and for what they were intended when placed upon a piece of timber in the ship-yard. I immediately commenced copying them, and in a short time was able to make the four letters named. After that, when I met with any boy who I knew could write, I would tell him I could write as well as he. The next word would be, "I don't believe you. Let me see you try it." I would then make the letters which I had been so fortunate as to learn, and ask him to beat that. In this way I got a good many lessons in writing, which it is quite possible I should never have gotten in any other way. During this time, my copy-book was the board fence, brick wall, and pavement; my pen and ink was a lump of chalk. With these, I learned mainly how to write. I then commenced and continued copying the Italics in Webster's Spelling Book,[3] until I could make them all without looking on the book. By this time, my little Master Thomas had gone to school, and learned how to write, and had written over a number of copy-books. These had been brought home, and shown to some of our near neighbors, and then laid aside. My mistress used to go to class meeting at the Wilk Street meeting-house every Monday afternoon, and leave me to take care of the house. When left thus, I used to spend the time in writing in the spaces left in Master Thomas's copy-book, copying what he had written. I continued to do this until I could write a hand very similar to that of Master Thomas. Thus, after a long, tedious effort for years, I finally succeeded in learning how to write.

Chapter VIII

In a very short time after I went to live at Baltimore, my old master's youngest son Richard died; and in about three years and six months after his death, my old master, Captain Anthony, died, leaving only his son, Andrew, and daughter, Lucretia, to share his

---

3. **Webster's Spelling Book:** First published in 1783 by the American lexicographer Noah Webster (1758–1843), his speller was the most popular and familiar book of its time, selling an estimated fifteen million copies by 1837. Using the speller, students proceeded from tables of easy-to-spell words to tables of more difficult words, in which italic characters indicated silent letters or an *s* pronounced as a *z*.

estate. He died while on a visit to see his daughter at Hillsborough. Cut off thus unexpectedly, he left no will as to the disposal of his property. It was therefore necessary to have a valuation of the property, that it might be equally divided between Mrs. Lucretia and Master Andrew. I was immediately sent for, to be valued with the other property. Here again my feelings rose up in detestation of slavery. I had now a new conception of my degraded condition. Prior to this, I had become, if not insensible to my lot, at least partly so. I left Baltimore with a young heart overborne with sadness, and a soul full of apprehension. I took passage with Captain Rowe, in the schooner Wild Cat, and, after a sail of about twenty-four hours, I found myself near the place of my birth. I had now been absent from it almost, if not quite, five years. I, however, remembered the place very well. I was only about five years old when I left it, to go and live with my old master on Colonel Lloyd's plantation; so that I was now between ten and eleven years old.

We were all ranked together at the valuation. Men and women, old and young, married and single, were ranked with horses, sheep, and swine. There were horses and men, cattle and women, pigs and children, all holding the same rank in the scale of being, and were all subjected to the same narrow examination. Silvery-headed age and sprightly youth, maids and matrons, had to undergo the same indelicate inspection. At this moment, I saw more clearly than ever the brutalizing effects of slavery upon both slave and slaveholder.

After the valuation, then came the division. I have no language to express the high excitement and deep anxiety which were felt among us poor slaves during this time. Our fate for life was now to be decided. We had no more voice in that decision than the brutes among whom we were ranked. A single word from the white men was enough — against all our wishes, prayers, and entreaties — to sunder forever the dearest friends, dearest kindred, and strongest ties known to human beings. In addition to the pain of separation, there was the horrid dread of falling into the hands of Master Andrew. He was known to us all as being a most cruel wretch, — a common drunkard, who had, by his reckless mismanagement and profligate dissipation, already wasted a large portion of his father's property. We all felt that we might as well be sold at once to the Georgia traders, as to pass into his hands; for we knew that that would be our inevitable condition, — a condition held by us all in the utmost horror and dread.

I suffered more anxiety than most of my fellow-slaves. I had known what it was to be kindly treated; they had known nothing of the kind. They had seen little or nothing of the world. They were in very deed men and women of sorrow, and acquainted with grief. Their backs had been made familiar with the bloody lash, so that they had become callous; mine was yet tender; for while at Baltimore I got few whippings, and few slaves could boast of a kinder master and mistress than myself, and the thought of passing out of their hands into those of Master Andrew — a man who, but a few days before, to give me a sample of his bloody disposition, took my little brother by the throat, threw him on the ground, and with the heel of his boot stamped upon his head till the blood gushed from his nose and ears — was well calculated to make me anxious as to my fate. After he had committed this savage outrage upon my brother, he turned to me, and said that was the way he meant to serve me one of these days, — meaning, I suppose, when I came into his possession.

Thanks to a kind Providence, I fell to the portion of Mrs. Lucretia, and was sent immediately back to Baltimore, to live again in the family of Master Hugh. Their joy at my return equalled their sorrow at my departure. It was a glad day to me. I had escaped a worse than lion's jaws. I was absent from Baltimore, for the purpose of valuation and division, just about one month, and it seemed to have been six.

Very soon after my return to Baltimore, my mistress, Lucretia, died, leaving her husband and one child, Amanda; and in a very short time after her death, Master Andrew died. Now all the property of my old master, slaves included, was in the hands of strangers, — strangers who had had nothing to do with accumulating it. Not a slave was left free. All remained slaves, from the youngest to the oldest. If any one thing in my experience, more than another, served to deepen my conviction of the infernal character of slavery, and to fill me with unutterable loathing of slaveholders, it was their base ingratitude to my poor old grandmother. She had served my old master faithfully from youth to old age. She had been the source of all his wealth; she had peopled his plantation with slaves; she had become a great grandmother in his service. She had rocked him in infancy, attended him in childhood, served him through life, and at his death wiped from his icy brow the cold death-sweat, and closed his eyes forever. She was nevertheless left a slave — a slave for life — a slave in the hands of strangers; and in their hands she saw her children, her grandchildren, and her great-grandchildren, divided, like so many sheep, without being gratified with the small privilege of a single word, as to their or her own destiny. And, to cap the climax of their base ingratitude and fiendish barbarity, my grandmother, who was now very old, having outlived my old master and all his children, having seen the beginning and end of all of them, and her present owners finding she was of but little value, her frame already racked with the pains of old age, and complete helplessness fast stealing over her once active limbs, they took her to the woods, built her a little hut, put up a little mud-chimney, and then made her welcome to the privilege of supporting herself there in perfect loneliness; thus virtually turning her out to die! If my poor old grandmother now lives, she lives to suffer in utter loneliness; she lives to remember and mourn over the loss of children, the loss of grandchildren, and the loss of great-grandchildren. They are, in the language of the slave's poet, Whittier, —

> Gone, gone, sold and gone
> To the rice swamp dank and lone
> Where the slave-whip ceaseless swings,
> Where the noisome insect stings,
> Where the fever-demon strews
> Poison with the falling dews,
> Where the sickly sunbeams glare
> Through the hot and misty air: —
>   Gone, gone, sold and gone
>   To the rice swamp dank and lone,
>   From Virginia hills and waters —
>   Woe is me, my stolen daughters![1]

---

1. **Gone . . . daughters!:** From "The Farewell: Of a Virginia Slave Mother to Her Daughter Sold into Southern Bondage" (1835), by the poet and abolitionist John Greenleaf Whittier (1807–1882). See page 960.

The hearth is desolate. The children, the unconscious children, who once sang and danced in her presence, are gone. She gropes her way, in the darkness of age, for a drink of water. Instead of the voices of her children she hears by day the moans of the dove, and by night the screams of the hideous owl. All is gloom. The grave is at the door. And now, when weighed down by the pains and aches of old age, when the head inclines to the feet, when the beginning and ending of human existence meet, and helpless infancy and painful old age combine together – at this time, this most needful time, the time for the exercise of that tenderness and affection which children only can exercise towards a declining parent – my poor old grandmother, the devoted mother of twelve children, is left all alone, in yonder little hut, before a few dim embers. She stands – she sits – she staggers – she falls – she groans – she dies – and there are none of her children or grandchildren present, to wipe from her wrinkled brow the cold sweat of death, or to place beneath the sod her fallen remains. Will not a righteous God visit for these things?[2]

In about two years after the death of Mrs. Lucretia, Master Thomas married his second wife. Her name was Rowena Hamilton. She was the eldest daughter of Mr. William Hamilton. Master now lived in St. Michael's. Not long after his marriage, a misunderstanding took place between himself and Master Hugh; and as a means of punishing his brother, he took me from him to live with himself at St. Michael's. Here I underwent another most painful separation. It, however, was not so severe as the one I dreaded at the division of property; for, during this interval, a great change had taken place in Master Hugh and his once kind and affectionate wife. The influence of brandy upon him, and of slavery upon her, had effected a disastrous change in the characters of both; so that, as far as they were concerned, I thought I had little to lose by the change. But it was not to them that I was attached. It was to those little Baltimore boys that I felt the strongest attachment. I had received many good lessons from them, and was still receiving them, and the thought of leaving them was painful indeed. I was leaving, too, without the hope of ever being allowed to return. Master Thomas had said he would never let me return again. The barrier betwixt himself and brother he considered impassable.

I then had to regret that I did not at least make the attempt to carry out my resolution to run away; for the chances of success are tenfold greater from the city than from the country.

I sailed from Baltimore for St. Michael's in the sloop Amanda, Captain Edward Dodson. On my passage, I paid particular attention to the direction which the steamboats took to go to Philadelphia. I found, instead of going down, on reaching North Point they went up the bay, in a north-easterly direction. I deemed this knowledge of the utmost importance. My determination to run away was again revived. I resolved to wait only so long as the offering of a favorable opportunity. When that came, I was determined to be off.

---

2. **Will not . . . these things?**: See Jeremiah 5:29: "Shall I not visit for these things? saith the Lord: shall not my soul be avenged on such a nation as this?"

Chapter IX

I have now reached a period of my life when I can give dates. I left Baltimore, and went to live with Master Thomas Auld, at St. Michael's, in March, 1832. It was now more than seven years since I lived with him in the family of my old master, on Colonel Lloyd's plantation. We of course were now almost entire strangers to each other. He was to me a new master, and I to him a new slave. I was ignorant of his temper and disposition; he was equally so of mine. A very short time, however, brought us into full acquaintance with each other. I was made acquainted with his wife not less than with himself. They were well matched, being equally mean and cruel. I was now, for the first time during a space of more than seven years, made to feel the painful gnawings of hunger—a something which I had not experienced before since I left Colonel Lloyd's plantation. It went hard enough with me then, when I could look back to no period at which I had enjoyed a sufficiency. It was tenfold harder after living in Master Hugh's family, where I had always had enough to eat, and of that which was good. I have said Master Thomas was a mean man. He was so. Not to give a slave enough to eat, is regarded as the most aggravated development of meanness even among slaveholders. The rule is, no matter how coarse the food, only let there be enough of it. This is the theory; and in the part of Maryland from which I came, it is the general practice,—though there are many exceptions. Master Thomas gave us enough of neither coarse nor fine food. There were four slaves of us in the kitchen—my sister Eliza, my aunt Priscilla, Henny, and myself; and we were allowed less than a half of a bushel of corn-meal per week, and very little else, either in the shape of meat or vegetables. It was not enough for us to subsist upon. We were therefore reduced to the wretched necessity of living at the expense of our neighbors. This we did by begging and stealing, whichever came handy in the time of need, the one being considered as legitimate as the other. A great many times have we poor creatures been nearly perishing with hunger, when food in abundance lay mouldering in the safe and smoke-house,[1] and our pious mistress was aware of the fact; and yet that mistress and her husband would kneel every morning, and pray that God would bless them in basket and store!

Bad as all slaveholders are, we seldom meet one destitute of every element of character commanding respect. My master was one of this rare sort. I do not know of one single noble act ever performed by him. The leading trait in his character was meanness; and if there were any other element in his nature, it was made subject to this. He was mean; and, like most other mean men, he lacked the ability to conceal his meanness. Captain Auld was not born a slaveholder. He had been a poor man, master only of a Bay craft. He came into possession of all his slaves by marriage; and of all men, adopted slaveholders are the worst. He was cruel, but cowardly. He commanded without firmness. In the enforcement of his rules, he was at times rigid, and at times lax. At times, he spoke to his slaves with the firmness of Napoleon and the fury of a demon; at other times, he might well be mistaken for an inquirer who had lost his way. He did nothing of himself. He might have passed for a lion, but for his ears. In all things noble which he

---

1. **the safe and smoke-house:** The meat safe, used for storing food, and a structure in which meat and fish were cured with smoke.

attempted, his own meanness shone most conspicuous. His airs, words, and actions, were the airs, words, and actions of born slaveholders, and, being assumed, were awkward enough. He was not even a good imitator. He possessed all the disposition to deceive, but wanted the power. Having no resources within himself, he was compelled to be the copyist of many, and being such, he was forever the victim of inconsistency; and of consequence he was an object of contempt, and was held as such even by his slaves. The luxury of having slaves of his own to wait upon him was something new and unprepared for. He was a slaveholder without the ability to hold slaves. He found himself incapable of managing his slaves either by force, fear, or fraud. We seldom called him "master;" we generally called him "Captain Auld," and were hardly disposed to title him at all. I doubt not that our conduct had much to do with making him appear awkward, and of consequence fretful. Our want of reverence for him must have perplexed him greatly. He wished to have us call him master, but lacked the firmness necessary to command us to do so. His wife used to insist upon our calling him so, but to no purpose. In August, 1832, my master attended a Methodist camp-meeting held in the Bay-side, Talbot county, and there experienced religion. I indulged a faint hope that his conversion would lead him to emancipate his slaves, and that, if he did not do this, it would, at any rate, make him more kind and humane. I was disappointed in both these respects. It neither made him to be humane to his slaves, nor to emancipate them. If it had any effect on his character, it made him more cruel and hateful in all his ways; for I believe him to have been a much worse man after his conversion than before. Prior to his conversion, he relied upon his own depravity to shield and sustain him in his savage barbarity; but after his conversion, he found religious sanction and support for his slaveholding cruelty. He made the greatest pretensions to piety. His house was the house of prayer. He prayed morning, noon, and night. He very soon distinguished himself among his brethren, and was soon made a class-leader and exhorter. His activity in revivals was great, and he proved himself an instrument in the hands of the church in converting many souls. His house was the preacher's home. They used to take great pleasure in coming there to put up; for while he starved us, he stuffed them. We have had three or four preachers there at a time. The names of those who used to come most frequently while I lived there, were Mr. Storks, Mr. Ewery, Mr. Humphry, and Mr. Hickey. I have also seen Mr. George Cookman[2] at our house. We slaves loved Mr. Cookman. We believed him to be a good man. We thought him instrumental in getting Mr. Samuel Harrison, a very rich slaveholder, to emancipate his slaves; and by some means got the impression that he was laboring to effect the emancipation of all the slaves. When he was at our house, we were sure to be called in to prayers. When the others were there, we were sometimes called in and sometimes not. Mr. Cookman took more notice of us than either of the other ministers. He could not come among us without betraying his sympathy for us, and, stupid as we were, we had the sagacity to see it.

    While I lived with my master in St. Michael's, there was a white young man, a Mr. Wilson, who proposed to keep a Sabbath school for the instruction of such slaves as might be disposed to learn to read the New Testament. We met but three times, when

---

2. **George Cookman:** The English-born American clergyman George M. Cookman (1800–1841), a prominent Methodist minister who later served as chaplain to Congress in 1838–39.

Mr. West and Mr. Fairbanks, both class-leaders, with many others, came upon us with sticks and other missiles, drove us off, and forbade us to meet again. Thus ended our little Sabbath school in the pious town of St. Michael's.

I have said my master found religious sanction for his cruelty. As an example, I will state one of many facts going to prove the charge. I have seen him tie up a lame young woman, and whip her with a heavy cowskin upon her naked shoulders, causing the warm red blood to drip; and, in justification of the bloody deed, he would quote this passage of Scripture — "He that knoweth his master's will, and doeth it not, shall be beaten with many stripes."[3]

Master would keep his lacerated young woman tied up in this horrid situation four or five hours at a time. I have known him to tie her up early in the morning, and whip her before breakfast; leave her, go to his store, return at dinner, and whip her again, cutting her in the places already made raw with his cruel lash. The secret of master's cruelty toward "Henny" is found in the fact of her being almost helpless. When quite a child, she fell into the fire, and burned herself horribly. Her hands were so burnt that she never got the use of them. She could do very little but bear heavy burdens. She was to master a bill of expense; and as he was a mean man, she was a constant offence to him. He seemed desirous of getting the poor girl out of existence. He gave her away once to his sister; but, being a poor gift, she was not disposed to keep her. Finally, my benevolent master, to use his own words, "set her adrift to take care of herself." Here was a recently-converted man, holding on upon the mother, and at the same time turning out her helpless child, to starve and die! Master Thomas was one of the many pious slaveholders who hold slaves for the very charitable purpose of taking care of them.

My master and myself had quite a number of differences. He found me unsuitable to his purpose. My city life, he said, had had a very pernicious effect upon me. It had almost ruined me for every good purpose, and fitted me for every thing which was bad. One of my greatest faults was that of letting his horse run away, and go down to his father-in-law's farm, which was about five miles from St. Michael's. I would then have to go after it. My reason for this kind of carelessness, or carefulness, was, that I could always get something to eat when I went there. Master William Hamilton, my master's father-in-law, always gave his slaves enough to eat. I never left there hungry, no matter how great the need of my speedy return. Master Thomas at length said he would stand it no longer. I had lived with him nine months, during which time he had given me a number of severe whippings, all to no good purpose. He resolved to put me out, as he said, to be broken; and, for this purpose, he let me for one year to a man named Edward Covey. Mr. Covey was a poor man, a farm-renter. He rented the place upon which he lived, as also the hands with which he tilled it. Mr. Covey had acquired a very high reputation for breaking young slaves, and this reputation was of immense value to him. It enabled him to get his farm tilled with much less expense to himself than he could have had it done without such a reputation. Some slaveholders thought it not much loss to allow Mr. Covey to have their slaves one year, for the sake of the training to which they were subjected, without any other compensation. He could hire young help with great ease, in consequence of this reputation. Added

---

3. "He . . . many stripes": Luke 12:47.

to the natural good qualities of Mr. Covey, he was a professor of religion – a pious soul – a member and a class-leader in the Methodist church. All of this added weight to his reputation as a "nigger-breaker." I was aware of all the facts, having been made acquainted with them by a young man who had lived there. I nevertheless made the change gladly; for I was sure of getting enough to eat, which is not the smallest consideration to a hungry man.

Chapter X

I left Master Thomas's house, and went to live with Mr. Covey, on the 1st of January, 1833. I was now, for the first time in my life, a field hand. In my new employment, I found myself even more awkward than a country boy appeared to be in a large city. I had been at my new home but one week before Mr. Covey gave me a very severe whipping, cutting my back causing the blood to run, and raising ridges on my flesh as large as my little finger. The details of this affair are as follows: Mr. Covey sent me, very early in the morning of one of our coldest days in the month of January, to the woods, to get a load of wood. He gave me a team of unbroken oxen. He told me which was the in-hand ox, and which the off-hand one. He then tied the end of a large rope around the horns of the in-hand ox, and gave me the other end of it, and told me, if the oxen started to run, that I must hold on upon the rope. I had never driven oxen before, and of course I was very awkward. I, however, succeeded in getting to the edge of the woods with little difficulty; but I had got a very few rods into the woods, when the oxen took fright, and started full tilt, carrying the cart against trees, and over stumps, in the most frightful manner. I expected every moment that my brains would be dashed out against the trees. After running thus for a considerable distance, they finally upset the cart, dashing it with great force against a tree, and threw themselves into a dense thicket. How I escaped death, I do not know. There I was, entirely alone, in a thick wood, in a place new to me. My cart was upset and shattered, my oxen were entangled among the young trees, and there was none to help me. After a long spell of effort, I succeeded in getting my cart righted, my oxen disentangled, and again yoked to the cart. I now proceeded with my team to the place where I had, the day before, been chopping wood, and loaded my cart pretty heavily, thinking in this way to tame my oxen. I then proceeded on my way home. I had now consumed one half of the day. I got out of the woods safely, and now felt out of danger. I stopped my oxen to open the woods gate; and just as I did so, before I could get hold of my ox-rope, the oxen again started, rushed through the gate, catching it between the wheel and the body of the cart, tearing it to pieces, and coming within a few inches of crushing me against the gate-post. Thus twice, in one short day, I escaped death by the merest chance. On my return, I told Mr. Covey what had happened and how it happened. He ordered me to return to the woods again immediately. I did so, and he followed on after me. Just as I got into the woods, he came up and told me to stop my cart, and that he would teach me how to trifle away my time, and break gates. He then went to a large gum tree, and with his axe cut three large switches, and, after trimming them up neatly with his pocket-knife, he ordered me to take off my clothes. I made him no answer, but stood with my clothes on. He repeated his order. I still made him no answer, nor did I move to strip myself. Upon this he rushed at me with the fierceness of a tiger, tore off my clothes, and lashed me till he had worn out his switches, cutting me so savagely as to leave the marks visible for a long time after. This whipping was the first of a number just like it, and for similar offences.

I lived with Mr. Covey one year. During the first six months, of that year, scarce a week passed without his whipping me. I was seldom free from a sore back. My awkwardness was almost always his excuse for whipping me. We were worked fully up to the point of endurance. Long before day we were up, our horses fed, and by the first approach of day we were off to the field with our hoes and ploughing teams. Mr. Covey gave us enough to eat, but scarce time to eat it. We were often less than five minutes taking our meals. We were often in the field from the first approach of day till its last lingering ray had left us; and at saving-fodder time, midnight often caught us in the field binding blades.[1]

Covey would be out with us. The way he used to stand it, was this. He would spend the most of his afternoons in bed. He would then come out fresh in the evening, ready to urge us on with his words, example, and frequently with the whip. Mr. Covey was one of the few slaveholders who could and did work with his hands. He was a hard-working man. He knew by himself just what a man or a boy could do. There was no deceiving him. His work went on in his absence almost as well as in his presence; and he had the faculty of making us feel that he was ever present with us. This he did by surprising us. He seldom approached the spot where we were at work openly, if he could do it secretly. He always aimed at taking us by surprise. Such was his cunning, that we used to call him, among ourselves, "the snake." When we were at work in the cornfield, he would sometimes crawl on his hands and knees to avoid detection, and all at once he would rise nearly in our midst, and scream out, "Ha, ha! Come, come! Dash on, dash on!" This being his mode of attack, it was never safe to stop a single minute. His comings were like a thief in the night. He appeared to us as being ever at hand. He was under every tree, behind every stump, in every bush, and at every window, on the plantation. He would sometimes mount his horse, as if bound to St. Michael's, a distance of seven miles, and in half an hour afterwards you would see him coiled up in the corner of the wood-fence, watching every motion of the slaves. He would, for this purpose, leave his horse tied up in the woods. Again, he would sometimes walk up to us, and give us orders as though he was upon the point of starting on a long journey, turn his back upon us, and make as though he was going to the house to get ready; and, before he would get half way thither, he would turn short and crawl into a fence-corner, or behind some tree, and there watch us till the going down of the sun.

Mr. Covey's *forte*[2] consisted in his power to deceive. His life was devoted to planning and perpetrating the grossest deceptions. Every thing he possessed in the shape of learning or religion, he made conform to his disposition to deceive. He seemed to think himself equal to deceiving the Almighty. He would make a short prayer in the morning, and a long prayer at night; and, strange as it may seem, few men would at times appear more devotional than he. The exercises of his family devotions were always commenced with singing; and, as he was a very poor singer himself, the duty of raising the hymn generally

---

1. **at saving-fodder time . . . binding blades:** That is, binding together sheaves of wheat at harvest time.
2. *forte*: Strong point (French).

came upon me. He would read his hymn, and nod at me to commence. I would at times do so; at others, I would not. My non-compliance would almost always produce much confusion. To show himself independent of me, he would start and stagger through with his hymn in the most discordant manner. In this state of mind, he prayed with more than ordinary spirit. Poor man! such was his disposition, and success at deceiving, I do verily believe that he sometimes deceived himself into the solemn belief, that he was a sincere worshipper of the most high God; and this, too, at a time when he may be said to have been guilty of compelling his woman slave to commit the sin of adultery. The facts in the case are these: Mr. Covey was a poor man; he was just commencing in life; he was only able to buy one slave; and, shocking as is the fact, he bought her, as he said, for a *breeder*. This woman was named Caroline. Mr. Covey bought her from Mr. Thomas Lowe, about six miles from St. Michael's. She was a large, able-bodied woman, about twenty years old. She had already given birth to one child, which proved her to be just what he wanted. After buying her, he hired a married man of Mr. Samuel Harrison, to live with him one year; and him he used to fasten up with her every night! The result was, that, at the end of the year, the miserable woman gave birth to twins. At this result Mr. Covey seemed to be highly pleased, both with the man and the wretched woman. Such was his joy, and that of his wife, that nothing they could do for Caroline during her confinement was too good, or too hard, to be done. The children were regarded as being quite an addition to his wealth.

If at any one time of my life more than another, I was made to drink the bitterest dregs of slavery, that time was during the first six months of my stay with Mr. Covey. We were worked in all weathers. It was never too hot or too cold; it could never rain, blow, hail, or snow, too hard for us to work in the field. Work, work, work, was scarcely more the order of the day than of the night. The longest days were too short for him, and the shortest nights too long for him. I was somewhat unmanageable when I first went there, but a few months of this discipline tamed me. Mr. Covey succeeded in breaking me. I was broken in body, soul, and spirit. My natural elasticity was crushed, my intellect languished, the disposition to read departed, the cheerful spark that lingered about my eye died; the dark night of slavery closed in upon me; and behold a man transformed into a brute!

Sunday was my only leisure time. I spent this in a sort of beast-like stupor, between sleep and wake, under some large tree. At times I would rise up, a flash of energetic freedom would dart through my soul, accompanied with a faint beam of hope, that flickered for a moment, and then vanished. I sank down again, mourning over my wretched condition. I was sometimes prompted to take my life, and that of Covey, but was prevented by a combination of hope and fear. My sufferings on this plantation seem now like a dream rather than a stern reality.

Our house stood within a few rods of the Chesapeake Bay, whose broad bosom was ever white with sails from every quarter of the habitable globe. Those beautiful vessels, robed in purest white, so delightful to the eye of freemen, were to me so many shrouded ghosts, to terrify and torment me with thoughts of my wretched condition. I have often, in the deep stillness of a summer's Sabbath, stood all alone upon the lofty banks of that noble bay, and traced, with saddened heart and tearful eye, the countless number of sails moving off to the mighty ocean. The sight of these always affected me powerfully. My thoughts would compel utterance; and there, with no audience but the Almighty, I would pour out my soul's complaint, in my rude way, with an apostrophe to the moving multitude of ships: —

"You are loosed from your moorings, and are free; I am fast in my chains, and am a slave! You move merrily before the gentle gale, and I sadly before the bloody whip! You are freedom's swift-winged angels, that fly round the world; I am confined in bands of iron! O that I were free! O, that I were on one of your gallant decks, and under your protecting wing! Alas! betwixt me and you, the turbid waters roll. Go on, go on. O that I could also go! Could I but swim! If I could fly! O, why was I born a man, of whom to make a brute! The glad ship is gone; she hides in the dim distance. I am left in the hottest hell of unending slavery. O God, save me! God, deliver me! Let me be free! Is there any God? Why am I a slave? I will run away. I will not stand it. Get caught, or get clear! I'll try it. I had as well die with ague as the fever. I have only one life to lose. I had as well be killed running as die standing. Only think of it; one hundred miles straight north, and I am free! Try it? Yes! God helping me, I will. It cannot be that I shall live and die a slave. I will take to the water. This very bay shall yet bear me into freedom. The steamboats steered in a north-east course from North Point. I will do the same; and when I get to the head of the bay, I will turn my canoe adrift, and walk straight through Delaware into Pennsylvania. When I get there, I shall not be required to have a pass; I can travel without being disturbed. Let but the first opportunity offer, and, come what will, I am off. Meanwhile, I will try to bear up under the yoke. I am not the only slave in the world. Why should I fret? I can bear as much as any of them. Besides, I am but a boy, and all boys are bound to some one. It may be that my misery in slavery will only increase my happiness when I get free. There is a better day coming."

Thus I used to think, and thus I used to speak to myself; goaded almost to madness at one moment, and at the next reconciling myself to my wretched lot.

I have already intimated that my condition was much worse, during the first six months of my stay at Mr. Covey's, than in the last six. The circumstances leading to the change in Mr. Covey's course toward me form an epoch in my humble history. You have seen how a man was made a slave; you shall see how a slave was made a man. On one of the hottest days of the month of August, 1833, Bill Smith, William Hughes, a slave named Eli, and myself, were engaged in fanning wheat.[3] Hughes was clearing the fanned wheat from before the fan, Eli was turning, Smith was feeding, and I was carrying wheat to the fan. The work was simple, requiring strength rather than intellect; yet, to one entirely unused to such work, it came very hard. About three o'clock of that day, I broke down; my strength failed me; I was seized with a violent aching of the head, attended with extreme dizziness; I trembled in every limb. Finding what was coming, I nerved myself up, feeling it would never do to stop work. I stood as long as I could stagger to the hopper with grain. When I could stand no longer, I fell, and felt as if held down by an immense weight. The fan of course stopped; every one had his own work to do; and no one could do the work of the other, and have his own go on at the same time.

Mr. Covey was at the house, about one hundred yards from the treading-yard where we were fanning. On hearing the fan stop, he left immediately, and came to the spot where we were. He hastily inquired what the matter was. Bill answered that I was sick, and there was no one to bring wheat to the fan. I had by this time crawled away under the

---

3. **fanning wheat:** Separating the wheat from the chaff with a fan.

side of the post and rail-fence by which the yard was enclosed, hoping to find relief by getting out of the sun. He then asked where I was. He was told by one of the hands. He came to the spot, and, after looking at me awhile, asked me what was the matter. I told him as well as I could, for I scarce had strength to speak. He then gave me a savage kick in the side, and told me to get up. I tried to do so, but fell back in the attempt. He gave me another kick, and again told me to rise. I again tried, and succeeded in gaining my feet; but, stooping to get the tub with which I was feeding the fan, I again staggered and fell. While down in this situation, Mr. Covey took up the hickory slat with which Hughes had been striking off the half-bushel measure, and with it gave me a heavy blow upon the head, making a large wound, and the blood ran freely; and with this again told me to get up. I made no effort to comply, having now made up my mind to let him do his worst. In a short time after receiving this blow, my head grew better. Mr. Covey had now left me to my fate. At this moment I resolved, for the first time, to go to my master, enter a complaint, and ask his protection. In order to [do] this, I must that afternoon walk seven miles; and this, under the circumstances, was truly a severe undertaking. I was exceedingly feeble; made so as much by the kicks and blows which I received, as by the severe fit of sickness to which I had been subjected. I, however, watched my chance, while Covey was looking in an opposite direction, and started for St. Michael's. I succeeded in getting a considerable distance on my way to the woods, when Covey discovered me, and called after me to come back, threatening what he would do if I did not come. I disregarded both his calls and his threats, and made my way to the woods as fast as my feeble state would allow; and thinking I might be overhauled by him if I kept the road, I walked through the woods, keeping far enough from the road to avoid detection, and near enough to prevent losing my way. I had not gone far before my little strength again failed me. I could go no farther. I fell down, and lay for a considerable time. The blood was yet oozing from the wound on my head. For a time I thought I should bleed to death; and think now that I should have done so, but that the blood so matted my hair as to stop the wound. After lying there about three quarters of an hour, I nerved myself up again, and started on my way, through bogs and briers, barefooted and bareheaded, tearing my feet sometimes at nearly every step; and after a journey of about seven miles, occupying some five hours to perform it, I arrived at master's store. I then presented an appearance enough to affect any but a heart of iron. From the crown of my head to my feet, I was covered with blood. My hair was all clotted with dust and blood; my shirt was stiff with blood. My legs and feet were torn in sundry places with briers and thorns, and were also covered with blood. I suppose I looked like a man who had escaped a den of wild beasts, and barely escaped them. In this state I appeared before my master, humbly entreating him to interpose his authority for my protection. I told him all the circumstances as well as I could, and it seemed, as I spoke, at times to affect him. He would then walk the floor, and seek to justify Covey by saying he expected I deserved it. He asked me what I wanted. I told him, to let me get a new home; that as sure as I lived with Mr. Covey again, I should live with but to die with him; that Covey would surely kill me; he was in a fair way for it. Master Thomas ridiculed the idea that there was any danger of Mr. Covey's killing me, and said that he knew Mr. Covey; that he was a good man, and that he could not think of taking me from him; that, should he do so, he would lose the whole year's wages; that

I belonged to Mr. Covey for one year, and that I must go back to him, come what might; and that I must not trouble him with any more stories, or that he would himself *get hold of me.* After threatening me thus, he gave me a very large dose of salts, telling me that I might remain in St. Michael's that night, (it being quite late,) but that I must be off back to Mr. Covey's early in the morning; and that if I did not, he would *get hold of me*, which meant that he would whip me. I remained all night, and, according to his orders, I started off to Covey's in the morning, (Saturday morning,) wearied in body and broken in spirit. I got no supper that night, or breakfast that morning. I reached Covey's about nine o'clock; and just as I was getting over the fence that divided Mrs. Kemp's fields from ours, out ran Covey with his cowskin, to give me another whipping. Before he could reach me, I succeeded in getting to the cornfield; and as the corn was very high, it afforded me the means of hiding. He seemed very angry, and searched for me a long time. My behavior was altogether unaccountable. He finally gave up the chase, thinking, I suppose, that I must come home for something to eat; he would give himself no further trouble in looking for me. I spent that day mostly in the woods, having the alternative before me, – to go home and be whipped to death, or stay in the woods and be starved to death. That night, I fell in with Sandy Jenkins, a slave with whom I was somewhat acquainted. Sandy had a free wife who lived about four miles from Mr. Covey's; and it being Saturday, he was on his way to see her. I told him my circumstances, and he very kindly invited me to go home with him. I went home with him, and talked this whole matter over, and got his advice as to what course it was best for me to pursue. I found Sandy an old adviser. He told me, with great solemnity, I must go back to Covey; but that before I went, I must go with him into another part of the woods, where there was a certain *root*, which, if I would take some of it with me, carrying it *always on my right side*, would render it impossible for Mr. Covey, or any other white man, to whip me. He said he had carried it for years; and since he had done so, he had never received a blow, and never expected to while he carried it. I at first rejected the idea, that the simple carrying of a root in my pocket would have any such effect as he had said, and was not disposed to take it; but Sandy impressed the necessity with much earnestness, telling me it could do no harm, if it did no good. To please him, I at length took the root, and, according to his direction, carried it upon my right side. This was Sunday morning. I immediately started for home; and upon entering the yard gate, out came Mr. Covey on his way to meeting. He spoke to me very kindly, made me drive the pigs from a lot near by, and passed on towards the church. Now, this singular conduct of Mr. Covey really made me begin to think that there was something in the *root* which Sandy had given me; and had it been on any other day than Sunday, I could have attributed the conduct to no other cause than the influence of that root; and as it was, I was half inclined to think the *root* to be something more than I at first had taken it to be. All went well till Monday morning. On this morning, the virtue of the *root* was fully tested. Long before daylight, I was called to go and rub, curry, and feed, the horses. I obeyed, and was glad to obey. But whilst thus engaged, whilst in the act of throwing down some blades from the loft, Mr. Covey entered the stable with a long rope; and just as I was half out of the loft, he caught hold of my legs, and was about tying me. As soon as I found what he was up to, I gave a sudden spring, and as I did so, he holding to my legs, I was brought sprawling on the stable floor.

Mr. Covey seemed now to think he had me, and could do what he pleased; but at this moment – from whence came the spirit I don't know – I resolved to fight; and, suiting my action to the resolution, I seized Covey hard by the throat; and as I did so, I rose. He held on to me, and I to him. My resistance was so entirely unexpected, that Covey seemed taken all aback. He trembled like a leaf. This gave me assurance, and I held him uneasy, causing the blood to run where I touched him with the ends of my fingers. Mr. Covey soon called out to Hughes for help. Hughes came, and, while Covey held me, attempted to tie my right hand. While he was in the act of doing so, I watched my chance, and gave him a heavy kick close under the ribs. This kick fairly sickened Hughes, so that he left me in the hands of Mr. Covey. This kick had the effect of not only weakening Hughes, but Covey also. When he saw Hughes bending over with pain, his courage quailed. He asked me if I meant to persist in my resistance. I told him I did, come what might; that he had used me like a brute for six months, and that I was determined to be used so no longer. With that, he strove to drag me to a stick that was lying just out of the stable door. He meant to knock me down. But just as he was leaning over to get the stick, I seized him with both hands by his collar, and brought him by a sudden snatch to the ground. By this time, Bill came. Covey called upon him for assistance. Bill wanted to know what he could do. Covey said, "Take hold of him, take hold of him!" Bill said his master hired him out to work, and not to help to whip me; so he left Covey and myself to fight our own battle out. We were at it for nearly two hours. Covey at length let me go, puffing and blowing at a great rate, saying that if I had not resisted, he would not have whipped me half so much. The truth was, that he had not whipped me at all. I considered him as getting entirely the worst end of the bargain; for he had drawn no blood from me, but I had from him. The whole six months afterwards, that I spent with Mr. Covey, he never laid the weight of his finger upon me in anger. He would occasionally say, he didn't want to get hold of me again. "No," thought I, "you need not; for you will come off worse than you did before."

This battle with Mr. Covey was the turning-point in my career as a slave. It rekindled the few expiring embers of freedom, and revived within me a sense of my own manhood. It recalled the departed self-confidence, and inspired me again with a determination to be free. The gratification afforded by the triumph was a full compensation for whatever else might follow, even death itself. He only can understand the deep satisfaction which I experienced, who has himself repelled by force the bloody arm of slavery. I felt as I never felt before. It was a glorious resurrection, from the tomb of slavery, to the heaven of freedom. My long-crushed spirit rose, cowardice departed, bold defiance took its place; and I now resolved that, however long I might remain a slave in form, the day had passed forever when I could be a slave in fact. I did not hesitate to let it be known of me, that the white man who expected to succeed in whipping, must also succeed in killing me.

From this time I was never again what might be called fairly whipped, though I remained a slave four years afterwards. I had several fights, but was never whipped.

It was for a long time a matter of surprise to me why Mr. Covey did not immediately have me taken by the constable to the whipping-post, and there regularly whipped for the crime of raising my hand against a white man in defence of myself. And the only explanation I can now think of does not entirely satisfy me; but such as it is, I will give it. Mr. Covey enjoyed the most unbounded reputation for being a first-rate overseer and negro-breaker. It was of considerable importance to him. That reputation was at stake; and had he sent me – a boy about sixteen years old – to the public whipping-post, his reputation would have been lost; so, to save his reputation, he suffered me to go unpunished.

My term of actual service to Mr. Edward Covey ended on Christmas day, 1833. The days between Christmas and New Year's day are allowed as holidays; and, accordingly, we were not required to perform any labor, more than to feed and take care of the stock. This time we regarded as our own, by the grace of our masters; and we therefore used or abused it nearly as we pleased. Those of us who had families at a distance, were generally allowed to spend the whole six days in their society. This time, however, was spent in various ways. The staid, sober, thinking and industrious ones of our number would employ themselves in making corn-brooms, mats, horse-collars, and baskets; and another class of us would spend the time in hunting opossums, hares, and coons. But by far the larger part engaged in such sports and merriments as playing ball, wrestling, running footraces, fiddling, dancing, and drinking whisky; and this latter mode of spending the time was by far the most agreeable to the feelings of our masters. A slave who would work during the holidays was considered by our masters as scarcely deserving them. He was regarded as one who rejected the favor of his master. It was deemed a disgrace not to get drunk at Christmas; and he was regarded as lazy indeed, who had not provided himself with the necessary means, during the year, to get whisky enough to last him through Christmas.

From what I know of the effect of these holidays upon the slave, I believe them to be among the most effective means in the hands of the slaveholder in keeping down the spirit of insurrection. Were the slaveholders at once to abandon this practice, I have not the slightest doubt it would lead to an immediate insurrection among the slaves. These holidays serve as conductors, or safety-valves, to carry off the rebellious spirit of enslaved humanity. But for these, the slave would be forced up to the wildest desperation; and woe betide the slaveholder, the day he ventures to remove or hinder the operation of those conductors! I warn him that, in such an event, a spirit will go forth in their midst, more to be dreaded than the most appalling earthquake.

The holidays are part and parcel of the gross fraud, wrong, and inhumanity of slavery. They are professedly a custom established by the benevolence of the slaveholders; but I undertake to say, it is the result of selfishness, and one of the grossest frauds committed upon the downtrodden slave. They do not give the slaves this time because they would not like to have their work during its continuance, but because they know it would be unsafe to deprive them of it. This will be seen by the fact, that the slaveholders like to have their slaves spend those days just in such a manner as to make them as glad of their ending as of their beginning. Their object seems to be, to disgust their slaves with freedom, by plunging them into the lowest depths of dissipation. For instance, the slaveholders not only like to see the slave drink of his own accord, but will adopt various plans to make him drunk. One plan is, to make bets on their slaves, as to who can drink the most whisky without getting drunk; and in this way they succeed in getting whole multitudes to drink to excess. Thus, when the slave asks for virtuous freedom, the cunning slaveholder, knowing his ignorance, cheats him with a dose of vicious dissipation, artfully labelled with the name of liberty. The most of us used to drink it down, and the result was just what might be supposed: many of us were led to think that there was little to choose between liberty and slavery. We felt, and very properly too, that we had almost as well be slaves to man as to rum. So, when the holidays ended, we staggered up from the filth of our wallowing, took a long breath, and marched to the field, – feeling, upon the whole, rather glad to go, from what our master had deceived us into a belief was freedom, back to the arms of slavery.

I have said that this mode of treatment is a part of the whole system of fraud and inhumanity of slavery. It is so. The mode here adopted to disgust the slave with freedom, by allowing him to see only the abuse of it, is carried out in other things. For instance, a slave loves molasses; he steals some. His master, in many cases, goes off to town, and buys a large quantity; he returns, takes his whip, and commands the slave to eat the molasses, until the poor fellow is made sick at the very mention of it. The same mode is sometimes adopted to make the slaves refrain from asking for more food than their regular allowance. A slave runs through his allowance, and applies for more. His master is enraged at him; but, not willing to send him off without food, gives him more than is necessary, and compels him to eat it within a given time. Then, if he complains that he cannot eat it, he is said to be satisfied neither full or fasting, and is whipped for being hard to please! I have an abundance of such illustrations of the same principle, drawn from my own observation, but think the cases I have cited sufficient. The practice is a very common one.

On the first of January, 1834, I left Mr. Covey, and went to live with Mr. William Freeland, who lived about three miles from St. Michael's. I soon found Mr. Freeland a very different man from Mr. Covey. Though not rich, he was what would be called an educated southern gentleman. Mr. Covey, as I have shown, was a well-trained negro-breaker and slavedriver. The former (slaveholder though he was) seemed to possess some regard for honor, some reverence for justice, and some respect for humanity. The latter seemed totally insensible to all such sentiments. Mr. Freeland had many of the faults peculiar to slaveholders, such as being very passionate and fretful; but I must do him the justice to say, that he was exceedingly free from those degrading vices to which Mr. Covey was constantly addicted. The one was open and frank, and we always knew where to find him. The other was a most artful deceiver, and could be understood only by such as were skilful enough to detect his cunningly-devised frauds. Another advantage I gained in my new master was, he made no pretensions to, or profession of, religion; and this, in my opinion, was truly a great advantage. I assert most unhesitatingly, that the religion of the south is a mere covering for the most horrid crimes, – a justifier of the most appalling barbarity, – a sanctifier of the most hateful frauds, – and a dark shelter under which the darkest, foulest, grossest, and most infernal deeds of slaveholders find the strongest protection. Were I to be again reduced to the chains of slavery, next to that enslavement, I should regard being the slave of a religious master the greatest calamity that could befall me. For of all slaveholders with whom I have ever met, religious slaveholders are the worst. I have ever found them the meanest and basest, the most cruel and cowardly, of all others. It was my unhappy lot not only to belong to a religious slaveholder, but to live in a community of such religionists. Very near Mr. Freeland lived the

Rev. Daniel Weeden, and in the same neighborhood lived the Rev. Rigby Hopkins. These were members and ministers in the Reformed Methodist Church. Mr. Weeden owned, among others, a woman slave, whose name I have forgotten. This woman's back, for weeks, was kept literally raw, made so by the lash of this merciless, *religious* wretch. He used to hire hands. His maxim was, Behave well or behave ill, it is the duty of a master occasionally to whip a slave, to remind him of his master's authority. Such was his theory, and such his practice.

Mr. Hopkins was even worse than Mr. Weeden. His chief boast was his ability to manage slaves. The peculiar feature of his government was that of whipping slaves in advance of deserving it. He always managed to have one or more of his slaves to whip every Monday morning. He did this to alarm their fears, and strike terror into those who escaped. His plan was to whip for the smallest offences, to prevent the commission of large ones. Mr. Hopkins could always find some excuse for whipping a slave. It would astonish one, unaccustomed to a slaveholding life, to see with what wonderful ease a slaveholder can find things, of which to make occasion to whip a slave. A mere look, word, or motion,—a mistake, accident, or want of power,—are all matters for which a slave may be whipped at any time. Does a slave look dissatisfied? It is said, he has the devil in him, and it must be whipped out. Does he speak loudly when spoken to by his master? Then he is getting high-minded, and should be taken down a button-hole lower. Does he forget to pull off his hat at the approach of a white person? Then he is wanting in reverence, and should be whipped for it. Does he ever venture to vindicate his conduct, when censured for it? Then he is guilty of impudence,—one of the greatest crimes of which a slave can be guilty. Does he ever venture to suggest a different mode of doing things from that pointed out by his master? He is indeed presumptuous, and getting above himself; and nothing less than a flogging will do for him. Does he, while ploughing, break a plough,—or, while hoeing, break a hoe? It is owing to his carelessness, and for it a slave must always be whipped. Mr. Hopkins could always find something of this sort to justify the use of the lash, and he seldom failed to embrace such opportunities. There was not a man in the whole county, with whom the slaves who had the getting their own home, would not prefer to live, rather than with this Rev. Mr. Hopkins. And yet there was not a man any where round, who made higher professions of religion, or was more active in revivals,—more attentive to the class, love-feast, prayer and preaching meetings, or more devotional in his family,—that prayed earlier, later, louder, and longer,—than this same reverend slave-driver, Rigby Hopkins.

But to return to Mr. Freeland, and to my experience while in his employment. He, like Mr. Covey, gave us enough to eat; but, unlike Mr. Covey, he also gave us sufficient time to take our meals. He worked us hard, but always between sunrise and sunset. He required a good deal of work to be done, but gave us good tools with which to work. His farm was large, but he employed hands enough to work it, and with ease, compared with many of his neighbors. My treatment, while in his employment, was heavenly, compared with what I experienced at the hands of Mr. Edward Covey.

Mr. Freeland was himself the owner of but two slaves. Their names were Henry Harris and John Harris. The rest of his hands he hired. These consisted of myself,

Sandy Jenkins,[1] and Handy Caldwell. Henry and John were quite intelligent, and in a very little while after I went there, I succeeded in creating in them a strong desire to learn how to read. This desire soon sprang up in the others also. They very soon mustered up some old spelling-books, and nothing would do but that I must keep a Sabbath school. I agreed to do so, and accordingly devoted my Sundays to teaching these my loved fellow-slaves how to read. Neither of them knew his letters when I went there. Some of the slaves of the neighboring farms found what was going on, and also availed themselves of this little opportunity to learn to read. It was understood, among all who came, that there must be as little display about it as possible. It was necessary to keep our religious masters at St. Michael's unacquainted with the fact, that, instead of spending the Sabbath in wrestling, boxing, and drinking whisky, we were trying to learn how to read the will of God; for they had much rather see us engaged in those degrading sports, than to see us behaving like intellectual, moral, and accountable beings. My blood boils as I think of the bloody manner in which Messrs. Wright Fairbanks and Garrison West, both class-leaders, in connection with many others, rushed in upon us with sticks and stones, and broke up our virtuous little Sabbath school, at St. Michael's — all calling themselves Christians! humble followers of the Lord Jesus Christ! But I am again digressing.

I held my Sabbath school at the house of a free colored man, whose name I deem it imprudent to mention; for should it be known, it might embarrass him greatly, though the crime of holding the school was committed ten years ago. I had at one time over forty scholars, and those of the right sort, ardently desiring to learn. They were of all ages, though mostly men and women. I look back to those Sundays with an amount of pleasure not to be expressed. They were great days to my soul. The work of instructing my dear fellow-slaves was the sweetest engagement with which I was ever blessed. We loved each other, and to leave them at the close of the Sabbath was a severe cross indeed. When I think that these precious souls are to-day shut up in the prison-house of slavery, my feelings overcome me, and I am almost ready to ask, "Does a righteous God govern the universe? and for what does he hold the thunders in his right hand, if not to smite the oppressor, and deliver the spoiled out of the hand of the spoiler?"[2] These dear souls came not to Sabbath school because it was popular to do so, nor did I teach them because it was reputable to be thus engaged. Every moment they spent in that school, they were liable to be taken up, and given thirty-nine lashes. They came because they wished to learn. Their minds had been starved by their cruel masters. They had been shut up in mental darkness. I taught them, because it was the delight of my soul to be doing something that looked like bettering the condition of my race. I kept up my school nearly the

---

1. **Sandy Jenkins:** This is the same man who gave me the roots to prevent my being whipped by Mr. Covey. He was a "clever soul." We used frequently to talk about the fight with Covey, and as often as we did so, he would claim my success as the result of the roots which he gave me. This superstition is very common among the more ignorant slaves. A slave seldom dies but that his death is attributed to trickery. [Douglass's note]

2. **"Does a righteous God . . . spoiler?":** Douglass echoes several biblical passages, including Exodus 15:6–17 and Isaiah 33:1: "Woe to thee that spoilest . . . when thou shalt cease to spoil, thou shalt be spoiled."

whole year I lived with Mr. Freeland; and, beside my Sabbath school, I devoted three evenings in the week, during the winter, to teaching the slaves at home. And I have the happiness to know, that several of those who came to Sabbath school learned how to read; and that one, at least, is now free through my agency.

The year passed off smoothly. It seemed only about half as long as the year which preceded it. I went through it without receiving a single blow. I will give Mr. Freeland the credit of being the best master I ever had, *till I became my own master.* For the ease with which I passed the year, I was, however, somewhat indebted to the society of my fellow-slaves. They were noble souls; they not only possessed loving hearts, but brave ones. We were linked and interlinked with each other. I loved them with a love stronger than any thing I have experienced since. It is sometimes said that we slaves do not love and confide in each other. In answer to this assertion, I can say, I never loved any or confided in any people more than my fellow-slaves, and especially those with whom I lived at Mr. Freeland's. I believe we would have died for each other. We never undertook to do any thing, of any importance, without a mutual consultation. We never moved separately. We were one; and as much so by our tempers and dispositions, as by the mutual hardships to which we were necessarily subjected by our condition as slaves.

At the close of the year 1834, Mr. Freeland again hired me of my master, for the year 1835. But, by this time, I began to want to live *upon free land* as well as *with Freeland*; and I was no longer content, therefore, to live with him or any other slaveholder. I began, with the commencement of the year, to prepare myself for a final struggle, which should decide my fate one way or the other. My tendency was upward. I was fast approaching manhood, and year after year had passed, and I was still a slave. These thoughts roused me — I must do something. I therefore resolved that 1835 should not pass without witnessing an attempt, on my part, to secure my liberty. But I was not willing to cherish this determination alone. My fellow-slaves were dear to me. I was anxious to have them participate with me in this, my life-giving determination. I therefore, though with great prudence, commenced early to ascertain their views and feelings in regard to their condition, and to imbue their minds with thoughts of freedom. I bent myself to devising ways and means for our escape, and meanwhile strove, on all fitting occasions, to impress them with the gross fraud and inhumanity of slavery. I went first to Henry, next to John, then to the others. I found, in them all, warm hearts and noble spirits. They were ready to hear, and ready to act when a feasible plan should be proposed. This was what I wanted. I talked to them of our want of manhood, if we submitted to our enslavement without at least one noble effort to be free. We met often, and consulted frequently, and told our hopes and fears, recounted the difficulties, real and imagined, which we should be called on to meet. At times we were almost disposed to give up, and try to content ourselves with our wretched lot; at others, we were firm and unbending in our determination to go. Whenever we suggested any plan, there was shrinking — the odds were fearful. Our path was beset with the greatest obstacles; and if we succeeded in gaining the end of it, our right to be free was yet questionable — we were yet liable to be returned to bondage. We could see no spot this side of the ocean, where we could be free. We knew nothing about Canada.

Our knowledge of the north did not extend farther than New York; and to go there, and be forever harassed with the frightful liability of being returned to slavery – with the certainty of being treated tenfold worse than before – the thought was truly a horrible one, and one which it was not easy to overcome. The case sometimes stood thus: At every gate through which we were to pass, we saw a watchman – at every ferry a guard – on every bridge a sentinel – and in every wood a patrol. We were hemmed in upon every side. Here were the difficulties, real or imagined – the good to be sought, and the evil to be shunned. On the one hand, there stood slavery, a stern reality, glaring frightfully upon us, – its robes already crimsoned with the blood of millions, and even now feasting itself greedily upon our own flesh. On the other hand, away back in the dim distance, under the flickering light of the north star, behind some craggy hill or snow-covered mountain, stood a doubtful freedom – half frozen – beckoning us to come and share its hospitality. This in itself was sometimes enough to stagger us; but when we permitted ourselves to survey the road, we were frequently appalled. Upon either side we saw grim death, assuming the most horrid shapes. Now it was starvation, causing us to eat our own flesh; – now we were contending with the waves, and were drowned; – now we were overtaken, and torn to pieces by the fangs of the terrible bloodhound. We were stung by scorpions, chased by wild beasts, bitten by snakes, and finally, after having nearly reached the desired spot, – after swimming rivers, encountering wild beasts, sleeping in the woods suffering hunger and nakedness, – we were overtaken by our pursuers, and, in our resistance, we were shot dead upon the spot! I say, this picture sometimes appalled us, and made us

> rather bear those ills we had,
> Than fly to others, that we knew not of.[3]

In coming to a fixed determination to run away, we did more than Patrick Henry, when he resolved upon liberty or death. With us it was a doubtful liberty at most, and almost certain death if we failed. For my part, I should prefer death to hopeless bondage.

Sandy, one of our number, gave up the notion, but still encouraged us. Our company then consisted of Henry Harris, John Harris, Henry Bailey, Charles Roberts, and myself. Henry Bailey was my uncle, and belonged to my master. Charles married my aunt: he belonged to my master's father-in-law, Mr. William Hamilton.

The plan we finally concluded upon was, to get a large canoe belonging to Mr. Hamilton, and upon the Saturday night previous to Easter holidays, paddle directly up the Chesapeake Bay. On our arrival at the head of the bay, a distance of seventy or eighty miles from where we lived, it was our purpose to turn our canoe adrift, and follow the guidance of the north star till we got beyond the limits of Maryland. Our reason for taking the water route was, that we were less liable to be suspected as runaways; we hoped to be regarded as fishermen; whereas, if we should take the land route, we should be subjected to interruptions of almost every kind. Any one having a white face, and being so disposed, could stop us, and subject us to examination.

---

3. rather . . . knew not of: Shakespeare, *Hamlet*, 3.1.81–82.

The week before our intended start, I wrote several protections, one for each of us. As well as I can remember, they were in the following words, to wit: —

This is to certify that I, the undersigned, have given the bearer, my servant, full liberty to go to Baltimore, and spend the Easter holidays. Written with mine own hand, &c., 1835.

William Hamilton

Near St. Michael's, in Talbot county, Maryland

We were not going to Baltimore; but, in going up the bay, we went toward Baltimore, and these protections were only intended to protect us while on the bay.

As the time drew near for our departure, our anxiety became more and more intense. It was truly a matter of life and death with us. The strength of our determination was about to be fully tested. At this time, I was very active in explaining every difficulty, removing every doubt, dispelling every fear, and inspiring all with the firmness indispensable to success in our undertaking; assuring them that half was gained the instant we made the move; we had talked long enough; we were now ready to move; if not now, we never should be; and if we did not intend to move now, we had as well fold our arms, sit down, and acknowledge ourselves fit only to be slaves. This, none of us were prepared to acknowledge. Every man stood firm; and at our last meeting, we pledged ourselves afresh, in the most solemn manner, that, at the time appointed, we would certainly start in pursuit of freedom. This was in the middle of the week, at the end of which we were to be off. We went, as usual, to our several fields of labor, but with bosoms highly agitated with thoughts of our truly hazardous undertaking. We tried to conceal our feelings as much as possible; and I think we succeeded very well.

After a painful waiting, the Saturday morning, whose night was to witness our departure, came. I hailed it with joy, bring what of sadness it might. Friday night was a sleepless one for me. I probably felt more anxious than the rest, because I was, by common consent, at the head of the whole affair. The responsibility of success or failure lay heavily upon me. The glory of the one, and the confusion of the other, were alike mine. The first two hours of that morning were such as I never experienced before, and hope never to again. Early in the morning, we went, as usual, to the field. We were spreading manure: and all at once, while thus engaged, I was overwhelmed with an indescribable feeling, in the fulness of which I turned to Sandy, who was near by, and said, "We are betrayed!" "Well," said he, "that thought has this moment struck me." We said no more. I was never more certain of any thing.

The horn was blown as usual, and we went up from the field to the house for breakfast. I went for the form, more than for want of any thing to eat that morning. Just as I got to the house, in looking out at the lane gate, I saw four white men, with two colored men. The white men were on horseback, and the colored ones were walking behind, as if tied. I watched them a few moments till they got up to our lane gate. Here they halted, and tied the colored men to the gate-post. I was not yet certain as to what the matter was. In a few moments, in rode Mr. Hamilton, with a speed betokening great excitement. He came to the door, and inquired if Master William was in. He was told he was at the barn. Mr. Hamilton, without dismounting, rode up to the barn with extraordinary speed. In a few moments, he and Mr. Freeland returned to the house. By this time, the three constables rode up, and in great haste dismounted, tied their horses, and met Master William and Mr. Hamilton returning from the barn; and after talking awhile, they all walked up to the kitchen door. There was no one in the kitchen but myself and John. Henry and Sandy were up at the barn. Mr. Freeland put his head in at the door, and called me by name, saying, there were some gentlemen at the door who wished to see me. I stepped to the door, and inquired what they wanted. They at once seized me, and, without giving me any satisfaction, tied me — lashing my hands closely together. I insisted upon knowing what the matter was. They at length said, that they had learned I had been in a "scrape," and that I was to be examined before my master; and if their information proved false, I should not be hurt.

In a few moments, they succeeded in tying John. They then turned to Henry, who had by this time returned, and commanded him to cross his hands. "I won't!" said Henry, in a firm tone, indicating his readiness to meet the consequences of his refusal. "Won't you?" said Tom Graham, the constable. "No. I won't!" said Henry, in a still stronger tone. With this, two of the constables pulled out their shining pistols, and swore, by their Creator, that they would make him cross his hands or kill him. Each cocked his pistol, and, with fingers on the trigger, walked up to Henry, saying, at the same time, if he did not cross his hands, they would blow his damned heart out. "Shoot me! shoot me!" said Henry; "you can't kill me but once. Shoot, shoot, — and be damned! *I won't be tied!*" This he said in a tone of loud defiance; and at the same time, with a motion as quick as lightning, he with one single stroke dashed the pistols from the hand of each constable. As he did this, all hands fell upon him, and, after beating him some time, they finally overpowered him, and got him tied.

During the scuffle, I managed, I know not how, to get my pass out, and, without being discovered, put it into the fire. We were all now tied; and just as we were to leave for Easton jail, Betsy Freeland, mother of William Freeland, came to the door with her hands full of biscuits, and divided them between Henry and John. She then delivered herself of a speech, to the following effect: — addressing herself to me, she said, "*You devil! You yellow devil!* it was you that put it into the heads of Henry and John to run away. But for you, you long-legged mulatto devil! Henry nor John would never have thought of such a thing." I made no reply, and was immediately hurried off towards St. Michael's. Just a moment previous to the scuffle with Henry, Mr. Hamilton suggested the propriety of making a search for the protections which he had understood Frederick had written for himself and the rest. But, just at the moment he was about carrying his proposal into effect, his aid was needed in helping to tie Henry; and the excitement attending the scuffle caused them either to forget, or to deem it unsafe, under the circumstances, to search. So we were not yet convicted of the intention to run away.

When we got about half way to St. Michael's, while the constables having us in charge were looking ahead, Henry inquired of me what he should do with his pass. I told him to eat it with his biscuit, and own nothing; and we passed the word around, "*Own nothing;*" and "*Own nothing!*" said we all. Our confidence in each other was unshaken. We were resolved to succeed or fail together, after the calamity had befallen us as much as before. We were now prepared for any thing. We were to be dragged that morning fifteen miles behind horses, and then to be placed in the Easton jail. When we reached St. Michael's, we underwent a sort of examination. We all denied that we ever intended to run away. We did this more to bring out the evidence against us, than from any hope of getting clear of being sold; for, as I have said, we were ready for that. The fact was, we cared but little where we went, so we went together. Our greatest concern was about separation. We dreaded that more than any thing this side of death. We found the evidence against us to be the testimony of one person; our master would not tell who it was; but we came to a unanimous decision among ourselves as to who their informant was. We were sent off to the jail at Easton. When we got there, we were delivered up to the sheriff, Mr. Joseph Graham, and by him placed in jail. Henry, John, and myself, were placed in one room together – Charles, and Henry Bailey, in another. Their object in separating us was to hinder concert.

We had been in jail scarcely twenty minutes, when a swarm of slave traders, and agents for slave traders, flocked into jail to look at us, and to ascertain if we were for sale. Such a set of beings I never saw before! I felt myself surrounded by so many fiends from perdition. A band of pirates never looked more like their father, the devil. They laughed and grinned over us, saying, "Ah, my boys! we have got you, haven't we." And after taunting us in various ways, they one by one went into an examination of us, with intent to ascertain our value. They would impudently ask us if we would not like to have them for our masters. We would make them no answer, and leave them to find out as best they could. Then they would curse and swear at us, telling us that they could take the devil out of us in a very little while, if we were only in their hands.

While in jail, we found ourselves in much more comfortable quarters than we expected when we went there. We did not get much to eat, nor that which was very good; but we had a good clean room, from the windows of which we could see what was going on in the street, which was very much better than though we had been placed in one of the dark, damp cells. Upon the whole, we got along very well, so far as the jail and its keeper were concerned. Immediately after the holidays were over, contrary to all our expectations, Mr. Hamilton and Mr. Freeland came up to Easton, and took Charles, the two Henrys, and John, out of jail, and carried them home, leaving me alone. I regarded this separation as a final one. It caused me more pain than any thing else in the whole transaction. I was ready for any thing rather than separation. I supposed that they had consulted together, and had decided that, as I was the whole cause of the intention of the others to run away, it was hard to make the innocent suffer with the guilty; and that they had, therefore, concluded to take the others home, and sell me, as a warning to the others that remained. It is due to the noble Henry to say, he seemed almost as reluctant at leaving the prison as at leaving home to come to the prison. But we knew we should, in all probability, be separated, if we were sold; and since he was in their hands, he concluded to go peaceably home.

I was now left to my fate. I was all alone, and within the walls of a stone prison. But a few days before, and I was full of hope. I expected to have been safe in a land of freedom; but now I was covered with gloom, sunk down to the utmost despair. I thought the possibility of freedom was gone. I was kept in this way about one week, at the end of which, Captain Auld, my master, to my surprise and utter astonishment, came up, and took me out, with the intention of sending me, with a gentleman of his acquaintance, into

Alabama. But, from some cause or other, he did not send me to Alabama, but concluded to send me back to Baltimore, to live again with his brother Hugh, and to learn a trade.

Thus, after an absence of three years and one month, I was once more permitted to return to my old home at Baltimore. My master sent me away, because there existed against me a very great prejudice in the community, and he feared I might be killed.

In a few weeks after I went to Baltimore, Master Hugh hired me to Mr. William Gardner, an extensive ship-builder, on Fell's Point. I was put there to learn how to calk.[4] It, however, proved a very unfavorable place for the accomplishment of this object. Mr. Gardner was engaged that spring in building two large man-of-war brigs, professedly for the Mexican government. The vessels were to be launched in the July of that year, and in failure thereof, Mr. Gardner was to lose a considerable sum; so that when I entered, all was hurry. There was no time to learn any thing. Every man had to do that which he knew how to do. In entering the ship-yard, my orders from Mr. Gardner were, to do whatever the carpenters commanded me to do. This was placing me at the beck and call of about seventy-five men. I was to regard all these as masters. Their word was to be my law. My situation was a most trying one. At times I needed a dozen pair of hands. I was called a dozen ways in the space of a single minute. Three or four voices would strike my ear at the same moment. It was – "Fred., come help me to cant this timber here." – "Fred., come carry this timber yonder." – "Fred., bring that roller here." – "Fred., go get a fresh can of water." – "Fred., come help saw off the end of this timber." – "Fred., go quick, and get the crowbar." – "Fred., hold on the end of this fall."[5] – "Fred., go to the blacksmith's shop, and get a new punch." – "Hurra, Fred.! run and bring me a cold chisel." – "I say, Fred., bear a hand, and get up a fire as quick as lightning under that steam-box." – "Halloo, nigger! come, turn this grindstone." – "Come, come! move, move! and bowse[6] this timber forward." – "I say, darky, blast your eyes, why don't you heat up some pitch?" – "Halloo! halloo! halloo!" (Three voices at the same time.) "Come here! – Go there! – Hold on where you are! Damn you, if you move, I'll knock your brains out!"

This was my school for eight months; and I might have remained there longer, but for a most horrid fight I had with four of the white apprentices, in which my left eye was nearly knocked out, and I was horribly mangled in other respects. The facts in the case were these: Until a very little while after I went there, white and black ship-carpenters worked side by side, and no one seemed to see any impropriety in it. All hands seemed to be very well satisfied. Many of the black carpenters were freemen. Things seemed to be going on very well. All at once, the white carpenters knocked off, and said they would not work with free colored workmen. Their reason for this, as alleged, was, that if free colored carpenters were encouraged, they would soon take the trade into their own hands, and poor white men would be thrown out of employment. They therefore felt called upon at once to put a stop to it. And, taking advantage of Mr. Gardner's necessities, they broke off, swearing they would work no longer, unless he would discharge his black carpenters. Now, though this did not extend to me in form, it did reach me in fact. My fellow-apprentices very soon began to feel it degrading to them to work with me.

---

4. **calk:** Now usually spelled *caulk*; to seal the cracks and joints in the hull of a ship to prevent leakage.
5. **fall:** The free end of the rope of a tackle or other hoisting device.
6. **bowse:** To pull or haul, as on a tackle or other hoisting device.

They began to put on airs, and talk about the "niggers" taking the country, saying we all ought to be killed; and, being encouraged by the journeymen, they commenced making my condition as hard as they could, by hectoring me around, and sometimes striking me. I, of course, kept the vow I made after the fight with Mr. Covey, and struck back again, regardless of consequences; and while I kept them from combining, I succeeded very well; for I could whip the whole of them, taking them separately. They, however, at length combined, and came upon me, armed with sticks, stones, and heavy handspikes. One came in front with a half brick. There was one at each side of me, and one behind me. While I was attending to those in front, and on either side, the one behind ran up with the handspike, and struck me a heavy blow upon the head. It stunned me. I fell, and with this they all ran upon me, and fell to beating me with their fists. I let them lay on for a while, gathering strength. In an instant, I gave a sudden surge, and rose to my hands and knees. Just as I did that, one of their number gave me, with his heavy boot, a power-ful kick in the left eye. My eyeball seemed to have burst. When they saw my eye closed, and badly swollen, they left me. With this I seized the handspike, and for a time pursued them. But here the carpenters interfered, and I thought I might as well give it up. It was impossible to stand my hand against so many. All this took place in sight of not less than fifty white ship-carpenters, and not one interposed a friendly word; but some cried, "Kill the damned nigger! Kill him! kill him! He struck a white person." I found my only chance for life was in flight. I succeeded in getting away without an additional blow, and barely so; for to strike a white man is death by Lynch law,[7] — and that was the law in Mr. Gardner's ship-yard; nor is there much of any other out of Mr. Gardner's ship-yard.

I went directly home, and told the story of my wrongs to Master Hugh; and I am happy to say of him, irreligious as he was, his conduct was heavenly, compared with that of his brother Thomas under similar circumstances. He listened attentively to my narration of the circumstances leading to the savage outrage, and gave many proofs of his strong indignation at it. The heart of my once overkind mistress was again melted into pity. My puffed-out eye and blood-covered face moved her to tears. She took a chair by me, washed the blood from my face, and, with a mother's tenderness, bound up my head, covering the wounded eye with a lean piece of fresh beef. It was almost compensation for my suffering to witness, once more, a manifestation of kindness from this, my once affectionate old mistress. Master Hugh was very much enraged. He gave expression to his feelings by pouring out curses upon the heads of those who did the deed. As soon as I got a little the better of my bruises, he took me with him to Esquire Watson's, on Bond Street, to see what could be done about the matter. Mr. Watson inquired who saw the assault committed. Master Hugh told him it was done in Mr. Gardner's ship-yard, at midday, where there were a large company of men at work. "As to that," he said, "the deed was done, and there was no question as to who did it." His answer was, he could do nothing in the case, unless some white man would come forward and testify. He could issue no warrant on my word. If I had been killed in the presence of a thousand colored people, their testimony combined would have been insufficient to have arrested one of the murderers. Master Hugh, for once, was compelled to say this state of things was too

---

7. **Lynch law:** The practice of executing an individual by mob action without due process of law.

bad. Of course, it was impossible to get any white man to volunteer his testimony in my behalf, and against the white young men. Even those who may have sympathized with me were not prepared to do this. It required a degree of courage unknown to them to do so; for just at that time, the slightest manifestation of humanity toward a colored person was denounced as abolitionism, and that name subjected its bearer to frightful liabilities. The watchwords of the bloody-minded in that region, and in those days, were, "Damn the abolitionists!" and "Damn the niggers!" There was nothing done, and probably nothing would have been done if I had been killed. Such was, and such remains, the state of things in the Christian city of Baltimore.

Master Hugh, finding he could get no redress, refused to let me go back again to Mr. Gardner. He kept me himself, and his wife dressed my wound till I was again restored to health. He then took me into the ship-yard of which he was foreman, in the employment of Mr. Walter Price. There I was immediately set to calking, and very soon learned the art of using my mallet and irons. In the course of one year from the time I left Mr. Gardner's, I was able to command the highest wages given to the most experienced calkers. I was now of some importance to my master. I was bringing him from six to seven dollars per week. I sometimes brought him nine dollars per week: my wages were a dollar and a half a day. After learning how to calk, I sought my own employment, made my own contracts, and collected the money which I earned. My pathway became much more smooth than before; my condition was now much more comfortable. When I could get no calking to do, I did nothing. During these leisure times, those old notions about freedom would steal over me again. When in Mr. Gardner's employment, I was kept in such a perpetual whirl of excitement, I could think of nothing, scarcely, but my life; and in thinking of my life, I almost forgot my liberty. I have observed this in my experience of slavery, – that whenever my condition was improved, instead of its increasing my contentment, it only increased my desire to be free, and set me to thinking of plans to gain my freedom. I have found that, to make a contented slave, it is necessary to make a thoughtless one. It is necessary to darken his moral and mental vision, and, as far as possible, to annihilate the power of reason. He must be able to detect no inconsistencies in slavery; he must be made to feel that slavery is right; and he can be brought to that only when he ceases to be a man.

I was now getting, as I have said, one dollar and fifty cents per day. I contracted for it; I earned it; it was paid to me; it was rightfully my own; yet, upon each returning Saturday night, I was compelled to deliver every cent of that money to Master Hugh. And why? Not because he earned it, – not because he had any hand in earning it, – not because I owed it to him, – not because he possessed the slightest shadow of a right to it; but solely because he had the power to compel me to give it up. The right of the grim-visaged pirate upon the high seas is exactly the same.

Chapter XI

I now come to that part of my life during which I planned, and finally succeeded in making, my escape from slavery. But before narrating any of the peculiar circumstances, I deem it proper to make known my intention not to state all the facts connected with the transaction. My reasons for pursuing this course may be understood from the following: First, were I to give a minute statement of all the facts, it is not only possible, but quite probable, that others would thereby be involved in the most embarrassing difficulties. Secondly, such a statement would most undoubtedly induce greater vigilance on the part of slaveholders than has existed heretofore among them; which would, of course be the means of guarding a door whereby some dear brother bondman might escape his galling chains. I deeply regret the necessity that impels me to suppress any thing of importance connected with my experience in slavery. It would afford me great pleasure indeed, as well as materially add to the interest of my narrative, were I at liberty to gratify a curiosity, which I know exists in the minds of many, by an accurate statement of all the facts pertaining to my most fortunate escape. But I must deprive myself of this pleasure, and the curious of the gratification which such a statement would afford. I would allow myself to suffer under the greatest imputations which evil-minded men might suggest, rather than exculpate myself, and thereby run the hazard of closing the slightest avenue by which a brother slave might clear himself of the chains and fetters of slavery.

I have never approved of the very public manner in which some of our western friends have conducted what they call the *underground railroad*, but which, I think, by their open declarations, has been made most emphatically the *upper-ground railroad*. I honor those good men and women for their noble daring, and applaud them for willingly subjecting themselves to bloody persecution, by openly avowing their participation in the escape of slaves. I, however, can see very little good resulting from such a course, either to themselves or the slaves escaping; while, upon the other hand, I see and feel assured that those open declarations are a positive evil to the slaves remaining, who are seeking to escape. They do nothing towards enlightening the slave, whilst they do much towards enlightening the master. They stimulate him to greater watchfulness, and enhance his power to capture his slave. We owe something to the slaves south of the line as well as to those north of it; and in aiding the latter on their way to freedom, we should be careful to do nothing which would be likely to hinder the former from escaping from slavery. I would keep the merciless slaveholder profoundly ignorant of the means of flight adopted by the slave. I would leave him to imagine himself surrounded by myriads of invisible tormentors, ever ready to snatch from his infernal grasp his trembling prey. Let him be left to feel his way in the dark; let darkness commensurate with his crime hover over him; and let him feel that at every step he takes, in pursuit of the flying bondman, he is running the frightful risk of having his hot brains dashed out by an invisible agency. Let us render the tyrant no aid; let us not hold the light by which he can trace the footprints of our flying brother. But enough of this. I will now proceed to the statement of those facts, connected with my escape, for which I am alone responsible and for which no one can be made to suffer but myself.

In the early part of the year 1838, I became quite restless. I could see no reason why I should, at the end of each week, pour the reward of my toil into the purse of my master. When I carried to him my weekly wages, he would, after counting the money, look me in the face with a robber-like fierceness, and ask, "Is this all?" He was satisfied with nothing less than the last cent. He would, however, when I made him six dollars, sometimes give me six cents, to encourage me. It had the opposite effect. I regarded it as a sort of admission of my right to the whole. The fact that he gave me any part of my wages was proof, to my mind, that he believed me entitled to the whole of them. I always felt worse for having received any thing; for I feared that the giving me a few cents would ease his conscience, and make him feel himself to be a pretty honorable sort of robber. My discontent grew upon me. I was ever on the look-out for means of escape; and, finding no direct means, I determined to try to hire my time, with a view of getting money with which to make my escape. In the spring of 1838, when Master Thomas came to Baltimore to purchase his spring goods, I got an opportunity, and applied to him to allow me to hire my time. He unhesitatingly refused my request, and told me this was another stratagem by which to escape. He told me I could go nowhere but that he could get me; and that, in the event of my running away, he should spare no pains in his efforts to catch me. He exhorted me to content myself, and be obedient. He told me, if I would be happy, I must lay out no plans for the future. He said, if I behaved myself properly, he would take care of me. Indeed, he advised me to complete thoughtlessness of the future, and taught me to depend solely upon him for happiness. He seemed to see fully the pressing necessity of setting aside my intellectual nature, in order to find contentment in slavery. But in spite of him, and even in spite of myself, I continued to think, and to think about the injustice of my enslavement, and the means of escape.

About two months after this, I applied to Master Hugh for the privilege of hiring my time. He was not acquainted with the fact that I had applied to Master Thomas, and had been refused. He too, at first, seemed disposed to refuse; but, after some reflection, he granted me the privilege, and proposed the following term: I was to be allowed all my time, make all contracts with those for whom I worked, and find my own employment; and, in return for this liberty, I was to pay him three dollars at the end of each week; find myself in calking tools, and in board and clothing. My board was two dollars and a half per week. This, with the wear and tear of clothing and calking tools, made my regular expenses about six dollars per week. This amount I was compelled to make up, or relinquish the privilege of hiring my time. Rain or shine, work or no work, at the end of each week the money must be forthcoming, or I must give up my privilege. This arrangement, it will be perceived, was decidedly in my master's favor. It relieved him of all need of looking after me. His money was sure. He received all the benefits of slaveholding without its evils; while I endured all the evils of a slave, and suffered all the care and anxiety of a freeman. I found it a hard bargain. But, hard as it was, I thought it better than the old mode of getting along. It was a step towards freedom to be allowed to bear the responsibilities of a freeman, and I was determined to hold on upon it. I bent myself to the work of making money. I was ready to work at night as well as day, and by the most untiring perseverance and industry, I made enough to meet my expenses, and lay up a little money every week. I went on thus from May till August. Master Hugh then refused to allow me to hire my time longer. The ground for his refusal was a failure on my part, one Saturday night, to pay him for my week's time. This failure was occasioned by my attending a camp meeting about ten miles from Baltimore. During the week, I had entered into an engagement with a number of young friends to start from Baltimore to the camp ground early Saturday evening; and being detained by my employer, I was unable to get down to Master Hugh's without disappointing the company. I knew that

Master Hugh was in no special need of the money that night. I therefore decided to go to camp meeting, and upon my return pay him the three dollars. I staid at the camp meeting one day longer than I intended when I left. But as soon as I returned, I called upon him to pay him what he considered his due. I found him very angry; he could scarce restrain his wrath. He said he had a great mind to give me a severe whipping. He wished to know how I dared go out of the city without asking his permission. I told him I hired my time, and while I paid him the price which he asked for it, I did not know that I was bound to ask him when and where I should go. This reply troubled him; and, after reflecting a few moments, he turned to me, and said I should hire my time no longer; that the next thing he should know of, I would be running away. Upon the same plea, he told me to bring my tools and clothing home forthwith. I did so; but instead of seeking work, as I had been accustomed to do previously to hiring my time, I spent the whole week without the performance of a single stroke of work. I did this in retaliation. Saturday night, he called upon me as usual for my week's wages. I told him I had no wages; I had done no work that week. Here we were upon the point of coming to blows. He raved, and swore his determination to get hold of me. I did not allow myself a single word; but was resolved, if he laid the weight of his hand upon me, it should be blow for blow. He did not strike me, but told me that he would find me in constant employment in future. I thought the matter over during the next day, Sunday, and finally resolved upon the third day of September, as the day upon which I would make a second attempt to secure my freedom. I now had three weeks during which to prepare for my journey. Early on Monday morning, before Master Hugh had time to make any engagement for me, I went out and got employment of Mr. Butler, at his ship-yard near the drawbridge, upon what is called the City Block, thus making it unnecessary for him to seek employment for me. At the end of the week, I brought him between eight and nine dollars. He seemed very well pleased, and asked me why I did not do the same the week before. He little knew what my plans were. My object in working steadily was to remove any suspicion he might entertain of my intent to run away; and in this I succeeded admirably. I suppose he thought I was never better satisfied with my condition than at the very time during which I was planning my escape. The second week passed, and again I carried him my full wages; and so well pleased was he, that he gave me twenty-five cents, (quite a large sum for a slaveholder to give a slave,) and bade me to make a good use of it. I told him I would.

Things went on without very smoothly indeed, but within there was trouble. It is impossible for me to describe my feelings as the time of my contemplated start drew near. I had a number of warm-hearted friends in Baltimore, — friends that I loved almost as I did my life, — and the thought of being separated from them forever was painful beyond expression. It is my opinion that thousands would escape from slavery, who now remain, but for the strong cords of affection that bind them to their friends. The thought of leaving my friends was decidedly the most painful thought with which I had to contend. The love of them was my tender point, and shook my decision more than all things else. Besides the pain of separation, the dread and apprehension of a failure exceeded what I had experienced at my first attempt. The appalling defeat I then sustained returned to torment me. I felt assured that, if I failed in this attempt, my case would be a hopeless one – it would seal my fate as a slave forever. I could not hope to get off with anything less than the severest punishment, and being placed beyond the means of escape. It required no very vivid imagination to depict the most frightful scenes through which I should have to pass, in case I failed. The wretchedness of slavery, and the blessedness of freedom, were perpetually before me. It was life and death with me. But I remained firm, and, according to my resolution, on the third day of September, 1838, I left my chains, and succeeded in reaching New York without the slightest interruption of any kind. How I did so, – what means I adopted, – what direction I travelled, and by what mode of conveyance, – I must leave unexplained, for the reasons before mentioned.

I have been frequently asked how I felt when I found myself in a free State. I have never been able to answer the question with any satisfaction to myself. It was a moment of the highest excitement I ever experienced. I suppose I felt as one may imagine the unarmed mariner to feel when he is rescued by a friendly man-of-war from the pursuit of a pirate. In writing to a dear friend, immediately after my arrival at New York, I said I felt like one who had escaped a den of hungry lions. This state of mind, however, very soon subsided; and I was again seized with a feeling of great insecurity and loneliness. I was yet liable to be taken back, and subjected to all the tortures of slavery. This in itself was enough to damp the ardor of my enthusiasm. But the loneliness overcame me. There I was in the midst of thousands, and yet a perfect stranger; without home and without friends, in the midst of thousands of my own brethren – children of a common Father, and yet I dared not to unfold to any one of them my sad condition. I was afraid to speak to any one for fear of speaking to the wrong one, and thereby falling into the hands of money-loving kidnappers, whose business it was to lie in wait for the panting fugitive, as the ferocious beasts of the forest lie in wait for their prey. The motto which I adopted when I started from slavery was this – "Trust no man!" I saw in every white man an enemy, and in almost every colored man cause for distrust. It was a most painful situation; and, to understand it, one must needs experience it, or imagine himself in similar circumstances. Let him be a fugitive slave in a strange land – a land given up to be the hunting-ground for slaveholders – whose inhabitants are legalized kidnappers – where he is every moment subjected to the terrible liability of being seized upon by his fellowmen, as the hideous crocodile seizes upon his prey! – I say, let him place himself in my situation – without home or friends – without money or credit – wanting shelter, and no one to give it – wanting bread, and no money to buy it, – and at the same time let him feel that he is pursued by merciless men-hunters, and in total darkness as to what to do, where to go, or where to stay, – perfectly helpless both as to the means of defence and means of escape, – in the midst of plenty, yet suffering the terrible gnawings of hunger, – in the midst of houses, yet having no home, – among fellow-men, yet feeling as if in the midst of wild beasts, whose greediness to swallow up the trembling and half-famished fugitive is only equalled by that with which the monsters of the deep swallow up the helpless fish upon which they subsist, – I say, let him be placed in this most trying situation, – the situation in which I was placed, – then, and not till then, will he fully appreciate the hardships of, and know how to sympathize with, the toil worn and whip-scarred fugitive slave.

Thank Heaven, I remained but a short time in this distressed situation. I was relieved from it by the humane hand of Mr. David Ruggles,[1] whose vigilance, kindness, and perseverance, I shall never forget. I am glad of an opportunity to express, as far as words can, the love and gratitude I bear him. Mr. Ruggles is now afflicted with blindness, and is himself in need of the same kind offices which he was once so forward in the performance of toward others. I had been in New York but a few days, when Mr. Ruggles sought me out, and very kindly took me to his boarding-house at the corner of Church and Lespenard Streets. Mr. Ruggles was then very deeply engaged in the memorable *Darg* case,[2] as well as attending to a number of other fugitive slaves, devising ways and means for their successful escape; and, though watched and hemmed in on almost every side, he seemed to be more than a match for his enemies.

Very soon after I went to Mr. Ruggles, he wished to know of me where I wanted to go; as he deemed it unsafe for me to remain in New York. I told him I was a calker, and should like to go where I could get work. I thought of going to Canada; but he decided against it, and in favor of my going to New Bedford, thinking I should be able to get work there at my trade. At this time, Anna,[3] my intended wife, came on; for I wrote to her immediately after my arrival at New York, (notwithstanding my homeless, houseless, and helpless condition,) informing her of my successful flight, and wishing her to come on forthwith. In a few days after her arrival, Mr. Ruggles called in the Rev. J. W. C. Pennington, who, in the presence of Mr. Ruggles, Mrs. Michaels, and two or three others, performed the marriage ceremony, and gave us a certificate, of which the following is an exact copy: —

This may certify, that I joined together in holy matrimony Frederick Johnson[4] and Anna Murray, as man and wife, in the presence of Mr. David Ruggles and Mrs. Michaels.

James W. C. Pennington[5]

New York, Sept. 15, 1838

Upon receiving this certificate, and a five-dollar bill from Mr. Ruggles, I shouldered one part of our baggage, and Anna took up the other, and we set out forthwith to take passage on board of the steamboat John W. Richmond for Newport, on our way to New Bedford. Mr. Ruggles gave me a letter to a Mr. Shaw in Newport, and told me, in case my money did not serve me to New Bedford, to stop in Newport and obtain further assistance; but upon our arrival at Newport, we were so anxious to get to a place of safety, that, notwithstanding we lacked the necessary money to pay our fare, we decided to take seats in the stage, and promise to pay when we got to New Bedford. We were encouraged to do this by two excellent gentlemen, residents of New Bedford, whose names I afterward ascertained to be Joseph Ricketson and William C. Taber. They seemed at once to

---

1. **Mr. David Ruggles:** Ruggles (1810–1849), a free black abolitionist, was the founder of the New York Vigilance Committee, an organization established to aid fugitive slaves.
2. *Darg* **case:** In 1838, Ruggles was briefly jailed for his involvement in the case of an escaped slave who had been brought to New York City by his master, John P. Darg of Virginia.
3. **Anna:** She was free. [Douglass's note]
4. **Frederick Johnson:** I had changed my name from Frederick *Bailey* to that of *Johnson.* [Douglass's note]
5. *James W. C. Pennington:* Pennington (1807–1870), who escaped from slavery in Maryland in 1827, later became a Presbyterian minister.

understand our circumstances, and gave us such assurance of their friendliness as put us fully at ease in their presence. It was good indeed to meet with such friends, at such a time. Upon reaching New Bedford, we were directed to the house of Mr. Nathan Johnson, by whom we were kindly received, and hospitably provided for. Both Mr. and Mrs. Johnson took a deep and lively interest in our welfare. They proved themselves quite worthy of the name of abolitionists. When the stage-driver found us unable to pay our fare, he held on upon our baggage as security for the debt. I had but to mention the fact to Mr. Johnson, and he forthwith advanced the money.

We now began to feel a degree of safety, and to prepare ourselves for the duties and responsibilities of a life of freedom. On the morning after our arrival at New Bedford, while at the breakfast-table, the question arose as to what name I should be called by. The name given me by my mother was, "Frederick Augustus Washington Bailey." I, however, had dispensed with the two middle names long before I left Maryland so that I was generally known by the name of "Frederick Bailey." I started from Baltimore bearing the name of "Stanley." When I got to New York, I again changed my name to "Frederick Johnson," and thought that would be the last change. But when I got to New Bedford, I found it necessary again to change my name. The reason of this necessity was, that there were so many Johnsons in New Bedford, it was already quite difficult to distinguish between them. I gave Mr. Johnson the privilege of choosing me a name, but told him he must not take from me the name of "Frederick." I must hold on to that, to preserve a sense of my identity. Mr. Johnson had just been reading the "Lady of the Lake," and at once suggested that my name be "Douglass."[6] From that time until now I have been called "Frederick Douglass"; and as I am more widely known by that name than by either of the others, I shall continue to use it as my own.

I was quite disappointed at the general appearance of things in New Bedford. The impression which I had received respecting the character and condition of the people of the north, I found to be singularly erroneous. I had very strangely supposed, while in slavery, that few of the comforts, and scarcely any of the luxuries, of life were enjoyed at the north, compared with what were enjoyed by the slaveholders of the south. I probably came to this conclusion from the fact that northern people owned no slaves. I supposed that they were about upon a level with the non-slaveholding population of the south. I knew *they* were exceedingly poor, and I had been accustomed to regard their poverty as the necessary consequence of their being non-slaveholders. I had somehow imbibed the opinion that, in the absence of slaves, there could be no wealth, and very little refinement. And upon coming to the north, I expected to meet with a rough, hard-handed, and uncultivated population, living in the most Spartan-like simplicity, knowing nothing of the ease, luxury, pomp, and grandeur of southern slaveholders. Such being my conjectures, any one acquainted with the appearance of New Bedford may very readily infer how palpably I must have seen my mistake.

In the afternoon of the day when I reached New Bedford, I visited the wharves, to take a view of the shipping. Here I found myself surrounded with the strongest proofs of

---

6. "**Douglass**": James of Douglas, the Earl of Bothwell, is the hero of *The Lady of the Lake*, a popular Romantic poem by Sir Walter Scott (1771-1832).

wealth. Lying at the wharves, and riding in the stream, I saw many ships of the finest model, in the best order, and of the largest size. Upon the right and left, I was walled in by granite warehouses of the widest dimensions, stowed to their utmost capacity with the necessaries and comforts of life. Added to this, almost every body seemed to be at work, but noiselessly so, compared with what I had been accustomed to in Baltimore. There were no loud songs heard from those engaged in loading and unloading ships. I heard no deep oaths or horrid curses on the laborer. I saw no whipping of men; but all seemed to go smoothly on. Every man appeared to understand his work, and went at it with a sober, yet cheerful earnestness, which betokened the deep interest which he felt in what he was doing, as well as a sense of his own dignity as a man. To me this looked exceedingly strange. From the wharves I strolled around and over the town, gazing with wonder and admiration at the splendid churches, beautiful dwellings, and finely-cultivated gardens; evincing an amount of wealth, comfort, taste, and refinement, such as I had never seen in any part of slaveholding Maryland.

Every thing looked clean, new and beautiful. I saw few or no dilapidated houses, with poverty-stricken inmates; no half-naked children and barefooted women, such as I had been accustomed to see in Hillsborough, Easton, St. Michael's, and Baltimore. The people looked more able, stronger, healthier, and happier, than those of Maryland. I was for once made glad by a view of extreme wealth, without being saddened by seeing extreme poverty. But the most astonishing as well as the most interesting thing to me was the condition of the colored people, a great many of whom, like myself, had escaped thither as a refuge from the hunters of men. I found many, who had not been seven years out of their chains, living in finer houses, and evidently enjoying more of the comforts of life, than the average of slaveholders in Maryland. I will venture to assert that my friend Mr. Nathan Johnson (of whom I can say with a grateful heart, "I was hungry, and he gave me meat; I was, thirsty, and he gave me drink; I was a stranger, and he took me in"[7]) lived in a neater house; dined at a better table; took, paid for, and read, more newspapers; better understood the moral, religious, and political character of the nation, – than nine tenths of the slaveholders in Talbot county, Maryland. Yet Mr. Johnson was a working man. His hands were hardened by toil, and not his alone, but those also of Mrs. Johnson. I found the colored people much more spirited than I had supposed they would be. I found among them a determination to protect each other from the blood-thirsty kidnapper, at all hazards. Soon after my arrival, I was told of a circumstance which illustrated their spirit. A colored man and a fugitive slave were on unfriendly terms. The former was heard to threaten the latter with informing his master of his whereabouts. Straightway a meeting was called among the colored people, under the stereotyped notice, "Business of importance!" The betrayer was invited to attend. The people came at the appointed hour, and organized the meeting by appointing a very religious old gentleman as president, who, I believe, made a prayer, after which he addressed the meeting as follows: *"Friends, we have got him here, and I would recommend that you young men just take him outside the door, and kill him!"* With this, a number of them bolted at him; but they were

---

7. "**I was hungry . . . he took me in**": Matthew 25:35.

intercepted by some more timid than themselves, and the betrayer escaped their vengeance, and has not been seen in New Bedford since. I believe there have been no more such
threats, and should there be hereafter, I doubt not that death would be the consequence.

I found employment, the third day after my arrival, in stowing a sloop with a load of
oil. It was new, dirty, and hard work for me; but I went at it with a glad heart and a willing hand. I was now my own master. It was a happy moment, the rapture of which can
be understood only by those who have been slaves. It was the first work, the reward of
which was to be entirely my own. There was no Master Hugh standing ready, the moment
I earned the money, to rob me of it. I worked that day with a pleasure I had never before
experienced. I was at work for myself and newly-married wife. It was to me the starting-
point of a new existence. When I got through with that job, I went in pursuit of a job of
calking; but such was the strength of prejudice against color, among the white calkers,
that they refused to work with me, and of course I could get no employment.[8] Finding
my trade of no immediate benefit, I threw off my calking habiliments, and prepared
myself to do any kind of work I could get to do. Mr. Johnson kindly let me have his wood-
horse and saw, and I very soon found myself a plenty of work. There was no work too
hard — none too dirty. I was ready to saw wood, shovel coal, carry the hod, sweep the
chimney, or roll oil casks, — all of which I did for nearly three years in New Bedford,
before I became known to the antislavery world.

In about four months after I went to New Bedford, there came a young man to me, and
inquired if I did not wish to take the "Liberator."[9] I told him I did; but, just having made
my escape from slavery, I remarked that I was unable to pay for it then. I, however,
finally became a subscriber to it. The paper came, and I read it from week to week
with such feelings as it would be quite idle for me to attempt to describe. The paper
became my meat and my drink. My soul was set all on fire. Its sympathy for my brethren
in bonds — its scathing denunciations of slaveholders — its faithful exposures of slavery — and its powerful attacks upon the upholders of the institution — sent a thrill of joy
through my soul, such as I had never felt before!

I had not long been a reader of the "Liberator," before I got a pretty correct idea of the
principles, measures and spirit of the anti-slavery reform. I took right hold of the cause.
I could do but little; but what I could, I did with a joyful heart, and never felt happier
than when in an anti-slavery meeting. I seldom had much to say at the meetings,
because what I wanted to say was said so much better by others. But, while attending an
anti-slavery convention at Nantucket, on the 11th of August, 1841, I felt strongly moved
to speak, and was at the same time much urged to do so by Mr. William C. Coffin, a gentleman who had heard me speak in the colored people's meeting at New Bedford. It was a
severe cross, and I took it up reluctantly. The truth was, I felt myself a slave, and the idea
of speaking to white people weighed me down. I spoke but a few moments, when I felt a
degree of freedom, and said what I desired with considerable ease. From that time until
now, I have been engaged in pleading the cause of my brethren — with what success, and
with what devotion, I leave those acquainted with my labors to decide.

---

8. **employment:** I am told that colored persons can now get employment at calking in New Bedford — a result
of anti-slavery effort. [Douglass's note]
9. **"Liberator":** Antislavery newspaper edited by William Lloyd Garrison.

Appendix

I find, since reading over the foregoing Narrative that I have, in several instances, spoken in such a tone and manner, respecting religion, as may possibly lead those unacquainted with my religious views to suppose me an opponent of all religion. To remove the liability of such misapprehension, I deem it proper to append the following brief explanation. What I have said respecting and against religion, I mean strictly to apply to the slaveholding religion of this land, and with no possible reference to Christianity proper; for, between the Christianity of this land, and the Christianity of Christ, I recognize the widest possible difference—so wide, that to receive the one as good, pure, and holy, is of necessity to reject the other as bad, corrupt, and wicked. To be the friend of the one, is of necessity to be the enemy of the other. I love the pure, peaceable, and impartial Christianity of Christ: I therefore hate the corrupt, slaveholding, women-whipping, cradle-plundering, partial and hypocritical Christianity of this land. Indeed, I can see no reason, but the most deceitful one, for calling the religion of this land Christianity. I look upon it as the climax of all misnomers, the boldest of all frauds, and the grossest of all libels. Never was there a clearer case of "stealing the livery of the court of heaven to serve the devil in."[1] I am filled with unutterable loathing when I contemplate the religious pomp and show, together with the horrible inconsistencies, which every where surround me. We have men-stealers for ministers, women-whippers for missionaries, and cradle-plunderers for church members. The man who wields the blood-clotted cowskin during the week fills the pulpit on Sunday, and claims to be a minister of the meek and lowly Jesus. The man who robs me of my earnings at the end of each week meets me as a class-leader on Sunday morning, to show me the way of life, and the path of salvation. He who sells my sister, for purposes of prostitution, stands forth as the pious advocate of purity. He who proclaims it a religious duty to read the Bible denies me the right of learning to read the name of the God who made me. He who is the religious advocate of marriage robs whole millions of its sacred influence, and leaves them to the ravages of wholesale pollution. The warm defender of the sacredness of the family relation is the same that scatters whole families,—sundering husbands and wives, parents and children, sisters and brothers,—leaving the hut vacant, and the hearth desolate. We see the thief preaching against theft, and the adulterer against adultery. We have men sold to build churches, women sold to support the gospel, and babes sold to purchase Bibles for the *poor heathen! all for the glory of God and the good of souls!* The slave auctioneer's bell and the church-going bell chime in with each other, and the bitter cries of the heart-broken slave are drowned in the religious shouts of his pious master. Revivals of religion and revivals in the slave-trade go hand in hand together. The slave prison and the church stand near each other. The clanking of fetters and the rattling of chains in the prison, and the pious psalm and solemn prayer in the church, may be heard at the same time. The dealers in the bodies and souls of men erect their stand in the presence of the pulpit, and they mutually help each other. The dealer gives his blood-stained gold to support the pulpit, and the pulpit, in return, covers his infernal business with the garb

---

1. "stealing . . . to serve the devil in": From book 8 of *The Course of Time* (1827), a phenomenally popular religious poem by Scottish poet Robert Pollok (1798–1827).

of Christianity. Here we have religion and robbery the allies of each other – devils dressed in angels' robes, and hell presenting the semblance of paradise.

> Just God![2] and these are they,
>   Who minister at thine altar, God of right!
> Men who their hands, with prayer and blessing, lay
>   On Israel's ark of light.[3]
>
> What! preach, and kidnap men?
>   Give thanks, and rob thy own afflicted poor?
> Talk of thy glorious liberty, and then
>   Bolt hard the captive's door?
>
> What! servants of thy own
>   Merciful Son, who came to seek and save
> The homeless and the outcast, fettering down
>   The tasked and plundered slave!
>
> Pilate and Herod friends![4]
>   Chief priests and rulers, as of old, combine!
> Just God and holy! is that church which lends
>   Strength to the spoiler thine?

The Christianity of America is a Christianity, of whose votaries it may be as truly said, as it was of the ancient scribes and Pharisees,[5] "They bind heavy burdens, and grievous to be borne, and lay them on men's shoulders, but they themselves will not move them with one of their fingers. All their works they do for to be seen of men. — They love the uppermost rooms at feasts, and the chief seats in the synagogues, ... and to be called of men, Rabbi, Rabbi. — But woe unto you, scribes and Pharisees, hypocrites! for ye shut up the kingdom of heaven against men; for ye neither go in yourselves, neither suffer ye them that are entering to go in. Ye devour widows' houses, and for a pretence make long prayers; therefore ye shall receive the greater damnation. Ye compass sea and land to make one proselyte, and when he is made, ye make him twofold more the child of hell than yourselves. — Woe unto you, scribes and Pharisees, hypocrites! for ye pay tithe of mint, and anise, and cumin, and have omitted the weightier matters of the law, judgment,

---

2. **Just God!:** The following are the first four stanzas of "Clerical Oppressors" by John Greenleaf Whittier, who prefaced the poem with the note: "In the report of the celebrated proslavery meeting in Charleston, S.C., on the 4th of the ninth month [September 4], 1835, published in the *Courier* of that city, it is stated: 'The clergy of all denominations attended in a body, lending their sanction to the proceedings, and adding by their presence to the impressive character of the scene!'"

3. **Israel's ark of light:** The Ark of the Covenant, containing the stone tablets upon which the Ten Commandments were inscribed, here used as a symbol of sacred religious law.

4. **Pilate and Herod friends!:** The unholy alliance of civil and religious authority as represented by Pontius Pilate, the Roman governor who condemned Jesus; and Herod Antipas, the Jewish ruler of Galilee involved in events leading to the executions of both John the Baptist and Jesus.

5. **ancient scribes and Pharisees:** The scribes were scholars and professional interpreters of religious laws in Jewish synagogues; the Pharisees were members of a sect that emphasized strict adherence to both the written laws and oral traditions of Judaism. In the following paragraph, Douglass quotes and draws heavily upon Christ's denunciation of the "hypocrisy and iniquity" of the scribes and Pharisees in Matthew 23.

mercy, and faith; these ought ye to have done, and not to leave the other undone. Ye blind guides! which strain at a gnat, and swallow a camel. Woe unto you, scribes and Pharisees, hypocrites! for ye make clean the outside of the cup and of the platter, but within, they are full of extortion and excess. — Woe unto you, scribes and Pharisees, hypocrites! for ye are like unto whited sepulchres, which indeed appear beautiful outward, but are within full of dead men's bones, and of all uncleanness. Even so ye also outwardly appear righteous unto men, but within ye are full of hypocrisy and iniquity."

Dark and terrible as is this picture, I hold it to be strictly true of the overwhelming mass of professed Christians in America. They strain at a gnat, and swallow a camel. Could any thing be more true of our churches? They would be shocked at the proposition of fellowshipping a *sheep*-stealer; and at the same time they hug to their communion a *man*-stealer, and brand me with being an infidel, if I find fault with them for it. They attend with Pharisaical strictness to the outward forms of religion, and at the same time neglect the weightier matters of the law, judgment, mercy, and faith. They are always ready to sacrifice, but seldom to show mercy. They are they who are represented as professing to love God whom they have not seen, whilst they hate their brother whom they have seen. They love the heathen on the other side of the globe. They can pray for him, pay money to have the Bible put into his hand, and missionaries to instruct him; while they despise and totally neglect the heathen at their own doors.

Such is, very briefly, my view of the religion of this land; and to avoid any misunderstanding, growing out of the use of general terms, I mean, by the religion of this land, that which is revealed in the words, deeds, and actions, of those bodies, north and south, calling themselves Christian churches, and yet in union with slaveholders. It is against religion, as presented by these bodies, that I have felt it my duty to testify.

I conclude these remarks by copying the following portrait of the religion of the south, (which is, by communion and fellowship, the religion of the north,) which I soberly affirm is "true to the life," and without caricature or the slightest exaggeration. It is said to have been drawn, several years before the present anti-slavery agitation began, by a northern Methodist preacher, who, while residing at the south, had an opportunity to see slaveholding morals, manners, and piety, with his own eyes. "Shall I not visit for these things? saith the Lord. Shall not my soul be avenged on such a nation as this?"[6]

A PARODY[7]

> Come, saints and sinners, hear me tell
> How pious priests whip Jack and Nell,
> And women buy and children sell,
> And preach all sinners down to hell,
>   And sing of heavenly union.
>
> They'll bleat and baa, [go on] like goats,
> Gorge down black sheep, and strain at motes,

---

6. "Shall . . . a nation as this?": Jeremiah 5:9.
7. A PARODY: This parody of the popular southern hymn "Heavenly Union" was apparently written by Douglass, who was famous for his ability to mimic Southern clergymen.

Array their backs in fine black coats,
Then seize their negroes by their throats,
    And choke, for heavenly union.

They'll church you if you sip a dram,
And damn you if you steal a lamb;
Yet rob old Tony, Doll, and Sam,
Of human rights, and bread and ham;
    Kidnapper's heavenly union.

They'll loudly talk of Christ's reward,
And bind his image with a cord,
And scold, and swing the lash abhorred,
And sell their brother in the Lord
    To handcuffed heavenly union.

They'll read and sing a sacred song,
And make a prayer both loud and long,
And teach the right and do the wrong,
Hailing the brother, sister throng,
    With words of heavenly union.

We wonder how such saints can sing,
Or praise the Lord upon the wing,
Who roar, and scold, and whip, and sting,
And to their slaves and mammon cling,
    In guilty conscience union.

They'll raise tobacco, corn, and rye,
And drive, and thieve, and cheat, and lie,
And lay up treasures in the sky,
By making switch and cowskin fly,
    In hope of heavenly union.

They'll crack old Tony on the skull,
And preach and roar like Bashan bull,[8]
Or braying ass, of mischief full,
Then seize old Jacob by the wool,
    And pull for heavenly union.

A roaring, ranting, sleek man-thief,
Who lived on mutton, veal, and beef,
Yet never would afford relief
To needy, sable sons of grief,
    Was big with heavenly union.

"Love not the world," the preacher said,
And winked his eye, and shook his head;

---

8. **Bashan bull:** See Psalms 22:12-13: "Be not far from me; for trouble is near; for there is none to help. Many bulls have compassed me: strong bulls of Bashan have beset me round."

He seized on Tom, and Dick, and Ned,
Cut short their meat, and clothes, and bread,
 Yet still loved heavenly union.

Another preacher whining spoke
Of One whose heart for sinners broke:
He tied old Nanny to an oak,
And drew the blood at every stroke,
 And prayed for heavenly union.

Two others oped their iron jaws,
And waved their children-stealing paws;
There sat their children in gewgaws;
By stinting negroes' backs and maws,
 They kept up heavenly union.

All good from Jack another takes,
And entertains their flirts and rakes
Who dress as sleek as glossy snakes,
And cram their mouths with sweetened cakes;
 And this goes down for union.

Sincerely and earnestly hoping that this little book may do something toward throwing light on the American slave system, and hastening the glad day of deliverance to the millions of my brethren in bonds — faithfully relying upon the power of truth, love, and justice, for success in my humble efforts — and solemnly pledging myself anew to the sacred cause, — I subscribe myself,

Frederick Douglass

Lynn, Mass., April 28, 1845

[1845]

Douglass through a Modern Lens

FREDERICK DOUGLASS was the most respected African American writer of the nineteenth century, and during the last forty years his *Narrative* has come to be viewed as one of the central texts of the American Renaissance. Nonetheless, his importance was not then and is not now simply or even primarily literary. In an

Frederick Douglass Monument
This statue of Douglass by Sidney Wells Edwards, the first monument to an African American in the United States, was unveiled in Rochester, New York, in 1899. Since then, numerous memorials to the writer, orator, abolitionist, and human rights leader have been established, including one dedicated in 2011 in front of the courthouse in Talbot County, Maryland, where Douglass was born into slavery in 1818.

introduction to Douglass's second autobiography, *My Bondage and My Freedom* (1855), the distinguished African American doctor James M'Cune Smith hailed him as "a representative American man – a type of his countrymen." Few then could have accepted a man of mixed African American and Caucasian heritage as a representative American, but Smith recognized that in his life and writings Douglass embodied the fundamental social and political values of the country. "I shall place this book in the hands of the only child spared me, bidding him to strive to emulate its noble example," Smith continued. "You may do likewise. It is an American book, for Americans, in the fullest sense of the idea." That "idea" was an ideal of freedom and equality, not simply for slaves in the South or people of color in the North, but for all Americans. When he died in 1895, Douglass himself no doubt recognized the deep divide between his dream of a truly egalitarian and fully integrated society and the realities of life in the United States. But his life and writings have remained an inspiration to those who have shared that dream, including the African American poet Robert Hayden (1913-1980). Appropriately,

Hayden published the following poem in 1962, at the height of a renewed struggle to fulfill Douglass's dream, and just two years before the passage of what was in its own way another tribute to him, the Civil Rights Act of 1964.

The text is taken from Hayden's *Collected Poems*, edited by Frederick Glaysher (1985).

Robert Hayden

[1913–1980]

FREDERICK DOUGLASS

When it is finally ours, this freedom, this liberty, this beautiful
and terrible thing, needful to man as air,
usable as earth; when it belongs at last to all,
when it is truly instinct, brain matter, diastole, systole,
reflex action; when it is finally won; when it is more   5
than the gaudy mumbo jumbo of politicians:
this man, this Douglass, this former slave, this Negro
beaten to his knees, exiled, visioning a world
where none is lonely, none hunted, alien,
this man, superb in love and logic, this man   10
shall be remembered. Oh, not with statues' rhetoric,
not with legends and poems and wreaths of bronze alone,
but with the lives grown out of his life, the lives
fleshing his dream of the beautiful, needful thing.

[1962, 1985]

American Facts
and American Fiction

IN 1837, JULIA A. PARKER, a schoolteacher from Vermont, wrote to a friend, "I have spent the winter very, very pleasantly, – with my books has the time been mostly passed; what very kind friends they are; my reading has been both entertaining and instructive." By then, reading "entertaining and instructive" material was becoming an important pastime that was made possible in ways it had never been before. More efficient methods for producing printed materials, rising literacy rates, the lower cost of books, increased leisure time, especially for middle-class women, and the growing number of circulating libraries all contributed to the rapid growth of

◀ **Fetridge and Company's Periodical Arcade**

By the 1850s, there was growing demand for books and periodicals, both of which became important commodities in the emerging consumer society of the United States. This engraving from an 1852 issue of *Gleason's Pictorial Drawing Room Companion* shows the bustling interior of Fetridge and Company's Periodical Arcade in Boston, where men, women, and children could find newspapers and magazines designed for every age and interest, as well as general-interest periodicals such as *Gleason's*.

771

reading in the United States. For fiction writers, however, finding readers remained a challenge. With its emphasis on the imaginary as opposed to the real, fiction was viewed with suspicion by many Americans, especially those imbued with the persistent Puritan attitudes of colonial America. For fiction and fiction writers, however, the period from 1830 through the Civil War was marked by significant developments that would forever alter the literary marketplace in the United States.

Although the United States had been independent for more than fifty years in 1830, the development of a national literature, especially fiction, still faced many obstacles. One of the most formidable was the serious competition of celebrated British writers. In the absence of an international copyright law, American publishers could obtain copies of British books, print, and sell them without paying any royalties to the authors. The Harper Brothers, for example, built their successful firm primarily by publishing cheap reprints of mostly British novels, rather than publishing works by untried American writers. By far the most celebrated fiction writer in the United States during the first half of the nineteenth century was Sir Walter Scott, the Scottish poet and author of historical romances that were entertaining and instructive by almost any reader's standards. Scott's twenty-seven novels, beginning with *Waverly* (1814) and ending with *Castle Dangerous* (1831), were all reprinted in the United States immediately after their publication in Great Britain. Magazines and newspapers lavishly praised his novels in lengthy reviews. American writers, even successful ones, faced constant comparisons with the British: James Fenimore Cooper was dubbed the "American Scott." When the greatly mourned Scott died in 1832, another British fiction writer was already emerging to take his place. By the mid-1830s, Charles Dickens's short fiction, *Sketches by Boz*, began to appear in American magazines. When Dickens began to write novels, beginning with *The Pickwick Papers* (1836–37), American readers demanded more. Soon Dickens's novels were taking America by storm — appearing as serials in periodicals, listed with booksellers, and widely available in circulating libraries. As other British fiction writers emerged in the 1840s and 1850s — such as Charles Reade, Charlotte and Emily Brontë, Wilkie Collins, and William Makepeace Thackeray — their works were also widely reprinted and avidly read in the United States.

In the view of many writers and intellectuals, the popularity of the British writers made the need for an American literature all the more pressing. Calls for the development of a national literature were amplified by Ralph Waldo Emerson, Margaret Fuller, and other transcendentalists in and around Boston. But few of them displayed much interest in fiction. The establishment of a powerful tradition of American fiction depended not only on ideas but also on the actions of a group of editors and writers who could make their cultural commitments work in the marketplace. A nationalistic group of editors and writers in New York City, who described their movement as "Young America," took the lead in promoting American writers. The group included Evert and George Duyckinck, editors of the *Literary World*, and emerging prose writers of similar literary interests and with strongly Democratic sympathies, such as Herman Melville and a Southern writer, William Gilmore Simms. Other writers trying to claim a place in the literary marketplace were also involved in the movement, including Edgar Allan Poe, though he did not share the Democratic politics and principles of some of the leaders of Young America.

Periodicals were viewed by many as an important means of developing a national literature, and several magazines founded in the 1830s were expressly designed to support new works and help American writers become established. In the first issue of the *Knickerbocker*, founded in New York City in 1833, a reviewer called on writers to focus on the "natural beauty of our delightful country" instead of the "exhausted fields of Europe." The editors of the magazine thus solicited the work of popular fiction writers like Washington Irving and James Kirke Paulding, as well as that of the young Nathaniel Hawthorne.

A reviewer called on writers to focus on the "natural beauty of our delightful country" instead of the "exhausted fields of Europe."

If there was a leader of the Young America movement, it was probably Hawthorne's friend John L. O'Sullivan. In 1837, he helped establish the *United States Magazine and Democratic Review* in order to advance the interests of the Democratic Party and combat what O'Sullivan referred to as the "literary toryism" (in other words, the conservative British emphasis) of other American magazines. A variety of emerging fiction writers appeared in the pages of the magazine, including the young Walt Whitman, who was not then writing much poetry but who published eight stories in the magazine during 1841-42. Hawthorne published nearly twenty-five essays and stories in the *Democratic Review* (as it was usually called), which also featured the regional work of writers like Henry William Herbert, who wrote as "Frank Forester."

Much of the fiction published in both the *Knickerbocker* and the *Democratic Review* tended to be based on history, which underscored the nationalistic dimension of such works even as it made them seem closer to reality. Indeed, many pieces published in magazines were called "tales" or "sketches," blurring the boundaries between fiction and reality in such works and consequently making them all the more appealing to readers who had lingering concerns about the value of imaginative literature.

Despite such resistance, writers of fiction began to explore a range of subject matter and played a major role in the development of the short story. The popularity of European writers who wrote novels and stories about magic, mystery, and psychological terror prompted many American writers to adopt what was described as "gothic" elements in their work. Hawthorne blended such elements into his historical fictions, while Poe wrote stories with sensational plots and horrific details, designed to startle and captivate readers.

Nicolino Calyo, *Reading Room of the Astor House*

This satirical watercolor, painted around 1840, shows three men absorbed in their newspapers in the reading room of the Astor House, which opened in New York City in 1836 and which for many years was considered the finest hotel in the United States.

Domestic fiction was also becoming an increasingly popular staple of periodical literature during the 1830s and 1840s. In 1830, Louis A. Godey began the publication of *Godey's Lady's Book*, a periodical that became the most popular magazine for women before the Civil War. The magazine was intended to be a "mirror of woman's mind," and its editor for forty years, Sarah Josepha Hale, filled *Godey's* with fashion illustrations, sheet music, recipes, reviews, and advice as well as articles on travel and the arts. But the magazine also published a wide range of American writers. Alongside the works of Hawthorne, Poe, and the young Harriet Beecher Stowe were stories by now-forgotten writers who adhered to a standard plot line: A peaceful domestic household is threatened by an errant husband, relative, or child — rarely a wife — and eventually order is restored by the actions of Christian characters. Although such stories were deeply rooted in the day-to-day realities of domestic life, for women readers they were anything but dull. On the contrary, domestic fiction provided many middle-class women with solace and companionship during long hours spent within the confines of "woman's sphere," especially as men began to spend a growing number of hours away from the home. Women, who achieved the same literacy rates as men by midcentury, were becoming important consumers and increasingly vital producers of reading material. Smart publishers and editors studied and catered to the tastes and interests of this influential group of readers.

A Reading Party

"The young ladies are no longer dependent upon the other sex for literary information, but converse with as much facility upon the merits of modern writers as the male portion of the community," a writer for the *Philadelphia Album and Ladies Literary Portfolio* observed in 1827. During the following decades, reading became an even more important form of recreation and self-improvement for middle-class women, both individually and socially, as indicated by this illustration from an 1846 issue of *Godey's Lady's Book.*

At the same time, some very different trends were also emerging in American fiction. Just as literacy rates for women were increasing, so were the numbers of working-class Americans who could read. One of the best-selling books of the 1840s was the journalist George Lippard's *The Monks of Monk Hall* (later called *The Quaker City*), a sensational account of life and crime in Philadelphia. Forerunners of the "true crime" genre so popular today, stories about urban depravity became a staple in some periodicals. Temperance fiction, designed to demonstrate the evils of drink, was equally vivid in its representation of urban squalor. Walt Whitman published a temperance novel, *Franklin Evans* (1842), which was printed in an extra edition of the *New World.* Many other writers, such as Stowe, published stories with similar themes. In contrast, another respected woman author Louisa May Alcott wrote dozens of melodramatic thrillers (always under a pen name) during her long career. Sensational fiction was aimed mainly at lower-class audiences. It was cheap, it sold well, and it was consequently regarded with deep suspicion by editors and writers who wanted something more substantial for American literature.

Periodicals designed for a more educated and cultured audience exerted a powerful force on the shaping of American fiction. Making a bid for the audience that *Godey's* was attracting (but also pointedly including men in the title), *Graham's Lady's and Gentleman's Magazine* was established in 1841 for the purpose of publishing American writers. For nine years, *Graham's* was the best and the most popular literary magazine in the country. It published not only domestic fiction by women writers but also stories by Poe (who briefly edited the magazine) and Hawthorne. In 1844, Robert Bonner, an Irish immigrant, founded the *New York Ledger* as a family story-paper designed to provide weekly entertainment within the home. Determined to devote the *Ledger* to "choice literature, romance, the news, and commerce," Bonner sought out lively and informative works by the best writers he could afford. When Fanny Fern was becoming a household name for her witty columns in other periodicals, Bonner recruited her by publishing her novella, *Fanny Ford* (1855). He also employed a number of the increasingly popular women writers who were making a name for themselves in periodicals, including Alcott, Grace Greenwood, and E.D.E.N. Southworth.

Several of the literary magazines established in the 1850s had an even more lasting effect on American fiction. *Harper's New Monthly Magazine* (1850), *Putnam's Monthly* (1853), and the *Atlantic Monthly* (1857) were considered the most important venues for writers of American fiction, but they differed in some fundamental ways. Although it published some shorter works by American writers, including Melville and Elizabeth Barstow Stoddard, *Harper's* heavily relied on serializations of British novels. In contrast, *Putnam's* strongly promoted American writers. It also tended to publish shorter works, rather than offering an alternative to books by publishing lengthy serializations. Wishing to engage a broad national audience, the editors of *Putnam's* invited Charles Dudley Warner to write about California and John Pendleton Kennedy to write about the South. The *Atlantic Monthly* ultimately provided an even more distinguished and enduring home for the new American literature. With the inspiration of writers such as Ralph Waldo Emerson, Oliver Wendell Holmes, and James Russell Lowell, the magazine was established as a monthly journal whose cultural mission was to guide the age in literature, politics, science, and the arts.

Periodicals designed for a more educated and cultured audience exerted a powerful force on the shaping of American fiction.

Originally, however, it focused narrowly on New England, publishing writers such as Hawthorne and Stowe. After the *Atlantic* was purchased in 1859 by the publishing company of Ticknor and Fields, the magazine sought to break out of the Northeast by including writers from other geographic locations, especially women such as Rebecca Harding Davis of West Virginia, whose *Life in the Iron-Mills* appeared in 1861. One other literary magazine established in the 1850s was the *Anglo-African*

Sunnyside

A mass-circulation magazine targeted at a national audience, *Harper's* often included lavish illustrations, especially for its numerous travel essays and articles on famous places like "Sunnyside," the house on the Hudson River where Washington Irving lived until his death in 1859. Despite its tribute to that most revered and successful of earlier American writers, most of the fiction published in *Harper's* consisted of reprints of works by popular British novelists, especially Charles Dickens, who offered formidable competition to his counterparts in the United States.

Magazine (1859). The first magazine devoted exclusively to publishing the works of African American writers such as Martin Delany and Frances E. W. Harper, it was specifically intended to compete with magazines devoted to white writers.

By the beginning of the Civil War, American fiction was firmly established as a significant part of American culture, in large part due to the influence of periodicals. For young, unknown writers, publishing in magazines and newspapers offered a way to achieve a literary reputation. In fact, of all the writers represented in this section, only Melville started off by writing a series of novels. He turned to writing periodical fiction after his career as a novelist faltered. But most American novelists began by writing primarily for periodicals. Although he published an immature novel in 1828, the dozens of sketches and stories Hawthorne wrote for magazines during the 1830s and 1840s paved the way for the major novels he published in the 1850s, including *The Scarlet Letter* (1850), *The House of the Seven Gables* (1851), and *The Blithedale Romance* (1852). The enthusiastic reception of a sketch Donald Grant Mitchell ("Ik Marvel") published in the *Southern Literary Messenger* prompted him to expand it into *Reveries of a Bachelor* (1850), one of the most enduringly popular books of the nineteenth century. Because of Stowe's success as a regular writer of short sketches for magazines and newspapers, the editor of the *National Era* invited her to submit installments of the story that would eventually become the best-selling novel of the 1850s, *Uncle Tom's Cabin*. A temperance novel by Timothy Shay Arthur, *Ten Nights in a Bar Room* (1854), was another bestseller and came close to rivaling the sales of Stowe's hugely successful novel. *Uncle Tom's Cabin* radically altered the literary landscape, establishing the novel as the most popular of all kinds of writing in the United States. Stowe's novel also gained a wide audience in England, where Queen Victoria was among the many enthusiastic readers of an edition published in London in 1852.

Novels by American women dominated fiction in the United States during the 1850s, when the best-selling novelists included Susan Warner,

America's First Blockbuster

Stowe's best-selling novel sold 300,000 copies during its first year of book publication in 1852. As this bookseller's advertisement indicates, the novel was available in different languages and various editions, priced from 37½¢ to $5.

author of *The Wide, Wide World* (1852), and Maria Susanna Cummins, author of *The Lamplighter* (1854). Their popularity led a rather bitter Hawthorne to complain to his editor about the success of such "scribbling women." At the same time, periodicals continued to be the preferred place of publication for prominent writers such as Fanny Fern, even as literary magazines offered a crucial outlet for the work of young writers like Alcott, Davis, and Elizabeth Barstow Stoddard in the years before and during the Civil War. In whatever form, whether in novels or stories published in periodicals, American fiction had finally become a powerful presence in the literary marketplace.

Nathaniel Hawthorne

[1804-1864]

Nathaniel Hawthorne was born on July 4, 1804, in Salem, Massachusetts, the descendant of a family that on his father's side could trace its lineage back to the earliest founding of New England. Hawthorne developed an intense awareness of his Puritan ancestors, including a judge who persecuted the Quakers and one of the magistrates at the Salem witch trials. His father, a sea captain, died in Dutch Guiana when Hawthorne was four years old, and he spent most of what he later called his "lonely youth" living with his two sisters and grieving mother in a small house in Salem. He was educated at local schools and then attended Bowdoin College in Maine, where his classmates included Franklin Pierce, later the thirteenth president, and Henry Wadsworth Longfellow, who went on to become the most popular poet in the United States.

Nathaniel Hawthorne

Charles Osgood painted this portrait in 1840, when Hawthorne was thirty-six and working in the Boston Custom House. Hawthorne had the portrait sent to his family in Salem, joking that since they had the likeness they might "very well dispense with the original."

After his graduation from Bowdoin in 1825, Hawthorne also set out to become a professional writer. He returned to Salem and lived with his mother and sisters for the next twelve years, during which time Hawthorne wrote constantly. In 1828, he anonymously published his first novel, *Fanshawe*, a melodramatic tale of sexual intrigue and undergraduate life set in an isolated college in New England around the middle of the eighteenth century. The reviews were mixed, and Hawthorne himself was deeply dissatisfied with the novel, so much so that he later tried to conceal his authorship. But the novel gained him some attention, and Hawthorne was far more successful in the historical sketches and stories he soon began to publish in periodicals such as the *American Monthly Magazine* and the *New-England Magazine.* He hoped to publish a sequence of historical stories to be called *Provincial Tales* but reluctantly allowed them to be published individually in *The Token: Christmas and New Year's Present*, a finely bound and lavishly illustrated annual edited by Samuel G. Goodrich.

Goodrich paid Hawthorne less than a dollar a page for the twenty-seven sketches and tales he contributed to *The Token* between 1831 and 1837. Nonetheless, it was a respectable place to publish, especially for a young, unknown writer. Although all of his contributions to *The Token* appeared anonymously, Hawthorne gradually made a name for himself in the world of periodicals, then an important step in the careers of most writers. In 1837, this time under his own name, Hawthorne published *Twice-Told Tales*, a collection of his early sketches and stories. The positive reception of the book — "It comes from the hand of a man of genius," Longfellow exclaimed in the *North American Review* — generated renewed demand for Hawthorne's work, which he began to publish in prominent magazines like the *Knickerbocker* and the *Democratic Review*. Nonetheless, having already met his future wife, Sophia Peabody, Hawthorne worried that his income from writing would not allow him to marry and begin a family. Consequently, in 1839, he took a minor position in the Boston Custom House, the first of three government jobs he would hold.

Hawthorne produced serious literary work only during periods when he was not employed in those jobs. In his two years of work at the Boston Custom House, he managed to publish a few sketches and three children's books: *Grandfather's Chair, Famous Old People*, and *Liberty Tree*. After resigning his position in 1841, Hawthorne invested his meager savings in Brook Farm, an experimental utopian community outside Boston. Finding communal life unsatisfying, Hawthorne once again determined to make a living as a full-time writer. In 1842, he published an expanded edition of *Twice-Told Tales*. In a lengthy review, Edgar Allan Poe emphasized what few others fully recognized, the innovative quality of the tales, observing that "Mr. Hawthorne's distinctive trait is invention, creation, imagination, originality." Although sales of the volume were disappointing, Hawthorne felt confident and financially secure enough to marry Sophia in July 1842. The couple moved to Concord, Massachusetts, where they rented a house, the "Old Manse," owned by the Ralph Waldo Emerson family. Through Emerson, Hawthorne met many members of the transcendental circle, including Margaret Fuller and Henry David Thoreau. During four years in Concord, Hawthorne published numerous sketches and stories, many of which he gathered in another highly regarded collection, *Mosses from an Old Manse*, published in 1846. Still struggling to earn enough from writing to support his growing family, however, he accepted the well-paid and undemanding position of surveyor in the Salem Custom House. The position was a choice piece of political patronage; and Hawthorne, who was active in local Democratic politics, was dismissed after a Whig, Zachary Taylor, became president in 1849.

Having written almost nothing during the previous few years, Hawthorne worked at a furious pace during the following three. He immediately began a long tale that developed into the most famous of all novels about the Puritans, *The Scarlet Letter*, which created a sensation when it appeared in 1850. Widely acclaimed as the most important

In the field of letters, Hawthorne is the most valuable example of the American genius.

—Henry James

author of prose fiction in the country, Hawthorne moved his family to Lenox, Massachusetts, where he met a young writer who also aspired to literary greatness, Herman Melville. The two writers became close friends, and Melville dedicated his novel *Moby-Dick* (1851) to Hawthorne, "In Token of My Admiration for His Genius." Following up on the success of *The Scarlet Letter*, Hawthorne in 1851 published two collections of his early stories — a new edition of *Twice-Told Tales* and *The Snow-Image, and Other Twice-Told Tales* — as well as *The House of the Seven Gables*, a novel set in New England during the 1840s. He then wrote a sequence of stories for children, *A Wonder-Book for Girls and Boys*, and a novel loosely based on his experiences at Brook Farm, *The Blithedale Romance*, both of which Hawthorne published in 1852.

But his remarkable period of productivity was short lived. In 1852, Hawthorne agreed to write a campaign biography of his old college friend Franklin Pierce, the Democratic nominee for president. After Pierce was elected, he appointed Hawthorne to the lucrative position of American consul in Liverpool, England. Hawthorne and his family lived in Europe for the rest of the decade, first in England and then, after his consular term ended in 1857, in Italy. Drawing upon his experiences there, he wrote *The Marble Faun*, a novel published shortly before Hawthorne returned with his family to the United States in June 1860. Settling in Concord, he wrote articles for the *Atlantic Monthly* and a collection of sketches based on his years in England, *Our Old Home* (1863). Hawthorne also began several novels, but his failing health and declining creative powers prevented him from completing them before his death on May 19, 1864.

bedfordstmartins.com/ americanlit for research links on Hawthorne

Reading Hawthorne's "My Kinsman, Major Molineux." This is probably the most celebrated of the sequence of early stories Hawthorne initially hoped to publish in a collection called *Provincial Tales* but instead allowed Samuel G. Goodrich to print individually in his popular annual, *The Token: Christmas and New Year's Present.* Set in the turbulent period before the American Revolution, "My Kinsman, Major Molineux" is in part an ironic coming-of-age story, for both its protagonist, Robin, and the country he may be understood to represent. As Robin confronts the darker sides of colonial life in his search for his relative, Hawthorne explores some of the key themes of his early fiction, especially the nature of innocence and of experience, as well as the relation between appearance and reality in the dreamlike and moon-drenched setting of the story. Hawthorne did not include this challenging story in his earliest collections, *Twice-Told Tales* (1837, 1842), but he later included it in *The Snow-Image, and Other Twice-Told Tales* (1851). The text is taken from the first printing in *The Token* (1832), where it appeared along with three of Hawthorne's other stories, and where it was ascribed to "the author of 'Sights from a Steeple,'" a sketch Hawthorne had published in the annual the previous year.

My Kinsman, Major Molineux

After the kings of Great Britain had assumed the right of appointing the colonial governors, the measures of the latter seldom met with the ready and general approbation, which had been paid to those of their predecessors, under the original charters.[1] The people looked with most jealous scrutiny to the exercise of power, which did not emanate from themselves, and they usually rewarded the rulers with slender gratitude, for the compliances, by which, in softening their instructions from beyond the sea, they had incurred the reprehension of those who gave them. The annals of Massachusetts Bay will inform us, that of six governors, in the space of about forty years from the surrender of the old charter, under James II., two were imprisoned by a popular insurrection; a third, as Hutchinson[2] inclines to believe, was driven from the province by the whizzing of a musket ball; a fourth, in the opinion of the same historian, was hastened to his grave by continual bickerings with the house of representatives; and the remaining two, as well as their successors, till the Revolution,[3] were favored with few and brief intervals of peaceful sway. The inferior members of the court party,[4] in times of high political excitement, led scarcely a more desirable life. These remarks may serve as preface to the following adventures, which chanced upon a summer night, not far from a hundred years ago.[5] The reader, in order to avoid a long and dry detail of colonial affairs, is requested to dispense with an account of the train of circumstances, that had caused much temporary inflammation of the popular mind.

It was near nine o'clock of a moonlight evening, when a boat crossed the ferry with a single passenger, who had obtained his conveyance, at that unusual hour, by the promise of an extra fare. While he stood on the landing-place, searching in either pocket for the means of fulfilling his agreement, the ferryman lifted a lantern, by the aid of which, and the newly risen moon, he took a very accurate survey of the stranger's figure. He was a youth of barely eighteen years, evidently country-bred, and now, as it should seem, upon his first visit to town. He was clad in a coarse grey coat, well worn, but in excellent repair; his under garments were durably constructed of leather, and sat tight to a pair of serviceable and well-shaped limbs; his stockings of blue yarn, were the incontrovertible handiwork of a mother or a sister; and on his head was a three-cornered hat, which in its better days had perhaps sheltered the graver brow of the lad's father. Under his left arm was a heavy cudgel, formed of an oak sapling, and retaining a part of the hardened root; and his equipment was completed by a wallet,[6] not so abundantly stocked as to incommode the vigorous shoulders on which it hung. Brown curly hair, well-shaped features,

---

1. **original charters:** In 1684, the charter of the Massachusetts Bay Colony, which had allowed it to function as a self-governing commonwealth, was annulled by the Court of Chancery in England. The royal charter issued in 1691 incorporated Plymouth and Maine into the province of Massachusetts Bay and provided for a governor to be appointed by the crown.
2. **Hutchinson:** Thomas Hutchinson (1711-1780), the last royal governor of Massachusetts Bay; he wrote *The History of the Colony and Province of Massachusetts-Bay* (1764, 1767).
3. **Revolution:** The American Revolution, which began with the battles of Lexington and Concord in April 1775.
4. **court party:** Supporters of the British royal government.
5. **a hundred years ago:** The story is set in the early 1730s.
6. **wallet:** Knapsack.

and bright, cheerful eyes, were nature's gifts, and worth all that art could have done for his adornment.

The youth, one of whose names was Robin, finally drew from his pocket the half of a little province-bill[7] of five shillings, which, in the depreciation of that sort of currency, did but satisfy the ferryman's demand, with the surplus of a sexangular piece of parchment valued at three pence. He then walked forward into the town, with as light a step, as if his day's journey had not already exceeded thirty miles, and with as eager an eye, as if he were entering London city, instead of the little metropolis of a New England colony. Before Robin had proceeded far, however, it occurred to him, that he knew not whither to direct his steps; so he paused, and looked up and down the narrow street, scrutinizing the small and mean wooden buildings, that were scattered on either side.

"This low hovel cannot be my kinsman's dwelling," thought he, "nor yonder old house, where the moonlight enters at the broken casement; and truly I see none hereabouts that might be worthy of him. It would have been wise to inquire my way of the ferryman, and doubtless he would have gone with me, and earned a shilling from the Major for his pains. But the next man I meet will do as well."

He resumed his walk, and was glad to perceive that the street now became wider, and the houses more respectable in their appearance. He soon discerned a figure moving on moderately in advance, and hastened his steps to overtake it. As Robin drew nigh, he saw that the passenger was a man in years, with a full periwig of grey hair, a wide-skirted coat of dark cloth, and silk stockings rolled about his knees. He carried a long and polished cane, which he struck down perpendicularly before him, at every step; and at regular intervals he uttered two successive hems, of a peculiarly solemn and sepulchral intonation. Having made these observations, Robin laid hold of the skirt of the old man's coat, just when the light from the open door and windows of a barber's shop, fell upon both their figures.

"Good evening to you, honored Sir," said he, making a low bow, and still retaining his hold of the skirt. "I pray you to tell me whereabouts is the dwelling of my kinsman, Major Molineux?"

The youth's question was uttered very loudly; and one of the barbers, whose razor was descending on a well-soaped chin, and another who was dressing a Ramillies wig,[8] left their occupations, and came to the door. The citizen, in the meantime, turned a long favored countenance upon Robin, and answered him in a tone of excessive anger and annoyance. His two sepulchral hems, however, broke into the very centre of his rebuke, with most singular effect, like a thought of the cold grave obtruding among wrathful passions.

"Let go my garment, fellow! I tell you. I know not the man you speak of. What! I have authority, I have – hem, hem – authority; and if this be the respect you show your betters, your feet shall be brought acquainted with the stocks,[9] by daylight, tomorrow morning!"

---

7. **province-bill:** Paper money issued in the colonies.
8. **Ramillies wig:** An elaborate wig with a braid, named in honor of a decisive British victory over the French in Ramillies, Belgium, during the War of Spanish Succession, May 23, 1706.
9. **stocks:** A wooden frame with holes for securing a person's ankles and wrists, in which criminals were exposed to public punishment and ridicule.

Robin released the old man's skirt, and hastened away, pursued by an ill-mannered roar of laughter from the barber's shop. He was at first considerably surprised by the result of his question, but, being a shrewd youth, soon thought himself able to account for the mystery.

"This is some country representative," was his conclusion, "who has never seen the inside of my kinsman's door, and lacks the breeding to answer a stranger civilly. The man is old, or verily – I might be tempted to turn back and smite him on the nose. Ah, Robin, Robin! even the barber's boys laugh at you, for choosing such a guide! You will be wiser in time, friend Robin."

He now became entangled in a succession of crooked and narrow streets, which crossed each other, and meandered at no great distance from the water-side. The smell of tar was obvious to his nostrils, the masts of vessels pierced the moonlight above the tops of the buildings, and the numerous signs, which Robin paused to read, informed him that he was near the centre of business. But the streets were empty, the shops were closed, and lights were visible only in the second stories of a few dwelling-houses. At length, on the corner of a narrow lane, through which he was passing, he beheld the broad counte-nance of a British hero swinging before the door of an inn,[10] whence proceeded the voices of many guests. The casement of one of the lower windows was thrown back, and a very thin curtain permitted Robin to distinguish a party at supper, round a well-furnished table. The fragrance of the good cheer steamed forth into the outer air, and the youth could not fail to recollect, that the last remnant of his travelling stock of provision had yielded to his morning appetite, and that noon had found, and left him, dinnerless.

"Oh, that a parchment three-penny might give me a right to sit down at yonder table," said Robin, with a sigh. "But the Major will make me welcome to the best of his victuals; so I will even step boldly in, and inquire my way to his dwelling."

He entered the tavern, and was guided by the murmur of voices, and fumes of tobacco, to the public room. It was a long and low apartment, with oaken walls, grown dark in the continual smoke, and a floor, which was thickly sanded, but of no immacu-late purity. A number of persons, the larger part of whom appeared to be mariners, or in some way connected with the sea, occupied the wooden benches, or leather-bottomed chairs, conversing on various matters, and occasionally lending their attention to some topic of general interest. Three or four little groups were draining as many bowls of punch, which the great West India trade had long since made a familiar drink in the colony. Others, who had the aspect of men who lived by regular and laborious handi-craft, preferred the insulated bliss of an unshared potation, and became more taciturn under its influence. Nearly all, in short, evinced a predilection for the Good Creature[11] in some of its various shapes, for this is a vice, to which, as the Fast-day sermons[12] of a hundred years ago will testify, we have a long hereditary claim. The only guests to whom Robin's sympathies inclined him, were two or three sheepish countrymen, who were using the inn somewhat after the fashion of a Turkish Caravansary;[13] they had

---

10. **door of an inn:** Hanging signboards with images were used to designate the nature of a business.
11. **Good Creature:** A reference to rum, which was consumed at the rate of 12 million gallons per year in British North America.
12. **Fast-day sermons:** Sermons given on days set aside for public penitence.
13. **Turkish Caravansary:** An inn built around a large courtyard to accommodate a group of travelers journeying together.

gotten themselves into the darkest corner of the room, and, heedless of the Nicotian atmosphere,[14] were supping on the bread of their own ovens, and the bacon cured in their own chimney-smoke. But though Robin felt a sort of brotherhood with these strangers, his eyes were attracted from them, to a person who stood near the door, holding whispered conversation with a group of ill-dressed associates. His features were separately striking almost to grotesqueness, and the whole face left a deep impression in the memory. The forehead bulged out into a double prominence, with a vale between; the nose came boldly forth in an irregular curve, and its bridge was of more than a finger's breadth; the eyebrows were deep and shaggy, and the eyes glowed beneath them like fire in a cave.

While Robin deliberated of whom to inquire respecting his kinsman's dwelling, he was accosted by the innkeeper, a little man in a stained white apron, who had come to pay his professional welcome to the stranger. Being in the second generation from a French protestant, he seemed to have inherited the courtesy of his parent nation; but no variety of circumstance was ever known to change his voice from the one shrill note in which he now addressed Robin.

"From the country, I presume, Sir?" said he, with a profound bow. "Beg to congratulate you on your arrival, and trust you intend a long stay with us. Fine town here, Sir, beautiful buildings, and much that may interest a stranger. May I hope for the honor of your commands in respect to supper?"

"The man sees a family likeness! the rogue has guessed that I am related to the Major!" thought Robin, who had hitherto experienced little superfluous civility.

All eyes were now turned on the country lad, standing at the door, in his worn three-cornered hat, grey coat, leather breeches, and blue yarn stockings, leaning on an oaken cudgel, and bearing a wallet on his back. Robin replied to the courteous innkeeper, with such an assumption of consequence, as befitted the Major's relative.

"My honest friend," he said, "I shall make it a point to patronise your house on some occasion, when —" here he could not help lowering his voice — "I may have more than a parchment three-pence in my pocket. My present business," continued he, speaking with lofty confidence, "is merely to inquire the way to the dwelling of my kinsman, Major Molineux."

There was a sudden and general movement in the room, which Robin interpreted as expressing the eagerness of each individual to become his guide. But the innkeeper turned his eyes to a written paper on the wall, which he read, or seemed to read, with occasional recurrences to the young man's figure.

"What have we here?" said he, breaking his speech into little dry fragments. "'Left the house of the subscriber, bounden servant,'[15] Hezekiah Mudge — had on when he went away, grey coat, leather breeches, master's third best hat. One pound currency reward to whoever shall lodge him in any jail in the province.' Better trudge, boy, better trudge."

Robin had begun to draw his hand towards the lighter end of the oak cudgel, but a strange hostility in every countenance, induced him to relinquish his purpose of

---

14. **Nicotian atmosphere:** Smoky with tobacco fumes; Jean Nicot introduced tobacco into France in 1559.
15. **bounden servant:** An indentured servant, bound by a contract to serve for a period of years in repayment for transportation to the colonies.

breaking the courteous innkeeper's head. As he turned to leave the room, he encountered a sneering glance from the bold-featured personage whom he had before noticed; and no sooner was he beyond the door, than he heard a general laugh, in which the innkeeper's voice might be distinguished, like the dropping of small stones into a kettle.

"Now is it not strange," thought Robin, with his usual shrewdness, "is it not strange, that the confession of an empty pocket, should outweigh the name of my kinsman, Major Molineux? Oh, if I had one of these grinning rascals in the woods, where I and my oak sapling grew up together, I would teach him that my arm is heavy, though my purse be light!"

On turning the corner of the narrow lane, Robin found himself in a spacious street, with an unbroken line of lofty houses on each side, and a steepled building at the upper end, whence the ringing of a bell announced the hour of nine. The light of the moon, and the lamps from numerous shop windows, discovered people promenading on the pavement, and amongst them, Robin hoped to recognise his hitherto inscrutable relative. The result of his former inquiries made him unwilling to hazard another, in a scene of such publicity, and he determined to walk slowly and silently up the street, thrusting his face close to that of every elderly gentleman, in search of the Major's lineaments. In his progress, Robin encountered many gay and gallant figures. Embroidered garments, of showy colors, enormous periwigs, gold-laced hats, and silver hilted swords, glided past him and dazzled his optics. Travelled youths, imitators of the European fine gentlemen of the period, trod jauntily along, half-dancing to the fashionable tunes which they hummed, and making poor Robin ashamed of his quiet and natural gait. At length, after many pauses to examine the gorgeous display of goods in the shop windows, and after suffering some rebukes for the impertinence of his scrutiny into people's faces, the Major's kinsman found himself near the steepled building, still unsuccessful in his search. As yet, however, he had seen only one side of the thronged street; so Robin crossed, and continued the same sort of inquisition down the opposite pavement, with stronger hopes than the philosopher seeking an honest man,[16] but with no better fortune. He had arrived about midway towards the lower end, from which his course began, when he overheard the approach of some one, who struck down a cane on the flag-stones at every step, uttering, at regular intervals, two sepulchral hems.

"Mercy on us!" quoth Robin, recognising the sound.

Turning a corner, which chanced to be close at his right hand, he hastened to pursue his researches, in some other part of the town. His patience was now wearing low, and he seemed to feel more fatigue from his rambles since he crossed the ferry, than from his journey of several days on the other side. Hunger also pleaded loudly within him, and Robin began to balance the propriety of demanding, violently and with lifted cudgel, the necessary guidance from the first solitary passenger, whom he should meet.

---

16. **honest man:** Diogenes (412?-323 BCE) was a Greek philosopher who carried a lantern with him in his futile search to find an honest man.

While a resolution to this effect was gaining strength, he entered a street of mean appearance, on either side of which, a row of ill-built houses was straggling towards the harbor. The moonlight fell upon no passenger along the whole extent, but in the third domicile which Robin passed, there was a half-opened door, and his keen glance detected a woman's garment within.

"My luck may be better here," said he to himself.

Accordingly, he approached the door, and beheld it shut closer as he did so; yet an open space remained, sufficing for the fair occupant to observe the stranger, without a corresponding display on her part. All that Robin could discern was a strip of scarlet petticoat,[17] and the occasional sparkle of an eye, as if the moonbeams were trembling on some bright thing.

"Pretty mistress," — for I may call her so with a good conscience, thought the shrewd youth, since I know nothing to the contrary — "my sweet pretty mistress, will you be kind enough to tell me whereabouts I must seek the dwelling of my kinsman, Major Molineux?"

Robin's voice was plaintive and winning, and the female, seeing nothing to be shunned in the handsome country youth, thrust open the door, and came forth into the moonlight. She was a dainty little figure, with a white neck, round arms, and a slender waist, at the extremity of which her scarlet petticoat jutted out over a hoop, as if she were standing in a balloon. Moreover, her face was oval and pretty, her hair dark beneath the little cap, and her bright eyes possessed a sly freedom, which triumphed over those of Robin.

"Major Molineux dwells here," said this fair woman.

Now her voice was the sweetest Robin had heard that night, the airy counterpart of a stream of melted silver; yet he could not help doubting whether that sweet voice spoke gospel truth. He looked up and down the mean street, and then surveyed the house before which they stood. It was a small, dark edifice of two stories, the second of which projected over the lower floor; and the front apartment had the aspect of a shop for petty commodities.

"Now truly I am in luck," replied Robin, cunningly, "and so indeed is my kinsman, the Major, in having so pretty a housekeeper. But I prithee trouble him to step to the door; I will deliver him a message from his friends in the country, and then go back to my lodgings at the inn."

"Nay, the Major has been a-bed this hour or more," said the lady of the scarlet petticoat; "and it would be to little purpose to disturb him to night, seeing his evening draught was of the strongest. But he is a kind-hearted man, and it would be as much as my life's worth, to let a kinsman of his turn away from the door. You are the good old gentleman's very picture, and I could swear that was his rainy-weather hat. Also, he has garments very much resembling those leather — But come in, I pray, for I bid you hearty welcome in his name."

---

17. **scarlet petticoat:** Red underskirts were often worn by prostitutes.

So saying, the fair and hospitable dame took our hero by the hand; and though the touch was light, and the force was gentleness, and though Robin read in her eyes what he did not hear in her words, yet the slender waisted woman, in the scarlet petticoat, proved stronger than the athletic country youth. She had drawn his half-willing footsteps nearly to the threshold, when the opening of a door in the neighborhood, startled the Major's housekeeper, and, leaving the Major's kinsman, she vanished speedily into her own domicile. A heavy yawn preceded the appearance of a man, who, like the Moonshine of Pyramus and Thisbe,[18] carried a lantern, needlessly aiding his sister luminary in the heavens. As he walked sleepily up the street, he turned his broad, dull face on Robin, and displayed a long staff, spiked at the end.

"Home, vagabond, home!" said the watchman, in accents that seemed to fall asleep as soon as they were uttered. "Home, or we'll set you in the stocks by peep of day!"

"This is the second hint of the kind," thought Robin. "I wish they would end my difficulties, by setting me there to-night."

Nevertheless, the youth felt an instinctive antipathy towards the guardian of midnight order, which at first prevented him from asking his usual question. But just when the man was about to vanish behind the corner, Robin resolved not to lose the opportunity, and shouted lustily after him —

"I say, friend! will you guide me to the house of my kinsman, Major Molineux?"

The watchman made no reply, but turned the corner and was gone; yet Robin seemed to hear the sound of drowsy laughter stealing along the solitary street. At that moment, also, a pleasant titter saluted him from the open window above his head; he looked up, and caught the sparkle of a saucy eye; a round arm beckoned to him, and next he heard light footsteps descending the staircase within. But Robin, being of the household of a New England clergyman, was a good youth, as well as a shrewd one; so he resisted temptation, and fled away.

He now roamed desperately, and at random, through the town, almost ready to believe that a spell was on him, like that, by which a wizard of his country, had once kept three pursuers wandering, a whole winter night, within twenty paces of the cottage which they sought. The streets lay before him, strange and desolate, and the lights were extinguished in almost every house. Twice, however, little parties of men, among whom Robin distinguished individuals in outlandish attire, came hurrying along, but though on both occasions they paused to address him, such intercourse did not at all enlighten his perplexity. They did but utter a few words in some language of which Robin knew nothing, and perceiving his inability to answer, bestowed a curse upon him in plain English, and hastened away. Finally, the lad determined to knock at the door of every mansion that might appear worthy to be occupied by his kinsman, trusting that perseverance would overcome the fatality which had hitherto thwarted him. Firm in this resolve, he was passing beneath the walls of a church, which formed the corner of two

---

18. **Moonshine of Pyramus and Thisbe:** In act 5 of Shakespeare's *A Midsummer Night's Dream*, amateurs produce a hilarious version of the tragic tale of Pyramus and Thisbe in which one character dresses as the moon and carries a lantern in order to represent the moonshine under which the lovers meet.

streets, when, as he turned into the shade of its steeple, he encountered a bulky stranger, muffled in a cloak. The man was proceeding with the speed of earnest business, but Robin planted himself full before him, holding the oak cudgel with both hands across his body, as a bar to further passage.

"Halt, honest man, and answer me a question," said he, very resolutely. "Tell me, this instant, whereabouts is the dwelling of my kinsman, Major Molineux?"

"Keep your tongue between your teeth, fool, and let me pass," said a deep, gruff voice, which Robin partly remembered. "Let me pass, I say, or I'll strike you to the earth!"

"No, no, neighbor!" cried Robin, flourishing his cudgel, and then thrusting its larger end close to the man's muffled face. "No, no, I'm not the fool you take me for, nor do you pass, till I have an answer to my question. Whereabouts is the dwelling of my kinsman, Major Molineux?"

The stranger, instead of attempting to force his passage, stept back into the moonlight, unmuffled his own face and stared full into that of Robin.

"Watch here an hour and Major Molineux will pass by," said he.

Robin gazed with dismay and astonishment, on the unprecedented physiognomy of the speaker. The forehead with its double prominence, the broad-hooked nose, the shaggy eyebrows, and fiery eyes, were those which he had noticed at the inn, but the man's complexion had undergone a singular, or more properly, a two-fold change. One side of the face blazed of an intense red, while the other was black as midnight, the division line being in the broad bridge of the nose; and a mouth, which seemed to extend from ear to ear, was black or red, in contrast to the color of the cheek. The effect was as if two individual devils, a fiend of fire and a fiend of darkness, had united themselves to form this infernal visage. The stranger grinned in Robin's face, muffled his party-colored features, and was out of sight in a moment.

"Strange things we travellers see!" ejaculated Robin.

He seated himself, however, upon the steps of the church-door, resolving to wait the appointed time for his kinsman's appearance. A few moments were consumed in philosophical speculations, upon the species of the *genus homo*,[19] who had just left him, but having settled this point shrewdly, rationally, and satisfactorily, he was compelled to look elsewhere for amusement. And first he threw his eyes along the street; it was of more respectable appearance than most of those into which he had wandered, and the moon, "creating, like the imaginative power, a beautiful strangeness in familiar objects," gave something of romance to a scene, that might not have possessed it in the light of day. The irregular, and often quaint architecture of the houses, some of whose roofs were broken into numerous little peaks; while others ascended, steep and narrow, into a single point; and others again were square; the pure milk-white of some of their complexions, the aged darkness of others, and the thousand sparklings, reflected from bright substances in the plastered walls of many; these matters engaged Robin's attention for awhile, and then began to grow wearisome. Next he endeavored to define the

19. *genus homo*: Human being (Latin).

forms of distant objects, starting away with almost ghostly indistinctness, just as his eye appeared to grasp them; and finally he took a minute survey of an edifice, which stood on the opposite side of the street, directly in front of the church-door, where he was stationed. It was a large square mansion, distinguished from its neighbors by a balcony, which rested on tall pillars, and by an elaborate gothic window, communicating therewith.

"Perhaps this is the very house I have been seeking," thought Robin.

Then he strove to speed away the time, by listening to a murmur, which swept continually along the street, yet was scarcely audible, except to an unaccustomed ear like his; it was a low, dull, dreamy sound, compounded of many noises, each of which was at too great a distance to be separately heard. Robin marvelled at this snore of a sleeping town, and marvelled more, whenever its continuity was broken, by now and then a distant shout, apparently loud where it originated. But altogether it was a sleep-inspiring sound, and to shake off its drowsy influence, Robin arose, and climbed a window-frame, that he might view the interior of the church. There the moonbeams came trembling in, and fell down upon the deserted pews, and extended along the quiet aisles. A fainter, yet more awful radiance, was hovering round the pulpit, and one solitary ray had dared to rest upon the opened page of the great bible. Had Nature, in that deep hour, become a worshipper in the house, which man had builded? Or was that heavenly light the visible sanctity of the place, visible because no earthly and impure feet were within the walls? The scene made Robin's heart shiver with a sensation of loneliness, stronger than he had ever felt in the remotest depths of his native woods; so he turned away, and sat down again before the door. There were graves around the church, and now an uneasy thought obtruded into Robin's breast. What if the object of his search, which had been so often and so strangely thwarted, were all the time mouldering in his shroud? What if his kinsman should glide through yonder gate, and nod and smile to him in passing dimly by?

"Oh, that any breathing thing were here with me!" said Robin.

Recalling his thoughts from this uncomfortable track, he sent them over forest, hill, and stream, and attempted to imagine how that evening of ambiguity and weariness, had been spent by his father's household. He pictured them assembled at the door, beneath the tree, the great old tree, which had been spared for its huge twisted trunk, and venerable shade, when a thousand leafy brethren fell. There, at the going down of the summer sun, it was his father's custom to perform domestic worship, that the neighbors might come and join with him like brothers of the family, and that the wayfaring man might pause to drink at that fountain, and keep his heart pure by freshening the memory of home. Robin distinguished the seat of every individual of the little audience; he saw the good man in the midst, holding the scriptures in the golden light that shone from the western clouds; he beheld him close the book, and all rise up to pray. He heard the old thanksgiving for daily mercies, the old supplications for their continuance, to which he had so often listened in weariness, but which were now among his dear remembrances. He perceived the slight inequality of his father's voice when he came to speak of the Absent One; he noted how his mother turned her face to the broad and knotted trunk, how his elder brother scorned, because the beard was rough upon his upper lip, to permit his features to be moved; how his younger sister drew down a low hanging branch before her eyes; and how the little one of all, whose sports had hitherto broken the decorum of the scene, understood the prayer for her playmate, and burst into clamorous grief. Then he saw them go in at the door; and when Robin would have entered also, the latch tinkled into its place, and he was excluded from his home.

"Am I here, or there?" cried Robin, starting; for all at once, when his thoughts had become visible and audible in a dream, the long, wide, solitary street shone out before him.

He aroused himself, and endeavored to fix his attention steadily upon the large edifice which he had surveyed before. But still his mind kept vibrating between fancy and reality; by turns, the pillars of the balcony lengthened into the tall, bare stems of pines, dwindled down to human figures, settled again in their true shape and size, and then commenced a new succession of changes. For a single moment, when he deemed himself awake, he could have sworn that a visage, one which he seemed to remember, yet could not absolutely name as his kinsman's, was looking towards him from the Gothic window. A deeper sleep wrestled with, and nearly overcame him, but fled at the sound of footsteps along the opposite pavement. Robin rubbed his eyes, discerned a man passing at the foot of the balcony, and addressed him in a loud, peevish, and lamentable cry.

"Halloo, friend! must I wait here all night for my kinsman, Major Molineux?"

The sleeping echoes awoke, and answered the voice; and the passenger, barely able to discern a figure sitting in the oblique shade of the steeple, traversed the street to obtain a nearer view. He was himself a gentleman in his prime, of open, intelligent, cheerful, and altogether prepossessing countenance. Perceiving a country youth, apparently homeless and without friends, he accosted him in a tone of real kindness, which had become strange to Robin's ears.

"Well, my good lad, why are you sitting here?" inquired he. "Can I be of service to you in any way?"

"I am afraid not, Sir," replied Robin, despondingly; "yet I shall take it kindly, if you'll answer me a single question. I've been searching half the night for one Major Molineux; now, Sir, is there really such a person in these parts, or am I dreaming?"

"Major Molineux! The name is not altogether strange to me," said the gentleman, smiling. "Have you any objection to telling me the nature of your business with him?"

Then Robin briefly related that his father was a clergyman, settled on a small salary, at a long distance back in the country, and that he and Major Molineux were brothers' children. The Major, having inherited riches, and acquired civil and military rank, had visited his cousin in great pomp a year or two before; had manifested much interest in Robin and an elder brother, and, being childless himself, had thrown out hints respecting the future establishment of one of them in life. The elder brother was destined to succeed to the farm, which his father cultivated, in the interval of sacred duties; it was therefore determined that Robin should profit by his kinsman's generous intentions, especially as he had seemed to be rather the favorite, and was thought to possess other necessary endowments.

"For I have the name of being a shrewd youth," observed Robin, in this part of his story.

"I doubt not you deserve it," replied his new friend, good naturedly; "but pray proceed."

"Well, Sir, being nearly eighteen years old, and well grown, as you see," continued Robin, raising himself to his full height, "I thought it high time to begin the world. So my mother and sister put me in handsome trim, and my father gave me half the remnant of his last year's salary, and five days ago I started for this place, to pay the Major a visit. But would you believe it, Sir? I crossed the ferry a little after dusk, and have yet found nobody that would show me the way to his dwelling; only an hour or two since, I was told to wait here, and Major Molineux would pass by."

"Can you describe the man who told you this?" inquired the gentleman.

"Oh, he was a very ill-favored fellow, Sir," replied Robin, "with two great bumps on his forehead, a hook nose, fiery eyes, and, what struck me as the strangest, his face was of two different colors. Do you happen to know such a man, Sir?"

"Not intimately," answered the stranger, "but I chanced to meet him a little time previous to your stopping me. I believe you may trust his word, and that the Major will very shortly pass through this street. In the mean time, as I have a singular curiosity to witness your meeting, I will sit down here upon the steps, and bear you company."

He seated himself accordingly, and soon engaged his companion in animated discourse. It was but of brief continuance, however, for a noise of shouting, which had long been remotely audible, drew so much nearer, that Robin inquired its cause.

"What may be the meaning of this uproar?" asked he. "Truly, if your town be always as noisy, I shall find little sleep, while I am an inhabitant."

"Why, indeed, friend Robin, there do appear to be three or four riotous fellows abroad to-night," replied the gentleman. "You must not expect all the stillness of your native woods, here in our streets. But the watch will shortly be at the heels of these lads, and —"

"Aye, and set them in the stocks by peep of day," interrupted Robin, recollecting his own encounter with the drowsy lantern-bearer. "But, dear Sir, if I may trust my ears, an army of watchmen would never make head against such a multitude of rioters. There were at least a thousand voices went to make up that one shout."

"May not one man have several voices, Robin, as well as two complexions?" said his friend.

"Perhaps a man may; but heaven forbid that a woman should!" responded the shrewd youth, thinking of the seductive tones of the Major's housekeeper.

The sounds of a trumpet in some neighboring street, now became so evident and continual, that Robin's curiosity was strongly excited. In addition to the shouts, he heard frequent bursts from many instruments of discord, and a wild and confused laughter filled up the intervals. Robin rose from the steps, and looked wistfully towards a point, whither several people seemed to be hastening.

"Surely some prodigious merrymaking is going on," exclaimed he. "I have laughed very little since I left home, Sir, and should be sorry to lose an opportunity. Shall we just step round the corner by that darkish house, and take our share of the fun?"

"Sit down again, sit down, good Robin," replied the gentleman, laying his hand on the skirt of the grey coat. "You forget that we must wait here for your kinsman; and there is reason to believe that he will pass by, in the course of a very few moments."

The near approach of the uproar had now disturbed the neighborhood; windows flew open on all sides; and many heads, in the attire of the pillow, and confused by sleep suddenly broken, were protruded to the gaze of whoever had leisure to observe them. Eager voices hailed each other from house to house, all demanding the explanation, which not a soul could give. Half-dressed men hurried towards the unknown commotion, stumbling as they went over the stone steps, that thrust themselves into the narrow footwalk. The shouts, the laughter, and the tuneless bray, the antipodes of music, came onward with increasing din, till scattered individuals, and then denser bodies, began to appear round a corner, at the distance of a hundred yards.

"Will you recognise your kinsman, Robin, if he passes in this crowd?" inquired the gentleman.

"Indeed, I can't warrant it, Sir; but I'll take my stand here, and keep a bright look out," answered Robin, descending to the outer edge of the pavement.

A mighty stream of people now emptied into the street, and came rolling slowly towards the church. A single horseman wheeled the corner in the midst of them, and close behind him came a band of fearful wind-instruments, sending forth a fresher discord, now that no intervening buildings keep it from the ear. Then a redder light disturbed the moonbeams, and a dense multitude of torches shone along the street, concealing by their glare whatever object they illuminated. The single horseman, clad in a military dress, and bearing a drawn sword, rode onward as the leader, and, by his fierce and variegated countenance, appeared like war personified; the red of one cheek was an emblem of fire and sword; the blackness of the other betokened the mourning which attends them. In his train, were wild figures in the Indian dress, and many fantastic shapes without a model, giving the whole march a visionary air, as if a dream had broken forth from some feverish brain, and were sweeping visibly through the midnight streets. A mass of people, inactive, except as applauding spectators, hemmed the procession in, and several women ran along the sidewalks, piercing the confusion of heavier sounds, with their shrill voices of mirth or terror.

"The double-faced fellow has his eye upon me," muttered Robin, with an indefinite but uncomfortable idea, that he was himself to bear a part in the pageantry.

The leader turned himself in the saddle, and fixed his glance full upon the country youth, as the steed went slowly by. When Robin had freed his eyes from those fiery ones, the musicians were passing before him, and the torches were close at hand; but the unsteady brightness of the latter formed a veil which he could not penetrate. The rattling of wheels over the stones sometimes found its way to his ear, and confused traces of a human form appeared at intervals, and then melted into the vivid light. A moment more, and the leader thundered a command to halt; the trumpets vomited a horrid breath, and held their peace; the shouts and laughter of the people died away, and there remained only an universal hum, nearly allied to silence. Right before Robin's eyes was an uncovered cart. There the torches blazed the brightest, there the moon shone out like day, and there, in tar-and-feathery dignity, sate his kinsman, Major Molineux!

He was an elderly man, of large and majestic person, and strong, square features, betokening a steady soul; but steady as it was, his enemies had found the means to shake it. His face was pale as death, and far more ghastly; the broad forehead was contracted in his agony, so that the eyebrows formed one dark grey line; his eyes were red and wild, and the foam hung white upon his quivering lip. His whole frame was agitated by a quick, and continual tremor, which his pride strove to quell, even in those circumstances of overwhelming humiliation. But perhaps the bitterest pang of all was when his eyes met those of Robin; for he evidently knew him on the instant, as the youth stood witnessing the foul disgrace of a head that had grown grey in honor. They stared at each other in silence, and Robin's knees shook, and his hair bristled, with a mixture of pity and terror. Soon, however, a bewildering excitement began to seize upon his mind; the preceding adventures of the night, the unexpected appearance of the crowd, the torches, the confused din, and the hush that followed, the spectre of his kinsman reviled by that great multitude, all this, and more than all, a perception of tremendous ridicule in the whole scene, affected him with a sort of mental inebriety. At that moment a voice of sluggish merriment saluted Robin's ears; he turned instinctively, and just behind the corner of the church stood the lantern-bearer, rubbing his eyes, and drowsily enjoying the lad's amazement. Then he heard a peal of laughter like the ringing of silvery bells; a woman twitched his arm, a saucy eye met his, and he saw the lady of the scarlet petticoat. A sharp, dry cachinnation appealed to his memory, and, standing on tiptoe in the crowd, with his white apron over his head, he beheld the courteous little innkeeper. And lastly, there sailed over the heads of the multitude a great, broad laugh, broken in the midst by two deep sepulchral hems; thus —

"Haw, haw, haw — hem, hem — haw, haw, haw, haw!"

The sound proceeded from the balcony of the opposite edifice, and thither Robin turned his eyes. In front of the Gothic window stood the old citizen, wrapped in a wide gown, his grey periwig exchanged for a nightcap, which was thrust back from his forehead, and his silk stockings hanging down about his legs. He supported himself on his polished cane in a fit of convulsive merriment, which manifested itself on his solemn old features, like a funny inscription on a tomb-stone. Then Robin seemed to hear the voices of the barbers; of the guests of the inn; and of all who had made sport of him that night. The contagion was spreading among the multitude, when, all at once, it seized upon Robin, and he sent forth a shout of laughter that echoed through the street; every man shook his sides, every man emptied his lungs, but Robin's shout was the loudest there. The cloud-spirits peeped from their silvery islands, as the congregated mirth went roaring up the sky! The Man in the Moon heard the far bellow; "Oho," quoth he, "the old Earth is frolicsome to-night!"

When there was a momentary calm in that tempestuous sea of sound, the leader gave the sign, and the procession resumed its march. On they went, like fiends that throng in mockery round some dead potentate, mighty no more, but majestic still in his agony. On they went, in counterfeited pomp, in senseless uproar, in frenzied merriment, trampling all on an old man's heart. On swept the tumult, and left a silent street behind.

"Well, Robin, are, you dreaming?" inquired the gentleman, laying his hand on the youth's shoulder.

Robin started, and withdrew his arm from the stone post, to which he had instinctively clung, while the living stream rolled by him. His cheek was somewhat pale, and his eye not quite so lively as in the earlier part of the evening.

"Will you be kind enough to show me the way to the Ferry?" said he, after a moment's pause.

"You have then adopted a new subject of inquiry?" observed his companion, with a smile.

"Why, yes, Sir," replied Robin, rather dryly. "Thanks to you, and to my other friends, I have at last met my kinsman, and he will scarce desire to see my face again. I begin to grow weary of a town life, Sir. Will you show me the way to the Ferry?"

"No, my good friend Robin, not to-night, at least," said the gentleman. "Some few days hence, if you continue to wish it, I will speed you on your journey. Or, if you prefer to remain with us, perhaps, as you are a shrewd youth, you may rise in the world, without the help of your kinsman, Major Molineux."

[1832]

Reading Hawthorne's "Young Goodman Brown."   Probably the most famous of Hawthorne's early stories of the Puritans, "Young Goodman Brown" was one of seventeen sketches and stories he published anonymously in the *New-England Magazine*. Established in 1831 as a vehicle for New England writers, the magazine enjoyed early success but failed as a result of declining sales in 1835. The editors attracted a variety of well-known writers, including Oliver Wendell Holmes, Henry Wadsworth Longfellow, and Lydia Sigourney, as well as virtual unknowns like Hawthorne. Although it paid only $1 per page for his contributions, publishing in the magazine was a boon to Hawthorne, who was seeking to establish himself as a writer. Like many of his other pieces in the magazine, "Young Goodman Brown" is set in colonial New England and refers to actual events, including the most infamous episode in the history of Hawthorne's native town, the Salem witch trials of 1692. Indeed, the story may be read, not only as a powerful exploration of the corrosive effects of the Puritan conscience, but also as a probing analysis of the moral psychology of a Puritan community in which people could believe their neighbors were witches in league with the devil. Hawthorne did not include the sobering story in his earliest collections, *Twice-Told Tales* (1837, 1842), but he later included it in *Mosses from an Old Manse* (1846). The text is taken from the first printing in the *New-England Magazine* (April 1835), where it was ascribed to "the author of 'The Gray Champion,'" a story Hawthorne had published in the magazine three months earlier.

YOUNG GOODMAN BROWN

Young goodman[1] Brown came forth, at sunset, into the street of Salem village, but put his head back, after crossing the threshold, to exchange a parting kiss with his young wife. And Faith, as the wife was aptly named, thrust her own pretty head into the street, letting the wind play with the pink ribbons of her cap, while she called to goodman Brown.

"Dearest heart," whispered she, softly and rather sadly, when her lips were close to his ear, "pr'y thee, put off your journey until sunrise, and sleep in your own bed to-night. A lone woman is troubled with such dreams and such thoughts, that she's afeard of herself, sometimes. Pray, tarry with me this night, dear husband, of all nights in the year!"

"My love and my Faith," replied young goodman Brown, "of all nights in the year, this one night must I tarry away from thee. My journey, as thou callest it, forth and back again, must needs be done 'twixt now and sunrise. What, my sweet, pretty wife, dost thou doubt me already, and we but three months married!"

"Then, God bless you!" said Faith, with the pink ribbons, "and may you find all well, when you come back."

"Amen!" cried goodman Brown. "Say thy prayers, dear Faith, and go to bed at dusk, and no harm will come to thee."

So they parted; and the young man pursued his way, until, being about to turn the corner by the meeting-house, he looked back, and saw the head of Faith still peeping after him, with a melancholy air, in spite of her pink ribbons.

"Poor little Faith!" thought be, for his heart smote him. "What a wretch am I, to leave her on such an errand! She talks of dreams, too. Methought, as she spoke, there was trouble in her face, as if a dream had warned her what work is to be done to-night. But, no, no! 'twould kill her to think it. Well; she's a blessed angel on earth; and after this one night, I'll cling to her skirts and follow her to Heaven."

With this excellent resolve for the future, goodman Brown felt himself justified in making more haste on his present evil purpose. He had taken a dreary road, darkened by all the gloomiest trees of the forest, which barely stood aside to let the narrow path creep through, and closed immediately behind. It was all as lonely as could be; and there is this peculiarity in such a solitude, that the traveler knows not who may be concealed by the innumerable trunks and the thick boughs overhead; so that, with lonely footsteps, he may yet be passing through an unseen multitude.

"There may be a devilish Indian behind every tree," said goodman Brown, to himself; and he glanced fearfully behind him, as he added, "What if the devil himself should be at my very elbow!"

His head being turned back, he passed a crook of the road, and looking forward again, beheld the figure of a man, in grave and decent attire, seated at the foot of an old tree. He arose, at goodman Brown's approach, and walked onward, side by side with him.

---

1. **goodman:** A courteous title for a man of humble birth.

"You are late, goodman Brown," said he. "The clock of the Old South[2] was striking as I came through Boston; and that is full fifteen minutes agone."

"Faith kept me back awhile," replied the young man, with a tremor in his voice, caused by the sudden appearance of his companion, though not wholly unexpected.

It was now deep dusk in the forest, and deepest in that part of it where these two were journeying. As nearly as could be discerned, the second traveler was about fifty years old, apparently in the same rank of life as goodman Brown, and bearing a considerable resemblance to him, though perhaps more in expression than features. Still, they might have been taken for father and son. And yet, though the elder person was as simply clad as the younger, and as simple in manner too, he had an indescribable air of one who knew the world, and would not have felt abashed at the governor's dinner-table, or in king William's court,[3] were it possible that his affairs should call him thither. But the only thing about him, that could be fixed upon as remarkable, was his staff, which bore the likeness of a great black snake, so curiously wrought, that it might almost be seen to twist and wriggle itself, like a living serpent. This, of course, must have been an ocular deception, assisted by the uncertain light.

"Come, goodman Brown!" cried his fellow-traveler, "this is a dull pace for the beginning of a journey. Take my staff, if you are so soon weary."

"Friend," said the other, exchanging his slow pace for a full stop, "having kept covenant by meeting thee here, it is my purpose now to return whence I came. I have scruples, touching the matter thou wot'st of."

"Sayest thou so?" replied he of the serpent, smiling apart. "Let us walk on, nevertheless, reasoning as we go, and if I convince thee not, thou shalt turn back. We are but a little way in the forest, yet."

"Too far, too far!" exclaimed the goodman, unconsciously resuming his walk. "My father never went into the woods on such an errand, nor his father before him. We have been a race of honest men and good Christians, since the days of the martyrs.[4] And shall I be the first of the name of Brown, that ever took this path, and kept" —

"Such company, thou wouldst say," observed the elder person, interpreting his pause. "Good, goodman Brown! I have been as well acquainted with your family as with ever a one among the Puritans; and that's no trifle to say. I helped your grandfather, the constable, when he lashed the Quaker woman so smartly through the streets of Salem. And it was I that brought your father a pitch-pine knot, kindled at my own hearth, to set fire to an Indian village, in king Philip's war.[5] They were my good friends, both; and many a pleasant walk have we had along this path, and returned merrily after midnight. I would fain be friends with you, for their sake."

---

2. **Old South:** The Old South Church in Boston; since one could not travel from Boston to Salem in fifteen minutes, the speed suggests a supernatural force.
3. **king William's court:** King William II and Queen Mary II were the joint rulers of England from 1689 to 1702.
4. **days of the martyrs:** Protestant martyrs executed in England during the reign of the Catholic queen Mary Tudor (1553-1558).
5. **king Philip's war:** The chief of the Wampanoag, called "King Philip" by the colonists, led uprisings against them during 1675-1676.

"If it be as thou sayest," replied goodman Brown, "I marvel they never spoke of these matters. Or, verily, I marvel not, seeing that the least rumor of the sort would have driven them from New-England. We are a people of prayer, and good works, to boot, and abide no such wickedness."

"Wickedness or not," said the traveler with the twisted staff, "I have a very general acquaintance here in New-England. The deacons of many a church have drunk the communion wine with me; the selectmen, of divers towns, make me their chairman; and a majority of the Great and General Court[6] are firm supporters of my interest. The governor and I, too — but these are state-secrets."

"Can this be so!" cried goodman Brown, with a stare of amazement at his undisturbed companion. "Howbeit, I have nothing to do with the governor and council; they have their own ways, and are no rule for a simple husbandman,[7] like me. But, were I to go on with thee, how should I meet the eye of that good old man, our minister, at Salem village? Oh, his voice would make me tremble, both Sabbath-day and lecture-day!"[8]

Thus far, the elder traveler had listened with due gravity, but now burst into a fit of irrepressible mirth, shaking himself so violently, that his snake-like staff actually seemed to wriggle in sympathy.

"Ha! ha! ha!" shouted he, again and again; then composing himself, "Well, go on, goodman Brown, go on; but, pr'y thee, don't kill me with laughing!"

"Well, then, to end the matter at once," said goodman Brown, considerably nettled, "there is my wife, Faith. It would break her dear little heart; and I'd rather break my own!"

"Nay, if that be the case," answered the other, "e'en go thy ways, goodman Brown. I would not, for twenty old women like the one hobbling before us, that Faith should come to any harm."

As he spoke, he pointed his staff at a female figure on the path, in whom goodman Brown recognized a very pious and exemplary dame, who had taught him his catechism, in youth, and was still his moral and spiritual adviser, jointly with the minister and deacon Gookin.

"A marvel, truly, that goody Cloyse[9] should be so far in the wilderness, at night-fall!" said he. "But, with your leave, friend, I shall take a cut through the woods, until we have left this Christian woman behind. Being a stranger to you, she might ask whom I was consorting with, and whither I was going."

"Be it so," said his fellow-traveler. "Betake you to the woods, and let me keep the path."

Accordingly, the young man turned aside, but took care to watch his companion, who advanced softly along the road, until he had come within a staff's length of the old dame.

---

6. **Great and General Court:** The colonial legislature.
7. **husbandman:** Farmer.
8. **lecture-day:** Sermon delivered on a weekday.
9. **goody Cloyse:** *Goody* was a shortened form of *goodwife*, a courteous form of address for a married woman of humble status. Cloyse and "goody Cory," referred to later in this passage, were the names of women sentenced to death during the Salem witch trials of 1692.

She, meanwhile, was making the best of her way, with singular speed for so aged a woman, and mumbling some indistinct words, a prayer, doubtless, as she went. The traveler put forth his staff, and touched her withered neck with what seemed the serpent's tail.

"The devil!" screamed the pious old lady.

"Then goody Cloyse knows her old friend?" observed the traveler, confronting her, and leaning on his writhing stick.

"Ah, forsooth, and is it your worship, indeed?" cried the good dame. "Yea, truly is it, and in the very image of my old gossip, goodman Brown, the grandfather of the silly fellow that now is. But, would your worship believe it? my broomstick hath strangely disappeared, stolen, as I suspect, by that unhanged witch, goody Cory, and that, too, when I was all anointed with the juice of smallage and cinque-foil and wolf's-bane" — [10]

"Mingled with fine wheat and the fat of a new-born babe," said the shape of old goodman Brown.

"Ah, your worship knows the receipt," cried the old lady, cackling aloud. "So, as I was saying, being all ready for the meeting, and no horse to ride on, I made up my mind to foot it; for they tell me, there is a nice young man to be taken into communion to-night. But now your good worship will lend me your arm, and we shall be there in a twinkling."

"That can hardly be," answered her friend. "I may not spare you my arm, goody Cloyse, but here is my staff, if you will."

So saying, he threw it down at her feet, where, perhaps, it assumed life, being one of the rods which its owner had formerly lent to the Egyptian Magi.[11] Of this fact, however, goodman Brown could not take cognizance. He had cast up his eyes in astonishment, and looking down again, beheld neither goody Cloyse nor the serpentine staff, but his fellow-traveler alone, who waited for him as calmly as if nothing had happened.

"That old woman taught me my catechism!" said the young man; and there was a world of meaning in this simple comment.

They continued to walk onward, while the elder traveler exhorted his companion to make good speed and persevere in the path, discoursing so aptly, that his arguments seemed rather to spring up in the bosom of his auditor, than to be suggested by himself. As they went, he plucked a branch of maple, to serve for a walking-stick, and began to strip it of the twigs and little boughs, which were wet with evening dew. The moment his fingers touched them, they became strangely withered and dried up, as with a week's sunshine. Thus the pair proceeded, at a good free pace, until suddenly, in a gloomy hollow of the road, goodman Brown sat himself down on the stump of a tree, and refused to go any farther.

---

10. **smallage . . . wolf's-bane:** Wild plants, some of them poisonous, associated with witchcraft.

11. **Egyptian Magi:** In the Old Testament, Aaron demonstrates the power of God to the Pharaoh by turning his staff into a serpent. When the Pharaoh's magicians replicate the feat, Aaron's staff swallows theirs (Exodus 7:8-13).

"Friend," said he, stubbornly, "my mind is made up. Not another step will I budge on this errand. What if a wretched old woman do choose to go to the devil, when I thought she was going to Heaven! Is that any reason why I should quit my dear Faith, and go after her?"

"You will think better of this, by-and-by," said his acquaintance, composedly. "Sit here and rest yourself awhile; and when you feel like moving again, there is my staff to help you along."

Without more words, he threw his companion the maple stick, and was as speedily out of sight, as if he had vanished into the deepening gloom. The young man sat a few moments, by the road-side, applauding himself greatly, and thinking with how clear a conscience he should meet the minister, in his morning-walk, nor shrink from the eye of good old deacon Gookin. And what calm sleep would be his, that very night, which was to have been spent so wickedly, but purely and sweetly now, in the arms of Faith! Amidst these pleasant and praiseworthy meditations, goodman Brown heard the tramp of horses along the road, and deemed it advisable to conceal himself within the verge of the forest, conscious of the guilty purpose that had brought him thither, though now so happily turned from it.

On came the hoof-tramps and the voices of the riders, two grave old voices, conversing soberly as they drew near. These mingled sounds appeared to pass along the road, within a few yards of the young man's hiding-place; but owing, doubtless, to the depth of the gloom, at that particular spot, neither the travelers nor their steeds were visible. Though their figures brushed the small boughs by the way-side, it could not be seen that they intercepted, even for a moment, the faint gleam from the strip of bright sky, athwart which they must have passed. Goodman Brown alternately crouched and stood on tip-toe, pulling aside the branches, and thrusting forth his head as far as he durst, without discerning so much as a shadow. It vexed him the more, because he could have sworn, were such a thing possible, that he recognized the voices of the minister and deacon Gookin, jogging along quietly, as they were wont to do, when bound to some ordination or ecclesiastical council. While yet within hearing, one of the riders stopped to pluck a switch.

"Of the two, reverend Sir," said the voice like the deacon's, "I had rather miss an ordination-dinner than to-night's meeting. They tell me that some of our community are to be here from Falmouth[12] and beyond, and others from Connecticut and Rhode-Island; besides several of the Indian powows,[13] who, after their fashion, know almost as much deviltry as the best of us. Moreover, there is a goodly young woman to be taken into communion."

"Mighty well, deacon Gookin!" replied the solemn old tones of the minister. "Spur up, or we shall be late. Nothing can be done, you know, until I get on the ground."

The hoofs clattered again, and the voices, talking so strangely in the empty air, passed on through the forest, where no church had ever been gathered, nor solitary

---

12. **Falmouth:** A town on Cape Cod in Massachusetts.
13. **Indian powows:** Medicine men. A powwow is a conference or gathering.

Christian prayed. Whither, then, could these holy men be journeying, so deep into the heathen wilderness? Young goodman Brown caught hold of a tree, for support, being ready to sink down on the ground, faint and overburthened with the heavy sickness of his heart. He looked up to the sky, doubting whether there really was a Heaven above him. Yet, there was the blue arch, and the stars brightening in it.

"With Heaven above, and Faith below, I will yet stand firm against the devil!" cried goodman Brown.

While he still gazed upward, into the deep arch of the firmament, and had lifted his hands to pray, a cloud, though no wind was stirring, hurried across the zenith, and hid the brightening stars. The blue sky was still visible, except directly overhead, where this black mass of cloud was sweeping swiftly northward. Aloft in the air, as if from the depths of the cloud, came a confused and doubtful sound of voices. Once, the listener fancied that he could distinguish the accents of town's-people of his own, men and women, both pious and ungodly, many of whom he had met at the communion-table, and had seen others rioting at the tavern. The next moment, so indistinct were the sounds, he doubted whether he had heard aught but the murmur of the old forest, whispering without a wind. Then came a stronger swell of those familiar tones, heard daily in the sunshine, at Salem village, but never, until now, from a cloud of night. There was one voice, of a young woman, uttering lamentations, yet with an uncertain sorrow, and entreating for some favor, which, perhaps, it would grieve her to obtain. And all the unseen multitude, both saints and sinners, seemed to encourage her onward.

"Faith!" shouted goodman Brown, in a voice of agony and desperation; and the echoes of the forest mocked him, crying – "Faith! Faith!" as if bewildered wretches were seeking her, all through the wilderness.

The cry of grief, rage, and terror, was yet piercing the night, when the unhappy husband held his breath for a response. There was a scream, drowned immediately in a louder murmur of voices, fading into far-off laughter, as the dark cloud swept away, leaving the clear and silent sky above goodman Brown. But something fluttered lightly down through the air, and caught on the branch of a tree. The young man seized it, and beheld a pink ribbon.

"My Faith is gone!" cried he, after one stupefied moment. "There is no good on earth; and sin is but a name. Come, devil! for to thee is this world given."

And maddened with despair, so that he laughed loud and long, did goodman Brown grasp his staff and set forth again, at such a rate, that he seemed to fly along the forest-path, rather than to walk or run. The road grew wilder and drearier, and more faintly traced, and vanished at length, leaving him in the heart of the dark wilderness, still rushing onward, with the instinct that guides mortal man to evil. The whole forest was peopled with frightful sounds; the creaking of the trees, the howling of wild beasts, and the yell of Indians; while, sometimes, the wind tolled like a distant church-bell, and sometimes gave a broad roar around the traveler, as if all Nature were laughing him to scorn. But he was himself the chief horror of the scene, and shrank not from its other horrors.

"Ha! ha! ha!" roared goodman Brown, when the wind laughed at him. "Let us hear which will laugh loudest! Think not to frighten me with your deviltry! Come witch, come wizard, come Indian powow, come devil himself! and here comes goodman Brown. You may as well fear him as he fear you!"

In truth, all through the haunted forest, there could be nothing more frightful than the figure of goodman Brown. On he flew, among the black pines, brandishing his staff with frenzied gestures, now giving vent to an inspiration of horrid blasphemy, and now shouting forth such laughter, as set all the echoes of the forest laughing like demons around him. The fiend in his own shape is less hideous, than when he rages in the breast of man. Thus sped the demoniac on his course, until, quivering among the trees, he saw a red light before him, as when the felled trunks and branches of a clearing have been set on fire, and throw up their lurid blaze against the sky, at the hour of midnight. He paused, in a lull of the tempest that had driven him onward, and heard the swell of what seemed a hymn, rolling solemnly from a distance, with the weight of many voices. He knew the tune; it was a familiar one in the choir of the village meeting-house. The verse died heavily away, and was lengthened by a chorus, not of human voices, but of all the sounds of the benighted wilderness, pealing in awful harmony together. Goodman Brown cried out; and his cry was lost to his own ear, by its unison with the cry of the desert.

In the interval of silence, he stole forward, until the light glared full upon his eyes. At one extremity of an open space, hemmed in by the dark wall of the forest, arose a rock, bearing some rude, natural resemblance either to an altar or a pulpit, and surrounded by four blazing pines, their tops a flame, their stems untouched, like candles at an evening meeting. The mass of foliage, that had overgrown the summit of the rock, was all on fire, blazing high into the night, and fitfully illuminating the whole field. Each pendent twig and leafy festoon was in a blaze. As the red light arose and fell, a numerous congregation alternately shone forth, then disappeared in shadow, and again grew, as it were, out of the darkness, peopling the heart of the solitary woods at once.

"A grave and dark-clad company!" quoth goodman Brown.

In truth, they were such. Among them, quivering to-and-fro, between gloom and splendor, appeared faces that would be seen, next day, at the council-board of the province, and others which, Sabbath after Sabbath, looked devoutly heavenward, and benignantly over the crowded pews, from the holiest pulpits in the land. Some affirm, that the lady of the governor was there. At least, there were high dames well known to her, and wives of honored husbands, and widows, a great multitude, and ancient maidens, all of excellent repute, and fair young girls, who trembled, lest their mothers should espy them. Either the sudden gleams of light, flashing over the obscure field, bedazzled goodman Brown, or he recognized a score of the church-members of Salem village, famous for their especial sanctity. Good old deacon Gookin had arrived, and waited at the skirts of that venerable saint, his revered pastor. But, irreverently consorting with these grave, reputable, and pious people, these elders of the church, these chaste dames and dewy virgins, there were men of dissolute lives and women of spotted fame, wretches given over to all mean and filthy vice, and suspected even of horrid crimes. It was strange to see, that the good shrank not from the wicked, nor were the sinners abashed by the saints. Scattered, also, among their pale-faced enemies, were the Indian priests, or pow-ows, who had often scared their native forest with more hideous incantations than any known to English witchcraft.

"But, where is Faith?" thought goodman Brown; and, as hope came into his heart, he trembled.

Another verse of the hymn arose, a slow and solemn strain, such as the pious love, but joined to words which expressed all that our nature can conceive of sin, and darkly hinted at far more. Unfathomable to mere mortals is the lore of fiends. Verse after verse was sung, and still the chorus of the desert swelled between, like the deepest tone of a mighty organ. And, with the final peal of that dreadful anthem, there came a sound, as if the roaring wind, the rushing streams, the howling beasts, and every other voice of the unconverted wilderness, were mingling and according with the voice of guilty man, in homage to the prince of all. The four blazing pines threw up a loftier flame, and obscurely discovered shapes and visages of horror on the smoke-wreaths, above the impious assembly. At the same moment, the fire on the rock shot redly forth, and formed a glowing arch above its base, where now appeared a figure. With reverence be it spoken, the apparition bore no slight similitude, both in garb and manner, to some grave divine of the New-England churches.

"Bring forth the converts!" cried a voice, that echoed through the field and rolled into the forest.

At the word, goodman Brown stept forth from the shadow of the trees, and approached the congregation, with whom he felt a loathful brotherhood, by the sympathy of all that was wicked in his heart. He could have well nigh sworn, that the shape of his own dead father beckoned him to advance, looking downward from a smoke-wreath, while a woman, with dim features of despair, threw out her hand to warn him back. Was it his mother? But he had no power to retreat one step, nor to resist, even in thought, when the minister and good old deacon Gookin, seized his arms, and led him to the blazing rock. Thither came also the slender form of a veiled female, led between Goody Cloyse, that pious teacher of the catechism, and Martha Carrier,[14] who had received the devil's prom-ise to be queen of hell. A rampant hag was she! And there stood the proselytes, beneath the canopy of fire.

"Welcome, my children," said the dark figure, "to the communion of your race! Ye have found, thus young, your nature and your destiny. My children, look behind you!"

They turned; and flashing forth, as it were, in a sheet of flame, the fiend-worshippers were seen; the smile of welcome gleamed darkly on every visage.

"There," resumed the sable form, "are all whom ye have reverenced from youth. Ye deemed them holier than yourselves, and shrank from your own sin, contrasting it with their lives of righteousness, and prayerful aspirations heavenward. Yet, here are they all, in my worshipping assembly! This night it shall be granted you to know their secret deeds; how hoary-bearded elders of the church have whispered wanton words to

---

14. **Martha Carrier:** At the Salem witch trials, Martha Carrier was tried and convicted of being a witch. She was condemned to death and hanged on August 19, 1692.

the young maids of their households; how many a woman, eager for widow's weeds, has given her husband a drink at bed-time, and let him sleep his last sleep in her bosom; how beardless youths have made haste to inherit their fathers' wealth; and how fair damsels – blush not, sweet ones! – have dug little graves in the garden, and bidden me, the sole guest, to an infant's funeral. By the sympathy of your human hearts for sin, ye shall scent out all the places – whether in church, bed-chamber, street, field, or forest – where crime has been committed, and shall exult to behold the whole earth one stain of guilt, one mighty blood-spot. Far more than this! It shall be yours to penetrate, in every bosom, the deep mystery of sin, the fountain of all wicked arts, and which, inexhaustibly supplies more evil impulses than human power – than my power, at its utmost! – can make manifest in deeds. And now, my children, look upon each other."

They did so; and, by the blaze of the hell-kindled torches, the wretched man beheld his Faith, and the wife her husband, trembling before that unhallowed altar.

"Lo! there ye stand, my children," said the figure, in a deep and solemn tone, almost sad, with its despairing awfulness, as if his once angelic nature could yet mourn for our miserable race. "Depending upon one another's hearts, ye had still hoped, that virtue were not all a dream. Now are ye undeceived! Evil is the nature of mankind. Evil must be your only happiness. Welcome, again, my children, to the communion of your race!"

"Welcome!" repeated the fiend-worshippers, in one cry of despair and triumph.

And there they stood, the only pair, as it seemed, who were yet hesitating on the verge of wickedness, in this dark world. A basin was hollowed, naturally, in the rock. Did it contain water, reddened by the lurid light? or was it blood? or, perchance, a liquid flame? Herein did the Shape of Evil dip his hand, and prepare to lay the mark of baptism upon their foreheads, that they might be partakers of the mystery of sin, more conscious of the secret guilt of others, both in deed and thought, than they could now be of their own. The husband cast one look at his pale wife, and Faith at him. What polluted wretches would the next glance shew them to each other, shuddering alike at what they disclosed and what they saw!

"Faith! Faith!" cried the husband. "Look up to Heaven, and resist the Wicked One!"

Whether Faith obeyed, he knew not. Hardly had he spoken, when he found himself amid calm night and solitude, listening to a roar of wind, which died heavily away through the forest. He staggered against the rock and felt it chill and damp, while a hanging twig, that had been all on fire, besprinkled his cheek with the coldest dew.

The next morning, young goodman Brown came slowly into the street of Salem village, staring around him like a bewildered man. The good old minister was taking a walk along the graveyard, to get an appetite for breakfast and meditate his sermon, and bestowed a blessing, as he passed, on goodman Brown. He shrank from the venerable saint, as if to avoid an anathema. Old deacon Gookin was at domestic worship, and the holy words of his prayer were heard through the open window. "What God doth the wizard pray to?" quoth goodman Brown. Goody Cloyse, that excellent old Christian, stood in the early sunshine, at her own lattice, catechising a little girl, who had brought her a pint of morning's milk. Goodman Brown snatched away the child, as from the grasp of the fiend himself. Turning the corner by the meeting-house, he spied the head of Faith, with the pink ribbons, gazing anxiously forth, and bursting into such joy at sight of him, that she skipt along the street, and almost kissed her husband before the whole village. But, goodman Brown looked sternly and sadly into her face, and passed on without a greeting.

Had goodman Brown fallen asleep in the forest, and only dreamed a wild dream of a witch-meeting?

Be it so, if you will. But, alas! it was a dream of evil omen for young goodman Brown. A stern, a sad, a darkly meditative, a distrustful, if not a desperate man, did he become, from the night of that fearful dream. On the Sabbath-day, when the congregation were singing a holy psalm, he could not listen, because an anthem of sin rushed loudly upon his ear, and drowned all the blessed strain. When the minister spoke from the pulpit, with power and fervid eloquence, and, with his hand on the open bible, of the sacred truths of our religion, and of saint-like lives and triumphant deaths, and of future bliss or misery unutterable, then did goodman Brown turn pale, dreading, lest the roof should thunder down upon the gray blasphemer and his hearers. Often, awaking suddenly at midnight, he shrank from the bosom of Faith, and at morning or eventide, when the family knelt down at prayer, he scowled, and muttered to himself, and gazed sternly at his wife, and turned away. And when he had lived long, and was borne to his grave, a hoary corpse, followed by Faith, an aged woman, and children and grand-children, a goodly procession, besides neighbors, not a few, they carved no hopeful verse upon his tomb-stone; for his dying hour was gloom.

[1835]

Reading Hawthorne's "Rappaccini's Daughter."   This unusual story was first published in the *United States Magazine and Democratic Review*, usually called the *Democratic Review*, a progressive political and literary journal edited by Hawthorne's friend John L. O'Sullivan. Committed to the development of a distinctly American literature, O'Sullivan published more stories by Hawthorne than by any other writer. Although "Rappaccini's Daughter" is set in medieval Italy, it reveals a marked shift in Hawthorne's interests during the early 1840s: from the past and its relation to the present — the primary concern of many of his early stories about New England — to contemporary social issues. Among the developments that he observed most closely was the emergence of such pseudosciences as mesmerism, phrenology, and spiritualism, viewed by many of their proponents as means of reforming or perfecting the individual and society. For the skeptical Hawthorne, however, such efforts at human engineering raised troubling questions about the exercise of power over others and the consequent threats to personal autonomy and the integrity of the self. Rappaccini was one of a number of "mad scientists" who appeared in Hawthorne's stories, characters who demonstrate the dark side of science and technology. Readers of "Rappaccini's Daughter," much of which takes place in an enclosed garden, have also called attention to Hawthorne's complex and seemingly conflicting views of women, nature, and human nature. The text of the story is taken from its first printing in the *Democratic Review*, December 1844.

RAPPACCINI'S DAUGHTER

Writings of Aubépine[1]

We do not remember to have seen any translated specimens of the productions of M. de l'Aubépine; a fact the less to be wondered at, as his very name is unknown to many of his own countrymen, as well as to the student of foreign literature. As a writer, he seems to occupy an unfortunate position between the Transcendentalists[2] (who, under one name or another, have their share in all the current literature of the world), and the great body of pen-and-ink men who address the intellect and sympathies of the multitude. If not too refined, at all events too remote, too shadowy and unsubstantial in his modes of development, to suit the taste of the latter class, and yet too popular to satisfy the spiritual or metaphysical requisitions of the former, he must necessarily find himself without an audience; except here and there an individual, or possibly an isolated clique. His writings, to do them justice, are not altogether destitute of fancy and originality; they might have won him greater reputation but for an inveterate love of allegory, which is apt to invest his plots and characters with the aspect of scenery and people in the clouds, and to steal away the human warmth out of his conceptions. His fictions are sometimes historical, sometimes of the present day, and sometimes, so far as can be discovered, have little or no reference either to time or space. In any case, he generally contents himself with a very slight embroidery of outward manners, – the faintest possible counterfeit of real life, – and endeavors to create an interest by some less obvious peculiarity of the subject. Occasionally, a breath of nature, a rain-drop of pathos and tenderness, or a gleam of humor, will find its way into the midst of his fantastic imagery, and make us feel as if, after all, we were yet within the limits of our native earth. We will only add to this very cursory notice, that M. de l'Aubépine's productions, if the reader chance to take them in precisely the proper point of view, may amuse a leisure hour as well as those of a brighter man; if otherwise, they can hardly fail to look excessively like nonsense.

Our author is voluminous; he continues to write and publish with as much praiseworthy and indefatigable prolixity, as if his efforts were crowned with the brilliant success that so justly attends those of Eugene Sue.[3] His first appearance was by a collection of stories, in a long series of volumes, entitled "*Contes deux fois racontées.*"[4] The titles of some of his more recent works (we quote from memory) are as follows: – "*Le Voyage*

---

1. **Writings of Aubépine:** This story was originally published with this preface, a thinly veiled, satirical account of Hawthorne's literary career. *Aubépine*, the French word for the bush known in English as the hawthorn, is the way in which Hawthorne signed a number of early love letters to his wife, Sophia Peabody Hawthorne.

2. **Transcendentalists:** Writers such as Ralph Waldo Emerson, Margaret Fuller, and Henry David Thoreau, with whom Hawthorne became personally acquainted while living in Concord, Massachusetts, during the period 1842–1846.

3. **Eugene Sue:** French author (1803–1857) whose works included the popular novel *The Wandering Jew* (1844).

4. **"*Contes deux fois racontées*":** *Twice-Told Tales* (French), the name of Hawthorne's first collection of short stories, published in 1837.

Céleste à Chemin de Fer," 3 tom. 1838. *"Le nouveau père Adam et la nouvelle mère Eve,"* 2 tom. 1839. *"Roderic; ou le Serpent à l'estomac,"* 2 tom. 1840. *"Le Culte du Feu,"* a folio volume of ponderous research into the religion and ritual of the old Persian Ghebers, published in 1841. *"La Soirée du Chateau en Espagne,"* 1 tom. 8vo. 1842; and *"L'Artiste du Beau; ou le Papillon Mécanique,"* 5 tom. 4vo. 1843.[5] Our somewhat wearisome perusal of this startling catalogue of volumes has left behind it a certain personal affection and sympathy, though by no means admiration, for M. de l'Aubépine; and we would fain do the little in our power towards introducing him favorably to the American public. The ensuing tale is a translation of his *"Beatrice; ou La Belle Empoisonneuse,"* recently published in *"La Revue Anti-Aristocratique."*[6] This journal, edited by the Comte de Bearhaven,[7] has, for some years past, led the defence of liberal principles and popular rights, with a faithfulness and ability worthy of all praise.

Rappaccini's Daughter

A young man, named Giovanni Guasconti, came, very long ago, from the more southern region of Italy, to pursue his studies at the University of Padua. Giovanni, who had but a scanty supply of gold ducats[8] in his pocket, took lodgings in a high and gloomy chamber of an old edifice, which looked not unworthy to have been the palace of a Paduan noble, and which, in fact, exhibited over its entrance the armorial bearings of a family long since extinct. The young stranger, who was not unstudied in the great poem of his country, recollected that one of the ancestors of this family, and perhaps an occupant of this very mansion, had been pictured by Dante as a partaker of the immortal agonies of his Inferno.[9] These reminiscences and associations, together with the tendency to heart-break natural to a young man for the first time out of his native sphere, caused Giovanni to sigh heavily, as he looked around the desolate and ill-furnished apartment.

---

5. **The titles . . . 1843:** With self-deprecating humor, Hawthorne provides bibliographic citations in French for several of his own writings, suggesting that they are much longer works by using the French abbreviation for volume, *tom*, as well as abbreviations for the size of volumes, "8 vo." and "4 vo.," standing for octavio and quarto. With the exception of "The Evening in a Castle in Spain," the only one that is not the title of a work by Hawthorne, all of the publications cited are sketches or short stories he had earlier published in magazines: "The Celestial Railroad," "The New Adam and Eve," "Egotism; or The Bosom-Serpent," "Fire-Worship," and "The Artist of the Beautiful."

6. **"Beatrice . . . Anti-Aristocratique":** Here Hawthorne provides an alternative version of the story's title as "Beatrice; or the Poisonous Beauty." *La Revue Anti-Aristocratique*, or *The Anti-Aristocratic Magazine*, is Hawthorne's ironic French title for the *Democratic Review*, the magazine in which he originally published "Rappaccini's Daughter."

7. **Comte de Bearhaven:** The editor of the *Democratic Review* was Hawthorne's close friend John L. O'Sullivan (1813-1895). "Bearhaven" is an affectionate reference to O'Sullivan's Irish ancestry and the aristocratic title claimed by his family from Berehaven, now more commonly known as Castletownbere, a town in County Cork, Ireland.

8. **gold ducats:** Coins formerly used in European countries.

9. **Dante . . . Inferno:** The Italian poet Dante Alighieri (1265-1321), author of *The Divine Comedy* (c. 1309-20), an epic poem in three books describing his allegorical journey through *Inferno* (hell), *Purgatorio* (purgatory), and *Paradiso* (paradise).

"Holy Virgin, signor," cried old dame Lisabetta, who, won by the youth's remarkable beauty of person, was kindly endeavoring to give the chamber a habitable air, "what a sigh was that to come out of a young man's heart! Do you find this old mansion gloomy? For the love of heaven, then, put your head out of the window, and you will see as bright sunshine as you have left in Naples."

Guasconti mechanically did as the old woman advised, but could not quite agree with her that the Lombard sunshine was as cheerful as that of southern Italy. Such as it was, however, it fell upon a garden beneath the window, and expended its fostering influences on a variety of plants, which seemed to have been cultivated with exceeding care.

"Does this garden belong to the house?" asked Giovanni.

"Heaven forbid, signor! – unless it were fruitful of better pot-herbs than any that grow there now," answered old Lisabetta. "No: that garden is cultivated by the own hands of Signor Giacomo Rappaccini, the famous Doctor, who, I warrant him, has been heard of as far as Naples. It is said he distils these plants into medicines that are as potent as a charm. Oftentimes you may see the signor Doctor at work, and perchance the signora his daughter, too, gathering the strange flowers that grow in the garden."

The old woman had now done what she could for the aspect of the chamber, and, commending the young man to the protection of the saints, took her departure.

Giovanni still found no better occupation than to look down into the garden beneath his window. From its appearance, he judged it to be one of those botanic gardens, which were of earlier date in Padua than elsewhere in Italy, or in the world. Or, not improbably, it might once have been the pleasure-place of an opulent family; for there was the ruin of a marble fountain in the centre, sculptured with rare art, but so wofully shattered that it was impossible to trace the original design from the chaos of remaining fragments. The water, however, continued to gush and sparkle into the sunbeams as cheerfully as ever. A little gurgling sound ascended to the young man's window, and made him feel as if the fountain were an immortal spirit, that sung its song unceasingly, and without heeding the vicissitudes around it; while one century embodied it in marble, and another scattered the garniture on the soil. All about the pool into which the water subsided, grew various plants, that seemed to require a plentiful supply of moisture for the nourishment of gigantic leaves, and, in some instances, flowers gorgeously magnificent. There was one shrub in particular, set in a marble vase in the midst of the pool, that bore a profusion of purple blossoms, each of which had the lustre and richness of a gem; and the whole together made a show so resplendent that it seemed enough to illuminate the garden, even had there been no sunshine. Every portion of the soil was peopled with plants and herbs, which, if less beautiful, still bore tokens of assiduous care; as if all had their individual virtues, known to the scientific mind that fostered them. Some were placed in urns, rich with old carving, and others in common garden-pots; some crept serpent-like along the ground, or climbed on high, using whatever means of ascent was offered them. One plant had wreathed itself round a statue of Vertumnus,[10] which was thus quite veiled

---

10. **Vertumnus:** The Roman god of the seasons, gardens, and fruit trees.

and shrouded in a drapery of hanging foliage, so happily arranged that it might have served a sculptor for a study.

While Giovanni stood at the window, he heard a rustling behind a screen of leaves, and became aware that a person was at work in the garden. His figure soon emerged into view, and showed itself to be that of no common laborer, but a tall, emaciated, sallow, and sickly-looking man, dressed in a scholar's garb of black. He was beyond the middle term of life, with grey hair, a thin grey beard, and a face singularly marked with intellect and cultivation, but which could never, even in his more youthful days, have expressed much warmth of heart.

Nothing could exceed the intentness with which this scientific gardener examined every shrub which grew in his path; it seemed as if he was looking into their inmost nature, making observations in regard to their creative essence, and discovering why one leaf grew in this shape, and another in that, and wherefore such and such flowers differed among themselves in hue and perfume. Nevertheless, in spite of the deep intelligence on his part, there was no approach to intimacy between himself and these vegetable existences. On the contrary, he avoided their actual touch, or the direct inhaling of their odors, with a caution that impressed Giovanni most disagreeably; for the man's demeanor was that of one walking among malignant influences, such as savage beasts, or deadly snakes, or evil spirits, which, should he allow them one moment of license, would wreak upon him some terrible fatality. It was strangely frightful to the young man's imagination, to see this air of insecurity in a person cultivating a garden, that most simple and innocent of human toils, and which had been alike the joy and labor of the unfallen parents of the race. Was this garden, then, the Eden of the present world? — and this man, with such a perception of harm in what his own hands caused to grow, was he the Adam?

The distrustful gardener, while plucking away the dead leaves or pruning the too luxuriant growth of the shrubs, defended his hands with a pair of thick gloves. Nor were these his only armor. When, in his walk through the garden, he came to the magnificent plant that hung its purple gems beside the marble fountain, he placed a kind of mask over his mouth and nostrils, as if all this beauty did but conceal a deadlier malice. But finding his task still too dangerous, he drew back, removed the mask, and called loudly, but in the infirm voice of a person affected with inward disease:

"Beatrice! — Beatrice!"[11]

"Here am I, my father! What would you?" cried a rich and youthful voice from the window of the opposite house; a voice as rich as a tropical sunset, and which made Giovanni, though he knew not why, think of deep hues of purple or crimson, and of perfumes heavily delectable. — "Are you in the garden?"

"Yes, Beatrice," answered the gardener, "and I need your help."

Soon there emerged from under a sculptured portal the figure of a young girl, arrayed with as much richness of taste as the most splendid of the flowers, beautiful as the day,

---

11. **Beatrice:** Hawthorne may have named his central character for the woman Dante loved, Beatrice Portinari (1266–1290), the inspiration for the idealized Beatrice who guides Dante through paradise in *The Divine Comedy* (see note 9). The name *Beatrice* means happy or the bringer of joy (Latin).

and with a bloom so deep and vivid that one shade more would have been too much. She looked redundant with life, health, and energy; all of which attributes were bound down and compressed, as it were, and girdled tensely, in their luxuriance, by her virgin zone.[12] Yet Giovanni's fancy must have grown morbid, while he looked down into the garden; for the impression which the fair stranger made upon him was as if here were another flower, the human sister of those vegetable ones, as beautiful as they — more beautiful than the richest of them — but still to be touched only with a glove, nor to be approached without a mask. As Beatrice came down the garden-path, it was observable that she handled and inhaled the odor of several of the plants, which her father had most sedulously avoided.

"Here, Beatrice," said the latter, — "see how many needful offices require to be done to our chief treasure. Yet, shattered as I am, my life might pay the penalty of approaching it so closely as circumstances demand. Henceforth, I fear, this plant must be consigned to your sole charge."

"And gladly will I undertake it," cried again the rich tones of the young lady, as she bent towards the magnificent plant, and opened her arms as if to embrace it. "Yes, my sister, my splendor, it shall be Beatrice's task to nurse and serve thee; and thou shalt reward her with thy kisses and perfumed breath, which to her is as the breath of life!"

Then, with all the tenderness in her manner that was so strikingly expressed in her words, she busied herself with such attentions as the plant seemed to require; and Giovanni, at his lofty window, rubbed his eyes, and almost doubted whether it were a girl tending her favorite flower, or one sister performing the duties of affection to another. The scene soon terminated. Whether Doctor Rappaccini had finished his labors in the garden, or that his watchful eye had caught the stranger's face, he now took his daughter's arm and retired. Night was already closing in; oppressive exhalations seemed to proceed from the plants, and steal upward past the open window; and Giovanni, closing the lattice, went to his couch, and dreamed of a rich flower and beautiful girl. Flower and maiden were different and yet the same, and fraught with some strange peril in either shape.

But there is an influence in the light of morning that tends to rectify whatever errors of fancy, or even of judgment, we may have incurred during the sun's decline, or among the shadows of the night, or in the less wholesome glow of moonshine. Giovanni's first movement on starting from sleep, was to throw open the window, and gaze down into the garden which his dreams had made so fertile of mysteries. He was surprised, and a little ashamed, to find how real and matter-of-fact an affair it proved to be, in the first rays of the sun, which gilded the dew-drops that hung upon leaf and blossom, and, while giving a brighter beauty to each rare flower, brought everything within the limits of ordinary experience. The young man rejoiced, that, in the heart of the barren city, he had the privilege of overlooking this spot of lovely and luxuriant vegetation. It would serve, he said to himself, as a symbolic language, to keep him in communion with nature. Neither the sickly and thoughtworn Doctor Giacomo Rappaccini, it is true, nor his brilliant daughter were now visible; so that Giovanni could not determine how much

12. girdled . . . virgin zone: That is, encircled around her waist, as with a cord or wide belt.

of the singularity which he attributed to both, was due to their own qualities, and how much to his wonder-working fancy. But he was inclined to take a most rational view of the whole matter.

In the course of the day, he paid his respects to Signor Pietro Baglioni, professor of medicine in the University, a physician of eminent repute, to whom Giovanni had brought a letter of introduction. The professor was an elderly personage, apparently of genial nature, and habits that might almost be called jovial; he kept the young man to dinner, and made himself very agreeable by the freedom and liveliness of his conversation, especially when warmed by a flask or two of Tuscan wine. Giovanni, conceiving that men of science, inhabitants of the same city, must needs be on familiar terms with one another, took an opportunity to mention the name of Dr. Rappaccini. But the professor did not respond with so much cordiality as he had anticipated.

"Ill would it become a teacher of the divine art of medicine," said Professor Pietro Baglioni, in answer to a question of Giovanni, "to withhold due and well-considered praise of a physician so eminently skilled as Rappaccini. But, on the other hand, I should answer it but scantily to my conscience, were I to permit a worthy youth like yourself, Signor Giovanni, the son of an ancient friend, to imbibe erroneous ideas respecting a man who might hereafter chance to hold your life and death in his hands. The truth is, our worshipful Doctor Rappaccini has as much science as any member of the faculty — with perhaps one single exception — in Padua, or all Italy. But there are certain grave objections to his professional character."

"And what are they?" asked the young man.

"Has my friend Giovanni any disease of body or heart, that he is so inquisitive about physicians?" said the Professor, with a smile. "But as for Rappaccini, it is said of him — and I, who know the man well, can answer for its truth — that he cares infinitely more for science than for mankind. His patients are interesting to him only as subjects for some new experiment. He would sacrifice human life, his own among the rest, or whatever else was dearest to him, for the sake of adding so much as a grain of mustard-seed to the great heap of his accumulated knowledge."

"Methinks he is an awful man,[13] indeed," remarked Guasconti, mentally recalling the cold and purely intellectual aspect of Rappaccini. "And yet, worshipful Professor, is it not a noble spirit? Are there many men capable of so spiritual a love of science?"

"God forbid," answered the Professor, somewhat testily — "at least, unless they take sounder views of the healing art than those adopted by Rappaccini. It is his theory, that all medicinal virtues are comprised within those substances which we term vegetable poisons. These he cultivates with his own hands, and is said even to have produced new varieties of poison, more horribly deleterious than Nature, without the assistance of this learned person, would ever have plagued the world with. That the signor Doctor does less mischief than might be expected, with such dangerous substances, is undeniable. Now and then, it must be owned, he has effected — or seemed to effect — a marvellous cure. But, to tell you my private mind, Signor Giovanni, he should receive little

---

13. **awful man:** One inspiring wonder or fear.

credit for such instances of success – they being probably the work of chance – but should be held strictly accountable for his failures, which may justly be considered his own work."

The youth might have taken Baglioni's opinions with many grains of allowance, had he known that there was a professional warfare of long continuance between him and Doctor Rappaccini, in which the latter was generally thought to have gained the advantage. If the reader be inclined to judge for himself, we refer him to certain black-letter tracts on both sides,[14] preserved in the medical department of the University of Padua.

"I know not, most learned Professor," returned Giovanni, after musing on what had been said of Rappaccini's exclusive zeal for science – "I know not how dearly this physician may love his art; but surely there is one object more dear to him. He has a daughter."

"Aha!" cries the Professor with a laugh. "So now our friend Giovanni's secret is out. You have heard of this daughter, whom all the young men in Padua are wild about, though not half a dozen have ever had the good hap to see her face. I know little of the Signora Beatrice, save that Rappaccini is said to have instructed her deeply in his science, and that, young and beautiful as fame reports her, she is already qualified to fill a professor's chair. Perchance her father destines her for mine! Other absurd rumors there be, not worth talking about, or listening to. So now, Signor Giovanni, drink off your glass of Lacryma."[15]

Guasconti returned to his lodgings somewhat heated with the wine he had quaffed, and which caused his brain to swim with strange fantasies in reference to Doctor Rappaccini and the beautiful Beatrice. On his way, happening to pass by a florist's, he bought a fresh bouquet of flowers.

Ascending to his chamber, he seated himself near the window, but within the shadow thrown by the depth of the wall, so that he could look down into the garden with little risk of being discovered. All beneath his eye was a solitude. The strange plants were basking in the sunshine, and now and then nodding gently to one another, as if in acknowledgment of sympathy and kindred. In the midst, by the shattered fountain, grew the magnificent shrub, with its purple gems clustering all over it; they glowed in the air, and gleamed back again out of the depths of the pool, which thus seemed to overflow with colored radiance from the rich reflection that was steeped in it. At first, as we have said, the garden was a solitude. Soon, however, – as Giovanni had half-hoped, half-feared, would be the case, – a figure appeared beneath the antique sculptured portal, and came down between the rows of plants, inhaling their various perfumes, as if she were one of those beings of old classic fable, that lived upon sweet odors. On again beholding Beatrice, the young man was even startled to perceive how much her beauty exceeded his recollection of it; so brilliant, so vivid in its character,

---

14. **black-letter tracts on both sides:** Formal papers printed in ornate, black type, designed to be kept as records.

15. **Lacryma:** Lacryma Christi, literally the "tear of Christ" (Italian), a wine made from grapes planted on the slopes of Mount Vesuvius in Italy.

that she glowed amid the sunlight, and, as Giovanni whispered to himself, positively illuminated the more shadowy intervals of the garden path. Her face being now more revealed than on the former occasion, he was struck by its expression of simplicity and sweetness; qualities that had not entered into his idea of her character, and which made him ask anew, what manner of mortal she might be. Nor did he fail again to observe, or imagine, an analogy between the beautiful girl and the gorgeous shrub that hung its gem-like flowers over the fountain; a resemblance which Beatrice seemed to have indulged a fantastic humor in heightening, both by the arrangement of her dress and the selection of its hues.

Approaching the shrub, she threw open her arms, as with a passionate ardor, and drew its branches into an intimate embrace; so intimate, that her features were hidden in its leafy bosom, and her glistening ringlets all intermingled with the flowers.

"Give me thy breath, my sister," exclaimed Beatrice; "for I am faint with common air! And give me this flower of thine, which I separate with gentlest fingers from the stem, and place it close beside my heart."

With these words, the beautiful daughter of Rappaccini plucked one of the richest blossoms of the shrub, and was about to fasten it in her bosom. But now, unless Giovanni's draughts of wine had bewildered his senses, a singular incident occurred. A small orange-colored reptile of the lizard or chameleon species, chanced to be creeping along the path, just at the feet of Beatrice. It appeared to Giovanni – but, at the distance from which he gazed, he could scarcely have seen anything so minute – it appeared to him, however, that a drop or two of moisture from the broken stem of the flower descended upon the lizard's head. For an instant, the reptile contorted itself violently, and then lay motionless in the sunshine. Beatrice observed this remarkable phenomenon, and crossed herself, sadly, but without surprise; nor did she therefore hesitate to arrange the fatal flower in her bosom. There it blushed, and almost glimmered with the dazzling effect of a precious stone, adding to her dress and aspect the one appropriate charm, which nothing else in the world could have supplied. But Giovanni, out of the shadow of his window bent forward and shrank back, and murmured and trembled.

"Am I awake? Have I my senses?" said he to himself. "What is this being? – beautiful, shall I call her? – or inexpressibly terrible?"

Beatrice now strayed carelessly through the garden, approaching closer beneath Giovanni's window, so that he was compelled to thrust his head quite out of its concealment in order to gratify the intense and painful curiosity which she excited. At this moment, there came a beautiful insect over the garden wall; it had perhaps wandered through the city and found no flowers nor verdure among those antique haunts of men, until the heavy perfumes of Doctor Rappaccini's shrubs had lured it from afar. Without alighting on the flowers, this winged brightness seemed to be attracted by Beatrice, and lingered in the air and fluttered about her head. Now here it could not be but that Giovanni Guasconti's eyes deceived him. Be that as it might, he fancied that while Beatrice was gazing at the insect with childish delight, it grew faint and fell at her feet! – its bright wings shivered! it was dead! – from no cause that he could discern, unless it were the atmosphere of her breath. Again Beatrice crossed herself and sighed heavily, as she bent over the dead insect.

An impulsive movement of Giovanni drew her eyes to the window. There she beheld the beautiful head of the young man — rather a Grecian than an Italian head, with fair, regular features, and a glistening of gold among his ringlets — gazing down upon her like a being that hovered in mid-air. Scarcely knowing what he did, Giovanni threw down the bouquet which he had hitherto held in his hand.

"Singnora," said he, "there are pure and healthful flowers. Wear them for the sake of Giovanni Guasconti!"

"Thanks, Signor," replied Beatrice, with her rich voice, that came forth as it were like a gush of music; and with a mirthful expression half childish and half woman-like. "I accept your gift, and would fain recompense it with this precious purple flower; but if I toss it into the air, it will not reach you. So Signor Guasconti must even content himself with my thanks."

She lifted the bouquet from the ground, and then as if inwardly ashamed at having stepped aside from her maidenly reserve to respond to a stranger's greeting, passed swiftly homeward through the garden. But, few as the moments were, it seemed to Giovanni when she was on the point of vanishing beneath the sculptured portal, that his beautiful bouquet was already beginning to wither in her grasp. It was an idle thought; there could be no possibility of distinguishing a faded flower from a fresh one at so great a distance.

For many days after the incident, the young man avoided the window that looked into Doctor Rappaccini's garden, as if something ugly and monstrous would have blasted his eye-sight, had he been betrayed into a glance. He felt conscious of having put himself, to a certain extent, within the influence of an unintelligible power, by the communication which he had opened with Beatrice. The wisest course would have been, if his heart were in any real danger, to quit his lodgings and Padua itself, at once; the next wiser, to have accustomed himself, as far as possible, to the familiar and day-light view of Beatrice; thus bringing her rigidly and systematically within the limits of ordinary experience. Least of all, while avoiding her sight, should Giovanni have remained so near this extraordinary being, that the proximity and possibility even of intercourse, should give a kind of substance and reality to the wild vagaries which his imagination ran riot continually in producing. Guasconti had not a deep heart — or at all events, its depths were not sounded now — but he had a quick fancy, and an ardent southern temperament, which rose every instant to a higher fever-pitch. Whether or no Beatrice possessed those terrible attributes — that fatal breath — the affinity with those so beautiful and deadly flowers — which were indicated by what Giovanni had witnessed, she had at least instilled a fierce and subtle poison into his system. It was not love, although her rich beauty was a madness to him; nor horror, even while he fancied her spirit to be imbued with the same baneful essence that seemed to pervade her physical frame; but a wild offspring of both love and horror that had each parent in it, and burned like one and shivered like the other. Giovanni knew not what to dread; still less did he know what to hope; *hope* and *dread* kept a continual warfare in his breast, alternately vanquishing one another and starting up afresh to renew the contest. Blessed are all simple emotions, be they dark or bright! It is the lurid intermixture of the two that produces the illuminating blaze of the infernal regions.

Sometimes he endeavored to assuage the fever of his spirit by a rapid walk through the streets of Padua, or beyond its gates; his footsteps kept time with the throbbings of his brain, so that the walk was apt to accelerate itself to a race. One day, he found himself arrested; his arm was seized by a portly personage who had turned back on recognizing the young man, and expended much breath in overtaking him.

"Signor Giovanni! – stay, my young friend!" cried he. "Have you forgotten me? That might well be the case, if I were as much altered as yourself."

It was Baglioni, whom Giovanni had avoided, ever since their first meeting, from a doubt that the professor's sagacity would look too deeply into his secrets. Endeavoring to recover himself, he stared forth wildly from his inner world into the outer one, and spoke like a man in a dream:

"Yes; I am Giovanni Guasconti. You are Professor Pietro Baglioni. Now let me pass!"

"Not yet – not yet, Signor Giovanni Guasconti," said the Professor, smiling, but at the same time scrutinizing the youth with an earnest glance. – "What; did I grow up side by side with your father, and shall his son pass me like a stranger, in these old streets of Padua? Stand still, Signor Giovanni; for we must have a word or two, before we part."

"Speedily, then, most worshipful Professor, speedily!" said Giovanni, with feverish impatience. "Does not your worship see that I am in haste?"

Now, while he was speaking, there came a man in black along the street, stooping and moving feebly, like a person in inferior health. His face was all overspread with a most sickly and sallow hue, but yet so pervaded with an expression of piercing and active intellect, that an observer might easily have overlooked the merely physical attributes, and have seen only this wonderful energy. As he passed, this person exchanged a cold and distant salutation with Baglioni, but fixed his eyes upon Giovanni with an intentness that seemed to bring out whatever was within him worthy of notice. Nevertheless, there was a peculiar quietness in the look, as if taking merely a speculative, not a human interest, in the young man.

"It is Doctor Rappaccini!" whispered the Professor, when the stranger had passed. – "Has he ever seen your face before?"

"Not that I know," answered Giovanni, starting at the name.

"He *has* seen you! – he must have seen you!" said Baglioni, hastily. "For some purpose or other, this man of science is making a study of you. I know that look of his! It is the same that coldly illuminates his face, as he bends over a bird, a mouse, or a butterfly, which, in pursuance of some experiment, he has killed by the perfume of a flower; – a look as deep as nature itself, but without nature's warmth of love. Signor Giovanni, I will stake my life upon it, you are the subject of one of Rappaccini's experiments!"

"Will you make a fool of me?" cried Giovanni, passionately. "*That*, Signor Professor, were an untoward experiment."

"Patience, patience!" replied the imperturbable Professor. – "I tell thee, my poor Giovanni, that Rappaccini has a scientific interest in thee. Thou hast fallen into fearful hands! And the Signora Beatrice? What part does she act in this mystery?"

But Guasconti, finding Baglioni's pertinacity intolerable, here broke away, and was gone before the Professor could again seize his arm. He looked after the young man intently, and shook his head.

"This must not be," said Baglioni to himself. "The youth is the son of my old friend, and should not come to any harm from which the arcana of medical science can preserve him. Besides, it is too insufferable an impertinence in Rappaccini, thus to snatch the bud out of my own hands, as I may say, and make use of him for his infernal experiments. This daughter of his! It shall be looked to. Perchance, most learned Rappaccini, I may foil you where you little dream of it!"

Meanwhile, Giovanni had pursued a circuitous route, and at length found himself at the door of his lodgings. As he crossed the threshold, he was met by old Lisabetta, who smirked and smiled, and was evidently desirous to attract his attention; vainly, however, as the ebullition of his feelings had momentarily subsided into a cold and dull vacuity. He turned his eyes full upon the withered face that was puckering itself into a smile, but seemed to behold it not. The old dame, therefore, laid her grasp upon his cloak.

"Signor! – Signor!" whispered she, still with a smile over the whole breadth of her visage, so that it looked not unlike a grotesque carving in wood, darkened by centuries – "Listen, Signor! There is a private entrance into the garden!"

"What do you say?" exclaimed Giovanni, turning quickly about, as if an inanimate thing should start into feverish life. – "A private entrance into Doctor Rappaccini's garden!"

"Hush! hush! – not so loud!" whispered Lisabetta, putting her hand over his mouth. "Yes; into the worshipful Doctor's garden, where you may see all his fine shrubbery. Many a young man in Padua would give gold to be admitted among those flowers."

Giovanni put a piece of gold into her hand.

"Show me the way," said he.

A surmise, probably excited by his conversation with Baglioni, crossed his mind, that this interposition of old Lisabetta might perchance be connected with the intrigue, whatever were its nature, in which the Professor seemed to suppose that Doctor Rappaccini was involving him. But such a suspicion, though it disturbed Giovanni, was inadequate to restrain him. The instant he was aware of the possibility of approaching Beatrice, it seemed an absolute necessity of his existence to do so. It mattered not whether she were angel or demon; he was irrevocably within her sphere, and must obey the law that whirled him onward, in ever lessening circles, towards a result which he did not attempt to foreshadow. And yet, strange to say, there came across him a sudden doubt, whether this intense interest on his part were not delusory – whether it were really of so deep and positive a nature as to justify him in now thrusting himself into an incalculable position – whether it were not merely the fantasy of a young man's brain, only slightly, or not at all, connected with his heart!

He paused – hesitated – turned half about – but again went on. His withered guide led him along several obscure passages, and finally undid a door, through which, as it was opened, there came the sight and sound of rustling leaves, with the broken sunshine glimmering among them. Giovanni stepped forth, and forcing himself through the entanglement of a shrub that wreathed its tendrils over the hidden entrance, he stood beneath his own window, in the open area of Doctor Rappaccini's garden.

How often is it the case, that, when impossibilities have come to pass, and dreams have condensed their misty substance into tangible realities, we find ourselves calm, and even coldly self-possessed, amid circumstances which it would have been a delirium of joy or agony to anticipate! Fate delights to thwart us thus. Passion will choose his own time to rush upon the scene, and lingers sluggishly behind, when an appropriate adjustment of events would seem to summon his appearance. So was it now with Giovanni. Day after day, his pulses had throbbed with feverish blood, at the improbable idea of an interview with Beatrice, and of standing with her, face to face, in this very garden, basking in the oriental sunshine of her beauty, and snatching from her full gaze the mystery which he deemed the riddle of his own existence. But now there was a singular and untimely equanimity within his breast. He threw a glance around the garden to discover if Beatrice or her father were present, and perceiving that he was alone, began a critical observation of the plants.

The aspect of one and all of them dissatisfied him; their gorgeousness seemed fierce, passionate, and even unnatural. There was hardly an individual shrub which a wanderer, straying by himself through a forest, would not have been startled to find growing wild, as if an unearthly face had glared at him out of the thicket. Several, also, would have shocked a delicate instinct by an appearance of artificialness, indicating that there had been such commixture, and, as it were, adultery of various vegetable species, that the production was no longer of God's making, but the monstrous offspring of man's depraved fancy, glowing with only an evil mockery of beauty. They were probably the result of experiment, which, in one or two cases, had succeeded in mingling plants individually lovely into a compound possessing the questionable and ominous character that distinguished the whole growth of the garden. In fine, Giovanni recognized but two or three plants in the collection, and those of a kind that he well knew to be poisonous. While busy with these contemplations, he heard the rustling of a silken garment, and turning, beheld Beatrice emerging from beneath the sculptured portal.

Giovanni had not considered with himself what should be his deportment; whether he should apologize for his intrusion into the garden, or assume that he was there with the privity, at least, if not the desire of Doctor Rappaccini or his daughter. But Beatrice's manner placed him at his ease, though leaving him still in doubt by what agency he had gained admittance. She came lightly along the path, and met him near the broken fountain. There was surprise in her face, but brightened by a simple and kind expression of pleasure.

"You are a connoisseur in flowers, Signor," said Beatrice with a smile, alluding to the bouquet which he had flung her from the window. "It is no marvel, therefore, if the sight of my father's rare collection has tempted you to take a nearer view. If he were here, he could tell you many strange and interesting facts as to the nature and habits of these shrubs, for he has spent a life-time in such studies, and this garden is his world."

"And yourself, lady" — observed Giovanni — "if fame says true — you, likewise, are deeply skilled in the virtues indicated by these rich blossoms, and these spicy perfumes. Would you deign to be my instructress, I should prove an apter scholar than under Signor Rappaccini himself."

"Are there such idle rumors?" asked Beatrice, with the music of a pleasant laugh. "Do people say that I am skilled in my father's science of plants? What a jest is there! No; though I have grown up among these flowers, I know no more of them than their hues and perfume; and sometimes, methinks I would fain rid myself of even that small knowledge. There are many flowers here, and those not the least brilliant, that shock and offend me, when they meet my eye. But, pray, Signor, do not believe these stories about my science. Believe nothing of me save what you see with your own eyes."

"And must I believe all that I have seen with my own eyes?" asked Giovanni pointedly, while the recollection of former scenes made him shrink. "No, Signora, you demand too little of me. Bid me believe nothing, save what comes from your own lips."

It would appear that Beatrice understood him. There came a deep flush to her cheek; but she looked full into Giovanni's eyes, and responded to his gaze of uneasy suspicion with a queenlike haughtiness.

"I do so bid you, Signor!" she replied. "Forget whatever you may have fancied in regard to me. If true to the outward senses, still it may be false in its essence. But the words of Beatrice Rappaccini's lips are true from the heart outward. Those you may believe!"

A fervor glowed in her whole aspect, and beamed upon Giovanni's consciousness like the light of truth itself. But while she spoke, there was a fragrance in the atmosphere around her, rich and delightful, though evanescent, yet which the young man, from an indefinable reluctance, scarcely dared to draw into his lungs. It might be the odor of the flowers. Could it be Beatrice's breath, which thus embalmed her words with a strange richness, as if by steeping them in her heart? A faintness passed like a shadow over Giovanni, and flitted away; he seemed to gaze through the beautiful girl's eyes into her transparent soul, and felt no more doubt or fear.

The tinge of passion that had colored Beatrice's manner vanished; she became gay, and appeared to derive a pure delight from her communion with the youth, not unlike what the maiden of a lonely island might have felt, conversing with a voyager from the civilized world. Evidently her experience of life had been confined within the limits of that garden. She talked now about matters as simple as the day-light or summer-clouds, and now asked questions in reference to the city, or Giovanni's distant home, his friends, his mother, and his sisters; questions indicating such seclusion, and such lack of familiarity with modes and forms, that Giovanni responded as if to an infant. Her spirit gushed out before him like a fresh rill, that was just catching its first glimpse of the sunlight, and wondering at the reflections of earth and sky which were flung into its bosom. There came thoughts, too, from a deep source, and fantasies of a gem-like brilliancy, as if diamonds and rubies sparkled upward among the bubbles of the fountain. Ever and anon, there gleamed across the young man's mind a sense of wonder, that he should be walking side by side with the being who had so wrought upon his imagination – whom he had idealized in such hues of terror – in whom he had positively witnessed such manifestations of dreadful attributes – that he should be conversing with Beatrice like a brother, and should find her so human and so maiden-like. But such reflections were only momentary; the effect of her character was too real, not to make itself familiar at once.

In this free intercourse, they had strayed through the garden, and now, after many turns among its avenues, were come to the shattered fountain, beside which grew the magnificent shrub with its treasury of glowing blossoms. A fragrance was diffused from it, which Giovanni recognized as identical with that which he had attributed to Beatrice's breath, but incomparably more powerful. As her eyes fell upon it, Giovanni beheld her press her hand to her bosom, as if her heart were throbbing suddenly and painfully.

"For the first time in my life," murmured she, addressing the shrub, "I had forgotten thee!"

"I remember, Signora," said Giovanni, "that you once promised to reward me with one of these living gems for the bouquet, which I had the happy boldness to fling to your feet. Permit me now to pluck it as a memorial of this interview."

He made a step towards the shrub, with extended hand. But Beatrice darted forward, uttering a shriek that went through his heart like a dagger. She caught his hand, and drew it back with the whole force of her slender figure. Giovanni felt her touch thrilling through his fibres.

"Touch it not!" exclaimed she, in a voice of agony. "Not for thy life! It is fatal!"

Then, hiding her face, she fled from him, and vanished beneath the sculptured portal. As Giovanni followed her with his eyes, he beheld the emaciated figure and pale intelligence of Doctor Rappaccini, who had been watching the scene, he knew not how long, within the shadow of the entrance.

No sooner was Guasconti alone in his chamber, than the image of Beatrice came back to his passionate musings, invested with all the witchery that had been gathering around it ever since his first glimpse of her, and now likewise imbued with a tender warmth of girlish womanhood. She was human: her nature was endowed with all gentle and feminine qualities; she was worthiest to be worshipped; she was capable, surely, on her part, of the height and heroism of love. Those tokens, which he had hitherto considered as proofs of a frightful peculiarity in her physical and moral system, were now either forgotten, or, by the subtle sophistry of passion, transmuted into a golden crown of enchantment, rendering Beatrice the more admirable, by so much as she was the more unique. Whatever had looked ugly, was now beautiful; or, if incapable of such a change, it stole away and hid itself among those shapeless half-ideas, which throng the dim region beyond the daylight of our perfect consciousness. Thus did Giovanni spend the night, nor fell asleep, until the dawn had begun to awake the slumbering flowers in Doctor Rappaccini's garden, whither his dreams doubtless led him. Up rose the sun in his due season, and flinging his beams upon the young man's eyelids, awoke him to a sense of pain. When thoroughly aroused, he became sensible of a burning and tingling agony in his hand – in his right hand – the very hand which Beatrice had grasped in her own, when he was on the point of plucking one of the gem-like flowers. On the back of that hand there was now a purple print, like that of four small fingers, and the likeness of a slender thumb upon his wrist.

Oh, how stubbornly does love – or even that cunning semblance of love which flourishes in the imagination, but strikes no depth of root into the heart – how stubbornly does it hold its faith, until the moment come, when it is doomed to vanish into thin mist! Giovanni wrapt a handkerchief about his head, and wondered what evil thing had stung him, and soon forgot his pain in a reverie of Beatrice.

After the first interview, a second was in the inevitable course of what we call fate. A third; a fourth; and a meeting with Beatrice in the garden was no longer an incident in Giovanni's daily life, but the whole space in which he might be said to live; for the anticipation and memory of that ecstatic hour made up the remainder. Nor was it otherwise with the daughter of Rappaccini. She watched for the youth's appearance, and flew to his side with confidence as unreserved as if they had been playmates from early infancy – as if they were such playmates still. If, by any unwonted chance, he failed to come at the appointed moment, she stood beneath the window, and sent up the rich sweetness of her tones to float around him in his chamber, and echo and reverberate throughout his heart – "Giovanni! Giovanni! Why tarriest thou? Come down!" – And down he hastened into that Eden of poisonous flowers.

But, with all this intimate familiarity, there was still a reserve in Beatrice's demeanor, so rigidly and invariably sustained, that the idea of infringing it scarcely occurred to his imagination. By all appreciable signs, they loved; they had looked love, with eyes that conveyed the holy secret from the depths of one soul into the depths of the other, as if it were too sacred to be whispered by the way; they had even spoken love, in those gushes of passion when their spirits darted forth in articulated breath, like tongues of long-hidden flame; and yet there had been no seal of lips, no clasp of hands, nor any slightest caress, such as love claims and hallows. He had never touched one of the gleaming ringlets of her hair; her garment – so marked was the physical barrier between them – had never been waved against him by a breeze. On the few occasions when Giovanni had seemed tempted to overstep the limit, Beatrice grew so sad, so stern, and withal wore such a look of desolate separation, shuddering at itself, that not a spoken word was requisite to repel him. At such times, he was startled at the horrible suspicions that rose, monster-like, out of the caverns of his heart, and stared him in the face; his love grew thin and faint as the morning-mist; his doubts alone had substance. But when Beatrice's face brightened again, after the momentary shadow, she was transformed at once from the mysterious, questionable being, whom he had watched with so much awe and horror; she was now the beautiful and unsophisticated girl, whom he felt that his spirit knew with a certainty beyond all other knowledge.

A considerable time had now passed since Giovanni's last meeting with Baglioni. One morning, however, he was disagreeably surprised by a visit from the Professor, whom he had scarcely thought of for whole weeks, and would willingly have forgotten still longer. Given up, as he had long been, to a pervading excitement, he could tolerate no companions, except upon condition of their perfect sympathy with his present state of feeling. Such sympathy was not to be expected from Professor Baglioni.

The visitor chatted carelessly, for a few moments, about the gossip of the city and the University, and then took up another topic.

"I have been reading an old classic author lately," said he, "and met with a story that strangely interested me. Possibly you may remember it. It is of an Indian prince, who sent a beautiful woman as a present to Alexander the Great.[16] She was as lovely as the dawn, and gorgeous as the sunset; but what especially distinguished her was a certain rich perfume in her breath — richer than a garden of Persian roses. Alexander, as was natural to a youthful conqueror, fell in love at first sight with this magnificent stranger. But a certain age physician, happening to be present, discovered a terrible secret in regard to her."

"And what was that?" asked Giovanni, turning his eyes downward to avoid those of the Professor.

"That this lovely woman," continued Baglioni, with emphasis, "had been nourished with poisons from her birth upward, until her whole nature was so imbued with them, that she herself had become the deadliest poison in existence. Poison was her element of life. With that rich perfume of her breath, she blasted the very air. Her love would have been poison! — her embrace death! Is not this a marvellous tale?"

"A childish fable," answered Giovanni, nervously starting from his chair. "I marvel how your worship finds time to read such nonsense, among your graver studies."

"By the by," said the Professor, looking uneasily about him, "what singular fragrance is this in your apartment? Is it the perfume of your gloves? It is faint, but delicious, and yet, after all, by no means agreeable. Were I to breathe it long, methinks it would make me ill. It is like the breath of a flower — but I see no flowers in the chamber."

"Nor are there any," replied Giovanni, who had turned pale as the Professor spoke; "nor, I think, is there any fragrance, except in your worship's imagination. Odors, being a sort of element combined of the sensual and the spiritual, are apt to deceive us in this manner. The recollection of a perfume — the bare idea of it — may easily be mistaken for a present reality."

"Aye; but my sober imagination does not often play such tricks," said Baglioni; "and were I to fancy any kind of odor, it would be that of some vile apothecary drug, wherewith my fingers are likely enough to be imbued. Our worshipful friend Rappaccini, as I have heard, tinctures his medicaments with odors richer than those of Araby. Doubtless, likewise, the fair and learned Signora Beatrice would minister to her patients with draughts as sweet as a maiden's breath. But wo to him that sips them!"

Giovanni's face evinced many contending emotions. The tone in which the Professor alluded to the pure and lovely daughter of Rappaccini was a torture to his soul; and yet, the intimation of a view of her character, opposite to his own, gave instantaneous distinctness to a thousand dim suspicions, which now grinned at him like so many demons. But he strove hard to quell them, and to respond to Baglioni with a true lover's perfect faith.

"Signor Professor," said he, "you were my father's friend — perchance, too, it is your purpose to act a friendly part towards his son. I would fain feel nothing towards you, save respect and deference. But I pray you to observe, Signor, that there is one subject on which we must not speak. You know not the Signora Beatrice. You cannot, therefore, estimate the wrong — the blasphemy, I may even say — that is offered to her character by a light or injurious word."

---

16. **Alexander the Great:** King of Macedonia (356–323 BCE), a famous military leader who conquered the Persian Empire. The story is told in book VII of *Vulgar Errors* (1646) by the English author Sir Thomas Browne (1605–1682).

"Giovanni! – my poor Giovanni!" answered the Professor, with a calm expression of pity, "I know this wretched girl far better than yourself. You shall hear the truth in respect to the poisoner Rappaccini, and his poisonous daughter. Yes; poisonous as she is beautiful! Listen; for even should you do violence to my grey hairs, it shall not silence me. That old fable of the Indian woman has become a truth, by the deep and deadly science of Rappaccini, and in the person of the lovely Beatrice!"

Giovanni groaned and hid his face.

"Her father," continued Baglioni, "was not restrained by natural affection from offering up his child, in this horrible manner, as the victim of his insane zeal for science. For – let us do him justice – he is as true a man of science as ever distilled his own heart in an alembic.[17] What, then, will be your fate? Beyond a doubt, you are selected as the material of some new experiment. Perhaps the result is to be death – perhaps a fate more awful still! Rappaccini, with what he calls the interest of science before his eyes, will hesitate at nothing."

"It is a dream!" muttered Giovanni to himself, "surely it is a dream!"

"But," resumed the professor, "be of good cheer, son of my friend! It is not yet too late for the rescue. Possibly, we may even succeed in bringing back this miserable child within the limits of ordinary nature, from which her father's madness has estranged her. Behold this little silver vase! It was wrought by the hands of the renowned Benvenuto Cellini,[18] and is well worthy to be a love-gift to the fairest dame in Italy. But its contents are invaluable. One little sip of this antidote would have rendered the most virulent poisons of the Borgias[19] innocuous. Doubt not that it will be as efficacious against those of Rappaccini. Bestow the vase, and the precious liquid within it, on your Beatrice, and hopefully await the result."

Baglioni laid a small, exquisitely wrought silver phial on the table, and withdrew, leaving what he had said to produce its effect upon the young man's mind.

"We will thwart Rappaccini yet!" thought he, chuckling to himself, as he descended the stairs. "But, let us confess the truth of him, he is a wonderful man! – a wonderful man indeed! A vile empiric,[20] however, in his practice, and therefore not to be tolerated by those who respect the good old rules of the medical profession!"

Throughout Giovanni's whole acquaintance with Beatrice, he had occasionally, as we have said, been haunted by dark surmises as to her character. Yet, so thoroughly had she made herself felt by him as a simple, natural, most affectionate and guileless creature, that the image now held up by Professor Baglioni, looked as strange and incredible, as if it were not in accordance with his own original conception. True, there were ugly recollections connected with his first glimpses of the beautiful girl; he could not quite forget the bouquet that withered in her grasp, and the insect that

---

17. **alembic:** An early apparatus for distilling liquids.
18. **Benvenuto Cellini:** Famous Italian artist and goldsmith (1500-1571).
19. **poisons of the Borgias:** The Borgias were a powerful and ruthless Italian Renaissance family that included the infamous Lucrezia Borgia (1480-1519), who was subject to widespread rumors of sexual corruption, poisoning, and murder.
20. **empiric:** An early term for a scientist who relies solely on observation and experiment, rather than theory.

perished amid the sunny air, by no ostensible agency, save the fragrance of her breath. These incidents, however, dissolving in the pure light of her character, had no longer the efficacy of facts, but were acknowledged as mistaken fantasies, by whatever testimony of the senses they might appear to be substantiated. There is something truer and more real, than what we can see with the eyes, and touch with the finger. On such better evidence, had Giovanni founded his confidence in Beatrice, though rather by the necessary force of her high attributes, than by any deep and generous faith, on his part. But, now, his spirit was incapable of sustaining itself at the height to which the early enthusiasm of passion had exalted it; he fell down, grovelling among earthly doubts, and defiled therewith the pure whiteness of Beatrice's image. Not that he gave her up; he did but distrust. He resolved to institute some decisive test that should satisfy him, once for all, whether there were those dreadful peculiarities in her physical nature, which could not be supposed to exist without some corresponding monstrosity of soul. His eyes, gazing down afar, might have deceived him as to the lizard, the insect, and the flowers. But if he could witness, at the distance of a few paces, the sudden blight of one fresh and healthful flower in Beatrice's hand, there would be room for no further question. With this idea, he hastened to the florist's, and purchased a bouquet that was still gemmed with the morning dew-drops.

It was now the customary hour of his daily interview with Beatrice. Before descending into the garden, Giovanni failed not to look at his figure in the mirror; a vanity to be expected in a beautiful young man, yet, as displaying itself at that troubled and feverish moment, the token of a certain shallowness of feeling and insincerity of character. He did gaze, however, and said to himself, that his features had never before possessed so rich a grace, nor his eyes such vivacity, nor his cheeks so warm a hue of superabundant life.

"At least," thought he, "her poison has not yet insinuated itself into my system. I am no flower to perish in her grasp!"

With that thought, he turned his eyes on the bouquet, which he had never once laid aside from his hand. A thrill of indefinable horror shot through his frame, on perceiving that those dewy flowers were already beginning to droop; they wore the aspect of things that had been fresh and lovely, yesterday. Giovanni grew white as marble, and stood motionless before the mirror, staring at his own reflection there, as at the likeness of something frightful. He remembered Baglioni's remark about the fragrance that seemed to pervade the chamber. It must have been the poison in his breath! Then he shuddered — shuddered at himself! Recovering from his stupor, he began to watch, with curious eye, a spider that was busily at work, hanging its web from the antique cornice of the apartment, crossing and re-crossing the artful system of interwoven lines, as vigorous and active a spider as ever dangled from an old ceiling. Giovanni bent towards the insect, and emitted a deep, long breath. The spider suddenly ceased its toil; the web vibrated with a tremor originating in the body of the small artizan. Again Giovanni sent forth a breath, deeper, longer, and imbued with a venomous feeling out of his heart; he knew not whether he were wicked or only desperate. The spider made a convulsive gripe with his limbs, and hung dead across the window.

"Accursed! Accursed!" muttered Giovanni, addressing himself. "Hast thou grown so poisonous, that this deadly insect perishes by thy breath?"

At that moment, a rich, sweet voice came floating up from the garden: —

"Giovanni! Giovanni! It is past the hour! Why tarriest thou! Come down!"

"Yes," muttered Giovanni again. "She is the only being whom my breath may not slay! Would that it might!"

He rushed down, and in an instant, was standing before the bright and loving eyes of Beatrice. A moment ago, his wrath and despair had been so fierce that he could have desired nothing so much as to wither her by a glance. But, with her actual presence, there came influences which had too real an existence to be at once shaken off; recollections of the delicate and benign power of her feminine nature, which had so often enveloped him in a religious calm; recollections of many a holy and passionate outgush of her heart, when the pure fountain had been unsealed from its depths, and made visible in its transparency to his mental eye; recollections which, had Giovanni known how to estimate them, would have assured him that all this ugly mystery was but an earthly illusion, and that, whatever mist of evil might seem to have gathered over her, the real Beatrice was a heavenly angel. Incapable as he was of such high faith, still her presence had not utterly lost its magic. Giovanni's rage was quelled into an aspect of sullen insensibility. Beatrice, with a quick spiritual sense, immediately felt that there was a gulf of blackness between them, which neither he nor she could pass. They walked on together, sad and silent, and came thus to the marble fountain, and to its pool of water on the ground, in the midst of which grew the shrub that bore gem-like blossoms. Giovanni was affrighted at the eager enjoyment — the appetite, as it were — with which he found himself inhaling the fragrance of the flowers.

"Beatrice," asked he abruptly, "whence came this shrub?"

"My father created it," answered she, with simplicity.

"Created it! created it!" repeated Giovanni. "What mean you, Beatrice?"

"He is a man fearfully acquainted with the secrets of nature," replied Beatrice; "and, at the hour when I first drew breath, this plant sprang from the soil, the offspring of his science, of his intellect, while I was but his earthly child. Approach it not!" continued she, observing with terror that Giovanni was drawing nearer to the shrub. "It has qualities that you little dream of. But I, dearest Giovanni, — I grew up and blossomed with the plant, and was nourished with its breath. It was my sister, and I loved it with a human affection: for — alas! hast thou not suspected it? there was an awful doom."

Here Giovanni frowned so darkly upon her that Beatrice paused and trembled. But her faith in his tenderness re-assured her, and made her blush that she had doubted for an instant.

"There was an awful doom," she continued, — "the effect of my father's fatal love of science — which estranged me from all society of any kind. Until Heaven sent thee, dearest Giovanni, Oh! how lonely was thy poor Beatrice!"

"Was it a hard doom?" asked Giovanni, fixing his eyes upon her.

"Only of late have I known how hard it was," answered she tenderly." Oh, yes; but my heart was torpid, and therefore quiet."

Giovanni's rage broke forth from his sullen gloom like a lightning-flash out of a dark cloud.

"Accursed one!" cried he, with venomous scorn and anger. "And finding thy solitude wearisome, thou hast severed me, likewise, from all the warmth of life, and enticed me into thy region of unspeakable horror!"

"Giovanni!" exclaimed Beatrice, turning her large bright eyes upon his face. The force of his words had not found its way into her mind; she was merely wonder-struck.

"Yes, poisonous thing!" repeated Giovanni, beside himself with passion. "Thou hast done it! Thou hast blasted me! Thou hast filled my veins with poison! Thou hast made me as hateful, as ugly, as loathsome and deadly a creature as thyself, — a world's wonder of hideous monstrosity! Now — if our breath be happily as fatal to ourselves as to all others — let us join our lips in one kiss of unutterable hatred, and so die!"

"What has befallen me?" murmured Beatrice, with a low moan out of her heart, "Holy Virgin pity me, a poor heart-broken child!"

"Thou! Dost thou pray?" cried Giovanni, still with the same fiendish scorn. "Thy very prayers, as they come from thy lips, taint the atmosphere with death. Yes, yes; let us pray! Let us to church, and dip our fingers in the holy water at the portal! They that come after us will perish as by a pestilence. Let us sign crosses in the air! It will be scattering curses abroad in the likeness of holy symbols!"

"Giovanni," said Beatrice calmly, for her grief was beyond passion, "why dost thou join thyself with me thus in those terrible words? I, it is true, am the horrible thing thou namest me. But thou! — what hast thou to do, save with one other shudder at my hideous misery, to go forth out of the garden and mingle with thy race, and forget that there ever crawled on earth such a monster as poor Beatrice?"

"Dost thou pretend ignorance?" asked Giovanni, scowling upon her, "Behold! This power have I gained from the pure daughter of Rappaccini!"

There was a swarm of summer-insects flitting through the air, in search of the food promised by the flower-odors of the fatal garden. They circled round Giovanni's head, and were evidently attracted towards him by the same influence which had drawn them, for an instant, within the sphere of several of the shrubs. He sent forth a breath among them, and smiled bitterly at Beatrice, as at least a score of the insects fell dead upon the ground.

"I see it! I see it!" shrieked Beatrice. "It is my father's fatal science? No, no, Giovanni; it was not I! Never, never! I dreamed only to love thee, and be with thee a little time, and so to let thee pass away, leaving but thine image in mine heart. For, Giovanni — believe it — though my body be nourished with poison, my spirit is God's creature, and craves love as its daily food. But my father! — he has united us in this fearful sympathy. Yes; spurn me! — tread upon me! — kill me! Oh, what is death, after such words as thine? But it was not I! Not for a world of bliss would I have done it!"

Giovanni's passion had exhausted itself in its outburst from his lips. There now came across him a sense, mournful, and not without tenderness, of the intimate and peculiar relationship between Beatrice and himself. They stood, as it were, in an utter solitude, which would be made none the less solitary by the densest throng of human life. Ought not, then, the desert of humanity around them to press this insulated pair close together? If they should be cruel to one another, who was there to be kind to them? Besides, thought Giovanni, might there not still be a hope of his returning within the limits of ordinary nature, and leading Beatrice – the redeemed Beatrice – by the hand? Oh, weak, and selfish, and unworthy spirit, that could dream of an earthly union and earthly happiness as possible, after such deep love had been so bitterly wronged as was Beatrice's love by Giovanni's blighting words! No, no; there could be no such hope. She must pass heavily, with that broken heart, across the borders – she must bathe her hurts in some fount of Paradise, and forget her grief in the light of immortality – and *there* be well!

But Giovanni did not know it.

"Dear Beatrice," said he, approaching her, while she shrank away, as always at his approach, but now with a different impulse – "dearest Beatrice, our fate is not yet so desperate. Behold! There is a medicine, potent, as a wise physician has assured me, and almost divine in its efficacy. It is composed of ingredients the most opposite to those by which thy awful father has brought this calamity upon thee and me. It is distilled of blessed herbs. Shall we not quaff it together, and thus be purified from evil?"

"Give it me!" said Beatrice, extending her hand to receive the little silver phial which Giovanni took from his bosom. She added, with a peculiar emphasis; "I will drink – but do thou await the result."

She put Baglioni's antidote to her lips; and, at the same moment, the figure of Rappaccini emerged from the portal, and came slowly towards the marble fountain. As he drew near, the pale man of science seemed to gaze with a triumphant expression at the beautiful youth and maiden, as might an artist who should spend his life in achieving a picture or a group of statuary, and finally be satisfied with his success. He paused – his bent form grew erect with conscious power, he spread out his hand over them, in the attitude of a father imploring a blessing upon his children. But those were the same hands that had thrown poison into the stream of their lives! Giovanni trembled. Beatrice shuddered nervously, and pressed her hand upon her heart.

"My daughter," said Rappaccini, "thou art no longer lonely in the world! Pluck one of those precious gems from thy sister shrub, and bid thy bridegroom wear it in his bosom. It will not harm him now! My science, and the sympathy between thee and him, have so wrought within his system, that he now stands apart from common men, as thou dost, daughter of my pride and triumph, from ordinary women. Pass on, then, through the world, most dear to one another, and dreadful to all besides!"

"My father," said Beatrice, feebly – and still, as she spoke, she kept her hand upon her heart – "wherefore didst thou inflict this miserable doom upon thy child?"

"Miserable!" exclaimed Rappaccini, "What mean you, foolish girl? Dost thou deem it misery to be endowed with marvellous gifts, against which no power nor strength could avail an enemy? Misery, to be able to quell the mightiest with a breath? Misery, to be as terrible as thou art beautiful? Wouldst thou, then, have preferred the condition of a weak woman, exposed to all evil, and capable of none?"

"I would fain have been loved, not feared," murmured Beatrice, sinking down upon the ground. – "But now it matters not; I am going, father, where the evil, which thou hast striven to mingle with my being, will pass away like a dream – like the fragrance of these poisonous flowers, which will no longer taint my breath among the flowers of

Eden. Farewell, Giovanni! Thy words of hatred are like lead within my heart — but they, too, will fall away as I ascend. Oh, was there not, from the first, more poison in thy nature than in mine?"

To Beatrice — so radically had her earthly part been wrought upon by Rappaccini's skill — as poison had been life, so the powerful antidote was death. And thus the poor victim of man's ingenuity and of thwarted nature, and of the fatality that attends all such efforts of perverted wisdom, perished there, at the feet of her father and Giovanni. Just at that moment, Professor Pietro Baglioni looked forth from the window, and called loudly, in a tone of triumph mixed with horror, to the thunder-stricken man of science:

"Rappaccini! Rappaccini! And is *this* the upshot of your experiment?"

[1844]

Edgar Allan Poe

[1809-1849]

Edgar Allan Poe was born on January 19, 1809, in Boston, Massachusetts, the second of three children of David and Elizabeth Arnold Poe, actors in a theatrical company. Shortly after the birth of their third child, the alcoholic David Poe abandoned the family and disappeared. Elizabeth Poe, a well-known leading lady, supported the family until her own death in December 1811 in Richmond, Virginia. The penniless children were sent to live with different foster parents. Although Poe was not legally adopted by John Allan, a prosperous merchant, and his wife Frances, they raised him as their son. In 1815, the Allans went to live in England, and Poe was sent to school in London. Five years later, the family returned to Richmond, where Poe continued his education until he entered the University of Virginia in February 1826.

Edgar Allan Poe

This daguerreotype of Poe was made less than a year before his early death on October 7, 1849.

The following years were marked by growing conflicts between John Allan and Poe, over both his behavior and his choice of career. During his first year at the University of Virginia, Poe was a good student, especially in Latin and French. Believing that the allowance he received from Allan was not adequate, however, he soon began to gamble and lost $2,000. An angry Allan refused to honor the debt or to send Poe back to the university for the spring semester of 1827. Bitter, humiliated, and increasingly estranged from his foster father, Poe left home shortly after his eighteenth birthday. By then, he had already written a good deal of poetry, and Poe immediately arranged for the publication of his book *Tamerlane and Other Poems* (1827), which he later revised and expanded as *Al Aaraaf, Tamerlane, and Minor Poems* (1829). But he had no prospect of earning a living as a poet, so in 1827 he enlisted in the army as "Edgar A. Perry." Poe enjoyed some advancement in the military, reaching the rank of sergeant major. He was also partially reconciled with John Allan, who refused to support Poe's literary aspirations but who helped him obtain an appointment to the United States Military Academy at West Point in 1830. Although he had no real interest in a military career, Poe hoped that success there would prompt Allan to make him his heir. But Poe's sympathetic foster mother was now dead, and Allan was out of patience with his foster son. After he dashed Poe's hopes for an inheritance once more, Poe deliberately disobeyed rules, received a court-martial, and was expelled from West Point in 1831.

The break with his foster father was now irreparable, and Poe determined to make his way as a professional writer. His friends at West Point helped him pay for the publication of a third book, *Poems: Second Edition* (1831). He then moved to Baltimore, where he lived in poverty with his aunt, Maria Clemm, and her daughter Virginia, whom Poe secretly married in 1835, when she was thirteen, and publicly remarried in 1836. Meanwhile, he had become a regular contributor to the Philadelphia *Saturday Courier*, where Poe's first story was published anonymously in 1832. Three years later, he moved back to Richmond, where he became the assistant editor of a new journal, the *Southern Literary Messenger*, to which he contributed reviews and stories. Before he was fired early in 1837, the journal also ran the first two installments of his novel *The Narrative of Arthur Gordon Pym*, which was published as a book in 1838. By then, Poe had moved with his wife and aunt, first to New York City and then to Philadelphia, where he continued to eke out a precarious living by writing criticism and stories for periodicals like the *American Museum of Literature and the Arts* and, as its coeditor, for *Burton's Gentleman's Magazine*. In 1839, a two-volume collection of his early stories was published as *Tales of the Grotesque and Arabesque*. Although it sold poorly, Poe was becoming a significant literary figure, known for both his stories and his reviews of poetry and fiction. After a brief stint as editor of *Graham's Magazine*, a distinguished literary monthly, Poe in 1844 moved his family back to New York City. There, he earned a living by writing journalism and doing editorial work. But he achieved his greatest literary success with the publication early in 1845 of "The Raven," a poem that caused a sensation in the United States and Europe.

The astonishing success of that poem made Poe a literary celebrity. Within a few months of its appearance, two collections of his writings were published: *Tales*, a collection of eighteen stories, and *The Raven and Other Poems*. Poe embarked on a lecture tour, offering a series of talks on "Poets and Poetry of America." He also became the editor and then owner of the *Broadway Journal*. But his reviews, often quite negative and even vindictive, alienated many members of the literary establishment, including Nathaniel Hawthorne and Henry Wadsworth Longfellow, whom Poe accused of plagiarism in an extended series of combative articles in the *Broadway Journal*. After the journal failed in 1846, Poe's financial difficulties were compounded by personal problems, especially the serious illness of his wife, Virginia, who died in 1847. Poe himself was often ill and

His greatness is that he turned his back and faced inland, to originality, with the identical gesture of a [Daniel] Boone.
—William Carlos Williams

depressed, and he drank frequently. Nonetheless, he wrote constantly, publishing criticism, poetry, and stories, as well as a book-length prose poem, *Eureka* (1848). He also continued to lecture, partly in an ongoing effort to gain backing for a new journal he had long planned to call the *Stylus*. Returning in the fall of 1849 from a visit to Richmond, where he lectured and was received with acclaim, Poe stopped off in Baltimore. What happened to him there remains a mystery. Within a week, he was found lying in the street, barely conscious and extremely disoriented. Poe died a few days later, on October 7, 1849.

Reading Poe's "The Fall of the House of Usher."   Perhaps the most familiar of Poe's celebrated tales of psychological terror, "The Fall of the House of Usher" first appeared in *Burton's Gentleman's Magazine and American Monthly Review*. Founded by William Evans Burton (1804-1860) and published under several titles between July 1837 and November 1840, the magazine was designed specifically for "gentlemen" readers, and its tone and subject matter were distinctly male. Outdoor recreations for men, such as archery and hunting, were frequent topics, as were articles on travel and brief biographies of important men in American history. Poe became the coeditor of the magazine in July 1839. Under his direction, the magazine became more diverse and published poetry and tales of a much higher quality, including several of Poe's own stories. Unhappy with the direction that the magazine was taking, however, Burton reassumed full editorship in June 1840. "The Fall of the House of Usher" was included in both *Tales of the Grotesque and Arabesque* (1839) and *Tales* (1845). The text is taken from its first printing in *Burton's Gentleman's Magazine*, September 1839.

bedfordstmartins.com/ americanlit for research links on Poe

THE FALL OF THE HOUSE OF USHER

During the whole of a dull, dark, and soundless day in the autumn of the year, when the clouds hung oppressively low in the heavens, I had been passing alone, on horseback, through a singularly dreary tract of country; and at length found myself, as the shades of the evening drew on, within view of the melancholy House of Usher. I know not how it was — but, with the first glimpse of the building, a sense of insufferable gloom pervaded my spirit. I say insufferable; for the feeling was unrelieved by any of that half-pleasurable, because poetic, sentiment, with which the mind usually receives even the sternest natural images of the desolate or terrible. I looked upon the scene before me — upon the mere house, and the simple landscape features of the domain — upon the bleak walls — upon the vacant eye-like windows — upon a few rank sedges — and upon a few white trunks of decayed trees — with an utter depression of soul which I can compare to no earthly sensation more properly than to the after-dream of the reveller upon opium – the bitter lapse into common life – the hideous dropping off of the veil. There was an iciness, a sinking, a sickening of the heart – an unredeemed dreariness of thought which no goading of the imagination could torture into aught of the sublime. What was it – I paused to think – what was it that so unnerved me in the contemplation of the House of Usher? It was a mystery all insoluble; nor could I grapple with the shadowy fancies that crowded upon me as I pondered. I was forced to fall back upon the unsatisfactory conclusion, that while, beyond doubt, there *are* combinations of very simple natural objects which have the power of thus affecting us, still the reason, and the analysis, of this power, lie among considerations beyond our depth. It was possible, I reflected, that a mere different arrangement of the particulars of the scene, of the details of the picture, would be sufficient to modify, or perhaps to annihilate its capacity for sorrowful impression; and, acting upon this idea, I reined my horse to the precipitous brink of a black and lurid tarn[1] that lay in unruffled lustre by the dwelling, and gazed down – but with a shudder even more thrilling than before – upon the remodelled and inverted images of the gray sedge, and the ghastly tree-stems, and the vacant and eye-like windows.

Nevertheless, in this mansion of gloom I now proposed to myself a sojourn of some weeks. Its proprietor, Roderick Usher, had been one of my boon companions in boyhood; but many years had elapsed since our last meeting. A letter, however, had lately reached me in a distant part of the country – a letter from him – which, in its wildly importunate nature, had admitted of no other than a personal reply. The MS.[2] gave evidence of nervous agitation. The writer spoke of acute bodily illness – of a pitiable mental idiosyncrasy which oppressed him – and of an earnest desire to see me, as his best, and indeed, his only personal friend, with a view of attempting, by the cheerfulness of my society, some alleviation of his malady. It was the manner in which all this, and much more, was said – it was the apparent *heart* that went with his request – which allowed me no room for hesitation – and I accordingly obeyed, what I still considered a very singular summons, forthwith.

Although, as boys, we had been even intimate associates, yet I really knew little of my friend. His reserve had been always excessive and habitual. I was aware, however, that his very ancient family had been noted, time out of mind, for a peculiar sensibility of temperament, displaying itself, through long ages, in many works of exalted art, and manifested, of late, in repeated deeds of munificent yet unobtrusive charity, as well as in a passionate devotion to the intricacies, perhaps even more than to the orthodox and easily recognizable beauties, of musical science. I had learned, too, the very remarkable fact, that the stem of the Usher race, all time-honored as it was, had put forth, at no period, any enduring branch; in other words, that the entire family lay in the direct line of descent, and had always, with very trifling and very temporary variation, so lain. It was this deficiency, I considered, while running over in thought the perfect keeping of the character of the premises with the accredited character of the people, and while speculating upon the possible influence which the one, in the long lapse of centuries,

---

1. **tarn:** Small mountain lake.
2. **MS.:** Standard editorial abbreviation for "manuscript."

might have exercised upon the other — it was this deficiency, perhaps, of collateral issue, and the consequent undeviating transmission, from sire to son, of the patrimony with the name, which had, at length, so identified the two as to merge the original title of the estate in the quaint and equivocal appellation of the "House of Usher" — an appellation which seemed to include, in the minds of the peasantry who used it, both the family and the family mansion.

I have said that the sole effect of my somewhat childish experiment, of looking down within the tarn, had been to deepen the first singular impression. There can be no doubt that the consciousness of the rapid increase of my superstition — for why should I not so term it? — served mainly to accelerate the increase itself. Such, I have long known, is the paradoxical law of all sentiments having terror as a basis. And it might have been for this reason only, that, when I again uplifted my eyes to the house itself, from its image in the pool, there grew in my mind a strange fancy — a fancy so ridiculous, indeed, that I but mention it to show the vivid force of the sensations which oppressed me. I had so worked upon my imagination as really to believe that around about the whole mansion and domain there hung an atmosphere peculiar to themselves and their immediate vicinity — an atmosphere which had no affinity with the air of heaven, but which had reeked up from the decayed trees, and the gray walls, and the silent tarn, in the form of an inelastic vapor or gas — dull, sluggish, faintly discernible, and leaden-hued. Shaking off from my spirit what *must* have been a dream, I scanned more narrowly the real aspect of the building. Its principal feature seemed to be that of an excessive antiquity. The discoloration of ages had been great. Minute fungi overspread the whole exterior, hanging in a fine tangled web-work from the eaves. Yet all this was apart from any extraordinary dilapidation. No portion of the masonry had fallen; and there appeared to be a wild inconsistency between its still perfect adaptation of parts, and the utterly porous, and evidently decayed condition of the individual stones. In this there was much that reminded me of the specious totality of old wood-work which has rotted for long years in some neglected vault, with no disturbance from the breath of the external air. Beyond this indication of extensive decay, however, the fabric gave little token of instability. Perhaps the eye of a scrutinizing observer might have discovered a barely perceptible fissure, which, extending from the roof of the building in front, made its way down the wall in a zig-zag direction, until it became lost in the sullen waters of the tarn.

Noticing these things, I rode over a short causeway to the house. A servant in waiting took my horse, and I entered the Gothic archway of the hall. A valet, of stealthy step, thence conducted me, in silence, through many dark and intricate passages in my progress to the studio of his master. Much that I encountered on the way contributed, I know not how, to heighten the vague sentiments of which I have already spoken. While the objects around me — while the carvings of the ceilings, the sombre tapestries of the walls, the ebon blackness of the floors, and the phantasmagoric armorial trophies which rattled as I strode, were but matters to which, or to such as which, I had been accustomed from my infancy — while I hesitated not to acknowledge how familiar was all this — I still wondered to find how unfamiliar were the fancies which ordinary images were stirring up. On one of the staircases, I met the physician of the family. His countenance, I thought, wore a mingled expression of low cunning and perplexity. He accosted me with trepidation and passed on. The valet now threw open a door and ushered me into the presence of his master.

The room in which I found myself was very large and excessively lofty. The windows were long, narrow, and pointed, and at so vast a distance from the black oaken floor as to be altogether inaccessible from within. Feeble gleams of encrimsoned light made their way through the trelliced panes, and served to render sufficiently distinct the more prominent objects around; the eye, however, struggled in vain to reach the remoter angles of the chamber, or the recesses of the vaulted and fretted ceiling. Dark draperies hung upon the walls. The general furniture was profuse, comfortless, antique, and tattered. Many books and musical instruments lay scattered about, but failed to give any vitality to the scene. I felt that I breathed an atmosphere of sorrow. An air of stern, deep, and irredeemable gloom hung over and pervaded all.

Upon my entrance, Usher arose from a sofa upon which he had been lying at full length, and greeted me with a vivacious warmth which had much in it, I at first thought of an overdone cordiality — of the constrained effort of the ennuyé[3] man of the world. A glance, however, at his countenance convinced me of his perfect sincerity. We sat down; and for some moments, while he spoke not, I gazed upon him with a feeling half of pity, half of awe. Surely, man had never before so terribly altered, in so brief a period, as had Roderick Usher! It was with difficulty that I could bring myself to admit the identity of the wan being before me with the companion of my early boyhood. Yet the character of his face had been at all times remarkable. A cadaverousness of complexion; an eye large, liquid, and luminous beyond comparison; lips somewhat thin and very pallid, but of a surpassingly beautiful curve; a nose of a delicate Hebrew model, but with a breadth of nostril unusual in similar formations; a finely moulded chin, speaking, in its want of prominence, of a want of moral energy; hair of a more than web-like softness and tenuity; these features, with an inordinate expansion above the regions of the temple, made up altogether a countenance not easily to be forgotten. And now in the mere exaggeration of the prevailing character of these features, and of the expression they were wont to convey, lay so much of change that I doubted to whom I spoke. The now ghastly pallor of the skin, and the now miraculous lustre of the eye, above all things startled and even awed me. The silken hair, too, had been suffered to grow all unheeded, and as, in its wild gossamer texture, it floated rather than fell about the face, I could not, even with effort, connect its arabesque expression with any idea of simple humanity.

In the manner of my friend I was at once struck with an incoherence — an inconsistency; and I soon found this to arise from a series of feeble and futile struggles to overcome an habitual trepidancy, an excessive nervous agitation. For something of this nature I had indeed been prepared, no less by his letter, than by reminiscences of certain boyish traits and by conclusions deduced from his peculiar physical conformation and temperament. His action was alternately vivacious and sullen. His voice varied rapidly from a tremulous indecision (when the animal spirits seemed utterly in abeyance) to that species of energetic concision — that abrupt, weighty, unhurried, and hollow-sounding enunciation — that leaden, self-balanced and perfectly modulated guttural utterance, which may

---

3. **ennuyé:** Bored (French).

be observed in the moments of the intensest excitement of the lost drunkard, or the irreclaimable eater of opium.

It was thus that he spoke of the object of my visit, of his earnest desire to see me, and of the solace he expected me to afford him. He entered, at some length, into what he conceived to be the nature of his malady. It was, he said, a constitutional and a family evil, and one for which he despaired to find a remedy — a mere nervous affection, he immediately added, which would undoubtedly soon pass off. It displayed itself in a host of unnatural sensations. Some of these, as he detailed them, interested and bewildered me — although, perhaps, the terms, and the general manner of the narration had their weight. He suffered much from a morbid acuteness of the senses; the most insipid food was alone endurable; he could wear only garments of certain texture; the odors of all flowers were oppressive; his eyes were tortured by even a faint light; and there were but peculiar sounds, and those from stringed instruments, which did not inspire him with horror.

To an anomalous species of terror I found him a bounden slave. "I shall perish," said he, "I *must* perish in this deplorable folly. Thus, thus, and not otherwise, shall I be lost. I dread the events of the future, not in themselves, but in their results. I shudder at the thought of any, even the most trivial, incident, which may operate upon this intolerable agitation of soul. I have, indeed, no abhorrence of danger, except in its absolute effect — in terror. In this unnerved — in this pitiable condition — I feel that I must inevitably abandon life and reason together in my struggles with some fatal demon of fear."

I learned, moreover, at intervals, and through broken and equivocal hints, another singular feature of his mental condition. He was enchained by certain superstitious impressions in regard to the dwelling which he tenanted, and from which, for many years, he had never ventured forth — in regard to an influence whose supposititious force was conveyed in terms too shadowy here to be restated — an influence which some peculiarities in the mere form and substance of his family mansion, had, by dint of long sufferance, he said, obtained over his spirit — an effect which the *physique* of the gray walls and turrets, and of the dim tarn into which they all looked down, had, at length, brought about upon the *morale* of his existence.

He admitted, however, although with hesitation, that much of the peculiar gloom which thus afflicted him could be traced to a more natural and far more palpable origin — to the severe and long-continued illness — indeed to the evidently approaching dissolution — of a tenderly beloved sister; his sole companion for long years — his last and only relative on earth. "Her decease," he said, with a bitterness which I can never forget, "would leave him (him the hopeless and the frail) the last of the ancient race of the Ushers." As he spoke, the lady Madeline (for so was she called) passed slowly through a remote portion of the apartment, and, without having noticed my presence, disappeared. I regarded her with an utter astonishment not unmingled with dread. Her figure, her air, her features — all, in their very minutest development were those — were identically (I can use no other sufficient term) were identically those of the Roderick Usher who sat beside me. A feeling of stupor oppressed me, as my eyes followed her retreating steps. As a door, at length, closed upon her exit, my glance sought instinctively and eagerly the countenance of the brother — but he had buried his face in his hands, and I could only perceive that a far more than ordinary wanness had overspread the emaciated fingers through which trickled many passionate tears.

The disease of the lady Madeline had long baffled the skill of her physicians. A settled apathy, a gradual wasting away of the person, and frequent although transient affections of a partially cataleptical character,[4] were the unusual diagnosis. Hitherto she had steadily borne up against the pressure of her malady, and had not betaken herself finally to bed; but, on the closing in of the evening of my arrival at the house, she succumbed, as her brother told me at night with inexpressible agitation, to the prostrating power of the destroyer — and I learned that the glimpse I had obtained of her person would thus probably be the last I should obtain — that the lady, at least while living, would be seen by me no more.

For several days ensuing, her name was unmentioned by either Usher or myself; and, during this period, I was buried in earnest endeavors to alleviate the melancholy of my friend. We painted and read together — or I listened, as if in a dream, to the wild improvisations of his speaking guitar. And thus, as a closer and still closer intimacy admitted me more unreservedly into the recesses of his spirit, the more bitterly did I perceive the futility of all attempt at cheering a mind from which darkness, as if an inherent positive quality, poured forth upon all objects of the moral and physical universe, in one unceasing radiation of gloom.

I shall ever bear about me, as Moslems in their shrouds at Mecca,[5] a memory of the many solemn hours I thus spent alone with the master of the House of Usher. Yet I should fail in any attempt to convey an idea of the exact character of the studies, or of the occupations, in which he involved me, or led me the way. An excited and highly distempered ideality threw a sulphurous lustre over all. His long improvised dirges will ring for ever in my ears. Among other things, I bear painfully in mind a certain singular perversion and amplification of the wild air of the last waltz of Von Weber.[6] From the paintings over which his elaborate fancy brooded, and which grew, touch by touch, into vaguenesses at which I shuddered the more thrillingly, because I shuddered knowing not why, from these paintings (vivid as their images now are before me) I would in vain endeavor to educe more than a small portion which should lie within the compass of merely written words. By the utter simplicity, by the nakedness, of his designs, he arrested and over-awed attention. If ever mortal painted an idea, that mortal was Roderick Usher. For me at least — in the circumstances then surrounding me — there arose out of the pure abstractions which the hypochondriac contrived to throw upon his canvas, an intensity of intolerable awe, no shadow of which felt I ever yet in the contemplation of the certainly glowing yet too concrete reveries of Fuseli.[7]

One of the phantasmagoric conceptions of my friend, partaking not so rigidly of the spirit of abstraction, may be shadowed forth, although feebly, in words. A small picture

---

4. **cataleptical character:** A condition characterized by muscular rigidity and a lack of response to external stimuli.

5. **Moslems . . . Mecca:** Once in their lives, Muslims are required to make a pilgrimage to Mecca, where they exchange their outer garments for a plain white shroud, a symbol of equality in which they will later be buried.

6. **Von Weber:** Carl Maria von Weber (1786–1826), German composer of Romantic operas. The popular piano piece known as "Weber's Last Waltz" was actually composed by Carl Gottlieb Reissiger (1798–1859), but a manuscript copy of the work was found among Weber's papers after his death and mistakenly attributed to him.

7. **Fuseli:** Henry Fuseli (1741–1825), Swiss painter of fantastic, Gothic subjects and themes.

presented the interior of an immensely long and rectangular vault or tunnel, with low walls, smooth, white, and without interruption or device. Certain accessory points of the design served well to convey the idea that this excavation lay at an exceeding depth below the surface of the earth. No outlet was observed in any portion of its vast extent, and no torch, or other artificial source of light was discernible – yet a flood of intense rays rolled throughout, and bathed the whole in a ghastly and inappropriate splendor.

I have just spoken of that morbid condition of the auditory nerve which rendered all music intolerable to the sufferer, with the exception of certain effects of stringed instruments. It was, perhaps, the narrow limits to which he thus confined himself upon the guitar, which gave birth, in great measure, to the fantastic character of his performances. But the fervid *facility* of his impromptus could not be so accounted for. They must have been, and were, in the notes, as well as in the words of his wild fantasias, (for he not unfrequently accompanied himself with rhymed verbal improvisations,) the result of that intense mental collectedness and concentration to which I have previously alluded as observable only in particular moments of the highest artificial excitement. The words of one of these rhapsodies I have easily borne away in memory. I was, perhaps, the more forcibly impressed with it, as he gave it, because, in the under or mystic current of its meaning, I fancied that I perceived, and for the first time, a full consciousness on the part of Usher, of the tottering of his lofty reason upon her throne. The verses, which were entitled "The Haunted Palace," ran very nearly, if not accurately, thus:

I

In the greenest of our valleys,
   By good angels tenanted,
Once a fair and stately palace –
   Snow-white palace – reared its head.
In the monarch Thought's dominion –
   It stood there!
Never seraph spread a pinion
   Over fabric half so fair.

II

Banners yellow, glorious, golden,
   On its roof did float and flow;
(This – all this – was in the olden
   Time long ago)
And every gentle air that dallied,
   In that sweet day,
Along the ramparts plumed and pallid,
   A winged odor went away.

III

Wanderers in that happy valley
   Through two luminous windows saw

Spirits moving musically
    To a lute's well-tunéd law,
Round about a throne, where sitting
    (Porphyrogene!)[8]
In state his glory well befitting,
    The sovereign of the realm was seen.

IV

And all with pearl and ruby glowing
    Was the fair palace door,
Through which came flowing, flowing, flowing,
    And sparkling evermore,
A troop of Echoes whose sole duty
    Was but to sing,
In voices of surpassing beauty,
    The wit and wisdom of their king.

V

But evil things, in robes of sorrow,
    Assailed the monarch's high estate;
(Ah, let us mourn, for never morrow
    Shall dawn upon him, desolate!)
And, round about his home, the glory
    That blushed and bloomed
Is but a dim-remembered story
    Of the old time entombed.

VI

And travellers now within that valley,
    Through the red-litten windows, see
Vast forms that move fantastically
    To a discordant melody;
While, like a rapid ghastly river,
    Through the pale door,
A hideous throng rush out forever,
    And laugh — but smile no more.[9]

I well remember that suggestions arising from this ballad led us into a train of thought wherein there became manifest an opinion of Usher's which I mention not so

---

8. **Porphyrogene:** Born in the purple, of royalty.
9. **In the greenest . . . but smile no more:** The poem is by Poe; in the first printing of "The Fall of the House of Usher," the story was followed by an editorial note: "The ballad of 'The Haunted Palace,' introduced in this tale, was published separately, some months ago, in the Baltimore 'Museum.'" That magazine was the *American Museum*, published in Baltimore, Maryland.

much on account of its novelty, (for other men have thought thus,) as on account of the pertinacity with which he maintained it. This opinion, in its general form, was that of the sentience of all vegetable things. But, in his disordered fancy, the idea had assumed a more daring character, and trespassed, under certain conditions, upon the kingdom of inorganization. I lack words to express the full extent, or the earnest *abandon* of his persuasion. The belief, however, was connected (as I have previously hinted) with the gray stones of the home of his forefathers. The condition of the sentience had been here, he imagined, fulfilled in the method of collocation of these stones – in the order of their arrangement, as well as in that of the many fungi which overspread them, and of the decayed trees which stood around – above all, in the long undisturbed endurance of this arrangement, and in its reduplication in the still waters of the tarn. Its evidence – the evidence of the sentience – was to be seen, he said, (and I here started as he spoke,) in *the gradual yet certain condensation of an atmosphere of their own about the waters and the walls.* The result was discoverable, he added, in that silent, yet importunate and terrible influence which for centuries had moulded the destinies of his family, and which made *him* what I now saw him – what he was. Such opinions need no comment, and I will make none.

Our books – the books which, for years, had formed no small portion of the mental existence of the invalid – were, as might be supposed, in strict keeping with this character of phantasm.[10] We pored together over such works as the Ververt et Chartreuse of Gresset; the Belphegor of Machiavelli; the Selenography of Brewster; the Heaven and Hell of Swedenborg; the Subterranean Voyage of Nicholas Klimm de Holberg; the Chiromancy of Robert Flud, of Jean d'Indaginé, and of De la Chambre; the Journey into the Blue Distance of Tieck; and the City of the Sun of Campanella. One favorite volume was a small octavo edition of the Directorium Inquisitorium, by the Dominican Eymeric de Gironne; and there were passages in Pomponius Mela, about the old African Satyrs and Oegipans, over which Usher would sit dreaming for hours. His chief delight, however, was found in the earnest and repeated perusal of an exceedingly rare and curious book in quarto Gothic – the manual of a forgotten church – the *Vigilae Mortuorum secundum Chorum Ecclesiae Maguntinae.*

I could not help thinking of the wild ritual of this work, and of its probable influence upon the hypochondriac, when, one evening, having informed me abruptly that the lady Madeline was no more, he stated his intention of preserving her corpse for a fortnight, previously to its final interment, in one of the numerous vaults within the main walls of the building. The wordly reason, however, assigned for this singular proceeding, was one which I did not feel at liberty to dispute. The brother had been led to his resolution (so he told me) by considerations of the unusual character of the malady of the deceased, of certain obtrusive and eager inquiries on the part of her medical men, and of the remote and exposed situation of the burial ground of the family. I will not deny that when I called to mind the sinister countenance of the person whom I met upon the

---

10. **Our books . . . phantasm:** All the titles listed here are real books dealing with demonism, the occult, and other aspects of pseudoscience.

staircase, on the day of my arrival at the house, I had no desire to oppose what I regarded as at best but a harmless, and not by any means an unnatural precaution.[11]

At the request of Usher, I personally aided him in the arrangements for the temporary entombment. The body having been encoffined, we two alone bore it to its rest. The vault in which we placed it (and which had been so long unopened that our torches, half smothered in its oppressive atmosphere, gave us little opportunity for investigation) was small, damp, and utterly without means of admission for light; lying, at great depth, immediately beneath that portion of the building in which was my own sleeping apartment. It had been used, apparently, in remote feudal times, for the worst purposes of a donjon-keep, and, in later days, as a place of deposit for powder, or other highly combustible substance, as a portion of its floor, and the whole interior of a long archway through which we reached it, were carefully sheathed with copper. The door, of massive iron, had been, also, similarly protected. Its immense weight caused an unusually sharp grating sound, as it moved upon its hinges.

Having deposited our mournful burden upon tressels[12] within the region of horror, we partially turned aside the yet unscrewed lid of the coffin, and looked upon the face of the tenant. The exact similitude between the brother and sister even here again startled and confounded me. Usher, divining, perhaps, my thoughts, murmured out some few words from which I learned that the deceased and himself had been twins, and that sympathies of a scarcely intelligible nature had always existed between them. Our glances, however, rested not long upon the dead — for we could not regard her unawed. The disease which had thus entombed the lady in the maturity of youth, had left, as usual in all maladies of a strictly cataleptical character, the mockery of a faint blush upon the bosom and the face, and that suspiciously lingering smile upon the lip which is so terrible in death. We replaced and screwed down the lid, and, having secured the door of iron, made our way, with toil, into the scarcely less gloomy apartments of the upper portion of the house.

And now, some days of bitter grief having elapsed, an observable change came over the features of the mental disorder of my friend. His ordinary manner had vanished. His ordinary occupations were neglected or forgotten. He roamed from chamber to chamber with hurried, unequal, and objectless step. The pallor of his countenance had assumed, if possible, a more ghastly hue — but the luminousness of his eye had utterly gone out. The once occasional huskiness of his tone was heard no more; and a tremulous quaver, as if of extreme terror, habitually characterized his utterance. — There were times, indeed, when I thought his unceasingly agitated mind was laboring with an oppressive secret, to divulge which he struggled for the necessary courage. At times, again, I was obliged to resolve all into the mere inexplicable vagaries of madness, as I beheld him gazing upon vacancy for long hours, in an attitude of the profoundest attention, as if listening to some imaginary sound. It was no wonder that his condition terrified — that

---

11. **precaution:** Usher fears that, if Madeline is buried immediately, her corpse will be dug up and sold to the interested "medical men" for dissection, a common occurrence in the early nineteenth century.

12. **tressels:** Trestles, a braced framework used to raise and support the coffin.

it infected me. I felt creeping upon me, by slow yet certain degrees, the wild influences of his own fantastic yet impressive superstitions.

It was, most especially, upon retiring to bed late in the night of the seventh or eighth day after the entombment of the lady Madeline, that I experienced the full power of such feelings. Sleep came not near my couch — while the hours waned and waned away. I struggled to reason off the nervousness which had dominion over me. I endeavored to believe that much, if not all of what I felt, was due to the phantasmagoric influence of the gloomy furniture of the room — of the dark and tattered draperies, which, tortured into motion by the breath of a rising tempest, swayed fitfully to and fro upon the walls, and rustled uneasily about the decorations of the bed. But my efforts were fruitless. An irrepressible tremor gradually pervaded my frame; and, at length, there sat upon my very heart an incubus[13] of utterly causeless alarm. Shaking this off with a gasp and a struggle, I uplifted myself upon the pillows, and, peering earnestly within the intense darkness of the chamber, harkened — I know not why, except that an instinctive spirit prompted me — to certain low and indefinite sounds which came, through the pauses of the storm, at long intervals, I knew not whence. Overpowered by an intense sentiment of horror unaccountable yet unendurable, I threw on my clothes with haste, for I felt that I should sleep no more during the night, and endeavored to arouse myself from the pitiable condition into which I had fallen, by pacing rapidly to and fro through the apartment.

I had taken but few turns in this manner, when a light step on an adjoining staircase arrested my attention. I presently recognized it as that of Usher. In an instant afterwards he rapped, with a gentle touch, at my door, and entered, bearing a lamp. His countenance was, as usual, cadaverously wan — but there was a species of mad hilarity in his eyes — an evidently restrained hysteria in his whole demeanor. His air appalled me — but any thing was preferable to the solitude which I had so long endured, and I even welcomed his presence as a relief.

"And you have not seen it!" he said abruptly, after having stared about him for some moments in silence — "you have not then seen it? — but, stay! you shall." Thus speaking, and having carefully shaded his lamp, he hurried to one of the gigantic casements, and threw it freely open to the storm.

The impetuous fury of the entering gust nearly lifted us from our feet. It was, indeed, a tempestuous yet sternly beautiful night, and one wildly singular in its terror and its beauty. A whirlwind had apparently collected its force in our vicinity; for here were frequent and violent alterations in the direction of the wind; and the exceeding density of the clouds (which hung so low as to press upon the turrets of the house) did not prevent our perceiving the life-like velocity with which they flew careering from all points against each other, without passing away into the distance. I say that even their exceeding density did not prevent our perceiving this — yet we had no glimpse of the moon or stars — nor was there any flashing forth of the lightning. But the under surfaces of the huge masses of agitated vapor, as well as all terrestrial objects immediately around us,

---

13. **incubus:** A demon or evil spirit who according to legend lies upon people in their sleep.

were glowing in the unnatural light of a faintly luminous and distinctly visible gaseous exhalation which hung about and enshrouded the mansion.

"You must not — you shall not behold this!" said I, shudderingly, to Usher, as I led him, with a gentle violence, from the window to a seat. "These appearances, which bewilder you, are merely electrical phenomena not uncommon — or it may be that they have their ghastly origin in the rank miasma of the tarn. Let us close this casement — the air is chilling and dangerous to your frame. Here is one of your favorite romances. I will read, and you shall listen — and so we will pass away this terrible night together."

The antique volume which I had taken up was the "Mad Trist" of Sir Launcelot Canning[14] — but I had called it a favorite of Usher's more in sad jest than in earnest; for, in truth, there is little in its uncouth and unimaginative prolixity which could have had interest for the lofty and spiritual ideality of my friend. It was, however, the only book immediately at hand; and I indulged a vague hope that the excitement which now agitated the hypochondriac might find relief (for the history of mental disorder is full of similar anomalies) even in the extremeness of the folly which I should read. Could I have judged, indeed, by the wild, overstrained air of vivacity with which he harkened, or apparently harkened, to the words of the tale, I might have well congratulated myself upon the success of my design.

I had arrived at that well-known portion of the story where Ethelred, the hero of the Trist, having sought in vain for peaceable admission into the dwelling of the hermit, proceeds to make good an entrance by force. Here, it will be remembered, the words of the narrative run thus —

"And Ethelred, who was by nature of a doughty heart, and who was now mighty withal, on account of the powerfulness of the wine which he had drunken, waited no longer to hold parley with the hermit, who, in sooth, was of an obstinate and maliceful turn, but, feeling the rain upon his shoulders, and fearing the rising of the tempest, uplifted his mace outright, and, with blows, made quickly room in the plankings of the door for his gauntleted hand, and now pulling therewith sturdily, he so cracked, and ripped, and tore all asunder, that the noise of the dry and hollow-sounding wood alarummed and reverberated throughout the forest."

At the termination of this sentence I started, and, for a moment, paused; for it appeared to me (although I at once concluded that my excited fancy had deceived me) — it appeared to me that, from some very remote portion of the mansion or of its vicinity, there came, indistinctly, to my ears, what might have been, in its exact similarity of character, the echo (but a stifled and dull one certainly) of the very cracking and ripping sound which Sir Launcelot had so particularly described. It was, beyond doubt, the coincidence alone which had arrested my attention; for, amid the rattling of the sashes of the casements, and the ordinary commingled noises of the still increasing

---

14. **"Mad Trist"** . . . **Canning:** The author and title of the tale are apparently fictitious, though its hero bears the name of an early English king, Ethelred (968?–1016). A trist is a secret or prearranged meeting.

storm, the sound, in itself, had nothing, surely, which should have interested or disturbed me. I continued the story.

"But the good champion Ethelred, now entering within the door, was sore enraged and amazed to perceive no signal of the maliceful hermit; but, in the stead thereof, a dragon of a scaly and prodigious demeanor, and of a fiery tongue, which sate in guard before a palace of gold, with a floor of silver; and upon the wall there hung a shield of shining brass with this legend enwritten –

> Who entereth herein, a conqueror hath bin,
> Who slayeth the dragon, the shield he shall win.

And Ethelred uplifted his mace, and struck upon the head of the dragon, which fell before him, and gave up his pesty breath, with a shriek so horrid and harsh, and withal so piercing, that Ethelred had fain to close his ears with his hands against the dreadful noise of it, the like whereof was never before heard."

Here again I paused abruptly, and now with a feeling of wild amazement – for there could be no doubt whatever that, in this instance, I did actually hear (although from what direction it proceeded I found it impossible to say) a low and apparently distant, but harsh, protracted, and most unusual screaming or grating sound – the exact counterpart of what my fancy had already conjured up as the sound of the dragon's unnatural shriek as described by the romancer.

Oppressed, as I certainly was, upon the occurrence of this second and most extraordinary coincidence, by a thousand conflicting sensations, in which wonder and extreme terror were predominant, I still retained sufficient presence of mind to avoid exciting, by any observation, the sensitive nervousness of my companion. I was by no means certain that he had noticed the sounds in question; although, assuredly, a strange alteration had, during the last few minutes, taken place in his demeanor. From a position fronting my own, he had gradually brought round his chair, so as to sit with his face to the door of the chamber, and thus I could but partially perceive his features, although I saw that his lips trembled as if he were murmuring inaudibly. His head had dropped upon his breast – yet I knew that he was not asleep, from the wide and rigid opening of the eye, as I caught a glance of it in profile. The motion of his body, too, was at variance with this idea – for he rocked from side to side with a gentle yet constant and uniform sway. Having rapidly taken notice of all this, I resumed the narrative of Sir Launcelot, which thus proceeded: –

"And now, the champion, having escaped from the terrible fury of the dragon, bethinking himself of the brazen shield, and of the breaking up of the enchantment which was upon it, removed the carcass from out of the way before him, and approached valorously over the silver pavement of the castle to where the shield was upon the wall; which in sooth tarried not for his full coming, but fell down at his feet upon the silver floor, with a mighty great and terrible ringing sound."

No sooner had these syllables passed my lips, than – as if a shield of brass had indeed, at the moment, fallen heavily upon a floor of silver – I became aware of a distinct, hollow, metallic, and clangorous, yet apparently muffled reverberation. Completely unnerved, I started convulsively to my feet, but the measured rocking movement of Usher was undisturbed. I rushed to the chair in which he sat. His eyes were bent fixedly before him, and throughout his whole countenance there reigned a more than stony rigidity. But, as I laid my hand upon his shoulder, there came a strong shudder over his frame; a sickly smile quivered about his lips; and I saw that he spoke in a low, hurried, and gibbering murmur, as if unconscious of my presence. Bending closely over his person, I at length drank in the hideous import of his words.

"Not hear it? – yes, I hear it, and *have* heard it. Long – long – long – many minutes, many hours, many days, have I heard it – yet I dared not – oh, pity me, miserable wretch that I am! – I dared not – *I dared* not speak! *We have put her living in the tomb!* Said I not that my senses were acute? – I *now* tell you that I heard her first feeble movements in the hollow coffin. I heard them – many, many days ago – yet I dared not – *I dared not speak!* And now – to-night – Ethelred – ha! ha! – the breaking of the hermit's door, and the death-cry of the dragon, and the clangor of the shield – say, rather, the rending of the coffin, and the grating of the iron hinges, and her struggles within the coppered archway of the vault! Oh whither shall I fly? Will she not be here anon? Is she not hurrying to upbraid me for my haste? Have I not heard her footsteps on the stair? Do I not distinguish that heavy and horrible beating of her heart? Madman!" – here he sprung violently to his feet, and shrieked out his syllables, as if in the effort he were giving up his soul – "Madman! *I tell you that she now stands without the door!*"

As if in the superhuman energy of his utterance there had been found the potency of a spell – the huge antique pannels to which the speaker pointed, threw slowly back, upon the instant, their ponderous and ebony jaws. It was the work of the rushing gust – but then without those doors there *did* stand the lofty and enshrouded figure of the lady Madeline of Usher. There was blood upon her white robes, and the evidence of some bitter struggle upon every portion of her emaciated frame. For a moment she remained trembling and reeling to and fro upon the threshold – then, with a low moaning cry, fell heavily inward upon the person of her brother, and in her horrible and now final death-agonies, bore him to the floor a corpse, and a victim to the terrors he had dreaded.

From that chamber, and from that mansion, I fled aghast. The storm was still abroad in all its wrath as I found myself crossing the old causeway. Suddenly there shot along the path a wild light, and I turned to see whence a gleam so unusual could have issued – for the vast house and its shadows were alone behind me. The radiance was that of the full, setting, and blood-red moon, which now shone vividly through that once barely-discernible fissure, of which I have before spoken, as extending from the roof of the building, in a zig-zag direction, to the base. While I gazed, this fissure rapidly widened – there came a fierce breath of the whirlwind – the entire orb of the satellite burst at once upon my sight – my brain reeled as I saw the mighty walls rushing asunder – there was a long tumultuous shouting sound like the voice of a thousand waters – and the deep and dank tarn at my feet closed sullenly and silently over the fragments of the "*House of Usher.*"

[1839]

Reading Poe's "The Tell-Tale Heart."   This powerfully compressed tale, one of the shortest Poe wrote, was first published in the *Pioneer: A Literary and Critical Magazine*, a monthly established by the poet James Russell Lowell. Lowell's lofty ambitions for the magazine included the idea that it should "take as high an aim in art as may be" and that the contributors would have the freedom to publish what they pleased, free of any editorial meddling or restrictions. In a letter inviting Poe to contribute, Lowell promised him "*carte blanche* for prose or verse as may best please you" and offered $10 for each contribution – a reasonable sum at a time when many magazines paid contributors very little, or nothing at all. Poe's macabre tale of guilt and obsession, essentially a monologue in which an accused murderer protests his sanity, appeared alongside poems by Lowell and articles on Beethoven and the Boston Athenaeum, one of the oldest libraries and art galleries in the United States. Poe published one more story as well as an essay during the short run of the magazine, which ended in March 1843 – barely four months after it was established – when Lowell had insufficient funds to pay the printers and authors with whom he had contracts. The text of "The Tell-Tale Heart" is taken from its first printing in the *Pioneer*, January 1843.

THE TELL-TALE HEART

Art is long and Time is fleeting,
  And our hearts, though stout and brave,
Still, like muffled drums, are beating
  Funeral marches to the grave.
                    -Longfellow[1]

True! – nervous – very, very dreadfully nervous I had been, and am; but why *will* you say that I am mad? The disease had sharpened my senses – not destroyed – not dulled them. Above all was the sense of hearing acute. I heard all things in the heaven and in the earth. I heard many things in hell. How, then, am I mad? Harken! and observe how healthily – how calmly I can tell you the whole story.

It is impossible to say how first the idea entered my brain; but, once conceived, it haunted me day and night. Object there was none. Passion there was none. I loved the old man. He had never wronged me. He had never given me insult. For his gold I had no desire. I think it was his eye! – yes, it was this! He had the eye of a vulture – a pale blue eye, with a film over it. Whenever it fell upon me, my blood ran cold; and so, by degrees – very gradually – I made up my mind to take the life of the old man, and thus rid myself of the eye forever.

---

1. *Longfellow*: The epigraph is from "A Psalm of Life" by Henry Wadsworth Longfellow (1807-1882).

Now this is the point. You fancy me mad. Madmen know nothing. But you should have seen *me*. You should have seen how wisely I proceeded – with what caution – with what foresight – with what dissimulation I went to work! I was never kinder to the old man than during the whole week before I killed him. And every night, about midnight, I turned the latch of his door and opened it – oh so gently! And then, when I had made an opening sufficient for my head, I first put in a dark lantern,[2] all closed, closed, so that no light shone out, and then I thrust in my head. Oh, you would have laughed to see how cunningly I thrust it in! I moved it slowly – very, very slowly, so that I might not disturb the old man's sleep. It took me an hour to place my whole head within the opening so far that I could see the old man as he lay upon his bed. Ha! – would a madman have been so wise as this? And then, when my head was well in the room, I undid the lantern cautiously – oh, so cautiously (for the hinges creaked) – I undid it just so much that a single thin ray fell upon the vulture eye. And this I did for seven long nights – every night just at midnight – but I found the eye always closed; and so it was impossible to do the work; for it was not the old man who vexed me, but his Evil Eye. And every morning, when the day broke, I went boldly into his chamber, and spoke courageously to him, calling him by name in a hearty tone, and inquiring how he had passed the night. So you see he would have been a very profound old man, indeed, to suspect that every night, just at twelve, I looked in upon him while he slept.

Upon the eighth night I was more than usually cautious in opening the door. A watch's minute-hand moves more quickly than did mine. Never, before that night, had I *felt* the extent of my own powers – of my sagacity. I could scarcely contain my feelings of triumph. To think that there I was, opening the door, little by little, and the old man not even to dream of my secret deeds or thoughts. I fairly chuckled at the idea. And perhaps the old man heard me; for he moved in the bed suddenly, as if startled. Now you may think that I drew back – but no. His room was as black as pitch with the thick darkness, (for the shutters were close fastened, through fear of robbers,) and so I knew that he could not see the opening of the door, and I kept on pushing it steadily, steadily.

I had got my head in, and was about to open the lantern, when my thumb slipped upon the tin fastening, and the old man sprang up in the bed, crying out – "Who's there?"

I kept quite still and said nothing. For another hour I did not move a muscle, and in the meantime I did not hear the old man lie down. He was still sitting up in the bed, listening; – just as I have done, night after night, hearkening to the death-watches in the wall.[3]

Presently I heard a slight groan, and I knew that it was the groan of mortal terror. It was not a groan of pain, or of grief – oh, no! – it was the low, stifled sound that arises

---

2. **dark lantern:** A lantern with a single pane that may be covered by a sliding panel to conceal the light.
3. **death-watches in the wall:** Several kinds of beetles make a clicking sound by striking their heads against wood, which was sometimes thought to be predictive of death.

from the bottom of the soul when overcharged with *awe*. I knew the sound well. Many a night, just at midnight, when all the world slept, it has welled up from my own bosom, deepening, with its dreadful echo, the terrors that distracted me. I say I knew it well. I knew what the old man felt, and pitied him, although I chuckled at heart. I knew that he had been lying awake ever since the first slight noise, when he had turned in the bed. His fears had been, ever since, growing upon him. He had been trying to fancy them causeless, but could not. He had been saying to himself – "It is nothing but the wind in the chimney – it is only a mouse crossing the floor," or "it is merely a cricket which has made a single chirp." Yes, he had been trying to comfort himself with these suppositions; but he had found all in vain. *All in vain*: because death, in approaching the old man, had stalked with his black shadow before him, and the shadow had now reached and enveloped the victim. And it was the mournful influence of the unperceived shadow that caused him to feel – although he neither saw nor heard me – to *feel* the presence of my head within the room.

When I had waited a long time, very patiently, without hearing the old man lie down, I resolved to open a little – a very, very little crevice in the lantern. So I opened it – you cannot imagine how stealthily, stealthily – until, at length, a single dim ray, like the thread of the spider, shot from out the crevice and fell full upon the vulture eye.

It was open – wide, wide open – and I grew furious as I gazed upon it. I saw it with perfect distinctness – all a dull blue, with a hideous veil over it that chilled the very marrow in my bones; but I could see nothing else of the old man's face or person; for I had directed the ray, as if by instinct, precisely upon the damned spot.

And now – have I not told you that what you mistake for madness is but over acuteness of the senses? – now, I say, there came to my ears *a low dull, quick sound — much such a sound as a watch makes when enveloped in cotton.* I knew *that* sound well, too. It was the beating of the old man's heart. It increased my fury, as the beating of a drum stimulates the soldier into courage.

But even yet I refrained and kept still. I scarcely breathed. I held the lantern motionless. I tried how steadily I could maintain the ray upon the eye. Meantime the hellish tattoo[4] of the heart increased. It grew quicker, and louder and louder every instant. The old man's terror *must* have been extreme! It grew louder, I say, louder every moment: – do you mark me well? I have told you that I am nervous: – so I am. And now, at the dead hour of night, and amid the dreadful silence of that old house, so strange a noise as this excited me to uncontrollable wrath. Yet, for some minutes longer, I refrained and kept still. But the beating grew louder, *louder*! I thought the heart must burst! And now a new anxiety seized me – the sound would be heard by a neighbor! The old man's hour had come! With a loud yell, I threw open the lantern and leaped into the room. He shrieked once – once only. In an instant I dragged him to the floor, and pulled the heavy bed[5] over him. I then sat upon the bed and smiled gaily, to find the deed so far done. But,

---

4. **tattoo:** A drumbeat used to recall soldiers to their quarters at night.
5. **heavy bed:** A heavy comforter often used as a mattress.

for many minutes, the heart beat on, with a muffled sound. This, however, did not vex me; it would not be heard through the walls. At length it ceased. The old man was dead. I removed the bed and examined the corpse. Yes, he was stone, stone dead. I placed my hand upon the heart and held it there many minutes. There was no pulsation. The old man was stone dead. His eye would trouble *me* no more.

If, still, you think me mad, you will think so no longer when I describe the wise precautions I took for the concealment of the body. The night waned, and I worked hastily, but in silence. First of all I dismembered the corpse. I cut off the head and the arms and the legs. I then took up three planks from the flooring of the chamber, and deposited all between the scantlings.[6] I then replaced the boards so cleverly, so cunningly, that no human eye — not even *his* — could have detected anything wrong. There was nothing to wash out — no stain of any kind — no blood-spot whatever. I had been too wary for that. A tub had caught all — ha! ha!

When I had made an end of these labors, it was four o'clock — still dark as midnight. As the bell sounded the hour, there came a knocking at the street door. I went down to open it with a light heart, — for what had I *now* to fear? There entered three men, who introduced themselves, with perfect suavity, as officers of the police. A shriek had been heard by a neighbor during the night; suspicion of foul play had been aroused; information had been lodged at the police-office, and they (the officers) had been deputed to search the premises.

I smiled, — for *what* had I to fear? I bade the gentlemen welcome. The shriek, I said, was my own in a dream. The old man, I mentioned, was absent in the country. I took my visiters all over the house. I bade them search — search *well*. I led them, at length, to *his* chamber. I showed them his treasures, secure, undisturbed. In the enthusiasm of my confidence, I brought chairs into the room, and desired them *here* to rest from their fatigues; while I myself, in the wild audacity of my perfect triumph, placed my own seat upon the very spot beneath which reposed the corpse of the victim.

The officers were satisfied. My *manner* had convinced them. I was singularly at ease. They sat, and, while I answered cheerily, they chatted of familiar things. But, ere long, I felt myself getting pale and wished them gone. My head ached, and I fancied a ringing in my ears: but still they sat and still chatted. The ringing became more distinct: I talked more freely, to get rid of the feeling; but it continued and gained definitiveness — until, at length, I found that the noise was *not* within my ears.

No doubt I now grew *very* pale; — but I talked more fluently, and with a heightened voice. Yet the sound increased — and what could I do? It was *a low, dull, quick sound — much such a sound as a watch makes when enveloped in cotton.* I gasped for breath — and yet the officers heard it not. I talked more quickly — more vehemently; — but the noise steadily increased. I arose, and argued about trifles, in a high key and with violent gesticulations; — but the noise steadily increased. Why *would* they not be gone? I paced the floor to and fro, with heavy strides, as if excited to fury by the observations of the men; — but the noise steadily increased. Oh God! what *could* I do? I foamed — I raved — I swore! I swung

---

6. **scantlings:** Narrow planks used to support the flooring.

the chair upon which I had sat, and grated it upon the boards; — but the noise arose over all and continually increased. It grew louder — louder — *louder*! And still the men chatted pleasantly, and smiled. Was it possible they heard not? Almighty God! — no, no! They heard! — they suspected! — they *knew*! — they were making a mockery of my horror! — this I thought, and this I think. But anything better than this agony! Anything was more tolerable than this derision! I could bear those hypocritical smiles no longer! I felt that I must scream or die! — and now — again! — hark! louder! louder! louder! *louder*! —

"Villains!" I shrieked, "dissemble no more! I admit the deed! — tear up the planks! — here, here! — it is the beating of his hideous heart!"

[1843]

Reading Poe's "The Purloined Letter."   This story is among the more famous of Poe's "tales of ratiocination," stories based on logical and methodical reasoning. Poe is considered by many to be the first writer of American detective stories, and his amateur detective, C. Auguste Dupin, is the forerunner of Sherlock Holmes, the enormously popular detective later created by the English writer Arthur Conan Doyle. In fact, Holmes mentions reading Poe and admiring his work in Doyle's story "The Cardboard Box" (1893). "The Purloined Letter," the third story to feature Dupin, first appeared in *The Gift*, one of the series of popular gift books published from the mid-1820s through the Civil War. Such literary annuals were beautifully bound and illustrated volumes that usually appeared late in the year (with the following year's publication date), just in time to be given as Christmas presents. By the mid-1840s, about sixty such gift books were being published each year. *The Gift* for 1845 included poetry by Henry Wadsworth Longfellow, Lydia Sigourney, and Ralph Waldo Emerson, as well as stories by Caroline Kirkland, Nathaniel P. Willis, and Poe. "The Purloined Letter" was included in Poe's second collection of stories, *Tales* (1845). The text is taken from its first printing in *The Gift* (1845).

THE PURLOINED LETTER

At Paris, just after dark one gusty evening in the autumn of 18—, I was enjoying the twofold luxury of meditation and a meerschaum,[1] in company with my friend C. Auguste Dupin, in his little back library, or book-closet, *au troisième*,[2] No. 33, *Rue Dunôt, Faubourg St. Germain.* For one hour at least we had maintained a profound silence; while each, to

---

1. **meerschaum:** A tobacco pipe carved from a soft, white mineral.
2. ***au troisième***: On the third floor; since the French do not number the ground floor, an American would locate Dupin's apartment on the fourth floor.

any casual observer, might have seemed intently and exclusively occupied with the curling eddies of smoke that oppressed the atmosphere of the chamber. For myself, however, I was mentally discussing certain topics which had formed matter for conversation between us at an earlier period of the evening; I mean the affair of the Rue Morgue, and the mystery attending the murder of Marie Roget.[3] I looked upon it, therefore, as something of a coincidence, when the door of our apartment was thrown open and admitted our old acquaintance, Monsieur G——, the Prefect of the Parisian police.

We gave him a hearty welcome; for there was nearly half as much of the entertaining as of the contemptible about the man, and we had not seen him for several years. We had been sitting in the dark, and Dupin now arose for the purpose of lighting a lamp, but sat down again, without doing so, upon G.'s saying that he had called to consult us, or rather to ask the opinion of my friend, about some official business which had occasioned a great deal of trouble.

"If it is any point requiring reflection," observed Dupin, as he forbore to enkindle the wick, "we shall examine it to better purpose in the dark."

"That is another of your odd notions," said the Prefect, who had a fashion of calling every thing "odd" that was beyond his comprehension, and thus lived amid an absolute legion of "oddities."

"Very true," said Dupin, as he supplied his visiter with a pipe, and rolled towards him a very comfortable chair.

"And what is the difficulty now?" I asked. "Nothing more in the assassination way, I hope?"

"Oh no; nothing of that nature. The fact is, the business is *very* simple indeed, and I make no doubt that we can manage it sufficiently well ourselves; but then I thought Dupin would like to hear the details of it, because it is so excessively *odd.*"

"Simple and odd," said Dupin.

"Why, yes; and not exactly that, either. The fact is, we have all been a good deal puzzled because the affair *is* so simple, and yet baffles us altogether."

"Perhaps it is the very simplicity of the thing which puts you at fault," said my friend.

"What nonsense you *do* talk!" replied the Prefect, laughing heartily.

"Perhaps the mystery is a little *too* plain," said Dupin.

"Oh, good heavens! who ever heard of such an idea?"

"A little *too* self-evident."

"Ha! ha! ha! – ha! ha! ha! – ho! ho! ho!" roared out our visiter, profoundly amused, "oh, Dupin, you will be the death of me yet!"

"And what, after all, *is* the matter on hand?" I asked.

"Why, I will tell you," replied the Prefect, as he gave a long, steady, and contemplative puff, and settled himself in his chair. "I will tell you in a few words; but, before I begin, let me caution you that this is an affair demanding the greatest secrecy, and that I should most probably lose the position I now hold, were it known that I confided it to any one."

---

3. **Rue Morgue . . . Marie Roget:** Other cases solved by Dupin, as described in Poe's two earlier stories about the detective: "The Murders in the Rue Morgue" (1841) and "The Mystery of Marie Rôget" (1842).

"Proceed," said I.

"Or not," said Dupin.

"Well, then; I have received personal information, from a very high quarter, that a certain document of the last importance, has been purloined from the royal apartments. The individual who purloined it is known; this beyond a doubt; he was seen to take it. It is known, also, that it still remains in his possession."

"How is this known?" asked Dupin.

"It is clearly inferred," replied the Prefect, "from the nature of the document, and from the non-appearance of certain results which would at once arise from its passing *out* of the robber's possession; — that is to say, from his employing it as he must design in the end to employ it."

"Be a little more explicit," I said.

"Well, I may venture so far as to say that the paper gives its holder a certain power in a certain quarter where such power is immensely valuable." The Prefect was fond of the cant of diplomacy.

"Still I do not quite understand," said Dupin.

"No? Well; the disclosure of the document to a third person, who shall be nameless, would bring in question the honour of a personage of most exalted station; and this fact gives the holder of the document an ascendancy over the illustrious personage whose honour and peace are so jeopardized."

"But this ascendancy," I interposed, "would depend upon the robber's knowledge of the loser's knowledge of the robber. Who would dare —"

"The thief," said G, "is the — Minister D——, who dares all things, those unbecoming as well as those becoming a man. The method of the theft was not less ingenious than bold. The document in question — a letter, to be frank — had been received by the personage robbed while alone in the royal *boudoir*. During its perusal she was suddenly interrupted by the entrance of the other exalted personage from whom especially it was her wish to conceal it. After a hurried and vain endeavour to thrust it in a drawer, she was forced to place it, open as it was, upon a table. The address, however, was uppermost, and the contents thus unexposed, the letter escaped notice. At this juncture enters the Minister D——. His lynx eye immediately perceives the paper, recognises the handwriting of the address, observes the confusion of the personage addressed, and fathoms her secret. After some business transactions, hurried through in his ordinary manner, he produces a letter somewhat similar to the one in question, opens it, pretends to read it, and then places it in close juxtaposition to the other. Again he converses, for some fifteen minutes, upon the public affairs. At length, in taking leave, he takes also from the table the letter to which he had no claim. Its rightful owner saw, but, of course, dared not call attention to the act, in the presence of the third personage who stood at her elbow. The minister decamped; leaving his own letter — one of no importance — upon the table."

"Here, then," said Dupin to me, "you have precisely what you demand to make the ascendancy complete — the robber's knowledge of the loser's knowledge of the robber."

"Yes," replied the Prefect; "and the power thus attained has, for some months past, been wielded, for political purposes, to a very dangerous extent. The personage robbed is more thoroughly convinced, every day, of the necessity of reclaiming her letter. But this, of course, cannot be done openly. In fine, driven to despair, she has committed the matter to me."

"Than whom," said Dupin, amid a perfect whirlwind of smoke, "no more sagacious agent could, I suppose, be desired, or even imagined."

"You flatter me," replied the Prefect; "but it is possible that some such opinion may have been entertained."

"It is clear," said I, "as you observe, that the letter is still in possession of the minister; since it is this possession, and not any employment, of the letter, which bestows the power. With the employment the power departs."

"True," said G——; "and upon this conviction I proceeded. My first care was to make thorough search of the minister's hotel; and here my chief embarrassment lay in the necessity of searching without his knowledge. Beyond all things, I have been warned of the danger which would result from giving him reason to suspect our design."

"But," said I, "you are quite *au fait*[4] in these investigations. The Parisian police have done this thing often before."

"O yes; and for this reason I did not despair. The habits of the minister gave me, too, a great advantage. He is frequently absent from home all night. His servants are by no means numerous. They sleep at a distance from their master's apartments, and, being chiefly Neapolitans, are readily made drunk. I have keys, as you know, with which I can open any chamber or cabinet in Paris. For three months a night has not passed, during the greater part of which I have not been engaged, personally, in ransacking the D—— Hotel. My honour is interested, and, to mention a great secret, the reward is enormous. So I did not abandon the search until I had become fully satisfied that the thief is a more astute man than myself. I fancy that I have investigated every nook and corner of the premises in which it is possible that the paper can be concealed."

"But is it not possible," I suggested, "that although the letter may be in possession of the minister, as it unquestionably is, he may have concealed it elsewhere than upon his own premises?"

"This is barely possible," said Dupin. "The present peculiar condition of affairs at court, and especially of those intrigues in which D—— is known to be involved, would render the instant availability of the document — its susceptibility of being produced at a moment's notice — a point of nearly equal importance with its possession."

"Its susceptibility of being produced?" said I.

"That is to say, of being *destroyed*," said Dupin.

"True," I observed; "the paper is clearly then upon the premises. As for its being upon the person of the minister, we may consider that as out of the question."

"Entirely," said the Prefect. "He has been twice waylaid, as if by footpads[5] and his person rigorously searched under my own inspection."

"You might have spared yourself this trouble," said Dupin. "D——, I presume, is not altogether a fool, and, if not, must have anticipated these waylayings, as a matter of course."

---

4. *au fait*: Informed (French).
5. **footpads**: Early term for street robbers on foot.

"Not *altogether* a fool," said G——, "but then he's a poet, which I take to be only one remove from a fool."

"True;" said Dupin, after a long and thoughtful whiff from his meerschaum, "although I have been guilty of certain doggerel myself."

"Suppose you detail," said I, "the particulars of your search."

"Why the fact is, we took our time, and we searched *every where*. I have had long experience in these affairs. I took the entire building, room by room; devoting the nights of a whole week to each. We examined, first, the furniture of each apartment. We opened every possible drawer; and I presume you know that, to a properly trained police agent, such a thing as a *secret* drawer is impossible. Any man is a dolt who permits a 'secret' drawer to escape him in a search of this kind. The thing is *so* plain. There is a certain amount of bulk — of space — to be accounted for in every cabinet. Then we have accurate rules. The fiftieth part of a line could not escape us. After the cabinets we took the chairs. The cushions we probed with the fine long needles you have seen me employ. From the tables we removed the tops."

"Why so?"

"Sometimes the top of a table, or other similarly arranged piece of furniture, is removed by the person wishing to conceal an article; then the leg is excavated, the article deposited within the cavity, and the top replaced. The bottoms and tops of bedposts are employed in the same way."

"But could not the cavity be detected by sounding?" I asked.

"By no means, if, when the article is deposited, a sufficient wadding of cotton be placed around it. Besides, in our case, we were obliged to proceed without noise."

"But you could not have removed — you could not have taken to pieces *all* articles of furniture in which it would have been possible to make a deposit in the manner you mention. A letter may be compressed into a thin spiral roll, not differing much in shape or bulk from a large knitting-needle, and in this form it might be inserted into the rung of a chair, for example. You did not take to pieces all the chairs?"

"Certainly not; but we did better — we examined the rungs of every chair in the hotel, and, indeed, the jointings of every description of furniture, by the aid of a most powerful microscope.[6] Had there been any traces of recent disturbance we should not have failed to detect it *instanter*.[7] A single grain of gimlet-dust, or saw-dust, for example, would have been as obvious as an apple. Any disorder in the glueing — any unusual gaping in the joints — would have sufficed to insure detection."

"Of course you looked to the mirrors, between the boards and the plates, and you probed the beds and the bed-clothes, as well as the curtains and carpets."

"That of course; and when we had absolutely completed every particle of the furniture in this way, then we examined the house itself. We divided its entire surface into compartments, which we numbered, so that none might be missed; then we scrutinized each individual square inch throughout the premises, including the two houses immediately adjoining, with the microscope, as before."

---

6. **microscope:** Magnifying glass.
7. *instanter*: At the instant; instantly (French).

"The two houses adjoining!" I exclaimed; "you must have had a great deal of trouble."

"We had; but the reward offered is prodigious."

"You include the *grounds* about the houses?"

"All the grounds are paved with brick. They gave us comparatively little trouble. We examined the moss between the bricks, and found it undisturbed."

"And the roofs?"

"We surveyed every inch of the external surface, and probed carefully beneath every tile."

"You looked among D——'s papers, of course, and into the books of the library?"

"Certainly; we opened every package and parcel; we not only opened every book, but we turned over every leaf in each volume, not contenting ourselves with a mere shake, according to the fashion of some of our police officers. We also measured the thickness of every book-*cover*, with the most accurate admeasurement, and applied to them the most jealous scrutiny of the microscope. Had any of the bindings been recently meddled with, it would have been utterly impossible that the fact should have escaped observation. Some five or six volumes, just from the hands of the binder, we carefully probed, longitudinally, with the needles."

"You explored the floors beneath the carpets?"

"Beyond doubt. We removed every carpet, and examined the boards with the microscope."

"And the paper on the walls?"

"Yes."

"You looked into the cellars?"

"We did; and, as time and labour were no objects, we dug up every one of them to the depth of four feet."

"Then," I said, "you have been making a miscalculation, and the letter is *not* upon the premises, as you suppose."

"I fear you are right there," said the Prefect. "And now, Dupin, what would you advise me to do?"

"To make a thorough re-search of the premises."

"That is absolutely needless," replied G——. "I am not more sure that I breathe than I am that the letter is not at the Hotel."

"I have no better advice to give you," said Dupin. "You have, of course, an accurate description of the letter?"

"Oh yes!" – And here the Prefect, producing a memorandum-book, proceeded to read aloud a minute account of the internal, and especially of the external, appearance of the missing document. Soon after finishing the perusal of this description, he took his departure, more entirely depressed in spirits than I had ever known the good gentleman before.

In about a month afterwards he paid us another visit, and found us occupied very nearly as before. He took a pipe and a chair, and entered into some ordinary conversation. At length I said, –

"Well, but G——, what of the purloined letter? I presume you have at last made up your mind that there is no such thing as overreaching the Minister?"

"Confound him, say I — yes; I made the re-examination, however, as Dupin suggested — but it was all labour lost, as I knew it would be."

"How much was the reward offered, did you say?" asked Dupin.

"Why, a very great deal — a *very* liberal reward — I don't like to say how much, precisely; but one thing I *will* say, that I wouldn't mind giving my individual check for fifty thousand francs to any one who could obtain me that letter. The fact is, it is becoming of more and more importance every day; and the reward has been lately doubled. If it were trebled, however, I could do no more than I have done."

"Why, yes," said Dupin, drawlingly, between the whiffs of his meerschaum, "I really — think, G—, you have not exerted yourself — to the utmost in this matter. You might — do a little more, I think, eh?"

"How? — in what way?"

"Why — puff, puff — you might — puff, puff — employ counsel in the matter, eh? — puff, puff, puff. Do you remember the story they tell of Abernethy?"[8]

"No; hang Abernethy!"

"To be sure! hang him and welcome. But, once upon a time, a certain rich miser conceived the design of spunging upon this Abernethy for a medical opinion. Getting up, for this purpose, an ordinary conversation in a private company, he insinuated his case to the physician, as that of an imaginary individual.

"'We will suppose,' said the miser, 'that his symptoms are such and such; now, doctor, what would *you* have directed him to take?'

"'Take!' said Abernethy, 'why, take *advice*, to be sure.'"

"But," said the Prefect, a little discomposed, "I am *perfectly* willing to take advice, and to pay for it. I would *really* give fifty thousand francs, every *centime* of it, to any one who would aid me in the matter!"

"In that case," replied Dupin, opening a drawer, and producing a check-book, "you may as well fill me up a check for the amount mentioned. When you have signed it, I will hand you the letter."

I was astounded. The Prefect appeared absolutely thunder-stricken. For some minutes he remained speechless and motionless, looking incredulously at my friend with open mouth, and eyes that seemed starting from their sockets; then, apparently recovering himself in some measure, he seized a pen, and after several pauses and vacant stares, finally filled up and signed a check for fifty thousand francs, and handed it across the table to Dupin. The latter examined it carefully and deposited it in his pocketbook; then, unlocking an *escritoire*,[9] took thence a letter and gave it to the Prefect. This functionary grasped it in a perfect agony of joy, opened it with a trembling hand, cast a rapid glance at its contents, and then, scrambling and struggling to the door, rushed at length unceremoniously from the room and from the house, without having uttered a solitary syllable since Dupin had requested him to fill up the check.

When he had gone, my friend entered into some explanation.

----

8. **Abernethy:** Probably a reference to the famous English surgeon John Abernethy (1764–1831), who was known for being blunt and sometimes even rude to his patients.

9. *escritoire*: Writing desk (French).

"The Parisian police," he said, "are exceedingly able in their way. They are persevering, ingenious, cunning, and thoroughly versed in the knowledge which their duties seem chiefly to demand. Thus, when G— detailed to us his mode of searching the premises at the Hotel D—, I felt entire confidence in his having made a satisfactory investigation – so far as his labours extended."

"So far as his labours extended?" said I.

"Yes," said Dupin. "The measures adopted were not only the best of their kind, but carried out to absolute perfection. Had the letter been deposited within the range of their search, these fellows would, beyond a question, have found it."

I merely laughed – but he seemed quite serious in all that he said.

"The measures, then," he continued, "were good in their kind, and well executed; their defect lay in their being inapplicable to the case, and to the man. A certain set of highly ingenious resources are, with the Prefect, a sort of Procrustean bed,[10] to which he forcibly adapts his designs. But he perpetually errs by being too deep or too shallow, for the matter in hand; and many a schoolboy is a better reasoner than he. I knew one about eight years of age, whose success at guessing in the game of 'even and odd' attracted universal admiration. This game is simple, and is played with marbles. One player holds in his hand a number of these toys, and demands of another whether that number is even or odd. If the guess is right, the guesser wins one; if wrong, he loses one. The boy to whom I allude won all the marbles of the school. Of course he had some principle of guessing; and this lay in mere observation and admeasurement of the astuteness of his opponents. For example, an arrant simpleton is his opponent, and, holding up his closed hand, asks, 'are they even or odd?' Our schoolboy replies, 'odd,' and loses; but upon the second trial he wins, for he then says to himself, 'the simpleton had them even upon the first trial, and his amount of cunning is just sufficient to make him have them odd upon the second; I will therefore guess odd;' – he guesses odd, and wins. Now, with a simpleton a degree above the first, he would have reasoned thus: 'this fellow finds that in the first instance I guessed odd, and, in the second, he will propose to himself, upon the first impulse, a simple variation from even to odd, as did the first simpleton; but then a second thought will suggest that this is too simple a variation, and finally he will decide upon putting it even as before. I will therefore guess even;' – he guesses even, and wins. Now this mode of reasoning in the schoolboy, whom his fellows termed 'lucky,' – what, in its last analysis, is it?"

"It is merely," I said, "an identification of the reasoner's intellect with that of his opponent."

"It is," said Dupin; "and, upon inquiring of the boy by what means he effected the *thorough* identification in which his success consisted, I received answer as follows: 'When I wish to find out how wise, or how stupid, or how good, or how wicked is any one, or what are his thoughts at the moment, I fashion the expression of my face, as accurately as possible, in accordance with the expression of his, and then wait to see what thoughts or sentiments arise in my mind or heart, as if to match or correspond with the expression.'

---

10. **Procrustean bed**: In Greek mythology, Procrustes was a robber who forced travelers to lie on a bed and either cut off parts of their limbs or stretched them to fit; *procrustean* means the enforcement of conformity by arbitrary means and without regard for natural variation.

This response of the schoolboy lies at the bottom of all the spurious profundity which has been attributed to Rochefoucault, to La Bougive, to Machiavelli, and to Campanella."[11]

"And the identification," I said, "of the reasoner's intellect with that of his opponent, depends, if I understand you aright, upon the accuracy with which the opponent's intellect is admeasured."

"For its practical value it depends upon this," replied Dupin; "and the Prefect and his cohort fail so frequently, first, by default of this identification, and, secondly, by ill-admeasurement, or rather through non-admeasurement, of the intellect with which they are engaged. They consider only their *own* ideas of ingenuity; and, in searching for any thing hidden, advert only to the modes in which *they* would have hidden it. They are right in this much — that their own ingenuity is a faithful representative of that of *the mass*; but when the cunning of the individual felon is diverse in character from their own, the felon foils them, of course. This always happens when it is above their own, and very usually when it is below. They have no variation of principle in their investigations; at best, when urged by some unusual emergency — by some extraordinary reward — they extend or exaggerate their old modes of *practice*, without touching their principles. What, for example, in this case of D——, has been done to vary the principle of action? What is all this boring, and probing, and sounding, and scrutinizing with the microscope, and dividing the surface of the building into registered square inches — what is it all but an exaggeration *of the application* of the one principle or set of principles of search, which are based upon the one set of notions regarding human ingenuity, to which the Prefect, in the long routine of his duty, has been accustomed? Do you not see he has taken it for granted that *all* men proceed to conceal a letter, — not exactly in a gimlet-hole bored in a chair-leg — but, at least, in *some* out-of-the-way hole or corner suggested by the same tenor of thought which would urge a man to secrete a letter in a gimlet-hole bored in a chair-leg? And do you not see also, that such *recherches*[12] nooks for concealment are adapted only for ordinary occasions, and would be adopted only by ordinary intellects; for, in all cases of concealment, a disposal of the article concealed — a disposal of it in this *recherché* manner, — is, in the very first instance, presumed and presumable; and thus its discovery depends, not at all upon the acumen, but altogether upon the mere care, patience, and determination of the seekers; and where the case is of importance — or, what amounts to the same thing in the policial eyes, when the reward is of magnitude, the qualities in question have *never* been known to fail. You will now understand what I meant in suggesting that, had the purloined letter been hidden any where within the limits of the Prefect's examination — in other words, had the principle of its concealment been comprehended within the principles of the Prefect — its discovery would have been a matter altogether beyond question. This

---

11. **Rochefoucault . . . Campanella:** Printer's errors in this passage may account for some misspellings. François La Rochefoucauld (1613-1680) was a French writer known for his epigrams and pithy sayings. La Bougive is probably Jean La Bruyére (1645-1696), a French writer of maxims and character sketches. Niccolò Machiavelli (1469-1527) was an Italian political writer, best known for *The Prince*, a treatise on the uses of power and the art of ruling. Tommaso Campanella (1568-1639) was an Italian philosopher.
12. *recherches*: Exotic or obscure (French).

functionary, however, has been thoroughly mystified; and the remote source of his defeat lies in the supposition that the Minister is a fool, because he has acquired renown as a poet. All fools are poets; this the Prefect *feels*; and he is merely guilty of a *non distributio medii*[13] in thence inferring that all poets are fools."

"But is this really the poet?" I asked. "There are two brothers, I know; and both have attained reputation in letters. The Minister I believe has written learnedly on the Differential Calculus. He is a mathematician, and no poet."

"You are mistaken; I know him well; he is both. As poet *and* mathematician, he would reason well; as poet, profoundly; as mere mathematician, he could not have reasoned at all, and thus would have been at the mercy of the Prefect."

"You surprise me," I said, "by these opinions, which have been contradicted by the voice of the world. You do not mean to set at naught the well-digested idea of centuries. The mathematical reason has been long regarded as *the* reason *par excellence*."

"'Il y a à parièr,' replied Dupin, quoting from Chamfort, 'que toute idée publique, toute convention reçue, est une sottise, car elle a convenue au plus grand nombre.'[14] The mathematicians, I grant you, have done their best to promulgate the popular error to which you allude, and which is none the less an error for its promulgation as truth. With an art worthy a better cause, for example, they have insinuated the term 'analysis' into application to algebra. The French are the originators of this particular deception; but if a term is of any importance — if words derive any value from applicability — then 'analysis' conveys 'algebra' about as much as, in Latin '*ambitus*' implies 'ambition,' '*religio*' 'religion,' or '*homines honesti*,' a set of *honourable* men."

"You have a quarrel on hand, I see," said I, "with some of the algebraists of Paris; but proceed."

"I dispute the availability, and thus the value, of that reason which is cultivated in any especial form other than the abstractly logical. I dispute, in particular, the reason educed by mathematical study. The mathematics are the science of form and quantity; mathematical reasoning is merely logic applied to observation upon form and quantity. The great error lies in supposing that even the truths of what is called *pure* algebra, are abstract or general truths. And this error is so egregious that I am confounded at the universality with which it has been received. Mathematical axioms are *not* axioms of general truth. What is true of *relation* — of form and quantity — is often grossly false in regard to morals, for example. In this latter science it is very usually *un*true that the aggregated parts are equal to the whole. In chemistry also the axiom fails. In the consideration of motive it fails; for two motives, each of a given value, have not, necessarily, a value when united, equal to the sum of their values apart. There are numerous other mathematical truths which are only truths within the limits of *relation*. But the mathematician argues, from his *finite truths*, through habit, as if they were

---

13. *non distributio medii*: The undistributed middle (Latin) refers to a fallacy in formal logic in which the two premises of a syllogism do not justify the conclusion.
14. 'Il y a . . . nombre': From a maxim of the French writer Sébastien Roch Nicolas Chamfort (1741–1794): "The odds are that every common notion, every accepted convention, is nonsense, precisely because it has suited itself to the majority."

of an absolutely general applicability – as the world indeed imagines them to be. Bryant,[15] in his very learned 'Mythology,' mentions an analogous source of error, when he says that 'although the Pagan fables are not believed, yet we forget ourselves continually, and make inferences from them as existing realities.' With the algebraist, however, who are Pagans themselves, the 'Pagan fables' *are* believed, and the inferences are made, not so much through lapse of memory, as through an unaccountable addling of the brains. In short, I never yet encountered the mere mathematician who could be trusted out of equal roots, or one who did not clandestinely hold it as a point of his faith that $x^2 + px$ was absolutely and unconditionally equal to q. Say to one of these gentlemen, by way of experiment, if you please, that you believe occasions may occur where $x^2 + px$ is *not* altogether equal to q, and, having made him understand what you mean, get out of his reach as speedily as convenient, for, beyond doubt, he will endeavour to knock you down.

"I mean to say," continued Dupin, while I merely laughed at his last observations, "that if the Minister had been no more than a mathematician, the Prefect would have been under no necessity of giving me this check. Had he been no more than a poet, I think it probable that he would have foiled us all. I knew him, however, as both mathematician and poet, and my measures were adapted to his capacity, with reference to the circumstances by which he was surrounded. I knew him as a courtier, too, and as a bold *intriguant*.[16] Such a man, I considered, could not fail to be aware of the ordinary policial modes of action. He could not have failed to anticipate – and events have proved that he did not fail to anticipate – the waylayings to which he was subjected. He must have foreseen, I reflected, the secret investigations of his premises. His frequent absences from home at night, which were hailed by the Prefect as certain aids to his success, I regarded only as *ruses*, to afford opportunity for thorough search to the police, and thus the sooner to impress them with the conviction to which G—, in fact, did finally arrive – the conviction that the letter was not upon the premises. I felt, also, that the whole train of thought, which I was at some pains in detailing to you just now, concerning the invariable principle of policial action in searches for articles concealed – I felt that this whole train of thought would necessarily pass through the mind of the Minister. It would imperatively lead him to despise all the ordinary *nooks* of concealment. *He* could not, I reflected, be so weak as not to see that the most intricate and remote recess of his hotel would be as open as his commonest closets to the eyes, to the probes, to the gimlets, and to the microscopes of the Prefect. I saw, in fine, that he would be driven, as a matter of course, to *simplicity*, if not deliberately induced to it as a matter of choice. You will remember, perhaps, how desperately the Prefect laughed when I suggested, upon our first interview, that it was just possible this mystery troubled him so much on account of its being so *very* self-evident."

"Yes," said I, "I remember his merriment well. I really thought he would have fallen into convulsions."

---

15. **Bryant**: Jacob Bryant (1715–1804), English author of *A New System; or, An Analysis of Ancient Mythology* (1774).
16. **intriguant**: Usually *intrigant*, a person who engages in intrigue (French).

"The material world," continued Dupin, "abounds with very strict analogies to the immaterial; and thus some colour of truth has been given to the rhetorical dogma, that metaphor, or simile, may be made to strengthen an argument, as well as to embellish a description. The principle of the *vis inertiae*,[17] for example, with the amount of *momentum* proportionate with it and consequent upon it, seems to be identical in physics and metaphysics. It is not more true in the former, that a large body is with more difficulty set in motion than a smaller one, and that its subsequent *impetus* is commensurate with this difficulty, than it is, in the latter, that intellects of the vaster capacity, while more forcible, more constant, and more eventful in their movements than those of inferior grade, are yet the less readily moved, and more embarrassed and full of hesitation in the first few steps of their progress. Again: have you ever noticed which of the street signs, over the shop-doors, are the most attractive of attention?"

"I have never given the matter a thought," I said.

"There is a game of puzzles," he resumed, "which is played upon a map. One party playing requires another to find a given word — the name of town, river, state, or empire — any word, in short, upon the motley and perplexed surface of the chart. A novice in the game generally seeks to embarrass his opponents by giving them the most minutely lettered names; but the adept selects such words as stretch, in large characters, from one end of the chart to the other. These, like the over-largely lettered signs and placards of the street, escape observation by dint of being excessively obvious; and here the physical oversight is precisely analogous with the moral inapprehension by which the intellect suffers to pass unnoticed those considerations which are too obtrusively and too palpably self-evident. But this is a point, it appears, somewhat above or beneath the understanding of the Prefect. He never once thought it probable, or possible, that the Minister had deposited the letter immediately beneath the nose of the whole world, by way of best preventing any portion of that world from perceiving it.

"But the more I reflected upon the daring, dashing, and discriminating ingenuity of D—; upon the fact that the document must always have been *at hand*, if he intended to use it to good purpose; and upon the decisive evidence, obtained by the Prefect, that it was not hidden within the limits of that dignitary's ordinary search — the more satisfied I became that, to conceal this letter, the Minister had resorted to the comprehensive and sagacious expedient of not attempting to conceal it at all.

"Full of these ideas, I prepared myself with a pair of green spectacles, and called one fine morning, quite by accident, at the ministerial hotel. I found D— at home, yawning, lounging, and dawdling as usual, and pretending to be in the last extremity of *ennui*.[18] He is, perhaps, the most really energetic human being now alive — but that is only when nobody sees him.

"To be even with him, I complained of my weak eyes, and lamented the necessity of the spectacles, under cover of which I cautiously and thoroughly surveyed the whole apartment, while seemingly intent only upon the conversation of my host.

---

17. *vis inertiae*: The power of inertia (Latin).
18. *ennui*: Boredom (French).

"I paid especial attention to a large writing-table near which he sat, and upon which lay confusedly, some miscellaneous letters and other papers, with one or two musical instruments and a few books. Here, however, after a long and very deliberate scrutiny, I saw nothing to excite particular suspicion.

"At length my eyes, in going the circuit of the room, fell upon a trumpery fillagree card-rack of pasteboard, that hung dangling by a dirty blue riband, from a little brass knob just beneath the middle of the mantel-piece. In this rack, which had three or four compartments, were five or six visiting-cards, and a solitary letter. This last was much soiled and crumpled. It was torn nearly in two, across the middle – as if a design, in the first instance, to tear it entirely up as worthless, had been altered, or stayed, in the second. It had a large black seal, bearing the D— cipher *very* conspicuously, and was addressed, in a diminutive female hand, to D—, the minister, himself. It was thrust carelessly, and even, as it seemed, contemptuously, into one of the uppermost divisions of the rack.

"No sooner had I glanced at this letter, than I concluded it to be that of which I was in search. To be sure, it was, to all appearance, radically different from the one of which the Prefect had read us so minute a description. Here the seal was large and black, with the D— cipher; there, it was small and red, with the ducal arms of the S— family. Here, the address, to the minister, was diminutive and feminine; there, the superscription, to a certain royal personage, was markedly bold and decided; the size alone formed a point of correspondence. But, then, the *radicalness* of these differences, which was excessive; the dirt, the soiled and torn condition of the paper, so inconsistent with the *true* methodical habits of D—, and so suggestive of a design to delude the beholder into an idea of the worthlessness of the document; these things, together with the hyperobtrusive situation of this document, full in the view of every visiter, and thus exactly in accordance with the conclusions to which I had previously arrived; these things, I say, were strongly corroborative of suspicion, in one who came with the intention to suspect.

"I protracted my visit as long as possible, and, while I maintained a most animated discussion with the minister, upon a topic which I knew well had never failed to interest and excite him, I kept my attention really riveted upon the letter. In this examination, I committed to memory its external appearance and arrangement in the rack; and also fell, at length, upon a discovery which set at rest whatever trivial doubt I might have entertained. In scrutinizing the edges of the paper, I observed them to be more *chafed* than seemed necessary. They presented the *broken* appearance which is manifested when a stiff paper, having been once folded and pressed with a folder, is refolded in a reversed direction, in the same creases or edges which had formed the original fold. This discovery was sufficient. It was clear to me that the letter had been turned, as a glove, inside out, re-directed, and re-sealed. I bade the minister good morning, and took my departure at once, leaving a gold snuff-box upon the table.

"The next morning I called for the snuff-box, when we resumed, quite eagerly, the conversation of the preceding day. While thus engaged, however, a loud report, as if of a pistol, was heard immediately beneath the windows of the hotel, and was succeeded by a series of fearful screams, and the shoutings of a terrified mob. D— rushed to a case-ment, threw it open, and looked out. In the meantime, I stepped to the card-rack, took the letter, put it in my pocket, and replaced it by a *fac-simile*, which I had carefully prepared at my lodgings – imitating the D— cipher, very readily, by means of a seal formed of bread.

"The disturbance in the street had been occasioned by the frantic behaviour of a man with a musket. He had fired it among a crowd of women and children. It proved, however, to have been without ball, and the fellow was suffered to go his way as a lunatic or a drunkard. When he had gone, D— came from the window, whither I had followed him immediately upon securing the object in view. Soon afterwards I bade him farewell. The pretended lunatic was a man in my own pay."

"But what purpose had you," I asked, "in replacing the letter by a *fac-simile?* Would it not have been better, at the first visit, to have seized it openly, and departed?"

"D—," replied Dupin, "is a desperate man, and a man of nerve. His hotel, too, is not without attendants devoted to his interests. Had I made the wild attempt you suggest, I should never have left the ministerial presence alive. The good people of Paris would have heard of me no more. But I had an object apart from these considerations. You know my political prepossessions. In this matter, I act as a partisan of the lady concerned. For eighteen months the minister has had her in his power. She has now him in hers – since, being unaware that the letter is not in his possession, he will proceed with his exactions as if it was. Thus will he inevitably commit himself, at once, to his political destruction. His downfall, too, will not be more precipitate than awkward. It is all very well to talk about the *facilis descensus Averni*;[19] but in all kinds of climbing, as Catalini[20] said of singing, it is far more easy to get up than to come down. In the present instance I have no sympathy – at least no pity – for him who descends. He is that *monstrum horrendum*,[21] an unprincipled man of genius. I confess, however, that I should like very well to know the precise character of his thoughts, when, being defied by her whom the Prefect terms 'a certain personage,' he is reduced to opening the letter which I left for him in the card-rack."

"How? did you put any thing particular in it?"

"Why – it did not seem altogether right to leave the interior blank – that would have been insulting. To be sure, D—, at Vienna once, did me an evil turn, which I told him, quite good-humouredly, that I should remember. So, as I knew he would feel some curiosity in regard to the identity of the person who had outwitted him, I thought it a pity not to give him a clue. He is well acquainted with my MS., and I just copied into the middle of the blank sheet the words,

> "'—Un dessein si funeste,
> S'il n'est digne d'Atrée, est digne de Thyeste.'

They are to be found in Crébillon's 'Atrée.'"[22]

[1845]

---

19. *facilis descensus Averni*: From the *Aeneid* by the Roman poet Virgil (70–19 BCE), meaning the descent to hell is easy (Latin).

20. **Catalini**: Probably a printer's error for Angelica Catalani (1780–1849), an Italian singer.

21. *monstrum horrendum*: Frightful monster (Latin). Virgil's name for Polyphemus, a one-eyed, man-eating giant.

22. "**Un dessein** . . . 'Atrée'": "A design so deadly, if not worthy of Atreus is worthy of Thyestes," from *Atrée et Thyeste* by Prosper Jolyot de Crébillon (1674–1762). In the tragedy, Thyestes seduces Atreus's wife and, in revenge, Atreus kills Thyestes's sons and serves them to him at a dinner.

Reading Poe's Poetry.   Although he is now best known for his short stories, Poe initially set out to become a poet, publishing three collections of verse between 1827 and 1831. Finding that he could not earn a living as a poet, Poe later supported himself by editing and writing for periodicals, in which most of his prose pieces appeared. It was not until 1845, when he published "The Raven," that Poe finally gained the fame as a poet for which he had so long hungered. On the strength of that poem, which caused a sensation, Poe immediately published *The Raven and Other Poems* (1845). But he published only a few more poems before his death in 1849. Like his poetry, Poe's poetic theory was at odds with dominant conceptions of the role of poetry during the period. Poe rejected didactic poetry, insisting that poetry should appeal strictly to a sense of beauty, inducing in the reader an almost hypnotic state in which mood triumphed over thought. The texts of the first three of the following poems are taken from the first edition of *The Raven and Other Poems* (1845); the text of his final poem, "Annabel Lee," is taken from the *Southern Literary Messenger*, where it appeared shortly after Poe's death in 1849.

SONNET — TO SCIENCE[1]

SCIENCE! true daughter of Old Time thou art!
   Who alterest all things with thy peering eyes.
Why preyest thou thus upon the poet's heart,
   Vulture, whose wings are dull realities?
How should he love thee? or how deem thee wise,   5
   Who wouldst not leave him in his wandering
To seek for treasure in the jewelled skies,
   Albeit he soared with an undaunted wing?
Hast thou not dragged Diana[2] from her car?
   And driven the Hamadryad[3] from the wood   10
To seek a shelter in some happier star?
   Hast thou not torn the Naiad[4] from her flood,
The Elfin from the green grass, and from me
   The summer dream beneath the tamarind tree?

                                    [1827, 1845]

---

1. **Sonnet—to Science:** In the first printing in *Al Aaraaf* (1829), the poem was untitled. Poe later reprinted it several times, sometimes as "Sonnet" and finally in 1845 as "Sonnet — to Science," the title by which it is widely known today.
2. **Diana:** Roman goddess of the moon, her "car."
3. **Hamadryad:** Nymphs of Roman and Greek mythology who lived in trees.
4. **Naiad:** Water nymphs of Greek mythology who lived in freshwater lakes, rivers, springs, and fountains.

TO HELEN

HELEN, thy beauty is to me
　　Like those Nicéan barks[1] of yore,
That gently, o'er a perfumed sea,
　　The weary, way-worn wanderer bore
To his own native shore.   5

On desperate seas long wont to roam.
　　Thy hyacinth hair,[2] thy classic face,
Thy Naiad[3] airs have brought me home
　　To the glory that was Greece,
And the grandeur that was Rome.   10

Lo! in yon brilliant window-niche
　　How statue-like I see thee stand,
　　The agate lamp within thy hand!
Ah, Psyche, from the regions which
　　Are Holy-Land!   15

[1831, 1845]

---

1. **Nicéan barks:** Ships from the ancient Greek city of Nicea.
2. **hyacinth hair:** The Greek god Apollo created the hyacinth, a flower, after the death of a beautiful young man, Hyacinthus.
3. **Naiad:** Water nymphs of Greek mythology who lived in freshwater lakes, rivers, springs, and fountains.

THE RAVEN[1]

ONCE upon a midnight dreary, while I pondered, weak and weary,
Over many a quaint and curious volume of forgotten lore,
While I nodded, nearly napping, suddenly there came a tapping,
As of some one gently rapping, rapping at my chamber door.
" 'Tis some visiter," I muttered, "tapping at my chamber door —   5
　　　　　　　　　Only this, and nothing more."

Ah, distinctly I remember it was in the bleak December,
And each separate dying ember wrought its ghost upon the floor.
Eagerly I wished the morrow; — vainly I had sought to borrow
From my books surcease of sorrow — sorrow for the lost Lenore —   10
For the rare and radiant maiden whom the angels name Lenore —
　　　　　　　　　Nameless here for evermore.

---

1. **The Raven:** The poem was first published anonymously in the *American Review*, where it was identified as "By — Quarles." In a long and laudatory note preceding the poem, the editor emphasized the ways in which it illustrated the alliterative, rhythmical, and metrical resources of the English language.

And the silken sad uncertain rustling of each purple curtain
Thrilled me — filled me with fantastic terrors never felt before;
So that now, to still the beating of my heart, I stood repeating   15
"'Tis some visiter entreating entrance at my chamber door —
Some late visiter entreating entrance at my chamber door; —
      This it is, and nothing more."

Presently my soul grew stronger; hesitating then no longer,
"Sir," said I, "or Madam, truly your forgiveness I implore;   20
But the fact is I was napping, and so gently you came rapping,
And so faintly you came tapping, tapping at my chamber door,
That I scarce was sure I heard you" — here I opened wide the door; ——
      Darkness there, and nothing more.

Deep into that darkness peering, long I stood there wondering, fearing,   25
Doubting, dreaming dreams no mortal ever dared to dream before;
But the silence was unbroken, and the darkness gave no token,
And the only word there spoken was the whispered word, "Lenore!"
This I whispered, and an echo murmured back the word, "Lenore!"
      Merely this, and nothing more.   30

Back into the chamber turning, all my soul within me burning,
Soon I heard again a tapping somewhat louder than before.
"Surely," said I, "surely that is something at my window lattice;
Let me see, then, what thereat is, and this mystery explore —
Let my heart be still a moment and this mystery explore; —   35
      'Tis the wind and nothing more!"

Open here I flung the shutter, when, with many a flirt and flutter,
In there stepped a stately raven of the saintly days of yore;
Not the least obeisance made he; not an instant stopped or stayed he;
But, with mien of lord or lady, perched above my chamber door —   40
Perched upon a bust of Pallas[2] just above my chamber door —
      Perched, and sat, and nothing more.

Then this ebony bird beguiling my sad fancy into smiling,
By the grave and stern decorum of the countenance it wore,
"Though thy crest be shorn and shaven, thou," I said, "art sure no craven,   45
Ghastly grim and ancient raven wandering from the Nightly shore —
Tell me what thy lordly name is on the Night's Plutonian shore!"[3]
      Quoth the raven, "Nevermore."

---

2. **bust of Pallas:** Pallas Athena, the Greek goddess of wisdom and the arts.
3. **Night's Plutonian shore:** In Greek mythology, Pluto (or Hades) was the god of the underworld, his dark kingdom.

Much I marvelled this ungainly fowl to hear discourse so plainly,
Though its answer little meaning — little relevancy bore;   50
For we cannot help agreeing that no living human being
Ever yet was blessed with seeing bird above his chamber door —
Bird or beast upon the sculptured bust above his chamber door,
                                    With such name as "Nevermore."

But the raven, sitting lonely on the placid bust, spoke only   55
That one word, as if his soul in that one word he did outpour.
Nothing farther then he uttered — not a feather then he fluttered —
Till I scarcely more than muttered "Other friends have flown before —
On the morrow *he* will leave me, as my hopes have flown before."
                                    Then the bird said "Nevermore."   60

Startled at the stillness broken by reply so aptly spoken,
"Doubtless," said I, "what it utters is its only stock and store
Caught from some unhappy master whom unmerciful Disaster
Followed fast and followed faster till his songs one burden bore —
Till the dirges of his Hope that melancholy burden bore   65
                                    Of 'Never — nevermore.'"

But the raven still beguiling all my sad soul into smiling,
Straight I wheeled a cushioned seat in front of bird, and bust and door;
Then, upon the velvet sinking, I betook myself to linking
Fancy unto fancy, thinking what this ominous bird of yore —   70
What this grim, ungainly, ghastly, gaunt, and ominous bird of yore
                                    Meant in croaking "Nevermore."

This I sat engaged in guessing, but no syllable expressing
To the fowl whose fiery eyes now burned into my bosom's core;
This and more I sat divining, with my head at ease reclining   75
On the cushion's velvet lining that the lamplight gloated o'er,
But whose velvet violet lining with the lamplight gloating o'er.
                                    She shall press, ah, nevermore!

Then, methought, the air grew denser, perfumed from an unseen censer
Swung by angels whose faint foot-falls tinkled on the tufted floor.   80
"Wretch," I cried, "thy God hath lent thee — by these angels he hath sent thee
Respite — respite and nepenthe[4] from thy memories of Lenore!
Quaff, oh quaff this kind nepenthe and forget this lost Lenore!"
                                    Quoth the raven, "Nevermore."

"Prophet!" said I, "thing of evil! — prophet still, if bird or devil! —   85
Whether Tempter sent, or whether tempest tossed thee here ashore,

---

4. **nepenthe:** Ancient drug used to ease pain or grief.

Desolate yet all undaunted, on this desert land enchanted —
On this home by Horror haunted — tell me truly, I implore —
Is there — *is* there balm in Gilead?[5] — tell me — tell me, I implore!"

        Quoth the raven, "Nevermore."   90

"Prophet!" said I, "thing of evil — prophet still, if bird or devil!
By that Heaven that bends above us — by that God we both adore —
Tell this soul with sorrow laden if, within the distant Aidenn,[6]
It shall clasp a sainted maiden whom the angels name Lenore —
Clasp a rare and radiant maiden whom the angels name Lenore."   95

        Quoth the raven, "Nevermore."

"Be that word our sign of parting, bird or fiend!" I shrieked, upstarting —
"Get thee back into the tempest and the Night's Plutonian shore!
Leave no black plume as a token of that lie thy soul hath spoken!
Leave my loneliness unbroken — quit the bust above my door!   100
Take thy beak from out my heart, and take thy form from off my door!"

        Quoth the raven, "Nevermore."

And the raven, never flitting, still is sitting, still is sitting
On the pallid bust of Pallas just above my chamber door;
And his eyes have all the seeming of a demon's that is dreaming,   105
And the lamp-light o'er him streaming throws his shadow on the floor;
And my soul from out that shadow that lies floating on the floor

       Shall be lifted — nevermore!

           [1845]

---

5. **Gilead:** See Jeremiah 46:11: "Is there no balm in Gilead, no physician there?" The evergreens in Gilead, a mountainous region of Jordan, were thought to have medicinal powers.
6. **Aidenn:** Probably an alternative spelling of *Eden.*

ANNABEL LEE

It was many and many a year ago,
 In a kingdom by the sea,
That a maiden there lived whom you may know
 By the name of Annabel Lee; —
And this maiden she lived with no other thought   5
 Than to love and be loved by me.

She was a child and *I* was a child,
 In this kingdom by the sea,
But we loved with a love that was more than love —
 I and my Annabel Lee —   10

With a love that the wingéd seraphs of Heaven
   Coveted her and me.

And this was the reason that, long ago,
   In this kingdom by the sea,
A wind blew out of a cloud by night   15
   Chilling my Annabel Lee;
So that her high-born kinsmen came
   And bore her away from me,
To shut her up in a sepulchre
   In this kingdom by the sea.   20

The angels, not half so happy in Heaven,
   Went envying her and me;
Yes! that was the reason (as all men know,
   In this kingdom by the sea)
That the wind came out of the cloud, chilling   25
   And killing my Annabel Lee.

But our love it was stronger by far than the love
   Of those who were older than we —
   Of many far wiser than we —
And neither the angels in Heaven above   30
   Nor the demons down under the sea
Can ever dissever my soul from the soul
   Of the beautiful Annabel Lee: —

For the moon never beams without bringing me dreams
   Of the beautiful Annabel Lee;   35
And the stars never rise but I see the bright eyes
   Of the beautiful Annabel Lee;
And so, all the night-tide, I lie down by the side
Of my darling, my darling, my life and my bride
   In her sepulchre there by the sea —   40
   In her tomb by the side of the sea.

                                   [1849]

Fanny Fern
(Sara Payson Willis Parton)

[1811–1872]

Fanny Fern was born Sara Payson Willis on July 9, 1811, in Portland, Maine,
the daughter of Nathaniel and Hannah Parker Willis. Fern's family was
deeply involved in periodical publication. Her father founded the *Boston*

Recorder, the first religious newspaper in the United States, and the *Youth's Companion*, the first children's newspaper. Fern's older brother, the popular poet and writer Nathaniel P. Willis, was the influential editor of the *New York Mirror* and later the *Home Journal*. Educated at Catherine E. Beecher's Female Seminary in Hartford, Connecticut, Fern also proved to be adept at writing and occasionally published articles in the *Hartford Courant*. In 1837, she married Charles Harrington Eldredge, a cashier at a Boston bank. When Eldredge died of typhoid fever in 1846, Fern and her two young daughters were left nearly penniless. Receiving only limited support from her father and father-in-law, Fern tried unsuccessfully to find work as a teacher and then as a seamstress. In 1849, under pressure from her father, she married Samuel P. Farrington, a cruel and jealous man, whom Fern left after two years. Farrington obtained a divorce on the grounds of desertion in 1852, a drastic measure in the mid-nineteenth century.

Facing the censure of her relatives and determined to make a living for herself and her children, Fern decided to follow in the family tradition of journalism. After months of effort, she sold her first article to a popular family newspaper, the *Olive Branch*, where "The Model Husband" appeared on June 28, 1851. She was soon writing reviews and articles on a variety of domestic and social topics for both the *Olive Branch* and another family newspaper, the *True Flag*. By the fall of 1851, her work was appearing under the name of "Fanny Fern," which she took as her legal name. In September 1852, when she entered into an

Everybody buys Fern Leaves, big Ferns and little Ferns, and everybody reads, and everybody laughs and cries over it.
– Frederick Douglass

Sketch of Fanny Fern

This sketch of Fanny Fern reading was drawn by her daughter Ellen around 1860. The text at the base of the sketch reads: "*Sara Willis Parton –* copied from a 'picture that little Nellie drew' of her mother; described by her sister Grace as 'a very bad likeness – yet funnily like, too, in some respects.'"
(Sophia Smith Collection, Smith College.)

bedfordstmartins.com/
americanlit *for research*
links on Fern

agreement to write a weekly article for the *Musical World and Times*, she became the first weekly newspaper columnist in the United States. Her first collection of articles, *Fern Leaves from Fanny's Port-Folio*, was published in June 1853 and sold an astonishing 70,000 copies in the first year. *Little Ferns for Fanny's Little Friends*, a collection of essays for children, appeared later that year; and *Fern Leaves from Fanny's Port-Folio*, Second Series, appeared in 1854. Now a highly successful journalist, Fern moved to New York City. There, she wrote for a variety of prominent periodicals. Taking advantage of her growing fame, she also published a novel, *Ruth Hall* (1854), a thinly veiled account of her difficult early life. After reading the novel, Nathaniel Hawthorne declared, "The woman writes as if the devil was in her," an admiring reference to Fern's rejection of the social and stylistic conventions governing many works written by women during the period. Two other works of fiction followed: *Fanny Ford* (1855), a serialized novella, and *Rose Clarke* (1856).

By then, Fern was the best-paid writer, male or female, in the United States. On January 5, 1856, she married James Parton, a writer and biographer. In an act that was almost unheard of at the time, when a married woman had no legal right to her own earnings, the couple signed a prenuptial agreement stipulating that the income Fern made from her writing was her own. Fern had just signed a contract to write exclusively for the *New York Ledger*, where her first weekly column appeared on her wedding day. Some of her enormously popular columns, devoted to witty cultural commentary and sharp social criticism, were subsequently collected in *Fresh Leaves* (1857), *Folly as It Flies* (1868), *Ginger Snaps* (1870), and *Caper-Sauce* (1872). During almost seventeen years, Fern never missed a deadline for the *Ledger*, where her final weekly column appeared two days after her death from cancer on October 10, 1872.

Reading Fern's Early Journalism.   The following three articles first appeared in the *Olive Branch*, a popular family newspaper published in Boston. Short articles and stories printed in the newspaper were frequently read aloud by families gathered for evening amusement, and Fern developed a breezy, colloquial style designed to engage a broad audience. Her columns were often witty commentaries on marriage and the domestic lives of women. Fern was paid $2 for each of her articles, which were often reprinted without her knowledge or permission in other periodicals, since copyright laws did not prevent such "copying" of periodical writings. "Hints to Young Wives" appeared on February 14, 1852; "The Tear of a Wife" on August 28, 1852; and "The Sober Husband" on April 9, 1853. The texts, which were not given titles until they were collected for publication in books, are taken from their first printings in the *Olive Branch*.

HINTS TO YOUNG WIVES

Mr. Norris.[1] — Shouldn't I like to make a bon-fire of all the "Hints to Young Wives," "Married Woman's Friend," and throw in the authors after them? I have a little neighbor who believes all they tell her is gospel truth, and lives up to it. The minute she sees her husband coming up street, she makes for the door, as if she hadn't another minute to live, stands in the entry with her teeth chattering in her head till he gets all his coats and mufflers, and overshoes, and what-do-you-call-'ems off, then chases round (like a cat in a fit) after the boot-jack; warms his slippers and puts 'em on, and dislocates her wrist carving at table for fear it will tire him.

Poor little innocent fool! she imagines that's the way to preserve his affection. Preserve a fiddlestick! The consequence is, he's sick of the sight of her; snubs her when she asks him a question, and after he has eaten her good dinners takes himself off as soon as possible, bearing in mind the old proverb "that too much of a good thing is good for nothing." Now the truth is just this, and I wish all the women on earth had but one ear in common, so that I could put this little bit of gospel into it: — Just so long as a man isn't quite as sure as if he knew for certain, whether nothing on earth could ever disturb your affection for him, he is your humble servant, but the very second he finds out (or thinks he does) that he has possession of every inch of your heart, and no neutral territory — he will turn on his heel and march off whistling "Yankee Doodle!"[2]

Now it's no use to take your pocket handkerchief and go snivelling round the house with a pink nose and red eyes; not a bit of it! If you have made the interesting discovery that you were married for a sort of upper servant or housekeeper, just *fill that place and no other*, keep your temper, keep all his strings and buttons and straps on; and then keep him at a distance as a housekeeper should — "them's my sentiments!" I have seen one or two men in my life who could bear to be loved (as a woman with a soul knows how,) without being spoiled by it, or converted into a tyrant — but they are rare birds, and should be caught, stuffed and handed to Barnum![3] Now as the ministers say, "I'll close with an interesting little incident that came under my observation."

Mr. Fern[4] came home one day when I had such a crucifying headache that I couldn't have told whether I was married or single, and threw an old coat into my lap to mend. Well, I tied a wet bandage over my forehead, "left all flying," and sat down to it — he might as well have asked me to make a *new* one; however I new lined the sleeves, mended all the button-holes, sewed on new buttons down the front, and all over the coat tails — when finally it occurred to me (I believe it was a suggestion of Satan,) that the *pocket* might need mending; so I turned it inside out, and *what do you think I found? A love-letter from him to my dress-maker!!* I dropped the coat, I dropped the work-basket, I

---

1. **Mr. Norris:** Unidentified; Fern often began her articles by responding to an article or story she had read in a newspaper.
2. **"Yankee Doodle!":** A popular patriotic ditty that begins "Yankee Doodle went to town."
3. **Barnum:** P. T. Barnum (1810–1891), the American promoter and showman who displayed natural and human curiosities in his American Museum in New York City.
4. **Mr. Fern:** Fern was not married at this time in her life.

dropped the buttons, I dropped the baby (it was a *female*, and I thought it just as well to put her out of future misery) and then I hopped up into a chair front of the looking-glass, and remarked to the young woman I saw there, "*F-a-n-n-y F-e-r-n! if you – are – ever – such – a – confounded – fool – again*" – *and I wasn't!!*

[1852]

The Tear of a Wife

"The tear of a loving girl is like a dew drop on a rose; but on the cheek of a *wife*, is a drop of poison to her husband."[1]

It's "an ill wind that blows *nobody* any good!" Papas will be happy to hear that twenty-five dollar pocket-handkerchiefs can be dispensed with *now*, in the bridal *trousseau*.[2] Their "occupation's gone"! Matrimonial tears "are poison." There's no knowing what you'll do, girls, with that escape valve shut off; but that's no more to the point than – whether you have anything to smile at or not; one thing is settled – *you must not cry!* Never mind back-aches, and sideaches, and headaches, and dropsical complaints, and smoky chimneys, and old coats, and young babies! *Smile! It flatters your husband.* He wants to be CONSIDERED the source of your happiness, whether he was baptized *Nero* or *Moses!* Your mind *never* being supposed to be occupied with any other subject than himself, of course a tear is a tacit reproach. Besides, you miserable little whimperer, what have you to cry for? *A-i-n-t y-o-u m-a-r-r-i-e-d?* Isn't that the *summum bonum*,[3] – the *height* of feminine ambition? You *can't* get beyond *that!!* It's the *jumping-off place!* You've ARRIV! – got to the end of your journey! Stage puts up *there!* You've nothing to do but retire on your laurels, and spend the rest of your life endeavoring to be thankful that you are *Mrs.* John Smith! "*Smile!*" *you simpleton!*

[1852]

---

1. **"The tear . . . husband":** The quotation is unidentified, but the sentiment was a common one in the nineteenth century.
2. *trousseau:* Clothing for a bride (French).
3. *summum bonum:* The greatest or supreme good (Latin).

The Sober Husband

"If your husband looks grave, let him alone; don't disturb or annoy him."

Oh, pshaw! when I'm married, the soberer my husband looked, the more fun I'd rattle about his ears. "*Don't disturb him!*" I guess so! I'd salt his coffee – and pepper his tea – and sugar his beefsteak – and tread on his toes – and hide his newspaper – and sew up his pockets – and put pins in his slippers – and dip his cigars in water – and I wouldn't stop for the Great Mogul,[1] till I had shortened his long face to my liking.

---

1. **Great Mogul:** A common expression meaning a very important person, derived from the powerful emperors of the Mogul Empire of south Asia (including most of present-day India), who ruled from 1527 to 1857.

Certainly, he'd "get vexed," there wouldn't be any fun in teasing him if he didn't, and that would give his melancholy blood a good, healthful start, and his eyes would snap and sparkle, and he'd say, "Fanny, WILL you be quiet or not?" and I should laugh, and pull his whiskers, and say, decidedly, "*Not!*" and then I should tell him he hadn't the slightest idea how handsome he looked when he was vexed, and then he would pretend not to hear the compliment — but would pull up his dickey, and take a sly peep in the glass (for all that!) and then he'd begin to grow amiable, and get off his stilts, and be just as agreeable all the rest of the evening *as if he wasn't my husband*, and all because I didn't follow that stupid bit of advice "to let him alone." Just as if *I* didn't know! Just imagine ME, Fanny, sitting down on a cricket[2] in the corner, with my forefinger in my mouth, looking out the sides of my eyes, and waiting till that man got ready to speak to me! You can see at once it would be — be — . Well, the amount of it is, *I shouldn't do it!*

[1853]

---

2. **sitting down on a cricket:** A cricket was a low, wooden footstool.

Reading Fern's Writings for the *New York Ledger*. Beginning with her first column on January 5, 1856, Fern wrote exclusively for the *New York Ledger*, a weekly edited by Robert Bonner. Although the family story-paper was designed to provide entertainment within the home, Bonner had no interest in dull, conventional material. Determined to make the *Ledger* a first-rate literary periodical, he set about hiring the best writers he could sign, including Lydia Sigourney, John Greenleaf Whittier, Henry Wadsworth Longfellow, and Louisa May Alcott. Unlike many other editors of the day, who paid little or nothing for irregular contributions from both known and unknown writers, Bonner developed a system of exclusive contracts for regular contributors, who earned fixed and generous salaries. When "Fanny Fern" was becoming a household name for her articles in several competing periodicals, Bonner secured such a contract with her. At the end of 1855, when Bonner proudly announced that Fern would become an exclusive writer for the *Ledger*, its circulation stood at 100,000; during the following year, it grew to 180,000. By 1860, circulation topped 400,000, in large part as a result of the powerful appeal of Fern's weekly columns. The following columns indicate some of Fern's characteristic concerns, especially the condition and rights of women, which she variously addressed in "Male Criticism on Ladies' Books" (May 23, 1857); "A Law More Nice Than Just" (July 10, 1858); "The 'Coming' Woman" (February 12, 1859); and "Independence" (July 30, 1859). The texts are taken from the first printings of the columns in the *New York Ledger*.

MALE CRITICISM ON LADIES' BOOKS

"Courtship and marriage, servants and children, these are the great objects of a woman's thoughts, and they necessarily form the staple topics of their writing and their conversation. We have no right to expect anything else in a woman's book." — N. Y. Times[1]

Is it in feminine novels *only* that courtship, marriage, servants, and children are the staple? Is not this true of all novels? — of Dickens, of Thackeray, of Bulwer[2] and a host of others? Is it peculiar to feminine pens, most astute and liberal of critics? Would a novel be a novel if it did not treat of courtship and marriage? and if it could be so recognized, would it find readers? When I see such a narrow, snarling criticism as the above, I always say to myself, the writer is some unhappy man, who has come up without the refining influence of mother, or sister, or reputable female friends; who has divided his migratory life between boarding-houses, restaurants, and the outskirts of editorial sanctums; and who knows as much about reviewing a woman's book, as I do about navigating a ship, or engineering an omnibus from the South Ferry, through Broadway, to Union Park.[3] I think I see him writing that paragraph in fit of spleen — of *male* spleen — in his small boarding-house upper chamber, by the cheerful light of a solitary candle, flickering alternately on cobwebbed walls, dusty wash-stand, begrimed bowl and pitcher, refuse cigar stumps, boot-jacks, old hats, buttonless coats, muddy trousers, and all the wretched accompaniments of solitary, selfish male existence, not to speak of his own puckered, unkissable face; perhaps, in addition, his boots hurt, his cravat-bow persists in slipping under his ear for want of a pin, and a wife to pin it (poor wretch!) or he has been refused by some pretty girl, as he deserved to be (narrow-minded old vinegar-cruet!) or snubbed by some lady authoress; or, more trying than all to the male constitution, has had a weak cup of coffee for that morning's breakfast.

But seriously — we have had quite enough of this shallow criticism (?) on lady-books. Whether the book which called forth the remark above quoted, was a good book or a bad one, I know not: I should be inclined to think the *former* from the dispraise of such a pen. Whether ladies can write novels or not, is a question I do not intend to discuss; but that some of them have no difficulty in finding either publishers or readers is a matter of history; and that gentlemen often write over feminine signatures would seem also to argue that feminine literature is, after all, in good odor with the reading public. Granting that lady-novels are not all that they should be — is such shallow, unfair, wholesale, sneering criticism (?) the way to reform them? Would it not be better and more manly to point out a better way kindly, justly, *and, above all, respectfully?* or — what would be a much harder task for such critics — write a better book!

[1857]

---

1. **N. Y. Times:** The quotation is from "Books of the Week," a regular book-review column in the *New York Times*, from April 22, 1857.
2. **Dickens . . . Bulwer:** Courtship, marriage, and domestic life were staples of nineteenth-century fiction, including the works of the popular British novelists Charles Dickens (1812–1870), William Makepeace Thackeray (1811–1863), and Edward Bulwer-Lytton (1803–1873).
3. **South Ferry . . . Union Park:** That is, from the southern tip of Manhattan to Union Square Park, at the intersection of Broadway and what is now Fourth Avenue.

A LAW MORE NICE THAN JUST

Here I have been sitting twiddling the morning paper between my fingers this half hour, reflecting upon the following paragraph in it: "Emma Wilson was arrested yesterday for wearing man's apparel."[1] Now, why this should be an actionable offense is past my finding out, or where's the harm in it, I am as much at a loss to see. Think of the old maids (and weep) who have to stay at home evening after evening, when, if they provided themselves with a coat, pants and hat, they might go abroad, instead of sitting there with their noses flattened against the window-pane, looking vainly for "the Coming Man." Think of the married women who stay at home after their day's toil is done, waiting wearily for their thoughtless, truant husbands, when they might be taking the much needed independent walk in trousers, which custom forbids to petticoats. And this, I fancy, may be the secret of this famous law — who knows? It *wouldn't* be pleasant for some of them to be surprised by a touch on the shoulder from some dapper young fellow, whose familiar treble voice belied his corduroys. That's it, now. What a fool I was not to think of it — not to remember that men who make the laws, make them to meet all these little emergencies.

Everybody knows what an everlasting drizzle of rain we have had lately, but nobody but a woman, and a woman who lives on fresh air and out-door exercise, knows the thraldom of taking her daily walk through a three weeks' rain, with skirts to hold up, and umbrella to hold down, and puddles to skip over, and gutters to walk round, and all the time in a fright lest, in an unguarded moment, her calves should become visible to some one of those rainy-day philanthropists who are interested in the public study of female anatomy.

One evening, after a long rainy day of scribbling, when my nerves were in double-twisted knots, and I felt as if myriads of little ants were leisurely traveling over me, and all for want of the walk which is my daily salvation, I stood at the window, looking at the slanting, persistent rain, and took my resolve: "*I'll do it,*" said I, audibly, planting my slipper upon the carpet. "Do what?" asked Mr. Fern, looking up from a big book. "Put on a suit of your clothes and take a tramp with you," was the answer. "You dare not," was the rejoinder; "you are a little coward, only saucy on paper." It was the work of a moment, with such a challenge, to fly up stairs and overhaul my philosopher's wardrobe. Of course we had fun. Tailors must be a stingy set, I remarked, to be so sparing of their cloth, as I struggled into a pair of their handiwork, undeterred by the vociferous laughter of the wretch who had solemnly vowed to "cherish me" through all my tribulations. "Upon my word, everything seems to be narrow where it ought to be broad, and the waist of this coat might be made for a hogshead; and, ugh! this shirt collar is cutting my ears off, and you have not a decent cravat in the whole lot, and your vests are frights, and what am I to do with my hair?" Still no reply from Mr. Fern, who lay on the floor, faintly ejaculating, between his fits of laughter, "Oh, my! by Jove! — oh! by Jupiter!"

---

1. **"Emma Wilson . . . man's apparel":** By custom and law, women were not permitted to wear trousers in public.

Was that to hinder me? Of course not. Strings and pins, women's never-failing resort, soon brought broadcloth and kerseymere[2] to terms. I parted my hair on one side, rolled it under, and then secured it with hair-pins; chose the best fitting coat, and capping the climax with one of those soft, cosy hats, looked in the glass, where I beheld the very facsimile of a certain musical gentleman, whose photograph hangs this minute in Brady's entry.[3]

Well, Mr. Fern seized his hat, and out we went together. "Fanny," said he, "you must not take my arm; you are a fellow." "True," said I, "I forgot; and you must not help me over the puddles, as you did just now, and do, for mercy's sake, stop laughing. There, there goes your hat — I mean *my* hat; confound the wind! and down comes my hair; lucky 'tis dark, isn't it?" But oh, the delicious freedom of that walk; after we were well started! No skirts to hold up, or to draggle their wet folds against my ankles; no stifling vail flapping in my face, and blinding my eyes; no umbrella to turn inside out, but instead, the cool rain driving slap into my face, and the resurrectionized blood coursing through my veins, and tingling in my cheeks. To be sure, Mr. Fern occasionally loitered behind, and leaned up against the side of a house to enjoy a little private "guffaw," and I could now and then hear a gasping "Oh, Fanny!" "Oh, my!" but none of these things moved me, and if I don't have a nicely-fitting suit of my own to wear rainy evenings, it is because — well, there *are* difficulties in the way. Who's the best tailor?

Now, if any male or female Miss Nancy who reads this feels shocked, let 'em! Any woman who likes, may stay at home during a three weeks' rain, till her skin looks like parchment, and her eyes like those of a dead fish, or she may go out and get a consumption dragging round wet petticoats; I won't — I positively declare I won't. I shall begin *evenings* when *that* suit is made, and take private walking lessons with Mr. Fern, and they who choose may crook their backs at home for fashion, and then send for the doctor to straighten them; I prefer to patronize my shoe-maker and tailor. I've as good a right to preserve the healthy body God gave me, as if I were not a woman.

[1858]

---

2. **broadcloth and kerseymere:** Different weaves of woolen cloth.

3. **a certain musical gentleman . . . in Brady's entry:** A reference to Fern's younger brother, the composer and music critic Richard Storrs Willis (1819–1900), whose portrait was apparently displayed in the studio of the prominent photographer Mathew Brady (1822?–1896).

THE "COMING" WOMAN

Men often say, "When *I* marry, my wife must be this, that and the other," enumerating all physical, mental, and moral perfections. One cannot but smile to look at the men who say these things; smile to think of the equivalent they will bring for all the amiability, beauty, health, intellectuality, domesticity and faithfulness they so modestly require; smile to think of the perforated hearts, damaged morals, broken-down constitutions, and irritable temper, which this bright, pure, innocent girl is to receive with her wedding ring. If one-half the girls knew the previous life of the men they marry, the list of old maids would be wonderfully increased.

Doubted? Well, if there is room for a doubt now, thank God the "coming" woman's Alpha and Omega[1] will not be matrimony. *She* will not of necessity sour into a pink-nosed old maid, or throw herself at any rickety old shell of humanity, whose clothes are as much out of repair as his morals. No, the future man has got to "step lively;" *this* wife is not to be had for the whistling. He will have a long canter round the pasture for her, and then she will leap the fence and leave him limping on the ground. Thick-soled boots and skating are coming in, and "nerves," novels and sentiment (by consequence) are going out. The coming woman, as I see her, is not to throw aside her needle; neither is she to sit embroidering worsted dogs and cats, or singing doubtful love ditties, and rolling up her eyes to "the chaste moon."

Heaven forbid she should stamp round with a cigar in her mouth, elbowing her *fellows*, and puffing smoke in their faces; or stand on the free-love platform, *public or private — call it by what specious name you will —* wooing men who, low as they may have sunk in their own self-respect, would die before they would introduce her to the unsullied sister who shared their cradle.

Heaven forbid the coming woman should not have warm blood in her veins, quick to rush to her cheek, or tingle at her fingers' ends when her heart is astir. No, the coming woman shall be no cold, angular, flat-chested, narrow-shouldered, *skimpy*, sharp-visaged Betsey, but she shall be a bright-eyed, full-chested, broad-shouldered, large-souled, intellectual being; able to walk, able to eat, able to fulfill her maternal destiny, and able — if it so please God — to go to her grave happy, self-poised and serene, though unwedded; for this world, though it may do for men, is, after all, but a narrow place for a woman's heart to beat in. That many die and make no sign, is no proof that martyrdom died out with John Rogers.[2]

[1859]

---

1. **Alpha and Omega:** The first and last letters of the Greek alphabet, frequently used to mean "the beginning and the end."

2. **John Rogers:** During the reign of the Roman Catholic queen Mary I of England, the Protestant martyr John Rogers (c. 1500–1555), a former Catholic priest who converted to Protestantism, was burned at the stake for his faith.

"INDEPENDENCE"

"Fourth of July." Well — I don't feel patriotic. Perhaps I might if they would stop that deafening racket. Washington was very well, if he *couldn't* spell,[1] and I'm glad we are all free; but as a woman — I shouldn't know it, didn't some orator tell me. Can I go out of an evening without a hat at my side? Can I go out with one on my head without danger of a stationhouse? Can I clap my hands at some public speaker when I am nearly bursting with delight? Can I signify the contrary when my hair stands on end with vexation? Can I stand up in the cars "like a gentleman" without being immediately invited "to sit down"? Can I

---

1. **Washington . . . spell:** It was sometimes said that George Washington's early education was so neglected that he never learned to spell.

get into an omnibus without having my sixpence taken from my hand and given to the driver? Can I cross Broadway without having a policeman tackled to my helpless elbow? Can I go to see anything *pleasant,* like an execution or a dissection? Can I drive that splendid "Lantern,"[2] distancing – like his owners – all competitors? Can I have the nomination for "Governor of Vermont," like our other contributor, John G. Saxe?[3] Can I be a Senator, that I may hurry up that millennial International Copyright Law?[4] Can I *even* be "President?" Bah – you know I can't. "*Free!*" Humph!

[1859]

---

2. **Lantern:** The name of a famous trotting horse owned by the editor of the *New York Ledger*, Robert Bonner (1824–1899).
3. **John G. Saxe:** John Godfrey Saxe (1816–1887), a poet and a satirist who was twice defeated in bids to become the governor of Vermont.
4. **International Copyright Law:** An act designed to protect authors and publishers from having their books republished outside of the United States without payment was not passed by Congress until 1891.

Herman Melville

[1819–1891]

Herman Melville was born on August 1, 1819, in New York City to Allan and Maria Gansevoort Melvill, the spelling of which the family later altered to Melville. He attended the New-York Male High School until 1830, when his father's business as an importer and wholesale merchant collapsed. The family then moved to Albany, New York, where their fortunes improved enough for Melville to enroll in the Albany Academy. By late 1831, the family business failed again; and in January 1832 an ill and exhausted Allan Melvill died. As the older sons tried to recoup the family finances, the thirteen-year-old Melville was taken out of school and apprenticed as a clerk in an Albany bank. For the next five years, he worked in the bank, as a helper on his uncle's farm in Pittsfield, Massachusetts, and then as an assistant in his brother's store. After briefly returning to school in Albany, where he joined a reading and debating club, Melville taught for a single term in 1837 in a school near Pittsfield. Still vainly searching for a career, however, he decided to study surveying and engineering at the Lansingburgh Academy, near Albany, in order to prepare for a job working on the Erie Canal.

In fact, he would spend most of the following five years, not on that canal between Albany and Buffalo, New York, but on the high seas, gaining experiences that would finally lead him to become a writer. Unable to find a job in 1839, Melville agreed to his brother's proposal that they join the crew of the *St. Lawrence*, which sailed regularly between New York and Liverpool, England. The voyage was deeply disturbing to the youthful Melville, who was shocked by the sometimes brutal behavior of the sailors. Nonetheless, after returning to New York and another brief stint as a

He can neither believe, nor be comfortable in his unbelief; and he is too honest and courageous not to try to do one or the other.

–Nathaniel Hawthorne

teacher, in January 1839 Melville signed up for a four-year voyage aboard the *Acushnet*, a whaling ship bound from New Bedford, Massachusetts, to the South Seas. The lack of success in finding whales and the captain's low spirits made morale on board very bad. In company with another crewman, Melville deserted his ship on the Marquesas Islands, where they stayed for a month, fearful of cannibalism. Melville joined the crew of another whaler, the *Lucy Ann*; was briefly held in Tahiti as a mutineer; and finally sailed to Hawaii, where he spent several months before shipping home as a common seaman aboard the navy frigate *United States*.

By October 1844, Melville was back in Lansingburgh, New York, his career as a sailor now over and his work as a writer about to begin. Within a couple of months, he began his first book, published in 1846 as *Typee; or, A Peep at Polynesian Life*. That Romantic and highly colored account of the brief period he had spent among the "cannibals" in the Marquesas was an immediate commercial and critical success. An influential reviewer and later one of Melville's closest friends, Evert Duyckinck, observed that the book was "a happy hit whichever way you look at it, whether as travels, romance, poetry, or humor." Swiftly following up on his success, Melville immediately wrote a sequel, *Omoo* (1847), which proved to be yet another hit. Increasingly ambitious, however, he followed that with *Mardi* (1849), a long, complex, allegorical work that sold poorly and generated considerable critical resistance. Chastened by the response, Melville — now married to Elizabeth Shaw and a new father — swiftly produced two books in his earlier mode, *Redburn* (1849) and *White-Jacket* (1850), both of which proved to be enormously popular with readers and reviewers alike.

But Melville's popularity did not last and his finances remained precarious. In 1850, he moved his family to a farm, Arrowhead, near Pittsfield, Massachusetts. There, he became friendly with Nathaniel Hawthorne, who had just published *The Scarlet Letter*. Melville himself was beginning work on yet another autobiographical narrative, this one based on his early experiences aboard the whaling ship *Acushnet*. Partly inspired by the presence of Hawthorne, to whom he later dedicated *Moby-Dick*, Melville began to transform the novel into something far different, even as he recognized the risks he was running by doing so. "Dollars damn me," he wrote to Hawthorne in 1851. "What I most feel moved to write, that is banned, — it will not sell. Yet, altogether, write the *other* way I cannot. So the product is a final hash, and all my books are botches." Although his powerful novel was anything but a hash, Melville was all too prophetic about what would result if he indulged his taste for metaphysical speculation and his hunger for literary greatness, as he did in *Moby-Dick* (1851). Despite a few admiring reviews, most critics were deeply hostile, and they were even more outraged by what many of them viewed as the immorality and sacrilege of his next novel, *Pierre* (1852). The reviewer for the *New York Herald* spoke for many when he flatly stated that "Mr. Melville has written himself out."

In an effort to revive his flagging literary career, Melville began to publish stories and sketches in two recently established literary journals, *Putnam's Monthly Magazine* and *Harper's New Monthly Magazine*. Those efforts resulted in his next two books: *Israel Potter* (1855), a satirical

Herman Melville
This portrait of the successful young author was painted by Asa W. Twitchell in 1847, when Melville was twenty-eight. Friends nicknamed him "Typee," a reference to his first and most popular book, published in 1846.

historical novel first serialized in *Putnam's*; and a collection of shorter pieces Melville had also published there, *The Piazza Tales* (1856). That collection included his novella *Benito Cereno*, an enigmatic meditation on slavery based on an American sea captain's earlier account of a slave insurrection aboard a Spanish ship. Emboldened by the modest success of such works, Melville then wrote *The Confidence-Man* (1857), a biting satire of American values and life in the United States. The book was a commercial and critical disaster that effectively marked the end of Melville's career as a novelist. During the remaining twenty-four years of his life, he published only two more major works: *Battle-Pieces and Aspects of the War* (1866), a collection of Civil War poems; and *Clarel* (1876), a long narrative poem about the quest for religious faith. He also privately published two small collections of poems, in 1888 and 1891. Melville spent most of those years working as a deputy inspector of customs in New York City, where he died in obscurity and relative poverty on September 28, 1891. His final work of fiction, *Billy Budd, Sailor*, was not published until 1924, when Melville finally began to gain the recognition and literary reputation that had eluded him during his lifetime.

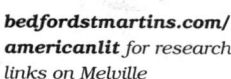

bedfordstmartins.com/ americanlit *for research links on Melville*

Reading Melville's "Bartleby, the Scrivener."

Following the poor reception of *Moby-Dick* (1851) and *Pierre* (1852), Melville decided to enter the periodical marketplace in an effort to boost his sagging reputation and make a living for his family. The first story he published in a periodical was "Bartleby, the Scrivener: A Story of Wall-Street," which appeared in *Putnam's Monthly Magazine.* When George Palmer Putnam decided that his publishing company would start a magazine, Melville was one of the writers to whom he appealed to help him establish *Putnam's*, which appeared in January 1853. Putnam and the first editor, Charles Briggs, wanted to publish a magazine of American literature rather than relying on British and European writings, as many of the other periodicals did. The magazine published fiction, poetry, reviews of literature and the arts, social criticism, and travel writing by such authors as William Cullen Bryant, Caroline

Wall Street

In this 1847 lithograph, Trinity Church, the fashionable Episcopalian church, is seen at the western end of Wall Street, where it intersects with Broadway.

Kirkland, Henry Wadsworth Longfellow, and Henry David Thoreau. Among the many social concerns addressed in *Putnam's* were urbanization and the changing world of work in the United States, concerns that were also reflected in Melville's story of Wall Street. Although it was published anonymously, the story attracted a great deal of attention, and it was soon well known that Melville was the author. He later included it in *The Piazza Tales*, a collection of his periodical fiction Melville published in 1856. "Bartleby, the Scrivener" has remained one of his most widely read and frequently debated stories. A central source of critical controversy over the story is its haunting principal character, who has been variously interpreted as a veiled portrait of the author, an example of passive resistance to unjust authority, and a representative of alienated workers in modern commercial society. The text is taken from its first printing as a two-part story in *Putnam's Monthly Magazine*, November and December 1853.

BARTLEBY, THE SCRIVENER[1]

A Story of Wall-Street

I am a rather elderly man. The nature of my avocations for the last thirty years has brought me into more than ordinary contact with what would seem an interesting and somewhat singular set of men, of whom as yet nothing that I know of has ever been written: — I mean the law-copyists or scriveners. I have known very many of them, professionally and privately, and if I pleased, could relate divers histories, at which good-natured gentlemen might smile, and sentimental souls might weep. But I waive the biographies of all other scriveners for a few passages in the life of Bartleby, who was a scrivener the strangest I ever saw or heard of. While of other law-copyists I might write the complete life, of Bartleby nothing of that sort can be done. I believe that no materials exist for a full and satisfactory biography of this man. It is an irreparable loss to literature. Bartleby was one of those beings of whom nothing is ascertainable, except from the original sources, and in his case those are very small. What my own astonished eyes saw of Bartleby, *that* is all I know of him, except, indeed, one vague report which will appear in the sequel.

Ere introducing the scrivener, as he first appeared to me, it is fit I make some mention of myself, my *employés*, my business, my chambers, and general surroundings; because some such description is indispensable to an adequate understanding of the chief character about to be presented.

Imprimis:[2] I am a man who, from his youth upwards, has been filled with a profound conviction that the easiest way of life is the best. Hence, though I belong to a profession proverbially energetic and nervous, even to turbulence, at times, yet nothing of that sort have I ever suffered to invade my peace. I am one of those unambitious lawyers who

---

1. **Scrivener:** An early term for a scribe, or someone who copies documents.
2. **Imprimis:** First of all (Latin).

never addresses a jury, or in any way draws down public applause; but in the cool tranquillity of a snug retreat, do a snug business among rich men's bonds and mortgages and title-deeds. All who know me, consider me an eminently *safe* man. The late John Jacob Astor,[3] a personage little given to poetic enthusiasm, had no hesitation in pronouncing my first grand point to be prudence; my next, method. I do not speak it in vanity, but simply record the fact, that I was not unemployed in my profession by the late John Jacob Astor; a name which, I admit, I love to repeat, for it hath a rounded and orbicular sound to it, and rings like unto bullion. I will freely add, that I was not insensible to the late John Jacob Astor's good opinion.

Some time prior to the period at which this little history begins, my avocations had been largely increased. The good old office, now extinct in the State of New-York, of a Master in Chancery,[4] had been conferred upon me. It was not a very arduous office, but very pleasantly remunerative. I seldom lose my temper; much more seldom indulge in dangerous indignation at wrongs and outrages; but I must be permitted to be rash here and declare, that I consider the sudden and violent abrogation of the office of Master in Chancery, by the new Constitution, as a — premature act; inasmuch as I had counted upon a life-lease of the profits, whereas I only received those of a few short years. But this is by the way.

My chambers were up stairs at No. — Wall-street. At one end they looked upon the white wall of the interior of a spacious sky-light shaft, penetrating the building from top to bottom. This view might have been considered rather tame than otherwise, deficient in what landscape painters call "life." But if so, the view from the other end of my chambers offered, at least, a contrast, if nothing more. In that direction my windows commanded an unobstructed view of a lofty brick wall, black by age and everlasting shade; which wall required no spy-glass to bring out its lurking beauties, but for the benefit of all near-sighted spectators, was pushed up to within ten feet of my window panes. Owing to the great height of the surrounding buildings, and my chambers being on the second floor, the interval between this wall and mine not a little resembled a huge square cistern.

At the period just preceding the advent of Bartleby, I had two persons as copyists in my employment, and a promising lad as an office-boy. First, Turkey; second, Nippers; third, Ginger Nut. These may seem names, the like of which are not usually found in the Directory. In truth they were nicknames, mutually conferred upon each other by my three clerks, and were deemed expressive of their respective persons or characters. Turkey was a short, pursy[5] Englishman of about my own age, that is, somewhere not far from sixty. In the morning, one might say, his face was of a fine florid hue, but

---

3. **John Jacob Astor:** German-born fur trader (1763–1848) who amassed a fortune through his business and real-estate dealings. In his will, he provided for $350,000 toward the founding of the New York Public Library.
4. **Master in Chancery:** A position in the Court of Chancery, or equity, in which the officeholder often received lucrative fees while cases over property rights were needlessly prolonged. The position was abolished when the New York State constitution was revised in 1846.
5. **pursy:** Short-winded because of obesity.

after twelve o'clock, meridian – his dinner hour – it blazed like a grate full of Christmas coals; and continued blazing – but, as it were, with a gradual wane – till 6 o'clock, P.M. or thereabouts, after which I saw no more of the proprietor of the face, which gaining its meridian with the sun, seemed to set with it, to rise, culminate, and decline the following day, with the like regularity and undiminished glory. There are many singular coincidences I have known in the course of my life, not the least among which was the fact, that exactly when Turkey displayed his fullest beams from his red and radiant countenance, just then, too, at that critical moment, began the daily period when I considered his business capacities as seriously disturbed for the remainder of the twenty-four hours. Not that he was absolutely idle, or averse to business then; far from it. The difficulty was, he was apt to be altogether too energetic. There was a strange, inflamed, flurried, flighty recklessness of activity about him. He would be incautious in dipping his pen into his inkstand. All his blots upon my documents, were dropped there after twelve o'clock, meridian. Indeed, not only would he be reckless and sadly given to making blots in the afternoon, but some days he went further, and was rather noisy. At such times, too, his face flamed with augmented blazonry, as if cannel coal had been heaped on anthracite.[6] He made an unpleasant racket with his chair; spilled his sand-box;[7] in mending his pens, impatiently split them all to pieces, and threw them on the floor in a sudden passion; stood up and leaned over his table, boxing his papers about in a most indecorous manner, very sad to behold in an elderly man like him. Nevertheless, as he was in many ways a most valuable person to me, and all the time before twelve o'clock, meridian, was the quickest, steadiest creature too, accomplishing a great deal of work in a style not easy to be matched – for these reasons, I was willing to overlook his eccentricities, though indeed, occasionally, I remonstrated with him. I did this very gently, however, because, though the civilest, nay, the blandest and most reverential of men in the morning, yet in the afternoon he was disposed, upon provocation, to be slightly rash with his tongue, in fact, insolent. Now, valuing his morning services as I did, and resolved not to lose them; yet, at the same time made uncomfortable by his inflamed ways after twelve o'clock; and being a man of peace, unwilling by my admonitions to call forth unseemly retorts from him; I took upon me, one Saturday noon (he was always worse on Saturdays), to hint to him, very kindly, that perhaps now that he was growing old, it might be well to abridge his labors; in short, he need not come to my chambers after twelve o'clock, but, dinner over, had best go home to his lodgings and rest himself till tea-time. But no; he insisted upon his afternoon devotions. His countenance became intolerably fervid, as he oratorically assured me – gesticulating with a long ruler at the other end of the room – that if his services in the morning were useful, how indispensable, then, in the afternoon?

---

6. **cannel coal . . . anthracite:** Cannel coal is highly volatile; when it is heaped on anthracite, a hard coal with little volatility, both burn with a bright flame.
7. **sand-box:** Sand was used for blotting ink on documents.

"With submission, sir," said Turkey on this occasion, "I consider myself your right-hand man. In the morning I but marshal and deploy my columns; but in the afternoon I put myself at their head, and gallantly charge the foe, thus!" — and he made a violent thrust with the ruler.

"But the blots, Turkey," intimated I.

"True, — but, with submission, sir, behold these hairs! I am getting old. Surely, sir, a blot or two of a warm afternoon is not to be severely urged against gray hairs. Old age — even if it blot the page — is honorable. With submission, sir, we *both* are getting old."

This appeal to my fellow-feeling was hardly to be resisted. At all events, I saw that go he would not. So I made up my mind to let him stay, resolving, nevertheless, to see to it, that during the afternoon he had to do with my less important papers.

Nippers, the second on my list, was a whiskered, sallow, and, upon the whole, rather piratical-looking young man of about five and twenty. I always deemed him the victim of two evil powers — ambition and indigestion. The ambition was evinced by a certain impatience of the duties of a mere copyist, an unwarrantable usurpation of strictly professional affairs, such as the original drawing up of legal documents. The indigestion seemed betokened in an occasional nervous testiness and grinning irritability, causing the teeth to audibly grind together over mistakes committed in copying; unnecessary maledictions, hissed, rather than spoken, in the heat of business; and especially by a continual discontent with the height of the table where he worked. Though of a very ingenious mechanical turn, Nippers could never get this table to suit him. He put chips under it, blocks of various sorts, bits of pasteboard, and at last went so far as to attempt an exquisite adjustment by final pieces of folded blotting-paper. But no invention would answer. If, for the sake of easing his back, he brought the table lid at a sharp angle well up towards his chin, and wrote there like a man using the steep roof of a Dutch house for his desk: — then he declared that it stopped the circulation in his arms. If now he lowered the table to his waistbands, and stooped over it in writing, then there was a sore aching in his back. In short, the truth of the matter was, Nippers knew not what he wanted. Or, if he wanted any thing, it was to be rid of a scrivener's table altogether. Among the manifestations of his diseased ambition was a fondness he had for receiving visits from certain ambiguous-looking fellows in seedy coats, whom he called his clients. Indeed I was aware that not only was he, at times, consider-able of a ward-politician, but he occasionally did a little business at the Justices' courts, and was not unknown on the steps of the Tombs.[8] I have good reason to believe, how-ever that one individual who called upon him at my chambers, and who, with a grand air, he insisted was his client, was no other than a dun,[9] and the alleged title-deed, a bill. But with all his failings, and the annoyances he caused me, Nippers, like his com-patriot Turkey, was a very useful man to me; wrote a neat, swift hand; and, when he

---

8. **the Tombs:** Informal name for the Halls of Justice and House of Detention, a prison built in New York City in 1840. The massive structure was designed to look like an ancient Egyptian tomb.
9. **dun:** Slang name for a bill collector.

chose, was not deficient in a gentlemanly sort of deportment. Added to this, he always dressed in a gentlemanly sort of way; and so, incidentally, reflected credit upon my chambers. Whereas with respect to Turkey, I had much ado to keep him from being a reproach to me. His clothes were apt to look oily and smell of eating-houses. He wore his pantaloons very loose and baggy in summer. His coats were execrable; his hat not to be handled. But while the hat was a thing of indifference to me, inasmuch as his natural civility and deference, as a dependent Englishman, always led him to doff it the moment he entered the room, yet his coat was another matter. Concerning his coats, I reasoned with him; but with no effect. The truth was, I suppose, that a man with so small an income, could not afford to sport such a lustrous face and a lustrous coat at one and the same time. As Nippers once observed, Turkey's money went chiefly for red ink. One winter day I presented Turkey with a highly-respectable looking coat of my own, a padded gray coat, of a most comfortable warmth, and which buttoned straight up from the knee to the neck. I thought Turkey would appreciate the favor, and abate his rashness and obstreperousness of afternoons. But no. I verily believe that buttoning himself up in so downy and blanket-like a coat had a pernicious effect upon him; upon the same principle that too much oats are bad for horses. In fact, precisely as a rash, restive horse is said to feel his oats, so Turkey felt his coat. It made him insolent. He was a man whom prosperity harmed.

Though concerning the self-indulgent habits of Turkey I had my own private surmises, yet touching Nippers I was well persuaded that whatever might be his faults in other respects, he was, at least, a temperate young man. But indeed, nature herself seemed to have been his vintner, and at his birth charged him so thoroughly with an irritable, brandy-like disposition, that all subsequent potations were needless. When I consider how, amid the stillness of my chambers, Nippers would sometimes impatiently rise from his seat, and stooping over his table, spread his arms wide apart, seize the whole desk, and move it, and jerk it, with a grim, grinding motion on the floor, as if the table were a perverse voluntary agent, intent on thwarting and vexing him; I plainly perceive that for Nippers, brandy and water were altogether superfluous.

It was fortunate for me that, owing to its peculiar cause – indigestion – the irritability and consequent nervousness of Nippers, were mainly observable in the morning, while in the afternoon he was comparatively mild. So that Turkey's paroxysms only coming on about twelve o'clock, I never had to do with their eccentricities at one time. Their fits relieved each other like guards. When Nippers' was on, Turkey's was off; and *vice versa.* This was a good natural arrangement under the circumstances.

Ginger Nut, the third on my list, was a lad some twelve years old. His father was a carman,[10] ambitious of seeing his son on the bench instead of a cart, before he died. So he sent him to my office as student at law, errand boy, and cleaner and sweeper, at the rate of one dollar a week. He had a little desk to himself, but he did not use it much. Upon inspection, the drawer exhibited a great array of the shells of various sorts of nuts. Indeed, to this quick-witted youth the whole noble science of the law was contained in a

---

10. **carman:** A streetcar driver or conductor.

nut-shell. Not the least among the employments of Ginger Nut, as well as one which he discharged with the most alacrity, was his duty as cake and apple purveyor for Turkey and Nippers. Copying law papers being proverbially a dry, husky sort of business, my two scriveners were fain to moisten their mouths very often with Spitzenbergs[11] to be had at the numerous stalls nigh the Custom House and Post Office. Also, they sent Ginger Nut very frequently for that peculiar cake – small, flat, round, and very spicy – after which he had been named by them. Of a cold morning when business was but dull, Turkey would gobble up scores of these cakes, as if they were mere wafers – indeed they sell them at the rate of six or eight for a penny – the scrape of his pen blending with the crunching of the crisp particles in his mouth. Of all the fiery after-noon blunders and flurried rashnesses of Turkey, was his once moistening a ginger-cake between his lips, and clapping it on to a mortgage for a seal.[12] I came within an ace of dismissing him then. But he mollified me by making an oriental bow, and saying – "With submission, sir, it was generous of me to find you in stationery on my own account."

Now my original business – that of a conveyancer and title hunter,[13] and drawer-up of recondite documents of all sorts – was considerably increased by receiving the mas-ter's office. There was now great work for scriveners. Not only must I push the clerks already with me, but I must have additional help. In answer to my advertisement, a motionless young man one morning, stood upon my office threshold, the door being open, for it was summer. I can see that figure now – pallidly neat, pitiably respectable, incurably forlorn! It was Bartleby.

After a few words touching his qualifications, I engaged him, glad to have among my corps of copyists a man of so singularly sedate an aspect, which I thought might operate beneficially upon the flighty temper of Turkey, and the fiery one of Nippers.

I should have stated before that ground glass folding-doors divided my premises into two parts, one of which was occupied by my scriveners, the other by myself. According to my humor I threw open these doors, or closed them. I resolved to assign Bartleby a cor-ner by the folding-doors, but on my side of them, so as to have this quiet man within easy call, in case any trifling thing was to be done. I placed his desk close up to a small side-window in that part of the room, a window which originally had afforded a lateral view of certain grimy back-yards and bricks, but which, owing to subsequent erections, com-manded at present no view at all, though it gave some light. Within three feet of the panes was a wall, and the light came down from far above, between two lofty buildings, as from a very small opening in a dome. Still further to a satisfactory arrangement, I procured a high green folding screen, which might entirely isolate Bartleby from my

---

11. **Spitzenbergs:** A variety of apple grown in New York State.
12. **a ginger-cake . . . for a seal:** That is, Turkey mistakes a small round cake for one of the wax wafers then used for sealing documents.
13. **conveyancer and title hunter:** A lawyer who arranges documents for the transfer of property, ensuring that the title is free of any encumbrances.

sight, though not remove him from my voice. And thus, in a manner, privacy and society were conjoined.

At first Bartleby did an extraordinary quantity of writing. As if long famishing for something to copy, he seemed to gorge himself on my documents. There was no pause for digestion. He ran a day and night line, copying by sun-light and by candle-light. I should have been quite delighted with his application, had he been cheerfully industrious. But he wrote on silently, palely, mechanically.

It is, of course, an indispensable part of a scrivener's business to verify the accuracy of his copy, word by word. Where there are two or more scriveners in an office, they assist each other in this examination, one reading from the copy, the other holding the original. It is a very dull, wearisome, and lethargic affair. I can readily imagine that to some sanguine temperaments it would be altogether intolerable. For example, I cannot credit that the mettlesome poet Byron[14] would have contentedly sat down with Bartleby to examine a law document of, say five hundred pages, closely written in a crimpy hand.

Now and then, in the haste of business, it had been my habit to assist in comparing some brief document myself, calling Turkey or Nippers for this purpose. One object I had in placing Bartleby so handy to me behind the screen, was to avail myself of his services on such trivial occasions. It was on the third day, I think, of his being with me, and before any necessity had arisen for having his own writing examined that, being much hurried to complete a small affair I had in hand, I abruptly called to Bartleby. In my haste and natural expectancy of instant compliance, I sat with my head bent over the original on my desk, and my right hand sideways, and somewhat nervously extended with the copy, so that immediately upon emerging from his retreat, Bartleby might snatch it and proceed to business without the least delay.

In this very attitude did I sit when I called to him, rapidly stating what it was I wanted him to do — namely, to examine a small paper with me. Imagine my surprise, nay, my consternation, when without moving from his privacy, Bartleby in a singularly mild, firm voice, replied, "I would prefer not to."

I sat awhile in perfect silence, rallying my stunned faculties. Immediately it occurred to me that my ears had deceived me, or Bartleby had entirely misunderstood my meaning. I repeated my request in the clearest tone I could assume. But in quite as clear a one came the previous reply, "I would prefer not to."

"Prefer not to," echoed I, rising in high excitement, and crossing the room with a stride. "What do you mean? Are you moon-struck? I want you to help me compare this sheet here — take it," and I thrust it towards him.

"I would prefer not to," said he.

---

14. **the mettlesome poet Byron:** The English poet George Gordon, Lord Byron (1788–1824), a central figure in the Romantic movement who was renowned for his daring and contempt for convention.

I looked at him steadfastly. His face was leanly composed; his gray eye dimly calm. Not a wrinkle of agitation rippled him. Had there been the least uneasiness, anger, impatience or impertinence in his manner; in other words, had there been any thing ordinarily human about him, doubtless I should have violently dismissed him from the premises. But as it was, I should have as soon thought of turning my pale plaster-of-paris bust of Cicero[15] out of doors. I stood gazing at him awhile, as he went on with his own writing, and then reseated myself at my desk. This is very strange, thought I. What had one best do? But my business hurried me. I concluded to forget the matter for the present, reserving it for my future leisure. So calling Nippers from the other room, the paper was speedily examined.

A few days after this, Bartleby concluded four lengthy documents, being quadruplicates of a week's testimony taken before me in my High Court of Chancery. It became necessary to examine them. It was an important suit, and great accuracy was imperative. Having all things arranged I called Turkey, Nippers and Ginger Nut from the next room, meaning to place the four copies in the hands of my four clerks, while I should read from the original. Accordingly Turkey, Nippers and Ginger Nut had taken their seats in a row, each with his document in hand, when I called to Bartleby to join this interesting group.

"Bartleby! quick, I am waiting."

I heard a slow scrape of his chair legs on the uncarpeted floor, and soon he appeared standing at the entrance of his hermitage.

"What is wanted?" said he mildly.

"The copies, the copies," said I hurriedly. "We are going to examine them. There" — and I held towards him the fourth quadruplicate.

"I would prefer not to," he said, and gently disappeared behind the screen.

For a few moments I was turned into a pillar of salt,[16] standing at the head of my seated column of clerks. Recovering myself, I advanced towards the screen and demanded the reason for such extraordinary conduct.

"*Why* do you refuse?"

"I would prefer not to."

With any other man I should have flown outright into a dreadful passion, scorned all further words, and thrust him ignominiously from my presence. But there was something about Bartleby that not only strangely disarmed me, but in a wonderful manner touched and disconcerted me. I began to reason with him.

"These are your own copies we are about to examine. It is labor saving to you, because one examination will answer for your four papers. It is common usage. Every copyist is bound to help examine his copy. Is it not so? Will you not speak? Answer!"

"I prefer not to," he replied in a flute-like tone. It seemed to me that while I had been addressing him, he carefully revolved every statement that I made; fully comprehended the meaning; could not gainsay the irresistible conclusion; but, at the same time, some paramount consideration prevailed with him to reply as he did.

---

15. **Cicero:** Roman orator and politician (106–42 BCE).

16. **pillar of salt:** In the Old Testament story, Lot's wife is turned into a pillar of salt when she disobeys a command from God not to turn and look back upon the destruction of the cities of Sodom and Gomorrah (Genesis 19:26).

"You are decided, then, not to comply with my request — a request made according to common usage and common sense?"

He briefly gave me to understand that on that point my judgment was sound. Yes: his decision was irreversible.

It is not seldom the case that when a man is browbeaten in some unprecedented and violently unreasonable way, he begins to stagger in his own plainest faith. He begins, as it were, vaguely to surmise that, wonderful as it may be, all the justice and all the reason is on the other side. Accordingly, if any disinterested persons are present, he turns to them for some reinforcement for his own faltering mind.

"Turkey," said I, "what do you think of this? Am I not right?"

"With submission, sir," said Turkey, with his blandest tone, "I think that you are."

"Nippers," said I, "what do *you* think of it?"

"I think I should kick him out of the office."

(The reader of nice perceptions will here perceive that, it being morning, Turkey's answer is couched in polite and tranquil terms, but Nippers replies in ill-tempered ones. Or, to repeat a previous sentence, Nippers's ugly mood was on duty, and Turkey's off.)

"Ginger Nut," said I, willing to enlist the smallest suffrage in my behalf, "what do *you* think of it?"

"I think, sir, he's a little *luny*," replied Ginger Nut, with a grin.

"You hear what they say," said I, turning towards the screen, "come forth and do your duty."

But he vouchsafed no reply. I pondered a moment in sore perplexity. But once more business hurried me. I determined again to postpone the consideration of this dilemma to my future leisure. With a little trouble we made out to examine the papers without Bartleby, though at every page or two, Turkey deferentially dropped his opinion that this proceeding was quite out of the common; while Nippers, twitching in his chair with a dyspeptic nervousness, ground out between his set teeth occasional hissing maledictions against the stubborn oaf behind the screen. And for his (Nippers's) part, this was the first and the last time he would do another man's business without pay.

Meanwhile Bartleby sat in his hermitage, oblivious to every thing but his own peculiar business there.

Some days passed, the scrivener being employed upon another lengthy work. His late remarkable conduct led me to regard his ways narrowly. I observed that he never went to dinner; indeed that he never went any where. As yet I had never of my personal knowledge known him to be outside of my office. He was a perpetual sentry in the corner. At about eleven o'clock though, in the morning, I noticed that Ginger Nut would advance toward the opening in Bartleby's screen, as if silently beckoned thither by a gesture invisible to me where I sat. The boy would then leave the office jingling a few pence, and reappear with a handful of ginger-nuts which he delivered in the hermitage, receiving two of the cakes for his trouble.

He lives, then, on ginger-nuts, thought I; never eats a dinner, properly speaking; he must be a vegetarian then; but no; he never eats even vegetables, he eats nothing but ginger-nuts. My mind then ran on in reveries concerning the probable effects upon the human constitution of living entirely on ginger-nuts. Ginger-nuts are so called because they contain ginger as one of their peculiar constituents, and the final flavoring one. Now what was ginger? A hot, spicy thing. Was Bartleby hot and spicy? Not at all. Ginger, then, had no effect upon Bartleby. Probably he preferred it should have none.

Nothing so aggravates an earnest person as a passive resistance. If the individual so resisted be of a not inhumane temper, and the resisting one perfectly harmless in his passivity; then, in the better moods of the former, he will endeavor charitably to construe to his imagination what proves impossible to be solved by his judgment. Even so, for the most part, I regarded Bartleby and his ways. Poor fellow! thought I, he means no mischief; it is plain he intends no insolence; his aspect sufficiently evinces that his eccentricities are involuntary. He is useful to me. I can get along with him. If I turn him away, the chances are he will fall in with some less indulgent employer, and then he will be rudely treated, and perhaps driven forth miserably to starve. Yes. Here I can cheaply purchase a delicious self-approval. To befriend Bartleby; to humor him in his strange wilfulness, will cost me little or nothing, while I lay up in my soul what will eventually prove a sweet morsel for my conscience. But this mood was not invariable with me. The passiveness of Bartleby sometimes irritated me. I felt strangely goaded on to encounter him in new opposition, to elicit some angry spark from him answerable to my own. But indeed I might as well have essayed to strike fire with my knuckles against a bit of Windsor soap. But one afternoon the evil impulse in me mastered me, and the following little scene ensued:

"Bartleby," said I, "when those papers are all copied, I will compare them with you."

"I would prefer not to."

"How? Surely you do not mean to persist in that mulish vagary?"

No answer.

I threw open the folding-doors near by, and turning upon Turkey and Nippers, exclaimed in an excited manner —

"He says, a second time, he won't examine his papers. What do you think of it, Turkey?"

It was afternoon, be it remembered. Turkey sat glowing like a brass boiler, his bald head steaming, his hands reeling among his blotted papers.

"Think of it?" roared Turkey; "I think I'll just step behind his screen, and black his eyes for him!"

So saying, Turkey rose to his feet and threw his arms into a pugilistic position. He was hurrying away to make good his promise, when I detained him, alarmed at the effect of incautiously rousing Turkey's combativeness after dinner.

"Sit down, Turkey," said I, "and hear what Nippers has to say. What do you think of it, Nippers? Would I not be justified in immediately dismissing Bartleby?"

"Excuse me, that is for you to decide, sir. I think his conduct quite unusual, and indeed unjust, as regards Turkey and myself. But it may only be a passing whim."

"Ah," exclaimed I, "you have strangely changed your mind then — you speak very gently of him now."

"All beer," cried Turkey; "gentleness is effects of beer — Nippers and I dined together to-day. You see how gentle I am, sir. Shall I go and black his eyes?"

"You refer to Bartleby, I suppose. No, not to-day, Turkey," I replied; "pray, put up your fists."

I closed the doors, and again advanced towards Bartleby. I felt additional incentives tempting me to my fate. I burned to be rebelled against again. I remembered that Bartleby never left the office.

"Bartleby," said I, "Ginger Nut is away; just step round to the Post Office, won't you? (it was but a three minutes walk,) and see if there is any thing for me."

"I would prefer not to."

"You *will* not?"

"I *prefer* not."

I staggered to my desk, and sat there in a deep study. My blind inveteracy returned. Was there any other thing in which I could procure myself to be ignominiously repulsed by this lean, penniless wight? — my hired clerk? What added thing is there, perfectly reasonable, that he will be sure to refuse to do?

"Bartleby!"

No answer.

"Bartleby," in a louder tone.

No answer.

"Bartleby," I roared.

Like a very ghost, agreeably to the laws of magical invocation, at the third summons, he appeared at the entrance of his hermitage.

"Go to the next room, and tell Nippers to come to me."

"I prefer not to," he respectfully and slowly said, and mildly disappeared.

"Very good, Bartleby," said I, in a quiet sort of serenely severe self-possessed tone, intimating the unalterable purpose of some terrible retribution very close at hand. At the moment I half intended something of the kind. But upon the whole, as it was drawing towards my dinner-hour, I thought it best to put on my hat and walk home for the day, suffering much from perplexity and distress of mind.

Shall I acknowledge it? The conclusion of this whole business was, that it soon became a fixed fact of my chambers, that a pale young scrivener, by the name of Bartleby, had a desk there; that he copied for me at the usual rate of four cents a folio (one hundred words); but he was permanently exempt from examining the work done by him, that duty being transferred to Turkey and Nippers, out of compliment doubtless to their superior acuteness; moreover, said Bartleby was never on any account to be dispatched on the most trivial errand of any sort; and that even if entreated to take upon him such a matter, it was generally understood that he would prefer not to — in other words, that he would refuse point-blank.

As days passed on, I became considerably reconciled to Bartleby. His steadiness, his freedom from all dissipation, his incessant industry (except when he chose to throw himself into a standing revery behind his screen), his great stillness, his unalterableness of demeanor under all circumstances, made him a valuable acquisition. One prime thing was this, — *he was always there*; — first in the morning, continually through the day, and the last at night. I had a singular confidence in his honesty. I felt my most precious papers perfectly safe in his hands. Sometimes to be sure I could not, for the very soul of me, avoid falling into sudden spasmodic passions with him. For it was exceeding difficult to bear in mind all the time those strange peculiarities, privileges, and unheard of exemptions, forming the tacit stipulations on Bartleby's part under which he remained in my office. Now and then, in the eagerness of dispatching pressing business, I would inadvertently summon Bartleby, in a short, rapid tone, to put his finger, say, on the incipient tie of a bit of red tape with which I was about compressing some papers. Of course, from behind the screen the usual answer, "I prefer not to," was sure to come; and then, how could a human creature with the common infirmities of our nature, refrain from bitterly exclaiming upon such perverseness — such unreasonableness. However, every added repulse of this sort which I received only tended to lessen the probability of my repeating the inadvertence.

Here it must be said, that according to the custom of most legal gentlemen occupying chambers in densely-populated law buildings, there were several keys to my door. One was kept by a woman residing in the attic, which person weekly scrubbed and daily swept and dusted my apartments. Another was kept by Turkey for convenience sake. The third I sometimes carried in my own pocket. The fourth I knew not who had.

Now, one Sunday morning I happened to go to Trinity Church, to hear a celebrated preacher, and finding myself rather early on the ground, I thought I would walk round to my chambers for a while. Luckily I had my key with me; but upon applying it to the lock, I found it resisted by something inserted from the inside. Quite surprised, I called out; when to my consternation a key was turned from within; and thrusting his lean visage at me, and holding the door ajar, the apparition of Bartleby appeared, in his shirt sleeves, and otherwise in a strangely tattered dishabille, saying quietly that he was sorry, but he was deeply engaged just then, and — preferred not admitting me at present. In a brief word or two, he moreover added, that perhaps I had better walk round the block two or three times, and by that time he would probably have concluded his affairs.

Now, the utterly unsurmised appearance of Bartleby, tenanting my law-chambers of a Sunday morning, with his cadaverously gentlemanly *nonchalance*, yet withal firm and self-possessed, had such a strange effect upon me, that incontinently I slunk away from my own door, and did as desired. But not without sundry twinges of impotent rebellion against the mild effrontery of this unaccountable scrivener. Indeed, it was his wonderful mildness chiefly, which not only disarmed me, but unmanned me, as it were. For I consider that one, for the time, is a sort of unmanned when he tranquilly permits his hired clerk to dictate to him and order him away from his own premises. Furthermore, I was full of uneasiness as to what Bartleby could possibly be doing in my office in his shirt sleeves, and in an otherwise dismantled condition of a Sunday morning. Was any thing amiss going on? Nay, that was out of the question. It was not to be thought of for a moment that Bartleby was an immoral person. But what could he be doing there? — copying? Nay again, whatever might be his eccentricities, Bartleby was an eminently decorous person. He would be the last man to sit down to his desk in any state approaching to nudity. Besides, it was Sunday; and there was something about Bartleby that forbade the supposition that he would by any secular occupation violate the proprieties of the day.

Nevertheless, my mind was not pacified; and full of a restless curiosity, at last I returned to the door. Without hindrance I inserted my key, opened it, and entered.

Bartleby was not to be seen. I looked round anxiously, peeped behind his screen; but it was very plain that he was gone. Upon more closely examining the place, I surmised that for an indefinite period Bartleby must have ate, dressed, and slept in my office, and that too without plate, mirror, or bed. The cushioned seat of a ricketty old sofa in one corner bore the faint impress of a lean, reclining form. Rolled away under his desk, I found a blanket; under the empty grate, a blacking box and brush; on a chair, a tin basin, with soap and a ragged towel; in a newspaper a few crumbs of ginger-nuts and a morsel of cheese. Yes, thought I, it is evident enough that Bartleby has been making his home here, keeping bachelor's hall all by himself. Immediately then the thought came sweeping across me, What miserable friendlessness and loneliness are here revealed! His poverty is great; but his solitude, how horrible! Think of it. Of a Sunday, Wall-street is deserted as Petra;[17] and every night of every day it is an emptiness. This building too, which of week-days hums with industry and life, at nightfall echoes with sheer vacancy, and all through Sunday is forlorn. And here Bartleby makes his home; sole spectator of a solitude which he has seen all populous — a sort of innocent and transformed Marius brooding among the ruins of Carthage![18]

For the first time in my life a feeling of overpowering stinging melancholy seized me. Before, I had never experienced aught but a not-unpleasing sadness. The bond of a common humanity now drew me irresistibly to gloom. A fraternal melancholy! For both I and Bartleby were sons of Adam. I remembered the bright silks and sparkling faces I had seen that day, in gala trim, swan-like sailing down the Mississippi of Broadway; and I contrasted them with the pallid copyist, and thought to myself, Ah, happiness courts the light, so we deem the world is gay; but misery hides aloof, so we deem that misery there is none. These sad fancyings — chimeras, doubtless, of a sick and silly brain — led on to other and more special thoughts, concerning the eccentricities of Bartleby. Presentiments of strange discoveries hovered round me. The scrivener's pale form appeared to me laid out, among uncaring strangers, in its shivering winding sheet.

Suddenly I was attracted by Bartleby's closed desk, the key in open sight left in the lock.

I mean no mischief, seek the gratification of no heartless curiosity, thought I; besides, the desk is mine, and its contents too, so I will make bold to look within. Every thing was methodically arranged, the papers smoothly placed. The pigeon holes were deep, and removing the files of documents, I groped into their recesses. Presently I felt something there, and dragged it out. It was an old bandanna handkerchief, heavy and knotted. I opened it, and saw it was a savings' bank.

I now recalled all the quiet mysteries which I had noted in the man. I remembered that he never spoke but to answer; that though at intervals he had considerable time to himself, yet I had never seen him reading — no, not even a newspaper; that for long

---

17. **Petra:** The ruins of an ancient city, located in present-day Jordan, were discovered by European explorers in 1812.
18. **Marius . . . Carthage:** Gaius Marius (157–86 BCE), powerful Roman general and politician who lost favor and was sent into exile in North Africa.

periods he would stand looking out, at his pale window behind the screen, upon the dead brick wall; I was quite sure he never visited any refectory or eating house; while his pale face clearly indicated that he never drank beer like Turkey, or tea and coffee even, like other men; that he never went any where in particular that I could learn; never went out for a walk, unless indeed that was the case at present; that he had declined telling who he was, or whence he came, or whether he had any relatives in the world; that though so thin and pale, he never complained of ill health. And more than all, I remembered a certain unconscious air of pallid – how shall I call it? – of pallid haughtiness, say, or rather an austere reserve about him, which had positively awed me into my tame compliance with his eccentricities, when I had feared to ask him to do the slightest incidental thing for me, even though I might know, from his long-continued motionlessness, that behind his screen he must be standing in one of those dead-wall reveries of his.

Revolving all these things, and coupling them with the recently discovered fact that he made my office his constant abiding place and home, and not forgetful of his morbid moodiness; revolving all these things, a prudential feeling began to steal over me. My first emotions had been those of pure melancholy and sincerest pity; but just in proportion as the forlornness of Bartleby grew and grew to my imagination, did that same melancholy merge into fear, that pity into repulsion. So true it is, and so terrible too, that up to a certain point the thought or sight of misery enlists our best affections; but, in certain special cases, beyond that point it does not. They err who would assert that invariably this is owing to the inherent selfishness of the human heart. It rather proceeds from a certain hopelessness of remedying excessive and organic ill. To a sensitive being, pity is not seldom pain. And when at last it is perceived that such pity cannot lead to effectual succor, common sense bids the soul be rid of it. What I saw that morning persuaded me that the scrivener was the victim of innate and incurable disorder. I might give alms to his body; but his body did not pain him; it was his soul that suffered, and his soul I could not reach.

I did not accomplish the purpose of going to Trinity Church that morning. Somehow, the things I had seen disqualified me for the time from church-going. I walked homeward, thinking what I would do with Bartleby. Finally, I resolved upon this; – I would put certain calm questions to him the next morning, touching his history, &c., and if he declined to answer them openly and unreservedly (and I supposed he would prefer not), then to give him a twenty dollar bill over and above whatever I might owe him, and tell him his services were no longer required; but that if in any other way I could assist him, I would be happy to do so, especially if he desired to return to his native place, wherever that might be, I would willingly help to defray the expenses. Moreover, if, after reaching home, he found himself at any time in want of aid, a letter from him would be sure of a reply.

The next morning came.

"Bartleby," said I, gently calling to him behind his screen.

No reply.

"Bartleby," said I, in a still gentler tone, "come here; I am not going to ask you to do any thing you would prefer not to do – I simply wish to speak to you."

Upon this he noiselessly slid into view.

"Will you tell me, Bartleby, where you were born?"

"I would prefer not to."

"Will you tell me *any thing* about yourself?"

"I would prefer not to."

"But what reasonable objection can you have to speak to me? I feel friendly towards you."

He did not look at me while I spoke, but kept his glance fixed upon my bust of Cicero, which as I then sat, was directly behind me, some six inches above my head.

"What is your answer, Bartleby?" said I, after waiting a considerable time for a reply, during which his countenance remained immovable, only there was the faintest conceivable tremor of the white attenuated mouth.

"At present I prefer to give no answer," he said, and retired into his hermitage.

It was rather weak in me I confess, but his manner on this occasion nettled me. Not only did there seem to lurk in it a certain calm disdain, but his perverseness seemed ungrateful, considering the undeniable good usage and indulgence he had received from me.

Again I sat ruminating what I should do. Mortified as I was at his behavior, and resolved as I had been to dismiss him when I entered my office, nevertheless I strangely felt something superstitious knocking at my heart, and forbidding me to carry out my purpose, and denouncing me for a villain if I dared to breathe one bitter word against this forlornest of mankind. At last, familiarly drawing my chair behind his screen, I sat down and said: "Bartleby, never mind then about revealing your history; but let me entreat you, as a friend, to comply as far as may be with the usages of this office. Say now you will help to examine papers to-morrow or next day: in short, say now that in a day or two you will begin to be a little reasonable: — say so, Bartleby."

"At present I would prefer not to be a little reasonable," was his mildly cadaverous reply.

Just then the folding-doors opened, and Nippers approached. He seemed suffering from an unusually bad night's rest, induced by severer indigestion than common. He overheard those final words of Bartleby.

"*Prefer not*, eh?" gritted Nippers — "I'd *prefer* him, if I were you, sir," addressing me — "I'd *prefer* him; I'd give him preferences, the stubborn mule! What is it, sir, pray, that he *prefers* not to do now?"

Bartleby moved not a limb.

"Mr. Nippers," said I, "I'd prefer that you would withdraw for the present."

Somehow, of late I had got into the way of involuntarily using this word "prefer" upon all sorts of not exactly suitable occasions. And I trembled to think that my contact with the scrivener had already and seriously affected me in a mental way. And what further and deeper aberration might it not yet produce? This apprehension had not been without efficacy in determining me to summary means.

As Nippers, looking very sour and sulky, was departing, Turkey blandly and deferentially approached.

"With submission, sir," said he, "yesterday I was thinking about Bartleby here, and I think that if he would but prefer to take a quart of good ale every day, it would do much towards mending him, and enabling him to assist in examining his papers."

"So you have got the word too," said I, slightly excited.

"With submission, what word, sir," asked Turkey, respectfully crowding himself into the contracted space behind the screen, and by so doing, making me jostle the scrivener. "What word, sir?"

"I would prefer to be left alone here," said Bartleby, as if offended at being mobbed in his privacy.

"*That's* the word, Turkey," said I – "*that's* it."

"Oh, *prefer?* oh yes – queer word. I never use it myself. But, sir, as I was saying, if he would but prefer –"

"Turkey," interrupted I, "you will please withdraw."

"Oh certainly, sir, if you prefer that I should."

As he opened the folding-door to retire, Nippers at his desk caught a glimpse of me, and asked whether I would prefer to have a certain paper copied on blue paper or white. He did not in the least roguishly accent the word prefer. It was plain that it involuntarily rolled from his tongue. I thought to myself, surely I must get rid of a demented man, who already has in some degree turned the tongues, if not the heads of myself and clerks. But I thought it prudent not to break the dismission at once.

The next day I noticed that Bartleby did nothing but stand at his window in his dead-wall revery. Upon asking him why he did not write, he said that he had decided upon doing no more writing.

"Why, how now? what next?" exclaimed I, "do no more writing?"

"No more."

"And what is the reason?"

"Do you not see the reason for yourself," he indifferently replied.

I looked steadfastly at him, and perceived that his eyes looked dull and glazed. Instantly it occurred to me, that his unexampled diligence in copying by his dim window for the first few weeks of his stay with me might have temporarily impaired his vision.

I was touched. I said something in condolence with him. I hinted that of course he did wisely in abstaining from writing for a while; and urged him to embrace that opportunity of taking wholesome exercise in the open air. This, however, he did not do. A few days after this, my other clerks being absent, and being in a great hurry to dispatch certain letters by the mail, I thought that, having nothing else earthly to do, Bartleby would surely be less inflexible than usual, and carry these letters to the post-office. But he blankly declined. So, much to my inconvenience, I went myself.

Still added days went by. Whether Bartleby's eyes improved or not, I could not say. To all appearance, I thought they did. But when I asked him if they did, he vouchsafed no answer. At all events, he would do no copying. At last, in reply to my urgings, he informed me that he had permanently given up copying.

"What!" exclaimed I; "suppose your eyes should get entirely well – better than ever before – would you not copy then?"

"I have given up copying," he answered, and slid aside.

He remained as ever, a fixture in my chamber. Nay – if that were possible – he became still more of a fixture than before. What was to be done? He would do nothing in the office: why should he stay there? In plain fact, he had now become a millstone to me, not only useless as a necklace, but afflictive to bear. Yet I was sorry for him. I speak less than truth when I say that, on his own account, he occasioned me uneasiness. If he would but have named a single relative or friend, I would instantly have written, and urged their taking the poor fellow away to some convenient retreat. But he seemed alone, absolutely alone in the universe. A bit of wreck in the mid Atlantic. At length, necessities connected with my business tyrannized over all other considerations. Decently as I could I told Bartleby that in six days' time he must unconditionally leave the office. I warned him to take measures, in the interval, for procuring some other abode. I offered to assist him in this endeavor, if he himself would but take the first step towards a removal. "And when you finally quit me, Bartleby," added I, "I shall see that you go not away entirely unprovided. Six days from this hour, remember."

At the expiration of that period, I peeped behind the screen, and lo! Bartleby was there.

I buttoned up my coat, balanced myself; advanced slowly towards him, touched his shoulder, and said, "The time has come; you must quit this place; I am sorry for you; here is money; but you must go."

"I would prefer not," he replied, with his back still towards me.

"You *must.*"

He remained silent.

Now I had an unbounded confidence in this man's common honesty. He had frequently restored to me sixpences and shillings carelessly dropped upon the floor, for I am apt to be very reckless in such shirt-button affairs. The proceeding then which followed will not be deemed extraordinary.

"Bartleby," said I, "I owe you twelve dollars on account; here are thirty-two; the odd twenty are yours. – Will you take it?" and handed the bills towards him.

But he made no motion.

"I will leave them here then," putting them under a weight on the table. Then taking my hat and cane and going to the door I tranquilly turned and added – "After you have removed your things from these offices, Bartleby, you will of course lock the door – since every one is now gone for the day but you – and if you please, slip your key underneath the mat, so that I may have it in the morning. I shall not see you again; so good-bye to you. If hereafter in your new place of abode I can be of any service to you, do not fail to advise me by letter. Good-bye, Bartleby, and fare you well."

But he answered not a word; like the last column of some ruined temple, he remained standing mute and solitary in the middle of the otherwise deserted room.

As I walked home in a pensive mood, my vanity got the better of my pity. I could not but highly plume myself on my masterly management in getting rid of Bartleby. Masterly I call it, and such it must appear to any dispassionate thinker. The beauty of my procedure seemed to consist in its perfect quietness. There was no vulgar bullying, no bravado of any sort, no choleric hectoring, and striding to and fro across the apartment, jerking out vehement commands for Bartleby to bundle himself off with his beggarly traps. Nothing of the kind. Without loudly bidding Bartleby depart — as an inferior genius might have done — I *assumed* the ground that depart he must; and upon that assumption built all I had to say. The more I thought over my procedure, the more I was charmed with it. Nevertheless, next morning, upon awakening, I had my doubts, — I had somehow slept off the fumes of vanity. One of the coolest and wisest hours a man has, is just after he awakes in the morning. My procedure seemed as sagacious ever, — but only in theory. How it would prove in practice — there was the rub. It was truly a beautiful thought to have assumed Bartleby's departure; but, after all, that assumption was simply my own, and none of Bartleby's. The great point was, not whether I had assumed that he would quit me, but whether he would prefer so to do. He was more a man of preferences than assumptions.[19]

After breakfast, I walked down town, arguing the probabilities *pro* and *con.* One moment I thought it would prove a miserable failure, and Bartleby would be found all alive at my office as usual; the next moment it seemed certain that I should see his chair empty. And so I kept veering about. At the corner of Broadway and Canal-street, I saw quite an excited group of people standing in earnest conversation.

"I'll take odds he doesn't," said a voice as I passed.

"Doesn't go? — done!" said I, "put up your money."

I was instinctively putting my hand in my pocket to produce my own, when I remembered that this was an election day. The words I had overheard bore no reference to Bartleby, but to the success or non-success of some candidate for the mayoralty. In my intent frame of mind, I had, as it were, imagined that all Broadway shared in my excitement, and were debating the same question with me. I passed on, very thankful that the uproar of the street screened my momentary absent-mindedness.

As I had intended, I was earlier than usual at my office door. I stood listening for a moment. All was still. He must he gone. I tried the knob. The door was locked. Yes, my procedure had worked to a charm; he indeed must be vanished. Yet a certain melancholy mixed with this: I was almost sorry for my brilliant success. I was fumbling under the door mat for the key, which Bartleby was to have left there for me, when accidentally my knee knocked against a panel, producing a summoning sound, and in response a voice came to me from within — "Not yet; I am occupied."

It was Bartleby.

I was thunderstruck. For an instant I stood like the man who, pipe in mouth, was killed one cloudless afternoon long ago in Virginia, by summer lightning; at his own warm open window he was killed, and remained leaning out there upon the dreamy afternoon, till some one touched him, when he fell.

"Not gone!" I murmured at last. But again obeying that wondrous ascendancy which the inscrutable scrivener had over me, and from which ascendancy, for all my chafing, I could not completely escape, I slowly went down stairs and out into the street, and while walking round the block, considered what I should next do in this unheard-of perplexity.

---

19. **assumptions:** In the original printing in *Putnam's*, the first part of "Bartleby" ended at this point. The story continued in the next month's issue.

Turn the man out by an actual thrusting I could not; to drive him away by calling him hard names would not do; calling in the police was an unpleasant idea; and yet, permit him to enjoy his cadaverous triumph over me, – this too I could not think of. What was to be done? or, if nothing could be done, was there any thing further that I could *assume* in the matter? Yes, as before I had prospectively assumed that Bartleby would depart, so now I might retrospectively assume that departed he was. In the legitimate carrying out of this assumption, I might enter my office in a great hurry, and pretending not to see Bartleby at all, walk straight against him as if he were air. Such a proceeding would in a singular degree have the appearance of a home-thrust. It was hardly possible that Bartleby could withstand such an application of the doctrine of assumptions. But upon second thoughts the success of the plan seemed rather dubious. I resolved to argue the matter over with him again.

"Bartleby," said I, entering the office, with a quietly severe expression, "I am seriously displeased. I am pained, Bartleby. I had thought better of you. I had imagined you of such a gentlemanly organization, that in any delicate dilemma a slight hint would suffice – in short, an assumption. But it appears I am deceived. Why," I added, unaffectedly starting, "you have not even touched that money yet," pointing to it, just where I had left it the evening previous.

He answered nothing.

"Will you, or will you not, quit me?" I now demanded in a sudden passion, advancing close to him.

"I would prefer *not* to quit you," he replied, gently emphasizing the *not.*

"What earthly right have you to stay here? Do you pay any rent? Do you pay my taxes? Or is this property yours?"

He answered nothing.

"Are you ready to go on and write now? Are your eyes recovered? Could you copy a small paper for me this morning? or help examine a few lines? or step round to the post-office? In a word, will you do any thing at all, to give a coloring to your refusal to depart the premises?"

He silently retired into his hermitage.

I was now in such a state of nervous resentment that I thought it but prudent to check myself at present from further demonstrations. Bartleby and I were alone. I remembered the tragedy of the unfortunate Adams and the still more unfortunate Colt[20] in the solitary office of the latter; and how poor Colt, being dreadfully incensed by Adams, and imprudently permitting himself to get wildly excited, was at unawares hurried into his fatal act – an act which certainly no man could possibly deplore more than the actor himself. Often it had occurred to me in my ponderings upon the subject, that

---

20. **Adams . . . Colt:** John C. Colt was a wealthy New York businessman who murdered a printer, Samuel Adams, in 1841. Adams had visited Colt in his lower Manhattan office to collect a debt, and Colt killed Adams with a hatchet. To cover up the crime, Colt crated the body for shipment to New Orleans, but it was discovered and Colt was arrested and sentenced for the murder. Claiming that the crime was an act of self-defense, Colt stabbed himself to death in the Tombs before he was to be hanged on November 18, 1842.

had that altercation taken place in the public street, or at a private residence, it would not have terminated as it did. It was the circumstance of being alone in a solitary office, up stairs, of a building entirely unhallowed by humanizing domestic associations — an uncarpeted office, doubtless, of a dusty, haggard sort of appearance; — this it must have been, which greatly helped to enhance the irritable desperation of the hapless Colt.

But when this old Adam of resentment rose in me and tempted me concerning Bartleby, I grappled him and threw him. How? Why, simply by recalling the divine injunction: "A new commandment give I unto you, that ye love one another."[21] Yes, this it was that saved me. Aside from higher considerations, charity often operates as a vastly wise and prudent principle — a great safeguard to its possessor. Men have committed murder for jealousy's sake, and anger's sake, and hatred's sake, and selfishness' sake, and spiritual pride's sake; but no man that ever I heard of, ever committed a diabolical murder for sweet charity's sake. Mere self-interest, then, if no better motive can be enlisted, should, especially with high-tempered men, prompt all beings to charity and philanthropy. At any rate, upon the occasion in question, I strove to drown my exasperated feelings towards the scrivener by benevolently construing his conduct. Poor fellow, poor fellow! thought I, he don't mean any thing; and besides, he has seen hard times, and ought to be indulged.

I endeavored also immediately to occupy myself, and at the same time to comfort my despondency. I tried to fancy that in the course of the morning, at such time as might prove agreeable to him, Bartleby, of his own free accord, would emerge from his hermitage, and take up some decided line of march in the direction of the door. But no. Half-past twelve o'clock came; Turkey began to glow in the face, overturn his inkstand, and become generally obstreperous; Nippers abated down into quietude and courtesy; Ginger Nut munched his noon apple; and Bartleby remained standing at his window in one of his profoundest dead-wall reveries. Will it be credited? Ought I to acknowledge it? That afternoon I left the office without saying one further word to him.

Some days now passed, during which, at leisure intervals I looked a little into "Edwards on the Will," and "Priestley on Necessity."[22] Under the circumstances, those books induced a salutary feeling. Gradually I slid into the persuasion that these troubles of mine touching the scrivener, had been all predestinated from eternity, and Bartleby was billeted upon me for some mysterious purpose of an all-wise Providence, which it was not for a mere mortal like me to fathom. Yes, Bartleby, stay there behind your screen, thought I; I shall persecute you no more; you are harmless and noiseless as any of these old chairs; in short, I never feel so private as when I know you are here. At last I see it, I feel it; I penetrate to the predestinated purpose of my life. I am content. Others may have loftier parts to enact; but my mission in this world, Bartleby, is to furnish you with office-room for such period as you may see fit to remain.

---

21. "A new commandment . . . love one another": Jesus's words to his disciples in John 13:34.
22. "Edwards on the Will," and "Priestley on Necessity": Jonathan Edwards (1703-1758), a colonial American clergyman and theologian, was the author of *Freedom of the Will* (1754); Joseph Priestley (1733-1804), a British scientist and clergyman, wrote *Doctrine of Philosophical Necessity Illustrated* (1777). Both writers argued that events were predestined and that human beings have no free will.

I believe that this wise and blessed frame of mind would have continued with me, had it not been for the unsolicited and uncharitable remarks obtruded upon me by my professional friends who visited the rooms. But thus it often is, that the constant friction of illiberal minds wears out at last the best resolves of the more generous. Though to be sure, when I reflected upon it, it was not strange that people entering my office should be struck by the peculiar aspect of the unaccountable Bartleby, and so be tempted to throw out some sinister observations concerning him. Sometimes an attorney having business with me, and calling at my office, and finding no one but the scrivener there, would undertake to obtain some sort of precise information from him touching my whereabouts; but without heeding his idle talk, Bartleby would remain standing immovable in the middle of the room. So after contemplating him in that position for a time, the attorney would depart, no wiser than he came.

Also, when a Reference[23] was going on, and the room full of lawyers and witnesses and business was driving fast; some deeply occupied legal gentleman present, seeing Bartleby wholly unemployed, would request him to run round to his (the legal gentleman's) office and fetch some papers for him. Thereupon, Bartleby would tranquilly decline, and yet remain idle as before. Then the lawyer would give a great stare, and turn to me. And what could I say? At last I was made aware that all through the circle of my professional acquaintance, a whisper of wonder was running round, having reference to the strange creature I kept at my office. This worried me very much. And as the idea came upon me of his possibly turning out a long-lived man, and keep occupying my chambers, and denying my authority; and perplexing my visitors; and scandalizing my professional reputation; and casting a general gloom over the premises; keeping soul and body together to the last upon his saving (for doubtless he spent but half a dime a day), and in the end perhaps outlive me, and claim possession of my office by right of his perpetual occupancy: as all these dark anticipations crowded upon me more and more, and my friends continually intruded their relentless remarks upon the apparition in my room; a great change was wrought in me. I resolved to gather all my faculties together, and for ever rid me of this intolerable incubus.

Ere revolving any complicated project, however, adapted to this end, I first simply suggested to Bartleby the propriety of his permanent departure. In a calm and serious tone, I commended the idea to his careful and mature consideration. But having taken three days to meditate upon it, he apprised me that his original determination remained the same; in short, that he still preferred to abide with me.

What shall I do? I now said to myself, buttoning up my coat to the last button. What shall I do? what ought I to do? what does conscience say I *should* do with this man, or rather ghost. Rid myself of him, I must; go, he shall. But how? You will not thrust him, the poor, pale, passive mortal, — you will not thrust such a helpless creature out of your door? you will not dishonor yourself by such cruelty? No, I will not, I cannot do that. Rather would I let him live and die here, and then mason up his remains in the wall. What then will you do? For all your coaxing, he will not budge. Bribes he leaves under

---

23. **Reference:** A legal proceeding in which a dispute is argued before a referee.

your own paperweight on your table; in short, it is quite plain that he prefers to cling to you.

Then something severe, something unusual must be done. What! surely you will not have him collared by a constable, and commit his innocent pallor to the common jail? And upon what ground could you procure such a thing to be done? — a vagrant, is he? What! he a vagrant, a wanderer, who refuses to budge? It is because he will *not* be a vagrant, then, that you seek to count him *as* a vagrant. That is too absurd. No visible means of support: there I have him. Wrong again: for indubitably he *does* support himself, and that is the only unanswerable proof that any man can show of his possessing the means so to do. No more then. Since he will not quit me, I must quit him. I will change my offices; I will move elsewhere; and give him fair notice that if I find him on my new premises I will then proceed against him as a common trespasser.

Acting accordingly, next day I thus addressed him: "I find these chambers too far from the City Hall; the air is unwholesome. In a word, I propose to remove my offices next week, and shall no longer require your services. I tell you this now, in order that you may seek another place."

He made no reply, and nothing more was said.

On the appointed day I engaged carts and men, proceeded to my chambers, and having but little furniture, every thing was removed in a few hours. Throughout, the scrivener remained standing behind the screen, which I directed to be removed the last thing. It was withdrawn; and being folded up like a huge folio, left him the motionless occupant of a naked room. I stood in the entry watching him a moment, while something from within me upbraided me.

I re-entered, with my hand in my pocket — and — and my heart in my mouth.

"Good-bye, Bartleby; I am going — good-bye, and God some way bless you; and take that," slipping something in his hand. But it dropped upon the floor, and then, — strange to say — I tore myself from him whom I had so longed to be rid of.

Established in my new quarters, for a day or two I kept the door locked, and started at every footfall in the passages. When I returned to my rooms after any little absence, I would pause at the threshold for an instant, and attentively listen, ere applying my key. But these fears were needless. Bartleby never came nigh me.

I thought all was going well, when a perturbed looking stranger visited me, inquiring whether I was the person who had recently occupied rooms at No. — Wall-street.

Full of forebodings, I replied that I was.

"Then sir," said the stranger, who proved a lawyer, "you are responsible for the man you left there. He refuses to do any copying; he refuses to do any thing; he says he prefers not to; and he refuses to quit the premises."

"I am very sorry, sir," said I, with assumed tranquillity, but an inward tremor, "but, really, the man you allude to is nothing to me — he is no relation or apprentice of mine, that you should hold me responsible for him."

"In mercy's name, who is he?"

"I certainly cannot inform you. I know nothing about him. Formerly I employed him as a copyist; but he has done nothing for me now for some time past."

"I shall settle him then, — good morning, sir."

Several days passed, and I heard nothing more; and though I often felt a charitable prompting to call at the place and see poor Bartleby, yet a certain squeamishness of I know not what withheld me.

All is over with him, by this time, thought I at last, when through another week no further intelligence reached me. But coming to my room the day after, I found several persons waiting at my door in a high state of nervous excitement.

"That's the man — here he comes," cried the foremost one, whom I recognized as the lawyer who had previously called upon me alone.

"You must take him away, sir, at once," cried a portly person among them, advancing upon me, and whom I knew to be the landlord of No. – Wall-street. "These gentlemen, my tenants, cannot stand it any longer; Mr. B—" pointing to the lawyer, "has turned him out of his room, and he now persists in haunting the building generally, sitting upon the banisters of the stairs by day, and sleeping in the entry by night. Every body is concerned; clients are leaving the offices; some fears are entertained of a mob; something you must do, and that without delay."

Aghast at this torrent, I fell back before it, and would fain have locked myself in my new quarters. In vain I persisted that Bartleby was nothing to me — no more than to any-one else. In vain: — I was the last person known to have any thing to do with him, and they held me to the terrible account. Fearful then of being exposed in the papers (as one person present obscurely threatened) I considered the matter, and at length said, that if the lawyer could give me a confidential interview with the scrivener, in his (the lawyer's) own room, I would that afternoon strive my best to rid them of the nuisance they complained of.

Going up stairs to my old haunt, there was Bartleby silently sitting upon the banister at the landing.

"What are you doing here, Bartleby?"

"Sitting upon the banister," he mildly replied.

I motioned him into the lawyer's room, who then left us.

"Bartleby," said I, "are you aware that you are the cause of great tribulation to me, by persisting in occupying the entry after being dismissed from the office?"

No answer.

"Now one of two things must take place. Either you must do something, or something must be done to you. Now what sort of business would you like to engage in? Would you like to re-engage in copying for some one?"

"No; I would prefer not to make any change."

"Would you like a clerkship in a dry-goods store?"

"There is too much confinement about that. No, I would not like a clerkship; but I am not particular."

"Too much confinement," I cried, "why you keep yourself confined all the time!"

"I would prefer not to take a clerkship," he rejoined, as if to settle that little item at once.

"How would a bar-tender's business suit you? There is no trying of the eyesight in that."

"I would not like it at all; though, as I said before, I am not particular."

His unwonted wordiness inspirited me. I returned to the charge.

"Well then, would you like to travel through the country collecting bills for the merchants? That would improve your health."

"No, I would prefer to be doing something else."

"How then would going as a companion to Europe, to entertain some young gentleman with your conversation, – how would that suit you?"

"Not at all. It does not strike me that there is any thing definite about that. I like to be stationary. But I am not particular."

"Stationary you shall be then," I cried, now losing all patience, and for the first time in all my exasperating connection with him fairly flying into a passion. "If you do not go away from these premises before night, I shall feel bound – indeed I *am* bound – to – to – to quit the premises myself!" I rather absurdly concluded, knowing not with what possible threat to try to frighten his immobility into compliance. Despairing of all further efforts, I was precipitately leaving him, when a final thought occurred to me – one which had not been wholly unindulged before.

"Bartleby," said I, in the kindest tone I could assume under such exciting circumstances, "will you go home with me now – not to my office, but my dwelling – and remain there till we can conclude upon some convenient arrangement for you at our leisure? Come, let us start now, right away."

"No: at present I would prefer not to make any change at all."

I answered nothing; but effectually dodging every one by the suddenness and rapidity of my flight, rushed from the building, ran up Wall-street towards Broadway, and jumping into the first omnibus was soon removed from pursuit. As soon as tranquillity returned I distinctly perceived that I had now done all that I possibly could, both in respect to the demands of the landlord and his tenants, and with regard to my own desire and sense of duty, to benefit Bartleby, and shield him from rude persecution. I now strove to be entirely care-free and quiescent; and my conscience justified me in the attempt; though indeed it was not so successful as I could have wished. So fearful was I of being again hunted out by the incensed landlord and his exasperated tenants, that, surrendering my business to Nippers, for a few days I drove about the upper part of the town and through the suburbs, in my rockaway;[24] crossed over to Jersey City and Hoboken, and paid fugitive visits to Manhattanville and Astoria. In fact I almost lived in my rockaway for the time.

When again I entered my office, lo, a note from the landlord lay upon the desk. I opened it with trembling hands. It informed me that the writer had sent to the police, and had Bartleby removed to the Tombs as a vagrant. Moreover, since I knew more about him than any one else, he wished me to appear at that place, and make a suitable statement of the facts. These tidings had a conflicting effect upon me. At first I was indignant; but at last almost approved. The landlord's energetic, summary disposition had led him to adopt a procedure which I do not think I would have decided upon myself; and yet as a last resort, under such peculiar circumstances, it seemed the only plan.

---

24. **rockaway:** A four-wheeled, enclosed carriage with two seats inside.

As I afterwards learned, the poor scrivener, when told that he must be conducted to the Tombs, offered not the slightest obstacle, but in his pale unmoving way, silently acquiesced.

Some of the compassionate and curious bystanders joined the party; and headed by one of the constables arm in arm with Bartleby, the silent procession filed its way through all the noise, and heat, and joy of the roaring thoroughfares at noon.

The same day I received the note I went to the Tombs, or to speak more properly, the Halls of Justice. Seeking the right officer, I stated the purpose of my call, and was informed that the individual I described was indeed within. I then assured the functionary that Bartleby was a perfectly honest man, and greatly to be compassionated, however unaccountably eccentric. I narrated all I knew, and closed by suggesting the idea of letting him remain in as indulgent confinement as possible till something less harsh might be done — though indeed I hardly knew what. At all events, if nothing else could be decided upon, the alms-house must receive him. I then begged to have an interview.

Being under no disgraceful charge, and quite serene and harmless in all his ways, they had permitted him freely to wander about the prison, and especially in the inclosed grass-platted yards thereof. And so I found him there, standing all alone in the quietest of the yards, his face towards a high wall, while all around, from the narrow slits of the jail windows, I thought I saw peering out upon him the eyes of murderers and thieves.

"Bartleby!"

"I know you," he said, without looking round, — "and I want nothing to say to you."

"It was not I that brought you here, Bartleby," said I, keenly pained at his implied suspicion. "And to you, this should not be so vile a place. Nothing reproachful attaches to you by being here. And see, it is not so sad a place as one might think. Look, there is the sky, and here is the grass."

"I know where I am," he replied, but would say nothing more, and so I left him.

As I entered the corridor again, a broad meat-like man, in an apron, accosted me, and jerking his thumb over his shoulder said — "Is that your friend?"

"Yes."

"Does he want to starve? If he does, let him live on the prison fare, that's all."

"Who are you?" asked I, not knowing what to make of such an unofficially speaking person in such a place.

"I am the grub-man. Such gentlemen as have friends here, hire me to provide them with something good to eat."

"Is this so?" said I, turning to the turnkey.

He said it was.

"Well then," said I, slipping some silver into the grub-man's hands (for so they called him). "I want you to give particular attention to my friend there; let him have the best dinner you can get. And you must be as polite to him as possible."

"Introduce me, will you?" said the grub-man, looking at me with an expression which seem to say he was all impatience for an opportunity to give a specimen of his breeding.

Thinking it would prove of benefit to the scrivener, I acquiesced; and asking the grub-man his name, went up with him to Bartleby.

"Bartleby, this is Mr. Cutlets; you will find him very useful to you."

"Your sarvant, sir, your sarvant," said the grub-man, making a low salutation behind his apron. "Hope you find it pleasant here, sir; — spacious grounds — cool apartments, sir — hope you'll stay with us some time — try to make it agreeable. May Mrs. Cutlets and I have the pleasure of your company to dinner, sir, in Mrs. Cutlets' private room?"

"I prefer not to dine to-day," said Bartleby, turning away. "It would disagree with me; I am unused to dinners." So saying he slowly moved to the other side of the inclosure, and took up a position fronting the dead-wall.

"How's this?" said the grub-man, addressing me with a stare of astonishment. "He's odd, aint he?"

"I think he is a little deranged," said I, sadly.

"Deranged? deranged is it? Well now, upon my word, I thought that friend of yourn was a gentleman forger; they are always pale and genteel-like, them forgers. I can't help pity 'em — can't help it, sir. Did you know Monroe Edwards?"[25] he added touchingly, and paused. Then, laying his hand pityingly on my shoulder, sighed, "he died of consumption at Sing-Sing. So you weren't acquainted with Monroe?"

"No. I was never socially acquainted with any forgers. But I cannot stop longer. Look to my friend yonder. You will not lose by it. I will see you again."

Some few days after this, I again obtained admission to the Tombs, and went through the corridors in quest of Bartleby; but without finding him.

"I saw him coming from his cell not long ago," said a turnkey, "may be he's gone to loiter in the yards."

So I went in that direction.

"Are you looking for the silent man?" said another turnkey passing me. "Yonder he lies — sleeping in the yard there. 'Tis not twenty minutes since I saw him lie down."

The yard was entirely quiet. It was not accessible to the common prisoners. The surrounding walls, of amazing thickness, kept off all sounds behind them. The Egyptian character of the masonry weighed upon me with its gloom. But a soft imprisoned turf grew under foot. The heart of the eternal pyramids, it seemed, wherein, by some strange magic, through the clefts, grass-seed, dropped by birds, had sprung.

Strangely huddled at the base of the wall, his knees drawn up, and lying on his side, his head touching the cold stones, I saw the wasted Bartleby. But nothing stirred. I paused; then went close up to him; stooped over, and saw that his dim eyes were open; otherwise he seemed profoundly sleeping. Something prompted me to touch him. I felt his hand, when a tingling shiver ran up my arm and down my spine to my feet.

The round face of the grub-man peered upon me now. "His dinner is ready. Won't he dine to-day, either? Or does he live without dining?"

"Lives without dining," said I, and closed the eyes.

---

25. **Monroe Edwards:** Edwards (1803?–1847) was a swindler and forger who notoriously defrauded several New York banks with bogus letters of credit. In 1842, he was arrested, convicted, and sentenced to ten years at Sing Sing, a brutal, "no-frills" prison on the banks of the Hudson River north of New York City — thus the expression "sent up the river." After an unsuccessful attempt to commit suicide and another to escape, Edwards died in the prison.

"Eh! – He's asleep, aint he?"

"With kings and counsellors,"[26] murmured I.

There would seem little need for proceeding further in this history. Imagination will readily supply the meagre recital of poor Bartleby's interment. But ere parting with the reader, let me say, that if this little narrative has sufficiently interested him, to awaken curiosity as to who Bartleby was, and what manner of life he led prior to the present narrator's making his acquaintance, I can only reply, that in such curiosity I fully share, but am wholly unable to gratify it. Yet here I hardly know whether I should divulge one little item of rumor, which came to my ear a few months after the scrivener's decease. Upon what basis it rested, I could never ascertain; and hence, how true it is I cannot now tell. But inasmuch as this vague report has not been without a certain strange suggestive interest to me, however sad, it may prove the same with some others; and so I will briefly mention it. The report was this: that Bartleby had been a subordinate clerk in the Dead Letter Office[27] at Washington, from which he had been suddenly removed by a change in the administration. When I think over this rumor, I cannot adequately express the emotions which seize me. Dead letters! does it not sound like dead men? Conceive a man by nature and misfortune prone to a pallid hopelessness, can any business seem more fitted to heighten it than that of continually handling these dead letters, and sorting them for the flames? For by the cart-load they are annually burned. Sometimes from out the folded paper the pale clerk takes a ring: – the finger it was meant for, perhaps, moulders in the grave; a bank-note sent in swiftest charity: – he whom it would relieve, nor eats nor hungers any more; pardon for those who died despairing; hope for those who died unhoping; good tidings for those who died stifled by unrelieved calamities. On errands of life, these letters speed to death.

Ah Bartleby! Ah humanity!

[1853]

---

26. **kings and counsellors:** In the Old Testament, the afflicted Job curses the day he was born and asks: "Why died I not from the womb? Why did I not give up the ghost when I came out of the belly? Why did the knees prevent me? or why the breasts that I should suck? For now should I have lain still and been quiet, I should have slept: then had I been at rest, With kings and counsellors of the earth, which build desolate places for themselves" (Job 3:11-14).

27. **Dead Letter Office:** A room or department in the post office for letters that are undeliverable and unreturnable because of partial or incorrect addresses.

Rebecca Harding Davis

[1831–1910]

Rebecca Harding Davis was born on June 24, 1831. She was the first of five children of Richard W. Harding, a cultivated Englishman who had come to America seeking to make his fortune in business, and Rebecca Leet

Rebecca Harding Davis

This photograph was taken when Davis was about thirty years old, around the same time that her first major work, *Life in the Iron-Mills*, appeared in the prestigious *Atlantic Monthly*.

Her pioneering firsts in subject matter are unequaled. She extended the realm of fiction.
—Tillie Olsen

Harding, the well-educated daughter of a prominent family in western Pennsylvania. Davis was born in her mother's family home in Washington, a small town south of Pittsburgh, but she spent her earliest years in Alabama, where her father had first settled. In 1836, Richard Harding moved his family to Wheeling, in the northwestern and pro-Union part of Virginia that became West Virginia during the Civil War. Davis grew up there in an affluent, cultured home in which she was given an extensive education by tutors and her mother. When Davis was fourteen, she was sent to the Washington Female Seminary in Pennsylvania, where she studied a wide range of subjects, including art and music, English literature, French, philosophy, and religion. After graduating as the valedictorian of her class in 1848, Davis returned home and lived with her family for the next fourteen years, helping with the education of her younger siblings and occasionally writing for the *Wheeling Intelligencer*, the largest newspaper in western Virginia.

Although she had a long and productive literary career, Davis's first significant publication is widely regarded as her best and most enduring work. When her first story, *Life in the Iron-Mills*, was published anonymously in the *Atlantic Monthly* in April 1861, it was immediately hailed as an outstanding work by a talented new writer. In accepting the story for publication, the editor of the *Atlantic*, James T. Fields, sent Davis a check for $50 and offered her $100 for another contribution. She sent him another grimly realistic story, "The Deaf and the Dumb," about a woman who is abandoned by her lover and works in the mills to support her parents. Fields thought it was too gloomy and asked her to change the title and the ending. In an example of what many critics view as a primary source of the flaws in much of her work — her willingness to tailor it to suit popular taste — Davis obliged by ending the story with the promise of a happy marriage and changing its title to "A Story of To-day." The revised and expanded version was serialized in the *Atlantic* and then published as her first novel, *Margret Howth: A Story of To-day* (1862). That year, she traveled to New England and met Ralph Waldo Emerson, Louisa May Alcott, and Nathaniel Hawthorne, who had written her a congratulatory note about *Life in the Iron-Mills* and whose work Davis particularly respected. (She later observed that Hawthorne's short stories had inspired her own style of writing.) In 1863, she met one of her admiring readers, L. Clarke Davis, who had begun corresponding with her after reading her work. The couple soon married. L. Clarke Davis, a lawyer, later became the prominent editor of the *Philadelphia Inquirer* and then the *Philadelphia Public Ledger*. Throughout their long marriage and the births of three children, Davis published steadily and produced some other significant works such as *Waiting for the Verdict* (1868), an ambitious novel about the Civil War. But her later writings are more distinguished by their bulk than by their quality. Scholars estimate that Davis published nearly five hundred works — including nine novels; numerous short stories and novellas; and many works of nonfiction, notably her entertaining autobiography, *Bits of Gossip* (1904), which appeared six years before her death in 1910.

Wheeling Iron Works

This view of the Top Mill of the Wheeling Iron and Nail Company, with smoke belching from its forest of tall chimneys, appeared in the *Illustrated Atlas of the Upper Ohio River and Valley* (1877).

Reading Davis's *Life in the Iron-Mills.*   In her autobiography, Davis described the fires of bituminous coal that burned in each room of her family home in Wheeling, Virginia. "These flames and grey ashes have always burned in my memory," she observed. They are also a constant motif in *Life in the Iron-Mills*, her realistic and richly symbolic depiction of a nightmarish world not very distant and yet far removed from her family's comfortable home. Davis wrote the story in 1860, an election year in which sectional divisions over slavery were leading the country toward disunion. But she focused on the sufferings of another oppressed group, the immigrant laborers in industrial centers like Wheeling, where Davis had spent most of her life and which she had frequently explored on long rambling walks around that grimy mill town on the Ohio River. An unknown writer, Davis boldly submitted the story to the most prestigious literary journal in the country, the *Atlantic Monthly*. Established in 1857 by a group of luminaries including Ralph Waldo Emerson, Oliver Wendell Holmes, and James Russell Lowell, the *Atlantic* was designed to promote American literature by publishing the work of the best writers in the country – both established figures and emerging talents, many of whom were women. Recognizing the story as a pioneering work in the emerging mode of realistic fiction, James T. Fields eagerly accepted *Life in the Iron-Mills* for publication in the *Atlantic*. It appeared there in April 1861, the month the Civil War began. After Virginia seceded from the Union, a pro-Union government was organized in Wheeling, which ultimately became the capital of the new state of West Virginia (1863). The following text is taken from the story's first printing in the *Atlantic Monthly*.

bedfordstmartins.com/
americanlit for research
links on Davis

LIFE IN THE IRON-MILLS

"Is this the end?
   O Life, as futile, then, as frail!
   What hope of answer or redress?"[1]

A cloudy day: do you know what that is in a town of iron-works?[2] The sky sank down before dawn, muddy, flat, immovable. The air is thick, clammy with the breath of crowded human beings. It stifles me. I open the window, and, looking out, can scarcely see through the rain the grocer's shop opposite, where a crowd of drunken Irishmen are puffing Lynchburg tobacco[3] in their pipes. I can detect the scent through all the foul smells ranging loose in the air.

The idiosyncrasy of this town is smoke. It rolls sullenly in slow folds from the great chimneys of the iron-foundries, and settles down in black, slimy pools on the muddy streets. Smoke on the wharves, smoke on the dingy boats, on the yellow river, — clinging in a coating of greasy soot to the house-front, the two faded poplars, the faces of the passers-by. The long train of mules, dragging masses of pig-iron[4] through the narrow street, have a foul vapor hanging to their reeking sides. Here, inside, is a little broken figure of an angel pointing upward from the mantel-shelf; but even its wings are covered with smoke, clotted and black. Smoke everywhere! A dirty canary chirps desolately in a cage beside me. Its dream of green fields and sunshine is a very old dream, — almost worn out, I think.

From the back-window I can see a narrow brick-yard sloping down to the river-side, strewed with rain-butts[5] and tubs. The river, dull and tawny-colored, (*la belle rivière!*)[6] drags itself sluggishly along, tired of the heavy weight of boats and coal-barges. What wonder? When I was a child, I used to fancy a look of weary, dumb appeal upon the face of the negro-like river slavishly bearing its burden day after day. Something of the same idle notion comes to me to-day, when from the street-window I look on the slow stream of human life creeping past, night and morning, to the great mills. Masses of men, with dull, besotted faces bent to the ground, sharpened here and there by pain or cunning; skin and muscle and flesh begrimed with smoke and ashes; stooping all night over boiling

---

1. **"Is this the end? . . . redress?":** The epigraph is adapted from two sections of the popular, long elegiac poem, *In Memoriam A.H.H.* (1850), by the English poet Alfred, Lord Tennyson (1809-1892), who wrote it to commemorate the untimely death of his friend, Arthur Henry Hallam. The first line is from section 12, lines 14-16: "'Is this the end of all my care?' / And circle moaning in the air: / 'Is this the end? Is this the end?'" The second two lines are taken from section 56, lines 25-29: "O life as futile, then, as frail! / O for thy voice to soothe and bless! / What hope of answer, or redress? / Behind the veil, behind the veil."
2. **town of iron-works:** Although the exact location is not specified in the story, Davis portrays the pollution and economic hardships of many towns like Wheeling, Virginia (later West Virginia), where she grew up and witnessed such conditions firsthand.
3. **Lynchburg tobacco:** In the mid-1800s, Lynchburg, Virginia, had the largest market share of dark-leaf tobacco, considered inferior to lighter varieties.
4. **pig-iron:** Crude form of iron cast in molds to form small ingots or blocks.
5. **rain-butts:** Large barrels designed to capture rainwater for domestic and industrial use.
6. *la belle rivière!*: The beautiful river (French); an ironic commentary on the polluted state of the Ohio River in the mid-nineteenth century.

caldrons of metal, laired by day in dens of drunkenness and infamy; breathing from infancy to death an air saturated with fog and grease and soot, vileness for soul and body. What do you make of a case like that, amateur psychologist? You call it an altogether serious thing to be alive: to these men it is a drunken jest, a joke, – horrible to angels perhaps, to them commonplace enough. My fancy about the river was an idle one: it is no type of such a life. What if it be stagnant and slimy here? It knows that beyond there waits for it odorous sunlight, – quaint old gardens, dusky with soft, green foliage of apple-trees, and flushing crimson with roses, – air, and fields, and mountains. The future of the Welsh puddler[7] passing just now is not so pleasant. To be stowed away, after his grimy work is done, in a hole in the muddy graveyard, and after that, – *not* air, nor green fields, nor curious roses.

Can you see how foggy the day is? As I stand here, idly tapping the window-pane, and looking out through the rain at the dirty back-yard and the coal-boats below, fragments of an old story float up before me, – a story of this old house into which I happened to come to-day. You may think it a tiresome story enough, as foggy as the day, sharpened by no sudden flashes of pain or pleasure. – I know: only the outline of a dull life, that long since, with thousands of dull lives like its own, was vainly lived and lost: thousands of them, – massed, vile, slimy lives, like those of the torpid lizards in yonder stagnant water-butt. – Lost? There is a curious point for you to settle, my friend, who study psychology in a lazy, *dilettante* way. Stop a moment. I am going to be honest. This is what I want you to do. I want you to hide your disgust, take no heed to your clean clothes, and come right down with me, – here, into the thickest of the fog and mud and foul effluvia. I want you to hear this story. There is a secret down here, in this nightmare fog, that has lain dumb for centuries: I want to make it a real thing to you. You, Egoist, or Pantheist, or Arminian,[8] busy in making straight paths for your feet on the hills, do not see it clearly, – this terrible question which men here have gone mad and died trying to answer. I dare not put this secret into words. I told you it was dumb. These men, going by with drunken faces and brains full of unawakened power, do not ask it of Society or of God. Their lives ask it; their deaths ask it. There is no reply. I will tell you plainly that I have a great hope; and I bring it to you to be tested. It is this: that this terrible dumb question is its own reply; that it is not the sentence of death we think it, but, from the very extremity of its darkness, the most solemn prophecy which the world has known of the Hope to come. I dare make my meaning no clearer, but will only tell my story. It will, perhaps, seem to you as foul and dark as this thick vapor about us, and as pregnant with death; but if your eyes are free as mine are to look deeper, no perfume-tinted dawn will be so fair with promise of the day that shall surely come.

My story is very simple, – only what I remember of the life of one of these men, – a furnace-tender in one of Kirby & John's rolling-mills, – Hugh Wolfe. You know the mills?

---

7. **puddler:** A worker who produces steel by stirring iron oxide into a molten vat of "pig iron."
8. **Egoist, or Pantheist, or Arminian:** An egoist is one who is devoted to self-cultivation, which in turn leads to the improvement of all. A pantheist finds the Deity in nature; an Arminian is one who follows the teachings of Jacobus Arminius (1560-1601), a theologian who opposed the Calvinist notion of predestination.

They took the great order for the Lower Virginia railroads there last winter; run usually with about a thousand men. I cannot tell why I choose the half-forgotten story of this Wolfe more than that of myriads of these furnace-hands. Perhaps because there is a secret underlying sympathy between that story and this day with its impure fog and thwarted sunshine, — or perhaps simply for the reason that this house is the one where the Wolfes lived. There were the father and son, — both hands, as I said, in one of Kirby & John's mills for making railroad-iron, — and Deborah, their cousin, a picker[9] in some of the cotton-mills. The house was rented then to half a dozen families. The Wolfes had two of the cellar-rooms. The old man, like many of the puddlers and feeders[10] of the mills, was Welsh, — had spent half of his life in the Cornish tin-mines. You may pick the Welsh emigrants, Cornish miners, out of the throng passing the windows, any day. They are a trifle more filthy; their muscles are not so brawny; they stoop more. When they are drunk, they neither yell, nor shout, nor stagger, but skulk along like beaten hounds. A pure, unmixed blood, I fancy: shows itself in the slight angular bodies and sharply-cut facial lines. It is nearly thirty years since the Wolfes lived here. Their lives were like those of their class: incessant labor, sleeping in kennel-like rooms, eating rank pork and molasses, drinking — God and the distillers only know what; with an occasional night in jail, to atone for some drunken excess. Is that all of their lives? — of the portion given to them and these their duplicates swarming the streets to-day? — nothing beneath? — all? So many a political reformer will tell you, — and many a private reformer, too, who has gone among them with a heart tender with Christ's charity, and come out outraged, hardened.

One rainy night, about eleven o'clock, a crowd of half-clothed women stopped outside of the cellar-door. They were going home from the cotton-mill.

"Good-night, Deb," said one, a mulatto, steadying herself against the gas-post. She needed the post to steady her. So did more than one of them.

"Dah 's a ball to Miss Potts' to-night. Ye 'd best come."

"Inteet, Deb, if hur 'll[11] come, hur 'll hef fun," said a shrill Welsh voice in the crowd.

Two or three dirty hands were thrust out to catch the gown of the woman, who was groping for the latch of the door.

"No."

"No? Where 's Kit Small, then?"

"Begorra![12] on the spools. Alleys behint, though we helped her, we dud. An wid ye! Let Deb alone! It 's ondacent frettin' a quite body. Be the powers, an' we 'll have a night of it! there 'll be lasbin's o' drink, — the Vargent[13] be blessed and praised for 't!"

They went on, the mulatto inclining for a moment to show fight, and drag the woman Wolfe off with them; but, being pacified, she staggered away.

---

9. **picker:** A worker in a cotton mill who operates a machine that separates cotton fibers.
10. **feeders:** Workers who slowly feed molten metal into the casting form in order to prevent air bubbles from forming, which would weaken the hardened iron.
11. **hur 'll:** *Hur* is a dialect pronoun used to mean she, he, her, or him.
12. **"Begorra! . . . spools":** *Begorra* is an English-Irish expression meaning "by God"; spools are spindles in the cotton mill on which the cotton is stretched and then wound by the spinning machine.
13. **Vargent:** Contracted form of *Virgin Mary.*

Deborah groped her way into the cellar, and, after considerable stumbling, kindled a match, and lighted a tallow dip, that sent a yellow glimmer over the room. It was low, damp, — the earthen floor covered with a green, slimy moss, — a fetid air smothering the breath. Old Wolfe lay asleep on a heap of straw, wrapped in a torn horse-blanket. He was a pale, meek little man, with a white face and red rabbit-eyes. The woman Deborah was like him; only her face was even more ghastly, her lips bluer, her eyes more watery. She wore a faded cotton gown and a slouching bonnet. When she walked, one could see that she was deformed, almost a hunchback. She trod softly, so as not to waken him, and went through into the room beyond. There she found by the half-extinguished fire an iron saucepan filled with cold boiled potatoes, which she put upon a broken chair with a pint-cup of ale. Placing the old candlestick beside this dainty repast, she untied her bonnet, which hung limp and wet over her face, and prepared to eat her supper. It was the first food that had touched her lips since morning. There was enough of it, however: there is not always. She was hungry, — one could see that easily enough, — and not drunk, as most of her companions would have been found at this hour. She did not drink, this woman, — her face told that, too, — nothing stronger than ale. Perhaps the weak, flaccid wretch had some stimulant in her pale life to keep her up, — some love or hope, it might be, or urgent need. When that stimulant was gone, she would take to whiskey. Man cannot live by work alone. While she was skinning the potatoes, and munching them, a noise behind her made her stop.

"Janey!" she called, lifting the candle and peering into the darkness. "Janey, are you there?"

A heap of ragged coats was heaved up, and the face of a young girl emerged, staring sleepily at the woman.

"Deborah," she said, at last, "I'm here the night."

"Yes, child. Hur's welcome," she said, quietly eating on.

The girl's face was haggard and sickly; her eyes were heavy with sleep and hunger: real Milesian eyes[14] they were, dark, delicate blue, glooming out from black shadows with a pitiful fright.

"I was alone," she said, timidly.

"Where's the father?" asked Deborah, holding out a potato, which the girl greedily seized.

"He's beyant — wid Haley, — in the stone house." (Did you ever hear the word *jail* from an Irish mouth?) "I came here. Hugh told me never to stay me-lone."

"Hugh?"

"Yes."

A vexed frown crossed her face. The girl saw it, and added quickly, —

"I have not seen Hugh the day, Deb. The old man says his watch lasts till the mornin'."

The woman sprang up, and hastily began to arrange some bread and flitch[15] in a tin

---

14. **Milesian eyes:** Irish eyes.
15. **flitch:** Salted and cured bacon.

pail, and to pour her own measure of ale into a bottle. Tying on her bonnet, she blew out the candle.

"Lay ye down, Janey dear," she said, gently, covering her with the old rags. "Hur can eat the potatoes, if hur 's hungry."

"Where are ye goin', Deb? The rain 's sharp."

"To the mill, with Hugh's supper."

"Let him bide till th' morn. Sit ye down."

"No, no," – sharply pushing her off. "The boy 'll starve."

She hurried from the cellar, while the child wearily coiled herself up for sleep. The rain was falling heavily, as the woman, pail in hand, emerged from the mouth of the alley, and turned down the narrow street, that stretched out, long and black, miles before her. Here and there a flicker of gas lighted an uncertain space of muddy footwalk and gutter; the long rows of houses, except an occasional lager-bier shop, were closed; now and then she met a band of mill-hands skulking to or from their work.

Not many even of the inhabitants of a manufacturing town know the vast machinery of system by which the bodies of workmen are governed, that goes on unceasingly from year to year. The hands of each mill are divided into watches that relieve each other as regularly as the sentinels of an army. By night and day the work goes on, the unsleeping engines groan and shriek, the fiery pools of metal boil and surge. Only for a day in the week, in half-courtesy to public censure, the fires are partially veiled; but as soon as the clock strikes midnight, the great furnaces break forth with renewed fury, the clamor begins with fresh, breathless vigor, the engines sob and shriek like "gods in pain."

As Deborah hurried down through the heavy rain, the noise of these thousand engines sounded through the sleep and shadow of the city like far-off thunder. The mill to which she was going lay on the river, a mile below the city-limits. It was far, and she was weak, aching from standing twelve hours at the spools. Yet it was her almost nightly walk to take this man his supper, though at every square she sat down to rest, and she knew she should receive small word of thanks.

Perhaps, if she had possessed an artist's eye, the picturesque oddity of the scene might have made her step stagger less, and the path seem shorter; but to her the mills were only "summat deilish to look at by night."

The road leading to the mills had been quarried from the solid rock, which rose abrupt and bare on one side of the cinder-covered road, while the river, sluggish and black, crept past on the other. The mills for rolling iron are simply immense tent-like roofs, covering acres of ground, open on every side. Beneath these roofs Deborah looked in on a city of fires, that burned hot and fiercely in the night. Fire in every horrible form: pits of flame waving in the wind; liquid metal-flames writhing in tortuous streams through the sand; wide caldrons filled with boiling fire, over which bent ghastly wretches stirring the strange brewing; and through all, crowds of half-clad men, looking like revengeful ghosts in the red light, hurried, throwing masses of glittering fire. It was like a street in Hell. Even Deborah muttered, as she crept through, "'T looks like t' Devil's place!" It did, – in more ways than one.

She found the man she was looking for, at last, heaping coal on a furnace. He had not time to eat his supper; so she went behind the furnace, and waited. Only a few men were with him, and they noticed her only by a "Hyur comes t' hunchback, Wolfe."

Deborah was stupid with sleep; her back pained her sharply; and her teeth chattered with cold, with the rain that soaked her clothes and dripped from her at every step. She stood, however, patiently holding the pail, and waiting.

"Hout, woman! ye look like a drowned cat. Come near to the fire," – said one of the men, approaching to scrape away the ashes.

She shook her head. Wolfe had forgotten her. He turned, hearing the man, and came closer.

"I did no' think; gi' me my supper, woman."

She watched him eat with a painful eagerness. With a woman's quick instinct, she saw that he was not hungry, – was eating to please her. Her pale, watery eyes began to gather a strange light.

"Is 't good, Hugh? T' ale was a bit sour, I feared."

"No, good enough." He hesitated a moment. "Ye're tired, poor lass! Bide here till I go. Lay down there on that heap of ash, and go to sleep."

He threw her an old coat for a pillow, and turned to his work. The heap was the refuse of the burnt iron, and was not a hard bed; the half-smothered warmth, too, penetrated her limbs, dulling their pain and cold shiver.

Miserable enough she looked, lying there on the ashes like a limp, dirty rag, – yet not an unfitting figure to crown the scene of hopeless discomfort and veiled crime: more fitting, if one looked deeper into the heart of things, – at her thwarted woman's form, her colorless life, her waking stupor that smothered pain and hunger, – even more fit to be a type of her class. Deeper yet if one could look, was there nothing worth reading in this wet, faded thing, half-covered with ashes? no story of a soul filled with groping passionate love, heroic unselfishness, fierce jealousy? of years of weary trying to please the one human being whom she loved, to gain one look of real heart-kindness from him? If anything like this were hidden beneath the pale, bleared eyes, and dull, washed-out-looking face, no one had ever taken the trouble to read its faint signs: not the half-clothed furnace-tender, Wolfe, certainly. Yet he was kind to her: it was his nature to be kind, even to the very rats that swarmed in the cellar: kind to her in just the same way. She knew that. And it might be that very knowledge had given to her face its apathy and vacancy more than her low, torpid life. One sees that dead, vacant look steal sometimes over the rarest, finest of women's faces, – in the very midst, it may be, of their warmest summer's day; and then one can guess at the secret of intolerable solitude that lies hid beneath the delicate laces and brilliant smile. There was no warmth, no brilliancy, no summer for this woman; so the stupor and vacancy had time to gnaw into her face perpetually. She was young, too, though no one guessed it; so the gnawing was the fiercer.

She lay quiet in the dark corner, listening, through the monotonous din and uncertain glare of the works, to the dull plash of the rain in the far distance, – shrinking back whenever the man Wolfe happened to look towards her. She knew, in spite of all his kindness, that there was that in her face and form which made him loathe the sight of her. She felt by instinct, although she could not comprehend it, the finer nature of the man, which made him among his fellow-workmen something unique, set apart. She knew, that, down under all the vileness and coarseness of his life, there was a groping passion for whatever was beautiful and pure, — that his soul sickened with disgust at her deformity, even when his words were kindest. Through this dull consciousness, which never left her, came, like a sting, the recollection of the dark blue eyes and lithe figure of the little Irish girl she had left in the cellar. The recollection struck through even her stupid intellect with a vivid glow of beauty and of grace. Little Janey, timid, helpless, clinging to Hugh as her only friend: that was the sharp thought, the bitter thought, that drove into the glazed eyes a fierce light of pain. You laugh at it? Are pain and jealousy less savage realities down here in this place I am taking you to than in your own house or your own heart, — your heart, which they clutch at sometimes? The note is the same, I fancy, be the octave high or low.

If you could go into this mill where Deborah lay, and drag out from the hearts of these men the terrible tragedy of their lives, taking it as a symptom of the disease of their class, no ghost Horror would terrify you more. A reality of soul-starvation, of living death, that meets you every day under the besotted faces on the street, — I can paint nothing of this, only give you the outside outlines of a night, a crisis in the life of one man: whatever muddy depth of soul-history lies beneath you can read according to the eyes God has given you.

Wolfe, while Deborah watched him as a spaniel its master, bent over the furnace with his iron pole, unconscious of her scrutiny, only stopping to receive orders. Physically, Nature had promised the man but little. He had already lost the strength and instinct vigor of a man, his muscles were thin, his nerves weak, his face (a meek, woman's face) haggard, yellow with consumption. In the mill he was known as one of the girl-men: "Molly Wolfe" was his *sobriquet*.[16] He was never seen in the cockpit,[17] did not own a terrier, drank but seldom; when he did, desperately. He fought sometimes, but was always thrashed, pommelled to a jelly. The man was game enough, when his blood was up: but he was no favorite in the mill; he had the taint of school-learning on him, — not to a dangerous extent, only a quarter or so in the free-school in fact, but enough to ruin him as a good hand in a fight.

For other reasons, too, he was not popular. Not one of themselves, they felt that, though outwardly as filthy and ash-covered; silent, with foreign thoughts and longings breaking out through his quietness in innumerable curious ways: this one, for instance. In the neighboring furnace-buildings lay great heaps of the refuse from the ore after the pig-metal is run. *Korl* we call it here: a light, porous substance, of a delicate, waxen, flesh-colored tinge. Out of the blocks of this korl, Wolfe, in his off-hours from the furnace, had a habit of chipping and moulding figures, — hideous, fantastic enough, but sometimes strangely beautiful: even the mill-men saw that, while they jeered at him. It was a curious fancy in the man, almost a passion. The few hours for rest he spent hewing and hacking with his blunt knife, never speaking, until his watch came again, —

16. *sobriquet*: Nickname (French).
17. cockpit: An arena where fighting roosters, called cocks, are set against one another.

working at one figure for months, and, when it was finished, breaking it to pieces perhaps, in a fit of disappointment. A morbid, gloomy man, untaught, unled, left to feed his soul in grossness and crime, and hard, grinding labor.

I want you to come down and look at this Wolfe, standing there among the lowest of his kind, and see him just as he is, that you may judge him justly when you hear the story of this night. I want you to look back, as he does every day, at his birth in vice, his starved infancy; to remember the heavy years he has groped through as boy and man, — the slow, heavy years of constant, hot work. So long ago he began, that he thinks sometimes he has worked there for ages. There is no hope that it will ever end. Think that God put into this man's soul a fierce thirst for beauty, — to know it, to create it; to *be* — something, he knows not what, — other than he is. There are moments when a passing cloud, the sun glinting on the purple thistles, a kindly smile, a child's face, will rouse him to a passion of pain, — when his nature starts up with a mad cry of rage against God, man, whoever it is that has forced this vile, slimy life upon him. With all this groping, this mad desire, a great blind intellect stumbling through wrong, a loving poet's heart, the man was by habit only a coarse, vulgar laborer, familiar with sights and words you would blush to name. Be just: when I tell you about this night, see him as he is. Be just, — not like man's law, which seizes on one isolated fact, but like God's judging angel, whose clear, sad eye saw all the countless cankering days of this man's life, all the countless nights, when, sick with starving, his soul fainted in him, before it judged him for this night, the saddest of all.

I called this night the crisis of his life. If it was, it stole on him unawares. These great turning-days of life cast no shadow before, slip by unconsciously. Only a trifle, a little turn of the rudder, and the ship goes to heaven or hell.

Wolfe, while Deborah watched him, dug into the furnace of melting iron with his pole, dully thinking only how many rails the lump would yield. It was late, nearly Sunday morning; another hour, and the heavy work would be done, — only the furnaces to replenish and cover for the next day. The workmen were growing more noisy, shouting, as they had to do, to be heard over the deep clamor of the mills. Suddenly they grew less boisterous, — at the far end, entirely silent. Something unusual had happened. After a moment, the silence came nearer; the men stopped their jeers and drunken choruses. Deborah, stupidly lifting up her head, saw the cause of the quiet. A group of five or six men were slowly approaching, stopping to examine each furnace as they came. Visitors often came to see the mills after night: except by growing less noisy, the men took no notice of them. The furnace where Wolfe worked was near the bounds of the works; they halted there hot and tired: a walk over one of these great foundries is no trifling task. The woman, drawing out of sight, turned over to sleep. Wolfe, seeing them stop, suddenly roused from his indifferent stupor, and watched them keenly. He knew some of them: the overseer, Clarke, — a son of Kirby, one of the mill-owners, — and a Doctor May, one of the town-physicians. The other two were strangers. Wolfe came closer. He seized eagerly every chance that brought him into contact with this mysterious class that shone down on him perpetually with the glamour of another order of being. What made the difference between them? That was the mystery of his life. He had a vague notion that perhaps to-night he could find it out. One of the strangers sat down on a pile of bricks, and beckoned young Kirby to his side.

"This *is* hot, with a vengeance. A match, please?" – lighting his cigar. "But the walk is worth the trouble. If it were not that you must have heard it so often, Kirby, I would tell you that your works look like Dante's Inferno."[18]

Kirby laughed.

"Yes. Yonder is Farinata[19] himself in the burning tomb," – pointing to some figure in the shimmering shadows.

"Judging from some of the faces of your men," said the other, "they bid fair to try the reality of Dante's vision, some day."

Young Kirby looked curiously around, as if seeing the faces of his hands for the first time.

"They're bad enough, that's true. A desperate set, I fancy. Eh, Clarke?"

The overseer did not hear him. He was talking of net profits just then, – giving, in fact, a schedule of the annual business of the firm to a sharp peering little Yankee, who jotted down notes on a paper laid on the crown of his hat: a reporter for one of the city-papers, getting up a series of reviews of the leading manufactories. The other gentle-men had accompanied them merely for amusement. They were silent until the notes were finished, drying their feet at the furnaces, and sheltering their faces from the intolerable heat. At last the overseer concluded with –

"I believe that is a pretty fair estimate, Captain."

"Here, some of you men!" said Kirby, "bring up those boards. We may as well sit down, gentlemen, until the rain is over. It cannot last much longer at this rate."

"Pig-metal," – mumbled the reporter, – "um! – coal facilities, – um! – hands em-ployed, twelve hundred, – bitumen, – um! – all right, I believe, Mr. Clarke; – sinking-fund, – what did you say was your sinking-fund?"[20]

"Twelve hundred hands?" said the stranger, the young man who had first spoken. "Do you control their votes, Kirby?"

"Control? No." The young man smiled complacently. "But my father brought seven hundred votes to the polls for his candidate last November. No force-work, you under-stand, – only a speech or two, a hint to form themselves into a society, and a bit of red and blue bunting to make them a flag. The Invincible Roughs, – I believe that is their name. I forget the motto: 'Our country's hope,' I think."

There was a laugh. The young man talking to Kirby sat with an amused light in his cool gray eye, surveying critically the half-clothed figures of the puddlers, and the slow swing of their brawny muscles. He was a stranger in the city, – spending a couple of months in the borders of a Slave State, to study the institutions of the South, – a brother-in-law of Kirby's, – Mitchell. He was an amateur gymnast, – hence his anatomical eye; a patron, in a *blasé* way, of the prize-ring; a man who sucked the essence out of a science

---

18. **Dante's Inferno:** The first book of *The Divine Comedy* by the Italian poet Dante Alighieri (1265–1321).
19. **Farinata:** A character in the *Inferno*; a heretic who was a leader of the Florentines.
20. **sinking-fund:** Money collected for paying corporate debts.

or philosophy in an indifferent, gentlemanly way; who took Kant, Novalis, Humboldt,[21] for what they were worth in his own scales; accepting all, despising nothing, in heaven, earth, or hell, but one-idead men; with a temper yielding and brilliant as summer water, until his Self was touched, when it was ice, though brilliant still. Such men are not rare in the States.

As he knocked the ashes from his cigar, Wolfe caught with a quick pleasure the contour of the white hand, the blood-glow of a red ring he wore. His voice, too, and that of Kirby's, touched him like music, — low, even, with chording cadences. About this man Mitchell hung the impalpable atmosphere belonging to the thorough-bred gentleman. Wolfe, scraping away the ashes beside him, was conscious of it, did obeisance to it with his artist sense, unconscious that he did so.

The rain did not cease. Clarke and the reporter left the mills; the others, comfortably seated near the furnace, lingered, smoking and talking in a desultory way. Greek would not have been more unintelligible to the furnace-tenders, whose presence they soon forgot entirely. Kirby drew out a newspaper from his pocket and read aloud some article, which they discussed eagerly. At every sentence, Wolfe listened more and more like a dumb, hopeless animal, with a duller, more stolid look creeping over his face, glancing now and then at Mitchell, marking acutely every smallest sign of refinement, then back to himself, seeing as in a mirror his filthy body, his more stained soul.

Never! He had no words for such a thought, but he knew now, in all the sharpness of the bitter certainty, that between them there was a great gulf never to be passed.[22] Never!

The bell of the mills rang for midnight. Sunday morning had dawned. Whatever hidden message lay in the tolling bells floated past these men unknown. Yet it was there. Veiled in the solemn music ushering the risen Saviour was a key-note to solve the darkest secrets of a world gone wrong, — even this social riddle which the brain of the grimy puddler grappled with madly to-night.

The men began to withdraw the metal from the caldrons. The mills were deserted on Sundays, except by the hands who fed the fires, and those who had no lodgings and slept usually on the ash-heaps. The three strangers sat still during the next hour, watching the men cover the furnaces, laughing now and then at some jest of Kirby's.

"Do you know," said Mitchell, "I like this view of the works better than when the glare was fiercest? These heavy shadows and the amphitheatre of smothered fires are ghostly, unreal. One could fancy these red smouldering lights to be the half-shut eyes of wild beasts, and the spectral figures their victims in the den."

---

21. **Kant, Novalis, Humboldt:** Immanuel Kant (1724-1804), German philosopher; Novalis, the pseudonym for the German poet Friedrich von Hardenberg (1772-1801); Alexander von Humboldt (1769-1859), German naturalist and explorer.

22. **great gulf . . . passed:** In a parable Christ tells his disciples, Lazarus, a beggar, finds comfort in heaven while the rich man is tormented in hell. When the rich man appeals for mercy, Abraham, in heaven with Lazarus, replies: "Between us and you there is a great gulf fixed: so that they which would pass from hence to you cannot; neither can they pass to us, that would come from thence" (Luke 16:26).

Kirby laughed. "You are fanciful. Come, let us get out of the den. The spectral figures, as you call them, are a little too real for me to fancy a close proximity in the darkness, – unarmed, too."

The others rose, buttoning their overcoats, and lighting cigars.

"Raining, still," said Doctor May, "and hard. Where did we leave the coach, Mitchell?"

"At the other side of the works. – Kirby, what's that?"

Mitchell started back, half-frightened, as, suddenly turning a corner, the white figure of a woman faced him in the darkness, – a woman, white, of giant proportions, crouching on the ground, her arms flung out in some wild gesture of warning.

"Stop! Make that fire burn there!" cried Kirby, stopping short.

The flame burst out, flashing the gaunt figure into bold relief.

Mitchell drew a long breath.

"I thought it was alive," he said, going up curiously.

The others followed.

"Not marble, eh?" asked Kirby, touching it.

One of the lower overseers stopped.

"Korl, Sir."

"Who did it?"

"Can't say. Some of the hands; chipped it out in off-hours."

"Chipped to some purpose, I should say. What a flesh-tint the stuff has! Do you see, Mitchell?"

"I see."

He had stepped aside where the light fell boldest on the figure, looking at it in silence. There was not one line of beauty or grace in it: a nude woman's form, muscular, grown coarse with labor, the powerful limbs instinct with some one poignant longing. One idea: there it was in the tense, rigid muscles, the clutching hands, the wild, eager face, like that of a starving wolf's. Kirby and Doctor May walked around it, critical, curious. Mitchell stood aloof, silent. The figure touched him strangely.

"Not badly done," said Doctor May. "Where did the fellow learn that sweep of the muscles in the arm and hand? Look at them! They are groping, – do you see? – clutching: the peculiar action of a man dying of thirst."

"They have ample facilities for studying anatomy," sneered Kirby, glancing at the half-naked figures.

"Look," continued the Doctor, "at this bony wrist, and the strained sinews of the instep! A working-woman, – the very type of her class."

"God forbid!" muttered Mitchell.

"Why?" demanded May. "What does the fellow intend by the figure? I cannot catch the meaning."

"Ask him," said the other, dryly. "There he stands," – pointing to Wolfe, who stood with a group of men, leaning on his ash-rake.

The Doctor beckoned him with the affable smile which kind-hearted men put on, when talking to these people.

"Mr. Mitchell has picked you out as the man who did this, – I'm sure I don't know why. But what did you mean by it?"

"She be hungry."

Wolfe's eyes answered Mitchell, not the Doctor.

"Oh-h! But what a mistake you have made, my fine fellow! You have given no sign of starvation to the body. It is strong, — terribly strong. It has the mad, half-despairing gesture of drowning."

Wolfe stammered, glanced appealingly at Mitchell, who saw the soul of the thing, he knew. But the cool, probing eyes were turned on himself now, — mocking, cruel, relentless.

"Not hungry for meat," the furnace-tender said at last.

"What then? Whiskey?" jeered Kirby, with a coarse laugh.

Wolfe was silent a moment, thinking.

"I dunno," he said, with a bewildered look. "It mebbe. Summat to make her live, I think, — like you. Whiskey ull do it, in a way."

The young man laughed again. Mitchell flashed a look of disgust somewhere, — not at Wolfe.

"May," he broke out impatiently, "are you blind? Look at that woman's face! It asks questions of God, and says, 'I have a right to know.' Good God, how hungry it is!"

They looked a moment; then May turned to the mill-owner: —

"Have you many such hands as this? What are you going to do with them? Keep them at puddling iron?"

Kirby shrugged his shoulders. Mitchell's look had irritated him.

"*Ce n'est pas mon affaire.*[23] I have no fancy for nursing infant geniuses. I suppose there are some stray gleams of mind and soul among these wretches. The Lord will take care of his own; or else they can work out their own salvation. I have heard you call our American system a ladder which any man can scale. Do you doubt it? Or perhaps you want to banish all social ladders, and put us all on a flat table-land, — eh, May?"

The Doctor looked vexed, puzzled. Some terrible problem lay hid in this woman's face, and troubled these men. Kirby waited for an answer, and, receiving none, went on, warming with his subject.

"I tell you, there's something wrong that no talk of *'Liberté'* or *'Égalité'*[24] will do away. If I had the making of men, these men who do the lowest part of the world's work should be machines, — nothing more, — hands. It would be kindness. God help them! What are taste, reason, to creatures who must live such lives as that?" He pointed to Deborah, sleeping on the ash-heap. "So many nerves to sting them to pain. What if God had put your brain, with all its agony of touch, into your fingers, and bid you work and strike with that?"

"You think you could govern the world better?" laughed the Doctor.

"I do not think at all."

"That is true philosophy. Drift with the stream, because you cannot dive deep enough to find bottom, eh?"

---

23. *Ce n'est pas mon affaire*: It's none of my business (French).
24. *'Liberté'* or *'Égalité'*: A reference to the slogan of the French Revolution, "Liberty, Equality, Fraternity!"

"Exactly," rejoined Kirby. "I do not think. I wash my hands of all social problems, — slavery, caste, white or black. My duty to my operatives has a narrow limit, — the pay-hour on Saturday night. Outside of that, if they cut korl, or cut each other's throats, (the more popular amusement of the two,) I am not responsible."

The Doctor sighed, — a good honest sigh, from the depths of his stomach.

"God help us! Who is responsible?"

"Not I, I tell you," said Kirby, testily. "What has the man who pays them money to do with their souls' concerns, more than the grocer or butcher who takes it?"

"And yet," said Mitchell's cynical voice, "look at her! How hungry she is!"

Kirby tapped his boot with his cane. No one spoke. Only the dumb face of the rough image looking into their faces with the awful question, "What shall we do to be saved?" Only Wolfe's face, with its heavy weight of brain, its weak, uncertain mouth, its desperate eyes, out of which looked the soul of his class, — only Wolfe's face turned towards Kirby's. Mitchell laughed, — a cool, musical laugh.

"Money has spoken!" he said, seating himself lightly on a stone with the air of an amused spectator at a play. "Are you answered?" — turning to Wolfe his clear, magnetic face.

Bright and deep and cold as Arctic air, the soul of the man lay tranquil beneath. He looked at the furnace-tender as he had looked at a rare mosaic in the morning; only the man was the more amusing study of the two.

"Are you answered? Why, May, look at him! 'De profundis clamavi.'[25] Or, to quote in English, 'Hungry and thirsty, his soul faints in him.' And so Money sends back its answer into the depths through you, Kirby! Very clear the answer, too! — I think I remember reading the same words somewhere: — washing your hands in Eau de Cologne, and saying, 'I am innocent of the blood of this man. See ye to it!'"[26]

Kirby flushed angrily.

"You quote Scripture freely."

"Do I not quote correctly? I think I remember another line, which may amend my meaning: 'Inasmuch as ye did it unto one of the least of these, ye did it unto me.'[27] Deist?[28] Bless you, man, I was raised on the milk of the Word. Now, Doctor, the pocket of the world having uttered its voice, what has the heart to say? You are a philanthropist, in a small way, — n'est ce pas?[29] Here, boy, this gentleman can show you how to cut korl better, — or your destiny. Go on, May!"

"I think a mocking devil possesses you to-night," rejoined the Doctor, seriously.

He went to Wolfe and put his hand kindly on his arm. Something of a vague idea possessed the Doctor's brain that much good was to be done here by a friendly word or two:

---

25. 'De profundis clamavi': Latin version of the opening words of Psalm 130, "Out of the depths have I cried unto thee, O Lord."

26. 'I am innocent . . . to it!': Pontius Pilate, the Roman governor, reluctantly agreed to crucify Jesus and renounced his responsibility by washing his hands before the mob (Matthew 27:24–26).

27. 'Inasmuch . . . unto me': Jesus's parable of the sheep and the goats. See Matthew 25:31–45.

28. Deist: Believer in a God who created the world but exercises no control over it.

29. n'est ce pas?: Isn't that so? (French).

a latent genius to be warmed into life by a waited-for sunbeam. Here it was: he had brought it. So he went on complacently: –

"Do you know, boy, you have it in you to be a great sculptor, a great man? – do you understand?" (talking down to the capacity of his hearer: it is a way people have with children, and men like Wolfe,) – "to live a better, stronger life than I, or Mr. Kirby here? A man may make himself anything he chooses. God has given you stronger powers than many men, – me, for instance."

May stopped, heated, glowing with his own magnanimity. And it was magnanimous. The puddler had drunk in every word, looking through the Doctor's flurry, and generous heat, and self-approval, into his will, with those slow, absorbing eyes of his.

"Make yourself what you will. It is your right."

"I know," quietly. "Will you help me?"

Mitchell laughed again. The Doctor turned now, in a passion, –

"You know, Mitchell, I have not the means. You know, if I had, it is in my heart to take this boy and educate him for" —

"The glory of God, and the glory of John May."

May did not speak for a moment; then, controlled, he said, –

"Why should one be raised, when myriads are left? – I have not the money, boy," to Wolfe, shortly.

"Money?" He said it over slowly, as one repeats the guessed answer to a riddle, doubtfully. "That is it? Money?"

"Yes, money, – that is it," said Mitchell, rising, and drawing his furred coat about him. "You've found the cure for all the world's diseases. – Come, May, find your good-humor, and come home. This damp wind chills my very bones. Come and preach our Saint-Simonian doctrines[30] to-morrow to Kirby's hands. Let them have a clear idea of the rights of the soul, and I'll venture next week they'll strike for higher wages. That will be the end of it."

"Will you send the coach-driver to this side of the mills?" asked Kirby, turning to Wolfe.

He spoke kindly: it was his habit to do so. Deborah, seeing the puddler go, crept after him. The three men waited outside. Doctor May walked up and down, chafed. Suddenly he stopped.

"Go back, Mitchell! You say the pocket and the heart of the world speak without meaning to these people. What has its head to say? Taste, culture, refinement? Go!"

Mitchell was leaning against a brick wall. He turned his head indolently, and looked into the mills. There hung about the place a thick, unclean odor. The slightest motion of his hand marked that he perceived it, and his insufferable disgust. That was all. May said nothing, only quickened his angry tramp.

"Besides," added Mitchell, giving a corollary to his answer, "it would be of no use. I am not one of them."

---

30. **Saint-Simonian doctrines:** Claude Henry de Rouvroy, comte de Saint-Simon (1760–1825), was a French philosopher who taught that the public control of production, the principle of common property, and the end of inheritances were the remedies for social ills.

"You do not mean" — said May, facing him.

"Yes, I mean just that. Reform is born of need, not pity. No vital movement of the people's has worked down, for good or evil; fermented, instead, carried up the heaving, cloggy mass. Think back through history, and you will know it. What will this lowest deep — thieves, Magdalens,[31] negroes — do with the light filtered through ponderous Church creeds, Baconian theories, Goethe schemes?[32] Some day, out of their bitter need will be thrown up their own light-bringer, — their Jean Paul, their Cromwell,[33] their Messiah."

"Bah!" was the Doctor's inward criticism. However, in practice, he adopted the theory; for, when, night and morning, afterwards, he prayed that power might be given these degraded souls to rise, he glowed at heart, recognizing an accomplished duty.

Wolfe and the woman had stood in the shadow of the works as the coach drove off. The Doctor had held out his hand in a frank, generous way, telling him to "take care of himself, and to remember it was his right to rise." Mitchell had simply touched his hat, as to an equal, with a quiet look of thorough recognition. Kirby had thrown Deborah some money, which she found, and clutched eagerly enough. They were gone now, all of them. The man sat down on the cinder-road, looking up into the murky sky.

" 'T be late, Hugh. Wunnot hur come?"

He shook his head doggedly, and the woman crouched out of his sight against the wall. Do you remember rare moments when a sudden light flashed over yourself, your world, God? when you stood on a mountain-peak, seeing your life as it might have been, as it is? one quick instant, when custom lost its force and every-day usage? when your friend, wife, brother, stood in a new light? your soul was bared, and the grave, — a fore-taste of the nakedness of the Judgment-Day? So it came before him, his life, that night. The slow tides of pain he had borne gathered themselves up and surged against his soul. His squalid daily life, the brutal coarseness eating into his brain, as the ashes into his skin: before, these things had been a dull aching into his consciousness; to-night, they were reality. He griped the filthy red shirt that clung, stiff with soot, about him, and tore it savagely from his arm. The flesh beneath was muddy with grease and ashes, — and the heart beneath that! And the soul? God knows.

Then flashed before his vivid poetic sense the man who had left him, — the pure face, the delicate, sinewy limbs, in harmony with all he knew of beauty or truth. In his cloudy fancy he had pictured a Something like this. He had found it in this Mitchell, even

---

31. **Magdalens:** Reformed prostitutes, after Mary Magdalene, a purported prostitute and a follower of Jesus.
32. **Baconian theories, Goethe schemes:** Sir Francis Bacon (1561-1626), English philosopher who stressed the importance of systematizing empirical information about the natural world; Johann Wolfgang von Goethe (1749-1832), German writer and philosopher who celebrated the power of the individual and emphasized the limitations of eighteenth-century rationalism.
33. **their Jean Paul, their Cromwell:** Mitchell refers to two famous saviors of the people. The Swiss-born Jean-Paul Marat (1743-1793) was a revolutionary journalist who wrote *The Chains of Slavery* (1774) and edited a radical newspaper, the *Friend of the People* (1789-1793), in support of the French Revolution. Oliver Cromwell (1599-1658) was the military leader of the Puritan Revolution that led to the overthrow and execution of King Charles I and the establishment of the Puritan Commonwealth in England.

when he idly scoffed at his pain: a Man all-knowing, all-seeing, crowned by Nature, reigning, — the keen glance of his eye falling like a sceptre on other men. And yet his instinct taught him that he too — He! He looked at himself with sudden loathing, sick, wrung his hands with a cry, and then was silent. With all the phantoms of his heated, ignorant fancy, Wolfe had not been vague in his ambitions. They were practical, slowly built up before him out of his knowledge of what he could do. Through years he had day by day made this hope a real thing to himself, — a clear, projected figure of himself, as he might become.

Able to speak, to know what was best, to raise these men and women working at his side up with him: sometimes he forgot this defined hope in the frantic anguish to escape, — only to escape, — out of the wet, the pain, the ashes, somewhere, any-where, — only for one moment of free air on a hill-side, to lie down and let his sick soul throb itself out in the sunshine. But to-night he panted for life. The savage strength of his nature was roused; his cry was fierce to God for justice.

"Look at me!" he said to Deborah, with a low, bitter laugh, striking his puny chest savagely. "What am I worth, Deb? Is it my fault that I am no better? My fault? My fault?"

He stopped, stung with a sudden remorse, seeing her hunchback shape writhing with sobs. For Deborah was crying thankless tears, according to the fashion of women.

"God forgi' me, woman! Things go harder wi' you nor me. It 's a worse share."

He got up and helped her to rise; and they went doggedly down the muddy street, side by side.

"It 's all wrong," he muttered, slowly, — "all wrong! I dunnot understan'. But it 'll end some day."

"Come home, Hugh!" she said, coaxingly; for he had stopped, looking around bewil-dered.

"Home, — and back to the mill!" He went on saying this over to himself, as if he would mutter down every pain in this dull despair.

She followed him through the fog, her blue lips chattering with cold. They reached the cellar at last. Old Wolfe had been drinking since she went out, and had crept nearer the door. The girl Janey slept heavily in the corner. He went up to her, touching softly the worn white arm with his fingers. Some bitterer thought stung him, as he stood there. He wiped the drops from his forehead, and went into the room beyond, livid, trembling. A hope, trifling, perhaps, but very dear, had died just then out of the poor puddler's life, as he looked at the sleeping, innocent girl, — some plan for the future, in which she had borne a part. He gave it up that moment, then and forever. Only a trifle, perhaps, to us: his face grew a shade paler, — that was all. But, somehow, the man's soul, as God and the angels looked down on it, never was the same afterwards.

Deborah followed him into the inner room. She carried a candle, which she placed on the floor, closing the door after her. She had seen the look on his face, as he turned away: her own grew deadly. Yet, as she came up to him, her eyes glowed. He was seated on an old chest, quiet, holding his face in his hands.

"Hugh!" she said, softly.

He did not speak.

"Hugh, did hur hear what the man said, – him with the clear voice? Did hur hear? Money, money, – that it wud do all?"

He pushed her away, – gently, but he was worn out; her rasping tone fretted him.

"Hugh!"

The candle flared a pale yellow light over the cobwebbed brick walls, and the woman standing there. He looked at her. She was young, in deadly earnest; her faded eyes, and wet, ragged figure caught from their frantic eagerness a power akin to beauty.

"Hugh, it is true! Money ull do it! Oh, Hugh, boy, listen till me! He said is true! It is money!"

"I know. Go back! I do not want you here."

"Hugh, it is t' last time. I 'll never worrit hur again."

There were tears in her voice now, but she choked them back.

"Hear till me only to-night! If one of t' witch people wud come, them we heard of t' home, and gif hur all hur wants, what then? Say, Hugh!"

"What do you mean?"

"I mean money."

Her whisper shrilled through his brain.

"If one of t' witch dwarfs wud come from t' lane moors to-night, and gif hur money, to go out, – *out*, I say, – out, lad, where t' sun shines, and t' heath grows, and t' ladies walk in silken gownds, and God stays all t' time, – where t' man lives that talked to us to-night, – Hugh knows, – Hugh could walk there like a king!"

He thought the woman mad, tried to check her, but she went on, fierce in her eager haste.

"If *I* were t' witch dwarf, if I had t' money, wud hur thank me? Wud hur take me out o' this place wid hur and Janey? I wud not come into the gran' house hur wud build, to vex hur wid t' hunch, – only at night, when t' shadows were dark, stand far off to see hur."

Mad? Yes! Are many of us mad in this way?

"Poor Deb! poor Deb!" he said, soothingly.

"It is here," she said, suddenly jerking into his hand a small roll. "I took it! I did it! Me, me! – not hur! I shall be hanged, I shall be burnt in hell, if anybody knows I took it! Out of his pocket, as he leaned against t' bricks. Hur knows?"

She thrust it into his hand, and then, her errand done, began to gather chips together to make a fire, choking down hysteric sobs.

"Has it come to this?"

That was all he said. The Welsh Wolfe blood was honest. The roll was a small green pocket-book containing one or two gold pieces, and a check for an incredible amount, as it seemed to the poor puddler. He laid it down, hiding his face again in his hands.

"Hugh, don't be angry wud me! It 's only poor Deb, – hur knows?"

He took the long skinny fingers kindly in his.

"Angry? God help me, no! Let me sleep. I am tired."

He threw himself heavily down on the wooden bench, stunned with pain and weariness. She brought some old rags to cover him.

It was late on Sunday evening before he awoke. I tell God's truth, when I say he had then no thought of keeping this money. Deborah had hid it in his pocket. He found it there. She watched him eagerly, as he took it out.

"I must gif it to him," he said, reading her face.

"Hur knows," she said with a bitter sigh of disappointment. "But it is hur right to keep it."

His right! The word struck him. Doctor May had used the same. He washed himself, and went out to find this man Mitchell. His right! Why did this chance word cling to him so obstinately? Do you hear the fierce devils whisper in his ear, as he went slowly down the darkening street?

The evening came on, slow and calm. He seated himself at the end of an alley leading into one of the larger streets. His brain was clear to-night, keen, intent, mastering. It would not start back, cowardly, from any hellish temptation, but meet it face to face. Therefore the great temptation of his life came to him veiled by no sophistry, but bold, defiant, owning its own vile name, trusting to one bold blow for victory.

He did not deceive himself. Theft! That was it. At first the word sickened him; then he grappled with it. Sitting there on a broken cart-wheel, the fading day, the noisy groups, the church-bells' tolling passed before him like a panorama,[34] while the sharp struggle went on within. This money! He took it out, and looked at it. If he gave it back, what then? He was going to be cool about it.

People going by to church saw only a sickly mill-boy watching them quietly at the alley's mouth. They did not know that he was mad, or they would not have gone by so quietly: mad with hunger; stretching out his hands to the world, that had given so much to them, for leave to live the life God meant him to live. His soul within him was smothering to death; he wanted so much, thought so much, and *knew* – nothing. There was nothing of which he was certain, except the mill and things there. Of God and heaven he had heard so little, that they were to him what fairy-land is to a child: something real, but not here; very far off. His brain, greedy, dwarfed, full of thwarted energy and unused powers, questioned these men and women going by, coldly, bitterly, that night. Was it not his right to live as they, – a pure life, a good, true-hearted life, full of beauty and kind words? He only wanted to know how to use the strength within him. His heart warmed, as he thought of it. He suffered himself to think of it longer. If he took the money?

Then he saw himself as he might be, strong, helpful, kindly. The night crept on, as this one image slowly evolved itself from the crowd of other thoughts and stood triumphant. He looked at it. As he might be! What wonder, if it blinded him to delirium, – the madness that underlies all revolution, all progress, and all fall?

---

34. **panorama:** A series of large paintings attached to one another in a long roll. Popular entertainments in the nineteenth century, panoramas of natural wonders, such as Niagara Falls, would be unrolled with commentary and musical accompaniment in front of an audience.

You laugh at the shallow temptation? You see the error underlying its argument so clearly, — that to him a true life was one of full development rather than self-restraint? that he was deaf to the higher tone in a cry of voluntary suffering for truth's sake than in the fullest flow of spontaneous harmony? I do not plead his cause. I only want to show you the mote in my brother's eye: then you can see clearly to take it out.[35]

The money, — there it lay on his knee, a little blotted slip of paper, nothing in itself; used to raise him out of the pit; something straight from God's hand. A thief! Well, what was it to be a thief? He met the question at last, face to face, wiping the clammy drops of sweat from his forehead. God made this money — the fresh air, too — for his children's use. He never made the difference between poor and rich. The Something who looked down on him that moment through the cool gray sky had a kindly face, he knew, — loved his children alike. Oh, he knew that!

There were times when the soft floods of color in the crimson and purple flames, or the clear depth of amber in the water below the bridge, had somehow given him a glimpse of another world than this, — of an infinite depth of beauty and of quiet some-where, — somewhere, — a depth of quiet and rest and love. Looking up now, it became strangely real. The sun had sunk quite below the hills, but his last rays struck upward, touching the zenith. The fog had risen, and the town and river were steeped in its thick, gray damp; but overhead, the sun-touched smoke-clouds opened like a cleft ocean, — shifting, rolling seas of crimson mist, waves of billowy silver veined with blood-scarlet, inner depths unfathomable of glancing light. Wolfe's artist-eye grew drunk with color. The gates of that other world! Fading, flashing before him now! What, in that world of Beauty, Content, and Right, were the petty laws, the mine and thine, of mill-owners and mill-hands?

A consciousness of power stirred within him. He stood up. A man, — he thought, stretching out his hands, — free to work, to live, to love! Free! His right! He folded the scrap of paper in his hand. As his nervous fingers took it in, limp and blotted, so his soul took in the mean temptation, lapped it in fancied rights, in dreams of improved exis-tences, drifting and endless as the cloud-seas of color. Clutching it, as if the tightness of his hold would strengthen his sense of possession, he went aimlessly down the street. It was his watch at the mill. He need not go, need never go again, thank God! — shaking off the thought with unbreakable loathing.

Shall I go over the history of the hours of that night? how the man wandered from one to another of his old haunts, with a half-consciousness of bidding them farewell, — lanes and alleys and backyards where the mill-hands lodged, — noting, with a new eagerness, the filth and drunkenness, the pig-pens, the ash-heaps covered with potato-skins, the bloated, pimpled women at the doors, — with a new disgust, a new sense of sudden

---

35. **show you the mote . . . take it out:** See Matthew 7:3-5: "And why beholdest thou the mote that is in thy brother's eye, but considerest not the beam that is in thine own eye? Or how wilt thou say to thy brother, Let me pull out the mote out of thine eye; and, behold, a beam is in thine own eye? Thou hypocrite, first cast out the beam out of thine own eye; and then shalt thou see clearly to cast out the mote out of thy brother's eye."

triumph, and, under all, a new, vague dread, unknown before, smothered down, kept under, but still there? It left him but once during the night, when, for the second time in his life, he entered a church. It was a sombre Gothic pile, where the stained light lost itself in far-retreating arches; built to meet the requirements and sympathies of a far other class than Wolfe's. Yet it touched, moved him uncontrollably. The distances, the shadows, the still, marble figures, the mass of silent kneeling worshippers, the mysterious music, thrilled, lifted his soul with a wonderful rain. Wolfe forgot himself, forgot the new life he was going to live, the mean terror gnawing underneath. The voice of the speaker strengthened the charm; it was clear, feeling, full, strong. An old man, who had lived much, suffered much; whose brain was keenly alive, dominant; whose heart was summer-warm with charity. He taught it to-night. He held up Humanity in its grand total; showed the great world-cancer to his people. Who could show it better? He was a Christian reformer; he had studied the age thoroughly; his outlook at man had been free, world-wide, over all time. His faith stood sublime upon the Rock of Ages; his fiery zeal guided vast schemes by which the gospel was to be preached to all nations. How did he preach it to-night? In burning, light-laden words he painted the incarnate Life, Love, the universal Man: words that became reality in the lives of these people, – that lived again in beautiful words and actions, trifling, but heroic. Sin, as he defied it, was a real foe to them; their trials, temptations, were his. His words passed far over the furnace-tender's grasp, toned to suit another class of culture; they sounded in his ears a very pleasant song in an unknown tongue. He meant to cure this world-cancer with a steady eye that had never glared with hunger, and a hand that neither poverty nor strychnine-whiskey[36] had taught to shake. In this morbid, distorted heart of the Welsh puddler he had failed.

Wolfe rose at last, and turned from the church down the street. He looked up; the night had come on foggy, damp; the golden mists had vanished, and the sky lay dull and ash-colored. He wandered again aimlessly down the street, idly wondering what had become of the cloud-sea of crimson and scarlet. The trial-day of this man's life was over, and he had lost the victory. What followed was mere drifting circumstance, – a quicker walking over the path, – that was all. Do you want to hear the end of it? You wish me to make a tragic story out of it? Why, in the police-reports of the morning paper you can find a dozen such tragedies: hints of shipwrecks unlike any that ever befell on the high seas; hints that here a power was lost to heaven, – that there a soul went down where no tide can ebb or flow. Commonplace enough the hints are, – jocose sometimes, done up in rhyme.

Doctor May, a month after the night I have told you of, was reading to his wife at breakfast from this fourth column of the morning-paper: an unusual thing, – these police-reports not being, in general, choice reading for ladies; but it was only one item he read.

---

36. **strychnine-whiskey:** Whiskey treated with a few drops of strychnine, used in the nineteenth century to stimulate the central nervous system.

"Oh, my dear! You remember that man I told you of, that we saw at Kirby's mill? — that was arrested for robbing Mitchell? Here he is; just listen: — 'Circuit Court. Judge Day. Hugh Wolfe, operative in Kirby & John's Loudon Mills. Charge, grand larceny. Sentence, nineteen years hard labor in penitentiary.' — Scoundrel! Serves him right! After all our kindness that night! Picking Mitchell's pocket at the very time!"

His wife said something about the ingratitude of that kind of people, and then they began to talk of something else.

Nineteen years! How easy that was to read! What a simple word for Judge Day to utter! Nineteen years! Half a lifetime!

Hugh Wolfe sat on the window-ledge of his cell, looking out. His ankles were ironed. Not usual in such cases; but he had made two desperate efforts to escape. "Well," as Haley, the jailer, said, "small blame to him! Nineteen years' imprisonment was not a pleasant thing to look forward to." Haley was very good-natured about it, though Wolfe had fought him savagely.

"When he was first caught," the jailer said afterwards, in telling the story, "before the trial, the fellow was cut down at once, — laid there on that pallet like a dead man, with his hands over his eyes. Never saw a man so cut down in my life. Time of the trial, too, came the queerest dodge of any customer I ever had. Would choose no lawyer. Judge gave him one, of course. Gibson it was. He tried to prove the fellow crazy; but it wouldn't go. Thing was plain as daylight: money found on him. 'T was a hard sentence, — all the law allows; but it was for 'xample's sake. These mill-hands are gettin' onbearable. When the sentence was read, he just looked up, and said the money was his by rights, and that all the world had gone wrong. That night, after the trial, a gentleman came to see him here, name of Mitchell, — him as he stole from. Talked to him for an hour. Thought he came for curiosity, like. After he was gone, thought Wolfe was remarkable quiet, and went into his cell. Found him very low; bed all bloody. Doctor said he had been bleeding at the lungs. He was as weak as a cat; yet, if ye'll b'lieve me, he tried to get a-past me and get out. I just carried him like a baby, and threw him on the pallet. Three days after, he tried it again: that time reached the wall. Lord help you! he fought like a tiger, — giv' some terrible blows. Fightin' for life, you see; for he can't live long, shut up in the stone crib down yonder. Got a death-cough now. 'T took two of us to bring him down that day; so I just put the irons on his feet. There he sits, in there. Goin' to-morrow, with a batch more of 'em. That woman, hunchback, tried with him, — you remember? — she's only got three years. 'Complice. But *she's* a woman, you know. He's been quiet ever since I put on irons: giv' up, I suppose. Looks white, sick-lookin'. It acts different on 'em, bein' sentenced. Most of 'em gets reckless, devilish-like. Some prays awful, and sings them vile songs of the mills, all in a breath. That woman, now, she's desper't. Been beggin' to see Hugh, as she calls him, for three days. I'm a-goin' to let her in. She don't go with him. Here she is in this next cell. I'm a-goin' now to let her in."

He let her in. Wolfe did not see her. She crept into a corner of the cell, and stood watching him. He was scratching the iron bars of the window with a piece of tin which he had picked up, with an idle, uncertain, vacant stare, just as a child or idiot would do.

"Tryin' to get out, old boy?" laughed Haley. "Them irons will need a crowbar beside your tin, before you can open 'em."

Wolfe laughed, too, in a senseless way.

"I think I'll get out," he said.

"I believe his brain's touched," said Haley, when he came out.

The puddler scraped away with the tin for half an hour. Still Deborah did not speak. At last she ventured nearer, and touched his arm.

"Blood?" she said, looking at some spots on his coat with a shudder.

He looked up at her. "Why, Deb!" he said, smiling, – such a bright, boyish smile, that it went to poor Deborah's heart directly, and she sobbed and cried out loud.

"Oh, Hugh, lad! Hugh! dunnot look at me, when it wur my fault! To think I brought hur to it! And I loved hur so! Oh, lad, I dud!"

The confession, even in this wretch, came with the woman's blush through the sharp cry.

He did not seem to hear her, – scraping away diligently at the bars with the bit of tin.

Was he going mad? She peered closely into his face. Something she saw there made her draw suddenly back, – something which Haley had not seen, that lay beneath the pinched, vacant look it had caught since the trial, or the curious gray shadow that rested on it. That gray shadow, – yes, she knew what that meant. She had often seen it creeping over women's faces for months, who died at last of slow hunger or consumption. That meant death, distant, lingering: but this – Whatever it was the woman saw, or thought she saw, used as she was to crime and misery, seemed to make her sick with a new horror. Forgetting her fear of him, she caught his shoulders, and looked keenly, steadily, into his eyes.

"Hugh!" she cried, in a desperate whisper, – "oh, boy, not that! for God's sake, not *that!*"

The vacant laugh went off his face, and he answered her in a muttered word or two that drove her away. Yet the words were kindly enough. Sitting there on his pallet, she cried silently a hopeless sort of tears, but did not speak again. The man looked up furtively at her now and then. Whatever his own trouble was, her distress vexed him with a momentary sting.

It was market-day. The narrow window of the jail looked down directly on the carts and wagons drawn up in a long line, where they had unloaded. He could see, too, and hear distinctly the clink of money as it changed hands, the busy crowd of whites and blacks shoving, pushing one another, and the chaffering and swearing at the stalls. Somehow, the sound, more than anything else had done, wakened him up, – made the whole real to him. He was done with the world and the business of it. He let the tin fall, and looked out, pressing his face close to the rusty bars. How they crowded and pushed! And he, – he should never walk that pavement again! There came Neff Sanders, one of the feeders at the mill, with a basket on his arm. Sure enough, Neff was married the other week. He whistled, hoping he would look up; but he did not. He wondered if Neff remembered he was there, if any of the boys thought of him up there, and thought that he never was to go down that old cinder-road again. Never again! He had not quite understood it before; but now he did. Not for days or years, but never! – that was it.

How clear the light fell on that stall in front of the market! and how like a picture it was, the dark-green heaps of corn, and the crimson beets, and golden melons! There was another with game: how the light flickered on that pheasant's breast, with the purplish blood dripping over the brown feathers! He could see the red shining of the drops, it was so near. In one minute he could be down there. It was just a step. So easy, as it seemed, so natural to go! Yet it could never be – not in all the thousands of years to come – that he should put his foot on that street again! He thought of himself with a sorrowful pity, as of some one else. There was a dog down in the market, walking after his master with such a stately, grave look! – only a dog, yet he could go backwards and forwards just as he pleased: he had good luck! Why, the very vilest cur, yelping there in the gutter, had not lived his life, had been free to act out whatever thought God had put into his brain; while he – No, he would not think of that! He tried to put the thought away, and to listen to a dispute between a countryman and a woman about some meat; but it would come back. He, what had he done to bear this?

Then came the sudden picture of what might have been, and now. He knew what it was to be in the penitentiary, – how it went with men there. He knew how in these long years he should slowly die, but not until soul and body had become corrupt and rotten, – how, when he came out, if he lived to come, even the lowest of the mill-hands would jeer him, – how his hands would be weak, and his brain senseless and stupid. He believed he was almost that now. He put his hand to his head, with a puzzled, weary look. It ached, his head, with thinking. He tried to quiet himself. It was only right, perhaps; he had done wrong. But was there right or wrong for such as he? What was right? And who had ever taught him? He thrust the whole matter away. A dark, cold quiet crept through his brain. It was all wrong; but let it be! It was nothing to him more than the others. Let it be!

The door grated, as Haley opened it.

"Come, my woman! Must lock up for t' night. Come, stir yerself!"

She went up and took Hugh's hand.

"Good-night, Deb," he said, carelessly.

She had not hoped he would say more; but the tired pain on her mouth just then was bitterer than death. She took his passive hand and kissed it.

"Hur'll never see Deb again!" she ventured, her lips growing colder and more bloodless.

What did she say that for? Did he not know it? Yet he would not be impatient with poor old Deb. She had trouble of her own, as well as he.

"No, never again," he said, trying to be cheerful.

She stood just a moment, looking at him. Do you laugh at her, standing there, with her hunchback, her rags, her bleared, withered face, and the great despised love tugging at her heart?

"Come, you!" called Haley, impatiently.

She did not move.

"Hugh!" she whispered.

It was to be her last word. What was it?

"Hugh, boy, not THAT!"

He did not answer. She wrung her hands, trying to be silent, looking in his face in an agony of entreaty. He smiled again, kindly.

"It is best, Deb. I cannot bear to be hurted any more."

"Hur knows," she said, humbly.

"Tell my father good-bye; and – and kiss little Janey."

She nodded, saying nothing, looked in his face again, and went out of the door. As she went, she staggered.

"Drinkin' to-day?" broke out Haley, pushing her before him. "Where the Devil did you get it? Here, in with ye!" and he shoved her into her cell, next to Wolfe's, and shut the door.

Along the wall of her cell there was a crack low down by the floor, through which she could see the light from Wolfe's. She had discovered it days before. She hurried in now, and, kneeling down by it, listened, hoping to hear some sound. Nothing but the rasping of the tin on the bars. He was at his old amusement again. Something in the noise jarred on her ear, for she shivered as she heard it. Hugh rasped away at the bars. A dull old bit of tin, not fit to cut korl with.

He looked out of the window again. People were leaving the market now. A tall mulatto girl, following her mistress, her basket on her head, crossed the street just below, and looked up. She was laughing; but, when she caught sight of the haggard face peering out through the bars, suddenly grew grave, and hurried by. A free, firm step, a clear-cut olive face, with a scarlet turban tied on one side, dark, shining eyes, and on the head the basket poised, filled with fruit and flowers, under which the scarlet turban and bright eyes looked out half-shadowed. The picture caught his eye. It was good to see a face like that. He would try to-morrow, and cut one like it. *To-morrow!* He threw down the tin, trembling, and covered his face with his hands. When he looked up again, the daylight was gone.

Deborah, crouching near by on the other side of the wall, heard no noise. He sat on the side of the low pallet, thinking. Whatever was the mystery which the woman had seen on his face, it came out now slowly, in the dark there, and became fixed, – a something never seen on his face before. The evening was darkening fast. The market had been over for an hour; the rumbling of the carts over the pavement grew more infrequent: he listened to each, as it passed, because he thought it was to be for the last time. For the same reason, it was, I suppose, that he strained his eyes to catch a glimpse of each passer-by, wondering who they were, what kind of homes they were going to, if they had children, – listening eagerly to every chance word in the street, as if – (God be merciful to the man! what strange fancy was this?) – as if he never should hear human voices again.

It was quite dark at last. The street was a lonely one. The last passenger, he thought, was gone. No, – there was a quick step: Joe Hill, lighting the lamps. Joe was a good old chap; never passed a fellow without some joke or other. He remembered once seeing the place where he lived with his wife. "Granny Hill" the boys called her. Bedridden she was;

but so kind as Joe was to her! kept the room so clean! — and the old woman, when he was there, was laughing at "some of t' lad's foolishness." The step was far down the street; but he could see him place the ladder, run up, and light the gas. A longing seized him to be spoken to once more.

"Joe!" he called, out of the grating. "Good-bye, Joe!"

The old man stopped a moment, listening uncertainly; then hurried on. The prisoner thrust his hand out of the window, and called again, louder; but Joe was too far down the street. It was a little thing; but it hurt him, — this disappointment.

"Good-bye, Joe!" he called, sorrowfully enough.

"Be quiet!" said one of the jailers, passing the door, striking on it with his club.

Oh, that was the last, was it?

There was an inexpressible bitterness on his face, as he lay down on the bed, taking the bit of tin, which he had rasped to a tolerable degree of sharpness, in his hand, — to play with, it may be. He bared his arms, looking intently at their corded veins and sinews. Deborah, listening in the next cell, heard a slight clicking sound, often repeated. She shut her lips tightly, that she might not scream; the cold drops of sweat broke over her, in her dumb agony.

"Hur knows best," she muttered at last, fiercely clutching the boards where she lay.

If she could have seen Wolfe, there was nothing about him to frighten her. He lay quite still, his arms outstretched, looking at the pearly stream of moonlight coming into the window. I think in that one hour that came then he lived back over all the years that had gone before. I think that all the low, vile life, all his wrongs, all his starved hopes, came then, and stung him with a farewell poison that made him sick unto death. He made neither moan nor cry, only turned his worn face now and then to the pure light, that seemed so far off, as one that said, "How long, O Lord? how long?"

The hour was over at last. The moon, passing over her nightly path, slowly came nearer, and threw the light across his bed on his feet. He watched it steadily, as it crept up, inch by inch, slowly. It seemed to him to carry with it a great silence. He had been so hot and tired there always in the mills! The years had been so fierce and cruel! There was coming now quiet and coolness and sleep. His tense limbs relaxed, and settled in a calm languor. The blood ran fainter and slow from his heart. He did not think now with a savage anger of what might be and was not; he was conscious only of deep stillness creeping over him. At first he saw a sea of faces: the mill-men, — women he had known, drunken and bloated, — Janeys timid and pitiful, — poor old Debs: then they floated together like a mist, and faded away, leaving only the clear, pearly moonlight.

Whether, as the pure light crept up the stretched-out figure, it brought with it calm and peace, who shall say? His dumb soul was alone with God in judgment. A Voice may have spoken for it from far-off Calvary, "Father, forgive them, for they know not what they do!"[37] Who dare say? Fainter and fainter the heart rose and fell, slower and slower the moon floated from behind a cloud, until, when at last its full

---

37. "Father . . . do!": The words of Jesus as he is crucified at Calvary (Luke 23:34).

tide of white splendor swept over the cell, it seemed to wrap and fold into a deeper stillness the dead figure that never should move again. Silence deeper than the Night! Nothing that moved, save the black, nauseous stream of blood dripping slowly from the pallet to the floor!

There was outcry and crowd enough in the cell the next day. The coroner and his jury, the local editors, Kirby himself, and boys with their hands thrust knowingly into their pockets and heads on one side, jammed into the corners. Coming and going all day. Only one woman. She came late, and outstayed them all. A Quaker, or Friend, as they call themselves. I think this woman was known by that name in heaven. A homely body, coarsely dressed in gray and white. Deborah (for Haley had let her in) took notice of her. She watched them all – sitting on the end of the pallet, holding his head in her arms – with the ferocity of a watch-dog, if any of them touched the body. There was no meekness, no sorrow, in her face; the stuff out of which murderers are made, instead. All the time Haley and the woman were laying straight the limbs and cleaning the cell, Deborah sat still, keenly watching the Quaker's face. Of all the crowd there that day, this woman alone had not spoken to her, – only once or twice had put some cordial to her lips. After they all were gone, the woman, in the same still, gentle way, brought a vase of wood-leaves and berries, and placed it by the pallet, then opened the narrow window. The fresh air blew in, and swept the woody fragrance over the dead face. Deborah looked up with a quick wonder.

"Did hur know my boy wud like it? Did hur know Hugh?"

"I know Hugh now."

The white fingers passed in a slow, pitiful way over the dead, worn face. There was a heavy shadow in the quiet eyes.

"Did hur know where they 'll bury Hugh?" said Deborah in a shrill tone, catching her arm.

This had been the question hanging on her lips all day.

"In t' town-yard? Under t' mud and ash? T' lad 'll smother, woman! He wur born on t' lane moor, where t' air is frick and strong. Take hur out, for God's sake, take hur out where t' air blows!"

The Quaker hesitated, but only for a moment. She put her strong arm around Deborah and led her to the window.

"Thee sees the hills, friend, over the river? Thee sees how the light lies warm there, and the winds of God blow all the day? I live there, – where the blue smoke is, by the trees. Look at me." She turned Deborah's face to her own, clear and earnest. "Thee will believe me? I will take Hugh and bury him there to-morrow."

Deborah did not doubt her. As the evening wore on, she leaned against the iron bars, looking at the hills that rose far off, through the thick sodden clouds, like a bright, unattainable calm. As she looked, a shadow of their solemn repose fell on her face: its fierce discontent faded into a pitiful, humble quiet. Slow, solemn tears gathered in her eyes: the poor weak eyes turned so hopelessly to the place where Hugh was to rest, the grave heights looking higher and brighter and more solemn than ever before. The Quaker watched her keenly. She came to her at last, and touched her arm.

934   AMERICAN FACTS AND AMERICAN FICTION

"When thee comes back," she said, in a low, sorrowful tone, like one who speaks from a strong heart deeply moved with remorse or pity, "thee shall begin thy life again, – there on the hills. I came too late; but not for thee, – by God's help, it may be."

Not too late. Three years after, the Quaker began her work. I end my story here. At evening-time it was light. There is no need to tire you with the long years of sunshine, and fresh air, and slow, patient Christ-love, needed to make healthy and hopeful this impure body and soul. There is a homely pine house, on one of these hills, whose windows overlook broad, wooded slopes and clover-crimsoned meadows, – niched into the very place where the light is warmest, the air freest. It is the Friends' meeting-house.[38] Once a week they sit there, in their grave, earnest way, waiting for the Spirit of Love to speak, opening their simple hearts to receive His words. There is a woman, old, deformed, who takes a humble place among them: waiting like them: in her gray dress, her worn face, pure and meek, turned now and then to the sky. A woman much loved by these silent, restful people; more silent than they, more humble, more loving. Waiting: with her eyes turned to hills higher and purer than these on which she lives, – dim and far off now, but to be reached some day. There may be in her heart some latent hope to meet there the love denied her here, – that she shall find him whom she lost, and that then she will not be all-unworthy. Who blames her? Something is lost in the passage of every soul from one eternity to the other, – something pure and beautiful, which might have been and was not: a hope, a talent, a love, over which the soul mourns, like Esau deprived of his birthright.[39] What blame to the meek Quaker, if she took her lost hope to make the hills of heaven more fair?

Nothing remains to tell that the poor Welsh puddler once lived, but this figure of the mill-woman cut in korl. I have it here in a corner of my library. I keep it hid behind a curtain, – it is such a rough, ungainly thing. Yet there are about it touches, grand sweeps of outline, that show a master's hand. Sometimes, – to-night, for instance, – the curtain is accidentally drawn back, and I see a bare arm stretched out imploringly in the darkness, and an eager, wolfish face watching mine: a wan, woful face, through which the spirit of the dead korl-cutter looks out, with its thwarted life, its mighty hunger, its unfinished work. Its pale, vague lips seem to tremble with a terrible question. "Is this the End?" they say, – "nothing beyond? – no more?" Why, you tell me you have seen that look in the eyes of dumb brutes, – horses dying under the lash. I know.

The deep of the night is passing while I write. The gas-light wakens from the shadows here and there the objects which lie scattered through the room: only faintly, though; for they belong to the open sunlight. As I glance at them, they each recall some task or pleasure of the coming day. A half-moulded child's head; Aphrodite;[40] a bough of forest-leaves; music; work; homely fragments, in which lie the secrets of all eternal truth and

---

38. **Friends' meeting-house:** Quakers are members of the Religious Society of Friends.
39. **Esau deprived of his birthright:** Esau, the twin brother of Jacob and the son of Isaac and Rebekah, gave his birthright to his brother in exchange for food (Genesis 25:33-34).
40. **Aphrodite:** Ancient Greek goddess of love, called Venus by the Romans.

beauty. Prophetic all! Only this dumb, woful face seems to belong to and end with the night. I turn to look at it. Has the power of its desperate need commanded the darkness away? While the room is yet steeped in heavy shadow, a cool, gray light suddenly touches its head like a blessing hand, and its groping arm points through the broken cloud to the far East, where, in the flickering, nebulous crimson, God has set the promise of the Dawn.

[1861]

SELECT POEMS

BY

MRS. L. H. SIGOURNEY.

Engraved by W.E. Tucker.

PHILADELPHIA

CAREY AND HART.

New Poetic Voices

IN THE NINETEENTH CENTURY, educated people considered poetry the highest literary form; and poetic achievement was viewed as the standard by which a national culture was measured. The desire to create a distinctly American literature consequently took on a special urgency in the realm of poetry. Nonetheless, the creation of truly indigenous poetry faced formidable obstacles in the United States. One was the dominance of the rich tradition of English poetry. Chaucer, Shakespeare, Milton, and especially the British Romantic poets — such as William Wordsworth, John Keats, and Percy Bysshe Shelley — exerted a powerful influence on American poets of the period. But surely, many reasoned, a nation without its own

◀ Title page of *Select Poems* (1848) by Lydia Sigourney

As technological developments lowered the cost of printing engravings, publishers often sought to enhance their books by adding illustrations, including portraits of the authors and elaborate title pages like this one from *Select Poems* (1848) by Lydia Sigourney. Here, a variety of flowers and plants are intertwined around a lyre, the musical instrument played by ancient poets and the Greek god Orpheus, son of Calliope, the Muse of epic poetry.

poets and poetry could not be a real nation. At the same time, some critics and writers were concerned that the democratic institutions and especially the material conditions in the United States were adverse to the development of the arts in general and poetry in particular. In response to what many perceived as the national necessity for poetry, the editor of the *Southern Quarterly Review*, Daniel Whitaker, simply announced that American poetry in fact existed. As he exclaimed in 1842: "Poetry! Why, America is *all* poetry. The pages of our Constitution, — the deeds of our patriot sires, — the deliberations of our sages and statesmen, — the civilization and progress of our people, — the wisdom of our laws, — the greatness of our name, are all covered over with the living fire of poetry."

> *"Poetry! Why, America is all poetry. The pages of our Constitution, — the deeds of our patriot sires, — the deliberations of our sages and statesmen, — the civilization and progress of our people, — the wisdom of our laws, — the greatness of our name, are all covered over with the living fire of poetry."*

Just as Whitaker viewed such notable achievements as poetic acts, so did many others view the writing of poetry as a patriotic act, a necessary part of building a new and culturally independent country. In the preface to the first edition of his highly successful anthology *The Poets and Poetry of America* (1842), Rufus Griswold stated that his intention was "to exhibit the progress and condition of Poetry in the United States." Affirming that "Literature, not less than wealth, adds to a nation's happiness and greatness," Griswold reprinted the works of dozens of poets, many of whom had become popular with readers through their frequent appearances in periodicals. Both magazines and newspapers published poetry in the nineteenth century. By midcentury, it was not uncommon for readers to find poems on the front pages of even national newspapers like the influential *New-York Tribune*. Families often read poetry aloud for evening entertainment, and in schools the memorization of poetry was an early part of training in reading. Although poetry never gained the share of the literary marketplace claimed by prose works, especially short stories and novels, the publication of books of poetry written by Americans rose steadily in the period before the Civil War. During the decade of 1830–40, some two hundred of these books of poetry were published in New York City alone. In the following decade, that number tripled, and the number of volumes of poetry written by Americans and published in the United States continued to climb during the 1850s.

As in the case of fiction and other prose writings, women claimed a significant share of the market for poetry. The much-admired Lydia Sigourney, who in 1830 was regularly writing for at least twenty magazines and newspapers, published more than fifty books during her lifetime. Most of those books were collections of her poems, which sold quite well. Sigourney's poems ranged from popular, sentimental accounts of the deaths of children to witty and often barbed political commentaries, including her opposition to federal policies for the removal of the Cherokee from their native lands in Georgia. Other women poets also gained a good deal of success. Elizabeth Oakes Smith published "The Sinless Child," a long narrative poem on a frequent nineteenth-century topic – the death of an innocent, young child – in the *Southern Literary Messenger* in 1842. The popularity of that poem and her other frequent contributions to periodicals prompted the publication of Smith's first book, *The Sinless Child and Other Poems*, in 1843. A complete edition of her poems followed in 1845, with a preface by the increasingly influential Rufus Griswold, who continued to publish his successful anthologies of poetry throughout the 1840s and 1850s. Like many other writers of the period, Smith published both poetry and prose; so did the popular short-story writer Rose Terry Cooke, whose *Poems* appeared in 1861, a decade after her first poem was published in the *New-York Tribune*.

Male writers also profited from the growing demand for poetry. In an earlier generation, it had not been economically feasible to make a career of writing poetry. Despite the acclaim generated by his poem "Thanatopsis" and the warm critical reception of his first collection of poetry, published in 1821, William Cullen Bryant had turned from poetry to work as a newspaper editor in order to earn a living. Like Bryant, Oliver Wendell Holmes gained early success with poems he began to publish in periodicals shortly after his graduation from Harvard in 1829. Although he published his first collection, *Poems*, in 1836, poetry remained an avocation for Holmes, who supported himself through the practice and later the teaching of medicine. When James Russell Lowell graduated from Harvard in 1839, his elders there strongly discouraged him from pursuing a career as a poet, and he dutifully went on to Harvard Law School. "Our stout Yankee nation would swap all the poems that ever were penned for a treatise on ventilation," Lowell gloomily observed in 1840. But times truly had changed during the previous few years, largely as a result of the establishment of important new literary periodicals like *Graham's Magazine* and the *Southern Literary Messenger*. In fact, the poems Lowell began to publish in such periodicals gained such immediate favor with audiences that he was soon able to publish the first of his many popular volumes of poetry, *A Year's Life* (1841). The critical success of that volume – one reviewer proclaimed that, in Lowell, the country had at last produced a poet who would write the great American poem and thus silence "the sneers of foreigners" – made his work all the more attractive to periodicals and allowed him to abandon the law for a career in literature.

The checkered career of Edgar Allan Poe illustrated the shifting position of poets and poetry in the United States. Poe was so determined to become a poet that in 1827, at the age of eighteen, he left his home in Virginia and made his way to Boston, then the center of publishing in the United States. There, he paid for the publication of his first volume of poetry, *Tamerlane and Other Poems* (1827). He published additional volumes of verse in 1829 and 1831, but the commercial failure of those collections obliged Poe to earn his living by editing magazines and writing critical articles and short stories. He continued to publish some poetry in periodicals, however, and in 1845 his poem "The Raven" caused a sensation when it was published in a New York City newspaper and then in the *American Review*. As a consequence, Poe began to lecture on American poets, became a principal reviewer for the *Broadway Journal*, and swiftly published *The Raven and Other Poems* (1845). The poems collected in that volume and a few other poems he published during the remaining four years of his life gained Poe far greater fame, both at home and abroad, than the short stories for which he is now principally known and valued as a writer.

In his critical statements on poetry, Poe insisted that its sole end was beauty, not truth. He consequently tended to dismiss forms of poetry that sought to convey ideas, teach lessons, or tell stories — that is, virtually all of the kinds of poetry that were most popular during the period. Certainly, many American poets would have challenged Poe's formulation. Much of the poetry written during the period was devoted to moral, political, or social ends. Among those who clearly recognized and early sought to exploit the growing popularity of poetry were the abolitionists, brilliant propagandists who used every form of communication at their disposal. One of the most prolific of the abolitionist poets was John Pierpont, a Harvard-educated Unitarian minister whose conservative Boston congregation accused him of wasting his time in "the making of Books," including *The Anti-Slavery Poems of John Pierpont* (1843). Pierpont was a close friend of the radical abolitionist William Lloyd Garrison — editor of the *Liberator* — and so was another notable antislavery poet, John Greenleaf Whittier, the author of *Poems Written during the Progress of the Abolition Question* (1838) and *Voices of Freedom* (1846). Garrison and other abolitionists also heavily promoted the work of Frances E. W. Harper, an African American woman whose antislavery collection *Poems on Miscellaneous Subjects* sold twelve thousand copies in 1854. The most popular poet of the period, Henry Wadsworth Longfellow, contributed to the cause with his early collection *Poems on Slavery*, published in 1842. But he gained international renown through ballads, lyrics, and especially a series of long narrative poems with American settings and themes, two of which were more successful than any volumes of poetry previously published in the United States: *Hiawatha*, which sold an astonishing forty-three thousand copies within a year of its publication in 1855; and *The Courtship of Miles Standish* (1858), which on its first day of publication sold fifteen thousand copies in Boston and London.

Longfellow was but one of many poets who answered the call for "literature by native authors," as the editor of the *American Review* put it in 1845. The "Fireside Poets," as Bryant, Holmes, Longfellow, Lowell, and Whittier were sometimes called, frequently invoked the comforts of hearth and home. The accessibility, didacticism, and moral seriousness of much of their

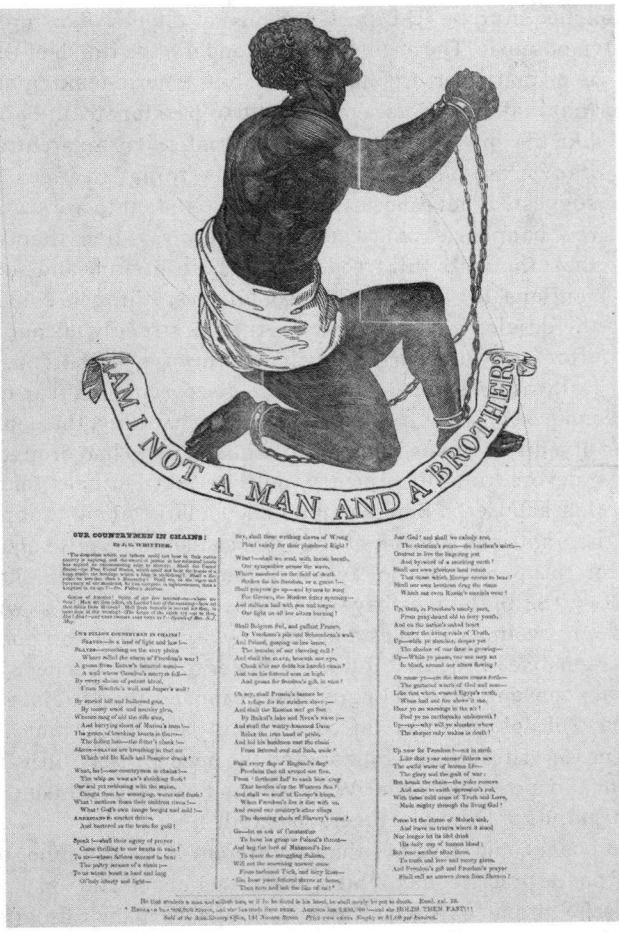

Am I Not a Man and a Brother?

This woodcut image of a supplicant male slave in chains appeared on the 1837 broadside publication of John Greenleaf Whittier's antislavery poem "Our Countrymen in Chains." The design was originally adopted as the seal of the Society for the Abolition of Slavery in England during the 1780s.

poetry accounted for a later description of the group, the "Schoolroom Poets." Although readers loved the rhythms and rhymes of their poems and enjoyed the patriotic pride they inspired, some critics lamented the lack of innovation and originality in the poetry written and published in the United States. "We hear, through all the varied music, the ground-tone of conventional life," Ralph Waldo Emerson observed in "The Poet," an essay published in 1844. "Our poets are men of talents who sing, and not the children of music. The argument is secondary, the finish of the verses is primary. For it is not metres, but a metre-making argument that makes a poem, – a thought so passionate and alive, that, like the spirit of a plant or an animal, it has an architecture of its own, and adorns nature with a new thing." In effect, Emerson suggested that American poets were content to work within narrow boundaries and established forms, rather than allowing their thoughts full freedom from both literary and social conventions. For his part, Emerson did everything he could to spur the development of a new poetry. He strongly encouraged the efforts of young writers such as Henry David Thoreau, who initially aspired to be a poet before discovering his true talent for narrative and poetic prose, and William Ellery Channing, the nephew and namesake of a distinguished Unitarian minister, who had dropped out of Harvard to devote himself to poetry and later settled near Emerson in Concord, Massachusetts. Emerson published a large amount of poetry in the *Dial*, the unofficial journal of the transcendentalists. He also helped arrange for the publication of two different collections of Channing's *Poems* (1843, 1848), though they were eclipsed by Emerson's own *Poems* (1847). Like his young disciples and so many other American poets, however, Emerson discovered that it was far easier to assert the need to break with literary conventions and English poetic models than to discover compelling ways of doing so. He was consequently less important as a poet than as a prose writer whose emphasis on the need for self-cultivation and self-reliance inspired both Walt Whitman and Emily Dickinson to claim the various kinds of freedoms Emerson extolled.

> *"For it is not metres, but a metre-making argument that makes a poem, – a thought so passionate and alive, that, like the spirit of a plant or an animal, it has an architecture of its own, and adorns nature with a new thing."*

No two poets could have been more different in background, temperament, and poetic practice than Whitman and Dickinson. The son of a farmer and laborer, Whitman quit school at the age of eleven and was largely self-educated. By the standards for women at the time, Dickinson was well educated, and the affluence of her distinguished family allowed her much free time for study and writing. One of Whitman's New York friends observed that he belonged to the "crowded thoroughfare," and few writers of the period so relished the sights and sounds of urban life. The reclusive Dickinson was happiest in an upstairs room in her family's comfortable house in Amherst, a rural town in western Massachusetts. Although both devoted most of their lives to writing poetry, their poems were strikingly different, as were their attitudes toward publication. Dickinson preferred to "publish" her poems in letters to friends and relatives. Of the nearly 1,800 poems she wrote by the time of her death in 1886, Dickinson published only a handful in periodicals. In contrast, Whitman constantly published his poems, in both periodicals and books, notably in the multiple editions of *Leaves of Grass* he published between 1855 and his death in 1892.

As unalike as they were, Whitman and Dickinson were united by the radical differences between their poetry and virtually all of the other poetry written during the period. Emerson warmly greeted the appearance of the first edition of *Leaves of Grass*, which he called "the most extraordinary piece of wit and wisdom that America has yet produced." Fanny Fern, the popular newspaper columnist, also praised Whitman's book for its challenge to the "forced, stiff, Parnassian exotics" of other poets. But most early reviewers fiercely condemned Whitman's iconoclastic approach to form and content, especially what they described as the "coarseness" and "sensuality" of *Leaves of Grass*. One of Whitman's harshest critics was Rufus Griswold, who in the mid-1850s was publishing anthologies of American poetry for use in schoolrooms. "It is impossible to imagine how any man's fancy could have conceived of such a mass of stupid filth," Griswold angrily exclaimed in his savage review of *Leaves of Grass*. Its poems were considered particularly unsuitable for female readers. Dickinson herself later playfully said that she had never read Whitman's book "but was told that he was disgraceful." Nonetheless, as she no doubt recognized, if Dickinson had sought a wider audience for her poetry she, too, would have faced stiff resistance from critics. Although her poems would not have been viewed as violating moral laws or the laws against obscenity, Dickinson defiantly violated the metrical laws of poetry even as she subverted conventional religious values and beliefs. Indeed, if her poetry had ever been read by Griswold, the self-styled arbiter of poetic taste in the United States, he would no doubt have rejected it almost as forcefully as he rejected *Leaves of Grass*. Certainly, neither the editor nor the many readers of *The Poets and Poetry of America* could then have recognized that in Whitman and Dickinson the country had produced its first great poets, whose work would later be viewed as among the most notable achievements of nineteenth-century American literature.

American Contexts

THE AMERICAN MUSE:
POETRY AT MIDCENTURY

WHITMAN AND DICKINSON have come to overshadow all other American poets of the nineteenth century, especially those of the period 1830–65. For readers at that time, however, Whitman was an obscure figure until he published the first edition of *Leaves of Grass* in 1855. After that, he was more notorious than famous. Dickinson was completely unknown until the first collection of her poems appeared in 1890, four years after her death. The following selections from the work of eight poets exemplify some of the various kinds of American poetry most widely distributed and read in the United States during the decades before the Civil War. Not surprisingly, the influence of eighteenth- and early nineteenth-century British poets like William Cowper, James Thomson, and William Wordsworth can be felt strongly here, especially in the ways in which many of these poems deal with everyday subjects, the lives of ordinary people, and the details of the natural world. The topics of the poems are various, ranging from abstract philosophical issues such as immortality to topical issues like slavery, the plight of Native Americans, and the role of women in society. For the most part, however, poets of the period employed conventional forms. Emerson persistently tried to expand those forms, while Poe sought special, unconventional effects. But most of the popular poets took fairly predictable approaches to rhythm and rhyme. In fact, even at that time, some critics complained about the conventionality of much of the poetry written and published in the United States. Nonetheless, the poets represented here and many others writing during the period laid an important and cultural foundation. With the aid of periodicals, in which all of them published, these writers helped develop an audience for poetry in the United States, a place which many critics at home and especially abroad viewed as inhospitable or even hostile to the arts. In fact, some of the very elements of style and subject matter that made and make poetry from this time seem so conventional allowed it to communicate directly and often with genuine force to large numbers of readers. Certainly, the poems presented in the following section indicate why Whitman's poetry never found favor with the mass audience he craved and why Dickinson mainly shared her poems with friends and relatives rather than subject her work to the pressures of a literary marketplace shaped by markedly different kinds of poetry.

bedfordstmartins.com/ americanlit for research links on the authors in this section

Lydia Sigourney

[1791–1865]

One of the most popular and prolific writers of the period, Lydia Howard Huntley Sigourney was born in Norwich, Connecticut, where she was raised in a devoutly Christian home. Deeply committed to female education, she opened a school for young women, first in Norwich and then in Hartford, Connecticut, which would become her lifelong home. She published her first work, *Moral Pieces in Prose and Verse*, in 1815. During the remaining fifty years of her life, she published more than fifty additional books of poetry and prose, both fiction and nonfictional works like the *History of the Condition of Women* (1837). Nonetheless, she was best known as a poet, "the sweet singer of Hartford," as she was often called in the periodicals where her works so frequently appeared. Sigourney was a popular

Lydia Sigourney

Based on a portrait by Alonzo Chappel, this engraving was printed around 1820, five years after Sigourney published the first of her many popular books, *Miscellaneous Pieces, in Prose and Verse*.

poet who used conventional forms, writing elegies to honor dead friends and lyrics about nature. But she also wrote about social and political problems in the United States. Two of her frequent topics were the status of women and the plight of Native Americans. The texts of the following poems are taken from her *Select Poems* (1848).

INDIAN NAMES

"How can the Red men be forgotten, while so many of our states and territories, bays, lakes and rivers, are indelibly stamped by names of their giving?"

Ye say, they all have passed away,[1]
   That noble race and brave,
That their light canoes have vanished
   From off the crested wave;
That 'mid the forests where they roamed   5
   There rings no hunter's shout;
But their name is on your waters,
   Ye may not wash it out.

'Tis where Ontario's billow
   Lake Ocean's surge is curl'd,   10
Where strong Niagara's thunders wake
   The echo of the world,
Where red Missouri bringeth
   Rich tributes from the west,
And Rappahannock[2] sweetly sleeps   15
   On green Virginia's breast.

Ye say, their cone-like cabins,
   That clustered o'er the vale,
Have fled away like withered leaves
   Before the autumn gale: 20
But their memory liveth on your hills
   Their baptism on your shore,
Your everlasting rivers speak
   Their dialect of yore.

---

1. **passed away:** Sigourney wrote several poems about the treatment of Native Americans in the United States. She was opposed to the Removal Act of 1830, which required five tribes to give up their native lands in the southeastern United States and move to the "Indian Territory," now the state of Oklahoma. In addition to writing poems, Sigourney organized a petition on behalf of a women's association and published it in 1831 as an open letter in the *Cherokee Phoenix*, the first periodical published by Native Americans.
2. **Rappahannock:** Now spelled "Rappahanock," a river that flows through Virginia and empties into the Chesapeake Bay. Sigourney emphasizes the number of Native American names used for rivers, states, and mountains in the United States.

Old Massachusetts wears it   25
    Within her lordly crown,
And broad Ohio bears it
    Amid her young renown;
Connecticut hath wreathed it
    Where her quiet foliage waves,   30
And bold Kentucky breathed it hoarse
    Through all her ancient caves.

Wachuset hides its lingering voice
    Within his rocky heart,
And Alleghany graves its tone   35
    Throughout his lofty chart;
Monadnock[3] on his forehead hoar
    Doth seal the sacred trust,
Your mountains build their monument,
    Though ye destroy their dust.   40

                        [1834, 1848]

---

3. **Wachuset . . . Alleghany . . . Monadnock:** A mountain in central Massachusetts, now spelled "Wachusett"; a mountain range in the eastern United States; and a mountain in southwestern New Hampshire.

TO A SHRED OF LINEN

Would they swept cleaner! –
                      Here's a littering shred
Of linen left behind – a vile reproach
To all good housewifery. Right glad am I,
That no neat lady, train'd in ancient times
Of pudding-making, and of sampler-work,   5
And speckless sanctity of household care,
Hath happened here, to spy thee. She, no doubt,
Keen looking through her spectacles, would say,
"*This comes of reading books:*" – or some spruce beau
Essenc'd and lily-handed, had he chanc'd   10
To scan thy slight superfices,[1] 'twould be
"*This comes of writing poetry.*" – Well – well –
Come forth – offender! – hast thou aught to say?
Canst thou by merry thought, or quaint conceit,

---

1. **superfices:** The surface or exterior of a thing.

Repay this risk, that I have run for thee?   15
— Begin at alpha, and resolve thyself
Into thine elements. I see the stalk
And bright, blue flower of flax, which erst o'erspread
That fertile land, where mighty Moses stretch'd
His rod miraculous. I see thy bloom   20
Tinging, too scantly, these New England vales.
But, lo! the sturdy farmer lifts his flail,
To crush thy bones unpitying, and his wife
With 'kerchief'd head, and eyes brimful of dust,
Thy fibrous nerves, with hatchel-tooth divides.   25
— I hear a voice of music — and behold!
The ruddy damsel singeth at her wheel,[2]
While by her side the rustic lover sits.
Perchance, his shrewd eye secretly doth count
The mass of skeins, which, hanging on the wall,   30
Increaseth day by day. Perchance his thought,
(For men have deeper minds than women — sure!)
Is calculating what a thrifty wife
The maid will make; and how his dairy shelves
Shall groan beneath the weight of golden cheese,   35
Made by her dexterous hand, while many a keg
And pot of butter, to the market borne,
May, transmigrated, on his back appear,
In new thanksgiving coats.
                              Fain would I ask,
Mine own New England, for thy once loved wheel,   40
By sofa and piano quite displac'd.
Why dost thou banish from thy parlor-hearth
That old Hygeian harp, whose magic rul'd
Dyspepsia, as the minstrel-shepherd's skill
Exorcis'd Saul's ennui?[3] There was no need,   45
In those good times, of callisthenics, sure,
And there was less of gadding, and far more
Of home-born, heart-felt comfort, rooted strong
In industry, and bearing such rare fruit,
As wealth might never purchase.
                              But come back,   50

---

2. **wheel:** A spinning wheel, used for spinning yarn or thread from natural fibers such as flax.
3. **Hygeian harp . . . Saul's ennui?:** Hygeia, the Greek goddess of health, provided relief from dyspepsia or indigestion; David's playing upon the harp refreshed King Saul when "the evil spirit" was upon him (1 Samuel 16:23).

Thou shred of linen. I did let thee drop,
In my harangue, as wiser ones have lost
The thread of their discourse. What was thy lot
When the rough battery of the loom had stretch'd
And knit thy sinews, and the chemist sun   55
Thy brown complexion bleach'd?
                                    Methinks I scan
Some idiosyncrasy, that marks thee out
A defunct pillow-case. — Did the trim guest,
To the best chamber usher'd, e'er admire
The snowy whiteness of thy freshen'd youth   60
Feeding thy vanity? or some sweet babe
Pour its pure dream of innocence on thee?
Say, hast thou listen'd to the sick one's moan,
When there was none to comfort? — or shrunk back
From the dire tossings of the proud man's brow?   65
Or gather'd from young beauty's restless sigh
A tale of untold love?
                              Still, close and mute! —
Wilt tell no secrets, ha? — Well then, go down,
With all thy churl-kept hoard of curious lore,
In majesty and mystery, go down   70
Into the paper-mill,[4] and from its jaws,
Stainless and smooth, emerge. — Happy shall be
The renovation, if on thy fair page
Wisdom and truth, their hallow'd lineaments
Trace for posterity. So shall thine end   75
Be better than thy birth, and worthier bard
Thine apotheosis immortalise.

                                                   [1848]

---

4. **paper-mill:** Before a process for pulping wood was invented, paper was made from the pulp of cotton or linen rags.

Elizabeth Oakes Smith

[1806–1893]

Widely known in her day as both a writer and a leader of the crusade for women's rights, Elizabeth Oakes Smith was born and educated in North Yarmouth, Maine. In 1823, she married Seba Smith, the editor of the *Eastern Argus*, a weekly newspaper published in Portland, Maine. In order

Elizabeth Oakes Smith

This portrait of Smith appeared as the frontispiece of Thomas B. Read's anthology *The Female Poets of America* (1849).

to help her husband, Smith wrote constantly for the *Argus*, often anonymously and occasionally over the signature *E*. After Seba Smith lost most of the family savings in failed investments, the couple and their six children moved to New York City. There, Smith began to publish novels and stories under the pseudonym "Ernest Helfenstein" or as "Mrs. Seba Smith." Earning a reputation for her frequent contributions to literary magazines, she gained her greatest success with a long poem, "The Sinless Child," published serially in the *Southern Literary Messenger* in 1842. That was the title poem of a collection of poetry she published the following year; in 1845, it was followed by *The Poetical Writings of Elizabeth Oakes Smith*, which included a laudatory preface by Rufus Griswold, the successful editor of the influential anthology *The Poets and Poetry of America*. Her poems, largely conventional in style, dealt with popular themes: the deaths of innocent children; the stages of life; and the importance of the home, religious faith, and self-reliance. The following texts are taken from the second edition of her *Poetical Writings*, published in 1846.

THE UNATTAINED

And is this life? and are we born for this?
To follow phantoms that elude the grasp,
Or whatsoe'er secured, within our clasp
To withering lie, as if each earthly kiss
Were doomed death's shuddering touch alone to meet.   5
O Life! hast thou reserved no cup of bliss?
Must still THE UNATTAINED beguile our feet?
The UNATTAINED with yearnings fill the breast,
That rob, for aye, the spirit of its rest?
Yes, this is Life; and everywhere we meet,   10
Not victor crowns, but wailings of defeat;
Yet faint thou not, thou dost apply a test,
That shall incite thee onward, upward still,
The present can not sate, or e'er thy spirit fill.

[1843, 1846]

THE DROWNED MARINER[1]

A mariner sat on the shrouds one night,
 The wind was piping free,
Now bright, now dimmed was the moonlight pale,
And the phosphor gleamed in the wake of the whale,
 As he floundered in the sea;   5
The scud was flying athwart the sky,
The gathering winds went whistling by,
And the wave as it towered, then fell in spray,
Looked an emerald wall in the moonlight ray.
The mariner swayed and rocked on the mast,   10
 But the tumult pleased him well,
Down the yawning wave his eye he cast,
And the monsters watched as they hurried past,
 Or lightly rose and fell;
For their broad, damp fins were under the tide,   15
And they lashed as they passed the vessel's side,
And their filmy eyes, all huge and grim,
Glared fiercely up, and they glared at him.

Now freshens the gale, and the brave ship goes
 Like an uncurbed steed along.   20
A sheet of flame is the spray she throws,
As her gallant prow the water plows —
 But the ship is fleet and strong:
The topsails are reefed and the sails are furled,
And onward she sweeps o'er the watery world,   25
And dippeth her spars in the surging flood;
But there came no chill to the mariner's blood.

Wildly she rocks, but he swingeth at ease,
 And holds him by the shroud;
And as she careens to the crowding breeze,   30
The gaping deep the mariner sees,
 And the surging heareth loud.
Was that a face, looking up at him,
With its pallid cheek and its cold eyes dim?
Did it beckon him down? did it call his name?   35
Now rolleth the ship the way whence it came.

---

1. **The Drowned Mariner:** A mariner is a sailor. Among the nautical terms used in the poem are *shrouds*, a set of ropes that stretch from the masthead to the sides of a ship for the support of the mast, and *spars*, the poles that support the riggings on a ship.

The mariner looked, and he saw with dread,
    A face he knew too well;
And the cold eyes glared, the eyes of the dead,
And its long hair out on the wave was spread.   40
    Was there a tale to tell?
The stout ship rocked with a reeling speed,
And the mariner groaned, as well he need,
For ever down, as she plunged on her side,
The dead face gleamed from the briny tide.   45

Bethink thee, mariner, well of the past,
    A voice calls loud for thee —
There's a stifled prayer, the first, the last,
The plunging ship on her beam is cast,
    Oh, where shall thy burial be?   50
Bethink thee of oaths that were lightly spoken,
Bethink thee of vows that were lightly broken,
Bethink thee of all that is dear to thee —
For thou art alone on the raging sea:

Alone in the dark, alone on the wave,   55
    To buffet the storm alone —
To struggle aghast at thy watery grave,
To struggle, and feel there is none to save —
    God shield thee, helpless one!
The stout limbs yield, for their strength is past,   60
The trembling hands on the deep are cast,
The white brow gleams a moment more,
Then slowly sinks — the struggle is o'er.

Down, down where the storm is hushed to sleep,
    Where the sea its dirge shall swell,   65
Where the amber drops for thee shall weep,
And the rose-lipped shell her music keep,
    There thou shalt slumber well.
The gem and the pearl lie heaped at thy side,
They fell from the neck of the beautiful bride,   70
From the strong man's hand, from the maiden's brow,
As they slowly sunk to the wave below.

A peopled home is the ocean bed,
    The mother and child are there —
The fervent youth and the hoary head,   75
The maid, with her floating locks outspread,
    The babe with its silken hair,

As the water moveth they lightly sway,
And the tranquil lights on their features play;
And there is each cherished and beautiful form,   80
Away from decay, and away from the storm.

[1845, 1846]

Henry Wadsworth Longfellow

[1807–1882]

The most revered poet of the period, Henry Wads-worth Longfellow was born in Portland, Maine, and educated at Bowdoin College, where he was the classmate of Nathaniel Hawthorne. Skilled at languages, Longfellow studied German, French, Italian, and Spanish during extended stays in Europe. He accepted a professorship first at Bowdoin and later at Harvard, where he taught until 1854. Adapting a wide range of European poetic techniques, Longfellow was known for his careful prosody and polished style. Always popular for his direct and graceful treatment of common themes such as the importance of cour-age and the beauty of nature, Longfellow scored his greatest commercial successes with a series of book-length narrative poems about early American history, especially *The Song of Hia-watha* (1855) and *The Courtship of Miles Standish* (1858). His poems were popular with a wide audience, who read them aloud and memorized them for recitation in school and on public occa-sions. He also published shorter poems in all the major literary magazines. The texts of the fol-lowing poems are taken from *Putnam's Monthly*, where they were first published in 1854 and 1855.

Henry Wadsworth Longfellow

This photograph of Longfellow was taken in Boston in 1860 or 1861, by which time he had become the most popular poet in the United States.

THE JEWISH CEMETERY AT NEWPORT[1]

How strange it seems! These Hebrews in their graves,
    Close by the street of this fair sea-port town;
Silent beside the never-silent waves,
    At rest in all this moving up and down!

The trees are white with dust, that o'er their sleep   5
    Wave their broad curtains in the south-wind's breath,
While underneath such leafy tents they keep
    The long, mysterious Exodus of Death.

And these sepulchral stones, so old and brown,
    That pave with level flags their burial-place,   10
Are like the tablets of the Law, thrown down
    And broken by Moses at the mountain's base.[2]

The very names recorded here are strange,
    Of foreign accent, and of different climes;
Alvares and Rivera interchange   15
    With Abraham and Jacob of old times.

"Blessed be God! for he created Death!"
    The mourners said: "and Death is rest and peace."
Then added, in the certainty of faith:
    "And giveth Life, that never more shall cease."   20

Closed are the portals of their Synagogue,
    No Psalms of David now the silence break,
No rabbi reads the ancient Decalogue[3]
    In the grand dialect the Prophets spake.

Gone are the living, but the dead remain,   25
    And not neglected, for a hand unseen,
Scattering its bounty, like a summer rain,
    Still keeps their graves and their remembrance green.

How came they here? What burst of Christian hate;
    What persecution, merciless, and blind,   30

---

1. **Newport:** In the seventeenth century, Rhode Island was the only colony that permitted Jewish immigration. The first permanent Jewish settlement was in Newport, home of the oldest synagogue in the United States.
2. **And these sepulchral stones . . . at the mountain's base:** The "level flags" are flagstones, used as grave stones. Longfellow compares them to the stone tablets on which the Ten Commandments were written, which Moses cast down in anger when he returned from Mount Sinai to find the people of Israel worshipping the golden calf (Exodus 20:1-17).
3. **Decalogue:** The Ten Commandments.

Drove o'er the sea, — that desert, desolate —
    These Ishmaels and Hagars[4] of mankind?

They lived in narrow streets and lanes obscure,
    Ghetto or Judenstrass,[5] in mirk and mire;
Taught in the school of patience to endure   35
    The life of anguish and the death of fire.

All their lives long, with the unleavened bread
    And bitter herbs of exile and its fears,
The wasting famine of the heart they fed,
    And slaked its thirst with marah of their tears.[6]   40

Anathema maranatha![7] was the cry
    That rang from town to town, from street to street;
At every gate the accursed Mordecai[8]
    Was mocked, and jeered, and spurned by Christian feet.

Pride and humiliation hand in hand   45
    Walked with them through the world, where'er they went;
Trampled and beaten were they as the sand,
    And yet unshaken as the continent.

For in the back-ground, figures vague and vast,
    Of patriarchs and of prophets rose sublime,   50
And all the great traditions of the Past
    They saw reflected in the coming time.

And thus for ever with reverted look,
    The mystic volume of the world they read,
Spelling it backward like a Hebrew book,[9]   55
    Till Life became a Legend of the Dead.

But ah! what once has been shall be no more!
    The groaning earth in travail and in pain
Brings forth its races, but does not restore,
    And the dead nations never rise again.   60

[1854]

---

4. **Ishmaels and Hagars:** Outcasts. When Abraham's son, Isaac, was born to his wife Sarah, she had Abraham's mistress, the slave girl Hagar, and Hagar's son Ishmael driven from their home. See Genesis 21.
5. **Ghetto or Judenstrass:** *Ghetto* (Italian) originally meant a section of a city to which Jews were restricted; *Judenstrass* is German for street of the Jews.
6. **marah of their tears:** The Hebrews wandered in the wilderness for three days without water before they arrived at a place where the water was too bitter to drink: "therefore the name of it was called Marah" (Exodus 15:23).
7. **Anathema maranatha!:** Cursed by God. See 1 Corinthians 16:22: "If any man love not the Lord Jesus Christ, let him be Anathema Maranatha."
8. **Mordecai:** Jewish leader persecuted by the Persians. See Esther 2–8.
9. **Hebrew book:** The text of a Hebrew book is read from right to left.

MY LOST YOUTH

Often I think of the beautiful town
　　That is seated by the sea;
Often in thought go up and down
The pleasant streets of that dear old town,
　　And my youth comes back to me.　　　　　　　　　　　　5
　　　　And a verse of a Lapland song[1]
　　　　Is haunting my memory still:
　　"A boy's will is the wind's will,
And the thoughts of youth are long, long thoughts."

I can see the shadowy lines of its trees,　　　　　　　　　10
　　And catch, in sudden gleams,
The sheen of the far-surrounding seas,
And islands that were the Hesperides[2]
　　Of all my boyish dreams.
　　　　And the burden of that old song,　　　　　　　　15
　　　　It murmurs and whispers still:
　　"A boy's will is the wind's will,
And the thoughts of youth are long, long thoughts."

I remember the black wharves and the slips,
　　And the sea-tides tossing free;　　　　　　　　　　　20
And Spanish sailors with bearded lips,
And the beauty and mystery of the ships,
　　And the magic of the sea.
　　　　And the voice of that wayward song
　　　　Is singing and saying still:　　　　　　　　　　25
　　"A boy's will is the wind's will,
And the thoughts of youth are long, long thoughts."

I remember the bulwarks by the shore,
　　And the fort upon the hill;
The sun-rise gun, with its hollow roar,　　　　　　　　30
The drum-beat repeated o'er and o'er,
　　And the bugle wild and shrill.
　　　　And the music of that old song
　　　　Throbs in my memory still:
　　"A boy's will is the wind's will,　　　　　　　　　35
And the thoughts of youth are long, long thoughts."

---

1. **Lapland song:** Longfellow took the refrain of this poem from a song translated in John Scheffer's *The History of Lapland* (1674).
2. **Hesperides:** In Greek mythology, three nymphs, the Hesperides, maintained a beautiful garden at the far western end of the world.

I remember the sea-fight far away,[3]
   How it thundered o'er the tide!
And the dead captains, as they lay
In their graves, o'erlooking the tranquil bay,   40
   Where they in battle died.
      And the sound of that mournful song
      Goes through me with a thrill:
  "A boy's will is the wind's will,
And the thoughts of youth are long, long thoughts."   45

I can see the breezy dome of groves,
   The shadows of Deering's Woods;[4]
And the friendships old and the early loves
Come back with a Sabbath sound, as of doves
   In quiet neighborhoods.   50
      And the verse of that sweet old song,
      It flutters and murmurs still:
  "A boy's will is the wind's will,
And the thoughts of youth are long, long thoughts."

I remember the gleams and glooms that dart   55
   Across the schoolboy's brain;
The song and the silence in the heart,
That in part are prophecies, and in part
   Are longings wild and vain.
      And the voice of that fitful song   60
      Sings on, and is never still:
  "A boy's will is the wind's will,
And the thoughts of youth are long, long thoughts."

There are things of which I may not speak;
   There are dreams that cannot die;   65
There are thoughts that make the strong heart weak,
And bring a pallor into the cheek,
   And a mist before the eye.
      And the words of that fatal song
      Come over me like a chill: 70
  "A boy's will is the wind's will,
And the thoughts of youth are long, long thoughts."

Strange to me now are the forms I meet
   When I visit the dear old town;

---

3. **sea-fight far away:** Longfellow wrote this poem about his hometown, Portland, Maine, off the shore of which the American *Enterprise* and the British *Boxer* fought a sea battle during the War of 1812.
4. **Deering's Woods:** This undeveloped tract of land, famous for its white oaks, was enjoyed as a peaceful retreat from the city of Portland, Maine, for decades before it became a public park in 1879.

But the native air is pure and sweet,   75
And the trees that o'ershadow each well-known street,
   As they balance up and down,
     Are singing the beautiful song,
     Are sighing and whispering still:
  "A boy's will is the wind's will,   80
And the thoughts of youth are long, long thoughts."

And Deering's Woods are fresh and fair,
   And with joy that is almost pain
My heart goes back to wander there,
And among the dreams of the days that were,   85
   I find my lost youth again.
     And the strange and beautiful song,
     The groves are repeating it still:
  "A boy's will is the wind's will,
And the thoughts of youth are long, long thoughts."   90

[1855]

John Greenleaf Whittier

[1807–1892]

John Greenleaf Whittier

This portrait of Whittier holding a book in his right hand was made in the early 1850s.

The son of Quakers whose values he fully embraced, John Greenleaf Whittier was born on a farm near Haverhill, Massachusetts. His first book, *Legends of New England in Prose and in Verse* (1831), reflected his deep interest in American folklore and history. But his attention was soon drawn to the injustices of his own time, especially slavery. Whittier announced himself an abolitionist in a pamphlet, *Justice and Expediency* (1833). From that year through the end of the Civil War, he devoted himself wholeheartedly to the antislavery crusade as both an editor and author — leaving "the Muses' haunt to turn the crank of an opinion mill," as Whittier himself later put it. By then, he had earned a reputation as one of the Fireside Poets and was the celebrated author of such works as *Snow-Bound* (1866), a nostalgic evocation of the rural New England of his childhood. But the subject matter for which Whittier was best known during the antebellum period is indicated by the titles of collections like *Poems Written during the Progress of the Abolition Question* (1838) and *Voices of Freedom* (1846). Many of the poems in those collections were initially published in antislavery newspapers such as the *Liberator*, where the first of the following poems appeared in 1835, and the *Pennsylvania Freeman*, which Whittier edited and where the second poem appeared in 1838. The texts are taken from *The Complete Works of John Greenleaf Whittier* (1892).

THE HUNTERS OF MEN[1]

Have ye heard of our hunting, o'er mountain and glen,
Through cane-brake and forest, — the hunting of men?
The lords of our land to this hunting have gone,
As the fox-hunter follows the sound of the horn;
Hark! the cheer and the hallo! the crack of the whip, 5
And the yell of the hound as he fastens his grip!
All blithe are our hunters, and noble their match,
Though hundreds are caught, there are millions to catch.
So speed to their hunting, o'er mountain and glen,
Through cane-brake and forest, — the hunting of men! 10

Gay luck to our hunters! how nobly they ride
In the glow of their zeal, and the strength of their pride!
The priest with his cassock flung back on the wind,
Just screening the politic statesman behind;
The saint and the sinner, with cursing and prayer, 15
The drunk and the sober, ride merrily there.
And woman, kind woman, wife, widow, and maid,
For the good of the hunted, is lending her aid:
Her foot 's in the stirrup, her hand on the rein,
How blithely she rides to the hunting of men! 20

Oh, goodly and grand is our hunting to see,
In this "land of the brave and this home of the free."
Priest, warrior, and statesman, from Georgia to Maine,
All mounting the saddle, all grasping the rein;
Right merrily hunting the black man, whose sin 25
Is the curl of his hair and the hue of his skin!

---

1. **The Hunters of Men:** In a headnote to the poem, Whittier later explained: "These lines were written when the orators of the American Colonization Society were demanding that the free black should be sent to Africa, and opposing Emancipation unless expatriation followed. See the report of the proceedings of the society at its annual meeting in 1834." Like many abolitionists, Whittier favored emancipation and education for slaves and strongly opposed the idea of mandatory colonization in Africa.

Woe, now, to the hunted who turns him at bay!
Will our hunters be turned from their purpose and prey?
Will their hearts fail within them? their nerves tremble, when
All roughly they ride to the hunting of men?   30

Ho! alms for our hunters! all weary and faint,
Wax the curse of the sinner and prayer of the saint.
The horn is wound faintly,[2] the echoes are still,
Over cane-brake and river, and forest and hill.
Haste, alms for our hunters! the hunted once more   35
Have turned from their flight with their backs to the shore:
What right have they here in the home of the white,
Shadowed o'er by our banner of Freedom and Right?
Ho! alms for the hunters! or never again
Will they ride in their pomp to the hunting of men!   40

Alms, alms for our hunters! why will ye delay,
When their pride and their glory are melting away?
The parson has turned; for, on charge of his own,
Who goeth a warfare, or hunting, alone?
The politic statesman looks back with a sigh,   45
There is doubt in his heart, there is fear in his eye.
Oh, haste, lest that doubting and fear shall prevail,
And the head of his steed take the place of the tail.
Oh, haste, ere he leave us! for who will ride then,
For pleasure or gain, to the hunting of men?   50

[1835, 1892]

---

2. **wound faintly**: Blown softly.

THE FAREWELL
OF A VIRGINIA SLAVE MOTHER TO HER DAUGHTERS
SOLD INTO SOUTHERN BONDAGE

Gone, gone, — sold and gone,
  To the rice-swamp dank and lone.
Where the slave-whip ceaseless swings,
Where the noisome insect stings,
Where the fever demon strews   5
Poison with the falling dews,

Where the sickly sunbeams glare
Through the hot and misty air;
   Gone, gone, — sold and gone,
   To the rice-swamp dank and lone,   10
   From Virginia's hills and waters;
   Woe is me, my stolen daughters!

   Gone, gone, — sold and gone,
   To the rice-swamp dank and lone.
There no mother's eye is near them,   15
There no mother's ear can hear them;
Never, when the torturing lash
Seams their back with many a gash,
Shall a mother's kindness bless them,
Or a mother's arms caress them.   20
   Gone, gone, — sold and gone,
   To the rice-swamp dank and lone,
   From Virginia's hills and waters;
   Woe is me, my stolen daughters!

   Gone, gone, — sold and gone,   25
   To the rice-swamp dank and lone.
Oh, when weary, sad, and slow,
From the fields at night they go,
Faint with toil, and racked with pain,
To their cheerless homes again,   30
There no brother's voice shall greet them
There no father's welcome meet them.
   Gone, gone, — sold and gone,
   To the rice-swamp dank and lone,
   From Virginia's hills and waters;   35
   Woe is me, my stolen daughters!

   Gone, gone, — sold and gone,
   To the rice-swamp dank and lone.
From the tree whose shadow lay
On their childhood's place of play;   40
From the cool spring where they drank;
Rock, and hill, and rivulet bank;
From the solemn house of prayer,
And the holy counsels there;
   Gone, gone, — sold and gone,   45
   To the rice-swamp dank and lone,
   From Virginia's hills and waters;
   Woe is me, my stolen daughters!

Gone, gone, — sold and gone,
   To the rice-swamp dank and lone;   50
Toiling through the weary day,
And at night the spoiler's prey.
Oh, that they had earlier died,
Sleeping calmly, side by side,
Where the tyrant's power is o'er,   55
And the fetter galls no more!
   Gone, gone, — sold and gone,
   To the rice-swamp dank and lone,
   From Virginia's hills and waters;
   Woe is me, my stolen daughters!   60

   Gone, gone, — sold and gone,
   To the rice-swamp dank and lone.
By the holy love He beareth;
By the bruised reed He spareth;
Oh, may He, to whom alone   65
All their cruel wrongs are known,
Still their hope and refuge prove,
With a more than mother's love.
   Gone, gone, — sold and gone,
   To the rice-swamp dank and lone,   70
   From Virginia's hills and waters;
   Woe is me, my stolen daughters!

[1838, 1892]

Frances E. W. Harper

[1825–1911]

Among the first and most wide-ranging of African American women writers, Frances Ellen Watkins Harper was the only child born to her free parents in Baltimore, Maryland. Forced by economic pressures to leave school at thirteen, Harper educated herself and later taught school in Ohio. Her first volume of poetry, *Forest Leaves*, appeared in 1845. With the encouragement of abolitionists, Harper later published *Poems on Miscellaneous Subjects*. Heavily promoted by William Lloyd Garrison, the editor of the abolitionist newspaper the *Liberator*, the volume sold twelve thousand copies when it was published in 1854. That same year, Harper joined the underground railroad and became a traveling lecturer for the Maine Anti-Slavery Society. She also published poems, essays, and stories in a variety of periodicals, including the new *Anglo-African Magazine*, established in 1859 to showcase the works of African American writers. After the Civil War, Harper worked for the education and enfranchisement of African Americans. She also published stories and a novel, *Iola Leroy; or, Shadows Uplifted* (1892). The texts of the following poems are taken from *Poems on Miscellaneous Subjects* (1854).

Frances E. W. Harper
This undated photograph, which was later used as the frontispiece of her *Poems* (1898), is the only known portrait of Harper.

The Slave Mother

Heard you that shriek? It rose
    So wildly on the air,
It seemed as if a burden'd heart
    Was breaking in despair.

Saw you those hands so sadly clasped —   5
    The bowed and feeble head —
The shuddering of that fragile form —
    That look of grief and dread?

Saw you the sad, imploring eye?
    Its every glance was pain,   10
As if a storm of agony
    Were sweeping through the brain.

She is a mother, pale with fear,
    Her boy clings to her side,
And in her kirtle[1] vainly tries   15
    His trembling form to hide.

He is not hers,[2] although she bore
    For him a mother's pains;

---

1. **kirtle:** A woman's long dress or skirt.
2. **He is not hers:** By law, the status of the mother determined whether a child was free or a slave.

He is not hers, although her blood
   Is coursing through his veins!   20

He is not hers, for cruel hands
   May rudely tear apart
The only wreath of household love
   That binds her breaking heart.

His love has been a joyous light   25
   That o'er her pathway smiled,
A fountain gushing ever new,
   Amid life's desert wild.

His lightest word has been a tone
   Of music round her heart,   30
Their lives a streamlet blent in one —
   Oh, Father! must they part?

They tear him from her circling arms,
   Her last and fond embrace.
Oh! never more may her sad eyes   35
   Gaze on his mournful face.

No marvel, then, these bitter shrieks
   Disturb the listening air:
She is a mother, and her heart
   Is breaking in despair.   40

                  [1854]

ETHIOPIA[1]

Yes! Ethiopia yet shall stretch
   Her bleeding hands abroad;
Her cry of agony shall reach
   The burning throne of God.

The tyrant's yoke from off her neck,   5
   His fetters from her soul,
The mighty hand of God shall break,
   And spurn the base control.

---

1. **Ethiopia:** A country in northeastern Africa; in the nineteenth century, *Ethiopia* was frequently synonymous with black Africa.

Redeemed from dust and freed from chains,
   Her sons shall lift their eyes;   10
From cloud-capt hills and verdant plains
   Shall shouts of triumph rise.

Upon her dark, despairing brow,
   Shall play a smile of peace;
For God shall bend unto her wo,   15
   And bid her sorrows cease.

'Neath sheltering vines and stately palms
   Shall laughing children play,
And aged sires with joyous psalms
   Shall gladden every day.   20

Secure by night, and blest by day,
   Shall pass her happy hours;
Nor human tigers hunt for prey
   Within her peaceful bowers.

Then, Ethiopia! stretch, oh! stretch   25
   Thy bleeding hands abroad;
Thy cry of agony shall reach
   And find redress from God.

                                      [1854]

Rose Terry Cooke

[1827–1892]

Born in Connecticut, Rose Terry Cooke was educated at the Hartford Female Seminary and worked briefly as a teacher and a governess. When she received an inheritance in 1847, she was free to devote herself to writing. Her short stories began to appear regularly in the leading literary magazines, *Putnam's Monthly* and *Harper's Monthly.* When the *Atlantic Monthly* was established in 1857, one of her stories was the lead work of fiction in the first issue; thereafter, Cooke published frequently in the *Atlantic.* While she is now known primarily for her short stories, Cooke also wrote hundreds of poems on a variety of popular themes ranging from the changing seasons to the death of children, as well as ballads about historical events in the United States. The texts of the following poems are taken from her *Poems* (1861).

Rose Terry Cooke

This undated portrait of Cooke was apparently made after the Civil War.

HERE

Sweet summer-night, beside the sea,
Cast all thy sweet life over me!
Thy silence and serenity,
   Thy healing and content;
The rushing waves that fall and break   5
Unutterable music make,
And words that no man ever spake
   Are to its measure lent.

The salt wind kisses into rest
Both languid eye and fevered breast,   10
The cool gray rock, with sea-weeds drest,
   Gives shadow, still with strength;
The bitter and baptismal sea
With living water sprinkles me,
Slow patience sets her bondsman[1] free,   15
   And blesses him at length.

There is a time in every tide
When surf and billow both subside,
And on the outward current glide
   Both shark and pirate sail;
The shipwrecked sailor, cast ashore,   20
Perceives afar that lessening roar,
And gives one desperate struggle more.
   Ah! shall that struggle fail?

[1861]

---

1. **bondsman:** A servant forced to work without wages; a slave.

CAPTIVE

The Summer comes, the Summer dies,
   Red leaves whirl idly from the tree,
But no more cleaving of the skies,
   No southward sunshine waits for me!

You shut me in a gilded cage,   5
   You deck the bars with tropic flowers,
Nor know that freedom's living rage
   Defies you through the listless hours.

What passion fierce, what service true,
    Could ever such a wrong requite?   10
What gift, or clasp, or kiss from you
    Were worth an hour of soaring flight?

I beat my wings against the wire,
    I pant my trammelled heart away;
The fever of one mad desire   15
    Burns and consumes me all the day.

What care I for your tedious love,
    For tender word or fond caress?
I die for one free flight above,
    One rapture of the wilderness!   20

[1861]

"THE HARVEST IS PAST"[1]

Go, dead Summer, o'er the seas away;
Autumn at her vespers[2] now will kneel and pray,
Sunlit vapors on the mountains stray,
Red grows the round moon, — Summer goes away.

Go, dead Summer! the birds will care,   5
They will follow on the soft sea-air,
While the south-wind breathes a low prayer,
And the perfumed pine-leaves thy shroud prepare.

Go, dead Summer! go, to come again.
All things rise but madness and pain.   10
New green grasses flicker on the plain,
Only a lost life comes not again.

One dead Summer never shall return.
In its ashes no red embers burn.
Over it vainly the tired soul may yearn.   15
It is dead, wept, buried: how can it return?

[1861]

---

1. **"The . . . Past"**: "The harvest is past, the summer is ended, and we are not saved" (Jeremiah 8:20).
2. **vespers**: Worship services held in the late afternoon or evening.

Walt Whitman

[1819–1892]

The poet familiarly known as Walt Whitman was born on May 31, 1819, on Long Island, New York, one of nine children born to a farmer, Walter Whitman Sr., and his wife, Louisa Van Velsor Whitman. In 1823 the family moved to Brooklyn, where Whitman spent his childhood, such as it was. By the age of eleven, he had left school to work as an office boy in a law firm; by fifteen, he was mostly supporting himself by working in the printing trade, perhaps initially as a compositor (a typesetter) in New York. After a devastating fire destroyed much of the publishing district in 1835, Whitman rejoined his family, which had by then moved back to Long Island. Although he taught sporadically at several schools there, Whitman was clearly not suited to the classroom. In 1838 he started his own weekly newspaper, the *Long Islander*, and by the early 1840s he had left teaching altogether. For the next several years, he worked as a printer in New York; edited a daily paper, the *Aurora*; and returned to Brooklyn, first to write for the *Long Island Star* and then to edit the *Brooklyn Daily Eagle*. Whitman was also writing, primarily prose pieces like the numerous literary and art reviews he printed in the *Eagle*, but also some poetry. Fired from the *Eagle* in 1848 for his free-soil politics — like a growing number of Democrats in the North, he strongly opposed the extension of slavery into territories gained during the Mexican War — Whitman was hired to be the first editor of the *Crescent*, a newspaper in New Orleans, where he headed along with his younger brother Jeff. By the end of the year, Whitman was again in New York, where he immersed himself in the pulsing life of that rising metropolis: riding the streets in horse-drawn buses or enjoying rambling walks around the city; attending the opera, which he loved, and going to museums; and spending time with his eclectic group of friends, who ranged from workingmen to artists. Whitman supported himself by working as a carpenter, but he increasingly devoted himself to reading, studying, and writing poetry, for which he finally gave up all other forms of labor.

In 1855, Whitman published the first edition of *Leaves of Grass*, which was thereafter the primary focus of his life and work. Whitman himself set the type for his self-published book, which he vigorously promoted by writing several anonymous reviews. He also sent a copy to Ralph Waldo Emerson, who in a congratulatory letter to Whitman exclaimed, "I greet you at the beginning of a great career, which yet must have had a long foreground somewhere, for such a start." If the Harvard-educated Emerson had then known about the unlikely foreground of *Leaves of Grass*, he would surely have been even more astonished by Whitman's remarkable poems. But few shared Emerson's appreciation of *Leaves of Grass*, which was attacked for what critics viewed as its crudeness, its vulgar language, and its scandalous subject matter. Undaunted, Whitman continued to work on the volume, adding new poems and publishing a second edition in 1856. By the beginning of the following year, he was already planning

Leaves

of

Grass.

5/50.

Brooklyn, New York:
1855.

The First Edition of *Leaves of Grass* (1855)

This portrait of Whitman was engraved from a daguerreotype made in 1854, when he was thirty-five. In contrast to the portraits of most other literary figures, who were customarily depicted in formal attire and equally formal poses, Whitman projected an image of himself as a workingman and man of the people. In an anonymous self-review of *Leaves of Grass*, Whitman described the poet portrayed in the frontispiece as "One of the roughs, his costume manly and free, his face sunburnt and bearded, his posture strong and erect."

another edition, but Whitman apparently wrote relatively few poems while he was editor of the *Brooklyn Daily Times* from March 1857 to June 1859. Freed of those editorial responsibilities, he began to expand and reconstruct *Leaves of Grass*, which a firm in Boston published in 1860. When the Civil War broke out the following year, Whitman moved to Washington, D.C., where he did volunteer work as a nurse in army hospitals and wrote the poems published as *Drum-Taps* early in 1865. Working with the wounded men made a profound impression on Whitman. In his letters to his mother and other family members, Whitman wrote frequently about the bravery of "my soldier boys," as he sometimes called them. Deeply affected by the assassination of Abraham Lincoln, whom he viewed as the representative democratic man and the martyred savior of the Union, Whitman wrote several poems on the death of the president. Those poems, along with those from *Drum-Taps*, were incorporated in the 1867 edition of *Leaves of Grass*, which was followed by yet another edition in 1871.

During those years, Whitman remained in Washington, where he worked as a clerk in the office of the attorney general. After suffering a debilitating stroke in 1873, Whitman left Washington and moved to Camden, New Jersey, where his small house at 328 Mickle Street became a kind of pilgrimage site for a growing number of admirers and disciples. Although he was often in ill health, he continued to see his many friends, to carry on an extensive international correspondence, and to put the final touches on *Leaves of Grass*. When a Boston firm published a new edition in 1881, the local district attorney threatened to sue the publisher for obscenity. By then, however, Whitman had largely won his long battle for recognition in the United States and especially in England, where some of the most influential literary figures of the period expressed lavish admiration for the poet and his *Leaves of Grass*. During the following decade, he published two shorter collections of poems, *November Boughs* (1888) and *Good-bye, My Fancy* (1891), both of which Whitman incorporated into the final edition of *Leaves of Grass*, published shortly before he died on March 26, 1892.

bedfordstmartins.com/
americanlit for research
links on Whitman

Reading Whitman's *Leaves of Grass.*　From the first publication of *Leaves of Grass* in 1855, Whitman worked on his book, adding new poems and sections, as well as rethinking the organization and structure of the volume. His continual revisions have made the history of the publication of *Leaves of Grass* quite complicated. From the first edition in 1855 until his death in 1892, there were five more separate American editions and at least two other reprintings of earlier editions, including what has come to be called the "Deathbed Edition" (1891–92), the last version of *Leaves of Grass* printed during his lifetime. The first edition included a preface and twelve untitled poems, one of which — later called "Song of Myself" — occupied more than half of the volume. Although Whitman's name appeared in the copyright notice, it was not announced on the title page of the volume. Instead, Whitman included a portrait of himself in a rough shirt and slouch hat. In the second edition published in 1856, Whitman added some new poems and gave titles to all of the poems in the volume, though he would later alter many of those titles. He made far more extensive changes in the 1860 edition, in which Whitman first began to transform *Leaves of Grass* from a collection of miscellaneous poems into a carefully articulated and orchestrated whole. In addition to revising the poems published in the first two editions and adding a large number of new poems, Whitman grouped many of the poems in thematic clusters, including the procreation poems of "Enfans d'Adam," later "Children of Adam," and the love poems about male relationships collectively entitled "Calamus."

In later editions, Whitman increasingly employed such clusters as central organizational and structural devices in *Leaves of Grass.* He achieved the final form of the volume through a long and complex process that included the continuous revision of individual poems, the omission of earlier poems and addition of new ones, and the constant rearrangement of poems within individual clusters and the volume as a whole. The 1881

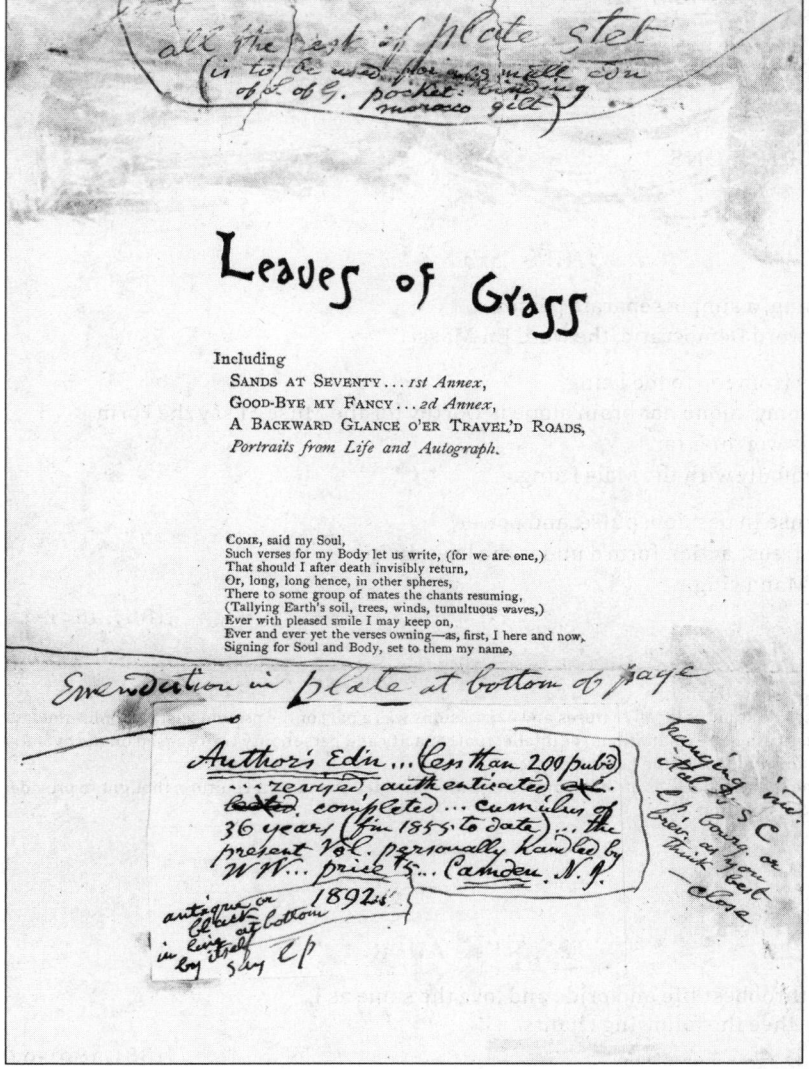

The "Deathbed Edition" of *Leaves of Grass* (1891–92)

Whitman's annotations on this trial title page of the final edition he saw through to press reveal his involvement in every stage of publication, from designing to publicizing the volume. Two months before he died, Whitman announced that he "would like this new 1892 edition to absolutely supercede all previous ones."

edition thus began with a group of prefatory "Inscriptions" and ended with "Songs of Parting," suggesting the overall movement from birth to death, as the poet retires from life and his lifelong work in verses such as the opening poem of the final chapter, "As the Time Draws Nigh." Although he later added two brief "annexes," Whitman made no other changes in the final or Deathbed Edition, where he noted: "As there are now several editions of L. of G., different texts and dates, I wish to say that I prefer this present one." The texts of the following poems are taken from — and the poems are printed here in the order they appear in — that edition of *Leaves of Grass* (1891-92).

From INSCRIPTIONS

ONE'S-SELF I SING

One's-Self I sing, a simple separate person,
Yet utter the word Democratic, the word En-Masse.[1]

Of physiology from top to toe I sing,
Not physiognomy[2] alone nor brain alone is worthy for the Muse,[3] I say the Form
    complete is worthier far,
The Female equally with the Male I sing.

Of Life immense in passion, pulse, and power,
Cheerful, for freest action form'd under the laws divine,
The Modern Man I sing.

[1867, 1891-92]

---

1. **En-Masse:** As a whole (French).
2. **physiognomy:** The study of facial features and expressions was a part of the pseudoscience of phrenology, which purported to provide explanations for intellectual capacity and personality traits based on the overall shape and position of bumps of the head.
3. **Muse:** Any one of the goddesses of Greek mythology who presided over art and culture, thought to provide poetic or artistic inspiration.

THOU READER

Thou reader throbbest life and pride and love the same as I,
Therefore for thee the following chants.

[1881, 1891-92]

SONG OF MYSELF[1]

1

I celebrate myself, and sing myself,
And what I assume you shall assume,
For every atom belonging to me as good belongs to you.

I loafe and invite my soul,
I lean and loafe at my ease observing a spear of summer grass.   5

My tongue, every atom of my blood, form'd from this soil, this air,
Born here of parents born here from parents the same, and their parents the same,
I, now thirty-seven years old in perfect health begin,
Hoping to cease not till death.

Creeds and schools in abeyance,   10
Retiring back a while suffced at what they are, but never forgotten,
I harbor for good or bad, I permit to speak at every hazard,
Nature without check with original energy.

2

Houses and rooms are full of perfumes, the shelves are crowded with perfumes,
I breathe the fragrance myself and know it and like it,   15
The distillation would intoxicate me also, but I shall not let it.

The atmosphere is not a perfume, it has no taste of the distillation, it is odorless,
It is for my mouth forever, I am in love with it,
I will go to the bank by the wood and become undisguised and naked,
I am mad for it to be in contact with me.   20

The smoke of my own breath,
Echoes, ripples, buzz'd whispers, love-root, silk-thread, crotch and vine,
My respiration and inspiration, the beating of my heart, the passing of blood and
    air through my lungs,
The sniff of green leaves and dry leaves, and of the shore and dark-color'd
    sea-rocks, and of hay in the barn,
The sound of the belch'd words of my voice loos'd to the eddies of the wind,   25
A few light kisses, a few embraces, a reaching around of arms,
The play of shine and shade on the trees as the supple boughs wag,
The delight alone or in the rush of the streets, or along the fields and hill-sides,

---

1. **"Song of Myself"**: This poem, untitled and undivided into sections in the first edition, was in later editions
variously titled "Poem of Walt Whitman, an American," "Walt Whitman," and finally "Song of Myself."

The feeling of health, the full-noon trill, the song of me rising from bed and
    meeting the sun.

Have you reckon'd a thousand acres much? have you reckon'd the earth much?   30
Have you practis'd so long to learn to read?
Have you felt so proud to get at the meaning of poems?

Stop this day and night with me and you shall possess the origin of all poems,
You shall possess the good of the earth and sun, (there are millions of suns left,)
You shall no longer take things at second or third hand, nor look through the eyes
    of the dead, nor feed on the spectres in books,   35
You shall not look through my eyes either, nor take things from me,
You shall listen to all sides and filter them from your self.

3

I have heard what the talkers were talking, the talk of the beginning and the end,
But I do not talk of the beginning or the end.

There was never any more inception than there is now,   40
Nor any more youth or age than there is now,
And will never be any more perfection than there is now,
Nor any more heaven or hell than there is now.

Urge and urge and urge,
Always the procreant urge of the world.   45

Out of the dimness opposite equals advance, always substance and increase,
    always sex,
Always a knit of identity, always distinction, always a breed of life.

To elaborate is no avail, learn'd and unlearn'd feel that it is so.

Sure as the most certain sure, plumb in the uprights, well entretied,[2] braced in the
    beams,
Stout as a horse, affectionate, haughty, electrical,   50
I and this mystery here we stand.

Clear and sweet is my soul, and clear and sweet is all that is not my soul.

Lack one lacks both, and the unseen is proved by the seen,
Till that becomes unseen and receives proof in its turn.

Showing the best and dividing it from the worst age vexes age,   55
Knowing the perfect fitness and equanimity of things, while they discuss I am
    silent, and go bathe and admire myself.

---

2. **entretied:** A carpenter's term meaning "cross-braced."

Welcome is every organ and attribute of me, and of any man hearty and clean,
Not an inch nor a particle of an inch is vile, and none shall be less familiar than
the rest.

I am satisfied — I see, dance, laugh, sing;
As the hugging and loving bed-fellow sleeps at my side through the night, and
withdraws at the peep of the day with stealthy tread,   60
Leaving me baskets cover'd with white towels swelling the house with their plenty,
Shall I postpone my acceptation and realization and scream at my eyes,
That they turn from gazing after and down the road,
And forthwith cipher[3] and show me to a cent,
Exactly the value of one and exactly the value of two, and which is ahead?   65

4

Trippers and askers surround me,
People I meet, the effect upon me of my early life or the ward and city I live in, or
the nation,
The latest dates, discoveries, inventions, societies, authors old and new,
My dinner, dress, associates, looks, compliments, dues,
The real or fancied indifference of some man or woman I love,   70
The sickness of one of my folks or of myself, or ill-doing or loss or lack of money,
or depressions or exaltations,
Battles, the horrors of fratricidal war, the fever of doubtful news, the fitful
events;
These come to me days and nights and go from me again,
But they are not the Me myself.

Apart from the pulling and hauling stands what I am,   75
Stands amused, complacent, compassionating, idle, unitary,
Looks down, is erect, or bends an arm on an impalpable certain rest,
Looking with side-curved head curious what will come next,
Both in and out of the game and watching and wondering at it.

Backward I see in my own days where I sweated through fog with linguists and
contenders,
I have no mockings or arguments, I witness and wait.   80

5

I believe in you my soul, the other I am must not abase itself to you,
And you must not be abased to the other.

---

3. **cipher:** To calculate or compute.

Loafe with me on the grass, loose the stop from your throat,
Not words, not music or rhyme I want, not custom or lecture, not even the best,   85
Only the lull I like, the hum of your valvèd voice.

I mind how once we lay such a transparent summer morning,
How you settled your head athwart my hips and gently turn'd over upon me,
And parted the shirt from my bosom-bone, and plunged your tongue to my
   bare-stript heart,
And reach'd till you felt my beard, and reach'd till you held my feet.   90

Swiftly arose and spread around me the peace and knowledge that pass all the
   argument of the earth,
And I know that the hand of God is the promise of my own,
And I know that the spirit of God is the brother of my own,
And that all the men ever born are also my brothers, and the women my sisters
   and lovers,
And that a kelson[4] of the creation is love,   95
And limitless are leaves stiff or drooping in the fields,
And brown ants in the little wells beneath them,
And mossy scabs of the worm fence,[5] heap'd stones, elder, mullein and poke-weed.

6

A child said *What is the grass?* fetching it to me with full hands;
How could I answer the child? I do not know what it is any more than he.   100

I guess it must be the flag of my disposition, out of hopeful green stuff woven.

Or I guess it is the handkerchief of the Lord,
A scented gift and remembrancer designedly dropt,
Bearing the owner's name someway in the corners, that we may see and remark,
   and say *Whose?*

Or I guess the grass is itself a child, the produced babe of the vegetation.   105

Or I guess it is a uniform hieroglyphic,
And it means, Sprouting alike in broad zones and narrow zones,
Growing among black folks as among white,
Kanuck, Tuckahoe, Congressman, Cuff,[6] I give them the same, receive them the
   same.

And now it seems to me the beautiful uncut hair of graves.   110

---

4. **kelson:** A nautical term referring to the girder that fastens to the keel of a ship for extra support.
5. **worm fence:** A fence made of split logs forming a zigzag pattern.
6. **Kanuck, Tuckahoe ... Cuff:** Nineteenth-century slang terms for a French Canadian, a Virginian, and an African American, from *cuffee*.

Tenderly will I use you curling grass,
It may be you transpire from the breasts of young men,
It may be if I had known them I would have loved them,
It may be you are from old people, or from offspring taken soon out of their
    mothers' laps,
And here you are the mothers' laps. 115

This grass is very dark to be from the white heads of old mothers,
Darker than the colorless beards of old men,
Dark to come from under the faint red roofs of mouths.

O I perceive after all so many uttering tongues,
And I perceive they do not come from the roofs of mouths for nothing. 120

I wish I could translate the hints about the dead young men and women,
And the hints about old men and mothers, and the offspring taken soon out of
    their laps.

What do you think has become of the young and old men?
And what do you think has become of the women and children?

They are alive and well somewhere, 125
The smallest sprout shows there is really no death,
And if ever there was it led forward life, and does not wait at the end to arrest it,
And ceas'd the moment life appear'd.

All goes onward and outward, nothing collapses,
And to die is different from what any one supposed, and luckier. 130

7

Has any one supposed it lucky to be born?
I hasten to inform him or her it is just as lucky to die, and I know it.

I pass death with the dying and birth with the new-wash'd babe, and am not
    contain'd between my hat and boots,
And peruse manifold objects, no two alike and every one good,
The earth good and the stars good, and their adjuncts all good. 135

I am not an earth nor an adjunct of an earth,
I am the mate and companion of people, all just as immortal and fathomless as
    myself,
(They do not know how immortal, but I know.)

Every kind for itself and its own, for me mine male and female,
For me those that have been boys and that love women, 140
For me the man that is proud and feels how it stings to be slighted,
For me the sweet-heart and the old maid, for me mothers and the mothers of
    mothers,

For me lips that have smiled, eyes that have shed tears,
For me children and the begetters of children.

Undrape! you are not guilty to me, nor stale nor discarded,   145
I see through the broadcloth and gingham whether or no,
And am around, tenacious, acquisitive, tireless, and cannot be shaken away.

8

The little one sleeps in its cradle,
I lift the gauze and look a long time, and silently brush away flies with my hand.

The youngster and the red-faced girl turn aside up the bushy hill,   150
I peeringly view them from the top.

The suicide sprawls on the bloody floor of the bedroom,
I witness the corpse with its dabbled hair, I note where the pistol has fallen.

The blab of the pave, tires of carts, sluff of boot-soles, talk of the promenaders,
The heavy omnibus, the driver with his interrogating thumb, the clank of the
    shod horses on the granite floor,   155
The snow-sleighs, clinking, shouted jokes, pelts of snow-balls,
The hurrahs for popular favorites, the fury of rous'd mobs,
The flap of the curtain'd litter, a sick man inside borne to the hospital,
The meeting of enemies, the sudden oath, the blows and fall,
The excited crowd, the policeman with his star quickly working his passage to the
    centre of the crowd,   160
The impassive stones that receive and return so many echoes,
What groans of over-fed or half-starv'd who fall sunstruck or in fits,
What exclamations of women taken suddenly who hurry home and give birth to
    babes,
What living and buried speech is always vibrating here, what howls restrain'd by
    decorum,
Arrests of criminals, slights, adulterous offers made, acceptances, rejections with
    convex lips,   165
I mind them or the show or resonance of them — I come and I depart.

9

The big doors of the country barn stand open and ready,
The dried grass of the harvest-time loads the slow-drawn wagon,
The clear light plays on the brown gray and green intertinged,
The armfuls are pack'd to the sagging mow.   170

I am there, I help, I came stretch'd atop of the load,
I felt its soft jolts, one leg reclined on the other,

I jump from the cross-beams and seize the clover and timothy,
And roll head over heels and tangle my hair full of wisps.

10

Alone far in the wilds and mountains I hunt,   175
Wandering amazed at my own lightness and glee,
In the late afternoon choosing a safe spot to pass the night,
Kindling a fire and broiling the fresh-kill'd game,
Falling asleep on the gather'd leaves with my dog and gun by my side.

The Yankee clipper is under her sky-sails, she cuts the sparkle and scud,   180
My eyes settle the land, I bend at her prow or shout joyously from the deck.

The boatmen and clam-diggers arose early and stopt for me,
I tuck'd my trowser-ends in my boots and went and had a good time;
You should have been with us that day round the chowder-kettle.

I saw the marriage of the trapper in the open air in the far west, the bride was a
    red girl,   185
Her father and his friends sat near cross-legged and dumbly smoking, they had
    moccasins to their feet and large thick blankets hanging from their shoulders,
On a bank lounged the trapper, he was drest mostly in skins, his luxuriant beard
    and curls protected his neck, he held his bride by the hand,
She had long eyelashes, her head was bare, her coarse straight locks descended
    upon her voluptuous limbs and reach'd to her feet.

The runaway slave came to my house and stopt outside,
I heard his motions crackling the twigs of the woodpile,   190
Through the swung half-door of the kitchen I saw him limpsy[7] and weak,
And went where he sat on a log and led him in and assured him,
And brought water and fill'd a tub for his sweated body and bruis'd feet,
And gave him a room that enter'd from my own, and gave him some coarse clean
    clothes,
And remember perfectly well his revolving eyes and his awkwardness,   195
And remember putting plasters on the galls of his neck and ankles;
He staid with me a week before he was recuperated and pass'd north,
I had him sit next me at table, my fire-lock lean'd in the corner.

11

Twenty-eight young men bathe by the shore,
Twenty-eight young men and all so friendly;   200
Twenty-eight years of womanly life and all so lonesome.

----

7. **limpsy:** A variant of *limp*; that is, lacking energy or vigor.

She owns the fine house by the rise of the bank,
She hides handsome and richly drest aft the blinds of the window.

Which of the young men does she like the best?
Ah the homeliest of them is beautiful to her. 205

Where are you off to, lady? for I see you,
You splash in the water there, yet stay stock still in your room.

Dancing and laughing along the beach came the twenty-ninth bather,
The rest did not see her, but she saw them and loved them.

The beards of the young men glisten'd with wet, it ran from their long hair, 210
Little streams pass'd all over their bodies.

An unseen hand also pass'd over their bodies,
It descended tremblingly from their temples and ribs.

The young men float on their backs, their white bellies bulge to the sun, they do
    not ask who seizes fast to them,
They do not know who puffs and declines with pendant and bending arch, 215
They do not think whom they souse with spray.

12

The butcher-boy puts off his killing-clothes, or sharpens his knife at the stall in
    the market,
I loiter enjoying his repartee and his shuffle and break-down.[8]

Blacksmiths with grimed and hairy chests environ the anvil,
Each has his main-sledge, they are all out, there is a great heat in the fire. 220

From the cinder-strew'd threshold I follow their movements,
The lithe sheer of their waists plays even with their massive arms,
Overhand the hammers swing, overhand so slow, overhand so sure,
They do not hasten, each man hits in his place.

13

The negro holds firmly the reins of his four horses, the block swags underneath
    on its tied-over chain, 225
The negro that drives the long dray of the stone-yard, steady and tall he stands
    pois'd on one leg on the string-piece,[9]
His blue shirt exposes his ample neck and breast and loosens over his hip-band,

---

8. **shuffle and break-down:** Popular dance steps in minstrel shows.
9. **string-piece:** Heavy timber used in a wagon to keep a load in place.

His glance is calm and commanding, he tosses the slouch of his hat away from
    his forehead,
The sun falls on his crispy hair and mustache, falls on the black of his polish'd
    and perfect limbs.

I behold the picturesque giant and love him, and I do not stop there,   230
I go with the team also.

In me the caresser of life wherever moving, backward as well as forward sluing,[10]
To niches aside and junior bending,[11] not a person or object missing,
Absorbing all to myself and for this song.

Oxen that rattle the yoke and chain or halt in the leafy shade, what is that you
    express in your eyes?   235
It seems to me more than all the print I have read in my life.

My tread scares the wood-drake and wood-duck[12] on my distant and day-long ramble,
They rise together, they slowly circle around.

I believe in those wing'd purposes,
And acknowledge red, yellow, white, playing within me,   240
And consider green and violet and the tufted crown intentional,
And do not call the tortoise unworthy because she is not something else,
And the jay in the woods never studied the gamut,[13] yet trills pretty well to me,
And the look of the bay mare shames silliness out of me.

14

The wild gander leads his flock through the cool night,   245
Ya-honk he says, and sounds it down to me like an invitation,
The pert may suppose it meaningless, but I listening close,
Find its purpose and place up there toward the wintry sky.

The sharp-hoof'd moose of the north, the cat on the house-sill, the chickadee, the
    prairie-dog,
The litter of the grunting sow as they tug at her teats,   250
The brood of the turkey-hen and she with her half-spread wings,
I see in them and myself the same old law.

The press of my foot to the earth springs a hundred affections,
They scorn the best I can do to relate them.

---

10. **sluing:** Turning or twisting around, as on a pivot.
11. **To niches aside and junior bending:** That is, stooping to smaller, out-of-the-way places.
12. **wood-drake and wood-duck:** The male and female of the wood duck, among the most colorful and beautiful of all waterfowl.
13. **gamut:** The complete musical scale.

I am enamour'd of growing out-doors, 255
Of men that live among cattle or taste of the ocean or woods,
Of the builders and steerers of ships and the wielders of axes and mauls, and the
　　drivers of horses,
I can eat and sleep with them week in and week out.

What is commonest, cheapest, nearest, easiest, is Me,
Me going in for my chances, spending for vast returns, 260
Adorning myself to bestow myself on the first that will take me,
Not asking the sky to come down to my good will,
Scattering it freely forever.

15

The pure contralto sings in the organ loft,
The carpenter dresses his plank, the tongue of his foreplane whistles its wild
　　ascending lisp, 265
The married and unmarried children ride home to their Thanksgiving dinner,
The pilot seizes the king-pin,[14] he heaves down with a strong arm,
The mate stands braced in the whale-boat, lance and harpoon are ready,
The duck-shooter walks by silent and cautious stretches,
The deacons are ordain'd with cross'd hands at the altar, 270
The spinning-girl retreats and advances to the hum of the big wheel,
The farmer stops by the bars as he walks on a First-day[15] loafe and looks at the
　　oats and rye,
The lunatic is carried at last to the asylum a confirm'd case,
(He will never sleep any more as he did in the cot in his mother's bed-room;)
The jour printer with gray head and gaunt jaws works at his case,[16] 275
He turns his quid of tobacco while his eyes blurr with the manuscript;
The malform'd limbs are tied to the surgeon's table,
What is removed drops horribly in a pail;
The quadroon girl is sold at the auction-stand, the drunkard nods by the bar-room
　　stove,
The machinist rolls up his sleeves, the policeman travels his beat, the gate-keeper
　　marks who pass, 280
The young fellow drives the express-wagon, (I love him, though I do not know
　　him;)
The half-breed straps on his light boots to compete in the race,
The western turkey-shooting draws old and young, some lean on their rifles, some
　　sit on logs,

---

14. **king-pin:** An extended spoke of a ship's wheel, designed to provide the pilot greater leverage in steering
through rough waters.
15. **bars . . . First-day:** The bars are the rails of a fence; First-day is the Quaker name for Sunday.
16. **jour printer . . . case:** A journeyman printer working at his case, or tray of printing type.

Out from the crowd steps the marksman, takes his position, levels his piece;
The groups of newly-come immigrants cover the wharf or levee,   285
As the woolly-pates hoe in the sugarfield, the overseer views them from his
    saddle,
The bugle calls in the ball-room, the gentlemen run for their partners, the
    dancers bow to each other,
The youth lies awake in the cedar-roof'd garret and harks to the musical rain,
The Wolverine[17] sets traps on the creek that helps fill the Huron,
The squaw wrapt in her yellow-hemm'd cloth is offering moccasins and bead-bags
    for sale,   290
The connoisseur peers along the exhibition-gallery with half-shut eyes bent
    sideways,
As the deck-hands make fast the steamboat the plank is thrown for the shore-
    going passengers,
The young sister holds out the skein while the elder sister winds it off in a ball,
    and stops now and then for the knots,
The one-year wife is recovering and happy having a week ago borne her first
    child,
The clean-hair'd Yankee girl works with her sewing-machine or in the factory or
    mill,   295
The paving-man leans on his two-handed rammer,[18] the reporter's lead flies swiftly
    over the note-book, the sign-painter is lettering with blue and gold,
The canal boy trots on the tow-path, the book-keeper counts at his desk, the
    shoemaker waxes his thread,
The conductor beats time for the band and all the performers follow him,
The child is baptized, the convert is making his first professions,
The regatta is spread on the bay, the race is begun, (how the white sails sparkle!)   300
The drover watching his drove sings out to them that would stray,
The pedler sweats with his pack on his back, (the purchaser higgling about the
    odd cent;)
The bride unrumples her white dress, the minute-hand of the clock moves slowly,
The opium-eater reclines with rigid head and just-open'd lips,
The prostitute draggles her shawl, her bonnet bobs on her tipsy and pimpled neck,   305
The crowd laugh at her blackguard oaths, the men jeer and wink to each other,
(Miserable! I do not laugh at your oaths nor jeer you;)
The President holding a cabinet council is surrounded by the great Secretaries,
On the piazza walk three matrons stately and friendly with twined arms,
The crew of the fish-smack pack repeated layers of halibut in the hold,   310
The Missourian crosses the plains toting his wares and his cattle,
As the fare-collector goes through the train he gives notice by the jingling of loose
    change,

---

17. **Wolverine:** A native of Michigan.
18. **two-handed rammer:** Tool used to set paving blocks in the construction of streets.

The floor-men are laying the floor, the tinners are tinning the roof, the masons are
  calling for mortar,
In single file each shouldering his hod pass onward the laborers;
Seasons pursuing each other the indescribable crowd is gather'd, it is the fourth
  of Seventh-month, (what salutes of cannon and small arms!)   315
Seasons pursuing each other the plougher ploughs, the mower mows, and the
  winter-grain falls in the ground;
Off on the lakes the pike-fisher watches and waits by the hole in the frozen
  surface,
The stumps stand thick round the clearing, the squatter strikes deep with his axe,
Flatboatmen make fast towards dusk near the cotton-wood or pecan-trees,
Coon-seekers go through the regions of the Red river or through those drain'd by
  the Tennessee, or through those of the Arkansas,   320
Torches shine in the dark that hangs on the Chattahooche or Altamahaw,[19]
Patriarchs sit at supper with sons and grandsons and great-grandsons around
  them,
In walls of adobie, in canvas tents, rest hunters and trappers after their day's
  sport,
The city sleeps and the country sleeps,
The living sleep for their time, the dead sleep for their time,   325
The old husband sleeps by his wife and the young husband sleeps by his wife;
And these tend inward to me, and I tend outward to them,
And such as it is to be of these more or less I am,
And of these one and all I weave the song of myself.

16

I am of old and young, of the foolish as much as the wise,   330
Regardless of others, ever regardful of others,
Maternal as well as paternal, a child as well as a man,
Stuff'd with the stuff that is coarse and stuff'd with the stuff that is fine,
One of the Nation of many nations, the smallest the same and the largest the
  same,
A Southerner soon as a Northerner, a planter nonchalant and hospitable down
  by the Oconee[20] I live,   335
A Yankee bound my own way ready for trade, my joints the limberest joints on
  earth and the sternest joints on earth,
A Kentuckian walking the vale of the Elkhorn[21] in my deer-skin leggings, a
  Louisianian or Georgian,

---

19. **Chattahooche or Altamahaw:** Rivers in Georgia.
20. **Oconee:** River in central Georgia.
21. **Elkhorn:** Elkhorn Creek, where Daniel Boone took his first steps in what is now Kentucky during a
hunting expedition in 1767-68.

A boatman over lakes or bays or along coasts, a Hoosier, Badger, Buckeye;[22]
At home on Kanadian snow-shoes or up in the bush, or with fishermen off
    Newfoundland,
At home in the fleet of ice-boats, sailing with the rest and tacking,   340
At home on the hills of Vermont or in the woods of Maine, or the Texas ranch,
Comrade of Californians, comrade of free North-Westerners, (loving their big
    proportions,)
Comrade of raftsmen and coalmen, comrade of all who shake hands and welcome
    to drink and meat,
A learner with the simplest, a teacher of the thoughtfullest,
A novice beginning yet experient of myriads of seasons,   345
Of every hue and caste am I, of every rank and religion,
A farmer, mechanic, artist, gentleman, sailor, quaker,
Prisoner, fancy-man, rowdy, lawyer, physician, priest.

I resist any thing better than my own diversity,
Breathe the air but leave plenty after me,   350
And am not stuck up, and am in my place.

(The moth and the fish-eggs are in their place,
The bright suns I see and the dark suns I cannot see are in their place,
The palpable is in its place and the impalpable is in its place.)

17

These are really the thoughts of all men in all ages and lands, they are not
    original with me,   355
If they are not yours as much as mine they are nothing, or next to nothing,
If they are not the riddle and the untying of the riddle they are nothing,
If they are not just as close as they are distant they are nothing.

This is the grass that grows wherever the land is and the water is,
This the common air that bathes the globe.   360

18

With music strong I come, with my cornets and my drums,
I play not marches for accepted victors only, I play marches for conquer'd and
    slain persons.

Have you heard that it was good to gain the day?
I also say it is good to fall, battles are lost in the same spirit in which they are
    won.

---

22. **Hoosier, Badger, Buckeye:** Natives of Indiana, Wisconsin, and Ohio.

I beat and pound for the dead,   365
I blow through my embouchures²³ my loudest and gayest for them.

Vivas to those who have fail'd!
And to those whose war-vessels sank in the sea!
And to those themselves who sank in the sea!
And to all generals that lost engagements, and all overcome heroes!   370
And the numberless unknown heroes equal to the greatest heroes known!

19

This is the meal equally set, this the meat for natural hunger,
It is for the wicked just the same as the righteous, I make appointments with all,
I will not have a single person slighted or left away,
The kept-woman, sponger, thief, are hereby invited,
The heavy-lipp'd slave is invited, the venerealee²⁴ is invited;   375
There shall be no difference between them and the rest.

This is the press of a bashful hand, this the float and odor of hair,
This the touch of my lips to yours, this the murmur of yearning,
This the far-off depth and height reflecting my own face,   380
This the thoughtful merge of myself, and the outlet again.

Do you guess I have some intricate purpose?
Well I have, for the Fourth-month showers have, and the mica on the side of a
    rock has.
Do you take it I would astonish?
Does the daylight astonish? does the early redstart twittering through the woods?   385
Do I astonish more than they?

This hour I tell things in confidence,
I might not tell everybody, but I will tell you.

20

Who goes there? hankering, gross, mystical, nude;
How is it I extract strength from the beef I eat?   390

What is a man anyhow? what am I? what are you?

----

23. **embouchures:** Either the mouthpieces of wind instruments or the shape of the mouth and lips when blowing through such instruments.
24. **venerealee:** A person suffering from a venereal (sexually transmitted) disease.

All I mark as my own you shall offset it with your own,
Else it were time lost listening to me.

I do not snivel that snivel the world over,
That months are vacuums and the ground but wallow and filth   395

Whimpering and truckling fold with powders[25] for invalids, conformity goes to the
    fourth-remov'd,
I wear my hat as I please indoors or out.

Why should I pray? why should I venerate and be ceremonious?

Having pried through the strata, analyzed to a hair, counsel'd with doctors and
    calculated close,
I find no sweeter fat than sticks to my own bones.   400

In all people I see myself, none more and not one a barley-corn[26] less,
And the good or bad I say of myself I say of them.

I know I am solid and sound,
To me the converging objects of the universe perpetually flow,
All are written to me, and I must get what the writing means.   405

I know I am deathless,
I know this orbit of mine cannot be swept by a carpenter's compass,
I know I shall not pass like a child's carlacue[27] cut with a burnt stick at night.

I know I am august,
I do not trouble my spirit to vindicate itself or be understood,   410
I see that the elementary laws never apologize,
(I reckon I behave no prouder than the level I plant my house by, after all.)
I exist as I am, that is enough,
If no other in the world be aware I sit content,
And if each and all be aware I sit content.   415

One world is aware and by far the largest to me, and that is myself,
And whether I come to my own to-day or in ten thousand or ten million years,
I can cheerfully take it now, or with equal cheerfulness I can wait.

My foothold is tenon'd and mortis'd[28] in granite,
I laugh at what you call dissolution,   420
And I know the amplitude of time.

---

25. **fold with powders:** Physicians then often wrapped powdered medications in twists of paper.
26. **barley-corn:** A grain of barley also used as a unit of measurement equal to roughly one-third of an inch.
27. **carlacue:** A curlicue made in the air with a lighted stick.
28. **tenon'd and mortis'd:** Mortise and tenon is a strong joint used by carpenters to join two pieces of wood at a ninety-degree angle.

21

I am the poet of the Body and I am the poet of the Soul,
The pleasures of heaven are with me and the pains of hell are with me,
The first I graft and increase upon myself, the latter I translate into a new
    tongue.

I am the poet of the woman the same as the man,   425
And I say it is as great to be a woman as to be a man,
And I say there is nothing greater than the mother of men.

I chant the chant of dilation or pride,
We have had ducking and deprecating about enough,
I show that size is only development.   430

Have you outstript the rest? are you the President?
It is a trifle, they will more than arrive there every one, and still pass on.

I am he that walks with the tender and growing night,
I call to the earth and sea half-held by the night.

Press close bare-bosom'd night — press close magnetic nourishing night!   435
Night of south winds — night of the large few stars!
Still nodding night — mad naked summer night.

Smile O voluptuous cool-breath'd earth!
Earth of the slumbering and liquid trees!
Earth of departed sunset — earth of the mountains misty-topt!   440
Earth of the vitreous pour of the full moon just tinged with blue!
Earth of shine and dark mottling the tide of the river!
Earth of the limpid gray of clouds brighter and clearer for my sake!
Far-swooping elbow'd earth — rich apple-blossom'd earth!
Smile, for your lover comes.   445

Prodigal, you have given me love — therefore I to you give love!
O unspeakable passionate love.

22

You sea! I resign myself to you also — I guess what you mean,
I behold from the beach your crooked inviting fingers,
I believe you refuse to go back without feeling of me,   450
We must have a turn together, I undress, hurry me out of sight of the land,
Cushion me soft, rock me in billowy drowse,
Dash me with amorous wet, I can repay you.

Sea of stretch'd ground-swells,
Sea breathing broad and convulsive breaths,   455

Sea of the brine of life and of unshovell'd yet always-ready graves,
Howler and scooper of storms, capricious and dainty sea,
I am integral with you, I too am of one phase and of all phases.

Partaker of influx and efflux I, extoller of hate and conciliation,
Extoller of amies[29] and those that sleep in each others' arms.   460

I am he attesting sympathy,
(Shall I make my list of things in the house and skip the house that supports
    them?)

I am not the poet of goodness only, I do not decline to be the poet of wickedness
    also.

What blurt is this about virtue and about vice?
Evil propels me and reform of evil propels me, I stand indifferent,   465
My gait is no fault-finder's or rejecter's gait,
I moisten the roots of all that has grown.

Did you fear some scrofula[30] out of the unflagging pregnancy?
Did you guess the celestial laws are yet to be work'd over and rectified?

I find one side a balance and the antipodal side a balance,   470
Soft doctrine as steady help as stable doctrine,
Thoughts and deeds of the present our rouse and early start.

This minute that comes to me over the past decillions,
There is no better than it and now.

What behaved well in the past or behaves well to-day is not such a wonder,   475
The wonder is always and always how there can be a mean man or an infidel.

                                    23

Endless unfolding of words of ages!
And mine a word of the modern, the word En-Masse.

A word of the faith that never balks,
Here or henceforward it is all the same to me, I accept Time absolutely.   480

It alone is without flaw, it alone rounds and completes all,
That mystic baffling wonder alone completes all.

I accept Reality and dare not question it,
Materialism first and last imbuing.

---

29. **amies:** Friends (French).
30. **scrofula:** A form of tuberculosis characterized by swelling of the lymph nodes in the neck and elsewhere
in the body.

Hurrah for positive science! long live exact demonstration!   485
Fetch stonecrop mixt with cedar and branches of lilac,[31]
This is the lexicographer, this the chemist, this made a grammar of the old
     cartouches,[32]
These mariners put the ship through dangerous unknown seas,
This is the geologist, this works with the scalpel, and this is a mathematician.

Gentlemen, to you the first honors always!   490
Your facts are useful, and yet they are not my dwelling,
I but enter by them to an area of my dwelling.

Less the reminders of properties told my words,
And more the reminders they of life untold, and of freedom and extrication,
And make short account of neuters and geldings, and favor men and women fully
     equipt,   495
And beat the gong of revolt, and stop with fugitives and them that plot and
     conspire.

24

Walt Whitman, a kosmos, of Manhattan the son,
Turbulent, fleshy, sensual, eating, drinking and breeding,
No sentimentalist, no stander above men and women or apart from them,
No more modest than immodest.   500

Unscrew the locks from the doors!
Unscrew the doors themselves from their jambs!

Whoever degrades another degrades me,
And whatever is done or said returns at last to me.

Through me the afflatus[33] surging and surging, through me the current and
     index.   505

I speak the pass-word primeval, I give the sign of democracy,
By God! I will accept nothing which all cannot have their counterpart of on the
     same terms.

Through me many long dumb voices,
Voices of the interminable generations of prisoners and slaves,
Voices of the diseas'd and despairing and of thieves and dwarfs,   510
Voices of cycles of preparation and accretion,

---

31. **Fetch . . . branches of lilac:** Stonecrop, a fleshy-leaved plant long used for healing wounds, is here "mixt with cedar," an evergreen tree associated with graveyards that represents eternal life. In the Victorian language of flowers, the lilac, with its heart-shaped leaves, symbolized love.
32. **cartouches:** Stone tablets inscribed in ancient languages.
33. **afflatus:** From the Latin *afflare, afflatum,* to breathe or blow on, here suggesting divine inspiration.

And of the threads that connect the stars, and of wombs and of the father-stuff,
And of the rights of them the others are down upon,
Of the deform'd, trivial, flat, foolish, despised,
Fog in the air, beetles rolling balls of dung. 515

Through me forbidden voices,
Voices of sexes and lusts, voices veil'd and I remove the veil,
Voices indecent by me clarified and transfigur'd.

I do not press my fingers across my mouth,
I keep as delicate around the bowels as around the head and heart, 520
Copulation is no more rank to me than death is.

I believe in the flesh and the appetites,
Seeing, hearing, feeling, are miracles, and each part and tag of me is a miracle.

Divine am I inside and out, and I make holy whatever I touch or am touch'd from,
The scent of these arm-pits aroma finer than prayer, 525
This head more than churches, bibles, and all the creeds.

If I worship one thing more than another it shall be the spread of my own body,
    or any part of it,
Translucent mould of me it shall be you!
Shaded ledges and rests it shall be you!
Firm masculine colter[34] it shall be you! 530
Whatever goes to the tilth[35] of me it shall be you!
You my rich blood! your milky stream pale strippings of my life!
Breast that presses against other breasts it shall be you!
My brain it shall be your occult convolutions!
Root of wash'd sweet-flag! timorous pond-snipe! nest of guarded duplicate eggs!
    it shall be you! 535
Mix'd tussled hay of head, beard, brawn, it shall be you!

Trickling sap of maple, fibre of manly wheat, it shall be you!
Sun so generous it shall be you!
Vapors lighting and shading my face it shall be you!
You sweaty brooks and dews it shall be you! 540
Winds whose soft-tickling genitals rub against me it shall be you!
Broad muscular fields, branches of live oak, loving lounger in my winding paths,
    it shall be you!
Hands I have taken, face I have kiss'd, mortal I have ever touch'd, it shall be you.

I dote on myself, there is that lot of me and all so luscious,
Each moment and whatever happens thrills me with joy, 545

---

34. **colter:** Blade of a plow.
35. **tilth:** Plowing or cultivation.

I cannot tell how my ankles bend, nor whence the cause of my faintest wish,
Nor the cause of the friendship I emit, nor the cause of the friendship I take again.

That I walk up my stoop, I pause to consider if it really be,
A morning-glory at my window satisfies me more than the metaphysics of books.

To behold the day-break!   550
The little light fades the immense and diaphanous shadows,
The air tastes good to my palate.

Hefts[36] of the moving world at innocent gambols silently rising freshly exuding,
Scooting obliquely high and low.

Something I cannot see puts upward libidinous prongs,   555
Seas of bright juice suffuse heaven.

The earth by the sky staid with, the daily close of their junction.
The heav'd challenge from the east that moment over my head,
The mocking taunt, See then whether you shall be master!

25

Dazzling and tremendous how quick the sun-rise would kill me,   560
If I could not now and always send sun-rise out of me.

We also ascend dazzling and tremendous as the sun,
We found our own O my soul in the calm and cool of the day-break.

My voice goes after what my eyes cannot reach,
With the twirl of my tongue I encompass worlds and volumes of worlds.   565

Speech is the twin of my vision, it is unequal to measure itself,
It provokes me forever, it says sarcastically,
Walt you contain enough, why don't you let it out then?

Come now I will not be tantalized, you conceive too much of articulation,
Do you not know O speech how the buds beneath you are folded?   570
Waiting in gloom, protected by frost,
The dirt receding before my prophetical screams,
I underlying causes to balance them at last,
My knowledge my live parts, it keeping tally with the meaning of all things,
Happiness, (which whoever hears me let him or her set out in search of this day.)   575

My final merit I refuse you, I refuse putting from me what I really am,
Encompass worlds, but never try to encompass me,
I crowd your sleekest and best by simply looking toward you.

---

36. **Hefts:** Here used in the sense of something heaved or lifted upward.

Writing and talk do not prove me,
I carry the plenum[37] of proof and every thing else in my face,   580
With the hush of my lips I wholly confound the skeptic.

26

Now I will do nothing but listen,
To accrue what I hear into this song, to let sounds contribute toward it.

I hear bravuras of birds, bustle of growing wheat, gossip of flames, clack of
   sticks cooking my meals,
I hear the sound I love, the sound of the human voice,   585
I hear all sounds running together, combined, fused or following,
Sounds of the city and sounds out of the city, sounds of the day and night,
Talkative young ones to those that like them, the loud laugh of work-people at
   their meals,
The angry base of disjointed friendship, the faint tones of the sick,
The judge with hands tight to the desk, his pallid lips pronouncing a
   death-sentence,   590
The heave'e'yo of stevedores unlading ships by the wharves, the refrain of the
   anchor-lifters,
The ring of alarm-bells, the cry of fire, the whirr of swift-streaking engines and
   hose-carts with premonitory tinkles and color'd lights,
The steam whistle, the solid roll of the train of approaching cars,
The slow march play'd at the head of the association marching two and two,
(They go to guard some corpse, the flag-tops are draped with black muslin.)   595

I hear the violoncello, ('tis the young man's heart's complaint,)
I hear the key'd cornet, it glides quickly in through my ears,
It shakes mad-sweet pangs through my belly and breast.

I hear the chorus, it is a grand opera,
Ah this indeed is music — this suits me.   600

A tenor large and fresh as the creation fills me,
The orbic flex of his mouth is pouring and filling me full.
I hear the train'd soprano (what work with hers is this?)
The orchestra whirls me wider than Uranus flies,[38]
It wrenches such ardors from me I did not know I possess'd them.   605
It sails me. I dab with bare feet, they are lick'd by the indolent waves,
I am cut by bitter and angry hail, I lose my breath,

---

37. **plenum:** Fullness or completeness.
38. **wider than Uranus flies:** Uranus, the seventh planet in our solar system, was long thought to be the most distant from the sun.

Steep'd amid honey'd morphine, my windpipe throttled in fakes[39] of death,
At length let up again to feel the puzzle of puzzles,
And that we call Being.   610

27

To be in any form, what is that?
(Round and round we go, all of us, and ever come back thither,)
If nothing lay more develop'd the quahaug[40] in its callous shell were enough.

Mine is no callous shell,
I have instant conductors all over me whether I pass or stop,   615
They seize every object and lead it harmlessly through me.

I merely stir, press, feel with my fingers, and am happy,
To touch my person to some one else's is about as much as I can stand.

28

Is this then a touch? quivering me to a new identity,
Flames and ether making a rush for my veins,   620
Treacherous tip of me reaching and crowding to help them,
My flesh and blood playing out lightning to strike what is hardly different from
    myself,
On all sides prurient provokers stiffening my limbs,
Straining the udder of my heart for its withheld drip,
Behaving licentious toward me, taking no denial,   625
Depriving me of my best as for a purpose,
Unbuttoning my clothes, holding me by the bare waist,
Deluding my confusion with the calm of the sunlight and pasture-fields,
Immodestly sliding the fellow-senses away,
They bribed to swap off with touch and go and graze at the edges of me,   630
No consideration, no regard for my draining strength or my anger,

Fetching the rest of the herd around to enjoy them a while,
Then all uniting to stand on a headland and worry me.

The sentries desert every other part of me,
They have left me helpless to a red marauder,   635
They all come to the headland to witness and assist against me.

I am given up by traitors,
I talk wildly, I have lost my wits, I and nobody else am the greatest traitor,
I went myself first to the headland, my own hands carried me there.

---

39. **fakes:** Coils of rope.
40. **quahaug:** A clam.

Your villain touch! what are you doing? my breath is tight in its throat,   640
Unclench your floodgates, you are too much for me.

29

Blind loving wrestling touch, sheath'd hooded sharp-tooth'd touch!
Did it make you ache so, leaving me?

Parting track'd by arriving, perpetual payment of perpetual loan,
Rich showering rain, and recompense richer afterward.   645

Sprouts take and accumulate, stand by the curb prolific and vital,
Landscapes projected masculine, full-sized and golden.

30

All truths wait in all things,
They neither hasten their own delivery nor resist it,
They do not need the obstetric forceps of the surgeon,   650
The insignificant is as big to me as any,
(What is less or more than a touch?)

Logic and sermons never convince,
The damp of the night drives deeper into my soul.

(Only what proves itself to every man and woman is so,   655
Only what nobody denies is so.)

A minute and a drop of me settle my brain,
I believe the soggy clods shall become lovers and lamps,
And a compend[41] of compends is the meat of a man or woman,
And a summit and flower there is the feeling they have for each other,   660
And they are to branch boundlessly out of that lesson until it becomes
     omnific,[42]
And until one and all shall delight us, and we them.

31

I believe a leaf of grass is no less than the journey-work of the stars,
And the pismire[43] is equally perfect, and a grain of sand, and the egg of the wren,
And the tree-toad is a chef-d'oeuvre[44] for the highest,   665

---

41. **compend:** A compendium, a concise compilation of a body of knowledge or summary of a larger work.
42. **omnific:** Creating all things; all-encompassing.
43. **pismire:** An early term for an ant.
44. **chef-d'oeuvre:** A masterpiece, especially in art or literature (French).

And the running blackberry would adorn the parlors of heaven,
And the narrowest hinge in my hand puts to scorn all machinery.
And the cow crunching with depress'd head surpasses any statue,
And a mouse is miracle enough to stagger sextillions of infidels.

I find I incorporate gneiss,[45] coal, long-threaded moss, fruits, grains, esculent
    roots,   670
And am stucco'd with quadrupeds and birds all over,
And have distanced what is behind me for good reasons,
But call any thing back again when I desire it.

In vain the speeding or shyness,
In vain the plutonic rocks[46] send their old heat against my approach,   675
In vain the mastodon retreats beneath its own powder'd bones,
In vain objects stand leagues off and assume manifold shapes,
In vain the ocean settling in hollows and the great monsters lying low,
In vain the buzzard houses herself with the sky,
In vain the snake slides through the creepers and logs,   680
In vain the elk takes to the inner passes of the woods,
In vain the razor-bill'd auk sails far north to Labrador,
I follow quickly, I ascend to the nest in the fissure of the cliff.

32

I think I could turn and live with animals, they are so placid and self-contain'd,
I stand and look at them long and long.   685

They do not sweat and whine about their condition,
They do not lie awake in the dark and weep for their sins,
They do not make me sick discussing their duty to God,
Not one is dissatisfied, not one is demented with the mania of owning things,
Not one kneels to another, nor to his kind that lived thousands of years ago,   690
Not one is respectable or unhappy over the whole earth.

So they show their relations to me and I accept them,
They bring me tokens of myself, they evince them plainly in their possession.

I wonder where they get those tokens,
Did I pass that way huge times ago and negligently drop them?   695

Myself moving forward then and now and forever,
Gathering and showing more always and with velocity,
Infinite and omnigenous,[47] and the like of these among them,

---

45. **gneiss:** Metamorphic rock.
46. **plutonic rocks:** Igneous rocks formed by solidification deep beneath the surface of the earth.
47. **omnigenous:** Of all kinds; belonging to every form of life.

Not too exclusive toward the reachers of my remembrancers,
Picking out here one that I love, and now go with him on brotherly terms.　700

A gigantic beauty of a stallion, fresh and responsive to my caresses,
Head high in the forehead, wide between the ears,
Limbs glossy and supple, tail dusting the ground,
Eyes full of sparkling wickedness, ears finely cut, flexibly moving.

His nostrils dilate as my heels embrace him,　705
His well-built limbs tremble with pleasure as we race around and return.

I but use you a minute, then I resign you, stallion,
Why do I need your paces when I myself out-gallop them?
Even as I stand or sit passing faster than you.

33

Space and Time! now I see it is true, what I guess'd at,　710
What I guess'd when I loaf'd on the grass,
What I guess'd while I lay alone in my bed,
And again as I walk'd the beach under the paling stars of the morning.

My ties and ballasts leave me, my elbows rest in sea-gaps,[48]
I skirt sierras, my palms cover continents,　715
I am afoot with my vision.

By the city's quadrangular houses – in log huts, camping with lumbermen,
Along the ruts of the turnpike, along the dry gulch and rivulet bed,
Weeding my onion-patch or hoeing rows of carrots and parsnips, crossing
　savannas, trailing in forests,
Prospecting, gold-digging, girdling the trees of a new purchase,　720
Scorch'd ankle-deep by the hot sand, hauling my boat down the shallow river,
Where the panther walks to and fro on a limb overhead, where the buck turns
　furiously at the hunter,
Where the rattlesnake suns by flabby length on a rock, where the otter is feeding
　on fish,
Where the alligator in his tough pimples sleeps by the bayou,
Where the black bear is searching for roots or honey, where the beaver pats the
　mud with his paddle-shaped tail;　725
Over the growing sugar, over the yellow-flower'd cotton plant, over the rice in its
　low moist field,
Over the sharp-peak'd farm house, with its scallop'd scum and slender shoots
　from the gutters,[49]

---

48. **sea-gaps:** Bays or estuaries.
49. **scallop'd scum . . . gutters:** That is, the debris and sediment on the roofs of old farmhouses in which
plants could take root.

Over the western persimmon, over the long-leav'd corn, over the delicate
    blue-flower flax,
Over the white and brown buckwheat, a hummer and buzzer there with the rest,
Over the dusky green of the rye as it ripples and shades in the breeze;   730
Scaling mountains, pulling myself cautiously up, holding on by low scragged
    limbs,
Walking the path worn in the grass and beat through the leaves of the brush,
Where the quail is whistling betwixt the woods and the wheat-lot,
Where the bat flies in the Seventh-month eve, where the great gold-bug[50] drops
    through the dark,
Where the brook puts out of the roots of the old tree and flows to the meadow,   735
Where cattle stand and shake away flies with the tremulous shuddering of their
    hides,
Where the cheese-cloth hangs in the kitchen, where andirons straddle the
    hearth-slab, where cobwebs fall in festoons from the rafters;
Where trip-hammers crash, where the press is whirling its cylinders,
Wherever the human heart beats with terrible throes under its ribs,
Where the pear-shaped balloon is floating aloft, (floating in it myself and looking
    composedly down,)   740
Where the life-car[51] is drawn on the slip-noose, where the heat hatches pale-green
    eggs in the dented sand,
Where the she-whale swims with her calf and never forsakes it,
Where the steam-ship trails hind-ways its long pennant of smoke,
Where the fin of the shark cuts like a black chip out of the water,
Where the half-burn'd brig is riding on unknown currents,   745
Where shells grow to her slimy deck, where the dead are corrupting below;
Where the dense-starr'd flag is borne at the head of the regiments,
Approaching Manhattan up by the long-stretching island,
Under Niagara, the cataract falling like a veil over my countenance,
Upon a door-step, upon the horse-block of hard wood outside,   750
Upon the race-course, or enjoying picnics or jigs or a good game of base-ball,
At he-festivals, with blackguard gibes, ironical license, bull-dances,[52] drinking,
    laughter,
At the cider-mill tasting the sweets of the brown mash, sucking the juice through
    a straw,
At apple-peelings wanting kisses for all the red fruit I find,
At musters, beach-parties, friendly bees,[53] huskings, house-raisings;   755
Where the mocking-bird sounds his delicious gurgles, cackles, screams, weeps,

---

50. **gold-bug:** Common name for the golden tortoise beetle.
51. **life-car:** Compartment suspended on a rope for transferring passengers from a ship in distress to another ship.
52. **bull-dances:** Country dances where men partner with men.
53. **friendly bees:** Occasions for work and socializing with neighbors.

Where the hay-rick stands in the barn-yard, where the dry-stalks are scatter'd,
    where the brood-cow waits in the hovel,
Where the bull advances to do his masculine work, where the stud to the mare,
    where the cock is treading the hen,
Where the heifers browse, where geese nip their food with short jerks,
Where sun-down shadows lengthen over the limitless and lonesome prairie,   760
Where herds of buffalo make a crawling spread of the square miles far and near,
Where the humming-bird shimmers, where the neck of the long-lived swan is
    curving and winding,
Where the laughing-gull scoots by the shore, where she laughs her near-human
    laugh,
Where bee-hives range on a gray bench in the garden half hid by the high weeds,
Where band-neck'd partridges roost in a ring on the ground with their heads out,   765
Where burial coaches enter the arch'd gates of a cemetery,
Where winter wolves bark amid wastes of snow and icicled trees,
Where the yellow-crown'd heron comes to the edge of the marsh at night and
    feeds upon small crabs,
Where the splash of swimmers and divers cools the warm noon,
Where the katy-did works her chromatic reed[54] on the walnut-tree over the well,   770
Through patches of citrons and cucumbers with silver-wired leaves,
Through the salt-lick or orange glade, or under conical firs,
Through the gymnasium, through the curtain'd saloon, through the office or
    public hall;
Pleas'd with the native and pleas'd with the foreign, pleas'd with the new and old,
Pleas'd with the homely woman as well as the handsome,   775
Pleas'd with the quakeress as she puts off her bonnet and talks melodiously,
Pleas'd with the tune of the choir of the whitewash'd church,
Pleas'd with the earnest words of the sweating Methodist preacher, impress'd
    seriously at the camp-meeting;
Looking in at the shop-windows of Broadway the whole forenoon, flatting the
    flesh of my nose on the thick plate glass,
Wandering the same afternoon with my face turn'd up to the clouds, or down a
    lane or along the beach,   780
My right and left arms round the sides of two friends, and I in the middle;
Coming home with the silent and dark-cheek'd bush-boy, (behind me he rides at
    the drape of the day,)[55]
Far from the settlements studying the print of animals' feet, or the moccasin
    print,
By the cot in the hospital reaching lemonade to a feverish patient,
Nigh the coffin'd corpse when all is still, examining with a candle;   785

---

54. **katy-did . . . chromatic reed:** Katydids, insects related to grasshoppers and crickets, rub their front wings together to produce a rasping "song."
55. **drape of the day:** Close of the day.

Voyaging to every port to dicker and adventure.
Hurrying with the modern crowd as eager and fickle as any,
Hot toward one I hate, ready in my madness to knife him,
Solitary at midnight in my back yard, my thoughts gone from me a long while,
Walking the old hills of Judaea with the beautiful gentle God by my side,   790
Speeding through space, speeding through heaven and the stars,
Speeding amid the seven satellites[56] and the broad ring, and the diameter of
    eighty thousand miles,
Speeding with tail'd meteors, throwing fire-balls like the rest,
Carrying the crescent child that carries its own full mother in its belly,[57]
Storming, enjoying, planning, loving, cautioning,   795
Backing and filling, appearing and disappearing,
I tread day and night such roads.

I visit the orchards of spheres and look at the product,
And look at quintillions ripen'd and look at quintillions green.

I fly those flights of a fluid and swallowing soul,   800
My course runs below the soundings of plummets.

I help myself to material and immaterial,
No guard can shut me off, no law prevent me.

I anchor my ship for a little while only,
My messengers continually cruise away or bring their returns to me.   805

I go hunting polar furs and the seal, leaping chasms with a pike-pointed staff,
    clinging to topples of brittle and blue.[58]

I ascend to the foretruck,
I take my place late at night in the crow's-nest,[59]
We sail the arctic sea, it is plenty light enough,
Through the clear atmosphere I stretch around on the wonderful beauty,   810
The enormous masses of ice pass me and I pass them, the scenery is plain in all
    directions,
The white-topt mountains show in the distance, I fling out my fancies toward
    them,
We are approaching some great battle-field in which we are soon to be
    engaged,
We pass the colossal outposts of the encampment, we pass with still feet and
    caution,

---

56. **seven satellites:** Known moons of Saturn.
57. **Carrying . . . in its belly:** An image of the crescent moon with the full moon still faintly visible.
58. **topples of brittle and blue:** Large cakes of ice that are pressed upward, sometimes to great heights, before toppling over.
59. **I ascend . . . crow's-nest:** The foretruck is a platform at the head of the foremast, and the crow's nest is a structure used as a lookout point on the upper part of the mainmast of a ship.

Or we are entering by the suburbs some vast and ruin'd city, 815
The blocks and fallen architecture more than all the living cities of the globe.

I am a free companion, I bivouac by invading watchfires,
I turn the bridegroom out of bed and stay with the bride myself,
I tighten her all night to my thighs and lips.

My voice is the wife's voice, the screech by the rail of the stairs, 820
They fetch my man's body up dripping and drown'd.

I understand the large hearts of heroes,
The courage of present times and all times,
How the skipper saw the crowded and rudderless wreck of the steam-ship,[60] and
    Death chasing it up and down the storm,
How he knuckled tight and gave not back an inch, and was faithful of days and
    faithful of nights, 825
And chalk'd in large letters on a board, *Be of good cheer, we will not desert you;*
How he follow'd with them and tack'd with them three days and would not give
    it up,
How he saved the drifting company at last,
How the lank loose-gown'd women look'd when boated from the side of their
    prepared graves,
How the silent old-faced infants and the lifted sick, and the sharp-lipp'd
    unshaved men; 830
All this I swallow, it tastes good, I like it well, it becomes mine,
I am the man, I suffer'd, I was there.

The disdain and calmness of martyrs,
The mother of old, condemn'd for a witch, burnt with dry wood, her children
    gazing on,
The hounded slave that flags in the race, leans by the fence, blowing, cover'd
    with sweat, 835
The twinges that sting like needles his legs and neck, the murderous buckshot
    and the bullets,
All these I feel or am.

I am the hounded slave, I wince at the bite of the dogs,
Hell and despair are upon me, crack and again crack the marksmen,
I clutch the rails of the fence, my gore dribs, thinn'd with the ooze of my skin,[61] 840
I fall on the weeds and stones,
The riders spur their unwilling horses, haul close,

---

60. **How the skipper . . . rudderless wreck of the steam-ship:** The following passage is based on the widely reported wreck of the *San Francisco*, which sailed from New York on December 22, 1853, was caught in a violent storm, and drifted helplessly until early January. More than 150 people died before survivors were rescued by various ships, though Whitman focuses on Captain Creighton of the *Three Bells*, who in the *New York Times* was described as "a hero, deserving the highest honors of public reception."
61. **my gore dribs . . . ooze of my skin:** That is, his blood dribbles down, diluted with sweat.

Taunt my dizzy ears and beat me violently over the head with whip-stocks.
Agonies are one of my changes of garments,
I do not ask the wounded person how he feels, I myself become the wounded
    person,   845
My hurts turn livid upon me as I lean on a cane and observe.

I am the mash'd fireman with breast-bone broken,
Tumbling walls buried me in their debris,
Heat and smoke I inspired, I heard the yelling shouts of my comrades,
I heard the distant click of their picks and shovels,   850
They have clear'd the beams away, they tenderly lift me forth.

I lie in the night air in my red shirt, the pervading hush is for my sake,
Painless after all I lie exhausted but not so unhappy,
White and beautiful are the faces around me, the heads are bared of their
    fire-caps,
The kneeling crowd fades with the light of the torches.   855

Distant and dead resuscitate,
They show as the dial or move as the hands of me, I am the clock myself.

I am an old artillerist, I tell of my fort's bombardment,
I am there again.

Again the long roll of the drummers,   860
Again the attacking cannon, mortars,
Again to my listening ears the cannon responsive.

I take part, I see and hear the whole,
The cries, curses, roar, the plaudits for well-aim'd shots,
The ambulanza slowly passing trailing its red drip,   865
Workmen searching after damages, making indispensable repairs,
The fall of grenades through the rent roof, the fan-shaped explosion,
The whizz of limbs, heads, stone, wood, iron, high in the air.

Again gurgles the mouth of my dying general, he furiously waves with his
    hand,
He gasps through the clot *Mind not me — mind — the entrenchments.*   870

34

Now I tell what I knew in Texas in my early youth,
(I tell not the fall of Alamo,[62]

---

62. **I tell not the fall of Alamo:** On March 6, 1836, the Alamo, a stronghold of Anglo-American colonists revolting against Mexican rule, was stormed by an army under the command of Santa Anna, and all 187 men inside the fort died. Whitman, however, here describes a less well-known event that occurred three weeks later, when a company of Texans was massacred after their surrender to Mexican forces at Goliad.

Not one escaped to tell the fall of Alamo,
The hundred and fifty are dumb yet at Alamo,)
'Tis the tale of the murder in cold blood of four hundred and twelve young men.   875

Retreating they had form'd in a hollow square with their baggage for
    breastworks,
Nine hundred lives out of the surrounding enemy's, nine times their number,
    was the price they took in advance,
Their colonel was wounded and their ammunition gone,
They treated for an honorable capitulation, receiv'd writing and seal, gave up
    their arms and march'd back prisoners of war.

They were the glory of the race of rangers,   880
Matchless with horse, rifle, song, supper, courtship,
Large, turbulent, generous, handsome, proud, and affectionate,
Bearded, sunburnt, drest in the free costume of hunters,
Not a single one over thirty years of age.

The second First-day morning they were brought out in squads and massacred,
    it was beautiful early summer,   885
The work commenced about five o'clock and was over by eight.

None obey'd the command to kneel,
Some made a mad and helpless rush, some stood stark and straight,
A few fell at once, shot in the temple or heart, the living and dead lay together,
The maim'd and mangled dug in the dirt, the new-comers saw them there,   890
Some half-kill'd attempted to crawl away,
These were despatch'd with bayonets or batter'd with the blunts of muskets,
A youth not seventeen years old seiz'd his assassin till two more came to release
    him,
The three were all torn and cover'd with the boy's blood.

At eleven o'clock began the burning of the bodies;   895
That is the tale of the murder of the four hundred and twelve young men.

35

Would you hear of an old-time sea-fight?[63]
Would you learn who won by the light of the moon and stars?
List to the yarn, as my grandmother's father the sailor told it to me.
Our foe was no skulk in his ship I tell you, (said he,)   900

---

63. **old-time sea-fight:** A famous battle during the Revolutionary War between the American *Bon Homme Richard*, commanded by John Paul Jones, and the British *Serapis* in the North Sea.

His was the surly English pluck, and there is no tougher or truer, and never was,
    and never will be;
Along the lower'd eve he came horribly raking us.

We closed with him, the yards entangled, the cannon touch'd,
My captain lash'd fast with his own hands.

We had receiv'd some eighteen pound shots under the water,   905
On our lower-gun-deck two large pieces had burst at the first fire, killing all
    around and blowing up overhead.

Fighting at sun-down, fighting at dark,
Ten o'clock at night, the full moon well up, our leaks on the gain, and five feet of
    water reported,
The master-at-arms loosing the prisoners confined in the after-hold to give
    them a chance for themselves.

The transit to and from the magazine[64] is now stopt by the sentinels,   910
They see so many strange faces they do not know whom to trust.

Our frigate takes fire,
The other asks if we demand quarter?
If our colors are struck and the fighting done?

Now I laugh content, for I hear the voice of my little captain,   915
We have not struck, he composedly cries, *we have just begun our part of the
    fighting.*

Only three guns are in use,
One is directed by the captain himself against the enemy's mainmast,
Two well serv'd with grape and canister[65] silence his musketry and clear his
    decks.

The tops alone second the fire of this little battery, especially the main-top,[66]   920
They hold out bravely during the whole of the action.

Not a moment's cease,
The leaks gain fast on the pumps, the fire eats toward the powder-magazine.

One of the pumps has been shot away, it is generally thought we are sinking.

Serene stands the little captain,   925
He is not hurried, his voice is neither high nor low,
His eyes give more light to us than our battle-lanterns.

---

64. **magazine:** The powder magazine, where ammunition was stored.
65. **grape and canister:** Grapeshot, small iron balls packed inside metal cylinders fired from canons, was used against troops at short range.
66. **The tops . . . main-top:** Solid wooden platforms on the masts from which sharpshooters could fire down at the deck of the opposing ship.

Toward twelve there in the beams of the moon they surrender to us.

36

Stretch'd and still lies the midnight,
Two great hulls motionless on the breast of the darkness, 930
Our vessel riddled and slowly sinking, preparations to pass to the one we have
    conquer'd,
The captain on the quarter-deck coldly giving his orders through a countenance
    white as a sheet,
Near by the corpse of the child that serv'd in the cabin,
The dead face of an old salt with long white hair and carefully curl'd whiskers,
The flames spite of all that can be done flickering aloft and below, 935
The husky voices of the two or three officers yet fit for duty,
Formless stacks of bodies and bodies by themselves, dabs of flesh upon the masts
    and spars,
Cut of cordage, dangle of rigging, slight shock of the soothe of waves,
Black and impassive guns, litter of powder-parcels, strong scent,
A few large stars overhead, silent and mournful shining, 940
Delicate sniffs of sea-breeze, smells of sedgy grass and fields by the shore,
    death-messages given in charge to survivors,
The hiss of the surgeon's knife, the gnawing teeth of his saw,
Wheeze, cluck, swash of falling blood, short wild scream, and long, dull, tapering
    groan,
These so, these irretrievable.

37

You laggards there on guard! look to your arms! 945
In at the conquer'd doors they crowd! I am possess'd!
Embody all presences outlaw'd or suffering,
See myself in prison shaped like another man,
And feel the dull unintermitted pain.

For me the keepers of convicts shoulder their carbines and keep watch, 950
It is I let out in the morning and barr'd at night.

Not a mutineer walks handcuff'd to jail but I am handcuff'd to him and walk by
    his side,
(I am less the jolly one there, and more the silent one with sweat on my twitching
    lips.)

Not a youngster is taken for larceny but I go up too, and am tried and sentenced.

Not a cholera patient lies at the last gasp but I also lie at the last gasp, 955
My face is ash-color'd, my sinews gnarl, away from me people retreat.

Askers embody themselves in me and I am embodied in them,
I project my hat, sit shame-faced, and beg.

38

Enough! enough! enough!
Somehow I have been stunn'd. Stand back!   960
Give me a little time beyond my cuff'd head, slumbers, dreams, gaping,
I discover myself on the verge of a usual mistake.

That I could forget the mockers and insults!
That I could forget the trickling tears and the blows of the bludgeons and
    hammers!
That I could look with a separate look on my own crucifixion and bloody
    crowning.   965

I remember now,
I resume the overstaid fraction,
The grave of rock multiplies what has been confided to it, or to any graves,
Corpses rise, gashes heal, fastenings roll from me.

I troop forth replenish'd with supreme power, one of an average unending
    procession,   970
Inland and sea-coast we go, and pass all boundary lines,
Our swift ordinances on their way over the whole earth,
The blossoms we wear in our hats the growth of thousands of years.

Eleves,[67] I salute you! come forward!
Continue your annotations, continue your questionings.   975

39

The friendly and flowing savage, who is he?
Is he waiting for civilization, or past it and mastering it?

Is he some Southwesterner rais'd out-doors? is he Kanadian?
Is he from the Mississippi country? Iowa, Oregon, California?
The mountains? prairie-life, bush-life? or sailor from the sea? 980

Wherever he goes men and women accept and desire him,
They desire he should like them, touch them, speak to them, stay with them.

Behavior lawless as snow-flakes, words simple as grass, uncomb'd head,
    laughter, and naivetè,

---

67. **Eleves:** Students (French).

Slow-stepping feet, common features, common modes and emanations,
They descend in new forms from the tips of his fingers,   985
They are wafted with the odor of his body or breath, they fly out of the glance of
    his eyes.

40

Flaunt of the sunshine I need not your bask — lie over!
You light surfaces only, I force surfaces and depths also.

Earth! you seem to look for something at my hands,
Say, old top-knot,[68] what do you want?   990

Man or woman, I might tell how I like you, but cannot,
And might tell what it is in me and what it is in you, but cannot,
And might tell that pining I have, that pulse of my nights and days.

Behold, I do not give lectures or a little charity,
When I give I give myself.   995

You there, impotent, loose in the knees,
Open your scarf'd chops[69] till I blow grit within you,
Spread your palms and lift the flaps of your pockets,
I am not to be denied, I compel, I have stores plenty and to spare,
And any thing I have I bestow.   1000

I do not ask who you are, that is not important to me,
You can do nothing and be nothing but what I will infold you.

To cotton-field drudge or cleaner of privies I lean,
On his right cheek I put the family kiss,
And in my soul I swear I never will deny him.   1005

On women fit for conception I start bigger and nimbler babes,
(This day I am jetting the stuff of far more arrogant republics.)

To any one dying, thither I speed and twist the knob of the door,
Turn the bed-clothes toward the foot of the bed,
Let the physician and the priest go home.   1010

I seize the descending man and raise him with resistless will,
O despairer, here is my neck,
By God, you shall not go down! hang your whole weight upon me.

---

68. **old top-knot:** A top-knot is a crest or knot of hair worn on the crown of the head, but Whitman appears
to use the term as part of a familiar epithet, perhaps akin to "old pal."
69. **scarf'd chops:** Worn or lined area around the mouth.

I dilate you with tremendous breath, I buoy you up,
Every room of the house do I fill with an arm'd force,   1015
Lovers of me, bafflers of graves.

Sleep — I and they keep guard all night,
Not doubt, not decease shall dare to lay finger upon you,
I have embraced you, and henceforth possess you to myself,
And when you rise in the morning you will find what I tell you is so.   1020

41

I am he bringing help for the sick as they pant on their backs,
And for strong upright men I bring yet more needed help.

I heard what was said of the universe,
Heard it and heard it of several thousand years;
It is middling well as far as it goes — but is that all?   1025

Magnifying and applying come I,
Outbidding at the start the old cautious hucksters,
Taking myself the exact dimensions of Jehovah,
Lithographing Kronos, Zeus his son, and Hercules his grandson,
Buying drafts of Osiris, Isis, Belus, Brahma, Buddha,   1030
In my portfolio placing Manito loose, Allah on a leaf, the crucifix engraved,
With Odin and the hideous-faced Mexitli and every idol and image,[70]
Taking them all for what they are worth and not a cent more,
Admitting they were alive and did the work of their days,
(They bore mites as for unfledg'd birds who have now to rise and fly and sing for
     themselves,)   1035
Accepting the rough deific sketches to fill out better in myself, bestowing them
     freely on each man and woman I see,
Discovering as much or more in a framer framing a house,
Putting higher claims for him there with his roll'd-up sleeves driving the mallet
     and chisel,
Not objecting to special revelations, considering a curl of smoke or a hair on the
     back of my hand just as curious as any revelation,
Lads ahold of fire-engines and hook-and-ladder ropes no less to me than the gods
     of the antique wars,   1040
Minding their voices peal through the crash of destruction,

---

70. **Taking . . . every idol and image:** Whitman refers to a series of myths from several cultures. In Greek mythology, Kronos ruled the universe until he was dethroned by Zeus. Hercules won immortality by completing twelve notable acts. Osiris was the Egyptian god of nature and fertility and Isis was his wife and sister, the goddess of fertility. Belus was an Assyrian god. Brahma is the Hindu creator. Manito was the nature god of the Algonkin tribes. Allah is the supreme being in Islam. Odin was the chief Norse god. Mexitli was an Aztec war god.

Their brawny limbs passing safe over charr'd laths, their white foreheads whole
    and unhurt out of the flames;
By the mechanic's wife with her babe at her nipple interceding for every person
    born,
Three scythes at harvest whizzing in a row from three lusty angels with shirts
    bagg'd out at their waists,
The snag-tooth'd hostler with red hair redeeming sins past and to come,   1045
Selling all he possesses, traveling on foot to fee lawyers for his brother and sit by
    him while he is tried for forgery;
What was strewn in the amplest strewing the square rod about me, and not filling
    the square rod then,
The bull and the bug never worshipp'd half enough,
Dung and dirt more admirable than was dream'd,
The supernatural of no account, myself waiting my time to be one of the
    supremes,   1050
The day getting ready for me when I shall do as much good as the best, and be as
    prodigious;
By my life-lumps![71] becoming already a creator,
Putting myself here and now to the ambush'd womb of the shadows.

42

A call in the midst of the crowd,
My own voice, orotund sweeping and final.   1055

Come my children,
Come my boys and girls, my women, household and intimates,
Now the performer launches his nerve, he has pass'd his prelude on the reeds
    within.

Easily written loose-finger'd chords — I feel the thrum of your climax and close.

My head slues round on my neck,   1060
Music rolls, but not from the organ,
Folks are around me, but they are no household of mine.

Ever the hard unsunk ground,
Ever the eaters and drinkers, ever the upward and downward sun, ever the air and
    the ceaseless tides,
Ever myself and my neighbors, refreshing, wicked, real,   1065
Ever the old inexplicable query, ever that thorn'd thumb,[72] that breath of itches and
    thirsts,

---

71. **life-lumps:** Testicles.
72. **thorn'd thumb:** A variant of the common expression "a thorn in the side," or a source of constant irritation.

Ever the vexer's *hoot! hoot!* till we find where the sly one hides and bring him forth,
Ever love, ever the sobbing liquid of life,
Ever the bandage under the chin, ever the trestles of death.[73]

Here and there with dimes on the eyes[74] walking,   1070
To feed the greed of the belly the brains liberally spooning,
Tickets buying, taking, selling, but in to the feast never once going,
Many sweating, ploughing, thrashing, and then the chaff for payment receiving,
A few idly owning, and they the wheat continually claiming.

This is the city and I am one of the citizens,   1075
Whatever interests the rest interests me, politics, wars, markets, newspapers, schools,
The mayor and councils, banks, tariffs, steamships, factories, stocks, stores, real
    estate and personal estate.

The little plentiful manikins skipping around in collars and tail'd coats,
I am aware who they are, (they are positively not worms or fleas,)
I acknowledge the duplicates of myself, the weakest and shallowest is deathless
    with me,   1080
What I do and say the same waits for them,
Every thought that flounders in me the same flounders in them.

I know perfectly well my own egotism,
Know my omnivorous lines and must not write any less,
And would fetch you whoever you are flush with myself.   1085

Not words of routine this song of mine,
But abruptly to question, to leap beyond yet nearer bring;
This printed and bound book — but the printer and the printing-office boy?
The well-taken photographs — but your wife or friend close and solid in your arms?
The black ship mail'd with iron, her mighty guns in her turrets — but the pluck of
    the captain and engineers?   1090
In the houses the dishes and fare and furniture — but the host and hostess, and
    the look out of their eyes?
The sky up there — yet here or next door, or across the way?
The saints and sages in history — but you yourself?
Sermons, creeds, theology — but the fathomless human brain,
And what is reason? and what is love? and what is life?   1095

43

I do not despise you priests, all time, the world over,
My faith is the greatest of faiths and the least of faiths,

---

73. **trestles of death:** Supports upon which coffins are placed.
74. **dimes on the eyes:** Coins were used to keep the eyes of the dead closed.

Enclosing worship ancient and modern and all between ancient and modern,
Believing I shall come again upon the earth after five thousand years,
Waiting responses from oracles, honoring the gods, saluting the sun,   1100
Making a fetich of the first rock or stump, powowing with sticks in the circle of
    obis,75
Helping the llama or brahmin as he trims the lamps of the idols,
Dancing yet through the streets in a phallic procession, rapt and austere in the
    woods a gymnosophist,76
Drinking mead from the skull-cap, to Shastas and Vedas admirant, minding the
    Koran,77
Walking the teokallis, spotted with gore from the stone and knife, beating the
    serpent-skin drum,   1105
Accepting the Gospels, accepting him that was crucified, knowing assuredly that
    he is divine,
To the mass kneeling or the puritan's prayer rising, or sitting patiently in a pew,
Ranting and frothing in my insane crisis, or waiting dead-like till my spirit
    arouses me,
Looking forth on pavement and land, or outside of pavement and land,
Belonging to the winders of the circuit of circuits.   1110

One of that centripetal and centrifugal gang I turn and talk like a man leaving
    charges before a journey.

Down-hearted doubters dull and excluded,
Frivolous, sullen, moping, angry, affected, dishearten'd, atheistical,
I know every one of you, I know the sea of torment, doubt, despair and unbelief.

How the flukes splash!   1115
How they contort rapid as lightning, with spasms and spouts of blood!78

Be at peace bloody flukes of doubters and sullen mopers,
I take my place among you as much as among any,
The past is the push of you, me, all, precisely the same,
And what is yet untried and afterward is for you, me, all, precisely the same.   1120

I do not know what is untried and afterward,
But I know it will in its turn prove sufficient, and cannot fail.

Each who passes is consider'd, each who stops is consider'd, not a single one can
    it fail.

---

75. **Making a fetich . . . circle of obis:** A fetich or fetish is an object of worship or a charm; obis or obeahs is a
form of religious belief practiced in Africa and the West Indies.
76. **gymnosophist:** Member of an ancient Hindu sect.
77. **Shastas . . . Koran:** Shastas and Vedas are ancient Hindu books; the Koran is the sacred text of Islam.
78. **How the flukes . . . spouts of blood:** Flukes are the tail fins of a whale, whose death throes are here used
metaphorically to suggest the torment of the "doubters."

It cannot fail the young man who died and was buried,
Nor the young woman who died and was put by his side,   1125
Nor the little child that peep'd in at the door, and then drew back and was never
  seen again,
Nor the old man who has lived without purpose, and feels it with bitterness worse
  than gall,
Nor him in the poor house tubercled by rum and the bad disorder,
Nor the numberless slaughter'd and wreck'd, nor the brutish koboo[79] call'd the
  ordure of humanity,
Nor the sacs merely floating with open mouths for food to slip in,   1130
Nor any thing in the earth, or down in the oldest graves of the earth,
Nor any thing in the myriads of spheres, nor the myriads of myriads that inhabit
  them,
Nor the present, nor the least wisp that is known.

44

It is time to explain myself — let us stand up.

What is known I strip away,   1135
I launch all men and women forward with me into the Unknown.

The clock indicates the moment — but what does eternity indicate?

We have thus far exhausted trillions of winters and summers,
There are trillions ahead, and trillions ahead of them.

Births have brought us richness and variety,   1140
And other births will bring us richness and variety.

I do not call one greater and one smaller,
That which fills its period and place is equal to any.

Were mankind murderous or jealous upon you, my brother, my sister?
I am sorry for you, they are not murderous or jealous upon me,   1145
All has been gentle with me, I keep no account with lamentation,
(What have I to do with lamentation?)

I am an acme of things accomplish'd, and I an encloser of things to be.

My feet strike an apex of the apices of the stairs,
On every step bunches of ages, and larger bunches between the steps,   1150
All below duly travel'd, and still I mount and mount.

---

79. **koboo:** Native of Sumatra, an island of Indonesia.

Rise after rise bow the phantoms behind me,
Afar down I see the huge first Nothing, I know I was even there,
I waited unseen and always, and slept through the lethargic mist,
And took my time, and took no hurt from the fetid carbon.   1155

Long I was hugg'd close — long and long.

Immense have been the preparations for me,
Faithful and friendly the arms that have help'd me.

Cycles ferried my cradle, rowing and rowing like cheerful boatmen,
For room to me stars kept aside in their own rings,   1160
They sent influences to look after what was to hold me.

Before I was born out of my mother generations guided me,
My embryo has never been torpid, nothing could overlay it.

For it the nebula cohered to an orb,
The long slow strata piled to rest it on,   1165
Vast vegetables gave it sustenance,
Monstrous sauroids transported it in their mouths and deposited it with care.[80]

All forces have been steadily employ'd to complete and delight me,
Now on this spot I stand with my robust soul.

45

O span of youth! ever-push'd elasticity!   1170
O manhood, balanced, florid and full.

My lovers suffocate me,
Crowding my lips, thick in the pores of my skin,
Jostling me through streets and public halls, coming naked to me at night,
Crying by day *Ahoy!* from the rocks of the river, swinging and chirping over my
        head,   1175
Calling my name from flower-beds, vines, tangled underbrush,
Lighting on every moment of my life,
Bussing[81] my body with soft balsamic busses,
Noiselessly passing handfuls out of their hearts and giving them to be mine.

Old age superbly rising! O welcome, ineffable grace of dying days!   1180

Every condition promulges[82] not only itself, it promulges what grows after and out
        of itself,

---

80. **Monstrous sauroids . . . care:** According to legend, Sauria – prehistoric reptiles – carried their eggs in
their mouths.
81. **Bussing:** Kissing.
82. **promulges:** Promulgates; announces.

And the dark hush promulges as much as any.

I open my scuttle[83] at night and see the far-sprinkled systems,
And all I see multiplied as high as I can cipher edge but the rim of the farther
    systems.

Wider and wider they spread, expanding, always expanding,   1185
Outward and outward and forever outward.

My sun has his sun and round him obediently wheels,
He joins with his partners a group of superior circuit,
And greater sets follow, making specks of the greatest inside them.

There is no stoppage and never can be stoppage,   1190
If I, you, and the worlds, and all beneath or upon their surfaces, were this moment
    reduced back to a pallid float,[84] it would not avail in the long run.

We should surely bring up again where we now stand,
And surely go as much farther, and then farther and farther.

A few quadrillions of eras, a few octillions of cubic leagues, do not hazard the
    span or make it impatient,
They are but parts, any thing is but a part.   1195

See ever so far, there is limitless space outside of that,
Count ever so much, there is limitless time around that.

My rendezvous is appointed, it is certain,
The Lord will be there and wait till I come on perfect terms,
The great Camerado, the lover true for whom I pine will be there.   1200

46

I know I have the best of time and space, and was never measured and never will
    be measured.

I tramp a perpetual journey, (come listen all!)
My signs are a rain-proof coat, good shoes, and a staff cut from the woods,
No friend of mine takes his ease in my chair,
I have no chair, no church, no philosophy,   1205
I lead no man to a dinner-table, library, exchange,[85]
But each man and each woman of you I lead upon a knoll,
My left hand hooking you round the waist,
My right hand pointing to landscapes of continents and the public road.

---

83. **scuttle:** A small opening in the wall or roof of a house.
84. **pallid float:** That is, the period before the formation of the solar system.
85. **exchange:** Stock exchange.

Not I, not any one else can travel that road for you,   1210
You must travel it for yourself.

It is not far, it is within reach,
Perhaps you have been on it since you were born and did not know,
Perhaps it is everywhere on water and on land.

Shoulder your duds dear son, and I will mine, and let us hasten forth,   1215
Wonderful cities and free nations we shall fetch as we go.

If you tire, give me both burdens, and rest the chuff[86] of your hand on my hip,
And in due time you shall repay the same service to me,
For after we start we never lie by again.

This day before dawn I ascended a hill and look'd at the crowded heaven,   1220
And I said to my spirit *When we become the enfolders of those orbs, and the*
     pleasure and knowledge of every thing in them, shall we be fill'd and satisfied
     then?
And my spirit said *No, we but level that lift to pass and continue beyond.*

You are also asking me questions and I hear you,
I answer that I cannot answer, you must find out for yourself.

Sit a while dear son,   1225
Here are biscuits to eat and here is milk to drink,
But as soon as you sleep and renew yourself in sweet clothes, I kiss you with a
     good-by kiss and open the gate for your egress hence.

Long enough have you dream'd contemptible dreams,
Now I wash the gum from your eyes,
You must habit yourself to the dazzle of the light and of every moment of your life.   1230

Long have you timidly waded holding a plank by the shore,
Now I will you to be a bold swimmer,
To jump off in the midst of the sea, rise again, nod to me, shout, and laughingly
     dash with your hair.

47

I am the teacher of athletes,
He that by me spreads a wider breast than my own proves the width of my own,   1235
He most honors my style who learns under it to destroy the teacher.

The boy I love, the same becomes a man not through derived power, but in his own
     right,
Wicked rather than virtuous out of conformity or fear,

---

86. **chuff**: Palm.

Fond of his sweetheart, relishing well his steak,
Unrequited love or a slight cutting him worse than sharp steel cuts,   1240
First-rate to ride, to fight, to hit the bull's eye, to sail a skiff, to sing a song or play
    on the banjo,
Preferring scars and the beard and faces pitted with small-pox over all latherers,
And those well-tann'd to those that keep out of the sun.

I teach straying from me, yet who can stray from me?
I follow you whoever you are from the present hour,   1245
My words itch at your ears till you understand them.

I do not say these things for a dollar or to fill up the time while I wait for a boat,
(It is you talking just as much as myself, I act as the tongue of you,
Tied in your mouth, in mine it begins to be loosen'd.)

I swear I will never again mention love or death inside a house,   1250
And I swear I will never translate myself at all, only to him or her who privately
    stays with me in the open air.

If you would understand me go to the heights or water-shore,
The nearest gnat is an explanation, and a drop or motion of waves a key,
The maul, the oar, the hand-saw, second my words.

No shutter'd room or school can commune with me,   1255
But roughs and little children better than they.

The young mechanic is closest to me, he knows me well,
The woodman that takes his axe and jug with him shall take me with him all day,
The farm-boy ploughing in the field feels good at the sound of my voice,
In vessels that sail my words sail, I go with fishermen and seamen and love them.   1260

The soldier camp'd or upon the march is mine,
On the night ere the pending battle many seek me, and I do not fail them,
On that solemn night (it may be their last) those that know me seek me.

My face rubs to the hunter's face when he lies down alone in his blanket,
The driver thinking of me does not mind the jolt of his wagon,   1265
The young mother and old mother comprehend me,
The girl and the wife rest the needle a moment and forget where they are,
They and all would resume what I have told them.

48

I have said that the soul is not more than the body,
And I have said that the body is not more than the soul,   1270
And nothing, not God, is greater to one than one's self is,
And whoever walks a furlong without sympathy walks to his own funeral drest in
    his shroud,

And I or you pocketless of a dime may purchase the pick of the earth,
And to glance with an eye or show a bean in its pod confounds the learning of all
    times,
And there is no trade or employment but the young man following it may become
    a hero,   1275
And there is no object so soft but it makes a hub for the wheel'd universe,
And I say to any man or woman, Let your soul stand cool and composed before a
    million universes.

And I say to mankind, Be not curious about God,
For I who am curious about each am not curious about God,
(No array of terms can say how much I am at peace about God and about death.)   1280

I hear and behold God on every object, yet understand God not in the least,
Nor do I understand who there can be more wonderful than myself.

Why should I wish to see God better than this day?
I see something of God each hour of the twenty-four, and each moment then,
In the faces of men and women I see God, and in my own face in the glass,   1285
I find letters from God dropt in the street, and every one is sign'd by God's name,
And I leave them where they are, for I know that wheresoe'er I go,
Others will punctually come for ever and ever.

49

And as to you Death, and you bitter hug of mortality, it is idle to try to alarm me.

To his work without flinching the accoucheur[87] comes,   1290
I see the elder-hand pressing receiving supporting,
I recline by the sills of the exquisite flexible doors,
And mark the outlet, and mark the relief and escape.

And as to you Corpse I think you are good manure, but that does not offend me,
I smell the white roses sweet-scented and growing,   1295
I reach to the leafy lips, I reach to the polish'd breasts of melons.

And as to you Life I reckon you are the leavings of many deaths,
(No doubt I have died myself ten thousand times before.)

I hear you whispering there O stars of heaven,
O suns – O grass of graves – O perpetual transfers and promotions,   1300
If you do not say any thing how can I say any thing?

Of the turbid pool that lies in the autumn forest,
Of the moon that descends the steeps of the soughing twilight,

---

87. **accoucheur:** Early French term for an obstetrician or midwife.

Toss, sparkles of day and dusk — toss on the black stems that decay in the muck,
Toss to the moaning gibberish of the dry limbs.   1305

I ascend from the moon, I ascend from the night,
I perceive that the ghastly glimmer is noonday sunbeams reflected,
And debouch[88] to the steady and central from the offspring great or small.

50

There is that in me — I do not know what it is — but I know it is in me.

Wrench'd and sweaty — calm and cool then my body becomes,   1310
I sleep — I sleep long.

I do not know it — it is without name — it is a word unsaid,
It is not in any dictionary, utterance, symbol.

Something it swings on more than the earth I swing on,
To it the creation is the friend whose embracing awakes me.   1315

Perhaps I might tell more. Outlines! I plead for my brothers and sisters.

Do you see O my brothers and sisters?
It is not chaos or death — it is form, union, plan — it is eternal life — it is
    Happiness.

51

The past and present wilt — I have fill'd them, emptied them,
And proceed to fill my next fold of the future.   1320

Listener up there! what have you to confide to me?
Look in my face while I snuff the sidle of evening,[89]
(Talk honestly, no one else hears you, and I stay only a minute longer.)

Do I contradict myself?
Very well then I contradict myself,   1325
(I am large, I contain multitudes.)

I concentrate toward them that are nigh, I wait on the door-slab.

Who has done his day's work? who will soonest be through with his supper?
Who wishes to walk with me?

Will you speak before I am gone? will you prove already too late?   1330

---

88. **debouch:** Emerge, often in the sense of issuing from a confined into an open area.
89. **snuff the sidle of evening:** To extinguish — in the sense of "snuffing out" a candle — the last, sidelong, or fading light of day.

52

The spotted hawk swoops by and accuses me, he complains of my gab and my
    loitering.

I too am not a bit tamed, I too am untranslatable,
I sound my barbaric yawp over the roofs of the world.

The last scud[90] of day holds back for me,
It flings my likeness after the rest and true as any on the shadow'd wilds,   1335
It coaxes me to the vapor and the dusk.

I depart as air, I shake my white locks at the runaway sun,
I effuse my flesh in eddies, and drift it in lacy jags,[91]

I bequeath myself to the dirt to grow from the grass I love,
If you want me again look for me under your boot-soles.   1340

You will hardly know who I am or what I mean,
But I shall be good health to you nevertheless,
And filter and fibre your blood.

Failing to fetch me at first keep encouraged,
Missing me one place search another,   1345
I stop somewhere waiting for you.

                [1855, 1891–92]

---

90. **scud:** A gust of wind or wind-driven clouds and mist.
91. **I effuse . . . lacy jags:** To *effuse* is to pour out or pour forth; *jags* are fragments, scraps, or tatters.

From CHILDREN OF ADAM

ONCE I PASS'D THROUGH A POPULOUS CITY

Once I pass'd through a populous city imprinting my brain for future use with its
    shows, architecture, customs, traditions,
Yet now of all that city I remember only a woman I casually met there who
    detain'd me for love of me,
Day by day and night by night we were together — all else has long been forgotten
    by me,
I remember I say only that woman who passionately clung to me,
Again we wander, we love, we separate again,
Again she holds me by the hand, I must not go,
I see her close beside me with silent lips sad and tremulous.

                [1860, 1891–92]

AS ADAM EARLY IN THE MORNING

As Adam early in the morning,
Walking forth from the bower refresh'd with sleep,
Behold me where I pass, hear my voice, approach,
Touch me, touch the palm of your hand to my body as I pass,
Be not afraid of my body.

[1860, 1891-92]

From CALAMUS[1]

IN PATHS UNTRODDEN

In paths untrodden,
In the growth by margins of pond-waters,
Escaped from the life that exhibits itself,
From all the standards hitherto publish'd, from the pleasures, profits,
    conformities,
Which too long I was offering to feed my soul,   5
Clear to me now standards not yet publish'd, clear to me that my soul,
That the soul of the man I speak for rejoices in comrades,
Here by myself away from the clank of the world,
Tallying and talk'd to here by tongues aromatic,
Breast-sorrel and pinks of love, fingers that wind around tighter than vines,   10
Gushes from the throats of birds hid in the foliage of trees as the sun is risen,
Breezes of land and love set from living shores to you on the living sea, to you
    O sailors!
Frost-mellow'd berries and Third-month twigs offer'd fresh to young persons
    wandering out in the fields when the winter breaks up,
Love-buds put before you and within you whoever you are,
Buds to be unfolded on the old terms,   15
If you bring the warmth of the sun to them they will open and bring form, color,
    perfume, to you,
If you become the aliment and the wet they will become flowers, fruits, tall
    branches and trees.

[1860, 1891-92]

---

1. CALAMUS: Another term for sweet-flag, an aromatic grass whose erect spears sometimes grow to as much as three feet in height.

CITY OF ORGIES

City of orgies, walks and joys,
City whom that I have lived and sung in your midst will one day make you
    illustrious,
Not the pageants of you, not your shifting tableaus, your spectacles, repay me,
Not the interminable rows of your houses, nor the ships at the wharves,
Nor the processions in the streets, nor the bright windows with goods in them,
Nor to converse with learn'd persons, or bear my share in the soiree or feast;
Not those, but as I pass O Manhattan, your frequent and swift flash of eyes
    offering me love,
Offering response to my own — these repay me,
Lovers, continual lovers, only repay me.

[1860, 1891-92]

I SAW IN LOUISIANA A LIVE-OAK GROWING

I saw in Louisiana a live-oak growing,
All alone stood it and the moss hung down from the branches,
Without any companion it grew there uttering joyous leaves of dark green,
And its look, rude, unbending, lusty, made me think of myself,
But I wonder'd how it could utter joyous leaves standing alone there without its
    friend near, for I knew I could not,   5
And I broke off a twig with a certain number of leaves upon it, and twined around
    it a little moss,
And brought it away, and I have placed it in sight in my room,
It is not needed to remind me as of my own dear friends,
(For I believe lately I think of little else than of them,)
Yet it remains to me a curious token, it makes me think of manly love;   10
For all that, and though the live-oak glistens there in Louisiana solitary in a wide
    flat space,
Uttering joyous leaves all its life without a friend a lover near,
I know very well I could not.

[1860, 1891-92]

HERE THE FRAILEST LEAVES OF ME

Here the frailest leaves of me and yet my strongest lasting,
Here I shade and hide my thoughts, I myself do not expose them,
And yet they expose me more than all my other poems.

[1860, 1891-92]

From SEA-DRIFT

OUT OF THE CRADLE ENDLESSLY ROCKING[1]

Out of the cradle endlessly rocking,
Out of the mocking-bird's throat, the musical shuttle,
Out of the Ninth-month[2] midnight,
Over the sterile sands and the fields beyond, where the child leaving his bed
    wander'd alone, bareheaded, barefoot,
Down from the shower'd halo,   5
Up from the mystic play of shadows twining and twisting as if they were alive,
Out from the patches of briers and blackberries,
From the memories of the bird that chanted to me,
From your memories sad brother, from the fitful risings and fallings I heard,
From under that yellow half-moon late-risen and swollen as if with tears,   10
From those beginning notes of yearning and love there in the mist,
From the thousand responses of my heart never to cease,
From the myriad thence-arous'd words,
From the word stronger and more delicious than any,
From such as now they start the scene revisiting,   15
As a flock, twittering, rising, or overhead passing,
Borne hither, ere all eludes me, hurriedly,
A man, yet by these tears a little boy again,
Throwing myself on the sand, confronting the waves,
I, chanter of pains and joys, uniter of here and hereafter,   20
Taking all hints to use them, but swiftly leaping beyond them,
A reminiscence sing.

Once Paumanok,[3]
When the lilac-scent was in the air and Fifth-month grass was growing,
Up this seashore in some briers,   25
Two feather'd guests from Alabama, two together,
And their nest, and four light-green eggs spotted with brown,
And every day the he-bird to and fro near at hand,
And every day the she-bird crouch'd on her nest, silent, with bright eyes,
And every day I, a curious boy, never too close, never disturbing them,   30
Cautiously peering, absorbing, translating.

---

1. **"Out of the Cradle Endlessly Rocking"**: This poem was first published as "A Child's Reminiscence" in the *New York Saturday Press* on December 24, 1859. An editorial notice in the weekly newspaper noted that "Our readers may, if they choose, consider as our Christmas or New Year's present to them [this] curious warble, by Walt Whitman." The poem was titled "A Word Out of the Sea" in the 1860 and 1867 editions and "Out of the Cradle Endlessly Rocking" in all later editions of *Leaves of Grass*.
2. **Ninth-month**: September. Whitman followed the practice of the Quakers, who referred to the days and months by their numbers because they objected to using names derived from pagan deities.
3. **Paumanok**: Native American name for Long Island.

Shine! shine! shine!
Pour down your warmth, great sun!
While we bask, we two together.

Two together!   35
Winds blow south, or winds blow north,
Day come white, or night come black,
Home, or rivers and mountains from home,
Singing all time, minding no time,
While we two keep together.   40

Till of a sudden,
May-be kill'd, unknown to her mate,
One forenoon the she-bird crouch'd not on the nest,
Nor return'd that afternoon, nor the next,
Nor ever appear'd again.   45

And thenceforward all summer in the sound of the sea,
And at night under the full of the moon in calmer weather,
Over the hoarse surging of the sea,
Or flitting from brier to brier by day,
I saw, I heard at intervals the remaining one, the he-bird,   50
The solitary guest from Alabama.

Blow! blow! blow!
Blow up sea-winds along Paumanok's shore;
I wait and I wait till you blow my mate to me.

Yes, when the stars glisten'd,   55
All night long on the prong of a moss-scallop'd stake,
Down almost amid the slapping waves,
Sat the lone singer wonderful causing tears.

He call'd on his mate,
He pour'd forth the meanings which I of all men know.   60

Yes my brother I know,
The rest might not, but I have treasur'd every note,
For more than once dimly down to the beach gliding,
Silent, avoiding the moonbeams, blending myself with the shadows,
Recalling now the obscure shapes, the echoes, the sounds and sights after their
    sorts,   65
The white arms out in the breakers tirelessly tossing,
I, with bare feet, a child, the wind wafting my hair,
Listen'd long and long.

Listen'd to keep, to sing, now translating the notes,
Following you my brother.   70

Soothe! soothe! soothe!
Close on its wave soothes the wave behind,
And again another behind embracing and lapping, every one close,
But my love soothes not me, not me.

Low hangs the moon, it rose late,   75
It is lagging — O I think it is heavy with love, with love.

O madly the sea pushes upon the land,
With love, with love.

O night! do I not see my love fluttering out among the breakers?
What is that little black thing I see there in the white?   80

Loud! loud! loud!
Loud I call to you, my love!

High and clear I shoot my voice over the waves,
Surely you must know who is here, is here,
You must know who I am, my love.   85

Low-hanging moon!
What is that dusky spot in your brown yellow?
O it is the shape, the shape of my mate!
O moon do not keep her from me any longer.

Land! land! O land!   90
Whichever way I turn, O I think you could give me my mate back again if you
* only would,*
For I am almost sure I see her dimly whichever way I look.

O rising stars!
Perhaps the one I want so much will rise, will rise with some of you.

O throat! O trembling throat!   95
Sound clearer through the atmosphere!
Pierce the woods, the earth,
Somewhere listening to catch you must be the one I want.

Shake out carols!
Solitary here, the night's carols!   100
Carols of lonesome love! death's carols!
Carols under that lagging, yellow, waning moon!
O under that moon where she droops almost down into the sea!
O reckless despairing carols.

But soft! sink low!   105
Soft! let me just murmur,
And do you wait a moment you husky-nois'd sea,
For somewhere I believe I heard my mate responding to me,

So faint, I must be still, be still to listen,
But not altogether still, for then she might not come immediately to me.   110

Hither my love!
Here I am! here!
With this just-sustain'd note I announce myself to you,
This gentle call is for you my love, for you.

Do not be decoy'd elsewhere,   115
That is the whistle of the wind, it is not my voice,
That is the fluttering, the fluttering of the spray,
Those are the shadows of leaves.

O darkness! O in vain!
O I am very sick and sorrowful.   120

O brown halo in the sky near the moon, drooping upon the sea!
O troubled reflection in the sea!
O throat! O throbbing heart!
And I singing uselessly, uselessly all the night.

O past! O happy life! O songs of joy!   125
In the air, in the woods, over fields,
Loved! loved! loved! loved! loved!
But my mate no more, no more with me!
We two together no more.

The aria sinking,   130
All else continuing, the stars shining,
The winds blowing, the notes of the bird continuous echoing,
With angry moans the fierce old mother incessantly moaning,
On the sands of Paumanok's shore gray and rustling,
The yellow half-moon enlarged, sagging down, drooping, the face of the sea
   almost touching,   135
The boy ecstatic, with his bare feet the waves, with his hair the atmosphere
   dallying,
The love in the heart long pent, now loose, now at last tumultuously bursting,
The aria's meaning, the ears, the soul, swiftly depositing,
The strange tears down the cheeks coursing,
The colloquy there, the trio, each uttering,   140
The undertone, the savage old mother incessantly crying,
To the boy's soul's questions sullenly timing, some drown'd secret hissing,
To the outsetting bard.

Demon or bird! (said the boy's soul,)
Is it indeed toward your mate you sing? or is it really to me?   145
For I, that was a child, my tongue's use sleeping, now I have heard you,
Now in a moment I know what I am for, I awake,

And already a thousand singers, a thousand songs, clearer, louder and more
    sorrowful than yours,
A thousand warbling echoes have started to life within me, never to die.

O you singer solitary, singing by yourself, projecting me,   150
O solitary me listening, never more shall I cease perpetuating you,
Never more shall I escape, never more the reverberations,
Never more the cries of unsatisfied love be absent from me,
Never again leave me to be the peaceful child I was before what there in the
    night,
By the sea under the yellow and sagging moon,   155
The messenger there arous'd, the fire, the sweet hell within,
The unknown want, the destiny of me.

O give me the clew! (it lurks in the night here somewhere,)
O if I am to have so much, let me have more!

A word then, (for I will conquer it,)   160
The word final, superior to all,
Subtle, sent up — what is it? — I listen;
Are you whispering it, and have been all the time, you sea-waves?
Is that it from your liquid rims and wet sands?

Whereto answering, the sea,   165
Delaying not, hurrying not,
Whisper'd me through the night, and very plainly before day-break.
Lisp'd to me the low and delicious word death,
And again death, death, death, death,
Hissing melodious, neither like the bird nor like my arous'd child's heart,   170
But edging near as privately for me rustling at my feet,
Creeping thence steadily up to my ears and laving me softly all over,
Death, death, death, death, death.

Which I do not forget,
But fuse the song of my dusky demon and brother,   175
That he sang to me in the moonlight on Paumanok's gray beach,
With the thousand responsive songs at random,
My own songs awaked from that hour,
And with them the key, the word up from the waves,
The word of the sweetest song and all songs,   180
That strong and delicious word which, creeping to my feet,
(Or like some old crone rocking the cradle, swathed in sweet garments, bending
    aside,)
The sea whisper'd me.

                                  [1860, 1891-92]

From DRUM-TAPS

BEAT! BEAT! DRUMS!

Beat! beat! drums! — blow! bugles! blow!
Through the windows — through doors — burst like a ruthless force,
Into the solemn church, and scatter the congregation,
Into the school where the scholar is studying;
Leave not the bridegroom quiet — no happiness must he have now with his bride,   5
Nor the peaceful farmer any peace, ploughing his field or gathering his grain,
So fierce you whirr and pound you drums — so shrill you bugles blow.

Beat! beat! drums! — blow! bugles! blow!
Over the traffic of cities — over the rumble of wheels in the streets;
Are beds prepared for sleepers at night in the houses? no sleepers must sleep in
     those beds,   10
No bargainers' bargains by day — no brokers or speculators — would they
     continue?
Would the talkers be talking? would the singer attempt to sing?
Would the lawyer rise in the court to state his case before the judge?
Then rattle quicker, heavier drums — you bugles wilder blow.

Beat! beat! drums! — blow! bugles! blow!   15
Make no parley — stop for no expostulation,
Mind not the timid — mind not the weeper or prayer,
Mind not the old man beseeching the young man,
Let not the child's voice be heard, nor the mother's entreaties,
Make even the trestles to shake the dead where they lie awaiting the hearses,   20
So strong you thump O terrible drums — so loud you bugles blow.

[1865, 1891-92]

CAVALRY CROSSING A FORD

A line in long array here they wind betwixt green islands,
They take a serpentine course, their arms flash in the sun — hark to the musical
     clank,
Behold the silvery river, in it the splashing horses loitering stop to drink,
Behold the brown-faced men, each group, each person a picture, the negligent
     rest on the saddles,
Some emerge on the opposite bank, others are just entering the ford — while,
Scarlet and blue and snowy white,
The guidon flags[1] flutter gayly in the wind.

[1865, 1891-92]

---

1. **guidon flags:** Small flags or standards used to signify the designation of a military unit.

VIGIL STRANGE I KEPT ON THE FIELD ONE NIGHT

Vigil strange I kept on the field one night;
When you my son and my comrade dropt at my side that day,
One look I but gave which your dear eyes return'd with a look I shall never forget,
One touch of your hand to mine O boy, reach'd up as you lay on the ground,
Then onward I sped in the battle, the even-contested battle,   5
Till late in the night reliev'd to the place at last again I made my way,
Found you in death so cold dear comrade, found your body son of responding
    kisses, (never again on earth responding,)
Bared your face in the starlight, curious the scene, cool blew the moderate
    night-wind,
Long there and then in vigil I stood, dimly around me the battle-field spreading,
Vigil wondrous and vigil sweet there in the fragrant silent night,   10
But not a tear fell, not even a long-drawn sigh, long, long I gazed,
Then on the earth partially reclining sat by your side leaning my chin in my
    hands,
Passing sweet hours, immortal and mystic hours with you dearest comrade — not
    a tear, not a word,
Vigil of silence, love and death, vigil for you my son and my soldier,
As onward silently stars aloft, eastward new ones upward stole,   15
Vigil final for you brave boy, (I could not save you, swift was your death,
I faithfully loved you and cared for you living, I think we shall surely meet
    again,)
Till at latest lingering of the night, indeed just as the dawn appear'd,
My comrade I wrapt in his blanket, envelop'd well his form,
Folded the blanket well, tucking it carefully over head and carefully under feet,   20
And there and then and bathed by the rising sun, my son in his grave, in his
    rude-dug grave I deposited,
Ending my vigil strange with that, vigil of night and battle-field dim,
Vigil for boy of responding kisses, (never again on earth responding,)
Vigil for comrade swiftly slain, vigil I never forget, how as day brighten'd,
I rose from the chill ground and folded my soldier well in his blanket,   25
And buried him where he fell.

[1865, 1891–92]

A SIGHT IN CAMP IN THE DAYBREAK GRAY AND DIM

A sight in camp in the daybreak gray and dim,
As from my tent I emerge so early sleepless,
As slow I walk in the cool fresh air the path near by the hospital tent,

Three forms I see on stretchers lying, brought out there untended lying,
Over each the blanket spread, ample brownish woolen blanket,
Gray and heavy blanket, folding, covering all.

Curious I halt and silent stand,
Then with light fingers I from the face of the nearest the first just lift the blanket;
Who are you elderly man so gaunt and grim, with well-gray'd hair, and flesh all
    sunken about the eyes?
Who are you my dear comrade?

Then to the second I step — and who are you my child and darling?
Who are you sweet boy with cheeks yet blooming?

Then to the third — a face nor child nor old, very calm, as of beautiful yellow-white
    ivory;
Young man I think I know you — I think this face is the face of the Christ himself,
Dead and divine and brother of all, and here again he lies.

[1865, 1891-92]

THE WOUND-DRESSER

1

An old man bending I come among new faces,
Years looking backward resuming in answer to children,
Come tell us old man, as from young men and maidens that love me,
(Arous'd and angry, I'd thought to beat the alarum, and urge relentless war,
But soon my fingers fail'd me, my face droop'd and I resign'd myself,
To sit by the wounded and soothe them, or silently watch the dead;)
Years hence of these scenes, of these furious passions, these chances,
Of unsurpass'd heroes, (was one side so brave? the other was equally brave;)
Now be witness again, paint the mightiest armies of earth,
Of those armies so rapid so wondrous what saw you to tell us?
What stays with you latest and deepest? of curious panics,
Of hard-fought engagements or sieges tremendous what deepest remains?

2

O maidens and young men I love and that love me,
What you ask of my days those the strangest and sudden your talking recalls,
Soldier alert I arrive after a long march cover'd with sweat and dust,
In the nick of time I come, plunge in the fight, loudly shout in the rush of
    successful charge,

Enter the captur'd works¹ — yet lo, like a swift-running river they fade,
Pass and are gone they fade — I dwell not on soldiers' perils or soldiers' joys,
(Both I remember well — many the hardships, few the joys, yet I was content.)

But in silence, in dreams' projections,   20
While the world of gain and appearance and mirth goes on,
So soon what is over forgotten, and waves wash the imprints off, the sand,
With hinged knees returning I enter the doors, (while for you up there,
Whoever you are, follow without noise and be of strong heart.)

Bearing the bandages, water and sponge,   25
Straight and swift to my wounded I go,
Where they lie on the ground after the battle brought in,
Where their priceless blood reddens the grass the ground,
Or to the rows of the hospital tent, or under the roof'd hospital,
To the long rows of cots up and down each side I return,   30
To each and all one after another I draw near, not one do I miss,
An attendant follows holding a tray, he carries a refuse pail,
Soon to be fill'd with clotted rags and blood, emptied, and fill'd again.

I onward go, I stop,
With hinged knees and steady hand to dress wounds,   35
I am firm with each, the pangs are sharp yet unavoidable,
One turns to me his appealing eyes — poor boy! I never knew you,
Yet I think I could not refuse this moment to die for you, if that would save you.

                                    3

On, on I go, (open doors of time! open hospital doors!)
The crush'd head I dress, (poor crazed hand tear not the bandage away,)   40
The neck of the cavalry-man with the bullet through and through I examine,
Hard the breathing rattles, quite glazed already the eye, yet life struggles hard,
(Come sweet death! be persuaded O beautiful death!
In mercy come quickly.)

From the stump of the arm, the amputated hand,   45
I undo the clotted lint, remove the slough, wash off the matter and blood,
Back on his pillow the soldier bends with curv'd neck and side-falling head,
His eyes are closed, his face is pale, he dares not look on the bloody stump,
And has not yet look'd on it.

---

1. **captur'd works:** Breastworks; usually earthwork thrown up to breast height as a temporary fortification.

I dress a wound in the side, deep, deep,   50
But a day or two more, for see the frame all wasted and sinking,
And the yellow-blue countenance see.

I dress the perforated shoulder, the foot with the bullet-wound,
Cleanse the one with a gnawing and putrid gangrene, so sickening, so offensive,
While the attendant stands behind aside me holding the tray and pail.   55

I am faithful, I do not give out,
The fractur'd thigh, the knee, the wound in the abdomen,
These and more I dress with impassive hand, (yet deep in my breast a fire, a burning
    flame.)

                                    4

Thus in silence in dreams' projections,
Returning, resuming, I thread my way through the hospitals,   60
The hurt and wounded I pacify with soothing hand,
I sit by the restless all the dark night, some are so young,
Some suffer so much, I recall the experience sweet and sad,
(Many a soldier's loving arms about this neck have cross'd and rested,
Many a soldier's kiss dwells on these bearded lips.)   65

                                                          [1865, 1891-92]

RECONCILIATION

Word over all, beautiful as the sky,
Beautiful that war and all its deeds of carnage must in time be utterly lost,
That the hands of the sisters Death and Night incessantly softly wash again, and ever
    again, this soil'd world;
For my enemy is dead, a man divine as myself is dead,
I look where he lies white-faced and still in the coffin — I draw near,
Bend down and touch lightly with my lips the white face in the coffin.

                                                          [1865-66, 1891-92]

———

From MEMORIES OF PRESIDENT LINCOLN

WHEN LILACS LAST IN THE DOORYARD BLOOM'D[1]

1

When lilacs last in the dooryard bloom'd,
And the great star[2] early droop'd in the western sky in the night,
I mourn'd, and yet shall mourn with ever-returning spring.

Ever-returning spring, trinity sure to me you bring,
Lilac blooming perennial and drooping star in the west,   5
And thought of him I love.

2

O powerful western fallen star!
O shades of night — O moody, tearful night!
O great star disappear'd — O the black murk that hides the star!
O cruel hands that hold me powerless — O helpless soul of me!   10
O harsh surrounding cloud that will not free my soul.

3

In the dooryard fronting an old farm-house near the white-wash'd palings,
Stands the lilac-bush tall-growing with heart-shaped leaves of rich green,
With many a pointed blossom rising delicate, with the perfume strong I love,
With every leaf a miracle — and from this bush in the dooryard,   15
With delicate-color'd blossoms and heart-shaped leaves of rich green,
A sprig with its flower I break.

4

In the swamp in secluded recesses,
A shy and hidden bird is warbling a song.

---

1. **"When Lilacs Last in the Dooryard Bloom'd"**: Whitman wrote his elegy to Abraham Lincoln in the weeks following the president's assassination on April 14, 1865. The poem was first published in a "Sequel" to *Drum-Taps* (1865), Whitman's collection of poetry on the Civil War. He later incorporated it into *Leaves of Grass*, initially in a cluster headed "President Lincoln's Burial Hymn" and later titled "Memories of President Lincoln."
2. **great star**: Venus.

Solitary the thrush, 20
The hermit withdrawn to himself, avoiding the settlements,
Sings by himself a song.

Song of the bleeding throat,
Death's outlet song of life, (for well dear brother I know,
If thou wast not granted to sing thou would'st surely die.) 25

5

Over the breast of the spring, the land, amid cities,
Amid lanes and through old woods, where lately the violets peep'd from the
    ground, spotting the gray debris,
Amid the grass in the fields each side of the lanes, passing the endless grass,
Passing the yellow-spear'd wheat, every grain from its shroud in the dark-brown
    fields uprisen,
Passing the apple-tree blows[3] of white and pink in the orchards, 30
Carrying a corpse to where it shall rest in the grave,
Night and day journeys a coffin.[4]

6

Coffin that passes through lanes and streets,
Through day and night with the great cloud darkening the land,
With the pomp of the inloop'd flags with the cities draped in black, 35
With the show of the States themselves as of crape-veil'd women standing,
With processions long and winding and the flambeaus[5] of the night,
With the countless torches lit, with the silent sea of faces and the unbared heads,
With the waiting depot, the arriving coffin, and the sombre faces,
With dirges through the night, with the thousand voices rising strong and
    solemn, 40
With all the mournful voices of the dirges pour'd around the coffin,
The dim-lit churches and the shuddering organs — where amid these you journey,
With the tolling tolling bells' perpetual clang,
Here, coffin that slowly passes,
I give you my sprig of lilac. 45

---

3. **blows:** Blossoms.
4. **Over . . . journeys a coffin:** After lying in state in Washington, D.C., Lincoln's body was taken by a special train for burial in Springfield, Illinois. The funeral train made numerous stops and was seen by millions of people during its long journey, which retraced the route Lincoln had traveled to his first inauguration in 1861 and which lasted from April 21 to May 3, 1865.
5. **flambeaus:** Flaming torches.

7

(Nor for you, for one alone,
Blossoms and branches green to coffins all I bring,
For fresh as the morning, thus would I chant a song for you O sane and sacred
    death.

All over bouquets of roses,
O death, I cover you over with roses and early lilies,   50
But mostly and now the lilac that blooms the first,
Copious I break, I break the sprigs from the bushes,
With loaded arms I come, pouring for you,
For you and the coffins all of you O death.)

8

O western orb sailing the heaven,   55
Now I know what you must have meant as a month since I walk'd,
As I walk'd in silence the transparent shadowy night,
As I saw you had something to tell as you bent to me night after night,
As you droop'd from the sky low down as if to my side, (while the other stars all
    look'd on,)
As we wander'd together the solemn night, (for something I know not what kept
    me from sleep,)   60
As the night advanced, and I saw on the rim of the west how full you were of woe,
As I stood on the rising ground in the breeze in the cool transparent night,
As I watch'd where you pass'd and was lost in the netherward black of the night,
As my soul in its trouble dissatisfied sank, as where you sad orb,
Concluded, dropt in the night, and was gone.   65

9

Sing on there in the swamp,
O singer bashful and tender, I hear your notes, I hear your call,
I hear, I come presently, I understand you,
But a moment I linger, for the lustrous star has detain'd me,
The star my departing comrade holds and detains me.   70

10

O how shall I warble myself for the dead one there I loved?
And how shall I deck my song for the large sweet soul that has gone?
And what shall my perfume be for the grave of him I love?

Sea-winds blown from east and west,
Blown from the Eastern sea and blown from the Western sea, till there on the
    prairies meeting,   75

These and with these and the breath of my chant,
I'll perfume the grave of him I love.

11

O what shall I hang on the chamber walls?
And what shall the pictures be that I hang on the walls,
To adorn the burial-house of him I love?   80

Pictures of growing spring and farms and homes,
With the Fourth-month[6] eve at sundown, and the gray smoke lucid and bright,
With floods of the yellow gold of the gorgeous, indolent, sinking sun, burning,
    expanding the air,
With the fresh sweet herbage under foot, and the pale green leaves of the trees
    prolific,
In the distance the flowing glaze, the breast of the river, with a wind-dapple here
    and there,   85
With ranging hills on the banks, with many a line against the sky, and shadows,
And the city at hand with dwellings so dense, and stacks of chimneys,
And all the scenes of life and the workshops, and the workmen homeward
    returning.

12

Lo, body and soul — this land,
My own Manhattan with spires, and the sparkling and hurrying tides, and the
    ships,   90
The varied and ample land, the South and the North in the light, Ohio's shores
    and flashing Missouri,
And ever the far-spreading prairies cover'd with grass and corn.

Lo, the most excellent sun so calm and haughty,
The violet and purple morn with just-felt breezes,
The gentle soft-born measureless light,   95
The miracle spreading bathing all, the fulfill'd noon,
The coming eve delicious, the welcome night and the stars,
Over my cities shining all, enveloping man and land.

13

Sing on, sing on you gray-brown bird,
Sing from the swamps, the recesses, pour your chant from the bushes,   100
Limitless out of the dusk, out of the cedars and pines.

---

6. **Fourth-month:** April. Whitman followed the practice of the Quakers, who referred to the days and months by their numbers because they objected to using names derived from pagan deities.

Sing on dearest brother, warble your reedy song,
Loud human song, with voice of uttermost woe.

O liquid and free and tender!
O wild and loose to my soul — O wondrous singer! 105

You only I hear — yet the star holds me, (but will soon depart,)
Yet the lilac with mastering odor holds me.

14

Now while I sat in the day and look'd forth,
In the close of the day with its light and the fields of spring, and the farmers
    preparing their crops,
In the large unconscious scenery of my land with its lakes and forests, 110
In the heavenly aerial beauty, (after the perturb'd winds and the storms,)
Under the arching heavens of the afternoon swift passing, and the voices of
    children and women,
The many-moving sea-tides, and I saw the ships how they sail'd,
And the summer approaching with richness, and the fields all busy with labor,
And the infinite separate houses, how they all went on, each with its meals and
    minutia of daily usages, 115
And the streets how their throbbings throbb'd, and the cities pent — lo, then and
    there,
Falling upon them all and among them all, enveloping me with the rest,
Appear'd the cloud, appear'd the long black trail,
And I knew death, its thought, and the sacred knowledge of death.

Then with the knowledge of death as walking one side of me, 120
And the thought of death close-walking the other side of me,
And I in the middle as with companions, and as holding the hands of
    companions,
I fled forth to the hiding receiving night that talks not,
Down to the shores of the water, the path by the swamp in the dimness,
To the solemn shadowy cedars and ghostly pines so still. 125

And the singer so shy to the rest receiv'd me,
The gray-brown bird I know receiv'd us comrades three,
And he sang the carol of death, and a verse for him I love.

From deep secluded recesses,
From the fragrant cedars and the ghostly pines so still, 130
Came the carol of the bird.

And the charm of the carol rapt me,
As I held as if by their hands my comrades in the night,
And the voice of my spirit tallied the song of the bird.

Come lovely and soothing death,   135
Undulate round the world, serenely arriving, arriving,
In the day, in the night, to all, to each,
Sooner or later delicate death.

Prais'd be the fathomless universe,
For life and joy, and for objects and knowledge curious,   140
And for love, sweet love — but praise! praise! praise!
For the sure-enwinding arms of cool-enfolding death.

Dark mother always gliding near with soft feet,
Have none chanted for thee a chant of fullest welcome?
Then I chant it for thee, I glorify thee above all,   145
I bring thee a song that when thou must indeed come, come unfalteringly.

Approach strong deliveress,
When it is so, when thou hast taken them I joyously sing the dead,
Lost in the loving floating ocean of thee,
Laved in the flood of thy bliss O death.   150

From me to thee glad serenades,
Dances for thee I propose saluting thee, adornments and feastings for thee,
And the sights of the open landscape and the high-spread sky are fitting,
And life and the fields, and the huge and thoughtful night.

The night in silence under many a star,   155
The ocean shore and the husky whispering wave whose voice I know,
And the soul turning to thee O vast and well-veil'd death,
And the body gratefully nestling close to thee.

Over the tree-tops I float thee a song,
Over the rising and sinking waves, over the myriad fields and the prairies
*   wide,*   160
Over the dense-pack'd cities all and the teeming wharves and ways,
I float this carol with joy, with joy to thee O death.

15

To the tally of my soul,
Loud and strong kept up the gray-brown bird,
With pure deliberate notes spreading filling the night.   165

Loud in the pines and cedars dim,
Clear in the freshness moist and the swamp-perfume,
And I with my comrades there in the night.

While my sight that was bound in my eyes unclosed,
As to long panoramas of visions.   170

And I saw askant[7] the armies,
I saw as in noiseless dreams hundreds of battle-flags,
Borne through the smoke of the battles and pierc'd with missiles I saw them,
And carried hither and yon through the smoke, and torn and bloody,
And at last but a few shreds left on the staffs, (and all in silence,)   175
And the staffs all splinter'd and broken.

I saw battle-corpses, myriads of them,
And the white skeletons of young men, I saw them,
I saw the debris and debris of all the slain soldiers of the war,
But I saw they were not as was thought,   180
They themselves were fully at rest, they suffer'd not,
The living remain'd and suffer'd, the mother suffer'd,
And the wife and the child and the musing comrade suffer'd,
And the armies that remain'd suffer'd.

16

Passing the visions, passing the night,   185
Passing, unloosing the hold of my comrades' hands,
Passing the song of the hermit bird and the tallying song of my soul,
Victorious song, death's outlet song, yet varying ever-altering song,
As low and wailing, yet clear the notes, rising and falling, flooding the night,
Sadly sinking and fainting, as warning and warning, and yet again bursting with
    joy,   190
Covering the earth and filling the spread of the heaven,
As that powerful psalm in the night I heard from recesses,
Passing, I leave thee lilac with heart-shaped leaves,
I leave thee there in the door-yard, blooming, returning with spring.

I cease from my song for thee,   195
From my gaze on thee in the west, fronting the west, communing with thee,
O comrade lustrous with silver face in the night.

Yet each to keep and all, retrievements out of the night,
The song, the wondrous chant of the gray-brown bird,
And the tallying chant, the echo arous'd in my soul,   200
With the lustrous and drooping star with the countenance full of woe,
With the holders holding my hand nearing the call of the bird,
Comrades mine and I in the midst, and their memory ever to keep, for the dead I
    loved so well,
For the sweetest, wisest soul of all my days and lands — and this for his dear sake,

---

7. **askant:** Early term meaning "sideways" or "obliquely."

Lilac and star and bird twined with the chant of my soul,   205
There in the fragrant pines and the cedars dusk and dim.

[1865-66, 1891-92]

———

From WHISPERS OF HEAVENLY DEATH

A NOISELESS PATIENT SPIDER

A noiseless patient spider,
I mark'd where on a little promontory it stood isolated,
Mark'd how to explore the vacant vast surrounding,
It launch'd forth filament, filament, filament, out of itself,
Ever unreeling them, ever tirelessly speeding them.   5

And you O my soul where you stand,
Surrounded, detached, in measureless oceans of space,
Ceaselessly musing, venturing, throwing, seeking the spheres to connect them,
Till the bridge you will need be form'd, till the ductile anchor hold,
Till the gossamer thread you fling catch somewhere, O my soul.   10

[1868, 1891-92]

———

From SONGS OF PARTING

AS THE TIME DRAWS NIGH

As the time draws nigh glooming a cloud,
A dread beyond of I know not what darkens me.

I shall go forth,
I shall traverse the States awhile, but I cannot tell whither or how long,
Perhaps soon some day or night while I am singing my voice will suddenly cease.

O book, O chants! must all then amount to but this?
Must we barely arrive at this beginning of us? — and yet it is enough, O soul;
O soul, we have positively appear'd — that is enough.

[1860, 1891-92]

Whitman through a Modern Lens

THROUGHOUT HIS LONG LIFE, Walt Whitman sought a wide audience for his writings, especially for *Leaves of Grass*, numerous editions of which he published between 1855 and his death in 1892. But, as a writer for the *Critic* observed in 1881:

> One great anomaly of Whitman's case has been that while he is an aggressive champion of democracy and of the working-man, in a broad sense of the term working-man, his admirers have been almost exclusively of a class the furthest possibly removed from that which labors for daily bread by manual work. Whitman has always been truly caviare to the multitude. It was only those that knew much of poetry and loved it greatly who penetrated the singular shell of his verses and rejoiced in the rich, pulpy kernel.

Certainly his work has had a powerful and profound impact on other American poets, for whom Whitman has been a steady source of inspiration and stimulation. In a poem commemorating Whitman's death in 1892, Edgar Arlington Robinson wrote:

His piercing and eternal cadence rings
Too pure for us — too powerfully pure,
Too lovingly triumphant, and too large;
But there are some that hear him, and they
    know
That he shall sing to-morrow for all men,
And that all time shall listen.

Thomas Eakins, *Walt Whitman*

A friend and admirer of Whitman, Eakins in 1887 made an unannounced visit to the poet's house to paint this portrait. Whitman, in turn, admired the painting for its realistic depiction of him in old age. As he observed, Eakins was the only artist Whitman knew "who could resist the temptation to see what they ought to be rather than what is."

Twentieth-century poets have heard diverse notes in Whitman's verse, some of which are recorded in the following two poems, written at the time of centennial celebrations of the publication of the first edition of *Leaves of Grass* in 1855. The first poem is by Langston Hughes (1902-1967), perhaps the most admired of all African American poets. The text is taken from *Poems: 1951-1967* (2001), in the *Collected Works of Langston Hughes.* The second poem is by Allen Ginsberg (1926-1997), the iconoclastic poet of the Beat generation. The text is taken from his *Collected Poems 1947-1980* (1984).

Langston Hughes

[1902-1967]

OLD WALT

Old Walt Whitman
Went finding and seeking,
Finding less than sought
Seeking more than found,
Every detail minding   5
Of the seeking or the finding.

Pleasured equally
In seeking as in finding,
Each detail minding,
Old Walt went seeking   10
And finding.

[1954, 2001]

Allen Ginsberg

[1926-1997]

A SUPERMARKET IN CALIFORNIA

What thoughts I have of you tonight, Walt Whitman, for I walked down the sidestreets under the trees with a headache self-conscious looking at the full moon.

In my hungry fatigue, and shopping for images, I went into the neon fruit supermarket, dreaming of your enumerations!

What peaches and what penumbras![1] Whole families shopping at night! Aisles full of husbands! Wives in the avocados, babies in the tomatoes! — and you, García Lorca,[2] what were you doing down by the watermelons?

I saw you, Walt Whitman, childless, lonely old grubber, poking among the meats in the refrigerator and eyeing the grocery boys.

I heard you asking questions of each: Who killed the pork chops? What price bananas? Are you my Angel?   5

I wandered in and out of the brilliant stacks of cans following you, and followed in my imagination by the store detective.

We strode down the open corridors together in our solitary fancy tasting artichokes, possessing every frozen delicacy, and never passing the cashier.

Where are we going, Walt Whitman? The doors close in an hour. Which way does your beard point tonight?

(I touch your book and dream of our odyssey in the supermarket and feel absurd.)

Will we walk all night through solitary streets? The trees add shade to shade, lights out in the houses, we'll both be lonely.   10

Will we stroll dreaming of the lost America of love past blue automobiles in driveways, home to our silent cottage?

Ah, dear father, graybeard, lonely old courage-teacher, what America did you have when Charon quit poling his ferry and you got out on a smoking bank and stood watching the boat disappear on the black waters of Lethe?[3]

Berkeley, 1955

[1956, 1984]

---

1. **penumbras:** Partial shadows; things that shroud or obscure.
2. **García Lorca:** Federico García Lorca (1898–1936), Spanish poet and dramatist.
3. **Charon . . . Lethe?:** In Greek mythology, Charon ferried the dead across the Lethe, the river of forgetfulness that flows through the underworld.

Emily Dickinson

[1830-1886]

Emily Dickinson was born on December 10, 1830, in Amherst, Massachusetts. At a time when the country was becoming increasingly urban, Dickinson cherished the rural, small-town atmosphere of Amherst. She left her home there only occasionally: for a year at Mount Holyoke Female Seminary in 1847-48; for trips to Washington, D.C., and Philadelphia with her family; and for short visits to Boston for treatment of ongoing problems with her eyesight. As she grew older, Dickinson was increasingly reluctant to leave her house, called "The Homestead," a large and imposing mansion which had been built by her grandfather in 1813. Dickinson was in her element in her comfortable room on its second floor, where she wrote roughly 1,789 poems and thousands of letters.

Dickinson's world was thoroughly domestic, at least to all outward appearances. Although neither she nor her sister, Lavinia, ever married, they lived together in the midst of family and friends, taking pride in light housekeeping, caring for relatives, and spending time in the substantial gardens surrounding the Homestead. The period of Dickinson's adolescence and young adulthood was a time of religious revivalism in Amherst and throughout New England, but she remained skeptical of conventional religion. She was especially suspicious of the puritanical doctrines of the First Church of Christ, which her mother joined in 1832 and her father and sister joined in 1850. Although she persistently explored religious issues in her poetry, Dickinson resolutely refused to join or attend church, preferring to establish a community for herself in other ways. That community was formed by a wide circle of family members and friends, with whom she enjoyed a lively, extensive correspondence throughout her life. Dickinson's father and her brother, Austin, both attorneys, were deeply involved with Amherst College, which had been founded by her grandfather and others in 1821. The Homestead was consequently a social center in Amherst. When Austin married Dickinson's dearest friend, Susan Gilbert, in 1856, the couple moved into "The Evergreens," the house next door, which had been built by Dickinson's father in order to keep the family close together. During the Civil War, Dickinson was at her most prolific, writing hundreds of poems and corresponding with dozens of new friends,

Emily Dickinson

This daguerreotype was taken between 1846 and 1848, when Dickinson was sixteen or seventeen and a student at the Mount Holyoke Female Seminary.
(Amherst College Archives and Special Collections.)

Emily Dickinson wrote about the kinds of experience few poets have the daring to explore or the genius to sing.

– Galway Kinnell

including prominent writers and reformers such as Thomas Wentworth Higginson and Helen Hunt Jackson.

After the war, Dickinson's life was saddened by the death of those closest to her. Her father died in 1874 and her mother in 1882. In addition, Austin began a long affair with Mabel Loomis Todd. Dickinson, who continued to have an intensely intimate relationship with Austin's wife, "Sue" – as Dickinson called her – found that relationship strained by the inevitable tensions brought about by the increasingly well-known affair. One of the most traumatic events of Dickinson's later years was the death of her beloved eight-year-old nephew, Gilbert, in 1883. Dickinson herself was increasingly ill in these last years and died from kidney disease on May 15, 1886.

Reading Dickinson's Poems.   Although the larger reading public did not have access to Dickinson's poems during her lifetime, she was to become the most widely read woman poet in the United States. At least eleven of Dickinson's poems were published in newspapers and magazines during her lifetime, but her attitude toward publication was complex. "Publication – is the Auction / Of the Mind," she declared in one of her poems (see p. 1059). Yet, as many scholars have pointed out, she "published" her poems by sending them to friends and family members, often enclosed with or incorporated into letters, such as those to Thomas Wentworth Higginson. Of the approximately 1,789 poems we have today, Dickinson sent about one-third of them in letters to friends and relatives, and the proportion is probably much higher since only a small percentage of her letters have survived.

After Dickinson's death, her sister, Lavinia, found more than a thousand poems in her desk, most of them bound into small packets called "fascicles," collections of the manuscripts of the poems. Many of them were first published through the efforts of Mabel Loomis Todd, who began to transcribe the poems at Lavinia's request and who then enlisted the aid of Higginson in editing the first collection of Dickinson's *Poems* (1890). That was followed by a second series of *Poems* (1891), edited by Higginson and Todd, and a third series of *Poems* (1896), edited by Todd, who was largely responsible for bringing Dickinson's work to the attention of critics and the public. That effort was continued by Dickinson's niece, Martha Dickinson Bianchi, who published eight more volumes of poems between 1914 and 1937. In 1945, more than six hundred new poems were published as *Bolts of Melody*, edited by Bianchi and Millicent Todd Bingham, who had inherited the manuscripts from her mother, Mabel Loomis Todd. Ten years later, Thomas H. Johnson published a three-volume "variorum" edition of all Dickinson's poems, identifying them by numbers in what he viewed as their chronological order. More recently, R. W. Franklin published a new edition of the poems, establishing a different chronological arrangement and correcting some editorial errors in the earlier edition. The texts of the

bedfordstmartins.com/ americanlit *for research* links on Dickinson

Manuscript version of "These are the days when Birds come back —"

poems included here are taken from Thomas H. Johnson's one-volume edition of *The Complete Poems of Emily Dickinson* (1960). With the exception of the first poem, the poems appear here in the order established by Johnson, with his number followed in square brackets by the number of the poem in *The Poems of Emily Dickinson* (1999), edited by R. W. Franklin.

Since Dickinson did not prepare her poems for print publication, all editors have confronted the task of deciphering her difficult handwriting and interpreting other features of her manuscripts. Some of those editorial complications are illustrated by the first poem reprinted here: "These are the days when Birds come back —" (130; Fr 122). There were several manuscript versions of this poem; the manuscript reproduced here is the copy found by Lavinia. Dickinson had sent another manuscript of the poem to Susan Dickinson, probably in 1859; yet another copy was clearly sent to the editor of the newspaper *Drum Beat*, where the poem was published as "October" on March 11, 1864. It is not known, however, who sent the poem to the newspaper. The manuscript of the poem is reproduced here along with two published versions, one from the first collection of *Poems by Emily Dickinson* (1890) and the other from Johnson's 1960 edition. Comparing the various versions of the poem demonstrates some of the liberties the early editors took, adding a title and altering some words of the manuscript. Such a comparison also illustrates the ways in which different editors have handled Dickinson's idiosyncratic capitalization and punctuation, two of the most striking features of her poems.

INDIAN SUMMER

These are the days when birds come
    back,
A very few, a bird or two,
To take a backward look.

These are the days when skies put on
The old, old sophistries of June, —
A blue and gold mistake.

Oh, fraud that cannot cheat the bee,
Almost thy plausibility
Induces my belief,

Till ranks of seeds their witness bear,
And softly through the altered air
Hurries a timid leaf!

Oh, sacrament of summer days,
Oh, last communion in the haze,
Permit a child to join,

Thy sacred emblems to partake,
Thy consecrated bread to break,
Taste thine immortal wine!

[c. 1859, 1890]

130 [FR 122]

These are the days when Birds come
    back —
A very few — a Bird or two —
To take a backward look.

These are the days when skies resume
The old — old sophistries of June —   5
A blue and gold mistake.

Oh fraud that cannot cheat the Bee —
Almost thy plausibility
Induces my belief.

Till ranks of seeds their witness bear —   10
And softly thro' the altered air
Hurries a timid leaf.

Oh Sacrament of summer days,
Oh Last Communion in the Haze —
Permit a child to join.   15

Thy sacred emblems to partake —
Thy consecrated bread to take
And thine immortal wine!

[c. 1859, 1960]

49 [FR 39]

I never lost as much but twice,
And that was in the sod.
Twice have I stood a beggar
Before the door of God!

Angels — twice descending
Reimbursed my store —
Burglar! Banker — Father!
I am poor once more!

[c. 1858, 1960]

67 [FR 112]

Success is counted sweetest
By those who ne'er succeed.
To comprehend a nectar
Requires sorest need.

Not one of all the purple Host   5
Who took the Flag today
Can tell the definition
So clear of Victory

As he defeated – dying –
On whose forbidden ear   10
The distant strains of triumph
Burst agonized and clear!

[c. 1859, 1960]

185 [FR 202]

"Faith" is a fine invention
When Gentlemen can *see* –
But *Microscopes* are prudent
In an Emergency.

[c. 1860, 1960]

199 [FR 225]

I'm "wife" – I've finished that –
That other state –
I'm Czar – I'm "Woman" now –
It's safer so –

How odd the Girl's life looks   5
Behind this soft Eclipse –
I think that Earth feels so
To folks in Heaven – now –

This being comfort – then
That other kind – was pain –   10
But why compare?
I'm "Wife"! Stop there!

[c. 1860, 1960]

214 [FR 207]

I taste a liquor never brewed –
From Tankards scooped in Pearl –
Not all the Vats upon the Rhine[1]
Yield such an Alcohol!

Inebriate of Air – am I –   5
And Debauchee of Dew –
Reeling – thro endless summer days –
From inns of Molten Blue –
When "Landlords" turn the drunken Bee
Out of the Foxglove's door –   10
When Butterflies – renounce their "drams" –
I shall but drink the more!

Till Seraphs[2] swing their snowy Hats –
And Saints – to windows run –
To see the little Tippler   15
Leaning against the – Sun –

                                                    [c. 1860, 1960]

216 [FR 124]

Safe in their Alabaster Chambers[3] –
Untouched by Morning
And untouched by Noon –
Sleep the meek members of the Resurrection –
Rafter of satin,   5
And Roof of stone.

Light laughs the breeze
In her Castle above them –
Babbles the Bee in a stolid Ear,
Pipe the Sweet Birds in ignorant cadence –   10
Ah, what sagacity perished here!

                                          [version of 1859, 1960]

Safe in their Alabaster Chambers –
Untouched by Morning –
And untouched by Noon –

---

1. **Rhine:** The Rhine River flows through major wine-producing areas in Germany.
2. **Seraphs:** Angels guarding God's throne.
3. **Alabaster Chambers:** Crypts made of translucent white marble.

Lie the meek members of the Resurrection —
Rafter of Satin — and Roof of Stone!   5

Grand go the Years — in the Crescent — above them —
Worlds scoop their Arcs —
And Firmaments — row —
Diadems — drop — and Doges[4] — surrender —
Soundless as dots — on a Disc of Snow —   10

[version of 1861, 1960]

241 [FR 339]

I like a look of Agony,
Because I know it's true —
Men do not sham Convulsion,
Nor simulate, a Throe —

The Eyes glaze once — and that is Death —
Impossible to feign
The Beads upon the Forehead
By homely Anguish strung.

[c. 1861, 1960]

249 [FR 269]

Wild Nights — Wild Nights!
Were I with thee
Wild Nights should be
Our luxury!

Futile — the Winds —   5
To a Heart in port —
Done with the Compass —
Done with the Chart![5]

Rowing in Eden —
Ah, the Sea!   10
Might I but moor — Tonight —
In Thee!

[c. 1861, 1960]

---

4. **Doges:** Powerful magistrates serving in the Italian republics of Venice and Genoa from the eleventh through the sixteenth centuries.
5. **Chart:** A navigational map used by sailors.

252 [FR 312]

I can wade Grief —
Whole Pools of it —
I'm used to that —
But the least push of Joy
Breaks up my feet —   5
And I tip — drunken —
Let no Pebble — smile —
'Twas the New Liquor —
That was all!

Power is only Pain —   10
Stranded, thro' Discipline,
Till Weights — will hang —
Give Balm — to Giants —
And they'll wit, like Men —
Give Himmaleh[6] —   15
They'll Carry — Him!

                                                    [c. 1861, 1960]

258 [FR 320]

There's a certain Slant of light,
Winter Afternoons —
That oppresses, like the Heft
Of Cathedral Tunes —

Heavenly Hurt, it gives us —   5
We can find no scar,
But internal difference,
Where the Meanings, are —

None may teach it — Any —
'Tis the Seal Despair —   10
An imperial affliction
Sent us of the Air —

When it comes, the Landscape listens —
Shadows — hold their breath —
When it goes, 'tis like the Distance   15
On the look of Death —

                                                    [c. 1861, 1960]

---

6. **Himmaleh:** The Himalayas, a vast mountain range in Asia that includes some of the highest peaks in the world.

280 [FR 340]

I felt a Funeral, in my Brain,
And Mourners to and fro
Kept treading – treading – till it seemed
That Sense was breaking through –

And when they all were seated,   5
A Service, like a Drum –
Kept beating – beating – till I thought
My Mind was going numb –

And then I heard them lift a Box
And creak across my Soul   10
With those same Boots of Lead, again,
Then Space – began to toll,

As all the Heavens were a Bell,
And Being, but an Ear,
And I, and Silence, some strange Race   15
Wrecked, solitary, here –

And then a Plank in Reason, broke,
And I dropped down, and down –
And hit a World, at every plunge,
And Finished knowing – then –   20
[c. 1861, 1960]

288 [FR 260]

I'm Nobody! Who are you?
Are you – Nobody – Too?
Then there's a pair of us?
Don't tell! they'd advertise – you know!

How dreary – to be – Somebody!
How public – like a Frog –
To tell one's name – the livelong June –
To an admiring Bog!

[c. 1861, 1960]

303 [FR 409]

The Soul selects her own Society –
Then – shuts the Door –
To her divine Majority –
Present no more –

Unmoved – she notes the Chariots – pausing –   5
At her low Gate –
Unmoved – an Emperor be kneeling
Upon her Mat –

I've known her – from an ample nation –
Choose One –   10
Then – close the Valves of her attention –
Like Stone –

      [c. 1862, 1960]

324 [FR 236]

Some keep the Sabbath going to Church –
I keep it, staying at Home –
With a Bobolink for a Chorister –
And an Orchard, for a Dome –

Some keep the Sabbath in Surplice[7] –   5
I just wear my Wings –
And instead of tolling the Bell, for Church,
Our little Sexton[8] – sings.

God preaches, a noted Clergyman –
And the sermon is never long,   10
So instead of getting to Heaven, at last –
I'm going, all along.

      [c. 1860, 1960]

341 [FR 372]

After great pain, a formal feeling comes –
The Nerves sit ceremonious, like Tombs –
The stiff Heart questions was it He, that bore,
And Yesterday, or Centuries before?

The Feet, mechanical, go round –   5
Of Ground, or Air, or Ought –
A Wooden way
Regardless grown,
A Quartz contentment, like a stone –

---

7. **Surplice:** A loose-fitting white gown worn by clergymen, acolytes, and choristers during Christian church services.
8. **Sexton:** An employee of a church responsible for ringing the bells to call the congregation to services.

This is the Hour of Lead —   10
Remembered, if outlived,
As Freezing persons, recollect the Snow —
First — Chill — then Stupor — then the letting go —

[c. 1862, 1960]

357 [Fr 615]

God is a distant — stately Lover —
Woos, as He states us — by His Son —
Verily, a Vicarious Courtship —
"Miles", and "Priscilla",[9] were such an One —

But, lest the Soul — like fair "Priscilla"
Choose the Envoy — and spurn the Groom —
Vouches, with hyperbolic archness —
"Miles", and "John Alden" were Synonym —

[c. 1862, 1960]

401 [Fr 675]

What Soft — Cherubic Creatures —
These Gentlewomen are —
One would as soon assault a Plush —
Or violate a Star —

Such Dimity Convictions[10] —   5
A Horror so refined
Of freckled Human Nature —
Of Deity — ashamed —

It's such a common — Glory —
A Fisherman's — Degree —   10
Redemption — Brittle Lady —
Be so — ashamed of Thee —

[c. 1862, 1960]

---

9. "Miles", and "Priscilla": A reference to Henry Wadsworth Longfellow's popular narrative poem about the Pilgrims, *The Courtship of Miles Standish* (1858), in which Miles Standish asks John Alden to propose for him to Priscilla Mullens, who famously asks John to speak for himself.

10. **Dimity Convictions**: Dimity, a cotton cloth woven with raised stripes or fancy figures, was then often used to make bedcovers, curtains, and dresses. Dickinson's ironic phrase seems to suggest self-consciously dainty or genteel convictions.

409 [FR 545]

They dropped like Flakes —
They dropped like Stars —
Like Petals from a Rose —
When suddenly across the June
A wind with fingers — goes —
They perished in the Seamless Grass —
No eye could find the place —
But God can summon every face
On his Repealless — List.

[c. 1862, 1960]

435 [FR 620]

Much Madness is divinest Sense
To a discerning Eye —
Much Sense — the starkest Madness —
'Tis the Majority
In this, as All, prevail —
Assent — and you are sane —
Demur — you're straightway dangerous —
And handled with a Chain —

[c. 1862, 1960]

441 [FR 519]

This is my letter to the World
That never wrote to Me —
The simple News that Nature told —
With tender Majesty

Her Message is committed
To Hands I cannot see —
For love of Her — Sweet — countrymen —
Judge tenderly — of Me

[c. 1862, 1960]

444 [FR 524]

It feels a shame to be Alive —
When Men so brave — are dead —
One envies the Distinguished Dust —
Permitted — such a Head —

The Stone — that tells defending Whom   5
This Spartan put away
What little of Him we — possessed
In Pawn for Liberty —

The price is great — Sublimely paid —
Do we deserve — a Thing —   10
That lives — like Dollars — must be piled
Before we may obtain?

Are we that wait — sufficient worth —
That such Enormous Pearl
As life — dissolved be — for Us —   15
In Battle's — horrid Bowl?

It may be — a Renown to live —
I think the Men who die —
Those unsustained — Saviors —
Present Divinity —   20

                                    [c. 1862, 1960]

448 [FR 446]

This was a Poet — It is That
Distills amazing sense
From ordinary Meanings —
And Attar[11] so immense

From the familiar species   5
That perished by the Door —
We wonder it was not Ourselves
Arrested it — before —

Of Pictures, the Discloser —
The Poet — it is He —   10
Entitles Us — by Contrast —
To ceaseless Poverty —

Of Portion — so unconscious —
The Robbing — could not harm —
Himself — to Him — a Fortune —   15
Exterior — to Time —

                                    [c. 1862, 1960]

---

11. **Attar:** Oil extracted from flowers and used to make perfume.

465 [FR 591]

I heard a Fly buzz — when I died —
The Stillness in the Room
Was like the Stillness in the Air —
Between the Heaves of Storm —

The Eyes around — had wrung them dry —   5
And Breaths were gathering firm
For that last Onset — when the King
Be witnessed — in the Room —

I willed my Keepsakes — Signed away
What portion of me be   10
Assignable — and then it was
There interposed a Fly —

With Blue — uncertain stumbling Buzz —
Between the light — and me —
And then the Windows failed — and then   15
I could not see to see —

                                              [c. 1862, 1960]

501 [FR 373]

This World is not Conclusion.
A Species stands beyond —
Invisible, as Music —
But positive, as Sound —
It beckons, and it baffles —   5
Philosophy — don't know —
And through a Riddle, at the last —
Sagacity, must go —
To guess it, puzzles scholars —
To gain it, Men have borne   10
Contempt of Generations
And Crucifixion, shown —
Faith slips — and laughs, and rallies —
Blushes, if any see —
Plucks at a twig of Evidence —   15
And asks a Vane,[12] the way —
Much Gesture, from the Pulpit —

---

12. **Vane:** A weathervane, a revolving device mounted on buildings that shows the direction of the wind.

Strong Hallelujahs roll —
Narcotics cannot still the Tooth
That nibbles at the soul —   20

                                                    [c. 1862, 1960]

508 [FR 353]

I'm ceded — I've stopped being Theirs —
The name They dropped upon my face
With water, in the country church
Is finished using, now,

And They can put it with my Dolls,   5
My childhood, and the string of spools,
I've finished threading — too —

Baptized, before, without the choice,
But this time, consciously, of Grace —
Unto supremest name —   10
Called to my Full — The Crescent dropped —
Existence's whole Arc, filled up,
With one small Diadem.

My second Rank — too small the first —
Crowned — Crowing — on my Father's breast —   15
A half unconscious Queen —
But this time — Adequate — Erect,
With Will to choose, or to reject,
And I choose, just a Crown —

                                                    [c. 1862, 1960]

512 [FR 360]

The Soul has Bandaged moments —
When too appalled to stir —
She feels some ghastly Fright come up
And stop to look at her —

Salute her — with long fingers —   5
Caress her freezing hair —
Sip, Goblin, from the very lips
The Lover — hovered — o'er —
Unworthy, that a thought so mean
Accost a Theme — so — fair —   10

The soul has moments of Escape —
When bursting all the doors —
She dances like a Bomb, abroad,
And swings upon the Hours,

As do the Bee — delirious borne —   15
Long Dungeoned from his Rose —
Touch Liberty — then know no more,
But Noon, and Paradise —

The Soul's retaken moments —
When, Felon led along,   20
With shackles on the plumed feet,
And staples, in the Song,

The Horror welcomes her, again,
These, are not brayed of Tongue —

                      [c. 1862, 1960]

605 [FR 513]

The Spider holds a Silver Ball
In unperceived Hands —
And dancing softly to Himself
His Yarn of Pearl — unwinds —

He plies from Nought to Nought —   5
In unsubstantial Trade —
Supplants our Tapestries with His —
In half the period —

An Hour to rear supreme
His Continents of Light —   10
Then dangle from the Housewife's Broom —
His Boundaries — forgot —

                      [c. 1862, 1960]

632 [FR 598]

The Brain — is wider than the Sky —
For — put them side by side —
The one the other will contain
With ease — and You — beside —

The Brain is deeper than the sea —   5
For — hold them — Blue to Blue —

The one the other will absorb –
As Sponges – Buckets – do –

The Brain is just the weight of God –
For – Heft them – Pound for Pound –   10
Nor We so much as check our speech –
Nor stop to cross Ourselves –

[c. 1862, 1960]

650 [FR 760]

Pain – has an Element of Blank –
It cannot recollect
When it begun – or if there were
A time when it was not –

It has no Future – but itself –
Its Infinite contain
Its Past – enlightened to perceive
New Periods – of Pain.

[c. 1862, 1960]

657 [FR 466]

I dwell in Possibility –
A fairer House than Prose –
More numerous of Windows –
Superior – for Doors –

Of Chambers as the Cedars –   5
Impregnable of Eye –
And for an Everlasting Roof
The Gambrels[13] of the Sky –

Of Visitors – the fairest –
For Occupation – This –   10
The spreading wide my narrow Hands
To gather Paradise –

[c. 1862, 1960]

709 [FR 788]

Publication – is the Auction
Of the Mind of Man –

---

13. **Gambrels:** A ridged roof with two sloping sides, one with a higher pitch.

Poverty — be justifying
For so foul a thing

Possibly — but We — would rather   5
From Our Garret go
White — Unto the White Creator —
Than invest — Our Snow —

Thought belong to Him who gave it —
Then — to Him Who bear   10
Its Corporeal illustration — Sell
The Royal Air —

In the Parcel — Be the Merchant
Of the Heavenly Grace —
But reduce no Human Spirit   15
To Disgrace of Price —

[c. 1863, 1960]

712 [FR 479]

Because I could not stop for Death —
He kindly stopped for me —
The Carriage held but just Ourselves —
And Immortality.

We slowly drove — He knew no haste   5
And I had put away
My labor and my leisure too,
For His Civility —

We passed the School, where Children strove
At Recess — in the Ring —   10
We passed the Fields of Gazing Grain —
We passed the Setting Sun —

Or rather — He passed Us —
The Dews drew quivering and chill —
For only Gossamer, my Gown —   15
My Tippet — only Tulle[14] —

We paused before a House that seemed
A Swelling of the Ground —
The Roof was scarcely visible —
The Cornice — in the Ground —   20

---

14. **Gossamer . . . Tulle:** Light clothing, including a dress made of fine, gauzy fabric and a shawl made of
stiffly netted silk.

Since then — 'tis Centuries — and yet
Feels shorter than the Day
I first surmised the Horses' Heads
Were toward Eternity —

[c. 1863, 1960]

754 [FR 764]

My Life had stood — a Loaded Gun —
In Corners — till a Day
The Owner passed — identified —
And carried Me away —

And now We roam in Sovereign Woods —   5
And now We hunt the Doe —
And every time I speak for Him —
The Mountains straight reply —

And do I smile, such cordial light
Upon the Valley glow —   10
It is as a Vesuvian face[15]
Had let its pleasure through —

And when at Night — Our good Day done —
I guard My Master's Head —
'Tis better than the Eider-Duck's   15
Deep Pillow — to have shared —

To foe of His — I'm deadly foe —
None stir the second time —
On whom I lay a Yellow Eye —
Or an emphatic Thumb —   20

Though I than He — may longer live
He longer must — than I —
For I have but the power to kill,
Without — the power to die —

[c. 1863, 1960]

883 [FR 930]

The Poets light but Lamps —
Themselves — go out —
The Wicks they stimulate —
If vital Light

---

15. **a Vesuvian face:** The famous eruption of Mount Vesuvius in Italy in 79 CE completely destroyed the Roman towns of Herculaneum and Pompeii.

Inhere as do the Suns —
Each Age a Lens
Disseminating their
Circumference —

[c. 1864, 1960]

986 [FR 1096]

A narrow Fellow in the Grass
Occasionally rides —
You may have met Him — did you not
His notice sudden is —

The Grass divides as with a Comb —   5
A spotted shaft is seen —
And then it closes at your feet
And opens further on —

He likes a Boggy Acre
A Floor too cool for Corn —   10
Yet when a Boy, and Barefoot —
I more than once at Noon
Have passed, I thought, a Whip lash
Unbraiding in the Sun
When stooping to secure it   15
It wrinkled, and was gone —

Several of Nature's People
I know, and they know me —
I feel for them a transport
Of cordiality —   20

But never met this Fellow
Attended, or alone
Without a tighter breathing
And Zero at the Bone —

[c. 1865, 1960]

1052 [FR 800]

I never saw a Moor[16] —
I never saw the Sea —
Yet know I how the Heather looks
And what a Billow be.

---

16. **Moor:** A tract of open wasteland sometimes covered with heather, a small flowering shrub.

I never spoke with God
Nor visited in Heaven –
Yet certain am I of the spot
As if the Checks were given –

[c. 1865, 1960]

1072 [FR 194]

Title divine – is mine!
The Wife – without the Sign!
Acute Degree – conferred on me –
Empress of Calvary![17]
Royal – all but the Crown!   5
Betrothed – without the swoon
God sends us Women –
When you – hold – Garnet to Garnet –
Gold – to Gold –
Born – Bridalled – Shrouded –   10
In a Day –
Tri Victory
"My Husband" – women say –
Stroking the Melody –
Is *this* – the way?   15

[c. 1862, 1960]

1078 [FR 1108]

The Bustle in a House
The Morning after Death
Is solemnest of industries
Enacted upon Earth –

The Sweeping up the Heart
And putting Love away
We shall not want to use again
Until Eternity.

[c. 1866, 1960]

1082 [FR 1044]

Revolution is the Pod
Systems rattle from

---

17. **Calvary:** The hill outside Jerusalem where Christ was crucified.

When the Winds of Will are stirred
Excellent is Bloom

But except its Russet Base   5
Every Summer be
The Entomber of itself,
So of Liberty —

Left inactive on the Stalk
All its Purple fled   10
Revolution shakes it for
Test if it be dead.

[c. 1866, 1960]

1129 [FR 1263]

Tell all the Truth but tell it slant —
Success in Circuit lies
Too bright for our infirm Delight
The Truth's superb surprise
As Lightning to the Children eased
With explanation kind
The Truth must dazzle gradually
Or every man be blind —

[c. 1868, 1960]

1463 [FR 1489]

A Route of Evanescence
With a revolving Wheel —
A Resonance of Emerald —
A Rush of Cochineal[18] —
And every Blossom on the Bush
Adjusts its tumbled Head —
The mail from Tunis,[19] probably,
An easy Morning's Ride —

[c. 1879, 1960]

1651 [FR 1715]

A Word made Flesh[20] is seldom
And tremblingly partook

---

18. **Cochineal:** A brilliant red dye made from the bodies of insects.
19. **Tunis:** The capital city of the North African country of Tunisia.
20. **A Word made Flesh:** See John 1:14: "And the Word was made flesh, and dwelt among us, (and we beheld his glory, the glory as of the only begotten of the Father,) full of grace and truth."

Nor then perhaps reported
But have I not mistook
Each one of us has tasted   5
With ecstasies of stealth
The very food debated
To our specific strength —

A Word that breathes distinctly
Has not the power to die   10
Cohesive as the Spirit
It may expire if He —
"Made Flesh and dwelt among us"
Could condescension be
Like this consent of Language   15
This loved Philology.

                                                [?, 1960]

1732 [FR 1773]

My life closed twice before its close —
It yet remains to see
If Immortality unveil
A third event to me

So huge, so hopeless to conceive
As these that twice befell.
Parting is all we know of heaven,
And all we need of hell.

                                                [?, 1960]

1737 [FR 267]

Rearrange a "Wife's" affection!
When they dislocate my Brain!
Amputate my freckled Bosom!
Make me bearded like a man!

Blush, my spirit, in thy Fastness —   5
Blush, my unacknowledged clay —
Seven years of troth have taught thee
More than Wifehood ever may!

Love that never leaped its socket —
Trust entrenched in narrow pain —   10

Constancy thro' fire — awarded —
Anguish — bare of anodyne![21]

Burden — borne so far triumphant —
None suspect me of the crown,
For I wear the "Thorns" till *Sunset* —   15
Then — my Diadem put on.

Big my Secret but it's *bandaged* —
It will never get away
Till the Day its Weary Keeper
Leads it through the Grave to thee.   20

[?, 1960]

1760 [FR 1590]

Elysium[22] is as far as to
The very nearest Room
If in that Room a Friend await
Felicity or Doom —

What fortitude the Soul contains,
That it can so endure
The accent of a coming Foot —
The opening of a Door —

[c. 1882, 1960]

---

21. **anodyne:** Something that soothes or relieves.
22. **Elysium:** In Greek mythology, the home of the blessed in the afterlife; also called the Elysium of Elysian Fields.

Reading Dickinson's Letters.   Dickinson wrote thousands of letters to a series of correspondents. Her most frequent correspondent was her sister-in-law, Susan Gilbert Dickinson, with whom Dickinson had a close, intense relationship for much of her adult life. The exchange between Dickinson and her sister-in-law reprinted here demonstrates the way in which Dickinson revised one of her poems in light of Susan's suggestions. Another of Dickinson's most important correspondents was writer and reformer Thomas Wentworth Higginson. Dickinson first wrote to him in response to his "Letter to a Young Contributor," an article published in the *Atlantic Monthly* in April 1862 in which Higginson offered practical advice to potential contributors to the magazine. In her first letter to him, Dickinson included four of her poems and asked Higginson, "Are you too deeply occupied to say if my Verse is alive?" In her second letter, Dickinson thanked him for his "surgery" — that is, Higginson's comments on the poems — and sent along some others, as he had requested. In response to his comments on that second group of poems, Dickinson wrote the letter printed here. As it suggests, Dickinson frequently adopted an ironic or playful tone in her letters to Higginson, who became one of her closest friends and, after her death, the coeditor of the first collections of her poems. The texts of the two letters are taken from *The Letters of Emily Dickinson*, edited by Thomas H. Johnson (1958).

EXCHANGE WITH SUSAN GILBERT DICKINSON

[To Susan Gilbert Dickinson   summer 1861]

Safe in their Alabaster Chambers,
Untouched by morning
And untouched by noon,
Sleep the meek members of the Resurrection,
Rafter of satin
And Roof of stone.

Light laughs the breeze
In her Castle above them,
Babbles the Bee in a stolid Ear,
Pipe the Sweet Birds in ignorant cadence, —
Ah, what sagacity perished here!

[The earlier version, above, ED sent to Sue during the summer of 1861. Sue appears to have objected to the second stanza, for ED sent her the following:]

Safe in their Alabaster Chambers,
Untouched by Morning —
And untouched by Noon —
Lie the meek members of the Resurrection —
Rafter of Satin — and Roof of Stone —

Grand go the Years — in the Crescent — about them —
Worlds scoop their Arcs —
And Firmaments — row —
Diadems — drop — and Doges — surrender —
Soundless as dots — on a Disc of Snow —

Perhaps this verse would please you better — Sue —

Emily —

[The new version elicited an immediate response:]

I am not suited dear Emily with the second verse — It is remarkable as the chain lightening that blinds us hot nights in the Southern sky but it does not go with the ghostly shimmer of the first verse as well as the other one — It just occurs to me that the first verse is complete in itself it needs no other, and can't be coupled — Strange things always go alone — as there is only one Gabriel and one Sun — You never made a peer for that verse, and I *guess* you[r] kingdom does'nt hold one — I always go to the fire and get warm after thinking of it, but I never *can* again — The flowers are sweet and bright and look as if they would kiss one — ah, they expect a humming-bird — Thanks for them of course — and not thanks only recognition either — Did it ever occur to you that is all there is here after all — "Lord that I may receive my sight" —

Susan is tired making *bibs* for her bird — her ring-dove — he will paint my cheeks when I am old to pay me —

Sue —

Pony Express

[ED answered thus:]

Is *this frostier?*

> Springs — shake the sills —
> But — the Echoes — stiffen —
> Hoar — is the Window —
> And numb — the Door —
> Tribes of Eclipse — in Tents of Marble —
> Staples of Ages — have buckled — there —

Dear Sue —

Your praise is good — to me — because I *know* it *knows* — and *suppose* — it *means* —

Could I make you and Austin[1] — proud — sometime — a great way off — 'twould give me taller feet —

Here is a crumb — for the "Ring dove" — and a spray for *his Nest,* a little while ago — *just* — "Sue."

Emily.

To Thomas Wentworth Higginson

[To T. W. Higginson   *7 June 1862*]

Dear friend.

Your letter gave no Drunkenness, because I tasted Rum before — Domingo[2] comes but once — yet I have had few pleasures so deep as your opinion, and if I tried to thank you, my tears would block my tongue —

---

1. **Austin:** Austin Dickinson (1829–1895), Susan's husband and Emily Dickinson's brother.
2. **Rum . . . Domingo:** Rum, alcoholic liquor manufactured in the Caribbean, is here used synonymously with *Domingo,* which in the nineteenth century referred to San Domingo, or Haiti.

My dying Tutor[3] told me that he would like to live till I had been a poet, but Death was much of Mob as I could master – then – And when far afterward – a sudden light on Orchards, or a new fashion in the wind troubled my attention – I felt a palsy, here – the Verses just relieve –

Your second letter surprised me, and for a moment, swung – I had not supposed it. Your first – gave no dishonor, because the True – are not ashamed – I thanked you for your justice – but could not drop the Bells whose jingling cooled my Tramp – Perhaps the Balm, seemed better, because you bled me, first.

I smile when you suggest that I delay "to publish" – that being foreign to my thought, as Firmament to Fin –

If fame belonged to me, I could not escape her – if she did not, the longest day would pass me on the chase – and the approbation of my Dog, would forsake me – then – My Barefoot-Rank is better –

You think my gait "spasmodic" – I am in danger – Sir –

You think me "uncontrolled" – I have no Tribunal.[4]

Would you have time to be the "friend" you should think I need? I have a little shape – it would not crowd your Desk – nor make much Racket as the Mouse, that dents your Galleries –

If I might bring you what I do – not so frequent to trouble you – and ask you if I told it clear – 'twould be control, to me –

The Sailor cannot see the North – but knows the Needle can –

The "hand you stretch me in the Dark," I put mine in, and turn away – I have no Saxon,[5] now –

> As if I asked a common Alms,
> And in my wondering hand
> A Stranger pressed a Kingdom,
> And I, bewildered, stand –
> As if I asked the Orient
> Had it for me a Morn –
> And it should lift it's purple Dikes,
> And shatter me with Dawn!

But, will you be my Preceptor,[6] Mr Higginson?

Your friend
E Dickinson –

---

3. **My dying Tutor:** Benjamin Franklin Newton (1821–1853), a law student in Edward Dickinson's office from 1847 to 1849, encouraged Dickinson's interest in poetry and later sent her a copy of Ralph Waldo Emerson's *Poems* (1847). His death at age thirty-two was a blow to Dickinson.
4. **Tribunal:** A panel of judges.
5. **I have no Saxon:** The editor of the letters, Thomas H. Johnson, points out that this phrase means "language fails me."
6. **Preceptor:** A teacher or an instructor.

Dickinson through a Modern Lens

IN AN EPIGRAPH to a collection of poems inspired by the life and work of Emily Dickinson, the poet Robert Francis observed, "In Amherst when someone leans out of a car window and asks the way to Emily's grave, one does not ask, 'Emily who?'" Indeed, Dickinson is so frequently read and taught that she, along with Walt Whitman and Robert Frost, is surely among the most familiar of all American poets. Frost, who as a teenager read Dickinson's posthumously published *Poems* shortly after the volume appeared in 1890, was drawn to the formal qualities of her verse and fascinated by the fact that she, too, was "troubled by many things" about death. Her poetry has been admired by modernist poets as different as Hart Crane and Marianne Moore. Moore, who was sometimes

The Homestead

Dickinson was born and lived most of her life in this house, her family home in Amherst, Massachusetts.

compared to Dickinson, told a friend in 1924 that "to be associated with Emily Dickinson's rigorous splendor is rare and trembling praise." Crane paid tribute to her lifelong poetic quest in his posthumously published poem "To Emily Dickinson" (1933). A variety of more recent poets have also written poems about her, including Galway Kinnell, Maxine Kumin, Joyce Carol Oates, and Billy Collins, the poet laureate of the United States during 2001-03. The following two poems reveal Dickinson's far-flung influence on women poets of different generations and diverse backgrounds. The first, by the feminist poet and social critic Adrienne Rich (1929-2012), is from her *Collected Early Poems, 1950-1977* (1993). The second is from *The Land of Bliss* (2001), the fourth collection of poems by the Hawaii-born Cathy Song (b. 1955).

Adrienne Rich

[1929-2012]

"I Am in Danger — Sir —"[1]

"Half-cracked" to Higginson, living,
afterward famous in garbled versions,[2]
your hoard of dazzling scraps a battlefield,
now your old snood

mothballed at Harvard[3]   5
and you in your variorum monument
equivocal to the end —
who are you?

---

1. "I . . . Sir —": A sentence from Dickinson's letter to Thomas Wentworth Higginson (1823-1911), a well-known writer who had critiqued some poems she had sent him in 1862 (see p. 1068). In the first line of the poem, Rich alludes to a letter in which Higginson described Dickinson as "my partially cracked Poetess at Amherst."
2. **garbled versions:** The editors of the early collections of Dickinson's poems frequently took liberties with the manuscripts, adding titles and altering her punctuation and frequently her wording. The "variorum monument" referred to in the following stanza is a reference to the three-volume *Poems of Emily Dickinson*, a scholarly edition edited by Thomas H. Johnson (1955).
3. **your old snood . . . Harvard:** A snood is an ornamental hairnet worn over the back of a woman's head; many of Dickinson's manuscripts, letters, and personal belongings are at the Houghton Library, Harvard University.

Gardening the day-lily,
wiping the wine-glass stems,   10
your thought pulsed on behind
a forehead battered paper-thin,

you, woman, masculine
in single-mindedness,
for whom the word was more   15
than a symptom —

a condition of being.
Till the air buzzing with spoiled language
sang in your ears
of Perjury   20

and in your half-cracked way you chose
silence for entertainment,
chose to have it out at last
on your own premises.

                                                    [1964, 1993]

Cathy Song

[b. 1955]

A POET IN THE HOUSE

Emily's job was to think.
She was the only one of us
who had that to do.
    – Lavinia Dickinson[1]

Seemingly small her work,
minute to the point of invisibility —
she vanished daily into paper, famished,
hungry for her next encounter —

---

1. **Lavinia Dickinson:** Dickinson's sister, who lived with her and conducted most of the domestic
affairs in their family house in Amherst, Massachusetts.

but she opened with a string of humble   5
words necessity,
necessary as the humble work
of bringing well to water, roast to knife, cake to frost,
the coarse, loud, grunting labor of the rest of us
who complained not at all   10
for the noises she heard
we deemed divine, if
claustrophobic and esoteric —
and contented ourselves to the apparent,
the menial, set our heads   15
to the task of daily maintenance,
the simple order at the kitchen table,
while she struggled with a different thing —
the pressure seized upon her mind —
we could ourselves not bear such strain   20
and, in gratitude, heaved the bucket,
squeezed the rag, breathed the sweet,
homely odor of soap.
Lifting dirt from the floor
I swear   25
we could hear her thinking.

[2001]

American Contexts

"MINE EYES HAVE SEEN THE GLORY": THE MEANINGS OF THE CIVIL WAR

THE CIVIL WAR WAS A SEISMIC EVENT in American history, the reverberations of which are still widely felt in the United States. One consequence of the war was to transform the *United States*, which had previously always been used in the plural, into a singular noun, a grammatical shift signaling that it was "one nation, indivisible," in the words of the Pledge of Allegiance. As the following documents illustrate, however, the meaning of the conflict between the North and the South was deeply contested — before, during, and after the Civil War. The war was the culmination of decades of growing sectional divisions. Those divisions were deepened by the strife between proslavery and antislavery settlers in Kansas during 1855–57, as well as by the attack led by John Brown at Harpers Ferry in 1859. By then, many radical abolitionists had concluded that violent means were justified in the struggle to end slavery — that, as Brown put it in a note written before his execution, "the crimes of this guilty land will never be purged away but with blood." Brown's final speech is reprinted here, as are important speeches by the political leaders of the opposing sides in the Civil War. In his inaugural address, the president of the Confederacy, Jefferson Davis, appealed to the political ideals outlined in the Declaration of Independence. In fact, southern secessionists frequently compared their struggle to the American Revolution. Abraham Lincoln, whose election as president in 1860 led to the secession of the southern states, initially insisted that his sole purpose in going to war was not to end slavery but to preserve the Union established by the Founding Fathers. Even the Emancipation Proclamation, which Lincoln issued in 1863, freed slaves only in areas that were not then under the control of the federal government. But in his Gettysburg Address, Lincoln affirmed that the war was being fought to bring about "a new birth of freedom," a fulfillment of the promise of the Declaration of Independence. In his second inaugural address, delivered near the end of the war, Lincoln thus suggested that the carnage was the price exacted for 250 years of slavery in what became the United States.

Although Lincoln's famous speeches are among the most memorable efforts to explicate the meaning of the war, the conflict generated a wide range of expression, from poems and songs to diaries, editorials, and sermons. The other documents included here also reveal some of the

John Steuart Curry, *Tragic Prelude*

Curry, whose ancestors were abolitionists, painted this allegorical mural at the State Capitol Building in Topeka, Kansas, between 1937 and 1942. The mural is dominated by the larger-than-life image of John Brown, a Moses-like figure with his arms outstretched, holding a rifle in one hand and a Bible in the other. He is flanked by contending antislavery and proslavery settlers, whose violent clashes in Kansas are represented as the "tragic prelude" to the Civil War. The tornado and prairie fire in the background suggest the destructive forces unleashed by the struggle over slavery, while the two prone figures in the foreground symbolize the million dead and wounded of the Civil War.

complexities and contradictions generated by the war. The most popular southern song was "Dixie's Land," a blackface minstrel song composed and originally performed in dialect by a Northerner, Daniel Emmett. Meanwhile, northern soldiers marched to "John Brown's Body" and the "Battle Hymn of the Republic," both of which were written to the tune of a popular southern camp-meeting song, "Say, Brothers, Will You Meet Us?" Near the end of the war, the influential African American minister Henry Highland Garnet hoped that the end of slavery would be the first step toward full equality between the races. Meanwhile, the Southerner Mary Chesnut mourned the loss of a way of life that depended on slavery. For Chesnut, the assassination of Lincoln was "a warning to tyrants." For the poet William Cullen Bryant and most Northerners, the fallen president was a martyr for the cause of freedom and the Union. Following the war, poets gave expression to similarly conflicting attitudes and emotions. Indeed, the only things that all Americans held in common after the war were rituals of mourning and an understanding of the terrible toll it had taken in human lives. In the final document in this section, Walt Whitman thus suggests that the shared grief for those who had died fighting in the war might serve as a powerful bond among all Americans, finally helping to reunite the North and the South.

bedfordstmartins.com/ **americanlit** *for research links on the authors in this section*

John Brown

[1800-1859]

Born in Connecticut and raised in Ohio, John Brown was unsuccessful at farming and business before he found his true vocation in the antislavery crusade, work for which he believed he had been called upon by God. He was active in the underground railroad and in groups organized to protect fugitive slaves. But he first gained national attention during 1855–57, when Brown emerged as a militant leader of free-soil settlers in their struggle with proslavery militia for control of the Kansas Territory. Returning east, where he met and gained the sympathetic support of writers such as Emerson and Thoreau, Brown began to plan a direct attack on slavery in the South. Despite the warnings of Frederick Douglass — who argued that the plan was suicidal — on October 16, 1859, Brown and eighteen followers, including three of his sons, seized the federal arsenal at Harpers Ferry, Virginia (now West Virginia). Although he repeatedly denies it in the following speech, it is thought that Brown hoped to start an insurrection that would attract large numbers of slaves to his small band. Within two days, however, his men were either killed or captured, as Brown was, by federal troops under the command of Brevet Colonel Robert E. Lee. Accused of treason, murder, and conspiring with slaves to rebel, Brown was swiftly tried, convicted, and sentenced to hang. Before his sentence was read, Brown delivered the following speech, which — along with the numerous letters he wrote from prison in the month between his sentencing and execution on December 2, 1859 — gained him tremendous sympathy in the North, where he was widely hailed as a Christlike martyr of the antislavery cause. The text of the speech is taken from Robert M. Dewitt, *The Life, Trial and Conviction of Capt. John Brown* (1860).

JOHN BROWN'S LAST SPEECH

I have, may it please the Court, a few words to say. In the first place, I deny everything but what I have all along admitted, of a design on my part to free slaves. I intended certainly to have made a clean thing of that matter, as I did last winter when I went into Missouri, and there took slaves without the snapping of a gun on either side, moving them through the country, and finally leaving them in Canada.[1] I designed to have done the same thing again on a larger scale. That was all I intended to do. I never did intend murder or treason, or the destruction of property, or to excite or incite the slaves to rebellion, or to make insurrection. I have another objection, and that is that it is unjust that I should suffer such a penalty. Had I interfered in the manner which I admit, and which I admit has been fairly proved — for I admire the truthfulness and candor of the greater portion of the witnesses who have testified in this case — had I so interfered in behalf of the rich, the powerful, the intelligent, the so-called great, or in behalf of any of their friends, either father, mother, brother, sister, wife, or children, or any of that class, and suffered and sacrificed what I have in this interference, it would have been all right, and every man in this Court would have deemed it an act worthy of reward rather than punishment. This Court acknowledges, too, as I suppose, the validity of the law of God. I see a book kissed, which I suppose to be the Bible, or at least the New Testament, which teaches me that all things whatsoever I would that men should do to me, I should do even so to them.[2] It teaches me further to remember them that are in bonds as bound with them.[3] I endeavored to act up to that instruction. I say I am yet too

---

1. **I went into Missouri . . . leaving them in Canada:** In December 1858, Brown led a group of men on a raid into Missouri. There, they attacked two homesteads, confiscating property and liberating eleven slaves, whom Brown conducted to freedom in Canada.

2. **whatsoever . . . to them:** See Christ's words in Matthew 7:12: "Therefore all things whatsoever ye would that men should do to you, do ye even so to them: for this is the law and the prophets."

3. **It teaches . . . bound with them:** See Hebrews 13:3: "Remember them that are in bonds, as bound with them."

young to understand that God is any respecter of persons. I believe that to have interfered as I have done, as I have always freely admitted I have done in behalf of His despised poor, is no wrong, but right. Now, if it is deemed necessary that I should forfeit my life for the furtherance of the ends of justice, and mingle my blood further with the blood of my children and with the blood of millions in this slave country whose rights are disregarded by wicked, cruel, and unjust enactments, I say let it be done. Let me say one word further. I feel entirely satisfied with the treatment I have received on my trial. Considering all the circumstances, it has been more generous than I expected. But I feel no consciousness of guilt. I have stated from the first what was my intention, and what was not. I never had any design against the liberty of any person, nor any disposition to commit treason or excite slaves to rebel or make any general insurrection. I never encouraged any man to do so, but always discouraged any idea of that kind. Let me say also in regard to the statements made by some of those who were connected with me, I fear it has been stated by some of them that I have induced them to join me, but the contrary is true. I do not say this to injure them, but as regretting their weakness. Not one but joined me of his own accord, and the greater part at their own expense. A number of them I never saw, and never had a word of conversation with till the day they came to me, and that was for the purpose I have stated. Now, I am done.

[1859, 1860]

Jefferson Davis

[1808-1889]

Jefferson Davis

This photograph was apparently taken in 1861, around the time Davis became president of the Confederate States of America.

Born in Kentucky, Jefferson Davis initially seemed destined for a distinguished career in the military. His father and uncles had been soldiers in the Revolutionary War, and his three older brothers served in the War of 1812. After his graduation from the military academy at West Point, Davis himself served at various wilderness outposts in the Northwest before he resigned from the army in 1835. He then became a successful cotton planter in Mississippi, where he entered politics in 1845. Elected to the House of Representatives, he left to serve as an officer in the Mexican War (1846-48). He was later appointed secretary of war (1853-57) by Franklin Pierce and elected for two terms in the Senate (1847-51, 1857-61), from which he resigned when Mississippi seceded from the Union. After being named the head of the provisional government by the Congress of the Confederate States, he was elected to a six-year term as president of the Confederate States of America. At the end of the war, he was captured, charged with war crimes, and imprisoned for two years in Virginia. But he was never tried, though he had demanded a trial. After his release from prison, Davis retired to Biloxi, Mississippi, where he wrote *The Rise and Fall of the Confederacy* (1878–81). Davis delivered his inaugural address on February 18, 1861, in Montgomery, Alabama, the first capital of the Confederacy. The text is taken from *Southern Historical Society Papers*, Vol. 1, No. 1 (January 1876).

JEFFERSON DAVIS'S INAUGURAL ADDRESS

Gentlemen of the Congress of the Confederate States of America:

Called to the difficult and responsible station of Executive Chief of the Provisional Government which you have instituted, I approach the discharge of the duties assigned me with an humble distrust of my abilities, but with a sustaining confidence in the wisdom of those who are to aid and guide me in the administration of public affairs, and an abiding faith in the patriotism and virtue of the people. Looking forward to the speedy establishment of a provisional government to take the place of the present one, and which, by its great moral and physical powers, will be better able to contend with the difficulties which arise from the conflicting incidents of separate nations, I enter upon the duties of the office for which I have been chosen with the hope that the beginning of our career as a Confederacy may not be obstructed by hostile opposition to the enjoyment of that separate and independent existence which we have asserted, and which, with the blessing of Providence, we intend to maintain.

Our present position has been achieved in a manner unprecedented in the history of nations. It illustrates the American idea that government rests upon the consent of the governed, and that it is the right of the people to alter or abolish a government whenever it becomes destructive of the ends for which it was established.[1] The declared purposes of the compact of Union from which we have withdrawn were to establish justice, insure domestic tranquillity, to provide for the common defence, to promote the general welfare, and to secure the blessings of liberty for ourselves and our posterity; and when in the judgment of the sovereign States now comprising this

---

1. **government . . . for which it was established:** Here, as elsewhere in his speech, Davis paraphrases the Declaration of Independence: "That to secure these rights, Governments are instituted among Men, deriving their just powers from the consent of the governed, – That whenever any Form of Government becomes destructive of these ends, it is the Right of the People to alter or to abolish it, and to institute new Government, laying its foundation on such principles and organizing its powers in such form, as to them shall seem most likely to effect their Safety and Happiness." The full text of the Declaration of Independence is printed on pages 389-93.

Confederacy it had been perverted from the purposes for which it was ordained, and had ceased to answer the ends for which it was established, an appeal to the ballot box declared that so far as they were concerned the government created by that compact should cease to exist. In this they merely asserted a right which the Declaration of Independence of 1776 defined to be inalienable. Of the time and occasion for its exercise, they, as sovereign, were the final judges each for itself. The impartial and enlightened verdict of mankind will vindicate the rectitude of our conduct, and He who knows the hearts of men will judge the sincerity with which we have labored to preserve the government of our fathers, in its spirit and in those rights inherent in it, which were solemnly proclaimed at the birth of the States, and which have been affirmed and reaffirmed in the Bills of Rights of the several States. When they entered into the Union of 1789, it was with the undeniable recognition of the power of the people to resume the authority delegated for the purposes of that government whenever, in their opinion, its functions were perverted and its ends defeated. By virtue of this authority, the time and occasion requiring them to exercise it having arrived, the sovereign States here represented have seceded from that Union, and it is a gross abuse of language to denominate the act rebellion or revolution. They have formed a new alliance, but in each State its government has remained as before. The rights of person and property have not been disturbed. The agency through which they have communicated with foreign powers has been changed, but this does not necessarily interrupt their international relations.

Sustained by a consciousness that our transition from the former Union to the present Confederacy has not proceeded from any disregard on our part of our just obligations, or any failure to perform every constitutional duty — moved by no intention or design to invade the rights of others — anxious to cultivate peace and commerce with all nations — if we may not hope to avoid war, we may at least expect that posterity will acquit us of having needlessly engaged in it. We are doubly justified by the absence of wrong on our part, and by wanton aggression on the part of others. There can be no cause to doubt that the courage and patriotism of the people of the Confederate States will be found equal to any measure of defence which may be required for their security. Devoted to agricultural pursuits, their chief interest is the export of a commodity required in every manufacturing country.[2] Our policy is peace, and the freest trade our necessities will permit. It is alike our interest, and that of all those to whom we would sell and from whom we would buy, that there should be the fewest practicable restrictions upon interchange of commodities. There can be but little rivalry between us and any manufacturing or navigating community, such as the Northwestern States of the American Union.

It must follow, therefore, that mutual interest would invite good will and kindness between them and us. If, however, passion or lust of dominion should cloud the judgment and inflame the ambition of these States, we must prepare to meet the emergency, and maintain, by the final arbitrament of the sword, the position we have assumed

---

2. a commodity . . . country: Cotton, the major product of the South, was an important element in the emerging global economy of the period. By 1860, the southern states exported two-thirds of the world's supply of cotton and three-fourths of the cotton used in the lucrative textile industries of France and Great Britain.

among the nations of the earth. We have now entered upon our career of independence, and it must be inflexibly pursued.

Through many years of controversy with our late associates, the Northern States, we have vainly endeavored to secure tranquillity and obtain respect for the rights to which we were entitled. As a necessity, not a choice we have resorted to separation, and henceforth our energies must be devoted to the conducting of our own affairs, and perpetuating the Confederacy we have formed. If a just perception of mutual interest shall permit us peaceably to pursue our separate political career, my most earnest desire will have been fulfilled. But if this be denied us, and the integrity and jurisdiction of our territory be assailed, it will but remain for us with a firm resolve to appeal to arms and invoke the blessings of Providence upon a just cause.

As a consequence of our new constitution, and with a view to meet our anticipated wants, it will be necessary to provide a speedy and efficient organization of the several branches of the executive departments having special charge of our foreign intercourse, financial and military affairs, and postal service. For purposes of defence, the Confederate States may, under ordinary circumstances rely mainly upon their militia; but it is deemed advisable, in the present condition of affairs, that there should be a well instructed, disciplined army, more numerous than would be usually required for a peace establishment.

I also suggest that for the protection of our harbors and commerce on the high seas, a navy adapted to those objects be built up. These necessities have doubtless engaged the attention of Congress.

With a constitution differing only in form from that of our forefathers, in so far as it is explanatory of their well known intents, freed from sectional conflicts which have so much interfered with the pursuits of the general welfare, it is not unreasonable to expect that the States from which we have parted may seek to unite their fortunes with ours under the government we have instituted. For this your constitution has made adequate provision, but beyond this, if I mistake not the judgment and will of the people, our reunion with the States from which we have separated is neither practicable nor desirable. To increase power, develop the resources, and promote the happiness of this Confederacy, it is necessary that there should be so much homogeneity as that the welfare of every portion be the aim of the whole. When this homogeneity does not exist, antagonisms are engendered which must and should result in separation.

Actuated solely by a desire to protect and preserve our own rights and promote our own welfare, the secession of the Confederate States has been marked by no aggression upon others, and followed by no domestic convulsion. Our industrial pursuits have received no check; the cultivation of our fields has progressed as heretofore; and even should we be involved in war, there would be no considerable diminution in the production of the great staple which constitutes our exports, and in which the commercial world has an interest scarcely less than our own. This common interest of producer and consumer can only be interrupted by external force, which would obstruct shipments to foreign markets — a course of conduct which would be detrimental to manufacturing and commercial interests abroad. Should reason guide the action of the government from which we have separated, a policy so injurious to the civilized world, the Northern

States included, could not be dictated even by the strongest desire to inflict injury upon us; but if otherwise, a terrible responsibility will rest upon it, and the suffering of millions will bear testimony to the folly and wickedness of our aggressors. In the meantime there will remain to us, besides the ordinary remedies before suggested, the well known resources for retaliation upon the commerce of our enemy.

Experience in public stations of subordinate grade to this which your kindness has conferred on me, has taught me that care and toil and disappointments are the price of official elevation. You will have many errors to forgive, many deficiencies to tolerate, but you will not find in me either a want of zeal or fidelity to a cause that has my highest hopes and most enduring affection. Your generosity has bestowed upon me an undeserved distinction, one which neither sought nor desired. Upon the continuance of that sentiment, and upon your wisdom and patriotism, I rely to direct and support me in the performance of the duties required at my hands. We have changed the constituent parts, not the system of our government. The constitution formed by our fathers is the constitution of the "Confederate States." In *their* exposition of it, and in the judicial constructions it has received, it has a light that reveals its true meaning. Thus instructed as to the just interpretations of that instrument, and ever remembering that all public offices are but trusts, held for the benefit of the people, and that delegated powers are to be strictly construed, I will hope that by due diligence in the discharge of my duties, though I may disappoint your expectations, yet to retain, when retiring, something of the good will and confidence which welcome my entrance into office. It is joyous in perilous times to look around upon a people united in heart, who are animated and actuated by one and the same purpose and high resolve, with whom the sacrifices to be made are not weighed in the balance against honor, right, liberty and equality. Obstacles may retard, but cannot prevent their progressive movements. Sanctified by justice and sustained by a virtuous people, let me reverently invoke the God of our fathers to guide and protect us in our efforts to perpetuate the principles which by HIS blessing they were able to vindicate, establish and transmit to their posterity, and with the continuance of HIS favor, ever to be gratefully acknowledged, let us look hopefully forward to success, to peace, and to prosperity.

[1861, 1876]

Civil War Songs

Dozens of songs were composed during the Civil War, ranging from marching songs to inspirational songs sung in both army camps and on the home fronts. One of the most familiar of the Southern songs, "Dixie" or "Dixie's Land," was composed by a Northerner, Daniel Emmett (1815–1904). A member of several popular minstrel bands, groups of white musicians who performed in blackface and sang in heavy dialect, Emmett composed the song in 1859 for Bryant's Minstrels in New York City. Although it was also popular in the North, after the outbreak of the Civil War (and to the dismay of Emmett) the song became almost exclusively associated with the South. By the time the war began, Union soldiers were already singing "John Brown's Body," whose anonymous author apparently wrote the lyrics to the tune of a popular camp-meeting song composed in 1856 by William Steffe of South Carolina. The most famous of all Union songs was written later to the same tune. During a visit to a Union army camp in 1861, Julia Ward Howe and her friend James Freeman Clarke heard the troops sing "John Brown's Body." In response to Clarke's challenge that she compose more dignified and noble lyrics for the song, Howe wrote "Battle Hymn of the Republic," a poem that appeared on the first page of the February 1862 issue of the *Atlantic Monthly*. The lyrics swiftly supplanted those of "John Brown's Body," though the chorus of that song was adapted for the "Battle Hymn of the Republic." None of the five stanzas of Howe's poem was followed by a chorus. But the song is traditionally sung and is here printed with the stirring chorus beginning "Glory, Glory Hallelujah," a phrase that in itself conveys the passion and religious fervor that ran through so many of the songs sung in both the North and the South during the Civil War.

DIXIE'S LAND

I wish I was in the land of cotton,
Old times there are not forgotten;
   Look away! Look away! Look away, Dixie's Land!
In Dixie's Land where I was born in,
Early on one frosty morning,   5
   Look away! Look away! Look away, Dixie's Land!

(Chorus)
Then I wish I was in Dixie! Hooray! Hooray!
In Dixie's Land I'll take my stand, to live and die in Dixie!
Away! Away! Away down South in Dixie!
Away! Away! Away down South in Dixie!   10

Old Missus married "Will the Weaver";
William was a gay deceiver!
   Look away! Look away! Look away, Dixie's Land!
But when he put his arm around her,
Smiled as fierce as a forty-pounder![1]   15
   Look away! Look away! Look away, Dixie's Land!
(Chorus)

---

1. **forty-pounder:** Nickname for a large cannon.

His face was sharp as a butcher's cleaver;
But that did not seem to grieve her!
    Look away! Look away! Look away, Dixie's Land!
Old Missus acted the foolish part   20
And died for a man that broke her heart!
    Look away! Look away! Look away, Dixie's Land!
(Chorus)

Now here's a health to the next old missus
And all the gals that want to kiss us!
    Look away! Look away! Look away, Dixie's Land!   25
But if you want to drive away sorrow,
Come and hear this song tomorrow!
    Look away! Look away! Look away, Dixie's Land!
(Chorus)

There's buckwheat cakes and Injin batter,[2]
Makes you fat or a little fatter!   30
    Look away! Look away! Look away, Dixie's Land!
Then hoe it down and scratch your gravel,
To Dixie's Land I'm bound to travel!
    Look away! Look away! Look away, Dixie's Land!
(Chorus)

[1859]

---

2. **Injin batter:** Mixture of corn meal, molasses, and yeast, used to make small cakes.

JOHN BROWN'S BODY

John Brown's body lies a-mouldering in the grave,
John Brown's body lies a-mouldering in the grave,
John Brown's body lies a-mouldering in the grave,
But his soul goes marching on.

(Chorus)
Glory, glory, hallelujah,   5
Glory, glory, hallelujah,
Glory, glory, hallelujah,
His soul goes marching on.

He's gone to be a soldier in the Army of the Lord,
He's gone to be a soldier in the Army of the Lord,   10
He's gone to be a soldier in the Army of the Lord,
His soul goes marching on.
(Chorus)

John Brown's knapsack is strapped upon his back,
John Brown's knapsack is strapped upon his back,
John Brown's knapsack is strapped upon his back,   15
His soul goes marching on.
(Chorus)

John Brown died that the slaves might be free,
John Brown died that the slaves might be free,
John Brown died that the slaves might be free,
But his soul goes marching on.   20
(Chorus)

The stars above in Heaven now are looking kindly down,
The stars above in Heaven now are looking kindly down,
The stars above in Heaven now are looking kindly down,
On the grave of old John Brown.
(Chorus)

[1860-61]

BATTLE HYMN OF THE REPUBLIC

Mine eyes have seen the glory of the coming of the Lord;
He is trampling out the vintage where the grapes of wrath are stored;
He hath loosed the fateful lightning of his terrible swift sword,
His truth is marching on.

(Chorus)
Glory, Glory Hallelujah,   5
Glory, Glory Hallelujah,
Glory, Glory Hallelujah,
His truth is marching on.

I have seen Him in the watch fires of a hundred circling camps;
They have builded Him an altar in the evening dews and damps;   10
I can read his righteous sentence by the dim and flaring lamps,
His day is marching on.
(Chorus)

I have read a fiery gospel writ in burnished rows of steel:
"As ye deal with My contemners, so with you My Grace shall deal;
Let the Hero, born of woman, crush the serpent with his heel,   15
Since God is marching on."
(Chorus)

He has sounded forth the trumpet that shall never call retreat;
He is sifting out the hearts of men before His Judgement Seat;
Oh! be swift, my soul, to answer Him, be jubilant, my feet!
Our God is marching on.   20
(Chorus)

In the beauty of the lilies Christ was born across the sea,
With a glory in his bosom that transfigures you and me;
As He died to make men holy, let us die to make men free,
While God is marching on.
(Chorus)

[1862]

Abraham Lincoln

[1809–1865]

Abraham Lincoln
This photograph of Lincoln was taken in 1864 by the renowned photographer Mathew Brady.

Abraham Lincoln, the sixteenth president of the United States, was born on a farm in Kentucky in 1809. His family moved first to Indiana and then to Illinois. Largely self-educated, Lincoln worked on farms and in stores and studied law as an apprentice. He served in the Illinois legislature and then in the U.S. House of Representatives, slowly gaining a national reputation that finally earned him the Republican nomination for president in 1860. Lincoln carried all eighteen free states but failed to gain a single electoral vote in any of the fourteen slave states, eleven of which seceded within three months of his election. The Civil War began a month after his inauguration in March 1861 and ended only a few days before his assassination in April 1865. Major sources of Lincoln's success as a politician and as a wartime leader were his abilities as a writer and his powerful rhetoric, as illustrated by the following two addresses. Both are among the most famous speeches in American history. The addresses are also among the most eloquent expositions of what the war ultimately meant to Lincoln and many others in the North, as the initial effort to preserve the Union also became a mission to end slavery in the United States.

Reading Lincoln's Gettysburg Address. From July 1-3, 1863, one of the bloodiest and most decisive battles of the Civil War was fought at Gettysburg, Pennsylvania, where roughly ninety thousand Union troops repulsed an invading army of more than seventy thousand led by General Robert E. Lee. The thousands of Union dead were buried in the Soldiers National Cemetery, established on the grounds of the battlefield and dedicated in November 1863. The major speaker was the acclaimed orator Everett Emerson of Massachusetts, who delivered a two-hour address. Lincoln was invited to offer what the program simply described as "Remarks," but he made the most of the occasion. Speaking for only two or three minutes, Lincoln movingly dedicated the cemetery at Gettysburg. He also dedicated the nation to the principle that "all men are created equal," the phrase from the Declaration of Independence quoted in the first sentence of the Gettysburg Address. The text of the speech, which was widely reprinted in newspapers, is that of the "final text" printed in volume 7 of *The Collected Works of Abraham Lincoln*, edited by Roy P. Basler (1953).

The Battle of Gettysburg

A photograph of Union dead on the battleground at Gettysburg, where over three thousand Union troops and nearly four thousand Confederate troops were killed in three days of fighting in July 1863.

THE GETTYSBURG ADDRESS

Address Delivered at the Dedication of the Cemetery at Gettysburg, November 19, 1863

Four score and seven years ago our fathers brought forth on this continent, a new nation, conceived in Liberty, and dedicated to the proposition that all men are created equal.

Now we are engaged in a great civil war, testing whether that nation, or any nation so conceived and so dedicated, can long endure. We are met on a great battle-field of that war. We have come to dedicate a portion of that field, as a final resting place for those who here gave their lives that that nation might live. It is altogether fitting and proper that we should do this.

But, in a larger sense, we can not dedicate — we can not consecrate — we can not hallow — this ground. The brave men, living and dead, who struggled here, have consecrated it, far above our poor power to add or detract. The world will little note, nor long remember what we say here, but it can never forget what they did here. It is for us the living, rather, to be dedicated here to the unfinished work which they who fought here have thus far so nobly advanced. It is rather for us to be here dedicated to the great task remaining before us — that from these honored dead we take increased devotion to that cause for which they gave the last full measure of devotion — that we here highly resolve that these dead shall not have died in vain — that this nation, under God, shall have a new birth of freedom — and that government of the people, by the people, for the people, shall not perish from the earth.

[1863, 1953]

Reading Lincoln's Second Inaugural Address. After winning election to a second term in 1864, Lincoln delivered his second inaugural address on March 4, 1865. By then, a series of military victories by Union forces clearly indicated that the Civil War was drawing to a close. It was equally clear by then just how costly the war had been: together, the number of dead on both sides of the conflict exceeded 600,000, more than in all the other wars in American history combined. Mindful of that terrible toll, Lincoln at once sought to articulate the meaning of the war and to lay the groundwork for peace, reconstruction, and reunification. The text of the address is taken from volume 8 of *The Collected Works of Abraham Lincoln*, edited by Roy P. Basler (1953).

SECOND INAUGURAL ADDRESS, MARCH 4, 1865

At this second appearing to take the oath of the presidential office, there is less occasion for an extended address than there was at the first.[1] Then a statement, somewhat in detail, of a course to be pursued, seemed fitting and proper. Now, at the expiration of four years, during which public declarations have been constantly called forth on every

---

1. **at the first:** Lincoln's first and much-longer inaugural address was delivered on March 4, 1861.

point and phase of the great contest which still absorbs the attention, and engrosses the energies of the nation, little that is new could be presented. The progress of our arms, upon which all else chiefly depends, is as well known to the public as to myself; and it is, I trust, reasonably satisfactory and encouraging to all. With high hope for the future, no prediction in regard to it is ventured.

On the occasion corresponding to this four years ago, all thoughts were anxiously directed to an impending civil-war. All dreaded it — all sought to avert it. While the inaugeral address was being delivered from this place, devoted altogether to *saving* the Union without war, insurgent agents were in the city seeking to *destroy* it without war — seeking to dissolve the Union, and divide effects, by negotiation. Both parties deprecated war; but one of them would *make* war rather than let the nation survive; and the other would *accept* war rather than let it perish. And the war came.

One eighth of the whole population were colored slaves, not distributed generally over the Union, but localized in the Southern part of it. These slaves constituted a peculiar and powerful interest. All knew that this interest was, somehow, the cause of the war. To strengthen, perpetuate, and extend this interest was the object for which the insurgents would rend the Union, even by war; while the government claimed no right to do more than to restrict the territorial enlargement of it. Neither party expected for the war, the magnitude, or the duration, which it has already attained. Neither anticipated that the *cause* of the conflict might cease with, or even before, the conflict itself should cease. Each looked for an easier triumph, and a result less fundamental and astounding. Both read the same Bible, and pray to the same God; and each invokes His aid against the other. It may seem strange that any men should dare to ask a just God's assistance in wringing their bread from the sweat of other men's faces; but let us judge not that we be not judged.[2] The prayers of both could not be answered; that of neither has been answered fully. The Almighty has His own purposes. "Woe unto the world because of offences! for it must needs be that offences come; but woe to that man by whom the offence cometh!"[3] If we shall suppose that American Slavery is one of those offences which, in the providence of God, must needs come, but which, having continued through His appointed time, He now wills to remove, and that He gives to both North and South, this terrible war, as the woe due to those by whom the offence came, shall we discern therein any departure from those divine attributes which the believers in a Living God always ascribe to Him? Fondly do we hope — fervently do we pray — that this mighty scourge of war may speedily pass away. Yet, if God wills that it continue, until all the wealth piled by the bond-man's two hundred and fifty years of unrequited toil shall be sunk, and until every drop of blood drawn with the lash, shall be paid by another drawn with the sword, as was said three thousand years ago, so still it must be said "the judgments of the Lord, are true and righteous altogether."[4]

---

2. **judge not . . . judged:** See Christ's words in the Sermon on the Mount: "Judge not, that ye be not judged" (Matthew 7:1).

3. **"Woe . . . cometh!":** Matthew 18:7. In that chapter of Matthew, Christ teaches his disciples humility, forgiveness, and compassion for others.

4. **"the judgments . . . altogether":** See Psalms 19:9: "The fear of the LORD is clean, enduring forever: the judgments of the LORD are true and righteous altogether."

With malice toward none; with charity for all; with firmness in the right, as God gives us to see the right, let us strive on to finish the work we are in; to bind up the nation's wounds; to care for him who shall have borne the battle, and for his widow, and his orphan — to do all which may achieve and cherish a just, and a lasting peace, among ourselves, and with all nations.

[1865, 1953]

Henry Highland Garnet

[1815–1882]

Henry Highland Garnet

This photograph was taken not long after Garnet became the first African American to deliver a sermon (or any other address) to the assembled members of Congress in 1865.

Henry Highland Garnet was born into slavery in Maryland. When he was nine years old, Garnet's entire family escaped to New York City. He received an excellent education there, and Garnet continued his studies at a school in New Hampshire and then at the Oneida Institute in central New York, where he prepared for the ministry. Garnet became the minister of a predominantly white Presbyterian church in Troy, New York, in 1842. The following year he delivered "An Address to the Slaves of the United States," in which Garnet exhorted his enslaved brethren to rise and strike for "their lives and liberties." During the following two decades, his militant position was endorsed by a growing number of abolitionists, and Garnet was among the first to press the government to enlist African American troops to fight in the Civil War. In 1864, Garnet became the pastor of the influential Fifteenth Street Presbyterian Church in Washington, D.C. Following the passage of the Thirteenth Amendment to the Constitution, which ended slavery in the United States, President Lincoln invited Garnet to deliver a sermon at the House of Representatives, the first time an African American had ever done so. In his "Memorial Discourse," Garnet reviewed the history of slavery and praised the assembled members of Congress for their passage of the Thirteenth Amendment. In his final exhortation, printed on p. 1090, he urged the legislators to go even further, erasing all distinctions based on race from the laws and Constitution of the United States. The text of the selection is taken from *A Memorial Discourse; by Rev. Henry Highland Garnet, Delivered in the Hall of the House of Representatives, Washington, D.C. on Sabbath, February 12, 1865* (1865).

From A MEMORIAL DISCOURSE

It is often asked when and where will the demands of the reformers of this and coming ages end? It is a fair question, and I will answer.

When all unjust and heavy burdens shall be removed from every man in the land. When all invidious and proscriptive distinctions shall be blotted out from our laws, whether they be constitutional, statute, or municipal laws. When emancipation shall be followed by enfranchisement, and all men holding allegiance to the government shall enjoy every right of American citizenship.[1] When our brave and gallant soldiers shall have justice done unto them. When the men who endure the sufferings and perils of the battle-field in the defence of their country, and in order to keep our rulers in their places, shall enjoy the well-earned privilege of voting for them. When in the army and navy, and in every legitimate and honorable occupation, promotion shall smile upon merit without the slightest regard to the complexion of a man's face. When there shall be no more class-legislation, and no more trouble concerning the black man and his rights, than there is in regard to other American citizens. When, in every respect, he shall be equal before the law, and shall be left to make his own way in the social walks of life.

We ask, and only ask, that when our poor frail barks are launched on life's ocean —

> "Bound on a voyage of awful length
> And dangers little known,"[2]

that, in common with others, we may be furnished with rudder, helm, and sails, and charts, and compass. Give us good pilots to conduct us to the open seas; lift no false lights along the dangerous coasts, and if it shall please God to send us propitious winds, or fearful gales, we shall survive or perish as our energies or neglect shall determine. We ask no special favors, but we plead for justice. While we scorn unmanly dependence; in the name of God, the universal Father, we demand the right to live, and labor, and to enjoy the fruits of our toil. The good work which God has assigned for the ages to come, will be finished, when our national literature shall be so purified as to reflect a faithful and a just light upon the character and social habits of our race, and the brush, and

---

1. **When emancipation . . . citizenship:** All those born or naturalized in the United States were later declared to be citizens by the Fourteenth Amendment (1868); "enfranchisement," or the right to vote, was finally guaranteed to black men by the Fifteenth Amendment (1870).
2. **"Bound . . . know":** The lines are from "Human Frailty," by the English poet William Cowper (1731-1800): "Bound on a voyage of awful length / And dangers little known, / A stranger to superior strength, / Man vainly trusts his own."

pencil, and chisel, and Lyre of Art, shall refuse to lend their aid to scoff at the afflictions of the poor, or to caricature, or ridicule a long-suffering people. When caste and prejudice in Christian churches shall be utterly destroyed, and shall be regarded as totally unworthy of Christians, and at variance with the principles of the gospel. When the blessings of the Christian religion, and of sound, religious education, shall be freely offered to all, then, and not till then, shall the effectual labors of God's people and God's instruments cease.

If slavery has been destroyed merely from *necessity*, let every class be enfranchised at the dictation of *justice.* Then we shall have a Constitution that shall be reverenced by all: rulers who shall be honored, and revered, and a Union that shall be sincerely loved by a brave and patriotic people, and which can never be severed.

Great sacrifices have been made by the people; yet, greater still are demanded ere atonement can be made for our national sins. Eternal justice holds heavy mortgages against us, and will require the payment of the last farthing.[3] We have involved ourselves in the sin of unrighteous gain, stimulated by luxury, and pride, and the love of power and oppression; and prosperity and peace can be purchased only by blood, and with tears of repentance. We have paid some of the fearful installments, but there are other heavy obligations to be met.

The great day of the nation's judgment has come, and who shall be able to stand? Even we, whose ancestors have suffered the afflictions which are inseparable from a condition of slavery, for the period of two centuries and a half, now pity our land and weep with those who weep.

Upon the total and complete destruction of this accursed sin depends the safety and perpetuity of our Republic and its excellent institutions.

Let slavery die. It has had a long and fair trial. God himself has pleaded against it. The enlightened nations of the earth have condemned it. Its death warrant is signed by God and man. Do not commute its sentence. Give it no respite, but let it be ignominiously executed.

Honorable Senators and Representatives! illustrious rulers of this great nation! I cannot refrain this day from invoking upon you, in God's name, the blessings of millions who were ready to perish, but to whom a new and better life has been opened by your humanity, justice, and patriotism. You have said, "Let the Constitution of the country be so amended that slavery and involuntary servitude shall no longer exist in the United States, except in punishment for crime."[4] Surely, an act so sublime could not escape Divine notice; and doubtless the deed has been recorded in the archives of heaven. Volumes may be appropriated to your praise and renown in the history of the world. Genius and art may perpetuate the glorious act on canvass and in marble, but certain and more lasting monuments in commemoration of your decision are already erected in the hearts and memories of a grateful people.

---

3. **farthing:** Formerly a coin in Great Britain, equal to a quarter of a penny.
4. **"Let . . . crime":** A close paraphrase of the Thirteenth Amendment, which had been adopted two months earlier, in December 1864.

The nation has begun its exodus from worse than Egyptian bondage; and I beseech you that you say to the people, "*that they go forward.*" With the assurance of God's favor in all things done in obedience to his righteous will, and guided by day and by night by the pillars of cloud and fire, let us not pause until we have reached the other and safe side of the stormy and crimson sea.[5] Let freemen and patriots mete out complete and equal justice to all men, and thus prove to mankind the superiority of our Democratic, Republican Government.

Favored men, and honored of God as his instruments, speedily finish the work which he has given you to do. *Emancipate, Enfranchise, Educate, and give the blessings of the gospel to every American citizen.* . . .

Then before us a path of prosperity will open, and upon us will descend the mercies and favors of God. Then shall the people of other countries, who are standing tip-toe on the shores of every ocean, earnestly looking to see the end of this amazing conflict, behold a Republic that is sufficiently strong to outlive the ruin and desolations of civil war, having the magnanimity to do justice to the poorest and weakest of her citizens. Thus shall we give to the world the form of a model Republic, founded on the principles of justice, and humanity, and Christianity, in which the burdens of war and the blessings of peace are equally borne and enjoyed by all.

[1865]

---

5. **The nation . . . crimson sea:** Garnet refers to Exodus: 14:15, in which God led the ancient Israelites from Egypt toward the promised land with a pillar of cloud by day and a pillar of fire by night, first dividing the Red Sea to allow them to escape from the pursuing Egyptians. As the Israelites approached the sea, terrified by the approach of the Pharaoh's army, Moses declared that God would fight for them: "And the LORD said unto Moses, Wherefore criest thou unto me? speak unto the children of Israel, that they go forward" (14:15).

Mary Boykin Miller Chesnut

[1823–1886]

Mary Boykin Miller, the daughter of Southern planters, married James Chesnut Jr., a lawyer, in 1840. They lived in comfort at Mulberry, a plantation owned by James Chesnut's parents near the small town of Camden, South Carolina. Even before the state seceded from the Union, James Chesnut resigned his U.S. Senate seat in order to support the Confederacy, soon becoming an aide to President Jefferson Davis. On November 8, 1860, Mary Chesnut began a diary that she kept throughout the war, writing her final entry on August 2, 1865. Although she was devoted to the Southern cause, Chesnut clearly had mixed feelings about slavery. At Mulberry, she had taught some of the slaves to read and write; in her diary, she speculated about the fate of female slaves sold at auction. At the same time, she viewed slavery as crucial to the Southern way of life, to which Chesnut was deeply committed. "Slavery has to go, of course, and joy go with it," she asserts in an entry in her diary. "These Yankees may kill us and lay waste our land for a while, but conquer us — never!" Late in her life, Chesnut decided to edit the diary for publication, but she died before completing her work on it. The text of the following selections is taken from *A Diary from Dixie, as written by Mary Boykin Chesnut, wife of James Chesnut, Jr., United States Senator from South Carolina, 1859–1861, and afterward an Aide to Jefferson Davis and a Brigadier-General in the Confederate Army,* edited by Isabella D. Martin and Myrta Lockett Avary (1905).

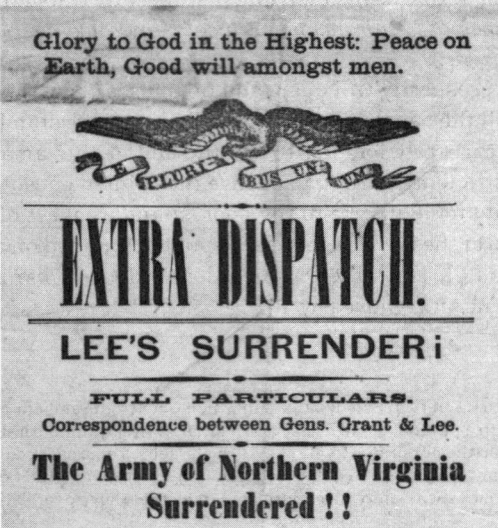

Lee's Surrender

The headline from a special edition of the Philadelphia *Evening Dispatch* announcing the surrender of General Robert E. Lee and his Confederate army in April 1865. (Chicago Historical Society [ICHi-22119].)

A DIARY FROM DIXIE, APRIL 19–22, 1865

April 19th [1865]. Just now, when Mr. Clay dashed up-stairs, pale as a sheet, saying, "General Lee has capitulated," I saw it reflected in Mary Darby's face before I heard him speak. She staggered to the table, sat down, and wept aloud. Mr. Clay's eyes were not dry. Quite beside herself Mary shrieked, "Now we belong to negroes and Yankees!" Buck said, "I do not believe it."

How different from ours of them is their estimate of us. How contradictory is their attitude toward us. To keep the despised and iniquitous South within their borders, as part of their country, they are willing to enlist millions of men at home and abroad, and to spend billions, and we know they do not love fighting *per se*, nor spending money. They are perfectly willing to have three killed for our one. We hear they have all grown rich, through "shoddy,"[1] whatever that is. Genuine Yankees can make a fortune trading jack-knives.

---

1. **"shoddy":** During the Civil War, fortunes were made by those who produced poor-quality supplies for the armies. Such supplies were generally called "shoddy," originally a term for an inferior-quality fabric made from waste woolen cloth.

"Somehow it is borne in on me that we will have to pay the piper," was remarked to-day. "No; blood can not be squeezed from a turnip. You can not pour anything out of an empty cup. We have no money even for taxes or to be confiscated."

While the Preston girls are here, my dining-room is given up to them, and we camp on the landing, with our one table and six chairs. Beds are made on the dining-room floor. Otherwise there is no furniture, except buckets of water and bath-tubs in their improvised chamber. Night and day this landing and these steps are crowded with the *élite* of the Confederacy, going and coming, and when night comes, or rather, bedtime, more beds are made on the floor of the landing-place for the war-worn soldiers to rest upon. The whole house is a bivouac. As Pickens[2] said of South Carolina in 1861, we are "an armed camp."

My husband is rarely at home. I sleep with the girls, and my room is given up to sol-diers. General Lee's few, but undismayed, his remnant of an army, or the part from the South and West, sad and crestfallen, pass through Chester.[3] Many discomfited heroes find their way up these stairs. They say Johnston will not be caught as Lee was. He can retreat; that is his trade. If he would not fight Sherman in the hill country of Georgia, what will he do but retreat in the plains of North Carolina with Grant, Sherman, and Thomas all to the fore?[4]

We are to stay here. Running is useless now; so we mean to bide a Yankee raid, which they say is imminent. Why fly? They are everywhere, these Yankees, like red ants, like the locusts and frogs which were the plagues of Egypt.[5]

The plucky way in which our men keep up is beyond praise. There is no howling, and our poverty is made a matter of laughing. We deride our own penury. Of the country we try not to speak at all.

April 22d. This yellow Confederate quire of paper,[6] my journal, blotted by entries, has been buried three days with the silver sugar-dish, teapot, milk-jug, and a few spoons and forks that follow my fortunes as I wander. With these valuables was Hood's silver cup, which was partly crushed when he was wounded at Chickamauga.[7]

It has been a wild three days, with aides galloping around with messages, Yankees hanging over us like a sword of Damocles.[8] We have been in queer straits. We sat up at Mrs. Bedon's dressed, without once going to bed for forty-eight hours, and we were aweary.

---

2. **Pickens:** Francis Wilkinson Pickens (1805–1869), the governor of South Carolina from 1860 to 1862.
3. **Chester:** A town just south of Richmond, Virginia, and a major shipping point on the Petersburg Railroad until Union forces destroyed the tracks in 1864. During most of the war, the Chesnuts lived in a hotel in Richmond, the capital of the Confederacy.
4. **They say Johnston . . . to the fore?:** Chesnut refers to a number of key military leaders in the final stages of the war: Confederate general Joseph Eggleston Johnston (1807–1891); Union general William Tecumseh Sherman (1820–1891); Union general Ulysses S. Grant (1822–1885); and Union general Edward Lloyd Thomas (1825–1898).
5. **plagues of Egypt:** The calamities visited on the Egyptians by God in order to force the Pharaoh to allow the Israelites to leave and seek the promised land, as described in Exodus 7–10.
6. **quire of paper:** Four sheets of paper folded in half to form eight pages.
7. **Hood's silver cup . . . Chickamauga:** Confederate general John Bell Hood (1831–1879) was severely wounded and lost his right leg in the battle of Chickamauga, in September 1863.
8. **sword of Damocles:** In order to teach his talkative official a lesson, the ancient Greek tyrant Dionysius had a sword suspended by a thread over Damocles's seat at a banquet. The sword of Damocles came to refer to the constant possibility of disaster or doom.

Colonel Cadwallader Jones came with a despatch, a sealed secret despatch. It was for General Chesnut. I opened it. Lincoln, old Abe Lincoln, has been killed, murdered, and Seward wounded![9] Why? By whom? It is simply maddening, all this.

I sent off messenger after messenger for General Chesnut. I have not the faintest idea where he is, but I know this foul murder will bring upon us worse miseries. Mary Darby says, "But they murdered him themselves. No Confederates are in Washington." "But if they see fit to accuse us of instigating it?" "Who murdered him? Who knows?" "See if they don't take vengeance on us, now that we are ruined and can not repel them any longer."

The death of Lincoln I call a warning to tyrants.[10] He will not be the last President put to death in the capital, though he is the first.

[1865, 1905]

---

9. **Lincoln . . . and Seward wounded!:** Lincoln was shot by John Wilkes Booth on April 14, 1865, while the president and his wife attended a play at Ford's Theatre in Washington, D.C. The assassination was part of a conspiracy to avenge the defeat of the Confederacy by assassinating Lincoln, Vice President Andrew Johnson, and William Seward, the secretary of state. Lincoln died early in the morning of April 15. Seward suffered stab wounds at the hands of one of the co-conspirators, but he was not seriously hurt. Johnson was not attacked.
10. **warning to tyrants:** Chesnut expressed a sentiment common among Southerners and sympathizers with their cause. After John Wilkes Booth shot President Lincoln and leaped to the stage of Ford's Theatre, many in the audience thought they heard him proclaim "*sic semper tyrannis*" — Latin for "as always to tyrants" and the motto of the state of Virginia.

William Cullen Bryant

[1794-1878]

William Cullen Bryant, whose life and works are described in more detail on page 467 of this volume, was a staunch abolitionist throughout his career as a poet and an editor of the influential New York *Evening Post*. He was also a great admirer of President Lincoln, whose assassination in April 1865 — only five days after Robert E. Lee surrendered his Confederate army to Ulysses S. Grant at Appomattox Court House, Virginia — generated profound shock and an outpouring of grief in the North. Lincoln was shot by John Wilkes Booth on April 14, Good Friday. His death early the following morning transformed him in the eyes of many into a Christlike figure, a martyr who had sacrificed his life to free the slaves and to preserve the Union. The first of many funeral services was conducted on April 19 at the White House, after which a horse-drawn hearse carrying Lincoln's remains was accompanied by a procession to the Capitol, where he lay in state in the rotunda. Two days later, his coffin was placed aboard a special train that stopped for funeral services in ten cities on its twelve-day journey to Springfield, Illinois, where Lincoln was buried on May 4. Many poets wrote tributes to the slain president, among the most famous of which are Walt Whitman's "When Lilacs Last in the Dooryard Bloom'd," printed on page 1032, and Bryant's more public elegy, "The Death of Lincoln." The text is taken from *Poems, by William Cullen Bryant. Collected and arranged by the author* (1876).

Lincoln's Funeral Procession

In this photograph of the funeral procession in Washington, D.C., a horse-drawn hearse carries Lincoln's coffin from the White House to the Capitol, where he lay in state in the rotunda.

THE DEATH OF LINCOLN

Oh, slow to smite and swift to spare,
    Gentle and merciful and just!
Who, in the fear of God, didst bear
    The sword of power, a nation's trust!

In sorrow by thy bier[1] we stand,   5
    Amid the awe that hushes all,
And speak the anguish of a land
    That shook with horror at thy fall.

Thy task is done; the bond[2] are free:
    We bear thee to an honored grave.   10
Whose proudest monument shall be
    The broken fetters of the slave.

Pure was thy life: its bloody close
    Hath placed thee with the sons of light,
Among the noble host of those   15
    Who perished in the cause of Right.

                    [1865, 1876]

---

1. **bier:** A movable frame on which a coffin is placed for movement to a burial ground.
2. **bond:** An alternate term for *bondsmen*, or slaves.

Walt Whitman

[1819-1892]

Walt Whitman, whose life and work are described in more detail on page 968 of this volume, is the American writer most closely associated with the Civil War. His *Drum-Taps* (1865) is the most famous collection of poetry to emerge from the war, and Whitman wrote a series of celebrated elegies on the death of his hero President Lincoln. During the war, Whitman also kept notebooks in which he jotted down the impressions he gathered as a volunteer nurse in army hospitals in and around Washington, D.C. A decade after the end of the war, Whitman gathered together and published those jottings as *Memoranda during the War.* As he noted in an introduction to the small book, most of it consisted of verbatim transcripts of the notes he had made between 1862 and 1865. At the end of the book, however, Whitman sought to summarize the experience of the war, both his own and that of his country. As the nation approached its centennial, Whitman was deeply concerned with the continuing bitterness and divisions between the North and the South. Memories of the war were a major source of those divisions, but Whitman suggested that the shared sense of grief and the ongoing mourning for all those who had died in the conflict might serve as a means of reuniting the nation. Appealing to the restorative powers of nature, he thus concluded his book with images of healing and on a note of reconciliation between the North and the South. The text of the following selections is taken from the first edition of *Memoranda during the War* (1875-76).

From MEMORANDA DURING THE WAR

Three Years Summ'd Up

During my past three years in Hospital, camp or field, I made over 600 visits or tours, and went, as I estimate, among from 80,000 to 100,000 of the wounded and sick, as sustainer of spirit and body in some degree, in time of need. These visits varied from an hour or two, to all day or night; for with dear or critical cases I always watch'd all night. Sometimes I took up my quarters in the Hospital, and slept or watch'd there several nights in succession. Those three years I consider the greatest privilege and satisfaction, (with all their feverish excitements and physical deprivations and lamentable sights,) and, of course, the most profound lesson and reminiscence, of my life. I can say that in my ministerings I comprehended all, whoever came in my way, Northern or Southern, and slighted none. It afforded me, too, the perusal of those subtlest, rarest, divinest volumes of Humanity, laid bare in its inmost recesses, and of actual life and death, better than the finest, most labor'd narratives, histories, poems in the libraries. It arous'd and brought out and decided undream'd-of depths of emotion. It has given me my plainest and most fervent views of the true *ensemble* and extent of The States. While I was with wounded and sick in thousands of cases from the New England States, and from New York, New Jersey, and

Pennsylvania, and from Michigan, Wisconsin, Ohio, Indiana, Illinois, and all the Western States, was with more or less from all the States, North and South, without exception. I was with many from the Border States, especially from Maryland and Virginia; and found, during those lurid years 1862-65, far more Union Southerners, especially Tennesseans, than is supposed. I was with many rebel officers and men among our wounded, and gave them always what I had, and tried to cheer them the same as any. I was among the army teamsters considerably, and, indeed, always found myself drawn to them. Among the black soldiers, wounded or sick, and in the contraband camps, I also took my way whenever in their neighborhood, and did what I could for them.

The Million Dead, Too, Summ'd Up — the Unknown

The Dead in this War — there they lie, strewing the fields and woods and valleys and battle-fields of the South — Virginia, the Peninsula — Malvern Hill and Fair Oaks — the banks of the Chickahominy — the terraces of Fredericksburgh — Antietam bridge — the grisly ravines of Manassas — the bloody promenade of the Wilderness — the varieties of the *strayed* dead, (the estimate of the War Department is 25,000 National soldiers kill'd in battle and never buried at all, 5,000 drown'd — 15,000 inhumed strangers or on the march in haste, in hitherto unfound localities — 2,000 graves cover'd by sand and mud, by Mississippi freshets, 3,000 carried away by caving-in of banks, &c.,) — Gettysburgh, the West, Southwest — Vicksburg — Chattanooga — the trenches of Petersburgh — the numberless battles, camps, Hospitals everywhere pass'd away since that War, and its wholesale deaths, burials, graves. (*They* make indeed the true Memoranda of the War — mute, subtle, immortal.) From ten years' rain and snow, in their seasons — grass, clover, pine trees, orchards, forests — from all the noiseless miracles of soil and sun and running streams — how peaceful and how beautiful appear to-day even the Battle-Trenches, and the many hundred thousand Cemetery mounds! Even at Andersonville,[1] to-day, innocence and a smile. (A late account says, "The stockade has fallen to decay, is grown upon, and a season more will efface it entirely, except from our hearts and memories. The *dead line*, over which so many brave soldiers pass'd to the freedom of eternity rather than endure the misery of life, can only be traced here and there, for most of the old marks the last ten years have obliterated. The thirty-five wells, which the prisoners dug with cups and spoons, remain just as they were left. And the wonderful spring which was discover'd one morning, after a thunder storm, flowing down the hillside, still yields its sweet, pure water as freely now as then. The Cemetery, with its thirteen thousand graves, is on the slope of a beautiful hill. Over the quiet spot already trees give the cool shade which would have been so gratefully sought by the poor fellows whose lives were ended under the scorching sun.")

And now, to thought of these — on these graves of the dead of the War, as on an altar — to memory of these, or North or South, I close and dedicate my book.

[1875-76]

1. **Andersonville:** Built in Georgia in 1864, Andersonville was one of the largest and the most infamous of the Confederate military prisons. Of the forty-five thousand Union prisoners confined there during the fourteen months the prison existed, thirteen thousand died of disease, exposure, or malnutrition.

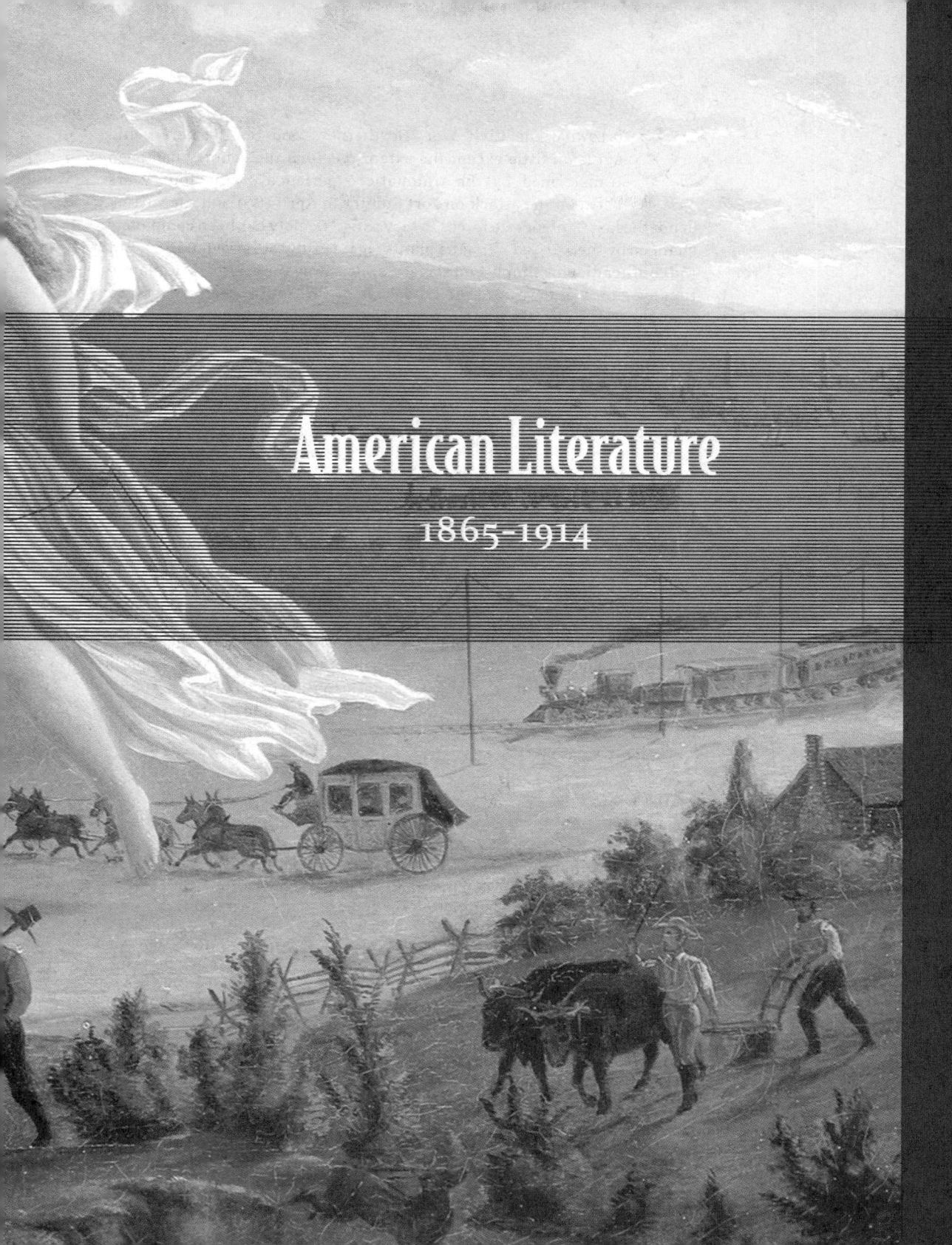

American Literature

1865–1914

$\mathcal{F}$ OLLOWING the Civil War, Northerners and Southerners could agree on little except the extent to which the country had been transformed by the traumatic experience of the four years between the attack on Fort Sumter in April 1861 and the surrender of the last Confederate forces in May 1865. "Society has been completely changed by the war," a Louisiana planter mournfully observed in 1865. But the conflict did not simply end slavery, sweep away the aristocratic plantation system, and devastate the landscape of the South. It also hastened changes that radically transformed life in the North. George Ticknor, a retired professor at Harvard College, wrote in 1868 that the war had created a "great gulf between what happened before in our century and what has happened since, or what is likely to happen hereafter. It does not seem to me as if I were living in the country in which I was born." The gulf between life before and after the war continued to expand during the following decades, as millions of settlers moved into the West and as unprecedented levels of immigration stimulated rapid industrialization in the North. Paradoxically, even as the reunited country developed into a world power, it was increasingly divided along lines of class, ethnicity, and race in a period that ushered in a modern and ever more multicultural America.

The Aftermath of the Civil War

In the years immediately following the end of hostilities, the nation struggled to come to terms with the terrible toll of the Civil War. Experts estimate that as many as 620,000 Americans died in the war, roughly 360,000 Union and 260,000 Confederate troops, and that more than

◀ (OVERLEAF)

American Progress

This chromolithograph, based on an 1872 painting of the same title by John Gast, reveals the conceptions many Americans then shared about "manifest destiny." In an elaborate explanation of the patriotic symbolism of the picture, the publisher described it as an illustration of "the grand drama of Progress in the civilization, settlement and history of our civilization," personified by a female figure "floating westward through the air bearing on her forehead 'The Star of Empire.'" In one hand she carries a book, "the emblem of Education and the testimonial of our national enlightenment," while with the other hand she stretches out the wires of the telegraph. She hovers over forms of technology and transportation, including the newly completed transcontinental railroad, and hunters, miners, and homesteaders crossing the Great Plains. Before them, "fleeing from 'Progress,'" are wild game and Indians, "moving Westward, ever Westward." In fact, many Indian tribes fought to retain their traditional homelands until the federal army finally forced them onto reservations to make room for the millions of settlers who poured into the West during the decades following the Civil War.

400,000 were wounded. Walt Whitman and Herman Melville published elegiac volumes of poetry about the war, and Elizabeth Stuart Phelps offered consolation to the grief-stricken country in her novel *The Gates Ajar*, in which a young woman mourning the death of her brother, killed in the war, finds comfort in the Spiritualist belief that those who have gone to heaven retain a vital link to their loved ones left behind on earth. Phelps's best-selling novel was published in 1868, the year that General John Logan, commander of the Grand Army of the Republic, issued a proclamation designating May 30 as a memorial day "for the purpose of strewing with flowers or otherwise decorating the graves of comrades who died in defense of their country during the late rebellion, and whose bodies now lie in almost every city, village, and hamlet churchyard in the land." Even before his official proclamation, the decoration of the graves of soldiers who had died in the war had become a common ritual of mourning in the North and the South. L. Nella Sweet's hymn "Kneel Where Our Loved Ones Are Sleeping,"

Charles S. Reinhart, "The Floral Tribute to the Nation's Dead"

This engraving of families mourning those who died in military service during the Civil War appeared in *Harper's Weekly* in 1870, by which time the ritual of decorating the graves of "Our Fallen Heroes" was well established in both the North and the South. Although neither the image nor the caption explicitly states on which side these war dead fought, the inscription on the stone marker at the lower left – "These Shall Not Have Died In Vain," a line from Lincoln's Gettysburg Address – indicates that they fought and died for the Union.

which was published in 1867, was thus dedicated "To the Ladies of the South who are Decorating the Graves of the 'Confederate Dead.'"

Even as the nation mourned, it struggled with questions about how and under what terms to unite the North and the South. In his final speech, delivered a few days before his assassination in April 1865, Abraham Lincoln described the daunting task of bringing together the bitterly divided country and of reconstructing the South. "No one man has authority to give up the rebellion for any other man," Lincoln somberly observed. "We simply must begin with, and mould from, disorganized and discordant elements. Nor is it a small additional embarrassment that we, the loyal people, differ among ourselves as to the mode, manner, and means of reconstruction." The differences in the North over the "means of reconstruction" became even more apparent after Lincoln's death, as Congress wrangled with the new president, Andrew Johnson of Tennessee, who reportedly declared, "This is a country for white men, and as long as I am president, it shall be a government for white men." In 1866, Johnson vetoed the Fourteenth Amendment, which would have granted citizenship to all persons born in the United States, including former slaves. The veto outraged moderates and generated growing support in Congress for the "Radical Republicans," who favored greater support for former slaves and a more "radical" reconstruction of the South. Overriding the veto of the amendment, which was formally adopted by the states two years later, Congress passed the first of the Reconstruction Acts in 1867.

"We simply must begin with, and mould from, disorganized and discordant elements. Nor is it a small additional embarrassment that we, the loyal people, differ among ourselves as to the mode, manner, and means of reconstruction."

African Americans made strong gains during the following decade of Reconstruction. President Johnson's repeated vetoes of civil-rights legislation led to his impeachment by an angry Congress. He survived by a single vote, but in 1868 the Republican Party replaced Johnson as their presidential nominee with General Ulysses S. Grant, the Civil War hero who subsequently served two terms as president. Grant presided over the passage of the Fifteenth Amendment (1870), which provided voting rights to all qualified adult males, regardless of race or previous condition of servitude. The amendment enabled African American men to participate fully in the political process, both as voters and as representatives on the state and national levels, and several African Americans were consequently elected to Congress. Reconstruction reached its high-water mark when Congress passed the sweeping Civil Rights Act of 1875. The law guaranteed all Americans, regardless of their race, access to public accommodations and facilities — such as restaurants, theaters, trains, and other public transportation — and protected their right to serve on juries.

The following year, however, Reconstruction came to an abrupt end as a result of the disputed presidential election of 1876. Samuel J. Tilden, a Democrat from New York, won the popular vote but fell one vote short of the necessary majority of the electoral vote because of disputed returns in four states, three of them in the South. An electoral commission set up by

Congress awarded the four states and the election to the Republican candidate, Rutherford B. Hayes. In what became known as the Compromise of 1877, the Republicans gained support for the commission's decision by offering southern Democrats in Congress a number of concessions, including the withdrawal of federal troops from the South.

The withdrawal of the troops, which had been deployed to ensure free elections and to protect black populations from attacks by whites who were determined to retain political power in the South, delivered a fatal blow to the civil rights and political aspirations of African Americans. The federal government effectively ceased to enforce the Fourteenth and Fifteenth Amendments, and the Supreme Court declared the Civil Rights Act of 1875 unconstitutional in 1883. Southern states soon began to enact legal codes—the so-called Jim Crow laws, named after a grotesque character who performed in "blackface" in popular minstrel shows—that legalized segregation. The states also adopted poll taxes and discriminatory literacy tests that disenfranchised many black voters. The African American activist Ida B. Wells led a crusade against lynching, but Congress refused to pass an antilynching law, and African Americans suffered growing violence at the hands of organized white terror groups such as the Ku Klux Klan. In 1896 the Supreme Court affirmed the legality of segregation laws in the case of *Plessy v. Ferguson*, which challenged a Louisiana law that required blacks to ride in separate railroad cars, ruling that the law was constitutional and that such "separate but equal" accommodations did not stamp the "colored race with the badge of inferiority."

African Americans suffered cultural as well as legislative and judicial setbacks. The growing indifference of many white Americans to the struggle for freedom and racial equality was revealed in changing interpretations of the meaning of the Civil War. John W. De Forest announced his pro-Union plot and theme in the title of his early novel about the war, *Miss Ravenel's Conversion from Secession to Loyalty* (1867), in which one of the central characters defined the conflict as the culminating act in "the drama of human liberty" a "struggle for the freedom of all men, without distinction of race and color." In Albion Tourgée's popular novel *A Fool's Errand* (1879), he attributes the ultimate defeat of that larger struggle to Southern racial bias and recalcitrance, indicting the federal government for its failure to check the crimes of the Ku Klux Klan and to transform the culture of the South during Reconstruction. But writers and publishers soon shifted their attention from the bitter aftermath of the conflict to the battles of the Civil War. In innumerable works—such as *The Personal Memoirs of U. S. Grant* (1885), which sold more than 300,000 copies within a year—former Union and Confederate soldiers recalled the fortitude and heroism displayed by combatants (almost invariably white soldiers and leaders) on both sides of the conflict. Concepts such as "honor" and "glory," which the authors of those accounts frequently evoked, had no place in Ambrose Bierce's unflinching short stories about the horrors of battle or

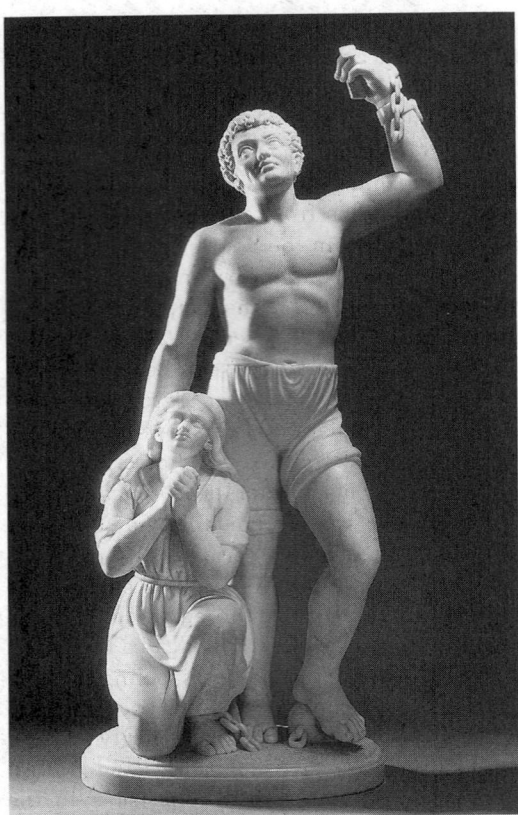

Edmonia Lewis, *Forever Free*

In this sculptural group, originally called *The Morning of Liberty*, the figures of two slaves, with their chains broken, rejoice in and offer prayerful thanks for the Emancipation Proclamation of 1863. Lewis, of mixed African American and Native American ancestry, sculpted the figures in 1867, at a time when many Americans hoped that Reconstruction would usher in a new era of freedom and equality in the United States.

in the most famous and best-selling novel about the war, Stephen Crane's *The Red Badge of Courage* (1895). Like most of the authors of histories, memoirs, and other popular writings about the Civil War at that time, however, Bierce and Crane largely ignored the causes and consequences of the war, which many white Americans came to view as a tragic and unnecessary conflict that had destroyed an idyllic plantation system in the South.

That "plantation myth" and its attendant racial stereotypes took deep root in American culture. A host of white writers contributed to the development of the myth, including Joel Chandler Harris, who published several collections of his popular *Uncle Remus* stories between 1881 and 1906, and especially Thomas Nelson Page, a white supremacist who in essays, poetry, novels, and stories such as those collected in *Ole Virginia* (1887) evoked a world of contented slaves and their benign masters in the antebellum South. In response to Page and his many imitators, the African American writer Charles W. Chesnutt sought to subvert the plantation myth by writing a series of stories about slavery, some of which were collected in *The Conjure Woman* (1899). Another African American writer, Pauline Hopkins, traced the bitter fortunes of a black family before and after the Civil War in her most famous novel, *Contending Forces; or, A Romance Illustrative of Negro Life North and South* (1900). But their realistic portrayals of slavery and the experiences of African Americans were overshadowed by romantic depictions of the "old South," as well as by works such as Thomas Dixon's hugely popular and viciously racist "Clan Trilogy" (1902–07), novels about Reconstruction in which the villains are emancipated slaves and the heroic defender of Aryan civilization is the Ku Klux Klan. The emerging technology of film also perpetuated the plantation

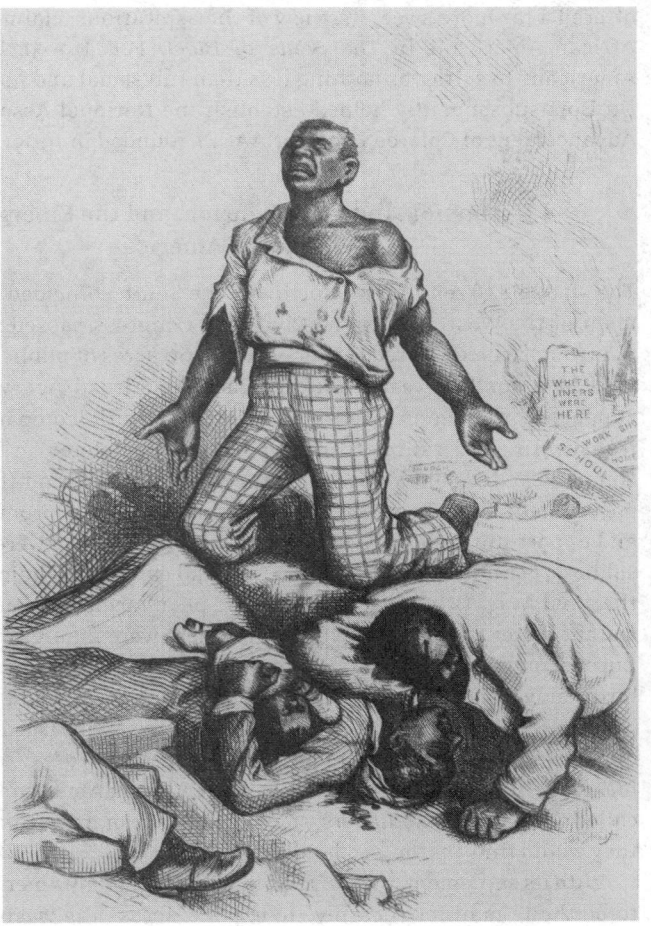

Thomas Nast, "Is This a Republican Form of Government?"

Published in *Harper's Weekly* in 1876, this engraving of a man kneeling by the bodies of murdered African Americans protests the federal government's failure to protect black populations from growing violence in the South. In the background — behind debris labeled "Work Shop," "School," and "Home" — a sign reads, "The White Liners Were Here," a reference to one of a number of white terrorist groups, which also included the White League and the Ku Klux Klan. The caption below the drawing reads, "Is this a republican form of government? Is this protecting life, liberty, or property? Is this equal protection under the laws?"

myth. Based on popular "Tom Shows," one of the first feature films was *Uncle Tom's Cabin*, subtitled *Slavery Days*, a distorted version of Harriet Beecher Stowe's antislavery novel in which even at a slave auction the slaves were shown "singing, dancing, shooting craps, and otherwise enjoying themselves," as the scene in the movie was described in the catalog for the film published by the Thomas A. Edison Company in 1903.

In the face of widespread racism and discrimination, African Americans divided over the ways in which they might seek to gain equality and civil rights in the United States. In numerous speeches and writings, including his warmly received autobiography, *Up from Slavery* (1901), Booker T. Washington affirmed that African Americans should devote their energies to economic and educational advancement, rather than pressing for social equality and political rights. W. E. B. Du Bois, who rejected Washington's accommodation to the attitudes and values of white America, offered a far-more sweeping view of the aspirations, claims, and rights of African Americans in *The Souls of Black Folk* (1903). Urging African Americans to settle for nothing less than full social and political equality, Du Bois subsequently helped establish the National Association for the Advancement of Colored People (NAACP), founded in 1909.

Expansion, Industrialization, and the Emergence of Modern America

The struggle to reunite the North and the South coincided with the settlement of the West. During the Civil War, Congress passed the Homestead Act (1862), which offered settlers title to 160 acres of public land after they worked it for five years, and the Pacific Railroad Act, which provided support to the Union Pacific and Central Pacific companies to build a transcontinental railroad line, which was completed in 1869. Railroad companies also sold at low rates the vast tracts of land they received as government subsidies. Lured by cheap land and the promise of freedom and opportunity, millions of settlers went west. Some were former Union soldiers, claiming the land grants they had earned for their service during the Civil War. Others were jobless or poor farmers from the East who sought better lands in the West. Still others were immigrants from across Europe, many of whom settled in areas that were viewed as harsh and inhospitable, especially the arid Great Plains. After the end of Reconstruction in 1877, thousands of African Americans sought freedom from racial oppression in the South by moving west, especially to Kansas. Led by a former slave, Benjamin "Pap" Singleton, the African American homesteaders called themselves *Exodusters*, sharing the hope of many other settlers that they would find a promised land in the West.

With its settlement, the country fulfilled what many Americans conceived to be their "manifest destiny" to expand across the western part of the continent, large portions of which had become U.S. territory as part of the treaty ending the Mexican War in 1848. American artists celebrated manifest destiny in paintings and stories of heroic pioneers bringing "civilization" to the West. But that process was viewed in a far different light by one of the first Mexican American writers to publish in English, María Amparo Ruiz de Burton. Describing her response to the term *manifest destiny* in a letter written in 1871, Ruiz de Burton angrily exclaimed: "Of all the evil phrases ever invented in order to create buffoons, there is not one phrase more detestable for me than that one, the most offensive, the most insulting; my blood rises to the top of my head when I hear it, and I see as if in a photographic instance, all that the Yankees have done to make Mexicans suffer—the robbery of Texas; war; [and] the robbery of California." As railroads reached into more and more areas that had once been part of Mexico,

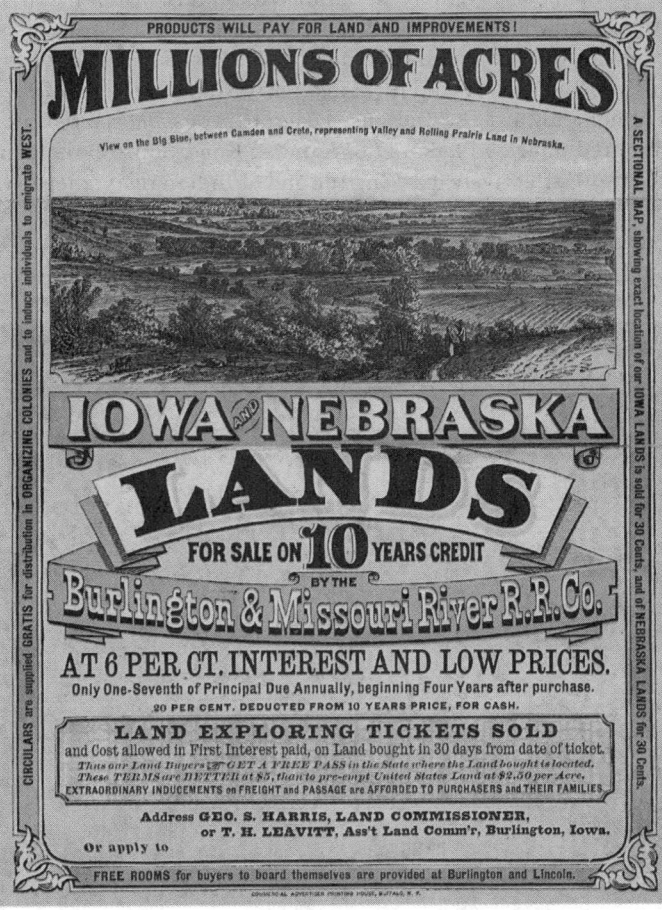

Advertisement for Western Lands

Railroad companies lured passengers and settlers by selling land in the West. By the time this poster was printed in 1872, the Burlington & Missouri Railroad Company ran from Chicago across Illinois and Iowa and deep into Nebraska.

Anglo-Americans arrived in large numbers, overwhelming and further marginalizing the Mexican American population, especially in southern California. In her novel *The Squatter and the Don* (1885), Ruiz de Burton dramatized the cultural clashes, racial tensions, and struggles over land between Anglo-American squatters and a Mexican American landowner in California.

The settlement of the West proved to be even more disastrous for Native Americans. In a last-ditch effort to preserve their way of life and to protect their lands from the relentless encroachment of white settlers, the Lakota (Sioux) and Cheyenne fought and won the battle of Little Bighorn in 1876. But the federal government swiftly overcame their resistance and redrew the boundary lines of Indian reservations, opening up vast portions of them to American settlers. The white reformer Helen Hunt Jackson documented the brutal history of the mistreatment of Native Americans in *A Century of Dishonor* (1883), a copy of which she sent to every member of Congress. Sarah Winnemucca Hopkins, the first Native American woman to publish a book in the United States, also pleaded the cause of the Indians in *Life among the Piutes: Their Wrongs and Claims* (1883). Such efforts did little to alter the harsh policies of the federal government toward the Indians. Federal troops massacred more than one hundred unarmed Lakota at Wounded Knee, South Dakota, on December 29, 1890, effectively marking the end of Indian resistance to the army and policies of the United States. After that, the struggle for Indian rights increasingly shifted to politics and print culture. Charles A. Eastman (Ohiyesa) began his literary career with a popular account of his traditional

San Carlos Apache Indian Reservation

Many bands of Apache were forcibly relocated from their traditional homelands, which once extended across Arizona and New Mexico, to this reservation in southeastern Arizona, established in 1872. Katherine Taylor Dodge took this photograph of men, women, and children waiting in line for supplies outside an agency building on "issue day" in 1899.

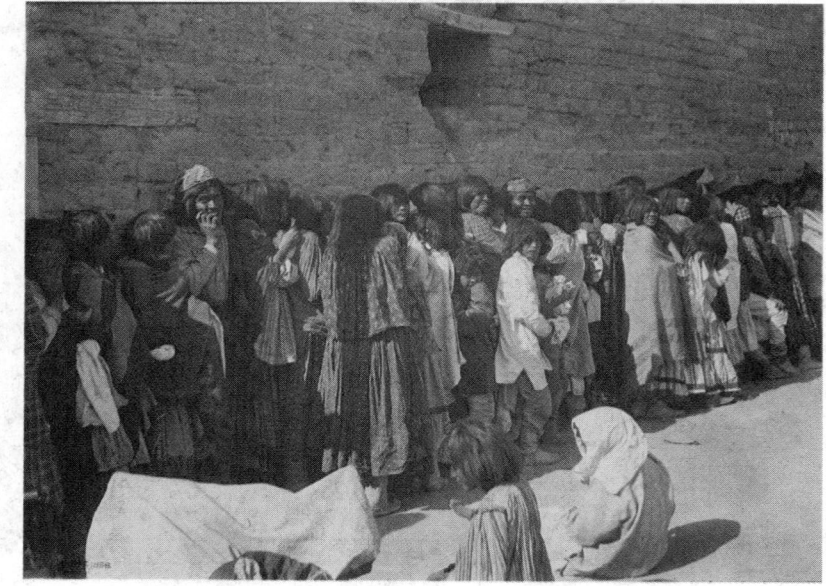

Lakota upbringing, *Indian Boyhood* (1902). Another indigenous writer, Zitkala-Ša, exploited the literacy she had gained in English at an "assimilation school" for Indians to challenge the policies of assimilation and to preserve the traditions of Native Americans.

Immigration also raised questions about how the so-called alien populations might be assimilated into American society and culture. In the period from 1865 to 1914, during which the population of the country grew from fewer than 40 million to over 100 million people, more than 25 million immigrants arrived in the United States. The most profound symbol of America's welcome to immigrants ultimately became the Statue of Liberty, given by the people of France in honor of the celebration of the U.S. centennial in 1876. But many Americans contested the meaning of the monument, which was not erected in New York harbor until 1886. The dignitaries who spoke at the opening ceremonies emphasized the

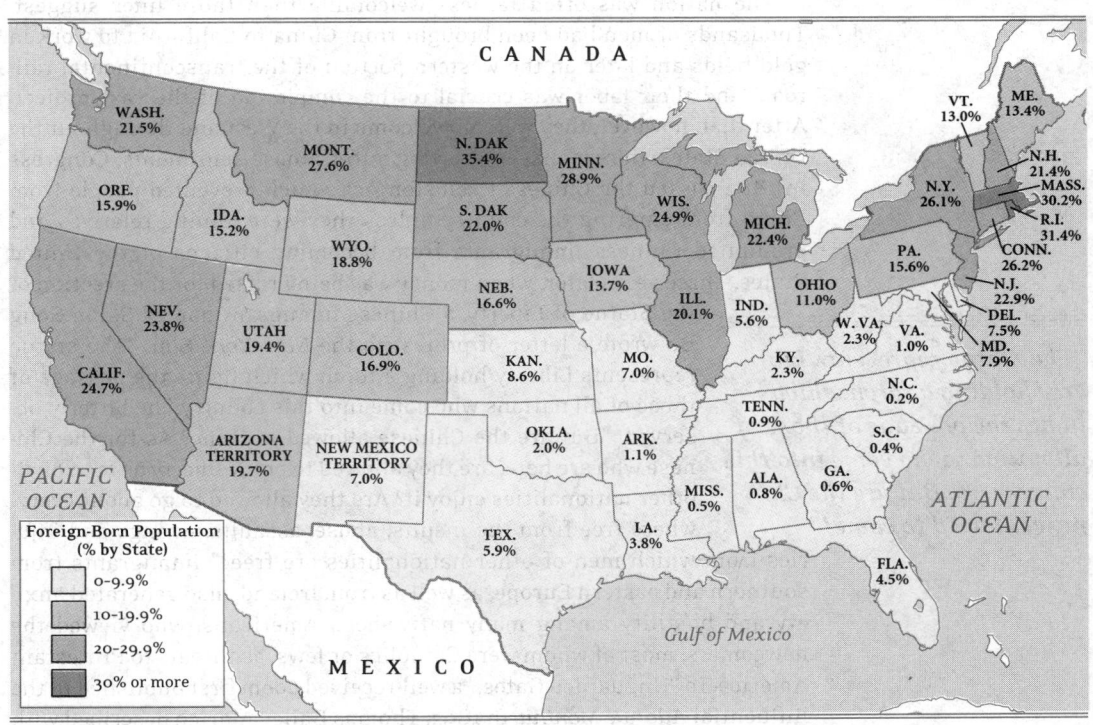

Immigrants in the United States, 1900

As this map illustrates, most of the millions of immigrants who arrived in the United States in the decades following the Civil War settled in the East, Midwest, and West, and foreign-born inhabitants exceeded 30 percent of the population of some states in 1900.

political symbolism of the statue, which was then called *Liberty Enlightening the World.* As early as 1883, however, the Jewish American poet Emma Lazarus affirmed a different meaning of the monument in her poem "The New Colossus." For Lazarus, the uplifted torch that *Liberty* holds was not a symbol of political enlightenment but a guiding light and welcoming gesture to immigrants from Europe. The words of "The New Colossus" were eventually inscribed on a bronze plaque that was attached to a wall in the base of the Statue of Liberty. Many subsequently came to understand the statue to be speaking the concluding lines of the famous poem:

> Give me your tired, your poor,
> Your huddled masses yearning to breathe free,
> The wretched refuse of your teeming shore.
> Send these, the homeless, tempest-tost, to me,
> I lift my lamp beside the golden door!

The nation was often far-less welcoming than those lines suggest. Thousands of men had been brought from China to California to work in gold fields and later on the western portion of the transcontinental railroad, and their labor was crucial to the completion of the vast project. After that, however, they were unwelcome in the West and throughout the United States. In response to growing anti-Chinese sentiments, Congress in 1882 passed the Chinese Exclusion Act, which prevented people from China from entering the country unless they were joining relatives and prohibited Chinese immigrants from becoming citizens of the United States. Three years later, when money was being raised for the erection of the Statue of Liberty, a Chinese immigrant named Saum Song Bo wrote a letter of protest to the *New York Sun.* "The statue represents Liberty holding a torch which lights the passage of those of all nations who come into this country," he bitterly observed. "But are the Chinese allowed to come? As for the Chinese who are here, are they allowed to enjoy liberty as men of all other nationalities enjoy it? Are they allowed to go about everywhere free from the insults, abuse, assaults, wrongs and injuries from which men of other nationalities are free?" Immigrants from southern and eastern Europe, as well as from Ireland, also generated anxiety and hostility among many native-born Americans, who viewed the newcomers, most of whom were Catholics or Jews, as threats to Protestant America. In "Unguarded Gates," a well-received poem first published in the influential *Atlantic Monthly* in 1892, Thomas Bailey Aldrich described with dismay the "wild motley throng" passing through New York harbor, bringing with them "unknown gods and rites," "tiger passions, here to stretch their claws," and "strange tongues . . . alien to our air." Aldrich's concern about the impact of the new arrivals on American culture and society was echoed in numerous magazine and newspaper articles on "the immigration question" and what it meant to be an "American."

"The statue represents Liberty holding a torch which lights the passage of those of all nations who come into this country. . . . But are the Chinese allowed to come?"

VOL. 17 NO. 440   MARCH 22 1890.   PRICE 10 CENTS.

Judge

ENTERED AT THE POST OFFICE AT NEW YORK AS SECOND CLASS MATTER.   COPYRIGHT 1890 BY THE JUDGE PUBLISHING CO.

THE PROPOSED EMIGRANT DUMPING SITE.

STATUE OF LIBERTY.—"Mr. Windom, if you are going to make this island a garbage heap, I am going back to France."

"The Proposed Emigrant Dumping Site"

In this anti-immigration cartoon, used on the cover of the conservative magazine *Judge* in 1890, a frowning Statue of Liberty lifts her skirts as new immigrants are "dumped" onto her already overcrowded island, a symbol of the United States.

Immigration and rapid industrialization also generated growing conflicts between labor and corporations, or trusts, controlled by a few wealthy men. During what historians call "the Gilded Age," industrialists such as Andrew Carnegie, J. P. Morgan, and John D. Rockefeller amassed huge fortunes through cutthroat business practices and exploitation of labor. The flood of immigrants created a massive surplus of labor in the United States, where wages further declined during the depressions following the financial panics of 1873, 1884, and 1893. The low wages and long hours, as well as the appalling living and working conditions of most laborers, led to calls for political reform and the emergence of trade

"The Anarchist Riot in Chicago — A Dynamite Bomb Exploding among the Police"

This engraving of the violent confrontation between Chicago police and labor protestors gathered at Haymarket Square appeared almost two weeks after the clash, on May 15, 1886, in *Harper's Weekly.* That popular illustrated newspaper catered primarily to middle-class readers, and its coverage of the McCormick strike and the Haymarket affair was patently hostile to the striking laborers, most of whom were impoverished immigrants from Europe.

unions, including the Federation of Organized Trades and Labor Unions (later renamed the American Federation of Labor) in 1881. Five years later, the federation initiated a call for a national strike for an eight-hour work-day. After strikers clashed with replacement workers at the McCormick Machine Harvesting Plant in Chicago, police retaliated by killing two of the striking workers. At a protest meeting called the following day at Haymarket Square, a bomb exploded, killing eight policemen. The arrest, trial, and conviction of eight men accused of the bombing, all of whom the judge sentenced to death, radicalized trade unionists such as Emma Goldman, a Jewish immigrant from Russia who became a leader of the anarchist move-ment in the United States. In 1894, the president of the American Railway Union, Eugene Debs, was imprisoned during the Pullman strike in Chi-cago. Debs, who came to believe that Americans should replace capitalism with a new cooperative system, subsequently helped form the Socialist Party, running for president five times on that ticket.

Chicago, the site of some of the most bitter and violent labor disputes of the period, came to symbolize both the dark realities and what many viewed as the bright promise of urban and industrial America. Harsh conditions in rural America prompted many on farms and in small towns to seek better lives in Chicago. Immigrants from abroad also swelled the population of the booming metropolis, which rose from roughly 100,000 in 1860 to nearly two million by 1900. Swiftly rebuilding after the "Great Fire" of 1871, the city won a competition to host the World's Columbian Exposition of 1893, a celebration of the four hundredth anniversary of Columbus's landing in America. But the exposition actually celebrated Chicago's economic power and the industrial advances of the United States. Twenty-seven million people visited the exposition, drawn there by the debut of the Ferris wheel, one of the most popular attractions; the nightly electric light shows powered by the huge dynamos displayed in the Palace of Mechanic Arts; and five thousand exhibits in the nearly two hundred buildings erected on landfill along the shore of Lake Michigan. The centerpiece of the exposition was the Court of Honor, a massive complex

World's Columbian Exposition, Chicago
Frances B. Johnston took this photograph of crowds of people touring the exposition grounds, including portions of the "Great White City," in 1893.

of plaster-clad, neoclassical buildings arranged around a vast reflecting pool, which came to be known as the "Great White City." That gleaming city bore little resemblance to the sprawling metropolis beyond the gates of the exposition or to other cities in the United States. Indeed, while millions were flocking to the Columbian Exposition, the social reformer Jane Addams and her associates published *Hull House Maps and Papers*, a study of the grim living and working conditions in the industrial area around Hull House, a settlement house that provided educational programs and other services to immigrants in Chicago.

Writers of fiction also began to explore the realities of the new urban and industrial order in the United States. The tumultuous life of American cities was the subject of a growing number of stories and novels, including Stephen Crane's *Maggie: A Girl of the Streets (A Story of New York)* (1893), Frank Norris's *McTeague: A Story of San Francisco* (1899), and Theodore Dreiser's *Sister Carrie* (1900). Novelists also focused on corrupt practices of corporations, which were the primary focus of journalists and writers known as "muckrakers," a reference to their digging in the dirt, or "muck," to uncover corruption in politics and big business. One of the most influential of their works was Upton Sinclair's *The Jungle* (1906), a best-selling novel he wrote when the socialist newspaper *Appeal to Reason* commissioned him to investigate the exploitation of immigrant workers in the meat-packing industry in Chicago. Writers such as Abraham Cahan, a Jewish immigrant from Russia, drew upon their own direct experiences to illuminate the lives of new arrivals. In *Yekl: A Tale of the New York Ghetto* (1896) and *The Imported Bridegroom and Other Stories of the New York Ghetto* (1898), Cahan revealed just how difficult conditions were for many of those who passed through the "golden door" into the United States.

Even as millions of immigrants came to America from countries around the world, the United States aggressively sought to expand its influence and territory abroad. In 1893, American sugar-plantation owners deposed Queen Liliʻuokalani of Hawaiʻi, which the United States annexed in 1898. That year, the country demonstrated its growing industrial and military might in the Spanish-American War. In the treaty that ended the brief war, Spain ceded control of Cuba, Puerto Rico, Guam, and the Philippines to the United States. Although it reluctantly granted independence to Cuba, the United States annexed Puerto Rico, Guam, and the Philippines. Anti-imperialists protested the betrayal of American political traditions, and many of those who had supported the war as an effort to liberate Spanish colonies opposed their annexation and were appalled by the brutal tactics employed by U.S. forces against Filipino guerillas during the Philippine-American War of 1899–1902. Revealing the attitudes of many Protestant Anglo-Americans toward "alien" groups at home and abroad, however, President McKinley argued that the Philippines "were unfit for self-government," so "there was nothing left for us to do but to take them all, and to educate the Filipinos, and uplift and civilize and Christianize them."

Innovation, Technology, and the Literary Marketplace

The industrialization that led to the country's emergence as a world power was accelerated by developments in technology that also transformed virtually every aspect of life in the United States. A host of new inventions were introduced between 1865 and 1914, including the lightbulb, the telephone, the typewriter, the radio, the motion picture, the automobile, and the airplane. There were equally significant changes in the technology of publishing, ranging from new methods of making paper to innovations in printing illustrations, the use of automated presses, and especially Ottmar Mergenthaler's invention in 1882 of the linotype machine, a revolutionary typesetting machine that Thomas Edison hailed as the "Eighth Wonder of the World."

Along with improved methods of distribution, those technologies helped a growing number of publishers meet the ever-increasing demand for printed materials of all kinds. One of the most striking developments in the period following the Civil War was the surge in reading, which was encouraged by the growing number of libraries in the United States. In 1876, when statistics on libraries were first compiled, there were 2,500 libraries housing twelve million volumes. By 1900, the number of libraries had doubled, and their holdings had increased to forty million volumes. Those who could afford to purchase books had increasing access to them, especially in cities. Although as many as 90 percent of books published before World War I were sold by other means, including by subscription,

W. R. Leigh, *A Modern Composing Room*
This illustration of linotype machines appeared in a series of articles, "The Business of a Newspaper," in *Scribner's Magazine* in 1897. In the accompanying text, the author explains, "Instead of type set from a case by hand there is now used the linotype machine, so called because it casts a line of type at a time. . . . One operator on such a machine can do the work of five or six hand compositors."

bookstores grew in number and size by 1900. Since literacy rates were high, the population was expanding rapidly, and nearly 80 percent of all children attended school by the end of the century, publishers were assured of a steady supply of readers for both books and periodicals in the United States. As publishing became a big business, the term *bestseller* entered the American language, apparently coined for the lists that *Bookman Magazine* began to publish in 1895.

Not all kinds of writing benefited equally from the expansion of the literary marketplace, in which poetry assumed a diminishing role. Many of the poets who had been popular before the Civil War continued to publish, including Rose Terry Cooke and Sarah Morgan Bryan Piatt, and especially Henry Wadsworth Longfellow and John Greenleaf Whittier, who gained his greatest fame with the publication of *Snow-Bound* (1866), a nostalgic evocation of a simpler, rural world that had been destroyed by the Civil War. The child-oriented work of "schoolroom poets" such as Longfellow and Whittier, as well as of popular poets such as Eugene Field and James Whitcomb Riley, strongly shaped public taste in poetry, making it difficult for more challenging and unconventional poets to gain an audience. Few read Walt Whitman, who published the first edition of his *Leaves of Grass* in 1855 and who revised and expanded the volume of poems through six more editions, including the final "deathbed" edition of 1891–92. After Emily Dickinson's death, Mabel Loomis Todd and Thomas Wentworth Higginson published the first of three volumes of her poems in 1890. The volumes sold well, as did the work of the pioneering African American poet Paul Laurence Dunbar, though he reached an even larger audience through his stories and novels. So did many white authors who wrote both poetry and fiction, including Stephen Crane, who published two collections of his poems, and Willa Cather, whose first book was a volume of poems, *April Twilights* (1903). One of the few American writers who devoted himself exclusively to poetry, Edwin Arlington Robinson struggled to earn a living. Certainly, the limited market for poetry was discouraging to established and would-be poets. "Poetry may get printed in newspapers, but no man makes money by it for the simple reason that nobody cares a fig for it," the revered poet William Cullen Bryant sourly observed shortly before his death in 1878. "The taste for it is something old-fashioned; the march of the age is in another direction; mankind are occupied with politics, railroads, and steamboats."

"Poetry may get printed in newspapers, but no man makes money by it for the simple reason that nobody cares a fig for it."

In contrast to poetry, fiction thrived in the new mechanical age. By the turn of the century, the novel had become the most popular of all literary genres, accounting for more than 25 percent of book production in the United States. In 1860, Ann Sophia Stephens published the first of the so-called dime novels, *Malaeska: The Indian Wife of the White Hunter*. Such mass-produced tales of adventure—which authors churned out in as little as a week and which frequently cost only a nickel—sold millions of copies during the following

A PATIENT RAILROAD TRAVELER.

Thomas Nast, "A Patient Railroad Traveler"

The transportation boom of the late 1800s created a new place for reading, the railroad car, as illustrated in this humorous engraving in *Harper's Weekly.* The image depicts a common practice of newsboys, who would drop books and magazines on the laps of travelers, later returning to collect either the unwanted copies or the purchase price.

decades. Horatio Alger's *Ragged Dick* series, urban versions of the rags-to-riches story, were also enormously popular, as were family novels such as Louisa May Alcott's *Little Women* (1868-69) and its many sequels. One of the most famous writers of the period and the first celebrity author in the United States was Mark Twain, who made a fortune from his series of bestsellers, including *Adventures of Huckleberry Finn* (1885). Other bestsellers ranged from historical romances such as Lew Wallace's biblical epic *Ben-Hur* (1880) to *The Call of the Wild* (1903), Jack London's internationally acclaimed novel about a sled dog in the wilds of the Klondike. European and especially English writers such as Arthur Conan Doyle and Rudyard Kipling continued to provide stiff competition, but American novelists benefited by the passage in 1891 of the Chase Act, which brought the United States into accord with an agreement for copyright protection signed in 1886 by a number of nations in Europe. The adoption of international copyright laws finally put European and American writers on a more equal footing, since American publishers thereafter had to pay royalties to authors whose works were first published outside the United States.

American fiction was also nourished by the growth of periodicals in the decades following the Civil War. During the war years, there were roughly 400 daily newspapers in the United States. By 1880, there were 850, and

"Mark Twain
Incorporated" (detail)
The name *Mark Twain*
gained such cultural
currency that Samuel
Clemens registered it as
a trademark and incorpo-
rated himself as a com-
mercial enterprise in
1908. He thus sought to
secure perpetual copy-
right for his work by
assigning all his copy-
rights, along with his
pseudonym, to the Mark
Twain Company. The *New
York World* satirized the
event in a cartoon in
which Twain – dressed
in his signature white
suit and holding his cus-
tomary cigar – is shown
joining a small and seedy-
looking group of capital-
ists, labeled "The
Malefactors of Great
Wealth Club."

that number reached 1,400 by the turn of the century. Newspapers devoted
a good deal of space to poetry and especially to prose fiction, which was a
staple of a multiplying number of magazines in the United States. After
struggling during the war years, when periodicals published in the North
lost most of their Southern readers, magazines rebounded swiftly. Almost
immediately, the dominance of the *Atlantic Monthly* and *Harper's Monthly*,
both of which had been established during the 1850s, was challenged by a
series of prominent new literary magazines, including the *Galaxy* (1866),
Lippincott's (1868), and *Scribner's Monthly* (1870), all published in the East;
and the *Overland Monthly* (1868), which was published in San Francisco
and featured writing about the West. During the following decades, the
number of magazines exploded, from 700 during the Civil War to 2,400 in
1880 to roughly 3,500 at the turn of the century, by which time magazines
had an estimated readership of sixty-five million people in the United
States. Readers were attracted by the colorful covers, lavish illustrations,
and modest cost of magazines such as *McClure's*, *Munsey's*, and the *Saturday Evening Post*, which achieved huge circulations by lowering their
cover prices and funding themselves primarily through advertisements.
Magazines became such a prominent feature of American life during the
period that it has been described as the era of the magazine, then the primary vehicle for the public expression of culture in the United States.

The growth of periodicals gave added impetus to the development of one
of the most vital forms of American literature, the short story. The story
that launched Twain's lucrative career, "Jim Smiley and His Jumping Frog,"
was published in the *New York Saturday Press* in 1865, the year Henry
James published his first signed work, "The Story of a Year," in the *Atlantic
Monthly*. The first editor of the *Overland Monthly* was Bret Harte, whose
enormously popular short stories helped create the vogue for regional or
"local color" fiction in the United States. The short story soon became recognized as one of the major contributions of prose writers in the United
States. "Almost as soon as America began to have any literature at all it had
good short stories," Brander Matthew observed in 1885; "for fifty years the
American short story has had a supremacy which any competent critic
could not but acknowledge." Although newspapers and magazines continued to serialize novels, the short story became the most popular literary
feature of periodicals. Suggesting that American writers had "brought the
short story nearer perfection in an all around sense than almost any other
people," the influential writer and critic William Dean Howells attributed
that development to the commercial success and "excellence" of American
magazines, adding, "[I]t is probable that, aside from the pictures, it is the
short stories that please the readers of our best magazines."

Magazines also revealed the important role of women as both consumers and producers of culture in the United States. The women's rights
movement received a major setback in 1870, when the Fifteenth Amendment extended suffrage to African American men but not to black or white

women. Thereafter, the movement increasingly focused its attention on the right of women to vote, which was not gained until the "Susan B. Anthony Amendment," first introduced in Congress in 1878, was finally adopted as the Nineteenth Amendment in 1920. Even as the American suffragists agitated through marches and public protests, activists such as Charlotte Perkins Gilman pursued a wide range of feminist issues in print. Gilman, for example, wrote for national periodicals such as the *New-England Magazine* and for her own journal, the *Forerunner*. Women faced strong opposition in their struggle for political rights and social equality, and they remained economically subordinate to men. By the end of the century, however, female education was expanding rapidly, at both the high-school and college levels, and a growing number of women were joining the labor force and entering professions that had previously been barred to them. The expanding economic and cultural roles of women were illustrated by the emergence of a series of magazines specifically designed to appeal to their interests and tastes. The most important women's magazine of the antebellum period, *Godey's Lady's Book*, ultimately succumbed to competition from a host of prominent magazines, including *Harper's Bazar* (1866), later renamed *Harper's Bazaar, Good Housekeeping* (1885), and *Ladies' Home Journal* (1883), the first magazine of any kind to circulate a million copies of a single issue, in February 1903. In addition to advertisements for women's clothing and accessories, as well as a wide

"Almost as soon as America began to have any literature at all it had good short stories."

Advertising Poster for *Harper's*

In the stiff competition for readers, many popular magazines distributed brightly colored advertising posters such as the one Edward Penfield designed for the November 1894 issue of *Harper's*. The poster shows a fashionably dressed young woman walking with a man whose sweater is emblazoned with the letter "Y," for Yale. A sign in the background announces a football game between Yale and Harvard.

range of articles on fashion, housekeeping, medicine, politics, and the arts, women's magazines published a good deal of short fiction, vigorously competing for readers with other mass-market magazines.

The growth of periodicals and the popularity of short stories offered opportunities for a wide range of American authors who emerged between the 1880s and the beginning of World War I. White women writers claimed a growing share of the market for fiction, including Edith Wharton, Sarah Orne Jewett, Mary E. Wilkins Freeman, Kate Chopin, Willa Cather, and Mary Austin. All of those writers produced novels as well as short fiction. But all of them began their careers by writing for newspapers or magazines and continued to do so, as did white male writers such as Ambrose Bierce and the novelists Stephen Crane, Theodore Dreiser, Jack London, and Frank Norris. At the same time, periodicals began to reflect the growing diversity of the country. The work of a few African American writers appeared in prominent national magazines. In 1887, Charles W. Chesnutt became the first African American writer to be published in the prestigious *Atlantic Monthly*, and Paul Laurence Dunbar later published stories in *Harper's Weekly* and the *Saturday Evening Post*. In 1900, Pauline Hopkins helped establish the *Colored American Magazine*, designed to feature the work and celebrate the achievements of African Americans. The following year, the *Outlook* serialized Booker T. Washington's *Up from Slavery*, even as W. E. B. Du Bois published a critique of Washington's leadership in the *Dial*, later revising the essay for *The Souls of Black Folk* (1903). The Native American writer Zitkala-Ša published essays and stories in several national magazines, as did Sui Sin Far, an immigrant of mixed Chinese and English ancestry who later collected some of her stories in *Mrs. Spring Fragrance* (1912). Following in the footsteps of immigrant writers such as Abraham Cahan, Mary Antin wrote an autobiographical account of what she described as her "assimilation into American ways," *The Promised Land*, which was serialized in the *Atlantic Monthly* in 1912.

By then, the United States bore little resemblance to the exhausted and grieving country that had emerged from the Civil War. In the summer of 1913, 50,000 white veterans of the war, former soldiers of both the Union and the Confederacy, gathered for a grand reunion commemorating the fiftieth anniversary of the Battle of Gettysburg. "Nothing could possibly be more impressive or more inspiring to the younger generation than this gathering," a journalist observed in the *Washington Post*. "But even more touching must be the emotions of these time-worn veterans, as they assemble on an occasion that in itself constitutes a greater victory than that of half a century ago, and one too, in which every section of a reunited country has common part." Indeed, as the reunion symbolized, many of the sectional divisions between the North and the South had been overcome, though largely at the expense of African Americans. The frontier had closed with the settlement of the West, largely at the expense of

The Gettysburg Reunion

This photograph, titled "Under Blue & Gray, Gettysburg," shows Union and Confederate veterans gathered at the Great Reunion of July 1913, which commemorated the fiftieth anniversary of the Battle of Gettysburg.

Mexican Americans and Native Americans. At the same time, immigration, industrialization, and urbanization had generated growing divisions in the country between wealth and poverty, as well as along lines of religion and ethnicity. The primarily agricultural country of the antebellum years gave way to an industrial colossus, whose military might and imperialistic ambitions had been demonstrated in the Spanish-American War of 1898. Many American writers had earlier used the Civil War as a symbol of what came to be called the "loss of American innocence." Certainly, if that "innocence" was not lost, it was at least deeply shaken by the traumatic conflict that ended in 1865. As many of the writings published during the following decades illustrate, it was further undermined by the tumultuous cultural, economic, political, and social developments of the half century between the end of the Civil War and the beginning of World War I, in August 1914.

COMPARATIVE TIMELINE, 1865-1914

Dates	American Literature	History and Politics	Developments in Culture, Science, and Technology
1865-1869	**1865** Walt Whitman, *Drum-Taps* **1865** Henry James, "The Story of a Year," his first signed story, in the *Atlantic Monthly* **1865** Mark Twain, "Jim Smiley and His Jumping Frog" in the *New York Saturday Press*	**1865** Thirteenth Amendment abolishes slavery in the United States **1865** Confederate general Robert E. Lee surrenders at Appomattox Courthouse **1865** Abraham Lincoln is assassinated and Andrew Johnson becomes president	**1865** *The Nation* begins publication in New York City **1865** William Booth founds religious group later named Salvation Army
	1866 Herman Melville, *Battle-Pieces and Aspects of the War* **1866** John Greenleaf Whittier, *Snow-Bound* **1867** John W. De Forest, *Miss Ravenel's Conversion from Secession to Loyalty* **1868** Elizabeth Stuart Phelps, *The Gates Ajar*	**1866** Ku Klux Klan is formed **1867** Congress passes first of the Reconstruction Acts **1868** Fourteenth Amendment grants citizenship to all persons born in the United States, including former slaves **1868** Ulysses S. Grant elected president **1869** Elizabeth Cady Stanton and Susan B. Anthony establish the National Woman Suffrage Association	**1866** Metropolitan Museum of Art founded in New York City **1867** Karl Marx, *Das Kapital* **1868** *Overland Monthly* begins publication in San Francisco **1869** Union Pacific and Central Pacific Railroads form transcontinental rail system **1869** Opening of Suez Canal
1870-1879	**1870** Bret Harte, *The Luck of Roaring Camp and Other Sketches*	**1870** U.S. population: 39,818,449 **1870** Fifteenth Amendment grants voting right to all qualified males, regardless of race or previous condition of servitude **1871** "Great Fire" of Chicago **1871** Revolution in France following defeat in Franco-Prussian War **1872** Congress designates Yellowstone as the first national park	**1870** First meteorological report issued by Weather Bureau, later National Weather Service **1871** P. T. Barnum opens "Greatest Show on Earth" in Brooklyn **1872** Claude Monet's painting *Impression, Sunrise* prompts first reference to Impressionists

COMPARATIVE TIMELINE, 1865–1914

Dates	American Literature	History and Politics	Developments in Culture, Science, and Technology
1870–1879 (cont.)	**1873** Mark Twain and Charles Dudley Warner, *The Gilded Age* 	**1873** Financial panic leads to economic depression in United States	**1873** Christopher Latham Sholes patents first typewriter **1874** Joseph F. Glidden patents barbed wire
		1875 Civil Rights Act guarantees all Americans, regardless of race, equal access to public accommodations	
	1876 Mark Twain, *The Adventures of Tom Sawyer*	**1876** Lakota (Sioux) and Cheyenne defeat Colonel Custer and his troops at battle of Little Bighorn **1876** Rutherford B. Hayes elected president	**1876** American technological advances, including telephone, displayed at Centennial Exhibition in Philadelphia **1876** Founding of National League of Professional Baseball Clubs
	1877 Sarah Orne Jewett, *Deephaven*	**1877** Withdrawal of federal troops from the South signals end of Reconstruction	**1877** All-England Lawn Championship is first played at Wimbledon, England
	1878 Henry James, *Daisy Miller* 	**1878** "Susan B. Anthony Amendment" granting women right to vote is introduced in Congress **1879** Congress enacts law permitting women lawyers to argue cases before Supreme Court	**1878** A. A. Pope manufactures first bicycles, called *wheels* **1879** Thomas Edison invents lightbulb
1880–1889	**1880** José Martí, *Impressions of America*	**1880** U.S. population: 50,155,783 **1880** James A. Garfield elected president	
	1881 Joel Chandler Harris, *Uncle Remus* **1881** Henry James, *The Portrait of a Lady*	**1881** Garfield is assassinated and Chester Arthur becomes president **1881** Founding of Federation of Organized Trades and Labor Union, later known as American Federation of Labor **1882** Chinese Exclusion Act	**1881** Booker T. Washington organizes Normal and Industrial Institute for Negroes, later Tuskegee Institute **1882** Ottmar Mergenthaler invents linotype machine

COMPARATIVE TIMELINE, 1865–1914

Dates	American Literature	History and Politics	Developments in Culture, Science, and Technology
1880–1889 (cont.)	**1883** Sarah Winnemucca Hopkins, *Life among the Piutes*	**1883** Supreme Court declares Civil Rights Act of 1875 unconstitutional **1884** Grover Cleveland elected president **1884** Financial panic leads to economic depression in United States	**1883** First performance of Buffalo Bill's Wild West Show **1884** Completion of Washington Monument
	1885 María Amparo Ruiz de Burton, *The Squatter and the Don* **1885** Mark Twain, *Adventures of Huckleberry Finn* **1886** Sarah Orne Jewett, *A White Heron and Other Stories*	**1886** "Haymarket Affair," culmination of violent labor strife in Chicago **1887** "Golden Jubilee" marking fiftieth year of Queen Victoria's reign in England **1888** Benjamin Harrison elected president	**1885** *Good Housekeeping* magazine begins publication in Holyoke, Massachusetts **1886** Dedication of Statue of Liberty in New York harbor **1888** George Eastman patents Kodak camera
	1889 Mark Twain, *A Connecticut Yankee in King Arthur's Court*	**1889** Oklahoma land rush as "Indian Territory" is opened to white settlers	**1889** Jane Addams founds Hull House, settlement house in Chicago
1890–1899	**1890** Emily Dickinson, *Poems*	**1890** U.S. population: 62,947,714 **1890** Massacre of Lakota (Sioux) by federal troops at Wounded Knee, South Dakota **1890** Wyoming is first state to give women right to vote	**1890** Jacob Riis, *How the Other Half Lives: Studies among the Tenements of New York*
	1891 William Dean Howells, *Criticism and Fiction*		**1891** The Music Hall, now Carnegie Hall, opens in New York City
	1891 Mary E. Wilkins Freeman, *A New England Nun and Other Stories* **1892** Ambrose Bierce, *Tales of Soldiers and Civilians* **1892** Charlotte Perkins Gilman, "The Yellow Wallpaper"	**1892** Grover Cleveland elected president **1892** Federal immigration center opens at Ellis Island in New York harbor	**1892** Pledge of Allegiance is first recited in public schools on Columbus Day **1892** *Vogue* magazine begins publication in New York City

COMPARATIVE TIMELINE, 1865–1914

Dates	American Literature	History and Politics	Developments in Culture, Science, and Technology
1890–1899 (cont.)	**1893** Stephen Crane, *Maggie: A Girl of the Streets (A Story of New York)*	**1893** American plantation owners depose Queen Liliʻuokalani of Hawaiʻi; land later annexed by United States (1898)	**1893** *McClure's Magazine*, famous for "muckraking" journalism, begins publication in New York City
			1893 World's Columbian Exposition in Chicago
	1894 Kate Chopin, *Bayou Folk*	**1894** Eugene Debs, president of the American Railway Union, is jailed during Pullman strike in Chicago	
	1895 Stephen Crane, *The Red Badge of Courage*	**1895** Cuban war of independence from Spain begins	**1895** *Bookman Magazine* coins term *bestseller*
	1896 Paul Laurence Dunbar, *Lyrics of Lowly Life*	**1896** Supreme Court affirms constitutionality of "separate but equal" accommodations for whites and African Americans in *Plessy v. Ferguson*	**1896** *Everybody's Magazine* begins publication in New York City
		1896 William McKinley is elected president	
	1897 E. A. Robinson, *Children of the Night*		**1897** Sigmund Freud defines Oedipus complex
	1898 Abraham Cahan, *The Imported Bridegroom and Other Stories of the New York Ghetto*	**1898** Spain cedes Cuba, Puerto Rico, Guam, and the Philippines to United States in treaty ending Spanish-American War	**1898** Marie Curie discovers elements polonium and radium, coining term *radioactivity*
	1899 Charles W. Chesnutt, *The Wife of His Youth and Other Stories of the Color Line*	**1899–1902** Boer War between British and descendants of Dutch settlers in South Africa	
	1899 Kate Chopin, *The Awakening*	**1899–1913** Philippine Insurrection	
	1899 Frank Norris, *McTeague: A Story of San Francisco*		
1900–1909	**1900** Theodore Dreiser, *Sister Carrie*	**1900** U.S. population: 75,994,575	**1900** Number of daily newspapers in United States is 1,400; there are 3,500 magazines, with estimated readership of 65 million
	1900 Pauline Hopkins, *Contending Forces; or, A Romance Illustrative of Negro Life North and South*	**1900** U.S. troops help suppress Boxer Rebellion against foreign presence in China	

COMPARATIVE TIMELINE, 1865–1914

Dates	American Literature	History and Politics	Developments in Culture, Science, and Technology
1900–1909 (cont.)	**1901** Booker T. Washington, *Up from Slavery*	**1901** McKinley is assassinated and Theodore Roosevelt becomes president	**1900** *Colored American Magazine* begins publication in Boston
	1902 Zitkala-Ša, *Old Indian Legends* **1903** Mary Austin, *The Land of Little Rain* **1903** Jack London, *The Call of the Wild* **1903** W. E. B. Du Bois, *The Souls of Black Folk*	**1902** Cuba gains independence	**1902** First movie theater opens in Los Angeles **1903** Wright brothers' first flight at Kitty Hawk, North Carolina **1903** *Ladies' Home Journal* becomes first magazine to circulate one million copies of a single issue
		1904 Theodore Roosevelt elected president **1905** First Russian Revolution	
	1905 Edith Wharton, *The House of Mirth* **1905** Willa Cather, *The Troll Garden* **1906** Upton Sinclair, *The Jungle* **1907** *The Education of Henry Adams*	**1906** San Francisco earthquake and fire **1908** William Howard Taft elected president **1909** Formation of National Association for the Advancement of Colored People (NAACP)	**1907** First radio broadcast **1908** Henry Ford introduces Model T **1909** Charlotte Perkins Gilman begins publication of *Forerunner*
1910–1914		**1910** U.S. population: 91,972,266 **1910** Beginning of Mexican Revolution **1911** Death of 146 women in Triangle Factory fire in New York City generates support of workers' unions and reform of labor laws	

COMPARATIVE TIMELINE, 1865–1914

Dates	American Literature	History and Politics	Developments in Culture, Science, and Technology
1910–1914 (cont.)	**1912** Mary Antin, *The Promised Land* **1912** Sui Sin Far, *Mrs. Spring Fragrance* **1913** Willa Cather, *O Pioneers!*	**1912** Woodrow Wilson elected president **1914** World War I begins in Europe	**1912** *Titanic* sinks with loss of more than 1,500 lives **1912** *Poetry: A Magazine of Verse* begins publication in Chicago **1913** Armory Show of modern art in New York City **1914** Opening of Panama Canal

Realism, Regionalism, and Naturalism

IN ADDITION TO TRIGGERING MASSIVE economic, political, and social dislocations, the Civil War generated a seismic cultural shift. The aftershocks were clearly registered in American literature, as writers responded to the altered circumstances, landscapes, and mood of the country during the decades following the war. The disillusionment and skepticism generated by the bloody conflict and its aftermath helped spur the development of a literary movement known as "realism." With its emphasis on representing things as they actually are, realism may be understood as a reaction against idealism, the representation of things as they should be, and

◄ John Sloan, *A Woman's Work* (1912)

Sloan was a member of the Ashcan School, a group of painters committed to portraying the reality of city life in the early twentieth century. Here, he offers a snapshot of and finds beauty in one of the most commonplace urban sights of the period, a woman pinning laundry on clotheslines strung between the fire escapes of tenement houses in New York City.

romanticism, both in the common sense of that term and in the narrower literary sense of writings that emphasize emotion, imagination, intuition, and the primacy of the individual. Just as there were realistic elements in many of the writings of the "Romantic Period" of American literature, from roughly 1830 to 1865, so were there romantic elements in many of the writings of the "Realistic Period," from roughly 1865 to the beginning of World War I. Nonetheless, most realists challenged or at least questioned some of the fundamental tenets of romanticism — the belief in the nobility and inherent goodness of the individual, an expansive faith in human progress, and the idealization of nature. Certainly, the Romantic idealism of earlier writers such as Ralph Waldo Emerson, Margaret Fuller, Henry

Thomas Anshutz, *The Ironworkers' Noontime* (1880)

Realism became a significant force in American painting as well as in literature in the decades following the Civil War. In what is widely regarded as the first realistic (especially by the standards of the time) and fully realized treatment of industrial subject matter by an American painter, Thomas Anshutz here depicts the noontime break of workers at a nail factory in Wheeling, West Virginia.

David Thoreau, and other transcendentalists proved to be difficult to sustain in the face of the carnage of the Civil War and the actualities of the new urban and industrial order in the United States.

Broader cultural movements spurred the development of American literary realism. What historians sometimes call the "second scientific revolution" strengthened the belief that new knowledge could be gained only through close observation of the natural world and that truth must be based on empirical evidence. The scientific method influenced the literary methods of the realists, who emphasized the importance of objectivity, observation, and the unbiased or unsentimental reporting of the observed phenomena of American life. The writings of the realists were related to and stimulated by the work of late-nineteenth-century American philosophers such as Charles Sanders Peirce, William James, and other participants in the philosophical movement called "pragmatism," the doctrine that the value of any belief, idea, or theory is dependent on its outcome or utility. Pragmatists reject moral absolutes, measuring the value of any truth, or conception, by its practical consequences and outcomes, as manifested in the conduct, ethical choices, and experiences of those who accept that conception as the "truth." American literary realism was also influenced by the work of British novelists such as Charles Dickens, George Eliot, and Anthony Trollope, as well as by the writings of a wide range of European writers, including Honoré de Balzac, Gustave Flaubert, Guy de Maupassant, and Ivan Turgenev. With their emphasis on the development of characters, their use of common language, their close attention to the details of specific locales, and their choice of plots mirroring the realities of ordinary lives, such fiction writers were popular among both authors and audiences in the United States.

The emergence of realism inspired a lively debate in postwar periodicals about the purposes and goals of American literature. The pages of literary magazines and even many newspapers were full of articles and commentaries on what constituted realism in fiction. George Parsons Lathrop, a critic and writer, offered the following definition in the *Atlantic Monthly* in 1874:

> Realism sets itself at work to consider characters and events which are apparently the most ordinary and uninteresting, in order to extract from these their full value and true meaning. It would apprehend in all particulars the connection between the familiar and the extraordinary, and the seen and the unseen of human nature. Beneath the deceptive cloak of outwardly uneventful days, it detects and endeavors to trace the outlines of the spirits that are hidden there; to measure the changes in their growth, to watch the symptoms of moral decay or regeneration, to fathom their histories of passionate or intellectual problems. In short, realism reveals. Where we thought nothing worthy of notice, it shows everything to be rife with significance.

Lathrop defined realism in a way that made it particularly useful and appealing to writers in the United States. During the decades before the Civil War, American writers had frequently commented on the difficulty of writing a romance in their native country, where "there is no shadow, no antiquity, no mystery, no picturesque and gloomy wrong, nor anything but a commonplace prosperity, in broad and simple daylight," as Nathaniel Hawthorne put it in his preface to *The Marble Faun* (1861). By suggesting that the materials of realism were "characters and events which are apparently the most ordinary and uninteresting," Lathrop affirmed the literary value of what Hawthorne and others had described as the commonplace actualities of life in the United States. Indeed, experiences and situations that others might dismiss as merely trivial or uneventful were for Lathrop potentially "rife with significance," a rich resource for writers committed to the faithful representation of everyday aspects of American life.

One of the earliest and most influential proponents of literary realism in the United States was the critic and novelist William Dean Howells. Born and raised in Ohio, where he worked as a journalist and printer, Howells became a major figure in the eastern literary establishment, first as an assistant editor (1866-70) and then as editor of the prestigious *Atlantic Monthly* (1871-81). During his years at the *Atlantic,* he advanced the cause of realism through his own fiction and by publishing the works of numerous writers from across the nation. Howells later promoted realism in his regular columns for another influential periodical, *Harper's Monthly.* "Realism is nothing more and nothing less than the truthful treatment of material," he succinctly stated in 1889. Throughout his long career, Howells tirelessly sought to guide the literary tastes of the American public away from the Romantic and sentimental toward what he viewed as the ordinary and true. "Let fiction cease to lie about life; let it portray men and women as they are, actuated by the motives and the passions in the measure we all know," he urged; "let it not put on fine literary airs; let it speak the dialect, the language, that most Americans know — the language of unaffected people everywhere — and there can be no doubt of an unlimited future, not only of delightfulness but of usefulness, for it."

> *"Let fiction cease to lie about life; let it portray men and women as they are, actuated by the motives and the passions in the measure we all know; . . . let it not put on fine literary airs; let it speak the dialect, the language, that most Americans know — the language of unaffected people everywhere — and there can be no doubt of an unlimited future, not only of delightfulness but of usefulness, for it."*

Two of the many writers Howells championed illustrate the breadth of his literary sympathies as well as the range of literary realism in the United States. When he was an assistant editor of the *Atlantic Monthly,* Howells was asked by the senior editor whether the magazine should publish an early story by Henry James. "Yes, and all the stories you can get from the writer," Howells replied, explaining in one of his later essays: "I admired, as we must in all that Mr. James has written, the finished workmanship in which there is no loss of vigor; the luminous and uncommon use of words, the originality of phrase, the whole clear and beautiful style." Howells was an equally strong supporter of the work of the other most famous American realist, Mark Twain, who in background and literary practice could not have been more different from James. The cosmopolitan James, who was born in New York City and spent much of his life in Europe, is best known for his novels and stories of Americans traveling abroad, including *Daisy Miller* (1878). Twain, who grew up on the frontier in Missouri and served his literary apprenticeship in the far West, emerged out of the tradition of "Southwestern humor," humorous sketches and tall tales told in thick regional dialects. Although many critics tended to dismiss Twain's popular writings as mere entertainment, Howells invited Twain to contribute to the *Atlantic Monthly*, where his series of autobiographical sketches *Old Times on the Mississippi* appeared in 1876. Along with many other writers of the period, Twain looked back to the time before the Civil War, which he nostalgically re-created in his first novel, *The Adventures of Tom Sawyer* (1876). Twain, however, offered a far more complex and darker version of that past in his *Adventures of Huckleberry Finn* (1885).

Twain's writings illustrate a number of features of "regionalism," a broad movement that encompassed a wide range of writers in various parts of the United States. As the nation's expanding population became more diverse and spread out across the continent, American writers began to redraw the literary map of the country. Twain's earliest work was influenced by Bret Harte, whose stories of miners, gamblers, and other "low-life" characters in California helped usher in the vogue of what was known as "local-color" writing, which became a staple of national, mass-circulation magazines after 1880. As some scholars have emphasized, local-color writing was in part a response to the growing pressures and threats of rapid social change during the late decades of the nineteenth century. By representing the characters and customs, as well as the peculiarities of dialect, dress, and manners of a specific region, local-color writers sought to preserve traditions threatened by the new urban and industrial order that emerged after the Civil War. Sarah Orne Jewett's sketches appealed to yearnings for the simpler life of provincial New England, while Mary Austin vividly described the remote and unspoiled landscapes of the far West. At the same time, Jewett and Austin emphasized the ways in which the natural environment shapes the lives of individuals, while other regional writers exposed the difficult conditions of life in various parts of the United States. The popular local-color writer Mary E. Wilkins Freeman and the poet Edwin Arlington Robinson, for example, dramatized the economic, emotional, and psychological struggles of people living in rural areas and decaying towns in the interior of New England. Willa Cather, who was celebrated for her pioneering stories of life in her native Nebraska, often evoked the claustrophobic world of the small town, the sameness of rural routines, and the grinding poverty experienced by many settlers on the Great Plains.

Eastman Johnson, *Cranberry Harvest, Nantucket Island* (1880)

Many writers and painters responded to rapid social change in the United States by depicting ways of life that were threatened by industrialization and urbanization, including this communal scene in which families of men, women, and children work together harvesting cranberries on the isolated and as yet undeveloped island of Nantucket.

Both realism and regionalism were frequently vehicles for social criticism and satire. Ambrose Bierce debunked romantic myths about the nobility and grandeur of the Civil War by exposing the horrors of battle in his *Tales of Soldiers and Civilians* (1892). Early in her career, the feminist and activist Charlotte Perkins Gilman adopted the strategies of psychological realism in "The Yellow Wall-Paper" (1892), a harrowing story that illustrates the confinement and oppression of women in American society at that time. Her concern with the restricted role of women in a patriarchal society was shared by Kate Chopin, who developed that theme in local-color stories about Creole life in Louisiana and in her controversial novel *The Awakening* (1899), and by Edith Wharton, who wrote a series of stories and novels in which she satirized the debased values and hollow lives of the wealthy elite of New York City. In a different part of the city and at the other end of the social scale, the Jewish American writer and journalist Abraham Cahan depicted life in the "Ghetto," the area in the Lower East Side of New York City where more than a million Jews fleeing persecution in Russia and eastern Europe settled between the 1880s and 1914. Another immigrant writer, Sui Sin Far, focused on the trials of Chinese Americans, who were widely viewed as "heathens" and often subjected to hostility and violence in cities such as San Francisco. At the same time, African American writers such as Charles W. Chesnutt and the poet Paul Laurence Dunbar sought to subvert romanticized visions of slavery and denigrating stereotypes of black people, while Pauline Hopkins revealed the grim consequences of racial discrimination and hatred in the numerous stories and novels she published in the *Colored American Magazine.*

Even as writers enriched the diversity and extended the range of American realism, some of its basic assumptions were challenged by writers who participated in a new literary movement called "naturalism." A major force behind the emergence of naturalism was the work of Charles Darwin, especially the "social Darwinism" popularized by the English philosopher Herbert Spencer. Spencer held that Darwin's theories of evolution through natural selection also apply to individuals or groups within society, which consequently operate under the natural law of "survival of the fittest." In effect, as the naturalists understood Darwin

Winslow Homer, *The Gulf Stream* (1899)

Homer's famous painting, which a critic in 1906 described as a powerful depiction of human isolation and vulnerability amidst "the cruelty of the elements and the elemental creatures of the sea," has much in common with the contemporary writings of the naturalists, who frequently depicted the struggle of characters for survival against the hostile forces of nature and the environment.

and Spencer, man is simply an animal struggling for survival in a competitive jungle and driven by the same internal and external forces that operate on other animals. As the French novelist Émile Zola famously put it in *The Experimental Novel* (1880), the fullest theoretical statement of the principles of naturalism, human beings are "human beasts." Zola also affirmed that the novel is a scientific experiment that arrives at the truth about humanity and society by demonstrating the determining effects of a changing environment on a particular hereditary makeup. Although the line between realism and naturalism is often blurred, realists tend to emphasize the role of individual choice or volition, while naturalists emphasize the ways in which human behavior is determined by biological, economic, and environmental forces, both social and natural. Rather than a source of solace or a spiritual resource, naturalists view "nature" as an indifferent backdrop for the struggles and strivings of human beings. Indeed, in many naturalistic works characters struggle for survival against the seemingly hostile forces of nature, symbolized by the threatening ocean waves in Stephen Crane's "The Open Boat" (1897) and the harsh climate of the Klondike in Jack London's "The Law of Life" (1901).

The naturalists were also determined to depict experiences and explore places that had for the most part remained outside the boundaries of realism. An important site of naturalistic writing was the city, or urban "jungle," which was both the setting and a central metaphor in works by Crane, Theodore Dreiser, and Frank Norris. In a review of Norris's *McTeague* (1899), which was based on a sensational murder case in San Francisco, William Dean Howells suggested that the brutal work raised fundamental questions about the future of fiction in the United States. "Whether we shall abandon the old-fashioned American ideal of the novel as something which may be read by all ages and sexes, for the European notion of it as something fit only for age and experience, and for men rather than women; whether we shall keep to the bounds of the provincial proprieties, or shall include within the imperial territory of fiction the passions and motives of the savage world which underlies as well as environs civilization, are points which this book sums up and puts concretely," Howells observed. Disturbed and deeply ambivalent about such an "expansion" of the subject matter of the American novel, Howells argued that Norris's "true picture of life is not true, because it leaves beauty out." But the naturalists insisted that realists such as Howells left out far more, from sexual drives to the socioeconomic forces that so powerfully shaped the lives of the great mass of people struggling for survival in the United States.

". . . whether we shall keep to the bounds of the provincial proprieties, or shall include within the imperial territory of fiction the passions and motives of the savage world which underlies as well as environs civilization, are points which this book sums up and puts concretely."

The naturalists, or what some critics then called "new realists," offered a dark and disturbing vision of American life at the turn of the twentieth century. Even as they aspired to scientific objectivity and disclaimed any moral or ethical purpose, however, many naturalists also sought to arouse concern and indignation about the conditions they described. Their depictions of urban life had much in common with shocking exposés such as *How the Other Half Lives: Studies among the Tenements of New York* (1890), by the Danish immigrant and reformer Jacob Riis; and the documentary photographs of Lewis Hine, a sociologist and crusader against child labor in the United States. Some naturalistic writings also overlapped the investigative journalism of the muckrakers, who exposed the abuses of corporations and corruption in government in an effort to bring about reform. In his final novels and stories, Frank Norris thus focused on the ruthless practices of the railroad monopolies and speculators who controlled the price of wheat, hoping that his writings would encourage the public to turn against big business and consequently "get fair treatment and not be abused." Indeed, in their efforts to engage truthfully the actualities of American life, including the experiences of women, minorities, and immigrants crowded into urban slums, both realists and naturalists often gave added force to efforts on behalf of social reform in the United States.

Lewis Hine, "Small newsie down-town"

Hine, who was one of the first to use the camera as a tool for social reform, took this photograph in St. Louis, Missouri, on the afternoon of Saturday, May 7, 1910. *Newsies* was the nickname for newsboys, many of them desperately poor homeless children who slept in the streets.

American Contexts

"THE AMERICA OF THE MIND": CRITICS, WRITERS, AND THE REPRESENTATION OF REALITY

DURING THE DECADES FOLLOWING the Revolution, writers in the United States persistently called for the creation of a distinctly American literature, one that would establish the new nation's cultural independence from England and Europe. After the Civil War, in what Henry James termed the "era of discussion," the debate over what would constitute such a literature escalated. In an article published in the *Nation* in January 1868, John William De Forest wondered whether the "Great American Novel," which he defined as "the picture of the ordinary emotions and manners of American existence," might not now be at hand. De Forest was skeptical, and some other critics doubted that the novelist could find sufficiently rich materials amid the mundane realities of life in the United States. In response to such doubts, James Herbert Morse in an 1883 essay emphasized the vitality of "American life," which had "mastered a continent and developed its enormous resources," "freed a nation of slaves," and "survived a war of almost incredible disintegrating properties." Affirming that "such a life is rich enough to meet the largest demands of the novelist," Morse concluded: "America has much to learn from Europe. We cannot greatly boast abroad of ease and elegance in social life, of art and learning, of fine culture and manners; but of variety of movement, of free action and growth, of that satisfaction that comes from being alive all over, we have enough and to spare. Life here is not thin, except to the thin."

Morse's sense of the opportunities available to American authors was shared by many critics and writers during the decades following the Civil War. As the selections included in the following section indicate, however, there was wide disagreement about the nature, purpose, and scope of American fiction. In response to those who insisted that writers should focus solely on American scenes and themes, Julian Hawthorne objected: "It is silly and childish to make the boundaries of the America of the mind coincide with those of the United States." Hawthorne was defending writers of the so-called international school, especially Henry James, who emphasized the fiction writer's imaginative freedom to explore a wide range of experiences and situations. At the same time, Hamlin Garland protested what he viewed as the ongoing domination of New England in American fiction, which he argued must include the experiences and perspectives of writers from the South and the West. Although the critical debate was dominated by white males, a "Lady from Philadelphia" suggested that "The Coming American Novelist" might well be a woman and an African American. There was a growing consensus that American fiction would be characterized by realism, or truth about the experience of life in the United States, a position championed by the influential critic and novelist William Dean Howells. In a famous statement, Howells suggested that realists should focus on "the more smiling aspects of life, which are the more American." But the limits of realism were challenged by naturalists such as Frank Norris, who was determined to treat the widest range of experience, from life in the slums to "the mystery of sex," areas into which American literature had rarely ventured. Indeed, as American society was transformed by growing immigration, industrialization, and urbanization, critics and writers increasingly questioned what constituted the true reality of life in the United States.

bedfordstmartins.com/
americanlit for research links on the authors in this section

Julian Hawthorne

[1846-1934]

Julian Hawthorne

This engraving is based on an undated photograph, probably taken during the 1870s.

The son of the novelist Nathaniel Hawthorne, Julian Hawthorne was educated in the United States but spent much of his early life in England. Hawthorne was the author of popular novels such as *Bresant* (1873) and *Garth* (1877), as well as books about his famous father, *Nathaniel Hawthorne and His Wife* (1884) and *Hawthorne and His Circle* (1903). Hawthorne was also a frequent contributor to a variety of literary magazines, including the *Atlantic Monthly*, *Harper's New Monthly Magazine*, the *Century Magazine*, and the *North American Review*, where he published "The American Element in Fiction." In the essay, Hawthorne vigorously defends writers of what was then called the "international school," especially Henry James, whose stories and novels frequently concerned the experiences of Americans traveling in Europe. In opposition to those who insisted that works of American literature must be set in the United States, Hawthorne argues that authors who brought an American perspective to bear on their characters and material were also creating a distinctly national literature. The text is taken from the first printing of the essay in the *North American Review*, August 1884.

From THE AMERICAN ELEMENT IN FICTION

That must be a very shallow literature which depends for its national flavor and character upon its topography and its dialect; and the criticism which can conceive of no deeper Americanism than this is shallower still. What is an American book? It is a book written by an American, and by one who writes as an American, that is, unaffectedly. So an English book is a book written by an unaffected Englishman. What difference can it make what the subject of the writing is? Mr. Henry James lately brought out a volume of essays on "French Poets and Novelists."[1] Mr. E. C. Stedman recently published a series of monographs on "The Victorian Poets."[2] Are these books French and English, or are they nondescript, or are they American? Not only are they American, but they are more essentially American than if they had been disquisitions upon American literature. And the reason is, of course, that they subject the things of the old world to the tests of the new, and thereby vindicate and illustrate the characteristic mission of America to mankind. We are here to hold up European conventionalisms and prejudices in the light of the

---

1. **"French Poets and Novelists"**:   A collection of literary essays published in 1878 by the American novelist Henry James (1843-1916).
2. **"The Victorian Poets"**:   A volume of literary criticism on British writers published in 1875 by the American critic Edmund C. Stedman (1833-1908).

new day, and thus afford everybody the opportunity, never heretofore enjoyed, of judging them by other standards, and in other surroundings than those amidst which they came into existence. In the same way, Emerson's "English Traits"[3] is an American thing, and it gives categorical reasons why American things should be. And what is an American novel except a novel treating of persons, places, and ideas from an American point of view? The point of view is *the* point, not the thing seen from it.

But it is said that "the great American novel," in order fully to deserve its name, ought to have American scenery. . . . It is silly and childish to make the boundaries of the America of the mind coincide with those of the United States. We need not dispute about free trade and protection here; literature is not commerce, nor is it politics. America is not a petty nationality, like France, England, and Germany; but whatever in such nationalities tends toward enlightenment and freedom is American. Let us not, therefore, confirm ourselves in a false and ignoble conception of our meaning and mission in the world. Let us not carry into the temple of the Muse[4] the jealousies, the prejudice, the ignorance, the selfishness of our "Senate" and "Representatives," strangely so called! Let us not refuse to breathe the air of Heaven, lest there be something European or Asian in it. If we cannot have a national literature in the narrow, geographical sense of the phrase, it is because our inheritance transcends all geographical definitions. The great American novel may not be written this year, or even in this century. Meanwhile, let us not fear to ride, and ride to death, whatever species of Pegasus[5] we can catch. It can do us no harm, and it may help us to acquire a firmer seat against the time when our own, our very own winged steed makes his appearance.

[1884]

---

3. **Emerson's "English Traits":** A travel book and work of cultural criticism published in 1856 by Ralph Waldo Emerson (1803–1882), who by the time of his death was widely considered to be one of the major American writers.
4. **the temple of the Muse:** In Greek and Roman mythology, the Muses were the nine goddesses who presided over the arts and sciences.
5. **Pegasus:** The winged horse of Greek mythology, a favorite of the nine Muses and a symbol of poetic inspiration.

Henry James

[1843–1916]

Although he is best known for his short stories and novels, Henry James was also a prolific writer of literary criticism who sought to establish fiction, often dismissed as trivial entertainment, as a significant art form (see James, p. 1207). His most famous critical essay is "The Art of Fiction," first published in the English journal *Longman's Magazine* and reprinted in James's collection *Partial Portraits* (1888). Responding to the "laws of fiction" that had been laid down in an essay by the English novelist Walter Besant, James delivers his most significant statement of the general principles governing the writing of fiction. In the following excerpt, probably the most famous passage in the essay, he addresses two of Besant's central points: that, as James summarizes them, "the novelist must write from his experience, [and] that his 'characters must be real and such as might be met with in actual life.'" The text is taken from the first printing in *Longman's Magazine*, September 1884.

From THE ART OF FICTION

It goes without saying that you will not write a good novel unless you possess the sense of reality; but it will be difficult to give you a recipe for calling that sense into being. Humanity is immense and reality has a myriad forms; the most one can affirm is that some of the flowers of fiction have the odour of it, and others have not; as for telling you in advance how your nosegay should be composed, that is another affair. It is equally excellent and inclusive to say that one must write from experience; to our supposititious aspirant such a declaration might savour of mockery. What kind of experience is intended, and where does it begin and end? Experience is never limited and it is never complete; it is an immense sensibility, a kind of huge spider-web, of the finest silken threads, suspended in the chamber of consciousness and catching every airborne particle in its tissue. It is the very atmosphere of the mind; and when the mind is imaginative—much more when it happens to be that of a man of genius—it takes to itself the faintest hints of life, it converts the very pulses of the air into revelations. The young lady living in a village has only to be a damsel upon whom nothing is lost to make it quite unfair (as it seems to me) to declare to her that she shall have nothing to say about the military. Greater miracles have been seen than that, imagination assisting, she should speak the truth about some of these gentlemen. I remember an English novelist, a woman of genius, telling me that she was much commended for the impression she had managed to give in one of her tales of the nature and way of life of the French Protestant youth. She had been asked where she learned so much about this recondite being; she had been congratulated on her peculiar opportunities. These opportunities consisted in her having once, in Paris, as she ascended a staircase, passed an open door where, in the household of a *pasteur*,[1] some of the young Protestants were seated at table round a finished meal. The glimpse made a picture; it lasted only a moment, but that moment was experience. She had got her impression, and she evolved her type. She knew what youth was, and what Protestantism; she also had the advantage of having seen what it was to be French; so that she converted these ideas into a concrete image and produced a reality. Above all, however, she was blessed with the faculty which when you give it an inch takes an ell,[2] and which for the artist is a much greater source of

---

1. *pasteur*: Minister or pastor (French).
2. **an ell**: A former measure of length, approximately 45 inches.

strength than any accident of residence or of place in the social scale. The power to guess the unseen from the seen, to trace the implication of things, to judge the whole piece by the pattern, the condition of feeling life, in general, so completely that you are well on your way to knowing any particular corner of it—this cluster of gifts may almost be said to constitute experience, and they occur in country and in town, and in the most differing stages of education. If experience consists of impressions, it may be said that impressions *are* experience, just as (have we not seen it?) they are the very air we breathe. Therefore, if I should certainly say to a novice, "Write from experience, and experience only," I should feel that this was a rather tantalising monition if I were not careful immediately to add, "Try to be one of the people on whom nothing is lost!"

[1884]

Anonymous
(A "Lady from Philadelphia")

This article was published in "Our Monthly Gossip," a regular feature offering literary news and commentary in *Lippincott's Magazine.* During the 1880s, *Lippincott's* was a successful national literary magazine published in Philadelphia. The magazine regularly printed serializations of novels, including popular English works such as Oscar Wilde's *The Picture of Dorian Gray* and Arthur Conan Doyle's late Sherlock Holmes tale *The Sign of the Four. Lippincott's* also published the work of American fiction writers, including Henry James, Julian Hawthorne, and Rebecca Harding Davis, as well as the African American poet Paul Laurence Dunbar. The following excerpt from the article in "Our Monthly Gossip," identified in the table of contents as the work of a "Lady from Philadelphia," was among the first suggestions that the "Coming American Novelist" might well be not only an African American but also a woman. The text is taken from the first printing in *Lippincott's Magazine*, April 1886.

From THE COMING AMERICAN NOVELIST

When we come to formulate our demands of the Coming American Novelist, we will agree that he must be native-born. His ancestors may come from where they will, but we must give him a birthplace and have the raising of him. Still, the longer his family has been here the better he will represent us. Suppose he should have no country but ours, no traditions but those he has learned here, no longings apart from us, no future except in our future—the orphan of the world, he finds with us his home. And with all this, suppose he refuses to be fused into that grand conglomerate we call the "American type."

***Lippincott's* Monthly Magazine**

In this poster advertising the January 1895 issue of *Lippincott's*, a woman is shown meditating on something she has just read in the popular magazine, which she still holds open in her hand.

With us, he is not of us. He is original, he has humor, he is tender, he is passive and fiery, he has been taught what we call justice, and he has his own opinion about it. He has suffered everything a poet, a dramatist, a novelist need suffer before he comes to have his lips anointed. And with it all he is in one sense a spectator, a little out of the race. How would these conditions go towards forming an original development? In a word, suppose the coming novelist is of African origin? When one comes to consider the subject, there is no improbability in it. One thing is certain — our great novel will not be written by the typical American. After a time the Yankee type will be replaced by some new combination from the effect of our life on the nations swarming to our shores; and, as far as nationality goes, The Novel might as well then be written by the African as by this new combination. Thus far he has given us the only national music we have ever had. Indeed, we may go further and assert that the plantation-songs are the only melodies in our day that are not growths from Handel or Beethoven. They are far more original than Wagner, because he is a legitimate result of a progress in logical lines. Given Gluck and

Beethoven, and Wagner is certain after a time.[1] Of course by "plantation-songs" such music as Foster's "Old Folks at Home" is not meant,[2] but the song of the African himself, not the one written for him and then sung by the white people. Whether the peculiar swing and rhythm of his melodies is a vague recollection of Africa or the offspring of his civilization, it is distinctive in musical history. . . .

Yet farther: I have used the generic masculine pronoun because it is convenient; but Fate keeps revenges in store. It was a woman who, taking the wrongs of the African as her theme, wrote the novel that awakened the world to their reality,[3] and why should not the coming novelist be a woman as well as an African? She — the woman of that race — has some claims on Fate which are not yet paid up.

[1886]

---

1. **Given Gluck . . . and Wagner is certain after a time:** The author traces a direct line of descent through a series of influential German composers, from Christoph Willibald von Gluck (1714-1787) and George Frederick Handel (1685-1759) through Ludwig von Beethoven (1770-1827) to Richard Wagner (1813-1883), then viewed by many as the most advanced and innovative composer of the period.

2. **Foster's "Old Folks at Home" is not meant:** "Old Folks at Home" was an enormously popular ballad published in 1851 by Stephen Collins Foster (1826-1864), a white Northerner who wrote many songs about plantation life, as distinct from what came to be called "Negro spirituals," songs composed and originally sung by slaves in the South. Such "slave songs" were growing in popularity through performances throughout the North by the Jubilee Singers, a vocal group organized at Fisk University in 1871.

3. **It was a woman . . . reality:** The author refers to Harriet Beecher Stowe, author of the enormously popular and influential antislavery novel *Uncle Tom's Cabin* (1851-52).

William Dean Howells

[1837-1920]

William Dean Howells was at once a major novelist and the most influential American literary critic of the late nineteenth century (see Howells, p. 1187). His fullest statement about the art of fiction was *Criticism and Fiction*, based in large part on the "Editor's Study" columns he wrote for *Harper's New Monthly Magazine* from 1886 until 1892. As he said in the first of those monthly columns, Howells proposed to "talk over with the reader — who will always be welcome here — such matters of literary interest as may come up from time to time, whether suggested by the new books of the day or other accidents of the literary life." Howells was a strong and consistent champion of realism, which he defined as the "truthful treatment of material." In the following commentary on the nature of American fiction, revised in part from his "Editor's Study" of September 1886, Howells suggests that such a truthful representation of American life would inevitably focus on its "more smiling aspects," since the actualities of life in the United States were sharply different from those in England and Europe. The text is taken from the first edition of *Criticism and Fiction* (1891).

From CRITICISM AND FICTION

It is the difference of the American novelist's ideals from those of the English novelist that gives him his advantage, and seems to promise him the future. The love of the passionate and the heroic, as the Englishman has it, is such a crude and unwholesome thing, so deaf and blind to all the most delicate and important facts of art and life, so insensible to the subtle values in either that its presence or absence makes the whole difference, and enables one who is not obsessed by it to thank Heaven that he is not as that other man is.

There can be little question that many refinements of thought and spirit which every American is sensible of in the fiction of this continent, are necessarily lost upon our good kin beyond seas, whose thumb-fingered apprehension requires something gross and palpable for its assurance of reality. This is not their fault, and I am not sure that it is wholly their misfortune: they are made so as not to miss what they do not find, and they are simply content without those subtleties of life and character which it gives us so keen a pleasure to have noted in literature. If they perceive them at all it is as something vague and diaphanous, something that filmily wavers before their sense and teases them, much as the beings of an invisible world might mock one of our material frame by intimations of their presence. It is with reason, therefore, on the part of an Englishman, that Mr. Henley[1] complains of our fiction as a shadow-land, though we find more and more in it the faithful report of our life, its motives and emotions, and all the comparatively etherealized passions and ideals that influence it.

In fact, the American who chooses to enjoy his birthright to the full, lives in a world wholly different from the Englishman's, and speaks (too often through his nose) another language: he breathes a rarefied and nimble air full of shining possibilities and radiant promises which the fog-and-soot-clogged lungs of those less-favored islanders struggle in vain to fill themselves with. But he ought to be modest in his advantage, and patient with the coughing and sputtering of his cousin who complains of finding himself in an exhausted receiver[2] on plunging into one of our novels. To be quite just to the poor fellow, I have had some such experience as that myself in the atmosphere of some of our more attenuated romances.

Yet every now and then I read a book with perfect comfort and much exhilaration, whose scenes the average Englishman would gasp in. Nothing happens; that is, nobody murders or debauches anybody else; there is no arson or pillage of any sort; there is not a ghost, or a ravening beast, or a hair-breadth escape, or a shipwreck, or a monster of

---

1. **Mr. Henley:** The English poet and critic William Ernest Henley (1849–1903).
2. **an exhausted receiver:** That is, a container from which all of the air has been withdrawn, or a vacuum.

self-sacrifice, or a lady five thousand years old in the whole course of the story; "no promenade, no band of music, nossing!" as Mr. Du Maurier's Frenchman said of the meet for a fox-hunt.[3] Yet it is all alive with the keenest interest for those who enjoy the study of individual traits and general conditions as they make themselves known to American experience.

These conditions have been so favorable hitherto (though they are becoming always less so) that they easily account for the optimistic faith of our novel which Mr. Hughes notices.[4] It used to be one of the disadvantages of the practice of romance in America, which Hawthorne more or less whimsically lamented,[5] that there were so few shadows and inequalities in our broad level of prosperity; and it is one of the reflections suggested by Dostoïevsky's novel, The Crime and the Punishment,[6] that whoever struck a note so profoundly tragic in American fiction would do a false and mistaken thing — as false and as mistaken in its way as dealing in American fiction with certain nudities which the Latin peoples seem to find edifying. Whatever their deserts, very few American novelists have been led out to be shot, or finally exiled to the rigors of a winter at Duluth; and in a land where journeymen carpenters and plumbers strike for four dollars a day the sum of hunger and cold is comparatively small, and the wrong from class to class has been almost inappreciable, though all this is changing for the worse. Our novelists, therefore, concern themselves with the more smiling aspects of life, which are the more American, and seek the universal in the individual rather than the social interests. It is worth while, even at the risk of being called commonplace, to be true to our well-to-do actualities; the very passions themselves seem to be softened and modified by conditions which formerly at least could not be said to wrong any one, to cramp endeavor, or to cross lawful desire. Sin and suffering and shame there must always be in the world, I suppose, but I believe that in this new world of ours it is still mainly from one to another one, and oftener still from one to one's self. We have death too in America, and a great deal of disagreeable and painful disease, which the multiplicity of our patent medicines does not seem to cure; but this is tragedy that comes in the very nature of things, and is not peculiarly American, as the large, cheerful average of health and success and happy life is. It will not do to boast, but it is well to be true to the facts, and to see that, apart from these purely mortal troubles, the race here has enjoyed conditions in which most of the ills that have darkened its annals might be averted by honest work and unselfish behavior.

America's reality is not as tragic as other countries (Russia)

---

3. **Mr. Du Maurier's Frenchman . . . fox-hunt:** A scene in *Pictures of English Society* (1884), by the popular English writer George du Maurier (1834–1896).

4. **Mr. Hughes notices:** The English critic Eilian Hughes, in his essay "Present Day Novels: English versus American" (1899).

5. **Hawthorne . . . lamented:** Nathaniel Hawthorne (1804–1864), in the preface to his final novel, *The Marble Faun* (1864), which is set in Italy.

6. **The Crime and the Punishment:** *Crime and Punishment* (1866), a tragic tale of poverty, suffering, murder, and redemption by the Russian novelist Fyodor Dostoevsky (1821–1881). In the following passage, Howells alludes to a central event in the life of Dostoevsky, who in 1849 was arrested for his involvement in revolutionary politics, sentenced to death, and placed before a firing squad. His sentence was commuted at the last moment, and he was instead exiled to Siberia.

Fine artists we have among us, and right-minded as far as they go; and we must not forget this at evil moments when it seems as if all the women had taken to writing hysterical improprieties, and some of the men were trying to be at least as hysterical in despair of being as improper. If we kept to the complexion of a certain school — which sadly needs a school-master — we might very well be despondent; but, after all, that school is not representative of our conditions or our intentions. Other traits are much more characteristic of our life and our fiction. In most American novels, vivid and graphic as the best of them are, the people are segregated if not sequestered, and the scene is sparsely populated. The effect may be in instinctive response to the vacancy of our social life, and I shall not make haste to blame it. There are few places, few occasions among us, in which a novelist can get a large number of polite people together, or at least keep them together. Unless he carries a snap-camera his picture of them has no probability; they affect one like the figures perfunctorily associated in such deadly old engravings as that of "Washington Irving and his Friends."[7] Perhaps it is for this reason that we excel in small pieces with three or four figures, or in studies of rustic communities, where there is propinquity if not society. Our grasp of more urbane life is feeble; most attempts to assemble it in our pictures are failures, possibly because it is too transitory, too intangible in its nature with us, to be truthfully represented as really existent.

[1891]

---

7. "Washington Irving and his Friends": A popular engraving based on the painting *Washington Irving and His Literary Friends at Sunnyside* by Christian Schussele, who depicted an imaginary gathering of fifteen American writers at Irving's home, though Irving and three of the other writers were dead by the time the picture was painted in 1863.

Hamlin Garland

[1860–1940]

Hamlin Garland

This undated photograph was apparently taken during the 1890s.

Born in Wisconsin, Hamlin Garland later lived for extended periods in both Boston and southern California. His early experiences of the rigors of midwestern farm life shaped his prolific literary career, during which he published nearly fifty books and five hundred articles in a wide range of newspapers and literary magazines. His best-known works are *Main-Travelled Roads* (1891), a collection of short stories; *Crumbling Idols* (1894), a collection of essays on American literature; and his autobiographies, *A Son of the Middle Border* (1917) and *A Daughter of the Middle Border* (1921), for which he won the Pulitzer Prize. Garland firmly supported realism and local color in fiction, believing that the writer "spontaneously reflects the life which goes on around him." In "Literary Emancipation of the West," Garland advocates a "literature of national scope." Challenging the supremacy that Boston had claimed and held "in

American literature for more than a half a century," Garland sought to promote writers of the South and the West: "The horizon widens each year, including more cities, more writers, more lovers of light and song, more makers of literature." The text of the following excerpt from the end of the essay is taken from the first printing in the *Forum*, October 1893.

From LITERARY EMANCIPATION OF THE WEST

Original creation moves in cycles. Each age of strong creative capability reveals life in its own fashion. That is, each creative age in the past uttered its own truth as over against the conventionalized dogmas of its teachers. I believe such a period of literary breaking-away has come in America. Whitman announced it, but could not exemplify it in popular form.[1] He voiced its force, its love of liberty and love of comrades, but he was the prophet, not the exemplar. He said well that the real literature of America could not be a polite literature. The nation is too great, too sincere. There is coming in this land the mightiest assertion in art of the rights of man and the glory of the physical universe ever made in the world. It will be done not by one man, but by many men and women. It will be born not of drawing-room culture, nor of imitation, nor of fear of masters, nor will it come from homes of great wealth. It will come from the average American home in the city, as well as in the country. It will deal with all kinds and conditions. It will be born of the mingling seas of men in the vast interior of America, because there the problem of the perpetuity of our democracy, the question of the liberty as well as the nationality of our art, will be fought out. This literature will be too great to submit to the domination of any literary centre or literary master. With cities of half-a-million inhabitants scattered from Pittsburg to Seattle, New York and Chicago will alike be made humble. Stand up, O young man and woman of the West! Stand erect! Face the future with a song on your lips and the light of a broader day in your eyes. Turn your back on the past, not in scorn, but in justice to the future. Reject the scholasticism of the East. Cease trying to be correct, and become creative. This is our day. The past is not vital. It is a highway of dust, and Homer, Aeschylus, Sophocles, Dante, Shakespeare are milestones.[2] Libraries do not create great poets and artists; they seldom aid, and they often warp and destroy them. To know Shakespeare is good. To know your fellow-men is better. All that Shakespeare

---

1. **Whitman announced . . . popular form:** In the preface to *Leaves of Grass* (1855), Walt Whitman (1819-1892) proclaims, "The American bard shall delineate no class of persons nor one or two out of the strata of interests nor love most nor truth most nor the soul most nor the body most . . . and not be for the eastern states more than the western or the northern states more than the southern." Although he was revered by many writers, during his lifetime Whitman never gained a wide audience in the United States.

2. **It is a highway of dust . . . milestones:** Garland associates what he earlier calls "the scholasticism of the East" with what he views as a sterile tradition of European literature from ancient epic poet Homer, who lived about 850 BCE, and the Greek dramatists Aeschylus (526-456 BCE) and Sophocles (c. 496-406 BCE) through the Italian poet Dante Alighieri (1265-1321) to William Shakespeare (1564-1616), who was by then considered to be the greatest writer in English.

knew of his fellows you may know of your fellows, but not at second-hand, not through Shakespeare, not through the eyes of the dead, but at first hand.

In closing let me say: I hope I have made it clear that our position is not one of attacking the East, or Eastern literary men. We are simply attacking the false and fatal idea of culture, based upon past models rather than upon truth. We are speaking for a broader outlook for American literature. We are standing for a literature which shall rise above culture, above library centres and literary masters, to sincerity of accent and to native democracy of sentiment, and, above all, to creative candor.

[1893]

Frank Norris

[1870-1902]

Frank Norris was deeply influenced by the naturalism of the French novelist Émile Zola, who argued that novelists should use methods of scientific objectivity to study human beings in relation to their surroundings. Zola's work influenced Norris's major novels, especially *McTeague* (1899), as well as his numerous literary essays, some of which were collected in *The Responsibilities of the Novelist*, published posthumously in 1903. Among the most famous of those essays is "A Plea for Romantic Fiction," which first appeared in the Boston *Evening Transcript*, the newspaper in which Norris published many of his critical statements. In the essay, Norris rejects the realism of writers such as William Dean Howells, who argued that American novelists should represent "the more smiling aspects of life" in the United States. In contrast, Norris urges the advantages of "Romance," not in the common sense of amorous tales of adventure, but as a form of the novel that "takes cognizance of the variations from the type of normal life," including the "sordid" and the "unlovely." This text is taken from the first printing in the Boston *Evening Transcript*, December 18, 1901.

A PLEA FOR ROMANTIC FICTION

Let us at the start make a distinction. Observe that one speaks of Romanticism and not of sentimentalism. One claims that the latter is as distinct from the former as is that other form of art which is called Realism. Romance has been often put-upon and overburdened by being forced to bear the onus of abuse that by right should fall to sentiment; but the two should be kept very distinct, for a very high and illustrious place will be claimed for Romance, while sentiment will be handed down the scullery stairs.

[handwritten margin note: KEEP them DISTINCT / ROMANTICISM ≥ SENTIMENTALISM]

Many people today are composing mere sentimentalism, and calling it and causing it to be called Romance, so that with those who are too busy to think much upon these subjects, but who none the less love honest literature, Romance too has fallen into disrepute. Consider now the cut-and-thrust stories. They are all labelled Romances, and it is very easy to get the impression that Romance must be an affair of cloaks and daggers, or moonlight and golden hair. But this is not so at all. The true Romance is a more serious business than this. It is not merely a conjurer's trick box, full of flimsy quackeries, tinsel and clap traps, meant only to amuse, and relying upon deception to do even that. Is it not something better than this? Can we not see in it an instrument, keen, finely tempered, flawless — an instrument with which we may go straight through clothes and tissues and wrappings of flesh down deep into the red living heart of things?

Is all this too subtle, too merely speculative and intrinsic, too "precieuse"[1] and nice and "literary"? Devoutly one hopes the contrary. So much is made of so-called Romanticism in present day fiction, that the subject seems worthy of discussion, and a protest against the misuse of a really noble and honest formula of literature appears to be timely — misuse, that is, in the sense of limited use. Let us suppose for the moment that a Romance can be made out of the cut-and-thrust business. Good heavens, are there no other things that are romantic, even in this — falsely, falsely called — humdrum world of today? Why should it be that so soon as the novelist addresses himself — seriously — to the consideration of contemporary life he must abandon Romance and take up that harsh, loveless, colorless, blunt tool called Realism?

Now, let us understand at once what is meant by Romance and what by Realism. Romance — I take it — is the kind of fiction that takes cognizance of variations from the type of normal life. Realism is the kind of fiction that confines itself to the types of normal life. According to this definition, then, Romance may even treat of the sordid, the unlovely — as for instance, the novels of M. Zola.[2] (Zola has been dubbed a Realist, but he is, on the contrary, the very head of the Romanticists.) Also, Realism, used as it sometimes is as a term of reproach, need not be in the remotest sense or degree offensive, but on the other hand respectable as a church, and proper as a deacon — as, for instance, the novels of Mr. Howells.[3]

The reason why one claims so much for Romance, and quarrels so pointedly with Realism, is that Realism stultifies itself. It notes only the surface of things. For it Beauty is not even skin-deep, but only a geometrical plane, without dimensions of depth, a mere outside. Realism is very excellent so far as it goes, but it goes no farther than the Realist himself can actually see, or actually hear. Realism is minute, it is the drama of a broken tea-cup, the tragedy of a walk down the block, the excitement of an afternoon call, the adventure of an invitation to dinner. It is the visit to my neighbor's house, a formal visit, from which I may draw no conclusions. I see my neighbor and his friends — very, oh, such very! probable people — and that is all. Realism bows upon the doormat and goes away

---

1. "precieuse": Precious, in the sense of fastidious or overrefined (French).
2. M. Zola: Émile Zola (1840–1902), French writer whose naturalistic novels strongly influenced Norris.
3. Mr. Howells: William Dean Howells (1837–1920), American novelist, editor, critic, and champion of realism.

and says to me, as we link arms on the sidewalk: "That is life." And I say it is not. It is not, as you would very well see if you took Romance with you to call upon my neighbor.

Lately you have been taking Romance a weary journey across the water — ages and the flood of years — and haling her into the fubsy, musty, worm-eaten, moth-riddled, rust-corroded "Grandes Salles"[4] of the Middle Ages and the Renaissance, and she has found the drama of a bygone age for you there. But would you take her across the street to your neighbor's front parlor (with the bisque[5] fisher boy on the mantel and the photograph of Niagara Falls on glass hanging in the front window) would you introduce her there? Not you. Would you take a walk with her in Fifth avenue, or Beacon street, or Michigan avenue?[6] No indeed. Would you choose her for a companion of a morning spent in Wall Street, or an afternoon in the Waldorf-Astoria?[7] You just guess you would not.

She would be out of place, you say, inappropriate. She might be awkward in my neighbor's front parlor, and knock over the little bisque fisher boy. Well, she might. If she did, you might find underneath the base of the statuette hidden away, tucked away — what? God knows. But something which would be a complete revelation of my neighbor's secretest life.

So you think Romance would stop in the front parlor and discuss medicated flannels and mineral waters with the ladies? Not for more than five minutes. She would be off upstairs with you, prying, peeping, peering into the closets of the bedroom, into the nursery, into the sitting-room; yes, and into that little iron box screwed to the lower shelf of the closet in the library; and into those compartments and pigeon-holes of the "secretaire"[8] in the study. She would find a heartache (may-be) between the pillows of the mistress's bed, and a memory carefully secreted in the master's deedbox. She would come upon a great hope amid the books and papers of the study table of the young man's room, and — perhaps — who knows — an affair, or, great heavens, an intrigue, in the scented ribbons and gloves and hairpins of the young lady's bureau. And she would pick here a little and there a little, making up a bag of hopes and fears, and a package of joys and sorrows — great ones, mind you — and then come down to the front door, and stepping out into the street, hand you the bags and package, and say to you — "That is Life!"

However it may be abroad, in America so many women are taking advantage of the educational opportunities offered them that a number of colleges and universities are growing apprehensive lest the preponderance of their students be of the feminine gender, and in at least two universities there is talk of limiting the attendance of women.[9] For even here the prejudice exists to such an extent that it is felt to be a shame to a university to have more women than men in it.

---

4. "Grandes Salles": Large halls or rooms (French).
5. bisque: Delicate porcelain.
6. Fifth avenue, or Beacon street, or Michigan avenue: Fashionable residential streets in New York City, Boston, and Chicago.
7. Waldorf-Astoria: Elegant hotel in New York City.
8. "secretaire": Desk (French). A secretary is a type of desk with cubbies and shelves often hidden by a hinged door that opens to form a work surface.
9. However it may be abroad . . . women: The following three paragraphs on the education and capacities of women were omitted from the version of Norris's essay published posthumously in *The Responsibilities of the Novelist and Other Literary Essays* (1903).

But it is not "manlike education" which they are trying to secure. It is merely education. It is knowledge—facts—theories—truth—speculation—all of which belongs to anyone with eyes to see and ears to hear, and muliebrity[10] is no bar to the acquirement of these things.

As to the foundress of the Babylonian wall and the builder of the Pyramid, Mr. Lang[11] has us on the hip. We cherished the belief that certain excellent ancient ladies did these things, but we can relinquish that fond faith. He might, however, have dealt one blow at a time. It would have been more endurable. In regard to Jean d'Arc,[12] however—can even Mr. Lang be sure that another such as she will not appear?

Romance does very well in the castles of the Middle Ages and the Renaissance chateaux, and she has the entrée[13] there and is very well received. That is all well and good. But let us protest against limiting her to such places and such times. You will find her, I grant you, in the chatelaine's chamber and the dungeon of the man-at-arms;[14] but, if you choose to look for her, you will find her equally at home in the brownstone house on the corner and in the office building downtown. And this very day, in this very hour, she is sitting among the rags and wretchedness, the dirt and despair of the tenements of the East Side of New York.

"What?" I hear you say, "look for Romance—the lady of the silken robes and golden crown, our beautiful, chaste maiden of soft voice and gentle eyes—look for her among the vicious ruffians, male and female, of Allen street and Mulberry Bend?"[15] I tell you she is there, and to your shame be it said that you will not know her in those surroundings. You, the aristocrats, who demand the fine linen and the purple in your fiction; you, the sensitive, the delicate, who will associate with your Romance only so long as she wears a silken gown. You will not follow her to the slums, for you believe that Romance should only amuse and entertain you, singing you sweet songs and touching the harp of silver strings with rosy-tipped fingers. If haply she should call to you from the squalor of a dive, or the awful degradation of a disorderly house, crying: "Look, listen! This, too, is life. These, too, are my children, look at them, know them and, knowing, help!" Should she call thus, you would stop your ears; you would avert your eyes, and you would answer, "Come from there, Romance. Your place is not there!" And you would make of her a harlequin, a tumbler, a sword dancer, when, as a matter of fact, she should be by right divine a teacher sent from god.

---

10. **muliebrity:** The quality or characteristics of being a woman. The English word was coined to supply the missing opposite of *virility*.

11. **Mr. Lang:** Andrew Lang (1844-1912), prolific British writer and scholar whose most famous work on folklore and primitive religions was *Myth, Ritual and Religion* (1887). The magnificent city of Babylon, which was surrounded by a massive wall, and the pyramids of Egypt were among the architectural wonders of the ancient world.

12. **Jean d'Arc:** St. Joan of Arc (1412-1431), the religious and military leader who led French troops to a series of stunning military victories over the English. Later burned at the stake as a heretic, she was canonized in 1920.

13. **entrée:** The right to enter or be included (French).

14. **chatelaine's chamber and the dungeon of the man-at-arms:** The private room of the mistress of a castle and the prison cell of a medieval cavalryman.

15. **Allen street and Mulberry Bend:** Streets in the slums of New York City.

She will not always wear the robe of silk, the gold crown, the jewelled shoon,[16] will not always sweep the silver harp. An iron note is hers if so she choose, and coarse garments, and stained hands, and, meeting her thus, it is for you to know her as she passes—know her for the same young queen of the blue mantle and lilies.[17] She can teach you, if you will be humble to learn. Teach you by showing, God help you, if at last you take from Romance her mission of teaching, if you do not believe that she has a purpose, a nobler purpose and a mightier than mere amusement, mere entertainment. Let Realism do the entertaining with its meticulous presentation of tea-cups, rag carpets, wall paper and hair-cloth sofas, stopping with these, going no deeper than it sees, choosing the ordinary, the untroubled, the commonplace.

But to Romance belongs the wide world for range, and the unplumbed depths of the human heart, and the mystery of sex, and the problems of life, and the black, unsearched penetralia of the soul of man. You, the indolent, must not always be amused. What matter the silken clothes, what matter the prince's houses? Romance, too, is a teacher, and if—throwing aside the purple—she wears the camel's hair and feeds upon the locusts, it is to cry aloud unto the people, "Prepare ye the way of the Lord, make straight his path."[18]

[1901]

---

16. **shoon:** An early plural form of *shoe.*
17. **queen of the blue mantle and lilies:** The Virgin Mary, who is traditionally depicted wearing a blue mantle and who is associated with the purity of the lily.
18. **"Prepare . . . path":** See Matthew 3:3. The words are spoken by the prophet John the Baptist, who is clothed in camel's hair and who survives on locusts and wild honey.

Mark Twain
(Samuel L. Clemens)

[1835-1910]

"Mark Twain," probably the most familiar figure in American literary history, first came before the public in 1863, when an itinerant journalist named Samuel L. Clemens adopted that pen name to sign his letters in the *Territorial Enterprise*, an obscure newspaper published in what was then the Nevada Territory. Clemens had been born nearly twenty-eight years earlier, on November 30, 1835, in Florida, Missouri. His family later moved to Hannibal, a town on the Mississippi River. There, in what he later described as "a heavenly place for a boy," Clemens unconsciously began to gather material for some of his most memorable works. He also began to gain the journalistic experience that would ultimately lead him to a career in writing. Shortly after his father's death in 1847, Clemens was apprenticed to a local printer. In 1851 he went to work for his brother, who had bought a newspaper in Hannibal. When Clemens was eighteen, he left home and drifted around the country for several years, still supporting himself as a printer and journalist. In 1857, however, Clemens pursued his childhood dream of becoming a steamboat pilot, a lucrative trade he plied until the outbreak of the Civil War in 1861 effectively ended commercial traffic on the Mississippi River. Following a brief stint in a pro-Southern militia unit in Missouri, Clemens turned his back on the war and headed west, his mind full of get-rich schemes. When those failed, he once again took up the pen, first in a series of unsigned letters and then as "Mark Twain." "It is an old river term, a leads-man's call, signifying two fathoms — twelve feet," Clemens explained to the editor of the *Territorial Enterprise*. "It has a richness about it; it was always a pleasant sound for a pilot to hear on a dark night; it meant safe water."

It was as "Mark Twain" — initially his literary persona and increasingly his public role — that Clemens would thereafter be known. He followed the spreading fame of that name from Nevada across the Sierra Nevada to California and finally back across the country to New York City. But he was then either celebrated or dismissed as a popular entertainer, the prolific generator of humorous newspaper sketches rather than serious literary work. His first book was a collection of such sketches, while his second book was a direct outgrowth of his newspaper work: *The Innocents Abroad* (1869), a comic and satirical account of a tour of Europe and the Holy Land based on letters originally published in the *Alta California* and the *New-York Tribune*. Flush with confidence and the substantial proceeds from that book, Twain in 1870 married Olivia Langdon, daughter of a wealthy family from Elmira, New York. The couple soon began a family and moved into a mansion in Hartford, Connecticut, where one of their neighbors was Harriet Beecher Stowe, the revered author best known for

Mark Twain

This photograph of Samuel L. Clemens was taken in 1867, shortly after he gained fame as "Mark Twain."

All modern American literature comes from one book by Mark Twain called Huckleberry Finn.
—Ernest Hemingway

her influential antislavery novel *Uncle Tom's Cabin* (1851). Only then, having worked his way up to affluence and social respectability in the East, did Twain begin to explore and exploit his wide experience and vivid memories of life along the Mississippi River in the years before the Civil War. Twain first wrote *Old Times on the Mississippi* (1875), a series of magazine sketches about his years as a steamboat pilot that he later incorporated into a book, *Life on the Mississippi* (1883). He followed those sketches with his first novel, *The Adventures of Tom Sawyer* (1876). In that popular "boy's book," as the genre was known, Twain told the story from the point of view of a genteel adult narrator. Twain took a different approach in the sequel he began to write in 1876. Using Tom Sawyer's disreputable and semiliterate friend Huck Finn as the narrator of the novel, Twain offered a triumphant demonstration of the power of colloquial speech in *Adventures of Huckleberry Finn*, which he finally published in 1885.

That acclaimed book ultimately overshadowed Twain's other writings, but during the following decades he produced a wide range of work, including novels, stories, and travel books. Although many of those works were set in the past or in distant places, or both, Twain remained deeply engaged in contemporary life in the United States. In a novel set in medieval England, *A Connecticut Yankee in King Arthur's Court* (1889), he mounted a thinly veiled attack on the social injustices and political inequalities generated by the growing disparity between the rich and the poor in the industrial North. Twain explored the implications of miscegenation and the corrosive effects of slavery and racism in *The Tragedy of Pudd'nhead Wilson* (1895), a novel set in the antebellum South. He protested the ongoing oppression of African Americans even more directly in an extended essay, "The United States of Lyncherdom" (1901), a bitter response to the wave of violence that had been unleashed against blacks in the South after the end of Reconstruction. Indeed, the writer from a slaveholding state who had earlier worked so hard to become a respected figure in Northern society and its literary culture — and whom many would come to view as the most quintessentially "American" of all the country's authors — became one of the sharpest critics of society and politics in the United States, both in the North and in the South. During the final decade of his life, Twain composed his lengthy *Autobiography*, some chapters of which he published in the *North American Review* in 1906-07. Organizing the work in the sequence in which his memories surfaced, rather than as a chronological narrative, Twain recalled scenes and events ranging from his joyous boyhood in Missouri to the devastating loss of his wife in 1904 and the deaths of two of his three daughters, one from meningitis in 1896 and the other from heart failure brought on by an epileptic seizure in December 1909. Shortly after describing those agonizing experiences in his *Autobiography*, Twain died at his home in Redding, Connecticut, on April 21, 1910.

bedfordstmartins.com/ americanlit for research links on Twain

Reading Twain's "Jim Smiley and His Jumping Frog."   This sketch spread the fame of "Mark Twain" beyond the West. He had heard a version of this often-told story at a gold camp in California and wrote it down at the request of his friend "Artemus Ward," the pen name of C. F. Browne, a popular comic writer who was putting together a collection of sketches in 1865. When the story arrived too late to be included in the volume, it was published in the *New York Saturday Press*, from which it was widely reprinted in newspapers all around the United States. Twain subsequently revised it several times, notably as the title story of his first book, *The Celebrated Jumping Frog of Calaveras County and Other Sketches* (1867), and even more substantially for his *Sketches, New and Old* (1875). In all of the versions, however, a key element is the ironic interplay between the two narrators: the condescending stand-in for the educated audience — "Mark Twain" in the earliest version — and the garrulous old Simon Wheeler, the colloquial teller of the tale, who may well have the last laugh. The text is taken from the first printing in the *New York Saturday Press*, November 18, 1865.

JIM SMILEY AND HIS JUMPING FROG[1]

Mr. A. Ward,

Dear Sir: — Well, I called on good-natured garrulous old Simon Wheeler, and I inquired after your friend Leonidas W. Smiley, as you requested me to do, and I hereunto append the result. If you can get any information out of it you are cordially welcome to it. I have a lurking suspicion that your Leonidas W. Smiley is a myth — that you never knew such a personage, and that you only conjectured that if I asked old Wheeler about him it would remind him of his infamous *Jim* Smiley, and he would go to work and bore me nearly to death with some infernal reminiscence of him as long and tedious as it should be useless to me. If that was your design, Mr. Ward, it will gratify you to know that it succeeded.

I found Simon Wheeler dozing comfortably by the bar-room stove of the little old dilapidated tavern in the ancient mining camp of Boomerang, and I noticed that he was fat and bald-headed, and had an expression of winning gentleness and simplicity upon his tranquil countenance. He roused up and gave me good-day. I told him a friend of mine had commissioned me to make some inquiries about a cherished companion of his boyhood named Leonidas W. Smiley — Rev. Leonidas W. Smiley — a young minister of the gospel, who he had heard was at one time a resident of this village of Boomerang. I added that if Mr. Wheeler could tell me anything about this Rev. Leonidas W. Smiley, I would feel under many obligations to him.

---

1. Jim Smiley and His Jumping Frog: When Twain later revised the story, he altered the title to "The Notorious Jumping Frog of Calaveras County." The county, which is in the foothills of the Sierra Nevada, directly east of San Francisco, was the center of mining activity during the California gold rush of 1849.

Simon Wheeler backed me into a corner and blockaded me there with his chair – and then sat down and reeled off the monotonous narrative which follows this paragraph. He never smiled, he never frowned, he never changed his voice from the quiet, gently-flowing key to which he turned the initial sentence, he never betrayed the slightest suspicion of enthusiasm – but all through the interminable narrative there ran a vein of impressive earnestness and sincerity, which showed me plainly that so far from his imagining that there was anything ridiculous or funny about his story, he regarded it as a really important matter, and admired its two heroes as men of transcendent genius in finesse . . . To me, the spectacle of a man drifting serenely along through such a queer yarn without ever smiling was exquisitely absurd. As I said before, I asked him to tell me what he knew of Rev. Leonidas W. Smiley, and he replied as follows. I let him go on in his own way, and never interrupted him once:

There was a feller here once by the name of *Jim* Smiley, in the winter of '49 – or maybe it was the spring of '50 – I don't recollect exactly, somehow, though what makes me think it was one or the other is because I remember the big flume wasn't finished when he first come to the camp; but anyway, he was the curiousest man about always betting on anything that turned up you ever see, if he could get anybody to bet on the other side, and if he couldn't he'd change sides – any way that suited the other man would suit *him* – any way just so's he got a bet, *he* was satisfied. But still, he was lucky – uncommon lucky; he most always come out winner. He was always ready and laying for a chance; there couldn't be no solitry thing mentioned but what that feller'd offer to bet on it – and take any side you please, as I was just telling you: if there was a horse race, you'd find him flush or you find him busted at the end of it; if there was a dog-fight, he'd bet on it; if there was a cat-fight, he'd bet on it; if there was a chicken-fight, he'd bet on it; why if there was two birds setting on a fence, he would bet you which one would fly first – or if there was a camp-meeting he would be there reglar to bet on parson Walker, which he judged to be the best exhorter about here, and so he was, too, and a good man; if he even see a straddle-bug start to go anywheres, he would bet you how long it would take him to get wherever he was going to, and if you took him up he would foller that straddle-bug to Mexico but what he would find out where he was bound for and how long he was on the road. Lots of the boys here has seen that Smiley and can tell you about him. Why, it never made no difference to *him* – he would bet on *anything* – the dangdest feller. Parson Walker's wife laid very sick, once, for a good while, and it seemed as if they warn't going to save her; but one morning he come in and Smiley asked him how she was, and he said she was considerable better – thank the Lord for his inf'nit mercy – and coming on so smart that with the blessing of Providence she'd get well yet – and Smiley, before he thought, says, "Well, I'll resk two-and-a-half that she don't, anyway."

Thish-yer Smiley had a mare – the boys called her the fifteen-minute nag, but that was only in fun, you know, because, of course, she was faster than that – and he used to win money on that horse, for all she was so slow and always had the asthma, or the distemper, or the consumption, or something of that kind. They used to give her two or three hundred yards' start, and then pass her under way; but always at the fag-end[2] of

---

2. **fag-end**: Tiring or exhausting conclusion of an event or occasion.

the race she'd get excited and desperate-like, and come cavorting and spraddling up, and scattering her legs around limber, sometimes in the air, and sometimes out to one side amongst the fences, and kicking up m-o-r-e dust, and raising m-o-r-e racket with her coughing and sneezing and blowing her nose — and always fetch up at the stand just about a neck ahead, as near as you could cipher it down.

And he had a little small bull-pup, that to look at him you'd think he warn't worth a cent, but to set around and look ornery, and lay for a chance to steal something. But as soon as money was up on him he was a different dog — his under-jaw'd begin to stick out like the for'castle of a steamboat, and his teeth would uncover, and shine savage like the furnaces. And a dog might tackle him, and bully-rag him, and bite him, and throw him over his shoulder two or three times, and Andrew Jackson[3] — which was the name of the pup — Andrew Jackson would never let on but what he was satisfied, and hadn't expected nothing else — and the bets being doubled and doubled on the other side all the time, till the money was all up — and then all of a sudden he would grab that other dog just by the joint of his hind legs and freeze to it — not chaw, you understand, but only just grip and hang on till they throwed up on the sponge, if it was a year. Smiley always came out winner on that pup till he harnessed a dog once that didn't have no hind legs, because they'd been sawed off in a circular saw, and when the thing had gone along far enough, and the money was all up, and he came to make a snatch for his pet holt, he saw in a minute how he'd been imposed on, and how the other dog had him in the door, so to speak, and he 'peared surprised, and then he looked sorter discouraged like, and didn't try no more to win the fight, and so he got shucked out bad. He gave Smiley a look as much as to say his heart was broke, and it was *his* fault, for putting up a dog that hadn't no hind legs for him to take holt of, which was his main dependence in a fight, and then he limped off a piece, and laid down and died. It was a good pup, was that Andrew Jackson, and would have made a name for hisself if he'd lived, for the stuff was in him, and he had genius — I know it, because he hadn't had no opportunities to speak of, and it don't stand to reason that a dog could make such a fight as he could under them circumstances, if he hadn't no talent. It always makes me feel sorry when I think of that last fight of his'on, and the way it turned out.

Well, thish-yer Smiley had rat-terriers and chicken cocks, and tom-cats, and all them kind of things, till you couldn't rest, and you couldn't fetch nothing for him to bet on but he'd match you. He ketched a frog one day and took him home and said he cal'lated to educate him; and so he never done nothing for three months but set in his back yard and learn that frog to jump. And you bet you he *did* learn him, too. He'd give him a little hunch behind, and the next minute you'd see that frog whirling in the air like a doughnut — see him turn one summerset, or maybe a couple, if he got a good start, and come down flat-footed and all right, like a cat. He got him up so in the matter of ketching flies, and kept him in practice so constant, that he'd nail a fly every time as far as he could see him. Smiley said all a frog wanted was education, and he could do most anything — and I believe him. Why, I've seen him set Dan'l Webster[4] down here on this floor — Dan'l Webster

---

3. **Andrew Jackson:** Nicknamed "Old Hickory" for his toughness and tenacity, Andrew Jackson (1767–1845) was a famous general and the seventh president of the United States.
4. **Dan'l Webster:** Daniel Webster (1782–1852), a senator from Massachusetts, was a well-known orator and Whig politician who led the opposition to President Andrew Jackson and the Democratic Party.

was the name of the frog—and sing out, "Flies! Dan'l, flies," and quicker'n you could wink, he'd spring straight up, and snake a fly off'n the counter there, and flop down on the floor again as solid as a gob of mud, and fall to scratching the side of his head with his hind foot as indifferent as if he hadn't no idea he'd done any more'n any frog might do. You never see a frog so modest and straightfor'ard as he was, for all he was so gifted. And when it come to fair-and-square jumping on a dead level, he could get over more ground at one straddle than any animal of his breed you ever see. Jumping on a dead level was his strong suit, you understand, and when it come to that, Smiley would ante up money on him as long as he had a red.[5] Smiley was monstrous proud of his frog, and well he might be, for fellers that had travelled and ben everywheres all said he laid over any frog that ever *they* see.

Well, Smiley kept the beast in a little lattice box, and he used to fetch him downtown sometimes and lay for a bet. One day a feller—a stranger in the camp, he was—come across him with his box, and says:

"What might it be that you've got in the box?"

And Smiley says, sorter indifferent like, "It might be a parrot, or it might be a canary, maybe, but it ain't—it's only just a frog."

And the feller took it, and looked at it careful, and turned it round this way and that, and says, "H'm—so 'tis. Well, what's *he* good for?"

"Well," Smiley says, easy and careless, "he's good enough for *one* thing I should judge—he can out-jump any frog in Calaveras county."

The feller took the box again, and took another long, particular look, and give it back to Smiley and says, very deliberate, "Well—I don't see no points about that frog that's any better'n any other frog."

"Maybe you don't," Smiley says. "Maybe you understand frogs, and maybe you don't understand 'em; maybe you've had experience, and maybe you ain't only a amature, as it were. Anyways, I've got *my* opinion, and I'll resk forty dollars that he can out-jump any frog in Calaveras county."

And the feller studied a minute, and then says, kinder sad, like, "Well—I'm only a stranger here, and I ain't got no frog—but if I had a frog I'd bet you."

And then Smiley says, "That's all right—that's all right—if you'll hold my box a minute I'll go and get you a frog"; and so the feller took the box, and put up his forty dollars along with Smiley's, and set down to wait.

So he set there a good while thinking and thinking to hisself, and then he got the frog out and prized his mouth open and took a teaspoon and filled him full of quail-shot—filled him pretty near up to his chin—and set him on the floor. Smiley he went out to the swamp and slopped around in the mud for a long time, and finally he ketched a frog and fetched him in and give him to this feller and says:

"Now if you're ready, set him alongside of Dan'l, with his fore-paws just even with Dan'l's, and I'll give the word." Then he says, "One—two—three—jump!" and him and the feller touched up the frogs from behind, and the new frog hopped off lively, but Dan'l give a heave, and hysted up his shoulders—so—like a Frenchman, but it wasn't no use—he couldn't budge; he was planted as solid as a anvil, and he couldn't no more stir

---

5. **red:** That is, a "red cent," so called because of the high copper content in the penny before the Civil War.

than if he was anchored out. Smiley was a good deal surprised, and he was disgusted too, but he didn't have no idea what the matter was, of course.

The feller took the money and started away, and when he was going out at the door he sorter jerked his thumb over his shoulder – this way – at Dan'l, and says again, very deliberate, "Well – *I* don't see no points about that frog that's any better'n any other frog."

Smiley he stood scratching his head and looking down at Dan'l a long time, and at last he says, "I do wonder what in the nation that frog throwed off for – I wonder if there ain't something the matter with him – he 'pears to look mighty baggy, somehow" – and he ketched Dan'l by the nap of the neck, and lifted him up and says, "Why blame my cats if he don't weigh five pounds" – and turned him upside down, and he belched out about a double-handful of shot. And then he see how it was, and he was the maddest man – he set the frog down and took out after that feller, but he never ketched him. And —

[Here Simon Wheeler heard his name called from the front-yard, and got up to go and see what was wanted.] And turning to me as he moved away, he said: "Just sit where you are, stranger, and rest easy – I ain't going to be gone a second."

But by your leave, I did not think that a continuation of the history of the enterprising vagabond Jim Smiley would be likely to afford me much information concerning the Rev. Leonidas W. Smiley, and so I started away.

At the door I met the sociable Wheeler returning, and he buttonholed me and recommenced:

"Well, thish-yer Smiley had a yaller one-eyed cow that didn't have no tail only just a short stump like a bannanner, and —"

"O, curse Smiley and his afflicted cow!" I muttered, good-naturedly, and bidding the old gentleman good-day, I departed.

Yours, truly,

Mark Twain
[1865]

Reading Twain's "A True Story, Repeated Word for Word as I Heard It." This story was told to Twain by a cook at Quarry Farm in Elmira, New York, where the Clemenses spent their summers. The printed version was particularly significant because it was the first piece Twain published in the most distinguished periodical in the United States, the *Atlantic Monthly*, where it appeared in 1874. Its editor, William Dean Howells, was then virtually the only member of the literary establishment who took Twain seriously as a writer, and the periodical consequently opened up to him a new and radically different audience. In response, the humorist offered a piece that was anything but funny, the poignant account of a former slave. Such stories, often transcribed by Northern abolitionists, had been a staple of the antislavery crusade before the Civil War. Here, in the waning period of Reconstruction, the story was transcribed by a writer who had grown up in a slave state, whose family had owned a slave, and who had briefly served in a pro-Southern militia unit in Missouri before moving west and finally settling in the East. At the same time, Twain's ear for southern vernacular speech gave the story a particular force and authenticity, anticipating his masterly deployment of such speech in *Adventures of Huckleberry Finn*. The text is taken from the first printing in the *Atlantic Monthly*, November 1874.

A TRUE STORY, REPEATED
WORD FOR WORD AS I HEARD IT

It was summer time, and twilight. We were sitting on the porch of the farm-house, on the summit of the hill, and "Aunt Rachel" was sitting respectfully below our level, on the steps, – for she was our servant, and colored. She was of mighty frame and stature; she was sixty years old, but her eye was undimmed and her strength unabated. She was a cheerful, hearty soul, and it was no more trouble for her to laugh than it is for a bird to sing. She was under fire, now, as usual when the day was done. That is to say, she was being chaffed without mercy, and was enjoying it. She would let off peal after peal of laughter, and then sit with her face in her hands and shake with throes of enjoyment which she could no longer get breath enough to express. At such a moment as this a thought occurred to me, and I said: –

"Aunt Rachel, how is that you've lived sixty years and never had any trouble?"

She stopped quaking. She paused, and there was a moment of silence. She turned her face over her shoulder toward me, and said, without even a smile in her voice: –

"Misto C —, is you in 'arnest?"

It surprised me a good deal; and it sobered my manner and my speech, too. I said: –

"Why, I thought – that is, I meant – why, you *can't* have had any trouble. I've never heard you sigh, and never seen your eye when there wasn't a laugh in it."

She faced fairly around, now, and was full of earnestness.

"Has I had any trouble? Misto C —, I's gwyne to tell you, den I leave it to you. I was bawn down 'mongst de slaves; I knows all 'bout slavery, 'case I ben one of 'em my own se'f. Well, sah, my ole man – dat's my husban' – he was lovin' an' kind to me, jist as kind as you is to yo' own wife. An' we had chil'en – seven chil'en – an' we loved dem chil'en jist de same as you loves yo' chil'en. Dey was black, but de Lord can't make no chil'en so black but what dey mother loves 'em an' wouldn't give 'em up, no, not for anything dat's in dis whole world.

"Well, sah, I was raised in ole Fo'ginny, but my mother she was raised in Maryland; an' my *souls!* she was turrible when she'd git started! My *lan'!* but she'd make de fur fly! When she'd git into dem tantrums, she always had one word dat she said. She'd straighten herse'f up an' put her fists in her hips an' say, 'I want you to understan' dat I wa' n't bawn in de mash to be fool' by trash! I 's one o' de ole Blue Hen's Chickens, *I* is!' 'Ca'se, you see, dat's what folks dat's bawn in Maryland calls deyselves, an' dey's proud of it. Well, dat was her word. I don't ever forgit it, beca'se she said it so much, an' beca'se she said it one day when my little Henry tore his wris' awful, an' most busted his head, right up at de top of his forehead, an' de niggers didn't fly aroun' fas' enough to 'tend to him. An' when dey talk' back at her, she up an' she says, 'Look-a-heah!' she says, 'I want you niggers to understan' dat I wa' n't bawn in de mash to be fool' by trash! I 's one o' de ole Blue Hen's Chickens, *I* is!' an' den she clar' dat kitchen an' bandage' up de chile herse'f. So I says dat word, too, when I's riled.

"Well, bymeby my ole mistis say she's broke, an' she got to sell all de niggers on de place. An' when I heah dat dey gwyne to sell us all off at oction in Richmon', oh de good gracious! I know what dat mean!"

Aunt Rachel had gradually risen, while she warmed to her subject, and now she towered above us, black against the stars.

"Dey put chains on us an' put us on a stan' as high as dis po'ch, — twenty foot high, — an' all de people stood aroun', crowds an' crowds. An' dey 'd come up dah an' look at us all roun', an' squeeze our arm, an' make us git up an' walk, an' den say, 'Dis one too ole,' or 'Dis one lame,' or 'Dis one don't 'mount to much.' An' dey sole my ole man, an' took him away, an' dey begin to sell my chil'en an' take *dem* away, an' I begin to cry; an' de man say, 'Shet up yo' dam blubberin',' an' hit me on de mouf wid his han'. An' when de las' one was gone but my little Henry, I grab *him* clost up to my breas' so, an' I ris up an' says, 'You shan't take him away,' I says; 'I'll kill de man dat totches him!' I says. But my little Henry whisper an' say, 'I gwyne to run away, an' den I work an' buy yo' freedom.' Oh, bless de chile, he always so good! But dey got him — dey got him, de men did; but I took and tear de clo'es mos' off of 'em, an' beat 'em over de head wid my chain; an' *dey* give it to *me*, too, but I didn't mine dat.

"Well, dah was my ole man gone, an' all my chil'en, all my seven chil'en — an' six of 'em I haint set eyes on ag'in to dis day, an' dat 's twenty-two year ago las' Easter. De man dat bought me b'long' in Newbern, an' he took me dah. Well, bymeby de years roll on an' de waw come. My marster he was a Confedrit colonel, an' I was his family's cook. So when de Unions took dat town, dey all run away an' lef' me all by myse'f wid de other niggers in dat mons'us big house. So de big Union officers move in dah, an' dey ask me would I cook for *dem*. 'Lord bless you,' says I, 'dat 's what I 's *for*.'

"Dey wa' n't no small-fry officers, mine you, dey was de biggest dey *is*; an' de way dey made dem sojers mosey roun'! De Gen'l he tole me to boss dat kitchen; an' he say, 'If anybody come meddlin' wid you, you jist make 'em walk chalk; don't you be afeard,' he say; 'you's 'mong frens, now.'

"Well, I thinks to myse'f, if my little Henry ever got a chance to run away, he'd make to de Norf, o' course. So one day I comes in dah whah de big officers was, in de parlor, an' I drops a kurtchy, so, an' I up an' tole 'em 'bout my Henry, dey a-listenin' to my troubles jist de same as if I was white folks; an' I says, 'What I come for is beca'se if he got away and got up Norf whah you gemmen comes from, you might 'a' seen him, maybe, an' could tell me so as I could fine him ag'in; he was very little, an' he had a sk-yar on his lef' wris', an' at de top of his forehad.' Den dey look mournful, an' de Gen'l say, 'How long sence you los' him?' an' I say, 'Thirteen year.' Den de Gen'l say, 'He wouldn't be little no mo', now — he's a man!'

"I never thought o' dat befo'! He was only dat little feller to *me*, yit. I never thought 'bout him growin' up an' bein' big. But I see it den. None o' de gemmen had run acrost him, so dey couldn't do nothin' for me. But all dat time, do' *I* didn't know it, my Henry *was* run off to de Norf, years an' years, an' he was a barber, too, an' worked for hisse'f. An' bymeby, when de waw come, he ups an' he says, 'I 's done barberin',' he says; 'I 's gwyne to fine my ole mammy, less'n she's dead.' So he sole out an' went to whah dey was recruitin', an' hired hisse'f out to de colonel for his servant; an' den he went all froo de battles everywhah, huntin' for his ole mammy; yes indeedy, he'd hire to fust one officer an' den another, tell he'd ransacked de whole Souf; but you see *I* didn't know nuffin 'bout *dis*. How was *I* gwyne to know it?

"Well, one night we had a big sojer ball; de sojers dah at Newbern was always havin' balls an' carryin' on. Dey had 'em in my kitchen, heaps o' times, 'ca'se it was so big. Mine you, I was *down* on sich doin's; beca'se my place was wid de officers, an' it rasp' me to have dem common sojers cavortin' roun' my kitchen like dat. But I alway' stood aroun' an' kep' things straight, I did; an' sometimes dey'd git my dander up, an' den I'd make 'em clar dat kitchen, mine I *tell* you!

"Well, one night – it was a Friday night – dey comes a whole plattoon f'm a *nigger* ridgment dat was on guard at de house, – de house was headquarters, you know, – an' den I was jist a-*bilin'!* Mad? I was jist a-*boomin'!* I swelled aroun', an' swelled aroun'; I jist was a-itchin' for 'em to do somefin for to start me. *An'* dey was a-walzin' an a-dancin'! *my!* but dey was havin' a time! an' I jist a-swellin' an' a-swellin' up! Pooty soon, 'long comes *sich* a spruce young nigger a-sailin' down de room wid a yaller wench roun' de wais'; an' roun' an' roun' an' roun' dey went, enough to make a body drunk to look at 'em; an' when dey got abreas' o' me, dey went to kin' o' balancin' aroun', fust on one leg an' den on t'other, an' smilin' at my big red turban, an' makin' fun, an' I ups an' says, '*Git* along wid you! – rub-bage!' De young man's face kin' o' changed, all of a sudden, for 'bout a second, but den he went to smilin' ag'in, same as he was befo'. Well, 'bout dis time, in comes some niggers dat played music an' b'long' to de ban', an' dey *never* could git along widout puttin' on airs. An' de very fust air dey put on dat night, I lit into 'em! Dey laughed, an' dat made me wuss. De res' o' de niggers got to laughin', an' den my soul *alive* but I was hot! My eye was jist a-blazin'! I jist straightened myself up, so, – jist as I is now, plum to de ceilin', mos', – an' I digs my fists into my hips, an' I says, 'Look-a-heah!' I says, 'I want you niggers to under-stan' dat I wa'n't bawn in de mash to be fool' by trash! I 's one o' de ole Blue Hen's Chick-ens, *I* is!' an' den I see dat young man stan' a-starin' an' stiff, lookin' kin' o' up at de ceilin' like he fo'got somefin, an' couldn't 'member it no mo'. Well, I jist march' on dem nig-gers, – so, lookin' like a gen'l, – an' dey jist cave' away befo' me an' out at de do'. An' as dis young man was a-goin' out, I heah him say to another nigger, 'Jim,' he says, 'you go 'long an' tell de cap'n I be on han' 'bout eight o'clock in de mawnin'; dey's somefin on my mine,' he says; 'I don't sleep no mo' dis night. You go 'long,' he says, 'an' leave me by my own se'f.'

"Dis was 'bout one o'clock in de mawnin'. Well, 'bout seven, I was up an' on han', git-tin' de officers' breakfast. I was a-stoopin' down by de stove, – jist so, same as if yo' foot was de stove, – an' I'd opened de stove do wid my right han', – so, pushin' it back, jist as I pushes yo' foot, – an' I'd jist got de pan o' hot biscuits in my han' an' was 'bout to raise up, when I see a black face come aroun' under mine, an' de eyes a-lookin' up into mine, jist as I 's a-lookin' up clost under yo' face now; an' I jist stopped *right dah*, an' never budged! jist gazed, an' gazed, so; an' de pan begin to tremble, an' all of a sudden I *knowed!* De pan drop' on de flo' an' I grab his lef' han' an' shove back his sleeve, – jist so, as I 's doin' to you, – an' den I goes for his forehead an' push de hair back, so, an' 'Boy!' I says, 'if you an't my Henry, what is you doin' wid dis welt on yo' wris' an' dat sk-yar on yo' forehead? De Lord God ob heaven be praise', I got my own ag'in!'

"Oh, no, Misto C ——, *I* hain't had no trouble. An' no *joy!*"

[1874]

Reading Twain's "The Private History of a Campaign That Failed." This account of Twain's brief experience in the pro-Southern militia in his home state of Missouri was published in 1885 in the *Century Illustrated Monthly Magazine*, which had begun publication four years earlier as a successor to *Scribner's Monthly Magazine*. From the beginning, the *Century* featured numerous articles about the Civil War, and in November 1884 the magazine launched an ambitious series of lavishly illustrated reminiscences written by soldiers who had fought on both sides of the conflict. Dozens of their accounts appeared in the magazine before the Century Company published a four-volume set based on the series, *Battles and Leaders of the Civil War* (1887–88), which became the best-selling and most frequently cited of all works on the Civil War. Twain's contribution to the series, which was not included in the published set, was distinctive in several ways. "Decisive battles, the leading characteristics of army life on each side of the lines, and the lives of the most prominent commanders, North and South, will be the subjects of the papers," the editors observed when announcing the commencement of the series in the *Century*. Twain's subject was far different, and the antiheroic tone of "The Private History of a Campaign That Failed" was in sharp opposition to the overall tone of the series, which the editors hoped would teach the generation that had grown up since the war "how the men who were divided on a question of principle and State fealty, and who fought the war which must remain the pivotal period of our history, won by equal devotion and valor that respect for each other which is the strongest bond of a reunited people." The text and one of its accompanying illustrations are taken from the first printing in the *Century*, December 1885.

THE PRIVATE HISTORY
OF A CAMPAIGN THAT FAILED

You have heard from a great many people who did something in the war; is it not fair and right that you listen a little moment to one who started out to do something in it, but didn't? Thousands entered the war, got just a taste of it, and then stepped out again, permanently. These, by their very numbers, are respectable, and are therefore entitled to a sort of voice, not a loud one, but a modest one; not a boastful one, but an apologetic one. They ought not to be allowed much space among better people — people who did something — I grant that; but they ought at least to be allowed to state why they didn't do anything, and also to explain the process by which they didn't do anything. Surely this kind of light must have a sort of value.

Out West there was a good deal of confusion in men's minds during the first months of the great trouble — a good deal of unsettledness, of leaning first this way, then that, then the other way. It was hard for us to get our bearings. I call to mind an instance of this. I was piloting on the Mississippi when the news came that South Carolina had gone out of the Union on the 20th of December, 1860. My pilot-mate was a New Yorker. He was strong

for the Union; so was I. But he would not listen to me with any patience; my loyalty was smirched, to his eye, because my father had owned slaves. I said, in palliation of this dark fact, that I had heard my father say, some years before he died, that slavery was a great wrong, and that he would free the solitary negro he then owned if he could think it right to give away the property of the family when he was so straitened in means. My mate retorted that a mere impulse was nothing—anybody could pretend to a good impulse; and went on decrying my Unionism and libeling my ancestry. A month later the secession atmosphere had considerably thickened on the Lower Mississippi, and I became a rebel; so did he. We were together in New Orleans, the 26th of January, when Louisiana went out of the Union. He did his full share of the rebel shouting, but was bitterly opposed to letting me do mine. He said that I came of bad stock—of a father who had been willing to set slaves free. In the following summer he was piloting a Federal gun-boat and shouting for the Union again, and I was in the Confederate army. I held his note for some borrowed money. He was one of the most upright men I ever knew; but he repudiated that note without hesitation, because I was a rebel, and the son of a man who owned slaves.

In that summer—of 1861—the first wash of the wave of war broke upon the shores of Missouri. Our State was invaded by the Union forces. They took possession of St. Louis, Jefferson Barracks, and some other points. The Governor, Claib Jackson, issued his proclamation calling out fifty thousand militia to repel the invader.[1]

I was visiting in the small town where my boyhood had been spent—Hannibal, Marion County. Several of us got together in a secret place by night and formed ourselves into a military company. One Tom Lyman, a young fellow of a good deal of spirit but of no military experience, was made captain; I was made second lieutenant. We had no first lieutenant; I do not know why; it was long ago. There were fifteen of us. By the advice of an innocent connected with the organization, we called ourselves the Marion Rangers. I do not remember that any one found fault with the name. I did not; I thought

---

1. **The Governor . . . to repel the invader:** Claiborne F. Jackson (1806–1862), the governor of Missouri from 1861 to 1862, was a staunch secessionist who tried to lead the state out of the Union. The delegates to a convention held in St. Louis in March 1861 voted overwhelmingly against both secession and coercive efforts to force the Southern states back into the Union. Even as federal troops occupied the state, Jackson reorganized its militia into the Missouri State Guard, which was supplied with arms by the Confederacy. In June, after federal troops attacked the state guard's gathering at "Camp Jackson," the governor called out 5,000 militiamen "to defend the state from invasion." In response, Twain joined a pro-Southern militia unit, though he and others technically pledged their support to the state and federal constitutions, not to the Confederacy. In fact, there was considerable confusion and uncertainty among some men in the state guard, since Missouri remained part of the Union despite the ongoing efforts of the governor. During his brief time in the militia, which he abandoned at the end of July, Twain did not participate in any of the battles between federal troops and the state guard.

it sounded quite well. The young fellow who proposed this title was perhaps a fair sample of the kind of stuff we were made of. He was young, ignorant, good-natured, well-meaning, trivial, full of romance, and given to reading chivalric novels and singing forlorn love-ditties. He had some pathetic little nickel-plated aristocratic instincts, and detested his name, which was Dunlap; detested it, partly because it was nearly as common in that region as Smith, but mainly because it had a plebeian sound to his ear. So he tried to ennoble it by writing it in this way: *d'Unlap.* That contented his eye, but left his ear unsatisfied, for people gave the new name the same old pronunciation – emphasis on the front end of it. He then did the bravest thing that can be imagined, a thing to make one shiver when one remembers how the world is given to resenting shams and affectations; he began to write his name so: *d'Un Lap.* And he waited patiently through the long storm of mud that was flung at this work of art, and he had his reward at last; for he lived to see that name accepted, and the emphasis put where he wanted it, by people who had known him all his life, and to whom the tribe of Dunlaps had been as familiar as the rain and the sunshine for forty years. So sure of victory at last is the courage that can wait. He said he had found, by consulting some ancient French chronicles, that the name was rightly and originally written d'Un Lap; and said that if it were translated into English it would mean Peterson: *Lap,* Latin or Greek, he said, for stone or rock, same as the French *pierre,* that is to say, Peter; *d',* of or from; *un,* a or one; hence, d'Un Lap, of or from a stone or a Peter; that is to say, one who is the son of a stone, the son of a Peter – Peterson. Our militia company were not learned, and the explanation confused them; so they called him Peterson Dunlap. He proved useful to us in his way; he named our camps for us, and he generally struck a name that was "no slouch," as the boys said.

That is one sample of us. Another was Ed Stevens, son of the town jeweler, – trim-built, handsome, graceful, neat as a cat; bright, educated, but given over entirely to fun. There was nothing serious in life to him. As far as he was concerned, this military expedition of ours was simply a holiday. I should say that about half of us looked upon it in the same way; not consciously, perhaps, but unconsciously. We did not think; we were not capable of it. As for myself, I was full of unreasoning joy to be done with turning out of bed at midnight and four in the morning, for a while; grateful to have a change, new scenes, new occupations, a new interest. In my thoughts that was as far as I went; I did not go into the details; as a rule one doesn't at twenty-four.

Another sample was Smith, the blacksmith's apprentice. This vast donkey had some pluck, of a slow and sluggish nature, but a soft heart; at one time he would knock a horse down for some impropriety, and at another he would get homesick and cry. However, he had one ultimate credit to his account which some of us hadn't: he stuck to the war, and was killed in battle at last.

Jo Bowers, another sample, was a huge, good-natured, flax-headed lubber; lazy, sentimental, full of harmless brag, a grumbler by nature; an experienced, industrious, ambitious, and often quite picturesque liar, and yet not a successful one, for he had had no intelligent training, but was allowed to come up just any way. This life was serious enough to him, and seldom satisfactory. But he was a good fellow anyway, and the boys all liked him. He was made orderly sergeant; Stevens was made corporal.

These samples will answer — and they are quite fair ones. Well, this herd of cattle started for the war. What could you expect of them? They did as well as they knew how, but really what was justly to be expected of them? Nothing, I should say. That is what they did.

We waited for a dark night, for caution and secrecy were necessary; then, toward midnight, we stole in couples and from various directions to the Griffith place, beyond the town; from that point we set out together on foot. Hannibal lies at the extreme south-eastern corner of Marion County, on the Mississippi River; our objective point was the hamlet of New London, ten miles away, in Ralls County.

The first hour was all fun, all idle nonsense and laughter. But that could not be kept up. The steady trudging came to be like work; the play had somehow oozed out of it; the stillness of the woods and the somberness of the night began to throw a depressing influence over the spirits of the boys, and presently the talking died out and each person shut himself up in his own thoughts. During the last half of the second hour nobody said a word.

Now we approached a log farm-house where, according to report, there was a guard of five Union soldiers. Lyman called a halt; and there, in the deep gloom of the overhanging branches, he began to whisper a plan of assault upon that house, which made the gloom more depressing than it was before. It was a crucial moment; we realized, with a cold suddenness, that here was no jest — we were standing face to face with actual war. We were equal to the occasion. In our response there was no hesitation, no indecision: we said that if Lyman wanted to meddle with those soldiers, he could go ahead and do it; but if he waited for us to follow him, he would wait a long time.

Lyman urged, pleaded, tried to shame us, but it had no effect. Our course was plain, our minds were made up: we would flank the farm-house — go out around. And that is what we did.

We struck into the woods and entered upon a rough time, stumbling over roots, getting tangled in vines, and torn by briers. At last we reached an open place in a safe region, and sat down, blown and hot, to cool off and nurse our scratches and bruises. Lyman was annoyed, but the rest of us were cheerful; we had flanked the farm-house, we had made our first military movement, and it was a success; we had nothing to fret about, we were feeling just the other way. Horse-play and laughing began again; the expedition was become a holiday frolic once more.

Then we had two more hours of dull trudging and ultimate silence and depression; then, about dawn, we struggled into New London, soiled, heel-blistered, fagged with our little march, and all of us except Stevens in a sour and raspy humor and privately down on the war. We stacked our shabby old shot-guns in Colonel Ralls's barn, and then went in a body and breakfasted with that veteran of the Mexican war.[2] Afterwards he took us to a distant meadow, and there in the shade of a tree we listened to an old-fashioned speech from him, full of gunpowder and glory, full of that adjective-piling, mixed metaphor, and windy declamation which was regarded as eloquence in that ancient time and that remote region; and then he swore us on the Bible to be faithful to the State of

---

2. **Mexican war:** The Mexican War (1846-48), at the conclusion of which the United States gained California and a vast territory in the Southwest, was a training ground for many soldiers and officers who later fought in the Civil War, including Ulysses S. Grant and Robert E. Lee.

Missouri and drive all invaders from her soil, no matter whence they might come or under what flag they might march. This mixed us considerably, and we could not make out just what service we were embarked in; but Colonel Ralls, the practiced politician and phrase-juggler, was not similarly in doubt; he knew quite clearly that he had invested us in the cause of the Southern Confederacy. He closed the solemnities by belting around me the sword which his neighbor, Colonel Brown, had worn at Buena Vista and Molino del Rey;[3] and he accompanied this act with another impressive blast.

Then we formed in line of battle and marched four miles to a shady and pleasant piece of woods on the border of the far-reaching expanses of a flowery prairie. It was an enchanting region for war — our kind of war.

We pierced the forest about half a mile, and took up a strong position, with some low, rocky, and wooded hills behind us, and a purling, limpid creek in front. Straightway half the command were in swimming, and the other half fishing. The ass with the French name gave this position a romantic title, but it was too long, so the boys shortened and simplified it to Camp Ralls.

We occupied an old maple-sugar camp, whose half-rotted troughs were still propped against the trees. A long corn-crib served for sleeping quarters for the battalion. On our left, half a mile away, was Mason's farm and house; and he was a friend to the cause. Shortly after noon the farmers began to arrive from several directions, with mules and horses for our use, and these they lent us for as long as the war might last, which they judged would be about three months. The animals were of all sizes, all colors, and all breeds. They were mainly young and frisky, and nobody in the command could stay on them long at a time; for we were town boys, and ignorant of horsemanship. The creature that fell to my share was a very small mule, and yet so quick and active that it could throw me without difficulty; and it did this whenever I got on it. Then it would bray — stretching its neck out, laying its ears back, and spreading its jaws till you could see down to its works. It was a disagreeable animal, in every way. If I took it by the bridle and tried to lead it off the grounds, it would sit down and brace back, and no one could budge it. However, I was not entirely destitute of military resources, and I did presently manage to spoil this game; for I had seen many a steamboat aground in my time, and knew a trick or two which even a grounded mule would be obliged to respect. There was a well by the corn-crib; so I substituted thirty fathom of rope for the bridle, and fetched him home with the windlass.

I will anticipate here sufficiently to say that we did learn to ride, after some days' practice, but never well. We could not learn to like our animals; they were not choice ones, and most of them had annoying peculiarities of one kind or another. Stevens's horse would carry him, when he was not noticing, under the huge excrescences which form on the trunks of oak-trees, and wipe him out of the saddle; in this way Stevens got several bad hurts. Sergeant Bowers's horse was very large and tall, with slim, long legs, and looked like a railroad bridge. His size enabled him to reach all about, and as far as he wanted to, with his head; so he was always biting Bowers's legs. On the march, in the

---

3. **Buena Vista and Molino del Rey:** Decisive American victories in the Mexican War.

sun, Bowers slept a good deal; and as soon as the horse recognized that he was asleep he would reach around and bite him on the leg. His legs were black and blue with bites. This was the only thing that could ever make him swear, but this always did; whenever the horse bit him he always swore, and of course Stevens, who laughed at everything, laughed at this, and would even get into such convulsions over it as to lose his balance and fall off his horse; and then Bowers, already irritated by the pain of the horse-bite, would resent the laughter with hard language, and there would be a quarrel; so that horse made no end of trouble and bad blood in the command.

However, I will get back to where I was — our first afternoon in the sugar-camp. The sugar-troughs came very handy as horse-troughs, and we had plenty of corn to fill them with. I ordered Sergeant Bowers to feed my mule; but he said that if I reckoned he went to war to be dry-nurse to a mule, it wouldn't take me very long to find out my mistake. I believed that this was insubordination, but I was full of uncertainties about everything military, and so I let the thing pass, and went and ordered Smith, the blacksmith's apprentice, to feed the mule; but he merely gave me a large, cold, sarcastic grin, such as an ostensibly seven-year-old horse gives you when you lift his lip and find he is fourteen, and turned his back on me. I then went to the captain, and asked if it was not right and proper and military for me to have an orderly. He said it was, but as there was only one orderly in the corps, it was but right that he himself should have Bowers on his staff. Bowers said he wouldn't serve on anybody's staff; and if anybody thought he could make him, let him try it. So, of course, the thing had to be dropped; there was no other way.

Next, nobody would cook; it was considered a degradation; so we had no dinner. We lazied the rest of the pleasant afternoon away, some dozing under the trees, some smoking cob-pipes and talking sweethearts and war, some playing games. By late suppertime all hands were famished; and to meet the difficulty all hands turned to, on an equal footing, and gathered wood, built fires, and cooked the meal. Afterward everything was smooth for a while; then trouble broke out between the corporal and the sergeant, each claiming to rank the other. Nobody knew which was the higher office; so Lyman had to settle the matter by making the rank of both officers equal. The commander of an ignorant crew like that has many troubles and vexations which probably do not occur in the regular army at all. However, with the song-singing and yarn-spinning around the campfire, everything presently became serene again; and by and by we raked the corn down level in one end of the crib, and all went to bed on it, tying a horse to the door, so that he would neigh if any one tried to get in.[4]

We had some horsemanship drill every forenoon; then, afternoons, we rode off here and there in squads a few miles, and visited the farmers' girls, and had a youthful good time, and got an honest good dinner or supper, and then home again to camp, happy and content.

---

4. **tying a horse . . . get in:** It was always my impression that that was what the horse was there for, and I know that it was also the impression of at least one other of the command, for we talked about it at the time, and admired the military ingenuity of the device; but when I was out West three years ago I was told by Mr. A. G. Fuqua, a member of our company, that the horse was his, that the leaving him tied at the door was a matter of mere forgetfulness, and that to attribute it to intelligent invention was to give him quite too much credit. In support of his position, he called my attention to the suggestive fact that the artifice was not employed again. I had not thought of that before. [Twain's note]

For a time, life was idly delicious, it was perfect; there was nothing to mar it. Then came some farmers with an alarm one day. They said it was rumored that the enemy were advancing in our direction, from over Hyde's prairie. The result was a sharp stir among us, and general consternation. It was a rude awakening from our pleasant trance. The rumor was but a rumor—nothing definite about it; so, in the confusion, we did not know which way to retreat. Lyman was for not retreating at all, in these uncertain circumstances; but he found that if he tried to maintain that attitude he would fare badly, for the command were in no humor to put up with insubordination. So he yielded the point and called a council of war—to consist of himself and the three other officers; but the privates made such a fuss about being left out, that we had to allow them to be present. I mean we had to allow them to remain, for they were already present, and doing the most of the talking too. The question was, which way to retreat; but all were so flurried that nobody seemed to have even a guess to offer. Except Lyman. He explained in a few calm words, that inasmuch as the enemy were approaching from over Hyde's prairie, our course was simple: all we had to do was not to retreat *toward* him; any other direction would answer our needs perfectly. Everybody saw in a moment how true this was, and how wise; so Lyman got a great many compliments. It was now decided that we should fall back on Mason's farm.

It was after dark by this time, and as we could not know how soon the enemy might arrive, it did not seem best to try to take the horses and things with us; so we only took the guns and ammunition, and started at once. The route was very rough and hilly and rocky, and presently the night grew very black and rain began to fall; so we had a troublesome time of it, struggling and stumbling along in the dark; and soon some person slipped and fell, and then the next person behind stumbled over him and fell, and so did the rest, one after the other; and then Bowers came with the keg of powder in his arms, whilst the command were all mixed together, arms and legs, on the muddy slope; and so he fell, of course, with the keg, and this started the whole detachment down the hill in a body, and they landed in the brook at the bottom in a pile, and each that was undermost pulling the hair and scratching and biting those that were on top of him; and those that were being scratched and bitten scratching and biting the rest in their turn, and all saying they would die before they would ever go to war again if they ever got out of this brook this time, and the invader might rot for all they cared, and the country along with him—and all such talk as that, which was dismal to hear and take part in, in such smothered, low voices, and such a grisly dark place and so wet, and the enemy may be coming any moment.

The keg of powder was lost, and the guns too; so the growling and complaining continued straight along whilst the brigade pawed around the pasty hillside and slopped around in the brook hunting for these things; consequently we lost considerable time at this; and then we heard a sound, and held our breath and listened, and it seemed to be the enemy coming, though it could have been a cow, for it had a cough like a cow; but we did not wait, but left a couple of guns behind and struck out for Mason's again as briskly as we could scramble along in the dark. But we got lost presently among the rugged little ravines, and wasted a deal of time finding the way again, so it was after nine when we reached Mason's stile at last; and then before we could open our mouths to give the countersign, several dogs came bounding over the fence, with great riot and noise, and each of them took a soldier by the slack of his trousers and began to back away with him. We could not shoot the dogs without endangering the persons they were attached to; so we had to look on, helpless, at what was perhaps the most mortifying spectacle of the civil war. There was light enough, and to spare, for the Masons had now run out on the porch with candles in their hands. The old man and his son came and undid the dogs without difficulty, all but Bowers's; but they couldn't undo his dog, they didn't know his combination; he was of the bull kind, and seemed to be set with a Yale time-lock; but they got him loose at last with some scalding water, of which Bowers got his share and returned thanks. Peterson Dunlap afterwards made up a fine name for this engagement, and also for the night march which preceded it, but both have long ago faded out of my memory.

We now went into the house, and they began to ask us a world of questions, whereby it presently came out that we did not know anything concerning who or what we were running from; so the old gentleman made himself very frank, and said we were a curious breed of soldiers, and guessed we could be depended on to end up the war in time, because no government could stand the expense of the shoe-leather we should cost it trying to follow us around. "Marion *Rangers!* good name, b'gosh!" said he. And wanted to know why we hadn't had a picket-guard at the place where the road entered the prairie, and why we hadn't sent out a scouting party to spy out the enemy and bring us an account of his strength, and so on, before jumping up and stampeding out of a strong position upon a mere vague rumor—and so on and so forth, till he made us all feel shabbier than the dogs had done, not half so enthusiastically welcome. So we went to bed shamed and low-spirited; except Stevens. Soon Stevens began to devise a garment for Bowers which could be made to automatically display his battle-scars to the grateful, or conceal them from the envious, according to his occasions; but Bowers was in no humor for this, so there was a fight, and when it was over Stevens had some battle-scars of his own to think about.

Then we got a little sleep. But after all we had gone through, our activities were not over for the night; for about two o'clock in the morning we heard a shout of warning from down the lane, accompanied by a chorus from all the dogs, and in a moment everybody was up and flying around to find out what the alarm was about. The alarmist was a horseman who gave notice that a detachment of Union soldiers was on its way from Hannibal with orders to capture and hang any bands like ours which it could find, and said we had no time to lose. Farmer Mason was in a flurry this time, himself. He hurried us out of the house with all haste, and sent one of his negroes with us to show us where to hide ourselves and our tell-tale guns among the ravines half a mile away. It was raining heavily.

We struck down the lane, then across some rocky pasture-land which offered good advantages for stumbling; consequently we were down in the mud most of the time, and every time a man went down he blackguarded the war, and the people that started it, and everybody connected with it, and gave himself the master dose of all for being so foolish as to go into it. At last we reached the wooded mouth of a ravine, and there we huddled ourselves under the streaming trees, and sent the negro back home. It was a dismal and heart-breaking time. We were like to be drowned with the rain, deafened with the howling wind and the booming thunder, and blinded by the lightning. It was indeed a wild night. The drenching we were getting was misery enough, but a deeper misery still was the reflection that the halter might end us before we were a day older. A death of this shameful sort had not occurred to us as being among the possibilities of war. It took the romance all out of the campaign, and turned our dreams of glory into a repulsive night-mare. As for doubting that so barbarous an order had been given, not one of us did that.

The long night wore itself out at last, and then the negro came to us with the news that the alarm had manifestly been a false one, and that breakfast would soon be ready. Straight-way we were lighted-hearted again, and the world was bright, and life as full of hope and promise as ever — for we were young then. How long ago that was! Twenty-four years.

The mongrel child of philology named the night's refuge Camp Devastation, and no soul objected. The Masons gave us a Missouri country breakfast, in Missourian abun-dance, and we needed it: hot biscuits; hot "wheat bread" prettily criss-crossed in a lat-tice pattern on top; hot corn pone; fried chicken; bacon, coffee, eggs, milk, buttermilk, etc.; and the world may be confidently challenged to furnish the equal to such a break-fast, as it is cooked in the South.

We staid several days at Mason's; and after all these years the memory of the dull-ness, the stillness and lifelessness of that slumberous farm-house still oppresses my spirit as with a sense of the presence of death and mourning. There was nothing to do, nothing to think about; there was no interest in life. The male part of the household were away in the fields all day, the women were busy and out of our sight; there was no sound but the plaintive wailing of a spinning-wheel, forever moaning out from some distant room, the most lonesome sound in nature, a sound steeped and sodden with homesickness and the emptiness of life. The family went to bed about dark every night, and as we were not invited to intrude any new customs, we naturally followed theirs. Those nights were a hundred years long to youths accustomed to being up till twelve. We lay awake and miserable till that hour every time, and grew old and decrepit waiting through the still eternities for the clock-strikes. This was no place for town boys. So at last it was with something very like joy that we received news that the enemy were on our track again. With a new birth of the old warrior spirit, we sprang to our places in line of battle and fell back on Camp Ralls.

Captain Lyman had taken a hint from Mason's talk, and he now gave orders that our camp should be guarded against surprise by the posting of pickets. I was ordered to place a picket at the forks of the road in Hyde's prairie. Night shut down black and threatening. I told Sergeant Bowers to go out to that place and stay till midnight; and, just as I was ex-pecting, he said he wouldn't do it. I tried to get others to go, but all refused. Some excused themselves on account of the weather; but the rest were frank enough to say they wouldn't go in any kind of weather. This kind of thing sounds odd now, and impossible, but there was no surprise in it at the time. On the contrary, it seemed a perfectly natural thing to do. There were scores of little camps scattered over Missouri where the same thing was happening. These camps were composed of young men who had been born and reared to a sturdy independence, and who did not know what it meant to be ordered around by Tom, Dick, and Harry, whom they had known familiarly all their lives, in the village or on the farm. It is quite within the probabilities that this same thing was hap-pening all over the South. James Redpath recognized the justice of this assumption, and furnished the following instance in support of it. During a short stay in East Tennessee he was in a citizen colonel's tent one day, talking, when a big private appeared at the door, and without salute or other circumlocution said to the colonel:

"Say, Jim, I'm a-goin' home for a few days."

"What for?"

"Well, I hain't b'en there for a right smart while, and I'd like to see how things is comin' on."

"How long are you going to be gone?"

"'Bout two weeks."

"Well, don't be gone longer than that; and get back sooner if you can."

That was all, and the citizen officer resumed his conversation where the private had broken it off. This was in the first months of the war, of course. The camps in our part of Missouri were under Brigadier-General Thomas H. Harris. He was a townsman of ours, a first-rate fellow, and well liked; but we had all familiarly known him as the sole and modest-salaried operator in our telegraph office, where he had to send about one dispatch a week in ordinary times, and two when there was a rush of business; consequently, when he appeared in our midst one day, on the wing, and delivered a military command of some sort, in a large military fashion, nobody was surprised at the response which he got from the assembled soldiery:

"Oh, now, what'll you take to *don't*, Tom Harris!"

It was quite the natural thing. One might justly imagine that we were hopeless material for war. And so we seemed, in our ignorant state; but there were those among us who afterward learned the grim trade; learned to obey like machines; became valuable soldiers; fought all through the war, and came out at the end with excellent records. One of the very boys who refused to go out on picket duty that night, and called me an ass for thinking he would expose himself to danger in such a foolhardy way, had become distinguished for intrepidity before he was a year older.

I did secure my picket that night—not by authority, but by diplomacy. I got Bowers to go, by agreeing to exchange ranks with him for the time being, and go along and stand the watch with him as his subordinate. We staid out there a couple of dreary hours in the pitchy darkness and the rain, with nothing to modify the dreariness but Bowers's monotonous growlings at the war and the weather; then we began to nod, and presently found it next to impossible to stay in the saddle; so we gave up the tedious job, and went back to the camp without waiting for the relief guard. We rode into camp without interruption or objection from anybody, and the enemy could have done the same, for there were no sentries. Everybody was asleep; at midnight there was nobody to send out another picket, so none was sent. We never tried to establish a watch at night again, as far as I remember, but we generally kept a picket out in the daytime.

In that camp the whole command slept on the corn in the big corn-crib; and there was usually a general row before morning, for the place was full of rats, and they would scramble over the boys' bodies and faces, annoying and irritating everybody; and now and then they would bite some one's toe, and the person who owned the toe would start up and magnify his English and begin to throw corn in the dark. The ears were half as heavy as bricks, and when they struck they hurt. The persons struck would respond, and inside of five minutes every man would be locked in a death-grip with his neighbor. There was a grievous deal of blood shed in the corn-crib, but this was all that was spilt while I was in the war. No, that is not quite true. But for one circumstance it would have been all. I will come to that now.

Our scares were frequent. Every few days rumors would come that the enemy were approaching. In these cases we always fell back on some other camp of ours; we never staid where we were. But the rumors always turned out to be false; so at last even we began to grow indifferent to them. One night a negro was sent to our corn-crib with the same old warning: the enemy was hovering in our neighborhood. We all said let him hover. We resolved to stay still and be comfortable. It was a fine warlike resolution, and no doubt we all felt the stir of it in our veins – for a moment. We had been having a very jolly time, that was full of horse-play and school-boy hilarity; but that cooled down now, and presently the fast-waning fire of forced jokes and forced laughs died out altogether, and the company became silent. Silent and nervous. And soon uneasy – worried – apprehensive. We had said we would stay, and we were committed. We could have been persuaded to go, but there was nobody brave enough to suggest it. An almost noiseless movement presently began in the dark, by a general but unvoiced impulse. When the movement was completed, each man knew that he was not the only person who had crept to the front wall and had his eye at a crack between the logs. No, we were all there; all there with our hearts in our throats, and staring out toward the sugar-troughs where the forest foot-path came through. It was late, and there was a deep woodsy stillness everywhere. There was a veiled moonlight, which was only just strong enough to enable us to mark the general shape of objects. Presently a muffled sound caught our ears, and we recognized it as the hoof-beats of a horse or horses. And right away a figure appeared in the forest path; it could have been made of smoke, its mass had so little sharpness of outline. It was a man on horseback; and it seemed to me that there were others behind him. I got hold of a gun in the dark, and pushed it through a crack between the logs, hardly knowing what I was doing, I was so dazed with fright. Somebody said "Fire!" I pulled the trigger. I seemed to see a hundred flashes and hear a hundred reports, then I saw the man fall down out of the saddle. My first feeling was of surprised gratification; my first impulse was an apprentice-sportsman's impulse to run and pick up his game. Somebody said, hardly audibly, "Good – we've got him – wait for the rest." But the rest did not come. We waited – listened – still no more came. There was not a sound, not the whisper of a leaf; just perfect stillness; an uncanny kind of stillness, which was all the more uncanny on account of the damp, earthy, late-night smells now rising and pervading it. Then, wondering, we crept stealthily out, and approached the man. When we got to him the moon revealed him distinctly. He was lying on his back, with his arms abroad; his mouth was open and his chest heaving with long gasps, and his white shirt-front was all splashed with blood. The thought shot through me that I was a murderer; that I had killed a man – a man who had never done me any harm. That was the coldest sensation that ever went through my marrow. I was down by him in a moment, helplessly stroking his forehead; and I would have given anything then – my own life freely – to make him again what he had been five minutes before. And all the boys seemed to be feeling in the same way; they hung over him, full of pitying interest, and tried all they could to help him, and said all sorts of regretful things. They had forgotten all about the enemy; they thought only of this one forlorn unit of the foe. Once my imagination persuaded me that the dying man gave me a reproachful look out of his shadowy eyes, and it seemed to me that I would rather he had stabbed me than done that. He muttered and mumbled like a dreamer in his sleep, about his wife and his child; and I thought with a new despair, "This thing that I have done does not end with him; it falls upon *them* too, and they never did me any harm, any more than he."

In a little while the man was dead. He was killed in war; killed in fair and legitimate war; killed in battle, as you may say; and yet he was as sincerely mourned by the opposing force as if he had been their brother. The boys stood there a half hour sorrowing over him, and recalling the details of the tragedy, and wondering who he might be, and if he were a spy, and saying that if it were to do over again they would not hurt him unless he attacked them first. It soon came out that mine was not the only shot fired; there were five others,—a division of the guilt which was a grateful relief to me, since it in some degree lightened and diminished the burden I was carrying. There were six shots fired at once; but I was not in my right mind at the time, and my heated imagination had magnified my one shot into a volley.

The man was not in uniform, and was not armed. He was a stranger in the country; that was all we ever found out about him. The thought of him got to preying upon me every night; I could not get rid of it. I could not drive it away, the taking of that unoffending life seemed such a wanton thing. And it seemed an epitome of war; that all war must be just that—the killing of strangers against whom you feel no personal animosity; strangers whom, in other circumstances, you would help if you found them in trouble, and who would help you if you needed it. My campaign was spoiled. It seemed to me that I was not rightly equipped for this awful business; that war was intended for men, and I for a child's nurse. I resolved to retire from this avocation of sham soldiership while I could save some remnant of my self-respect. These morbid thoughts clung to me against reason; for at bottom I did not believe I had touched that man. The law of probabilities decreed me guiltless of his blood; for in all my small experience with guns I had never hit anything I had tried to hit, and I knew I had done my best to hit him. Yet there was no solace in the thought. Against a diseased imagination, demonstration goes for nothing.

The rest of my war experience was of a piece with what I have already told of it. We kept monotonously falling back upon one camp or another, and eating up the country. I marvel now at the patience of the farmers and their families. They ought to have shot us; on the contrary, they were as hospitably kind and courteous to us as if we had deserved it. In one of these camps we found Ab Grimes, an Upper Mississippi pilot, who afterwards became famous as a dare-devil rebel spy, whose career bristled with desperate adventures. The look and style of his comrades suggested that they had not come into the war to play, and their deeds made good the conjecture later. They were fine horsemen and good revolver-shots; but their favorite arm was the lasso. Each had one at his pommel, and could snatch a man out of the saddle with it every time, on a full gallop, at any reasonable distance.

In another camp the chief was a fierce and profane old blacksmith of sixty, and he had furnished his twenty recruits with gigantic home-made bowie-knives, to be swung with the two hands, like the *machetes* of the Isthmus.[5] It was a grisly spectacle to see

---

5. the *machetes* of the Isthmus: The heavy, broad-bladed knives used to cut paths through the dense jungles of the Isthmus of Panama.

that earnest band practicing their murderous cuts and slashes under the eye of that remorseless old fanatic.

The last camp which we fell back upon was in a hollow near the village of Florida, where I was born — in Monroe County. Here we were warned, one day, that a Union colonel was sweeping down on us with a whole regiment at his heels. This looked decidedly serious. Our boys went apart and consulted; then we went back and told the other companies present that the war was a disappointment to us and we were going to disband. They were getting ready, themselves, to fall back on some place or other, and were only waiting for General Tom Harris, who was expected to arrive at any moment; so they tried to persuade us to wait a little while, but the majority of us said no, we were accustomed to falling back, and didn't need any of Tom Harris's help; we could get along perfectly well without him — and save time too. So about half of our fifteen, including myself, mounted and left on the instant; the others yielded to persuasion and staid — staid through the war.

An hour later we met General Harris on the road, with two or three people in his company — his staff, probably, but we could not tell; none of them were in uniform; uniforms had not come into vogue among us yet. Harris ordered us back; but we told him there was a Union colonel coming with a whole regiment in his wake, and it looked as if there was going to be a disturbance; so we had concluded to go home. He raged a little, but it was of no use; our minds were made up. We had done our share; had killed one man, exterminated one army, such as it was; let him go and kill the rest, and that would end the war. I did not see that brisk young general again until last year; then he was wearing white hair and whiskers.

In time I came to know that Union colonel whose coming frightened me out of the war and crippled the Southern cause to that extent — General Grant.[6] I came within a few hours of seeing him when he was as unknown as I was myself; at a time when anybody could have said, "Grant? — Ulysses S. Grant? I do not remember hearing the name before." It seems difficult to realize that there was once a time when such a remark could be rationally made; but there *was*, and I was within a few miles of the place and the occasion too, though proceeding in the other direction.

The thoughtful will not throw this war-paper of mine lightly aside as being valueless. It has this value: it is a not unfair picture of what went on in many and many a militia camp in the first months of the rebellion, when the green recruits were without discipline, without the steadying and heartening influence of trained leaders; when all their circumstances were new and strange, and charged with exaggerated terrors, and before the invaluable experience of actual collision in the field had turned them from rabbits into soldiers. If this side of the picture of that early day has not before been put into history, then history has been to that degree incomplete, for it had and has its rightful place there. There was more Bull Run material scattered through the early camps of this country than exhibited itself at Bull Run.[7] And yet it learned its trade presently, and

---

6. **General Grant:** Ulysses S. Grant (1822–1885), who was virtually unknown at the beginning of the Civil War, swiftly rose from obscurity to general-in-chief of the Union armies and then to president of the United States.
7. **Bull Run:** At the first battle of Bull Run in July 1861, the first major land battle of the Civil War, Confederate forces routed Union troops, many of whom fled in disorder from northern Virginia back to Washington, D.C.

helped to fight the great battles later. I could have become a soldier myself, if I had waited. I had got part of it learned; I knew more about retreating than the man that invented retreating.

[1885]

Reading Twain's "The War Prayer."   Twain was generally supportive of the Spanish-American War of 1898, which he viewed as an effort to liberate subject peoples from the despotism of Spanish rule, especially in Cuba. Under the terms of the treaty that ended the brief, eight-month war, Cuba gained independence, but Spain ceded Puerto Rico and Guam to the United States, which was also allowed to purchase the Philippine Islands. The war was consequently followed by the Philippine-American War (formerly known as the "Philippine Insurrection"), a bloody and protracted conflict between American troops and Filipinos seeking independence from the United States. Twain was appalled by his country's brutal military occupation of the islands, where between 250,000 and a million Filipinos, the vast majority of them civilians, died before the rebellion finally subsided at the end of 1913. "There must be two Americas," Twain bitterly observed early in the conflict, "one that sets the captive free, and one that takes a once-captive's new freedom away from him, and picks a quarrel with him with nothing to found it on; then kills him to get his land." His response to the Philippine-American War is also revealed in "The War Prayer," which Twain dictated in 1904-05 and then submitted to *Harper's Bazar* (later named *Harper's Bazaar*). After the editor rejected it as "not quite suited to a woman's magazine," Twain told a friend that he did not think the story would be published in his lifetime, adding, "None but the dead are permitted to tell the truth." Indeed, since he was under contract to write exclusively for the publishing firm of Harper & Brothers, Twain could not publish "The War Prayer" elsewhere, and the story did not appear until several years after Twain's death. The text is taken from its first printing in the collection *Europe and Elsewhere* (1923), edited by Twain's literary executor Albert Bigelow Paine.

Philippine-American War

This photograph of American troops firing from a trench was taken in 1899, before the Philippine insurgents shifted from conventional tactics to guerilla warfare, which continued for more than a decade after the war officially ended on July 4, 1902.

THE WAR PRAYER

It was a time of great and exalting excitement. The country was up in arms, the war was on, in every breast burned the holy fire of patriotism; the drums were beating, the bands playing, the toy pistols popping, the bunched firecrackers hissing and spluttering; on every hand and far down the receding and fading spread of roofs and balconies a flutter-ing wilderness of flags flashed in the sun; daily the young volunteers marched down the wide avenue gay and fine in their new uniforms, the proud fathers and mothers and sis-ters and sweethearts cheering them with voices choked with happy emotion as they swung by; nightly the packed mass meetings listened, panting, to patriot oratory which stirred the deepest deeps of their hearts, and which they interrupted at briefest inter-vals with cyclones of applause, the tears running down their cheeks the while; in the churches the pastors preached devotion to flag and country, and invoked the God of Battles, beseeching His aid in our good cause in outpouring of fervid eloquence which moved every listener. It was indeed a glad and gracious time, and the half dozen rash spirits that ventured to disapprove of the war and cast a doubt upon its righteousness straightway got such a stern and angry warning that for their personal safety's sake they quickly shrank out of sight and offended no more in that way.

Sunday morning came—next day the battalions would leave for the front; the church was filled; the volunteers were there, their young faces alight with martial dreams—visions of the stern advance, the gathering momentum, the rushing charge, the flashing sabers, the flight of the foe, the tumult, the enveloping smoke, the fierce pursuit, the surrender!—them home from the war, bronzed heroes, welcomed, adored, submerged in golden seas of glory! With the volunteers sat their dear ones, proud, happy, and envied by the neighbors and friends who had no sons and brothers to send forth to the field of honor, there to win for the flag, or, failing, die the noblest of noble deaths. The service proceeded; a war chapter from the Old Testament was read; the first prayer was said; it was followed by an organ burst that shook the building, and with one impulse the house rose, with glowing eyes and beating hearts, and poured out that tremendous invocation—

> "God the all-terrible! Thou who ordainest,
> Thunder thy clarion and lightning thy sword!"[1]

Then came the "long" prayer. None could remember the like of it for passionate pleading and moving and beautiful language. The burden of its supplication was, that an ever-merciful and benignant Father of us all would watch over our noble young soldiers, and aid, comfort, and encourage them in their patriotic work; bless them, shield them in the day of battle and the hour of peril, bear them in His mighty hand, make them strong and confident, invincible in the bloody onset; help them to crush the foe, grant to them and to their flag and country imperishable honor and glory—

---

1. **"God . . . sword!"**: A variant of the opening lines of a familiar Protestant hymn: "God the All-terrible! King, who ordainest / Thunder thy clarion, the lightning thy sword, / Show forth thy pity on high where thou reignest; / Give to us peace in our time, O Lord."

An aged stranger entered and moved with slow and noiseless step up the main aisle, his eyes fixed upon the minister, his long body clothed in a robe that reached to his feet, his head bare, his white hair descending in a frothy cataract to his shoulders, his seamy face unnaturally pale, pale even to ghastliness. With all eyes following him and wondering, he made his silent way; without pausing, he ascended to the preacher's side and stood there, waiting. With shut lids the preacher, unconscious of his presence, continued his moving prayer, and at last finished it with the words, uttered in fervent appeal, "Bless our arms, grant us the victory, O Lord our God, Father and Protector of our land and flag!"

The stranger touched his arm, motioned him to step aside – which the startled minister did – and took his place. During some moments he surveyed the spellbound audience with solemn eyes, in which burned an uncanny light; then in a deep voice he said:

"I come from the Throne – bearing a message from Almighty God!" The words smote the house with a shock; if the stranger perceived it he gave no attention. "He has heard the prayer of His servant your shepherd, and will grant it if such shall be your desire after I, His messenger, shall have explained to you its import – that is to say, its full import. For it is like unto many of the prayers of men, in that it asks for more than he who utters it is aware of – except he pause and think.

"God's servant and yours has prayed his prayer. Has he paused and taken thought? Is it one prayer? No, it is two – one uttered, the other not. Both have reached the ear of Him Who hearest all supplications, the spoken and the unspoken. Ponder this – keep it in mind. If you would beseech a blessing upon yourself, beware! lest without intent you invoke a curse upon a neighbor at the same time. If you pray for the blessing of rain upon your crop which needs it, by that act you are possibly praying for a curse upon some neighbor's crop which may not need rain and can be injured by it.

"You have heard your servant's prayer – the uttered part of it. I am commissioned of God to put into words the other part of it – that part which the pastor – and also you in your hearts – fervently prayed silently. And ignorantly and unthinkingly? God grant that it was so! You heard these words: 'Grant us the victory, O Lord our God!' That is sufficient. The *whole* of the uttered prayer is compact into those pregnant words. Elaborations were not necessary. When you have prayed for victory you have prayed for many unmentioned results which follow victory – *must* follow it, cannot help but follow it. Upon the listening spirit of God the Father fell also the unspoken part of the prayer. He commandeth me to put it into words. Listen!

"O Lord our Father, our young patriots, idols of our hearts, go forth to battle – be Thou near them! With them – in spirit – we also go forth from the sweet peace of our beloved firesides to smite the foe. O Lord our God, help us to tear their soldiers to bloody shreds with our shells; help us to cover their smiling fields with the pale forms of their patriot dead; help us to drown the thunder of the guns with the shrieks of their wounded, writhing in pain; help us to lay waste their humble homes with a hurricane of fire; help us to wring the hearts of their unoffending widows with unavailing grief; help us to turn them out roofless with their little children to wander unfriended the wastes of their desolated land in rags and hunger and thirst, sports of the sun flames of summer and the icy winds of winter, broken in spirit, worn with travail, imploring Thee for the refuge of the grave and denied it – for our sakes who adore Thee, Lord, blast their hopes, blight their lives, protract their bitter pilgrimage, make heavy their steps, water their way with their tears, stain the white snow with the blood of their wounded feet! We ask it, in the spirit of love, of Him Who is the Source of Love, and Who is the ever-faithful refuge and friend of all that are sore beset and seek His aid with humble and contrite hearts. Amen."

(*After a pause.*) "Ye have prayed it; if ye still desire it, speak! The messenger of the Most High waits."

It was believed afterward that the man was a lunatic, because there was no sense in what he said.

[1904-05, 1923]

Writers on Writers: Arthur Miller on Mark Twain

In 1996, near the end of his distinguished literary career, the American play-wright Arthur Miller (1915-2005) wrote the introduction to a reprint of a series of autobiographical writings Mark Twain had published near the end of his own long and successful career, in 1906-07. Miller recalled that as a teenager he had read Twain's novel *A Connecticut Yankee in King Arthur's Court*, one of the books that tore him "from the football field to the library," and one that made him "a friend of Mark Twain for life." Miller, whose most famous play, *Death of a Salesman*, was conceived as a tragedy of the common man, admiringly added that Twain had "somehow managed – despite a steady underlying seriousness few writers have matched – to step around the pit of self-importance and to keep his membership in the ordinary human race in front of his mind and writing." Having achieved commercial success and widespread notoriety, both personal and professional, Miller also clearly recognized the pitfalls confronted by celebrity authors such as Twain. In the following passage, the final para-graphs of his introduction, Miller thus speculates on what might have become of a popular entertainer such as Twain in the age of television, which could have offered him wealth and fame as a comedian but only at the cost of blunting his satire and compromising his art. The text is taken from the Introduction to *Chapters from My Autobiography*, in The *Oxford Mark Twain* (1996).

ARTHUR MILLER

[1915-2005]

From Introduction to *Chapters from My Autobiography*

Mark Twain was a performer, obviously, a man drawn happily toward center stage. Almost from the start of his career he moved about the country from one lecture platform to another, telling his stories, cracking his jokes. It was years before he was taken seriously – or took himself seriously – as an artist, let alone a major one who would be looked to for insights into America's always uncertain moral life and its shifting but everlasting hypocrisies. One has to wonder what would have become of him in our television age, when he may well have found fame as essentially a comedian, like Will Rogers, or a character with his own program, perhaps like Jack Benny or Bob Hope.[1] Sam Clemens did not disdain money, not at all, and TV could have made him very rich, could have addicted him to the compromises that come and must come with that territory, could have fed his appetite for soft celebrity rather than the hard bed of art. He would have been pressured to round the edges of his satire so as to emphasize uplift for the folks, perhaps to spare some fraudulent politician his lash whose subcommittee might make trouble for the broadcasting industry. Or even simpler, he would have been told in very clear tones, as I and doubtless other writers have been told by a network producer, that American television does not want "art." (They pronounce the quotation marks.) And that he must eliminate diversions from the main drive of his stories and simplify his syntax lest the audience lose track of a too-lengthy sentence. One way or another he would surely have ended in a head-on crash on the information superhighway, there can be no doubt of that.

It isn't easy to say how strong his resistance would have been to the suborning of his talent by his own declared wish to capture the big audience rather than settling for a far easier triumph with a narrower and more elegant supportive clique that already agreed with him. That big audience today is facing the TV screen, not the book or the lecture platform. My own inclination is in his favor; I think he would certainly have fallen for the power and emoluments of national TV celebrity, but would have found his way home again. Because he was an artist, and one who fed upon his own soul as much as on what he observed, and the call of the soul was the most powerful emotion he knew.

Of course this estimate may be wrong. Orson Welles,[2] another man of brilliance and also a performer, was basically neutered by the American entertainment

---

1. **Will Rogers . . . Jack Benny or Bob Hope:** Miller cites three of the most popular entertainers of the twentieth century. Born on the Cherokee Indian Reservation in Oklahoma, William Penn Adair Rogers (1879-1935) was an actor, humorist, and writer who became one of the best-known celebrities of the 1920s and 30s, widely celebrated for the wit and down-home wisdom of his simple cowboy persona, "Will" Rogers. Jack Benny, born Benjamin Kubelsky (1894-1974), and Bob Hope (1903-2003) had long careers in show business and were among the pioneers of television, starring in the comedy series *The Jack Benny Show* and *The Bob Hope Show*. Also known for his humanitarian work, Hope hosted nearly 200 shows to entertain American troops serving in combat zones from World War II through the Persian Gulf War (1990-91).

2. **Orson Welles:** George Orson Welles (1915-1985) was an actor, director, and writer whose early successes included *Citizen Kane* (1941), regarded by many film critics as the best film ever made. In later years, however, Welles had difficulty financing his own projects and turned increasingly to making commercials and appearing on television talk shows, prompting many to suggest that he had squandered his prodigious talents.

business, and spent most of his creative powers at poolside thrilling other artists with his culture, his knowledge and the spectacle of a greatness that was always on the verge of retaking the stage but could not be reborn, at least in my
opinion, because it had no spiritual support in a country where few people knew
enough to want what he could give. All that is certain is that the country by and
by would have tired of listening to the Mark Twain Weekly Hour; and if he wanted
to remain a national prime-time asset, the bubbling up of his genuine material
would have slowed in due time and he would have had to begin clawing at himself, scouring his memories to feed into the television maw, and would have
ended in a wealthy, self-contemptuous defeat.

   We had Mark Twain when it was still possible to have him as an artist intent
on addressing the whole country without having to pay the price of celebrity and
the inevitable desiccation of his talent. We had Mark Twain when it was still possible to have him as the celebrity he was and the respected artist at the same
time; the culture would support such a phenomenon still. That he might have
survived intact the crush of the bottom line of mass communications—which in
theory would have attracted him—is not easy to imagine. So the treasure is intact, and our American luck, at least in this case, has held.

[1996]

William Dean Howells

[1837–1920]

William Dean Howells was born in Martinsville (now Martin's Ferry), Ohio, on March 1, 1837, the son of a printer and publisher, William Cooper Howells, and his wife, Mary Dean Howells. Their increasingly large family moved from town to town in Ohio, as the utopian Socialist and abolitionist William Cooper Howells struggled to earn a living in the precarious newspaper business. Howells later recalled that from the age of twelve to nineteen he had "worked pretty steadily 'at case,'" that is, setting type. "I have to lament an almost entire want of schooling," he added. "However, my father had ardent literary tastes, and an excellent library and I studied and read as I could. . . . I learned with little or no help Spanish and German, a trifle of Latin and a soupçon of Greek." Inspired by his voracious and wide-ranging reading in drama, especially Shakespeare, fiction, and poetry, Howells began to write at an early age. By the time he was fifteen, he was working as a reporter for a newspaper edited by his father in Columbus, the *Ohio State Journal*, in which Howells's first poem was published in 1852. Although he was initially distressed that his proud father had printed the poem without his knowledge, Howells promptly began submitting his poems for publication. He published his first story in yet another newspaper edited by his father, the *Ashtabula Sentinel*, where Howells's "A Tale of Love and Politics," subtitled "Adventures of a Printer Boy," appeared in 1857.

Howells's youthful apprenticeship in the newspaper business soon began to pay dividends. He wrote a regular column from the state capitol in Columbus for the *Daily Cincinnati Gazette* and then joined the editorial staff of the *Ohio State Journal*, for which he wrote reviews, poems, and stories. Howells also published poems in more prominent eastern periodicals, including the *New York Saturday Press*. But his greatest early triumph came in August 1859, when James Russell Lowell accepted one of Howells's poems for publication in the prestigious *Atlantic Monthly*. In 1860, Howells published his first book, *Poems of Two Friends*, with his fellow journalist James John Piatt. A strong supporter of the Republican Party, Howells was hired to write a campaign biography of its presidential candidate, Abraham Lincoln. Having earned enough money for a trip east, Howells visited Boston, where he met Lowell and other members of the literary establishment in New England, including Henry Wadsworth Longfellow, Ralph Waldo Emerson, Nathaniel Hawthorne, and Henry David Thoreau. Howells then went to New York City, where he sought out Walt Whitman. Soon after Howells went back home, he met his future wife, Elinor Mead, a transplanted easterner who was impressed that someone from Ohio had published a poem in the *Atlantic Monthly*. When Lincoln became president in 1861, he rewarded Howells by appointing

William Dean Howells

This engraving of a photograph of Howells was published in 1877, during his time as editor of the influential *Atlantic Monthly*.

him American consul to Venice, Italy, where he remained throughout the Civil War.

Following his return to the United States in 1865, Howells emerged as one of the country's most influential critics, editors, and writers. Now married and a new father, Howells first moved to New York and then settled his family in Boston. Revising articles he had written for the *Boston Daily Advertiser* during his years in Venice, a city he loved, Howells wrote *Venetian Life*, a major commercial success published in 1866. That year, he was hired to work at the *Atlantic Monthly*, first as an assistant editor (1866–71) and then as its editor (1871–81). During his years at the magazine, Howells published the work of a wide range of American writers, including his friends Henry James and Mark Twain. Beginning with his first novel, *Their Wedding Journey* (1871), Howells also serialized some of his own work in the magazine. After he left the editorship of the *Atlantic Monthly* to devote himself to writing fiction, Howells published two of his most celebrated novels, *A Modern Instance* (1882) and *The Rise of Silas Lapham* (1885). He also continued to write for periodicals, including *Cosmopolitan*, the *Nation*, and especially *Harper's New Monthly Magazine.* His move from Boston to New York City, where he became the associate editor of *Harper's* in 1886, represented a seismic shift in American publishing away from its traditional center in New England. In his monthly columns for the magazine, the "Editor's Study" (1886–92) and the "Editor's Easy Chair" (1899–1909), Howells promoted the work of a host of emerging writers from around the country, including Abraham Cahan, Charles W. Chesnutt, Stephen Crane, Paul Laurence Dunbar, Mary E. Wilkins Freeman, Sarah Orne Jewett, Frank Norris, and Edith Wharton.

During the final decades of his life, Howells became deeply involved in political and social issues. Those concerns are reflected in *Annie Kilburn* (1888), which exposes the human costs of industrialization; *A Hazard of New Fortunes* (1890), with its emphasis on the stark contrasts between wealth and poverty in New York City; and *A Traveler from Altruria* (1894), in which Howells satirizes life in the United States from the point of view of a visitor from a utopian republic. An outspoken critic of the Spanish-American War of 1898, Howells also strongly supported radical causes, including trade unionism, women's rights, and racial equality, becoming one of the founding members of the National Association for the Advancement of Colored People (NAACP) in 1909. When he turned seventy-five in 1912, he was asked to prepare a statement to be read to the schoolchildren in New York City. "While I would wish you to love America most because it's your home, I would have you love the whole world and think of all the people in it as your countrymen," Howells responded with his characteristic candor and clarity. "You will hear people more foolish than wicked say 'Our country, right or wrong,' but that is a false patriotism and bad Americanism. When our country is wrong she is worse than other countries when they are wrong, for she has more light than other countries, and we somehow ought to make her feel that we are sorry and ashamed for her."

Just as his social and political views mirrored the earlier radicalism of his father, Howells at the end of his long life explored his Ohio boyhood in a volume of reminiscences, *Years of My Youth* (1915), and two semiautobiographical novels, *New Leaf Mills* (1913) and *The Leatherwood God* (1916). The author of over one hundred books of drama, fiction, poetry, travel writing, and literary criticism, Howells died at the age of eighty-three on May 11, 1920.

bedfordstmartins.com/
americanlit for research links on Howells

Reading Howells's "Editha." Writing about the short story, Howells observed that American writers had perfected the genre, in part because of the popularity of magazines and the public demand for brief, readable works. Although he preferred to write novels, Howells also wrote dozens of short stories. Few of them were as pointed or as political as "Editha," which Howells wrote in response to the Spanish-American War of 1898, an example of what he and other critics decried as the growing imperialism of the

Editha

This illustration is one of three that appeared in the first printing of Howells's story in *Harper's*. Its caption read, "Keep it – keep it – and read it sometime."

United States. The war was in part generated by American support for the Cuban struggle for independence from Spain during the 1890s. The brutal suppression of the Cuban revolt aroused strong anti-Spanish sentiment in the United States, where public opinion was further inflamed by sensational coverage in the press. In February 1898, the U.S. battleship *Maine* blew up in Havana harbor, killing 266 American sailors. Blaming Spain, the press clamored for intervention, and two months later Congress declared what came to be called the "Newspaper War." Howells, who condemned the war as "a wicked, wanton thing," protested by signing petitions and later by writing "Editha." The story was published in *Harper's New Monthly Magazine*, for which Howells also wrote a monthly editorial column, and which devoted more space to political and social commentary after it came under new leadership in 1900. The text, including one of the three original illustrations, is taken from the first printing of the story in the January 1905 issue of *Harper's*.

EDITHA

The air was thick with the war feeling, like the electricity of a storm which has not yet burst. Editha sat looking out into the hot spring afternoon, with her lips parted, and panting with the intensity of the question whether she could let him go. She had decided that she could not let him stay, when she saw him at the end of the still leafless avenue, making slowly up toward the house, with his head down, and his figure relaxed. She ran impatiently out on the veranda, to the edge of the steps, and imperatively demanded greater haste of him with her will before she called aloud to him, "George!"

He had quickened his pace in mystical response to her mystical urgence, before he could have heard her; now he looked up and answered, "Well?"

"Oh, how united we are!" she exulted, and then she swooped down the steps to him. "What is it?" she cried.

"It's war," he said, and he pulled her up to him, and kissed her.

She kissed him back intensely, but irrelevantly, as to their passion, and uttered from deep in her throat, "How glorious!"

"It's war," he repeated, without consenting to her sense of it; and she did not know just what to think at first. She never knew what to think of him; that made his mystery, his charm. All through their courtship, which was contemporaneous with the growth of the war feeling, she had been puzzled by his want of seriousness about it. He seemed to despise it even more than he abhorred it. She could have understood his abhorring any sort of bloodshed; that would have been a survival of his old life when he thought he would be a minister, and before he changed and took up the law. But making light of a cause so high and noble seemed to show a want of earnestness at the core of his being. Not but that she felt herself able to cope with a congenital defect of that sort, and make his love for her save him from himself. Now perhaps the miracle was already wrought in him. In the presence of the tremendous fact that he announced, all triviality seemed to have gone out of him; she began to feel that. He sank down on the top step, and wiped his forehead with his handkerchief, while she poured out upon him her question of the origin and authenticity of his news.

All the while, in her duplex emotioning, she was aware that now at the very beginning she must put a guard upon herself against urging him, by any word or act, to take the part that her whole soul willed him to take, for the completion of her ideal of him. He was very nearly perfect as he was, and he must be allowed to perfect himself. But he was peculiar, and he might very well be reasoned out of his peculiarity. Before her reasoning went her emotioning: her nature pulling upon his nature, her womanhood upon his manhood, without her knowing the means she was using to the end she was willing. She had always supposed that the man who won her would have done something to win her; she did not know what, but something. George Gearson had simply asked her for her love, on the way home from a concert, and she gave her love to him, without, as it were, thinking. But now, it flashed upon her, if he could do something worthy to *have* won her – be a hero, *her* hero – it would be even better than if he had done it before asking her; it would be grander. Besides, she had believed in the war from the beginning.

"But don't you see, dearest," she said, "that it wouldn't have come to this, if it hadn't been in the order of Providence? And I call any war glorious that is for the liberation of people who have been struggling for years against the cruelest oppression. Don't you think so, too?"

"I suppose so," he returned, languidly. "But war! Is it glorious to break the peace of the world?"

"That ignoble peace! It was no peace at all, with that crime and shame at our very gates." She was conscious of parroting the current phrases of the newspapers, but it was no time to pick and choose her words. She must sacrifice anything to the high ideal she had for him, and after a good deal of rapid argument she ended with the climax: "But now it doesn't matter about the how or why. Since the war has come, all that is gone. There are no two sides, any more. There is nothing now but our country."

He sat with his eyes closed and his head leant back against the veranda, and he said with a vague smile, as if musing aloud, "Our country – right or wrong."

"Yes, right or wrong!" she returned fervidly. "I'll go and get you some lemonade." She rose rustling, and whisked away; when she came back with two tall glasses of clouded liquid, on a tray, and the ice clucking in them, he still sat as she had left him, and she said as if there had been no interruption: "But there is no question of wrong in this case. I call it a sacred war. A war for liberty, and humanity, if ever there was one. And I know you will see it just as I do, yet."

He took half the lemonade at a gulp, and he answered as he set the glass down: "I know you always have the highest ideal. When I differ from you, I ought to doubt myself."

A generous sob rose in Editha's throat for the humility of a man, so very nearly perfect, who was willing to put himself below her.

Besides she felt, more subliminally, that he was never so near slipping through her fingers as when he took that meek way.

"You shall not say that! Only, for once I happen to be right." She seized his hand in her two hands, and poured her soul from her eyes into his. "Don't you think so?" she entreated him.

He released his hand and drank the rest of his lemonade, and she added, "Have mine, too," but he shook his head in answering, "I've no business to think so, unless I act so, too."

Her heart stopped a beat, before it pulsed on with leaps that she felt in her neck. She had noticed that strange thing in men; they seemed to feel bound to do what they believed, and not think a thing was finished when they said it, as girls did. She knew what was in his mind, but she pretended not, and she said, "Oh, I am not sure," and then faltered.

He went on as if to himself without apparently heeding her, "There's only one way of proving one's faith in a thing like this."

She could not say that she understood, but she did understand.

He went on again. "If I believed—if I felt as you do about this war—Do you wish me to feel as you do?"

Now he was really not sure; so she said, "George, I don't know what you mean."

He seemed to muse away from her as before. "There is a sort of fascination in it. I suppose that at the bottom of his heart every man would like at times to have his courage tested; to see how he would act."

"How can you talk in that ghastly way!"

"It *is* rather morbid. Still, that's what it comes to, unless you're swept away by ambition, or driven by conviction. I haven't the conviction or the ambition, and the other thing is what it comes to with me. I ought to have been a preacher, after all; then I couldn't have asked it of myself, as I must, now I'm a lawyer. And you believe it's a holy war, Editha?" he suddenly addressed her. "Or, I know you do! But you wish me to believe so, too?"

She hardly knew whether he was mocking or not, in the ironical way he always had with her plainer mind. But the only thing was to be outspoken with him.

"George, I wish you to believe whatever you think is true, at any and every cost. If I've tried to talk you into anything, I take it all back."

"Oh, I know that, Editha. I know how sincere you are, and how—I wish I had your undoubting spirit! I'll think it over; I'd like to believe as you do. But I don't, now; I don't, indeed. It isn't this war alone; though this seems peculiarly wanton and needless; but it's every war—so stupid; it makes me sick. Why shouldn't this thing have been settled reasonably?"

"Because," she said, very throatily again, "God meant it to be war."

"You think it was God? Yes, I suppose that is what people will say."

"Do you suppose it would have been war if God hadn't meant it?"

"I don't know. Sometimes it seems as if God had put this world into men's keeping to work it as they pleased."

"Now, George, that is blasphemy."

"Well, I won't blaspheme. I'll try to believe in your pocket Providence," he said, and then he rose to go.

"Why don't you stay to dinner?" Dinner at Balcom's Works was at one o'clock.

"I'll come back to supper, if you'll let me. Perhaps I shall bring you a convert."

"Well, you may come back, on that condition."

"All right. If I don't come, you'll understand."

He went away without kissing her, and she felt it a suspension of their engagement. It all interested her intensely; she was undergoing a tremendous experience, and she was being equal to it. While she stood looking after him, her mother came out through one of the long windows, on to the veranda, with a catlike softness and vagueness.

"Why didn't he stay to dinner?"

"Because – because – war has been declared," Editha pronounced, without turning.

Her mother said, "Oh, my!" and then said nothing more until she had sat down in one of the large Shaker chairs, and rocked herself for some time. Then she closed whatever tacit passage of thought there had been in her mind with the spoken words, "Well, I hope *he* won't go.

"And *I* hope he *will*," the girl said, and confronted her mother with a stormy exaltation that would have frightened any creature less unimpressionable than a cat.

Her mother rocked herself again for an interval of cogitation. What she arrived at in speech was, "Well, I guess you've done a wicked thing, Editha Balcom."

The girl said, as she passed indoors through the same window her mother had come out by, "I haven't done anything – yet."

In her room, she put together all her letters and gifts from Gearson, down to the withered petals of the first flower he had offered, with that timidity of his veiled in that irony of his. In the heart of the packet she enshrined her engagement ring which she had restored to the pretty box he had brought it for her in. Then she sat down, if not calmly yet strongly, and wrote:

"George: I understood – when you left me. But I think we had better emphasize your meaning that if we cannot be one in everything we had better be one in nothing. So I am sending these things for your keeping till you have made up your mind.

"I shall always love you, and therefore I shall never marry any one else. But the man I marry must love his country first of all, and be able to say to me,

'I could not love thee, dear, so much,
Loved I not honor more.'[1]

"There is no honor above America with me. In this great hour there is no other honor.

"Your heart will make my words clear to you. I had never expected to say so much, but it has come upon me that I must say the utmost.   Editha"

She thought she had worded her letter well, worded it in a way that could not be bettered; all had been implied and nothing expressed.

She had it ready to send with the packet she had tied with red, white, and blue ribbon, when it occurred to her that she was not just to him, that she was not giving him a fair chance. He had said he would go and think it over, and she was not waiting. She was pushing, threatening, compelling. That was not a woman's part. She must leave him free, free, free. She could not accept for her country or herself a forced sacrifice.

_____

1. I . . . more: The famous lines are from "To Lucasta, Going to the Wars," by the English poet Richard Lovelace (1618-1658).

In writing her letter she had satisfied the impulse from which it sprang; she could well afford to wait till he had thought it over. She put the packet and the letter by, and rested serene in the consciousness of having done what was laid upon her by her love itself to do, and yet used patience, mercy, justice.

She had her reward. Gearson did not come to tea, but she had given him till morning, when, late at night there came up from the village the sound of a fife and drum with a tumult of voices, in shouting, singing, and laughing. The noise drew nearer and nearer; it reached the street end of the avenue; there it silenced itself, and one voice, the voice she knew best, rose over the silence. It fell; the air was filled with cheers; the fife and drum struck up, with the shouting singing, and laughing again, but now retreating; and a single figure came hurrying up the avenue.

She ran down to meet her lover and clung to him. He was very gay, and he put his arm round her with a boisterous laugh. "Well, you must call me Captain, now; or Cap, if you prefer; that's what the boys call me. Yes, we've had a meeting at the town hall, and everybody has volunteered; and they selected me for captain, and I'm going to the war, the big war, the glorious war, the holy war ordained by the pocket Providence that blesses butchery. Come along; let's tell the whole family about it. Call them from their downy beds, father, mother, Aunt Hitty, and all the folks!"

But when they mounted the veranda steps he did not wait for a larger audience; he poured the story out upon Editha alone.

"There was a lot of speaking, and then some of the fools set up a shout for me. It was all going one way, and I thought it would be a good joke to sprinkle a little cold water on them. But you can't do that with a crowd that adores you. The first thing I knew I was sprinkling hell-fire on them. 'Cry havoc, and let slip the dogs of war.'[2] That was the style. Now that it had come to the fight, there were no two parties; there was one country, and the thing was to fight the fight to a finish as quick as possible. I suggested volunteering then and there, and I wrote my name first of all on the roster. Then they elected me—that's all. I wish I had some ice-water!"

She left him walking up and down the veranda, while she ran for the ice-pitcher and goblet, and when she came back he was still walking up and down, shouting the story he had told her to her father and mother, who had come out more sketchily dressed than they commonly were by day. He drank goblet after goblet of the ice-water without noticing who was giving it, and kept on talking, and laughing through his talk wildly. "It's astonishing," he said, "how well the worse reason looks when you try to make it appear the better. Why, I believe I was the first convert to the war in that crowd to-night! I never thought I should like to kill a man; but now, I shouldn't care; and the smokeless powder lets you see the man drop that you kill. It's all for the country! What a thing it is to have a country that *can't* be wrong, but if it is, is right anyway!"

Editha had a great, vital thought, an inspiration. She set down the ice-pitcher on the veranda floor, and ran up-stairs and got the letter she had written him. When at last he noisily bade her father and mother, "Well, good night. I forgot I woke you up; I sha'n't want any sleep myself," she followed him down the avenue to the gate. There, after the whirling words that

---

2. 'Cry . . . war': The line is from Mark Antony's soliloquy following the assassination of Caesar in Shakespeare's *Julius Caesar*, 3.1.273.

seemed to fly away from her thoughts and refuse to serve them, she made a last effort to solemnize the moment that seemed so crazy, and pressed the letter she had written upon him.

"What's this?" he said. "Want me to mail?"

"No, no. It's for you. I wrote it after you went this morning. Keep it – keep it – and read it sometime –" She thought, and then her inspiration came: "Read it if ever you doubt what you've done, or fear that I regret your having done it. Read it after you've started."

They strained each other in embraces that seemed as ineffective as their words, and he kissed her face with quick, hot breaths that were so unlike him, that made her feel as if she had lost her old lover and found a stranger in his place. The stranger said, "What a gorgeous flower you are, with your red hair, and your blue eyes that look black now, and your face with the color painted out by the white moonshine! Let me hold you under my chin, to see whether I love blood, you tiger-lily!" Then he laughed Gearson's laugh, and released her, scared and giddy. Within her wilfulness she had been frightened by a sense of subtler force in him, and mystically mastered as she had never been before.

She ran all the way back to the house, and mounted the steps panting. Her mother and father were talking of the great affair. Her mother said: "Wa'n't Mr. Gearson in rather of an excited state of mind? Didn't you think he acted curious?"

"Well, not for a man who'd just been elected captain and had to set 'em up for the whole of Company A," her father chuckled back.

"What in the world do you mean, Mr. Balcom? Oh! There's Editha!" She offered to follow the girl indoors.

"Don't come, mother!" Editha called, vanishing.

Mrs. Balcom remained to reproach her husband. "I don't see much of anything to laugh at."

"Well, it's catching. Caught it from Gearson. I guess it won't be much of a war, and I guess Gearson don't think so, either. The other fellows will back down as soon as they see we mean it. I wouldn't lose any sleep over it. I'm going back to bed, myself."

Gearson came again next afternoon, looking pale, and rather sick, but quite himself, even to his languid irony. "I guess I'd better tell you, Editha, that I consecrated myself to your god of battles last night by pouring too many libations to him down my own throat. But I'm all right, now. One has to carry off the excitement, somehow."

"Promise me," she commanded, "that you'll never touch it again!"

"What! Not let the cannikin clink? Not let the soldier drink?[3] Well, I promise."

"You don't belong to yourself now; you don't even belong to *me*. You belong to your country, and you have a sacred charge to keep yourself strong and well for your country's sake. I have been thinking, thinking all night and all day long."

"You look as if you had been crying a little, too," he said with his queer smile.

"That's all past. I've been thinking, and worshipping you. Don't you suppose I know all that you've been through, to come to this? I've followed you every step from your old theories and opinions."

---

3. **Not let . . . the soldier drink?:** See the drinking song in Shakespeare's *Othello*, 3.2.72–76: "And let me the canakin clink, clink; / And let me the canakin clink: / A soldier's but a man; / A life's but a span; / Why then let a soldier drink." A canakin, later spelled *cannikin*, was an early term for a small can or drinking vessel.

"Well, you've had a long row to hoe."

"And I know you've done this from the highest motives –"

"Oh, there won't be much pettifogging to do till this cruel war is –"

"And you haven't simply done it for my sake. I couldn't respect you if you had."

"Well, then we'll say I haven't. A man that hasn't got his own respect intact wants the respect of all the other people he can corner. But we won't go into that. I'm in for the thing now, and we've got to face our future. My idea is that this isn't going to be a very protracted struggle; we shall just scare the enemy to death before it comes to a fight at all. But we must provide for contingencies, Editha. If anything happens to me –"

"Oh, George!" She clung to him sobbing.

"I don't want you to feel foolishly bound to my memory. I should hate that, wherever I happened to be."

"I am yours, for time and eternity – time and eternity." She liked the words; they satisfied her famine for phrases.

"Well, say eternity; that's all right; but time's another thing; and I'm talking about time. But there is something! My mother! If anything happens –"

She winced, and he laughed. "You're not the bold soldier-girl of yesterday!" Then he sobered. "If anything happens, I want you to help my mother out. She won't like my doing this thing. She brought me up to think war a fool thing as well as a bad thing. My father was in the civil war; all through it; lost his arm in it." She thrilled with the sense of the arm round her; what if that should be lost? He laughed as if divining her: "Oh, it doesn't run in the family, as far as I know!" Then he added, gravely, "He came home with misgivings about war, and they grew on him. I guess he and mother agreed between them that I was to be brought up in his final mind about it; but that was before my time. I only knew him from my mother's report of him and his opinions; I don't know whether they were hers first; but they were hers last. This will be a blow to her. I shall have to write and tell her –"

He stopped, and she asked, "Would you like me to write, too, George?"

"I don't believe that would do. No, I'll do the writing. She'll understand a little if I say that I thought the way to minimize it was to make war on the largest possible scale at once – that I felt I must have been helping on the war somehow if I hadn't helped keep it from coming, and I knew I hadn't; when it came, I had no right to stay out of it."

Whether his sophistries satisfied him or not, they satisfied her. She clung to his breast, and whispered, with closed eyes and quivering lips, "Yes, yes, yes!"

"But if anything should happen, you might go to her, and see what you could do for her. You know? It's rather far off; she can't leave her chair –"

"Oh, I'll go, if it's the ends of the earth! But nothing will happen! Nothing *can!* I –"

She felt herself lifted with his rising, and Gearson was saying, with his arm still round her, to her father: "Well, we're off at once, Mr. Balcom. We're to be formally accepted at the capital, and then bunched up with the rest somehow, and sent into camp somewhere, and got to the front as soon as possible. We all want to be in the van, of course; we're the first company to report to the Governor. I came to tell Editha, but I hadn't got round to it."

She saw him again for a moment at the capital, in the station, just before the train started southward with his regiment. He looked well, in his uniform, and very soldierly, but somehow girlish, too, with his clean-shaven face and slim figure. The manly eyes and the strong voice satisfied her, and his preoccupation with some unexpected details of duty flattered her. Other girls were weeping and bemoaning themselves, but she felt a sort of noble distinction in the abstraction, the almost unconsciousness, with which they parted. Only at the last moment he said, "Don't forget my mother. It mayn't be such a walk-over as I supposed," and he laughed at the notion.

He waved his hand to her, as the train moved off – she knew it among a score of hands that were waved to other girls from the platform of the car, for it held a letter which she knew was hers. Then he went inside the car to read it, doubtless, and she did not see him again. But she felt safe for him through the strength of what she called her love. What she called her God, always speaking the name in a deep voice and with the implication of a mutual understanding, would watch over him and keep him and bring him back to her. If with an empty sleeve, then he should have three arms instead of two, for both of hers should be his for life. She did not see, though, why she should always be thinking of the arm his father had lost.

There were not many letters from him, but they were such as she could have wished, and she put her whole strength into making hers such as she imagined he could have wished, glorifying and supporting him. She wrote to his mother glorifying him as their hero, but the brief answer she got was merely to the effect that Mrs. Gearson was not well enough to write herself, and thanking her for her letter by the hand of some one who called herself "Yrs truly, Mrs. W. J. Andrews."

Editha determined not to be hurt, but to write again quite as if the answer had been all she expected. But before it seemed as if she could have written, there came news of the first skirmish, and in the list of the killed which was telegraphed as a trifling loss on our side, was Gearson's name. There was a frantic time of trying to make out that it might be, must be, some other Gearson; but the name, and the company and the regiment, and the State were too definitely given.

Then there was a lapse into depths out of which it seemed as if she never could rise again; then a lift into clouds far above all grief, black clouds, that blotted out the sun, but where she soared with him, with George, George! She had the fever that she expected of herself, but she did not die in it; she was not even delirious, and it did not last long. When she was well enough to leave her bed, her one thought was of George's mother, of his strangely worded wish that she should go to her and see what she could do for her. In the exaltation of the duty laid upon her – it buoyed her up instead of burdening her – she rapidly recovered.

Her father went with her on the long railroad journey from northern New York to western Iowa; he had business out at Davenport, and he said he could just as well go then as any other time; and he went with her to the little country town where George's mother lived in a little house on the edge of illimitable corn-fields, under trees pushed to a top of the rolling prairie. George's father had settled there after the civil war, as so many other old soldiers had done; but they were Eastern people, and Editha fancied touches of the East in the June rose overhanging the front door, and the garden with early summer flowers stretching from the gate of the paling fence.

It was very low inside the house, and so dim, with the closed blinds, that they could scarcely see one another: Editha tall and black in her crapes which filled the air with the smell of their dyes; her father standing decorously apart with his hat on his forearm, as at funerals; a woman rested in a deep armchair, and the woman who had let the strangers in stood behind the chair.

The seated woman turned her head round and up, and asked the woman behind her chair, "*Who* did you say?"

Editha, if she had done what she expected of herself, would have gone down on her knees at the feet of the seated figure and said, "I am George's Editha," for answer.

But instead of her own voice she heard that other woman's voice, saying, "Well, I don't know as I *did* get the name just right. I guess I'll have to make a little more light in here," and she went and pushed two of the shutters ajar.

Then Editha's father said in his public will-now-address-a-few-remarks tone, "My name is Balcom, ma'am; Junius H. Balcom, of Balcom's Works, New York; my daughter —"

"Oh!" The seated woman broke in, with a powerful voice, the voice that always surprised Editha from Gearson's slender frame. "Let me see you! Stand round where the light can strike on your face," and Editha dumbly obeyed. "So, you're Editha Balcom," she sighed.

"Yes," Editha said, more like a culprit than a comforter.

"What did you come for?" Mrs. Gearson asked.

Editha's face quivered, and her knees shook. "I came — because — because George —" She could go no farther.

"Yes," the mother said, "he told me he had asked you to come if he got killed. You didn't expect that, I suppose, when you sent him."

"I would rather have died myself than done it!" Editha said with more truth in her deep voice than she ordinarily found in it. "I tried to leave him free —"

"Yes, that letter of yours, that came back with his other things, left him free."

Editha saw now where George's irony came from.

"It was not to be read before — unless — until — I told him so," she faltered.

"Of course, he wouldn't read a letter of yours, under the circumstances, till he thought you wanted him to. Been sick?" the woman abruptly demanded.

"Very sick," Editha said, with self-pity.

"Daughter's life," her father interposed, "was almost despaired of, at one time."

Mrs. Gearson gave him no heed. "I suppose you would have been glad to die, such a brave person as you! I don't believe *he* was glad to die. He was always a timid boy, that way; he was afraid of a good many things; but if he was afraid he did what he made up his mind to. I suppose he made up his mind to go, but I knew what it cost him, by what it cost me when I heard of it. I had been through *one* war before. When you sent him you didn't expect he would get killed."

The voice seemed to compassionate Editha, and it was time. "No," she huskily murmured.

"No, girls don't; women don't, when they give their men up to their country. They think they'll come marching back, somehow, just as gay as they went, or if it's an empty sleeve, or even an empty pantaloon, it's all the more glory, and they're so much the prouder of them, poor things."

The tears began to run down Editha's face; she had not wept till then; but it was now such a relief to be understood that the tears came.

"No, you didn't expect him to get killed," Mrs. Gearson repeated in a voice which was startlingly like George's again. "You just expected him to kill some one else, some of those foreigners, that weren't there because they had any say about it, but because they had to be there, poor wretches—conscripts, or whatever they call 'em. You thought it would be all right for my George, *your* George, to kill the sons of those miserable mothers and the husbands of those girls that you would never see the faces of." The woman lifted her powerful voice in a psalmlike note. "I thank my God he didn't live to do it! I thank my God they killed him first, and that he ain't livin' with their blood on his hands!" She dropped her eyes which she had raised with her voice, and glared at Editha. "What you got that black on for?" She lifted herself by her powerful arms so high that her helpless body seemed to hang limp its full length. "Take it off, take it off, before I tear it from your back!"

The lady who was passing the summer near Balcom's Works was sketching Editha's beauty, which lent itself wonderfully to the effects of a colorist. It had come to that confidence which is rather apt to grow between artist and sitter, and Editha had told her everything.

"To think of your having such a tragedy in your life!" the lady said. She added: "I suppose there are people who feel that way about war. But when you consider the good this war has done—how much it has done for the country! I can't understand such people, for my part. And when you had come all the way out there to console her—got up out of a sick bed! Well!"

"I think," Editha said, magnanimously, "she wasn't quite in her right mind; and so did papa."

"Yes," the lady said, looking at Editha's lips in nature and then at her lips in art, and giving an empirical touch to them in the picture. "But how dreadful of her! How perfectly—excuse me—how *vulgar!*"

A light broke upon Editha in the darkness which she felt had been without a gleam of brightness for weeks and months. The mystery that had bewildered her was solved by the word; and from that moment she rose from grovelling in shame and self-pity, and began to live again in the ideal.

[1905]

Ambrose Bierce

[1842-1914?]

Ambrose Gwinnett Bierce was born in Horse Cave Creek, in southeastern Ohio, on June 24, 1842. He was the youngest of the ten surviving children of Laura and Marcus Aurelius Bierce, both of whom could trace their ancestors to the earliest settlers in New England. Bierce's father, who struggled to earn a living by farming and working at various trades, was an avid reader and collector of books. By some accounts, he had the largest

[Bierce] acknowledges no debt and pays no tribute.... His originality defies imitation.
  —Kate Chopin

personal library in Kosciusko County, Indiana, where the family moved in 1846. Bierce attended school there for a time, but in 1857 he left home and moved to Warsaw, Indiana, to work as an apprentice in the print shop of an antislavery newspaper, the *Northern Indianan*. His apprenticeship ended abruptly, perhaps because of a disagreement with the publisher, and the alienated young man went to live with his uncle Lucius Verus Bierce, a politician and militant abolitionist, in Akron, Ohio. Bierce later attended the Kentucky Military Institute for a year before dropping out and returning to Indiana. In April 1861, almost immediately after the Civil War broke out

Ambrose Bierce

J. H. E. Partington painted this dramatic portrait of Bierce — posed with his elbow leaning on a table next to a skull, the symbol of mortality, transience, and the vanity of life — in the 1890s.

and two months before his nineteenth birthday, Bierce enlisted in the Ninth Indiana Volunteers of the Union army. Rising to the rank of brevet captain, he fought with distinction in some of the bloodiest battles of the Civil War: Shiloh, Chickamauga, Missionary Ridge, and Kennesaw Mountain, site of some of the heaviest fighting in General Sherman's Atlanta campaign, where Bierce received a serious head wound in June 1864.

Those harsh war experiences profoundly shaped his outlook on life, as well as his satirical and often bitter writings. After being discharged from the army in January 1865, Bierce worked as a federal treasury agent in the South before joining a military expedition to inspect forts and outposts across the West. In 1867, he arrived in San Francisco, which by then had become an important center of publication and a magnet for aspiring journalists and writers. Bierce, who later met Mark Twain and who became friends with Bret Harte and other writers of the "San Francisco Circle," soon began to publish poems and essays in the *Californian*, a weekly literary journal, and the *San Francisco News-Letter and California Advertiser*. In 1868, he became editor of the *News-Letter*, for which he also wrote a popular column, "The Town Crier." Bierce published his first short story in the most prestigious of western literary journals, the *Overland Monthly*, in 1871. That year, he married Mary Ellen Day, the daughter of a wealthy miner, and the couple moved to England. There, Bierce wrote regularly for two popular magazines of humor and satire, *Fun* and *Figaro*, and published three collections of his journalistic writings under the pen name "Dod Grile." After returning to the United States in 1875, Bierce worked at various jobs before resuming his career as a journalist in San Francisco. In 1881, he became the editor of the aptly named *Wasp*, in which Bierce became increasingly notorious for his sting-ing reviews. One of them was a single sentence: "The covers of this book are too far apart." Although Bierce was generous to beginning writers, he was often irreverent about established ones, attacking such respected figures as William Dean Howells, Henry James, and even the much-loved English novelist Charles Dickens.

Well known even by the initials with which he frequently signed his journalism, "A.G.B.," Bierce's influence became so great that his numer-ous enemies derisively called him "Almighty God Bierce." In 1887, he accepted a position as a columnist and editorial writer for William Randolph Hearst's popular, scandalous, and sensational *San Francisco Examiner*. For the next ten years, Bierce wrote for the *Examiner* and other Hearst publications, producing a wide variety of work, including short stories on subjects ranging from the supernatural to the Civil War. His collection of war stories, *Tales of Soldiers and Civilians*, appeared in 1892. His other most famous work was *The Cynic's Word Book* (1906), a collection of aphorisms and epigrams he later titled *The Devil's Diction-ary* (1911). In it, he satirically reinterpreted words such as *history*, which Bierce defined as "[a]n account mostly false, of events mostly unim-portant, which are brought about by rulers mostly knaves, and soldiers mostly fools." At the same time, his personal history was shadowed by his estrangement from his wife and the death of his two sons. In 1913, the seventy-one-year-old Bierce bid good-bye to his friends and his daugh-ter and set off to meet Pancho Villa, one of the leaders of the Mexican Revolution. "To be a Gringo in Mexico—ah, that is euthanasia," Bierce observed in a letter. At the end of December 1913, he disappeared and was never heard from or seen again. "The old gringo came to Mexico to die," is the simple explanation offered by a character in *The Old Gringo* (1985), a fictionalized account of Bierce's final months by the Mexican novelist Carlos Fuentes.

bedfordstmartins.com/ *americanlit* for research links on Bierce

Reading Bierce's "Chickamauga."   First published on the front page of the Sunday edition of William Randolph Hearst's influential *San Francisco Examiner*, "Chickamauga" is among the most powerful anti-war stories in American literature. The story is set during the battle of Chickamauga, September 18-20, 1863, fought in northern Georgia as part of the fierce struggle for control of Chattanooga, a key rail center at the heart of the Confederacy. The bloody battle, which claimed an esti-mated 35,000 casualties, ended with the rout and retreat of the Union troops, including the twenty-one-year-old Bierce. Although he accurately describes the landscape of the battle, Bierce in "Chickamauga" does not focus on military goals and tactics or even directly on the experiences of soldiers. Instead, he adopts the perspective of a young Southern boy, confused by what he encounters during the course of an afternoon and

Battle of Chickamauga

Published in 1890 by a firm that specialized in commemorative prints, especially battle scenes of the Civil War, this lithograph is an idealized representation of the repeated Confederate assaults on the Union line during the bloody two-day battle in Georgia.

evening near his plantation home. Bierce's grim story was probably not wholly surprising to the readers of the *San Francisco Examiner*, who were accustomed to the newspaper's graphic, even sensational reporting of local, national, and international events. In fact, the story appeared at a time when the United States was on the brink of a war with Germany over American interests in the Samoan Islands. Most newspaper coverage of the potential conflict tended to romanticize the idea of war, but Bierce had extensive, firsthand knowledge of its terrible reality, which he vividly captures in "Chickamauga." The text of the story is taken from its first printing in the *San Francisco Examiner*, January 20, 1889.

CHICKAMAUGA

One sunny Autumn afternoon a child strayed away from its rude home in a small field and entered a forest unobserved. It was happy in a new sense of freedom from control — happy in the opportunity of exploration and adventure; for this child's spirit, in bodies of its ancestors, had for many thousands of years been trained to memorable feats of discovery and conquest — notorious in battles whose critical moments were centuries, whose victors' camps were great cities of hewn stone. From the cradle of its race it had conquered its way through two continents and, passing a great sea, had penetrated a third, there to be born to war and dominance as a heritage.

The child was a boy, aged about six years; the son of a poor planter. In his younger manhood the father had been a soldier; had fought against naked savages and followed the flag of his country into the capital of a civilized race to the far South.[1] In the peaceful life of a planter the warrior-fire survived; once kindled it is never extinguished. The man loved military books and pictures, and the boy had understood enough to make himself a wooden sword, though even the eye of his father would hardly have known it for what it was. This weapon he now bore bravely, as became the son of an heroic race, and pausing now and again in the sunny interspaces of the forest assumed, with some exaggeration, the postures of aggression and defense that he had been taught by the engraver's art. Made reckless by the ease with which he overcame invisible foes attempting to stay his advance, he committed the common enough military error of pushing the pursuit to a dangerous extreme, until he found himself upon the margin of a wide but shallow brook, whose rapid waters barred his direct advance against the flying foe who had crossed with illogical ease. But the intrepid victor was not to be baffled: the spirit of the race which had passed the great sea burned unconquerable in that small breast and would not be denied. Finding a place where some bowlders in the bed of the stream lay but a step or a leap apart, he made his way across and fell again upon the rear-guard of his imaginary foe, putting all to the sword.

Now that the battle had been won, prudence required that he withdraw to his base of operations. Alas! like many a mightier conquerer, and like one, the mightiest, he could not

> curb the lust for war,
> Nor learn that tempted Fate will leave the loftiest star.[2]

Advancing from the bank of the creek, he suddenly found himself confronted with a new and more formidable enemy: in the path that he was following, bolt upright, with ears erect and paws suspended before it, sat a rabbit! With a startled cry the child turned and fled, he knew not in what direction, calling upon his mother, weeping, stumbling, his tender skin cruelly torn by brambles, his little heart beating hard with terror — breathless, blind with tears — lost in the forest! Then, for more than an hour, he wandered with aimless feet through the tangled under-growth, till at last, overcome with

---

1. **followed the flag . . . to the far South:** That is, fought with the American troops who captured Mexico City in September 1847, during the Mexican War of 1846-48.
2. **curb . . . star:** The lines are from *Childe Harold's Pilgrimage*, canto 3, 38:341-42, by the English poet George Gordon, Lord Byron (1788-1824).

fatigue, he lay down between two rocks within a few yards of the stream and, still grasping his toy sword, no longer a weapon but a companion, sobbed himself to sleep. The wood-birds sang merrily above his head, the squirrels, whisking their bravery of tail, ran barking from tree to tree, unconscious of the pity of it, and from somewhere far away came a strange, muffled thunder, as if the partridges were drumming in celebration of Nature's victory over the son of her immemorial enslavers. And back at the little plantation, where white men and black were hastily searching the fields and hedgerows in alarm, a mother's heart was breaking for her missing child.

Hours passed, and then the little sleeper rose to his feet. The chill of the evening was in his limbs, the fear of the gloom in his heart. But he had rested, and he no longer wept. With some blind instinct which impelled to action, he struggled through the undergrowth about him and came to a more open ground — on his right the brook, to the left a gentle acclivity studded with infrequent trees; over all, the gathering gloom of twilight. A thin ghostly mist rose along the water. It frightened and repelled him; instead of recrossing, in the direction whence he came, he turned his back upon it and went forward toward the dark inclosing wood. Suddenly he saw before him a strange moving object, which he took to be some large animal — a dog, a pig — he could not name it; perhaps it was a bear. He had seen pictures of bears, but knew of nothing to their discredit, and had vaguely wished to meet one. But something in form or movement of this object — something in the awkwardness of its approach told him that it was not a bear, and curiosity was stayed by fear. He stood still, and as it came slowly on, gained courage every moment, for he saw that it had not the long, menacing ears of the rabbit. Possibly his impressionable mind was half-conscious of something familiar in its shambling, awkward gait. Before it had approached near enough to resolve his doubts he saw that it was followed by another — and another. To right and to left were many more: the whole open space about him was alive with them — all moving forward toward the brook.

They were men. They crept upon their hands and knees; they used their hands only, dragging their legs; they used their knees only, their arms hanging useless at their sides; they strove to rise to their feet, but fell prone in the attempt. They did nothing naturally, and nothing alike, save only to advance foot by foot in the same direction. Singly, in pairs and in little groups, they came on through the gloom, some halting now and again while others crept slowly past them, then resuming their movement. They came by dozens and by hundreds: as far on either hand as one could see in the deepening gloom they extended, and the black wood behind them appeared to be inexhaustible. The very ground seemed in motion toward the creek. Occasionally one who had paused did not again go on, but lay as dead. He was dead. Some, pausing, made strange gestures with their hands; erected their arms and lowered them again; clasped their heads; spread their palms upward, as men are sometimes seen to do in public prayer.

Not all of this did the child note; it is what would have been noted by an older observer; he saw little but that these were men, yet crept like babes. Being men, they were not terrible, though some of them were singularly clad. He moved among them freely, going from one to another and peering into their faces with childish curiosity. All their faces were singularly white and many were streaked and gouted with red. Something in this — something, too, perhaps, in their grotesque attitudes and movements — reminded him of the painted clown whom he had seen last summer in the circus, and he laughed as he watched them. But on and ever on they crept, these maimed and bleeding men, as heedless as he of the dramatic contrast between his laughter and their own ghastly gravity. To him it was a merry spectacle. He had seen his father's negroes creep upon their hands and knees for his amusement—had ridden them so, fancying them his horses. He now approached one of these crawling figures from behind and with an agile movement mounted it astride. The man sank upon his breast, recovered, flung the small body fiercely to the ground as an unbroken colt might have done, then turned upon him a face that lacked a lower jaw—from the upper teeth to the throat was a great red gap fringed with hanging shreds of flesh and splinters of bone. The unnatural prominence of nose, the absence of chin, the fierce eyes, gave this man the appearance of a great bird of prey crimsoned in throat and breast by the blood of its quarry. He rose to his knees, the child to his feet. The man shook his fist at the child; the child, terrified at last, ran to a tree near by, got upon the farther side of it and took a more serious view of the situation. And so the uncanny multitude dragged itself slowly and painfully along in hideous pantomime—moved forward down the slope like a swarm of great black beetles, with never a sound of going—in silence profound, absolute.

Instead of darkening, the haunted landscape began to brighten. Through the belt of trees beyond the brook shone a strange red light, the trunks and branches of the trees making a black lacework against it. It struck the creeping figures and gave them monstrous shadows which caricatured their movements on the lit grass. It fell upon their faces, touching their whiteness with a ruddy tinge, accentuating the stains with which so many of them were freaked and maculated.[3] It sparkled on buttons and bits of metal in their clothing. Instinctively the child turned toward the growing splendor and moved down the slope with his horrible companions; in a few moments had passed the foremost of the throng—not much of a feat considering his advantages. He placed himself in the lead, his wooden sword still in hand, and solemnly directed the march, conforming his pace to theirs and occasionally turning as if to see that his forces did not straggle. Surely such a leader never before had such a following.

Scattered about upon the ground, now slowly narrowing by the encroachment of this awful march to water, were certain articles to which, in the leader's mind, were coupled no significant associations: an occasional blanket, tightly rolled lengthwise, doubled and the ends bound together with a string; a heavy knapsack here, and there a broken musket—such things, in short, as are found in the rear of retreating troops: the "spoor"[4] of men flying from their hunters. Everywhere near the creek, which here had a margin of lowland, the earth was trodden into mud by the feet of men and horses. An observer of better experience in the use of his eyes would have noticed that these footprints pointed in both directions: the ground had been twice passed over—in advance and in retreat. A few hours before, these desperately stricken men, with their more fortunate and now distant comrades, had penetrated the forest in thousands. Their successive battalions' lines, breaking into swarms and reforming in lines, had passed the child on every

---

3. **the stains . . . maculated:** Marked with unusual spots or blotches.
4. **"spoor":** A track or trail, especially that of a wild animal pursued as game.

side — had almost trodden on him as he slept. The rustle and murmur of their march had not awakened him. Almost within a stone's throw of where he lay they had fought a battle; but all unheard by him were the roar of the musketry, the shock of cannon, "the thunder of the captains and the shouting,"[5] He had slept through it all, grasping his little wooden sword with perhaps a tighter clutch in unconscious sympathy with his martial environment, but as hoodless of the grandeur of the struggle as the dead who died to make the glory.

The fire beyond the belt of woods on the farther side of the creek, reflected to earth from the canopy of its own smoke, was now suffusing the whole landscape. It transformed the sinuous line of mist to the vapor of gold. The water gleamed with dashes of red, and red, too, were many of the stones protruding above the surface. But that was blood; the less desperately wounded had stained them in crossing. On them, too, the child now crossed with eager steps: he was going to the fire. As he stood upon the farther bank he turned about to look at the companions of his march. The advance was arriving at the creek. The stronger had already drawn themselves to the brink and plunged their faces in the flood. Three or four who lay without motion appeared to have no heads. At this the child's eyes expanded with wonder: even his hospitable understanding could not accept a phenomenon implying such vitality as that. After slaking their thirst these men had not had the strength to back away from the water, nor to keep their heads above it. They were drowned. In rear of these, the open spaces of the forest showed the leader as many formless figures of his grim command as at first; but not half so many were in motion. He waved his cap for their encouragement and smiling pointed with his weapon in the direction of the guiding light — a pillar of fire to this strange exodus.[6]

Confident of the fidelity of his forces, he now entered the belt of woods, passed through it easily in the red illumination of its interspaces, climbed a fence, ran across a field, turning now and again to coquet with his responsive shadow, and so approached the blazing ruin of a dwelling. Desolation everywhere. In all the wide glare not a living thing was visible. He cared nothing for that; the spectacle pleased, and he danced with glee in imitation of the wavering flames. He ran about collecting fuel, but every object that he found was too heavy for him to cast it in his approach. In despair he flung in his sword — a surrender to the superior forces of nature. His military career was at an end.

Shifting his position, his eyes fell upon some outbuildings, which had an oddly familiar appearance, as if he had dreamed of them. He stood considering them with wonder, when suddenly the entire plantation, with its enclosing forest, seemed to turn as if upon a pivot. His little world swung half around; the points of the compass were reversed. He recognized the blazing building as his own home.

For a moment he stood stupefied by the power of the revelation; then ran with aimless feet, making a half circuit of the ruin. There, conspicuous, in the light of the conflagration, lay the dead body of a woman — the white face turned upward, the hands thrown

---

5. **"the thunder . . . shouting"**: See Job 39:25: "He saith among the trumpets, Ha, ha; and he smelleth the battle afar off, the thunder of the captains, and the shouting."
6. **a pillar of fire to this strange exodus**: See the description of God leading the Israelites out of slavery in Egypt: "And the Lord went before them by day in a pillar of a cloud, to lead them the way; and by night in a pillar of fire, to give them light; to go by day and night" (Exodus 13:21).

all abroad and clutched full of grass, the clothing deranged, the long dark hair in tangles and full of clotted blood. The greater part of the forehead was torn away and from the jagged hole the brain protruded, overflowing the temple, a frothy mass of gray, crowned with clusters of crimson bubbles. The work of a shell.

The child moved his little hands, making wild, uncertain gestures. He uttered a series of inarticulate and indescribable cries — something between the chattering of an ape and the gobbling of a turkey — a startling, soulless, unholy sound — the language of a devil. He was a deaf mute.

Then he stood motionless, with quivering lips, looking down upon the wreck.

[1889]

Henry James

[1843-1916]

Henry James was born in New York City on April 15, 1843, the second child of affluent and cosmopolitan parents, Henry James Sr. and Mary Walsh James. Henry James Sr., a well-known writer who was deeply absorbed in philosophical and theological issues, was friendly with a number of prominent literary figures, including Ralph Waldo Emerson. James and his four siblings — including his elder brother, William, who would become one of America's foremost philosophers and psychologists, and his talented sister, Alice, whose vivid diary was finally published more than forty years after her tragically early death in 1892 — were initially educated by tutors and in private schools in New York City. Seeking to provide his children with greater cultural and educational opportunities, however, and dreading what he described as "those inevitable habits of extravagance and insubordination which appear to be the characteristics of American youth," James's father moved the family to Europe in 1855. During most of the following five years, James attended schools in England, France, Switzerland, and Germany — reading widely, learning to speak French and German, and becoming familiar with cathedrals, galleries, and theaters in cities across Europe. Shortly after the family returned to the United States in 1860, the country was plunged into the Civil War. Although his two younger brothers later enlisted in the Union army, James suffered a back injury that apparently precluded military service. Instead, he enrolled in Harvard Law School in the fall of 1862.

James, however, soon embarked on a literary career. He withdrew from Harvard in 1863, remained in Boston, and began writing reviews, sketches, and stories for two of the country's most influential literary journals, the *North American Review* and the *Atlantic Monthly*, as well as for the *Nation*, a magazine established in New York City in 1865. James also traveled

Henry James

This photograph was taken in the early 1880s, when James was about forty years old and living in London.

extensively in Europe, writing travel sketches and collecting impressions that would become an important source of material for his later fiction. In a letter home to his mother in 1869, he observed:

> We [Americans] seem a people of *character*, we seem to have energy, capacity, and intellectual stuff in equal measure. What I have pointed out as our vices are the elements of the modern man with *culture* quite left out. It's the absolute and incredible lack of *culture* that strikes you in common traveling Americans.

At the same time, James suggested that one of the responsibilities of being an American was "fighting against a superstitious valuation of Europe," as he put it in a letter written in 1870. James thus began to develop what is called his "international theme," a central topic of his early fiction, in which he often focused on the experiences of Americans living or traveling in Europe. James charts the comic misadventures and sometimes tragic fates of such characters in the pieces collected as *A Passionate Pilgrim, and Other Tales* (1875) and *Transatlantic Sketches* (1875), as well as in his first two novels, *Roderick Hudson* (1875) and *The American* (1876). The novels were first serialized in the *Atlantic Monthly*, which by then was edited by his close friend William Dean Howells. James also cultivated friendships with distinguished European authors, especially Ivan Turgenev and Gustave Flaubert, whom he met during an extended stay in Paris during 1875-76.

In 1876, James decided to settle in London, where be became a major presence in the city's vibrant literary community. But he wrote for audiences on both sides of the Atlantic. James continued to explore the international theme in what are widely regarded as the most successful of his early works of fiction: *Daisy Miller: A Study* (1878), the novella that made him famous; and another remarkable "study" of a young American woman in Europe, *The Portrait of a Lady*, which was serialized in London's *Macmillan's Magazine* and the *Atlantic Monthly* during 1880-81. In those works, James displays his mastery of "The Art of Fiction," the title of an important essay he published in 1884. As both a critic and a prolific practitioner of that art, James helped raise fiction writing to a new level of seriousness. Yet none of his subsequent works achieved the popularity of *Daisy Miller* or *The Portrait of a Lady*. During trips home to Boston, where both of his parents died in 1882, James determined "to write a very *American* tale, a tale very characteristic of our social conditions," as he described *The Bostonians* (1886). Serialized in New York's *Century Magazine*, the novel was sharply criticized for its satire of reformers and Boston culture. James was no more successful with *The Princess Casamassima* (1886) and *The Tragic Muse* (1889), naturalistic novels in which he turned his attention to politics and social conditions in England. Discouraged by the tepid reception and poor sales of his novels, James spent the years between 1890 and 1895 seeking to become a successful playwright. Two of his plays were produced in London, but both were commercial and critical failures. With

I can think of but one English-speaking author who is really keeping his self-respect and sticking for perfection. Of course I refer to that mighty master of language and keen student of human actions and motives, Henry James.

—Willa Cather

the strong encouragement of William Dean Howells, who assured him that there was still an audience for his work in America as well as in England, James once again determined to make his living by writing fiction.

In 1897, James moved from London to his new home in the English countryside, Lamb House, where he lived and worked for the rest of his life. He continued his wide correspondence with other literary figures and formed close friendships with several younger American writers, including Stephen Crane and especially Edith Wharton. In what is sometimes called his "major phase," James at the turn of the century returned to the international theme in three long and complex novels: *The Wings of the Dove* (1902), *The Ambassadors* (1903), and *The Golden Bowl* (1904). Following an extended visit to the United States during 1904-05, after an absence of more than twenty years, James wrote a penetrating social and cultural critique of what had become "a vast, crude democracy of trade," as he describes the country in *The American Scene* (1907). James also prepared a collected edition of his works, revising many of them and writing prefaces to those he selected for inclusion in the New York edition of his *Novels and Tales* (1907-10). The twenty-six-volume edition testified to his artistic achievement, but the expensive set was not a commercial success, and very few of his individual novels and collections of stories were still in print. James was also troubled by health problems and saddened by the passing of friends and his brothers William and Robertson, both of whom died in 1910. The only surviving member of his family, James was spurred to begin writing autobiographical books, *A Small Boy and Others* (1913), *Notes of a Son and Brother* (1914), and the posthumously published *The Middle Years* (1917). Distressed by the failure of the United States to join the Allied cause at the opening of World War I, James became a naturalized British citizen shortly before his death in London in 1916.

bedfordstmartins.com/
americanlit for research
links on James

Reading James's "The Real Thing."   James later explained that this story was inspired by an anecdote told to him by his friend George du Maurier, an illustrator on the staff of the popular British magazine *Punch*. Du Maurier, who employed a working-class couple as models for his weekly "social" illustrations in the magazine, had been approached by a society couple who had suffered financial reverses and sought work as models for the illustrations, reasoning that they would not need to "make believe" in order to portray members of the upper class. From that anecdote and the questions it raised about the nature of representation and the relationship of art to life, "'The Real Thing' sprang at a bound," as James recalled. Appropriately, his story of an illustrator confronted by the aristocratic Major and Mrs. Monarch was first published in *Black and White: A Weekly Illustrated Record and Review*. Established in London in 1891, the journal was designed to feature single-color illustrations (called "black-and-whites") of articles and current literary works. "The three pillars of our enterprise are good art, good literature, and good printing," the editors announced in the first issue of *Black and White*. They consequently published "The Real Thing" along with illustrations by the artist Rudolf Blind, and new illustrations were provided by in-house artists when the story was reprinted in American periodicals later in 1892. The illustrations were omitted, as was standard practice, when the story was reprinted in *The Real Thing and Other Tales* (1893). The text, including the three original illustrations, is taken from the first printing in *Black and White*, April 16, 1892.

THE REAL THING

I

When the porter's wife (she used to answer the house-bell) announced, "A gentleman—with a lady, sir," I had, as I often had in those days, for the wish was father to the thought, an immediate vision of sitters. Sitters my visitors in this case proved to be; but not in the sense I should have preferred. However, there was nothing at first to indicate that they might not have come for a portrait. The gentleman, a man of fifty, very high and very straight, with a moustache slightly grizzled and a dark grey walking-coat admirably fitted, both of which I noted professionally—I don't mean either as a barber or a tailor—would have struck me as a celebrity if celebrities often were striking. It was a truth of which I had for some time been conscious that a figure with a good deal of frontage was, as one might say, almost never a public institution. A glance at the lady helped to remind me of this paradoxical law: she also looked too distinguished to be a "personality." Moreover one would scarcely come across two variations together.

Neither of the pair spoke immediately—they only prolonged the preliminary gaze which suggested that each wished to give the other a chance. They were visibly shy; they stood there letting me take them in—which, as I afterwards perceived, was the most practical thing they could have done. In this way their embarrassment served their cause. I had seen people painfully reluctant to mention that they desired anything so gross as to be represented on canvas; but the scruples of my new friends appeared almost insurmountable. Yet the gentleman might have said, "I should like a portrait of my wife"; and the lady might have said, "I should like a portrait of my husband." Perhaps they were not husband and wife—this naturally would make the matter more delicate. Perhaps they wished to be done together—in which case they ought to have brought a third person to break the news.

"We come from Mr. Rivet," the lady said at last, with a dim smile which had the effect of a moist sponge passed over a "sunk" piece of painting,[1] as well as of a vague allusion to vanished beauty. She was as tall and straight, in her degree as her companion, and with ten years less to carry. She looked as sad as a woman could look whose face was not charged with expression; that is, her tinted oval mask showed friction, as an exposed

---

1. a "sunk" piece of painting: An improperly prepared surface of a painting where the paint has seeped into the canvas and the color is consequently diminished.

surface shows it. The hand of time had played over her freely, but only to simplify. She was slim and stiff, and so well-dressed, in dark blue cloth, with lappets[2] and pockets and buttons, that it was clear she employed the same tailor as her husband. The couple had an indefinable air of prosperous thrift—they evidently got a good deal of luxury for their money. If I was to be one of their luxuries it would behove me to consider my terms.

"Ah, Claude Rivet recommended me?" I enquired; and I added that it was very kind of him, though I could reflect that, as he only painted landscape, this was not a sacrifice.

The lady looked very hard at the gentleman, and the gentleman looked round the room. Then staring at the floor a moment and stroking his moustache, he rested his pleasant eyes on me with the remark: "He said you were the right one."

"I try to be, when people want to sit."

"Yes, we should like to," said the lady, anxiously.

"Do you mean together?"

My visitors exchanged a glance. "If you could do anything with *me*, I suppose it would be double," the gentleman stammered.

"Oh yes, you naturally make a higher charge for two figures than for one."

"We should like to make it pay," the husband confessed.

"That's very good of you," I returned, appreciating so unwonted a sympathy—for I supposed he meant pay the artist.

A sense of strangeness seemed to dawn on the lady. "We mean for the illustrations—Mr. Rivet said you might put one in."

"Put one in—an illustration?" I was equally confused.

"Sketch her off, you know," said the gentleman, colouring.

It was only then that I understood the service Claude Rivet had rendered me; he had told them that I worked in black and white, for magazines, for story-books, for sketches of contemporary life, and consequently had frequent employment for models. These things were true, but it was not less true that (I may confess it now—whether because the aspiration was to lead to everything or to nothing I leave the reader to guess) I couldn't get the honours, to say nothing of the emoluments, of a great painter of portraits out of my head. My "illustrations" were my pot-boilers; I looked to a different branch of art (far and away the most interesting it had always seemed to me) to perpetuate my fame. There was no shame in looking to it also to make my fortune; but that fortune was by so much further from being made, from the moment my visitors wished to be "done" for nothing. I was disappointed; for, in the pictorial sense, I had immediately *seen* them. I had seized their type—I had already settled what I would do with it. Something that wouldn't absolutely have pleased them, I afterwards reflected. But that's nothing; a portrait is almost always bad in direct proportion as it gratifies the original or his friends. He himself can please his friends; the triumph of the painter is to please his enemies; they can't get over that. At any rate the delight of the sitter is in general a bad note.

"Ah, you're—you're—a—?" I began, as soon as I had mastered my surprise. I couldn't bring out the dingy word "models"; it seemed to fit the case so little.

"We haven't had much practice," said the lady.

---

2. **lappets:** Decorative flaps or lapels.

"We've got to do something, and we've thought that an artist, in your line, might perhaps make something of us," her husband threw off. He further mentioned that they didn't know many artists and that they had gone first, on the off chance (he painted views of course, but sometimes put in figures—perhaps I remembered), to Mr. Rivet, whom they had met a few years before at a place in Norfolk where he was sketching.

"We used to sketch a little ourselves," the lady recalled.

"It's very awkward, but we absolutely *must* do something," her husband went on.

"Of course, we're not so *very* young," she admitted, with a wan smile.

With the remark that I might as well know something more about them, the husband had handed me a card, extracted from a neat new pocket-book (their appurtenances were all of the freshest), and inscribed with the words, "Major Monarch." Impressive as these words were, they didn't carry my knowledge much further; but my visitor presently added: "I've left the army, and we've had the misfortune to lose our money. In fact, our means are extremely small."

"It's an awful bore," said Mrs. Monarch.

They evidently wished to be discreet—to take care not to swagger because they were gentlefolks. I perceived they would have been willing to recognise this as something of a drawback, at the same time that I guessed at an underlying sense—their consolation in adversity—that they *had* their points. They certainly had; but these advantages struck me as preponderantly social; such, for instance, as would help to make a drawing-room look well. However, a drawing-room was always, or ought to be, a picture.

In consequence of his wife's allusion to their age Major Monarch remarked: "Naturally, it's more for the figure that we thought of going in. We can still hold ourselves up." On the instant, I saw that the figure was indeed their strong point. His "naturally" didn't sound vain, but it lighted up the question. "*She* has got the best," he continued, nodding at his wife, with a pleasant after-dinner absence of circumlocution. I could only reply, as if we were in fact sitting over our wine, that this didn't prevent his own from being very good; which led him, in turn, to rejoin. "We thought that if you ever have to do people like us, we might be something like it. *She*, particularly—for a lady in a book, you know."

I was so amused by them that, to get more of it, I did my best to take their point of view; and though it was an embarrassment to find myself appraising physically, as if they were animals on hire or useful blacks, a pair whom I should have expected to meet only in one of the relations in which criticism is tacit, I looked at Mrs. Monarch judicially enough to be able to exclaim, after a moment, with conviction: "Oh yes, a lady in a book!" She was singularly like a bad illustration.

"We'll stand up, if you like," said the Major; and he raised himself before me with a really grand air.

I could take his measure at a glance—he was six feet two and a perfect gentleman. It would have paid any club, in process of formation and in want of a stamp, to engage him, at a salary, to stand in the principal window. What struck me immediately was that in coming to me they had rather missed their vocation; they could surely have been turned to better account for advertising purposes. I couldn't, of course, see the thing in detail; but I could see them make someone's fortune—I don't mean their own. There was something in them for a waistcoat-maker, an hotel-keeper or a soap-vendor. I could imagine "We always use it" pinned on their bosoms with the greatest effect; I had a vision of the promptitude with which they would launch a *table d'hôte.*[3]

Mrs. Monarch sat still, not from pride but from shyness, and presently her husband said to her: "Get up my dear and show how smart you are." She obeyed, but she had to need to get up to show it. She walked to the end of the studio, and then she came back blushing, with her fluttered eyes on her husband. I was reminded of an incident I had accidentally had a glimpse of in Paris—being with a friend there, a dramatist about to produce a play—when an actress came to him to ask to be entrusted with a part. She went through her paces before him, walked up and down as Mrs. Monarch was doing. Mrs. Monarch did it quite as well, but I abstained from applauding. It was very odd to see such people apply for such poor pay. She looked as if she had ten thousand a year. Her husband had used the word that described her: she was, in the London current jargon, essentially and typically "smart." Her figure was, in the same order of ideas, conspicuously and irreproachably "good." For a woman of her age her waist was surprisingly small; her elbow, moreover, had the orthodox crook. She held her head at the conventional angle; but why did she come to *me?* She ought to have tried on jackets at a big shop. I feared my visitors were not only destitute, but "artistic"—which would be a great complication. When she sat down again I thanked her, observing that what a draughtsman most valued in his model was the faculty for keeping quiet.

"MRS. MONARCH WENT THROUGH HER PACES BEFORE ME, AND DID IT QUITE WELL."

---

3. *table d'hôte*: Literally, "host's table"; a communal dining table for guests at a hotel (French).

"Oh *she* can keep quiet," said Major Monarch. Then he added, jocosely: "I've always kept her quiet."

"I'm not a nasty fidget, am I?" Mrs. Monarch appealed to her husband.

He addressed his answer to me. "Perhaps it isn't out of place to mention — because we ought to be quite business-like, oughtn't we? — that when I married her she was known as the Beautiful Statue."

"Oh dear!" said Mrs. Monarch, ruefully.

"Of course I should want a certain amount of expression," I rejoined.

"Of *course!*" they both exclaimed.

"And then I suppose you know that you'll get awfully tired."

"Oh, we *never* get tired!" they eagerly cried.

"Have you had any kind of practice?"

They hesitated — they looked at each other. "We've been photographed, *immensely,*" said Mrs. Monarch.

"She means the fellows have asked us," added the Major.

"I see — because you're so good-looking."

"I don't know what they thought, but they were always after us."

"We always got our photographs for nothing," smiled Mrs. Monarch.

"We might have bought some, my dear," her husband remarked.

"I'm not sure we have any left. We've given quantities away," she explained to me.

"With our autographs and that sort of thing," said the Major.

"Are they to be got in the shops?" I enquired, as a harmless pleasantry.

"Oh, yes; *hers* — they used to be."

"Not now," said Mrs. Monarch, with her eyes on the floor.

II

I could fancy the "sort of thing" they put on the presentation copies of their photographs, and I was sure they wrote a beautiful hand. It was odd how quickly I was sure of everything that concerned them. If they were now so poor as to have to earn shillings and pence, they never had had much of a margin. Their good looks had been their capital, and they had good-humouredly made the most of the career that this resource marked out for them. It was in their faces, the blankness, the deep intellectual repose of the twenty years of country-house visiting which had given them pleasant intonations. I could see the sunny drawing-rooms, sprinkled with periodicals she didn't read, in which Mrs. Monarch had continuously sat; I could see the wet shrubberies in which she had walked, equipped to admiration for either exercise. I could see the rich covers[4] the major had helped to shoot, and the wonderful garments in which, late at night, he repaired to the smoking-room to talk about them. I could imagine their leggings and waterproofs, their knowing tweeds and rugs, their rolls of sticks and cases of tackle and neat umbrellas; and I could evoke the exact appearance of their two servants and the compact variety of their luggage on the platforms of country stations.

---

4. **covers:** Game birds shot in their cover, or place of concealment.

They gave small tips, but they were liked; they didn't do anything themselves, but they were welcome. They looked so well everywhere; they gratified the general relish for stature, complexion and "form." They knew it without fatuity or vulgarity, and they respected themselves in consequence. They were not superficial; they were thorough and kept themselves up—it had been their line. Respectable people had to have some line. I could feel how, even in a dull house, they could have been counted upon for cheerfulness. At present something had happened—it didn't matter what, their little income had grown less, it had grown least—and they had to do something for pocket-money. Their friends liked them, but didn't like to support them. There was something about them that represented credit—their clothes, their manners, their type; but if credit is a large empty pocket in which an occasional chink reverberates, the chink at least must be audible. What they wanted of me was to help to make it so. Fortunately they had no children—I soon divined that. They would also perhaps wish our relations to be kept secret; this was why it was "for the figure"—the reproduction of the face would betray them.

I liked them—they were so simple; and I had no objection to them if they would suit. But, somehow, with all their perfections I didn't easily believe in them. After all, they were amateurs, and the ruling passion of my life was the detestation of the amateur. Combined with this was another perversity—an innate preference for the represented subject over the real one. The defect of the real one was so apt to be a lack of representation. I liked things that appeared; then one was sure. Whether they were or not was a subordinate, and almost always a tiresome question. There were other considerations, the first of which was that I already had two or three people in use, notably a young person with big feet, in alpaca, from Kilburn, who, for a couple of years, had come to me regularly for my illustrations, and with whom I was still—perhaps ignobly—satisfied. I frankly explained to my visitors how the case stood; but they had taken more precautions than I supposed. They had reasoned out their opportunity, for Claude Rivet had told them of the projected *édition de luxe* of one of the writers of our day—the rarest of the novelists—who, long neglected by the multitudinous vulgar and dearly prized by the attentive (need I mention Philip Vincent?), had had the happy fortune of seeing, late in life, the dawn and then the full light of a higher criticism—an estimate in which on the part of the public, there was something really of expiation. The edition in question, planned by a publisher of taste, was practically an act of high reparation; the wood-cuts with which it was to be enriched were the homage of English art to one of the most independent representatives of English letters. Major and Mrs. Monarch confessed to me that they had hoped I might be able to work *them* into my share of the enterprise. They knew I was to do the first of the books, "Rutland Ramsay," but I had to make clear to them that my participation in the rest of the affair—this first book was to be a test—was to depend on the satisfaction I should give. If this should be limited my employers would drop me without a scruple. It was therefore a crisis for me, and naturally I was making special preparations, looking about for new people, if they should be necessary, and securing the best types. I admitted, however, that I should like to settle down to two or three good models who would do for everything.

"Should we have often to—a—put on special clothes?" Mrs. Monarch timidly demanded.

"Dear, yes – that's half the business."

"And should we be expected to supply our own costumes?"

"Oh, no; I've got a lot of things. A painter's model put on – or put off – anything he likes."

"And do you mean – a – the same?"

"The same?"

Mrs. Monarch looked at her husband again.

"Oh, she was just wondering," he explained, "if the costumes are in *general* use." I had to confess that they were and I mentioned further that some of them (I had a lot of genuine, greasy last-century things), had served their time, a hundred years ago, on living, world-stained men and women. "We'll put on anything that *fits*," said the Major.

"Oh, I arrange that – they fit in the pictures."

"I'm afraid I should do better for the modern books. I would come as you like," said Mrs. Monarch.

"She has got a lot of clothes at home; they might do for contemporary life," her husband continued.

"Oh, I can fancy scenes in which you'd be quite at home." And indeed I could see the slipshod rearrangements of stale properties – the stories I tried to produce pictures for without the exasperation of reading them – whose sandy tracts the good lady might help to people. But I had to return to the fact that for this sort of work – the daily mechanical grind – I was already equipped; the people I was working with were quite adequate.

"We only thought we might be more like *some* characters," said Mrs. Monarch mildly, getting up.

Her husband also rose; he stood looking at me with a dim wistfulness that was touching in so fine a man. "Wouldn't it be rather a pull sometimes to have – a – to have –?" He hung fire; he wanted me to help him by phrasing what he meant. But I couldn't – I didn't know. So he brought it out, awkwardly; "The *real* thing; a gentleman, you know, or a lady." I was quite ready to give a general assent – I admitted that there was a great deal in that. This encouraged Major Monarch to say, following up his appeal with an unacted gulp: "It's awfully hard – we've tried everything." The gulp was communicative; it proved too much for his wife. Before I knew it Mrs. Monarch had dropped again upon a divan and burst into tears. Her husband sat down beside her, holding one of her hands; whereupon she quickly dried her eyes with the other, while I felt embarrassed as she looked up at me. "There isn't a confounded job I haven't applied for – waited for – prayed for. You can fancy we'd be pretty bad first. Secretaryships and that sort of thing? You might as well ask for a peerage. I'd be *anything* – I'm strong; a messenger or a coal-heaver. I'd put on a gold-laced cap and open carriage-doors in front of the haberdashers; I'd hang about a station, to carry portmanteaus;[5] I'd be a postman. But they won't *look* at you; there are thousands, as good as yourself, already on the ground. *Gentlemen*, poor beggars, that have drunk their wine, that have kept their hunters!"

---

5. **portmanteaus:** Large trunks or suitcases (French).

I was as reassuring as I knew how to be, and my visitors were presently on their feet again while, for the experiment, we agreed on an hour. We were discussing it when the door opened and Miss Churm came in with a wet umbrella. Miss Churm had to take the omnibus to Maida Vale[6] and then walk half a mile. She looked a trifle blowsy and slightly splashed. I scarcely ever saw her come in without thinking afresh how odd it was that, being so little in herself, she should yet be so much in others. She was a meagre little Miss Churm, but she was an ample heroine of romance. She was a freckled cockney[7] girl, but she could represent everything, from a fine lady to a shepherdess; she had the faculty, as she might have had a fine voice or long hair. She couldn't spell, and she loved beer, but she had two or three "points," and practice, and a knack, and mother-wit, and a kind of whimsical sensibility, and a love of the theatre, and seven sisters, and not an ounce of respect, especially for the *h*.[8] The first thing my visitors saw was that her umbrella was wet, and in their spotless perfection they visibly winced at it. The rain had come on since their arrival.

"I'm all in a soak; there *was* a mess of people in the bus. I wish you lived near a station," said Miss Churm. I requested her to get ready as quickly as possible, and she passed into the room in which she always changed her dress. But before going out she asked me what she was to get into this time.

"It's the Russian princess, don't you know?" I answered; "the one with the 'golden eyes,' in black velvet, for the long thing in the *Cheapside*."[9]

"Golden eyes? I *say!*" cried Miss Churm, while my companions watched her, with intensity, as she withdrew. She always arranged herself, when she was late, before I could turn round; and I kept my visitors a little, on purpose, so that they might get an idea, from seeing her, what would be expected of themselves. I mentioned that she was quite my notion of an excellent model – she was really very clever.

"Do you think she looks like a Russian princess?" Major Monarch asked, with lurking alarm.

"When I make her, yes."

"Oh, if you have to *make* her –" he reasoned, acutely.

"That's the most you can ask. There are so many that are not makeable."

"Well now, *here's* a lady" – and with a persuasive smile he passed his arm into his wife's – "who's already made!"

"Oh, I'm not a Russian princess," Mrs. Monarch protested, a little coldly. I could see that she had known some and didn't like them. There, immediately, was a complication of a kind that I never had to fear with Miss Churm.

This young lady came back in black velvet – the gown was rather rusty and very low on her lean shoulders – and with a Japanese fan in her red hands. I reminded her that in the scene I was doing she had to look over someone's head. "I forget whose it is; but it doesn't matter. Just look over a head."

---

6. **Maida Vale:** Then a predominantly Jewish district in northwest London.
7. **cockney:** A working-class inhabitant of London, especially one from the East End.
8. **the *h*:** A feature of the cockney dialect was the dropping of the sound of the *h* in a word: for example, pronouncing half as "'alf."
9. ***Cheapside:*** A fictitious illustrated periodical named after Cheapside, meaning "market-place," a street long associated with produce markets and related businesses in London.

"MISS CHURM TOOK HER STATION NEAR THE FIRE. SHE FELL INTO POSITION AND SETTLED HERSELF INTO A TALL ATTITUDE."

"I'd rather look over a stove," said Miss Churm; and she took her station near the fire. She fell into position, settled herself into a tall attitude, gave a certain backward inclination to her head and a certain forward droop to her fan, and looked, at least to my prejudiced sense, distinguished and charming, foreign and dangerous. We left her looking so, while I went downstairs with Major and Mrs. Monarch. "I think I could come as near to it as that," said Mrs. Monarch.

"Oh, you think she's shabby, but you must allow for the alchemy of art." However they went off with an evident increase of comfort, founded on their demonstrable advantage in being the real thing, I could fancy them shuddering over Miss Churm. She was very droll about them when I went back, for I told her what they wanted.

"Well, if *she* can sit I'll tyke to bookkeeping," said my model.

"She's very lady-like," I replied, as an innocent form of aggravation.

"So much the worse for *you*. That means she can't turn round."

"She'll do for the fashionable novels."

"Oh yes, she'll *do* for them!" my model humorously declared. "Ain't they bad enough without her?" I had often sociably denounced them to Miss Churm.

III

It was for the elucidation of a mystery in one of these works that I first tried Mrs. Monarch. Her husband came with her, to be useful if necessary—it was sufficiently clear that as a general thing he would prefer to come with her. At first I wondered if this were for "propriety's" sake—if he were going to be jealous and meddling. The idea was too tiresome, and if it had been confirmed it would speedily have brought our acquaintance to a close. But I soon saw there was nothing in it, and that if he accompanied Mrs. Monarch it was (in addition to the chance of being wanted), simply because he had nothing else to do. When she was away from him his occupation was gone—she never *had* been away from him. I judged, rightly, that in their awkward situation their close union was their main comfort, and that this union had no weak spot. It was a real marriage, an encouragement to the hesitating, a nut for pessimists to crack. Their address was humble (I remember afterwards thinking it had been the only thing about them that was really professional), and I could fancy the lamentable lodgings in which the Major would have been left alone. He could bear them with his wife—he couldn't bear them without her.

He had too much tact to try and make himself agreeable when he couldn't be useful; so he simply sat and waited, when I was too absorbed in my work to talk. But I liked to make him talk—it made my work, when it didn't interrupt it, less sordid, less special. To listen to him was to combine the excitement of going out with the economy of staying at home. There was only one hindrance: that I seemed not to know any of the people he and his wife had known. I think he wondered extremely, during the term of our intercourse, whom the deuce I *did* know. He hadn't a stray sixpence of an idea to fumble for; so we didn't spin it very fine—we confined ourselves to questions of leather and even of liquor (saddlers and breeches-makers and how to get good claret cheap), and matters like "good trains" and the habits of small game. His lore on these last subjects was astonishing—he was a mixture of the station-master and the ornithologist. When he couldn't talk about greater things he could talk cheerfully about smaller, and since I couldn't accompany him into reminiscences of the fashionable world he could lower the conversation without a visible effort to my level.

So earnest a desire to please was touching in a man who could so easily have knocked one down. He looked after the fire and had an opinion on the draught of the stove, without my asking him, and I could see that he thought many of my arrangements not half clever enough. I remember telling him that if I were only rich I would offer him a salary to come and teach me how to live. Sometimes he gave a random sigh, of which the essence was: "Give me even such a bare old barrack as *this*, and I'd do something with it!" When I wanted to use him he came alone—which was an illustration of the superior courage of women. His wife could bear her solitary second floor, and she was, in general, more discreet; showing by various small reserves that she was alive to the propriety of keeping our relations markedly professional—not letting them slide into sociability. She wished it to remain clear that she and the Major were employed, not cultivated, and if she approved of me as a superior, where I could be kept in my place, she never thought me quite good enough for an equal.

She sat with great intensity, giving the whole of her mind to it, and was capable of remaining for an hour almost as motionless as if she were before a photographer's lens. I could see she had been photographed often, but somehow the very habit that made her good for that purpose unfitted her for mine. At first I was extremely pleased with her lady-like airs, and it was a satisfaction, on coming to follow her lines, to see how good they were and how far they took one. But after a few times I began to find her rather irritatingly stiff; do what I would with it my drawing looked like a photograph or a copy of a photograph. Her figure had no variety of expression—she herself had no sense of variety. You may say that this was my business, was only a question of placing her. I placed her in every conceivable position, but she managed to obliterate their differences. She was always a lady, certainly, and, into the bargain, was always the same lady. She was the real thing, but always the same thing. There were moments when I was oppressed by the serenity of her confidence that she *was* the real thing. All her dealings with me, and all her husband's, were an implication that this was lucky for *me*. Meanwhile I found myself

[margin handwritten note:] Being the REAL THING interrupts her ability to imagine what THE REAL THING might be like. She is too close to it to really see it or 'dress' herself in it.

trying to invent types that approached her own, instead of making her own transform itself—in the clever way that was not impossible, for instance, to poor Miss Churm. Arrange as I would and take the precautions I would, she always, in my pictures, came out too tall—landing me in the dilemma of having represented a fascinating woman as seven feet high, which, out of respect perhaps to my own very much scantier inches, was far from my idea of such a personage.

The case was worse with the Major—nothing I could do would keep *him* down, so that he became useful only for the representation of brawny giants. I adored variety and range, I cherished human accidents, the illustrative note; I wanted to characterise closely, and the thing in the world I most hated was the danger of being ridden by a type. I had quarrelled with some of my friends about it—I had parted company with them for maintaining that one *had* to be, and that if the type was beautiful (witness Raphael and Leonardo),[10] the subjection was only a gain. I was neither Leonardo nor Raphael; I was only a possibly presumptuous young modern searcher; I held that everything was to be sacrificed sooner than character. When they averred that the haunting type in question might easily be character, I retorted, perhaps superficially: "Whose?" It couldn't be everybody's—it might end in being nobody's.

After I had drawn Mrs. Monarch a dozen times I perceived more clearly than before that the value of such a model as Miss Churm resided precisely in the fact that she had no positive stamp, combined of course with the other fact that what she did have was a curious and inexplicable talent for imitation. Her usual appearance was like a curtain, which she could draw up, at request, for a kind of regular performance. This performance was simply suggestive; but it was a word to the wise—it was vivid and pretty. Sometimes, even, I thought it, though she was plain herself, too insipidly pretty; I made it a reproach to her that the figures drawn from her were monotonously (*bêtement,*[11] as we used to say) graceful. Nothing made her more angry; it was so much her pride to feel that she could sit for characters that had nothing in common with each other. She would accuse me at such moments of taking away her "reputytion."

It suffered a certain shrinkage, this queer quantity, from the repeated visits of my new friends. Miss Churm was greatly in demand, never in want of employment, so I had no scruple in putting her off occasionally, to try them more at my ease. It was certainly amusing, at first, to do the real thing—it was amusing to do Major Monarch's trousers. They *were* the real thing, even if he did come out colossal. It was amusing to do his wife's back hair (it was so mathematically neat,) and the particular "smart" tension of her tight stays. She lent herself especially to positions in which the face was somewhat averted or blurred; she abounded in lady-like back views and *profils perdus.*[12] When she stood erect she took naturally one of the attitudes in which

---

10. **Raphael and Leonardo:** Raffaello Sanzio or Santi (1483–1520) and Leonardo da Vinci (1452–1519), master painters of the Italian Renaissance.
11. *bêtement:* Foolishly (French).
12. *profils perdus:* Lost profiles (French); views showing more of the back of the head than the profile of the face.

court painters represent queens and princesses; so that I found myself wondering whether, to draw out this accomplishment, I couldn't get the editor of the *Cheapside* to publish a truly royal romance, "A Tale of Buckingham Palace." Sometimes, however, the real thing and the make-believe came into contact; by which I mean that Miss Churm, keeping an appointment, or coming to make one on days when I had much work in hand, encountered her imposing rivals. The encounter was not on their part, for they noticed her no more than if she had been the housemaid; not from intentional loftiness, but simply because, as yet, professionally, they didn't know how to fraternise, as I could guess that they would have liked to, or at least that the Major would. They couldn't talk about the omnibus — they always walked; and they didn't know what else to try — she wasn't interested in good trains or cheap claret. Besides, they must have felt — in the air — that she was amused at them, secretly derisive of their ever knowing how. She was not a person to conceal her scepticism if she had had a chance to show it. On the other hand Mrs. Monarch didn't think her tidy; for why else did she take pains to say to me (it was going out of the way, for Mrs. Monarch), that she didn't like dirty women?

One day, when my young lady happened to be present with my other sisters (she even dropped in, when it was convenient, for a chat), I asked her to be so good as to lend a hand in getting tea — a service with which she was familiar and which was one of a class that, living as I did in a small way, with slender domestic resources, I often appealed to my models to render. They liked to lay hands on my property, to break the sitting — I made them feel Bohemian. The next time I saw Miss Churm after this incident she surprised me greatly by making a scene about it — she accused me of having wished to humiliate her. She had not resented the outrage at the time, but had seemed obliging and amused, enjoying the comedy of asking Mrs. Monarch, who sat dull and silent, whether she would have cream and sugar, and putting an exaggerated simper into the question. She had tried intonations — as if she too wished to pass for the real thing; till I was afraid my other visitors would take offence.

Oh, *they* were determined not to do this; and their really touching patience was the measure of their great need. They would sit by the hour, uncomplaining, till I was ready to use them; they would come back on the chance of being wanted and would walk away cheerfully if they were not. I used to go to the door with them to see in what magnificent order they retreated. I tried to find other employment for them — I introduced them to several artists. But they didn't "take," for reasons I could appreciate, and I became conscious, rather anxiously, that after such disappointments, they fell back upon me with a heavier weight. They did me the honour to think that it was I who was most *their* form. They were not picturesque enough for the painters, and in those days there were not so many serious workers in black and white. Besides, they had an eye to the great job I had mentioned to them — they had secretly set their hearts on supplying the right essence for my pictorial vindication of our high national novelist. They knew that for this undertaking I should want no costume-effects, none of the frippery of past ages — that it was a case in which everything would be contemporary and satirical and, presumably, genteel. If I could work them into it their future would be assured, for the labour would of course be long.

One day Mrs. Monarch came without her husband—she explained his absence by his having had to go to the City.[13] While she sat there in her usual anxious stiffness there came, at the door, a knock which I immediately recognised as the subdued appeal of a model out of work. It was followed by the entrance of a young man whom I easily perceived to be a foreigner, and who proved in fact to be an Italian acquainted with no English word but my name, which he uttered in a way that made it seem to include all others. I had not then visited his country, nor was I proficient in his tongue; but as he was not so poorly constituted—what Italian is?—as to depend upon that alone for expression, he conveyed to me, in familiar but graceful mimicry, that he was in search of exactly the employment in which the lady before me was engaged. I was not struck with him at first, and while I continued to draw I emitted vague sounds of discouragement and dismissal. He stood his ground, however, not importunately, but with a dumb, dog-like fidelity in his eyes which amounted to innocent impudence—the manner of a devoted servant (he might have been in the house for years), unjustly suspected. Suddenly I saw that this very attitude and expression made a picture, whereupon I told him to sit down and wait till I should be free. There was another picture in the way he obeyed me, and I observed as I worked that there were others still in the way he looked wonderingly, with his head thrown back, about the high studio. He might have been crossing himself in St. Peter's. Before I finished I said to myself: "The fellow's a bankrupt orange-monger, but he's a treasure."

When Mrs. Monarch withdrew he passed across the room like a flash to open the door for her, standing there with the rapt, pure gaze of the young Dante spellbound by the young Beatrice.[14] As I never insisted, in such situations, on the blankness of the British domestic, I reflected that he had the making of a servant (and I needed one, but couldn't pay him to be only that), as well as of a model; in short I made up my mind to adopt my insinuating visitor if he would agree to officiate in the double capacity. He jumped at my offer, and in the event my rashness (for I had known nothing about him), was not brought home to me. He proved a sympathetic though a desultory ministrant, and had in a wonderful degree the *sentiment de la pose*.[15] It was uncultivated, instinctive; a part of the happy instinct which had guided him to my door and helped him to spell out my name on the card nailed to it. He had had no other introduction to me than a guess, from the shape of my high north window, seen outside, that my place was a studio, and that as a studio it would contain an artist. He had wandered to England in search of fortune, like other itinerants, and had embarked, with a partner and a small green handcart, on the sale of penny ices. The ices had melted away and the partner had dissolved in their train. My young man wore tight yellow trousers with reddish stripes and his name was Oronte. He was sallow but fair, and when I put him into some old clothes of my own he looked like an Englishman. He was as good as Miss Churm, who could look, when required, like an Italian.

---

13. **the City:** The central banking and commercial area of London.
14. **Dante . . . Beatrice:** From the time the Italian poet Dante Alighieri (1265–1321) first saw Beatrice Polinari, when both of them were nine years old, she was his ideal and inspiration, finally becoming the symbol of God's love and salvation in his epic poem *The Divine Comedy* (c. 1309–20).
15. *sentiment de la pose*: Feeling for a pose (French).

IV

I thought Mrs. Monarch's face slightly convulsed when, on her coming back with her husband, she found Oronte installed. It was strange to have to recognise in a little Neapolitan cad a competitor to her magnificent Major. It was she who scented danger first, for the Major was anecdotically unconscious. But Oronte gave us tea, with a hundred eager confusions (he had never seen such a queer process), and I think she thought better of me for having at last an "establishment." They saw a couple of drawings that I had made of the establishment, and Mrs. Monarch hinted that it never would have struck her that he had sat for them. "Now, the drawings you make from *us*, they look exactly like us," she reminded me, smiling in triumph; and I recognised that this was indeed just their defect. When I drew the Monarchs I couldn't, somehow, get away from them—get into the character I wanted to represent; and I had not the least desire my model should be discoverable in my picture. Miss Churm never was, and Mrs. Monarch thought I hid her, very properly, because she was vulgar; whereas if she was lost it was only as the dead who go to heaven are lost—in the gain of an angel the more.

By this time I had got a certain start with "Rutland Ramsay," the first novel in the great projected series; that is, I had produced a dozen drawings, several with the help of the Major and his wife, and I had sent them in for approval. My understanding with the publishers, as I have already hinted, had been that I was to be left to do my work, in this particular case, as I liked, with the whole book committed to me: but my connection with the rest of the series was only contingent. There were moments when, frankly, it *was* a comfort to have the real thing under one's hand; for there were characters in "Rutland Ramsay" that were very much like it. There were people presumably as straight as the Major and women of as good a fashion as Mrs. Monarch. There was a great deal of country-house life—treated, it is true, in a fine, fanciful, ironical, generalised way—and there was a considerable implication of knickerbockers and kilts.[16] There were certain things I had to settle at the outset; such things, for instance, as the exact appearance of the hero, the particular bloom of the heroine. The author, of course, gave me a lead, but there was a margin for interpretation. I took the Monarchs into my confidence, I told them frankly what I was about, I mentioned my embarrassments and alternatives. "Oh, take *him!*" Mrs. Monarch murmured sweetly, looking at her husband; and "What could you want better than my wife?" the Major inquired, with the comfortable candour that now prevailed between us.

I was not obliged to answer these remarks—I was only obliged to place my sitters. I was not easy in mind, and I postponed, a little timidly perhaps, the solution of the question. The book was a large canvas, the other figures were numerous, and I worked off at first some of the episodes in which the hero and the heroine were not concerned. When once I had set *them* up I should have to stick to them—I couldn't make my young man seven feet high in one place and five feet nine in another. I inclined on the whole to the latter measurement, though the Major more than once reminded me that *he* looked about as

---

16. **knickerbockers and kilts:** Short pants gathered above the knee and knee-length, pleated skirts, both of which would have been suitable "casual" attire for men at English country houses.

young as anyone. It was indeed quite possible to arrange him for the figure so that it would have been difficult to detect his age. After my young friend Oronte had been with me a month, and after I had given him to understand several different times that his laz-zarone[17] habits would presently constitute an insurmountable barrier to our further in-tercourse, I waked to a sense of his heroic capacity. He was only five feet seven, but the other inches could be managed. I tried him almost secretly at first, for I was really rather afraid of the judgment my other models would pass on such a choice. If they regarded Miss Churm as little better than a snare, what would they think of the representation by a person so little the real thing as an Italian street-vendor, of a protagonist formed by a public school?

If I went a little in fear of them it was not because they bullied me, because they had got an oppressive foothold, but because, in their really pathetic decorum and mysteri-ously maintained newness, they counted on me so intensely. I was therefore very glad when Jack Hawley came home: he was always of such good counsel. He painted badly himself, but there was no one like him for putting his finger on the place. He had been absent from England for a year; he had been somewhere — I don't remember where — to get a fresh eye. I was in a good deal of dread of any such organ, but we were old friends; he had been away for months and a sense of emptiness was creeping into my life. I hadn't winced for a year.

He came back with a fresh eye, but with the same old black velvet jacket, and the first evening he spent in my studio we smoked cigarettes till the small hours. He had done no work himself, he had only got the eye; so the field was clear for the production of my own things. He wanted to see what I had done for the *Cheapside*, but he was unable to recog-nise that I had gone much further. That at least seemed the meaning of two or three comprehensive groans which, as he lounged on my big divan, on a folded leg, looking at my latest drawings, issued from his lips with the smoke of his cigarette.

"What's the matter with you?" I asked.

"What's the matter with *you?*"

"Nothing save that I'm mystified."

"You are indeed. You're quite off the hinge. What's the meaning of this new fad?" And he tossed me, with visible irreverence, a drawing in which I happened to have depicted both my majestic models. I asked if he didn't think it good, and he replied that it struck him as execrable, given the sort of thing I had always represented myself to him as wishing to arrive at; but I let that pass, I was so anxious to see exactly what he meant. The two figures in the picture looked colossal, but I supposed this was *not* what he meant, inasmuch as, for aught he knew to the contrary, I might have been try-ing for that. I maintained that I was working exactly in the same way as when he last had done me the honour to commend me. "Well, there's a muddle somewhere," he an-swered; "wait a bit and I'll make it out." I depended upon him to do so: where else was the fresh eye? But he produced at last nothing more luminous than "I don't know — I don't like your types." This was lame, for a critic who had never consented to discuss

---

17. **lazzarone:** Originally a beggar in Naples, Italy, the term was then more generally used to refer to a person who lives on the streets.

with me anything but the question of execution, the direction of strokes and the mystery of values.

"In the drawings you've been looking at I think my types are very handsome."

"Oh, they won't do."

"I've had a couple of new models."

"I see you have. *They* won't do."

"Are you very sure of that?"

"Absolutely – they're stupid."

"You mean *I* am – for I ought to get round that."

"You *can't* – with such people. Who are they?"

I told him, as far as was necessary, and he declared, heartlessly: *"Ce sont des gens qu'il faut mettre à la porte."*[18]

"You've never seen them: they're awfully good," I compassionately objected.

"Not seen them? Why, all this recent work of yours drops to pieces with them. It's all I want to see of them."

"No one else has said anything against it – the *Cheapside* people are pleased."

"Everyone else is an ass, and the *Cheapside* people the biggest asses of all. Come, don't pretend, at this time of day, to have pretty illusions about the public, especially about publishers and editors. It's not for *such* animals you work – it's for those who know. Keep straight for them; keep straight for *me* if you can't keep straight for yourself. There's a certain sort of thing you tried for from the first – and a very good thing it is. But this twaddle isn't *in* it." When I talked with Hawley, later, about "Rutland Ramsay" and its possible successors, he declared that I must get back into my boat again or I would go to the bottom. His voice, in short, was the voice of warning.

I noted the warning, but I didn't turn my friends out of doors. They bored me a good deal; but the very fact that they bored me admonished me not to sacrifice them – if there was anything to be done with them – simply to irritation. As I look back at this phase they seem to me to have pervaded my life not a little. I have a vision of them as most of the time in my studio, seated, against the wall, on an old velvet bench to be out of the way, and looking like a pair of patient courtiers in a royal ante-chamber. I am convinced that during the coldest weeks of the winter they held their ground because it saved them fire. Their newness was losing its gloss, and it was impossible not to feel that they were objects of charity. Whenever Miss Churm arrived they went away, and after I was fairly launched in "Rutland Ramsay" Miss Churm arrived pretty often. They managed to express to me, tacitly, that they supposed I wanted her for the low life of the book, and I let them suppose it, since they had attempted to study the work – it was lying about the studio – without discovering that it dealt only with the highest circles. They had dipped into the most brilliant of our novelists without deciphering many passages. I still took an hour from them, now and again, in spite of Jack Hawley's warning: it would be time enough to dismiss them, if dismissal should be necessary, when the rigour of the season was over. Hawley had made their acquaintance – he had met them at my fireside – and thought them a blighting apparition. Learning that he was a painter, they

18. *Ce . . . porte*: They are people who should be shown the door (French).

tried to approach him, to show him too that they were the real thing; but he looked at them, across the big room, as if they were miles away: they were a compendium of everything that he most objected to in the social system of his country. Such people as that, all convention and patent-leather, with ejaculations that stopped conversation, had no business in a studio; a studio was a place to learn to see, and how could you see through a pair of feather beds?

The main inconvenience I suffered at their hands was that, at first, I was shy of letting them discover that my artful little servant was sitting to me for "Rutland Ramsay." They knew that I had been odd enough (they were prepared, by this time, to allow oddity to artists,) to pick a foreign vagabond out of the streets, when I might have had a person with whiskers and credentials; but it was some time before they learned how high I rated his accomplishments. They found him sitting to me more than once, but they never doubted I was doing him as an organ-grinder. There were several things they never guessed, and one of them was that for a striking scene in the novel, in which a footman briefly figured, it occurred to me to make use of Major Monarch as the menial. I kept putting this off, I didn't like to ask him to don the livery – besides the difficulty of finding a livery to fit him. At last, one day late in the winter, when I was at work on the despised Oronte (he caught one's idea in an instant), and was in the glow of feeling that I was going very straight, they came in, the Major and his wife, with their society laugh about nothing (there was less and less to laugh at), like country-callers – they always reminded me of that – who have walked across after church and are presently persuaded to stay to luncheon. Luncheon was over, but they could stay to tea – I knew they wanted it. The fit was on me, however, and I couldn't let my ardour cool and my work wait, with the fading daylight, while my model prepared it. So I asked Mrs. Monarch if she could mind laying it out – a request which, for an instant, brought all the blood to her face. Her eyes were on her husband's for a second, and some mute telegraphy passed between them. Their folly was over the next instant; his cheerful shrewdness put an end to it. So far from pitying their wounded pride, I must add, I was moved to give it as complete a lesson as I could. They bustled about together and got out the cups and saucers and made the kettle boil. I know they felt as if they were waiting on my servant, and when the tea was prepared I said: "He'll have a cup, please – he's tired." Mrs. Monarch brought him one where he stood, and he took it from her as if he had been a gentleman at a party, squeezing a crush-hat with an elbow.

Then it came over me that she had made a great effort for me – made it with a kind of nobleness – and that I owed her a compensation. Each time I saw her, after this, I wondered what the compensation could be. I couldn't go on doing the wrong thing to oblige them. Oh, it *was* the wrong thing, the stamp of the work for which they sat – Hawley was not the only person to say it now. I sent in a large number of the drawings I had made for "Rutland Ramsay" and I received a warning that was more to the point than Hawley's. The artistic adviser of the house for which I was working was of opinion that many of my illustrations were not what had been looked for. Most of these illustrations were the subjects in which the Monarchs had figured. Without going into the question of what *had* been looked for, I saw at this rate I shouldn't get the other books to do. I hurled myself, in despair, upon Miss Churm, and I put her through all her paces. I not only adopted

Oronte publicly as my hero, but one morning when the Major looked in to see if I didn't require him to finish a figure for the *Cheapside*, for which he had begun to sit the week before, I told him that I had changed my mind—I would do the drawing from my man. At this my visitor turned pale and stood looking at me. "Is *he* your idea of an English gentleman?" he asked.

I was disappointed, I was nervous, I wanted to get on with my work; so I replied, with irritation: "Oh, my dear Major—I can't be ruined for *you!*"

He stood another moment; then, without a word, he quitted the studio. I drew a long breath when he was gone, for I said to myself that I shouldn't see him again. I had not told him defi-

"MRS. MONARCH BROUGHT THE MODEL A CUP OF TEA, AND HE TOOK IT FROM HER AS IF HE HAD BEEN A GENTLEMAN AT A PARTY, SQUEEZING A CRUSH HAT WITH HIS ELBOW"

nitely that I was in danger of having my work rejected, but I was vexed at his not having felt the catastrophe in the air, read with me the moral of our fruitless collaboration, the lesson that, in the deceptive atmosphere of art, even the highest respectability may fail of being plastic.

I didn't owe my friends money, but I did see them again. They re-appeared together, three days later, and under the circumstances there was something tragic in the fact. It was a proof to me that they could find nothing else in life to do. They had threshed the matter out in a dismal conference—they had digested the bad news that they were not in for the series. If they were not useful to me even for the *Cheapside* their function seemed difficult to determine, and I could only judge at first, that they had come, forgivingly, decorously, to take a last leave. This made me rejoice, in secret, that I had little leisure for a scene; for I had placed both my other models in position together and I was pegging away at a drawing from which I hoped to derive glory. It had been suggested by the passage in which Rutland Ramsay, drawing up a chair to Artemisin's piano stool, says memorable things to her while she ostensibly fingers out a difficult piece of music. I had done Miss Churm at the piano before—it was an attitude in which she knew how to take on an absolutely poetic grace. I wished the two figures to "compose" together, intensely, and my little Italian had entered perfectly into my conception. The pair were therefore before me, the piano had been pulled out; it was a charming picture of blended youth and murmured love, which I had only to catch and keep. My visitors stood and looked at it, and I said friendly things to them over my shoulder.

They made no response, but I was used to silent company and went on with my work, only a little disconcerted (even though exhilarated with the sense that *this* was at least the ideal thing) at not having got rid of them after all. Presently I heard Mrs. Monarch's sweet voice beside, or rather above, me: "I wish her hair was a little better done." I looked up and she was staring with a strange fixedness at Miss Churm, whose back was turned to her. "Do you mind my just touching it?" she went on—a question which made me spring up for an instant, as with the instinctive fear that she might do the young lady a harm. But she quieted me with a glance I shall never forget—I confess I should like to have been able to draw *that*—and went for a moment to my model. She spoke to her softly, laying a hand upon her shoulder and bending over her; and as the girl, understanding, gratefully assented, she disposed her rough curls, with a few quick passes, in such a way as to make Miss Churm's head twice as charming. It was one of the most heroic personal services I have ever seen rendered. Then Mrs. Monarch turned away with a low sigh, and looking about her, as if for something to do, stooped to the floor, with a noble humility, and picked up a dirty rag that had dropped out of my paint box.

The Major, meanwhile, had also been looking for something to do, and, wandering to the other end of the studio, saw before him my breakfast things, neglected, unremoved. "I say, can't I be useful *here*?" he called out to me, with an irrepressible quaver. I assented, with a laugh that I fear was awkward, and for the next ten minutes, while I worked, I heard the light clatter of china and the tinkle of spoons and glass. Mrs. Monarch assisted her husband—they washed up my crockery—they put it away. They wandered off into my little scullery, and I afterwards found that they had cleaned my knives and that my slender stock of plate had an unprecedented surface. When it came over me, the latent eloquence of what they were doing, I confess that my drawing was blurred for a moment—the picture swam. They had accepted their failure, but they couldn't accept their fate. They had bowed their heads, in bewilderment, to the perverse and cruel law in virtue of which the real thing could be so much less precious than the unreal; but they didn't want to starve. If my servants were my models, my models might be my servants. They would reverse the parts—the others would sit for the ladies and gentlemen and *they* would do the work. They would still be in the studio—it was an intense dumb appeal to me not to turn them out. "Take us on," they wanted to say—"we'll do anything."

When all this hung before me the *afflatus*[19] vanished—my pencil dropped from my hand. My sitting was spoiled and I got rid of my sitters, who were also evidently rather mystified and awestruck. Then, alone with the Major and his wife, I had a most uncomfortable moment. He put their prayer into a single sentence: "I say, you know—just let *us* do for you, can't you?" I couldn't—it was dreadful to see them emptying my slops; but I pretended I could, to oblige them, for about a week. Then I gave them a sum of money to go away; and I never saw them again. I obtained the remaining books, but my friend Hawley repeats that Major and Mrs. Monarch did me a permanent harm—got me into a second-rate trick. If it be true I am content to have paid the price—for the memory.

[1892]

---

19. *afflatus*: A divine creative impulse or inspiration.

Reading James's "The Jolly Corner."   In 1904 James returned to the
United States for the first time in more than twenty years, during which
he had lived in London and then bought a house in the ancient town of Rye
on the south coast of England. During his extended 1904 American lecture
tour, James visited the graves of his parents and sister for the first time,
and he was deeply distressed to discover that his childhood home in the
Washington Square area of "Old" New York had been torn down and a new
building had been erected on the site by New York University. Drawing on
this experience, the year after James returned to England he wrote "The
Jolly Corner," the story of Spencer Brydon, an American who returns to
New York after living abroad for thirty-three years. As James had done,
Brydon experiences the strangeness of returning to a city that had
changed dramatically: The population had grown from 942,000 in 1870 to
nearly 3.5 million in 1900, by which time the world's first skyscraper district began to rise in New York. In fact, Brydon participates in the city's
rapid commercial development, overseeing the conversion of one of his
properties into a block of high-rise apartments. In the company of his
friend Alice Staverton, he contemplates the kind of life he might have led
if he had never left New York. Determined to confront his "alter ego," his
imagined second self who had remained in the city, each night Brydon
prowls the dark and empty rooms of his childhood home on "a jolly

Alfred Stieglitz, "Old and New York"

This famous 1910
photograph of the
changing New York
cityscape shows the
under-construction
Vanderbilt Hotel, a
twenty-two-story
skyscraper completed
three years later, already
looming over townhouses
and mansions on Park
Avenue South.

corner," in a district that clearly resembles Washington Square. In what is widely considered one of his finest ghost stories, James also explores one of his most persistent themes, the contrast between what he viewed as the hollow commercialism of the United States and the highly developed artistic culture of Europe. "The Jolly Corner" was published in the first issue of the *English Review*, established as a venue for challenging modern writers, such as the novelists Joseph Conrad, John Galsworthy, and Thomas Hardy. The text is taken from the first printing in the *English Review*, December 1908.

THE JOLLY CORNER

I

"Every one asks me what I 'think' of everything," said Spencer Brydon; "and I make answer as I can—begging or dodging the question, putting them off with any nonsense. It wouldn't matter to any of them really," he went on, "for, even were it possible to meet in that stand-and-deliver way[1] so silly a demand on so big a subject, my 'thoughts' would still be almost altogether about something that concerns only myself." He was talking to Miss Staverton, with whom, for a couple of months now, he had availed himself of every possible occasion to talk; this disposition and this resource, this comfort and support, as the matter in fact presented itself, having promptly enough taken the first place among the surprises, as he would have called them, attending his so strangely belated return to America. Everything was somehow a surprise; and that might be natural when one had so long and so consistently neglected everything, taken pains to give surprises so much margin for preparation. He had given them more than thirty years—thirty-three, to be exact; and they now seemed to him to have organised their performance quite on the scale of that licence. He had been twenty-three on leaving New York—he was fifty-six to-day: unless indeed he were to reckon as he had sometimes, since his repatriation, found himself feeling, in which case he would have lived longer than is often allotted to man.[2] It would have taken a century, he repeatedly said to himself, and said also to Alice Staverton, it would have taken a longer absence and a more averted mind than those even of which he had been guilty, to pile up the differences, the newnesses, the queernesses, above all the bignesses, for the better or the worse, that at present assaulted his vision wherever he looked.

The great fact all the while, however, had been the incalculability; since he *had* supposed himself, from decade to decade, to be allowing, and in the most liberal and intelligent manner, for brilliancy of change. He actually saw that he had allowed for nothing;

---

1. **stand-and-deliver way:** *Stand and deliver*, a phrase that dates back to the sixteenth century, was used by highwaymen to command travelers to halt and surrender their possessions.
2. **lived longer . . . allotted to man:** "The days of our years are threescore years and ten," or seventy years (Psalms 90:10).

he missed what he would have been sure of finding, he found what he would never have imagined. Proportions and values were upside-down; the ugly things he had expected, the ugly things of his far-away youth, when he had too promptly waked up to a sense of the ugly—these uncanny phenomena placed him rather, as it happened, under the charm; whereas the "swagger" things, the modern, the monstrous, the famous things, those he had more particularly, like thousands of ingenuous inquirers every year, come over to see, were exactly his sources of dismay. They were as so many set traps for displeasure, above all for reaction, of which his restless tread was constantly pressing the spring. It was interesting, doubtless, the whole show, but it would have been too disconcerting had not a certain finer truth saved the situation. He had distinctly not, in this steadier light, come over *all* for the monstrosities; he had come, not only in the last analysis but quite on the face of the act, under an impulse with which they had nothing to do. He had come (putting the thing pompously) to look at his "property," which he had thus, for a third of a century, not been within four thousand miles of; or, expressing it less sordidly, he had yielded to the humour of seeing again his house on the jolly corner, as he usually, and quite fondly, described it—the one in which he had first seen the light, in which various members of his family had lived and had died, in which the holidays of his overschooled boyhood had been passed and the few social flowers of his chilled adolescence gathered, and which, alienated then for so long a period, had, through the successive deaths of his two brothers and the termination of old arrangements, come wholly into his hands. He was the owner of another not quite so "good"— the jolly corner having been, from far back, superlatively extended and consecrated; and the value of the pair represented his main capital, with an income consisting, in these later years, of their respective rents, which (thanks precisely to their original excellent type) had never been depressingly low. He could live in "Europe," as he had been in the habit of living, on the product of these flourishing New York leases, and all the better since that of the second structure, the mere number in its long row, having within a twelvemonth fallen in, renovation at a high advance had proved beautifully possible.

These were items of property indeed, but he had found himself since his arrival distinguishing more than ever between them. The house within the street, two bristling stretches westward, was already in course of reconstruction as a tall mass of flats:[3] he had acceded some time before to overtures for this conversion—in which, now that it was going forward, it had been not the least of his astonishments to find himself able, on the spot and though without an ounce of such experience, to participate with a certain intelligence, almost with a certain competence. He had lived his life with his back so turned to such concerns and his face addressed to those of so different an order, that he scarce knew what to make of this lively stir, in a compartment of his mind never yet

---

3. **a tall mass of flats:** An apartment building. Affluent New Yorkers lived in private houses until "French flats" were introduced shortly after the Civil War. In contrast to the cramped quarters in the tenement houses of the lower classes, such large and luxurious apartments had all of the modern conveniences, including indoor plumbing. In fact, the new residential concept proved to be so attractive that roughly half of all middle-class people in the city were living in multiple-dwelling units by 1900.

penetrated, of a capacity for business and a sense for construction. These virtues, so common all round him now, had been dormant in his own organism – where it might be said of them perhaps that they had slept the sleep of the just. At present, in the splendid autumn weather – the autumn at least *was* a pure boon in the terrible place – he loafed about his "work" undeterred, secretly agitated; not in the least "minding" that the whole proposition, as they said, was vulgar and sordid, and ready to climb ladders, to walk the plank, to handle materials and look wise about them, to ask questions, in fine, and challenge explanations and really "go into" figures.

It amused, it verily quite charmed; and, by the same stroke, it amused, and even more, Alice Staverton, though perhaps charming her perceptibly less. She wasn't, however, going to be better off for it, as *he* was – and so astonishingly much: nothing was now likely, he knew, ever to make her better off than she found herself, in the afternoon of life, as the delicately frugal possessor and tenant of the small house in Irving Place[4] to which she had subtly managed to cling through her almost unbroken New York career. If he knew the way to it now better than to any other address among the dreadful multiplied numberings which seemed to him to reduce the whole place to some vast ledger-page, overgrown, fantastic, of ruled and criss-crossed lines and figures – if he had formed, for his consolation, that habit, it was really not a little because of the charm of his having encountered and recognised in the vast wilderness of the wholesale, breaking through the mere gross generalisation of wealth and force and success, a small, still scene where items and shades, all delicate things, kept the sharpness of the notes of a high voice perfectly trained, and where economy hung about like the scent of a garden. His old friend lived with one maid and herself dusted her relics and trimmed her lamps and polished her silver; she stood off, in the awful modern crush, when she could, but she sallied forth and did battle when the challenge was really to "spirit," the spirit she after all confessed to, proudly and a little shyly, as to that of the better time, that of *their* common, their quite far-away and antediluvian social period and order. She made use of the street-cars when need be, the terrible things that people scrambled for as the panic-stricken at sea scramble for the boats; she affronted inscrutably, under stress, all the public concussions and ordeals; and yet with that slim mystifying grace of her appearance, which defied you to say if she were a fair young woman who looked older through trouble, or a fine smooth older one who looked young through successful indifference; with her precious reference, above all, to memories and histories into which he could enter, she was exquisite for him like some pale pressed flower (a rarity to begin with), and, failing other sweetnesses, she was a sufficient reward of his effort. They had communities of knowledge, "their" knowledge (this discriminating possessive was always on her lips) of presences of the other age, presences all overlaid, in his case, by the experience of a man and the freedom of a wanderer, overlaid by pleasure, by infidelity, by passages of life that were strange and dim to her, just by "Europe" in short, but still unobscured, still exposed and cherished, under that pious visitation of the spirit from which she had never been diverted.

---

4. **Irving Place:** During the nineteenth century, the area around Irving Place – from 14th to 20th streets at Gramercy Park – became one of the most sought-after residential neighborhoods in New York.

She had come with him one day to see how his "apartment-house" was rising; he had helped her over gaps and explained to her plans, and while they were there had happened to have, before her, a brief but lively discussion with the man in charge, the representative of the building firm that had undertaken his work. He had found himself quite "standing up" to this personage over a failure on the latter's part to observe some detail of one of their noted conditions, and had so lucidly argued his case that, besides ever so prettily flushing, at the time, for sympathy in his triumph, she had afterwards said to him (though to a slightly greater effect of irony) that he had clearly for too many years neglected a real gift. If he had but stayed at home he would have anticipated the inventor of the sky-scraper. If he had but stayed at home he would have discovered his genius in time really to develop streets and to harvest a fortune. He was to remember these words, while the weeks elapsed, for the little silver ring with which he might feel that they had died away in the queerest and deepest of his own lately most disguised and most muffled vibrations.

It had begun to be present to him after the first fortnight, it had broken out with the oddest abruptness, this particular wanton wonderment: it met him there — and this was the image under which he himself judged the matter, or at least, not a little, thrilled and flushed with it — very much as he might have been met by some strange figure, some unexpected occupant, at a turn of one of the dim passages of an empty house. The quaint analogy quite hauntingly remained with him, when he didn't indeed rather improve it by a still intenser form: that of his opening a door behind which he would have made sure of finding nothing, a door into a room shuttered and void, and yet so coming, with a great suppressed start, on some quite erect confronting presence, something planted in the middle of the place and facing him through the dusk. After that visit to the house in construction he walked with his companion to see the other and always so much the better one, which, in the eastward direction, formed one of the corners of the street now so generally dishonoured and disfigured in its westward reaches and of the comparatively conservative Avenue. The Avenue had still pretensions, as Miss Staverton said, to decency; the old people had gone, mostly, the old names were unknown, and here and there an old association seemed to stray, all vaguely, like some very aged person, out too late, whom you might meet and feel the impulse to watch or follow, in kindness, for safe restoration to shelter.

They went in together, our friends; he admitted himself with his key, as he kept no one there, he explained, preferring, for his reasons, to leave the place empty, under a simple arrangement with a good woman living in the neighbourhood who came for a daily hour to open windows and dust and sweep. Spencer Brydon had his reasons, and was growingly aware of them; they seemed to him better each time he arrived, though he didn't name them all to his companion, any more than he told her as yet how often, how quite absurdly often, he himself came. He only let her see for the present, while they walked through the great blank rooms, that absolute vacancy reigned and that, from top to bottom, there was nothing but Mrs. Muldoody's broomstick, in a corner, to tempt the burglar. Mrs. Muldoody was then on the premises, and she loquaciously attended the visitors, preceding them from room to room and pushing back shutters and throwing up sashes — all to show them, as she remarked, how little there was to see. There was little indeed to see in the great gaunt shell, where the main dispositions and the general apportionment of space, the style of an age of ampler allowances, had nevertheless, for its master, their honest, pleading message, affecting him as some good old servant's, some life-long retainer's appeal for a character, or even for a retiring pension; yet it was also a remark of Mrs. Muldoody's that, glad as she was to oblige him by her noonday round, there was a request she greatly hoped he would never make of her. If he should wish her for any reason to come in after dark she would just tell him, if he "plased," that he must ask it of somebody else.

The fact that there was nothing to see didn't militate, for the worthy woman, against what one *might* see, and she put it frankly to Miss Staverton that no lady could be expected to like – could she? – "craping up to thim top storeys in the ayvil hours." The gas and the electric light were off the house, and she fairly evoked a gruesome vision of her march through the great grey rooms – so many of them as there were too! – with her glimmering taper. Miss Staverton met her honest glare with a smile and the profession that she herself certainly would recoil from such an adventure. Spencer Brydon meanwhile held his peace – for the moment; the question of the "evil" hours in his old home had already become too grave for him. He had begun some time since to "crape," and he knew just why a packet of candles, addressed to that pursuit, had been stowed by his own hand, three weeks before, at the back of a drawer of the fine old sideboard that occupied as a "fixture" the deep recess in the dining-room. For the present he laughed at his companions – quickly, however, changing the subject; for the reason that in the first place his laugh struck him even at that moment as starting the odd echo, the conscious human resonance (he scarce knew how to qualify it) that sounds made while he was there alone sent back to his ear or his fancy; and that in the second he imagined Alice Staverton, for the instant, on the point of asking him, with a divination, if he ever so prowled. There were divinations he was unprepared for, and he had at all events averted inquiry by the time Mrs. Muldoody had left them, passing on to other parts.

There was happily enough to say, on so consecrated a spot, that could be said freely and fairly; so that a whole train of declarations was precipitated by his friend's having herself broken out, after a yearning look round: "But I hope you don't mean they want to pull *this* to pieces!" His answer came, promptly, with his reawakened wrath: it was of course exactly what they wanted and what they were "at" him for, daily, with the pertinacity of people who couldn't for their life understand a man's having a decent feeling. He had found the place, just as it stood and beyond what he could express, an interest and a joy. There were values other than the beastly rent-values, and in short, in short ——! But it was here that Miss Staverton took him up. "In short you're to make so good a thing of your sky-scraper that, living in luxury on *those* ill-gotten gains, you can afford for a while to be sentimental here!" Her smile had for him, with the words, the particular mild irony with which he found half her talk suffused; an irony without bitterness and that came, exactly, from her having so much imagination – not, like the cheap sarcasms with which one heard most people, about the world of "society," bid for the reputation of cleverness, from nobody's really having any. It was agreeable to him at this very moment to be sure that when he had answered, after a brief demur, "Well, yes: so, precisely, you may put it!" her imagination would still do him justice. He explained that even if never a dollar were to come to him from the other house he would nevertheless cherish this one; and he dwelt, further, while they lingered and wandered, on the fact of the stupefaction he was already exciting, the positive mystification he felt himself create.

He spoke of the value of all he read into it, into the mere sight of the walls, mere shapes of the rooms, mere sound of the floors, mere feel, in his hand, of the old silver-plated knobs of the several mahogany doors, which suggested the pressure of the palms of the dead; the seventy years of the past, in short, that these things represented, the annals of nearly three generations, counting his grandfather's, the one that had ended there, and the impalpable ashes of his long-extinct youth, afloat in the very air like microscopic motes. She listened to everything; she was a woman who answered but who didn't chatter. She scattered abroad therefore no cloud of words; she could assent, she could agree, above all she could encourage, without doing that. Only at the last she went a little further than he had done himself. "And then how do you know? You may still, after all, want to live here." It rather indeed pulled him up, for it wasn't what he had been thinking, at least in her sense of the words. "You mean I may decide to stay on for the sake of it?"

"Well, *with* such a home——!" But, quite beautifully, she had too much tact to dot so monstrous an i, and it was precisely an illustration of the way she didn't rattle. How could any one – of any wit – insist on any one else's "wanting" to live in New York?

"Oh," he said, "I *might* have lived here (since I had my opportunity early in life); I might have put in here all these years. Then everything would have been different enough – and I daresay 'funny' enough. But that's another matter. And then the beauty of it – I mean of my perversity, of my refusal to agree to a 'deal' – is just in the total absence of a reason. Don't you see that if I had a reason about the matter at all it would *have* to be the other way and would then be inevitably a reason of dollars? There are no reasons here *but* of dollars. Let us therefore have none whatever – not the ghost of one."

They were thus back in the hall for departure, but from where they stood the vista was large, through an open door, into the great square main saloon, with its almost antique felicity of brave intervals between windows. Her eyes quitted that long reach and met his own a moment. "Are you very sure the 'ghost' of one doesn't much rather serve ——?"

He had a positive sense of turning pale. But it was as near as they were then to come. For he made answer, he believed, between a glare and a grin: "Oh, ghosts – of course the place must swarm with them! I should be ashamed of it if it didn't. Poor Mrs. Muldoody's right, and it's why I haven't asked her to do more than look in."

Miss Staverton's gaze again lost itself, and things that she didn't utter, it was clear, came and went in her mind. She might even for the minute, off there in the fine room, have imagined some element dimly gathering. Simplified like the death-mask of a handsome face, it perhaps produced for her just then an effect akin to the stir of an expression in the "set" commemorative plaster. Yet whatever her impression may have been she uttered instead of it a vague platitude. "Well, if it were only furnished and lived in ——!"

She appeared to imply that in case of its being still furnished he might have been a little less opposed to the idea of a return. But she passed straight into the vestibule, as if to leave her words behind her, and the next moment he had opened the house-door and was standing with her on the steps. He closed the door and while he repocketed his key, looking up and down, they took in the comparatively harsh actuality of the Avenue, which reminded him of the assault of the outer light of the Desert on the traveller emerging from an Egyptian tomb. But he risked before they stepped into the street his gathered answer to her speech. "For me it *is* lived in. For me it *is* furnished." At which it was easy for her to sigh "Ah yes ——!" very vaguely and discreetly, since his parents and his favourite sister, to say nothing of other kin, in numbers, had run their course and met their end there. That represented, within the walls, ineffaceable life.

It was a few days after this that, during an hour passed with her again, he had expressed his impatience of the too flattering curiosity – among the people he met – about his appreciation of New York. He had arrived at none at all that was socially producible, and as for that matter of his "thinking" (thinking the better or the worse of anything there) he was wholly taken up with one subject of thought. It was mere vain egoism, and it was moreover, if she liked, a morbid obsession. He found all things come back to the question of what he personally might have been, how he might have led his life and "turned out," if he had not so at the outset given it up. And confessing for the first time to the intensity within him of this absurd speculation – which but proved too, no doubt, the habit of selfishly thinking – be affirmed the impotence there of any other source of interest, any other local appeal. "What would it have made of me, what would it have made of me? I keep for ever wondering, all idiotically; as if I could possibly know! I see what it has made of dozens of others, those I meet, and it positively aches within me, to the point of exasperation, that it would have made something of me as well. Only I can't make out *what*, and the worry of it, the small rage of curiosity, never to be satisfied, brings back what I remember to have felt once or twice after judging best, for reasons, to burn some important letter unopened. I've been sorry, I've hated it – I've never known what was in the letter. You may of course say it's a trifle ——!"

"I don't say it's a trifle," Miss Staverton gravely interrupted.

She was seated by her fire, and before her, on his feet and restless, he turned to and fro between this intensity of his idea and a fitful and unseeing inspection, through his single eye-glass, of the dear little old objects on her chimneypiece. Her interruption made him for an instant look at her harder. "I shouldn't care if you did!" he laughed, however; "and it's only a figure, at any rate, for the way I now feel. *Not* to have followed my perverse young course – and almost in the teeth of my father's curse, as I may say; not to have kept it up so, 'over there,' from that day to this, without a doubt or a pang; not, above all, to have liked it, to have loved it, so much, loved it, naturally, with such an abysmal *conceit* of my own preference: some variation from *that*, I say, must have produced some different effect for my life and for my 'form.' I should have stuck here – if it had been possible; and I was too young, at twenty-three, to judge, *pour deux sous*,[5] whether it *were* possible. If I had waited I might have seen it was, and then I might have been, by staying here, something nearer to one of these types who have been hammered

---

5. *pour deux sous*: For two pennies (French).

so hard and made so keen by their conditions. It isn't that I admire them so much—the question of any charm in them, or of any charm beyond that of the rank money-passion exerted by their conditions *for* them, has nothing to do with the matter; it's only a question of what fantastic, yet perfectly possible, development of my own nature I may not have missed. It comes over me that I had then a strange *alter ego*[6] deep down somewhere within me, as the full-blown flower is in the small tight bud, and that I just took the course, I just transferred him to the climate, that blighted him at once and for ever."

"And you wonder about the flower," Miss Staverton said. "So do I, if you want to know; and so I've been wondering these several weeks. I believe in the flower," she continued. "I feel that it would have been quite splendid, quite huge and monstrous."

"Monstrous above all!" her visitor echoed; "and I imagine, by the same stroke, quite hideous and offensive."

"You don't believe that," she returned; "if you did you wouldn't wonder. You'd know, and that would be enough for you. What you feel—and what I feel for you—if that you'd have had power."

"You'd have liked me that way?" he asked.

She barely hung fire. "How should I not have liked you?"

"I see. You'd have liked me, have preferred me, a billionaire!"

"How should I not have liked you?" she simply again asked. He stood before her still—her question kept him motionless. He took it in, so much there was of it; and indeed his not otherwise meeting it testified to that. "I know at least what I am," he simply went on; "the other side of the medal is clear enough. I've not been edifying—I believe I'm thought in a hundred quarters to have been barely decent. I've followed strange paths and worshipped strange gods;[7] it must have come to you again and again—in fact you've admitted to me as much—that I was leading, at any time these thirty years, a selfish, frivolous, scandalous life. And you see what it has made of me."

She just waited, smiling at him. "You see what it has made of *me*."

"Oh, you're a person whom nothing can have altered. You were born to be what you are, anywhere, anyway: you've the perfection nothing else could have touched. And don't you see how, without my exile, I shouldn't have been waiting till now——? "But he pulled up for the strange pang.

"The great thing to see," she presently said, "seems to me to be that it has spoiled nothing. It hasn't spoiled your being here at last. It hasn't spoiled this. It hasn't spoiled your speaking——" She also, however, faltered.

He wondered at everything her controlled emotion might mean. "Do you believe then—too dreadfully!—that I *am* as good as I might ever have been?"

"Oh no! Far from it!" With which she got up from her chair and was nearer him. "But I don't care," she smiled.

"You mean I'm good enough?"

---

6. *alter ego*: Literally, "the other I" (Latin), a second self distinct from an individual's normal or original personality.

7. worshipped strange gods: An echo of numerous passages in the Old Testament, including God's command in Psalms 81:9: "There shall no strange god be in thee; neither shalt thou worship any strange god."

She considered a little. "Will you believe it if I say so? I mean will you let that settle your question for you?" And then as if making out in his face that he drew back from this, that he had some idea which, however absurd, he couldn't yet bargain away: "Oh, you don't care either – but very differently: you don't care for anything but yourself."

Spencer Brydon recognised it – it was in fact what he had absolutely professed. Yet he importantly qualified. "*He* isn't myself. He's the just so totally other person. But I do want to see him," he added. "And I can. And I shall."

Their eyes met for a minute while he guessed from something in hers that she divined his strange sense. But neither of them otherwise expressed it, and her apparent understanding, with no protesting shock, no easy derision, touched him more deeply than anything yet, constituting for his stifled perversity, on the spot, an element that was like breathable air. What she said, however, was unexpected. "Well, *I've* seen him."

"You – ?"

"I've seen him in a dream."

"Oh, a 'dream' ——!" It let him down.

"But twice over," she continued. "I saw him as I see you now."

"You've dreamed the same dream ——?"

"Twice over," she repeated. "The very same."

This did somehow a little speak to him, as it also pleased him.

"You dream about me at that rate?"

"Ah, about *him!*" she smiled.

His eyes again sounded her. "Then you know all about him." And as she said nothing more: "What's the wretch like?"

She hesitated, and it was as if he were pressing her so hard that, resisting for reasons of her own, she had to turn away. "I'll tell you some other time!"

II

It was after this that there was most of a virtue for him most of a cultivated charm, most of a preposterous secret thrill, in the particular form of surrender to his obsession and of address to what he more and more believed to be his privilege. It was what in these weeks he was living for – since he really felt life to begin but after Mrs. Muldoody had retired from the scene and, visiting the ample house from attic to cellar, making sure he was alone, he knew himself in safe possession and, as he tacitly expressed it, let himself go. He sometimes came twice in the twenty-four hours; the moments he liked best were those of gathering dusk, of the short autumn twilight; this was the time of which, again and again, he found himself hoping most. Then he could, as seemed to him, most intimately wander and wait, linger and listen, feel his fine attention, never in his life before so fine, on the pulse of the great vague place: he preferred the lampless hour and only wished he might have prolonged, each day, the deep crepuscular[8] magic. Later – rarely much before midnight, but then for a

---

8. **crepuscular:** Twilight or dim light.

considerable vigil – he watched with his glimmering light; moving slowly, holding it high, playing it far, rejoicing above all, as much as he might, in open vistas, reaches of communication between rooms and along passages; the long, straight chance or show, as he would have called it, for the revelation he pretended to invite. It was a practice he found he could perfectly "work" without exciting remark; no one was in the least the wiser for it; even Alice Staverton, who was moreover a well of discretion, didn't quite fully imagine.

He let himself in and let himself out with the assurance of calm proprietorship; and accident so far favoured him that if a fat Avenue "officer"[9] had happened on occasion to see him entering at eleven-thirty, he had never yet, to the best of his belief, been noticed as emerging at two. He walked there on the crisp November nights, arrived regularly at the evening's end; it was as easy to do this after dining out as to take his way to a club or to his hotel. When he left his club, if he had not been dining out, it was ostensibly to go to his hotel; and when he left his hotel, if he had spent a part of the evening there, it was ostensibly to go to his club. Everything was easy in fine; everything conspired and promoted: there was truly even in the quality of his experience something that glossed over, something that salved and simplified all the rest of consciousness. He circulated, talked, renewed, loosely and pleasantly, old relations – met indeed, so far as he could, new expectations and seemed to make out on the whole that in spite of the career, of such different contacts, which he had spoken of to Miss Staverton as ministering so little, for those who might have watched it, to edification, he was positively rather liked than not. He was a dim secondary social success – and all with people who had truly not an idea of him. It was all mere surface sound, this murmur of their welcome, this popping of their corks – just as his gestures of response were the extravagant shadows, emphatic in proportion as they meant little, of some game of *ombres chinoises*.[10] He projected himself all day, in thought, straight over the bristling line of hard unconscious heads and into the other, the real, the waiting life; the life that, as soon as he had heard behind him the click of his great house-door, began for him as beguilingly as the slow opening bars of some rich music follows the tap of the conductor's wand.

He always caught the first effect of the steel point of his stick on the old marble of the hall pavement, large black and white squares that he remembered as the admiration of his childhood and that had then made in him, as he now saw, for the growth of an early conception of style. This effect was the thin reverberating tinkle as of some far-off bell hung who should say where? – in the depths of the house, in the past of that mystical other world that might have been for him had he not, for weal or woe, abandoned it. On this impression he did ever the same thing; he put his stick all noiselessly away in a corner – feeling the place once more in the likeness of some great glass bowl, all precious concave crystal, set delicately humming by the play of a moist finger round its

---

9. **Avenue "officer"**: A police officer on foot patrol.
10. *ombres chinoises*: Literally, "Chinese shadows" (French), from an ancient Chinese form of storytelling in which opaque figures are placed in front of an illuminated screen and moved from below to create the illusion of moving figures.

edge. The concave crystal held, as it were, this mystical other world, and the indescribably fine murmur of its rim was the sigh there, the scarce audible pathetic wail, to his strained ear, of all the old baffled forsworn possibilities. What he did therefore by this appeal of his hushed presence was to wake them into such measure of ghostly life as they might still enjoy. They were shy, all but unappeasably shy, but they weren't really sinister; at least they weren't as he had hitherto felt them — before they had taken the Form he so yearned to make them take, the Form he at moments saw himself in the light of fairly hunting, on tiptoe, the points of his evening-shoes, from room to room and from storey to storey.

That was the essence of his vision — which was all rank folly, if one would, while he was out of the house and otherwise occupied, but which took on the last verisimilitude as soon as he was isolated. He knew what he meant and what he wanted; it was as clear as the figure on a cheque presented in demand for cash. His *alter ego* "walked" — that was the note of his image of him, and his image of his motive for his own odd pastime was the desire to waylay him and meet him. He roamed slowly, warily, but all restlessly, he himself did — Mrs. Muldoody had been absolutely right with her figure of their "craping"; and the presence he watched for would roam restlessly too. But it would be as cautious and as shifty; the conviction of its probable, in fact its already quite sensible, quite audible evasion of pursuit grew for him from night to night, laying on him finally a spell to which nothing in his life had been comparable. It had been the theory of many superficially judging persons, he knew, that he was wasting that life in a surrender to sensations; but he had tasted of no pleasure as fine as his actual tension, had been introduced to no sport that demanded at once the patience and the nerve of this stalking of a creature more subtle, yet at bay perhaps more formidable, than any beast of the forest. The terms, the comparisons, the very practices of the chase came again positively into play; there were even moments when passages of his occasional experience as a sportsman, stirred memories, from his younger time, of moor and mountain and desert, revived for him — and to the increase of his keenness — by the tremendous force of analogy. He found himself at moments — once he had placed his single light on some mantelshelf or in some recess — stepping back into shelter or shade, effacing himself behind a door or in an embrasure as he had sought of old the vantage of rock and tree; he found himself holding his breath and living in the joy of the instant, the supreme suspense created by big game alone.

He wasn't afraid (though putting himself the question as he believed gentlemen on Bengal tiger-shoots or in close quarters with the great bear of the Rockies had been known to confess to having put it); and this indeed — since here at least he might be frank! — because of the impression, so intimate and so strange, that he himself produced as yet a dread, produced certainly a strain, beyond the liveliest he was likely to feel. They fell for him into categories, they fairly became familiar, the signs, for his own perception, of the alarm his presence and his vigilance created; though leaving him always to remark portentously on his probably having formed a relation, his probably enjoying a consciousness, unique in the experience of man. People enough, first and last, had been in terror of apparitions, but who had ever before so turned the tables and become himself, in the apparitional world, an incalculable terror? He might have found this sublime had he quite dared to think of it; but he didn't too much insist, truly, on that side of his privilege. With habit and repetition he gained to an extraordinary degree the power to penetrate the dusk of distances and the darkness of corners, to resolve back into their innocence the treacheries of uncertain light, the evil-looking forms taken in the gloom by mere shadows, by accidents of the air, by shifting effects of perspective; putting down his dim luminary, he could still wander on without it, pass into other rooms and, only knowing it was there behind him in case of need, see his way about, project visually, for his purpose, a comparative clearness. It made him feel, this acquired faculty, like some monstrous stealthy cat; he wondered if he would have appeared to have at these moments large shining yellow eyes, and what it mightn't verily be for the poor hard-pressed *alter ego* to be confronted with such a face.

He liked, however, the open shutters; he opened everywhere those Mrs. Muldoody had closed, closing them as carefully afterwards, so that she shouldn't notice; he liked — oh this he did like and above all in the upper rooms! — the sense of the hard silver of the autumn stars through the window-panes, and scarcely less the flare of the street-lamps below, the white electric lustre which it would have taken curtains to keep out. This was human, actual, social; this was of the world he had lived in, and he was more at his ease certainly for the countenance, coldly general and impersonal, that, all the while and in spite of his detachment, it seemed to give him. He had support of course mostly in the rooms at the wide front and the prolonged side; it failed him considerably in the parts of the back. But if he sometimes, on his rounds, was glad of his optical reach, so none the less often the rear of the house affected him as the very jungle of his prey. The place was there more subdivided, a large "extension," in particular, where small rooms for servants had been multiplied, abounded in nooks and corners, in closets and passages, in the ramifications especially of an ample back-staircase over which he leaned, many a time, to look far down — not deterred from his gravity even while aware that he might for a spectator have figured some solemn simpleton playing at hide-and-seek. He himself, outside, might in fact make that ironic *rapprochement;*[11] but within the walls, and in spite of the clear windows, his consistency was proof against the cynical light of New York.

It had been in the nature of that measure of the exasperated consciousness of his victim to become a real test for him; since he had quite put it to himself from the first that, oh distinctly! he could "cultivate" his whole perception. He had felt it as above all open to cultivation — which indeed was but another name for his manner of spending his time. He was bringing it on, bringing it to perfection, by practice, the expenditure by which it had grown so fine that he was now aware of impressions, attestations of his general postulate, that couldn't have broken upon him at once. This was the case more specifically with a phenomenon at last quite frequent for him in the upper rooms, the recognition — absolutely unmistakable and by a turn dating from a particular hour, his resumption of his campaign after a diplomatic drop, a calculated absence of three nights — of his being followed at a distance carefully taken and to the express end that he should the

---

11. *rapprochement*: A coming together (French).

less confidently, less arrogantly, appear to himself merely to pursue. It worried, it finally quite broke him up, for it proved, of all the conceivable impressions, the one that least suited his book. He was kept in sight while remaining himself – as regards the essence of his position – sightless, and his only recourse then was in abrupt turns, rapid recoveries of ground. He wheeled about, retracing his steps, as if he might so catch in his face at least the stirred air of some other quick revolution. It was indeed true that his fully dislocalised thought of these manœuvres recalled to him Pantaloon, at the Christmas farce, buffeted and tricked from behind by ubiquitous Harlequin;[12] but it remained wholly without prejudice to the influence of the conditions themselves, each time he was re-exposed to them, so that in fact this association, had he suffered it to become constant, would on a certain side have but ministered to his intenser gravity. He had made, as I have said, to create on the premises the baseless sense of a reprieve, his three absences; and the result of the third was to confirm the after-effect of the second.

On his return, that night – the night succeeding his last intermission – he stood in the hall and looked up the staircase with a certainty more intimate than any he had yet known. "He's *there*, at the top, and waiting – not, as in general, falling back for disappearance. He's holding his ground, and it's the first time – which is a proof, isn't it? that something has happened for him." So Brydon argued with his hand on the banister and his foot on the lowest stair; in which position he felt, as never before, the air chilled by his logic. He himself turned cold in it, for he seemed of a sudden to know what now was involved. "Harder pressed? – yes, he takes it in, with its thus making clear to him that I've come, as they say, 'to stay.' He doesn't like it, at last: in the sense, I mean, that his wrath, his menaced interest, now balances with his dread. I've hunted him till he has 'turned': that, up there, is what has happened – he's the fanged or the antlered animal brought at last to bay." There came to him, as I say – but determined by an influence beyond my notation! – the acuteness of this certainty; under which, however, the next moment, he had broken into a sweat that he would as little have consented to attribute to fear as he would have dared immediately to act upon it for a sign of exaltation. It marked none the less a prodigious thrill, a thrill that represented sudden dismay, no doubt, but also represented, and with the selfsame throb, the strangest, the most joyous, possibly the next minute almost the proudest, duplication of consciousness.

"He has been dodging, retreating, hiding, but now, worked up to anger, he'll fight!" – this intense impression made a single mouthful as it were, of terror and applause. But what was wondrous was that the applause, for the felt fact, was so eager, since if it was his other self he was running to earth this ineffable identity was thus in the last resort not unworthy of him. It bristled there – somewhere near at hand, however unseen still – as the hunted thing, even as the trodden worm of the adage, *must* at last

---

12. **Pantaloon . . . Harlequin:** An allusion to the *Commedia dell'arte* (a comedy of art or craft), an Italian theatrical performance originating in the sixteenth century involving five characters including Harlequin, the comic central character who becomes enmeshed in complicated situations; and Pantaloon, a gullible character who is easily tricked.

bristle; and Brydon at this instant tasted probably of a sensation more complex than had ever before found itself consistent with sanity. It was as if it would have shamed him that a character so associated with his own should triumphantly succeed in just skulking, should to the end not dare to face him; so that the drop of this danger was, on the spot, a great lift of the whole situation. Yet by another rare shift of the same subtlety he was already trying to ascertain how much more he himself might now be in peril of fear; rejoicing thus that he could, in another form, actively inspire that fear, and simultaneously quaking for the form in which he might passively know it.

The apprehension of knowing it must after a little have grown in him, and the strangest moment of his adventure perhaps, the most memorable or really most interesting, afterwards, of his crisis, was the lapse of a sharp spasm of concentrated conscious *combat*, the sense of a need to hold on to something, even after the manner of a man slipping and slipping on some awful incline; the vivid impulse, above all, to move, to act, to charge somehow and upon something—to show himself, in a word, that he wasn't afraid. The state of "holding-on" was thus the state to which he was momentarily reduced; if there had been anything in the great vacancy to seize he would have been presently aware of having clutched it as, under a shock at home, he might have clutched the nearest chair-back. He had been surprised at any rate—of this he *was* aware—into something unprecedented since his original appropriation of the place; he had closed his eyes, held them tight for a long minute, as with that instinct of dismay and that terror of vision. When he opened them the room, the other contiguous rooms, extraordinarily, seemed lighter—so light, almost, that at first he thought it was day. He stood firm, however that might be, just where he had paused; his resistance had helped him—it was as if there were something he had tided over. He knew after a little what this was—it had been in the imminent danger of flight. He had stiffened his will against going, without which he would have made for the stairs; and it seemed to him that, still with his eyes closed, he would have descended them, would have known how, straight and swiftly to the bottom.

Well, as he had held out here he was—still at the top, among the more intricate upper rooms and with the gauntlet of the others, of all the rest of the house, still to run when it should be his time to go. He would go at his time—only at his time: didn't he go every night at very much the same hour? He took out his watch—there was light for that: it was scarcely a quarter past one, and he had never retreated so soon. He reached his lodgings for the most part at two—with his walk of a quarter of an hour. He would wait for the last quarter—he wouldn't stir till then; and he kept his watch there with his eyes on it, reflecting while he held it that this deliberate wait, a wait with an effort which he recognised, would serve perfectly for the attestation he desired to make. It would prove his courage—unless indeed the latter might most be proved by his budging at last from his place. What he mainly felt now was that, since he hadn't originally scuttled, he had his dignities—which had never in his life seemed so many—all to preserve and to carry aloft. This was before him in truth as a physical image, an image almost worthy of an age of greater romance. That remark indeed glimmered for him only to glow the next instant with a finer light; since what age of romance, after all, could have matched either the state of his mind or, "objectively" as they said, the wonder of his situation? The only difference would have been that, brandishing his dignities over his head as in a parchment scroll, he might then — that is in the heroic time — have proceeded downstairs with a drawn sword in his other grasp.

At present, really, the light he had set down on the mantel of the next room would have to figure his sword; which utensil, in the course of a minute, he had taken the requisite number of steps to possess himself of. The door between the rooms was open, and from the second another door opened to a third. These rooms, as he remembered, gave all three upon a common corridor as well, but there was a fourth beyond them without issue save through the preceding. To have moved, to have heard his step again, was appreciably a help; though even in recognising this he lingered once more a little by the chimney-piece on which his light had rested. When he next moved, hesitating a little where to turn, he found himself considering a circumstance that, after his first and comparatively vague apprehension of it, produced in him the start that often attends some pang of recollection, the violent shock of having ceased happily to forget. He had come into sight of the door in which the brief chain of communication ended, and which he now looked at from the nearer threshold, the one not directly facing it. Placed at some distance to the left of this point, it would have admitted him to the last room of the four, the room without other approach or egress, had it not, to his intimate conviction, been closed *since* his former visitation, the matter probably of a quarter of an hour before. He stared with all his eyes at the wonder of the fact, arrested again where he stood and again holding his breath while he sounded its sense. Surely it had *been* closed — that is it had been on his previous passage indubitably open!

He took it full in the face that something had happened between — that he couldn't have noticed before (by which he meant on his original tour of all the rooms that evening) that such a barrier had exceptionally presented itself. He had indeed since that moment undergone an agitation so extraordinary that it might have muddled for him any earlier view; and he tried to think that he might perhaps have then gone into the room and inadvertently, automatically, on coming out, have drawn the door after him. The difficulty was that this, exactly, was what he never did; it was against his whole policy as he might have said, the essence of which was to keep vistas clear. He had had them from the first, he was well aware, quite on the brain: the strange apparition, at the far end of one of them, of his baffled "prey" (which had become by so sharp an irony so little the term now to apply) was the form of success his imagination had most cherished, projecting into it always a refinement of beauty. He had known fifty times the start of perception that had afterwards dropped; had fifty times gasped to himself "There!" under some fond brief hallucination. The house, as the case stood, admirably lent itself; he might wonder at the taste, the native architecture of the particular time, which could rejoice so in the multiplication of doors — the opposite extreme to the modern, the actual, almost complete proscription of them; but it had fairly contributed to provoke this obsession of the presence encountered telescopically, as he might say, focussed and studied in diminishing perspective and as by a rest for the elbow.

It was with these considerations that his present attention was charged — they perfectly availed to make what he saw portentous. He *couldn't* by any lapse have blocked that aperture; and if he hadn't, if it was unthinkable, why what else was clear but that there had been another agent? Another agent? – he had been catching, as he felt a moment back, the very breath of him; but when had he been so close as in this simple, this logical, this completely personal act? It was so logical, that is, that one might have *taken* it for personal; yet for what did Brydon take it, he asked himself while, softly panting, he felt his eyes almost leave their sockets. Ah this time at last they *were*, the two, the opposed projections of him, in presence; and this time, as much as one would, the question of danger loomed. With it rose as not before the question of courage – for what he knew the blank face of the door to say to him was "Show us how much you have!" It stared, it glared back at him with that challenge; it put to him the two alternatives: should he just push it open or not? Oh, to have this consciousness was to *think* – and to think, Brydon knew as he stood there, was, with the lapsing moments, not to have acted! Not to have acted – that was the misery and the pang – was even still not to act; was in fact all to feel the thing in another, in a new and terrible way. How long did he pause and how long did he debate? There was presently nothing to measure it; for his vibration had already changed – as just by the effect of its intensity. Shut up there, at bay, defiant, and with the prodigy of the thing palpably, provably *done* thus giving notice like some stark signboard – under that accession of accent the situation itself had turned; and Brydon at last remarkably made up his mind on what it had turned to.

It had turned altogether to a different admonition; to a supreme hint for him of the value of Discretion! This slowly-dawned, no doubt – for it could take its time; so perfectly, on his threshold, had he been stayed, so little, as yet, had he either advanced or retreated. It was the strangest of all things that now when, by his taking ten steps and applying his hand to a latch, or even his shoulder and his knee, if necessary, to a panel, all the hunger of his prime need might have been met, his high curiosity crowned, his unrest assuaged – it was amazing, but it was also exquisite and rare, that insistence should have, at a touch, quite dropped from him. Discretion – he jumped at that; and yet not, verily, at such a pitch, because it saved his nerves or his skin, but because, much more valuably, it saved the situation. When I say he "jumped" at it I feel the consonance of this term with the fact that – at the end indeed of I know not how long – he did move again, he crossed straight to the door. He wouldn't touch it – it seemed now that he might *if* he would: he would only just wait there a little to show, to prove that he wouldn't. He had thus another station close to the thin partition by which revelation was denied him; but with his eyes bent and his hands held off in a mere intensity of stillness. He listened as if there had been something to hear, but this attitude, while it lasted, was his own communication. "If you won't then – good: I spare you and I give up. You affect me as by the appeal, positively, for pity: you convince me that, for reasons rigid and sublime – what do I know? – we both of us should have suffered. I respect them then, and, though moved and privileged as, I believe, it has never been given to man, I retire, I renounce – and never, on my honour, to try again. So rest for ever – and let *me!*"

That, for Brydon, was the deep sense of this last demonstration – solemn, measured, directed as he felt it to be. He brought it to a close, he turned away; and now verily he knew how deeply he had been stirred. He retraced his steps, taking up his candle, burnt, he observed, well-nigh to the socket, and marking again, lighten it as he would, the distinctness of his footfall; after which he in a moment knew himself at the other side of the house. He did here what he had not yet done at these hours — he opened half a case-ment, one of those in the front, and let in the air of the night; a thing he would have taken at any time previous for a sharp rupture of his spell. His spell was broken now, and it didn't matter — broken by his concession and his surrender, which made it idle henceforth that he should ever come back. The empty street, with its other life so marked even by the great lamplit vacancy, was within call, within touch; he stayed there as to be in it again, high above it though he was still perched; he watched as for some comforting common fact, some vulgar human note, the passage of a scavenger or a thief, some night-bird however base. He would have blessed that sign of life; he would have welcomed, positively, the slow approach of his friend the policeman, whom he had hitherto only sought to avoid, and wasn't sure that if the patrol had come into sight he mightn't have felt the impulse to get into relation with it, to hail it on some pretext from his fourth floor.

The pretext that wouldn't have been too silly or too compromising, the explanation that would have saved his dignity and kept his name, in such a case, out of the papers, was not definite to him: he was so occupied with the thought of recording his Discre-tion — as an effect of the vow he had just uttered to his intimate adversary — that the im-portance of this loomed large and something had overtaken, all ironically, his sense of proportion. If there had been a ladder applied to the front of the house, even one of the vertiginous perpendiculars employed by painters and roofers and sometimes left stand-ing overnight, he would have managed somehow, astride of the window-sill, to compass by outstretched leg and arm that mode of descent. If there had been some such uncanny thing as he had found in his room at hotels, a workable fire-escape in the form of notched cable or canvas shoot,[13] he would have availed himself of it as a proof — well, of his pres-ent delicacy. He nursed that sentiment, as the question stood, a little in vain, and even — at the end of he scarce knew once more how long — found it, as by the action on his mind of the failure of response of the outer world, sinking back to vague anguish. It seemed to him he had waited an age for some stir of the great grim hush; the life of the town was itself under a spell — so unnaturally, up and down the whole prospect of known and rather ugly objects, the blankness and the silence lasted. Had they ever, he asked himself, the hard-faced houses which had begun to look livid in the dim dawn, had they ever spoken so little to any need of his spirit? Great builded voids, great crowded still-nesses put on often, in the heart of cities, for the small hours, a sort of sinister mask, and it was of this large collective negation that Brydon presently became conscious — all the more that the break of day was, almost incredibly, now at hand, proving to him what a night he had made of it.

He looked again at his watch, saw what had become of his time-values (he had taken hours for minutes — not, as in other tense situations, minutes for hours) and the strange air of the streets was but the weak, the sullen flush of a dawn in which everything was still locked up. His choked appeal from his own open window had been the sole note of

---

13. **notched cable or canvas shoot**: A cable with a braking device or a long chute made of canvas, devices allowing people to escape from the upper stories of a burning building.

life, and he could but break off at last as for a worse despair. Yet while so deeply demor-
alised he was capable again of an impulse denoting – at least by his present measure –
extraordinary resolution; of retracing his steps to the spot where he had turned cold
with the extinction of his last pulse of doubt as to there being in the place another presence than his own. This required an effort strong enough to sicken him; but he had his
reason, which over-mastered for the moment everything else. There was the whole of the
rest of the house to traverse, and how should he screw himself to that if the door he had
seen closed were at present open? He could hold to the idea that the closing had practically been for him an act of mercy, a chance offered him to descend, depart, get off the
ground and never again profane it. This conception held together, it worked; but what it
meant for him depended now clearly on the amount of forbearance his recent action, or
rather his recent inaction, had engendered. The image of the "presence," whatever it
was, waiting there for him to go – this image had not yet been so concrete for his nerves
as when he stopped short of the point at which certainty would have come to him. For
with all his resolution, or more exactly with all his dread, he did stop short – he hung
back from really seeing. The risk was too great and his fear too definite: it took at this
moment an awful specific form.

He knew – yes, as he had never known anything – that, *should* he see the door open it
would all too abjectly be the end of him. It would mean that the agent of his shame – his
shame being the deep abjection – was once more at large and in general possession;
and what glared him thus in the face was the act that this would determine for him. It
would send him straight about to the window he had left open, and by that window, be
the long ladder or the dangling rope as absent as it would, he saw himself uncontrollably, insanely, fatally take his way to the street. The hideous chance of this he at least
could avert; but he could only avert it by recoiling in time from assurance. He had the
whole house to traverse – this fact was still there; only he now knew that uncertainty
alone could start him. He stole back from where he had checked himself – merely to do
so was suddenly like safety – and, making blindly for the greater staircase, left gaping
rooms and sounding passages behind. Here was the top of the stairs, with a fine large
dim descent and three spacious landings to deal with. His instinct was all for mildness,
but his feet were harsh on the floors, and, strangely, when he had in a couple of minutes become aware of this, it counted somehow for help. He couldn't have spoken, the
tone of his voice would have scared him and the common conceit or resource of "whistling in the dark" (whether literally or figuratively) have appeared basely vulgar; yet he
liked none the less to hear himself go, and when he had reached his first landing – taking it all with no rush, but quite steadily – that stage of success drew from him a gasp
of relief.

The house withal seemed immense, the scale of space again inordinate; the open
rooms, to no one of which his eyes deflected, gloomed in their shuttered state like
mouths of caverns; only the high skylight that formed the crown of the deep well created
for him a medium in which he could advance but which might have been, for queerness
of colour, some watery under-world. He tried to think of something noble, as that his
property was really grand, a splendid possession; but this nobleness took the form too
of the clear delight with which he was finally to sacrifice it. They might come in now, the

builders, the destroyers—they might come as soon as they would. At the end of two flights he had dropped to another zone, and from the middle of the third, with only one more left, he recognised the influence of the lower windows, of half-drawn blinds, of the occasional gleam of street-lamps, of the glazed spaces of the vestibule. This was the bottom of the sea, which showed an illumination of its own and which he even saw paved—when at a given moment he drew up to sink a long look over the banisters—with the marble squares of his childhood. By that time, indubitably, he felt, as he might have said in a commoner caused better; it had allowed him to stop and take breath, and the case increased with the sight of the old black-and-white slabs. But what he most felt was that now surely, with the element of impunity moving him on as by hard firm hands, the case was settled for what he might have seen above had he dared that last look. The closed door, blessedly remote now, was still closed—and he had only in short to reach that of the house.

He came down further, he crossed the passage forming the access to the last flight; and if here again he stopped an instant it was almost for the sharpness of the thrill of assured escape. It made him shut his eyes—which opened again to the straight descent of the remainder of the stairs. Here was impunity still, but impunity almost excessive; inasmuch as the sidelights and the high fan-tracery[14] of the entrance were glimmering straight into the hall; an appearance produced, he the next instant saw, by the fact that the vestibule gaped wide, that the hinged halves of the inner door had been thrown far back. Out of that again the *question* sprang at him, making his eyes, as he felt, half start from his head as they had done at the top of the house before the sign of the other door. If he had left that one open hadn't he left this one closed, and wasn't he now in *most* immediate presence of some inconceivable occult activity? It was as sharp, the question, as a knife in his side, but the answer hung fire still and seemed to lose itself in the vague darkness to which the thin admitted dawn, glimmering archwise over the whole outer door, made a semicircular margin, a cold, silvery nimbus that seemed to play a little as he looked, to shift and expand and contract.

It was as if there had been something within it protected by indistinctness and corresponding in extent with the opaque surface behind, the painted panels of the last barrier to his escape, of which the key was in his pocket. The indistinctness mocked him even while he stared, affected him as somehow shrouding or challenging certitude, so that after faltering an instant on his step he let himself go with the sense that here *was* at last something to meet, to touch, to take, to know—something all unnatural and dreadful, but to advance upon which was the condition for him either of liberation or of supreme defeat. The penumbra,[15] dense and dark, was the virtual screen of a figure which stood in it as still as some image erect in a niche or as some black-vizored sentinel guarding a treasure. Brydon was to know afterwards, was to recall and make out, the particular thing he had believed during the rest of his descent. He saw, in its

---

14. **sidelights . . . fan-tracery:** Narrow vertical windows flanking the front door and the elaborate carving on the wooden vaulting over the entryway.
15. **penumbra:** A partially shaded area.

great grey glimmering margin, the central vagueness diminish, and he felt it to be taking the very form toward which for so many days the passion of his curiosity had yearned. It gloomed, it loomed, it was something, it was somebody, the prodigy of a personal presence.

Rigid and conscious, spectral yet human, a man of his own substance and stature waited there to measure himself with his power to dismay. This only could it be—this only till he recognised, with his advance, that what made the face dim was the pair of raised hands that covered it and in which, so far from being offered in defiance, it was buried as for dark deprecation. So Brydon, before him, took him in; with every fact of him now, in the higher light, hard and acute—his planted stillness, his vivid truth, his grizzled bent head and white masking hands, his queer actuality of evening-dress, of dangling double eyeglass, of gleaming silk lappet[16] and white linen, of pearl button and gold watchguard and polished shoe. No portrait by a great modern master could have presented him with more intensity, thrust him out of his frame with more art, as if there had been "treatment," of the consummate sort, in his every shade and salience. The revulsion, for our friend, had become, before he knew it, immense—this drop, in the act of apprehension, to the sense of his adversary's inscrutable manoeuvre. That meaning at least, while he gaped, it offered him; for he could but gape at his other self in this other anguish, gape as a proof that *he*, standing there for the achieved, the enjoyed, the triumphant life, couldn't be faced in his triumph. Wasn't the proof in the splendid covering hands, strong and completely spread?—so spread and so intentional that, in spite of a special verity that surpassed every other, the fact that one of these hands had lost two fingers, which were reduced to stumps, as if accidentally shot away, the face was effectually guarded and saved.

"Saved," though, *would* it be?—Brydon breathed his wonder till the very impunity of his attitude and the very insistence of his eyes produced, as he felt, a sudden stir which showed, the next instant, for a deeper portent, while the head raised itself, the betrayal of a braver purpose. The hands, as he looked, began to move, to open; then, as if deciding in a flash, dropped from the face and left it uncovered and presented. Horror, with the sight, had leaped into Brydon's throat, gasping there in a sound he couldn't utter; for the bared identity was too hideous as *his*, and his glare was the passion of his protest. The face, *that* face, Spencer Brydon's?—he searched it still, but looking away from it in dismay and denial, falling straight from his height of sublimity. It was unknown, inconceivable, awful, disconnected from any possibility——! He had been "sold," he inwardly moaned, stalking such game as this: the presence before him was a presence, the horror within him was a horror, but the waste of his nights had been only grotesque and the success of his adventure an irony. Such an identity fitted his at *no* point, made its alternative monstrous. A thousand times yes, as it came upon him nearer now—the face was the face of a stranger. It came upon him nearer now, quite as one of those expanding fantastic images projected by the magic-lantern of childhood; for the stranger, whoever he might be, evil, odious, blatant, vulgar, had advanced as for

---

16. **lappet:** A decorative flap or lapel.

aggression, and he knew himself give ground. Then harder pressed still, sick with the force of his shock and falling back as under the hot breath and the roused passion of a life larger than his own, a rage of personality before which his own collapsed, he felt the whole vision turn to darkness and his very feet give way. His head went round; he was going; he had gone.

III

What had next brought him back, clearly – though after how long? – was Mrs. Muldoody's voice, coming to him from quite near, from so near that he seemed presently to see her as kneeling on the ground before him while he lay looking up at her; himself not wholly on the ground, but half raised and upheld – conscious, yes, of tenderness of support and more particularly of a head pillowed in extraordinary softness and faintly refreshing fragrance. He considered, he wondered, his wit but half at his service; then another face intervened, bending more directly over him, and he finally knew that Alice Staverton had made her lap an ample and perfect cushion to him, and that she had to this end seated herself on the lowest degree of the staircase, the rest of his long person remaining stretched on his old black and white slabs. They were cold, these marble squares of his youth; but *he* somehow was not, in this rich return of consciousness – the most wonderful hour, little by little, that he had ever known, leaving him, as it did, so gratefully, so abysmally passive, and yet as with a treasure of intelligence waiting, all round him, for quiet appropriation; dissolved, he might call it, in the air of the place and producing the golden glow of a late autumn afternoon. He had come back, yes – come back from further away than any man but himself had ever travelled; yet it was strange how, with this sense, what he had come back *to* seemed really the great thing, and as if his prodigious journey had been all for the sake of it. Slowly and surely his consciousness grew, his vision of his state thus completing itself: he had been miraculously *carried* back – lifted and carefully borne as from where he had been picked up, the uttermost end of an interminable grey passage. Even with this he had been suffered to rest, and what had now brought him to knowledge was the break in the long, mild motion.

It had brought him to knowledge, to knowledge – yes, this was the beauty of his state; which came to resemble more and more that of a man who, going to sleep on some news of a great inheritance, has then, after dreaming it away, after profaning it with matters strange to it, waked up again to full serenity of certitude and has only to lie and see it shine. This was the drift of his patience – that he had only to let it shine steadily. He must moreover, with intermissions, still have been lifted and borne; since why and how else should he have known himself, later on, with the afternoon glow intenser, no longer at the foot of his stairs – situated as these now seemed at that dark other end of his tunnel – but on a deep window-bench of his high saloon, over which had been spread, couch-fashion, a mantle of soft stuff lined with grey fur that was familiar to his eyes and that one of his hands kept fondly feeling as if for its pledge of truth. Mrs. Muldoody's face had gone, but the other, the second he had recognised, hung over him in a way that showed how he was still propped and pillowed. He took it all in, and the more he took it in the more it seemed to suffice: he was as much at peace as if he had had food and drink. It was the two women who had found him, on Mrs. Muldoody's having plied, at her usual hour, her latch-key—and on her having above all arrived while Miss Staverton still lingered near the house. She had been turning away, all anxiety, from worrying the vain bell-handle—her calculation having been of the hour of the good woman's visit; but the latter, blessedly, had come up in time not to miss her, and they had entered together. He had then lain, beyond the vestibule, very much as he was lying now—quite, that is, as he appeared to have fallen, but all so wondrously without bruise or gash; only in a depth of stupor. What he most took in, however, at present, with the steadier clearance, was that Alice Staverton had, for a long unspeakable moment, not doubted he was dead.

"It must have been that I *was*." He made it out as she held him. "Yes—I can only have died. You brought me literally to life. Only," he wondered, his eyes rising to her, "only, in the name of all the benedictions, how?"

It took her but an instant to bend her face and kiss him, and something in the manner of it, and in the way her hands clasped and locked his head while he felt the cool charity and virtue of her lips, something in all this beatitude somehow answered everything. "And now I keep you," she said.

Oh keep me, keep me!" he pleaded while her face still hung over him; in response to which it dropped again and stayed close, clingingly close. It was the seal of their situation—of which he tasted the impress for a long blissful moment in silence. But he came back. "Yet how did you know ——?"

"I was uneasy. You were to have come, you remember—and you had sent no word."

"Yes, I remember—I was to have gone to you at one to-day." It caught on to their "old" life and relation—which were so near and so far. "I was still out there in my strange darkness—where was it, what was it? I must have stayed there so long." He could but wonder at the depth and the duration of his swoon.

"Since last night?" she asked with a shade of fear for her possible indiscretion.

"Since this morning—it must have been: the cold dim dawn of to-day. Where have I been," he vaguely wailed, "where have I been?" He felt her hold him close, and it was as if this helped him now to make in all security his mild moan. "What a long dark day!"

All in her tenderness she had waited a moment. "In the cold dim dawn?" she quavered.

But he had already gone on, piecing together the parts of the whole prodigy. "As I didn't turn up, you came straight ——?"

She barely hesitated. "I went first to your hotel—where they told me of your absence. You had dined out last evening and had not been back since. But they appeared to know you had been at your club."

"So you had the idea of *this* ——?"

"Of what?" she asked in a moment.

"Well—of what has happened."

"I believed at least you'd have been here. I've known, all along," she said, "that you've been coming."

"'Known' it —— ?"

"Well, I've believed it. I said nothing to you after that talk we had a month ago – but I felt sure. I knew you *would,*" she declared.

"That I would persist, you mean?"

"That you'd see him."

"Ah, but I didn't!" cried Brydon with his long wail. "There's somebody – an awful beast; whom I brought, too horribly, to bay. But it's not me."

At this she bent over him again, and her eyes were in his eyes. "No – it's not you." And it was as if, while her face hovered, he might have made out in it, had it not been so near, some particular meaning blurred by a smile. "No, thank heaven," she repeated – "it's not you! Of course it wasn't to have been."

"Ah, but it *was,*" he gently insisted. And he stared before him now as he had been staring for so many weeks. "I was to have known myself."

"You couldn't!" she returned consolingly. And then reverting, and as if to account further for what she had herself done, "But it wasn't only *that,* that you hadn't been at home," she went on. "I waited till the hour at which we had found Mrs. Muldoody that day of your bringing me; and she arrived, as I've told you, while, failing to bring any one to the door, I waited, in my despair, on the steps. After a little, if she hadn't come by such a mercy, I should have found means to hunt her up. But it wasn't," said Alice Staverton, as if once more with her fine intention – "it wasn't only that."

His eyes, as he lay, turned back to her. "What more then?"

She met it, the wonder she had stirred. "In the cold dim dawn, you say? Well, in the cold dim dawn of this morning I too saw you."

"Saw *me* —— ?"

"Saw *him,*" said Alice Staverton. "It must have been at the same moment."

He lay an instant taking it in – as if he wished to be quite reasonable. "At the same moment?"

"Yes – in my dream again, the same one I've named to you. He came back to me. Then I knew it for a sign. He had come to you."

At this Brydon raised himself; he had to see her better. She helped him when she understood his movement, and he sat up, steadying himself beside her there on the window-bench and with his right hand grasping her left. "He didn't come to me."

"You came to yourself," she beautifully smiled.

"Ah, I've come to myself now – thanks to you, dearest. But this brute, with his awful face – this brute's a black stranger. He's none of *me,* even as I *might* have been," Brydon sturdily contended.

But she kept her clearness. "Isn't the whole point that you'd have been different?"

He almost scowled for it. "As different as *that?* —— ?"

Her lucid look seemed to bathe him. "Haven't you exactly wanted to know *how* different? So this morning," she said, "you appeared to me."

"Like *him?*"

"A black stranger!"

"Then how did you know it was I?"

"Because, as I told you weeks ago, my mind, my imagination, had worked so over what you might, what you mightn't have been – to show you, you see, how I've thought of you. In the midst of that you came to me – that my wonder might be answered. So I knew," she went on; "and believed that, since the question held you too so fast, as you told me that day, you too would see for yourself. And when this morning I again saw I knew it would be because you had – and also then, from the first moment, because you somehow wanted me. *He* seemed to tell me of that. So why," she strangely smiled, "shouldn't I like him?"

It brought Spencer Brydon to his feet. "You 'like' that horror ——?"

"I *could* have liked him. And to me," she said, "he was no horror. I had accepted him."

" 'Accepted' ——?" Brydon oddly sounded.

"Before, for the interest of his difference – yes. And as I didn't disown him, as I knew him – which you at last, confronted with him in his difference, so cruelly didn't, my dear – well, he must have been, you see, less dreadful to me. And it may have pleased him that I pitied him."

She was beside him on her feet, but still holding his hand – still with her arm supporting him. Yet though it all brought for him thus a dim light, "You 'pitied' him?" he grudgingly, resentfully asked.

"He has been unhappy, he has been ravaged," she said.

"And haven't I been unhappy? Am not I – you've only to look at me! – ravaged?"

"Ah I don't say I like him *better*," she granted after a thought. "But he's grim, he's worn – and things have happened to him. He doesn't make shift, for sight, with your charming monocle."

"No" – it struck Brydon: "I couldn't have sported mine 'down town.' They'd have guyed me there."[17]

"His great convex pince-nez[18] – I saw it, I recognised the kind – is for his poor ruined sight. And his poor right hand!"

"Aie!" Brydon winced – whether for his proved identity or for his lost fingers. Then "He has a million a year," he lucidly added. "But he hasn't you."

"And he isn't – no, he isn't – *you!*" she murmured as he drew her to his breast.

[1908]

---

17. **"They'd have guyed me there"**: That is, they would have made a joke of him for wearing his monocle, a corrective lens worn over one eye that was associated with wealthy, upper-class men.
18. **pince-nez**: Spectacles without earpieces that were supported by pinching the bridge of the nose.

Sarah Orne Jewett

[1849-1909]

Sarah Orne Jewett was born on September 3, 1849, the second of the three daughters of Caroline Perry Jewett and Theodore H. Jewett, an obstetrician and country doctor in South Berwick, Maine. The affluent family had deep roots in New England, where Jewett's paternal ancestors had arrived in 1638, part of the great Puritan migration from England. Although she later traveled extensively, Jewett always considered home to be her family's large house in the center of South Berwick, an old river town near the seacoast in southern Maine. "My local attachments are stronger than any cat's that ever meowed," she once quipped. She was educated there at Miss Raynes School and then at the Berwick Academy, from which Jewett graduated in 1865. Encouraged by her parents, Jewett read widely in English, Continental, and American literature, apparently determined from an early age to become a writer. Her first published story, "Jenny Garrow's Lovers," appeared under the pen name "A. C. Eliot" in the *Flag of Our Union*, a weekly magazine, in January 1868. Later that year, she also published a poem in a magazine for children, *Our Young Folks*.

Jewett herself dated the beginning of her career as a writer with the publication of a story in the *Atlantic Monthly*, the most respected literary journal of the day, in December 1869. She had earlier submitted two stories to the journal, both of which were rejected. Undaunted, and responding to some encouragement from the young assistant editor of the *Atlantic*, William Dean Howells, she submitted another story, "Mr. Bruce." To her great delight, it was accepted. "I came as near being utterly satisfied & happy as I can," Jewett wrote in her diary. Although she continued to write poems and stories for children, many of which were published in the *Riverside Magazine for Young People*, Jewett increasingly turned her attention to writing for adults. She became friendly with Howells, who assumed the editorship of the *Atlantic* in 1871. He recognized Jewett's talent and pressed her to develop the plots of her stories. "I don't believe I could write a long story as he suggested," Jewett responded in a letter to another of her editors in 1873. "In the first place I have no dramatic talent. The story would have no plot. I should have to fill it out with descriptions of character and meditations. It seems to me I can furnish the theatre, and show you the actors, and the scenery, and the audience, but there is never any play!" Jewett finally won her point with Howells, who published her nearly plotless sketch "The Shore House" in the *Atlantic* in 1873. It was the first of a series of sketches Jewett later collected and connected within a fictional framework in her first book, *Deephaven* (1877), a novel about a young woman's summer in a coastal village in New England.

Through her growing mastery of what was called "local-color" writing, Jewett became one of the most respected authors in the United States. Following the success of *Deephaven*, she became a regular contributor to the *Atlantic* and other prominent periodicals, in which Jewett first published many of the sketches and stories collected in *Old Friends and*

New (1879) and *Country By-Ways* (1881). She also came to know writers and leaders of the literary establishment in Boston, including the editor and publisher James T. Fields and his wife, Annie Fields, a literary force in her own right. After Annie Fields's husband died in 1881, she became Jewett's lifelong companion in what was then called a "Boston marriage," a term for a marriage-like relationship between two women who lived together independent of male support. The pair traveled throughout Europe, and they associated with a wide range of celebrated writers, including Howells, Henry James, Mark Twain, Louisa May Alcott, Mary E. Wilkins Freeman, and Harriet Beecher Stowe, whom Jewett called "the mother of us all." Stowe's earlier novels about village life in New England strongly influenced Jewett, who explored similar terrain in two of her own novels: *A Country Doctor* (1884), about a young woman who chooses to attend medical school rather than to marry, and *A Marsh Island* (1885). She was best known for her numerous collections of shorter works, notably *A White Heron and Other Stories* (1886) and *The Country of the Pointed Firs* (1896), a series of related sketches set in Dunnet Landing, a fishing village in Maine. At the height of her fame, Jewett sustained serious injuries in a carriage accident in 1902. She never fully recovered, and Jewett wrote only a handful of additional works before she died at her home in Maine in 1909. During the last years of her life, however, she met and mentored Willa Cather, who dedicated her novel *O Pioneers!* (1913) to the memory of Jewett, "in whose beautiful and delicate work there is perfection that endures."

It is that kind of honesty, that earnest endeavor to tell truly the thing that haunts the mind, that I love in Miss Jewett's own work.

—Willa Cather

Reading Jewett's "A White Heron."
In a letter written in early 1886 to her companion, Annie Fields, Jewett expressed concern about the reception of a story she had recently completed:

> Mr. Howells thinks that this age frowns upon the romantic, that it is no use to write romance any more; but dear me, how much of it there is left in everyday life after all. It must be the fault of the writers that such writing is dull, but what shall I do with my 'White heron' now she is written? She isn't a very good magazine story, but I love her, and I mean to keep her for the beginning of my next book.

Imagining the response of William Dean Howells, a champion of realism who had published many of her works in the *Atlantic Monthly*, Jewett decided that "A White Heron" was too "romantic" to please editors and readers of magazines. True to the story she loved, however, Jewett placed it at the opening of a collection she published later that year, *A White Heron and Other Stories*. An anonymous reviewer for the *Overland Monthly* praised the beauty and simplicity of all the stories in the collection, observing that the title story was

bedfordstmartins.com/ americanlit *for research links on Jewett*

> perfect in its way — a tiny classic. One little episode of child life, among birds and woods, makes it up; and the secret soul of a child, the appeal of the bird to its instinctive honor and tenderness, never were interpreted with more beauty and insight.

Indeed, the story that Jewett did not venture to submit to magazines became her best-known and most frequently anthologized work. The text is taken from the first printing in *A White Heron and Other Stories* (1886).

A WHITE HERON

I

The woods were already filled with shadows one June evening, just before eight o'clock, though a bright sunset still glimmered faintly among the trunks of the trees. A little girl was driving home her cow, a plodding, dilatory, provoking creature in her behavior, but a valued companion for all that. They were going away from whatever light there was, and striking deep into the woods, but their feet were familiar with the path, and it was no matter whether their eyes could see it or not.

There was hardly a night the summer through when the old cow could be found waiting at the pasture bars; on the contrary, it was her greatest pleasure to hide herself away among the huckleberry bushes, and though she wore a loud bell she had made the discovery that if one stood perfectly still it would not ring. So Sylvia had to hunt for her until she found her, and call Co'! Co'! with never an answering Moo, until her childish patience was quite spent. If the creature had not given good milk and plenty of it, the case would have seemed very different to her owners. Besides, Sylvia had all the time there was, and very little use to make of it. Sometimes in pleasant weather it was a consolation to look upon the cow's pranks as an intelligent attempt to play hide and seek, and as the child had no playmates she lent herself to this amusement with a good deal of zest. Though this chase had been so long that the wary animal herself had given an unusual signal of her whereabouts, Sylvia had only laughed when she came upon Mistress Moolly at the swampside, and urged her affectionately homeward with a twig of birch leaves. The old cow was not inclined to wander farther, she even turned in the right direction for once as they left the pasture, and stepped along the road at a good pace. She was quite ready to be milked now, and seldom stopped to browse. Sylvia wondered what her grandmother would say because they were so late. It was a great while since she had left home at half-past five o'clock, but everybody knew the difficulty of making this errand a short one. Mrs. Tilley had chased the hornéd torment too many summer evenings herself to blame any one else for lingering, and was only thankful as she waited that she had Sylvia, nowadays, to give such valuable assistance. The good woman suspected that Sylvia loitered occasionally on her own account; there never was such a child for straying about out-of-doors since the world was made! Everybody said that it was a good change for a little maid who had tried to grow for eight years in a crowded manufacturing town, but, as for Sylvia herself, it seemed as if she never had been alive at all before she came to live at the farm. She thought often with wistful compassion of a wretched geranium that belonged to a town neighbor.

" 'Afraid of folks,' " old Mrs. Tilley said to herself, with a smile, after she had made the unlikely choice of Sylvia from her daughter's houseful of children, and was returning to the farm. "'Afraid of folks,' they said! I guess she won't be troubled no great with 'em up to the old place!" When they reached the door of the lonely house and stopped to unlock it, and the cat came to purr loudly, and rub against them, a deserted pussy, indeed, but fat with young robins, Sylvia whispered that this was a beautiful place to live in, and she never should wish to go home.

The companions followed the shady wood-road, the cow taking slow steps and the child very fast ones. The cow stopped long at the brook to drink, as if the pasture were not half a swamp, and Sylvia stood still and waited, letting her bare feet cool themselves in the shoal water, while the great twilight moths struck softly against her. She waded on through the brook as the cow moved away, and listened to the thrushes with a heart that beat fast with pleasure. There was a stirring in the great boughs overhead. They were full of little birds and beasts that seemed to be wide awake, and going about their world, or else saying good-night to each other in sleepy twitters. Sylvia herself felt sleepy as she walked along. However, it was not much farther to the house, and the air was soft and sweet. She was not often in the woods so late as this, and it made her feel as if she were a part of the gray shadows and the moving leaves. She was just thinking how long it seemed since she first came to the farm a year ago, and wondering if everything went on in the noisy town just the same as when she was there; the thought of the great red-faced boy who used to chase and frighten her made her hurry along the path to escape from the shadow of the trees.

Suddenly this little woods-girl is horror-stricken to hear a clear whistle not very far away. Not a bird's-whistle, which would have a sort of friendliness, but a boy's whistle, determined, and somewhat aggressive. Sylvia left the cow to whatever sad fate might await her, and stepped discreetly aside into the bushes, but she was just too late. The enemy had discovered her, and called out in a very cheerful and persuasive tone, "Halloa, little girl, how far is it to the road?" and trembling Sylvia answered almost inaudibly, "A good ways."

She did not dare to look boldly at the tall young man, who carried a gun over his shoulder, but she came out of her bush and again followed the cow, while he walked alongside.

"I have been hunting for some birds," the stranger said kindly, "and I have lost my way, and need a friend very much. Don't be afraid," he added gallantly. "Speak up and tell me what your name is, and whether you think I can spend the night at your house, and go out gunning early in the morning."

Sylvia was more alarmed than before. Would not her grandmother consider her much to blame? But who could have foreseen such an accident as this? It did not seem to be her fault, and she hung her head as if the stem of it were broken, but managed to answer "Sylvy," with much effort when her companion again asked her name.

Mrs. Tilley was standing in the doorway when the trio came into view. The cow gave a loud moo by way of explanation.

"Yes, you'd better speak up for yourself, you old trial! Where'd she tucked herself away this time, Sylvy?" But Sylvia kept an awed silence; she knew by instinct that her grandmother did not comprehend the gravity of the situation. She must be mistaking the stranger for one of the farmer-lads of the region.

The young man stood his gun beside the door, and dropped a lumpy game-bag beside it; then he bade Mrs. Tilley good-evening, and repeated his wayfarer's story, and asked if he could have a night's lodging.

"Put me anywhere you like," he said. "I must be off early in the morning, before day; but I am very hungry, indeed. You can give me some milk at any rate, that's plain."

"Dear sakes, yes," responded the hostess, whose long slumbering hospitality seemed to be easily awakened. "You might fare better if you went out to the main road a mile or so, but you're welcome to what we've got. I'll milk right off, and you make yourself at home. You can sleep on husks or feathers," she proffered graciously. "I raised them all myself. There's good pasturing for geese just below here towards the ma'sh. Now step round and set a plate for the gentleman, Sylvy!" And Sylvia promptly stepped. She was glad to have something to do, and she was hungry herself.

It was a surprise to find so clean and comfortable a little dwelling in this New England wilderness. The young man had known the horrors of its most primitive housekeeping, and the dreary squalor of that level of society which does not rebel at the companionship of hens. This was the best thrift of an old-fashioned farmstead, though on such a small scale that it seemed like a hermitage. He listened eagerly to the old woman's quaint talk, he watched Sylvia's pale face and shining gray eyes with ever growing enthusiasm, and insisted that this was the best supper he had eaten for a month, and afterward the new-made friends sat down in the door-way together while the moon came up.

Soon it would be berry-time, and Sylvia was a great help at picking. The cow was a good milker, though a plaguy thing to keep track of, the hostess gossiped frankly, adding presently that she had buried four children, so Sylvia's mother, and a son (who might be dead) in California were all the children she had left. "Dan, my boy, was a great hand to go gunning," she explained sadly. "I never wanted for pa'tridges or gray squer'ls while he was to home. He's been a great wand'rer, I expect, and he's no hand to write letters. There, I don't blame him, I'd ha' seen the world myself if it had been so I could."

"Sylvy takes after him," the grandmother continued affectionately, after a minute's pause. "There ain't a foot o' ground she don't know her way over, and the wild creaturs counts her one o' themselves. Squer'ls she'll tame to come an' feed right out o' her hands, and all sorts o' birds. Last winter she got the jay-birds to bangeing[1] here, and I believe she'd 'a' scanted herself of her own meals to have plenty to throw out amongst 'em, if I hadn't kep' watch. Anything but crows, I tell her, I'm willin' to help support – though Dan he had a tamed one o' them that did seem to have reason same as folks. It was round here a good spell after he went away. Dan an' his father they didn't hitch, – but he never held up his head ag'in after Dan had dared him an' gone off."

The guest did not notice this hint of family sorrows in his eager interest in something else.

"So Sylvy knows all about birds, does she?" he exclaimed, as he looked round at the little girl who sat, very demure but increasingly sleepy, in the moonlight. "I am making a collection of birds myself. I have been at it ever since I was a boy." (Mrs. Tilley smiled.)

---

1. **bangeing:** Maine dialect word for hanging about.

"There are two or three very rare ones I have been hunting for these five years. I mean to get them on my own ground if they can be found."

"Do you cage 'em up?" asked Mrs. Tilley doubtfully, in response to this enthusiastic announcement.

"Oh no, they're stuffed and preserved, dozens and dozens of them," said the ornithologist, "and I have shot or snared every one myself. I caught a glimpse of a white heron a few miles from here on Saturday, and I have followed it in this direction. They have never been found in this district at all. The little white heron, it is," and he turned again to look at Sylvia with the hope of discovering that the rare bird was one of her acquaintances.

But Sylvia was watching a hop-toad in the narrow footpath.

"You would know the heron if you saw it," the stranger continued eagerly. "A queer tall white bird with soft feathers and long thin legs. And it would have a nest perhaps in the top of a high tree, made of sticks, something like a hawk's nest."

Sylvia's heart gave a wild beat; she knew that strange white bird, and had once stolen softly near where it stood in some bright green swamp grass, away over at the other side of the woods. There was an open place where the sunshine always seemed strangely yellow and hot, where tall, nodding rushes grew, and her grandmother had warned her that she might sink in the soft black mud underneath and never be heard of more. Not far beyond were the salt marshes just this side the sea itself, which Sylvia wondered and dreamed much about, but never had seen, whose great voice could sometimes be heard above the noise of the woods on stormy nights.

"I can't think of anything I should like so much as to find that heron's nest," the handsome stranger was saying. "I would give ten dollars to anybody who could show it to me," he added desperately, "and I mean to spend my whole vacation hunting for it if need be. Perhaps it was only migrating, or had been chased out of its own region by some bird of prey."

Mrs. Tilley gave amazed attention to all this, but Sylvia still watched the toad, not divining, as she might have done at some calmer time, that the creature wished to get to its hole under the door-step, and was much hindered by the unusual spectators at that hour of the evening. No amount of thought, that night, could decide how many wished-for treasures the ten dollars, so lightly spoken of, would buy.

The next day the young sportsman hovered about the woods, and Sylvia kept him company, having lost her first fear of the friendly lad, who proved to be most kind and sympathetic. He told her many things about the birds and what they knew and where they lived and what they did with themselves. And he gave her a jack-knife, which she thought as great a treasure as if she were a desert-islander. All day long he did not once make her troubled or afraid except when he brought down some unsuspecting singing creature from its bough. Sylvia would have liked him vastly better without his gun; she could not understand why he killed the very birds he seemed to like so much. But as the day waned, Sylvia still watched the young man with loving admiration. She had never seen anybody so charming and delightful; the woman's heart, asleep in the child, was vaguely thrilled by a dream of love. Some premonition of that great power stirred and swayed these young creatures who traversed the solemn woodlands with soft-footed silent care. They stopped to listen to a bird's song; they pressed forward again eagerly, parting the branches – speaking to each other rarely and in whispers; the young man going first and Sylvia following, fascinated, a few steps behind, with her gray eyes dark with excitement.

She grieved because the longed-for white heron was elusive, but she did not lead the guest, she only followed, and there was no such thing as speaking first. The sound of her own unquestioned voice would have terrified her – it was hard enough to answer yes or no when there was need of that. At last evening began to fall, and they drove the cow home together, and Sylvia smiled with pleasure when they came to the place where she heard the whistle and was afraid only the night before.

II

Half a mile from home, at the farther edge of the woods, where the land was highest, a great pine-tree stood, the last of its generation. Whether it was left for a boundary mark, or for what reason, no one could say; the wood-choppers who had felled its mates were dead and gone long ago, and a whole forest of sturdy trees, pines and oaks and maples, had grown again. But the stately head of this old pine towered above them all and made a landmark for sea and shore miles and miles away. Sylvia knew it well. She had always believed that whoever climbed to the top of it could see the ocean; and the little girl had often laid her hand on the great rough trunk and looked up wistfully at those dark boughs that the wind always stirred, no matter how hot and still the air might be below. Now she thought of the tree with a new excitement, for why, if one climbed it at break of day could not one see all the world, and easily discover from whence the white heron flew, and mark the place, and find the hidden nest?

What a spirit of adventure, what wild ambition! What fancied triumph and delight and glory for the later morning when she could make known the secret! It was almost too real and too great for the childish heart to bear.

All night the door of the little house stood open and the whippoorwills came and sang upon the very step. The young sportsman and his old hostess were sound asleep, but Sylvia's great design kept her broad awake and watching. She forgot to think of sleep. The short summer night seemed as long as the winter darkness, and at last when the whippoorwills ceased, and she was afraid the morning would after all come too soon, she stole out of the house and followed the pasture path through the woods, hastening toward the open ground beyond, listening with a sense of comfort and companionship to the drowsy twitter of a half-awakened bird, whose perch she had jarred in passing. Alas, if the great wave of human interest which flooded for the first time this dull little life should sweep away the satisfactions of an existence heart to heart with nature and the dumb life of the forest!

There was the huge tree asleep yet in the paling moonlight, and small and silly Sylvia began with utmost bravery to mount to the top of it, with tingling, eager blood coursing the channels of her whole frame, with her bare feet and fingers, that pinched and held like bird's claws to the monstrous ladder reaching up, up, almost to the sky itself. First she must mount the white oak tree that grew alongside, where she was almost lost among the dark branches and the green leaves heavy and wet with dew; a bird fluttered off its nest, and a red squirrel ran to and fro and scolded pettishly at the harmless house-breaker. Sylvia felt her way easily. She had often climbed there, and knew that higher still one of the oak's upper branches chafed against the pine trunk, just where its lower boughs were set close together. There, when she made the dangerous pass from one tree to the other, the great enterprise would really begin.

She crept out along the swaying oak limb at last, and took the daring step across into the old pine-tree. The way was harder than she thought; she must reach far and hold fast, the sharp dry twigs caught and held her and scratched her like angry talons, the pitch made her thin little fingers clumsy and stiff as she went round and round the tree's great stem, higher and higher upward. The sparrows and robins in the woods below were beginning to wake and twitter to the dawn, yet it seemed much lighter there aloft in the pine-tree, and the child knew she must hurry if her project were to be of any use.

The tree seemed to lengthen itself out as she went up, and to reach farther and far-ther upward. It was like a great main-mast to the voyaging earth; it must truly have been amazed that morning through all its ponderous frame as it felt this determined spark of human spirit wending its way from higher branch to branch. Who knows how steadily the least twigs held themselves to advantage this light, weak creature on her way! The old pine must have loved his new dependent. More than all the hawks, and bats, and moths, and even the sweet voiced thrushes, was the brave, beating heart of the solitary gray-eyed child. And the tree stood still and frowned away the winds that June morning while the dawn grew bright in the east.

Sylvia's face was like a pale star, if one had seen it from the ground, when the last thorny bough was past, and she stood trembling and tired but wholly triumphant, high in the tree-top. Yes, there was the sea with the dawning sun making a golden dazzle over it, and toward that glorious east flew two hawks with slow-moving pinions. How low they looked in the air from that height when one had only seen them before far up, and dark against the blue sky. Their gray feathers were as soft as moths; they seemed only a little way from the tree, and Sylvia felt as if she too could go flying away among the clouds. Westward, the woodlands and farms reached miles and miles into the distance; here and there were church steeples, and white villages, truly it was a vast and awe-some world!

The birds sang louder and louder. At last the sun came up bewilderingly bright. Sylvia could see the white sails of ships out at sea, and the clouds that were purple and rose-colored and yellow at first began to fade away. Where was the white heron's nest in the sea of green branches, and was this wonderful sight and pageant of the world the only reward for having climbed to such a giddy height? Now look down again, Sylvia, where the green marsh is set among the shining birches and dark hem-locks; there where you saw the white heron once you will see him again; look, look! a white spot of him like a single floating feather comes up from the dead hemlock and grows larger, and rises, and comes close at last, and goes by the landmark pine with steady sweep of wing and outstretched slender neck and crested head. And wait! wait! do not move a foot or a finger, little girl, do not send an arrow of light and consciousness from your two eager eyes, for the heron has perched on a pine bough not far beyond yours, and cries back to his mate on the nest and plumes his feathers for the new day!

The child gives a long sigh a minute later when a company of shouting cat-birds comes also to the tree, and vexed by their fluttering and lawlessness the solemn heron goes away. She knows his secret now, the wild, light, slender bird that floats and wavers, and goes back like an arrow presently to his home in the green world beneath. Then Sylvia, well satisfied, makes her perilous way down again, not daring to look far below the branch she stands on, ready to cry sometimes because her fingers ache and her lamed feet slip. Wondering over and over again what the stranger would say to her, and what he would think when she told him how to find his way straight to the heron's nest.

"Sylvy, Sylvy!" called the busy old grandmother again and again, but nobody answered, and the small husk bed was empty and Sylvia had disappeared.

The guest waked from a dream, and remembering his day's pleasure hurried to dress himself that might it sooner begin. He was sure from the way the shy little girl looked once or twice yesterday that she had at least seen the white heron, and now she must really be made to tell. Here she comes now, paler than ever, and her worn old frock is torn and tattered, and smeared with pine pitch. The grandmother and the sportsman stand in the door together and question her, and the splendid moment has come to speak of the dead hemlock-tree by the green marsh.

But Sylvia does not speak after all, though the old grandmother fretfully rebukes her, and the young man's kind, appealing eyes are looking straight in her own. He can make them rich with money; he has promised it, and they are poor now. He is so well worth making happy, and he waits to hear the story she can tell.

No, she must keep silence! What is it that suddenly forbids her and makes her dumb? Has she been nine years growing and now, when the great world for the first time puts out a hand to her, must she thrust it aside for a bird's sake? The murmur of the pine's green branches is in her ears, she remembers how the white heron came flying through the golden air and how they watched the sea and the morning together, and Sylvia cannot speak; she cannot tell the heron's secret and give its life away.

Dear loyalty, that suffered a sharp pang as the guest went away disappointed later in the day, that could have served and followed him and loved him as a dog loves! Many a night Sylvia heard the echo of his whistle haunting the pasture path as she came home with the loitering cow. She forgot even her sorrow at the sharp report of his gun and the sight of thrushes and sparrows dropping silent to the ground, their songs hushed and their pretty feathers stained and wet with blood. Were the birds better friends than their hunter might have been—who can tell? Whatever treasures were lost to her, woodlands and summer-time, remember! Bring your gifts and graces and tell your secrets to this lonely country child!

[1886]

Kate Chopin

[1850–1904]

Kate Chopin was born Katherine O'Flaherty on February 8, 1850, in St. Louis, Missouri. Her parents were Thomas O'Flaherty, an Irish immigrant who had become a prosperous merchant, and his second wife, Eliza Faris, a Creole, the term then widely used for aristocratic descendants of the early French settlers of Louisiana and the Gulf Coast of the United States. Chopin grew up in comfortable circumstances and attended a Catholic girls' school, the Academy of the Sacred Heart. But her early years were shadowed by the death of her father in a railroad accident in 1855 and the loss of her half-brother, who died of typhoid fever while serving as a Confederate soldier in the Civil War. After she graduated from high school in 1868, Chopin began her life as a fashionable young debutante in St. Louis, though in her diary she privately complained that "parties, operas, concerts, skating and amusements ad infinitum have so taken up all my time that my dear reading and writing that I love so well have suffered much neglect." During this time, she wrote her first-known story, a brief account of an unspecified animal that escapes from a cage into the larger world, which Chopin suggestively entitled "Emancipation: A Life Fable."

Kate Chopin

This photograph was taken while Chopin was living in Louisiana, the setting of much of her later fiction about life among the Creoles.

The story was never published, however, and Chopin did not embark on a literary career for nearly twenty years. She soon met and married Oscar Chopin, the son of plantation owners in Natchitoches Parish, Louisiana, who was studying banking in St. Louis. In 1870, the couple settled in New Orleans, where Oscar became a successful cotton broker. Although Chopin wrote a lively account of their honeymoon in Europe, she had little time for writing in her role of wife and mother to the six children she bore during the next eight years. Following serious financial reverses, the family moved to the small town of Cloutierville, Louisiana, where Oscar Chopin died suddenly of malaria in December 1882. By all accounts, the couple's marriage had been a happy one, and Chopin was grief stricken. Returning to St. Louis in 1884, she and her children lived with her mother, whose death the following year was another blow to Chopin. To supplement her now diminished income, to deal with grief and loneliness, and to satisfy friends who encouraged her to pursue her literary interests, Chopin finally began to write seriously during 1888. She published her first work, a short poem "If It Might Be," in a well-regarded Chicago magazine, *America*, in January 1889. The poem was followed by her first published story—"A Point at Issue!"—which appeared in the St. Louis *Post-Dispatch* in October 1889. In it, Chopin developed a theme that would become increasingly central to her writing, that of a woman torn between the demands of marriage and the desire to maintain her freedom and autonomy.

Chopin soon began to draw upon a vital source for her fiction, her fourteen years in Louisiana. In her first novel, written during 1889-90, she told the story of a young Creole widow who manages a Louisiana plantation inherited from her husband. When a publisher rejected the novel, whose plot involves alcoholism and divorce, Chopin published it at her own expense as *At Fault* (1890). While most reviews were mixed, several praised her depiction of life among the Creoles in Louisiana, which was also the setting of "For Marse Chouchoute," published in the *Youth's Companion* in August 1891. Chopin found a ready market for such stories, which she regularly published in other prominent magazines, including the *Century* and the *Atlantic Monthly*. Her first collection of stories, *Bayou Folk*, appeared in 1894, and a second collection, *A Night in Acadie*, followed in 1897. Those volumes established Chopin as an accomplished author of "local-color" fiction, one who was frequently compared to popular regional writers such as Mary E. Wilkins Freeman, Joel Chandler Harris, and George Washington Cable. Chopin "tells a story like a poet, and reproduces the spirit of a landscape like a painter," a reviewer admiringly observed in the *Nation* in June 1898. By then, Chopin had begun her major work, *The Awakening*, the story of Edna Pontellier, a New Orleans wife and mother who falls in love with another man, takes a third man as a lover, and ultimately rejects the claims of her husband and children by swimming out to her death in the ocean off Grand Isle, Louisiana.

The storm of controversy generated by the publication of *The Awakening* in 1899 virtually ended Chopin's promising literary career. Although many recognized her artistry and praised her luminous prose style, most reviewers were aghast at the subject matter of the novel. Writing for the St. Louis *Post-Dispatch* in May 1899, a reviewer called Edna Pontellier "a derelict in a moral ocean, whose chart she had never studied," declaring that the novel was "sad and mad, and bad, but it is all consummate art." The negative criticism caused Chopin's publisher to withdraw a collection of stories, *A Vocation and a Voice*, which was to follow *The Awakening*. Chopin continued to publish an occasional story and was still regarded as a literary celebrity in St. Louis. But the reaction to *The Awakening* had severely damaged her national reputation, and the pace of her literary production fell off dramatically after 1900. When she died of a brain hemorrhage on August 22, 1904, obituaries largely ignored *The Awakening* and praised Chopin for her colorful stories of Creole life in Louisiana.

bedfordstmartins.com/ americanlit *for research links on Chopin*

Reading Chopin's "At the 'Cadian Ball." In her careful manuscript-account book, Chopin recorded that "At the 'Cadian Ball" was written during three days, July 15-17, and immediately submitted for publication on July 18, 1892. She sent the story to a short-lived weekly magazine published in Boston, *Two Tales*, each issue of which contained two original short stories "by the best authors," as its title page proclaimed. Chopin recorded that she received a payment of forty dollars for the story, which appeared in the October 1892 issue. The story was among twenty-three Chopin gathered together the following year into what she called her "collection of Creole stories," which the prominent Boston firm Houghton Mifflin published as *Bayou Folk* (1894). Reviewers generally praised the stories in the collection, emphasizing its "flavor of quaint and picturesque life among the Creole folk of the Louisiana bayous," as well as Chopin's "faithful, artistic transcripts of picturesque local life." In the midst of the rich descriptions of the southern setting, the accomplished use of dialect, and the presentation of unusual characters, however, alert readers might also have discovered suggestions of social criticism in "At the 'Cadian Ball," which subtly exposes the hierarchical nature of Creole society, especially the attitudes toward and position of women within that society. The text is taken from the first printing in *Two Tales*, October 1892.

AT THE 'CADIAN BALL[1]

Bobinôt—that big, brown, good-natured Bobinôt—had no intention of going to the ball, even though he knew Calixta would be there. For what came of those balls but heartache, and a sickening disinclination for work the whole week through, till Saturday night came again and his tortures began afresh? Why could he not have loved Ozéina, who would marry him to-morrow; or Fronie, or any one of a dozen others, rather than that little Spanish vixen? Calixta's slender foot had never touched Cuban soil; but her mother's had, and the Spanish was in her blood all the same. For that reason the prairie people forgave her much that they would not have overlooked in their own daughters or sisters.

Her eyes—Bobinôt thought of her eyes, and weakened—the bluest, the drowsiest, most tantalizing that ever looked into a man's; her flaxen hair that kinked worse than a mulatto's close to her head; that broad, smiling mouth and tip-tilted nose, that full figure; that voice like a rich contralto song, with cadences in it that must have been taught by Satan, for there had been no one else to teach her tricks on that 'Cadian prairie. Bobinôt thought of them all as he ploughed his rows of cane.

---

1. **At the 'Cadian Ball:** The Acadians were the original French settlers of what is now Nova Scotia, from which most of them were expelled by the British authorities during the French and Indian War (1754-63). Some of the exiled Acadians settled in what was then the Spanish, but soon became the French, colony of Louisiana. Their descendants are called "Cajuns," an English corruption of the French word *acadien*, after *Acadia*, the original name of their ancestral region in Nova Scotia.

There had even been a breath of scandal whispered about her a year ago, when she went to Assumption[2] – but why talk of it? No one did now. *"C'est Espagnol, ça,"*[3] most of them said with lenient shoulder-shrugs. *"Bon chien tient de race,"*[4] the old men mumbled over their pipes, stirred by recollections. Nothing was made of it, except that Fronie threw it up to Calixta when the two quarrelled and fought on the church steps after mass one Sunday, about a lover. Calixta swore roundly in fine 'Cadian French and with true Spanish spirit, and slapped Fronie's face. Fronie had slapped her back: *"Tiens, cocotte, va!"* *"Espèce de lionèse; prends ça, et ça!"*[5] till the curé[6] himself was obliged to hasten and make peace between them. Bobinôt thought of it all, and would not go to the ball.

But in the afternoon, over at Friedheimer's store, where he was buying a trace-chain,[7] he heard some one say that Alcée Laballière would be there. Then wild horses could not have kept him away. He knew how it would be – or rather he did not know how it would be – if the handsome young planter came over to the ball as he sometimes did. If Alcée happened to be in a serious mood, he might only go to the card-room and play a round or two; or he might stand out on the galleries talking crops and politics with the old people. But there was no telling. A drink or two could put the devil in his head – that was what Bobinôt said to himself, as he wiped the sweat from his brow with his red bandanna; a gleam from Calixta's eyes, a flash of her ankle, a twirl of her skirts could do the same. Yes, Bobinôt would go to the ball.

That was the year Alcée Laballière put nine hundred acres in rice. It was putting a good deal of money into the ground, but the returns promised to be glorious. Old Madame Laballière, sailing about the spacious galleries in her white *volante*,[8] figured it all out in her head. Clarisse, her god-daughter, helped her a little, and together they built more air-castles than enough. Alcée worked like a mule that time; and if he did not kill himself, it was because his constitution was an iron one. It was an every-day affair for him to come in from the field well nigh exhausted, and wet to the waist. He did not mind if there were visitors; he left them to his mother and Clarisse. There were often visitors. Young men and women who came up from the city, which was but a few hours away, to see his beautiful kinswoman. She was worth going a good deal farther than that to see. Dainty as a lily; hardy as a sunflower; slim, tall, graceful like one of the reeds that grew in the marsh. Cold and kind and cruel by turn, and everything that was aggravating to Alcée.

He would have liked to sweep the place of those visitors, often. The men above all, with their ways and their manners; their swaying of fans like women, and dandling about hammocks. He could have pitched them over the levee into the river, if it hadn't meant murder. That was Alcée. But he must have been crazy the day he came in from the

---

2. **Assumption:** Assumption Parish (county), at the heart of "Cajun Country" in southern Louisiana.
3. *"C'est Espagnol, ça"*: That's a Spaniard for you (French).
4. *"Bon . . . race"*: Just like her mother (French).
5. *"Tiens, cocotte, va! Espèce . . . ça!"*: Listen, you flirt, get out! You dirty she-cat; take that and that! (French).
6. **curé:** Parish priest (French).
7. **trace-chain:** Chains on the sides of a harness, used to attach a horse to a vehicle.
8. *volante*: A flounced gown (French).

rice-field, and, toil-stained as he was, clasped Clarisse by the arms and panted a volley of hot, blistering love-words into her face. No man had ever spoken love to her like that.

"Monsieur!" she exclaimed, looking him full in the eyes, without a quiver. Alcée's hands dropped and his glance wavered before the chill of her calm, clear eyes.

"Par exemple!"[9] she muttered disdainfully, as she turned from him, deftly adjusting the careful toilet that he had so brutally disarranged.

That happened a day or two before the cyclone came that cut into the rice like fine steel. It was an awful thing – coming so swiftly, without a moment's warning in which to light a holy candle or set a piece of blessed palm burning. Old madame wept openly and said her beads, just as her son Lidié, the New Orleans one, would have done. If such a thing had happened to Alphonse, the Laballière planting cotton up in Natchitoches,[10] he would have raved and stormed like a second cyclone and made his surroundings unbearable for a day or two. But Alcée took the misfortune differently. He looked ill and gray, after it, and said nothing. His speechlessness was frightful. Clarisse's heart grew as tender as a kitten's; but when she offered her soft, purring words of condolence, he accepted them with mute indifference. Then she and nainaine[11] wept afresh in each other's arms.

A night or two later, when Clarisse went to her window to kneel there in the moonlight and say her prayers before retiring, she saw that Bruce, Alcée's negro servant, had led his master's saddle-horse noiselessly along the edge of the sward that bordered the gravel-path, and stood holding him near by. Presently, she heard Alcée quit his room, which was beneath her own, and traverse the lower portico. As he emerged from the shadow and crossed the strip of moonlight, she perceived that he carried a pair of well-filled saddle-bags which he at once flung across the animal's back. He then lost no time in mounting, and after a brief exchange of words with Bruce, went cantering away, taking no precaution to avoid the noisy gravel as the negro had done.

Clarisse had never suspected that it might be Alcée's custom to sally forth from the plantation secretly, and at such an hour; for it was nearly midnight. And had it not been for the tell-tale saddle-bags, she would only have crept to bed, to wonder, to fret and dream unpleasant dreams. But her impatience and anxiety would not be held in check. Hastily unbolting the shutters of her door that opened upon the gallery, she stepped outside and called softly to the old negro.

"Gre't Peter! Miss Clarisse. I wasn' sho it was a ghos' o' w'at, stan'in' up dah, plumb in de night, dataway."

He mounted half-way up the long, broad flight of stairs. She was standing at the top of them.

"Bruce, w'ere has Monsieur Alcée gone?" she asked.

"W'y, he gone 'bout he business, I reckin," replied Bruce, striving to be non-committal at the outset.

---

9. *"Par exemple!"*: Literally, "For example!" (French). In this instance, the exclamation means "Take hold of yourself!"

10. **Natchitoches**: Parish (county) in northwestern Louisiana.

11. **nainaine**: A dialect term for a godmother or older woman companion (French).

"W'ere has Monsieur Alcée gone?" she reiterated, stamping her bare foot. "I won't stan' any nonsense or any lies; mine, Bruce."

"I don' ric'lic ez I eva tole you lie *yit*, Miss Clarisse. Mista Alcée, he all broke up, sho."

"W'ere – has – he gone? *Ah Sainte Vierge! faut de la patience! butor, va!*"[12]

"W'en I was in he room, a-breshin' off he clo'es to-day," the darkey began, settling himself against the stair-rail, "he look dat speechless an' down, I say, 'You 'pear tu me like some pussun w'at gwine have a spell o' sickness, Mista Alcée.' He say, 'You reckin.' An' he git up, go look hisse'f stidy in de glass. Den he go to de chimbly an' jerk up de quinine bottle an po' a gre't hoss-dose onto he han'. An' he swalla dat mess in a wink, an' wash hit down wid a big dram o' whisky w'at he keep in he room, agin he come all soppin' wet outen de fiel'.

"He lows, 'No, I ain' gwine be sick, Bruce.' Den he square off. He say, 'I kin mak out to stan' up an' gi' an' take wid any man I knows, lessen hit's John L. Sulvun.[13] But w'en God A'mighty an' a 'oman jines fo'ces agin me, dats one too many fur me.' I tell 'im jis so, whils' I'se makin' out to bresh a spot off w'at ain' dah, on he coat colla. I tell 'im, 'You wants li'le res', suh.' He say, 'No, I wants li'le fling; dats w'at I wants; an I gwine git it. Pitch me a fis' ful o' clo'es in dem 'ar saddle-bags.' Dat w'at he say. Don't you bodda, missy. He jis gone a caperin' yonda tu de Cajun ball. Uh – uh – de skeeters is fair' a-swarmin' like bees roun' yo' foots!"

The mosquitoes were indeed attacking Clarisse's white feet savagely. She had unconsciously been alternately rubbing one foot over the other while hearing the darkey's recital.

"The 'Cadian ball," she repeated contemptuously. "Humph! *Par exemple!*[14] Nice conduc' for a Laballière. An' he needs a saddle-bag, fill' with clothes, to go to the 'Cadian ball!"

"Oh, Miss Clarisse; you go on tu bed, chile; git yo' soun' sleep. He 'low he come back in couple weeks o' so. I kiarn be repeatin' lot o' truck w'at young mans say, out heah face o' a young gol."

Clarisse said no more but flashed back into the house.

"You done talk too much wid yo' mouf a'ready, you ole fool nigga, you," muttered Bruce to himself as he walked away.

Alcée reached the ball very late, of course – too late for the chicken gombo which had been served at midnight.

The big, low-ceiled room – they called it a hall – was packed with men and women dancing to the music of three fiddles. There were broad galleries all around it. There was a room at one side where sober-faced men were playing cards. Another in which babies were sleeping, called *le parc aux petits*.[15] Any one who is white may go to a 'Cadian ball, but he must pay for his lemonade, his coffee and chicken gombo. And he must behave

---

12. *"Ah Sainte Vierge! . . . butor, va!"*: Ah Blessed Virgin! Give me patience! Go, lout! (French).
13. **John L. Sulvun**: John L. Sullivan (1855–1918), a legendary boxer and the first American sports celebrity.
14. *"Par exemple!"*: Literally, "For example!" (French). In this instance, the exclamation means "What an example!" (See note 9.)
15. *le parc aux petits*: Playroom (French).

himself like a 'Cadian. Grosboeuf was giving this ball. He had been giving them since he was a young man, and he was a middle-aged one, now. In that time he could recall but one disturbance, and that was caused by American railroaders, who were not in touch with their surroundings and had no business there. *"Ces maudits gens du raiderode,"*[16] Grosboeuf called them.

Alcée Laballière's presence at the ball caused a flutter even among the men, who could not but admire his grit after such a misfortune befalling him. To be sure, they knew the Laballières were rich — that there were resources East, and more again in the city. But they felt it took a *brave homme*[17] to stand a blow like that philosophically. One old gentleman, who was in the habit of reading a Paris newspaper and knew things, chuckled gleefully to everybody that Alcée's conduct was altogether *chic, mais chic.*[18] That he had more *panache*[19] than Boulanger. Well, perhaps he had.

But what he did not show outwardly was that he was in a mood for ugly things tonight. Poor Bobinôt alone felt it, vaguely. He discerned a gleam of it in Alcée's handsome eyes as the young planter stood in the doorway looking with rather feverish glance upon the assembly, while he laughed and talked with a 'Cadian farmer who was beside him.

Bobinôt himself was dull-looking and clumsy. Most of the men were. But the young women were very beautiful. The eyes that glanced into Alcée's as they passed him, were big, dark, soft as those of the young heifers' standing out in the cool prairie grass.

But the belle was Calixta. Her white dress was not nearly so handsome or well made as Fronie's (she and Fronie had quite forgotten the battle on the church steps, and were friends again), nor were her slippers so stylish as those of Ozéina; and she fanned herself with a handkerchief, since she had broken her red fan at the last ball, and her aunts and uncles were not willing to give her another. But all the men agreed she was at her best to-night. Such animation! such *abandon!* such flashes of wit!

"Né, Bobinôt! *Mais*[20] w'ats the matta? W'at you standin' *planté là*[21] like ole Ma'ame Tina's cow in the bog, you?"

That was good. That was an excellent thrust at Bobinôt, who had forgotten the figure of the dance, with his mind bent on other things, and it started a clamor of laughter at his expense. He joined good-naturedly. It was better to receive even such notice as that from Calixta than none at all. But Madame Suzonne, sitting in a corner, whispered to her neighbor that if Ozéina were to conduct herself in such manner, she should immediately be taken out to the mule-cart and driven home. The women did not always approve of Calixta.

Now and then were short lulls in the dance, when couples flocked out upon the galleries for a brief respite and a breath of air. The moon had gone down pale in the west, and

---

16. *"Ces maudits gens du raiderode"*: Those cursed railroad people (French).
17. *brave homme*: Brave man (French).
18. *chic, mais chic*: Stylish, just stylish (French).
19. more *panache* than Boulanger: That is, more style than General George Boulanger (1837–1891), a popular French politician who had gone into exile to avoid being arrested on the charge of treason, and who ultimately committed suicide by shooting himself in the head by the grave of his mistress, with whom he was then interred in 1891.
20. *"Mais"*: But (French).
21. *"planté là"*: Rooted there (French).

in the east was yet no promise of day. After such an interval, when the dancers again assembled to resume the interrupted quadrille, Calixta was not among them.

She was sitting out upon a bench in the shadow, with Alcée beside her. They were acting like fools. He had attempted to take a little gold ring from her finger; just for the fun of it, for there was nothing he could have done with the ring but replace it again. But she clinched her hand tight. He had pretended that it was a very difficult matter to open it. Then he kept the hand in his. They seemed to forget about it. He played with her ear-ring, a thin crescent of gold hanging from her small, brown ear. He caught a whisp of the kinky hair that had escaped its fastening, and rubbed the ends of it against his shaven cheek.

"You know, last year in Assumption, Calixta." They belonged to the younger generation, so preferred to speak English.

"Don't come say Assumption to me, M'sieur Alcée. I done yeard Assumption till I'm plumb sick."

"Yes, I know. The idiots! Because you were in Assumption, and I happened to go to Assumption, they must have it that we went together. But it was nice — *hein*,[22] Calixta? — in Assumption?"

They saw Bobinôt emerge from the hall and stand a moment outside the lighted doorway, peering uneasily and searchingly into the darkness. He did not see them, and went slowly back.

"There is Bobinôt looking for you. You are going to set poor Bobinôt crazy. You'll marry him some day; *hein*, Calixta?"

"I don't say, no, me," she replied, striving to withdraw her hand, which he held more firmly for the attempt.

"But, come, Calixta; you know you said you would go back to Assumption, just to spite them."

"No, I never said that, me. You mus' dreamt that."

"Oh, I thought you did. You know I'm going down to the city."

"W'en?"

"To-night."

"You betta make has'e, then; it's mos't day."

"Well, to-morrow'll do."

"W'at you goin' do, yonda?"

"I don't know. Drown myself in the lake, maybe; unless you go down there to visit your uncle."

Calixta's senses were reeling; and they well-nigh left her when she felt Alcée's lips brush her ear like the touch of a rose.

"Mista Alcée! Is dat Mista Alcée?" the thick voice of a negro was asking, who stood on the ground holding to the banister-rails near which the couple sat.

"W'at do you want, now?" cried Alcée impatiently. "Can't I have a moment of peace?"

"I ben huntin' you high an' low, suh," said the man. "Dey — dey some one in de road, onda de mulbare-tree, want see you a minute."

---

22. *hein*:   Eh (French).

"I wouldn't go out to the road to see the Angel Gabriel. And if you come back here with any more talk, I'll have to break your neck." The negro turned mumbling away.

Alcée and Calixta laughed softly about it. Her boisterousness was all gone. They talked low, and laughed softly, as lovers do.

"Alcée! Alcée Laballière!"

It was not the negro's voice this time; but one that went through Alcée's body like an electric shock, bringing him to his feet.

It was Clarisse standing there in her riding-habit, where the negro had stood. For an instant confusion reigned in Alcée's thoughts, like one who awakes suddenly from a dream. But he felt that something of serious import had brought her to the ball in the dead of night.

"W'at does this mean, Clarisse?" he asked.

"It means something has happen' at home. You mus' come."

"Happened to maman?" he questioned, in alarm.

"No; nainaine is well, and asleep. It is something else. Not to fr'ghten you. But you mus' come. Come with me, Alcée."

There was no need for the imploring note. He would have followed the voice anywhere.

She had now recognized the girl sitting back on the bench.

"*Ah, c'est vous, Calixta? Comment ça va, mon enfant?*"[23]

"*Tcha va b'en; et vous, mam'zélle?*"[24]

Alcée swung himself over the low rail and started to follow Clarisse, without a word, without a glance back at the girl. He had forgotten he was leaving her there. But Clarisse whispered something to him and he turned back to say "good night, Calixta," and offer his hand to press through the railing. She pretended not to see it.

"How come that? You settin' yere by yo'se'f, Calixta?" It was Bobinôt who had found her there alone. The dancers had not yet come out. She looked ghastly in the faint, gray light that was struggling out of the east.

"Yes, that's me. Go yonda in the *parc aux petits* an' ask aunt Olisse fu' my hat. She knows w'ere 'tis. I want ter go home, me."

"How you came?"

"I come afoot, with the Cateaus. But I'm goin' now. I ent going' wait fu' 'em. I'm plumb wo' out, me."

"Kin I go with you, Calixta?"

"I don' care."

They went together across the open prairie and along the edge of the fields, stumbling in the uncertain light. He told her to lift her dress that was getting wet and bedraggled; for she was pulling at the weeds and grasses with her hands.

---

23. "*Ah . . . enfant?*": Ah, is it you, Calixta? How's it going, my little one? (French).

24. "*Tcha . . . mam'zélle?*": I'm fine; and you, miss? (French). In the exchange between the two young women, Chopin distinguishes between Clarisse's more refined French and Calixta's Acadian dialect, in which the standard French phrase *Ça va bien* (I'm fine) is pronounced "Tcha va b'en."

"I don' care; it's got to go in the tub, anyway. You been sayin' all along you want to marry me, Bobinôt. Well, if you want, yet, I don' care, me."

The glow of sudden and overwhelming happiness shone out in the brown, rugged face of the young Acadian. He could not speak, for very joy. It choked him.

"Oh well, if you don' want," snapped Calixta, flippantly, pretending to be piqued at his silence.

"*Bon Dieu!*[25] You know that makes me crazy, w'at you sayin'. You mean that, Calixta? You ent goin' turn roun' agin?"

"I neva tole you that much *yet,* Bobinôt. I mean that. *Tiens,*"[26] and she held out her hand in the business-like manner of a man who clinches a bargain with a hand-clasp. Bobinôt grew bold with happiness and asked Calixta to kiss him. She turned her face, that looked almost ugly after the night's dissipation, and looked steadily into his.

"I don' want ter kiss you, Bobinôt," she said, turning away again, "not to-day. Some other time. *Bonté divine!*[27] ent you satisfy, *yet!*"

"Oh, I'm satisfy, Calixta," he said.

Riding through a patch of wood, Clarisse's saddle became ungirted, and she and Alcée dismounted to readjust it.

For the twentieth time he asked her what had happened at home.

"But, Clarisse, w'at is it? Is it a misfortune?"

"*Ah, Dieu sait!*[28] It's only something that happen' to me."

"To you!"

"I saw you go away las' night, Alcée, with those saddle-bags," she said, haltingly, striving to arrange something about the saddle, "an' I made Bruce tell me. He said you had gone to the ball, an' wouldn' be home for weeks an' weeks. I thought, Alcée — maybe you were going to — to Assumption. I got wild. An' then I knew if you didn't come back, *now,* to-night, I would die. I couldn' stan' it — again."

She had her face hidden in her arm that she was resting against the saddle when she said that.

He began to wonder if this meant love. But she had to tell him so, before he believed it. And when she told him, he thought the face of the Universe was changed — just like Bobinôt. Was it last week the cyclone had well-nigh ruined him? The cyclone seemed a huge joke, now. It was he, then, who, an hour ago was kissing little Calixta's ear and whispering nonsense into it. Calixta was like a myth, now. The one, only, great reality in the world was Clarisse standing before him, telling him that she loved him.

In the distance they heard the rapid discharge of pistol-shots; but it did not disturb them. They knew it was only the negro musicians who had gone into the yard to fire their pistols into the air, as the custom is, and to announce *"le bal est fini."*[29]

[1892]

---

25. *"Bon Dieu!"*: Good God! (French).
26. *"Tiens"*: Well? (French).
27. *Bonté divine!*: Goodness gracious! (French).
28. *Dieu sait!*: God knows! (French).
29. *"le bal est fini"*: The ball is ended (French).

Charles W. Chesnutt

[1858-1932]

Charles Waddell Chesnutt was born in Cleveland, Ohio, on June 20, 1858. He was the first child of Andrew Jackson ("Jack") Chesnutt, the son of a white man and a black woman, and Ann Maria Sampson Chesnutt, whose parents were of mixed racial heritage. The young couple had fallen in love in 1856, during an arduous wagon-train trip organized by a group of free blacks escaping growing racial oppression in their home town of Fayetteville, North Carolina. After arriving in the North, Jack Chesnutt and Ann Maria Sampson married and settled in Cleveland. During the Civil War, Jack Chesnutt served as a teamster in the Union army. After the war, and over his wife's objections to returning to North Carolina, he accepted his father's offer to set him up in the grocery business in Fayetteville, where the family moved in 1866.

Charles W. Chesnutt

This photograph was taken around 1899, the year Chesnutt published two collections of his stories about slavery and the "color line" in the United States.

Charles Chesnutt consequently spent much of his childhood and young adulthood in the tense and racially troubled South. He initially attended the Howard School. After the death of his mother and the failure of his father's grocery business in 1871, when Chesnutt was thirteen, he was forced to drop out of school and go to work. Chesnutt, who had been an excellent student, practiced composition by keeping a journal and remained an avid reader. Following a careful course of study and self-improvement, he began teaching in 1875. Two years later, he became an assistant to the principal of the State Colored Normal School in Fayetteville, the first state-supported teacher-training school for African Americans. Chesnutt married a fellow teacher, Susan Perry, and he became the principal of the school in 1879. Gaining that respected and remunerative position was a signal achievement, but Chesnutt felt that he had reached the limit of what an African American man could do in Fayetteville. By then, his experience as a person of mixed racial heritage living in the South led him to challenge the increasingly complex and corrosive system of discrimination based on color, or what Chesnutt called "caste," in the United States. "I think I must write a book," he wrote in his journal in May 1880:

> I shall write for a purpose, a high, holy purpose, and this will inspire me to greater effort. The object of my writings would be not so much the elevation of the colored people as the elevation of the whites — for I consider the unjust spirit of caste which is so insidious as to pervade a whole nation, and so powerful as to subject a whole race and all connected with it to scorn and social ostracism — I consider this a barrier to the moral progress of the American people; and I would be one of the first to head a determined, organized crusade against it.

Committed to becoming a writer and to make a better life for his family, Chesnutt resigned his comfortable position and moved north in 1883. His family joined him the following year, after Chesnutt found a job as a clerk and stenographer in a law office in Cleveland. He studied law in the office even as he began his literary career. His first story, "Uncle Peter's House," appeared in the *Cleveland News and Herald* and other newspapers, through which Chesnutt gained a foothold in the literary marketplace. In 1887, the same year he passed the Ohio bar examination, Chesnutt published "The Goophered Grapevine" in the *Atlantic Monthly*. It was the first story published in that prestigious magazine by an African American, though Chesnutt's racial identity was not then known to the editor or widely known among readers and reviewers until 1899. During the intervening years, Chesnutt published numerous works in periodicals, including several more stories in the *Atlantic*. He also became friendly with one of the editors of the magazine, Walter Hines Page, who helped arrange for the publication of Chesnutt's first book, *The Conjure Woman* (1899). That acclaimed collection of dialect stories was such a hit that the publisher swiftly released a second collection of stories, *The Wife of His Youth and Other Stories of the Color Line* (1899). The title echoed "The Color Line," a famous essay on racial prejudice Frederick Douglass had published in 1881. Chesnutt wrote a biography of Douglass, and he exposed the effects of such prejudice in two novels: *The House behind the Cedars* (1900), the story of a brother and sister of mixed racial heritage who seek to pass for white in the increasingly segregated South; and *The Marrow of Tradition* (1901), inspired by an 1898 riot in which more than twenty blacks had been killed by white supremacists seeking to overthrow the government of Wilmington, North Carolina. Discouraged by the frequently hostile critical reception and the poor sales of those books, however, Chesnutt published only one more novel, *The Colonel's Dream* (1905).

Like his fictional colonel, who is forced to abandon his "dream" of reforming the economic and educational system of the South, Chesnutt for the most part abandoned his own dream of reforming American society through his fiction. Instead, he increasingly devoted his energies and pen to more direct political efforts to end racial discrimination, both in Cleveland and nationally through his work in organizations such as the National Association for the Advancement of Colored People (NAACP). In the remaining years of his life, Chesnutt wrote only a handful of stories and two novels, both of which were rejected by publishers. His contributions to African American literature were recognized in 1928, when the NAACP awarded Chesnutt its Springarn Medal for his "pioneer work as a literary artist depicting the life and struggles of Americans of Negro descent, and for his long and useful career as scholar, worker, and freeman of one of America's greatest cities." Chesnutt died at his home in Cleveland in November 1932.

bedfordstmartins.com/
americanlit for research
links on Chesnutt

Reading Chesnutt's "The Passing of Grandison." Following the success of *The Conjure Woman*, Chesnutt's first collection of stories, his Boston publisher rushed *The Wife of His Youth and Other Stories of the Color Line* into print in December 1899, so that the book would be available for the holiday season. Only three of the stories had previously been published, including the popular title story, "The Wife of His Youth," which had appeared in the prestigious *Atlantic Monthly*. Walter Hines Page, a prominent editor and friend of Chesnutt, had suggested the addition of "and Other Stories of the Color Line" to the title of the collection. In a letter to his publisher, Chesnutt observed that the title would "very aptly characterize the volume," which he hoped would "throw a little light upon the great problem on which the stories are strung." That "great problem" was racial prejudice, the manifestations of which Chesnutt exposed in stories about the African American community, in which lighter-colored skin was often considered a badge of superiority, and in a wide range of other stories about divisions between the races in the United States. As he recognized, racial discrimination and segregation in the country was gaining added support from the emergence of the "plantation myth," especially through popular and proliferating fictions depicting loyal slaves and their benign masters in the antebellum South. Chesnutt sought to subvert that myth in *The Conjure Woman*, dialect stories of plantation life told to transplanted Northerners by a former slave, and in "The Passing of Grandison," the only story in his second collection set before the Civil War. The text is taken from the first printing in *The Wife of His Youth and Other Stories of the Color Line* (1899).

THE PASSING OF GRANDISON

I

When it is said that it was done to please a woman, there ought perhaps to be enough said to explain anything; for what a man will not do to please a woman is yet to be discovered. Nevertheless, it might be well to state a few preliminary facts to make it clear why young Dick Owens tried to run one of his father's negro men off to Canada.

In the early fifties, when the growth of anti-slavery sentiment and the constant drain of fugitive slaves into the North had so alarmed the slaveholders of the border States as to lead to the passage of the Fugitive Slave Law,[1] a young white man from Ohio, moved by compassion for the sufferings of a certain bondman who happened to have a "hard master," essayed to help the slave to freedom. The attempt was discovered and frustrated; the abductor was tried and convicted for slave-stealing, and sentenced to a term of imprisonment in the penitentiary. His death, after the expiration of only a small part of the sentence, from cholera contracted while nursing stricken fellow prisoners, lent to the case a melancholy interest that made it famous in anti-slavery annals.

Dick Owens had attended the trial. He was a youth of about twenty-two, intelligent, handsome, and amiable, but extremely indolent, in a graceful and gentlemanly way; or,

---

1. **Fugitive Slave Law:** The most controversial provision of the Compromise of 1850, this law required all U.S. citizens to aid in the capture and return of runaway slaves to their masters in the South.

as old Judge Fenderson put it more than once, he was lazy as the Devil, a mere figure of speech, of course, and not one that did justice to the Enemy of Mankind. When asked why he never did anything serious, Dick would good-naturedly reply, with a well-modulated drawl, that he didn't have to. His father was rich; there was but one other child, an unmarried daughter, who because of poor health would probably never marry, and Dick was therefore heir presumptive to a large estate. Wealth or social position he did not need to seek, for he was born to both. Charity Lomax had shamed him into studying law, but notwithstanding an hour or so a day spent at old Judge Fenderson's office, he did not make remarkable headway in his legal studies.

"What Dick needs," said the judge, who was fond of tropes, as became a scholar, and of horses, as was befitting a Kentuckian, "is the whip of necessity, or the spur of ambition. If he had either, he would soon need the snaffle[2] to hold him back."

But all Dick required, in fact, to prompt him to the most remarkable thing he accomplished before he was twenty-five, was a mere suggestion from Charity Lomax. The story was never really known to but two persons until after the war, when it came out because it was a good story and there was no particular reason for its concealment.

Young Owens had attended the trial of this slave-stealer, or martyr—either or both—and, when it was over, had gone to call on Charity Lomax, and, while they sat on the veranda after sundown, had told her all about the trial. He was a good talker, as his career in later years disclosed, and described the proceedings very graphically.

"I confess," he admitted, "that while my principles were against the prisoner, my sympathies were on his side. It appeared that he was of good family, and that he had an old father and mother, respectable people, dependent upon him for support and comfort in their declining years. He had been led into the matter by pity for a negro whose master ought to have been run out of the county long ago for abusing his slaves. If it had been merely a question of old Sam Briggs's negro, nobody would have cared anything about it. But father and the rest of them stood on the principle of the thing, and told the judge so, and the fellow was sentenced to three years in the penitentiary."

Miss Lomax had listened with lively interest.

"I've always hated old Sam Briggs," she said emphatically, "ever since the time he broke a negro's leg with a piece of cordwood. When I hear of a cruel deed it makes the Quaker blood that came from my grandmother assert itself. Personally I wish that all Sam Briggs's negroes would run away. As for the young man, I regard him as a hero. He dared something for humanity. I could love a man who would take such chances for the sake of others."

"Could you love me, Charity, if I did something heroic?"

"You never will, Dick. You're too lazy for any use. You'll never do anything harder than playing cards or fox-hunting."

"Oh, come now, sweetheart! I've been courting you for a year, and it's the hardest work imaginable. Are you never going to love me?" he pleaded.

His hand sought hers, but she drew it back beyond his reach.

---

2. **snaffle:** A bit on a bridle used with a single set of reins to control a horse.

"I'll never love you, Dick Owens, until you have done something. When that time comes, I'll think about it."

"But it takes so long to do anything worth mentioning, and I don't want to wait. One must read two years to become a lawyer, and work five more to make a reputation. We shall both be gray by then."

"Oh, I don't know," she rejoined. "It doesn't require a lifetime for a man to prove that he is a man. This one did something, or at least tried to."

"Well, I'm willing to attempt as much as any other man. What do you want me to do, sweetheart? Give me a test."

"Oh, dear me!" said Charity, "I don't care what you *do*, so you do *something*. Really, come to think of it, why should I care whether you do anything or not?"

"I'm sure I don't know why you should, Charity," rejoined Dick humbly, "for I'm aware that I'm not worthy of it."

"Except that I do hate," she added, relenting slightly, "to see a really clever man so utterly lazy and good for nothing."

"Thank you, my dear; a word of praise from you has sharpened my wits already. I have an idea! Will you love me if *I* run a negro off to Canada?"

"What nonsense!" said Charity scornfully. "You must be losing your wits. Steal another man's slave, indeed, while your father owns a hundred!"

"Oh, there'll be no trouble about that," responded Dick lightly; "I'll run off one of the old man's; we've got too many anyway. It may not be quite as difficult as the other man found it, but it will be just as unlawful, and will demonstrate what I am capable of."

"Seeing's believing," replied Charity. "Of course, what you are talking about now is merely absurd. I'm going away for three weeks, to visit my aunt in Tennessee. If you're able to tell me, when I return, that you've done something to prove your quality, I'll—well, you may come and tell me about it."

II

Young Owens got up about nine o'clock next morning, and while making his toilet put some questions to his personal attendant, a rather bright looking young mulatto of about his own age.

"Tom," said Dick.

"Yas, Mars Dick," responded the servant.

"I'm going on a trip North. Would you like to go with me?"

Now, if there was anything that Tom would have liked to make, it was a trip North. It was something he had long contemplated in the abstract, but had never been able to muster up sufficient courage to attempt in the concrete. He was prudent enough, however, to dissemble his feelings.

"I wouldn't min' it, Mars Dick, ez long ez you'd take keer er me an' fetch me home all right."

Tom's eyes belied his words, however, and his young master felt well assured that Tom needed only a good opportunity to make him run away. Having a comfortable home, and a dismal prospect in case of failure, Tom was not likely to take any desperate chances; but young Owens was satisfied that in a free State but little persuasion would be required to lead Tom astray. With a very logical and characteristic desire to gain his end with the least necessary expenditure of effort, he decided to take Tom with him, if his father did not object.

Colonel Owens had left the house when Dick went to breakfast, so Dick did not see his father till luncheon.

"Father," he remarked casually to the colonel, over the fried chicken, "I'm feeling a trifle run down. I imagine my health would be improved somewhat by a little travel and change of scene."

"Why don't you take a trip North?" suggested his father. The colonel added to paternal affection a considerable respect for his son as the heir of a large estate. He himself had been "raised" in comparative poverty, and had laid the foundations of his fortune by hard work; and while he despised the ladder by which he had climbed, he could not entirely forget it, and unconsciously manifested, in his intercourse with his son, some of the poor man's deference toward the wealthy and well-born.

"I think I'll adopt your suggestion, sir," replied the son, "and run up to New York; and after I've been there awhile I may go on to Boston for a week or so. I've never been there, you know."

"There are some matters you can talk over with my factor in New York,"[3] rejoined the colonel, "and while you are up there among the Yankees, I hope you'll keep your eyes and ears open to find out what the rascally abolitionists are saying and doing. They're becoming altogether too active for our comfort, and entirely too many ungrateful niggers are running away. I hope the conviction of that fellow yesterday may discourage the rest of the breed. I'd just like to catch any one trying to run off one of my darkeys. He'd get short shrift; I don't think any Court would have a chance to try him."

"They are a pestiferous lot," assented Dick, "and dangerous to our institutions. But say, father, if I go North I shall want to take Tom with me."

Now, the colonel, while a very indulgent father, had pronounced views on the subject of negroes, having studied them, as he often said, for a great many years, and, as he asserted oftener still, understanding them perfectly. It is scarcely worth while to say, either, that he valued more highly than if he had inherited them the slaves he had toiled and schemed for.

"I don't think it safe to take Tom up North," he declared, with promptness and decision. "He's a good enough boy, but too smart to trust among those low-down abolitionists. I strongly suspect him of having learned to read, though I can't imagine how. I saw him with a newspaper the other day, and while he pretended to be looking at a woodcut,[4] I'm almost sure he was reading the paper. I think it by no means safe to take him."

Dick did not insist, because he knew it was useless. The colonel would have obliged his son in any other matter, but his negroes were the outward and visible sign of his wealth and station, and therefore sacred to him.

---

3. **factor in New York:** A factor was an agent for the sale of goods, in this case cotton, much of which was exported to textile mills in Great Britain via New York City.
4. **woodcut:** Nineteenth-century newspapers contained illustrations made from prints or designs cut in a block of wood and imprinted on the pages.

"Whom do you think it safe to take?" asked Dick. "I suppose I'll have to have a body-servant."

"What's the matter with Grandison?" suggested the colonel. "He's handy enough, and I reckon we can trust him. He's too fond of good eating, to risk losing his regular meals; besides, he's sweet on your mother's maid, Betty, and I've promised to let 'em get married before long. I'll have Grandison up, and we'll talk to him. Here, you boy Jack," called the colonel to a yellow youth[5] in the next room who was catching flies and pulling their wings off to pass the time, "go down to the barn and tell Grandison to come here."

"Grandison," said the colonel, when the negro stood before him, hat in hand.

"Yas, marster."

"Haven't I always treated you right?"

"Yas, marster."

"Haven't you always got all you wanted to eat?"

"Yas, marster."

"And as much whiskey and tobacco as was good for you, Grandison?"

"Y-a-s, marster."

"I should just like to know, Grandison, whether you don't think yourself a great deal better off than those poor free negroes down by the plank road, with no kind master to look after them and no mistress to give them medicine when they're sick and – and" –

"Well, I sh'd jes' reckon I is better off, suh, dan dem low-down free niggers, suh! Ef anybody ax 'em who dey b'long ter, dey has ter say nobody, er e'se lie erbout it. Anybody ax me who I b'longs ter, I ain' got no 'casion ter be shame' ter tell 'em, no, suh, 'deed I ain', suh!"

The colonel was beaming. This was true gratitude, and his feudal heart thrilled at such appreciative homage. What cold-blooded, heartless monsters they were who would break up this blissful relationship of kindly protection on the one hand, of wise subordination and loyal dependence on the other! The colonel always became indignant at the mere thought of such wickedness.

"Grandison," the colonel continued, "your young master Dick is going North for a few weeks, and I am thinking of letting him take you along. I shall send you on this trip, Grandison, in order that you may take care of your young master. He will need some one to wait on him, and no one can ever do it so well as one of the boys brought up with him on the old plantation. I am going to trust him in your hands, and I'm sure you'll do your duty faithfully, and bring him back home safe and sound – to old Kentucky."

Grandison grinned. "Oh yas, marster, I'll take keer er young Mars Dick."

"I want to warn you, though, Grandison," continued the colonel impressively, "against these cussed abolitionists, who try to entice servants from their comfortable homes and their indulgent masters, from the blue skies, the green fields, and the warm sunlight of their southern home, and send them away off yonder to Canada, a dreary country, where the woods are full of wildcats and wolves and bears, where the snow lies up to the

---

5. **yellow youth:** A mixed-race youth with a light complexion.

eaves of the houses for six months of the year, and the cold is so severe that it freezes your breath and curdles your blood; and where, when runaway niggers get sick and can't work, they are turned out to starve and die, unloved and uncared for. I reckon, Grandison, that you have too much sense to permit yourself to be led astray by any such foolish and wicked people."

" 'Deed, suh, I would n' 'low none er dem cussed, low-down abolitioners ter come nigh me, suh. I'd — I'd — would I be 'lowed ter hit 'em, suh?"

"Certainly, Grandison," replied the colonel, chuckling, "hit 'em as hard as you can. I reckon they'd rather like it. Begad, I believe they would! It would serve 'em right to be hit by a nigger!"

"Er ef I didn't hit 'em, suh," continued Grandison reflectively, "I'd tell Mars Dick, en *he'd* fix 'em. He'd smash de face off'n 'em, suh, I jes' knows he would."

"Oh yes, Grandison, your young master will protect you. You need fear no harm while he is near."

"Dey won't try ter steal me, will dey, marster?" asked the negro, with sudden alarm.

"I don't know, Grandison," replied the colonel, lighting a fresh cigar. "They're a desperate set of lunatics, and there's no telling what they may resort to. But if you stick close to your young master, and remember always that he is your best friend, and understands your real needs, and has your true interests at heart, and if you will be careful to avoid strangers who try to talk to you, you'll stand a fair chance of getting back to your home and your friends. And if you please your master Dick, he'll buy you a present, and a string of beads for Betty to wear when you and she get married in the fall."

"Thanky, marster, thanky, suh," replied Grandison, oozing gratitude at every pore; "you is a good marster, to be sho', suh; yas, 'deed you is. You kin jes' bet me and Mars Dick gwine git 'long jes' lack I wuz own boy ter Mars Dick. En it won't be my fault ef he don' want me fer his boy all de time, w'en we come back home ag'in."

"All right, Grandison, you may go now. You needn't work any more to-day, and here's a piece of tobacco for you off my own plug."

"Thanky, marster, thanky, marster! You is de bes' marster any nigger ever had in dis worl'." And Grandison bowed and scraped and disappeared round the corner, his jaws closing around a large section of the colonel's best tobacco.

"You may take Grandison," said the colonel to his son. "I allow he's abolitionist-proof."

III

Richard Owens, Esq., and servant, from Kentucky, registered at the fashionable New York hostelry for Southerners in those days, a hotel where an atmosphere congenial to Southern institutions was sedulously maintained. But there were negro waiters in the dining-room, and mulatto bell-boys, and Dick had no doubt that Grandison, with the native gregariousness and garrulousness of his race, would foregather and palaver with them sooner or later, and Dick hoped that they would speedily inoculate him with the virus of freedom. For it was not Dick's intention to say anything to his servant about his plan to free him, for obvious reasons. To mention one of them, if Grandison should go away, and by legal process be recaptured, his young master's part in the matter would doubtless become known, which would be embarrassing to Dick, to say the least. If, on the other hand, he should merely give Grandison sufficient latitude, he had no doubt he would eventually lose him. For while not exactly skeptical about Grandison's perfervid loyalty, Dick had been a somewhat keen observer of human nature, in his own indolent way, and based his expectations upon the force of the example and argument that his servant could scarcely fail to encounter. Grandison should have a fair chance to become free by his own initiative; if it should become necessary to adopt other measures to get rid of him, it would be time enough to act when the necessity arose; and Dick Owens was not the youth to take needless trouble.

The young master renewed some acquaintances and made others, and spent a week or two very pleasantly in the best society of the metropolis, easily accessible to a wealthy, well-bred young Southerner, with proper introductions. Young women smiled on him, and young men of convivial habits pressed their hospitalities; but the memory of Charity's sweet, strong face and clear blue eyes made him proof against the blandishments of the one sex and the persuasions of the other. Meanwhile he kept Grandison supplied with pocket-money, and left him mainly to his own devices. Every night when Dick came in he hoped he might have to wait upon himself, and every morning he looked forward with pleasure to the prospect of making his toilet unaided. His hopes, however, were doomed to disappointment, for every night when he came in Grandison was on hand with a bootjack,[6] and a nightcap mixed for his young master as the colonel had taught him to mix it, and every morning Grandison appeared with his master's boots blacked and his clothes brushed, and laid his linen out for the day.

"Grandison," said Dick one morning, after finishing his toilet, "this is the chance of your life to go around among your own people and see how they live. Have you met any of them?"

"Yas, suh, I's seen some of 'em. But I don' keer nuffin fer 'em, suh. Dey're diffe'nt f'm de niggers down ou' way. Dey 'lows dey're free, but dey ain' got sense 'nuff ter know dey ain' half as well off as dey would be down Souf, whar dey'd be 'preciated."

When two weeks had passed without any apparent effect of evil example upon Grandison, Dick resolved to go on to Boston, where he thought the atmosphere might prove more favorable to his ends. After he had been at the Revere House[7] for a day or two without losing Grandison, he decided upon slightly different tactics.

Having ascertained from a city directory the addresses of several well-known abolitionists, he wrote them each a letter something like this: —

DEAR FRIEND AND BROTHER: —
A wicked slaveholder from Kentucky, stopping at the Revere House, has dared to insult the liberty-loving people of Boston by bringing his slave into their midst. Shall this be tolerated? Or shall steps be taken in the name of liberty to rescue a fellow-man from bondage? For obvious reasons I can only sign myself,

A FRIEND OF HUMANITY

---

6. **bootjack:** A device for removing tight boots.
7. **Revere House:** Built in 1847 and named after the Revolutionary War hero Paul Revere, this prestigious hotel was frequented by celebrities and other prominent visitors to Boston.

That his letter might have an opportunity to prove effective, Dick made it a point to send Grandison away from the hotel on various errands. On one of these occasions Dick watched him for quite a distance down the street. Grandison had scarcely left the hotel when a long-haired, sharp-featured man came out behind him, followed him, soon overtook him, and kept along beside him until they turned the next corner. Dick's hopes were roused by this spectacle, but sank correspondingly when Grandison returned to the hotel. Grandison said nothing about the encounter. Dick hoped there might be some self-consciousness behind this unexpected reticence, the results of which might develop later on.

But Grandison was on hand again when his master came back to the hotel at night, and was in attendance again in the morning, with hot water, to assist at his master's toilet. Dick sent him on further errands from day to day, and upon one occasion came squarely up to him — inadvertently of course — while Grandison was engaged in conversation with a young white man in clerical garb. When Grandison saw Dick approaching, he edged away from the preacher and hastened toward his master, with a very evident expression of relief upon his countenance.

"Mars Dick," he said, "dese yer abolitioners is jes' pesterin' de life out er me tryin' ter git me ter run away. I don' pay no 'tention ter 'em, but dey riles me so sometimes dat I'm feared I'll hit some of 'em some er dese days, an' dat mought git me inter trouble. I ain' said nuffin' ter you 'bout it, Mars Dick, fer I did n' wanter 'sturb yo' min'; but I don' like it, suh; no, suh, I don'! Is we gwine back home 'fo' long, Mars Dick?"

"We'll be going back soon enough," replied Dick somewhat shortly, while he inwardly cursed the stupidity of a slave who could be free and would not, and registered a secret vow that if he were unable to get rid of Grandison without assassinating him, and were therefore compelled to take him back to Kentucky, he would see that Grandison got a taste of an article of slavery that would make him regret his wasted opportunities. Meanwhile he determined to tempt his servant yet more strongly.

"Grandison," he said next morning, "I'm going away for a day or two, but I shall leave you here. I shall lock up a hundred dollars in this drawer and give you the key. If you need any of it, use it and enjoy yourself, — spend it all if you like, — for this is probably the last chance you'll have for some time to be in a free State, and you'd better enjoy your liberty while you may."

When he came back a couple of days later and found the faithful Grandison at his post, and the hundred dollars intact, Dick felt seriously annoyed. His vexation was increased by the fact that he could not express his feelings adequately. He did not even scold Grandison; how could he, indeed, find fault with one who so sensibly recognized his true place in the economy of civilization, and kept it with such touching fidelity?

"I can't say a thing to him," groaned Dick. "He deserves a leather medal, made out of his own hide tanned. I reckon I'll write to father and let him know what a model servant he has given me."

He wrote his father a letter which made the colonel swell with pride and pleasure. "I really think," the colonel observed to one of his friends, "that Dick ought to have the nigger interviewed by the Boston papers, so that they may see how contented and happy our darkeys really are."

Dick also wrote a long letter to Charity Lomax, in which he said, among many other things, that if she knew how hard he was working, and under what difficulties, to accomplish something serious for her sake, she would no longer keep him in suspense, but overwhelm him with love and admiration.

Having thus exhausted without result the more obvious methods of getting rid of Grandison, and diplomacy having also proved a failure, Dick was forced to consider more radical measures. Of course he might run away himself, and abandon Grandison, but this would be merely to leave him in the United States, where he was still a slave, and where, with his notions of loyalty, he would speedily be reclaimed. It was necessary, in order to accomplish the purpose of his trip to the North, to leave Grandison permanently in Canada, where he would be legally free.

"I might extend my trip to Canada," he reflected, "but that would be too palpable. I have it! I'll visit Niagara Falls on the way home, and lose him on the Canada side. When he once realizes that he is actually free, I'll warrant that he'll stay."

So the next day saw them westward bound, and in due course of time, by the somewhat slow conveyances of the period, they found themselves at Niagara. Dick walked and drove about the Falls for several days, taking Grandison along with him on most occasions. One morning they stood on the Canadian side, watching the wild whirl of the waters below them.

"Grandison," said Dick, raising his voice above the roar of the cataract, "do you know where you are now?"

"I's wid you, Mars Dick; dat's all I keers."

"You are now in Canada, Grandison, where your people go when they run away from their masters. If you wished, Grandison, you might walk away from me this very minute, and I could not lay my hand upon you to take you back."

Grandison looked around uneasily.

"Let's go back ober de ribber, Mars Dick. I's feared I'll lose you ovuh heah, an' den I won' hab no marster, an' won't nebber be able to git back home no mo'."

Discouraged, but not yet hopeless, Dick said, a few minutes later, —

"Grandison, I'm going up the road a bit, to the inn over yonder. You stay here until I return. I'll not be gone a great while."

Grandison's eyes opened wide and he looked somewhat fearful.

"Is dey any er dem dadblasted abolitioners roun' heah, Mars Dick?"

"I don't imagine that there are," replied his master, hoping there might be. "But I'm not afraid of *your* running away, Grandison. I only wish I were," he added to himself.

Dick walked leisurely down the road to where the whitewashed inn, built of stone, with true British solidity, loomed up through the trees by the roadside. Arrived there he ordered a glass of ale and a sandwich, and took a seat at a table by a window, from which he could see Grandison in the distance. For a while he hoped that the seed he had sown might have fallen on fertile ground, and that Grandison, relieved from the restraining power of a master's eye, and finding himself in a free country, might get up and walk away; but the hope was vain, for Grandison remained faithfully at his post, awaiting his master's return. He had seated himself on a broad flat stone, and, turning his eyes away from the grand and awe-inspiring spectacle that lay close at hand, was looking anxiously toward the inn where his master sat cursing his ill-timed fidelity.

By and by a girl came into the room to serve his order, and Dick very naturally glanced at her; and as she was young and pretty and remained in attendance, it was some minutes before he looked for Grandison. When he did so his faithful servant had disappeared.

To pay his reckoning and go away without the change was a matter quickly accomplished. Retracing his footsteps toward the Falls, he saw, to his great disgust, as he approached the spot where he had left Grandison, the familiar form of his servant stretched out on the ground, his face to the sun, his mouth open, sleeping the time away, oblivious alike to the grandeur of the scenery, the thunderous roar of the cataract, or the insidious voice of sentiment.

"Grandison," soliloquized his master, as he stood gazing down at his ebony encumbrance, "I do not deserve to be an American citizen; I ought not to have the advantages I possess over you; and I certainly am not worthy of Charity Lomax, if I am not smart enough to get rid of you. I have an idea! You shall yet be free, and I will be the instrument of your deliverance. Sleep on, faithful and affectionate servitor, and dream of the blue grass and the bright skies of old Kentucky, for it is only in your dreams that you will ever see them again!"

Dick retraced his footsteps towards the inn. The young woman chanced to look out of the window and saw the handsome young gentleman she had waited on a few minutes before, standing in the road a short distance away, apparently engaged in earnest conversation with a colored man employed as hostler[8] for the inn. She thought she saw something pass from the white man to the other, but at that moment her duties called her away from the window, and when she looked out again the young gentleman had disappeared, and the hostler, with two other young men of the neighborhood, one white and one colored, were walking rapidly towards the Falls.

IV

Dick made the journey homeward alone, and as rapidly as the conveyances of the day would permit. As he drew near home his conduct in going back without Grandison took on a more serious aspect than it had borne at any previous time, and although he had prepared the colonel by a letter sent several days ahead, there was still the prospect of a bad quarter of an hour with him; not, indeed, that his father would upbraid him, but he was likely to make searching inquiries. And notwithstanding the vein of quiet recklessness that had carried Dick through his preposterous scheme, he was a very poor liar, having rarely had occasion or inclination to tell anything but the truth. Any reluctance to meet his father was more than offset, however, by a stronger force drawing him homeward, for Charity Lomax must long since have returned from her visit to her aunt in Tennessee.

Dick got off easier than he had expected. He told a straight story, and a truthful one, so far as it went.

The colonel raged at first, but rage soon subsided into anger, and anger moderated into annoyance, and annoyance into a sort of garrulous sense of injury. The colonel thought he had been hardly used; he had trusted this negro, and he had broken faith.

---

8. **hostler:** A man who cares for the horses of people staying at an inn.

Yet, after all, he did not blame Grandison so much as he did the abolitionists, who were undoubtedly at the bottom of it.

As for Charity Lomax, Dick told her, privately of course, that he had run his father's man, Grandison, off to Canada, and left him there.

"Oh, Dick," she had said with shuddering alarm, "what have you done? If they knew it they'd send you to the penitentiary, like they did that Yankee."

"But they don't know it," he had replied seriously; adding, with an injured tone, "you don't seem to appreciate my heroism like you did that of the Yankee; perhaps it's because I wasn't caught and sent to the penitentiary. I thought you wanted me to do it."

"Why, Dick Owens!" she exclaimed. "You know I never dreamed of any such outrageous proceeding.

"But I presume I'll have to marry you," she concluded, after some insistence on Dick's part, "if only to take care of you. You are too reckless for anything; and a man who goes chasing all over the North, being entertained by New York and Boston society and having negroes to throw away, needs some one to look after him."

"It's a most remarkable thing," replied Dick fervently, "that your views correspond exactly with my profoundest convictions. It proves beyond question that we were made for one another."

They were married three weeks later. As each of them had just returned from a journey, they spent their honeymoon at home.

A week after the wedding they were seated, one afternoon, on the piazza of the colonel's house, where Dick had taken his bride, when a negro from the yard ran down the lane and threw open the big gate for the colonel's buggy to enter. The colonel was not alone. Beside him, ragged and travel-stained, bowed with weariness, and upon his face a haggard look that told of hardship and privation, sat the lost Grandison.

The colonel alighted at the steps.

"Take the lines, Tom," he said to the man who had opened the gate, "and drive round to the barn. Help Grandison down — poor devil, he's so stiff he can hardly move! — and get a tub of water and wash him and rub him down, and feed him, and give him a big drink of whiskey, and then let him come round and see his young master and his new mistress."

The colonel's face wore an expression compounded of joy and indignation — joy at the restoration of a valuable piece of property; indignation for reasons he proceeded to state.

"It's astounding, the depths of depravity the human heart is capable of! I was coming along the road three miles away, when I heard some one call me from the roadside. I pulled up the mare, and who should come out of the woods but Grandison. The poor nigger could hardly crawl along, with the help of a broken limb. I was never more astonished in my life. You could have knocked me down with a feather. He seemed pretty far gone — he could hardly talk above a whisper — and I had to give him a mouthful of whiskey to brace him up so he could tell his story. It's just as I thought from the beginning, Dick; Grandison had no notion of running away; he knew when he was well off, and where his friends were. All the persuasions of abolition liars and runaway niggers did not move him. But the desperation of those fanatics knew no bounds; their guilty consciences gave them no rest. They got the notion somehow that Grandison belonged to a nigger-catcher, and had been brought North as a spy to help capture ungrateful run-away servants. They actually kidnaped him – just think if it! – and gagged him and bound him and threw him rudely into a wagon, and carried him into the gloomy depths of a Canadian forest, and locked him in a lonely hut, and fed him on bread and water for three weeks. One of the scoundrels wanted to kill him, and persuaded the others that it ought to be done; but they got to quarreling about how they should do it, and before they had their minds made up Grandison escaped, and, keeping his back steadily to the North Star, made his way, after suffering incredible hardships, back to the old planta-tion, back to his master, his friends, and his home. Why, it's as good as one of Scott's novels![9] Mr. Simms[10] or some other one of our Southern authors ought to write it up."

"Don't you think, sir," suggested Dick, who had calmly smoked his cigar throughout the colonel's animated recital, "that that kidnaping yarn sounds a little improbable? Isn't there some more likely explanation?"

"Nonsense, Dick; it's the gospel truth! Those infernal abolitionists are capable of anything – everything! Just think of their locking the poor, faithful nigger up, beating him, kicking him, depriving him of his liberty, keeping him on bread and water for three long, lonesome weeks, and he all the time pining for the old plantation!"

There were almost tears in the colonel's eyes at the picture of Grandison's sufferings that he conjured up. Dick still professed to be slightly skeptical, and met Charity's se-verely questioning eye with bland unconsciousness.

The colonel killed the fatted calf[11] for Grandison, and for two or three weeks the returned wanderer's life was a slave's dream of pleasure. His fame spread throughout the county, and the colonel gave him a permanent place among the house servants, where he could always have him conveniently at hand to relate his adventures to admir-ing visitors.

About three weeks after Grandison's return the colonel's faith in sable humanity was rudely shaken, and its foundations almost broken up. He came near losing his belief in the fidelity of the negro to his master, – the servile virtue most highly prized and most sedulously cultivated by the colonel and his kind. One Monday morning Grandison was missing. And not only Grandison, but his wife, Betty the maid; his mother, aunt Eunice; his father, uncle Ike; his brothers, Tom and John, and his little sister Elsie, were likewise absent from the plantation; and a hurried search and in-quiry in the neighborhood resulted in no information as to their whereabouts. So much valuable property could not be lost without an effort to recover it, and the wholesale nature of the transaction carried consternation to the hearts of those whose ledgers were chiefly bound in black. Extremely energetic measures were taken by the colonel and his friends. The fugitives were traced, and followed from point to

---

9. **Scott's novels:** The acclaimed historical romances of the British novelist Sir Walter Scott (1771-1832) were bestsellers in the United States.

10. **Mr. Simms:** William Gilmore Simms (1806-1870), a popular Southern writer.

11. **fatted calf:** An allusion to the parable of the prodigal son, whose father celebrates his return home by ordering the killing of a calf fattened up for a feast (Luke 15:11-33).

point, on their northward run through Ohio. Several times the hunters were close upon their heels, but the magnitude of the escaping party begot unusual vigilance on the part of those who sympathized with the fugitives, and strangely enough, the underground railroad seemed to have had its tracks cleared and signals set for this particular train. Once, twice, the colonel thought he had them, but they slipped through his fingers.

One last glimpse he caught of his vanishing property, as he stood, accompanied by a United States marshal, on a wharf at a port on the south shore of Lake Erie. On the stern of a small steamboat which was receding rapidly from the wharf, with her nose pointing toward Canada, there stood a group of familiar dark faces, and the look they cast backward was not one of longing for the fleshpots of Egypt.[12] The colonel saw Grandison point him out to one of the crew of the vessel, who waved his hand derisively toward the colonel. The latter shook his fist impotently – and the incident was closed.

[1899]

---

12. **fleshpots of Egypt:** As Moses led the Israelites out of slavery to the promised land, they endured such great hunger in the wilderness that they declared, "Would to God we had died by the hand of the Lord in the land of Egypt, when we sat by the flesh pots, and when we did eat bread to the full" (Exodus 16:3).

Pauline E. Hopkins

[1859-1930]

Pauline Elizabeth Hopkins, who has been hailed as "the Dean of African American women writers," was born in Portland, Maine, in 1859. Her father died when Hopkins was a young child, and her mother married William A. Hopkins, a tailor and a veteran of the Civil War. The family moved to Boston, where Hopkins attended public schools and developed an interest in writing. When she was fifteen, Hopkins won first prize in an essay contest sponsored in part by William Wells Brown, the abolitionist, activist, and author of *Clotel* (1853), the first novel published by an African American. After her graduation from Boston Girls High School, Hopkins, her mother, and her stepfather formed a theatrical troupe, the Hopkins Colored Troubadours. In 1880, the group performed a play written by Hopkins, *Peculiar Sam; or, The Underground Railroad*, one of the earliest musical dramas in the history of black theater in the United States. An accomplished singer, Hopkins toured with the troupe for twelve years, becoming widely known as "Boston's Favorite Soprano." Early in the 1890s, however, she left the troupe and trained as a stenographer to support herself while she pursued a career in writing. Hopkins soon began to earn a reputation as a speaker, lecturing on African American history at churches and reading her fiction at women's clubs in Boston.

Pauline E. Hopkins
This photograph appeared in the supplement to the March 1904 issue of the *Colored American Magazine.*

Within a decade, Hopkins reached the zenith of her brief but remarkable literary career. In 1900, she published her first and best-known novel, *Contending Forces; or, A Romance Illustrative of Negro Life North and South*, the saga of the injustices suffered by several generations of a black family before and after the Civil War. The epigraph to the novel, which she took from Ralph Waldo Emerson's 1844 "Address on the Emancipation in the British West Indies," expresses a central thesis in all of Hopkins's work: "The civility of no race can be perfect whilst another race is degraded." The year the novel was published, Hopkins helped found the *Colored American Magazine* in Boston. As an announcement read, the new magazine was designed to be *"Of the Race, By the Race, For the Race,"* an echo of the closing lines of Abraham Lincoln's Gettysburg Address. When Hopkins became its editor in 1903, she stated that the magazine was

> intended to show that the colored people can advance on all the lines of progress known to other races, that they can be more than tillers of the soils, hewers of wood and drawers of water—that they can attain to eminence (both the men and women among them) as thinkers, writers, as doctors, as lawyers, as clergymen, as singers, musicians, artists, actors, and also as successful business men, in the conduct of enterprises of importance.

[Pauline Hopkins] has given us a sense of her day, a clue *collection, and we can use the light of it to clarify our understanding and our intuition. We can take the building blocks she does supply us and use them to fill in old gaps.*

—Gwendolyn Brooks

Hopkins was also the major contributor to the *Colored American Magazine*. True to her goal of illustrating the potential of African Americans and instilling pride in their achievements, Hopkins wrote two extended series of essays for the magazine, *Famous Men of the Negro Race* (1900-01) and *Famous Women of the Negro Race* (1901-02). She also published a substantial amount of fiction in the magazine, seven stories and three serialized novels: *Hagar's Daughter: A Story of Southern Caste Prejudice* (1901-02); *Winona: A Tale of Negro Life in the South and Southwest* (1902); and *Of One Blood; or, The Hidden Self* (1902-03).

Following that prolific period of creativity, Hopkins's literary career virtually ended. In 1904, the *Colored American Magazine* came under the control of Booker T. Washington, who strongly disapproved of what he considered to be Hopkins's radical politics and her commitment to the doctrine of racial uplift espoused by African American leaders such as W. E. B. Du Bois. Hopkins was consequently ousted from the editorship of the magazine, in which no more of her works appeared. Despite that painful rebuff, she published two groundbreaking historical works the following year: a pamphlet entitled *A Primer of Facts Pertaining to the Early Greatness of the African Race and the Possibility of Restoration by Its Descendants* and "The Dark Races of the Twentieth Century," a four-part series of essays on the global African community that appeared in *The Voice of the Negro*. More than a decade later, in 1916, she published a two-part essay in another African American magazine, the *New Era*. But she apparently did little other writing. Hopkins died in 1930 in a house fire at her home in Cambridge, Massachusetts, where she was working as a stenographer for the Massachusetts Institute of Technology.

Reading Hopkins's "'As the Lord Lives, He Is One of Our Mother's Children.'"   This story was one of Hopkins's final contributions to the *Colored American Magazine*. Although it was primarily literary, the magazine included a wide range of essays on the past and present experiences of African Americans, as well as articles on current social issues in the United States. Many of the stories and serialized novels published in the magazine were also strongly shaped by social activism. A major concern was lynching, most often the hanging of black men for their alleged crimes by lawless white mobs. The number of such lynchings, which were rampant in the South for five decades after the end of Reconstruction in 1876, peaked during the 1890s. In "'As the Lord Lives, He Is One of Our Mother's Children,'" Hopkins offers a powerful indictment of that murderous manifestation of racial prejudice and the hatred of blacks in the United States, what the antilynching activist Ida B. Wells called "our country's national crime." The text is taken from the first printing in the *Colored American Magazine*, November 1903.

bedfordstmartins.com/ americanlit for research links on Hopkins

The *Colored American Magazine*

Even before she became its editor, Hopkins was the major contributor to the *Colored American Magazine*, in which she frequently highlighted the civic and cultural activities of middle-class women, as in the featured article in this issue, and the achievements of other African Americans.

"AS THE LORD LIVES,
HE IS ONE OF OUR MOTHER'S CHILDREN"[1]

It was Saturday afternoon in a large Western town, and the Rev. Septimus Stevens sat in his study writing down the headings for his Sunday sermon. It was slow work; somehow the words would not flow with their usual ease, although his brain was teeming with ideas. He had written for his heading at the top of the sheet these words for a text: "As I live, he is one of our mother's children." It was to be a great effort on the Negro question,[2] and the reverend gentleman, with his New England training, was in full sympathy with his subject. He had jotted down a few headings under it, when he came to a full stop; his mind simply refused to work. Finally, with a sigh, he opened the compartment in his desk where his sermons were packed and began turning over those old creations in search of something suitable for the morrow.

Suddenly the whistles in all directions began to blow wildly. The Rev. Septimus hurried to the window, threw it open and leaned out, anxious to learn the cause of the wild clamor. Could it be another of the terrible "cave-ins," that were the terror of every mining district? Men were pouring out of the mines as fast as they could come up. The crowds which surged through the streets night and day were rushing to meet them. Hundreds of policemen were about; each corner was guarded by a squad commanded by a sergeant. The police and the mob were evidently working together. Tramp, tramp, on they rushed; down the serpentine boulevard for nearly two miles they went swelling like an angry torrent. In front of the open window where stood the white-faced clergyman they paused. A man mounted the empty barrel and harangued the crowd: "I am from Dover City, gentlemen, and I have come here to-day to assist you in teaching the blacks a lesson. I have killed a nigger before," he yelled, "and in revenge of the wrong wrought upon you and yours I am willing to kill again. The only way you can teach these niggers a lesson is to go to the jail and lynch these men as an object lesson. String them up! That is the only thing to do. Kill them, string them up, lynch them! I will lead you. On to the prison and lynch Jones and Wilson, the black fiends!" With a hoarse shout, in which were mingled cries like the screams of enraged hyenas and the snarls of tigers, they rushed on.

Nora, the cook, burst open the study door, pale as a sheet, and dropped at the minister's feet. "Mother of God!" she cried, "and is it the end of the wurruld?"

On the maddened men rushed from north, south, east and west, armed with everything from a brick to a horse-pistol.[3] In the melee a man was shot down. Somebody planted a long knife in the body of a little black newsboy for no apparent reason. Every now and then a Negro would be overwhelmed somewhere on the outskirts of the crowd and left beaten to a pulp. Then they reached the jail and battered in the door.

---

1. **"As the Lord Lives . . . Children"**: Although this is not a biblical quotation, the expressions "As the Lord lives" and "As I live, saith the Lord" are frequently used in the Bible.
2. **The Negro question**: The general term for debates concerning race and the place of African Americans in the social, political, and economic life of the United States.
3. **horse-pistol**: A larger revolver usually carried in a holster by horsemen.

The solitary watcher at the window tried to move, but could not; terror had stricken his very soul, and his white lips moved in articulate prayer. The crowd surged back. In the midst was only one man; for some reason, the other was missing. A rope was knotted about his neck—charged with murder, himself about to be murdered. The hands which drew the rope were too swift, and, half-strangled, the victim fell. The crowd halted, lifted him up, loosened the rope and let the wretch breathe.

He was a grand man—physically—black as ebony, tall, straight, deep-chested, every fibre full of that life so soon to be quenched. Lucifer, just about to be cast out of heaven, could not have thrown around a glance of more scornful pride.[4] What might not such a man have been, if—but it was too late. "Run fair, boys," said the prisoner, calmly, "run fair! You keep up your end of the rope and I'll keep up mine."

The crowd moved a little more slowly, and the minister saw the tall form "keeping up" its end without a tremor of hesitation. As they neared the telegraph pole, with its outstretched arm, the watcher summoned up his lost strength, grasped the curtain and pulled it down to shut out the dreadful sight. Then came a moment of ominous silence. The man of God sank upon his knees to pray for the passing soul. A thousand-voiced cry of brutal triumph arose in cheers for the work that had been done, and curses and imprecations, and they who had hunted a man out of life hurried off to hunt for gold.

To and fro on the white curtain swung the black silhouette of what had been a man.

For months the minister heard in the silence of the night phantom echoes of those frightful voices, and awoke, shuddering, from some dream whose vista was closed by that black figure swinging in the air.

About a month after this happening, the rector was returning from a miner's cabin in the mountains where a child lay dying. The child haunted him; he thought of his own motherless boy and a fountain of pity overflowed in his heart. He had dismounted and was walking along the road to the ford at the creek which just here cut the path fairly in two.

The storm of the previous night had refreshed all nature and had brought out the rugged beauty of the landscape in all its grandeur. The sun had withdrawn his last dazzling rays from the eastern highlands upon which the lone traveler gazed, and now they were fast veiling themselves in purple night shadows that rendered them momentarily more grand and mysterious. The man of God stood a moment with uncovered head repeating aloud some lines from a great Russian poet:

> "O Thou eternal One! whose presence bright
> All space doth occupy, all motion guide;
> Unchanged through time's all devastating flight;
> Thou only God! There is no God beside
> Being above all beings, Mighty One!
> Whom none can comprehend and none, explore."[5]

---

4. **Lucifer . . . pride:** The account of Lucifer, or Satan, being cast out of heaven for the sin of pride is found in Isaiah 14:12–15, though Hopkins probably had in mind the famous account of Satan's failed rebellion against God depicted in book I of *Paradise Lost* by the English poet John Milton (1608–1674).
5. **"O Thou . . . explore":** The lines are from a translation of "God," by the Russian poet Gavrila Romanovich Derzhavin (1743–1816).

Another moment passed in silent reverence of the All-Wonderful, before he turned to remount his horse and enter the waters of the creek. The creek was very much swollen and he found it hard to keep the ford. Just as he was midway the stream he saw something lying half in the water on the other bank. Approaching nearer he discovered it to be a man, apparently unconscious. Again dismounting, he tied his horse to a sapling, and went up to the inert figure, ready, like the Samaritan of old,[6] to succor the wayside fallen. The man opened his deep-set eyes and looked at him keenly. He was gaunt, haggard and despairing, and soaking wet.

"Well, my man, what is the matter?" Rev. Mr. Stevens had a very direct way of going at things.

"Nothing," was the sullen response.

"Can't I help you? You seem ill. Why are you lying in the water?"

"I must have fainted and fallen in the creek," replied the man, answering the last question first. "I've tramped from Colorado hunting for work. I'm penniless, have no home, haven't had much to eat for a week, and now I've got a touch of your d— mountain fever." He shivered as if with a chill, and smiled faintly.

The man, from his speech, was well educated, and in spite of his pitiful situation, had an air of good breeding, barring his profanity.

"What's your name?" asked Stevens, glancing him over sharply as he knelt beside the man and deftly felt his pulse and laid a cool hand on the fevered brow.

"Stone — George Stone."

Stevens got up. "Well, Stone, try to get on my horse and I'll take you to the rectory. My housekeeper and I together will manage to make you more comfortable."

So it happened that George Stone became a guest at the parsonage, and later, sexton of the church. In that gold-mining region, where new people came and went constantly and new excitements were things of everyday occurrence, and new faces as plenty as old ones, nobody asked or cared where the new sexton came from. He did his work quietly and thoroughly, and quite won Nora's heart by his handy ways about the house. He had a room under the eaves, and seemed thankful and content. Little Flip, the rector's son, took a special liking to him, and he, on his side, worshipped the golden-haired child and was never tired of playing with him and inventing things for his amusement.

"The reverend sets a heap by the boy," he said to Nora one day in reply to her accusation that he spoiled the boy and there was no living with him since Stone's advent. "He won't let me thank him for what he's done for me, but he can't keep me from loving the child."

One day in September, while passing along the street, Rev. Stevens had his attention called to a flaming poster on the side of a fence by the remarks of a crowd of men near him. He turned and read it:

$1,500 REWARD!

"The above reward will be paid for information leading to the arrest of 'Gentleman Jim,' charged with complicity in the murder of Jerry Mason. This nigger is six feet, three inches

---

6. **the Samaritan of old**: Jesus tells the parable of a Samaritan, an inhabitant of Samaria, who aids a traveler who has been beaten, robbed, and left for dead by the side of a road, in Luke 10:29-37.

tall, weight one hundred and sixty pounds. He escaped from jail when his pal was lynched two months ago by a citizen's committee. It is thought that he is in the mountains, etc. He is well educated, and might be taken for a white man. Wore, when last seen, blue jumper and overalls and cowhide boots."

He read it the second time, and he was dimly conscious of seeing, like a vision in the brain, a man playing about the parsonage with little Flip.

"I knowed him. I worked a spell with him over in Lone Tree Gulch before he got down on his luck," spoke a man at his side who was reading the poster with him. "Jones and him was two of the smartest and peaceablest niggers I ever seed. But Jerry Mason kinder sot on 'em both; never could tell why, only some white men can't 'bide a nigger eny mo' than a dog can a cat; it's a natural antiperthy. I'm free to say the niggers seemed harmless, but you can't tell what a man'll do when his blood's up."

He turned to the speaker. "What will happen if they catch him?"

"Lynch him sure, there's been a lot of trouble over there lately. I wouldn't give a tossup for him if they get their hands on him once more."

Rev. Stevens pushed his way through the crowd, and went slowly down the street to the church. He found Stone there sweeping and dusting. Saying that he wanted to speak with him, he led the way to the study. Facing around upon him suddenly, Stevens said, gravely: "I want you to tell me the truth. Is your real name 'Stone,' and are you a Negro?"

A shudder passed over Stone's strong frame, then he answered, while his eyes never left the troubled face before him, "I am a Negro, and my name is not Stone."

"You said that you had tramped from Colorado."

"I hadn't. I was hiding in the woods; I had been there a month ago. I lied to you."

"Is it all a lie?"

Stone hesitated, and then said: "I was meaning to tell you the first night, but somehow I couldn't. I was afraid you'd turn me out; and I was sick and miserable —"

"Tell me the truth now."

"I will; I'll tell you the God's truth."

He leaned his hand on the back of a chair to steady himself; he was trembling violently. "I came out West from Wilmington, North Carolina,[7] Jones and I together. We were both college men and chums from childhood. All our savings were in the business we had at home when the leading men of the town conceived the idea of driving the Negroes out, and the Wilmington tragedy began. Jones was unmarried, but I lost wife and children that night – burned to death when the mob fired our home. When we got out here we took up claims in the mountains. They were a rough crowd after we struck pay dirt, but Jones and I kept to ourselves and got along all right until Mason joined the crowd. He was from Wilmington; knew us, and took delight in tormenting us. He was a fighting man, but we wouldn't let him push us into trouble."

---

7. **Wilmington, North Carolina**: The site of a race riot in November 1898, during which a mob of white supremacists murdered dozens of African Americans, burned the offices of a black newspaper, and overthrew the elected city government in what is widely viewed as the only realized coup d'état in American history.

"You didn't quarrel with him, then?"

The minister gazed at Stone keenly. He seemed a man to trust. "Yes, I did. We didn't want trouble, but we couldn't let Mason rob us. We three had hot words before a big crowd; that was all there was to it that night. In the morning Mason lay dead upon our claim. He'd been shot by some one. My partner and I were arrested, brought to this city and lodged in the jail over there. Jones was lynched! God, can I ever forget that hooting, yelling crowd, and the terrible fight to get away! Somehow I did it — you know the rest."

"Stone, there's a reward for you, and a description of you as you were the night I found you."

Gentleman Jim's face was ashy. "I'll never be taken alive. They'll kill me for what I never did!"

"Not unless I speak. I am in sore doubt what course to take. If I give you up the Vigalantes will hang you."

"I'm a lost man," said the Negro, helplessly, "but I'll never be taken alive."

Stevens walked up and down the room once or twice. It was a human life in his hands. If left to the law to decide, even then in this particular case the Negro stood no chance. It was an awful question to decide. One more turn up and down the little room and suddenly stopping, he flung himself upon his knees in the middle of the room, and raising his clasped hands, cried aloud for heavenly guidance. Such a prayer as followed, the startled listener had never before heard anywhere. There was nothing of rhetorical phrases, nothing of careful thought in the construction of sentences, it was the outpouring of a pure soul asking for help from its Heavenly Father with all the trustfulness of a little child. It came in a torrent, a flood; it wrestled mightily for the blessing it sought. Rising to his feet when his prayer was finished, Rev. Stevens said, "Stone, — you are to remain Stone, you know — it is best to leave things as they are. Go back to work."

The man raised his bowed head.

"You mean you're not going to give me up?"

"Stay here till the danger is past; then leave for other parts."

Stone's face turned red, then pale, his voice trembled and tears were in the gray eyes. "I can't thank you, Mr. Stevens, but if ever I get the chance you'll find me grateful."

"All right, Stone, all right," and the minister went back to his writing.

That fall the Rev. Septimus Stevens went to visit his old New England home — he and Flip. He was returning home the day before Thanksgiving, with his widowed mother, who had elected to leave old associations and take charge of her son's home. It was a dim-colored day.

Engineers were laying out a new road near a place of swamps and oozy ground and dead, wet grass, over-arched by leafless, desolate boughs. They were eating their lunch now, seated about on the trunks of fallen trees. The jokes were few, scarcely a pun seasoned the meal. The day was a dampener; that the morrow was a holiday did not kindle merriment.

Stone sat a little apart from the rest. He had left Rev. Stevens when he got this job in another state. They had voted him moody and unsociable long ago — a man who broods forever upon his wrongs is not a comfortable companion; he never gave any one a key to his moods. He shut himself up in his haunted room – haunted by memory – and no one interfered with him.

The afternoon brought a change in the weather. There was a strange hush, as if Nature were holding her breath. But it was as a wild beast holds its breath before a spring. Suddenly a little chattering wind ran along the ground. It was too weak to lift the sodden leaves, yet it made itself heard in some way, and grew stronger. It seemed dizzy, and ran about in a circle. There was a pale light over all, a brassy, yellow light, that gave all things a wild look. The chief of the party took an observation and said: "We'd better get home."

Stone lingered. He was paler, older.

The wind had grown vigorous now and began to tear angrily at the trees, twisting the saplings about with invisible hands. There was a rush and a roar that seemed to spread about in every direction. A tree was furiously uprooted and fell directly in front of him; Stone noticed the storm for the first time.

He looked about him in a dazed way and muttered, "He's coming on this train, he and the kid!"

The brassy light deepened into darkness. Stone went upon the railroad track, and stumbled over something that lay directly over it. It was a huge tree that the wind had lifted in its great strength and whirled over there like thistledown. He raised himself slowly, a little confused by the fall. He took hold of the tree mechanically, but the huge bulk would not yield an inch.

He looked about in the gathering darkness; it was five miles to the station where he might get help. His companions were too far on their way to recall, and there lay a huge mass, directly in the way of the coming train. He had no watch, but he knew it must be nearly six. Soon – very soon – upon the iron pathway, a great train, freighted with life, would dash around the curve to wreck and ruin! Again he muttered, "Coming on this train, he and the kid!" He pictured the faces of his benefactor and the little child, so like his own lost one, cold in death; the life crushed out by the cruel wheels. What was it that seemed to strike across the storm and all its whirl of sound – a child's laugh? Nay, something fainter still – the memory of a child's laugh. It was like a breath of spring flowers in the desolate winter – a touch of heart music amid the revel of the storm. A vision of other fathers with children climbing upon their knees, a soft babble of baby voices assailed him.

"God help me to save them!" he cried.

Again and again he tugged at the tree. It would not move. Then he hastened and got an iron bar from among the tools. Again he strove – once – twice – thrice. With a groan the nearest end gave way. Eureka! If only his strength would hold out. He felt it ebbing slowly from him, something seemed to clutch at his heart; his head swam. Again and yet again he exerted all his strength. There came a prolonged shriek that awoke the echoes. The train was coming. The tree was moving! It was almost off the other rail. The leafless trees seemed to enfold him – to hold him with skeleton arms. "Oh, God save them!" he gasped. "Our times are in Thy hand!"

Something struck him a terrible blow. The agony was ended. Stone was dead.

Rev. Stevens closed his eyes, with a deadly faintness creeping over him, when he saw how near the trainload of people had been to destruction. Only God had saved them at the eleventh hour through the heroism of Stone, who lay dead upon the track, the life crushed out of him by the engine. An inarticulate thanksgiving rose to his lips as soft and clear came the sound of distant church bells, calling to weekly prayer, like "horns of Elfland softly blowing."[8]

Sunday, a week later, Rev. Septimus Stevens preached the greatest sermon of his life. They had found the true murderer of Jerry Mason, and Jones and Gentleman Jim were publicly exonerated by a repentant community.

On this Sunday Rev. Stevens preached the funeral sermon of Gentleman Jim. The church was packed to suffocation by a motley assemblage of men in all stages of dress and undress, but there was sincerity in their hearts as they listened to the preacher's burning words: "As the Lord lives, he is one of our mother's children."

[1903]

---

8. **"horns . . . blowing"**: From *The Princess*, by the English poet Alfred, Lord Tennyson (1809-1892): "O hark, O hear! how thin and clear, / And thinner, clearer, farther going! / O sweet and far from cliff and scar / The horns of Elfland faintly blowing!" (IV:7-10).

Charlotte Perkins Gilman

[1860-1935]

Charlotte Perkins Gilman was born Charlotte Anna Perkins in Hartford, Connecticut, on July 3, 1860. She was the daughter of Mary Westcott and Frederick Beecher Perkins, a nephew of Harriet Beecher Stowe, the famous author of *Uncle Tom's Cabin*. After Frederick Perkins abandoned his family, his destitute wife took their two young children to Providence, Rhode Island, where Gilman briefly attended school. Although she preferred drawing and writing poetry to academic studies, Gilman developed an abiding interest in science. In a chapter in her autobiography titled "Girlhood – If Any," Gilman later assessed her character and intellectual condition at "Sixteen, with a life to build":

> My mother's profound religious tendency and implacable sense of duty; my father's intellectual appetite; a will power, well developed, from both; a passion of my own for scientific knowledge, for real laws of life; an insatiable demand for perfection in everything, and that proven process of mine for acquiring habits.

Alluding to Henry Wadsworth Longfellow's sentimental poem "Maidenhood," in which a meek and timid maiden stands poised on the brink of "womanhood," Gilman concluded that "instead of 'Standing with reluctant feet where the brook and river meet,' I plunged in and swam."

The unconventional Gilman increasingly found herself swimming against the main currents of American culture and society. When she was eighteen and still seeking a way to "build" her life, Gilman pursued her interest in art by studying at the Rhode Island School of Design. Determined to become independent, she supported herself by teaching art, designing greeting cards, and working as a governess. In 1882, she met a promising local artist, Charles Walter Stetson. After a two-year courtship, during which Gilman constantly questioned whether she could pursue a career if she became a wife and mother, she married Stetson. Following the birth of their daughter, Katherine, in 1885, Gilman became so severely depressed that she sought treatment from Silas Weir Mitchell, a physician who had developed the "rest cure" for what were then called "nervous diseases," a diagnosis more frequently applied to women patients. Mitchell's direction that she should sharply limit her intellectual activity brought Gilman "near the border line of utter mental ruin," as she later observed. She consequently went back to work, writing articles on dress reform and other women's issues. In 1888, she left her husband, whom she later divorced, and moved with her daughter to Pasadena, California. There, she wrote and lectured on a wide range of topics, including "The Labor Movement." Her poem "Similar Cases" (1890), a satire of those who opposed social change and human progress, brought her wide recognition and led to the publication of the first of her two volumes of poetry, *In This Our World* (1893). Gilman also wrote the earliest of her almost two hundred stories, the best known of which, "The Yellow Wall-Paper," appeared in 1892. Two years later, after sending her daughter back East to live with her former husband and his new wife, Gilman moved to San Francisco to edit the radical *Impress*, the organ of the Pacific Coast Woman's Press Association. When the paper failed in 1895, Gilman accepted an invitation from the social and labor reformer Jane Addams to live at Hull House, the famous settlement house for recent immigrants in Chicago.

Gilman devoted the rest of her life to lecturing, writing, and other work on behalf of women and social reform. In 1898, she published her major sociological work, *Women and Economics: A Study of the Economic Relation between Men and Women as a Factor in Social Evolution*. Two years later, Gilman married a younger cousin, George Houghton Gilman, with whom she was by all accounts very happy. During the following decade, she extended her feminist analysis of American culture and institutions in a series of books: *Concerning Children* (1900); *The Home: Its Work and Influence* (1903); *Human Work* (1904); and *The Man-Made World; or, Our Androcentric Culture* (1911). She also published hundreds of works in periodicals ranging from women's magazines to the *American Journal of Sociology*, as well as in the *Forerunner*, a monthly magazine Gilman edited from 1909 to 1916. Many of her short stories and all of her longer fictional works first appeared in the magazine, including serializations of her feminist utopian novels *Herland* (1915) and its sequel, *With Her in Ourland* (1916). A Socialist and pacifist who helped form the Women's Peace Party in 1915, Gilman also tirelessly campaigned for social causes, including the right of women to have unrestricted access to birth control and their right to vote, which was finally gained in 1920. Her later writings included *His*

Charlotte Perkins Gilman

When this photograph was taken in 1896, Gilman was already widely known as a writer, social reformer, and feminist.

bedfordstmartins.com/ americanlit *for research links on Gilman*

Religion and Hers (1923), a sweeping critique of Christian theology and male-dominated conceptions of morality, and her posthumously published autobiography, *The Living of Charlotte Perkins Gilman* (1935). After the death of her husband in 1934, Gilman discovered that she had breast cancer. Committed to "The Right to Die," the title of her final article, Gilman committed suicide by taking an overdose of chloroform on August 17, 1935.

Reading Gilman's "The Yellow Wall-Paper."   On August 28, 1890, Gilman recorded in her diary that she had sent "The Yellow Wall-Paper" to William Dean Howells, who had earlier written her an admiring letter about one of her poems, "Similar Cases." Howells, who later described Gilman's story as "terrible and too wholly dire" and "too terribly good to be printed," sent it to Horace Scudder, the editor of the *Atlantic Monthly*. Scudder rejected the story, which he returned to Gilman along with a brief note: "Dear Madam, Mr. Howells has handed me this story. I could not forgive myself if I made others as miserable as I have made myself!" Undaunted, Gilman sent the story to the *National Review*, where it was also rejected, and then to the *New England Magazine*, where it finally appeared in 1892. In an article titled "Why I Wrote *The Yellow Wall-Paper*?" published in 1916 in her magazine, the *Forerunner*, Gilman explained that the story was based on her own treatment for "melancholia," or depression, under the care of "a noted specialist in nervous

"I am sitting by the Window in this Atrocious Nursery."

The Yellow Wall-Paper

This illustration appeared above the title of Gilman's story in the first printing in the *New England Magazine*.

diseases, the best known in the country." He had "applied the rest cure" and then sent her home "with solemn advice to 'live as domestic a life as far as possible,' to 'have but two hours' intellectual life a day,' and 'never to touch pen, brush or pencil again.'" Observing that she had sent a copy of "The Yellow Wall-Paper" to "the physician who so nearly drove me mad," and who had consequently altered his treatment, Gilman triumphantly concluded that the story "was not intended to drive people crazy, but to save people from being driven crazy, and it worked." But the gothic story of a woman's descent into madness is more than an indictment of nineteenth-century medical practices. It is also a study of the politics of marriage and the restrictive roles then assigned to women in the United States. The text is taken from the first printing in the *New England Magazine*, January 1892.

THE YELLOW WALL-PAPER

It is very seldom that mere ordinary people like John and myself secure ancestral halls for the summer.

A colonial mansion, a hereditary estate, I would say a haunted house, and reach the height of romantic felicity – but that would be asking too much of fate!

Still I will proudly declare that there is something queer about it.

Else, why should it be let so cheaply? And why have stood so long untenanted?

John laughs at me, of course, but one expects that in marriage.

John is practical in the extreme. He has no patience with faith, an intense horror of superstition, and he scoffs openly at any talk of things not to be felt and seen and put down in figures.

John is a physician, and *perhaps* – (I would not say it to a living soul, of course, but this is dead paper and a great relief to my mind) – *perhaps* that is one reason I do not get well faster.

You see, he does not believe I am sick!

And what can one do?

If a physician of high standing, and one's own husband, assures friends and relatives that there is really nothing the matter with one but temporary nervous depression – a slight hysterical tendency[1] – what is one to do?

My brother is also a physician, and also of high standing, and he says the same thing.

---

1. **hysterical tendency:** In the nineteenth century, hysteria (from the Greek *husterikos*, meaning "of the womb") was thought to be an emotional disorder suffered exclusively by women, resulting in a variety of physical symptoms such as overdramatic behavior, selective amnesia, fatigue, and depression.

So I take phosphates or phosphites[2] – whichever it is, and tonics, and journeys, and air, and exercise, and am absolutely forbidden to "work" until I am well again.

Personally, I disagree with their ideas.

Personally, I believe that congenial work, with excitement and change, would do me good.

But what is one to do?

I did write for a while in spite of them; but it *does* exhaust me a good deal – having to be so sly about it, or else meet with heavy opposition.

I sometimes fancy that in my condition if I had less opposition and more society and stimulus – but John says the very worst thing I can do is to think about my condition, and I confess it always makes me feel bad.

So I will let it alone and talk about the house.

The most beautiful place! It is quite alone, standing well back from the road, quite three miles from the village. It makes me think of English places that you read about, for there are hedges and walls and gates that lock, and lots of separate little houses for the gardeners and people.

There is a *delicious* garden! I never saw such a garden – large and shady, full of box-bordered paths, and lined with long grape-covered arbors with seats under them.

There were greenhouses, too, but they are all broken now.

There was some legal trouble, I believe, something about the heirs and co-heirs; anyhow, the place has been empty for years.

That spoils my ghostliness, I am afraid, but I don't care – there is something strange about the house – I can feel it.

I even said so to John one moonlight evening, but he said what I felt was a *draught*, and shut the window.

I get unreasonably angry with John sometimes. I'm sure I never used to be so sensitive. I think it is due to this nervous condition.

But John says if I feel so, I shall neglect proper self-control; so I take pains to control myself – before him, at least, and that makes me very tired.

I don't like our room a bit. I wanted one downstairs that opened on the piazza and had roses all over the window, and such pretty old-fashioned chintz hangings! but John would not hear of it.

He said there was only one window and not room for two beds, and no near room for him if he took another.

He is very careful and loving, and hardly lets me stir without special direction.

I have a schedule prescription for each hour in the day; he takes all care from me, and so I feel basely ungrateful not to value it more.

He said we came here solely on my account, that I was to have perfect rest and all the air I could get. "Your exercise depends on your strength, my dear," said he, "and your

---

2. **phosphates or phosphites:** Derived from phosphoric acid, these compounds were used to treat forms of exhaustion in the nineteenth century.

food somewhat on your appetite; but air you can absorb all the time." So we took the nursery at the top of the house.

It is a big, airy room, the whole floor nearly, with windows that look all ways, and air and sunshine galore. It was nursery first and then playroom and gymnasium, I should judge; for the windows are barred for little children, and there are rings and things in the walls.

The paint and paper look as if a boys' school had used it. It is stripped off – the paper – in great patches all around the head of my bed, about as far as I can reach, and in a great place on the other side of the room low down. I never saw a worse paper in my life.

One of those sprawling flamboyant patterns committing every artistic sin.

It is dull enough to confuse the eye in following, pronounced enough to constantly irritate and provoke study, and when you follow the lame uncertain curves for a little distance they suddenly commit suicide – plunge off at outrageous angles, destroy themselves in unheard of contradictions.

The color is repellant, almost revolting; a smouldering unclean yellow, strangely faded by the slow-turning sunlight.

It is a dull yet lurid orange in some places, a sickly sulphur tint in others.

No wonder the children hated it! I should hate it myself if I had to live in this room long.

There comes John, and I must put this away, – he hates to have me write a word.

We have been here two weeks, and I haven't felt like writing before, since that first day.

I am sitting by the window now, up in this atrocious nursery, and there is nothing to hinder my writing as much as I please, save lack of strength.

John is away all day, and even some nights when his cases are serious.

I am glad my case is not serious!

But these nervous troubles are dreadfully depressing.

John does not know how much I really suffer. He knows there is no *reason* to suffer, and that satisfies him.

Of course it is only nervousness. It does weigh on me so not to do my duty in any way!

I meant to be such a help to John, such a real rest and comfort, and here I am a comparative burden already!

Nobody would believe what an effort it is to do what little I am able, – to dress and entertain, and order things.

It is fortunate Mary is so good with the baby. Such a dear baby!

And yet I *cannot* be with him, it makes me so nervous.

I suppose John never was nervous in his life. He laughs at me so about this wall-paper!

At first he meant to repaper the room, but afterward he said that I was letting it get the better of me, and that nothing was worse for a nervous patient than to give way to such fancies.

He said that after the wall-paper was changed it would be the heavy bedstead, and then the barred windows, and then that gate at the head of the stairs, and so on.

"You know the place is doing you good," he said, "and really, dear, I don't care to renovate the house just for a three months' rental."

"Then do let us go downstairs," I said, "there are such pretty rooms there."

Then he took me in his arms and called me a blessed little goose, and said he would go down cellar, if I wished, and have it whitewashed into the bargain.

But he is right enough about the beds and windows and things.

It is an airy and comfortable room as any one need wish, and, of course, I would not be so silly as to make him uncomfortable just for a whim.

I'm really getting quite fond of the big room, all but that horrid paper.

Out of one window I can see the garden, those mysterious deep-shaded arbors, the riotous old-fashioned flowers, and bushes and gnarly trees.

Out of another I get a lovely view of the bay and a little private wharf belonging to the estate. There is a beautiful shaded lane that runs down there from the house. I always fancy I see people walking in these numerous paths and arbors, but John has cautioned me not to give way to fancy in the least. He says that with my imaginative power and habit of story-making, a nervous weakness like mine is sure to lead to all manner of excited fancies, and that I ought to use my will and good sense to check the tendency. So I try.

I think sometimes that if I were only well enough to write a little it would relieve the press of ideas and rest me.

But I find I get pretty tired when I try.

It is so discouraging not to have any advice and companionship about my work. When I get really well, John says we will ask Cousin Henry and Julia down for a long visit; but he says he would as soon put fireworks in my pillow-case as to let me have those stimulating people about now.

I wish I could get well faster.

But I must not think about that. This paper looks to me as if it *knew* what a vicious influence it had!

There is a recurrent spot where the pattern lolls like a broken neck and two bulbous eyes stare at you upside down.

I get positively angry with the impertinence of it and the everlastingness. Up and down and sideways they crawl, and those absurd, unblinking eyes are everywhere. There is one place where two breadths didn't match, and the eyes go all up and down the line, one a little higher than the other.

I never saw so much expression in an inanimate thing before, and we all know how much expression they have! I used to lie awake as a child and get more entertainment and terror out of blank walls and plain furniture than most children could find in a toy-store.

I remember what a kindly wink the knobs of our big, old bureau used to have, and there was one chair that always seemed like a strong friend.

I used to feel that if any of the other things looked too fierce I could always hop into that chair and be safe.

The furniture in this room is no worse than inharmonious, however, for we had to bring it all from downstairs. I suppose when this was used as a playroom they had to take the nursery things out, and no wonder! I never saw such ravages as the children have made here.

The wall-paper, as I said before, is torn off in spots, and it sticketh closer than a brother — they must have had perseverance as well as hatred.

Then the floor is scratched and gouged and splintered, the plaster itself is dug out here and there, and this great heavy bed which is all we found in the room, looks as if it had been through the wars.

But I don't mind it a bit — only the paper.

There comes John's sister. Such a dear girl as she is, and so careful of me! I must not let her find me writing.

She is a perfect and enthusiastic house-keeper, and hopes for no better profession. I verily believe she thinks it is the writing which made me sick!

But I can write when she is out, and see her a long way off from these windows.

There is one that commands the road, a lovely shaded winding road, and one that just looks off over the country. A lovely country, too, full of great elms and velvet meadows.

This wallpaper has a kind of sub-pattern in a different shade, a particularly irritating one, for you can only see it in certain lights, and not clearly then.

But in the places where it isn't faded and where the sun is just so — I can see a strange, provoking, formless sort of figure, that seems to skulk about behind that silly and conspicuous front design.

There's sister on the stairs!

Well, the Fourth of July is over! The people are all gone and I am tired out. John thought it might do me good to see a little company, so we just had mother and Nellie and the children down for a week.

Of course I didn't do a thing. Jennie sees to everything now.

But it tired me all the same.

John says if I don't pick up faster he shall send me to Weir Mitchell[3] in the fall.

But I don't want to go there at all. I had a friend who was in his hands once, and she says he is just like John and my brother, only more so!

Besides, it is such an undertaking to go so far.

I don't feel as if it was worth while to turn my hand over for anything, and I'm getting dreadfully fretful and querulous.

I cry at nothing, and cry most of the time.

Of course I don't when John is here, or anybody else, but when I am alone.

And I am alone a good deal just now. John is kept in town very often by serious cases, and Jennie is good and lets me alone when I want her to.

So I walk a little in the garden or down that lovely lane, sit on the porch under the roses, and lie down up here a good deal.

---

3. **Weir Mitchell:** Silas Weir Mitchell (1829-1914) was a physician and author who specialized in the treatment of what were called "nervous diseases." During the Civil War, he treated shell-shocked soldiers and those suffering "phantom" pains from amputated limbs. Afterwards, he became interested in emotional disorders more generally and developed the "rest cure," a widely used treatment involving bed rest, isolation, and severely limited physical activity.

I'm getting really fond of the room in spite of the wall-paper. Perhaps *because* of the wallpaper.

It dwells in my mind so!

I lie here on this great immovable bed – it is nailed down, I believe – and follow that pattern about by the hour. It is as good as gymnastics, I assure you. I start, we'll say, at the bottom, down in the corner over there where it has not been touched, and I determine for the thousandth time that I *will* follow that pointless pattern to some sort of a conclusion.

I know a little of the principle of design, and I know this thing was not arranged on any laws of radiation, or alternation, or repetition, or symmetry, or anything else that I ever heard of.

It is repeated, of course, by the breadths, but not otherwise.

Looked at in one way each breadth stands alone, the bloated curves and flourishes – a kind of "debased Romanesque" with *delirium tremens*[4] – go waddling up and down in isolated columns of fatuity.

But, on the other hand, they connect diagonally, and the sprawling outlines run off in great slanting waves of optic horror, like a lot of wallowing seaweeds in full chase.

The whole thing goes horizontally, too, at least it seems so, and I exhaust myself in trying to distinguish the order of its going in that direction.

They have used a horizontal breadth for a frieze, and that adds wonderfully to the confusion.

There is one end of the room where it is almost intact, and there, when the cross-lights fade and the low sun shines directly upon it, I can almost fancy radiation after all, – the interminable grotesques seem to form around a common centre and rush off in headlong plunges of equal distraction.

It makes me tired to follow it. I will take a nap I guess.

I don't know why I should write this.

I don't want to.

I don't feel able.

And I know John would think it absurd. But I *must* say what I feel and think in some way – it is such a relief!

But the effort is getting to be greater than the relief.

Half the time now I am awfully lazy, and lie down ever so much.

John says I mustn't lose my strength, and has me take cod liver oil and lots of tonics and things, to say nothing of ale and wine and rare meat.

Dear John! He loves me very dearly, and hates to have me sick. I tried to have a real earnest reasonable talk with him the other day, and tell him how I wish he would let me go and make a visit to Cousin Henry and Julia.

---

4. **"debased Romanesque" with *delirium tremens*:** Romanesque was an early style of architecture in Western Europe characterized by elaborate ornamentation; *delirium tremens*, Latin for "shaking frenzy," is an extreme form of alcohol withdrawal manifested by symptoms such as agitation, confusion, and hallucinations.

But he said I wasn't able to go, nor able to stand it after I got there; and I did not make out a very good case for myself, for I was crying before I had finished.

It is getting to be a great effort for me to think straight. Just this nervous weakness I suppose.

And dear John gathered me up in his arms, and just carried me upstairs and laid me on the bed, and sat by me and read to me till it tired my head.

He said I was his darling and his comfort and all he had, and that I must take care of myself for his sake, and keep well.

He says no one but myself can help me out of it, that I must use my will and self-control and not let any silly fancies run away with me.

There's one comfort, the baby is well and happy, and does not have to occupy this nursery with the horrid wall-paper.

If we had not used it, that blessed child would have! What a fortunate escape! Why, I wouldn't have a child of mine, an impressionable little thing, live in such a room for worlds.

I never thought of it before, but it is lucky that John kept me here after all, I can stand it so much easier than a baby, you see.

Of course I never mention it to them any more—I am too wise—but I keep watch of it all the same.

There are things in that paper that nobody knows but me, or ever will.

Behind that outside pattern the dim shapes get clearer every day.

It is always the same shape, only very numerous.

And it is like a woman stooping down and creeping about behind that pattern. I don't like it a bit. I wonder—I begin to think—I wish John would take me away from here!

It is so hard to talk with John about my case, because he is so wise, and because he loves me so.

But I tried it last night.

It was moonlight. The moon shines in all around just as the sun does.

I hate to see it sometimes, it creeps so slowly, and always comes in by one window or another.

John was asleep and I hated to waken him, so I kept still and watched the moonlight on that undulating wall-paper till I felt creepy.

The faint figure behind seemed to shake the pattern, just as if she wanted to get out.

I got up softly and went to feel and see if the paper *did* move, and when I came back John was awake.

"What is it, little girl?" he said. "Don't go walking about like that—you'll get cold."

I thought it was a good time to talk, so I told him that I really was not gaining here, and that I wished he would take me away.

"Why, darling!" said he, "our lease will be up in three weeks, and I can't see how to leave before.

"The repairs are not done at home, and I cannot possibly leave town just now. Of course if you were in any danger, I could and would, but you really are better, dear, whether you can see it or not. I am a doctor, dear, and I know. You are gaining flesh and color, your appetite is better, I feel really much easier about you."

"I don't weigh a bit more," said I, "nor as much; and my appetite may be better in the evening when you are here, but it is worse in the morning when you are away!"

"Bless her little heart!" said he with a big hug, "she shall be as sick as she pleases! But now let's improve the shining hours[5] by going to sleep, and talk about it in the morning!"

"And you won't go away?" I asked gloomily.

"Why, how can I, dear? It is only three weeks more and then we will take a nice little trip of a few days while Jennie is getting the house ready. Really dear you are better!"

"Better in body perhaps —" I began, and stopped short, for he sat up straight and looked at me with such a stern, reproachful look that I could not say another word.

"My darling," said he, "I beg you, for my sake and for our child's sake, as well as for your own, that you will never for one instant let that idea enter your mind! There is nothing so dangerous, so fascinating, to a temperament like yours. It is a false and foolish fancy. Can you trust me as a physician when I tell you so?"

So of course I said no more on that score, and we went to sleep before long. He thought I was asleep first, but I wasn't, and lay there for hours trying to decide whether that front pattern and the back pattern really did move together or separately.

On a pattern like this, by daylight, there is a lack of sequence, a defiance of law, that is a constant irritant to a normal mind.

The color is hideous enough, and unreliable enough, and infuriating enough, but the pattern is torturing.

You think you have mastered it, but just as you get well underway in following, it turns a back-somersault and there you are. It slaps you in the face, knocks you down, and tramples upon you. It is like a bad dream.

The outside pattern is a florid arabesque, reminding one of a fungus. If you can imagine a toadstool in joints, an interminable string of toadstools, budding and sprouting in endless convolutions — why, that is something like it.

That is, sometimes!

There is one marked peculiarity about this paper, a thing nobody seems to notice but myself, and that is that it changes as the light changes.

When the sun shoots in through the east window — I always watch for that first long, straight ray — it changes so quickly that I never can quite believe it.

That is why I watch it always.

By moonlight — the moon shines in all night when there is a moon — I wouldn't know it was the same paper.

At night in any kind of light, in twilight, candlelight, lamplight, and worst of all by moonlight, it becomes bars! The outside pattern I mean, and the woman behind it is as plain as can be.

---

5. **improve the shining hours**: An allusion to the first stanza of a popular song written for children, "Against Idleness and Mischief," by Isaac Watts (1674-1748): "How doth the little busy Bee / Improve each shining Hour, / And gather Honey all the day / From every opening Flower!"

I didn't realize for a long time what the thing was that showed behind, that dim sub-pattern, but now I am quite sure it is a woman.

By daylight she is subdued, quiet. I fancy it is the pattern that keeps her so still. It is so puzzling. It keeps me quiet by the hour.

I lie down ever so much now. John says it is good for me, and to sleep all I can.

Indeed he started the habit by making me lie down for an hour after each meal.

It is a very bad habit I am convinced, for you see I don't sleep.

And that cultivates deceit, for I don't tell them I'm awake – O, no!

The fact is I am getting a little afraid of John.

He seems very queer sometimes, and even Jennie has an inexplicable look.

It strikes me occasionally, just as a scientific hypothesis, – that perhaps it is the paper!

I have watched John when he did not know I was looking, and come into the room suddenly on the most innocent excuses, and I've caught him several times *looking at the paper*! And Jennie too. I caught Jennie with her hand on it once.

She didn't know I was in the room, and when I asked her in a quiet, a very quiet voice, with the most restrained manner possible, what she was doing with the paper – she turned around as if she had been caught stealing, and looked quite angry – asked me why I should frighten her so!

Then she said that the paper stained everything it touched, that she had found yellow smooches on all my clothes and John's, and she wished we would be more careful!

Did not that sound innocent? But I know she was studying that pattern, and I am determined that nobody shall find it out but myself!

Life is very much more exciting now than it used to be. You see I have something more to expect, to look forward to, to watch. I really do eat better, and am more quiet than I was.

John is so pleased to see me improve! He laughed a little the other day, and said I seemed to be flourishing in spite of my wall-paper.

I turned it off with a laugh. I had no intention of telling him it was *because* of the wall-paper – he would make fun of me. He might even want to take me away.

I don't want to leave now until I have found it out. There is a week more, and I think that will be enough.

I'm feeling ever so much better! I don't sleep much at night, for it is so interesting to watch developments; but I sleep a good deal in the daytime.

In the daytime it is tiresome and perplexing.

There are always new shoots on the fungus, and new shades of yellow all over it. I cannot keep count of them, though I have tried conscientiously.

It is the strangest yellow, that wall-paper! It makes me think of all the yellow things I ever saw – not beautiful ones like buttercups, but old foul, bad yellow things.

But there is something else about that paper – the smell! I noticed it the moment we came into the room, but with so much air and sun it was not bad. Now we have had a week of fog and rain, and whether the windows are open or not, the smell is here.

It creeps all over the house.

I find it hovering in the dining-room, skulking in the parlor, hiding in the hall, lying in wait for me on the stairs.

It gets into my hair.

Even when I go to ride, if I turn my head suddenly and surprise it – there is that smell!

Such a peculiar odor, too! I have spent hours in trying to analyze it, to find what it smelled like.

It is not bad – at first, and very gentle, but quite the subtlest, most enduring odor I ever met.

In this damp weather it is awful, I wake up in the night and find it hanging over me.

It used to disturb me at first. I thought seriously of burning the house – to reach the smell.

But now I am used to it. The only thing I can think of that it is like is the *color* of the paper! A yellow smell.

There is a very funny mark on this wall, low down, near the mopboard. A streak that runs round the room. It goes behind every piece of furniture, except the bed, a long, straight, even *smooch*, as if it had been rubbed over and over.

I wonder how it was done and who did it, and what they did it for. Round and round and round – round and round and round – it makes me dizzy!

I really have discovered something at last.

Through watching so much at night, when it changes so, I have finally found out.

The front pattern *does* move – and no wonder! The woman behind shakes it!

Sometimes I think there are a great many women behind, and sometimes only one, and she crawls around fast, and her crawling shakes it all over.

Then in the very bright spots she keeps still, and in the very shady spots she just takes hold of the bars and shakes them hard.

And she is all the time trying to climb through. But nobody could climb through that pattern – it strangles so; I think that is why it has so many heads.

They get through, and then the pattern strangles them off and turns them upside down, and makes their eyes white!

If those heads were covered or taken off it would not be half so bad.

I think that woman gets out in the daytime!

And I'll tell you why – privately – I've seen her!

I can see her out of every one of my windows!

It is the same woman, I know, for she is always creeping, and most women do not creep by daylight.

I see her in that long shaded lane, creeping up and down. I see her in those dark grape arbors, creeping all around the garden.

I see her on that long road under the trees, creeping along, and when a carriage comes she hides under the blackberry vines.

I don't blame her a bit. It must be very humiliating to be caught creeping by day-light!

I always lock the door when I creep by daylight. I can't do it at night, for I know John would suspect something at once.

And John is so queer now, that I don't want to irritate him. I wish he would take another room! Besides, I don't want anybody to get that woman out at night but myself.

I often wonder if I could see her out of all the windows at once.

But, turn as fast as I can, I can only see out of one at one time.

And though I always see her, she *may* be able to creep faster than I can turn!

I have watched her sometimes away off in the open country, creeping as fast as a cloud shadow in a high wind.

If only that top pattern could be gotten off from the under one! I mean to try it, little by little.

I have found out another funny thing, but I shan't tell it this time! It does not do to trust people too much.

There are only two more days to get this paper off, and I believe John is beginning to notice. I don't like the look in his eyes.

And I heard him ask Jennie a lot of professional questions about me. She had a very good report to give.

She said I slept a good deal in the daytime.

John knows I don't sleep very well at night, for all I'm so quiet!

He asked me all sorts of questions, too, and pretended to be very loving and kind.

As if I couldn't see through him!

Still, I don't wonder he acts so, sleeping under this paper for three months.

It only interests me, but I feel sure John and Jennie are secretly affected by it.

Hurrah! This is the last day, but it is enough. John to stay in town over night, and won't be out until this evening.

Jennie wanted to sleep with me – the sly thing! But I told her I should undoubtedly rest better for a night all alone.

That was clever, for really I wasn't alone a bit! As soon as it was moonlight and that poor thing began to crawl and shake the pattern, I got up and ran to help her.

I pulled and she shook, I shook and she pulled, and before morning we had peeled off yards of that paper.

A strip about as high as my head and half around the room.

And then when the sun came and that awful pattern began to laugh at me, I declared I would finish it to-day!

We go away to-morrow, and they are moving all my furniture down again to leave things as they were before.

Jennie looked at the wall in amazement, but I told her merrily that I did it out of pure spite at the vicious thing.

She laughed and said she wouldn't mind doing it herself, but I must not get tired.

How she betrayed herself that time!

But I am here, and no person touches this paper but me, – not *alive!*

She tried to get me out of the room – it was too patent! But I said it was so quiet and empty and clean now that I believed I would lie down again and sleep all I could; and not to wake me even for dinner – I would call when I woke.

So now she is gone, and the servants are gone, and the things are gone, and there is nothing left but that great bedstead nailed down, with the canvas mattress we found on it.

We shall sleep downstairs to-night, and take the boat home to-morrow.

I quite enjoy the room, now it is bare again.

How those children did tear about here!

This bedstead is fairly gnawed!

But I must get to work.

I have locked the door and thrown the key down into the front path.

I don't want to go out, and I don't want to have anybody come in, till John comes.

I want to astonish him.

I've got a rope up here that even Jennie did not find. If that woman does get out, and tries to get away, I can tie her!

But I forgot I could not reach far without anything to stand on!

This bed will *not* move!

I tried to lift and push it until I was lame, and then I got so angry I bit off a little piece at one corner – but it hurt my teeth.

Then I peeled off all the paper I could reach standing on the floor. It sticks horribly and the pattern just enjoys it! All those strangled heads and bulbous eyes and waddling fungus growths just shriek with derision!

I am getting angry enough to do something desperate. To jump out of the window would be admirable exercise, but the bars are too strong even to try.

Besides I wouldn't do it. Of course not. I know well enough that a step like that is improper and might be misconstrued.

I don't like to *look* out of the windows even – there are so many of those creeping women, and they creep so fast.

I wonder if they all come out of that wall-paper as I did?

But I am securely fastened now by my well-hidden rope – you don't get *me* out in the road there!

I suppose I shall have to get back behind the pattern when it comes night, and that is hard!

It is so pleasant to be out in this great room and creep around as I please!

I don't want to go outside. I won't, even if Jennie asks me to.

For outside you have to creep on the ground, and everything is green instead of yellow.

But here I can creep smoothly on the floor, and my shoulder just fits in that long smooch around the wall, so I cannot lose my way.

Why, there's John at the door!

It is no use, young man, you can't open it!

How he does call and pound!

Now he's crying for an axe.

It would be a shame to break down that beautiful door!

"John dear!" said I in the gentlest voice, "the key is down by the front steps, under a plantain leaf!"

That silenced him for a few moments.

Then he said — very quietly indeed, "Open the door, my darling!"

"I can't," said I. "The key is down by the front door under a plantain leaf!"

And then I said it again, several times, very gently and slowly, and said it so often that he had to go and see, and he got it of course, and came in. He stopped short by the door.

"What is the matter?" he cried. "For God's sake, what are you doing!"

I kept on creeping just the same, but I looked at him over my shoulder.

"I've got out at last," said I, "in spite of you and Jane![6] And I've pulled off most of the paper, so you can't put me back!"

Now why should that man have fainted? But he did, and right across my path by the wall, so that I had to creep over him every time!

[1892]

---

6. **in spite of you and Jane!:** Jane, who has not previously been introduced in the story, is possibly the name of the narrator herself or an oblique reference to Charlotte Brontë's well-known gothic romance, *Jane Eyre* (1847). The title character is a governess who falls in love and agrees to marry her employer, Mr. Rochester. But she learns that he is already married to Bertha Mason, who has gone mad and is kept locked away in a hidden room on the third floor of Rochester's manor house, Thornfield Hall. (In one harrowing scene, Bertha is described scurrying around the room on all fours and growling like an animal.) After Bertha dies in a fire she sets to the house, Jane eventually marries Rochester. In the first published version of Gilman's story in the *New England Magazine*, the narrator's statement ends with a question mark, and in later printings it ends with a period. We have followed the punctuation in Gilman's manuscript, in which the statement ends with an exclamation point that the original compositor evidently mistook for a question mark.

Edith Wharton

[1862–1937]

Edith Wharton was born Edith Newbold Jones on January 24, 1862, in New York City. Both of her socially prominent parents, George F. Jones and Lucretia Stevens Rhinelander Jones, could trace their family histories back more than two hundred years to the earliest settlement of colonial New York. Wharton grew up in a world of wealth and privilege — of European travel, summers spent in the fashionable resort of Newport, Rhode Island, and winters at the family home on Fifth Avenue in Manhattan. She was educated by private tutors, learning five languages and becoming a voracious reader. As she later recalled, "By the time I was seventeen, though I had not read every book in my father's library, I had looked into them all." That "all" included texts ranging from the Bible and Elizabethan drama to Washington Irving's stories and the poems of Henry Wadsworth Longfellow, as well as a long list of books on art,

I met [Wharton] in New York and she's a very distinguished grande dame who fought the good fight with bronze age weapons when there were very few people in the line at all.
        —F. Scott Fitzgerald

Edith Wharton

The prominent photographer A. F. Bradley took this portrait of Wharton around 1900, when she was committing herself to a career of writing.

architecture, history, philosophy, and travel. Wharton also began writing at an early age. When she was fifteen, she adopted the pseudonym "Mr. Olivieri," writing a novella, *Fast and Loose*, and a very negative review of it, which she imagined might appear in the influential magazine the *Nation*. The novella was not published, but her mother arranged for the private publication of a collection of Wharton's poems, *Verses* (1878).

Wharton was increasingly torn between her literary ambitions and the demands of her social position. At the age of seventeen, she duly made her debut in New York City. Six years later, in 1885, she married Edward ("Teddy") Wharton, a thirty-four-year-old friend of her brother. Although it was soon clear that she and her socially prominent husband had little in common, Wharton dutifully sought to adapt to the role of society matron. At the same time, she was unwilling to give up completely her writing. Beginning in 1889, she published several poems in the *Atlantic Monthly* and *Scribner's*, where her first story appeared in 1891. Finding her marriage stressful and the continual rounds of parties and other social events exhausting, Wharton suffered bouts of depression and wrote little more until 1897, when she and the architect Ogden Codman published *The Decoration of Houses*. The following year, she sought out the services of Silas Weir Mitchell, a prominent physician who specialized in "rest cures" for what were then called "nervous diseases." Another of Mitchell's patients, Charlotte Perkins Gilman, had already published a story about the devastating effects of such enforced inactivity, "The Yellow Wall-Paper" (1892), but the rest cure helped Wharton gain the solitude and space she needed for her writing. Her first collection of stories, *The Greater Inclination* (1899), was followed by *The Valley of Decision* (1902), a historical novel set in eighteenth-century Italy. The novel received generally positive reviews and an enthusiastic reception from readers, including Henry James. In one of his earliest letters to Wharton, however, James urged her to write about the "American Subject," as he called it. "There it is round you," James exhorted her. "Don't pass it by. . . . Take hold of it & keep hold & let it pull you where it will. . . . DO NEW YORK!"

Although she treated many other subjects, Wharton achieved her greatest fame as a chronicler of the fashionable world she knew so well. In 1902, she and her husband built the Mount, a magnificent estate and gardens Wharton designed in Lenox, Massachusetts. There, she perceptively explored the complex dynamics and narrow restrictions of upper-class society in numerous stories and in *The House of Mirth* (1905), an acclaimed novel about an unconventional young woman who is destroyed in her attempt to gain a secure place among the corrupt, nouveau riche of New York City. By then, Wharton's marriage had become severely strained, especially by her husband's numerous extramarital affairs. After the unhappy couple moved to France in 1907, Wharton found love and solace in the company of Morton Fullerton, a journalist with whom she had an affair that lasted from 1908 to 1910. Wharton wrote that she had tried "to adjust herself" to her marriage, which finally ended in divorce in 1913, but that she "was overmastered by the longing to meet people who shared my interests." One of those people was an old friend, Walter Berry, an American lawyer who became Wharton's long-term companion and the person she most relied on for editorial advice about her work. Nonetheless, like her close friend Henry James, Wharton enjoyed greater intellectual companionship among artists and writers in Europe than in the United States. Even after she moved permanently to France in 1910, however, Wharton continued to explore American scenes and themes in works such as *Ethan Frome* (1911), *The Custom of the Country* (1913), *Summer* (1917), and *The Age of Innocence* (1920), a novel of "Old New York" that earned her the Pulitzer Prize.

During the remainder of her career, Wharton was overshadowed by a younger generation of novelists, including her admirers F. Scott Fitzgerald and Sinclair Lewis. But she remained a revered and widely read writer. In 1923, she became the first woman to be awarded an honorary doctorate of letters by Yale University, and in 1929 she received the Gold Medal of the American Academy of Arts and Letters. She also continued to write steadily until her death from a stroke on August 11, 1937, by which time Wharton had produced a remarkable body of work: dozens of reviews and magazine articles, three volumes of poetry, more than eighty-five short stories in eleven collections, twenty-seven novellas and novels, and nine nonfictional works, including her vivid autobiography, *A Backward Glance* (1934).

bedfordstmartins.com/ americanlit for research links on Wharton

Reading Wharton's "The Quicksand."   This story was first published in the prestigious *Harper's Monthly* in 1902. Founded in June 1850 and still in publication today, *Harper's* is the oldest general-interest monthly magazine in the United States. In Wharton's day, it published many of the most established American writers, including Henry James and Mark Twain, as well as younger writers such as Jack London and Wharton. As in much of her fiction, Wharton in "The Quicksand" offers glimpses into the lives of affluent New Yorkers, and

Metropolitan Museum of Art

This photograph of the museum, on Fifth Avenue at 82nd Street on the Upper East Side of Manhattan, was taken shortly after the neoclassical facade and central pavilion were completed in 1902.

like many of her other stories it focuses on what one critic has called "The Marriage Question." Wharton explores the subject of marriage through a series of conversations and debates between a wealthy widow, her son, and a young woman who hesitates to marry him because, like his father before him, he runs a powerful but disreputable newspaper, *The Radiator*. Indeed, the story registers the impact of what was called "yellow journalism," the sensationalizing of the news associated with the circulation wars between Joseph Pulitzer's *New York World* and William Randolph Hearst's *New York Journal* in the late 1890s. But Wharton's story is finally less concerned with journalistic ethics than with individual moral choices, especially the complex choices faced by women whose autonomy is limited by powerful social and economic forces. The text is taken from the first printing in *Harper's Monthly*, June 1902.

THE QUICKSAND

I

As Mrs. Quentin's victoria,[1] driving homeward, turned from the Park into Fifth Avenue, she divined her son's tall figure walking ahead of her in the twilight. His long stride covered the ground more rapidly than usual, and she had a premonition that, if he were going home at that hour, it was because he wanted to see her.

Mrs. Quentin, though not a fanciful woman, was sometimes aware of a sixth sense enabling her to detect the faintest vibrations of her son's impulses. She was too shrewd to fancy herself the one mother in possession of this faculty, but she permitted herself to think that few could exercise it more discreetly. If she could not help overhearing Alan's thoughts, she had the courage to keep her discoveries to herself, the tact to take for granted nothing that lay below the surface of their spoken intercourse: she knew that most people would rather have their letters read than their thoughts. For this superfeminine discretion Alan repaid her by — being Alan. There could have been no completer reward. He was the key to the meaning of life, the justification of what must have seemed as incomprehensible as it was odious, had it not all-sufficingly ended in himself. He was a perfect son, and Mrs. Quentin had always hungered for perfection.

Her house, in a minor way, bore witness to the craving. One felt it to be the result of a series of eliminations: there was nothing fortuitous in its blending of line and color. The almost morbid finish of every material detail of her life suggested the possibility that a diversity of energies had, by some pressure of circumstance, been forced into the channel of a narrow dilettanteism. Mrs. Quentin's fastidiousness had, indeed, the flaw of being too one-sided. Her friends were not always worthy of the chairs they sat in, and she overlooked in her associates defects she would not have tolerated in her bric-à-brac.[2] Her house was, in fact, never so distinguished as when it was empty; and it was at its best in the warm fire-lit silence that now received her.

Her son, who had overtaken her on the door-step, followed her into the drawing-room, and threw himself into an arm-chair near the fire, while she laid off her furs and busied herself about the tea table. For a while neither spoke; but glancing at him across the kettle, his mother noticed that he sat staring at the embers with a look she had never seen on his face, though its arrogant young outline was as familiar to her as her own thoughts. The look extended itself to his negligent attitude, to the droop of his long fine hands, the dejected tilt of his head against the cushions. It was like the moral

---

1. **victoria:** Named for Queen Victoria, monarch of the United Kingdom of Great Britain and Ireland from 1837 until her death in 1901, a victoria was a four-wheeled, horse-drawn carriage with a collapsible hood, an elevated seat for a driver, and seats for two passengers. Mrs. Quentin is coming from Central Park, which is bordered on the east by Fifth Avenue, then and now one of the most fashionable residential areas in New York City.
2. **bric-à-brac:** A miscellaneous collection of small decorative objects.

equivalent of physical fatigue: he looked, as he himself would have phrased it, dead-beat, played out. Such an air was so foreign to his usual bright indomitableness that Mrs. Quentin had the sense of an unfamiliar presence, in which she must observe herself, must raise hurried barriers against an alien approach. It was one of the drawbacks of their excessive intimacy that any break in it seemed a chasm.

She was accustomed to let his thoughts circle about her before they settled into speech, and she now sat in motionless expectancy, as though a sound might frighten them away.

At length, without turning his eyes from the fire, he said: "I'm so glad you're a nice old-fashioned intuitive woman. It's painful to see them think."

Her apprehension had already preceded him. "Hope Fenno—?" she faltered.

He nodded. "She's been thinking—hard. It was very painful—to me, at least; and I don't believe she enjoyed it: she said she didn't," He stretched his feet to the fire. "The result of her cogitations is that she won't have me. She arrived at this by pure ratiocination—it's not a question of feeling, you understand. I'm the only man she's ever loved—but she won't have me. What novels did you read when you were young, dear? I'm convinced it all turns on that. If she'd been brought up on Trollope and Whyte-Melville, instead of Tolstoi and Mrs. Ward,[3] we should have now been vulgarly sitting on a sofa, trying on the engagement-ring."

Mrs. Quentin at first was kept silent by the mother's instinctive anger that the girl she has not wanted for her son should have dared to refuse him. Then she said, "Tell me, dear."

"My good woman, she has scruples."

"Scruples?"

"Against the paper. She objects to me in my official capacity as owner of the *Radiator*."

His mother did not echo his laugh.

"She had found a solution, of course—she overflows with expedients. I was to chuck the paper, and we were to live happily ever afterward on canned food and virtue. She even had an alternative ready—women are so full of resources! I was to turn the *Radiator* into an independent organ, and run it at a loss to show the public what a model newspaper ought to be. On the whole, I think she fancied this plan more than the other—it commended itself to her as being more uncomfortable and aggressive. It's not the fashion nowadays to be good by stealth."

Mrs. Quentin said to herself, "I didn't know how much he cared!" Aloud she murmured, "You must give her time."

"Time?"

"To move out the old prejudices and make room for new ones."

---

3. **Trollope . . . Mrs. Ward:** Anthony Trollope (1815–1882) was a prolific, popular British fiction writer, best known for his domestic novels set in the imaginary county of Barsetshire; George Whyte-Melville (1821–1878) was a Scottish novelist who wrote mainly about the popular British sport of fox-hunting. The second set of writers dealt with more serious themes: Leo Tolstoi or Tolstoy (1828–1910), a Russian novelist, moralist, and social reformer; and Mary August Arnold Ward, who published under her married name as Mrs. Humphry Ward (1851–1920), the author of numerous novels addressing political and religious issues.

"My dear mother, those she has are brand-new; that's the trouble with them. She's tremendously up-to-date. She takes in all the moral fashion-papers, and wears the newest thing in ethics."

Her resentment lost its way in the intricacies of his metaphor. "Is she so very religious?"

"You dear archaic woman! She's hopelessly irreligious; that's the difficulty. You can make a religious woman believe almost anything: there's the habit of credulity to work on. But when a girl's faith in the Deluge[4] has been shaken, it's very hard to inspire her with confidence. She makes you feel that, before believing in you, it's her duty as a conscientious agnostic to find out whether you're not obsolete, or whether the text isn't corrupt, or somebody hasn't proved conclusively that you never existed, anyhow."

Mrs. Quentin was again silent. The two moved in that atmosphere of implications and assumptions where the lightest word may shake down the dust of countless stored impressions; and speech was sometimes more difficult between them than had their union been less close.

Presently she ventured, "It's impossible?"

"Impossible?"

She seemed to use her words cautiously, like weapons that might slip and inflict a cut. "What she suggests."

Her son, raising himself, turned to look at her for the first time. Their glance met in a shock of comprehension. He was with her against the girl, then! Her satisfaction overflowed in a murmur of tenderness.

"Of course not, dear. One can't change—change one's life. . . ."

"One's self," he emended. "That's what I tell her. What's the use of my giving up the paper if I keep my point of view?"

The psychological distinction attracted her. "Which is it she minds most?"

"Oh, the paper—for the present. She undertakes to modify the point of view afterward. All she asks is that I shall renounce my heresy: the gift of grace will come later."

Mrs. Quentin sat gazing into her untouched cup. Her son's first words had produced in her the hallucinated sense of struggling in the thick of a crowd that he could not see. It was horrible to feel herself hemmed in by influences imperceptible to him; yet if anything could have increased her misery it would have been the discovery that her ghosts had become visible.

As though to divert his attention, she precipitately asked, "And you—?"

His answer carried the shock of an evocation. "I merely asked her what she thought of *you*."

"Of me?"

"She admires you immensely, you know."

---

4. **faith in the Deluge:** A reference to the episode described in Genesis 6–9, in which a great flood washed away the wickedness that God saw on earth, leaving Noah, his family, and pairs of animals who survived in an ark. Scientific discoveries and historical scholarship of the nineteenth century tended to undermine belief in the worldwide flood.

For a moment Mrs. Quentin's cheek showed the lingering light of girlhood: praise transmitted by her son acquired something of the transmitter's merit. "Well—?" she smiled.

"Well—you didn't make my father give up the *Radiator*, did you?"

His mother, stiffening, made a circuitous return: "She never comes here. How can she know me?"

"She's so poor! She goes out so little." He rose and leaned against the mantel-piece, dislodging with impatient fingers a slender bronze wrestler poised on a porphyry base, between two warm-toned Spanish ivories. "And then her mother—" he added, as if involuntarily.

"Her mother has never visited me," Mrs. Quentin finished for him.

He shrugged his shoulders. "Mrs. Fenno has the scope of a wax doll. Her rule of conduct is taken from her grandmother's sampler."[5]

"But the daughter is so modern—and yet—"

"The result is the same? Not exactly. *She* admires you—oh, immensely!" He replaced the bronze and turned to his mother with a smile. "Aren't you on some hospital committee together? What especially strikes her is your way of doing good. She says philanthropy is not a line of conduct, but a state of mind—and it appears that you are one of the elect."

As, in the vague diffusion of physical pain, relief seems to come with the acuter pang of a single nerve, Mrs. Quentin felt herself suddenly eased by a rush of anger against the girl. "If she loved you—" she began.

His gesture checked her. "I'm not asking you to get her to do that."

The two were again silent, facing each other in the disarray of a common catastrophe—as though their thoughts, at the summons of danger, had rushed naked into action. Mrs. Quentin, at this revealing moment, saw for the first time how many elements of her son's character had seemed comprehensible simply because they were familiar: as, in reading a foreign language, we take the meaning of certain words for granted till the context corrects us. Often as, in a given case, her maternal musings had figured his conduct, she now found herself at a loss to forecast it; and with this failure of intuition came a sense of the subserviency which had hitherto made her counsels but the anticipation of his wish. Her despair escaped in the moan, "What *is* it you ask me?"

"To talk to her."

"Talk to her?"

"Show her—tell her—make her understand that the paper has always been a thing outside your life—that hasn't touched you—that needn't touch *her*. Only, let her hear you—watch you—be with you—she'll see . . . she can't help seeing . . ."

His mother faltered. "But if she's given you her reasons—?"

"Let her give them to you! If she can—when she sees you. . . ." His impatient hand again displaced the wrestler. "I care abominably," he confessed.

---

5. **her grandmother's sampler:** Samplers were embroidered pieces of fabric that often included moral verses.

II

On the Fenno threshold a sudden sense of the futility of the attempt had almost driven Mrs. Quentin back to her carriage; but the door was already opening, and a parlor-maid who believed that Miss Fenno was in led the way to the depressing drawing-room. It was the kind of room in which no member of the family is likely to be found except after dinner or after death. The chairs and tables looked like poor relations who had repaid their keep by a long career of grudging usefulness: they seemed banded together against intruders in a sullen conspiracy of discomfort. Mrs. Quentin, keenly susceptible to such influences, read failure in every angle of the upholstery. She was incapable of the vulgar error of thinking that Hope Fenno might be induced to marry Alan for his money; but between this assumption and the inference that the girl's imagination might be touched by the finer possibilities of wealth, good taste admitted a distinction. The Fenno furniture, however, presented to such reasoning the obtuseness of its black-walnut chamferings;[6] and something in its attitude suggested that its owners would be as uncompromising. The room showed none of the modern attempts at palliation, no apologetic draping of facts; and Mrs. Quentin, provisionally perched on a green-reps Gothic sofa[7] with which it was clearly impossible to establish any closer relations, concluded that, had Mrs. Fenno needed another seat of the same size, she would have set out placidly to match the one on which her visitor now languished.

To Mrs. Quentin's fancy, Hope Fenno's opinions, presently imparted in a clear young voice from the opposite angle of the Gothic sofa, partook of the character of their surroundings. The girl's mind was like a large light empty place, scantily furnished with a few massive prejudices, not designed to add to any one's comfort but too ponderous to be easily moved. Mrs. Quentin's own intelligence, in which its owner, in an artistically shaded half-light, had so long moved amid a delicate complexity of sensations, seemed in comparison suddenly close and crowded; and in taking refuge there from the glare of the young girl's candor, the older woman found herself stumbling in an unwonted obscurity. Her uneasiness resolved itself into a sense of irritation against her listener. Mrs. Quentin knew that the momentary value of any argument lies in the capacity of the mind to which it is addressed; and as her shafts of persuasion spent themselves against Miss Fenno's obduracy, she said to herself that, since conduct is governed by emotions rather than ideas, the really strong people are those who mistake their sensations for opinions. Viewed in this light, Miss Fenno was certainly very strong: there was an unmistakable ring of finality in the tone with which she declared, "It's impossible."

Mrs. Quentin's answer veiled the least shade of feminine resentment. "I told Alan that, where he had failed, there was no chance of my making an impression."

Hope Fenno laid on her visitor's an almost reverential hand. "Dear Mrs. Quentin, it's the impression you make that confirms the impossibility."

---

6. **chamferings:** Beveled, or slanted, edges.
7. **green-reps Gothic sofa:** A massive divan or couch in a highly ornamented style evoking the medieval period, covered in a green-colored woven fabric with a ribbed surface. Such Gothic Revival furniture had earlier been popular in England and the United States.

Mrs. Quentin waited a moment: she was perfectly aware that, where her feelings were concerned, her sense of humor was not to be relied on. "Do I make such an odious impression?" she asked at length, with a smile that seemed to give the girl her choice of two meanings.

"You make such a beautiful one! It's too beautiful – it obscures my judgment."

Mrs. Quentin looked at her thoughtfully. "Would it be permissible, I wonder, for an older woman to suggest that, at your age, it isn't always a misfortune to have what one calls one's judgment temporarily obscured?"

Miss Fenno flushed. "I try not to judge others – "

"You judge Alan."

"Ah, *he* is not others," she murmured, with an accent that touched the older woman.

"You judge his mother."

"I don't; I don't!"

Mrs. Quentin pressed her point. "You judge yourself, then, as you would be in my position – and your verdict condemns me."

"How can you think it? It's because I appreciate the difference in our point of view that I find it so difficult to defend myself – "

"Against what?"

"The temptation to imagine that I might be as *you* are – feeling as I do."

Mrs. Quentin rose with a sigh. "My child, in my day love was less subtle." She added, after a moment, "Alan is a perfect son."

"Ah, that again – that makes it worse!"

"Worse?"

"Just as your goodness does, your sweetness, your immense indulgence in letting me discuss things with you in a way that must seem almost an impertinence."

Mrs. Quentin's smile was not without irony. "You must remember that I do it for Alan."

"That's what I love you for!" the girl instantly returned; and again her tone touched her listener.

"And yet you're sacrificing him – and to an idea!"

"Isn't it to ideas that all the sacrifices that were worth while have been made?"

"One may sacrifice one's self."

Miss Fenno's color rose. "That's what I'm doing," she said gently.

Mrs. Quentin took her hand. "I believe you are," she answered. "And it isn't true that I speak only for Alan. Perhaps I did when I began; but now I want to plead for you too – against yourself." She paused, and then went on with a deeper note: "I have let you, as you say, speak your mind to me in terms that some women might have resented, because I wanted to show you how little, as the years go on, theories, ideas, abstract conceptions of life, weigh against the actual, against the particular way in which life presents itself to us – to women especially. To decide beforehand exactly how one ought to behave in given circumstances is like deciding that one will follow a certain direction in crossing an unexplored country. Afterward we find that we must turn out for the obstacles – cross the rivers where they're shallowest – take the tracks that others have beaten – make all sorts of unexpected concessions. Life is made up of compromises:

that is what youth refuses to understand. I've lived long enough to doubt whether any real good ever came of sacrificing beautiful facts to even more beautiful theories. Do I seem casuistical?[8] I don't know—there may be losses either way...but the love of the man one loves . . . of the child one loves . . . that makes up for everything. . . ."

She had spoken with a thrill which seemed to communicate itself to the hand her listener had left in hers. Her eyes filled suddenly, but through their dimness she saw the girl's lips shape a last desperate denial:

"Don't you see it's because I feel all this that I mustn't—that I can't?"

III

Mrs. Quentin, in the late spring afternoon, had turned in at the doors of the Metropolitan Museum.[9] She had been walking in the Park, in a solitude oppressed by the ever-present sense of her son's trouble, and had suddenly remembered that some one had added a Beltraffio[10] to the collection. It was an old habit of Mrs. Quentin's to seek in the enjoyment of the beautiful the distraction that most of her acquaintances appeared to find in each other's company. She had few friends, and their society was welcome to her only in her more superficial moods; but she could drug anxiety with a picture as some women can soothe it with a bonnet.

During the six months that had elapsed since her visit to Miss Fenno she had been conscious of a pain of which she had supposed herself no longer capable: as a man will continue to feel the ache of an amputated arm. She had fancied that all her centres of feeling had been transferred to Alan; but she now found herself subject to a kind of dual suffering, in which her individual pang was the keener in that it divided her from her son's. Alan had surprised her: she had not foreseen that he would take a sentimental rebuff so hard. His disappointment took the uncommunicative form of a sterner application to work. He threw himself into the concerns of the *Radiator* with an aggressiveness that almost betrayed itself in the paper. Mrs. Quentin never read the *Radiator*, but from the glimpses of it reflected in the other journals she gathered that it was at least not being subjected to the moral reconstruction which had been one of Miss Fenno's alternatives.

Mrs. Quentin never spoke to her son of what had happened. She was superior to the cheap satisfaction of avenging his injury by depreciating its cause. She knew that in sentimental sorrows such consolations are as salt in the wound. The avoidance of a subject so vividly present to both could not but affect the closeness of their relation. An invisible presence hampered their liberty of speech and thought. The girl was always between them; and to hide the sense of her intrusion they began to be less frequently

---

8. **casuistical:** Practicing casuistry, overly subtle arguments or reasoning.
9. **Metropolitan Museum:** The Metropolitan Museum of Art, which opened in 1870 and moved to its current location on Fifth Avenue at 82nd Street in 1880. The museum abuts Central Park, the extensive landscaped grounds that had opened in 1859.
10. **Beltraffio:** The Italian painter Giovanni Antonio Beltraffio or Boltraffio (1466–1516), a follower of Leonardo da Vinci. A painting donated to the museum in 1890, *Girl with Cherries*, may have been painted by Boltraffio, but the background of that portrait does not match the one described in the story.

together. It was then that Mrs. Quentin measured the extent of her isolation. Had she ever dared to forecast such a situation, she would have proceeded on the conventional theory that her son's suffering must draw her nearer to him; and this was precisely the relief that was denied her. Alan's uncommunicativeness extended below the level of speech, and his mother, reduced to the helplessness of dead-reckoning, had not even the solace of adapting her sympathy to his needs. She did not know what he felt: his course was incalculable to her. She sometimes wondered if she had become as incomprehensible to him; and it was to find a moment's refuge from the dogging misery of such conjectures that she had now turned in at the Museum.

The long line of mellow canvases seemed to receive her into the rich calm of an autumn twilight. She might have been walking in an enchanted wood where the footfall of care never sounded. So deep was the sense of seclusion that, as she turned from her prolonged communion with the new Beltraffio, it was a surprise to find she was not alone.

A young lady who had risen from the central ottoman stood in suspended flight as Mrs. Quentin faced her. The older woman was the first to regain her self-possession.

"Miss Fenno!" she said.

The girl advanced with a blush. As it faded, Mrs. Quentin noticed a change in her. There had always been something bright and bannerlike in her aspect, but now her look drooped, and she hung at half-mast, as it were. Mrs. Quentin, in the embarrassment of surprising a secret that its possessor was doubtless unconscious of betraying, reverted hurriedly to the Beltraffio.

"I came to see this," she said. "It's very beautiful."

Miss Fenno's eye travelled incuriously over the mystic blue reaches of the landscape. "I suppose so," she assented; adding, after another tentative pause, "You come here often, don't you?"

"Very often," Mrs. Quentin answered. "I find pictures a great help."

"A help?"

"A rest, I mean . . . if one is tired or out of sorts."

"Ah," Miss Fenno murmured, looking down.

"This Beltraffio is new, you know," Mrs. Quentin continued. "What a wonderful background, isn't it? Is he a painter who interests you?"

The girl glanced again at the dusky canvas, as though in a final endeavor to extract from it a clue to the consolations of art. "I don't know," she said at length; "I'm afraid I don't understand pictures." She moved nearer to Mrs. Quentin and held out her hand.

"You're going?"

"Yes."

Mrs. Quentin looked at her. "Let me drive you home," she said, impulsively. She was feeling, with a shock of surprise, that it gave her, after all, no pleasure to see how much the girl had suffered.

Miss Fenno stiffened perceptibly. "Thank you; I shall like the walk."

Mrs. Quentin dropped her hand with a corresponding movement of withdrawal, and a momentary wave of antagonism seemed to sweep the two women apart. Then, as Mrs. Quentin, bowing slightly, again addressed herself to the picture, she felt a sudden touch on her arm.

"Mrs. Quentin," the girl faltered, "I really came here because I saw your carriage." Her eyes sank, and then fluttered back to her hearer's face. "I've been horribly unhappy!" she exclaimed.

Mrs. Quentin was silent. If Hope Fenno had expected an immediate response to her appeal, she was disappointed. The older woman's face was like a veil dropped before her thoughts.

"I've thought so often," the girl went on precipitately, "of what you said that day you came to see me last autumn. I think I understand now what you meant—what you tried to make me see. . . . ? Oh, Mrs. Quentin," she broke out, "I didn't mean to tell you this—I never dreamed of it till this moment—but you *do* remember what you said, don't you? You must remember it! And now that I've met you in this way, I can't help telling you that I believe—I begin to believe—that you were right, after all."

Mrs. Quentin had listened without moving; but now she raised her eyes with a slight smile. "Do you wish me to say this to Alan?" she asked.

The girl flushed, but her glance braved the smile. "Would he still care to hear it?" she said fearlessly.

Mrs. Quentin took momentary refuge in a renewed inspection of the Beltraffio; then, turning, she said, with a kind of reluctance: "He would still care."

"Ah!" broke from the girl.

During this exchange of words the two speakers had drifted unconsciously toward one of the benches. Mrs. Quentin glanced about her: a custodian who had been hovering in the doorway sauntered into the adjoining gallery, and they remained alone among the silvery Vandykes and flushed bituminous Halses.[11] Mrs. Quentin sank down on the bench and reached a hand to the girl.

"Sit by me," she said.

Miss Fenno dropped beside her. In both women the stress of emotion was too strong for speech. The girl was still trembling, and Mrs. Quentin was the first to regain her composure.

"You say you've suffered," she began at last. "Do you suppose *I* haven't?"

"I knew you had. That made it so much worse for me—that I should have been the cause of your suffering for Alan!"

Mrs. Quentin drew a deep breath. "Not for Alan only," she said. Miss Fenno turned on her a wondering glance. "Not for Alan only. *That* pain every woman expects—and knows how to bear. We all know our children must have such disappointments, and to suffer with them is not the deepest pain. It's the suffering apart—in ways they don't understand." She breathed deeply. "I want you to know what I mean. You were right—that day—and I was wrong."

"Oh," the girl faltered.

Mrs. Quentin went on in a voice of passionate lucidity. "I knew it then—I knew it even while I was trying to argue with you—I've always known it! I didn't want my son to marry

---

11. **Vandykes . . . Halses:** The Flemish painter Anthony van Dyke or van Dyck (1599-1641), many of whose portraits have lush backgrounds; and the Dutch portrait painter Frans Hals (1580-1666), whose subjects are often painted against dark backgrounds.

you till I heard your reasons for refusing him; and then—then I longed to see you his wife!"

"Oh, Mrs. Quentin!"

"I longed for it; but I knew it mustn't be."

"Mustn't be?"

Mrs. Quentin shook her head sadly, and the girl, gaining courage from this mute negation, cried with an uncontrollable escape of feeling:

"It's because you thought me hard, obstinate, narrow-minded? Oh, I understand that so well! My self-righteousness must have seemed so petty! A girl who could sacrifice a man's future to her own moral vanity—for it *was* a form of vanity; you showed me that plainly enough—how you must have despised me! But I am not that girl now—indeed I'm not. I'm not impulsive—I think things out. I've thought this out. I know Alan loves me—I know *how* he loves me—and I believe I can help him—oh, not in the ways I had fancied before—but just merely by loving him." She paused, but Mrs. Quentin made no sign. "I see it all so differently now. I see what an influence love itself may be—how my believing in him, loving him, accepting him just as he is, might help him more than any theories, any arguments. I might have seen this long ago in looking at *you*—as he often told me—in seeing how you'd kept yourself apart from—from—Mr. Quentin's work and his—been always the beautiful side of life to them—kept their faith alive in spite of themselves—not by interfering, preaching, reforming, but by—just loving them and being there—" She looked at Mrs. Quentin with a simple nobleness. "It isn't as if I cared for the money, you know; if I cared for that, I should be afraid—"

"You will care for it in time," Mrs. Quentin said suddenly.

Miss Fenno drew back, releasing her hand. "In time?"

"Yes; when there's nothing else left." She stared a moment at the pictures. "My poor child," she broke out, "I've heard all you say so often before!"

"You've heard it?"

"Yes—from myself. I felt as you do, I argued as you do, I acted as I mean to prevent your doing, when I married Alan's father."

The long empty gallery seemed to reverberate with the girl's startled exclamation—"Oh, Mrs. Quentin—"

"Hush; let me speak. Do you suppose I'd do this if you were the kind of pink-and-white idiot he ought to have married? It's because I see you're alive, as I was, tingling with beliefs, ambitions, energies, as I was—that I can't see you walled up alive, as I was, without stretching out a hand to save you!" She sat gazing rigidly forward, her eyes on the pictures, speaking in the low precipitate tone of one who tries to press the meaning of a lifetime into a few breathless sentences.

"When I met Alan's father," she went on, "I knew nothing of his—his work. We met abroad, where I had been living with my mother. That was twenty-six years ago, when the *Radiator* was less—less notorious than it is now. I knew my husband owned a newspaper—a great newspaper—and nothing more. I had never seen a copy of the *Radiator*; I had no notion what it stood for, in politics—or in other ways. We were married in Europe, and a few months afterward we came to live here. People were already beginning to talk about the *Radiator*. My husband, on leaving college, had bought it with some money an old uncle had left him, and the public at first was merely curious to see what an ambitious, stirring young man without any experience of journalism was going to make out of his experiment. They found first of all that he was going to make a great deal of money out of it. I found that out too. I was so happy in other ways that it didn't make much difference at first; though it was pleasant to be able to help my mother, to be generous and charitable, to live in a nice house, and wear the handsome gowns he liked to see me in. But still it didn't really count—it counted so little that when, one day, I learned what the *Radiator* was, I would have gone out into the streets barefooted rather than live another hour on the money it brought in. . . ." Her voice sank, and she paused to steady it. The girl at her side did not speak or move. "I shall never forget that day," she began again. "The paper had stripped bare some family scandal—some miserable bleeding secret that a dozen unhappy people had been struggling to keep out of print—that *would* have been kept out if my husband had not—Oh, you must guess the rest! I can't go on!"

She felt a hand on hers. "You mustn't go on, Mrs. Quentin," the girl whispered.

"Yes, I must—I must! You must be made to understand." She drew a deep breath. "My husband was not like Alan. When he found out how I felt about it he was surprised at first—but gradually he began to see—or at least I fancied he saw—the hatefulness of it. At any rate he saw how I suffered, and he offered to give up the whole thing—to sell the paper. It couldn't be done all of a sudden, of course—he made me see that—for he had put all his money in it, and he had no special aptitude for any other kind of work. He was a born journalist—like Alan. It was a great sacrifice for him to give up the paper, but he promised to do it—in time—when a good opportunity offered. Meanwhile, of course, he wanted to build it up, to increase the circulation—and to do that he had to keep on in the same way—he made that clear to me. I saw that we were in a vicious circle. The paper, to sell well, had to be made more and more detestable and disgraceful. At first I rebelled—but somehow—I can't tell you how it was—after that first concession the ground seemed to give under me: with every struggle I sank deeper. And then—then Alan was born. He was such a delicate baby that there was very little hope of saving him. But money did it—the money from the paper. I took him abroad to see the best physicians—I took him to a warm climate every winter. In hot weather the doctors recommended sea air, and we had a yacht and cruised every summer. I owed his life to the *Radiator*. And when he began to grow stronger the habit was formed—the habit of luxury. He could not get on without the things he had always been used to. He pined in bad air; he drooped under monotony and discomfort; he throve on variety, amusement, travel, every kind of novelty and excitement. And all I wanted for him his inexhaustible foster-mother was there to give!

"My husband said nothing, but he must have seen how things were going. There was no more talk of giving up the *Radiator*. He never reproached me with my inconsistency, but I thought he must despise me, and the thought made me reckless. I determined to ignore the paper altogether—to take what it gave as though I didn't know where it came from. And to excuse this I invented the theory that one may, so to speak, purify money by putting it to good uses. I gave away a great deal in charity—I indulged myself very little at first. All the money that was not spent on Alan I tried to do good with. But gradually, as my boy grew up, the problem became more complicated. How was I to protect Alan from the contamination I had let him live in? I couldn't preach by example—couldn't hold up his father as a warning, or denounce the money we were living on. All I could do was to disguise the inner ugliness of life by making it beautiful outside—to build a wall of beauty between him and the facts of life, turn his tastes and interests another way, hide the *Radiator* from him as a smiling woman at a ball may hide a cancer in her breast! Just as Alan was entering college his father died. Then I saw my way clear. I had loved my husband—and yet I drew my first free breath in years. For the *Radiator* had been left to Alan outright—there was nothing on earth to prevent his selling it when he came of age. And there was no excuse for his not selling it. I had brought him up to depend on money, but the paper had given us enough money to gratify all his tastes. At last we could turn on the monster that had nourished us. I felt a savage joy in the thought—I could hardly bear to wait till Alan came of age. But I had never spoken to him of the paper, and I didn't dare speak of it now. Some false shame kept me back, some vague belief in his ignorance. I would wait till he was twenty-one, and then we should be free.

"I waited—the day came, and I spoke. You can guess his answer, I suppose. He had no idea of selling the *Radiator*. It wasn't the money he cared for—it was the career that tempted him. He was a born journalist, and his ambition, ever since he could remember, had been to carry on his father's work, to develop, to surpass it. There was nothing in the world as interesting as modern journalism. He couldn't imagine any other kind of life that wouldn't bore him to death. A newspaper like the *Radiator* might be made one of the biggest powers on earth, and he loved power, and meant to have all he could get. I listened to him in a kind of trance. I couldn't find a word to say. His father had had scruples—he had none. I seemed to realize at once that argument would be useless. I don't know that I even tried to plead with him—he was so bright and hard and inaccessible! Then I saw that he was, after all, what I had made him—the creature of my concessions, my connivances, my evasions. That was the price I had paid for him—I had kept him at that cost!

"Well—I *had* kept him, at any rate. That was the feeling that survived. He was my boy, my son, my very own—till some other woman took him. Meanwhile the old life must go on as it could. I gave up the struggle. If at that point he was inaccessible, at others he was close to me. He has always been a perfect son. Our tastes grew together—we enjoyed the same books, the same pictures, the same people. All I had to do was to look at him in profile to see the side of him that was really mine. At first I kept thinking of the dreadful other side—but gradually the impression faded, and I kept my mind turned from it, as one does from a deformity in a face one loves. I thought I had made my last compromise with life—had hit on a *modus vivendi*[12] that would last my time.

"And then he met you. I had always been prepared for his marrying, but not a girl like you. I thought he would choose a sweet thing who would never pry into his closets—he hated women with ideas! But as soon as I saw you I knew the struggle would have to

---

12. **modus vivendi**: A temporary agreement or truce between contending parties (Latin).

begin again. He is so much stronger than his father – he is full of the most monstrous convictions. And he has the courage of them, too – you saw last year that his love for you never made him waver. He believes in his work; he adores it – it is a kind of hideous idol to which he would make human sacrifices! He loves you still – I've been honest with you – but his love wouldn't change him. It is you who would have to change – to die gradually, as I have died, till there is only one live point left in me. Ah, if one died completely – that's simple enough! But something persists – remember that – a single point, an aching nerve of truth. Now and then you may drug it – but a touch wakes it again, as your face has waked it in me. There's always enough of one's old self left to suffer with. . . ."

She stood up and faced the girl abruptly. "What shall I tell Alan?" she said.

Miss Fenno sat motionless, her eyes on the ground. Twilight was falling on the gallery – a twilight which seemed to emanate not so much from the glass dome overhead as from the crepuscular depths into which the faces of the pictures were receding. The custodian's step sounded warningly down the corridor. When the girl looked up she was alone.

[1902]

Sui Sin Far
(Edith Maud Eaton)

[1865–1914]

Sui Sin Far, who adopted that pen name as an assertion of her Chinese identity, was born Edith Maud Eaton in Macclesfield, England, on March 15, 1865. She was the second child of Edward Eaton, the son of an English silk merchant, and Lotus Blossom Trefusis, a young Chinese woman who had been adopted by an English couple and educated in England before returning to China. The couple met and married there sometime in the early 1860s. After the birth of their first child, a son, they returned to Edward Eaton's family home in Macclesfield, the center of the silk trade in England. A marriage between a British man and a Chinese woman was virtually unheard of in England, and the Eatons were clearly undecided about where to make their home. They moved to New York for a time and then returned to Macclesfield in 1868 or 1869. During her childhood, Sui Sin Far received frequent reminders of her "difference" from other children, but she attended a private school and was brought up to think of herself as English. By the time she was about six years old, the silk industry in England was declining, and the growing family emigrated to North America, settling first near New York City and then in Montreal. Although he worked as a clerk, Edward Eaton devoted himself to painting, and Sui Sin Far later recalled that her mother was a "fascinating story teller."

Indeed, art and books were an integral part of
the family life that fueled her literary interests and ultimately led her to become one
of the first authors of Asian descent to be
published in North America.

More immediately, however, as
the second oldest of fourteen surviving children, Sui Sin Far was expected
to help support the poverty-stricken
family. When she was about eleven
years old, her formal education
ended, and she went to work. She
began to sell lace she made and her
father's paintings on the streets of
Montreal. In 1883, she found a job in
the composing room of the *Montreal
Daily Star* and set about to learn
to type and take shorthand, office
skills that were providing thousands
of young women new opportunities for
work at the end of the nineteenth century. She was soon proficient enough to
secure a job in a law firm. She began to write
in her spare time and to publish articles in
local and regional newspapers. In 1888–89, she
published several stories in the *Dominion Illustrated*, a new Canadian periodical that primarily featured romantic tales directed at women. These
early works were signed "Edith Eaton" or "E.E." By the mid-1890s, she had
established her own stenographic agency in Montreal. She also traveled
widely, to the American Midwest and to Jamaica, where she joined her sister, Winnifred Eaton, a writer who had assumed a Japanese pen name,
Onoto Watanna. When Sui Sin Far returned to Montreal, ill with malaria
from which she would never fully recover, she decided to resettle in the
United States. She moved to San Francisco and then to Seattle, Washington, where she easily found work in its growing "Chinatown."

Taking as her pen name the Cantonese word for "Narcissus," in the late
1890s Sui Sin Far began to publish articles and stories in which she
directly confronted the pervasive prejudice and frequent violence directed
against Chinese immigrants in the United States. During the following decade, her writings began to gain national attention. In 1909, she published
an autobiographical essay, "Leaves from the Mental Portfolio of an Eur-
asian," in a prominent New York newspaper, the *Independent*, where four
of her stories subsequently appeared. Sui Sin Far moved to Boston, where
she gained a firm foothold in the literary marketplace of the East, publishing her writings in *Good Housekeeping, Hampton's Magazine*, and the
New-England Magazine. She also published a collection of her stories,
Mrs. Spring Fragrance (1912). A reviewer for the *New York Times* observed
that Sui Sin Far had "struck a new note in fiction," while the reviewer for

the *Boston Globe* emphasized the ways in which she subverted stereotypes of Chinese people:

> The tales are told with a sympathy that strikes straight to one's heart; to say they are convincing is weak praise, and they show the Chinese with feelings absolutely indistinguishable from those of white people – only the Chinese seem to have more delicate sensibilities, and more acute ways of handling their problems.

bedfordstmartins.com/ americanlit for research links on Sui Sin Far

Despite such positive reviews, the book did not sell well. Sui Sin Far, who was in poor health, returned to Montreal, where she died of heart failure in 1914. The manuscript of a novel she was working on at the time of her death was apparently lost, and her published writings soon fell into oblivion, but Sui Sin Far has recently come to be recognized as one of the founders of the tradition of Asian American literature in both Canada and the United States.

Reading Sui Sin Far's "'Its Wavering Image.'"   This was the fourth story in Sui Sin Far's only published volume, the collection *Mrs. Spring Fragrance.* When the book was published, the admiring reviewer for the *New York Times* reserved special praise for the stories in which she portrayed "for readers of the white race the lives, feelings, sentiments of the Americanized Chinese of the Pacific coast, or those who have intermarried with them and of the children who have sprung from such unions." Of all the stories in the collection, "'Its Wavering Image'" was probably the most autobiographical, or at least what one critic had described as the most "self-referential." Certainly, Sui Sin Far, the daughter of a Caucasian father and a Chinese mother, is reflected in the story's central character, Pan, the daughter of a Chinese father and a Caucasian mother. As the narrator of the story immediately observes, Pan begins to ponder the "mystery of her nature" only after becoming involved with "her first white friend," Mark Carson, a reporter researching an article about Chinatown. The article he subsequently writes is thus framed by the story of his romantic relationship with Pan, who struggles to retain her sense of biracial and bicultural identity in the face of his insistence that she must be either

Arnold Genthe, **"Dressed for the Feast, Chinatown, San Francisco"**

This image of two young women in holiday dress was one of numerous photographs Genthe took in Chinatown, some of which he first collected in *Pictures of Old Chinatown* (1908).

"white" or Chinese. Indeed, like much of Sui Sin Far's fiction, "'Its Wavering Image'" powerfully suggests the racial and cultural barriers both Chinese immigrants and Eurasians faced in their struggle to gain acceptance in the United States. The text of the story is taken from *Mrs. Spring Fragrance* (1912).

"Its Wavering Image"[1]

I

Pan was a half white, half Chinese girl. Her mother was dead, and Pan lived with her father who kept an Oriental Bazaar on Dupont Street. All her life had Pan lived in Chinatown,[2] and if she were different in any sense from those around her, she gave little thought to it. It was only after the coming of Mark Carson that the mystery of her nature began to trouble her.

They met at the time of the boycott of the Sam Yups by the See Yups.[3] After the heat and dust and unsavoriness of the highways and byways of Chinatown, the young reporter who had been sent to find a story, had stepped across the threshold of a cool, deep room, fragrant with the odor of dried lilies and sandalwood, and found Pan.

She did not speak to him, nor he to her. His business was with the spectacled merchant, who, with a pointed brush, was making up accounts in brown paper books and rolling balls in an abacus box.[4] As to Pan, she always turned from whites. With her father's people she was natural and at home; but in the presence of her mother's she felt strange and constrained, shrinking from their curious scrutiny as she would from the sharp edge of a sword.

When Mark Carson returned to the office, he asked some questions concerning the girl who had puzzled him. What was she? Chinese or white? The city editor answered him, adding: "She is an unusually bright girl, and could tell more stories about the Chinese than any other person in this city — if she would."

---

1. **"Its Wavering Image"**: The title is from the final line of "The Bridge," a melancholy poem about love and loss published by Henry Wadsworth Longfellow in *The Belfry of Bruges and Other Poems* (1845). Several stanzas were set to music by the English composer Maria Lindsay (1827-1898).

2. **Chinatown**: The area of downtown San Francisco known as Chinatown was densely populated by Chinese immigrants, who had been coming to California since the California gold rush of 1848-55.

3. **Sam Yups . . . See Yups**: Although most of the Chinese immigrants were from the Canton region of China, they spoke different dialects and identified with different families or "companies." The Sam Yups were merchants who controlled the retail shops of Chinatown, while the See Yups were laborers. Their interests were often at odds, and in August 1895 the See Yups began a boycott of retail shops owned by the Sam Yups that resulted in violence in the Chinatowns of several U.S. cities.

4. **abacus box**: A computing device consisting of rods designating a given denomination and strung with moveable beads or balls representing a digit or a specific number of digits.

Mark Carson had a determined chin, clever eyes, and a tone to his voice which easily won for him the confidence of the unwary. In the reporter's room he was spoken of as "a man who would sell his soul for a story."

After Pan's first shyness had worn off, he found her bewilderingly frank and free with him; but he had all the instincts of a gentleman save one, and made no ordinary mistake about her. He was Pan's first white friend. She was born a Bohemian,[5] exempt from the conventional restrictions imposed upon either the white or Chinese woman; and the Oriental who was her father mingled with his affection for his child so great a respect for and trust in the daughter of the dead white woman, that everything she did or said was right to him. And Pan herself! A white woman might pass over an insult; a Chinese woman fail to see one. But Pan! He would be a brave man indeed who offered one to childish little Pan.

All this Mark Carson's clear eyes perceived, and with delicate tact and subtlety he taught the young girl that, all unconscious until his coming, she had lived her life alone. So well did she learn this lesson that it seemed at times as if her white self must entirely dominate and trample under foot her Chinese.

Meanwhile, in full trust and confidence, she led him about Chinatown, initiating him into the simple mystery and history of many things, for which she, being of her father's race, had tender regard and pride. For her sake he was received as a brother by the yellow-robed priest in the joss house,[6] the Astrologer of Prospect Place, and other conservative Chinese. The Water Lily Club opened its doors to him when she knocked, and the Sublimely Pure Brothers' organization[7] admitted him as one of its honorary members, thereby enabling him not only to see but to take part in a ceremony in which no American had ever before participated. With her by his side, he was welcomed wherever he went. Even the little Chinese women in the midst of their babies, received him with gentle smiles, and the children solemnly munched his candies and repeated nursery rhymes for his edification.

He enjoyed it all, and so did Pan. They were both young and light-hearted. And when the afternoon was spent, there was always that high room open to the stars, with its China bowls full of flowers and its big colored lanterns, shedding a mellow light.

Sometimes there was music. A Chinese band played three evenings a week in the gilded restaurant beneath them, and the louder the gongs sounded and the fiddlers fiddled, the more delighted was Pan. Just below the restaurant was her father's bazaar. Occasionally Mun You would stroll upstairs and inquire of the young couple if there was anything needed to complete their felicity, and Pan would answer: "Thou only." Pan was very proud of her Chinese father. "I would rather have a Chinese for a father than a white man," she often told Mark Carson. The last time she had said that he had asked whom she would prefer for a husband, a white man or a Chinese. And Pan, for the first time since he had known her, had no answer for him.

---

5. **Bohemian:** A person who lives an unconventional life; a term often applied to an artist or writer.

6. **joss house:** An American term for a temple or house of worship in Chinatown.

7. **Sublimely Pure Brothers' organization:** A brotherhood or secret society.

II

It was a cool, quiet evening, after a hot day. A new moon was in the sky.

"How beautiful above! How unbeautiful below!" exclaimed Mark Carson involuntarily.

He and Pan had been gazing down from their open retreat into the lantern-lighted, motley-thronged street beneath them.

"Perhaps it isn't very beautiful," replied Pan, "but it is here I live. It is my home." Her voice quivered a little.

He leaned towards her suddenly and grasped her hands.

"Pan," he cried, "you do not belong here. You are white — white."

"No! no!" protested Pan.

"You are," he asserted. "You have no right to be here."

"I was born here," she answered, "and the Chinese people look upon me as their own."

"But they do not understand you," he went on. "Your real self is alien to them. What interest have they in the books you read — the thoughts you think?"

"They have an interest in me," answered faithful Pan. "Oh, do not speak in that way any more."

"But I must," the young man persisted. "Pan, don't you see that you have got to decide what you will be — Chinese or white? You cannot be both."

"Hush! Hush!" bade Pan. "I do not love you when you talk to me like that."

A little Chinese boy brought tea and saffron cakes. He was a picturesque little fellow with a quaint manner of speech. Mark Carson jested merrily with him, while Pan holding a tea-bowl between her two small hands laughed and sipped.

When they were alone again, the silver stream and the crescent moon became the objects of their study. It was a very beautiful evening.

After a while Mark Carson, his hand on Pan's shoulder, sang:

> "And forever, and forever,
> As long as the river flows,
> As long as the heart has passions,
> As long as life has woes,
> The moon and its broken reflection,
> And its shadows shall appear,
> As the symbol of love in heaven,
> And its wavering image here."[8]

Listening to that irresistible voice singing her heart away, the girl broke down and wept. She was so young and so happy.

"Look up at me," bade Mark Carson. "Oh, Pan! Pan! Those tears prove that you are white." Pan lifted her wet face.

"Kiss me, Pan," said he. It was the first time.

Next morning Mark Carson began work on the special-feature article which he had been promising his paper for some weeks.

---

8. **"And ... here"**: The final stanza of "The Bridge," a popular Victorian parlor song by Maria Lindsay (see note 1).

III

"Cursed be his ancestors," bayed Man You.

He cast a paper at his daughter's feet and left the room.

Startled by her father's unwonted passion, Pan picked up the paper, and in the clear passionless light of the afternoon read that which forever after was blotted upon her memory.

"Betrayed! Betrayed! Betrayed to be a betrayer!"

It burnt red hot; agony unrelieved by words, unassuaged by tears.

So till evening fell. Then she stumbled up the dark stairs which led to the high room open to the stars and tried to think it out. Someone had hurt her. Who was it? She raised her eyes. There shone: "Its Wavering Image." It helped her to lucidity. He had done it. Was it unconsciously dealt – that cruel blow? Ah, well did he know that the sword which pierced her through others, would carry with it to her own heart, the pain of all those others. None knew better than he that she, whom he had called "a white girl, a white woman," would rather that her own naked body and soul had been exposed, than that things, sacred and secret to those who loved her, should be cruelly unveiled and ruthlessly spread before the ridiculing and uncomprehending foreigner. And knowing all this so well, so well, he had carelessly sung her heart away, and with her kiss upon his lips, had smilingly turned and stabbed her. She, who was of the race that remembers.

IV

Mark Carson, back in the city after an absence of two months, thought of Pan. He would see her that very evening. Dear little Pan, pretty Pan, clever Pan, amusing Pan; who was always so frankly glad to have him come to her; so eager to hear all that he was doing; so appreciative, so inspiring, so loving. She would have forgotten that article by now. Why should a white woman care about such things? Her true self was above it all. Had he not taught her *that* during the weeks in which they had seen so much of one another? True, his last lesson had been a little harsh, and as yet he knew not how she had taken it; but even if its roughness had hurt and irritated, there was a healing balm, a wizard's oil which none knew so well as he how to apply.

But for all these soothing reflections, there was an undercurrent of feeling which caused his steps to falter on his way to Pan. He turned into Portsmouth square and took a seat on one of the benches facing the fountain erected in memory of Robert Louis Stevenson.[9] Why had Pan failed to answer the note he had written telling her of the assignment which would keep him out of town for a couple of months and giving her his address? Would Robert Louis Stevenson have known why? Yes – and so did Mark Carson. But though Robert Louis Stevenson would have boldly answered himself the question, Mark Carson thrust it aside, arose, and pressed up the hill.

---

9. **Robert Louis Stevenson:** The Scottish author (1850–1894) of the popular novels *Treasure Island, Kidnapped,* and *The Strange Case of Dr Jekyll and Mr Hyde.* Following his death, a memorial fountain was erected in his honor in Portland Square, between Chinatown and the Latin District, a small park Stevenson had frequented during his visit to San Francisco in 1889–90.

"I knew they would not blame you, Pan!"

"Yes."

"And there was no word of you, dear. I was careful about that, not only for your sake, but for mine."

Silence.

"It is mere superstition anyway. These things have got to be exposed and done away with."

Still silence.

Mark Carson felt strangely chilled. Pan was not herself tonight. She did not even look herself. He had been accustomed to seeing her in American dress. Tonight she wore the Chinese costume. But for her clear-cut features she might have been a Chinese girl. He shivered.

"Pan," he asked, "why do you wear that dress?"

Within her sleeves Pan's small hands struggled together; but her face and voice were calm.

"Because I am a Chinese woman," she answered.

"You are not," cried Mark Carson, fiercely. "You cannot say that now, Pan. You are a white woman — white. Did your kiss not promise me that?"

"A white woman!" echoed Pan, her voice rising high and clear to the stars above them. "I would not be a white woman for all the world. *You* are a white man. And *what* is a promise to a white man!"

When she was lying low, the element of Fire having raged so fiercely within her that it had almost shriveled up the childish frame, there came to the house of Man You a little toddler who could scarcely speak. Climbing upon Pan's couch, she pressed her head upon the sick girl's bosom. The feel of that little head brought tears.

"Lo!" said the mother of the toddler. "Thou wilt bear a child thyself some day, and all the bitterness of this will pass away."

And Pan, being a Chinese woman, was comforted.

[1912]

Edwin Arlington Robinson

[1869-1935]

Edwin Arlington Robinson was born on December 22, 1869, in Head Tide, Maine. He was the third son of Edward Robinson, a prosperous timber merchant, and his wife, Mary Palmer Robinson, a distant descendant of the colonial American poet Anne Bradstreet. The following year, the family moved to Gardiner, Maine — the Tilbury Town of many of Robinson's later poems — where he spent a happy and secure childhood. When he was about eleven, Robinson joined a group of local poets, and after his graduation from Gardiner High School in 1889 he spent a year writing poetry and studying the work of the classical Roman poet Horace and the English poet John Milton. Robinson later recalled that by the time he was twenty he felt "doomed, or elected, or sentenced for life, to the writing of poetry." In 1891, he enrolled at Harvard, where Robinson published a few poems in the *Harvard Advocate*, but his education was interrupted when his father died in 1892. After the Panic of 1893, the worst economic crisis the country had yet experienced, his family's financial difficulties forced Robinson to leave Harvard for good and return home to Gardiner.

Robinson spent much of his time there working on short stories and writing poetry, his enduring literary love. At the end of one of his first published poems, "Sonnet," which

E. A. Robinson

By the time Lilla Cabot Perry painted this portrait in 1916, Robinson had established himself as one of the foremost poets in the United States.

appeared in the *Critic* in 1894, Robinson posed a question that revealed his aspiration to become the poet, "the beacon bright," whose work would illuminate and give meaning to the gray and poetically barren age in the United States: "Shall not one bard arise / To wrench one banner from the western skies, / And mark it with his fame for evermore?" Robinson gathered "Sonnet" together with some of his other early poems and sought a publisher for a manuscript he called *The Tavern and the Night Before*. When it was rejected, he retitled the slim volume *The Torrent and the Night Before*, which he privately printed with the financial help of an uncle in 1896. Robinson sent copies to friends, critics he thought might review the book, and writers he admired, including Edward Eggleston, the author of the popular novel *The Hoosier Schoolmaster* (1871). Robinson was thrilled when Eggleston replied, "You have given me a rare sensation: you have sent me a book that I can read, and for that I thank you. I am a very busy man, but you have sent me a book I cannot help reading and for that I forgive you." Although the volume did not attract much critical attention, Robinson was sufficiently encouraged to pay the printing costs of a second collection of his poems, *The Children of the Night* (1897).

After the death of his mother, Robinson felt that he needed a change of scene and moved to New York City, where he had a few acquaintances from his years at Harvard. He initially lived on the small income from his mother's estate, but the financial reverses that continued to plague his family soon dried up that source of money, and Robinson supported himself through a string of odd jobs and with some help from friends. In 1905, he received a major break when President Theodore Roosevelt read and admired *The Children of the Night*. Roosevelt, who wrote an enthusiastic review of the volume, arranged a job for Robinson in the New York Custom House. With virtually no duties beyond spending a few hours a day at the office, he could devote himself to poetry, and when Roosevelt left office Robinson quit the job in order to write full time. After he published *The*

[Robinson] understood loneliness in all its many forms and deities and was thus less interested in its conventional poetic aspects than he was in the loneliness of the man in the crowd.

-James Dickey

Town Down the River (1909), a Boston newspaper called him "America's Foremost Poet." Despite his use of traditional poetic forms, his reputation was advanced by proponents of the "new" verse like Harriet Munroe, who published his poem "Eros Turannos" in her magazine *Poetry*, and experimental poets like Amy Lowell, who observed that Robinson's collection *The Man against the Sky* (1916) was "dynamic with experience and knowledge of life." The popularity of Robert Frost's early poetry also helped generate a growing audience for Robinson's explorations of rural life in New England. In his next volume of poetry, however, he turned from the characters and settings of Tilbury Town to the medieval past in a long narrative poem based on the legends of King Arthur, *Merlin* (1917).

Robinson's final years were filled with honors. His work was often embraced by those who were hostile to more radical departures in poetry and the arts. In a review of his collection *The Three Taverns* (1920), for example, a critic approvingly described it as a volume that makes "no compromise with vers libre, imagism, polyphonic prose and so on." Robinson subsequently received three Pulitzer Prizes, for his *Collected Poems* (1921), *The Man Who Died Twice* (1924), and his best-selling *Tristram* (1927), another long narrative poem based on Arthurian legends. At the time of his death in New York on April 6, 1935, Robinson had not only achieved his dream of becoming a leading American poet, but he was also among the first to earn a living by writing poetry in the United States.

Reading Robinson's Poetry.

As his reputation grew, Robinson published some of his poems in prominent periodicals such as the *Nation*, the *New Republic*, *Poetry*, and *Scribner's Magazine*. But most of his poetry first appeared in books, one of which had the unique distinction of being reviewed by a sitting president of the United States. Theodore Roosevelt so admired Robinson's second book of poetry, *The Children of the Night* (1897), that he wrote a review of the volume for *Outlook* in 1905. Bemoaning the current public taste in poetry, Roosevelt praised Robinson's "curious simplicity and good taste." Although the president admitted that he did not entirely understand "Luke Havergal," he declared: "I am entirely sure that I like it." Roosevelt also admired "Richard Cory," which he said "illustrates a very ancient but very profound philosophy of life with a curiously local touch."

bedfordstmartins.com/ americanlit *for research links on Robinson*

That "local touch" was characteristic of the best poems Robinson wrote throughout his career, represented by the following selection of poems published between 1896 and 1919. Just as he frequently evoked the distant past, Robinson favored traditional poetic forms, especially the sonnet, and his poems generally follow conventional (though often highly complex) metrical patterns and rhyme schemes. At the same time, Robinson employed a plain, vernacular language in his often stark explorations of life and characters in his fictional Tilbury Town. Indeed, Robinson's work was influenced by the realism and emerging naturalism of much of the American fiction written around the turn of the century. Certainly, he avoided the romanticism and sentimentality characteristic of so much popular poetry of the period. While some readers consequently found his tone too despairing, others have emphasized Robinson's pervasive and complex use of irony. "We don't despair — not quite — and neither does Robinson," the poet Archibald MacLeish observed. "But we don't hope either, as we used to, and Robinson, with no bitterness, has put hope by as well. His is the after voice, the evening voice, and we neither accept it nor reject it but we know the thing it means." The texts of the following poems are taken from the *Collected Poems of Edwin Arlington Robinson* (1921).

LUKE HAVERGAL

Go to the western gate, Luke Havergal,
There where the vines cling crimson on the wall,
And in the twilight wait for what will come.
The leaves will whisper there of her, and some,
Like flying words, will strike you as they fall;   5
But go, and if you listen she will call.
Go to the western gate, Luke Havergal —
Luke Havergal.

No, there is not a dawn in eastern skies
To rift the fiery night that's in your eyes;   10
But there, where western glooms are gathering,
The dark will end the dark, if anything:
God slays Himself with every leaf that flies,
And hell is more than half of paradise.
No, there is not a dawn in eastern skies —   15
In eastern skies.

Out of a grave I come to tell you this,
Out of a grave I come to quench the kiss
That flames upon your forehead with a glow
That blinds you to the way that you must go.   20
Yes, there is yet one way to where she is,
Bitter, but one that faith may never miss.
Out of a grave I come to tell you this —
To tell you this.

There is the western gate, Luke Havergal,   25
There are the crimson leaves upon the wall.
Go, for the winds are tearing them away, —
Nor think to riddle the dead words they say,
Nor any more to feel them as they fall;
But go, and if you trust her she will call.   30
There is the western gate, Luke Havergal —
Luke Havergal.

[1896, 1921]

RICHARD CORY

Whenever Richard Cory went down town,
We people on the pavement looked at him:
He was a gentleman from sole to crown,
Clean favored, and imperially slim.

And he was always quietly arrayed,   5
And he was always human when he talked;
But still he fluttered pulses when he said,
"Good-morning," and he glittered when he walked.

And he was rich — yes, richer than a king —
And admirably schooled in every grace: 10
In fine, we thought that he was everything
To make us wish that we were in his place.

So on we worked, and waited for the light,
And went without the meat, and cursed the bread;
And Richard Cory, one calm summer night,   15
Went home and put a bullet through his head.

[1897, 1921]

MINIVER CHEEVY

Miniver Cheevy, child of scorn,
    Grew lean while he assailed the seasons;
He wept that he was ever born,
    And he had reasons.
Miniver loved the days of old   5
    When swords were bright and steeds were prancing;
The vision of a warrior bold
    Would set him dancing.

Miniver sighed for what was not,
    And dreamed, and rested from his labors;   10
He dreamed of Thebes and Camelot,
    And Priam's neighbors.[1]

---

1. **He dreamed . . . Priam's neighbors:** Thebes, an ancient city that figures in many Greek myths, was destroyed by Alexander the Great in 336 BCE. Camelot was the home of King Arthur, the legendary king of medieval England. Priam was the king of Troy, whose "neighbors" included Aeneas, Achilles, and other heroic figures of the Trojan War as described in Homer's epic poem the *Iliad*.

Miniver mourned the ripe renown
    That made so many a name so fragrant;
He mourned Romance, now on the town,   15
    And Art, a vagrant.

Miniver loved the Medici,[2]
    Albeit he had never seen one;
He would have sinned incessantly
    Could he have been one.   20

Miniver cursed the commonplace
    And eyed a khaki suit with loathing;
He missed the mediaeval grace
    Of iron clothing.

Miniver scorned the gold he sought,   25
    But sore annoyed was he without it;
Miniver thought, and thought, and thought,
    And thought about it.

Miniver Cheevy, born too late,
    Scratched his head and kept on thinking;   30
Miniver coughed, and called it fate,
    And kept on drinking.

[1907, 1921]

---

2. **the Medici:** The powerful family that ruled Florence for much of the fifteenth century, during the Italian Renaissance.

THE MILL

The miller's wife had waited long,
    The tea was cold, the fire was dead;
And there might yet be nothing wrong
    In how he went and what he said:
"There are no millers any more,"   5
    Was all that she had heard him say;
And he had lingered at the door
    So long that it seemed yesterday.

Sick with a fear that had no form
    She knew that she was there at last;   10
And in the mill there was a warm
    And mealy fragrance of the past.

What else there was would only seem
    To say again what he had meant;
And what was hanging from a beam   15
    Would not have heeded where she went.

And if she thought it followed her,
    She may have reasoned in the dark
That one way of the few there were
    Would hide her and would leave no mark: 20
Black water, smooth above the weir
    Like starry velvet in the night,
Though ruffled once, would soon appear
    The same as ever to the sight.

[1919, 1921]

Stephen Crane

[1871–1900]

Stephen Crane

This photograph was taken while Crane was working as a war correspondent in Greece in 1897.

Stephen Crane was born on November 1, 1871, in Newark, New Jersey. He was the fourteenth child of the Reverend Dr. Jonathan Townley Crane, a Methodist minister and church official, and his wife, Mary Helen Peck Crane, the daughter of a Methodist minister who was herself deeply involved in church affairs as a journalist and lecturer. The family moved several times, following the ministerial work of Crane's father, who died in 1880. Three years later, the family settled in Asbury Park, New Jersey. When Crane was about sixteen, he began to work as a copy boy for his older brother's summer news bureau, which supplied articles about the New Jersey shore to the *New-York Tribune* and to the Associated Press. Crane attended Pennington Seminary before transferring to the Claverack College and Hudson River Institute, a military academy and prep school. Crane published his first signed sketch in the school magazine, the *Vidette*, in February 1890. That fall, he entered Lafayette College as an engineering student but withdrew after his first semester. In January 1891, he enrolled as a special student at Syracuse University. As a writer for the *Philadelphia Press* wryly observed in 1896, "Mr. Crane studied more or less at Lafayette College and Syracuse University, but took no degree. Like several authors not unknown to fame, he appears to have found it hard to stick to the curriculum."

In fact, Crane was already eager to launch his literary career. During his one semester at Syracuse University, where he was a star on the varsity baseball team, he contributed to the student newspaper, worked as a local correspondent for the *New-York Tribune*, and began to write a novel about a slum girl driven to prostitution and suicide, *Maggie: A Girl of the Streets*. In May 1891, Crane left college for good and moved to New York City. Working as a journalist, he endured poverty and deprivation for several years. When he was unable to find a publisher for *Maggie*, Crane paid for the printing of the novel in 1893. In a review, the noted writer Hamlin Garland lauded Crane's "truthful and unhackneyed study of the slums," observing that the novel was "pictorial, graphic, [and] terrible in its directness." The book did not sell, but Crane pressed on, writing articles, stories, and *The Red Badge of Courage*, a novel about the Civil War. Although he was born after the war, Crane had read at least one of the proliferating accounts of the conflict in the popular series "The Battles and Leaders of the Civil War," which ran in *Century Magazine* during the 1880s. *The Red Badge of Courage* first appeared in a shorter version as a serial published by the Bacheller Syndicate, which supplied literary materials to more than 700 small newspapers across the country—Willa Cather, then a college senior, read the novel in the pages of the *Nebraska State Journal* in December 1894. Hired by Bacheller as a reporter and travel writer, Crane took an extended tour of the West and Mexico. In addition to the articles and stories he wrote during his travels, Crane also published a collection of his experimental poetry, *The Black Riders and Other Lines* (1895).

The reviews of his poetry were mixed, but the publication of *The Red Badge of Courage* in book form gained Crane international acclaim by 1896. Describing its reception in England, the novelist Joseph Conrad later recalled that the "small volume" detonated "with the impact of a twelve inch shell charged with a very high explosive." In response to the growing demand for his work, Crane in 1896 published a new edition of *Maggie* and a collection of stories, *The Little Regiment and Other Episodes of the Amercian Civil War*. He swiftly wrote two works of fiction, one about the humdrum life of a workingman in New York, *George's Mother* (1896); and the other about a young artist, *The Third Violet* (1897). The success of *The Red Badge of Courage* also provided Crane with an opportunity to become a war correspondent. During a voyage from Jacksonville, Florida, to cover the ongoing revolution against Spanish rule in Cuba, Crane narrowly survived a shipwreck that he described in a newspaper account and then in his most famous short story, "The Open Boat." In Jacksonville, Crane met Cora Taylor, whose nightclub, the Hotel de Dream, was reputed to be a house of prostitution. Taylor accompanied Crane to Greece, where he covered the Greco-Turkish War of 1897, and then to England. She remained there, handling his correspondence, when Crane left for Cuba to cover the Spanish-American War of 1898. That year, he published *The Open Boat and Other Tales of Adventure*, as well as some highly regarded dispatches from Cuba. Suffering from malaria, he rejoined Taylor in England, where in 1899 Crane prepared a collection of stories and two other books for publication: his second volume of poetry, *War Is Kind*; and a satirical novel about a war correspondent, *Active Service*. Despite the

[Crane's] was a costly vision, won through personal suffering, hard living and harsh artistic discipline; and by the time of his death, at twenty-nine, he was recognized as one of the important innovators of American fictional prose and master of a powerful and original style.

–Ralph Ellison

bedfordstmartins.com /americanlit *for research links on Crane*

tubercular hemorrhage he suffered later that year, Crane continued a relentless work schedule, publishing two additional collections of sketches and stories before he died on June 5, 1900, in Germany, where he had gone seeking a cure.

Reading Crane's "The Open Boat."   Eagerly accepting an offer to become a war correspondent for a newspaper syndicate, Crane signed on as an "able seaman" aboard the *Commodore*, a steamship smuggling munitions from Jacksonville, Florida, to the *insurrectos* who were rebelling against Spanish rule in Cuba. After the *Commodore* sank on January 2, 1897, Crane and three other survivors spent thirty hours in a ten-foot dinghy before they reached shore at Daytona Beach. His detailed report of the shipwreck, which made national news, was swiftly published as "Stephen Crane's Own Story" in the *New York Press* on January 7, 1897. At the end of the article, after describing his escape from the sinking *Commodore* along with the ship's captain and two members of the crew, Crane observed: "The history of life in an open boat for thirty hours would no doubt be instructive for the young, but none is to be told here and now." He soon offered an account of those "thirty hours" in "The Open Boat." As the poet John Berryman notes in his biography of Crane, "To take 'The Open Boat,' however, as a *report* is to misunderstand the nature of his work: it is an action of his art upon the remembered possibility of death. The death is so close that the story is warm." The artistry of Crane's story of human brotherhood in the face of an indifferent and seemingly hostile nature has been admired by many authors, including Ernest Hemingway, who in a 1935 interview included "The Open Boat" among the works he said every writer should read. The text is taken from the first printing in *Scribner's Magazine*, June 1897.

THE OPEN BOAT

A Tale Intended to Be After the Fact. Being the Experience of Four Men from the Sunk Steamer *Commodore*

I

None of them knew the color of the sky. Their eyes glanced level, and were fastened upon the waves that swept toward them. These waves were of the hue of slate, save for the tops, which were of foaming white, and all of the men knew the colors of the sea. The horizon narrowed and widened, and dipped and rose, and at all times its edge was jagged with waves that seemed thrust up in points like rocks.

Many a man ought to have a bath-tub larger than the boat which here rode upon the sea. These waves were most wrongfully and barbarously abrupt and tall, and each froth-top was a problem in small boat navigation.

The cook squatted in the bottom and looked with both eyes at the six inches of gunwale which separated him from the ocean. His sleeves were rolled over his fat forearms, and the two flaps of his unbuttoned vest dangled as he bent to bail out the boat. Often he said: "Gawd! That was a narrow clip." As he remarked it he invariably gazed eastward over the broken sea.

The oiler,[1] steering with one of the two oars in the boat, sometimes raised himself suddenly to keep clear of water that swirled in over the stern. It was a thin little oar and it seemed often ready to snap.

The correspondent, pulling at the other oar, watched the waves and wondered why he was there.

The injured captain, lying in the bow, was at this time buried in that profound dejection and indifference which comes, temporarily at least, to even the bravest and most enduring when, willy nilly, the firm fails, the army loses, the ship goes down. The mind of the master of a vessel is rooted deep in the timbers of her, though he command for a day or a decade, and this captain had on him the stern impression of a scene in the grays of dawn of seven turned faces, and later a stump of a top-mast with a white ball on it that slashed to and fro at the waves, went low and lower, and down. Thereafter there was something strange in his voice. Although steady, it was deep with mourning, and of a quality beyond oration or tears.

"Keep'er a little more south, Billie," said he.

"'A little more south,' sir," said the oiler in the stern.

A seat in this boat was not unlike a seat upon a bucking broncho, and, by the same token, a broncho is not much smaller. The craft pranced and reared, and plunged like an animal. As each wave came, and she rose for it, she seemed like a horse making at a fence outrageously high. The manner of her scramble over these walls of water is a mystic thing, and, moreover, at the top of them were ordinarily these problems in white water, the foam racing down from the summit of each wave, requiring a new leap, and a leap from the air. Then, after scornfully bumping a crest, she would slide, and race, and splash down a long incline and arrive bobbing and nodding in front of the next menace.

A singular disadvantage of the sea lies in the fact that after successfully surmounting one wave you discover that there is another behind it just as important and just as nervously anxious to do something effective in the way of swamping boats. In a ten-foot dingey one can get an idea of the resources of the sea in the line of waves that is not probable to the average experience, which is never at sea in a dingey. As each slaty wall of water approached, it shut all else from the view of the men in the boat, and it was not difficult to imagine that this particular wave was the final outburst of the ocean, the last effort of the grim water. There was a terrible grace in the move of the waves, and they came in silence, save for the snarling of the crests.

In the wan light, the faces of the men must have been gray. Their eyes must have glinted in strange ways as they gazed steadily astern. Viewed from a balcony, the whole thing would doubtlessly have been weirdly picturesque. But the men in the boat had

---

1. **oiler:** The person who oils machinery in the engine room of a ship.

no time to see it, and if they had had leisure there were other things to occupy their minds. The sun swung steadily up the sky, and they knew it was broad day because the color of the sea changed from slate to emerald-green, streaked with amber lights, and the foam was like tumbling snow. The process of the breaking day was unknown to them. They were aware only of this effect upon the color of the waves that rolled toward them.

In disjointed sentences the cook and the correspondent argued as to the difference between a life-saving station and a house of refuge. The cook had said: "There's a house of refuge just north of the Mosquito Inlet Light, and as soon as they see us, they'll come off in their boat and pick us up."

"As soon as who see us?" said the correspondent.

"The crew," said the cook.

"Houses of refuge don't have crews," said the correspondent. "As I understand them, they are only places where clothes and grub are stored for the benefit of shipwrecked people. They don't carry crews."

"Oh, yes, they do," said the cook.

"No, they don't," said the correspondent.

"Well, we're not there yet, anyhow," said the oiler, in the stern.

"Well," said the cook, "perhaps it's not a house of refuge that I'm thinking of as being near Mosquito Inlet Light. Perhaps it's a life-saving station."

"We're not there yet," said the oiler, in the stern.

II

As the boat bounced from the top of each wave, the wind tore through the hair of the hatless men, and as the craft plopped her stern down again the spray slashed past them. The crest of each of these waves was a hill, from the top of which the men surveyed, for a moment, a broad tumultuous expanse; shining and wind-riven. It was probably splendid. It was probably glorious, this play of the free sea, wild with lights of emerald and white and amber.

"Bully good thing it's an on-shore wind," said the cook. "If not, where would we be? Wouldn't have a show."

"That's right," said the correspondent.

The busy oiler nodded his assent.

Then the captain, in the bow, chuckled in a way that expressed humor, contempt, tragedy, all in one. "Do you think we've got much of a show, now, boys?" said he.

Whereupon the three were silent, save for a trifle of hemming and hawing. To express any particular optimism at this time they felt to be childish and stupid, but they all doubtless possessed this sense of the situation in their mind. A young man thinks doggedly at such times. On the other hand, the ethics of their condition was decidedly against any open suggestion of hopelessness. So they were silent.

"Oh, well," said the captain, soothing his children, "we'll get ashore all right."

But there was that in his tone which made them think, so the oiler quoth: "Yes! If this wind holds!"

The cook was bailing: "Yes! If we don't catch hell in the surf."

Canton flannel gulls[2] flew near and far. Sometimes they sat down on the sea, near patches of brown sea-weed that rolled over the waves with a movement like carpets on a line in a gale. The birds sat comfortably in groups, and they were envied by some in the dingey, for the wrath of the sea was no more to them than it was to a covey of prairie chickens a thousand miles inland. Often they came very close and stared at the men with black beadlike eyes. At these times they were uncanny and sinister in their unblinking scrutiny, and the men hooted angrily at them, telling them to be gone. One came, and evidently decided to alight on the top of the captain's head. The bird flew parallel to the boat and did not circle, but made short sidelong jumps in the air in chicken-fashion. His black eyes were wistfully fixed upon the captain's head. "Ugly brute," said the oiler to the bird. "You look as if you were made with a jackknife." The cook and the correspondent swore darkly at the creature. The captain naturally wished to knock it away with the end of the heavy painter,[3] but he did not dare do it, because anything resembling an emphatic gesture would have capsized this freighted boat, and so with his open hand, the captain gently and carefully waved the gull away. After it had been discouraged from the pursuit the captain breathed easier on account of his hair, and others breathed easier because the bird struck their minds at this time as being somehow grewsome and ominous.

In the meantime the oiler and the correspondent rowed. And also they rowed.

They sat together in the same seat, and each rowed an oar. Then the oiler took both oars; then the correspondent took both oars; then the oiler; then the correspondent. They rowed and they rowed. The very ticklish part of the business was when the time came for the reclining one in the stern to take his turn at the oars. By the very last star of truth, it is easier to steal eggs from under a hen than it was to change seats in the dingey. First the man in the stern slid his hand along the thwart and moved with care, as if he were of Sèvres.[4] Then the man in the rowing seat slid his hand along the other thwart. It was all done with the most extraordinary care. As the two sidled past each other, the whole party kept watchful eyes on the coming wave, and the captain cried: "Look out now! Steady there!"

The brown mats of sea-weed that appeared from time to time were like islands, bits of earth. They were travelling, apparently, neither one way nor the other. They were, to all intents, stationary. They informed the men in the boat that it was making progress slowly toward the land.

The captain, rearing cautiously in the bow, after the dingey soared on a great swell, said that he had seen the lighthouse at Mosquito Inlet. Presently the cook remarked that he had seen it. The correspondent was at the oars, then, and for some reason he too wished to look at the lighthouse, but his back was toward the far shore and the waves

---

2. **Canton flannel gulls:** Canton flannel is a strong, warm cotton fabric, probably used here to suggest the imperviousness of the seagulls to the harsh elements.
3. **painter:** A rope attached to the bow of a boat for tying it to a dock.
4. **Sèvres:** A delicate, ornately decorated French porcelain made near Paris.

were important, and for some time he could not seize an opportunity to turn his head. But at last there came a wave more gentle than the others, and when at the crest of it he swiftly scoured the western horizon.

"See it?" said the captain.

"No," said the correspondent, slowly, "I didn't see anything."

"Look again," said the captain. He pointed. "It's exactly in that direction."

At the top of another wave, the correspondent did as he was bid, and this time his eyes chanced on a small still thing on the edge of the swaying horizon. It was precisely like the point of a pin. It took an anxious eye to find a lighthouse so tiny.

"Think we'll make it, captain?"

"If this wind holds and the boat don't swamp, we can't do much else," said the captain.

The little boat, lifted by each towering sea, and splashed viciously by the crests, made progress that in the absence of sea-weed was not apparent to those in her. She seemed just a wee thing wallowing, miraculously, top-up, at the mercy of five oceans. Occasionally, a great spread of water, like white flames, swarmed into her.

"Bail her, cook," said the captain, serenely.

"All right, captain," said the cheerful cook.

III

It would be difficult to describe the subtle brotherhood of men that was here established on the seas. No one said that it was so. No one mentioned it. But it dwelt in the boat, and each man felt it warm him. They were a captain, an oiler, a cook, and a correspondent, and they were friends, friends in a more curiously iron-bound degree than may be common. The hurt captain, lying against the water-jar in the bow, spoke always in a low voice and calmly, but he could never command a more ready and swiftly obedient crew than the motley three of the dingey. It was more than a mere recognition of what was best for the common safety. There was surely in it a quality that was personal and heart-felt. And after this devotion to the commander of the boat there was this comradeship that the correspondent, for instance, who had been taught to be cynical of men, knew even at the time was the best experience of his life. But no one said that it was so. No one mentioned it.

"I wish we had a sail," remarked the captain. "We might try my overcoat on the end of an oar and give you two boys a chance to rest." So the cook and the correspondent held the mast and spread wide the overcoat. The oiler steered, and the little boat made good way with her new rig. Sometimes the oiler had to scull sharply to keep a sea from breaking into the boat, but otherwise sailing was a success.

Meanwhile the light-house had been growing slowly larger. It had now almost assumed color, and appeared like a little gray shadow on the sky. The man at the oars could not be prevented from turning his head rather often to try for a glimpse of this little gray shadow.

At last, from the top of each wave the men in the tossing boat could see land. Even as the light-house was an upright shadow on the sky, this land seemed but a long black shadow on the sea. It certainly was thinner than paper. "We must be about opposite New

Smyrna,"[5] said the cook, who had coasted this shore often in schooners. "Captain, by the way, I believe they abandoned that life-saving station there about a year ago."

"Did they?" said the captain.

The wind slowly died away. The cook and the correspondent were not now obliged to slave in order to hold high the oar. But the waves continued their old impetuous swooping at the dingey, and the little craft, no longer under way, struggled woundily over them. The oiler or the correspondent took the oars again.

Shipwrecks are *apropos* of nothing. If men could only train for them and have them occur when the men had reached pink condition, there would be less drowning at sea. Of the four in the dingey none had slept any time worth mentioning for two days and two nights previous to embarking in the dingey, and in the excitement of clambering about the deck of a foundering ship they had also forgotten to eat heartily.

For these reasons, and for others, neither the oiler nor the correspondent was fond of rowing at this time. The correspondent wondered ingenuously how in the name of all that was sane could there be people who thought it amusing to row a boat. It was not an amusement; it was a diabolical punishment, and even a genius of mental aberrations could never conclude that it was anything but a horror to the muscles and a crime against the back. He mentioned to the boat in general how the amusement of rowing struck him, and the weary-faced oiler smiled in full sympathy. Previously to the foundering, by the way, the oiler had worked double-watch in the engine-room of the ship.

"Take her easy, now, boys," said the captain. "Don't spend yourselves. If we have to run a surf you'll need all your strength, because we'll sure have to swim for it. Take your time."

Slowly the land arose from the sea. From a black line it became a line of black and a line of white, trees, and sand. Finally, the captain said that he could make out a house on the shore. "That's the house of refuge, sure," said the cook. "They'll see us before long, and come out after us."

The distant light-house reared high. "The keeper ought to be able to make us out now, if he's looking through a glass," said the captain. "He'll notify the life-saving people."

"None of those other boats could have got ashore to give word of the wreck," said the oiler, in a low voice. "Else the life-boat would be out hunting us."

Slowly and beautifully the land loomed out of the sea. The wind came again. It had veered from the northeast to the southeast. Finally, a new sound struck the ears of the men in the boat. It was the low thunder of the surf on the shore. "We'll never be able to make the light-house now," said the captain. "Swing her head a little more north, Billie," said the captain.

" 'A little more north,' sir," said the oiler.

Whereupon the little boat turned her nose once more down the wind, and all but the oarsman watched the shore grow. Under the influence of this expansion doubt and direful apprehension was leaving the minds of the men. The management of the boat was still most absorbing, but it could not prevent a quiet cheerfulness. In an hour perhaps, they would be ashore.

---

5. **New Smyrna:** A town on the Florida coast, south of Daytona Beach.

Their back-bones had become thoroughly used to balancing in the boat and they now rode this wild colt of a dingey like circus men. The correspondent thought that he had been drenched to the skin, but happening to feel in the top pocket of his coat, he found therein eight cigars. Four of them were soaked with sea-water; four were perfectly scatheless. After a search, somebody produced three dry matches, and thereupon the four waifs rode in their little boat, and with an assurance of an impending rescue shining in their eyes, puffed at the big cigars and judged well and ill of all men. Everybody took a drink of water.

IV

"Cook," remarked the captain, "there don't seem to be any signs of life about your house of refuge."

"No," replied the cook. "Funny they don't see us!"

A broad stretch of lowly coast lay before the eyes of the men. It was of low dunes topped with dark vegetation. The roar of the surf was plain, and sometimes they could see the white lip of a wave as it spun up the beach. A tiny house was blocked out black upon the sky. Southward, the slim light-house lifted its little gray length.

Tide, wind, and waves were swinging the dingey northward. "Funny they don't see us," said the men.

The surf's roar was here dulled, but its tone was, nevertheless, thunderous and mighty. As the boat swam over the great rollers, the men sat listening to this roar.

"We'll swamp sure," said everybody.

It is fair to say here that there was not a life-saving station within twenty miles in either direction, but the men did not know this fact and in consequence they made dark and opprobrious remarks concerning the eyesight of the nation's life-savers. Four scowling men sat in the dingey and surpassed records in the invention of epithets.

"Funny they don't see us."

The light-heartedness of a former time had completely faded. To their sharpened minds it was easy to conjure pictures of all kinds of incompetency and blindness and, indeed, cowardice. There was the shore of the populous land, and it was bitter and bitter to them that from it came no sign.

"Well," said the captain, ultimately, "I suppose we'll have to make a try ourselves. If we stay out here too long we'll none of us have strength left to swim after the boat swamps."

And so the oiler, who was at the oars, turned the boat straight for the shore. There was a sudden tightening of muscles. There was some thinking.

"If we don't all get ashore —," said the captain. "If we don't all get ashore, I suppose you fellows know where to send news of my finish?"

They then briefly exchanged some addresses and admonitions. As for the reflections of the men, there was a great deal of rage in them. Perchance they might be formulated thus: "If I am going to be drowned — if I am going to be drowned — if I am going to be drowned, why, in the name of the seven mad gods who rule the sea, was I allowed to come thus far and contemplate sand and trees? Was I brought here merely to have my nose dragged away as I was about to nibble the sacred cheese of life? It is preposterous. If this old ninny-woman, Fate, cannot do better than this, she should be deprived of the management of men's fortunes. She is an old hen who knows not her intention. If she has decided to drown me, why did she not do it in the beginning and save me all this trouble. The whole affair is absurd. . . . But, no, she cannot mean to drown me. She dare not drown me. She cannot drown me. Not after all this work." Afterward the man might have had an impulse to shake his fist at the clouds: "Just you drown me, now, and then hear what I call you!"

The billows that came at this time were more formidable. They seemed always just about to break and roll over the little boat in a turmoil of foam. There was a preparatory and long growl in the speech of them. No mind unused to the sea would have concluded that the dingey could ascend these sheer heights in time. The shore was still afar. The oiler was a wily surfman. "Boys," he said, swiftly, "she won't live three minutes more and we're too far out to swim. Shall I take her to sea again, captain?"

"Yes! Go ahead!" said the captain.

This oiler, by a series of quick miracles, and fast and steady oarsmanship, turned the boat in the middle of the surf and took her safely to sea again.

There was a considerable silence as the boat bumped over the furrowed sea to deeper water. Then somebody in gloom spoke. "Well, anyhow, they must have seen us from the shore by now."

The gulls went in slanting flight up the wind toward the gray desolate east. A squall, marked by dingy clouds, and clouds brick-red, like smoke from a burning building, appeared from the southeast.

"What do you think of those life-saving people? Ain't they peaches?"

"Funny they haven't seen us."

"Maybe they think we're out here for sport! Maybe they think were fishin'. Maybe they think we're damned fools."

It was a long afternoon. A changed tide tried to force them southward, but wind and wave said northward. Far ahead, where coast-line, sea, and sky formed their mighty angle, there were little dots which seemed to indicate a city on the shore.

"St. Augustine?"

The captain shook his head. "Too near Mosquito Inlet."

And the oiler rowed, and then the correspondent rowed. Then the oiler rowed. It was a weary business. The human back can become the seat of more aches and pains than are registered in books for the composite anatomy of a regiment. It is a limited area, but it can become the theatre of innumerable muscular conflicts, tangles, wrenches, knots, and other comforts.

"Did you ever like to row, Billie?" asked the correspondent.

"No," said the oiler. "Hang it."

When one exchanged the rowing-seat for a place in the bottom of the boat, he suffered a bodily depression that caused him to be careless of everything save an obligation to wiggle one finger. There was cold sea-water swashing to and fro in the boat, and he lay in it. His head, pillowed on a thwart, was within an inch of the swirl of a wave crest, and sometimes a particularly obstreperous sea came in-board and drenched him once more. But these matters did not annoy him. It is almost certain that if the boat had capsized he would have tumbled comfortably out upon the ocean as if he felt sure that it was a great soft mattress.

"Look! There's a man on the shore!"

"Where?"

"There! See 'im? See 'im?"

"Yes, sure! He's walking along."

"Now he's stopped. Look! He's facing us!"

"He's waving at us!"

"So he is! By thunder!"

"Ah, now, we're all right! Now we're all right! There'll be a boat out here for us half an hour."

"He's going on. He's running. He's going up to that house there."

The remote beach seemed lower than the sea, and it required a searching glance to discern the little black figure. The captain saw a floating stick and they rowed to it. A bath-towel was by some weird chance in the boat, and, tying this on the stick, the captain waved it. The oarsman did not dare turn his head, so he was obliged to ask questions.

"What's he doing now?"

"He's standing still again. He's looking, I think. . . . There he goes again. Toward the house. . . . Now he's stopped again."

"Is he waving at us?"

"No, not now! He was, though."

"Look! There comes another man!"

"He's running."

"Look at him go, would you."

"Why, he's on a bicycle. Now he's met the other man. They're both waving at us. Look!"

"There comes something up the beach."

"What the devil is that thing?"

"Why, it looks like a boat."

"Why, certainly it's a boat."

"No, it's on wheels."

"Yes, so it is. Well, that must be the life-boat. They drag them along shore on a wagon."

"That's the life-boat, sure."

"No, by —, it's – it's an omnibus."

"I tell you it's a life-boat."

"It is not! It's an omnibus. I can see it plain. See? One of these big hotel omnibuses."

"By thunder, you're right. It's an omnibus, sure as fate. What do you suppose they are doing with an omnibus? Maybe they are going around collecting the life-crew, hey?"

"That's it, likely. Look! There's a fellow waving a little black flag. He's standing on the steps of the omnibus. There come those other two fellows. Now they're all talking together. Look at the fellow with the flag. Maybe he ain't waving it."

"That ain't a flag, is it? That's his coat. Why, certainly, that's his coat."

"So it is. It's his coat. He's taken it off and is waving it around his head. But would you look at him swing it."

"Oh, say, there isn't any life-saving station there. That's just a winter resort hotel omnibus that has brought over some of the boarders to see us drown."

"What's that idiot with the coat mean? What's he signaling, anyhow?"

"It looks as if he were trying to tell us to go north. There must be a life-saving station up there."

"No! He thinks we're fishing. Just giving us a merry hand. See? Ah, there, Willie."

"Well, I wish I could make something out of those signals. What do you suppose he means?"

"He don't mean anything. He's just playing."

"Well, if he'd just signal us to try the surf again, or to go to sea and wait, or go north, or go south, or go to hell—there would be some reason in it. But look at him. He just stands there and keeps his coat revolving like a wheel. The ass!"

"There come more people."

"Now there's quite a mob. Look! Isn't that a boat?"

"Where? Oh, I see where you mean. No, that's no boat."

"That fellow is still waving his coat."

"He must think we like to see him do that. Why don't he quit it. It don't mean anything."

"I don't know. I think he is trying to make us go north. It must be that there's a life-saving station there somewhere."

"Say, he ain't tired yet. Look at 'im wave."

"Wonder how long he can keep that up. He's been revolving his coat ever since he caught sight of us. He's an idiot. Why aren't they getting men to bring a boat out. A fishing boat—one of those big yawls—could come out here all right. Why don't he do something?"

"Oh, it's all right, now."

"They'll have a boat out here for us in less than no time, now that they've seen us."

A faint yellow tone came into the sky over the low land. The shadows on the sea slowly deepened. The wind bore coldness with it, and the men began to shiver.

"Holy smoke!" said one, allowing his voice to express his impious mood, "if we keep on monkeying out here! If we've got to flounder out here all night!"

"Oh, we'll never have to stay here all night! Don't you worry. They've seen us now, and it won't be long before they'll come chasing out after us."

The shore grew dusky. The man waving a coat blended gradually into this gloom, and it swallowed in the same manner the omnibus and the group of people. The spray, when it dashed uproariously over the side, made the voyagers shrink and swear like men who were being branded.

"I'd like to catch the chump who waved the coat. I feel like soaking him one, just for luck."

"Why? What did he do?"

"Oh, nothing, but then he seemed so damned cheerful."

In the meantime the oiler rowed, and then the correspondent rowed, and then oiler rowed. Gray-faced and bowed forward, they mechanically, turn by turn, plied the leaden oars. The form of the light-house had vanished from the southern horizon, but finally a pale star appeared, just lifting from the sea. The streaked saffron in the west passed before the all-merging darkness, and the sea to the east was black. The land had vanished, and was expressed only by the low and drear thunder of the surf.

"If I am going to be drowned – if I am going to be drowned – if I am going to be drowned, why, in the name of the seven mad gods, who rule the sea, was I allowed to come thus far and contemplate sand and trees? Was I brought here merely to have my nose dragged away as I was about to nibble the sacred cheese of life?"

The patient captain, drooped over the water-jar, was sometimes obliged to speak to the oarsman.

"Keep her head up! Keep her head up!"

" 'Keep her head up,' sir." The voices were weary and low.

This was surely a quiet evening. All save the oarsman lay heavily and listlessly in the boat's bottom. As for him, his eyes were just capable of noting the tall black waves that swept forward in a most sinister silence, save for an occasional subdued growl of a crest.

The cook's head was on a thwart, and he looked without interest at the water under his nose. He was deep in other scenes. Finally he spoke. "Billie," he murmured, dreamfully, "what kind of pie do you like best?"

V

"Pie," said the oiler and the correspondent, agitatedly. "Don't talk about those things, blast you!"

"Well," said the cook, "I was just thinking about ham sandwiches, and —"

A night on the sea in an open boat is a long night. As darkness settled finally, the shine of the light, lifting from the sea in the south, changed to full gold. On the northern horizon a new light appeared, a small bluish gleam on the edge of the waters. These two lights were the furniture of the world. Otherwise there was nothing but waves.

Two men huddled in the stern, and distances were so magnificent in the dingey that the rower was enabled to keep his feet partly warmed by thrusting them under his companions. Their legs indeed extended far under the rowing-seat until they touched the feet of the captain forward. Sometimes, despite the efforts of the tired oarsman, a wave came piling into the boat, an icy wave of the night, and the chilling water soaked them anew. They would twist their bodies for a moment and groan, and sleep the dead sleep once more, while the water in the boat gurgled about them as the craft rocked.

The plan of the oiler and the correspondent was for one to row until he lost the ability, and then arouse the other from his sea-water couch in the bottom of the boat.

The oiler plied the oars until his head drooped forward, and the overpowering sleep blinded him. And he rowed yet afterward. Then he touched a man in the bottom of the boat, and called his name. "Will you spell me for a little while?" he said, meekly.

"Sure, Billie," said the correspondent, awakening and dragging himself to a sitting position. They exchanged places carefully, and the oiler, cuddling down in the sea-water at the cook's side, seemed to go to sleep instantly.

The particular violence of the sea had ceased. The waves came without snarling. The obligation of the man at the oars was to keep the boat headed so that the tilt of the rollers would not capsize her, and to preserve her from filling when the crests rushed past. The black waves were silent and hard to be seen in the darkness. Often one was almost upon the boat before the oarsman was aware.

In a low voice the correspondent addressed the captain. He was not sure that the captain was awake, although this iron man seemed to be always awake. "Captain, shall I keep her making for that light north, sir?"

The same steady voice answered him. "Yes. Keep it about two points off the port bow."

The cook had tied a life-belt around himself in order to get even the warmth which this clumsy cork contrivance could donate, and he seemed almost stove-like when a rower, whose teeth invariably chattered wildly as soon as he ceased his labor, dropped down to sleep.

The correspondent, as he rowed, looked down at the two men sleeping under foot. The cook's arm was around the oiler's shoulders, and, with their fragmentary clothing and haggard faces, they were the babes of the sea, a grotesque rendering of the old babes in the wood.

Later he must have grown stupid at his work, for suddenly there was a growling of water, and a crest came with a roar and a swash into the boat, and it was a wonder that it did not set the cook afloat in his life-belt. The cook continued to sleep, but the oiler sat up, blinking his eyes and shaking with the new cold.

"Oh, I'm awful sorry, Billie," said the correspondent, contritely.

"That's all right, old boy," said the oiler, and lay down again and was asleep.

Presently it seemed that even the captain dozed, and the correspondent thought that he was the one man afloat on all the oceans. The wind had a voice as it came over the waves, and it was sadder than the end.

There was a long, loud swishing astern of the boat, and a gleaming trail of phosphorescence, like blue flame, was furrowed on the black waters. It might have been made by a monstrous knife.

Then there came a stillness, while the correspondent breathed with the open mouth and looked at the sea.

Suddenly there was another swish and another long flash of bluish light, and this time it was alongside the boat, and might almost have been reached with an oar. The correspondent saw an enormous fin speed like a shadow through the water, hurling the crystalline spray and leaving the long glowing trail.

The correspondent looked over his shoulder at the captain. His face was hidden, and he seemed to be asleep. He looked at the babes of the sea. They certainly were asleep. So, being bereft of sympathy, he leaned a little way to one side and swore softly into the sea.

But the thing did not then leave the vicinity of the boat. Ahead or astern, on one side or the other, at intervals long or short, fled the long sparkling streak, and there was to be heard the whiroo of the dark fin. The speed and power of the thing was greatly to be admired. It cut the water like a gigantic and keen projectile.

The presence of this biding thing did not affect the man with the same horror that it would if he had been a picnicker. He simply looked at the sea dully and swore in an undertone.

Nevertheless, it is true that he did not wish to be alone with the thing. He wished one of his companions to awaken by chance and keep him company with it. But the captain hung motionless over the water-jar and the oiler and the cook in the bottom of the boat were plunged in slumber.

VI

"If I am going to be drowned — if I am going to be drowned — if I am going to be drowned, why, in the name of the seven mad gods, who rule the sea, was I allowed to come thus far and contemplate sand and trees?"

During this dismal night, it may be remarked that a man would conclude that it was really the intention of the seven mad gods to drown him, despite the abominable injustice of it. For it was certainly an abominable injustice to drown a man who had worked so hard. The man felt it would be a crime most unnatural. Other people had drowned at sea since galleys swarmed with painted sails, but still —

When it occurs to a man that nature does not regard him as important, and that she feels she would not maim the universe by disposing of him, he at first wishes to throw bricks at the temple, and hates deeply the fact that there are no bricks and no temples. Any visible expression of nature would surely be pelleted with his jeers.

Then, if there be no tangible thing to hoot he feels, perhaps, the desire to confront a personification and indulge in pleas, bowed to one knee, and with hands supplicant, saying: "Yes, but I love myself."

A high cold star on a winter's night is the word he feels that she says to him. Thereafter he knows the pathos of his situation.

The men in the dingey had not discussed these matters, but each had, no doubt, reflected upon them in silence and according to his mind. There was seldom any expression upon their faces save the general one of complete weariness. Speech was devoted to the business of the boat.

To chime the notes of his emotion, a verse mysteriously entered the correspondent's head. He had even forgotten that he had forgotten this verse, but it suddenly was in his mind.

A soldier of the Legion lay dying in Algiers,
There was lack of woman's nursing, there was dearth of woman's tears;
But a comrade stood beside him, and he took that comrade's hand
And he said: "I shall never see my own, my native land."[6]

---

6. A soldier . . . land: Crane is loosely quoting the first stanza of the popular poem about the death of a French legionnaire, "Bingen on the Rhine" (1883), by Caroline E. S. Norton (1808-1877): "A soldier of the Legion lay dying in Algiers, / There was a lack of woman's nursing, there was dearth of woman's tears; / But a comrade stood beside him, while his lifeblood ebbed away, / And bent with pitying glances, to hear what he might say. / The dying soldier faltered, and he took that comrade's hand, / And he said, "I nevermore shall see my own, my native land: / Take a message, and a token, to some distant friends of mine, / For I was born at Bingen, — at Bingen on the Rhine."

In his childhood, the correspondent had been made acquainted with the fact that a soldier of the Legion lay dying in Algiers, but he had never regarded the fact as important. Myriads of his school-fellows had informed him of the soldier's plight, but the dinning had naturally ended by making him perfectly indifferent. He had never considered it his affair that a soldier of the Legion lay dying in Algiers, nor had it appeared to him as a matter for sorrow. It was less to him than the breaking of a pencil's point.

Now, however, it quaintly came to him as a human, living thing. It was no longer merely a picture of a few throes in the breast of a poet, meanwhile drinking tea and warming his feet at the grate; it was an actuality – stern, mournful, and fine.

The correspondent plainly saw the soldier. He lay on the sand with his feet out straight and still. While his pale left hand was upon his chest in an attempt to thwart the going of his life, the blood came between his fingers. In the far Algerian distance, a city of low square forms was set against a sky that was faint with the last sunset hues. The correspondent, plying the oars and dreaming of the slow and slower movements of the lips of the soldier, was moved by a profound and perfectly impersonal comprehension. He was sorry for the soldier of the Legion who lay dying in Algiers.

The thing which had followed the boat and waited had evidently grown bored at the delay. There was no longer to be heard the slash of the cut-water, and there was no longer the flame of the long trail. The light in the north still glimmered, but it was apparently no nearer to the boat. Sometimes the boom of the surf rang in the correspondent's ears, and he turned the craft seaward then and rowed harder. Southward, someone had evidently built a watch-fire on the beach. It was too low and too far to be seen, but it made a shimmering, roseate reflection upon the bluff back of it, and this could be discerned from the boat. The wind came stronger, and sometimes a wave suddenly raged out like a mountain-cat and there was to be seen the sheen and sparkle of a broken crest.

The captain, in the bow, moved on his water-jar and sat erect. "Pretty long night," he observed to the correspondent. He looked at the shore. "Those life-saving people take their time."

"Did you see that shark playing around?"

"Yes, I saw him. He was a big fellow, all right."

"Wish I had known you were awake."

Later the correspondent spoke into the bottom of the boat.

"Billie!" There was a slow and gradual disentanglement. "Billie, will you spell me?"

"Sure," said the oiler.

As soon as the correspondent touched the cold comfortable sea-water in the bottom of the boat, and had huddled close to the cook's life-belt he was deep in sleep, despite the fact that his teeth played all the popular airs. This sleep was so good to him that it was but a moment before he heard a voice call his name in a tone that demonstrated the last stages of exhaustion. "Will you spell me?"

"Sure, Billie."

The light in the north had mysteriously vanished, but the correspondent took his course from the wide-awake captain.

Later in the night they took the boat farther out to sea, and the captain directed the cook to take one oar at the stern and keep the boat facing the seas. He was to call out if he should hear the thunder of the surf. This plan enabled the oiler and the correspondent to get respite together. "We'll give those boys a chance to get into shape again," said the captain. They curled down and, after a few preliminary chatterings and trembles, slept once more the dead sleep. Neither knew they had bequeathed to the cook the company of another shark, or perhaps the same shark.

As the boat caroused on the waves, spray occasionally bumped over the side and gave them a fresh soaking, but this had no power to break their repose. The ominous slash of the wind and the water affected them as it would have affected mummies.

"Boys," said the cook, with the notes of every reluctance in his voice, "she's drifted in pretty close. I guess one of you had better take her to sea again." The correspondent, aroused, heard the crash of the toppled crests.

As he was rowing, the captain gave him some whiskey and water, and this steadied the chills out of him. "If I ever get ashore and anybody shows me even a photograph of an oar —"

At last there was a short conversation.

"Billie. . . . Billie, will you spell me?"

"Sure," said the oiler.

VII

When the correspondent again opened his eyes, the sea and the sky were each of the gray hue of the dawning. Later, carmine and gold was painted upon the waters. The morning appeared finally, in its splendor, with a sky of pure blue, and the sunlight flamed on the tips of the waves.

On the distant dunes were set many little black cottages, and a tall white wind-mill reared above them. No man, nor dog, nor bicycle appeared on the beach. The cottages might have formed a deserted village.

The voyagers scanned the shore. A conference was held in the boat. "Well," said the captain, "if no help is coming, we might better try a run through the surf right away. If we stay out here much longer we will be too weak to do anything for ourselves at all." The others silently acquiesced in this reasoning. The boat was headed for the beach. The correspondent wondered if none ever ascended the tall wind-tower, and if then they never looked seaward. This tower was a giant, standing with its back to the plight of the ants. It represented in a degree, to the correspondent, the serenity of nature amid the struggles of the individual—nature in the wind, and nature in the vision of men. She did not seem cruel to him then, nor beneficent, nor treacherous, nor wise. But she was indifferent, flatly indifferent. It is, perhaps, plausible that a man in this situation pressed with the unconcern of the universe, should see the innumerable flaws of his life and have them taste wickedly in his mind and wish for another chance. A distinction between right and wrong seems absurdly clear to him, then, in this new ignorance of the grave-edge, and he understands that if he were given another opportunity he would mend his conduct and his words, and be better and brighter during an introduction, or at a tea.

"Now, boys," said the captain, "she is going to swamp sure. All we can do is to work her in as far as possible, and then when she swamps, pile out and scramble for the beach. Keep cool now and don't jump until she swamps sure."

The oiler took the oars. Over his shoulders he scanned the surf. "Captain," he said, "I think I'd better bring her about, and keep her head-on to the seas and back her in."

"All right, Billie," said the captain. "Back her in." The oiler swung the boat then and, seated in the stern, the cook and the correspondent were obliged to look over their shoulders to contemplate the lonely and indifferent shore.

The monstrous inshore rollers heaved the boat high until the men were again enabled to see the white sheets of water scudding up the slanted beach. "We won't get in very close," said the captain. Each time a man could wrest his attention from the rollers, he turned his glance toward the shore, and in the expression of the eyes during this contemplation there was a singular quality. The correspondent, observing the others, knew that they were not afraid, but the full meaning of their glances was shrouded.

As for himself, he was too tired to grapple fundamentally with the fact. He tried to coerce his mind into thinking of it, but the mind was dominated at this time by the muscles, and the muscles said they did not care. It merely occurred to him that if he should drown it would be a shame.

There were no hurried words, no pallor, no plain agitation. The men simply looked at the shore. "Now, remember to get well clear of the boat when you jump," said the captain.

Seaward the crest of a roller suddenly fell with a thunderous crash, and the long white comber came roaring down upon the boat.

"Steady now," said the captain. The men were silent. They turned their eyes from the shore to the comber and waited. The boat slid up the incline, leaped at the furious top, bounced over it, and swung down the long back of the waves. Some water had been shipped and the cook bailed it out.

But the next crest crashed also. The tumbling boiling flood of white water caught the boat and whirled it almost perpendicular. Water swarmed in from all sides. The correspondent had his hands on the gunwale[7] at this time, and when the water entered at that place he swiftly withdrew his fingers, as if he objected to wetting them.

The little boat, drunken with this weight of water, reeled and snuggled deeper into the sea.

"Bail her out, cook! Bail her out," said the captain.

"All right, captain," said the cook.

"Now, boys, the next one will do for sure," said the oiler. "Mind to jump clear of the boat."

The third wave moved forward, huge, furious, implacable. It fairly swallowed the dingey, and almost simultaneously the men tumbled into the sea. A piece of life-belt had lain in the bottom of the boat, and as the correspondent went overboard he held this to his chest with his left hand.

The January water was icy, and he reflected immediately that it was colder than he had expected to find it off the coast of Florida. This appeared to his dazed mind as a fact

---

7. **gunwale:** The upper edge of the side of the boat.

important enough to be noted at the time. The coldness of the water was sad; it was tragic. This fact was somehow mixed and confused with his opinion of his own situation that it seemed almost a proper reason for tears. The water was cold.

When he came to the surface he was conscious of little but the noisy water. Afterward he saw his companions in the sea. The oiler was ahead in the race. He was swimming strongly and rapidly. Off to correspondent's left, the cook's great white and corked back bulged out of the water, and in the rear the captain was hanging with his one good hand to the keel of the overturned dingey.

There is a certain immovable quality to a shore, and the correspondent wondered at it amid the confusion of the sea.

It seemed also very attractive, but the correspondent knew that it was a long journey, and he paddled leisurely. The piece of life-preserver lay under him, and sometimes he whirled down the incline of a wave as if he were on a hand-sled.

But finally he arrived at a place in the sea where travel was beset with difficulty. He did not pause swimming to inquire what manner of current had caught him, but there his progress ceased. The shore was set before him like a bit of scenery on a stage, and he looked at it and understood with his eyes each detail of it.

As the cook passed, much farther to the left, the captain was calling to him, "Turn over on your back, cook! Turn over on your back and use the oar."

"All right, sir." The cook turned on his back, and, paddling with an oar, went ahead as if he were a canoe.

Presently the boat also passed to the left of the correspondent with the captain clinging with one hand to the keel. He would have appeared like a man raising himself to look over a board fence, if it were not for the extraordinary gymnastics of the boat. The correspondent marvelled that the captain could still hold it.

They passed on, nearer to shore — the oiler, the cook, the captain — and following them went the water-jar, bouncing gayly over the seas.

The correspondent remained in the grip of this strange new enemy — a current. The shore, with its white slope of sand and its green bluff, topped with little silent cottages, was spread like a picture before him. It was very near to him then, but he was impressed as one who in a gallery looks at a scene from Brittany or Algiers.

He thought: "I am going to drown? Can it be possible? Can it be possible? Can it be possible?" Perhaps an individual must consider his own death to be the final phenomenon of nature.

But later a wave perhaps whirled him out of this small deadly current, for he found suddenly that he could again make progress toward the shore. Later still, he was aware that the captain, clinging with one hand to the keel of the dingey, had his face turned away from the shore and toward him, and was calling his name. "Come to the boat! Come to the boat!"

In his struggle to reach the captain and the boat, he reflected that when one gets properly wearied, drowning must really be a comfortable arrangement, a cessation of hostilities accompanied by a large degree of relief, and he was glad of it, for the main thing in his mind for some moments had been horror of the temporary agony. He did not wish to be hurt.

Presently he saw a man running along the shore. He was undressing w
markable speed. Coat, trousers, shirt, everything flew magically off him.

"Come to the boat," called the captain.

"All right, captain." As the correspondent paddled, he saw the captain
down to bottom and leave the boat. Then the correspondent performed I
marvel of the voyage. A large wave caught him and flung him with ease ɛ
speed completely over the boat and far beyond it. It struck him even then a
gymnastics, and a true miracle of the sea. An overturned boat in the surf
thing to a swimming man.

The correspondent arrived in water that reached only to his waist, but his condition did not enable him to stand for more than a moment. Each wave knocked him into a heap, and the under-tow pulled at him.

Then he saw the man who had been running and undressing, and undressing and running, come bounding into the water. He dragged ashore the cook, and then waded toward the captain, but the captain waved him away, and sent him to the correspondent. He was naked, naked as a tree in winter, but a halo was about his head, and he shone like a saint. He gave a strong pull, and a long drag, and a bully heave at the correspondent's hand. The correspondent, schooled in the minor formulae, said: "Thanks, old man." But suddenly the man cried: "What's that?" He pointed a swift finger. The correspondent said: "Go."

In the shallows, face downward, lay the oiler. His forehead touched sand that was periodically, between each wave, clear of the sea.

The correspondent did not know all that transpired afterward. When he achieved safe ground he fell, striking the sand with each particular part of his body. It was as if he had dropped from a roof, but the thud was grateful to him.

It seems that instantly the beach was populated with men with blankets, clothes, and flasks, and women with coffee-pots and all the remedies sacred to their minds. The welcome of the land to the men from the sea was warm and generous, but a still and dripping shape was carried slowly up the beach, and the land's welcome for it could only be the different and sinister hospitality of the grave.

When it came night, the white waves paced to and fro in the moonlight, and the wind brought the sound of the great sea's voice to the men on shore, and they felt that they could then be interpreters.

[1897]

Reading Crane's Poetry.   Although he was and is best known for his fiction, Crane expressed a higher opinion of his poems, which he said "give my ideas of life as a whole, so far as I know it." Probably inspired by the free verse of Walt Whitman and especially by the compressed, epigrammatic style of Emily Dickinson's poetry, which Crane discovered in 1893, he began to write his own innovative poems, or what he called "lines," further distancing his verse from the formal and metrical conventions of poetry in English. Like Dickinson, Crane did not title his poems, which were printed in all capital letters in his first collection, *The Black Riders and Other Lines* (1895), though not in his second collection, *War Is Kind* (1899). Many of the poems were equally unconventional in the views Crane expressed about human life, nature, and God. The publisher of *Black Riders* consequently asked him to expunge many of the poems in the volume, especially those referring to God. Crane protested that the publisher was seeking to "cut all the ethical sense out of the book," all of its "anarchy," adding: "It is the anarchy which I particularly insist on." Crane finally agreed to the omission of seven poems from *Black Riders*. A number of critics objected to the bitterness and cynicism displayed in Crane's poems, which many reviewers dismissed as eccentric and formless. But other reviewers emphasized the freshness and originality of the poems in *Black Riders* and *War Is Kind*. Indeed, the spare language and striking imagery of those poems anticipated the work of Carl Sandburg, who in his poem "Letters to Dead Imagists" (1916) paid homage to Dickinson and Crane; as well as that of Amy Lowell, who viewed Crane as an important precursor of modernist verse in the United States. The texts are taken from *Poems and Literary Remains*, edited by Fredson Bowers (1975), volume 10 of *The Works of Stephen Crane*.

From THE BLACK RIDERS AND OTHER LINES

I

Black riders came from the sea.
There was clang and clang of spear and shield,
And clash and clash of hoof and heel,
Wild shouts and the wave of hair
In the rush upon the wind:
Thus the ride of sin.

[1895, 1975]

XIV

There was crimson clash of war.
Lands turned black and bare;
Women wept;
Babes ran, wondering.
There came one who understood not these things.
He said, "Why is this?"
Whereupon a million strove to answer him.
There was such intricate clamor of tongues,
That still the reason was not.

[1895, 1975]

XIX

A god in wrath
Was beating a man;
He cuffed him loudly
With thunderous blows
That rang and rolled over the earth.   5
All people came running.
The man screamed and struggled,
And bit madly at the feet of the god.
The people cried,
"Ah, what a wicked man!"   10
And —
"Ah, what a redoubtable god!"

[1895, 1975]

XXIV

I saw a man pursuing the horizon;
Round and round they sped.
I was disturbed at this;
I accosted the man.
"It is futile," I said,
"You can never —"

"You lie," he cried,
And ran on.

[1895, 1975]

———

From WAR IS KIND

I [DO NOT WEEP, MAIDEN, FOR WAR IS KIND]

Do not weep, maiden, for war is kind.
Because your lover threw wild hands toward the sky
And the affrighted steed ran on alone,
Do not weep.

War is kind.   5

    Hoarse, booming drums of the regiment
    Little souls who thirst for fight,
    These men were born to drill and die
    The unexplained glory flies above them
    Great is the battle-god, great, and his kingdom —   10
    A field where a thousand corpses lie.

Do not weep, babe, for war is kind.
Because your father tumbled in the yellow trenches,
Raged at his breast, gulped and died,
Do not weep.   15
War is kind.

    Swift, blazing flag of the regiment
    Eagle with crest of red and gold,
    These men were born to drill and die
    Point for them the virtue of slaughter   20
    Make plain to them the excellence of killing
    And a field where a thousand corpses lie.

Mother whose heart hung humble as a button
On the bright splendid shroud of your son,
Do not weep.   25
War is kind.

[1896, 1899, 1975]

Theodore Dreiser

[1871-1945]

Theodore Dreiser was born in Terre Haute, Indiana, on August 27, 1871. He was the twelfth of thirteen children of the German-born John Paul Dreiser and his wife, Sarah Schänäb Dreiser, the descendant of Czechoslovakian immigrants. The couple's eldest surviving son, a popular entertainer who adopted the stage name Paul Dresser, later gained wealth and fame as the composer of nostalgic songs like "On the Banks of the Wabash, Far Away." But the family home in Indiana was anything but idyllic, and Dreiser's older siblings frequently rebelled against the strict rules imposed by their father, a deeply pious Roman Catholic. One of Dreiser's sisters, abandoned by the son of a wealthy family, bore an illegitimate child, and another sister ran away with a married man who had stolen money from his employer to finance their trip to Canada. During his difficult and impoverished childhood, Dreiser had little formal education until the family moved to

Warsaw, Indiana, where he attended school from 1883 to 1887. That year, at the age of sixteen, he left home to seek a better life in Chicago. He worked as a laborer for two years, until one of his former teachers from Warsaw arranged for Dreiser to enroll as a special student at Indiana University. Although he did well enough to continue his studies, Dreiser did not feel that he fit into college life, so he dropped out after two semesters and returned to Chicago. In 1892, he was hired as a reporter for the *Daily Globe.* While on an assignment for the newspaper in 1893, he met Sara White, a schoolteacher from Missouri, whom Dreiser married in 1898. During their extended courtship, he worked as an itinerant journalist throughout the Midwest, as the editor of a music magazine in New York City, and as a freelance writer for popular magazines such as *Cosmopolitan, McClure's, Metropolitan,* and *Munsey's.*

After churning out magazine articles for several years, Dreiser began to write fiction in 1899. He first experimented with several short stories and then started work on a novel, *Sister Carrie,* in which Dreiser told the story of a country girl who goes to Chicago, where she escapes work in a sweatshop by becoming the mistress of a traveling salesman before running away with a married saloon manager, finally abandoning him for a successful career on Broadway. Dreiser's determination to "tell about life as it is," as he said in an interview, especially about the powerful force of sexuality in human life, brought him into immediate conflict with literary conventions and the realities of the literary marketplace. Harper & Brothers firmly rejected the novel, explaining that Dreiser's handling of "the continued illicit relations of the heroine" would offend readers, especially "the feminine readers who control the destinies of so many novels." Dreiser submitted a revised version to Doubleday, Page and Company, which had recently published Frank Norris's graphic and naturalistic novel *McTeague* (1899). Norris, who reviewed manuscripts for the company, helped Dreiser secure a contract for the publication of *Sister Carrie.* After the owner of the company, Frank Doubleday, read the manuscript, he sought to block publication of the "immoral" novel. When that proved to be impossible, the company grudgingly published but refused to market *Sister Carrie* (1900). Despite a few positive reviews in the United States and a generally favorable reception in England, the novel sold fewer than five hundred copies, earning Dreiser less than seventy dollars. Bitterly disappointed, he virtually gave up writing fiction for nearly a decade, during which time he worked as the editor of various women's magazines until an in-office affair forced him to resign in 1910.

By then, *Sister Carrie* had been reissued, and Dreiser once again turned from journalism to fiction. In his second novel, *Jennie Gerhardt* (1911), he tells the tragic story of a poor young woman who, after bearing the illegitimate child of a U.S. senator, becomes the mistress of a wealthy socialite. Dreiser then wrote *The Financier* (1911) and *The Titan* (1914), the first two novels of a trilogy about the rise and fall of a Chicago industrialist. (The final novel of the trilogy, *The Stoic,* was published posthumously in 1947.) The sale of Dreiser's most autobiographical novel, *The "Genius"* (1915), was prohibited in New York City by the Society for the Suppression of Vice. At

Theodore Dreiser

This youthful sketch of Dreiser appeared in *Contemporary Portraits: Second Series* (1919) by Frank Harris.

For Dreiser is a true hyphenate, a product of that conglomerate Americanism that springs from other roots than the English tradition. Do we realize how rare it is to find a talent that is thoroughly American and wholly un-English?

–Randolph Bourne

the same time, his novels were hailed by younger writers who were determined to challenge the standards of propriety imposed on American fiction. Having separated from his wife a decade earlier, Dreiser in 1919 began a long-term affair with his cousin Helen Richardson, with whom he moved to California. There, he wrote *An American Tragedy* (1925), based on an actual story of a poor young man who drowned his pregnant girlfriend in order to pursue his "American dream" of wealth and success. The novel was widely hailed as a masterpiece, but it was banned in Boston, and Dreiser's writings continued to generate outrage. In 1935, the library trustees of Warsaw, Indiana, which was as close to a hometown as he had, ordered the burning of all the library's books by Dreiser. A year before his death on December 18, 1945, however, Dreiser received the Award of Merit from the American Academy of Arts and Sciences, not only for his literary achievement, but also for his "courage and integrity in breaking trail as a pioneer in the presentation of fiction of real human beings in a real America."

Reading Dreiser's "Butcher Rogaum's Door."   This was one of several stories Dreiser completed during the summer of 1899, shortly before he began to write *Sister Carrie* (1900). Anticipating many of the themes of that novel, the early stories reveal his determination to confront the hard facts and darker aspects of life in the United States. In "Butcher Rogaum's Door," he explores what a reviewer described as the "dangers of innocent girlhood in the slums of New York." The spare and gritty story was inspired by Dreiser's experience as a police reporter, as well as by his memories of conflicts between his sisters and his stern, German-born father. "Butcher Rogaum's Door" was first published in a St. Louis weekly magazine, the *Mirror*, edited by the iconoclastic William Marion Reedy, whom the poet Edgar Lee Masters described as the "Literary Boss of the Middle West." Seeking to dismantle what he viewed as the "genteel" literary tradition of the East in order to develop a more vital and indigenous tradition of writing in the United States, Reedy published work by a remarkable range of American authors, including poetry by Stephen Crane and Edwin Arlington Robinson, as well as the experimental verse of emerging poets such as T. S. Eliot, Amy Lowell, Edna St. Vincent Millay, Ezra Pound, and Carl Sandburg. Under Reedy's leadership, the circulation of the *Mirror* eventually surpassed that of several venerable literary magazines published in the East, including the *Atlantic Monthly* and the *Nation*. The text of "Butcher Rogaum's Door," which Dreiser later revised as "Old Rogaum and His Theresa" for his collection *Free and Other Stories* (1918), is taken from the first printing in the *Mirror*, December 12, 1901.

bedfordstmartins.com/
americanlit for research
links on Dreiser

BUTCHER ROGAUM'S DOOR

In all Bleecker Street[1] was no more comfortable doorway than that of the butcher Rogaum, even if the first floor was given over to meat market purposes. It was to one side of the main entrance, which gave ingress to the butcher shop, and from it led up a flight of steps, at least five feet wide, to the living rooms above. A little portico stood out in front of it, railed on either side, and within was a second or final door, forming, with the outer or storm door, a little area, where Mrs. Rogaum and her children frequently sat of a summer's evening. The outer door was never locked, owing to the inconvenience it would inflict on Mr. Rogaum, who had no other way of getting upstairs. In winter, when all had gone to bed, there had been cases in which belated travelers had taken refuge there from the snow or sleet. One or two newsboys occasionally slept there, until routed out by Officer Maguire, who, seeing it half open at two o'clock one morning, took occasion to look in. He jogged the newsboys sharply with his stick and then, when they were gone, tried the inner door which was locked.

"You ought to keep that outer door locked, Rogaum," he observed to the sedate butcher, the next evening, as he was passing, "people might get in there. A couple of kids were sleeping there last night."

"Ach, dat is no difference," answered Rogaum, pleasantly. "I haf de inner door locked, yet. Dat iss no difference."

"Better lock it," said the officer, more to vindicate his authority than anything else. "Something will happen there yet."

The door was never locked, however, and now of a summer evening Mrs. Rogaum and the children made pleasant use of its recess, watching the route of street cars and occasionally belated trucks go by. The children played on the sidewalk, all except the budding Theresa (eighteen just turning), who, with one companion of the neighborhood, the pretty Kenrihan girl, walked up and down the block, laughing, glancing, watching the boys. Old Mrs. Kenrihan lived in the next block and there, sometimes, the two stopped. There, also, they more frequently pretended to be when talking with the boys in the intervening side street. Young "Connie" Almerting and George Goujon were the bright particular mashers[2] who held the attention of this block. These two made their acquaintance in the customary bold, boyish way and thereafter the girls had an urgent desire to be out in the street together after eight and to linger where the boys could see and overtake them.

Old Mrs. Rogaum never knew. She was a particularly fat, old, German lady, completely dominated by her liege and portly lord, and at nine o'clock regularly, as he had long ago deemed mete and fit, she was wont to betake her way upward and so to bed. Old Rogaum, at that hour, himself closed the market and went to his chamber.

---

1. **Bleecker Street:** A major thoroughfare in Greenwich Village, then a crowded tenement district in lower Manhattan.
2. **mashers:** A late-nineteenth-century slang term for men who make aggressive sexual advances to women in public places.

All the children were called sharply, once from the doorstep below and once from the window above, only Mrs. Rogaum did it first and Rogaum last. It had come, because of a shade of lenience, not wholly apparent in the father's nature, that the older of the children needed two callings and sometimes three. Theresa, now that she had got in with the Kenrihan maiden, needed that many calls and even more.

She loved to walk up and down in the as yet bright street, where were voices and laughter, and occasionally moonlight streaming down. What a nuisance it was to be called at nine, anyhow. What old foggies her parents were. Mrs. Kenrihan was not so strict with her daughter. It made her pettish when Rogaum insisted, calling as he often did, in German, "Come you now," in a very hoarse and belligerent voice.

She came, eventually, frowning and wretched, all the moonlight calling her, all the voices of the night urging her to come back. Her objection made the coming later and later, however, until now, by August of this, her eighteenth year, it was nearly ten when she entered and Rogaum was almost invariably angry.

"I vill lock you oudt," he declared, in strongly accented English, while she tried to slip by him each time, "I vill show you. Du sollst[3] come ven I say yet. Hear now."

"I'll not," answered Theresa, but it was always under her breath.

Poor Mrs. Rogaum hated to hear the wrath of her husband's voice. It spoke of harder and fiercer times which had been with her. Still she was not powerful enough in the family councils to put in a weighty word. So Rogaum fumed unrestricted.

There were other nights, however, many of them, and now that the young sparks of the neighborhood had enlisted the girl's attention, it was a more trying time than ever. Theresa had a tender eye for the dashing Almerting. What a fine fellow he was, indeed! What authority! His cigarette was always cocked at a high angle, in her presence, and his hat had the least suggestion of being set to one side. He had a shrewd way of winking one eye, was strong and athletic and worked in a tobacco factory. His was a trade, indeed, nearly acquired, as he said, and his jingling pockets attested that he had money of his own. Altogether he was very captivating.

"Ah, what do you want to go in for?" he used to say to her, tossing his head gaily on one side to listen, as old Rogaum called. "Tell him you didn't hear."

"No, I've got to go," said the little girl.

"Well, you don't have to just yet. Stay another minute. George, what was that fellow's name that tried to sass us the other day?"

"Theresa!" roared old Rogaum, forcefully. "If you do not now come! Ve will see."

"I've got to go," observed Theresa with a faint effort at starting.

Thus the moments slipped away and delight was sipped in the moonlight. Both the young men would follow to the corner, almost in sight of the irate old butcher.

"Let him call," said young Almerting one night, catching hold of her soft, white fingers and causing her body to quiver thereby.

"Oh, no," she gasped nervously.

---

3. **Du sollst:** You shall (German).

"Well, good-night, then," he said and with a flip of the heel had his arm around her and his soft lips against her burning cheeks.

"Get out," she murmured, pushing.

He jumped away and strolled gaily off, Goujon having been equally successful. Then Theresa went home.

"Vy don'd you come ven I call?" said old Rogaum wrathfully. "Muss ich all my time spenden calling, mit you on the streeds oudt? In now. I vill show you."

"I wasn't," snapped Theresa, even as his fat hand reached her back.

"Take dot now," he exclaimed. "Und come you yussed vunce more at dis time—Ve vill see if I am boss in my own house, aber! Komst du vun minute nach[4] ten to-morrow und you vill see vat you vill get. I vill the door lock. Du sollst not in kommen. Mark! Oudt sollst du stayen—oudt!"[5] And he glared wrathfully after her retreating form.

He was angry, but equally determined. It was not that he imagined that she was as yet in bad company, but he wished to forefend against possible danger. He knew she only walked from his shop to the door of the Kenrihans' and back again. Had not his wife told him so? If he had thought upon what far pilgrimage her feet had already ventured or ever seeing the dashing Almerting hanging near, then had there been wrath and tears. As it was, his mind was more or less at ease.

On the following eve it was much the same story, only this time the nervous Theresa got in on time. Other evenings and for many, she was safe, but soon "Connie" claimed her more sharply for his "steady," and bought her ice-cream. In the range of the short block it was all done, lingering by the curbstone and strolling a block or two away from the corner, until she had offended seriously at home and the threat was reflected anew. Then came another blow and another threat—that she should not get in at all.

Well enough she meant to obey, on this radiant night, but somehow the time fled too fast.

"Ah, wait a minute," said "Connie." "Stand still. He won't lock you out."

"But he will, though," said Theresa. "You don't know him."

"Well, if he does, come back to me. I will be here."

There was a sinister grin on the youth's face.

"Well, wait, anyhow," insisted the blade.

Longer and longer she waited and now no voice came.

She began to feel that something was wrong—a greater strain than if old Rogaum's voice had been filling the whole neighborhood.

"I've got to go," she said.

"You're a great card, you are," said he, derisively.

Still, he caught her as she went, kissing her soundly and then standing and looking after.

"I wish he would lock her out," he thought.

---

4. **nach:** After (German).
5. **"Du sollst not in kommen. . . . oudt!":** "You shall not come in. Notice! You shall stay out!—Out!" (German).

At her own doorstep she paused momentarily, more to soften her progress than anything. The outer door she opened and then the inner – or tried to. It was locked. For a moment she paused, cold fear racing over her body, and then knocked.

No answer.

Again she rattled the door, this time nervously and was about to cry out.

Still no answer.

"Let her go, now," said Rogaum, savagely, sitting in his front room, where she could not hear. "I vill her a lesson teach."

"Hadn't you better let her in now, yet?" pleaded Mrs. Rogaum faintly.

"No, no," said Mr. Rogaum. "Nefer. Let her vait awhile."

His voice was rich in wrath and he was saving up a good beating for her. She should wait and wait and plead and when she was thoroughly wretched and subdued he would let her in and beat her – such a beating as she had never received in all her born days.

Again the door rattled and still she got no answer. Not even her call brought a sound.

Now, strangely, a new element, not heretofore apparent in her nature, but, nevertheless wholly there, was called into life, springing in action as Diana,[6] full formed. The cold chill left her and she wavered angrily.

"All right," she said, some old German stubbornness springing up, "I won't knock. You don't need to let me in."

Suggestions of tears were in her eyes, but she backed firmly out onto the stoop and sat down, hesitating. Old Rogaum saw her, lowering down from the lattice, but said nothing. He would teach her for once what were proper hours.

At the corner, standing, Almerting also saw. He recognized the simple white dress and paused steadily, a strange thrill racing over him. Really they had locked her out. Gee, this was new. He had never before had a girl on his hands at this hour. There she was, white, quiet, shut out, waiting at her father's doorstep.

Sitting thus, Theresa pondered a moment and girlish anger and rashness dominated in her. Her pride was hurt and she felt revengeful. They would shut her out, would they? All right, she would go out and they should look to it how they would get her back – the old curmudgeons. He would beat her, but that did not matter. It was a thing afar off.

Getting up, she stepped on the now quieting sidewalk and strolled up the street. It was a rather nervous procedure, however. There were street cars and stores lighted and people passing, but soon these would not be and she was locked out. Into the side streets were already long silent walks and gleaming rows of lamps.

At the corner her youthful lover almost pounced upon her.

"Locked out are you?" he said, his eyes shining.

For the moment she was delighted to see him, for a nameless dread had somehow gotten a hold of her.

"Yes," she answered.

"Well, let's stroll on a little," said the boy.

---

6. **Diana:** In Roman mythology, the goddess of the moon and of the hunt, who was especially revered by women.

At the farther corner up, they passed Officer Maguire and Officer Delehanty, idly swinging their clubs and discussing politics.

"'Tis a shame," said Officer Delehanty, "the way things do now be run."

"Isn't that Rogaum's girl there, though, with Almerting?" asked Maguire, interrupting.

"It is that," said Delehanty, looking after.

"Well, I think he'd better be keeping an eye on her," said Officer Maguire. "'Tis no time for a decent girl to be out."

"That's a sharp lad, that, with her," observed Delehanty. "I know him. He works over here in a tobacco factory. He's up to no good, I'll warrant ye."

"Teach 'em a lesson, I would," said Almerting to her. "Stroll around awhile and make 'em think you mean business. They won't lock you out any more. If they don't let you in when we come back, I'll find you a place all right."

His sharp eyes were gleaming as he looked around into her own and now he fairly carried her on.

Old butcher Rogaum saw her go, marveling at her audacity, but thought she would soon come back. At half-past ten he stuck his head out of the open window and at eleven walked the floor.

He was first wrathful and then nervous – then nervous and wrathful – and finally, all nervous, without a scintilla of wrath. His stout wife sat up in bed and began to wring her hands.

"Lie down!" he commanded. "You make me sick. I know vot I am doing."

"Is she still at the door?" pleaded the mother.

"I think so," he said.

His nerve was weakening, however, and now it finally collapsed.

"She has the street gone up," he said, anxiously. "I will go after."

Slipping on his coat he went down the stairs and out into the streets. It was growing late and the stillness and gloom of midnight was nearing. Nowhere in sight was his Theresa. First one way and then another he went, looking here, there, everywhere, finally groaning.

"Ach, Gott!" he said, the sweat bursting out on his brow, "What in Teufel's[7] name iss dis?"

He thought he would seek a policeman, but there was no policeman. Officer Maguire had long since gone for a quiet game in one of the neighboring saloons. Still old Rogaum hunted on, worrying more and more.

Finally he thought to hasten home, for she must have got back. Mrs. Rogaum, too, would be frantic. If she were not there, he would hunt up the police in earnest. This thing could not go on.

As he turned into his own corner, he almost ran, coming up to the little portico wet and panting. At a puffing step, he turned and almost fell over a white body at his feet, a prone and writhing figure of a woman.

---

7. **Teufel's:** Devil's (German).

"Ach, Gott!" he cried, shouting aloud in his distress and excitement. "Theresa, what iss dis? Wilhelmina, a light now. Bring a light now, I say, for himmel's sake. De vooman hat sich *umgebracht*.[8] Help!"

He had fallen on his knees, and was turning over a writhing, groaning figure.

"Um," said the woman weakly. "Ah."

Almost by the pale light of the street, he could see that it was not his Theresa, and yet there was something very like in the figure. It cut the fiercest cords of his intensity, but there was something else about the situation which made him forget his own troubles.

Mrs. Rogaum, loudly admonished, almost tumbled down the stairs. At the foot, she held the light and then nearly dropped it. A beautiful figure, more girl than woman, rich in all the physical charms that characterize a certain type, lay near to dying. Her soft hair had fallen back over a good forehead now quite white. Her pretty hands, well decked with rings, were clutched tightly in an agonized grip. At her neck, a blue silk shirtwaist and light, lace collar were torn away where she had clutched herself, and on the white flesh was a yellow stain as of one who had been burned. A strange odor reeked in the area, and in one corner was a spilled bottle.

"Ach, Gott!" exclaimed Mrs. Rogaum. "It iss a vooman. She have herself gekilt. Run for de police. Oh, my! Oh, my!"

Rogaum did not kneel for more than a moment. He bounded up and jumping out in front of his door, began to yell lustily for the police. Officer Maguire heard the very first cry, and, leaving his social game, came running.

"What's the matter here, now?" he exclaimed, rushing up, full and ready for murder, robbery, fire, or, indeed, anything in the whole roster of human calamities.

"A vooman!" said Rogaum, excitedly. "She have herself *umgebracht*. She iss dying. Ach, Gott! in my own doorstep, yet."

"Vere iss de hospital?" put in Mrs. Rogaum, thinking clearly of an ambulance, but not being able to express it.

"She is gekilt, sure, Oh! Oh!" and bending over her, the poor, old motherly soul stroked the tightened hands and trickled tears upon the blue shirtwaist. "Ach, vy did you do dot?" she said. "Ach, for vy?"

Officer Maguire was essentially a man of action. He jumped out upon the sidewalk, amid the gathering company, and beat loudly with his club upon the stone flagging.

"Go, telephone for an ambulance," he said roughly to Rogaum, but others beat the old butcher to the corner. Even while Officer Delehanty, hearing the peculiar ring of the stick upon the stone in the night, came running from afar, Maguire held up a passing milk-wagon, making its way up from the Jersey ferry, with a few tons of fresh milk, and demanded a helping.

"Give us a quart there, will you?" he said authoritatively. "A woman's swallowed acid in here."

"Sure," said the driver, dying to get in on the excitement. "Where is a glass?"

---

8. hat sich *umgebracht*: Has killed herself (German).

Maguire ran back and returned, bearing a glass from an excited neighbor. Fat Mrs. Rogaum stood looking nervously on, while the wieldy officer raised the golden head, and poured the milk.

"Here, now, drink this," he said.

The girl, a fair blonde of the type which the world so readily ignores, only opened her eyes, and looked, groaning a little.

"Drink it," shouted the officer fiercely. "Do you want to die? Open your mouth."

Used to a fear of the law in all her days, she obeyed now, even in death. The lips parted, the fresh milk was drained to the end, some spilling on neck and cheek.

While they were so working, old Rogaum came back and stood looking on, by the side of his wife.

"Ach, ach," he said, rather distractedly, "und she iss oudt yet? I could not find her. Oh, oh!"

There was a clang of a gong up the street, as the racing ambulance turned rapidly in. A young hospital surgeon dismounted and, seeing the woman's condition, ordered immediate removal. Both officers and the surgeon helped her in the ambulance, and, after a moment, the lone bell, ringing wildly in the night, was all the evidence remaining that a tragedy had been.

"Do you know how she came here?" said Officer Delehanty, coming back to get Rogaum's testimony for the police.

"No, no," answered Rogaum, wretchedly. "She was here alretty. I was for my daughter look. Ach, himmel, I have my daughter lost. She vass avay."

Mrs. Rogaum also chattered.

The officer did not at first get the significance of this. He was only interested in the facts of the present case.

"You say she was here when you came? Where were you?"

"I say I vass for my daughter look. I come here, undt de vooman vass here now alretty."

"What time was this?"

"Only now yet. Yussed a half-hour."

Officer Maguire had strolled up, after chasing away the crowd with fierce and unholy threats. He noticed the peculiar perturbation of the usual placid German couple.

"What about your daughter?" he said, catching a word as to that.

Both old people raised their voices at once.

"She have gone. She have run avay. Ach, himmel, we must for her look. Quick – she could not get in. We haf de door shut."

"That's the girl I saw walking with young Almerting, do ye mind? The one in the white dress," said Maguire to Delehanty.

"White dress, yah," echoed Rogaum, and then the fact of her walking with some one came home like a blow.

"Dit you hear dot?" he exclaimed, even as Mrs. Rogaum did likewise, *"Mein Gott, hast du das gehoert?"*[9]

---

9. *"Mein . . . gehoert?"*: "My God, did you hear that?" (German).

He fairly bounded as he said it. His hands flew up to his stout and ruddy head.

"Why do you let her out for nights?" observed Officer Maguire roughly, catching the drift of the situation. "That's no time for young girls to be out."

"Ich?" exclaimed poor Rogaum. "Me, yet. Ho, ho, ho!" His voice was almost hysteric.

"Well, go in now," said Officer Delehanty. "There's no use standing out here. Give us a description of the girl, and we'll look for her."

"Never mind," said Maguire. "I know her. I can tip them off."

The two men turned away, leaving the old German couple in the throe of distress. A time-worn, old church clock near by now chimed out one and then two. The notes cut like knives. Mrs. Rogaum began fearfully to cry. Rogaum walked and blustered to himself.

"It's a queer case, that," said Officer Delehanty, referring to the outcast of the doorway, so recently sent away. "I think I know that woman. She didn't come there by herself."

"Not a bit of it," said Maguire. "She was put there all right."

He tipped his nose up significantly, and cocked his eye serenely. "I think I know the one that did it. Let's go round to 68."

Around the corner the significant red light over the transom at that number told a story of its own. The two policemen strolled up and leisurely knocked. At the very first sound, a painted denizen of the half-world opened the door.

"Where is Adele?" said Maguire as the two officers stepped in.

"She's gone to bed."

"Tell her to come down."

They seated themselves deliberately in the gaudy mirrored parlor, and waited, conversing between themselves. Presently a sleepy-looking woman of forty appeared in an elegant robe and slippered in red.

"We're here about that case you had to-night."

"What case?" said the lady.

"You know," put in Maguire. "How did she come to take poison?"

"I don't know what you're talking about," said the woman.

"Come now," said Delehanty. "We know you've got a pull, but we've got to know about this case. It won't be published. What made her take the poison?"

The woman hesitated, under the steady eye of the officer, but finally weakened.

"Why, her lover went back on her – that's all."

"What was his name?"

"I don't know. You never can tell that."

"Was her name Annie," said Maguire.

"No – Emily."

"Well, how did she get over there?" inquired Delehanty pleasantly.

"George took her."

Little by little, as they sat there, the whole miserable story came out – miserable as all the error and suffering of the world.

"She did love him, did she?" inquired Maguire, rather surprised.

"Of course, she did – she was crazy over him."

"And he wouldn't come back?"

"That's what he said."

Wonderful, wonderful this to the policeman. He would never get it through his head. Great, surging, maddening passion, that would rather die in a doorway than lose. He shook his head.

"How old was she?"

"Oh, twenty-one."

"Think o' that," said Delehanty, who had a pretty daughter the same age.

"Well, where'd she come from?"

"Oh, here in New York. Her family locked her out, one night, I think."

Something in the way the woman said this brought old Rogaum back to Maguire's mind. He had forgotten all about that pretty German's disappearance.

"I'll tell old Rogaum that," he said facetiously to Delehanty. "He locked his girl out tonight."

The two men inquired a little farther, and then went away.

"Let's go by and see if the girl has got back yet," said Maguire, as they came out and around the corner, disturbed but little by the tragedies of life.

"Is your daughter back again," asked Maguire, beating soundly on the door.

"Ach, no," said the hysterical Mrs. Rogaum, who was quite alone. "My husband he haf gone out again to look vunce. Oh, my, oh, my!"

"That's what you get for locking her out," said Maguire masterfully. "That other woman down here," and he pointed to the still acid-stained area, "was also locked out. You oughtn't to do that."

It was carrying coals to Newcastle,[10] however. Her grief was great enough.

They returned to the station, and sent out a hurry call:

"Look out for girl, Theresa Rogaum. Aged 18; height, about 5, 3; light hair, blue eyes, cotton dress, trimmed with blue ribbon. Last seen with lad named Almerting, about 21 years of age."

There were other details even more pointed and conclusive. As each station received the message, the men were informed when called up. From Battery to Harlem,[11] and far beyond, policemen were scanning the long streets, in the dim shadows of the night, for a girl in a white dress, and a youth of 21.

Officer Halsey got the message, after he had reported for a third time from his beat, which took in a portion of Washington Square. He had seen a good many couples this pleasant summer evening, but none that answered this description. He went out and idled about the corner until Officer Paisly came up, and then the matter was discussed.

"I saw that couple, I bet you, not over an hour and a half ago," said the latter interestedly. "She was dressed in white, and looked to me as if she didn't want to go. I remember

---

10. **carrying coals to Newcastle:** Newcastle upon Tyne was known as the major exporter of coal mined in the surrounding area in northern England. The expression means to do something pointless or unnecessary.

11. **From Battery to Harlem:** That is, from the Lower East Side to the Upper West Side of Manhattan.

looking at the fellow with her. They acted sort of funny. They went in this park down at the Eighth street end there."

"Supposing we beat it," said Halsey, weary for something to do.

"Sure," said the other quickly.

Together they began a careful search, kicking around in the moonlight, under the trees. The moon was leaning moderately toward the West, and all the branches were silvered with light and dew. Among the flowers, past clumps of bushes, near the fountain they searched, each one going his way alone. At last, the wandering Halsey paused beside a thick clump of flaming bushes, ruddy, slightly, even in the night. A murmur of voices greeted him, and something very much like the sound of a sob.

"What's that," he said, mentally, drawing near and listening.

"Why don't you come on now," said the first of the voices heard. "They won't let you in. What's the use crying?"

No answer to this, but no sobs. She must have been crying silently.

"Come on. I can take care of you. We can live in Hoboken.[12] That's all right."

There was a movement as if the speaker were patting her on the shoulder.

"What's the use crying? Don't you believe I love you?"

The officer stole quietly around to get a better view. He wanted to see for himself. In the moonlight, from a comfortable distance he could see them seated, now that his eyes were searching. The tall bushes were almost all about the bench. In his arm was a girl – a pretty girl, in white, held very close. Dropping down to get a better view, he saw him kiss her and hold her – hold her in such a way that she could but yield to him, whatever her slight disinclination.

It was a common affair at earlier hours, but rather startling now. The officer was delighted, as he crept nearer, to break it up.

Suddenly he appeared before them very quickly, and with a sinister look. "What are you two doing here?" he inquired, as if he had not seen.

The girl tumbled out of her compromising position, speechless and blushing violently.

"We're just sitting in the Park," returned the lean-faced youth, with considerable *sang froid*.[13]

"Well, we don't allow this. You'll have to come along with me."

The boy stood up. "What for?" he said.

"Never mind," said Halsey, "come along now. I want you both. That's all."

At the other end of the Park, Paisly joined them and, at the station house, the girl was given a chair. She was all tears and melancholy.

"Send them down here," said the man at the Bleecker Street Station, who had heard from Maguire of old Rogaum's grief. "We want to send her home."

By four in the morning, the twain were down in Bleecker Street, and Rogaum rushing stationward.

---

12. **Hoboken:** Town in New Jersey, across the Hudson River from Manhattan.
13. *sang froid:* Literally "cold blood" (French), the term suggests calm or coolness in trying circumstances.

"Ach, Gott, now!" he said, as he saw his daughter again, "what haf you done? Oh, oh!" and he gathered her in his arms.

"You, you!" he said, glaring at the imperturbable Almerting, "come not near my tochter any more. I vill preak your effery pone, du teufel, du!"

He made a move toward the incarcerated lover, but here the Sergeant interfered.

"Stop that," he said now. "Take your daughter out of here, and go home, or I'll lock you both up. D'ye hear? We'll do whatever punishing's to be done."

"I didn't do nawthin," said Almerting, cynically. "They locked her out."

"You shut up," said the Sergeant, irritably. Still he called after the butcher angrily:

"Keep your daughter off the streets hereafter, do you hear?"

Old Rogaum heard nothing. He was in a mixture of wondrous feelings. What to do was beyond him.

At the corner near the butcher shop, the wakeful Maguire was still idling as they passed.

"Don't lock her out any more," he called, significantly. "That's what brought the other girl to your door."

"What is dot?" said Rogaum.

"I say the other girl was locked out. That's why she committed suicide."

"Ach, I know," said the husky German, under his breath, but he had no intention of locking her out. He did not know what he would do until they were in the presence of his crying wife, who fell upon Theresa weeping.

"She vass like you," said the old mother to the wandering Theresa, ignorant of the important lesson brought to their very door. "She vass loog like you."

"I will not vip you now," said the old butcher, solemnly, too delighted to think of punishment, "aber,[14] go not avay any more. Dot loafer, aber – let him come here no more. I vill fix him."

"She wouldn't run away no more yet, no," said the fat mother, tearfully.

"No," said Theresa, in tears, "he wouldn't let me come back, that was all. I hope they arrest him."

"I vill fix him," said Rogaum, unloading now on the lover freely. "De penitentiary he should have."

"Don't you ever bother that girl again," said the Sergeant to young Almerting, as he turned him loose after an hour. "If you do, we'll get you, and you won't get off under six months."

"I don't want her," said the boy, cynically. "Let him have his old daughter. They had better not lock her out, though – that's all I say. I don't want her," and away he went.

[1901]

---

14. **aber:** But or though (German).

Paul Laurence Dunbar

[1872–1906]

Paul Laurence Dunbar

This photograph was taken around 1900, only a few years before Dunbar's premature death ended the career of the most famous African American writer of his generation.

Paul Laurence Dunbar was born in Dayton, Ohio, on June 27, 1872, the child of two former slaves from Kentucky. His father, Joshua Dunbar, had escaped to Canada by way of the underground railroad before the Civil War, during which he returned to enlist in the Fifty-fifth Massachusetts Infantry Regiment. He married Matilda J. Murphy, a widow with two young sons, and the couple had two children before they divorced in 1876. Dunbar was raised by his mother, who worked as a washerwoman to support her children. She inspired them with a love of poetry, songs, and storytelling, especially the rich oral traditions of African Americans. The family moved several times while Dunbar was growing up in Dayton, where he attended predominantly white schools and was the only African American in his class at Central High School. An outgoing and talented student, Dunbar experienced relatively little racial prejudice at school, where he was encouraged to develop his extraordinary literary abilities. He read a variety of British poets, including John Keats and William Wordsworth, as well as popular American poets such as Henry Wadsworth Longfellow and John Greenleaf Whittier. Dunbar edited the school newspaper and published his first poem, "Our Martyred Soldiers," in the *Dayton Herald* on June 8, 1888. Some of his verses also appeared in a smaller local newspaper published by his friends Orville and Wilbur Wright, known later as the famous Wright brothers, who started a printing shop in Dayton in 1888.

When he graduated from high school in 1891, however, Dunbar confronted the narrowly limited opportunities available to African Americans in late-nineteenth-century America. Unable to find more suitable work, he took a job as an elevator operator in a building in Dayton. But he continued to write poetry, which soon opened up a new world to Dunbar. After one of his high school teachers arranged for him to recite a welcoming address at the meeting of the Western Association of Writers in 1892, he began to publish poems in local newspapers, and the following year Dunbar took a loan to pay for the publication of his first volume of poetry, *Oak and Ivy* (1893). His notoriety in Dayton, where he was known as the "elevator boy poet," and growing reputation in the Midwest led to an invitation for Dunbar to recite a poem on "Negro American Day" at the World's Colombian Exposition, which opened in 1893 in Chicago. There, he met a number of influential African Americans, including the antilynching crusader Ida B. Wells and Frederick Douglass, then the U.S. ambassador to Haiti. Taking an immediate interest in Dunbar, whom he called "the most promising young colored man in America," Douglass secured him a job as a clerk in the Haitian pavilion at the exposition. Dunbar also gained the patronage of two white admirers from Toledo, Ohio: the lawyer Charles A. Thatcher and the psychiatrist Henry A. Tobey, who promoted his career and paid for the publication of his second book of poetry, *Majors and Minors* (1895). The volume was enthusiastically reviewed by William Dean Howells, who subsequently wrote the preface to Dunbar's first commercially produced volume of poetry, *Lyrics of Lowly Life* (1896).

That bestseller gained Dunbar a wide audience for his work, which was read and praised by both blacks and whites in the United States. Propelled by the enthusiastic reception of *Lyrics of Lowly Life*, Dunbar gave numerous readings in eastern cities and then during a successful tour of England. Following his return in 1897, he moved to Washington, D.C., where Dunbar worked for a time as an assistant in the Reading Room of the Library of Congress. During the following years, his writings appeared in prominent national periodicals such as the *Atlantic Monthly*, *Century*, *Lipincott's*, and the *Saturday Evening Post*, which were eager to publish Dunbar's poetry as well as the fiction he soon began to write. His earliest stories were collected in *Folks from Dixie* (1898), published the same year as his first novel, *The Uncalled*. He also wrote plays for black performers and collaborated on the Broadway musicals *Clorindy* and *In Dahomey*. In 1898, he married Alice Ruth Moore, who would later become well known as Alice Dunbar-Nelson for her stories of Creole life in New Orleans. But the couple separated four years later, partly as a result of Dunbar's heavy drinking to ease the pain in his lungs from tuberculosis, which he contracted around 1899. Nonetheless, he continued to write and publish at a furious pace until he finally succumbed to the disease on February 9, 1906. During the mere thirteen years since his first book appeared in 1893, Dunbar had produced a staggering amount of work, including numerous essays, four novels, four collections of short stories, and thirteen collections of the poems for which he was hailed as "The Poet Laureate of the Negro Race" by the influential African American leader Booker T. Washington.

Reading Dunbar's Poetry. During his lifetime, Dunbar became what the literary scholar Henry Louis Gates Jr. has described as "the most famous black writer in the world." Dunbar first gained serious attention when his second book, *Majors and Minors* (1895), was reviewed by William Dean Howells in *Harper's Weekly* in June 1896. That influential critic was struck by the humor and lyrical quality of the poems in the volume, as well as by Dunbar's versatility in using both the dialect of southern blacks and what Howells called "our American English." But he was careful to add: "I am speaking of him as a black poet, when I should be speaking of him as a poet." In his introduction to *Lyrics of Lowly Life* (1896), however, Howells emphasizes the poet's racial identity, observing that Dunbar was "the first instance of an American negro who had evinced innate distinction in literature," by which he evidently meant the first African American writer of unmixed racial heritage to do so. Dunbar's contributions to and his role in shaping a distinctive African American literary tradition were later deeply contested, especially among black poets and critics. His friend and contemporary James Weldon Johnson suggested that Dunbar's

FOR PAUL LAURENCE DUNBAR
Born of the sorrowful of
  heart,
Mirth was a crown upon
  his head;
Pride kept his twisted
  lips apart
In jest, to hide a heart
  that bled
    –Countee Cullen

bedfordstmartins.com/
americanlit *for research*
links on Dunbar

dialect poetry had helped promote the racist plantation myth promulgated by popular white writers who evoked a world of benign masters and contented slaves in the antebellum South. Nonetheless, Johnson was a self-described disciple of Dunbar, whose work also influenced poets of the Harlem Renaissance as different as Langston Hughes and Countee Cullen. More recently, critics have tended to focus increasing attention on the veiled social commentary offered in some of Dunbar's dialect poems, as well as on the sensitive exploration of the plight of African Americans in many of the poems he wrote in standard English. The texts of "An Ante-bellum Sermon" and "We Wear the Mask" are taken from *Lyrics of Lowly Life* (1896). The text of "Sympathy," one of Dunbar's most famous poems and the source of the title of Maya Angelou's best-selling autobiography, *I Know Why the Caged Bird Sings* (1970), is taken from *Lyrics of the Hearthside* (1899).

AN ANTE-BELLUM[1] SERMON

We is gathahed hyeah, my brothahs,
    In dis howlin' wildaness,
Fu' to speak some words of comfo't
    To each othah in distress.
An' we chooses fu' ouah subjic'   5
    Dis—we'll 'splain it by an' by;
"An' de Lawd said, 'Moses, Moses,'[2]
    An' de man said, 'Hyeah am I.'"

Now ole Pher'oh, down in Egypt,
    Was de wuss man evah bo'n,   10
An' he had de Hebrew chillun
    Down dah wukin' in his co'n;
'T well de Lawd got tiahed o' his foolin',
    An' sez he: "I 'll let him know—
Look hyeah, Moses, go tell Pher'oh   15
    Fu' to let dem chillun go."

"An' ef he refuse to do it,
    I will make him rue de houah,
Fu' I 'll empty down on Egypt
    All de vials of my powah."   20

---

1. **Ante-bellum:** Literally, "before the war" (Latin), though in American history *antebellum* (as it is now spelled) almost always refers to the period before the Civil War.
2. **Moses:** The Hebrew prophet who led the Israelites out of slavery in Egypt to the promised land (Exodus 20). Slaves often compared themselves to the ancient Israelites, especially in the slave songs or "Negro spirituals" that became popular in the decades following the Civil War.

Yes, he did – an' Pher'oh's ahmy
    Was n't wuth a ha'f a dime;
Fu' de Lawd will he'p his chillun,
    You kin trust him evah time.

An' yo' enemies may 'sail you   25
    In de back an' in de front;
But de Lawd is all aroun' you,
    Fu' to ba' de battle's brunt.
Dey kin fo'ge yo' chains an shackles
    F'om de mountains to de sea;   30
But de Lawd will sen' some Moses
    Fu' to set his chillun free.

An' de lan' shall hyeah his thundah,
    Lak a blas' f'om Gab'el's ho'n,[3]
Fu' de Lawd of hosts is mighty   35
    When he girds his ahmor on.
But fu' feah some one mistakes me,
    I will pause right hyeah to say,
Dat I 'm still a-preachin' ancient,
    I ain't talkin' 'bout to-day.   40

But I tell you, fellah christuns,
    Things 'll happen mighty strange;
Now, de Lawd done dis fu' Isrul,
    An' his ways don't nevah change,
An' de love he showed to Isrul   45
    Was n't all on Isrul spent;
Now don't run an' tell yo' mastahs
    Dat I 's preachin' discontent.

'Cause I is n't; I 'se a-judgin'
    Bible people by deir ac's;   50
I 'se a-givin' you de Scriptuah,
    I 'se a-handin' you de fac's.
Cose ole Pher'oh b'lieved in slav'ry.
    But de Lawd he let him see,
Dat de people he put bref in, –   55
    Evah mothah's son was free.

---

3. **Gab'el's ho'n:** Gabriel's horn, a reference to the archangel who announces good news by blowing his horn, which according to Christian doctrine will announce the Last Judgment.

An' dahs othahs thinks lak Pher'oh,
    But dey calls de Scriptuah liar,
Fu' de Bible says "a servant
    Is a-worthy of his hire."[4]   60
An' you cain't git roun' nor thoo dat,
    An' you cain't git ovah it,
Fu' whatevah place you git in,
    Dis hyeah Bible too 'll fit.

So you see de Lawd's intention,   65
    Evah sence de worl' began,
Was dat His almighty freedom
    Should belong to evah man,
But I think it would be bettah,
    Ef I 'd pause agin to say,   70
Dat I 'm talkin' 'bout ouah freedom
    In a Bibleistic way.

But de Moses is a-comin',
    an' he's comin, suah and fas'
We kin hyeah his feet a-trompin,   75
    We kin hyeah his trumpit blas'.
But I want to wa'n you people,
    Don't you git too brigity;[5]
An' don't you git to braggin'
    'Bout dese things, you wait an' see.   80

But when Moses wif his powah
    Comes an' sets us chillun free,
We will praise de gracious Mastah,[6]
    Dat has gin us liberty;
An' we'll shout ouah halleluyahs,   85
    On dat mighty reck'nin' day,
When we'se reco'nised ez citiz' —
    Huh uh! Chillun, let us pray!

          [1896]

---

4. "a servant . . . his hire": A reference to the biblical injunction against withholding wages from a servant — for example, in Leviticus 19:13 and Deuteronomy 24:15 — and an indictment of slavery as contrary to the scriptures.
5. brigity: Biggity, or boastful.
6. Mastah: Jesus Christ.

WE WEAR THE MASK

We wear the mask that grins and lies,
It hides our cheeks and shades our eyes, –
This debt we pay to human guile;
With torn and bleeding hearts we smile,
And mouth with myriad subtleties.   5

Why should the world be over-wise,
In counting all our tears and sighs?
Nay, let them only see us, while
   We wear the mask.

We smile, but, O great Christ, our cries   10
To thee from tortured souls arise.
We sing, but oh the clay is vile
Beneath our feet, and long the mile;
But let the world dream otherwise,
   We wear the mask!   15
                   [1896]

SYMPATHY

I know what the caged bird feels, alas!
   When the sun is bright on the upland slopes;
When the wind stirs soft through the springing grass,
And the river flows like a stream of glass;
   When the first bird sings and the first bud opes,   5
And the faint perfume from its chalice steals –
I know what the caged bird feels!

I know why the caged bird beats his wing
   Till its blood is red on the cruel bars;
For he must fly back to his perch and cling   10
When he fain would be on the bough a-swing;
   And a pain still throbs in the old, old scars
And they pulse again with a keener sting –
I know why he beats his wing!

I know why the caged bird sings, ah me,   15
   When his wing is bruised and his bosom sore, –
When he beats his bars and he would be free;
It is not a carol of joy or glee,
   But a prayer that he sends from his heart's deep core,
But a plea, that upward to Heaven he flings –   20
I know why the caged bird sings!
                   [1899]

Willa Cather

[1873-1947]

Wilella Sibert Cather was born in Back Creek Valley, west of Winchester, Virginia, on December 7, 1873, the first child of Mary Virginia Boak and Charles Cather. Often called "Willie" by her family, Cather later adopted the name "Willa." When a fire destroyed part of their farm in 1883, her family left Virginia to join relatives who had established a homestead on high ground, the "Divide" as it was called, between the Little Blue and Republican rivers in southeastern Nebraska. In an interview in 1913, Cather recalled her vivid first impressions of the stark landscape: "[T]he roads were mostly faint trails over the bunch grass in those days. The land was open range and there was almost no fencing. As we drove further and further out into the country, I felt a good deal as if we had come to the end of everything." The remote area was populated by large numbers of European immigrants from Germany, Denmark, Sweden, and Russia, whose customs and language also made a strong impression on Cather. After two years on the homestead, Charles Cather moved his family to the bustling railroad town of Red Cloud, Nebraska, where he opened an insurance and real-estate business. Cather attended public schools, wrote plays, and participated in dramatic performances (often taking male roles) in the town's new Opera House. After graduating from high school in 1890, she studied for a year at the Latin School, a college preparatory school in Lincoln, before enrolling at the University of Nebraska in the fall of 1891. At the time, relatively few women attended the university, and Cather further challenged gender roles by arriving there dressed as what she called her "twin brother," William Cather.

An excellent student, Cather soon determined to become a professional writer. Her first story appeared in a campus literary magazine in 1892. In addition to editing the student newspaper, she became a regular contributor to the local Lincoln newspaper, the *Nebraska State Journal,* writing reviews and a weekly drama column. After she graduated in 1895, Cather worked for Nebraska newspapers, but the ambitious young writer was eager to be a part of a larger literary scene. In 1896, she accepted an offer to become the editor of the *Home Monthly,* a small magazine published in Pittsburgh, Pennsylvania. After a year with the *Home Monthly*, the pages of which were filled with works Cather published under various pen names, she took a job with the *Pittsburgh Leader*. She resigned from the newspaper in 1900, about the time one of her stories was published in *Cosmopolitan*, then a family magazine and one of the major markets for fiction in the United States. By then, she had begun to develop a close relationship with Isabelle McClung, the daughter of a wealthy Pittsburgh judge, who invited Cather to move into the family's large house in the spring of 1901. She lived there for the next five years, teaching English and Latin at high schools and devoting her free time to writing. Cather's first book was a collection of poetry, *April Twilights* (1903). Her stories appeared in prominent periodicals such as *Everybody's Magazine*, the *Saturday Evening Post*, and *Scribner's*, paving the way for the publication of her first collection of short fiction, *The Troll Garden*, in 1905. The following year, she moved to New York City to take a position on the editorial staff of *McClure's Magazine*. She worked for that influential magazine for six years, publishing numerous stories and rising to the position of managing editor before resigning to devote herself full time to writing in 1912.

During the remainder of her long career, Cather became a highly admired novelist. Her first novel, *Alexander's Bridge* (1912), was set in the East and revealed the strong influence of Henry James and Edith Wharton. Cather explored a very different terrain in *O Pioneers!* (1913), a novel in which she drew heavily on her early experiences in Nebraska. Living in New York City with Edith Lewis, her long-term companion, Cather subsequently wrote a series of acclaimed novels about life on the Great Plains, including *The Song of the Lark* (1915), *My Ántonia* (1918), and *A Lost Lady* (1923). In an interview, however, Cather said that she did not want to become too identified with the West, since "using one setting all the time is very like planting a field with corn season after season. I believe in rotation of crops. If the public ties me down to the cornfield too much I'm afraid I'll leave that scene entirely." Cather, who traveled widely with Edith Lewis, broke new ground with *The Professor's House* (1925), which was set in Michigan and the Southwest, and *Death Comes for the Archbishop* (1927), a novel about the Spanish settlement of New Mexico. In her later novels, she ventured equally far afield: to the early settlement of Canada in *Shadows on the Rock* (1931); forward to the early twentieth century in *Lucy Gayheart* (1935), the action of which shifts between a small town on the Great Plains and urban Chicago; and back to antebellum Virginia, where she was born, in her final novel, *Sapphira and the Slave Girl* (1940). Cather died at her home in New York City on April 24, 1947.

We have nothing better than [Willa Cather]. She takes so much pains to conceal her sophistication that it is easy to miss her quality.
—Wallace Stevens

Reading Cather's "A Wagner Matinée." This story was first published in *Everybody's Magazine*. Founded in 1896, the illustrated monthly developed a reputation for its investigative (what its critics called "muckraking") journalism, as well as for publishing works by a variety of

American writers, including Frank Norris, who contributed exposés of corrupt business practices. Seeking the broadest possible audience, the magazine also featured articles designed to appeal to women and fiction by popular authors such as Mary E. Wilkins Freeman. At the time "A Wagner Matinée" was published in the magazine, the controversial operas of Richard Wagner were being widely performed in the United States. The story generated controversy, drawing the ire of friends and family members who objected to Cather's bleak depiction of life in Nebraska. In an editorial in the *Nebraska State Journal*, her old friend Will Jones observed: "If the writers of fiction who use western Nebraska as material would look up now and then and not keep their eyes and noses in the cattle yards, they might be more agreeable company." In response to such criticism, Cather slightly revised the story before publishing it in her collection *The Troll*

Homesteaders in Nebraska

This photograph of the David Hilton family was taken in 1887 near Weissert, in central Nebraska. The photographer noted that the family "did not want to show the old sod house to friends back east, but the young lady and mother wanted to prove they had an organ."

Garden (1905), toning down the harsh description of the narrator's aunt Georgiana, a figure loosely based on her Boston-born aunt, Frances Cather, who had moved with her husband to Nebraska. Some biographers have suggested that as Cather grew older she became increasingly charitable about her early experiences in Nebraska, and she further altered "A Wagner Matinée" in the version published in her collection *Youth and the Bright Medusa* (1920), as well as in the final version published in 1937. The following text is taken from the first printing in *Everybody's Magazine*, February 1904.

bedfordstmartins.com/ americanlit for research links on Cather

A WAGNER MATINÉE

I received one morning a letter written in pale ink, on glassy, blue-lined notepaper, and bearing the postmark of a little Nebraska village. This communication, worn and rubbed, looking as though it had been carried for some days in a coat-pocket that was none too clean, was from my Uncle Howard. It informed me that his wife had been left a small legacy by a bachelor relative who had recently died, and that it had become necessary for her to come to Boston to attend to the settling of the estate. He requested me to meet her at the station, and render her whatever services might prove necessary. On examining the date indicated as that of her arrival, I found it no later than to-morrow. He had characteristically delayed writing until, had I been away from home for a day, I must have missed the good woman altogether.

The name of my Aunt Georgiana called up not alone her own figure, at once pathetic and grotesque, but opened before my feet a gulf of recollections so wide and deep that, as the letter dropped from my hand, I felt suddenly a stranger to all the present conditions of my existence, wholly ill at ease and out of place amid the surroundings of my study. I became, in short, the gangling farmer-boy my aunt had known, scourged with chilblains[1] and bashfulness, my hands cracked and raw from the corn-husking. I felt the knuckles of my thumb tentatively, as though they were raw again. I sat again before her parlor organ, thumbing the scales with my stiff, red hands, while she beside me made canvas mittens for the huskers.[2]

The next morning, after preparing my landlady somewhat, I set out for the station. When the train arrived I had some difficulty in finding my aunt. She was the last of the passengers to alight, and when I got her into the carriage she looked not unlike one of those charred, smoked bodies that firemen lift from the *débris* of a burned building. She had come all the way in a day coach; her linen duster[3] had become black with soot and her black bonnet gray with dust during the journey. When we arrived at my boarding-house the landlady put her to bed at once, and I did not see her again until the next morning.

---

1. **chilblains:** Itchy, painful swellings on the skin, caused by exposure to cold.
2. **huskers:** People employed to remove the husks, or coverings, from ears of corn.
3. **linen duster:** A long, loose, and lightweight coat worn by women in the early 1900s for traveling.

Whatever shock Mrs. Springer experienced at my aunt's appearance she considerately concealed. Myself, I saw my aunt's misshapen figure with that feeling of awe and respect with which we behold explorers who have left their ears and fingers north of Franz Josef Land, or their health somewhere along the Upper Congo.[4] My Aunt Georgiana had been a music-teacher at the Boston Conservatory, somewhere back in the latter sixties. One summer, which she had spent in the little village in the Green Mountains where her ancestors had dwelt for generations, she had kindled the callow fancy of the most idle and shiftless of all the village lads, and had conceived for this Howard Carpenter one of those absurd and extravagant passions which a handsome country boy of twenty-one sometimes inspires in a plain, angular, spectacled woman of thirty. When she returned to her duties in Boston, Howard followed her; and the upshot of this inexplicable infatuation was that she eloped with him, eluding the reproaches of her family and the criticism of her friends by going with him to the Nebraska frontier. Carpenter, who of course had no money, took a homestead[5] in Red Willow County, fifty miles from the railroad. There they measured off their eighty acres by driving across the prairie in a wagon, to the wheel of which they had tied a red cotton handkerchief, and counting its revolutions. They built a dugout in the red hillside, one of those cave dwellings whose inmates usually reverted to the conditions of primitive savagery. Their water they got from the lagoons where the buffalo drank, and their slender stock of provisions was always at the mercy of bands of roving Indians. For thirty years my aunt had not been farther than fifty miles from the homestead.

But Mrs. Springer knew nothing of all this, and must have been considerably shocked at what was left of my kinswoman. Beneath the soiled linen duster, which on her arrival was the most conspicuous feature of her costume, she wore a black stuff dress whose ornamentation showed that she had surrendered herself unquestioningly into the hands of a country dressmaker. My poor aunt's figure, however, would have presented astonishing difficulties to any dressmaker. Her skin was yellow as a Mongolian's from constant exposure to a pitiless wind, and to the alkaline water, which transforms the most transparent cuticle into a sort of flexible leather. She wore ill-fitting false teeth. The most striking thing about her physiognomy, however, was an incessant twitching of the mouth and eyebrows, a form of nervous disorder resulting from isolation and monotony, and from frequent physical suffering.

In my boyhood this affliction had possessed a sort of horrible fascination for me, of which I was secretly very much ashamed, for in those days I owed to this woman most of the good that ever came my way, and had a reverential affection for her. During the three winters when I was riding herd for my uncle, my aunt, after cooking three meals for half a dozen farm-hands, and putting the six children to bed, would often stand until midnight at her ironing-board, hearing me at the kitchen table beside her recite Latin

---

4. **Franz Josef Land . . . Upper Congo:** An archipelago in the far north of Russia, and the Lualaba or Upper Congo River, an area in central Africa that was not explored by Europeans until the 1860s.
5. **homestead:** The federal Homestead Act of 1862 provided parcels of public land in the West to those willing to settle and farm the land for at least five years.

declensions and conjugations, and gently shaking me when my drowsy head sank down over a page of irregular verbs. It was to her, at her ironing or mending, that I read my first Shakespeare; and her old text-book of mythology was the first that ever came into my empty hands. She taught me my scales and exercises, too, on the little parlor organ which her husband had bought her after fifteen years, during which she had not so much as seen any instrument except an accordion, that belonged to one of the Norwegian farm-hands. She would sit beside me by the hour, darning and counting, while I struggled with the "Harmonious Blacksmith";[6] but she seldom talked to me about music, and I understood why. She was a pious woman; she had the consolation of religion; and to her at least her martyrdom was not wholly sordid. Once when I had been doggedly beating out some passages from an old score of "Euryanthe"[7] I had found among her music-books, she came up to me and, putting her hand over my eyes, gently drew my head back upon her shoulder, saying tremulously, "Don't love it so well, Clark, or it may be taken from you. Oh! dear boy, pray that whatever your sacrifice be it is not that."

When my aunt appeared on the morning after her arrival, she was still in a semi-somnambulant state. She seemed not to realize that she was in the city where she had spent her youth, the place longed for hungrily for half a lifetime. She had been so wretchedly train-sick throughout the journey that she had no recollection of anything but her discomfort, and, to all intents and purposes, there were but a few hours of nightmare between the farm in Red Willow County and my study on Newbury Street. I had planned a little pleasure for her that afternoon, to repay her for some of the glorious moments she had given me when we used to milk together in the straw-thatched cowshed, and she, because I was more than usually tired, or because her husband had spoken sharply to me, would tell me of the splendid performance of Meyerbeer's "Huguenots"[8] she had seen in Paris in her youth. At two o'clock the Boston Symphony Orchestra was to give a Wagner programme,[9] and I intended to take my aunt, though as I conversed with her I grew doubtful about her enjoyment of it. Indeed, for her own sake, I could only wish her taste for such things quite dead, and the long struggle mercifully ended at last. I suggested our visiting the Conservatory and the Common before lunch, but she seemed altogether too timid to wish to venture out. She questioned me absently about various changes in the city, but she was chiefly concerned that she had forgotten to leave instructions about feeding half-skimmed milk to a certain weakling calf, "Old Maggie's calf, you know, Clark," she explained, evidently having forgotten how long I had been away. She was further troubled because she had neglected to tell her daughter about the freshly opened kit of mackerel in the cellar, that would spoil if it were not used directly.

---

6. **"Harmonious Blacksmith":** A musical composition by the German composer and pianist Robert Schumann (1810–1856).
7. **"Euryanthe":** Set in twelfth-century France, this romantic opera about a tragic love affair was composed by Carl Maria von Weber (1786–1826) and first performed in 1823.
8. **"Huguenots":** *Les Huguenots* (1836), an opera about the massacre of Huguenots (Protestants) by Catholics in Paris in 1572, was composed by Giacomo Meyerbeer (1791–1864).
9. **Wagner programme:** Selections from the music of Richard Wagner (1813–1883), the acclaimed German composer of thirteen major operas and numerous other works.

I asked her whether she had ever heard any of the Wagnerian operas, and found that she had not, though she was perfectly familiar with their respective situations and had once possessed the piano score of "The Flying Dutchman."[10] I began to think it would have been best to get her back to Red Willow County without waking her, and regretted having suggested the concert.

From the time we entered the concert-hall, however, she was a trifle less passive and inert, and seemed to begin to perceive her surroundings. I had felt some trepidation lest she might become aware of the absurdities of her attire, or might experience some painful embarrassment at stepping suddenly into the world to which she had been dead for a quarter of a century. But again I found how superficially I had judged her. She sat looking about her with eyes as impersonal, almost as stony as those with which the granite Rameses in a museum[11] watches the froth and fret that ebbs and flows about his pedestal, separated from it by the lonely stretch of centuries. I have seen this same aloofness in old miners who drift into the Brown Hotel at Denver, their pockets full of bullion, their linen soiled, their haggard faces unshorn, and who stand in the thronged corridors as solitary as though they were still in a frozen camp on the Yukon, or in the yellow blaze of the Arizona desert, conscious that certain experiences have isolated them from their fellows by a gulf no haberdasher could conceal.

The audience was made up chiefly of women. One lost the contour of faces and figures, indeed any effect of line whatever, and there was only the color contrast of bodices past counting, the shimmer and shading of fabrics soft and firm, silky and sheer, resisting and yielding: red, mauve, pink, blue, lilac, purple, ecru, rose, yellow, cream, and white, all the colors that an impressionist finds in a sunlit landscape, with here and there the dead black shadow of a frock-coat. My Aunt Georgiana regarded them as though they had been so many daubs of tube paint on a palette.

When the musicians came out and took their places, she gave a little stir of anticipation, and looked with quickening interest down over the rail at that invariable grouping; perhaps the first wholly familiar thing that had greeted her eye since she had left old Maggie and her weakling calf. I could feel how all those details sank into her soul, for I had not forgotten how they had sunk into mine when I came fresh from ploughing forever and forever between green aisles of corn, where, as in a treadmill, one might walk from daybreak to dusk without perceiving a shadow of change in one's environment. I reminded myself of the impression made on me by the clean profiles of the musicians, the gloss of their linen, the dull black of their coats, the beloved shapes of the instruments, the patches of yellow light thrown by the green-shaded stand-lamps on the smooth, varnished bellies of the 'cellos and the bass viols in the rear, the restless, wind-tossed forest of fiddle necks and bows; I recalled how, in the first orchestra I had

---

10. **"The Flying Dutchman"**: Wagner's early opera, inspired by the legend of a ship that sails the seas but can never find its way home, was first performed in 1843.
11. **granite Rameses in a museum**: Rameses, or Ramses, was the name of eleven different Egyptian pharaohs, most of whom were commemorated in statues that had been removed to various museums in the nineteenth century.

ever heard, those long bow strokes seemed to draw the soul out of me, as a conjuror's stick reels out paper ribbon from a hat.

The first number was the Tannhäuser overture.[12] When the violins drew out the first strain of the Pilgrims' chorus, my Aunt Georgiana clutched my coat-sleeve. Then it was that I first realized that for her this singing of basses and stinging frenzy of lighter strings broke a silence of thirty years, the inconceivable silence of the plains. With the battle between the two motifs, with the bitter frenzy of the Venusberg theme[13] and its ripping of strings, came to me an overwhelming sense of the waste and wear we are so powerless to combat. I saw again the tall, naked house on the prairie, black and grim as a wooden fortress; the black pond where I had learned to swim, the rain-gullied clay about the naked house; the four dwarf ash-seedlings on which the dishcloths were always hung to dry before the kitchen door. The world there is the flat world of the ancients; to the east, a cornfield that stretched to daybreak; to the west, a corral that stretched to sunset; between, the sordid conquests of peace, more merciless than those of war.

The overture closed. My aunt released my coat-sleeve, but she said nothing. She sat staring at the orchestra through a dullness of thirty years, through the films made, little by little, by each of the three hundred and sixty-five days in every one of them. What, I wondered, did she get from it? She had been a good pianist in her day, I knew, and her musical education had been broader than that of most music-teachers of a quarter of a century ago. She had often told me of Mozart's operas and Meyerbeer's, and I could remember hearing her sing, years ago, certain melodies of Verdi's.[14] When I had fallen ill with a fever she used to sit by my cot in the evening, while the cool night wind blew in through the faded mosquito-netting tacked over the window, and I lay watching a bright star that burned red above the cornfield, and sing "Home to our mountains, oh, let us return!"[15] in a way fit to break the heart of a Vermont boy near dead of homesickness already.

I watched her closely through the prelude to Tristan and Isolde,[16] trying vainly to conjecture what that warfare of motifs, that seething turmoil of strings and winds, might mean to her. Had this music any message for her? Did or did not a new planet swim into her ken? Wagner had been a sealed book to Americans before the sixties. Had she anything left with which to comprehend this glory that had flashed around the world since she had gone from it? I was in a fever of curiosity, but Aunt Georgiana sat silent upon

---

12. **Tannhäuser overture:** The musical introduction to Wagner's opera *Tannhäuser* (1843-44).

13. **Venusberg theme:** The bacchanalian music associated in the opera with Venusberg, a mountain in Germany that according to Teutonic legend housed the court of Venus, the goddess of love.

14. **Mozart's operas . . . melodies of Verdi's:** The most famous operas of Wolfgang Amadeus Mozart (1756-1791) are *The Marriage of Figaro* (1786), *Don Giovanni* (1787), *Cosi fan tutte* (1790), and *The Magic Flute* (1791). The operas of the Italian composer Giuseppe Verdi (1813-1901) were admired for their beautiful and numerous melodies, many of which were widely known and sung.

15. **"Home to our mountains, oh, let us return!":** A translation of "Ai nostri monti ritoneremo" (Italian), a poignant and touching aria sung by Azucena to her son Manrico, both imprisoned, near the end of Verdi's popular opera *Il Trovatore* (1853).

16. **Tristan and Isolde:** This medieval romance was the basis for Wagner's opera, first performed in 1856.

her peak in Darien.[17] She preserved this utter immobility throughout the numbers from the "Flying Dutchman," though her fingers worked mechanically upon her black dress, as though of themselves they were recalling the piano score they had once played. Poor old hands! They were stretched and pulled and twisted into mere tentacles to hold, and lift, and knead with; the palms unduly swollen, the fingers bent and knotted, on one of them a thin worn band that had once been a wedding-ring. As I pressed and gently quieted one of those groping hands, I remembered, with quivering eyelids, their services for me in other days.

Soon after the tenor began the Prize Song,[18] I heard a quick-drawn breath, and turned to my aunt. Her eyes were closed, but the tears were glistening on her cheeks, and I think in a moment more they were in my eyes as well. It never really dies, then, the soul? It withers to the outward eye only, like that strange moss which can lie on a dusty shelf half a century and yet, if placed in water, grows green again. My aunt wept gently throughout the development and elaboration of the melody.

During the intermission before the second half of the concert, I questioned my aunt and found that the Prize Song was not new to her. Some years before there had drifted to the farm in Red Willow County a young German, a tramp cow-puncher, who had sung in the chorus at Baireuth[19] when he was a boy, along with the other peasant boys and girls. Of a Sunday morning he used to sit on his blue gingham-sheeted bed in the hands' bedroom, which opened off the kitchen, cleaning the leather of his boots and saddle, and singing the Prize Song, while my aunt went about her work in the kitchen. She had hovered about him until she had prevailed upon him to join the country church, though his sole fitness for this step, so far as I could gather, lay in his boyish face and his possession of this divine melody. Shortly afterward he had gone to town on the Fourth of July, been drunk for several days, lost his money at a faro-table,[20] ridden a saddled Texas steer on a bet, and disappeared with a fractured collar-bone.

"Well, we have come to better things than the old Trovatore[21] at any rate, Aunt Georgie?" I queried, with well-meant jocularity.

Her lip quivered and she hastily put her handkerchief up to her mouth. From behind it she murmured, "And you've been hearing this ever since you left me, Clark?" Her question was the gentlest and saddest of reproaches.

"But do you get it, Aunt Georgiana, the astonishing structure of it all?" I persisted.

"Who could?" she said, absently; "why should one?"

---

17. **peak in Darien:** The Darien Peak is a thin peninsula of land connecting Central and South America. From this vantage point, the Spanish explorer and conquistador Vasco Núñez de Balboa (1475-1519) is said to have simultaneously viewed the Atlantic and Pacific oceans.
18. **Prize Song:** A song from *Die Meistersinger von Nürnberg* (1868), one of Wagner's most popular operas.
19. **Baireuth:** A town in Germany, usually spelled *Bayreuth*, where an opera house was especially constructed for the performance of Wagner's operas and where the monthlong Richard Wagner Festival was inaugurated in 1876.
20. **faro-table:** Faro is a card game in which players bet on the order in which the cards will appear.
21. **better things than the old Trovatore:** Admirers of Wagner's complex and demanding music often dismissed Verdi's operas, especially enormously popular ones like *Il Trovatore* (see note 15).

The second half of the programme consisted of four numbers from the Ring.[22] This was followed by the forest music from Siegfried, and the programme closed with Siegfried's funeral march. My aunt wept quietly, but almost continuously. I was perplexed as to what measure of musical comprehension was left to her, to her who had heard nothing for so many years but the singing of gospel hymns in Methodist services at the square frame school-house on Section Thirteen. I was unable to gauge how much of it had been dissolved in soapsuds, or worked into bread, or milked into the bottom of a pail.

The deluge of sound poured on and on; I never knew what she found in the shining current of it; I never knew how far it bore her, or past what happy islands, or under what skies. From the trembling of her face I could well believe that the Siegfried march, at least, carried her out where the myriad graves are, out into the gray, burying-grounds of the sea; or into some world of death vaster yet, where, from the beginning of the world, hope has lain down with hope, and dream with dream and, renouncing, slept.

The concert was over; the people filed out of the hall chattering and laughing, glad to relax and find the living level again, but my kinswoman made no effort to rise. I spoke gently to her. She burst into tears and sobbed pleadingly, "I don't want to go, Clark, I don't want to go!"

I understood. For her, just outside the door of the concert-hall, lay the black pond with the cattle-tracked bluffs, the tall, unpainted house, naked as a tower, with weather-curled boards; the crook-backed ash-seedlings where the dishcloths hung to dry, the gaunt, moulting turkeys picking up refuse about the kitchen door.

[1904]

---

22. **the Ring:** Wagner's *Der Ring des Nibelungen* is a sequence of four operas – *Das Rheingold, Die Walküre, Siegfried*, and *Götterdämmerung* – which premiered in 1876. As indicated, the program concludes with two scenes from *Siegfried*, both of them among Wagner's most celebrated compositions: the delicate "Forest Murmurs" from act 2 and the powerful "Funeral March."

Writing "American" Lives

IN 1782, J. HECTOR ST. JOHN DE CRÈVECOEUR, a French immigrant who had settled in New York before returning to Europe during the Revolutionary War, published a series of essays about life in the British colonies in North America, *Letters from an American Farmer.* The book was an immediate success in England, France, and the newly constituted United States, where an expanded version appeared in 1884. In one of its most famous passages, Crèvecoeur describes the process by which people from different backgrounds and countries were transformed by their experiences in the colonies — the "great American asylum" — and asks, "What then is the American?" In America, Crèvecoeur suggests, "individuals of all nations are melted into a new race of men, whose labors and posterity will one day cause great changes in the world."

◀ Alfred Stieglitz, *The Steerage* (1907)

Often thought to capture the drama of poor immigrants bound for America in steerage, the lowest and least-costly levels of ships, Stieglitz actually took this famous photograph aboard a ship sailing to Europe. By some estimates, more than 15 percent of immigrants returned to their homelands, many of them disillusioned by the harsh conditions of life in the United States.

The Melting Pot

By offering an image of the melting-pot metaphor, the cover design of this program for Israel Zangwill's popular play perhaps inadvertently suggests how painful the process of assimilation might be for immigrants in the United States.

Crèvecoeur was among the first to develop the idea of America as what would come to be called the "melting pot." That metaphor gained enormous cultural currency through a popular play, *The Melting Pot* (1908), by Israel Zangwill, the London-born son of eastern European immigrants who frequently wrote about Jewish immigrant life in England and the United States. In the play, which opened to great acclaim in Washington, D.C., Zangwill depicted the life of members of a Jewish family who escaped discrimination and growing violence against Jews in czarist Russia and came to America, where they achieved success through hard work and assimilation. "America is God's Crucible," Zangwill exclaimed, "the great Melting-Pot where all the races of Europe are melting and reforming!" The idea that immigrants should be reformed through assimilation into American ways was widely shared in the United States. President Theodore Roosevelt, who viewed hyphenations such as *Polish-American* as a form of "moral treason," is reported to have shouted, "That's a great play!" at the end of a performance of *The Melting Pot*.

Even at the time, however, some questioned the melting-pot ideal. In "Trans-National America" (1916), written during World War I, the social critic Randolph Bourne ironically observed:

No reverberatory effect of the great war has caused American public opinion more solicitude than the failure of the "melting-pot." . . . We have had to listen to publicists who express themselves as stunned by the evidence of vigorous nationalistic movements in this country among Germans, Scandinavians,

Bohemians, and Poles, while in the same breath they insist that the alien shall be forcibly assimilated to that Anglo-Saxon tradition which they unquestioningly label "American."

Challenging that narrow definition of *American*, Bourne encouraged Americans to pursue a "higher ideal" than the melting pot, which he believed would produce a culture "washed out into a tasteless, colorless fluid of uniformity." In contrast to those who viewed such assimilation as crucial to the process of Americanization, Bourne affirmed that "the failure of the melting-pot, far from closing the great American democratic experiment, means that it has only just begun."

As the selections in the following section illustrate, a diverse range of writers engaged the questions Bourne raised about what it meant to be an American, as well as about the development of culture and society in the United States. José Martí, an immigrant from Cuba who had been exiled from his native island because of his revolutionary activities against the Spanish government there, challenged the idea that the United States represented "America" and held exclusive claim to the term *Americans*. In his "Impressions of America," a series of essays he wrote shortly after his arrival in New York City in 1880, and in his later articles for Spanish-language newspapers throughout Latin America, Martí explored every aspect of society and culture in the United States. Committed to the struggle for independence in Cuba, Martí was alarmed by the desire of many in the United States to take possession of the Spanish colony and to exert economic and political control throughout the Americas. He was also concerned about the social and cultural consequences of American imperialism, since he recognized that the United States had little knowledge of or respect for the indigenous traditions of its neighbors in Latin America. Indeed, just as the melting-pot metaphor implied that the Anglo-American was the only model of the American, Martí feared that what he described as "Anglo-Saxon America" would arrogantly impose a similar national model on the diverse nations of the Americas.

> *"The failure of the melting-pot, far from closing the great American democratic experiment, means that it has only just begun."*

The Anglo-American conception of the melting pot posed an even more direct and immediate threat to the indigenous traditions of Native Americans. Forced onto reservations, members of Native American groups struggled to retain their traditions and ways of life in a country in which most white people were accustomed to thinking of the Indians as "savages" who needed to be "civilized" before they could become "Americans." Many Native American children were consequently sent to "assimilation schools" in the East. Zitkala-Ša, who was born on the Pine Ridge Reservation in present-day South Dakota, describes that harsh process of reeducation and forced assimilation in "The School Days of an Indian Girl" (1900), one of a series of autobiographical sketches she published in the

Carlisle Indian Industrial School

This is a photograph taken in 1892 of the student body assembled on the grounds of the best known of the assimilation schools for Indian children, founded in Carlisle, Pennsylvania, in 1879. Students were required to convert to Christianity, speak only English, and wear uniforms at the school, the motto of which was "Kill the Indian, save the man."

Atlantic Monthly in 1900. Zitkala-Ša consequently found herself torn between two worlds, the indigenous culture of her birth and the Anglo-American culture in which she was educated. But she used her literacy in English to plead the Indian cause and to preserve Native American traditions, through both short stories and the Sioux tales she collected in *Old Indian Legends* (1902). Zitkala-Ša later became an activist for Indian rights, including the right of citizenship, which Native Americans finally gained in 1924.

African Americans also struggled for equal rights and recognition as Americans. In the face of pervasive racial discrimination and hatred, especially in the South, the former slave and influential educator Booker T. Washington wrote *Up from Slavery* (1901), an autobiography in which he offered his own life as an example to white America of the capacities of African Americans. But he also argued that African Americans should seek white support for their economic and educational initiatives rather than agitate for social equality and full political rights. Another prominent African American educator, W. E. B. Du Bois, sharply criticized Washington's

Founders of the Niagara Movement

In July 1905, a group of twenty-nine African American businessmen and intellectual leaders—including W. E. B. Du Bois (second row, second from the right)—held a series of secret meetings near Niagara Falls. They met on the Canadian side of the falls, since no hotel on the American side would allow them to register. Rejecting Booker T. Washington's policy of accommodation, they formed the Niagara Movement, named after the location and because they hoped to unleash a "mighty current" of protest against racial discrimination and segregation in the United States. In his address to the first public meeting of the organization, which included women as well as men, Du Bois in 1906 declared, "The battle we wage is not for ourselves alone but for all true Americans."

conciliatory approach to white America. In *The Souls of Black Folk* (1903), Du Bois asserted that African Americans must strive for all of the rights proclaimed in the Declaration of Independence. Pointing out that a slave ship arrived in Jamestown, Virginia, in 1619, a year before the *Mayflower* landed at Plymouth Rock, Du Bois also challenged the foundational myth of white America: "Your country? How came it yours? Before the Pilgrims landed we were here. . . . Would America have been America without her Negro people?"

> *"Your country? How came it yours? Before the Pilgrims landed we were here. . . . Would America have been America without her Negro people?"*

Four years after Du Bois published his influential book, Henry Adams privately printed his autobiography, *The Education of Henry Adams*. The two writers had several things in common. Both were born and raised in Massachusetts, and both were Harvard-educated historians who produced major works in the field. But they approached American history from radically different backgrounds and perspectives. Determined to explore episodes in the nation's past that many white Americans were eager to forget, Du Bois wrote histories of the slave trade to the United States and of Reconstruction. Adams, the descendant of wealthy and distinguished New England families and of two presidents — his great-grandfather, John Adams, and his grandfather, John Quincy Adams — wrote a nine-volume history of the presidential administrations of Jefferson and Madison. Although Du Bois and Adams apparently never met, both attended the Paris Universal Exposition in 1900. Du Bois won a gold medal for the exhibit he organized on the history, condition, and achievements of African Americans, while Adams spent much of his time at the exposition in fascinated study and contemplation of the powerful, electricity-generating machines in the Hall of Dynamos.

The differing backgrounds and experiences of the two writers shaped their conceptions of American society and of the challenges facing the country at the turn of the century. In *The Souls of Black Folk*, Du Bois famously and prophetically proclaimed, "The problem of the Twentieth Century is the problem of the color line." For the alienated Adams, a man of an earlier era who had gloomily witnessed the transformation of the United States into an industrial nation dominated by the forces of a rapacious capitalism, the central problem of the new age was the blind worship of machines. The result in the twentieth century, he predicted, would be a world in which accelerating advances in science and technology would outstrip the ability of human beings to control the mechanical and dehumanizing forces they had unleashed.

Despite such forebodings and the sobering realities of the new urban and industrial order, many continued to view America as a land of freedom and opportunity, symbolized by the Statue of Liberty. Certainly, that hopeful vision was affirmed by the final writer represented in this section, Mary Antin, whose family immigrated to the United States along with many other

The Promised Land

The cover design of Antin's autobiography used the Statue of Liberty as a symbol of the country's welcome of immigrants to the "promised land" of America.

Jews fleeing persecution and discriminatory laws in czarist Russia. Published in the aftermath of the early performances of *The Melting Pot* and with the personal encouragement of Israel Zangwill, Antin's best-selling autobiography, *The Promised Land* (1912), offered a reassuring message about the efficacy and value of assimilation. "The ghost of the *Mayflower* pilots every immigrant ship," she declared, "and Ellis Island is another name for Plymouth Rock." But some Anglo-Americans firmly rejected her analogy between the small band of Pilgrims at Plymouth and the millions of immigrants passing through the portal of Ellis Island, which had opened in New York harbor in 1892. Conservative critics also strongly objected to Antin's use of the phrase "our forefathers" for the Pilgrims and heroes of the American Revolution, questioning her description of herself as an American. Moreover, even many of those who sought to redefine *American* in order to include white European immigrants were reluctant to extend the term to immigrants from Africa, Asia, and Latin America, or to Native Americans and African Americans. Indeed, by the early twentieth century the question Crèvecoeur had so confidently answered more than a century earlier – "What then is the American?" – had become a deeply contested question of *who* is an American.

> *"The ghost of the* Mayflower *pilots every immigrant ship, . . . and Ellis Island is another name for Plymouth Rock."*

José Martí

[1853-1895]

Don José Julián Martí y Peréz was born in Havana, Cuba, on January 28, 1853. He was the eldest of eight children born to Mariano Martí y Navarro, a Spaniard serving in an artillery unit of the Spanish army, and Leonor Pérez Cabrera, from Tenerife in the Canary Islands. In 1857, the family moved back to Spain but returned to Havana in 1859. Martí regarded Cuba as his homeland, and its long struggle for independence from Spain strongly shaped his life and writings. Although his family was very poor, his mother strongly believed in education, and Martí attended school in Havana. Encouraged by one of his teachers, he began to write at an early age, publishing his first poem in a local newspaper in 1868. That year also marked the beginning of the first armed revolt against Spanish rule in Cuba, a protracted conflict that came to be known as the Ten Years' War. Martí soon began to write political articles for a friend's newspaper and then established his own paper, *La Patria Libre* ("The Free Homeland"). In the only issue of the newspaper, which appeared five days before his sixteenth birthday, Martí published a poetic allegory celebrating the heroism of the Cuban rebels. Still in high school, he was arrested on charges of disloyalty to Spain and sentenced to six years of hard labor in a military prison. After six months of punishing work in the stone quarries of

José Martí

This photograph was taken in Brooklyn around 1885, several years after Martí's arrival in the United States.

Havana, where he suffered a severe leg injury, he was granted clemency and deported to Spain.

Martí lived in exile for virtually the rest of his life. Soon after he arrived in Spain, he published *El Presidio Político en Cuba* ("The Political Prison in Cuba"), a tract in which he appealed directly to the Spanish people to end the atrocities committed in their name in Cuba. Martí continued his studies, first in Madrid and then at the University of Zaragoza, from which he graduated in 1874 with degrees in law, philosophy, and letters. Leaving Spain, he toured several European cities before rejoining his family, which had moved to Mexico. There, he taught high school and became known as a journalist and playwright. In 1875, he became engaged to Carmen Zayas-Bazán, a Cuban living in Mexico. They were married in 1877, after Martí had accepted a position as a professor of French, English, Italian, and German literature at a university in Guatemala. In late 1878, the couple returned to Cuba, where their son was born and Martí taught in a private school in Havana. The following year, he was arrested for conspiring against the Spanish government of Cuba and deported, without his family, to Spain. In 1880, he made his way to New York City. He was briefly joined by his wife, but she disliked the city and soon returned with their son to Cuba. Martí lived in New York for most of the next fifteen years, teaching, writing for English- and Spanish-language periodicals, and editing *La América*, through which Martí hoped, as he put it, "to explain the mind of the United States of the North to those who are in spirit, and will someday be in form, the United States of South America." He also wrote articles on virtually every aspect of life in the United States as a foreign correspondent for newspapers in Venezuela, Argentina, Uruguay, Honduras, and Mexico. During the same period, Martí published a novel and two innovative and widely acclaimed volumes of poetry, *Ismaelillo* ("Little Ishmael," 1882), inspired by his absent son, and *Versos sensillos* ("Simple Verses," 1891).

> *He was a man of genius, of imagination, of hope, and of courage.*
> —Charles A. Dana

Martí's achievements in prose and verse placed him among the leading writers in the Spanish language, but he ultimately gave up many of his literary pursuits to devote himself to the cause of Cuban independence. In 1891, he gave speeches in Florida in an effort to generate support among Cubans living there for a revolt against Spanish rule in Cuba. As Martí recognized, genuine independence also meant resisting the efforts of the United States to exert economic and political control over Cuba. In one of the many notebooks he kept throughout this life, he affirmed that "Cuba must be free—of Spain and of the United States." In his most famous essay, "Nuestra América" ("Our America," 1891), he passionately affirmed the need for "Anglo-Saxon America" to understand the nature and diversity of Latin American countries, which must be allowed to develop their own social, political, and cultural identities, free of the domination of the United States. Fearing that the United States would annex Cuba before it could gain independence, as some American politicians desired, in 1892 Martí organized and was elected *delgado* (leader) of the Cuban Revolutionary Party. He also established a newspaper that became the official organ of the party, *Patria*. Through his articles and speeches, Martí tirelessly promoted and raised money for a war of independence, which began in Cuba early in 1895. "I called for this war, and my responsibility does not end with its onset, but begins," Martí wrote in March 1895. The following month, he and a small group of exiles landed in Cuba, where Martí was killed in a skirmish with Spanish troops on March 25, 1895.

Martí was later hailed as the father of Cuban independence, but genuine independence proved to be elusive in Cuba. The brutal efforts of the Spanish government to suppress the rebellion there inflamed public opinion in the United States and helped spark the Spanish-American War of 1898. In the treaty that ended the war, Spain ceded control of Guam, the Philippines, Puerto Rico, and Cuba to the United States. Instead of allowing Martí's revolutionary government to take control of Cuba, the United States established a military government and its troops occupied the island until 1901. In order to end the occupation and gain independence, Cuban leaders had to agree to incorporate provisions into Cuba's constitution that made the new republic a virtual colony of the United States. With the exception of a permanent lease of the Guantanamo Bay Naval Base, which the United States has steadily declined to yield, most of those provisions were abrogated in 1934 at the order of President Franklin Delano Roosevelt as part of his "Good Neighbor Policy." In 1965, on the seventieth anniversary of Martí's death in battle, a statue honoring him was placed in Central Park in New York City, fittingly at the head of the Avenue of the Americas.

bedfordstmartins.com/ americanlit for research links on Martí

Reading Martí's "Impressions of America."   Soon after he arrived in the United States in January 1880, Martí wrote numerous essays for the *Hour*, a weekly literary magazine established by Charles A. Dana, the editor of the influential daily newspaper the *New York Sun*. Most of the essays were originally written in French, but Martí wrote a series of essays, "Impressions of America," in English. All of the essays in the series carried the byline "By a Very Fresh Spaniard," possibly to exploit the popularity of writings by European visitors about life in the United States. At the same time, the Cuban-born Martí was "fresh" from Spain, where he had been deported from Cuba in 1879, as well as "fresh," or youthful and inexperienced, in the United States. Whatever the reason for the byline, Martí used his position as a recent arrival in New York City to comment satirically on both the United States and Spain. Certainly, he displayed considerable knowledge of American culture, even alluding to popular American writers such as Mark Twain and his newly published book, *A Tramp Abroad* (1880). "Impressions of America," in which Martí offered a critical perspective on life in the country to readers in the United States, anticipated many of his later journalistic writings, in which he reported on life and developments in the United States for newspapers throughout Latin America. Indeed, even as he expressed his admiration for certain aspects of life in the United States, Martí in his early "Impressions of America" called attention to its pervasive materialism, the gulf between wealth and poverty in the country, and the indifference to the kind of suffering he witnessed in the growing slums of New York City. The texts of the following essays, the first and third in the series, are taken from the first printing in the *Hour*, July 10 and October 23, 1880.

IMPRESSIONS OF AMERICA

I

I am, at last, in a country where every one looks like his own master. One can breathe freely, freedom being here the foundation, the shield, the essence of life. One can be proud of his species here. Every one works; every one reads. Only does every one feel in the same degree that they read and work? Man, as a strong creature—made to support on his shoulders the burden of misfortune, never bent, never tired, never dismaying—is unrivalled here. Are women, those beings that we, the Southern people,[1] like,—feeble and souple, tender and voluptuous,—as perfect, in their way, as men are to theirs? Activity, devoted to trade, is truly immense. I was never surprised in any country of the world I have visited. Here, I was surprised. As I arrived, in one of this summer-days, when the face of hasty business men are at the same moment fountains and volcanoes; when, bag in hand, the vest open, the neck-tye detached, I saw the diligent New Yorkers running up and down, buying here, selling there, transpiring, working, going ahead; when I remarked that no one stood quietly in the corners, no door was shut an instant, no man was quiet, I stopped myself, I looked respectfully on this people, and I said goodbye for ever to that lazy life and poetical inutility of our European countries. I remembered a sentence of an old Spaniard, a healthy countryman, father of thirty-six sons: "Only those who dig their bread, have a right to eat it; and, as if they dig most deeply, they will eat it whiter." But is this activity devoted in the same extent to the development of these high and noble anxieties of soul, that cannot be forgotten by a people who want to escape from unavoidable ruin, and strepitous definitive crumbling? When the days of poverty may arrive—what richness, if not that of spiritual strength and intellectual comfort, will help this people in its colossal misfortune? Material power, as that of Carthage,[2] if it rapidly increases, rapidly falls down. If this love of richness is not tempered and dignified by the ardent love of intellectual pleasures,—if kindness toward men, passion for all what is great, devotion to all what means sacrifice and glory, are not as developed as fervorous and absorbent passion for money, where shall they go? where shall they find sufficient cause to excuse this hard burden of life and feel relief to their sorrow? Life wants permanent roots; life is unpleasant without the comfort of intelligence, the pleasures of art and the internal gratification that the goodness of the soul and the exquisiteness of taste produce to us.

---

1. **Southern people:** That is, the inhabitants of southern, or Mediterranean, Europe, including Spain.
2. **Carthage:** A powerful and wealthy city on the coast of North Africa founded by the Phoenicians (c. 814 BCE) and destroyed by the Romans in 146 BCE.

I am deeply obliged to this country, where the friendless find always a friend and a kind hand is always found by those who look honestly for work. A good idea finds always here a suitable, soft, grateful ground. You must be intelligent; that is all. Give something useful. You will have all what you want. Doors are shut for those who are dull and lazy; life is sure to those who are faithful to the law of work. When I was a child, I read with admiration, – born as I am in a country where there is no field for individual activity, a series of biographies as those who are called here with a magnificent simplicity – *self-made men.* My childhood was not entirely gone out when I admired again, in British Honduras,[3] a wealthy Southern family brought by misfortune to painful scanti-ness, – and raising by their hands, in the thick *bossom* of forest, a clean, elegant, pros-perous sugar plantation. The father, an ancient governor of a powerful State, was the engineer; the charming mother, very simply dressed, with a perpetual smile on her lips, – the smile of those who are courageous enough to support human sufferings, – was the most skillful housekeeper I have ever seen. Hot cakes, fine pastry, fresh milk, sweet jelly – were always on hand. When she came to me, the noble face illuminated by the most pure look, the curled silver hair carefully dressed, a waiter with exquisite dishes in her wrinkled hands – the sweetest feelings filled my heart, and tears of pleasure came to my eyes. The sons helped the father in all kinds of labors; they ploughed the field – saw the sugar-cane, burn the woods, build a new "sweet home" – and as slightly dressed as miserable countrymen in those far forests do – very early in the morning, merrily sing-ing, they drove the oxen to the hardest work of the plantation. And they were elegant, gentle, learned young men. I will study a most original country at its birth – in the school; at its development – in the family; at its pleasures – in the theatre, in the clubs, in Fourteenth Street,[4] in large and small family party. I will go, in a brilliant Sun-day, walking down the fashionable Fifth Avenue, to the crowded church to hear a preacher – the word of peace – speaking about politics or the field of war. I will see many nonsenses, many high deeds; the politicians, who save the country, when they could – without any effort go back to the days of arrogant militarism, violation of the public will, corruption of the political morality; I will see benevolent faces of men, defi-ant faces of women, the most capricious and uncommendable fancies, all the greatness of freedom and all the miseries of prejudices; here, a powerful originality, there a vulgar imitation of transatlantic extravagances. Liberty in politics, in customs, in enterprises; humble slavery in taste. Frenchmen give the sacred word; great names, and not great works are looked for. As there is not a fixed mind on art, the most striking is the most loved. There is no taste for the sweet beauty of Hélène or Galaethea[5] – the taste being all devoted to old imperfect works of China and Japan. If a scientific object would have been

---

3. **British Honduras:** Then a colony of Great Britain, now the country of Belize, in Central America. Martí vis-ited the colony as a child in 1863.
4. **Fourteenth Street:** In the late nineteenth century, the area south of Fourteenth Street was the poorest and most densely populated district in New York City.
5. **Hélène or Galaethea:** In Greek mythology, Hélène was the trusted friend of Venus, the goddess of love; Galatea (as it is also spelled) was a beautiful sea nymph whose lover was killed by the cyclops Polyphemus in a jealous rage.

intended by the owners of these *bibelots*,[6] it would be a matter of praise. But it is only for the censurable pleasure of indiscreetly holding foreign goods bought at a high price.

At a first glance what else can I tell? I have all my impressions vividly awaken. The crowds of Broadway; the quietness of the evenings; the character of men; the most curious and noteworthy character of women; the life in the hotel, that will never be understood for us; that young lady, physically and mentally stronger than the young man who courts her; that old gentleman, full of wisdom and capacity who writes in a sobrious[7] language for a hundred newspapers; this feverish life; this astonishing movement; this splendid sick people, in one side wonderfully extended, in other side – that of intellectual pleasures – childish and poor; this colossal giant, candorous and credulous; these women, too richly dressed to be happy; these men, too devoted to business of pocket, with remarkable neglectness of the spiritual business, – all is, at the same time, coming to my lips, and begging to be prepared in this brief account of my impressions.

Size and number: these are here the elements of greatness. Nothing is absolutely neglected, however. If the common people, increased every day by a thirsty foreign population, that must not be confounded with the true American people, shows that anxious desire for money, and fights frightfully in this way, – the true Americans preserve national greatness, constitutional rights, old and honorable names, from the vulgar storm of immigration, that brings in strength and possibilities of wealth, what they lack of intellectual height, and moral deepness. In the columns of a newspaper, in the page of a magazine, in the familiar chit-chat, the most pure feelings, noble aspirations, and generous ideas bravely fight for the rapid improvement of the country, in the sense of moral development.

It will be reached. It has not yet been reached, because many strangers bring here their odiums, their wounds, their moral ulcers. What a terrible enemy the desperate want of money is for the achievement of virtues! How great a nation must be, to conduct in a quiet way, these bands of wolves, hungry and thirsty, these excrescences of old poor countries, ferocious or unuseful there, – and here, under the influence of work, good, kind and tame!

And, for the *mot de la fin*,[8] let me tell you what it happened to me, as I came, a week ago, from Cape May,[9] a charming watering-place, to Philadelphia. The train near to the station jumped off the tracks; the car where I was, fell side-way. The accident was without consequence; but, as everybody was compelled by the shaking and pulling of the car to abandon violently their seats, the moment was a solemn one. Women became deadly pale. Men forgot women, looking for their own salvation. I thought, first, what must occur to a man under such a case, and, in the same instant, I saw rolling a poor eighty years' woman on the floor. I ran to her, offering her my hands. The old lady, very elegant indeed, notwithstanding her large amount of years, looked at me gratefully, tended her

---

6. *bibelots*: Rare objects or curios (French).
7. sobrious: This is probably a mistake or a typographical error, though Martí may have coined a term combining the words *sober* and *serious*.
8. *mot de la fin*: Final word or line (French).
9. Cape May: A vacation resort on the southern shore of New Jersey.

hands toward me; – but, as she touched the extreme of my fingers with their own, she told me, with expressive frightened grimaces:

"By the hands, no! Go away! Go away!"

Was she an old Puritan?

III

We read in Europe many wonderful statements about this country. The splendor of life, the abundance of money, the violent struggles for its possession, the golden currents, that dazzle and blind the vulgar people, the excellencies of instruction, the habit of working, the vision of that new country arising above the ruins of old nations, excite the attention of thoughtful men, who are anxiously looking for the definitive settlement of all the destructive forces that began during the last century to lay the foundations of a new era of mankind. This could be, and ought to be, the transcendental significance of the United States. But have the States the elements they are supposed to have? Can they do what they are expected to do? Do they impose their own character, or do they suffer the imposition of the character on others? Is America going to Europe or Europe coming to America? Error, both in politics and religion, has been worshipped in the Old World. Truth, liberty and dignity are supposed to have reached, at last, a sure hearth in the New World. We must ask for a response to these secrets of the home-life from the benches of the schoolrooms, the daily newspaper and conversation in society. Eloquent answers to all mystifications strike the observer as he goes through the streets. We must ask women for the natural end of their unextinguishable thirst for pleasure and amuse-ment. We must ask them if a being so exclusively devoted to the possession of silk dresses, dazzling diamonds and all kinds of costly fancies could afterwards carry into their homes those solid virtues, those sweet feelings, that kind resignation, that evan-gelic power of consolation which can only keep up a hearth shaken by misfortune, and inspire children with contempt for regular pleasures and the love of internal satisfac-tions that make men happy and strong, as they did Ismael,[10] against the days of poverty. We must ask a boy of fourteen what he knows and what he is taught. We must observe in the newspapers what they place before the public – news or ideas. We must look at what people read, what they applaud, and what they love. And, as these problems cannot be answered in a page, or understood and remembered by a new-comer, I have taken here and there some memoranda. Here, from my notebook, are some:

"What do I see? A girl seven years old goes to school. She talks with unusual ease to other girls; this miniature of a woman has all the self-control of a married woman; she looks and smiles at me as if she could know all the mysteries of mankind. Her ears are adorned with heavy earrings; her little fingers with rings. Where can this wonderful volubility come from? What will this little girl, so fond of jewelry at seven years, do for it at sixteen? Slavery would be better than this kind of liberty; ignorance would be better than this dangerous science."

---

10. **Ismael:** Usually spelled *Ishmael*, the son of Abraham and his wife's maid Hagar. Ishmael and his mother were driven away after the birth of Isaac, the son of Abraham and his wife, Sarah (Genesis 16:12).

"I went down town by the elevated railroad. As I travelled by this perilous but seductive way, I lost all hope of understanding Americans when I heard the name of a street, *'Chamber Street!' Cham, Chem, Chamber* or *Chember?* Is it *Houston, House* or *Hous?* Is it *Franklin, Frank* or *Frenk?* It is curious to observe that I can always understand an Englishman when he speaks to me; but among the Americans a word is a whisper; a sentence is an electric commotion. And if somebody asks me how can I know if a language that I so badly write, is badly spoken, I will tell frankly that it is very frequent that critics speak about what they absolutely ignore. There is, among the Americans, an excellent writer, the humorist Mark Twain – and has he not presented the gifted king of Bavaria, a poet, an enthusiast, a knight of old times, as a savage who obliges the singers of his theatre to play the same opera twice in a night, under the most terrible rain that could fall over the poor Bavarians?[11] He astonishes himself with the mastodontic composition of German words. All conversation is here in a single word: no breathe, no pause; not a distinct sound. We see that we are in the land of railroads. 'That's all' – 'did'nt' – 'won't' – 'ain't' – 'indeed' – 'Nice weather' – 'Very pleasant' – 'Coney Island'[12] – 'Excursion.' That is all that I can seize, when I listen with anxious attention, to the average American. When I listened to men and women of culture I have been able to appreciate how the correctness of Addison can be mingled with the acuteness of Swift, and the strength of Carlyle with the charming melody of Longfellow.[13]

"Among women, as their usual kindness inclines them to soften the asperity of their language, in order to be easily understood by the foreigner, the English tongue appears exceptionally harmonious. Everything could be pardoned to these indefatigable talkers, if they would speak in such a way, in order to employ the time that seems to be always short for them; but if – by a marvel – you can fathom the sense of those whirling words, you will remark that a vulgar subject is, commonly, too extensively developed."

"I love silence and quietness. Poor Chatterton[14] was right when he desperately longed for the delights of solitude. The pleasures of cities begin for me when the motives which make pleasure for others are fading away. The true day for my soul dawns in the midst of the night. As I took yesterday evening my usual nocturne walk, many pitiful sights made a painful impression upon me. One old man, dressed in that style which reveals at the same time that good fortune we have had and the bad times that begin for us, steps silently under a street-lamp. His eyes, fixed upon the passers by, were full of tears; his

---

11. **Mark Twain . . . Bavarians?:** In early 1880, Twain published *A Tramp Abroad,* a humorous account of his walking tour of central and southern Europe that includes his account of the king of Bavaria.

12. **Coney Island:** An amusement park in Brooklyn, on the southern shore of Long Island.

13. **Addison . . . Longfellow:** Martí describes the characteristics frequently associated with the writings of four well-known writers: the English essayist Joseph Addison (1672–1719); the English satirist Jonathan Swift (1667–1745), author of *Gulliver's Travels* (1726); Thomas Carlyle (1795–1881), the influential Scottish philosopher and man of letters; and the popular American poet Henry Wadsworth Longfellow (1807–1882).

14. **Chatterton:** The English poet Thomas Chatterton (1752–1770), a child prodigy who committed suicide at age seventeen, leaving behind a large number of his poems.

hand held a poor handkerchief. He could not articulate a single word. His sighs, not his words, begged for assistance. A little farther on, in Fourteenth Street, a periodic sound, as a distant lamentation, sprang from the shadow. A poor woman knelt on the sidewalk, as if looking for her grave, or for strength to lift on her shoulders the hoarse organ whose crank her dying hand was turning. I passed through Madison Square,[15] and I saw a hundred robust men, evidently suffering from the pangs of misery. They moved painfully, as if they wished to blot out of their minds their sorrowful thoughts — and were all lying down on the grass or seated on the benches, shoeless, foodless, concealing their anguish under their dilapidated hats."

[1880]

---

15. **Madison Square:** A six-acre public park in midtown Manhattan.

Zitkala-Ša
(Gertrude Simmons Bonnin)
[1876-1938]

Zitkala-Ša (Red Bird), the name she took during her teens in an assertion of her Indian identity, was born Gertrude Simmons on the Pine Ridge Reservation in present-day South Dakota in 1876. She was the daughter of a white man, about whom little is known, and a Dakota mother, Ellen Tate 'Iyohiwin (Reaches for the Wind) Simmons. In the aftermath of the battle of Little Bighorn in 1876, the Dakota, Lakota, and Nakota, who formed the large, loosely constructed group that came to be known collectively as the Sioux, were driven into increasingly smaller reservations to make room for the growing number of white homesteaders on the Great Plains. Like other Native American groups across the United States, the Sioux also struggled to preserve tribal cultures and traditions that the federal government was determined to eradicate. Many Native American children were consequently recruited by missionary schools designed to assimilate them into white culture. In 1884, Zitkala-Ša

Zitkala-Ša

For this portrait, one of a series of photographs Gertrude Käsebier took of her in 1898, Zitkala-Ša posed in a European-style dress but clutched an Indian basket to her chest, representing her mixed ancestry and her dual identity as both a white person and a Dakota (Sioux).

enrolled at White's Manual Institute, a Quaker boarding school in Wabash, Indiana. Unhappy at school and restless at home on the reservation, where Zitkala-Ša spent four years during the following decade, she graduated from White's in 1894. Despite her mother's wish that she return to the reservation, she then studied at Earlham College in Richmond, Indiana, from 1895 to 1897.

After leaving college, Zitkala-Ša devoted herself to teaching, writing, and music. Seeking to provide a more sympathetic education to Native American children, she accepted a teaching position at the Carlisle Indian Industrial School in western Pennsylvania. But the independent-minded young woman objected to the military-like discipline of the school. She was also sharply critical of its director, Richard Henry Pratt, who had earlier written to a group of Baptist ministers, "In Indian civilization I am a Baptist, because I believe in immersing the Indians in our civilization and when we get them under holding them there until they are thoroughly soaked." In response to such attitudes toward Native American life and culture, Zitkala-Ša wrote a series of autobiographical essays about her childhood, education, and experiences as a teacher, which appeared in the *Atlantic Monthly* in 1900. The magazine also published her essay "Why I Am a Pagan," a firm rejection of Christianity and the efforts of missionaries to convert Native Americans. Her short stories about the situation of Indians like herself, torn between the claims of their native traditions and enforced assimilation into white culture, soon began to appear in other prominent periodicals such as *Harper's Magazine* and *Everybody's Magazine*. An accomplished musician, Zitkala-Ša left the Carlisle School and studied at the Boston Conservatory of Music during 1900–01. In 1902, she published a collection of Sioux tales, *Old Indian Legends*, in an effort to use the literary tools of white culture to preserve the traditions of Native Americans. Later that year, she married Raymond T. Bonnin, a Yankton Sioux who worked for the Bureau of Indian Affairs, and moved with him to the Uintah and Ouray Reservation in Utah. The demands of family life and her work on the reservation left Zitkala-Ša little time for other pursuits, but with William Hanson she wrote an opera about Indian life, *The Sun Dance* (1913), yet another attempt to fuse the artistic forms of white culture with the traditions of Native Americans.

During the final twenty-five years of her life, Zitkala-Ša became a leading activist in the crusade for the rights of Native Americans. In 1916, she and her husband moved to Washington, D.C., where they continued to work for the reform of education policies concerning Native Americans and to gain for them the rights of citizenship and the protection of land rights. Zitkala-Ša was deeply involved in various organizations, including the Society of American Indians, editing and writing articles for its journal, the *American Indian Magazine*, from 1917 to 1920. She also published a collection of essays and sketches, *American Indian Stories* (1921). After going to Oklahoma to investigate the conditions on reservations there, Zitkala-Ša, Charles H. Fabens, and Matthew K. Sniffen wrote an exposé of the abuses, *Oklahoma's Poor Rich Indians: An Orgy of Graft and Exploitation of the Five*

bedfordstmartins.com/
americanlit *for research*
links on Zitkala-Ša

Civilized Tribes—Legalized Robbery (1924). That year, Native Americans were finally granted citizenship in the United States. In 1926, Zitkala-Ša founded the National Council of American Indians, serving as its president until her death in Washington, on January 26, 1938.

Reading Zitkala-Ša's "The School Days of an Indian Girl." Zitkala-Ša's first publications appeared in the prominent literary magazine the *Atlantic Monthly.* Because it was rapidly losing ground to popular monthlies like the *Century Magazine* and *Scribner's Magazine,* a new editor of the *Atlantic,* Bliss Perry, decided to introduce more current and controversial material. In addition to publishing political commentaries by Theodore Roosevelt and Woodrow Wilson, Perry featured new literary voices such as Mary Austin and Paul Laurence Dunbar. From January through March 1900, the *Atlantic* also published three autobiographical essays written by Zitkala-Ša. In the first, "Impressions of an Indian Childhood," she described her early life on the Pine Ridge Reservation in South Dakota, focusing most of her attention on the customs and legends of the Sioux. The second essay, reprinted below, was "The School Days of an Indian Girl," in which Zitkala-Ša offered a vivid account of her difficult experiences at White's Manual Labor Institute, the Quaker school she had attended for six years in Wabash, Indiana. The result of that "civilizing machine," as she described the school, was to make Zitkala-Ša "neither a wild Indian nor a tame one." In the third of the essays, "An Indian Teacher among Indians," she described her experiences at yet another "civilizing machine," the Carlisle Indian Industrial School in Pennsylvania. Zitkala-Ša later included all three of the autobiographical essays in her collection *American Indian Legends* (1921). The text is taken from the first printing in the *Atlantic Monthly,* February 1900.

THE SCHOOL DAYS OF AN INDIAN GIRL

I. The Land of Red Apples

There were eight in our party of bronzed children who were going East with the missionaries. Among us were three young braves, two tall girls, and we three little ones, Judéwin, Thowin, and I.

We had been very impatient to start on our journey to the Red Apple Country, which, we were told, lay a little beyond the great circular horizon of the Western prairie. Under a sky of rosy apples we dreamt of roaming as freely and happily as we had chased the cloud shadows on the Dakota plains. We had anticipated much pleasure from a ride on the iron horse, but the throngs of staring palefaces disturbed and troubled us.

On the train, fair women, with tottering babies on each arm, stopped their haste and scrutinized the children of absent mothers. Large men, with heavy bundles in their hands, halted near by, and riveted their glassy blue eyes upon us.

I sank deep into the corner of my seat, for I resented being watched. Directly in front of me, children who were no larger than I hung themselves upon the backs of their seats, with their bold white faces toward me. Sometimes they took their forefingers out of their mouths and pointed at my moccasined feet. Their mothers, instead of reproving such rude curiosity, looked closely at me, and attracted their children's further notice to my blanket. This embarrassed me, and kept me constantly on the verge of tears.

I sat perfectly still, with my eyes downcast, daring only now and then to shoot long glances around me. Chancing to turn to the window at my side, I was quite breathless upon seeing one familiar object. It was the telegraph pole which strode by at short paces. Very near my mother's dwelling, along the edge of a road thickly bordered with wild sunflowers, some poles like these had been planted by white men. Often I had stopped, on my way down the road, to hold my ear against the pole, and, hearing its low moaning, I used to wonder what the paleface had done to hurt it. Now I sat watching for each pole that glided by to be the last one.

In this way I had forgotten my uncomfortable surroundings, when I heard one of my comrades call out my name. I saw the missionary standing very near, tossing candies and gums into our midst. This amused us all, and we tried to see who could catch the most of the sweetmeats. The missionary's generous distribution of candies was impressed upon my memory by a disastrous result which followed. I had caught more than my share of candies and gums, and soon after our arrival at the school I had a chance to disgrace myself, which, I am ashamed to say, I did.

Though we rode several days inside of the iron horse, I do not recall a single thing about our luncheons.

It was night when we reached the school grounds. The lights from the windows of the large buildings fell upon some of the icicled trees that stood beneath them. We were led toward an open door, where the brightness of the lights within flooded out over the heads of the excited palefaces who blocked the way. My body trembled more from fear than from the snow I trod upon.

Entering the house, I stood close against the wall. The strong glaring light in the large whitewashed room dazzled my eyes. The noisy hurrying of hard shoes upon a bare wooden floor increased the whirring in my ears. My only safety seemed to be in keeping next to the wall. As I was wondering in which direction to escape from all this confusion, two warm hands grasped me firmly, and in the same moment I was tossed high in mid-air. A rosy-cheeked paleface woman caught me in her arms. I was both frightened and insulted by such trifling. I stared into her eyes, wishing her to let me stand on my own feet, but she jumped me up and down with increasing enthusiasm. My mother had never made a plaything of her wee daughter. Remembering this I began to cry aloud.

They misunderstood the cause of my tears, and placed me at a white table loaded with food. There our party were united again. As I did not hush my crying, one of the older ones whispered to me, "Wait until you are alone in the night."

It was very little I could swallow besides my sobs, that evening.

"Oh, I want my mother and my brother Dawee! I want to go to my aunt!" I pleaded; but the ears of the palefaces could not hear me.

From the table we were taken along an upward incline of wooden boxes, which I learned afterward to call a stairway. At the top was a quiet hall, dimly lighted. Many narrow beds were in one straight line down the entire length of the wall. In them lay sleeping brown faces, which peeped just out of the coverings. I was tucked into bed with one of the tall girls, because she talked to me in my mother tongue and seemed to soothe me.

I had arrived in the wonderful land of rosy skies, but I was not happy, as I had thought I should be. My long travel and the bewildering sights had exhausted me. I fell asleep, heaving deep, tired sobs. My tears were left to dry themselves in streaks, because neither my aunt nor my mother was near to wipe them away.

II. The Cutting of My Long Hair

The first day in the land of apples was a bitter-cold one; for the snow still covered the ground, and the trees were bare. A large bell rang for breakfast, its loud metallic voice crashing through the belfry overhead and into our sensitive ears. The annoying clatter of shoes on bare floors gave us no peace. The constant clash of harsh noises, with an undercurrent of many voices murmuring an unknown tongue, made a bedlam within which I was securely tied. And though my spirit tore itself in struggling for its lost freedom, all was useless.

A paleface woman, with white hair, came up after us. We were placed in a line of girls who were marching into the dining room. These were Indian girls, in stiff shoes and closely clinging dresses. The small girls wore sleeved aprons and shingled hair.[1] As I walked noiselessly in my soft moccasins, I felt like sinking to the floor, for my blanket had been stripped from my shoulders. I looked hard at the Indian girls, who seemed not to care that they were even more immodestly dressed than I, in their tightly fitting clothes. While we marched in, the boys entered at an opposite door. I watched for the three young braves who came in our party. I spied them in the rear ranks, looking as uncomfortable as I felt.

A small bell was tapped, and each of the pupils drew a chair from under the table. Supposing this act meant they were to be seated, I pulled out mine and at once slipped into it from one side. But when I turned my head, I saw that I was the only one seated, and all the rest at our table remained standing. Just as I began to rise, looking shyly around to see how chairs were to be used, a second bell was sounded. All were seated at last, and I had to crawl back into my chair again. I heard a man's voice at one end of the hall, and I looked around to see him. But all the others hung their heads over their plates. As I glanced at the long chain of tables, I caught the eyes of a paleface woman upon me. Immediately I dropped my eyes, wondering why I was so keenly watched by the

---

1. **shingled hair:** An early twentieth-century term for a woman's close-cropped haircut, which is layered in the back like a man's haircut.

strange woman. The man ceased his mutterings, and then a third bell was tapped. Every one picked up his knife and fork and began eating. I began crying instead, for by this time I was afraid to venture anything more.

But this eating by formula was not the hardest trial in that first day. Late in the morning, my friend Judéwin gave me a terrible warning. Judéwin knew a few words in English; and she had overheard the paleface woman talk about cutting our long, heavy hair. Our mothers had taught us that only unskilled warriors who were captured had their hair shingled by the enemy. Among our people, short hair was worn by mourners, and shingled hair by cowards!

We discussed our fate some moments, and when Judéwin said, "We have to submit, because they are strong," I rebelled.

"No, I will not submit! I will struggle first!" I answered.

I watched my chance, and when no one noticed I disappeared. I crept up the stairs as quietly as I could in my squeaking shoes, — my moccasins had been exchanged for shoes. Along the hall I passed, without knowing whither I was going. Turning aside to an open door, I found a large room with three white beds in it. The windows were covered with dark green curtains, which made the room very dim. Thankful that no one was there, I directed my steps toward the corner farthest from the door. On my hands and knees I crawled under the bed, and cuddled myself in the dark corner.

From my hiding place I peered out, shuddering with fear whenever I heard footsteps near by. Though in the hall loud voices were calling my name, and I knew that even Judéwin was searching for me, I did not open my mouth to answer. Then the steps were quickened and the voices became excited. The sounds came nearer and nearer. Women and girls entered the room. I held my breath, and watched them open closet doors and peep behind large trunks. Some one threw up the curtains, and the room was filled with sudden light. What caused them to stoop and look under the bed I do not know. I remember being dragged out, though I resisted by kicking and scratching wildly. In spite of myself, I was carried downstairs and tied fast in a chair.

I cried aloud, shaking my head all the while until I felt the cold blades of the scissors against my neck, and heard them gnaw off one of my thick braids. Then I lost my spirit. Since the day I was taken from my mother I had suffered extreme indignities. People had stared at me. I had been tossed about in the air like a wooden puppet. And now my long hair was shingled like a coward's! In my anguish I moaned for my mother, but no one came to comfort me. Not a soul reasoned quietly with me, as my own mother used to do; for now I was only one of many little animals driven by a herder.

III. The Snow Episode

A short time after our arrival we three Dakotas were playing in the snowdrifts. We were all still deaf to the English language, excepting Judéwin, who always heard such puzzling things. One morning we learned through her ears that we were forbidden to fall lengthwise in the snow, as we had been doing, to see our own impressions, However, before many hours we had forgotten the order, and were having great sport in the snow, when a shrill voice called us. Looking up, we saw an imperative hand beckoning us into the house. We shook the snow off ourselves, and started toward the woman as slowly as we dared.

Judéwin said: "Now the paleface is angry with us. She is going to punish us for falling into the snow. If she looks straight into your eyes and talks loudly, you must wait until she stops. Then, after a tiny pause, say, 'No.'" The rest of the way we practiced upon the little word "no."

As it happened, Thowin was summoned to judgment first. The door shut behind her with a click.

Judéwin and I stood silently listening at the keyhole. The paleface woman talked in very severe tones. Her words fell from her lips like crackling embers, and her inflection ran up like the small end of a switch. I understood her voice better than the things she was saying. I was certain we had made her very impatient with us. Judéwin heard enough of the words to realize all too late that she had taught us the wrong reply.

"Oh, poor Thowin!" she gasped, as she put both hands over her ears.

Just then I heard Thowin's tremulous answer, "No."

With an angry exclamation, the woman gave her a hard spanking. Then she stopped to say something. Judéwin said it was this: "Are you going to obey my word the next time?"

Thowin answered again with the only word at her command, "No."

This time the woman meant her blows to smart, for the poor frightened girl shrieked at the top of her voice. In the midst of the whipping the blows ceased abruptly, and the woman asked another question: "Are you going to fall in the snow again?"

Thowin gave her bad password another trial. We heard her say feebly, "No! No!"

With this the woman hid away her half-worn slipper, and led the child out, stroking her black shorn head. Perhaps it occurred to her that brute force is not the solution for such a problem. She did nothing to Judéwin nor to me. She only returned to us our unhappy comrade, and left us alone in the room.

During the first two or three seasons misunderstandings as ridiculous as this one of the snow episode frequently took place, bringing unjustifiable frights and punishments into our little lives.

Within a year I was able to express myself somewhat in broken English. As soon as I comprehended a part of what was said and done, a mischievous spirit of revenge possessed me. One day I was called in from my play for some misconduct. I had disregarded a rule which seemed to me very needlessly binding. I was sent into the kitchen to mash the turnips for dinner. It was noon, and steaming dishes were hastily carried into the dining room. I hated turnips, and their odor which came from the brown jar was offensive to me. With fire in my heart, I took the wooden tool that the paleface woman held out to me. I stood upon a step, and, grasping the handle with both hands, I bent in hot rage over the turnips. I worked my vengeance upon them. All were so busily occupied that no one noticed me. I saw that the turnips were in a pulp, and that further beating could not improve them; but the order was, "Mash these turnips," and mash them I would! I renewed my energy; and as I sent the masher into the bottom of the jar, I felt a satisfying sensation that the weight of my body had gone into it.

Just here a paleface woman came up to my table. As she looked into the jar, she shoved my hands roughly aside. I stood fearless and angry. She placed her red hands upon the rim of the jar. Then she gave one lift and a stride away from the table. But lo! the pulpy contents fell through the crumbled bottom to the floor! She spared me no scolding phrases that I had earned. I did not heed them. I felt triumphant in my revenge, though deep within me I was a wee bit sorry to have broken the jar.

As I sat eating my dinner, and saw that no turnips were served, I whooped in my heart for having once asserted the rebellion within me.

IV. The Devil

Among the legends the old warriors used to tell me were many stories of evil spirits. But I was taught to fear them no more than those who stalked about in material guise. I never knew there was an insolent chieftain among the bad spirits, who dared to array his forces against the Great Spirit, until I heard this white man's legend from a paleface woman.

Out of a large book she showed me a picture of the white man's devil. I looked in horror upon the strong claws that grew out of his fur-covered fingers. His feet were like his hands. Trailing at his heels was a scaly tail tipped with a serpent's open jaws. His face was a patchwork: he had bearded cheeks, like some I had seen palefaces wear; his nose was an eagle's bill, and his sharp-pointed ears were pricked up like those of a sly fox. Above them a pair of cow's horns curved upward. I trembled with awe, and my heart throbbed in my throat, as I looked at the king of evil spirits. Then I heard the paleface woman say that this terrible creature roamed loose in the world, and that little girls who disobeyed school regulations were to be tortured by him.

That night I dreamt about this evil divinity. Once again I seemed to be in my mother's cottage. An Indian woman had come to visit my mother. On opposite sides of the kitchen stove, which stood in the centre of the small house, my mother and her guest were seated in straight-backed chairs. I played with a train of empty spools hitched together on a string. It was night, and the wick burned feebly. Suddenly I heard some one turn our door-knob from without.

My mother and the woman hushed their talk, and both looked toward the door. It opened gradually. I waited behind the stove. The hinges squeaked as the door was slowly, very slowly pushed inward.

Then in rushed the devil! He was tall! He looked exactly like the picture I had seen of him in the white man's papers. He did not speak to my mother, because he did not know the Indian language, but his glittering yellow eyes were fastened upon me. He took long strides around the stove, passing behind the woman's chair. I threw down my spools, and ran to my mother. He did not fear her, but followed closely after me. Then I ran round and round the stove, crying aloud for help. But my mother and the woman seemed not to know my danger. They sat still, looking quietly upon the devil's chase after me. At last I grew dizzy. My head revolved as on a hidden pivot. My knees became numb, and doubled under my weight like a pair of knife blades without a spring. Beside my mother's chair I fell in a heap. Just as the devil stooped over me with outstretched claws my mother awoke from her quiet indifference, and lifted me on her lap. Whereupon the devil vanished, and I was awake.

On the following morning I took my revenge upon the devil. Stealing into the room where a wall of shelves was filled with books, I drew forth The Stories of the Bible. With a broken slate pencil I carried in my apron pocket, I began by scratching out his wicked eyes. A few moments later, when I was ready to leave the room, there was a ragged hole in the page where the picture of the devil had once been.

V. Iron Routine

A loud-clamoring bell awakened us at half past six in the cold winter mornings. From happy dreams of Western rolling lands and unlassoed freedom we tumbled out upon chilly bare floors back again into a paleface day. We had short time to jump into our shoes and clothes, and wet our eyes with icy water, before a small hand bell was vigorously rung for roll call.

There were too many drowsy children and too numerous orders for the day to waste a moment in any apology to nature for giving her children such a shock in the early morning. We rushed downstairs, bounding over two high steps at a time, to land in the assembly room.

A paleface woman, with a yellow-covered roll book open on her arm and a gnawed pencil in her hand, appeared at the door. Her small, tired face was coldly lighted with a pair of large gray eyes.

She stood still in a halo of authority, while over the rim of her spectacles her eyes pried nervously about the room. Having glanced at her long list of names and called out the first one, she tossed up her chin and peered through the crystals of her spectacles to make sure of the answer "Here."

Relentlessly her pencil black-marked our daily records if we were not present to respond to our names, and no chum of ours had done it successfully for us. No matter if a dull headache or the painful cough of slow consumption had delayed the absentee, there was only time enough to mark the tardiness. It was next to impossible to leave the iron routine after the civilizing machine had once begun its day's buzzing; and as it was inbred in me to suffer in silence rather than to appeal to the ears of one whose open eyes could not see my pain, I have many times trudged in the day's harness heavy-footed, like a dumb sick brute.

Once I lost a dear classmate. I remember well how she used to mope along at my side, until one morning she could not raise her head from her pillow. At her deathbed I stood weeping, as the paleface woman sat near her moistening the dry lips. Among the folds of the bedclothes I saw the open pages of the white man's Bible. The dying Indian girl talked disconnectedly of Jesus the Christ and the paleface who was cooling her swollen hands and feet.

I grew bitter, and censured the woman for cruel neglect of our physical ills. I despised the pencils that moved automatically, and the one teaspoon which dealt out, from a large bottle, healing to a row of variously ailing Indian children. I blamed the hard-working, well-meaning, ignorant woman who was inculcating in our hearts her superstitious ideas. Though I was sullen in all my little troubles, as soon as I felt better I was ready again to smile upon the cruel woman. Within a week I was again actively testing the chains which tightly bound my individuality like a mummy for burial.

The melancholy of those black days has left so long a shadow that it darkens the path of years that have since gone by. These sad memories rise above those of smoothly grinding school days. Perhaps my Indian nature is the moaning wind which stirs them now for their present record. But, however tempestuous this is within me, it comes out as the low voice of a curiously colored seashell, which is only for those ears that are bent with compassion to hear it.

VI. Four Strange Summers

After my first three years of school, I roamed again in the Western country through four strange summers.

During this time I seemed to hang in the heart of chaos, beyond the touch or voice of human aid. My brother, being almost ten years my senior, did not quite understand my feelings. My mother had never gone inside of a schoolhouse, and so she was not capable of comforting her daughter who could read and write. Even nature seemed to have no place for me. I was neither a wee girl nor a tall one; neither a wild Indian nor a tame one. This deplorable situation was the effect of my brief course in the East, and the unsatisfactory "teenth" in a girl's years.

It was under these trying conditions that, one bright afternoon, as I sat restless and unhappy in my mother's cabin, I caught the sound of the spirited step of my brother's pony on the road which passed by our dwelling. Soon I heard the wheels of a light buckboard, and Dawee's familiar "Ho!" to his pony. He alighted upon the bare ground in front of our house. Tying his pony to one of the projecting corner logs of the low-roofed cottage, he stepped upon the wooden doorstep.

I met him there with a hurried greeting, and, as I passed by, he looked a quiet "What?" into my eyes.

When he began talking with my mother, I slipped the rope from the pony's bridle. Seizing the reins and bracing my feet against the dashboard, I wheeled around in an instant. The pony was ever ready to try his speed. Looking backward, I saw Dawee waving his hand to me. I turned with the curve in the road and disappeared. I followed the winding road which crawled upward between the bases of little hillocks. Deep water-worn ditches ran parallel on either side. A strong wind blew against my cheeks and fluttered my sleeves. The pony reached the top of the highest hill, and began an even race on the level lands. There was nothing moving within that great circular horizon of the Dakota prairies save the tall grasses, over which the wind blew and rolled off in long, shadowy waves.

Within this vast wigwam of blue and green I rode reckless and insignificant. It satisfied my small consciousness to see the white foam fly from the pony's mouth.

Suddenly, out of the earth a coyote came forth at a swinging trot that was taking the cunning thief toward the hills and the village beyond. Upon the moment's impulse, I gave him a long chase and a wholesome fright. As I turned away to go back to the village, the wolf sank down upon his haunches for rest, for it was a hot summer day; and as I drove slowly homeward, I saw his sharp nose still pointed at me, until I vanished below the margin of the hilltops.

In a little while I came in sight of my mother's house. Dawee stood in the yard, laughing at an old warrior who was pointing his forefinger, and again waving his whole hand, toward the hills. With his blanket drawn over one shoulder, he talked and motioned excitedly. Dawee turned the old man by the shoulder and pointed me out to him.

"Oh han!" (Oh yes) the warrior muttered, and went his way. He had climbed the top of his favorite barren hill to survey the surrounding prairies, when he spied my chase after the coyote. His keen eyes recognized the pony and driver. At once uneasy for my safety, he had come running to my mother's cabin to give her warning. I did not appreciate his kindly interest, for there was an unrest gnawing at my heart.

As soon as he went away, I asked Dawee about something else.

"No, my baby sister, I cannot take you with me to the party to-night," he replied. Though I was not far from fifteen, and I felt that before long I should enjoy all the privileges of my tall cousin, Dawee persisted in calling me his baby sister.

That moonlight night, I cried in my mother's presence when I heard the jolly young people pass by our cottage. They were no more young braves in blankets and eagle plumes, nor Indian maids with prettily painted cheeks. They had gone three years to school in the East, and had become civilized. The young men wore the white man's coat and trousers, with bright neckties. The girls wore tight muslin dresses, with ribbons at neck and waist. At these gatherings they talked English. I could speak English almost as well as my brother, but I was not properly dressed to be taken along. I had no hat, no ribbons, and no close-fitting gown. Since my return from school I had thrown away my shoes, and wore again the soft moccasins.

While Dawee was busily preparing to go I controlled my tears. But when I heard him bounding away on his pony, I buried my face in my arms and cried hot tears.

My mother was troubled by my unhappiness. Coming to my side, she offered me the only printed matter we had in our home. It was an Indian Bible, given her some years ago by a missionary. She tried to console me. "Here, my child, are the white man's papers. Read a little from them," she said most piously.

I took it from her hand, for her sake; but my enraged spirit felt more like burning the book, which afforded me no help, and was a perfect delusion to my mother. I did not read it, but laid it unopened on the floor, where I sat on my feet. The dim yellow light of the braided muslin burning in a small vessel of oil flickered and sizzled in the awful silent storm which followed my rejection of the Bible.

Now my wrath against the fates consumed my tears before they reached my eyes. I sat stony, with a bowed head. My mother threw a shawl over her head and shoulders, and stepped out into the night.

After an uncertain solitude, I was suddenly aroused by a loud cry piercing the night. It was my mother's voice wailing among the barren hills which held the bones of buried warriors. She called aloud for her brothers' spirits to support her in her helpless misery. My fingers grew icy cold, as I realized that my unrestrained tears had betrayed my suffering to her, and she was grieving for me.

Before she returned, though I knew she was on her way, for she had ceased her weeping, I extinguished the light, and leaned my head on the window sill.

Many schemes of running away from my surroundings hovered about in my mind. A few more moons of such a turmoil drove me away to the Eastern school. I rode on the white man's iron steed, thinking it would bring me back to my mother in a few winters, when I should be grown tall, and there would be congenial friends awaiting me.

VII. Incurring My Mother's Displeasure

In the second journey to the East I had not come without some precautions. I had a secret interview with one of our best medicine men, and when I left his wigwam I carried securely in my sleeve a tiny bunch of magic roots. This possession assured me of friends wherever I should go. So absolutely did I believe in its charms that I wore it through all the school routine for more than a year. Then, before I lost my faith in the dead roots, I lost the little buckskin bag containing all my good luck.

At the close of this second term of three years I was the proud owner of my first diploma. The following autumn I ventured upon a college career against my mother's will.

I had written for her approval, but in her reply I found no encouragement. She called my notice to her neighbors' children, who had completed their education in three years. They had returned to their homes, and were then talking English with the frontier settlers. Her few words hinted that I had better give up my slow attempt to learn the white man's ways, and be content to roam over the prairies and find my living upon wild roots. I silenced her by deliberate disobedience.

Thus, homeless and heavy-hearted, I began anew my life among strangers.

As I hid myself in my little room in the college dormitory, away from the scornful and yet curious eyes of the students, I pined for sympathy. Often I wept in secret, wishing I had gone West, to be nourished by my mother's love, instead of remaining among a cold race whose hearts were frozen hard with prejudice.

During the fall and winter seasons I scarcely had a real friend, though by that time several of my classmates were courteous to me at a safe distance.

My mother had not yet forgiven my rudeness to her, and I had no moment for letter-writing. By daylight and lamplight, I spun with reeds and thistles, until my hands were tired from their weaving, the magic design which promised me the white man's respect.

At length, in the spring term, I entered an oratorical contest among the various classes. As the day of competition approached, it did not seem possible that the event was so near at hand, but it came. In the chapel the classes assembled together, with their invited guests. The high platform was carpeted, and gayly festooned with college colors. A bright white light illumined the room, and outlined clearly the great polished beams that arched the domed ceiling. The assembled crowds filled the air with pulsating murmurs. When the hour for speaking arrived all were hushed. But on the wall the old clock which pointed out the trying moment ticked calmly on.

One after another I saw and heard the orators. Still, I could not realize that they longed for the favorable decision of the judges as much as I did. Each contestant received a loud burst of applause, and some were cheered heartily. Too soon my turn came, and I paused a moment behind the curtains for a deep breath. After my concluding words, I heard the same applause that the others had called out.

Upon my retreating steps, I was astounded to receive from my fellow students a large bouquet of roses tied with flowing ribbons. With the lovely flowers I fled from the stage. This friendly token was a rebuke to me for the hard feelings I had borne them.

Later, the decision of the judges awarded me the first place. Then there was a mad uproar in the hall, where my classmates sang and shouted my name at the top of their lungs; and the disappointed students howled and brayed in fearfully dissonant tin trumpets. In this excitement, happy students rushed forward to offer their congratulations. And I could not conceal a smile when they wished to escort me in a procession to the students' parlor, where all were going to calm themselves. Thanking them for the kind spirit which prompted them to make such a proposition, I walked alone with the night to my own little room.

A few weeks afterward, I appeared as the college representative in another contest. This time the competition was among orators from different colleges in our state. It was held at the state capital, in one of the largest opera houses.

Here again was a strong prejudice against my people. In the evening, as the great audience filled the house, the student bodies began warring among themselves. Fortunately, I was spared witnessing any of the noisy wrangling before the contest began. The slurs against the Indian that stained the lips of our opponents were already burning like a dry fever within my breast.

But after the orations were delivered a deeper burn awaited me. There, before that vast ocean of eyes, some college rowdies threw out a large white flag, with a drawing of a most forlorn Indian girl on it. Under this they had printed in bold black letters words that ridiculed the college which was represented by a "squaw." Such worse than barbarian rudeness embittered me. While we waited for the verdict of the judges, I gleamed fiercely upon the throngs of palefaces. My teeth were hard set, as I saw the white flag still floating insolently in the air.

Then anxiously we watched the man carry toward the stage the envelope containing the final decision.

There were two prizes given, that night, and one of them was mine!

The evil spirit laughed within me when the white flag dropped out of sight, and the hands which furled it hung limp in defeat.

Leaving the crowd as quickly as possible, I was soon in my room. The rest of the night I sat in an armchair and gazed into the crackling fire. I laughed no more in triumph when thus alone. The little taste of victory did not satisfy a hunger in my heart. In my mind I saw my mother far away on the Western plains, and she was holding a charge against me.

[1900]

Booker T. Washington

[1856-1915]

Booker Taliferro Washington was born on a small farm near Hale's Ford, Virginia, probably in the spring of 1856. He was the son of a slave, Jane, who never revealed the identity of his white father. She later married

Booker T. Washington

When this photograph was taken around 1903, Washington was the most influential and widely known African American spokesperson in the United States.

another slave, Washington Ferguson, whose first name Washington took as his last name. Emancipated during the Civil War, in the summer of 1865 the family moved to Malden, West Virginia, where Washington Ferguson had found a job in a salt factory. Washington and his brother also went to work in the factory, packing salt into barrels. In his autobiography, Washington recalls that the first word he learned to read was actually a number, 18, the number assigned to his stepfather at the factory. Possessed by what he called "an intense longing to learn to read," Washington used a spelling book his mother found for him to learn the alphabet and a few words. Before and after his long hours of work at the factory, he also began to

attend a school for freed slaves. In 1872, now sixteen and working in a coal mine, Washington enrolled at the Hampton Normal and Agricultural Institute, founded by the American Missionary Association as an experimental school for African Americans. Paying his way by working as a janitor in the school, Washington was deeply influenced by its principal, Samuel Chapman Armstrong, a leader in the movement for "industrial," or vocational, education as a way to improve the lot of former slaves. After graduating in 1875, Washington returned home and taught for two years at a school in Malden. He then studied for a year at the Wayland Seminary in Washington, D.C., before accepting a teaching position in a program for Native Americans at Hampton in 1878.

Three years later, Armstrong recommended the twenty-five-year-old Washington for the position of director of a new school for African Americans in Tuskegee, Alabama. For the rest of his life, Washington was closely associated with the Tuskegee Normal School and Industrial Institute, as well as with what came to be called the "Tuskegee Machine," a network of students, alumni, and supporters who formed a political coalition that worked to advance the interests of African Americans. Washington shrewdly handled the institute's affairs, buying land and relying on private contributions so that the school would not be indebted to the state and consequently subject to its control and changing property laws in Alabama. He also established a working farm and later a brickyard, which eventually became the mainstay of several industries established at the institute. Students took classes and worked in the industries, where they were trained to pursue a variety of occupations. The school's emphasis on vocational training was criticized by those who advocated a full liberal arts education for African Americans. Washington, however, successfully promoted his views through extended lecture tours, gaining the support of many wealthy white donors for the Institute. But his professional successes during these years were shadowed by the deaths of his first two wives, Fanny Norton Smith and Olivia A. Davidson. A widower with three children, he married Margaret J. Murray, with whom he would spend the rest of his life, in 1893.

During the following decade, Washington became the most prominent and powerful spokesperson for African Americans. In 1895, he was invited to speak at the opening of the Cotton States and International Exposition, a showcase of agriculture, manufacturing, technology, and transportation designed to promote Atlanta as the center of the "new" South. In his "Atlanta Exposition Address," Washington urged members of both races to "cast down your bucket where you are," declaring: "In all things that are purely social we can be as separate as the fingers, yet one as the hand in all things essential to mutual progress." In effect, he proposed that African Americans should accommodate themselves to racial segregation and political disenfranchisement in order to enjoy a greater degree of economic security. The address outraged some blacks, including John Hope, then a young professor at Roger Williams University in Nashville, who in a passionate rebuttal to Washington angrily asked: "If we are not striving for equality, in heaven's name for what are we living?" But whites cheered the address, which was published in newspapers across the country and which made Washington a celebrity. The following year, he became the first African American to receive an honorary degree from Harvard University, and he was lauded by President William McKinley, who visited Tuskegee and warmly praised Washington's efforts. In a further effort to improve the economic conditions of African Americans, Washington in 1900 founded the National Business League, arguing that blacks should "leave political and civil rights alone" in order to "make a businessman of the Negro." Washington amplified his argument and extended his influence through his growing control of the African American press, his numerous articles in influential white periodicals, and the publication of his best-selling and widely acclaimed autobiography, *Up from Slavery* (1901).

Washington's conservative positions and his conciliatory posture toward white America generated growing controversy among African Americans. He continued to promote industrial education and to preach the gospel of the gradual economic advancement of his race in numerous lectures and in his writings, including *Tuskegee and Its People* (1905), *The Story of the Negro* (1909), and *The Man Farthest Down: A Record of*

It is no ordinary tribute to this man's tact and power, that, steering as he must amid so many diverse interests and opinions, he to-day commands not simply the applause of those who believe in his theories, but also the respect of those who do not.

—W. E. B. Du Bois

Observation and Study in Europe (1912), in which he affirmed that African Americans were better off than impoverished whites in Europe. In response, many African American leaders protested that Washington was ignoring the violence directed at blacks, especially the epidemic of lynching in the South, as well as the pervasive political and social inequality among the races in the United States. Although he privately contributed funds for legal challenges to the segregation and disenfranchisement of blacks, Washington publicly avoided politics and strongly opposed the militant Niagara Movement and its successor, the National Association for the Advancement of Colored People (NAACP), which was founded in 1909. The following year, his longtime critic W. E. B. Du Bois and twenty-two other African American leaders signed a statement in which they asserted that "Mr. Washington's large financial responsibilities have made him dependent on the rich charitable public and that, for this reason, he has for years been compelled to tell, not the whole truth, but that part of it which certain powerful interests in America wish to appear as the whole truth." Despite mounting criticism of his views, when Washington died at Tuskegee on November 14, 1915, he was widely honored as what the obituary in the *New York Times* described as the "foremost teacher and leader of the negro race."

bedfordstmartins.com/ americanlit for research links on Washington

Reading Washington's *Up from Slavery*.   As he explains in the preface, Washington's autobiography began as a series of articles published during 1900-01 in the *Outlook*, a weekly magazine with a circulation of 100,000 that featured autobiography, biography, literary criticism, and essays on national affairs. Its editor, Lyman Abbott, had strongly encouraged Washington to write the account, observing in a letter to him: "The pictorial side of your life, the incidents which you have seen, out of which your own generalizations have grown, will be of the first interest and value to your readers." The series was widely read, and *Up from Slavery* was consequently published to great acclaim as a book in 1901. The influential writer and critic William Dean Howells published an enthusiastic article about the book and its author, "An Exemplary Citizen." Indeed, the account was frequently compared to the most famous of American "rags-to-riches" stories, the *Autobiography* of Benjamin Franklin. Widely viewed in the eyes of white America as the foremost representative of his race, Washington in *Up from Slavery* exploits that position to challenge denigrating stereotypes about the capacities of African Americans. At the same time, Washington had gained his prominent position largely by saying what most white Americans wanted to hear, and the following chapter on the speech that made him famous contains some of his most controversial statements about the role of African Americans in the United States. The text is taken from the first edition of *Up from Slavery* (1901), in which Washington altered the serialized version in the *Outlook* by insisting on the capitalization of the word *Negro* and by using the British spellings for words such as *coloured.*

UP FROM SLAVERY

Chapter XIV
The Atlanta Exposition Address

The Atlanta Exposition, at which I had been asked to make an address as a representative of the Negro race, . . . was opened with a short address from Governor Bullock.[1] After other interesting exercises, including an invocation from Bishop Nelson, of Georgia, a dedicatory ode by Albert Howell, Jr., and addresses by the President of the Exposition and Mrs. Joseph Thompson, the President of the Woman's Board, Governor Bullock introduced me with the words, "We have with us to-day a representative of Negro enterprise and Negro civilization."

When I arose to speak, there was considerable cheering, especially from the coloured people. As I remember it now, the thing that was uppermost in my mind was the desire to say something that would cement the friendship of the races and bring about hearty coöperation between them. So far as my outward surroundings were concerned, the only thing that I recall distinctly now is that when I got up, I saw thousands of eyes looking intently in my face. The following is the address which I delivered: –

MR. PRESIDENT AND GENTLEMEN OF THE BOARD OF DIRECTORS AND CITIZENS.

One-third of the population of the South is of the Negro race. No enterprise seeking the material, civil, or moral welfare of this section can disregard this element of our population and reach the highest success. I but convey to you, Mr. President and Directors, the sentiment of the masses of my race when I say that in no way have the value and manhood of the American Negro been more fittingly and generously recognized than by the managers of this magnificent Exposition at every stage of its progress. It is a recognition that will do more to cement the friendship of the two races than any occurrence since the dawn of our freedom.

Not only this, but the opportunity here afforded will awaken among us a new era of industrial progress. Ignorant and inexperienced, it is not strange that in the first years of our new life we began at the top instead of at the bottom; that a seat in Congress or the state legislature was more sought than real estate or industrial skill; that the political convention of stump speaking had more attractions than starting a dairy farm or truck garden.

A ship lost at sea for many days suddenly sighted a friendly vessel. From the mast of the unfortunate vessel was seen a signal, "Water, water; we die of thirst!" The answer from the friendly vessel at once came back, "Cast down your bucket where you are." A

---

1. **Governor Bullock:** Rufus Bullock (1834–1907), a businessman from New York who had cooperated with the Confederacy, was elected the first Republican governor of Georgia in 1868. His unpopular Reconstruction policies and his support for African American equality infuriated the powerful Ku Klux Klan, which ran a smear campaign accusing Bullock of corruption, malfeasance, and fraud. He was consequently forced from office in 1871. Tried twice in Atlanta and acquitted on all charges, Bullock restored his reputation and became a prominent citizen. In 1895, he was instrumental in organizing the Atlanta Exposition, inviting Washington to give an address and serving as the master of ceremonies on opening day of the exposition.

second time the signal, "Water, water; send us water!" ran up from the distressed vessel, and was answered, "Cast down your bucket where you are." And a third and fourth signal for water was answered, "Cast down your bucket where you are." The captain of the distressed vessel, at last heeding the injunction, cast down his bucket, and it came up full of fresh, sparkling water from the mouth of the Amazon River. To those of my race who depend on bettering their condition in a foreign land or who underestimate the importance of cultivating friendly relations with the Southern white man, who is their next-door neighbour, I would say: "Cast down your bucket where you are" — cast it down in making friends in every manly way of the people of all races by whom we are surrounded.

Cast it down in agriculture, mechanics, in commerce, in domestic service, and in the professions. And in this connection it is well to bear in mind that whatever other sins the South may be called to bear, when it comes to business, pure and simple, it is in the South that the Negro is given a man's chance in the commercial world, and in nothing is this Exposition more eloquent than in emphasizing this chance. Our greatest danger is that in the great leap from slavery to freedom we may overlook the fact that the masses of us are to live by the productions of our hands, and fail to keep in mind that we shall prosper in proportion as we learn to dignify and glorify common labour and put brains and skill into the common occupations of life; shall prosper in proportion as we learn to draw the line between the superficial and the substantial, the ornamental gewgaws of life and the useful. No race can prosper till it learns that there is as much dignity in tilling a field as in writing a poem. It is at the bottom of life we must begin, and not at the top. Nor should we permit our grievances to overshadow our opportunities.

To those of the white race who look to the incoming of those of foreign birth and strange tongue and habits for the prosperity of the South, were I permitted I would repeat what I say to my own race, "Cast down your bucket where you are." Cast it down among the eight millions of Negroes whose habits you know, whose fidelity and love you have tested in days when to have proved treacherous meant the ruin of your firesides. Cast down your bucket among these people who have, without strikes and labour wars, tilled your fields, cleared your forests, builded your railroads and cities, and brought forth treasures from the bowels of the earth, and helped make possible this magnificent representation of the progress of the South. Casting down your bucket among my people, helping and encouraging them as you are doing on these grounds, and to education of head, hand, and heart, you will find that they will buy your surplus land, make blossom the waste places in your fields, and run your factories. While doing this, you can be sure in the future, as in the past, that you and your families will be surrounded by the most patient, faithful, law-abiding, and unresentful people that the world has seen. As we have proved our loyalty to you in the past, in nursing your children, watching by the sick-bed of your mothers and fathers, and often following them with tear-dimmed eyes to their graves, so in the future, in our humble way, we shall stand by you with a devotion that no foreigner can approach, ready to lay down our lives, if need be, in defence of yours, interlacing our industrial, commercial, civil, and religious life with yours in a way that shall make the interests of both races one. In all things that are purely social we can be as separate as the fingers, yet one as the hand in all things essential to mutual progress.

There is no defence or security for any of us except in the highest intelligence and development of all. If anywhere there are efforts tending to curtail the fullest growth of the Negro, let these efforts be turned into stimulating, encouraging, and making him the most useful and intelligent citizen. Effort or means so invested will pay a thousand percent interest. These efforts will be twice blessed – "blessing him that gives and him that takes."[2]

There is no escape through law of man or God from the inevitable:

> The laws of changeless justice bind
>   Oppressor with oppressed;
> And close as sin and suffering joined
>   We march to fate abreast.[3]

Nearly sixteen millions of hands will aid you in pulling the load upward, or they will pull against you the load downward. We shall constitute one-third and more of the ignorance and crime of the South, or one-third its intelligence and progress; we shall contribute one-third to the business and industrial prosperity of the South, or we shall prove a veritable body of death, stagnating, depressing, retarding every effort to advance the body politic.

Gentlemen of the Exposition, as we present to you our humble effort at an exhibition of our progress, you must not expect overmuch. Starting thirty years ago with ownership here and there in a few quilts and pumpkins and chickens (gathered from miscellaneous sources), remember the path that has led from these to the inventions and production of agricultural implements, buggies, steam-engines, newspapers, books, statuary, carving, paintings, the management of drug-stores and banks, has not been trodden without contact with thorns and thistles. While we take pride in what we exhibit as a result of our independent efforts, we do not for a moment forget that our part in this exhibition would fall far short of your expectations but for the constant help that has come to our educational life, not only from the Southern states, but especially from Northern philanthropists, who have made their gifts a constant stream of blessing and encouragement.

The wisest among my race understand that the agitation of questions of social equality is the extremest folly, and that progress in the enjoyment of all the privileges that will come to us must be the result of severe and constant struggle rather than of artificial forcing. No race that has anything to contribute to the markets of the world is long in any degree ostracized. It is important and right that all privileges of the law be ours, but it is vastly more important that we be prepared for the exercises of these privileges. The opportunity to earn a dollar in a factory just now is worth infinitely more than the opportunity to spend a dollar in a opera-house.

---

2. **"blessing . . . takes"**: Washington is quoting loosely from Shakespeare's *The Merchant of Venice* 4.1.187: "It blesseth him that gives and him that takes."
3. **The laws . . . abreast**: From "Song of the Negro Boatman at Port Royal" (1863), with lyrics by the abolitionist poet John Greenleaf Whittier and music by E. W. Kellogg.

In conclusion, may I repeat that nothing in thirty years has given us more hope and encouragement, and drawn us so near to you of the white race, as this opportunity offered by the Exposition; and here bending, as it were, over the altar that represents the results of the struggles of your race and mine, both starting practically empty-handed three decades ago, I pledge that in your effort to work out the great and intricate problem which God has laid at the doors of the South, you shall have at all times the patient, sympathetic help of my race; only let this be constantly in mind, that, while from representations in these buildings of the product of field, of forest, of mine, of factory, letters, and art, much good will come, yet far above and beyond material benefits will be that higher good, that, let us pray God, will come, in a blotting out of sectional differences and racial animosities and suspicions, in a determination to administer absolute justice, in a willing obedience among all classes to the mandates of law. This, this, coupled with our material prosperity, will bring into our beloved South a new heaven and a new earth.[4]

The first thing that I remember, after I had finished speaking, was that Governor Bullock rushed across the platform and took me by the hand, and that others did the same. I received so many and such hearty congratulations that I found it difficult to get out of the building. I did not appreciate to any degree, however, the impression which my address seemed to have made, until the next morning, when I went into the business part of the city. As soon as I was recognized, I was surprised to find myself pointed out and surrounded by a crowd of men who wished to shake hands with me. This was kept up on every street on to which I went, to an extent which embarrassed me so much that I went back to my boarding-place. The next morning I returned to Tuskegee. At the station in Atlanta, and at almost all of the stations at which the train stopped between that city and Tuskegee, I found a crowd of people anxious to shake hands with me.

The papers in all parts of the United States published the address in full, and for months afterward there were complimentary editorial references to it. Mr. Clark Howell, the editor of the Atlanta *Constitution*, telegraphed to a New York paper, among other words, the following, "I do not exaggerate when I say that Professor Booker T. Washington's address yesterday was one of the most notable speeches, both as to character and as to the warmth of its reception, ever delivered to a Southern audience. The address was a revelation. The whole speech is a platform upon which blacks and whites can stand with full justice to each other."

The Boston *Transcript* said editorially: "The speech of Booker T. Washington at the Atlanta Exposition, this week, seems to have dwarfed all the other proceedings and the Exposition itself. The sensation that it has caused in the press has never been equalled."

I very soon began receiving all kinds of propositions from lecture bureaus, and editors of magazines and papers, to take the lecture platform, and to write articles. One lecture bureau offered me fifty thousand dollars, or two hundred dollars a night and expenses, if I would place my services at its disposal for a given period. To all these communications I replied that my life-work was at Tuskegee; and that whenever I spoke it

---

4. **a new heaven and a new earth:** See the opening verse of John of Patmos's final vision of the New Jerusalem: "And I saw a new heaven and a new earth: for the first heaven and the first earth were passed away" (Revelation 21:1).

must be in the interests of the Tuskegee school and my race, and that I would enter into no arrangements that seemed to place a mere commercial value upon my services.

Some days after its delivery I sent a copy of my address to the President of the United States, the Hon. Grover Cleveland.[5] I received from him the following autograph reply:

GRAY GABLES, BUZZARD'S BAY, MASS.,
OCTOBER 6, 1895

BOOKER T. WASHINGTON, ESQ.:

MY DEAR SIR: I thank you for sending me a copy of your address delivered at the Atlanta Exposition.

I thank you with much enthusiasm for making the address. I have read it with intense interest, and I think the Exposition would be fully justified if it did not do more than furnish the opportunity for its delivery. Your words cannot fail to delight and encourage all who wish well for your race; and if our coloured fellow-citizens do not from your utterances gather new hope and form new determinations to gain every valuable advantage offered them by their citizenship, it will be strange indeed.

Yours very truly,
GROVER CLEVELAND

Later I met Mr. Cleveland, for the first time, when, as President, he visited the Atlanta Exposition. At the request of myself and others he consented to spend an hour in the Negro Building, for the purpose of inspecting the Negro exhibit and of giving the coloured people in attendance an opportunity to shake hands with him. As soon as I met Mr. Cleveland I became impressed with his simplicity, greatness, and rugged honesty. I have met him many times since then, both at public functions and at his private residence in Princeton, and the more I see of him the more I admire him. When he visited the Negro Building in Atlanta he seemed to give himself up wholly, for that hour, to the coloured people. He seemed to be as careful to shake hands with some old coloured "auntie" clad partially in rags, and to take as much pleasure in doing so, as if he were greeting some millionaire. Many of the coloured people took advantage of the occasion to get him to write his name in a book or on a slip of paper. He was as careful and patient in doing this as if he were putting his signature to some great state document.

Mr. Cleveland has not only shown his friendship for me in many personal ways, but has always consented to do anything I have asked of him for our school. This he has done, whether it was to make a personal donation or to use his influence in securing the donations of others. Judging from my personal acquaintance with Mr. Cleveland, I do not believe that he is conscious of possessing any colour prejudice. He is too great for that. In my contact with people I find that, as a rule, it is only the little, narrow people who live for themselves, who never read good books, who do not travel, who never open up their souls in a way to permit them to come into contact with other souls — with the great outside world. No man whose vision is bounded by colour can come into contact with what is highest and best in the world. In meeting men, in many places, I have found that the happiest people are those who do the most for others; the most miserable are those who do the least. I have also found that few things, if any, are capable of making

---

5. **Hon. Grover Cleveland:** Stephen Grover Cleveland (1837–1908) served as president of the United States for two nonconsecutive terms: 1886–89 and 1893–97.

one so blind and narrow as race prejudice. I often say to our students, in the course of my talks to them on Sunday evenings in the chapel, that the longer I live and the more experience I have of the world, the more I am convinced that, after all, the one thing that is most worth living for—and dying for, if need be—is the opportunity of making some one else more happy and more useful.

The coloured people and the coloured newspapers at first seemed to be greatly pleased with the character of my Atlanta address, as well as with its reception. But after the first burst of enthusiasm began to die away, and the coloured people began reading the speech in cold type, some of them seemed to feel that they had been hypnotized. They seemed to feel that I had been too liberal in my remarks toward the Southern whites, and that I had not spoken out strongly enough for what they termed the "rights" of the race. For a while there was a reaction, so far as a certain element of my own race was concerned, but later these reactionary ones seemed to have been won over to my way of believing and acting.

While speaking of changes in public sentiment, I recall that about ten years after the school at Tuskegee was established, I had an experience that I shall never forget. Dr. Lyman Abbott, then the pastor of Plymouth Church, and also editor of the *Outlook* (then the *Christian Union*), asked me to write a letter for his paper giving my opinion of the exact condition, mental and moral, of the coloured ministers in the South, as based upon my observations. I wrote the letter, giving the exact facts as I conceived them to be. The picture painted was a rather black one—or, since I am black, shall I say "white"? It could not be otherwise with a race but a few years out of slavery, a race which had not had time or opportunity to produce a competent ministry.

What I said soon reached every Negro minister in the country, I think, and the letters of condemnation which I received from them were not few. I think that for a year after the publication of this article every association and every conference or religious body of any kind, of any race, that met, did not fail before adjourning to pass a resolution condemning me, or calling upon me to retract or modify what I had said. Many of these organizations went so far in their resolutions as to advise parents to cease sending their children to Tuskegee. One association even appointed a "missionary" whose duty it was to warn the people against sending their children to Tuskegee. This missionary had a son in the school, and I noticed that, whatever the "missionary" might have said or done with regard to others, he was careful not to take his son away from the institution. Many of the coloured papers, especially those that were the organs of religious bodies, joined in the general chorus of condemnation or demands for retraction.

During the whole time of the excitement, and through all the criticism, I did not utter a word of explanation or retraction. I knew that I was right, and that time and the sober second thought of the people would vindicate me. It was not long before the bishops and other church leaders began to make a careful investigation of the conditions of the ministry, and they found out that I was right. In fact, the oldest and most influential bishop in one branch of the Methodist Church said that my words were far too mild. Very soon public sentiment began making itself felt, in demanding a purifying of the ministry. While this is not yet complete by any means, I think I may say, without egotism, and I have been told by many of our most influential ministers, that my words had much to do with starting a demand for the placing of a higher type of men in the pulpit. I have had the satisfaction of having many who once condemned me thank me heartily for my frank words.

The change of the attitude of the Negro ministry, so far as regards myself, is so complete that at the present time I have no warmer friends among any class than I have among the clergymen. The improvement in the character and life of the Negro ministers is one of the most gratifying evidences of the progress of the race. My experience with them, as well as other events in my life, convince me that the thing to do, when one feels sure that he has said or done the right thing, and is condemned, is to stand still and keep quiet. If he is right, time will show it.

In the midst of the discussion which was going on concerning my Atlanta speech, I received the letter which I give below, from Dr. Gilman, the President of Johns Hopkins University, who had been made chairman of the judges of award in connection with the Atlanta Exposition: —

> Johns Hopkins University, Baltimore,
> President's Office, September 30, 1895
>
> Dear Mr. Washington: Would it be agreeable to you to be one of the Judges of Award in the Department of Education at Atlanta? If so, I shall be glad to place your name upon the list. A line by telegraph will be welcomed.
>
> Yours very truly,
> D. C. Gilman

I think I was even more surprised to receive this invitation than I had been to receive the invitation to speak at the opening of the Exposition. It was to be a part of my duty, as one of the jurors, to pass not only upon the exhibits of the coloured schools, but also upon those of the white schools. I accepted the position, and spent a month in Atlanta in performance of the duties which it entailed. The board of jurors was a large one, consisting in all of sixty members. It was about equally divided between Southern white people and Northern white people. Among them were college presidents, leading scientists and men of letters, and specialists in many subjects. When the group of jurors to which I was assigned met for organization, Mr. Thomas Nelson Page,[6] who was one of the number, moved that I be made secretary of that division, and the motion was unanimously adopted. Nearly half of our division were Southern people. In performing my duties in the inspection of the exhibits of white schools I was in every case treated with respect, and at the close of our labours I parted from my associates with regret.

I am often asked to express myself more freely than I do upon the political condition and the political future of my race. These recollections of my experience in Atlanta give me the opportunity to do so briefly. My own belief is, although I have never before said so in so many words, that the time will come when the Negro in the South will be accorded all the political rights which his ability, character, and material possessions

---

6. **Mr. Thomas Nelson Page:** Southern writer (1853–1922) who helped popularize romantic myths about slavery and plantation life in collections of stories such as *In Ole Virginia* (1887).

entitle him to. I think, though, that the opportunity to freely exercise such political rights will not come in any large degree through outside or artificial forcing, but will be accorded to the Negro by the Southern white people themselves, and that they will protect him in the exercise of those rights. Just as soon as the South gets over the old feeling that it is being forced by "foreigners," or "aliens," to do something which it does not want to do, I believe that the change in the direction that I have indicated is going to begin. In fact, there are indications that it is already beginning in a slight degree.

Let me illustrate my meaning. Suppose that some months before the opening of the Atlanta Exposition there had been a general demand from the press and public platform outside the South that a Negro be given a place on the opening programme, and that a Negro be placed upon the board of jurors of award. Would any such recognition of the race have taken place? I do not think so. The Atlanta officials went as far as they did because they felt it to be a pleasure, as well as a duty, to reward what they considered merit in the Negro race. Say what we will, there is something in human nature which we cannot blot out, which makes one man, in the end, recognize and reward merit in another, regardless of colour or race.

I believe it is the duty of the Negro—as the greater part of the race is already doing—to deport himself modestly in regard to political claims, depending upon the slow but sure influences that proceed from the possession of property, intelligence, and high character for the full recognition of his political rights. I think that the according of the full exercise of political rights is going to be a matter of natural, slow growth, not an over-night, gourd-vine affair. I do not believe that the Negro should cease voting, for a man cannot learn the exercise of self-government by ceasing to vote any more than a boy can learn to swim by keeping out of the water, but I do believe that in his voting he should more and more be influenced by those of intelligence and character who are his next-door neighbours.

I know coloured men who, through the encouragement, help, and advice of Southern white people, have accumulated thousands of dollars' worth of property, but who, at the same time, would never think of going to those same persons for advice concerning the casting of their ballots. This, it seems to me, is unwise and unreasonable, and should cease. In saying this I do not mean that the Negro should truckle, or not vote from principle, for the instant he ceases to vote from principle he loses the confidence and respect of the Southern white man even.

I do not believe that any state should make a law that permits an ignorant and poverty-stricken white man to vote, and prevents a black man in the same condition from voting. Such a law is not only unjust, but it will react, as all unjust laws do, in time; for the effect of such a law is to encourage the Negro to secure education and property, and at the same time it encourages the white man to remain in ignorance and poverty. I believe that in time, through the operation of intelligence and friendly race relations, all cheating at the ballot box in the South will cease. It will become apparent that the white man who begins by cheating a Negro out of his ballot soon learns to cheat a white man out of his, and that the man who does this ends his career of dishonesty by the theft of property or by some equally serious crime. In my opinion, the time will come when the South will encourage all of its citizens to vote. It will see that it pays better, from every standpoint, to have healthy, vigorous life than to have that political stagnation which always results when one-half of the population has no share and no interest in the Government.

As a rule, I believe in universal, free suffrage, but I believe that in the South we are confronted with peculiar conditions that justify the protection of the ballot in many of the states, for a while at least, either by an educational test, a property test, or by both combined; but whatever tests are required, they should be made to apply with equal and exact justice to both races.

[1901]

W. E. B. Du Bois

[1868–1963]

William Edward Burghardt Du Bois was born on February 23, 1868, in Great Barrington, a small town in the Berkshire Mountains of western Massachusetts. The birth certificate incorrectly spelled his name "Duboise," and Du Bois frequently had to explain that his name was pronounced "*Due Boyss*, with the accent on the last syllable." His father, Alfred Du Bois, was born in Haiti, the descendant of free people of color. During the 1850s, a period of social and political turmoil in Haiti, Alfred Du Bois immigrated to the United States. He briefly served in the Union army before moving to Great Barrington, where he married Mary Burghardt, of mixed African and Dutch ancestry. Alfred Du Bois left the family when Du Bois was about two years old, and he was subsequently raised by his mother, who worked as a domestic servant to provide for herself and her son. Du Bois attended the town school in Great Barrington, where he was such an

W. E. B. Du Bois

This photograph of Du Bois was used as the frontispiece of his influential book *The Souls of Black Folk* (1903).

exceptional student that he soon began to write professionally for African American newspapers such as the *New York Age* and the *New York Globe*. Elected valedictorian of his high-school class, Du Bois delivered his graduation speech on the white abolitionist and reformer Wendell Phillips, who had steadily fought against all forms of racial injustice in the United States.

Du Bois's mother died a few months after his graduation in 1884, but local ministers and teachers raised money for a scholarship that enabled him to enroll at Fisk University in Nashville, Tennessee, in 1885. While he was invigorated by his studies and by his fellow African American students at the all-black college, Du Bois was shocked by the racism he experienced in Nashville and during the summers he spent teaching in rural Tennessee. After he graduated from Fisk in 1888, he was awarded a grant from Harvard University, where Du Bois earned a second B.A. in 1890. He then received a grant for European travel and study at the University of Berlin. Returning to the United States in 1895, Du Bois earned the first Ph.D. awarded by Harvard to an African American. Trained primarily as a historian, he turned down a job offer from Booker T. Washington at the Tuskegee Institute. Du Bois instead accepted a position at another institution founded by African Americans, Wilberforce University in Ohio, where he completed his first book, *The Suppression of the African Slave Trade to the United States of America, 1638–1870* (1896). Based on his doctoral dissertation and still considered a foundational study of the slave trade, the book was the first of his many publications designed to recover the history of African Americans. At Wilberforce, Du Bois met and married Nina Gomer, and the two moved to Philadelphia in 1896 when he accepted an appointment from the University of Pennsylvania to research and write a study of the black population of the city, *The Philadelphia Negro* (1899). In it, Du Bois virtually invented the field of urban sociology, and he accepted an offer to assume the leadership of the Atlanta Sociological Laboratory, a research program at the all-black Atlanta University.

> *My earliest memories of written words are those of Du Bois and the Bible.*
> *—Langston Hughes*

In Atlanta, Du Bois began to work closely with other black intellectuals, a group he called the "Talented Tenth." Through his own work as the editor of a sociological series on African Americans, *Atlanta University Studies*, and by holding yearly conferences on topics such as "The Social and Physical Condition of Negroes in Cities," Du Bois began to challenge the conservative views of Booker T. Washington, then the most influential African American leader in the United States. Du Bois offered his most vigorous challenge to Washington's leadership in a chapter in *The Souls of Black Folk* (1903), a collection of essays, stories, and meditations on the history and condition of African Americans. The inspirational book helped Du Bois launch the Niagara Movement, organized in 1905 to fight for the civil rights of African Americans. Du Bois also founded two periodicals, the *Moon* and *Horizon*, in an effort to promote the activities of the Niagara Movement, which paved the way for the founding of an even larger organization, the National Association for the Advancement of Colored People (NAACP), in 1909. Du Bois resigned his position at Atlanta University and moved to New York City, where he became head of publications for the NAACP. In 1910, he founded its official journal, the *Crisis*, which Du Bois firmly declared would "stand for the rights of men, irrespective of color or race, for the highest ideals of American democracy, and for reasonable but earnest and persistent attempts to gain these rights and realize these ideals." Under his editorship, which lasted for almost twenty-five years, the *Crisis* became the most prestigious African American periodical in the United States.

During the final decades of his life, however, Du Bois became increasingly disillusioned with both American society and the activities of the NAACP. Believing that the organization was focusing its attention on middle-class blacks rather than on those living in desperate poverty, Du Bois left the NAACP in 1934 and returned to Atlanta University. During the following decade, he wrote three books on civil rights: *Black Reconstruction in America* (1935), *Dusk of Dawn: An Essay toward an Autobiography of a Race Concept* (1940), and *Colour and Democracy* (1945). After he retired from the university in 1944, Du Bois rejoined the NAACP as the director of special research, serving as the organization's representative at the conference that founded the United Nations. But his radical politics placed him at odds with the more-moderate leadership of the NAACP. In 1948, he became associated with the Council on African Affairs, which was considered by the U.S. attorney general to be a subversive, Communist-front organization. Du Bois, who was also deeply involved in the left-wing Progressive Party, was indicted in 1951 as "an agent of a foreign principal," the Soviet Union. Although he was eventually acquitted of the charges, Du Bois felt that he had not received firm support from his former colleagues in the NAACP. Embittered by the experience and by what he viewed as the lack of progress in the struggle for civil rights, Du Bois joined the Communist Party in 1961, stating on his application for membership: "Capitalism cannot reform itself." That year, he renounced his American citizenship and moved to Ghana, where he died on August 27, 1963.

One of the most graceful tributes to the lifelong crusader for civil rights was offered the following day, at the "March on Washington for Jobs and Freedom," where the president of the NAACP, Roy Wilkins, told the huge crowd gathered at the Lincoln Memorial:

> Remember that this has been a long fight. We were reminded of it by the news of the death yesterday in Africa of Dr. W. E. B. Du Bois. Now, regardless of the fact that in recent years Dr. Du Bois chose another path, it is incontrovertible that at the dawn of the twentieth century his was the voice that was calling you to gather here today in this cause. If you want to read something that applies to 1963 go back and get a volume of *The Souls of Black Folk* by Du Bois published in 1903.

bedfordstmartins.com/ americanlit for research links on Du Bois

Reading Du Bois's *The Souls of Black Folk*. Revising previously published articles and adding new material, Du Bois put together a collection of what the original subtitle called "Essays and Sketches" and what he later described as "bits of history and biography, some descriptions of scenes and persons, something of controversy and criticism, some statistics and a bit of story-telling." The complex book, which defied and still defies easy description, caused a sensation when it was published in 1903. The publisher had to arrange a third printing within two months, and *The Souls of Black Folk* sold roughly ten thousand copies within five years. Although it was ignored or sharply criticized by most Southern newspapers — one declared that the book was "dangerous for the Negro to read" — it was widely and favorably reviewed in the North. The book had a particularly profound effect on African American activists and writers such as the poet James Weldon Johnson, who observed on the thirtieth anniversary of the publication of *The Souls of Black Folk* that its impact was "greater upon and within the Negro race than any other single book published in this country since *Uncle Tom's Cabin*," Harriet Beecher Stowe's blockbuster novel of the 1850s. The two chapters presented here are probably the most famous in *The Souls of Black Folk*. "Of Our Spiritual Strivings" was based on "Strivings of the Negro People," which had appeared in the *Atlantic Monthly* in 1897. In that chapter, Du Bois recounted his first experience of racism as a child in school and meditated on the "double-consciousness" of being "an American, a Negro." The chapter that generated much of the commentary on and controversy about *The Souls of Black Folk* was "Of Mr. Booker T. Washington and Others," a revised and expanded version of a much shorter essay, "The Evolution of Negro Leadership," which had appeared in the *Dial* in 1901. In that chapter, Du Bois challenged what he viewed as Washington's accommodation to legalized segregation and the disenfranchisement of black people in the South. In contrast, Du Bois insisted that black people must "strive for the rights which the world accords to men," accepting nothing less than full social and political equality in the United States. The text of the two chapters is taken from the first edition of *The Souls of Black Folk* (1903).

THE SOULS OF BLACK FOLK

I

Of Our Spiritual Strivings

O water, voice of my heart, crying in the sand,
    All night long crying with a mournful cry,
As I lie and listen, and cannot understand
        The voice of my heart in my side or the voice of the sea,
    O water, crying for rest, is it I, is it I?
    All night long the water is crying to me.

Unresting water, there shall never be rest
    Till the last moon droop and the last tide fail,
And the fire of the end begin to burn in the west;
        And the heart shall be weary and wonder and cry like the sea,
    All life long crying without avail,
        As the water all night long is crying to me.

—ARTHUR SYMONS[1]

---

1. **Arthur Symons:** Welsh critic and poet (1865–1945); the title of the poem is "The Crying of Water."

Between me and the other world there is ever an unasked question: unasked by some through feelings of delicacy; by others through the difficulty of rightly framing it. All, nevertheless, flutter round it. They approach me in a half-hesitant sort of way, eye me curiously or compassionately, and then, instead of saying directly, How does it feel to be a problem? they say, I know an excellent colored man in my town; or, I fought at Mechanicsville;[3] or, Do not these Southern outrages make your blood boil? At these I smile, or am interested, or reduce the boiling to a simmer, as the occasion may require. To the real question, How does it feel to be a problem? I answer seldom a word.

And yet, being a problem is a strange experience, – peculiar even for one who has never been anything else, save perhaps, in babyhood and in Europe. It is in the early days of rollicking boyhood that the revelation first bursts upon one, all in a day, as it were. I remember well when the shadow swept across me. I was a little thing, away up in the hills of New England, where the dark Housatonic winds between Hoosac and Taghkanic to the sea.[4] In a wee wooden schoolhouse, something put it into the boys' and girls' heads to buy gorgeous visiting-cards – ten cents a package – and exchange. The exchange was merry, till one girl, a tall newcomer, refused my card, – refused it peremptorily, with a glance. Then it dawned upon me with a certain suddenness that I was different from the others; or like, mayhap, in heart and life and longing, but shut out from their world by a vast veil. I had thereafter no desire to tear down that veil, to creep through; I held all beyond it in common contempt, and lived above it in a region of blue sky and great wandering shadows. That sky was bluest when I could beat my mates at examination-time, or beat them at a foot-race, or even beat their stringy heads. Alas, with the years all this fine contempt began to fade; for the worlds I longed for, and all their dazzling opportunities, were theirs, not mine. But they should not keep these prizes, I said; some, all, I would wrest from them. Just how I would do it I could never decide: by reading law, by healing the sick, by telling the wonderful tales that swam in my head, – some way. With other black boys the strife was not so fiercely sunny: their youth shrunk into tasteless sycophancy, or into silent hatred of the pale world about them and mocking distrust of everything white; or wasted itself in a bitter cry, Why did God make

---

2. [musical notation]: As Du Bois notes in his preface, "The Forethought," each chapter of the book is introduced by a bar of music from what he called the "Sorrow Songs," or African American slave songs, "some echo of haunting melody from the only American music which welled up from black souls in the past." The bar of music here is from "Nobody Knows the Trouble I've Seen."

3. Mechanicsville: Virginia site of a Civil War battle in which an attack by Confederate troops was severely repulsed by Union forces on June 26, 1862.

4. Housatonic . . . to the sea: The Housatonic River flows from western Massachusetts through the Hoosac and Taconic mountain ranges before emptying into Long Island Sound at Milford Point, Connecticut.

me an outcast and a stranger in mine own house? The shades of the prison-house closed round about us all:[5] walls strait and stubborn to the whitest, but relentlessly narrow, tall, and unscalable to sons of night who must plod darkly on in resignation, or beat unavailing palms against the stone, or steadily, half hopelessly, watch the streak of blue above.

After the Egyptian and Indian, the Greek and Roman, the Teuton and Mongolian, the Negro is a sort of seventh son, born with a veil, and gifted with second-sight in this American world, — a world which yields him no true self-consciousness, but only lets him see himself through the revelation of the other world. It is a peculiar sensation, this double-consciousness, this sense of always looking at one's self through the eyes of others, of measuring one's soul by the tape of a world that looks on in amused contempt and pity. One ever feels his two-ness, — an American, a Negro; two souls, two thoughts, two unreconciled strivings; two warring ideals in one dark body, whose dogged strength alone keeps it from being torn asunder.

The history of the American Negro is the history of this strife, — this longing to attain self-conscious manhood, to merge his double self into a better and truer self. In this merging he wishes neither of the older selves to be lost. He would not Africanize America, for America has too much to teach the world and Africa. He would not bleach his Negro soul in a flood of white Americanism, for he knows that Negro blood has a message for the world. He simply wishes to make it possible for a man to be both a Negro and an American, without being cursed and spit upon by his fellows, without having the doors of Opportunity closed roughly in his face.

This, then, is the end of his striving: to be a co-worker in the kingdom of culture, to escape both death and isolation, to husband and use his best powers and his latent genius. These powers of body and mind have in the past been strangely wasted, dispersed, or forgotten. The shadow of a mighty Negro past flits through the tale of Ethiopia the Shadowy and of Egypt the Sphinx. Throughout history, the powers of single black men flash here and there like falling stars, and die sometimes before the world has rightly gauged their brightness. Here in America, in a few days since Emancipation, the black man's turning hither and thither in hesitant and doubtful striving has often made his very strength to lose effectiveness, to seem like absence of power, like weakness. And yet it is not weakness, — it is the contradiction of double aims. The double-aimed struggle of the black artisan — on the one hand to escape white contempt for a nation of mere hewers of wood and drawers of water, and on the other hand to plough and nail and dig for a poverty-stricken horde — could only result in making him a poor craftsman, for he had but half a heart in either cause. By the poverty and ignorance of his people, the Negro minister or doctor was tempted toward quackery and demagogy; and by the criticism of the other world, toward ideals that made him ashamed of his lowly tasks. The would-be

---

5. **The shades . . . about us all:** Du Bois is loosely quoting from "Ode: Intimations of Immortality from Recollections of Early Childhood," by the English poet William Wordsworth (1770–1850): "But trailing clouds of glory do we come / From God, who is our home: / Heaven lies about us in our infancy! / Shades of the prison-house begin to close / Upon the growing Boy."

black *savant*[6] was confronted by the paradox that the knowledge his people needed was a twice-told tale to his white neighbors, while the knowledge which would teach the white world was Greek to his own flesh and blood. The innate love of harmony and beauty that set the ruder souls of his people a-dancing and a-singing raised but confusion and doubt in the soul of the black artist; for the beauty revealed to him was the soul-beauty of a race which his larger audience despised, and he could not articulate the message of another people. This waste of double aims, this seeking to satisfy two unreconciled ideals, has wrought sad havoc with the courage and faith and deeds of ten thousand thousand people, — has sent them often wooing false gods and invoking false means of salvation, and at times has even seemed about to make them ashamed of themselves.

Away back in the days of bondage they thought to see in one divine event the end of all doubt and disappointment; few men ever worshipped Freedom with half such unquestioning faith as did the American Negro for two centuries. To him, so far as he thought and dreamed, slavery was indeed the sum of all villainies, the cause of all sorrow, the root of all prejudice; Emancipation was the key to a promised land of sweeter beauty than ever stretched before the eyes of wearied Israelites. In song and exhortation swelled one refrain — Liberty; in his tears and curses the God he implored had Freedom in his right hand. At last it came, — suddenly, fearfully, like a dream. With one wild carnival of blood and passion came the message in his own plaintive cadences: —

> "Shout, O children!
> Shout, you 're free!
> For God has bought your liberty!"[7]

Years have passed away since then, — ten, twenty, forty; forty years of national life, forty years of renewal and development, and yet the swarthy spectre sits in its accustomed seat at the Nation's feast. In vain do we cry to this our vastest social problem: —

> "Take any shape but that, and my firm nerves
> Shall never tremble!"[8]

The Nation has not yet found peace from its sins; the freedman has not yet found in freedom his promised land. Whatever of good may have come in these years of change, the shadow of a deep disappointment rests upon the Negro people, — a disappointment all the more bitter because the unattained ideal was unbounded save by the simple ignorance of a lowly people.

The first decade was merely a prolongation of the vain search for freedom, the boon that seemed ever barely to elude their grasp, — like a tantalizing will-o'-the-wisp, maddening and misleading the headless host. The holocaust of war, the terrors of the Ku-Klux Klan, the lies of carpet-baggers, the disorganization of industry, and the contradictory advice of friends and foes, left the bewildered serf with no new watchword

---

6. *savant*: A learned person (French).
7. "Shout . . . liberty!": From an early nineteenth-century African American slave song.
8. "Take . . . tremble!": From Shakespeare's *Macbeth*, 3.4.120–21.

beyond the old cry for freedom. As the time flew, however, he began to grasp a new idea. The ideal of liberty demanded for its attainment powerful means, and these the Fifteenth Amendment[9] gave him. The ballot, which before he had looked upon as a visible sign of freedom, he now regarded as the chief means of gaining and perfecting the liberty with which war had partially endowed him. And why not? Had not votes made war and emancipated millions? Had not votes enfranchised the freedmen? Was anything impossible to a power that had done all this? A million black men started with renewed zeal to vote themselves into the kingdom. So the decade flew away, the revolution of 1876[10] came, and left the half-free serf weary, wondering, but still inspired. Slowly but steadily, in the following years, a new vision began gradually to replace the dream of political power, – a powerful movement, the rise of another ideal to guide the unguided, another pillar of fire by night after a clouded day. It was the ideal of "book-learning"; the curiosity, born of compulsory ignorance, to know and test the power of the cabalistic letters of the white man, the longing to know. Here at last seemed to have been discovered the mountain path to Canaan;[11] longer than the highway of Emancipation and law, steep and rugged, but straight, leading to heights high enough to overlook life.

Up the new path the advance guard toiled, slowly, heavily, doggedly; only those who have watched and guided the faltering feet, the misty minds, the dull understandings, of the dark pupils of these schools know how faithfully, how piteously, this people strove to learn. It was weary work. The cold statistician wrote down the inches of progress here and there, noted also where here and there a foot had slipped or some one had fallen. To the tired climbers, the horizon was ever dark, the mists were often cold, the Canaan was always dim and far away. If, however, the vistas disclosed as yet no goal, no resting-place, little but flattery and criticism, the journey at least gave leisure for reflection and self-examination; it changed the child of Emancipation to the youth with dawning self-consciousness, self-realization, self-respect. In those sombre forests of his striving his own soul rose before him, and he saw himself, – darkly as through a veil; and yet he saw in himself some faint revelation of his power, of his mission. He began to have a dim feeling that, to attain his place in the world, he must be himself, and not another. For the first time he sought to analyze the burden he bore upon his back, that dead-weight of social degradation partially masked behind a half-named Negro problem. He felt his poverty; without a cent, without a home, without land, tools, or savings, he had entered into competition with rich, landed, skilled neighbors. To be a poor man is hard, but to be a poor race in a land of dollars is the very bottom of hardships. He felt the weight of his ignorance, – not simply of letters, but of life, of business, of the humanities; the accu-

---

9. **Fifteenth Amendment**: "The right of citizens of the United States to vote shall not be denied or abridged by the United States or by any state on account of race, color, or previous condition of servitude." Ratified on February 3, 1870, the amendment thus enfranchised men who had formerly been slaves.
10. **revolution of 1876**: Despite the fact that both the popular and Electoral College votes in the presidential election of 1876 went to Samuel J. Tilden, a Democrat, after months of wrangling and challenges from Southern states the Electoral College awarded the election to Rutherford B. Hayes, a Republican. As part of the so-called Compromise of 1877, federal troops were withdrawn from the Southern states, effectively ending Reconstruction and dealing a blow to new black voters and civil rights in the South.
11. **Canaan**: The promised land of the ancient Israelites.

mulated sloth and shirking and awkwardness of decades and centuries shackled his hands and feet. Nor was his burden all poverty and ignorance. The red stain of bastardy, which two centuries of systematic legal defilement of Negro women had stamped upon his race, meant not only the loss of ancient African chastity, but also the hereditary weight of a mass of corruption from white adulterers, threatening almost the obliteration of the Negro home.

A people thus handicapped ought not to be asked to race with the world, but rather allowed to give all its time and thought to its own social problems. But alas! while sociologists gleefully count his bastards and his prostitutes, the very soul of the toiling, sweating black man is darkened by the shadow of a vast despair. Men call the shadow prejudice, and learnedly explain it as the natural defence of culture against barbarism, learning against ignorance, purity against crime, the "higher" against the "lower" races. To which the Negro cries Amen! and swears that to so much of this strange prejudice as is founded on just homage to civilization, culture, righteousness, and progress, he humbly bows and meekly does obeisance. But before that nameless prejudice that leaps beyond all this he stands helpless, dismayed, and well-nigh speechless; before that personal disrespect and mockery, the ridicule and systematic humiliation, the distortion of fact and wanton license of fancy, the cynical ignoring of the better and the boisterous welcoming of the worse, the all-pervading desire to inculcate disdain for everything black, from Toussaint[12] to the devil, — before this there rises a sickening despair that would disarm and discourage any nation save that black host to whom "discouragement" is an unwritten word.

But the facing of so vast a prejudice could not but bring the inevitable self-questioning, self-disparagement, and lowering of ideals which ever accompany repression and breed in an atmosphere of contempt and hate. Whisperings and portents came borne upon the four winds: Lo! we are diseased and dying, cried the dark hosts; we cannot write, our voting is vain; what need of education, since we must always cook and serve? And the Nation echoed and enforced this self-criticism, saying: Be content to be servants, and nothing more; what need of higher culture for half-men? Away with the black man's ballot, by force or fraud, — and behold the suicide of a race! Nevertheless, out of the evil came something of good, — the more careful adjustment of education to real life, the clearer perception of the Negroes' social responsibilities, and the sobering realization of the meaning of progress.

So dawned the time of *Sturm und Drang:*[13] storm and stress to-day rocks our little boat on the mad waters of the world-sea; there is within and without the sound of conflict, the burning of body and rending of soul, inspiration strives with doubt, and faith with vain questionings. The bright ideals of the past, — physical freedom, political power, the training of brains and the training of hands, — all these in turn have waxed and waned, until even the last grows dim and overcast. Are they all wrong, — all false?

---

12. **Toussaint:** Toussaint Louverture (1743–1803), former slave who led the successful Haitian revolution against the French in 1791.
13. *Sturm und Drang:* Storm and stress (German).

No, not that, but each alone was over-simple and incomplete, – the dreams of a credulous race-childhood, or the fond imaginings of the other world which does not know and does not want to know our power. To be really true, all these ideals must be melted and welded into one. The training of the schools we need to-day more than ever, – the training of deft hands, quick eyes and ears, and above all the broader, deeper, higher culture of gifted minds and pure hearts. The power of the ballot we need in sheer self-defence, – else what shall save us from a second slavery? Freedom, too, the long-sought, we still seek, – the freedom of life and limb, the freedom to work and think, the freedom to love and aspire. Work, culture, liberty, – all these we need, not singly but together, not successively but together, each growing and aiding each, and all striving toward that vaster ideal that swims before the Negro people, the ideal of human brotherhood, gained through the unifying ideal of Race; the ideal of fostering and developing the traits and talents of the Negro, not in opposition to or contempt for other races, but rather in large conformity to the greater ideals of the American Republic, in order that some day on American soil two world-races may give each to each those characteristics both so sadly lack. We the darker ones come even now not altogether empty-handed: there are to-day no truer exponents of the pure human spirit of the Declaration of Independence than the American Negroes; there is no true American music but the wild sweet melodies of the Negro slave; the American fairy tales and folk-lore are Indian and African; and, all in all, we black men seem the sole oasis of simple faith and reverence in a dusty desert of dollars and smartness. Will America be poorer if she replace her brutal dyspeptic blundering with light-hearted but determined Negro humility? or her coarse and cruel wit with loving jovial good-humor? or her vulgar music with the soul of the Sorrow Songs?

Merely a concrete test of the underlying principles of the great republic is the Negro Problem, and the spiritual striving of the freedmen's sons is the travail of souls whose burden is almost beyond the measure of their strength, but who bear it in the name of an historic race, in the name of this the land of their fathers' fathers, and in the name of human opportunity.

And now what I have briefly sketched in large outline let me on coming pages tell again in many ways, with loving emphasis and deeper detail, that men may listen to the striving in the souls of black folk.

III
Of Mr. Booker T. Washington and Others

From birth till death enslaved; in word, in deed, unmanned!
. . . .
Hereditary bondsmen! Know ye not
Who would be free themselves must strike the blow?

–Byron[14]

---

14. **Byron:** The lines are from *Childe Harold's Pilgrimage*, 2.74.710 and 2.76.720–21, by the English poet George Gordon, Lord Byron (1788–1824).

Easily the most striking thing in the history of the American Negro since 1876 is the ascendancy of Mr. Booker T. Washington. It began at the time when war memories and ideals were rapidly passing; a day of astonishing commercial development was dawning; a sense of doubt and hesitation overtook the freedmen's sons, — then it was that his leading began. Mr. Washington came, with a simple definite programme, at the psychological moment when the nation was a little ashamed of having bestowed so much sentiment on Negroes, and was concentrating its energies on Dollars. His programme of industrial education, conciliation of the South, and submission and silence as to civil and political rights, was not wholly original; the Free Negroes from 1830 up to war-time had striven to build industrial schools, and the American Missionary Association[16] had from the first taught various trades; and Price[17] and others had sought a way of honorable alliance with the best of the Southerners. But Mr. Washington first indissolubly linked these things; he put enthusiasm, unlimited energy, and perfect faith into this programme, and changed it from a by-path into a veritable Way of Life. And the tale of the methods by which he did this is a fascinating study of human life.

It startled the nation to hear a Negro advocating such a programme after many decades of bitter complaint; it startled and won the applause of the South, it interested and won the admiration of the North; and after a confused murmur of protest, it silenced if it did not convert the Negroes themselves.

To gain the sympathy and coöperation of the various elements comprising the white South was Mr. Washington's first task; and this, at the time Tuskegee was founded, seemed, for a black man, well-nigh impossible. And yet ten years later it was done in the word spoken at Atlanta: "In all things purely social we can be as separate as the five fingers, and yet one as the hand in all things essential to mutual progress." This "Atlanta Compromise"[18] is by

---

15. [musical notation]: The music is from the African American slave song "There's a Great Camp Meeting in the Promised Land," also known as "Walk Together Children" (see also note 2).
16. **American Missionary Association**: Founded in 1846 as a missionary and abolitionist society, the organization was first formed to educate and train African Americans. Following Emancipation, the AMA founded a number of schools, including the Hampton Institute, attended by Booker T. Washington, as well as Fisk and Dillard universities.
17. **Price**: Joseph C. Price (1854-1893), scholar, minister, and influential African American leader who helped establish the Zion Wesley Institute, which, with the help of his fundraising, became Livingstone College, where he served as its first president.
18. **"Atlanta Compromise"**: Du Bois's characterization of Washington's most famous speech, "The Atlanta Exposition Address" (see pp. 1423-26). In it, Washington essentially withdrew demands for the full social and political equality of blacks in order to gain support for their technical training and access to jobs in the South.

all odds the most notable thing in Mr. Washington's career. The South interpreted it in different ways: the radicals received it as a complete surrender of the demand for civil and political equality; the conservatives, as a generously conceived working basis for mutual understanding. So both approved it, and to-day its author is certainly the most distinguished Southerner since Jefferson Davis,[19] and the one with the largest personal following.

Next to this achievement comes Mr. Washington's work in gaining place and consideration in the North. Others less shrewd and tactful had formerly essayed to sit on these two stools and had fallen between them; but as Mr. Washington knew the heart of the South from birth and training, so by singular insight he intuitively grasped the spirit of the age which was dominating the North. And so thoroughly did he learn the speech and thought of triumphant commercialism, and the ideals of material prosperity, that the picture of a lone black boy poring over a French grammar amid the weeds and dirt of a neglected home soon seemed to him the acme of absurdities.[20] One wonders what Socrates and St. Francis of Assisi would say to this.[21]

And yet this very singleness of vision and thorough oneness with his age is a mark of the successful man. It is as though Nature must needs make men narrow in order to give them force. So Mr. Washington's cult has gained unquestioning followers, his work has wonderfully prospered, his friends are legion, and his enemies are confounded. To-day he stands as the one recognized spokesman of his ten million fellows, and one of the most notable figures in a nation of seventy millions. One hesitates, therefore, to criticise a life which, beginning with so little, has done so much. And yet the time is come when one may speak in all sincerity and utter courtesy of the mistakes and shortcomings of Mr. Washington's career, as well as of his triumphs, without being thought captious or envious, and without forgetting that it is easier to do ill than well in the world.

The criticism that has hitherto met Mr. Washington has not always been of this broad character. In the South especially has he had to walk warily to avoid the harshest judgments, — and naturally so, for he is dealing with the one subject of deepest sensitiveness to that section. Twice — once when at the Chicago celebration of the Spanish-American War he alluded to the color-prejudice that is "eating away the vitals of the South,"[22] and

---

19. **Jefferson Davis**: Davis (1808-1889) was the president of the Confederate States of America during the Civil War.
20. **the acme of absurdities**: In his popular autobiography, *Up from Slavery* (1901), Washington illustrates what he viewed as the absurdity of educational practices that did not yield practical results and material gains by describing "a young man, who had attended some high school, sitting down in a one-room cabin, with grease on his clothing, filth all around him, and weeds in the garden, engaged in studying a French grammar."
21. **what Socrates . . . say to this**: Socrates, an ancient Greek philosopher (469-399 BCE), and St. Francis of Assisi, the Italian monk (c. 1181-1226) who founded the Franciscan order. Each would have rejected what Du Bois characterizes as Washington's "ideals of material prosperity," the former in his quest for knowledge and the latter in his quest for spirituality.
22. **"eating away . . . the South"**: In a speech to a crowd of 16,000 people at a Spanish-American War Peace Jubilee in Chicago in 1898, Washington asserted that the United States had won all its battles but one, "the effort to conquer ourselves in the blotting out of racial prejudice," adding: "Until we thus conquer ourselves, I make no empty statement when I say that we shall have, especially in the Southern part of our country, a cancer gnawing at the heart of the Republic, that shall one day prove as dangerous as an attack from an army without or within."

once when he dined with President Roosevelt[23] – has the resulting Southern criticism been violent enough to threaten seriously his popularity. In the North the feeling has several times forced itself into words, that Mr. Washington's counsels of submission overlooked certain elements of true manhood, and that his educational programme was unnecessarily narrow. Usually, however, such criticism has not found open expression, although, too, the spiritual sons of the Abolitionists have not been prepared to acknowledge that the schools founded before Tuskegee, by men of broad ideals and self-sacrificing spirit, were wholly failures or worthy of ridicule. While, then, criticism has not failed to follow Mr. Washington, yet the prevailing public opinion of the land has been but too willing to deliver the solution of a wearisome problem into his hands, and say, "If that is all you and your race ask, take it."

Among his own people, however, Mr. Washington has encountered the strongest and most lasting opposition, amounting at times to bitterness, and even to-day continuing strong and insistent even though largely silenced in outward expression by the public opinion of the nation. Some of this opposition is, of course, mere envy; the disappointment of displaced demagogues and the spite of narrow minds. But aside from this, there is among educated and thoughtful colored men in all parts of the land a feeling of deep regret, sorrow, and apprehension at the wide currency and ascendancy which some of Mr. Washington's theories have gained. These same men admire his sincerity of purpose, and are willing to forgive much to honest endeavor which is doing something worth the doing. They coöperate with Mr. Washington as far as they conscientiously can; and, indeed, it is no ordinary tribute to this man's tact and power that, steering as he must between so many diverse interests and opinions, he so largely retains the respect of all.

But the hushing of the criticism of honest opponents is a dangerous thing. It leads some of the best of the critics to unfortunate silence and paralysis of effort, and others to burst into speech so passionately and intemperately as to lose listeners. Honest and earnest criticism from those whose interests are most nearly touched, – criticism of writers by readers, of government by those governed, of leaders by those led, – this is the soul of democracy and the safeguard of modern society. If the best of the American Negroes receive by outer pressure a leader whom they had not recognized before, manifestly there is here a certain palpable gain. Yet there is also irreparable loss, – a loss of that peculiarly valuable education which a group receives when by search and criticism it finds and commissions its own leaders. The way in which this is done is at once the most elementary and the nicest problem of social growth. History is but the record of such group-leadership; and yet how infinitely changeful is its type and character! And of all types and kinds, what can be more instructive than the leadership of a group within a group? – that curious double movement where real progress may be negative

---

23. **when he dined with President Roosevelt:** Many white Southerners were outraged when President Theodore Roosevelt invited Washington to visit him in the White House in 1901. In an editorial, one newspaper editor wrote: "With our long-matured views on the subject of social intercourse between blacks and whites, the least we can say now is that we deplore the President's taste, and we distrust his wisdom."

and actual advance be relative retrogression. All this is the social student's inspiration and despair.

Now in the past the American Negro has had instructive experience in the choosing of group leaders, founding thus a peculiar dynasty which in the light of present conditions is worth while studying. When sticks and stones and beasts form the sole environment of a people, their attitude is largely one of determined opposition to and conquest of natural forces. But when to earth and brute is added an environment of men and ideas, then the attitude of the imprisoned group may take three main forms, — a feeling of revolt and revenge; an attempt to adjust all thought and action to the will of the greater group; or, finally, a determined effort at self-realization and self-development despite environing opinion. The influence of all of these attitudes at various times can be traced in the history of the American Negro, and in the evolution of his successive leaders.

Before 1750, while the fire of African freedom still burned in the veins of the slaves, there was in all leadership or attempted leadership but the one motive of revolt and revenge, — typified in the terrible Maroons, the Danish blacks, and Cato of Stono,[24] and veiling all the Americas in fear of insurrection. The liberalizing tendencies of the latter half of the eighteenth century brought, along with kindlier relations between black and white, thoughts of ultimate adjustment and assimilation. Such aspiration was especially voiced in the earnest songs of Phyllis, in the martyrdom of Attucks, the fighting of Salem and Poor, the intellectual accomplishments of Banneker and Derham, and the political demands of the Cuffes.[25]

Stern financial and social stress after the war cooled much of the previous humanitarian ardor. The disappointment and impatience of the Negroes at the persistence of slavery and serfdom voiced itself in two movements. The slaves in the South, aroused undoubtedly by vague rumors of the Haytian revolt, made three fierce attempts at insurrection, — in 1800 under Gabriel in Virginia, in 1822 under Vesey in Carolina, and in 1831

---

24. **the terrible Maroons, the Danish blacks, and Cato of Stono:** Du Bois refers to a series of famous slave rebellions. Maroons were escaped slaves and their descendants in Jamaica, where they fought off British troops from their settlements high in the mountains and gained their freedom through a bloody campaign known as the first Maroon War, which ended with a peace treaty in 1739. Thousands of Africans were also taken as slaves to the Danish West Indies (now the Virgin Islands), established as a colony for sugar plantations in 1672. Many of the slaves revolted in 1733, and another revolt finally ended slavery in the colony in 1848. Cato, a slave near Stono, South Carolina, organized nearly eighty slaves in a rebellion against their white masters in 1739. Called "Cato's Conspiracy," the incident led to fears of slave rebellions throughout the British colonies in North America.

25. **Such aspiration . . . political demands of the Cuffes:** Du Bois refers to a series of celebrated African Americans. Phillis Wheatley (1753-1784), who was brought to Boston as a slave, was the author of the first book published by an African American, *Poems on Various Subjects, Religious and Moral* (1773). Crispus Attucks (1723-1770), an escaped slave who was shot and killed by British troops in the Boston Massacre of 1770, was considered to be the first casualty of the American Revolution. Peter Salem (1750-1816) and Salem Poor (b. 1740s-?) were among some three dozen African Americans who fought with the colonists against the British in the battle of Bunker Hill in 1775. Benjamin Banneker (1731-1806) was an African American mathematician and astronomer; and James Derham (1762-?) was the first African American physician. Paul Cuffe (1759-1817) was an African American merchant and sea captain who fought for the rights of free blacks in Massachusetts and organized an effort to resettle them in colonies in Africa.

again in Virginia under the terrible Nat Turner.[26] In the Free States, on the other hand, a new and curious attempt at self-development was made. In Philadelphia and New York color-prescription led to a withdrawal of Negro communicants from white churches and the formation of a peculiar socio-religious institution among the Negroes known as the African Church, — an organization still living and controlling in its various branches over a million of men.

Walker's wild appeal[27] against the trend of the times showed how the world was changing after the coming of the cotton-gin. By 1830 slavery seemed hopelessly fastened on the South, and the slaves thoroughly cowed into submission. The free Negroes of the North, inspired by the mulatto immigrants from the West Indies, began to change the basis of their demands; they recognized the slavery of slaves, but insisted that they themselves were freemen, and sought assimilation and amalgamation with the nation on the same terms with other men. Thus, Forten and Purvis of Philadelphia, Shad of Wilmington, Du Bois of New Haven, Barbadoes of Boston, and others,[28] strove singly and together as men, they said, not slaves; as "people of color," not as "Negroes." The trend of the times, however, refused them recognition save in individual and exceptional cases, considered them as one with all the despised blacks, and they soon found themselves striving to keep even the rights they formerly had of voting and working and moving as freemen. Schemes of migration and colonization arose among them; but these they refused to entertain, and they eventually turned to the Abolition movement as a final refuge.[29]

Here, led by Remond, Nell, Wells-Brown, and Douglass,[30] a new period of self-assertion and self-development dawned. To be sure, ultimate freedom and assimilation was the

---

26. **The slaves in the South . . . Nat Turner:** The successful revolution in Haiti, beginning with a slave uprising in 1791, influenced three widely publicized slave revolts in the United States. The first was led by Gabriel Prosser (c. 1775–1800), who was executed for his role in an unsuccessful revolt in Richmond, Virginia, on October 7, 1800. Denmark Vesey (1767–1822), a former slave who planned a rebellion in Charleston, South Carolina, was charged with plotting to overthrow slavery and executed on June 23, 1822. Nat Turner (1800–1831), who led a bloody rebellion in Southampton County, Virginia, was captured and executed on November 11, 1831.

27. **Walker's wild appeal:** David Walker (1796–1830), a free person of color in Boston, published a militant antislavery tract, *Appeal in Four Articles; Together with a Preamble, To the Coloured Citizens of the World, but in Particular, and Very Expressly, to Those of the United States of America,* in 1829.

28. **Forten and Purvis . . . and others:** African American leaders of efforts to secure the rights of free people of color in the North: James Forten (1766–1842), Robert Purvis (1810–1898), Abraham Shadd (1801–1882), James G. Barbadoes (1796–1841), and Du Bois's paternal grandfather, Alexander Du Bois (1803–1888), who emigrated from Haiti to the United States. Forten, Purvis, Shadd, and Barbadoes were present in 1830 at the first National Negro Convention, out of which emerged a number of other organizations with similar goals, including the "American Society of Free People of Colour for improving their condition in the United States."

29. **they eventually turned . . . as a final refuge:** In fact, Forten, Purvis, Shadd, and Barbadoes were active abolitionists who became involved in the American Anti-Slavery Society as early as the 1830s.

30. **led by Remond . . . and Douglass:** Four influential African American activists and writers: Charles Lenox Remond (1810–1893), a free black who became an important abolitionist lecturer and later a recruiter of African American soldiers during the Civil War; William Cooper Nell (1816–1874), a historian and author of *Colored Patriots of the American Revolution, With Sketches of Several Distinguished Colored Persons: To Which Is Added a Brief Survey of the Condition and Prospects of Colored Americans* (1855); William Wells Brown (1814–1884), author of numerous works, including the *Narrative of William W. Brown, a*

ideal before the leaders, but the assertion of the manhood rights of the Negro by himself was the main reliance, and John Brown's raid was the extreme of its logic. After the war and emancipation, the great form of Frederick Douglass, the greatest of American Negro leaders, still led the host. Self-assertion, especially in political lines, was the main programme, and behind Douglass came Elliot, Bruce, and Langston, and the Reconstruction politicians, and, less conspicuous but of greater social significance Alexander Crummell and Bishop Daniel Payne.[31]

Then came the Revolution of 1876, the suppression of the Negro votes, the changing and shifting of ideals, and the seeking of new lights in the great night. Douglass, in his old age, still bravely stood for the ideals of his early manhood, – ultimate assimilation *through* self-assertion, and on no other terms. For a time Price arose as a new leader, destined, it seemed, not to give up, but to re-state the old ideals in a form less repugnant to the white South. But he passed away in his prime. Then came the new leader. Nearly all the former ones had become leaders by the silent suffrage of their fellows, had sought to lead their own people alone, and were usually, save Douglass, little known outside their race. But Booker T. Washington arose as essentially the leader not of one race but of two, – a compromiser between the South, the North, and the Negro. Naturally the Negroes resented, at first bitterly, signs of compromise which surrendered their civil and political rights, even though this was to be exchanged for larger chances of economic development. The rich and dominating North, however, was not only weary of the race problem, but was investing largely in Southern enterprises, and welcomed any method of peaceful coöperation. Thus, by national opinion, the Negroes began to recognize Mr. Washington's leadership; and the voice of criticism was hushed.

Mr. Washington represents in Negro thought the old attitude of adjustment and submission; but adjustment at such a peculiar time as to make his programme unique. This is an age of unusual economic development, and Mr. Washington's programme naturally takes an economic cast, becoming a gospel of Work and Money to such an extent as apparently almost completely to overshadow the higher aims of life. Moreover, this is an age when the more advanced races are coming in closer contact with the less developed races, and the race-feeling is therefore intensified; and Mr. Washington's programme practically accepts the alleged inferiority of the Negro races. Again, in our own land, the reaction from the sentiment of war time has given impetus to race-prejudice against Negroes, and Mr. Washington withdraws many of the high demands of Negroes as men

---

Fugitive Slave (1847) and the first novel published by an African American, *Clotel; or, The President's Daughter* (1853); and Frederick Douglass, the celebrated abolitionist, lecturer, and author of *Narrative of the Life of Frederick Douglass* (1845), *My Bondage and My Freedom* (1855), and several editions of *The Life and Times of Frederick Douglass*.

31. **Elliot . . . Payne:** African American political and social leaders during the period following the Civil War: Robert Brown Eliot (1841–1884), a U.S. congressman from South Carolina; Blanche K. Bruce (1841–1898), a Republican from Mississippi and the first African American elected to the Senate; John Mercer Langston (1829–1897), Virginia's first African American congressman; Alexander Crummell (1819–1898), an Anglican minister educated at Cambridge University in England and a founder of the American Negro Academy; and Daniel Payne (1811–1893), the first African American college president (Wilberforce College) and a bishop of the African Methodist Episcopal Church.

and American citizens. In other periods of intensified prejudice all the Negro's tendency to self-assertion has been called forth; at this period a policy of submission is advocated. In the history of nearly all other races and peoples the doctrine preached at such crises has been that manly self-respect is worth more than lands and houses, and that a people who voluntarily surrender such respect, or cease striving for it, are not worth civilizing.

In answer to this, it has been claimed that the Negro can survive only through submission. Mr. Washington distinctly asks that black people give up, at least for the present, three things, —

First, political power,

Second, insistence on civil rights,

Third, higher education of Negro youth, —

and concentrate all their energies on industrial education, the accumulation of wealth, and the conciliation of the South. This policy has been courageously and insistently advocated for over fifteen years, and has been triumphant for perhaps ten years. As a result of this tender of the palm-branch, what has been the return? In these years there have occurred:

1. The disfranchisement of the Negro.

2. The legal creation of a distinct status of civil inferiority for the Negro.

3. The steady withdrawal of aid from institutions for the higher training of the Negro.

These movements are not, to be sure, direct results of Mr. Washington's teachings; but his propaganda has, without a shadow of doubt, helped their speedier accomplishment. The question then comes: Is it possible, and probable, that nine millions of men can make effective progress in economic lines if they are deprived of political rights, made a servile caste, and allowed only the most meagre chance for developing their exceptional men? If history and reason give any distinct answer to these questions, it is an emphatic *No.* And Mr. Washington thus faces the triple paradox of his career:

1. He is striving nobly to make Negro artisans business men and property-owners; but it is utterly impossible, under modern competitive methods, for workingmen and property-owners to defend their rights and exist without the right of suffrage.

2. He insists on thrift and self-respect, but at the same time counsels a silent submission to civic inferiority such as is bound to sap the manhood of any race in the long run.

3. He advocates common-school and industrial training, and depreciates institutions of higher learning; but neither the Negro common-schools, nor Tuskegee itself, could remain open a day were it not for teachers trained in Negro colleges, or trained by their graduates.

This triple paradox in Mr. Washington's position is the object of criticism by two classes of colored Americans. One class is spiritually descended from Toussaint the Savior, through Gabriel, Vesey, and Turner, and they represent the attitude of revolt and revenge; they hate the white South blindly and distrust the white race generally, and so far as they agree on definite action, think that the Negro's only hope lies in emigration beyond the borders of the United States. And yet, by the irony of fate, nothing has more effectually made this programme seem hopeless than the recent course of the United States toward weaker and darker peoples in the West Indies, Hawaii, and the Philippines, – for where in the world may we go and be safe from lying and brute force?[32]

The other class of Negroes who cannot agree with Mr. Washington has hitherto said little aloud. They deprecate the sight of scattered counsels, of internal disagreement; and especially the dislike making their just criticism of a useful and earnest man an excuse for a general discharge of venom from small-minded opponents. Nevertheless, the questions involved are so fundamental and serious that it is difficult to see how men like the Grimkes, Kelly Miller, J. W. E. Bowen,[33] and other representatives of this group, can much longer be silent. Such men feel in conscience bound to ask of this nation three things:

1. The right to vote.
2. Civic equality.
3. The education of youth according to ability.

They acknowledge Mr. Washington's invaluable service in counselling patience and courtesy in such demands; they do not ask that ignorant black men vote when ignorant whites are debarred, or that any reasonable restrictions in the suffrage should not be applied; they know that the low social level of the mass of the race is responsible for much discrimination against it, but they also know, and the nation knows, that relentless color-prejudice is more often a cause than a result of the Negro's degradation; they seek the abatement of this relic of barbarism, and not its systematic encouragement and pampering by all agencies of social power from the Associated Press to the Church of Christ. They advocate, with Mr. Washington, a broad system of Negro common schools supplemented by thorough industrial training; but they are surprised that a man of Mr. Washington's insight cannot see that no such educational system ever has rested or can rest on any other basis than that of the well-equipped college and university, and they insist that there is a demand for a few such institutions throughout the South to train the best of the Negro youth as teachers, professional men, and leaders.

This group of men honor Mr. Washington for his attitude of conciliation toward the white South; they accept the "Atlanta Compromise" in its broadest interpretation; they recognize, with him, many signs of promise, many men of high purpose and fair judgment, in this section; they know that no easy task has been laid upon a region already tottering under heavy burdens. But, nevertheless, they insist that the way to truth and

---

32. **And yet, . . . brute force?:** Several examples of American aggression toward "weaker and darker peoples": the overthrow of the royal government and consequent annexation of Hawai'i in 1898; the invasion of Puerto Rico during the Spanish-American War, at the conclusion of which Spain ceded the island to the United States in 1898; and the brutal suppression of the Filipino insurrection during the Philippine-American War (1899-1902).

33. **Grimkes . . . Bowen:** African American civic, educational, and religious leaders of the period: Archibald H. Grimké (1849-1930), a prominent lawyer and later one of the founders of the NAACP; his brother Francis J. Grimké (1850-1937), the celebrated pastor of the Fifteenth Street Presbyterian Church in Washington, D.C.; Kelly Miller (1863-1939), dean of Howard University; and John Wesley Edward Bowen (1855-1933), president of Gammon Theological Seminary in Atlanta.

right lies in straightforward honesty, not in indiscriminate flattery; in praising those of the South who do well and criticising uncompromisingly those who do ill; in taking advantage of the opportunities at hand and urging their fellows to do the same, but at the same time in remembering that only a firm adherence to their higher ideals and aspirations will ever keep those ideals within the realm of possibility. They do not expect that the free right to vote, to enjoy civic rights, and to be educated, will come in a moment; they do not expect to see the bias and prejudices of years disappear at the blast of a trumpet; but they are absolutely certain that the way for a people to gain their reasonable rights is not by voluntarily throwing them away and insisting that they do not want them; that the way for a people to gain respect is not by continually belittling and ridiculing themselves; that, on the contrary, Negroes must insist continually, in season and out of season, that voting is necessary to modern manhood, that color discrimination is barbarism, and that black boys need education as well as white boys.

In failing thus to state plainly and unequivocally the legitimate demands of their people, even at the cost of opposing an honored leader, the thinking classes of American Negroes would shirk a heavy responsibility, — a responsibility to themselves, a responsibility to the struggling masses, a responsibility to the darker races of men whose future depends so largely on this American experiment, but especially a responsibility to this nation, — this common Fatherland. It is wrong to encourage a man or a people in evil-doing; it is wrong to aid and abet a national crime simply because it is unpopular not to do so. The growing spirit of kindliness and reconciliation between the North and South after the frightful differences of a generation ago ought to be a source of deep congratulation to all, and especially to those whose mistreatment caused the war; but if that reconciliation is to be marked by the industrial slavery and civic death of those same black men, with permanent legislation into a position of inferiority, then those black men, if they are really men, are called upon by every consideration of patriotism and loyalty to oppose such a course by all civilized methods, even though such opposition involves disagreement with Mr. Booker T. Washington. We have no right to sit silently by while the inevitable seeds are sown for a harvest of disaster to our children, black and white.

First, it is the duty of black men to judge the South discriminatingly. The present generation of Southerners are not responsible for the past, and they should not be blindly hated or blamed for it. Furthermore, to no class is the indiscriminate endorsement of the recent course of the South toward Negroes more nauseating than to the best thought of the South. The South is not "solid"; it is a land in the ferment of social change, wherein forces of all kinds are fighting for supremacy; and to praise the ill the South is to-day perpetrating is just as wrong as to condemn the good. Discriminating and broad-minded criticism is what the South needs, — needs it for the sake of her own white sons and daughters, and for the insurance of robust, healthy mental and moral development.

To-day even the attitude of the Southern whites toward the blacks is not, as so many assume, in all cases the same; the ignorant Southerner hates the Negro, the workingmen fear his competition, the money-makers wish to use him as a laborer, some of the educated see a menace in his upward development, while others – usually the sons of the masters – wish to help him to rise. National opinion has enabled this last class to maintain the Negro common schools, and to protect the Negro partially in property, life, and limb. Through the pressure of the money-makers, the Negro is in danger of being reduced to semi-slavery, especially in the country districts; the workingmen, and those of the educated who fear the Negro, have united to disfranchise him, and some have urged his deportation; while the passions of the ignorant are easily aroused to lynch and abuse any black man. To praise this intricate whirl of thought and prejudice is nonsense; to inveigh indiscriminately against "the South" is unjust; but to use the same breath in praising Governor Aycock, exposing Senator Morgan, arguing with Mr. Thomas Nelson Page, and denouncing Senator Ben Tillman,[34] is not only sane, but the imperative duty of thinking black men.

It would be unjust to Mr. Washington not to acknowledge that in several instances he has opposed movements in the South which were unjust to the Negro; he sent memorials to the Louisiana and Alabama constitutional conventions, he has spoken against lynching, and in other ways has openly or silently set his influence against sinister schemes and unfortunate happenings. Notwithstanding this, it is equally true to assert that on the whole the distinct impression left by Mr. Washington's propaganda is, first, that the South is justified in its present attitude toward the Negro because of the Negro's degradation; secondly, that the prime cause of the Negro's failure to rise more quickly is his wrong education in the past; and, thirdly, that his future rise depends primarily on his own efforts. Each of these propositions is a dangerous half-truth. The supplementary truths must never be lost sight of: first, slavery and race-prejudice are potent if not sufficient causes of the Negro's position; second, industrial and common-school training were necessarily slow in planting because they had to await the black teachers trained by higher institutions, – it being extremely doubtful if any essentially different development was possible, and certainly a Tuskegee was unthinkable before 1880; and, third, while it is a great truth to say that the Negro must strive and strive mightily to help himself, it is equally true that unless his striving be not simply seconded, but rather aroused and encouraged, by the initiative of the richer and wiser environing group, he cannot hope for great success.

In his failure to realize and impress this last point, Mr. Washington is especially to be criticised. His doctrine has tended to make the whites, North and South, shift the burden of the Negro problem to the Negro's shoulders and stand aside as critical and

---

34. **praising Governor Aycock . . . denouncing Senator Ben Tillman:** Charles B. Aycock (1859–1912) was a strong supporter of local schools and universal education who came to be known as the "Education Governor" of North Carolina (1901–05). Du Bois also refers to three southerners known for their racist attitudes toward African Americans: John Tyler Morgan (1824–1907), a former Confederate general who continued to support the doctrine of states' rights during Reconstruction and who was instrumental in developing the ideology of white supremacy during his long service as a U.S. senator from Alabama (1877–1907); Thomas Nelson Page (1853–1922), a southern writer who helped popularize romantic myths about slavery and plantation life in collections of stories such as *In Ole Virginia* (1887); and Benjamin R. ("Pitchfork Ben") Tillman (1847–1918), a racial demagogue who advocated segregation and the disenfranchisement of black voters as governor of South Carolina (1890–94) and as a U.S. senator (1895–1918).

rather pessimistic spectators; when in fact the burden belongs to the nation, and the hands of none of us are clean if we bend not our energies to righting these great wrongs.

The South ought to be led, by candid and honest criticism, to assert her better self and do her full duty to the race she has cruelly wronged and is still wronging. The North – her co-partner in guilt – cannot salve her conscience by plastering it with gold. We cannot settle this problem by diplomacy and suaveness, by "policy" alone. If worse come to worst, can the moral fibre of this country survive the slow throttling and murder of nine millions of men?

The black men of America have a duty to perform, a duty stern and delicate, – a forward movement to oppose a part of the work of their greatest leader. So far as Mr. Washington preaches Thrift, Patience, and Industrial Training for the masses, we must hold up his hands and strive with him, rejoicing in his honors and glorying in the strength of this Joshua called of God and of man to lead the headless host. But so far as Mr. Washington apologizes for injustice, North or South, does not rightly value the privilege and duty of voting, belittles the emasculating effects of caste distinctions, and opposes the higher training and ambition of our brighter minds, – so far as he, the South, or the Nation, does this, – we must unceasingly and firmly oppose them. By every civilized and peaceful method we must strive for the rights which the world accords to men, clinging unwaveringly to those great words which the sons of the Fathers would fain forget: "We hold these truths to be self-evident: That all men are created equal; that they are endowed by their Creator with certain unalienable rights; that among these are life, liberty, and the pursuit of happiness."[35]

[1903]

---

35. "**We . . . happiness**": From the preamble to the Declaration of Independence (1776), which in the original reads "inalienable" rights not "unalienable" rights.

Henry Adams

[1838–1918]

Henry Brooks Adams was born in Boston, Massachusetts, on February 16, 1838. Speaking of himself in the third person, Adams in his autobiography later observed: "Probably no child, born in the year, held better cards than he." His mother, Abigail Brown Brooks Adams, was from one of the wealthiest and most distinguished families in Boston, and his father, Charles Francis Adams, was the grandson of the second president, John Adams, and the son of the sixth president, John Quincy Adams. Henry Adams grew up in a world of comfort and culture in his family home, which contained the largest private library in Boston, and

His true function was to ask questions, not to answer them; his true function was to provoke speculation, not to satisfy it.

–Henry Steele Commager

Henry Adams

This photograph was taken in the 1870s, while Adams was teaching history at Harvard.

was a frequent visitor to the home of his grandfather John Quincy Adams in Quincy, Massachusetts. Adams recalled that one day while he was staying there he adamantly refused to go to school. Without saying a word, the former president took his grandson's hand, silently walked him to school and, still without speaking, left him seated in a classroom. Despite Adams's aversion to formal education, he duly attended private schools and enrolled at Harvard College in 1854. Although he earned mediocre grades, primarily for tardiness and other violations of school rules, he acted in theatrical performances, wrote for the *Harvard Magazine*, and was popular with other students, who elected him to deliver the class oration of 1858.

Adams spent most of the following decade studying and working abroad. "As yet he knew nothing," Adams observed of himself at the time of his graduation from Harvard. "Education had not begun." Eager to learn modern languages and to see the world, he joined several of his classmates on what was then a part of every wealthy young man's education, a grand tour of Europe. Adams studied civil law in Germany, taking time off to tour Austria, Switzerland, and Italy, from which he wrote travel letters published in the *Boston Daily Courier*. He finally returned to the United States in October 1860, on the eve of the Civil War. Adams took a position as a secretary to his father, now a congressman from Massachusetts, in Washington, D.C. When President Lincoln appointed his father minister to Great Britain, Adams accompanied him to London and continued to serve as his secretary there until May 1868. Adams became a foreign correspondent for the *New York Times*, reporting on the British reaction to the Civil War. He also began to write more substantial pieces for the distinguished Boston journal the *North American Review*, including "Captaine John Smith" (1867), a rigorous historical analysis in which Adams demonstrates that Smith had invented the romantic story of his rescue from death by the love-struck Pocahontas.

After his return home in 1868, Adams devoted himself to the study of American history and current events in the United States. He initially worked as a journalist in Washington, D.C., where he championed causes such as currency reform and the overhaul of the "spoils system" of civil service. Appalled by the spreading corruption during the Gilded Age, as exemplified by the financier Jay Gould's effort to corner the market on gold and the financial chicanery involved in the struggle for control of the Erie Railroad, Adams and his older brother, Charles Francis Adams Jr., studied those scandals in articles they gathered together as *Chapters of Erie and Other Essays*, published in 1871. By then, the once-reluctant student had accepted positions as assistant professor of history at Harvard and as editor of the *North American Review*. In 1872, he married Marian ("Clover") Hooper, the accomplished daughter of a prominent Boston physician, and the couple embarked on a yearlong wedding journey to Europe and Egypt. They lived in Boston until 1877, when Adams resigned from Harvard to edit the papers of Albert Gallatin, Thomas

Jefferson's secretary of the treasury, at the State Department Archives in Washington, D.C. In addition to a biography of Gallatin and an edition of his writings, Adams anonymously published *Democracy: An American Novel* (1880), a best-selling satire of political corruption in Washington; and *Esther; A Novel* (1884), which appeared under the pseudonym Frances Snow Compton. Adams also began work on his major project, the nine-volume *History of the United States during the Administration of Thomas Jefferson and James Madison* (1889–91).

While Adams was working on the project, his happy and productive life in Washington was shattered by the loss of his wife, who committed suicide in December 1885. During the remaining years of his life, the grief-stricken Adams traveled extensively: to the American West; to Mexico and the Caribbean, including Cuba; to Japan, where he studied Buddhism, and later across the South Pacific to Hawaii, Fiji, Australia, and Ceylon; to Egypt, Turkey, and Russia; and throughout Europe. Adams became fascinated by medieval culture, especially the architecture of Gothic cathedrals in northern France, the central focus of his book *Mont-Saint-Michel and Chartres*, which he privately printed in 1904 and later authorized the American Institute of Architects to publish in 1913. He also wrote *The Education of Henry Adams*, an autobiography he privately printed in 1907. In it, Adams introduced his "Dynamic Theory of History," a complex formulation of the gravitational pull or "attractive force" of various concepts that had shaped the evolution of human beings from their earliest beginnings to 1900. Adams reformulated his theory in several later works, including "A Letter to American Teachers of History," a pamphlet he distributed to college librarians and history professors in 1910. Although he was partially paralyzed by a stroke in 1912, Adams continued to travel and entertain friends at his home in Washington, where he died on March 27, 1918. He was buried beside his wife in Rock Creek Cemetery, where Adams had earlier commissioned a now-famous memorial to mark their plots, asking the sculptor Augustus Saint-Gaudens to create a statue that symbolized "the acceptance, intellectually, of the inevitable."

bedfordstmartins.com/ americanlit for research links on Adams

Reading Adams's *The Education of Henry Adams*.   Adams began working on his autobiography in 1903 and completed it in 1905. In 1907, he paid for a printing of one hundred copies, which he circulated for comment and correction among those mentioned in the book, including his brothers and his friend President Theodore Roosevelt. Although Adams made a few corrections, he remained dissatisfied with the book, which he would not allow to be reprinted during his lifetime. A second edition, which appeared six months after his death in 1918, was awarded the Pulitzer Prize. Adopting the unusual narrative strategy of writing about himself in the third person, Adams describes the events of his life with the objectivity of a historian and, frequently, with ironic detachment. As the title of his autobiography indicates, and as Adams emphasizes in his Preface, printed below, the central focus of the work is his education, or rather the failure of his traditional education to prepare him for the modern world. Among his most revelatory confrontations with that world were his visits to the World's Columbian Exposition in Chicago in 1893 and the Paris Exposition in 1900, where he was fascinated by the advances in technology displayed in the Hall of Dynamos. Adams, who had been reading medieval philosophy and studying Gothic architecture for several years, began to ponder the relation between the dynamo, the recently invented mechanical producer of electrical energy, and the power of the Catholic Church during the Middle Ages. He pursued that question in the famous chapter also printed below, "The Virgin and the Dynamo," in which he suggests that by 1900 a belief in scientific progress and technology, symbolized by the dynamo, had come to exert the same force over the minds of human beings that had once been exerted by the medieval church, symbolized by the Virgin Mary. The text is taken from the second edition of *The Education of Henry Adams: An Autobiography* (1918).

Palace of Electricity

This lantern slide of the interior of the Palace of Electricity shows one of the huge dynamos (lower left) that fascinated Henry Adams during his visit to the Paris Universal Exposition in 1900. Lantern slides were frequently used in educational lectures and popular entertainments in which photographic images were displayed on a wall or a screen.

THE EDUCATION OF HENRY ADAMS

Preface

Jean Jacques Rousseau began his famous "Confessions"[1] by a vehement appeal to the Deity: "I have shown myself as I was; contemptible and vile when I was so; good, generous, sublime when I was so; I have unveiled my interior such as Thou thyself hast seen it, Eternal Father! Collect about me the innumerable swarm of my fellows; let them hear my confessions; let them groan at my unworthiness; let them blush at my meannesses! Let each of them discover his heart in his turn at the foot of thy throne with the same sincerity; and then let any one of them tell thee if he dares: 'I was a better man!'"

Jean Jacques was a very great educator in the manner of the eighteenth century, and has been commonly thought to have had more influence than any other teacher of his time; but his peculiar method of improving human nature has not been universally admired. Most educators of the nineteenth century have declined to show themselves before their scholars as objects more vile or contemptible than necessary, and even the humblest teacher hides, if possible, the faults with which nature has generously embellished us all, as it did Jean Jacques, thinking, as most religious minds are apt to do, that the Eternal Father himself may not feel unmixed pleasure at our thrusting under his eyes chiefly the least agreeable details of his creation.

As an unfortunate result the twentieth century finds few recent guides to avoid, or to follow. American literature offers scarcely one working model for high education. The student must go back, beyond Jean Jacques, to Benjamin Franklin, to find a model even of self-teaching. Except in the abandoned sphere of the dead languages, no one has discussed what part of education has, in his personal experience, turned out to be useful, and what not. This volume attempts to discuss it.

As educator, Jean Jacques was, in one respect, easily first; he erected a monument of warning against the Ego. Since his time, and largely thanks to him, the Ego has steadily tended to efface itself, and, for purposes of model, to become a manikin on which the toilet of education is to be draped in order to show the fit or misfit of the clothes. The object of study is the garment, not the figure. The tailor adapts the manikin as well as the clothes to his patron's wants. The tailor's object, in this volume, is to fit young men, in universities or elsewhere, to be men of the world, equipped for any emergency; and the garment offered to them is meant to show the faults of the patchwork fitted on their fathers.

At the utmost, the active-minded young man should ask of his teacher only mastery of his tools. The young man himself, the subject of education, is a certain form of energy; the object to be gained is economy of his force; the training is partly the clearing away of

---

1. **Rousseau ... "Confessions":** The French writer, philosopher, and education reformer Jean Jacques Rousseau (1712-1778) persistently describes his failings and imperfections in his remarkably candid autobiography, *The Confessions*, published posthumously in 1782.

obstacles, partly the direct application of effort. Once acquired, the tools and models may be thrown away.

The manikin, therefore, has the same value as any other geometrical figure of three or more dimensions, which is used for the study of relation. For that purpose it cannot be spared; it is the only measure of motion, of proportion, of human condition; it must have the air of reality; must be taken for real; must be treated as though it had life. Who knows? Possibly it had!

February 16, 1907

Chapter XXV
The Dynamo and the Virgin (1900)

Until the Great Exposition of 1900[2] closed its doors in November, Adams haunted it, aching to absorb knowledge, and helpless to find it. He would have liked to know how much of it could have been grasped by the best-informed man in the world. While he was thus meditating chaos, Langley[3] came by, and showed it to him. At Langley's behest, the Exhibition dropped its superfluous rags and stripped itself to the skin, for Langley knew what to study, and why, and how; while Adams might as well have stood outside in the night, staring at the Milky Way. Yet Langley said nothing new, and taught nothing that one might not have learned from Lord Bacon,[4] three hundred years before; but though one should have known the "Advancement of Science" as well as one knew the "Comedy of Errors,"[5] the literary knowledge counted for nothing until some teacher should show how to apply it. Bacon took a vast deal of trouble in teaching King James I and his subjects, American or other, towards the year 1620, that true science was the development or economy of forces; yet an elderly American in 1900 knew neither the formula nor the forces; or even so much as to say to himself that his historical business in the Exposition concerned only the economies or developments of force since 1893, when he began the study at Chicago.[6]

Nothing in education is so astonishing as the amount of ignorance it accumulates in the form of inert facts. Adams had looked at most of the accumulations of art in the

---

2. **Great Exposition of 1900**: The Paris Universal Exposition, held from April to November 1900, attracted over fifty-seven million visitors from around the world.

3. **Langley**: Samuel P. Langley (1834-1906), professor of astronomy and secretary of the Smithsonian Institution. He invented an "aerodrome," a flying machine that failed after several attempts, including one just a few days before the Wright brothers successfully flew a plane at Kitty Hawk on December 17, 1903.

4. **Lord Bacon**: Sir Francis Bacon (1561-1626), English philosopher and author of *The Advancement of Learning*, which he presented to King James I in 1605, and the *Novum Organum*, variously translated as "New Organ" or "New Instrument," an important work in the development of the scientific method first published in 1620. His belief that truth is discovered through empirical observation strongly influenced Adams, who observed that Bacon "urged society to lay aside the idea of evolving the universe from a thought, and to try evolving thought from the universe."

5. **"Comedy of Errors"**: An early play (1594) by William Shakespeare (1564-1616).

6. **Chicago**: Adams attended the World's Columbian Exposition of 1893 in Chicago, where he became interested in force as both a scientific and philosophical concept.

storehouses called Art Museums; yet he did not know how to look at the art exhibits of 1900. He had studied Karl Marx and his doctrines of history[7] with profound attention, yet he could not apply them at Paris. Langley, with the ease of a great master of experiment, threw out of the field every exhibit that did not reveal a new application of force, and naturally threw out, to begin with, almost the whole art exhibit. Equally, he ignored almost the whole industrial exhibit. He led his pupil directly to the forces. His chief interest was in new motors to make his airship feasible, and he taught Adams the astonishing complexities of the new Daimler motor,[8] and of the automobile, which, since 1893, had become a nightmare at a hundred kilometres an hour, almost as destructive as the electric tram which was only ten years older; and threatening to become as terrible as the locomotive steam-engine itself, which was almost exactly Adams's own age.

Then he showed his scholar the great hall of dynamos, and explained how little he knew about electricity or force of any kind, even of his own special sun, which spouted heat in inconceivable volume, but which, as far as he knew, might spout less or more, at any time, for all the certainty he felt in it. To him, the dynamo itself was but an ingenious channel for conveying somewhere the heat latent in a few tons of poor coal hidden in a dirty engine-house carefully kept out of sight; but to Adams the dynamo became a symbol of infinity. As he grew accustomed to the great gallery of machines, he began to feel the forty-foot dynamos as a moral force, much as the early Christians felt the Cross. The planet itself seemed less impressive, in its old-fashioned, deliberate, annual or daily revolution, than this huge wheel, revolving within arm's-length at some vertiginous speed, and barely murmuring — scarcely humming an audible warning to stand a hair's-breadth further for respect of power — while it would not wake the baby lying close against its frame. Before the end, one began to pray to it; inherited instinct taught the natural expression of man before silent and infinite force. Among the thousand symbols of ultimate energy, the dynamo was not so human as some, but it was the most expressive.

Yet the dynamo, next to the steam-engine, was the most familiar of exhibits. For Adams's objects its value lay chiefly in its occult mechanism. Between the dynamo in the gallery of machines and the engine-house outside, the break of continuity amounted to abysmal fracture for a historian's objects. No more relation could he discover between the steam and the electric current than between the Cross and the cathedral. The forces were interchangeable if not reversible, but he could see only an absolute *fiat* in electricity as in faith. Langley could not help him. Indeed, Langley seemed to be worried by the same trouble, for he constantly repeated that the new forces were anarchical, and especially that he was not responsible for the new rays, that were little short of parricidal in their wicked spirit towards science. His own rays, with which he had doubled the solar

---

7. **Marx and his doctrines of history:** The influential German philosopher and social scientist Karl Marx (1818–1883) viewed social conflict as a driving force in the historical process.
8. **the new Daimler motor:** A famous high-speed internal combustion engine invented by the German engineer and automotive pioneer Gottlieb Daimler (1834–1900). A car fitted with the engine won the first auto race in history, from Paris to Rouen, in 1894.

spectrum, were altogether harmless and beneficent; but Radium denied its God – or, what was to Langley the same thing, denied the truths of his Science.[9] The force was wholly new.

A historian who asked only to learn enough to be as futile as Langley or Kelvin,[10] made rapid progress under this teaching, and mixed himself up in the tangle of ideas until he achieved a sort of Paradise of ignorance vastly consoling to his fatigued senses. He wrapped himself in vibrations and rays which were new, and he would have hugged Marconi and Branly[11] had he met them, as he hugged the dynamo; while he lost his arithmetic in trying to figure out the equation between the discoveries and the economies of force. The economies, like the discoveries, were absolute, supersensual, occult; incapable of expression in horse-power. What mathematical equivalent could he suggest as the value of a Branly coherer? Frozen air, or the electric furnace, had some scale of measurement, no doubt, if somebody could invent a thermometer adequate to the purpose; but X-rays had played no part whatever in man's consciousness, and the atom itself had figured only as a fiction of thought. In these seven years man had translated himself into a new universe which had no common scale of measurement with the old. He had entered a supersensual world, in which he could measure nothing except by chance collisions of movements imperceptible to his senses, perhaps even imperceptible to his instruments, but perceptible to each other, and so to some known ray at the end of the scale. Langley seemed prepared for anything, even for an indeterminable number of universes interfused – physics stark mad in metaphysics.

Historians undertake to arrange sequences, – called stories, or histories – assuming in silence a relation of cause and effect. These assumptions, hidden in the depths of dusty libraries, have been astounding, but commonly unconscious and childlike; so much so, that if any captious critic were to drag them to light, historians would probably reply, with one voice, that they had never supposed themselves required to know what they were talking about. Adams, for one, had toiled in vain to find out what he meant. He had even published a dozen volumes of American history for no other purpose than to satisfy himself whether, by the severest process of stating, with the least possible comment, such facts as seemed sure, in such order as seemed rigorously consequent, he could fix for a familiar moment a necessary sequence of human movement. The result had satisfied him as little as at Harvard College. Where he saw sequence, other men saw something quite different, and no one saw the same unit of measure. He cared little about his experiments and less about his statesmen, who seemed to him quite as igno-

---

9. **His own rays . . . the truths of his Science:** In 1878, Langley invented the bolometer, a device that allowed him to measure the intensity of electromagnetic radiation, invisible heat rays in the infrared spectrum. Radium, an extremely radioactive element that challenged traditional scientific ideas about matter and energy, was discovered by Marie and Pierre Curie in 1898.
10. **Kelvin:** 1st Baron William Thomson Kelvin (1824-1907), Irish-Scottish engineer, physicist, and inventor who made significant contributions to the mathematical analysis of electricity and thermodynamics during the nineteenth century.
11. **Marconi and Branly:** Guglielmo Marconi (1874-1937), Italian electrical engineer who developed wireless telegraphy and invented the radio in 1895. Eugène Édouard Désiré Branly (1844-1940), French physicist who invented the coherer, a device for detecting radio waves.

rant as himself and, as a rule, no more honest; but he insisted on a relation of sequence, and if he could not reach it by one method, he would try as many methods as science knew. Satisfied that the sequence of men led to nothing and that the sequence of their society could lead no further, while the mere sequence of time was artificial, and the sequence of thought was chaos, he turned at last to the sequence of force; and thus it happened that, after ten years' pursuit, he found himself lying in the Gallery of Machines at the Great Exposition of 1900, his historical neck broken by the sudden irruption of forces totally new.

Since no one else showed much concern, an elderly person without other cares had no need to betray alarm. The year 1900 was not the first to upset schoolmasters. Copernicus and Galileo had broken many professorial necks about 1600;[12] Columbus had stood the world on its head towards 1500;[13] but the nearest approach to the revolution of 1900 was that of 310, when Constantine set up the Cross.[14] The rays that Langley disowned, as well as those which he fathered, were occult, supersensual, irrational; they were a revelation of mysterious energy like that of the Cross; they were what, in terms of mediaeval science, were called immediate modes of the divine substance.

The historian was thus reduced to his last resources. Clearly if he was bound to reduce all these forces to a common value, this common value could have no measure but that of their attraction on his own mind. He must treat them as they had been felt; as convertible, reversible, interchangeable attractions on thought. He made up his mind to venture it; he would risk translating rays into faith. Such a reversible process would vastly amuse a chemist, but the chemist could not deny that he, or some of his fellow physicists, could feel the force of both. When Adams was a boy in Boston, the best chemist in the place had probably never heard of Venus except by way of scandal, or of the Virgin except as idolatry;[15] neither had he heard of dynamos or automobiles or radium; yet his mind was ready to feel the force of all, though the rays were unborn and the women were dead.

Here opened another totally new education, which promised to be by far the most hazardous of all. The knife-edge along which he must crawl, like Sir Lancelot[16] in the twelfth century, divided two kingdoms of force which had nothing in common but

---

12. **Copernicus and Galileo . . . 1600:** The Polish astronomer Nicolaus Copernicus (1473-1543) proved that the earth rotates around the sun, a theory supported by the Italian astronomer Galileo Galilei (1564-1642), who was consequently condemned by the Inquisition.

13. **Columbus . . . 1500:** The four voyages the Italian navigator and explorer Christopher Columbus (1451-1506) undertook between 1492 and 1504 initiated the European exploration and colonization of the Americas, what was then a "New World" to Europeans.

14. **Constantine set up the Cross:** Constantine I, or Constantine the Great (c. 272-337), the first Roman emperor to embrace Christianity, issued the Edict of Milan in 313, ending government-sanctioned persecution of Christians.

15. **Venus . . . idolatry:** Adams suggests that a chemist, or pharmacist, knows about the effects of Venus, the Greek goddess of love, through the treatment of sexually transmitted diseases. The centrality of the Virgin Mary to Catholicism was often denigrated as idolatry by Protestants.

16. **Sir Lancelot:** In the medieval legends of King Arthur and the Knights of the Round Table, Sir Lancelot is a great knight who tragically destroys the kingdom because of his illicit relationship with Arthur's wife, Guinevere. In one of his many legendary exploits, Lancelot rescues Guinevere after crawling across a bridge made of a sword.

attraction. They were as different as a magnet is from gravitation, supposing one knew what a magnet was, or gravitation, or love. The force of the Virgin was still felt at Lourdes,[17] and seemed to be as potent as X-rays; but in America neither Venus nor Virgin ever had value as force—at most as sentiment. No American had ever been truly afraid of either.

This problem in dynamics gravely perplexed an American historian. The Woman had once been supreme; in France she still seemed potent, not merely as a sentiment, but as a force. Why was she unknown in America? For evidently America was ashamed of her, and she was ashamed of herself, otherwise they would not have strewn fig-leaves so profusely all over her. When she was a true force, she was ignorant of fig-leaves, but the monthly-magazine-made American female had not a feature that would have been recognized by Adam. The trait was notorious, and often humorous, but any one brought up among Puritans knew that sex was sin. In any previous age, sex was strength. Neither art nor beauty was needed. Every one, even among Puritans, knew that neither Diana of the Ephesians[18] nor any of the Oriental goddesses was worshipped for her beauty. She was goddess because of her force; she was the animated dynamo; she was reproduction—the greatest and most mysterious of all energies; all she needed was to be fecund. Singularly enough, not one of Adams's many schools of education had ever drawn his attention to the opening lines of Lucretius, though they were perhaps the finest in all Latin literature, where the poet invoked Venus exactly as Dante invoked the Virgin:—

"Quae quoniam rerum naturam *sola* gubernas."[19]

The Venus of Epicurean philosophy survived in the Virgin of the Schools:—

"Donna, sei tanto grande, e tanto vali,
Che qual vuol grazia, e a te non ricorre,
Sua disianza vuol volar senz' ali."[20]

All this was to American thought as though it had never existed. The true American knew something of the facts, but nothing of the feelings; he read the letter, but he never felt the law. Before this historical chasm, a mind like that of Adams felt itself helpless; he turned from the Virgin to the Dynamo as though he were a Branly coherer. On one side, at the Louvre and at Chartres,[21] as he knew by the record of work actually done and still before his eyes, was the highest energy ever known to man, the creator of four-fifths

17. **Lourdes:** Town in southwestern France that became an important pilgrimage site for Catholics in 1858 when a young girl claimed to have had visions of the Virgin Mary in a grotto there.
18. **Diana of the Ephesians:** Diana, a goddess in Roman mythology associated with hunting and virginity, was a principal deity of Ephesus, an ancient city in Asia Minor.
19. **"Quae . . . gubernas":** *On the Nature of Things*, by the Roman poet Lucretius (c. 99–55 BCE), begins with a long invocation and tribute to Venus. This line may be translated "Since *you alone* govern the nature of things."
20. **"Donna . . . ali":** The lines from the last canto of *Paradiso*, the final volume of the *Divine Comedy* by the Italian poet Dante Alighieri (1265–1321), may be translated: "Thou, Lady, art so great and so prevailing that whoso would have grace and does not turn to thee, his desire would seek to fly without wings" (33.13–15). What Adams calls the "Virgin of the Schools" is a reference to the Scholastic school of medieval theology.
21. **Louvre . . . Chartres:** The Louvre Museum in Paris, one of the largest and most renowned museums in the world; and Chartres Cathedral in northern France, a beautifully preserved Gothic cathedral constructed in the early thirteenth century and dedicated to the Virgin Mary.

of his noblest art, exercising vastly more attraction over the human mind than all the steam-engines and dynamos ever dreamed of; and yet this energy was unknown to the American mind. An American Virgin would never dare command; an American Venus would never dare exist.

The question, which to any plain American of the nineteenth century seemed as remote as it did to Adams, drew him almost violently to study, once it was posed; and on this point Langleys were as useless as though they were Herbert Spencers[22] or dynamos. The idea survived only as art. There one turned as naturally as though the artist were himself a woman. Adams began to ponder, asking himself whether he knew of any American artist who had ever insisted on the power of sex, as every classic had always done; but he could think only of Walt Whitman;[23] Bret Harte,[24] as far as the magazines would let him venture; and one or two painters, for the flesh-tones. All the rest had used sex for sentiment, never for force; to them, Eve was a tender flower, and Herodias[25] an unfeminine horror. American art, like the American language and American education, was as far as possible sexless. Society regarded this victory over sex as its greatest triumph, and the historian readily admitted it, since the moral issue, for the moment, did not concern one who was studying the relations of unmoral force. He cared nothing for the sex of the dynamo until he could measure its energy.

Vaguely seeking a clue, he wandered through the art exhibit, and, in his stroll, stopped almost every day before St. Gaudens's General Sherman,[26] which had been given the central post of honor. St. Gaudens himself was in Paris, putting on the work his usual interminable last touches, and listening to the usual contradictory suggestions of brother sculptors. Of all the American artists who gave to American art whatever life it breathed in the seventies, St. Gaudens was perhaps the most sympathetic, but certainly the most inarticulate. General Grant or Don Cameron[27] had scarcely less instinct of rhetoric than he. All the others—the Hunts, Richardson, John La Farge, Stanford White[28]—were exuberant; only St. Gaudens could never discuss or dilate on an

---

22. **Herbert Spencers:** Spencer (1820–1903) was an influential English philosopher best known for applying Darwin's evolutionary theory to other areas, including psychology and the study of society.

23. **Walt Whitman:** Whitman (1819–1892) was notorious and often censured for the unabashed celebration of sexuality and the human body in his poetry.

24. **Bret Harte:** Harte (1836–1902) was a popular author of Western local-color stories, whose cast of characters frequently included gamblers, miners, and prostitutes.

25. **Herodias:** The wife of King Herod who in the biblical account arranges for her daughter Salome to dance before the king and ask for the head of John the Baptist as a reward (Mark 6:21–27).

26. **St. Gaudens's General Sherman:** *General Sherman Led by Lady Victory,* one of several Civil War monuments sculpted by Augustus Saint-Gaudens (1848–1907), was exhibited at the Paris Exposition before being erected in New York City.

27. **General Grant or Don Cameron:** Adams once said that General Ulysses S. Grant (who later served as U.S. president from 1869 to 1877) was "pre-intellectual, archaic, and would have seemed so even to the cave-dwellers." James Donald Cameron (1833–1918), Grant's secretary of war, became a U.S. senator (1877–97) and the head of a powerful political machine in Pennsylvania.

28. **the Hunts . . . White:** Several noted American artists and designers: the painter William Morris Hunt (1824–1879) and his brother, the architect Richard Morris Hunt (1828–1895); the architect Henry Hobson Richardson (1838–1886); John La Farge (1835–1910), a painter and designer of stained glass windows; and the architect Stanford White (1853–1906).

emotion, or suggest artistic arguments for giving to his work the forms that he felt. He never laid down the law, or affected the despot, or became brutalized like Whistler[29] by the brutalities of his world. He required no incense; he was no egoist; his simplicity of thought was excessive; he could not imitate, or give any form but his own to the creations of his hand. No one felt more strongly than he the strength of other men, but the idea that they could affect him never stirred an image in his mind.

This summer his health was poor and his spirits were low. For such a temper, Adams was not the best companion, since his own gaiety was not *folle*;[30] but he risked going now and then to the studio on Mont Parnasse to draw him out for a stroll in the Bois de Boulogne,[31] or dinner as pleased his moods, and in return St. Gaudens sometimes let Adams go about in his company.

Once St. Gaudens took him down to Amiens, with a party of Frenchmen, to see the cathedral.[32] Not until they found themselves actually studying the sculpture of the western portal, did it dawn on Adams's mind that, for his purposes, St. Gaudens on that spot had more interest to him than the cathedral itself. Great men before great monuments express great truths, provided they are not taken too solemnly. Adams never tired of quoting the supreme phrase of his idol Gibbon,[33] before the Gothic cathedrals: "I darted a contemptuous look on the stately monuments of superstition." Even in the footnotes of his history, Gibbon had never inserted a bit of humor more human than this, and one would have paid largely for a photograph of the fat little historian, on the background of Notre Dame of Amiens, trying to persuade his readers — perhaps himself — that he was darting a contemptuous look on the stately monument, for which he felt in fact the respect which every man of his vast study and active mind always feels before objects worthy of it; but besides the humor, one felt also the relation. Gibbon ignored the Virgin, because in 1789 religious monuments were out of fashion. In 1900 his remark sounded fresh and simple as the green fields to ears that had heard a hundred years of other remarks, mostly no more fresh and certainly less simple. Without malice, one might find it more instructive than a whole lecture of Ruskin.[34] One sees what one brings, and at that moment Gibbon brought the French Revolution. Ruskin brought reaction against the Revolution. St. Gaudens had passed beyond all. He liked the stately monuments much more than he liked Gibbon or Ruskin; he loved their dignity; their unity; their scale; their lines; their lights and shadows; their decorative sculpture; but he was even

---

29. **Whistler:** James Abbott MacNeill Whistler (1834-1903), American painter known for his biting wit and his frequent conflicts with critics and patrons.
30. *folle:* Wild or excessive (French).
31. **Mont Parnasse . . . Bois de Boulogne:** The former is an area of Paris frequented by artists and writers, and the latter is a large wooded park on the outskirts of Paris.
32. **Amiens . . . cathedral:** This Gothic cathedral in northern France is particularly renowned for the richly carved figures in the portals of the west facade, constructed in the early thirteenth century.
33. **Gibbon:** Edward Gibbon (1737-1794), English historian best known for his magisterial *The Decline and Fall of the Roman Empire* (1776-88).
34. **Ruskin:** John Ruskin (1819-1900), English art critic who became a convert to the medieval style of architecture and an influential proponent of the so-called Gothic Revival that swept across England and the United States between roughly 1830 and 1880.

less conscious than they of the force that created it all – the Virgin, the Woman – by whose genius "the stately monuments of superstition" were built, through which she was expressed. He would have seen more meaning in Isis with the cow's horns, at Edfoo,[35] who expressed the same thought. The art remained, but the energy was lost even upon the artist.

Yet in mind and person St. Gaudens was a survival of the 1500; he bore the stamp of the Renaissance, and should have carried an image of the Virgin round his neck, or stuck in his hat, like Louis XI.[36] In mere time he was a lost soul that had strayed by chance into the twentieth century, and forgotten where it came from. He writhed and cursed at his ignorance, much as Adams did at his own, but in the opposite sense. St. Gaudens was a child of Benvenuto Cellini,[37] smothered in an American cradle. Adams was a quintessence of Boston, devoured by curiosity to think like Benvenuto. St. Gaudens's art was starved from birth, and Adams's instinct was blighted from babyhood. Each had but half of a nature, and when they came together before the Virgin of Amiens they ought both to have felt in her the force that made them one; but it was not so. To Adams she became more than ever a channel of force; to St. Gaudens she remained as before a channel of taste.

For a symbol of power, St. Gaudens instinctively preferred the horse, as was plain in his horse and Victory of the Sherman monument. Doubtless Sherman also felt it so. The attitude was so American that, for at least forty years, Adams had never realized that any other could be in sound taste. How many years had he taken to admit a notion of what Michael Angelo and Rubens[38] were driving at? He could not say; but he knew that only since 1895 had he begun to feel the Virgin or Venus as force, and not everywhere even so. At Chartres – perhaps at Lourdes – possibly at Cnidos if one could still find there the divinely naked Aphrodite of Praxiteles – but otherwise one must look for force to the goddesses of Indian mythology.[39] The idea died out long ago in the German and English stock. St. Gaudens at Amiens was hardly less sensitive to the force of the female energy than Matthew Arnold at the Grande Chartreuse.[40] Neither of them felt

---

35. **Isis . . . at Edfoo:** While traveling in Egypt, Adams saw a statue of Isis, the Egyptian earth-mother goddess renowned for her magical powers, at Edfu, on the banks of the Nile.

36. **Louis XI:** Although he unified the country and laid the foundation for an absolute monarchy in France, the powerful Louis the Prudent (1423-1483), as he was called, dressed like a poor pilgrim and wore an old felt hat upon which the sole ornament was the lead figure of a saint.

37. **Benvenuto Cellini:** Cellini (1500-1571), volatile Italian sculptor who gave an account of his tempestuous life in his posthumously published autobiography.

38. **Michael Angelo and Rubens:** The Italian Renaissance painter and sculptor Michelangelo Buonarroti (1475-1564) and the baroque Flemish painter Peter Paul Rubens (1577-1640), both of whom were famous for their renderings of the human body.

39. **the divinely naked Aphrodite . . . goddesses of Indian mythology:** Called Venus by the Romans, Aphrodite was the goddess of love in Greek mythology. The renowned Greek sculptor Praxiteles (c. 350 BCE) carved a life-size statue of Aphrodite stepping from a bath for a shrine in Cnidus (Knidos), a city in Asia Minor. (The torso of the sculpture, whose head and extremities are now missing, is in the Vatican Museum in Rome.) Ancient stone temples in India were often decorated with erotic sculptures, and Hindu goddesses such as Parvati were represented as beautiful, graceful, and voluptuous figures.

40. **Grande Chartreuse:** The English poet and critic Matthew Arnold (1822-1888) wrote a meditation on the loss of faith, "Stanzas from the Grande Chartreuse," while he was staying at a Carthusian monastery, the serenity of which he contrasted with the modern industrial world.

goddesses as power—only as reflected emotion, human expression, beauty, purity, taste, scarcely even as sympathy. They felt a railway train as power; yet they, and all other artists, constantly complained that the power embodied in a railway train could never be embodied in art. All the steam in the world could not, like the Virgin, build Chartres.

Yet in mechanics, whatever the mechanicians might think, both energies acted as interchangeable forces on man, and by action on man all known force may be measured. Indeed, few men of science measured force in any other way. After once admitting that a straight line was the shortest distance between two points, no serious mathematician cared to deny anything that suited his convenience, and rejected no symbol, unproved or unproveable, that helped him to accomplish work. The symbol was force, as a compass-needle or a triangle was force, as the mechanist might prove by losing it, and nothing could be gained by ignoring their value. Symbol or energy, the Virgin had acted as the greatest force the Western world ever felt, and had drawn man's activities to herself more strongly than any other power, natural or supernatural, had ever done; the historian's business was to follow the track of the energy; to find where it came from and where it went to; its complex source and shifting channels; its values, equivalents, conversions. It could scarcely be more complex than radium; it could hardly be deflected, diverted, polarized, absorbed more perplexingly than other radiant matter. Adams knew nothing about any of them, but as a mathematical problem of influence on human progress, though all were occult, all reacted on his mind, and he rather inclined to think the Virgin easiest to handle.

The pursuit turned out to be long and tortuous, leading at last into the vast forests of scholastic science. From Zeno to Descartes, hand in hand with Thomas Aquinas, Montaigne, and Pascal, one stumbled as stupidly as though one were still a German student of 1860.[41] Only with the instinct of despair could one force one's self into this old thicket of ignorance after having been repulsed at a score of entrances more promising and more popular. Thus far, no path had led anywhere, unless perhaps to an exceedingly modest living. Forty-five years of study had proved to be quite futile for the pursuit of power; one controlled no more force in 1900 than in 1850, although the amount of force controlled by society had enormously increased. The secret of education still hid itself somewhere behind ignorance, and one fumbled over it as feebly as ever. In such labyrinths, the staff is a force almost more necessary than the legs; the pen becomes a sort

---

41. **From Zeno . . . 1860:** Adams was a student in Germany from 1858 to 1860. Here, he mentions the diverse thinkers and writers he later studied: the Greek philosopher Zeno of Cithium (366-264 BCE), the founder of Stoicism; René Descartes (1596-1650), French philosopher and mathematician said to be the inventor of analytic geometry; the Scholastic Catholic theologian Thomas Aquinas (c. 1225-1274), the subject of the final chapter of Adams's *Mont-Saint-Michel and Chartres* (1904); Michel Eyquem de Montaigne (1533-1592), skeptical French philosopher and writer famous for his personal essays; and Blaise Pascal (1623-1662), influential French mathematician and physicist who late in life turned to writing about philosophy and religion, strongly defending the Christian faith.

of blind-man's dog, to keep him from falling into the gutters. The pen works for itself, and acts like a hand, modelling the plastic material over and over again to the form that suits it best. The form is never arbitrary, but is a sort of growth like crystallization, as any artist knows too well; for often the pencil or pen runs into side-paths and shapelessness, loses its relations, stops or is bogged. Then it has to return on its trail, and recover, if it can, its line of force. The result of a year's work depends more on what is struck out than on what is left in; on the sequence of the main lines of thought, than on their play or variety. Compelled once more to lean heavily on this support, Adams covered more thousands of pages with figures as formal as though they were algebra, laboriously striking out, altering, burning, experimenting, until the year had expired, the Exposition had long been closed, and winter drawing to its end, before he sailed from Cherbourg, on January 19, 1901, for home.

[1907, 1918]

Mary Antin

[1881-1949]

Mary Antin was born Maryashe Antin in Polotzk, Russia, on June 13, 1881, the second of four children born to Esther and Israel Antin. Beginning with the reign of Czar Alexander II in the mid-nineteenth century and continuing under the reigns of Alexander III and Nicolas II, life for Jewish families was extremely difficult in Russia. Anti-Jewish riots, or "pogroms," were common, and the government passed discriminatory laws limiting the access of Jews to education and narrowly restricting the areas in which they could live in Russia. Even within that "Pale of Settlement," where the Antins lived, Jews were subjected to harassment and attacks, as well as to the forced induction of young Jewish boys into the Russian army. As a result, hundreds of thousands of Jews immigrated to western Europe and the United States. Like many Jewish men, Israel Antin went ahead of his family to find a job and a place to live, leaving for Boston in 1891. Trained in Russia as a rabbi, and having worked there in the family business, he was ill suited to the menial jobs available to immigrants. Israel Antin nonetheless believed that his family's future would be more secure in the United States, so he sent for his wife and children, who arrived in Boston in 1894.

Residing in various "wrong ends" of the city, as Antin later described the slum areas occupied by immigrants, the family struggled economically but took advantage of free education in Boston. To help support the family, Antin's older sister went to work in a garment factory, or "sweatshop." Antin and her two younger siblings were enrolled in the Chelsea

Mary Antin

This photograph of Antin, holding the flag and talking to a group of schoolchildren, was taken in 1916, four years after the publication of her popular autobiography, *The Promised Land*.

Public School. A gifted student, Antin completed the first four grades in half of a school year, and she soon began to win prizes for her writing. Her first publication was "Snow," an essay printed in *Primary Education* in 1893. Antin's teacher sent it to the journal, noting, "This is the uncorrected paper of a Russian child twelve years old, who had studied English only four months." Antin's second publication was a poem on George Washington, which appeared in the *Boston Herald* in 1895. Her success at school and her writing skills gained her the attention of caseworkers at the Hebrew Immigrant Aid Society, through whom Antin met Josephine Lazarus (the sister of the poet Emma Lazarus) and the writer and Jewish leader Israel Zangwill. Deeply impressed by a letter about her family's life in the United States that Antin had written to an uncle in Russia, Zangwill encouraged her to translate it from Yiddish into English. He also helped arrange for its publication as *From Plotsk to Boston* (the name of Antin's birthplace in Russia was misspelled), a pamphlet that appeared in 1899. While she was in high school, Antin worked as a secretary to Amadeus William Grabau, a German immigrant who had become a geology professor at Columbia University. They married in 1901, and Antin left school and moved with her husband to New York City.

Although she took some courses there, Antin did not complete a degree. Instead, she devoted herself to writing, especially to work on an autobiography focusing on her experiences as an immigrant in the United States. By 1910, Antin had completed much of the manuscript of a book she thought to call "The Making of an American." But she discovered that the title had already been taken by the Danish immigrant Jacob Riis, an influential photojournalist and author of a series of muckraking books on life in the slums of New York City, as well as his autobiography, *The Making of an American* (1901). Antin therefore called her autobiography *The Promised Land*, a resonant phrase suggesting that for Jewish immigrants the land God promised the ancient Israelites was now the new land of America. Published in installments in the *Atlantic Monthly* before it appeared in book form in 1912, *The Promised Land* was an immediate success, ultimately going through thirty-four printings and selling eighty-five thousand copies. In her introduction, Antin announces her central theme, the transformation of an immigrant into an American: "I was born, I have lived, and I have been made over." Indeed, the success of her book was in large part due to her positive message about the reality and her own realization of the American dream. At the end of her account, Antin thus proclaims: "America is the youngest of the nations and inherits all that went before in history. And I am the youngest of America's children, and into my hands is given all her priceless heritage, to the last white star espied through the telescope, to the last great thought of the philosopher. Mine is the whole majestic past, and mine is the shining future."

The success of *The Promised Land* did indeed provide Antin with a "shining future," but only for a short time. She swiftly became a public figure, writing articles for numerous periodicals and delivering lectures across the country about her own experiences and on the broader subject of immigration. Challenging efforts to restrict immigration, Antin published *They Who Knock at Our Gates, A Complete Gospel of Immigration* (1914), in which she emphasized the vital contributions immigrants made to the success of the United States. She also became a fervent supporter of Zionism, the movement to establish a Jewish homeland in Palestine. During World War I, she supported the Allies, but her husband strongly supported Germany. After the United States entered the war in 1917, his pro-German stance and statements led to his dismissal from his position at Columbia. Under increasing emotional and financial pressures, the couple separated. Antin began to suffer from an unidentified mental illness, possibly bipolar disorder, which eventually led to her residence at the Austen Riggs Psychiatric Center in Massachusetts in the early 1920s. Although she kept up an extensive correspondence and sporadically sought to resume her literary career, Antin published little during the last two decades of her life. Her final published work was "House of the Father" (1941), an essay in which she affirmed her identity as both a Jew and an American. After a battle with cancer, Antin died at a nursing home on May 15, 1949.

bedfordstmartins.com/
americanlit *for research links on Antin*

Reading Antin's *The Promised Land.* In June 1911, Antin began to correspond with Ellery Sedgwick, the editor of the *Atlantic Monthly,* who had accepted one of her short stories and expressed an interest in publishing her autobiography. Although she was drawn to the prestige of appearing in the prominent magazine, Antin was determined that serial publication would not deprive her of a larger audience. "I can assure you, I am not aiming at the pages of the *Atlantic Monthly,*" she wrote to Sedgwick. "I am aiming, if you must know, at the heart of the world." After she received a book contract from Houghton Mifflin, the parent company of the *Atlantic,* the first part of her autobiography appeared in the magazine in October 1911 as "Within the Pale," an account of her early life in the "Pale of Settlement," the confined area in which Jews were forced to live in Russia. Six additional installments were published monthly from November 1911 through April 1912, after which the revised and expanded text was divided into twenty chapters and published as *The Promised Land.* Chapter VIII, "The Exodus," is an account of the six-week journey she, her mother, and her three siblings made from their home in Polotzk, Russia, by train to Hamburg, Germany, and from there by steamer to Boston, where they were

Mashke and Fetchke

Taken when they were small children in Russia, this photograph of Antin and her older sister, whose names were changed to Mary and Frieda after they arrived in the United States, was used as the frontispiece of *The Promised Land.*

reunited with her father, Israel Antin. In the following sections from chapter IX, "The Promised Land," Antin describes the family's early struggles in Boston, culminating in the day she and her two younger siblings were led to school by their father, who in the act of enrolling them "took possession of America." The text is taken from the first edition of *The Promised Land* (1912).

From THE PROMISED LAND

From Chapter IX

Having made such good time across the ocean, I ought to be able to proceed no less rapidly on *terra firma*, where, after all, I am more at home. And yet here is where I falter. Not that I hesitated, even for the space of a breath, in my first steps in America. There was no time to hesitate. The most ignorant immigrant, on landing, proceeds to give and receive greetings, to eat, sleep, and rise, after the manner of his own country; wherein he is corrected, admonished, and laughed at, whether by interested friends or the most indifferent strangers; and his American experience is thus begun. The process is spontaneous on all sides, like the education of the child by the family circle. But while the most stupid nursery maid is able to contribute her part toward the result, we do not expect an analysis of the process to be furnished by any member of the family, least of all by the engaging infant. The philosophical maiden aunt alone, or some other witness equally psychological and aloof, is able to trace the myriad efforts by which the little Johnnie or Nellie acquires a secure hold on the disjointed parts of the huge plaything, life.

Now I was not exactly an infant when I was set down, on a May day some fifteen years ago, in this pleasant nursery of America. I had long since acquired the use of my faculties, and had collected some bits of experience, practical and emotional, and had even learned to give an account of them. Still, I had very little perspective, and my observations and comparisons were superficial. I was too much carried away to analyze the forces that were moving me. My Polotzk I knew well before I began to judge it and experiment with it. America was bewilderingly strange, unimaginably complex, delightfully unexplored. I rushed impetuously out of the cage of my provincialism and looked eagerly about the brilliant universe. My question was, What have we here? — not, What does this mean? That query came much later. When I now become retrospectively introspective, I fall into the predicament of the centipede in the rhyme, who got along very smoothly until he was asked which leg came after which, whereupon he became so rattled that he couldn't take a step. I know I have come on a thousand feet, on wings, winds, and American machines, — I have leaped and run and climbed and crawled, — but to tell which step came after which I find a puzzling matter. Plenty of maiden aunts were present during my second infancy, in the guise of immigrant officials, school-teachers, settlement workers, and sundry other unprejudiced and critical observers. Their statistics

I might properly borrow to fill the gaps in my recollections, but I am prevented by my sense of harmony. The individual, we know, is a creature unknown to the statistician; whereas I undertook to give the personal view of everything. So I am bound to unravel, as well as I can, the tangle of events, outer and inner, which made up the first breathless years of my American life.

During his three years of probation, my father had made a number of false starts in business. His history for that period is the history of thousands who come to America, like him, with pockets empty, hands untrained to the use of tools, minds cramped by centuries of repression in their native land. Dozens of these men pass under your eyes every day, my American friend, too absorbed in their honest affairs to notice the looks of suspicion which you cast at them, the repugnance with which you shrink from their touch. You see them shuffle from door to door with a basket of spools and buttons, or bending over the sizzling irons in a basement tailor shop, or rummaging in your ash can, or moving a pushcart from curb to curb, at the command of the burly policeman. "The Jew peddler!" you say, and dismiss him from your premises and from your thoughts, never dreaming that the sordid drama of his days may have a moral that concerns you. What if the creature with the untidy beard carries in his bosom his citizenship papers? What if the cross-legged tailor is supporting a boy in college who is one day going to mend your state constitution for you? What if the ragpicker's daughters are hastening over the ocean to teach your children in the public schools? Think, every time you pass the greasy alien on the street, that he was born thousands of years before the oldest native American; and he may have something to communicate to you, when you two shall have learned a common language. Remember that his very physiognomy is a cipher, the key to which it behooves you to search for most diligently.

By the time we joined my father, he had surveyed many avenues of approach toward the coveted citadel fortune. One of these, heretofore untried, he now proposed to essay, armed with new courage, and cheered on by the presence of his family. In partnership with an energetic little man who had an English chapter in his history, he prepared to set up a refreshment booth on Crescent Beach. But while he was completing arrangements at the beach we remained in town, where we enjoyed the educational advantages of a thickly populated neighborhood; namely, Wall Street, in the West End of Boston.

Anybody who knows Boston knows that the West and North Ends are the wrong ends of that city. They form the tenement district, or, in the newer phrase, the slums of Boston. Anybody who is acquainted with the slums of any American metropolis knows that that is the quarter where poor immigrants foregather, to live, for the most part, as unkempt, half-washed, toiling, unaspiring foreigners; pitiful in the eyes of social missionaries, the despair of boards of health, the hope of ward politicians, the touchstone of American democracy. The well-versed metropolitan knows the slums as a sort of house of detention for poor aliens, where they live on probation till they can show a certificate of good citizenship.

He may know all this and yet not guess how Wall Street, the West End, appears in the eyes of a little immigrant from Polotzk. What would the sophisticated sight-seer say about Union Place, off Wall Street, where my new home waited for me? He would say that it is no place at all, but a short box of an alley. Two rows of three-story tenements are its sides, a stingy strip of sky is its lid, a littered pavement is the floor, and a narrow mouth its exit.

But I saw a very different picture on my introduction to Union Place. I saw two imposing rows of brick buildings, loftier than any dwelling I had ever lived in. Brick was even on the ground for me to tread on, instead of common earth or boards. Many friendly windows stood open, filled with uncovered heads of women and children. I thought the people were interested in us, which was very neighborly. I looked up to the topmost row of windows, and my eyes were filled with the May blue of an American sky!

In our days of affluence in Russia we had been accustomed to upholstered parlors, embroidered linen, silver spoons and candlesticks, goblets of gold, kitchen shelves shining with copper and brass. We had featherbeds heaped halfway to the ceiling; we had clothes presses dusky with velvet and silk and fine woollen. The three small rooms into which my father now ushered us, up one flight of stairs, contained only the necessary beds, with lean mattresses; a few wooden chairs; a table or two; a mysterious iron structure, which later turned out to be a stove; a couple of unornamental kerosene lamps; and a scanty array of cooking-utensils and crockery. And yet we were impressed with our new home and its furniture. It was not only because we had just passed through our seven lean years, cooking in earthen vessels, eating black bread on holidays and wearing cotton; it was chiefly because these wooden chairs and tin pans were American chairs and pans that they shone glorious in our eyes. And if there was anything lacking for comfort or decoration we expected it to be presently supplied — at least, we children did. Perhaps my mother alone, of us newcomers, appreciated the shabbiness of the little apartment, and realized that for her there was as yet no laying down of the burden of poverty.

Our initiation into American ways began with the first step on the new soil. My father found occasion to instruct or correct us even on the way from the pier to Wall Street, which journey we made crowded together in a rickety cab. He told us not to lean out of the windows, not to point, and explained the word "greenhorn." We did not want to be "greenhorns," and gave the strictest attention to my father's instructions. I do not know when my parents found opportunity to review together the history of Polotzk in the three years past, for we children had no patience with the subject; my mother's narrative was constantly interrupted by irrelevant questions, interjections, and explanations.

The first meal was an object lesson of much variety. My father produced several kinds of food, ready to eat, without any cooking, from little tin cans that had printing all over them. He attempted to introduce us to a queer, slippery kind of fruit, which he called "banana," but had to give it up for the time being. After the meal, he had better luck with a curious piece of furniture on runners, which he called "rocking-chair." There were five of us newcomers, and we found five different ways of getting into the American machine of perpetual motion, and as many ways of getting out of it. One born and bred to the use of a rocking-chair cannot imagine how ludicrous people can make themselves when attempting to use it for the first time. We laughed immoderately over our various experiments with the novelty, which was a wholesome way of letting off steam after the unusual excitement of the day.

In our flat we did not think of such a thing as storing the coal in the bathtub. There was no bathtub. So in the evening of the first day my father conducted us to the public baths. As we moved along in a little procession, I was delighted with the illumination of the streets. So many lamps, and they burned until morning, my father said, and so people did not need to carry lanterns. In America, then, everything was free, as we had heard in Russia. Light was free; the streets were as bright as a synagogue on a holy day. Music was free; we had been serenaded, to our gaping delight, by a brass band of many pieces, soon after our installation on Union Place.

Education was free. That subject my father had written about repeatedly, as comprising his chief hope for us children, the essence of American opportunity, the treasure that no thief could touch, not even misfortune or poverty. It was the one thing that he was able to promise us when he sent for us; surer, safer than bread or shelter. On our second day I was thrilled with the realization of what this freedom of education meant. A little girl from across the alley came and offered to conduct us to school. My father was out, but we five between us had a few words of English by this time. We knew the word school. We understood. This child, who had never seen us till yesterday, who could not pronounce our names, who was not much better dressed than we, was able to offer us the freedom of the schools of Boston! No application made, no questions asked, no examinations, rulings, exclusions; no machinations, no fees. The doors stood open for every one of us. The smallest child could show us the way.

This incident impressed me more than anything I had heard in advance of the freedom of education in America. It was a concrete proof — almost the thing itself. One had to experience it to understand it.

It was a great disappointment to be told by my father that we were not to enter upon our school career at once. It was too near the end of the term, he said, and we were going to move to Crescent Beach[1] in a week or so. We had to wait until the opening of the schools in September. What a loss of precious time — from May till September!

Not that the time was really lost. Even the interval on Union Place was crowded with lessons and experiences. We had to visit the stores and be dressed from head to foot in American clothing; we had to learn the mysteries of the iron stove, the washboard, and

---

1. **Crescent Beach:** A long, crescent-shaped beach facing Massachusetts Bay five miles north of Boston; it later became the Revere Beach Reservation, established in 1896 as the first public beach in the United States. Antin's father and his partner ran a refreshment stand there during the summer of 1894. After licensing problems and damage from a storm forced them to close the stand, Antin's family moved to Chelsea, then an industrial city across the Mystic River from Boston.

the speaking-tube; we had to learn to trade with the fruit peddler through the window, and not to be afraid of the policeman; and, above all, we had to learn English.

The kind people who assisted us in these important matters form a group by themselves in the gallery of my friends. If I had never seen them from those early days till now, I should still have remembered them with gratitude. When I enumerate the long list of my American teachers, I must begin with those who came to us on Wall Street and taught us our first steps. To my mother, in her perplexity over the cookstove, the woman who showed her how to make the fire was an angel of deliverance. A fairy godmother to us children was she who led us to a wonderful country called "uptown," where, in a dazzlingly beautiful palace called a "department store," we exchanged our hateful homemade European costumes, which pointed us out as "greenhorns" to the children on the street, for real American machine-made garments, and issued forth glorified in each other's eyes.

With our despised immigrant clothing we shed also our impossible Hebrew names. A committee of our friends, several years ahead of us in American experience, put their heads together and concocted American names for us all. Those of our real names that had no pleasing American equivalents they ruthlessly discarded, content if they retained the initials. My mother, possessing a name that was not easily translatable, was punished with the undignified nickname of Annie. Fetchke, Joseph, and Deborah issued as Frieda, Joseph, and Dora, respectively. As for poor me, I was simply cheated. The name they gave me was hardly new. My Hebrew name being Maryashe in full, Mashke for short, Russianized into Marya (*Mar-ya*), my friends said that it would hold good in English as *Mary*; which was very disappointing, as I longed to possess a strange-sounding American name like the others.

I am forgetting the consolation I had, in this matter of names, from the use of my surname, which I have had no occasion to mention until now. I found on my arrival that my father was "Mr. Antin" on the slightest provocation, and not, as in Polotzk, on state occasions alone. And so I was "Mary Antin," and I felt very important to answer to such a dignified title. It was just like America that even plain people should wear their surnames on week days.

As a family we were so diligent under instruction, so adaptable, and so clever in hiding our deficiencies, that when we made the journey to Crescent Beach, in the wake of our small wagon-load of household goods, my father had very little occasion to admonish us on the way, and I am sure he was not ashamed of us. So much we had achieved toward our Americanization during the two weeks since our landing.

In Polotzk we had supposed that "America" was practically synonymous with "Boston." When we landed in Boston, the horizon was pushed back, and we annexed Crescent Beach. And now, espying other lands of promise, we took possession of the province of Chelsea, in the name of our necessity.

In Chelsea, as in Boston, we made our stand in the wrong end of the town. Arlington Street was inhabited by poor Jews, poor Negroes, and a sprinkling of poor Irish. The side streets leading from it were occupied by more poor Jews and Negroes. It was a proper locality for a man without capital to do business. My father rented a tenement with a store in the basement. He put in a few barrels of flour and of sugar, a few boxes of crackers, a few gallons of kerosene, an assortment of soap of the "save the coupon" brands; in the cellar, a few barrels of potatoes, and a pyramid of kindling-wood; in the showcase, an alluring display of penny candy. He put out his sign, with a gilt-lettered warning of "Strictly Cash," and proceeded to give credit indiscriminately. That was the regular way to do business on Arlington Street. My father, in his three years' apprenticeship, had learned the tricks of many trades. He knew when and how to "bluff." The legend of "Strictly Cash" was a protection against notoriously irresponsible customers; while none of the "good" customers, who had a record for paying regularly on Saturday, hesitated to enter the store with empty purses.

If my father knew the tricks of the trade, my mother could be counted on to throw all her talent and tact into the business. Of course she had no English yet, but as she could perform the acts of weighing, measuring, and mental computation of fractions mechanically, she was able to give her whole attention to the dark mysteries of the language, as intercourse with her customers gave her opportunity. In this she made such rapid progress that she soon lost all sense of disadvantage, and conducted herself behind the counter very much as if she were back in her old store in Polotzk. It was far more cosey than Polotzk — at least, so it seemed to me; for behind the store was the kitchen, where, in the intervals of slack trade, she did her cooking and washing. Arlington Street customers were used to waiting while the storekeeper salted the soup or rescued a loaf from the oven.

Once more Fortune favored my family with a thin little smile, and my father, in reply to a friendly inquiry, would say, "One makes a living," with a shrug of the shoulders that added "but nothing to boast of." It was characteristic of my attitude toward bread-and-butter matters that this contented me, and I felt free to devote myself to the conquest of my new world. Looking back to those critical first years, I see myself always behaving like a child let loose in a garden to play and dig and chase the butterflies. Occasionally, indeed, I was stung by the wasp of family trouble; but I knew a healing ointment — my faith in America. My father had come to America to make a living. America, which was free and fair and kind, must presently yield him what he sought. I had come to America to see a new world, and I followed my own ends with the utmost assiduity; only, as I ran out to explore, I would look back to see if my house were in order behind me — if my family still kept its head above water.

In after years, when I passed as an American among Americans, if I was suddenly made aware of the past that lay forgotten, — if a letter from Russia, or a paragraph in the newspaper, or a conversation overheard in the street-car, suddenly reminded me of what I might have been, — I thought it miracle enough that I, Mashke, the granddaughter of Raphael the Russian, born to a humble destiny, should be at home in an American metropolis, be free to fashion my own life, and should dream my dreams in English phrases. But in the beginning my admiration was spent on more concrete embodiments of the splendors of America; such as fine houses, gay shops, electric engines and apparatus, public buildings, illuminations, and parades. My early letters to my Russian friends were filled with boastful descriptions of these glories of my new country. No native citizen of Chelsea took such pride and delight in its institutions as I did. It required no fife and drum corps, no Fourth of July procession, to set me tingling with patriotism. Even the common agents and instruments of municipal life, such as the letter carrier and the fire engine, I regarded with a measure of respect. I know what I thought of people who said that Chelsea was a very small, dull, unaspiring town, with no discernible excuse for a separate name or existence.

The apex of my civic pride and personal contentment was reached on the bright September morning when I entered the public school. That day I must always remember, even if I live to be so old that I cannot tell my name. To most people their first day at school is a memorable occasion. In my case the importance of the day was a hundred times magnified, on account of the years I had waited, the road I had come, and the conscious ambitions I entertained.

I am wearily aware that I am speaking in extreme figures, in superlatives. I wish I knew some other way to render the mental life of the immigrant child of reasoning age. I may have been ever so much an exception in acuteness of observation, powers of comparison, and abnormal self-consciousness; none the less were my thoughts and conduct typical of the attitude of the intelligent immigrant child toward American institutions. And what the child thinks and feels is a reflection of the hopes, desires, and purposes of the parents who brought him overseas, no matter how precocious and independent the child may be. Your immigrant inspectors will tell you what poverty the foreigner brings in his baggage, what want in his pockets. Let the overgrown boy of twelve, reverently drawing his letters in the baby class, testify to the noble dreams and high ideals that may be hidden beneath the greasy caftan of the immigrant. Speaking for the Jews, at least, I know I am safe in inviting such an investigation.

Who were my companions on my first day at school? Whose hand was in mine, as I stood, overcome with awe, by the teacher's desk, and whispered my name as my father prompted? Was it Frieda's steady, capable hand? Was it her loyal heart that throbbed, beat for beat with mine, as it had done through all our childish adventures? Frieda's heart did throb that day, but not with my emotions. My heart pulsed with joy and pride and ambition; in her heart longing fought with abnegation. For I was led to the schoolroom, with its sunshine and its singing and the teacher's cheery smile; while she was led to the workshop, with its foul air, care-lined faces, and the foreman's stern command. Our going to school was the fulfilment of my father's best promises to us, and Frieda's share in it was to fashion and fit the calico frocks in which the baby sister and I made our first appearance in a public schoolroom.

I remember to this day the gray pattern of the calico, so affectionately did I regard it as it hung upon the wall—my consecration robe awaiting the beatific day. And Frieda, I am sure, remembers it, too, so longingly did she regard it as the crisp, starchy breadths of it slid between her fingers. But whatever were her longings, she said nothing of them; she bent over the sewing-machine humming an Old-World melody. In every straight, smooth seam, perhaps, she tucked away some lingering impulse of childhood; but she matched the scrolls and flowers with the utmost care. If a sudden shock of rebellion made her straighten up for an instant, the next instant she was bending to adjust a ruffle to the best advantage. And when the momentous day arrived, and the little sister and I stood up to be arrayed, it was Frieda herself who patted and smoothed my stiff new calico; who made me turn round and round, to see that I was perfect; who stooped to pull out a disfiguring basting-thread. If there was anything in her heart besides sisterly love and pride and good-will, as we parted that morning, it was a sense of loss and a woman's acquiescence in her fate; for we had been close friends, and now our ways would lie apart. Longing she felt, but no envy. She did not grudge me what she was denied. Until that morning we had been children together, but now, at the fiat of her destiny, she became a woman, with all a woman's cares; whilst I, so little younger than she, was bidden to dance at the May festival of untroubled childhood.

I wish, for my comfort, that I could say that I had some notion of the difference in our lots, some sense of the injustice to her, of the indulgence to me. I wish I could even say that I gave serious thought to the matter. There had always been a distinction between us rather out of proportion to the difference in our years. Her good health and domestic instincts had made it natural for her to become my mother's right hand, in the years preceding the emigration, when there were no more servants or dependents. Then there was the family tradition that Mary was the quicker, the brighter of the two, and that hers could be no common lot. Frieda was relied upon for help, and her sister for glory. And when I failed as a milliner's apprentice, while Frieda made excellent progress at the dressmaker's, our fates, indeed, were sealed. It was understood, even before we reached Boston, that she would go to work and I to school. In view of the family prejudices, it was the inevitable course. No injustice was intended. My father sent us hand in hand to school, before he had ever thought of America. If, in America, he had been able to support his family unaided, it would have been the culmination of his best hopes to see all his children at school, with equal advantages at home. But when he had done his best, and was still unable to provide even bread and shelter for us all, he was compelled to make us children self-supporting as fast as it was practicable. There was no choosing possible; Frieda was the oldest, the strongest, the best prepared, and the only one who was of legal age to be put to work.

My father has nothing to answer for. He divided the world between his children in accordance with the laws of the country and the compulsion of his circumstances. I have no need of defending him. It is myself that I would like to defend, and I cannot. I remember that I accepted the arrangements made for my sister and me without much reflection, and everything that was planned for my advantage I took as a matter of course. I was no heartless monster, but a decidedly self-centered child. If my sister had seemed unhappy it would have troubled me; but I am ashamed to recall that I did not consider how little it was that contented her. I was so preoccupied with my own happiness that I did not half perceive the splendid devotion of her attitude towards me, the sweetness of her joy in my good luck. She not only stood by approvingly when I was helped to everything; she cheerfully waited on me herself. And I took everything from her hand as if it were my due.

The two of us stood a moment in the doorway of the tenement house on Arlington Street, that wonderful September morning when I first went to school. It was I that ran away, on winged feet of joy and expectation; it was she whose feet were bound in the treadmill of daily toil. And I was so blind that I did not see that the glory lay on her, and not on me.

Father himself conducted us to school. He would not have delegated that mission to the President of the United States. He had awaited the day with impatience equal to mine, and the visions he saw as he hurried us over the sun-flecked pavements transcended all my dreams. Almost his first act on landing on American soil, three years before, had been his application for naturalization. He had taken the remaining steps in the process with eager promptness, and at the earliest moment allowed by the law, he became a citizen of the United States. It is true that he had left home in search of bread for his hungry family, but he went blessing the necessity that drove him to America. The boasted freedom of the New World meant to him far more than the right to reside, travel, and work wherever he pleased; it meant the freedom to speak his thoughts, to throw off the shackles of superstition, to test his own fate, unhindered by political or religious tyranny. He was only a young man when he landed – thirty-two; and most of his life he had been held in leading-strings. He was hungry for his untasted manhood.

Three years passed in sordid struggle and disappointment. He was not prepared to make a living even in America, where the day laborer eats wheat instead of rye. Apparently the American flag could not protect him against the pursuing Nemesis[2] of his limitations; he must expiate the sins of his fathers who slept across the seas. He had been endowed at birth with a poor constitution, a nervous, restless temperament, and an abundance of hindering prejudices. In his boyhood his body was starved, that his mind might be stuffed with useless learning. In his youth this dearly gotten learning was sold, and the price was the bread and salt which he had not been trained to earn for himself. Under the wedding canopy he was bound for life to a girl whose features were still strange to him; and he was bidden to multiply himself, that sacred learning might be perpetuated in his sons, to the glory of the God of his fathers. All this while he had been led about as a creature without a will, a chattel, an instrument. In his maturity he awoke, and found himself poor in health, poor in purse, poor in useful knowledge, and hampered on all sides. At the first nod of opportunity he broke away from his prison, and strove to atone for his wasted youth by a life of useful labor; while at the same time he sought to lighten the gloom of his narrow scholarship by freely partaking of modern ideas. But his utmost endeavor still left him far from his goal. In business, nothing prospered with him. Some fault of hand or mind or temperament led him to failure where other men found success. Wherever the blame for his disabilities be placed, he reaped

---

2. **Nemesis:** The spirit of divine retribution in Greek mythology, often personified as a relentless pursuing goddess.

their bitter fruit. "Give me bread!" he cried to America. "What will you do to earn it?" the challenge came back. And he found that he was master of no art, of no trade; that even his precious learning was of no avail, because he had only the most antiquated methods of communicating it.

So in his primary quest he had failed. There was left him the compensation of intellectual freedom. That he sought to realize in every possible way. He had very little opportunity to prosecute his education, which, in truth, had never been begun. His struggle for a bare living left him no time to take advantage of the public evening school; but he lost nothing of what was to be learned through reading, through attendance at public meetings, through exercising the rights of citizenship. Even here he was hindered by a natural inability to acquire the English language. In time, indeed, he learned to read, to follow a conversation or lecture; but he never learned to write correctly, and his pronunciation remains extremely foreign to this day.

If education, culture, the higher life were shining things to be worshiped from afar, he had still a mean left whereby he could draw one step nearer to them. He could send his children to school, to learn all those things that he knew by fame to be desirable. The common school, at least, perhaps high school; for one or two, perhaps even college! His children should be students, should fill his house with books and intellectual company; and thus he would walk by proxy in the Elysian Fields[3] of liberal learning. As for the children themselves, he knew no surer way to their advancement and happiness.

So it was with a heart full of longing and hope that my father led us to school on that first day. He took long strides in his eagerness, the rest of us running and hopping to keep up.

At last the four of us stood around the teacher's desk; and my father, in his impossible English, gave us over in her charge, with some broken word of his hopes for us that his swelling heart could no longer contain. I venture to say that Miss Nixon was struck by something uncommon in the group we made, something outside of Semitic features and the abashed manner of the alien. My little sister was as pretty as a doll, with her clear pink-and-white face, short golden curls, and eyes like blue violets when you caught them looking up. My brother might have been a girl, too, with his cherubic contours of face, rich red color, glossy black hair, and fine eyebrows. Whatever secret fears were in his heart, remembering his former teachers, who had taught with the rod, he stood up straight and uncringing before the American teacher, his cap respectfully doffed. Next to him stood a starved-looking girl with eyes ready to pop out, and short dark curls that would not have made much of a wig for a Jewish bride.

All three children carried themselves rather better than the common run of "green" pupils that were brought to Miss Nixon. But the figure that challenged attention to the group was the tall, straight father, with his earnest face and fine forehead, nervous hands eloquent in gesture, and a voice full of feeling. This foreigner, who brought his children to school as if it were an act of consecration, who regarded the teacher of the primer class with reverence, who spoke of visions, like a man inspired, in a common

---

3. **Elysian Fields:** The paradise of the gods in Greek mythology.

schoolroom, was not like other aliens, who brought their children in dull obedience to the law; was not like the native fathers, who brought their unmanageable boys, glad to be relieved of their care. I think Miss Nixon guessed what my father's best English could not convey. I think she divined that by the simple act of delivering our school certificates to her he took possession of America.

[1912]

American Literature

1914–1945

The architectural photographer Samuel H. Gottscho took this photograph of the financial district of Manhattan, framed by the Brooklyn Bridge, in 1934. The bridge connecting Brooklyn and Manhattan became a symbol of technological progress, and New York City emerged as the quintessential modern metropolis and a center of modernism during the period 1914-45.

O N MARCH 3, 1913, the day before Woodrow Wilson's inauguration for his first term as president, hundreds of thousands of the people gathered in the nation's capital witnessed a very different spectacle: the great "Woman Suffrage Procession." At the time, women had gained the right to vote in only ten states, all of them in the Midwest and West. Impatient with the slow progress of the state-by-state campaign, many activists pressed for a renewed effort to gain passage of a women's suffrage amendment to the Constitution. In an effort to attract media attention to the cause, more than five thousand women from around the country marched down Pennsylvania Avenue from the Capitol past the White House. When the procession reached the Treasury Building, women and children presented an allegorical pageant to display "those ideals toward which both men and women have been struggling through the ages and toward which, in co-operation and equality, they will continue to

"Woman Suffrage Procession"

The author, feminist, socialite, and *Titanic* survivor Helen Churchill Hungerford Candee, center, rode on horseback near the head of the 1913 women's suffrage procession in Washington, D.C. Accompanied by heralds, nine bands, and more than twenty floats, thousands of suffragists marched down Pennsylvania Avenue, with the Capitol in the background, demanding the passage of a women's suffrage amendment to the Constitution.

strive." But the carefully organized and orchestrated event revealed the deep antagonism toward women's suffrage among many men in the country. Crowds of jeering men along the parade route blocked the participants, more than one hundred of whom were taken to the local emergency room after being jostled, shoved, or tripped. In fact, the widely publicized treatment of the marchers and the failure of the police to intervene did more than the procession itself to generate support for the cause of women's suffrage in the United States. Nonetheless, it would take seven more years of demonstrations, parades, protests, and concerted political action before women gained the vote after Congress passed, and the required thirty-six states ratified, the Nineteenth Amendment in 1920.

Art and Society in the Era of the Great War

The intensifying struggle for women's suffrage demonstrated only one aspect of the social and cultural ferment in the United States during the period from the eve of World War I to 1920. In February 1913, only a month before the Woman Suffrage Procession in Washington and eighteen months before what contemporaries called the "Great War" began in Europe, the International Exhibition of Modern Art opened in New York City. Called the Armory Show because it was held in the Sixty-ninth Regiment Armory on Madison Avenue, the exhibition brought together a vast array of American and European art, including innovative works by Henri Matisse, the leader of the fauves ("wild beasts"), and Pablo Picasso, the central figure in the development of cubism. By the time the Armory Show finished its runs in New York, Chicago, and Boston, more than 300,000 Americans had viewed the exhibition. Most greeted the avant-garde art in the show with derision and hostility, as did many critics. In an editorial, the influential *New York Times* ominously warned that cubism "is surely a part of the general movement, discernable all over the world, to disrupt and degrade, if not to destroy, not only art, but literature and society, too." But the exhibition exerted a profound impact on American artists and writers. Reviewing the Armory Show for the *Chicago Tribune* in April 1913, the art critic, editor, and poet Harriet Monroe observed that the rebellious European artists "represent a search for new beauty, impatience with formulae, a reaching out toward the inexpressible, a longing for new versions of truth."

As Monroe recognized, the Armory Show revealed a revolutionary spirit in the arts that had already begun to transform American literature. As early as 1903, Gertrude Stein moved to Paris, where she became closely associated with artists such as Picasso, who painted her portrait in 1906. Stein subsequently began to undertake a series of radical experiments in prose, including the brief, nonrepresentational word-portraits "Matisse" and "Picasso." Stein's sketches were published in 1912 in a special issue of *Camera Work* (1903–17), an influential journal of modern art edited by

Marcel Duchamp,
*Nude Descending
a Staircase, No. 2*

Duchamp's 1912 work was
the most controversial
among the 1,250 paint-
ings, sculptures, and
pieces of decorative art
exhibited at the Armory
Show. Conservative
viewers were shocked and
outraged by the cubist
painting, which one critic
described as "an explo-
sion in a shingle factory."

Alfred Stieglitz in New York City. But the major developments in American
literature in the years before World War I were in poetry. Ironically, the
first center of a "new" American poetry was London, England, where the
young expatriate Ezra Pound moved in 1908. In addition to publishing
several volumes of his own poetry, Pound strongly supported the work of
other American poets, including H.D. (Hilda Doolittle), who settled in London in 1911, and Robert Frost. In a final effort to become a professional
poet, Frost moved his family to London in 1912. With the help of Pound and
other writers Frost met there, the New Englander whom many view as the
most quintessentially "American" of modern poets published his first two
volumes of poetry in London.

The literary scene that drove Frost to seek an audience for his work overseas also spurred the creation of new outlets for writers in the United States. In 1912, a few months before Harriet Monroe wrote her review of the Armory Show, she founded *Poetry: A Magazine of Verse*. The magazine initially featured the innovative poetry of Pound, H.D., and other "imagists," whose work inspired Amy Lowell to join the movement and to edit three collections of imagist poetry between 1915 and 1917. The first professionally published verse by a wide range of poets also appeared in *Poetry*, including that of Carl Sandburg, T. S. Eliot, and the Japanese-born Jun Fujita, who moved to Chicago in 1915. Generally regarded as the first of the "little magazines," small-circulation literary magazines featuring the experimental work of little-known writers, *Poetry* inspired others to begin similar ventures. In the spring of 1914, Margaret Anderson founded an even more progressive journal of the arts in Chicago, the *Little Review*, which published under the banner, "Making No Compromises with Public Taste." True to those words, Anderson and her companion and coeditor, Jane Heap, printed a serialization of James Joyce's novel *Ulysses*, for which they were later convicted of publishing obscenity. "Who were the bourgeoisie?" the journalist and writer Ben Hecht asked. "Anyone who didn't read the *Little Review*."

During the second decade of the twentieth century, Chicago became what the influential editor and critic H. L. Mencken hailed as "The Literary Capital of the United States." Another literary center and the undisputed capital of bohemian life was Greenwich Village, an area on the Lower West Side of Manhattan. After moving there from Iowa in 1914, the writers Susan Glaspell and George Cram Cook, her husband, became deeply interested in the experimental theater pioneered by the recently created Washington Square Players. Along with friends from Greenwich Village who spent their summers in Provincetown, Massachusetts, Cook and Glaspell formed a small theater group, the Provincetown Players, in 1915. Performing plays by Glaspell, the then-unknown Eugene O'Neill, and many other young dramatists and writers, the Provincetown Players revolutionized theater in the United States. Bohemian life in Greenwich Village was also energized by artists from abroad, including the French painter Marcel Duchamp, whose *Nude Descending a Staircase* had created an uproar at the Armory Show, and the expatriate English painter and poet Mina Loy, who had lived in Paris and Florence before coming to New York in 1916. Loy and American poets such as Marianne Moore, Wallace Stevens, and William Carlos Williams found a ready outlet for their innovative work in a slew of avant-garde magazines published in Greenwich Village, especially *Others: A Magazine of the New Verse*, whose motto was, "The Old Expressions Are with Us Always/And There Are Always Others."

For many writers, artistic innovation went hand in hand with revolutionary politics. The most prominent outlet for the radical intellectual community was the *Masses*, founded in Greenwich Village in 1911 as

We were wild enough to believe that the artists and critics could dominate America.

"A Monthly Magazine Devoted to the Interests of the Working People." Although it published poetry and fiction, the *Masses* sought to promote social and economic change primarily through articles and editorials. Plotting an equivalent revolution in the arts, James Oppenheim, Waldo Frank, and Paul Rosenfield established the *Seven Arts* in 1916. As Oppenheim later recalled, "we were wild enough to believe that the artists and critics could dominate America." In an essay "America in the Arts," published in the first issue of the magazine, the radical French writer and pacifist Romain Rolland insisted that artists all across the United States "must dare to express themselves, freely, sincerely, entirely, in art. . . . They must be careless of form. They must be fearless of opinion." One writer who embraced that credo was the Chicago-based Sherwood Anderson, who had recently published several experimental stories about life in a small midwestern town in the *Little Review* and the *Masses*. Anderson subsequently became the most frequent contributor to the *Seven Arts*, where four more of the interrelated stories appeared before he collected them as *Winesburg, Ohio*, published in 1919.

By then, both the *Masses* and the *Seven Arts* had succumbed to the jingoism and anti-German hysteria that swept the country during World War I. The United States maintained an official policy of neutrality after the war began in August 1914, pitting the Allied Powers – led by Great Britain, France, Russia, and later Italy – against the Central Powers – led by Germany, Austria-Hungary, and the Ottoman Empire. Max Eastman, the Marxist editor of the *Masses*, attacked both sides in the conflict, which he and many other radicals viewed as an inevitable result of Western imperialism and the competitive capitalist system. After the United States declared war on the Central Powers in April 1917, the *Masses* continued to oppose the war, as did the *Seven Arts*, which published a series of pacifist essays by the radical cultural critic Randolph Bourne. The *New-York Tribune* consequently branded the *Seven Arts* as "an enemy within," and the magazine folded after its major financial backer withdrew her support. The *Masses* was forced to cease publication after it was banned from the U.S. mail for violating the Espionage Act, which gave the postal service the authority to revoke the mailing privilege of any newspaper or magazine that published material critical of the war effort. In July 1917, Eastman and several of his colleagues were indicted under the act. The jury in the first trial was hopelessly deadlocked, and the jury in the second trial voted to acquit them in October 1918, a month before the armistice ended hostilities in World War I.

Because of its late entry into the war, the United States was spared the full brunt of the catastrophic conflict. Total military casualties in the war exceeded thirty million, including nearly ten million dead or missing. Russia, which pulled out of the war following the Bolshevik Revolution of 1917, suffered the largest number of casualties, nearly seven million. It was

The Masses

This left-wing magazine published the work of many radical writers and visual artists, including Robert Minor, who provided the cover illustration for this 1916 issue devoted to President Wilson's policy of "preparedness." Although Wilson won reelection in 1916 on the slogan "He kept us out of the war," he had already begun a military buildup that many believed would inevitably lead to the country's entry into World War I.

THE MASSES

JULY, 1916   10 CENTS

PREPAREDNESS NUMBER

"AT THE THROAT OF THE REPUBLIC"
John Reed Exposes the Whole Preparedness Plot

Jim Larkin on the Irish Rebellion

Lincoln Steffens on Mexico

Max Eastman at the White House

Dante Barton Describes the Pittsburg Strike

Pictures By

BOARDMAN ROBINSON   MAURICE BECKER
ROBERT MINOR   K. R. CHAMBERLAIN
GEORGE BELLOWS   ART YOUNG
CORNELIA BARNS   KARL PEARSON
           JO DAVIDSON

followed by Germany, France, and Austria-Hungary, all with more than five million, and Great Britain, with three million. Ezra Pound, who observed the war at close range from his vantage point in London and lost some of his closest friends in the fighting on the western front, wrote an epitaph for a generation of men in his poem "Hugh Selwyn Mauberly" (1920). Remembering those who "walked knee deep in hell," the soldiers who had experienced the horrors of trench warfare in France, Pound bitterly declared:

> There died a myriad,
> And of the best, among them,
> For an old bitch gone in the teeth,
> For a botched civilization.

Pound's revulsion for the war, which he believed exposed the bankrupt values and debased culture of the civilization that had given rise to the conflict, was shared by many writers on both sides of the Atlantic. Certainly, the war profoundly shaped the attitudes and work of the American writers who emerged during the following decade, including Ernest Hemingway, who was seriously wounded while serving in an ambulance corps in Italy. Compared with the appalling losses in Europe, however, American casualties were relatively light: Of the 3.5 million men mobilized in the United States, roughly 70,000 died or were missing in action and 190,000 were wounded, amounting to less than 2 percent of the total military casualties in World War I.

Ironically, the end of hostilities marked the beginning of one of the darkest years in American history. As the war began to wind down in Europe in the fall of 1918, a virulent strain of influenza erupted, the beginning of a pandemic that killed between twenty and forty million people worldwide during 1918-19. The disease affected over 25 percent of the American population, causing the deaths of more than 600,000 people, almost ten times the number of American soldiers who died during World War I. The pandemic left many families and neighborhoods shattered, and the country was further convulsed by labor strife. There were thousands of strikes in 1919, the largest of which was mounted by 350,000 recently organized workers against the United States Steel Corporation. They failed to gain any concessions, partly because many Americans viewed the predominantly foreign-born strikers as "alien" revolutionaries in league with the Bolsheviks in Russia. The labor agitation fueled the "Red scare," a period of antiradical hysteria during which Attorney General A. Mitchell Palmer led raids on labor unions and other leftist organizations, arresting more than 4,000 alleged Communists.

The Famous 369th Arrive in New York City

The 369th Infantry Regiment, nicknamed the Harlem Hellcats, was one of several African American units that achieved distinction on the battlefield during World War I. This photograph shows the unit arriving home in New York City, where they paraded through the streets in February 1919, only three months before race riots broke out in cities across the United States.

Many white Americans also believed that "Bolshevik" agitation among African Americans was the cause of growing racial tensions in the United States. More than 700,000 African American men had registered for military service and 380,000 had served during World War I. They hoped that by fighting for their country they might earn their full rights as citizens. Instead, the recruits found themselves in segregated military units and often assigned to labor battalions. When they returned home, they found racial prejudice and segregation unabated, in both the northern and southern states. During what became known as the "Red Summer" of 1919, race riots erupted in numerous towns and cities, including Charleston, South Carolina; Washington, D.C.; Omaha, Nebraska; East St. Louis, Illinois; and Chicago. In contrast to earlier riots, this time African Americans fought back against white mobs. The militant mood of African Americans was most forcefully expressed by the Jamaican immigrant Claude McKay in his poem "If We Must Die." First published in the *Liberator*, founded in 1919 by Max Eastman and other writers who had earlier been associated with the *Masses*, McKay's call to arms was reprinted in African American newspapers all across the United States.

American Culture in the 1920s

The upheavals of 1919 revealed the strains created by sweeping changes in American society during and immediately after World War I. According to the census of 1920, nearly 14 million of the roughly 106 million people in the country were foreign born. Although immigration from Europe declined during the war, between 1910 and 1920 the population of the country was swelled by 890,000 immigrants fleeing the political and economic turmoil of the Mexican Revolution. The influx generated stronger cultural connections between artists in the United States and Mexico. It also created a market for stories about Mexico by María Cristina Mena, the first Mexican American woman writer to publish in a major magazine in the United States, and later for the work of writers such as the Texas-born Katherine Anne Porter. But there was widespread bias against immigrants from Mexico, as well as against those from southern and eastern Europe, most of them Catholic, who were virtually excluded from the country by a series of restrictive immigration laws passed in the early 1920s. As the deeply conservative president Calvin Coolidge decreed in his State of the Union address in 1923, "America must be kept American." The shortage of workers in northern factories created by the decline in immigration from Europe created new job opportunities for African Americans seeking escape from Jim Crow laws, racial violence, and a depressed rural economy in the South. From roughly 1914 to 1930, as many as 1.5 million African Americans joined the "great migration," creating the first large urban black communities in cities such as Chicago, Cleveland, Detroit, and New York.

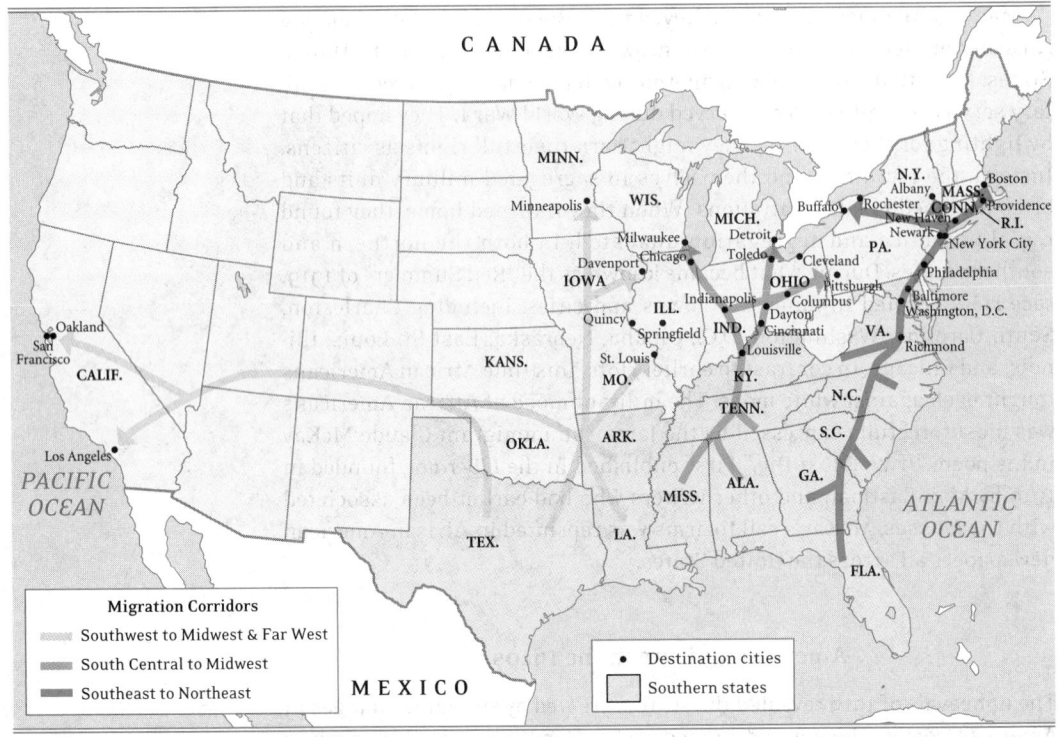

The Great Migration, 1914-1930

This map illustrates the main corridors along which as many as 1.5 million African Americans moved from the rural South to cities in the East, Midwest, and West during what is known as the first great migration, which lasted from roughly the beginning of World War I in Europe to the onset of the Great Depression.

The migration gave rise to what the poet Langston Hughes described as "Manhattan's black Renaissance," a remarkable flowering of African American art, literature, and music beginning in the early 1920s. At the time, most of those involved in the cultural upsurge called it the "New Negro Movement." Centered in Harlem, the movement is now best known as the Harlem Renaissance. From 1914 through 1925, the African American population of Harlem grew from 14,000 to over 175,000, and the congested area became a magnet for activists, artists, and writers. In March 1925, the *Survey Graphic* published a special issue entitled *Harlem: Mecca of the New Negro*, edited by Alain Locke, a professor at Howard University. In his introductory essay, "Enter the New Negro," Locke observed: "The migrant masses, shifting from countryside to city, hurdle several generations of experience at a leap, but more important, the same thing happens spiritually in the life-attitudes and self-expression of the Young Negro, in his poetry, his art, his education, and his new outlook."

African American writers benefited from growing interest in and expanding outlets for their work. Georgia Douglas Johnson first gained attention when three of her poems were published in and she subsequently appeared on the cover of the *Crisis*, the magazine of the National Association for the Advancement of Colored People (NAACP). Its editor, W. E. B. Du Bois, who viewed literature as a powerful weapon in the struggle for racial equality, regularly published, promoted, and reviewed the work of African American writers. James Weldon Johnson, who became the chief executive officer of the NAACP in 1920, showcased the work of thirty-one poets, most of them contemporary, in his pioneering anthology, *The Book of American Negro Poetry* (1922). In 1923, the National Urban League founded *Opportunity: A Journal of Negro Life*, whose motto was, "Not alms, but opportunity." Zora Neale Hurston's first professionally published story and Sterling A. Brown's earliest published poems appeared in *Opportunity*, which became a driving force in the art and literature of the Harlem Renaissance. White publishing companies took note of the growing market for works by African American writers. Boni & Liveright, founded in 1916 to bring modernist works to the American reading public, published *Cane* (1923), an experimental volume of poems, sketches, and stories by Jean Toomer. The prestigious firm of Harper and Brothers published four volumes of verse by Countee Cullen, one of the most popular poets of the 1920s. After Langston Hughes won a prize sponsored by *Opportunity*, his first volume of poetry was accepted by Alfred A. Knopf, Inc., which was at the forefront of new literary trends and which also later published Nella Larsen's novels *Quicksand* (1928) and *Passing* (1929).

As impressive as the literary achievements of the Harlem Renaissance were, African American music exerted a far more pervasive influence during the 1920s, often called the "Jazz Age." The ratification of the Eighteenth, or "Prohibition," Amendment – which took effect in January 1920 – led to the establishment of huge numbers of illegal bars, called "speakeasies," in urban centers throughout the United States. To attract customers, speakeasies often provided live entertainment, especially jazz – music that was widely associated with lawlessness and lack of inhibition. Jazz was also performed at venues such as the legendary Harlem nightspot the Cotton Club. "The Charleston," the anthem and the most popular dance of the Jazz Age, was introduced in the all-black musical *Runnin' Wild*, which opened on Broadway in 1923. Jazz was also carried far beyond Broadway, clubs, and speakeasies by the radio and by phonograph records. A decade after the first commercial radio station began broadcasting in 1919, more than ten million homes had radios, and the sales of record players reached five million in 1929. The white bandleader Paul Whiteman, the self-proclaimed "King of Jazz," called jazz "the folk music

Josephine Baker

Josephine Baker

Jazz, which became an international cultural phenomenon, was carried to Europe by performers such as the celebrated singer and dancer Josephine Baker, pictured here doing the Charleston at the Folies Bergère, Paris, in 1926.

of the machine age." Meanwhile, jazz was decried as a threat to morality and the social order in the pulpit and the press, including the *New York American*, which prophesied, "Moral disaster is coming to hundreds of young American girls through the pathological, nerve-irritating, sex-exciting music of jazz orchestras."

If jazz provided the soundtrack of the 1920s, the decade's most prominent actor was the "flapper," the very symbol of the Jazz Age. Women, who had taken the places of many men in the labor force during World War I, were increasingly involved in the public sphere, and their educational and employment opportunities continued to grow at a steady rate. By 1920, when the ratification of the Nineteenth Amendment granted women the right to vote, they represented 60 percent of all the high-school graduates and nearly 15 percent of the country's workforce. During the following decade, many young women also claimed unprecedented social and sexual freedom – driving cars, smoking in public, applying "kiss-proof" makeup, and wearing revealing clothing that shocked their elders. The image of the liberated "flapper," with her close-cut or "bobbed" hair, short skirts, and

Farm Family Listening to Their Radio

Between 1923 and 1930, 60 percent of American families purchased radios, which became a primary source of entertainment and information, especially in isolated rural areas. As the writer E. B. White observed, "When [people in a rural community] say 'The Radio,'" they "refer to a pervading and somewhat godlike presence which has come into their lives and homes."

silk stockings rolled to just above the knee, was a staple of popular fiction, notably the stories in F. Scott Fitzgerald's collections *Flappers and Philosophers* (1921) and *Tales of the Jazz Age* (1922). She also appeared in advertisements, cartoons, fashion magazines, and movies such as *The Flapper* (1920) and *Flaming Youth* (1924). Indeed, movies dominated the mass-entertainment industry during the 1920s. In 1929, two years after the release of the first of the full-length "talkies," *The Jazz Singer*, the weekly attendance at movies exceeded ninety million, roughly three-quarters of the population of the United States.

Despite the competition of the radio, movies, and other leisure-time activities, including the growing popularity of professional sports, American literature flourished during the 1920s. The most popular poet of the decade was Edna St. Vincent Millay, whose work embodied the political, social, and sexual rebellion of the "modern woman." Millay was the first woman to be awarded the Pulitzer Prize for Poetry, for her collection *The Harp-Weaver and Other Poems* (1922). Meanwhile, the work of more

Tales of the Jazz Age

Boldly designed, brightly colored dust jackets were rare until the 1920s, when publishers began to realize that such protective covers could also attract the attention of potential buyers to books displayed on counters or in shop windows. The dust jacket of Fitzgerald's second collection of short stories was designed by the popular illustrator John Held Jr., best known for satirical depictions of "flaming youth," notably Betty Coed, the prototypical flapper, and her friend Joe College.

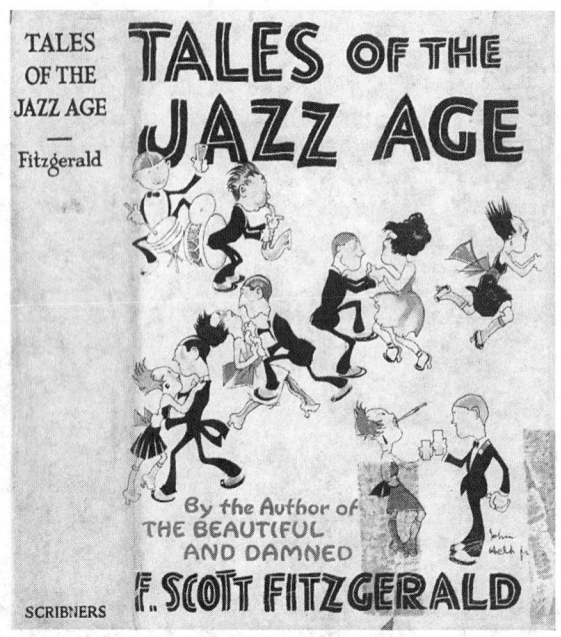

experimental poets appeared in proliferating little magazines, as well as more substantial journals such as the *Dial*, which the wealthy art patron Scofield Thayer had purchased in 1919. Determined to transform the *Dial* into the preeminent international journal of the arts, Thayer published avant-garde work by both European and American writers, including the most influential poem of the decade, T. S. Eliot's *The Waste Land* (1922). Thayer also established the prestigious Dial Prize and the Dial Press, which published collections of poetry by two of the major contributors to the *Dial*, E. E. Cummings and Marianne Moore. In Paris, to which many alienated American artists and writers had flocked after World War I, the writer Robert McAlmon established Contact Editions, devoted to publishing books "not likely to be printed . . . for commercial or legislative reasons" – that is, because they either would not be expected to sell or would be deemed immoral or obscene in the United States. McAlmon subsequently published Mina Loy's *Lunar Baedecker* (1923), William Carlos Williams's *Spring and All* (1923), and Ernest Hemingway's first book, *Three Stories & Ten Poems* (1923).

Although the market for experimental poetry and prose was limited, there was a strong demand for more mainstream literary productions. In 1900, only 10 percent of young people aged fourteen to seventeen attended high school. By 1929, the number exceeded 40 percent, and a million students were enrolled in college. People also had the money to buy books and magazines. Sophisticated urban readers turned to *Vanity Fair*, a magazine of culture and fashion established in 1914, which later vied with the upstart *New Yorker*, begun in 1925. The bible of rebellious youth was *Smart Set*, "A Magazine of Cleverness," edited from 1914 to 1923 by H. L. Mencken and George Jean Nathan. The iconoclastic editors, who proclaimed that "One civilized reader is worth a thousand boneheads," published challenging works by established authors and younger writers such as F. Scott Fitzgerald, whose first professionally published story appeared in *Smart Set* in 1919. Fitzgerald, however, made far more money by writing stories for mass-circulation family magazines such as *Collier's*, *Cosmopolitan*, *Redbook*, and especially the *Saturday Evening Post*.

Mass-market magazines and other periodicals were sustained by the enormous growth of advertising during the 1920s. The decade's economic boom was in large part generated by the emerging consumer culture in which print advertising played an important role. The *Saturday Evening Post* was able to pay writers top dollar and to keep the cover price of the expensively produced "glossy" at five cents because the annual advertising revenues of the magazine exceeded 50 million dollars by the end of the

Through her dealings as business manager of the home, the modern woman brings sound commercial sense to bear on her judgment of a Ford closed car.

She knows that its low first cost, its small upkeep and operation costs, and its long-sustained usefulness make it a genuine economy. She is aware that the ease

with which she can get expert attention for it anywhere and at any time is an asset of great dollar-and-cents value to her.

And she is delighted to find this value in a car that she drives so easily, and whose outward style and inward comfort she so whole-heartedly approves.

TUDOR SEDAN, $590   FORDOR SEDAN, $685   COUPE, $525   (All prices f. o. b. Detroit)

Ford
CLOSED CARS

Ford Car Advertisement

Led by Ford's legendary Model T, and with the help of modern advertising, cars became the most powerful force in the prosperity of the 1920s. This image appeared in a full-page advertisement in the *Ladies' Home Journal* in 1924. The prominent role of women in the consumer economy of the decade is also evident in the text of the advertisement, which reads in part: "Through her dealings as business manager of the home, the modern woman brings sound commercial sense to bear on her judgment of a Ford closed car."

1920s. The pages of magazines and newspapers were filled with advertisements for cars, the mainstay of the American economy during the decade, as well as innumerable other consumer products, especially those for women and the home. The visual images in advertisements powerfully shaped American culture, and advertising agencies claimed that they provided an important source of information to the American public. In "The Power of the Printed Word," an advertisement reprinted in the collection *In Behalf of Advertising* (1929), a copywriter for the firm of N. W. Ayer & Son exclaimed,

> Twenty-five million American families buy twenty-nine million newspapers every day, not to mention the periodicals they receive by the week and the month. Out of the magazines and newspapers they glean the ideas that are to rule their daily lives. They read the printed page with confidence. Its advertising carries conviction!

Book publishing also flourished during the 1920s. The number of libraries increased dramatically, and the creation of subscription book clubs expanded the reading public in the United States. The most famous was the Book-of-the-Month Club, established by Henry Scherman in 1926. Scherman assembled a panel of literary scholars to select the "the best new books published each month," which were then distributed by mail to subscribers, many of whom either did not have ready access to bookstores or were uncertain about which books they should read. This effort to secure a place for serious works of literature in the expanding consumer economy was immediately successful, and the Book-of-the-Month Club had 110,000 subscribers by 1929. There was a particularly strong demand for novels, and the production of new books of fiction doubled during the decade. "The sales department always wants a novel," the influential Scribner's editor Maxwell Perkins wryly observed: "They want to turn everything into a novel. They would have turned the New Testament into one, if it had come to us for publication." Certainly, there were novels on every possible subject for readers of widely varying tastes. Two of the most popular novelists of the day were Edgar Rice Burroughs, who wrote two dozen sequels to his story *Tarzan of the Apes* (1914), and Zane Grey, a prolific author of action-packed stories about the Old West. Writers who had begun their careers around the turn of the century enjoyed significant success during the decade, including the widely respected novelists Willa Cather and Edith Wharton, as well as their controversial contemporary Theodore Dreiser, whose best-selling work was *An American Tragedy* (1925).

They want to turn everything into a novel. They would have turned the New Testament into one, if it had come to us for publication.

A new generation of novelists also emerged. Following the publication of his first novel, *Main Street* (1920), Sinclair Lewis continued to top the bestseller lists with a series of satirical portraits of middle-class life in the Midwest. In 1930, Lewis became the first American to be awarded the

Nobel Prize for Literature. The fame of F. Scott Fitzgerald, one of the other bright stars to emerge in 1920, began to fade after the publication of his third novel, *The Great Gatsby* (1925). The following year, Ernest Hemingway published his first major novel, *The Sun Also Rises* (1926), a story about expatriates in Paris that the *New York Times* hailed as "one of the events of an unusually rich year in literature." The year also saw the publication of William Faulkner's first novel, *Soldier's Pay* (1926), whose central figure is a dying aviator wounded in World War I. The novel created little stir, and despite the profound impact of the war, the actualities of its battles were rarely the subject of popular novels until 1929. That year, a decade after the signing of the treaty that formally ended hostilities, two antiwar novels gained a wide readership in the United States: Hemingway's *A Farewell to Arms* and the internationally acclaimed *All Quiet on the Western Front*, a translation of *Im Westen Nichts Neues* by the German novelist Erich Maria Remarque, perhaps the most grimly realistic of all depictions of the horror and futility of what many hopefully referred to as "The War to End All Wars."

From the Great Depression to World War II

The prosperity and productivity of the 1920s came to an abrupt end in October 1929. Although the stock market rallied briefly after a massive sell-off on "Black Thursday," October 24, the prices of stocks tumbled again the following week, on "Black Monday" and "Black Tuesday," which marked the beginning of what came to be called the "Great Depression." The economic downturn soon affected European countries, and a depression spread throughout the world. In the United States, the stock market continued to fall until July 1932, by which time the Dow Jones Industrial Average was down nearly 90 percent from its high point before the crash in 1929. More than 10,000 of the country's 25,000 banks failed, and industrial output plummeted, leading to massive unemployment. By 1934, over 15 million people, more than 25 percent of the workforce, were unemployed. The economic and human crisis was exacerbated by a series of devastating droughts and dust storms that left 500,000 people homeless in the "Dust Bowl" of Texas, Arkansas, Oklahoma, and the Great Plains.

The Great Depression deeply undermined the optimism that had been generated by the seemingly limitless economic growth of the 1920s. During his successful election campaign in 1928, the Republican Herbert Hoover confidently asserted, "We shall soon with the help of God be in sight of the day when poverty will be banished from this land." Ironically, during Hoover's presidency the most common images of urban life in the United States were men selling apples on street corners, beggars, and "bread lines," long lines of people waiting for food outside relief offices and charitable organizations. Describing the bleak scenes in New York City and the

Bread Line

One of the most common scenes and iconic images of the Great Depression was the "bread line," as illustrated by this photograph of a long line of jobless and homeless men waiting for food outside the municipal lodging house in New York City, during the winter of 1932-33.

dark mood of the country in 1932, the English visitor Mary Agnes Hamilton observed: "The American people, unfamiliar with suffering, with none of that long history of catastrophe and calamity behind it which makes the experience of European nations, is outraged and baffled by misfortune. Depression blocks its view; they cannot see around it." As Hamilton also observed, the nation's loss of confidence had resulted in "a despair of any and every kind of leadership," including that of the conservative Hoover, who was soundly defeated by Franklin D. Roosevelt in the presidential election of 1932. In an effort to restore the morale of the people and bring about "a new deal for the forgotten man," Roosevelt created a number of new agencies, the largest of which was the Works Progress Administration or WPA. The agency provided jobs for millions of destitute people, including unemployed writers and artists who worked on cultural programs sponsored by the Federal Theater Project and the Federal Writers' Project.

Many American writers became deeply involved in radical politics during the Great Depression. In his retrospective essay "Echoes of the Jazz Age" (1931), F. Scott Fitzgerald observed, "It was characteristic of the Jazz Age that it had no interest in politics at all." Although that was an exaggeration, Fitzgerald rightly gauged the seismic cultural and political shift generated by the stock market crash of 1929. During the 1920s, writers such as John Dos Passos maintained an interest in radical causes, and he and several other writers became involved in the case of Nicola Sacco and Bartolomeo Vanzetti, two Italian immigrants and anarchists who many believed were wrongfully convicted of murder and executed in Massachusetts in 1927. One of the leaders of the protests against their execution was Michael Gold, the Marxist editor of the recently established journal the *New Masses*. Gold was later active in the international campaign to "Free the Scottsboro Boys," nine black teenagers convicted of raping two white girls on a freight train bound from Tennessee to Alabama on March 25, 1931. The case had far-reaching consequences, dividing the country along sectional and racial lines, giving impetus to more militant tactics in the struggle for civil rights, and generating support in the black community for radical political groups, including the Communist Party. The Party's involvement in the case and its commitment to racial equality also attracted writers such as Langston Hughes, who exposed the injustices of the American legal and economic system in poems and a verse play, *Scottsboro Limited* (1932).

American writing was also influenced by the "proletarian literature" movement of the 1930s. For Marxist critics and writers, such socially engaged literature was a vital instrument in the class struggle. In his

Scottsboro Limited

Prentiss Taylor, an artist who collaborated with Hughes on several projects, created the lithograph used on the cover of this 1932 collection of works inspired by the case of the "Scottsboro Boys," nine black teenagers falsely accused of raping two white girls. All-white juries in the small town of Scottsboro, Alabama, swiftly convicted all nine defendants, eight of whom were sentenced to death. After a long legal and political battle, the defendants who had not escaped or died in prison were released.

introduction to the anthology *Proletarian Literature of the United States* (1935), Joseph Freeman emphasized that writing "on the people's side" promised to introduce new areas of feeling and experience into the dominant culture of the United States. In the *U.S.A.* trilogy (1930–36), a sweeping chronicle of American life from the turn of the century through the stock market crash of 1929, Dos Passos revealed both the corrosive effects of materialism and the harsh realities of life for working-class people in the United States. The Great Depression inspired Sandburg to write his epic poem *The People, Yes* (1936), which was hailed as a visionary affirmation of the need to build a social revolution upon "the belief in the people," as the radical poet Archibald MacLeish put it in a review in the *New Masses*. That belief was at the core of perhaps the most famous American novel of the 1930s, *The Grapes of Wrath* (1939), John Steinbeck's saga of the ordeal of the Joads, an impoverished tenant-farmer family joining the mass exodus from the Dust Bowl of Oklahoma to California. Michael Gold hailed Steinbeck as a champion of the "people's culture," and the best-selling book was made into a popular movie in 1940. That year, Richard Wright captured the misery and poverty endured by African Americans living in a slum on the South Side of Chicago in *Native Son* (1940), the first Book-of-the-Month Club selection written by an African American.

Dorothea Lange, *Migrant Mother* (California, 1936)

The human crisis created by the Dust Bowl, which John Steinbeck dramatizes in his novel *The Grapes of Wrath* (1939), was also documented by photojournalists from the Farm Security Administration, including the former fashion and portrait photographer Dorothea Lange. Lange took this famous photograph of an impoverished Oklahoma woman and her children during a brief stop at a pea-picker's camp in Nipomo, California.

Social protest formed only one aspect of the literature of the 1930s. In contrast to Wright, Zora Neale Hurston offered a far more positive vision of African American life in stories and her first novel, *Their Eyes Were Watching God* (1937). Although the Florida-born Hurston is most often associated with the Harlem Renaissance, she was also part of what came to be known as the Southern Literary Renaissance. The most critically acclaimed southern writer of the 1930s was William Faulkner, who explored the region's troubled past and its legacy in a wide range of stories and novels, including *Absalom, Absalom!* (1936). But that complex and challenging work was completely overshadowed by another southern novel about the Civil War and Reconstruction that was published the same year, Margaret Mitchell's *Gone with the Wind* (1936). Although the hefty, thousand-page book cost two dollars, a substantial sum in the midst of the Depression, Mitchell's blockbuster sold more than one million copies within a year, won a Pulitzer Prize in 1937, and was made into a smash-hit movie starring Clark Gable and Vivien Leigh in 1939.

Like the motion pictures, publishing weathered the hard financial times of the Great Depression far better than most other businesses. Initially, many little magazines ceased publication, and book production dropped 50 percent between 1929 and 1933. But production later rallied, and other kinds of reading materials flourished. Mass-circulation family magazines continued to attract large numbers of readers, and the 1930s was the heyday of "pulps," so called because of the cheap, wood-pulp paper of which these popular magazines were made. Successors to the dime novels of the late nineteenth century, pulps specialized in various fictional genres, including westerns, romances, and science fiction. Among the most famous of the pulps was the crime-fiction magazine *Black Mask*, which published the pioneering stories and novels of Dashiell Hammett, including *The Maltese Falcon* (1930). *Black Mask* and other pulps later succumbed to competition from comic books and paperback novels. Although there were many earlier paperbound books, the first mass-market paperback novels published in the United States were the Pocket Books. Designed to fit into a man's coat pocket and priced at only twenty-five cents, Pocket Books were introduced in 1939. To test-market the books, the publisher reprinted *The Good Earth* (1931), a popular novel by Pearl Buck, who had won the Nobel Prize in 1938. The first run of two thousand copies sold out quickly at untraditional outlets for books, including Macy's Department Store and a corner cigar store in New York City. Thus, Pocket Books began a revolution not only in publishing but also in the marketing of books in the United States.

Paperbacks and other kinds of books assumed a prominent role during World War II. The confident theme of the New York World's Fair of 1939 was "Building the World of Tomorrow." The fair celebrated new technologies, including television, but further development of that

Newsstand in
Omaha, Nebraska

Newsstand in
Omaha, Nebraska

John Vachon, a photogra-
pher for the Farm Secu-
rity Administration, took
this photograph while on
assignment in Nebraska
in November 1938. The
photograph displays a
range of interests and
tastes catered to by American periodicals, including
an array of "pulps" and
mass-circulation family
magazines, as well as the
first all-photography news-
magazine, the recently
created and tremendously
popular *Life*.

formidable competitor to books was interrupted by the beginning of the
war in Europe in September 1939. The war generated industrial production in the United States, which then finally emerged from the Great
Depression. After the country entered the global conflict in December
1941, providing books to members of the armed forces became a prominent part of the war effort. The American Library Association, the Red
Cross, and the United Service Organizations (USO) sponsored the Victory Book Campaign, which collected millions of books for distribution
to military camps. At the same time, rationing of paper curtailed the
printing of traditional, hard-backed books, spurring the development
of cheaply produced paperbacks. Early in 1942, a group of publishers
founded the Council on Books in Wartime, which distributed inexpensive, five-by-four-inch paperbacks called the Armed Services Editions.
By the end of the war, the council had distributed 123.5 million copies
of more than 1,300 different books to American troops at home and
overseas.

   In addition to raising the morale of the troops, books came to symbolize
the ideological struggle between the United States and the Axis Powers. In
his State of the Union address in January 1941, commonly known as his
"Four Freedoms Speech," President Roosevelt outlined the fundamental

liberties that all people should enjoy: freedom of speech, freedom of worship, freedom from want, and freedom from fear. Many Americans subsequently came to view World War II as a struggle to defend those freedoms from the onslaught of the military dictatorship in Japan and the Fascist regimes in Germany and Italy. Early in 1942, a group of American authors formed the Writers' War Board, a government-subsidized organization that adopted the slogan "Books Are Weapons in the War of Ideas." The board coordinated the work of hundreds of authors who fought the war with their pens, including Edna St. Vincent Millay, a former pacifist who had been deeply involved in the Sacco and Vanzetti case in the 1920s, and Langston Hughes, who had written some of the most revolutionary political poetry of the 1930s. Indeed, many writers who had earlier been among the harshest critics of American politics and society strongly supported the war, in which President Roosevelt affirmed that Americans were fighting "for a better day for all mankind."

World War II Poster

This poster was distributed to U.S. libraries by the Office of War Information. The giant book, with its quotation from a 1942 speech by President Roosevelt, looms over a scene that evokes the Nazi book burnings that began in May 1933, when university students burned 25,000 "un-German" books in a ceremony held in Munich. To rally Americans around the war effort, groups such as the Writers' War Board sponsored annual commemorations of the book burnings, and in a massive Flag Day parade in 1942, "New York at War," city librarians marched under the banner "Fascism Burns Books, Democracy Reads Books."

COMPARATIVE TIMELINE, 1914–1945

Dates	American Literature	Historical Events	Developments in Culture, Science, and Technology
1914–1919	**1914** Frost, *North of Boston* **1914** Pound publishes the poetry anthology *Des Imagistes* **1914** Stein, *Tender Buttons* **1914** Lowell, *Sword Blades and Poppy Seeds* **1914** Mena's "The Vine-Leaf" is published in *Century* **1915** Lowell publishes first of three poetry anthologies, *Some Imagist Poets* **1915** Pound, *Cathay* **1916** Glaspell, *Trifles* **1916** Sandburg, *Chicago Poems* **1916** H.D., *Sea Garden* **1917** Williams, *Al Que Quiere!* **1917** Eliot, *Prufrock and Other Observations* **1917** Millay, *Renascence and Other Poems* **1918** G. D. Johnson, *The Heart of a Woman*	**1914** World War I begins in Europe **1914–30** More than one million African Americans join the great migration, moving from small towns in the South to cities in the North **1916** Wilson elected to second term as president **1917** United States declares war on Central Powers, thus entering World War I **1917** Bolshevik Revolution in Russia **1917** Immigration acts exclude all Asian workers except Japanese **1918** Armistice signed, ending World War I **1918** Eighteenth Amendment prohibits manufacture, sale, and transportation of alcohol **1918–19** Influenza pandemic kills between 20 and 40 million people worldwide	**1914** Opening of Panama Canal **1914** Babe Ruth makes Major League debut with Red Sox **1914** First transcontinental phone call **1914** *Little Review, Smart Set, Blast, Vanity Fair*, and *New Republic* all begin publication **1914** W. C. Handy publishes "St. Louis Blues" **1915** Max Weber paints *Grand Central Terminal* **1915** Alfred Kreymborg founds *Others* **1916** Provincetown Players give first public performances **1916** *Seven Arts* founded **1917** Pulitzer Prizes established **1917** Original Dixieland Jazz Band makes first jazz recording

COMPARATIVE TIMELINE, 1914–1945

Dates	American Literature	History and Politics	Developments in Culture, Science, and Technology
1914–1919 (cont.)	**1919** Moore, *Observations* **1919** Anderson, *Winesburg, Ohio* 	**1919** Race riots erupt across United States **1919** Treaty of Versailles and formation of the League of Nations **1919** Steelworkers strike U.S. Steel	**1919** *Dial* is purchased by wealthy art patron Scofield Thayer **1919** *Liberator* is founded by Max Eastman and other writers once associated with *Masses*
1920–1929	**1920** O'Neill, *The Emperor Jones* **1920** Millay, *A Few Figs from Thistles* **1920** Fitzgerald, *This Side of Paradise*	**1920** U.S. population: 105,710,620. Some 14,000,000 are foreign-born, and urban population exceeds rural population for first time **1920** "Red scare" prompts fears of Communists and foreign-born radicals **1920** Harding elected president **1920** Nineteenth Amendment grants women right to vote 	**1920s** Stein and Toklas host expatriate American artists and writers at their home in Paris
	1921 Fitzgerald, *Flappers and Philosophers* **1921** Dos Passos, *Three Soldiers* **1922** Eliot, *The Waste Land* **1922** Fitzgerald, *Tales of the Jazz Age* **1922** Millay, *The Harp-Weaver and Other Poems*, awarded Pulitzer Prize **1922** G. D. Johnson, *Bronze: A Book of Verse* **1922** McKay, *Harlem Shadows* **1922** Stein, *Geography and Plays* **1922** J. W. Johnson, *The Book of American Negro Poetry*	**1921** Emergency Quota Act temporarily restricts immigration from Europe to the U.S.	**1921** Regular radio broadcasts begin **1922** *Reader's Digest* founded **1922** James Joyce, *Ulysses* **1922** *Fugitive* and *Soil* founded **1922** Louis Armstrong joins Creole Jazz Band in Chicago

COMPARATIVE TIMELINE, 1914–1945

Dates	American Literature	Historical Events	Developments in Culture, Science, and Technology
1920–1929 (cont.)	**1923** Loy, *Lunar Baedecker* **1923** Frost, *New Hampshire*, awarded Pulitzer Prize **1923** Hemingway, *Three Stories and Ten Poems* **1923** Stevens, *Harmonium* **1923** Fujita, *Tanka: Poems in Exile* **1923** Cummings, *Tulips and Chimneys* **1923** Williams, *Spring and All* **1923** Toomer, *Cane*	**1923** Coolidge becomes president after Harding dies in office	**1923** *Time* magazine established **1923** National Urban League founds *Opportunity* OPPORTUNITY **1923** Former members of the Provincetown Players form Experimental Theatre
	1925 Hemingway, *In Our Time* **1925** Fitzgerald, *The Great Gatsby* **1925** Pound, *A Draft of XVI Cantos* **1925** Alain Locke publishes *The New Negro*, an anthology of the Harlem Renaissance **1925** Cullen, *Color* **1925** Cummings, *XLI Poems. &.*	**1924** First women governors elected in Wyoming and Texas **1924** Indian Citizenship Act grants citizenship to Native Americans **1924** National Origins Act reduces quotas of immigrants from Europe and disallows immigration from Japan **1925** John Scopes is convicted for violating state law forbidding teaching of evolution in Tennessee	**1924** Paul Whiteman, the "King of Jazz," commissions George Gershwin's *Rhapsody in Blue* **1925** *New Yorker* is founded **1925** *Grand Ole Opry* makes radio debut and eventually becomes longest-running live music show

COMPARATIVE TIMELINE, 1914–1945

Dates	American Literature	Historical Events	Developments in Culture, Science, and Technology
1920–1929 (cont.)	**1926** Hemingway, *The Sun Also Rises* **1926** Crane, *White Buildings* **1926** Hughes, *The Weary Blues* **1926** Faulkner, *Soldier's Pay* **1927** J. W. Johnson, *God's Trombones* **1927** Cullen publishes *Caroling Dusk: An Anthology of Verse by Negro Poets* **1928** Larsen, *Quicksand* **1929** Hemingway, *A Farewell to Arms* **1929** Cullen, *The Black Christ and Other Poems* **1929** Faulkner, *The Sound and the Fury*	**1926** Ford introduces eight-hour, five-day work week **1927** Italian immigrants Sacco and Vanzetti are executed in Massachusetts after being convicted of first-degree murder **1928** Herbert Hoover elected president **1929** Stock market crash leads to decade-long depression in the United States and spreads worldwide 	**1926** Henry Scherman establishes Book-of-the-Month Club **1927** Duke Ellington's dance band begins performing at Harlem's Cotton Club **1927** First transatlantic telephone call **1927** Charles Lindbergh completes his solo, nonstop flight across Atlantic Ocean **1927** *The Jazz Singer* is first full-length "talkie" motion picture **1927** Ford introduces Model A car and ends production of successful Model T **1928** Penicillin discovered **1928–29** Erich Maria Remarque's best-selling *All Quiet on the Western Front* first published in Germany, then translated into English **1929** More than ten million homes have radios **1929** Museum of Modern Art opens in New York City **1929** More than 40 percent of young people attend high school and a million students are enrolled in college
1930–1939	**1930–36** Dos Passos, *U.S.A.* trilogy **1930** Crane, *The Bridge* **1930** Porter, *Flowering Judas and Other Stories*	**1930** U.S. population: 122,775,046	**1930** Aaron Douglas paints Symbolic Negro History Series at Fisk University **1930** Sinclair Lewis becomes first American to be awarded Nobel Prize for Literature

COMPARATIVE TIMELINE, 1914–1945

Dates	American Literature	Historical Events	Developments in Culture, Science, and Technology
1930–1939 (cont.)	1930 Larson's "Sanctuary" appears in *Forum* 1930 Twelve Southerners, *I'll Take My Stand* 1931 Hughes, *Scottsboro Limited* 1931 Faulkner, *These 13*	1931 Nine African American teenagers are convicted of rape, igniting a legal and political campaign to "Free the Scottsboro Boys"	1931 "The Star-Spangled Banner" becomes official national anthem 1931 Empire State Building opens 1931 *Story* magazine founded
	1932 Brown, *Southern Road*	1932 Franklin D. Roosevelt elected president	1932 San Francisco Opera House opens 1932 Amelia Earhart is first woman to complete a solo, nonstop flight across Atlantic Ocean.
	1933 Hurston's "The Gilded Six-Bits" appears in *Story* 1933 Stein, *The Autobiography of Alice B. Toklas*	1933–37 Roosevelt's New Deal programs include Social Security, welfare, and unemployment insurance 1933 Nazis stage massive public book burnings 1933 Twenty-first Amendment ends Prohibition 1934 Adolf Hitler becomes Führer of Germany 1934–39 Dust Bowl in Midwest	1933 *Newsweek* founded 1933 Albert Einstein arrives in United States as refugee from Nazi Germany 1934 Apollo Theater opens in Harlem
	1935 Stevens, *Ideas of Order* 1935 Le Sueur, "Annunciation" 1935 Moore, *Selected Poems*	1935 Harlem race riot 1935 Wagner Act protects workers' rights to form unions and bargain collectively	1935 Federal Writers' Project established as part of Works Progress Administration (WPA)
	1936 Mitchell, *Gone with the Wind* 1936 Faulkner, *Absalom, Absalom!* 1936 Sandburg, *The People, Yes*	1936 Roosevelt reelected president 1936–39 Spanish civil war	1936 Dorothea Lange's photograph *Migrant Mother* 1936 Birth control legalized 1936 Hoover Dam completed 1936 *Life* magazine founded 1936 O'Neill awarded Nobel Prize for Literature

Comparative Timeline, 1914–1945

Dates	American Literature	Historical Events	Developments in Culture, Science, and Technology
1930–1939 (cont.)	**1937** Frost, *A Farther Range*, awarded Pulitzer Prize **1937** Hurston, *Their Eyes Were Watching God* **1938** Steinbeck's "Flight" appears in *The Long Valley* **1938** Wright, *Uncle Tom's Children* **1939** Steinbeck, *The Grapes of Wrath*, awarded Pulitzer Prize **1939** Faulkner's "Barn Burning" appears in *Harper's*	**1939** New York World's Fair **1939–45** World War II and the Holocaust	**1938** Ballpoint pen invented **1939** *The Wizard of Oz* premieres at Capitol Theatre in New York City **1939** Pocket Books begin publication
1940–1945	**1940** Hemingway, *For Whom the Bell Tolls* **1940** Wright, *Native Son* **1941** Welty, *A Curtain of Green and Other Stories* **1941** Reznikoff, *Going To and Fro and Walking Up and Down* **1942** Hughes, *Shakespeare in Harlem* **1943** Eliot, *Four Quartets* **1943** Welty, *The Wide Net and Other Stories* **1944** Porter, *The Leaning Tower and Other Stories* **1944** Williams, *The Wedge* **1944** Bulosan's "The End of the War" appears in the *New Yorker*	**1940** U.S. population: 131,669,275 **1940** Beginning of second great migration of African Americans from the South to cities in the North and West **1941** United States enters World War II following Japanese attack on Pearl Harbor **1941** Roosevelt's "Four Freedoms" speech **1944** Roosevelt reelected president **1944** D day: Allied invasion of Normandy, France **1945** Truman becomes president after death of Roosevelt **1945** United States drops atomic bombs on Hiroshima and Nagasaki; Japan surrenders, ending World War II	**1940** Color television invented **1941** Development of Z3, first computer controlled by software **1941** Development of bop or bebop as offshoot of jazz **1942–43** Victory Book Campaign provides millions of books to soldiers **1942–45** Publication of paperback American Service Editions

Modernisms
in American Poetry

IN RECENT YEARS, many critics and scholars have begun to refer to "modernism" as "modernisms," a term that perhaps more clearly suggests the lively disagreements, multiplicity of styles, and plurality of movements within the broad revolution in the arts that took place during the early decades of the twentieth century in Europe and the United States. Certainly, there was no single style of modern American poetry, which was characterized by widely differing aesthetic values, literary purposes, and poetic techniques. Spurred in part by experiments in the visual arts, many poets were committed to formal innovation, including two of the earliest and most energetic proponents of what was often called the "new poetry," Ezra Pound and Amy Lowell.

◀ Aaron Douglas, *Poetry*

This mural is part of the Symbolic Negro History Series, which Douglas created in 1930 for a new library at the historically black Fisk University in Nashville, Tennessee. During the previous decade, Douglas had emerged as one of the major figures of the Harlem Renaissance, in which writers and visual artists worked closely together, as they did in centers of modernism from New York City to London and Paris.

But both poets admired the work of Robert Frost, who adapted the conventional forms and meters of English poetry. The traditional sonnet was a favorite form of the most popular American poet of the period 1914-45, Edna St. Vincent Millay, as well as of two poets associated with the Harlem Renaissance, Claude McKay and Countee Cullen. In contrast, another poet associated with the movement, Langston Hughes, drew inspiration from the forms and rhythms of jazz and the blues. Hughes was also influenced by the vernacular verse of the white poet Carl Sandburg, whose rough-hewn work differed dramatically from the highly polished verse of contemporary poets such as Mina Loy, Marianne Moore, and Wallace Stevens. Indeed, the modernisms of modern American poets were frequently at odds, sometimes almost violently so, as is evident in the work of two of the most influential poets of the period, the expatriate T. S. Eliot and his homebound and self-declared literary opponent William Carlos Williams.

At the same time, modern American poets were connected in a number of ways. All of them passionately believed in the necessity of poetry, its vital role in culture and society. "Times change and forms and their meanings alter," Stevens wrote in 1937. "Thus new poems are necessary. Their forms must be discovered in the spoken, the living language of their day, or old forms, embodying exploded concepts, will tyrannize over the imagination, depriving us of its greatest benefits." Although they lived in far-flung areas, many poets worked closely together in cities such as Chicago, New York, London, and Paris. Many were also connected by a network of friendships and literary alliances. Eliot and Williams, for example, were friends of Ezra Pound, who was in close contact or correspondence with writers on both sides of the Atlantic. Finally, virtually all of the poets of the period benefited from the emergence of new periodicals, especially little magazines, which were designed to provide a venue and generate an audience for experimental writing. The motto of the first of those magazines, *Poetry: A Magazine of Verse*, was a line from Walt Whitman: "To have great poets we must have great audiences too."

> *Thus new poems are necessary. Their forms must be discovered in the spoken, the living language of their day, or old forms, embodying exploded concepts, will tyrannize over the imagination, depriving us of its greatest benefits.*

Few individuals were as crucial to the development of modern American poetry as the founder and editor of *Poetry*, Harriet Monroe. Born into an affluent Chicago family, the well-educated Monroe traveled widely in the United States and Europe and visited China during 1910-11. Returning to Chicago, where she worked as an art critic, Monroe was deeply frustrated by the lack of cultural depth and the lowly status of poetry in the United States. She consequently set out to establish a new kind of literary magazine devoted exclusively to poetry. "My idea of 'direction,'" Monroe recalled in her autobiography, "was to offer good poems to set against the 'piles of rubbish' which bemired the poetic landscape in newspapers and popular magazines." To raise the funds for a new magazine, Monroe visited or wrote to over one hundred prominent Chicagoans, asking for pledges of fifty dollars a year for five years to support the venture. When she had the $5,000 she needed, Monroe wrote letters to poets promising that "this magazine will appeal to, and it may be hoped will develop, a public primarily interested in poetry as an art, as the highest, most complete human expression of truth and beauty." As a next step, she wrote to Pound, then living in London, and invited him to participate. Pound, who agreed to serve as a "Foreign Correspondent" to the magazine, enthusiastically told Monroe that the revolution in American poetry would "make the Italian Renaissance look like a tempest in a teapot!"

The publication of the first issue of *Poetry* in October 1912 marked the beginning of a new era for poetry in the United States. Pound soon sent Monroe several poems by his two closest associates in London, the English poet Richard Aldington and a young American poet living in London, Hilda Doolittle, who published under her initials "H.D." Pound identified them as "imagistes," thus christening the first organized movement in modern English poetry, which he called "imagisme." In brief essays in the March 1913 issue of *Poetry*, he and F. S. Flint outlined the fundamental characteristics of the movement: direct treatment of the "thing," or object; the use of spare, concrete language; and *vers libre*, or free verse, composition – as opposed to the conventional meters of English poetry. As Pound affirmed in "Ikon," a prose poem he published later in 1913, "It is in art the highest business to create the beautiful image; to create order and profusion of images that we may furnish the life of our minds with a noble surrounding." Pound soon edited the first anthology to feature the work of the group, *Des Imagistes* (1914). The volume included several poems by a zealous convert to the movement, Amy Lowell. After she and Pound divided over the direction of the movement, which Lowell sought to democratize and popularize as "imagism," she subsequently edited and published three additional anthologies, *Some Imagist Poets* (1915, 1916, and 1917).

In their revolt against conventional poetic practices, the imagists and other modernist American poets drew inspiration from a wide range of non-English literary models. They were strongly influenced by the experimental techniques of the symbolists and other late-nineteenth-century French poets, who had introduced the term *vers libre* and sought to evoke inner realities through the use of symbolic images. Imagists such as H.D. were drawn to classical poetry, especially the lyrics of the ancient Greek poet Sappho of Lesbos, and Pound championed a wide range of earlier verse, including Anglo-Saxon poetry and work of medieval troubadour poets such as Arnaut Daniel and Guido Cavalcanti. Pound and many others were also deeply interested in the arts of Asia. Defining the

Harriet Monroe

This photograph was taken in 1911, about the time Monroe founded *Poetry: A Magazine of Verse*. She was dressed in clothing purchased during her recent trip to China, the art of which strongly influenced modern poets and painters in Europe and the United States.

It is in art the highest business to create the beautiful image; to create order and profusion of images that we may furnish the life of our minds with a noble surrounding.

Artists and Writers in Paris

This group portrait was taken in the early 1920s. The figure at the far right in the second row is the expatriate American poet Ezra Pound, who moved from London to Paris in 1920. The poet Mina Loy, at the center of the front row, is looking at the American painter and photographer Man Ray, who is squatting and holding a camera.

single most important element in the revolution in American poetry, Harriet Monroe in 1917 declared that "these poets have bowed to the winds from the East." Among the writers who introduced Japanese poetic forms to American audiences were the bilingual poet and critic Yone Noguchi and Jun Fujita, a Japanese immigrant who became a frequent contributor to *Poetry*. Pound adapted the form of the Japanese haiku in his most famous imagist poem, the two-line "In a Station at the Metro," which appeared in the magazine in 1913. He subsequently published an acclaimed collection of translations of ancient Chinese poems, *Cathay* (1915). The imagist poet John Gould Fletcher later observed that the publication of Pound's free-verse translations was the "pivotal moment" in the development of the "new poetry" in English.

Pound also generously promoted the careers of a wide variety of American poets in England and the United States. In 1913, he helped his friend William Carlos Williams publish a collection of poems in London, where Pound also helped arrange for the publication of Robert Frost's first two books of poetry, *A Boy's Will* (1913) and *North of Boston* (1914). The work of the two poets suggested the range of both the new poetry and Pound's aesthetic sympathies, since Williams's experimental poems about the everyday lives of common people in suburban New Jersey bore little similarity to Frost's more traditional verse, which was deeply rooted in rural New England. Both, however, sought to develop a new, distinctively American idiom in poetry, as did the Chicago journalist Carl Sandburg. In 1914, Harriet Monroe published a group of Sandburg's raw and realistic poems about life in an industrial city, and Pound encouraged Sandburg to publish his first book, *Chicago Poems* (1916). The modern urban landscape was also at the center of the work of a very different poet, T. S. Eliot, for whom Pound reserved his greatest praise. "He is the only American I know of who has made what I can call adequate preparation for writing," Pound observed after he met the highly educated and widely read Eliot in London in 1914. Through Pound's influence, Eliot's first professionally published poem, "The Love Song of J. Alfred Prufrock," appeared in *Poetry* in 1915.

The example of *Poetry* and the proliferating alliances and movements within modernism inspired the establishment of a number of other little magazines. In London, Pound helped the British writer and painter Wyndham Lewis found *Blast*, an experimental magazine that Lewis described as the "battering ram" for a loosely defined movement called "Vorticism." In New York City, the poet Alfred Kreymborg established *Others: A Magazine of the New Verse*, a rival to *Poetry*, in 1915. But little magazines were plagued by economic problems resulting from small circulations and limited support from advertisers. Seeking to overcome the general indifference to magazines such as *Others*, a reviewer admiringly observed that the first issues of the magazine "are among the live things being done in America just now," adding,

> *The new poetry is revolutionary. It is the expression of a democracy of feeling rebelling against an aristocracy of form.*

> Perhaps you are unfamiliar with this "new poetry" that is called "revolutionary." Perhaps you've heard that it is queer and have let it go at that. Perhaps if you tried it you'd find that a side of you that has been sleeping would come awake again. It is worth the price of a Wednesday matinée to find out. By the way, the new poetry is revolutionary. It is the expression of a democracy of feeling rebelling against an aristocracy of form.

Others displayed the full array of new voices in American poetry, from expatriates such as Pound, Eliot, and H.D. to Kreymborg's friends and associates in and around New York City, including Mina Loy, Marianne Moore, Wallace Stevens, and William Carlos Williams.

Although such "revolutionary" poets seemed to present a united front, they were increasingly divided about the nature and direction of the new poetry. After *Others* ceased publication, Williams and his friend Robert McAlmon established a new magazine designed to feature cutting-edge writing, *Contact*. The title reflected their conviction that successful writing is "indigenous," a direct expression of the artist's immediate experiences

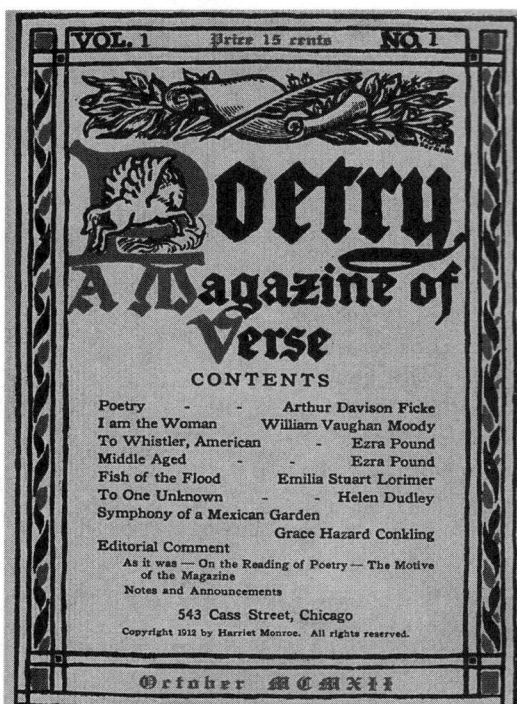

and perceptions of local conditions. Williams, who was convinced that European literary traditions posed a serious obstacle to the development of modern American poetry, was particularly hostile to T. S. Eliot, whom he viewed as an academic, backward-looking poet who had abandoned America. Williams was consequently devastated by the fame and widespread influence of Eliot's *The Waste Land* (1922), which was published in the United States in the most prominent literary journal of the period, the *Dial*, and then as a book by the modernist firm Boni & Liveright. Describing the impact of Eliot's learned and richly allusive poem, "the great catastrophe to our letters," Williams bitterly recalled, "I felt at once that it has set us back twenty years, and I'm sure it did. Critically Eliot had returned us to the classroom just at the moment when I felt we were on the point of an escape to matters much closer to the essence of a new art form itself — rooted in the locality which should give it fruit."

The Waste Land formed only one prominent feature of the complex literary landscape of the 1920s. The Pulitzer Prize for 1922, the year Eliot's poem was published, was awarded to the popular poet Edna St. Vincent Millay, for her collection *The Harp-Weaver and Other Poems.* Another popular poet, Robert Frost, received the first of his four Pulitzer Prizes for his collection *New Hampshire* (1923). Together with the older American poet Edwin Arlington Robinson, who received three Pulitzer Prizes during the 1920s, Millay and Frost greatly expanded the audience for poetry in the United States. At the same time, critics praised the "stylistic innovations" and "feeling for American speech" displayed by E. E. Cummings in his first collection, *Tulips and Chimneys* (1923). That year, Wallace Stevens published his acclaimed first collection, *Harmonium*, and Mina Loy's first collection, *Lunar Baedecker*, was published by Robert McAlamon's Contact Press in Paris. The Dial Press, a publishing offshoot of the *Dial*, published Marianne Moore's second volume of poetry, *Observations* (1924). Volumes by two of the most active and influential of the imagist poets appeared in 1925: H.D.'s *Collected Poems* and Amy Lowell's final collection, *What's O'Clock*, for which she was posthumously awarded a Pulitzer Prize. Hart Crane, who was influenced by many English and American poets, including the imagists and other modern poets as diverse as Cummings, Eliot, Pound, Stevens, and Williams, further extended the boundaries of

◀ Little Magazines

The proliferation of little magazines spurred the development of modernism in Europe and the United States. Two were devoted exclusively to verse: *Poetry*, founded in Chicago in 1912; and *Others*, founded in New York City in 1915. The short-lived *Blast*, two issues of which were published during 1914-15, was the journal of the movement called Vorticism. *Opportunity*, founded in New York City by the National Urban League in 1923, assumed a vital role in the Harlem Renaissance.

poetic language and subject matter in his first collection, *White Buildings* (1926).

American verse was also enriched by poets of the Harlem Renaissance. James Weldon Johnson was inspired by African American preaching to write "The Creation" (1920), the first of the poems he later collected in *God's Trombones: Seven Negro Sermons in Verse* (1927). Claude McKay, an immigrant from Jamaica, employed the traditional form of the sonnet in politically charged works such as "If We Must Die" and other poems in his collection *Harlem Shadows* (1922). Other poets also adapted traditional lyric forms to evoke the scenes and themes of African American life, including Georgia Douglas Johnson, especially in her collection *Bronze: A Book of Verse* (1922), and Countee Cullen, whose first collection of poems was entitled *Color* (1925). Some of the poems in that collection also appeared in Alain Locke's influential anthology, *The New Negro* (1925), and the work of many young poets was published in the *Crisis*, the official magazine of the National Association for the Advancement of Colored People (NAACP), and in *Opportunity: A Journal of Negro Life*. In 1925, Langston Hughes won first prize in a literary contest sponsored by *Opportunity*, leading to the publication of his first collection of poetry, *The Weary Blues* (1926). Hughes employed black vernacular language and the rhythms of jazz and the blues to depict the essence of African American life in the urban North. Sterling A. Brown employed similar elements, but he drew upon the dialect, experience, and folklore of rural black people in his collection *Southern Road* (1932).

Following the artistic and economic boom of the 1920s, however, poets and poetry confronted major obstacles during the Great Depression and World War II. Millay and Frost remained popular, as did Carl Sandburg, who responded to the economic crisis of the early 1930s in his epic poem *The People, Yes* (1936). Cummings, Stevens, and some other prominent modernist poets also published important collections during the decade. But the declining interest in and market for poetry had a profound effect on some lesser-known poets. Despite the critical success of *Southern Road*, for example, Brown could not interest a publisher in his second collection of poetry, and he subsequently devoted himself to criticism and scholarship. Other African American poets turned to writing more commercially viable work. In addition to political poetry in support of various radical causes, Langston Hughes wrote fiction and several plays during the Great Depression. T. S. Eliot, who also sought to gain a broader audience by writing drama, completed only one major poetic project after 1930, his *Four Quartets* (1943). Ezra Pound, who had settled in Italy in 1924, continued to work on his long poem *The Cantos*, but he devoted much of his energy to writing treatises on culture, economics, and politics during the 1930s.

Even as Pound embraced the right-wing Italian political movement called "Fascism," he became closely associated with an avant-garde group of left-wing poets in the United States. In 1931, he helped arrange for the young poet Louis Zukovsky to edit a special issue of *Poetry* devoted to the work of the "objectivists." Much like the earlier imagists, the objectivists were committed to everyday language and to writing as a form "of seeing, of thinking, with the things as they exist," as Zukovsky put it. But in contrast to the imagists, many of whom were drawn to nature and mythology, the radical objectivists sought to document the urban proletarian experience during the Great Depression. Zukovsky's editorial work led to the establishment of the Objectivist Press, which published works by Charles Reznikoff, who had previously published most of his work at his own expense, and William Carlos Williams. After the press collapsed under financial pressure in 1936, Williams began a long association with James Laughlin, whom Pound encouraged to establish a publishing house committed to experimental writing, New Directions Press.

Laughlin's successful venture and the establishment of college-based literary journals such as *Prairie Schooner*, the *Southern Review*, and the *Kenyon Review* helped fill the gap left by the demise of the many little magazines that folded during the Great Depression. A notable exception was *Poetry*, which survived even after Harriet Monroe's death in 1936. The staff of the magazine immediately arranged for a memorial issue that included tributes by poets such as Ezra Pound, Marianne Moore, Carl Sandburg, and Wallace Stevens. "No one in our time or in any other time has served the cause of art with greater devotion," Pound gracefully observed of Monroe. In another tribute to the importance of her editorship of *Poetry*, the poet and critic Malcolm Cowley observed that there had "been whole years during which she edited the only magazine in America that would print intelligent poetry and give the authors of it the idea that they were not singing in a soundproof room entirely cut off from the world." Indeed, by nurturing the belief that there was an outlet and an audience for even the most experimental verse, little magazines such as *Poetry* had played a vital role in what Cowley aptly described as the "poetic renaissance" that began around the time Monroe established the magazine in 1912.

American Contexts

"MAKE IT NEW":
THEORIES OF MODERN POETRY

IN HIS TRANSLATION OF THE *TA HIO* ("The Great Learning") of the ancient Chinese philosopher Confucius, the influential modern poet and critic Ezra Pound reaffirmed, "Renew thyself daily, utterly, make it new, and again new, make it new." The exhortation "make it new," a phrase that Pound later used as the title of a collection of his essays, consequently became a kind of shorthand for the complex and often conflicting agendas of American poets during the early decades of the twentieth century.

As the following commentaries by poets suggest, there was considerable disagreement among them about the ways in which poetry could be made new and what constituted the new poetry. In her introductory essay in the first issue of *Poetry: A Magazine of Verse* in 1912, its founder and editor Harriet Monroe affirmed that "all forms, whether narrative, dramatic, or lyric, will be acceptable." Monroe subsequently published a wide range of poetry in her magazine, which strongly encouraged both established and emerging poets in the United States. During the decades following the founding of *Poetry*, however, all of the elements of poetry — form, language, rhythm, rhyme, and subject matter — were topics of serious discussion and debate. Divisions emerged even within the first organized group of modern poets writing in English, the imagistes or imagists. Pound, the first leader of the group, described their fundamental aesthetic values and poetic techniques in an essay published in *Poetry* in 1913. But he soon came into conflict with Amy Lowell, who was determined to democratize what Pound, using the French term, called imagisme and she called imagism, primarily in an effort to make such modern poetry seem less foreign or alien to audiences in the United States. As Lowell embarked on a crusade for imagism in essays such as "The New Manner in Modern Poetry," Pound moved in other directions, working with other new poets such as T. S. Eliot. In his 1919 essay "Tradition and the Individual Talent," Eliot challenged poets and critics who rejected "tradition" by emphasizing the vital connections between modern poets and poets of the past, a European tradition extending back to the ancient Greek poet Homer.

DES IMAGISTES

THE ΓΛΕΒΕ

VOLUME I
NUMBER 5

FEBRUARY
1914

SUBSCRIPTION
Three Dollars Yearly
THIS ISSUE 50 CENTS

AN ANTHOLOGY

Des Imagistes

Ezra Pound edited the first anthology of the imagists, which first appeared as a special issue of the little magazine the *Glebe* and was published as a book in 1914.

During the period from the 1920s through World War II, many poets grappled with questions about the function and status of poetry in the modern age. For poets of the Harlem Renaissance, questions about the language, sources, and subject matter of poetry were central to the contested issue of whether there was or could be what Langston Hughes described as "any true Negro Art in America." James Weldon Johnson rejected the tradition of dialect poetry, which he argued was not "capable of giving expression to the varied conditions of Negro life in America." Hughes, who frequently wrote in dialect, encouraged African American poets to produce work that was racial in both subject and treatment, drawing inspiration from indigenous traditions of music such as spirituals and jazz. Hart Crane suggested that urban life and technological advances opened new subjects for poets, exploring what in his 1930 essay "Modern Poetry" he described as the "function of poetry in a Machine Age." The poet most closely associated with rural New England, Robert Frost, reaffirmed some of the traditional forms and functions of poetry in the essay "The Figure a Poem Makes" (1939), published near the end of the Great Depression.

bedfordstmartins.com/ americanlit for research links on the authors in this section

Harriet Monroe

[1860-1936]

Although she published several volumes of her poetry and a collection of critical essays on other poets, Harriet Monroe was and is best known as the founder of *Poetry: A Magazine of Verse*, which she edited from 1912 until her death in 1936. Generally regarded as the most influential little magazine published in the United States, *Poetry* featured the work of a broad spectrum of American poets, including T. S. Eliot, Robert Frost, Amy Lowell, Edna St. Vincent Millay, Marianne Moore, Carl Sandburg, and Wallace Stevens. Monroe also published poets who were associated with the Harlem Renaissance, including Countee Cullen and Langston Hughes, as well as the work of recent immigrants such as Jun Fujita, a Japanese-born poet living in Chicago. *Poetry* had a transnational flavor, publishing English translations of the work of Rabindranath Tagore, the Bengali poet who won the Nobel Prize in 1913. Although the eclectic Monroe was receptive to diverse styles of poetry, she could be quite conservative. She published Joyce Kilmer's conventional "Trees," which became one of the most popular of all American poems, but rejected the innovative work of E. E. Cummings. Despite such occasional lapses, Monroe brilliantly fulfilled her stated purpose of establishing a magazine that would "give to poetry her own place, her own voice," as she put it in her introductory essay "The Motive of the Magazine." The text of the essay is taken from the first issue of *Poetry: A Magazine of Verse*, October 1912.

THE MOTIVE OF THE MAGAZINE

In the huge democracy of our age no interest is too slight to have an organ. Every sport, every little industry requires its own corner, its own voice, that it may find its friends, greet them, welcome them.

The arts especially have need of each an entrenched place, a voice of power, if they are to do their work and be heard. For as the world grows greater day by day, as every member of it, through something he buys or knows or loves, reaches out to the ends of the earth, things precious to the race, things rare and delicate, may be overpowered, lost in the criss-cross of modern currents, the confusion of modern immensities.

Painting, sculpture, music are housed in palaces in the great cities of the world; and every week or two a new periodical is born to speak for one or the other of them, and tenderly nursed at some guardian's expense. Architecture, responding to commercial and social demands, is whipped into shape by the rough and tumble of life and fostered, willy-nilly, by men's material needs. Poetry alone, of all the fine arts, has been left to shift for herself in a world unaware of its immediate and desperate need of her, a world whose great deeds, whose triumphs over matter, over the wilderness, over racial enmities and distances, require her ever-living voice to give them glory and glamour.

Poetry has been left to herself and blamed for inefficiency, a process as unreasonable as blaming the desert for barrenness. This art, like every other, is not a miracle of direct creation, but a reciprocal relation between the artist and his public. The people must do their part if the poet is to tell their story to the future; they must cultivate and irrigate the soil if the desert is to blossom as the rose.

The present venture is a modest effort to give to poetry her own place, her own voice. The popular magazines can afford her but scant courtesy—a Cinderella corner in the ashes[1]—because they seek a large public which is not hers, a public which buys them not for their verse but for their stories, pictures, journalism, rarely for their literature, even in prose. Most magazine editors say that there is no public for poetry in America; one of them wrote to a young poet that the verse his monthly accepted "must appeal to the barber's wife of the Middle West," and others prove their distrust by printing less verse from year to year, and that rarely beyond page-end length and importance.

We believe that there is a public for poetry, that it will grow, and that as it becomes more numerous and appreciative the work produced in this art will grow in power, in beauty, in significance. In this belief we have been encouraged by the generous enthusiasm of many subscribers to our fund, by the sympathy of other lovers of the art, and by the quick response of many prominent poets, both American and English, who have sent or promised contributions.

We hope to publish in *Poetry* some of the best work now being done in English verse. Within space limitations set at present by the small size of our monthly sheaf, we shall be able to print poems longer, and of more intimate and serious character, than the popular magazines can afford to use. The test, limited by ever-fallible human judgment, is to be quality alone; all forms, whether narrative, dramatic, or lyric, will be acceptable. We hope to offer our subscribers a place of refuge, a green isle in the sea, where Beauty may plant her gardens, and Truth, austere revealer of joy and sorrow, of hidden delights and despairs, may follow her brave quest unafraid.

[1912]

---

1. **a Cinderella corner in the ashes:** A reference to the famous folktale about a beautiful young girl whose cruel stepmother and stepsisters dress her in rags and make her sleep on the floor by the hearth. Because she is always covered in ashes and cinders, they mockingly call her *Cinderella.*

Ezra Pound

[1885-1972]

Ezra Pound was one of the central figures in the development of modern poetry in England and the United States (see Pound, p. 1597). In addition to writing poetry, reviews, and manifestos, he helped establish and edit several little magazines. He also advised and encouraged numerous other poets, including H.D., T. S. Eliot, Robert Frost, Amy Lowell, Marianne Moore, and William Carlos Williams. Pound was the organizer of the imagistes, a group of British and American poets based in London. When Harriet Monroe, the editor of *Poetry: A Magazine of Verse*, began to receive letters from readers asking for information about the imagistes, she invited Pound to respond. He and the English poet and translator F. S. Flint provided commentaries that Monroe published in March 1913. Flint contributed a brief opening statement, "Imagisme," while Pound contributed "A Few Don'ts by an Imagiste." In it, he gave a series of practical and witty suggestions about the use of imagery, language, rhyme, and rhythm for those beginning to write verse, offering a short course in modern poetic technique and the procedures of the imagistes. The text is taken from the first printing of the essay in *Poetry: A Magazine of Verse*, March 1913.

From A Few Don'ts by an Imagiste

An "Image" is that which presents an intellectual and emotional complex in an instant of time. I use the term "complex" rather in the technical sense employed by the newer psychologists, such as Hart,[1] though we might not agree absolutely in our application.

It is the presentation of such a "complex" instantaneously which gives that sense of sudden liberation; that sense of freedom from time limits and space limits; that sense of sudden growth, which we experience in the presence of the greatest works of art.

It is better to present one Image in a lifetime than to produce voluminous works.

All this, however, some may consider open to debate. The immediate necessity is to tabulate a list of don'ts for those beginning to write verses. But I cannot put all of them into Mosaic negative.

To begin with, consider the three rules recorded by Mr. Flint,[2] not as dogma—never consider anything as dogma—but as the result of long contemplation, which, even if it is someone else's contemplation, may be worth consideration.

Pay no attention to the criticism of men who have never themselves written a notable work. Consider the discrepancies between the actual writing of the Greek poets and dramatists, and the theories of the Graeco-Roman grammarians, concocted to explain their metres.

Language

Use no superfluous word, no adjective, which does not reveal something.

Don't use such an expression as "dim lands *of peace.*" It dulls the image. It mixes an abstraction with the concrete. It comes from the writer's not realizing that the natural object is always the *adequate* symbol.

---

1. **the newer psychologists, such as Hart:** Dr. Bernard Hart was an English interpreter of the theories of the Austrian founder of psychotherapy, Sigmund Freud. Describing "the general conception underlying Freud's teaching," Hart in a 1911 essay explained: "Unconscious ideas are agglomerated into groups with accompanying effects, the systems thus being formed being termed 'complexes.'"
2. **the three rules recorded by Mr. Flint:** In the preceding essay, F. S. Flint summarized the general rules followed by the imagistes: "1. Direct treatment of the 'thing,' whether subjective or objective. 2. To use absolutely no word that did not contribute to the presentation. 3. As regarding rhythm: to compose in sequence of the musical phrase, not in sequence of a metronome."

Go in fear of abstractions. Don't retell in mediocre verse what has already been done in good prose. Don't think any intelligent person is going to be deceived when you try to shirk all the difficulties of the unspeakably difficult art of good prose by chopping your composition into line lengths.

What the expert is tired of today the public will be tired of tomorrow.

Don't imagine that the art of poetry is any simpler than the art of music, or that you can please the expert before you have spent at least as much effort on the art of verse as the average piano teacher spends on the art of music.

Be influenced by as many great artists as you can, but have the decency either to acknowledge the debt outright, or to try to conceal it.

Don't allow "influence" to mean merely that you mop up the particular decorative vocabulary of some one or two poets whom you happen to admire. A Turkish war correspondent was recently caught red-handed babbling in his dispatches of "dove-gray" hills, or else it was "pearl-pale," I cannot remember.

Use either no ornament or good ornament.

Rhythm and Rhyme

Let the candidate fill his mind with the finest cadences he can discover, preferably in a foreign language so that the meaning of the words may be less likely to divert his attention from the movement; e.g., Saxon charms, Hebridean Folk Songs, the verse of Dante,[3] and the lyrics of Shakespeare — if he can dissociate the vocabulary from the cadence. Let him dissect the lyrics of Goethe[4] coldly into their component sound values, syllables long and short, stressed and unstressed, into vowels and consonants.

It is not necessary that a poem should rely on its music, but if it does rely on its music that music must be such as will delight the expert.

Let the neophyte know assonance and alliteration, rhyme immediate and delayed, simple and polyphonic, as a musician would expect to know harmony and counterpoint and all the minutiae of his craft. No time is too great to give to these matters or to any one of them, even if the artist seldom has need of them.

Don't imagine that a thing will "go" in verse just because it's too dull to go in prose.

Don't be "viewy" — leave that to the writers of pretty little philosophic essays. Don't be descriptive; remember that the painter can describe a landscape much better than you can, and that he has to know a deal more about it.

---

3. **Saxon charms, Hebridean Folk Songs, the verse of Dante:** Pound refers to the cadences of verse written in languages other than standard English: Anglo-Saxon poetry written in Old English, the Germanic language of the ancient Saxons; the dialect poems and songs of the inhabitants of the Hebrides, an isolated group of islands off the northwestern coast of Scotland; and the work of the Italian poet Dante Alighieri (1265-1321), author of the epic poem *The Divine Comedy.*
4. **Goethe:** The German poet, novelist, and dramatist Johann Wolfgang von Goethe (1749-1832).

When Shakespeare talks of the "Dawn in russet mantle clad"[5] he presents something which the painter does not present. There is in this line of his nothing that one can call description; he presents.

Consider the way of the scientists rather than the way of an advertising agent for a new soap.

The scientist does not expect to be acclaimed as a great scientist until he has *discovered* something. He begins by learning what has been discovered already. He goes from that point onward. He does not bank on being a charming fellow personally. He does not expect his friends to applaud the results of his freshman class work. Freshmen in poetry are unfortunately not confined to a definite and recognizable classroom. They are "all over the shop." Is it any wonder "the public is indifferent to poetry"?

Don't chop your stuff into separate *iambs*.[6] Don't make each line stop dead at the end, and then begin every next line with a heave. Let the beginning of the next line catch the rise of the rhythm wave, unless you want a definite longish pause.

In short, behave as a musician, a good musician, when dealing with that phase of your art which has exact parallels in music. The same laws govern, and you are bound by no others.

[1913]

---

5. "**Dawn . . . clad**": A reference to familiar lines in Shakespeare's *Hamlet*: "But, look, the morn in russet mantle clad, / Walks o'er the dew of yon high eastern hill" (1.1.166-67).
6. **separate *iambs***: The most common metrical form in English poetry is iambic verse, in which lines are divided into a set number of metrical feet called iambs, each of which consists of an unstressed syllable followed by a stressed syllable.

Amy Lowell

[1874-1925]

Amy Lowell supplanted Ezra Pound as the driving force in what he called imagisme and she called imagism (see Lowell, p. 1551). After Pound published his anthology *Des Imagistes* (1914), which included some of Lowell's poems, she began to plan an anthology that would include additional new poets and create a wider audience for imagism. To her disappointment, Pound refused to participate in the project, arguing that having the poems selected by a committee, as Lowell planned, would inevitably lower the standards of the anthology. In a letter to Lowell, Pound asserted that he wanted "the name 'Imagisme' to retain some sort of meaning. It stands, or I should like it to stand for hard light, clear edges. I cannot trust any democratized committee to maintain that standard." Lowell persisted, however, and the first of her three anthologies, *Some Imagist Poets*, appeared in April 1915. Even as Pound derided the movement as "Amygism," Lowell promoted imagism and what was called "the new poetry" at her countless readings and lectures, as well as in essays such as "The New Manner in Modern Poetry." Seeking to pave the way for a wider acceptance of modern poetry in the United States, a country that embraced change and celebrated progress, Lowell in the essay emphasized that the "new manner" was "an inevitable change, reflecting the evolution of life." The text is taken from the first printing of the essay in the *New Republic*, March 4, 1916.

THE NEW MANNER IN MODERN POETRY

We hear so much about "the new poetry" to-day, and see it so injudiciously lauded in publishers' catalogues, and so non-understandingly reviled and jeered at in the daily press, that it is no wonder if most people think it a mere advertising term, with no basis in fact.

This is most unfair and uncritical, for there is a "new manner" in the poetry of to-day which sets it quite apart from the poetry immediately preceding it. I am not referring to the extreme fads so prevalent in Europe before the war, such as futurism, headed by Marinetti, with its pronunciamento that verbs should only be used in the infinitive, and its algebraic signs of "plus" and "minus," etc., to eke out a language it had intentionally impoverished; or "Fantaisisme," with Guillaume Apolinaire as chief priest, who wrote so-called "ideographic poetry," or poems printed so as to represent a picture of a railroad train with puffing smoke, or some other thing of the sort.[1] That these "notions" (to borrow a phrase from the country shopkeeper) will survive the war is inconceivable, but that the real, sane "new manner" will persist cannot admit of a doubt. For the new manner is not a dress assumed at will, it is the result of changed surroundings, of a changed attitude toward life.

The "new manner" is made up of so many elements that to give all these elements one specific name is little difficult, but elsewhere I have called it "externality," and that name will quite suffice to show its antagonism to the "internality" which is the most marked quality in the poetry of the 'nineties.

There is not space in a brief paper to show the steps by which poetry arrived at the introspective state against which the "new manner" is a protest. That the poets of the late Victorian epoch were extraordinarily subjective, no one will deny. And this subjectivity led to a refining and ever refining upon their emotions, until the emotions themselves became somewhat tenuous. With this, growing all the time, went a most beautiful technique. There seems to have been something a little faded about these men; perhaps jaded would be a better term. Were they really so melancholy, or was it just a fashion? Some of them were pensively sad, some were despairingly enraged, they looked at grey and old-rose landscapes and sighed a languid appreciation, or they whipped up their jaded mental appetites with minute descriptions of artificial, insinuated suggestions of quite ordinary vulgarities. But whatever they did they made beautiful, literary backgrounds

---

1. **I am not referring . . . or some other thing of the sort:** Lowell dismisses as "fads" two of the most radical movements in the modern arts: Italian futurism, initially a literary movement created by Filippo Tommaso Marinetti (1876–1944), who published the manifesto *Le Futurisme* in 1909; and "Fantaisisme," or "Surnaturalisme" (surrealism), the literary method of the influential French poet and critic Guillaume Apollinaire (1880–1918).

for a gigantic ego. Each man's ego was swollen to a quite abnormal size, and he was wor-shipped by his other self, the author, with every conceivable literary device and subtlety.

Egoism may be a crime in the world of morals, but in the world of the arts it is per-fectly permissible. It makes very good and very interesting poetry. In mentioning it I am not condemning it, I am only labelling it. It was the manner of the 'nineties, it is not the manner of to-day.

Now, by "externality" I mean the attitude of being interested in things for themselves and not because of the effect they have upon oneself. The poet of the "new manner" paints landscapes because landscapes are beautiful, not because they chime with his mood. He tells stories because stories are interesting, and not to prove a thesis. He writes narrative poems because his range embraces the world and is not confined to himself. He is ironic, grotesque, ugly at times, because he has the feeling of the univer-sality of life.

Some critics are forever measuring the modernity of poetry by what they call its "so-cial consciousness." When a poet really writes in the "modern manner," social con-sciousness becomes one facet of his feeling of universality. The greater includes the less, and "externality" includes the universe and everything in it. But Milton and Dante[2] were universal, it may be said, were they therefore modern? Certainly not. They were universal, but they were not "external." Man stuck out in high relief all over their work. Man and his destiny—man completely out of focus, in short—was their theme. The "new manner" attempts to put man in his proper place in the picture; that is why it is so at variance with the method of the so-called "cosmic" poet.[3]

Now "externality" shows itself in two ways: in choice of subject matter, and in treat-ment; and this last again may be subdivided into general arrangement and ordering of particulars, and style.

First, as to subject matter. "Externality" is the main trend of the "new manner," but of course that does not mean that no poet ever writes subjective verses. He could hardly be universal if he excluded himself. It is a fact, however, that modern poetry of the new kind does not concern itself primarily with introspection.

Another characteristic of the "new manner" is humor. Pensive melancholy is no lon-ger inevitably to be worn, like a badge of office. It has gone, with many other obvious fripperies, such as leonine hair and visioning eyes. Is it because poets are more sincere to-day, that they have less "side"?[4] I do not know, but certainly in the 'nineties, in Eng-land at least, they were a very carefully put together lot. It is this sincerity, I believe, which has brought back humor. To many poets of the preceding generation, melancholy must have been a fashion. I really think that if there is a fashion to-day it is sincerity.

---

2. **Milton and Dante:** The English poet John Milton (1608–1674), author of the epic poem *Paradise Lost*, and the Italian poet Dante Alighieri (1265–1321), author of the epic poem *The Divine Comedy*.
3. **the so-called "cosmic" poet:** The American poet Walt Whitman (1819–1892). In his popular book *Cosmic Consciousness* (1901), Richard Maurice Bucke included Whitman among the few notable individuals in his-tory who had attained such a mystical, all-embracing state of being, which represented the next stage in the evolution of the human mind.
4. **"side":** Slang for pretentiousness or conceit.

Another striking tendency of the "new manner" is its insistence upon the poetry in unpoetic things. The new poet is never tired of finding colors in a dust-heap, and shouting about them. Sometimes the colors so occupy him that he takes them separately, unrelated to the dust-heap, as it were. This taking colors, and light and shade, in planes and cubes, with practically no insistence on the substances which produce them, be they men or houses or trees or water, is often called futurism by the ignorant. Probably because the real futurists, Marinetti and his followers, never employ it.

The poets of the "new manner" have another distinguishing mark. They endeavor to write poetry in the syntax of prose. Inversions are abhorrent to them, except when used purposely for accent. They try to write in the ordinary phrase construction of everyday speech and make it poetry just the same. How difficult this is, only those who have tried it know. When at a loss for a rhyme they do not permit themselves to drop suddenly into a simile for three lines — a cunning simile, neatly devised to give the necessary rhyme. They use colloquial language; "poetic diction" has sunk into ill repute, only newspaper poets and their ilk employ it. Poets no longer "fain" to do anything, nor "ope" their eyes to the "ethiope splendor of the spangled night," when "they themselves have lain upon a couch to woo reluctant slumber."

Still a third characteristic is the presentation of facts and images without comment. If there is one thing which the "new manner" is more against than another, it is preaching in a poem. And this care not to point a moral is one of the most pronounced features of the "new manner." It is this very thing which leads so many poetry lovers of the older generation to find it cold. An old-fashioned editor once said to me that what he missed in modern poetry was its lack of noble thoughts. The poetry which is a pepsin to weak intellects to whom crude life is indigestible, has nothing in common with the "new manner." "Noble thoughts," neat little uplift labels wrapped in the tinfoil of pretty verse, has its place in the scheme of existence, no doubt, but to the modern poet it is anathema. He seeks to give life, the world, as it is, as he sees it, at any rate; and the lesson of his poem, if there be one, must be inherent in the poem itself. He takes the intelligence of his readers for granted, and trusts to their getting the meaning of the poem as it unfolds, refusing to bellow it at them through a megaphone in impertinent asides.

Why do people refuse to take art as organic, and insist upon considering it as merely explanatory? When these same people walk in the garden on a fine morning, do they feel chilled and depressed because the little flower-buds are not tagged with texts? But there! We shall never agree, and for people who like to be drugged with fine, conventional sentiments there is no cure in heaven or earth, that I am aware of.

Now as to form. It is the belief of most people that interest in metrical experiments is a distinguishing feature of the "new manner." But do you suppose that there has ever been a time when real poets were not interested in metrical experiments? Poets have been widening and deepening and freeing their prosody ever since there was a prosody to tinker with. In experimenting, the modern poet is merely following tradition.

As the word "new" has been "wished on" to contemporary poetry, so are its metrical experiments dubbed and condemned as "new." *Vers libre* in particular is constantly called "new" and hooted at; or poets who employ it are told that they think it is new, and it is not. Of course it is not, only the paragraph writers in the newspapers ever supposed it was. So far as I know, the only metrical experiment which is in the least new is "polyphonic prose," and that had its beginnings in France, in the work of Gustave Kahn, and Saint-Pol-Roux, and Paul Fort.[5] I believe I am the first poet who has ever employed it in English, and it had to be so adapted in bringing it over from one language to another that it only retains a partial resemblance to the French form.

Now the "new manner" does not consist solely in any one of these characteristics; it consists in all. Some poets have one of them, some another; it may be subject, it may be form. The "new manner" is as characteristic as the manner of differing peoples. All Americans are not alike, but all Americans have something which sets them together, and apart from other nationalities. So the change in poetry is easily distinguished. And it is an inevitable change, reflecting the evolution of life.

[1916]

---

5. **"polyphonic prose,"** . . . **Paul Fort:** Lowell traces her own experiments in polyphonic prose — rhythmical prose that employs elements of verse, especially alliteration, assonance, and rhyme — back to the work of three influential French symbolist poets: Gustave Kahn (1859–1936), who claimed to have invented the term *vers libre*, or free verse; Saint-Pol-Roux (1861–1940); and Paul Fort (1872–1960).

T. S. Eliot

[1888–1965]

T. S. Eliot was one of the most influential poets and literary critics of the twentieth century (see Eliot, p. 1623). One of his most famous essays, "Tradition and the Individual Talent," was first published in two parts in the *Egoist: An Individualist Review*. The feminist and anarchist Dora Marsden established the radical magazine in 1911 as the *Freewoman*, later the *New Freewoman*, whose purpose was "to expound a doctrine of philosophical individualism." After Ezra Pound became the literary editor in 1913, the name of the magazine was changed to the *Egoist*, which he helped transform into a prominent avant-garde literary journal. It subsequently published the work of many new writers, including James Joyce and Eliot, who served as the assistant editor from 1917 through 1919. During the same period, there was a growing tension within literary circles between tradition and innovation, between those who advocated a firm break with the conventions, language, and forms of earlier poetry and those who found inspiration, models, and subjects in the past, notably Eliot and Pound. In "Tradition and the Individual Talent," Eliot offered a complex formulation of the relation between the modern poet and the European literary tradition beginning with Homer. Even as he emphasized the poet's responsibility to develop "the consciousness of the past," Eliot challenged the conventional understanding of "tradition," which in his view was not fixed but fluid, subject to transformation by the introduction of each genuinely *new* work of art. The text of the following selection, the first part and the opening of the second part of the essay, is taken from its first printing in the *Egoist* in September and December 1919.

From TRADITION AND THE INDIVIDUAL TALENT

In English writing we seldom speak of tradition, though we occasionally apply its name in deploring its absence. We cannot refer to "the tradition" or to "a tradition"; at most, we employ the adjective in saying that the poetry of So-and-So is "traditional" or even "too traditional." Seldom, perhaps, does the word appear except in a phrase of censure. If otherwise, it is vaguely approbative, with the implication, as to the work approved, of some pleasing archaeological reconstruction. You can hardly make the word agreeable to English ears without this comfortable reference to the reassuring science of archaeology.

Certainly the word is not likely to appear in our appreciations of living or dead writers. Every nation, every race, has not only its own creative, but its own critical turn of mind; and is even more oblivious of the shortcomings and limitations of its critical habits than of those of its creative genius. We know, or think we know, from the enormous mass of critical writing that has appeared in the French language the critical method or habit of the French; we only conclude (we are such unconscious people) that the French are "more critical" than we, and sometimes even plume ourselves a little with the fact, as if the French were the less spontaneous. Perhaps they are; but we might remind ourselves that criticism is as inevitable as breathing, and that we should be none the worse for articulating what passes in our minds when we read a book and feel an emotion about it, for criticising our own minds in their work of criticism. One of the facts that might come to light in this process is our tendency to insist, when we praise a poet, upon those aspects of his work in which he least resembles anyone else. In these aspects or parts of his work we pretend to find what is individual, what is the peculiar essence of the man. We dwell with satisfaction upon the poet's difference from his predecessors, especially his immediate predecessors; we endeavour to find something that can be isolated in order to be enjoyed. Whereas if we approach a poet without this prejudice we shall often find that not only the best, but the most individual parts of his work may be those in which the dead poets, his ancestors, assert their immortality most vigorously. And I do not intend the impressionable period of adolescence, but the period of full maturity.

Yet if the only form of tradition, of handing down, consisted in following the ways of the immediate generation before us in a blind or timid adherence to its successes, "tradition" should positively be discouraged. We have seen many such simple currents soon lost in the sand; and novelty is better than repetition. Tradition is a matter of much wider significance. It cannot be inherited, and if you want it you must obtain it by great labour. It involves, in the first place, the historical sense, which we may call nearly indispensable to anyone who would continue to be a poet beyond his twenty-fifth year; and the historical sense involves a perception, not only of the pastness of the past, but of its presence; the historical sense compels a man to write not merely with his own generation in his bones, but with a feeling that the whole of the literature of Europe from Homer and within it the whole of the literature of his own country has a simultaneous existence and composes a simultaneous order. This historical sense, which is a sense of the timeless as well as of the temporal and of the timeless and of the temporal together, is what makes a writer traditional. And it is at the same time what makes a writer most acutely conscious of his place in time, of his contemporaneity.

No poet, no artist of any art, has his complete meaning alone. His significance, his appreciation is the appreciation of his relation to the dead poets and artists. You cannot value him alone; you must set him, for contrast and comparison, among the dead. I mean this as a principle of aesthetic, not merely historical, criticism. The necessity that he shall conform, that he shall cohere, is not one-sided; what happens when a new work of art is created is something that happens simultaneously to all the works of art which preceded it. The existing monuments form an ideal order among themselves, which is modified by the introduction of the new (the really new) work of art among them. The existing order is complete before the new work arrives; for order to persist after the supervention of novelty, the *whole* existing order must be, if ever so slightly, altered; and so the relations, proportions, values of each work of art toward the whole are readjusted; and this is conformity between the old and the new. Whoever has approved this idea of order, of the form of European, of English literature, will not find it preposterous that the past should be altered by the present as much as the present is directed by the past. And the poet who is aware of this will be aware of great difficulties and responsibilities.

In a peculiar sense he will be aware also that he must inevitably be judged by the standards of the past. I say judged by, not amputated, by them; not judged to be as good as, or worse or better than, the dead; and certainly not judged by the canons of dead critics. It is a judgment, a comparison in which two things are measured by each other. To conform merely would be for the new work not really to conform at all; it would not be new, and would therefore not be a work of art. And we do not quite say that the new is more valuable because it fits in; but its fitting in is a test of its value—a test, it is true, which can only be slowly and cautiously applied, for we are none of us infallible judges of conformity. We say: it appears to conform, and is perhaps individual, or it appears individual, and may conform; but we are hardly likely to find that it is one and not the other.

To proceed to a more intelligible exposition of the relation of the poet to the past: he can neither take the past as a lump, an indiscriminate bolus, nor can he form himself wholly on one or two private admirations, nor can he form himself wholly upon one preferred period. The first course is inadmissible, the second is an important experience of youth, and the third is a pleasant and highly desirable supplement. The poet must be very conscious of the main current, which does not at all flow invariably through the most distinguished reputations. He must be quite aware of the obvious fact that art never improves, but that the material of art is never quite the same. He must be aware that the mind of Europe—the mind of his own country—a mind which he learns in time to be much more important than his own private mind—is a mind which changes, and that this change is a development which abandons nothing *en route*, which does not superannuate either Shakespeare or Homer or the rock drawing of the Magdalenian draughtsmen.[1] That this development, refinement perhaps, complication certainly, is not, from the point of view of the artist, any improvement. Perhaps not even an improvement from the point of view of the psychologist or not to the extent which we imagine; perhaps only in the end based upon a complication in economics and machinery. But the difference between the present and the past is that the conscious present is an awareness of the past in a way and to an extent which the past's awareness of itself cannot show.

Someone said: "The dead writers are remote from us because we *know* so much more than they did." Precisely, and they are that which we know.

I am alive to a usual objection to what is clearly part of my programme for the *métier*[2] of poetry. The objection is that the doctrine requires a ridiculous amount of erudition (pedantry), a claim which can be rejected by appeal to the lives of poets in any pantheon. It will even be affirmed that much learning deadens or perverts poetic sensibility. While, however, we persist in believing that a poet ought to know as much as will not encroach upon his necessary receptivity and necessary laziness, it is not desirable to confine knowledge to whatever can be put into a useful shape for examinations, drawing rooms, or the still more pretentious modes of publicity. Some can absorb knowledge, the more tardy must sweat for it. Shakespeare acquired more essential history from Plutarch than most men could from the whole British Museum.[3] What is to be insisted upon is that the poet must develop or procure the consciousness of the past and that he should continue to develop this consciousness throughout his career.

What happens is a continual surrender of himself as he is at the moment to something which is more valuable. The progress of an artist is a continual self-sacrifice, a continual extinction of personality.

There remains to define this process of depersonalisation and its relation to the sense of tradition. It is in this depersonalisation that art may be said to approach the condition of science. I shall, therefore, invite you to consider, as a suggestive analogy, the action which takes place when a bit of finely filiated platinum is introduced into a chamber containing oxygen and sulphur dioxide.[4]

---

1. **the rock drawing of the Magdalenian draughtsmen:** The Magdalenians were peoples who flourished in Europe from 18,000 to 10,000 BCE. Their celebrated cave art, primarily engravings and paintings of various species of animals, was discovered in the 1860s but not accepted as genuine by anthropologists and historians until 1902.
2. *métier*: An activity or occupation, especially work for which a person is particularly suited (French).
3. **Shakespeare . . . British Museum:** One of the major sources of Shakespeare's history plays was Plutarch's *Parallel Lives*, biographies of eminent Greeks and Romans, which Sir Thomas North translated into English in 1579. The British Museum in London has extensive collections that cover world cultures from prehistory to the present day.
4. **the action . . . oxygen and sulphur dioxide:** The platinum acts as a catalyst. Eliot explains the analogy in the second paragraph of part 2 of the essay, printed below.

II

The upshot of this article and of the article which preceded it is this: that honest criticism and sensitive appreciation is directed not upon the poet but upon the poetry. If we attend to the confused cries of the newspaper critics and the susurrus[5] of popular repetition that follows, we shall hear the names of poets in great number; if we seek not blue-book knowledge[6] but the enjoyment of poetry, and ask for a poem, we shall seldom find it. In the last article I tried to point out the importance of the relation of the poem to other poems by other authors, and suggested the conception of poetry as a living whole of all the poetry that has ever been written. The other aspect of this Impersonal theory of poetry is the relation of the poem to its author. And I hinted, by an analogy, that the mind of the mature poet differs from that of the immature one not precisely in any valuation of "personality," not being necessarily more interesting, or having "more to say," but rather by being a more finely perfected medium in which special, or very varied, feelings are at liberty to enter into new combinations.

The analogy was that of the catalyst. When the two gases previously mentioned are mixed in the presence of a filament of platinum, they form sulphurous acid. This combination takes place only if the platinum is present; nevertheless the newly formed acid contains no trace of platinum, and the platinum itself is apparently unaffected; has remained inert, passive and unchanged. The mind of the poet is the shred of platinum. It may partly or exclusively operate upon the experience of the man himself; but, the more perfect the artist, the more completely separate in him will be the man who suffers and the mind which creates; the more perfectly will the mind digest and transmute the passions which are its material.

[1919]

---

5. **susurrus:** A poetic term for murmuring or rustling.
6. **blue-book knowledge:** Blue books are official guidebooks.

James Weldon Johnson

[1871–1938]

James Weldon Johnson was a novelist, poet, and tireless promoter of the work of other African American writers during the Harlem Renaissance (see Johnson, p. 1546). In his often-quoted preface to *The Book of American Negro Poetry: Chosen and Edited with an Essay on the Negro's Creative Genius* (1922), he observed, "The public, generally speaking, does not know that there are American Negro poets." Johnson designed his anthology as a corrective that would demonstrate the richness and range of modern African American poetry. "The final measure of the greatness of all peoples is the amount and standard of the literature and art they have produced," he affirmed. "The world does not know that a people is great until that people produces great literature and art." The anthology included the work of more than thirty poets, beginning with Paul Laurence Dunbar

(1872–1906), whose "Negro dialect poems" had gained and continued to enjoy widespread popularity. In the following passage from the Preface, Johnson explained why so few of the contemporary poets included in his anthology wrote in dialect, which he argued was not "capable of giving expression to the varied conditions of Negro life in America." The text is taken from the first printing of *The Book of American Negro Poetry* (1922).

From PREFACE TO
THE BOOK OF AMERICAN NEGRO POETRY

It may be surprising to many to see how little of the poetry being written by Negro poets to-day is being written in Negro dialect. The newer Negro poets show a tendency to discard dialect; much of the subject-matter which went into the making of traditional dialect poetry, 'possums, watermelons, etc., they have discarded altogether, at least, as poetic material. This tendency will, no doubt, be regretted by the majority of white readers; and, indeed, it would be a distinct loss if the American Negro poets threw away this quaint and musical folk-speech as a medium of expression. And yet, after all, these poets are working through a problem not realized by the reader, and, perhaps, by many of these poets themselves not realized consciously. They are trying to break away from, not Negro dialect itself, but the limitations on Negro dialect imposed by the fixing effects of long convention.

The Negro in the United States has achieved or been placed in a certain artistic niche. When he is thought of artistically, it is as a happy-go-lucky, singing, shuffling, banjo-picking being or as a more or less pathetic figure. The picture of him is in a log cabin amid fields of cotton or along the levees. Negro dialect is naturally and by long association the exact instrument for voicing this phase of Negro life; and by that very exactness it is an instrument with but two full stops, humor and pathos. So even when he confines himself to purely racial themes, the Aframerican poet realizes that there are phases of Negro life in the United States which cannot be treated in the dialect either adequately or artistically. Take, for example, the phases rising out of life in Harlem, that most wonderful Negro city in the world. I do not deny that a Negro in a log cabin is more picturesque than a Negro in a Harlem flat, but the Negro in the Harlem flat is here, and he is but part of a group growing everywhere in the country, a group whose ideals are becoming increasingly more vital than those of the traditionally artistic group, even if its members are less picturesque.

What the colored poet in the United States needs to do is something like what Synge did for the Irish;[1] he needs to find a form that will express the racial spirit by symbols from within rather than by symbols from without, such as the mere mutilation of English spelling and pronunciation. He needs a form that is freer and larger than dialect, but which will still hold the racial flavor; a form expressing the imagery, the idioms, the

---

1. **Synge did for the Irish:** The poet and dramatist John Millington Synge (1871–1909) was a central figure in the Irish literary renaissance at the end of the nineteenth and beginning of the twentieth centuries.

peculiar turns of thought, and the distinctive humor and pathos, too, of the Negro, but which will also be capable of voicing the deepest and highest emotions and aspirations, and allow of the widest range of subjects and the widest scope of treatment.

Negro dialect is at present a medium that is not capable of giving expression to the varied conditions of Negro life in America, and much less is it capable of giving the fullest interpretation of Negro character and psychology. This is no indictment against the dialect as dialect, but against the mould of convention in which Negro dialect in the United States has been set. In time these conventions may become lost, and the colored poet in the United States may sit down to write in dialect without feeling that his first line will put the general reader in a frame of mind which demands that the poem be humorous or pathetic. In the meantime, there is no reason why these poets should not continue to do the beautiful things that can be done, and done best, in the dialect.

In stating the need for Aframerican poets in the United States to work out a new and distinctive form of expression I do not wish to be understood to hold any theory that they should limit themselves to Negro poetry, to racial themes; the sooner they are able to write *American* poetry spontaneously, the better. Nevertheless, I believe that the richest contribution the Negro poet can make to the American literature of the future will be the fusion into it of his own individual artistic gifts.

[1922]

Langston Hughes

[1902-1967]

Langston Hughes was one of the major literary figures that emerged during the Harlem Renaissance (see Hughes, p. 743). His famous manifesto, "The Negro Artist and the Racial Mountain," appeared in the *Nation* in 1926. Only one week earlier, the magazine had published "The Negro-Art Hokum," a provocative essay by the African American cultural critic George Schuyler (1895-1977). Dismissing the idea that there could be such a thing as "Negro art" in the United States, Schuyler observed: "As for the literature, painting, and sculpture of Aframericans — such as there is — it is identical in kind with the literature, painting, and sculpture of white Americans: that is, it shows more or less evidence of European influence." He thus argued that, far from being shaped by different experiences or displaying a distinctive psychology, "your American Negro is just plain American." In sharp contrast, Hughes asserted that the "desire" to run away from one's race "is the mountain standing in the way of any true Negro art in America." He therefore urged the would-be "racial artist" to explore the full range of African American life, including the experiences of the urban poor in the North. He also celebrated indigenous forms of African American culture, especially jazz, "one of the inherent expressions of Negro life in America." The text is taken from the first printing of the essay in the *Nation*, June 23, 1926.

THE NEGRO ARTIST AND THE RACIAL MOUNTAIN

One of the most promising of the young Negro poets[1] said to me once, "I want to be a poet—not a Negro poet," meaning, I believe, "I want to write like a white poet"; meaning subconsciously, "I would like to be a white poet"; meaning behind that, "I would like to be white." And I was sorry the young man said that, for no great poet has ever been afraid of being himself. And I doubted then that, with his desire to run away spiritually from his race, this boy would ever be a great poet. But this is the mountain standing in the way of any true Negro art in America—this urge within the race toward whiteness, the desire to pour racial individuality into the mold of American standardization, and to be as little Negro and as much American as possible.

But let us look at the immediate background of this young poet. His family is of what I suppose one would call the Negro middle class: people who are by no means rich yet never uncomfortable nor hungry—smug, contented, respectable folk, members of the Baptist church. The father goes to work every morning. He is a chief steward at a large white club. The mother sometimes does fancy sewing or supervises parties for the rich families of the town. The children go to a mixed school. In the home they read white papers and magazines. And the mother often says "Don't be like niggers" when the children are bad. A frequent phrase from the father is, "Look how well a white man does things." And so the word *white* comes to be unconsciously a symbol of all the virtues. It holds for the children beauty, morality, and money. The whisper of "I want to be white" runs silently through their minds. This young poet's home is, I believe, a fairly typical home of the colored middle class. One sees immediately how difficult it would be for an artist born in such a home to interest himself in interpreting the beauty of his own people. He is never taught to see that beauty. He is taught rather not to see it, or if he does, to be ashamed of it when it is not according to Caucasian patterns.

For racial culture the home of a self-styled "high-class" Negro has nothing better to offer. Instead there will perhaps be more aping of things white than in a less cultured or less wealthy home. The father is perhaps a doctor, lawyer, landowner, or politician. The mother may be a social worker, or a teacher, or she may do nothing and have a maid. Father is often dark but he has usually married the lightest woman he could find. The family attend a fashionable church where few really colored faces are to be found. And they themselves draw a color line. In the North they go to white theaters and white movies. And in the South they have at least two cars and a house "like white folks." Nordic manners, Nordic faces, Nordic hair, Nordic art (if any), and an Episcopal heaven. A very high mountain indeed for the would-be racial artist to climb in order to discover himself and his people.

But then there are the low-down folks, the so-called common element, and they are the majority—may the Lord be praised! The people who have their nip of gin on Saturday nights and are not too important to themselves or the community, or too well fed, or too learned to watch the lazy world go round. They live on Seventh Street in Washington or

---

1. **the most promising of the young Negro poets:** Hughes was probably referring to his friend and rival, Countee Cullen, by far the most popular African American poet of the 1920s. In a 1924 interview, Cullen had declared that he wanted "to be POET and not NEGRO POET."

State Street in Chicago and they do not particularly care whether they are like white folks or anybody else. Their joy runs, bang! into ecstasy. Their religion soars to a shout. Work maybe a little today, rest a little tomorrow. Play awhile. Sing awhile. O, let's dance! These common people are not afraid of spirituals, as for a long time their more intellectual brethren were, and jazz is their child. They furnish a wealth of colorful, distinctive material for any artist because they still hold their own individuality in the face of American standardizations. And perhaps these common people will give to the world its truly great Negro artist, the one who is not afraid to be himself. Whereas the better-class Negro would tell the artist what to do, the people at least let him alone when he does appear. And they are not ashamed of him — if they know he exists at all. And they accept what beauty is their own without question.

Certainly there is, for the American Negro artist who can escape the restrictions the more advanced among his own group would put upon him, a great field of unused material ready for his art. Without going outside his race, and even among the better classes with their "white" culture and conscious American manners, but still Negro enough to be different, there is sufficient matter to furnish a black artist with a lifetime of creative work. And when he chooses to touch on the relations between Negroes and whites in this country with their innumerable overtones and undertones, surely, and especially for literature and the drama, there is an inexhaustible supply of themes at hand. To these the Negro artist can give his racial individuality, his heritage of rhythm and warmth, and his incongruous humor that so often, as in the Blues, becomes ironic laughter mixed with tears. But let us look again at the mountain.

A prominent Negro clubwoman in Philadelphia paid eleven dollars to hear Raquel Meller[2] sing Andalusian popular songs. But she told me a few weeks before she would not think of going to hear "that woman," Clara Smith,[3] a great black artist, sing Negro folksongs. And many an upper-class Negro church, even now, would not dream of employing a spiritual in its services. The drab melodies in white folks' hymnbooks are much to be preferred. "We want to worship the Lord correctly and quietly. We don't believe in 'shouting.' Let's be dull like the Nordics," they say, in effect.

The road for the serious black artist, then, who would produce a racial art is most certainly rocky and the mountain is high. Until recently he received almost no encouragement for his work from either white or colored people. The fine novels of Chestnutt[4] go out of print with neither race noticing their passing. The quaint charm and humor of Dunbar's dialect verse[5] brought to him, in his day, largely the same kind of encouragement one would give a sideshow freak (A colored man writing poetry! How odd!) or a clown (How amusing!).

---

2. **Raquel Meller:** Meller (1888–1962), a celebrated Spanish singer and recording artist whose concerts broke box-office records in cities throughout the United States, sang only in Spanish.
3. **Clara Smith:** Smith (1894–1935), billed as the "Queen of the Moaners," was a popular blues singer who performed on the segregated vaudeville circuit for African American artists and audiences during the 1920s.
4. **Chestnutt:** Charles W. Chesnutt (1858–1932) gained popularity with his early short stories, but his later novels exploring the theme of racial hatred and prejudice sold so poorly that he virtually ceased writing fiction. (See pp. 1273–86.)
5. **Dunbar's dialect verse:** The enormously popular poems written in "Negro dialect" by Paul Laurence Dunbar (1872–1906). (See pp. 1376–81.)

The present vogue in things Negro, although it may do as much harm as good for the budding colored artist, has at least done this: it has brought him forcibly to the attention of his own people among whom for so long, unless the other race had noticed him beforehand, he was a prophet with little honor. I understand that Charles Gilpin[6] acted for years in Negro theaters without any special acclaim from his own, but when Broadway gave him eight curtain calls, Negroes, too, began to beat a tin pan in his honor. I know a young colored writer, a manual worker by day, who had been writing well for the colored magazines for some years, but it was not until he recently broke into the white publications and his first book was accepted by a prominent New York publisher that the "best" Negroes in his city took the trouble to discover that he lived there. Then almost immediately they decided to give a grand dinner for him. But the society ladies were careful to whisper to his mother that perhaps she'd better not come. They were not sure she would have an evening gown.

The Negro artist works against an undertow of sharp criticism and misunderstanding from his own group and unintentional bribes from the whites. "O, be respectable, write about nice people, show how good we are," say the Negroes. "Be stereotyped, don't go too far, don't shatter our illusions about you, don't amuse us too seriously. We will pay you," say the whites. Both would have told Jean Toomer not to write "Cane."[7] The colored people did not praise it. The white people did not buy it. Most of the colored people who did read "Cane" hate it. They are afraid of it. Although the critics gave it good reviews the public remained indifferent. Yet (excepting the work of Du Bois) "Cane" contains the finest prose written by a Negro in America. And like the singing of Robeson,[8] it is truly racial.

But in spite of the Nordicized Negro intelligentsia and the desires of some white editors we have an honest American Negro literature already with us. Now I await the rise of the Negro theater. Our folk music, having achieved world-wide fame, offers itself to the genius of the great individual American Negro composer who is to come. And within the next decade I expect to see the work of a growing school of colored artists who paint and model the beauty of dark faces and create with new technique the expressions of their own soul-world. And the Negro dancers who will dance like flame and the singers who will continue to carry our songs to all who listen — they will be with us in even greater numbers tomorrow.

Most of my own poems are racial in theme and treatment, derived from the life I know. In many of them I try to grasp and hold some of the meanings and rhythms of jazz. I am sincere as I know how to be in these poems and yet after every reading I answer questions like these from my own people: Do you think Negroes should always write about Negroes? I wish you wouldn't read some of your poems to white folks. How do you find anything interesting in a place like a cabaret? Why do you write about black people? You aren't black. What makes you do so many jazz poems?

---

6. **Charles Gilpin:** Gilpin (1878–1930) was the first African American actor to appear in a leading role in an all-white theater, in the title role of Eugene O'Neill's *The Emperor Jones* (1920). For his critically acclaimed performance in the play, the NAACP awarded Gilpin its annual Springarn Medal for outstanding achievement by an African American. (See photo on p. 1712.)

7. **"Cane":** A critically acclaimed collection of poems, sketches, and stories exploring African American culture in the North and the South by Jean Toomer (1894–1967). (See pp. 1809–18.)

8. **the singing of Robeson:** Paul Robeson (1898–1976) was a singer, actor, and activist famed for his concert performances of "Negro spirituals" and folk songs in New York and later in cities throughout Europe. He succeeded Charles Gilpin in the title role of *The Emperor Jones* (see note 6).

But jazz to me is one of the inherent expressions of Negro life in America: the eternal tom-tom beating in the Negro soul—the tom-tom of revolt against weariness in a white world, a world of subway trains, and work, work, work; the tom-tom of joy and laughter, and pain swallowed in a smile. Yet the Philadelphia clubwoman is ashamed to say that her race created it and she does not like me to write about it. The old subconscious "white is best" runs through her mind. Years of study under white teachers, a lifetime of white books, pictures, and papers, and white manners, morals, and Puritan standards made her dislike the spirituals. And now she turns up her nose at jazz and all its manifestations—likewise almost everything else distinctly racial. She doesn't care for the Winold Reiss[9] portraits of Negroes because they are "too Negro." She does not want a true picture of herself from anybody. She wants the artist to flatter her, to make the white world believe that all Negroes are as smug and as near white in soul as she wants to be. But, to my mind, it is the duty of the younger Negro artist, if he accepts any duties at all from outsiders, to change through the force of his art that old whispering "I want to be white," hidden in the aspirations of his people, to "Why should I want to be white? I am a Negro—and beautiful!"

So I am ashamed for the black poet who says, "I want to be a poet, not a Negro poet," as though his own racial world were not as interesting as any other world. I am ashamed, too, for the colored artist who runs from the painting of Negro faces to the painting of sunsets after the manner of the academicians because he fears the strange un-whiteness of his own features. An artist must be free to choose what he does, certainly, but he must also never be afraid to do what he might choose.

Let the blare of Negro jazz bands and the bellowing voice of Bessie Smith[10] singing Blues penetrate the closed ears of the colored near-intellectuals until they listen and perhaps understand. Let Paul Robeson singing Water Boy, and Rudolph Fisher[11] writing about the streets of Harlem, and Jean Toomer holding the heart of Georgia in his hands, and Aaron Douglas[12] drawing strange black fantasies cause the smug Negro middle class to turn from their white, respectable, ordinary books and papers to catch a glimmer of their own beauty. We younger Negro artists who create now intend to express our individual dark-skinned selves without fear or shame. If white people are pleased we are glad. If they are not, it doesn't matter. We know we are beautiful. And ugly too. The tom-tom cries and the tom-tom laughs. If colored people are pleased we are glad. If they are not, their displeasure doesn't matter either. We build our temples for tomorrow, strong as we know how, and we stand on top of the mountain, free within ourselves.

[1926]

---

9. **Winold Reiss:** Reiss (1886–1953), a German immigrant, was a designer and artist well known for his portraits of African Americans in Harlem during the 1920s.

10. **Bessie Smith:** Smith (1892–1937), still regarded as the "Queen of the Blues," was the most famous and influential blues singer of the 1920s.

11. **Rudolph Fisher:** Fisher (1897–1934), who later published two novels set in Harlem, was then known for his first short story, "The City of Refuge," which was published in the prestigious *Atlantic Monthly* in 1925.

12. **Aaron Douglas:** The African American painter and illustrator Aaron Douglas (1900–1979), who drew his inspiration from jazz, folk culture, and African art, became the leading visual artist of the Harlem Renaissance. In addition to his black-and-white drawings in African American periodicals such as the *Crisis* and *Opportunity*, Douglas's illustrations had appeared in Alain Locke's famous anthology, *The New Negro* (1925).

Hart Crane

[1899-1932]

Hart Crane published "Modern Poetry" two years before his early death in 1932 (see Crane, p. 1676). The essay, one of his few works of formal criticism, appeared in *Revolt in the Arts: A Survey of the Creation, Distribution and Appreciation of Art in America* (1930), a collection of essays on art, literature, and culture edited by the well-known drama critic Oliver M. Sayler. As he explained in the preface, Sayler collected essays by "thirty-six representative authorities," including Crane, who had recently gained considerable fame and notoriety with the publication of his poetic sequence *The Bridge* (1930). Inspired by the Brooklyn Bridge, a symbol of the modern technological age, Crane in *The Bridge* sought to achieve what he called "a new cultural synthesis" of America. In "Modern Poetry," he suggested that poets in a "Machine Age" must seek a similar synthesis, absorbing the seemingly antipoetic influences of science, technology, and urban life in the United States. The text is taken from the first printing of the essay in *Revolt in the Arts* (1930).

From MODERN POETRY

The function of poetry in a Machine Age is identical to its function in any other age; and its capacities for presenting the most complete synthesis of human values remain essentially immune from any of the so-called inroads of science. The emotional stimulus of machinery is on an entirely different psychic plane from that of poetry. Its only menace lies in its capacities for facile entertainment, so easily accessible as to arrest the development of any but the most negligible esthetic responses. The ultimate influence of machinery in this respect remains to be seen, but its firm entrenchment in our lives has already produced a series of challenging new responsibilities for the poet.

For unless poetry can absorb the machine, i.e., *acclimatize* it as naturally and casually as trees, cattle, galleons, castles, and all other human associations of the past, then poetry has failed of its full contemporary function. This process does not infer any program of lyrical pandering to the taste of those obsessed by the importance of machinery; nor does it essentially involve even the specific mention of a single mechanical contrivance. It demands, however, along with the traditional qualifications of the poet, an extraordinary capacity for surrender, at least temporarily, to the sensations of urban life. This presupposes, of course, that the poet possesses sufficient spontaneity and gusto to convert this experience into positive terms. Machinery will tend to lose its sensational glamour and appear in its true subsidiary order in human life as use and continual poetic allusion subdue its novelty. For, contrary to general prejudice, the wonderment experienced in watching nose dives is of less immediate creative promise to poetry than the familiar gesture of a motorist in the modest act of shifting gears. I mean to say that mere romantic speculation on the power and beauty of machinery keeps it at a continual remove; it can not act creatively in our lives until, like the unconscious nervous responses of our bodies, its connotations emanate from within—forming as spontaneous a terminology of poetic reference as the bucolic world of pasture, plow, and barn.

The familiar contention that science is inimical to poetry is no more tenable than the kindred notion that theology has been proverbially hostile—with the "Commedia" of Dante[1] to prove the contrary. That "truth" which science pursues is radically different from the metaphorical, extra-logical "truth" of the poet. When Blake wrote that "a tear is an intellectual thing, And a sigh is the sword of an Angel King"[2]—he was not in any logical conflict with the principles of the Newtonian Universe. Similarly, poetic prophecy in the case of the seer, has nothing to do with factual prediction or with futurity. It is a peculiar type of perception, capable of apprehending some absolute and timeless concept of the imagination with astounding clarity and conviction.

That the modern poet can profitably assume the roles of philosopher or theologian is questionable at best. Science, the uncanonized Deity of the times, seems to have automatically displaced the hierarchies of both Academy and Church. It is pertinent to cite the authors of the "Commedia" and "Paradise Lost"[3] as poets whose verse survives the religious dogmas and philosophies of their respective periods, but it is fallacious to assume that either of these poets could have written important religious verse without the fully developed and articulated religious dogmas that each was heir to.

The future of American poetry is too complicated a speculation to be more than approached in this limited space. Involved in it are the host of considerations relative to the comparative influences of science, machinery, and other factors which I have merely touched upon;—besides those influential traditions of early English prosody which form points of departure, at least, for any indigenous rhythms and forms which may emerge. The most typical and valid expression of the American *psychosis* seems to me still to be found in Whitman.[4] His faults as a technician, and his clumsy and indiscriminate enthusiasm are somewhat beside the point. He, better than any other, was able to coordinate those forces in America which seem most intractable, fusing them into a universal vision which takes on additional significance as time goes on. He was a revolutionist beyond the strict meaning of Coleridge's definition of genius,[5] but his bequest is still to be realized in all its implications.

[1930]

---

1. **"Commedia" of Dante:** *The Divine Comedy*, a Christian epic by the Italian poet Dante Alighieri (1265-1321).
2. **"a tear . . . King":** The lines are from "The Grey Monk," by the English poet William Blake (1757-1827).
3. **"Paradise Lost":** An epic poem that tells the Christian story of the Fall of man, by the English poet John Milton (1608-1674).
4. **American *psychosis* . . . Whitman:** Crane appears to use the word *psychosis* in the sense of the American mind or soul, which many critics and writers believed had found its fullest expression in the poetry of Walt Whitman (1819-1892).
5. **Coleridge's definition of genius:** In his lectures on Shakespeare, the English poet and critic Samuel Taylor Coleridge (1772-1834) famously observed: "As it must not, so genius cannot, be lawless: for it is even this that constitutes its genius—the power of acting creatively under laws of its own origination."

Robert Frost

[1874-1963]

By the time Robert Frost wrote "The Figure a Poem Makes," the preface to the first edition of his *Collected Poems* (1939), he was among the most famous poets in the United States (see Frost, p. 1556). Already the winner of three Pulitzer Prizes for Poetry (he would eventually win four), Frost was a college dropout who had recently accepted a two-year position as a professor at Harvard University. Although he gave numerous readings and talks, Frost wrote only a few formal commentaries on other poets or on poetry, of which the best known is "The Figure a Poem Makes." In the brief essay, which is itself a kind of prose poem, Frost discussed the resources available to poets and meditated on the nature of the poem. Writing at the end of the Great Depression, during which many critics and writers had insisted that literature must assume a social role, Frost assigned the poem a very different function. "It begins in delight and ends in wisdom," he memorably declared. To distinguish such "wisdom" from the beliefs embraced by members of political, philosophical, or religious groups, Frost added that the poem "ends in a clarification of life — not necessarily a great clarification, such as sects and cults are founded on, but in a momentary stay against confusion." The text of the essay, which was subsequently reprinted as the preface to many editions of his poems, is taken from the *Collected Poems of Robert Frost* (1939).

THE FIGURE A POEM MAKES

Abstraction is an old story with the philosophers, but it has been like a new toy in the hands of the artists of our day. Why can't we have any one quality of poetry we choose by itself? We can have in thought. Then it will go hard if we can't in practice. Our lives for it.

Granted no one but a humanist much cares how sound a poem is if it is only *a* sound. The sound is the gold in the ore. Then we will have the sound out alone and dispense with the inessential. We do till we make the discovery that the object in writing poetry is to make all poems sound as different as possible from each other, and the resources for that of vowels, consonants, punctuation, syntax, words, sentences, meter are not enough. We need the help of context — meaning — subject matter. That is the greatest help towards variety. All that can be done with words is soon told. So also with meters — particularly in our language where there are virtually but two, strict iambic and loose iambic. The ancients with many were still poor if they depended on meters for all tune. It is painful to watch our sprung-rhythmists[1] straining at the point of omitting one

---

1. **sprung-rhythmists:** *Sprung rhythm*, a term coined by the English poet Gerard Manley Hopkins (1844-1889), is a poetic meter approximating the natural patterns of English speech in which each line has the same number of stressed syllables but each stressed syllable is followed by a variable number of unstressed syllables, from zero to three. Frost wrote iambic verse, in which lines are divided into a set number of metrical feet called *iambs*, each of which consists of an unstressed syllable followed by a stressed syllable.

short from a foot for relief from monotony. The possibilities for tune from the dramatic tones of meaning struck across the rigidity of a limited meter are endless. And we are back in poetry as merely one more art of having something to say, sound or unsound. Probably better if sound, because deeper and from wider experience.

Then there is this wildness whereof it is spoken. Granted again that it has an equal claim with sound to being a poem's better half. If it is a wild tune, it is a poem. Our problem then is, as modern abstractionists, to have the wildness pure; to be wild with nothing to be wild about. We bring up as aberrationists, giving way to undirected associations and kicking ourselves from one chance suggestion to another in all directions as of a hot afternoon in the life of a grasshopper. Theme alone can steady us down. Just as the first mystery was how a poem could have a tune in such a straightness as meter, so the second mystery is how a poem can have wildness and at the same time a subject that shall be fulfilled.

It should be of the pleasure of a poem itself to tell how it can. The figure a poem makes. It begins in delight and ends in wisdom. The figure is the same as for love. No one can really hold that the ecstasy should be static and stand still in one place. It begins in delight, it inclines to the impulse, it assumes direction with the first line laid down, it runs a course of lucky events, and ends in a clarification of life — not necessarily a great clarification, such as sects and cults are founded on, but in a momentary stay against confusion. It has denouement. It has an outcome that though unforeseen was predestined from the first image of the original mood — and indeed from the very mood. It is but a trick poem and no poem at all if the best of it was thought of first and saved for the last. It finds its own name as it goes and discovers the best waiting for it in some final phrase at once wise and sad — the happy-sad blend of the drinking song.

No tears in the writer, no tears in the reader. No surprise for the writer, no surprise for the reader. For me the initial delight is in the surprise of remembering something I didn't know I knew. I am in a place, in a situation, as if I had materialized from cloud or risen out of the ground. There is a glad recognition of the long lost and the rest follows. Step by step the wonder of unexpected supply keeps growing. The impressions most useful to my purpose seem always those I was unaware of and so made no note of at the time when taken, and the conclusion is come to that like giants we are always hurling experience ahead of us to pave the future with against the day when we may want to strike a line of purpose across it for somewhere. The line will have the more charm for not being mechanically straight. We enjoy the straight crookedness of a good walking stick. Modern instruments of precision are being used to make things crooked as if by eye and hand in the old days.

I tell how there may be a better wildness of logic than of inconsequence. But the logic is backward, in retrospect, after the act. It must be more felt than seen ahead like prophecy. It must be a revelation, or a series of revelations, as much for the poet as for the reader. For it to be that there must have been the greatest freedom of the material to move about in it and to establish relations in it regardless of time and space, previous relation, and everything but affinity. We prate of freedom. We call our schools free because we are not free to stay away from them till we are sixteen years of age. I have given up my democratic prejudices and now willingly set the lower classes free to be completely taken care of by the upper classes. Political freedom is nothing to me. I bestow it right and left. All I would keep for myself is the freedom of my material — the condition of body and mind now and then to summons aptly from the vast chaos of all I have lived through.

Scholars and artists thrown together are often annoyed at the puzzle of where they differ. Both work from knowledge; but I suspect they differ most importantly in the way their knowledge is come by. Scholars get theirs with conscientious thoroughness along projected lines of logic; poets theirs cavalierly and as it happens in and out of books. They stick to nothing deliberately, but let what will stick to them like burrs where they walk in the fields. No acquirement is on assignment, or even self-assignment. Knowledge of the second kind is much more available in the wild free ways of wit and art. A school boy may be defined as one who can tell you what he knows in the order in which he learned it. The artist must value himself as he snatches a thing from some previous order in time and space into a new order with not so much as a ligature clinging to it of the old place where it was organic.

More than once I should have lost my soul to radicalism if it had been the originality it was mistaken for by its young converts. Originality and initiative are what I ask for my country. For myself the originality need be no more than the freshness of a poem run in the way I have described: from delight to wisdom. The figure is the same as for love. Like a piece of ice on a hot stove the poem must ride on its own melting. A poem may be worked over once it is in being, but may not be worried into being. Its most precious quality will remain its having run itself and carried away the poet with it. Read it a hundred times: it will forever keep its freshness as a metal keeps its fragrance. It can never lose its sense of a meaning that once unfolded by surprise as it went.

[1939]

James Weldon Johnson

[1871–1938]

James William Johnson, who later changed his middle name to Weldon, was born in Jacksonville, Florida, on June 17, 1871. He was the first child of James Johnson, the headwaiter at a first-class resort hotel, and Helen Dillet Johnson, a schoolteacher. Johnson's mother was born and raised in the Bahamas, where her father was for many years a member of the House of Assembly. After she married James Johnson, the couple lived in the Bahamas until 1866, when they moved to Jacksonville. Johnson grew up there in a comfortable and cultured home. His father was fond of reciting passages from Shakespeare's plays, and his artistic mother played the piano, sang, and wrote poetry. Johnson and his brother, John Rosamond Johnson, took music lessons and attended the Stanton Grammar School, the only school open to African Americans in Jacksonville. Johnson later recalled that as a child he was especially stirred by a speech delivered by his hero Frederick Douglass, who "moved a large audience of white and colored people by his supreme eloquence." After he graduated from Stanton in 1887, Johnson attended the preparatory school and then the college division of the all-black Atlanta University, where he worked in the printing office and received a solid education in literature, mathematics, and science, as well as in Latin and Greek. He published his first poem in the university's *Bulletin* and won an oratory contest for his speech "The Best Methods of Removing the Disabilities of Caste from the Negro." Gaining the attention of influential African Americans, in 1893 he was introduced to Booker T. Washington at the Columbian Exposition in Chicago, where Johnson also met the poet Paul Laurence Dunbar.

The talented and energetic Johnson pursued a number of different careers following his graduation from college in 1894. Returning home to Jacksonville, he became the principal of the Stanton School. He also established a newspaper, the *Daily American*, to be "published chiefly in the interest of the colored people of Florida and the South." Despite a large number of subscribers, the costs of publishing a newspaper proved to be prohibitive, and he reluctantly ended the venture after eight months. He then decided to study law, and in 1898 he became the first African American to be admitted to the Florida Bar since the end of Reconstruction. After his brother, a composer, graduated from the New England Conservatory of Music in 1897, Johnson wrote the lyrics for some of his songs. In

1900, the brothers collaborated on "Lift Ev'ry Voice and Sing," a lyric about the experiences and aspirations of African Americans that Johnson originally wrote for a celebration of Abraham Lincoln's birthday at the Stanton School. The song became popular throughout the South, and the National Association for the Advancement of Colored People (NAACP) later adopted it as the "Negro National Anthem." In 1902, Johnson resigned his position at the Stanton School, closed his successful law practice, and left for New York City. Working with his brother as a songwriting team—together, they wrote two hundred songs for Broadway musicals—Johnson met a variety of artists and producers, as well as his future wife, Grace Nail, the daughter of a Harlem businessman. Johnson also published essays and made friends in political circles. He gave up Broadway in 1906, when President Theodore Roosevelt appointed Johnson American consul in Venezuela, from which he moved to a similar diplomatic post in Nicaragua in 1909.

During the following two decades, Johnson gained prominence as an author and as an activist in the NAACP. In 1912, he anonymously published a novel, *The Autobiography of an Ex-Colored Man* (1912), ostensibly the "confession" of a light-skinned African American who "passes" for white in turn-of-the-century New York City. The novel generated little interest, but Johnson's literary career received a major boost when his "Fifty Years," a long poem celebrating the fiftieth anniversary of the Emancipation Proclamation, appeared in the *New York Times*. The distinguished African American novelist Charles W. Chesnutt called the poem "the finest thing I ever read on the subject," and its popularity led to the publication of Johnson's first collection of poetry, *Fifty Years and Other Poems* (1917). Meanwhile, frustrated by the lack of advancement in the consular service, Johnson resigned in 1913, and he and his wife settled in Harlem. Johnson became an editor of the crusading African American newspaper the *New York Age*. He also joined the NAACP. Elected field secretary, he was active in antilynching campaigns and established many new branches of the organization, which appointed him executive secretary in 1920. Johnson was also a major figure in the Harlem Renaissance, showcasing African American cultural achievements in three major anthologies: *The Book of American Negro Poetry* (1922), *The Book of American Negro Spirituals* (1925), and *The Second Book of American Negro Spirituals* (1926). In 1927, Johnson published his major poetic work, *God's Trombones: Seven Negro Sermons in Verse*.

Although he was encouraged to run for public office, Johnson preferred to spend his time writing and encouraging young African American artists and authors. In 1931, he accepted a position as a professor of literature and creative writing at Fisk University. In addition to poems, he wrote his autobiography, *Along This Way* (1933). Johnson also published a collection of his lectures, *Negro Americans, What Now?* (1934), in which he argued that integration was the only viable solution to racial problems in the United States. During a vacation in Maine, Johnson died in a car accident on June 26, 1938. More than 2,500 people, white and black, attended his funeral services, and hundreds more gathered to pay their respects outside the church in Harlem.

James Weldon Johnson aptly, deeply, with love and humor and a powerful rhyming tongue, has told our story and sung our song.

–Maya Angelou

Reading Johnson's "The Creation."   Subtitled "A Negro Sermon," this poem was first published in 1920 in the *Freeman*, a short-lived journal of social commentary that was also widely regarded as one of the most vibrant literary magazines of the 1920s. Johnson later included "The Creation" in his anthology *The Book of American Negro Poetry* (1922) and then in his collection *God's Trombones: Seven Negro Sermons in Verse* (1927). In the preface to the collection, Johnson explained that the poems were partially based on his early memories of sermons delivered by the "old-time preachers," but that he was directly inspired by a more recent occasion in Kansas City. There, he had heard a famed visiting preacher deliver a sermon in a "wonderful voice" that sounded like a trombone, "the instrument possessing above all others the power to express the wide and varied range of emotions encompassed by the human voice—and with greater amplitude." Johnson stated that he began to jot down some ideas for "The Creation" even before the preacher finished his sermon. Johnson was also familiar with earlier poems such as Paul Laurence Dunbar's "An Antebellum Sermon" (1896). Johnson, however, was concerned that such dialect poems perpetuated stereotypes and limited the expressive range of African Americans. He thus explained that "The Creation" was intended to move beyond dialect to capture the emotional resonance and rhetorical power of African American sermons, "a fusion of Negro idioms with Bible English"—that is, the rich language of the creation story in the King James Version of the Bible (Genesis 1:1-27). The text is taken from *God's Trombones* (1927).

bedfordstmartins.com/ *americanlit* for research links on *Johnson*

"The Creation"

In an effort to fuse literature and art, and to display the achievements of African Americans in both areas, Johnson's poems in *God's Trombones* were accompanied by titles lettered by C. B. Falls and drawings by Aaron Douglas, a leading artist of the Harlem Renaissance.

THE CREATION

And God stepped out on space,
And he looked around and said:
I'm lonely —
I'll make me a world.

And far as the eye of God could see   5
Darkness covered everything,
Blacker than a hundred midnights
Down in a cypress swamp.

Then God smiled,
And the light broke,   10
And the darkness rolled up on one side,
And the light stood shining on the other,
And God said: That's good!

Then God reached out and took the light in his hands,
And God rolled the light around in his hands   15
Until he made the sun;
And he set that sun a-blazing in the heavens.
And the light that was left from making the sun
God gathered it up in a shining ball
And flung it against the darkness,   20
Spangling the night with the moon and stars.
Then down between
The darkness and the light
He hurled the world;
And God said: That's good!   25

Then God himself stepped down —
And the sun was on his right hand,
And the moon was on his left;
The stars were clustered about his head,
And the earth was under his feet.   30
And God walked, and where he trod
His footsteps hollowed the valleys out
And bulged the mountains up.

Then he stopped and looked and saw
That the earth was hot and barren.   35
So God stepped over to the edge of the world
And he spat out the seven seas —
He batted his eyes, and the lightnings flashed —
He clapped his hands, and the thunders rolled —

And the waters above the earth came down,   40
The cooling waters came down.

Then the green grass sprouted,
And the little red flowers blossomed,
The pine tree pointed his finger to the sky,
And the oak spread out his arms,   45
The lakes cuddled down in the hollows of the ground,
And the rivers ran down to the sea;
And God smiled again,
And the rainbow appeared,
And curled itself around his shoulder.   50

Then God raised his arm and he waved his hand
Over the sea and over the land,
And he said: Bring forth! Bring forth!
And quicker than God could drop his hand,
Fishes and fowls   55
And beasts and birds
Swam the rivers and the seas,
Roamed the forests and the woods,
And split the air with their wings.
And God said: That's good!   60

Then God walked around,
And God looked around
On all that he had made.
He looked at his sun,
And he looked at his moon,   65
And he looked at his little stars;
He looked on his world
With all its living things,
And God said: I'm lonely still.

Then God sat down—   70
On the side of a hill where he could think;
By a deep, wide river he sat down;
With his head in his hands,
God thought and thought,
Till he thought: I'll make me a man!   75

Up from the bed of the river
God scooped the clay;
And by the bank of the river
He kneeled him down;
And there the great God Almighty   80

Who lit the sun and fixed it in the sky,
Who flung the stars to the most far corner of the n
Who rounded the earth in the middle of his hand;
This Great God,
Like a mammy bending over her baby,
Kneeled down in the dust
Toiling over a lump of clay
Till he shaped it in his own image;

Then into it he blew the breath of life,
And man became a living soul.   90
Amen.   Amen.

                                    [1920, 1927]

Amy Lowell

[1874-1925]

Amy Lowell was born on February 9, 1874, in Brookline, Massachusetts. She was the daughter of Augustus and Katherine Lawrence Lowell and a descendant of one of the most prominent families in New England, which included James Russell Lowell, the well-known nineteenth-century poet and the first editor of the presti-gious *Atlantic Monthly.* Her wealthy and cultured parents carefully over-saw the education of their five gifted children, and Lowell was taught by an English governess before being sent to a private school. From an early age, she also enjoyed reading in the extensive library of her fami-ly's magnificent home, Sevenels, which was filled with Asian art and surrounded by eight acres of gardens in a fashionable section of Boston. Lowell was a good student, but she disliked rote learning and ended her formal education when she was seventeen, in 1891. With-drawn, lonely, and deeply self-conscious about her weight, she reluctantly bowed to social conventions and became a debutante, going to parties and

Amy Lowell

This photograph of Lowell enjoying a rare moment of relaxation in the gardens at her estate, Sevenels, was taken in 1922, when she was at the height of her fame as a poet and tireless pro-moter of the "new poetry" in the United States.

other social events. After her mother's death in 1895, Lowell traveled extensively in Europe and to Africa. When her father died in 1900, she inherited Sevenels, which Lowell lovingly maintained. Although she continued to read deeply and was especially drawn to the work of the British Romantic poets, Lowell evidently had no idea of becoming a poet until she attended a performance by the Italian actress Eleonora Duse in 1902. Lowell was so moved that when she got home she wrote a poem, "Eleonora Duse."

Lowell subsequently began seriously to study and write poetry. Her first published poem appeared in the *Atlantic Monthly* in 1910, two years before she published her first collection of verse, *A Dome of Many Coloured Glass* (1912). The conventional volume created little stir, but Lowell's life and poetry soon changed dramatically. In 1912, she met Ada Dwyer Russell, a professional actress who was separated from her husband. Lowell invited her to visit Sevenels, where Russell moved permanently in 1913. With Russell's supportive help, Lowell maintained her life as a full-time writer and began to explore new directions in her poetry. She became fascinated by the work of a small group of experimental English and American poets led by Ezra Pound—the imagistes, as they called themselves in London, or imagists, as they came to be called in the United States. After reading some poems by H.D. (Hilda Doolittle) in the January 1913 issue of *Poetry* magazine, Lowell realized, "Why, I, too am an *Imagiste*!" She went to London to meet Pound and H.D., and she began to write her own imagist verse, which appeared in magazines and in her experimental collection of poems, *Sword Blades and Poppy Seeds* (1914). During the following decade, Lowell became an important force in American poetry, editing three collections of imagist poetry between 1915 and 1917 and publishing ten additional collections of her own poetry, including *Men, Women, and Ghosts* (1916), *Can Grande Castle* (1918), *Pictures of the Floating World* (1919), and finally *What's O'Clock* (1925).

Lowell also became well known as a public personality and crusader for modern poetry. Flamboyant, iconoclastic, and theatrical, she smoked cigars freely and lived openly with Ada Dwyer Russell, to whom Lowell wrote a series of erotic love poems. She also engaged in a heated public debate with Pound over the future of imagism, which he subsequently dismissed as "Amygism." Although that episode later undermined her place in histories on modernism, Lowell tirelessly promoted the new verse in essays and during her extensive speaking tours in the United States. Undaunted by the derision and hostility she frequently encountered at her thronged readings and lectures, she insisted that the experimental poetry many critics condemned as foreign or alien was a natural outgrowth of American progress in all areas, from the arts to science and technology. Lowell also emphasized the vital role poetry might play in the development of a national identity, the ongoing effort "to free ourselves from the tutelage of another nation," adding: "I might say with perfect truth that the most national things we have are skyscrapers, ice water, and the New Poetry, and each of these means more than appears on the surface." Indeed, perhaps no other poet of her time worked so hard

The force which Miss Lowell's New England ancestors put into founding and running cotton-mills, or belike into saving souls, she puts into conquering an art and making it express and serve her.

–Harriet Monroe

to express what poetry might mean to Americans. During the final years of her life, however, Lowell's vigor and productivity were undermined by ill health, and she died prematurely at the age of fifty-one, on May 12, 1925.

Reading Lowell's Poetry.   Early in her career, Lowell was heavily influenced by the English Romantic poets, especially John Keats. After discovering the experimental work of the imagists, however, she adopted their forms and techniques, including their embrace of *vers libre*, verse freed from the conventional metrical patterns and rhyme schemes of traditional poetry in English. In "Amy Lowell and the Art of Poetry," a survey of her achievement published in the *North American Review* shortly before her death in 1925, the American poet and critic Archibald MacLeish praised her sharply defined visual images, her use of conversational language, and especially the rhythmical freedom of her poetry. By then, Lowell's poetry was being overshadowed by the work of younger poets, especially T. S. Eliot's *The Waste Land.* MacLeish, however, concluded his graceful tribute to Lowell with a simple description of the aspect of her best work that would ensure it enduring fame: "It is the quality of her art." Certainly, that quality is illustrated in the following selection of her poems. "The Taxi" and "Aubade," two of her early experiments in free verse, or what Lowell called "unrhymed cadence," were published in her second collection, *Sword Blades and Poppy Seeds* (1914). The other poems included here were published in *Pictures of the Floating World* (1919) — a translation of ukiyo-e, Japanese visual arts that were at once highly sophisticated and readily accessible to common people. The texts of all of the poems are taken from *The Complete Poetical Works of Amy Lowell* (1955).

bedfordstmartins.com/ **americanlit** *for research links on Lowell*

THE TAXI

When I go away from you
The world beats dead
Like a slackened drum.
I call out for you against the jutted stars
And shout into the ridges of the wind.   5
Streets coming fast,
One after the other,
Wedge you away from me,
And the lamps of the city prick my eyes
So that I can no longer see your face.   10
Why should I leave you,
To wound myself upon the sharp edges of the night?

[1914, 1955]

AUBADE[1]

As I would free the white almond from the green husk
So would I strip your trappings off,
Beloved.
And fingering the smooth and polished kernel
I should see that in my hands glittered a gem beyond counting.

[1914, 1955]

---

1. **Aubade:** A lyric about dawn or about lovers parting at morning.

VENUS TRANSIENS[1]

Tell me,
Was Venus more beautiful
Than you are,
When she topped
The crinkled waves,   5
Drifting shoreward
On her plaited shell?
Was Botticelli's vision[2]
Fairer than mine;
And were the painted rosebuds   10
He tossed his lady,
Of better worth
Than the words I blow about you
To cover your too great loveliness
As with a gauze   15
Of misted silver?
For me,
You stand poised
In the blue and buoyant air,
Cinctured by bright winds,   20
Treading the sunlight.
And the waves which precede you
Ripple and stir
The sands at my feet.

[1919, 1955]

---

1. **Venus Transiens:**   Venus [the Roman goddess of love] passing over (Latin).
2. **Botticelli's vision:** Sandro Botticelli (1445–1510), Italian painter known for his mythological works,
notably *The Birth of Venus* (c. 1480), which depicts the beautiful goddess floating ashore on a seashell
amidst a shower of roses.

MADONNA OF THE EVENING FLOWERS[1]

All day long I have been working,
Now I am tired.
I call: "Where are you?"
But there is only the oak-tree rustling in the wind.
The house is very quiet,   5
The sun shines in on your books,
On your scissors and thimble just put down,
But you are not there.
Suddenly I am lonely:
Where are you?   10
I go about searching.

Then I see you,
Standing under a spire of pale blue larkspur,
With a basket of roses on your arm.
You are cool, like silver,   15
And you smile.
I think the Canterbury bells[2] are playing little tunes.

You tell me that the peonies need spraying,
That the columbines have overrun all bounds,
That the pyrus japonica[3] should be cut back and rounded.   20
You tell me these things.
But I look at you, heart of silver,
White heart-flame of polished silver,
Burning beneath the blue steeples of the larkspur,
And I long to kneel instantly at your feet,   25
While all about us peal the loud, sweet *Te Deums*[4] of the Canterbury bells.

[1919, 1955]

_____

1. **Madonna of the Evening Flowers:** The title makes a play on the various meanings of *Madonna*, usually a reference to the Virgin Mary but also a shortened form of the Madonna or Annunciation lily (*Lilium candidum*), a plant bearing fragrant white flowers that yield oil used in perfumes.
2. **Canterbury bells:** The common name for *Campanula medium*, a tall plant with bell-shaped flowers.
3. **pyrus japonica:** Japanese quince, a flowering shrub from eastern Asia.
4. *Te Deums*: Shortened form of an ancient Latin hymn, *Te deum laudamus*, "We praise thee, God."

A DECADE

When you came, you were like red wine and honey,
And the taste of you burnt my mouth with its sweetness.
Now you are like morning bread,
Smooth and pleasant.

I hardly taste you at all for I know your savour,
But I am completely nourished.

[1919, 1955]

Robert Frost

[1874-1963]

Robert Frost

This photograph was taken in 1913 in England, where Frost first gained wide acclaim as a poet.

Robert Lee Frost was born in San Francisco, California, on March 26, 1874. Although he was named after the famous Confederate general, Frost's parents were transplanted northerners: Isabelle Moodie Frost, a former teacher from a deeply religious family in Ohio, and William Prescott Frost Jr., an ambitious Harvard-educated journalist seeking fame and fortune in the West. Their marriage was deeply troubled, and while Isabelle Frost was pregnant with her second child she fled with her young son back to her in-laws in Lawrence, Massachusetts. Eventually she and her two children returned to San Francisco, where Frost's father was seriously ill with tuberculosis. After his death in 1885, the family returned to Lawrence. Encouraged by his mother, who frequently read poetry aloud to her children, Frost published poems in his high-school newspaper and secretly began to plan a poetic career for himself. After his graduation in 1892, he enrolled at Dartmouth College, but Frost was so unhappy there that he dropped out before the end of his first semester and returned home to Lawrence.

During the following years, Frost took various jobs while pursuing his dream of becoming a poet. He taught school, worked in one of the textile mills in Lawrence and as a reporter for a local newspaper, and wrote poetry in his spare time. His first professional publication was "My Butterfly," a poem that appeared in a New York newspaper, the *Independent*, in 1894. Frost, who was elated by the fifteen dollars he received, subsequently paid for the printing of two copies of a collection of his poems, *Twilight*, one for himself and the other for his high-school sweetheart, Elinor White, whom he married in 1895. After they had the first of their six children, two of whom died in infancy, Frost sought a more secure way of supporting his family. Deciding to train to become a high-school teacher of Greek and Latin, he enrolled at Harvard University in 1897. But he withdrew before he finished his second year, and with the help of his grandfather Frost and his wife bought a farm in Derry, New Hampshire, in 1900. Although his experiences would later provide rich resources for his poetry, life on the isolated farm was difficult, and Frost returned to full-time teaching in 1906. He also returned to serious work on his poems, several of which were published in the *Independent*, the *Youth's Companion*, and the *New England Magazine*.

In 1911, when he was thirty-seven, Frost determined to make a final effort to become a professional poet. He sold the farm in Derry, left his teaching position at the end of the academic year, and took his family to England in the summer of 1912. The bold gamble paid off, since the connections he made among other poets there, especially Ezra Pound, led to the publication of Frost's first collection of poetry, *A Boy's Will* (1913). In a review of the volume published in the Chicago-based little magazine *Poetry*, Pound described Frost's work as "a little raw" but observed that the volume had "the tang of the New Hampshire woods, and it has just this utter sincerity." *A Boy's Will* also received several favorable reviews in England, leading to the publication of a second collection of Frost's poems, *North of Boston* (1914). After war broke out in Europe in August 1914, he decided to bring his family back to the United States. By the time they returned in 1915, an American publishing firm had brought out editions of *A Boy's Will* and *North of Boston*, largely through the efforts of Amy Lowell, who had discovered Frost's work during a visit to London and who wrote a rave review of the two volumes for the *New Republic*. Frost soon published another collection, *Mountain Interval* (1916), which was followed by *New Hampshire* (1923). That volume was awarded the Pulitzer Prize, which Frost also received for his *Collected Poems* (1931), *A Farther Range* (1937), and *A Witness Tree* (1943). Indeed, along with his own favorite, Emily Dickinson, Frost became the best-known poet in the United States.

During the last two decades of his life, he secured that position less by the poetry he published than by his accomplished public performances in the role of the poet. Frost gave innumerable readings of his work, taught poetry at a number of colleges and universities, and was awarded more than forty honorary degrees, including those conferred on him by the two institutions from which he had dropped out, Dartmouth and Harvard. During the 1950s, Frost made visits to England and South America sponsored by the State Department. At the request of President Kennedy, Frost in 1962 visited the Soviet Union, where he chided Premier Khrushchev by reading his poem "Mending Wall," offering a subtle denunciation of the recently erected Berlin Wall. But his most memorable public moment occurred at Kennedy's inauguration the previous year, in January 1961. When the wind and bright sunlight made it impossible for the eighty-six-year-old Frost to read the poem that he had written for the occasion, he hesitated briefly and then recited from memory an earlier poem, "The Gift Outright." The deeply moving moment was in many ways the climax of the long career of a man who had from the beginning sought to make poetry an integral part of life in the United States. His final collection of poems, *In the Clearing*, was published in 1962, the year he was awarded the Congressional "Gold" Medal by President Kennedy. Frost died on January 29, 1963, and, as a clear indication of the household name he had become, his obituary was printed on the front page of newspapers across the United States.

Reading Frost's Poetry.

In her influential 1915 review of *A Boy's Will* and *North of Boston*, Amy Lowell emphasized some of the fundamental qualities of Frost's poetry: his "great and beautiful simplicity of phrase," the liberties he took with "classical metres," written "in a way to set the

This man has the good sense to speak naturally and to paint the thing, the thing as he sees it.

–Ezra Pound

teeth of all the poets of the older schools on edge," and his use of a "blank verse which does not hesitate to leave out a syllable or put one in." Lowell also praised what she described as Frost's "photographic" realism. Indeed, Frost was often celebrated for his unsentimental depictions of rural life and ordinary people, though he once observed: "There are two types of realist — the one who offers a good deal of dirt with his potato to show that it is a real one; and the one who is satisfied with the potato brushed clean. . . . To me, the thing that art does for life is to clean it, to strip it to form." Later, when an interviewer asked him if poetry was an escape from life, Frost responded, "No, it's a way of taking life by the throat." The following selection of poems charts Frost's ongoing and often fierce engagement with life over a nearly thirty-year period. The earliest of these — "Mending Wall" and "After Apple-Picking" — were first published in *North of Boston* (1914). After that, Frost's work frequently appeared in prominent periodicals such as the *Atlantic Monthly*, where his well-known poems "The Road Not Taken" and "Birches" were published in 1915. He first collected those poems in *Mountain Interval* (1916). All of the later poems in the following selection first appeared in periodicals, and they are ordered and dated according to their initial publication rather than in the order in which they were published in later volumes. The texts of all of the poems are taken from *The Poetry of Robert Frost*, edited by Edward Connery Lathem (1969).

bedfordstmartins.com/
americanlit *for research*
links on Frost

MENDING WALL

Something there is that doesn't love a wall,
That sends the frozen-ground-swell under it
And spills the upper boulders in the sun,
And makes gaps even two can pass abreast.
The work of hunters is another thing: 5
I have come after them and made repair
Where they have left not one stone on a stone,
But they would have the rabbit out of hiding,
To please the yelping dogs. The gaps I mean,
No one has seen them made or heard them made,   10
But at spring mending-time we find them there.
I let my neighbor know beyond the hill;
And on a day we meet to walk the line
And set the wall between us once again.
We keep the wall between us as we go.   15
To each the boulders that have fallen to each.
And some are loaves and some so nearly balls
We have to use a spell to make them balance:
"Stay where you are until our backs are turned!"

We wear our fingers rough with handling them.   20
Oh, just another kind of outdoor game,
One on a side. It comes to little more:
There where it is we do not need the wall:
He is all pine and I am apple orchard.
My apple trees will never get across   25
And eat the cones under his pines, I tell him.
He only says, "Good fences make good neighbors."
Spring is the mischief in me, and I wonder
If I could put a notion in his head:
"*Why* do they make good neighbors? Isn't it   30
Where there are cows? But here there are no cows.
Before I built a wall I'd ask to know
What I was walling in or walling out,
And to whom I was like to give offense.
Something there is that doesn't love a wall,   35
That wants it down." I could say "Elves" to him,
But it's not elves exactly, and I'd rather
He said it for himself. I see him there,
Bringing a stone grasped firmly by the top
In each hand, like an old-stone savage armed.   40
He moves in darkness as it seems to me,
Not of woods only and the shade of trees.
He will not go behind his father's saying,
And he likes having thought of it so well
He says again, "Good fences make good neighbors."   45

                                        [1914, 1969]

AFTER APPLE-PICKING

My long two-pointed ladder's sticking through a tree
Toward heaven still,
And there's a barrel that I didn't fill
Beside it, and there may be two or three
Apples I didn't pick upon some bough.   5
But I am done with apple-picking now.
Essence of winter sleep is on the night,
The scent of apples: I am drowsing off.
I cannot rub the strangeness from my sight
I got from looking through a pane of glass   10
I skimmed this morning from the drinking trough
And held against the world of hoary grass.

It melted, and I let it fall and break.
But I was well
Upon my way to sleep before it fell, 15
And I could tell
What form my dreaming was about to take.
Magnified apples appear and disappear,
Stem end and blossom end,
And every fleck of russet showing clear. 20
My instep arch not only keeps the ache,
It keeps the pressure of a ladder-round.
I feel the ladder sway as the boughs bend.
And I keep hearing from the cellar bin
The rumbling sound 25
Of load on load of apples coming in.
For I have had too much
Of apple-picking: I am overtired
Of the great harvest I myself desired.
There were ten thousand thousand fruit to touch, 30
Cherish in hand, lift down, and not let fall.
For all
That struck the earth,
No matter if not bruised or spiked with stubble,
Went surely to the cider-apple heap 35
As of no worth.
One can see what will trouble
This sleep of mine, whatever sleep it is.
Were he not gone,
The woodchuck could say whether it's like his 40
Long sleep, as I describe its coming on,
Or just some human sleep.

[1914, 1969]

THE ROAD NOT TAKEN

Two roads diverged in a yellow wood,
And sorry I could not travel both
And be one traveler, long I stood
And looked down one as far as I could
To where it bent in the undergrowth; 5

Then took the other, as just as fair,
And having perhaps the better claim,

Because it was grassy and wanted wear;
Though as for that, the passing there
Had worn them really about the same,   10

And both that morning equally lay
In leaves no step had trodden black.
Oh, I kept the first for another day!
Yet knowing how way leads on to way,
I doubted if I should ever come back.   15

I shall be telling this with a sigh
Somewhere ages and ages hence:
Two roads diverged in a wood, and I
I took the one less traveled by,
And that has made all the difference.   20

[1915, 1969]

BIRCHES

When I see birches bend to left and right
Across the lines of straighter darker trees,
I like to think some boy's been swinging them.
But swinging doesn't bend them down to stay
As ice storms do. Often you must have seen them   5
Loaded with ice a sunny winter morning
After a rain. They click upon themselves
As the breeze rises, and turn many-colored
As the stir cracks and crazes their enamel.
Soon the sun's warmth makes them shed crystal shells   10
Shattering and avalanching on the snow crust —
Such heaps of broken glass to sweep away
You'd think the inner dome of heaven had fallen.
They are dragged to the withered bracken by the load,
And they seem not to break; though once they are bowed 15
So low for long, they never right themselves:
You may see their trunks arching in the woods
Years afterwards, trailing their leaves on the ground
Like girls on hands and knees that throw their hair
Before them over their heads to dry in the sun.   20
But I was going to say when Truth broke in
With all her matter of fact about the ice storm,
I should prefer to have some boy bend them
As he went out and in to fetch the cows —

Some boy too far from town to learn baseball,   25
Whose only play was what he found himself,
Summer or winter, and could play alone.
One by one he subdued his father's trees
By riding them down over and over again
Until he took the stiffness out of them,   30
And not one but hung limp, not one was left
For him to conquer. He learned all there was
To learn about not launching out too soon
And so not carrying the tree away
Clear to the ground. He always kept his poise   35
To the top branches, climbing carefully
With the same pains you use to fill a cup
Up to the brim, and even above the brim.
Then he flung outward, feet first, with a swish,
Kicking his way down through the air to the ground.   40
So was I once myself a swinger of birches.
And so I dream of going back to be.
It's when I'm weary of considerations,
And life is too much like a pathless wood
Where your face burns and tickles with the cobwebs   45
Broken across it, and one eye is weeping
From a twig's having lashed across it open.
I'd like to get away from earth awhile
And then come back to it and begin over.
May no fate willfully misunderstand me   50
And half grant what I wish and snatch me away
Not to return. Earth's the right place for love:
I don't know where it's likely to go better.
I'd like to go by climbing a birch tree,
And climb black branches up a snow-white trunk   55
Toward heaven, till the tree could bear no more,
But dipped its top and set me down again.
That would be good both going and coming back.
One could do worse than be a swinger of birches.

                                                              [1915, 1969]

FIRE AND ICE

Some say the world will end in fire,
Some say in ice.
From what I've tasted of desire

I hold with those who favor fire.
But if it had to perish twice,
I think I know enough of hate
To say that for destruction ice
Is also great
And would suffice.

[1920, 1969]

NOTHING GOLD CAN STAY

Nature's first green is gold,
Her hardest hue to hold.
Her early leaf's a flower;
But only so an hour.
Then leaf subsides to leaf.
So Eden sank to grief,
So dawn goes down to day.
Nothing gold can stay.

[1923, 1969]

STOPPING BY WOODS ON A SNOWY EVENING

Whose woods these are I think I know.
His house is in the village, though;
He will not see me stopping here
To watch his woods fill up with snow.

My little horse must think it queer   5
To stop without a farmhouse near
Between the woods and frozen lake
The darkest evening of the year.

He gives his harness bells a shake
To ask if there is some mistake.   10
The only other sound's the sweep
Of easy wind and downy flake.

The woods are lovely, dark, and deep,
But I have promises to keep,
And miles to go before I sleep,   15
And miles to go before I sleep.

[1923, 1969]

ACQUAINTED WITH THE NIGHT

I have been one acquainted with the night.
I have walked out in rain – and back in rain.
I have outwalked the furthest city light.

I have looked down the saddest city lane.
I have passed by the watchman on his beat   5
And dropped my eyes, unwilling to explain.

I have stood still and stopped the sound of feet
When far away an interrupted cry
Came over houses from another street,

But not to call me back or say good-by;   10
And further still at an unearthly height
One luminary clock against the sky

Proclaimed the time was neither wrong nor right.
I have been one acquainted with the night.

[1928, 1969]

DESERT PLACES

Snow falling and night falling fast, oh, fast
In a field I looked into going past,
And the ground almost covered smooth in snow,
But a few weeds and stubble showing last.

The woods around it have it – it is theirs.   5
All animals are smothered in their lairs.
I am too absent-spirited to count;
The loneliness includes me unawares.

And lonely as it is, that loneliness
Will be more lonely ere it will be less –   10
A blanker whiteness of benighted snow
With no expression, nothing to express.

They cannot scare me with their empty spaces
Between stars – on stars where no human race is.
I have it in me so much nearer home   15
To scare myself with my own desert places.

[1934, 1969]

THE GIFT OUTRIGHT

The land was ours before we were the land's.
She was our land more than a hundred years
Before we were her people. She was ours
In Massachusetts, in Virginia,
But we were England's, still colonials,   5
Possessing what we still were unpossessed by,
Possessed by what we now no more possessed.
Something we were withholding made us weak
Until we found out that it was ourselves
We were withholding from our land of living,   10
And forthwith found salvation in surrender.
Such as we were we gave ourselves outright
(The deed of gift was many deeds of war)
To the land vaguely realizing westward,
But still unstoried, artless, unenhanced,   15
Such as she was, such as she would become.[1]

[1942, 1969]

1. **Such . . . would become:** In the earliest version of this poem, which Frost thought of as a brief history of the United States and which was first published in the *Virginia Quarterly Review* in 1942, the final line read: "Such as she was, such as she might become." Frost later altered "might become" to "would become." When president-elect John F. Kennedy invited Frost to read a poem at his inauguration in January 1961, he requested that, if the poet did not plan to write a new poem for the occasion, he read "The Gift Outright." He also asked that, if Frost read the poem, he change the last line to read "Such as she was, such as she will become," better to reflect the optimism of his new presidency. Frost did write a new poem for the occasion, but when bright sunlight prevented him from reading it, he instead recited from memory "The Gift Outright." When he came to the final line, he first said "would become" but then paused and said "will become," noting that he had changed the line for the occasion.

Carl Sandburg

[1878-1967]

Carl August Sandburg was born in Galesburg, Illinois, on January 6, 1878, the son of Clara Anderson, a former hotel maid, and August Sandburg, who worked for a railroad line. Both were Swedish immigrants, and Sandburg grew up in a household in which he spoke both Swedish and English. Sandburg later recalled that he decided to become "a person of letters"

Carl Sandburg

This photograph of Sandburg was taken in 1905, about the time that the struggling young poet first moved to Chicago.

when he first learned the alphabet, at the age of six. But he left school after graduating from the eighth grade in order to help support the growing family. For the next several years, he took a series of odd jobs, delivering milk, selling fruit on street corners, shining shoes at a barber shop, and working as a stagehand at the opera house. Eager to see more of the world, the restless nineteen-year-old set off as a hobo in the summer of 1897 on a trip through Iowa, Missouri, Kansas, Nebraska, and Colorado. Along the way, he supported himself by taking a long list of temporary jobs, from waiting on tables and washing dishes to working on a railroad and in the wheat fields. Sandburg also kept notebooks in which he jotted down anecdotes, impressions, and lists of words and phrases. Shortly after he returned home in 1898, he enlisted in the Sixth Illinois Regiment, which was part of the force that occupied Puerto Rico during the Spanish-American War.

Following his brief stint as a soldier, Sandburg once again returned to Galesburg, where he took his first steps toward a literary career. As a veteran of the war, he was entitled to free tuition at Lombard College, where he attended classes from 1898 until 1902. Although he did not earn a degree, he met Philip Green Wright, a professor who strongly encouraged and inspired Sandburg. Using his own handpress, Wright later printed small runs of Sandburg's first collections of poems and other writings, *In Reckless Ecstasy* (1904), *Incidentals* (1906), and *The Plaint of a Rose* (1908). After leaving college, Sandburg pursued a career on the lecture circuit, delivering talks on his heroes Walt Whitman and Abraham Lincoln, and as a journalist in Chicago, where he moved in 1906. He became deeply involved with the prolabor Social Democratic Party and consequently moved to Milwaukee, where he worked as a party organizer and wrote for progressive periodicals such as *La Follette's Weekly*. He also met Lillian Steichen, whom he married in July 1908. Sandburg later observed that, in addition to his mentor Wright, the most important influences on his life were his artistic wife, a Phi Beta Kappa graduate of the University of Chicago, and her older brother, the celebrated photographer Edward Steichen. In 1912, Sandburg took his family back to Chicago, where he worked as a reporter for various progressive newspapers. Throughout his years as an activist and journalist, however, Sandburg continued to write poetry. Early in 1914, he sent a group of nine poems to Harriet Monroe, who swiftly published them in her magazine *Poetry*. Although the reception of his raw verse on unpoetical subjects was almost violently mixed, a young publishing agent, Alfred Harcourt, was so impressed with Sandburg's work that he encouraged Monroe to "steer Carl my way." Harcourt's firm, Henry Holt, published Sandburg's first major collection, *Chicago Poems*, in 1916.

The volume launched Sandburg's successful career as a poet, though he became almost equally well known for his many other writings. In 1917, he took a job with the *Chicago Daily News*, where he worked as a reporter and later as a film critic until 1930. His coverage of one of the ugliest episodes in the city's history led to the publication of his most important journalistic work, *The Chicago Race Riots, July 1919*. He also found time to write the poems collected in *Cornhuskers* (1918), *Smoke and Steel* (1920), *Slabs of the Sunburnt West* (1922), and *Good Morning, America* (1928). The popularity of a series of books for children he published during the 1920s, the *Rootabaga* stories, prompted Sandburg to begin work on another book for children, a biography of Abraham Lincoln. But the project developed into something far more ambitious, the two-volume *Abraham Lincoln: The Prairie Years* (1926). The onset of the Depression inspired Sandburg to write his impassioned epic poem *The People, Yes* (1936). Sandburg also completed his four-volume *Abraham Lincoln: The War Years* (1939), which was awarded the Pulitzer Prize for History. Other awards and honors followed, including numerous honorary degrees and a second Pulitzer Prize for his *Complete Poems* (1950). Characteristically, however, Sandburg continued to experiment with a variety of genres, writing a novel, *Remembrance Rock* (1948); a lyrical account of his early years, *Always the Young Strangers* (1953); and the exhibition catalog for *The Family of Man* (1955), a collection of photographs of people from sixty-eight countries taken by Edward Steichen. Sandburg's final book of poetry, *Honey and Salt*, was published in 1963. A few months after he died on July 23, 1967, a memorial service was held for Sandburg at the Lincoln Memorial in Washington, D.C., where the thousands of mourners were led by President Lyndon B. Johnson.

Reading Sandburg's Poetry.   Sandburg's first professionally published poems appeared in *Poetry: A Magazine of Verse*, established in 1912 in an effort to change the character of American poetry by featuring new and innovative work. The editor, Harriet Monroe, was reportedly "shocked" by the rough style and subject matter of the poems, but she admired the authenticity of Sandburg's voice. One of the poems included in the following selection, "Chicago," was among the nine "Chicago Poems" that appeared at the opening of the March 1914 issue of *Poetry*. Although the poems outraged some reviewers, including one who called them an "affront to the poetry-loving public," Sandburg was later awarded the prize for the best poems published during the year in *Poetry*. His appearance in the magazine also led to the publication of his collection *Chicago Poems* (1916). In addition to the poems that had appeared in *Poetry*, the volume included "A Fence" and "Fog." "Grass" was published in Sandburg's next book, *Cornhuskers* (1918). Together, these poems reveal his debt to Walt Whitman, who helped inspire Sandburg's experiments in free verse and explorations of the seemingly unpoetical realities of urban and rural life in the Midwest. In a graceful tribute to Sandburg published in 1924, Monroe defined "love" as the central and controlling motive of his poems — "love of the prairie country, the prairie towns and city, and the people who struggle through toilsome lives there." She also praised the artistry of Sandburg's best poems, which had "greatly widened the rhythmic range of English poetry," as well as his use of the vernacular: "It is enough to say that any writer who can use the common speech of the people for beauty thereby enriches and revivifies the language." The texts are taken from *The Complete Poems of Carl Sandburg* (1970).

CHICAGO

Hog Butcher for the World,
Tool Maker, Stacker of Wheat,
Player with Railroads and the Nation's Freight Handler;
Stormy, husky, brawling,
City of the Big Shoulders: 5

They tell me you are wicked and I believe them, for I have seen your painted
    women under the gas lamps luring the farm boys.
And they tell me you are crooked and I answer: Yes, it is true I have seen the
    gunman kill and go free to kill again.
And they tell me you are brutal and my reply is: On the faces of women and
    children I have seen the marks of wanton hunger.
And having answered so I turn once more to those who sneer at this my city, and
    I give them back the sneer and say to them:
Come and show me another city with lifted head singing so proud to be alive and
    coarse and strong and cunning.   10
Flinging magnetic curses amid the toil of piling job on job, here is a tall bold
    slugger set vivid against the little soft cities;
Fierce as a dog with tongue lapping for action, cunning as a savage pitted against
    the wilderness,
        Bareheaded,
        Shoveling,
        Wrecking,   15
        Planning,
        Building, breaking, rebuilding,
Under the smoke, dust all over his mouth, laughing with white teeth,
Under the terrible burden of destiny laughing as a young man laughs,
Laughing even as an ignorant fighter laughs who has never lost a battle,   20
Bragging and laughing that under his wrist is the pulse, and under his ribs the
    heart of the people,
                Laughing!
Laughing the stormy, husky, brawling laughter of Youth, half-naked, sweating,
    proud to be Hog Butcher, Tool Maker, Stacker of Wheat, Player with Railroads
    and Freight Handler to the Nation.

[1914, 1970]

A FENCE

Now the stone house on the lake front[1] is finished and the workmen are beginning
    the fence.
The palings are made of iron bars with steel points that can stab the life out of any
    man who falls on them.

---

1. **lake front:** Along the shore of Lake Michigan, where many wealthy people built houses in Chicago.

As a fence, it is a masterpiece, and will shut off the rabble and all vagabonds and
    hungry men and all wandering children looking for a place to play.
Passing through the bars and over the steel points will go nothing except Death
    and the Rain and Tomorrow.

[1916, 1970]

FOG

The fog comes
on little cat feet.

It sits looking
over harbor and city
on silent haunches
and then moves on.

[1916, 1970]

GRASS

Pile the bodies high at Austerlitz and Waterloo.[1]
Shovel them under and let me work —
    I am the grass; I cover all.

And pile them high at Gettysburg[2]
And pile them high at Ypres and Verdun.[3]

5

Shovel them under and let me work.
Two years, ten years, and passengers ask the conductor:
    What place is this?
    Where are we now?

    I am the grass.

10

    Let me work.

[1918, 1970]

---

1. **Austerlitz and Waterloo:** Napoleon and his French army defeated the Austrians and Russians at the town
of Austerlitz, in the present-day Czech Republic, in 1805. A decade later, Napoleon's forces were defeated by
the British in the decisive battle of Waterloo, near a town in Belgium.
2. **Gettysburg:** A bloody battle of the Civil War fought in 1863 in Pennsylvania, where the Union Army
defeated Confederate troops led by General Robert E. Lee.
3. **Ypres and Verdun:** Among the bloodiest battles of World War I, the former fought near a town in Belgium
between 1914 and 1917 and the latter fought in northeastern France in 1916.

Wallace Stevens

[1879–1955]

Wallace Stevens was born on October 2, 1879, in Reading, Pennsylvania. He was the second of five children born to Garrett Stevens, a lawyer, and Margaretha Catharine Zeller Stevens, a former schoolteacher and deeply religious person who was active in the Presbyterian Church. Stevens attended a Lutheran grammar school and then the Reading Boys' School. In 1897, he enrolled at Harvard University as a "special student" — that is, one whose academic abilities and financial need qualified him to complete his degree in three rather than four years. Stevens took courses with an eye to law school, for which his father wanted him to prepare. He also pursued his deep interests in art and literature, both in his academic courses and in his work for the college's literary magazine, the *Harvard Advocate.* Concerned about the amount of time Stevens was devoting to literary pursuits, especially to writing the numerous poems he published in the *Harvard Advocate*, Garrett Stevens in a letter admonished his son: "Keep hammering at your real work . . . for a fellow never knows what's in store — and time mis-spent now counts heavily."

For the most part, Stevens followed his father's advice, even as he sought to become a poet. After he left Harvard in 1900, he moved to New York City, where Stevens worked as a journalist on the night shift at the *New York Tribune*. He enjoyed life in the city, and Stevens became so deeply absorbed in the theater that he wanted to quit his job at the *Tribune* in order to write plays. Instead, in 1901 he reluctantly agreed to his father's plans for him and enrolled in the New York Law School. Stevens graduated in 1903, worked as a clerk in a law firm, and was admitted to the New York State Bar in 1904. During a visit home that summer, he met Elsie Viola Moll, a piano teacher Stevens described as "the prettiest girl in Reading." While working at a series of law offices, Stevens frequently visited and wrote to Elsie, presenting her with a handwritten collection of his verses on her birthday in 1908 and again in 1909. Despite the objections of his father, who viewed the Moll family as socially inferior, Stevens married her in the summer of 1909, after he landed a seemingly secure job on the legal staff of an insurance company in New York City. Following the death of his father in 1911 and his mother in 1912, Stevens once again began to write poetry. In 1914, his first professionally published poems appeared in

The music of his lines and the dusk of implications in the phrases stays on and delivers its effect for me always.

– Carl Sandburg

the little magazine *Trend*, edited by an old friend from Harvard, Pitts Sanborn. Stevens also met a number of avant-garde artists, musicians, and writers, including the poets Mina Loy, Marianne Moore, and William Carlos Williams. Stimulated by his new friends, Stevens became a regular contributor to various little magazines. *Poetry* published several of his poems and his first play, *Three Travelers Watch a Sunrise*, which won the magazine's award for verse drama in 1916.

That year also marked a crucial turning point in his life. When his employer went bankrupt, Stevens accepted a position with the Hartford Accident and Indemnity Company. Although he did not want to leave New York City, Stevens and his wife moved permanently to Hartford, Connecticut, in March 1916. Initially, he made frequent trips to New York City, and he continued to write a steady stream of poetry, some of which Stevens collected in his first book, *Harmonium* (1923). A few critics recognized the originality of the volume, but the reception was otherwise rather tepid, and the book was a commercial failure; Stevens reportedly received a first royalty check for $6.70. During the following few years, he devoted himself to his job at the insurance company, where Stevens was so successful that he became recognized as one of the masters of the surety-bond business in the United States. Around 1930, however, he returned to serious work on his poetry, soon publishing an expanded edition of *Harmonium* (1931). During the following two decades, Stevens published several more collections, including *Ideas of Order* (1935), *The Man with the Blue Guitar* (1937), *Parts of a World* (1942), *Transport to Summer* (1947), and *The Auroras of Autumn* (1950). Although he rarely gave readings of his work, Stevens delivered a number of lectures on poetry, some of which were published as *The Necessary Angel* (1951). He also received several awards, including the prestigious Bollingen Prize in Poetry in 1950 and the Pulitzer Prize for his *Collected Poems* (1954). Stevens died at his home in Hartford on August 2, 1955.

Reading Stevens's Poetry.   In 1914, when Stevens was thirty-five, his poems began to appear in little magazines such as *Trend; Rogue; Others: A Magazine of the New Verse*; and *Poetry*, where portions of his most famous poem, "Sunday Morning," appeared later in 1915. Stevens subsequently included both poems in his first collection, *Harmonium* (1923), the title of which suggests his emphasis on the harmonious order that could be achieved only through the power of the poetic imagination. Most of the other poems in the following selection were also first collected in *Harmonium*, which was described by some critics as the most remarkable first book by any modernist poet and has been compared in originality and innovation to Walt Whitman's first edition of *Leaves of Grass* (1855). In a review of the volume in *Poetry*, Harriet Monroe advised her readers: "If one seeks sheer beauty of sound, phrase, rhythm, packed with prismatically colored ideas by a mind at once wise and whimsical, one should open one's eyes and ears, sharpen one's wits, widen one's sympathies to include rare and exquisite aspects of life, and then run for this volume of iridescent poems." In 1931, Stevens published a second edition of *Harmonium*, in which he

bedfordstmartins.com/ americanlit for research links on Stevens omitted some poems and added fourteen others, including his World War I poem "The Death of a Soldier." The poise, restraint, and relative austerity of that early poem anticipated the characteristics of much of his later work, represented in the following selection by "Of Modern Poetry" (1940) – among the poems that most forcefully convey his conception of the role of the poet and poetry in the twentieth century. The texts are taken from *The Collected Poems of Wallace Stevens* (1954).

SUNDAY MORNING[1]

I

Complacencies of the peignoir,[2] and late
Coffee and oranges in a sunny chair,
And the green freedom of a cockatoo
Upon a rug mingle to dissipate
The holy hush of ancient sacrifice.   5
She dreams a little, and she feels the dark
Encroachment of that old catastrophe,
As a calm darkens among water-lights.
The pungent oranges and bright, green wings
Seem things in some procession of the dead,   10
Winding across wide water, without sound.
The day is like wide water, without sound,
Stilled for the passing of her dreaming feet
Over the seas, to silent Palestine,
Dominion of the blood and sepulchre.[3]   15

II

Why should she give her bounty to the dead?
What is divinity if it can come
Only in silent shadows and in dreams?
Shall she not find in comforts of the sun,
In pungent fruit and bright, green wings, or else   20

---

1. **Sunday Morning:** Harriet Monroe omitted stanzas II, III, and VI when she published the poem in the November 1915 issue of her magazine, *Poetry*. Stevens agreed to the omissions but suggested that the remaining stanzas be printed I, VIII, IV, V, and VII, the order in which they appeared in *Poetry*. But he restored the omitted stanzas and the original order of the stanzas when he published the poem in his first collection, *Harmonium* (1923).
2. **peignoir:** A woman's light dressing gown or robe.
3. **sepulchre:** The tomb in Palestine where Christ's body was placed after his crucifixion, the "ancient sacrifice" alluded to in line 5 of the stanza.

In any balm or beauty of the earth,
Things to be cherished like the thought of heaven?
Divinity must live within herself:
Passions of rain, or moods in falling snow;
Grievings in loneliness, or unsubdued   25
Elations when the forest blooms; gusty
Emotions on wet roads on autumn nights;
All pleasures and all pains, remembering
The bough of summer and the winter branch.
These are the measures destined for her soul.   30

III

Jove[4] in the clouds had his inhuman birth.
No mother suckled him, no sweet land gave
Large-mannered motions to his mythy mind
He moved among us, as a muttering king,
Magnificent, would move among his hinds,   35
Until our blood, commingling, virginal,
With heaven, brought such requital to desire
The very hinds discerned it, in a star.[5]
Shall our blood fail? Or shall it come to be
The blood of paradise? And shall the earth   40
Seem all of paradise that we shall know?
The sky will be much friendlier then than now,
A part of labor and a part of pain,
And next in glory to enduring love,
Not this dividing and indifferent blue.   45

IV

She says, "I am content when wakened birds,
Before they fly, test the reality
Of misty fields, by their sweet questionings;
But when the birds are gone, and their warm fields
Return no more, where, then, is paradise?"   50
There is not any haunt of prophecy,
Nor any old chimera[6] of the grave,
Neither the golden underground, nor isle

---

4. **Jove:** The English name for Jupiter, the lord of the sky and ruler of the gods in Roman mythology.
5. **hinds . . . in a star:** *Hinds* is an archaic term for peasants or rustics, an allusion to the shepherds who came to the manger to see Joseph, Mary, and the newly born Jesus, whose birth was signaled by the star of Bethlehem.
6. **chimera:** A savage, fire-breathing monster in Greek mythology.

Melodious, where spirits gat them home,
Nor visionary south, nor cloudy palm   55
Remote on heaven's hill, that has endured
As April's green endures; or will endure
Like her remembrance of awakened birds,
Or her desire for June and evening, tipped
By the consummation of the swallow's wings.   60

V

She says, "But in contentment I still feel
The need of some imperishable bliss."
Death is the mother of beauty; hence from her,
Alone, shall come fulfilment to our dreams
And our desires. Although she strews the leaves   65
Of sure obliteration on our paths,
The path sick sorrow took, the many paths
Where triumph rang its brassy phrase, or love
Whispered a little out of tenderness,
She makes the willow shiver in the sun   70
For maidens who were wont to sit and gaze
Upon the grass, relinquished to their feet.
She causes boys to pile new plums and pears
On disregarded plate. The maidens taste
And stray impassioned in the littering leaves.   75

VI

Is there no change of death in paradise?
Does ripe fruit never fall? Or do the boughs
Hang always heavy in that perfect sky,
Unchanging, yet so like our perishing earth,
With rivers like our own that seek for seas   80
They never find, the same receding shores
That never touch with inarticulate pang?
Why set the pear upon those river-banks
Or spice the shores with odors of the plum?
Alas, that they should wear our colors there,   85
The silken weavings of our afternoons,
And pick the strings of our insipid lutes!
Death is the mother of beauty, mystical,
Within whose burning bosom we devise
Our earthly mothers waiting, sleeplessly.   90

VII

Supple and turbulent, a ring of men
Shall chant in orgy on a summer morn
Their boisterous devotion to the sun,
Not as a god, but as a god might be,
Naked among them, like a savage source.   95
Their chant shall be a chant of paradise,
Out of their blood, returning to the sky;
And in their chant shall enter, voice by voice,
The windy lake wherein their lord delights,
The trees, like serafin,[7] and echoing hills,   100
That choir among themselves long afterward.
They shall know well the heavenly fellowship
Of men that perish and of summer morn.
And whence they came and whither they shall go
The dew upon their feet shall manifest.   105

VIII

She hears, upon that water without sound,
A voice that cries, "The tomb in Palestine
Is not the porch of spirits lingering.
It is the grave of Jesus, where he lay."
We live in an old chaos of the sun,   110
Or old dependency of day and night,
Or island solitude, unsponsored, free,
Of that wide water, inescapable.
Deer walk upon our mountains, and the quail
Whistle about us their spontaneous cries;   115
Sweet berries ripen in the wilderness;
And, in the isolation of the sky,
At evening, casual flocks of pigeons make
Ambiguous undulations as they sink,
Downward to darkness, on extended wings.   120

[1915, 1954]

---

7. **serafin:** Usually spelled *seraphim*, angels who in Christian theology occupy the highest rank of the celestial hierarchy.

THIRTEEN WAYS OF LOOKING
AT A BLACKBIRD

I

Among twenty snowy mountains,
The only moving thing
Was the eye of the blackbird.

II

I was of three minds,
Like a tree   5
In which there are three blackbirds.

III

The blackbird whirled in the autumn winds.
It was a small part of the pantomime.

IV

A man and a woman
Are one.   10
A man and a woman and a blackbird
Are one.

V

I do not know which to prefer,
The beauty of inflections
Or the beauty of innuendoes,   15
The blackbird whistling
Or just after.

VI

Icicles filled the long window
With barbaric glass.
The shadow of the blackbird   20
Crossed it, to and fro.
The mood
Traced in the shadow
An indecipherable cause.

VII

O thin men of Haddam,[1]   25
Why do you imagine golden birds?
Do you not see how the blackbird
Walks around the feet
Of the women about you?

VIII

I know noble accents   30
And lucid, inescapable rhythms;
But I know, too,
That the blackbird is involved
In what I know.

IX

When the blackbird flew out of sight,   35
It marked the edge
Of one of many circles.

X

At the sight of blackbirds
Flying in a green light,
Even the bawds of euphony   40
Would cry out sharply.

XI

He rode over Connecticut
In a glass coach.
Once, a fear pierced him,
In that he mistook   45
The shadow of his equipage
For blackbirds.

---

1. **Haddam:** A city in Connecticut. In a letter written in 1953, Stevens explained: "The thin men of Haddam are entirely fictitious although some years ago one of the citizens of that place wrote to ask what I had in mind. I just liked the name."

XII

The river is moving.
The blackbird must be flying.

XIII

It was evening all afternoon.   50
It was snowing
And it was going to snow.
The blackbird sat
In the cedar-limbs.

[1917, 1954]

THE DEATH OF A SOLDIER[1]

Life contracts and death is expected,
As in a season of autumn.
The soldier falls.

He does not become a three-days personage,
Imposing his separation,   5
Calling for pomp.

Death is absolute and without memorial,
As in a season of autumn,
When the wind stops,

When the wind stops and, over the heavens,   10
The clouds go, nevertheless,
In their direction.

[1918, 1954]

---

1. **The Death of a Soldier:** This poem was originally part of a poetic sequence, "Lettres d'un Soldat," published in *Poetry* in May 1918. Stevens was inspired by and drew upon his reading of *Lettres d'un soldat*, a collection of letters from the trenches written by Eugène Lemercier, a young French painter who was killed at the front in World War I.

ANECDOTE OF THE JAR

I placed a jar in Tennessee,
And round it was, upon a hill.
It made the slovenly wilderness
Surround that hill.

The wilderness rose up to it,   5
And sprawled around, no longer wild.
The jar was round upon the ground
And tall and of a port in air.

It took dominion everywhere.
The jar was gray and bare.   10
It did not give of bird or bush,
Like nothing else in Tennessee.

[1919, 1954]

THE SNOW MAN

One must have a mind of winter
To regard the frost and the boughs
Of the pine-trees crusted with snow;

And have been cold a long time
To behold the junipers shagged with ice,   5
The spruces rough in the distant glitter

Of the January sun; and not to think
Of any misery in the sound of the wind,
In the sound of a few leaves,

Which is the sound of the land   10
Full of the same wind
That is blowing in the same bare place

For the listener, who listens in the snow,
And, nothing himself, beholds
Nothing that is not there and the nothing that is.   15

[1921, 1954]

TEA AT THE PALAZ OF HOON[1]

Not less because in purple[2] I descended
The western day through what you called
The loneliest air, not less was I myself.

What was the ointment sprinkled on my beard?[3]

---

1. **Tea at the Palaz of Hoon:** The title suggests a tea ceremony or the ritual of afternoon tea at the palatial residence of the poem's narrator, an imaginary character named Hoon.
2. **in purple:** Dressed in purple, the color of royalty.
3. **ointment . . . beard:** The ointment is suggestive of the anointing oil Moses sprinkles on the head of Aaron to consecrate him as the first High Priest (Leviticus 8:12).

What were the hymns that buzzed beside my ears?   5
What was the sea whose tide swept through me there?

Out of my mind the golden ointment rained,
And my ears made the blowing hymns they heard.
I was myself the compass of that sea:

I was the world in which I walked, and what I saw   10
Or heard or felt came not but from myself;
And there I found myself more truly and more strange.

[1921, 1954]

THE EMPEROR OF ICE-CREAM

Call the roller of big cigars,
The muscular one, and bid him whip
In kitchen cups concupiscent curds.[1]
Let the wenches dawdle in such dress
As they are used to wear, and let the boys   5
Bring flowers in last month's newspapers.
Let be be finale of seem.
The only emperor is the emperor of ice-cream.

Take from the dresser of deal,[2]
Lacking the three glass knobs, that sheet   10
On which she embroidered fantails[3] once
And spread it so as to cover her face.
If her horny feet protrude, they come
To show how cold she is, and dumb.
Let the lamp affix its beam.   15
The only emperor is the emperor of ice-cream.

[1922, 1954]

---

1. **concupiscent curds:** That is, lustful *curds*, a soft white substance formed by curdling or coagulating milk.
2. **deal:** Inexpensive fir or pine wood.
3. **fantails:** Pigeons with broad, fan-shaped tails.

OF MODERN POETRY

The poem of the mind in the act of finding
What will suffice. It has not always had
To find: the scene was set; it repeated what
Was in the script.
          Then the theatre was changed   5
To something else. Its past was a souvenir.
It has to be living, to learn the speech of the place.
It has to face the men of the time and to meet
The women of the time. It has to think about war
And it has to find what will suffice. It has   10
To construct a new stage. It has to be on that stage
And, like an insatiable actor, slowly and
With meditation, speak words that in the ear,
In the delicatest ear of the mind, repeat,
Exactly, that which it wants to hear, at the sound   15
Of which, an invisible audience listens,
Not to the play, but to itself, expressed
In an emotion as of two people, as of two
Emotions becoming one. The actor is
A metaphysician in the dark, twanging   20
An instrument, twanging a wily string that gives
Sounds passing through sudden rightnesses, wholly
Containing the mind, below which it cannot descend,
Beyond which it has no will to rise,
          It must   25
Be the finding of a satisfaction, and may
Be of a man skating, a woman dancing, a woman
Combing. The poem of the act of the mind.

[1940, 1954]

Mina Loy

[1882-1966]

Born Mina Gertrude Lowy in London on December 27, 1882, Loy was the daughter of Julia Bryan, a Protestant, and Sigmund Lowy, a prosperous Jewish tailor whose ancestors had emigrated from Hungary. Loy and her younger sister were educated at home by governesses and then briefly sent to school. From an early age, she was drawn to art, an interest that her

Mina Loy

This passport photo was taken in the 1920s, about the time Loy published her first book of poetry, *Lunar Baedecker* (1923).

father encouraged. But her mother objected that studying art was not a suitable activity for a young society woman, who should stay at home and prepare for marriage. Nonetheless, after Loy finished her minimal formal education in 1896, her parents permitted her to attend art school, first in London and later for a year in Munich, Germany. In 1900, she returned home to London, where she continued her studies and met another young art student, Stephen Haweis. They moved to Paris and were married there in 1903. Instead of taking his name, however, she changed her name to Loy. She later told her daughters that the name was derived from the French word *loi*, or law, implicitly asserting that she would be a law unto herself.

Loy and Haweis became deeply involved in new movements in the arts in Europe. Through Gertrude Stein, Loy met other avant-garde artists, and in 1906 she was elected as a member of the Salon d'Automne (Autumn Salon), an annual exhibition that featured the work of the most innovative painters of the period, including Henri Matisse and Pablo Picasso. That year, she and Haweis moved to Florence, where Loy gave birth to a daughter in 1907 and a son in 1909. But she and her husband were increasingly estranged. Loy was drawn into an expatriate group that gathered around Mabel Dodge, a wealthy patron of the arts, at whose villa Loy met a number of American intellectuals and writers, including Carl Van Vechten, who would later serve as her informal literary agent in New York City. After Haweis left her in 1913, Loy had brief affairs with Filippo Marinetti and Giovanni Papini, two of the leaders of Italian futurism, a revolutionary movement that ridiculed tradition and called upon artists to embrace the new realities of urban and industrial life. Inspired by the movement, Loy in 1914 published her first poem, "Aphorisms on Futurism," in *Camera Work*, edited by Van Vechten's friend Alfred Stieglitz. At the same time, Loy deeply resented the misogynistic attitudes common among the male futurists. Adopting their hostile posture toward tradition and their strategy of promoting futurism by publishing militant manifestos, Loy wrote a "Feminist Manifesto," in which she advised women: "If you want to realize yourselves . . . all your pet illusions must be unmasked. The lies of centuries have got to be discarded."

Although she continued to paint, Loy gained greater notoriety as a poet and a public personality. She exploded on the literary scene when her four-part "Love Songs" appeared in the July 1915 issue of *Others: A Magazine of the New Verse*, published in New York City. After she moved there in the fall of 1916, Loy became known for both her iconoclastic poetry and her bohemian lifestyle in Greenwich Village, and she was soon profiled in an article in the *New York Evening Sun* as the representative "Modern Woman." She met Marianne Moore, Wallace Stevens, and William Carlos

Williams and other contributors to *Others*. Loy was also involved with a group of avant-garde European artists and writers who fled to Greenwich Village during World War I, including Arthur Cravan, an English writer and professional boxer associated with the nihilistic, antibourgeois movement Dada, or Dadaism. When Loy's divorce from Haweis was final in late 1917, she and Cravan traveled to Mexico, where they were married in 1918. After World War I ended, the poverty-stricken couple decided to return to Europe. Loy, who was pregnant, took a hospital ship to Buenos Aires. Since they could only afford one ticket, Cravan tried to sail there in his own small boat and was apparently lost at sea. Loy went on to London, where she gave birth to their daughter in 1919. Seeking information about Cravan's fate, she returned to the United States before settling with her children in Paris. There, she published her first book of poetry, *Lunar Baedecker* (1923), as well as extended portions of an ambitious poetic allegory of her life, *Anglo-Mongrels and the Rose*, which appeared in 1923 and 1925.

Those publications represented the high point of Loy's career as a poet. To support herself and her children, she opened a retail shop to sell lighting fixtures and other decorative objects she designed. She later worked as the Paris agent for her son-in-law's art gallery in New York City. Her friends there organized exhibitions of her paintings in 1925 and again in 1933. She returned to the United States three years later, becoming a citizen in 1946. Although she continued to write poetry during these years, Loy displayed little interest in publication, and her second book did not appear until 1958, when *Lunar Baedecker & Time-Tables* was published with an introduction by William Carlos Williams. Loy also produced three-dimensional assemblages, what she called "experiments in junk," found objects from the streets of the Bowery, or "Skid Row," the impoverished area where she lived in New York City. Some of them were exhibited there as "Constructions" in 1959. Loy died in Aspen, Colorado, where she had moved to be near her daughters, on September 25, 1966.

Mina Loy was endowed from birth with a first-rate intelligence and a sensibility which has plagued her all her life facing a shoddy world.
– William Carlos Williams

Reading Loy's *Love Songs*. Loy began to write this poetic sequence early in 1915, when she was living in Florence in the aftermath of her failed marriage and two painful affairs. The first four poems in the sequence were a record of her "utter defeat in the sex war," as Loy described them, and she was initially hesitant about having them published. In a letter to Carl Van Vechten, she worried that the poems were "rather pretty – rather mawkish – probably a little indecent." Nonetheless, the four poems appeared as "Love Songs" in the first issue of the little magazine *Others* (July 1915) and in *Others, An Anthology of the New Verse*, published in 1916. When she moved to New York City later that year, Loy discovered that the poems had excited considerable controversy. Many of her fellow modernists admired her experimental verse and her candid exploration of female desire and the sexual experience of women. But most critics dismissed the poems as lewd and artistically crude. Undeterred, Loy wrote an extended, thirty-four-poem sequence that was published as *Songs to Joannes* in the

Mina Loy, *Consider Your Grandmother's Stays*

Loy's satirical drawing dates from 1916, the year after she published the first version of *Love Songs*. The Victorian corset, with its vertical whalebone "stays," was a rigid undergarment that was tightly cinched with laces in order to create an exaggerated "hourglass" figure. For many modern women, the painfully uncomfortable corset was a symbol of female confinement and the restricted roles women were forced to play.

bedfordstmartins.com/
americanlit for research
links on Loy

April 1917 issue of *Others*. In 1923, Loy published a revised and compressed version of that sequence as *Love Songs* in her collection *Lunar Baedecker*. Throughout her revisions, Loy maintained her commitment to a radical subversion, not only of the male-dominated tradition of love poetry, but also of conventional poetic forms. Certainly, all three versions of the poetic sequence display some of the most striking aspects of her verse, including her ironic wit, her startling imagery, and her unusual vocabulary, an often-dizzying combination of archaic, colloquial, foreign, poetic, and scientific words. The following text of *Love Songs* is that of the first version, as published in *Others: A Magazine of the New Verse* (July 1915).

LOVE SONGS

I

Spawn of fantasies
Sifting the appraisable
Pig Cupid[1]   his rosy snout

---

1. **Cupid:** A variation of *cupido*, or desire (Latin), Cupid was the Roman god of love, usually represented as a cherubic, winged boy with a bow and an arrow.

Rooting erotic garbage
"Once upon a time"   5
Pulls a weed   white star-topped
Among wild oats sown in mucous membrane
I would   an eye in a Bengal light[2]
Eternity in a sky-rocket
Constellations in an ocean   10
Whose rivers run no fresher
Than a trickle of saliva

These are suspect places

I must live in my lantern
Trimming subliminal flicker   15
Virginal   to the bellows
Of experience
                    Colored glass.

II

        The skin-sack
In which a wanton duality
Packed   20
All the completions of my infructuous[3] impulses
Something the shape of a man
To the casual vulgarity of the merely observant
More of a clock-work mechanism
Running down against time   25
To which I am not paced
    My finger-tips are numb from fretting your hair
A God's door-mat
    On the threshold of your mind.

III

We might have coupled   30
In the bed-ridden monopoly of a moment
Or broken flesh with one another
At the profane communion table
Where wine is spilled on promiscuous lips

---

2. **Bengal light**: A colored signal flare.
3. **infructuous**: An early term meaning barren, unfruitful, or unprofitable, rarely used after the nineteenth century.

We might have given birth to a butterfly 35
With the daily news
Printed in blood on its wings.

IV

Once in a *mezzanino*[4]
The starry ceiling
Vaulted an unimaginable family 40
Bird-like abortions
With human throats
And wisdom's eyes
Who wore lamp-shade red dresses
And woolen hair 45

One bore a baby
In a padded *porte-enfant*[5]
Tied with a sarsanet[6] ribbon
To her goose's wings
But for the abominable shadows 50
I would have lived
Among their fearful furniture
To teach them to tell me their secrets
For I had guessed mine
That if I should find YOU 55
And bring you with me
The brood would be swept clean out.

[1915]

---

4. *mezzanino*: Either an apartment one-half story up from the ground floor or, more usually, the lowest balcony of a theater (Italian).
5. *porte-enfant*: Baby carriage (French).
6. sarsanet: Probably a misprint of *sarsenet*, sometimes spelled *sarcenet*, a soft silk fabric.

William Carlos Williams

[1883-1963]

William Carlos Williams was born in Rutherford, a suburb of Paterson, New Jersey, on September 17, 1883. He was the oldest son of recent immigrants, Raquel Hélène Rose Hoheb, of mixed Basque, French, and Jewish descent; and the English-born William George Williams, who had been raised in Puerto Rico. After meeting and marrying there, the couple had moved to the United States in 1882. Named after his father, an advertising executive, and his mother's brother, Carlos Hoheb, a physician, Williams was raised in a culturally diverse family that maintained close ties to friends and relatives in the Caribbean. During his childhood, French and especially Spanish were spoken at home as often as English. He attended public schools in Rutherford and later, while his father was in South America on business, spent two years at boarding schools in Geneva, Switzerland, and Paris. After he returned home in 1899, Williams commuted to Horace Mann High School in New York City, from which he graduated in 1902. His mother had studied painting for three years in Paris, and "her interest in art became my interest in art," as Williams said in his *Autobiography* (1951). He also began keeping notebooks of his writings and "Whitmanesque thoughts," as he called them. Determined to become a writer, he was equally determined to free himself from the necessity of earning a living by writing, so in 1902 Williams enrolled in the School of Dentistry before switching to the School of Medicine at the University of Pennsylvania.

William Carlos Williams

The painter and photographer Charles Sheeler took this portrait of his friend and fellow artist in 1926, by which time Williams was firmly established as a modernist poet and a physician in private practice in Rutherford, New Jersey.

The following decade was crucial to his development as a writer. In Philadelphia, he met the painter Charles Demuth, Hilda Doolittle (who later published as H.D.), and Ezra Pound, who "used to assault me . . . for my lack of education and reading," as Williams humorously recalled. He participated fully in the cultural life of the university, writing poems, playing the violin, and becoming the arts editor of his yearbook. He also diligently prepared himself for a career in medicine, beginning an internship in obstetrics and pediatrics in New York City after his graduation in 1906. Disgusted with corrupt hospital policies, Williams resigned in 1909 and spent the next year studying pediatrics in Germany. After he returned home, Williams began a private medical practice in Rutherford, where he married his fiancée of several years, Florence Herman, in 1912. Although their relationship was later strained by his extramarital affairs, they remained together and raised two sons. As he would do for the next forty years, Williams attended to both his patients and his poetry. He had earlier paid for the publication of his first book, *Poems* (1909), and with Pound's help a second volume, *The Tempers*, was privately printed in London in 1913. That year, Williams published several poems in Harriet Monroe's influential magazine, *Poetry*, and he later became a regular contributor to *Others: A Magazine of the New Verse*. Williams also began to enjoy the company of artists and poets associated with *Others*, including Mina Loy, Marianne Moore, and Wallace Stevens, whom he met during frequent weekend visits to New York City.

Williams will make a poem of a bare fact — just to show you something he noticed.

–Mina Loy

Williams gained a growing reputation for his rough-hewn and home-grown brand of modernism, an extension of the effort to develop a distinctly American poetry begun by Walt Whitman. A note printed on the dust jacket of *Al Que Quiere!* (1917) – "To Him Who Wants It!" – aggressively proclaimed, "This book is a collection of poems by William Carlos Williams. You, gentle reader, will probably not like it, because it is brutally powerful and scornfully crude." He sought to influence the course of American modernism through his poetry, including a collection of prose poems, *Kora in Hell* (1918), and *Sour Grapes* (1921), as well as by joining with the writer Robert McAlmon to start a new magazine, *Contact*, which Williams coedited from 1920 to 1923. But the small-circulation magazine, which was designed to promote the work of what Williams pointedly described as "native artists," and his own writings were far overshadowed by the influential work of the expatriate T. S. Eliot, *The Waste Land* (1922). In an immediate and furious response to Eliot's dense and learned poem, Williams wrote an innovative collection of poems and interspersed prose commentaries, *Spring and All* (1923). He also attempted to counter Eliot's emphasis on European cultural traditions by taking a year off from his medical practice to do the research for *In the American Grain* (1925), an impressionistic book of historical essays in which Williams sought to construct a vital, indigenous tradition for Americans.

During the following decades, Williams tenaciously demonstrated the resources of the American scene for writers in the United States. He continued to publish poems, as well as numerous plays, short stories, and novels, notably *White Mule* (1937), *In the Money* (1940), and *The Build-Up* (1952), a trilogy in which Williams traced the fortunes of several generations of an immigrant family in New Jersey. Still deeply committed to what in an early essay he had described as the writer's "own locality," he explored the history and modern realities of an industrial city in New Jersey in his most ambitious poem, *Paterson*, which was published in five volumes from 1946 to 1958. For American poets seeking an alternative to the dominant tradition of modernism represented by Eliot and Pound, Williams became a hero and role model, the true heir of Walt Whitman. During the 1950s, a series of strokes slowed his work, but Williams continued to write, publishing his final volume of poetry, *Pictures from Brueghel*, in 1962. The volume was awarded the Pulitzer Prize the following year, when the "Doctor-Poet," as he was described in the obituary in the *New York Times*, died at his home in Rutherford on March 4, 1963.

*bedfordstmartins.com/
americanlit for research
links on Williams*

Reading Williams's Poetry.   After his second volume of poetry was published in London in 1913, Williams became a regular contributor to little magazines such as *Poetry, Others*, and the *Dial*. Most of the poems in the following section were first published in those magazines, alongside the work of the other pioneering modernists and practitioners of the "new verse." Certainly, Williams was influenced by the swirl of new

Charles Demuth,
The Figure 5 in Gold
(1928)

Demuth's abstract por-
trait of his close friend
Williams – note the poet's
initials and the names
"Bill" and "Carlos" in the
painting – is a visual
interpretation of and
homage to his poem "The
Great Figure" (1921).

developments in poetry, including imagism. In his *Autobiography* (1951),
however, Williams said that imagism "ran quickly out," and that he
became committed to what he later defined as "objectivism," observing:
"The poem being an object (like a symphony or cubist painting) it must be
the purpose of the poet to make of his words a new form: to invent, that is,
an object consonant with his day." As his reference to cubism indicates,
Williams was deeply interested in developments in the visual arts, and his
poetry reveals his concentrated powers of observation and, often, his
painterly handling of scenes or subjects. His statement also calls attention to his deep commitment to the craft of poetry. Rejecting conventional
metrical patterns and traditional poetic forms, Williams sought to invent
new rhythms, or measures, as well as new forms "consonant with his day."
For him, that meant inventing forms and developing a language, what he
called an "American idiom," in agreement or harmony with the frequently
discordant elements of his own time and place, modern urban and industrial America. Indeed, few twentieth-century poets were so committed to
engaging, finding beauty in, and wresting meaning from the material and
social conditions of life in the United States. The texts of the following
poems are taken from *The Collected Poems of William Carlos Williams*,
Volume 1, edited by A. Walton Litz and Christopher MacGowan (1986); and
Volume 2, edited by Christoper MacGowan (1988).

THE YOUNG HOUSEWIFE

At ten A.M. the young housewife
moves about in negligee[1] behind
the wooden walls of her husband's house.
I pass solitary in my car.

Then again she comes to the curb   5
to call the ice-man, fish-man, and stands
shy, uncorseted, tucking in
stray ends of hair, and I compare her
to a fallen leaf.

The noiseless wheels of my car   10
rush with a crackling sound over
dried leaves as I bow and pass smiling.

[1916, 1986]

---

1. **negligee:** A woman's light dressing gown, often made from a sheer fabric, from *négliger*, "to neglect" (French).

DANSE RUSSE[1]

If I when my wife is sleeping
and the baby and Kathleen[2]
are sleeping
and the sun is a flame-white disc
in silken mists   5
above shining trees, –
if I in my north room
dance naked, grotesquely
before my mirror
waving my shirt round my head   10
and singing softly to myself:
"I am lonely, lonely.
I was born to be lonely,
I am best so!"
If I admire my arms, my face,   15
my shoulders, flanks, buttocks
against the yellow drawn shades, –

---

1. **Danse Russe:** Russian dance (French). Williams, who attended a performance of Sergei Diaghilev's *Ballet Russe* in 1916, especially admired the dancing of the most acclaimed member of the group, Vaslav Nijinsky.
2. **Kathleen:** Kathleen McBride, a young woman who worked in the Williams family home.

Who shall say I am not
the happy genius of my household?

[1916, 1986]

PORTRAIT OF A LADY

Your thighs are appletrees
whose blossoms touch the sky.
Which sky? The sky
where Watteau hung a lady's
slipper. Your knees   5
are a southern breeze – or
a gust of snow. Agh! what
sort of man was Fragonard?[1]
– as if that answered
anything. Ah, yes – below   10
the knees, since the tune
drops that way, it is
one of those white summer days,
the tall grass of your ankles
flickers upon the shore –   15
Which shore? –
the sand clings to my lips –
Which shore?
Agh, petals maybe. How
should I know?   20
Which shore? Which shore?
I said petals from an appletree.

[1920, 1986]

---

1. **Watteau . . . Fragonard:** As the disruptive voice in the poem implies, *The Swing* (c. 1767) – a famous French baroque painting in which a young woman tosses off her slipper as she swings above her semiprone and impassioned lover, who gazes up at her exposed legs – was painted by Jean-Honoré Fragonard (1732-1806), not by his precursor Jean-Antoine Watteau (1684-1721).

WILLOW POEM

It is a willow when summer is over,
a willow by the river
from which no leaf has fallen nor
bitten by the sun
turned orange or crimson.   5
The leaves cling and grow paler,

swing and grow paler
over the swirling waters of the river
as if loath to let go,
they are so cool, so drunk with   10
the swirl of the wind and of the river —
oblivious to winter,
the last to let go and fall
into the water and on the ground.

[1920, 1986]

QUEEN-ANNE'S-LACE

Her body is not so white as
anemone petals nor so smooth — nor
so remote a thing. It is a field
of the wild carrot[1] taking
the field by force; the grass   5
does not raise above it.
Here is no question of whiteness,
white as can be, with a purple mole
at the center of each flower.
Each flower is a hand's span   10
of her whiteness. Wherever
his hand has lain there is
a tiny purple blemish. Each part
is a blossom under his touch
to which the fibres of her being   15
stem one by one, each to its end,
until the whole field is a
white desire, empty, a single stem,
a cluster, flower by flower,
a pious wish to whiteness gone over —   20
or nothing.

[1921, 1986]

---

1. **wild carrot:** A wildflower with broad round heads of tiny white flowers; commonly called Queen Anne's lace.

THE WIDOW'S LAMENT IN SPRINGTIME

Sorrow is my own yard
where the new grass
flames as it has flamed

often before but not
with the cold fire   5
that closes round me this year.
Thirtyfive years
I lived with my husband.
The plumtree is white today
with masses of flowers.   10
Masses of flowers
load the cherry branches
and color some bushes
yellow and some red
but the grief in my heart   15
is stronger than they
for though they were my joy
formerly, today I notice them
and turn away forgetting.
Today my son told me   20
that in the meadows,
at the edge of the heavy woods
in the distance, he saw
trees of white flowers.
I feel that I would like   25
to go there
and fall into those flowers
and sink into the marsh near them.

                                              [1921, 1986]

THE GREAT FIGURE

Among the rain
and lights
I saw the figure 5
in gold
on a red   5
firetruck
moving
tense
unheeded
to gong clangs   10
siren howls
and wheels rumbling
through the dark city.

                                              [1921, 1986]

TO ELSIE[1]

The pure products of America
go crazy —
mountain folk from Kentucky

or the ribbed north end of
Jersey   5
with its isolate lakes and

valleys, its deaf-mutes, thieves
old names
and promiscuity between

devil-may-care men who have taken   10
to railroading
out of sheer lust of adventure —

and young slatterns, bathed
in filth
from Monday to Saturday   15

to be tricked out that night
with gauds[2]
from imaginations which have no

peasant traditions to give them
character   20
but flutter and flaunt

sheer rags — succumbing without
emotion
save numbed terror

under some hedge of choke-cherry   25
or viburnum — [3]
which they cannot express —

Unless it be that marriage
perhaps
with a dash of Indian blood   30

---

1. **To Elsie:** This poem was first published as "XVIII" in Williams's collection of numbered poems and interspersed prose commentaries, *Spring and All* (1923). Elsie was a young, mentally impaired woman from the state orphanage who worked for the Williams family after Kathleen (see "Danse Russe," note 2).
2. **gauds:** Cheap, showy ornaments or trinkets.
3. **choke-cherry or viburnum:** Familiar names of two of the most common flowering and fruit-bearing shrubs indigenous to North America.

will throw up a girl so desolate
so hemmed round
with disease or murder

that she'll be rescued by an
agent —   35
reared by the state and

sent out at fifteen to work in
some hard-pressed
house in the suburbs —

some doctor's family, some Elsie —   40
voluptuous water
expressing with broken

brain the truth about us —
her great
ungainly hips and flopping breasts   45

addressed to cheap
jewelry
and rich young men with fine eyes

as if the earth under our feet
were   50
an excrement of some sky

and we degraded prisoners
destined
to hunger until we eat filth

while the imagination strains   55
after deer
going by fields of goldenrod in

the stifling heat of September
Somehow
it seems to destroy us   60

It is only in isolate flecks that
something
is given off

No one
to witness   65
and adjust, no one to drive the car

[1923, 1986]

THE RED WHEELBARROW[1]

so much depends
upon

a red wheel
barrow

glazed with rain
water

beside the white
chickens

[1923, 1986]

---

1. **The Red Wheelbarrow:** This poem was first published as "XXII" in Williams's collection of numbered poems and interspersed prose commentaries, *Spring and All* (1923).

THIS IS JUST TO SAY

I have eaten
the plums
that were in
the icebox

and which   5
you were probably
saving
for breakfast

Forgive me
they were delicious   10
so sweet
and so cold

[1934, 1986]

A SORT OF A SONG[1]

Let the snake wait under
his weed
and the writing
be of words, slow and quick, sharp
to strike, quiet to wait,   5
sleepless.

---

1. **A Sort of a Song:** Williams changed the title of this poem, which he first published as "A Possible Sort of Song" in the *Old Line* (April 1943), when he collected it in *The Wedge* (1944).

    – through metaphor to reconcile
    the people and the stones.
    Compose. (No ideas
    but in things) Invent!   10
    Saxifrage[2] is my flower that splits
    the rocks.

                                      [1943, 1988]

---

2. **Saxifrage:** A low-growing plant with small white, yellow, or red flowers and succulent leaves, often found growing in narrow crevices in rocks.

Ezra Pound

[1885–1972]

Ezra Loomis Pound was born in October 1885, in Hailey, Idaho, where his father worked in the Government Land Grant Office. His mother, a New Yorker, found life on the frontier difficult, and when Pound was about eighteen months old she took him back East, where his father was subsequently appointed as an assayer in the U.S. Mint in Philadelphia. Pound was raised and educated in suburban Wyncote. He was a precocious student, earning the nickname "Professor" when he was just six years old and publishing his first poem in a local newspaper in 1896. In 1901, a month before his sixteenth birthday, Pound entered the University of Pennsylvania. There, he met Hilda Doolittle (who later published under the initials "H.D."), with whom he became romantically involved, and an aspiring poet who became his lifelong friend, William Carlos Williams. Pound immersed himself in the study of Greek, Latin, and German, but he was indifferent to subjects that did not interest him. Concerned about his mediocre academic record, Pound and his parents decided that he should transfer to Hamilton College, in central New York, where he studied Romance languages, Hebrew, and Anglo-Saxon. After his graduation in 1905, he returned to the University of Pennsylvania on a graduate fellowship and traveled to Spain, Italy, and France. When the fellowship was not renewed, Pound accepted a position teaching Romance languages at Wabash College in Indiana. Dismissed at the end of the first semester for his behavior (a woman evidently spent a night in his room), Pound asked his disappointed but supportive parents to loan him money for a trip to Europe, where he sailed in the summer of 1908.

    During the following years, Pound emerged as a major force in modern poetry. He briefly settled in Venice, where he put together and paid eight dollars for the printing of his first book of poems, *A Lume Spento* ["With Tapers Quenched"] (1908). He then moved on to London, where he met the artist Dorothy Shakespear, whom Pound later married, and a number of major literary figures, including Henry James and the Irish poet William

Ezra Pound

This photograph of Pound, which the prominent photographer Alvin Langdon Coburn took in London in 1913, later appeared in Coburn's book *Men of Mark* (1922).

Butler Yeats. Pound's early collections of poetry attracted critical attention, and he generously encouraged other poets, including T. S. Eliot,
Robert Frost, H.D., and William Carlos Williams, helping them publish and
writing reviews of their work. Pound became the "foreign correspondent"
for and a frequent contributor to Harriet Monroe's Chicago-based *Poetry:
A Magazine of Verse*, and he helped edit other avant-garde literary magazines in London. Pound also organized the imagists, the first modernist
literary group in England and the United States. He edited an anthology of
their poems, *Des Imagistes*, which was published in New York City in 1914,
and a number of his compressed imagist poems later appeared in *Lustra*
(1916). By then, however, Pound had moved away from imagism and helped
launch "vorticism," joining with the English painter Wyndham Lewis and
the young sculptor Henri Gaudier-Brzeska to establish the short-lived
journal of the movement, *Blast* (1914-15). As Pound described it, the
revolutionary movement promised to put "the arts in their rightful place
as the acknowledged guide and lamp of civilization."

That broadly political goal became central to Pound's poetry and other
writings. During World War I, he published *Cathay* (1915), loose translations of ancient Chinese poems, and another work of literary and cultural
translation, *Homage to Sextus Propertius* (1917). In 1920, Pound and his
wife moved from London to Paris, where they lived until 1924, and then on
to Rapallo, Italy. On the Continent, he became close to numerous expatriate artists and writers, including Gertrude Stein and Ernest Hemingway.
Pound also met Olga Rudge, a violinist with whom he had an affair that
lasted until the end of his life. They had a daughter, Mary, in 1926, a few
months before Pound and his wife had a son, Omar. *Personae: The Collected Poems of Ezra Pound* appeared in 1926, but his major poetic project
was the *Cantos*, an epic poem he worked on for nearly fifty years, publishing it in stages before the complete text appeared in 1969. During the
1930s, Pound also published numerous prose works on politics, economics, and culture, including *ABC of Economics* (1933), *ABC of Reading* (1934),
and *Guide to Kulchur* (1938). During the same period, he embraced the Italian movement called "Fascism" – after *fasces*, or bound sticks, the symbol
of political power in ancient Rome – led by Benito Mussolini. Pound's admiration for Mussolini led him to broadcast a series of pro-Axis radio programs from Rome during World War II. In 1943, he was indicted in absentia
for treason by a grand jury in Washington, D.C. At the end of the war, Pound
surrendered in Italy, where he was imprisoned in an American detention
camp in Pisa before being extradited to stand trial in the United States.

Pound's career and literary legacy were consequently defined by the
tension between his political beliefs and his poetic achievements. At his
trial, he was found to be of "unsound mind" and committed to St. Elizabeth's Hospital in Washington, D.C. Although most of his friends had
been repulsed by his pro-Fascist and anti-Semitic statements before and
during the war, Pound was supported by many of the writers he had earlier championed, including T. S. Eliot, Robert Frost, Ernest Hemingway,
Marianne Moore, and William Carlos Williams. In a move that aroused
considerable controversy, Pound was awarded the prestigious Bollingen

Prize for his *Pisan Cantos* (1948), written while he was in prison in Italy, and he later received the Academy of American Poets Award. After the government withdrew the indictment against him in 1958, Pound returned to Italy, where he lived with his wife, close by Olga Rudge, until his death in 1972.

Reading Pound's Early Poetry.   Reflecting on his early career, Pound recalled that the English novelist Ford Maddox Ford had literally rolled on the floor in derision of the stilted, archaic, and self-consciously poetical language of his *Canzoni* (1911). "That roll saved me at least two years, maybe more," Pound added. "It sent me back to my own proper effort, namely, toward using the living tongue." His effort to use "the living tongue"—to employ what Ford characterized as "natural language"—is revealed in the following poems, one of which Pound published in his next collection, *Ripostes* (1912). In a review of the volume, one critic observed that Pound's work was "a vehement protest" against simplistic notions of poetry as merely versification. Pound adapted traditional meters and forms, including blank verse ("Portrait d'une Femme") and the sonnet, even as he began to experiment with freer rhythmical structures. In the final two poems of this group—"A Pact" and "The Rest," both first published in 1913—Pound adopted the free verse of his poetic forefather Walt Whitman to express his reconciliation with Whitman and to address directly contemporary American poets from his triumphant "exile" in London. The texts of the poems are taken from *Personae: The Collected Poems of Ezra Pound* (1949).

Ripostes

Dorothy Shakespear's abstract design for the cover of this early reprint of *Ripostes* (1912) reflects Pound's effort to develop a more modern idiom in the poetry he wrote during the period 1912–13.

PORTRAIT D'UNE FEMME[1]

Your mind and you are our Sargasso Sea,[2]
London has swept about you this score years
And bright ships left you this or that in fee:

---

1. **Portrait d'une Femme:** Portrait of a lady (French).
2. **Sargasso Sea:** A generally calm region of the Atlantic Ocean between the Azores and the Caribbean Sea, so called because of the brown seaweed (also known as *sargassum* weed) floating in the water.

Ideas, old gossip, oddments of all things,
Strange spars of knowledge and dimmed wares of price.   5
Great minds have sought you — lacking someone else.
You have been second always. Tragical?
No. You preferred it to the usual thing:
One dull man, dulling and uxorious,
One average mind — with one thought less, each year.   10
Oh, you are patient, I have seen you sit
Hours, where something might have floated up.
And now you pay one. Yes, you richly pay.
You are a person of some interest, one comes to you
And takes strange gain away: 15
Trophies fished up; some curious suggestion;
Fact that leads nowhere; and a tale or two,
Pregnant with mandrakes,[3] or with something else
That might prove useful and yet never proves,
That never fits a corner or shows use,   20
Or finds its hour upon the loom of days:
The tarnished, gaudy, wonderful old work;
Idols and ambergris and rare inlays,
These are your riches, your great store; and yet
For all this sea-hoard of deciduous things,   25
Strange woods half sodden, and new brighter stuff:
In the slow float of differing light and deep,
No! there is nothing ! In the whole and all,
Nothing that's quite your own.
                    Yet this is you.   30

[1912, 1949]

3. **mandrakes:** A Mediterranean plant with white or purple flowers, large yellow berries, and a forked fleshy root that bears a resemblance to the human form. In early times, the plant was widely used for medicinal and magical purposes.

A Pact[1]

I make a pact with you, Walt Whitman —
I have detested you long enough.
I come to you as a grown child

1. **A Pact:** Pound was deeply ambivalent about Walt Whitman (1819–1892), to whom he offered this "pact," or formal agreement. In a 1909 essay, "What I Feel about Walt Whitman," Pound acknowledged: "The vital part of my message, taken from the sap and fibre of America, is the same as his." At the same time, Pound was sharply critical of what he viewed as the artistic crudity of Whitman's poetry, observing in a letter to his father in 1913 that "it is impossible to read [*Leaves of Grass*] without swearing at the author almost continuously."

Who has had a pig-headed father;
I am old enough now to make friends.
It was you that broke the new wood,
Now is a time for carving.
We have one sap and one root —
Let there be commerce between us.

[1913, 1949]

THE REST

O helpless few in my country,
O remnant enslaved!

Artists broken against her,
A-stray, lost in the villages,
Mistrusted, spoken-against,   5

Lovers of beauty, starved,
Thwarted with systems,
Helpless against the control;

You who can not wear yourselves out
By persisting to successes,   10
You who can only speak,
Who can not steel yourselves into reiteration;

You of the finer sense,
Broken against false knowledge,
You who can know at first hand,   15
Hated, shut in, mistrusted:

Take thought:
I have weathered the storm,
I have beaten out my exile.

[1913, 1949]

Reading Pound's "In a Station of the Metro."   This is probably the
most famous of all imagist poems. According to Pound, it was inspired by
a fleeting moment "in the Paris Underground," or subway system, where in
the jostle he "saw a beautiful face, and then, turning suddenly, another and
another, and then a beautiful child's face, and then another beautiful
face." But he could not "find words" for what that made him feel, or discover a way "to tell the adventure," until he thought to follow the example
of poets in Japan, "where sixteen syllables are counted enough for a poem
if you arrange and punctuate them properly." Adapting the form of the Japanese haiku or hokku, Pound made a poem of nineteen syllables, the first
and final versions of which are printed below. The text of the first version,

with its unusual spacing and punctuation, is taken from *Poetry* (April 1913), where Pound included it among twelve poems he published as "Contemporania." The text of the final version, which first appeared in *Lustra* (1916), is taken from *Personae: The Collected Poems of Ezra Pound* (1949).

IN A STATION OF THE METRO

The apparition   of these faces   in the crowd   :
Petals   on a wet, black   bough   .

[1913]

IN A STATION OF THE METRO

The apparition of these faces in the crowd;
Petals on a wet, black bough.

[1916, 1949]

Reading Pound's *Cathay.*   T. S. Eliot called Pound "the inventor of Chinese poetry for our time," a tribute to the influence of the "translations" he collected in *Cathay* (1915). Pound's free-verse translations were based on literal versions of classical Chinese poems in the notebooks of the American scholar Ernest Fenollosa. Pound, who had read Fenollosa's essays on Chinese poetry in *Poetry*, met his widow in London in 1913. He subsequently became Fenollosa's literary executor and edited some of his work, including an essay "The Chinese Written Character as a Medium for Poetry" (1919). Pound was especially drawn to the work of the eighth-century Tang dynasty poet Li Po, the author of the four poems printed below. (Pound refers to him as *Rihaku*, a transliteration of the Japanese spelling of his name.) In a headnote to a reprint of "The River Merchant's Wife: A Letter" in the journal *Current Opinion*, the editor observed, "Any poem that has come down to us through twelve centuries of chance and change has an appeal to our curiosity," as well as "an appeal to the unchanging heart of mankind." At the same time, Pound's free-verse lyrics were in many ways strikingly contemporary in poetic technique and subject matter. As scholars have suggested, in selecting and translating Li Po's poems about leave-taking, separation, and the sorrows of men fighting on the frontiers of a collapsing kingdom, Pound in *Cathay* used the ancient Chinese texts to give expression to the experiences and feelings of many Europeans during the first year of World War I. Shortly before his death in the trenches in France, the sculptor Henri Gaudier-Brzeska wrote his friend Pound that he had read parts of *Cathay* to his troops and that "the poems depict our situation in a wonderful way." The texts are taken from *Personae: The Collected Poems of Ezra Pound* (1949).

From CATHAY

THE RIVER-MERCHANT'S WIFE: A LETTER

While my hair was still cut straight across my forehead
I played about the front gate, pulling flowers.
You came by on bamboo stilts, playing horse,
You walked about my seat, playing with blue plums.
And we went on living in the village of Chokan:[1]   5
Two small people, without dislike or suspicion.

At fourteen I married My Lord you.
I never laughed, being bashful.
Lowering my head, I looked at the wall.
Called to, a thousand times, I never looked back.   10

At fifteen I stopped scowling,
I desired my dust to be mingled with yours
Forever and forever and forever.
Why should I climb the look out?

At sixteen you departed,   15
You went into far Ku-to-yen,[2] by the river of swirling eddies,
And you have been gone five months.
The monkeys make sorrowful noise overhead.

You dragged your feet when you went out.
By the gate now, the moss is grown, the different mosses,   20
Too deep to clear them away!
The leaves fall early this autumn, in wind.
The paired butterflies are already yellow with August
Over the grass in the West garden;
They hurt me. I grow older.   25
If you are coming down through the narrows of the river Kiang,[3]
Please let me know beforehand,
And I will come out to meet you
            As far as Cho-fu-Sa.[4]

                              By Rihaku
                              [1915, 1949]

---

1. **Chokan:** The Japanese spelling of *Ch'ang-kan*, a village near Nanjing, China, on the south bank of the Yangtze River.
2. **Ku-to-yen:** An island on the Ch'u-t'ang River.
3. **Kiang:** The Japanese spelling of the Ch'u-t'ang River (see note 2).
4. **Cho-fu-Sa:** Ch'ang-feng-sha, a beach several hundred miles upstream from Nanjing (see note 1).

THE JEWEL STAIRS' GRIEVANCE

The jewelled steps are already quite white with dew,
It is so late that the dew soaks my gauze stockings,
And I let down the crystal curtain
And watch the moon through the clear autumn.

By Rihaku

Note — Jewel stairs, therefore a palace. Grievance, therefore
there is something to complain of. Gauze stockings, therefore a
court lady, not a servant who complains. Clear autumn, therefore he has no excuse on account of weather. Also she has come
early, for the dew has not merely whitened the stairs, but has
soaked her stockings. The poem is especially prized because she
utters no direct reproach.[1]

[1915, 1949]

---

1. **Jewel . . . reproach:** Pound's note is here printed following the poem, as it was in *Cathay.*

LAMENT OF THE FRONTIER GUARD

By the North Gate, the wind blows full of sand,
Lonely from the beginning of time until now!
Trees fall, the grass goes yellow with autumn.
I climb the towers and towers
      to watch out the barbarous land: 5
Desolate castle, the sky, the wide desert.
There is no wall left to this village.
Bones white with a thousand frosts,
High heaps, covered with trees and grass;
Who brought this to pass?   10
Who has brought the flaming imperial anger?
Who has brought the army with drums and with kettle-drums?
Barbarous kings.
A gracious spring, turned to blood-ravenous autumn,
A turmoil of wars-men, spread over the middle kingdom,   15
Three hundred and sixty thousand,
And sorrow, sorrow like rain.
Sorrow to go, and sorrow, sorrow returning.
Desolate, desolate fields,
And no children of warfare upon them,   20
      No longer the men for offence and defence.
Ah, how shall you know the dreary sorrow at the North Gate,

With Rihoku's na
And we guardsme

By Rihaku
[1915, 1949]

---

1. **Rihoku's name forg**　　　　　　　　ling of the name of the famous Chinese general Li
Mu, who died in a bat　　　　　　　3 BCE.

H.D. (Hilda Doolittle)

[1886-1961]

The poet and novelist who signed her name H.D. was born Hilda Doolittle on September 10, 1886, in Bethlehem, Pennsylvania. She was the daughter of Charles Leander Doolittle, a professor of astronomy at Lehigh University, and Helen Eugenia Wolle Doolittle. H.D.'s mother, a teacher of painting and music, was a descendant of the founders of Bethlehem, the first Moravian settlement in North America. H.D. spent her formative years in the midst of the tight-knit and deeply religious Moravian community, whose mystical traditions she explored in her later autobiographical writings. In 1895, her family moved to Philadelphia, where her father became the director of the Flower Observatory at the University

H.D.

Inscribed to her close friend Marianne Moore, this photograph was taken about 1921, by which time Hilda Doolittle had firmly established her literary identity as the innovative modernist poet H.D.

of Pennsylvania. H.D. recalled that the move for her was traumatic and "drove me in, introverted me," as she put it. When she was fifteen, H.D. met Ezra Pound, then sixteen and a student at the University of Pennsylvania. After graduating from a Quaker school, H.D. enrolled as a day student at Bryn Mawr College in 1904. She made a number of friends, including Marianne Moore and William Carlos Williams, and apparently fell in love with Frances Gregg, a young artist studying at the Pennsylvania Academy of Fine Arts. In 1905, after Pound completed his undergraduate degree at Hamilton College and returned to do graduate work at the University of Pennsylvania, he and H.D. announced their engagement. Complaining of ill health and discouraged by her poor grades, H.D. withdrew from Bryn Mawr. She lived at home for the next five years, writing some stories that she published under the pen name Edith Gray.

The year 1910 marked a turning point for H.D. Her on-again, off-again engagement to Pound was renewed, and he convinced her to join him in London. After she settled there in 1911, she discovered that Pound was engaged to another woman, Dorothy Shakespear. Despite the urging of H.D.'s protective parents, who wanted her to return home, she insisted on staying in London. She remained close to Pound, who introduced her to a number of literary figures, including the English poet and novelist Richard Aldington. H.D., Pound, and Aldington worked and studied together, writing innovative poetry that came to be known as "imagist" verse. After Pound became the foreign correspondent for the Chicago-based *Poetry: A Magazine of Verse*, edited by Harriet Monroe, he sent her three of H.D.'s poems, which he signed "H.D., *Imagiste*." The poems appeared under that distinctive signature in the January 1913 issue of *Poetry*. She and Aldington were married later that year, and they became prominent members of a London literary circle that included the English novelist and poet D. H. Lawrence, with whom H.D. exchanged manuscripts. Her work appeared along with that of a range of English and American poets in *Des Imagistes* (1914), an anthology edited by Pound. She was caught in the middle of the struggle for control of the movement waged between Pound and his rival Amy Lowell, who included H.D.'s poems in her annual anthologies, *Some Imagist Poets* (1915–17). Those anthologies helped establish H.D.'s literary reputation, and in 1916 she published her first book of poems, *Sea Garden*. When Aldington was drafted into the army, H.D. took over his position as literary editor of the *Egoist*, publishing poems and seeking to keep the spark of modern poetry alive in England during the bleak years of World War I.

After the war, H.D. asserted growing personal and professional independence. In 1918, her "modern" marriage to Aldington collapsed, undermined by the stillbirth of their only child, Aldington's infidelities, and their wartime separation. H.D. subsequently had an affair with the painter Cecil Gray, the father of her daughter, Frances Perdita Aldington, born in 1919. By then, H.D. had met and fallen in love with the wealthy heiress and writer Winifred Ellerman, who published under the name Bryher. Although they frequently kept different residences and had numerous other relationships, including Bryher's two marriages, she and H.D. became lifelong companions. Together, they moved to Paris, where they were actively involved in the expatriate community of artists and writers drawn there during the 1920s. H.D. published *Hymen* (1921), *Heliodora* (1924), and her *Collected Poems* (1925), as well as a play, *Hippolytus Temporizes* (1927). She also wrote novels, notably *HERmione* (written in 1927, published in 1981), in which H.D. explored the conflicts between heterosexual and lesbian love and desire in her early relationships with Pound and Frances Gregg. As a result of Bryher's involvement in POOL Productions, H.D. also appeared in two films, *Foothills* (1927) and *Borderline* (1930). She and Bryher later lived in Switzerland and traveled throughout Europe. During 1933 and 1934, H.D. became a patient and pupil of Sigmund Freud in Vienna. She broke away from her earlier imagist verse in *Trilogy* (1944–46), a three-part poem inspired by her experiences during the London blitz. During the final fifteen years of her life, H.D. wrote steadily, publishing memoirs, novels, and poetry, including *Helen in Egypt* (1961), a feminist retelling of the origins of the Trojan War. In 1960, H.D. became the first woman to receive the Award of Merit Medal for Poetry of the American Academy of Arts and Letters. She died in Zurich, Switzerland, on September 28, 1961.

bedfordstmartins.com/ americanlit for research links on H.D.

Reading H.D.'s Poetry.   In a letter accompanying the three poems by H.D. he sent to Harriet Monroe in 1912, Ezra Pound described the work as "some *modern* stuff by an American," adding: "I say modern, for it is the laconic speech of the Imagistes, even if the subject is classic. . . . It's straight talk, straight as the Greeks!" Pound called attention to some of the most striking aspects of H.D.'s early poetry. As he indicated, it was "modern" because she rejected the verbosity and slackness that Pound and other modernists associated with late Victorian poetry in England. As Pound also indicated, the subject of many of H.D.'s poems was "classic," though she often challenged the patriarchal foundations of ancient myths such as the story of Helen of Troy. For H.D., however, the "Greeks" were not simply a source of subject matter, since she also found aesthetic inspiration in classical poetry, especially in the directness and simple treatment of images characteristic of the surviving fragments of the ancient Greek poet Sappho of Lesbos (c. 630 BCE). Like those fragments, H.D.'s early poems are characterized by their precise language and concentration on a single image or set of related images. She rejected conventional poetic forms, experimenting with both rhythmical patterns and stanza forms in an effort to develop a new poetic idiom. As she observed in a 1919 essay, H.D. thus sought to help readers "get out of the murky, dead, old, thousand-times-explored old world, the dead world of overworked emotions and thoughts." Most of the following poems were first published in the *Egoist*, and several of the other selections appeared in little magazines such as *Poetry*, before H.D. collected them in her first three volumes of poetry, *Sea Garden* (1916), *Hymen* (1921), and *Heliodora* (1924). The texts are taken from her *Collected Poems, 1912-1944*, edited by Louis Martz (1983).

OREAD[1]

> Whirl up, sea —
> whirl your pointed pines,
> splash your great pines
> on our rocks,
> hurl your green over us,
> cover us with your pools of fir.

[1914, 1983]

---

1. **Oread:**   A mountain nymph in Greek mythology.

THE POOL

Are you alive?
I touch you.
You quiver like a sea-fish.
I cover you with my net.
What are you — banded[1] one?

[1915, 1983]

---

1. **banded**: Bound or fastened, as with a band or manacle.

GARDEN[1]

I

You are clear
O rose, cut in rock,
hard as the descent of hail.

I could scrape the colour
from the petals   5
like spilt dye from a rock.

If I could break you
I could break a tree.

If I could stir
I could break a tree —   10
I could break you.

II

O wind, rend open the heat,
cut apart the heat,
rend it to tatters.

Fruit cannot drop   15
through this thick air —
fruit cannot fall into heat
that presses up and blunts
the points of pears
and rounds the grapes.   20

---

1. **Garden**: The poem was initially printed in this two-part format, first in *Poetry* (March 1915) and then in *Sea Garden* (1916). The second section is often printed alone under the title "Heat."

Cut the heat —
plough through it,
turning it on either side
of your path.

[1915, 1983]

SEA ROSE

Rose, harsh rose,
marred and with stint of petals,[1]
meagre flower, thin,
sparse of leaf,

more precious   5
than a wet rose
single on a stem —
you are caught in the drift.

Stunted, with small leaf,
you are flung on the sand,   10
you are lifted
in the crisp sand
that drives in the wind.

Can the spice-rose[2]
drip such acrid fragrance   15
hardened in a leaf?

[1916, 1983]

---

1. **stint of petals:** *Stint* is an early term for a small or limited amount.
2. **spice-rose:** A rose of unknown heritage, with pale pink blossoms and a fragrance that is often described as spicy or tea-like.

LEDA[1]

Where the slow river
meets the tide,
a red swan lifts red wings
and darker beak,
and underneath the purple down   5
of his soft breast
uncurls his coral feet.

---

1. **Leda:** The wife of Tyndareus, a king of Sparta, in Greek mythology. Zeus fell in love with Leda, whom he approached in the form of a swan. The offspring of their union included Helen of Troy.

Through the deep purple
of the dying heat
of sun and mist,   10
the level ray of sun-beam
has caressed
the lily with dark breast,
and flecked with richer gold
its golden crest.   15

Where the slow lifting
of the tide,
floats into the river
and slowly drifts
among the reeds,   20
and lifts the yellow flags,
he floats
where tide and river meet.

Ah kingly kiss —
no more regret   25
nor old deep memories
to mar the bliss;
where the low sedge is thick,
the gold day-lily
outspreads and rests   30
beneath soft fluttering
of red swan wings
and the warm quivering
of the red swan's breast.

[1919, 1983]

HELEN[1]

All Greece hates
the still eyes in the white face,
the lustre as of olives
where she stands,
and the white hands.   5

---

1. **Helen:** Helen of Troy, the beautiful daughter of Zeus and Leda, married King Menelaus of Sparta. Paris, the son of King Priam of Troy, either abducted Helen or convinced her to run away with him to Troy. Determined to bring her back, the Greeks assembled a mighty army and laid siege to Troy. At the end of the decade-long war, the city was destroyed, and Helen returned home with Menelaus.

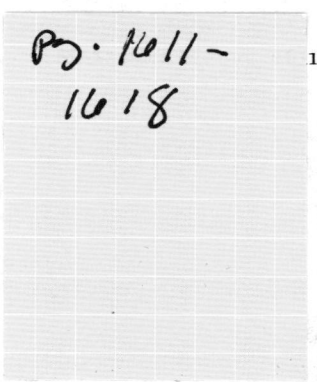

All Greece reviles
the wan face when she smiles,
hating it deeper still
when it grows wan and white,
remembering past enchantments
and past ills.

Greece sees unmoved,
God's daughter, born of love,
the beauty of cool feet
and slenderest knees,
could love indeed the maid,
only if she were laid,
white ash amid funereal cypresses.

15

[1923, 1983]

Marianne Moore
[1887-1972]

Marianne Craig Moore was born in Kirkwood, Missouri, on November 15, 1887, the second child of John and Mary Warner Moore. Several months before Moore's birth, her father was institutionalized for a nervous breakdown following the failure of one of his inventions, and her mother took the couple's year-old son, Warner, to live with her father, John Riddle Warner, a Presbyterian minister in Kirkwood. His deep religious faith strongly shaped his daughter and grandchildren, who lived with him until his death in 1894. Mary Moore then moved with her two children to Pittsburgh and later to Carlisle, Pennsylvania, where she took a job as an English teacher at a preparatory school for girls, the Metzger Institute. Determined to prepare both of her children for college, Mary Moore sent her son to a nearby school for boys and enrolled Moore at Metzger. In 1905, the year after her brother entered Yale, Moore was admitted to Bryn Mawr College. Discouraged by a professor from majoring in English, Moore studied history, law, and politics and minored in biology. But she was actively involved in the college literary magazine, where her earliest poems and stories appeared, and she met other students interested in literature, including Hilda Doolittle, who later published as H.D. During Moore's senior year, she submitted some poems to the *Literary Digest* and the prestigious *Atlantic Monthly*. Although both magazines rejected her work, Moore had already begun to set her sights on a literary career by the time she graduated from Bryn Mawr in 1909.

Marianne Moore

This photograph of Moore appeared in the *New York Times* shortly after the publication of her second collection of poems, *Observations* (1924).

Like other poets of her generation, Moore faced the challenge of finding ways to support herself and her writing. She returned home and enrolled in a secretarial course at Carlisle Commercial College. Following a trip with her mother to Europe, where Moore visited a long list of art museums, she took a job teaching secretarial courses and business English at the Carlisle Industrial Indian School. Moore became active in the suffrage movement and once "climbed a lamppost" in a demonstration for women's right to vote, as she later told her friend Elizabeth Bishop. Moore also continued to write poetry. In 1915, several of her poems appeared in two of the most prominent little magazines of the period, *Others* and *Poetry*. H.D., who became the literary editor of the London-based *Egoist*, published several more of Moore's poems in 1916. That year, she gave up her job in Carlisle and moved with her mother to Chatham, New Jersey, where they lived with and kept house for Moore's brother, the Presbyterian pastor of the Ogden Memorial Church. When he enlisted as a chaplain in the army two years later, Moore and her mother moved to New York City. Working there as a secretary and private tutor and later at a branch of the New York Public Library, Moore became friendly with several poets she admired, especially Wallace Stevens and William Carlos Williams. She also began to correspond with Ezra Pound and T. S. Eliot, both of whom warmly supported her work. In 1921, H.D. and her companion Bryher (the pen name of Winifred Ellerman) put together a collection of Moore's early verse, *Poems*, which was published in London.

More than any modern poet, she gives us the feeling that life is softly exploding around us, within easy reach.
— John Ashbery

Moore subsequently gained a secure foothold in the emerging world of modernist culture in the United States. She was a frequent contributor to the *Dial*, which became the nation's most prestigious journal of the arts after Scofield Thayer took it over in 1920. In 1924, Moore won the annual Dial Award of $2,000, established by Thayer to recognize special achievement in American letters and to provide "leisure through which at least one artist may serve God (or go to the Devil) according to his own lights." The Dial Press published Moore's second book of poetry, *Observations* (1924). She became the managing editor of the *Dial* in 1925 and assumed sole editorship when Thayer resigned in 1926. After the magazine ceased publication in 1929, Moore worked as a freelance writer. T. S. Eliot suggested that she publish a new collection of her work and offered advice about the arrangement of her *Selected Poems* (1935). In his introduction to the volume, Eliot observed that Moore's work formed "part of the small body of durable poetry written in our time." The book sold poorly, but Moore steadily published her poetry in the *Nation*, the *New Republic*, and the *Partisan Review*, as well as in a new generation of literary journals such as the *Kenyon Review*. She also periodically published collections of her poems, including *The Pangolin and Other Verse* (1938), *What Are Years* (1941), and *Nevertheless* (1944).

During the final decades of her life, Moore became widely known as a poet and a public figure. In 1947, the year her supportive and protective mother died, Moore was elected to the National Institute of Arts and Letters. Her *Collected Poems* (1951) won the Pulitzer Prize and the Bollingen

Prize. In addition to several more volumes of poetry, she published a translation of La Fontaine's *Fables* (1954), as well as a collection of essays, *Predilections* (1955). Moore was also adopted by the media, the subject of feature articles in magazines ranging from *Vogue* to *Sports Illustrated*. An ardent baseball fan, she was invited to throw out the first ball at the opening game of the season at Yankee Stadium in 1966. *The Complete Poems of Marianne Moore* was published to celebrate her eightieth birthday in 1967. Moore—"our beloved Marianne," as she was described in her obituary in the *New York Times*—died of a stroke less than five years later, on February 5, 1972.

*bedfordstmartins.com/
americanlit* for research
links on Moore

Reading Moore's Poetry.   Throughout her life, Moore kept notebooks in which she jotted down quotations from her reading, comments on sermons and lectures she heard, and descriptions of animals and the natural world. Drawing on her notebooks, Moore helped pioneer the modernist practice of weaving quotations into her poems, to which she sometimes added extended notes. Many of her poems focus on a single image or natural object, displaying an attentiveness to detail Moore in part attributed to her early interest in biology and laboratory science: "Precision, economy of statement, logic employed to ends that are disinterested, drawing and identifying, liberate—at least have some bearing on—imagination." The effect of her concentrated poems was perhaps best described by her friend William Carlos Williams, who in a 1925 essay observed that "in looking at some apparently small object, one feels the swirl of great events." Williams and other modernist poets also called attention to her metrical innovations. "Moore's versification is anything but 'free,'" T. S. Eliot observed in 1935. "Many of the poems are in exact, and sometimes complicated, formal patterns, and move with the elegance of a minuet." In some of her poems, those complex patterns are the result of her use of a metrical system called "syllabics," that is, lines of a fixed and carefully counted number of syllables, often resulting in unusual line breaks that may appear to disrupt the syntax of a passage. Moore was also known—in fact, she was notorious—for her constant revisions, as exemplified by her most famous poem, "Poetry." The original, thirty-line version of the poem appeared in *Others* in 1919. Moore slightly trimmed and altered the line breaks of the poem in various later versions before compressing it into a mere three lines in her *Complete Poems* (1967). Perhaps in response to those who questioned her radical cutting of the poem, Moore in the epigraph to that volume observed, "Omissions are not accidents." Both the original and the final version of "Poetry" are printed below. The texts of all final versions of the poems are taken from *The Complete Poems of Marianne Moore* (1980).

POETRY[1]

I too, dislike it: there are things that are important beyond all this fiddle.
 Reading it, however, with a perfect contempt for it, one discovers that there
    is in
  it after all, a place for the genuine.
   Hands that can grasp, eyes
    that can dilate, hair that can rise   5
     if it must, these things are important not because a

high sounding interpretation can be put upon them but because they are
 useful; when they become so derivative as to become unintelligible, the
 same thing may be said for all of us — that we
  do not admire what   10
  we cannot understand. The bat,
   holding on upside down or in quest of something to

eat, elephants pushing, a wild horse taking a roll, a tireless wolf under
 a tree, the immovable critic twinkling his skin like a horse that feels a flea,
   the base-
 ball fan, the statistician — case after case   15
  could be cited did
  one wish it; nor is it valid
   to discriminate against "business documents and

school-books"[2]; all these phenomena are important. One must make a
    distinction
 however: when dragged into prominence by half poets, the result is not poetry, 20
 nor till the autocrats[3] among us can be
  "literalists of
  the imagination"[4] — above
   insolence and triviality and can present

---

1. **Poetry:** The version printed here follows the text and format of the original, as it was published at the opening of the final issue of *Others* (July 1919), an issue of the magazine edited by William Carlos Williams.
2. **"business documents and school-books":** When she published the poem in her collection *Observations* (1924), Moore added a note in which she identified and quoted the full passage from the *Diary of Tolstoy:* "Where the boundary between prose and poetry lies, I shall never understand. The question is raised in manuals of style, yet the answer to it lies beyond me. Poetry is verse; prose is not verse. Or else poetry is everything with the exception of business documents and school books."
3. **autocrats:** In a later version published in her *Selected Poems* (1935), Moore altered this to *poets.*
4. **"literalists of the imagination":** When she published the poem in her collection *Observations* (1924), Moore added a note in which she identified and quoted the source of the phrase, W. B. Yeats's "William Blake and His Illustrations," in *Ideas of Good and Evil* (1903): "The limitation of his view was from the very intensity of his vision; he was a too literal realist of the imagination, as others are of nature; and because he believed that the figures seen by the mind's eye, when exalted by inspiration were 'eternal existences,' he hated every grace of style that might obscure their lineaments."

for inspection, imaginary gardens with real toads in them, shall we have   25
  it. In the meantime, if you demand on one hand, in defiance of their opinion —
  the raw material of poetry in
     all its rawness and
    that which is on the other hand,
      genuine then you are interested in poetry.   30

[1919]

POETRY[1]

I, too, dislike it.
  Reading it, however, with a perfect contempt for it, one discovers in
  it, after all, a place for the genuine.

[1919, 1980]

---

1. **Poetry:** The editors of *The Complete Poems of Marianne Moore* (1967), where this final version of the poem first appeared, convinced Moore to include what was described as the "Original version" in a note. In fact, the version printed in that note was an intermediate version published in her *Selected Poems* (1935), not the original version published in 1919 and reprinted above.

TO MILITARY PROGRESS[1]

You use your mind
like a millstone to grind
   chaff.
You polish it
and with your warped wit   5
   laugh

at your torso,
prostrate where the crow
   falls
on such faint hearts   10
as its god imparts,
   calls

and claps its wings
till the tumult brings
   more   15

---

1. **To Military Progress:** This poem, the first in which Moore addressed the carnage of World War I, was originally published as "To the Soul of 'Progress'" in the *Egoist* (April 1, 1915). With minor revisions, the poem then appeared in *Others: An Anthology of the New Verse* (1917). Moore changed the title and made some additional editorial and wording changes when she revised the poem for her second collection, *Observations* (1924).

black minute-men
to revive again,
   war

at little cost.
They cry for the lost   20
   head
and seek their prize
till the evening sky's
   red.

[1915, 1980]

THE FISH[1]

wade
through black jade.
   Of the crow-blue mussel-shells, one keeps
   adjusting the ash-heaps;
      opening and shutting itself like   5

an
injured fan.
   The barnacles which encrust the side
   of the wave, cannot hide
      there for the submerged shafts of the   10

sun,
split like spun
   glass, move themselves with spotlight swiftness
   into the crevices —
      in and out, illuminating   15

the
turquoise sea
   of bodies. The water drives a wedge
   of iron through the iron edge
      of the cliff; whereupon the stars,[2]   20

pink
rice-grains, ink-
   bespattered jelly-fish, crabs like green

---

1. **The Fish:** The title also serves as the first line of the poem, which was originally published in the London magazine *Egoist* (August 1918), then edited by the poet H.D.
2. **stars:** Abbreviated version of *starfish*.

lilies, and submarine
 toadstools, slide each on the other.   25
All
external
 marks of abuse are present on this
 defiant edifice —
  all the physical features of   30
ac-
cident — lack
 of cornice,[3] dynamite grooves, burns, and
 hatchet strokes, these things stand
  out on it; the chasm-side is   35
dead.
Repeated
 evidence has proved that it can live
 on what can not revive
  its youth. The sea grows old in it. 40

         [1918, 1980]

---

3. **cornice:** An overhanging mass, often of hardened snow, at the edge of a precipice.

TO A SNAIL

If "compression is the first grace of style,"[1]
you have it. Contractility is a virtue
as modesty is a virtue.
It is not the acquisition of any one thing
that is able to adorn,   5
or the incidental quality that occurs
as a concomitant of something well said,
that we value in style,
but the principle that is hid:
in the absence of feet, "a method of conclusions"; 10
"a knowledge of principles,"
in the curious phenomenon of your occipital[2] horn.

        [1924, 1980]

---

1. **"compression . . . style":** "The very first grace of style is that which comes from compression." *Demetrius on Style*, translated by W. Hamilton Fyfe (Heinemann, 1932). [Moore's note] The quotation is from an ancient Greek treatise on style, probably dating from the second century BCE.
2. **occipital:** At the back of the skull.

AN EGYPTIAN PULLED GLASS BOTTLE
IN THE SHAPE OF A FISH

Here we have thirst
and patience, from the first,
    and art, as in a wave held up for us to see
    in its essential perpendicularity;

not brittle but
intense — the spectrum, that
    spectacular and nimble animal the fish,
    whose scales turn aside the sun's sword by their polish.

[1924]

Fish-Shaped Glass Bottle

After Marianne Moore received the Dial Award for "service to literature," she
presented the *Dial* editor, Scofield Thayer, with a personally illustrated copy of her
collection *Observations* (1924). One of her additions to the volume was this tracing
of a black-and-white photograph of an ancient polychrome vase that had appeared
in 1921 in the *Illustrated London News*, the inspiration for her poem "An Egyptian
Pulled Glass Bottle in the Shape of a Fish."

Elizabeth Bishop (1911-1979), whose poetry can be found on pp. 1986-1992, was a great admirer of the work of Marianne Moore. As a student at Vassar College, she was deeply impressed by Moore's second collection of poems, *Observations* (1924); and in 1934 a college librarian arranged for Bishop to meet Moore in New York City. In an article she wrote for *Vanity Fair* in 1983, Bishop later recalled: "I sat down, and she began to talk. It seems to me that Marianne talked to me steadily for the next thirty-five years, but of course that is nonsensical. I was living far from New York many of those years and saw her at long intervals. She must have been one of the world's greatest talkers: entertaining, enlightening, fascinating, and memorable; her talk, like her poetry, was quite different from anyone else's in the world." As that account suggests, the two women became fast friends and remained so for the rest of Moore's life. In the following extract from "As We Like It," an essay that first appeared in the *Quarterly Review of Literature* (Spring 1948), Bishop discusses the connections between what she describes as "our two most original writers," Moore and Edgar Allan Poe (1809-1849). The text is taken from Elizabeth Bishop, *Prose*, edited by Lloyd Schwartz (2011).

ELIZABETH BISHOP

[1911-1979]

From As We Like It

Miss Moore has said in conversation that she has been influenced by Poe's prose,[1] and although it should not be pushed too far, an interesting study could be made of several points of comparison. Miss Moore and Poe are our two most original writers and one feels that Miss Moore would cheerfully subscribe to Poe's remark on Originality: "The extent to which this has been neglected in

---

1. **Poe's prose:** In addition to his poetry, Poe produced a large body of prose, including short stories, essays, and reviews.

versification is one of the most unaccountable things in the world," and his painful edict that "In general, to be found, it must be elaborately sought, and although a positive merit of the highest class, demands in its attainment less of invention than negation," and also that it is greatly assisted by "an extension of the application of the principles of rhyme and alliteration."[2]

In fact, although it might have surprised him, one might almost say that in some respects Miss Moore is Poe's Ideal Poet, the one he was unable to be himself.

Poe in his prose and Miss Moore in her strike a tone of complete truth-telling that is compelling and rare . . . .

They both take delight in their wide reading and in sharing it, and both are capable of making something unexpected and amusing out of the footnote, that usually unsmiling paragraph.

And both are virtuosi, Miss Moore, of course, to a much higher degree. I do not want to go into problems of versification and shall simply say that the more one reads Miss Moore the more one is inclined to give up such problems and merely exclaim, "How does she do it!" She is able to develop some completely "natural" idea with so many graces and effects of hesitation and changes of mood and pace that one is reminded of what little one knows of the peculiarities of Oriental music. This constant high level of technical skill must cost her incredible effort, although one is rarely aware of it; but what may be an effort for her would for most poets be an impossibility.

Sometimes I have thought that her individual verse forms, or "mannerisms" as they might be called, may have developed as much from a sense of modesty as from the demands of artistic expression; that actually she may be somewhat embarrassed by her own precocity and sensibilities and that her varied verse forms and rhyme schemes and syllabic logarithms are all a form of apology, are saying, "It really isn't as easy for me as I'm afraid you may think it is." The precocious child is often embarrassed by his own understanding and is capable of going to great lengths to act his part as a child properly; one feels that Miss Moore sometimes has to make things difficult for herself as a sort of *noblesse oblige*,[3] or self-imposed taxalion to keep everything "fair" in the world of poetry.

[1948, 2011]

---

2. **"The extent . . . alliteration"**: The quotations are from "The Philosophy of Composition" (1846), Poe's account of writing his most famous poem, "The Raven."

3. *noblesse oblige*: Literally, "nobility oblige" (French), usually signifying the generous behavior thought to be the responsibility of those of high birth or rank toward those who are less fortunate.

Jun Fujita

[1888-1963]

Jun Fujita was born near Hiroshima, Japan, on December 13, 1888. Few details are known about his early life in Japan. When he was about eighteen years old, his uncle employed him to photograph fishing and lumber industries in Canada, where Fujita lived until around 1915. He then moved to Chicago, initially planning to become an engineer. In order to support himself while studying at the Armour Institute, now the Illinois Institute of Technology, Fujita took a job as a photographer with the Chicago *Evening Post*. At the time, he was the only Japanese news photographer in the country, and he quickly gained a reputation for his portraits of people as diverse as Al Capone, Albert Einstein, Carl Sandburg, and several presidents, as well as for his photographs of sensational events such as the capsizing of the steamer *Eastland* in the Chicago River in 1915, the race riots in Chicago during the "Red Summer" of 1919, and the "St. Valentine's Day Massacre," in which Capone's criminal gang shot and killed seven members of a rival gang in 1929.

During these years, Fujita also began to write poetry. His poems appeared in various periodicals, including the avant-garde journal *Caprice*, published in Berkeley, California, and the Chicago-based magazines the *Wave* and *Poetry: A Magazine of Verse*, edited by Harriet Monroe. Fujita often wrote English variants of the tanka, an ancient form of Japanese poetry that also provided the title of his first and only book, *Tanka: Poems in Exile* (1923). Monroe wrote a favorable review of the volume for *Poetry*, and Llewellen Jones, the literary critic for the *Evening Post*, was even more enthusiastic, observing that "Mr. Fujita shows an extraordinary power of evoking a whole landscape with its emotional suggestions, from words as economically used as is the single line of the master etcher." But the book, which was published in a beautifully printed, limited edition of only 365 copies, gained little attention, and Fujita apparently published no more of his poetry after 1928, when several more of his tanka appeared in *Poetry*.

Fujita thereafter devoted himself to photography and painting. About 1928, he began to build a cabin near Ranier, Minnesota, on property bought by his longtime companion, Florence Carr, a secretary and social worker Fujita married in 1940. Carr bought the land because, as an "Asian alien," Fujita was prohibited by state law from owning property in Minnesota. Fujita, who loved the wilderness, often retreated to the cabin to sketch, paint watercolors, and take photographs of the natural world. After beginning a successful commercial photography business in the early 1930s, he was commissioned by the government to photograph Federal Works projects throughout the United States. Unlike most other people of Japanese ancestry in the country, the overwhelming majority of whom lived in Hawaii or on the West Coast, Fujita was able to avoid being sent to an internment camp during World War II by remaining in Chicago. Through a special act of Congress, he was granted U.S. citizenship in 1954. Remembered primarily for his photographic work, Fujita died at his home in Chicago on July 13, 1963.

Jun Fujita

This undated photograph is apparently one of the few portraits taken of Fujita, who was himself more widely known for his photography than for the poetry he published during the 1920s.

bedfordstmartins.com/
americanlit for research
links on Fujita

Reading Fujita's Poetry.   Between 1919 and 1928, Fujita published more than twenty poems and two reviews in Harriet Monroe's prominent magazine *Poetry*. In both his poems and reviews, Fujita sought to educate Americans about Japanese poetry and poetic forms, which were increasingly popular among poets and readers in the United States. In "A Japanese Cosmopolite" (1922), a review of the influential poetry of Yone Noguchi, the first Japanese national to publish poetry in English, Fujita observed:

> The so-called oriental influence in western literature today, I am afraid, is taking the form it has assumed in the other arts, which, to a great extent, have adopted the carcass of Japanese pictures and missed the essence.

For Fujita, the essence of Japanese poetry was what he defined as the creation of "poetic silence," the poet's ability to suggest a mood or a feeling without relying on extended description or explicit commentary. "Ten words of prose, once set down, do the duty of only ten words," he once observed. "But two words of poetry, with their suggestive power, can create a mood or paint a picture that in prose would require perhaps five hundred words." In many of his poems, including the first of the following selection, Fujita freely adapted the compressed form of the Japanese tanka, traditionally a thirty-one-syllable poem divided into five syllabic units, or lines. As the other poems in the selection indicate, he also wrote somewhat longer poems in free verse, including imagistic poems inspired by nighttime scenes in Chicago. The texts of the poems are taken from *Tanka: Poems in Exile* (1923).

DIMINUENDO[1]

Into the evening haze
Out of giant stacks, the smoke
Winds and fades.

Din and whistles have dwindled away
And stillness chants an empty echo.

[1923]

---

1. **Diminuendo:** A gradual decrease in the force or loudness in a musical passage.

MICHIGAN BOULEVARD[1]

A row of black tombs – tall and jagged,
The buildings stand in the drizzly night.
With vacant stare the boulevard lamps in rain
Amuse the green gleams they cast.

---

1. **Michigan Boulevard:** A major north and south thoroughfare, usually called Michigan Avenue, running parallel to Lake Michigan and through the central business and retail district of Chicago.

Beyond the lamps, among the tombs,
Drip, and drip,
The hollow sound rises.

[1923]

CHICAGO RIVER[1]

Slowly, by the slimy wooden wharves,
Through the stillness of rain
The Chicago River glides into night.
From the silhouette of a black iron bridge,
The watchman's light is dripping —   5
Dripping like melting tallow.
Out of darkness
Comes a woman,
Hellos to me; her wet face glares;
Casually she turns and goes   10
Into the darkness.

Through the stillness of rain
The Chicago River glides on.

[1923]

---

1. **Chicago River**: The river that flows through downtown Chicago. In a remarkable feat of engineering in 1900, the direction of the notoriously polluted river was changed to flow into the Chicago Sanitary and Ship Canal, in an effort to control the massive amounts of industrial waste and raw sewage that were contaminating Lake Michigan.

T. S. Eliot

[1888-1965]

Thomas Stearns Eliot was born on September 26, 1888, in St. Louis, Missouri. He was the youngest of seven children of Henry Ware Eliot, president of the Hydraulic-Press Brick Company, and Charlotte Chauncy Stearns Eliot, both of whom were descended from early English settlers of New England. Eliot's grandfather, William Greenleaf Eliot, graduated from Harvard Divinity School and moved to St. Louis in 1834. There, he helped found a Unitarian church and Washington University, which Eliot's father attended. After their marriage, Eliot's parents were active in St. Louis society, supporting the arts and various civic causes. The family lived in an urban neighborhood near the Mississippi River and spent the summers at their second home near Gloucester, Massachusetts. Eliot grew up in a household that valued "Religion, the Community, and

T. S. Eliot

The celebrity photographer E. O. Hoppé took this portrait of Eliot about 1920, when the rising young poet and critic was working at a branch of Lloyd's Bank in London.

Education," as he recalled in 1953. He was educated at private schools in St. Louis and attended Milton Academy in Massachusetts for a year before enrolling at Harvard University in 1906. Influenced by his mother, a former teacher and amateur poet whose work appeared in various religious journals, Eliot had begun to write poetry at an early age, and he published some of his work in the *Harvard Advocate*. He also read a book he described as a "revelation," Arthur Symon's *The Symbolist Movement in Literature* (1895), which introduced Eliot to the writings of French poets such as Jules Laforgue. By the time Eliot graduated from Harvard in 1910, having earned both a BA and an MA in English literature, he was writing poetry that departed sharply from the conventions of the nineteenth-century British poets who had earlier influenced his work.

Eliot was initially torn between an academic and a literary career. During the year 1910-11, which he spent in postgraduate study at the Sorbonne, Eliot copied into a notebook some of the poems that would later bring him considerable recognition, including "The Love Song of J. Alfred Prufrock." After his year in Paris, Eliot put aside his poetry and returned to Harvard, where he did three years of graduate work under the tutelage of its distinguished faculty in philosophy, including William James, Josiah Royce, George Santayana, and the visiting Bertrand Russell. Eliot also studied Hindu religion and Sanskrit. In 1914, he returned to Europe on a fellowship, briefly studying in Germany and then, after the beginning of World War I, moving on to Merton College, Oxford. In England, he met Ezra Pound, whose influence and help would prove to be invaluable to Eliot. In a letter to Harriet Monroe, the editor of the influential *Poetry: A Magazine of Verse*, Pound observed that Eliot "has actually trained himself *and* modernized himself *on his own.*" Pound urged Monroe to publish "The Love Song of J. Alfred Prufrock," the first of a number of Eliot's poems that appeared in *Poetry* in 1915 and 1916. In the meantime, Eliot met and impulsively married Vivien Haigh-Wood, the daughter of an affluent, upper-middle-class English family. From the beginning, they proved to be painfully incompatible, and their troubled union was further strained by financial difficulties. To support them, Eliot taught school, gave lectures, and wrote reviews. He also completed his doctoral dissertation, but Eliot never received his PhD because he did not return to Harvard for a required dissertation defense. In 1917, he became the assistant editor of an avant-garde literary magazine, the *Egoist*, and also found a job in the Foreign Department of Lloyds Bank.

Between 1917 and 1923, Eliot rose from obscurity to literary fame on both sides of the Atlantic. With the encouragement and financial support of Pound, Eliot published two collections of his poems in London, *Prufrock and Other Observations* (1917) and *Poems* (1919). The contents of the two collections were subsequently published in 1920 as *Poems* in New York City and in London as *Ara Vos Prec*. Eliot also wrote *Ezra Pound, His Metric and Poetry* (1918), as well as numerous articles and reviews, some of which he collected in *The Sacred Wood: Essays on Poetry and Criticism* (1920). In addition to one of Eliot's most famous and influential essays, "Tradition and the Individual Talent," the volume included commentaries on a wide array of literary subjects, including Greek and Elizabethan drama and poets ranging from Dante to the nineteenth-century British poets William Blake and Charles Algernon Swinburne. The whole of European culture, from ancient fertility myths to popular tunes of the Jazz Age, came within the purview of Eliot's most ambitious poem, *The Waste Land*, published in 1922. The poem first appeared in the inaugural issue of the *Criterion*, a new journal edited by Eliot in London, and then in an avant-garde literary magazine published in New York City, the *Dial*, which awarded Eliot its annual prize of two thousand dollars. Late in the year, *The Waste Land* was published as a book, which in later editions Eliot gratefully dedicated to Pound. Although its reception was mixed – one English critic dismissed the volume as "so much waste paper" – the poem catapulted Eliot into the forefront of modernist poets. In 1923, Eliot was also relieved of nagging financial concerns and the pressures of his job at the bank when the publishing firm of Faber and Gwyer (later Faber and Faber) offered him a position as its literary editor, an influential position he retained until his death in 1965.

In the late 1920s, Eliot made two decisions that profoundly shaped his later life and writings. Long dissatisfied with the Unitarianism in which his family was steeped and he was raised, Eliot joined the Church of England in June 1927. Later that year, he became a British citizen. In his preface to *For Lancelot Andrewes* (1928), a collection of essays dedicated to the renowned seventeenth-century Anglican bishop who had overseen the translation of the authorized King James Version of the Bible, Eliot described himself as "classicist in literature, royalist in politics, and anglo-catholic in religion." Many of Eliot's admirers were shocked by his reactionary political turn and devotion to the teachings of the church, a commitment that strongly shaped his life and writings. From the early 1930s through the 1950s, Eliot sought to reach a wider audience by writing plays, notably his acclaimed church drama *Murder in the Cathedral* (1935) and a play about sin and Christian redemption, *The Family Reunion* (1939). His preoccupation with human suffering and spirituality was also revealed in his last major poetic project, a group of four meditative poems that Eliot published separately and then as *Four Quartets* (1943). Partly on the strength of the volume, which some critics considered his masterpiece, Eliot was awarded the Nobel Prize for Literature in 1948. Many other awards and prizes followed, including numerous honorary degrees from universities in England and the United States, where he was in great demand as a lecturer. Long separated from his first wife, who was institutionalized for mental instability from 1938 until her death in 1947, Eliot married Valerie Fletcher in 1957. He died in London on January 4, 1965, and was buried in East Coker, the village from which his ancestors had emigrated to America.

He is the only American I know of who has made what I can call adequate preparation for writing. He has actually trained himself and modernized himself on his own.

–Ezra Pound

Reading Eliot's "The Love Song of J. Alfred Prufrock."   When Ezra Pound pressed Harriet Monroe to publish this poem in her magazine *Poetry*, he told her that he wanted Eliot's first published poem to be one that would immediately "differentiate him from everyone else, in the public mind." In a brief note at the end of the June 1915 issue of *Poetry*, in which the poem appeared, Monroe rather tersely identified the poet: "Mr. T. S. Eliot is a young American poet resident in England, who has published nothing hitherto in this country." Aside from some additional poems in *Poetry* and a single poem in another little magazine, *Others*, no more of Eliot's verse was published in the United States before 1920. But many reviewers on both sides of the Atlantic were openly hostile to the experimental verse collected in Eliot's first book, *Prufrock and Other Observations*, which was published in London in 1917. For the English reviewer Arthur Waugh, Eliot was yet another new poet who had forgotten that "the first essence of poetry is beauty," and who consequently produced "unmetrical, incoherent banalities." Pound quickly countered, describing the characters in Eliot's poems as "the stuff of the modern world" and praising the volume for its "fine tone, its humanity, and its realism." Although Eliot employed a popular nineteenth-century poetic form, the dramatic monologue, "The Love Song of J. Alfred Prufrock" was and remains a strikingly modern poem, with its urban setting and unpoetical imagery, its untraditional rhythms, and its mixture of colloquial language and allusions to Dante's *Inferno*, the Bible, and Shakespeare. The text is taken from Eliot's *Collected Poems 1909–1962* (1963).

bedfordstmartins.com/
americanlit *for research
links on Eliot*

THE LOVE SONG OF J. ALFRED PRUFROCK

*S'io credessi che mia risposta fosse
a persona che mai tornasse al mondo,
questa fiamma staria senza più scosse.
Ma per ciò che giammai di questo fondo
non tornò vivo alcun, s'i'odo il vero,
senza tema d'infamia ti rispondo.*[1]

Let us go then, you and I,
When the evening is spread out against the sky
Like a patient etherised upon a table;
Let us go, through certain half-deserted streets,
The muttering retreats   5
Of restless nights in one-night cheap hotels
And sawdust restaurants with oyster-shells:
Streets that follow like a tedious argument

---

1. **S'io . . . rispondo**: The lines are from the *Inferno*, by the Italian poet Dante Alighieri (1265–1321): "If I believed that my response was heard / by anyone returning to the world, / this flame would stand and never stir again, / But since no man has ever come alive / out of this gulf of Hell, if I hear true, / I'll answer, with no fear of infamy" (27.61–66, as translated by Anthony Esolen). The speaker is Guido da Montefeltro, whose spirit Dante encounters during his descent into hell. Since Guido assumes that Dante is also dead and therefore cannot return to the world, he is willing to confess to the sin of false counsel, for which he is punished by being encased in flame.

Of insidious intent
To lead you to an overwhelming question . . .   10
Oh, do not ask, "What is it?"
Let us go and make our visit.

In the room the women come and go
Talking of Michelangelo.[2]

The yellow fog that rubs its back upon the window-panes,   15
The yellow smoke that rubs its muzzle on the window-panes,
Licked its tongue into the corners of the evening,
Lingered upon the pools that stand in drains,
Let fall upon its back the soot that falls from chimneys,
Slipped by the terrace, made a sudden leap,   20
And seeing that it was a soft October night,
Curled once about the house, and fell asleep.

And indeed there will be time
For the yellow smoke that slides along the street
Rubbing its back upon the window-panes;   25
There will be time, there will be time
To prepare a face to meet the faces that you meet;
There will be time to murder and create,
And time for all the works and days of hands[3]
That lift and drop a question on your plate;   30
Time for you and time for me,
And time yet for a hundred indecisions,
And for a hundred visions and revisions,
Before the taking of a toast and tea.

In the room the women come and go   35
Talking of Michelangelo.

And indeed there will be time
To wonder, "Do I dare?" and, "Do I dare?"
Time to turn back and descend the stair,
With a bald spot in the middle of my hair —   40
(They will say: "How his hair is growing thin!")
My morning coat, my collar mounting firmly to the chin,

---

2. **Michelangelo:** The Italian sculptor and painter Michelangelo Buonarroti (1475–1564), a leading figure of
the Italian Renaissance.
3. **There will be time . . . works and days of hands:** *Works and Days* is a poem about agricultural work by the
Greek poet Hesiod (c. 700 BCE). Here and in several following lines, Eliot also echoes Ecclesiastes: "To every
thing there is a season, and a time to every purpose under the heaven: A time to be born, and a time to die; a
time to plant, and a time to pluck up that which is planted" (3:1–2).

My necktie rich and modest, but asserted by a simple pin –
(They will say: "But how his arms and legs are thin!")
Do I dare   45
Disturb the universe?
In a minute there is time
For decisions and revisions which a minute will reverse.

For I have known them all already, known them all –
Have known the evenings, mornings, afternoons,   50
I have measured out my life with coffee spoons;
I know the voices dying with a dying fall[4]
Beneath the music from a farther room.
    So how should I presume?

And I have known the eyes already, known them all –   55
The eyes that fix you in a formulated phrase,
And when I am formulated, sprawling on a pin,
When I am pinned and wriggling on the wall,
Then how should I begin
To spit out all the butt-ends of my days and ways?   60
    And how should I presume?

And I have known the arms already, known them all –
Arms that are braceleted and white and bare
(But in the lamplight, downed with light brown hair!)
Is it perfume from a dress   65
That makes me so digress?
Arms that lie along a table, or wrap about a shawl.
    And should I then presume?
    And how should I begin?
          .   .   .   .   .

Shall I say, I have gone at dusk through narrow streets   70
And watched the smoke that rises from the pipes
Of lonely men in shirt-sleeves, leaning out of windows? . . .

I should have been a pair of ragged claws
Scuttling across the floors of silent seas.
          .   .   .   .   .

And the afternoon, the evening, sleeps so peacefully!   75
Smoothed by long fingers,

---

4. **a dying fall**: A possible allusion to the opening lines of Shakespeare's *Twelfth Night:* "If music be the food of love, play on; / Give me excess of it, that, surfeiting, / The appetite may sicken, and so die. / That strain again! It had a dying fall."

Asleep ... tired ... or it malingers,
Stretched on the floor, here beside you and me.
Should I, after tea and cakes and ices,
Have the strength to force the moment to its crisis?   80
But though I have wept and fasted, wept and prayed,
Though I have seen my head (grown slightly bald) brought in upon
    a platter,[5]
I am no prophet – and here's no great matter;
I have seen the moment of my greatness flicker,
And I have seen the eternal Footman hold my coat, and snicker,   85
And in short, I was afraid.

And would it have been worth it, after all,
After the cups, the marmalade, the tea,
Among the porcelain, among some talk of you and me,
Would it have been worth while,   90
To have bitten off the matter with a smile,
To have squeezed the universe into a ball
To roll it towards some overwhelming question,
To say: "I am Lazarus,[6] come from the dead,
Come back to tell you all, I shall tell you all" –   95
If one, settling a pillow by her head,
    Should say: "That is not what I meant at all.
    That is not it, at all."

And would it have been worth it, after all,
Would it have been worth while,   100
After the sunsets and the dooryards and the sprinkled streets,
After the novels, after the teacups, after the skirts that trail along
    the floor –
And this, and so much more? –
It is impossible to say just what I mean!
But as if a magic lantern[7] threw the nerves in patterns on a screen: 105
Would it have been worth while
If one, settling a pillow or throwing off a shawl,
And turning toward the window, should say:
    "That is not it at all,

---

5. **head ... upon a platter**: The head of the prophet John the Baptist, who was executed by King Herod at the request of Princess Salome, was brought to Queen Herodias on a silver platter (Matthew 14:3-11).
6. **Lazarus**: The story of the resurrection of Lazarus is told in John 11:1-44.
7. **magic lantern**: A multilens forerunner of movie and slide projectors, used to project images on theater screens in popular magic-lantern shows.

That is not what I meant, at all."   110

    •   •   •   •   •

No! I am not Prince Hamlet,[8] nor was meant to be;
Am an attendant lord, one that will do
To swell a progress,[9] start a scene or two,
Advise the prince; no doubt, an easy tool,
Deferential, glad to be of use,   115
Politic, cautious, and meticulous;
Full of high sentence,[10] but a bit obtuse;
At times, indeed, almost ridiculous —
Almost, at times, the Fool.

I grow old . . . I grow old . . .   120
I shall wear the bottoms of my trousers rolled.

Shall I part my hair behind? Do I dare to eat a peach?
I shall wear white flannel trousers, and walk upon the beach.
I have heard the mermaids singing, each to each.

I do not think that they will sing to me.   125

I have seen them riding seaward on the waves
Combing the white hair of the waves blown back
When the wind blows the water white and black.

We have lingered in the chambers of the sea
By sea-girls wreathed with seaweed red and brown   130
Till human voices wake us, and we drown.

[1915, 1963]

---

8. **Prince Hamlet:** The famously indecisive title character of Shakespeare's *Hamlet, Prince of Denmark*.
9. **Am an attendant lord . . . swell a progress:** That is, a minor figure who simply increases the number of members of a royal court who are embarking on a journey.
10. **high sentence:** Sententiousness. The passage is probably an allusion to Polonius, the pompous dispenser of advice in *Hamlet*.

Reading Eliot's *The Waste Land*.   Recent scholarship suggests that Eliot wrote most of the first two parts of his famous poem early in 1921, a stressful period when he was working at Lloyd's Bank in London, entertaining his recently widowed mother and his siblings from St. Louis, and preparing to assume the editorship of a new journal, the *Criterion*. By the fall, both he and his wife were ill and exhausted, and Eliot took a leave of absence from the bank and went to Margate, a seaside resort in southeast England. From there, he went to Paris and then on to Lausanne, Switzerland. During his treatment at a sanitarium there, he wrote the final three sections of the poem. Uncertain about its value, when Eliot returned to Paris in January 1922 he asked Ezra Pound for his comments on the poem, then entitled "He Do the Police in Different Voices." When Pound read the manuscript, he noted that it was "a masterpiece; one of most important 19 pages in English." In what is widely viewed as a brilliant act of editorial intervention, and what Eliot himself described as "irrefutable evidence of Pound's critical genius," he offered extensive suggestions for revision, cutting several lengthy sections and deleting hundreds of words and phrases from the poem. *The Waste Land*, as it was retitled, was first published in England in the *Criterion* (October 1922), edited by Eliot, and then in the United States in the *Dial* (November 1922). In both magazines, the poem appeared without notes, which Eliot added when the poem was published as a book by the New York firm of Boni & Liveright at the end of 1922. Much later, in *The Frontiers of Criticism* (1956), Eliot explained, "I had at first intended only to put down all the references for my quotations, with a view to spiking the guns of critics of my earlier poems who had accused me of plagiarism." At the same time, Eliot continued, "it was discovered that the poem was inconveniently short, so I set to work to expand the notes, in order to provide a few more pages of printed matter, with the result that they became the remarkable exposition of bogus scholarship that is still on view today." Many scholars, however, view the notes as an integral part of the poem, and we have incorporated all of them and provided additional notes in an effort to help readers negotiate the complex cultural landscape of *The Waste Land*, which reveals Eliot's extensive reading of the Bible and other Christian texts, ancient Hindu scriptures, and European literature ranging from Greek and Roman classics to writings by his contemporaries. As some of the reviewers immediately recognized, Eliot's poem was at once a deeply personal and a radically modern work that expressed the pervasive sense of disillusionment and despair in the aftermath of World War I. In a review of *The Waste Land*, the American critic Edmund Wilson thus praised Eliot as "one of our only authentic poets," explaining: "For this new poem – which presents itself as so far his most considerable claim to eminence – not only recapitulates all his earlier and already familiar motifs, but it sounds for the first time in all their intensity, untempered by irony or disguise, the hunger for beauty and anguish at living which lie at the bottom of all his work." The text is taken from Eliot's *Collected Poems 1909-1962* (1963).

Original Typescript of *The Waste Land* (Overleaf) ▶

The first page of Eliot's typescript of the poem he initially called "He Do the Police in Different Voices" contains a fifty-four-line sequence depicting a drunken and rowdy night in Boston. After revising the sequence, Eliot omitted it at the urging of Ezra Pound. In the published version of *The Waste Land*, the first part of the poem, "The Burial of the Dead," consequently opens with the passage that originally followed on page 2 of the typescript, beginning "April is the cruellest month . . . ."

HE DO THE POLICE IN DIFFERENT VOICES: Part I.

THE BURIAL OF THE DEAD.

First we had a couple of feelers down at Tom's place,
There was old Tom, boiled to the eyes, blind,
(Don't you remember that time after a dance,
Top hats and all, we and Silk Hat Harry,
And old Tom took us behind, brought out a bottle of fizz,
With old Jane, Tom's wife; and we got Joe to sing
"I'm proud of all the Irish blood that's in me,
"There's not a man can say a word agin me").
Then we had dinner in good form, and a couple of Bengal lights.
When we got into the show, up in Row A,
I tried to put my foot in the drum, and didn't the girl squeal,
She never did take to me, a nice guy¯ but rough;
The next thing we were out in the street, Oh was it cold!
When will you be good! Blew in to the Opera Exchange,
Sopped up some gin, sat in to the cork game,
Mr. Fay was there, singing "The Maid of the Mill";
Then we thought we'd breeze along and take a walk.
Then we lost Steve.
("I turned up an hour later down at Myrtle's place.
What d'y' mean, she says, at two o'clock in the morning,
I'm not in business here for guys like you;
We've only had a raid last week, I've been warned twice.
~~Sergeant, I said~~, I've kept a decent house for twenty years,
There's three gents from the Buckingham Club upstairs now,
I'm going to retire and live on a farm, she says,
There's no money in it now, what with the damage done,
And the reputation the place gets, ~~on account~~ of a few bar-flies,
I've kept a clean house for twenty years, she says,
And the gents from the Buckingham Club know they're safe here;
You was well introduced, but this is the last of you.
Get me a woman, I said; you're too drunk, she said,
But she gave me a bed, and a bath, and ham and eggs,
And now you go get a shave, she said; I had a ~~good laugh~~,
Myrtle ~~was always a good sport~~).
We'd just gone up the alley, a fly cop came along,
Looking for trouble; committing a nuisance, he said,
You come on to the station. I'm sorry, I said,
It's no use being sorry, he said; let me get my hat, I said.
Well by a stroke of luck who came by but Mr. Donavan.
What's this, officer.   You're new on this beat, aint you?
~~I thought so. You know who I am~~ Yes, I do,
Saidd the fresh cop, ~~very peevish.~~ Then let it alone,
These gents are particular friends of mine.
Wasn't it luck? Then we went to the German Club,
~~We~~ and Mr. Donavan and his friend ~~Joe Leahy~~,
~~Found it shut.~~ I want to get home, said the cabman,
We all go the same way home, said Mr. Donavan,
Cheer up, Trixie and Stella; and put his foot through the window.
The next I know the old cab was hauled up on the avenue,
And the cabman and little Ben Levin the tailor,
The one who read George Meredith,
Were running a hundred yards on a bet,
And Mr. Donavan holding the watch.
So I got out to see the sunrise, and walked home.

THE WASTE LAND[1]

"Nam Sibyllam quidem Cumis ego ipse oculis meis vidi in ampulla pendere, et cum illi pueri dicerent: Σίβυλλα τί θέλεις; respondebat illa: ἀποθανεῖν θέλω."[2]

FOR EZRA POUND

IL MIGLIOR FABBRO.[3]

I. The Burial of the Dead[4]

April is the cruellest month, breeding
Lilacs out of the dead land, mixing
Memory and desire, stirring
Dull roots with spring rain.
Winter kept us warm, covering   5
Earth in forgetful snow, feeding
A little life with dried tubers.
Summer surprised us, coming over the Starnbergersee[5]
With a shower of rain; we stopped in the colonnade,
And went on in sunlight, into the Hofgarten,[6]   10
And drank coffee, and talked for an hour.
Bin gar keine Russin, stamm' aus Litauen, echt deutsch.[7]

---

1. **The Waste Land:** Not only the title, but the plan and a good deal of the incidental symbolism of the poem were suggested by Miss Jessie L. Weston's book on the Grail legend: *From Ritual to Romance* (Cambridge). Indeed, so deeply am I indebted, Miss Weston's book will elucidate the difficulties of the poem much better than my notes can do; and I recommend it (apart from the great interest of the book itself) to any who think such elucidation of the poem worth the trouble. To another work of anthropology I am indebted in general, one which has influenced our generation profoundly; I mean *The Golden Bough;* I have used especially the two volumes *Adonis, Attis, Osiris.* Anyone who is acquainted with these works will immediately recognise in the poem certain references to vegetation ceremonies. [Eliot's note] In *The Golden Bough: A Study in Magic and Religion,* first published in 1890, the British anthropologist James Frazer studied parallels between Christianity and ancient mystery religions, fertility cults that centered on the worship of a sacred king whose life and sacrificial death were reenacted in imitation of the natural cycles of death and rebirth in nature. Building on Frazer's work, Weston in *From Ritual to Romance* (1920) sought to establish connections between the mystery religions and Arthurian tales about the quest for the Holy Grail, the cup Christ used at the Last Supper. In the medieval tales, a knight from King Arthur's court goes in quest of the grail, which is held in the castle of the sexually maimed Fisher King. By asking the right question, the knight can heal the king and restore the fertility of his blighted realm, the Wasteland.
2. **[epigraph]:** The passage is from chapter 48 of the *Satyricon* by the Roman satirist Petronius (?-66 CE): "And as for the Sibyl, I saw her with my own eyes at Cumae, suspended in a bottle, and when boys asked her, 'Sibyl, what is your wish?,' she would reply, 'I want to die'" (translated by P. G. Walsh). According to Roman myth, Apollo granted the Sibyl immortality but not eternal youth, and as she grew older and older her body shriveled so much that she could fit into a bottle.
3. **[dedication]:** Eliot dedicated the poem to Ezra Pound, "the greater craftsman," originally a tribute to the thirteenth-century Provençal poet Arnaut Daniel in the *Purgatorio* (26.117) by the Italian poet Dante Alighieri (1265-1321). All translations of Dante in the following notes are by Anthony Esolen.
4. **The Burial of the Dead:** The title of the burial service in the Anglican *Book of Common Prayer.*
5. **Starnbergersee:** A large lake southwest of Munich, Germany, a popular destination for wealthy tourists.
6. **Hofgarten:** Court Garden (German), a public park with cafés in Munich.
7. **Bin . . . deutsch:** "I am not a Russian woman at all, I come from Lithuania, a real German" (German).

And when we were children, staying at the arch-duke's,
My cousin's, he took me out on a sled,
And I was frightened. He said, Marie,   15
Marie, hold on tight. And down we went.
In the mountains, there you feel free.
I read, much of the night, and go south in the winter.

What are the roots that clutch, what branches grow
Out of this stony rubbish? Son of man,[8]   20
You cannot say, or guess, for you know only
A heap of broken images, where the sun beats,
And the dead tree gives no shelter, the cricket no relief,[9]
And the dry stone no sound of water. Only
There is shadow under this red rock,[10]   25
(Come in under the shadow of this red rock),
And I will show you something different from either
Your shadow at morning striding behind you

Or your shadow at evening rising to meet you;

I will show you fear in a handful of dust.   30
      Frisch weht der Wind
      Der Heimat zu
      Mein Irisch Kind,
      Wo weilest du?[11]
"You gave me hyacinths[12] first a year ago;   35
"They called me the hyacinth girl."
  — Yet when we came back, late, from the hyacinth garden,
Your arms full, and your hair wet, I could not

---

8. **Son of man:** Cf. Ezekiel II, i. [Eliot's note] Here and in other notes, Eliot invites the reader to compare (abbreviated as *cf.*) a passage in his poem with a passage from another work, in this case a verse from Ezekiel: "And he [God] said unto me, Son of man, stand upon thy feet, and I will speak unto thee."

9. **And the dead tree . . . no relief:** Cf. Ecclesiastes XII, v. [Eliot's note] The verse, part of an allegory of old age in which the Preacher foretells "the evil days," reads: "Also when they shall be afraid of that which is high, and fears shall be in the way, and the almond tree shall flourish, and the grasshopper shall be a burden, and desire shall fail: because man goeth to his long home, and the mourners go about in the streets."

10. **There . . . red rock:** See the prophesy of the reign of the Messiah in Isaiah: "And a man shall be as an hiding place from the wind, and a covert from the tempest; as rivers of water in a dry place, as the shadow of a great rock in a weary land" (32:2).

11. ***Frisch . . . Wo weilest du?*:** V. *Tristan und Isolde,* I, verses 5–8. [Eliot's note] Here and in other notes, Eliot refers the reader (*v.* is an abbreviation of *vide,* "to see or consult") to a passage in another work, in this case a tragic opera about doomed lovers by German composer Richard Wagner (1813–1883). In the passage Eliot cites, a sailor sings of the lover he has left behind: "Fresh blows the wind / To the homeland; / My Irish child, / Where are you waiting?"

12. **hyacinths:** In Greek mythology, Apollo accidentally killed his beloved friend Hyacinthus, and purple flowers magically sprang where his blood touched the ground. The story is told in chapter 10 of the *Metamorphoses* by the Roman poet Ovid (43 BCE–17 CE).

Speak, and my eyes failed, I was neither
Living nor dead, and I knew nothing,   40
Looking into the heart of light, the silence.
Oed' und leer das Meer.[13]

Madame Sosostris, famous clairvoyante,
Had a bad cold, nevertheless
Is known to be the wisest woman in Europe,   45
With a wicked pack of cards.[14] Here, said she,
Is your card, the drowned Phoenician Sailor,
(Those are pearls that were his eyes.[15] Look!)
Here is Belladonna, the Lady of the Rocks,
The lady of situations.   50
Here is the man with three staves, and here the Wheel,
And here is the one-eyed merchant, and this card,
Which is blank, is something he carries on his back,
Which I am forbidden to see. I do not find
The Hanged Man. Fear death by water.   55
I see crowds of people, walking round in a ring.
Thank you. If you see dear Mrs. Equitone,
Tell her I bring the horoscope myself:
One must be so careful these days.
Unreal City,[16]   60
Under the brown fog of a winter dawn,
A crowd flowed over London Bridge, so many,

---

13. *Oed' . . . das Meer*: Id. [ibid] III, verse 24. [Eliot's note] Eliot again refers to *Tristan und Isolde* (see note 11). Tristan, who is dying and awaiting Isolde's arrival by ship, is told: "Desolate and empty [is] the sea."

14. **With a wicked pack of cards**: I am not familiar with the exact constitution of the Tarot pack of cards, from which I have obviously departed to suit my own convenience. The Hanged Man, a member of the traditional pack, fits my purpose in two ways: because he is associated in my mind with the Hanged God of Frazer, and because I associate him with the hooded figure in the passage of the disciples to Emmaus in Part V. The Phoenician Sailor and the Merchant appear later; also the "crowds of people," and Death by Water is executed in Part IV. The Man with Three Staves (an authentic member of the Tarot pack) I associate, quite arbitrarily, with the Fisher King himself. [Eliot's note] The Tarot deck, which includes cards with allegorical representations, is sometimes used for divination, or fortune-telling. Of the Tarot cards mentioned in the following passage, the Phoenician Sailor, Belladonna (Italian for "beautiful woman"), and the one-eyed merchant are Eliot's inventions.

15. **Those . . . eyes**: In Shakespeare's *The Tempest*, the sprite Ariel seeks to comfort Prince Ferdinand, who believes that his father has drowned in a shipwreck, by singing: "Full Fathom five thy father lies; / Of his bones are coral made: / Those are pearls that were his eyes: / Nothing of him that doth fade, / But doth suffer a sea-change / Into something rich and strange" (1.2.397–402).

16. **Unreal City**: Cf. Baudelaire: "Fourmillante cité, cité pleine de rêves, / Où le spectre en plein jour raccroche le passant." [Eliot's note] Eliot quotes the opening of "Les sept viellards" ("The Seven Old Men"), a poem about a ghostly encounter in the street by the French poet Charles Baudelaire (1821–1867): "Swarming city – city gorged with dreams, / Where ghosts by day accost the passer-by" (translated by Richard Howard). *The City* is the name of the financial district of London, where Eliot worked in a bank from 1917 to 1923.

I had not thought death had undone so many.[17]
Sighs, short and infrequent, were exhaled,[18]
And each man fixed his eyes before his feet.   65
Flowed up the hill and down King William Street,
To where Saint Mary Woolnoth[19] kept the hours
With a dead sound on the final stroke of nine.[20]
There I saw one I knew, and stopped him, crying: "Stetson!
"You who were with me in the ships at Mylae![21]   70
"That corpse you planted last year in your garden,
"Has it begun to sprout? Will it bloom this year?
"Or has the sudden frost disturbed its bed?
"O keep the Dog far hence, that's friend to men,
"Or with his nails he'll dig it up again![22]   75
"You! hypocrite lecteur! – mon semblable, – mon frère!"[23]

II. A Game of Chess[24]

The Chair she sat in, like a burnished throne,[25]
Glowed on the marble, where the glass

---

17. **I had not thought . . . so many:** Cf. *Inferno*, III, 55-57: "si lunga tratta / di gente, ch'io non avrei mai creduto / che morte tanta n'avesse disfatta." [Eliot's note] Eliot quotes Dante's description of the small-souled, the unnamed spirits of those who did neither good nor evil in life and who are therefore rejected by both heaven and hell: "in a long file / so numerous a host of people ran, / I had not thought death had unmade so many."
18. **Sighs . . . exhaled:** Cf. *Inferno*, IV, 25-27: "Quivi, secondo che per ascoltare, / non avea pianto, ma' che di-sospiri, / che l'aura eterna facevan tremare." [Eliot's note] Eliot quotes Dante's description of limbo, dwelling place of the spirits of unbaptized infants and virtuous people who lived before the advent of Christianity: "As far as I could tell by listening, here / there were no wails, but only sighs, that made / a trembling in the everlasting air."
19. **Saint Mary Woolnoth:** An Anglican church at the intersection of King William Street and Lombard Street in the City. The eighteenth-century church, which was built on a site that had been used for worship for two thousand years, had lost its parishioners and was then nearly derelict, since people no longer lived in the financial district.
20. **With a dead sound . . . stroke of nine:** A phenomenon which I have often noticed. [Eliot's note] Eliot passed by the church on his way to work at the nearby office of Lloyds Bank.
21. **Mylae:** A city in Sicily, off the coast of which Rome in 260 BCE won a decisive naval victory over Carthage in the first of the Punic Wars, fought for commercial domination of the Mediterranean.
22. **"O keep . . . dig it up again!":** Cf. the Dirge in Webster's *White Devil.* [Eliot's note] Eliot recasts lines from a play by the English dramatist John Webster (d. 1625), in which a mother sings a dirge over the body of her son, Marcello, who has been murdered by his brother, Flamineo: "But keep the wolf far thence, that's foe to men, / For with his nails he'll dig them up again."
23. **"hypocrite lecteur! . . . mon frère!":** V. Baudelaire, Preface to *Fleurs du Mal.* [Eliot's note] Eliot quotes the final line of the introductory poem to the volume, "Au Lecteur" ("To the Reader"): "hypocrite reader, – my alias, – my twin!" (translated by Richard Howard).
24. **A Game of Chess:** The title of a play by the English dramatist Thomas Middleton (1570-1627), a satirical account of England's long rivalry with Spain. In another play by Middleton, *Women Beware Women,* a game of chess is used to distract the attention of a woman responsible for watching over her son's beautiful young wife. The moves of the chess game played on the stage parallel the moves of the seduction played out on the balcony above. See note 35.
25. **The Chair . . . burnished throne:** Cf. *Antony and Cleopatra,* II, ii, l. 190. [Eliot's note] Eliot refers to the description in Shakespeare's play of Cleopatra floating on her ship to her first meeting with Antony: "The barge she sat in, like a burnish'd throne, / Burn'd on the water."

Held up by standards wrought with fruited vines
From which a golden Cupidon peeped out   80
(Another hid his eyes behind his wing)
Doubled the flames of sevenbranched candelabra
Reflecting light upon the table as
The glitter of her jewels rose to meet it,
From satin cases poured in rich profusion.   85
In vials of ivory and coloured glass
Unstoppered, lurked her strange synthetic perfumes,
Unguent, powdered, or liquid – troubled, confused
And drowned the sense in odours; stirred by the air
That freshened from the window, these ascended   90
In fattening the prolonged candle-flames,
Flung their smoke into the laquearia,²⁶
Stirring the pattern on the coffered ceiling.
Huge sea-wood fed with copper
Burned green and orange, framed by the coloured stone,   95
In which sad light a carvèd dolphin swam.
Above the antique mantel was displayed
As though a window gave upon the sylvan scene²⁷
The change of Philomel,²⁸ by the barbarous king
So rudely forced; yet there the nightingale²⁹   100
Filled all the desert with inviolable voice
And still she cried, and still the world pursues,
"Jug Jug" to dirty ears.³⁰

---

26. **laquearia**: V. *Aeneid*, I, 726: "dependent lychni laquearibus aureis incensi, et noctem flammis funalia vincunt." [Eliot's note] *Laquearia* is the plural form of the Latin word for a paneled ceiling, a reference to the description in Virgil's epic poem of the banquet hall where Queen Dido welcomes Aeneas and his men to Carthage: "Lighted lamps hung from the coffered ceiling / Rich with gold leaf, and torches with high flames / Prevailed over the night" (translated by Robert Fitzgerald).

27. **sylvan scene**: V. Milton, *Paradise Lost*, IV, 140. [Eliot's note] Eliot cites a line in a passage describing Satan's first view of Eden in the Christian epic by the English poet John Milton (1608-1674): "A Silvan Scene, and as the ranks ascend / Shade above shade, a woody Theatre / Of stateliest view."

28. **Philomel**: V. Ovid, *Metamorphoses*, VI, Philomela. [Eliot's note] Eliot refers to the story of Philomela, as told by the Roman poet Ovid (43 BCE-17 CE). In his version of the Greek myth, Philomela is raped by her sister's husband, the barbarian king Tereus of Thrace. Tereus cuts out Philomela's tongue to prevent her from telling the story, but she weaves a tapestry depicting the attack and sends it to her sister Procne. Together, the sisters take their revenge by killing Procne's son by Tereus, Itylus, and serving him as food to the king. When they reveal what he has eaten, Tereus pursues the sisters, and all three are transformed into birds. In some versions of the myth, Philomela becomes a nightingale; in others, she becomes a swallow.

29. **So rudely . . . nightingale**: Cf. Part III, l. 204. [Eliot's note] Eliot refers the reader ahead to line 204 of part III of the poem, "The Fire Sermon."

30. **"Jug Jug" to dirty ears**: "Jug, jug," the conventional poetic way of representing the nightingale's song, was also a crude slang expression for sexual intercourse. Here and in lines 204-6, Eliot echoes a song by the English poet and playwright John Lyly (1553-1606) about Philomela, "the ravish'd nightingale," who still cries out against the crime committed by King Tereus (Tereu): "Jug, jug, jug, jug, Tereu! She cries, / And still her woes at midnight rise."

And other withered stumps of time
Were told upon the walls; staring forms   105
Leaned out, leaning, hushing the room enclosed.
Footsteps shuffled on the stair.
Under the firelight, under the brush, her hair
Spread out in fiery points
Glowed into words, then would be savagely still.   110

"My nerves are bad to-night. Yes, bad. Stay with me.
"Speak to me. Why do you never speak. Speak.
    "What are you thinking of? What thinking? What?
"I never know what you are thinking. Think."

I think we are in rats' alley[31]   115
Where the dead men lost their bones.

"What is that noise?"
                    The wind under the door.[32]
"What is that noise now? What is the wind doing?"
                    Nothing again nothing.   120
                                                    "Do
"You know nothing? Do you see nothing? Do you remember
"Nothing?"

        I remember
Those are pearls that were his eyes.   125
"Are you alive, or not? Is there nothing in your head?"[33]
                                                    But

O O O O that Shakespearian Rag—
It's so elegant
So intelligent[34]   130
"What shall I do now? What shall I do?"
"I shall rush out as I am, and walk the street
"With my hair down, so. What shall we do tomorrow?
"What shall we ever do?"

---

31. **I think . . . rats' alley:** Cf. Part III, l. 195. [Eliot's note] Eliot refers the reader ahead to line 195 of part III of the poem, "The Fire Sermon."

32. **The wind under the door:** Cf. Webster: "Is the wind in that door still?" [Eliot's note] A doctor attending to a victim of an attack thus asks if the patient is still alive in *The Devil's Law Case,* a play by the English dramatist John Webster (d. 1625).

33. **Those are pearls . . . head?:** Cf. Part I, l. 37, 48. [Eliot's note] Eliot refers the reader back to lines 37[-40] and 48 of part I of the poem, "The Burial of the Dead." See note 15.

34. **O O O O . . . intelligent:** Eliot loosely quotes the refrain from a popular ragtime song published in 1912 and performed that year on Broadway in the Ziegfeld Follies: "That Shakespearian rag, / Most intelligent, very elegant."

The hot water at ten.   135

And if it rains, a closed car at four.
And we shall play a game of chess,
Pressing lidless eyes and waiting for a knock upon the door.[35]

When Lil's husband got demobbed,[36] I said —
I didn't mince my words, I said to her myself,   140
HURRY UP PLEASE ITS TIME[37]
Now Albert's coming back, make yourself a bit smart.
He'll want to know what you done with that money he gave you
To get yourself some teeth. He did, I was there.
You have them all out, Lil, and get a nice set,   145
He said, I swear, I can't bear to look at you.
And no more can't I, I said, and think of poor Albert,
He's been in the army four years, he wants a good time,
And if you don't give it him, there's others will, I said.
Oh is there, she said. Something o' that, I said.   150
Then I'll know who to thank, she said, and give me a straight look.
HURRY UP PLEASE ITS TIME
If you don't like it you can get on with it, I said.
Others can pick and choose if you can't.
But if Albert makes off, it won't be for lack of telling.   155
You ought to be ashamed, I said, to look so antique.
(And her only thirty-one.)
I can't help it, she said, pulling a long face,
It's them pills I took, to bring it off, she said.
(She's had five already, and nearly died of young George.)   160
The chemist[38] said it would be all right, but I've never been the same.
You *are* a proper fool, I said.
Well, if Albert won't leave you alone, there it is, I said,
What you get married for if you don't want children?
HURRY UP PLEASE ITS TIME   165
Well, that Sunday Albert was home, they had a hot gammon,
And they asked me in to dinner, to get the beauty of it hot —
HURRY UP PLEASE ITS TIME
HURRY UP PLEASE ITS TIME
Goonight Bill. Goonight Lou. Goonight May. Goonight.   170

---

35. **And we shall play . . . door:** Cf. the game of chess in Middleton's *Women beware Women*. [Eliot's note]
See note 24.
36. **demobbed:** British slang term for *demobilized*, to be released from military service.
37. **HURRY . . . TIME:** The expression customarily used by bartenders to announce closing time in an English public house (pub).
38. **chemist:** British term for a pharmacist, who has given her the pills "to bring it off," that is, to induce an abortion.

Ta ta. Goonight. Goonight.
Good night, ladies, good night, sweet ladies, good night, good night.[39]

III. The Fire Sermon[40]

The river's tent is broken; the last fingers of leaf
Clutch and sink into the wet bank. The wind
Crosses the brown land, unheard. The nymphs are departed.   175
Sweet Thames, run softly, till I end my song.[41]
The river bears no empty bottles, sandwich papers,
Silk handkerchiefs, cardboard boxes, cigarette ends
Or other testimony of summer nights. The nymphs are departed.
And their friends, the loitering heirs of City directors;   180
Departed, have left no addresses.
By the waters of Leman I sat down and wept[42] . . .
Sweet Thames, run softly till I end my song,
Sweet Thames, run softly, for I speak not loud or long.
But at my back in a cold blast I hear   185
The rattle of the bones, and chuckle spread from ear to ear.[43]

A rat crept softly through the vegetation
Dragging its slimy belly on the bank
While I was fishing in the dull canal
On a winter evening round behind the gashouse   190
Musing upon the king my brother's wreck
And on the king my father's death[44] before him.
White bodies naked on the low damp ground
And bones cast in a little low dry garret,
Rattled by the rat's foot only, year to year.   195

---

39. **Good night . . . good night:** Ophelia, who later drowns herself, speaks these words at the end of a speech in her mad scene in Shakespeare's *Hamlet* (4.5.72-73).

40. **The Fire Sermon:** This sermon by the renowned religious teacher Siddartha Gautama (c. 563-483 BCE), known as the Buddha or the Enlightened One, was available in a standard textbook, *Buddhism in Translation* (1896), by Henry Clarke Warren, a professor at Harvard. Instructing a congregation of "priests," or monks, on the need to free themselves from the things of this world, including ideas and impressions received by the eye or the mind, "the Blessed One" declares: "All things, O priests, are on fire. . . . With the fire of passion, say I, with the fire of hatred, with the fire of infatuation; with birth, old age, death, sorrow, lamentation, misery, grief, despair are they on fire."

41. **Sweet Thames . . . song:** V. Spenser, Prothalamion. [Eliot's note] Here and in lines 183-84, Eliot quotes the refrain to "Prothalamion," a poem celebrating marriage by the English poet Edmund Spenser (1552-1599).

42. **By . . . wept:** Compare Psalms 137:1: "By the rivers of Babylon, there we sat down, yea, we wept, when we remembered Zion." Eliot completed the first draft of *The Waste Land* during his stay at a sanatorium in Lausanne, a city on Lake Leman (another name for Lake Geneva) in Switzerland.

43. **But . . . ear to ear:** The lines echo lines 21-22 of "To His Coy Mistress" by the English poet Andrew Marvell (1621-1678): "But at my back I always hear / Time's wingèd chariot hurrying near."

44. **And on the king my father's death:** Cf. *The Tempest*, I, ii. [Eliot's note] In this scene in Shakespeare's play, following a shipwreck in which Prince Ferdinand believes that his father has drowned, he is comforted by the song of the sprite Ariel: "Sitting on a bank, / Weeping again the king my father's wrack, / This music crept by me upon the waters, / Allaying both their fury, and my passion, / With its sweet air" (1.2.387-91). See note 15.

But at my back from time to time I hear⁴⁵
The sound of horns and motors,⁴⁶ which shall bring
Sweeney to Mrs. Porter in the spring.
O the moon shone bright on Mrs. Porter
And on her daughter   200
They wash their feet in soda water⁴⁷
*Et O ces voix d'enfants, chantant dans la coupole!*⁴⁸

Twit twit twit
Jug jug jug jug jug jug
So rudely forc'd.   205
Tereu⁴⁹

Unreal City
Under the brown fog of a winter noon
Mr. Eugenides, the Smyrna merchant⁵⁰
Unshaven, with a pocket full of currants   210
C.i.f. London:⁵¹ documents at sight,
Asked me in demotic French⁵²
To luncheon at the Cannon Street Hotel
Followed by a weekend at the Metropole.⁵³

At the violet hour, when the eyes and back   215
Turn upward from the desk, when the human engine waits
Like a taxi throbbing waiting,

---

45. **But . . . I hear:** Cf. Marvell, "To His Coy Mistress." [Eliot's note] See note 43.
46. **The sound of horns and motors:** Cf. Day, *Parliament of Bees:* "When of the sudden, listening, you shall hear, / A noise of horns and hunting, which shall bring / Actaeon to Diana in the spring, / Where all shall see her naked skin . . . ." [Eliot's note] The lines are from a pastoral poem about "the doings, the births, the wars, the wooings" of bees by the English poet and playwright John Day (1574-1640). In Greek mythology, Actaeon was a hunter who was changed into a stag and killed by his own dogs as punishment for seeing the naked body of Artemis (Diana in Roman mythology), the goddess of virginity.
47. **O the moon . . . soda water:** I do not know the origin of the ballad from which these lines are taken: it was reported to me from Sydney, Australia. [Eliot's note] In his version of this so-called ballad, Eliot expurgated the lyrics of an obscene song popular with soldiers about the "madam" of a brothel whose prostitutes were notorious for infecting their clients with venereal disease.
48. **Et . . . coupole!:** V. Verlaine, *Parsifal.* [Eliot's note] Eliot quotes the last line of a sonnet by the French poet Paul Verlaine (1844-1896): "—And, o those voices of children singing in the dome!" Verlaine's sonnet refers to the final scene of Richard Wagner's opera *Parsifal,* in which the Arthurian knight recovers the Holy Spear that pierced Christ's side at the Crucifixion. Returning to the Grail Castle, Parsifal heals Amfortas, the Fisher King, with a touch of the Holy Spear.
49. **Jug jug . . . Tereu:** See note 30.
50. **Mr. Eugenides, the Smyrna merchant:** Smyrna, a port city on the coast of Asia Minor, was the focus of the Greco-Turkish War of 1919-22. After the Greek occupation force withdrew in 1921, Turkish troops massacred 30,000 Christian inhabitants of the city, present-day Izmir.
51. **C.i.f. London:** The currants were quoted at a price "carriage and insurance free to London"; and the Bill of Lading, etc., were to be handed to the buyer upon payment of the sight draft. [Eliot's note]
52. **demotic French:** Colloquial French, the speech used by ordinary people as opposed to correct or learned language.
53. **Cannon Street Hotel . . . Metropole:** A hotel then attached to the Cannon Street Station, a busy railroad terminal for travelers to and from the Continent, and a large resort hotel in Brighton, on the southern coast of England.

I Tiresias, though blind, throbbing between two lives,[54]
Old man with wrinkled female breasts, can see
At the violet hour, the evening hour that strives   220
Homeward, and brings the sailor home from sea,[55]
The typist home at teatime, clears her breakfast, lights
Her stove, and lays out food in tins.
Out of the window perilously spread
Her drying combinations[56] touched by the sun's last rays,   225
On the divan are piled (at night her bed)
Stockings, slippers, camisoles, and stays.
I Tiresias, old man with wrinkled dugs
Perceived the scene, and foretold the rest —
I too awaited the expected guest.   230
He, the young man carbuncular, arrives,
A small house agent's clerk, with one bold stare,
One of the low on whom assurance sits
As a silk hat on a Bradford millionaire.[57]
The time is now propitious, as he guesses,   235
The meal is ended, she is bored and tired,
Endeavours to engage her in caresses
Which still are unreproved, if undesired.
Flushed and decided, he assaults at once;
Exploring hands encounter no defence;   240
His vanity requires no response,

---

54. **I Tiresias . . . two lives:** Tiresias, although a mere spectator and not indeed a "character," is yet the most important personage in the poem, uniting all the rest. Just as the one-eyed merchant, seller of currants, melts into the Phoenician Sailor, and the latter is not wholly distinct from Ferdinand Prince of Naples, so all the women are one woman, and the two sexes meet in Tiresias. What Tiresias *sees,* in fact, is the substance of the poem. The whole passage from Ovid is of great anthropological interest. [Eliot's note] In the note, Eliot quotes in the original Latin the passage from "Tiresias" from the *Metamorphoses,* which A. D. Melville has translated: ". . . it chanced that Jove [Zeus], / Well warmed with nectar, laid his mighty cares / Aside and, Juno too in idle mood, / The pair were gaily joking, and Jove said / 'You women get more pleasure out of love / Than we men do, I'm sure.' She disagreed. / So they resolved to get the views of wise / Tiresias. He knew both sides of love. / For once in a green copse when two huge snakes / Were mating, he attacked them with his stick, / And was transformed (a miracle!) from man / To woman; and spent seven autumns so; / Till in the eighth he saw the snakes once more / And said 'If striking you has magic power / To change the striker to the other sex, / I'll strike you now again.' He struck the snakes / And so regained the shape he had at birth. / Asked then to give his judgment on the joke, / He found for Jove; and Juno (so it's said) / Took umbrage beyond reason, out of all / Proportion, and condemned her judge to live / In the black night of blindness evermore. / But the Almighty Father (since no god / Has the right to undo what any god has done) / For his lost sight gave him the gift to see / What things should come, the power and prophesy, / An honor to relieve that penalty."
55. **At the violet hour . . . from sea:** This may not appear as exact as Sappho's lines, but I had in mind the "longshore" or "dory" fisherman, who returns at nightfall. [Eliot's note] Eliot refers to a fragment of verse by the ancient Greek lyric poet Sappho: "Dusk and western star, / You gather / What glittering sunrise / Scattered far, / The ewe to fold, / Kid and nanny home, / But the daughter / You send wandering / From her mother" (translated by Guy Davenport).
56. **Her drying combinations:** *Combination* was a term for a woman's undergarment that combined a chemise and panties.
57. **Bradford millionaire:** Bradford, a textile center in Yorkshire, England, had boomed as a result of the demand for uniforms and blankets for the military during World War I.

And makes a welcome of indifference.
(And I Tiresias have foresuffered all
Enacted on this same divan or bed;
I who have sat by Thebes below the wall   245
And walked among the lowest of the dead.)
Bestows one final patronising kiss,
And gropes his way, finding the stairs unlit . . .

She turns and looks a moment in the glass,
Hardly aware of her departed lover;   250
Her brain allows one half-formed thought to pass:
"Well now that's done: and I'm glad it's over."
When lovely woman stoops to folly[58] and
Paces about her room again, alone,
She smoothes her hair with automatic hand,   255
And puts a record on the gramophone.

"This music crept by me upon the waters"[59]
And along the Strand, up Queen Victoria Street.
O City city, I can sometimes hear
Beside a public bar in Lower Thames Street,   260
The pleasant whining of a mandoline
And a clatter and a chatter from within
Where fishmen lounge at noon: where the walls
Of Magnus Martyr[60] hold
Inexplicable splendour of Ionian white and gold.   265

      The river sweats[61]
      Oil and tar

---

58. **When . . . stoops to folly:** V. Goldsmith, the song in *The Vicar of Wakefield*. [Eliot's note] In chapter 24 of the novel by the Irish author Oliver Goldsmith (1728-1774), the vicar's daughter Olivia sings a song about her seduction: "When Lovely woman stoops to folly, / And finds too late that men betray, / What charm can soothe her melancholy, / What art can wash her guilt away? / The only art her guilt to cover, / To hide her shame from every eye, / To give repentance to her lover, / And wring his bosom — is to die."

59. **"This . . . waters":** V. *The Tempest,* as above. [Eliot's note] See note 44. In the following passage, Eliot refers to streets in London running parallel to or toward the River Thames.

60. **Magnus Martyr:** The interior of St. Magnus Martyr is to my mind one of the finest among Wren's interiors. See *The Proposed Demolition of Nineteen City Churches* (P. S. King & Son, Ltd.). [Eliot's note] Eliot in the following line refers to the graceful Ionic columns in the interior of the church, designed by the celebrated English architect Sir Christopher Wren (1632-1723).

61. **The river sweats:** The Song of the (three) Thames-daughters begins here. From line 292 to 306 inclusive they speak in turn. V. *Götterdämmerung,* III, i: the Rhine-daughters. [Eliot's note] Eliot refers to an opera by the German composer Richard Wagner (1813-1883), *Die Götterdämmerung (The Twilight of the Gods).* In an earlier opera, *Das Rheingold,* the Rhine-daughters, guardians of a great lump of pure gold laid upon the highest rock in the river, swim around the rock and sing about the gold, repeatedly expressing their joy in the ecstatic cry "Weialala leia wallala leialala" (see lines 277-78 and 291-92). The gold is later stolen, and the Rhine-daughters reappear at the opening of act III of *Die Götterdämmerung,* where they sing of the beauty it had bestowed upon the river: "Once there was light, / When clear and fair / Our father's gold shone on the billows. / Rhinegold! / Gleaming gold! / How bright was once thy radiance, / Lovely star of the waters!"

The barges drift
With the turning tide
Red sails   270
Wide
To leeward, swing on the heavy spar.
The barges wash
Drifting logs
Down Greenwich reach   275
Past the Isla of Dogs.[62]
   Weialala leia
   Wallala leialala

Elizabeth and Leicester[63]
Beating oars   280
The stern was formed
A gilded shell
Red and gold
The brisk swell
Rippled both shores   285
Southwest wind
Carried down stream
The peal of bells
White towers
   Weialala leia   290
   Wallala leialala

"Trams and dusty trees.
Highbury bore me. Richmond and Kew
Undid me.[64] By Richmond I raised my knees
Supine on the floor of a narrow canoe."   295

"My feet are at Moorgate,[65] and my heart
Under my feet. After the event

---

62. **Isla of Dogs**: A peninsula in the estuary of the River Thames across from Greenwich. Past that point, the river is called the Greenwich Reach.

63. **Elizabeth and Leicester**: V. Froude, *Elizabeth*, Vol. I, ch. iv, letter of De Quadra to Philip of Spain: "In the afternoon we were in a barge, watching the games on the river. (The queen) was alone with Lord Robert and myself on the poop, when they began to talk nonsense, and went so far that Lord Robert at last said, as I was on the spot there was no reason why they should not be married if the queen pleased." [Eliot's note] Eliot refers to the *History of England from the Fall of Wolsey to the Death of Elizabeth* (1863) by James Anthony Froude (1818–1894), who translates an account by the Spanish ambassador at Queen Elizabeth's court of her flirtation with the Catholic Robert Dudley, Earl of Leicester.

64. **"Highbury bore me. Richmond and Kew / Undid me"**: Cf. *Purgatorio*, V. 133: "Ricorditi di me, che son la Pia; / Siena mi fe', disfecemi Maremma." [Eliot's note] Eliot refers to a passage in which the spirit of a woman who had been born in Sienna and murdered by her husband in Maremma, an area of southern Tuscany, asks Dante: "Kindly remember me – my name is Pia. / Maremma unmade what Sienna made." Highbury is a suburb of London; Richmond, a residential area along the Thames, is bordered by Kew, home of Kew Gardens.

65. **Moorgate**: A slum in east London.

He wept. He promised 'a new start.'
I made no comment. What should I resent?"

"On Margate Sands.[66]   300
I can connect
Nothing with nothing.
The broken fingernails of dirty hands.
My people humble people who expect
Nothing."   305
          la la

To Carthage then I came[67]

Burning burning burning burning[68]
O Lord Thou pluckest me out[69]
O Lord Thou pluckest   310

burning

IV. Death by Water

Phlebas the Phoenician,[70] a fortnight dead,
Forgot the cry of gulls, and the deep sea swell
And the profit and loss.

          A current under sea   315
Picked his bones in whispers. As he rose and fell
He passed the stages of his age and youth
Entering the whirlpool.

          Gentile or Jew
O you who turn the wheel and look to windward,   320
Consider Phlebas, who was once handsome and tall as you.

---

66. **Margate Sands:** The beach at Margate, a modest seaside resort on the estuary of the River Thames about seventy miles east of London.
67. **To Carthage . . . came:** V. St. Augustine's *Confessions:* "to Carthage then I came, where a cauldron of unholy loves sang all about mine ears." [Eliot's note] Eliot refers to a passage in the spiritual autobiography of St. Augustine (354–430), the bishop of Hippo in North Africa.
68. **Burning . . . burning:** The complete text of the Buddha's Fire Sermon (which corresponds in importance to the Sermon on the Mount) from which these words are taken, will be found translated in the late Henry Clarke Warren's *Buddhism in Translation* (Harvard Oriental Series). Mr. Warren was one of the great pioneers of Buddhist studies in the Occident. [Eliot's note] See note 40.
69. **O Lord . . . out:** From St. Augustine's *Confessions* again. The collocation of these two representatives of eastern and western asceticism, as the culmination of this part of the poem, is not an accident. [Eliot's note] See note 67.
70. **Phlebas the Phoenician:** Phoenicia, an ancient civilization centered in present-day Lebanon, rose to prominence through commerce and its extensive maritime trade in the Mediterranean. See "the drowned Phoenician sailor," one of the Tarot cards read by Madame Sosostris (line 47), and her warning "Fear death by water" (line 55).

V. What the Thunder Said[71]

After the torchlight red on sweaty faces
After the frosty silence in the gardens
After the agony in stony places
The shouting and the crying   325
Prison and palace and reverberation
Of thunder of spring over distant mountains
He who was living is now dead
We who were living are now dying
With a little patience[72]   330

Here is no water but only rock
Rock and no water and the sandy road
The road winding above among the mountains
Which are mountains of rock without water
If there were water we should stop and drink   335
Amongst the rock one cannot stop or think
Sweat is dry and feet are in the sand
If there were only water amongst the rock
Dead mountain mouth of carious teeth that cannot spit
Here one can neither stand nor lie nor sit   340
There is not even silence in the mountains
But dry sterile thunder without rain
There is not even solitude in the mountains
But red sullen faces sneer and snarl
From doors of mudcracked houses   345
                                        If there were water
    And no rock
    It there were rock
    And also water
    And water   350
    A spring
    A pool among the rock
    If there were the sound of water only
    Not the cicada

---

71. **What the Thunder Said:** In the first part of Part V three themes are employed: the journey to Emmaus, the approach to the Chapel Perilous (see Miss Weston's book), and the present decay of eastern Europe. [Eliot's note] In the chapter "The Perilous Chapel" in Jessie Weston's *From Ritual to Romance* (see note 1), she summarizes the dangers and terrors the heroes of Grail romances encounter in the Chapel Perilous, where "the general impression is that this is an adventure in which supernatural, and evil, forces are engaged." For the journey to Emmaus, during which the resurrected Jesus walks and converses with his disciples, who do not recognize him, see Luke 24:13-34.

72. **After the torchlight . . . patience:** This first stanza alludes to the biblical account of the arrest, imprisonment, trial, and crucifixion of Jesus.

And dry grass singing   355
But sound of water over a rock
Where the hermit-thrush[73] sings in the pine trees
Drip drop drip drop drop drop drop
But there is no water

Who is the third who walks always beside you?[74]   360
When I count, there are only you and I together
But when I look ahead up the white road
There is always another one walking beside you
Gliding wrapt in a brown mantle, hooded
I do not know whether a man or a woman   365
—But who is that on the other side of you?

What is that sound high in the air[75]
Murmur of maternal lamentation
Who are those hooded hordes swarming
Over endless plains, stumbling in cracked earth   370
Ringed by the flat horizon only
What is the city over the mountains
Cracks and reforms and bursts in the violet air
Falling towers
Jerusalem Athens Alexandria   375
Vienna London
Unreal

A woman drew her long black hair out tight
And fiddled whisper music on those strings
And bats with baby faces in the violet light   380
Whistled, and beat their wings
And crawled head downward down a blackened wall

---

73. **hermit-thrush**: This is *Turdus aonalaschkae pallasii,* the hermit-thrush which I have heard in Quebec County. Chapman says (*Handbook of Birds in Eastern North America*) "it is most at home in secluded woodland and thickety retreats. . . . Its notes are not remarkable for variety or volume, but in purity and sweetness of tone and exquisite modulation they are unequalled." Its "water-dripping song" is justly celebrated. [Eliot's note]
74. **Who . . . beside you?**: The following lines were stimulated by the account of one of the Antarctic expeditions (I forget which, but I think one of Shackleton's): "it was related that the party of explorers, at the extremity of their strength, had the constant delusion that there was *one more member* than could actually be counted." [Eliot's note] Sir Ernest Henry Shackleton (1874-1922) was a British explorer of the Antarctic.
75. **What . . . air**: Cf. Hermann Hesse, *Blick ins Chaos.* [Eliot's note] In the note, Eliot quotes in the original German a passage from an essay on the downfall of Europe in *Blick ins Chaos* (*In Sight of Chaos*) by the poet and novelist Hermann Hesse (1877-1962). The book so impressed Eliot that he encouraged his friend Sydney Schiff to translate it into English. Schiff, who published under the pseudonym Stephen Hudson, translated the passage: "Already half Europe, at all events half Eastern Europe, is on the road to Chaos. In a state of drunken illusion she is reeling into the abyss and, as she reels, she sings a drunken hymn such as Dmitri Karamazov sang [in Fyodor Dostoyevsky's novel *The Brothers Karamazov* (1882)]. The insulted citizen laughs that song to scorn, the saint and seer hear it with tears."

And upside down in air were towers
Tolling reminiscent bells, that kept the hours
And voices singing out of empty cisterns and exhausted wells 385

In this decayed hole among the mountains
In the faint moonlight, the grass is singing
Over the tumbled graves, about the chapel
There is the empty chapel, only the wind's home.
It has no windows, and the door swings, 390
Dry bones can harm no one.
Only a cock stood on the rooftree
Co co rico co co rico[76]
In a flash of lightning. Then a damp gust
Bringing rain 395

Ganga[77] was sunken, and the limp leaves
Waited for rain, while the black clouds
Gathered far distant, over Himavant.[78]
The jungle crouched, humped in silence.
Then spoke the thunder 400

Da
Datta:[79] what have we given?
My friend, blood shaking my heart
The awful daring of a moment's surrender
Which an age of prudence can never retract 405
By this, and this only, we have existed
Which is not to be found in our obituaries
Or in memories draped by the beneficent spider[80]
Or under seals broken by the lean solicitor
In our empty rooms 410
Da

---

76. **Co co rico co co rico:** *Cocorico* is a French and Italian word that approximates the sound of the crowing of a rooster, associated in folklore with the coming of dawn and the consequent departure of evil spirits.

77. **Ganga:** The Ganges, the sacred river in India, personified by the Hindu goddess Ganga.

78. **Himavant:** The Sanskrit word for *snowy*, applied to mountains in the Himalayas.

79. **Datta:** "Datta, dayadhvam, damyata" (Give, sympathise, control). The fable of the meaning of the Thunder is found in the *Brihadaranyaka—Upanishad* 5, 1. A translation is found in Deussen's *Sechzig Upanishads des Veda,* p. 489. [Eliot's note] Eliot refers to the fable of the Thunder in the Upanishads, ancient Hindu texts written in Sanskrit. In the fable, the Lord of Creation, Prajapati, utters the word *da* (the Sanskrit word representing the sound of thunder) to his three kinds of offspring: lesser gods, who understand it as "Control yourselves" (damyata); men, who understand it as "Give" (datta); and demons, who understand it as "Be compassionate" (dayadhvam).

80. **Or in memories . . . spider:** Cf. Webster, *The White Devil,* V, vi: ". . . they'll remarry / Ere the worm pierce your winding-sheet, ere the spider / Make a thin curtain for your epitaphs." [Eliot's note] The lines are spoken by the murderous villain of the play, Flamineo, who discovers that his sister has betrayed him and bitterly cautions men on their deathbeds not to trust their ostensibly grieving wives, who will swiftly find new husbands. See note 22.

Dayadhvam: I have heard the key[81]
Turn in the door once and turn once only
We think of the key, each in his prison
Thinking of the key, each confirms a prison   415
Only at nightfall, aethereal rumours
Revive for a moment a broken Coriolanus[82]
Da
Damyata: The boat responded
Gaily, to the hand expert with sail and oar   420
The sea was calm, your heart would have responded
Gaily, when invited, beating obedient
To controlling hands

I sat upon the shore
Fishing,[83] with the arid plain behind me   425
Shall I at least set my lands in order?[84]
London Bridge is falling down falling down falling down
Poi s'ascose nel foco che gli affina[85]
Quando fiam uti chelidon[86] – O swallow swallow
Le Prince d'Aquitaine à la tour abolie[87]   430
These fragments I have shored against my ruins

---

81. **I have heard the key:** Cf. *Inferno*, XXXIII, 46: "ed io sentii chiavar l'uscio di sotto / all'orribile torre." Also F. H. Bradley, *Appearance and Reality*, p. 346: "My external sensations are no less private to myself than are my thoughts or my feelings. In either case my experience falls within my own circle, a circle closed on the outside; and, with all its elements alike, every sphere is opaque to the others which surround it. . . . In brief, regarded as an existence which appears in a soul, the whole world for each is peculiar and private to that soul." [Eliot's note] The line from the *Inferno* is spoken by the traitor Ugolino, who tells Dante how his enemies imprisoned him and his children, leaving them to die of starvation: "And I could hear them nailing up the door / of the horrible tower." *Appearance and Reality: A Metaphysical Essay* (1893) was written by the English idealist philosopher Francis Herbert Bradley (1846-1924).
82. **Coriolanus:** The tragic hero of Shakespeare's play *Coriolanus* (1608), a proud and patrician Roman general who is driven into exile and seeks revenge by leading enemy forces against Rome.
83. **Fishing:** V. Weston, *From Ritual to Romance;* chapter on the Fisher King. [Eliot's note] See note 1.
84. **Shall I . . . order?:** See Isaiah 38:1: "Thus saith the LORD, Set thine house in order: for thou shalt die, and not live."
85. **Poi . . . affina:** V. *Purgatorio*, XXVI, 148. "'Ara vos prec per aquella valor / que vos guida al som de l'escalina, / sovegna vos a temps de ma dolor.' / Poi s'ascose nel foco che gli affina." [Eliot's note] The words are spoken to Dante by the spirit of the Provençal poet Arnaut Daniel, speaking amid the purifying flames of the ring of lust in purgatory: "'And so I beg of you, by that same power / that leads you to the summit of the stairs, / at the just time recall my sufferings.' / At that he hid in the refining fire." See note 3.
86. **Quando . . . chelidon:** V. *Pervigilium Veneris*. Cf. Philomela in Parts II and III. [Eliot's note] Eliot quotes part of a line from an anonymous, fourth-century Latin poem, "The Vigil of Venus," in which Philomela asks: "When shall I become like the swallow," continuing "that I cease to be silent?" See note 28.
87. **Le Prince . . . abolie:** V. Gerard de Nerval, Sonnet *El Desdichado.* [Eliot's note] Eliot quotes the second line from "The Disinherited," a sonnet by the French poet Gerard de Nerval (1808-1855), which begins: "I am the dark one, – the widower, – the unconsoled, / The Prince of Aquitaine at his stricken tower" (translated by Robert Duncan).

Why then Ile fit you. Hieronymo's mad againe.[88]
Datta. Dayadhvam. Damyata.
       Shantih   shantih   shantih[89]

[1922, 1963]

---

88. **Why then . . . mad againe:** V. Kyd's *Spanish Tragedy.* [Eliot's note] The subtitle of the play by the English dramatist Thomas Kyd (1557?-1595) is *Hieronymo Is Mad Againe.* When asked to write a play to entertain the Spanish court, Hieronimo readily agrees, saying: "Why then I'll fit [accommodate] you." He convinces the murderers of his son to act in the play, during the performance of which Hieronimo and a confederate kill them. Significantly, given the mingling of languages in *The Waste Land,* Hieronimo writes the various roles in the play in "unknown languages" – Greek, Latin, Italian, and French – "That it may breed the more variety."
89. **Shantih . . . shantih:** Repeated as here, a formal ending to an Upanishad. "The Peace which passeth understanding" is our equivalent to this word. [Eliot's note] The Upanishads are a series of Hindu treatises written in Sanskrit (c. 800-200 BCE). The ending of an Upanishad is similar to the benediction offered by Paul in Philippians 4:7: "And the peace of God, which passeth all understanding, shall keep your hearts and minds through Jesus Christ."

Reading Eliot's "Journey of the Magi." In June 1927, Eliot was baptized and confirmed in the Church of England. Later that year, this poem appeared as a pamphlet in a series, the Ariel poems, short works produced for the Christmas season by Eliot's London publisher, Faber and Faber. Like the later poems Eliot wrote for the series, which he gathered together in his *Collected Poems 1909-1935,* "The Journey of the Magi" concerns spiritual growth and a religious quest, in this case the journey of the three wise men who, according to the biblical account, witness the newborn Jesus. The dramatic monologue also anticipated a persistent concern in Eliot's later poetry and drama, the effects produced by the irruption of supernatural elements into everyday life. The text is taken from Eliot's *Collected Poems 1909-1962* (1963).

JOURNEY OF THE MAGI[1]

"A cold coming we had of it,
Just the worst time of the year
For a journey, and such a long journey:
The ways deep and the weather sharp,
The very dead of winter."[2]
And the camels galled, sore-footed, refractory,
Lying down in the melting snow.

5

---

1. **Magi:** The three wise men from the East who followed the star of Bethlehem and brought gifts to the infant Jesus (Matthew 2:1-12).
2. **"A cold coming . . . dead of winter":** The quotation is adapted from a famous Christmas sermon delivered in 1622 by Bishop Lancelot Andrewes, the renowned Anglican preacher and cleric who oversaw the translation of the authorized King James Version of the Bible.

There were times we regretted
The summer palaces on slopes, the terraces,
And the silken girls bringing sherbet.   10
Then the camel men cursing and grumbling
And running away, and wanting their liquor and women,
And the night-fires going out, and the lack of shelters,
And the cities hostile and the towns unfriendly
And the villages dirty and charging high prices: 15
A hard time we had of it.
At the end we preferred to travel all night,
Sleeping in snatches,
With the voices singing in our ears, saying
That this was all folly.   20

Then at dawn we came down to a temperate valley,
Wet, below the snow line, smelling of vegetation,
With a running stream and a water-mill beating the darkness,
And three trees on the low sky.
And an old white horse galloped away in the meadow.   25
Then we came to a tavern with vine-leaves over the lintel,
Six hands at an open door dicing for pieces of silver,
And feet kicking the empty wine-skins.
But there was no information, and so we continued
And arrived at evening, not a moment too soon   30
Finding the place; it was (you may say) satisfactory.

All this was a long time ago, I remember,
And I would do it again, but set down
This set down
This: were we led all that way for   35
Birth or Death? There was a Birth, certainly,
We had evidence and no doubt. I had seen birth and death,
But had thought they were different; this Birth was
Hard and bitter agony for us, like Death, our death.
We returned to our places, these Kingdoms,   40
But no longer at ease here, in the old dispensation,
With an alien people clutching their gods.
I should be glad of another death.

[1927, 1963]

Reading Eliot's "Burnt Norton."   Eliot wrote this poem soon after he
completed *Murder in the Cathedral* (1935), his verse play about the killing
in 1170 of Thomas Becket, the archbishop of Canterbury. The poem was
most directly inspired by Eliot's visit to Burnt Norton, an abandoned

eighteenth-century manor house in southern England, which he had toured during the summer of 1934. (The house was called Burnt Norton because the original structure had been destroyed by a fire set by its owner in 1737.) Eliot was especially taken with the extensive rose gardens, which figure prominently in "Burnt Norton." Eliot first published it as the final poem in his *Collected Poems 1909-1935*. At that point, he apparently did not conceive of the poem as the first in a series, but after World War II began in September 1939, Eliot wrote three additional poems similar in tone and structure to "Burnt Norton" – "East Coker," "The Dry Salvages," and "Little Gidding." He published the group of poems as *Four Quartets* (1943). In the later poems in the sequence, Eliot continued to explore the questions he meditated upon in "Burnt Norton," including the nature of time, the limitations of language and human knowledge, the consequent struggle for religious faith, and the Christian meaning of redemption. The text is taken from the first printing of the poem in Eliot's *Collected Poems 1909-1935* (1936).

Burnt Norton

τοῦ" λόγου δ'ἐόντο" ξυνοῦ ζώουσιν οἱ πολλοὶ
ὡς ἰδίαν ἔχοντες φρόνησιν.

I. p. 77. Fr. 2.

ὁδὸς ἄνω κάτω μία καὶ ὡυτή.

I. p. 89. Fr. 60.

Diels. *Die Fragmente der Vorsokratiker* (Herakleitos).[1]

I

Time present and time past
Are both perhaps present in time future,
And time future contained in time past.[2]
If all time is eternally present
All time is unredeemable.　　　　　　　　　　　　　　　5

---

1. [epigraphs]: The two epigraphs are from the surviving fragments of the writings of the Greek philosopher Heraclitus (c. 540-475 BCE), as compiled in 1903 by the German classical scholar Hermann Diels (1848-1922) in *Die Fragmente der Vorsokratiker* (*The Fragments of the Pre-Socratics*). Heraclitus argued that stability is illusory, since change is universal, and all things are in flux. As translated by Kathleen Freeman, the two passages Eliot quotes read: (1) "But although the Law is universal, the majority live as if they had understanding peculiar to themselves." (2) "The way up and down is one and the same."
2. **Time . . . in time past:** Eliot echoes Ecclesiastes 3:15: "That which hath been is now; and that which is to be hath already been; and God requireth that which is past."

What might have been is an abstraction
Remaining a perpetual possibility
Only in a world of speculation.
What might have been and what has been
Point to one end, which is always present.   10
Footfalls echo in the memory
Down the passage which we did not take
Towards the door we never opened
Into the rose-garden. My words echo
Thus, in your mind.   15
                    But to what purpose
Disturbing the dust on a bowl of rose-leaves
I do not know.
                    Other echoes
Inhabit the garden. Shall we follow?   20
Quick, said the bird, find them, find them,
Round the corner. Through the first gate,
Into our first world, shall we follow
The deception of the thrush? Into our first world.
There they were, dignified, invisible,   25
Moving without pressure, over the dead leaves,
In the autumn heat, through the vibrant air,
And the bird called, in response to
The unheard music hidden in the shrubbery,
And the unseen eyebeam crossed, for the roses   30
Had the look of flowers that are looked at.
There they were as our guests, accepted and accepting.
So we moved, and they, in a formal pattern,
Along the empty alley, into the box circle,[3]
To look down into the drained pool.   35
Dry the pool, dry concrete, brown edged,
And the pool was filled with water out of sunlight,
And the lotos rose,[4] quietly, quietly,
The surface glittered out of heart of light,[5]
And they were behind us, reflected in the pool.   40
Then a cloud passed, and the pool was empty.

---

3. **box circle:** Boxwood shrubs, planted in a circle.
4. **lotos rose:** The lotus is any of a large number of floating water plants, perhaps in this case the "sacred lotus," an Asiatic variety bearing dark pink flowers.
5. **out of heart of light:** Eliot alludes to a passage in *Paradiso*, the final volume of the *Divine Comedy* by the Italian poet Dante Alighieri (1265-1321), in which the poet passes upward among the blessed souls in the heaven of the Sun: "So from the heart of a new gleam of light / came a voice" (12.28-29, as translated by Anthony Esolen).

Go, said the bird, for the leaves were full of children,
Hidden excitedly, containing laughter.
Go, go, go, said the bird: human kind
Cannot bear very much reality.   45
Time past and time future
What might have been and what has been
Point to one end, which is always present.

II

Garlic and sapphires in the mud
Clot the bedded axle-tree.[6]   50
The trilling wire in the blood
Sings below inveterate scars
And reconciles forgotten wars.
The dance along the artery
The circulation of the lymph   55
Are figured in the drift of stars
Ascend to summer in the tree
We move above the moving tree
In light upon the figured leaf
And hear upon the sodden floor   60
Below, the boarhound and the boar
Pursue their pattern as before
But reconciled among the stars.

At the still point of the turning world. Neither flesh nor fleshless;
Neither from nor towards; at the still point, there the dance is, 65
But neither arrest nor movement. And do not call it fixity.
Where past and future are gathered. Neither movement from nor
    towards,
Neither ascent nor decline. Except for the point, the still point,
There would be no dance, and there is only the dance.
I can only say, *there* we have been: but I cannot say where.   70
And I cannot say, how long, for that is to place it in time.

The inner freedom from the practical desire,
The release from action and suffering, release from the inner
And the outer compulsion, yet surrounded
By a grace of sense, a white light still and moving,   75

---

6. **axle-tree:** A rod supporting a cart with terminal spindles on which the wheels turn; also, in Christian cosmology, the "axletree" of heaven, around which the universe revolves.

Erhebung[7] without motion, concentration
Without elimination, both a new world
And the old made explicit, understood
In the completion of its partial ecstasy,
The resolution of its partial horror.   80
Yet the enchainment of past and future
Woven in the weakness of the changing body,
Protects mankind from heaven and damnation
Which flesh cannot endure.
                Time past and time future   85
Allow but a little consciousness.
To be conscious is not to be in time
But only in time can the moment in the rose-garden,
The moment in the arbour where the rain beat,
The moment in the draughty church at smoke-fall   90
Be remembered; involved with past and future.
Only through time time is conquered.

III

Here is a place of disaffection
Time before and time after
In a dim light:[8] neither daylight   95
Investing form with lucid stillness
Turning shadow into transient beauty
With slow rotation suggesting permanence
Nor darkness to purify the soul
Emptying the sensual with deprivation   100
Cleansing affection from the temporal.
Neither plenitude nor vacancy. Only a flicker
Over the strained time-ridden faces
Distracted from distraction by distraction
Filled with fancies and empty of meaning   105
Tumid apathy with no concentration
Men and bits of paper, whirled by the cold wind
That blows before and after time,
Wind in and out of unwholesome lungs
Time before and time after.   110

---

7. *Erhebung*: Exaltation (German).
8. **Here . . . dim light:** This section of the poem is set in the London subway system, the Underground.

Eructation[9] of unhealthy souls
Into the faded air, the torpid
Driven on the wind that sweeps the gloomy hills of London,
Hampstead and Clerkenwell, Campden and Putney,
Highgate, Primrose and Ludgate.[10] Not here   115
Not here the darkness, in this twittering world.

Descend lower, descend only
Into the world of perpetual solitude,
World not world, but that which is not world,
Internal darkness, deprivation   120
And destitution of all property,
Dessication of the world of sense,
Evacuation of the world of fancy,
Inoperancy of the world of spirit;[11]
This is the one way, and the other   125
Is the same, not in movement
But abstention from movement; while the world moves
In appetency,[12] on its metalled ways
Of time past and time future.

IV

Time and the bell have buried the day,   130
The black cloud carries the sun away.
Will the sunflower turn to us, will the clematis
Stray down, bend to us; tendril and spray
Clutch and cling?
Chill   135
Fingers of yew be curled
Down on us?[13] After the kingfisher's wing

---

9. **Eructation:** Belching.
10. **Hampstead . . . Ludgate:** Names of various sections and neighborhoods in London.
11. **Descend lower . . . world of spirit:** In his treatise *Dark Night of the Soul*, the Spanish mystic St. John of the Cross (1542–1591) described a process of contemplation that "produces in spiritual persons two kinds of darkness or purgation," explaining: "And thus the one night or purgation will be sensual, wherein the soul is purged according to sense, which is subdued to the spirit; and the other is a night or purgation which is spiritual, wherein the soul is purged and stripped according to the spirit, and subdued and made ready for the union of love with God" (translated by E. Allison Peers).
12. **appetency:** An early term for longing or desire.
13. **Fingers of yew . . . on us?:** The yew is a long-lived coniferous tree often associated with graveyards, as in a famous passage from *In Memoriam* by the English poet Alfred, Lord Tennyson (1809–1892): "Old Yew, which graspest at the stones / That name the under-lying dead, / Thy fibres net the dreamless head, / Thy roots are wrapt about the bones" (II.1–4).

Has answered light to light, and is silent, the light is still
At the still point of the turning world.

V

Words move, music moves   140
Only in time; but that which is only living
Can only die. Words, after speech, reach
Into the silence. Only by the form, the pattern,
Can words or music reach
The stillness, as a Chinese jar still   145
Moves perpetually in its stillness.
Not the stillness of the violin, while the note lasts,
Not that only, but the co-existence,
Or say that the end precedes the beginning,
And the end and the beginning were always there   150
Before the beginning and after the end.
And all is always now. Words strain,
Crack and sometimes break, under the burden,
Under the tension, slip, slide, perish,
Decay with imprecision, will not stay in place,   155
Will not stay still. Shrieking voices
Scolding, mocking, or merely chattering,
Always assail them. The Word in the desert
Is most attacked by voices of temptation,[14]
The crying shadow in the funeral dance,   160
The loud lament of the disconsolate chimera.[15]

The detail of the pattern is movement,
As in the figure of the ten stairs.[16]
Desire itself is movement
Not in itself desirable;   165
Love is itself unmoving,
Only the cause and end of movement,
Timeless, and undesiring
Except in the aspect of time
Caught in the form of limitation   170

---

14. **The Word in the desert . . . temptation:** An allusion to Christ's forty days in the wilderness, where he was tempted by the devil, as described in Luke 4:1-4.
15. **chimera:** In Greek mythology, a fire-breathing female monster with body parts from several animals.
16. **the ten stairs:** An allusion to St. John of the Cross's model for the soul's ascent to God, "The Ten Degrees of the Mystical Ladder of the Divine Love." See note 11.

Between un-being and being.
Sudden in a shaft of sunlight
Even while the dust moves
There rises the hidden laughter
Of children in the foliage   175
Quick now, here, now, always –
Ridiculous the waste sad time
Stretching before and after.

[1936]

Claude McKay

[1889–1948]

Claude McKay

The writer and photographer Carl Van Vechten took this portrait of McKay in 1934, the year the poet returned to New York City after spending more than a decade in exile abroad.

Photo © Carl Van Vechten

Festus Claudius McKay was born in Sunny Ville, Jamaica, on September 15, 1889. He was the youngest of eleven children born to prosperous black farmers, Hannah Ann Elizabeth Edwards McKay and Thomas Francis McKay, who provided their children with solid educations and strong religious training in the Baptist Church. Initially educated by his brilliant older brother Uriah Theo McKay, a prominent schoolteacher and radical reformer, McKay was a gifted student. After he completed his secondary education, however, he decided that he did not want to follow the path of his older brothers, most of whom were teachers or preachers. Instead, he won a scholarship to the government trade school in Kingston. His training to be a wheelwright ended when an earthquake destroyed the school in 1907, and he soon went home to care for his ailing and beloved mother. When she died in 1909, McKay returned to Kingston, where he impulsively joined the Jamaica Constabulary. Soon realizing that he was completely unsuited to the harsh discipline and brutality of police work, McKay managed to extricate himself from the force after seventeen months – rather than the mandatory five years – through the influence of a wealthy English aristocrat, Walter Jekyll. The editor of a collection of indigenous writings, *Jamaican Song and Story* (1907), Jekyll encouraged McKay to write dialect verse in the local Creole language, some of which was published in a Jamaican newspaper, the *Daily Gleaner*. In 1912, Jekyll also arranged for the publication in London of McKay's first two collections of poetry, *Constab Ballads* and *Songs of Jamaica.*

Despite his success, McKay believed he would have greater opportunities in the United States. When a visitor told him about Booker T. Washington's Tuskegee Institute, the twenty-three-year-old McKay set off for Alabama in 1912. Shocked by what he later described as the "implacable hate of my race" he confronted in the South, and unhappy with the curriculum at Tuskegee, McKay soon transferred to Kansas State College. No happier there, he was rescued in 1914 by a financial gift from his friend Jekyll, which allowed McKay to move to New York City, invest in a restaurant, and marry Eulalie Imelda Lewars, a fellow Jamaican. Within a year, the restaurant failed, and their marriage ended. Supporting himself by working as a railroad porter, McKay lived in Harlem, where he became involved with other writers and intellectuals. In 1917, he submitted two poems in standard English, "The Harlem Dancer" and "Invocation," to an innovative little magazine, *Seven Arts*. Fearing that his reputation as a Jamaican dialect poet would hurt his chances with an American magazine, McKay submitted and the poems were published under the pseudonym "Eli Edwards." But his identity soon became known to Max Eastman, the editor of a radical socialist journal, the *Liberator*. During the explosive summer of 1919, when race riots erupted in both northern and southern cities across the United States, McKay published under his own name "If We Must Die" in the *Liberator*. The militant poem was widely reprinted in African American newspapers, and poets such as Langston Hughes and James Weldon Johnson later cited it as a major inspiration of the Harlem Renaissance.

McKay, however, strongly resisted being restricted to the role of a black protest poet. He soon moved to London, where he studied the writings of Karl Marx and worked for a socialist journal, the *Workers' Dreadnought*. He also published a book of poems, *Spring in New Hampshire* (1920). After returning to New York in 1921, he became the associate editor of the *Liberator* and published his acclaimed collection *Harlem Shadows* (1922). Although he was buoyed by his literary success, McKay was becoming increasingly disenchanted with the American social and political system. "Color-consciousness was the fundamental of my restlessness," he later observed. McKay decided to set off once again, this time to the Soviet Union, where he was warmly received. His sympathy with the Bolshevik Revolution brought him to the attention of the Federal Bureau of Investigation, which blocked McKay's return to the United States. For the next twelve years, he lived in Europe and North Africa. Turning from poetry to prose fiction, he wrote *Home to Harlem* (1928), a graphic account of the underside of Harlem life that McKay's hero W. E. B. Du Bois savagely attacked, observing that "after the dirtier parts of its filth I felt distinctly like taking a bath." But the best-selling novel, the first by a black writer in the United States, won the annual Harmon Gold Award for an outstanding work of literature by an African American. McKay followed it with three more works of fiction: *Banjo* (1929), a novel about black beach boys in Marseilles; *Gingertown* (1932), a collection of stories set in Harlem and Jamaica; and *Banana Bottom* (1933), a novel celebrating the folk culture of a village in Jamaica.

McKay published no more books of fiction or poetry after he returned to the United States in 1934. Now an opponent of Communism, he remained committed to socialism and wrote articles for progressive periodicals such as the *Nation*. He also continued to write poetry, but he could not interest a publisher in "Cities" (c. 1934), a sequence of poems charting his travels around the world, or a later collection of deeply personal and embittered poems, "The Cycle" (c. 1943). His final published books were works

[O]ut of a heterogeneity of experience with an underlying unity, Claude McKay, as wheelwright, constable, agriculturist, porter, longshoreman, waiter, vagabond, rebel, and penitent, created his best poems.

–Melvin Tolson

of nonfiction, *A Long Way from Home* (1937), an autobiography, and *Harlem: Negro Metropolis* (1940). In 1940, he became an American citizen, and McKay converted to Roman Catholicism in 1944. He spent much of the rest of his life in Chicago, where he worked for the Catholic Youth Organization and where he died on May 22, 1948. McKay, who had never returned to his native Jamaica, was buried in New York City.

Reading McKay's Poetry.   Early in his career, McKay earned a reputation as a Jamaican dialect poet, but he wrote poems only in standard English after he immigrated to the United States in 1912. Well acquainted with the Bible and steeped from an early age in the poetry of Shakespeare and British Romantic poets such as John Keats and Percy Bysshe Shelley, McKay was drawn to traditional lyric forms, especially the sonnet. In an "Author's Word" at the opening of *Harlem Shadows* (1922), widely regarded as his most significant collection of poetry, McKay explained: "I have adhered to such of the older traditions as I find adequate for my most lawless and revolutionary passions and moods." Certainly, there is a vital tension between the strict form and rhyme schemes of the sonnet, which commonly deals with the subject of love, and McKay's angry and defiant denunciations of racial hatred and social inequality in sonnets such as "If We Must Die" and "America," both of which were originally published in the revolutionary political and literary journal the *Liberator*. The texts of the following poems, all of which McKay collected in *Harlem Shadows*, are taken from his *Complete Poems*, edited by William J. Maxwell (2004).

bedfordstmartins.com/
americanlit *for research*
links on McKay

THE HARLEM DANCER[1]

Applauding youths laughed with young prostitutes
And watched her perfect, half-clothed body sway;
Her voice was like the sound of blended flutes
Blown by black players upon a picnic day.[2]
She sang and danced on gracefully and calm,   5
The light gauze hanging loose about her form;
To me she seemed a proudly-swaying palm
Grown lovelier for passing through a storm.
Upon her swarthy neck black shiny curls
Luxuriant fell; and tossing coins in praise,   10

---

1. **The Harlem Dancer:** McKay's first publication in the United States, this poem appeared as one of "Two Sonnets" in the influential but short-lived magazine *Seven Arts* (October 1917).
2. **blended flutes . . . picnic day:** An allusion to pan flutes, also known as panpipes, an ancient folk instrument associated with pastoral poetry.

The wine-flushed, bold-eyed boys, and even the girls,
Devoured her shape with eager, passionate gaze;
But looking at her falsely-smiling face,
I knew her self was not in that strange place.

[1917, 2004]

If We Must Die[1]

If we must die, let it not be like hogs
Hunted and penned in an inglorious spot,
While round us bark the mad and hungry dogs,
Making their mock at our accursèd lot.
If we must die, O let us nobly die,   5
So that our precious blood may not be shed
In vain; then even the monsters we defy
Shall be constrained to honor us though dead!
O kinsmen! we must meet the common foe!
Though far outnumbered let us show us brave,   10
And for their thousand blows deal one deathblow!
What though before us lies the open grave?
Like men we'll face the murderous, cowardly pack,[2]
Pressed to the wall, dying, but fighting back!

[1919, 2004]

1. **If We Must Die**: McKay wrote this poem in response to what James Weldon Johnson named the "Red Summer," a wave of antiblack riots and lynchings that took place in Chicago; Washington, D.C.; Omaha, Nebraska; and other northern and southern cities in the summer and fall of 1919. To the amazement of many white people and editorial writers, blacks fought back, displaying a new militancy that McKay also voiced in his poem, which was first published in the *Liberator*, a "Journal of Revolutionary Progress," in July 1919.
2. **cowardly pack**: According to historians, the riots were initiated by gangs of white segregationists, called *white hoodlums* by Carl Sandburg, who reported on the Chicago riots for the *Chicago Daily News*.

The Lynching

His Spirit in smoke ascended to high heaven.
His father, by the cruelest way of pain,
Had bidden him to his bosom once again;
The awful sin remained still unforgiven.[1]
All night a bright and solitary star   5

1. **His Spirit . . . unforgiven**: The scene recalls the crucifixion of Christ, who at the moment of death commits his spirit to his Father (Luke 23:46).

(Perchance the one that ever guided him,
Yet gave him up at last to Fate's wild whim)
Hung pitifully o'er the swinging char.[2]
Day dawned, and soon the mixed crowds came to view
The ghastly body swaying in the sun   10
The women thronged to look, but never a one
Showed sorrow in her eyes of steely blue;
And little lads, lynchers that were to be,
Danced round the dreadful thing in fiendish glee.

[1920, 2004]

2. **swinging char:** That is, the charred body swinging at the end of the rope. Many lynching victims were both hanged and burned.

AMERICA

Although she feeds me bread of bitterness,
And sinks into my throat her tiger's tooth,
Stealing my breath of life, I will confess
I love this cultured hell that tests my youth!
Her vigor flows like tides into my blood,   5
Giving me strength erect against her hate.
Her bigness sweeps my being like a flood.
Yet as a rebel fronts a king in state,
I stand within her walls with not a shred
Of terror, malice, not a word of jeer.   10
Darkly I gaze into the days ahead,
And see her might and granite wonders there,
Beneath the touch of Time's unerring hand,
Like priceless treasures sinking in the sand.[1]

[1921, 2004]

1. **Darkly I gaze . . . sinking in the sand:** The poet's foreboding vision of the nation's future decline echoes "Ozymandias," the Greek name for the pharaoh Ramses II, by the English poet Percy Bysshe Shelley (1792–1822). Shelley's sonnet about the arrogance and transience of power, as illustrated by the fragmentary remains of what was once the largest statue in Egypt, concludes: "Round the decay / Of that colossal Wreck, boundless and bare / The lone and level sands stretch far away."

AFRICA

The sun sought thy dim bed and brought forth light,
The sciences were sucklings at thy breast;
When all the world was young in pregnant night

Thy slaves toiled at thy monumental best.
Thou ancient treasure-land, thou modern prize, 5
New peoples marvel at thy pyramids!
The years roll on, thy sphinx of riddle eyes
Watches the mad world with immobile lids.
The Hebrews humbled them at Pharaoh's name.
Cradle of Power! Yet all things were in vain! 10
Honor and Glory, Arrogance and Fame!
They went. The darkness swallowed thee again.
Thou art the harlot, now thy time is done,
Of all the mighty nations of the sun.

[1921, 2004]

Edna St. Vincent Millay

[1892–1950]

Edna St. Vincent Millay was born in Rockland, Maine, on February 22, 1892, the first of the three daughters of Cora Buzzelle and Henry Tollman Millay. In 1900, Cora Millay left her husband, an improvident schoolteacher, and moved with her daughters into a small house in the poorest part of Camden, Maine, where she supported the family by working as a practical nurse. A former singer who frequently read poetry to her daughters, Cora Millay strongly encouraged their interests in literature and music. Edna St. Vincent Millay, who from an early age insisted on being called "Vincent," studied piano and wrote for a literary magazine she started in high school. When she was fourteen, she published her first poem in a popular illustrated magazine for children, *St. Nicholas*, and another of her early poems later appeared in *Current Literature*. Unable to afford college, Millay remained at home after her graduation from high school, helping to care for her younger sisters, occasionally working as a typist, and writing poetry. The publication of her long poem "Renascence" in the popular anthology *The Lyric Year* (1912) gained her

Edna St. Vincent Millay

The noted portrait photographer Arnold Genthe took this publicity photograph in 1914, after Millay had risen to fame on the basis of her early poem "Renascence."

national attention, and Millay consequently obtained a scholarship to Vassar College, which she entered in the fall of 1913. Although she defiantly flouted every rule of the small women's college, Millay seriously studied languages and literature, acted in plays, including one she wrote, and published her poetry in the Vassar *Miscellany*.

After her graduation from Vassar in 1917, Millay embarked on a highly successful literary career. She moved to New York City, where she published her warmly received first book, *Renascence and Other Poems* (1917). Free-spirited and fiercely independent, Millay lived a bohemian existence in Greenwich Village, where she enjoyed the company of other writers and artists, with many of whom she had affairs, and acted in plays produced by the Provincetown Players. In order to earn money, she published a series of short stories under the pen name Nancy Boyd in *Ainslee's Magazine*. In 1920, Millay published her second volume of poetry, *A Few Figs from Thistles*, which one reviewer favorably compared to Emily Dickinson's poetry, and *Aria da Capo*, a popular antiwar play that was produced by the Provincetown Players. Eagerly accepting a job with the cultural magazine *Vanity Fair*, Millay spent most of the following three years traveling in Europe, where she wrote articles for the magazine, plays, and poetry. Her third book of poetry, *Second April* (1921), was nominated for the Pulitzer Prize, which Millay was awarded for her next book, *The Harp-Weaver and Other Poems* (1922). The first woman to be awarded the Pulitzer Prize for Poetry, Millay was also a rarity among poets, male or female: She was earning a living by writing poetry. Indeed, by then she was the most popular and best-selling poet in the United States.

In 1923, Millay's life changed in two important ways. She entered into an "open" marriage with Eugen Jan Boissevain, the forty-three-year-old widower of Inez Milholland, a Vassar alumna and leader of the women's suffrage movement who had died in 1916. With Boissevain, by all accounts a remarkable person who strongly supported her career, Millay thereafter lived at Steepletop, a farmhouse they purchased in the Berkshire Mountains near Austerlitz, New York. At the same time, Millay began to assume a more prominent public role. She traveled across the country, enthralling audiences with theatrical readings in a rich contralto voice that was variously described as sounding like "a bronze bell" and "an axe on fresh wood." She also became increasingly active in social causes, including women's rights and the case of Nicola Sacco and Bartolomeo Vanzetti, two Italian-born anarchists who were convicted of robbery and murder in Massachusetts. Millay led other writers in a protest in Boston and made a last-minute appeal to the governor of Massachusetts to stay the execution, but Sacco and Vanzetti were electrocuted later that night, on August 23, 1927. The bitter aftertaste of that experience remained with Millay, who later told a fellow writer that the case had made her "more aware of the underground workings of forces alien to true democracy." For the first time, Millay included several poems of social protest in her next book, *The Buck in the Snow and Other Poems* (1928).

During the 1930s and 1940s, Millay's phenomenal success as a poet was shadowed by physical problems and personal losses. Her beloved mother died in 1931, the year Millay published *Fatal Interview*, a sonnet sequence

Her talent, with its diverting mixture of solemnity and levity, won the enthusiasm of a time bewildered intellectually and moving unsteadily towards an emotional attitude of its own.

—Allen Tate

inspired by her passionate and painful affair with George Dillon, a younger man she had met at a reading at the University of Chicago. That acclaimed volume, which sold thirty-five thousand copies within two weeks, was followed by *Wine from These Grapes* (1934) and *Huntsman, What Quarry?* (1939), collections of poems that revealed Millay's gloomy response to the growing threat of another world war and the rise of Fascism in Europe. Abandoning her earlier pacifism, Millay championed the Allied cause in articles and the poems collected in *Make Bright the Arrows* (1940). Although that volume and the other propagandistic poetry Millay wrote during World War II damaged her critical reputation, she was elected to the American Academy of Arts and Letters in 1940 and awarded the Gold Medal for lifetime achievement by the Poetry Society of America in 1943. Millay suffered a nervous breakdown in 1944, and her final years were marred by illness, addiction to alcohol and morphine, and the death of her husband in 1949. Millay died alone in her home of a heart attack on October 19, 1950.

bedfordstmartins.com/ americanlit for research links on Millay

Reading Millay's Poetry. In one of the many articles published in the aftermath of her sudden death, a writer for the *New York Times* described Millay as "'a poet's poet,' and a 'lover's poet,' and sometimes a crusader's poet as well." Unlike more experimental poets of her generation, including her female contemporaries H.D. and Marianne Moore, Millay most often wrote in conventional meters and adopted traditional forms such as the epigram, the quatrain, and especially the sonnet, upon which she placed her personal stamp. In a review of her third book of poetry, *Second April* (1921), the critic and writer Maxwell Anderson commented that many of her sonnets were "powerful, humanly moving, perfectly touched, said as only a first-class artist could say them." During her lifetime, Millay published seventeen collections of her poems, many of which first appeared in periodicals. "First Fig" and "Second Fig," the opening poems of her collection *A Few Figs from Thistles* (1920), were first published in Harriet Monroe's innovative, Chicago-based *Poetry: A Magazine of Verse* in 1918. Millay, who vastly expanded the audience for poetry in the United States, also published in national mass-circulation magazines, including the *Saturday Evening Post* and *Vanity Fair*. By 1927, her fame was so great that her protest poem "Justice Denied in Massachusetts" was printed under the boldface headline "POEM BY MISS MILLAY ON SACCO AND VANZETTI" in the *New York Times*. The texts of the poems are taken from her *Collected Poems*, edited by Norma Millay (1956).

FIRST FIG

My candle burns at both ends;
    It will not last the night;
But ah, my foes, and oh, my friends —
    It gives a lovely light!

[1918, 1956]

SECOND FIG

Safe upon the solid rock the ugly houses stand:
Come and see my shining palace built upon the sand!

[1918, 1956]

[I, BEING BORN A WOMAN AND DISTRESSED]

I, being born a woman and distressed
By all the needs and notions of my kind,
Am urged by your propinquity to find
Your person fair, and feel a certain zest
To bear your body's weight upon my breast: 5
So subtly is the fume of life designed,
To clarify the pulse and cloud the mind,
And leave me once again undone, possessed.
Think not for this, however, the poor treason
Of my stout blood against my staggering brain,   10
I shall remember you with love, or season
My scorn with pity, — let me make it plain:
I find this frenzy insufficient reason
For conversation when we meet again.

[1921, 1956]

[OH, OH, YOU WILL BE SORRY FOR THAT WORD!]

Oh, oh, you will be sorry for that word!
Give back my book and take my kiss instead.
Was it my enemy or my friend I heard,
"What a big book for such a little head!"
Come, I will show you now my newest hat,   5
And you may watch me purse my mouth and prink!
Oh, I shall love you still, and all of that.
I never again shall tell you what I think.
I shall be sweet and crafty, soft and sly;
You will not catch me reading any more: 10
I shall be called a wife to pattern by;
And some day when you knock and push the door,

Some sane day, not too bright and not too stormy,
I shall be gone, and you may whistle for me.

[1922, 1956]

JUSTICE DENIED IN MASSACHUSETTS[1]

Let us abandon then our gardens and go home
And sit in the sitting-room.
Shall the larkspur blossom or the corn grow under this cloud?
Sour to the fruitful seed
Is the cold earth under this cloud,   5
Fostering quack and weed, we have marched upon but cannot
    conquer;
We have bent the blades of our hoes against the stalks of them.

Let us go home, and sit in the sitting-room.
Not in our day
Shall the cloud go over and the sun rise as before,   10
Beneficent upon us
Out of the glittering bay,
And the warm winds be blown inward from the sea
Moving the blades of corn
With a peaceful sound.   15
Forlorn, forlorn,
Stands the blue hay-rack by the empty mow.
And the petals drop to the ground,
Leaving the tree unfruited.
The sun that warmed our stooping backs and withered the weed
    uprooted –   20
We shall not feel it again.
We shall die in darkness, and be buried in the rain.

What from the splendid dead
We have inherited –
Furrows sweet to the grain, and the weed subdued –   25
See now the slug and the mildew plunder.

---

1. **Justice Denied in Massachusetts:** Millay wrote this poem to protest the impending execution of Nicola Sacco and Bartolomeo Vanzetti, two Italian-born anarchists who were sentenced to death after being convicted of robbery and murder in Massachusetts. Many believed that the men had not received a fair trial because of hostility to Italian immigrants and the pervasive fear of "reds," or radicals, during the 1920s. Despite protests and appeals to the governor to stay the execution, Sacco and Vanzetti were put to death on August 22, 1927, the day Millay's poem was first published in the *New York Times*.

Evil does overwhelm
The larkspur and the corn;
We have seen them go under.

Let us sit here, sit still, 30
Here in the sitting-room until we die;
At the step of Death on the walk, rise and go;
Leaving to our children's children this beautiful doorway,
And this elm,
And a blighted earth to till 35
With a broken hoe.

[1927, 1956]

E. E. Cummings

[1894–1962]

Edward Estlin Cummings was born on October 14, 1894, in Cambridge, Massachusetts. He was the first child of Edward Cummings, a professor at Harvard University and later a Unitarian minister, and Rebecca Haswell Clarke Cummings, a descendant of Susanna Rowson, the author of *Charlotte Temple* (1791), one of the first best-selling novels published in the United States. The affluent family lived in a large house in Cambridge and at Joy Farm, their summer home on Silver Lake in New Hampshire. They often read together, especially the poetry of Henry Wadsworth Longfellow, the revered nineteenth-century American poet whom Cummings's mother particularly admired and wanted her son to emulate. Cummings, who wrote constantly, published poems and short stories in the literary magazine of the prestigious Cambridge Latin School. In 1911, he entered Harvard, where he excelled academically, earning a bachelor's degree with honors in Greek and English literature, and helped edit and contributed fairly traditional poems to the *Harvard Monthly*. But he was fascinated by "The New Art," the title of his

E. E. Cummings

This photograph of Cummings was taken while he was in Paris in 1923, the year his first book of poetry was published in New York City.

1915 graduation speech in which Cummings championed radical departures in art, music, and literature, including the imagist verse of Amy Lowell. After his graduation, he stayed on for an additional year at Harvard, earning a master's degree in 1916. From an early age, Cummings had enjoyed drawing and sketching, and he now began to paint seriously, heavily influenced by the new trends in art, especially cubism. He also wrote experimental poems, some of which were published in an anthology edited by one of his college friends, *Eight Harvard Poets* (1917).

Cummings's effort to join the ranks of modernist artists was temporarily disrupted by World War I. Leaving Cambridge, he took a job with a mail-order publishing firm in New York City, where he worked briefly before the United States entered the war in April 1917. To avoid being drafted, the pacifistic Cummings volunteered to serve in the Norton-Harjes Ambulance Corps and was sent to France. Five months later, Cummings and a friend, William Slater Brown, were arrested on suspicion of treason. The unfounded charges stemmed primarily from some mildly negative letters about the war that Brown had written home, as well as the two men's constant questioning of the authority of the chief of the ambulance corps. Nonetheless, Cummings and Brown were sent to a French detention camp for three months. Through the efforts of his father, Cummings was released in December 1917 and sent back to the United States. After living for six months in New York City, he was drafted into the infantry and sent for training to Camp Devens, Massachusetts. Fortunately for Cummings, who hated the army and the war, the conflict ended a few months later, and he was discharged and returned to New York City in January 1919.

Cummings soon found himself at the center of the cultural ferment of the early 1920s. He painted, wrote poetry, and enjoyed the company of a circle of artistic friends from his Harvard days, including the wealthy art patron Scofield Thayer. Cummings fell in love with Thayer's estranged wife, Elaine, who gave birth to their daughter in December 1919. Thayer was less concerned with their affair than with his purchase of the *Dial*, a prominent political and cultural magazine he was determined to transform into the preeminent journal of avant-garde art. Immediately after Thayer and his Harvard friend James Sibley Watson gained control of the magazine, they invited Cummings to contribute to the *Dial*, where four of his drawings and seven of his innovative poems appeared in January 1920. He also gained attention for his abstract paintings, two of which were exhibited at the Society of Independent Artists Exhibition in the spring of 1920. His relationship with Elaine Thayer was now strained, and Cummings soon left New York to study art in Paris. There, he wrote *The Enormous Room* (1922), a graphic and stylistically dizzying account of his imprisonment in France. He also continued to write poetry, which regularly appeared in the *Dial* and other little magazines such as *Broom*, *Secession*, and the *Little Review*. With the help of his friend John Dos Passos, Cummings published his exuberant first collection of poems, *Tulips and Chimneys* (1923). Returning to New York early in 1924, he married Elaine

One has in Mr. Cummings's work, a sense of the best dancing and of the best horticulture.
—Marianne Moore

Thayer, but they were divorced by the end of the year. Cummings immersed himself in work and soon published his second collection of poetry, *XLI Poems. &.* (1925). Five years after he published his first poems in the *Dial*, Cummings received the magazine's prestigious award "for distinguished service to American letters" in 1925.

During the following decades, Cummings gained popular as well as critical acclaim. He extended his experiments in language and typography in the poems collected in *is 5* (1926) – the title, he explained, revealed the difference between most people, who think that two and two is four, and the poet, who knows that it is 5 – and *ViVa* (1931). The versatile Cummings also wrote a play, *Him*, which was produced by the Provincetown Players in 1928, and published a controversial diary/memoir/novel about his 1931 trip to Russia, *Eimi* (1933). His unhappy second marriage, to Anne Barton, ended in divorce after five years, in 1934. That year, his personal life changed dramatically when he met Marion Morehouse, a former fashion model who lived with Cummings as his common-law wife until his death. Cummings regained some of his earlier humor and exuberance in the poems collected in *No Thanks* (1935), which he ironically dedicated to the fourteen publishers who had rejected the manuscript, *50 Poems* (1940), and *1 x 1* (1944). During his later years, he won the Harriet Monroe Prize from *Poetry* for *Xaipe* (1950), and his *Collected Poems* (1954) was given a special citation by the National Book Award, won that year by Wallace Stevens's *Collected Poems*. Cummings was awarded the Bollingen Prize in recognition of his lifetime achievement in 1958, the year he published his final volume of poetry, *95 Poems*. Especially popular among college students, Cummings gave hundreds of readings at universities across the country, and he and Morehouse traveled extensively in Europe. But they spent much of their time at Joy Farm, which Cummings inherited upon his father's death, and where he died of a stroke on September 3, 1962.

Reading Cummings's Poetry. Although he ultimately became one of the most beloved of twentieth-century American poets, Cummings was initially viewed as a radical innovator whose verse was considered extreme even by the standards of the "new poetry." In addition to erotic love poems and poems celebrating the beauty and freshness of nature, work that proved to be especially popular with readers, Cummings wrote sharply satirical poems and parodies of American culture, jingoism, and militarism. The form of his poems was equally innovative. An artist who produced drawings and paintings throughout his life, Cummings was deeply concerned with the visual appearance of a poem. In a notebook written late in his life, Cummings wrote that his early work, "the inaudible poem – the visual poem, the poem not for ears but eyes – moved me more." He constantly experimented with style and typography in his colloquial, free-verse poems, fusing together and creating new words, substituting one part of speech for another, breaking lines at unusual points, varying

bedfordstmartins.com/ americanlit for research links on Cummings

E. E. Cummings,
Noise Number 13

Cummings described this abstract 1925 painting as a "Forwardflung backwardSpinning hoop."

the spacing between words, and generally avoiding capitalizations. His eccentric typography, for which Cummings has often been called the "lowercase poet," later prompted some publishers and scholars to spell his name "e. e. cummings." Beginning after his death, that trend persisted for decades until the E. E. Cummings Society verified that there was no basis for the use of lowercase letters, since Cummings followed the usual convention of capitalizing his name in his personal correspondence, in signatures on the poems he published in magazines, and on the covers of the books published during his lifetime. From the beginning of his career, however, the idiosyncratic typography and punctuation of his poems created problems for editors. Shortly before his first poems were published in the *Dial* in 1920, for example, Cummings wrote the editor, Scofield Thayer: "Note punctuation exemplifying a theory in my soul that every 'word' *purely* considered implies its own punctuation." The texts of the following poems, which retain Cummings's original typography and punctuation, are taken from *E. E. Cummings: Complete Poems, 1904–1962*, edited by George J. Firmage (1991).

[IN JUST-]

in Just-
spring   when the world is mud-
luscious the little
lame balloonman

whistles   far   and wee   5

and eddieandbill come
running from marbles and
piracies and it's
spring

when the world is puddle-wonderful   10

the queer
old balloonman whistles
far   and   wee
and bettyandisbel come dancing

from hop-scotch and jump-rope and   15

it's
spring
and
        the

                goat-footed   20

balloonMan   whistles
far
and
wee

[1920, 1991]

[BUFFALO BILL 'S]

Buffalo Bill 's[1]
defunct
        who used to
        ride a watersmooth-silver
                        stallion   5

---

1. **Buffalo Bill 's:** The colorful William Cody (1846–1917), a Union soldier in the Civil War, was nicknamed Buffalo Bill for hunting and killing over 4,000 buffalo for the Kansas Pacific Railroad in the late 1860s. He later developed a popular traveling extravaganza, Buffalo Bill's Wild West Show, often advertised as "America's National Entertainment."

and break onetwothreefourfive pigeonsjustlikethat
　　　　　　　　　　　　Jesus

he was a handsome man
　　　　　　　　　and what i want to know is
how do you like your blueeyed boy　　　　　　　10
Mister Death

　　　　　　　　　　　　[1920, 1991]

[THE CAMBRIDGE LADIES WHO LIVE IN FURNISHED SOULS]

the Cambridge[1] ladies who live in furnished souls
are unbeautiful and have comfortable minds
(also, with the church's protestant blessings
daughters,unscented shapeless spirited)
they believe in Christ and Longfellow,[2]both dead,　　　5
are invariably interested in so many things –
at the present writing one still finds
delighted fingers knitting for the is it Poles?
perhaps.　　While permanent faces coyly bandy
scandal of Mrs. N and Professor D　　　　　　　10
. . . . the Cambridge ladies do not care,above
Cambridge if sometimes in its box of
sky lavender and cornerless,the
moon rattles like a fragment of angry candy

　　　　　　　　　　　　[1922, 1991]

---

1. **Cambridge:** Cummings was born and raised in Cambridge, Massachusetts, where he also attended Harvard University.
2. **Longfellow:** The poet Henry Wadsworth Longfellow (1807-1882) was among the most popular American poets in the nineteenth and early twentieth centuries.

["NEXT TO OF COURSE GOD AMERICA I[1]"]

"next to of course god america i
love you land of the pilgrims' and so forth oh
say can you see by the dawn's early my
country 'tis of centuries come and go

---

1. **"next to of course god america i:**　This poem was originally published as "The Patriot" in *Vanity Fair* (May 1925).

and are no more what of it we should worry   5
in every language even deafanddumb
thy sons acclaim your glorious name by gorry
by jingo by gee by gosh by gum
why talk of beauty what could be more beautiful than these heroic happy dead   10
who rushed like lions to the roaring slaughter
they did not stop to think they died instead
then shall the voice of liberty be mute?"

He spoke.   And drank rapidly a glass of water

[1926, 1991]

[I SING OF OLAF GLAD AND BIG]

i sing of Olaf glad and big
whose warmest heart recoiled at war:
a conscientious object-or

his wellbelovéd colonel(trig[1]
westpointer most succinctly bred)   5
took erring Olaf soon in hand;
but – though an host of overjoyed
noncoms[2](first knocking on the head
him)do through icy waters roll
that helplessness which others stroke   10
with brushes recently employed
anent this muddy toiletbowl,
while kindred intellects evoke
allegiance per blunt instruments –
Olaf(being to all intents   15
a corpse and wanting any rag
upon what God unto him gave)
responds,without getting annoyed
"I will not kiss your fucking flag"

straightway the silver bird[3] looked grave   20
(departing hurriedly to shave)

but – though all kinds of officers
(a yearning nation's blueeyed pride)

---

1. **trig:** Smart and neat in appearance.
2. **noncoms:** A military term for noncommissioned officers.
3. **silver bird:** The badge signifying the military rank of colonel.

their passive prey did kick and curse
until for wear their clarion   25
voices and boots were much the worse,
and egged the firstclassprivates on
his rectum wickedly to tease
by means of skilfully applied
bayonets roasted hot with heat —   30
Olaf(upon what were once knees)
does almost ceaselessly repeat
"there is some shit I will not eat"

our president,being of which
assertions duly notified   35
threw the yellowsonofabitch
into a dungeon,where he died

Christ(of His mercy infinite)
i pray to see;and Olaf,too

preponderatingly because   40
unless statistics lie he was
more brave than me:more blond than you.

                                        [1931, 1991]

[ANYONE LIVED IN A PRETTY HOW TOWN]

anyone lived in a pretty how town
(with up so floating many bells down)
spring summer autumn winter
he sang his didn't he danced his did.

Women and men(both little and small)   5
cared for anyone not at all
they sowed their isn't they reaped their same
sun moon stars rain

children guessed(but only a few
and down they forgot as up they grew   10
autumn winter spring summer)
that noone loved him more by more

when by now and tree by leaf
she laughed his joy she cried his grief
bird by snow and stir by still   15
anyone's any was all to her

someones married their everyones
laughed their cryings and did their dance
(sleep wake hope and then)they
said their nevers they slept their dream   20

stars rain sun moon
(and only the snow can begin to explain
how children are apt to forget to remember
with up so floating many bells down)

one day anyone died i guess   25
(and noone stooped to kiss his face)
busy folk buried them side by side
little by little and was by was

all by all and deep by deep
and more by more they dream their sleep   30
noone and anyone earth by april
wish by spirit and if by yes.

Women and men(both dong and ding)
summer autumn winter spring
reaped their sowing and went their came   35
sun moon stars rain

[1940, 1991]

Hart Crane

[1899-1932]

[Crane] was a born poet.
—E. E. Cummings

Harold Hart Crane was born on July 21, 1899, in Garrettsville, Ohio. He was the only child of Grace Hart, the daughter of an eminent and prosperous family, and Clarence Crane, an ambitious salesman who worked briefly for his father's maple-syrup company before starting a competing company in the nearby town of Warren, Ohio. In 1908, Crane's parents separated, and they sent their shy and withdrawn nine-year-old son to live with his maternal grandmother in Cleveland. When the couple reconciled, the family moved to Cleveland, where Crane's father established the Crane Company, a chain of successful candy shops featuring chocolates and a "summer candy" he invented, Life Savers. In the midst of this new stability, Crane began to attend school regularly and enrolled in East High School in 1913. Interested in music and an avid reader of poetry and drama, he soon began writing verses. But his parents' turbulent marriage faltered once again, and in 1915 Crane's mother took him out of school to visit his grandmother

Hart Crane

This photograph was taken on the roof of the building where Crane lived in 1924. The expansive view of the Brooklyn Bridge, shown in the background, inspired his most ambitious poem, *The Bridge* (1930).

at her vacation cottage on the Isle of Pines in the West Indies. When he and his mother returned to Cleveland later that year, Crane met Harriet Moody, the widow of the poet William Vaughn Moody. The friend of many emerging writers of the day, including Carl Sandburg, she offered Crane the first serious encouragement he had received about his writing. He subsequently sent a poem to a small magazine in New York City, *Bruno's Weekly*, which published Crane's "C 33" – a reference to the cell in London's Reading Gaol in which the Irish writer Oscar Wilde had been imprisoned for homosexual acts – in 1916.

For the next three years, the aspiring young poet struggled to gain a foothold in the literary world. After his parents divorced in 1916, Crane dropped out of high school and worked briefly at various sales jobs. His father then reluctantly provided him with an allowance that enabled Crane to move to New York City, where he was expected to study with tutors in preparation for admission to Columbia University. Crane lived a bohemian life in a series of rented rooms in Greenwich Village, where through Harriet Moody and family friends he met other writers and artists. Crane spent most of his time reading and writing, publishing several poems in the avant-garde magazine the *Pagan* in March 1917. At the urging of his mother, who strongly approved of his efforts to become a writer and wanted him to acknowledge her side of the family, he began to publish his work under the name "Hart Crane." During the following year, he became an associate editor of the *Pagan*, but the wartime economy and his father's refusal to fund what he no longer viewed as serious preparation for college forced Crane to return to Cleveland. There, he worked in a munitions plant and as a riveter in a shipyard until the end of World War I, when he became a reporter for the Cleveland *Plain Dealer*. In 1919, he returned to New York City, where he took a job as an advertising manager for the *Little Review*.

After a few months, the lack of money once again forced him back to the Midwest, this time to Akron, Ohio, where he worked as a clerk in one of the candy stores run by the Crane Company.

Although his father hoped that he would give up the "poetry nonsense," Crane produced his most significant work during the following decade. From 1919 to 1922, he worked for the Crane Company in Akron, Cleveland, and Washington, D.C. Dissatisfied with the work, he quit and found a job writing copy for an advertising company in Cleveland. At the same time, he corresponded with other writers, including Sherwood Anderson, and he gained a modest reputation by publishing poems in notable little magazines such as the *Dial* and the *Little Review*. In 1923, determined to make a final push to establish himself as a poet, Crane moved back to New York City. There he met numerous writers, including E. E. Cummings, Eugene O'Neill, and Jean Toomer, as well as the influential critics Malcolm Cowley and Waldo Frank. In 1924, Crane had a passionate love affair with Emil Opffer, a Danish sailor with whom he lived in a room overlooking the Brooklyn Bridge that had once been occupied by its famed architect, John Roebling. The intense experience inspired Crane's two most acclaimed poetic sequences: "Voyages," an ecstatic series of love poems, and *The Bridge*, an epic exploration of the history and mystical significance of America. A friend, the financier Otto Kahn, agreed to support Crane while he worked on his book-length poem, much of which he wrote during an extended stay at the Isle of Pines in 1926. But he struggled to complete *The Bridge*. After the publication of his first collection of poetry, *White Buildings* (1926), Crane worked primarily on shorter poems, especially a sequence he tentatively entitled "Key West." Finally, after he returned to New York City from a seven-month trip to England and France, he finished *The Bridge* in December 1929.

The publication of the poem early in 1930 effectively marked the end of Crane's brief and brilliant career. Now famous, he was awarded a Guggenheim Fellowship and went to Mexico, where he planned to write a historical epic about the Spanish overthrow of the Aztec Empire. Although he wrote a friend that he doubted that he would ever "change [his sexual orientation] very fundamentally," he began an affair with Peggy Baird, the former wife of Malcolm Cowley. According to those who met Crane in Mexico, including Katherine Anne Porter, he seemed to be in a downward spiral during the year he spent there, drinking heavily and writing little. He completed what proved to be his final poem, "The Broken Tower," shortly before he sailed from Vera Cruz aboard a passenger liner bound for New York City via Havana. At noon on April 26, 1932, in full view of many of the other passengers, Crane committed suicide by jumping from the main deck into the churning wake of the ship as it steamed at full speed in the Caribbean. His body was not recovered. *The Collected Poems of Hart Crane*, edited with an introduction by his friend and mentor Waldo Frank, was published in 1933.

bedfordstmartins.com/
americanlit for research
links on Crane

Reading Crane's Poetry.

In the introduction to Crane's first collection of poetry, *White Buildings* (1926), Allen Tate described Crane as "the poet of the complex urban civilization of his age." Certainly, life in the modern city was at the center of many of his poems, but his subjects were diverse, as were his poetic models. Largely self-educated, he read and admired Elizabethan poetry and drama; the work of British Romantic poets, especially John Keats and Percy Bysshe Shelley; and the nineteenth-century American poets as different as Walt Whitman, Edgar Allan Poe, and Emily Dickinson. Crane was also influenced by a wide range of contemporary poets, including E. E. Cummings, T. S. Eliot, Ezra Pound, and Wallace Stevens. Even compared with the challenging work of such poets, Crane's poetry struck many critics as difficult and obscure. Although he was in some ways a relatively traditional poet who most often wrote in regular meters and frequently used rhyme, Crane's poems are also characterized by their heightened diction, dense imagery, and complex metaphors. In a letter to the editor of *Poetry*, Harriet Monroe, who criticized the obscurity and apparent illogic of a poem he had submitted, Crane in 1926 emphasized that unlike other forms of writing, poetry derived its power from what he called "the logic of metaphor," explaining:

> I may very possibly be more interested in the so-called illogical impingements of the connotations of words on the consciousness (and their combinations and interplay in metaphor on this basis) than I am interested in the preservation of their logically rigid significations at the cost of limiting my subject matter and the perceptions involved in the poem.

The texts are taken from *The Complete Poems of Hart Crane*, edited by Marc Simon (2000).

VOYAGES[1]

I

Above the fresh ruffles of the surf
Bright striped urchins flay each other with sand.
They have contrived a conquest for shell shucks,
And their fingers crumble fragments of baked weed
Gaily digging and scattering.   5

And in answer to their treble interjections
The sun beats lightning on the waves,
The waves fold thunder on the sand;
And could they hear me I would tell them:

O brilliant kids, frisk with your dog,   10
Fondle your shells and sticks, bleached
By time and the elements; but there is a line

---

1. **Voyages:** Crane wrote most of these poems during the spring of 1924 for his lover Emil Opffer. After publishing four of the poems as "Voyages" in the *Little Review* (Spring 1926), Crane added two poems and published the expanded, six-poem sequence as "Voyages" at the end of his first book, *White Buildings* (1926).

You must not cross nor ever trust beyond it
Spry cordage of your bodies to caresses
Too lichen-faithful from too wide a breast.   15
The bottom of the sea is cruel.

II

— And yet this great wink of eternity,
Of rimless floods, unfettered leewardings,[2]
Samite[3] sheeted and processioned where
Her undinal[4] vast belly moonward bends,
Laughing the wrapt inflections of our love;   5

Take this Sea, whose diapason[5] knells
On scrolls of silver snowy sentences,
The sceptred terror of whose sessions rends
As her demeanors motion well or ill,
All but the pieties of lovers' hands.   10

And onward, as bells off San Salvador
Salute the crocus lustres of the stars,
In these poinsettia meadows of her tides, —
Adagios of islands,[6] O my Prodigal,
Complete the dark confessions her veins spell.   15

Mark how her turning shoulders wind the hours,
And hasten while her penniless rich palms
Pass superscription of bent foam and wave, —
Hasten, while they are true, — sleep, death, desire,
Close round one instant in one floating flower.   20

Bind us in time, O Seasons clear, and awe.
O minstrel galleons of Carib[7] fire,
Bequeath us to no earthly shore until
Is answered in the vortex of our grave
The seal's wide spindrift gaze toward paradise.   25

---

2. **leewardings:** From *leeward*, the side sheltered or away from the wind.
3. **Samite:** A silk fabric woven with gold and silver threads, used in the Middle Ages.
4. **undinal:** With the characteristics of a water nymph.
5. **diapason:** A poetic term for the entire scope or range of something, or figuratively, a swelling burst of harmony.
6. **Adagios of islands:** In "General Aims and Theories" (1937), an essay unpublished during his lifetime, Crane explained that he used this phrase to suggest "the motion of a boat through islands clustered thickly, the rhythm of the motion, etc.," adding that "it seems a much more direct and creative statement than any more logical employment of words such as 'coasting slowly through the islands,' besides ushering in a whole world of music."
7. **Carib:** Of or relating to the Caribs, the indigenous peoples of coastal areas of the Caribbean.

III

Infinite consanguinity[8] it bears —
This tendered theme of you that light
Retrieves from sea plains where the sky
Resigns a breast that every wave enthrones;
While ribboned water lanes I wind   5
Are laved and scattered with no stroke
Wide from your side, whereto this hour
The sea lifts, also, reliquary[9] hands.

And so, admitted through black swollen gates
That must arrest all distance otherwise, —   10
Past whirling pillars and lithe pediments,
Light wrestling there incessantly with light,
Star kissing star through wave on wave unto
Your body rocking!
                        and where death, if shed,   15
Presumes no carnage, but this single change, —
Upon the steep floor flung from dawn to dawn
The silken skilled transmemberment of song;

Permit me voyage, love, into your hands . . .

IV

Whose counted smile of hours and days, suppose
I know as spectrum of the sea and pledge
Vastly now parting gulf on gulf of wings
Whose circles bridge, I know, (from palms to the severe
Chilled albatross's white immutability)   5
No stream of greater love advancing now
Than, singing, this mortality alone
Through clay aflow immortally to you.

All fragrance irrefragably, and claim
Madly meeting logically in this hour   10
And region that is ours to wreathe again,
Portending eyes and lips and making told
The chancel port and portion of our June —

---

8. **consanguinity:** Familial relationship.
9. **reliquary:** A container for holy relics.

Shall they not stem and close in our own steps
Bright staves of flowers and quills today as I   15
Must first be lost in fatal tides to tell?

In signature of the incarnate word[10]
The harbor shoulders to resign in mingling
Mutual blood, transpiring as foreknown
And widening noon within your breast for gathering   20
All bright insinuations that my years have caught
For islands where must lead inviolably
Blue latitudes and levels of your eyes, –

In this expectant, still exclaim receive
The secret oar and petals of all love.   25

---

10. **the incarnate word:** The word embodied in human form, an allusion to John 1:14: "And the Word was made flesh, and dwelt among us." In a letter to Waldo Frank in April 1924, Crane wrote of his relationship to Emil Opffer: "I have seen the Word made Flesh. I mean nothing less, and I know now that there is such a thing as indestructibility."

TO BROOKLYN BRIDGE[1]

How many dawns, chill from his rippling rest
The seagull's wings shall dip and pivot him,
Shedding white rings of tumult, building high
Over the chained bay waters Liberty –

Then, with inviolate curve, forsake our eyes   5
As apparitional as sails that cross
Some page of figures to be filed away;
– Till elevators drop us from our day . . .

I think of cinemas, panoramic sleights
With multitudes bent toward some flashing scene   10
Never disclosed, but hastened to again,
Foretold to other eyes on the same screen;

And Thee, across the harbor, silver-paced
As though the sun took step of thee, yet left

---

1. **To Brooklyn Bridge:** Crane published this poem separately under this title in the *Dial* (June 1927) and later in italics as the opening section of *The Bridge* (1930). The Brooklyn Bridge, which Crane later described as "the matchless symbol of America and its destiny," spans the East River between Brooklyn and Manhattan Island. It was the longest suspension bridge in the world when it opened to great fanfare in 1883.

Some motion ever unspent in thy stride, –   15
Implicitly thy freedom staying thee!

Out of some subway scuttle, cell or loft
A bedlamite² speeds to thy parapets,
Tilting there momently, shrill shirt ballooning,
A jest falls from the speechless caravan.   20

Down Wall,³ from girder into street noon leaks,
A rip-tooth of the sky's acetylene;
All afternoon the cloud-flown derricks turn . . .
Thy cables breathe the North Atlantic still.

And obscure as that heaven of the Jews,   25
Thy guerdon⁴ . . . Accolade thou dost bestow
Of anonymity time cannot raise:
Vibrant reprieve and pardon thou dost show.

O harp and altar, of the fury fused,
(How could mere toil align thy choiring strings!)   30
Terrific threshold of the prophet's pledge,
Prayer of pariah, and the lover's cry, –

Again the traffic lights that skim thy swift
Unfractioned idiom, immaculate sigh of stars,
Beading thy path – condense eternity: 35
And we have seen night lifted in thine arms.

Under thy shadow by the piers I waited;
Only in darkness is thy shadow clear.
The City's fiery parcels all undone,
Already snow submerges an iron year . . .   40

O Sleepless as the river under thee,
Vaulting the sea, the prairies' dreaming sod,
Unto us lowliest sometime sweep, descend
And of the curveship lend a myth to God.

[1927, 2000]

---

2. **bedlamite:** An insane person; the term is derived from the inmates of Bedlam, the informal name for
St. Mary of Bethlehem, the notorious insane asylum in London.
3. **Wall:** Wall Street, the major financial district of New York City.
4. **guerdon:** An archaic term for *reward.*

Sterling A. Brown

[1901–1989]

Sterling A. Brown

This photograph of Brown was taken early in his distinguished career as a poet and professor of English at Howard University.

Sterling Allen Brown was born on May 1, 1901, in Washington, D.C. He was the youngest of six children of Adelaide Allen, a graduate of Fisk University, and Sterling Nelson Brown, a former slave who worked his way through Oberlin College and Fisk to become the minister of the Lincoln Temple Congregational Church and a professor of religion at Howard University. In a 1973 interview, Brown recalled that when he was a child his mother often read to him from the works of poets such as Henry Wadsworth Longfellow and Paul Laurence Dunbar: "I remember even now her stopping sweeping . . . now standing over that broom and reading poetry to me, and she was a good reader, great sense of rhythm." Brown attended Dunbar High School in Washington, where his teachers included Haley Douglass, grandson of Frederick Douglass, and Jessie Redmon Fauset, later a novelist and literary editor of the *Crisis*, the journal of the National Association for the Advancement of Colored People (NAACP). When he graduated in 1918, Brown went to Williams College, which each year granted a scholarship to the outstanding student from Dunbar. At the isolated college in northwestern Massachusetts, Brown was one of a small group of African American students who experienced racism in the form of "benign neglect," as he later described it. Brown graduated Phi Beta Kappa in 1922 and then enrolled at Harvard University, where he earned a master's degree in 1923.

At Harvard, Brown began to formulate the poetics that would shape his writing for the rest of his life. Fascinated by the formal and linguistic experiments of a new generation of poets, he was strongly influenced by the anthology *Modern American Poetry* (1921), which introduced him to the work of Amy Lowell, Robert Frost, Edwin Arlington Robinson, and Carl Sandburg. He was especially impressed by Frost and by Robinson, who, as Brown later observed, "took up the undistinguished, the failures, and showed the extraordinary in ordinary lives." He was also drawn to the work of Claude McKay, Langston Hughes, and other poets of the Harlem Renaissance. Convinced that the rural culture of southern blacks was the basis for modern African American literature, Brown began serious study of African American folkways after he left Harvard in 1923 and took his first position teaching English at Virginia Seminary and College. He continued his anthropological studies while teaching at Lincoln University in Missouri (1926–28), Fisk (1928–29), and Howard, where he moved in 1929. Meanwhile, he married Daisy Turnbull in 1927, the year Brown published his first poem, "When de Saints Go Marching Home," in *Opportunity: A Journal of Negro Life*. His poetry then began to appear regularly in *Opportunity*, in anthologies edited by his fellow poets Countee Cullen and James Weldon Johnson, and in *Folk-Say, A Regional Miscellany*, edited by the influential folklorist Benjamin A. Botkin.

During the following decades, Brown distinguished himself as a poet, literary critic, and scholar. In 1932, he published his first collection of poetry, *Southern Road*. In the preface to the volume, James Weldon Johnson called Brown's work "a distinctive contribution to American poetry," and *Southern Road* was praised by both white and black reviewers in periodicals as diverse as *Opportunity*, the *New Republic*, the *New York Times*, and the *Saturday Review of Literature*. But worsening economic conditions prevented the publication of Brown's second collection, *No Hiding Place*. He consequently turned to other projects, notably two influential books of literary criticism: *The Negro in American Fiction* and *Negro Poetry and Drama*, both published in 1937. He also coedited one of the most important anthologies of African American literature published in the first half of the twentieth century, *The Negro Caravan* (1941), which included the work of writers ranging from the eighteenth-century poet Phillis Wheatley to contemporary fiction writers such as Zora Neale Hurston and Richard Wright. During the five decades Brown taught at Howard, from which he retired in 1969, he also inspired generations of students, including the Nobel laureate Toni Morrison. In 1975, Brown published his second book of poems, *The Last Ride of Wild Bill and Eleven Narrative Poems*, and four years later he was named poet laureate of the District of Columbia. His various contributions gained increasing attention from critics and scholars, many of whom credited Brown with founding the field of African American studies. When he died on January 17, 1989, the obituary in the *Washington Post* observed that Brown had been "perhaps the most knowledgeable living person on the subject of American Negro literature, tradition, heritage, and thought."

He infused his poetry with genuine characteristic flavor by adopting as his medium the common, racy, living speech of the Negro in certain phases of real life.

–James Weldon Johnson

Reading Brown's Poetry.   The title of Brown's first collection of poetry, *Southern Road* (1932), indicated his departure from poets of the Harlem Renaissance, who were exploring the urban experience of African Americans in the North. In contrast, most of Brown's poems were rooted in the experience, folklore, and music of the rural black population of the South. Drawing inspiration from work songs, spirituals, and especially the blues, Brown wrote in black vernacular at a time when many other African American writers dismissed such language as a vestige of blackface minstrel shows and the "plantation myth." Brown was determined to liberate black vernacular from the burden of the plantation tradition even as he challenged the conventions of what was called "Negro dialect poetry," which had previously been the vehicle of exaggerated humor, pathos, or sentimentality. James Weldon Johnson, who a decade earlier had asserted that such poetry "was not capable of giving expression to the varied conditions of Negro life in America," testified to the success of Brown's experiments in language and subject matter in *Southern Road*. "Mr. Brown's work is not only fine, it is unique," Johnson observed in his preface to the volume. "He infused his poetry with genuine characteristic flavor by adopting as his medium the common, racy, living speech of the Negro in certain phases of *real* life. For his raw material he dug down into the deep mine of Negro folk poetry." The texts of the following poems from *Southern Road* are taken from *The Collected Poems of Sterling A. Brown* (1989).

bedfordstmartins.com/ americanlit *for research links on Brown*

Southern Road

E. Simms Campbell, a young African American artist who later became a successful cartoonist for mainstream magazines such as *Esquire*, provided four black-and-white illustrations for *Southern Road*. The letters in the background of this illustration, which preceded the section "Tin Roof Blues," form part of the words "FOR COLORED ONLY," a sign common throughout the segregated South.

SOUTHERN ROAD[1]

Swing dat hammer – hunh –
Steady, bo';
Swing dat hammer – hunh –
Steady, bo';
Ain't no rush, bebby,   5
Long ways to go.

---

1. **Southern Road:** The speaker of this poem is the leader of a chain gang, a group of black convicts shackled together and overseen by a white guard in the South. The word *hunh* at the end of the first and third lines of each stanza mimics the collective sound of their exhaled breaths or grunts as the men swing their hammers in unison to the rhythm of the work song.

Burner tore his – hunh –
Black heart away;
Burner tore his – hunh –
Black heart away;   10
Got me life,[2] bebby,
An' a day.

Gal's on Fifth Street – hunh –
Son done gone;[3]
Gal's on Fifth Street – hunh –   15
Son done gone;
Wife's in de ward, bebby,
Babe's not bo'n.

My ole man died – hunh –
Cussin' me;   20
My ole man died – hunh –
Cussin' me;
Ole lady rocks, bebby,
Huh misery.

Doubleshackled – hunh –   25
Guard behin';
Doubleshackled – hunh –
Guard behin';
Ball an' chain, bebby,
On my min'.   30

White man tells me – hunh –
Damn yo' soul;
White man tells me – hunh –
Damn yo' soul;
Got no need, bebby,   35
To be tole.

Chain gang nevah – hunh –
Let me go;
Chain gang nevah – hunh –
Let me go;   40
Po' los' boy, bebby,
Evahmo' . . .

[1931]

---

2. **Burner . . . Got me life:** He was sentenced to life imprisonment for shooting a man through the heart with his *burner*, a slang term for *gun*.
3. **Gal's on Fifth Street . . . Son done gone:** His daughter has become a prostitute and his son is already dead.

STRONG MEN

The young men keep coming on
The strong men keep coming on.
SANDBURG[1]

They dragged you from homeland,
They chained you in coffles,[2]
They huddled you spoon-fashion in filthy hatches,
They sold you to give a few gentlemen ease.

They broke you in like oxen,   5
They scourged you,
They branded you,
They made your women breeders,
They swelled your numbers with bastards. . . .
They taught you the religion they disgraced.   10

You sang:
    Keep a-inchin' along
    Lak a po' inch worm. . . .

You sang:
    Bye and bye   15
    I'm gonna lay down dis heaby load. . . .

You sang:
    Walk togedder, chillen,
    Dontcha git weary. . . .
      The strong men keep a-comin' on   20
      The strong men git stronger.

They point with pride to the roads you built for them,
They ride in comfort over the rails you laid for them.
They put hammers in your hands
And said—Drive so much before sundown.   25

You sang:
    Ain't no hammah
    In dis lan',
    Strikes lak mine, bebby,
    Strikes lak mine.   30

---

1. **Sandburg:** The epigraph is adapted from Carl Sandburg's "Upstream" (1922), which begins and ends with the line "The strong men keep coming on." Brown particularly admired Sandburg's use of colloquial speech and treatment of common subjects.
2. **coffles:** A line of animals or slaves fastened together.

They cooped you in their kitchens,
They penned you in their factories,
They gave you the jobs that they were too good for,
They tried to guarantee happiness to themselves
By shunting dirt and misery to you.   35

You sang:
    Me an' muh baby gonna shine, shine
    Me an' muh baby gonna shine.
      The strong men keep a-comin' on
      The strong men git stronger. . . .   40

They bought off some of your leaders
You stumbled, as blind men will . . .
They coaxed you, unwontedly soft-voiced. . . .
You followed a way.
Then laughed as usual.   45

They heard the laugh and wondered;
Uncomfortable,
Unadmitting a deeper terror. . . .
      The strong men keep a-comin' on
      Gittin' stronger. . . .   50

What, from the slums
Where they have hemmed you,
What, from the tiny huts
They could not keep from you—
What reaches them   55
Making them ill at ease, fearful?
Today they shout prohibition at you
"Thou shalt not this"
"Thou shalt not that"
"Reserved for whites only"   60
You laugh.

One thing they cannot prohibit—
      The strong men . . . coming on
      The strong men gittin' stronger.
      Strong men. . . .   65
      Stronger. . . .

                                      [1931, 1989]

Langston Hughes

[1902–1967]

James Langston Hughes was born on February 1, 1902, in Joplin, Missouri. He was the only child of Carrie Langston Hughes, a former schoolteacher, and James Nathaniel Hughes. In Hughes's autobiography, he explained that his parents were descendants of white slave owners and slave traders, slaves, free people of color, and Native Americans, observing: "There are lots of different kinds of blood in our family." When Hughes's father was denied the chance to take the Oklahoma Territory Bar examination because of his race, he left his family and went to live in Mexico. Carrie Hughes took her son back home to Lawrence, Kansas, where Hughes was raised primarily by his twice-widowed grandmother, Mary Langston. Her first husband was Lewis Sheridan Leary, who died in the abolitionist John Brown's raid at Harpers Ferry in 1859, and her second husband (and Hughes's grandfather) was Charles Langston, a well-known abolitionist and the brother of John Mercer Langston, a congressman from Virginia in the 1890s. Despite the family connections, Hughes's troubled childhood was spent in poverty. Encouraged to read by both his mother and grandmother, he recalled: "I began to believe in nothing but books and the wonderful world in books — where if people suffered, they suffered in beautiful language, not in monosyllables, as we did in Kansas." When he was thirteen, his grandmother died and Hughes joined his mother and her new husband in Lincoln, Illinois. In 1916, the family moved to Cleveland, Ohio, where Hughes attended Central High School. There, Hughes took an English class with Ethel Weimer, a memorable teacher who encouraged her students to read modern American poets such as Carl Sandburg and Edna St. Vincent Millay. It was in that class that Hughes began "to take poetry seriously," as he later recalled.

During the following decade, Hughes emerged as one of the most notable poets among the writers of the Harlem Renaissance. He wrote for his school's literary magazine, and in 1919 he published his first poems in *Brownie's Book*, a magazine for African American children founded by W. E. B. Du Bois. After Hughes graduated from high school in 1920, he lived for a year with his father in Mexico. In June 1921, nineteen-year-old Hughes gained acclaim when his poem "The Negro Speaks of Rivers" appeared in the *Crisis*, the magazine of the National Association for the Advancement of Colored People (NAACP), from which it was almost immediately reprinted in the influential *Literary Digest*. His father, who did not want him to become a writer, reluctantly agreed to help pay for a college education, and Hughes enrolled at Columbia University in New York City in the fall of 1921. Although he loved living in Harlem, he was unhappy at the nearly all-white university and withdrew in 1922. He spent the next three years working at a series of menial jobs, but he continued to write and publish poems regularly in the *Crisis*. Uncertain about his future, he joined the crew of a freighter bound for West Africa. He spent much of 1923 and 1924 visiting several African countries and working as a busboy in Paris. When he returned to the United States, he lived with his mother in Washington, D.C., before moving back to Harlem, where the gregarious Hughes associated with many other writers and artists, including Aaron Douglas, Countee Cullen, and Zora Neale Hurston. In 1925, "The Weary Blues," which Hughes called his "lucky poem," won first prize in a literary contest sponsored by *Opportunity: A Journal of Negro Life*, the recently founded magazine of the National Urban League. The prize paved the way for the publication of his first collection of poetry, *The Weary Blues* (1926).

With his literary career fully launched, Hughes struck out in new directions in his life and writings. Still determined to get a college education, he enrolled at the historically black Lincoln University in Pennsylvania, from which he graduated in 1929. In the meantime, he published his second book of poems, *Fine Clothes to the Jew* (1927), and began to write *Not Without Laughter* (1930), a novel based on his early life in the Midwest. During the 1930s, his writings reflected his growing political radicalism and disenchantment with life in the United States. After his return from a brief stay in Cuba and Haiti, Hughes published *Scottsboro Limited* (1931), a verse play protesting the sensational case of the "Scottsboro Boys," a group of black teenagers falsely accused and convicted of raping two white girls in Tennessee. During a year-long visit to Russia, Hughes published militant poems such as "Good Morning Revolution," hailing the revolution as "the very best friend / I ever had." When he returned to the United States, he wrote *The Ways of White Folks* (1934), a collection of satirical and often bitter stories about race relations in the United States. Hughes also began to write drama. The earliest of his plays was *Mulatto*, in which he drew upon his family history to explore the theme of miscegenation and racial divisions in the South. Encouraged by its successful run on Broadway in 1935, Hughes wrote several more plays, including *Troubled Island* (1936), a historical drama about the slave revolution against French rule in Haiti. During 1937, Hughes lived in Madrid, where he reported on the Spanish civil war for the *Baltimore Afro-American*. When he returned to the United States in 1938, he published a collection of his socialist poetry, *A New Song*, and founded the Harlem Suitcase Theater, a drama group that performed a play he wrote advocating black nationalism and revolution, *Don't You Want to Be Free?*

He pursues his way, scornful, in subject matter, in photography, and rhythmical treatment, of whatever obstructions time and tradition have placed before him.

–Countee Cullen

bedfordstmartins.com/ americanlit for research links on Hughes

Hughes later retreated from the revolutionary political positions he had assumed during the 1930s, but he continued to devote himself to the cause of full equality for African Americans. He also continued to extend the range of his writings. In 1940, he published the first volume of his autobiography, *The Big Sea* (1940), which was followed by two volumes of poetry, *Shakespeare in Harlem* (1942) and *Jim Crow's Last Stand* (1943). Struggling to support himself, Hughes wrote song lyrics and in 1942 began to write a weekly column for the crusading African American newspaper the *Chicago Defender*. Taking on the persona of a comic character in Harlem named "Simple" (later "Jesse B. Semple"), Hughes for more than twenty years provided pointed and often humorous commentary on civil rights and social mores in America. The popular column became the basis for five book collections, beginning in 1950 with *Simple Speaks His Mind* and ending in 1965 with *Simple's Uncle Sam*. Meanwhile, Hughes continued to write poetry, notably *Montage of a Dream Deferred* (1951), an acclaimed sequence of poems about Harlem. His later works included several more volumes of poetry, including the radically experimental *Ask Your Mama* (1962); the second volume of his autobiography, *I Wonder as I Wander* (1956); collections of short stories; a number of innovative plays fusing narrative and gospel music; and a series of books for children on African American history, life, and music, including *The First Book of Jazz* (1957). Eager to promote the careers of younger African American writers, Hughes in his final years edited *New Negro Poets USA* (1964) and *The Best Short Stories by Negro Writers* (1967). The author of more than fifty books, Hughes was working on several new projects when he died in New York City on May 22, 1967.

Reading Hughes's Poetry.   Identifying the central strand in his writings, probably the most diverse body of work produced by an American writer, Hughes once stated simply: "My writing has been largely concerned with the depicting of Negro life in America." His earliest poetic models were the dialect poems of African American poet Paul Laurence Dunbar and the fervently democratic work of the white poet Carl Sandburg, through whom Hughes discovered Walt Whitman. Blending the free verse of Whitman and Sandburg with the language of African American slave songs, or spirituals, Hughes announced the major theme of his future work in the first adult poem he published, "The Negro Speaks of Rivers" (1921). In other poems collected in his first book, *The Weary Blues* (1926), Hughes employed black vernacular, the form of the blues, and the rhythms of jazz to capture the essence of African American life, especially in the urban North. Sounding what a reviewer for the *New York Herald Tribune* called "a new note in contemporary American poetry," Hughes embarked on a lifelong effort to fuse writing and African American musical forms. He was also influenced by and worked closely with visual artists of the Harlem Renaissance, especially his friend Aaron Douglas. In an early essay, "The Negro Artist and the Racial Mountain" (1926), Hughes

The Weary Blues

The book jacket of Hughes's first collection of poems was designed by the young Mexican artist Miguel Covarrubias, who illustrated the work of a number of African American writers and who became a key figure in the vital cultural relations between Mexico and the United States during the 1920s.

proclaimed: "We younger Negro artists who create now intend to express our individual dark-skinned selves without fear or shame." Hughes continued to do that throughout his long and distinguished career, becoming an inspiration and a role model for new African American writers who emerged during the two decades before his death in 1967. The texts of the following poems are from *The Collected Poems of Langston Hughes*, edited by Arnold Rampersad (1994).

THE NEGRO SPEAKS OF RIVERS

I've known rivers:
I've known rivers ancient as the world and older than the flow of human blood
    in human veins.

My soul has grown deep like the rivers.

I bathed in the Euphrates when dawns were young.
I built my hut near the Congo and it lulled me to sleep.
I looked upon the Nile and raised the pyramids above it.   5

I heard the singing of the Mississippi when Abe Lincoln went down to New
Orleans,[1] and I've seen its muddy bosom turn all golden in the sunset.

I've known rivers:
Ancient, dusky rivers.

My soul has grown deep like the rivers.   10

[1921, 1994]

---

1. **Abe Lincoln . . . New Orleans:** Abraham Lincoln formed his antislavery views as a result of his firsthand
observation of the slave trade during boat trips down the Mississippi River to New Orleans in 1828 and 1831.

MOTHER TO SON

Well, son, I'll tell you.
Life for me ain't been no crystal stair.
It's had tacks in it,
And splinters,
And boards torn up,   5
And places with no carpet on the floor —
Bare.
But all the time
I'se been a-climbin' on,
And reachin' landin's,   10
And turnin' corners,
And sometimes goin' in the dark
Where there ain't been no light.
So boy, don't you turn back.
Don't you set down on the steps   15
'Cause you finds it's kinder hard.
Don't you fall now —
For I'se still goin', honey,
I'se still climbin',
And life for me ain't been no crystal stair.   20

[1922, 1994]

JAZZONIA[1]

Oh, silver tree!
Oh, shining rivers of the soul!

In a Harlem cabaret
Six long-headed jazzers play.

---

1. **Jazzonia:** The Greek suffix *onia* suggests the land or country of jazz, located here in a nightclub in Harlem.

A dancing girl whose eyes are bold   5
Lifts high a dress of silken gold.

Oh, singing tree!
Oh, shining rivers of the soul!

Were Eve's eyes
In the first garden   10
Just a bit too bold?[2]
Was Cleopatra gorgeous
In a gown of gold?[3]

Oh, shining tree!
Oh, silver rivers of the soul!   15

In a whirling cabaret
Six long-headed jazzers play.

[1923, 1994]

2. **Eve's eyes . . . bold?:** According to the Old Testament account, after Eve is tempted by the serpent and she and Adam eat the forbidden fruit of the tree of knowledge, "the eyes of them both were opened, and they knew that they were naked" (Genesis 3:7).
3. **Cleopatra . . . gold?:** The seductive queen Cleopatra of Egypt (69–30 BCE) was often associated with extravagance and sensuality, most famously in Shakespeare's *Antony and Cleopatra*.

I, Too

I, too, sing America.[1]

I am the darker brother.
They send me to eat in the kitchen
When company comes,
But I laugh,   5
And eat well,
And grow strong.

Tomorrow,
I'll be at the table[2]
When company comes.   10
Nobody'll dare
Say to me,

1. **I, too, sing America:** An allusion to "I Hear America Singing" by the white poet Walt Whitman (1819–1892), whom Hughes admired and who is often described as the "poet of America."
2. **I'll be at the table:** In early versions of this poem, including its first publication in the *Survey Graphic* (March 1, 1925), this line read: "I'll sit at the table."

"Eat in the kitchen,"
Then.

Besides,   15
They'll see how beautiful I am
And be ashamed —

I, too, am America.

                                                                          [1925, 1994]

THE WEARY BLUES

Droning a drowsy syncopated tune,
Rocking back and forth to a mellow croon,
   I heard a Negro play.
Down on Lenox Avenue the other night
By the pale dull pallor of an old gas light   5
   He did a lazy sway. . . .
   He did a lazy sway. . . .
To the tune o' those Weary Blues.
With his ebony hands on each ivory key
He made that poor piano moan with melody.   10
   O Blues!
Swaying to and fro on his rickety stool
He played that sad raggy tune like a musical fool.
   Sweet Blues!
Coming from a black man's soul.   15
   O Blues!
In a deep song voice with a melancholy tone
I heard that Negro sing, that old piano moan —
   "Ain't got nobody in all this world,
     Ain't got nobody but ma self.   20
     I's gwine to quit ma frownin'
     And put ma troubles on the shelf."
Thump, thump, thump, went his foot on the floor.
He played a few chords then he sang some more —
   "I got the Weary Blues   25
     And I can't be satisfied.
     Got the Weary Blues
     And can't be satisfied —
     I ain't happy no mo'
     And I wish that I had died."   30
And far into the night he crooned that tune.
The stars went out and so did the moon.

The singer stopped playing and went to bed
While the Weary Blues echoed through his head.
He slept like a rock or a man that's dead.   35

[1925, 1994]

CROSS

My old man's a white old man
And my old mother's black.
If ever I cursed my white old man
I take my curses back.

If ever I cursed my black old mother   5
And wished she were in hell,
I'm sorry for that evil wish
And now I wish her well.

My old man died in a fine big house.
My ma died in a shack.   10
I wonder where I'm gonna die,
Being neither white nor black?

[1925, 1994]

BRASS SPITTOONS[1]

Clean the spittoons, boy.
    Detroit,
    Chicago,
    Atlantic City,
    Palm Beach.   5
Clean the spittoons.
The steam in hotel kitchens,
And the smoke in hotel lobbies,
And the slime in hotel spittoons:
Part of my life.   10
    Hey, boy!
    A nickel,
    A dime,
    A dollar,
Two dollars a day.   15
    Hey, boy!

---

1. **Brass Spittoons:** These bowl-shaped receptacles for spitting into, especially by users of chewing tobacco, were then a fixture in hotel lobbies and other public places.

A nickel,
A dime,
A dollar,
Two dollars   20
Buys shoes for the baby.
House rent to pay.
Gin on Saturday,
Church on Sunday.
    My God!   25
Babies and gin and church
and women and Sunday
all mixed up with dimes and
dollars and clean spittoons
and house rent to pay.   30
    Hey, boy!
A bright bowl of brass is beautiful to the Lord
Bright polished brass like the cymbals
Of King David's dancers,
Like the wine cups of Solomon.[2]   35
    Hey, boy!
A clean spittoon on the altar of the Lord.
A clean bright spittoon all newly polished, –
At least I can offer that.
    Come 'ere, boy!   40

                                                        [1926, 1994]

---

2. **King David's dancers . . . cups of Solomon:** King David of Israel, who is thought by many to be the author of the Psalms, refers to dancing as a form of worship of the Lord: "Let them praise his name in the dance: let them sing praises unto him with the timbrel and harp" (Psalms 149:3). David's son and successor, the fabulously wealthy king Solomon, had gold wine vessels (1 Kings 10:21).

CHRIST IN ALABAMA[1]

Christ is a nigger,
Beaten and black:
Oh, bare your back!

---

1. **Christ in Alabama:** Hughes wrote this poem when a North Carolina magazine, *Contempo*, invited him to comment on the notorious case of the so-called Scottsboro Boys, nine black teenagers accused of raping two white girls on a freight train bound from Tennessee to Alabama on March 25, 1931. The publication of the poem in *Contempo* generated heated controversy, including protests and petitions in North Carolina. Coolly responding to the furor, especially over the first line of the poem, Hughes observed: "I meant my poem to be a protest against the domination of all stronger peoples over weaker ones."

Mary is His mother:
Mammy of the South,   5
Silence your mouth.

God is His father:
White Master above
Grant Him your love.

Most holy bastard   10
Of the bleeding mouth,
   Nigger Christ
   On the cross
   Of the South.

[1931, 1994]

HARLEM

What happens to a dream deferred?

   Does it dry up
   like a raisin in the sun?
   Or fester like a sore —
   And then run?   5
   Does it stink like rotten meat?
   Or crust and sugar over —
   like a syrupy sweet?

   Maybe it just sags
   like a heavy load.   10

   Or does it explode?

[1951, 1994]

Countee Cullen

[1903-1946]

Countee Cullen was born on March 30, 1903, to Elizabeth Thomas Lucas
in Louisville, Kentucky. The identity of his father and most other details
of his early life are unknown. He was raised by a woman named Amanda
Porter, possibly his paternal grandmother, who took him to New York
City. When she died in 1917, Cullen went to live with Reverend Frederick
Asbury Cullen, the popular minister of the largest church in Harlem, the
Salem Methodist Episcopal Church, and his wife, Carolyn Belle Mitchell
Cullen. Although the couple never formally adopted him, Cullen began to

Countee Cullen

Inscribed "with admiration" to James Weldon Johnson, this photograph was taken in the mid-1920s, when the young Cullen was one of the most popular poets in the United States.

The best of his poetry is motivated by race. He is always seeking to free himself and his art from these bonds.
-James Weldon Johnson

use their surname in 1918 and always referred to them as his parents. An outstanding student at DeWitt Clinton High School, Cullen helped edit the school newspaper and literary magazine. He also began to write poetry, winning a citywide contest for his poem "I Have a Rendezvous with Life." After high school, he attended New York University, where he excelled academically and regularly published poems in the school's literary magazine, the *Arch*, and later in prominent national magazines such as H. L. Mencken's *American Mercury*, the *Bookman*, the *Century*, *Harper's*, and the *Nation*. He also won a string of literary prizes, including the John Reed Memorial Prize awarded by *Poetry: A Magazine of Verse*.

The precocious Cullen soon became the most popular and acclaimed African American poet since Paul Laurence Dunbar. During his senior year of college, the prestigious firm of Harper and Brothers published Cullen's first collection of poems, *Color* (1925). Some of the poems in the volume also appeared in Alain Locke's influential anthology, *The New Negro* (1925). Locke joined in the chorus of praise for the author of *Color*, proclaiming in his review: "Ladies and Gentleman! A genius!" Meanwhile, Cullen graduated Phi Beta Kappa from New York University and continued his studies at Harvard. After he completed a master's degree in English and French, Cullen returned to New York City, where he assumed a central role in the Harlem Renaissance. Cullen became the assistant editor of *Opportunity*, the magazine of the National Urban League. In addition to writing a regular column for the magazine, "The Dark Tower," he published two more books of his early poetry, *Copper Sun* (1927) and *Ballad of the Brown Girl* (1928). Eager to promote the work of other African American poets, Cullen edited *Caroling Dusk: An Anthology of Verse by Negro Poets* (1927), which he hoped might serve as a prelude "to that fuller symphony which Negro poets will in time contribute to the national literature." He also enjoyed an active social life that included many well-known African American writers and artists, including Aaron Douglas, Langston Hughes, and Zora Neale Hurston. In a large and elaborate wedding, Cullen in 1928 married Nina Yolande Du Bois, the daughter of W. E. B. Du Bois. Soon after their marriage, which was deeply troubled and ended in divorce two years later, Cullen received one of the first Guggenheim Fellowships awarded to an African American. Along with his closest friend and companion, Harold Jackman, Cullen sailed for France, where he wrote *The Black Christ and Other Poems* (1929).

Cullen never again achieved the success he enjoyed during the 1920s. Turning from poetry to fiction, he wrote a satirical novel about African Americans in New York City, *One Way to Heaven* (1932). He also gave lectures and readings of his poetry across the United States. Although he was offered teaching positions at several historically black colleges, Cullen evidently preferred to remain in New York City. In 1934, he accepted a full-time teaching position at Frederick Douglass Junior High School. The job left him relatively little time for writing, but he published some new poems along with a translation of a classical Greek play by Euripides, *The Medea and Some Poems* (1935). Cullen married

Ida Mae Robertson in 1940, and he later published two books for children. Before he died from complications arising from high blood pressure on January 9, 1946, he began to compile the poems included in the posthumously published collection *On These I Stand: The Best Poems of Countee Cullen* (1947). Although his reputation had declined, his poetry continued to engage many readers, including the African American poet and novelist Owen Dodson, who in a tribute to Cullen observed: "If you ask any Negro what he found in Cullen's poetry, he would say: 'all my dilemmas are written here.'"

Reading Cullen's Poetry. In his anthology, *Caroling Dusk*, Cullen included a wide range of verse written by contemporary African American poets, from the jazz rhythms of Langston Hughes to the so-called Negro dialect poetry of Sterling A. Brown. In contrast, Cullen was a deeply traditional poet who said that verse emerged from him already "metered and rhymed." He was most strongly influenced by the British Romantic poets, especially John Keats. Cullen also deeply admired the lyrical work of his white contemporary Edna St. Vincent Millay, the subject of his undergraduate thesis at New York University. Like Millay, he was especially drawn to the sonnet, the form of two of his most famous poems, "Yet Do I Marvel" and "From the Dark Tower." But in those poems, as well as in the rhymed couplets of longer poems such as "Heritage," Cullen explored subjects far removed from the mainstream of British and American poetry, including prejudice, racial identity, and the consciousness of African Americans torn between the claims of America, or the Western tradition, and the cultural heritage of Africa. Although he declared in 1924 that he wanted "to be POET and not NEGRO POET," suggesting that the development of African American artists had been hindered by their exclusive "concern with their race," Cullen added

bedfordstmartins.com/ *americanlit* for research *links on Cullen*

> That is all very well, none of us can get away from it. I cannot at times. You will see it in my verse. The consciousness of this is too poignant at times. I cannot escape it. But what I mean is this: I shall not write of negro subjects for the purpose of propaganda. That is not what a poet is concerned with. Of course, when the emotion rising out of the fact that I am a negro is strong, I express it.

Certainly, he expressed those emotions in the following poems, the texts of which are taken from *My Soul's High Song: The Collected Writings of Countee Cullen, Voice of the Harlem Renaissance*, edited by Gerald Early (1991).

Yet Do I Marvel

I doubt not God is good, well-meaning, kind,
And did He stoop to quibble could tell why
The little buried mole continues blind,

Why flesh that mirrors Him must some day die,
Make plain the reason tortured Tantalus   5
Is baited by the fickle fruit, declare
If merely brute caprice dooms Sisyphus
To struggle up a never-ending stair.[1]
Inscrutable His ways are, and immune
To catechism by a mind too strewn   10
With petty cares to slightly understand
What awful brain compels His awful hand.
Yet do I marvel at this curious thing:
To make a poet black, and bid him sing!

[1924, 1991]

---

1. **Make plain . . . stair:** In Greek mythology, both Tantalus and Sisyphus were punished for their crimes by being sent to Hades. Tantalus, the son of Zeus, was forced to stand in chin-deep water with fruit hanging from branches over his head, but the fruit and water receded whenever he sought to eat or drink. Sisyphus was forced continually to roll a stone to the top of a hill, only to see it roll back down as soon as he completed the task.

HERITAGE

(For Harold Jackman)[1]

What is Africa to me:
Copper sun or scarlet sea,
Jungle star or jungle track,
Strong bronzed men, or regal black
Women from whose loins I sprang   5
When the birds of Eden sang?
One three centuries removed
From the scenes his fathers loved,
Spicy grove, cinnamon tree,
What is Africa to me?   10

So I lie, who all day long
Want no sound except the song
Sung by wild barbaric birds
Goading massive jungle herds,
Juggernauts[2] of flesh that pass   15

---

1. **For Harold Jackman:** Jackman (1901-1961), Cullen's longtime friend and companion, was a teacher and active supporter of many African American writers in New York City.
2. **Juggernauts:** Derived from the name for a sacred idol of the Hindu, the term also means a powerful, overwhelming force.

Trampling tall defiant grass
Where young forest lovers lie,
Plighting troth beneath the sky.
So I lie, who always hear,
Though I cram against my ear   20
Both my thumbs, and keep them there,
Great drums throbbing through the air.
So I lie, whose fount of pride,
Dear distress, and joy allied,
Is my somber flesh and skin,   25
With the dark blood dammed within
Like great pulsing tides of wine
That, I fear, must burst the fine
Channels of the chafing net
Where they surge and foam and fret.   30

Africa? A book one thumbs
Listlessly, till slumber comes.
Unremembered are her bats
Circling through the night, her cats
Crouching in the river reeds,   35
Stalking gentle flesh that feeds
By the river brink; no more
Does the bugle-throated roar
Cry that monarch claws have leapt
From the scabbards where they slept.   40
Silver snakes that once a year
Doff the lovely coats you wear,
Seek no covert in your fear
Lest a mortal eye should see;
What's your nakedness to me?   45
Here no leprous flowers rear
Fierce corollas in the air;
Here no bodies sleek and wet,
Dripping mingled rain and sweat,
Tread the savage measures of   50
Jungle boys and girls in love.
What is last year's snow to me,
Last year's anything? The tree
Budding yearly must forget
How its past arose or set—   55
Bough and blossom, flower, fruit,
Even what shy bird with mute
Wonder at her travail there,

Meekly labored in its hair.
One three centuries removed   60
From the scenes his fathers loved,
Spice grove, cinnamon tree,
What is Africa to me?

So I lie, who find no peace
Night or day, no slight release   65
From the unremittant beat
Made by cruel padded feet
Walking through my body's street.
Up and down they go, and back,
Treading out a jungle track.   70
So I lie, who never quite
Safely sleep from rain at night —
I can never rest at all
When the rain begins to fall;
Like a soul gone mad with pain   75
I must match its weird refrain;
Ever must I twist and squirm,
Writhing like a baited worm,
While its primal measures drip
Through my body, crying, "Strip!   80
Doff this new exuberance.
Come and dance the Lover's Dance!"
In an old remembered way
Rain works on me night and day.

Quaint, outlandish heathen gods   85
Black men fashion out of rods,
Clay, and brittle bits of stone,
In a likeness like their own,
My conversion came high-priced;
I belong to Jesus Christ,   90
Preacher of humility;
Heathen gods are naught to me.

Father, Son, and Holy Ghost,
So I make an idle boast;
Jesus of the twice-turned cheek,   95
Lamb of God, although I speak
With my mouth thus, in my heart
Do I play a double part.
Ever at Thy glowing altar
Must my heart grow sick and falter,   100

Wishing He I served were black,
Thinking then it would not lack
Precedent of pain to guide it,
Let who would or might deride it;
Surely then this flesh would know   105
Yours had borne a kindred woe.
Lord, I fashion dark gods, too,
Daring even to give You
Dark despairing features where,
Crowned with dark rebellious hair,   110
Patience wavers just so much as
Mortal grief compels, while touches
Quick and hot, of anger, rise
To smitten cheek and weary eyes.
Lord, forgive me if my need   115
Sometimes shapes a human creed.

All day long and all night through,
One thing only must I do:
Quench my pride and cool my blood,
Lest I perish in the flood.   120
Lest a hidden ember set
Timber that I thought was wet
Burning like the dryest flax,
Melting like the merest wax,
Lest the grave restore its dead.   125
Not yet has my heart or head
In the least way realized
They and I are civilized.

[1925, 1991]

The Emergence
of Modern American Drama

DURING THE EARLY DECADES of the twentieth century, "Broadway," the area around Times Square in New York City, at once symbolized and dominated theater in the United States. Many of the plays performed by hundreds of touring companies originated on Broadway, where the number of theatrical productions rose from seventy during the 1900-01 season to a peak of almost three hundred during 1926-27, after which the audience for theater was eroded by the growing popularity of "talkies" in movie theaters and the onset of the Great Depression. Operettas were especially popular on Broadway, as were musical extravaganzas such as Florenz Ziegfeld's *Follies*, which he produced virtually every year from 1907 through 1927.

◄ **The Great White Way**

Taken around 1910, this photograph shows Broadway at night, looking south from 42nd Street. The number and intensity of lights on theater marquees and billboard advertisements along the stretch of Broadway just north and south of 42nd Street inspired the nickname the "Great White Way."

During the same period, the Broadway musical emerged in shows such as those written, produced, and performed by George M. Cohan, whose string of hits made him the undisputed "king" of Broadway. Another major force in the American theater world was David Belasco, who wrote, directed, or produced more than one hundred Broadway plays before his death in 1931. Although his productions were known for their realistic, meticulously detailed sets, Belasco's plays epitomized the most popular form of American drama, the melodrama, with its stock characters (hero, villain, and damsel in distress) and formulaic plot.

The popularity of melodramas, which remained the staple of legitimate Broadway theater until after World War I, impeded the development of more modern forms of drama in the United States. Despite some energetic efforts, the revolution in European theater led by Norwegian playwright Henrik Ibsen, often called "the father of modern drama," did not spread to Broadway. American companies successfully produced works by the controversial Irish playwright George Bernard Shaw, a champion of Ibsen who was seeking to develop a vital "theatre of ideas" in England. There were also productions of a few of Ibsen's plays, notably those featuring the prominent actress Minnie Madden Fiske, who gained acclaim in *A Doll's House* in 1894 and later in *Hedda Gabler*. Describing her triumph in that play, "which is packing the house nightly," a reviewer in the *New York Times* observed in 1903: "It is a sight to bring disquiet to

That Ragtime Suffragette

This sheet music from the *Ziegfeld Follies* of 1913 at once reflected and satirized the increasingly militant campaign for women's suffrage in the United States. The lyrics included the verse: "That Ragtime Suffragette, / She's no household pet! / While her husband's waiting home to dine, / She is ragging up and down the line, / Shouting votes, votes, votes for women."

those reactionary folk who so long ago proclaimed that they had sealed the mausoleum of Ibsen." Nonetheless, there was deep and ongoing hostility to Ibsen's plays, in which he dealt realistically with subjects such as syphilis, euthanasia, and the confined role of women in marriage and society. Bemoaning the fact that "Mrs. Fiske," as she was widely known, had chosen to perform in Ibsen's plays, an influential American drama critic declared that "Ibsenism is rank, a deadly pessimism, is a disease, injurious to the Stage and the People."

Much of the impetus toward realism and modernism in American drama came from amateurs and theater people working away from (and many of them far away from) Broadway. One of the most significant artistic developments during the decade 1910–20 was the emergence of small groups that rejected the conventions of the commercial stage in favor of a new, experimental theater. Many of those groups were inspired by the American tour of Dublin's Abbey Players in 1911. Originally an amateur company, the Abbey Players developed into the Irish National Theatre and was renowned for naturalistic acting and simplified staging, two key elements of the movement known as the European Art Theatre. The first American art theater that sprang up in the wake of the Irish group's galvanizing tour was the Chicago Little Theatre, established in 1912 in an effort to elevate what many viewed as the "vulgar" taste in drama in the United States. Other short-lived groups followed in 1913, including the Toy Theatre in Boston and the Little Theatre in New York City, where the Washington Square Players undertook a more lasting and significant venture in 1915. Two other art theaters were established the following year, the Pasadena Playhouse and the Cleveland Play House.

Of all those little-theater groups, none had as profound an impact on the course of American drama as the Provincetown Players. The group was formed by artists, writers, and intellectuals based in the bohemian Greenwich Village section of New York City who spent their summers in the artists' colony of Provincetown, Massachusetts. Led by George Cram Cook and his wife, Susan Glaspell, the founding members of the group gave their first public performances in the summer of 1916 in a converted wooden fishing shack they christened the Wharf Theatre. Buoyed by their first season in Provincetown and inspired by Cook's dream of a new American theater, when they returned to New York City that fall members of the group converted a small space in an unheated building in Greenwich Village into the Provincetown Theatre, later called Provincetown Playhouse. In their first public statement in New York City, the Provincetown Players declared that their primary purpose was to maintain a "stage for free dramatic experiment in the true amateur spirit!"

The Wharf Theatre

In the summer of 1916, the Provincetown Players gave their first public performances in a converted, 25 × 35 foot fishing shack at the end of Lewis Wharf in Provincetown, Massachusetts. Members of the group rigged up rudimentary lighting, created benches by resting planks on sawhorses, and built a 10 × 12 foot stage in the ramshackle building, which many theater historians view as the birthplace of modern American drama.

In contrast to most other little-theater groups, which produced plays by modern European playwrights, the Provincetown Players were determined to perform only new works by American writers. In fact, Cook formed the group to "*cause* better American plays to be written," as Glaspell later recalled. Remarkably, given their limited financial resources, primitive theatrical spaces, and amateur productions, they did just that. Their initial season was notable for performances of Glaspell's first single-authored play, *Trifles*, as well as the first play by Eugene O'Neill to reach the stage, *Bound East for Cardiff*. Although the work of those two prolific playwrights was the mainstay of the Provincetown Players, they produced a wide range of drama—ninety-three new plays by forty-seven different American playwrights—between 1916 and 1922. Although they were primarily committed to realism and representational plays dealing with contemporary problems, the Provincetown Players were also imbued with the playful, iconoclastic spirit that characterized the cultural revolution that broke out on many fronts in Greenwich Village. During the group's first season in New York City, the lineup of plays it produced included *Lima Beans*, a "pantomime dance of automatons to an accompaniment of rhythmic words, in place of music," as the domestic farce was described by its author, Alfred Kreymborg, the editor of *Others: A Magazine of the New Verse.* The lead roles of the Wife and the Husband were performed by two contributors to that radical journal, the expatriate English poet Mina Loy, who had recently arrived in New York City; and the American poet William Carlos Williams, who commuted from his home and medical practice in Paterson, New Jersey. The role of the vegetable "Huckster" was played by the Lithuanian-born abstract painter William Zorach, who also designed the set and "The Curtain," adorned with bold "patterns of remarkable vegetables" and listed on the program as one of the play's four characters. The success of *Lima Beans* encouraged the Provincetown Players to undertake other experimental plays in verse, notably two produced during their 1919-20 season, Wallace Stevens's *Three Travelers Watch a Sunrise* and Edna St. Vincent Millay's satire of war and nationalism, *Aria de Capo.*

Eugene O'Neill's plays also reflected the experimental spirit of the Provincetown Players. O'Neill found himself catapulted to the forefront of American playwrights by his groundbreaking play *The Emperor Jones,* a smash hit first performed at the Provincetown Playhouse in November

Provincetown Players Playbill

The playbill logo of the Provincetown Players was based on a sketch of the set design for the group's 1916 production of Louise Bryant's one-act play *The Game.* The American painter and early exponent of modernism Marguerite Zorach had designed the backdrop, an abstract rendering of trees, the sea, and the moon, suggestive of Provincetown Harbor.

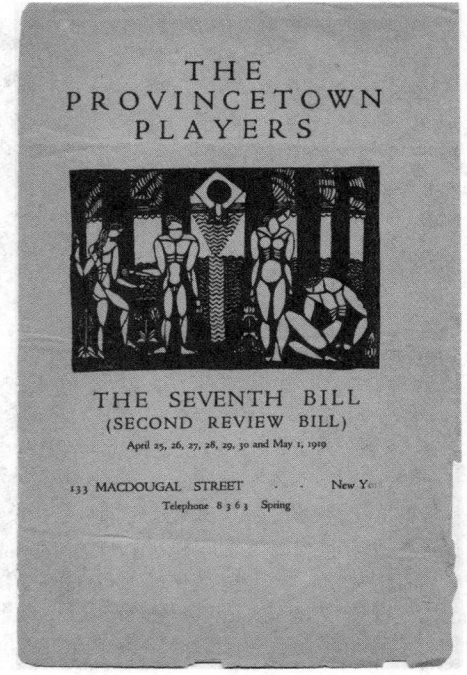

THE PROVINCETOWN PLAYERS

THE SEVENTH BILL
(SECOND REVIEW BILL)
April 25, 26, 27, 28, 29, 30 and May 1, 1919

133 MACDOUGAL STREET · · New Yo
Telephone 8363 Spring

1920. By insisting that the title role be played by a black actor, Charles Gilpin, rather than by a white actor in blackface, O'Neill and the Provincetown Players exerted what the African American poet and activist James Weldon Johnson described as "the initial and greatest force in opening up the way for the Negro on the dramatic stage." Gilpin's acclaimed performance in *The Emperor Jones* not only paved the way for other black actors to appear in productions by white theater companies, but also gave impetus to what came to be called the "Black Little Theatre Movement" of the 1920s.

The play opened up the American stage in other ways as well. Having earlier joined with Glaspell and other playwrights in the effort to establish realism and naturalism as vital forces in the American theater, O'Neill in *The Emperor Jones* adapted some of the dramatic forms of German expressionism, namely nonrepresentational action, dialogue, and sets designed to reveal the hidden lives of characters, especially their intense desires, fears, and memories. O'Neill continued his experiments with expressionistic techniques in *The Hairy Ape* – "a bitter, brutal, wildly fantastic play of nightmare hue and nightmare distortion," as one critic described it – which the Provincetown Players produced early in 1922.

Charles Gilpin in
The Emperor Jones

Gilpin, who had earlier performed with various African American theatrical groups, was the first black actor to star in a dramatic production in an all-white theater in the United States. For his critically acclaimed performance in O'Neill's play, the National Association for the Advancement of Colored People (NAACP) awarded Gilpin its annual Springarn Medal for outstanding achievement by an African American.

Ironically, their triumphant productions of O'Neill's two most experimental plays to date – both of which went on to play in larger theaters on Broadway – marked the beginning of the end of the Provincetown Players. Glaspell contributed to the success of the 1921-22 season with her own experiment with expressionistic techniques, *The Verge*. Following that season, however, she and Cook effectively withdrew from the group because of what they viewed as the growing commercialism and professionalism of the Provincetown Players. After the remaining members reorganized as the Experimental Theatre in 1923, the new company indicated its departure from its former practices by opening with an older European play, *The Spook Sonata*, by the Swedish dramatist August Strindberg, whom O'Neill in the playbill described as "the precursor of all modernity in our present theatre just as Ibsen . . . was the father of modernity of twenty years or so ago." The Experimental Theatre also produced important new plays by O'Neill, including *All God's Chillun Got Wings* and *Desire under the Elms*, both of which premiered in 1924, and *The Great God Brown* (1926). He thereafter became permanently associated with a larger and better financed group, the Theatre Guild. Established in 1918 by members of the former Washington Square Players, the Theatre Guild was a fully professional theatrical company that successfully balanced aesthetic and commercial considerations. From 1918 through the 1940s, the Theatre Guild established the most distinguished record of productions of any theatrical company in American history, while the final incarnation of the Provincetown Players, the Experimental Theatre, collapsed at the beginning of the Great Depression in 1929.

During their brief history, however, the Provincetown Players left an indelible mark on theater in the United States. As early as 1921, the influential English drama critic William Archer declared that one must look to the sand dunes of Cape Cod "for the real birthplace of the New American Drama." The impact of the Provincetown Players became even clearer as American drama continued to mature during the following decades. Almost forty years after the first performances of the Provincetown Players at the Wharf Theatre in 1916, one of their original members, the journalist Mary Heaton Vorse, recalled with a justifiable mixture of wonder and pride, "We had no idea that we were to help break through the traditions of Broadway and revolutionize and humanize the theatre of America."

> *We had no idea that we were to help break through the traditions of Broadway and revolutionize and humanize the theatre of America.*

Susan Glaspell

[1876-1948]

Susan Keating Glaspell was born in Davenport, Iowa, probably on July 1, 1876, the daughter of Elmer and Alice Keating Glaspell. Glaspell was educated at public schools in Davenport and briefly worked as a society columnist for a local newspaper before enrolling at Drake University in 1895. An outstanding journalism student, she graduated in 1899 and took a job with the *Des Moines Daily News*, the first newspaper in Iowa to hire women reporters. Assigned to cover the governor's office and the state legislature, Glaspell became steeped in the life and politics of the Midwest. She began to write her own column, "The News Girl," in which she initially offered commentary on local political issues but later wrote light essays in which she assumed the persona of an innocent and slightly silly young girl, whose naive understanding of the world was the central joke of the pieces. Encouraged by the publication of several of her stories in the *Youth's Companion*, Glaspell decided to devote herself to writing fiction and returned home to Davenport in 1901. During the following decade, her socially conscious stories appeared in prominent periodicals such as the *American Illustrated Magazine, Harper's Monthly*, and the *Ladies' Home Journal*. She also published her first two novels, *The Glory of the Conquered* (1909) and *The Visioning* (1911).

Around 1910, Glaspell became deeply involved with fellow novelist George Cram Cook, the well-educated and twice-divorced son of a wealthy Davenport family. After they married in 1914, Glaspell and Cook moved to

Susan Glaspell

This photograph of Glaspell at work in her Greenwich Village apartment was taken around 1920, when she was one of the leading figures in the experimental theater group the Provincetown Players.

New York City, joining a growing number of writers and intellectuals who were gravitating to the lively artistic community on the Lower West Side of Manhattan known as Greenwich Village. Attracted to the experimental theater that was beginning to emerge there, Glaspell and Cook coauthored a one-act play, *Suppressed Desires,* a satire of the new fad of Freudian psychoanalysis they hoped would be produced by the recently created Washington Square Players. When the company rejected the play as too "esoteric," Glaspell and Cook performed it for friends, first in their apartment in Greenwich Village and later in Provincetown, Massachusetts. Along with a number of other artists and writers who spent the summers there, Glaspell and Cook formed a small theater group, the Provincetown Players, which was soon joined by the then unknown Eugene O'Neill. As an actor, a director, and a dramatist, Glaspell was one of the most vital figures among the Provincetown Players, who produced nine of her plays between 1915 and 1922. The plays were remarkable for their range of characters and situations, as well as for the variety of dramatic techniques Glaspell employed. She frequently explored feminist themes in those works, including her first full-length play, *Bernice* (1919), which the reviewer for the *New York Times* praised for its "beautiful simplicity, rich characterizations, and deep insights into masculine vanity." In 1922, disillusioned by growing differences over the direction of the Provincetown Players, Glaspell and Cook withdrew from the group in order to pursue his dream of living and writing in Greece.

Cook's sudden death ended their sojourn, and a bereft Glaspell returned to Provincetown in 1924. When she was able to begin work again, she edited a collection of Cook's poems, *Greek Coins* (1926), and wrote an account of their relationship, *The Road to the Temple* (1927). With Norman Matson, a young writer with whom Glaspell lived for several years, she wrote *The Comic Artist* (1927), a full-length play that was later produced on Broadway. She also wrote two best-selling novels, *Brook Evans* (1928) and *Fugitive's Return* (1929), as well as a play based on the life and literary legacy of Emily Dickinson, *Alison's House* (1930), which was awarded the Pulitzer Prize for Drama. Although that was her last play, Glaspell maintained her involvement in the theater, directing the Midwest Play Bureau of the Federal Theatre Project in Chicago from 1936 to 1938. Frustrated by governmental red tape, she resigned her position and once again devoted herself to writing fiction, notably the novels *The Morning Is Near Us* (1939), *Norma Ashe* (1942), and *Judd Rankin's Daughter* (1945). By the time she died in Provincetown in 1948, Glaspell had produced a remarkable body of work in fiction and drama, including more than fifty short stories, nine novels, and ten plays, plus three dramas that she coauthored. Nonetheless, although her experimental techniques and innovative early plays had helped transform American drama, at the end of her life Glaspell was overshadowed by other playwrights, especially by the major figure to emerge from the Provincetown Players. The subheadline of her obituary in the *New York Times* thus announced: "Winner of Pulitzer Prize in 1930 with 'Alison's House' Dies — 'Discovered' Eugene O'Neill."

bedfordstmartins.com/ americanlit for research links on Glaspell

Reading Glaspell's *Trifles*.　While working as a reporter for the *Des Moines Daily News* from 1899 to 1901, Glaspell investigated the murder of an Iowa farmer and covered the trial of his wife, Margaret Hossack, who was accused of killing her sleeping husband with an axe. Although she was convicted, Hossack insisted that an intruder had killed her husband, and her conviction was overturned on appeal. The sensational crime and trial were covered by newspapers across the country, in which opinion was deeply divided over Hossack's guilt or innocence. Inspired by the case, and by her visit to the crime scene at the Hossack farmhouse, Glaspell later wrote *Trifles*, her first single-authored play, for the Provincetown Players. They first performed the one-act play at the Wharf Theatre on August 8, 1916, with Glaspell herself playing the role of one of the five characters, Mrs. Hale. The uncompromising play explores different ways of seeing and knowing, as men and women seek clues in a tragic case involving an isolated farm woman, Minnie Wright, who is suspected of having murdered her cold and abusive husband. Glaspell later revised the play into a short story, "A Jury of Her Peers," which was first published in the popular magazine *Every Week* and then in *The Best Short Stories of 1917*. Still the best

Trifles

This photograph of an early performance of *Trifles* illustrates how well suited Glaspell's play was to the small stage and spare productions of the Wharf Theatre, where it was first performed, and to the simplified staging characteristic of experimental theater in the United States.

known of all of her plays, *Trifles* became a popular feature of both amateur and professional theater groups and was widely performed throughout the twentieth century. The text is taken from the first edition of *Trifles* (1916).

TRIFLES

A Play in One Act

Presented by the Provincetown Players at the Wharf Theatre, Provincetown, Mass., August 8, 1916

GEORGE HENDERSON	*Robert Rogers*
HENRY PETERS	*Robert Conville*
LEWIS HALE	*George Cram Cook*
MRS. PETERS	*Alice Hall*
MRS. HALE	*Susan Glaspell*

SCENE

The kitchen in the now abandoned farmhouse of John Wright, a gloomy kitchen, plainly left without having been put in order—unwashed pans under the sink, a loaf of bread outside the bread-box, a dish-towel on the table—other signs of incompleted work. Door opens rear and enter sheriff followed by county attorney and Hale. The sheriff and Hale are men in middle life, the county attorney is a young man; all are much bundled up and go at once to the stove. They are followed by the two women—the sheriff's wife first; she is a slight wiry woman, a thin nervous face. Mrs. Hale is larger and would ordinarily be called more comfortable looking, but she is disturbed now and looks fearfully about as she enters. The women have come in slowly, and stand close together near the door.

COUNTY ATTORNEY: (*Rubbing his hands*) This feels good. Come up to the fire, ladies.

MRS. PETERS: (*Takes a step forward and looks around*) I'm not – cold.

SHERIFF: (*Unbuttoning his overcoat and stepping away from the stove as if to mark the beginning of official business*) Now, Mr. Hale, before we move things about, you explain to Mr. Henderson just what you saw when you came here yesterday morning.

COUNTY ATTORNEY: By the way, has anything been moved? Are things just as you left them yesterday?

SHERIFF: (*Looking all about*) It's just the same. When it dropped below zero last night I thought I'd better send Frank out this morning to make a fire for us – no use getting pneumonia with a big case on, but I told him not to touch anything except the stove – and you know Frank.

COUNTY ATTORNEY: Somebody should have been left here yesterday.

SHERIFF: Oh – yesterday. When I had to send Frank to Morris Center for that man who went crazy – I want you to know I had my hands full yesterday. I knew you could get back from Omaha by today and as long as I went over everything here myself —

COUNTY ATTORNEY: Well, Mr. Hale, tell just what happened when you came here yesterday morning.

HALE: Harry and I had started to town with a load of potatoes. We came along the road from my place and as I got here I said, "I'm going to see if I can't get John Wright to go in with me on a party telephone. I spoke to Wright about it once before and he put me off, saying folks talked too much anyway, and all he asked was peace and quiet — I guess you know about how much he talked himself, but I thought maybe if I went to the house and talked about it before his wife, though I said to Harry that I didn't know as what his wife wanted made much difference to John —

COUNTY ATTORNEY: Let's talk about that later, Mr. Hale. I do want to talk about that, but tell now just what happened when you got to the house.

HALE: I didn't hear or see anything; I knocked at the door, and still it was all quiet inside. I knew they must be up, it was past eight o'clock. So I knocked again, and I thought I heard somebody say "Come in." I wasn't sure, I'm not sure yet, but I opened the door – this door (*jerking a hand backward*) and there in that rocker – (*pointing to it*) sat Mrs. Wright. (*All look at the rocker*)

COUNTY ATTORNEY: What – was she doing?

HALE: She was rockin' back and forth. She had her apron in her hand and was kind of – pleating it.

COUNTY ATTORNEY: And how did she – look?

HALE: Well, she looked queer.

COUNTY ATTORNEY: How do you mean – queer?

HALE: Well, as if she didn't know what she was going to do next. And kind of done up.

COUNTY ATTORNEY: How did she seem to feel about your coming?

HALE: Why, I don't think she minded – one way or other. She didn't pay much attention. I said, "How do, Mrs. Wright, it's cold, ain't it?" And she said "Is it?" – and went on kind of pleating at her apron. Well, I was surprised; she didn't ask me to come up to the stove, or to set down, but just sat there, not even looking at me, so I said, "I want to see John." And then she – laughed. I guess you would call it a laugh. I thought of Harry and the team outside, so I said a little sharp: "Can't I see John?" "No," she says, kind o' dull like. "Ain't he home?" says I. "Yes," says she, "he's home." "Then why can't I see him?" I asked her, out of patience. "'Cause he's dead," says she. "*Dead?*" says I. She just nodded her head, not getting a bit excited, but rockin' back and forth. "Why – where is he?" says I, not knowing what to say. She just pointed upstairs – like that (*himself pointing to the room above*) I got up, with the idea of going up there. I walked from there to here – (*pointing*) – then I says, "Why, what did he die of?" "He died of a rope round his neck," says she, and just went on pleatin' at her apron. Well, I went out and called Harry. I thought I might – need help. We went upstairs and there he was – lyin' —

COUNTY ATTORNEY: I think I'd rather have you go into that upstairs, where you can point it all out. Just go on now with the rest of the story.

HALE: Well, my first thought was to get that rope off. It looked – (*stops, his face twitches*) – but Harry, he went up to him, and he said, "No, he's dead all right, and we'd better not touch anything." So we went back down stairs. She was still sitting that same way. "Has anybody been notified?" I asked. "No," says she, unconcerned. "Who did this, Mrs. Wright?" said Harry. He said it businesslike – and she stopped pleatin' of her apron. "I don't know," she says. "You don't *know?*" says Harry. "No," says she. "Weren't you sleepin' in the bed with him?" says Harry. "Yes," says she, "but I was on the inside." "Somebody slipped a rope round his neck and strangled him and you didn't wake up?" says Harry. "I didn't wake up," she said after him. We may have looked as if we didn't see how that could be, for after a minute she said, "I sleep sound." Harry was going to ask her more questions but I said maybe we ought to let her tell her story first to the coroner, or the sheriff, so Harry went fast as he could to Rivers' place, where there's a telephone.

COUNTY ATTORNEY: And what did Mrs. Wright do when she knew that you had gone for the coroner?

HALE: She moved from that chair to this one over here, (*pointing to a small chair in the corner*) and just sat there with her hands held together and looking down. I got a feeling that I ought to make some conversation, so I said I had come in to see if John wanted to put in a telephone, and at that she started to laugh, and then she stopped and looked at me — scared. (*County attorney, who has had his notebook out, makes a note*) I dunno, maybe it wasn't scared. I wouldn't like to say it was. Soon Harry got back, and then Dr. Lloyd came, and you, Mr. Peters, and so I guess that's all I know that you don't.

COUNTY ATTORNEY: (*Looking around*) I guess we'll go upstairs first — and then out to the barn and around there. (*To sheriff*) You're convinced that there was nothing important here — nothing that would point to any motive?

SHERIFF: Nothing here but kitchen things.

COUNTY ATTORNEY: (*Opens the door of a cupboard closet. Gets up on a chair and looks on a shelf. Pulls his hand away, sticky*) Here's a nice mess. (*The women draw nearer*)

MRS. PETERS: Oh, her fruit; it did freeze. (*To County Attorney*) She worried about that when it turned so cold. She said the fire'd go out and her jars would break.

SHERIFF: Well, can you beat the women! Held for murder and worrying about her preserves.

COUNTY ATTORNEY: (*Setting his lips firmly*) I guess before we are through she may have something more serious than preserves to worry about.

HALE: Well, women are used to worrying over trifles. (*The two women move a little closer together*)

COUNTY ATTORNEY: (*With the gallantry of a young politician*) And yet, for all their worries, what would we do without the ladies? (*The women do not unbend. He goes to sink, takes a dipperful of water from pail and pouring it into basin, washes his hands. Starts to wipe them on roller-towel, turns it for a cleaner place*) Dirty towels! (*Kicks his foot against pans under the sink*) Not much of a housekeeper, would you say, ladies?

MRS. HALE: (*Stiffly*) There's a great deal of work to be done on a farm.

COUNTY ATTORNEY: (*With conciliation*) To be sure. And yet (*with a little bow to her*) I know there are some Dickson county farmhouses which do not have such roller towels. (*Gives it a pull to expose its full length again*)

MRS. HALE: Those towels get dirty awful quick. Men's hands aren't always as clean as they might be.

COUNTY ATTORNEY: Ah, loyal to your sex, I see. But you and Mrs. Wright were neighbors. I suppose you were friends, too.

MRS. HALE: (*Shaking her head*) I've not seen much of her of late years. I've not been in this house — it's more than a year.

COUNTY ATTORNEY: And why was that? You didn't like her?

MRS. HALE: I liked her all well enough. Farmers' wives have their hands full, Mr. Henderson. And then —

COUNTY ATTORNEY: Yes —?

MRS. HALE: (*Looking about*) It never seemed a very cheerful place.

COUNTY ATTORNEY: No — it's not cheerful. I shouldn't say she had the homemaking instinct.

MRS. HALE: Well, I don't know as Wright had, either.

COUNTY ATTORNEY: You mean that they didn't get on very well?

MRS. HALE: No, I don't mean anything. But I don't think a place'd be any cheerfuller for John Wright's being in it.

COUNTY ATTORNEY: I'd like to talk more of that a little later. I want to get the lay of things upstairs now. (*Moves to stair-door, followed by the two men*)

SHERIFF: I suppose anything Mrs. Peters does'll be all right. She was to take in some clothes for her, you know, and a few little things. We left in such a hurry yesterday.

COUNTY ATTORNEY: Yes, but I would like to see what you take, Mrs. Peters, and keep an eye out for anything that might be of use to us.

MRS. PETERS: Yes, Mr. Henderson. (*The women listen to the men's steps on the stairs, then look about the kitchen*)

MRS. HALE: I'd hate to have men coming into my kitchen, snooping round and criticizing. (*Arranges pans under sink which the county attorney had shoved out of place*)

MRS. PETERS: Of course it's no more than their duty.

MRS. HALE: Duty's all right, but I guess that deputy sheriff that came out to make the fire might have got a little of this on. (*Gives roller towel a pull*) Wish I'd thought of that sooner. Seems mean to talk about her for not having things slicked up when she had to come away in such a hurry.

MRS. PETERS: (*Going to table at side, lifts one end of towel that covers a pan*) She had bread set. (*Stands still*)

MRS. HALE: (*Her eyes fixed on loaf of bread outside bread-box. Moves slowly toward it*) She was going to put this in there. (*Picks up loaf, then abruptly drops it. In a manner of returning to familiar things*) It's a shame about her fruit. I wonder if it's all gone. (*Gets up on a chair and looks*) I think there's some here that is all right, Mrs. Peters. Yes — here; (*holding it toward the window*) this is cherries, too. (*Looking again*) I declare I believe that's the only one. (*Gets down, bottle in her hand. Goes to sink and wipes it off on the outside*) She'll feel awful bad after all her hard work in the hot weather. I remember the afternoon I put up my cherries last summer. (*Puts bottle on table. With a sigh starts to sit down in rocking-chair. Before she is seated realizes what chair it is; with a slow look at it, steps back. The chair which she has touched rocks back and forth*)

MRS. PETERS: Well, I must get those things from the front room closet. (*Starts to door left, looks into the other room, steps back*) You coming with me, Mrs. Hale? You could help me carry them. (*Both women go out; reappear, Mrs. Peters carrying a dress and skirt, Mrs. Hale following with a pair of shoes*)

MRS. PETERS: My, it's cold in there. (*Puts clothes on table, goes up to stove*)

MRS. HALE: (*Holding up skirt and examining it*) Wright was close. I think maybe that's why she kept so much to herself. She didn't even belong to the Ladies' Aid. I suppose she felt she couldn't do her part, and then you don't enjoy things when you feel shabby. She used to wear pretty clothes and be lively, when she was Minnie Foster, one of the town girls singing in the choir. But that was – oh, that was thirty years ago. This all you was to take in?

MRS. PETERS: She said she wanted an apron. Funny thing to want, for there isn't much to get you dirty in jail, goodness knows. But I suppose just to make her feel more natural. She said they was in the top drawer in this cupboard. Yes, here. And then her little shawl that always hung behind the door. (*Looks on stair door*) Yes, here it is.

MRS. HALE: (*Abruptly moving toward her*) Mrs. Peters?

MRS. PETERS: Yes, Mrs. Hale?

MRS. HALE: Do you think she did it?

MRS. PETERS: (*In a frightened voice*) Oh, I don't know.

MRS. HALE: Well, I don't think she did. Asking for an apron and her little shawl. Worrying about her fruit.

MRS. PETERS: (*Starts to speak, glances up, where footsteps are heard in the room above. In a low voice*) Mr. Peters says it looks bad for her. Mr. Henderson is awful sarcastic in a speech and he'll make fun of her sayin' she didn't wake up.

MRS. HALE: Well, I guess John Wright didn't wake when they was slipping that rope under his neck.

MRS. PETERS: No, it's strange. It must have been done awful crafty and still. They say it was such a – funny way to kill a man, rigging it all up like that.

MRS. HALE: That's just what Mr. Hale said. There was a gun in the house. He says that's what he can't understand.

MRS. PETERS: Mr. Henderson said coming out that what was needed for the case was a motive; something to show anger, or – sudden feeling.

MRS. HALE: (*Standing by table*) Well, I don't see any signs of anger around here, but (*puts hand on dish towel in middle of table, stands looking at table, one half of which is clean, the other half messy*) It's wiped to here. (*Makes a move as if to finish work, then turns and looks at loaf of bread beside the breadbox. Drops towel. In that voice of coming back to familiar things*) Wonder how they are finding things upstairs. I hope she had it a little more red-up[1] up there. You know, it seems kind of *sneaking*. Locking her up in town and then coming out here and trying to get her own house to turn against her!

---

1. **red-up:** A country expression meaning tidied or cleaned up.

MRS. PETERS: But, Mrs. Hale, the law is the law.

MRS. HALE: I spose'tis. (*Unbuttoning her coat*) Better loosen up your things, Mrs. Peters. You won't feel them when you go out.

MRS. PETERS: (*Taking off fur tippet, goes to hang it on hook at back of the room, stands looking at the under part of the small table*) She was piecing a quilt. (*Brings large sewing basket to table front and they look at the bright pieces*)

MRS. HALE: It's log cabin pattern. Pretty, isn't it? I wonder if she was goin' to quilt it or just knot it? (*Footsteps have been heard coming down the stairs. The sheriff enters followed by Hale and Henderson*)

SHERIFF: They wonder if she was going to quilt it or just knot it. (*The men laugh, the women look abashed*)

COUNTY ATTORNEY: (*Rubbing his hands over the stove*) Frank's fire didn't do much up there, did it? Well, let's go out to the barn and get that cleared up. (*Exeunt men door rear*)

MRS. HALE: (*Resentfully*) I don't know as there's anything so strange, our takin' up our time with little things while we're waiting for them to get the evidence. (*Sits down, smoothing out block with decision*) I don't see as it's anything to laugh about.

MRS. PETERS: (*Apologetically*) Of course they've got awful important things on their minds. (*Pulls up a chair and sits by the table*)

MRS. HALE: (*Examining another block*) Mrs. Peters, look at this one. Here, this is the one she was working on, and look at the sewing! All the rest of it has been so nice and even. And look at this! It's all over the place! Why, it looks as if she didn't know what she was about! (*After she has said this they look at each other, then start to glance back at the door. After an instant Mrs. Hale has pulled at a knot and ripped the sewing*)

MRS. PETERS: Oh, what are you doing, Mrs. Hale?

MRS. HALE: (*Mildly*) Just pulling out a stitch or two that's not sewed very good. (*Threading a needle*) Bad sewing always made me fidgety.

MRS. PETERS: (*Nervously*) I don't think we ought to touch things.

MRS. HALE: I'll just finish up this end. (*Suddenly stopping and leaning forward*) Mrs. Peters?

MRS. PETERS: Yes, Mrs. Hale?

MRS. HALE: What do you suppose she was so nervous about?

MRS. PETERS: Oh – I don't know. I don't know as she was nervous. I sometimes sew awful queer when I'm just tired. (*Mrs. Hale starts to say something, looks at her, compresses her lips a little, goes on sewing*) Well I must get these things wrapped up. They may be through sooner than we think. (*Piling apron and other things up together*) I wonder where I can find a piece of paper, and string.

MRS. HALE: In that cupboard, maybe.

MRS. PETERS: (*Looking in cupboard*) Why, here's a bird-cage. (*Holds it up*) Did she have a bird, Mrs. Hale?

MRS. HALE: Why, I don't know whether she did or not – I've not been here for so long. There was a man around last year selling canaries cheap, but I don't know as she took one; maybe she did. She used to sing real pretty herself.

MRS. PETERS: (*Glancing around*) Seems funny to think of a bird here. But she must have had one, or why should she have had a cage? I wonder what happened to it.

MRS. HALE: I s'pose maybe the cat got it.

MRS. PETERS: No, she didn't have a cat. She's got that feeling some people have about cats – being afraid of them. My cat got in her room and she was real upset and asked me to take it out.

MRS. HALE: My sister Bessie was like that. Queer, ain't it?

MRS. PETERS: (*Examining cage*) Why, look at this door. It's broke. One hinge is pulled apart.

MRS. HALE: (*Looking, too*) Looks as if someone must have been rough with it.

MRS. PETERS: Why, yes. (*Puts cage on table*)

MRS. HALE: I wish if they're going to find any evidence they'd be about it. I don't like this place.

MRS. PETERS: But I'm awful glad you came with me, Mrs. Hale. It would be lonesome for me sitting here alone.

MRS. HALE: It would, wouldn't it? (*Dropping sewing, voice falling*) But I tell you what I do wish, Mrs. Peters. I wish I had come over some times when *she* was here. I – (*looking around the room*) – wish I had.

MRS. PETERS: But of course you were awful busy, Mrs. Hale – your house and your children.

MRS. HALE: I could've come. I stayed away because it weren't cheerful – and that's why I ought to have come. I – I've never liked this place. Maybe because it's down in a hollow and you don't see the road. I dunno what it is, but it's a lonesome place and always was. I wish I had come over to see Minnie Foster sometimes. I can see now – (*shakes her head*)

MRS. PETERS: Well, you mustn't reproach yourself, Mrs. Hale. Somehow we just don't see how it is with other folks until – something comes up.

MRS. HALE: Not having children makes less work – but it makes a quiet house, and Wright out to work all day, and no company when he did come in. Did you know John Wright, Mrs. Peters?

MRS. PETERS: Not to know him; I've seen him in town. They say he was a good man.

MRS. HALE: Yes – good; he didn't drink, and kept his word as well as most, I guess, and paid his debts. But he was a hard man, Mrs. Peters. Just to pass the time of day with him – (*shivers*) Like a raw wind that gets to the bone. (*Pauses, her eye falling on the cage*) I should think she would 'a wanted a bird. But what do you suppose went with it?

MRS. PETERS: I don't know, unless it got sick and died. (*She reaches over and swings the broken door, swings it again, both women watch it*)

MRS. HALE: You weren't raised round here, were you? (*Mrs. Peters shakes her head*) You didn't know – her?

MRS. PETERS: Not till they brought her yesterday.

MRS. HALE: She – come to think of it, she was kind of like a bird herself – real sweet and pretty, but kind of timid and – fluttery. How – she – did – change. (*Silence; then as if struck by a happy thought and relieved to get back to everyday things*) Tell you what, Mrs. Peters, why don't you take the quilt in with you? It might take up her mind.

MRS. PETERS: Why, I think that's a real nice idea, Mrs. Hale. There couldn't possibly be any objection to it, could there? Now, just what would I take? I wonder if her patches are in here – and her things. (*Both look in sewing basket*)

MRS. HALE: Here's some red. I expect this has got sewing things in it. (*Brings out a fancy box*) What a pretty box. Looks like something somebody would give you. Maybe her scissors are in here. (*Opens box. Suddenly puts her hand to her nose.*) Why – (*Mrs. Peters bends nearer, then turns her face away*) There's something wrapped up in this piece of silk.

MRS. PETERS: Why, this isn't her scissors.

MRS. HALE: (*Lifting the silk*) Oh, Mrs. Peters – it's (*Mrs. Peters bends closer*)

MRS. PETERS: It's the bird.

MRS. HALE: (*Jumping up*) But, Mrs. Peters – look at it! Its neck! Look at its neck! It's all – other side *to.*

MRS. PETERS: Somebody-wrung-its-neck. (*Their eyes meet. A look of growing comprehension, of horror. Steps are heard outside. Mrs. Hale slips box under quilt pieces, and sinks into her chair. Enter Sheriff and County Attorney. Mrs. Peters rises*)

COUNTY ATTORNEY: (*As one turning from serious things to little pleasantries*) Well, ladies, have you decided whether she was going to quilt it or knot it?

MRS. PETERS: We think she was going to – knot it.

COUNTY ATTORNEY: Well, that's interesting, I am sure. (*Looking at bird-cage*) Has the bird flown?

MRS. HALE: (*Piling more quilt pieces over the box*) We think the – cat got it.

COUNTY ATTORNEY: (*Preoccupied*) Is there a cat? (*Mrs. Hale glances in a quick covert way at Mrs. Peters*)

MRS. PETERS: Well, not *now.* They're superstitious, you know. They leave.

COUNTY ATTORNEY: (*To Peters, in the manner of continuing an interrupted conversation*) No sign at all of anyone having come from the outside. Their own rope. Now let's go up again and go over it piece by piece. (*They start upstairs*) It would have to have been someone who knew just the — (*Mrs. Peters sinks into her chair. The two women sit there not looking at one another, but as if peering into something and at the same time holding back. When they talk now it is in the manner of feeling their way over strange ground, as if afraid of what they are saying, but as if they cannot help saying it*)

MRS. HALE: She liked the bird. She was going to bury it in that pretty box.

MRS. PETERS: (*In a whisper*) When I was a girl – my kitten – there was a boy took a hatchet, and before my eyes – and before I could get there – (*covers her face an instant*) If they hadn't held me back I would have – (*catches herself, looks upstairs where steps are heard, falters weakly*) – hurt him.

MRS. HALE: (*With a slow look around her*) I wonder how it would seem never to have had any children around. (*Pause*) No, Wright wouldn't like the bird – a thing that sang. She used to sing. He killed that, too.

MRS. PETERS: (*Moving uneasily*) We don't know who killed the bird.

MRS. HALE: I knew John Wright.

MRS. PETERS: It was an awful thing was done in this house that night, Mrs. Hale. Killing a man while he slept, slipping a rope around his neck that choked the life out of him.

MRS. HALE: His neck. Choked the life out of him. (*Her hand goes out and rests on the bird-cage*)

MRS. PETERS: (*With rising voice*) We don't know who killed him. We don't *know*.

MRS. HALE: (*Her own feeling not interrupted*) If there'd been years and years of nothing, then a bird to sing to you, it would be awful – still, after the bird was still.

MRS. PETERS: (*Something within her speaking*) I know what stillness is. When we home-steaded in Dakota, and my first baby died – after he was two years old, and me with no other then —

MRS. HALE: (*Moving*) How soon do you suppose they'll be through, looking for the evidence?

MRS. PETERS: I know what stillness is. (*Pulling herself back*) The law has got to punish crime, Mrs. Hale.

MRS. HALE: (*Not as if answering that*) I wish you'd seen Minnie Foster when she wore a white dress with blue ribbons and stood up there in the choir and sang. (*Suddenly looking around the room*) Oh, I *wish* I'd come over here once in a while! That was a crime! That was a crime! Who's going to punish that?

MRS. PETERS: (*Looking upstairs*) We mustn't – take on.

MRS. HALE: I might have known she needed help! I know how things can be – for women. I tell you, it's queer, Mrs. Peters. We live close together and we live far apart. We all go through the same things – it's all just a different kind of the same thing – (*Brushes her eyes, then seeing the bottle of fruit, reaches out for it*) If I was you I wouldn't tell her her fruit was gone. Tell her it *ain't*. Tell her it's all right. Take this in to prove it to her. She – she may never know whether it was broke or not.

MRS. PETERS: (*Picks up the bottle, looks about for something to wrap it in; takes petticoat from clothes brought from front room, very nervously begins winding that around it. In a false voice*) My, it's a good thing the men couldn't hear us. Wouldn't they just laugh! Getting all stirred up over a little thing like a – dead canary. As if that could have any-thing to do with – with – wouldn't they *laugh!* (*The men are heard coming down stairs*)

MRS. HALE: (*Muttering*) Maybe they would – maybe they wouldn't.

COUNTY ATTORNEY: No, Peters, it's all perfectly clear except a reason for doing it. But you know juries when it comes to women. If there was some definite thing. Some-thing to show – something to make a story about – a thing that would connect up with this strange way of doing it – (*The women's eyes meet for an instant. Enter Hale from outer door*)

HALE: Well, I've got the team around. Pretty cold out there.

COUNTY ATTORNEY: I'm going to stay here a while by myself. (*To sheriff*) You can send Frank out for me, can't you? I want to go over everything. I'm not satisfied that we can't do better.

SHERIFF: Do you want to see what Mrs. Peters is going to take in?

COUNTY ATTORNEY: (*Goes to table. Picks up apron, laughs*) Oh, I guess they're not very dangerous things the ladies have picked out. (*Moves a few things about, disturbing quilt pieces which cover the box. Steps back*) No, Mrs. Peters doesn't need supervis-ing. For that matter, a sheriff's wife is married to the law. Ever think of it that way, Mrs. Peters?

MRS. PETERS: Not — just that way.

SHERIFF: (*Chuckling*) Married to the law. (*Moves toward front room*) I just want you to come in here a minute, George. We ought to take a look at these windows.

COUNTY ATTORNEY: Oh, windows!

SHERIFF: We'll be right out, Mr. Hale. (*Exit Hale door rear. Sheriff follows County Attorney through door left. The two women's eyes follow them out. Mrs. Hale rises, hands tightly together, looking intensely at Mrs. Peters, whose eyes make a slow turn, finally meeting Mrs. Hale's. A moment Mrs. Hale holds her, then her own eyes point the way to the spot where the box is concealed. Suddenly Mrs. Peters throws back quilt pieces and tries to put box in the bag she is wearing. It is too big. She opens box, starts to take bird out, cannot touch it, goes to pieces, stands there helpless. Sound of a knob turning in the other room. Mrs. Hale snatches box and puts it in the pocket of her big coat. Enter County Attorney and Sheriff*)

COUNTY ATTORNEY: (*Facetiously*) Well, Henry, at least we found out that she was not going to quilt it. She was going to — what is it you call it, ladies?

MRS. HALE: (*Hand against her pocket*) We call it — knot it, Mr. Henderson.

Curtain

[1916]

Eugene O'Neill

[1888-1953]

Eugene O'Neill . . . has done nothing much in American drama save to transform it utterly, in ten or twelve years, from a false world of neat and competent trickery to a world of splendor and fear and greatness.

—Sinclair Lewis

Eugene Gladstone O'Neill was born October 16, 1888, the third son of Mary Ellen Quinlan O'Neill, the devout daughter of Irish Catholic immigrants, and James O'Neill, an actor famous for his leading roles in romantic dramas, especially *The Count of Monte Cristo*. Although the couple owned a house in New London, Connecticut, they toured constantly, and O'Neill was born in a residential hotel in New York City. Following the early death of one of her sons, "Ella" O'Neill became addicted to morphine, and her flamboyant husband was a heavy drinker who enjoyed the company of many other women. During his traumatic early childhood, O'Neill witnessed frequent scenes of conflict between his parents. When he was seven, O'Neill was sent to a Catholic boarding school, and he subsequently lived with his parents only during summer vacations, often spending even holidays at school. After graduating from prep school in 1906, O'Neill enrolled at Princeton University, from which he was dismissed for poor academic performance before the end of his first year. Drifting aimlessly, he first worked as a secretary in New York City. When he learned that his girlfriend Kathleen Jenkins was pregnant, O'Neill married her, but he was unprepared for the responsibilities of being a husband and father. The restless O'Neill soon abandoned his family and went to prospect for gold in Honduras. He then signed on as a sailor aboard tramp steamers bound for ports in South America, South Africa, and England.

O'Neill discovered his calling after returning to New York City in 1912. He divorced Jenkins (granting her full custody of their son), tried acting with his father, and worked briefly as a reporter for a newspaper in New London. When he was diagnosed with tuberculosis, his father sent him to recover at a sanatorium. During the six months of enforced inactivity and solitude, O'Neill read constantly, especially Greek tragedies and the works of modern European dramatists such as Henrik Ibsen, George Bernard Shaw, and August Strindberg. Inspired by their work, O'Neill began to write short plays when he returned to New London in 1913. James O'Neill was so relieved that his son was finally making something of his life that he paid for the publication of five of those plays as "Thirst" and Other One Act Plays (1914). Although the volume generated little interest and sold poorly, O'Neill was now determined to become a playwright. After taking George Pierce Baker's pioneering course in playwriting at Harvard University during 1914-15, O'Neill moved to Provincetown, Massachusetts. There, he met George Cram Cook and his wife, Susan Glaspell, through whom O'Neill became involved in their theater group the Provincetown Players. After the group staged the first performance of a play by O'Neill, Bound East for Cardiff (1916), he was almost exclusively associated with the Provincetown Players, who produced ten more of his one-act plays during the period 1916-20. His first full-length play and first venture into the commercial theater was Beyond the Horizon (1920), a modest Broadway hit for which O'Neill received the first of his four Pulitzer Prizes.

O'Neill was soon catapulted into the forefront of American dramatists. His earliest plays were primarily and often grimly realistic, many of them based on his experiences as a sailor aboard ships or in seedy waterfront bars. But he began to experiment with the dramatic techniques of German expressionism, literally "the inner made outer," in his acclaimed play The Emperor Jones (1920). In an enthusiastic review, the influential drama critic Heywood Broun observed: "We never see a play by O'Neill without feeling that something of the sort will be done better within a season or so, and that O'Neill will do it." Indeed, he continued to challenge the theatrical conventions of the American theater, further experimenting with the use of expressionistic dialogue and action in The Hairy Ape (1922) and The Great God Brown (1926), meanwhile creating an uproar with a play about an interracial marriage, All God's Chillun Got Wings (1924). O'Neill also began to draw upon ancient Greek tragedies and Freudian psychology in plays focusing on destructive conflicts within families, including Desire under the Elms (1924) and his marathon, five-hour Strange Interlude (1928). But his professional success was shadowed by the death of his mother in 1920, his father in 1921, and his alcoholic older brother in 1923. His second

Eugene O'Neill

This photograph was taken in Provincetown, Massachusetts, in the early 1920s, at the time critics began to hail O'Neill as the foremost dramatist in the United States.

marriage, to the writer Agnes Bolton Burton in 1918, ended in a bitter divorce after O'Neill left her and their two children to be with the actress Carlotta Monterey, whom he married in 1929. Two years later, he published one of his most celebrated plays, *Mourning Becomes Electra* (1931), a retelling of Aeschylus's Orestia trilogy set in nineteenth-century New England.

bedfordstmartins.com/ americanlit for research links on O'Neill

Widely hailed as the founder of modern drama in the United States, O'Neill was the first American playwright to receive the Nobel Prize in Literature, in 1936. That triumph effectively marked the beginning of his long physical and professional decline. During the following years, O'Neill wrote some major plays, notably *The Iceman Cometh* (1939), which was produced on Broadway in 1946. But the four-hour play did poorly, and others he wrote during the period were not published or produced until after his death, including the Pulitzer Prize–winning *Long Day's Journey into Night* (1940). Because of the personal nature of the play, an autobiographical account of his troubled family, O'Neill instructed that it should be published posthumously, and it was not produced until 1957. Suffering from the progressive degenerative effects of a neurological disorder akin to Parkinson's disease, O'Neill was unable to write at all during the last decade of his life, and he spent his final years living in isolation with his wife in a residential hotel in Boston. Just before he died on November 27, 1953, he is reported to have said: "Born in a hotel room – and God damn it – died in a hotel room."

Reading O'Neill's *The Emperor Jones.*   First performed at their small theater in Greenwich Village on November 1, 1920, *The Emperor Jones* was the crowning success of the Provincetown Players. "They are turning away dozens," one enthusiastic reviewer reported. "People squat on their coats on the hard and not immaculate floors, or sit cheerfully on radiators, or stand patiently for two hours while the tragedy of fear of a Negro porter and ex-convict, turned primitive man again, unfolds itself before the fascinated imagination." In fact, the demand for tickets was so great that the play had to be moved to a larger theater uptown, where it ran for 204 performances on Broadway.

Although the play represented a challenge to the conventions of dramatic realism, O'Neill's story of the downfall and disintegration of the self-appointed "emperor" of a West Indian island was informed by well-known events in the tortured history of Haiti. The nation had gained its independence from France through a successful rebellion begun in 1791 and led by a former slave, Toussaint Louverture. Henri Christophe, who played a major role in the rebellion, became the president of northern Haiti in 1807. In 1811, he proclaimed himself king and established magnificent palaces and homes for himself. Fearing a coup, the autocratic and increasingly unpopular Christophe committed suicide by shooting himself with a silver bullet in 1820. O'Neill's first title for *The Emperor Jones* was "The Silver Bullet," and Brutus Jones, the Pullman porter who becomes a dictator, is a thinly veiled representation of Christophe. Contemporary audiences would have been reminded of the early history of Haiti by more recent events in the country, where an uprising against an unpopular dictator in 1915 had prompted the United States to send three hundred marines to Port-au-Prince to "protect American and foreign interests," as the official policy read. The ongoing military occupation of the country raised considerable opposition in the United States, where many may have drawn a connection between the American policy and Brutus Jones's effort to control and exploit the inhabitants of "an island in the West Indies as yet un-self-determined by White Marines," as O'Neill ironically describes the setting of *The Emperor Jones*.

The resonant play also gained force from its staging, casting, and innovations in language and dramatic structure. One of the founders and leading forces in the Provincetown Players, George Cram Cook, told Susan Glaspell that O'Neill wrote the play "to *compel* us to do the untried,

The Emperor Jones

Jesse Tarbox Beals, the first female photojournalist, took this photograph of the slave-market scene during the earliest performances of O'Neill's play at the Provincetown Playhouse, in November 1920.

to do the impossible." In response, Cook almost single-handedly built a white plaster dome over the stage of the Provincetown Playhouse. The diffused light reflected from the curved and polished surface of the dome gave an illusion of infinite depth to the shallow stage, where the increasingly hallucinatory action was enhanced by bold sets and punctuated by the persistent and quickening drumbeat heard throughout the play. But the most compelling element of the first production was the mesmerizing acting of Charles Gilpin, the first African American to be given a major role on the mainstream American stage, whose performance was hailed by critics as "the crown to a play that opens up the imagination of the American theatre." Indeed, *The Emperor Jones* was then and still is widely viewed as a defining moment in the theatrical history of the United States.

Despite its dramatic impact and historical importance, the play was and remains deeply controversial. Often credited with spurring the development of African American drama during the Harlem Renaissance, *The Emperor Jones* nonetheless raises fundamental questions about racial representation and stereotyping. The eight scenes of the play take Brutus Jones back in his imagination through incidents from both his own criminal past and the tragic history of African Americans, including a slave auction and the voyage of a slave ship, finally returning him to Africa. Langston Hughes reported that, when the play was performed in Harlem, some members of the audience objected so strongly to the portrait of a black man overcome by superstitious fears and reverting to his primitive self that they shouted: "Why don't you come out o' that jungle — back to Harlem where you belong?" Gilpin, however, strongly defended the play, as did his immediate successor in the role, the actor and activist Paul Robeson, who played Brutus Jones on Broadway and in the movie version produced in 1933. "This is undoubtedly one of '*the* great plays,' a true classic of the drama, American or otherwise," Robeson declared in an article in the African American journal *Opportunity* in 1924. In response to those who hoped that he would now get a role "portraying the finest type of Negro," Robeson asserted that he would probably never portray "a more heroically tragic figure than 'Brutus Jones, Emperor,' not excepting 'Othello.'" Certainly, the role continued to provide a powerful vehicle for distinguished black actors, including Ossie Davis, who made his television debut in *The Emperor Jones* in 1955; and James Earl Jones, who played the lead role in a radio version directed by Theodore Mann in 1990. The text of the play is taken from the first printing in *Theatre Arts Magazine* (January 1921).

THE EMPEROR JONES

CHARACTERS

BRUTUS JONES, *Emperor*

HENRY SMITHERS, *A Cockney Trader*[1]

AN OLD NATIVE WOMAN

LEM, *A Native Chief*

SOLDIERS, *Adherents of Lem*

The Little Formless Fears; Jeff; The Negro Convicts; The Prison Guard; The Planters;
   The Auctioneer; The Slaves; The Congo Witch-Doctor; The Crocodile God

The action of the play takes place on an island in the West Indies as yet un-self-determined by White Marines.[2] *The form of native government is, for the time being, an Empire.*

SCENE ONE

The audience chamber in the palace of the Emperor—a spacious, high-ceilinged room with bare, white-washed walls. The floor is of white tiles. In the rear, to the left of center, a wide archway giving out on a portico with white pillars. The palace is evidently situated on high ground, for beyond the portico nothing can be seen but a vista of distant hills, their summits crowned with thick groves of palm trees. In the right wall, center, a smaller arched doorway leading to the living quarters of the palace. The room is bare of furniture with the exception of one huge chair made of uncut wood which stands at center, its back to rear. This is very apparently the Emperor's throne. It is painted a dazzling, eye-smiting scarlet. There is a brilliant orange cushion on the seat and another smaller one is placed on the floor to serve as a footstool. Strips of matting, dyed scarlet, lead from the foot of the throne to the two entrances.

It is late afternoon but the sunlight still blazes yellowly beyond the portico and there is an oppressive burden of exhausting heat in the air.

As the curtain rises, a native negro woman sneaks in cautiously from the entrance on the right. She is very old, dressed in cheap calico, bare-footed, a red bandana handkerchief covering all but a few stray wisps of white hair. A bundle bound in colored cloth is carried over the shoulder on the end of a stick. She hesitates beside the doorway, peering back as if in extreme dread of being discovered. Then she begins to glide noiselessly, a step at a time, toward the doorway in the rear. At this moment, Smithers appears beneath the portico.

Smithers is a tall, stoop-shouldered man about forty. His bald head, perched on a long neck with an enormous Adam's apple, looks like an egg. The tropics have tanned his

---

1. **A Cockney Trader:** A trader from East London, England, an area known for the broad, distinctive accent of its inhabitants, often viewed as the epitome of working-class Londoners.

2. *an island . . . Marines:* Probably a reference to Haiti, which was occupied by U.S. Marines and effectively controlled by the American government from 1915 to 1934.

naturally pasty face with its small, sharp features to a sickly yellow, and Native Rum has painted his pointed nose to a startling red. His little, washy-blue eyes are red-rimmed and dart about him like a ferret's. His expression is one of unscrupulous meanness, cowardly and dangerous. His attitude toward Jones is that of one who will give vent to a nourished grudge against all superiority—as far as he dares. He is dressed in a worn riding suit of dirty white drill, puttees, spurs, and wears a white cork helmet. A cartridge belt with an automatic revolver is around his waist. He carries a riding whip in his hand. He sees the woman and stops to watch her suspiciously. Then, making up his mind, he steps quickly on tiptoe into the room. The woman, looking back over her shoulder continually, does not see him until it is too late. When she does, Smithers springs forward and grabs her firmly by the shoulder. She struggles to get away, fiercely but silently.

SMITHERS: (*tightening his grasp—roughly*) Easy! None o' that, me birdie. You can't wriggle out now. I got me 'ooks on yer.

WOMAN: (*seeing the uselessness of struggling, gives away to frantic terror, and sinks to the ground, embracing his knees supplicatingly*) No tell him! No tell him, Mister!

SMITHERS: (*with great curiosity*) Tell 'im? (*Then scornfully.*) Oh, you mean 'is bloomin' Majesty. What's the gaime, any 'ow? What are you sneakin' away for? Been stealin' a bit, I s'pose. (*He taps her bundle with his riding whip significantly.*)

WOMAN: (*shaking her head vehemently*) No, me no steal.

SMITHERS: Bloody liar! But tell me what's up. There's somethin' funny goin' on. I smelled it in the air first thing I got up this mornin.' You blacks are up to some devilment. This palace of 'is is like a bleedin' tomb. Where's all the 'ands? (*The woman keeps sullenly silent. Smithers raises his whip threateningly.*) Ow, yer won't, won't yer? I'll show yer what's what.

WOMAN: (*coweringly*) I tell, Mister. You no hit. They go—all go. (*She makes a sweeping gesture toward the hills in the distance.*)

SMITHERS: Run away—to the 'ills?

WOMAN: Yes, Mister. Him Emperor—Great Father—(*She touches her forehead to the floor with a quick mechanical jerk.*) Him sleep after eat. Then they go—all go. Me old woman. Me left only. Now, me go too.

SMITHERS: (*his astonishment giving way to an immense mean satisfaction*) Ow! So that's the ticket! Well, I know bloody well wot's in the air—when they runs orf to the 'ills. The tom-tom 'll be thumping out there bloomin' soon. (*With extreme vindictiveness.*) And I'm bloody glad of it, for one! Serve 'im right! Puttin' on airs, the stinkin' nigger! 'Is Majesty! Gawd blimey! I only 'opes I'm there when they takes 'im out to shoot 'im. (*Suddenly.*) 'E's still 'ere all right, ain't 'e?

WOMAN: Yes. Him sleep.

SMITHERS: 'E's bound to find out soon as 'e wakes up. 'E's cunnin' enough to know when 'is time's come. (*He goes to the doorway on right and whistles shrilly with his fingers in his mouth. The old woman springs to her feet and runs out of the doorway, rear. Smithers goes after her, reaching for his revolver.*) Stop or I'll shoot! (*Then stopping—indifferently.*) Pop orf then, if yer like, yer black cow! (*He stands in the doorway, looking after her.*)

(*Jones enters from the right. He is a tall, powerfully-built, full blooded negro of middle age. His features are typically negroid, yet there is something decidedly distinctive about his face—an underlying strength of will, a hardy, self-reliant confidence in himself that inspires respect. His eyes are alive with a keen, cunning intelligence. In manner, he is shrewd, suspicious, evasive. He wears a light blue uniform coat, sprayed with brass buttons, heavy gold chevrons on his shoulders, gold braid on the collar, cuffs, etc. His pants are bright red with a light blue stripe down the side. Patent leather laced boots with brass spurs, and a belt with a long-barreled, pearl-handled revolver in a holster complete his make up. Yet there is something not altogether ridiculous about his grandeur. He has a way of carrying it off.*)

JONES: (*not seeing anyone—greatly irritated and blinking sleepily shouts*) Who dare whistle dat way in my palace? Who dare wake up de Emperor? I'll git de hide frayled off some o' you niggers sho'!

SMITHERS: (*showing himself—in a manner half-afraid and half-defiant*) It was me whistled to yer. (*As Jones frowns angrily.*) I got news for yer.

JONES: (*putting on his suavest manner which fails to cover up his contempt for the white man*) Oh, it's you, Mister Smithers. (*He sits down on his throne with easy dignity.*) What news you got to tell me?

SMITHERS: (*coming close to enjoy his discomfiture*) Don't you notice nothin' funny today?

JONES: (*coldly*) Funny? No, I ain't perceived nothin' of de kind!

SMITHERS: Then you ain't so foxy as I thought you was. Where's all your court—(*Sarcastically.*) the Generals and the Cabinet Ministers and all?

JONES: (*imperturbably*) Where dey mostly runs to, minute I closes my eyes—drinkin' rum and talkin' big down in de town. (*Sarcastically.*) How come you don't know dat? Ain't you sousin' with 'em most every day?

SMITHERS: (*stung but pretending indifference—with a wink*) That's part of the day's work. I got ter—ain't I—in my business?

JONES: (*contemptuously*) Yo' business!

SMITHERS: (*imprudently enraged*) Gawd blimey,[3] you was glad enough for me ter take you in on it when you landed here first. You didn' 'ave no 'igh and mighty airs in them days!

JONES: (*his hand going to his revolver like a flash—menacingly*) Talk polite, white man! Talk polite, you heah me! I'm boss heah now, is you forgettin?' (*The Cockney seems about to challenge this last statement with the facts, but something in the other's eyes holds and cowes him.*)

SMITHERS: (*in a cowardly whine*) No 'arm meant, old top.

JONES: (*condescendingly*) I accepts yo' apology. (*Lets his hand fall from his revolver.*) No use'n you rakin' up ole times. What I was den is one thing. What I is now 's another. You didn't let me in on yo' crooked work out o' no kind feelin' dat time. I done de dirty work fo' you—and most o' de brain work, too, fo' dat matter—and I was wu'th money to you, dat's de reason.

---

3. **blimey:** A British term used to express surprise, excitement, or alarm.

SMITHERS: Well, blimey, I give yer a start, didn't I—when no one else would. I wasn't afraid to hire yer like the rest was—'count of the story about your breakin' jail back in the States.

JONES: No, you didn't have no s'cuse to look down on me fo' dat. You been in jail yo'self more'n once.

SMITHERS: (*furiously*) It's a lie! (*Then trying to pass it off by an attempt at scorn.*) Garn! Who told yer that fairy tale?

JONES: Dey's some things I ain't got to be tole. I kin see 'em in folk's eyes. (*Then after a pause—meditatively.*) Yes, you sho' give me a start. And it didn't take long from dat time to git dese fool woods' niggers right where I wanted dem. (*With pride.*) From stowaway to Emperor in two years! Dat's goin' some!

SMITHERS: (*with curiosity*) And I bet you got er pile o' money 'id safe someplace.

JONES: (*with satisfaction*) I sho' has! And it's in a foreign bank where no pusson don't ever get it out but me no matter what come. You don't s'pose I was holdin' down dis Emperor job for de glory in it, did you? Sho'! De fuss and glory part of it, dat's only to turn de heads o' de low-flung, bush niggers dat's here. Dey wants de big circus show for deir money. I gives it to 'em an' I gits de money. (*With a grin.*) De long green, dat's me every time! (*Then rebukingly.*) But you ain't got no kick agin me, Smithers. I'se paid you back all you done for me many times. Ain't I pertected you and winked at all de crooked tradin' you been doin' right out in de broad day. Sho' I has—and me makin' laws to stop it at de same time! (*He chuckles.*)

SMITHERS: (*grinning*) But, meanin' no 'arm, you been grabbin' right and left yourself, ain't you? Look at the taxes you've put on 'em! Blimey! You've squeezed 'em dry!

JONES: (*chuckling*) No dey ain't *all* dry yet. I'se still heah, ain't I?

SMITHERS: (*smiling at his secret thought*) They're dry right now, you'll find out. (*Changing the subject abruptly.*) And as for me breaking laws, you've broke 'em all yerself just as fast as yer made 'em.

JONES: Ain't I de Emperor? De laws don't go for him. (*Judicially.*) You heah what I tells you, Smithers. Dere's little stealin' like you does, and dere's big stealin' like I does. For de little stealin' dey gits you in jail soon or late. For de big stealin' dey makes you Emperor and puts you in de Hall o' Fame when you croaks. (*Reminiscently.*) If dey's one thing I learns in ten years on de Pullman ca's[4] listenin' to de white quality talk, it's dat same fact. And when I gits a chance to use it I winds up Emperor in two years.

SMITHERS: (*unable to repress the genuine admiration of the small fry for the large*) Yes, you turned the bleedin' trick, all right. Blimey, I never seen a bloke 'as 'ad the bloomin' luck you 'as.

JONES: (*severely*) Luck? What you mean—luck?

SMITHERS: I suppose you'll say as that swank about the silver bullet ain't luck—and that was what first got the fool blacks on yer side the time of the revolution, wasn't it?

---

4. **on de Pullman ca's:** Pullman railroad cars were equipped with sleeping berths and other amenities for long-distance train travel. By the 1920s, roughly twenty thousand African American men were employed as Pullman porters. Although they earned better wages than most African Americans and were respected members of their communities, porters worked long hours under degrading conditions, spurring the formation of the Brotherhood of Sleeping Car Porters in 1925.

JONES: (*with a laugh*) Oh, dat silver bullet! Sho' was luck! But I makes dat luck, you heah? I loads de dice! Yessuh! When dat murderin' nigger ole Lem hired to kill me takes aim ten feet away and his gun misses fire and I shoots him dead, what you heah me say?

SMITHERS: You said yer'd got a charm so's no lead bullet'd kill yer. You was so strong only a silver bullet could kill yer, you told 'em. Blimey, wasn't that swank for yer — and plain, fat-'eaded luck?

JONES: (*proudly*) I got brains and uses 'em quick. Dat ain't luck.

SMITHERS: Yer knew they wasn't 'ardly liable to get no silver bullets. And it was luck 'e didn't 'it you that time.

JONES: (*laughing*) And dere all dem fool bush niggers was kneelin' down and bumpin' deir heads on de ground like I was a miracle out o' de Bible. Oh Lawd, from dat time on I has dem all eatin' out of my hand. I cracks de whip and dey jumps through.

SMITHERS: (*with a sniff*) Yankee bluff done it.

JONES: Ain't a man's talkin' big what makes him big — long as he makes folks believe it. So', I talks large when I ain't got nothin' to back it up, but I ain't talkin' wild just de same. I knows I kin fool 'em — I *knows* it — and dat's backin' enough fo' my game. And ain't I got to learn deir lingo and teach some of dem English befo' I kin talk to 'em? Ain't dat wirk? You ain't never learned any word er it, Smithers, in de ten years you been heah, dough yo' knows it's money in yo' pocket tradin' wid 'em if you does. But yo' too shiftless to take de trouble.

SMITHERS: (*flushing*) Never mind about me. What's this I've 'eard about yer really 'avin' a silver bullet moulded for yourself?

JONES: It's playin' out my bluff. I has de silver bullet moulded and I tells 'em when de time comes I kills myself wid it. I tells 'em dat's 'cause I'm de on'y man in de world big enuff to git me. No use'n deir tryin'. And dey falls down and bumps deir heads. (*He laughs.*) I does dat so's I kin take a walk in peace widout no jealous nigger gunnin' at me from behind de trees.

SMITHERS: (*astonished*) Then you 'ad it made — 'onest?

JONES: Sho' did. Heah she be. (*He takes out his revolver, breaks it, and takes the silver bullet out of one chamber.*) Five lead an' dis silver baby at de last. Don't she shine pretty? (*He holds it in his hand, looking at it admiringly, as if strangely fascinated.*)

SMITHERS: Let me see. (*Reaches out his hand for it.*)

JONES: (*harshly*) Keep yo' hands whar dey b'long, white man. (*He replaces it in the chamber and puts the revolver back on his hip.*)

SMITHERS: (*snarling*) Gawd blimey! Think I'm a bleedin' thief, you would.

JONES: No. 'Tain't dat. I knows you'se scared to steal from me. On'y I ain't 'lowin' nary body to touch dis baby. She's my rabbit's foot.

SMITHERS: (*sneering*) A bloomin' charm, wot? (*Venomously.*) Well, you'll need all the bloody charms you 'as before long, s'elp me!

JONES: (*judicially*) Oh, I'se good for six months yit 'fore dey gits sick o' my game. Den, when I sees trouble comin,' I makes my getaway.

SMITHERS: Ho! You got it all planned, ain't yer?

JONES: I ain't no fool. I knows dis Emperor's time is sho't. Dat why I make hay when de sun shine. Was you thinkin' I'se aimin' to hold down dis job for life? No, suh! What good is gittin' money if you stays back in dis raggedy country? I wants action when I spends. And when I sees dese niggers gittin' up deir nerve to tu'n me out, and I'se got all de money in sight, I resigns on de spot and beats it quick.

SMITHERS: Where to?

JONES: None o' yo' business.

SMITHERS: Not back to the bloody States, I'll lay my oath.

JONES: (*suspiciously*) Why don't I? (*Then with an easy laugh.*) You mean 'count of dat story 'bout me breakin' from jail back dere? Dat's all talk.

SMITHERS: (*skeptically*) Ho, yes!

JONES: (*sharply*) You ain't 'sinuatin' I'se a liar, is you?

SMITHERS: (*hastily*) No, Gawd strike me! I was only thinkin' o' the bloody lies you told the blacks 'ere about killin' white men in the States.

JONES: (*angered*) How come dey're lies?

SMITHERS: You'd 'ave been in jail if you 'ad, wouldn't yer then? (*With venom.*) And from what I've 'eard, it ain't 'ealthy for a black to kill a white man in the States. They burn 'em in oil, don't they?

JONES: (*with cool deadliness*) You mean lynchin'[5] 'd scare me? Well, I tells you, Smithers, maybe I does kill one white man back dere. Maybe I does. And maybe I kills another right heah 'fore long if he don't look out.

SMITHERS: (*trying to force a laugh*) I was on'y spoofin' yer. Can't yer take a joke? And you was just sayin' you'd never been in jail.

JONES: (*in the same tone—slightly boastful*) Maybe I goes to jail dere for gettin' in an argument wid razors ovah a crap game. Maybe I gits twenty years when dat colored man die. Maybe I gits in 'nother argument wid de prison guard was overseer o' us when we're walkin' de roads. Maybe he hits me wid a whip an' I splits his head wid a shovel an' runs away an' files de chain off my leg an' gits away safe. Maybe I does all dat an' maybe I don't. It's a story I tells you so's you knows I'se de kind of man dat if you evah repeats one word of it, I ends yo' stealin' on dis yearth mighty damn quick!

SMITHERS: (*terrified*) Think I'd peach on yer? Not me! Ain't I always been yer friend?

JONES: (*suddenly relaxing*) Sho' you has — and you better be.

SMITHERS: (*recovering his composure—and with it his malice*) And just to show yer I'm yer friend, I'll tell yer that bit o' news I was goin' to.

JONES: Go ahead! Shoot de piece. Must be bad news from de happy way you look.

SMITHERS: (*warningly*) Maybe it's gettin' time for you to resign—with that bloomin' silver bullet, wot? (*He finishes with a mocking grin.*)

JONES: (*puzzled*) What's dat you say? Talk plain.

SMITHERS: Ain't noticed any of the guards or servants about the place today, I 'aven't.

JONES: (*carelessly*) Dey're all out in de garden sleepin' under de trees. When I sleeps, dey sneaks a sleep, too, and I pretends I never suspicions it. All I got to do is to ring de bell an' dey come flyin,' makin' a bluff dey was wukin' all de time.

---

5. **lynchin':** During what is called "The Lynching Era" (1880–1930), almost three thousand African Americans, mostly men, were killed by white mobs in the South, usually by hanging or burning, or both.

SMITHERS: (*in the same mocking tone*) Ring the bell now an' you'll bloody well see what I means.

JONES: (*startled to alertness, but preserving the same careless tone*) Sho' I rings. (*He reaches below the throne and pulls out a big common dinner bell which is painted the same vivid scarlet as the throne. He rings this vigorously – then stops to listen. Then he goes to both doors, rings again, and looks out.*)

SMITHERS: (*watching him with malicious satisfaction – after a pause – mockingly*) The bloody ship is sinkin' an' the bleedin' rats 'as slung their 'ooks.

JONES: (*in a sudden fit of anger flings the bells clattering into a corner*) Low-flung, woods' niggers! (*Then catching Smithers' eye on him, he controls himself and suddenly bursts into a low chuckling laugh.*) Reckon I overplays my hand dis once! A man can't take de pot on a bob-tailed flush[6] all de time. Was I sayin I'd sit in six months mo'? Well, I'se changed my mind den. I cashes in and resigns de job of Emperor right dis minute.

SMITHERS: (*with real admiration*) Blimey, but you're a cool bird, and no mistake.

JONES: No use'n fussin.' When I knows de game's up I kisses it goodbye widout no long waits. Dey've all run off to de hills, ain't dey?

SMITHERS: Yes – every bleedin' man jack of 'em.

JONES: Den de revolution is at de post. And de Emperor better git his feet smokin' up de trail. (*He starts for the door in rear.*)

SMITHERS: Goin' out to look for your 'orse? Yer won't find any. They steals the 'orses first thing. Mine was gone when I went for 'im this mornin'. That's wot first give me a suspicion of wot was up.

JONES: (*alarmed for a second, scratches his head, then philosophically*) Well, den I hoofs it. Feet, do yo' duty! (*He pulls out a gold watch and looks at it.*) Three-thuty. Sun-down's at six-thuty or dereabouts. (*Puts his watch back – with cool confidence.*) I got plenty o' time to make it easy.

SMITHERS: Don't be so bloomin' sure of it. They'll be after you 'ot and 'eavy. Ole Lem is at the bottom o' this business an' 'e 'ates you like 'ell. 'E'd rather do for you than eat 'is dinner, 'e would!

JONES: (*scornfully*) Dat fool no-count nigger! Does you think I'se scared o' him? I stands him on his thick head more'n once befo' dis, and I does it again if he come in my way – (*fiercely.*) And dis time I leave him a dead nigger fo' sho'!

SMITHERS: You'll 'ave to cut through the big forest – an' these blacks 'ere can sniff and follow a trail in the dark like 'ounds. You'd have to 'ustle to get through that forest in twelve hours even if you knew all the bloomin' trails like a native.

JONES: (*with indignant scorn*) Look-a-heah, white man! Does you think I'm a natural bo'n fool? Give me credit fo' havin' some sense, fo' Lawd's sake! Don't you s'pose I'se looked ahead and made sho' of all de chances? I'se gone out in dat big forest, pretend-in' to hunt, so many times dat I knows it high an' low like a book. I could go through on dem trails wid my eyes shut. (*With great contempt.*) Think dese ig'nerent bush nig-gers dat don't got brains enuff to know deir own names even can catch Brutus Jones?

---

6. **bob-tailed flush:** Four cards of the same suit, a relatively weak hand in a poker game.

Huh, I s'pects not! Not on yo' life! Why, man, de white men went after me wid blood-hounds where I come from an' I jes' laughs at 'em. It's a shame to fool dese black trash around heah, dey're so easy. You watch me, man'. I'll make dem look sick. I will. I'll be 'cross de plain to de edge of de forest by time dark comes. Once in de woods in de night, dey got a swell chance o' findin dis baby! Dawn tomorrow I'll be out at de oder side and on de coast whar dat French gun boat is stayin'. She picks me up, take me to the Martinique[7] when she go dar, and dere I is safe wid a mighty big bankroll in my jeans. It's easy as rollin' off a log.

SMITHERS: (*maliciously*) But s'posin' somethin' 'appens wrong an' they do nab yer?

JONES: (*decisively*) Dey don't. – Dat's de answer.

SMITHERS: But, just for argyments sake, – what'd you do?

JONES: (*frowning*) I'se got five lead bullets in dis gun good enuff fo' common bush niggers – an' after dat I got de silver bullet left to cheat 'em out o' gittin' me.

SMITHERS: (*jeeringly*) Ho, I was fergettin' that silver bullet. You'll bump yourself orf in style, won't yer? Blimey!

JONES: (*gloomily*) Yo' kin bet yo' whole roll on one thing, white man. Dis baby plays out his string to de end and when he quits, he quits wid a bang de way he ought. Silver bullet ain't none too good for him when he go, dat's a fac'! (*Then shaking off his nervousness – with a confident laugh.*) Sho'! What is I talkin' about? Ain't come to dat yit an' I never will – not wid trash niggers like dese yere. (*Boastfully.*) Silver bullet bring me luck anyway. I kin outguess, outrun, outfight, an' outplay de whole lot o' dem all ovah de board any time o' de day er night! Yo' watch me!

(*From the distant hills comes the faint, steady thump of a tom-tom, low and vibrating. It starts at a rate exactly corresponding to normal pulse beat—72 to the minute—and continues at a gradually accelerating rate from this point uninterruptedly to the very end of the play.*)

(*Jones starts at the sound; a strange look of apprehension creeps into his face for a moment as he listens. Then he asks, with an attempt to regain his most casual manner—*)

What's dat drum beatin' fo'?

SMITHERS: (*with a mean grin*) For you. That means the bleedin' ceremony 'as started. I've 'eard it b'fore and I knows.

JONES: Cer'mony? What cer'mony?

SMITHERS: The blacks is 'oldin' a bloody meetin,' 'avin' a war dance, gettin' their courage worked up b'fore they starts after you.

JONES: Let dem! Dey'll sho' need it!

SMITHERS: And they're there 'oldin' their 'eathen religious service – makin' no end of devil spells and charms to 'elp 'em agains your silver bullet. (*He guffaws loudly.*) Blimey, but they're balmy as 'ell.

---

7. **Martinique:** Another island in the Caribbean, south and east of Haiti.

JONES: (*a tiny bit awed and shaken in spite of himself*) Huh! Takes moren' dat to scare dis chicken!

SMITHERS: (*scenting the other's feeling—maliciously*) Ternight when it's pitch black in the forest, they'll 'ave their pet devils and ghosts 'oundin' after you. You'll find yer bloody 'air 'll be standin' on end before tomorrow mornin'. (*Seriously.*) It's a bleedin' queer place, that stinkin' forest, even in daylight. Yer don't know what might 'appen in there, it's that rotten still. Always sends the cold shivers down my back minute I gets in it.

JONES: (*with a contemptuous sniff*) I ain't no chicken-liver like you is. Trees an' me, we'se friends, an' dar's a full moon comin' bring me light. And let dem po' niggers make all de fool spells dey'se a min' to. Does yo' s'pect I'se silly enuff to b'lieve in ghosts an' han'nts an' all dat ole woman's talk? G'long, white man! You ain't talkin' to me. (*With a chuckle.*) Doesn't you knows dey's got to do wid a man' was member in good standin' o' de Baptist Church. Sho' I was dat when I was porter on de Pullman, an' befo' I gits into my little trouble. Let dem try deir heathen tricks. De Baptist Church done pertect me an' land dem all in hell. (*Then with more confident satisfaction.*) An' I'se got little silver bullet o' my own, don't forgit.

SMITHERS: Ho! You 'aven't give much 'eed to your Baptist Church since you been down 'ere. I've 'eard myself and 'ad turned her coat an' was takin' up with their blarsted witch-doctors, or whatever the 'ell yer calls the swine.

JONES: (*vehemently*) I pretends to! Sho' I pretends! Dat's part o' my game from de fust. If I finds out dem niggers believes dat black is white, den I yells it out louder 'n some deir loudest. It don't git me nothin' to do missionary work for de Baptist Church. I'se after de coin, an' I lays my Jesus on de shelf for de time bein'. (*Stops abruptly to look at his watch—alertly.*) But I ain't got de time to waste no moe fool talk wid you. I'se gwine away from heah dis secon'. (*He reaches in under the throne and pulls out an expensive Panama hat with a bright multi-colored band and sets it jauntily on his head.*) So long, white man! (*With a grin.*) See you in jail sometime, maybe!

SMITHERS: No me, you won't. Well, I wouldn't be in yer bloody boots for no bloomin' money, but 'ere's wishin' yer luck just the same.

JONES: (*contemptuously*) You're de frightenedest man evah I see! I tells you I'se safe 's'f I was in New York City. It take dem niggers from now to dark to git up de nerve to start somethin'. By dat time, I'se got a head start dey never ketch up wid.

SMITHERS: (*maliciously*) Give my regards to any ghosts yer meets up with.

JONES: (*grinning*) If dat ghost got money, I'll tell him never ha'nt you less'n he wants to lose it.

SMITHERS: (*flattered*) Garn! (*Then curiously*). Ain't yer takin' no luggage with yer?

JONES: I travels light when I wants to move fast. And I got tinned grub buried on de edge o' de forest. (*Boastfully.*) Now say dat I don't look ahead an' use my brains! (*With a wide, liberal gesture.*) I will all dat's left in de palace to you — an' you better grab all you kin sneak away wid befo' dey gits here.

SMITHERS: (*gratefully*) Righto — and thanks ter yer. (*As Jones walks toward the door in rear—cautioningly.*) Say! Look 'ere, you ain't goin' out that way, are yer?

JONES: Does you think I'd slink out de back door like a common nigger? I'se Emperor yit, ain't I? And de Emperor Jones leaves de way he comes, and dat black trash don't dare stop him—not yit, leastways. (*He stops for a moment in the doorway, listening to the far-off but insistent beat of the tom-tom.*) Listen to dat roll-call, will yo'? Must be mighty big drum carry dat far. (*Then with a laugh.*) Well, if dey ain't no whole brass band to see me off, I sho' got de drum part of it. So long, white man. (*He puts his hands in his pockets and with studied carelessness, whistling a tune, he saunters out of the doorway and off to the left.*)

SMITHERS: (*looks after him with a puzzled admiration*) 'E's got 'is bloomin' nerve with 'im, s'elp me! (*Then angrily.*) Ho—the bleedin' nigger—puttin' on 'is bloody airs! I 'opes they nabs 'im an' gives 'im what's what! (*Then putting business before the pleasure of his thought, looking around him with cupidity.*) A bloke ought to find a 'ole lot in this palace that' go for a bit of cash. Let's take a look, 'Arry, me lad. (*He starts for the doorway on right as*)

The Curtain Falls.

SCENE TWO

Nightfall. The end of the plain where the Great Forest begins. The foreground is sandy, level ground dotted by a few stones and clumps of stunted bushes cowering close against the earth to escape the buffeting of the trade wind. In the rear the forest is a wall of darkness dividing the world. Only when the eye becomes accustomed to the gloom can the outlines of separate trunks of the nearest trees be made out, enormous pillars of deeper blackness. A somber monotone of wind lost in the leaves moans in the air. Yet this sound serves but to intensify the impression of the forest's relentless immobility, to form a background throwing into relief, its brooding, implacable silence.

(*Jones enters from the left, walking rapidly. He stops as he nears the edge of the forest, looks around him quickly, peering into the dark as if searching for some familiar landmark. Then, apparently satisfied that he is where he ought to be, he throws himself on the ground, dog-tired.*)

Well, heah I is. In de nick o' time, too! Little mo' an' it'd be blacker'n de ace of spades heahabouts. (*He pulls a bandana handkerchief from his hip pocket and mops off his perspiring face.*) So'! Gimme air! I'se tuckered out sho' 'nuff. Dat soft Emperor job ain't no trainin' fo' a long hike ovah dat plain in de brilin' sun. (*Then with a chuckle.*) Cheah up, nigger, de worst is yet to come. (*He lifts his head and stares at the forest. His chuckle peters out abruptly. In a tone of awe.*) My goodness, look at dem woods, will you? Dat no-count Smithers said dey'd be black an' he sho' called de turn. (*Turning away from them quickly and looking down at his feet, he snatches at a chance to change the subject—solicitously.*) Feet, yo' is holdin' up yo' end fine an' I sutinly hopes you ain't blisterin' none. It's time you git a rest. (*He takes off his shoes, his eyes studiously avoiding the forest. He feels of the soles of his feet gingerly.*) You is still in de pink—only a little mite feverish. Cool you'selfs. Remember yo' done got a long journey yit befo' yo'. (*He sits in a weary attitude, listening to the rhythmic beating of the tom-tom. He grumbles in a loud tone to cover up a growing uneasiness.*) Bush niggers! Wonder dey wouldn't git sick o' beatin' dat drum. Sound louder, seem like. I wonder if dey's startin' after me? (*He scrambles to his feet, looking back across the plain.*) Couldn't see dem now, nohow, if dey was hundred feet away. (*Then shaking himself like a wet dog to get rid of these depressing thoughts.*) Sho', dey's miles an' miles behind. What yo' gittin' fidgetty about? (*But he sits down and begins to lace up his shoes in great haste, all the time muttering reassuringly.*) You know what? Yo' belly is empty, dat's what's de matter wid you. Come time to eat! Wid nothin' but wind on yo' stumach, o' course yo' feels juggedy. Well, we eats right heah an' now soon's I gits dese pesky shoes laced up. (*He finishes lacing up his shoes.*) Dere! Now le's see! (*Gets on his hands and knees and searches the ground around him with his eyes.*) White stone, white stone, where is yo'? (*He sees the first white stone and crawls to it—with satisfaction.*) Heah yo' is! I knowed dis was de right place. Box of grub, come to me. (*He turns over the stone and feels in under it—in a tone of dismay.*) Ain't heah! Gorry, is I in de right place or isn't I? Dere's 'nother stone. Guess dat's it. (*He scrambles to the next stone and turns it over.*) Ain't heah, neither! Grub, what is yo'? Ain't heah. Gorry, has I got to go hungry into dem woods—all de night? (*While he is talking he scrambles from one stone to another, turning them over in frantic haste. Finally he jumps to his feet excitedly.*) Is I lost de place? Must have! But how dat happen when I was followin' de trail across de plain in broad daylight? (*Almost plaintively.*) I'se hungry, I is! I gotta git my food. Whar's my strength gonna come from if I doesn't? Gorry, I gotta find dat grub high an' low somehow! Why it come dark so quick like dat? Can't see nothin'. (*He scratches a match on his trousers and peers about him. The rate of the beat of the far-off tom-tom increases perceptibly as he does so. He mutters in a bewildered voice.*) How come all dese white stones come heah when I only remembers one? (*Suddenly, with a frightened gasp, he flings the match on the ground and stamps on it.*) Nigger, is yo' gone crazy mad? Is you lightin' matches to show dem whar you is? Fo' Lawd's sake, use yo' haid. Gorry, I'se got to be careful! (*He stares at the plain behind him apprehensively, his hand on his revolver.*) But how come all dese white stones? And whar's dat tin box o' grub I hid all wrapped up in oil cloth?

(*While his back is turned, the Little Formless Fears creep out from the deeper blackness of the forest. They are black, shapeless, only their glittering little eyes can be seen. If they have any describable form at all it is that of a grubworm about the size of a creeping child. They move noiselessly, but with deliberate, painful effort, striving to raise themselves on end, failing and sinking prone again. Jones turns about to face the forest. He stares up at the tops of the trees, seeking vainly to discover his whereabouts by their conformation.*)

Can't tell nothin' from dem trees! Gorry, nothin' 'round heah look like I evah seed it befo'. I'se done lost de place sho' nuff! (*With mournful foreboding.*) It's mighty queer!

It's mighty queer! (*With sudden forced defiance—in an angry tone.*) Woods, is yo' tryin' to put somethin' ovah on me?

(*From the formless creatures on the ground in front of him comes a tiny gale of low mocking laughter like a rustling of leaves. They squirm upward toward him in twisted attitudes. Jones looks down, leaps backward with a yell of terror, yanking out his revolver as he does so—in a quavering voice.*)

What's dat? Who's dar? What's you? Git away from me befo' I shoots yo' up! Yo' don't? —

(*He fires. There is a flash, a loud report, then silence broken only by the far-off, quickened throb of the tom-tom. The formless creatures have scurried back into the forest. Jones remains fixed in his position, listening intently. The sound of the shot, the reassuring feel of the revolver in his hand have somewhat restored his shaken nerve. He addresses himself with renewed confidence.*)

Dey're gone. Dat shot fix 'em. Dey was only little animals—little wild pigs, I reckon. Dey've maybe rooted out yo' grub an' eat it. Sho', yo' fool nigger, what yo' think dey is—ha'nts? (*Excitedly.*) Gorry, you give de game away when yo' fire dat shot. Dem niggers heah dat fo' su'tin! Time yo' beat it in de woods widout no long waits. (*He starts for the forest—hesitates before the plunge—then urging himself in with manful resolution.*) Git in, nigger! What yo' skeered at? Ain't nothin' dere but de trees! Git in! (*He plunges boldly into the forest.*)

SCENE THREE

(*Nine o'clock. In the forest. The moon has just risen. Its beams drifting through the canopy of leaves, make a barely perceptible, suffused eerie glow. A dense low wall of underbrush and creepers is in the nearer foreground forming in a small triangular clearing. Beyond this is the massed blackness of the forest like an encompassing barrier. A path is dimly discerned leading down to the clearing from left, rear, and winding away from it again toward the right. As the scene opens nothing can be distinctly made out. Except for the beating of the tom-tom, which is a trifle louder and quicker than in the previous scene, there is silence broken every few seconds by a queer, clicking sound. Then gradually the figure of the negro, Jeff, can be discerned crouching on his haunches at the rear of the triangle. He is middle-aged, thin, brown in color, is dressed in a Pullman porter's uniform, cap, etc. He is throwing a pair of dice on the ground before him, picking them up, shaking them, casting them out with the regular, rigid, mechanical movements of an automaton. The heavy, plodding footsteps of someone approaching along the trail from the left are heard and Jones' voice, pitched in a slightly higher key and strained in a cheering effort to overcome its own tremors.*)

De moon's rizen. Does yo' heah dat, nigger? Yo' gits more light from dis out. No mo' buttin' yo' fool head agin' de trunks an' scratchin' de hide off yo' legs in de bushes. Now yo' sees whar yo'se gwine. So cheer up! From now on yo' has a snap. (*He steps just to the rear of the triangular clearing and mops off his face on his sleeve. He has lost his Panama hat. His face is scratched, his brilliant uniform shows several large rents.)* What time's it gittin' to be, I wonder? I dassent light no match to find out. Phoo'. It's wa'm an' dat's a fac'! (*Wearily.*) How long I been makin' tracks in dese woods? Must be hours an' hours. Seems like fo'evah! Yit can't be, when de moon's jes' riz. Dis am a long night fo' yo', yo' Majesty! (*With a mournful chuckle.*) Majesty! Der ain't much majesty 'bout dis baby now. (*With attempted cheerfulness.*) Never min'. It's all part o' de game. Dis night come to an end like everythin' else. An' when yo' gits dar safe an' has dat bankroll in yo' hands, yo' laughs at all dis. (*He starts to whistle but checks himself abruptly.*) What you' whistlin' for, yo' po' dope? Want all de worl' to heah yo'? (*He stops talking to listen.*) Heah dat ole drum! Sho' gits nearer from de sound. Dey're packin' it along wid 'em. Time fo' me to move. (*He takes a step forward, then stops — worriedly.*) What's dat odder queer clicketty sound I heah? Der it is! Sound close! Sound like — fo' God sake, sound like some nigger was shakin' crap! (*Frightenedly.*) I better beat it quick when I gits dem notions. (*He walks quickly into the clear space — then stands transfixed as he sees Jeff — in a terrified gasp.*) Who dar? Who dat? Is dat yo', Jeff? (*Starting toward the other, forgetful for a moment of his surroundings and really believing it is a living man that he sees — in a tone of happy relief.*) Jeff! I'se sho' mighty glad to see yo'! Dey tol' me yo' done died from dat razor cut I gives you. (*Stopping suddenly, bewilderedly.*) But how you come to be heah, nigger? (*He stares fascinatedly at the other who continues his mechanical play with the dice. Jones' eyes begin to roll wildly. He stutters.*) Ain't you gwine — look up — can't you speak to me? Is you — is you — a ha'nt? (*He jerks out his revolver in a frenzy of terrified rage.*) Nigger, I kills yo' dead once. Has I got to kill yo' agin? You take it den. (*He fires. When the smoke clears away Jeff has disappeared. Jones stands trembling — then with a certain reassurance.*) He's gone, anyway. Ha'nt or no ha'nt, dat shot fix him. (*The beat of the far-off tom-tom is perceptibly louder and more rapid. Jones becomes conscious of it — with a start, looking back over his shoulder.*) Dey's gittin' near! Dey'se comin' fast! An' heah I is shootin' shots to let 'em know jes' whar I is. Oh, Gorry, I'se got to run. (*Forgetting the path he plunges wildly into the underbrush in the rear and disappears in the shadow.*)

SCENE FOUR

(*Eleven o'clock. In the forest. A wide dirt road runs diagonally from right, front, to left, rear. Rising sheer on both sides the forest walls it in. The moon is now up. Under its light the road glimmers ghastly and unreal. It is as if the forest had stood aside momentarily to let the road pass through and accomplish its veiled purpose. This done, the forest will fold in upon itself again and the road will be no more. Jones stumbles in from the forest on the right. His uniform is ragged and torn. He looks about him with numbed surprise when he sees the road, his eyes blinking in the bright moonlight. He flops down exhaustedly and pants heavily for a while. Then with sudden anger.*)

I'm meltin' wid heat! Runnin' an' runnin' an' runnin'! Damn dis heah coat! Like a strait jacket! (*He tears off his coat and flings it away from him, revealing himself stripped to the waist.*) Dere! Dat's better! Now I kin breathe! (*Looking down at his feet, the spurs catch his eye.)* An' to hell wid dese high-fangled spurs. Dey're what's been a-trippin' me up an' breakin' my neck. (*He unstraps and flings them away disgustedly.*) Dere! I gits rid o' dem frippety Emperor trappin's an' I travels lighter. Lawd! I'se tired! (*After a pause, listening to the insistent beat of the tom-tom in the distance.*) I must 'a put some distance between myself an' dem—runnin' like dat—an' yet—dat damn drum sound jes' de same—nearer, even. Well, I guess I a'most holds my lead anyhow. Dey won't never cotch up. (*With a sigh.*) If on'y my fool legs stands up. Oh, I'se sorry I evah went in for dis. Dat Emperor job is sho' hard to shake. (*He looks around him suspiciously.*) How'd dis road evah git heah? Good level road, too. I never remembers seein' it befo.' (*Shaking his head apprehensively.*) Dese woods is sho' full o' de queerest things at night. (*With sudden terror.*) Lawd God, don't let me see no more o' dem ha'nts! Dey gits my goat! (*Then trying to talk himself into confidence.*) Ha'nts! Yo' fool nigger, dey ain't no such things! Don't de Baptist parson tell you dat many time? Is yo' civilized, or is yo' like dese ign'rent black niggers heah? Sho'! Dat was all in yo' own head. Wasn't nothin' there! Wasn't no Jeff! Know what? Yo' jus' get seein' dem things 'cause yo' belly's empty an' you's sick wid hunger inside. Hunger 'fects yo' head an' yo' eyes. Any fool know dat. (*Then pleading fervently.*) But Bless God I don't come across no more o' dem, whatever dey is! (*Then cautiously.*) Rest! Don't talk! Rest! You needs it. Den yo' gits on yo' way again. (*Looking at the moon.*) Night's half gone a' most. Yo' hits de coast in de mawning! Den you'se all safe.

(*From the right forward a small gang of negroes enter. They are dressed in striped convicts' suits, their heads are shaven, one leg drags limpingly, shackled to a heavy ball and chain. Some carry picks, the others shovels. They are followed by a white man dressed in the uniform of a prison guard. A Winchester rifle is slung across his shoulders and he carries a heavy whip. At a signal from the guard they stop on the road opposite where Jones is sitting. Jones, who has been staring up at the sky, unmindful of their noiseless approach, suddenly looks down and sees them. His eyes pop out, he tries to get to his feet and fly, but sinks back, too numbed by fright to move. His voice catches in a choking prayer.*)

Lawd Jesus!

(*The prison guard cracks his whip—noiselessly—and at that signal all the convicts start to work on the road. They swing their picks, they shovel, but not a sound comes from their labor. Their movements, like those of Jeff in the preceding scene, are those of automatons—rigid, slow and mechanical. The prison guard points sternly at Jones with his whip, motions him to take his place among the other shovellers. Jones gets to his feet in a hypnotized stupor. He mumbles subserviently.*)

Yes, suh! Yes, suh! I'se comin'!

(*As he shuffles, dragging one foot, over to his place, he curses under his breath with rage and hatred.*)

God damn yo' soul, I gits even wid yo' yit, sometime.

(*As if there was a shovel in his hands he goes through weary, mechanical gestures of digging up dirt, and throwing it to the roadside. Suddenly the guard approaches him angrily, threateningly. He raises his whip and lashes Jones viciously across the shoulders with it. Jones winces with pain and cowers abjectly. The guard turns his back on him and walks away contemptuously. Instantly Jones straightens up. With arms upraised as if his shovel were a club in his hands he springs murderously at the unsuspecting guard. In the act of crashing down his shovel on the white man's skull, Jones suddenly becomes aware that his hands are empty. He cries despairingly.*)

Whar's my shovel? Gimme my shovel 'till I splits his damn head! (*Appealing to his fellow convicts.*) Gimme a shovel, one o' yo' fo' God's sake!

(*They stand fixed in motionless attitudes, their eyes on the ground. The guard seems to wait expectantly, his back turned to the attacker. Jones bellows with baffled, terrified rage, tugging frantically at his revolver.*)

I kills you, you white debil, if it's de last thing I evah does! Ghost or debil, I kill you agin!

(*He frees the revolver and fires point blank at the guard's back. Instantly the walls of the forest close in from both sides, the road and the figures of the convict gang are blotted out in an enshrouding darkness. The only sounds are a crashing in the underbrush as Jones leaps away in mad flight and the throbbing boom of the tom-tom, still far distant, but increased in volume of sound and rapidity of beat.*)

SCENE FIVE

(*One o'clock. A large circular clearing, enclosed by the serried ranks of lofty, gigantic trunks of tall trees whose tops are lost to view. In the center is a big dead stump worn by time into a curious resemblance to an auction block. The moon floods the clearing with a clear light. Jones forces his way in through the forest on the left. He looks wildly about the clearing with hunted, fearful glances. His pants are in tatters, his shoes cut and misshapen, flapping about his feet. He slinks cautiously to the stump in the center and sits down in a tense position, ready for instant flight. Then he holds his head in his hands and rocks back and forth moaning to himself miserably.*)

Oh Lawd, Lawd! Oh Lawd, Lawd! (*Suddenly he throws himself on his knees and raises his clasped hands to the sky — in a voice of agonized pleading.*) Lawd, Jesus, heah my prayer! I'se a poor sinner, a poor sinner! I knows I done wrong, I knows it! When I cotches Jeff cheatin' wid loaded dice my anger overcomes me an' I kills him dead! Lawd, I done wrong! When dat guard hits me wid de whip, my anger overcomes me, and I kills him dead. Lawd, I done wrong! An' down heah whar dese fool bush niggers raises me up to the seat o' de mighty, I steals all I could grab. Lawd, I done wrong! I knows it! I'se sorry! Forgive me, Lawd! Forgive dis po' sinner! (*Then beseeching terrifiedly.*) An' keep dem away, Lawd! Keep dem away from me! An' stop dat drum soundin' in my ears! Dat begin to sound ha'nted, too. (*He gets to his feet, evidently slightly reassured by his prayer—with attempted confidence.*) De Lawd'll preserve me from dem ha'nts after dis. (*Sits down on the stump again.*) I ain't skeered o' real men. Let dem come. But dem odders—(*He shudders—then looks down at his feet, working his toes inside the shoes—with a groan.*) Oh, my po' feet! Dem shoes ain't no use no more 'ceptin' to hurt. I'se better off widout dem. (*He unlaces them and pulls them off—holds the wrecks of the shoes in his hand and regards them mournfully.*) You was real, A-one patin' leather, too. Look at yo' now. Emperor, you'se gittin' mighty low!

(*He sighs dejectedly and remains with bowed shoulders staring down at the shoes in his hands as if reluctant to throw them away. While his attention is thus occupied, a crowd of figures silently enter the clearing from all sides. All are dressed in Southern costumes of the period of the fifties of the last century. There are middle-aged men who are evidently well-to-do planters. There is one spruce, authoritative individual—the auctioneer. There are a crowd of curious spectators, chiefly young belles and dandies who have come to the slave-market for diversion. All exchange courtly greetings in dumb show and chat silently together. There is something stiff, rigid, unreal, marionettish about their movements. They group themselves about the stump. Finally a batch of slaves are led in from the left by an attendant—three men of different ages, two women, one with a baby in her arms, nursing. They are placed to the left of the stump, besides Jones.*

The white planters look them over appraisingly as if they were cattle, and exchange judgments on each. The dandies point with their fingers and make witty remarks. The belles titter bewitchingly. All this in silence save for the ominous throb of the tom-tom. The auctioneer holds up his hand, taking his place at the stump. The groups strain forward attentively. He touches Jones on the shoulder peremptorily, motioning for him to stand on the stump—the auction block.

Jones looks up, sees the figures on all sides, looks wildly for some opening to escape, sees none, screams and leaps madly to the top of the stump to get as far away from them as possible. He stands there, cowering, paralyzed with horror. The Auctioneer begins his silent spiel. He points to Jones, appeals to the planters to see for themselves. Here is a good field hand, sound in wind and limb as they can see. Very strong still in spite of his being middle-aged. Look at that back. Look at those shoulders. Look at the muscles in his arms and his sturdy legs. Capable of any amount of hard labor. Moreover, of a good disposition, intelligent and tractable. Will any gentleman start the bidding? The planters raise their fingers, make their bids. They are apparently all eager to possess Jones. The bidding is lively, the crowd interested. While this has been going on, Jones has been seized by the courage of desperation. He dares to look down and around him. Over his face abject terror gives way to mystification, to gradual realization—stutteringly.)

What yo' all doin,' white folks? What's all dis? What yo' all lookin' at me fo'? What yo' doin' wid me, anyhow? (*Suddenly convulsed with raging hatred and fear.*) Is dis a auction? Is yo' sellin' me like dey uster befo' de war? (*Jerking out his revolver just as the auctioneer knocks him down to one of the planters – glaring from him to the purchaser.*) An' you sells me? An' you buys me? I shows you I'se a free nigger, damn yo' souls! (*He fires at the auctioneer and at the planter with such rapidity that the two shots are almost simultaneous. As if this were a signal the walls of the forest fold in. – Only blackness remains and silence broken by Jones as he rushes off, crying with fear – and by the quickened, ever louder beat of the tom-tom.*)

SCENE SIX

(*Three o'clock. A cleared space in the forest. The limbs of the trees meet over it forming a low ceiling about five feet from the ground. The interlocked ropes of creepers reaching upward to entwine the tree trunks give an arched appearance to the sides. The space this encloses is like the dark, noisome hold of some ancient vessel. The moonlight is almost completely shut out and only a vague, wan light filters through. The scene is in complete darkness at first. There is the noise of someone approaching from the left, stumbling and crawling through the undergrowth. Jones' voice is heard, between chattering moans.*)

Oh Lawd, what I gwine do now? Ain't got no bullet left on'y de silver one. If mo' o' dem ha'nts come after me, how I gwine skeer dem away? Oh Lawd, on'y de silver one left – an' I gotta save dat fo' luck. If I shoots dat one I'm a goner sho'! Lawd, it's black heah! Whar's de moon? Oh, Lawd, don't dis night evah come to an end? (*By the sounds, he is feeling his way cautiously forward.*) Dere! Dis feels like a clear space. I gotta lie down an' rest. I don't care if dem niggers does catch me. I gotta rest.

(*He is well forward now where his figure can be dimly made out. His pants have been so torn away that what is left of them is no better than a breech cloth. He flings himself full length, face downward on the ground, panting with exhaustion. Gradually it seems to grow lighter in the enclosed space and two rows of seated figures can be seen behind Jones. They are sitting in crumpled, despairing attitudes, hunched facing one another with their backs touching the forest walls as if they were shackled to them. All are negroes, naked save for loincloths. At first they are silent and motionless. Then they begin to sway slowly forward toward each other and back again in unison, as if they were laxly letting themselves follow the long roll of a ship at sea. At the same time, a low, melancholy murmur rises among them, increasing gradually by rhythmic degrees which seem to be directed and controlled by the throb of the tom-tom in the distance, to a long, tremendous wail of despair that reaches a certain pitch, unbearably acute, then falls by slow gradations of tone into silence and is taken up again. Jones starts, looks up, sees the figures, and throws himself down again to shut off the sight. A shudder of terror shakes his whole body as the wail rises up about him again. But the next time, his voice, as if under some uncanny compulsion, starts with the others. As their chorus lifts he rises to a sitting posture similar to the others, swaying back and forth. His voice reaches the highest pitch of sorrow, of desolation. The light fades out, the other voices cease, and only darkness is left. Jones can be heard scrambling to his feet and running off, his voice*) *sinking down the scale and receding as he moves farther and farther away in the forest. The tom-tom beats louder, quicker, with a more insistent, triumphant pulsation.)*

SCENE SEVEN

(Five o'clock. The foot of a gigantic tree by the edge of a great river. A rough structure of boulders, like an altar, is by the tree. The raised river bank is in the nearer background. Beyond this the surface of the river spreads out, brilliant and unruffled in the moonlight, is blotted out and merged with a veil to bluish mist in the distance. Jones' voice is heard from the left rising and falling in the long, despairing wail of the chained slaves, to the rhythmic beat of the tom-tom. —As his voice sinks into silence, he enters the open space. —The expression of his face is fixed and stony, his eyes have an obsessed glare, he moves with a strange deliberation like a sleep-walker or one in a trance. He looks around at the tree, the rough stone altar, the moonlit surface of the river beyond and passes his hand over his head with a vague gesture of puzzled bewilderment. Then, as if in obedience to some obscure impulse, he goes into a kneeling, devotional posture before the altar. Then he seems to come to himself partly, to have an uncertain realization of what he is doing, for he straightens up and stares about him horrifiedly—in an incoherent mumble.)

What—what is I doin'? What is—dis place? Seems like—seems like I know dat tree—an' dem stones—an' de river. I remember—seems like I been heah befo'. *(Tremblingly.)* Oh, Gorry, I'se skeered in dis place! I'se skeered! Oh, Lawd, pertect dis sinner!

(Crawling away from the altar, he cowers close to the ground, his face hidden, his shoulders heaving with sobs of hysterical fright. From behind the trunk of the tree, as if he had sprung out of it, the figure of the Congo Witch-Doctor appears. He is wizened and old, naked except for the fur of some small animal tied about his waist, its bushy tail hanging down in front like a Highlander's. His body is stained all over a bright red. Antelope horns are on each side of his head, branching upward. In one hand he carries a bone rattle, in the other a charm stick with a bunch of white cockatoo feathers tied to the end. A great number of glass beads and bone ornaments are about his neck, ears, wrists, and ankles. He struts noiselessly with a queer prancing step to a position in the clear ground between Jones and the altar. Then with a preliminary, summoning stamp of his foot on the earth, he begins to dance and to chant. As if in response to his summons the beating of the tom-tom grows to a fierce, exultant boom whose throbs seem to fill the air with vibrating rhythm. Jones looks up, starts to spring to his feet, reaches a half-kneeling, half-squatting position and remains rigidly fixed there, paralyzed with awed fascination by this new apparition. The Witch-Doctor sways, stamping with his foot, his bone rattle clicking the time. His voice rises and falls in a weird, monotonous croon, without articulate word division. Gradually his dance becomes clearly one of a narrative in pantomime, his croon is an incantation, a charm to allay the fierceness of some implacable deity demanding sacrifice. He flees, he is pursued by devils, he hides, he flees again. Ever wilder and wilder becomes his flight, nearer and nearer draws the pursuing evil,

more and more the spirit of terror gains possession of him. His croon, rising to intensity, is punctuated by shrill cries. Jones has become completely hypnotized. His voice joins in the incantation, in the cries, he beats time with his hands and sways his body to and fro from the waist. The whole spirit and meaning of the dance has entered into him, has become his spirit. Finally the theme of the pantomime halts, on a howl of despair, and is taken up again in a note of savage hope. There is a salvation. The forces of evil demand sacrifice. They must be appeased. The Witch-Doctor points with his wand to the sacred tree, the river beyond, to the altar, and finally to Jones with a ferocious command. Jones seems to sense the meaning of this. It is he who must offer himself for sacrifice. He beats his forehead abjectly to the ground, moaning hysterically.)

Mercy, Oh Lawd! Mercy! Mercy on dis po' sinner!

(The Witch-Doctor springs to the river bank. He stretches out his arms and calls to some God within its depths. Then he starts backward slowly, his arms remaining out. A huge head of a crocodile appears over the bank and its eyes, glittering greenly, fasten upon Jones. He stares into them fascinatedly. The Witch-Doctor prances up to him, touches him with his wand, motions with hideous command toward the waiting monster. Jones squirms on his belly nearer and nearer, moaning continually.)

Mercy, Lawd! Mercy!

(The crocodile heaves more of his enormous hulk onto the land. Jones squirms toward him. The Witch-Doctor's voice shrills out in furious exultation, the tom-tom beats madly. Jones cries out in fierce, exhausted spasms of anguished pleading.)

Lawd, save me! Lawd Jesus, heah my prayer!

(Immediately, in answer to his prayer, comes the thought of the one bullet left him. He snatches at his hip, shouting defiantly.)

De silver bullet! Yo' don't git me yit!

(He fires at the green eyes in front of him. The head of the crocodile sinks back behind the river bank, the Witch-Doctor springs behind the sacred tree and disappears. Jones lies with his face to the ground, his arms outstretched, whimpering with fear as the throb of the tom-tom fills the silence about him with a somber pulsation, a baffled but revengeful power.)

SCENE EIGHT

(Dawn. Same as Scene Two, the dividing line of forest and plain. The nearest tree trunks are dimly revealed but the forest behind them is still a mass of glooming shadow. The tom-tom seems on the very spot, so loud and continuously vibrating are its beats. Lem enters from the left, followed by a small squad of his soldiers, and by the Cockney trader,

Smithers. Lem is a heavy-set, ape-faced old savage of the extreme African type, dressed only in a loin cloth. A revolver and cartridge belt are about his waist. His soldiers are in different degrees of rag-concealed nakedness. All wear broad palm leaf hats. Each one carries a rifle. Smithers is the same as in Scene One. One of the soldiers, evidently a tracker, is peering about keenly on the ground. He grunts and points to the spot where Jones entered the forest. Lem and Smithers come to look.)

SMITHERS: (*after a glance, turns away in disgust*) That's where 'e went in right enough. Much good it'll do yer. 'E's miles orf by this an' safe to the Coast, damn 'is 'ide! I tole yer yer'd lose 'im, didn't I? — wastin' the 'ole bloomin' night beatin' yer bloody drum and castin' yer silly spells! Gawd blimey, wot a pack!

LEM: (*gutturally*) We cotch him. You see. (*He makes a motion to his soldiers, who squat down on their haunches in a semicircle.*)

SMITHERS: (*exasperatedly*) Well, ain't yer goin' in an' 'unt 'im in the woods? What the 'ell's the good of waitin'?

LEM: (*imperturbably — squatting down himself*) We cotch him.

SMITHERS: (*turning away from him contemptuously*) Aw! Garn! 'E's a better man than the lot o' you put together. I 'ates the sight o' 'im but I'll say that for 'im.

(A sound of snapping twigs comes from the forest. The soldiers jump to their feet, cocking their rifles alertly. Lem remains sitting with an imperturbable expression, but listening intently. The sound from the woods is repeated. Lem makes a quick signal with his hand. His followers creep quickly but noiselessly into the forest, scattering so that each enters at a different spot.)

SMITHERS: (*in the silence that follows — in a contemptuous whisper*) You ain't thinkin' that would be 'im, I 'ope?

LEM: (*calmly*) We cotch him.

SMITHERS: Blarsted fat 'eads! (*Then after a second's thought — wonderingly.*) Still an' all, it might happen. If 'e lost 'is bloody way in these stinkin' woods 'e'd likely turn in a circle without 'is knowin' it. They all does.

LEM: (*peremptorily*) Ssshh!

(The report of several rifles sound from the forest, followed a second later by savage, exultant yells. The beating of the tom-tom abruptly ceases. Lem looks up at the white man with a grin of satisfaction.)

We cotch him. Him dead.

SMITHERS: (*with a snarl*) 'Ow d'yer know it's 'im an' 'ow d'yer know 'e's dead?

LEM: My men's dey got 'um silver bullets. Dey kill him shore.

SMITHERS: (*astonished*) They got silver bullets?

LEM: Lead bullet no kill him. He got um strong charm. I took um money, make um silver bullet, make um strong charm, too.

SMITHERS: (*light breaking upon him*) So that's wot you was up to all night, wot? You was scared to put after 'im till you'd moulded silver bullets, eh?

LEM: (*simply stating a fact*) Yes. Him got strong charm. Lead no good.

SMITHERS: (*slapping his thigh and guffawing*) Haw-haw! If yer don't beat all 'ell! (*Then recovering himself— scornfully.*) I'll bet you it ain't 'im they shot at all, yer bleedin' looney!

LEM: (*calmly*) Dey come bring him now.

(*The soldiers come out of the forest, carrying Jones' limp body. There is a little reddish-purple hole under his left breast. He is dead. They carry him to Lem, who examines his body with great satisfaction.*)

SMITHERS: (*leans over his shoulder— in a tone of frightened awe*) Well, they did for yer right enough, Jonesy, me lad! Dead as a 'erring! (*Mockingly.*) Where's yer 'igh an' mighty airs now, yer bloomin' Majesty? (*Then with a grin.*) Silver bullets! Gawd blimey, but yer died in the 'eight o' style, any'ow!

(*Lem makes a motion to the soldiers to carry the body out left. Smithers speaks to him sneeringly.*)

SMITHERS: And I s'pose you think it's yer bleedin' charms and yer silly beatin' the drum that made 'im run in a circle when 'e'd lost 'imself, don't yer? (*But Lem makes no reply, does not seem to hear the question, walks out left after his men. Smithers looks after him with contemptuous scorn.*) Stupid as 'ogs, the lot of 'em! Blarsted niggers!

Curtain Falls.

[1921]

At Home and Abroad: American Fiction between the Wars

AMERICAN FICTION CAME FULLY OF AGE between the beginning of World War I in 1914 and the end of World War II in 1945. Several of the writers who had earlier shaped the course of fiction continued to write and publish, including Edith Wharton, Willa Cather, and Theodore Dreiser, whose unflinching depictions of American life inspired a new generation of writers. The popular novelist Sinclair Lewis, who in 1930 became the first American to win the Nobel Prize for Literature, recalled that Dreiser's "great first novel," *Sister Carrie* (1900), "came to housebound and airless America like a great free Western wind, and to our stuffy domesticity gave us the first fresh air since Mark Twain and Whitman." The realism and naturalism that became dominant modes of American fiction around

◀ Pablo Picasso, *Portrait of Gertrude Stein*

Picasso completed this famous portrait, which foreshadows his adoption of cubism, in 1906. At the time, both the twenty-four-year-old Spanish painter and the thirty-two-year-old American writer were virtually unknown artists living in Paris.

1900 remained vital forces in the work of many of the younger writers who emerged during and immediately after World War I. But they also developed new styles of writing in response to radically altered conditions in the United States, as well as to the spirit of innovation and experimentation generated by the modernist revolution in the arts that began in Europe.

That revolution was nowhere more apparent than in the work of post-impressionist artists in France. After Gertrude Stein moved permanently to Paris in 1903, she began to collect avant-garde works by Paul Cezanne, widely regarded as the father of modern art, and younger artists such as Pablo Picasso, the central figure in the development of cubism. Stein subsequently began to write experimental prose in which she sought to adapt the visual strategies of cubism, especially the fragmentation and resynthesis of subjects viewed simultaneously from multiple perspectives. Just as the cubists rejected the conventions of realism in art, Stein challenged conceptions of literary realism, writing sketches and stories that disrupted chronology and linear narrative. "One must not forget that the reality of the twentieth century is not the reality of the nineteenth century, not at all, and Picasso was the only one in painting who felt it," Stein later observed in *Picasso* (1938). Other American writers were first introduced to cubism and other new movements in European painting at the Armory Show, an international exhibition of art that toured cities in the United States in 1913. Sherwood Anderson saw the show in Chicago, the year before he read Stein's *Tender Buttons* (1914). Energized by the revelatory artworks in the Armory Show and by Stein's verbal cubism, Anderson began to write the experimental stories he later collected in *Winesburg, Ohio* (1919).

Stein and Anderson, who became close friends, subsequently influenced a number of younger American writers. Inspired in part by reading *Winesburg, Ohio,* Jean Toomer wrote *Cane* (1923), a collection of poems, sketches, and stories about life in black communities in rural Georgia and in the urban North. In his innovative book, Toomer at once challenged generic categories and blurred the lines between poetry and prose, crafting impressionistic prose pieces that revealed the strong impact of contemporary poetry, especially the compressed verse of the imagists. Indeed, many fiction writers of the period also wrote poetry, including Ernest Hemingway, a young Chicago journalist Anderson encouraged to move to Paris and pursue a literary career. Under the tutelage of Stein and the poet Ezra Pound, Hemingway wrote and published his first two books there, *Three Stories and Ten Poems* (1923) and *In Our Time* (1925), a series of prose sketches of violent events that formed an ironic counterpoint to the prayer "Give us peace in our time, O Lord." As critics recognized, the simple diction and colloquial language of Hemingway's early work bore the strong stamp of his mentors Anderson and Stein. Hemingway found other models of artistic expression in the postimpressionist paintings he saw at Stein's

Max Weber, *Grand Central Terminal*

Max Weber, whose family emigrated from Russia to the United States when he was ten, was among the first painters to apply the principles of European modernism to American scenes, especially the contours of life in New York City. In this painting from 1915, he adopted the multiple perspectives and intersecting geometrical planes of cubist art to render the dynamism, motion, and speed of the city, as symbolized by its major railroad station, Grand Central Terminal.

studio and in galleries, especially the late semiabstract landscapes of Cezanne. In an extended meditation on art and writing that Hemingway omitted from his early story "Big Two-Hearted River," his character Nick Adams declares that he "wanted to write about country so it would be there like Cezanne had done it in painting. You had to do it from inside yourself." Hemingway sought to achieve a similar synthesis of naturalistic description and personal expression in the seemingly objective yet emotionally charged stories collected in his first book published in the United States, *In Our Time* (1925).

American writers were further influenced by broader cultural movements in Europe. The new theories advanced by Sigmund Freud and his disciple Carl Jung gave wide currency to concepts such as sexual repression, the significance of dreams, and the unconscious mind, opening up new ways for writers to understand and explore the interior lives of their characters. James Joyce, Marcel Proust, Virginia Woolf, and other modern European novelists offered new ways of seeing and representing the world. Joyce's first novel, *A Portrait of the Artist as a Young Man* (1916), was published to wide acclaim in the United States, where portions of his novel *Ulysses* (1922) first appeared in the *Little Review* between 1918 and 1920. Many American writers were fascinated by Joyce's innovations in language and literary form, especially his development of the interior monologue, a type of stream of consciousness in which the flow of thoughts, impressions, and associations reveals the inner life and individual consciousness of a character. After reading *Ulysses*, Phil Stone told his young friend William Faulkner that "anyone who wrote fiction must hereafter go to school in Joyce." The lesson was not lost on Faulkner, who later experimented with Joyce's stream-of-consciousness narrative style in his inventive novels *The Sound and the Fury* (1929) and *As I Lay Dying* (1930).

Novels also registered major changes in the social, physical, and cultural landscape of the United States. Hemingway, Faulkner, and the other novelists who emerged following World War I were part of a generation "grown up to find all Gods dead, all wars fought, all faiths in man shaken," as F. Scott Fitzgerald put it in his first novel, *This Side of Paradise* (1920). Industries boomed during and after the war, raising concerns about what Sherwood Anderson described as the "universal greyness" of life in an industrial society. The whole struggle for writers, Anderson observed, was "to save what may be saved of individuality." Technological innovations had a strong impact on American life and culture, which was transformed by the mass production of cars, the immense popularity of radio and the movies, and the fast pace of life in the cities. For the first time, the majority of Americans lived in urban areas in 1920, and the city assumed a prominent role in novels such as John Dos Passos's *Manhattan Transfer* (1925). In his "collective novel," Dos Passos adapted the techniques of cubist painting and film, especially abrupt cross-cutting from one scene to another, to expose the fragmentation of life in New York City. The novel revealed the impact of T. S. Eliot's influential poem *The Waste Land* (1922), a vision of urban desolation and sterility that left a strong imprint on F. Scott Fitzgerald's *The Great Gatsby* (1925). At the same time, the first great migration of African Americans from the rural South to northern cities created vibrant black communities, including Harlem, the complex racial and social realities of which Nella Larsen explored in her novels *Quicksand* (1929) and *Passing* (1929).

Although the novel dominated the literary marketplace, the short story remained an important form of literary expression. Most novelists also wrote short stories, a form well suited to the experimental work of Stein, Anderson, Toomer, and Hemingway, though the latter gained far greater commercial success with his novels *The Sun Also Rises* (1926) and *A Farewell to Arms* (1929). Short stories were published in avant-garde literary journals on both sides of the Atlantic, including the first magazine devoted exclusively to the form, *Story*. As the novelist Nelson Algren later observed, "*Story* was the most distinguished magazine of the short story in America at a time when the short story was at its peak as an art form internationally and when American short stories were read and admired the world over." Short stories also remained a

Story was the most distinguished magazine of the short story in America at a time when the short story was at its peak as an art form internationally and when American short stories were read and admired the world over.

staple of popular, mass-circulation magazines in the United States. Between 1913 and 1916, shortly after she emigrated from Mexico, María Cristina Mena published a series of stories about her native country in the *Century.* During the period of conflict and political unrest that followed the Mexican Revolution of 1910–17, the Texas-born writer Katherine Anne Porter published stories about Mexico in the *Century* and other magazines, including the title story of the collection that made her reputation, *Flowering Judas and Other Stories* (1930). F. Scott Fitzgerald published more than 150 magazine stories, nearly half of them in the most popular weekly magazine of the period, the *Saturday Evening Post,* whose circulation reached 2,750,000 during the economic boom of the 1920s.

The stock market crash of 1929 sharply altered the course of American fiction. As the deepening economic depression plunged hundreds of thousands of Americans into unemployment and homelessness, many writers were drawn to political causes. The new emphasis on social art, art that was at once socially responsible and accessible to a wide public, generated a broad reaction against literary experimentation. The Marxist critic Max Eastman attacked Gertrude Stein and other modernists in his famous essay "The Cult of Unintelligibility" (1929). After the publication of Stein's popular book *The Autobiography of Alice B. Toklas* (1933) and her subsequent lecture tour of the United States, the editor of the leftist magazine the *New Masses,* Michael Gold, responded to her sudden

Charles Demuth,
My Egypt

In the early decades of the twentieth century, many American writers and painters wrestled with the new industrial landscape in the United States. As the title of this 1927 painting suggests, Demuth invested the concrete grain towers in his hometown of Lancaster, Pennsylvania, with the monumental grandeur of the pyramids of ancient Egypt.

notoriety in an angry essay entitled "Gertrude Stein: A Literary Idiot." Describing her "as a forbidding priestess of a strange literary cult," Gold harshly observed that many Marxists "see in the work of Gertrude Stein extreme symptoms of the decay of capitalist culture. They view her work as the complete attempt to annihilate all relations between the artist and the society in which he lives." In opposition to such "idle art," which he dismissed as the literary equivalent of the "idle rich," Gold in other essays called for the development of a genuine "proletarian literature" focused on the economic and social struggles of the working class. One of the writers most closely associated with the proletarian movement was the feminist and Socialist Meridel Le Sueur, whose essays, reportage, and stories frequently focused on the struggles of the poor and dispossessed during the Great Depression.

Millard Sheets, *Tenement Flats*

In this 1934 painting, Sheets lovingly portrayed tenement life of Bunker Hill, a poor, working-class neighborhood in Los Angeles. Sheets, who was deeply involved in the first federal arts program established during the Great Depression, the Public Works of Art Project, gifted this painting to the United States.

Social criticism was also a central element of the work of several of the most prominent American novelists of the 1930s. John Dos Passos offered a sweeping critique of the bankruptcy of American values and the boom-and-bust economy that had led to the Great Depression in *U.S.A.* (1930–36). In his ambitious trilogy, Dos Passos continued the experimentation he had begun in his earlier novels, combining fictional narratives, short biographies, actual news stories, and bits of popular culture into the literary equivalent of a cinematic "montage" that revealed his strong interest in the pioneering films of the Russian director Sergei Eisenstein. In contrast, two novelists who emerged during the 1930s, John Steinbeck and Richard Wright, employed the traditional narrative forms of realism and naturalism. Steinbeck and Wright were also influenced by the photojournalism and documentary journalism that developed during the Great Depression, as exemplified by *Let Us*

John Steuart Curry, *Hoover and the Flood*

In 1940, *Life* magazine commissioned the prominent regionalist artist John Steuart Curry to create a series of paintings depicting modern American history. In part, this large painting of the disastrous Mississippi River flood of 1927 commemorated the work of then secretary of the commerce Herbert Hoover, who led the relief efforts and who is pictured on the right. But the artist mainly focused on the faith and endurance of the common people, both black and white, as symbolized by the man raising his hands to heaven and the mother nursing her child in a pose that recalls the Madonna.

Now Praise Famous Men (1939), an impassioned report on the condition of impoverished tenant farmers in the South written by James Agee and accompanied by the powerful photographs of Walker Evans. Steinbeck exposed the plight of displaced farmers fleeing the Dust Bowl in his best-selling novel *The Grapes of Wrath* (1939), while Wright gained critical acclaim for *Native Son*, a harrowing novel about black life in an urban ghetto published in 1940.

The concern with the trials of common people that spawned social realism gave a strong impetus to regional fiction. Most of Steinbeck's work was deeply rooted in California, including the early stories he collected in *The Long Valley* (1938), a reference to the Salinas Valley where he grew up in central California. Wright's first book was *Uncle Tom's Children* (1938), a collection of bitter stories about black life in the segregated South. The anthropologist and novelist Zora Neale Hurston, who grew up in Eatonville, Florida, drew upon her study of African American dialect and folk culture in her novels and in stories such as "The Gilded Six Bits," which was published in *Story* in 1933. White writers also discovered rich resources for fiction in the South. William Faulkner employed modernist literary techniques to explore what he described as his "own little postage stamp of native soil" in northern Mississippi, the setting of most of the novels and stories he wrote during the 1930s. His work inspired younger southern writers, including Eudora Welty, who recorded life in her native Mississippi in photographs and in stories she began to write in the mid-1930s. Welty was praised for her use of dialect and uncanny ability to capture speech patterns, as well as for her realistic depictions of life in the Depression-era South. But she displayed little interest in the social protest that fueled much of the American fiction of the 1930s. In her later essay "Must the Novelist Crusade?" (1965), she affirmed that "great fiction shows us not how to conduct our behavior but how to feel," a statement that might well have served as a motto of her first collection of stories, *A Curtain of Green* (1941).

Great fiction shows us not how to conduct our behavior but how to feel.

Although fiction remained popular during World War II, Americans were far more absorbed in journalistic reports from the front lines, especially after the United States entered the war in December 1941. But the Japanese invasion and conquest of the Philippines helped generate interest in the work of Carlos Bulosan, the first Filipino American writer to gain a wide readership in the United States. During the war, Bulosan began to publish his work in magazines such as the *New Yorker*, where his story "The End of the War" appeared in 1944. Along with the groundbreaking stories by the Mexican immigrant María Cristina Mena and the work of African American writers such as Jean Toomer, Nella Larsen, Zora Neale Hurston, and Richard Wright, Bulosan's stories were signs that American fiction had not only come of age, but also begun to mirror the rich diversity of the United States.

Gertrude Stein

[1874-1946]

Gertrude Stein was born on February 3, 1874, in Allegheny, a suburb of Pittsburgh, Pennsylvania. She was the seventh child of Daniel and Amelia Keyser Stein, middle-class German Jews who owned a textile firm with stores in Pittsburgh and Baltimore, Maryland. Following a disagreement with his brother, a co-owner of the firm, Daniel Stein relocated his business and moved his family to Vienna, Austria. The Steins lived there and in Paris until 1879, when they returned to the United States and settled in Oakland, California. Stein was educated by private tutors and then attended high school in Oakland. After the death of her mother in 1888 and her father in 1891, Stein and her siblings received small trust funds, and she withdrew from high school. In 1892, she went to live with an aunt in Baltimore, and her brother Leo enrolled at Harvard University. The next year, Stein enrolled as a special student at Harvard Annex, later called Radcliffe College, where she studied philosophy and psychology with William James, the brother of the novelist Henry James. Her first published work was a coauthored article on "automatic writing," a free-writing exercise used in therapy, which appeared in the *Psychological Review* in 1896. After graduating magna cum laude in 1898, she decided to continue her study of psychology at the Johns Hopkins School of Medicine in Baltimore. During her years there, she was "bored, frankly and openly bored," as Stein put it, and in 1903 she left medical school without taking a degree and joined her brother Leo, who had gone to study art in Paris.

Gertrude Stein

This photograph of Stein was taken in the studio of her apartment at 27 rue de Fleurus, about two years after she moved to Paris in 1903.

Stein lived there for most of the rest of her life. She and her brother found a two-story courtyard apartment with an attached studio on the rue de Fleurus in Montparnasse, the vibrant artistic and intellectual center of Paris. Stein immediately wrote *Q.E.D.* (c. 1903), a semiautobiographical novel about a failed lesbian love affair that was not published until after her death. She and Leo soon began to hold an open house on Saturday evenings, gatherings that developed into a famous salon for intellectuals, painters, and writers. Many also came to see the paintings she and Leo began to collect, including innovative works by emerging, avant-garde artists such as Henri Matisse and Pablo Picasso, who painted Stein's portrait

For me the work of
Gertrude Stein consists
in a rebuilding, an entire
new recasting of life, in
the city of words.
    –Sherwood Anderson

in 1906. According to Stein, during her long sittings for the portrait, which represented Picasso's first step toward the development of cubism, she mentally composed sentences for her experimental *Three Lives*. Before it was privately printed in 1909, she wrote *The Making of Americans*, a fictional account of the history of her family that grew into what Stein described as "the history of every kind and of every individual human being." While she was working on the thousand-page saga, which was not published until 1925, Stein met Alice B. Toklas, a thirty-year-old Californian who was visiting Paris. They were immediately drawn to each other, and early in 1910 Toklas moved into the apartment on the rue de Fleurus, becoming Stein's lifelong companion, lover, and secretary.

During the following decades, Stein became a major force among modernist writers in English. In 1910, she began writing a series of brief, non-representational "word portraits," including "Picasso" and "Matisse," both of which Alfred Stieglitz published in a special issue of his influential journal *Camera Work*. In 1913, her brother moved out of their apartment and left for Italy, and they divided their famous art collection, with Leo taking the paintings by Matisse and Stein keeping those by Picasso and other cubists. Stein privately published *Tender Buttons: Objects, Food, Rooms* (1914), still-life studies in which she attempted to create in words what the cubists created on canvas. During World War I, Stein bought and learned to drive a Ford truck, which she and Toklas used to transport supplies and to evacuate refugees for the American Fund for French Wounded. After the war, they hosted dozens of expatriate American artists and writers, including Sherwood Anderson, Zelda and F. Scott Fitzgerald, and Ernest Hemingway. Stein privately published *Geography and Plays* (1922), a collection of her word portraits and short plays, and her friends helped her find commercial publishers for *The Making of Americans* and *Composition as Explanation* (1926). She published a wide range of writings during the next few years, further solidifying her reputation for innovation and tireless experimentation. In her witty memoirs, *The Autobiography of Alice B. Toklas* (1933), Stein thus adopted the unconventional strategy of telling her own story from Toklas's point of view, focusing on their life together in Paris.

The Autobiography made Stein famous. The book was serialized in the prestigious *Atlantic Monthly*, and it became a bestseller as a selection of the Book-of-the-Month Club. At the same time, an equally unconventional opera she wrote with the American composer Virgil Thomson, *Four Saints in Three Acts*, began a successful run on Broadway in 1934. Suddenly in demand as a speaker, Stein embarked on an extended lecture tour of the United States. Stein further capitalized on the success of *The Autobiography* by writing a second volume of her memoirs, *Everybody's Autobiography* (1937). A series of other books followed, including *Picasso* (1938) and a children's book, *The World Is Round* (1939). During the German occupation of France, Stein and Toklas moved to the countryside, where they lived quietly throughout World War II in order to escape the organized persecution of Jews. Stein continued to write, publishing *Ida, a Novel* (1941) and another volume of her memoirs, *Wars I Have Seen* (1945). She also wrote

bedfordstmartins.com/
americanlit *for research*
links on Stein

another opera, *The Mother of Us All*, based on the life of pioneering feminist Susan B. Anthony. With Toklas at her side, Stein died of cancer on July 27, 1946. "The world will be a duller place without her," one of her many admirers observed in the *Nation*.

Reading Stein's "Ada." Stein composed this sketch, the first of her word portraits, in 1910. In the series of brief prose works, Stein sought to capture the essence of an individual's life and character without relying on physical description or detailed bio-graphical information. In "Ada," her sub-ject was her companion and lover, Alice Babette Toklas (1877-1967). Born in San Francisco, she was twenty when her mother died of cancer, and Toklas then served for a time as a housekeeper for her grandfa-ther, father, and brother. After inheriting some money from her grandfather, Toklas left home and went to Europe, where she met Stein at a party on the day she arrived in Paris in 1907. Early in 1910, they began living together and were lovers and com-panions until Stein's death in 1946. In many ways, "Ada" chronicles this narra-tive up to 1910, but Stein offered few con-crete details and changed all of the names of the people involved in the story. Alice, for example, has become Ada, a name with different meanings in various cultures, including "first daughter" (Nigerian), "ornament" (Hebrew), and "happy" (Old German). All of those meanings may fig-ure in "Ada," which may also be a playful allusion to Augusta Ada Byron, Lady Lovelace (1815-1852), the remarkable daughter of the British poet Lord Byron, who became one of the first women to be widely recognized as a mathematician and who helped pioneer the earliest forms of computer programming. In *The Autobiography of Alice B. Toklas* (1933), Stein says that when Toklas read "Ada" she initially thought Stein was making fun of her but that she was finally "terribly pleased with it." The text is taken from its first publication in *Geography and Plays* (1922).

Alice B. Toklas

The noted photographer Arnold Genthe took this portrait of Toklas in San Francisco in 1906, shortly before her trip to Europe.

ADA

Barnes Colhard did not say he would not do it but he did not do it. He did it and then he did not do it, he did not ever think about it. He just thought some time he might do something.

His father Mr. Abram Colhard spoke about it to every one and very many of them spoke to Barnes Colhard about it and he always listened to them.

Then Barnes fell in love with a very nice girl and she would not marry him. He cried then, his father Mr. Abram Colhard comforted him and they took a trip and Barnes promised he would do what his father wanted him to be doing. He did not do the thing, he thought he would do another thing, he did not do the other thing, his father Mr. Colhard did not want him to do the other thing. He really did not do anything then. When he was a good deal older he married a very rich girl. He had thought perhaps he would not propose to her but his sister wrote to him that it would be a good thing. He married the rich girl and she thought he was the most wonderful man and one who knew everything. Barnes never spent more than the income of the fortune he and his wife had then, that is to say they did not spend more than the income and this was a surprise to very many who knew about him and about his marrying the girl who had such a large fortune. He had a happy life while he was living and after he was dead his wife and children remembered him.

He had a sister who also was successful enough in being one being living. His sister was one who came to be happier than most people come to be in living. She came to be a completely happy one. She was twice as old as her brother. She had been a very good daughter to her mother. She and her mother had always told very pretty stories to each other. Many old men loved to hear her tell these stories to her mother. Every one who ever knew her mother liked her mother. Many were sorry later that not every one liked the daughter. Many did like the daughter but not every one as every one had liked the mother. The daughter was charming inside in her, it did not show outside in her to every one, it certainly did to some. She did sometimes think her mother would be pleased with a story that did not please her mother, when her mother later was sicker the daughter knew that there were some stories she could tell her that would not please her mother. Her mother died and really mostly altogether the mother and the daughter had told each other stories very happily together.

The daughter then kept house for her father and took care of her brother. There were many relations who lived with them. The daughter did not like them to live with them and she did not like them to die with them. The daughter, Ada they had called her after her grandmother who had delightful ways of smelling flowers and eating dates and sugar, did not like it at all then as she did not like so much dying and she did not like any of the living she was doing then. Every now and then some old gentlemen told delightful stories to her. Mostly then there were not nice stories told by any one then in her living. She told her father Mr. Abram Colhard that she did not like it at all being one being living then. He never said anything. She was afraid then, she was one needing charming stories and happy telling of them and not having that thing she was always trembling. Then every one who could live with them were dead and there were then the father and the son a young man then and the daughter coming to be that one then. Her grandfather had left some money to them each one of them. Ada said she was going to use it to go away from them. The father said nothing then, then he said something and she said nothing then, then they both said nothing and then it was that she went away from them. The father was quite tender then, she was his daughter then. He wrote her tender letters then, she wrote him tender letters then, she never went back to live with him. He wanted her to come and she wrote him tender letters then. He liked the tender letters she wrote to him. He wanted her to live with him. She answered him by writing tender letters to him and telling very nice stories indeed in them. He wrote nothing and then he wrote again and there was some waiting and then he wrote tender letters again and again.

She came to be happier than anybody else who was living then. It is easy to believe this thing. She was telling some one, who was loving every story that was charming. Some one who was living was almost always listening. Some one who was loving was almost always listening. That one who was loving was almost always listening. That one who was loving was telling about being one then listening. That one being loving was then telling stories having a beginning and a middle and an ending. That one was then one always completely listening. Ada was then one and all her living then one completely telling stories that were charming, completely listening to stories having a beginning and a middle and an ending. Trembling was all living, living was all loving, some one was then the other one. Certainly this one was loving this Ada then. And certainly Ada all her living then was happier in living than any one else who ever could, who was, who is, who ever will be living.

[c. 1910, 1922]

Reading Stein's "Picasso."   Stein first met Pablo Picasso (1881–1973), the Spanish painter and sculptor, at a gallery in Paris in 1905. They soon began a lifelong friendship based on mutual admiration. Stein and her brother Leo were early collectors of Picasso's paintings, including his famous 1906 portrait of Stein, which she bequeathed to the Metropolitan Museum of Art in New York City (see p. 1752). By the time Stein composed her word portrait of Picasso, probably in 1911, he and his friend Georges Braque had developed analytical cubism, a revolutionary movement in painting in which different aspects or facets of an object are seen simultaneously. During the period 1906–11, Stein was also seeking to break free of traditional modes of representation in prose. In his introduction to the special issue of *Camera Work* in which "Picasso" and Stein's contemporaneous portrait of the painter Henri Matisse first appeared, Alfred Stieglitz observed that "in these articles by Miss Stein, the Post-Impressionist spirit is found expressing itself in literary form." The portraits were accompanied by reproductions of works by both painters, but Stein does not describe Picasso as a painter, refer to any of his works, nor offer either a physical description or a biography of the artist. Instead, she seeks to capture the essence of his character and work, emphasizing his charisma, his originality, and his artistic fertility, manifested in his seemingly effortless creation of "something having meaning." The text is taken from the first printing in *Camera Work*, August 1912.

PICASSO

One whom some were certainly following was one who was completely charming. One whom some were certainly following was one who was charming. One whom some were following was one who was completely charming. One whom some were following was one who was certainly completely charming.

Some were certainly following and were certain that the one they were then following was one working and was one bringing out of himself then something. Some were certainly following and were certain that the one they were then following was one bringing out of himself then something that was coming to be a heavy thing, a solid thing and a complete thing.

One whom some were certainly following was one working and certainly was one bringing something out of himself then and was one who had been all his living had been one having something coming out of him.

Something had been coming out of him, certainly it had been coming out of him, certainly it was something, certainly it had been coming out of him and it had meaning, a charming meaning, a solid meaning, a struggling meaning, a clear meaning.

One whom some were certainly following and some were certainly following him, one whom some were certainly following was one certainly working.

One whom some were certainly following was one having something coming out of him something having meaning and this one was certainly working then.

This one was working and something was coming then, something was coming out of this one then. This one was one and always there was something coming out of this one and always there had been something coming out of this one. This one had never been one not having something coming out of this one. This one was one having something coming out of this one. This one had been one whom some were following. This one was one whom some were following. This one was being one whom some were following. This one was one who was working.

This one was one who was working. This one was one being one having something being coming out of him. This one was one going on having something come out of him. This one was one going on working. This one was one whom some were following. This one was one who was working.

This one always had something being coming out of this one. This one was working. This one always had been working. This one was always having something that was coming out of this one that was a solid thing, a charming thing, a lovely thing, a perplexing thing, a disconcerting thing, a simple thing, a clear thing, a complicated thing, an interesting thing, a disturbing thing, a repellant thing, a very pretty thing. This one was one certainly being one having something coming out of him. This one was one whom some were following. This one was one who was working.

This one was one who was working and certainly this one was needing to be working so as to be one being working. This one was one having something coming out of him. This one would be one all his living having something coming out of him. This one was working and then this one was working and this one was needing to be working, not to be one having something coming out of him something having meaning, but was needing to be working so as to be one working.

This one was certainly working and working was something this one was certain this one would be doing and this one was doing that thing, this one was working. This one was not one completely working. This one was not ever completely working. This one certainly was not completely working.

This one was one having always something being coming out of him, something having completely a real meaning. This one was one whom some were following. This one was one who was working. This one was one who was working and he was one needing this thing needing to be working so as to be one having some way of being one having some way of working. This one was one who was working. This one was one having something come out of him something having meaning. This one was one always having something come out of him and this thing the thing coming out of him always had real meaning. This one was one who was working. This one was one who was almost always working. This one was not one completely working. This one was one not ever completely working. This one was not one working to have anything come out of him. This one did have something having meaning that did come out of him. He always did have something come out of him. He was working, he was not ever completely working. He did have some following. They were always following him. Some were certainly following him. He was one who was working. He was one having something coming out of him something having meaning. He was not ever completely working.

[1912]

Sherwood Anderson

[1876–1941]

Sherwood Anderson was born in Camden, Ohio, on September 13, 1876. He was the third of the six children of Irwin Anderson, who had fought in the Union cavalry during the Civil War, and Emma Smith Anderson. The family moved to the village of Caledonia, where Irwin Anderson's harness-making business failed, before settling in Clyde, Ohio, in 1884. Anderson's childhood was spent in poverty, and he left high school before graduation in order to help support the family. After his mother died in 1895, Anderson left Clyde for Chicago, where he worked as a manual laborer until 1898. He then joined the Ohio National Guard and spent a year in Cuba during the Spanish-American War. When he returned to the United States, he completed high school at the Wittenberg Academy, a school on the campus of Wittenberg College in Springfield, Ohio. Although Anderson enjoyed his studies and wanted to begin college there, he was once again forced to find work, so he left after a year and returned to Chicago in 1900.

Sherwood Anderson

The writer and photographer Carl Van Vechten took this portrait of Anderson in 1933.

Discovering that he had a considerable flair for writing advertising copy, he worked for a publishing company and later in an advertising agency. In 1904, he married the first of his four wives, Cornelia Lane, the college-educated daughter of a wealthy businessman in Toledo, Ohio.

Anderson seemed well on the way to a successful career in business, the ambition of his youth, but he soon began to dream of becoming a writer.

Two years after their marriage, he and his wife relocated to Cleveland, where Anderson worked as the head of advertising for the United Factories Company before setting up his own mail-order firm in Elyria, Ohio, in 1907. For the next five years, he devoted himself to various business ventures. He also began to spend long hours writing in an upstairs room in the family home. Torn between his desire to write and the need to apply himself to business in order to support his growing family, which now included three children, Anderson collapsed from nervous exhaustion in 1912. He consequently abandoned business, separated from his family, and returned to Chicago, which was then becoming a vibrant literary center. Working in advertising to support himself and his writing, Anderson published two articles in a newly established Chicago-based literary magazine, the *Little Review*, in 1914. Later that year, he published his first short story in a prominent national magazine, *Harper's*. He then began work on a series of novels, including two stories of small-town boys who seek fame and fortune in Chicago, *Windy McPherson's Son* (1916) and *Marching Men* (1917). Meanwhile, Anderson was divorced from his first wife and married Tennessee Mitchell, with whom he moved to New York City in 1917. The following year, he published a volume of poems inspired by the work of Walt Whitman and the Chicago poet Carl Sandburg, *Mid-American Chants* (1918), most of which Anderson had written during 1914-15.

> *Winesburg, Ohio, when it first appeared, kept me up a whole night in a steady crescendo of emotion.*
>
> –Hart Crane

During the same period, he had also begun to write the kind of experimental prose that later brought him wide recognition. In his autobiography, Anderson recalled that he began to conceive of a new way of writing when he read Gertrude Stein's innovative book *Tender Buttons* in the summer of 1914: "Here was something purely experimental and dealing in words separated from sense—in the ordinary meaning of the word *sense*—an approach I was sure the poets must often be compelled to make. Was it an approach that would help me? I decided to try it." Even as he worked on more conventional novels and poems, Anderson wrote a series of impressionistic sketches about the lives of people in a small Midwestern town based on his memories of Clyde, Ohio. Several of the interrelated sketches were published individually in the *Little Review* and other avant-garde magazines before Anderson gathered them into a volume, *Winesburg, Ohio* (1919). By then, he had already begun a novel about a Midwestern town, *Poor White* (1920), which was followed by the first of several acclaimed collections of his short stories, *The Triumph of the Egg* (1921). Meanwhile, the restless Anderson frequently moved around the country, dividing most of his time between Chicago and New York City. In 1921, he made his first trip to Europe, where he met and began a lifelong friendship with Gertrude Stein. He also strongly encouraged younger writers, including Ernest Hemingway, a journalist he met in Chicago, and William Faulkner, whom Anderson later met in New Orleans.

Although he was increasingly overshadowed by emerging writers such as Hemingway and Faulkner, Anderson continued to write and publish until the end of his life. With his second marriage falling apart, he wrote a novel about a man's midlife crisis, *Many Marriages* (1923). In 1924, Anderson married his third wife, Elizabeth Prall, and published his highly regarded autobiography, *A Story-Teller's Story*. It was followed by his best-selling book *Dark Laughter* (1925), a novel in which Anderson contrasted the sterility of his neurotic white characters to what he conceived to be the spontaneous, unself-conscious sexuality of African Americans. In 1927, he settled in Troutdale, Virginia, and bought two small newspapers in nearby Marion. After he divorced Elizabeth Prall, Anderson in 1933 married the radical labor activist Eleanor Copenhaver, a much younger woman with whom he lived contentedly in Virginia. During the final decade of his life, he published a collection of stories and two novels, but he wrote mainly essays and other short, nonfictional works, including a collection of sketches about life in the Midwest and South during the Depression, *Puzzled America* (1935). Anderson devoted most of his efforts to his post-humously published *Memoirs*, which he did not complete before his death on March 8, 1941, while he and his wife were aboard a ship bound for South America.

bedfordstmartins.com/ americanlit for research links on Anderson

Reading Anderson's *Winesburg, Ohio*. Anderson's most famous book, which marked an important turning point in his career, is a collection of independent but interrelated stories set in a fictional town closely resembling Clyde, Ohio, where he grew up. He began to write the stories in 1915, when Anderson was just starting out as a writer in Chicago, and soon they started appearing in various little magazines. "Hands" appeared in the March 1916 issue of the *Masses*, a Socialist magazine of politics and literature published in New York City; and "Paper Pills" was

Clyde, Ohio

This photograph of Main Street in winter was taken in the 1880s, about the time Anderson's family moved to the village in northern Ohio.

first published as "The Philosopher" in the June–July 1916 issue of the *Little Review*. Other stories followed in those magazines and in the radical political and literary magazine *Seven Arts;* the collection, which also included previously unpublished stories was accepted by the respected New York publisher B. W. Huebsch, who had earlier published important works by modern writers such as James Joyce and D. H. Lawrence. The full title of Anderson's collection was *Winesburg, Ohio: A Group of Tales of Ohio Small Town Life*, and he dedicated the book to the memory of his mother, "Whose keen observations on the life about her first awoke in me the hunger to see beneath the surface of lives." In a publicity release, Huebsch declared that Anderson "lays bare the hearts and minds of the inhabitants of a typical American village. . . . It is the psychoanalytic method applied to literature." Certainly, Anderson was fascinated by psychology, especially the effects of repressed or thwarted sexuality. A few reviewers consequently condemned him for reducing "his material from human clay to plain dirt," as one put it in the New York *Sun*. But most of the reviews were positive, and several of them offered genuine insights into Anderson's literary methods. The reviewer for the *Chicago Daily Tribune*, for example, admiringly observed that Anderson "suggests rather than depicts," adding that "he respects the imaginative faculty of his reader by refusing to be explicit where overtones of emotion are already invoked by the reader." The text of the following stories is taken from the first edition of *Winesburg, Ohio* (1919).

From Winesburg, Ohio

Hands

Upon the half decayed veranda of a small frame house that stood near the edge of a ravine near the town of Winesburg, Ohio, a fat little old man walked nervously up and down. Across a long field that had been seeded for clover but that had produced only a dense crop of yellow mustard weeds, he could see the public highway along which went a wagon filled with berry pickers returning from the fields. The berry pickers, youths and maidens, laughed and shouted boisterously. A boy clad in a blue shirt leaped from the wagon and attempted to drag after him one of the maidens, who screamed and protested shrilly. The feet of the boy in the road kicked up a cloud of dust that floated across the face of the departing sun. Over the long field came a thin girlish voice. "Oh, you Wing Biddlebaum, comb your hair, it's falling into your eyes," commanded the voice to the man, who was bald and whose nervous little hands fiddled about the bare white forehead as though arranging a mass of tangled locks.

Wing Biddlebaum, forever frightened and beset by a ghostly band of doubts, did not think of himself as in any way a part of the life of the town where he had lived for twenty years. Among all the people of Winesburg but one had come close to him. With George Willard, son of Tom Willard, the proprietor of the New Willard House, he had formed something like a friendship. George Willard was the reporter on the *Winesburg Eagle* and sometimes in the evenings he walked out along the highway to Wing Biddlebaum's house. Now as the old man walked up and down on the veranda, his hands moving nervously about, he was hoping that George Willard would come and spend the evening with him. After the wagon containing the berry pickers had passed, he went across the field through the tall mustard weeds and climbing a rail fence peered anxiously along the road to the town. For a moment he stood thus, rubbing his hands together and looking up and down the road, and then, fear overcoming him, ran back to walk again upon the porch on his own house.

In the presence of George Willard, Wing Biddlebaum, who for twenty years had been the town mystery, lost something of his timidity, and his shadowy personality, submerged in a sea of doubts, came forth to look at the world. With the young reporter at his side, he ventured in the light of day into Main Street or strode up and down on the rickety front porch of his own house, talking excitedly. The voice that had been low and trembling became shrill and loud. The bent figure straightened. With a kind of wriggle, like a fish returned to the brook by the fisherman, Biddlebaum the silent began to talk, striving to put into words the ideas that had been accumulated by his mind during long years of silence.

Wing Biddlebaum talked much with his hands. The slender expressive fingers, forever active, forever striving to conceal themselves in his pockets or behind his back, came forth and became the piston rods of his machinery of expression.

The story of Wing Biddlebaum is a story of hands. Their restless activity, like unto the beating of the wings of an imprisoned bird, had given him his name. Some obscure poet of the town had thought of it. The hands alarmed their owner. He wanted to keep them hidden away and looked with amazement at the quiet inexpressive hands of other men who worked beside him in the fields, or passed, driving sleepy teams on country roads.

When he talked to George Willard, Wing Biddlebaum closed his fists and beat with them upon a table or on the walls of his house. The action made him more comfortable. If the desire to talk came to him when the two were walking in the fields, he sought out a stump or the top board of a fence and with his hands pounding busily talked with renewed ease.

The story of Wing Biddlebaum's hands is worth a book in itself. Sympathetically set forth it would tap many strange, beautiful qualities in obscure men. It is a job for a poet. In Winesburg the hands had attracted attention merely because of their activity. With them Wing Biddlebaum had picked as high as a hundred and forty quarts of strawberries in a day. They became his distinguishing feature, the source of his fame. Also they made more grotesque an already grotesque and elusive individuality. Winesburg was proud of the hands of Wing Biddlebaum in the same spirit in which it was proud of Banker White's new stone house and Wesley Moyer's bay stallion, Tony Tip, that had won the two-fifteen trot at the fall races in Cleveland.

As for George Willard, he had many times wanted to ask about the hands. At times an almost overwhelming curiosity had taken hold of him. He felt that there must be a reason for their strange activity and their inclination to keep hidden away and only a growing respect for Wing Biddlebaum kept him from blurting out the questions that were often in his mind.

Once he had been on the point of asking. The two were walking in the fields on a summer afternoon and had stopped to sit upon a grassy bank. All afternoon Wing Biddlebaum had talked as one inspired. By a fence he had stopped and beating like a giant woodpecker upon the top board had shouted at George Willard, condemning his tendency to be too much influenced by the people about him. "You are destroying yourself," he cried. "You have the inclination to be alone and to dream and you are afraid of dreams. You want to be like others in town here. You hear them talk and you try to imitate them."

On the grassy bank Wing Biddlebaum had tried again to drive his point home. His voice became soft and reminiscent, and with a sigh of contentment he launched into a long rambling talk, speaking as one lost in a dream.

Out of the dream Wing Biddlebaum made a picture for George Willard. In the picture men lived again in a kind of pastoral golden age. Across a green open country came clean-limbed young men, some afoot, some mounted upon horses. In crowds the young men came to gather about the feet of an old man who sat beneath a tree in a tiny garden and who talked to them.

Wing Biddlebaum became wholly inspired. For once he forgot the hands. Slowly they stole forth and lay upon George Willard's shoulders. Something new and bold came into the voice that talked. "You must try to forget all you have learned," said the old man. "You must begin to dream. From this time on you must shut your ears to the roaring of the voices."

Pausing in his speech, Wing Biddlebaum looked long and earnestly at George Willard. His eyes glowed. Again he raised the hands to caress the boy and then a look of horror swept over his face.

With a convulsive movement of his body, Wing Biddlebaum sprang to his feet and thrust his hands deep into his trousers pockets. Tears came to his eyes, "I must be getting along home. I can talk no more with you," he said nervously.

Without looking back, the old man had hurried down the hillside and across a meadow, leaving George Willard perplexed and frightened upon the grassy slope. With a shiver of dread the boy arose and went along the road toward town. "I'll not ask him about his hands," he thought, touched by the memory of the terror he had seen in the man's eyes. "There's something wrong, but I don't want to know what it is. His hands have something to do with his fear of me and of everyone."

And George Willard was right. Let us look briefly into the story of the hands. Perhaps our talking of them will arouse the poet who will tell the hidden wonder story of the influence for which the hands were but fluttering pennants of promise.

In his youth Wing Biddlebaum had been a school teacher in a town in Pennsylvania. He was not then known as Wing Biddlebaum, but went by the less euphonic name of Adolph Myers. As Adolph Myers he was much loved by the boys of his school.

Adolph Myers was meant by nature to be a teacher of youth. He was one of those rare, little-understood men who rule by a power so gentle that it passes as a lovable weakness. In their feeling for the boys under their charge such men are not unlike the finer sort of women in their love of men.

And yet that is but crudely stated. It needs the poet there. With the boys of his school, Adolph Myers had walked in the evening or had sat talking until dusk upon the schoolhouse steps lost in a kind of dream. Here and there went his hands, caressing the shoulders of the boys, playing about the tousled heads. As he talked his voice became soft and musical. There was a caress in that also. In a way the voice and the hands, the stroking of the shoulders and the touching of the hair were a part of the schoolmaster's effort to carry a dream into the young minds. By the caress that was in his fingers he expressed himself. He was one of those men in whom the force that creates life is diffused, not centralized. Under the caress of his hands doubt and disbelief went out of the minds of the boys and they began also to dream.

And then the tragedy. A half-witted boy of the school became enamored of the young master. In his bed at night he imagined unspeakable things and in the morning went forth to tell his dreams as facts. Strange, hideous accusations fell from his loose-hung lips. Through the Pennsylvania town went a shiver. Hidden, shadowy doubts that had been in men's minds concerning Adolph Myers were galvanized into beliefs.

The tragedy did not linger. Trembling lads were jerked out of bed and questioned. "He put his arms about me," said one. "His fingers were always playing in my hair," said another.

One afternoon a man of the town, Henry Bradford, who kept a saloon, came to the schoolhouse door. Calling Adolph Myers into the school yard he began to beat him with his fists. As his hard knuckles beat down into the frightened face of the schoolmaster, his wrath became more and more terrible. Screaming with dismay, the children ran here and there like disturbed insects. "I'll teach you to put your hands on my boy, you beast," roared the saloon keeper, who, tired of beating the master, had begun to kick him about the yard.

Adolph Myers was driven from the Pennsylvania town in the night. With lanterns in their hands a dozen men came to the door of the house where he lived alone and commanded that he dress and come forth. It was raining and one of the men had a rope in his hands. They had intended to hang the schoolmaster, but something in his figure, so small, white, and pitiful, touched their hearts and they let him escape. As he ran away into the darkness they repented of their weakness and ran after him, swearing and throwing sticks and great balls of soft mud at the figure that screamed and ran faster and faster into the darkness.

For twenty years Adolph Myers had lived alone in Winesburg. He was but forty but looked sixty-five. The name of Biddlebaum he got from a box of goods seen at a freight station as he hurried through an eastern Ohio town. He had an aunt in Winesburg, a black-toothed old woman who raised chickens, and with her he lived until she died. He had been ill for a year after the experience in Pennsylvania, and after his recovery worked as a day laborer in the fields, going timidly about and striving to conceal his hands. Although he did not understand what had happened he felt that the hands must be to blame. Again and again the fathers of the boys had talked of the hands. "Keep your hands to yourself," the saloon keeper had roared, dancing with fury in the schoolhouse yard.

Upon the veranda of his house by the ravine, Wing Biddlebaum continued to walk up and down until the sun had disappeared and the road beyond the field was lost in the grey shadows. Going into his house he cut slices of bread and spread honey upon them. When the rumble of the evening train that took away the express cars loaded with the day's harvest of berries had passed and restored the silence of the summer night, he went again to walk upon the veranda. In the darkness he could not see the hands and they became quiet. Although he still hungered for the presence of the boy, who was the medium through which he expressed his love of man, the hunger became again a part of his loneliness and his waiting. Lighting a lamp, Wing Biddlebaum washed the few dishes soiled by his simple meal and, setting up a folding cot by the screen door that led to the porch, prepared to undress for the night. A few stray white bread crumbs lay on the cleanly washed floor by the table; putting the lamp upon a low stool he began to pick up the crumbs, carrying them to his mouth one by one with unbelievable rapidity. In the dense blotch of light beneath the table, the kneeling figure looked like a priest engaged in some service of his church. The nervous expressive fingers, flashing in and out of the light, might well have been mistaken for the fingers of the devotee going swiftly through decade after decade of his rosary.[1]

[1916, 1919]

PAPER PILLS

He was an old man with a white beard and huge nose and hands. Long before the time during which we will know him, he was a doctor and drove a jaded white horse from house to house through the streets of Winesburg. Later he married a girl who had money. She had been left a large fertile farm when her father died. The girl was quiet, tall, and dark, and to many people she seemed very beautiful. Everyone in Winesburg wondered why she married the doctor. Within a year after the marriage she died.

The knuckles of the doctor's hands were extraordinarily large. When the hands were closed they looked like clusters of unpainted wooden balls as large as walnuts fastened together by steel rods. He smoked a cob pipe and after his wife's death sat all day in his empty office close by a window that was covered with cobwebs. He never opened the window. Once on a hot day in August he tried but found it stuck fast and after that he forgot all about it.

Winesburg had forgotten the old man, but in Doctor Reefy there were the seeds of something very fine. Alone in his musty office in the Heffner Block above the Paris Dry Goods Company's store, he worked ceaselessly, building up something that he himself

---

1. **the fingers of the devotee . . . rosary:** Rosary describes both a sequence of prayers, each set of which is known as a decade, and the string of beads used to keep count of the prayers in a Roman Catholic devotional exercise designed to venerate the Virgin Mary and contemplate the life of Christ.

destroyed. Little pyramids of truth he erected and after erecting knocked them down again that he might have the truths to erect other pyramids.

Doctor Reefy was a tall man who had worn one suit of clothes for ten years. It was frayed at the sleeves and little holes had appeared at the knees and elbows. In the office he wore also a linen duster with huge pockets into which he continually stuffed scraps of paper. After some weeks the scraps of paper became little hard round balls, and when the pockets were filled he dumped them out upon the floor. For ten years he had but one friend, another old man named John Spaniard who owned a tree nursery. Sometimes, in a playful mood, old Doctor Reefy took from his pockets a handful of the paper balls and threw them at the nursery man. "That is to confound you, you blithering old sentimentalist," he cried, shaking with laughter.

The story of Doctor Reefy and his courtship of the tall dark girl who became his wife and left her money to him is a very curious story. It is delicious, like the twisted little apples that grow in the orchards of Winesburg. In the fall one walks in the orchards and the ground is hard with frost underfoot. The apples have been taken from the trees by the pickers. They have been put in barrels and shipped to the cities where they will be eaten in apartments that are filled with books, magazines, furniture, and people. On the trees are only a few gnarled apples that the pickers have rejected. They look like the knuckles of Doctor Reefy's hands. One nibbles at them and they are delicious. Into a little round place at the side of the apple has been gathered all of its sweetness. One runs from tree to tree over the frosted ground picking the gnarled, twisted apples and filling his pockets with them. Only the few know the sweetness of the twisted apples.

The girl and Doctor Reefy began their courtship on a summer afternoon. He was forty-five then and already he had begun the practice of filling his pockets with the scraps of paper that became hard balls and were thrown away. The habit had been formed as he sat in his buggy behind the jaded white horse and went slowly along country roads. On the papers were written thoughts, ends of thoughts, beginnings of thoughts.

One by one the mind of Doctor Reefy had made the thoughts. Out of many of them he formed a truth that arose gigantic in his mind. The truth clouded the world. It became terrible and then faded away and the little thoughts began again.

The tall dark girl came to see Doctor Reefy because she was in the family way and had become frightened. She was in that condition because of a series of circumstances also curious.

The death of her father and mother and the rich acres of land that had come down to her had set a train of suitors on her heels. For two years she saw suitors almost every evening. Except two they were all alike. They talked to her of passion and there was a strained eager quality in their voices and in their eyes when they looked at her. The two who were different were much unlike each other. One of them, a slender young man with white hands, the son of a jeweler in Winesburg, talked continually of virginity. When he was with her he was never off the subject. The other, a black-haired boy with large ears, said nothing at all but always managed to get her into the darkness, where he began to kiss her.

For a time the tall dark girl thought she would marry the jeweler's son. For hours she sat in silence listening as he talked to her and then she began to be afraid of something.

Beneath his talk of virginity she began to think there was a lust greater than in all the others. At times it seemed to her that as he talked he was holding her body in his hands. She imagined him turning it slowly about in the white hands and staring at it. At night she dreamed that he had bitten into her body and that his jaws were dripping. She had the dream three times, then she became in the family way to the one who said nothing at all but who in the moment of his passion actually did bite her shoulder so that for days the marks of his teeth showed.

After the tall dark girl came to know Doctor Reefy it seemed to her that she never wanted to leave him again. She went into his office one morning and without her saying anything he seemed to know what had happened to her.

In the office of the doctor there was a woman, the wife of the man who kept the bookstore in Winesburg. Like all old-fashioned country practitioners, Doctor Reefy pulled teeth, and the woman who waited held a handkerchief to her teeth and groaned. Her husband was with her and when the tooth was taken out they both screamed and blood ran down on the woman's white dress. The tall dark girl did not pay any attention. When the woman and the man had gone the doctor smiled. "I will take you driving into the country with me," he said.

For several weeks the tall dark girl and the doctor were together almost every day. The condition that had brought her to him passed in an illness, but she was like one who has discovered the sweetness of the twisted apples, she could not get her mind fixed again upon the round perfect fruit that is eaten in the city apartments. In the fall after the beginning of her acquaintanceship with him she married Doctor Reefy and in the following spring she died. During the winter he read to her all of the odds and ends of thoughts he had scribbled on the bits of paper. After he had read them he laughed and stuffed them away in his pockets to become round hard balls.

[1916, 1919]

Katherine Anne Porter

[1890-1980]

Katherine Anne Porter was born Callista Russell Porter on May 15, 1890, in a two-room cabin in Indian Creek, a small community in central Texas. She was the fourth child of Harrison Porter, a farmer, and Mary Alice Jones Porter, a former schoolteacher. Although Porter's parents were well educated by the standards of the time, they were very poor. After Porter's mother died in 1892, the family went to live with her paternal grandmother, Catherine Porter, in her small house in Kyle, Texas, between Austin and San Marcos. As a young girl, Porter loved reading and listening to her grandmother's fascinating tales about the early days in Texas. When Catherine Porter died in 1901, the family moved on to San Antonio. Porter received the last of her formal education during a year at the Thomas School, a private girls' school where she studied singing, elocution, and acting. Along with her father and one of her sisters, Porter then moved again, this time to Victoria. There, she taught music and the dramatic arts and met the first of her four husbands, a railroad clerk named John Henry Koontz, whom Porter married in 1906, a month after her sixteenth birthday. Influenced by her husband's family, Porter converted from Methodism to Roman Catholicism. But she was increasingly unhappy, and she abruptly left Koontz in 1913 and went to Chicago. At the time of her divorce in 1915, she changed her legal name to Katherine Anne Porter.

Katherine Anne Porter

This photograph of Porter was taken in Mexico in 1930, the year she published *Flowering Judas and Other Stories*.

Porter soon began a career as a journalist and writer. After struggling to support herself in Chicago, where she had hoped to break into the movies, she returned to Texas. Ill and exhausted, she was diagnosed with tuberculosis late in 1915. During her recovery at a sanitarium, from which she was released in September 1917, she met a newspaperwoman who helped Porter get a job as a reporter for the Fort Worth *Critic*. For the next two years, she worked for that newspaper and as a columnist and drama critic for the *Rocky Mountain News* in Denver, Colorado. Determined to launch her literary career, late in 1919 she moved to New York City and settled happily into the vital artistic community of Greenwich Village. While she supported herself by working in the publicity department of a movie company, Porter began to write short stories, three of which were published in *Everyland*, a magazine sponsored by the Interchurch World Movement. She also met several Mexican artists, who helped Porter get a job with the *Magazine of Mexico*, an American-backed promotional magazine that sent her on assignment to Mexico City. During the first of her several extended visits to Mexico, she became actively involved in the educational and cultural reforms undertaken in the turbulent wake of the Mexican Revolution of 1910–17. Suspected by the government of being a Bolshevik and threatened with deportation, Porter left in June 1921 and returned to New York City, where she began to write about Mexico. Some of her essays appeared in the *Christian Science Monitor*, and her first major story, "María Concepción," was published in the *Century* in December 1922.

During the remainder of the 1920s and throughout the 1930s, Porter continued what she described as her "nomadic" life, even as she firmly established herself as a master of short fiction. She went back to Mexico to help organize a traveling exhibit of folk art and later to research and write articles on the country for a special issue of the magazine *Survey Graphic*, published in May 1924. Sensitized to social injustices by her experiences in Mexico, Porter also became associated with radicals and left-wing causes after she returned to the United States. In 1926, she married but soon separated from the English painter Ernest Stock. During the late 1920s, most of Porter's writings were book reviews, though she tried her hand at poetry and worked on a biography of the Puritan minister Cotton Mather. She also wrote several short stories, and some of her influential literary friends in New York City finally convinced Harcourt Brace to publish her first book, *Flowering Judas and Other Stories* (1930). Although it was published in a limited edition of six hundred copies and earned Porter only $100 in royalties, the collection made her reputation. Its publication also marked the beginning of her most productive decade as a writer.

Porter went to Mexico to work on a novel, and in 1931 she sailed from Vera Cruz to Bremen, Germany, accompanied by her third husband, the writer Eugene Pressley. They lived for a time in Berlin, where Porter witnessed with alarm the rise of Nazism, and then settled in Paris. After they returned to the United States in 1936, she divorced Pressley and married a young graduate student, Albert Erskine. The marriage was a fiasco, and they separated in 1938. In the midst of the chaos in her personal life, Porter wrote a series of autobiographical stories based on her early years in Texas, including the three novellas in her acclaimed collection *Pale Horse, Pale Rider* (1939).

The remainder of Porter's career was punctuated by a series of awards, honors, and literary successes. In 1944, the year she published *The Leaning Tower and Other Stories*, she was appointed to the prestigious Chair of Poetry and Literature at the Library of Congress. She later taught at Stanford and the University of Michigan. Still restlessly moving from place to place, she continued to work on a novel based in part on the log she wrote during her 1931 voyage to Germany, which was finally published as *Ship of Fools* in 1962. The reviews were generally enthusiastic, and Porter earned a million dollars from royalties and the film rights purchased by United Artists. *The Collected Stories of Katherine Anne Porter* (1965) was awarded the Pulitzer Prize for Fiction. In failing health, Porter wrote little and was increasingly reclusive in the years before her death at the age of ninety, on September 18, 1980.

Most good stories are about the interior of our lives, but Katherine Anne Porter's stories take place there.

—Eudora Welty

Reading Porter's "Flowering Judas." Explaining why she selected this story to represent her work in an anthology of American writing edited by Whit Burnett, *This Is My Best* (1942), Porter observed that she wrote it in one sitting "between seven o'clock and midnight of a very cold December, 1929, in Brooklyn." She added that the central character in "Flowering Judas," one of several stories inspired by Porter's experiences in Mexico during the 1920s, was based on an American schoolteacher friend whom she had once observed being serenaded by a Mexican labor leader: "In that glimpse, no more than a flash, I thought I understood, or perceived for the first time, the desperate complication of her mind and feelings, and I knew a story; perhaps not her true story, not even the real story of the whole situation, but all the same a story that seemed symbolic truth to me." Porter immediately sent the story to *Hound and Horn*, a distinguished literary magazine that published the works of several avant-garde writers such as Gertrude Stein, Ezra Pound, and T. S. Eliot. "Flowering Judas" appeared in the June-July 1930 issue of the magazine, and Porter then made it the title story of her breakthrough collection, *Flowering Judas and Other Stories* (1930).

bedfordstmartins.com /americanlit for research links on Porter

FLOWERING JUDAS[1]

Braggioni sits heaped upon the edge of a straight-backed chair much too small for him, and sings to Laura in a furry, mournful voice. Laura has begun to find reasons for avoiding her own house until the latest possible moment, for Braggioni is there almost every night. No matter how late she is, he will be sitting there with a surly, waiting expression, pulling at his kinky yellow hair, thumbing the strings of his guitar, snarling a tune under his breath. Lupe the Indian maid meets Laura at the door, and says with a flicker of a glance towards the upper room, "He waits."

Laura wishes to lie down, she is tired of her hairpins and the feel of her long tight sleeves, but she says to him, "Have you a new song for me this evening?" If he says yes, she asks him to sing it. If he says no, she remembers his favorite one, and asks him to sing it again. Lupe brings her a cup of chocolate and a plate of rice, and Laura eats at the small table under the lamp, first inviting Braggioni, whose answer is always the same: "I have eaten, and besides, chocolate thickens the voice."

Laura says, "Sing, then," and Braggioni heaves himself into song. He scratches the guitar familiarly as though it were a pet animal, and sings passionately off key, taking the high notes in a prolonged painful squeal. Laura, who haunts the markets listening to the ballad singers, and stops every day to hear the blind boy playing his reed-flute in Sixteenth of September Street,[2] listens to Braggioni with pitiless courtesy, because she dares not smile at his miserable performance. Nobody dares to smile at him. Braggioni is cruel to everyone, with a kind of specialized insolence, but he is so vain of his talents, and so sensitive to slights, it would require a cruelty and vanity greater than his own to lay a finger on the vast cureless wound of his self-esteem. It would require courage, too, for it is dangerous to offend him, and nobody has this courage.

Braggioni loves himself with such tenderness and amplitude and eternal charity that his followers—for he is a leader of men, a skilled revolutionist, and his skin has been punctured in honorable warfare—warm themselves in the reflected glow, and say to each other: "He has a real nobility, a love of humanity raised above mere personal affections." The excess of this self-love has flowed out, inconveniently for her, over Laura, who, with so many others, owes her comfortable situation and her salary to him. When he is in a very good humor, he tells her, "I am tempted to forgive you for being a *gringa*. *Gringita!*"[3] and Laura, burning, imagines herself leaning forward suddenly, and with a

---

1. **Flowering Judas:** A small tree native to the eastern Mediterranean, commonly known as the redbud or Judas tree. According to legend, it got its name because Judas Iscariot hanged himself on the tree after he betrayed Jesus. In various versions of the legend, the white flowers of the tree consequently turned red with shame or blood or because the tree became the body of Judas, who was said to have red hair. Porter took the title from and drew upon the imagery of T. S. Eliot's "Gerontion" (1920), a poem in which he evoked the apathy, inertia, and sterility of Europe in the aftermath of World War I: "In the juvescence of the year / Came Christ the tiger / In depraved May, dogwood and chestnut, flowering judas, / To be eaten, to be divided, to be drunk / Among whispers."

2. **Sixteenth of September Street:** This street in Mexico City, where the story is set, is named after Mexican Independence Day, commemorating the beginning of the ten-year war for independence from Spain on September 16, 1810.

3. *gringa. Gringita!:* Negative terms for non-Mexican females, especially Americans. The form *gringita* is used for a young girl, while *gringa* is used for a woman.

sound back-handed slap wiping the suety smile from his face. If he notices her eyes at these moments he gives no sign.

She knows what Braggioni would offer her, and she must resist tenaciously without appearing to resist, and if she could avoid it she would not admit even to herself the slow drift of his intention. During these long evenings which have spoiled a long month for her, she sits in her deep chair with an open book on her knees, resting her eyes on the consoling rigidity of the printed page when the sight and sound of Braggioni sing-ing threaten to identify themselves with all her remembered afflictions and to add their weight to her uneasy premonitions of the future. The gluttonous bulk of Brag-gioni has become a symbol of her many disillusions, for a revolutionist should be lean, animated by heroic faith, a vessel of abstract virtues. This is nonsense, she knows it now and is ashamed of it. Revolution must have leaders, and leadership is a career for energetic men. She is, her comrades tell her, full of romantic error, for what she defines as cynicism in them is merely "a developed sense of reality." She is almost too willing to say, "I am wrong, I suppose I don't really understand the principles," and afterward she makes a secret truce with herself, determined not to surrender her will to such expedi-ent logic. But she cannot help feeling that she has been betrayed irreparably by the dis-union between her way of living and her feeling of what life should be, and at times she is almost contented to rest in this sense of grievance as a private store of consolation. Sometimes she wishes to run away, but she stays. Now she longs to fly out of this room, down the narrow stairs, and into the street where the houses lean together like con-spirators under a single mottled lamp, and leave Braggioni singing to himself.

Instead she looks at Braggioni, frankly and clearly, like a good child who under-stands the rules of behavior. Her knees cling together under sound blue serge, and her round white collar is not purposely nun-like. She wears the uniform of an idea, and has renounced vanities. She was born Roman Catholic, and in spite of her fear of being seen by someone who might make a scandal of it, she slips now and again into some crum-bling little church, kneels on the chilly stone, and says a Hail Mary on the gold rosary she bought in Tehuantepec.[4] It is no good and she ends by examining the altar with its tinsel flowers and ragged brocades, and feels tender about the battered doll-shape of some male saint whose white, lace-trimmed drawers hang limply around his ankles below the hieratic dignity of his velvet robe. She has encased herself in a set of princi-ples derived from her early training, leaving no detail of gesture or of personal taste untouched, and for this reason she will not wear lace made on machines. This is her pri-vate heresy, for in her special group the machine is sacred, and will be the salvation of the workers. She loves fine lace, and there is a tiny edge of fluted cobweb on this collar, which is one of twenty precisely alike, folded in blue tissue paper in the upper drawer of her clothes chest.

---

4. **She was born Roman Catholic . . . Tehuantepec:** Being seen entering a church would create a "scandal" because the Roman Catholic Church opposed the Mexican Revolution of 1910–17. Hail Mary, or Ave Maria (Latin), a prayer for the intercession of the Virgin Mary, is frequently recited in sequences of ten repetitions, or decades, counted out on a string of beads called a rosary. Tehuantepec, a center of indigenous Zapotec culture in southern Mexico, is known for the traditional dress of its women and their important role in the city, which is sometimes described as a matriarchal society.

Braggioni catches her glance solidly as if he had been waiting for it, leans forward, balancing his paunch between his spread knees, and sings with tremendous emphasis, weighing his words. He has, the song relates, no father and no mother, nor even a friend to console him; lonely as a wave of the sea he comes and goes, lonely as a wave. His mouth opens round and yearns sideways, his balloon cheeks grow oily with the labor of song. He bulges marvelously in his expensive garments. Over his lavender collar, crushed upon a purple necktie, held by a diamond hoop: over his ammunition belt of tooled leather worked in silver, buckled cruelly around his gasping middle: over the tops of his glossy yellow shoes Braggioni swells with ominous ripeness, his mauve silk hose stretched taut, his ankles bound with the stout leather thongs of his shoes.

When he stretches his eyelids at Laura she notes again that his eyes are the true tawny yellow cat's eyes. He is rich, not in money, he tells her, but in power, and this power brings with it the blameless ownership of things, and the right to indulge his love of small luxuries. "I have a taste for the elegant refinements," he said once, flourishing a yellow silk handkerchief before her nose. "Smell that? It is Jockey Club,[5] imported from New York." Nonetheless he is wounded by life. He will say so presently. "It is true everything turns to dust in the hand, to gall on the tongue." He sighs and his leather belt creaks like a saddle girth. "I am disappointed in everything as it comes. Everything." He shakes his head. "You, poor thing, you will be disappointed, too. You are born for it. We are more alike than you realize in some things. Wait and see. Some day you will remember what I have told you, you will know that Braggioni was your friend."

Laura feels a slow chill, a purely physical sense of danger, a warning in her blood that violence, mutilation, a shocking death, wait for her with lessening patience. She has translated this fear into something homely, immediate, and sometimes hesitates before crossing the street. "My personal fate is nothing, except as the testimony of a mental attitude," she reminds herself, quoting from some forgotten philosophic primer, and is sensible enough to add, "Anyhow, I shall not be killed by an automobile if I can help it."

"It may be true I am as corrupt, in another way, as Braggioni," she thinks in spite of herself, "as callous, as incomplete," and if this is so, any kind of death seems preferable. Still she sits quietly, she does not run. Where could she go? Uninvited she has promised herself to this place; she can no longer imagine herself as living in another country, and there is no pleasure in remembering her life before she came here.

Precisely what is the nature of this devotion, its true motives, and what are its obligations? Laura cannot say. She spends part of her days in Xochimilco,[6] near by, teaching Indian children to say in English, "The cat is on the mat." When she appears in the classroom they crowd about her with smiles on their wise, innocent, clay-colored faces, crying, "Good morning, my titcher!" in immaculate voices, and they make of her desk a fresh garden of flowers every day.

---

5. **Jockey Club:** A fragrance then sold as both cologne and an extract for perfuming handkerchiefs.
6. **Xochimilco:** A borough south of the historic center of Mexico City. In a sketch published in 1921, Porter observed that the "Xochimilco Indians are a splendid remnant of the Aztec race," adding that the independent and self-sufficient inhabitants of the area grow their own food and "the loveliest flowers in Mexico."

During her leisure she goes to union meetings and listens to busy important voices quarreling over tactics, methods, internal politics. She visits the prisoners of her own political faith in their cells, where they entertain themselves with counting cockroaches, repenting of their indiscretions, composing their memoirs, writing out manifestoes and plans for their comrades who are still walking about free, hands in pockets, sniffing fresh air. Laura brings them food and cigarettes and a little money, and she brings messages disguised in equivocal phrases from the men outside who dare not set foot in the prison for fear of disappearing into the cells kept empty for them. If the prisoners confuse night and day, and complain, "Dear little Laura, time doesn't pass in this infernal hole, and I won't know when it is time to sleep unless I have a reminder," she brings them their favorite narcotics, and says in a tone that does not wound them with pity, "Tonight will really be night for you," and though her Spanish amuses them, they find her comforting, useful. If they lose patience and all faith, and curse the slowness of their friends in coming to their rescue with money and influence, they trust her not to repeat everything, and if she inquires, "Where do you think we can find money, or influence?" they are certain to answer, "Well, there is Braggioni, why doesn't he do something?"

She smuggles letters from headquarters to men hiding from firing squads in back streets in mildewed houses, where they sit in tumbled beds and talk bitterly as if all Mexico were at their heels, when Laura knows positively they might appear at the band concert in the Alameda[7] on Sunday morning, and no one would notice them. But Braggioni says, "Let them sweat a little. The next time they may be careful. It is very restful to have them out of the way for a while." She is not afraid to knock on any door in any street after midnight, and enter in the darkness, and say to one of these men who is really in danger: "They will be looking for you — seriously — tomorrow morning after six. Here is some money from Vicente. Go to Vera Cruz[8] and wait."

She borrows money from the Roumanian agitator to give to his bitter enemy the Polish agitator. The favor of Braggioni is their disputed territory, and Braggioni holds the balance nicely, for he can use them both. The Polish agitator talks love to her over café tables, hoping to exploit what he believes is her secret sentimental preference for him, and he gives her misinformation which he begs her to repeat as the solemn truth to certain persons. The Roumanian is more adroit. He is generous with his money in all good causes, and lies to her with an air of ingenuous candor, as if he were her good friend and confidant. She never repeats anything they may say. Braggioni never asks questions. He has other ways to discover all that he wishes to know about them.

Nobody touches her, but all praise her gray eyes, and the soft, round under lip which promises gayety, yet is always grave, nearly always firmly closed: and they cannot understand why she is in Mexico. She walks back and forth on her errands, with puzzled eyebrows, carrying her little folder of drawings and music and school papers. No dancer dances more beautifully than Laura walks, and she inspires some amusing, unexpected ardors, which cause little gossip, because nothing comes of them. A young captain who

---

7. **Alameda:** Alameda Central, the oldest and most popular public park in Mexico City.
8. **Vera Cruz:** Veracruz is a major port on the Gulf of Mexico, 250 miles east of Mexico City.

had been a soldier in Zapata's army[9] attempted, during a horseback ride near Cuernavaca,[10] to express his desire for her with the noble simplicity befitting a rude folkhero: but gently, because he was gentle. This gentleness was his defeat, for when he alighted, and removed her foot from the stirrup, and essayed to draw her down into his arms, her horse, ordinarily a tame one, shied fiercely, reared and plunged away. The young hero's horse careered blindly after his stable-mate, and the hero did not return to the hotel until rather late that evening. At breakfast he came to her table in full charro dress,[11] gray buckskin jacket and trousers with strings of silver buttons down the leg, and he was in a humorous, careless mood. "May I sit with you?" and "You are a wonderful rider. I was terrified that you might be thrown and dragged. I should never have forgiven myself. But I cannot admire you enough for your riding!"

"I learned to ride in Arizona," said Laura.

"If you will ride with me again this morning, I promise you a horse that will not shy with you," he said. But Laura remembered that she must return to Mexico City at noon.

Next morning the children made a celebration and spent their playtime writing on the blackboard, "We lov ar ticher," and with tinted chalks they drew wreaths of flowers around the words. The young hero wrote her a letter: "I am a very foolish, wasteful, impulsive man. I should have first said I love you, and then you would not have run away. But you shall see me again." Laura thought, "I must send him a box of colored crayons," but she was trying to forgive herself for having spurred her horse at the wrong moment.

A brown, shock-haired youth came and stood in her patio one night and sang like a lost soul for two hours, but Laura could think of nothing to do about it. The moonlight spread a wash of gauzy silver over the clear spaces of the garden, and the shadows were cobalt blue. The scarlet blossoms of the Judas tree were dull purple, and the names of the colors repeated themselves automatically in her mind, while she watched not the boy, but his shadow, fallen like a dark garment across the fountain rim, trailing in the water. Lupe came silently and whispered expert counsel in her ear: "If you will throw him one little flower, he will sing another song or two and go away." Laura threw the flower, and he sang a last song and went away with the flower tucked in the band of his hat. Lupe said, "He is one of the organizers of the Typographers Union,[12] and before that he sold corridos[13] in the Merced market, and before that, he came from Guanajuato, where I was born. I would not trust any man, but I trust least those from Guanajuato."[14]

She did not tell Laura that he would be back again the next night, and the next, nor that he would follow her at a certain fixed distance around the Merced market, through

---

9. **Zapata's army:** The war hero General Emiliano Zapata (1879-1919), a leader of the Mexican Revolution who championed the cause of peasants against the regime of the dictator Porfirio Díaz.

10. **Cuernavaca:** A popular resort town fifty miles south of Mexico City.

11. **charro dress:** The traditional dress of a Mexican horseman or cowboy.

12. **Typographers Union:** A labor union for workers involved in all aspects of the publishing business, part of the wider labor movement that coincided with the Mexican Revolution.

13. **corridos:** Song sheets of popular ballads, many of which were written in support of or to spread news about the Mexican Revolution.

14. **Guanajuato:** Capital of the state of the same name in central Mexico, this city is known for its narrow and winding streets.

the Zócalo, up Francisco I. Madero Avenue, and so along the Paseo de la Reforma to Chapultepec Park, and into the Philosopher's Footpath,[15] still with that flower withering in his hat, and an indivisible attention in his eyes.

Now Laura is accustomed to him, it means nothing except that he is nineteen years old and is observing a convention with all propriety, as though it were founded on a law of nature, which in the end it might well prove to be. He is beginning to write poems which he prints on a wooden press, and he leaves them stuck like handbills in her door. She is pleasantly disturbed by the abstract, unhurried watchfulness of his black eyes which will in time turn easily towards another object. She tells herself that throwing the flower was a mistake, for she is twenty-two years old and knows better; but she refuses to regret it, and persuades herself that her negation of all external events as they occur is a sign that she is gradually perfecting herself in the stoicism she strives to cultivate against that disaster she fears, though she cannot name it.

She is not at home in the world. Every day she teaches children who remain strangers to her, though she loves their tender round hands and their charming opportunist savagery. She knocks at unfamiliar doors not knowing whether a friend or a stranger shall answer, and even if a known face emerges from the sour gloom of that unknown interior, still it is the face of a stranger. No matter what this stranger says to her, nor what her message to him, the very cells of her flesh reject knowledge and kinship in one monotonous word. No. No. No. She draws her strength from this one holy talismanic word which does not suffer her to be led into evil. Denying everything, she may walk anywhere in safety, she looks at everything without amazement.

No, repeats this firm unchanging voice of her blood; and she looks at Braggioni without amazement. He is a great man, he wishes to impress this simple girl who covers her great round breasts with thick dark cloth, and who hides long, invaluably beautiful legs under a heavy skirt. She is almost thin except for the incomprehensible fullness of her breasts, like a nursing mother's, and Braggioni, who considers himself a judge of women, speculates again on the puzzle of her notorious virginity, and takes the liberty of speech which she permits without a sign of modesty, indeed, without any sort of sign, which is disconcerting.

"You think you are so cold, *gringita!* Wait and see. You will surprise yourself some day! May I be there to advise you!" He stretches his eyelids at her, and his ill-humored cat's eyes waver in a separate glance for the two points of light marking the opposite ends of a smoothly drawn path between the swollen curve of her breasts. He is not put off by that blue serge, nor by her resolutely fixed gaze. There is all the time in the world. His cheeks are bellying with the wind of song. "O girl with the dark eyes," he sings, and reconsiders. "But yours are not dark. I can change all that. O girl with the green eyes, you have stolen my heart away!" then his mind wanders to the song, and Laura feels the weight of his attention being shifted elsewhere. Singing thus, he seems harmless, he is quite harmless,

---

15. **Merced market . . . Philosopher's Footpath:** La Merced Market is in the historic center of Mexico City, east of the main plaza, or Zócalo. From there, they continue westward along major avenues for several miles across the city to Chapultepec Park, thought to have been laid out in the 1420s by Nezahualcóyotl, the philosopher king of the pre-Columbian city-state of Texcoco.

there is nothing to do but sit patiently and say "No," when the moment comes. She draws a full breath, and her mind wanders also, but not far. She dares not wander too far.

Not for nothing has Braggioni taken pains to be a good revolutionist and a professional lover of humanity. He will never die of it. He has the malice, the cleverness, the wickedness, the sharpness of wit, the hardness of heart, stipulated for loving the world profitably. *He will never die of it.* He will live to see himself kicked out from his feeding trough by other hungry world-saviors. Traditionally he must sing in spite of his life which drives him to bloodshed, he tells Laura, for his father was a Tuscany peasant who drifted to Yucatan and married a Maya woman[16]: a woman of race, an aristocrat. They gave him the love and knowledge of music, thus: and under the rip of his thumbnail, the strings of the instrument complain like exposed nerves.

Once he was called Delgadito[17] by all the girls and married women who ran after him; he was so scrawny all his bones showed under his thin cotton clothing, and he could squeeze his emptiness to the very backbone with his two hands. He was a poet and the revolution was only a dream then; too many women loved him and sapped away his youth, and he could never find enough to eat anywhere, anywhere! Now he is a leader of men, crafty men who whisper in his ear, hungry men who wait for hours outside his office for a word with him, emaciated men with wild faces who waylay him at the street gate with a timid, "Comrade, let me tell you . . ." and they blow the foul breath from their empty stomachs in his face.

He is always sympathetic. He gives them handfuls of small coins from his own pocket, he promises them work, there will be demonstrations, they must join the unions and attend the meetings, above all they must be on the watch for spies. They are closer to him than his own brothers, without them he can do nothing—until tomorrow, comrade!

Until tomorrow. "They are stupid, they are lazy, they are treacherous, they would cut my throat for nothing," he says to Laura. He has good food and abundant drink, he hires an automobile and drives in the Paseo[18] on Sunday morning, and enjoys plenty of sleep in a soft bed beside a wife who dares not disturb him; and he sits pampering his bones in easy billows of fat, singing to Laura, who knows and thinks these things about him. When he was fifteen, he tried to drown himself because he loved a girl, his first love, and she laughed at him. "A thousand women have paid for that," and his tight little mouth turns down at the corners. Now he perfumes his hair with Jockey Club, and confides to Laura: "One woman is really as good as another for me, in the dark. I prefer them all."

His wife organizes unions among the girls in the cigarette factories, and walks in picket lines, and even speaks at meetings in the evening. But she cannot be brought to acknowledge the benefits of true liberty. "I tell her I must have my freedom, net. She

---

16. **Tuscany peasant . . . Maya woman:** Tuscany is a region of central Italy. The Maya, ancient peoples of northern Central America, developed one of the most advanced and sophisticated civilizations of the pre-Columbian Americas.

17. **Delgadito:** Little Thin (Spanish).

18. **Paseo:** The Paseo de la Reforma, a wide avenue that runs diagonally across Mexico City. See note 15.

does not understand my point of view." Laura has heard this many times. Braggioni scratches the guitar and meditates. "She is an instinctively virtuous woman, pure gold, no doubt of that. If she were not, I should lock her up, and she knows it."

His wife, who works so hard for the good of the factory girls, employs part of her leisure lying on the floor weeping because there are so many women in the world, and only one husband for her, and she never knows where nor when to look for him. He told her: "Unless you can learn to cry when I am not here, I must go away for good." That day he went away and took a room at the Hotel Madrid.[19]

It is this month of separation for the sake of higher principles that has been spoiled not only for Mrs. Braggioni, whose sense of reality is beyond criticism, but for Laura, who feels herself bogged in a nightmare. Tonight Laura envies Mrs. Braggioni, who is alone, and free to weep as much as she pleases about a concrete wrong. Laura has just come from a visit to the prison, and she is waiting for tomorrow with a bitter anxiety as if tomorrow may not come, but time may be caught immovably in this hour, with herself transfixed, Braggioni singing on forever, and Eugenio's body not yet discovered by the guard.

Braggioni says: "Are you going to sleep?" Almost before she can shake her head, he begins telling her about the May-day disturbances coming on in Morelia,[20] for the Catholics hold a festival in honor of the Blessed Virgin, and the Socialists celebrate their martyrs on that day. "There will be two independent processions, starting from either end of town, and they will march until they meet, and the rest depends . . ." He asks her to oil and load his pistols. Standing up, he unbuckles his ammunition belt, and spreads it laden across her knees. Laura sits with the shells slipping through the cleaning cloth dipped in oil, and he says again he cannot understand why she works so hard for the revolutionary idea unless she loves some man who is in it. "Are you not in love with someone?" "No," says Laura. "And no one is in love with you?" "No." "Then it is your own fault. No woman need go begging. Why, what is the matter with you? The legless beggar woman in the Alameda has a perfectly faithful lover. Did you know that?"

Laura peers down the pistol barrel and says nothing, but a long, slow faintness rises and subsides in her; Braggioni curves his swollen fingers around the throat of the guitar and softly smothers the music out of it, and when she hears him again he seems to have forgotten her, and is speaking in the hypnotic voice he uses when talking in small rooms to a listening, close-gathered crowd. Some day this world, now seemingly so composed and eternal, to the edges of every sea shall be merely a tangle of gaping trenches, of crashing walls and broken bodies. Everything must be torn from its accustomed place where it has rotted for centuries, hurled skyward and distributed, cast down again clean as rain, without separate identity. Nothing shall survive that the stiffened hands of poverty have created for the rich and no one shall be left alive except the elect spirits

---

19. **Hotel Madrid:** The Hotel Plaza Madrid, in the center of Mexico City.
20. **May-day disturbances . . . Morelia:** May Day or May 1st, a celebration of the labor movement known as International Workers' Day, is also the day on which Catholics wear flowers in honor of the Virgin Mary, to whose devotion the month is dedicated by the Catholic Church. In May 1921 there were violent clashes between Socialists and Catholics in the streets of Morelia, a city 225 miles west of Mexico City.

destined to procreate a new world cleansed of cruelty and injustice, ruled by benevolent anarchy: "Pistols are good, I love them, cannon are even better, but in the end I pin my faith to good dynamite," he concludes, and strokes the pistol lying in her hands. "Once I dreamed of destroying this city, in case it offered resistance to General Ortíz,[21] but it fell into his hands like an over-ripe pear."

He is made restless by his own words, rises and stands waiting. Laura holds up the belt to him: "Put that on, and go kill somebody in Morelia, and you will be happier," she says softly. The presence of death in the room makes her bold. "Today, I found Eugenio going into a stupor. He refused to allow me to call the prison doctor. He had taken all the tablets I brought him yesterday. He said he took them because he was bored."

"He is a fool, and his death is his own business," says Braggioni, fastening his belt carefully.

"I told him if he had waited only a little while longer, you would have got him set free," says Laura. "He said he did not want to wait."

"He is a fool and we are well rid of him," says Braggioni, reaching for his hat.

He goes away. Laura knows his mood has changed, she will not see him any more for a while. He will send word when he needs her to go on errands into strange streets, to speak to the strange faces that will appear, like clay masks with the power of human speech, to mutter their thanks to Braggioni for his help. Now she is free, and she thinks, I must run while there is time. But she does not go.

Braggioni enters his own house where for a month his wife has spent many hours every night weeping and tangling her hair upon her pillow. She is weeping now, and she weeps more at the sight of him, the cause of all her sorrows. He looks about the room. Nothing is changed, the smells are good and familiar, he is well acquainted with the woman who comes toward him with no reproach except grief on her face. He says to her tenderly: "You are so good, please don't cry any more, you dear good creature." She says, "Are you tired, my angel? Sit here and I will wash your feet." She brings a bowl of water, and kneeling, unlaces his shoes, and when from her knees she raises her sad eyes under her blackened lids, he is sorry for everything, and bursts into tears. "Ah, yes, I am hungry, I am tired, let us eat something together," he says, between sobs. His wife leans her head on his arm and says, "Forgive me!" and this time he is refreshed by the solemn, endless rain of her tears.

Laura takes off her serge dress and puts on a white linen nightgown and goes to bed. She turns her head a little to one side, and lying still, reminds herself that it is time to sleep. Numbers tick in her brain like little clocks, soundless doors close of themselves around her. If you would sleep, you must not remember anything, the children will say tomorrow, good morning, my teacher, the poor prisoners who come every day bringing flowers to their jailor. 1-2-3-4-5 — it is monstrous to confuse love with revolution, night with day, life with death — ah, Eugenio!

---

21. **General Ortíz:** Eulalio Gutiérrez Ortíz (1881-1939), the provisional president of Mexico for a brief period in 1914-15, during which troops under the command of the revolutionary leaders Francisco ("Pancho") Villa and Emiliano Zapata took Mexico City.

The tolling of the midnight bell is a signal, but what does it mean? Get up, Laura, and follow me: come out of your sleep, out of your bed, out of this strange house. What are you doing in this house? Without a word, without fear she rose and reached for Eugenio's hand, but he eluded her with a sharp, sly smile and drifted away. This is not all, you shall see — Murderer, he said, follow me, I will show you a new country, but it is far away and we must hurry. No, said Laura, not unless you take my hand, no; and she clung first to the stair rail, and then to the topmost branch of the Judas tree that bent down slowly and set her upon the earth, and then to the rocky ledge of a cliff, and then to the jagged wave of a sea that was not water but a desert of crumbling stone. Where are you taking me, she asked in wonder but without fear. To death, and it is a long way off, and we must hurry, said Eugenio. No, said Laura, not unless you take my hand. Then eat these flowers, poor prisoner, said Eugenio in a voice of pity, take and eat: and from the Judas tree he stripped the warm bleeding flowers, and held them to her lips. She saw that his hand was fleshless, a cluster of small white petrified branches, and his eye sockets were without light, but she ate the flowers greedily for they satisfied both hunger and thirst. Murderer! said Eugenio, and Cannibal! This is my body and my blood. Laura cried No! and at the sound of her own voice, she awoke trembling, and was afraid to sleep again.

[1929, 1965]

Zora Neale Hurston

[1891–1960]

Zora Neale Hurston

Hurston's friend Carl Van Vechten took this photograph in 1934, the year she published her acclaimed first novel, *Jonah's Gourd Vine*.

Photo © Carl Van Vechten

Zora Neale Hurston was born on January 7, 1891, in Notasulga, Alabama, the fifth child of John Hurston, a farmer and Baptist minister, and Lucy Ann Potts Hurston, a former schoolteacher. The family soon moved to Eatonville, Florida, the first incorporated all-black community in the United States. Describing her happy early life there, Hurston recalled: "Mama exhorted her children at every opportunity to 'jump at de sun.' " Hurston's childhood ended abruptly when her mother died in 1904. She was sent to school in Jacksonville and rarely saw her father, who married a woman Hurston disliked. Although she lived with relatives in Sanford, Florida, and later in Memphis, Tennessee, Hurston was essentially on her own. She worked as a domestic servant, and in 1915 she became a wardrobe girl in a touring company that performed the light operas of Gilbert and Sullivan.

Hurston developed a deep love of music and theater before she left the company in Baltimore in 1917. She took high school courses at the Morgan Academy, graduated in 1918, and then enrolled at Howard University in Washington, D.C. Working as a manicurist and a waitress in order to pay for her tuition, Hurston majored in English and attended classes as she could afford them, from 1918 through 1924.

Hurston was swept up in the excitement of the Harlem Renaissance. At Howard, she joined the staff of the student literary magazine, the *Stylus,* in which she published her first story in 1921. Through her work on the magazine, she came into contact with the poet Georgia Douglas Johnson. At Johnson's "S Street Salon," called by its regulars the "Saturday Nighters Club," Hurston met Sterling Brown, Jean Toomer, and James Weldon Johnson. Hurston's writing came to the attention of Charles S. Johnson, founder of *Opportunity: A Journal of Negro Life,* the new magazine of the National Urban League. Buoyed by the publication of her story "Drenched in Light" in the December 1924 issue of *Opportunity,* Hurston decided to become a writer and moved to New York City early in 1925. A few months later, Johnson announced the *Opportunity* Literary Contest, and Hurston submitted four entries, two of which received Honorable Mention and two of which received prizes: "Color Struck" won the second prize for plays while "Spunk" won the second prize for short stories and was swiftly published in the June issue of *Opportunity.* One of the judges in the short story category, Alain Locke, subsequently included "Spunk" in his anthology *The New Negro: An Interpretation,* an influential compendium of African American culture published later in 1925. At the awards dinner given by *Opportunity,* Hurston received cash prizes totaling seventy dollars, money that she desperately needed; she also met other prize-winners, including the young African American poets Countee Cullen and Langston Hughes, as well as the influential white writers Carl Van Vechten and Fannie Hurst. Hurst offered her a job as a secretary, and another white writer, Annie Nathan Meyer, helped Hurston secure a scholarship to Barnard College, where she enrolled as the only black student in September 1926. Later that year, along with several of her friends, Hurston helped establish and contributed to a short-lived magazine, *Fire!! A Quarterly Devoted to Younger Negro Artists.*

Hurston began to pursue a dual career as a writer and an anthropologist. In 1927, she married Herbert Sheen, a physician and classmate from Howard, but they separated less than a year later. Meanwhile, she studied at Barnard with the distinguished anthropologist Franz Boas and did her first fieldwork in the South, a requirement for the degree in anthropology she earned in 1928. With the help of Boas, she was awarded a research fellowship to collect black folklore in the South and in the Bahamas. She published a scholarly article on her research, "Hoodoo in America," in the *Journal of American Folklore* (1931). She also wrote plays, including a collaboration with Langston Hughes, *Mule-Bone: A Comedy of Negro Life* (1931), and *The Great Day,* which was produced in New York in 1932. The following year, Hurston wrote her first novel, *Jonah's Gourd Vine* (1934), based on her family history in Florida. Even as she basked in the

[Hurston] was full of side-splitting anecdotes, humorous tales, and tragicomic stories, remembered out of her life in the South.... She could make you laugh one minute and cry the next.
–Langston Hughes

enthusiastic reviews of the novel, Hurston was awarded a fellowship from the Rosenwald Fund to do graduate work in anthropology at Columbia University, where she enrolled in January 1935. "Life has picked me up bodaciously and throwed me over the fence," she excitedly wrote to a friend. When the head of the Rosenwald Fund arbitrarily reduced her fellowship, the proud and independent Hurston stopped going to classes, but her reputation as an anthropologist was established by the publication of *Mules and Men* (1935), a study of African American dance, music, folklore, and religious practices in the South. On the strength of the work, Hurston was awarded a Guggenheim Fellowship, which she used to support her ethnographic research in Jamaica and Haiti. In addition to a book-length account of her work there, she wrote her best-selling and most famous novel, *Their Eyes Were Watching God* (1937).

During the final decades of her life, Hurston suffered both personal and professional setbacks. She married twice, in 1939 and 1944, but neither union lasted more than a year. Disappointed by the reception of her ambitious novel *Moses, Man of the Mountain* (1939), Hurston later scored a major hit with her memoir *Dust Tracks on the Road* (1942). Despite her sudden celebrity and the demand for her work, she published only one more book, *Seraph on the Suwanee* (1948), a novel about a family of white southerners that received good reviews and sold well. Almost immediately after it was published, however, Hurston was falsely accused of molesting the troubled young son of a former landlady in New York. Although the charges were dropped when Hurston was able to prove that she had been out of the country when the alleged crime occurred, she was devastated by the sensational publicity and decided to leave New York and return permanently to Florida. She completed two more novels, both of which were rejected by her publisher, and then worked on a revisionist biography of King Herod the Great. After it was rejected by her publisher in 1955, Hurston wrote little, supporting herself by working as a maid, a librarian, and sometimes as a substitute teacher. She died in a county welfare home on January 28, 1960, and was buried in an unmarked grave in a segregated cemetery in Fort Pierce, Florida. In 1973, the African American novelist Alice Walker located the grave and erected a marker in Hurston's honor. Taking a line from Jean Toomer's poem "Georgia Dusk," Walker had the marker inscribed:

Zora Neale Hurston
"A Genius of the South"
1901 [sic]-1960
Novelist, Folklorist
Anthropologist

bedfordstmartins.com/ americanlit for research links on Hurston

Reading Hurston's "The Gilded Six-Bits."   Hurston, who had not published any fiction since 1926, wrote this story while she was living in her hometown of Eatonville, Florida, in 1933. She sent it to her friend Robert Wunch, a professor of English at nearby Rollins College, who liked it so much that he read it to his writing class and then sent it to *Story: The Magazine of the Short Story.* Founded in 1931 by two Americans living in Vienna, Austria, Whit Burnett and Martha Foley, the successful and influential magazine subsequently published short fiction by prominent writers such as William Faulkner, Langston Hughes, Katherine Anne Porter, Gertrude Stein, and William Carlos Williams. "The Gilded Six-Bits" was published in the magazine just after it moved to New York City. An account of infidelity and forgiveness set in Eatonville, "The Gilded Six-Bits" proved to be one of Hurston's most popular stories. It also represented a turning point in her career, since the publisher Bernard Lippincott was so impressed by the story that he asked Hurston if she were working on a novel. As a result, she immediately wrote her first novel, *Jonah's Gourd Vine* (1934), and Hurston thereafter devoted most of her efforts to writing fiction. The text is taken from the first printing in *Story*, August 1933.

THE GILDED SIX-BITS

It was a Negro yard around a Negro house in a Negro settlement that looked to the payroll of the G and G Fertilizer works for its support.

But there was something happy about the place. The front yard was parted in the middle by a sidewalk from gate to door-step, a sidewalk edged on either side by quart bottles driven neck down into the ground on a slant. A mess of homey flowers planted without a plan but blooming cheerily from their helter-skelter places. The fence and house were whitewashed. The porch and steps scrubbed white.

The front door stood open to the sunshine so that the floor of the front room could finish drying after its weekly scouring. It was Saturday. Everything clean from the front gate to the privy house. Yard raked so that the strokes of the rake would make a pattern. Fresh newspaper cut in fancy edge on the kitchen shelves.

Missie May was bathing herself in the galvanized washtub in the bedroom. Her dark-brown skin glistened under the soapsuds that skittered down from her wash rag. Her stiff young breasts thrust forward aggressively like broad-based cones with the tips lacquered in black.

She heard men's voices in the distance and glanced at the dollar clock on the dresser.

"Humph! Ah'm way behind time t'day! Joe gointer be heah 'fore Ah git mah clothes on if Ah don't make haste."

She grabbed the clean meal sack at hand and dried herself hurriedly and began to dress. But before she could tie her slippers, there came the ring of singing metal on wood. Nine times.

Missie May grinned with delight. She had not seen the big tall man come stealing in the gate and creep up the walk grinning happily at the joyful mischief he was about to commit. But she knew that it was her husband throwing silver dollars in the door for her to pick up and pile beside her plate at dinner. It was this way every Saturday afternoon.

The nine dollars hurled into the open door, he scurried to a hiding place behind the cape jasmine bush and waited.

Missie May promptly appeared at the door in mock alarm.

"Who dat chunkin' money in mah do'way?" she demanded. No answer from the yard. She leaped off the porch and began to search the shrubbery. She peeped under the porch and hung over the gate to look up and down the road. While she did this, the man behind the jasmine darted to the china berry tree. She spied him and gave chase.

"Nobody ain't gointer be chunkin' money at me and Ah not do 'em nothin'," she shouted in mock anger. He ran around the house with Missie May at his heels. She overtook him at the kitchen door. He ran inside but could not close it after him before she crowded in and locked with him in a rough and tumble. For several minutes the two were a furious mass of male and female energy. Shouting, laughing, twisting, turning, tussling, tickling each other in the ribs; Missie May clutching onto Joe and Joe trying, but not too hard, to get away.

"Missie May, take yo' hand out mah pocket!" Joe shouted out between laughs.

"Ah ain't, Joe, not lessen you gwine gimme whateve' it is good you got in yo' pocket. Turn it go, Joe, do Ah'll tear yo' clothes."

"Go on tear 'em. You de one dat pushes de needles round heah. Move yo' hand Missie May."

"Lemme git dat paper sack out yo' pocket. Ah bet its candy kisses."

"Tain't. Move yo' hand. Woman ain't got no business in a man's clothes nohow. Go way."

Missie May gouged way down and gave an upward jerk and triumphed.

"Unhhunh! Ah got it. It 'tis so candy kisses. Ah knowed you had somethin' for me in yo' clothes. Now Ah got to see whut's in every pocket you got."

Joe smiled indulgently and let his wife go through all of his pockets and take out the things that he had hidden there for her to find. She bore off the chewing gum, the cake of sweet soap, the pocket handkerchief as if she had wrested them from him, as if they had not been bought for the sake of this friendly battle.

"Whew! dat play-fight done got me all warmed up." Joe exclaimed. "Got me some water in de kittle?"

"Yo' water is on de fire and yo' clean things is cross de bed. Hurry up and wash yo'self and git changed so we kin eat. Ah'm hongry." As Missie said this, she bore the steaming kettle into the bedroom.

"You ain't hongry, sugar," Joe contradicted her. "Youse jes' a little empty. Ah'm de one whut's hongry. Ah could eat up camp meetin', back off 'ssociation, and drink Jurdan dry.[1] Have it on de table when Ah git out de tub."

"Don't you mess wid mah business, man. You git in yo' clothes. Ah'm a real wife, not no dress and breath. Ah might not look lak one, but if you burn me, you won't git a thing but wife ashes."

---

1. **drink Jurdan dry:** The Jordan River, in which Jesus was baptized by John the Baptist, figures prominently in slave songs, or "Negro spirituals," including "One More River," which Joe ironically echoes: "O, Jordan stream will never run dry, / Dere ain't but one more river to cross."

Joe splashed in the bedroom and Missie May fanned around in the kitchen. A fresh red and white checked cloth on the table. Big pitcher of buttermilk beaded with pale drops of butter from the churn. Hot fried mullet, crackling bread, ham hock atop a mound of string beans and new potatoes, and perched on the window-sill a pone of spicy potato pudding.

Very little talk during the meal but that little consisted of banter that pretended to deny affection but in reality flaunted it. Like when Missie May reached for a second helping of the tater pone. Joe snatched it out of her reach.

After Missie May had made two or three unsuccessful grabs at the pan, she begged, "Aw, Joe gimme some mo' dat tater pone."

"Nope, sweetenin' is for us men-folks. Y'all pritty lil frail eels don't need nothin' lak dis. You too sweet already."

"Please, Joe."

"Naw, naw. Ah don't want you to git no sweeter than whut you is already. We goin' down de road a lil piece t'night so you go put on yo' Sunday go-to-meetin' things."

Missie May looked at her husband to see if he was playing some prank "Sho nuff, Joe?"

"Yeah. We goin' to de ice cream parlor."

"Where de ice cream parlor at, Joe?"

"A new man done come heah from Chicago and he done got a place and took and opened it up for a ice cream parlor, and bein' as it's real swell, Ah wants you to be one de first ladies to walk in dere and have some set down."

"Do Jesus, Ah ain't knowed nothin' 'bout it. Who de man done it?"

"Mister Otis D. Slemmons, of spots and places—Memphis, Chicago, Jacksonville, Philadelphia and so on."

"Dat heavy-set man wid his mouth full of gold teethes?"

"Yeah. Where did you see 'im at?"

"Ah went down to de sto' tuh git a box of lye and Ah seen 'im standin' on de corner talkin' to some of de mens, and Ah come on back and went to scrubbin' de floor, and he passed and tipped his hat whilst Ah was scourin' de steps. Ah thought Ah never seen *him* befo'."

Joe smiled pleasantly. "Yeah, he's up to date. He got de finest clothes Ah ever seen on a colored man's back."

"Aw, he don't look no better in his clothes than you do in yourn. He got a puzzlegut on 'im and he so chuckle-headed, he got a pone behind his neck."

Joe looked down at his own abdomen and said wistfully, "Wisht Ah had a build on me lak he got. He ain't puzzle-gutted, honey. He jes' got a corperation. Dat make 'm look lak a rich white man. All rich mens is got some belly on 'em."

"Ah seen de pitchers of Henry Ford and he's a spare-built man and Rockefeller[2] look lak he ain't got but one gut. But Ford and Rockefeller and dis Slemmons and all de rest kin be as many-gutted as dey please, Ah'm satisfied wid you jes' lak you is, baby. God

---

2. **Ford . . . Rockefeller:** The wealthy industrialists Henry Ford (1863–1947), the founder of the Ford Motor Company; and John D. Rockefeller (1839–1937), founder of the Standard Oil Company. As Missie May indicates, both men were very thin.

took pattern after a pine tree and built you noble. Youse a pritty man, and if Ah knowed any way to make you mo' pritty still Ah'd take and do it."

Joe reached over gently and toyed with Missie May's ear. "You jes' say dat cause you love me, but Ah know Ah can't hold no light to Otis D. Slemmons. Ah ain't never been nowhere and Ah ain't got nothin' but you."

Missie May got on his lap and kissed him and he kissed back in kind. Then he went on. "All de womens is crazy 'bout 'im everywhere he go."

"How you know dat, Joe?"

"He tole us so hisself."

"Dat don't make it so. His mouf is cut cross-ways, ain't it? Well, he kin lie jes' lak any-body else."

"Good Lawd, Missie! You womens sho is hard to sense into things. He's got a five-dollar gold piece for a stick-pin and he got a ten-dollar gold piece on his watch chain and his mouf is jes' crammed full of gold teethes. Sho wisht it wuz mine. And whut make it so cool, he got money 'cumulated. And womens give it all to 'im."

"Ah don't see whut de womens see on 'im. Ah wouldn't give 'im a wink if de sheriff wuz after 'im."

"Well, he tole us how de white womens in Chicago give 'im all dat gold money. So he don't 'low nobody to touch it at all. Not even put dey finger on it. Dey tole 'im not to. You kin make 'miration at it, but don't tetch it."

"Whyn't he stay up dere where dey so crazy 'bout 'im?"

"Ah reckon dey done made 'im vast-rich and he wants to travel some. He say dey wouldn't leave 'im hit a lick of work. He got mo' lady people crazy 'bout him than he kin shake a stick at."

"Joe, Ah hates to see you so dumb. Dat stray nigger jes' tell y'all anything and y'all b'lieve it."

"Go 'head on now, honey and put on yo' clothes. He talkin' 'bout his pritty womens — Ah want 'im to see *mine*."

Missie May went off to dress and Joe spent the time trying to make his stomach punch out like Slemmons' middle. He tried the rolling swagger of the stranger, but found that his tall bone-and-muscle stride fitted ill with it. He just had time to drop back into his seat before Missie May came in dressed to go.

On the way home that night Joe was exultant. "Didn't Ah say ole Otis was swell? Can't he talk Chicago talk? Wuzn't dat funny whut he said when great big fat ole Ida Armstrong come in? He asted me, 'Who is dat broad wid de forte shake?' Dat's a new word. Us always thought forty was a set of figgers but he showed us where it means a whole heap of things. Sometimes he don't say forty, he jes' say thirty-eight and two and dat mean de same thing. Know whut he tole me when Ah wuz payin' for our ice cream? He say, 'Ah have to hand it to you, Joe. Dat wife of yours is jes' thirty-eight and two. Yessuh, she's forte!' Ain't he killin'?"

"He'll do in case of a rush. But he sho is got uh heap uh gold on 'im. Dat's de first time Ah ever seed gold money. It lookted good on him sho nuff, but it'd look a whole heap bet-ter on you."

"Who, me? Missie May youse crazy! Where would a po' man lak me git gold money from?"

Missie May was silent for a minute, then she said, "Us might find some goin' long de road some time. Us could."

"Who would be losin' gold money round heah? We ain't even seen none dese white folks wearin' no gold money on dey watch chain. You must be figgerin' Mister Packard or Mister Cadillac goin' pass through heah."

"You don't know whut been lost 'round heah. Maybe somebody way back in memorial times lost they gold money and went on off and it ain't never been found. And then if we wuz to find it, you could wear some 'thout havin' no gang of womens lak dat Slemmons say he got."

Joe laughed and hugged her. "Don't be so wishful 'bout me. Ah'm satisfied de way Ah is. So long as Ah be yo' husband, Ah don't keer 'bout nothin' else. Ah'd ruther all de other womens in de world to be dead than for you to have de toothache. Less we go to bed and git our night rest."

It was Saturday night once more before Joe could parade his wife in Slemmons' ice cream parlor again. He worked the night shift and Saturday was his only night off. Every other evening around six o'clock he left home, and dying dawn saw him hustling home around the lake where the challenging sun flung a flaming sword from east to west across the trembling water.

That was the best part of life – going home to Missie May. Their whitewashed house, the mock battle on Saturday, the dinner and ice cream parlor afterwards, church on Sunday nights when Missie out-dressed any woman in town – all, everything was right.

One night around eleven the acid ran out at the G. and G. The foreman knocked off the crew and let the steam die down. As Joe rounded the lake on his way home, a lean moon rode the lake in a silver boat. If anybody had asked Joe about the moon on the lake, he would have said he hadn't paid it any attention. But he saw it with his feelings. It made him yearn painfully for Missie. Creation obsessed him. He thought about children. They had been married more than a year now. They had money put away. They ought to be making little feet for shoes. A little boy child would be about right.

He saw a dim light in the bedroom and decided to come in through the kitchen door. He could wash the fertilizer dust off himself before presenting himself to Missie May. It would be nice for her not to know that he was there until he slipped into his place in bed and hugged her back. She always liked that.

He eased the kitchen door open slowly and silently, but when he went to set his dinner bucket on the table he bumped it into a pile of dishes, and something crashed to the floor. He heard his wife gasp in fright and hurried to reassure her.

"Iss me, honey. Don't git skeered."

There was a quick, large movement in the bedroom. A rustle, a thud, and a stealthy silence. The light went out.

What? Robbers? Murderers? Some varmint attacking his helpless wife, perhaps. He struck a match, threw himself on guard and stepped over the door-sill into the bedroom.

The great belt on the wheel of Time slipped and eternity stood still. By the match light he could see the man's legs fighting with his breeches in his frantic desire to get them on. He had both chance and time to kill the intruder in his helpless condition – half in and half out of his pants – but he was too weak to take action. The shapeless enemies of humanity that live in the hours of Time had waylaid Joe. He was assaulted in his weakness. Like Samson awakening after his haircut.[3] So he just opened his mouth and laughed.

The match went out and he struck another and lit the lamp. A howling wind raced across his heart, but underneath its fury he heard his wife sobbing and Slemmons pleading for his life. Offering to buy it with all that he had. "Please, suh, don't kill me. Sixty-two dollars at de sto'. Gold money."

Joe just stood. Slemmons looked at the window, but it was screened. Joe stood out like a rough-backed mountain between him and the door. Barring him from escape, from sunrise, from life.

He considered a surprise attack upon the big clown that stood there laughing like a chessy cat. But before his fist could travel an inch, Joe's own rushed out to crush him like a battering ram. Then Joe stood over him.

"Git into yo' damn rags, Slemmons, and dat quick."

Slemmons scrambled to his feet and into his vest and coat. As he grabbed his hat, Joe's fury overrode his intentions and he grabbed at Slemmons with his left hand and struck at him with his right. The right landed. The left grazed the front of his vest. Slemmons was knocked a somersault into the kitchen and fled through the open door. Joe found himself alone with Missie May, with the golden watch charm clutched in his left fist. A short bit of broken chain dangled between his fingers.

Missie May was sobbing. Wails of weeping without words. Joe stood, and after awhile he found out that he had something in his hand. And then he stood and felt without thinking and without seeing with his natural eyes. Missie May kept on crying and Joe kept on feeling so much and not knowing what to do with all his feelings, he put Slemmons' watch charm in his pants pocket and took a good laugh and went to bed.

"Missie May, whut you cryin' for?"

"Cause Ah love you so hard and Ah know you don't love *me* no mo'."

Joe sank his face into the pillow for a spell then he said huskily, "You don't know de feelings of dat yet, Missie May."

"Oh Joe, honey, he said he wuz gointer give me dat gold money and he jes' kept on after me —"

Joe was very still and silent for a long time. Then he said, "Well, don't cry no mo', Missie May. Ah got yo' gold piece for you."

The hours went past on their rusty ankles. Joe still and quiet on one bed-rail and Missie May wrung dry of sobs on the other. Finally the sun's tide crept upon the shore of night and drowned all its hours. Missie May with her face stiff and streaked towards the window saw the dawn come into her yard. It was day. Nothing more. Joe wouldn't be coming home as usual. No need to fling open the front door and sweep off the porch, making it nice for Joe. Never no more breakfast to cook; no more washing and starching of Joe's jumper-jackets and pants. No more nothing. So why get up?

---

3. **Like Samson . . . haircut:** Samson is a biblical figure who is granted supernatural strength by God. While he sleeps, the seductress Delilah orders a servant to shave off Samson's hair, the source of his strength, and he awakens to find himself weak and helpless to defend himself from his enemies, the Philistines (Judges 13–16).

With this strange man in her bed, she felt embarrassed to get up and dress. She decided to wait till he had dressed and gone. Then she would get up, dress quickly and be gone forever beyond reach of Joe's looks and laughs. But he never moved. Red light turned to yellow, then white.

From beyond the no-man's land between them came a voice. A strange voice that yesterday had been Joe's.

"Missie May, ain't you gonna fix me no breakfus'?"

She sprang out of bed. "Yeah, Joe. Ah didn't reckon you wuz hongry."

No need to die today. Joe needed her for a few more minutes anyhow.

Soon there was a roaring fire in the cook stove. Water bucket full and two chickens killed. Joe loved fried chicken and rice. She didn't deserve a thing and good Joe was letting her cook him some breakfast. She rushed hot biscuits to the table as Joe took his seat.

He ate with his eyes in his plate. No laughter, no banter.

"Missie May, you ain't eatin' yo' breakfus'."

"Ah don't choose none, Ah thank yuh."

His coffee cup was empty. She sprang to refill it. When she turned from the stove and bent to set the cup beside Joe's plate, she saw the yellow coin on the table between them.

She slumped into her seat and wept into her arms.

Presently Joe said calmly, "Missie May, you cry too much. Don't look back lak Lot's wife and turn to salt."[4]

The sun, the hero of every day, the impersonal old man that beams as brightly on death as on birth, came up every morning and raced across the blue dome and dipped into the sea of fire every evening. Water ran down hill and birds nested.

Missie knew why she didn't leave Joe. She couldn't. She loved him too much, but she could not understand why Joe didn't leave her. He was polite, even kind at times, but aloof.

There were no more Saturday romps. No ringing silver dollars to stack beside her plate. No pockets to rifle. In fact the yellow coin in his trousers was like a monster hiding in the cave of his pockets to destroy her.

She often wondered if he still had it, but nothing could have induced her to ask nor yet to explore his pockets to see for herself. Its shadow was in the house whether or no.

One night Joe came home around midnight and complained of pains in the back. He asked Missie to rub him down with liniment. It had been three months since Missie had touched his body and it all seemed strange. But she rubbed him. Grateful for the chance. Before morning, youth triumphed and Missie exulted. But the next day, as she joyfully made up their bed, beneath her pillow she found the piece of money with the bit of chain attached.

Alone to herself, she looked at the thing with loathing, but look she must. She took it into her hands with trembling and saw first thing that it was no gold piece. It was a

---

4. **"Don't look back . . . salt"**: Despite warnings, as she is leaving her home in the doomed city of Sodom, Lot's wife looks back at the city and is turned into a pillar of salt (Genesis 19:26).

gilded half dollar. Then she knew why Slemmons had forbidden anyone to touch his gold. He trusted village eyes at a distance not to recognize his stick-pin as a gilded quarter, and his watch charm as a four-bit piece.

She was glad at first that Joe had left it there. Perhaps he was through with her punishment. They were man and wife again. Then another thought came clawing at her. He had come home to buy from her as if she were any woman in the long house. Fifty cents for her love. As if to say that he could pay as well as Slemmons. She slid the coin into his Sunday pants pocket and dressed herself and left his house.

Half way between her house and the quarters she met her husband's mother, and after a short talk she turned and went back home. Never would she admit defeat to that woman who prayed for it nightly. If she had not the substance of marriage she had the outside show. Joe must leave *her*. She let him see she didn't want his old gold four-bits, too.

She saw no more of the coin for some time though she knew that Joe could not help finding it in his pocket. But his health kept poor, and he came home at least every ten days to be rubbed.

The sun swept around the horizon, trailing its robes of weeks and days. One morning as Joe came in from work, he found Missie May chopping wood. Without a word he took the ax and chopped a huge pile before he stopped.

"You ain't got no business choppin' wood, and you know it."

"How come? Ah been choppin' it for de last longest."

"Ah ain't blind. You makin' feet for shoes."

"Won't you be glad to have a lil baby chile, Joe?"

"You know dat 'thout astin' me."

"Iss gointer be a boy chile and de very spit of you."

"You reckon, Missie May?"

"Who else could it look lak?"

Joe said nothing, but he thrust his hand deep into his pocket and fingered something there.

It was almost six months later Missie May took to bed and Joe went and got his mother to come wait on the house.

Missie May was delivered of a fine boy. Her travail was over when Joe came in from work one morning. His mother and the old women were drinking great bowls of coffee around the fire in the kitchen.

The minute Joe came into the room his mother called him aside.

"How did Missie May make out?" he asked quickly.

"Who, dat gal? She strong as a ox. She gointer have plenty mo'. We done fixed her wid de sugar and lard to sweeten her for de nex' one."

Joe stood silent awhile.

"You ain't ast 'bout de baby, Joe. You oughter be mighty proud cause he sho is de spittin' image of yuh, son. Dat's yourn all right, if you never git another one, dat un is yourn. And you know Ah'm mighty proud too, son, cause Ah never thought well of you marryin' Missie May cause her ma used tuh fan her foot round right smart and Ah been mighty skeered dat Missie May wuz gointer git misput on her road."

Joe said nothing. He fooled around the house till late in the day then just before he went to work, he went and stood at the foot of the bed and asked his wife how she felt. He did this every day during the week.

On Saturday he went to Orlando[5] to make his market. It had been a long time since he had done that.

Meat and lard, meal and flour, soap and starch. Cans of corn and tomatoes. All the staples. He fooled around town for awhile and bought bananas and apples. Way after while he went around to the candy store.

"Hello, Joe," the clerk greeted him. "Ain't seen you in a long time."

"Nope, Ah ain't been heah. Been round in spots and places."

"Want some of them molasses kisses you always buy?"

"Yessuh." He threw the gilded half dollar on the counter. "Will dat spend?"

"Whut is it, Joe? Well, I'll be doggone! A gold-plated four-bit piece. Where'd you git it, Joe?"

"Offen a stray nigger dat come through Eatonville. He had it on his watch chain for a charm—goin' round making out iss gold money. Ha ha! He had a quarter on his tie pin and it wuz all golded up too. Tryin' to fool people. Makin' out he so rich and everything. Ha! Ha! Tryin' to tole off folkses wives from home."

"How did you git it, Joe? Did he fool you, too?"

"Who, me? Naw suh! He ain't fooled me none. Know whut Ah done? He come round me wid his smart talk. Ah hauled off and knocked 'im down and took his old four-bits way from 'im. Gointer buy my wife some good ole lasses kisses wid it. Gimme fifty cents worth of dem candy kisses."

"Fifty cents buys a mighty lot of candy kisses, Joe. Why don't you split it up and take some chocolate bars, too. They eat good, too."

"Yessuh, dey do, but Ah wants all dat in kisses. Ah got a lil boy chile home now. Tain't a week old yet, but he kin suck a sugar tit and maybe eat one them kisses hisself."

Joe got his candy and left the store. The clerk turned to the next customer. "Wisht I could be like these darkies. Laughin' all the time. Nothin' worries 'em."

Back in Eatonville, Joe reached his own front door. There was the ring of singing metal on wood. Fifteen times. Missie May couldn't run to the door, but she crept there as quickly as she could.

"Joe Banks, Ah hear you chunkin' money in mah do'way. You wait till Ah got mah strength back and Ah'm gointer fix you for dat."

[1933]

•

---

5. **Orlando:** Orlando, Florida, six miles south of Eatonville.

Writers on Writers: Alice Walker on Zora Neale Hurston

The novelist and essayist Alice Walker (b. 1944), whose work can be found on pages 2234-2242, discovered Zora Neale Hurston while doing research for one of her own stories. Eager to learn more about a once-famous African American woman writer who had fallen into obscurity, Walker traveled to Florida, where Hurston had grown up and where she had died in 1960. There, Walker famously located Hurston's unmarked grave and paid to have a marker erected in honor of the "Novelist, Folklorist [and] Anthropologist." Walker wrote an extended essay about her experience for *MS. Magazine* and later published a biography of Hurston. In the following excerpt from her preface to the biography, Walker describes the appeal of Hurston's work, especially for African Americans. As Walker indicates, she first fully understood the central characteristic of Hurston's work after sharing it with her relatives, "typical black Americans . . . rapidly forgetting their southern cultural inheritance in the suburbs and ghettos of Boston and New York," who nonetheless "could not hold back the smiles, the laughter, the *joy* over who she was showing them to be: descendants of an inventive, joyous, courageous, and outrageous people." The text is taken from Alice Walker, *Zora Neale Hurston: A Literary Biography* (1977).

ALICE WALKER

(b. 1944)

From A Cautionary Tale and a Partisan View

This was my first indication of the quality I feel is most characteristic of Zora's work: racial health—a sense of black people as complete, complex, *undiminished* human beings, a sense that is lacking in so much black writing and literature. (In my opinion, only Du Bois[1] showed an equally consistent delight in the

---

1. Du Bois: W. E. B. Du Bois (1868-1963), the sociologist, historian, civil rights activist, and author of *The Souls of Black Folk* (1903). See page 1431.

beauty and spirit of black people, which is interesting when one considers that the angle of his vision was completely the opposite of Zora's.) Zora's pride in black people was so pronounced in the ersatz black twenties that it made other blacks suspicious and perhaps uncomfortable; after all, *they* were still infatuated with things European — *everything* European. Zora was interested in Africa, Haiti, Jamaica — and, for a little racial diversity (Indians), Honduras. She also had a confidence in herself as an individual that few people (anyone?), black or white, understood. This was because Zora grew up in a community of black people who had enormous respect for themselves and for their ability to *govern* themselves. Her own father had written the Eatonville town laws. This community affirmed her right to exist, and loved her as an extension of itself. For how many other black Americans is this true? It certainly isn't true for any that I know. In her easy self-acceptance, Zora was more like an uncolonized African than she was like her contemporary American blacks, most of whom believed, at least during their formative years, that their blackness was something wrong with them.

On the contrary, Zora's early work shows she grew up *pitying* whites because the ones she saw lacked "light" and soul. It is impossible to imagine Zora envying anyone (except tongue-in-cheek), and, least of all, a white person for being white. Which is, after all, if one is black, a clear and present calamity of the mind.

[1977]

María Cristina Mena

[1893-1965]

María Cristina Mena was born in Mexico City on April 3, 1893, into a wealthy, upper-class family. Her Spanish mother and Mexican father sent her to a Catholic convent school in Mexico City and later to a boarding school in England. Fluent in Spanish, English, French, and Italian, the precocious Mena began writing poetry as a child. Concerned about the increasing political turmoil in Mexico, and wishing their fourteen-year-old daughter to further her education, her parents sent Mena to live with family friends in New York City. There, she continued her studies and began to write stories inspired by her reading and her memories of Mexico. Few other details are known about her early years in New York City, but her experiences are illuminated by the outline of a story Mena later planned to write about

> a family of wealthy refugees from Mexico, with possibilities of rich comedy in their contact with American life, especially in relation to the gradual emancipation of their daughter, who in spite of efforts to keep her in pious subjection in accordance with Mexican tradition, takes to American freedom like a duck to water and blossoms into an ardently independent young woman.

Although that story was never written, Mena's early stories about life in Mexico found a ready audience in the United States. In November 1913, her first two stories were published during the same month: "The Gold Vanity Set" in *American* magazine and "John of God, the Water-Carrier," in *Century* magazine. The publication of the stories, both signed with her full name, marked the first time a Mexican American woman writer's work appeared in a major magazine in the United States. Writing in English, Mena sought to present realistic depictions of Mexican life, culture, and customs to an American audience accustomed to thinking of the country either as a quaint, exotic land or in terms of the ongoing Mexican Revolution, which had broken out in 1910. Indeed, her stories appeared at a time when there was growing bias and hostility among Anglo-Americans toward the hundreds of thousands of immigrants driven north by the economic and social upheaval in Mexico. Mena soon contracted to become a regular contributor to the *Century*, where seven more of her stories were published during 1914-16. From the beginning, however, Mena chafed at the efforts of the editors of the magazine to confine her writing to simple stories suffused with the "local color" of life in Mexico. Her resistance to such one-dimensional portraits of the land and its people is also revealed in the only essay Mena published in the *Century*, "Julian Carillo: The Herald of a Musical Monroe Doctrine" (1915), a sketch of the celebrated Mexican composer and conductor who had recently organized the American Symphony Orchestra in New York City. At the beginning of her essay, where she described Carillo's early life in a poor Mexican family, Mena pointedly observed: "This would seem to be a good place for 'local color,' but the writer resists that fatal allurement." In fact, scholars have commented on the ways in which Mena sought to present complex portrayals of Mexican characters that defied stereotypes, even as she offered subtle commentaries on American attitudes toward Mexico and Mexicans.

In 1916, Mena married Henry Kellet Chambers (1867–1935), an Australian-born journalist and author of several plays, including *Butterfly* and *An American Wedding*. Although she wrote little during the following twenty years, Mena remained active in literary circles. In 1927, she began to correspond with the English author D. H. Lawrence, whom she strongly defended when his controversial novel *Lady Chatterley's Lover*, privately printed in Italy in 1928, was banned in both England and the United States. The correspondence between the two writers began after Lawrence read Mena's early story "John of God, the Water-Carrier," which was republished in 1927 in the *Monthly Criterion*, a London-based literary journal edited by T. S. Eliot. The story was subsequently included in both the *Yearbook of the American Short Story* and *The Best Short Stories of 1928*. Perhaps inspired by the flurry of interest in her work, Mena wrote her final story, "A Son of the Tropics," a tale of the Mexican Revolution published in *Household Magazine* in 1931. After her husband died in 1935, Mena began to write books about Mexican life and history for children, publishing five of them between 1942 and 1953. She also worked with the blind, translating her own books and the work of others into Braille. Mena died at her home in Brooklyn on August 3, 1965. The brief obituary of "Mrs. Henry Chambers" in the *New York Times* described Mena as a writer "who dedicated her work 'to bringing to the American public the life of the Mexican people.'"

Reading Mena's "The Vine-Leaf." Written when Mena was only twenty-one, this was one of eight of her stories that appeared in the *Century Illustrated Monthly Magazine* from 1913 through 1916. Published in New York, the *Century* had developed a large national circulation through the publication of a wide variety of material, ranging from the popular 1880s series *Battles and Leaders of the Civil War* to highly regarded serializations of novels by William Dean Howells and Henry James, biographies of prominent Americans such as Abraham Lincoln, travel narratives, and stories about the American West. Although the magazine sought to present a variety of cultural experiences, during the years leading up to World War I it also published numerous articles and stories about the negative effects of immigration in the United States. Commissioned by the editors to write about Mexican life for the magazine, Mena was thus entering a complex literary and cultural terrain. While she was excited to be published in the *Century*, she resisted the efforts of its editors to shape her material. Her desire for artistic control and her resistance to male authority over her work is perhaps obliquely reflected in the character of the *marquesa* in "The Vine-Leaf." The text is taken from the first printing in the *Century*, December 1914.

bedfordstmartins.com/
americanlit for research
links on Mena

THE VINE-LEAF

It is a saying in the capital of Mexico that Dr. Malsufrido[1] carries more family secrets under his hat than any archbishop, which applies, of course, to family secrets of the rich. The poor have no family secrets, or none that Dr. Malsufrido would trouble to carry under his hat.

The doctor's hat is, appropriately enough, uncommonly capacious, rising very high, and sinking so low that it seems to be supported by his ears and eyebrows, and it has a furry look, as if it had been brushed the wrong way, which is perhaps what happens to it if it is ever brushed at all. When the doctor takes it off, the family secrets do not fly out like a flock of parrots, but remain nicely bottled up beneath a dome of old and highly polished ivory, which, with its unbroken fringe of dyed black hair, has the effect of a tonsure; and then Dr. Malsufrido looks like one of the early saints. I've forgotten which one.

So edifying is his personality that, when he marches into a sick-room, the forces of disease and infirmity march out of it, and do not dare to return until he has taken his leave. In fact, it is well known that none of his patients has ever had the bad manners to die in his presence.

If you will believe him, he is almost ninety years old, and everybody knows that he has been dosing good Mexicans for half a century. He is forgiven for being a Spaniard on account of a legend that he physicked royalty in his time, and that a certain princess — but that has nothing to do with this story.

It is sure he has a courtly way with him that captivates his female patients, of whom he speaks as his *penitentes*,[2] insisting on confession as a prerequisite of diagnosis, and declaring that the physician who undertakes to cure a woman's body without reference to her soul is a more abominable kill-healthy than the famous *Dr. Sangrado*, who taught medicine to *Gil Blas*.[3]

"Describe me the symptoms of your conscience, Señora," he will say. "Fix yourself that I shall forget one tenth of what you tell me."

"But what of the other nine tenths, Doctor?" the troubled lady will exclaim.

"The other nine tenths I shall take care not to believe," Dr. Malsufrido will reply, with a roar of laughter. And sometimes he will add:

"Do not confess your neighbor's sins; the doctor will have enough with your own."

When an inexperienced one fears to become a *penitente* lest that terrible old doctor betray her confidence, he reassures her as to his discretion, and at the same time takes her mind off her anxieties by telling her the story of his first patient.

"Figure you my prudence, Señora," he begins, "that, although she was my patient, I did not so much as see her face."

---

1. **Dr. Malsufrido**: The doctor's name means impatient or intolerant (Spanish).
2. *penitentes*: Repentant sinners (Spanish).
3. *Dr. Sangrado . . . Gil Blas*: Characters in the episodic novel *The Adventures of Gil Blas of Santillane* (1715-35), set in Spain and written in French by Alain-René LeSage (1668-1747). Dr. Sangrado practices medicine by only two methods: encouraging patients to drink hot water and bleeding them.

And then, having enjoyed the startled curiosity of his hearer, he continues:

"On that day of two crosses when I first undertook the mending of mortals, she arrived to me beneath a veil as impenetrable as that of a nun, saying:

"'To you I come, Señor Doctor, because no one knows you.'

"'Who would care for fame, Señorita,' said I, 'when obscurity brings such excellent fortune?'

"And the lady, in a voice which trembled slightly, returned:

"'If your knife is as apt as your tongue, and your discretion equal to both, I shall not regret my choice of a surgeon.'

"With suitable gravity I reassured her, and inquired how I might be privileged to serve her. She replied:

"'By ridding me of a blemish, if you are skilful enough to leave no trace on the skin.'

"'Of that I will judge, with the help of God, when the señorita shall have removed her veil.'

"'No, no; you shall not see my face. Praise the saints the blemish is not there!'

"'Wherever it be,' said I, resolutely, 'my science tells me that it must be seen before it can be well removed.'

"The lady answered with great simplicity that she had no anxiety on that account, but that, as she had neither duenna nor servant with her, I must help her. I had no objection, for a surgeon must needs be something of a lady's maid. I judged from the quality of her garments that she was of an excellent family, and I was ashamed of my clumsy fingers; but she was as patient as marble, caring only to keep her face closely covered. When at last I saw the blemish she had complained of, I was astonished, and said:

"'But it seems to me a blessed stigma, Señorita, this delicate, wine-red vine-leaf, staining a surface as pure as the petal of any magnolia. With permission, I should say that the God Bacchus[4] himself painted it here in the arch of this chaste back, where only the eyes of Cupid[5] could find it; for it is safely below the line of the most fashionable gown.'

"But she replied:

"'I have my reasons. Fix yourself that I am superstitious.'

"I tried to reason with her on that, but she lost her patience, and cried:

"'For favor, good surgeon, your knife!'

"Even in those days I had much sensibility, Señora, and I swear that my heart received more pain from the knife than did she. Neither the cutting nor the stitching brought a murmur from her. Only some strong ulterior thought could have armed a delicate woman with such valor. I beat my brains to construe the case, but without success. A caprice took me to refuse the fee she offered me.

"'No, Señorita,' I said, 'I have not seen your face, and if I were to take your money, it might pass that I should not see the face of a second patient, which would be a great misfortune. You are my first, and I am as superstitious as you.'

---

4. **Bacchus:** Greek god of wine.
5. **Cupid:** Roman god of love.

"I would have added that I had fallen in love with her, but I feared to appear ridiculous, having seen no more than her back.

"'You would place me under an obligation,' she said. I felt that her eyes studied me attentively through her veil. 'Very well, I can trust you the better for that. *Adiós*, Señor Surgeon.'

"She came once more to have me remove the stitches, as I had told her, and again her face was concealed, and again I refused payment; but I think she knew that the secret of the vine-leaf was buried in my heart."

"But that secret, what was it, Doctor? Did you ever see the mysterious lady again?"

"*Chist!*[6] Little by little one arrives to the *rancho*, Señora. Five years passed, and many patients arrived to me, but, although all showed me their faces, I loved none of them better than the first one. Partly through family influence, partly through well-chosen friendships, and perhaps a little through that diligence in the art of Hippocrates[7] for which in my old age I am favored by the most charming of Mexicans, I had prospered, and was no longer unknown.

"At a meeting of a learned society I became known to a certain *marqués*[8] who had been a great traveler in his younger days. We had a discussion on a point of anthropology, and he invited me to his house, to see the curiosities he had collected in various countries. Most of them recalled scenes of horror, for he had a morbid fancy.

"Having taken from my hand the sword with which he had seen five Chinese pirates sliced into small pieces, he led me toward a little door, saying:

"'Now you shall see the most mysterious and beautiful of my mementos, one which recalls a singular event in our own peaceful Madrid.'

"We entered a room lighted by a skylight, and containing little but an easel on which rested a large canvas. The *marqués* led me where the most auspicious light fell upon it. It was a nude, beautifully painted. The model stood poised divinely, with her back to the beholder, twisting flowers in her hair before a mirror. And there, in the arch of that chaste back, staining a surface as pure as the petal of any magnolia, what did my eyes see? Can you possibly imagine, Señora?"

"*Válgame Dios!*[9] The vine-leaf, Doctor!"

"What penetration of yours, Señora! It was veritably the vine-leaf, wine-red, as it had appeared to me before my knife barbarously extirpated it from the living flesh; but in the picture it seemed unduly conspicuous, as if Bacchus had been angry when he kissed. You may imagine how the sight startled me. But those who know Dr. Malsufrido need no assurance that even in those early days he never permitted himself one imprudent word. No, Señora; I only remarked, after praising the picture in proper terms:

"'What an interesting moon is that upon the divine creature's back!'

---

6. *Chist!*: Hush! (Spanish).
7. the art of Hippocrates: Hippocrates (c. 460–377 BCE), the Greek physician generally regarded as the founder of Western medicine, formulated a statement of medical conduct and ethics, the Hippocratic Oath.
8. *marqués*: A nobleman.
9. *Válgame Dios!*: "Bless me, God!" (Spanish).

"'Does it not resemble a young vine-leaf in early spring?' said the *marqués*, who contemplated the picture with the ardor of a connoisseur. I agreed politely, saying:

"'Now that you suggest it, *Marqués*, it has some of the form and color of a tender vine-leaf. But I could dispense me a better vine-leaf, with many bunches of grapes, to satisfy the curiosity I have to see such a well-formed lady's face. What a misfortune that it does not appear in that mirror, as the artist doubtless intended! The picture was never finished, then?'

"'I have reason to believe that it was finished,' he replied, 'but that the face painted in the mirror was obliterated. Observe that its surface is an opaque and disordered smudge of many pigments, showing no brush-work, but only marks of a rude rubbing that in some places has overlapped the justly painted frame of the mirror.'

"'This promises an excellent mystery,' I commented lightly. 'Was it the artist or his model who was dissatisfied with the likeness, *Marqués*?'

"'I suspect that the likeness was more probably too good than not good enough,' returned the *marqués*. 'Unfortunately, poor Andrade is not here to tell us.'

"'Andrade! The picture was his work?'

"'The last his hand touched. Do you remember when he was found murdered in his studio?'

"'With a knife sticking between his shoulders. I remember it very well.'

"The *marqués* continued:

"'I had asked him to let me have this picture. He was then working on that rich but subdued background. The figure was finished, but there was no vine-leaf, and the mirror was empty of all but a groundwork of paint, with a mere luminous suggestion of a face.

"'Andrade, however, refused to name me a price, and tried to put me off with excuses. His friends were jesting about the unknown model, whom no one had managed to see, and all suspected that he designed to keep the picture for himself. That made me the more determined to possess it. I wished to make it a betrothal gift to the beautiful Señorita Lisarda Monte Alegre, who had then accepted the offer of my hand, and who is now the *marquesa*.[10] When I have a desire, Doctor, it bites me, and I make it bite others. That poor Andrade, I gave him no peace.

"'He fell into one of his solitary fits, shutting himself in his studio, and seeing no one; but that did not prevent me from knocking at his door whenever I had nothing else to do. Well, one morning the door was open.'

"'Yes, yes!' I exclaimed. 'I remember now, *Marqués*, that it was you who found the body.'

"'You have said it. He was lying in front of this picture, having dragged himself across the studio. After assuring myself that he was beyond help, and while awaiting the police, I made certain observations. The first thing to strike my attention was this vine-leaf. The paint was fresh, whereas the rest of the figure was comparatively dry. Moreover, its color had not been mixed with Andrade's usual skill. Observe you, Doctor,

---

10. **marquesa**: A noblewoman, the wife or widow of a *marqués* (Spanish).

that the blemish is not of the texture of the skin, or bathed in its admirable atmosphere. It presents itself as an excrescence. And why? Because that color had been mixed and applied with feverish haste by the hand of a dying man, whose one thought was to denounce his assassin – she who undoubtedly bore such a mark on her body, and who had left him for dead, after carefully obliterating the portrait of herself which he had painted in the mirror.'

"'*Ay Dios!*[11] But the police, *Marqués* – they never reported these details so significant?'

"'Our admirable police are not connoisseurs of the painter's art, my friend. Moreover, I had taken the precaution to remove from the dead man's fingers the empurpled brush with which he had traced that accusing symbol.'

"'You wished to be the accomplice of an unknown assassin?'

"'Inevitably, Señor, rather than deliver that lovely body to the hands of the public executioner.'

"The *marqués* raised his lorgnette and gazed at the picture. And I – I was recovering from my agitation, Señora. I said:

"'It seems to me, *Marqués*, that if I were a woman and loved you, I should be jealous of that picture.'

"He smiled and replied:

"'It is true that the *marquesa* affects some jealousy on that account, and will not look at the picture. However, she is one who errs on the side of modesty, and prefers more austere objects of contemplation. She is excessively religious.'

"'I have been called superstitious,' pronounced a voice behind me.

"It was a voice that I had heard before. I turned, Señora, and I ask you to try to conceive whose face I now beheld."

"*Válgame la Virgen*,[12] Dr. Malsufrido, was it not the face of the good *marquesa*, and did she not happen to have been also your first patient?"

"Again such penetration, Señora, confounds me. It was she. The *marqués* did me the honor to present me to her.

"'I have heard of your talents, Señor Surgeon,' she said.

"'And I of your beauty, *Marquesa*,' I hastened to reply; 'but that tale was not well told.' And I added, 'If you are superstitious, I will be, too.'

"With one look from her beautiful and devout eyes she thanked me for that prudence which to this day, Señora, is at the service of my *penitentes*, little daughters of my affections and my prayers; and then she sighed and said:

"'Can you blame me for not loving this questionable lady of the vine-leaf, of whom my husband is such a gallant accomplice?'

"'Not for a moment,' I replied, 'for I am persuaded, *Marquesa*, that a lady of rare qualities may have power to bewitch an unfortunate man without showing him the light of her face.'"

[1914]

---

11. *Ay Dios!*: "Oh God!" (Spanish).
12. *Válgame la Virgen*: "Bless me, Mother of God" (Spanish).

Jean Toomer

[1894-1967]

Jean Toomer was born Nathan Eugene Pinchback Toomer on December 26, 1894, in Washington, D.C. His parents were Nathan Toomer, a planter, and Nina Pinchback Toomer, the daughter of a former governor of Louisiana, the first person of African American descent to hold that office in the United States. Shortly after Toomer was born, his father abandoned the family, and his mother took him to live with her parents in an affluent, predominantly white neighborhood in Washington. He attended elementary school there and at an all-white school in New Rochelle, New York, where his mother took him after she remarried in 1906. Toomer hated his stepfather, and he returned to live with his grandparents after his mother died in 1909. By then, his grandparents had been forced by financial pressures to move to a modest, black section of Washington. There, at the age of fifteen, the light-complexioned Toomer first learned about his ancestry and mixed racial heritage, which he later described as "seven blood mixtures: French, Dutch, Welsh, Negro, German, Jewish, and Indian." Shocked by the discovery, he attended an all-black high school, graduated in 1914, and enrolled at the University of Wisconsin. "I was again entering the white world," he recalled in an unpublished autobiography; "and though I personally had experienced no prejudice or exclusion from the whites or the colored people, I had seen enough to know that America viewed life as if it were divided into white and black."

Jean Toomer

This photograph of Toomer was taken in New York City in 1932.

Refusing to define himself as either black or white, Toomer struggled to discover a vocation and a place for himself in the racially divided United States. He withdrew from the University of Wisconsin after one semester and lived with his grandparents for a year before enrolling at the American College of Physical Training in Chicago in the spring of 1916. That fall, he enrolled at the City College of New York, where he studied history, psychology, and sociology. In December 1917, after the United States entered World War I, Toomer withdrew from college and tried to enlist, but he was turned down for military service because of an athletic injury. He subsequently worked briefly in Milwaukee and Chicago before returning to New York City in the spring of 1918. Living in the lively bohemian district of Greenwich Village, he met Lola Ridge, an editor of the avant-garde magazine *Broom*, who introduced Toomer to the influential white writer and cultural critic Waldo Frank. Encouraged by Frank to become a writer, and now calling himself Jean Toomer, in the summer of 1919 he returned to live with his grandparents in Washington. He began to read the work of modern American and European novelists, as well as poets ranging from William Blake, Charles Baudelaire, and Walt Whitman to Robert Frost and the imagists. Toomer studied other innovative work by reading little magazines such as the *Dial* and *Poetry: A Magazine of Verse.* He experimented with both poetry and prose, amassing what he described as literally "a trunk full of manuscripts" by 1921, when Toomer accepted a temporary appointment as the head of the Sparta Agricultural and Industrial Institute, an all-black school in Georgia.

The brief time he spent there profoundly shaped the course of Toomer's life and literary career. "A visit to Georgia last fall was the starting point of almost everything of worth," he declared in a letter to the editors of the *Liberator* in 1922.

> I heard folk-songs come from the lips of Negro peasants. I saw the rich dusk beauty that I had heard many false accents about, and of which, till then, I was somewhat skeptical. And a deep part of my nature, a part that I had repressed, sprang suddenly to life and responded to them. Now, I can not conceive of myself as aloof and separated. My point of view has not changed; it has deepened, it has widened.

Certainly no earlier volume of poetry or fiction or both had come close to expressing the ethos of the Negro in the southern setting as Cane *did.*
—Arna Bontemps

The experience inspired Toomer's earliest publications, a series of poems, sketches, and stories that he subsequently wove together in his first book, *Cane* (1923). Waldo Frank, who arranged for its publication and wrote a preface to the volume, observed: "For Toomer, the Southland is not a problem to be solved; it is a field of loveliness to be sung: the Georgia Negro is not a downtrodden soul to be uplifted; he is material for a gorgeous painting." Some reviewers were puzzled by the generic mixture of what one described as "an interesting, occasionally beautiful, and often queer book of exploration into old country and new ways of writing." But most critics praised the artistry and innovation displayed in *Cane*, which Toomer's publisher advertised as "a book about Negroes by a Negro." Although it sold poorly, the book had a powerful impact on young African American writers such as Sterling Brown, Langston Hughes, and Zora Neale Hurston, who credited *Cane* as a major impetus for the Harlem Renaissance.

Toomer, however, steadily withdrew from black literary circles and from writing about African Americans. He began to study the work of George Ivanovitch Gurdjieff, a Greek Armenian mystic who had established an institute in Fontainebleau, France. Toomer first attended the school in 1924, and most of his writings during the following years were based on Gurdjieff's theories of spiritual self-development. In 1930, when James Weldon Johnson asked for permission to reprint some of Toomer's poems in a new edition of *The Book of American Negro Poetry*, he flatly refused. "My poems are not Negro poems, nor are they Anglo-Saxon or white or English poems," Toomer sharply replied: "They are, first, mine. And, second, they spring from the result of racial blendings here in America which have produced a new race or stock." He developed his concept of racial fusion in *The Blue Meridian*, a visionary poem about the possibilities of a thoroughly democratic "New America." But he created a public furor when he married the first of his two white wives, the writer Margery Latimer, in 1932. After Latimer died giving birth to their first child, Toomer married Marjorie Content, the daughter of a wealthy Wall Street financier, in 1934. They moved to Doylestown, Pennsylvania, where he eventually became a Quaker. For the rest of his life, Toomer devoted himself to writing for Quaker journals, giving lectures, and continuing his study of philosophy and religion. He died on March 30, 1967.

Reading Toomer's *Cane.*   An experimental and innovative work that defies easy classification, *Cane* has been variously described as a novel, a novel-poem, and a collage or mosaic of imagistic poems, prose sketches, and short stories. Toomer began to write the pieces that make up the book after he returned to Washington, D.C., from a three-month stay in Sparta, Georgia, in 1921. He published his first poem in the *Crisis*, the magazine of the National Association for the Advancement of Colored People (NAACP), but many of the pieces in the book first appeared in avant-garde literary journals targeted at primarily white audiences, including *Broom*, the *Double Dealer*, the *Little Review*, the *Modern Review*, and *Prairie.* Encouraged by the reception of the individual works, Toomer began to conceive of them as part of a single book along the lines of Sherwood Anderson's short-story cycle *Winesburg, Ohio* (1919). Whereas Anderson explored the lives of ordinary white people in a fictional town in the Midwest, Toomer sought to capture the experience and folk culture of rural blacks in the fictional southern town of Sempter, Georgia,

bedfordstmartins.com/ americanlit for research links on Toomer

Cane

The design of the dust jacket of the first edition evokes an exotic, tropical locale that bears little resemblance to the actual setting of Toomer's poems, sketches, and stories about the cotton plantation country of central Georgia.

the setting of the various works in the first and third sections of *Cane*. When his publisher asked Toomer to expand the manuscript, he added the poems, sketches, and stories in the second section, set in the burgeoning black areas of Chicago and Washington, D.C. The text of the following selection — the final poem and story in the first section — is taken from the first edition of *Cane* (1923).

From CANE

PORTRAIT IN GEORGIA

Hair — braided chestnut,
coiled like a lyncher's rope,
Eyes — fagots,
Lips — old scars, or the first red blisters,
Breath — the last sweet scent of cane,
And her slim body, white as the ash
    of black flesh after flame.

[1923]

BLOOD-BURNING MOON

1

Up from the skeleton stone walls, up from the rotting floor boards and the solid hand-hewn beams of oak of the pre-war cotton factory, dusk came. Up from the dusk the full moon came. Glowing like a fired pine-knot, it illumined the great door and soft showered the Negro shanties aligned along the single street of factory town. The full moon in the great door was an omen. Negro women improvised songs against its spell.

Louisa sang as she came over the crest of the hill from the white folks' kitchen. Her skin was the color of oak leaves on young trees in fall. Her breasts, firm and up-pointed like ripe acorns. And her singing had the low murmur of winds in fig trees. Bob Stone, younger son of the people she worked for, loved her. By the way the world reckons things, he had won her. By measure of that warm glow which came into her mind at thought of him, he had won her. Tom Burwell whom the whole town called Big Boy, also loved her. But working in the fields all day, and far away from her, gave him no chance to show it. Though often enough of evenings he had tried to. Somehow, he never got along. Strong as he was with hands upon the ax or plow, he found it difficult to hold her. Or so he thought. But the fact was that he held her to factory town more firmly than he thought for. His black balanced, and pulled against, the white of Stone, when she thought of them. And her mind was vaguely upon them as she came over the crest of the hill, coming from the white folks' kitchen. As she sang softly at the evil face of the full moon.

A strange stir was in her. Indolently, she tried to fix upon Bob or Tom as the cause of it. To meet Bob in the canebrake, as she was going to do an hour or so later, was nothing new. And Tom's proposal which she felt on its way to her could be indefinitely put off. Separately, there was no unusual significance to either one. But for some reason, they jumbled when her eyes gazed vacantly at the rising moon. And from the jumble came the stir that was strangely within her. Her lips trembled. The slow rhythm of her song grew agitant and restless. Rusty black and tan spotted hounds, lying in the dark corners of porches or prowling around back yards, put their noses in the air and caught its tremor. They began plaintively to yelp and howl. Chickens woke up and cackled. Intermittently, all over the countryside dogs barked and roosters crowed as if heralding a weird dawn or some ungodly awakening. The women sang lustily. Their songs were cotton-wads to stop their ears. Louisa came down into factory town and sank wearily upon the step before her home. The moon was rising towards a thick cloud-bank which soon would hide it.

> Red nigger moon. Sinner!
> Blood-burning moon. Sinner!
> Come out that fact'ry door.

2

Up from the deep dusk of a cleared spot on the edge of the forest a mellow glow arose and spread fan-wise into the low-hanging heavens. And all around the air was heavy with the scent of boiling cane. A large pile of cane-stalks lay like ribboned shadows upon the ground. A mule, harnessed to a pole, trudged lazily round and round the pivot of the grinder. Beneath a swaying oil lamp, a Negro alternately whipped out at the mule, and fed cane-stalks to the grinder. A fat boy waddled pails of fresh ground juice between the grinder and the boiling stove. Steam came from the copper boiling pan. The scent of cane came from the copper pan and drenched the forest and the hill that sloped to factory town, beneath its fragrance. It drenched the men in circle seated around the stove. Some of them chewed at the white pulp of stalks, but there was no need for them to, if all they wanted was to taste the cane. One tasted it in factory town. And from factory town one could see the soft haze thrown by the glowing stove upon the low-hanging heavens.

Old David Georgia stirred the thickening syrup with a long ladle, and ever so often drew it off. Old David Georgia tended his stove and told tales about the white folks, about moonshining and cotton picking, and about sweet nigger gals, to the men who sat there about his stove to listen to him. Tom Burwell chewed cane-stalk and laughed with the others till someone mentioned Louisa. Till some one said something about Louisa and Bob Stone, about the silk stockings she must have gotten from him. Blood ran up Tom's neck hotter than the glow that flooded from the stove. He sprang up. Glared at the men and said, "She's my gal." Will Manning laughed. Tom strode over to him. Yanked him up and knocked him to the ground. Several of Manning's friends got up to fight for him. Tom whipped out a long knife and would have cut them to shreds if they hadnt ducked into the woods. Tom had had enough. He nodded to Old David Georgia and swung down the path to factory town. Just then, the dogs started barking and the roosters began to crow. Tom felt funny. Away from the fight, away from the stove, chill got to him. He shivered. He shuddered when he saw the full moon rising towards the cloud-bank. He who didnt give a godam for the fears of old women. He forced his mind to fasten on Louisa. Bob Stone. Better not be. He turned into the street and saw Louisa sitting before her home. He went towards her, ambling, touched the brim of a marvelously shaped, spotted, felt hat, said he wanted to say something to her, and then found that he didnt know what he had to say, or if he did, that he couldnt say it. He shoved his big fists in his overalls, grinned, and started to move off.

"Youall want me, Tom?"

"Thats what us wants, sho, Louisa."

"Well, here I am —"

"An here I is, but that aint ahelpin none, all th same."

"You wanted to say something? . ."

"I did that, sho. But words is like th spots on dice: no matter how y fumbles em, there's times when they jes wont come. I dunno why. Seems like th love I feels fo yo done stole m tongue. I got it now. Whee! Louisa, honey, I oughtnt tell y, I feel I oughtnt cause yo is young an goes t church an I has had other gals, but Louisa I sho do love y. Lil gal, Ise watched y from them first days when youall sat right here befo yo door befo th well an sang sometimes in a way that like t broke m heart. Ise carried y with me into th fields, day after day, an after that, an I sho can plow when yo is there, an I can pick cotton. Yassur! Come near beatin Barlo yesterday. I sho did. Yassur! An next year if ole Stone'll trust me, I'll have a farm. My own. My bales will buy yo what y gets from white folks now. Silk stockings an purple dresses — course I dont believe what some folks been whisperin as t how y gets them things now. White folks always did do for niggers what they likes. An they jes cant help alikin yo, Louisa. Bob Stone likes y. Course he does. But not th way folks is awhisperin. Does he, hon?"

"I dont know what you mean, Tom."

"Course y dont. Ise already cut two niggers. Had t hon, t tell em so. Niggers always tryin t make somethin out a nothin. An then besides, white folks aint up t them tricks so much nowadays. Godam better not be. Leastawise not with yo. Cause I wouldnt stand f it. Nassur."

"What would you do, Tom?"

"Cut him jes like I cut a nigger."

"No, Tom —"

"I said I would an there aint no mo to it. But that aint th talk f now. Sing, honey Louisa, an while I'm listenin t y I'll be makin love."

Tom took her hand in his. Against the tough thickness of his own, hers felt soft and small. His huge body slipped down to the step beside her. The full moon sank upward into the deep purple of the cloud-bank. An old woman brought a lighted lamp and hung it on the common well whose bulky shadow squatted in the middle of the road, opposite Tom and Louisa. The old woman lifted the well-lid, took hold the chain, and began drawing up the heavy bucket. As she did so, she sang. Figures shifted, restless-like, between lamp and window in the front rooms of the shanties. Shadows of the figures fought each other on the gray dust of the road. Figures raised the windows and joined the old woman in song. Louisa and Tom, the whole street, singing:

> Red nigger moon. Sinner!
> Blood-burning moon. Sinner!
> Come out that fact'ry door.

3

Bob Stone sauntered from his veranda out into the gloom of fir trees and magnolias. The clear white of his skin paled, and the flush of his cheeks turned purple. As if to balance this outer change, his mind became consciously a white man's. He passed the house with its huge open hearth which, in the days of slavery, was the plantation cookery. He saw Louisa bent over that hearth. He went in as a master should and took her. Direct, honest, bold. None of this sneaking that he had to go through now. The contrast was repulsive to him. His family had lost ground. Hell no, his family still owned the niggers, practically. Damned if they did, or he wouldnt have to duck around so. What would they think if they knew? His mother? His sister? He shouldnt mention them, shouldnt think of them in this connection. There in the dusk he blushed at doing so. Fellows about town were all right, but how about his friends up North? He could see them incredible, repulsed. They didnt know. The thought first made him laugh. Then, with their eyes still upon him, he began to feel embarrassed. He felt the need of explaining things to them. Explain hell. They wouldnt understand, and moreover, who ever heard of a Southerner getting on his knees to any Yankee, or anyone. No sir. He was going to see Louisa to-night, and love her. She was lovely—in her way. Nigger way. What way was that? Damned if he knew. Must know. He'd known her long enough to know. Was there something about niggers that you couldnt know? Listening to them at church didnt tell you anything. Looking at them didnt tell you anything. Talking to them didnt tell you anything—unless it was gossip, unless they wanted to talk. Of course, about farming, and licker, and craps—but those werent nigger. Nigger was something more. How much more? Something to be afraid of, more? Hell no. Who ever heard of being afraid of a nigger? Tom Burwell. Cartwell had told him that Tom went with Louisa after she reached home. No sir. No nigger had ever been with his girl. He'd like to see one try. Some position for him to be in. Him, Bob Stone, of the old Stone family, in a scrap with a nigger over a nigger girl. In the good old days. . . Ha! Those were the days. His family had lost ground. Not so much, though. Enough for him to have to cut through old Lemon's canefield by way of the woods, that he might meet her. She was worth it. Beautiful nigger gal. Why nigger? Why not, just gal? No, it was because she was nigger that he went to her. Sweet. . . The scent of boiling cane came to him. Then he saw the rich glow of the stove. He heard the voices of the men circled around it. He was about to skirt the clearing when he heard his own name mentioned. He stopped. Quivering. Leaning against a tree, he listened.

"Bad nigger. Yassur, he sho is one bad nigger when he gets started."

"Tom Burwell's been on th gang[1] three times fo cuttin men."

"What y think he's agwine t do t Bob Stone?"

"Dunno yet. He aint found out. When he does – Baby!"

"Aint no tellin."

"Young Stone aint no quitter an I ken tell y that. Blood of th old uns in his veins."

"Thats right. He'll scrap, sho."

"Be gettin too hot f niggers round this away."

"Shut up, nigger. Y dont know what y talkin bout."

Bob Stone's ears burned as though he had been holding them over the stove. Sizzling heat welled up within him. His feet felt as if they rested on red-hot coals. They stung him to quick movement. He circled the fringe of the glowing. Not a twig cracked beneath his feet. He reached the path that led to factory town. Plunged furiously down it. Halfway along, a blindness within him veered him aside. He crashed into the bordering cane-brake. Cane leaves cut his face and lips. He tasted blood. He threw himself down and dug his fingers in the ground. The earth was cool. Cane-roots took the fever from his hands. After a long while, or so it seemed to him, the thought came to him that it must be time to see Louisa. He got to his feet and walked calmly to their meeting place. No Louisa. Tom Burwell had her. Veins in his forehead bulged and distended. Saliva moistened the dried blood on his lips. He bit down on his lips. He tasted blood. Not his own blood; Tom Burwell's blood. Bob drove through the cane and out again upon the road. A hound swung down the path before him towards factory town. Bob couldnt see it. The dog loped aside to let him pass. Bob's blind rushing made him stumble over it. He fell with a thud that dazed him. The hound yelped. Answering yelps came from all over the countryside. Chickens cackled. Roosters crowed, heralding the bloodshot eyes of southern awaken-ing. Singers in the town were silenced. They shut their windows down. Palpitant be-tween the rooster crows, a chill hush settled upon the huddled forms of Tom and Louisa. A figure rushed from the shadow and stood before them. Tom popped to his feet.

"Whats y want?"

"I'm Bob Stone."

"Yassur – an I'm Tom Burwell. Whats y want?"

Bob lunged at him. Tom side-stepped, caught him by the shoulder, and flung him to the ground. Straddled him.

"Let me up."

"Yassur – but watch yo doins, Bob Stone."

A few dark figures, drawn by the sound of scuffle, stood about them. Bob sprang to his feet.

"Fight like a man, Tom Burwell, an I'll lick y."

Again he lunged. Tom side-stepped and flung him to the ground. Straddled him.

"Get off me, you godam nigger you."

"Yo sho has started somethin now. Get up."

---

1. **gang:** Chain gangs, groups of black convicts shackled together and working under the direct supervision of an armed guard, were then common in the South.

Tom yanked him up and began hammering at him. Each blow sounded as if it smashed into a precious, irreplaceable soft something. Beneath them, Bob staggered back. He reached in his pocket and whipped out a knife.

"Thats my game, sho."

Blue flash, a steel blade slashed across Bob Stone's throat. He had a sweetish sick feeling. Blood began to flow. Then he felt a sharp twitch of pain. He let his knife drop. He slapped one hand against his neck. He pressed the other on top of his head as if to hold it down. He groaned. He turned, and staggered towards the crest of the hill in the direction of white town. Negroes who had seen the fight slunk into their homes and blew the lamps out. Louisa, dazed, hysterical, refused to go indoors. She slipped, crumbled, her body loosely propped against the woodwork of the well. Tom Burwell leaned against it. He seemed rooted there.

Bob reached Broad Street. White men rushed up to him. He collapsed in their arms.

"Tom Burwell . . ."

White men like ants upon a forage rushed about. Except for the taut hum of their moving, all was silent. Shotguns, revolvers, rope, kerosene, torches. Two high-powered cars with glaring search-lights. They came together. The taut hum rose to a low roar. Then nothing could be heard but the flop of their feet in the thick dust of the road. The moving body of their silence preceded them over the crest of the hill into factory town. It flattened the Negroes beneath it. It rolled to the wall of the factory, where it stopped. Tom knew that they were coming. He couldnt move. And then he saw the search-lights of the two cars glaring down on him. A quick shock went through him. He stiffened. He started to run. A yell went up from the mob. Tom wheeled about and faced them. They poured down on him. They swarmed. A large man with dead-white face and flabby cheeks came to him and almost jabbed a gun-barrel through his guts.

"Hands behind y, nigger."

Tom's wrists were bound. The big man shoved him to the well. Burn him over it, and when the woodwork caved in, his body would drop to the bottom. Two deaths for a godam nigger. Louisa was driven back. The mob pushed in. Its pressure, its momentum was too great. Drag him to the factory. Wood and stakes already there. Tom moved in the direction indicated. But they had to drag him. They reached the great door. Too many to get in there. The mob divided and flowed around the walls to either side. The big man shoved him through the door. The mob pressed in from the sides. Taut humming. No words. A stake was sunk into the ground. Rotting floor boards piled around it. Kerosene poured on the rotting floor boards. Tom bound to the stake. His breast was bare. Nail scratches let little lines of blood trickle down and mat into the hair. His face, his eyes were set and stony. Except for irregular breathing, one would have thought him already dead. Torches were flung onto the pile. A great flare muffled in black smoke shot upward. The mob yelled. The mob was silent. Now Tom could be seen within the flames. Only his head, erect, lean, like a blackened stone. Stench of burning flesh soaked the air. Tom's eyes popped. His head settled downward. The mob yelled. Its yell echoed against the skeleton stone walls and sounded like a hundred yells. Like a hundred mobs yelling. Its yell thudded against the thick front wall and fell back. Ghost of a yell slipped through the flames and out the great door of the factory. It fluttered like a dying thing down the single street of factory town. Louisa, upon the step before her home, did not hear it, but her eyes opened slowly. They saw the full moon glowing in the great door. The full moon, an evil thing, an omen, soft showering the homes of folks she knew. Where were they, these people? She'd sing, and perhaps they'd come out and join her. Perhaps Tom Burwell would come. At any rate, the full moon in the great door was an omen which she must sing to:

> Red nigger moon. Sinner!
> Blood-burning moon. Sinner!
> Come out that fact'ry door.

[1923]

F. Scott Fitzgerald

[1896-1940]

F. Scott Fitzgerald

This photograph of Fitzgerald was taken during the 1920s, when he was at the height of his critical and commercial success as a writer.

Francis Scott Key Fitzgerald was born in St. Paul, Minnesota, on September 24, 1896. He was the first child of Edward Fitzgerald, a descendant of Francis Scott Key, the composer of "The Star Spangled Banner," and Mary McQuillan Fitzgerald, the devout daughter of a wealthy Irish Catholic family. In 1898, Edward Fitzgerald's furniture factory failed, and he moved the family to Buffalo, New York. When he lost his job in 1908, he came home from work "a completely broken man," as Fitzgerald described the traumatic event. The family returned to St. Paul, where they were largely supported by the McQuillans. Fitzgerald recalled that, by the age of twelve, he "wrote all through every class in school," and he published his first short story in the school's literary magazine in October 1909. In an effort to force him to study and improve his academic performance, the family sent him to a private preparatory school in New Jersey in September 1911. He continued to devote most of his efforts to writing, so his grades were mediocre, but he did well enough on his entrance exams to be admitted to Princeton University in the fall of 1913. He was drawn there by the Triangle Club, a musical-comedy troupe for which Fitzgerald wrote an operetta during his first year, and he was a regular contributor to the *Princeton Tiger,* a humor magazine, and the *Nassau Literary Magazine.* When his grades slipped and he was barred from extracurricular activities as a form of academic probation, Fitzgerald left Princeton without completing his degree. In the fall of 1917, after the United States entered World War I, he was granted an army commission and was sent for officer training to Fort Leavenworth, Kansas.

Despite the unpromising circumstances, Fitzgerald soon fulfilled his youthful dreams of literary success. At Fort Leavenworth, he worked feverishly on a semiautobiographical novel, *The Romantic Egoist,* which he submitted to the New York publisher Charles Scribner's Sons in the spring of 1918. Meanwhile, he was transferred to an army camp near Montgomery, Alabama, where he met his future wife, Zelda Sayre. That summer, Scribner's rejected Fitzgerald's novel, but the editor Maxwell Perkins strongly encouraged him to revise and resubmit it, observing that "no manuscript novel has come to us for a long time that seemed to display so much originality." The war ended before Fitzgerald could be shipped overseas, and he was discharged from the army. Zelda Sayre refused to marry him until he had "prospects," as she called them, and Fitzgerald went to New York City in February 1919. In an effort to earn enough money to support them, he took a job in advertising and wrote short stories at night. Discouraged by his failure to sell any of the stories, Fitzgerald returned home to St. Paul. There, he revised, retitled, and resubmitted his novel, which Scribner's published on March 26, 1920. One advertisement for the novel read: "Were you ever under thirty? Then read THIS SIDE OF PARADISE by F. Scott Fitzgerald." The first printing of three thousand copies sold out in three days, and sales were spurred by favorable and sometimes enthusiastic reviews, one of which described Fitzgerald as a "new American author of amazing potentialities." A triumphant Fitzgerald married Zelda Sayre in New York on April 3, 1920, and the young couple embarked on a nomadic and often notorious life that came to symbolize both the glamour and the excesses of what he soon dubbed the "Jazz Age."

The financial pressures to support their lavish lifestyle strongly shaped Fitzgerald's early career. *This Side of Paradise* sold more than forty thousand copies in 1920. Even during that year, however, he made significantly more money from stories he sold to magazines, especially the mass-circulation *Saturday Evening Post.* Although he deeply resented the time such writing took away from his work on novels, Fitzgerald ultimately produced more than 150 magazine stories, including some outstanding ones. Following the publication of his popular first collection of stories, *Flappers and Philosophers* (1920), he concentrated on his second novel, *The Beautiful and the Damned* (1922). Reviews were mixed, but the novel sold well, as did Fitzgerald's second collection of stories, *Tales of the Jazz Age* (1922). He then decided to write a play that "is to make my fortune," a farcical political satire published as *The Vegetable; or, From President to Postman.* But the out-of-town tryouts were disastrous, and the play never opened on Broadway. Now in debt, Fitzgerald swiftly produced ten stories early in 1923, earning enough money to support his work on a new novel he

He had one of the rarest qualities in all literature . . . a kind of subdued magic, controlled and exquisite, the sort of thing you get from good string quartets.

–Raymond Chandler

initially called "Among the Ash Heaps and Millionaires." After he and Zelda took their three-year-old daughter to live on the French Riviera in 1924, Fitzgerald completed the novel, which was published as *The Great Gatsby* (1925). Despite admiring reviews, the book sold poorly, though Fitzgerald earned a good deal of subsidiary income from a successful stage version and a silent movie made by the Famous Players Film Company. He also continued to command top dollar for his magazine stories, some of the best of which were included in his collection *All the Sad Young Men* (1926). "As F. Scott Fitzgerald continues to publish books, it becomes apparent that he is head and shoulders better than any writer of his generation," a reviewer observed in the *Bookman*.

Fitzgerald's productivity and reputation declined dramatically during the remainder of his career. In France, he became friends with and strongly promoted the work of Ernest Hemingway, who soon began to eclipse Fitzgerald. He began a new novel, but his progress was impeded by his heavy drinking and his strained relationship with Zelda. Overshadowed by her famous husband, and deeply frustrated by her futile effort to become a professional ballerina, she suffered the first of a series of mental breakdowns in 1930. Later diagnosed with schizophrenia, she was in and out of hospitals until her death in 1948, a period during which she wrote an autobiographical novel about her marriage to Fitzgerald, *Save Me the Waltz* (1932). After nearly eight years of sporadic work, Fitzgerald finally published a novel based on similar material, *Tender Is the Night* (1934). It received mixed reviews, and he published only one more book, a short-story collection appropriately entitled *Taps at Reveille* (1935). In 1936, after a series of his essays collectively known as "The Crack Up" appeared in *Esquire*, a writer for the *New York Post* brutally described Fitzgerald as a "washed up alcoholic." The following year, he moved to California, where he worked as a screenwriter for Metro-Goldwyn-Mayer. Fitzgerald continued to publish stories in magazines, primarily in *Esquire*, and he began work on a novel about Hollywood. But he had not yet completed the novel, posthumously published as *The Last Tycoon* (1941), when he died of a heart attack on December 21, 1940.

bedfordstmartins.com/ americanlit for research links on Fitzgerald

Reading Fitzgerald's "The Ice Palace." This was one of the earliest of the sixty-five stories Fitzgerald published in the *Saturday Evening Post* between 1920 and 1937. Originally established in 1821 as a four-page weekly newspaper, the *Post* was among the longest-running periodicals in the United States. During the 1920s, its circulation reached 2,750,000 copies a week, and the *Post* came to symbolize the tastes and values of middle-class America. The conservative magazine placed a premium on hard work and material success, and more than half of the roughly two hundred pages in each issue were devoted to advertisements, especially for cars. For only five cents an issue, readers also enjoyed a variety of articles on business, current affairs, and travel; humorous and human-interest stories; and fiction by the most popular writers of the period. The *Post* was also well known for its lavish illustrations by Norman Rockwell,

"The Ice Palace" was first published in this issue of the popular weekly, the cover of which projected the innocent, family-oriented image of the *Post*. Its Philadelphia publisher claimed that the magazine was descended from the *Pennsylvania Gazette*, founded in 1728 by Benjamin Franklin, but he had died more than thirty years before the first issue of the *Post* appeared in 1821.

Illustration © SEPS. Licensed by Curtis Licensing. All Rights Reserved.

THE SATURDAY EVENING POST

An Illustrated Weekly
Founded A.D. 1728 by Benj. Franklin

MAY 22, 1920   5¢. THE COPY
                      10¢. in Canada

Arthur Stringer—George Pattullo—Wallace Irwin—F. Scott Fitzgerald—Thomas Joyce
Nina Wilcox Putnam—Eleanor Franklin Egan—Donald Wilhelm—Ferdinand Reyher

who began working for the magazine in 1916; and by James H. Crank, who illustrated "The Ice Palace." Inspired by Fitzgerald's courtship of Zelda Sayre, who was born and raised in Montgomery, Alabama, the story concerns a journey of discovery undertaken by Sally Carrol Happer, a girl born in "southernmost Georgia," who is engaged to Harry Bellamy, a boy from a nameless northern city that closely resembles Fitzgerald's hometown of St. Paul, Minnesota. Through the conflict that emerges between the young couple, Fitzgerald explores the broader climatic, cultural, and historical divisions between the North and the South, where the graves of the Confederate dead exemplify the region's strong connections to the past and the legacy of the Civil War. The text of the story, which Fitzgerald included in his collection *Flappers and Philosophers* (1920), is taken from the first printing in the *Saturday Evening Post*, May 22, 1920.

THE ICE PALACE

[I]

The sunlight dripped over the house like golden paint over an art jar and the freckling shadows here and there only intensified the rigor of the bath of light. The Butterworth and Larkin houses flanking were intrenched behind great stodgy trees; only the Happer house took the full sun and all day long faced the dusty road-street with a tolerant kindly patience. This was the city of Tarleton in southernmost Georgia – September afternoon.

Up in her bedroom window Sally Carrol Happer rested her nineteen-year-old chin on a fifty-two-year-old sill and watched Clark Darrow's ancient flivver[1] turn the corner. The car was hot – being partly metallic it retained all the heat it absorbed or evolved – and Clark Darrow sitting bolt upright at the wheel wore a pained, strained expression as though he considered himself a spare part and rather likely to break. He laboriously crossed two dust ruts, the wheels squeaking indignantly at the encounter, and then with a terrifying expression he gave the steering gear a final wrench and deposited self and car approximately in front of the Happer steps. There was a plaintive heaving sound, a death rattle, followed by a short silence; and then the air was rent by a startling whistle.

Sally Carrol gazed down sleepily. She started to yawn, but finding this quite impossible unless she raised her chin from the window still changed her mind and continued silently to regard the car, whose owner sat brilliantly if perfunctorily at attention as he waited for an answer to his signal. After a moment the whistle once more split the dusty air.

"Good mawnin'."

With difficulty Clark twisted his tall body round and bent a distorted glance on the window.

"'Tain't mawnin', Sally Carrol."

"Isn't it, sure enough?"

"What you doin'?"

"Eatin' 'n apple."

"Come on go swimmin' – want to?"

"Reckon so."

"How 'bout hurryin' up?"

"Sure enough."

Sally Carrol sighed voluminously and raised herself with profound inertia from the floor, where she had been occupied in alternately destroying parts of a green apple and painting paper dolls for her younger sister. She approached a mirror, regarded her expression with a pleased and pleasant languor, dabbed two spots of rouge on her lips and a grain of powder on her nose and covered her bobbed corn-colored hair with a rose-littered sunbonnet. Then she kicked over the painting water, said, "Oh, damn!" – but let it lie – and left the room.

"How you, Clark?" she inquired a minute later as she slipped nimbly over the side of the car.

"Mighty fine, Sally Carrol."

"Where we go swimmin'?"

"Out to Walley's Pool. Told Marylyn we'd call by an' get her an' Joe Ewing."

Clark was dark and lean and when on foot was rather inclined to stoop. His eyes were ominous and his expression rather petulant except when startlingly illuminated by one

---

1. **flivver**: An informal word for a cheap, poorly maintained car.

of his frequent smiles. Clark had what was locally called "a income" – just enough to keep himself in ease and his car in gasoline – and he had spent the two years since he graduated from Georgia Tech in dozing round the lazy streets of his home town discussing how he could best invest his capital for an immediate fortune.

Hanging round he found not at all difficult; a crowd of little girls had grown up beautifully, the amazing Sally Carrol foremost among them; and they enjoyed being swum with and danced with and made love to in the flower-filled summery evenings – and they all liked Clark immensely. When feminine company palled there were half a dozen other youths who were always just about to do something and meanwhile were quite willing to join him in a few holes of golf or a game of billiards or the consumption of a quart of "hard yella licker." Every once in a while one of these contemporaries made a farewell round of calls before going up to New York or Philadelphia or Pittsburgh to go into business, but mostly they just stayed round in this languid paradise of dreamy skies and firefly evenings and noisy street fairs – and especially of gracious soft-voiced girls who were brought up on memories instead of money.

The flivver having been excited into a sort of restless resentful life Clark and Sally Carrol rolled and rattled down Valley Avenue into Jefferson Street, where the dust road became a pavement; along opiate Millicent Place, where there were half a dozen prosperous substantial mansions; and on into the downtown section.

Driving was perilous here, for it was shopping time; the population idled casually across the streets and a drove of low-moaning oxen were being urged along in front of a placid street car; even the shops seemed only yawning their doors and blinking their windows in the sunshine before retiring into a state of utter and finite coma.

"Sally Carrol," said Clark suddenly, "it a fact that you're engaged?"

She looked at him quickly.

"Where'd you hear that?"

"Sure enough, you engaged?"

"'At's a nice question to ask a girl!"

"Girl told me you were engaged to a Yankee you met up in Asheville last summah."

Sally Carrol sighed.

"Never saw such an old town faw rumors."

"Don't marry a Yankee, Sally Carrol. We need you round here."

Sally Carrol was silent a moment.

"Clark," she demanded suddenly, "who on earth shall I marry?"

"I offah my services."

"Honey, you couldn't suppawt a wife," she answered cheerfully. "Anyway, I know you too well to fall in love with you."

"'At doesn't mean you ought to marry a Yankee."

"S'pose I love him?"

He shook his head.

"You couldn't. He'd be a lot different from us, every way."

He broke off as he halted the car in front of a rambling dilapidated house. Marylyn Wade and Joe Ewing appeared in the doorway.

"'Lo, Sally Carrol."

"Hi!"

"How you-all?"

"Sally Carrol," demanded Marylyn as they started off again, "you engaged?"

"Lawdy, where'd all this start? Can't I look at a man 'thout everybody in town engagin' me to him?"

Clark stared straight in front of him at a bolt on the clattering wind shield.

"Sally Carrol," he said with a curious intensity, "don't you like us?"

"What?"

"Us down here?"

"Why, Clark, you know I do. I adore all you boys."

"Then why you gettin' engaged to a Yankee?"

"Clark, I don't know. I'm not sure what I'll do, but—well, I want to go places and see people. I want my mind to grow. I want to live where things happen on a big scale."

"What you mean?"

"Oh, Clark, I love you, and I love Joe here, and Ben Arrot, and you-all, but you'll—you'll—"

"We'll all be failures?"

"Yes. I don't mean only money failures but just sort of—of ineffectual and sad and—oh, how can I tell you?"

"You mean because we stay here in Tarleton?"

"Yes, Clark; and because you like it and never want to change things or think or go ahead."

He nodded and she reached over and pressed his hand.

"Clark," she said softly, "I wouldn't change you for the world. You're sweet the way you are. The things that'll make you fail I'll love always—the living in the past, the lazy days and nights you have, and all your carelessness and generosity."

"But you're goin' away?"

"Yes—because I couldn't ever marry you. You've a place in my heart no one else ever could have, but tied down here I'd get restless. I'd feel I was—wastin' myself. There's two sides to me, you see. There's the sleepy old side you love; an' there's a sawt of energy—the feelin' that makes me do wild things. That's the part of me that may be useful some-where, that'll last when I'm not beautiful any more."

She broke off with characteristic suddenness and sighed, "Oh, sweet cooky!" as her mood changed.

Half closing her eyes and tipping back her head till it rested on the seat back she let the savory breeze fan her eyes and ripple the fluffy curls of her bobbed hair. They were in the country now, hurrying between tangled growths of bright-green coppice and grass and tall trees that sent sprays of foliage to hang a cool welcome over the road. Here and there they passed a battered negro cabin, its oldest white-haired inhabitant smoking a corncob pipe beside the door and half a dozen scantily clothed pickaninnies[2] parading tattered dolls on the wild grown grass in front. Farther out were lazy cotton fields, where

---

2. **pickaninnies:** Probably derived from the Spanish word *pequeño*, meaning small or little, this now-offensive term was commonly used from the mid-nineteenth century until the 1930s to refer to African American children.

even the workers seemed intangible shadows lent by the sun to the earth not for toil but to while away some age-old tradition in the golden September fields. And round the drowsy picturesqueness, over the trees and shacks and muddy rivers, flowed the heat, never hostile, only comforting like a great warm nourishing bosom for the infant earth.

"Sally Carrol, we're here!"

"Poor chile's soun' asleep."

"Honey, you dead at last outa sheer laziness?"

"Water, Sally Carrol! Cool water waitin' faw you!"

Her eyes opened sleepily.

"Hi!" she murmured, smiling.

II

In November Harry Bellamy, tall, broad and brisk, came down from his Northern city to spend four days. His intention was to settle a matter that had been hanging fire since he and Sally Carrol had met in Asheville, North Carolina, in midsummer. The settlement took only a quiet afternoon and an evening in front of a glowing open fire, for Harry Bellamy had everything Sally Carrol wanted; and, besides, she loved him – loved him with that side of her she kept especially for loving. Sally Carrol had several rather clearly defined sides.

On his last afternoon they walked, and she found their steps tending half-unconsciously toward one of her favorite haunts, the cemetery. When it came in sight, gray-white and golden-green under the cheerful late sun, she paused irresolute by the iron gate.

"Are you mournful by nature, Harry?" she asked with a faint smile. "Mournful? Not I."

"Then let's go in here. It depresses some folks, but I like it."

They passed through the gateway and followed a path that led through a wavy valley of graves – dusty-gray and moldy for the fifties; quaintly carved with flowers and jars for the seventies; ornate and hideous for the nineties, with fat marble cherubs lying in sodden sleep on stone pillows, and great impossible growths of nameless granite flowers. Occasionally they saw a kneeling figure with tributary flowers, but over most of the graves lay silence and withered leaves with only the fragrance that their own shadowy memories could waken in living minds.

They reached the top of a hill where they were fronted by a tall round headstone, freckled with dark spots of damp and half grown over with vines.

"'Margery Lee,'" she read; "'1844-1873,' Wasn't she nice? She died when she was twenty-nine. Dear Margery Lee," she added softly. "Can't you see her, Harry?"

"Yes, Sally Carrol."

He felt a little hand insert itself into his.

"She was dark, I think; and she always wore her hair with a ribbon in it, and gorgeous hoopskirts of bright blue and old rose."

"Yes."

"Oh, she was sweet, Harry! And she was the sort of girl born to stand on a wide pillared porch and welcome folks in. I think perhaps a lot of men went away to war meanin' to come back to her; but maybe none of 'em ever did."

He stooped down close to the stone, hunting for any record of marriage.

"There's nothing here to show."

"Of course not. How could there be anything there better than just 'Margery Lee,' and that eloquent date?"

She drew close to him and an unexpected lump came into his throat as her yellow hair brushed his cheek.

"You see how she was, don't you, Harry?"

"I see," he agreed gently. "I see through your precious eyes. You're beautiful now, so I know she must have been."

Silent and close they stood, and he could feel her shoulders trembling a little. An ambling breeze swept up the hill and stirred the brim of her floppidy hat.

"Let's go down there!"

She was pointing to a flat stretch on the other side of the hill where along the green turf were a thousand grayish-white crosses stretching in endless ordered rows like the stacked-arms of a battalion.

"Those are the Confederate dead," said Sally Carrol simply.

They walked along and read the inscriptions, always only a name and a date, sometimes quite indecipherable.

"The last row is the saddest – see, 'way over there. Every cross has just a date on it and the word 'Unknown.'"

She looked at him and her eyes brimmed with tears.

"I can't tell you how real it is to me, darling – if you don't know."

"How you feel about it is beautiful to me."

"No, no, it's not me, it's them – that old time that I've tried to have live in me. These were just men, unimportant, evidently, or they wouldn't have been 'unknown'; but they died for the most beautiful thing in the world – the dead South. You see," she continued, her voice still husky, her eyes glistening with tears, "people have these dreams they fasten on to things, and I've always grown up with that dream. It was so easy because it was all dead and there weren't any disillusions comin' to me. I've tried in a way to live up to those past standards of noblesse oblige – there's just the last remnants of it, you know, like the roses of an old garden dying all round us – streaks of strange courtliness and chivalry in some of these boys an' stories I used to hear from a Confederate soldier who lived next door, and a few old darkies. Oh, Harry, there was something, there was something! I couldn't ever make you understand, but it was there."

"I understand," he assured her again quietly.

Sally Carrol smiled and dried her eyes on the tip of a handkerchief protruding from his breast pocket.

"You don't feel depressed, do you, lover? Even when I cry I'm happy here, and I get a sawt of strength from it."

Hand in hand they turned and walked slowly away. Finding soft grass she drew him down to a seat beside her with their backs against the remnants of a low broken wall.

"Wish those three old women would clear out," he complained. "I want to kiss you, Sally Carrol."

"Me, too."

They waited impatiently for the three bent figures to move off, and then she kissed him until the sky seemed to fade out, and all her smiles and tears to vanish in an ecstasy of eternal seconds.

Afterward they walked slowly back together, while on the corners twilight played at somnolent black-and-white checkers with the end of day.

"You'll be up about mid-January," he said, "and you've got to stay a month at least. It'll be slick. There's a winter carnival on, and if you've never really seen snow it'll be like fairyland to you. There'll be skating and skiing and tobogganing and sleigh riding and all sorts of torchlight parades on snowshoes. They haven't had one for years, so they're going to make it a knock-out."

"Will it be cold, Harry?" she asked suddenly.

"You certainly won't. You may freeze your nose, but you won't be shivery cold. It's hard and dry, you know."

"I guess I'm a summer child. I don't like any cold I've ever seen."

She broke off and they were both silent for a minute.

"Sally Carrol," he said very slowly, "what do you say to — March?"

"I say I love you."

"March?"

"March, Harry."

III

All night in the Pullman it was very cold. She rang for the porter to ask for another blanket, and when he couldn't give her one she tried vainly, by squeezing down into the bottom of her berth and doubling back the bedclothes, to snatch a few hours' sleep.

Sally Carrol wanted to look her best in the morning.

She rose at six and sliding uncomfortably into her clothes stumbled up to the diner for a cup of coffee. The snow had filtered into the vestibules and covered the floor with a slippery coating. It was intriguing, this cold, it crept in everywhere. Her breath was quite visible and she blew into the air with a naive enjoyment. Seated in the diner she stared out the window at white hills and valleys and scattered pines with each branch a green platter for a cold feast of snow.

Sometimes a solitary farmhouse would fly by, ugly and bleak and lone on the white waste; and with each one she had an instant of chill compassion for the souls shut in there waiting for spring.

As she left the diner and swayed back into the Pullman she experienced a surging rush of energy and wondered if she was feeling the bracing air of which Harry had spoken. This was the North, the North — her land now!

> *Then blow, ye winds, heigho!*
> *A-roving I will go.*[3]

---

3. *Then blow . . . I will go*: The opening lines of the chorus of a popular song frequently sung in elementary schools, "A Capital Ship," by Charles E. Carryl (1841-1920).

she chanted exultantly to herself.

"What's 'at?" inquired the porter politely.

"I said, 'Brush me off.'"

The long wires of the telegraph poles doubled: two tracks ran up beside the train – three – four; came a succession of white-roofed houses, a glimpse of a trolley car with frosted windows, streets – more streets – the city.

She stood for a dazed moment in the frosty station before she saw three fur-bundled figures descending upon her.

"There she is!"

"Oh, Sally Carrol!"

Sally Carrol dropped her bag.

"Hi!"

A faintly familiar icy-cold face kissed her, and then she was in a group of faces all apparently emitting great clouds of heavy smoke; she was shaking hands. There was Gordon, a short, eager man of thirty who looked like an amateur knocked-about model for Harry; and his wife Myra, a listless lady with flaxen hair under a fur automobile cap. Almost immediately Sally Carrol thought of her as vaguely Scandinavian. A cheerful chauffeur adopted her bag and amid ricochets of half phrases, exclamations and perfunctory, listless "my dear's" from Myra they swept each other from the station.

Then they were in a sedan bound through a crooked succession of snowy streets where dozens of little boys were hitching sleds behind grocery wagons and automobiles.

"Oh," cried Sally Carrol, "I want to do that! Can we, Harry?"

"That's for kids. But we might —"

"It looks like such a circus!" she said regretfully.

Home was a rambling frame house set on a white lap of snow, and there she met a big, gray-haired man of whom she approved, and a lady who was like an egg and who kissed her – these were Harry's parents. There was a breathless, indescribable hour crammed full of half sentences, hot water, bacon and eggs and confusion; and after that she was alone with Harry in the library asking him if she dared smoke.

It was a large room with a Madonna over the fireplace and rows upon rows of books in covers of light gold and dark gold and shiny red. All the chairs had little lace squares where one's head should rest, the couch was just comfortable, the books looked as if they had been read – some – and Sally Carrol had an instantaneous vision of the battered old library at home with her father's huge medical books and the oil paintings of her three great-uncles and the old couch that had been mended up for forty-five years and was still luxurious to dream in. This room struck her as being neither attractive nor particularly otherwise. It was simply a room with a lot of fairly expensive things in it that all looked about fifteen years old.

"What do you think of it up here?" demanded Harry eagerly. "Does it surprise you? Is it what you expected, I mean?"

"You are, Harry," she said quietly, and reached out her arms to him.

But after a brief kiss he seemed anxious to extort enthusiasm from her.

"The town, I mean. Do you like it? Can you feel the pep in the air?"

"Oh, Harry," she laughed, "you'll have to give me time. You can't just fling questions at me."

She puffed at her cigarette with a sigh of contentment.

"One thing I want to ask you," he began rather apologetically; "you Southerners put quite an emphasis on family and all that – not that it isn't quite all right, but you'll find it a little different here. I mean – you'll notice a lot of things that'll seem to you sort of vulgar display at first, Sally Carrol; but just remember that this is a three-generation town. Everybody has a father and about half of us have grandfathers. Back of that we don't go."

"Of course," she murmured.

"Our grandfathers, you see, founded the place, and a lot of them had to take some pretty queer jobs while they were doing the founding.

"For instance, there's one woman who at present is about the social model for the town; well, her father was the first public ash man – things like that."

"Why," said Sally Carrol, puzzled, "did you s'pose I was goin' to make remarks about people?"

"Not at all," interrupted Harry; "and I'm not apologizing for anyone either. It's just that – well, a Southern girl came up here last summer and said some unfortunate things, and – oh, I just thought I'd tell you."

Sally Carrol felt suddenly indignant – as though she had been unjustly spanked – but Harry evidently considered the subject closed, for he went on with a great surge of enthusiasm.

"It's carnival time, you know. First in ten years. And there's an ice palace they're building now that's the first they've had since eighty-five. Built out of blocks of the clearest ice they could find – on a tremendous scale."

She rose and walking to the window pushed aside the heavy Turkish portières and looked out.

"Oh!" she cried suddenly. "There's two little boys makin' a snow man! Harry, do you reckon I can go out an' help 'em?"

"You dream! Come here and kiss me."

She left the window rather reluctantly.

"I don't guess this is a very kissable climate, is it? I mean, it makes you so you don't want to sit round, doesn't it?"

"We're not going to. I've got a vacation for the first week you're here, and there's a dinner dance to-night."

"Oh, Harry," she confessed, subsiding in a heap, half in his lap, half in the pillows, "I sure do feel confused. I haven't got an idea whether I'll like it or not, an' I don't know what people expect or anythin'. You'll have to tell me, honey."

"I'll tell you," he said softly, "if you'll just tell me you're glad to be here."

"Glad – just awful glad!" she whispered, insinuating herself into his arms in her own peculiar way. "Where you are is home for me, Harry."

And as she said this she had the feeling for almost the first time in her life that she was acting a part.

That night, amid the gleaming candles of a dinner party where the men seemed to do most of the talking while the girls sat in a haughty and expensive aloofness, even Harry's presence on her left failed to make her feel at home.

"They're a good-looking crowd, don't you think?" he demanded. "Just look round. There's Spud Hubbard, tackle at Princeton last year, and Junie Morton—he and the red-haired fellow next to him were both Yale hockey captains; Junie was in my class. Why, the best athletes in the world come from these states round here. This is a man's country, I tell you. Look at John J. Fishburn!"

"Who's he?" asked Sally Carrol innocently.

"Don't you know?"

"I've heard the name."

"Greatest wheat man in the Northwest, and one of the greatest financiers in the country."

She turned suddenly to a voice on her right.

"I guess they forgot to introduce us. My name's Roger Patton."

"My name is Sally Carrol Happer," she said graciously.

"Yes, I know. Harry told me you were coming."

"You a relative?"

"No, I'm a professor."

"Oh," she laughed.

"At the university. You're from the South, aren't you?"

"Yes; Tarleton, Georgia."

She liked him immediately—a reddish-brown mustache under watery blue eyes that had something in them that these other eyes lacked, some quality of appreciation. They exchanged stray sentences through dinner and she made up her mind to see him again.

After coffee she was introduced to numerous good-looking young men who danced with conscious precision and seemed to take it for granted that she wanted to talk about nothing except Harry.

"Heavens," she thought, "they talk as if my being engaged made me older than they are—as if I'd tell their mothers on them!"

In the South an engaged girl, even a young married woman, expected the same amount of half-affectionate badinage[4] and flattery that would be accorded a débutante, but here all that seemed banned. One young man, after getting well started on the subject of Sally Carrol's eyes and how they had allured him ever since she entered the room, went into a violent confusion when he found she was visiting the Bellamys—was Harry's fiancée. He seemed to feel as though he had made some risqué and inexcusable blunder, became immediately formal and left her at the first opportunity.

She was rather glad when Roger Patton cut in on her, and suggested that they sit out a while.

"Well," he inquired, blinking cheerily, "how's Carmen from the South?"

---

4. **badinage:** Quick, witty conversation or small talk.

"Mighty fine. How's – how's Dangerous Dan McGrew?[5] Sorry, but he's the only Northerner I know much about."

He seemed to enjoy that.

"Of course," he confessed, "as a professor of literature I'm not supposed to have read Dangerous Dan McGrew."

"Are you a native?"

"No, I'm a Philadelphian. Imported from Harvard to teach seventeenth-century French. But I've been here ten years."

"Nine years, three hundred an' sixty-four days longer than me."

"Like it here?"

"Uh-huh. Sure do!"

"Really?"

"Well, why not? Don't I look as if I were havin' a good time?"

"I saw you look out the window a minute ago – and shiver."

"Just my imagination," laughed Sally Carrol. "I'm used to havin' everythin' quiet outside, an' sometimes I look out an' see a flurry of snow, an' it's just as if somethin' dead was movin'."

He nodded appreciatively.

"Ever been North before?"

"Spent two Julys in Asheville, North Carolina."

"Nice-looking crowd, aren't they?" suggested Patton, indicating the swirling floor.

Sally Carrol started. This had been Harry's remark.

"Sure are! They're – canine."

"What?"

She flushed.

"I'm sorry; that sounded worse than I meant it. You see I always think of people as feline or canine, irrespective of sex."

"Which are you?"

"I'm feline. So are you. So are most Southern men an' most of these girls here."

"What's Harry?"

"Harry's canine, distinctly. All the men I've met to-night seem to be canine."

"What does 'canine' imply? A certain conscious masculinity as opposed to subtlety?"

"Reckon so. I never analyzed it – only I just look at people an' say 'canine' or 'feline' right off. It's right absurd, I guess."

"Not at all. I'm interested. I used to have a theory about these people. I think they're freezing up."

"What?"

---

5. **Carmen from the South . . . Dangerous Dan McGrew:** Carmen, a Spanish name meaning "song," is most familiar as the name of the main character in the popular opera *Carmen*, by Georges Bizet (1838–1875). "The Shooting of Dan McGrew" was a popular narrative poem set during the Yukon gold rush by Robert W. Service (1874–1958).

"I think they're growing like Swedes — Ibsenesque, you know. Very gradually getting gloomy and melancholy. It's these long winters. Ever read any Ibsen?"[6]

She shook her head.

"Well, you find in his characters a certain brooding rigidity. They're righteous, narrow and cheerless, without infinite possibilities for great sorrow or joy."

"Without smiles or tears?"

"Exactly. That's my theory. You see there are thousands of Swedes up here. They come, I imagine, because the climate is very much like their own, and there's been a gradual mingling. They're probably not half a dozen here to-night, but — we've had four Swedish governors. Am I boring you?"

"I'm mighty interested."

"Your future sister-in-law is half Swedish. Personally I like her, but my theory is that Swedes react rather badly on us as a whole. Scandinavians, you know, have the largest suicide rate in the world."

"Why do you live here if it's so depressing?"

"Oh, it doesn't get me. I'm pretty well cloistered, and I suppose books mean more than people to me anyway."

"But writers all speak about the South being tragic. You know — Spanish señoritas, black hair and daggers an' hauntin' music."

He shook his head.

"No, the Northern races are the tragic races — they don't indulge in the cheering luxury of tears."

Sally Carrol thought of her graveyard. She supposed that that was vaguely what she had meant when she said it didn't depress her.

"The Italians are about the gayest people in the world — but it's a dull subject," he broke off. "Anyway, I want to tell you you're marrying a pretty fine man."

Sally Carrol was moved by an impulse of confidence.

"I know. I'm the sort of person who wants to be taken care of after a certain point, and I feel sure I will be."

"Shall we dance? You know," he continued as they rose, "it's encouraging to find a girl who knows what she's marrying for. Nine-tenths of them think of it as a sort of walking into a moving-picture sunset."

She laughed, and liked him immensely.

Two hours later on the way home she nestled near Harry in the back seat.

"Oh, Harry," she whispered, "it's so co-old!"

"But it's warm in here, darling girl."

"But outside it's cold; and oh, that howling wind!"

She buried her face deep in his fur coat and trembled involuntarily as his cold lips kissed the tip of her ear.

---

6. **Ibsen:** The Norwegian playwright Henrik Ibsen (1828–1906), known for his often grim portrayals of reality.

IV

The first week of her visit passed in a whirl. She had her promised toboggan ride at the back of an automobile through a chill January twilight. Swathed in furs she put in a morning tobogganing on the country-club hill; even tried skiing, to sail through the air for a glorious moment and then land in a tangled, laughing bundle on a soft snowdrift. She liked all the winter sports, except an afternoon spent snowshoeing over a glaring plain under pale yellow sunshine; but she soon realized that these things were for children—that she was being humored and that the enjoyment round her was only a reflection of her own.

At first the Bellamy family puzzled her. The men were reliable and she liked them; to Mr. Bellamy especially, with his iron-gray hair and energetic dignity, she took an immediate fancy once she found that he was born in Kentucky; this made of him a link between the old life and the new. But toward the women she felt a definite hostility. Myra, her future sister-in-law, seemed the essence of spiritless conventionality. Her conversation was so utterly devoid of personality that Sally Carrol, who came from a country where a certain amount of charm and assurance could be taken for granted in the women, was inclined to despise her.

"If those women aren't beautiful," she thought, "they're nothing. They just fade out when you look at them. They're glorified domestics. Men are the center of every mixed group."

Lastly there was Mrs. Bellamy, whom Sally Carrol detested. The first day's impression of an egg had been confirmed — an egg with a cracked, veiny voice and such an ungracious dumpiness of carriage that Sally Carrol felt that if she once fell she would surely scramble. In addition, Mrs. Bellamy seemed to typify the town in being innately hostile to strangers. She called Sally Carrol "Sally," and could not be persuaded that the double name was anything more than a tedious, ridiculous nickname. To Sally Carrol this shortening of her name was like presenting her to the public half clothed. She loved "Sally Carrol"; she loathed "Sally." She knew also that Harry's mother disapproved of her bobbed hair; and she had never dared smoke downstairs after that first day when Mrs. Bellamy had come into the library sniffing violently.

Of all the men she met she preferred Roger Patton, who was a frequent visitor at the house. He never again alluded to the Ibsenesque tendency of the populace, but when he came in one day and found her curled up on the sofa bent over Peer Gynt[7] he laughed and told her to forget what he'd said—that it was all rot.

And then one afternoon in her second week she and Harry hovered on the edge of a dangerously steep quarrel. She considered that he precipitated it entirely, though the Serbia in the case[8] was an unknown man who had not had his trousers pressed.

---

7. **Peer Gynt:** A poetic and satirical verse play by Henrik Ibsen. See note 6.
8. **the Serbia in the case:** The assassination of Archduke Franz Ferdinand, heir to the Austro-Hungarian throne, by members of a nationalist group in the small Balkan nation of Serbia set in motion a series of events that culminated in World War I, a global conflict that began in August 1914.

They had been walking homeward between mounds of high-piled snow and under a sun which Sally Carrol scarcely recognized. They passed a little girl done up in gray wool until she resembled a small Teddy bear, and Sally Carrol could not resist a gasp of maternal appreciation.

"Look! Harry!"

"What?"

"That little girl – did you see her face?"

"Yes, why?"

"It was red as a little strawberry. Oh, she was cute!"

"Why, your own face is almost as red as that already! Everybody's healthy here. We're out in the cold as soon as we're old enough to walk. Wonderful climate!"

She looked at him and had to agree. He was mighty healthy looking; so was his brother.

And she had noticed the new red in her own cheeks that very morning.

Suddenly their glances were caught and held and they stared for a moment at the street corner ahead of them. A man was standing there, his knees bent, his eyes gazing upward with a tense expression as though he were about to make a leap toward the chilly sky. And then they both exploded into a shout of laughter, for coming closer they discovered it had been a ludicrous momentary illusion produced by the extreme bagginess of the man's trousers.

"Reckon that's one on us," she laughed.

"He must be a Southerner, judging by those trousers," suggested Harry mischievously.

"Why, Harry!"

Her surprised look must have irritated him.

"Those damn Southerners!"

Sally Carrol's eyes flashed.

"Don't call 'em that!"

"I'm sorry, dear," said Harry, malignantly apologetic, "but you know what I think of them. They're sort of – sort of degenerates – not at all like the old Southerners. They've lived so long down there with all the colored people that they've gotten lazy and shiftless."

"Hush your mouth, Harry!" she cried angrily. "They're not! They may be lazy – anybody would be in that climate – but they're my best friends, an' I don't want to hear 'em criticized in any such sweepin' way. Some of 'em are the finest men in the world."

"Oh, I know. They're all right when they come North to college, but of all the hangdog, ill-dressed, slovenly lot I ever saw a bunch of small-town Southerners are the worst!"

Sally Carrol was clenching her gloved hands and biting her lip furiously.

"Why," continued Harry, "there was one in my class at New Haven and we all thought that at last we'd found the true type of Southern aristocrat, but it turned out that he wasn't an aristocrat at all – just the son of a Northern carpetbagger who owned about all the cotton round Birmingham."

"A Southerner wouldn't talk the way you're talking now," she said evenly.

"They haven't the energy!"

"Or the somethin' else."

"I'm sorry, Sally Carrol, but I've heard you say yourself that you'd never marry —"

"That's quite different. I told you I wouldn't want to tie my life to any of the boys that are round Tarleton now, but I never made any sweepin' generalities."

They walked along in silence.

"I probably spread it on a bit thick, Sally Carrol. I'm sorry."

She nodded, but made no answer. Five minutes later as they stood in the hallway she suddenly threw her arms round him.

"Oh, Harry," she cried, her eyes full of tears, "let's get married next week. I'm afraid of having fusses like that. I'm afraid, Harry. It wouldn't be that way if we were married."

But Harry being in the wrong was still irritated.

"That'd be idiotic. We decided on March."

The tears in Sally Carrol's eyes faded; her expression hardened slightly.

"Very well — I suppose I shouldn't have said that."

Harry melted.

"Dear little nut!" he cried. "Come and kiss me and let's forget."

That very night at the end of a vaudeville performance the orchestra played Dixie, and Sally Carrol felt something stronger and more enduring than her tears and smiles of the day brim up inside her. She leaned forward, gripping the arms of her chair until her face grew crimson.

"Sort of get you, dear?" whispered Harry.

But she did not hear him. To the spirited throb of the violins and the inspiring beat of the kettledrums her own old ghosts were marching by and on into the darkness, and as fifes whistled and sighed in the low encore they seemed so nearly out of sight that she could have waved good-by.

> *Away, away, away down South in Dixie!*
> *Away, away, away down South in Dixie!*[9]

V

It was a particularly cold night. A sudden thaw had nearly cleared the streets the day before, but now they were traversed again with a powdery wraith of loose snow that traveled in wavy lines before the feet of the wind and filled the lower air with a fine-particled mist. There was no sky — only a dark, ominous tent that draped in the tops of the streets and was in reality a vast approaching army of snowflakes — while over it all, chilling away the comfort from the brown-and-green glow of lighted windows and muffling the steady trot of the horse pulling their sleigh, interminably washed the north wind. It was a dismal town after all, she thought — dismal.

Sometimes at night it had seemed to her as though no one lived here — they had all gone long ago, leaving lighted houses to be covered in time by tombing heaps of sleet. Oh, if there should be snow on her grave! To be beneath great piles of it all winter long,

---

9. *Away . . . Dixie!*: The chorus of "Dixie," also known as "I Wish I Was in Dixie," the unofficial anthem of the Confederacy and the song that made *Dixie* a synonym for the South.

where even her headstone would be a light shadow against light shadows. Her grave – a grave that should be flower-strewn and washed with sun and rain.

She thought again of those isolated country houses that her train had passed, and of the life there the long winter through – the ceaseless glare through the windows, the crust forming on the soft drifts of snow, finally the slow, cheerless melting and the harsh spring of which Roger Patton had told her. Her spring – to lose it forever – with its lilacs and the lazy sweetness it stirred in her heart. She was laying away that spring – afterward she would lay away that sweetness.

With a gradual insistence the storm broke. Sally Carrol felt a film of flakes melt quickly on her eyelashes and Harry reached over a furry arm and drew down her complicated flannel cap. Then the small flakes came in skirmish line and the horse bent his neck patiently as a transparency of white appeared momentarily on his coat.

"Oh, he's cold, Harry," she said quickly.

"Who? The horse? Oh, no, he isn't. He likes it!"

After another ten minutes they turned a corner and came in sight of their destination. On a tall hill outlined in vivid glaring green against the wintry sky stood the ice palace. It was three stories in the air, with battlements and embrasures and narrow icicled windows, and the innumerable electric lights inside made a gorgeous transparency of the great central hall. Sally Carrol clutched Harry's hand under the fur robe.

"It's beautiful!" he cried excitedly. "My golly, it's beautiful, isn't it? They haven't had one here since eighty-five!"

Somehow the notion of there not having been one since eighty-five oppressed her. Ice was a ghost, and this mansion of it was surely peopled by those shades of the eighties, with pale faces and blurred snow-filled hair.

"Come on, dear," said Harry.

She followed him out of the sleigh and waited while he hitched the horse. A party of four – Gordon, Myra, Roger Patton and another girl – drew up beside them with a mighty jingle of bells. There was quite a crowd already, bundled in fur or sheepskin, shouting and calling to each other as they moved through the snow, which was now so thick that people could scarcely be distinguished a few yards away.

"It's a hundred and seventy feet tall," Harry was saying to a muffled figure beside him as they trudged toward the entrance; "covers six thousand square yards."

She caught snatches of conversation: "One main hall" – "walls twenty to forty inches thick" – "and the ice cave has almost a mile of" – "This Canuck[10] who built it —"

They found their way inside, and dazed by the magic of the great crystal walls Sally Carrol found herself repeating over and over two lines from Kubla Khan:

> It was a miracle of rare device,
> A sunny pleasure-dome with caves of ice![11]

---

10. **Canuck:** Informal and usually derogatory term for a Canadian.
11. **It was . . . caves of ice!:** The lines are from "Kubla Khan" (1816), a famous visionary poem by the English writer Samuel Taylor Coleridge (1772–1834).

In the great glittering cavern with the dark shut out she took a seat on a wooden bench, and the evening's oppression lifted. Harry was right — it was beautiful; and her gaze traveled the smooth surface of the walls, the blocks for which had been selected for their purity and clearness to obtain this opalescent, translucent effect.

"Look! Here we go — oh, boy!" cried Harry.

A band in a far corner struck up Hail, Hail, the Gang's All Here![12] which echoed over to them in wild muddled acoustics, and then the lights suddenly went out; silence seemed to flow down the icy sides and sweep over them. Sally Carrol could still see her white breath in the darkness, and a dim row of pale faces over on the other side.

The music eased to a sighing complaint, and from outside drifted in the full-throated resonant chant of the marching clubs. It grew louder like some paean of a viking tribe traversing an ancient wild; it swelled — they were coming nearer; then a row of torches appeared, and another and another, and keeping time with their moccasined feet a long column of gray-mackinawed[13] figures swept in, snowshoes slung at their shoulders, torches soaring and flickering as their voices rose along the great walls.

The gray column ended and another followed, the light streaming luridly this time over red toboggan caps and flaming crimson mackinaws, and as it entered it took up the refrain; then came a long platoon of blue and white, of green, of white, of brown and yellow.

"Those white ones are the Wacouta Club," whispered Harry eagerly. "Those are the men you've met round at dances."

The volume of the voices grew; the great cavern was a phantasmagoria of torches waving in great banks of fire, of colors and the rhythm of soft leather steps. The leading column turned and halted, platoon deployed in front of platoon until the whole procession made a solid flag of flame, and then from thousands of voices burst a mighty shout that filled the air like a crash of thunder and sent the torches wavering. It was magnificent, it was tremendous! To Sally Carrol it was the North offering sacrifices on some mighty altar to the gray pagan God of Snow.

As the shout died the band struck up again and there came more singing, and then long reverberating cheers by each club. She sat very quiet listening while the staccato cries rent the stillness; and then she started, for there was a volley of explosion, and great clouds of smoke went up here and there through the cavern — the flashlight photographers at work — and the council was over. With the band at their head the clubs formed in column once more, took up their chant and began to march out.

"Come on!" shouted Harry. "We want to see the labyrinths downstairs before they turn the lights off!"

They all rose and started toward the chute — Harry and Sally Carrol in the lead, her little glove buried in his big fur gauntlet. At the bottom of the chute was a long empty room of ice with the ceiling so low that they had to stoop — and their hands were parted. Before she realized what he intended Harry had darted down one of the half dozen

---

12. **Hail, Hail, the Gang's All Here!**: The phrase, which had earlier appeared in the chorus of the American standard "Alabama Jubilee" (1915), was the title of a popular song written in 1917 and set to a rollicking tune originally composed by Arthur Sullivan for the comic opera *The Pirates of Penzance* (1879).
13. **gray-mackinawed**: A mackinaw is a short coat or jacket, usually made of heavy wool.

glittering passages that opened into the room, and was only a vague receding blot against the green shimmer.

"Harry!" she called.

"Come on!" he cried back.

She looked round the empty chamber; the rest of the party had evidently decided to go home, were already outside somewhere in the blundering snow. She hesitated and then darted in after Harry.

"Harry!" she shouted.

She had reached a turning point thirty feet down; she heard a faint muffled answer far to the left, and with a touch of panic fled toward it. She passed another turning, two more yawning alleys.

"Harry!"

No answer. She started to run straight forward, and then turned like lightning and sped back the way she had come, enveloped in a sudden ice terror.

She reached a turn — was it here? — took the left and came to what should have been the outlet into the long low room, but it was only another glittering passage with darkness at the end. She called again, but the walls gave back a flat lifeless echo with no reverberations. Retracing her steps she turned another corner, this time following a wide passage. It was like the green lane between the parted waters of the Red Sea,[14] like a damp vault connecting empty tombs.

She slipped a little now as she walked, for ice had formed on the bottom of her overshoes; she had to run her gloves along the half-slippery, half-sticky walls to keep her balance.

"Harry!"

Still no answer. The sound she made bounced mockingly down to the end of the passage.

Then on an instant the lights went out and she was in complete darkness. She gave a small frightened cry and sank down into a cold little heap on the ice. She felt her left knee do something as she fell, but she scarcely noticed it as some deep terror far greater than any fear of being lost settled upon her. She was alone with this presence that came out of the North, the dreary loneliness that rose from ice-bound whalers in the Arctic seas, from smokeless trackless wastes where were strewn the whitened bones of adventure. It was an icy breath of death; it was rolling down low across the land to clutch at her.

With a furious despairing energy she rose again and started blindly down the darkness. She must get out. She might be lost in here for days, freeze to death and lie embedded in the ice like corpses she had read of, kept perfectly preserved until the melting of a glacier. Harry probably thought she had left with the others — he had gone by now; no one would know until late next day. She reached pitifully for the wall. Forty inches thick they had said — forty inches thick!

"Oh!"

---

14. **parted waters of the Red Sea:** In the biblical account, God gives Moses the power to part the Red Sea, allowing the Israelites to escape from Egypt to the promised land (Exodus 14).

On both sides of her along the walls she felt things creeping, damp souls that haunted this palace, this town, this North.

"Oh, send somebody – send somebody!" she cried aloud.

Clark Darrow – he would understand; or Joe Ewing; she couldn't be left here to wander forever – to be frozen, heart, body and soul. This her – this Sally Carrol. Why, she was a happy thing. She was a happy little girl. She liked warmth and summer and Dixie. These things were foreign – foreign.

"You're not crying," something said aloud. "You'll never cry any more. Your tears would just freeze; all tears freeze up here!"

She sprawled full length on the ice.

"O God!" she faltered.

A long single file of minutes went by, and with a great weariness she felt her eyes closing. Then someone seemed to sit down near her and take her face in warm soft hands. She looked up gratefully.

"Why, it's Margery Lee," she crooned softly to herself. "I knew you'd come." It really was Margery Lee, and she was just as Sally Carrol had known she would be, with a young white brow and wide welcoming eyes and a hoop skirt of some soft material that was quite comforting to rest on.

"Margery Lee."

It was getting darker now and darker – all those tombstones ought to be repainted, sure enough, only that would spoil 'em of course. Still, you ought to be able to see 'em.

Then after a succession of moments that went fast and then slow, but seemed to be ultimately resolving themselves into a multitude of blurred rays converging toward a pale yellow sun, she heard a great cracking noise break her new-found stillness.

It was the sun, it was a light; a torch, and a torch beyond that, and another one, and voices; a face took flesh below the torch, heavy arms raised her and she felt something on her cheek, it felt wet. Someone had seized her and was rubbing her face with snow. How ridiculous – with snow!

"Sally Carrol! Sally Carrol!"

It was Dangerous Dan McGrew; and two other faces she didn't know.

"Child, child! We've been looking for you two hours. Harry's half crazy!"

Things came rushing back into place – the singing, the torches, the great shout of the marching clubs. She squirmed in Patton's arms and gave a long low cry.

"Oh, I want to get out of here! I'm going back home. Take me home" – her voice rose to a scream that sent a chill to Harry's heart as he came racing down the next passage – "to-morrow!" she cried with delirious, unrestrained passion – "To-morrow! To-morrow! To-morrow!"

VI

The wealth of golden sunlight poured a quite enervating yet oddly comforting heat over the house where day long it faced the dusty stretch of road. Two birds were making a great to-do in a cool spot found among the branches of a tree next door, and down the

street a colored woman was announcing herself melodiously as a purveyor of strawberries. It was April afternoon.

Sally Carrol Happer, resting her chin on her arm and her arm on an old window seat,
gazed sleepily down over the spangled dust whence the heat waves were rising for the
first time this spring. She was watching a very ancient flivver turn a perilous corner and
rattle and groan to a jolting stop at the end of the walk. She made no sound, and in a
minute a strident familiar whistle rent the air. Sally Carrol smiled and blinked.

"Good mawnin'."

A head appeared tortuously from under the car top below.

" 'Taint mawnin', Sally Carrol."

"Sure enough," she said in affected surprise. "I guess maybe not."

"What you doin'?"

"Eatin' green peach. 'Spect to die any minute."

Clark twisted himself a last impossible notch to get a view of her face.

"Water's warm as a kettla steam, Sally Carrol. Wanta go swimmin'?"

"Hate to move," sighed Sally Carrol lazily, "but I reckon so."

[1920]

William Faulkner

[1897-1962]

William Faulkner was born William Cuthbert Falkner in New Albany,
Mississippi, on September 25, 1897. He was the first of four sons born to
Murry Falkner, a railroad administrator,
and Maud Butler Falkner. Faulkner was
named after his colorful great-grandfather,
William Clark Falkner, a Confederate colonel in the Civil War, a successful banker,
businessman, lawyer, and politician, and a
prolific author best known for his popular
novel *The White Rose of Memphis* (1881). As
a child, Faulkner reportedly exclaimed: "I
want to be a writer just like my great-grand-
daddy." He was educated in Oxford, home
of the University of Mississippi, where his
family moved in 1902. Bored with school,
he dropped out after the eleventh grade,
preferring to write verse and study poetry
with his older friend and mentor, Phil
Stone, a Yale graduate who introduced Faulkner to modernist literature. He
proposed to a local girl, Estelle Oldham, but her parents flatly rejected the
match, and she married another man early in 1918. Devastated by the loss,
Faulkner tried to enlist in the U.S. Air Corps. After he was rejected because
he was too short, he decided to try the Royal Air Force, which had a recruiting

William Faulkner

This photograph was
taken to accompany a
widely circulated news-
paper article on one of
Faulkner's few commer-
cial successes, *Sanctuary*
(1931). Uncomfortable
with the attention gener-
ated by the scandalous
novel, Faulkner wore an
old tweed jacket and
slacks spattered with
paint to the publicity
shoot.

office in New York City. Faulkner, who passed himself off as British, partly by adding a *u* to his last name, was enlisted as a cadet and sent to Canada. The war ended before he completed his pilot training there, and in December 1918 Faulkner returned to Oxford, walking with a cane and telling tall tales about his war wounds and exploits in combat.

Faulkner was aimless and adrift until he began to devote himself seriously to writing. As a "war veteran," he was allowed to enroll as a special student at the University of Mississippi. He contributed stories and verse to the campus newspaper, and one of his poems was published in the national magazine the *New Republic*. Faulkner dropped out of the university after three semesters and took a series of jobs, including one in a bookstore in New York City. Back in Oxford in 1922, he went to work as the university postmaster, but he was fired for losing and misplacing mail. With the help of Phil Stone, Faulkner published a collection of his poetry, *The Marble Faun* (1924). In 1925, he moved to New Orleans, where he was a contributor to the *Times-Picayune* and published essays and sketches in a new literary magazine, the *Double Dealer*. As Faulkner humorously recalled, he also became acquainted with the most prominent contributor to the magazine: "Met a man named Sherwood Anderson. Said, 'Why not write novels? Maybe won't have to work.'" Faulkner consequently wrote *Soldier's Pay*, a novel about a wounded aviator that was published with Anderson's help in 1926. After returning from a trip to Europe, he wrote a satirical novel about writers and intellectuals in New Orleans, *Mosquitoes* (1927). Anderson, however, gave Faulkner some additional advice that strongly shaped his literary career. He urged Faulkner to write about his native region in north Mississippi, advice that he took to heart in his next novel, *Sartoris* (1929). "Beginning with *Sartoris* I discovered that my own little postage stamp of native soil was worth writing about and that I would never live long enough to exhaust it," he observed in an interview in 1955. "It opened up a gold mine of other people, so I created a cosmos of my own."

The cosmos that Faulkner created was Yoknapatawpha County, Mississippi, the setting for most of his later fiction. Even as he found his true subject matter, he began to experiment with language and narrative structure in *The Sound and the Fury* (1929). Although not all the reviews were favorable, the *New York Times* called it a "daring experiment" written by a major new talent in American literature. Meanwhile, Faulkner had been seeing Estelle Oldham and her two sons during his visits to Oxford. Following her divorce, they were married in 1929. While working on the night shift at the university power plant, Faulkner swiftly wrote another experimental novel, *As I Lay Dying* (1930). After he and Estelle bought a rundown estate in Oxford, Faulkner set about earning money to support them by writing magazine stories, which became his primary source of income. His first collection of stories, *These Thirteen*, appeared in 1931, the year he published *Sanctuary*. The sensational novel, whose plot revolves around the kidnapping and rape of a coed by a bootlegger, was made into a movie and led to the first of what Faulkner called his numerous "tours of duty" as a screenwriter in Hollywood. Recoiling from producing a work designed to "sell," as he candidly described *Sanctuary*, Faulkner wrote his most

Faulkner sees with the eyes of the artist and can make us see what is here and at the same time see through it to the truth about it, the human truth.
–Eudora Welty

complex work to date, *Light in August* (1932), set in Depression-era Mississippi. He continued to explore issues of race, class, and the burden of Southern history in his ambitious modernist novel about the Civil War and its aftermath, *Absalom, Absalom!* (1936). Now regarded as one of his masterpieces, the novel sold poorly, and Faulkner followed it with *The Unvanquished* (1938), a novel based on a series of popular Civil War stories he had earlier published in the *Saturday Evening Post.*

Faulkner's career and reputation fluctuated widely during the following decade. Although he and his wife now had a daughter, their first daughter had died shortly after birth, and the couple's marriage was increasingly strained. The hard work and the constant effort to make money also began to take a toll on Faulkner, a heavy drinker who occasionally checked himself into a sanatorium in Oxford to recover from his binges. Nonetheless, he continued to write, though at a slower pace. In 1939, he published *The Wild Palms,* his best-selling novel to date, and began work on the first volume of a trilogy of novels about a poor white family of sharecroppers, *The Hamlet* (1940). (He did not complete the so-called Snopes trilogy until the late 1950s, when he published *The Town* and *The Mansion.*) He then revised a series of stories into what he described as a "novel" about the troubled history of racial relations in the South, *Go Down, Moses* (1942). With the sale of his books slumping and many of his works now out of print, Faulkner returned to work as a screenwriter in Hollywood. But his literary reputation received a major boost from the publication of *The Portable Faulkner* (1946), edited by the influential critic Malcolm Cowley. The Modern Library subsequently began to reissue Faulkner's earlier works, and his next novel, *Intruder in the Dust* (1948), was made into a major motion picture by MGM.

In his final years, Faulkner gained prominence as both a writer and as a spokesman for the South. In 1950, he was awarded the Nobel Prize for Literature for his "powerful and independent contribution in America's new literature of the novel," as the citation read, and his fame was heightened by the electrifying acceptance speech he delivered at the awards ceremony in Stockholm. As the struggle for civil rights intensified during the 1950s, Faulkner felt duty-bound to speak out against racial segregation, though his moderate position was attacked by both white segregationists and black activists. The reviews of his late works were mixed, but he was awarded the Pulitzer Prize for *A Fable* (1954) and for his final novel, *The Reivers* (1962). Shortly after it was published, Faulkner was injured in a fall from a horse in Oxford. While at a clinic, where he was also treated for alcoholism, he died of a heart attack on July 6, 1962.

Reading Faulkner's "That Evening Sun." This story was first published as "That Evening Sun Go Down," an even more direct reference to the opening line of W. C. Handy's famous song "St. Louis Blues" (1914): "I hate to see that evening sun go down." (Handy, the famous black trumpet player and "father of the blues," had frequently brought his band down from Memphis to perform at dances the teenage Faulkner attended in

Oxford, Mississippi.) The story first appeared in March 1931 in the lively *American Mercury*, a monthly magazine of literature and often satirical commentary on American life that also published the work of Sherwood Anderson, F. Scott Fitzgerald, and Sinclair Lewis. Despite the iconoclastic nature of the magazine, its editor, H. L. Mencken, was concerned that readers would object to a character named "Jesus." Mencken consequently asked Faulkner to alter the name and to soften the references to pregnancy in the story. Faulkner reluctantly agreed to the changes, but when he included the story in his first collection, *These Thirteen*, he shortened the title and restored both the name "Jesus" and the original language about the pregnancy of Jesus's wife, Nancy. "That Evening Sun," which includes the main characters from Faulkner's novel about the Compson family, *The Sound and the Fury* (1929), is narrated by Quentin Compson, who looks back on an episode from his childhood. The harrowing story of the isolated and vulnerable Nancy reveals the differing perspectives of adults and children, as well as the sharp contrasts between the worlds of white and black people in the South. The text is taken from *These Thirteen* (1931).

bedfordstmartins.com/ americanlit for research links on Faulkner

THAT EVENING SUN[1]

I

Monday is no different from any other week day in Jefferson now. The streets are paved now, and the telephone and electric companies are cutting down more and more of the shade trees — the water oaks, the maples and locusts and elms — to make room for iron poles bearing clusters of bloated and ghostly and bloodless grapes, and we have a city laundry which makes the rounds on Monday morning, gathering the bundles of clothes into bright-colored, specially-made motor cars: the soiled wearing of a whole week now flees apparitionlike behind alert and irritable electric horns, with a long diminishing noise of rubber and asphalt like tearing silk, and even the Negro women who still take in white people's washing after the old custom, fetch and deliver it in automobiles.

But fifteen years ago, on Monday morning the quiet dusty, shady streets would be full of Negro women with, balanced on their steady, turbaned heads, bundles of clothes tied up in sheets, almost as large as cotton bales, carried so without touch of hand between the kitchen door of the white house and the blackened washpot beside a cabin door in Negro Hollow.[2]

Nancy would set her bundle on the top of her head, then upon the bundle in turn she would set the black straw sailor hat which she wore winter and summer. She was tall,

---

1. **That Evening Sun:** Faulkner took the title of the story, which he first published as "That Evening Sun Go Down," from the opening of one of the most famous of all blues songs, W. C. Handy's "St. Louis Blues" (1914): "I hate to see that evening sun go down / I hate to see that evening sun go down / 'Cause my baby, he's done left this town."
2. **Negro Hollow:** A name given to the segregated sections of southern towns inhabited by African Americans.

with a high, sad face sunken a little where her teeth were missing. Sometimes we would go a part of the way down the lane and across the pasture with her, to watch the balanced bundle and the hat that never bobbed nor wavered, even when she walked down into the ditch and up the other side and stooped through the fence. She would go down on her hands and knees and crawl through the gap, her head rigid, uptilted, the bundle steady as a rock or a balloon, and rise to her feet again and go on.

Sometimes the husbands of the washing women would fetch and deliver the clothes, but Jesus never did that for Nancy, even before father told him to stay away from our house, even when Dilsey was sick and Nancy would come to cook for us.

And then about half the time we'd have to go down the lane to Nancy's cabin and tell her to come on and cook breakfast. We would stop at the ditch, because father told us to not have anything to do with Jesus — he was a short black man, with a razor scar down his face — and we would throw rocks at Nancy's house until she came to the door, leaning her head around it without any clothes on.

"What yawl mean, chunking my house?" Nancy said. "What you little devils mean?"

"Father says for you to come on and get breakfast," Caddy said. "Father says it's over a half an hour now, and you've got to come this minute."

"I aint studying no breakfast," Nancy said. "I going to get my sleep out."

"I bet you're drunk," Jason said. "Father says you're drunk. Are you drunk, Nancy?"

"Who says I is?" Nancy said. "I got to get my sleep out. I aint studying no breakfast."

So after a while we quit chunking the cabin and went back home. When she finally came, it was too late for me to go to school. So we thought it was whisky until that day they arrested her again and they were taking her to jail and they passed Mr Stovall. He was the cashier in the bank and a deacon in the Baptist church, and Nancy began to say:

"When you going to pay me, white man? When you going to pay me, white man? It's been three times now since you paid me a cent —" Mr Stovall knocked her down, but she kept on saying, "When you going to pay me, white man? It's been three times now since —" until Mr Stovall kicked her in the mouth with his heel and the marshal caught Mr Stovall back, and Nancy lying in the street, laughing. She turned her head and spat out some blood and teeth and said, "It's been three times now since he paid me a cent."

That was how she lost her teeth, and all that day they told about Nancy and Mr Stovall, and all that night the ones that passed the jail could hear Nancy singing and yelling. They could see her hands holding to the window bars, and a lot of them stopped along the fence, listening to her and to the jailer trying to make her stop. She didn't shut up until almost daylight, when the jailer began to hear a bumping and scraping upstairs and he went up there and found Nancy hanging from the window bar. He said that it was cocaine and not whisky, because no nigger would try to commit suicide unless he was full of cocaine, because a nigger full of cocaine wasn't a nigger any longer.

The jailer cut her down and revived her; then he beat her, whipped her. She had hung herself with her dress. She had fixed it all right, but when they arrested her she didn't have on anything except a dress and so she didn't have anything to tie her hands with and she couldn't make her hands let go of the window ledge. So the jailer heard the noise and ran up there and found Nancy hanging from the window, stark naked, her belly already swelling out a little, like a little balloon.

When Dilsey was sick in her cabin and Nancy was cooking for us, we could see her apron swelling out; that was before father told Jesus to stay away from the house. Jesus was in the kitchen, sitting behind the stove, with his razor scar on his black face like a piece of dirty string. He said it was a watermelon that Nancy had under her dress.

"It never come off of your vine, though," Nancy said.

"Off of what vine?" Caddy said.

"I can cut down the vine it did come off of," Jesus said.

"What makes you want to talk like that before these chillen?" Nancy said. "Whyn't you go on to work? You done et. You want Mr Jason to catch you hanging around his kitchen, talking that way before these chillen?"

"Talking what way?" Caddy said. "What vine?"

"I cant hang around white man's kitchen," Jesus said. "But white man can hang around mine. White man can come in my house, but I cant stop him. When white man want to come in my house, I aint got no house. I cant stop him, but he cant kick me outen it. He cant do that."

Dilsey was still sick in her cabin. Father told Jesus to stay off our place. Dilsey was still sick. It was a long time. We were in the library after supper.

"Isn't Nancy through in the kitchen yet?" mother said. "It seems to me that she has had plenty of time to have finished the dishes."

"Let Quentin go and see," father said. "Go and see if Nancy is through, Quentin. Tell her she can go on home."

I went to the kitchen. Nancy was through. The dishes were put away and the fire was out. Nancy was sitting in a chair, close to the cold stove. She looked at me.

"Mother wants to know if you are through," I said.

"Yes," Nancy said. She looked at me. "I done finished." She looked at me.

"What is it?" I said. "What is it?"

"I aint nothing but a nigger," Nancy said. "It aint none of my fault."

She looked at me, sitting in the chair before the cold stove, the sailor hat on her head. I went back to the library. It was the cold stove and all, when you think of a kitchen being warm and busy and cheerful. And with a cold stove and the dishes all put away, and nobody wanting to eat at that hour.

"Is she through?" mother said.

"Yessum," I said.

"What is she doing?" mother said.

"She's not doing anything. She's through."

"I'll go and see," father said.

"Maybe she's waiting for Jesus to come and take her home," Caddy said.

"Jesus is gone," I said. Nancy told us how one morning she woke up and Jesus was gone.

"He quit me," Nancy said. "Done gone to Memphis, I reckon. Dodging them city *po*lice for a while, I reckon."

"And a good riddance," father said. "I hope he stays there."

"Nancy's scaired of the dark," Jason said.

"So are you," Caddy said.

"I'm not," Jason said.

"Scairy cat," Caddy said.

"I'm not," Jason said.

"You, Candace!" mother said. Father came back.

"I am going to walk down the lane with Nancy," he said. "She says that Jesus is back."

"Has she seen him?" mother said.

"No. Some Negro sent her word that he was back in town. I wont be long."

"You'll leave me alone, to take Nancy home?" mother said. "Is her safety more precious to you than mine?"

"I wont be long," father said.

"You'll leave these children unprotected, with that Negro about?"

"I'm going too," Caddy said. "Let me go, Father."

"What would he do with them, if he were unfortunate enough to have them?" father said.

"I want to go, too," Jason said.

"Jason!" mother said. She was speaking to father. You could tell that by the way she said the name. Like she believed that all day father had been trying to think of doing the thing she wouldn't like the most, and that she knew all the time that after a while he would think of it. I stayed quiet, because father and I both knew that mother would want him to make me stay with her if she just thought of it in time. So father didn't look at me. I was the oldest. I was nine and Caddy was seven and Jason was five.

"Nonsense," father said. "We wont be long."

Nancy had her hat on. We came to the lane. "Jesus always been good to me," Nancy said. "Whenever he had two dollars, one of them was mine." We walked in the lane. "If I can just get through the lane," Nancy said, "I be all right then."

The lane was always dark. "This is where Jason got scared on Hallowe'en," Caddy said.

"I didn't," Jason said.

"Cant Aunt Rachel do anything with him?" father said. Aunt Rachel was old. She lived in a cabin beyond Nancy's, by herself. She had white hair and she smoked a pipe in the door, all day long; she didn't work any more. They said she was Jesus' mother. Sometimes she said she was and sometimes she said she wasn't any kin to Jesus.

"Yes you did," Caddy said. "You were scairder than Frony. You were scairder than T.P. even. Scairder than niggers."

"Cant nobody do nothing with him," Nancy said. "He say I done woke up the devil in him and aint but one thing going to lay it down again."

"Well, he's gone now," father said. "There's nothing for you to be afraid of now. And if you'd just let white men alone."

"Let what white men alone?" Caddy said. "How let them alone?"

"He aint gone nowhere," Nancy said. "I can feel him. I can feel him now, in this lane. He hearing us talk, every word, hid somewhere, waiting. I aint seen him, and I aint going to see him again but once more, with that razor in his mouth. That razor on that string down his back, inside his shirt. And then I aint going to be even surprised."

"I wasn't scaired," Jason said.

"If you'd behave yourself, you'd have kept out of this," father said. "But it's all right now. He's probably in St Louis now. Probably got another wife by now and forgot all about you."

"If he has, I better not find out about it," Nancy said. "I'd stand there right over them, and every time he wropped her, I'd cut that arm off. I'd cut his head off and I'd slit her belly and I'd shove —"

"Hush," father said.

"Slit whose belly, Nancy?" Caddy said.

"I wasn't scaired," Jason said. "I'd walk right down this lane by myself."

"Yah," Caddy said. "You wouldn't dare to put your foot down in it if we were not here too."

II

Dilsey was still sick, so we took Nancy home every night until mother said, "How much longer is this going on? I to be left alone in this big house while you take home a frightened Negro?"

We fixed a pallet in the kitchen for Nancy. One night we waked up, hearing the sound. It was not singing and it was not crying, coming up the dark stairs. There was a light in mother's room and we heard father going down the hall, down the back stairs, and Caddy and I went into the hall. The floor was cold. Our toes curled away from it while we listened to the sound. It was like singing and it wasn't like singing, like the sounds that Negroes make.

Then it stopped and we heard father going down the back stairs, and we went to the head of the stairs. Then the sound began again, in the stairway, not loud, and we could see Nancy's eyes halfway up the stairs, against the wall. They looked like cat's eyes do, like a big cat against the wall, watching us. When we came down the steps to where she was, she quit making the sound again, and we stood there until father came back up from the kitchen, with his pistol in his hand. He went back down with Nancy and they came back with Nancy's pallet.

We spread the pallet in our room. After the light in mother's room went off, we could see Nancy's eyes again. "Nancy," Caddy whispered, "are you asleep Nancy?"

Nancy whispered something. It was oh or no, I dont know which. Like nobody had made it, like it came from nowhere and went nowhere, until it was like Nancy was not there at all; that I had looked so hard at her eyes on the stairs that they had got printed on my eyeballs, like the sun does when you have closed your eyes and there is no sun. "Jesus," Nancy whispered. "Jesus."

"Was it Jesus?" Caddy said. "Did he try to come into the kitchen?"

"Jesus," Nancy said. Like this: Jeeeeeeeeeeeeeeeesus, until the sound went out, like a match or a candle does.

"It's the other Jesus she means," I said.

"Can you see us, Nancy?" Caddy whispered. "Can you see our eyes too?"

"I aint nothing but a nigger," Nancy said. "God knows. God knows."

"What did you see down there in the kitchen?" Caddy whispered. "What tried to get in?"

"God knows," Nancy said. We could see her eyes. "God knows."

Dilsey got well. She cooked dinner. "You'd better stay in bed a day or two longer," father said.

"What for?" Dilsey said. "If I had been a day later, this place would be to rack and ruin. Get on out of here now, and let me get my kitchen straight again."

Dilsey cooked supper too. And that night, just before dark, Nancy came into the kitchen.

"How do you know he's back?" Dilsey said. "You aint seen him."

"Jesus is a nigger," Jason said.

"I can feel him," Nancy said. "I can feel him laying yonder in the ditch."

"Tonight?" Dilsey said. "Is he there tonight?"

"Dilsey's a nigger too," Jason said.

"You try to eat something," Dilsey said.

"I dont want nothing," Nancy said.

"I aint a nigger," Jason said.

"Drink some coffee," Dilsey said. She poured a cup of coffee for Nancy. "Do you know he's out there tonight? How come you know it's tonight?"

"I know," Nancy said. "He's there, waiting. I know. I done lived with him too long. I know what he is fixing to do fore he know it himself."

"Drink some coffee," Dilsey said. Nancy held the cup to her mouth and blew into the cup. Her mouth pursed out like a spreading adder's, like a rubber mouth, like she had blown all the color out of her lips with blowing the coffee.

"I aint a nigger," Jason said. "Are you a nigger, Nancy?"

"I hellborn, child," Nancy said. "I wont be nothing soon. I going back where I come from soon."

III

She began to drink the coffee. While she was drinking, holding the cup in both hands, she began to make the sound again. She made the sound into the cup and the coffee sploshed out onto her hands and her dress. Her eyes looked at us and she sat there, her elbows on her knees, holding the cup in both hands, looking at us across the wet cup, making the sound.

"Look at Nancy," Jason said. "Nancy cant cook for us now. Dilsey's got well now."

"You hush up," Dilsey said. Nancy held the cup in both hands, looking at us, making the sound, like there were two of them: one looking at us and the other making the sound. "Whyn't you let Mr Jason telefoam the marshal?" Dilsey said. Nancy stopped then, holding the cup in her long brown hands. She tried to drink some coffee again, but it sploshed out of the cup, onto her hands and her dress, and she put the cup down. Jason watched her.

"I cant swallow it," Nancy said. "I swallows but it wont go down me."

"You go down to the cabin," Dilsey said. "Frony will fix you a pallet and I'll be there soon."

"Wont no nigger stop him," Nancy said.

"I aint a nigger," Jason said. "Am I, Dilsey?"

"I reckon not," Dilsey said. She looked at Nancy. "I dont reckon so. What you going to do, then?"

Nancy looked at us. Her eyes went fast, like she was afraid there wasn't time to look, without hardly moving at all. She looked at us, at all three of us at one time. "You member that night I stayed in yawls' room?" she said. She told about how we waked up early the next morning, and played. We had to play quiet, on her pallet, until father woke up and it was time to get breakfast. "Go and ask your maw to let me stay here tonight," Nancy said. "I wont need no pallet. We can play some more."

Caddy asked mother. Jason went too. "I cant have Negroes sleeping in the bedrooms," mother said. Jason cried. He cried until mother said he couldn't have any dessert for three days if he didn't stop. Then Jason said he would stop if Dilsey would make a chocolate cake. Father was there.

"Why dont you do something about it?" mother said. "What do we have officers for?"

"Why is Nancy afraid of Jesus?" Caddy said. "Are you afraid of father, Mother?"

"What could the officers do?" father said. "If Nancy hasn't seen him, how could the officers find him?"

"Then why is she afraid?" mother said.

"She says he is there. She says she knows he is there tonight."

"Yet we pay taxes," mother said. "I must wait here alone in this big house while you take a Negro woman home."

"You know that I am not lying outside with a razor," father said.

"I'll stop if Dilsey will make a chocolate cake," Jason said. Mother told us to go out and father said he didn't know if Jason would get a chocolate cake or not, but he knew what Jason was going to get in about a minute. We went back to the kitchen and told Nancy.

"Father said for you to go home and lock the door, and you'll be all right," Caddy said. "All right from what, Nancy? Is Jesus mad at you?" Nancy was holding the coffee cup in her hands again, her elbows on her knees and her hands holding the cup between her knees. She was looking into the cup. "What have you done that made Jesus mad?" Caddy said. Nancy let the cup go. It didn't break on the floor, but the coffee spilled out, and Nancy sat there with her hands still making the shape of the cup. She began to make the sound again, not loud. Not singing and not unsinging. We watched her.

"Here," Dilsey said. "You quit that, now. You get aholt of yourself. You wait here. I going to get Versh to walk home with you." Dilsey went out.

We looked at Nancy. Her shoulders kept shaking, but she quit making the sound. We watched her. "What's Jesus going to do to you?" Caddy said. "He went away."

Nancy looked at us. "We had fun that night I stayed in yawls' room, didn't we?"

"I didn't," Jason said. "I didn't have any fun."

"You were asleep in mother's room," Caddy said. "You were not there."

"Let's go down to my house and have some more fun," Nancy said.

"Mother wont let us," I said. "It's too late now."

"Dont bother her," Nancy said. "We can tell her in the morning. She wont mind."

"She wouldn't let us," I said.

"Dont ask her now," Nancy said. "Dont bother her now."

"She didn't say we couldn't go," Caddy said.

"We didn't ask," I said.

"If you go, I'll tell," Jason said.

"We'll have fun," Nancy said. "They wont mind, just to my house. I been working for yawl a long time. They wont mind."

"I'm not afraid to go," Caddy said. "Jason is the one that's afraid. He'll tell."

"I'm not," Jason said.

"Yes, you are," Caddy said. "You'll tell."

"I wont tell," Jason said. "I'm not afraid."

"Jason aint afraid to go with me," Nancy said. "Is you, Jason?"

"Jason is going to tell," Caddy said. The lane was dark. We passed the pasture gate. "I bet if something was to jump out from behind that gate, Jason would holler."

"I wouldn't," Jason said. We walked down the lane. Nancy was talking loud.

"What are you talking so loud for, Nancy?" Caddy said.

"Who; me?" Nancy said. "Listen at Quentin and Caddy and Jason saying I'm talking loud."

"You talk like there was five of us here," Caddy said. "You talk like father was here too."

"Who; me talking loud, Mr Jason?" Nancy said.

"Nancy called Jason 'Mister,'" Caddy said.

"Listen how Caddy and Quentin and Jason talk," Nancy said.

"We're not talking loud," Caddy said. "You're the one that's talking like father —"

"Hush," Nancy said; "hush, Mr. Jason."

"Nancy called Jason 'Mister' aguh —"

"Hush," Nancy said. She was talking loud when we crossed the ditch and stopped through the fence where she used to stoop through with the clothes on her head. Then we came to her house. We were going fast then. She opened the door. The smell of the house was like the lamp and the smell of Nancy was like the wick, like they were waiting for one another to begin to smell. She lit the lamp and closed the door and put the bar up. Then she quit talking loud, looking at us.

"What're we going to do?" Caddy said.

"What do yawl want to do?" Nancy said.

"You said we would have some fun," Caddy said.

There was something about Nancy's house; something you could smell besides Nancy and the house. Jason smelled it, even. "I dont want to stay here," he said. "I want to go home."

"Go home, then," Caddy said.

"I dont want to go by myself," Jason said.

"We're going to have some fun," Nancy said.

"How?" Caddy said.

Nancy stood by the door. She was looking at us, only it was like she had emptied her eyes, like she had quit using them. "What do you want to do?" she said.

"Tell us a story," Caddy said. "Can you tell a story?"

"Yes," Nancy said.

"Tell it," Caddy said. We looked at Nancy. "You dont know any stories."

"Yes," Nancy said. "Yes I do."

She came and sat in a chair before the hearth. There was a little fire there. Nancy built it up, when it was already hot inside. She built a good blaze. She told a story. She talked like her eyes looked, like her eyes watching us and her voice talking to us did not belong to her. Like she was living somewhere else, waiting somewhere else. She was outside the cabin. Her voice was inside and the shape of her, the Nancy that could stoop under a barbed wire fence with a bundle of clothes balanced on her head as though without weight, like a balloon, was there. But that was all. "And so this here queen come walking up to the ditch, where that bad man was hiding. She was walking up to the ditch, and she say, 'If I can just get past this here ditch,' was what she say . . ."

"What ditch?" Caddy said. "A ditch like that one out there? Why did a queen want to go into a ditch?"

"To get to her house," Nancy said. She looked at us. "She had to cross the ditch to get into her house quick and bar the door."

"Why did she want to go home and bar the door?" Caddy said.

IV

Nancy looked at us. She quit talking. She looked at us. Jason's legs stuck straight out of his pants where he sat on Nancy's lap. "I dont think that's a good story," he said. "I want to go home."

"Maybe we had better," Caddy said. She got up from the floor. "I bet they are looking for us right now." She went toward the door.

"No," Nancy said. "Dont open it." She got up quick and passed Caddy. She didn't touch the door, the wooden bar.

"Why not?" Caddy said.

"Come back to the lamp," Nancy said. "We'll have fun. You dont have to go."

"We ought to go," Caddy said. "Unless we have a lot of fun." She and Nancy came back to the fire, the lamp.

"I want to go home," Jason said. "I'm going to tell."

"I know another story," Nancy said. She stood close to the lamp. She looked at Caddy, like when your eyes look up at a stick balanced on your nose. She had to look down to see Caddy, but her eyes looked like that, like when you are balancing a stick.

"I wont listen to it," Jason said. "I'll bang on the floor."

"It's a good one," Nancy said. "It's better than the other one."

"What's it about?" Caddy said. Nancy was standing by the lamp. Her hand was on the lamp, against the light, long and brown.

"Your hand is on that hot globe," Caddy said. "Dont it feel hot to your hand?"

Nancy looked at her hand on the lamp chimney. She took her hand away, slow. She stood there, looking at Caddy, wringing her long hand as though it were tied to her wrist with a string.

"Let's do something else," Caddy said.

"I want to go home," Jason said.

"I got some popcorn," Nancy said. She looked at Caddy and then at Jason and then at me and then at Caddy again. "I got some popcorn."

"I dont like popcorn," Jason said. "I'd rather have candy."

Nancy looked at Jason. "You can hold the popper." She was still wringing her hand; it was long and limp and brown.

"All right," Jason said. "I'll stay a while if I can do that. Caddy cant hold it. I'll want to go home again if Caddy holds the popper."

Nancy built up the fire. "Look at Nancy putting her hands in the fire," Caddy said. "What's the matter with you, Nancy?"

"I got popcorn," Nancy said. "I got some." She took the popper from under the bed. It was broken. Jason began to cry.

"Now we cant have any popcorn," he said.

"We ought to go home, anyway," Caddy said. "Come on, Quentin."

"Wait," Nancy said; "wait. I can fix it. Dont you want to help me fix it?"

"I dont think I want any," Caddy said. "It's too late now."

"You help me, Jason," Nancy said. "Dont you want to help me?"

"No," Jason said. "I want to go home."

"Hush," Nancy said; "hush. Watch. Watch me. I can fix it so Jason can hold it and pop the corn." She got a piece of wire and fixed the popper.

"It wont hold good," Caddy said.

"Yes it will," Nancy said. "Yawl watch. Yawl help me shell some corn."

The popcorn was under the bed too. We shelled it into the popper and Nancy helped Jason hold the popper over the fire.

"It's not popping," Jason said. "I want to go home."

"You wait," Nancy said. "It'll begin to pop. We'll have fun then." She was sitting close to the fire. The lamp was turned up so high it was beginning to smoke.

"Why dont you turn it down some?" I said.

"It's all right," Nancy said. "I'll clean it. Yawl wait. The popcorn will start in a minute."

"I dont believe it's going to start," Caddy said. "We ought to start home, anyway. They'll be worried."

"No," Nancy said. "It's going to pop. Dilsey will tell um yawl with me. I been working for yawl long time. They wont mind if yawl at my house. You wait, now. It'll start popping any minute now."

Then Jason got some smoke in his eyes and he began to cry. He dropped the popper into the fire. Nancy got a wet rag and wiped Jason's face, but he didn't stop crying.

"Hush," she said. "Hush." But he didn't hush. Caddy took the popper out of the fire.

"It's burned up," she said. "You'll have to get some more popcorn, Nancy."

"Did you put all of it in?" Nancy said.

"Yes," Caddy said. Nancy looked at Caddy. Then she took the popper and opened it and poured the cinders into her apron and began to sort the grains, her hands long and brown, and we watching her.

"Haven't you got any more?" Caddy said.

"Yes," Nancy said; "yes. Look. This here aint burnt. All we need to do is—"

"I want to go home," Jason said. "I'm going to tell."

"Hush," Caddy said. We all listened. Nancy's head was already turned toward the barred door, her eyes filled with red lamplight. "Somebody is coming," Caddy said.

Then Nancy began to make that sound again, not loud, sitting there above the fire, her long hands dangling between her knees; all of a sudden water began to come out on her face in big drops, running down her face, carrying in each one a little turning ball of firelight like a spark until it dropped off her chin. "She's not crying," I said.

"I aint crying," Nancy said. Her eyes were closed. "I aint crying. Who is it?"

"I dont know," Caddy said. She went to the door and looked out. "We've got to go now," she said. "Here comes father."

"I'm going to tell," Jason said. "Yawl made me come."

The water still ran down Nancy's face. She turned in her chair. "Listen. Tell him. Tell him we going to have fun. Tell him I take good care of yawl until in the morning. Tell him to let me come home with yawl and sleep on the floor. Tell him I wont need no pallet. We'll have fun. You member last time how we had so much fun?"

"I didn't have fun," Jason said. "You hurt me. You put smoke in my eyes. I'm going to tell."

V

Father came in. He looked at us. Nancy did not get up.

"Tell him," she said.

"Caddy made us come down here," Jason said. "I didn't want to."

Father came to the fire. Nancy looked up at him. "Cant you go to Aunt Rachel's and stay?" he said. Nancy looked up at father, her hands between her knees. "He's not here," father said. "I would have seen him. There's not a soul in sight."

"He in the ditch," Nancy said. "He waiting in the ditch yonder."

"Nonsense," father said. He looked at Nancy. "Do you know he's there?"

"I got the sign," Nancy said.

"What sign?"

"I got it. It was on the table when I come in. It was a hogbone, with blood meat still on it, laying by the lamp. He's out there. When yawl walk out that door, I gone."

"Gone where, Nancy?" Caddy said.

"I'm not a tattletale," Jason said.

"Nonsense," father said.

"He out there," Nancy said. "He looking through that window this minute, waiting for yawl to go. Then I gone."

"Nonsense," father said. "Lock up your house and we'll take you on to Aunt Rachel's."

" 'Twont do no good," Nancy said. She didn't look at father now, but he looked down at her, at her long, limp, moving hands. "Putting it off wont do no good."

"Then what do you want to do?" father said.

"I dont know," Nancy said. "I cant do nothing. Just put it off. And that dont do no good. I reckon it belong to me. I reckon what I going to get aint no more than mine."

"Get what?" Caddy said. "What's yours?"

"Nothing," father said. "You all must get to bed."

"Caddy made me come," Jason said.

"Go on to Aunt Rachel's," father said.

"It wont do no good," Nancy said. She sat before the fire, her elbows on her knees, her long hands between her knees. "When even your own kitchen wouldn't do no good. When even if I was sleeping on the floor in the room with your chillen, and the next morning there I am, and blood —"

"Hush," father said. "Lock the door and put out the lamp and go to bed."

"I scared of the dark," Nancy said. "I scared for it to happen in the dark."

"You mean you're going to sit right here with the lamp lighted?" father said. Then Nancy began to make the sound again, sitting before the fire, her long hands between her knees. "Ah, damnation," father said. "Come along, chillen. It's past bedtime."

"When yawl go home, I gone," Nancy said. She talked quieter now, and her face looked quiet, like her hands. "Anyway, I got my coffin money saved up with Mr Lovelady." Mr Lovelady was a short, dirty man who collected the Negro insurance, coming around to the cabins or the kitchens every Saturday morning, to collect fifteen cents. He and his wife lived at the hotel. One morning his wife committed suicide. They had a child, a little girl. He and the child went away. After a week or two he came back alone. We would see him going along the lanes and the back streets on Saturday mornings.

"Nonsense," father said. "You'll be the first thing I'll see in the kitchen tomorrow morning."

"You'll see what you'll see, I reckon," Nancy said. "But it will take the Lord to say what that will be."

VI

We left her sitting before the fire.

"Come and put the bar up," father said. But she didn't move. She didn't look at us again, sitting quietly there between the lamp and the fire. From some distance down the lane we could look back and see her through the open door.

"What, Father?" Caddy said. "What's going to happen?"

"Nothing," father said. Jason was on father's back, so Jason was the tallest of all of us. We went down into the ditch. I looked at it, quiet. I couldn't see much where the moonlight and the shadows tangled.

"If Jesus is hid here, he can see us, cant he?" Caddy said.

"He's not there," father said. "He went away a long time ago."

"You made me come," Jason said, high; against the sky it looked like father had two heads, a little one and a big one. "I didn't want to."

We went up out of the ditch. We could still see Nancy's house and the open door, but we couldn't see Nancy now, sitting before the fire with the door open, because she was tired. "I just done got tired," she said. "I just a nigger. It aint no fault of mine."

But we could hear her, because she began just after we came up out of the ditch, the sound that was not singing and not unsinging. "Who will do our washing now, Father?" I said.

"I'm not a nigger," Jason said, high and close above father's head.

"You're worse," Caddy said, "you are a tattletale. If something was to jump out, you'd be scairder than a nigger."

"I wouldn't," Jason said.

"You'd cry," Caddy said.

"Caddy," father said.

"I wouldn't!" Jason said.

"Scairy cat," Caddy said.

"Candace!" father said.

[1931]

Reading Faulkner's "Barn Burning."   Although this story is one of Faulkner's most famous and widely anthologized, it was rejected by five different magazines before it was accepted by *Harper's,* where it first appeared in June 1939. Faulkner soon reworked the story for *The Hamlet* (1940), the first of his novels charting the rise of Flem Snopes, the eldest son of a poor white tenant family. But he appears only briefly in "Barn Burning," which focuses on the dilemma of his younger brother, Sarty Snopes. Sarty is named for Colonel John Sartoris, a Confederate army officer and wealthy landowner whose aristocratic family is the subject of two earlier novels by Faulkner, *Sartoris* (1929) and *The Unvanquished* (1938). As Sarty's name perhaps suggests, he is torn between loyalty to his father, Abner Snopes, and his allegiance to traditional values of community, decency, and truth. The text is taken from its first publication in a book, Faulkner's *Collected Stories* (1950).

BARN BURNING

The store in which the Justice of the Peace's court was sitting smelled of cheese. The boy, crouched on his nail keg at the back of the crowded room, knew he smelled cheese, and more: from where he sat he could see the ranked shelves close-packed with the solid, squat, dynamic shapes of tin cans whose labels his stomach read, not from the lettering which meant nothing to his mind but from the scarlet devils and the silver curve of fish – this, the cheese which he knew he smelled and the hermetic meat which his intestines believed he smelled coming in intermittent gusts momentary and brief between the other constant one, the smell and sense just a little of fear because mostly of despair and grief, the old fierce pull of blood. He could not see the table where the Justice sat and before which his father and his father's enemy (*our enemy* he thought in that despair; *ourn! mine and hisn both! He's my father!*) stood, but he could hear them, the two of them that is, because his father had said no word yet:

"But what proof have you, Mr. Harris?"

"I told you. The hog got into my corn. I caught it up and sent it back to him. He had no fence that would hold it. I told him so, warned him. The next time I put the hog in my pen. When he came to get it I gave him enough wire to patch up his pen. The next time I put the hog up and kept it. I rode down to his house and saw the wire I gave him still rolled on to the spool in his yard. I told him he could have the hog when he paid me a dollar pound fee. That evening a nigger came with the dollar and got the hog. He was a strange nigger. He said, 'He say to tell you wood and hay kin burn.' I said, 'What?' 'That whut he say to tell you,' the nigger said. 'Wood and hay kin burn.' That night my barn burned. I got the stock out but I lost the barn."

"Where is the nigger? Have you got him?"

"He was a strange nigger, I tell you. I don't know what became of him."

"But that's not proof. Don't you see that's not proof?"

"Get that boy up here. He knows." For a moment the boy thought too that the man meant his older brother until Harris said, "Not him. The little one. The boy," and, crouching, small for his age, small and wiry like his father, in patched and faded jeans even too small for him, with straight, uncombed, brown hair and eyes gray and wild as storm scud, he saw the men between himself and the table part and become a lane of grim faces, at the end of which he saw the Justice, a shabby, collarless, graying man in spectacles, beckoning him. He felt no floor under his bare feet; he seemed to walk beneath the palpable weight of the grim turning faces. His father, stiff in his black Sunday coat donned not for the trial but for the moving, did not even look at him. *He aims for me to lie*, he thought, again with that frantic grief and despair. *And I will have to do hit.*

"What's your name, boy?" the Justice said.

"Colonel Sartoris Snopes,"[1] the boy whispered.

"Hey?" the Justice said. "Talk louder. Colonel Sartoris? I reckon anybody named for Colonel Sartoris in this country can't help but tell the truth, can they?" The boy said nothing. *Enemy! Enemy!* he thought; for a moment he could not even see, could not see that the Justice's face was kindly nor discern that his voice was troubled when he spoke to the man named Harris: "Do you want me to question this boy?" But he could hear, and during those subsequent long seconds while there was absolutely no sound in the crowded little room save that of quiet and intent breathing it was as if he had swung outward at the end of a grape vine, over a ravine, and at the top of the swing had been caught in a prolonged instant of mesmerized gravity, weightless in time.

"No!" Harris said violently, explosively. "Damnation! Send him out of here!" Now time, the fluid world, rushed beneath him again, the voices coming to him again through the smell of cheese and sealed meat, the fear and despair and the old grief of blood:

"This case is closed. I can't find against you, Snopes, but I can give you advice. Leave this country and don't come back to it."

His father spoke for the first time, his voice cold and harsh, level, without emphasis: "I aim to. I don't figure to stay in a country among people who . . ." he said something unprintable and vile, addressed to no one.

---

1. **Colonel Sartoris Snopes:** Sarty is named after the character John Sartoris, a wealthy landowner and colonel in the Confederate army, whom Faulkner in other works depicted as a representative of the aristocratic "Old Order" in the South.

"That'll do," the Justice said. "Take your wagon and get out of this country before dark. Case dismissed."

His father turned, and he followed the stiff black coat, the wiry figure walking a little stiffly from where a Confederate provost's man's musket ball had taken him in the heel on a stolen horse thirty years ago,[2] followed the two backs now, since his older brother had appeared from somewhere in the crowd, no taller than the father but thicker, chewing tobacco steadily, between the two lines of grim-faced men and out of the store and across the worn gallery and down the sagging steps and among the dogs and half-grown boys in the mild May dust, where as he passed a voice hissed:

"Barn burner!"

Again he could not see, whirling; there was a face in a red haze, moonlike, bigger than the full moon, the owner of it half again his size, he leaping in the red haze toward the face, feeling no blow, feeling no shock when his head struck the earth, scrabbling up and leaping again, feeling no blow this time either and tasting no blood, scrabbling up to see the other boy in full flight and himself already leaping into pursuit as his father's hand jerked him back, the harsh, cold voice speaking above him: "Go get in the wagon."

It stood in a grove of locusts and mulberries across the road. His two hulking sisters in their Sunday dresses and his mother and her sister in calico and sunbonnets were already in it, sitting on and among the sorry residue of the dozen and more movings which even the boy could remember — the battered stove, the broken beds and chairs, the clock inlaid with mother-of-pearl, which would not run, stopped at some fourteen minutes past two o'clock of a dead and forgotten day and time, which had been his mother's dowry. She was crying, though when she saw him she drew her sleeve across her face and began to descend from the wagon. "Get back," the father said.

"He's hurt. I got to get some water and wash his . . ."

"Get back in the wagon," his father said. He got in too, over the tail-gate. His father mounted to the seat where the older brother already sat and struck the gaunt mules two savage blows with the peeled willow, but without heat. It was not even sadistic; it was exactly that same quality which in later years would cause his descendants to over-run the engine before putting a motor car into motion, striking and reining back in the same movement. The wagon went on, the store with its quiet crowd of grimly watching men dropped behind; a curve in the road hid it. *Forever* he thought. *Maybe he's done satisfied now, now that he has* . . . stopping himself, not to say it aloud even to himself. His mother's hand touched his shoulder.

"Does hit hurt?" she said.

"Naw," he said. "Hit don't hurt. Lemme be."

"Can't you wipe some of the blood off before hit dries?"

"I'll wash to-night," he said. "Lemme be, I tell you."

The wagon went on. He did not know where they were going. None of them ever did or ever asked, because it was always somewhere, always a house of sorts waiting for them a

---

2. **Confederate provost's . . . thirty years ago:** A provost was an officer in charge of a detachment of military police assigned to stop theft in the Confederate army. The story takes place in the early 1890s, thirty years after the Civil War.

day or two days or even three days away. Likely his father had already arranged to make a crop on another farm before he . . . Again he had to stop himself. He (the father) always did. There was something about his wolflike independence and even courage when the advantage was at least neutral which impressed strangers, as if they got from his latent ravening ferocity not so much a sense of dependability as a feeling that his ferocious conviction in the rightness of his own actions would be of advantage to all whose interest lay with his.

That night they camped, in a grove of oaks and beeches where a spring ran. The nights were still cool and they had a fire against it, of a rail lifted from a nearby fence and cut into lengths — a small fire, neat, niggard[3] almost, a shrewd fire; such fires were his father's habit and custom always, even in freezing weather. Older, the boy might have remarked this and wondered why not a big one; why should not a man who had not only seen the waste and extravagance of war, but who had in his blood an inherent voracious prodigality with material not his own, have burned everything in sight? Then he might have gone a step farther and thought that that was the reason: that niggard blaze was the living fruit of nights passed during those four years in the woods hiding from all men, blue or gray, with his strings of horses (captured horses, he called them). And older still, he might have divined the true reason: that the element of fire spoke to some deep mainspring of his father's being, as the element of steel or of powder spoke to other men, as the one weapon for the preservation of integrity, else breath were not worth the breathing, and hence to be regarded with respect and used with discretion.

But he did not think this now and he had seen those same niggard blazes all his life. He merely ate his supper beside it and was already half asleep over his iron plate when his father called him, and once more he followed the stiff back, the stiff and ruthless limp, up the slope and on to the starlit road where, turning, he could see his father against the stars but without face or depth — a shape black, flat, and bloodless as though cut from tin in the iron folds of the frockcoat which had not been made for him, the voice harsh like tin and without heat like tin:

"You were fixing to tell them. You would have told him." He didn't answer. His father struck him with the flat of his hand on the side of the head, hard but without heat, exactly as he had struck the two mules at the store, exactly as he would strike either of them with any stick in order to kill a horse fly, his voice still without heat or anger: "You're getting to be a man. You got to learn. You got to learn to stick to your own blood or you ain't going to have any blood to stick to you. Do you think either of them, any man there this morning, would? Don't you know all they wanted was a chance to get at me because they knew I had them beat? Eh?" Later, twenty years later, he was to tell himself, "If I had said they wanted only truth, justice, he would have hit me again." But now he said nothing. He was not crying. He just stood there. "Answer me," his father said.

"Yes," he whispered. His father turned.

"Get on to bed. We'll be there tomorrow."

To-morrow they were there. In the early afternoon the wagon stopped before a paintless two-room house identical almost with the dozen others it had stopped before even

---

3. **niggard:** A variant of an early English word meaning meager or scanty.

in the boy's ten years, and again, as on the other dozen occasions, his mother and aunt got down and began to unload the wagon, although his two sisters and his father and brother had not moved.

"Likely hit ain't fitten for hawgs," one of the sisters said.

"Nevertheless, fit it will and you'll hog it and like it," his father said. "Get out of them chairs and help your Ma unload."

The two sisters got down, big, bovine, in a flutter of cheap ribbons; one of them drew from the jumbled wagon bed a battered lantern, the other a worn broom. His father handed the reins to the older son and began to climb stiffly over the wheel. "When they get unloaded, take the team to the barn and feed them." Then he said, and at first the boy thought he was still speaking to his brother: "Come with me."

"Me?" he said.

"Yes," his father said. "You."

"Abner," his mother said. His father paused and looked back—the harsh level stare beneath the shaggy, graying, irascible brows.

"I reckon I'll have a word with the man that aims to begin to-morrow owning me body and soul for the next eight months."

They went back up the road. A week ago—or before last night, that is—he would have asked where they were going, but not now. His father had struck him before last night but never before had he paused afterward to explain why; it was as if the blow and the following calm, outrageous voice still rang, repercussed, divulging nothing to him save the terrible handicap of being young, the light weight of his few years, just heavy enough to prevent his soaring free of the world as it seemed to be ordered but not heavy enough to keep him footed solid in it, to resist it and try to change the course of its events.

Presently he could see the grove of oaks and cedars and the other flowering trees and shrubs where the house would be, though not the house yet. They walked beside a fence massed with honeysuckle and Cherokee roses and came to a gate swinging open between two brick pillars, and now, beyond a sweep of drive, he saw the house for the first time and at that instant he forgot his father and the terror and despair both, and even when he remembered his father again (who had not stopped) the terror and despair did not return. Because, for all the twelve movings, they had sojourned until now in a poor country, a land of small farms and fields and houses, and he had never seen a house like this before. *Hit's big as a courthouse,* he thought quietly, with a surge of peace and joy whose reason he could not have thought into words, being too young for that: *They are safe from him. People whose lives are a part of this peace and dignity are beyond his touch, he no more to them than a buzzing wasp: capable of stinging for a little moment but that's all; the spell of this peace and dignity rendering even the barns and stable and cribs which belong to it impervious to the puny flames he might contrive . . .* this, the peace and joy, ebbing for an instant as he looked again at the stiff black back, the stiff and implacable limp of the figure which was not dwarfed by the house, for the reason that it had never looked big anywhere and which now, against the serene columned backdrop, had more than ever that impervious quality of something cut ruthlessly from tin, depthless, as though, sidewise to the sun, it would cast no shadow. Watching him, the boy remarked the absolutely undeviating course which his father held and saw the stiff foot come squarely down in a pile of fresh droppings where a horse had stood in the drive and which his father could have avoided by a simple change of stride. But it ebbed only for a moment, though he could not have thought this into words either, walking on in the spell of the house, which he could even want but without envy, without sorrow, certainly never with that ravening and jealous rage which unknown to him walked in the ironlike black coat before him: *Maybe he will feel it too. Maybe it will even change him now from what maybe he couldn't help but be.*

They crossed the portico. Now he could hear his father's stiff foot as it came down on the boards with clocklike finality, a sound out of all proportion to the displacement of the body it bore and which was not dwarfed either by the white door before it, as though it had attained to a sort of vicious and ravening minimum not to be dwarfed by anything—the flat, wide, black hat, the formal coat of broadcloth which had once been black but which had now that friction-glazed greenish cast of the bodies of old house flies, the lifted sleeve which was too large, the lifted hand like a curled claw. The door opened so promptly that the boy knew the Negro must have been watching them all the time, an old man with neat grizzled hair, in a linen jacket, who stood barring the door with his body, saying, "Wipe yo foots, white man, fo you come in here. Major ain't home nohow."

"Get out of my way, nigger," his father said, without heat too, flinging the door back and the Negro also and entering, his hat still on his head. And now the boy saw the prints of the stiff foot on the doorjamb and saw them appear on the pale rug behind the machinelike deliberation of the foot which seemed to bear (or transmit) twice the weight which the body compassed. The Negro was shouting "Miss Lula! Miss Lula!" somewhere behind them, then the boy, deluged as though by a warm wave by a suave turn of carpeted stair and a pendant glitter of chandeliers and a mute gleam of gold frames, heard the swift feet and saw her too, a lady — perhaps he had never seen her like before either — in a gray, smooth gown with lace at the throat and an apron tied at the waist and the sleeves turned back, wiping cake or biscuit dough from her hands with a towel as she came up the hall, looking not at his father at all but at the tracks on the blond rug with an expression of incredulous amazement.

"I tried," the Negro cried. "I tole him to . . ."

"Will you please go away?" she said in a shaking voice. "Major de Spain is not at home. Will you please go away?"

His father had not spoken again. He did not speak again. He did not even look at her. He just stood stiff in the center of the rug, in his hat, the shaggy iron-gray brows twitching slightly above the pebble-colored eyes as he appeared to examine the house with brief deliberation. Then with the same deliberation he turned; the boy watched him pivot on the good leg and saw the stiff foot drag round the arc of the turning, leaving a final long and fading smear. His father never looked at it, he never once looked down at the rug. The Negro held the door. It closed behind them, upon the hysteric and indistinguishable woman-wail. His father stopped at the top of the steps and scraped his boot clean on the edge of it. At the gate he stopped again. He stood for a moment, planted stiffly on the stiff foot, looking back at the house. "Pretty and white, ain't it?" he said.

"That's sweat. Nigger sweat. Maybe it ain't white enough yet to suit him. Maybe he wants to mix some white sweat with it."

Two hours later the boy was chopping wood behind the house within which his mother and aunt and the two sisters (the mother and aunt, not the two girls, he knew that; even at this distance and muffled by walls the flat loud voices of the two girls emanated an incorrigible idle inertia) were setting up the stove to prepare a meal, when he heard the hooves and saw the linen-clad man on a fine sorrel mare, whom he recognized even before he saw the rolled rug in front of the Negro youth following on a fat bay carriage horse—a suffused, angry face vanishing, still at full gallop, beyond the corner of the house where his father and brother were sitting in the two tilted chairs; and a moment later, almost before he could have put the axe down, he heard the hooves again and watched the sorrel mare go back out of the yard, already galloping again. Then his father began to shout one of the sisters' names, who presently emerged backward from the kitchen door dragging the rolled rug along the ground by one end while the other sister walked behind it.

"If you ain't going to tote, go on and set up the wash pot," the first said.

"You, Sarty!" the second shouted. "Set up the wash pot!" His father appeared at the door, framed against that shabbiness, as he had been against that other bland perfection, impervious to either, the mother's anxious face at his shoulder.

"Go on," the father said. "Pick it up." The two sisters stooped, broad, lethargic; stooping, they presented an incredible expanse of pale cloth and a flutter of tawdry ribbons.

"If I thought enough of a rug to have to git hit all the way from France I wouldn't keep hit where folks coming in would have to tromp on hit," the first said. They raised the rug.

"Abner," the mother said. "Let me do it."

"You go back and git dinner," his father said. "I'll tend to this."

From the woodpile through the rest of the afternoon the boy watched them, the rug spread flat in the dust beside the bubbling wash-pot, the two sisters stooping over it with that profound and lethargic reluctance, while the father stood over them in turn, implacable and grim, driving them though never raising his voice again. He could smell the harsh homemade lye they were using; he saw his mother come to the door once and look toward them with an expression not anxious now but very like despair; he saw his father turn, and he fell to with the axe and saw from the corner of his eye his father raise from the ground a flattish fragment of field stone and examine it and return to the pot, and this time his mother actually spoke: "Abner. Abner. Please don't. Please, Abner."

Then he was done too. It was dusk; the whippoorwills had already begun. He could smell coffee from the room where they would presently eat the cold food remaining from the mid-afternoon meal, though when he entered the house he realized they were having coffee again probably because there was a fire on the hearth, before which the rug now lay spread over the backs of the two chairs. The tracks of his father's foot were gone. Where they had been were now long, water-cloudy scoriations resembling the sporadic course of a lilliputian mowing machine.

It still hung there while they ate the cold food and then went to bed, scattered without order or claim up and down the two rooms, his mother in one bed, where his father would later lie, the older brother in the other, himself, the aunt, and the two sisters on pallets on the floor. But his father was not in bed yet. The last thing the boy remembered was the depthless, harsh silhouette of the hat and coat bending over the rug and it seemed to him that he had not even closed his eyes when the silhouette was standing over him, the fire almost dead behind it, the stiff foot prodding him awake. "Catch up the mule," his father said.

When he returned with the mule his father was standing in the black door, the rolled rug over his shoulder. "Ain't you going to ride?" he said.

"No. Give me your foot."

He bent his knee into his father's hand, the wiry, surprising power flowed smoothly, rising, he rising with it, on to the mule's bare back (they had owned a saddle once; the boy could remember it though not when or where) and with the same effortlessness his father swung the rug up in front of him. Now in the starlight they retraced the afternoon's path, up the dusty road rife with honeysuckle, through the gate and up the black tunnel of the drive to the lightless house, where he sat on the mule and felt the rough warp of the rug drag across his thighs and vanish.

"Don't you want me to help?" he whispered. His father did not answer and now he heard again that stiff foot striking the hollow portico with that wooden and clocklike deliberation, that outrageous overstatement of the weight it carried. The rug, hunched, not flung (the boy could tell that even in the darkness) from his father's shoulder struck the angle of wall and floor with a sound unbelievably loud, thunderous, then the foot again, unhurried and enormous; a light came on in the house and the boy sat, tense, breathing steadily and quietly and just a little fast, though the foot itself did not increase its beat at all, descending the steps now; now the boy could see him.

"Don't you want to ride now?" he whispered. "We kin both ride now," the light within the house altering now, flaring up and sinking. *He's coming down the stairs now*, he thought. He had already ridden the mule up beside the horse block; presently his father was up behind him and he doubled the reins over and slashed the mule across the neck, but before the animal could begin to trot the hard, thin arm came round him, the hard, knotted hand jerking the mule back to a walk.

In the first red rays of the sun they were in the lot, putting plow gear on the mules. This time the sorrel mare was in the lot before he heard it at all, the rider collarless and even bareheaded, trembling, speaking in a shaking voice as the woman in the house had done, his father merely looking up once before stooping again to the hame he was buckling, so that the man on the mare spoke to his stooping back:

"You must realize you have ruined that rug. Wasn't there anybody here, any of your women . . ." he ceased, shaking, the boy watching him, the older brother leaning now in the stable door, chewing, blinking slowly and steadily at nothing apparently. "It cost a hundred dollars. But you never had a hundred dollars. You never will. So I'm going to charge you twenty bushels of corn against your crop. I'll add it in your contract and when you come to the commissary you can sign it. That won't keep Mrs. de Spain quiet but maybe it will teach you to wipe your feet off before you enter her house again."

Then he was gone. The boy looked at his father, who still had not spoken or even looked up again, who was now adjusting the logger-head in the hame.

"Pap," he said. His father looked at him—the inscrutable face, the shaggy brows beneath which the gray eyes glinted coldly. Suddenly the boy went toward him, fast, stopping as suddenly. "You done the best you could!" he cried. "If he wanted hit done different why didn't he wait and tell you how? He won't git no twenty bushels! He won't git none! We'll gether hit and hide hit! I kin watch . . ."

"Did you put the cutter back in that straight stock like I told you?"

"No, sir," he said.

"Then go do it."

That was Wednesday. During the rest of that week he worked steadily, at what was within his scope and some which was beyond it, with an industry that did not need to be driven nor even commanded twice; he had this from his mother, with the difference that some at least of what he did he liked to do, such as splitting wood with the half-size axe which his mother and aunt had earned, or saved money somehow, to present him with at Christmas. In company with the two older women (and on one afternoon, even one of the sisters), he built pens for the shoat and the cow which were a part of his father's contract with the landlord, and one afternoon, his father being absent, gone somewhere on one of the mules, he went to the field.

They were running a middle buster[4] now, his brother holding the plow straight while he handled the reins, and walking beside the straining mule, the rich black soil shearing cool and damp against his bare ankles, he thought *Maybe this is the end of it. Maybe even that twenty bushels that seems hard to have to pay for just a rug will be a cheap price for him to stop forever and always from being what he used to be;* thinking, dreaming now, so that his brother had to speak sharply to him to mind the mule: *Maybe he even won't collect the twenty bushels. Maybe it will all add up and balance and vanish—corn, rug, fire; the terror and grief, the being pulled two ways like between two teams of horses—gone, done with for ever and ever.*

Then it was Saturday; he looked up from beneath the mule he was harnessing and saw his father in the black coat and hat. "Not that," his father said. "The wagon gear." And then, two hours later, sitting in the wagon bed behind his father and brother on the seat, the wagon accomplished a final curve, and he saw the weathered paintless store with its tattered tobacco and patent-medicine posters and the tethered wagons and saddle animals below the gallery. He mounted the gnawed steps behind his father and brother, and there again was the lane of quiet, watching faces for the three of them to walk through. He saw the man in spectacles sitting at the plank table and he did not need to be told this was a Justice of the Peace; he sent one glare of fierce, exultant, partisan defiance at the man in collar and cravat now, whom he had seen but twice before in his life, and that on a galloping horse, who now wore on his face an expression not of rage but of amazed unbelief which the boy could not have known was at the incredible circumstance of being sued by one of his own tenants, and came and stood against his father and cried at the Justice: "He ain't done it! He ain't burnt . . ."

"Go back to the wagon," his father said.

---

4. **middle buster:** Usually "middlebuster," a two-bladed plow that turns the earth to both sides of a row.

"Burnt?" the Justice said. "Do I understand this rug was burned too?"

"Does anybody here claim it was?" his father said. "Go back to the wagon." But he did not, he merely retreated to the rear of the room, crowded as that other had been, but not to sit down this time, instead, to stand pressing among the motionless bodies, listening to the voices:

"And you claim twenty bushels of corn is too high for the damage you did to the rug?"

"He brought the rug to me and said he wanted the tracks washed out of it. I washed the tracks out and took the rug back to him."

"But you didn't carry the rug back to him in the same condition it was in before you made the tracks on it."

His father did not answer, and now for perhaps half a minute there was no sound at all save that of breathing, the faint, steady suspiration of complete and intent listening.

"You decline to answer that, Mr. Snopes?" Again his father did not answer. "I'm going to find against you, Mr. Snopes. I'm going to find that you were responsible for the injury to Major de Spain's rug and hold you liable for it. But twenty bushels of corn seems a little high for a man in your circumstances to have to pay. Major de Spain claims it cost a hundred dollars. October corn will be worth about fifty cents. I figure that if Major de Spain can stand a ninety-five dollar loss on something he paid cash for, you can stand a five-dollar loss you haven't earned yet. I hold you in damages to Major de Spain to the amount of ten bushels of corn over and above your contract with him, to be paid to him out of your crop at gathering time. Court adjourned."

It had taken no time hardly, the morning was but half begun. He thought they would return home and perhaps back to the field, since they were late, far behind all other farmers. But instead his father passed on behind the wagon, merely indicating with his hand for the older brother to follow with it, and crossed the road toward the blacksmith shop opposite, pressing on after his father, overtaking him, speaking, whispering up at the harsh, calm face beneath the weathered hat: "He won't git no ten bushels neither. He won't git one. We'll . . ." until his father glanced for an instant down at him, the face absolutely calm, the grizzled eyebrows tangled above the cold eyes, the voice almost pleasant, almost gentle:

"You think so? Well, we'll wait till October anyway."

The matter of the wagon—the setting of a spoke or two and the tightening of the tires—did not take long either, the business of the tires accomplished by driving the wagon into the spring branch behind the shop and letting it stand there, the mules nuzzling into the water from time to time, and the boy on the seat with the idle reins, looking up the slope and through the sooty tunnel of the shed where the slow hammer rang and where his father sat on an upended cypress bolt, easily, either talking or listening, still sitting there when the boy brought the dripping wagon up out of the branch and halted it before the door.

"Take them on to the shade and hitch," his father said. He did so and returned. His father and the smith and a third man squatting on his heels inside the door were talking, about crops and animals; the boy, squatting too in the ammoniac dust and hoof-parings and scales of rust, heard his father tell a long and unhurried story out of the time before the birth of the older brother even when he had been a professional horsetrader. And then his father came up beside him where he stood before a tattered last year's circus poster on the other side of the store, gazing rapt and quiet at the scarlet horses, the incredible poisings and convolutions of tulle and tights and the painted leers of comedians, and said, "It's time to eat."

But not at home. Squatting beside his brother against the front wall, he watched his father emerge from the store and produce from a paper sack a segment of cheese and divide it carefully and deliberately into three with his pocket knife and produce crackers from the same sack. They all three squatted on the gallery and ate, slowly, without talking; then in the store again, they drank from a tin dipper tepid water smelling of the cedar bucket and of living beech trees. And still they did not go home. It was a horse lot this time, a tall rail fence upon and along which men stood and sat and out of which one by one horses were led, to be walked and trotted and then cantered back and forth along the road while the slow swapping and buying went on and the sun began to slant westward, they—the three of them—watching and listening, the older brother with his muddy eyes and his steady, inevitable tobacco, the father commenting now and then on certain of the animals, to no one in particular.

It was after sundown when they reached home. They ate supper by lamplight, then, sitting on the doorstep, the boy watched the night fully accomplish, listening to the whippoorwills and the frogs, when he heard his mother's voice: "Abner! No! No! Oh, God. Oh, God. Abner!" and he rose, whirled, and saw the altered light through the door where a candle stub now burned in a bottle neck on the table and his father, still in the hat and coat, at once formal and burlesque as though dressed carefully for some shabby and ceremonial violence, emptying the reservoir of the lamp back into the five-gallon kerosene can from which it had been filled, while the mother tugged at his arm until he shifted the lamp to the other hand and flung her back, not savagely or viciously, just hard, into the wall, her hands flung out against the wall for balance, her mouth open and in her face the same quality of hopeless despair as had been in her voice. Then his father saw him standing in the door.

"Go to the barn and get that can of oil we were oiling the wagon with," he said. The boy did not move. Then he could speak.

"What . . ." he cried. "What are you . . ."

"Go get that oil," his father said. "Go."

Then he was moving, running, outside the house, toward the stable: this the old habit, the old blood which he had not been permitted to choose for himself, which had been bequeathed him willy nilly and which had run for so long (and who knew where, battening on what of outrage and savagery and lust) before it came to him. *I could keep on,* he thought. *I could run on and on and never look back, never need to see his face again. Only I can't. I can't,* the rusted can in his hand now, the liquid sploshing[5] in it as he ran back to the house and into it, into the sound of his mother's weeping in the next room, and handed the can to his father.

---

5. **sploshing:** Another term for splashing.

"Ain't you going to even send a nigger?" he cried. "At least you sent a nigger before!"

This time his father didn't strike him. The hand came even faster than the blow had, the same hand which had set the can on the table with almost excruciating care flashing from the can toward him too quick for him to follow it, gripping him by the back of his shirt and on to tiptoe before he had seen it quit the can, the face stooping at him in breathless and frozen ferocity, the cold, dead voice speaking over him to the older brother who leaned against the table, chewing with that steady, curious, sidewise motion of cows:

"Empty the can into the big one and go on. I'll catch up with you."

"Better tie him up to the bedpost," the brother said.

"Do like I told you," the father said. Then the boy was moving, his bunched shirt and the hard, bony hand between his shoulder-blades, his toes just touching the floor, across the room and into the other one, past the sisters sitting with spread heavy thighs in the two chairs over the cold hearth, and to where his mother and aunt sat side by side on the bed, the aunt's arms about his mother's shoulders.

"Hold him," the father said. The aunt made a startled movement. "Not you," the father said. "Lennie. Take hold of him. I want to see you do it." His mother took him by the wrist. "You'll hold him better than that. If he gets loose don't you know what he is going to do? He will go up yonder." He jerked his head toward the road. "Maybe I'd better tie him."

"I'll hold him," his mother whispered.

"See you do then." Then his father was gone, the stiff foot heavy and measured upon the boards, ceasing at last.

Then he began to struggle. His mother caught him in both arms, he jerking and wrenching at them. He would be stronger in the end, he knew that. But he had no time to wait for it. "Lemme go!" he cried. "I don't want to have to hit you!"

"Let him go!" the aunt said. "If he don't go, before God, I am going up there myself!"

"Don't you see I can't?" his mother cried. "Sarty! Sarty No! No! Help me, Lizzie!"

Then he was free. His aunt grasped at him but it was too late. He whirled, running, his mother stumbled forward or to her knees behind him, crying to the nearer sister: "Catch him, Net! Catch him!" But that was too late too, the sister (the sisters were twins, born at the same time, yet either of them now gave the impression of being, encompassing as much living meat and volume and weight as any other two of the family) not yet having begun to rise from the chair, her head, face, alone merely turned, presenting to him in the flying instant an astonishing expanse of young female features untroubled by any surprise even, wearing only an expression of bovine interest. Then he was out of the room, out of the house, in the mild dust of the starlit road and the heavy rifeness of honeysuckle, the pale ribbon unspooling with terrific slowness under his running feet, reaching the gate at last and turning in, running, his heart and lungs drumming, on up the drive toward the lighted house, the lighted door. He did not knock, he burst in, sobbing for breath, incapable for the moment of speech; he saw the astonished face of the Negro in the linen jacket without knowing when the Negro had appeared.

"De Spain!" he cried, panted. "Where's . . ." then he saw the white man too emerging from a white door down the hall. "Barn!" he cried. "Barn!"

"What?" the white man said. "Barn?"

"Yes!" the boy cried. "Barn!"

"Catch him!" the white man shouted.

But it was too late this time too. The Negro grasped his shirt, but the entire sleeve, rotten with washing, carried away, and he was out that door too and in the drive again, and had actually never ceased to run even while he was screaming into the white man's face.

Behind him the white man was shouting, "My horse! Fetch my horse!" and he thought for an instant of cutting across the park and climbing the fence into the road, but he did not know the park nor how high the vine-massed fence might be and he dared not risk it. So he ran on down the drive, blood and breath roaring; presently he was in the road again though he could not see it. He could not hear either: the galloping mare was almost upon him before he heard her, and even then he held his course, as if the very urgency of his wild grief and need must in a moment more find him wings, waiting until the ultimate instant to hurl himself aside and into the weed-choked roadside ditch as the horse thundered past and on, for an instant in furious silhouette against the stars, the tranquil early summer night sky which, even before the shape of the horse and rider vanished, stained abruptly and violently upward: a long, swirling roar incredible and soundless, blotting the stars, and he springing up and into the road again, running again, knowing it was too late yet still running even after he heard the shot and, an instant later, two shots, pausing now without knowing he had ceased to run, crying "Pap! Pap!", running again before he knew he had begun to run, stumbling, tripping over something and scrabbling up again without ceasing to run, looking backward over his shoulder at the glare as he got up, running on among the invisible trees, panting, sobbing, "Father! Father!"

At midnight he was sitting on the crest of a hill. He did not know it was midnight and he did not know how far he had come. But there was no glare behind him now and he sat now, his back toward what he had called home for four days anyhow, his face toward the dark woods which he would enter when breath was strong again, small, shaking steadily in the chill darkness, hugging himself into the remainder of his thin, rotten shirt, the grief and despair now no longer terror and fear but just grief and despair. *Father. My father,* he thought. "He was brave!" he cried suddenly, aloud but not loud, no more than a whisper: "He was! He was in the war! He was in Colonel Sartoris' cav'ry!" not knowing that his father had gone to that war a private in the fine old European sense, wearing no uniform, admitting the authority of and giving fidelity to no man or army or flag, going to war as Malbrouck[6] himself did: for booty — it meant nothing and less than nothing to him if it were enemy booty or his own.

The slow constellations wheeled on. It would be dawn and then sun-up after a while and he would be hungry. But that would be to-morrow and now he was only cold, and walking would cure that. His breathing was easier now and he decided to get up and go on, and then he found that he had been asleep because he knew it was almost dawn, the

---

6. **Malbrouck:** John Churchill (1650–1722), the first Duke of Marlborough, infamous for embezzlement and taking bribes, was the subject of a popular children's nursery song, "Malbrouck Goes Off to the War."

night almost over. He could tell that from the whippoorwills. They were everywhere now among the dark trees below him, constant and inflectioned and ceaseless, so that, as the instant for giving over to the day birds drew nearer and nearer, there was no interval at all between them. He got up. He was a little stiff, but walking would cure that too as it would the cold, and soon there would be the sun. He went on down the hill, toward the dark woods within which the liquid silver voices of the birds called unceasing – the rapid and urgent beating of the urgent and quiring[7] heart of the late spring night. He did not look back.

[1939, 1950]

---

7. **quiring:** A musical term for the sound of the singing of a choir.

Writers on Writers: Toni Morrison on William Faulkner

The novelist Toni Morrison (b. 1931), whose work can be found on pages 2151–2167, completed an MA thesis on Virginia Woolf and William Faulkner in 1955, five years after Faulkner won the Nobel Prize for Literature and forty years before Morrison became the first African American writer to win the coveted prize, in 1995. A decade earlier, Morrison was invited to participate in an international conference on Faulkner, held in Oxford, Mississippi. There, Morrison read from her work in progress, the novel that would become *Beloved* (1987). Following her reading, she agreed to answer questions from the audience. In response to a question about Faulkner's influence on her, Morrison in the following exchange discusses what she views as some of the sources of his power, including his courage and what she characterizes as his unblinking *gaze*, "a refusal-to-look-away approach in his writing." The text is taken from *Faulkner and Women* (1986), edited by Doreen Fowler and Ann J. Abadie.

TONI MORRISON

(b. 1931)

From Faulkner and Women

QUESTION: Ms. Morrison, you mentioned that you wrote a thesis on Faulkner. What effect did Faulkner have on your literary career?

MORRISON: Well, I'm not sure that he had any effect on my work. I am typical, I think, of all writers who are convinced that they are wholly original and that if they recognized an influence they would abandon it as quickly as possible. But as a reader in the '50s and later, of course (I said 1956 because that's when I was working on a thesis that had to do with him), I was concentrating on Faulkner. I don't think that my response was any different from any other student at that time, inasmuch as there was in Faulkner this power and courage—the courage of a writer, a special kind of courage. My reasons, I think, for being interested and deeply moved by all his subjects had something to do with my desire to find out something about this country and that artistic articulation of its past that was not available in history, which is what art and fiction can do but sometimes history refuses to do. I suppose history can humanize the past also, but it frequently refuses to do so for perfectly good reasons. But there was an articulate investigation of an era that one or two authors provided and Faulkner was certainly at the apex of that investigation. And there was something else about Faulkner which I can only call "gaze." He had a gaze that was different. It appeared, at that time, to be similar to a look, even a sort of staring, a refusal-to-look-away approach in his writing that I found admirable. At that time, in the '50s or the '60s, it never crossed my mind to write books. But then I did it, and I was very surprised myself that I was doing it, and I knew that I was doing it for some reasons that are not writerly ones. I don't really find strong connections between my work and Faulkner's. In an extraordinary kind of memorable way there are literary watersheds in one's life. In mine, there are four or five, and I hope they are all ones that meet every body's criteria of who should be read, but some of them don't. Some books are just awful in terms of technique but nevertheless they are terrific: they are too good to be correct. With Faulkner there was always something to surface. Besides, he could infuriate you in such wonderful ways. It wasn't just complete delight — there was also that other quality that is just as important as devotion: outrage. The point is that with Faulkner one was never indifferent.

[1986]

Ernest Hemingway

[1899-1961]

Ernest William Hemingway was born on July 21, 1899, in Oak Park, a comfortable suburb of Chicago, Illinois. He was the second child and first son of Dr. Clarence Edmonds Hemingway, an obstetrician and general practitioner, and Grace Hall Hemingway, a former singer and music teacher. Hemingway took music lessons with his mother and learned to fish and hunt with his father at the family's summer cottage in upper Michigan. He attended Oak Park High School, where he played football, wrote a weekly column for the school newspaper, and contributed poems and essays to the literary magazine, *Tabula*. The United States entered World War I shortly before his graduation in 1917, and Hemingway wanted to join the army. His father, who had hoped he would go to college to prepare for a career in medicine, felt that he was too young to enlist. Instead, with the help of an uncle, Hemingway got a job as a cub reporter on the prestigious *Kansas City Star*. For the next seven months, he covered crime stories and interviewed politicians and visiting celebrities. Although he was good at his job and later said that it taught him invaluable skills as a writer, he was still eager to enlist. Rejected by the army because of poor vision, he volunteered for the Red Cross ambulance corps. In May 1918, he sailed for Europe and began service as an ambulance driver in Italy. A few weeks after his arrival, Hemingway was seriously wounded by a mortar shell as he distributed cigarettes and chocolates to Italian soldiers. With over two hundred pieces of shrapnel in his legs, he spent the next several months recuperating in a hospital in Milan before returning to Oak Park in January 1919.

No longer interested in college, Hemingway began to chart a career as a writer. He worked as a journalist in Chicago, where he met Sherwood Anderson. Famous for his stories about the narrowness and oppressions of small-town life in the Midwest, Anderson urged Hemingway to go to Paris. Hemingway subsequently secured a job as the European correspondent of the *Toronto Star Weekly*. Shortly after he married Hadley Richardson in September 1921, the young couple sailed for Europe. Armed with letters of introduction from Anderson, who generously described his young and unknown friend as a writer of "extraordinary talent," Hemingway soon met many of the expatriate artists and writers living in Paris, including Gertrude Stein and his early mentor Ezra Pound. "He's teaching me to write," Hemingway excitedly reported, "and I'm teaching him to box." With Pound's help, he began to publish sketches and stories in the *Little Review* and Paris-based little magazines such as the *transatlantic review*. Pound also helped arrange for the publication in Paris of two small collections of Hemingway's apprentice work, *Three Stories and Ten Poems* (1923) and *In Our Time* (1924), a series of brief vignettes he incorporated into his collection of stories *In Our Time* (1925). The collection was published by the adventuresome American firm of Boni & Liveright.

Ernest Hemingway

This photograph was taken outside Hemingway's apartment building in Paris in 1924, shortly before he emerged as one of the foremost writers of what his friend Gertrude Stein called the "Lost Generation."

As Hemingway anticipated, however, the publisher was obliged to reject his lightweight novel *The Torrents of Spring* (1926), a parody of the work of the firm's most prominent author, Sherwood Anderson. Hemingway was consequently free to accept an offer from his friend F. Scott Fitzgerald's publisher, Charles Scribner's Sons. The distinguished firm soon published *The Sun Also Rises* (1926), Hemingway's acclaimed novel about expatriates in Europe, and a second collection of his stories, *Men without Women* (1927).

As one reviewer quipped about the rugged Hemingway, he was now "a big man in American letters." In 1926, he left his wife and their young son to live with Pauline Pfeifer, a wealthy fashion reporter Hemingway married in 1927. The following year, they left Paris and moved to Key West, Florida. Soon after they arrived, Hemingway learned that his father had committed suicide by shooting himself in the head with a revolver. Despite the personal turmoil, he completed *A Farewell to Arms* (1929), a best-selling novel loosely based on his experiences in World War I. Hemingway's next books were a study of bullfighting, *Death in the Afternoon* (1932), and another collection of his stories, *Winner Take Nothing* (1933). In 1934, he went on his first safari to Africa, which provided material for more stories and a nonfictional account of the trip, *Green Hills of Africa* (1935). While he was working on *To Have and Have Not* (1937), a socially conscious novel about a fishing-boat captain driven to smuggling by hard times during the Great Depression, Hemingway became deeply involved in the Spanish civil war. Along with other American writers, he worked on a propaganda film in support of the republican cause, *The Spanish Earth*. He also wrote a play, *The Fifth Column*, which many viewed as an attempt to justify the Communist Party's murderous purges of its leftist allies in the republican government in Spain. But Communist reviewers were infuriated by his novel *For Whom the Bell Tolls* (1940), in which Hemingway exposed the political infighting and the atrocities committed by both sides during the bitter civil war. The novel was sold to Paramount Pictures for $100,000, the highest price that had ever been paid for the film rights to a book, and it was a runaway bestseller for both Scribner's and as a main selection of the Book-of-the-Month Club.

Despite some later triumphs, Hemingway's career steadily declined after 1940. That year, soon after his divorce from Pauline Pfeifer, he married the writer Martha Gellhorn. During World War II, he worked as a war correspondent, covering D day and the liberation of Paris. He also began a relationship with an American journalist, Mary Welsh, whom Hemingway married immediately after Gellhorn divorced him in 1945. For the rest of his life, Hemingway divided his time between his homes in Cuba and Ketchum, Idaho. In 1950, he published his first novel in a decade, *Across the River and into the Trees*. Although the reviews of that novel were disappointing, Hemingway scored a critical and commercial hit with *The Old Man and the Sea* (1952). The beloved story of an infirm but indomitable Cuban fisherman, which was first published in an issue of *Life* magazine that sold over five million copies in two days, won the Pulitzer Prize. It also led to Hemingway's reception of the Nobel Prize for Literature, awarded in recognition of "his powerful, style-forming mastery of the art

Hemingway never retired from his life into his workshop.

—Tennessee Williams

of modern narration," in 1954. But he was not able to attend the awards ceremony in Stockholm, since he was recovering from serious injuries he had received earlier that year in a plane crash while on safari in Africa. The remaining years of his life were marred by ill health and bouts of serious depression. He worked on several projects, including novels and a posthumously published memoir, *A Moveable Feast* (1964). But the shock treatments he received for depression restricted his memory, and he wrote less and less. On July 2, 1961, a few weeks before his sixty-second birthday, Hemingway committed suicide by shooting himself in the head with a double-barreled shotgun at his house in Idaho. "Probably no other American writer of our time has set such a stamp on modern literature," the critic Alfred Kazin declared in a tribute to Hemingway in the *New York Times*.

bedfordstmartins.com/ americanlit for research links on Hemingway

Reading Hemingway's "Big Two-Hearted River." This story first appeared in the inaugural issue of *This Quarter*, a Paris-based literary monthly edited by the writer Ernest Walsh and the painter Ethel Moorhead. The distinguished issue was dedicated to Ezra Pound and included works by a number of avant-garde writers, including Gertrude Stein and the poets H.D. and William Carlos Williams. Hemingway originally wrote a

Hemingway in Michigan

In this photograph, which probably dates from the end of his high-school years, Hemingway is hiking through a second-growth forest in upper Michigan, the setting of his story "Big Two-Hearted River."

longer version of "Big Two-Hearted River," which concluded with an extended interior monologue by Nick Adams, a semiautobiographical character who appears in more than twenty of Hemingway's stories. But he omitted the monologue, which was published posthumously as "On Writing" in *The Nick Adams Stories* (1972), in order to focus "just on the straight fishing," as Hemingway wrote a friend in 1924. When he submitted the story to *This Quarter* early the following year, he told the editors that "it is the best thing I have done by a long shot," and many critics and writers agreed. In a review of Hemingway's early collection of stories *In Our Time* (1925), the critic and poet Allen Tate singled out "Big Two-Hearted River" for special praise, observing that "the passionate accuracy of particular observation, the intense monosyllabic diction, the fidelity to the internal demands of the subject—these qualities fuse in the most completely realized naturalistic fiction of the age." Hemingway's friend F. Scott Fitzgerald later said that he could think of few "contemporary American short stories as good as 'Big Two-Hearted River,'" adding: "It is the account of a boy on a fishing trip—he hikes, pitches his tent, cooks dinner, sleeps, and next morning casts for trout. Nothing more—but I read it with the most breathless unwilling interest I have experienced since [Joseph] Conrad first bent my reluctant eyes upon the sea." The text is taken from the first printing in *This Quarter*, May 1925.

BIG TWO-HEARTED RIVER[1]

[Part One]

The train went on up the track out of sight around one of the hills of burnt timber. Nick sat down on the bundle of canvas and bedding the baggage man had pitched out of the door of the baggage car. There was no town, nothing but the rails and the burnt over country. The thirteen saloons that had lined the one street of Seney had not left a trace. The foundations of the Mansion House hotel stuck up above the ground. The stone was chipped and split by the fire. It was all that was left of the town of Seney. Even the surface had been burned off the ground.

Nick looked at the burned over stretch of hillside where he had expected to find the scattered houses of the town and then walked down the railroad track to the bridge over the river. The river was there. It swirled against the log piles of the bridge. Nick looked down into the clear, brown water, coloured from the pebbly bottom, and watched the trout keeping themselves steady in the current with wavering fins. As he watched them they changed their positions by quick angles only to hold steady in the fast water again. Nick watched them a long time.

He watched them holding themselves with their noses into the current, many trout in deep fast moving water, slightly distorted as he watched far down through the glassy

1. **Big Two-Hearted River:** Hemingway originally published the story as "Big Two Hearted River," adding the hyphen in the title in his collection *In Our Time* (1925).

convex surface of the pool, its surface pushing and swelling smooth against the resistance of the log driven piles of the bridge. At the bottom of the pool were the big trout. Nick did not see them at first. Then he saw them at the bottom of the pool, big trout looking to hold themselves on the gravel bottom in a varying mist of gravel and sand raised in spurts by the current.

Nick looked down into the pool from the bridge. It was a hot day. A kingfisher flew up the stream. It was a long time since Nick had looked into a stream and seen trout. They were very satisfactory. As the shadow of the kingfisher moved up the stream a big trout shot up stream in a long angle, only his shadow marking the angle, then lost his shadow as he came through the surface of the water, caught the sun, and then, as he went back into the stream under the surface, his shadow seemed to float down the stream with the current, unresisting, to his post under the bridge where he tightened facing upstream.

Nick's heart tightened as the trout moved. He felt all the old feeling.

He turned and looked down the stream. It stretched away, pebbly bottomed with shallows and big boulders and a deep pool as it curved away around the foot of a bluff.

Nick walked back up the ties to where his pack lay in the cinders beside the railway track. He was happy. He adjusted the pack harness around the bundle, pulling straps tight, slung the pack on his back, got his arms through the shoulder straps and took some of the pull off his shoulders by leaning his forehead against the wide band of the tump line.[2] Still it was too heavy. It was much too heavy. He had his leather rod case in his hand and leaning forward to keep the weight of the pack high on his shoulders he walked along the road that paralleled the railway track, leaving the burned town behind in the heat, and then turned off around a hill with a high, fire scarred hill on either side onto a road that went back into the country. He walked along the road feeling the ache from the pull of the heavy pack. The road climbed steadily. It was hard work walking up hill. His muscles ached and the day was hot but Nick felt happy. He felt he had left everything behind, the need for thinking, the need to write, other needs. It was all back of him.

From the time he had gotten down off the train and the baggage man had thrown his pack out of the open car door things had been different. Seney was burnt, the country was burned over and changed, but it did not matter. It could not all be burned. He knew that. He hiked along the road, sweating in the sun, climbing to cross the range of hills that separated the railway from the pine plains.

The road ran on, dipping occasionally, but always climbing. Nick went on up. Finally the road after going parallel to the burnt high hillside reached the top. Nick leaned back against a stump and slipped out of the pack harness. Ahead of him as far as he could see was the pine plain. The burned country stopped off at the left with the range of hills. On ahead islands of dark pine trees rose out of the plain. Far off to the left was the line of the river. Nick followed it with his eye and caught glints of the water in the sun.

There was nothing but the pine plain ahead of him until the far blue hills that marked the Lake Superior height of land. He could hardly see them, faint and far away in the

---

2. **tump line:** Also spelled *tumpline* or *tump-line*, a strap placed across the forehead to help carry a heavy backpack.

heat light over the plain. If he looked too steadily they were gone. But if he only half looked they were there, the far off hills of the height of land.

Nick sat down against the charred stump and smoked a cigarette. His pack balanced on the top of the stump, harness holding ready, a hollow molded in it from his back. Nick sat smoking, looking out over the country. He did not need to get his map out. He knew where he was from the position of the river.

As he smoked, his legs stretched out in front of him, he noticed a grasshopper walk along the ground and up onto his woolen sock. The grasshopper was black. As he had walked along the road climbing he had started many grasshoppers from the dust. They were all black. They were not the big grasshoppers with yellow and black or red and black wings whirring out from their black wing sheathing and whirring as they fly up. These were just ordinary hoppers but all a sooty black in color. Nick had wondered about them as he walked without really thinking about them. Now as he watched the black hopper that was nibbling at the wool of his sock with its fourway lip, he realised that they had all turned black from living in the burned over land. He realised that the fire must have come the year before but the grasshoppers were all black now. He wondered how long they would stay that way.

Carefully he reached his hand down and took hold of the hopper by the wings. He turned him up, all his legs walking in the air, and looked at his jointed belly. Yes, it was black too, irridescent where the back and head were dusty.

"Go on Hopper," Nick said, speaking out loud for the first time, "Fly away somewhere."

He tossed the grasshopper up into the air and watched him sail away to a charcoal stump across the road.

Nick stood up. He leaned his back against the weight of his pack where it rested upright on the stump and got his arms through the shoulder straps. He stood with the pack on his back on the brow of the hill looking out across the country toward the distant river and then struck down the hillside away from the road. Under foot the ground was good walking. Two hundred yards down the hillside the fire line stopped. Then it was sweet fern, growing ankle high, to walk through and clumps of jack pines, a long undulating country with frequent rises and descents, sandy underfoot and the country alive again.

Nick kept his direction by the sun. He knew where he wanted to strike the river and he kept on through the pine plain, mounting small rises to see other rises ahead of him and sometimes from the top of a rise a great solid island of pines off to his right or his left. He broke off some sprigs of the heathery sweet fern, and put them under his pack straps. The chafing crushed it and he smelled it as he walked.

He was tired and very hot walking across the uneven, shadeless pine plain. At any time he knew he could strike the river by turning off to his left. It could not be more than a mile away. But he kept on toward the North to hit the river as far upstream as he could go in one day's walking.

For some time as he walked Nick had been in sight of one of the big islands of pine standing out above the rolling high ground he was crossing. He dipped down and then as he came slowly up to the crest of the ridge he turned and made toward the pine trees.

There was no underbrush in the island of pine trees. The trunks of the trees went straight up or slanted toward each other. The trunks were straight and brown without branches. The branches were high above. Some interlocked to make a solid shadow on the brown forest floor. Around the grove of trees was a bare space. It was brown and soft under foot as Nick walked on it. This was the over-lapping of the pine needle floor extending out beyond the width of the high branches. The trees had grown tall and the branches moved high, leaving in the sun this bare space they had once covered with shadow. Sharp at the edge of this extension of the forest floor commenced the sweet fern.

Nick slipped off his pack and lay down in the shade. He lay on his back and looked up into the pine trees. His neck and back and the small of his back rested as he stretched. The earth felt good against his back. He looked up at the sky through the branches and then shut his eyes. He opened them and looked up again. There was a wind high up in the branches. He shut his eyes again and went to sleep.

Nick woke stiff and cramped. The sun was nearly down. His pack was heavy and the straps painful as he lifted it on. He leaned over with the pack on and picked up the leather rod case and started out from the pine trees across the sweet fern swale toward the river. He knew it could not be more than a mile.

He came down a hillside covered with stumps into a meadow. At the edge of the meadow flowed the river. Nick was glad to get to the river. He walked up stream through the meadow. His trousers were soaked with the dew as he walked. After the hot day the dew had come quickly and heavily. The river made no sound. It was too fast and smooth. At the edge of the meadow, before he mounted to a piece of high ground to make camp, Nick looked down the river at the trout rising. They were rising to insects come from the swamp on the other side of the stream when the sun went down. The trout jumped out of water to take them. While Nick walked through the little stretch of meadow along side the stream trout had jumped high out of water. Now as he looked down the river the insects must be settling on the surface for the trout were feeding steadily all down the stream. As far down the long stretch as he could see the trout were rising, making circles all down the surface of the water as though it were starting to rain.

The ground rose, wooded and sandy, to overlook the meadow, the stretch of river and the swamp. Nick dropped his pack and rod case and looked for a level piece of ground. He was very hungry and he wanted to make his camp before he cooked. Between two jack pines the ground was quite level. He took the ax out of the pack and chopped out two projecting roots. That leveled a piece of ground large enough to sleep on. He smoothed out the sandy soil with his hand and pulled all the sweet fern bushes by their roots. His hands smelled good from the sweet fern. He smoothed the uprooted earth. He did not want anything making lumps under the blankets. When he had the ground smooth he spread his three blankets. One he folded double next to the ground. The other two he spread on top.

With the ax he slit off a bright slab of pine from one of the stumps and split it into pegs for the tent. He wanted them long and solid to hold in the ground. With the tent unpacked and spread on the ground, the pack, leaning against a jackpine, looked much smaller. Nick tied the rope that served the tent for a ridge-pole to the trunk of one of the pine trees and pulled the tent up off the ground with the other end of the rope and tied it to the other pine. The tent hung on the rope like a canvas blanket on a clothes line. Nick poked a pole he had cut up under the back peak of the canvas and then made it a tent by pegging out the sides. He pegged the sides out taut and drove the pegs deep, hitting them down into the ground with the flat of the ax until the rope loops were buried and the canvas was drum tight.

Across the open mouth of the tent Nick fixed cheese cloth to keep out mosquitoes. He crawled inside under the mosquito bar with various things from the pack to put at the head of the bed under the slant of the canvas. Inside the tent the light came through the brown canvas. It smelled pleasantly of canvas. Already there was something mysterious and homelike. Nick was happy as he crawled inside the tent. He had not been unhappy all day. This was different though. Now things were done. There had been this to do. Now it was done. It had been a hard trip. He was very tired. That was done. He had made his camp. He was settled. Nothing could touch him. It was a good place to camp. He was there, in the good place. He was in his home where he had made it. Now he was hungry.

He came out, crawling under the cheese cloth. It was quite dark outside. It was lighter in the tent.

Nick went over to the pack and found with his fingers a long nail in a paper sack of nails in the bottom of the pack. He drove it into the pine tree, holding it close and hitting it gently with the flat of the ax. He hung the pack up on the nail. All his supplies were in the pack. They were off the ground and sheltered now.

Nick was hungry. He did not believe he had ever been hungrier. He opened and emptied a can of pork and beans and a can of spaghetti into the frying pan.

"I've got a right to eat this kind of stuff if I'm willing to carry it," Nick said. His voice sounded strange in the darkening woods. He did not speak again.

He started a fire with some chunks of pine he got with the ax from a stump. Over the fire he stuck a wire grill, pushing the four legs down into the ground with his boot. Nick put the frying pan on the grill over the flames. He was hungrier. The beans and spaghetti warmed. Nick stirred them and mixed them together. They began to bubble, making little bubbles that rose with difficulty to the surface. There was a good smell. Nick got out a bottle of tomato catchup and cut four slices of bread. The little bubbles were coming faster now. Nick sat down beside the fire and lifted the frying pan off. He poured about half the contents out into the tin plate. It spread slowly on the plate. Nick knew it was too hot. He poured on some tomato catchup. He knew the beans and spaghetti were still too hot. He looked at the fire, then at the tent, he was not going to spoil it all by burning his tongue. For years he had never enjoyed fried bananas because he had never been able to wait for them to cool. His tongue was very sensitive. He was very hungry. Across the river in the swamp in the almost dark he saw a mist rising. He looked at the tent once more. All right. He took a full spoonful from the plate.

"Christ," Nick said, "Jesus Christ," he said happily.

He ate the whole plateful before he remembered the bread. Nick finished the second plateful with the bread, mopping the plate shiny. He had not eaten since a cup of coffee and a ham sandwich in the station restaurant at St. Ignace. It had been a very fine experience. He had been that hungry before but had not been able to satisfy it. He could have made camp hours before if he had wanted to. There were plenty of good places to camp on the river. But this was good.

Nick tucked two big chips of pine under the grill. The fire flared up. He had forgotten to get water for the coffee. Out of the pack he got a folding canvas bucket and walked down the hill across the edge of the meadow to the stream. The other bank was in the white mist. The grass was wet and cold as he knelt on the bank and dipped the canvas bucket into the stream. It bellied and pulled hard in the current. The water was ice cold. Nick rinsed the bucket and carried it full up to the camp. Up away from the stream it was not so cold.

Nick drove another big nail and hung the bucket full of water. He dipped the coffee pot half full, put some more chips under the grill onto the fire and put the pot on. He could not remember which way he made coffee. He could remember an argument about it with Hopkins but not which side he had taken. He decided to bring it to a boil. He remembered now that was Hopkins' way. He had once argued about everything with Hopkins. While he waited for the coffee to boil he opened a small can of apricots. He liked to open cans. He emptied the can of apricots out into a tin cup. While he watched the coffee on the fire he drank the juice syrup of the apricots, carefully at first to keep from spilling, then meditatively, sucking the apricots down. They were better than fresh apricots.

The coffee boiled as he watched. The lid came up and coffee and grounds ran down the side of the pot. Nick took it off the grill. It was a triumph for Hopkins. He put sugar in the empty apricot cup and poured some of the coffee out to cool. It was too hot to pour and he used his hat to hold the handle of the coffee pot. He would not let it steep in the pot at all. Not the first cup. It should be straight Hopkins all the way. Hop deserved that. He was a very serious coffee maker. He was the most serious man Nick had ever known. Not heavy; serious. That was a long time ago. Hopkins spoke without moving his lips. He had played polo. He made millions of dollars in Texas. He had borrowed carfare to go to Chicago when the wire came that his first big well had come in. He could have wired for money. That would have been too slow. They called Hop's girl the Blonde Venus. Hop did not mind because she was not his real girl. Hopkins said very confidently that none of them would make fun of his real girl. He was right. Hopkins went away when the telegram came. That was on the Black River. It took eight days for the telegram to reach him. Hopkins gave away his 22 caliber colt automatic pistol to Nick. He gave his camera to Bill. It was to remember him always by. They were all going fishing again next summer. The Hop Head[3] was rich. He would get a yacht and they would all cruise along the north shore of Lake Superior. He was excited but serious. They said good-bye and all felt bad. It broke up the trip. They never saw Hopkins again. That was a long time ago on the Black River.

Nick drank the coffee, the coffee according to Hopkins. The coffee was bitter. Nick laughed. It made a good ending to the story. His mind was starting to work. He knew he could choke it because he was tired enough. He spilled the coffee out of the pot and shook the grounds loose into the fire. He lit a cigarette and went inside the tent. He took off his shoes and trousers sitting on the blankets, rolled the shoes up inside the trousers for a pillow and got in between the blankets.

Out through the front of the tent he watched the glow of the fire when the night wind blew on it. It was a quiet night. The swamp was perfectly quiet. Nick stretched under the

---

3. **The Hop Head:** *Hop-head* was a slang term for a drug addict, especially one addicted to heroin. It was later used as the title of a song composed by Duke Ellington, "Hop Head," and recorded by his jazz band in 1927.

blanket comfortably. A mosquito hummed close to his ear. Nick sat up and lit a match. The mosquito was on the canvas over his head. Nick moved the match quickly up to it. The mosquito made a satisfactory hiss in the flame. The match went out. Nick lay down again under the blankets. He turned on his side and shut his eyes. He was sleepy. He felt sleep coming. He curled up under the blanket and went to sleep.

Part Two

In the morning the sun was up and the tent was starting to get hot. Nick crawled out under the mosquito netting stretched across the mouth of the tent to look at the morning. The grass was wet on his hands as he came out. He held his pants and his shoes in his hands. The sun was just up over the hill. There was the meadow, the river and the swamp. There were birch trees in the green of the swamp on the other side of the river.

The river was clear and smoothly fast in the early morning. Down about two hundred yards were three logs all the way across the stream. They made the water smooth and deep above them. As Nick watched a mink crossed the river on the logs and went into the swamp. Nick was excited. He was excited by the early morning and the river. He was really too hurried to eat breakfast but he knew he must. He built a little fire and put on the coffee pot. While the water was heating in the pot he took an empty bottle and went down over the edge of the high ground to the meadow. The meadow was wet with dew and Nick wanted to catch grasshoppers for bait before the sun dried the grass. He found plenty of good grasshoppers. They were at the base of the grass stems. Sometimes they clung to a grass stem. They were cold and wet with the dew and could not jump until the sun warmed them. Nick picked them up, taking only the medium sized brown ones, and put them in the bottle. He turned over a log and just under the shelter of the edge were several hundred hoppers. It was a grasshopper lodging house. Nick put about fifty of the medium browns into the bottle. While he was picking up the hoppers the others warmed in the sun and commenced to hop away. They flew when they hopped. At first they made one flight and stayed stiff when they landed as though they were dead.

Nick knew that by the time he was through with breakfast they would be as lively as ever. Without dew in the grass it would take him all day to catch a bottle full of good grasshoppers and he would have to crush many of them slamming at them with his hat. He washed his hands at the stream. He was excited to be near it. Then he walked up to the tent. The hoppers were already jumping stiffly in the grass. In the bottle, warmed by the sun, they were jumping in a mass. Nick put in a pine stick as a cork. It plugged the mouth of the bottle enough so the hoppers could not get out and left plenty of air passage.

He had rolled the log back and knew he could get grasshoppers there every morning.

Nick laid the bottle full of jumping grasshoppers against a pine trunk. Rapidly he mixed some buckwheat flour with water and stirred it smooth, one cup of flour one cup of water. He put a handful of coffee in the pot and dipped a lump of grease out of a can and slid it sputtering across the hot skillet. On the smoking skillet he poured smoothly the buckwheat batter. It spread like lava, the grease spitting sharply. Around the edges the buckwheat cake began to firm, then brown, then crisp. The surface was bubbling slowly to porousness. Nick pushed under the browned under surface with a fresh pine chip. He shook the skillet sideways and the cake was loose on the surface. I won't try and flop it, he thought. He slid the chip of clean wood all the way under the cake and flopped it over onto its face. It sputtered in the pan.

When it was cooked Nick re-greased the skillet. He used all the batter. It made another big flapjack and one smaller one.

Nick ate a big flapjack and a smaller one covered with apple butter. He put apple butter on the third cake, folded it over twice, wrapped it in oiled paper and put it in his shirt pocket. He put the apple butter jar back in the pack and cut bread for two sandwiches.

In the pack he found a big onion. He sliced it in two and peeled the silky outer skin. Then he cut one half into slices and made onion sandwiches. He wrapped them in oiled paper and buttoned them in the other pocket of his khaki shirt. He turned the skillet upside down on the grill, drank the coffee, sweetened and yellow brown with the condensed milk in it, and tidied up the camp. It was a nice little camp.

Nick took his fly rod out of the leather rod case, jointed it, and shoved the rod case back into the tent. He put on the reel and threaded the line through the guides. He had to hold it from hand to hand as he threaded it or it would slip back through its own weight. It was a heavy, double tapered fly line. Nick had paid eight dollars for it a long time ago. It was made heavy to lift back in the air and come forward flat and heavy and straight to make it possible to cast a fly which has no weight. Nick opened the aluminum leader box. The leaders were coiled between the damp flannel pads. Nick had wet the pads at the water cooler on the train up to St. Ignace. In the damp pads the gut leaders had softened and Nick unrolled one and tied it by a loop at the end to the heavy fly line. He fastened a hook on the end of the leader. It was a small hook; very thin and springy.

Nick took it from his hook book sitting with the rod across his lap. He tested the knot and the spring of the rod by pulling the line taut. It was a good feeling. He was careful not to let the hook bite into his finger.

He started down to the stream, holding his rod, the bottle of grasshoppers hung from his neck by a thong tied in half hitches around the neck of the bottle. His landing net hung by a hook from his belt. Over his shoulder was a long flour sack tied at each corner into an ear. The cord went over his shoulder. The sack flapped against his legs.

Nick felt awkard and professionally happy with all his equipment hanging from him. The grasshopper bottle swung against his chest. In his shirt the breast pockets bulged against him with the lunch and his fly book.

He stepped into the stream. It was a shock. His trousers clung tight to his legs. His shoes felt the gravel. The water was a rising cold shock.

Rushing, the current sucked against his legs. Where he stepped in the water was over his knees. He waded with the current. The gravel slid under his shoes. He looked down at the swirl of water below each leg and tipped up the bottle to get a grasshopper.

The first grasshopper gave a jump in the neck of the bottle and went out into the water. He was sucked under in the whirl by Nick's right leg and came to the surface a little way down stream. He floated rapidly, kicking. In a quick circle, breaking the smooth surface of the water, he disappeared. A trout had taken him.

Another hopper poked his head out of the bottle. His antennae wavered. He was getting his front legs out of the bottle to have a purchase to jump. Nick took him by the head and held him while he threaded the slim hook under his chin, down through his thorax and into the last segments of his abdomen. The grasshopper took hold of the hook with his front feet spitting tobacco juice on it. Nick dropped him into the water.

Holding the rod in his right hand he let out line against the pull of the grasshopper in the current. He stripped off line from the reel with his left hand and let it run free. He could see the hopper in the little waves of the current. It went out of sight.

There was a tug on the line. Nick pulled against the taut line. It was his first strike. Holding the now living rod across the current he brought in the line with his left hand. The rod bent in jerks, the trout pumping against the current. Nick knew it was a small one. He lifted the rod straight up in the air. It bowed with the pull.

He saw the trout in the water jerking with his head and body against the shifting tangent of the line in the stream.

Nick took the line in his left hand and pulled the trout, thumping tiredly against the current, to the surface. His back was mottled the clear, water-over-gravel color, his side flashing in the sun. The rod under his right arm Nick stooped, dipping his right hand into the current. He held the trout, never still, with his moist right hand while he unhooked the barb from his mouth, then dropped him back into the stream.

He hung unsteadily in the current, then settled to the bottom beside a stone. Nick reached down his hand to touch him, his arm to the elbow under water. The trout was steady in the moving stream, resting on the gravel, beside a stone. As Nick's fingers touched him, touched his smooth, cool, underwater feeling he was gone, gone in a shadow across the bottom of the stream.

He's all right, Nick thought. He was only tired.

He had wet his hand before he touched the trout so he would not disturb the delicate mucous that covered him. If a trout was touched with a dry hand a white fungous attacked the unprotected spot. Years before when he had fished crowded streams with fly fishermen ahead of him and behind him Nick had again and again come on dead trout, furry with white fungous, drifted against a rock, or floating belly up in some pool. Nick did not like to fish with other men on the river. Unless they were of your party they spoiled it.

He wallowed down the stream, above his knees in the current, through the fifty yards of shallow water above the pile of logs that crossed the stream. He did not rebait his hook and held it in his hand as he waded. He was certain he could catch small trout in the shallows but he did not want them. There would be no big trout in the shallows this time of day.

Now the water deepened up his thighs sharply and coldly. Ahead was the smooth dammed-back flood of water above the logs. The water was smooth and dark, on the left the lower edge of the meadow, on the right the swamp.

Nick leaned back against the current and took a hopper from the bottle. He threaded the hopper on the hook and spat on him for good luck. Then he pulled several yards of line from the reel and tossed the hopper out ahead onto the fast dark water. It floated down toward the logs, then the weight of the line pulled the bait under the surface. Nick held the rod in his right hand letting the line run out through his fingers.

There was a long tug. Nick struck and the rod came alive and dangerous, bent double, the line tightening, coming out of water, tightening, all in a heavy, dangerous, steady pull. Nick felt the moment when the leader would break if the strain increased and let the line go.

The reel ratcheted into a mechanical shriek as the line went out. Too fast. Nick could not check it, the line rushing out, the reel note rising as the line ran out.

With the core of the reel showing, his heart feeling stopped with the excitement, leaning back against the current that mounted icily his thighs, Nick thumbed the reel hard with his left hand. It was awkward getting his thumb inside the fly reel frame.

As he put on the pressure the line tightened into sudden hardness and beyond the logs a huge trout went high out of water. As he jumped Nick lowered the tip of the rod. But he felt as he dropped the tip to ease the strain the moment when the strain was too great; the hardness too tight. Of course the leader had broken. There was no mistaking the feeling when all spring left the line and it became dry and hard. Then it went slack.

His mouth dry, his heart down Nick reeled in. He had never seen so big a trout. There was a heaviness, a power not to be held, and then the bulk of him as he jumped. He looked as broad as a salmon.

Nick's hand was shaky. He reeled in slowly. The thrill had been too much. He felt, vaguely, a little sick, as though it would be better to sit down.

The leader had broken where the hook was tied to it. Nick took it in his hand. He thought of the trout somewhere on the bottom, holding himself steady over the gravel, far down below the light, under the logs, with the hook in his jaw. Nick knew the trout's teeth would cut through the snell of the hook. The hook would imbed itself in his jaw. He'd bet the trout was angry. Anything that size would be angry. That was a trout. He had been solidly hooked. Solid as a rock. He felt like a rock too before he started off. By God he was a big one. By God he was the biggest one I ever heard of.

Nick climbed out onto the meadow and stood, water running down his trousers and out of his shoes, his shoes squlchy. He went over and sat on the logs. He did not want to rush his sensations any.

He wriggled his toes in the water in his shoes and got out a cigarette from his breast pocket. He lit it and tossed the match into the fast water below the logs. A tiny trout rose at the match as it swung around in the fast current. Nick laughed. He would finish the cigarette.

He sat on the logs smoking, drying in the sun, the sun warm on his back, the river shallow ahead entering the woods, curving into the woods, shallows, light glittering, big watersmooth rocks, cedars along the bank and white birches, the logs warm in the sun, smooth to sit on, without bark, gray to the touch, slowly the feeling of disappointment left him. It went away slowly, the feeling of disappointment that came sharply after the thrill that made his shoulders ache. It was all right now. His rod lying out on the logs, Nick tied a new hook on the leader, pulling the gut tight until it grimped into itself in a hard knot.

He baited up, then picked up the rod and walked to the far end of the logs to get into the water where it was not too deep. Under and beyond the logs was a deep pool. Nick walked around the shallow shelf near the swamp shore until he came out on the shallow bed of the stream.

On the left, where the meadow ended and the woods began, a great elm tree was uprooted. Gone over in a storm it lay back into the woods, its roots clotted with dirt, grass growing in them, rising a solid bank beside the stream. The river cut to the edge of the uprooted tree. From where Nick stood he could see deep channels, like ruts, cut in the shallow bed of the stream by the flow of the current. Pebbly where he stood and pebbly and full of boulders beyond, where it curved near the tree roots the bed of the stream was marly and between the ruts of deep water green weed fronds swung in the current.

Nick swung the rod back over his shoulder and forward and the line, curving forward, laid the grasshopper down on one of the deep channels in the weeds. A trout struck and Nick hooked him.

Holding the rod far out toward the uprooted tree and sloshing backward in the current Nick worked the trout, plunging, the rod bending alive, out of the danger of the weeds into the open river. Holding the rod, pumping alive against the current, Nick brought the trout in. He rushed, but always came, the spring of the rod yielding to the rushes, sometimes jerking under water but always bringing him in. Nick eased downstream with the rushes. The rod above his head he led the trout over the net, then lifted.

The trout hung heavy in the net, mottled trout back and silver sides in the meshes. Nick unhooked him; heavy sides, good to hold, big undershot jaw, and slipped him, heaving and big sliding, into the long sack that hung from his shoulders in the water.

Nick spread the mouth of the sack against the current and it filled, heavy with water. He held it up, the bottom in the stream, and the water poured out through the sides. Inside at the bottom was the big trout, alive in the water.

Nick moved down stream. The sack out ahead of him, sunk, heavy in the water, pulling from his shoulders.

It was getting hot, the sun hot on the back of his neck.

Nick had one good trout. He did not care about getting many trout. Now the stream was shallow and wide. There were trees along both banks. The trees of the left bank made short shadows on the current in the forenoon sun. Nick knew there were trout in each shadow. In the afternoon, after the sun had crossed toward the hills, the trout would be in the cool shadows on the other side of the stream.

The very biggest ones would lie up close to the bank. You could always pick them up there on the Black River. When the sun was down they all moved out into the current. Just when the sun made the water blinding in the glare before it went down you were liable to strike a big trout anywhere in the current. It was almost impossible to fish then, the surface of the water was blinding as a mirror in the sun. Of course you could fish upstream, but in a stream like this or the Black you had to wallow against the current and in a deep place the water piled up on you. It was no fun to fish upstream with this much current.

Nick moved along through the shallow stretch watching the banks for deep holes. A beech tree grew close beside the river so that the branches hung down into the water. The stream went back in under the leaves. There were always trout in a place like that.

Nick did not care about fishing that hole. He was sure he would get hooked in the branches.

It looked deep though. He dropped the grasshopper so that the current took it under water, back in under the overhanging branch. The line pulled hard and Nick struck. The trout threshed heavily, half out of water in the leaves and branches. The line was caught. Nick pulled hard and the trout was off. He reeled in and holding the hook in his hand walked down the stream.

Ahead, close to the left bank, was a big log. Nick saw it was hollow. Pointing up stream the current entered it smoothly, only a little ripple spreading each side of the log. The top of the hollow log was grey and dry. It was partly in the shadow and the water deepened toward it.

Nick took the cork out of the grasshopper bottle and a hopper clung to it. He picked him off, hooked him and tossed him out onto the current. He held the rod far out so that the hopper on the water moved into the current flowing into the hollow log. Nick lowered the rod and the hopper floated in. There was a heavy strike. Nick swung the rod against the pull. It felt as though he were hooked into the log its-self except that what he was hooked to felt alive, alive and pulling.

He tried to force the fish out into the current. It came, heavily.

The line went slack and Nick thought the trout was gone. Then he saw him, very near, in the current, shaking his head, trying to get the hook out. His mouth was clamped shut. He was fighting the hook in the clear flowing current.

Looping in the line with his left hand Nick swung the rod to make the line taut and tried to lead the trout toward the net; but he was gone, out of sight, the line pumping. Nick fought him against the current, letting him thump in the water against the spring of the rod. He shifted the rod to his left hand, worked the trout upstream, holding his weight, fighting on the rod, and then let him down into the net. He lifted him clear of the water, a heavy half circle in the net, the net dripping, unhooked him and slid him into the sack.

He spread the mouth of the sack and looked down in at the two big trout alive in the water.

Through the deepening water Nick waded over to the hollow log. He took the sack off over his head, the trout flopping as it came out of water, and hung it so the trout were deep in the clear water. Then he pulled himself up on the log and sat, the water from his trousers and boots running down into the stream. He laid his rod down, moved along to the shady end of the log and took the sandwiches out of his pocket. He dipped the sandwiches in the cold water. The current carried away the crumbs. He ate the sandwiches and dipped his hat full of water to drink, the water running out through his hat just ahead of his drinking.

It was cool in the shade sitting on the log. He took a cigarette out and scratched a match to light it. The match sunk into the grey wood, making a tiny furrow. Nick leaned over the side of the log, found a hard place and lit the match. He sat smoking and watching the river.

Ahead the river narrowed and went into a swamp. The river became smooth and deep and the swamp looked solid with cedar trees, their trunks close, their branches together. It would not be possible to walk through a swamp like that. The branches grew so low. You would have to keep almost level with the ground to move at all. You could not make your way through the branches. That must be why the animals that live in swamps are built the way they are, Nick thought.

He wished he had brought something to read. He felt like reading. He did not feel like going on into the swamp. He looked down the river. A big cedar slanted all the way across the stream. Beyond that the river went into the swamp.

Nick did not want to go in there now. He felt a reaction against deep wading with the water deepening up under his armpits. He did not want to hook big trout in places impossible to land them. In the swamp the banks were bare, covered with cedar needles, the big cedars came together overhead, the sun did not come through except in patches. In the fast deep water in the half light the fishing would be tragic. In the swamp fishing was a tragic adventure. Nick did not want it. He did not want to go down the stream any further today.

He took out his knife, opened it, and stuck it in the log. Then he pulled up the sack, reached into it and brought out one of the trout. Holding him near the tail, hard to hold, alive in his hands, he whacked him against the log. The trout quivered, rigid. Nick laid him on the log in the shade and broke the neck of the other fish in the same way. He laid them side by side on the log. They were fine trout.

Nick cleaned them, slitting the belly from the ventral fin to the tip of the jaw. All the insides, the gills and tongues came out in one piece. They were both males with long grey white strips of milt,[4] smooth and clean. All the insides clean and compact, coming out all together. Nick tossed the offal ashore for the minks to find.

He washed the trout in the stream. When he held them back up in the water they looked like live fish. Their color had not yet gone. He washed his hands and dried them on the log. Then he laid the trout on the sack spread out on the log, rolled them up in it, tied it into a bundle and put it in the landing net. His knife was still standing, blade stuck in the log. He cleaned it on the wood and put it in his pocket.

Nick stood up on the log holding his rod, the landing net hanging heavy against his thighs, then stepped into the water and splashed ashore. He climbed the bank and cut up into the woods toward the high ground. He was going back to camp. He looked back. The river just showed through the trees. There were plenty of days coming when he could fish the swamp.

[1925]

---

4. **milt:** Semen from the reproductive gland of a fish.

John Steinbeck

[1902–1968]

John Ernst Steinbeck was born on February 27, 1902, in Salinas, a town in the central coastal region of California. He was the third of four children and the only son of Olive Hamilton Steinbeck, a former schoolteacher, and John Ernst Steinbeck, the manager of a flour mill who later became treasurer of Monterey County. As a child, Steinbeck was an avid reader whose favorite book was Sir Thomas Malory's *Morte d'Arthur,* a collection of the stories about the legendary King Arthur of England. Steinbeck attended Salinas High School, where he played baseball and wrote for the school newspaper, and worked during the summers on ranches and construction crews. After his graduation in 1919, he enrolled at Stanford University. Although his parents hoped he would pursue a technical degree, Steinbeck wanted to be a writer. He published satirical articles in the *Stanford Spectator,* the campus literary magazine, and especially enjoyed his creative-writing classes. He was otherwise an indifferent student who missed classes and preferred reading and writing what he chose. He tried taking time off from college, working as a manual laborer, before withdrawing from Stanford in 1925. Like other aspiring writers, he determined to go to New York City, working his way there aboard a freighter that sailed from San Francisco.

John Steinbeck

This photograph was taken in the mid-1930s, when critics began to hail Steinbeck as one of the major American writers to emerge during the Great Depression.

For the next ten years, Steinbeck struggled to establish himself as a professional author. A relative helped him get a job as a reporter for the *New York American,* but he was soon fired. "I think now that the $25 a week that they paid me was a total loss," Steinbeck humorously recalled. "They gave me stories to cover in Queens and Brooklyn and I would get lost and spend hours trying to find my way back." Since he also failed to find a publisher for a collection of his short stories, Steinbeck had little choice but to return to California, and he signed on aboard a freighter bound back to San Francisco. After his arrival, he took a series of undemanding jobs that left him ample time for writing. He completed several novels, only one of which—*Cup of Gold* (1929), a fictionalized history of the seventeenth-century pirate Henry Morgan—was published. In 1930, Steinbeck married his first wife, Carol Hennings, a social activist who helped sensitize him to the plight of the poor and unemployed during the Great Depression. The stock market crash hurt the publishing business, but Steinbeck obtained a New York literary agent who placed two more of his books, both set in California: a short-story cycle, *The Pastures of Heaven* (1932); and a novel, *To a God Unknown* (1933). Although neither book sold well, Steinbeck also published a series of stories in the *North American Review.* Readers of the prestigious journal responded with enthusiasm, and the stories brought Steinbeck to the attention of a New York publisher, Paul Covici. He read and immediately agreed to publish a novel that had been rejected by many other publishing firms: *Tortilla Flat* (1935), Steinbeck's comic story about a group of wastrels living in a dilapidated section of Monterey, California.

bedfordstmartins.com/
americanlit for research
links on Steinbeck

The royalties and sale of the film rights to the best-selling novel gave Steinbeck his first financial security, and he was "stunned and delighted" to learn that it had been awarded the prize for the best novel of 1935 by the Commonwealth Club of California.

Steinbeck earned even greater acclaim during the following five years. He soon published *In Dubious Battle* (1936), a novel about violent labor strife in the apple-growing industry, and *Of Mice and Men* (1937), a tragic novella about the broken dreams of two migrant laborers in California. Steinbeck sold the film rights of the novella, and his own dramatic adaptation was a hit on Broadway, winning the coveted New York Drama Critics' Circle Award for best play of 1938. At the urging of his publisher, Steinbeck followed up on his success by putting together a collection of his short stories, *The Long Valley* (1938), a highly regarded volume that sold briskly. He also began researching a novel about the plight of the "Okies," farmers driven from their homes in the Dust Bowl of Oklahoma to seek a new life in California. Following the main path of their great migration, Steinbeck drove west along Route 66 to California, where he was horrified by what he witnessed in the migrant camps. "The death of children by starvation in our valleys is simply staggering," he wrote his agent. Steinbeck poured his outrage and passion into his most ambitious novel, *The Grapes of Wrath* (1939). Angry businessmen and politicians called the book a pack of lies, and the controversial novel was banned by a number of school boards in states from New York to California. Nonetheless, Steinbeck was invited to the White House by President Franklin D. Roosevelt, whose socially conscious wife, Eleanor, publicly praised *The Grapes of Wrath*. It was the best-selling novel of 1939 and was awarded the Pulitzer Prize for Fiction. Steinbeck's fame was further spread by the 1940 film version starring Henry Fonda and directed by the legendary John Ford.

Steinbeck never again achieved the commercial and critical success of *The Grapes of Wrath*. In 1941, he left California and moved permanently to New York City. Under the pressures of his new life as a celebrity author, his marriage fell apart, and after his divorce Steinbeck married Gwyndolen Conger in 1943. Shortly thereafter, he went to Europe as a war correspondent for the *New York Herald Tribune*. In 1945, Steinbeck published a new novel, *Cannery Row*, an evocation of the lives of those living in a poor section of Monterey during the Depression. Although the book sold well, critics tended to dismiss the novel and those that followed, including *The Pearl* (1947) and *Burning Bright* (1950). After his second marriage ended, he married Elaine Anderson Scott, a former stage manager on Broadway, in 1950. By all accounts, they were very happy together, but Steinbeck was deeply hurt by the critical reception of his works, especially *East of Eden* (1952), a historical saga about two California families from 1900 to World War II. In a review in the *Nation*, Leo Gurko raised a question that many critics were asking, "why Steinbeck's talent has declined so rapidly and so far" since *The Grapes of Wrath*. Indeed, he was widely regarded as past his prime, an impression that seemed to be confirmed by his modest output during the remainder of the 1950s.

Steinbeck, however, ended his career on a far more triumphant note. His final novel was *The Winter of Our Discontent* (1961), a critique of

American materialism set in New England. Although some reviews were negative, many critics echoed the novelist Saul Bellow, who declared that Steinbeck had returned "to the high standards of *The Grapes of Wrath*." In 1962, he was awarded the Nobel Prize for Literature for "his realistic as well as imaginative writings, distinguished by a sympathetic humor and a keen social perception." That same year, Steinbeck published his enormously popular *Travels with Charley in Search of America*, an account of a cross-country trip with his "old French gentleman poodle," Charley. Steinbeck was awarded the Presidential Medal of Freedom in 1964, and he became a friend and strong supporter of President Lyndon Johnson during the Vietnam War. After suffering a stroke, Steinbeck died of a heart attack on December 20, 1968.

Reading Steinbeck's "Flight."   This story is set in the Santa Lucia Mountains, close to where Steinbeck grew up in central California. The stark and naturalistic tale was rejected by several magazines, including *Scribner's* and the *Saturday Evening Post*, before Steinbeck first published it in his collection *The Long Valley*. It was the only story in the collection that had not previously been published in a magazine, but most critics have affirmed Steinbeck's belief in the power and quality of "Flight." William Soskin singled out the story for special praise in a review of *The Long Valley* that appeared in the *New York Herald* in September 1938:

> Steinbeck is at his comfortable best in stories that demand careful reporting of detail — the agonizing detail of a hunted youth's flight into the mountains after he has killed a man, of increasing pain and thirst and desperate struggle and fear that remind you of one of William Faulkner's hunted creatures and of Eugene O'Neill's terror-stricken Emperor Jones.

Critics, however, have offered a range of interpretations of "Flight," which some read as an account of a human being's regression into an animal and others view as an allegory of initiation into the wilderness or of growth from childhood to adulthood. The text is taken from *The Long Valley* (1938).

FLIGHT

About fifteen miles below Monterey, on the wild coast,[1] the Torres family had their farm, a few sloping acres above a cliff that dropped to the brown reefs and to the hissing white waters of the ocean. Behind the farm the stone mountains stood up against the sky. The farm buildings huddled like little clinging aphids on the mountain skirts, crouched low to the ground as though the wind might blow them into the sea. The little shack, the

---

1. **Monterey, on the wild coast:** Monterey, the capital of California under Spanish and Mexican rule, is on the rugged central coast, where the Santa Lucia Mountains run close to the Pacific Ocean.

rattling, rotting barn were grey-bitten with sea salt, beaten by the damp wind until they had taken on the color of the granite hills. Two horses, a red cow and a red calf, half a dozen pigs and a flock of lean, multicolored chickens stocked the place. A little corn was raised on the sterile slope, and it grew short and thick under the wind, and all the cobs formed on the landward sides of the stalks.

Mama Torres, a lean, dry woman with ancient eyes, had ruled the farm for ten years, ever since her husband tripped over a stone in the field one day and fell full length on a rattlesnake. When one is bitten on the chest there is not much that can be done.

Mama Torres had three children, two undersized black ones of twelve and fourteen, Emilio and Rosy, whom Mama kept fishing on the rocks below the farm when the sea was kind and when the truant officer was in some distant part of Monterey County. And there was Pepé, the tall smiling son of nineteen, a gentle, affectionate boy, but very lazy. Pepé had a tall head, pointed at the top, and from its peak, coarse black hair grew down like a thatch all around. Over his smiling little eyes Mama cut a straight bang so he could see. Pepé had sharp Indian cheek bones and an eagle nose, but his mouth was as sweet and shapely as a girl's mouth, and his chin was fragile and chiseled. He was loose and gangling, all legs and feet and wrists, and he was very lazy. Mama thought him fine and brave, but she never told him so. She said, "Some lazy cow must have got into thy father's family, else how could I have a son like thee." And she said, "When I carried thee, a sneaking lazy coyote came out of the brush and looked at me one day. That must have made thee so."

Pepé smiled sheepishly and stabbed at the ground with his knife to keep the blade sharp and free from rust. It was his inheritance, that knife, his father's knife. The long heavy blade folded back into the black handle. There was a button on the handle. When Pepé pressed the button, the blade leaped out ready for use. The knife was with Pepé always, for it had been his father's knife.

One sunny morning when the sea below the cliff was glinting and blue and the white surf creamed on the reef, when even the stone mountains looked kindly, Mama Torres called out the door of the shack, "Pepé, I have a labor for thee."

There was no answer. Mama listened. From behind the barn she heard a burst of laughter. She lifted her full long skirt and walked in the direction of the noise.

Pepé was sitting on the ground with his back against a box. His white teeth glistened. On either side of him stood the two black ones, tense and expectant. Fifteen feet away a redwood post was set in the ground. Pepé's right hand lay limply in his lap, and in the palm the big black knife rested. The blade was closed back into the handle. Pepé looked smiling at the sky.

Suddenly Emilio cried, "Ya!"

Pepé's wrist flicked like the head of a snake. The blade seemed to fly open in mid-air, and with a thump the point dug into the redwood post, and the black handle quivered. The three burst into excited laughter. Rosy ran to the post and pulled out the knife and brought it back to Pepé. He closed the blade and settled the knife carefully in his listless palm again. He grinned self-consciously at the sky.

"Ya!"

The heavy knife lanced out and sunk into the post again. Mama moved forward like a ship and scattered the play.

"All day you do foolish things with the knife, like a toy-baby," she stormed. "Get up on thy huge feet that eat up shoes. Get up!" She took him by one loose shoulder and hoisted at him. Pepé grinned sheepishly and came half-heartedly to his feet. "Look!" Mama cried. "Big lazy, you must catch the horse and put on him thy father's saddle. You must ride to Monterey. The medicine bottle is empty. There is no salt. Go thou now, Peanut! Catch the horse."

A revolution took place in the relaxed figure of Pepé.

"To Monterey, me? Alone? *Si*,[2] Mama."

She scowled at him. "Do not think, big sheep, that you will buy candy. No, I will give you only enough for the medicine and the salt."

Pepé smiled. "Mama, you will put the hatband on the hat?"

She relented then. "Yes, Pepé. You may wear the hatband."

His voice grew insinuating, "And the green handkerchief, Mama?"

"Yes, if you go quickly and return with no trouble, the silk green handkerchief will go. If you make sure to take off the handkerchief when you eat so no spot may fall on it. . . ."

"*Si*, Mama. I will be careful. I am a man."

"Thou? A man? Thou art a peanut."

He went into the rickety barn and brought out a rope, and he walked agilely enough up the hill to catch the horse.

When he was ready and mounted before the door, mounted on his father's saddle that was so old that the oaken frame showed through torn leather in many places, then Mama brought out the round black hat with the tooled leather band, and she reached up and knotted the green silk handkerchief about his neck. Pepé's blue denim coat was much darker than his jeans, for it had been washed much less often.

Mama handed up the big medicine bottle and the silver coins. "That for the medicine," she said, "and that for the salt. That for a candle to burn for the papa. That for *dulces*[3] for the little ones. Our friend Mrs. Rodriguez will give you dinner and maybe a bed for the night. When you go to the church say only ten Paternosters and only twenty-five Ave Marias.[4] Oh! I know, big coyote. You would sit there flapping your mouth over Aves all day while you looked at the candles and the holy pictures. That is not good devotion to stare at the pretty things."

The black hat, covering the high pointed head and black thatched hair of Pepé, gave him dignity and age. He sat the rangy horse well. Mama thought how handsome he was, dark and lean and tall. "I would not send thee now alone, thou little one, except for the medicine," she said softly. "It is not good to have no medicine, for who knows when the toothache will come, or the sadness of the stomach. These things are."

"Adios, Mama," Pepé cried. "I will come back soon. You may send me often alone. I am a man."

---

2. **Si**: Yes (Spanish).

3. **dulces**: Candy (Spanish).

4. **Paternosters . . . Ave Marias:** These are two popular Roman Catholic prayers, frequently recited in a series as counted out on a string of prayer beads, known as a rosary: *Paternoster*, literally "Our Father" (Latin), the name of the Lord's Prayer; and *Ave Maria*, literally "Hail Mary" (Latin), the name of the prayer in honor of Mary, the mother of Jesus.

"Thou art a foolish chicken."

He straightened his shoulders, flipped the reins against the horse's shoulder and rode away. He turned once and saw that they still watched him, Emilio and Rosy and Mama. Pepé grinned with pride and gladness and lifted the tough buckskin horse to a trot.

When he had dropped out of sight over a little dip in the road, Mama turned to the black ones, but she spoke to herself. "He is nearly a man now," she said. "It will be a nice thing to have a man in the house again." Her eyes sharpened on the children. "Go to the rocks now. The tide is going out. There will be abalones to be found." She put the iron hooks into their hands and saw them down the steep trail to the reefs. She brought the smooth stone *metate*[5] to the doorway and sat grinding her corn to flour and looking occasionally at the road over which Pepé had gone. The noonday came and then the afternoon, when the little ones beat the abalones on a rock to make them tender and Mama patted the tortillas to make them thin. They ate their dinner as the red sun was plunging down toward the ocean. They sat on the doorsteps and watched the big white moon come over the mountain tops.

Mama said, "He is now at the house of our friend Mrs. Rodriguez. She will give him nice things to eat and maybe a present."

Emilio said, "Some day I too will ride to Monterey for medicine. Did Pepé come to be a man today?"

Mama said wisely, "A boy gets to be a man when a man is needed. Remember this thing. I have known boys forty years old because there was no need for a man."

Soon afterwards they retired, Mama in her big oak bed on one side of the room, Emilio and Rosy in their boxes full of straw and sheepskins on the other side of the room.

The moon went over the sky and the surf roared on the rocks. The roosters crowed the first call. The surf subsided to a whispering surge against the reef. The moon dropped toward the sea. The roosters crowed again.

The moon was near down to the water when Pepé rode on a winded horse to his home flat. His dog bounced out and circled the horse yelping with pleasure. Pepé slid off the saddle to the ground. The weathered little shack was silver in the moonlight and the square shadow of it was black to the north and east. Against the east the piling mountains were misty with light; their tops melted into the sky.

Pepé walked wearily up the three steps and into the house. It was dark inside. There was a rustle in the corner.

Mama cried out from her bed. "Who comes? Pepé, is it thou?"

"*Sí*, Mama."

"Did you get the medicine?"

"*Sí*, Mama."

"Well, go to sleep, then. I thought you would be sleeping at the house of Mrs. Rodriguez." Pepé stood silently in the dark room. "Why do you stand there, Pepé? Did you drink wine?"

---

5. **metate**: A flat stone on which grain is ground (Spanish).

"*Sí*, Mama."

"Well, go to bed then and sleep out the wine."

His voice was tired and patient, but very firm. "Light the candle, Mama. I must go away into the mountains."

"What is this, Pepé? You are crazy." Mama struck a sulphur match and held the little blue burr until the flame spread up the stick. She set light to the candle on the floor beside her bed. "Now, Pepé, what is this you say?" She looked anxiously into his face.

He was changed. The fragile quality seemed to have gone from his chin. His mouth was less full than it had been, the lines of the lips were straighter, but in his eyes the greatest change had taken place. There was no laughter in them any more, nor any bashfulness. They were sharp and bright and purposeful.

He told her in a tired monotone, told her everything just as it had happened. A few people came into the kitchen of Mrs. Rodriguez. There was wine to drink. Pepé drank wine. The little quarrel—the man started toward Pepé and then the knife—it went almost by itself.

It flew, it darted before Pepé knew it. As he talked, Mama's face grew stern, and it seemed to grow more lean. Pepé finished. "I am a man now, Mama. The man said names to me I could not allow."

Mama nodded. "Yes, thou art a man, my poor little Pepé. Thou art a man. I have seen it coming on thee. I have watched you throwing the knife into the post, and I have been afraid." For a moment her face had softened, but now it grew stern again. "Come! We must get you ready. Go. Awaken Emilio and Rosy. Go quickly."

Pepé stepped over to the corner where his brother and sister slept among the sheepskins. He leaned down and shook them gently. "Come, Rosy! Come, Emilio! The mama says you must arise."

The little black ones sat up and rubbed their eyes in the candlelight. Mama was out of bed now, her long black skirt over her nightgown. "Emilio," she cried. "Go up and catch the other horse for Pepé. Quickly, now! Quickly." Emilio put his legs in his overalls and stumbled sleepily out the door.

"You heard no one behind you on the road?" Mama demanded.

"No, Mama. I listened carefully. No one was on the road."

Mama darted like a bird about the room. From a nail on the wall she took a canvas water bag and threw it on the floor. She stripped a blanket from her bed and rolled it into a tight tube and tied the ends with string. From a box beside the stove she lifted a flour sack half full of black stringy jerky. "Your father's black coat, Pepé. Here, put it on."

Pepé stood in the middle of the floor watching her activity. She reached behind the door and brought out the rifle, a long 38-56, worn shiny the whole length of the barrel. Pepé took it from her and held it in the crook of his elbow. Mama brought a little leather bag and counted the cartridges into his hand. "Only ten left," she warned. "You must not waste them."

Emilio put his head in the door. "'*Qui 'st 'l caballo*,[6] Mama."

"Put on the saddle from the other horse. Tie on the blanket. Here, tie the jerky to the saddle horn."

---

6. '*Qui 'st 'l caballo*: Here's the horse (colloquial Spanish).

Still Pepé stood silently watching his mother's frantic activity. His chin looked hard, and his sweet mouth was drawn and thin. His little eyes followed Mama about the room almost suspiciously.

Rosy asked softly, "Where goes Pepé?"

Mama's eyes were fierce. "Pepé goes on a journey. Pepé is a man now. He has a man's thing to do."

Pepé straightened his shoulders. His mouth changed until he looked very much like Mama.

At last the preparation was finished. The loaded horse stood outside the door. The water bag dripped a line of moisture down the bay shoulder.

The moonlight was being thinned by the dawn and the big white moon was near down to the sea. The family stood by the shack. Mama confronted Pepé. "Look, my son! Do not stop until it is dark again. Do not sleep even though you are tired. Take care of the horse in order that he may not stop of weariness. Remember to be careful with the bullets—there are only ten. Do not fill thy stomach with jerky or it will make thee sick. Eat a little jerky and fill thy stomach with grass. When thou comest to the high mountains, if thou seest any of the dark watching men, go not near to them nor try to speak to them. And forget not thy prayers." She put her lean hands on Pepé's shoulders, stood on her toes and kissed him formally on both cheeks, and Pepé kissed her on both cheeks. Then he went to Emilio and Rosy and kissed both of their cheeks.

Pepé turned back to Mama. He seemed to look for a little softness, a little weakness in her. His eyes were searching, but Mama's face remained fierce. "Go now," she said. "Do not wait to be caught like a chicken."

Pepé pulled himself into the saddle. "I am a man," he said.

It was the first dawn when he rode up the hill toward the little canyon which let a trail into the mountains. Moonlight and daylight fought with each other, and the two warring qualities made it difficult to see. Before Pepé had gone a hundred yards, the outlines of his figure were misty; and long before he entered the canyon, he had become a grey, indefinite shadow.

Mama stood stiffly in front of her doorstep, and on either side of her stood Emilio and Rosy. They cast furtive glances at Mama now and then.

When the grey shape of Pepé melted into the hillside and disappeared, Mama relaxed. She began the high, whining keen of the death wail. "Our beautiful—our brave," she cried. "Our protector, our son is gone." Emilio and Rosy moaned beside her. "Our beautiful—our brave, he is gone." It was the formal wail. It rose to a high piercing whine and subsided to a moan. Mama raised it three times and then she turned and went into the house and shut the door.

Emilio and Rosy stood wondering in the dawn. They heard Mama whimpering in the house. They went out to sit on the cliff above the ocean. They touched shoulders. "When did Pepé come to be a man?" Emilio asked.

"Last night," said Rosy. "Last night in Monterey." The ocean clouds turned red with the sun that was behind the mountains.

"We will have no breakfast," said Emilio. "Mama will not want to cook." Rosy did not answer him. "Where is Pepé gone?" he asked.

Rosy looked around at him. She drew her knowledge from the quiet air. "He has gone on a journey. He will never come back."

"Is he dead? Do you think he is dead?"

Rosy looked back at the ocean again. A little steamer, drawing a line of smoke sat on the edge of the horizon. "He is not dead," Rosy explained. "Not yet."

Pepé rested the big rifle across the saddle in front of him. He let the horse walk up the hill and he didn't look back. The stony slope took on a coat of short brush so that Pepé found the entrance to a trail and entered it.

When he came to the canyon opening, he swung once in his saddle and looked back, but the houses were swallowed in the misty light. Pepé jerked forward again. The high shoulder of the canyon closed in on him. His horse stretched out its neck and sighed and settled to the trail.

It was a well-worn path, dark soft leaf-mould earth strewn with broken pieces of sandstone. The trail rounded the shoulder of the canyon and dropped steeply into the bed of the stream. In the shallows the water ran smoothly, glinting in the first morning sun. Small round stones on the bottom were as brown as rust with sun moss. In the sand along the edges of the stream the tall, rich wild mint grew, while in the water itself the cress, old and tough, had gone to heavy seed.

The path went into the stream and emerged on the other side. The horse sloshed into the water and stopped. Pepé dropped his bridle and let the beast drink of the running water.

Soon the canyon sides became steep and the first giant sentinel redwoods guarded the trail, great round red trunks bearing foliage as green and lacy as ferns. Once Pepé was among the trees, the sun was lost. A perfumed and purple light lay in the pale green of the underbrush. Gooseberry bushes and blackberries and tall ferns lined the stream, and overhead the branches of the redwoods met and cut off the sky.

Pepé drank from the water bag, and he reached into the flour sack and brought out a black string of jerky. His white teeth gnawed at the string until the tough meat parted. He chewed slowly and drank occasionally from the water bag. His little eyes were slumberous and tired, but the muscles of his face were hard set. The earth of the trail was black now. It gave up a hollow sound under the walking hoofbeats.

The stream fell more sharply. Little waterfalls splashed on the stones. Five-fingered ferns hung over the water and dripped spray from their fingertips. Pepé rode half over in his saddle, dangling one leg loosely. He picked a bay leaf from a tree beside the way and put it into his mouth for a moment to flavor the dry jerky. He held the gun loosely across the pommel.

Suddenly he squared in his saddle, swung the horse from the trail and kicked it hurriedly up behind a big redwood tree. He pulled up the reins tight against the bit to keep the horse from whinnying. His face was intent and his nostrils quivered a little.

A hollow pounding came down the trail, and a horseman rode by, a fat man with red cheeks and a white stubble beard. His horse put down its head and blubbered at the trail when it came to the place where Pepé had turned off. "Hold up!" said the man and he pulled up his horse's head.

When the last sound of the hoofs died away, Pepé came back into the trail again. He did not relax in the saddle any more. He lifted the big rifle and swung the lever to throw a shell into the chamber, and then he let down the hammer to half cock.

The trail grew very steep. Now the redwood trees were smaller and their tops were dead, bitten dead where the wind reached them. The horse plodded on; the sun went slowly overhead and started down toward the afternoon.

Where the stream came out of a side canyon, the trail left it. Pepé dismounted and watered his horse and filled up his water bag. As soon as the trail had parted from the stream, the trees were gone and only the thick brittle sage and manzanita and chaparral edged the trail. And the soft black earth was gone, too, leaving only the light tan broken rock for the trail bed. Lizards scampered away into the brush as the horse rattled over the little stones.

Pepé turned in his saddle and looked back. He was in the open now: he could be seen from a distance. As he ascended the trail the country grew more rough and terrible and dry. The way wound about the bases of great square rocks. Little grey rabbits skittered in the brush. A bird made a monotonous high creaking. Eastward the bare rock mountaintops were pale and powder-dry under the dropping sun. The horse plodded up and up the trail toward a little V in the ridge which was the pass.

Pepé looked suspiciously back every minute or so, and his eyes sought the tops of the ridges ahead. Once, on a white barren spur, he saw a black figure for a moment, but he looked quickly away, for it was one of the dark watchers. No one knew who the watchers were, nor where they lived, but it was better to ignore them and never to show interest in them. They did not bother one who stayed on the trail and minded his own business.

The air was parched and full of light dust blown by the breeze from the eroding mountains. Pepé drank sparingly from his bag and corked it tightly and hung it on the horn again. The trail moved up the dry shale hillside, avoiding rocks, dropping under clefts, climbing in and out of old water scars. When he arrived at the little pass he stopped and looked back for a long time. No dark watchers were to be seen now. The trail behind was empty. Only the high tops of the redwoods indicated where the stream flowed.

Pepé rode on through the pass. His little eyes were nearly closed with weariness, but his face was stern, relentless and manly. The high mountain wind coasted sighing through the pass and whistled on the edges of the big blocks of broken granite. In the air, a red-tailed hawk sailed over close to the ridge and screamed angrily. Pepé went slowly through the broken jagged pass and looked down on the other side.

The trail dropped quickly, staggering among broken rock. At the bottom of the slope there was a dark crease, thick with brush, and on the other side of the crease a little flat, in which a grove of oak trees grew. A scar of green grass cut across the flat. And behind the flat another mountain rose, desolate with dead rocks and starving little black bushes. Pepé drank from the bag again for the air was so dry that it encrusted his nostrils and burned his lips. He put the horse down the trail. The hooves slipped and struggled on the steep way, starting little stones that rolled off into the brush. The sun was gone behind the westward mountain now, but still it glowed brilliantly on the oaks and on the grassy flat. The rocks and the hillsides still sent up waves of the heat they had gathered from the day's sun.

Pepé looked up to the top of the next dry withered ridge. He saw a dark form against the sky, a man's figure standing on top of a rock, and he glanced away quickly not to appear curious. When a moment later he looked up again, the figure was gone.

Downward the trail was quickly covered. Sometimes the horse floundered for footing, sometimes set his feet and slid a little way. They came at last to the bottom where the dark chaparral was higher than Pepé's head. He held up his rifle on one side and his arm on the other to shield his face from the sharp brittle fingers of the brush.

Up and out of the crease he rode, and up a little cliff. The grassy flat was before him, and the round comfortable oaks. For a moment he studied the trail down which he had come, but there was no movement and no sound from it. Finally he rode out over the flat, to the green streak, and at the upper end of the damp he found a little spring welling out of the earth and dropping into a dug basin before it seeped out over the flat.

Pepé filled his bag first, and then he let the thirsty horse drink out of the pool. He led the horse to the clump of oaks, and in the middle of the grove, fairly protected from sight on all sides, he took off the saddle and the bridle and laid them on the ground. The horse stretched his jaws sideways and yawned. Pepé knotted the lead rope about the horse's neck and tied him to a sapling among the oaks, where he could graze in a fairly large circle.

When the horse was gnawing hungrily at the dry grass, Pepé went to the saddle and took a black string of jerky from the sack and strolled to an oak tree on the edge of the grove, from under which he could watch the trail. He sat down in the crisp dry oak leaves and automatically felt for his big black knife to cut the jerky, but he had no knife. He leaned back on his elbow and gnawed at the tough strong meat. His face was blank, but it was a man's face.

The bright evening light washed the eastern ridge, but the valley was darkening. Doves flew down from the hills to the spring, and the quail came running out of the brush and joined them, calling clearly to one another.

Out of the corner of his eye Pepé saw a shadow grow out of the bushy crease. He turned his head slowly. A big spotted wildcat was creeping toward the spring, belly to the ground, moving like thought.

Pepé cocked his rifle and edged the muzzle slowly around. Then he looked apprehensively up the trail and dropped the hammer again. From the ground beside him he picked an oak twig and threw it toward the spring. The quail flew up with a roar and the doves whistled away. The big cat stood up: for a long moment he looked at Pepé with cold yellow eyes, and then fearlessly walked back into the gulch.

The dusk gathered quickly in the deep valley. Pepé muttered his prayers, put his head down on his arm and went instantly to sleep.

The moon came up and filled the valley with cold blue light, and the wind swept rustling down from the peaks. The owls worked up and down the slopes looking for rabbits. Down in the brush of the gulch a coyote gabbled. The oak trees whispered softly in the night breeze.

Pepé started up, listening. His horse had whinnied. The moon was just slipping behind the western ridge, leaving the valley in darkness behind it. Pepé sat tensely gripping his rifle. From far up the trail he heard an answering whinny and the crash of shod hooves on the broken rock. He jumped to his feet, ran to his horse and led it under the trees. He threw on the saddle and cinched it tight for the steep trail, caught the unwilling head and forced the bit into the mouth. He felt the saddle to make sure the water bag and the sack of jerky were there. Then he mounted and turned up the hill.

It was velvet dark. The horse found the entrance to the trail where it left the flat; and started up, stumbling and slipping on the rocks. Pepé's hand rose up to his head. His hat was gone. He had left it under the oak tree.

The horse had struggled far up the trail when the first change of dawn came into the air, a steel greyness as light mixed thoroughly with dark. Gradually the sharp snaggled edge of the ridge stood out above them, rotten granite tortured and eaten by the winds of time. Pepé had dropped his reins on the horn, leaving direction to the horse. The brush grabbed at his legs in the dark until one knee of his jeans was ripped.

Gradually the light flowed down over the ridge. The starved brush and rocks stood out in the half light, strange and lonely in high perspective. Then there came warmth into the light. Pepé drew up and looked back, but he could see nothing in the darker valley below. The sky turned blue over the coming sun. In the waste of the mountainside, the poor dry brush grew only three feet high. Here and there, big outcroppings of unrotted granite stood up like mouldering houses. Pepé relaxed a little. He drank from his water bag and bit off a piece of jerky. A single eagle flew over, high in the light.

Without warning Pepé's horse screamed and fell on its side. He was almost down before the rifle crash echoed up from the valley. From a hole behind the struggling shoulder, a stream of bright crimson blood pumped and stopped and pumped and stopped. The hooves threshed on the ground. Pepé lay half stunned beside the horse. He looked slowly down the hill. A piece of sage clipped off beside his head and another crash echoed up from side to side of the canyon. Pepé flung himself frantically behind a bush.

He crawled up the hill on his knees and one hand. His right hand held the rifle up off the ground and pushed it ahead of him. He moved with the instinctive care of an animal. Rapidly he wormed his way toward one of the big outcroppings of granite on the hill above him. Where the brush was high he doubled up and ran, but where the cover was slight he wriggled forward on his stomach, pushing the rifle ahead of him. In the last little distance there was no cover at all. Pepé poised and then he darted across the space and flashed around the corner of the rock.

He leaned panting against the stone. When his breath came easier he moved along behind the big rock until he came to a narrow split that offered a thin section of vision down the hill. Pepé lay on his stomach and pushed the rifle barrel through the slit and waited.

The sun reddened the western ridges now. Already the buzzards were settling down toward the place where the horse lay. A small brown bird scratched in the dead sage leaves directly in front of the rifle muzzle. The coasting eagle flew back toward the rising sun.

Pepé saw a little movement in the brush far below. His grip tightened on the gun. A little brown doe stepped daintily out on the trail and crossed it and disappeared into the brush again. For a long time Pepé waited. Far below he could see the little flat and the oak trees and the slash of green. Suddenly his eyes flashed back at the trail again. A quarter of a mile down there had been a quick movement in the chaparral. The rifle swung over. The front sight nestled in the v of the rear sight. Pepé studied for a moment and then raised the rear sight a notch. The little movement in the brush came again. The sight settled on it. Pepé squeezed the trigger. The explosion crashed down the mountain and up the other side, and came rattling back. The whole side of the slope grew still. No more movement. And then a white streak cut into the granite of the slit and a bullet whined away and a crash sounded up from below. Pepé felt a sharp pain in his right hand. A sliver of granite was sticking out from between his first and second knuckles and the point protruded from his palm. Carefully he pulled out the sliver of stone. The wound bled evenly and gently. No vein nor artery was cut.

Pepé looked into a little dusty cave in the rock and gathered a handful of spider web, and he pressed the mass into the cut, plastering the soft web into the blood. The flow stopped almost at once.

The rifle was on the ground. Pepé picked it up, levered a new shell into the chamber. And then he slid into the brush on his stomach. Far to the right he crawled, and then up the hill, moving slowly and carefully, crawling to cover and resting and then crawling again.

In the mountains the sun is high in its arc before it penetrates the gorges. The hot face looked over the hill and brought instant heat with it. The white light beat on the rocks and reflected from them and rose up quivering from the earth again, and the rocks and bushes seemed to quiver behind the air.

Pepé crawled in the general direction of the ridge peak, zig-zagging for cover. The deep cut between his knuckles began to throb. He crawled close to a rattlesnake before he saw it, and when it raised its dry head and made a soft beginning whirr, he backed up and took another way. The quick grey lizards flashed in front of him, raising a tiny line of dust. He found another mass of spider web and pressed it against his throbbing hand.

Pepé was pushing the rifle with his left hand now. Little drops of sweat ran to the ends of his coarse black hair and rolled down his cheeks. His lips and tongue were growing thick and heavy. His lips writhed to draw saliva into his mouth. His little dark eyes were uneasy and suspicious. Once when a grey lizard paused in front of him on the parched ground and turned its head sideways he crushed it flat with a stone.

When the sun slid past noon he had not gone a mile. He crawled exhaustedly a last hundred yards to a patch of high sharp manzanita, crawled desperately, and when the patch was reached he wriggled in among the tough gnarly trunks and dropped his head on his left arm. There was little shade in the meager brush, but there was cover and safety. Pepé went to sleep as he lay and the sun beat on his back. A few little birds hopped close to him and peered and hopped away. Pepé squirmed in his sleep and he raised and dropped his wounded hand again and again.

The sun went down behind the peaks and the cool evening came, and then the dark. A coyote yelled from the hillside, Pepé started awake and looked about with misty eyes. His hand was swollen and heavy; a little thread of pain ran up the inside of his arm and settled in a pocket in his armpit. He peered about and then stood up, for the mountains were black and the moon had not yet risen. Pepé stood up in the dark. The coat of his father pressed on his arm. His tongue was swollen until it nearly filled his mouth. He wriggled out of the coat and dropped it in the brush, and then he struggled up the hill, falling over rocks and tearing his way through the brush. The rifle knocked against stones as he went. Little dry avalanches of gravel and shattered stone went whispering down the hill behind him.

After a while the old moon came up and showed the jagged ridge top ahead of him. By moonlight Pepé traveled more easily. He bent forward so that his throbbing arm hung away from his body. The journey uphill was made in dashes and rests, a frantic rush up a few yards and then a rest. The wind coasted down the slope rattling the dry stems of the bushes.

The moon was at meridian when Pepé came at last to the sharp backbone of the ridge top. On the last hundred yards of the rise no soil had clung under the wearing winds. The way was on solid rock. He clambered to the top and looked down on the other side. There was a draw like the last below him, misty with moonlight, brushed with dry struggling sage and chaparral. On the other side the hill rose up sharply and at the top the jagged rotten teeth of the mountain showed against the sky. At the bottom of the cut the brush was thick and dark.

Pepé stumbled down the hill. His throat was almost closed with thirst. At first he tried to run, but immediately he fell and rolled. After that he went more carefully. The moon was just disappearing behind the mountains when he came to the bottom. He crawled into the heavy brush feeling with his fingers for water. There was no water in the bed of the stream, only damp earth. Pepé laid his gun down and scooped up a handful of mud and put it in his mouth, and then he spluttered and scraped the earth from his tongue with his finger, for the mud drew at his mouth like a poultice. He dug a hole in the stream bed with his fingers, dug a little basin to catch water; but before it was very deep his head fell forward on the damp ground and he slept.

The dawn came and the heat of the day fell on the earth, and still Pepé slept. Late in the afternoon his head jerked up. He looked slowly around. His eyes were slits of wariness. Twenty feet away in the heavy brush a big tawny mountain lion stood looking at him. Its long thick tail waved gracefully, its ears were erect with interest, not laid back dangerously. The lion squatted down on its stomach and watched him.

Pepé looked at the hole he had dug in the earth. A half inch of muddy water had collected in the bottom. He tore the sleeve from his hurt arm, with his teeth ripped out a little square, soaked it in the water and put it in his mouth. Over and over he filled the cloth and sucked it.

Still the lion sat and watched him. The evening came down but there was no movement on the hills. No birds visited the dry bottom of the cut. Pepé looked occasionally at the lion. The eyes of the yellow beast drooped as though he were about to sleep. He yawned and his long thin red tongue curled out. Suddenly his head jerked around and his nostrils quivered. His big tail lashed. He stood up and slunk like a tawny shadow into the thick brush.

A moment later Pepé heard the sound, the faint far crash of horses' hooves on gravel. And he heard something else, a high whining yelp of a dog.

Pepé took his rifle in his left hand and he glided into the brush almost as quietly as the lion had. In the darkening evening he crouched up the hill toward the next ridge. Only when the dark came did he stand up. His energy was short. Once it was dark he fell over the rocks and slipped to his knees on the steep slope, but he moved on and on up the hill, climbing and scrabbling over the broken hillside.

When he was far up toward the top, he lay down and slept for a little while. The withered moon, shining on his face, awakened him. He stood up and moved up the hill. Fifty yards away he stopped and turned back, for he had forgotten his rifle. He walked heavily down and poked about in the brush, but he could not find his gun. At last he lay down to rest. The pocket of pain in his armpit had grown more sharp. His arm seemed to swell out and fall with every heartbeat. There was no position lying down where the heavy arm did not press against his armpit.

With the effort of a hurt beast, Pepé got up and moved again toward the top of the ridge. He held his swollen arm away from his body with his left hand. Up the steep hill he dragged himself, a few steps and a rest, and a few more steps. At last he was nearing the top. The moon showed the uneven sharp back of it against the sky.

Pepé's brain spun in a big spiral up and away from him. He slumped to the ground and lay still. The rock ridge top was only a hundred feet above him.

The moon moved over the sky. Pepé half turned on his back. His tongue tried to make words, but only a thick hissing came from between his lips.

When the dawn came, Pepé pulled himself up. His eyes were sane again. He drew his great puffed arm in front of him and looked at the angry wound. The black line ran up from his wrist to his armpit. Automatically he reached in his pocket for the big black knife, but it was not there. His eyes searched the ground. He picked up a sharp blade of stone and scraped at the wound, sawed at the proud flesh and then squeezed the green juice out in big drops. Instantly he threw back his head and whined like a dog. His whole right side shuddered at the pain, but the pain cleared his head.

In the grey light he struggled up the last slope to the ridge and crawled over and lay down behind a line of rocks. Below him lay a deep canyon exactly like the last, waterless and desolate. There was no flat, no oak trees, not even heavy brush in the bottom of it. And on the other side a sharp ridge stood up, thinly brushed with starving sage, littered with broken granite. Strewn over the hill there were giant outcroppings, and on the top the granite teeth stood out against the sky.

The new day was light now. The flame of the sun came over the ridge and fell on Pepé where he lay on the ground. His coarse black hair was littered with twigs and bits of spider web. His eyes had retreated back into his head. Between his lips the tip of his black tongue showed.

He sat up and dragged his great arm into his lap and nursed it, rocking his body and moaning in his throat. He threw back his head and looked up into the pale sky. A big black bird circled nearly out of sight, and far to the left another was sailing near.

He lifted his head to listen, for a familiar sound had come to him from the valley he had climbed out of; it was the crying yelp of hounds, excited and feverish, on a trail.

Pepé bowed his head quickly. He tried to speak rapid words but only a thick hiss came from his lips. He drew a shaky cross on his breast with his left hand. It was a long struggle to get to his feet. He crawled slowly and mechanically to the top of a big rock on the ridge peak. Once there, he arose slowly, swaying to his feet, and stood erect. Far below he could see the dark brush where he had slept. He braced his feet and stood there, black against the morning sky.

There came a ripping sound at his feet. A piece of stone flew up and a bullet droned off into the next gorge. The hollow crash echoed up from below. Pepé looked down for a moment and then pulled himself straight again.

His body jarred back. His left hand fluttered helplessly toward his breast. The second crash sounded from below. Pepé swung forward and toppled from the rock. His body struck and rolled over and over, starting a little avalanche. And when at last he stopped against a bush, the avalanche slid slowly down and covered up his head.

[1938]

Richard Wright

[1908–1960]

Richard Wright

The noted African American photographer Gordon Parks took this portrait of Wright in his study in 1943, when the novelist was one of the most acclaimed writers in the United States.

Richard Nathaniel Wright was born on September 4, 1908, on a plantation east of Natchez, Mississippi. He was the first of two sons born to Nathaniel Wright, an illiterate sharecropper, and Ella Wilson Wright, a former schoolteacher. In 1911, the impoverished family moved to Natchez, where they lived with Wright's maternal grandparents, and then on to Memphis, Tennessee. Wright's father abandoned the family, and Ella Wright was forced to place her sons in an orphanage before taking them to live with her sister and brother-in-law in Elaine, Arkansas, in 1915. For a time, the family enjoyed some stability. In 1917, however, Wright's prosperous uncle was murdered by a group of white men who wanted to take over his saloon, and the family fled to Jackson, Mississippi. Wright's mother suffered a stroke that left her paralyzed, and he was sent to live with relatives in Greenwood, Mississippi. He worked at odd jobs before returning to Jackson, where Wright began his first uninterrupted schooling. His earliest story, "The Voodoo of Hell's Half Acre," appeared in a local newspaper in 1924. The next year, he graduated from the ninth grade in the Smith-Robinson Public School as the class valedictorian. He briefly attended high school but dropped out and moved to Memphis, where he worked as a delivery boy and a dishwasher. Determined to escape racial hatred and segregation in the South, and hoping to find greater opportunities in the North, he boarded a train for Chicago in 1927.

Wright lived there for the next ten years. He took a series of menial jobs and was often unemployed after the onset of the Great Depression in 1929. At the same time, he wrote constantly and read widely in European and American literature, especially the works of Sherwood Anderson, Theodore Dreiser, and experimental modernists such as Gertrude Stein, James Joyce, and T. S. Eliot. Wright joined the John Reed Club, a literary organization affiliated with the Communist Party, and began to publish poetry in leftist magazines such as the *New Masses*. In a poem printed there in June 1934, after he officially joined the Communist Party, he proclaimed:

> I am black and have seen black hands
> Raised in fists of revolt, side by side with the white fists of white workers,
> And some day—and it is only this which sustains me—
> Some day there shall be millions and millions of them,
> One red day in a burst of fists on a new horizon!

Wright also wrote fiction, including two novels, *Lawd Today!* and *Tarbaby's Dawn*. He could not interest a publisher in either novel, but he made connections with other writers through his work for the Illinois Writers Project, part of the Federal Arts Project. In 1936, his story "Big Boy Leaves Home" was published in an anthology, *The New Caravan*. The story was singled out as the best story in the collection by reviewers in a number of influential periodicals, including the *Saturday Review of Literature* and the *New York Times*. Eager to pursue his literary career, and believing that it would be easier to find a publisher for his work in New York City, Wright moved there in 1937.

During the following decade, Wright enjoyed growing acclaim as a writer. Although he was increasingly disillusioned with Communism, he became the Harlem editor of the *Daily Worker*, a newspaper published by the Communist Party. Wright achieved his first major breakthrough as a writer when he won first prize in a competition sponsored by the prominent magazine *Story*. The award was five hundred dollars and the publication of his prize-winning collection, *Uncle Tom's Children* (1938). Almost without exception, critics hailed Wright's often-brutal stories about life in the segregated South as the work of a major new literary talent. In 1939, he married Dhima Rose Meadman, a white ballet dancer, and was awarded a Guggenheim Fellowship. Inspired in part by his research into the sensational case of an eighteen-year-old black youth who was convicted in Chicago of murdering a white woman,

Wright was one of the people who made me conscious of the need to struggle.

–Amiri Baraka

Wright soon completed a new novel, *Native Son* (1940). The raw story, a surprise Book-of-the-Month Club selection, was acclaimed by the *New Yorker* "as the most powerful American novel to appear since *The Grapes of Wrath*." While Wright was enjoying the success of *Native Son*, his marriage failed and he married Ellen Poplowitz, a white Communist organizer, in 1941. Wright, however, withdrew from the Communist Party. He later sharply criticized the party in "I Tried to Be a Communist," an essay published in the *Atlantic Monthly* in 1944. The essay was originally part of his autobiography, then called *American Hunger*, which ended with an account of his bitter experiences in Chicago. He omitted the Chicago section at the insistence of the Book-of-the-Month Club, and the first part of the book was subsequently published as *Black Boy*. W. E. B. Du Bois objected that Wright's "harsh and forbidding story" was a grotesquely distorted portrait of black family life in the South. But most reviewers praised *Black Boy*, which was a main selection of the Book-of-the-Month Club and a runaway bestseller in 1945.

Despite his fame and commercial success, Wright remained deeply angered by the intractable racism and segregation in the United States. Following a trip to France, where he was treated as a celebrity, Wright moved with his wife and their young daughter to Paris in 1947. For the rest of his life, he lived as an expatriate in France and traveled widely in Europe, Asia, and Africa. Nonetheless, he continued to write about life and racial relations in the United States, the setting of his ambitious philosophical novel about an alienated black intellectual, *The Outsider* (1953). The novel received mixed reviews, and Wright fared even less well with a sensational novel about a white man who marries and then brutally murders a prostitute, *Savage Holiday* (1954). His next books were *Black Power* (1954), a critical assessment of conditions in postcolonial Africa; and *The Color Curtain* (1956), an account of his attendance at the Bandung Conference in Indonesia, a meeting of twenty-nine nations from Africa and Asia. Because of his earlier membership in the Communist Party, his involvement in global politics, and his ongoing criticism of the United States, Wright was kept under surveillance by the Central Intelligence Agency. His international reputation continued to grow, however, and he gave a series of lectures on race that he published in 1957 as *White Man, Listen!* The following year, Wright published *The Long Dream*, the first in a projected trilogy of novels about a black community in Mississippi. He contracted dysentery during his travels and died of a heart attack in Paris on November 28, 1960.

bedfordstmartins.com/ americanlit for research links on Wright

Reading Wright's "Almos' a Man."   In 1937, shortly before he moved from Chicago to New York City, Wright completed a draft of *Tarbaby's Dawn*, a novel about a restless and rebellious black youth growing up in the rural South. Although numerous publishers praised the power and realism of the novel, all of them rejected the book, which, as one editor put it, "would have to surmount almost impossible commercial obstacles." In short, the publishers were convinced that the novel would not sell. Wright also failed to publish a story drawn from the final chapters of the novel, "Almos' a Man." But the enthusiastic reception of his collection of stories *Uncle Tom's Children* (1938) created a strong demand for his short fiction. He consequently revised "Almos' a Man," which appeared in *Harper's Bazaar,* a popular fashion magazine that was renowned for publishing groundbreaking fiction. In a publication note, the influential fiction editor of *Harper's Bazaar,* George Davis, described Wright as "one of our finest short story writers" and took the opportunity to promote his forthcoming novel, *Native Son* (1940). Twenty years later, during the last year of his life, Wright revised "Almos' a Man" as "The Man Who Was Almost a Man," the opening story in his posthumously published collection, *Eight Men* (1961). The text of the story is taken from its first printing in *Harper's Bazaar,* January 1940.

ALMOS' A MAN

Dave struck out across the fields, looking homeward through paling light. Whuts the usa talkin wid em niggers in the field? Anyhow, his mother was putting supper on the table. Them niggers can't understan *nothing.* One of these days he was going to get a gun and practise shooting, then they can't talk to him as though he were a little boy. He slowed, looking at the ground. Shucks, Ah ain scareda them even ef they are biggern me! Aw, Ah know whut Ahma do. . . . Ahm going by ol Joe's sto n git that Sears Roebuck catlog n look at them guns. Mabbe Ma will lemme buy one when she gits mah pay from ol man Hawkins. Ahma beg her t gimme some money. Ahm ol ernough to hava gun. Ahm seventeen. Almos a man. He strode, feeling his long, loose-jointed limbs. Shucks, a man oughta hava little gun aftah he done worked hard all day. . . .

He came in sight of Joe's store. A yellow lantern glowed on the front porch. He mounted steps and went through the screen door, hearing it bang behind him. There was a strong smell of coal oil and mackerel fish. He felt very confident until he saw fat Joe walk in through the rear door, then his courage began to ooze.

"Howdy, Dave! Whutcha want?"

"How yuh, Mistah Joe? Aw, Ah don wanna buy nothing. Ah jus wanted t see ef yuhd lemme look at tha ol catlog erwhile."

"Sure! You wanna see it here?"

"Nawsuh. Ah wans t take it home wid me. Ahll bring it back termorrow when Ah come in from the fiels."

"You plannin on buyin something?"

"Yessuh."

"Your ma letting you have your own money now?"

"Shucks. Mistah Joe, Ahm gittin t be a man like anybody else!"

Joe laughed and wiped his greasy white face with a red bandanna.

"Whut you plannin on buyin?"

Dave looked at the floor, scratched his head, scratched his thigh, and smiled. Then he looked up shyly.

"Ahll tell yuh, Mistah Joe, ef yuh promise yuh won't tell."

"I promise."

"Waal, Ahma buy a gun."

"A gun? Whut you want with a gun?"

"Ah wanna keep it."

"You ain't nothing but a boy. You don't need a gun."

"Aw, lemme have the catlog, Mistah Joe. Ahll bring it back."

Joe walked through the rear door. Dave was elated. He looked around at barrels of sugar and flour. He heard Joe coming back. He craned his neck to see if he were bringing the book. Yeah, he's got it! Gawddog, he's got it!

"Here; but be sure you bring it back. It's the only one I got."

"Sho, Mistah Joe."

"Say, if you wanna buy a gun, why don't you buy one from me. I gotta gun to sell."

"Will it shoot?"

"Sure it'll shoot."

"Whut kind is it?"

"Oh, it's kinda old. . . . A Lefthand Wheeler.[1] A pistol. A big one."

"Is it got bullets in it?"

"It's loaded."

"Kin Ah see it?"

"Where's your money?"

"Whut yuh wan fer it?"

"I'll let you have it for two dollars."

"Just *two* dollahs? Shucks, Ah could buy tha when Ah git mah pay."

"I'll have it here when you want it."

"Awright, suh. Ah be in fer it."

He went through the door, hearing it slam again behind him. Ahma git some money from Ma n buy me a gun! Only *two* dollahs! He tucked the thick catalogue under his arm and hurried.

"Where yuh been, boy?" His mother held a steaming dish of black-eyed peas.

"Aw, Ma, Ah jus stopped down the road t talk wid th boys."

"Yuh know bettah than t keep suppah waitin."

He sat down, resting the catalogue on the edge of the table.

"Yuh git up from there and git to the well n wash yosef! Ah ain feedin no hogs in mah house!"

She grabbed his shoulder and pushed him. He stumbled out of the room, then came back to get the catalogue.

"Whut this?"

---

1. **Lefthand Wheeler:** A large revolver with an automatic mechanism for rotating the cylinder around a central barrel, invented by Artemus Wheeler in 1818.

"Aw, Ma, it's jusa catlog."

"Who yuh git it from?"

"From Joe, down at the sto."

"Waal, thas good. We kin use it around the house."[2]

"Naw, Ma." He grabbed for it. "Gimme mah catlog, Ma." She held onto it and glared at him.

"Quit hollerin at me! Whuts wrong wid yuh? Yuh crazy?"

"But Ma, please. It ain mine! It's Joe's! He tol me t bring it back t im termorrow."

She gave up the book. He stumbled down the back steps, hugging the thick book under his arm. When he had splashed water on his face and hands, he groped back to the kitchen and fumbled in a corner for the towel. He bumped into a chair; it clattered to the floor. The catalogue sprawled at his feet. When he had dried his eyes he snatched up the book and held it again under his arm. His mother stood watching him.

"Now, ef yuh gonna acka fool over that ol book, Ahll take it n burn it up."

"Naw, Ma, please."

"Waal, set down n be still!"

He sat and drew the oil lamp close. He thumbed page after page, unaware of the food his mother set on the table. His father came in. Then his small brother.

"Whutcha got there, Dave?" his father asked.

"Jusa catlog," he answered, not looking up.

"Ywah, here they is!" His eyes glowed at blue and black revolvers. He glanced up, feeling sudden guilt. His father was watching him. He eased the book under the table and rested it on his knees. After the blessing was asked, he ate. He scooped up peas and swallowed fat meat without chewing. Buttermilk helped to wash it down. He did not want to mention money before his father. He would do much better by cornering his mother when she was alone. He looked at his father uneasily out of the edge of his eye.

"Boy, how come yuh don quit foolin wid tha book n eat yo suppah?"

"Yessuh."

"How yuh n ol man Hawkins gittin erlong?"

"Suh?"

"Can't yuh hear? Why don yuh lissen? Ah ast yuh how wuz yuh n ol man Hawkins gittin erlong?"

"Oh, swell, Pa. Ah plows mo lan than anybody over there."

"Waal, yuh oughta keep yo min on whuy yuh doin."

"Yessuh."

He poured his plate full of molasses and sopped at it slowly with a chunk of corn-bread. When all but his mother had left the kitchen, he still sat and looked again at the guns in the catalogue. Lawd, ef Ah only had tha pretty one! He could almost feel the

---

2. "**We kin use it around the house**": The thin pages of catalogs were frequently used as a substitute for toilet paper in outhouses.

slickness of the weapon with his fingers. If he had a gun like that he would polish it and keep it shining so it would never rust. N Ahd keep it loaded, by Gawd!

"Ma?"

"Hunh?"

"Ol man Hawkins give yuh mah money yit?"

"Yeah, but ain no usa yuh thinkin bout thowin nona it erway. Ahm keepin tha money sos yuh kin have cloes t go t school this winter."

He rose and went to her side with the open catalogue in his palms. She was washing dishes, her head bent low over a pan. Shyly he raised the open book. When he spoke his voice was husky, faint.

"Ma, Gawd knows Ah wans one of these."

"One of whut?" she asked, not raising her eyes.

"One of *these*," he said again, not daring even to point. She glanced up at the page, then at him with wide eyes.

"Nigger, is yuh gone plum crazy?"

"Aw, Ma —"

"Git outta here! Don yuh talk t me bout no gun! Yuh a fool!"

"Ma, Ah kin buy one fer *two* dollahs."

"Not ef Ah knows it yuh ain!"

"But yuh promised me one —"

"Ah don care whut Ah promised! Yuh ain nothing but a boy yit!"

"Ma, ef yuh lemme buy one Ahll *never* ast yuh fer nothing no mo."

"Ah tol yuh t git outta here! Yuh ain gonna toucha penny of tha money fer no gun! Thas how come Ah has Mistah Hawkins t pay yo wages t me, cause Ah knows yuh ain got no sense."

"But Ma, we needa gun. Pa ain got no gun. We needa gun in the house. Yuh kin never tell whut might happen."

"Now don yuh try to maka fool outta me, boy! Ef we did hava gun yuh wouldn't have it!"

He laid the catalogue down and slipped his arm around her waist.

"Aw, Ma, Ah done worked hard alla summer n ain ast yuh fer nothin, is Ah, now?"

"Thas whut yuh spose t do!"

"But Ma, Ah wans a gun. Yuh kin lemme have two dollahs outta mah money. Please, Ma. I kin give it to Pa. . . . Please, Ma! Ah loves yuh, Ma."

When she spoke her voice came soft and low.

"Whut yuh wan wida gun, Dave? Yuh don need no gun. Yuhll git in trouble. N ef yo Pa jus *thought* Ah let yuh have money t buy a gun he'd hava fit."

"Ahll hide it. Ma, it ain but two dollahs."

"Lawd, chil, whuts wrong wid yuh?"

"Ain nothing wrong, Ma. Ahm almos a man now. Ah wans a gun."

"Who gonna sell yuh a gun?"

"Ol Joe at the sto."

"N it don cos but two dollahs?"

"Thas all, Ma. Just two dollahs. Please, Ma."

She was stacking the plates away; her hands moved slowly, reflectively. Dave kept an anxious silence. Finally, she turned to him.

"Ahll let yuh git the gun ef yuh promise me one thing."

"Whuts tha, Ma?"

"Yuh bring it straight back t *me*, yuh hear? Itll be fer Pa."

"Yessum! Lemme go now, Ma."

She stooped, turned slightly to one side, raised the hem of her dress, rolled down the top of her stocking, and came up with a slender wad of bills.

"Here," she said. "Lawd knows yuh don need no gun. But yer Pa does. Yuh bring it right back t *me*, yuh hear? Ahma put it up. Now ef yuh don, Ahma have yuh Pa lick yuh so hard yuh won ferget it."

"Yessum."

He took the money, ran down the steps, and across the yard.

"Dave! Yuuuuuh Daaaaave!"

He heard, but he was not going to stop now. "Naw, Lawd!"

The first movement he made the following morning was to reach under his pillow for the gun. In the gray light of dawn he held it loosely, feeling a sense of power. Could killa man wida gun like this. Kill anybody, black er white. And if he were holding his gun in his hand nobody could run over him; they would have to respect him. It was a big gun, with a long barrel and a heavy handle. He raised and lowered it in his hand, marveling at its weight.

He had not come straight home with it as his mother had asked; instead he had stayed out in the fields, holding the weapon in his hand, aiming it now and then at some imaginary foe. But he had not fired it; he had been afraid that his father might hear. Also he was not sure he knew how to fire it.

To avoid surrendering the pistol he had not come into the house until he knew that all were asleep. When his mother had tiptoed to his bedside late that night and demanded the gun, he had first played 'possum; then he had told her that the gun was hidden outdoors, that he would bring it to her in the morning. Now he lay turning it slowly in his hands. He broke it, took out the cartridges, felt them, and then put them back.

He slid out of bed, got a long strip of old flannel from a trunk, wrapped the gun in it, and tied it to his naked thigh while it was still loaded. He did not go in to breakfast. Even though it was not yet daylight, he started for Jim Hawkins' plantation. Just as the sun was rising he reached the barns where the mules and plows were kept.

"Hey! That you, Dave?"

He turned. Jim Hawkins stood eyeing him suspiciously.

"Whatre yuh doing here so early?"

"Ah didn't know Ah wuz gittin up so early, Mistah Hawkins. Ah wuz fixin t hitch up ol Jenny n take her t the fiels."

"Good. Since you're here so early, how about plowing that stretch down by the woods?"

"Suits me, Mistah Hawkins."

"O.K. Go to it!"

He hitched Jenny to a plow and started across the fields. Hot dog! This was just what he wanted. If he could get down by the woods, he could shoot his gun and nobody would hear. He walked behind the plow, hearing the traces creaking, feeling the gun tied tight to his thigh.

When he reached the woods, he plowed two whole rows before he decided to take out the gun. Finally, he stopped, looked in all directions, then untied the gun and held it in his hand. He turned to the mule and smiled.

"Know whut this is, Jenny? Naw, yuh wouldn't know! Yuhs jusa ol mule! Anyhow, this is a gun, n it kin shoot, by Gawd!"

He held the gun at arm's length. Whut t hell, Ahma shoot this thing! He looked at Jenny again.

"Lissen here, Jenny! When Ah pull this ol trigger Ah don wan yuh t run n acka fool now."

Jenny stood with head down, her short ears pricked straight. Dave walked off about twenty feet, held the gun far out from him, at arm's length, and turned his head. Hell, he told himself, Ah ain afraid. The gun felt loose in his fingers; he waved it wildly for a moment. Then he shut his eyes and tightened his forefinger. *Blooom!* A report him and he thought his right hand was torn from his arm. He heard Jenny whinnying and galloping over the field, and he found himself on his knees, squeezing his fingers hard between his legs. His hand was numb; he jammed it into his mouth, trying to warm it, trying to stop the pain. The gun lay at his feet. He did not quite know what had happened. He stood up and stared at the gun as though it were a live thing. He gritted his teeth and kicked the gun. Yuh almos broke mah arm! He turned to look for Jenny; she was far over the fields, tossing her head and kicking wildly.

"Hol on there, ol mule!"

When he caught up with her she stood trembling, walling her big white eyes at him. The plow was far away; the traces had broken. Then Dave stopped short, looking, not believing. Jenny was bleeding. Her left side was red and wet with blood. He went closer. Lawd have mercy! Wondah did Ah shoot this mule? He grabbed for Jenny's mane. She flinched, snorted whirled, tossing her head.

"Hol on now! Hol on."

Then he saw the hole in Jenny's side, right between the ribs. It was round, wet, red. A crimson stream streaked down the front leg, flowing fast. Good Gawd! Ah wuznt shootin at tha mule. . . . He felt panic. He knew he had to stop that blood, or Jenny would bleed to death. He had never seen so much blood in all his life. He ran the mule for half a mile, trying to catch her. Finally she stopped, breathing hard, stumpy tail half arched. He caught her mane and led her back to where the plow and gun lay. Then he stopped and grabbed handfuls of damp black earth and tried to plug the bullet hole. Jenny shuddered, whinnied, and broke from him.

"Hol on! Hol on now!"

He tried to plug it again, but blood came anyhow. His fingers were hot and sticky. He rubbed dirt hard into his palms, trying to dry them. Then again he attempted to plug the bullet hole but Jenny shied away, kicking her heels high. He stood helpless. He had to do something. He ran at Jenny; she dodged him. He watched a red stream of blood flow down Jenny's leg and form a bright pool at her feet.

"Jenny . . . Jenny . . ." he called weakly.

His lips trembled. She's bleeding t death! He looked in the direction of home, wanting to go back, wanting to get help. But he saw the pistol lying in the damp black clay. He had a queer feeling that if he only did something, this would not be; Jenny would not be there bleeding to death.

When he went to her this time, she did not move. She stood with sleepy, dreamy eyes; and when he touched her she gave a low-pitched whinny and knelt to the ground, her front knees slopping in blood.

"Jenny . . . Jenny . . ." he whispered.

For a long time she held her neck erect; then her head sank, slowly. Her ribs swelled with a mighty heave and she went over.

Dave's stomach felt empty, very empty. He picked up the gun and held it gingerly between his thumb and forefinger. He buried it at the foot of a tree. He took a stick and tried to cover the pool of blood with dirt – but what was the use? There was Jenny lying with her mouth open and her eyes walled and glassy. He could not tell Jim Hawkins he had shot his mule. But he had to tell something. Yeah, Ahll tell em Jenny started gittin wil n fell on the joint of the plow. . . . But that would hardly happen to a mule. He walked across the field slowly, head down.

It was sunset. Two of Jim Hawkins' men were over near the edge of the woods digging a hole in which to bury Jenny. Dave was surrounded by a knot of people; all of them were looking down at the dead mule.

"I don't see how in the world it happened," said Jim Hawkins for the tenth time.

The crowd parted and Dave's mother, father, and small brother pushed into the center.

"Where Dave?" his mother called.

"There he is," said Jim Hawkins.

His mother grabbed him.

"Whut happened, Dave? Whut yuh done?"

"Nothing."

"C mon, boy, talk," his father said.

Dave took a deep breath and told the story he knew nobody believed.

"Waal," he drawled. "Ah brung ol Jenny down here sos Ah could do mah plowin. Ah plowed bout two rows, jus like yuh see." He stopped and pointed at the long rows of upturned earth. "Then something musta been wrong wid ol Jenny. She wouldn't ack right a-tall. She started snortin n kickin her heels. Ah tried to hol her, but she pulled erway, rearin n goin on. Then when the point of the plow was stickin up in the air, she swung erroun n twisted herself back on it. . . . She stuck herself n started t bleed. N fo Ah could do anything, she wuz dead."

"Did you ever hear of anything like that in all your life?" asked Jim Hawkins.

There were white and black standing in the crowd. They murmured. Dave's mother came close to him and looked hard into his face.

"Tell the truth, Dave," she said.

"Looks like a bullet hole ter me," said one man.

"Dave, whut yuh do wid tha gun?" his mother asked.

The crowd surged in, looking at him.

He jammed his hands into his pockets, shook his head slowly from left to right, and backed away. His eyes were wide and painful.

"Did he hava gun?" asked Jim Hawkins.

"By Gawd, Ah tol yuh tha wuz a *gun* wound," said a man, slapping his thigh.

His father caught his shoulders and shook him till his teeth rattled.

"Tell whut happened, yuh rascal! Tell whut . . ."

Dave looked at Jenny's stiff legs and began to cry.

"Whut yuh do wid tha gun?" his mother asked.

"Whut wuz he doin wida gun?" his father asked.

"Come on and tell the truth," said Hawkins. "Ain't nobody going to hurt you. . . ."

His mother crowded close to him.

"Did yuh shoot tha mule, Dave?"

Dave cried, seeing blurred white and black faces.

"Ahh ddinnt gggo tt sshoooot hher. . . . Ah ssswear ffo Gawd Ahh ddint. . . . Ah wuz a-trying t sssee ef the ol gggun would sshoot –"

"Where yuh git the gun from?" his father asked.

"Ah got it from Joe, at the sto."

"Where yuh git the money?"

"Ma give it t me."

"He kept worryin me, Bob. . . . Ah had t. . . . Ah tol im t bring the gun right back t me. . . . It was fer yuh, the gun."

"But how yuh happen to shoot that mule?" asked Jim Hawkins.

"Ah wuznt shootin at the mule, Mistah Hawkins. The gun jumped when Ah pulled the trigger. . . . N fo Ah knowed anything Jenny wuz there a-bleedin."

Somebody in the crowd laughed. Jim Hawkins walked close to Dave and looked into his face.

"Well, looks like you have bought you a mule, Dave."

"Ah swear fo Gawd, Ah didn't go t kill the mule, Mistah Hawkins!"

"But you killed her!"

All the crowd was laughing now. They stood on tiptoe and poked heads over one another's shoulders.

"Well, boy, looks like yuh done bought a dead mule! Hahaha!"

"Ain tha ershame."

"Hohohohoho."

Dave stood, head down, twisting his feet in the dirt.

"Well, you needn't worry about it, Bob," said Jim Hawkins to Dave's father. "Just let the boy keep on working and pay me two dollars a month."

"Whut yuh wan fer yo mule, Mistah Hawkins?"

Jim Hawkins screwed up his eyes.

"Fifty dollars."

"Whut yuh do wid tha gun?" Dave's father demanded.

Dave said nothing.

"Yuh wan me t take a tree lim n beat yuh till yuh talk!"

"Nawsuh!"

"Whut yuh do wid it?"

"Ah thowed it erway."

"Where?"

"Ah . . . Ah thowed it in the creek."

"Waal, c mon home. N firs thing in the mawnin git to tha creek n fin tha gun."

"Yessuh."

"Whut yuh pay fer it?"

"Two dollahs."

"Take tha gun n git yo money back n carry it t Mistah Hawkins, yuh hear? N don fergit Ahma lam yo black bottom good fer this! Now march yosef on home, suh!"

Dave turned and walked slowly. He heard people laughing. Dave glared, his eyes welling with tears. Hot anger bubbled in him. Then he swallowed and stumbled on.

That night Dave did not sleep. He was glad that he had gotten out of killing the mule so easily, but he was hurt. Something hot seemed to turn over inside him each time he remembered how they had laughed. He tossed on his bed, feeling his hard pillow. N Pa says he's gonna beat me. . . . He remembered other beatings, and his back quivered. Naw, naw, Ah sho don wan im t beat me tha way no mo. . . . Dam em *all!* Nobody ever gave him anything. All he did was work. They treat me lika mule. . . . N then they beat me. . . . He gritted his teeth. N Ma had t tell on me.

Well, if he had to, he would take old man Hawkins that two dollars. But that meant selling the gun. And he wanted to keep that gun. Fifty dollahs fer a dead mule.

He turned over, thinking of how he had fired the gun. He had an itch to fire it again. Ef other men kin shoota gun, by Gawd, Ah kin! He was still listening. Mebbe they all sleepin now. . . . The house was still. He heard the soft breathing of his brother. Yes, now! He would go down and get that gun and see if he could fire it! He eased out of bed and slipped into overalls.

The moon was bright. He ran almost all the way to the edge of the woods. He stumbled over the ground, looking for the spot where he had buried the gun. Yeah, here it is. Like a hungry dog scratching for a bone he pawed it up. He puffed his black cheeks and blew dirt from the trigger and barrel. He broke it and found four cartridges unshot. He looked around; the fields were filled with silence and moonlight. He clutched the gun stiff and hard in his fingers. But as soon as he wanted to pull the trigger, he shut his eyes and turned his head. Naw, Ah can't shoot wid mah eyes closed n mah head turned. With effort he held his eyes open; then he squeezed. *Blooooom!* He was stiff, not breathing. The gun was still in his hands. Dammit, he'd done it! He fired again. *Bloooom!* He smiled. *Bloooom! Blooooom! Click, click.* There! It was empty. If anybody could shoot a gun, he could. He put the gun into his hip pocket and started across the fields.

When he reached the top of a ridge he stood straight and proud in the moonlight, looking at Jim Hawkins' big white house, feeling the gun sagging in his pocket. Lawd, ef Ah had jus one mo bullet Ahd taka shot at tha house. Ahd like t scare ol man Hawkins jusa little. . . . Jussa enough t let im know Dave Sanders is a man.

To his left the road curved, running to the tracks of the Illinois Central. He jerked his head, listening. From far off came a faint *hoooof-hoooof; hoooof-hoooof; hoooof-hooof* . . . Tha's number eight. He took a swift look at Jim Hawkins' white house; he thought of pa, of ma, of his little brother, and the boys. He thought of the dead mule and heard *hoooof-hooof; hoooof-hoooof; hoooof-hoooof* . . . He stood rigid. Two dollahs a mont. Les see now. . . . Tha means itll take bout two years. Shucks! Ahll be dam!

He started down the road, toward the tracks. Yeah, here she comes! He stood beside the track and held himself stiffly. Here she comes, erroun the ben. . . . C mon, yuh slow poke! C mon! He had his hand on his gun; something quivered in his stomach. Then the train thundered past, the gray and brown box cars rumbling and clinking. He gripped the gun tightly; then he jerked his hand out of his pocket. Ah betcha Bill wouldn't do it! Ah betcha. . . . The cars slid past, steel grinding upon steel. Ahm riding yuh ternight so hep me Gawd! He was hot all over. He hesitated just a moment; then he grabbed, pulled atop of a car, and lay flat. He felt his pocket; the gun was still there. Ahead the long rails were glinting in moonlight, stretching away, away to somewhere, somewhere where he could be a man. . . .

[1940]

Eudora Welty

[1909-2001]

Eudora Welty

This photograph of Welty was taken in the 1930s, early in the career of the writer who later came to be called the "Voice of the American South."

Eudora Alice Welty was born on April 13, 1909, in Jackson, Mississippi. She was the first of three surviving children of Christian Webb Welty, a cashier for a life insurance company, and Mary Chestina Andrews Welty, a former schoolteacher, who after their marriage had moved to Jackson from their family homes in Ohio and West Virginia. Welty's happy childhood was filled with visits to her grandparents, summers at a nearby camp, music and art lessons, and extensive reading. While in high school, she published two poems in a national magazine for children, *St. Nicholas.* Following her graduation in 1925, she spent two years at the Mississippi State College for Women and then transferred to the University of Wisconsin, where she earned a BA in English literature in 1929. Welty then enrolled in an advertising course at Columbia University. The economic depression that gripped the nation made it impossible for her to find a full-time job in New York City, and she returned home to live with her mother after her father's sudden death in 1931. Although she frequently traveled around the country and to Europe, Welty lived for the rest of her life in the comfortable house her parents had built in suburban Jackson. She wrote for a local radio station and a newspaper, and then worked for three years as a publicity agent for a federal relief program, the Works Progress Administration. Welty, whose father had taught her to love photography, traveled and took photographs throughout Mississippi. She also drew upon her impressions in her first published story, "Death of a Traveling Salesman," which appeared in *Manuscript* magazine in 1936.

From that point on, Welty's literary reputation rose steadily. Her stories about isolated and lonely individuals in rural Mississippi appeared in prominent magazines and literary journals such as the *Southern Review*, *Prairie Schooner*, *Harper's Bazaar*, and the *Atlantic Monthly*. In 1939, she began a correspondence with Katherine Anne Porter, who wrote the introduction to Welty's first book, *A Curtain of Green and Other Stories* (1941). Although one reviewer felt that the stories showed "too great a preoccupation with the abnormal and grotesque," most critics and readers were enthusiastic about the collection, and the poet Louise Bogan compared Welty to William Faulkner. Following the publication of her novella *The Robber Bridegroom* (1942), a gothic fairy tale set "many many years ago in old Mississippi," Welty received a note of congratulations from Faulkner, who told her: "You're doing all right." She framed the note and hung it near her writing desk. Welty won first prize in the O. Henry Awards for the best American short stories of 1942 and of 1943, the year she published her second collection, *The Wide Net and Other Stories*. Unable to secure a position as a war correspondent, as she had hoped, Welty served on the staff of the *New York Times Book Review* in 1944. During the following decade, she wrote a richly symbolic short-story sequence, *The Golden Apples* (1949), and her first two novels: *Delta Wedding* (1946), a portrait of an exuberant family uniting for a large wedding in Mississippi; and *The Ponder Heart* (1954), a dramatic monologue in Southern dialect that won the William Dean Howells Medal as the most distinguished work of American fiction between 1950 and 1955.

Welty was later widely recognized for her contributions to American culture and letters. Following the publication of her final collection of stories, *The Bride of the Innisfallen* (1955), Welty wrote little fiction for the next fifteen years, during which she devoted herself to writing essays, teaching, lecturing, and nursing her mother through a final illness. She returned to fiction in *Losing Battles*, a comic novel about a family reunion published in 1970. The next year, she published *One Time, One Place*, a collection of what Welty diffidently described as the "snapshots" she had taken while working for the Works Progress Administration during the Great Depression. Her next book was *The Optimist's Daughter* (1972), a

She has simply an eye and an ear sharp, shrewd, and true as a tuning fork.
–Katherine Anne Porter

bedfordstmartins.com/
americanlit for research
links on Welty

semiautobiographical novel that won the Pulitzer Prize. Welty also received many other honors, including the Presidential Medal of Freedom, awarded to her by Jimmy Carter in 1980. In 1983, she gave a series of lectures at Harvard University, revising them as her best-selling autobiography, *One Writer's Beginnings* (1984). Observing that she was "a writer who came of a sheltered life," Welty affirmed: "A sheltered life can be a daring life as well. For all serious daring starts from within." Certainly, her daring work was admired by readers as diverse as the Southern novelist Flannery O'Connor and the computer programmer Steven Dorner, who was so taken with Welty's story "Why I Live at the P.O." that he named his widely used e-mail program *Eudora*. After a lengthy illness, Welty died at the age of ninety-two at her home in Jackson, Mississippi, on July 23, 2001.

Reading Welty's "Lily Daw and the Three Ladies."   Although she had been successful in publishing her work in magazines in the 1930s, Welty had difficulty in finding a publisher for a collection of her stories, which she sent to several publishing companies in New York City. Finally, in early 1941, the editors at Doubleday, Doran and Company accepted the collection, which they titled *A Curtain of Green and Other Stories*. The opening story was the previously unpublished "Lily Daw and the Three Ladies," which in her introduction to the volume Katherine Anne Porter succinctly summarized as an account of "a half-witted girl in the grip of social forces represented by a group of earnest ladies bent on doing the best thing for her, no matter what the consequences." Set in the fictional town of Victory, Mississippi, the story offers a shrewd portrait of small-town life, manners, and morals; it is also filled with Welty's characteristic humor, sharp satire, and keen eye for detail. Widely regarded as one of her finest short fictions, "Lily Daw and the Three Ladies" was one of the stories Welty chose to read to an enthusiastic audience in Washington, D.C., after she was named an honorary consultant in American letters at the Library of Congress in 1958. The text is taken from *A Curtain of Green and Other Stories* (1941).

LILY DAW AND THE THREE LADIES

Mrs Watts and Mrs Carson were both in the post office in Victory when the letter came from the Ellisville Institute for the Feeble Minded of Mississippi.[1] Aimee Slocum, with her hand still full of mail, ran out in front and handed it straight to Mrs Watts, and they all three read it together. Mrs Watts held it taut between her pink hands, and Mrs Carson

---

1. **Ellisville Institute for the Feeble Minded of Mississippi:** In 1920, Governor Lee Russell signed the "Law of Mental Deficiency" establishing the "Mississippi School and Colony for the Feebleminded," which opened at a site near Ellisville in 1921. The term *feebleminded* was used in the late nineteenth and early twentieth centuries for a wide range of loosely defined intellectual and developmental "deficiencies," and many states established such schools for the care and education of boys and girls. The name of the institution was changed to the Ellisville State School in 1929.

underscored each line slowly with her thimbled finger. Everybody else in the post office wondered what was up now.

"What will Lily say," beamed Mrs Carson at last, "when we tell her we're sending her to Ellisville!"

"She'll be tickled to death," said Mrs Watts, and added in a guttural voice to a deaf lady, "Lily Daw's getting in at Ellisville!"

"Don't you all dare go off and tell Lily without me!" called Aimee Slocum, trotting back to finish putting up the mail.

"Do you suppose they'll look after her down there?" Mrs Carson began to carry on a conversation with a group of Baptist ladies waiting in the post office. She was the Baptist preacher's wife.

"I've always heard it was lovely down there, but crowded," said one.

"Lily lets people walk over her so," said another.

"Last night at the tent show—" said another, and then popped her hand over her mouth.

"Don't mind me, I know there are such things in the world," said Mrs Carson, looking down and fingering the tape measure which hung over her bosom.

"Oh, Mrs Carson. Well, anyway, last night at the tent show, why, the man was just before making Lily buy a ticket to get in."

"A ticket!"

"Till my husband went up and explained she wasn't bright, and so did everybody else." The ladies all clucked their tongues.

"Oh, it was a very nice show," said the lady who had gone. "And Lily acted so nice. She was a perfect lady—just set in her seat and stared."

"Oh, she can be a lady—she can be," said Mrs Carson, shaking her head and turning her eyes up. "That's just what breaks your heart."

"Yes'm, she kept her eyes on—what's that thing makes all the commotion?—the xylophone," said the lady. "Didn't turn her head to the right or to the left the whole time. Set in front of me."

"The point is, what did she do after the show?" asked Mrs Watts practically. "Lily has gotten so she is very mature for her age."

"Oh, Etta!" protested Mrs Carson, looking at her wildly for a moment.

"And that's how come we are sending her to Ellisville," finished Mrs Watts.

"I'm ready, you all," said Aimee Slocum, running out with white powder all over her face. "Mail's up. I don't know how good it's up."

"Well, of course, I do hope it's for the best," said several of the other ladies. They did not go at once to take their mail out of their boxes; they felt a little left out.

The three women stood at the foot of the water tank.

"To find Lily is a different thing," said Aimee Slocum.

"Where in the wide world do you suppose she'd be?" It was Mrs Watts who was carrying the letter.

"I don't see a sign of her either on this side of the street or on the other side," Mrs Carson declared as they walked along.

Ed Newton was stringing Redbird school tablets[2] on the wire across the store.

"If you're after Lily, she come in here while ago and tole me she was fixin' to git married," he said.

"Ed Newton!" cried the ladies all together, clutching one another. Mrs Watts began to fan herself at once with the letter from Ellisville. She wore widow's black, and the least thing made her hot.

"Why she is not. She's going to Ellisville, Ed," said Mrs Carson gently. "Mrs Watts and I and Aimee Slocum are paying her way out of our own pockets. Besides, the boys of Victory are on their honor. Lily's not going to get married, that's just an idea she's got in her head."

"More power to you, ladies," said Ed Newton, spanking himself with a tablet.

When they came to the bridge over the railroad tracks, there was Estelle Mabers, sitting on a rail. She was slowly drinking an orange Ne-Hi.[3]

"Have you seen Lily?" they asked her.

"I'm supposed to be out here watching for her now," said the Mabers girl, as though she weren't there yet. "But for Jewel — Jewel says Lily come in the store while ago and picked out a two-ninety-eight hat and wore it off. Jewel wants to swap her something else for it."

"Oh, Estelle, Lily says she's going to get married!" cried Aimee Slocum.

"Well I declare," said Estelle; she never understood anything.

Loralee Adkins came riding by in her Willys-Knight,[4] tooting the horn to find out what they were talking about.

Aimee threw up her hands and ran out into the street. "Loralee, Loralee, you got to ride us up to Lily Daws'. She's up yonder fixing to get married!"

"Hop in, my land!"

"Well, that just goes to show you right now," said Mrs Watts, groaning as she was helped into the back seat. "What we've got to do is persuade Lily it will be nicer to go to Ellisville."

"Just to think!"

While they rode around the corner Mrs Carson was going on in her sad voice, sad as the soft noises in the hen house at twilight. "We buried Lily's poor defenseless mother. We gave Lily all her food and kindling and every stitch she had on. Sent her to Sunday school to learn the Lord's teachings, had her baptized a Baptist. And when her old father commenced beating her and tried to cut her head off with the butcher knife, why, we went and took her away from him and gave her a place to stay."

The paintless frame house with all the weather vanes was three stories high in places and had yellow and violet stained-glass windows in front and gingerbread around the

2. **Redbird school tablets:** A brand-name notebook, featuring a red cardinal on its cover, commonly used in schools in the 1930s.
3. **orange Ne-Hi:** An orange-flavored carbonated soft drink developed in the 1920s.
4. **Willys-Knight:** An automobile produced by the Willys-Overland Company between 1914 and 1933.

porch. It leaned steeply to one side, toward the railroad, and the front steps were gone. The car full of ladies drew up under the cedar tree.

"Now Lily's almost grown up," Mrs Carson continued. "In fact, she's grown," she concluded, getting out.

"Talking about getting married," said Mrs Watts disgustedly. "Thanks, Loralee, you run on home."

They climbed over the dusty zinnias onto the porch and walked through the open door without knocking.

"There certainly is always a funny smell in this house. I say it every time I come," said Aimee Slocum.

Lily was there, in the dark of the hall, kneeling on the floor by a small open trunk.

When she saw them she put a zinnia in her mouth, and held still.

"Hello, Lily," said Mrs Carson reproachfully.

"Hello," said Lily. In a minute she gave a suck on the zinnia stem that sounded exactly like a jay bird. There she sat, wearing a petticoat for a dress, one of the things Mrs Carson kept after her about. Her milky-yellow hair streamed freely down from under a new hat. You could see the wavy scar on her throat if you knew it was there.

Mrs Carson and Mrs Watts, the two fattest, sat in the double rocker. Aimee Slocum sat on the wire chair donated from the drugstore that burned.

"Well, what are you doing, Lily?" asked Mrs Watts, who led the rocking.

Lily smiled.

The trunk was old and lined with yellow and brown paper, with an asterisk pattern showing in darker circles and rings. Mutely the ladies indicated to each other that they did not know where in the world it had come from. It was empty except for two bars of soap and a green washcloth, which Lily was now trying to arrange in the bottom.

"Go on and tell us what you're doing, Lily," said Aimee Slocum.

"Packing, silly," said Lily.

"Where are you going?"

"Going to get married, and I bet you wish you was me now," said Lily. But shyness overcame her suddenly, and she popped the zinnia back into her mouth.

"Talk to me, dear," said Mrs Carson. "Tell old Mrs Carson why you want to get married."

"No," said Lily, after a moment's hesitation.

"Well, we've thought of something that will be so much nicer," said Mrs Carson. "Why don't you go to Ellisville!"

"Won't that be lovely?" said Mrs Watts. "Goodness, yes."

"It's a lovely place," said Aimee Slocum uncertainly.

"You've got bumps on your face," said Lily.

"Aimee, dear, you stay out of this, if you don't mind," said Mrs Carson anxiously. "I don't know what it is comes over Lily when you come around her."

Lily stared at Aimee Slocum meditatively.

"There! Wouldn't you like to go to Ellisville now?" asked Mrs Carson.

"No'm," said Lily.

"Why not?" All the ladies leaned down toward her in impressive astonishment.

"'Cause I'm goin' to get married," said Lily.

"Well, and who are you going to marry, dear?" asked Mrs Watts. She knew how to pin people down and make them deny what they'd already said.

Lily bit her lip and began to smile. She reached into the trunk and held up both cakes of soap and wagged them.

"Tell us," challenged Mrs Watts. "Who you're going to marry, now."

"A man last night."

There was a gasp from each lady. The possible reality of a lover descended suddenly like a summer hail over their heads. Mrs Watts stood up and balanced herself.

"One of those show fellows! A musician!" she cried.

Lily looked up in admiration.

"Did he – did he do anything to you?" In the long run, it was still only Mrs Watts who could take charge.

"Oh, yes'm," said Lily. She patted the cakes of soap fastidiously with the tips of her small fingers and tucked them in with the washcloth.

"What?" demanded Aimee Slocum, rising up and tottering before her scream. "What?" she called out in the hall.

"Don't ask her what," said Mrs Carson, coming up behind. "Tell me, Lily – just yes or no — are you the same as you were?"

"He had a red coat," said Lily graciously. "He took little sticks and went *ping-pong! ding-dong!*"

"Oh, I think I'm going to faint," said Aimee Slocum, but they said, "No, you're not."

"The xylophone!" cried Mrs Watts. "The xylophone player! Why, the coward, he ought to be run out of town on a rail!"

"Out of town? He is out of town, by now," cried Aimee. "Can't you read? — the sign in the café — Victory on the ninth, Como on the tenth? He's in Como. Como!"

"All right! We'll bring him back!" cried Mrs Watts. "He can't get away from me!"

"Hush," said Mrs Carson. "I don't think it's any use following that line of reasoning at all. It's better in the long run for him to be gone out of our lives for good and all. That kind of a man. He was after Lily's body alone and he wouldn't ever in this world make the poor little thing happy, even if we went out and forced him to marry her like he ought – at the point of a gun."

"Still —" began Aimee, her eyes widening.

"Shut up," said Mrs Watts. "Mrs Carson, you're right, I expect."

"This is my hope chest – see?" said Lily politely in the pause that followed. "You haven't even looked at it. I've already got soap and a washrag. And I have my hat – on. What are you all going to give me?"

"Lily," said Mrs Watts, starting over, "we'll give you lots of gorgeous things if you'll only go to Ellisville instead of getting married."

"What will you give me?" asked Lily.

"I'll give you a pair of hemstitched pillowcases," said Mrs Carson.

"I'll give you a big caramel cake," said Mrs Watts.

"I'll give you a souvenir from Jackson – a little toy bank," said Aimee Slocum. "Now will you go?"

"No," said Lily.

"I'll give you a pretty little Bible with your name on it in real gold," said Mrs Carson.

"What if I was to give you a pink crêpe de chine brassière[5] with adjustable shoulder straps?" asked Mrs Watts grimly.

"Oh, Etta."

"Well, she needs it," said Mrs Watts. "What would they think if she ran all over Ellisville in a petticoat looking like a Fiji?"[6]

"I wish *I* could go to Ellisville," said Aimee Slocum luringly.

"What will they have for me down there?" asked Lily softly.

"Oh! lots of things. You'll have baskets to weave, I expect. . . ." Mrs Carson looked vaguely at the others.

"Oh, yes indeed, they will let you make all sorts of baskets," said Mrs Watts; then her voice too trailed off.

"No'm, I'd rather get married," said Lily.

"Lily Daw! Now that's just plain stubbornness!" cried Mrs Watts. "You almost said you'd go and then you took it back!"

"We've all asked God, Lily," said Mrs Carson finally, "and God seemed to tell us – Mr Carson, too – that the place where you ought to be, so as to be happy, was Ellisville."

Lily looked reverent, but still stubborn.

"We've really just got to get her there – now!" screamed Aimee Slocum all at once. "Suppose — ! She can't stay here!"

"Oh no, no, no," said Mrs Carson hurriedly. "We mustn't think that."

They sat sunken in despair.

"Could I take my hope chest – to go to Ellisville?" asked Lily shyly, looking at them sidewise.

"Why, yes," said Mrs Carson blankly.

Silently they rose once more to their feet.

"Oh, if I could just take my hope chest!"

"All the time it was just her hope chest," Aimee whispered.

Mrs Watts struck her palms together. "It's settled!"

"Praise the fathers," murmured Mrs Carson.

Lily looked up at them, and her eyes gleamed. She cocked her head and spoke out in a proud imitation of someone – someone utterly unknown.

"O.K. – Toots!"[7]

The ladies had been nodding and smiling and backing away toward the door.

"I think I'd better stay," said Mrs Carson, stopping in her tracks. "Where – where could she have learned that terrible expression?"

---

5. **crêpe de chine brassière:** A woman's undergarment (commonly known as a bra) made of a light silk fabric (French).

6. **a Fiji:** A native of the Fiji Island in the South Pacific Ocean; here, the term is derogatory, suggesting that Lily will not be appropriately dressed.

7. **Toots:** Short for *tootsie*, a slang term of endearment equivalent to *babe* or *sweetie*.

"Pack up," said Mrs Watts. "Lily Daw is leaving for Ellisville on Number One."

In the station the train was puffing. Nearly everyone in Victory was hanging around waiting for it to leave. The Victory Civic Band had assembled without any orders and was scattered through the crowd. Ed Newton gave false signals to start on his bass horn. A crate full of baby chickens got loose on the platform. Everybody wanted to see Lily all dressed up, but Mrs Carson and Mrs Watts had sneaked her into the train from the other side of the tracks.

The two ladies were going to travel as far as Jackson to help Lily change trains and be sure she went in the right direction.

Lily sat between them on the plush seat with her hair combed and pinned up into a knot under a small blue hat which was Jewel's exchange for the pretty one. She wore a traveling dress made out of part of Mrs Watts's last summer's mourning. Pink straps glowed through. She had a purse and a Bible and a warm cake in a box, all in her lap.

Aimee Slocum had been getting the outgoing mail stamped and bundled. She stood in the aisle of the coach now, tears shaking from her eyes.

"Good-by, Lily," she said. She was the one who felt things.

"Good-by, silly," said Lily.

"Oh, dear, I hope they get our telegram to meet her in Ellisville!" Aimee cried sorrowfully, as she thought how far away it was. "And it was so hard to get it all in ten words, too."

"Get off, Aimee, before the train starts and you break your neck," said Mrs Watts, all settled and waving her dressy fan gaily. "I declare, it's so hot, as soon as we get a few miles out of town I'm going to slip my corset down."

"Oh, Lily, don't cry down there. Just be good, and do what they tell you — it's all because they love you." Aimee drew her mouth down. She was backing away, down the aisle.

Lily laughed. She pointed across Mrs Carson's bosom out the window toward a man. He had stepped off the train and just stood there, by himself. He was a stranger and wore a cap.

"Look," she said, laughing softly through her fingers.

"Don't — look," said Mrs Carson very distinctly, as if, out of all she had ever spoken, she would impress these two solemn words upon Lily's soft little brain. She added, "Don't look at anything till you get to Ellisville."

Outside, Aimee Slocum was crying so hard she almost ran into the stranger. He wore a cap and was short and seemed to have on perfume, if such a thing could be.

"Could you tell me, madam," he said, "where a little lady lives in this burg name of Miss Lily Daw?" He lifted his cap — and he had red hair.

"What do you want to know for?" Aimee asked before she knew it.

"Talk louder," said the stranger. He almost whispered, himself.

"She's gone away — she's gone to Ellisville!"

"Gone?"

"Gone to Ellisville!"

"Well, I like that!" The man stuck out his bottom lip and puffed till his hair jumped.

"What business did you have with Lily?" cried Aimee suddenly.

"We was only going to get married, that's all," said the man.

Aimee Slocum started to scream in front of all those people. She almost pointed to the long black box she saw lying on the ground at the man's feet. Then she jumped back in fright.

"The xylophone! The xylophone!" she cried, looking back and forth from the man to the hissing train. Which was more terrible? The bell began to ring hollowly, and the man was talking.

"Did you say Ellisville? That in the state of Mississippi?" Like lightning he had pulled out a red notebook entitled, "Permanent Facts & Data." He wrote down something. "I don't hear well."

Aimee nodded her head up and down, and circled around him.

Under "Ellis-Ville Miss" he was drawing a line; now he was flicking it with two little marks. "Maybe she didn't say she would. Maybe she said she wouldn't." He suddenly laughed very loudly, after the way he had whispered. Aimee jumped back. "Women! – Well, if we play anywheres near Ellisville, Miss., in the future I may look her up and I may not," he said.

The bass horn sounded the true signal for the band to begin. White steam rushed out of the engine. Usually the train stopped for only a minute in Victory, but the engineer knew Lily from waving at her, and he knew this was her big day.

"Wait!" Aimee Slocum did scream. "Wait, mister! I can get her for you. Wait, Mister Engineer! Don't go!"

Then there she was back on the train, screaming in Mrs Carson's and Mrs Watts's faces.

"The xylophone player! The xylophone player to marry her! Yonder he is!"

"Nonsense," murmured Mrs Watts, peering over the others to look where Aimee pointed. "If he's there I don't see him. Where is he? You're looking at One-Eye Beasley."

"The little man with the cap – no, with the red hair! Hurry!"

"Is that really him?" Mrs Carson asked Mrs Watts in wonder. "Mercy! He's small, isn't he?"

"Never saw him before in my life!" cried Mrs Watts. But suddenly she shut up her fan.

"Come on! This is a train we're on!" cried Aimee Slocum. Her nerves were all unstrung.

"All right, don't have a conniption fit, girl," said Mrs Watts. "Come on," she said thickly to Mrs Carson.

"Where are we going now?" asked Lily as they struggled down the aisle.

"We're taking you to get married," said Mrs. Watts. "Mrs Carson, you'd better phone up your husband right there in the station."

"But I don't want to git married," said Lily, beginning to whimper. "I'm going to Ellisville."

"Hush, and we'll all have some ice-cream cones later," whispered Mrs Carson.

Just as they climbed down the steps at the back end of the train, the band went into "Independence March."[8]

---

8. **"Independence March"**: "The Spirit of Independence" (1912), a stirring patriotic march composed by Abe Holzmann (1874–1939).

The xylophone player was still there, patting his foot. He came up and said, "Hello, Toots. What's up – tricks?" and kissed Lily with a smack, after which she hung her head.

"So you're the young man we've heard so much about," said Mrs Watts. Her smile was brilliant. "Here's your little Lily."

"What say?" asked the xylophone player.

"My husband happens to be the Baptist preacher of Victory," said Mrs Carson in a loud, clear voice. "Isn't that lucky? I can get him here in five minutes: I know exactly where he is."

They were in a circle around the xylophone player, all going into the white waiting room.

"Oh, I feel just like crying, at a time like this," said Aimee Slocum. She looked back and saw the train moving slowly away, going under the bridge at Main Street. Then it disappeared around the curve.

"Oh, the hope chest!" Aimee cried in a stricken voice.

"And whom have we the pleasure of addressing?" Mrs Watts was shouting, while Mrs Carson was ringing up the telephone.

The band went on playing. Some of the people thought Lily was on the train, and some swore she wasn't. Everybody cheered, though, and a straw hat was thrown into the telephone wires.

[1940]

Carlos Bulosan

[1911–1956]

Carlos Bulosan was born in Pangasinan, a province on the island of Luzon in the Philippines, on November 2, 1911, near the end of a tumultuous period in his country's history. In 1896, the Filipinos had begun a successful revolt against Spanish rule, and they expected to be granted independence after Spain ceded the Philippines to the United States in the treaty that ended the Spanish-American War of 1898. Instead, the United States annexed the islands, and American troops defeated Filipino guerillas during the Philippine-American War of 1899-1902, though fighting continued until 1913. The years of bloody conflict, during which an estimated two hundred thousand to one million civilians died of disease and starvation, left the country impoverished. Although little is known about his childhood, Bulosan recalled:

I lived in Mangusmana with my father until I was seven years old. We lived in a small grass hut; but it was sufficient because we were peasants. My father could not read or write, but he knew how to work his one hectare of land, which was the sole support of our big family.

Bulosan attended American-style schools, but he left high school after three semesters in order to work to help support the family. Like thousands of other Filipinos, including two older brothers who had gone to California, Bulosan believed that he would find greater freedom and economic opportunity in the United States. He consequently booked passage in steerage aboard a steamer bound for Seattle, Washington.

Bulosan arrived on July 22, 1930, at the beginning of the Great Depression. Along with other expatriate Filipino Americans – or "Pinoy," as they called themselves – he endured terrible poverty and hardship in his new country. In fact, it could not truly be his country, since as immigrants from an American colony Filipinos could not become citizens of the United States. Bulosan was quickly disillusioned by the violence, prejudice, and exploitation the Pinoy suffered as farm or cannery workers, virtually the only jobs available to them. "Do you know what a Filipino feels in America?" he wrote a friend during the 1930s. "He is the loneliest thing on earth. . . . He is enchained damnably to his race, his heritage. He is betrayed, my friend." As a migrant farmworker, Bulosan followed the crops from Washington through Oregon to California.

Carlos Bulosan

This undated photograph of Bulosan at what he called his "write spot" was apparently taken in the early 1940s, when he was becoming widely known for his articles, poems, and stories about the experiences of Filipino Americans.

After he reached Los Angeles, he helped organize the United Cannery, Agricultural, Packing, and Allied Workers of America. Bulosan edited the *New Tide*, a bimonthly magazine for workers, and began to write articles for various newspapers, including the *Philippine Commonwealth Times*. In 1936, he was diagnosed with tuberculosis and spent two years in the convalescent ward of the Los Angeles County Hospital. Friends provided him with dozens of periodicals and books, and he studied the works of Karl Marx and American writers from Walt Whitman to Theodore Dreiser, Sherwood Anderson, and their younger contemporaries William Faulkner, Ernest Hemingway, and John Steinbeck. Bulosan also wrote constantly, and his verse regularly appeared in little magazines such as the *Lyric* and *Poetry*, which published several groups of his poems between 1936 and 1942.

After the entry of the United States into World War II, Bulosan became the major literary voice of Filipino Americans. The war was a complicated issue for the Pinoy, who were intensely aware of the injustices in the United States but who were eager to participate in the effort to drive the Japanese from the conquered Philippines. At first, Filipino Americans were classified as aliens and denied admission to the military services. Bulosan and others worked to change the law, and President Franklin Roosevelt signed a special proclamation that led to the formation of the

Insignia of Filipino Battalions and Regiments

This military insignia was approved for all Filipino infantry units in 1942. The volcano represents the area in central California where the units trained before they were sent to the western Pacific, and the three stars represent the main islands in the Philippines — Luzon, Mindanao, and the Visayan Islands.

First and Second Filipino Regiments in the United States. Too frail to serve in the military, Bulosan fought the war with his pen. He published a collection of his poetry, *Letter from America* (1942), and *The Voice of Bataan* (1943), a poetic tribute to the American and Filipino soldiers who had died defending Bataan Island in the Philippines. Bulosan also began to publish stories in mainstream magazines such as *Harper's Bazaar,* the *New Yorker,* and *Town and Country.* He became even more widely known when his article "Freedom from Want" accompanied one of Norman Rockwell's famous "Four Freedoms" paintings, which were published in successive issues of the *Saturday Evening Post* in 1943. The following year, Bulosan's collection of short stories based on Filipino folktales, *The Laughter of My Father,* became an international bestseller. He then wrote his most famous book, the autobiographical *America Is in the Heart* (1946), an often grim depiction of the collective experience of Filipino Americans and an eloquent plea for the end of racism and intolerance in the United States.

During the final decade of his life, Bulosan struggled against illness and the anticommunist hysteria generated by the cold war. Despite his rising stature as a writer in the 1940s, Bulosan came under suspicion for his leftist views and labor activities, and he was investigated by the House of Representatives Un-American Activities Committee. Beginning in 1950, he was also under constant surveillance by the FBI, which effectively blacklisted Bulosan. Unable to find work, he spent the last years of his life in poverty and poor health, nursed by his companion, the labor activist Josephine Patrick. Looking back over his life and literary career, Bulosan in an autobiographical sketch written in 1955 observed that he had been impelled to write by his "grand dream of equality among men and freedom for all," as well as by his desire "to translate the desires and aspirations of the whole Filipino people in the Philippines and abroad in terms relevant to contemporary history." Bulosan died in Seattle of tuberculosis on September 11, 1956, leaving behind the manuscript of a posthumously published novel about the twentieth-century history of the Philippines, *The Cry and the Dedication* (1995).

bedfordstmartins.com/ americanlit *for research links on Bulosan*

Reading Bulosan's "The End of the War."   Set at Camp Beale, a training camp for the First Filipino Infantry near Sacramento, California, this story was first published in the prominent cultural magazine the *New Yorker.* Throughout the war, the magazine published articles, essays, and letters from foreign correspondents, mostly firsthand accounts of battles in Europe and the Pacific. "The End of the War" appeared in the magazine shortly before the long-anticipated American invasion of the Japanese-occupied Philippines, which began in October 1944. In Bulosan's story, a Filipino private has a dream in which the Japanese surrender as his regiment arrives on Mindanao, an island in the Philippines. As the story of the dream is repeated throughout the camp, it expands and grows. As in much of Bulosan's other fiction, "The End of the War" evokes different dreams, from the American dream of individual happiness and success, a dream denied to Filipino Americans, to their shared dream of justice and equality and the collective dream of Filipinos for a free and independent Philippines. The text is taken from the *New Yorker*, September 2, 1944.

THE END OF THE WAR

It was a fine Sunday morning and the First Filipino Infantry[1] was very quiet. Private Pascual Fidel, who was small even for a Filipino, opened his eyes and kicked the thick Army blankets off his body. His right hand reached for the shiny harmonica which was on the floor beside a pair of clean boots. He rubbed his eyes slowly and then began humming "Amor, Amor, Amor,"[2] which he had heard on the radio some nights before. He tapped the harmonica on his knee, out of habit, put it in his mouth, and fumbled for the first note. Suddenly his hands stopped and he jumped up and ran around the room from cot to cot, looking, but his comrades had already left. With nothing on but his undershorts, he rushed through the door of the barracks and out into the bright morning sunlight, screaming for his cousin, "Pitong! Sergeant Pitong Tongkol!"

Sergeant Tongkol, who was in the same company of the First Filipino Infantry, stood watching three men planting poppies in a vacant space nearby. He looked up and saw Private Fidel running toward him. Anxious to know what it was all about, Sergeant Tongkol started to meet his cousin. They met in front of the mess hall, where most of the soldiers were now assembled.

"What is it, Cousin?" Sergeant Tongkol asked.

"I had a dream," Private Fidel said, when he had caught his breath.

"A dream?" Sergeant Tongkol said.

"It is a big dream," Private Fidel said. "It is bigger than this whole camp." He stopped and looked beyond Sergeant Tongkol at the distant low brown hills of northern California. Then, turning around slowly, he scanned the vastness of the valley that surrounded Camp Beale.[3]

"What happened, Cousin?" Sergeant Tongkol asked.

---

1. **First Filipino Infantry:** Before World War II, Filipinos living in the United States were not permitted to serve in the military. After the Japanese attacks on Pearl Harbor and the Philippines in December 1941, President Roosevelt authorized the founding of a Filipino unit, which was formed at Camp San Luis Obispo, California, on March 4, 1942. After extensive training, the First Filipino Infantry Regiment finally left for the western Pacific in May 1944. Less than two months after Bulosan's story was published, on October 20, 1944, U.S. troops began the invasion of Leyte, an island in the Japanese-occupied Philippines. After landing on the island early in February 1945, the soldiers of the First Filipino Infantry engaged in fierce battles with the Japanese.
2. **"Amor, Amor, Amor":** Literally, "Love, Love, Love" (Spanish), a popular Latin melody of the period, also known as "Amor."
3. **Camp Beale:** In January 1943, the First Filipino Infantry Regiment was moved to Camp Beale, near Sacramento, California.

"We were approaching Mindanao[4] when it happened," Private Fidel said. "I remember it very well because I was playing *monte*[5] with my brother Malong and your brother Ponso when it happened. I had a poor hand, so I wanted to cheat, because it was my last dollar." He spread an imaginary hand of cards in front of his cousin, and while Sergeant Tongkol became more and more impatient, Private Fidel deliberated as if he were actually playing cards. Finally he said, "Your brother Ponso put two dollars in the pot, but my brother Malong raised the bet. I had a pair of threes, but there was another three under my left foot. I remember it well because my eyes were not on my cards; they were glued to the approaching shore of southern Mindanao. I saw Ponso's helmet move in the morning light when I reached for the hidden card. Then it happened, suddenly and without ceremony."

"What happened?" Sergeant Tongkol asked.

"I ran to the railing of the ship and looked," Private Fidel continued. "I stood there for quite some time, not believing what I saw. But it was true. They came to the shore and surrendered."

"What is true?" Sergeant Tongkol shouted. "Who surrendered? As your superior, Private Fidel, I order you to answer me!" He stepped back and stood at attention, waiting for his cousin to obey him.

"The Japs met us on the beach and surrendered," Private Fidel said. "A few minutes afterward, it was broadcast that Germany had also surrendered and the war came to a sudden end."

Sergeant Tongkol was stunned for a moment. Then, realizing the importance of the event, he grabbed his cousin and a rush of anxious words poured out of his mouth. "Are you sure, Cousin?" he asked. "Are you sure they were Japs? Did you see the large teeth of the yellow sons of the Rising Sun?[6] Did you *hear* the broadcast that the war came to an end?"

"I'm sure, Sergeant Tongkol!" Private Fidel shouted.

Sergeant Tongkol relaxed his hold. His face was filled with a sudden kindness. "Not so loud, Cousin," he said. "Here is my blouse. You might catch cold."

Private Fidel put the blouse on. It was so big that it hung like an overcoat. Filled now with the big dream, Sergeant Tongkol expanded his chest. Wild anticipation illumined his eyes and his dark face. He put his arm around Private Fidel, as though his cousin were a precious toy. "Let's tell the good news to my brother," Sergeant Tongkol said.

The two Filipino soldiers walked eagerly toward the mess hall, each with his arm around the other. It was always like that with Private Fidel and Sergeant Tongkol. They were the same age and in their native village, on the island of Luzon, they used to go together into the banana grove across the river and steal the choicest fruit. They sailed together to the United States when they were seventeen years old. They

---

4. **Mindanao:** Many had expected the U.S. invasion of the Philippines to begin on Mindanao, the southern and easternmost island in the archipelago, but American strategists finally decided to launch the attack on the central island of Leyte. See note 1.

5. *monte*: Short for the popular card game Spanish Monte.

6. **Did you see . . . Rising Sun?:** In the center of the flag of Japan is a large red disc, representing the rising sun. In war propaganda and racist caricatures of the period, the Japanese were depicted as men with bright yellow skin and large, bucked teeth.

had worked together on a farm most of the time since, and they were never separated from each other except when one of them was in jail for gambling or selling something that did not belong to him. When the war came, they had volunteered together. But it had been hard on Private Fidel when, some months after their enlistment, his cousin Pitong was promoted. Pitong had always been his inferior in civilian life, especially when they were working on the farm. Sergeant Tongkol had been just a field hand, cutting lettuce or picking tomatoes or doing some unimportant job like that, but he, Private Fidel, was a bookkeeper or timekeeper or had some other important job. He resented his cousin's promotion and he had tried many times to work against him, but every time he attempted to discredit his cousin, he himself was the one who was discredited. He had resigned himself to his fate and did not even try for a promotion, except in his dreams, where one promotion after another came to him.

Mess Sergeant Ponso Tongkol was chopping string beans into a barrel with a long butcher knife. When the two soldiers approached him, he started chopping faster. His feet danced rhythmically as he jabbed the knife up and down. It was a stunt they always enjoyed. The two soldiers stood watching him. Suddenly Sergeant Pitong grabbed his brother. "The war has ended, Ponso!" he said.

One of the dancing feet stopped in mid-air. The butcher knife stopped moving up and down. Slowly, Ponso looked up from the barrel of chopped string beans and his eyes fastened on his brother's face. "You are kidding, Brother," he said.

"But it is true, Ponso," Sergeant Pitong said.

Mess Sergeant Ponso sat down on the edge of the barrel and put the knife in his lap. "If it is true that the war has ended," he said, "why am I still preparing string beans for dinner?"

"It is in the dream that the war has ended," Private Fidel interrupted.

Sergeant Pitong pushed him away and planted himself in front of his brother. "We were approaching Mindanao when it happened," he began, glancing sideways at Private Fidel with a superior air. "I remember it vividly, because I was walking on the deck with his brother Malong."

"No, no!" Private Fidel protested. "*I* was there!"

"Let me tell it," Sergeant Pitong said. "This dream is not for a small potato like you, Private Fidel." Then he turned his back on him and faced the Mess Sergeant. "I was walking on the deck with Private Fidel's brother Malong when it happened. I was about to tell him about a champion gamecock I had when I was in Salinas, California.[7] That rooster had the most beautiful pair of legs. I made lots of money betting on him, but it was not the money that I enjoyed but his dancing feet when he was in the ring with an adversary. Well, then, it was at this moment that it happened. The Japs came to the shore and surrendered. Then it was broadcast that the war had ended."

---

7. **Salinas, California:** A town in the fertile Central Valley, where many Filipino immigrants worked as farm laborers. At the beginning of the Salinas lettuce strikes of 1934-36, a group of fifty vigilantes attacked and burned a labor camp run by a leader in the Filipino Labor Union (F.L.U.).

"Was the Son of Heaven with the soldiers?" Mess Sergeant Ponso asked.

"He was the first one to come to the shore," Sergeant Pitong said.

Private Fidel interrupted again. "He was *not* there. The Emperor was not there. I would have seen him and his white horse if they'd been there."

"He *was* there!" Sergeant Pitong said. "The Son of Heaven came to meet us with several generals. They were all smiling and willing to surrender."

"The salomabit!"[8] Mess Sergeant Ponso exclaimed. He gripped the handle of the butcher knife with both hands. "Then what did you do?"

"We started shouting and throwing away our guns," his brother said.

"Goddamit!" Mess Sergeant Ponso shouted, getting up from the barrel. Slowly he sat down again. "If I was only there," he said. The strong hands tightened around the knife. He was a much larger man than his brother. He got up once more and walked around a table, stabbing the air furiously with the knife.

"It was only a dream," Private Fidel said.

But Mess Sergeant Ponso did not hear him. He said, "Ten years I worked peacefully in America, minding my own business, when the salomabit come stabbing me at the back. Maybe it is not much I make, but I got the beautiful Ford from Detroit. When I come home at night from work, I ride it to town, pressing the horn and whistling. I ride and ride and I am happy. In the bank I got money—maybe not much, but it is my money. When I see the flag, I take the hat off and I say, 'Thank you very much!' I like the color of the flag and I work hard. Why the salomabit come?" He drove the knife into the edge of the table with a terrific blow. Then he looked at his brother and cousin. "If only I was there!"

Private Fidel stepped back. He was not afraid of his cousin, but he kept his eyes on the knife nevertheless. Mess Sergeant Ponso pulled the knife out and wiped it with his apron. Then he produced a bottle of wine from the rice bin and filled three glasses. "Let's celebrate," he said.

They emptied their glasses. As though he had noticed Private Fidel for the first time, Mess Sergeant Ponso pulled a pair of pants from a hook on the wall and gave it to him. "Here," he said, "put these on. And then let's tell the good news to your brother."

The three soldiers hurried from the mess hall and went to the latrine, where Private Malong Fidel was on duty. When he saw them rushing toward him, he dropped the handle of his mop.

"The war has come to an end, Malong," Mess Sergeant Ponso said.

Private Malong stepped back against the wall of the latrine. "Don't torture me," he said. "I'm too tired."

"But it's true!" Mess Sergeant Ponso shouted. "I saw the Son of Heaven himself and his wife—"

Sergeant Pitong tried to interrupt, but his brother prevented him by putting a huge hand over his mouth.

---

8. **"The salomabit!"**: "The son of a bitch!" (Filipino idiom).

"No, no!" Private Fidel cried. "*I* was there!" The loud voice of his cousin Ponso drowned him out. Private Fidel had dreamed the big dream, but it was too big for him to hold. It was a dream that belonged to no one now, yet it was a dream for every soldier. Hearing it told by another person, Private Fidel knew that it was not his dream any more. First it had become Sergeant Pitong's dream, then Mess Sergeant Ponso had taken it over. In a few minutes, it would be Malong's dream.

In utter defeat, Private Fidel backed out into the sunlight and returned to his barracks, where he sat on his cot. He was surprised to notice that the harmonica was still in his hand. He tapped it on his knee, out of habit, and started to play "Amor, Amor, Amor." After a while, he began playing with great joy and inspiration.

[1944]

American Literature

since 1945

ON AUGUST 14, 1945, three months after World War II ended in Europe, an excited crowd of 750,000 people gathered in Times Square in New York City, looking intently at the Monograph News Bulletin, the electronic message board on Times Tower. At 7:03 PM, the headline they had been anticipating finally flashed across the board: "OFFICIAL—TRUMAN ANNOUNCES JAPANESE SURRENDER." The crowd erupted with cheers, and within a few hours two million people filled Times Square, wildly celebrating "V-J" (Victory in Japan) day, the conclusion of a devastating, six-year conflict that took the lives of an estimated fifty to seventy million people and ushered in the nuclear age.

In fact, the formal end of hostilities in World War II marked the beginning of a new conflict that powerfully shaped life and politics in the United States. Even as the war ended, growing tensions between the former Allies over Russia's takeover of Eastern Europe set the stage for what soon became known as the "cold war," the decades-long economic, ideological, and political struggle between the Soviet Union and the Western democracies, led by the United States. As the cold war intensified, especially after the Soviet Union tested its first nuclear weapon in 1949, anticommunist hysteria was fueled by the House Un-American Activities Committee (HUAC), which conducted sensationalistic investigations of suspected Communist influences in education, the entertainment industry, and other institutions; and by Senator Joseph McCarthy of Wisconsin, who charged that Communists had infiltrated the U.S. Army, the State Department, and the administration of President Truman. In a famous Lincoln Day speech to the Republican Women's Club of Wheeling, West Virginia, McCarthy declared: "Today we are engaged in a final, all-out battle between communistic atheism and Christianity." Although McCarthy's personal influence waned after the Korean War (1950–53), the first sustained military effort to "contain" Communism, what became known as "McCarthyism" continued into the 1960s, by which time the United States was involved in one of the most divisive conflicts in its history, the Vietnam War.

◀ (OVERLEAF)

Suburban Sprawl

One of the most striking developments during the decades since World War II has been the rapid growth of suburbia, as illustrated by this photograph of housing developments spreading westward from Las Vegas toward the Spring Mountains of Nevada. In 1945, roughly 70 percent of Americans living in metropolitan areas lived in the central cities; by 1990, the figure had declined to 40 percent. That population shift has radically altered American life and the landscape of many parts of the country, generating both environmental and social concerns in the United States.

Celebration of Japan's Surrender

This photograph of the crowd filling Times Square was taken just after 7 PM on August 14, 1945. Moments later, the official news of the Japanese surrender was flashed on Times Tower, the building just behind a reproduction of the Statue of Liberty, which had been erected to encourage people to buy war bonds during World War II.

Culture and Society in the Age of Affluence

Those global and political events coincided with dramatic changes in American society and culture following World War II. The revolution in publishing that had begun shortly before the war gained strong momentum after 1945. That year, the earliest American publisher of mass-market paperbacks, Pocket Books, brought out the first two "instant" books: *FDR: A Memorial,* issued within days of the death of the beloved president Franklin Delano Roosevelt in April; and *The Atomic Age Opens,* which appeared only a few weeks after the United States dropped the first atomic bombs on the Japanese cities of Hiroshima and Nagasaki in August. At the time, Pocket Books' major competitor was the British firm Penguin Books, which by the end of the war was exporting a million volumes a month to the United States. In 1945, the firm's American distributors, Ian Ballantine and his wife, Betty, left Penguin and established Bantam Books. Determined "to change the reading habits of America" by publishing inexpensive editions of books "that mattered," as Ian Ballantine put it, Bantam began with a reprint of Mark Twain's *Life on the Mississippi*. But the Ballantines knew that they would have to publish popular books to succeed in business. In addition to a reprint of a high-quality literary work, every month Bantam also published a book in each of three popular genres: a hard-boiled detective novel, a mystery, and a western, all selling for twenty-five cents a copy. By 1950, the highly successful company had sold 38 million books, and in 1952 the Ballantines formed a new company, Ballantine Books, which published original books in paperback format. Its list included many works of science fiction, which emerged as one of the most popular of all paperback genres, and by 1960 the dollar sales of paperbacks surpassed that of hardbacks in the United States.

The market for books was spurred by the rapid expansion of the educational system, in which many aspiring writers found work. In 1944,

Bantam Books

One of the earliest Bantam books was this reprint of Fitzgerald's novel, originally published twenty years earlier, in 1925. As the publishers claimed, books in the new paperback series were recognizable by "tasteful pictures on the covers, by their famous authors, and by the tough bantam rooster on the front of all the books."

OFFICIAL STUDENT PUBLICATION

The COUGAR

Volume 15   Z 739   UNIVERSITY OF HOUSTON, HOUSTON, TEXAS   FRIDAY, FEBRUARY 8, 1946   Number 18

ENROLLMENT HITS ALL TIME PEAK

$1,000,000 Vet Center, $5,000,000 Building Project To Be Proposed

Vets Register

4600 Registered; 2900 Veterans

Three Ex-Cougar Scribes Return To Write Columns

Election of Cougar Staff Slated Today In Cougar Office

Impact of the GI Bill

The headline of this issue of the student newspaper of the University of Houston, dated February 8, 1946, indicates the impact that World War II veterans who went to college on the GI Bill had on the growth and development of higher education in the United States.

Congress passed the Serviceman's Readjustment Act, known as the GI Bill, which provided veterans with low-interest loans for housing, farms, and small businesses, as well as funds for job training and education. By 1956, over 2.2 million veterans of World War II and the Korean War, the vast majority of them male, had used government funds to attend college. Few colleges and universities were prepared to accommodate the overwhelming numbers of new students, and institutions of higher education expanded dramatically. State systems built new campuses, and almost all colleges responded to the demand by constructing new facilities, classrooms, and laboratories. The swelling enrollments created the need for additional faculty, and many writers supported themselves by teaching literature. The opportunity to do so was a particular boon for poets, who could seldom hope to make an adequate living by selling their work. In contrast to an earlier generation of American poets, very few of whom taught regularly, many of the those who emerged during or immediately after World War II found full-time jobs in the academic world, including the distinguished poet-teachers Theodore Roethke, Robert Hayden, and John Berryman.

The GI Bill had an even more dramatic impact on other aspects of life and culture in the United States. In fact, many historians have described it as the legislation that "made modern America," a testament to the enormous boost the bill provided to education, business, and housing, which in turn fueled the booming consumer economy and created a thriving white middle class in the United States. Millions of veterans used government loans to purchase or build homes, most of them in the burgeoning suburbs. Of the 13 million homes constructed during the 1950s, 11 million were in the suburbs, which were made accessible by a massive program of highway construction. One of the most famous suburbs was Levittown, built on former potato fields on Long Island, twenty-eight miles from New York City. Similarly, in Southern California developers laid out suburban tracts on ranch lands northwest of and in orange groves east of Los Angeles.

Growing prosperity began to dispel some of the darker shadows still cast by the Depression and World War II. An optimistic and upbeat note was sounded in popular self-help manuals such as Dale Carnegie's best-seller *How to Stop Worrying and Start Living* (1948) and Norman Vincent Peale's perennially popular *A Guide to Confident Living* (1948) and *The Power of Positive Thinking* (1952). Although such books promoted the idea that happiness and success were within reach of all Americans, writers and playwrights offered a far less rosy vision of life in the United States. In a series of hit plays beginning with *The Glass Menagerie* (1945), Tennessee Williams dramatized a forlorn world of lost hopes and unfulfilled promises, while his contemporary Arthur Miller exposed the hollowness of the American dream in his Pulitzer Prize–winning play *Death of a Salesman* (1949). In the face of outpourings of patriotic pride over the United States victory in World War II, Norman Mailer gained wide acclaim and commercial success with his grimly realistic novel about American soldiers fighting in the Pacific, *The Naked and the Dead* (1948). During the war, more than 100,000 people of Japanese extraction on the West Coast, most of them citizens, were interned in remote concentration camps, called "War Relocation Centers." One of the internees was the young writer Hisaye Yamamoto, who subsequently explored the experiences of Japanese immigrants and their American-born children in a series of stories published in magazines such as the prominent left-wing political and literary journal the *Partisan Review*. Knowledge of the Holocaust had a powerful impact, especially on Jewish American writers such as Bernard Malamud, who began to explore his Jewish identity and heritage, and Saul Bellow, who exposed anti-Semitism in a bleak novel set in postwar New York City, *The Victim* (1947). In what was perhaps a sign of changing times, however, Bellow achieved his greatest early success with *The Adventures of Augie March* (1952), an exuberant and optimistic coming-of-age novel set in Depression-era Chicago.

As many white residents moved to the suburbs, their place in cities such as Chicago was taken by increasing numbers of immigrants and African Americans. Nearly one million African Americans served in the military during World War II. But segregated troops remained the official policy of the U.S. Army, and the prospects of returning African American veterans were sharply limited. Despite the provisions of the GI Bill, suburban housing developments were often reserved "for whites only," and many colleges and universities routinely denied admission to nonwhite students. Meanwhile, during the first decade of what is known as the

"Kitchenette" Apartment House

The documentary photographer Edwin Rosskam took this photograph in 1941 in what was known as the "Black Belt," a chain of neighborhoods on the South Side of Chicago. Many of the African Americans who joined the second great migration to northern cities were crammed into rundown buildings such as this one, in which apartments were divided into one-room units, frequently occupied by entire families who shared kitchens and bathrooms with the residents of other units.

"second great migration," which began around 1940, an estimated 1.5 million African Americans moved from the South to cities in the North and the West. By the end of World War II, more African Americans lived in cities than in rural areas. The urban black experience was the subject of a series of notable works published during the following years, including Gwendolyn Brooks's collection of poems about life in a black ghetto in Chicago, *A Street in Bronzeville* (1945). Brooks won the Pulitzer Prize, the first awarded to an African American, for her next collection, *Annie Allen* (1949), and Ralph Ellison won the National Book Award for his novel *Invisible Man* (1952), which traced the movement of its anonymous protagonist through some of the major events of twentieth-century African American history.

Despite the prominence of those books, African Americans and other minority groups were, as Ellison suggested, largely invisible in many areas of American life and culture during much of the 1950s. The most dominant cultural force during the period was television, which profoundly shaped conceptions of what constituted reality in the United States. In 1950, a decade after the beginning of commercial television, roughly 10 percent of American homes had a television, and that number swiftly rose to 87 percent by 1960. With the exception of the comedy series *Amos 'n' Andy* (1951-53), which CBS was forced to withdraw because of African American protests against its caricatures of black people, television was dominated by popular shows about white suburban families—that is, a successful white-collar father, his contented stay-at-home wife, and their happy children—such as *The Adventures of Ozzie and Harriet* (1952-66), *Father Knows Best* (1954-63), and *Leave It to Beaver* (1957-63). Such shows not only avoided controversy, they were also carefully designed to suggest that there *were* no social problems and only the mildest of domestic tribulations in the United States. Another major bastion of the tastes of the white middle class was *The Ed Sullivan Show*, a Sunday-night institution that became the longest-running variety series in television history (1948–71). Ironically, however, it helped legitimize a major assault on the sensibilities of its adult audience when Sullivan first invited Elvis Presley, the "King of Rock 'n' Roll," on the show in 1956.

The subsequent explosion of rock 'n' roll was but one of the tremors of restlessness and discontent that began to shake American life during the

Elvis Presley

Presley recorded his first songs in 1954 for Sun Records in Memphis, Tennessee. Since some white audiences would not listen to black performers, the owner of the independent record label, Sam Phillips, sought a white man who could sing in the black rhythm-and-blues style. "Elvis the Pelvis," as he was nicknamed, is shown here performing on *The Ed Sullivan Show* in September 1956.

mid-1950s. One of the movie icons of the period was the actor James Dean, star of a cult classic about an alienated, misunderstood teenager, *Rebel Without a Cause* (1955). The year the movie appeared, Allen Ginsberg read his revolutionary poem *Howl*, often called the manifesto of the "Beat generation," in San Francisco. Through their graphic depictions of an urban underworld of crime, drugs, and homosexual acts, Ginsberg and the Beat novelists Jack Kerouac and William Burroughs vigorously challenged censorship laws and the values of Middle America, paving the way for the emergence of the counterculture of the 1960s. Middle-class values also came under attack from within, notably in Sloan Wilson's bestseller *The Man in the Grey Flannel Suit* (1955), a semiautobiographical novel about the sterile lives of businessmen in New York City. After John Updike moved to a town north of Boston in 1957, he began his long exploration of the discontents in upper-middle-class suburbia. At about the same time, a dramatist who had grown up in that world, Edward Albee, wrote a series of biting satires of consumerism and the American family, including *The American Dream* (1961), which he described as "a stand against the fiction that everything in this slipping land of ours is peachy keen." Meanwhile, the economist John Kenneth Galbraith emphasized the environmental and social costs of the consumerist society, especially the dangers of the widening gap between rich and poor, in his influential book *The Affluent Society* (1958).

But the greatest challenge to postwar complacency and the status quo came from the African American civil rights movement. Following the landmark decision in the case of *Brown v. the Board of Education of Topeka* (1954), in which the Supreme Court banned segregation in public schools, African American activists began a campaign of direct action in the South. On December 1, 1955, Rosa Parks made national headlines when she was arrested, tried, and convicted of disorderly conduct for refusing to give up her seat to a white person and move to the back of a bus in Montgomery, Alabama. Led by Martin Luther King Jr., the African American community boycotted the city's bus system for more than a year, until a federal court ordered the desegregation of the buses. The successful effort was followed by other boycotts, sit-ins at lunch counters and other segregated facilities, and "freedom rides" designed to desegregate interstate bus terminals in the South. Television news broadcast footage of the harassment and often brutal treatment of the nonviolent protesters, and some of the most vivid and disturbing images came from efforts to desegregate schools in the South. In 1957, President Dwight D. Eisenhower was forced to call in a thousand paratroopers to keep the peace in Little Rock, Arkansas, where angry white mobs threatened the first nine black students attempting to enroll at Central High School. In 1962, two people were killed and dozens were injured or wounded in rioting that erupted on the campus of the University of Mississippi when federal marshals enforced a court order to enroll its first black student, James Meredith.

March on Washington for Jobs and Freedom

The civil rights march in August 1963 was the largest demonstration ever held in the nation's capital. This photograph, taken by Warren K. Leffer from the Lincoln Memorial, shows the massive crowd fanning outward from the steps of the memorial, surrounding the reflecting pool, and continuing on to the Washington Monument.

Sympathetic news coverage and the eloquence of many of its leaders helped generate growing support for the civil rights movement. In 1963, President John F. Kennedy sent a modest civil rights bill to Congress. In an effort to persuade Congress to adopt the legislation, more than 250,000 people joined the March on Washington for Jobs and Freedom on August 28, 1963. Martin Luther King Jr. delivered the televised keynote address, widely regarded as the most important speech in the history of the civil rights movement. In his famous improvised conclusion to the speech, popularly known as "I have a dream," King realigned the American dream, so often associated with material success during the 1950s, with the country's highest ideals of freedom, justice, and equality for all people. The novelist James Baldwin, who a few months earlier had published one of the most devastating of all accounts of race relations in the United States, his best-selling *The Fire Next Time* (1963), later recalled about the March on Washington: "That day, for a moment, it almost seemed that we stood on a height, and could see our inheritance; perhaps we could make the kingdom real, perhaps the beloved community would not forever remain the dream one dreamed in agony." But the agony continued. Barely three weeks later, on September 15, 1963, four young African American girls were killed and twenty-three people were injured when a bomb set by a Ku Klux Klan splinter group

That day, for a moment, it almost seemed that we stood on a height, and could see our inheritance; perhaps we could make the kingdom real, perhaps the beloved community would not forever remain the dream one dreamed in agony.

blew up the Sixteenth Street Baptist Church, a meeting place for civil rights leaders in Birmingham, Alabama. In November, President Kennedy was assassinated, and his successor, Lyndon Johnson, pressed for the passage of and signed the Civil Rights Act in July 1964.

Conflicts at Home and Abroad

Despite that victory, the struggle for civil rights was hardly over, and the next decade brought increased agitation for radical reform in the United States. What was called the "Freedom Summer" of 1964, a campaign to register black voters during which several civil-rights workers were murdered in Mississippi, helped spur passage of the Voting Rights Act of 1965. The focus of the civil rights movement then shifted from the South to other parts of the country, and from legislative guarantees of equality to the economic and racial oppression of black people in urban ghettos in the North and the West, where riots broke out throughout the mid-1960s, most violently after the assassination of Martin Luther King Jr. in 1968. At the same time, King's nonviolent approach was challenged by black activists such as Malcolm X, a charismatic leader of the separatist Nation of Islam. Following his assassination in 1965, militant black separatists formed what came to be called the Black Power Movement and its cultural counterpart the Black Arts Movement, which was led by the poet and playwright Amiri Baraka. Although the political influence of the movement was limited, the emphasis on black identity, pride, and unity had a significant cultural impact. Robert Hayden, whose poetry finally gained wide recognition during the 1960s, remained aloof from the Black Arts Movement, but the movement gained the allegiance of the prominent poet Gwendolyn Brooks. She strongly supported the development of black publishing ventures such as Dudley Randall's Broadside Press, which printed work by Brooks and dozens of emerging black writers, including Audre Lorde. Brooks also championed younger African American poets such as Michael Harper, who in turn played a significant role in efforts to recover the rich tradition of African American literature, one of the major cultural consequences of the civil rights movement.

The movement also inspired other groups, including Mexican Americans. Large numbers of Mexican Americans served in the armed forces in World War II, during which the United States and Mexico developed the *bracero*, or laborer, program that brought Mexicans into the country to work as contract laborers on farms in the Southwest. Following the war, the government deported millions of the laborers, but many others remained in the United States, and immigration from Mexico rose rapidly during the 1950s and 1960s. In 1962, César Chávez, a farmworker and labor leader, and the activist Dolores Huerta founded the National Farm Workers Association, later known as the United Farm Workers Organizing Committee. In Texas, José Angel Gutierrez and others formed La Raza

Unida (The United Race), a political party designed to promote the interests of Mexican Americans. The cultural pride and sense of brotherhood generated by the Chicano movement found artistic expression in a wide range of works, including the famous poem *I Am Joaquín/Yo soy Joaquín*, a chronicle of the history and struggles of Mexican Americans by political activist Rodolfo "Corky" Gonzales. At the opening of the epic poem, which was printed as a bilingual pamphlet in 1967 and often circulated at community rallies, Gonzalez proclaimed:

> I am Joaquín, lost in a world of confusion,
> caught up in the whirl of gringo society,
> confused by the ruled, scorned by attitudes,
> suppressed by manipulation, and destroyed by modern society.

Gonzales subsequently gained a large following, including many of the 1,500 Mexican American students who in 1969 gathered in Denver, Colorado, for the Chicano Youth Liberation Conference. Demanding sweeping changes in American education designed to liberate Mexican American students from "Anglo concepts," the youths called for the creation of a new Chicano nation, Aztlán, their name for an area in the

Viva Chavez, Viva la Causa, Viva la Huelga

Paul Davis painted the portrait of a young laborer used on this poster announcing a benefit performance, at Carnegie Hall in New York City, for the California Grape Workers in 1968. The Spanish motto may be translated "Hurrah for Chavez, Hurrah for the Cause, Hurrah for the Strike," a reference to the labor leader César Chávez and the five-year Delano grape strike and boycott, which ultimately developed into a broader social movement known as *La Causa*, the Cause.

Southwest taken over by the United States after the Mexican-American War of 1846–48.

Native Americans also protested their long history of exploitation and oppression. Although divided by language, religion, and tribal affiliations, many Native Americans united to organize demonstrations against the federal government's decision in the early 1950s to "terminate" tribal organizations and refuse to recognize them as sovereign governments. In 1961, more than four hundred representatives of ninety tribal groups gathered in Chicago and prepared a shared statement of principles, the "Declaration of Indian Purpose," in which they affirmed their right to choose a way of life and to preserve their threatened heritage: "We believe in the inherent right of all people to retain spiritual and cultural values, and that the free exercise of these values is necessary to the normal development of any people." The Chicago meeting led to the establishment of other organizations, including the National Council of American Indians, which lobbied for the improvement of education for Native Americans, and the American Indian Movement (AIM). Founded in 1968 to promote and protect the interests of Native Americans living on reservations and in urban areas, AIM gained international attention in 1973, when members of the group occupied the village of Wounded Knee, South Dakota. AIM also established "survival schools" designed to preserve the history

The Siege at Wounded Knee

In 1973, activists in the American Indian Movement (AIM) and local residents occupied the village of Wounded Knee on the Pine Ridge Reservation in South Dakota, the site of an 1890 massacre in which troops of the Seventh Cavalry killed more than two hundred Lakota Sioux. The 1973 occupation and the subsequent seventy-one-day siege of the village by heavily armed federal marshals and FBI agents attracted worldwide attention to the cause of Indian rights and sovereignty in the United States.

and culture of Native Americans. Such efforts at cultural renewal gained impetus from the work of writers such as N. Scott Momaday, who became the first Native American to win a Pulitzer Prize, for his novel *House Made of Dawn* (1969). The groundbreaking book helped inspire a remarkable flowering of writings rooted in Native American life and traditions, including stories and novels by Leslie Marmon Silko, Gerald Vizenor, and James Welch, and the poetry of Paula Gunn Allen, Joy Harjo, and Simon Ortiz.

The women's liberation movement also strongly shaped American writing and society. During World War II, women had fought the war primarily on the home front, where they held manufacturing jobs in unprecedented numbers. After the war, however, most women were forced into lower-paying jobs or urged to withdraw from the workforce to accommodate the millions of male veterans returning from overseas. As one company newspaper proclaimed in 1945: "The Kitchen – Women's Big Post-War Goal." While the GI Bill dramatically expanded the educational opportunities for veterans, the enrollment figures for women in college lagged well behind those for men during the 1950s. In 1963, the extensive discrimination that women faced in employment and education was revealed in the report of the Presidential Commission on the Status of Women. But the major spur to the emergence of the modern feminist movement was the publication of Betty Friedan's *The Feminine Mystique* (1963). For an article on women's experiences, Friedan sent a questionnaire to her classmates at the prestigious women's school Smith College, from which she had graduated in 1942. When no magazine editor would accept the article, in which she reported that most of her classmates were deeply discontented with their narrow lives, Friedan developed it into *The Feminine Mystique*. In the opening chapter, "A Problem That Has No Name," she observed:

> The problem lay buried, unspoken, for many years in the minds of American women. It was a strange stirring, a dissatisfaction that women suffered in the middle of the twentieth century in the United States. Each suburban wife struggled with it alone. As she made the beds, shopped for groceries, matched slipcover material, ate peanut butter sandwiches with her children, chauffeured Cub Scouts and Brownies, lay beside her husband at night – she was afraid to ask even of herself the silent question – "Is this all?"

The Feminine Mystique hit a nerve, becoming a bestseller that eventually sold three million copies. When Friedan died in 2006, the *New York Times* called the book "one of the most influential nonfiction books of the twentieth century." Friedan helped establish and served as the first president of the National Organization for Women, whose membership grew from 1,000 in 1967 to 15,000 in 1971. (The contributing membership has now reached 500,000.) The movement was also advanced by the establishment of new publishing outlets. In 1970, a group of women established the

Women's Equality March

Betty Friedan, whose manifesto *The Feminine Mystique* laid the groundwork for the modern feminist movement, led ten thousand women in a march in New York City on August 26, 1970, the fiftieth anniversary of the passage of the Nineteenth Amendment granting women the right to vote in the United States. In the march, which was part of a nationwide "Women's Strike for Equality," demonstrators carried placards with such slogans as "Don't Iron While the March Is Hot."

Feminist Press, designed to bring back into print significant literary works by women. In addition to expanding and enriching the literary canon, the Feminist Press was instrumental in providing texts that spurred the development of women's studies in colleges and universities across the United States. In the midst of numerous women's magazines devoted primarily to domestic concerns, fashion, and light fiction, a new magazine, *Ms.*, was founded in 1972. Edited by Gloria Steinem, the magazine featured articles on a range of women's issues, including domestic abuse and abortion, as well as the work of writers such as Alice Walker and Angela Davis. Despite the predictions of prominent male newscasters and commentators, the first issue of 300,000 copies sold out in eight days and generated 26,000 subscription orders.

In its early stages, the women's movement primarily addressed the concerns of white, middle-class women, but radical feminists pressed for a multi-issue and multiracial approach to women's liberation. Together with other radical movements of the 1960s, the women's liberation movement helped inspire the formation of the Gay Liberation Front in the summer of 1969. Following a riot in New York City in the summer of 1969, when patrons of a gay bar called the Stonewall Inn fought back against ongoing police harassment, a group of men and women in the area founded a newspaper, *Come Out!* "We reject society's attempt to impose sexual roles and definitions of our nature," the editors wrote in the first issue in September 1969. "We are stepping outside these roles and simplistic myths. We are going to be who we are. At the same time, we are creating new social forms and relations, that is, relations based upon sisterhood, cooperation, human love and uninhibited sexuality." A major force in radicalizing other women and making gay and lesbian rights a central part of the women's movement was the poet Adrienne Rich, who began to write and speak out as a lesbian-feminist poet in the early 1970s. She was also instrumental in efforts to make the women's movement more welcoming to women of color. When Rich won the National Book Award for her collection *Diving into the Wreck* (1973), she declined to accept the honor as an individual. In a statement written with the other female nominees, the African American poets Audre Lorde and Alice Walker, Rich instead accepted the award on behalf of all silenced women. Indeed, one of the most significant results of the first decade of the feminist movement was to make women heard and to gain them an increasingly public role in the United States.

Feminists and many participants in other civil rights movements were also deeply involved in protests against the Vietnam War. In what was justified as an effort to counter the spread of Communism in Asia, President Kennedy sent 15,000 military advisers to South Vietnam in 1963. But there was little opposition to the war until 1965, when President Johnson authorized the bombing of North Vietnam and deployed 184,000 combat troops, whose number grew to 540,000 by 1968. The escalation triggered the earliest of innumerable demonstrations, rallies, and teach-ins against the war, a march on Washington, D.C., organized in April 1965 by the radical student group Students for a Democratic Society. That year, the poets Robert Bly and David Ray established American Writers Against the Vietnam War. Among those who participated in activities organized by the group were Adrienne Rich and two other prominent poets, Allen Ginsberg, the icon of the drug culture and counterculture, and the patrician Robert Lowell. The most famous demonstration against the war was mounted on October 21, 1967, when thousands of protesters marched on the Pentagon in Washington, D.C. Lowell participated in the march, and Ginsberg supplied the text of an "exorcism" protesters chanted in front of the Pentagon, "No Taxation Without Representation," which began: "Who represents my body in Pentagon? Who spends my spirit's billions for war manufacture? Who levies the majority to exult unwilling in Bomb Roar?" But the most powerful testimony against the war was ultimately offered by some of those who fought in Vietnam, including writers such as Tim O'Brien. Following his tour of duty as an

Viet Nam Moratorium

John Schneider designed this poster for the Ad Hoc Federal Employees Moratorium Committee, in support of the Moratorium to End the War in Vietnam, a nationwide demonstration that took place on October 15, 1969. The traditional peace symbol of the dove was used extensively by opponents of the war, who were known as "Doves."

infantryman in Vietnam, O'Brien wrote the first of a series of critically acclaimed works in which he drew upon his experiences there, *If I Die in a Combat Zone, Box Me Up and Ship Me Home* (1973). That year, the Paris Peace Accords finally ended what was then the longest conflict in the history of the United States.

Into the Twenty-First Century

Although many Americans simply wanted to forget the war, the defeat in Vietnam left a lasting legacy. The bitter loss seriously undermined morale and confidence in the country's political leaders, whose reputation was further damaged by the publication of the *Pentagon Papers* (1971), a top-secret document demonstrating that high-ranking officials had consistently lied about the Vietnam War; and by the Watergate crisis of 1973-74. The human costs of the war were enormous: more than 58,000 American troops were killed or missing in action and 300,000 were wounded during the brutal conflict, which claimed the lives of an estimated 1.5 million Vietnamese. In contrast to veterans of World War II, many Vietnam veterans felt neglected or ignored, at least until the war became the subject of *Vietnam: A Television History*, a thirteen-part series that premiered on PBS in 1983, as well as numerous books and movies during the 1980s. Treatments of the war in popular culture revealed ongoing divisions over its meaning and conduct. But even after the dissolution of the Soviet Union and the end of the cold war, of which the Vietnam War was the most serious and sustained conflict, the war remained a touchstone for those opposed to American military intervention in other countries. Opponents of the first Gulf War in 1991 argued that the United States went to war simply to advance its economic and political interests, just as it had done in Vietnam. For many, the Iraq War has also evoked memories of the Vietnam War. On March 17, 2007, thousands of antiwar protesters gathered in Washington to mark the fourth anniversary of the invasion of Iraq and what they billed as "the fortieth anniversary of the historic 1967 march to the Pentagon."

The Vietnam War and the turmoil of the 1960s also had other far-reaching social, economic, and cultural consequences. The financial cost of the war, estimated at 150 billion dollars, drained resources from the ambitious social programs initiated by President Johnson, who in his first State of the Union address in 1964 had declared a "War on Poverty." In large part, that effort was a response to Michael Harrington's influential book *The Other America* (1962), which exposed the grinding poverty experienced by one of every four Americans, ranging from black people living in urban ghettos to the white rural poor throughout Appalachia and the South. At the same time, the social movements of the 1960s and demonstrations against the Vietnam War generated deep resentments among many working-class white Americans, the "silent majority" to whom President Richard Nixon appealed for support in 1969. During the 1970s, however, both the poor and blue-collar workers were among those hit hardest by the end of the long economic boom that had lasted since shortly after World War II. The cost of the Vietnam War and the mounting deficit led to rapid inflation and growing unemployment, which were further increased by the oil embargo of 1973–74.

The consequent spur to the construction of nuclear power plants helped galvanize the environmental movement. In 1962, the same year Harrington published *The Other America* and only a year before the appearance of *The Feminine Mystique*, Rachel Carson published the book that is widely credited with launching the modern environmental movement, *Silent Spring*. The movement began to gain mass support after Earth Day was first celebrated on April 22, 1970. Modeled after the teach-ins that were held at college and university campuses against the Vietnam War and designed to make the environment a prominent part of the national agenda, the first Earth Day was celebrated by twenty million people at colleges, schools, and communities around the United States. The movement gained strength from a wide range of nature writings, including Annie Dillard's *A Pilgrim at Tinker's Creek* (1974) and Gary Snyder's collection of poetry *Turtle Island* (1974), both of which won Pulitzer Prizes. As Snyder explained, he took the title of his collection from "the old/new name for the continent, based on many creation myths of the people who have been living here for millennia." Indeed, ecological thinking was significantly enriched by Native American practices and perspectives. At a conference in 1977, for example, the Iroquois leader Oren Lyons spoke powerfully of

OUR NATIONAL PARKS

ANSEL ADAMS

Ansel Adams,
*The Tetons and
the Snake River*

A major focus of the modern environmental movement has been the preservation of the wilderness, a goal that has been advanced by nature writers and visual artists such as the renowned American landscape photographer Ansel Adams (1902–1984). His iconic image of Grand Teton National Park in Wyoming was reproduced on the cover of this collection of his photographs and writings, published to commemorate the 120th anniversary of the establishment of the first national park in 1872.

the connection between the human and the natural world: "I must warn you that the Creator made us all equal with one another. And not only human beings, but all life is equal. The equality of our life is what you must understand and the principles by which you must continue on behalf of the future of this world."

Despite significant resistance, environmentalism and other social movements have strongly shaped the social, political, and cultural landscape of the United States. Feminists suffered a major defeat when the equal rights amendment failed to gain ratification by the required number of states by 1982. The setback for the women's movement was but one sign of a broad conservative backlash and the growing influence of evangelical Christianity, signaled by the formation of political organizations such as the Moral Majority, founded in 1979, and its successor the Christian Coalition. The

I must warn you that the Creator made us all equal with one another. And not only human beings, but all life is equal. The equality of our life is what you must understand and the principles by which you must continue on behalf of the future of this world.

onset of the AIDS epidemic in the 1980s at once spurred the gay rights movement and intensified opposition to it, and the country was and remains deeply divided over other issues such as abortion and programs designed to increase opportunities for members of minority groups, including affirmative action. At the same time, immigration has continued to alter the demographics of the country during the last thirty years. The Vietnam War and the chaos it generated in neighboring Laos and Cambodia created millions of refugees, many of whom came to the United States. Immigration from other parts of Asia also increased rapidly during the 1980s, while immigrants from Mexico, Central America, and the Caribbean contributed to the growth of the Latino population, which reached thirty-one million, or 11 percent of the total population, in 2000.

The increasing pluralism of the country has had a profound impact on American life and literature. Rita Dove became the first African American Poet Laureate of the United States in 1993, the year Toni Morrison became the first African American to win the Nobel Prize. In its citation, the Nobel Prize committee described Morrison as a novelist who "gives life to an essential aspect of American reality," and other aspects of that reality have been the focus of a wide range of writers from radically different backgrounds and traditions. Indeed, the very concept of "American reality" has been and is being continually reshaped by Asian American, Latino/a, and Native American novelists and poets, among many other writers. In "The Future of American Fiction," an introduction to a special summer issue of the *New Yorker* in 1999, a gathering of stories by "20 Writers for the 21st Century," Bill Buford observed that their work "offers a satisfying picture of a highly accomplished group of writers robustly taking on stories of their own Americanness."

But literature faces formidable challenges in the twenty-first century. Cable television expanded rapidly after the introduction of pay TV in 1972. By the year 2000, there were sixty-five million cable subscribers, and that figure now exceeds one hundred million. The Apple Computer Company introduced the first affordable (at least to many middle-class Americans) personal computer in 1976, spurring the development of another popular form of entertainment, electronic games. In what came to be called "the electronic age," the use of computers became a common and, for many Americans, an indispensable part of life after the development of the Internet, one of the most revolutionary technological innovations in the period since World War II. The Internet and the rise of social media have changed the ways in which most Americans communicate, enroll in college classes, handle finances, and shop. It may also have reduced the amount of time people devote to reading. As early as 1994, in his influential book *The Gutenberg Elegies: The Fate of Reading in an Electronic Age*, Sven Birkerts argued that

This cartoon by James Whitworth humorously questions the role of printed books in a digital age.
www.CartoonStock.com

"IT CAN HOLD A THOUSAND BOOKS, WHATEVER "BOOKS" ARE..."

the ever-increasing use of technology would end reading, a crucial source of an individual's sense of identity and selfhood. A decade later, in the National Endowment for the Arts report "Reading at Risk" (2004), the authors cited television and other electronic media as the primary cause of an apparent decline of "literary reading" in the United States. The report, however, was criticized for its failure to take into account the electronic media as a venue for reading, as well as for its narrow definition of literary reading, which did not include popular nonfiction genres such as the memoir.

Although reading habits have certainly changed, as they did when paperbacks began to dominate the literary marketplace after World War II, reading and writing remain vital elements of American culture. As the report "Reading at Risk" also noted, the number of people in the United States who do some form of creative writing increased from eleven million in 1982 to fifteen million in 2002. The prestigious Writers' Workshop at the University of Iowa, the first graduate program in creative writing, was established in the 1930s and remained virtually the only program of its type through the 1950s. There are now more than three hundred similar programs, and creative writing is also a popular course of study at the undergraduate level. Since 1996, the television talk-show host Oprah Winfrey has launched new writers and spurred the formation of local reading groups through her popular Book Club, the interactive, online version of which is billed as "A Book Club for the Digital Age." Although many small independent bookstores and even some large chain bookstores have closed, online booksellers have become highly successful, and the number of new books published in the traditional way continues to climb each year, up from roughly 215,000 in 2002 to more than 350,000 in 2012. Since World War II, there has been a decline in mass-market magazines that feature poetry and fiction, which is now a prominent part of only a few high-profile magazines such as *Harper's* and the *New Yorker*. But there are numerous small literary magazines, through which emerging writers may hope to gain at least a modest readership and establish a reputation. Most of those magazines also publish online versions, which often provide supplements such as additional works by the writer not included in the print version, interviews, video clips of readings, and space for the comments by readers.

In fact, the Internet has supplemented rather than supplanted print publications. The advent of E-books and E-magazines available on E-readers such as tablets and smart phones has provided an entirely new venue for writers. Today, printed books and magazines are simply two of the sources of reading materials. Moreover, the Internet is regarded by many as a way of widening the possibilities for publishing. In the past, few people could hope to publish a print book, but the Internet allows any writer to bypass traditional publishers and post a book online. The number of such self-published books has grown from roughly 33,000 in 2002 to over a million in 2012. Other examples of new trends in publishing abound. The complex relationship between print culture and electronic publishing was illustrated shortly before the invasion of Iraq in 2003, when Sam Hamill led an effort to "reconstitute a Poets Against the War movement like the one organized to speak out against the war in Vietnam." Hamill edited an anthology, *Poets Against the War* (2003), which included contributions by well-known writers such as Rita Dove, Martín Espada, Joy Harjo, Ursula K. Le Guin, and Adrienne Rich, one of the veterans of the earlier American Writers Against the Vietnam War. But the poets in the anthology represented only a tiny fraction of those who responded to Hamill's call, so he and other volunteers subsequently created a Web site (www.poetsagainstthewar.org) to accommodate the initial and ongoing submissions, an online collection of twenty thousand works by writers from around the world billed as "the largest poetry anthology ever published." Whether such arrangements represent a genuine democratization of publishing or an implicit assertion of the status of the printed book remains to be seen. Nonetheless, it is clear that literature continues to matter and to be a matter of vital interest in the United States.

COMPARATIVE TIMELINE, AMERICAN LITERATURE SINCE 1945

Dates	American Literature	Historical Events	Developments in Culture, Science, and Technology
1945–1949	**1945** Williams, *The Glass Menagerie* **1945** Brooks, *A Street in Bronzeville* **1946** Bishop, *North and South* **1946** Lowell, *Lord Weary's Castle*, awarded Pulitzer Prize **1946** Williams, *Portrait of a Madonna* **1947** Williams, *A Streetcar Named Desire* **1947** Bellow, *The Victim* **1948** Hayden, *The Lion and the Archer* **1948** Roethke, *The Lost Son and Other Poems* **1949** Miller, *Death of a Salesman* **1949** Brooks, *Annie Allen*, awarded Pulitzer Prize **1949** Yamamoto, "Seventeen Syllables"	**1945** Harry S. Truman becomes president after death of Roosevelt **1945** United States drops atomic bombs on Hiroshima and Nagasaki; Japan surrenders, ending World War II **1947–50** Anticommunist investigations by Senator Joseph McCarthy and House Un-American Activities Committee **1948** State of Israel established **1948** Truman elected president **1949** Soviet Union tests its first nuclear weapon, intensifying the cold war **1949** Mao Zedong and Communist revolutionaries establish People's Republic of China	**1945** Bantam Books established **1945** First nuclear reactor is built **1945-55** Over two million U.S. veterans attend college on GI Bill **1947–51** Building of Levittown, New York **1947** Jackie Robinson is first African American player in major league baseball **1949** Philip Johnson, Glass House, New Canaan, Connecticut
1950–1959	**1950** Malamud, "The First Seven Years" **1951** Bellow, "Looking for Mr. Green"	**1950** U.S. population: 151,325,798; 10,033,385 are immigrants **1950–53** Korean War **1951** United Nations officially opens in New York City	**1950** Jackson Pollock, *Autumn Rhythm*

COMPARATIVE TIMELINE, AMERICAN LITERATURE SINCE 1945

Dates	American Literature	Historical Events	Developments in Culture, Science, and Technology
1950–1959 (cont.)	**1951** Rich, *A Change of World* **1952** Ellison, *Invisible Man* **1952** O'Connor, *Wise Blood* **1953** Bellow, *The Adventures of Augie March* **1953** Roethke, *The Waking, Poems*, awarded Pulitzer Prize **1953** Miller, *The Crucible* **1953** Baldwin, *Go Tell It on the Mountain*	**1952** Dwight D. Eisenhower elected president **1953** U.S. government begins Indian termination and relocation programs	**1953** Francis Crick and James D. Watson publish description of the double helix structure of DNA
	1955 Baldwin, *Notes of a Native Son* **1955** Kerouac, *On the Road* **1955** O'Connor, *A Good Man Is Hard to Find* **1956** Berryman, *Homage to Mistress Bradstreet* **1956** Ginsberg, *Howl and Other Poems* **1956** Ashbery, *Some Trees*	**1954** *Brown v. Board of Education* bans segregation in public schools **1954** United States begins aid program to newly independent government of South Vietnam **1955–56** Bus boycotts by African Americans in Montgomery, Alabama **1956** Eisenhower reelected president	**1954** Construction of the first commercial nuclear power plant begins in Pennsylvania **1955** First live television broadcast on NBC **1955** *Rebel Without a Cause* starring James Dean **1956** Elvis Presley, "King of Rock 'n' Roll," appears on *The Ed Sullivan Show*
	1957 Malamud, *The Assistant* **1959** Lowell, *Life Studies* **1959** Snyder, *Riprap*	**1957** Eisenhower sends U.S. troops to enforce integration of Little Rock Central High School, Arkansas **1958** National Aeronautics and Space Administration (NASA) founded **1959** Alaska and Hawaii become the forty-ninth and fiftieth states	**1957** Peak of postwar baby boom (4,300,000 births) **1957** Soviet Union launches *Sputnik*, first satellite to orbit Earth **1958** John Kenneth Galbraith, *The Affluent Society* **1959** Alfred Hitchcock's *North by Northwest* starring Cary Grant **1959** Barbie dolls are launched by Mattel

COMPARATIVE TIMELINE, AMERICAN LITERATURE SINCE 1945

Dates	American Literature	History and Politics	Developments in Culture, Science, and Technology
1960–1969	1960 Albee, *The Zoo Story* 1960 Plath, *The Colossus and Other Poems* 1960 Updike, *Rabbit, Run* 1960 Brooks, *The Bean Eaters* 1961 Olsen, *Tell Me a Riddle* 1961 Updike, "A & P" 1961 Albee, *The Sandbox* 1962 Hayden, *A Ballad of Remembrance* 1962 Albee, *Who's Afraid of Virginia Woolf?*	1960 U.S. population: 179,323,175; 10,347,000 are immigrants 1960 John F. Kennedy elected president 1960 The FDA approves sale of Enovid, the first birth control pill 1961 Berlin Wall erected 1961 Freedom Riders attempt to desegregate bus terminals and interstate transportation in South 1961 Ninety tribal groups prepare Declaration of Indian Purpose 1962 Cuban missile crisis 1962 César Chávez founds United Farm Workers Organizing Committee	1960 Women represent one-third of labor force 1960 87 percent of American homes have a television 1960 One-quarter of Americans live in suburbs 1961 John F. Kennedy establishes the Peace Corps 1962 John Glenn becomes the first American to orbit Earth 1962 Rachel Carson publishes *Silent Spring* 1963 Betty Friedan publishes *The Feminine Mystique*
	1964 Berryman, *77 Dream Songs* 1964 Lowell, *For the Union Dead* 1964 Barthelme, *Come Back, Dr. Caligari* 1964 Baraka, *Dutchman*	1963 March on Washington for Jobs and Freedom is largest civil rights demonstration in U.S. history 1963 President Kennedy sends 15,000 military advisers to South Vietnam 1963 Kennedy assassinated; Lyndon B. Johnson assumes presidency 1963 Limited nuclear test-ban treaty signed by United States and Soviet Union 1964 Civil Rights Act 1964 Johnson elected president 1964 Gulf of Tonkin Resolution authorizes U.S. military action in Vietnam	

COMPARATIVE TIMELINE, AMERICAN LITERATURE SINCE 1945

Dates	American Literature	History and Politics	Developments in Culture, Science, and Technology
1960–1969 (cont.)	1965 Bishop, *Questions of Travel* 1965 Plath, *Ariel*	1965 Malcolm X assassinated 1965 Civil rights march from Selma to Montgomery 1965 Voting Rights Act 1965 184,000 U.S. combat troops arrive in Vietnam 1966 National Organization for Women (NOW) founded 1967 100,000 march on Pentagon to protest Vietnam War	1965 The Beatles perform at Shea Stadium in New York 1965 American Writers Against the War founded 1965 Broadside Press founded 1967 "Summer of Love" in Haight-Ashbury district of San Francisco, center of counterculture 1967 Andy Warhol, *Marilyn*
	1968 Updike, *Couples* 1969 Le Guin, *The Left Hand of Darkness* 1969 Momaday, *House Made of Dawn*, awarded Pulitzer Prize	1968 Martin Luther King Jr. and Robert F. Kennedy assassinated 1968 Riot at Democratic National Convention in Chicago 1968 Richard M. Nixon elected president 1968 American Indian Movement (AIM) founded 1969 Stonewall riot leads to Gay and Lesbian Liberation Movement 1969 Chicano Youth Liberation Conference, Denver, Colorado	1969 Neil Armstrong and Buzz Aldrin land on the moon 1969–74 *The Brady Bunch* airs on TV 1969 Woodstock Music Festival in Bethel, New York
1970–1979	1970 Morrison, *The Bluest Eye* 1970 Harper, *Dear John, Dear Coltrane* 1971 DeLillo, *Americana* 1971 Rich, *The Will to Change*	1970 U.S. population: 203,211,926; 9,619,000 are immigrants 1970 Student protesters killed by national guard and police at Kent State and Jackson State universities 1970 Environmental Protection Agency established	1970 Earth Day first observed 1970 Feminist Press established

COMPARATIVE TIMELINE, AMERICAN LITERATURE SINCE 1945

Dates	American Literature	History and Politics	Developments in Culture, Science, and Technology
1970–1979 (cont.)		**1972** Nixon reelected president **1972–74** Watergate investigation **1972** Congress passes equal rights amendment; required number of states fail to ratify it by 1982 deadline **1972** Congress passes Title IX, banning gender discrimination in all aspects of education including hiring and athletics	**1972** *Ms. Magazine* founded **1972–83** *M.A.S.H.* airs on TV **1972** Introduction of pay TV spurs rapid expansion of cable television
	1973 O'Brien, *If I Die in a Combat Zone* **1973** Walker, *In Love and Trouble* 	**1973** The Paris Accords bring formal end to U.S. role in Vietnam **1973** *Roe v. Wade* protects a woman's right to abortion in early stages of pregnancy **1973–74** Arab oil embargo creates energy crisis in United States **1973** Members of American Indian Movement stage protest at Wounded Knee, South Dakota 	**1973** Pell grants program started to help low-income students attend college
	1974 Olsen, *Yonnondio* **1974** Barthelme, "The School" **1974** Snyder, *Turtle Island*, awarded Pulitzer Prize **1974** Silko, "Yellow Woman" **1975** Ashbery, *Self-Portrait in a Convex Mirror* 	**1974** Nixon resigns; Gerald Ford becomes president and pardons Nixon **1975** North Vietnamese launch final offensive and take over all of Vietnam, ending war	**1975–85** *The Jeffersons* is longest-running TV comedy starring African Americans
	1976 Lorde, *Coal* **1976** Carver, *Will You Please Be Quiet, Please?* **1976** Momaday, *The Names: A Memoir*	**1976** Jimmy Carter elected president	**1976** Apple Computer Company introduces the first personal computer

COMPARATIVE TIMELINE, AMERICAN LITERATURE SINCE 1945

Dates	American Literature	History and Politics	Developments in Culture, Science, and Technology
1970–1979 (cont.)	**1976** Kingston, *The Woman Warrior* **1977** Silko, *Ceremony*	**1979** American hostages seized at U.S. embassy in Tehran, Iran **1979** Energy crisis caused by decline of foreign oil production and price hikes by OPEC	**1977** *Star Wars* film saga begins **1979** ESPN begins twenty-four-hour sports broadcasting **1979** Sugar Hill Gang's hip-hop song "Rapper's Delight" reaches American Top 40 **1979** Moral Majority founded by Jerry Falwell
1980–1989	**1980** Dove, *The Yellow House on the Corner* **1981** Carver, *What We Talk About When We Talk About Love* **1982** Walker, *The Color Purple* **1982–2005** Wilson, *The Pittsburgh Cycle* **1983** Morrison, "Recitatif" **1983** Harjo, *She Had Some Horses* **1984** Rich, *The Fact of a Doorframe* **1984** Baraka, *The Autobiography of LeRoi Jones/Amiri Baraka* **1984** Cisneros, *The House on Mango Street* **1985** DeLillo, *White Noise* **1985** Le Guin, "She Unnames Them" **1985** Wilson, *The Janitor*	**1980** U.S. population: 226,545,805; 14,079,000 are immigrants **1980** Ronald Reagan elected president **1981** Sandra Day O'Connor first woman appointed to Supreme Court **1982** Unemployment approaches 11 percent **1982** United States invades Grenada and topples its Marxist government **1984** Reagan reelected president	**1980** *Pac-Man* video arcade game is released in United States **1981** MTV premieres **1981** IBM markets its first personal computer **1982** Vietnam Veterans Memorial dedicated in Washington, D.C. **1982** Michael Jackson's *Thriller* recording released **1982** U.S. Centers for Disease Control begins use of term *AIDS* for new disease **1983** First handheld mobile phone becomes commercially available **1983** *Vietnam: A Television History* airs on PBS **1984–92** *The Cosby Show* airs on TV **1985** Nintendo Entertainment System is released in the United States

COMPARATIVE TIMELINE, AMERICAN LITERATURE SINCE 1945

Dates	American Literature	History and Politics	Developments in Culture, Science, and Technology
1980–1989 (cont.)		**1986** Congress passes the Immigration Reform and Control Act, punishing employers who hire undocumented aliens	
	1987 Le Guin, *Buffalo Gals* **1987** Morrison, *Beloved* **1987** Anzaldúa, *Borderlands/La Frontera* **1987** Dillard, *An American Childhood*		**1987** Aretha Franklin becomes first woman inducted into Rock and Roll Hall of Fame
	1988 Komunyakka, *Dien Cai Dau*	**1988** George H.W. Bush elected president **1989** Berlin Wall falls, marking collapse of Communism in Eastern Europe	**1989** Christian Coalition founded by minister Pat Robertson
1990–1999	**1990** O'Brien, *The Things They Carried* **1990** Espada, *Rebellion Is the Circle of a Lover's Hands* **1991** Silko, *Almanac of the Dead* **1991** Cisneros, *Woman Hollering Creek* **1992** Lorde, *Undersong* **1992** Mamet, "The Rake"	**1990** U.S. population: 248,765,170; 19,763,000 are immigrants **1990–91** Persian Gulf War **1991** Dissolution of Soviet Union ends cold war **1991** Americans with Disabilities Act **1992** Bill Clinton elected president	**1990** 60 percent of married women with children work outside the home **1992** MTV airs first widely popular reality TV program, *The Real World* **1992** Mall of America opens in Bloomington, Minnesota
	1993 Alexie, *The Lone Ranger and Tonto Fistfight in Heaven*	**1993** North American Free Trade Agreement (NAFTA) **1993** Janet Reno appointed first female attorney general	**1993** Holocaust Memorial Museum dedicated in Washington, D.C. **1993** Toni Morrison becomes first African American to win Nobel Prize in Literature **1993** Rita Dove becomes first African American Poet Laureate
	1995 Alexie, *Reservation Blues* **1996** hooks, *Bone Black*	**1995** Radical militia members bomb federal buildings in Oklahoma City, killing 169 **1996** Clinton reelected president	**1996** 10 million Americans have Internet access

COMPARATIVE TIMELINE, AMERICAN LITERATURE SINCE 1945

Dates	American Literature	History and Politics	Developments in Culture, Science, and Technology
1990–1999 (cont.)	**1997** DeLillo, *Underworld*	**1997** Madeleine Albright becomes first female secretary of state	
	1999 Dove, *On the Bus with Rosa Parks*	**1999** U.S. troops join NATO peacekeeping force in Kosovo	**1999–2007** *The Sopranos* airs on HBO
2000–2009	**2000** Harper, *Songlines in Michaeltree* **2000** Soto, *The Effects of Knut Hamsun on a Fresno Boy*	**2000** U.S. population: 281,421,906 **2000** George W. Bush elected president	**2000** Metallica sues Napster for pirating music on Internet
		2001 Terrorists destroy New York's World Trade Center and attack Pentagon **2002** U.S. invasion of Afghanistan	**2001** Apple releases iPod **2001** Wikipedia goes online **2002** Microsoft launches Xbox Live
	2003 Espada, *Alabanza* **2003** Alexie, *Ten Little Indians*	**2003** Space shuttle *Columbia* disintegrates over Texas killing all seven astronauts onboard **2003** War in Iraq begins	
	2004 Harjo, *Native Joy for Real* **2004** Dove, *American Smooth*	**2004** George W. Bush re-elected president	**2004** Facebook is launched
		2005 Hurricane Katrina hits Gulf Coast	**2005** YouTube is launched **2005** Oprah Winfrey tops *Forbes* magazine's "Celebrity 100 Power List"
	2006 Bechdel, *Fun Home* **2006** Espada, *The Republic of Poetry* **2007** Updike, *Terrorist* **2007** DeLillo, *Falling Man*	**2006** Saddam Hussein, former Iraq president, is executed in Baghdad **2007** Virginia Tech massacre **2007** Global economic downturn **2008** Barack Obama elected president	**2006** Apple iTunes Store sells one-billionth song **2006** Twitter established **2007** Apple releases iPhone

COMPARATIVE TIMELINE, AMERICAN LITERATURE SINCE 1945

Dates	American Literature	History and Politics	Developments in Culture, Science, and Technology
2010 to Present	**2010** DeLillo, *Point Omega*	**2010** U.S. population: 308,745,538	
		2011 Osama bin Laden is killed in Pakistan	**2011** Apple releases iPad
			2011 Space shuttle fleet is retired
	2012 Harjo, *Crazy Brave: A Memoir*	**2012** Barack Obama reelected president	**2012** Science Rover lands on Mars
	2012 Cisneros, *Have You Seen Marie?*		**2012** Over 245 million Internet users in the United States
	2012 Alexie, *Blasphemy: New and Selected Stories*		
	2012 Morrison, *Home*		
	2012 Díaz, *This Is How You Lose Her*		

From Modernism
to Postmodernism

THE PERIOD FROM THE END OF World War II in 1945 to the present is frequently called the "age of postmodernism." Although the meaning of the term *postmodernism* is complicated and often contested, it generally refers to a movement in literature and the arts that followed and departed from modernism. Modernist writers had earlier sought to develop a language and new literary forms capable of representing the reality of modern life in the early twentieth century, an effort made all the more challenging by the carnage of World War I. Following World War II, with its attendant horrors of the Holocaust and the atomic bombs dropped on Hiroshima and Nagasaki, writers once again sought ways of representing

◄ Romare Bearden, *Summertime*

Inspired in part by the civil rights movement, Bearden began work on a celebrated series of collages, innovative works with connections to both modernist art, especially cubism, and the African American folk tradition of quilt making. Like his friend Ralph Ellison and the poets Gwendolyn Brooks and Robert Hayden, Bearden expressed the complexities of black identity and the richness of the African American experience from the rural South to the streets of Harlem, which he evoked in *Summertime* (1967).

Art © Romare Bearden Foundation/Licensed by VAGA, NY.

George Tooker, *Subway*

Despite growing prosperity and optimism after World War II, many artists remained disaffected with life in the United States. George Tooker adopted traditional painterly techniques, but he used them to explore the anxiety and isolation of life in the modern metropolis, as symbolized by the bleak underground world represented in surrealistic works such as *Subway* (1950).

a radically altered reality. Norman Mailer, who gained fame with his grim war novel *The Naked and the Dead* (1948), later observed: "Probably, we will never be able to determine the psychic havoc of the concentration camps and the atom bombs upon the unconscious minds of almost everyone alive in those years." American reality continued to change at a dizzying pace during the 1950s, giving rise to a new youth culture and a radical counterculture represented by the Beats, who rejected the dominant social, political, and cultural values in the United States. Received values and beliefs were further undermined by the radical social movements of the 1960s, the widespread opposition to the Vietnam War, the loss of political confidence following Watergate, the energy crisis and increasing degradation of the environment, and the technological challenges posed to earlier forms of art and communication in the postmodern age.

Although modernism and postmodernism share some characteristics, there are fundamental differences between the two broad and complex movements. In an effort to "make it new," in Ezra Pound's memorable phrase, modernist writers broke sharply with the past, rejecting traditional literary forms and modes of narration. In contrast, many postmodern writers have self-consciously appropriated, mixed, and parodied earlier styles or conventions of writing. Indeed, many of those writers have dismissed the very idea of creativity, invention, or originality, the key words of modernism. The distinction between elite and popular cultural forms, a tenet of modernism, has also been eroded in postmodern literature, which is often characterized by the blurring of generic boundaries and imagery drawn from consumer culture and the mass media. Although the fragmentation characteristic of both modern and postmodern literature reflects the breakdown of earlier systems of thought, modernist writers sought to achieve a new conceptual unity, while postmodern writers display a distrust of overarching theories and broad generalizations. Their interest is consequently in the local and provisional, rather than in the global or universal. Finally, just as postmodernism calls into question earlier notions of art and the primacy of the artist, it challenges the traditional conception of the social role of literature, its capacity either to represent reality or to bring about social change in the chaotic and fragmented world that has developed in the decades since World War II.

Jackson Pollock, *Autumn Rhythm (Number 30)*

Pollock's 1950 painting is one of the most famous works by a member of the "New York school" of artists, who became known as abstract expressionists. To create the ambitious work, he variously poured, flung, and dripped enamel paint onto a large canvas spread out on the floor of his studio. His emphasis on improvisation, process, stylistic innovation, and freedom of expression was characteristic of much of the new American art and literature produced during the decades following World War II.

But the landscape of American literature during this period is far more complex, crowded, and diverse than the term *postmodernism* suggests. Many of the writers of the period have challenged the assumptions and rejected or at least radically altered the practices of literary modernism. At the same time, some of the most prominent American modernist writers — including the novelists William Faulkner, Ernest Hemingway, Richard Wright, and Eudora Welty, as well as the poets T. S. Eliot, Marianne Moore, Ezra Pound, Wallace Stevens, and William Carlos Williams — continued to write and exert considerable influence after 1945. Most of the younger writers who emerged immediately after the war continued to work within the broad traditions of modernism and realism, and those movements remain vital to this day. In fact, relatively few American writers of the postwar period fall into neat categories, and some of them have tangential or even contested relations to the main concerns of postmodernism. Certainly, the works included in the following section of this anthology suggest the richness, as well as the complexity and diversity, of American literature since 1945.

Drama formed a prominent part of that literature in the immediate postwar years. During the Great Depression, American dramatists had for the most part abandoned the radical experimentation of earlier modernist drama in favor of a realistic style and more socially engaged plays. That trend remained visible in the work of the two dramatists who dominated the Broadway stage during the 1940s and 1950s, Tennessee Williams and Arthur Miller. But they blended realism with a more expressive dramatic idiom. Williams explored the role of memory in his early plays, including *Portrait of a Madonna*, a forerunner of his Pulitzer Prize–winning *A Streetcar Named Desire* (1947). Seeking ways to express the inner lives and psychology of his memorable female characters, Williams employed snatches of music, stylized sets, and poetic language, all of which combined to create what has variously been described as a poetic or subjective realism. Inspired in part by the experimental effects in Williams's plays, Miller said that he was determined not to be "encompassed by conventional realism" in his Pulitzer Prize–winning *Death of a Salesman*. Although it is essentially a domestic drama with roots in the protest literature of the 1930s, the play disrupts the conventions of time and space, as characters from the past and present interact in a stage setting with transparent walls. Miller first called the play "The Inside of His Head," and much of its action takes place within the mind and memory of its tragic Everyman, Willy Loman.

The growth of Off-Broadway theater spurred experimentation in American drama. Before Edward Albee had his first major Broadway hit, *Who's Afraid of Virginia Woolf?* (1962), he gained a reputation with a series of one-act plays produced Off-Broadway, including *The Sandbox* (1960). Influenced by an avant-garde movement in European drama variously characterized as the "theater of the absurd," the "new theater," and the "anti-theater," Albee's short plays illustrated the movement away from the conventions of realistic or representational drama in the late 1950s. *The Sandbox*, in which the flat characters Mommy and Daddy engage in a meaningless dialogue while they wait for Grandma to die, was also a biting satire of the American family, the icon of American life and culture during the 1950s. In 1964, Albee conducted a playwriting workshop that included the poet and radical social critic LeRoi Jones, later Amiri Baraka, who became a key figure in the Black Arts Movement. Like Albee, Baraka challenged social stereotypes and theatrical conventions in his angry, confrontational play *Dutchman* (1964), in which he used a chance meeting between a white woman and a black man in a subway car to expose the oppression and repressed black rage at the heart of race relations in the United States. August Wilson later explored issues of race and class in plays ranging from his one-act sketch *The Janitor* (1985) to an ambitious cycle of ten plays in which he charted the African American experience in the twentieth century, the *Pittsburgh Cycle* (1982-2003).

American poets also began to engage new subjects following World War II. The early work of the major American poets who emerged in the decade after the war revealed both their technical mastery of traditional verse forms and their debts to modernism. Gwendolyn Brooks, who was influenced by her study of modernist poets and the writers of the Harlem Renaissance, explored life in the urban black ghetto in her collections *A Street in Bronzeville* (1945) and *Annie Allen* (1949). Her contemporary Robert Hayden, who did not gain wide recognition until the 1960s, adapted modernist practices to explore African American history in poems such as "Middle Passage" (1945), in which the poet's voice mingles with voices from the past in a dense and allusive account of a slave mutiny in 1839. History and a profound sense of place blended in Elizabeth Bishop's poetry, which displayed the rhythmic subtlety, formal control, and close observation characteristic of the work of her mentor Marianne Moore. History also assumed a prominent role in the poetry of Robert Lowell, who explored his ancestry and the tangled history of New England; and John Berryman, whose complex dialogue with the seventeenth-century poet Anne Bradstreet, *Homage to Mistress Bradstreet* (1956), was hailed by many critics as the most successful long poem in English since T. S. Eliot's influential *The Waste Land* (1922).

By the mid-1950s, however, American poetry had already begun to move in directions that diverged sharply from the practices of poets such as Eliot. Where he and many other modernists followed what Eliot defined as the "impersonal theory of poetry," the work of many postwar poets became increasingly autobiographical. Theodore Roethke included a number of intense poems about his early life and relationship with his father in his breakthrough volume, *The Lost Son* (1948). After the publication of

Homage to Mistress Bradstreet, Berryman began his most ambitious poetic project, *The Dream Songs*. The tragicomic poems in the sequence were not only deeply personal, but also unconventional in form and language, an idiosyncratic blend of poetic diction, colloquial speech, and slang. Influenced in part by Berryman, and feeling that his own earlier work was too stiffly formal, Lowell began to experiment with freer forms and a more colloquial language in the autobiographical poems in his aptly named collection *Life Studies* (1959). Widely credited with giving major impetus to the "confessional" school of American poetry, the volume had a strong impact on the diction and subject matter of the late poetry of Sylvia Plath. During the year before she committed suicide in 1963, Plath imaginatively dramatized the details of her life—from her conflicted relationship with her father to her failed marriage and difficult experiences as a wife and mother—in the poems published in her posthumous collection *Ariel* (1965).

Other young American poets also began to test the boundaries of language and subject matter during the 1950s. The tendency toward more open forms and a concentrated, colloquial language was in large part a tribute to the American modernist William Carlos Williams, who was an important mentor of many younger poets, including Allen Ginsberg. Williams wrote the introduction to Ginsberg's most famous volume of poetry, the revolutionary *Howl and Other Poems* (1956), which thrust the young poet into the forefront of the Beat movement. As Ginsberg later explained, "The point of Beat is that you get beat down to a certain nakedness where you actually are able to see the world in a visionary way." For many, however, *Howl* was probably less notable for its beatific vision than for its graphic, incantatory language and its shocking depiction of the underside of American life, which caused a sensation when Ginsberg first read the poem at a group reading in San Francisco on October 7, 1955. One of the other poets who participated in that reading was Gary Snyder, who represented a very different side of the Beat movement. Inspired by his study of Zen Buddhism, Native American culture, and poetic models ranging from ancient Chinese poets to Williams and Ezra Pound, Snyder developed a meditative style through which he sought to capture the quiet rhythms of everyday life, manual labor, and the natural world.

In contrast to Snyder, who became a central figure in the environmental movement, the other Beats concentrated on urban life, as did John Ashbery, a member of a loosely associated group of poets called the "New York school." Whereas Snyder spent more than a decade in Japan, Ashbery spent a decade in Paris, and he was influenced by French surrealism as well as by postwar movements in American art, including abstract expressionism and pop art. Like many of the painters associated with those movements, Ashbery produced work notable for its experimentation, playfulness, and

The point of Beat is that you get beat down to a certain nakedness where you actually are able to see the world in a visionary way.

Roy Lichtenstein, *Blam*
Lichtenstein based his large-scale 1962 painting on a panel created by Russ Heath for the comic book *All American Men of War #89.* By copying a cartoon image, Lichtenstein subverted the distinction between high art and mass culture, challenging assumptions about originality and the role of the artist. His painting may also be seen as an ironic commentary on the pervasive images of violence in the mass media, part of a broad critique of American society mounted by numerous artists and writers during the 1960s.

spontaneity. And, like many of his contemporary poets, he developed a colloquial style, though Ashbery for the most part avoided the most common subjects and themes of postwar poetry. He displayed little interest in autobiography or history or what is commonly understood as events and experiences, whether actual or imagined. Instead, the focus of his self-reflective and fragmented poems is on language and the nature of perception and representation in a mundane world of commonplace particulars.

Widely regarded as the quintessential postmodern poet and the most influential poet of the last forty years, Ashbery has steadily challenged the reader's search for meaning or a message. But many of his contemporaries and younger poets have affirmed the social and political role of poetry. One of the most committed poets was Adrienne Rich, who, like Ashbery, was initially influenced by modernists such as Wallace Stevens. Her experiences of trying to balance her life as a traditional wife and mother with her career as a poet pushed her work in new directions, most clearly announced in her autobiographical volume *Snapshots of a Daughter-in-Law* (1963). As she observed about the poems in that collection, "I began trying, to the best of my ability, to face the hard questions of poetry and experience." Although her new work bore the stamp of confessional

> *I began trying, to the best of my ability, to face the hard questions of poetry and experience.*

poets such as Berryman, Lowell, and Plath, for Rich the personal and the political were becoming one. Further radicalized by the civil rights movement and the Vietnam War, Rich faced those "hard questions" even more directly and boldly in other volumes of poetry she published during the 1960s. At the beginning of the following decade, she announced her determination to make poetry a vehicle for personal and social change in the title of her collection *The Will to Change* (1971), and she explored a range of issues in her award-winning collection *Diving into the Wreck* (1973).

Political and social issues assumed a prominent place in the work of poets from different racial and ethnic backgrounds. In the early 1970s, Rich's friend Audre Lorde also began publishing poems in which she addressed subjects such as lesbianism and liberation from oppression. Lorde and other African American poets drew upon the resources of colloquial black speech, as well as the rich traditions of black music, which inspired many of the poems in Michael Harper's first collection, *Dear John, Dear Coltrane* (1970). Like Harper, Rita Dove explored African American history and culture and the painful legacies of slavery and racism in her first collection, *The Yellow House on the Corner* (1980); and Yusef Komunyakaa vividly chronicled the experiences of black soldiers in Vietnam in the poems in *Dien Cai Dau* (1988). The Native American poet Joy Harjo brought a powerful sense of history, memory, and place to poems in which she exposed the contemporary difficulties of Native Americans. Latino and Latina writers have further extended the range of American poetry and affirmed its potential to change American society. In her influential and innovative book *Borderlands/La Frontera* (1987), the cultural critic, feminist theorist, and writer Gloria Anzaldúa blended poetry and prose, English and Spanish, to explore the racial, sexual, and social "borderlands" within the United States. The work of the bilingual poet Martín Espada, whose father was brought as a child to the United States from Puerto Rico, is deeply rooted in the history and cultural traditions of Latin America. From the beginning of his career, Espada has been committed to a poetry of witness, empathy, and advocacy embracing all oppressed people, inside and outside the United States, including the immigrant food workers who died in the attack on the World Trade Center, the subject of his poem "Alabanza: In Praise of Local 100" (2003).

During the decades since World War II, American fiction has also displayed the regional, racial, and ethnic diversity of the United States. The experience of previously marginalized groups played a vital role in the fiction of the immediate postwar period. The African American novelists Ralph Ellison and James Baldwin were encouraged by the success of their mentor Richard Wright, whose protest novel *Native Son* (1940) and autobiographical *Black Boy* (1945) had achieved both critical and commercial success. Ellison and Baldwin, however, illustrated a shift in postwar fiction away from the social realism of Wright's books and many other works published during the Great Depression and World War II. Like Wright,

**WE HAVE BEEN NAUGHT—
WE SHALL BE ALL**

Emigdio Vasquez, *Obreros*

The Chicano artist and muralist Emigdio Vasquez works in a photo-realistic style
to document the daily life of working people in the *barrio*, the Mexican American
neighborhoods of East Los Angeles. As in numerous other works of postmodern
art and literature, previously marginalized groups and activities assume a central
place in his 1995 painting *Obreros* ("Workers").

Ellison and Baldwin exposed the pervasive racism of American society, but
they distanced themselves from the tradition of protest fiction. Both were
committed to rendering the complexity, contradictions, and range of African
American life in works characterized by poetic language, rich symbolism,
and complex narrative structures, including Ellison's novel *Invisible Man*
(1952) and Baldwin's first novel *Go Tell It on the Mountain* (1953), as well as
the autobiographical title essay of his collection *Notes of a Native Son* (1955).

Similar experiments in style and efforts to extend realism into new
areas of experience were undertaken by a wide range of other fiction writers during the decade following World War II. Jewish American writers
such as Bernard Malamud and Saul Bellow became significant forces in
American fiction, the postwar geography of which encompassed what was
formerly known as the "Jewish ghetto" on the Lower East Side of New York
City, the semimythical site of many of Malamud's stories and novels; and
poor neighborhoods in Bellow's adopted city, Chicago, the setting of his

memorable story "Looking for Mr. Green" (1951) and his breakthrough novel, *The Adventures of Augie March* (1953). Bellow's colloquial style, his mingling of high and low culture, and his fascination with characters adrift in a world of deceptive appearances displayed his kinship with a writer from a dramatically different background, Flannery O'Connor. A Catholic who was raised in and wrote about the predominantly Protestant South, O'Connor blended regional realism and symbolism, violence and grotesque humor, in novels and the morality tales collected in *A Good Man Is Hard to Find* (1955). Hisaye Yamamoto, the daughter of Japanese immigrants in California, drew upon her early life and experiences in a relocation center for Japanese Americans during World War II in stories such as "Seventeen Syllables" (1949). Tillie Olsen, the radical, working-class daughter of Jewish emigrants from Russia, also challenged stereotypes of life in the United States. The most famous of her autobiographical stories, "I Stand Here Ironing" (1956), is a first-person, stream-of-consciousness narrative told by a troubled mother of five who, abandoned by her husband, must work and raise her children, a situation that was deeply at odds with postwar complacency and images of middle-class suburban families during the 1950s. Jack Kerouac challenged the dominant values of the postwar era in his best-selling novel *On the Road* (1957), which blurred the boundaries between fiction and nonfiction; as well as in autobiographical essays such as "Alone on a Mountaintop," one of the nonfictional pieces in his collection *Lonesome Traveler* (1960).

Three influential writers who emerged during the 1960s and 1970s reveal some of the divergent tendencies in more recent American fiction. John Updike was widely admired for the fluid and often lyrical style of stories and novels in which he chronicled the changing patterns of life in middle-class suburbia, blending close observation with moral and social commentary. Updike was a consummate storyteller, but another frequent contributor to the prestigious *New Yorker*, Donald Barthelme, challenged readerly expectations of what constituted character and plot in literary fiction. Barthelme subverted traditional narrative forms in his inventive novels and patchwork stories, which are characterized by playfulness, pastiche, and irony. His work suggested that realism was "used up," as the novelist and critic John Barth put it in his essay "The Literature of Exhaustion" (1967). In contrast, Raymond Carver demonstrated the ongoing vitality of realistic fiction in stories he published in magazines such as *Esquire* and the *New Yorker*. Refining a spare "minimalist" style reminiscent of Ernest Hemingway's modernist prose, Carver told powerful and poignant stories rooted in the everyday lives and struggles of working-class people, and he was widely credited with reinvigorating and virtually reinventing the realistic short story in the United States.

Realism and postmodern modes of narration have coexisted and often mingled in fiction and other kinds of prose narratives published since the

Barbara Kruger,
Untitled (Your fictions
become history)

A graphic designer who
turned to photography,
Barbara Kruger appropri-
ates, transforms, and
comments upon familiar
images, as in this frag-
mented and roughly
reconstituted photograph
of the head of a classical
Greek statue, produced in
1983. Together, the com-
posite image and Kruger's
caption invite the viewer
to consider the nature of
representation, the power
of images to create stereotypes, and the role of such
fictions in the construc-
tion of history and indi-
vidual identity, issues
that are also central to
contemporary writings
ranging from memoirs to
postmodern works of
fiction.

*Copyright © Barbara Kruger,
Courtesy Mary Boone Gallery,
New York.*

1970s. The growing popularity of the contemporary memoir, an autobiographical form that the writer Patricia Hampl has called "the signature
genre of our age," has given new life to the realistic tradition, which is
grounded on the belief that language can represent life and society. In
style and structure, however, memoirs often display a kinship with postmodern narratives, as illustrated by two innovative examples of the genre:
N. Scott Momaday's *The Names: A Memoir* (1976), in which he employed
multiple voices and perspectives to tell the story of his complex origins;
and Maxine Hong Kingston's *The Woman Warrior: Memoirs of a Girlhood
among Ghosts* (1976), in which she freely mixed fact and fiction, legend
and fantasy, in a phantasmagoric account of her early life in a Chinese
American community in California. The growing prominence of the memoir has raised fundamental questions about identity, memory, and the relationship between truth, or authenticity, and the telling of stories. Those
questions are central to postmodern works such as Tim O'Brien's celebrated collection of stories about the Vietnam War, *The Things They Carried: A Work of Fiction* (1990), in which he casts himself as a character and

explores the complex relations among invention, lying, and truth-telling. The explosion of new technologies has also influenced the ways in which stories are told. Postmodern writers such as Don DeLillo find traditional realism inadequate to represent the changing conditions of contemporary life and what he sees as the deadening effects of electronic communication, information overload, and the constant barrage of images in a world of "technoculture." At the same time, the pressure of popular culture has narrowed the former division between literary and popular genres such as fantasy and science fiction, leading to growing recognition of writers such as Ursula K. Le Guin. Graphic books of various kinds have also gained wide popularity and acceptance, as exemplified by the success of Alison Bechdel's *Fun House: A Family Tragicomic*, an acclaimed graphic memoir that was named the Best Book of 2006 by *Time* magazine.

The breakdown of firm cultural categories and social boundaries characteristic of postmodernism has also opened up additional space for the stories of minority writers. In her essay "Postmodern Blackness" (1990), the memoirist and cultural theorist bell hooks observed that a postmodernism that challenges "notions of universality and static overdetermined identity within mass culture and mass consciousness can open up new possibilities for the construction of the self and the assertion of agency." Inspired in part by one of her neglected "foremothers," Zora Neale Hurston, the African American novelist Alice Walker gained considerable success with a series of stories and novels about the experiences of black women, including *The Color Purple* (1983). Toni Morrison, the first African American to win the Nobel Prize, has adapted postmodern literary practices in novels such as *Beloved* (1987), in which she told a harrowing story about slavery and its aftermath by mingling elements of fantasy, history, and magical realism. The Chicana writer Sandra Cisneros explored the "borderlands" occupied by Mexican Americans in her best-selling novel *The House on Mango Street* (1984) and her admired collection of stories *Woman Hollering Creek* (1991). Junot Díaz drew upon his own and the broader experience of immigrants from the Dominican Republic in his first novel, *The Brief Wondrous Life of Oscar Wao* (2007), for which he was awarded the Pulitzer Prize for Fiction; and in his collections of short stories, *Drown* (1996) and *This Is How You Lose Her* (2012). Native American writers have also received critical praise for works that reveal wide variations in style and subject matter. The work of Leslie Marmon Silko is deeply rooted in traditions of Native American history, myth, and storytelling, while Sherman Alexie has probed the realities of Indians on reservations and in cities, establishing the Native American presence in contemporary life and the culture of the United States.

Perhaps the only hallmark of American literature since 1945 is the range of literary imagination displayed in works of enormous diversity. That literary period may perhaps be described as postmodern only

1945-1977

insofar as a major principle of postmodernism is the u
overarching construct or single unified narrative of his
ers of the period have constructed competing narratives
ing and collapsing the distinction between elite and
adapting traditional forms and breaking generic boun
life to old stories and engaging subjects previously outs
of literature, and responding in complex and often div
ever-changing social, political, and cultural fabric of the

Theodore Roethke

[1908–1963]

Theodore Huebner Roethke was born on May 25, 1908, in Saginaw, Michigan, to Otto and Helen Huebner Roethke. Otto Roethke, the son of German immigrants, helped run the family business, a nursery with the most extensive greenhouses in the United States. "It was a wonderful place to grow up," Roethke recalled. "There were not only twenty-five acres in the town, mostly under glass and intensely cultivated, but farther out the last stand of virgin timber in the Saginaw Valley." But his early life was shadowed by his father's death from cancer in April 1923, shortly before Roethke turned fifteen. During high school, he spent most of his time reading, especially the work of nineteenth-century British and American prose writers, including Ralph Waldo Emerson and Henry David Thoreau. Describing his early literary aspirations, Roethke later said: "I really wanted, at fifteen and sixteen, to write the 'chiseled' prose as it was called in those days. . . . I bought my own editions of Emerson, Thoreau, and as God's my witness, subscribed to the *Dial*," the avant-garde literary magazine published in New York City. Roethke was also drawn to the poetry of Walt Whitman and the British Romantic poets William Blake and William Wordsworth. Against the wishes of his mother, who wanted him to remain close to home after his graduation from high school, Roethke enrolled in the University of Michigan in the fall of 1925. After he graduated magna cum laude in 1929, he dutifully enrolled at the university's law school. Increasingly engaged in writing poetry, he withdrew after a semester and began graduate study in English at Harvard in the fall of 1930.

Roethke supported himself by teaching while he pursued a career as a poet. At Harvard, the poet Robert Hillier strongly encouraged Roethke's poetic efforts, but he did not have enough money to continue his studies and left after a year to take a teaching job at Lafayette College in Pennsylvania. During his four years there, Roethke published his first poems in a little magazine, the *Harp*, and met a number of supportive poets, including Stanley Kunitz and Louise Bogan. In the fall of 1935, Roethke took a position at Michigan State College (now University). He was soon hospitalized

Theodore Roethke

This undated photograph of Roethke was apparently taken shortly before the sudden death of the famed poet-teacher on August 1, 1963.

for his first bout of bipolar disorder, then called manic depression. After his release from the hospital in January 1936, he earned an MA at the University of Michigan and took a teaching position at the Pennsylvania State College (now University), where the burly and athletic poet also coached the tennis team. He continued to work on his poems, several of which appeared in *Poetry: A Magazine of Verse* and prominent national magazines such as the *Atlantic Monthly*, the *Nation*, and the *New Yorker*. Roethke fell in love with a librarian at the college, Kitty Stokes, who encouraged him to publish his first book of poems, *Open House* (1941). In 1943, he took a leave of absence from Penn State to accept a visiting position at Bennington, a small women's college in Vermont. As a result of an affair with a student, Roethke was asked to leave Bennington in 1945. Struggling with depression, Roethke was once again hospitalized and given electroshock therapy. Following his release and a period of writing and recovery at home in Saginaw, made possible by a Guggenheim Fellowship, he returned to Penn State in 1947.

That summer, Roethke accepted a position as a professor and poet in residence at the University of Washington in Seattle, a position he held for the rest of his life. During his first year there, Roethke published what most critics view as his breakthrough volume, *The Lost Son and Other Poems* (1948). Buoyed by the enthusiastic reviews, Roethke began to work feverishly on his next book and was awarded a second Guggenheim Fellowship in 1950. Following the publication of *Praise to the End!* (1951), the National Institute of Arts and Letters awarded him a grant in recognition of "the vigor and originality of his style, the subtlety of his versification, and his faithful devotion over many years to the art of poetry both as a producer and a teacher." On a trip to New York for a series of readings, Roethke encountered one of his former Bennington students, Beatrice O'Connell. They were married within a month, in January 1953. Following their extended honeymoon in Europe, Roethke published his acclaimed collection *The Waking, Poems* (1953), which was awarded the Pulitzer Prize. He spent the academic year 1955-56 teaching on a Fulbright Scholarship in Italy before resuming his teaching schedule at the University of Washington. Although he suffered serious depressive episodes, for which he was twice hospitalized for extended periods in Seattle, he continued to write, publishing two more collections of poetry, *The Exorcism* (1957) and *Words for the Wind* (1958). The latter volume won a host of awards, including the prestigious Bollingen Prize, and he subsequently embarked on reading tours in the United States and Europe. Roethke was working on the revisions of what proved to be his final book, *The Far Field* (1964), when he died suddenly of a heart attack while swimming on August 1, 1963.

There is no poetry anywhere that is so valuably conscious of the human body as Roethke's; no poetry that can place the body in an environment.

–James Dickey

Reading Roethke's Poetry. Roethke admired and was influenced by a wide range of poets, including those he described as his "spiritual ancestors"—William Blake, William Wordsworth, and Walt Whitman—and modernist poets such as T. S. Eliot, Wallace Stevens, and William Butler Yeats. Like much of the work of Wordsworth, Whitman, and Yeats, Roethke's poetry is strongly autobiographical. In the early 1940s, he began an intense exploration of his personal past in poems such as "My Papa's Waltz," which was first published in *Harper's Bazaar* in 1942. In it, he expressed his deeply ambivalent and unresolved feelings about his dead father, Otto Roethke. "All the present has fallen," Roethke noted in his journal in 1944: "I am only what I remember." Among his most vivid memories of childhood were of playing and working in the acres of greenhouses of the family nursery, the setting of "Cuttings," "Cuttings (later)," and "Root Cellar," three of the poems from his famous sequence "The Greenhouse Poems" in *The Lost Son and Other Poems* (1948). Roethke experimented with a wide range of metrical and poetic forms, from free verse and unrhymed lyric stanzas to the complex form of the villanelle in "The Waking," the title poem of his Pulitzer Prize-winning collection, *The Waking, Poems* (1953). The texts of the poems are taken from *The Collected Poems of Theodore Roethke* (1966).

bedfordstmartins.com/ *americanlit* *for research links on Roethke*

MY PAPA'S WALTZ

The whiskey on your breath
Could make a small boy dizzy;
But I hung on like death:
Such waltzing was not easy.

We romped until the pans   5
Slid from the kitchen shelf;
My mother's countenance
Could not unfrown itself.

The hand that held my wrist
Was battered on one knuckle;   10
At every step you missed
My right ear scraped a buckle.

You beat time on my head
With a palm caked hard by dirt,
Then waltzed me off to bed   15
Still clinging to your shirt.

[1942, 1966]

CUTTINGS[1]

Sticks-in-a-drowse droop over sugary loam,
Their intricate stem-fur dries;
But still the delicate slips keep coaxing up water;
The small cells bulge;

One nub of growth
Nudges a sand-crumb loose,
Pokes through a musty sheath
Its pale tendrilous horn.[2]

[1948, 1966]

---

1. **Cuttings:** This poem was the first in a series Roethke first called "News of the Root" and later "The Green-house Poems," the first section of *The Lost Son and Other Poems* (1948). A cutting is a piece cut from a plant or tree, placed in a growing medium, and encouraged to develop roots in order to propagate the parent plant.
2. **tendrilous horn:** A sprout of growth covered with threadlike appendages that stretch out to attach to another plant or object for support.

CUTTINGS[1]

(later)

This urge, wrestle, resurrection of dry sticks,
Cut stems struggling to put down feet,
What saint strained so much,
Rose on such lopped limbs to a new life?

I can hear, underground, that sucking and sobbing,   5
In my veins, in my bones I feel it, —
The small waters seeping upward,
The tight grains parting at last.
When sprouts break out,
Slippery as fish,   10
I quail, lean to beginnings, sheath-wet.

[1948, 1966]

---

1. **Cuttings (later):** This poem, the second of "The Greenhouse Poems" in *The Lost Son and Other Poems*, was first published as "Cuttings" in *Harper's Bazaar* (1948).

ROOT CELLAR[1]

Nothing would sleep in that cellar, dank as a ditch,
Bulbs broke out of boxes hunting for chinks in the dark,
Shoots dangled and drooped,

---

1. **Root Cellar:** This poem, the third of "The Greenhouse Poems" in *The Lost Son and Other Poems* (1948), was first published as "Florist's Root Cellar" in *Poetry: A Magazine of Verse* (1943).

Lolling obscenely from mildewed crates,
Hung down long yellow evil necks, like tropical snakes.   5
And what a congress of stinks!—
Roots ripe as old bait,
Pulpy stems, rank, silo-rich,
Leaf-mold, manure, lime, piled against slippery planks.
Nothing would give up life: 10
Even the dirt kept breathing a small breath.

                                                [1943, 1966]

THE WAKING[1]

I wake to sleep, and take my waking slow.
I feel my fate in what I cannot fear.
I learn by going where I have to go.

We think by feeling. What is there to know?
I hear my being dance from ear to ear.   5
I wake to sleep, and take my waking slow.

Of those so close beside me, which are you?
God bless the Ground! I shall walk softly there,
And learn by going where I have to go.

Light takes the Tree; but who can tell us how?   10
The lowly worm climbs up a winding stair;
I wake to sleep, and take my waking slow.

Great Nature has another thing to do
To you and me; so take the lively air,
And, lovely, learn by going where to go.   15

This shaking keeps me steady. I should know.
What falls away is always. And is near.
I wake to sleep, and take my waking slow.
I learn by going where I have to go.

                                                [1953, 1966]

---

1. **The Waking:** This nineteen-line poem is a villanelle, a complex form composed of five triplets (a three-line stanza rhymed *a b a*) and a concluding quatrain (a four-line stanza rhymed *a b a b*). The form employs only two rhymes, and alternating stanzas end with the same last line.

The poet and novelist Sherman Alexie is among the best-known contemporary Native American writers (see page 2296). In an interview with fellow poet Diane Thiel for the Poetry Society of America, Alexie discussed his interest in poetics and his powerful response to Theodore Roethke's poem "My Papa's Waltz." The text of the following extract from the interview is taken from the transcription published on the Poetry Society Organization Web site, http://www.poetrysociety.org.

SHERMAN ALEXIE

[b. 1966]

From A Conversation: Sherman Alexie and Diane Thiel

SA: Although I would certainly be defined as a free verse poet, I have always worked in traditional and invented forms. Though I've never recognized it before, the fact that the title poem of my first book is a sestina says a lot about my varied ambitions.[1] My earliest interest in formalism came from individual poems rather than certain poets. Marvell's "To His Coy Mistress," Roethke's "My Papa's Waltz," Gwendolyn Brooks' "We Real Cool," and Langston Hughes' "A Dream Deferred" are poems that come to mind as early formal poems I admired.[2] Speaking both seriously and facetiously, I think I've spent my whole career rewriting "My Papa's Waltz" with an Indian twist. Lately, as I've been writing much more formally — with end rhyme, a tenuous dance with meter, and explicit

---

1. **the title poem . . . ambitions:** Alexie's first book was *The Business of Fancydancing: Stories and Poems* (1992). A sestina is a complex French verse form consisting of six sestets (six-line stanzas) and a final, three-line envoy.

2. **Marvell's "To His Coy Mistress" . . . poems I admired:** In addition to the famous poem by the English poet Andrew Marvell (1621–1678), Alexie cites three American poems included in this anthology: Roethke's "My Papa's Waltz" (p. 1979); Brooks's "We Real Cool" (p. 2071); and Hughes's "Harlem," which Alexie calls "A Dream Deferred," a phrase from the first line of the poem (p. 1699).

form – I've discovered that in writing toward that end rhyme, that accented or unaccented syllable, or that stanza break, I am constantly surprising myself with new ideas, new vocabulary, and new ways of looking at the world. The conscious use of form seems to have freed my subconscious.

DT: That's exactly how I feel about using form – that it has the power to free the subconscious. I've actually thought about Roethke's poem when reading your work. For me, too, it was one of the poems that startled me into poetry early on. It's an interesting poem to teach because of the range of reaction to it. Some – those who focus on the waltz and the horseplay – feel the tone to be much lighter. Others – those who concentrate more on the whisky on his breath, the way the child "hung on like death," and the ear scraping a buckle – feel that it's much darker. I think that the tug of the two different tones creates the true charge in the poem.

SA: I think the poem is incredibly sad and violent, and its sadness and violence is underscored by its gentle rhymes and rhythms. It's Mother Goose on acid,[3] maybe. I think that its gentle music is a form of denial about the terror contained in the poem, or maybe it's the way kids think, huh? My dad wasn't violent, but he would leave us to go drinking, and would sometimes be gone for a few weeks. He was completely undependable and unpredictable. My wife's father was a scary and unpredictable alcoholic, charming and funny one moment, violent and caustic the next. So Roethke's poem, I think, is all about the unpredictability of the alcoholic father.

---

3. **Mother Goose on acid:** Mother Goose is an imaginary author of nursery rhymes and fairy tales; *acid* is a slang term for the psychedelic drug LSD.

Elizabeth Bishop

[1911-1979]

Elizabeth Bishop

This Associated Press photograph was taken in 1956, the year Bishop was awarded the Pulitzer Prize for her second collection of poetry, *North and South* (1955).

Elizabeth Bishop was born on February 8, 1911, in Worcester, Massachusetts, to Gertrude May Boomer Bishop, a former teacher and nurse, and William Thomas Bishop, the heir to a successful construction business. Eight months later, Bishop's father died from Bright's disease, and Bishop's distraught mother returned with her daughter to live with her parents in Great Village, Nova Scotia. In 1916, after Bishop's mother had suffered a series of violent episodes of mental illness, the Boomers committed her to a hospital where she remained until her death in 1934. Bishop saw her mother only once more. In 1917, when she was six years old, she went to live with her paternal grandparents in Worcester. The wealthy Bishops wished to give their granddaughter a better education than the Boomers could provide in rural Nova Scotia, but she was lonely and miserable until her mother's sister, Bishop's beloved "Aunt Maud," took her to live in Boston. Her paternal grandparents died within a few days of one another in 1923, leaving Bishop a substantial trust fund. Throughout her life, Bishop suffered from asthma and other ailments, and during her frequent childhood illnesses she read widely and developed a strong interest in poetry. By 1924, her health had improved, and she began spending the summers at a nautical camp for girls on Cape Cod. Her supportive fellow campers recalled that "Bishy" had a favorite perch in an apple tree where she would write poems, songs, and skits they performed on Sunday evenings. After completing her final two years of high school at Walnut Hill, a boarding school in Natick, Bishop entered Vassar College in 1930.

It took Bishop nearly two decades to establish herself as a poet. At Vassar, she became friends with the future novelist Mary McCarthy, with whom Bishop founded *Con Spirito*, an avant-garde alternative to the college's literary magazine. During her senior year, she met the visiting poet Marianne Moore, who became Bishop's close friend and mentor. Moore encouraged Bishop, who was considering a medical career, to pursue her interest in writing. Financially independent, she went to New York City after her graduation in 1934. Moore recommended her poems to editors and chose three of them for inclusion in *Trial Balances* (1935), an anthology of the work of young writers selected and introduced by established writers. From 1935 to 1937, Bishop traveled in Europe and North Africa before settling in Key West, Florida, where she bought a house with her college friend Louise Crane. Their partnership was the first of Bishop's lesbian relationships, a part of her life about which she was deeply reticent. Bishop worked on her poems while she and Crane lived a highly social life, filled with music, friends, and visitors to their home. By 1941, however, their relationship was at an end, and Bishop divided her time between Key West and New York City during World War II. Through Moore, she met E. E. Cummings and other poets, but Bishop was depressed and frustrated by her inability to interest a publisher in her first collection of poetry. In 1945, with Moore's support, Bishop's manuscript won first place among more than eight hundred entries in a poetry contest sponsored by the prominent Boston firm Houghton Mifflin, which consequently published it as *North and South* (1946). The book received positive reviews from Moore and the young poet Robert Lowell, whom Bishop met in 1947. They became lifelong friends, and Lowell helped secure her the position of Consultant in Poetry to the Library of Congress, now called the Poet Laureate, for 1949–50.

Despite her slow pace of publication, Bishop's reputation rose steadily during the remainder of her career. On a trip to South America in 1951, she was captivated by Brazil, where she lived for the next eighteen years. She became involved with Lota de Macedo Soares, with whom Bishop lived in Rio de Janeiro and later bought a house at Ouro Prêto. She was awarded the Pulitzer Prize for her second collection, *Poems: North and South—A Cold Spring* (1955). Although she continued to struggle with illness and bouts of alcoholism, she also translated several books from Portuguese to English and wrote a travel book, *Brazil* (1962). "I think geography comes first in my work," Bishop told an interviewer late in her life, and Brazil was the setting of many of the poems in her third book, *Questions of Travel* (1965). She subsequently taught at the University of Washington, returned to Brazil, and then left again for the United States. Lota de Macedo Soares followed her there and died in New York City, possibly of an overdose of sedatives, in September 1967. Bishop lived for a time in San Francisco with an old friend, Suzanne Bowen, and briefly returned with her to Brazil. Bishop's *Complete Poems* (1969) won the National Book Award. In 1970, she began to teach at Harvard University, where she was poet in residence from 1973 to 1977. There, she met Alice Methfessel, her companion for the rest of her life. Bishop coedited *An Anthology of Twentieth-Century Brazilian Poetry* (1972), and her final volume of poems, *Geography III*, was published in 1976. She suffered a cerebral aneurysm and died in Boston on October 6, 1979.

It is this continually renewed sense of discovering the strangements, the unreality of our reality at the very moment of becoming conscious of it as reality, that is the great subject for Elizabeth Bishop.

–John Ashbery

Reading Bishop's Poetry. Bishop was a notorious perfectionist who often spent years and sometimes even decades working on a single poem. In 1956, the poetry editor of the *New Yorker*, with which Bishop had a first-reading contract and in which many of her poems were first published, wrote to her: "As usual, this letter is a plea to let us see some of the Elizabeth Bishop manuscripts that I feel certain are on your desk, all finished if only you could bring yourself to part with them." In fact, Bishop's notebooks reveal that she began hundreds of poems, some of which have recently been published in a controversial collection of her unfinished work, *Edgar Allan Poe and the Juke-Box: Uncollected Poems, Drafts, and Fragments* (2006), edited by Alice Quinn. Bishop, however, allowed only about ninety of her poems to be published during her long career. In them, she employed a range of poetic techniques, including demanding forms

bedfordstmartins.com/ americanlit *for research links on Bishop*

such as the sestina and the villanelle, and she is widely admired for the craftsmanship and rhythmic subtlety of her work. She is also admired for her powers of observation and description, as revealed in her precise and detailed renderings of animals and the natural world as well as the physical geography of the places she lived, especially Brazil, the setting of "The Armadillo." In contrast to her close friend and contemporary Robert Lowell, a central figure in the confessional school of American poetry, Bishop was an intensely private poet. But she drew upon sharply etched memories of her childhood in poems such as "Sestina" and "In the Waiting Room," and she indirectly evoked the often painful circumstances of her personal life in "One Art," a poignant meditation on loss published in her final collection. The texts are taken from *The Complete Poems, 1927–1979* (1983).

SESTINA[1]

September rain falls on the house.
In the failing light, the old grandmother
sits in the kitchen with the child
beside the Little Marvel Stove,[2]
reading the jokes from the almanac,   5
laughing and talking to hide her tears.

She thinks that her equinoctial tears
and the rain that beats on the roof of the house
were both foretold by the almanac,
but only known to a grandmother.   10
The iron kettle sings on the stove.
She cuts some bread and says to the child,

It's time for tea now; but the child
is watching the teakettle's small hard tears
dance like mad on the hot black stove,   15
the way the rain must dance on the house.
Tidying up, the old grandmother
hangs up the clever almanac

on its string. Birdlike, the almanac
hovers half open above the child,   20

---

1. **Sestina:** A complex French verse form consisting of six sestets (six-line stanzas) and a final, three-line envoy. The final words of the six lines in the first stanza are repeated in different sequences at the end of the lines of the succeeding stanzas, and all six words appear in the envoy, three of them in the middle of the lines, and three of them at the end of the lines.
2. **Little Marvel Stove:** This cast-iron woodstove, manufactured by the Magee Furnace Company in Boston, was a fixture in the kitchens of many late-nineteenth- and early-twentieth-century homes.

hovers above the old grandmother
and her teacup full of dark brown tears.
She shivers and says she thinks the house
feels chilly, and puts more wood in the stove.

It was to be, says the Marvel Stove.   25
I know what I know, says the almanac.
With crayons the child draws a rigid house
and a winding pathway. Then the child
puts in a man with buttons like tears
and shows it proudly to the grandmother.   30
But secretly, while the grandmother
busies herself about the stove,
the little moons fall down like tears
from between the pages of the almanac
into the flower bed the child   35
has carefully placed in the front of the house.

Time to plant tears, says the almanac.
The grandmother sings to the marvellous stove
and the child draws another inscrutable house.

[1956, 1983]

THE ARMADILLO

For Robert Lowell[1]

This is the time of year
when almost every night
the frail, illegal fire balloons appear.[2]
Climbing the mountain height,

rising toward a saint   5
still honored in these parts,
the paper chambers flush and fill with light
that comes and goes, like hearts.

Once up against the sky it's hard
to tell them from the star —   10
planets, that is — the tinted ones:
Venus going down, or Mars,

---

1. **Dedication:** Bishop dedicated her poem to her close friend Robert Lowell (see p. 2056).
2. **This is the time . . . illegal fire balloons appear:** In June, during the festivals of St. Anthony, St. John, and St. Peter, Brazilians in some regions celebrate by releasing miniature fire-propelled balloons. The paper devices are banned because they frequently crash to the earth and cause serious fires.

or the pale green one.[3] With a wind,
they flare and falter, wobble and toss;
but if it's still they steer between   15
the kite sticks of the Southern Cross,[4]

receding, dwindling, solemnly
and steadily forsaking us,
or, in the downdraft from a peak,
suddenly turning dangerous.   20

Last night another big one fell.
It splattered like an egg of fire
against the cliff behind the house.
The flame ran down. We saw the pair

of owls who nest there flying up   25
and up, their whirling black-and-white
stained bright pink underneath, until
they shrieked up out of sight.

The ancient owls' nest must have burned.
Hastily, all alone,   30
a glistening armadillo left the scene,
rose-flecked, head down, tail down,

and then a baby rabbit jumped out,
short-eared, to our surprise.
So soft! — a handful of intangible ash   35
with fixed, ignited eyes.

Too pretty, dreamlike mimicry!
O falling fire and piercing cry
and panic, and a weak mailed fist[5]
clenched ignorant against the sky!   40

[1957, 1983]

---

3. **the pale green one:** The planet Neptune.
4. **Southern Cross:** Also called the "Crux," a constellation of stars in the shape of a cross that is visible only in the Southern Hemisphere.
5. **mailed fist:** The armadillo, whose name is derived from the Spanish word *armado* ("armed man"), is covered in bony plates that resemble chain mail or body armor.

IN THE WAITING ROOM

In Worcester, Massachusetts,
I went with Aunt Consuelo
to keep her dentist's appointment
and sat and waited for her
in the dentist's waiting room.   5

It was winter. It got dark
early. The waiting room
was full of grown-up people,
arctics[1] and overcoats,
lamps and magazines.   10
My aunt was inside
what seemed like a long time
and while I waited I read
the *National Geographic*
(I could read) and carefully   15
studied the photographs:
the inside of a volcano,
black, and full of ashes;
then it was spilling over
in rivulets of fire.   20
Osa and Martin Johnson[2]
dressed in riding breeches,
laced boots, and pith helmets.
A dead man slung on a pole
—"Long Pig,"[3] the caption said.   25
Babies with pointed heads
wound round and round with string;
black, naked women with necks
wound round and round with wire
like the necks of light bulbs.   30
Their breasts were horrifying.
I read it right straight through.
I was too shy to stop.
And then I looked at the cover:
the yellow margins, the date.   35
Suddenly, from inside,
came an *oh!* of pain
—Aunt Consuelo's voice—
not very loud or long.
I wasn't at all surprised;   40
even then I knew she was

1. **arctics:** Waterproof overshoes.
2. **Osa and Martin Johnson:** Natives of Kansas, these explorers and naturalists traveled throughout Africa, Borneo, and the South Seas from 1917 through 1937, the year that Martin Johnson died in a plane crash. The famous couple published photographs in magazines such as *National Geographic*, wrote travel books, and produced feature films about Africa. Early in his career, Martin Johnson accompanied Jack London on a voyage to the South Pacific, recounted in *The Cruise of the Snark* (1911).
3. **"Long Pig":** In his popular account of his voyage to the South Pacific, *The Cruise of the Snark* (1911), Jack London explains: "Now long-pig is not pig. Long-pig is the Polynesian euphemism for human flesh; and these descendants of man-eaters, a king's son at their head, brought in the pigs to table as of old their grandfathers had brought in their slain enemies."

a foolish, timid woman.
I might have been embarrassed,
but wasn't. What took me
completely by surprise   45
was that it was *me*:
my voice, in my mouth.
Without thinking at all
I was my foolish aunt,
I — we — were falling, falling,   50
our eyes glued to the cover
of the *National Geographic*,
February, 1918.

I said to myself: three days
and you'll be seven years old.   55
I was saying it to stop
the sensation of falling off
the round, turning world
into cold, blue-black space.
But I felt: you are an *I*,   60
you are an *Elizabeth*,
you are one of *them*.
Why should you be one, too?
I scarcely dared to look
to see what it was I was.   65
I gave a sidelong glance
— I couldn't look any higher —
at shadowy gray knees,
trousers and skirts and boots
and different pairs of hands   70
lying under the lamps.
I knew that nothing stranger
had ever happened, that nothing
stranger could ever happen.

Why should I be my aunt,   75
or me, or anyone?
What similarities —
boots, hands, the family voice
I felt in my throat, or even
the *National Geographic*   80
and those awful hanging breasts —
held us all together
or made us all just one?
How — I didn't know any
word for it — how "unlikely" . . .   85

How had I come to be here,
like them, and overhear
a cry of pain that could have
got loud and worse but hadn't?

The waiting room was bright   90
and too hot. It was sliding
beneath a big black wave,
another, and another.

Then I was back in it.
The War was on. Outside,   95
in Worcester, Massachusetts,
were night and slush and cold,
and it was still the fifth
of February, 1918.[4]

[1971, 1983]

---

4. **the fifth of February, 1918:** On this date, the liner *Tuscania* was sunk by a German submarine off the coast of Scotland. More than two hundred men died in the sinking, the first of a ship carrying American troops to Europe. Outraged public opinion in the United States led to an escalation of American involvement in World War I, which the country had entered in April 1917.

ONE ART[1]

The art of losing isn't hard to master;
so many things seem filled with the intent
to be lost that their loss is no disaster.

Lose something every day. Accept the fluster
of lost door keys, the hour badly spent.   5
The art of losing isn't hard to master.

Then practice losing farther, losing faster:
places, and names, and where it was you meant
to travel. None of these will bring disaster.

I lost my mother's watch. And look! my last, or   10
next-to-last, of three loved houses went.
The art of losing isn't hard to master.

I lost two cities, lovely ones. And, vaster,
some realms I owned, two rivers, a continent.
I miss them, but it wasn't a disaster.   15

---

1. **One Art:** This nineteen-line poem is a villanelle, a complex form composed of five triplets (a three-line stanza rhymed *a b a*) and a concluding quatrain (a four-line stanza rhymed *a b a b*). The form employs only two rhymes, and alternating stanzas end with the same last line.

— Even losing you (the joking voice, a gesture
I love) I shan't have lied. It's evident
the art of losing's not too hard to master
though it may look like (*Write* it!) like disaster.

[1976, 1983]

Tennessee Williams

[1911-1983]

Thomas Lanier Williams was born on March 26, 1911, in Columbus, Mississippi. He was the first of three children born to Edwina Dakin Williams, the daughter of a minister, and Cornelius Coffin Williams, a traveling shoe salesman from Tennessee. Because his father was often away from home, the family lived with his mother's parents, with whom Williams became very close. In 1918, the family moved to an apartment in St. Louis, Missouri, where Cornelius Williams took a job as the manager of a shoe company. The Williamses' marriage became increasingly strained, and their children grew up in a contentious, sometimes violent household. Cornelius Williams often taunted his oldest son for siding with his mother, calling him "Miss Nancy." Using a typewriter his mother bought for him, Williams escaped into writing. "Our literary boy," as he was called in a yearbook, contributed stories to school newspapers and won third prize in an essay contest sponsored by the sophisticated magazine *Smart Set* in 1927. The following year, he published a horror story in the pulp magazine *Weird Tales*. After a tour of Europe with his grandfather in the summer of 1929, Williams enrolled in the University of Missouri. Bored by the courses required for his journalism major, he preferred studying poetry and drama, especially the plays of Eugene O'Neill and the Swedish playwright August Strindberg. In an effort to earn extra money, he submitted works to literary contests and won an honorable mention for his first play, *Beauty Is the Word.*

Despite his early successes and promising start, Williams struggled to make his way as a writer. His father, unhappy with his son's isolation and deep absorption in literature, insisted that Williams join a fraternity and take military training courses. When he failed those courses in his junior year, his angry father withdrew him from the university in 1932, and Williams was forced to return home to St. Louis. He worked in his father's

Tennessee Williams

This photograph of Williams was taken in the late 1940s, when he was at the height of his early fame as one of the major American dramatists to emerge in the years after World War II.

shoe factory during the day and wrote at night and on weekends, submitting his stories, plays, and poems to literary contests and magazines. In 1935, mentally and physically exhausted, he claimed that he had suffered a heart attack and went to recover at his grandparents' home in Memphis. While there, his one-act play "Cairo! Shanghai! Bombay!" was performed by a local theater, and Williams resolved to become a playwright. He returned to St. Louis, where with the financial help of his grandfather Williams enrolled at Washington University in the fall of 1936. Two of his plays were performed there, and Williams subsequently transferred to the University of Iowa, where he studied playwriting and production and graduated with a BA in 1938. Apparently because of his southern accent, the students there called him "Tennessee," a name Williams soon adopted to sign his work. In the meantime, the situation in the family home in St. Louis had further deteriorated as his sister, Rose, slipped into mental illness. Eager to be on his own and away from home, Williams took a short-term job with the Works Progress Administration in New Orleans. As he recalled in his *Memoirs* (1975), he first came out as a gay man while living a bohemian life in the French Quarter. In 1939, Williams finally achieved a major breakthrough when a group of his one-act plays, *American Blues*, won a special award in a play contest sponsored by the Group Theatre in New York City.

During the following five years, Williams fulfilled his dream of becoming a playwright. The head of the play department at the Group Theatre contacted the prominent literary agent Audrey Wood, who agreed to take Williams on and helped secure him a Rockefeller Foundation grant of $1,000. With the money, Williams went to New York City in 1940. He enrolled in a playwriting seminar at the New School for Social Research and wrote the autobiographical *Battle of Angels*, which was produced by the prestigious Theater Guild. The play opened in Boston, then notorious for the provincialism and intellectual snobbery of its critics, who dubbed the drama "Delta dirt" and described its author as a "hillbilly." Devastated by the failure, Williams left New York and returned to New Orleans. He visited St. Louis in 1943, after he learned that his sister had undergone a lobotomy, a procedure then used in extreme cases of schizophrenia. The operation reduced her to an infantile state, and she was institutionalized for the rest of her life. Williams was horrified by his parents' decision to allow the operation and deeply guilty about his failure to prevent it. He soon left home to take a job as a scriptwriter in Hollywood with MGM. The studio rejected several of his ideas for films, including a screen synopsis of what Williams recast as "A Memory Play," *The Glass Menagerie*. Loosely based on his sister's withdrawal from reality and his own efforts to escape their suffocating home in St. Louis, the play ran for 561 performances on Broadway during 1945-46. Shortly after it closed, he achieved even greater fame with *A Streetcar Named Desire*, which opened to universal acclaim in December 1947, ran for more than two years on Broadway, and was awarded the Pulitzer Prize.

Williams is a realistic writer . . . primarily interested in passion, in ecstasy, in creating a synthesis of his conflicting feelings.

–Arthur Miller

Although he remained a major force in American theater, Williams never again quite matched the critical and commercial success of his early triumphs. He soon began the most significant and long-lasting romantic relationship of his life with Frank Merlo, whom Williams met in New Orleans in 1947. For the first time, he was also financially secure, since he earned several million dollars from the royalties and the sale of screen rights to *A Streetcar Named Desire*. Many of his later plays were also made into successful movies, including his Broadway hits *Cat on a Hot Tin Roof* (1955), *Sweet Bird of Youth* (1959), and *The Night of the Iguana* (1961). During the 1960s, which Williams described in his *Memoirs* as his "lost decade," his years of drinking and drug abuse began to catch up with him. After Merlo died of lung cancer in 1963, Williams became so severely depressed that his brother, Dakin, committed him to a psychiatric hospital in 1969. There, Williams was temporarily forced to withdraw from drugs and alcohol, and he emerged from the hospital healthier than he had been for many years. But he found that tastes were changing in American drama, and his career was essentially over. Nonetheless, the prolific Williams continued to write steadily and completed his final play only a month before he died on February 24, 1983.

Reading Williams's *Portrait of a Madonna*.   In addition to forty-five full-length dramas, Williams wrote more than sixty one-act plays, of which one of the best known is *Portrait of a Madonna*. Alternately titled

Portrait of a Madonna

Jessica Tandy, who played Lucretia Collins in the first performance of *Portrait of a Madonna* in 1946, reprised the role on Broadway in 1959. With Tandy in this scene from that later production are Margot Stevenson as the Nurse and John Randolph as Mr. Abrams.

Port Mad or *The Leafless Block*, it was completed early in 1940, when Williams suggested to his agent that the play might "be bound with two other new ones, possibly under the inclusive title 'The Lonely Heart' as all three are about rather desolate people and nostalgic in atmosphere." Following the success of *The Glass Menagerie* on Broadway, *Portrait of a Madonna* was first performed in 1946 at the Actor's Laboratory Theater in Los Angeles, where it was staged by Hume Cronyn. The role of Lucretia Collins was played by Jessica Tandy, who once called *Portrait of a Madonna* a "superb play," adding: "It's got everything in it. It's a perfect little jewel of a play." Lucretia, an aging southern belle from New Orleans living in exile in an unnamed northern city and lost in memories of the past, was also the forerunner of Williams's most famous female character, Blanche DuBois, the tragic figure at the center of *A Streetcar Named Desire*. In fact, when Williams saw the Los Angeles production of *Portrait of a Madonna*, he immediately wanted Tandy for the role of Blanche DuBois, which she played when *A Streetcar Named Desire* opened on Broadway in 1947. The text of *Portrait of a Madonna* is taken from the first publication in *27 Wagons Full of Cotton and Other Plays* (1945).

bedfordstmartins.com/ americanlit *for research links on Williams*

PORTRAIT OF A MADONNA[1]

Respectfully dedicated to the talent and charm of Miss Lillian Gish.

CHARACTERS

MISS LUCRETIA COLLINS.   THE DOCTOR.

THE PORTER.[2]   THE NURSE.

THE ELEVATOR BOY.   MR. ABRAMS.

SCENE

The living room of a moderate-priced city apartment. The furnishings are old-fashioned and everything is in a state of neglect and disorder. There is a door in the back wall to a bedroom, and on the right to the outside hall.

MISS COLLINS: Richard! (*The door bursts open and Miss Collins rushes out, distractedly. She is a middle-aged spinster, very slight and hunched of figure with a desiccated face that is flushed with excitement. Her hair is arranged in curls that would become a young girl and she wears a frilly negligee[3] which might have come from an old hope chest of a period considerably earlier.*) No, no, no, no! I don't care if the whole church hears about it! (*She frenziedly snatches up the phone.*) Manager, I've got to

---

1. **Portrait of a Madonna:** In Christian art the Madonna is the Virgin Mary, who is usually shown holding the infant Jesus. Williams dedicated the play to Lillian Gish (1893–1993), a stage actor who became a star of silent films. Gish, who was renowned for her angelic beauty and acting skill, was often cast as an innocent victim who is rescued in the nick of time. Like many other actors, however, she was not able to make the transition to "talkies" when they developed in the late 1920s. She consequently returned to the theater and played Lucretia Collins in a production of *Portrait of a Madonna* in Berlin, Germany, in 1957.
2. **The Porter:** A person employed by an apartment building to monitor the main entrance.
3. *negligee*: A woman's robe, typically made of a light, translucent fabric.

speak to the manager! Hurry, oh, please hurry, there's a *man—*! (*wildly aside as if to an invisible figure*) Lost all respect, absolutely no respect! . . . Mr. Abrams? (*in a tense hushed voice*) I don't want any reporters to hear about this but something awful has been going on upstairs. Yes, this is Miss Collins' apartment on the top floor. I've refrained from making any complaint because of my connections with the church. I used to be assistant to the Sunday School superintendent and I once had the primary class. I helped them put on the Christmas pageant. I made the dress for the Virgin and Mother, made robes for the Wise Men. Yes, and now this has happened, I'm not responsible for it, but night after night after night this man has been coming into my apartment and—indulging his senses! Do you understand? Not once but repeatedly, Mr. Abrams! I don't know whether he comes in the door or the window or up the fire-escape or whether there's some secret entrance they know about at the church, but he's here now, in my bedroom, and I can't force him to leave, I'll have to have some assistance! No, he isn't a thief, Mr. Abrams, he comes of a very fine family in Webb, Mississippi, but this woman has ruined his character, she's destroyed his respect for ladies! Mr. Abrams? Mr. Abrams! Oh, goodness! (*She slams up the receiver and looks distractedly about for a moment; then rushes back into the bedroom.*) Richard! (*The door slams shut. After a few moments an old porter enters in drab gray cover-alls. He looks about with a sorrowfully humorous curiosity, then timidly calls.*)

PORTER: Miss Collins? (*The elevator door slams open in hall and the Elevator Boy, wearing a uniform, comes in.*)

ELEVATOR BOY: Where is she?

PORTER: Gone in 'er bedroom.

ELEVATOR BOY: (*grinning*) She got him in there with her?

PORTER: Sounds like it. (*Miss Collins' voice can be heard faintly protesting with the mysterious intruder.*)

ELEVATOR BOY: What'd Abrams tell yuh to do?

PORTER: Stay here an' keep a watch on 'er till they git here.

ELEVATOR BOY: Jesus.

PORTER: Close 'at door.

ELEVATOR BOY: I gotta leave it open a little so I can hear the buzzer. Ain't this place a holy sight though?

PORTER: Don't look like it's had a good cleaning in fifteen or twenty years. I bet it ain't either. Abrams'll bust a blood vessel when he takes a lookit them walls.

ELEVATOR BOY: How comes it's in this condition?

PORTER: She wouldn't let no one in.

ELEVATOR BOY: Not even the paper-hangers?

PORTER: Naw. Not even the plumbers. The plaster washed down in the bathroom underneath hers an' she admitted her plumbin' had been stopped up. Mr. Abrams had to let the plumber in with this here pass-key when she went out for a while.

ELEVATOR BOY: Holy Jeez. I wunner if she's got money stashed around here. A lotta freaks do stick away big sums of money in ole mattresses an' things.

PORTER: She ain't. She got a monthly pension check or something she always turned over to Mr. Abrams to dole it out to 'er. She tole him that Southern ladies was never brought up to manage finanshul affairs. Lately the checks quit comin'.

ELEVATOR BOY: Yeah?

PORTER: The pension give out or somethin'. Abrams says he got a contribution from the church to keep 'er on here without 'er knowin' about it. She's proud as a peacock's tail in spite of 'er awful appearance.

ELEVATOR BOY: Lissen to 'er in there!

PORTER: What's she sayin'?

ELEVATOR BOY: Apologizin' to him! For callin' the *police!*

PORTER: She thinks police 're comin'?

MISS COLLINS: (*from bedroom*) Stop it, it's got to stop!

ELEVATOR BOY: Fightin' to protect her honor again! What a commotion, no wunner folks are complainin'!

PORTER: (*lighting his pipe*) This here'll be the last time.

ELEVATOR BOY: She's goin' out, huh?

PORTER: (*blowing out the match*) Tonight.

ELEVATOR BOY: Where'll she go?

PORTER: (*slowly moving to the old gramophone*) She'll go to the state asylum.

ELEVATOR BOY: Holy G!

PORTER: Remember this ole number? (*He puts on a record of "I'm Forever Blowing Bubbles."*[4])

ELEVATOR BOY: Naw. When did that come out?

PORTER: Before your time, sonny boy. Machine needs oilin'. (*He takes out small oil-can and applies oil about the crank and other parts of gramophone.*)

ELEVATOR BOY: How long is the old girl been here?

PORTER: Abrams says she's been livin' here twenty-five, thirty years, since before he got to be manager even.

ELEVATOR BOY: Livin' alone all that time?

PORTER: She had an old mother died of an operation about fifteen years ago. Since then she ain't gone out of the place excep' on Sundays to church or Friday nights to some kind of religious meeting.

ELEVATOR BOY: Got an awful lot of ol' magazines piled aroun' here.

PORTER: She used to collect 'em. She'd go out in back and fish 'em out of the incinerator.

ELEVATOR BOY: What'n hell for?

PORTER: Mr. Abrams says she used to cut out the Campbell soup kids. Them red-tomato-headed kewpie dolls that go with the soup advertisements. You seen 'em, ain'tcha?

ELEVATOR BOY: Uh-huh.

PORTER: She made a collection of 'em. Filled a big lot of scrapbooks with them paper kiddies an' took 'em down to the Children's Hospitals on Xmas Eve an' Easter Sunday, exactly twicet a year. Sounds better, don't it? (*referring to gramophone, which resumes its faint, wheedling music*) Eliminated some a that crankin' noise . . .

ELEVATOR BOY: I didn't know that she'd been nuts *that* long.

PORTER: Who's nuts an' who ain't? If you ask me the world is populated with people that's just as peculiar as she is.

---

4. *"I'm Forever Blowing Bubbles"*: A widely performed, popular song composed by John Kellette for the Broadway musical revue *The Passing Show of 1918*.

ELEVATOR BOY: Hell. She don't have brain *one*.

PORTER: There's important people in Europe got less'n she's got. Tonight they're takin' her off 'n' lockin' her up. They'd do a lot better to leave 'er go an' lock up some a them maniacs over there. She's harmless; they ain't. They kill millions of people an' go scot free!

ELEVATOR BOY: An ole woman like her is disgusting, though, imaginin' somebody's raped her.

PORTER: Pitiful, not disgusting. Watch out for them cigarette ashes.

ELEVATOR BOY: What's uh diff'rence? So much dust you can't see it. All a this here goes out in the morning, don't it?

PORTER: Uh-huh.

ELEVATOR BOY: I think I'll take a couple a those ole records as curiosities for my girl friend. She's got a portable in 'er bedroom, she says it's better with music!

PORTER: Leave 'em alone. She's still got 'er property rights.

ELEVATOR BOY: Aw, she's got all she wants with them dream-lovers of hers!

PORTER: *Hush up!* (*He makes a warning gesture as Miss Collins enters from bedroom. Her appearance is that of a ravaged woman. She leans exhaustedly in the doorway, hands clasped over her flat, virginal bosom.*)

MISS COLLINS: (*breathlessly*) Oh, Richard — Richard . . .

PORTER: (*coughing*) Miss — Collins.

ELEVATOR BOY: Hello, Miss Collins.

MISS COLLINS: (*just noticing the men*) Goodness! You've arrived already! Mother didn't tell me you were here! (*Self-consciously she touches her ridiculous corkscrew curls with the faded pink ribbon tied through them. Her manner becomes that of a slightly coquettish but prim little Southern belle.*) I must ask you gentlemen to excuse the terrible disorder.

PORTER: That's all right, Miss Collins.

MISS COLLINS: It's the maid's day off. Your No'thern girls receive such excellent domestic training, but in the South it was never considered essential for a girl to have anything but prettiness and charm! (*She laughs girlishly.*) Please do sit down. Is it too close? Would you like a window open?

PORTER: No, Miss Collins.

MISS COLLINS: (*advancing with delicate grace to the sofa*) Mother will bring in something cool after while. . . . Oh, my! (*She touches her forehead.*)

PORTER: (*kindly*) Is anything wrong, Miss Collins?

MISS COLLINS: Oh, no, no, thank you, nothing! My head is a little bit heavy. I'm always a little bit — malarial[5] — this time of year! (*She sways dizzily as she starts to sink down on the sofa.*)

PORTER: (*helping her*) Careful there, Miss Collins.

MISS COLLINS: (*vaguely*) Yes, it is, I hadn't noticed before. (*She peers at them nearsightedly with a hesitant smile.*) You gentlemen have come from the church?

---

5. **malarial:** Malaria is a tropical disease characterized by an intermittent fever caused by parasites transmitted by mosquitoes.

PORTER: No, ma'am. I'm Nick, the porter, Miss Collins, and this boy here is Frank that runs the elevator.

MISS COLLINS: (*stiffening a little*) Oh? . . . I don't understand.

PORTER: (*gently*) Mr. Abrams just asked me to drop in here an' see if you was getting along all right.

MISS COLLINS: Oh! Then he must have informed you of what's been going on in here!

PORTER: He mentioned some kind of – disturbance.

MISS COLLINS: Yes! Isn't it outrageous? But it mustn't go any further, you understand. I mean you mustn't repeat it to other people.

PORTER: No, I wouldn't say nothing.

MISS COLLINS: Not a word of it, please!

ELEVATOR BOY: Is the man still here, Miss Collins?

MISS COLLINS: Oh, no. No, he's gone now.

ELEVATOR BOY: How did he go, out the bedroom window, Miss Collins?

MISS COLLINS: (*vaguely*) Yes. . . .

ELEVATOR BOY: I seen a guy that could do that once. He crawled straight up the side of the building. They called him The Human Fly! Gosh, that's a wonderful publicity angle, Miss Collins – "Beautiful Young Society Lady Raped by The Human Fly!"

PORTER: (*nudging him sharply*) Git back in your cracker box!

MISS COLLINS: Publicity? No! It would be so humiliating! Mr. Abrams surely hasn't reported it to the papers!

PORTER: No, ma'am. Don't listen to this smarty pants.

MISS COLLINS: (*touching her curls*) Will pictures be taken, you think? There's one of him on the mantel.

ELEVATOR BOY: (*going to the mantel*) This one here, Miss Collins?

MISS COLLINS: Yes. Of the Sunday School faculty picnic. I had the little kindergardeners that year and he had the older boys. We rode in the cab of a railroad locomotive from Webb to Crystal Springs. (*She covers her ears with a girlish grimace and toss of her curls.*) Oh, how the steam-whistle blew! Blew! (*giggling*) Blewwwww! It frightened me so, he put his arm round my shoulders! But she was there, too, though she had no business being. She grabbed his hat and stuck it on the back of her head and they – they *rassled* for it, they actually *rassled* together! Everyone said it was *shameless!* Don't you think that it was?

PORTER: Yes, Miss Collins.

MISS COLLINS: That's the picture, the one in the silver frame up there on the mantel. We cooled the watermelon in the springs and afterwards played games. She hid somewhere and he took ages to find her. It got to be dark and he hadn't found her yet and everyone whispered and giggled about it and finally they came back together – her hangin' on to his arm like a common little strumpet – and Daisy Belle Huston shrieked out, "Look, everybody, the seat of Evelyn's skirt!" It was – covered with – grass-stains! Did you ever hear of anything as outrageous? It didn't faze her, though, she laughed like it was something very, very amusing! Rather *triumphant* she was!

ELEVATOR BOY: Which one is him, Miss Collins?

MISS COLLINS: The tall one in the blue shirt holding onto one of my curls. He loved to play with them.

ELEVATOR BOY: Quite a Romeo — 1910 model, huh?

MISS COLLINS: (*vaguely*) Do you? It's nothing, really, but I like the lace on the collar. I said to Mother, "Even if I don't wear it, Mother, it will be *so* nice for my hope-chest!"[6]

ELEVATOR BOY: How was he dressed tonight when he climbed into your balcony, Miss Collins?

MISS COLLINS: Pardon?

ELEVATOR BOY: Did he still wear that nifty little stick-candy-striped blue shirt with the celluloid collar?

MISS COLLINS: He hasn't changed.

ELEVATOR BOY: Oughta be easy to pick him up in that. What color pants did he wear?

MISS COLLINS: (*vaguely*) I don't remember.

ELEVATOR BOY: Maybe he didn't wear any. Shimmied out of 'em on the way up the wall! You could get him on grounds of indecent exposure, Miss Collins!

PORTER: (*grasping his arm*) Cut that or git back in your cage! Understand?

ELEVATOR BOY: (*snickering*) Take it easy. She don't hear a thing.

PORTER: Well, you keep a decent tongue or get the hell out. Miss Collins here is a lady. You understand that?

ELEVATOR BOY: Okay. She's Shoiley Temple.[7]

PORTER: She's a *lady!*

ELEVATOR BOY: Yeah! (*He returns to the gramophone and looks through the records.*)

MISS COLLINS: I really shouldn't have created this disturbance. When the officers come I'll have to explain that to them. But you can understand my feelings, can't you?

PORTER: Sure, Miss Collins.

MISS COLLINS: When men take advantage of common white-trash women who smoke in public there is probably some excuse for it, but when it occurs to a lady who is single and always com-*pletely* above reproach in her moral behavior, there's really nothing to do but call for police protection! Unless of course the girl is fortunate enough to have a father and brothers who can take care of the matter privately without any scandal.

PORTER: Sure. That's right, Miss Collins.

MISS COLLINS: Of course it's bound to cause a great deal of very disagreeable talk. Especially 'round the *church!* Are you gentlemen Episcopalian?

PORTER: No, ma'am. Catholic, Miss Collins.

MISS COLLINS: Oh. Well, I suppose you know in England we're known as the English Catholic church. We have direct Apostolic succession through St. Paul who christened the Early Angles — which is what the original English people were called — and established the English branch of the Catholic church over there. So when you hear

---

6. **hope-chest:** A chest in which a young woman collects clothing and household items in anticipation of her marriage.

7. **Shoiley Temple:** Shirley Temple (b. 1928), an enormously popular child film star of the 1930s.

ignorant people claim that our church was founded by—by Henry the *Eighth*—that horrible, *lecher*ous old man who had so many wives—as many as *Blue*-beard they say!—you can see how ridiculous it *is* and how thoroughly ob*nox*-ious to anybody who really *knows* and under*stands* Church *His*tory!

PORTER: (*comfortingly*) Sure, Miss Collins. Everybody knows that.

MISS COLLINS: I wish they *did*, but they need to be in*structed*! Before he died, my father was Rector at the Church of St. Michael and St. George at Glorious Hill, Mississippi. . . . I've literally grown up right in the very *shadow* of the Episcopal church. At Pass Christian and Natchez, Biloxi, Gulfport, Port Gibson, Columbus and Glorious Hill![8] (*with gentle, bewildered sadness*) But you know I sometimes suspect that there has been some kind of spiritual schism in the modern church. These northern dioceses have completely departed from the good old church traditions. For instance our Rector at the Church of the Holy Communion has never darkened my door. It's a fashionable church and he's terribly busy, but even so you'd think he might have time to make a stranger in the congregation feel at home. But he doesn't though! Nobody seems to have the time any more. . . . (*She grows more excited as her mind sinks back into illusion.*) I ought not to mention this, but do you know they actually take a malicious de-*light* over there at the Holy Communion—where I've recently transferred my letter[9]—in what's been going on here at night in this apartment? *Yes!* (*She laughs wildly and throws up her hands.*) They take a malicious de*LIGHT* in it!! (*She catches her breath and gropes vaguely about her wrapper.*)

PORTER: You lookin' for somethin', Miss Collins?

MISS COLLINS: My—handkerchief . . . (*She is blinking her eyes against tears.*)

PORTER: (*removing a rag from his pocket*) Here. Use this, Miss Collins. It's just a rag but it's clean, except along that edge where I wiped off the phonograph handle.

MISS COLLINS: Thanks. You gentlemen are very kind. Mother will bring in something cool after while. . . .

ELEVATOR BOY: (*placing a record on machine*) This one is got some kind of foreign title. (*The record begins to play Tschaikowsky's "None But the Lonely Heart."[10]*)

MISS COLLINS: (*stuffing the rag daintily in her bosom*) Excuse me, please. Is the weather nice outside?

PORTER: (*huskily*) Yes, it's nice, Miss Collins.

MISS COLLINS: (*dreamily*) So wa'm for this time of year. I wore my little astrakhan cape[11] to service but had to *carry* it *home*, as the weight of it actually seemed *oppres*sive to me. (*Her eyes fall shut.*) The sidewalks seem so dreadfully long in summer. . . .

ELEVATOR BOY: This ain't summer, Miss Collins.

---

8. **Pass Christian . . . Glorious Hill:** All are cities in Mississippi except the fictional town of Glorious Hill.
9. **transferred my letter:** That is, transferred her church membership.
10. **"None But the Lonely Heart":** A melancholy romance for voice and piano by the Russian composer Pyotr Ilyich Tchaikovsky (1840–1893). An English translation of the poem to which the romance is set begins: "None but the lonely heart / Can know my sadness / Alone and parted / Far from joy and gladness."
11. **astrakhan cape:** A woman's wrap made of a cloth resembling the curly fleece of the young karakul lambs of central Asia.

MISS COLLINS: (*dreamily*) I used to think I'd never get to the end of that last block. And that's the block where all the trees went down in the big tornado. The walk is simply *glit*-tering with sunlight. (*pressing her eyelids*) Impossible to shade your face and I *do* perspire so freely! (*She touches her forehead daintily with the rag.*) Not a branch, not a leaf to give you a little protection! You simply *have* to en-*dure* it. Turn your hideous red face away from all the front-porches and walk as fast as you decently *can* till you get *by* them! Oh, dear, dear Savior, sometimes you're not so lucky and you *meet* people and have to *smile!* You can't *avoid* them unless you cut *across* and that's so *ob*-vious, you know. . . . People would say you're pe*cu*liar. . . . His house is right in the middle of that awful leafless block, *their* house, his and *hers*, and they have an auto-mobile and always get home early and sit on the porch and *watch* me walking by – Oh, Father in Heaven – with a ma*li*cious de*light!* (*She averts her face in remembered torture.*) She has such *penetrating* eyes, they look straight through me. She sees that terrible choking thing in my throat and the pain I have in *here* – (*touching her chest*) – and she points it out and laughs and whispers to him, "There she goes with her shiny big red nose, the poor old maid – that *loves* you!" (*She chokes and hides her face in the rag.*)

PORTER: Maybe you better forget all that, Miss Collins.

MISS COLLINS: Never, never forget it! Never, never! I left my parasol once – the one with long white fringe that belonged to Mother – I left it behind in the cloak-room at the church so I didn't have anything to cover my face with when I walked by, and I couldn't turn back either, with all those people behind me – giggling back of me, poking fun at my clothes! Oh, dear, dear! I had to walk straight forward – past the last elm tree and into that *merciless* sunlight. Oh! It beat down on me, *scorching* me! *Whips!* . . . Oh, Jesus! . . . Over my face and my body! . . . I tried to walk on fast but was dizzy and they kept closer behind me –! I stumbled, I nearly fell, and all of them burst out laughing! My face turned so *horribly* red, it got so red and wet, I knew how ugly it was in all that merciless glare – not a single shadow to hide in! And then – (*Her face contorts with fear.*) – their automobile drove up in front of their house, right where I had to pass by it, and *she* stepped out, in white, so fresh and easy, her stomach round with a baby, the first of the *six.* Oh, God! . . . And he stood smiling behind her, white and easy and cool, and they stood there waiting for me. *Waiting!* I had to keep on. What else could I do? I couldn't turn *back*, could I? *No!* I said dear *God*, strike me *dead!* He didn't, though. I put my head way down like I couldn't see them! You know what she did? She stretched out her hand to *stop* me! And *he* – he stepped up straight in front of me, *smiling*, block-ing the walk with his terrible big white body! *"Lucretia,"* he said, "Lucretia *Collins!"* I – I tried to speak but I couldn't, the breath went out of my body! I covered my face and – ran! . . . Ran! . . . Ran! (*beating the arm of the sofa*) Till I reached the end of the block – and the elm trees – *started* again. . . . Oh, Merciful Christ in Heaven, how *kind* they were! (*She leans back exhaustedly, her hand relaxed on sofa. She pauses and the music ends.*) I said to Mother, "Mother, we've got to leave town!" We *did* after that. And now after all these years he's finally remembered and come *back!* Moved away from that house and the woman and come *here* – I saw him in the back of the church one day. I wasn't sure – but it *was.* The night after that was the night that he first broke in — and indulged his senses with me. . . . He doesn't realize that I've changed, that I can't feel again the way that I used to feel, now that he's got six children by that Cincinnati girl — three in high-school already! Six! Think of that? Six children! I don't know what he'll say when he knows another one's coming! He'll probably blame *me* for it because a man always *does!* In spite of the fact that he *forced* me!

ELEVATOR BOY: (*grinning*) Did you say — a *baby,* Miss Collins?

MISS COLLINS: (*lowering her eyes but speaking with tenderness and pride*) Yes — I'm expecting a *child.*

ELEVATOR BOY: *Jeez!* (*He claps his hand over his mouth and turns away quickly.*)

MISS COLLINS: Even if it's not legitimate, I think it has a perfect right to its father's name — don't you?

PORTER: Yes. Sure, Miss Collins.

MISS COLLINS: A child is innocent and pure. No matter how it's conceived. And it must *not* be made to suffer! So I intend to dispose of the little property Cousin Ethel left me and give the child a private education where it won't come under the evil influence of the Christian church! I want to make sure that it doesn't grow up in the shadow of the cross and then have to walk along blocks that scorch you with terrible sunlight! (*The elevator buzzer sounds from the hall.*)

PORTER: Frank! Somebody wants to come up. (*The Elevator Boy goes out. The elevator door bangs shut. The Porter clears his throat.*) Yes, it'd be better — to go off some place else.

MISS COLLINS: If only I had the courage — but I don't. I've grown so used to it here, and people outside — it's always so *hard,* to *face* them!

PORTER: Maybe you won't — have to face nobody, Miss Collins. (*The elevator door clangs open.*)

MISS COLLINS: (*rising fearfully*) Is someone coming — here?

PORTER: You just take it easy, Miss Collins.

MISS COLLINS: If that's the officers coming for Richard, tell them to go away. I've decided not to prosecute Mr. Martin. (*Mr. Abrams enters with the Doctor and the Nurse. The Elevator Boy gawks from the doorway. The Doctor is the weary, professional type, the Nurse hard and efficient. Mr. Abrams is a small, kindly person, sincerely troubled by the situation.*)

MISS COLLINS: (*shrinking back, her voice faltering*) I've decided not to — prosecute Mr. Martin . . .

DOCTOR: Miss Collins?

MR. ABRAMS: (*with attempted heartiness*) Yes, this is the lady you wanted to meet, Dr. White.

DOCTOR: Hmmm. (*briskly to the Nurse*) Go in her bedroom and get a few things together.

NURSE: Yes, sir. (*She goes quickly across to the bedroom.*)

MISS COLLINS: (*fearfully shrinking*) Things?

DOCTOR: Yes, Miss Tyler will help you pack up an overnight bag. (*smiling mechanically*) A strange place always seems more homelike the first few days when we have a few of our little personal articles around us.

MISS COLLINS: A strange — place?

DOCTOR: (*carelessly, making a memorandum*) Don't be disturbed, Miss Collins.

MISS COLLINS: I know! (*excitedly*) You've come from the Holy Communion to place me under arrest! On moral charges!

MR. ABRAMS: Oh, no, Miss Collins, you got the wrong idea. This is a doctor who —

DOCTOR: (*impatiently*) Now, now, you're just going away for a while till things get straightened out. (*He glances at his watch.*) Two-twenty-five! Miss Tyler?

NURSE: Coming!

MISS COLLINS: (*with slow and sad comprehension*) Oh. . . . I'm going away. . . .

MR. ABRAMS: She was always a lady, Doctor, such a perfect lady.

DOCTOR: Yes. No doubt.

MR. ABRAMS: It seems too bad!

MISS COLLINS: Let me — write him a note. A pencil? Please?

MR. ABRAMS: Here, Miss Collins. (*She takes the pencil and crouches over the table. The Nurse comes out with a hard, forced smile, carrying a suitcase.*)

DOCTOR: Ready, Miss Tyler?

NURSE: All ready, Dr. White. (*She goes up to Miss Collins.*) Come along, dear, we can tend to that later!

MR. ABRAMS: (*sharply*) Let her finish the note!

MISS COLLINS: (*straightening with a frightened smile*) It's — finished.

NURSE: All right, dear, come along. (*She propels her firmly toward the door.*)

MISS COLLINS: (*turning suddenly back*) Oh, Mr. Abrams!

MR. ABRAMS: Yes, Miss Collins?

MISS COLLINS: If he should come again — and find me gone — I'd rather you didn't tell him — about the baby. . . . I think its better for *me* to tell him *that*. (*gently smiling*) You know how men *are*, don't you?

MR. ABRAMS: Yes, Miss Collins.

PORTER: Goodbye, Miss Collins. (*The Nurse pulls firmly at her arm. She smiles over her shoulder with a slight apologetic gesture.*)

MISS COLLINS: Mother will bring in — something cool — after while . . . (*She disappears down the hall with the Nurse. The elevator door clangs shut with the metallic sound of a locked cage. The wires hum.*)

MR. ABRAMS: She wrote him a note.

PORTER: What did she write, Mr. Abrams?

MR. ABRAMS: "Dear — Richard. I'm going away for a while. But don't worry, I'll be back. I have a secret to tell you. Love — Lucretia." (*He coughs.*) We got to clear out this stuff an' pile it down in the basement till I find out where it goes.

PORTER: (*dully*) Tonight, Mr. Abrams?

MR. ABRAMS: (*roughly to hide his feeling*) No, no, not tonight, you old fool. Enough has happened tonight! (*then gently*) We can do it tomorrow. Turn out that bedroom light — and close the window. (*Music playing softly becomes audible as the men go out slowly, closing the door, and the light fades out.*)

Curtain

[1945]

Robert Hayden

[1913-1980]

Robert Hayden was born Asa Bundy Sheffey on August 4, 1913, in Detroit, Michigan, to Asa Sheffey, a black laborer from Kentucky, and Ruth Finn Sheffey, a woman of mixed racial ancestry with theatrical ambitions. When Hayden was eighteen months old, his parents separated, and he was raised by an African American couple, William Hayden, a laborer, and Sue Ellen Hayden, a former maid. Although they never filed adoption papers, they rechristened the child Robert Earl Hayden. The Haydens, who were ill suited to one another and often without jobs, lived in a poor, primarily black section of Detroit called "Paradise Valley." As an escape from his difficult home life, Hayden read constantly, began writing stories, plays, and poems, and became actively involved in a dramatic group at the Second Baptist Church. When he was about sixteen, he began reading modern poetry, and he was especially drawn to the work of Carl Sandburg, Edna St. Vincent Millay, and the two most prominent poets of the Harlem Renaissance, Countee Cullen and Langston Hughes. With the financial help of a relative, Hayden also studied violin at the Detroit Institute of Musical Art. Because he was acutely nearsighted, he was sent to a special, predominantly white school during his senior year of high school. After he graduated in 1930, he published his first poem, "Africa," in a black literary magazine, *Abbot's Monthly*.

Robert Hayden

This undated photograph was probably taken around 1962, the year Hayden published his innovative collection, *A Ballad of Remembrance*.

Like many of his contemporaries, Hayden struggled to support himself and his writing during the Great Depression and World War II. Living at home, he secured a tuition scholarship to study at Detroit City College (now Wayne State University), where he enrolled in 1932. Four years later, when he was only one credit hour short of graduation, he was forced to withdraw in order to find work. Because he met the legal requirement of pauperism, he got a job as a writer and researcher for the Federal Writers' Project in Detroit. From 1936 to 1940, Hayden conducted research on African American history, the subject of many of his later poems. He also began to take graduate courses at the University of Michigan in Ann Arbor, where he won a prize for a collection of his poems, *Heart-Shape in the Dust*, which was subsequently published by a local press in 1940. That year, he left home and married Erma Inez Morris, a pianist and music teacher who strongly encouraged Hayden's aspirations as a poet. In 1941, he became a full-time student at Michigan, where Hayden studied with his most influential mentor, the distinguished British poet W. H. Auden. Hayden was awarded another prize for an unpublished collection of poems, "The Black Spear," some of which had previously appeared in the influential anthology *The Negro Caravan* (1941), edited by Sterling Brown. Long unhappy with the Baptist fundamentalism in which he was raised, Hayden converted to the Baha'i World Faith, a religion that promotes the unity of all human beings and world peace. In 1944, he was awarded an MA from Michigan, where he worked as a teaching assistant until he accepted a position as a professor of English at the historically black Fisk University in Nashville, Tennessee, in 1946.

Hayden was a consummate poet and a moral historian as well.
—Michael S. Harper

Hayden did not achieve widespread recognition as a poet until the final years of his life. His first poem in a major literary magazine, a tribute to the nineteenth-century African American leader Frederick Douglass, appeared in the *Atlantic Monthly* in 1947. During the following fifteen years, Hayden published only three slim volumes of verse: *The Lion and the Archer* (1948), *Figure of Time* (1955), and *A Ballad of Remembrance* (1962), a collection of lyrics about his family and early life together with historical narratives about slavery and racial relations in the United States. That groundbreaking volume, which was published in London, won the Grand Prize for Poetry at the First World Festival of Negro Arts in Dakar, Senegal, in 1966, and Hayden was subsequently named the Poet Laureate of Senegal. Following the publication of his *Selected Poems* (1966), Hayden was finally noticed by critics and reviewers in the United States. Although his poetry was deeply rooted in the history and the experiences of African Americans, during the 1960s Hayden came into conflict with militants because of his refusal to write what he considered to be political propaganda or to define himself as a black poet, a role he rejected on aesthetic grounds and because his commitment to the universalism of the Baha'i religion made it impossible for him to support separatist conceptions of racial art and identity. Hayden, who left Fisk to take a teaching position at the University of Michigan in 1969, enjoyed considerable success during the 1970s, publishing *Words in the Mourning Time* (1970), *The Night-Blooming Cereus* (1972), and *Angle of Ascent: New and Selected Poems* (1975). That year, he was elected Fellow of the Academy of American Poets, and in 1976 he became the first African American to be appointed Consultant in Poetry to the Library of Congress, a position later called Poet Laureate. Hayden died on February 25, 1980.

Reading Hayden's "Middle Passage." This poem was based on Hayden's research into the revolt aboard the *Amistad*, a Spanish ship transporting a group of kidnapped West Africans from the slave market of Havana, where they had been sold, to a sugar plantation farther along the coast of Cuba. On July 2, 1839, the captives, led by Cinqué, seized the ship, killing the captain, Ramón Ferrar, and three members of the crew. The Africans ordered the navigator and the surviving crew members to sail the ship back to Africa. But they steered northward, and the *Amistad* was captured by the U.S. Navy off the coast of Long Island and towed to

New London, Connecticut. When the captives were charged with mutiny and murder, American abolitionists formed the Amistad Committee, which filed countercharges of kidnapping, assault, and false imprisonment on behalf of the Africans. The case ultimately went to the Supreme Court, where they were defended by former president John Quincy Adams, then a representative from Massachusetts. On March 9, 1841, the justices decided in favor of the captives, who were freed. The famous event — which was dramatized in Steven Spielberg's popular 1997 film *Amistad* — was an important, early victory in the antislavery movement in the United States. Hayden narrates the story through a variety of voices, including both captives and captors, integrating passages from court depositions and alluding to hymns, myths, and literary works. In an interview, Hayden later observed that "although the horrors of the slave trade are common to all [three parts of the poem], each section develops a particular aspect of this horror, focuses on a particular theme or incident." Hayden, who worked slowly and constantly revised his poems, first published "Middle Passage" in 1945 in *Phylon*, a journal for the study of race and culture founded by W. E. B. Du Bois. A revised version appeared in *Cross Section 1945*, edited by Edwin Seaver. The third and final version of "Middle Passage" appeared at the opening of a series of poems tracing the history of slavery in *A Ballad of Remembrance* (1962). The following text is that of the final version, as printed in Hayden's *Collected Poems* (1985).

bedfordstmartins.com/ americanlit *for research links on Hayden*

MIDDLE PASSAGE[1]

I

Jesús, Estrella, Esperanza, Mercy:[2]

> Sails flashing to the wind like weapons,
> sharks following the moans the fever and the dying;
> horror the corposant and compass rose.[3]

Middle Passage:
> voyage through death
> > to life upon these shores.

5

> "10 April 1800 —
> Blacks rebellious. Crew uneasy. Our linguist says

---

1. **Middle Passage:** The name given to the route across the Atlantic Ocean taken by slave ships sailing from Africa to North or South America.
2. ***Jesús, Estrella, Esperanza, Mercy***: The names of slave ships; *Estrella* means star and *Esperanza* means hope (Spanish).
3. **corposant and compass rose:** *Corposant* is an early term for the appearance of St. Elmo's fire — a brush discharge of electricity sometimes observable during foul weather — on a mast or other structure of a ship. A compass rose is a circular emblem showing the directions printed on a chart or map.

their moaning is a prayer for death,   10
ours and their own. Some try to starve themselves,
Lost three this morning leaped with crazy laughter
to the waiting sharks, sang as they went under."

Desire, Adventure, Tartar, Ann:

Standing to America, bringing home   15
black gold, black ivory, black seed.

> *Deep in the festering hold thy father lies,*
> *of his bones New England pews are made,*
> *those are altar lights that were his eyes.*[4]

Jesus   Saviour   Pilot   Me   20
Over   Life's   Tempestuous   Sea[5]

We pray that Thou wilt grant, O Lord,
safe passage to our vessels bringing
heathen souls unto Thy chastening.

Jesus   Saviour   25

"8 bells. I cannot sleep, for I am sick
with fear, but writing eases fear a little
since still my eyes can see these words take shape
upon the page & so I write, as one
would turn to exorcism. 4 days scudding,   30
but now the sea is calm again. Misfortune
follows in our wake like sharks (our grinning
tutelary gods). Which one of us
has killed an albatross?[6] A plague among
our blacks — Ophthalmia: blindness — & we   35
have jettisoned the blind to no avail.
It spreads, the terrifying sickness spreads.
Its claws have scratched sight from the Capt.'s eyes
& there is blindness in the fo'c'sle[7]
& we must sail 3 weeks before we come   40
to port."

---

4. **Deep . . . eyes**: A reworking of a song from Shakespeare's *The Tempest*, in which the sprite Ariel seeks to comfort Prince Ferdinand, who believes that his father has drowned in a shipwreck, by singing: "Full Fathom five thy father lies: / Of his bones are coral made: / Those are pearls that were his eyes: / Nothing of him that doth fade, / But doth suffer a sea-change / Into something rich and strange" (1.2.397-402).
5. **Jesus . . . Sea**: The first two lines of a Protestant hymn, often called "The Sailor's Hymn," which was first published in the *Sailor's Magazine* (1871).
6. **albatross**: Sailors believed that killing one of these large oceanic birds brought bad luck.
7. **fo'c'sle**: Forecastle, the forward part of a ship below the deck, used as the crew's living quarters.

What port awaits us, Davy Jones'
or home? I've heard of slavers drifting, drifting,
playthings of wind and storm and chance, their crews
gone blind, the jungle hatred   45
crawling up on deck.

Thou   Who   Walked   On   Galilee

"Deponent[8] further sayeth *The Bella J*
left the Guinea Coast
with cargo of five hundred blacks and odd   50
for the barracoons[9] of Florida:

"That there was hardly room 'tween-decks for half
the sweltering cattle stowed spoon-fashion there;
that some went mad of thirst and tore their flesh
and sucked the blood: 55

"That Crew and Captain lusted with the comeliest
of the savage girls kept naked in the cabins;
that there was one they called The Guinea Rose
and they cast lots and fought to lie with her:

"That when the Bo's'n piped all hands,[10] the flames   60
spreading from starboard already were beyond
control, the negroes howling and their chains
entangled with the flames:

"That the burning blacks could not be reached,
that the Crew abandoned ship,   65
leaving their shrieking negresses behind,
that the Captain perished drunken with the wenches:

"Further Deponent sayeth not."

Pilot   Oh   Pilot   Me

II

Aye, lad, and I have seen those factories,   70
Gambia, Rio Pongo, Calabar;[11]
have watched the artful mongos[12] baiting traps
of war wherein the victor and the vanquished

---

8. **Deponent:** A legal term for a person who makes a deposition under oath.
9. **barracoons:** Crude enclosures where captives were held before being sold in the slave markets.
10. **Bo's'n piped all hands:** The boatswain manages the equipment and the crew, or "hands," whom he calls to work with a pipe, or whistle.
11. **Gambia, Rio Pongo, Calabar:** Gambia is a small country in West Africa on the coast of the Atlantic Ocean; the Rio Pongo is an important commercial river in West Africa; and Calabar is a coastal city in Nigeria.
12. **mongos:** One of the largest ethnic groups of the African country known today as the Democratic Republic of the Congo.

Were caught as prizes for our barracoons.
Have seen the nigger kings whose vanity   75
and greed turned wild black hides of Fellatah,
Mandingo, Ibo, Kru[13] to gold for us.

And there was one — King Anthracite we named him —
fetish face beneath French parasols
of brass and orange velvet, impudent mouth   80
whose cups were carven skulls of enemies:

He'd honor us with drum and feast and conjo
and palm-oil-glistening wenches deft in love,
and for tin crowns that shone with paste,
red calico and German-silver trinkets   85

Would have the drums talk war and send
his warriors to burn the sleeping villages
and kill the sick and old and lead the young
in coffles[14] to our factories.

Twenty years a trader, twenty years,   90
for there was wealth aplenty to be harvested
from those black fields, and I'd be trading still
but for the fevers melting down my bones.

                                   III[15]

Shuttles in the rocking loom of history,
the dark ships move, the dark ships move,   95
their bright ironical names
like jests of kindness on a murderer's mouth;
plough through thrashing glister toward
fata morgana's[16] lucent melting shore,

---

13. **Fellatah, Mandingo, Ibo, Kru:** The names of African tribes.
14. **coffles:** A line of slaves, prisoners, or animals, fastened together.
15. **III:** Part III follows, in the main, the account of the *Amistad* mutiny given by Muriel Rukeyser in her biography of Willard Gibbs. [Hayden's note] Rukeyser (1913–1980), an American poet and political activist, wrote *Willard Gibbs: American Genius* (1942), a biography of the nineteenth-century mathematician and physicist. In the second chapter of the book, Rukeyser tells the story of his father, also named Josiah Willard Gibbs, an abolitionist, linguist, and professor of theology at Yale University. Because the *Amistad* captives could not speak English, Gibbs learned to count to ten in their Mende language. He then went from boat to boat in the New York harbor, repeating the numbers in Mende until he found a sailor and former slave, James Covey, who could translate for the captives. Gibbs was also a defense witness at the trial of the captives in New Haven, Connecticut.
16. **fata morgana:** Literally "fairy Morgan" (Italian), a mirage at sea originally attributed to the enchantress Morgan Le Fay.

weave toward New World littorals[17] that are   100
mirage and myth and actual shore.

Voyage through death,
                    voyage whose chartings are unlove.

A charnel stench, effluvium of living death
spreads outward from the hold,   105
where the living and the dead, the horribly dying,
lie interlocked, lie foul with blood and excrement.

> *Deep in the festering hold thy father lies,*
> *the corpse of mercy rots with him,*
> *rats eat love's rotten gelid eyes.*   110

> *But, oh, the living look at you*
> *with human eyes whose suffering accuses you,*
> *whose hatred reaches through the swill of dark*
> *to strike you like a leper's claw.*

> *You cannot stare that hatred down*   115
> *or chain the fear that stalks the watches*
> *and breathes on you its fetid scorching breath;*
> *cannot kill the deep immortal human wish,*
> *the timeless will.*

> "But for the storm that flung up barriers   120
> of wind and wave, *The Amistad,*[18] señores,
> would have reached the port of Príncipe[19] in two,
> three days at most; but for the storm we should
> have been prepared for what befell.
> Swift as the puma's leap it came. There was   125
> that interval of moonless calm filled only
> with the water's and the rigging's usual sounds,
> then sudden movement, blows and snarling cries
> and they had fallen on us with machete
> and marlinspike. It was as though the very   130
> air, the night itself were striking us.
> Exhausted by the rigors of the storm,
> we were no match for them. Our men went down
> before the murderous Africans. Our loyal

---

17. **littorals:** Areas of land along a coast.
18. ***The Amistad:*** The Spanish slave ship that was the scene of the famous slave rebellion in 1839.
19. **Príncipe:** Port Príncipe in Cuba was the original destination of the *Amistad.*

Celestino[20] ran from below with gun   135
and lantern and I saw, before the cane-
knife's wounding flash, Cinquez,[21]
that surly brute who calls himself a prince,
directing, urging on the ghastly work.
He hacked the poor mulatto down, and then   140
he turned on me. The decks were slippery
when daylight finally came. It sickens me
to think of what I saw, of how these apes
threw overboard the butchered bodies of
our men, true Christians all, like so much jetsam.   145
Enough, enough. The rest is quickly told:
Cinquez was forced to spare the two of us
you see to steer the ship to Africa,
and we like phantoms doomed to rove the sea
voyaged east by day and west by night,   150
deceiving them, hoping for rescue,
prisoners on our own vessel, till
at length we drifted to the shores of this
your land, America, where we were freed
from our unspeakable misery. Now we   155
demand, good sirs, the extradition of
Cinquez and his accomplices to La
Havana.[22] And it distresses us to know
there are so many here who seem inclined
to justify the mutiny of these blacks.   160
We find it paradoxical indeed
that you whose wealth, whose tree of liberty
are rooted in the labor of your slaves
should suffer the august John Quincy Adams[23]
to speak with so much passion of the right   165
of chattel slaves to kill their lawful masters
and with his Roman rhetoric weave a hero's
garland for Cinquez. I tell you that
we are determined to return to Cuba
with our slaves and there see justice done. Cinquez — 170
or let us say 'the Prince' — Cinquez shall die."

---

20. **Celestino:** A "mulatto" slave owned by the ship's captain who worked as a cook aboard the *Amistad*.
21. **Cinquez:** Sengbe Pieh (known as *Cinquez* or *Cinqué*), a member of the Mende tribe, was kidnapped and sold into slavery in West Africa in 1839. He led the revolt aboard the *Amistad*.
22. **La Havana:** Havana, Cuba.
23. **John Quincy Adams:** The congressman from Massachusetts and former president helped defend the surviving captives of the *Amistad* when their case went before the Supreme Court in 1841.

The deep immortal human wish,
the timeless will:

Cinquez its deathless primaveral[24] image,
life that transfigures many lives.

Voyage through death
> to life upon these shores.

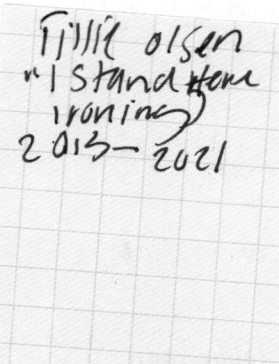

---

24. **primaveral:** A rare, figurative term for the early springtime.

Tillie Olsen

[1912?-2007]

Tillie Olsen was the second of six children born to Samuel and Ida Beber Lerner, Socialists and Jewish immigrants who fled Russia after the failed revolution of 1905. They did not obtain a birth certificate for their daughter, who was born in 1912 or 1913, probably in rural Nebraska. Olsen's father worked at a series of menial jobs in order to support his family, which moved frequently before settling in Omaha. A committed radical, he went to Tulsa, Oklahoma, to help African Americans rebuild their houses after the devastating race riot there in 1920, and he served for several years as the state secretary of the Nebraska Socialist Party. Olsen revered her hard-working, illiterate mother, whom she later described as "one of the most eloquent and one of the most brilliant human beings I've ever known." As a child, Olsen was deeply inspired by a speech delivered in Omaha by the labor leader and five-time Socialist Party presidential candidate Eugene V. Debs, who declared that "under socialism society would be like a great symphony with each person playing his own instrument." Olsen, who attended public schools, was a voracious reader of works ranging from the poetry of Edna St. Vincent Millay, Carl Sandburg, and Walt Whitman to the novels of Jack London, Upton Sinclair, and the South African feminist Olive Schreiner.

Olsen's own writings were strongly shaped by her difficult experiences as a radical, working-class woman with limited education and few prospects. In 1929, after she completed the eleventh grade, she left high school to go to work. Two years later, she joined the Young Communist League in Kansas City, Missouri, where she was jailed for a month after handing out leaflets to workers in a packinghouse. In 1932, ill and impoverished, she moved to a relative's home in Fairbault, Minnesota. She

Tillie Olsen

This photograph of Olsen was taken during the long hiatus in her writing career, in 1941, when she was president of the Parent Teacher Association (PTA) of an elementary school in San Francisco.

became pregnant and gave birth to her first daughter, Karla, named for Karl Marx. Olsen also began working on *Yonnondio*, a novel about the exploitation and struggles of a working-class family during the Great Depression. Olsen took her newborn to California in 1933, eventually settling in San Francisco. There, she met Jack Olsen, a longshoreman and labor organizer who was also involved in the Young Communist League. With him, Olsen was arrested and jailed during the violent San Francisco maritime strike of 1934. While she was serving her sentence, her story "The Iron Throat," the first chapter of her novel in progress, was published in the *Partisan Review*. The magazine subsequently published her essay "The Strike," and two essays she wrote about her arrest and sentencing appeared in another progressive magazine, the *New Republic*. The prominent New York publishing firm Random House offered her a monthly stipend to complete her novel, but Olsen abandoned the project and virtually ceased writing in order to devote herself to radical causes and the care of her family. In 1936, she and Jack Olsen began living together — they were married in 1943, when he was drafted into the army — and had three daughters between 1938 and 1948. Olsen also worked at various jobs, including stints as a waitress, a secretary, a meatpacker, and a punch-press operator.

During the 1950s, Olsen returned to writing, and her work subsequently gained considerable critical attention. She took a creative-writing course at San Francisco State College in 1953, about the time she began to write what became one of her most famous stories, "I Stand Here Ironing." An early version of the story won her a Wallace Stegner Fellowship at Stanford University in 1956, and Olsen received a Ford Foundation Grant in 1959. Olsen's other most famous story, "Tell Me a Riddle," won first prize in the O. Henry Awards for the best American short stories of 1961. That year, at the age of fifty, she published her first book, *Tell Me a Riddle* (1961). In recognition of her achievement in that acclaimed collection of stories, the prestigious $25,000 Rea Award for Short Fiction was later bestowed on Olsen, who in the words of the citation "had forced open the language of the short story, insisting that it include the domestic life of women, the passions and anguishes of maternity, the deep, gnarled roots of a long marriage, the hopes and frustrations of immigration, the shining charge of political commitment." Beginning in the early 1970s, Olsen was a writer in residence and visiting professor at a series of colleges and universities, including Amherst, Kenyon, MIT, Stanford, and UCLA. After her husband found the manuscript of her early, unfinished novel, Olsen edited but did not revise or complete the manuscript, which was published as *Yonnondio: From the Thirties* (1974). She wrote *Silences* (1978), a collection of essays and meditations on silences in literary history, including the silenced voices of women who "never came to writing," and edited a collection that included her own tribute to her mother, *Mother to Daughter, Daughter to Mother* (1984). Olsen continued to teach, give lectures, and collect a growing number of awards and honorary degrees until her death on January 1, 2007.

Tillie Olsen — a writer of such generosity and honesty, she literally saves lives.

—Alice Walker

Reading Olsen's "I Stand Here Ironing." This story, which was first published in 1956 as "Help Her to Believe" in a California magazine, the *Pacific Spectator,* was subsequently selected for inclusion in *The Best American Short Stories of 1957.* Olsen later changed its title and placed the story at the opening of her collection *Tell Me a Riddle* (1961). Concerned with the challenges of poverty, the demands of motherhood, the needs of children, and the plight of the woman writer, the semiautobiographical "I Stand Here Ironing" is one of Olsen's most admired and frequently anthologized stories. In her essay "Silences in Literature" (1962), Olsen explained the circumstances of writing the story, "which I was somehow able to carry around within me, through work, through home," in the early 1950s: "Time on the bus, even when I had to stand, was enough; the stolen moments at work, enough; the deep night hours for as long as I could stay awake, after the kids were in bed, after the household tasks were done, sometimes during. It is no accident that the first work I considered publishable began: 'I stand here ironing, and what you asked me moves tormented back and forth with the iron.'" The text is taken from *Tell Me a Riddle* (1961).

bedfordstmartins.com/ americanlit for research links on Olsen

I STAND HERE IRONING

I stand here ironing, and what you asked me moves tormented back and forth with the iron.

"I wish you would manage the time to come in and talk with me about your daughter. I'm sure you can help me understand her. She's a youngster who needs help and whom I'm deeply interested in helping."

"Who needs help." . . . Even if I came, what good would it do? You think because I am her mother I have a key, or that in some way you could use me as a key? She has lived for nineteen years. There is all that life that has happened outside of me, beyond me.

And when is there time to remember, to sift, to weigh, to estimate, to total? I will start and there will be an interruption and I will have to gather it all together again. Or I will become engulfed with all I did or did not do, with what should have been and what cannot be helped.

She was a beautiful baby. The first and only one of our five that was beautiful at birth. You do not guess how new and uneasy her tenancy in her now-loveliness. You did not know her all those years she was thought homely, or see her poring over her baby pictures, making me tell her over and over how beautiful she had been—and would be, I would tell her—and was now, to the seeing eye. But the seeing eyes were few or nonexistent. Including mine.

I nursed her. They feel that's important nowadays. I nursed all the children, but with her, with all the fierce rigidity of first motherhood, I did like the books then said. Though her cries battered me to trembling and my breasts ached with swollenness, I waited till the clock decreed.

Why do I put that first? I do not even know if it matters, or if it explains anything.

She was a beautiful baby. She blew shining bubbles of sound. She loved motion, loved light, loved color and music and textures. She would lie on the floor in her blue overalls patting the surface so hard in ecstasy her hands and feet would blur. She was a miracle to me, but when she was eight months old I had to leave her daytimes with the woman downstairs to whom she was no miracle at all, for I worked or looked for work and for Emily's father, who "could no longer endure" (he wrote in his good-bye note) "sharing want with us."

I was nineteen. It was the pre-relief, pre-WPA world of the depression.[1] I would start running as soon as I got off the streetcar, running up the stairs, the place smelling sour, and awake or asleep to startle awake, when she saw me she would break into a clogged weeping that could not be comforted, a weeping I can hear yet.

After a while I found a job hashing[2] at night so I could be with her days, and it was better. But it came to where I had to bring her to his family and leave her.

It took a long time to raise the money for her fare back. Then she got chicken pox and I had to wait longer. When she finally came, I hardly knew her, walking quick and nervous like her father, looking like her father, thin, and dressed in a shoddy red that yellowed her skin and glared at the pockmarks. All the baby loveliness gone.

She was two. Old enough for nursery school they said, and I did not know then what I know now — the fatigue of the long day, and the lacerations of group life in the kinds of nurseries that are only parking places for children.

Except that it would have made no difference if I had known. It was the only place there was. It was the only way we could be together, the only way I could hold a job.

And even without knowing, I knew. I knew the teacher that was evil because all these years it has curdled into my memory, the little boy hunched in the corner, her rasp, "why aren't you outside, because Alvin hits you? that's no reason, go out, scaredy." I knew Emily hated it even if she did not clutch and implore "don't go Mommy" like the other children, mornings.

She always had a reason why we should stay home. Momma, you look sick, Momma. I feel sick. Momma, the teachers aren't there today, they're sick. Momma, we can't go, there was a fire there last night. Momma, it's a holiday today, no school, they told me.

But never a direct protest, never rebellion. I think of our others in their three-, four-year-oldness — the explosions, the tempers, the denunciations, the demands — and I feel suddenly ill. I put the iron down. What in me demanded that goodness in her? And what was the cost, the cost to her of such goodness?

The old man living in the back once said in his gentle way: "You should smile at Emily more when you look at her." What *was* in my face when I looked at her? I loved her. There were all the acts of love.

---

1. **It was the pre-relief . . . depression:** In May 1935, President Franklin D. Roosevelt created a massive relief agency, the Works Progress Administration (WPA), which provided jobs to the unemployed during the Great Depression. Millions worked on public construction projects and cultural programs sponsored by the various divisions of the WPA.
2. **hashing:** Serving food in a café or diner.

It was only with the others I remembered what he said, and it was the face of joy, and not of care or tightness or worry I turned to them — too late for Emily. She does not smile easily, let alone almost always as her brothers and sisters do. Her face is closed and sombre, but when she wants, how fluid. You must have seen it in her pantomimes, you spoke of her rare gift for comedy on the stage that rouses a laughter out of the audience so dear they applaud and applaud and do not want to let her go.

Where does it come from, that comedy? There was none of it in her when she came back to me that second time, after I had had to send her away again. She had a new daddy now to learn to love, and I think perhaps it was a better time.

Except when we left her alone nights, telling ourselves she was old enough.

"Can't you go some other time, Mommy, like tomorrow?" she would ask. "Will it be just a little while you'll be gone? Do you promise?"

The time we came back, the front door open, the clock on the floor in the hall. She rigid awake. "It wasn't just a little while. I didn't cry. Three times I called you, just three times, and then I ran downstairs to open the door so you could come faster. The clock talked loud. I threw it away, it scared me what it talked."

She said the clock talked loud again that night I went to the hospital to have Susan. She was delirious with the fever that comes before red measles, but she was fully conscious all the week I was gone and the week after we were home when she could not come near the new baby or me.

She did not get well. She stayed skeleton thin, not wanting to eat, and night after night she had nightmares. She would call for me, and I would rouse from exhaustion to sleepily call back: "You're all right, darling, go to sleep, it's just a dream," and if she still called, in a sterner voice, "now go to sleep, Emily, there's nothing to hurt you." Twice, only twice, when I had to get up for Susan anyhow, I went in to sit with her.

Now when it is too late (as if she would let me hold and comfort her like I do the others) I get up and go to her at once at her moan or restless stirring. "Are you awake, Emily? Can I get you something?" And the answer is always the same: "No, I'm all right, go back to sleep, Mother."

They persuaded me at the clinic to send her away to a convalescent home in the country where "she can have the kind of food and care you can't manage for her, and you'll be free to concentrate on the new baby." They still send children to that place. I see pictures on the society page of sleek young women planning affairs to raise money for it, or dancing at the affairs, or decorating Easter eggs or filling Christmas stockings for the children.

They never have a picture of the children so I do not know if the girls still wear those gigantic red bows and the ravaged looks on the every other Sunday when parents can come to visit "unless otherwise notified" — as we were notified the first six weeks.

Oh it is a handsome place, green lawns and tall trees and fluted flower beds. High up on the balconies of each cottage the children stand, the girls in their red bows and white dresses, the boys in white suits and giant red ties. The parents stand below shrieking up to be heard and the children shriek down to be heard, and between them the invisible wall "Not To Be Contaminated by Parental Germs or Physical Affection."

There was a tiny girl who always stood hand in hand with Emily. Her parents never came. One visit she was gone. "They moved her to Rose Cottage" Emily shouted in explanation. "They don't like you to love anybody here."

She wrote once a week, the labored writing of a seven-year-old. "I am fine. How is the baby. If I write my leter nicly I will have a star. Love." There never was a star. We wrote every other day, letters she could never hold or keep but only hear read—once. "We simply do not have room for children to keep any personal possessions," they patiently explained when we pieced one Sunday's shrieking together to plead how much it would mean to Emily, who loved so to keep things, to be allowed to keep her letters and cards.

Each visit she looked frailer. "She isn't eating," they told us.

(They had runny eggs for breakfast or mush with lumps, Emily said later, I'd hold it in my mouth and not swallow. Nothing ever tasted good, just when they had chicken.)

It took us eight months to get her released home, and only the fact that she gained back so little of her seven lost pounds convinced the social worker.

I used to try to hold and love her after she came back, but her body would stay stiff, and after a while she'd push away. She ate little. Food sickened her, and I think much of life too. Oh she had physical lightness and brightness, twinkling by on skates, bouncing like a ball up and down up and down over the jump rope, skimming over the hill; but these were momentary.

She fretted about her appearance, thin and dark and foreign-looking at a time when every little girl was supposed to look or thought she should look a chubby blonde replica of Shirley Temple.[3] The doorbell sometimes rang for her, but no one seemed to come and play in the house or be a best friend. Maybe because we moved so much.

There was a boy she loved painfully through two school semesters. Months later she told me how she had taken pennies from my purse to buy him candy. "Licorice was his favorite and I brought him some every day, but he still liked Jennifer better'n me. Why, Mommy?" The kind of question for which there is no answer.

School was a worry to her. She was not glib or quick in a world where glibness and quickness were easily confused with ability to learn. To her overworked and exasperated teachers she was an overconscientious "slow learner" who kept trying to catch up and was absent entirely too often.

I let her be absent, though sometimes the illness was imaginary. How different from my now-strictness about attendance with the others. I wasn't working. We had a new baby, I was home anyhow. Sometimes, after Susan grew old enough. I would keep her home from school, too, to have them all together.

Mostly Emily had asthma, and her breathing, harsh and labored, would fill the house with a curiously tranquil sound. I would bring the two old dresser mirrors and her boxes of collections to her bed. She would select beads and single earrings, bottle tops and shells, dried flowers and pebbles, old postcards and scraps, all sorts of oddments; then she and Susan would play Kingdom, setting up landscapes and furniture, peopling them with action.

---

3. **Shirley Temple:** An enormously popular child film star of the 1930s.

Those were the only times of peaceful companionship between her and Susan. I have edged away from it, that poisonous feeling between them, that terrible balancing of hurts and needs I had to do between the two, and did so badly, those earlier years.

Oh there are conflicts between the others too, each one human, needing, demanding, hurting, taking—but only between Emily and Susan, no, Emily toward Susan that corroding resentment. It seems so obvious on the surface, yet it is not obvious. Susan, the second child, Susan, golden- and curly-haired and chubby, quick and articulate and assured, everything in appearance and manner Emily was not; Susan, not able to resist Emily's precious things, losing or sometimes clumsily breaking them; Susan telling jokes and riddles to company for applause while Emily sat silent (to say to me later: that was *my* riddle, Mother, I told it to Susan); Susan, who for all the five years' difference in age was just a year behind Emily in developing physically.

I am glad for that slow physical development that widened the difference between her and her contemporaries, though she suffered over it. She was too vulnerable for that terrible world of youthful competition, of preening and parading, of constant measuring of yourself against every other, of envy, "If I had that copper hair," "If I had that skin. . . ." She tormented herself enough about not looking like the others, there was enough of the unsureness, the having to be conscious of words before you speak, the constant caring—what are they thinking of me? without having it all magnified by the merciless physical drives.

Ronnie is calling. He is wet and I change him. It is rare there is such a cry now. That time of motherhood is almost behind me when the ear is not one's own but must always be racked and listening for the child cry, the child call. We sit for a while and I hold him, looking out over the city spread in charcoal with its soft aisles of light. *"Shoogily,"* he breathes and curls closer. I carry him back to bed, asleep. *Shoogily*. A funny word, a family word, inherited from Emily, invented by her to say: *comfort*.

In this and other ways she leaves her seal, I say aloud. And startle at my saying it. What do I mean? What did I start to gather together, to try and make coherent? I was at the terrible, growing years. War years. I do not remember them well. I was working, there were four smaller ones now, there was not time for her. She had to help be a mother, and housekeeper, and shopper. She had to set her seal. Mornings of crisis and near hysteria trying to get lunches packed, hair combed, coats and shoes found, everyone to school or Child Care on time, the baby ready for transportation. And always the paper scribbled on by a smaller one, the book looked at by Susan then mislaid, the homework not done. Running out to that huge school where she was one, she was lost, she was a drop; suffering over the unpreparedness, stammering and unsure in her classes.

There was so little time left at night after the kids were bedded down. She would struggle over books, always eating (it was in those years she developed her enormous appetite that is legendary in our family) and I would be ironing, or preparing food for the next day, or writing V-mail[4] to Bill, or tending the baby. Sometimes, to make me laugh, or out of her despair, she would imitate happenings or types at school.

---

4. **V-mail:** Victory mail, letters written on small forms (with space for roughly 100-300 words) that were delivered at no charge to members of the American armed forces stationed overseas during World War II.

I think I said once: "Why don't you do something like this in the school amateur show?" One morning she phoned me at work, hardly understandable through the weeping: "Mother, I did it. I won, I won; they gave me first prize; they clapped and clapped and wouldn't let me go."

Now suddenly she was Somebody, and as imprisoned in her difference as she had been in anonymity.

She began to be asked to perform at other high schools, even in colleges, then at city and statewide affairs. The first one we went to, I only recognized her that first moment when thin, shy, she almost drowned herself into the curtains. Then: Was this Emily? The control, the command, the convulsing and deadly clowning, the spell, then the roaring, stamping audience, unwilling to let this rare and precious laughter out of their lives.

Afterwards: You ought to do something about her with a gift like that – but without money or knowing how, what does one do? We have left it all to her, and the gift has as often eddied inside, clogged and clotted, as been used and growing.

She is coming. She runs up the stairs two at a time with her light graceful step, and I know she is happy tonight. Whatever it was that occasioned your call did not happen today.

"Aren't you ever going to finish the ironing, Mother? Whistler painted his mother in a rocker.[5] I'd have to paint mine standing over an ironing board." This is one of her communicative nights and she tells me everything and nothing as she fixes herself a plate of food out of the icebox.

She is so lovely. Why did you want me to come in at all? Why were you concerned? She will find her way.

She starts up the stairs to bed. "Don't get me up with the rest in the morning." "But I thought you were having midterms." "Oh, those," she comes back in, kisses me, and says quite lightly, "in a couple of years when we'll all be atom-dead[6] they won't matter a bit."

She has said it before. She *believes* it. But because I have been dredging the past, and all that compounds a human being is so heavy and meaningful in me, I cannot endure it tonight.

I will never total it all. I will never come in to say: She was a child seldom smiled at. Her father left me before she was a year old. I had to work her first six years when there was work, or I sent her home and to his relatives. There were years she had care she hated. She was dark and thin and foreign-looking in a world where the prestige went to blondeness and curly hair and dimples, she was slow where glibness was prized. She was a child of anxious, not proud, love. We were poor and could not afford for her the soil of easy growth. I was a young mother, I was a distracted mother. There were the other children pushing up, demanding. Her younger sister seemed all that she was not. There were years she did not want me to touch her. She kept too much in herself, her life was such she had to keep too much in herself. My wisdom came too late. She has much to her and probably little will come of it. She is a child of her age, of depression, of war, of fear.

---

5. **Whistler . . . in a rocker:** The American artist James McNeill Whistler (1834-1903) painted *Arrangement in Grey and Black: The Artist's Mother* (1871), a famous portrait of his mother seated in a rocking chair, commonly known as *Whistler's Mother*.
6. **atom-dead:** That is, killed by an atomic bomb.

Let her be. So all that is in her will not bloom — but in how many does it? There is still enough left to live by. Only help her to know — help make it so there is cause for her to know — that she is more than this dress on the ironing board, helpless before the iron.

[1956, 1961]

John Berryman

[1914-1972]

John Berryman was born John Allyn Smith on October 25, 1914. He was the son of Martha Little Smith, a former schoolteacher, and Allyn Smith, a bank manager in McAlester, Oklahoma. Berryman's father either resigned or was dismissed from the bank early in 1926, and he moved the family to Tampa, Florida. Despite the business boom there, Allyn Smith had little success and became so deeply depressed that he committed suicide by shooting himself on June 26, 1926. The trauma of his father's death haunted Berryman for the rest of his life. Later that year, his mother remarried and he took the last name of his stepfather, John Angus Berryman, their landlord in Florida. The new family moved to New York City, where Berryman's stepfather took a job as a bond salesman on Wall Street. Berryman was sent to a private boarding school in Connecticut. A rather withdrawn, slender, nearsighted boy, Berryman

John Berryman

Terence Spencer took this photograph in May 1957, when Berryman was at work on his ambitious poetic sequence *The Dream Songs* (1969).

suffered from bullying and teasing because of his poor performance in sports, a major part of the school's program. But he excelled at his academic work and won a partial scholarship at Columbia University, where he enrolled in 1932. He took classes with the poet and critic Mark Van Doren, whose encouragement and example "made me a poet," as Berryman later said. He published his first poems as well as reviews in the *Columbia Review*. After his graduation in 1936, he was awarded a fellowship for study at Cambridge University in England, where he met the prominent British poets W. H. Auden and Dylan Thomas.

After Berryman returned to the United States in 1938, he supported himself by teaching while pursuing a literary career. He worked briefly as the poetry editor of the *Nation* until he accepted a position at Wayne State University in Detroit, Michigan, in 1939. There, he became close friends with Bhain Campbell, a fellow poet whose death from cancer in 1940, at the age of only twenty-nine, was another traumatic loss for Berryman. Later that year, he accepted a position as an instructor at Harvard University. Twenty of his poems first appeared in *Five Young American Poets* (1940) and then in Berryman's first book, *Poems* (1942). But he was still struggling to find his own poetic voice, and the collection revealed the strong influence of Auden and the Irish poet William Butler Yeats. Berryman married Eileen Mulligan in 1942, the year before he became an instructor at Princeton University. During his years there, he met and became friends with a number of writers, including Robert Lowell and Saul Bellow. Although Berryman achieved considerable success as a teacher, he suffered from bouts of insecurity and began drinking heavily. One of the first of his many extramarital affairs, with the wife of a Princeton graduate student, inspired a remarkable series of poems, Berryman's finest work to that point in his career. But he did not publish them until twenty years later, in *Berryman's Sonnets* (1967), and in the meantime he received mixed reviews for the dense and difficult poems in his 1948 collection *The Dispossessed.* He also published critical and scholarly work on a wide range of writers, including "The Poetry of Ezra Pound" (1949), an influential essay on the controversial poet; and *Stephen Crane: A Critical Biography* (1950).

During the last two decades of his life, Berryman established himself as a major poet. Awarded his first Guggenheim Fellowship in 1952, he completed work on a poem inspired by the life and writings of the seventeenth-century American poet Anne Bradstreet, *Homage to Mistress Bradstreet*, which was published in the *Partisan Review* in 1953 and as a book in 1956. The influential critic Edmund Wilson called it "the most distinguished long poem by an American since [T. S. Eliot's] *The Waste Land*" (1922). Despite his now secure position as one of the foremost poets of his generation, Berryman continued to struggle with anxiety and alcohol. His wife left him in 1953, and the following year he was arrested and jailed for disorderly conduct while teaching at the Writers' Workshop at the University of Iowa. Dismissed from his position there, he accepted an invitation to teach at the University of Minnesota. In 1956, following his divorce, he married Elizabeth Ann Levine. After the birth of their son, they divorced in 1959, and Berryman married his third wife, Kathleen Donohue, in 1961. The couple had two daughters. Meanwhile, he worked on his most ambitious poetic project, an ongoing sequence of semiautobiographical poems he called "Dream Songs," which were published in book form as *77 Dream Songs* (1964) and a sequel, *His Toy, His Dream, His Rest* (1968). The complete sequence appeared as *The Dream Songs* in 1969, the year Berryman was awarded the prestigious Bollingen Prize in Poetry. In the view of most critics, he failed to sustain the intensity of those poems in his final collections, *Love and Fame* (1970) and *Delusions, Etc.* (1972), which was published a few months after Berryman committed suicide in Minneapolis, jumping off the Washington Avenue Bridge into the Mississippi River on January 7, 1972.

Like their hero, durable and battered Henry, The Dream Songs *are open everywhere; open, at the risk of total breakdown, to nothing less than the life that breathed them.*

–Adrienne Rich

Reading Berryman's *The Dream Songs.* Berryman, who had become interested in dream analysis, conceived of this poetic sequence in April 1955. Some of the earliest of his "Dream Songs" were published in England in the *Times Literary Supplement*, and many of the poems subsequently appeared in American magazines such as the *Atlantic, Harper's,* and *Poetry.* Although he did not adhere to his original plan of writing a poem every two days, the final sequence included 385 numbered poems in *The Dream Songs.* Most critics viewed the antihero of the seemingly confessional poems as a thinly veiled portrait of Berryman. In a prefatory note to *The Dream Songs,* however, he explained that the sequence "is essentially about an imaginary character (not the poet, not me) named Henry, a white American in early middle age sometimes in blackface, who has suffered an irreversible loss and talks about himself sometimes in the first person, sometimes in the third, sometimes even in the second; he has a friend, never named, who addresses him as Mr. Bones and variants thereof." Whatever their status as autobiography may be, *The Dream Songs* are remarkable for Berryman's stylistic innovations. In his speech accepting the National Book Award, he stated: "I set up *The Dream Songs* as hostile to every visible tendency in both American and English poetry." Although almost all of the poems of the sequence are composed of three, six-line stanzas, they are characterized by their unconventional colloquial diction — including what Berryman called the "coon talk" derived from the offensive tradition of black-faced minstrelsy — as well as by their fractured syntax and unconventional rhythms. The texts of the poems selected here are taken from *The Dream Songs* (1969).

bedfordstmartins.com/ americanlit *for research links on Berryman*

1

Huffy Henry hid   the day,
unappeasable Henry sulked.
I see his point, — a trying to put things over.
It was the thought that they thought
they could *do* it made Henry wicked and away.   5
But he should have come out and talked.

All the world like a woolen lover
once did seem on Henry's side.
Then came a departure.
Thereafter nothing fell out as it might or ought.   10
I don't see how Henry, pried
open for all the world to see, survived.

What he has now to say is a long
wonder the world can bear & be.
Once in a sycamore I was glad   15
all at the top, and I sang.

Hard on the land wears the strong sea
and empty grows every bed.

[1959, 1964, 1969]

4

Filling her compact & delicious body
with chicken páprika, she glanced at me
twice.
Fainting with interest, I hungered back
and only the fact of her husband & four other people   5
kept me from springing on her

or falling at her little feet and crying
"You are the hottest one for years of night
Henry's dazed eyes
have enjoyed, Brilliance." I advanced upon   10
(despairing) my spumoni. — Sir Bones: is stuffed,
de world, wif feeding girls.

— Black hair, complexion Latin, jewelled eyes
downcast . . . The slob beside her   feasts . . . What wonders is
she sitting on, over there?   15
The restaurant buzzes. She might as well be on Mars.
Where did it all go wrong? There ought to be a law against Henry.
— Mr Bones: there is.

[1963, 1964, 1969]

14

Life, friends, is boring. We must not say so.
After all, the sky flashes, the great sea yearns,
we ourselves flash and yearn,
and moreover my mother told me as a boy
(repeatingly) "Ever to confess you're bored   5
means you have no

Inner Resources." I conclude now I have no
inner resources, because I am heavy bored.
Peoples bore me,
literature bores me, especially great literature,   10
Henry bores me, with his plights & gripes
as bad as achilles,[1]

---

1. **achilles:** The Greek warrior Achilles, the hero of Homer's *Iliad* (eighth century BCE), sulked in his tent and temporarily refused to fight after he was insulted by Agamemnon, the leader of the Greeks in the Trojan War.

who loves people and valiant art, which bores me.
And the tranquil hills, & gin, look like a drag
and somehow a dog   15
has taken itself & its tail considerably away
into mountains or sea or sky, leaving
behind: me, wag.

[1963, 1964, 1969]

26

The glories of the world struck me, made me aria,[1] once.
— What happen then, Mr Bones?
if be you cares to say.
— Henry. Henry became interested in women's bodies,
his loins were & were the   scene of stupendous achievement.   5
Stupor. Knees, dear. Pray.

All the knobs & softnesses of, my God,
the ducking & trouble it swarm on Henry,
at one time.
— What happen then, Mr Bones?   10
you seems excited-like.
— Fell Henry back into   the original crime: art, rime

besides a sense of others, my God, my God,
and a jealousy for the honour (alive) of his country,
what can get more odd?   15
and discontent with the thriving gangs & pride.
— What happen then, Mr Bones?
— I had a most marvellous   piece of luck. I died.

[1964, 1969]

---

1. **aria:** An extended solo song in an opera or oratorio.

Ralph Ellison

[1913-1994]

Ralph Waldo Ellison was born March 1, 1913, in Oklahoma City, Oklahoma. He was the first of two sons born to Ida Millsap Ellison and Lewis Alfred Ellison, the owner of a small business selling ice and coal. Like thousands of other African Americans who migrated to the North and West, the couple had moved to Oklahoma to escape racism and segregation in the

Ralph Ellison

The noted African American photographer Gordon Parks took this portrait, which appeared on the dust jacket of Ellison's first and most renowned book, *Invisible Man* (1952).

South. Ellison's proud father, who wanted his first-born son to become a poet, named him after the revered nineteenth-century American author Ralph Waldo Emerson. When Ellison was three, his father died from injuries sustained in an accident, and his mother supported the family by working as a maid and as the sexton of the African Methodist Episcopal Church. She was also active in the Socialist Party and campaigned against segregation laws in Oklahoma. While attending the all-black Frederick Douglass High School, Ellison excitedly discovered the work of Langston Hughes, Countee Cullen, and other poets of the Harlem Renaissance. Initially, however, Ellison trained to be a musician. He took trumpet lessons and became interested in jazz and the blues. In 1933, a year after his graduation from high school, he was awarded a music scholarship to the Tuskegee Institute in Alabama. During his college years, Ellison began to write poetry and switched from music to English. He consequently lost his scholarship, and in the summer of 1936 he went to New York City, hoping to earn enough money to pay for his final year at Tuskegee.

Ellison decided instead to remain there in order to pursue a career as a writer. He was strongly encouraged by Richard Wright, who had recently moved from Chicago to pursue his own literary career in New York. Wright, who worked for the Communist Party's *Daily Worker* and coedited the Marxist literary magazine the *New Challenge*, invited Ellison to contribute to the magazine. In 1938, about the time Ellison married the actress and singer Rose Poindexter, Wright helped him secure a job researching African American history for the Federal Writers' Project. Ellison's first published story, "Slick Gonna Learn," appeared in *Direction* in 1939, and he wrote book reviews for radical magazines such as the *New Masses*. Along with Wright, Ellison began to distance himself from the Communist Party, which he no longer believed had much to offer African Americans. In 1942, he resigned from the Federal Writers' Project to edit the *Negro Quarterly*. Unwilling to serve in the segregated U.S. Army during World War II, Ellison enlisted and served for two years as a cook in the merchant marine. By the end of the war, he had published several more stories and critical essays. Now divorced from his first wife, Ellison in 1946 married Fanny McConnell, who supported them while he worked on his first novel, *Invisible Man* (1952). The novel, a first-person narrative by an unnamed protagonist whose life story mirrors the often-bitter history of African Americans during the first half of the twentieth century, was widely reviewed in the United States. Although one black reviewer called the novel "a vicious distortion of Negro life," Langston Hughes described it as "deep, beautifully written, provocative and moving." Many other reviewers, both black and white, hailed the artistry, courage, and psychological realism of *Invisible Man*, which became a bestseller and won the National Book Award.

The high expectations generated by the success of *Invisible Man* proved to be a heavy burden for Ellison. From 1955 to 1957, he was a fellow at the American Academy in Rome, and he taught at various colleges and universities after his return to the United States. Most of his writings during the period were essays and reviews, some of which were later collected in his highly regarded volume of cultural criticism, *Shadow and Act* (1964). As

Ellison explained in the introduction, the collection was tied together by three major themes: "Literature and folklore; Negro musical expression — especially jazz and the blues; and the complex relationship between the Negro American subculture and North American culture as a whole." In 1958, Ellison finally began his second novel, then called *And Hickman Arrives*, in which a black evangelist, now an old man, recalls his childhood experiences in the South. Ellison published several chapters as stories, always identifying them as excerpts "from a novel in progress." Embarrassed by his failure to complete the novel, Ellison claimed that the only copy of the manuscript was destroyed in a fire at his summer home in Massachusetts in 1967. In fact, he apparently lost only a small part of the ballooning manuscript, which had "become inordinately long . . . and complicated," as he told a friend in 1968. During the 1960s, his reputation declined, especially among more militant African Americans, who believed that Ellison was not doing enough to promote the civil rights movement. In 1970, he became the Albert Schweitzer Professor of Humanities at New York University, and he later received numerous awards and honors, including the Presidential Medal of the Arts from Ronald Reagan in 1985. Ellison published another collection of cultural criticism, *Going to the Territory* (1986). He also continued to work on his second novel, which ultimately expanded to a 2,000-page manuscript. An abridged version edited by his literary executor, John Callahan, was finally published as *Juneteenth* (1999), five years after Ellison died of pancreatic cancer in his Harlem apartment on April 16, 1994.

We are, readers and writers alike, buoyed and challenged by wave upon brilliant wave of Ellison's artistry.

–Toni Morrison

Reading Ellison's "The Invisible Man."

While staying with friends in Vermont in the summer of 1945, Ellison jotted down the sentence "I am an invisible man" in his notebook. The sentence was the germ of what became his most critically acclaimed work, *Invisible Man* (1952). The first chapter of the novel was published in 1947 as a story, "The Invisible Man," in the prominent British journal *Horizon.* It appeared in a special issue of that journal devoted to American art and culture that also included works by John Berryman, E. E. Cummings, Marianne Moore, and Wallace Stevens. The story was subsequently reprinted in the United States as "Battle Royal" in the 1948 edition of *Magazine of the Year.* The title of that version was changed to avoid some copyright issues, and the editors cut portions of an erotic passage in which the narrator describes his arousal by the sight of a white stripper performing at a "smoker." (Ellison restored the excised portions in *Invisible Man.*) Inspired in part by an episode in Richard Wright's autobiographical *Black Boy* (1945), "The Invisible Man" is a harrowing and ironic story of an African American youth's initiation into a world of racism, segregation, and violence. Taught to know his "place" by the leading white citizens of a small southern town, the protagonist takes his first step toward the discovery that he is "an invisible man." In some working notes for *Invisible Man*, Ellison wrote: "'Invisibility' . . . springs from two basic facts of American life: from the racial conditioning which often makes the white American interpret cultural, physical or psychological

bedfordstmartins.com/ americanlit *for research links on Ellison*

differences as signs of racial inferiority; and, on the other hand, it springs from a great formlessness of Negro life wherein all values are in flux, and where those institutions and patterns of life which mold the white American's personality are missing or not so immediate in their effect." The text of the story is taken from the first printing in *Horizon* (October 1947).

THE INVISIBLE MAN

It goes a long way back, some twenty years. All my life I had been looking for something, and everywhere I turned someone tried to tell me what it was. I accepted their answers, too, though they were often in contradiction and even self-contradictory. I was naïve. I was looking for myself and asking everyone except myself questions which I, and only I, could answer. It took me a long time and much painful boomeranging of my expectations to realize a matter everyone else appears to have been born with: that I am nobody but myself, an invisible man!

And yet I am no freak of nature, nor of history. I was in the cards, other things having been equal (or unequal) eighty-five years ago. I am not ashamed of my grandparents for having been slaves. I am only ashamed of myself for having at one time been ashamed.

About eighty-five years ago they were told that they were free, united with others of our country in everything pertaining to the common good, and, in everything social, separate like the fingers of the hand.[1] And they believed it. They exulted in it. They stayed in their place, worked hard, and brought up my father to do the same. But my grandfather is the one. He was an odd old guy — my grandfather, and I'm told I take after him. It was he who caused the trouble. On his deathbed he called my father to him and said, "Son, after I'm gone I want you to keep up the good fight. I never told you, but our life is a war and I have been a traitor all my born days, a spy in the enemy's country all my born days, ever since I give up my gun back in the Reconstruction.[2] Live with your head in the lion's mouth. I want you to overcome 'em with yesses, undermine 'em with grins, agree 'em to death and destruction, let 'em swoller you till they vomit or bust wide open." They thought the old man had gone out of his head. He had been the meekest of men. The younger children were rushed from the room, the shades drawn and the flame of the lamp turned so low that it sputtered on the wick like the old man's breathing. "Learn it to the young 'uns," he whispered fiercely. Then he died.

But my folks were more alarmed over his last words than over his dying. I was warned emphatically to forget it and, indeed, this is the first time it has been repeated outside the family circle. It had a tremendous effect upon me, however. I could never be sure of what he meant. Grandfather had been a meek old man who never made any trouble, yet on his deathbed he had called himself a traitor and a spy, and he had spoken of his meekness as a dangerous activity. It became a constant puzzle which lay unanswered in the back of my mind. And whenever things went well for me I remembered my grandfather and felt guilty, and uncomfortable. It was as though I was carrying out his advice in spite of myself. And to make it worse, everyone loved me for it. I was praised by the most lilywhite men of the town. I was considered an example of desirable conduct — just as my grandfather had been. And what puzzled me was that the old man had defined it as *treachery*. When I was praised for my conduct I felt a guilt that in some way I was doing something that was really against the wishes of the white folks, that if they had understood they would have desired me to act just the opposite, that I should have been sulky and bad and that really would have been what they wanted, even though they were fooled and thought they wanted me to act as I did. It made me very afraid that some day they would look upon me as a traitor and I would be lost. Still, I was afraid to act any other way because they didn't like that at all. The old man's words were like a curse. On my graduation day I delivered a paper in which I showed that humility was the secret, indeed, the very essence, of progress. (Not that I believed this. How could I, remembering my grandfather? I only knew that it worked.) It was a great success. Everyone praised me

---

1. **united . . . fingers of the hand:** The narrator alludes to "The Atlanta Exposition Address" by Booker T. Washington (1856-1915), the prominent African American educator and founder of the Tuskegee Institute in Alabama. In that 1895 speech Washington famously declared, "In all things that are purely social we can be as separate as the fingers, yet one as the hand in all things essential to mutual progress" (see p. 1423), effectively putting aside demands for the full social and political equality of African Americans in order to gain white support for technical training and access to jobs in the South.
2. **Reconstruction:** During Reconstruction (1865-1877), the period following the Civil War, a number of southern states prohibited African Americans from owning guns under laws called "Black Codes."

and I was invited to give the speech before the town's leading white citizens. It was a triumph for our whole community.

When I got there I discovered that it was on the occasion of a smoker, and I was told that since I was to be there anyway I might as well take part in the battle royal to be fought by some of my schoolmates as part of the entertainment.[3] The battle royal came first. It was in the main ballroom of the leading hotel. All the town's big shots were there in their tuxedos, wolfing down the buffet foods, drinking beer and whisky and smoking black cigars. It was a large room with a high ceiling. Chairs were arranged in neat rows around three sides of a portable boxing ring. The fourth side was clear, revealing a gleaming space of polished floor. I had some misgivings over the battle royal, by the way. Not from a distaste for fighting, but because I didn't care too much for the other fellows who were to take part. They were tough guys, who seemed to have no grandfather curses worrying their minds. No one could have mistaken their toughness. And besides, I suspected that fighting a battle royal might detract from the dignity of my speech. In those pre-invisible days I visualized myself a neo-Booker T. Washington. But the other fellows didn't care too much for me, either, and there were nine of them. I felt superior to them in my way, and I didn't like the manner in which we were all crowded together into the servants' elevator. Nor did they like my being there. In fact as the warmly lighted floors flashed past the elevator we had words over the fact that I, by taking part in the fight, had knocked one of their friends out of a night's work.

We were led out of the elevator through a rococo hall into an ante-room and told to get into our fighting togs. Each of us was issued with a pair of boxing gloves. Then we were told to go out into the ballroom and wait our turn. When ready we were ushered out and entered the big, mirrored hall as instructed, looking cautiously about us, and whispering lest we might accidentally be heard in the noise of the room. It was foggy with cigar smoke. And already the whisky was taking effect. I was shocked to see that some of the most important men of the town were tipsy. They were all there, bankers, lawyers, judges, doctors, fire chiefs, teachers, merchants. Even one of the more fashionable pastors. Something we could not see was going on up front. A clarinet was vibrating sensuously and the men were standing up and moving forward. We were a small tight group, clustered together, our bare upper bodies touching and shining with anticipatory sweat; while up front the big shots were becoming increasingly excited over something we could not see. Suddenly I heard the school superintendent who had told me to come yell, "Bring up the shines,[4] gentlemen! Bring up the little shines!"

We were rushed up to the front of the ballroom. It smelled strongly of tobacco and whisky and when we were pushed into place I almost wet my pants. A sea of faces, some hostile, some amused, ringed round us, and in the centre, facing us, stood a magnificent blonde, stark nude. There was dead silence. I felt a blast of cold air chill me. I tried to back away, but they were behind me and around me. Some of the boys stood with lowered

---

3. **occasion of a smoker . . . entertainment:** *Smoker* was a common term for an all-male social gathering. A "battle royal" is a free-for-all fight involving several combatants.
4. **shines:** A derogatory term for black people.

heads, trembling. I felt a wave of irrational guilt and fear. My teeth chattered, my skin turned to goose flesh, my knees knocked. Yet I was strongly attracted and looked in spite of myself. Had the price of looking been blindness, I would have looked. The hair was yellow like that of a circus kewpie doll, the face heavily powdered and rouged, as though to form an abstract mask, the eyes hollow and smeared a cool blue — the colour of a baboon's butt. I felt a compulsive desire to spit upon her as my eyes brushed slowly over her body. Her breasts were firm and round as the domes of East Indian temples, and I stood so close as to see the fine skin texture and beads of pearly perspiration glistening like dew around the pink and erected buds of her nipples. I wanted at one and the same time to run from the room, to sink through the floor, or go to her and cover her from my eyes and the eyes of the others with my body; to feel the soft thighs, to caress her and destroy her, to love her and murder her, to hide from her, and yet to stroke where below the small American flag tattooed upon her belly her thighs formed a clear, inverted V. I had a notion that of all in the room she saw only me with her impersonal eyes.

And then she began to dance, a slow sensuous movement; the smoke of a hundred cigars clinging to her like the thinnest of veils. She seemed like a fair bird-girl girdled in veils calling to me from the angry surface of some grey and threatening sea. I was transported. Then I became aware of a clarinet playing and the big shots yelling at us. Some threatened us if we looked and others if we did not. On my right I saw one boy faint and a man grabbed a silver pitcher from a table, stepping close as he dashed iced water upon him, then stood him up and forced two of us to support him as his head hung, and moans issued from his thick bluish lips. Another boy began to plead to go home. He was the largest of the group, wearing dark-red fighting tights much too small to conceal the erection which projected from him as though in answer to the insinuating low-registered moaning of the clarinet. He tried to hide himself with his boxing gloves. And all the while the blonde continued dancing, smiling faintly at the big shots who watched her with fascination, and faintly smiling at our fear. I noticed a certain merchant who followed her hungrily, his lips loose and drooling. He was a large man who wore diamond studs in a shirtfront, which swelled with the ample pouch underneath, and each time the blonde swayed her undulating hips he ran his hand through the thin hair of his bald head and, with his arms upheld, his posture clumsy like that of an intoxicated panda, wound his belly in a slow and obscene grind. This creature was completely hypnotized. The music had quickened. The dancer flung herself about with detached facial expression, the men began reaching out to touch her. I could see their beefy fingers sink into the soft flesh. Some of the others tried to stop them and she began to move around the floor in graceful circles as they gave chase, slipping and sliding over the polished floor. It was mad. Chairs went crashing, beer was spilt as they ran laughing and howling after her. They caught her just as she reached a door, raised her from the floor, and tossed her as college boys are tossed at a hazing, and above her red, fixed-smiling lips I saw the terror and disgust in her eyes, almost like my own terror and that I saw in some of the other boys, as I watched. They tossed her twice and her soft breasts seemed to flatten against the air and her legs flung wildly as she spun. Some of the more sober ones helped her to escape. And I started off the floor, heading for the ante-room with the rest of the boys.

Some were still crying and in hysteria. But as we tried to leave we were stopped and ordered to get into the ring. There was nothing to do but what we were told. All ten of us climbed under the ropes and allowed ourselves to be blindfolded with broad bands of white cloth. One of the men seemed to feel a bit sympathetic and tried to cheer us up as we stood with our backs against the ropes. Some of us tried to grin. "See that boy over there?" one of the men said. "I want you to run across at the bell and give it to him right in the belly. If you don't get him, I'm going to get you. I don't like his looks." Each of us was told the same. The blindfolds were put on. Yet even then I had been going over my speech. In my mind each word was as bright as flame. I felt the cloth pressed into place and frowned so that it would be loosened when I relaxed.

But now I felt a sudden fit of blind terror. I was unused to darkness. It was as though I had suddenly found myself in a dark room filled with poisonous cottonmouths. I could hear the bleary voices yelling insistently for the battle royal to begin.

"Get going in there!"

"Let me at that big nigger!"

I strained to pick out the school superintendent's voice, as though to squeeze some security out of that slightly more familiar sound.

"Let me at those black sonsabitches!" someone yelled.

"No, Jackson, no!" another voice yelled . . . "Here, somebody help me hold Jack."

"I want to get at that ginger-coloured bugger. Tear him limb from limb," the first voice yelled.

I stood against the ropes trembling. For in those days I was what they called ginger-coloured and he sounded as though he might crunch me between his teeth like a crisp ginger cookie. Quite a struggle was going on. Chairs were being kicked about and I could hear voices grunting as with a terrific effort. I wanted to see, to see more desperately than ever before. But the blindfold was tight as a thick, skin-puckering scab and when I raised my gloved hand to push the layers of white aside a voice yelled, "Oh, no you don't, black bastard! Leave that alone!"

"Ring the bell before Jackson kills him a coon!" someone boomed in the sudden silence. And I heard the bell clang and the sound of the feet scuffling forward.

A glove smacked against my head. I pivoted, striking out stiffly as someone went past, and felt the jar ripple along the length of my arm to my shoulder. Then it seemed as though all nine of the boys had turned upon me at once. Blows pounded me from all sides while I struck out as best I could. So many blows landed upon me that I wondered if I were not the only blindfolded fighter in the ring, or if the man called Jackson hadn't succeeded in getting me after all.

Blindfolded, I sensed that I could not control my motions and that I had no dignity. I stumbled about like a baby or a drunken man. The smoke had become thicker and with each new blow it seemed to sear and further restrict my lungs. My saliva became like hot bitter glue. A glove connected with my head, filling my mouth with warm blood. It was everywhere. I could not tell if the moisture I felt upon my body was sweat or blood. A blow landed hard against the nape of my neck. I felt myself going over, my head hitting the floor. Streaks of blue light filled the black world behind the blindfold. I lay prone pretending that I was knocked out, but felt myself seized by hands and yanked to my feet. "Get going, black boy! Mix it up!" My arms were like lead, my head smarting from blows. I managed to feel my way to the ropes and held on trying to catch my breath. A glove landed in my mid-section and I went over again feeling as though the smoke had become a knife jabbed into my guts. Pushed this way and that by the legs milling around me, I finally pulled erect and discovered that I could see. The blindfold had slipped a fraction and I could see the black, sweat-washed forms weaving in the smoky-blue atmosphere like drunken dancers weaving to the rapid drum-like thuds of blows. Everyone fought hysterically. It was complete anarchy. Everybody fought everybody else. No group fought together for long. Two, three, four, fought one, then turned to fight each other, were themselves attacked. Blows landed below the belt and in the kidney, with the gloves open as well as closed. My eye was partly opened now and there was not so much terror. I moved carefully, avoiding blows, although not too many to attract attention, fighting from group to group. The boys groped about like blind, cautious crabs, crouching to protect their mid-sections, their heads pulled in short against their shoulders, their arms stretched nervously before them with their fists testing the smoke-filled air like the knobbed feelers of hypersensitive snails. In one corner I glimpsed a boy violently punching the air and heard him scream in pain as he smashed his hand against a ring post. For a second I saw him bent over, holding his hand, then going down as a blow caught his unprotected head. I played one group against the other, slipping in and throwing a punch then stepping out of range while pushing the others into the mêlée to take the blows blindly aimed at me. The smoke was agonizing and there were no rounds, no bells at four-minute intervals to relieve our exhaustion. The room spun round me, a swirl of lights, smoke, sweating bodies – surrounded by tense white faces. I bled from both nose and mouth, the blood spattered from time to time upon my chest. The men kept yelling, "Slug him, black boy. Knock his guts out!"

"Uppercut him. Kill that big boy!"

Taking a fake fall, I saw a boy going down heavily beside me as though he were felled by a single blow, saw a sneaker-clad foot shoot into his groin as the two who had knocked him down stumbled upon him as I rolled out of range.

The harder we fought the more threatening the men became. And yet I had begun to worry about my speech again. How would it go? Would they recognize my ability? What would they give me?

I was fighting automatically when suddenly I noticed that one after another of the boys was leaving the ring. I was surprised, filled with panic, as though I had been left alone with an unknown danger. Then I understood. The boys had arranged it among themselves. It was the custom for the two men left in the ring to slug it out for the winner's prize. I discovered this too late. When the bell sounded two men in tuxedos leaped into the ring and removed the blindfold. I found myself facing Tatlock, the biggest of the gang. I felt sick at my stomach. Hardly had the bell stopped ringing in my ears than it clanged again and I saw him moving swiftly towards me. Thinking of nothing else to do I hit him smash on the nose. He kept coming, bringing the sharp violence of rank sweat. His face was a black blank of a face, only his eyes alive – with hate of me, and aglow with a feverish terror from what had happened to us all. I became anxious. I wanted to deliver my speech and he came at me as though he meant to beat it out of me. I smashed him again and again, taking his blows as they came. Then on a sudden impulse I struck him lightly and as we clinched, I whispered, "Fake like I knocked you out, you can have the prize."

"I'll break your behind," he whispered hoarsely.

"For *them?*"

"For *me*, sonofabitch!"

They were yelling for us to break it up and Tatlock spun me half around with a blow, and as a joggled camera sweeps in a reeling scene, I saw the howling red faces crouching tense beneath the clouds of blue-grey smoke. For a moment the world wavered, unravelled, flowed, then my head cleared and Tatlock bounced before me. That fluttering shadow before my eyes was his jabbing left hand. Then falling forward, my head against his damp shoulder, I whispered,

"I'll make it five dollars more."

"Go to hell!"

But his muscles relaxed a trifle beneath my pressure and I breathed, "Seven!"

"Give it to your ma," he said, ripping me beneath the heart. And while I still held him I butted him and moved away. I felt myself bombarded with punches. I fought back with hopeless desperation. I wanted to deliver my speech more than anything else in the world, because I felt that only these men could judge truly my ability, and now this stupid clown was ruining my chances. I began fighting carefully now, moving in to punch him and out again with my faster speed. A lucky blow to his chin and I had him going too — until I heard a loud voice yell, "I got my money on the big boy." Hearing this I almost dropped my guard. I was confused: should I try to win against the voice out there? Would not this go against my speech, and was not this a moment for humility, for non-resistance? A blow to my head as I danced about sent my right eye popping like a jack-in-the-box and settled my dilemma. The room went red as I fell. It was a dream fall, my body languid and fastidious as to where to land, until the floor became impatient and smashed up to meet me. A moment later I came to. An hypnotic voice said "FIVE" . . . emphatically. And I lay there, hazily watching a dark red spot of my own blood shaping itself into a butterfly, glistening and soaking into the soiled grey world of the canvas.

When the voice drawled "TEN" I was lifted up and dragged to a chair. I sat dazed. My eye pained and swelled with each throb of my pounding heart and I wondered if now I would be allowed to speak. I was wringing wet, my mouth still bleeding. We were grouped along the wall now. The other boys ignored me as they congratulated Tatlock and speculated as to how much they would be paid. One boy whimpered over his smashed hand. Looking up front, I saw attendants in white jackets rolling the portable ring away and placing a small square rug in the vacant space surrounded by chairs. "Perhaps," I thought, "I will stand on the rug to deliver my speech."

Then the M.C. called to us. My heart fell when he said,

"Come on up here, boys, and get your money."

We ran forward to where the men laughed and talked in their chairs, waiting. Everyone seemed friendly now.

"There it is on the rug," the man said. I saw the rug covered with coins of all dimensions and a few crumpled bills. But what excited me, scattered here and there were gleaming pieces of gold.

"Boys, it's all yours," the man said. "That's right, Sambo," a blond man said, winking at me confidentially.

I trembled with excitement, forgetting my pain. I would get the gold and the bills, I thought. I would use both hands. I would throw my body against the others to block them from the gold.

"Get down around the rug now," the man commanded, "and don't anyone touch it until I give the signal."

"This ought to be good," I heard.

As told, we got around the square rug on our knees. Slowly the man raised his freckled hand and we followed it upwards with our eyes.

I heard, "These niggers look like they're about to pray!"

Then, "Ready," the man said, "Go!"

I lunged for a yellow coin lying on the blue design of the carpet, touching it and sending a surprised shriek to join those rising around me. I tried frantically to remove my hand but could not let go. A hot violent force tore through my body, shaking me like a wet rat. The rug was electrified. The hair bristled up on my head as I shook myself free. My muscles jumped, my nerves jangled, writhed. But I saw that this was not stopping the other boys. Laughing in fear and embarrassment some were holding back and scooping up the coins knocked off by the painful contortions of the others. The men roared above us as we struggled.

"Pick it up, goddamit, pick it up!" someone called like a bass-voiced parrot. "Go on, get it!"

I crawled rapidly around the floor, picking up the coins, trying to avoid the coppers and to get greenbacks and the gold. Ignoring the shock by laughing, as I brushed the coins off quickly I discovered that I could contain the electricity—a contradiction, but it works. Then the men began to push us upon the rug. Laughing embarrassedly, we struggled out of their hands and kept after the coins. We were all wet and slippery and hard to hold. Suddenly I saw a boy lifted into the air, glistening with sweat like a circus seal, and dropped, his wet back landing flush upon the electrically charged rug, heard him yell and saw him literally dance upon his back, his elbows beating a frenzied rhythm upon the floor, his muscles twitching like the flesh of a horse stung by many flies. When he finally rolled off, his face was grey and no one stopped him when he ran from the floor amid booming laughter.

"Get that money," the M.C. called. "That's good, hard American cash!"

And we snatched and grabbed, snatched and grabbed. I was careful not to come too close to the rug now, and when I felt the hot whisky breath descend upon me like a cloud of foul air, I reached out and grabbed the leg of a chair. It was occupied, and I held on desperately.

"Leggo, nigger! Leggo!"

The huge face wavered down to mine as he tried to push me free. But my body was slippery and he was too drunk. It was Mr. Colcord, who owned a chain of movie houses and entertainment palaces. Each time he grabbed me I slipped out of his hands. It became a real struggle. I feared the rug more than I did the drunk, so I held on, surprising myself for a moment by trying to topple *him* upon the rug. It was such an enormous idea that I found myself actually carrying it out. I tried not to be obvious, yet trying to tumble him out of the chair I grabbed his leg, when he raised up roaring with laughter, and, looking me dead in the eye, kicked me viciously in the chest. The chair leg flew out of my hand and I felt myself going and rolled. It was as though I had rolled through a bed of hot coals. It seemed a whole century would pass before I would roll free, a century in which I was seared through the deepest levels of my body to the fearful breath within me, and the breath seared and heated to the point of explosion. "It'll all be over in a flash," I thought, as I rolled clear.

"All be over in a flash." But not yet. The men on the other side were waiting, red faces swollen as though from apoplexy as they bent forward in their chairs. Seeing their fingers coming towards me I rolled away, as a fumbled football rolls off the receiver's fingertips, back into the coals. That time I luckily sent the rug sliding out of place and heard the coins ringing against the floor and the boys scuffling to pick them up and the M.C. calling, "All right, boys, that's all. Go get dressed and get your money."

I was limp as a dishrag. My back felt as though it had been beaten with wires. When we had dressed, the M.C. came in and gave us each five dollars, except Tatlock, who got ten for being last in the ring. Then he told us to leave. I was not to get a chance to deliver my speech, I thought. I was going out into the dim garbage-filled alley in despair when I was stopped and told to go back. When I went back the men were pushing back their chairs and gathering in groups to talk. The M.C. knocked on a table for quiet.

"Gentlemen," he said, "we almost forgot an important part of the programme. A *most* serious part, gentlemen. This boy was brought here to deliver a speech which he made at his graduation yesterday . . ."

"Bravo!"

"I'm told that he is the smartest boy we've got out there in Milltown. I'm told that he knows more big words than a pocket-sized dictionary."

Much applause and laughter.

"So now, gentlemen, I want you to give him your attention."

There was still laughter as I faced them, my mouth was dry, my eye throbbing. I began slowly, but evidently my throat was tense, because they began shouting, "Louder! Louder!"

I began again, tensing my diaphragm to project my voice, although it ached from the many blows to my solar plexus.

"We of the younger generation extol the wisdom of that great leader and educator," I shouted, "who first spoke these flaming words of wisdom:[5] 'A ship lost at sea for many days suddenly sighted a friendly vessel. From the mast of the unfortunate vessel was seen a signal: "Water, water: we die of thirst!" The answer from the friendly vessel came back: "Cast down your bucket where you are." The captain of the distressed vessel, at last heeding the injunction, cast down his bucket, and it came up full of fresh sparkling water from the mouth of the Amazon River.' And like him I say, and in his words, 'To those of my race who depend upon bettering their condition in a foreign land, or who

---

5. **these flaming words of wisdom**: What follows is an often-quoted passage from Booker T. Washington's Atlanta Exposition Address. See note 1.

undertake the importance of cultivating friendly relations with the Southern white man, who is his next-door neighbour, I would say: "Cast down your bucket where you are" – cast it down in making friends in every manly way of the people of all races by whom we are surrounded . . .'"

I spoke automatically and with such fervour that I did not realize that the men were still talking and laughing until my dry mouth filling up with blood from the cut, almost strangled me. I coughed, wanting to stop and go to one of the tall brass, sand-filled spittoons to relieve myself, but a few of the men, especially the superintendent, were listening, and I was afraid, so I gulped it down, blood, saliva and all, and continued. What powers of endurance I had during those days! What enthusiasm! What a belief in the rightness of things! I spoke even louder in spite of the pain. But they still talked and still they laughed as though with cotton in dirty ears. So I spoke with greater emotional emphasis. I closed my ears and swallowed blood until I was nauseated. The speech seemed a hundred times as long as before, but I could not leave out a single word. All had to be said, each memorized nuance considered, rendered. Nor was that all. Whenever I uttered a word of three or more syllables a group of voices would yell, for me to repeat it. I used the phrase "social responsibility" and they yelled:

"What's that word you say, boy?"

"Social responsibility," I said.

"What?"

"Social . . ."

"Louder . . ."

"Responsibility."

"More!"

"Responsi——"

"Repeat!"

"——bility."

The room filled with the uproar of laughter until, no doubt, distracted by having to gulp down my blood, I made a mistake and yelled a phrase I had often seen denounced in newspaper editorials, heard debated in private.

"Social . . ."

"What?" they yelled.

"Equality."

The laughter hung smoke-like in the sudden stillness. I opened my eyes, puzzled. Sounds of displeasure filled the room. The M.C. rushed forward. They shouted hostile phrases at me. But I did not understand. A small, dry, moustached man in the front row blared out, "Say that slowly, son!"

"What, sir?"

"What you just said."

"Social responsibility, sir," I said.

"You weren't being smart, were you, boy?" he said not unkindly.

"No, sir!"

"You sure that about equality was a mistake?"

"Yes, sir," I said. "I was swallowing blood."

"Well, you had better speak more slowly so we can understand. We mean to do right by you but you've got to know your place at all times. All right, now, go on with your speech."

I was afraid. I wanted to leave but I wanted also to speak, and I was afraid they'd snatch me down. "Thank you, sir," I said, beginning where I had left off, and having them ignore me as before.

Yet when I finished there was a thunderous applause. I was surprised to see the superintendent come forth with a package wrapped in white tissue paper, and gesturing for quiet, address the men.

"Gentlemen, you see that I did not over-praise this boy. He makes a good speech and some day he'll lead his people and we will find him useful. And I don't have to tell you that that is important in these days and times. This is a good, smart boy, and so to encourage him in the right direction, in the name of the Board of Education I wish to present him with a prize in the form of this . . ."

He paused, removing the tissue paper and revealing a gleaming calfskin briefcase.

"In the form of this first-class article from Shad Whitmore's shop."

"Boy," he said, addressing me. "Take this prize and keep it well. Consider it a badge of office. Prize it. Keep developing as you are and some day it will be filled with important papers that will help shape the destiny of your people."

I was so moved that I could hardly express my thanks. A rope of bloody saliva drooled upon the leather, forming a shape like an undiscovered continent, and I wiped it quickly away. I felt an importance that I had never dreamed before.

"Open it and see what's inside," I was told.

My fingers atremble, I complied, smelling the fresh leather and seeing an official-looking document inside. It was a scholarship to the state college for Negroes. My eyes filled with tears and I ran awkwardly off the floor. I was overjoyed. I did not even mind when I discovered that the gold pieces I had scrambled for were brass pocket tokens advertising a certain make of Detroit automobile.

When I reached home everyone was excited. Next day the neighbours came to congratulate me. I even felt safe from my grandfather, whose deathbed curse usually spoiled my triumphs. I stood beneath his photograph with my briefcase in hand and smiled triumphantly into his stolid, black, peasant's face. It was a face that fascinated me. The eyes seemed to follow everywhere I went. That night I dreamed I was at a circus with him and that he refused to laugh at the clowns no matter what they did, then later he told me to open my briefcase and read what was inside and I did, finding an official envelope stamped with the state seal and inside the envelope I found another and another, endlessly, and I thought I would fall of weariness. "Them's yours," he said. "Now open that one," and I did and in it I found an engraved document containing a short message in letters of gold: "Read it," my grandfather said. "Out loud!"

"To Whom it May Concern," I intoned. "Keep This Nigger-Boy Running." I awoke with the old man's laughter ringing in my ears.

[1947]

Saul Bellow

[1915–2005]

Saul Bellow was born on June 10, 1915, in Lachine, Canada, a w[...] town near Montreal. His parents were Abraham and Lescha Be[...] immigrants from St. Petersburg, Russia. Bellow was the cou[...] child and the first to be born in Canada. Like other immigrant [...] Bellows struggled to make a living, and in 1918 they moved to an impoverished Jewish section of Montreal. Bellow, who grew up speaking English, French, and Yiddish, studied Hebrew and by the age of four could recite long passages from the Pentateuch. When he was eight years old, he was hospitalized for six months as a result of complications from an emergency appendectomy. The experience had a profound effect on Bellow, who in a 1990 interview said that he developed an early sense of the fragility of life. In 1924, after Bellow's father failed at yet another business venture, the family left Canada to join relatives in Chicago, where they found a place to live in the predominantly Polish and Jewish section of Humboldt Park. When he was not in school or working at odd jobs, Bellow spent long hours reading at a public library. During his senior year at Tuley High School, Bellow's mother died of cancer. "My life was never the same," he recalled. After his graduation in 1933, he attended Crane Junior College for a semester and then enrolled at the University of Chicago. In 1935, when his father could no longer afford to pay his tuition and living expenses, Bellow moved back home and transferred to nearby Northwestern University.

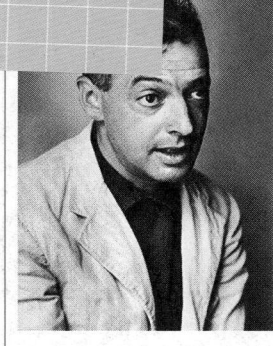

Saul Bellow

This photograph was taken in 1953, the year Bellow published his breakthrough novel *The Adventures of Augie March*.

 Bellow struggled to make his way as a writer. Although he published a short story in the *Daily Northwestern* in February 1936, he received little encouragement from professors in the English Department. Bellow maintained that they believed that a Jew could never fully understand English literature, so he instead studied sociology and anthropology. When he graduated in 1937, he was awarded a fellowship for graduate study at the University of Wisconsin, Madison. But he withdrew after a year, later explaining, "Every time I worked on my thesis, it turned out to be a story." Bellow, who returned to Chicago in 1938, also recalled that his father was so frustrated by his ambition to become a writer that he once exclaimed: "You write and then you erase; you call that a profession?" Nonetheless, Bellow persevered, initially supporting himself by working for the Federal Writers' Project. He married the first of his five wives and later took a variety of jobs, including doing editorial work for the *Encyclopedia Britannica* and teaching at Pestalozzi-Froebel Teacher's College. His first published story appeared in the prestigious *Partisan Review* in 1941. After the United States entered World War II, Bellow became an American citizen in 1942. He was eventually rejected by the army because of a hernia, and he joined the merchant marine. While waiting for his own military service to begin, he wrote a novel about a man about to be inducted into the army, *Dangling Man* (1944). From 1946 to 1948, Bellow taught at the University of Minnesota in Minneapolis, where he wrote *The Victim* (1947), a novel about a Jewish man coping with anti-Semitism in the aftermath of World War II. In 1948, Bellow was awarded a Guggenheim Fellowship, and he lived for two years in Paris. There, he began work on *The Adventures of Augie March* (1953), the story of a young Jew coming of age in Depression-era Chicago.

That novel won the National Book Award and firmly established Bellow as a "writer of consequence," as he was described in the *New York Times.* Now living in New York City, he published reviews and short fiction in a variety of prominent magazines. For the next several years, he also taught courses at New York University, Princeton, and Bard College. His collection *Seize the Day* (1956), was followed by *Henderson, the Rain King* (1959), a satiric novel about a man who goes on a spiritual pilgrimage to Africa. *Herzog* (1964), the story of a middle-aged Jewish professor's complicated response to a failed marriage and a failing career, was on the *New York Times* bestseller list for a year. Bellow returned to live in Chicago in 1967, when he accepted a position at the University of Chicago. Within the next decade, he published *Mosby's Memoirs and Other Stories* (1968) and two novels: *Mr. Sammler's Planet* (1970), the story of a Holocaust survivor living in New York; and *Humboldt's Gift* (1975), a sharp critique of American capitalist values that won the Pulitzer Prize. In 1976, Bellow was awarded the Nobel Prize for Literature. The citation praised him "for the human understanding and subtle analysis of contemporary culture that are combined in his work." Bellow continued that analysis of the state of contemporary culture in several of his later works, notably *The Dean's December* (1982), a novel about the decay of urban America; and *Ravelstein* (2000), inspired by the life and death from an AIDS-related illness of his closest friend, the philosopher and controversial education critic Allan Bloom. Hailed as a writer who "breathed new life into the American novel," Bellow died in Boston on April 5, 2005.

bedfordstmartins.com/ americanlit for research links on Bellow

Reading Bellow's "Looking for Mr. Green."   Regarded by many critics as Bellow's finest short story, "Looking for Mr. Green" first appeared in 1951 in *Commentary,* an influential magazine of literature and politics published by the American Jewish Committee. Bellow included the story in his first collection, *Seize the Day* (1956), and later revised it for publication in *Mosby's Memoirs and Other Stories* (1968). Several of the stories in that much-admired collection are accounts of quests, like the one in "Looking for Mr. Green," which is set in Depression-era Chicago. Its central character is George Grebe, an unemployed white college graduate who is forced to take a job with a government agency, delivering relief checks in an impoverished black ghetto on the South Side. As he searches for an elusive man named Tulliver Green, Grebe confronts the hard realities of life in urban Chicago, the site of Bellow's complex exploration of the ways in which human beings make connections in what he describes as the "layers of ruin" of the modern urban world. The text is taken from *Mosby's Memoirs and Other Stories* (1968).

LOOKING FOR MR. GREEN

Whatsoever thy hand findeth to do, do it with thy might. . . .[1]

Hard work? No, it wasn't really so hard. He wasn't used to walking and stair-climbing, but the physical difficulty of his new job was not what George Grebe felt most. He was delivering relief checks in the Negro district, and although he was a native Chicagoan this was not a part of the city he knew much about — it needed a depression to introduce him to it. No, it wasn't literally hard work, not as reckoned in foot-pounds, but yet he was beginning to feel the strain of it, to grow aware of its peculiar difficulty. He could find the streets and numbers, but the clients were not where they were supposed to be, and he felt like a hunter inexperienced in the camouflage of his game. It was an unfavorable day, too — fall, and cold, dark weather, windy. But, anyway, instead of shells in his deep trenchcoat pocket he had the cardboard of checks, punctured for the spindles of the file, the holes reminding him of the holes in player-piano paper. And he didn't look much like a hunter, either; his was a city figure entirely, belted up in this Irish conspirator's coat. He was slender without being tall, stiff in the back, his legs looking shabby in a pair of old tweed pants gone through and fringy at the cuffs. With this stiffness, he kept his head forward, so that his face was red from the sharpness of the weather; and it was an indoors sort of face with gray eyes that persisted in some kind of thought and yet seemed to avoid definiteness of conclusion. He wore sideburns that surprised you some-what by the tough curl of the blond hair and the effect of assertion in their length. He was not so mild as he looked, nor so youthful; and nevertheless there was no effort on his part to seem what he was not. He was an educated man; he was a bachelor; he was in some ways simple; without lushing, he liked a drink; his luck had not been good. Nothing was deliberately hidden.

He felt that his luck was better than usual today. When he had reported for work that morning he had expected to be shut up in the relief office at a clerk's job, for he had been hired downtown as a clerk, and he was glad to have, instead, the freedom of the streets and welcomed, at least at first, the vigor of the cold and even the blowing of the hard wind. But on the other hand he was not getting on with the distribution of the checks. It was true that it was a city job; nobody expected you to push too hard at a city job. His supervisor, that young Mr. Raynor, had practically told him that. Still, he wanted to do well at it. For one thing, when he knew how quickly he could deliver a batch of checks, he would know also how much time he could expect to clip for himself. And then, too, the clients would be waiting for their money. That was not the most important consideration, though it certainly mattered to him. No, but he wanted to do well, simply for doing-well's sake, to acquit himself decently of a job because he so rarely had a job to do that required just this sort of energy. Of this peculiar energy he now had a superabundance; once it had started to flow, it flowed all too heavily. And, for the time being anyway, he was balked. He could not find Mr. Green.

So he stood in his big-skirted trenchcoat with a large envelope in his hand and papers showing from his pocket, wondering why people should be so hard to locate who were

---

1. **Whatsoever . . . with thy might**: The opening of Ecclesiastes 9:10, which concludes: "for there is no work, nor device, nor knowledge, nor wisdom, in the grave, whither thou goest."

too feeble or sick to come to the station to collect their own checks. But Raynor had told him that tracking them down was not easy at first and had offered him some advice on how to proceed. "If you can see the postman, he's your first man to ask, and your best bet. If you can't connect with him, try the stores and tradespeople around. Then the janitor and the neighbors. But you'll find the closer you come to your man the less people will tell you. They don't want to tell you anything."

"Because I'm a stranger."

"Because you're white. We ought to have a Negro doing this, but we don't at the moment, and of course you've got to eat, too, and this is public employment. Jobs have to be made. Oh, that holds for me too. Mind you, I'm not letting myself out. I've got three years of seniority on you, that's all. And a law degree. Otherwise, you might be back of the desk and I might be going out into the field this cold day. The same dough pays us both and for the same, exact, identical reason. What's my law degree got to do with it? But you have to pass out these checks, Mr. Grebe, and it'll help if you're stubborn, so I hope you are."

"Yes, I'm fairly stubborn."

Raynor sketched hard with an eraser in the old dirt of his desk, left-handed, and said, "Sure, what else can you answer to such a question. Anyhow, the trouble you're going to have is that they don't like to give information about anybody. They think you're a plainclothes dick or an installment collector, or summons-server or something like that. Till you've been seen around the neighborhood for a few months and people know you're only from the relief."

It was dark, ground-freezing, pre-Thanksgiving weather; the wind played hob with the smoke, rushing it down, and Grebe missed his gloves, which he had left in Raynor's office. And no one would admit knowing Green. It was past three o'clock and the postman had made his last delivery. The nearest grocer, himself a Negro, had never heard the name Tulliver Green, or said he hadn't. Grebe was inclined to think that it was true, that he had in the end convinced the man that he wanted only to deliver a check. But he wasn't sure. He needed experience in interpreting looks and signs and, even more, the will not to be put off or denied and even the force to bully if need be. If the grocer did know, he had got rid of him easily. But since most of his trade was with reliefers, why should he prevent the delivery of a check? Maybe Green, or Mrs. Green, if there was a Mrs. Green, patronized another grocer. And was there a Mrs. Green? It was one of Grebe's great handicaps that he hadn't looked at any of the case records. Raynor should have let him read files for a few hours. But he apparently saw no need for that, probably considering the job unimportant. Why prepare systematically to deliver a few checks?

But now it was time to look for the janitor. Grebe took in the building in the wind and gloom of the late November day—trampled, frost-hardened lots on one side; on the other, an automobile junk yard and then the infinite work of Elevated frames, weak-looking, gaping with rubbish fires; two sets of leaning brick porches three stories high and a flight of cement stairs to the cellar. Descending, he entered the underground passage, where he tried the doors until one opened and he found himself in the furnace room. There someone rose toward him and approached, scraping on the coal grit and bending under the canvas-jacketed pipes.

"Are you the janitor?"

"What do you want?"

"I'm looking for a man who's supposed to be living here. Green."

"What Green?"

"Oh, you maybe have more than one Green?" said Grebe with new, pleasant hope. "This is Tulliver Green."

"I don't think I c'n help you, mister. I don't know any."

"A crippled man."

The janitor stood bent before him. Could it be that he was crippled? Oh, God! what if he was. Grebe's gray eyes sought with excited difficulty to see. But no, he was only very short and stooped. A head awakened from meditation, a strong-haired beard, low, wide shoulders. A staleness of sweat and coal rose from his black shirt and the burlap sack he wore as an apron.

"Crippled how?"

Grebe thought and then answered with the light voice of unmixed candor, "I don't know. I've never seen him." This was damaging, but his only other choice was to make a lying guess, and he was not up to it. "I'm delivering checks for the relief to shut-in cases. If he weren't crippled he'd come to collect himself. That's why I said crippled. Bedridden, chair-ridden — is there anybody like that?"

This sort of frankness was one of Grebe's oldest talents, going back to childhood. But it gained him nothing here.

"No suh. I've got four buildin's same as this that I take care of. I don' know all the tenants, leave alone the tenants' tenants. The rooms turn over so fast, people movin' in and out every day. I can't tell you."

The janitor opened his grimy lips but Grebe did not hear him in the piping of the valves and the consuming pull of air to flame in the body of the furnace. He knew, however, what he had said.

"Well, all the same, thanks. Sorry I bothered you. I'll prowl around upstairs again and see if I can turn up someone who knows him."

Once more in the cold air and early darkness he made the short circle from the cellarway to the entrance crowded between the brickwork pillars and began to climb to the third floor. Pieces of plaster ground under his feet; strips of brass tape from which the carpeting had been torn away marked old boundaries at the sides. In the passage, the cold reached him worse than in the street; it touched him to the bone. The hall toilets ran like springs. He thought grimly as he heard the wind burning around the building with a sound like that of the furnace, that this was a great piece of constructed shelter. Then he struck a match in the gloom and searched for names and numbers among the writings and scribbles on the walls. He saw WHOODY-DOODY GO TO JESUS, and zigzags, caricatures, sexual scrawls, and curses. So the sealed rooms of pyramids were also decorated, and the caves of human dawn.

The information on his card was, TULLIVER GREEN — APT 3D. There were no names, however, and no numbers. His shoulders drawn up, tears of cold in his eyes, breathing vapor, he went the length of the corridor and told himself that if he had been lucky enough to have the temperament for it he would bang on one of the doors and bawl out

"Tulliver Green!" until he got results. But it wasn't in him to make an uproar and he continued to burn matches, passing the light over the walls. At the rear, in a corner off the hall, he discovered a door he had not seen before and he thought it best to investigate. It sounded empty when he knocked, but a young Negress answered, hardly more than a girl. She opened only a bit, to guard the warmth of the room.

"Yes suh?"

"I'm from the district relief station on Prairie Avenue. I'm looking for a man named Tulliver Green to give him his check. Do you know him?"

No, she didn't; but he thought she had not understood anything of what he had said. She had a dream-bound, dream-blind face, very soft and black, shut off. She wore a man's jacket and pulled the ends together at her throat. Her hair was parted in three directions, at the sides and transversely, standing up at the front in a dull puff.

"Is there somebody around here who might know?"

"I jus' taken this room las' week."

He observed that she shivered, but even her shiver was somnambulistic and there was no sharp consciousness of cold in the big smooth eyes of her handsome face.

"All right, miss, thank you. Thanks," he said, and went to try another place.

Here he was admitted. He was grateful, for the room was warm. It was full of people, and they were silent as he entered — ten people, or a dozen, perhaps more, sitting on benches like a parliament. There was no light, properly speaking, but a tempered darkness that the window gave, and everyone seemed to him enormous, the men padded out in heavy work clothes and winter coats, and the women huge, too, in their sweaters, hats, and old furs. And, besides, bed and bedding, a black cooking range, a piano piled towering to the ceiling with papers, a dining-room table of the old style of prosperous Chicago. Among these people Grebe, with his cold-heightened fresh color and his smaller stature, entered like a schoolboy. Even though he was met with smiles and good will, he knew, before a single word was spoken, that all the currents ran against him and that he would make no headway. Nevertheless he began. "Does anybody here know how I can deliver a check to Mr. Tulliver Green?"

"Green?" It was the man that had let him in who answered. He was in short sleeves, in a checkered shirt, and had a queer, high head, profusely overgrown and long as a shako;[2] the veins entered it strongly from his forehead. "I never heard mention of him. Is this where he live?"

"This is the address they gave me at the station. He's a sick man, and he'll need his check. Can't anybody tell me where to find him?"

He stood his ground and waited for a reply, his crimson wool scarf wound about his neck and drooping outside his trenchcoat, pockets weighted with the block of checks and official forms. They must have realized that he was not a college boy employed afternoons by a bill collector, trying foxily to pass for a relief clerk, recognized that he was an older man who knew himself what need was, who had had more than an average

---

2. **shako:** A tall, plumed military hat.

seasoning in hardship. It was evident enough if you looked at the marks under his eyes
and at the sides of his mouth.

"Anybody know this sick man?"

"No, suh." On all sides he saw heads shaken and smiles of denial. No one knew. And
maybe it was true, he considered, standing silent in the earthen, musky human gloom of
the place as the rumble continued. But he could never really be sure.

"What's the matter with this man?" said shako-head.

"I've never seen him. All I can tell you is that he can't come in person for his money.
It's my first day in this district."

"Maybe they given you the wrong number?"

"I don't believe so. But where else can I ask about him?" He felt that this persistence
amused them deeply, and in a way he shared their amusement that he should stand up
so tenaciously to them. Though smaller, though slight, he was his own man, he retracted
nothing about himself, and he looked back at them, gray-eyed, with amusement and also
with a sort of courage. On the bench some man spoke in his throat, the words impossible
to catch, and a woman answered with a wild, shrieking laugh, which was quickly cut off.

"Well, so nobody will tell me?"

"Ain't nobody who knows."

"At least, if he lives here, he pays rent to someone. Who manages the building?"

"Greatham Company. That's on Thirty-ninth Street."

Grebe wrote it in his pad. But, in the street again, a sheet of wind-driven paper clinging to his leg while he deliberated what direction to take next, it seemed a feeble lead to
follow. Probably this Green didn't rent a flat, but a room. Sometimes there were as many
as twenty people in an apartment; the real-estate agent would know only the lessee. And
not even the agent could tell you who the renters were. In some places the beds were
even used in shifts, watchmen or jitney drivers or short-order cooks in night joints turning out after a day's sleep and surrendering their beds to a sister, a nephew, or perhaps a
stranger, just off the bus. There were large numbers of newcomers in this terrific, blight-
bitten portion of the city between Cottage Grove and Ashland, wandering from house to
house and room to room. When you saw them, how could you know them? They didn't
carry bundles on their backs or look picturesque. You only saw a man, a Negro, walking
in the street or riding in the car, like everyone else, with his thumb closed on a transfer.
And therefore how were you supposed to tell? Grebe thought the Greatham agent would
only laugh at his question.

But how much it would have simplified the job to be able to say that Green was old, or
blind, or consumptive. An hour in the files, taking a few notes, and he needn't have been
at such a disadvantage. When Raynor gave him the block of checks he asked, "How much
should I know about these people?" Then Raynor had looked as though he were preparing
to accuse him of trying to make the job more important than it was. He smiled, because
by then they were on fine terms, but nevertheless he had been getting ready to say something like that when the confusion began in the station over Staika and her children.

Grebe had waited a long time for this job. It came to him through the pull of an old
schoolmate in the Corporation Counsel's office, never a close friend, but suddenly
sympathetic and interested—pleased to show, moreover, how well he had done, how

strongly he was coming on even in these miserable times. Well, he was coming through strongly, along with the Democratic administration itself. Grebe had gone to see him in City Hall, and they had had a counter lunch or beers at least once a month for a year, and finally it had been possible to swing the job. He didn't mind being assigned the lowest clerical grade, nor even being a messenger, though Raynor thought he did.

This Raynor was an original sort of guy and Grebe had taken to him immediately. As was proper on the first day, Grebe had come early, but he waited long, for Raynor was late. At last he darted into his cubicle of an office as though he had just jumped from one of those hurtling huge red Indian Avenue cars. His thin, rough face was wind-stung and he was grinning and saying something breathlessly to himself. In his hat, a small fedora, and his coat, the velvet collar a neat fit about his neck, and his silk muffler that set off the nervous twist of his chin, he swayed and turned himself in his swivel chair, feet leaving the ground; so that he pranced a little as he sat. Meanwhile he took Grebe's measure out of his eyes, eyes of an unusual vertical length and slightly sardonic. So the two men sat for a while, saying nothing, while the supervisor raised his hat from his miscombed hair and put it in his lap. His cold-darkened hands were not clean. A steel beam passed through the little makeshift room, from which machine belts once had hung. The building was an old factory.

"I'm younger than you; I hope you won't find it hard taking orders from me," said Raynor. "But I don't make them up, either. You're how old, about?"

"Thirty-five."

"And you thought you'd be inside doing paper work. But it so happens I have to send you out."

"I don't mind."

"And it's mostly a Negro load we have in this district."

"So I thought it would be."

"Fine. You'll get along. *C'est un bon boulot.*[3] Do you know French?"

"Some."

"I thought you'd be a university man."

"Have you been in France?" said Grebe.

"No, that's the French of the Berlitz School. I've been at it for more than a year, just as I'm sure people have been, all over the world, office boys in China and braves in Tanganyika.[4] In fact, I damn well know it. Such is the attractive power of civilization. It's overrated, but what do you want? *Que voulez-vous?*[5] I get *Le Rire*[6] and all the spicy papers, just like in Tanganyika. It must be mystifying, out there. But my reason is that I'm aiming at the diplomatic service. I have a cousin who's a courier, and the way he describes it is awfully attractive. He rides in the *wagon-lits*[7] and reads books. While we — What did you do before?"

---

3. *C'est un bon boulot*: It's a good job (French).
4. *Tanganyika*: A British territory in East Africa that gained its independence in 1961.
5. *Que voulez-vous?*: What do you want? (French).
6. *Le Rire*: *Laughter* (French), a weekly humor magazine that was founded in Paris in 1894 and published in various forms through the 1950s.
7. *wagon-lits*: Sleeping cars on a train (French).

"I sold."

"Where?"

"Canned meat at Stop and Shop. In the basement."

"And before that?"

"Window shades, at Goldblatt's."

"Steady work?"

"No, Thursdays and Saturdays. I also sold shoes."

"You've been a shoe-dog too. Well. And prior to that? Here it is in your folder." He opened the record. "Saint Olaf's College, instructor in classical languages. Fellow, University of Chicago, 1926-27. I've had Latin, too. Let's trade quotations – '*Dum spiro spero.*' "[8]

" '*Da dextram misero.*' "[9]

" '*Alea jacta est.*' "[10]

" '*Excelsior.*' "[11]

Raynor shouted with laughter, and other workers came to look at him over the partition. Grebe also laughed, feeling pleased and easy. The luxury of fun on a nervous morning.

When they were done and no one was watching or listening, Raynor said rather seriously, "What made you study Latin in the first place? Was it for the priesthood?"

"No."

"Just for the hell of it? For the culture? Oh, the things people think they can pull!" He made his cry hilarious and tragic. "I ran my pants off so I could study for the bar, and I've passed the bar, so I get twelve dollars a week more than you as a bonus for having seen life straight and whole. I'll tell you, as a man of culture, that even though nothing looks to be real, and everything stands for something else, and that thing for another thing, and that thing for a still further one – there ain't any comparison between twenty-five and thirty-seven dollars a week, regardless of the last reality. Don't you think that was clear to your Greeks? They were a thoughtful people, but they didn't part with their slaves."

This was a great deal more than Grebe had looked for in his first interview with his supervisor. He was too shy to show all the astonishment he felt. He laughed a little, aroused, and brushed at the sunbeam that covered his head with its dust. "Do you think my mistake was so terrible?"

"Damn right it was terrible, and you know it now that you've had the whip of hard times laid on your back. You should have been preparing yourself for trouble. Your people must have been well off to send you to the university. Stop me, if I'm stepping on your toes. Did your mother pamper you? Did your father give in to you? Were you brought up tenderly, with permission to go and find out what were the last things that everything else stands for while everybody else labored in the fallen world of appearances?"

---

8. '*Dum spiro spero*': Where there's life there's hope (Latin).
9. '*Da dextram misero*': Give the right hand to the wretched (Latin).
10. '*Alea jacta est*': The die is cast (Latin).
11. '*Excelsior*': Higher (Latin).

"Well, no, it wasn't exactly like that." Grebe smiled. *The fallen world of appearances!*[12] no less. But now it was his turn to deliver a surprise. "We weren't rich. My father was the last genuine English butler in Chicago—"

"Are you kidding?"

"Why should I be?"

"In a livery?"

"In livery. Up on the Gold Coast."[13]

"And he wanted you to be educated like a gentleman?"

"He did not. He sent me to the Armour Institute to study chemical engineering. But when he died I changed schools."

He stopped himself, and considered how quickly Raynor had reached him. In no time he had your valise on the table and all your stuff unpacked. And afterward, in the streets, he was still reviewing how far he might have gone, and how much he might have been led to tell if they had not been interrupted by Mrs. Staika's great noise.

But just then a young woman, one of Raynor's workers, ran into the cubicle exclaiming, "Haven't you heard all the fuss?"

"We haven't heard anything."

"It's Staika, giving out with all her might. The reporters are coming. She said she phoned the papers, and you know she did."

"But what is she up to?" said Raynor.

"She brought her wash and she's ironing it here, with our current, because the relief won't pay her electric bill. She has her ironing board set up by the admitting desk, and her kids are with her, all six. They never are in school more than once a week. She's always dragging them around with her because of her reputation."

"I don't want to miss any of this," said Raynor, jumping up. Grebe, as he followed with the secretary, said, "Who is this Staika?"

"They call her the 'Blood Mother of Federal Street.' She's a professional donor at the hospitals. I think they pay ten dollars a pint. Of course it's no joke, but she makes a very big thing out of it and she and the kids are in the papers all the time."

A small crowd, staff and clients divided by a plywood barrier, stood in the narrow space of the entrance, and Staika was shouting in a gruff, mannish voice, plunging the iron on the board and slamming it on the metal rest.

"My father and mother came in a steerage, and I was born in our house, Robey by Huron. I'm no dirty immigrant. I'm a U.S. citizen. My husband is a gassed veteran from France with lungs weaker'n paper, that hardly can he go to the toilet by himself. These six children of mine, I have to buy the shoes for their feet with my own blood. Even a

---

12. **The fallen world of appearances!**: As Grebe evidently recognizes, his supervisor has alluded to Augustine of Hippo (354–430), later St. Augustine, an influential theologian of the early Roman Catholic Church. Augustine developed the concept that human beings live in two worlds: the realm of appearances, of things as they seem, and the higher reality of things as they are. In order to leave behind the sinful or fallen realm of appearances, human beings must seek divine salvation and spiritual liberation in the higher reality.

13. **Gold Coast**: A wealthy neighborhood along the lakefront north of downtown Chicago. Livery is a special uniform worn by a servant.

lousy little white Communion necktie, that's a couple of drops of blood; a little piece of mosquito veil for my Vadja so she won't be ashamed in church for the other girls, they take my blood for it by Goldblatt. That's how I keep goin'. A fine thing if I had to depend on the relief. And there's plenty of people on the rolls – fakes! There's nothin' *they* can't get, that can go and wrap bacon at Swift and Armour any time. They're lookin' for them by the Yards. They never have to be out of work. Only they rather lay in their lousy beds and eat the public's money." She was not afraid, in a predominantly Negro station, to shout this way about Negroes.

Grebe and Raynor worked themselves forward to get a closer view of the woman. She was flaming with anger and with pleasure at herself, broad and huge, a golden-headed woman who wore a cotton cap laced with pink ribbon. She was barelegged and had on black gym shoes, her Hoover apron[14] was open and her great breasts, not much re-strained by a man's undershirt, hampered her arms as she worked at the kid's dress on the ironing board. And the children, silent and white, with a kind of locked obstinacy, in sheepskins and lumberjackets, stood behind her. She had captured the station, and the pleasure this gave her was enormous. Yet her grievances were true grievances. She was telling the truth. But she behaved like a liar. The look of her small eyes was hidden, and while she raged she also seemed to be spinning and planning.

"They send me out college case workers in silk pants to talk me out of what I got comin'. Are they better'n me? Who told them? Fire them. Let 'em go and get married, and then you won't have to cut electric from people's budget."

The chief supervisor, Mr. Ewing, couldn't silence her and he stood with folded arms at the head of his staff, bald, bald-headed, saying to his subordinates like the ex-school principal he was, "Pretty soon she'll be tired and go."

"No she won't," said Raynor to Grebe. "She'll get what she wants. She knows more about the relief even than Ewing. She's been on the rolls for years, and she always gets what she wants because she puts on a noisy show. Ewing knows it. He'll give in soon. He's only saving face. If he gets bad publicity, the Commissioner'll have him on the car-pet, downtown. She's got him submerged; she'll submerge everybody in time, and that includes nations and governments."

Grebe replied with his characteristic smile, disagreeing completely. Who would take Staika's orders, and what changes could her yelling ever bring about?

No, what Grebe saw in her, the power that made people listen, was that her cry expressed the war of flesh and blood, perhaps turned a little crazy and certainly ugly, on this place and this condition. And at first, when he went out, the spirit of Staika some-how presided over the whole district for him, and it took color from her; he saw her color, in the spotty curb fires, and the fires under the El,[15] the straight alley of flamy gloom. Later, too, when he went into a tavern for a shot of rye, the sweat of beer, association with West Side Polish streets, made him think of her again.

---

14. **Hoover apron:** A popular, wrap-around apron invented by the wife of Herbert Hoover, who was appointed as the first director of the U.S. Food Administration when the United States entered World War I in 1917 and who was elected president in 1928, the year before the onset of the Great Depression.
15. **El:** The common name of the elevated train system in Chicago.

He wiped the corners of his mouth with his muffler, his handkerchief being inconvenient to reach for, and went out again to get on with the delivery of his checks. The air bit cold and hard and a few flakes of snow formed near him. A train struck by and left a quiver in the frames and a bristling icy hiss over the rails.

Crossing the street, he descended a flight of board steps into a basement grocery, setting off a little bell. It was a dark, long store and it caught you with its stinks of smoked meat, soap, dried peaches, and fish. There was a fire wrinkling and flapping in the little stove, and the proprietor was waiting, an Italian with a long, hollow face and stubborn bristles. He kept his hands warm under his apron.

No, he didn't know Green. You knew people but not names. The same man might not have the same name twice. The police didn't know, either, and mostly didn't care. When somebody was shot or knifed they took the body away and didn't look for the murderer. In the first place, nobody would tell them anything. So they made up a name for the coroner and called it quits. And in the second place, they didn't give a goddamn anyhow. But they couldn't get to the bottom of a thing even if they wanted to. Nobody would get to know even a tenth of what went on among these people. They stabbed and stole, they did every crime and abomination you ever heard of, men and men, women and women, parents and children, worse than the animals. They carried on their own way, and the horrors passed off like a smoke. There was never anything like it in the history of the whole world.

It was a long speech, deepening with every word in its fantasy and passion and becoming increasingly senseless and terrible: a swarm amassed by suggestion and invention, a huge, hugging, despairing knot, a human wheel of heads, legs, bellies, arms, rolling through his shop.

Grebe felt that he must interrupt him. He said sharply, "What are you talking about! All I asked was whether you knew this man."

"That isn't even the half of it. I been here six years. You probably don't want to believe this. But suppose it's true?"

"All the same," said Grebe, "there must be a way to find a person."

The Italian's close-spaced eyes had been queerly concentrated, as were his muscles, while he leaned across the counter trying to convince Grebe. Now he gave up the effort and sat down on his stool. "Oh — I suppose. Once in a while. But I been telling you, even the cops don't get anywhere."

"They're always after somebody. It's not the same thing."

"Well, keep trying if you want. I can't help you."

But he didn't keep trying. He had no more time to spend on Green. He slipped Green's check to the back of the block. The next name on the list was FIELD, WINSTON.

He found the back-yard bungalow without the least trouble; it shared a lot with another house, a few feet of yard between. Grebe knew these two-shack arrangements. They had been built in vast numbers in the days before the swamps were filled and the streets raised, and they were all the same — a boardwalk along the fence, well under street level, three or four ball-headed posts for clotheslines, greening wood, dead shingles, and a long, long flight of stairs to the rear door.

A twelve-year-old boy let him into the kitchen, and there the old man was, sitting by the table in a wheel chair.

"Oh, it's d' Government man," he said to the boy when Grebe drew out his checks. "Go bring me my box of papers." He cleared a space on the table.

"Oh, you don't have to go to all that trouble," said Grebe. But Field laid out his papers: Social Security card, relief certification, letters from the state hospital in Manteno, and a naval discharge dated San Diego, 1920.

"That's plenty," Grebe said. "Just sign."

"You got to know who I am," the old man said. "You're from the Government. It's not your check, it's a Government check and you got no business to hand it over till everything is proved."

He loved the ceremony of it, and Grebe made no more objections. Field emptied his box and finished out the circle of cards and letters.

"There's everything I done and been. Just the death certificate and they can close book on me." He said this with a certain happy pride and magnificence. Still he did not sign; he merely held the little pen upright on the golden-green corduroy of his thigh. Grebe did not hurry him. He felt the old man's hunger for conversation.

"I got to get better coal," he said. "I send my little gran'son to the yard with my order and they fill his wagon with screening. The stove ain't made for it. It fall through the grate. The order says Franklin County egg-size coal."

"I'll report it and see what can be done."

"Nothing can be done, I expect. You know and I know. There ain't no little ways to make things better, and the only big thing is money. That's the only sunbeams, money. Nothing is black where it shines, and the only place you see black is where it ain't shining. What we colored have to have is our own rich. There ain't no other way."

Grebe sat, his reddened forehead bridged levelly by his close-cut hair and his cheeks lowered in the wings of his collar—the caked fire shone hard within the isinglass-and-iron frames[16] but the room was not comfortable—sat and listened while the old man unfolded his scheme. This was to create one Negro millionaire a month by subscription. One clever, good-hearted young fellow elected every month would sign a contract to use the money to start a business employing Negroes. This would be advertised by chain letters and word of mouth, and every Negro wage earner would contribute a dollar a month. Within five years there would be sixty millionaires.

"That'll fetch respect," he said with a throat-stopped sound that came out like a foreign syllable. "You got to take and organize all the money that gets thrown away on the policy wheel and horse race. As long as they can take it away from you, they got no respect for you. Money, that's d' sun of human kind!" Field was a Negro of mixed blood, perhaps Cherokee, or Natchez; his skin was reddish. And he sounded, speaking about a golden sun in this dark room, and looked, shaggy and slab-headed, with the mingled blood of his face and broad lips, the little pen still upright in his hand, like one of the underground kings of mythology, old judge Minos[17] himself.

---

16. **isinglass-and-iron frames:** The firebox of the coal stove is made of isinglass—thin, transparent sheets of mica—framed in strips of iron.

17. **Minos:** A king of Crete who after his death was the judge of the dead in Hades, the underworld in Greek mythology.

And now he accepted the check and signed. Not to soil the slip, he held it down with his knuckles. The table budged and creaked, the center of the gloomy, heathen midden of the kitchen covered with bread, meat, and cans, and the scramble of papers.

"Don't you think my scheme'd work?"

"It's worth thinking about. Something ought to be done, I agree."

"It'll work if people will do it. That's all. That's the only thing, any time. When they understand it in the same way, all of them."

"That's true," said Grebe, rising. His glance met the old man's.

"I know you got to go," he said. "Well, God bless you, boy, you ain't been sly with me. I can tell it in a minute."

He went back through the buried yard. Someone nursed a candle in a shed, where a man unloaded kindling wood from a sprawl-wheeled baby buggy and two voices carried on a high conversation. As he came up the sheltered passage he heard the hard boost of the wind in the branches and against the house fronts, and then, reaching the sidewalk, he saw the needle-eye red of cable towers in the open icy height hundreds of feet above the river and the factories—those keen points. From here, his view was obstructed all the way to the South Branch and its timber banks, and the cranes beside the water. Rebuilt after the Great Fire,[18] this part of the city was, not fifty years later, in ruins again, factories boarded up, buildings deserted or fallen, gaps of prairie between. But it wasn't desolation that this made you feel, but rather a faltering of organization that set free a huge energy, an escaped, unattached, unregulated power from the giant raw place. Not only must people feel it but, it seemed to Grebe, they were compelled to match it. In their very bodies. He no less than others, he realized. Say that his parents had been servants in their time, whereas he was not supposed to be one. He thought that they had never done any service like this, which no one visible asked for, and probably flesh and blood could not even perform. Nor could anyone show why it should be performed; or see where the performance would lead. That did not mean that he wanted to be released from it, he realized with a grimly pensive face. On the contrary. He had something to do. To be compelled to feel this energy and yet have no task to do—that was horrible; that was suffering; he knew what that was. It was now quitting time. Six o'clock. He could go home if he liked, to his room, that is, to wash in hot water, to pour a drink, lie down on his quilt, read the paper, eat some liver paste on crackers before going out to dinner. But to think of this actually made him feel a little sick, as though he had swallowed hard air. He had six checks left, and he was determined to deliver at least one of these: Mr. Green's check.

So he started again. He had four or five dark blocks to go, past open lots, condemned houses, old foundations, closed schools, black churches, mounds, and he reflected that there must be many people alive who had once seen the neighborhood rebuilt and new. Now there was a second layer of ruins; centuries of history accomplished through human massing. Numbers had given the place forced growth; enormous numbers had also broken it down. Objects once so new, so concrete that it could have occurred to anyone they stood for other things, had crumbled. Therefore, reflected Grebe, the secret of them was out. It was that they stood for themselves by agreement, and were natural and not

---

18. **Great Fire:** The disastrous fire that burned October 8–10, 1871, destroying four square miles of the city and killing hundreds of people in Chicago.

unnatural by agreement, and when the things themselves collapsed the agreement became visible. What was it, otherwise, that kept cities from looking peculiar? Rome, that was almost permanent, did not give rise to thoughts like these. And was it abidingly real? But in Chicago, where the cycles were so fast and the familiar died out, and again rose changed, and died again in thirty years, you saw the common agreement or covenant, and you were forced to think about appearances and realities. (He remembered Raynor and he smiled. Raynor was a clever boy.) Once you had grasped this, a great many things became intelligible. For instance, why Mr. Field should conceive such a scheme. Of course, if people were to agree to create a millionaire, a real millionaire would come into existence. And if you wanted to know how Mr. Field was inspired to think of this, why, he had within sight of his kitchen window the chart, the very bones of a successful scheme—the El with its blue and green confetti of signals. People consented to pay dimes and ride the crash-box cars, and so it was a success. Yet how absurd it looked; how little reality there was to start with. And yet Yerkes, the great financier who built it, had known that he could get people to agree to do it. Viewed as itself, what a scheme of a scheme it seemed, how close to an appearance. Then why wonder at Mr. Field's idea? He had grasped a principle. And then Grebe remembered, too, that Mr. Yerkes had established the Yerkes Observatory and endowed it with millions.[19] Now how did the notion come to him in his New York museum of a palace or his Aegean-bound yacht to give money to astronomers? Was he awed by the success of his bizarre enterprise and therefore ready to spend money to find out where in the universe being and seeming were identical? Yes, he wanted to know what abides; and whether flesh is Bible grass; and he offered money to be burned in the fire of suns. Okay, then, Grebe thought further, these things exist because people consent to exist with them—we have got so far—and also there is a reality which doesn't depend on consent but within which consent is a game. But what about need, the need that keeps so many vast thousands in position? You tell me that, you *private* little gentleman and *decent* soul—he used these words against himself scornfully. Why is the consent given to misery? And why so painfully ugly? Because there is *something* that is dismal and permanently ugly? Here he sighed and gave it up, and thought it was enough for the present moment that he had a real check in his pocket for a Mr. Green who must be real beyond question. If only his neighbors didn't think they had to conceal him.

This time he stopped at the second floor. He struck a match and found a door. Presently a man answered his knock and Grebe had the check ready and showed it even before he began. "Does Tulliver Green live here? I'm from the relief."

The man narrowed the opening and spoke to someone at his back.

"Does he live here?"

"Uh-uh. No."

"Or anywhere in this building? He's a sick man and he can't come for his dough." He exhibited the check in the light, which was smoky—the air smelled of charred lard—and the man held off the brim of his cap to study it.

"Uh-uh. Never seen the name."

---

19. **Mr. Yerkes . . . millions:** Charles Tyson Yerkes (1837–1905) was an American financier who played a major role in developing Chicago's mass-transit system. In an effort to improve his public image, he funded the University of Chicago's Yerkes Observatory, which housed the world's largest telescope when it opened in 1897.

"There's nobody around here that uses crutches?"

He seemed to think, but it was Grebe's impression that he was simply waiting for a decent interval to pass.

"No, suh. Nobody I ever see."

"I've been looking for this man all afternoon" – Grebe spoke out with sudden force – "and I'm going to have to carry this check back to the station. It seems strange not to be able to find a person to *give* him something when you're looking for him for a good reason. I suppose if I had bad news for him I'd find him quick enough."

There was a responsive motion in the other man's face. "That's right, I reckon."

"It almost doesn't do any good to have a name if you can't be found by it. It doesn't stand for anything. He might as well not have any," he went on, smiling. It was as much of a concession as he could make to his desire to laugh.

"Well, now, there's a little old knot-back man I see once in a while. He might be the one you lookin' for. Downstairs."

"Where? Right side or left? Which door?"

"I don't know which. Thin-face little knot-back with a stick."

But no one answered at any of the doors on the first floor. He went to the end of the corridor, searching by matchlight, and found only a stairless exit to the yard, a drop of about six feet. But there was a bungalow near the alley, an old house like Mr. Field's. To jump was unsafe. He ran from the front door, through the underground passage and into the yard. The place was occupied. There was a light through the curtains, upstairs. The name on the ticket under the broken, scoop-shaped mailbox was Green! He exultantly rang the bell and pressed against the locked door. Then the lock clicked faintly and a long staircase opened before him. Someone was slowly coming down – a woman. He had the impression in the weak light that she was shaping her hair as she came, making herself presentable, for he saw her arms raised. But it was for support that they were raised; she was feeling her way downward, down the wall, stumbling. Next he wondered about the pressure of her feet on the treads; she did not seem to be wearing shoes. And it was a freezing stairway. His ring had got her out of bed, perhaps, and she had forgotten to put them on. And then he saw that she was not only shoeless but naked; she was entirely naked, climbing down while she talked to herself, a heavy woman, naked and drunk. She blundered into him. The contact of her breasts, though they touched only his coat, made him go back against the door with a blind shock. See what he had tracked down, in his hunting game!

The woman was saying to herself, furious with insult, "So I cain't ——k, huh? I'll show that son-of-a-bitch kin I, cain't I."

What should he do now? Grebe asked himself. Why, he should go. He should turn away and go. He couldn't talk to this woman. He couldn't keep her standing naked in the cold. But when he tried he found himself unable to turn away.

He said, "Is this where Mr. Green lives?"

But she was still talking to herself and did not hear him.

"Is this Mr. Green's house?"

At last she turned her furious drunken glance on him. "What do you want?"

Again her eyes wandered from him; there was a dot of blood in their enraged brilliance. He wondered why she didn't feel the cold.

"I'm from the relief."

"Awright, what?"

"I've got a check for Tulliver Green."

This time she heard him and put out her hand.

"No, no, for *Mr.* Green. He's got to sign," he said. How was he going to get Green's signature tonight!

"I'll take it. He cain't."

He desperately shook his head, thinking of Mr. Field's precautions about identification. "I can't let you have it. It's for him. Are you Mrs. Green?"

"Maybe I is, and maybe I ain't. Who want to know?"

"Is he upstairs?"

"Awright. Take it up yourself, you goddamn fool."

Sure, he was a goddamn fool. Of course he could not go up because Green would probably be drunk and naked, too. And perhaps he would appear on the landing soon. He looked eagerly upward. Under the light was a high narrow brown wall. Empty! It remained empty!

"Hell with you, then!" he heard her cry. To deliver a check for coal and clothes, he was keeping her in the cold. She did not feel it, but his face was burning with frost and self-ridicule. He backed away from her.

"I'll come tomorrow, tell him."

"Ah, hell with you. Don' never come. What you doin' here in the nighttime? Don' come back." She yelled so that he saw the breadth of her tongue. She stood astride in the long cold box of the hall and held on to the banister and the wall. The bungalow itself was shaped something like a box, a clumsy, high box pointing into the freezing air with its sharp, wintry lights.

"If you are Mrs. Green, I'll give you the check," he said, changing his mind.

"Give here, then." She took it, took the pen offered with it in her left hand, and tried to sign the receipt on the wall. He looked around, almost as though to see whether his madness was being observed, and came near believing that someone was standing on a mountain of used tires in the auto-junking shop next door.

"But are you Mrs. Green?" he now thought to ask. But she was already climbing the stairs with the check, and it was too late, if he had made an error, if he was now in trouble, to undo the thing. But he wasn't going to worry about it. Though she might not be Mrs. Green, he was convinced that Mr. Green was upstairs. Whoever she was, the woman stood for Green, whom he was not to see this time. Well, you silly bastard, he said to himself, so you think you found him. So what? Maybe you really did find him — what of it? But it was important that there was a real Mr. Green whom they could not keep him from reaching because he seemed to come as an emissary from hostile appearances. And though the self-ridicule was slow to diminish, and his face still blazed with it, he had, nevertheless, a feeling of elation, too. "For after all," he said, "he *could* be found!"

[1951, 1968]

Robert Lowell

[1917-1977]

Robert Traill Spence Lowell Jr. was born on March 1, 1917, in Boston, Massachusetts. He was the only child of Robert Lowell Sr., an officer in the U.S. Navy, and Charlotte Winslow Lowell. Lowell's mother was descended from Edward Winslow, who came to America on the *Mayflower* in 1620, while his father was related to the poet Amy Lowell and was a descendant of James Russell Lowell, a poet and the first editor of the *Atlantic Monthly*. In 1924, Lowell was enrolled at the Brimmer School in Boston and later attended St. Mark's School in Southborough,

Robert Lowell

This photograph of Lowell at his writing desk was taken in 1951, by which time he had already gained widespread recognition as one of the major young poets in the United States.

Massachusetts. He was a rebellious student who often settled differences through fistfights, earning himself the lifelong nickname "Cal," derived from *Caliban*, an unruly character in Shakespeare's *The Tempest*, and from the name of the mad Roman emperor *Caligula*. One of his teachers at St. Mark's was the poet Richard Eberhart, and Lowell published his first poem in the school's literary magazine in 1935. That fall, he enrolled at Harvard University. There were no poets on the faculty, and Lowell became bitterly unhappy. He infuriated his parents by becoming engaged to a writer a few years older than himself, and during a heated argument about her Lowell punched his father and knocked him down. His parents sent him to a family friend and psychiatrist who sympathetically arranged for him to go to Tennessee to meet the poet Allen Tate, then teaching at Vanderbilt University. Lowell spent the summer of 1937 living in a tent on the lawn of Tate's home and writing poetry. On Tate's advice, he transferred to Kenyon College, where he studied with the poet and critic John Crowe Ransom. Lowell graduated summa cum laude in 1940.

By the end of the decade, Lowell was firmly established as a poet. Following his graduation, he married the writer Jean Stafford, converted to Roman Catholicism, took graduate courses at Louisiana State University with the poet Robert Penn Warren, and worked briefly as an editorial assistant in New York City. After the United States entered World War II, Lowell twice volunteered for military service but was rejected because of his poor eyesight. When he was drafted in 1943, however, he "respectfully declined to serve," as he stated in a public letter to President Franklin D. Roosevelt, citing what Lowell viewed as the brutality and immorality of the Allied bombing of civilian populations in Germany.

For refusing induction, Lowell was sentenced to the legal minimum of a year in jail, of which he served five months in a federal prison in Danbury, Connecticut. By then, his poems had begun to appear in prominent literary journals such as the *Partisan Review*, the *Kenyon Review*, and the *Sewanee Review*, and his first book of poems, *Land of Unlikeness*, was published by a small press shortly before his parole in 1944. Lowell and his wife moved to New York City, where he radically revised and expanded the collection, which was republished as *Lord Weary's Castle* (1946). The acclaimed volume won the Pulitzer Prize, and Lowell was awarded a Guggenheim Fellowship and the American Academy of Arts and Letters Prize. At the age of only thirty, he was appointed Consultant in Poetry at the Library of Congress, a position now called Poet Laureate, for 1947-48.

Lowell's later work was shaped by his personal struggles and growing political engagement. In 1949, a year after his divorce from Jean Stafford, he married the writer and critic Elizabeth Hardwick. They lived in Europe from 1950 through 1952, during which Lowell published a collection of dense dramatic monologues, *The Mills of the Kavanaughs* (1951). After their return to the United States, Lowell accepted visiting positions at a series of colleges, including Boston University, where he taught from 1954 to 1960. During the 1950s, Lowell lost his faith in Catholicism and suffered bouts of severe depression, a result of the bipolar disorder for which he was hospitalized at intervals throughout his adult life. On the advice of psychiatrists, he began writing about his childhood. The first result was "91 Revere Street," a prose memoir published in the *Partisan Review* in 1956. Lowell later included it in *Life Studies* (1959), a revolutionary collection of intensely autobiographical poems that won the National Book Award. In 1960, Lowell returned to New York City, where he published *Imitations* (1961), loose translations of a wide range of ancient and modern European poems, and *The Old Glory* (1964), three plays based on stories by Nathaniel Hawthorne and Herman Melville. At the same time, Lowell directly addressed contemporary social issues in the title poem and many of the other poems in *For the Union Dead* (1964). In 1965, he wrote his second public letter to a president, Lyndon B. Johnson, declining an invitation to the White House as a protest against the escalation of the Vietnam War. The turbulence of the 1960s was reflected in the poems and translations in his collection *Near the Ocean* (1967), published the year Lowell also joined Norman Mailer and many other writers in a massive antiwar demonstration and march on the Pentagon in Washington, D.C.

By then, Lowell was the most famous and influential poet writing in English. In 1970, disillusioned by events in the United States, he accepted a visiting position at Essex University in England. There, he began an affair with the writer Lady Caroline Blackwood, who gave birth to their son in 1971. A year later, Lowell divorced Elizabeth Hardwick and married Blackwood. Revising the poems in his poetic journal *Notebooks 1967–68* (1969) and writing new poems, he published three collections of unrhymed

In the person and poetry of Robert Lowell, the whole scope and efficacy of the artistic endeavour was exemplified and affirmed. And his death shook the frame of poetry.
—Seamus Heaney

sonnets in 1973: *History; For Lizzie and Harriet*, about his second wife, Elizabeth Hardwick, and their daughter, Harriet; and *The Dolphin*, about his new life in England. For the latter volume, Lowell was awarded his second Pulitzer Prize. Shortly after the publication of his final collection, *Day by Day* (1977), Lowell decided to return to Hardwick and the United States. He died of a heart attack in a cab on the way into New York City from the airport on September 12, 1977.

Reading Lowell's Poetry.　Lowell, who majored in classics in college and later translated works from a range of languages, once said in an interview: "From the beginning I was preoccupied with technique, fascinated by the past and tempted by other languages." His early poems were highly formal, dense with allusions to literature and history. Dissatisfied

The Robert Gould Shaw Memorial

This famous Civil War memorial, which was created by the sculptor Augustus Saint-Gaudens and dedicated in Boston in 1897, figures prominently in Lowell's poem "For the Union Dead." The larger-than-life bronze relief depicts the mounted white officer Colonel Robert Gould Shaw amid the marching African American troops under his command, the Fifty-fourth Regiment of the Massachusetts Volunteer Infantry. Shaw died and his regiment suffered heavy casualties during an assault on Fort Wagner, near Charleston, South Carolina, in July 1863.

with the formal rhetoric and traditional metrics of his earlier poetry, and inspired by the work of his friends John Berryman and William Carlos Williams, Lowell in the late 1950s began to write deeply personal poems in a looser, more colloquial style. The result was *Life Studies* (1959), a volume that helped inaugurate what came to be called the "confessional" style of American poetry. Two of the following poems were first published in that volume: "Memories of West Street and Lepke," inspired by Lowell's imprisonment for refusing induction into the military during World War II; and his famous poem, "Skunk Hour." In June 1960, less than a year after the publication of *Life Studies*, Lowell read an early version of what is widely regarded as his finest public poem, "For the Union Dead," before an audience of thousands gathered for an arts festival at the Boston Public Garden. "I've always wanted to write a northern Civil War poem," Lowell remarked in an interview with the southern poet Robert Penn Warren. "And finally at forty-three I did and it's about Colonel Shaw who commanded the first Negro regiment from Boston." The poem is also a commentary on the distressing state of the union one hundred years after the beginning of the Civil War. Lowell, who in a 1971 interview remarked that "revision is inspiration," compulsively revised his poems, many of which exist in multiple versions. The texts of the following poems are those of the final versions, as published in his *Collected Poems* (2003), edited by Frank Bidart and David Gewanter.

**bedfordstmartins.com/
americanlit** *for research
links on Lowell*

MEMORIES OF WEST STREET AND LEPKE[1]

Only teaching on Tuesdays, book-worming
in pajamas fresh from the washer each morning,
I hog a whole house on Boston's
"hardly passionate Marlborough Street,"[2]
where even the man
scavenging filth in the back alley trash cans,
has two children, a beach wagon, a helpmate,
and is a "young Republican."
I have a nine months' daughter,

5

---

1. **Memories of West Street and Lepke:** In 1943, Lowell refused induction into the army in protest of the Allied bombing of civilians in Germany and outlined his objections to the war in a public letter to President Franklin D. Roosevelt. Lowell, who was sentenced to a year in prison, spent ten days in New York City's West Street Jail and five months in the federal prison at Danbury, Connecticut. His fellow inmate at the West Street Jail was Louis Buchalter (1897–1944), called "Lepke," from the Yiddish *Lepkeleh*, or "Little Louis." The head of the Murder Inc. crime syndicate, Lepke was convicted of murder in 1941 and executed in the electric chair in 1944. The poem, an early version of which was published as "My Season in Hell" in the *Partisan Review* (1958), first appeared under the present title in 1959.
2. **"hardly passionate Marlborough Street":** In a 1957 letter inviting William Carlos Williams and his wife to visit him in his quiet neighborhood in Boston, Lowell wrote: "It might be pleasant for you both to be here on Marlboro St. (William James once gave his classes this example of understatement: 'Marlboro Street is hardly a passionate street.')."

young enough to be my granddaughter.   10
Like the sun she rises in her flame-flamingo infants' wear.

These are the tranquillized *Fifties*,
and I am forty. Ought I to regret my seedtime?
I was a fire-breathing Catholic C.O.,[3]
and made my manic statement,   15
telling off the state and president, and then
sat waiting sentence in the bull pen
beside a Negro boy with curlicues
of marijuana in his hair.

Given a year,   20
I walked on the roof of the West Street Jail, a short
enclosure like my school soccer court,
and saw the Hudson River once a day
through sooty clothesline entanglements
and bleaching khaki tenements.   25
Strolling, I yammered metaphysics with Abramowitz,
a jaundice-yellow ("it's really tan")
and fly-weight pacifist,
so vegetarian,
he wore rope shoes and preferred fallen fruit.   30
He tried to convert Bioff and Brown,
the Hollywood pimps, to his diet.
Hairy, muscular, suburban,
wearing chocolate double-breasted suits,
they blew their tops and beat him black and blue.   35

I was so out of things, I'd never heard
of the Jehovah's Witnesses.[4]
"Are you a C.O.?" I asked a fellow jailbird.
"No," he answered, "I'm a J.W."
He taught me the "hospital tuck,"[5]   40
and pointed out the T-shirted back
of *Murder Incorporated*'s Czar Lepke,[6]
there piling towels on a rack,
or dawdling off to his little segregated cell full
of things forbidden the common man: 45

---

3. **C.O.**: Conscientious objector.
4. **Jehovah's Witnesses**: A pacifist Christian denomination whose members were jailed or persecuted in many countries because they refused to serve in the military during World War II.
5. **"hospital tuck"**: A method of putting a flat (rather than a fitted) sheet on a mattress.
6. **Czar Lepke**: See note 1.

a portable radio, a dresser, two toy American
flags tied together with a ribbon of Easter palm.
Flabby, bald, lobotomized,
he drifted in a sheepish calm,
where no agonizing reappraisal   50
jarred his concentration on the electric chair —
hanging like an oasis in his air
of lost connections. . . .

[1958, 2003]

SKUNK HOUR

(for Elizabeth Bishop)[1]

Nautilus Island's hermit
heiress still lives through winter in her Spartan cottage;
her sheep still graze above the sea.
Her son's a bishop. Her farmer
is first selectman in our village;   5
she's in her dotage.[2]

Thirsting for
the hierarchic privacy
of Queen Victoria's century,
she buys up all   10
the eyesores facing her shore,
and lets them fall.

The season's ill —
we've lost our summer millionaire,
who seemed to leap from an L. L. Bean   15
catalogue. His nine-knot yawl[3]
was auctioned off to lobstermen.
A red fox stain covers Blue Hill.

And now our fairy
decorator brightens his shop for fall;   20

---

1. **Dedication:** Lowell dedicated the poem to the poet Elizabeth Bishop "because rereading her suggested a way of breaking through the shell of my old manner," as he observed in 1962. Lowell added that he had modeled "Skunk Hour" on her "much better" poem "The Armadillo," printed on page 1117. Both poems, Lowell noted, "use short line stanzas, start with drifting description, and end with a single animal."
2. **Nautilus Island's hermit . . . dotage:** The island is near what Lowell described as the "declining" seacoast village of Castine, Maine, where he spent the summer of 1957. A selectman is a member of the village's governing board.
3. **nine-knot yawl:** A fast, two-masted sailboat.

his fishnet's filled with orange cork,
orange, his cobbler's bench and awl;
there is no money in his work,
he'd rather marry.

One dark night,[4]   25
my Tudor Ford climbed the hill's skull;
I watched for love-cars. Lights turned down,
they lay together, hull to hull,
where the graveyard shelves on the town. . . .
My mind's not right.   30

A car radio bleats,
"Love, O careless Love. . . ."[5] I hear
my ill-spirit sob in each blood cell,
as if my hand were at its throat. . . .
I myself am hell;[6]   35
nobody's here —

only skunks, that search
in the moonlight for a bite to eat.
They march on their soles up Main Street:
white stripes, moonstruck eyes' red fire   40
under the chalk-dry and spar spire
of the Trinitarian Church.

I stand on top
of our back steps and breathe the rich air —
a mother skunk with her column of kittens swills the garbage pail.   45
She jabs her wedge-head in a cup
of sour cream, drops her ostrich tail,
and will not scare.

[1958, 2003]

---

4. **One dark night:** Describing the shift from the first four stanzas to stanzas five and six, Lowell observed: "This is the dark night. I hoped my readers would remember John of the Cross's poem. My night is not gracious, but secular, puritan, and agnostic. An Existentialist night." The poem "The Dark Night of the Soul" by the Catholic mystic St. John of the Cross (1542-1591) describes a spiritual purging that prepares the soul for its union with God.

5. **"Love, O careless Love. . . .":** "Careless Love," a song dating from the late 1800s, was recorded by a number of blues and country singers during the 1950s.

6. **I myself am hell:** An allusion to *Paradise Lost* by the English poet John Milton (1608-1674), in which Satan exclaims: "Which way I fly is Hell; my self am Hell" (IV.75).

FOR THE UNION DEAD[1]

"Relinquunt Omnia Servare Rem Publicam."[2]

The old South Boston Aquarium stands
in a Sahara of snow now. Its broken windows are boarded.
The bronze weathervane cod has lost half its scales.
The airy tanks are dry.[3]

Once my nose crawled like a snail on the glass;   5
my hand tingled
to burst the bubbles
drifting from the noses of the cowed, compliant fish.

My hand draws back. I often sigh still
for the dark downward and vegetating kingdom   10
of the fish and reptile. One morning last March,
I pressed against the new barbed and galvanized

fence on the Boston Common.[4] Behind their cage,
yellow dinosaur steamshovels were grunting
as they cropped up tons of mush and grass   15
to gouge their underworld garage.

Parking spaces luxuriate like civic
sandpiles in the heart of Boston.
A girdle of orange, Puritan-pumpkin colored girders
braces the tingling Statehouse,[5]   20

---

1. **For the Union Dead:** In June 1960, in his first public reading of this poem at the Boston Arts Festival, Lowell explained that it "is about childhood memories, the evisceration of our modern cities, civil rights, nuclear warfare and more particularly, Colonel Robert Shaw and his Negro regiment, the Massachusetts Fifty-fourth. I brought in early personal memories because I wanted to avoid the fixed, brazen tone of the set-piece and official ode." Colonel Robert Gould Shaw was the white commander of one of the first African American units organized during the Civil War, the Fifty-fourth Regiment of the Massachusetts Volunteer Infantry. The twenty-six-year-old Shaw, a member of a prominent Boston family deeply involved in the anti-slavery movement, died leading his troops in a heroic but unsuccessful assault on Confederate fortifications at Fort Wagner, South Carolina, in 1863. Lowell's great-great uncle, James Russell Lowell, commemorated Shaw's life and death in "Memoriae Positum R. G. S.," an ode published in the *Atlantic Monthly* in 1864. "For the Union Dead," which Lowell earlier published as "Colonel Shaw and the Massachusetts' 54th," appeared in the *Atlantic Monthly* in 1960.
2. **"Relinquunt . . . Publicam":** "They give up everything to serve the Republic" (Latin). Lowell adapted an inscription on Augustus Saint-Gaudens's famous *Memorial to Robert Gould Shaw*, altering the Latin so that "he" becomes "they," thus recognizing the sacrifice of the two hundred fifty African American troops who also died or were wounded in the assault on Fort Wagner. See note 1 and the illustration on p. 2058.
3. **The old . . . dry:** The grand South Boston Aquarium, which was inaugurated on Thanksgiving Day in 1912, fell into disrepair before the city finally decided to close the decrepit building in 1954. The cod, which became the official symbol of the state in 1974, was an emblem of the importance of the fishing industry from the earliest days of the Commonwealth of Massachusetts.
4. **Boston Common:** Dating from 1634, the fifty-acre common is one of the oldest public parks in the United States.
5. **Statehouse:** The Massachusetts State House, across the street from the Boston Common.

shaking over the excavations, as it faces Colonel Shaw
and his bell-cheeked Negro infantry
on St. Gaudens' shaking Civil War relief,
propped by a plank splint against the garage's earthquake.

Two months after marching through Boston,   25
half the regiment was dead;
at the dedication,
William James could almost hear the bronze Negroes breathe.[6]

Their monument sticks like a fishbone
in the city's throat.   30
Its Colonel is as lean
as a compass-needle.

He has an angry wrenlike vigilance,
a greyhound's gentle tautness;
he seems to wince at pleasure,   35
and suffocate for privacy.

He is out of bounds now. He rejoices in man's lovely,
peculiar power to choose life and die —
when he leads his black soldiers to death,
he cannot bend his back.   40

On a thousand small town New England greens,
the old white churches hold their air
of sparse, sincere rebellion; frayed flags
quilt the graveyards of the Grand Army of the Republic.[7]

The stone statues of the abstract Union Soldier   45
grow slimmer and younger each year —
wasp-waisted, they doze over muskets
and muse through their sideburns . . .

Shaw's father wanted no monument
except the ditch,   50
where his son's body was thrown
and lost with his "niggers."[8]

---

6. **William James . . . breathe:** In an address delivered upon the occasion of the unveiling of the *Robert Gould Shaw Memorial* on May 31, 1897, the philosopher and psychologist William James (1842–1910) declared: "There they march, warm-blooded champions of a better day for man."
7. **Grand Army of the Republic:** The Union army in the Civil War. Hundreds of towns and villages in New England and throughout the North erected memorials to those who fought in the Civil War, usually represented by a stone or bronze statue of a Union soldier standing at attention and holding a musket. Similar memorials to Confederate soldiers were erected throughout the South.
8. **Shaw's father . . . "niggers":** After the battle at Fort Wagner, stories circulated that the Confederate commander ordered his men to bury Shaw in a mass grave along "with his niggers."

The ditch is nearer.
There are no statues for the last war here;
on Boylston Street, a commercial photograph   55
shows Hiroshima boiling

over a Mosler Safe, the "Rock of Ages"
that survived the blast.[9] Space is nearer.
When I crouch to my television set,
the drained faces of Negro school-children rise like balloons.[10]   60

Colonel Shaw
is riding on his bubble,
he waits
for the blessèd break.

The Aquarium is gone. Everywhere,   65
giant finned cars nose forward like fish;
a savage servility
slides by on grease.

[1960, 2003]

---

9. **Mosler Safe . . . survived the blast:** The United States dropped the first atomic bomb on Hiroshima, Japan, on August 6, 1945. The Mosler Safe Company advertised that one of its safes had survived the blast, which killed an estimated 140,000 people, including 60,000 people who later died from injuries or radiation poisoning.
10. **the drained faces . . . like balloons:** After the Supreme Court's ruling in the 1954 case of *Brown v. Board of Education of Topeka* that segregation in public schools was unconstitutional, enforced integration often led to conflict in the South. One of the most televised confrontations occurred in Little Rock, Arkansas, in 1957. Governor Orville Faubus ordered the Arkansas National Guard to prevent nine African American students from entering Central High School, and President Eisenhower responded by sending in federal troops to enforce the integration of the school and to protect the safety of the "Little Rock Nine."

Gwendolyn Brooks

[1917-2000]

Gwendolyn Elizabeth Brooks was born in Topeka, Kansas, on June 7, 1917. She was the first child of Keziah Wims Brooks, a former schoolteacher, and David Anderson Brooks, a janitor for a music company in Chicago. Brooks's mother, who had returned to her parents' home in Topeka to give birth to her daughter, soon rejoined her husband in Chicago, where Brooks grew up in a predominantly black neighborhood on the South Side. She remembered a happy childhood in which her father, who had been forced by financial pressures to withdraw from Fisk University, recited poetry to her, while her mother composed songs for which Brooks wrote the words. As a wedding present, her father had given her mother a collection of the Harvard Classics, a fifty-one-volume set advertised as the "World's Great Books." The set included what Brooks later called "white treasures," including the essays

[Brooks] has accorded heroic stature to the lives of women in the African American community, while never ceasing to speak for and to that community as a whole. Her poetry holds up a mirror to the American experience entire, its dreams, self-delusions and nightmares.

–Adrienne Rich

of Ralph Waldo Emerson, collections of British poetry, and translations of Greek drama. "Very early in life I became fascinated with the wonders language can achieve," Brooks recalled. "And I began playing with words." As she also recalled, her mother often told her: "You're going to be the *lady* Paul Laurence Dunbar." The precocious Brooks published her first poem at the age of thirteen in *American Childhood Magazine*. When Langston Hughes and James Weldon Johnson gave readings at neighborhood churches, her mother introduced her to the poets, and Brooks sent them her poems. Johnson advised her to read modernist poets such as T. S. Eliot, E. E. Cummings, and Ezra Pound, and Hughes was encouraging, telling her: "You're very talented! Keep writing! Some day you'll have a book published!"

Despite the economic and social obstacles confronting her, Brooks was determined to fulfill Hughes's prophesy. By the time she graduated from high school in 1934, she had published over one hundred poems in her weekly column in the prominent African American newspaper the *Chicago Defender*. She enrolled at nearby Wilson Junior College, from which she graduated in 1936. She had difficulty finding a job during the Depression and worked as a maid and a secretary until 1937, when she became the publicity director of a local youth group sponsored by the National Association for the Advancement of Colored People (NAACP). At its gatherings, she met a number of activists and writers, including the poet Henry Blakely. In 1938, Brooks married Blakely, with whom she later had two children, and they moved into a small apartment on the South Side. She won the Midwestern Writers' Conference Poetry Award in 1943, and some of her poems

Gwendolyn Brooks

Slim Aarons took this photograph of Brooks on the back steps of her apartment in Chicago in 1960, the year she published her groundbreaking collection *The Bean Eaters*.

were subsequently published in the Chicago-based *Poetry: A Magazine of Verse* and the national magazine *Harper's*. On the advice of friends, she sent a collection of poems set in her South Side neighborhood to Harper and Row in New York City. Richard Wright, who read her manuscript for the publisher, wrote that the poems "are hard and real, right out of the central core of Black Belt Negro life in urban areas." Reviewers were enthusiastic about the collection, published as *A Street in Bronzeville* (1945), and Brooks won a grant from the American Academy of Arts and Letters and a Guggenheim Fellowship. In 1949, she published *Annie Allen*, poems about a young woman growing up amid poverty and racism in Bronzeville. The volume won the Pulitzer Prize, the first ever awarded to an African American.

Although she continued to develop the themes of her popular Bronzeville poems, Brooks later addressed racial prejudice and social inequality much more directly. She wrote *Maud Martha* (1953), a semiautobiographical novel about a black woman's childhood and marriage, and a collection of children's poetry, *Bronzeville Girls and Boys* (1956). In some of the poems published in *The Bean Eaters* (1960), Brooks looked beyond her Chicago neighborhood to subjects such as the struggle for school desegregation in the South. In 1967, Brooks attended the Second Fisk University Writers Conference, where she met Amiri Baraka and other writers involved in the Black Arts Movement, a cultural counterpart of the militant Black Power Movement. The conference marked a crucial turning point for Brooks, who in her autobiography *Report from Part One* (1972) said that her goal was thereafter to write poems that would "somehow successfully 'call' all black people: black people in taverns, black people in alleys, black people in gutters, schools, offices, factories, prison, the consulate." In the title poem of her next collection, *In the Mecca* (1968), Brooks explored the grim realities of black life in and around the Mecca, a tenement in Chicago. She dedicated the collection to the memory of Langston Hughes and to her contemporaries James Baldwin and Amiri Baraka. In an effort to support the development of black presses, Brooks then ended her long association with Harper and Row, and her numerous collections of poetry were later published by the small Broadside Press in Detroit and the Third World Press in Chicago.

During the final decades of her life, Brooks assumed a prominent public role. In 1968, she succeeded Carl Sandburg as the Poet Laureate of Illinois, a position in which she established initiatives to take poetry to the people through public readings and school programs. She traveled widely, giving readings, teaching workshops, and receiving honorary degrees at colleges and universities across the United States. She also visited Africa, England, France, and Russia. In 1985, she was appointed Consultant in Poetry at the Library of Congress, a position now called Poet Laureate. The year after the publication of her collected poems, *Blacks* (1987), she was awarded the Frost Medal for lifetime achievement by the Poetry Society of America. In 1994, she was named the National Endowment for the Humanities Jefferson Lecturer, the highest honor in the humanities in the United States. Her final book, *Report from Part Two* (1996), was a continuation of her autobiography. Brooks died at her home in Chicago on December 3, 2000.

bedfordstmartins.com/ americanlit for research links on Brooks

Reading Brooks's Poetry. "I wrote about what I saw and heard in the street," Brooks once said in an interview. Certainly, life in the black neighborhoods of Chicago was a central subject of her work from her earliest published poems to her somber final collection, *Children Coming Home* (1991), dramatic monologues in the voices of children living in a world of drugs, poverty, and violence. Brooks, who read widely English and American poetry as a young girl, was praised for her innovative use of traditional poetic forms in her first collection, *A Street in Bronzeville* (1945). The first three poems in the following selection first appeared in that volume, including her controversial poem "the mother," about a woman who has had several abortions. Asked about the poem in an interview, Brooks affirmed: "It has a kind of joy and life. . . . And I feel that it shouldn't be called 'an abortion poem' as it is so often called. I have a little catalog here of the qualities of motherhood, which I hope are not customarily missed." The selection also includes two of her best-known poems, the title poem of *The Bean Eaters* (1960) and another poem from that volume, "We Real Cool," a compressed urban ballad that has been cited as a poetical precursor to hip-hop or rap music. The impact of the Black Arts and Black Power Movements on Brooks is illustrated by the final poem in this selection, "Malcolm X," a tribute to the slain Black Nationalist leader that was first published in her collection *In the Mecca* (1968). The texts of all of the poems are taken from her collected poems, *Blacks* (1987).

From A STREET IN BRONZEVILLE

kitchenette building[1]

We are things of dry hours and the involuntary plan,
Grayed in, and gray. "Dream" makes a giddy sound, not strong
Like "rent," "feeding a wife," "satisfying a man."

But could a dream send up through onion fumes
Its white and violet, fight with fried potatoes   5
And yesterday's garbage ripening in the hall,
Flutter, or sing an aria down these rooms

Even if we were willing to let it in,
Had time to warm it, keep it very clean,
Anticipate a message, let it begin?   10

---

1. **kitchenette building:** A term associated with buildings in what was known as the "Black Belt" and other areas occupied by African Americans, in which apartments were divided into one-room units, frequently occupied by entire families who shared kitchens and bathrooms with the residents of other units.

We wonder. But not well! not for a minute!
Since Number Five is out of the bathroom now,
We think of lukewarm water, hope to get in it.

[1945, 1987]

the mother

Abortions will not let you forget.
You remember the children you got that you did not get,
The damp small pulps with a little or with no hair,
The singers and workers that never handled the air.
You will never neglect or beat   5
Them, or silence or buy with a sweet.
You will never wind up the sucking-thumb
Or scuttle off ghosts that come.
You will never leave them, controlling your luscious sigh,
Return for a snack of them, with gobbling mother-eye.   10

I have heard in the voices of the wind the voices of my dim killed children.
I have contracted. I have eased
My dim dears at the breasts they could never suck.
I have said, Sweets, if I sinned, if I seized
Your luck   15
And your lives from your unfinished reach,
If I stole your births and your names,
Your straight baby tears and your games,
Your stilted or lovely loves, your tumults, your marriages, aches, and your deaths,
If I poisoned the beginnings of your breaths,   20
Believe that even in my deliberateness I was not deliberate.
Though why should I whine,
Whine that the crime was other than mine? –
Since anyhow you are dead.
Or rather, or instead,   25
You were never made.
But that too, I am afraid,
Is faulty: oh, what shall I say, how is the truth to be said?
You were born, you had body, you died.
It is just that you never giggled or planned or cried.   30

Believe me, I loved you all.
Believe me, I knew you, though faintly, and I loved, I loved you
All.

[1945, 1987]

a song in the front yard

I've stayed in the front yard all my life.
I want a peek at the back
Where it's rough and untended and hungry weed grows.
A girl gets sick of a rose.

I want to go in the back yard now   5
And maybe down the alley,
To where the charity children play.
I want a good time today.

They do some wonderful things.
They have some wonderful fun.   10
My mother sneers, but I say it's fine
How they don't have to go in at quarter to nine.

My mother, she tells me that Johnnie Mae
Will grow up to be a bad woman.
That George'll be taken to Jail soon or late   15
(On account of last winter he sold our back gate.)

But I say it's fine. Honest, I do.
And I'd like to be a bad woman, too,
And wear the brave stockings of night-black lace
And strut down the streets with paint on my face.   20

[1945, 1987]

THE BEAN EATERS

They eat beans mostly, this old yellow pair.
Dinner is a casual affair.
Plain chipware on a plain and creaking wood,
Tin flatware.

Two who are Mostly Good.   5
Two who have lived their day,
But keep on putting on their clothes
And putting things away.

And remembering . . .
Remembering, with twinklings and twinges,   10
As they lean over the beans in their rented back room that
        is full of beads and receipts and dolls and cloths,
        tobacco crumbs, vases and fringes.

[1960, 1987]

WE REAL COOL

THE POOL PLAYERS.
SEVEN AT THE GOLDEN SHOVEL.

We real cool. We
Left school. We

Lurk late. We
Strike straight. We

Sing sin. We
Thin gin. We

Jazz June. We
Die soon.

[1960, 1987]

MALCOLM X[1]

For Dudley Randall.[2]

Original.
Ragged-round.
Rich-robust.

He had the hawk-man's eyes.
We gasped. We saw the maleness.   5
The maleness raking out and making guttural the air
and pushing us to walls.

And in a soft and fundamental hour
a sorcery devout and vertical
beguiled the world.   10

He opened us —
who was a key,

who was a man.

[1968, 1987]

---

1. **Malcolm X:** Malcolm Little (1925–1965), later Malcolm X, a Black Nationalist and human-rights leader who became a Black Muslim minister, was assassinated in New York City.
2. **Dedication:** Brooks dedicated the poem to the poet and editor Dudley Randall (1914–2000), a pioneer in African American book publishing who founded the Broadside Press.

Hisaye Yamamoto

[1921–2011]

Hisaye Yamamoto was born in Redondo Beach, California, on August 23, 1921. Her parents were immigrant farmers from Kumamoto, Japan. As a Nisei, the term for children born to Japanese immigrants (known as Issei),

Hisaye Yamamoto

This photograph shows Yamamoto standing in front of a shop in Little Tokyo, the Japanese American district in downtown Los Angeles. In the window, the shop displays an American flag and a portrait of the family that founded the business.

Yamamoto spoke Japanese at home and began to learn English only when she entered kindergarten. Yamamoto later recalled that, while her parents "eked out a living" by growing strawberries, she quickly learned English and became an avid reader. She began writing stories and sketches when she was a teenager and published frequently in the English sections of Japanese-language newspapers, often using the pen name "Napoleon." As she said in a 1987 interview, "On weekends [the papers] would have a feature page, where people would send in all kinds of things. They'd print anything, so that's how I got started, and I haven't stopped yet!" After Yamamoto graduated from Excelsior Union High School in 1938, she enrolled at Compton Junior College, where she majored in foreign languages and was the class salutatorian at her graduation in 1940.

The lives of Yamamoto and other Japanese Americans changed dramatically in the aftermath of the bombing of Pearl Harbor on December 7, 1941. Strong anti-Japanese sentiment in the United States prompted President Franklin D. Roosevelt to issue the Japanese Relocation Order of February 1942. Roughly 110,000 people of Japanese extraction living on the West Coast, almost two-thirds of them American citizens, were consequently rounded up and forcibly removed to remote concentration camps, called "War Relocation Centers." The Yamamotos lost their farm and were sent to the Poston Relocation Center on the Colorado Indian Reservation in Arizona. Yamamoto wrote for a daily newspaper established to help combat the monotony of life at the camp, the *Poston Chronicle*, in which she published her first works of fiction, including a serialized mystery, "Death Rides the Rails to Poston." In 1944, she and two of her brothers were allowed to leave the camp to seek jobs in Massachusetts, where Yamamoto worked as a cook, but they returned after learning that another brother had died in combat in Italy. When the family was finally released from the camp in 1945, they moved back to California, where Yamamoto worked for three years for the African American newspaper the *Los Angeles Tribune*. She also became deeply involved with the civil rights movement, participating in demonstrations sponsored by the Congress of Racial Equality (CORE).

Yamamoto subsequently became one of the first Japanese American writers to gain recognition in the United States. She quit her job at the *Tribune* in order to care for a baby born into her family. She also began to write essays and stories based on her childhood memories, her family's bitter wartime experiences in the camp, and her life as a Nisei in Los Angeles. Her first national publication, "The High-Heeled Shoes: A Memoir," a series of linked sketches dramatizing the sexual harassment of women, appeared in the *Partisan Review* in 1948. Her most famous story, "Seventeen Syllables," appeared in the magazine the following year, and Yamamoto also published stories in other prominent periodicals such as *Harper's Bazaar* and the *Kenyon Review*. The John Hay Whitney Foundation awarded her a fellowship for a year of full-time writing in 1950. Meanwhile, she had been reading the *Catholic Worker*, the publication of the Catholic Worker Movement, founded in 1933 by the radical social activist Dorothy Day. Passing up a writing fellowship at Stanford University, Yamamoto in 1953 went to live at one of the movement's cooperative farms on Staten Island, New York. There, she met and married Anthony DeSoto. In 1955, the couple returned to Los Angeles, where they eventually had four children. Although she devoted most of her time to her family, Yamamoto continued to publish stories and other writings, most of which appeared in the widely read Japanese American newspaper *Rafu Shimpo*. Her first collection of stories, *Seventeen Syllables: Five Stories of Japanese American Life*, was published in Japan in 1985, three years before *Seventeen Syllables and Other Stories* was published by a small press in the United States. In 1986, Yamamoto was awarded the American Book Award for Lifetime Achievement from the Before Columbus Foundation. Yamamoto lived in her home in northeast Los Angeles—writing occasionally, tending her garden, and enjoying her grandchildren—until she suffered a stroke in 2010. Her health failed, and she died in her sleep at the age of eighty-nine on January 30, 2011.

bedfordstmartins.com/ americanlit for research links on Yamamoto

Reading Yamamoto's "Seventeen Syllables." This story first appeared in one of the most influential political and cultural journals of the postwar period, the *Partisan Review*, whose cosmopolitan editors published the work of a wide range of American and European authors. The issue in which Yamamoto's story appeared, for example, also included works by Saul Bellow, Theodore Roethke, and the French author Albert Camus. In "Seventeen Syllables," which takes place before World War II, the third-person narrator tells the story through the eyes of its adolescent main character, Rosie. The daughter of Japanese immigrants, Rosie witnesses without fully comprehending the conflict between her father, a hard-working farmer, and her artistic mother, who writes haiku, an ancient form of Japanese poetry traditionally consisting of seventeen syllables divided into lines of five, seven, and five syllables. The need for self-expression is a central theme in the story, which also concerns the failure of communication, not only between the husband and wife, but also between them and their acculturated, English-speaking daughter. The text is taken from the first printing of the story in the *Partisan Review*, November 1949.

SEVENTEEN SYLLABLES

The first Rosie knew that her mother had taken to writing poems was one evening when she finished one and read it aloud for her daughter's approval. It was about cats, and Rosie pretended to understand it thoroughly and appreciate it no end, partly because she hesitated to disillusion her mother about the quantity and quality of Japanese she had learned in all the years now that she had been going to Japanese school every Saturday (and Wednesday, too, in the summer). Even so, her mother must have been skeptical about the depth of Rosie's understanding, because she explained afterwards about the kind of poem she was trying to write.

See, Rosie, she said, it was a *haiku*, a poem in which she must pack all her meaning into seventeen syllables only, which were divided into three lines of five, seven, and five syllables. In the one she had just read, she had tried to capture the charm of a kitten, as well as comment on the superstition that owning a cat of three colors meant good luck.

"Yes, yes, I understand. How utterly lovely," Rosie said, and her mother, either satisfied or seeing through the deception and resigned, went back to composing.

The truth was that Rosie was lazy; English lay ready on the tongue but Japanese had to be searched for and examined, and even then put forth tentatively (probably to meet with laughter). It was so much easier to say yes, yes, even when one meant no, no. Besides, this was what was in her mind to say: I was looking through one of your magazines from Japan last night, Mother, and towards the back I found some *haiku* in English that delighted me. There was one that made me giggle off and on until I fell asleep —

> It is morning, and lo!
> I lie awake, comme il faut,[1]
> sighing for some dough.

Now, how to reach her mother, how to communicate the melancholy song? Rosie knew formal Japanese by fits and starts, her mother had even less English, no French. It was much more possible to say yes, yes.

It developed that her mother was writing the *haiku* for a daily newspaper, the *Mainichi Shinbun*,[2] that was published in San Francisco. Los Angeles, to be sure, was closer to the farming community in which the Hayashi family lived and several Japanese vernaculars were printed there, but Rosie's parents said they preferred the tone of the northern paper. Once a week, the *Mainichi* would have a section devoted to *haiku*, and her mother

---

1. **comme il faut**: According to custom (French).
2. **Mainichi Shinbun**: Daily Newspaper (Japanese), named after the largest newspaper in Japan.

became an extravagant contributor, taking for herself the blossoming pen name, Umé Hanazono.[3]

So Rosie and her father lived for awhile with two women, her mother and Umé Hanazono. Her mother (Tomé Hayashi by name) kept house, cooked, washed, and, along with her husband and the Carrascos, the Mexican family hired for the harvest, did her ample share of picking tomatoes out in the sweltering fields and boxing them in tidy strata in the cool packing shed. Umé Hanazono, who came to life after the dinner dishes were done, was an earnest, muttering stranger who often neglected speaking when spoken to and stayed busy at the parlor table as late as midnight scribbling with pencil on scratch paper or carefully copying characters on good paper with her fat, pale green Parker.[4]

This new interest had some repercussions on the household routine. Before, Rosie had been accustomed to her parents and herself taking their hot baths early and going to bed almost immediately afterwards, unless her parents challenged each other to a game of flower cards[5] or unless company dropped in. Now, if her father wanted to play cards, he had to resort to solitaire (at which he always cheated fearlessly), and if a group of friends came over, it was bound to contain someone who was also writing *haiku*, and the small assemblage would be split in two, her father entertaining the nonliterary members and her mother comparing ecstatic notes with the visiting poet.

If they went out, it was more of the same thing. But Umé Hanazono's life span, even for a poet's, was very brief – perhaps three months at most.

One night they went over to see the Hayano family in the neighboring town to the west, an adventure both painful and attractive to Rosie. It was attractive because there were four Hayano girls, all lovely and each one named after a season of the year (Haru, Natsu, Aki, Fuyu), painful because something had been wrong with Mrs. Hayano ever since the birth of her first child. Rosie would sometimes watch Mrs. Hayano, reputed to have been the belle of her native village, making her way about a room, stooped, slowly shuffling, violently trembling (*always* trembling), and she would be reminded that this woman, in this same condition, had carried and given issue to three babies. She would look wonderingly at Mr. Hayano, handsome, tall, and strong, and she would look at her four pretty friends. But it was not a matter she could come to any decision about.

On this visit, however, Mrs. Hayano sat all evening in the rocker, as motionless and unobtrusive as it was possible for her to be, and Rosie found the greater part of the evening practically anaesthetic. Too, Rosie spent most of it in the girls' room, because Haru, the garrulous one, said almost as soon as the bows and other greetings were over, "Oh, you must see my new coat!"

It was a pale plaid of grey, sand, and blue, with an enormous collar, and Rosie, seeing nothing special in it, said, "Gee, how nice."

---

3. **Umé Hanazono:** Plum-tree Flower Garden (Japanese).
4. **Parker:** A high-quality fountain pen made by the Parker Pen Company.
5. **flower cards:** Playing cards of Japanese origin used in a number of games.

"Nice?" said Haru, indignantly. "Is that all you can say about it? It's gorgeous! And so cheap, too. Only seventeen-ninety-eight, because it was a sale. The saleslady said it was twenty-five dollars regular."

"Gee," said Rosie. Natsu, who never said much and when she said anything said it shyly, fingered the coat covetously and Haru pulled it away.

"Mine," she said, putting it on. She minced in the aisle between the two large beds and smiled happily. "Let's see how your mother likes it."

She broke into the front room and the adult conversation, and went to stand in front of Rosie's mother, while the rest watched from the door. Rosie's mother was properly envious. "May I inherit it when you're through with it?"

Haru, pleased, giggled and said yes, she could, but Natsu reminded gravely from the door, "You promised me, Haru."

Everyone laughed but Natsu, who shamefacedly retreated into the bedroom. Haru came in laughing, taking off the coat. "We were only kidding, Natsu," she said. "Here, you try it on now."

After Natsu buttoned herself into the coat, inspected herself solemnly in the bureau mirror, and reluctantly shed it, Rosie, Aki, and Fuyu got their turns, and Fuyu, who was eight, drowned in it while her sisters and Rosie doubled up in amusement. They all went into the front room later, because Haru's mother quaveringly called to her to fix the tea and rice cakes and open a can of sliced peaches for everybody. Rosie noticed that her mother and Mr. Hayano were talking together at the little table — they were discussing a *haiku* that Mr. Hayano was planning to send to the *Mainichi,* while her father was sitting at one end of the sofa looking through a copy of *Life,* the new picture magazine.[6] Occasionally, her father would comment on a photograph, holding it toward Mrs. Hayano and speaking to her as he always did — loudly, as though he thought someone such as she must surely be at least a trifle deaf also.

The five girls had their refreshments at the kitchen table, and it was while Rosie was showing the sisters her trick of swallowing peach slices without chewing (she chased each slippery crescent down with a swig of tea) that her father brought his empty teacup and untouched saucer to the sink and said, "Come on, Rosie, we're going home now."

"Already?" asked Rosie.

"Work tomorrow," he said.

He sounded irritated, and Rosie, puzzled, gulped one last yellow slice and stood up to go, while the sisters began protesting, as was their wont.

"We have to get up at five-thirty," he told them, going into the front room quickly, so that they did not have their usual chance to hang onto his hands and plead for an extension of time.

Rosie, following, saw that her mother and Mr. Hayano were sipping tea and still talking together, while Mrs. Hayano concentrated, quivering, on raising the handleless Japanese cup to her lips with both her hands and lowering it back to her lap. Her father,

---

6. *Life* . . . magazine: The publisher Henry Luce introduced this popular all-photography news magazine in 1936.

saying nothing, went out the door, onto the bright porch, and down the steps. Her mother looked up and asked, "Where is he going?"

"Where is he going?" Rosie said. "He said we were going home now."

"Going home?" Her mother looked with embarrassment at Mr. Hayano and his absorbed wife and then forced a smile. "He must be tired," she said.

Haru was not giving up yet. "May Rosie stay overnight?" she asked, and Natsu, Aki, and Fuyu came to reinforce their sister's plea by helping her make a circle around Rosie's mother. Rosie, for once, having no desire to stay, was relieved when her mother, apologizing to the perturbed Mr. and Mrs. Hayano for her father's abruptness at the same time, managed to shake her head no at the quartet, kindly but adamant, so that they broke their circle to let her go.

Rosie's father looked ahead into the windshield as the two joined him. "I'm sorry," her mother said. "You must be tired." Her father, stepping on the starter, said nothing. "You know how I get when it's *haiku*," she continued, "I forget what time it is." He only grunted.

As they rode homeward, silently, Rosie, sitting between, felt a rush of hate for both, for her mother for begging, for her father for denying her mother. I wish this old Ford would crash, right now, she thought, then immediately, no, no, I wish my father would laugh, but it was too late: already the vision had passed through her mind of the green pick-up crumpled in the dark against one of the mighty eucalyptus trees they were just riding past, of the three contorted, bleeding bodies, one of them hers.

Rosie ran between two patches of tomatoes, her heart working more rambunctiously than she had ever known it to. How lucky it was that Aunt Taka and Uncle Gimpachi had come tonight, though, how very lucky. Otherwise, she might not have really kept her half-promise to meet Jesús Carrasco. Jesús, who was going to be a senior in September at the same school she went to, and his parents were the ones helping with the tomatoes this year. She and Jesús, who hardly remembered seeing each other at Cleveland High, where there were so many other people and two whole grades between them, had become great friends this summer — he always had a joke for her when he periodically drove the loaded pick-up up from the fields to the shed where she was usually sorting while her mother and father did the packing, and they laughed a great deal together over infinitesimal repartee during the afternoon break for chilled watermelon or ice cream in the shade of the shed.

What she enjoyed most was racing him to see which could finish picking a double row first. He, who could work faster, would tease her by slowing down until she thought she would surely pass him this time, then speeding up furiously to leave her several sprawling vines behind. Once he had made her screech hideously by crossing over, while her back was turned, to place atop the tomatoes in her green-stained bucket a truly monstrous, pale green worm (it had looked more like an infant snake). And it was when they had finished a contest this morning, after she had pantingly pointed a green finger at the immature tomatoes evident in the lugs at the end of his row and he had returned the accusation (with justice), that he had startlingly brought up the matter of their possibly meeting outside the range of both their parents' dubious eyes.

"What for?" she had asked.

"I've got a secret I want to tell you," he said.

"Tell me now," she demanded.

"It won't be ready till tonight," he said.

She laughed. "Tell me tomorrow then."

"It'll be gone tomorrow," he threatened.

"Well, for seven hakes,[7] what is it?" she had asked, more than twice, and when he had suggested that the packing shed would be an appropriate place to find out, she had cautiously answered maybe. She had not been certain she was going to keep the appointment until the arrival of her mother's sister and her husband. Their coming seemed a sort of signal of permission, of grace, and she had definitely made up her mind to lie and leave as she was bowing them welcome.

So, as soon as everyone appeared settled back for the evening, she announced loudly that she was going to the privy outside, "I'm going to the *benjo!*"[8] and slipped out the door. And now that she was actually on her way, her heart pumped in such an undisciplined way that she could hear it with her ears. It's because I'm running, she told herself, slowing to a walk. The shed was up ahead, one more patch away, in the middle of the fields. Its bulk, looming in the dimness, took on a sinisterness that was funny when Rosie reminded herself that it was only a wooden frame with a canvas roof and three canvas walls that made a slapping noise on breezy days.

Jesús was sitting on the narrow plank that was the sorting platform and she went around to the other side and jumped backwards to seat herself on the rim of a packing stand. "Well, tell me," she said, without greeting, thinking her voice sounded reassuringly familiar.

"I saw you coming out the door," Jesús said. "I heard you running part of the way, too."

"Uh-huh," Rosie said. "Now tell me the secret."

"I was afraid you wouldn't come," he said.

Rosie delved around on the chicken-wire bottom of the stall for number two tomatoes, ripe, which she was sitting beside, and came up with a left-over that felt edible. She bit into it and began sucking out the pulp and seeds. "I'm here," she pointed out.

"Rosie, are you sorry you came?"

"Sorry? What for?" she said. "You said you were going to tell me something."

"I will, I will," Jesús said, but his voice contained disappointment, and Rosie, fleetingly, felt the older of the two, realizing a brand-new power which vanished without category under her recognition.

"I have to go back in a minute," she said. "My aunt and uncle are here from Wintersburg. I told them I was going to the privy."

Jesús laughed. "You funny thing," he said. "You slay me!"

"Just because you have a bathroom *inside*," Rosie said. "Come on, tell me."

---

7. **for seven hakes:** A comically garbled version of the expression "for heaven's sake."
8. *benjo*: Outhouse or privy (Japanese).

Chuckling, Jesús came around to lean on the stand facing her. They still could not see each other very clearly, but Rosie noticed that Jesús became very sober again as he took the hollow tomato from her hand and dropped it back into the stall. When he took hold of her empty hand, she could find no words to protest; her vocabulary had become distressingly constricted and she thought desperately that all that remained intact now was yes and no and oh, and even these few sounds would not easily out. Thus, kissed by Jesús, Rosie fell, for the first time, entirely victim to a helplessness delectable beyond speech. But the terrible, beautiful sensation lasted no more than a second, and the reality of Jesús's lips and tongue and teeth and hands made her pull away with such strength that she nearly tumbled.

Rosie stopped running as she approached the lights from the windows of home. How long since she had left? She could not guess, but gasping yet, she went to the privy in back and locked herself in. Her own breathing deafened her in the dark, close space, and she sat and waited until she could hear at last the nightly calling of the frogs and crickets. Even then, all she could think to say was oh, my, and the pressure of Jesús's face against her face would not leave.

No one had missed her in the parlor, however, and Rosie walked in and through quickly, announcing that she was next going to take a bath. "Your father's in the bathhouse," her mother said, and Rosie, in her room, recalled that she had not seen him when she entered. There had been only Aunt Taka and Uncle Gimpachi with her mother at the table, drinking tea. She got her robe and straw sandals and crossed the parlor again to go outside. Her mother was telling them about the *haiku* competition in the *Mainichi* and the poem she had entered.

Rosie met her father coming out of the bathhouse. "Are you through, Father?" she asked. "I was going to ask you to scrub my back."

"Scrub your own back," he said shortly, going toward the main house.

"What have I done now?" she yelled after him. She suddenly felt like doing a lot of yelling. But he did not answer, and she went into the bathhouse. Turning on the dangling light, she removed her denims and T-shirt and threw them in the big carton for dirty clothes standing next to the washing machine. Her other things she took with her into the bath compartment to wash after her bath. After she had scooped a basin of hot water from the square wooden tub, she sat on the grey cement of the floor and soaped herself at exaggerated leisure, singing, "Red Sails in the Sunset"[9] at the top of her voice and using da-da-da where she suspected her words. Then, standing, still singing, for she was possessed by the notion that any attempt now to analyze would result in spoilage and she believed that the larger her volume the less she would be able to hear herself think, she obtained more hot water and poured it on until she was free of lather. Only then did she allow herself to step into the steaming vat, one leg first, then the remainder of her body inch by inch until the water no longer stung and she could move around at will.

---

9. **"Red Sails in the Sunset":** A hit song recorded by both the popular singer Bing Crosby (1903–1977) and the bandleader Guy Lombardo (1902–1977) in 1935.

She took a long time soaking, afterwards remembering to go around outside to stoke the embers of the tin-lined fireplace beneath the tub and to throw on a few more sticks so that the water might keep its heat for her mother, and when she finally returned to the parlor, she found her mother still talking *haiku* with her aunt and uncle, the three of them on another round of tea. Her father was nowhere in sight.

At Japanese school the next day (Wednesday, it was), Rosie was grave and giddy by turns. Preoccupied at her desk in the row for students on Book Eight, she made up for it at recess by performing wild mimicry for the benefit of her friend Chizuko. She held her nose and whined a witticism or two in what she considered was the manner of Fred Allen; she assumed intoxication and a British accent to go over the climax of the Rudy Vallee recording of the pub conversation about William Ewart Gladstone; she was the child Shirley Temple piping, "On the Good Ship Lollipop"; she was the gentleman soprano of the Four Inkspots trilling, "If I Didn't Care."[10] And she felt reasonably satisfied when Chizuko wept and gasped, "Oh, Rosie, you ought to be in the movies!"

Her father came after her at noon, bringing her sandwiches of minced ham and two nectarines to eat while she rode, so that she could pitch right into the sorting when they got home. The lugs were piling up, he said, and the ripe tomatoes in them would probably have to be taken to the cannery tomorrow if they were not ready for the produce haulers tonight. "This heat's not doing them any good. And we've got no time for a break today."

It *was* hot, probably the hottest day of the year, and Rosie's blouse stuck damply to her back even under the protection of the canvas. But she worked as efficiently as a flawless machine and kept the stalls heaped, with one part of her mind listening in to the parental murmuring about the heat and the tomatoes and with another part planning the exact words she would say to Jesús when he drove up with the first load of the afternoon. But when at last she saw that the pick-up was coming, her hands went berserk and the tomatoes started falling in the wrong stalls, and her father said, "Hey, hey! Rosie, watch what you're doing!"

"Well, I have to go to the *benjo*," she said, hiding panic.

"Go in the weeds over there," he said, only half-joking.

"Oh, Father!" she protested.

"Oh, go on home," her mother said. "We'll make out for awhile."

In the privy, Rosie peered through a knothole toward the fields, watching as much as she could of Jesús. Happily she thought she saw him look in the direction of the

---

10. **She held her nose and whined ... "If I Didn't Care":** Rosie mimics a number of American radio, recording, and movie stars of the period: the comedian Fred Allen (1894-1956), the host of a popular radio show from 1934-1949; the singer and bandleader Rudy Vallee (1901-1986), a famous mimic whose recordings included songs and comic bits such as a drunken conversation in an English pub about the British political leader William Ewart Gladstone (1809-1898); Shirley Temple (b. 1928), the beloved child actor whose recording of her signature song "On the Good Ship Lollipop" sold 500,000 copies after she first sang it in the movie *Bright Eyes* (1934); and the Ink Spots, a pioneering black vocal group whose first smash hit was "If I Didn't Care" (1939), featuring the high tenor voice of their lead singer, Bill Kenny.

house from time to time before he finished unloading and went back toward the patch where his mother and father worked. As she was heading for the shed, a very presentable black car purred up the dirt driveway to the house and its driver motioned to her. Was this the Hayashi home, he wanted to know. She nodded. Was she a Hayashi? Yes, she said, thinking that he was a good-looking man. He got out of the car with a huge, flat package and she saw that he warmly wore a business suit. "I have something here for your mother then," he said, in a more elegant Japanese than she was used to.

She told him where her mother was and he came along with her, patting his face with an immaculate white handkerchief and saying something about the coolness of San Francisco. To her surprised mother and father, he bowed and introduced himself as, among other things, the *haiku* editor of the *Mainichi Shinbun*, saying that since he had been coming as far as Los Angeles anyway, he had decided to bring her the first prize she had won in the recent contest.

"First prize?" her mother echoed, believing and not believing, pleased and overwhelmed. Handed the package with a bow, she bobbed her head up and down numerous times to express her utter gratitude.

"It is nothing much," he added, "but I hope it will serve as a token of our great appreciation for your contributions and our great admiration of your considerable talent."

"I am not worthy," she said, falling easily into his style. "It is I who should make some sign of my humble thanks for being permitted to contribute."

"No, no, to the contrary," he said, bowing again.

But Rosie's mother insisted, and then saying that she knew she was being unorthodox, she asked if she might open the package because her curiosity was so great. Certainly she might. In fact, he would like her reaction to it, for personally, it was one of his favorite *Hiroshiges*.[11]

Rosie thought it was a pleasant picture, which looked to have been sketched with delicate quickness. There were pink clouds, containing some graceful calligraphy, and a sea, that was a pale blue except at the edges, containing four sampans with indications of people in them. Pines edged the water and on the far-off beach there was a cluster of thatched huts towered over by pine-dotted mountains of grey and blue. The frame was scalloped and gilt.

After Rosie's mother pronounced it without peer and somewhat prodded her father into nodding agreement, she said Mr. Kuroda must at least have a cup of tea, after coming all this way, and although Mr. Kuroda did not want to impose, he soon agreed that a cup of tea would be refreshing and went along with her to the house, carrying the picture for her.

"Ha, your mother's crazy!" Rosie's father said, and Rosie laughed uneasily as she resumed judgment on the tomatoes. She had emptied six lugs when he broke into an imaginary conversation with Jesús to tell her to go and remind her mother of the tomatoes, and she went slowly.

---

11. ***Hiroshiges***: Woodcut prints by Ando Hiroshige (1797–1858), a well-known Japanese landscape artist.

Mr. Kuroda was in his shirtsleeves expounding some *haiku* theory as he munched a rice cake, and her mother was rapt. Abashed in the great man's presence, Rosie stood next to her mother's chair until her mother looked up inquiringly, and then she started to whisper the message, but her mother pushed her gently away and reproached, "You are not being very polite to our guest."

"Father says the tomatoes . . ." Rosie said aloud, smiling foolishly.

"Tell him I shall only be a minute," her mother said, speaking the language of Mr. Kuroda.

When Rosie carried the reply to her father, he did not seem to hear and she said again, "Mother says she'll be back in a minute."

"All right, all right," he nodded, and they worked again in silence. But suddenly, her father uttered an incredible noise, exactly like the cork of a bottle popping, and the next Rosie knew, he was stalking angrily toward the house, almost running, in fact, and she chased after him crying, "Father! Father! What are you going to do?"

He stopped long enough to order her back to the shed. "Never mind!" he shouted. "Get on with the sorting!"

And from the place in the fields where she stood, frightened and vacillating, Rosie saw her father enter the house. Soon Mr. Kuroda came out alone, putting on his coat. Mr. Kuroda got into his car and backed out down the driveway, onto the highway. Next her father emerged, also alone, something in his arms (it was the picture, she realized), and, going over to the bathhouse woodpile, he threw the picture on the ground and picked up the axe. Smashing the picture, glass and all (she heard the explosion faintly), he reached over for the kerosene that was used to encourage the bath fire and poured it over the wreckage. I am dreaming, Rosie said to herself, I am dreaming, but her father, having made sure that his act of cremation was irrevocable, was even then returning to the fields.

Rosie ran past him and toward the house. What had become of her mother? She burst into the parlor and found her mother at the back window, watching the dying fire. They watched together until there remained only a feeble smoke under the blazing sun. Her mother was very calm.

"Do you know why I married your father?" she said, without turning.

"No," said Rosie. It was the most frightening question she had ever been called upon to answer. Don't tell me now, she wanted to say, tell me tomorrow, tell me next week, don't tell me today. But she knew she would be told now, that the telling would combine with the other violence of the hot afternoon to level her life, her world (so various, so beautiful, so new?[12])to the very ground.

It was like a story out of the magazines, illustrated in sepia, which she had consumed so greedily for a period until the information had somehow reached her that those wretchedly unhappy autobiographies, offered to her as the testimonials of living men

---

12. **so various, so beautiful, so new?:** A reference to the opening of the final stanza of "Dover Beach" by the English poet Matthew Arnold (1822–1888): "Ah, love, let us be true / To one another! for the world, which seems / To lie before us like a land of dreams, / So various, so beautiful, so new, / Hath really neither joy, nor love, nor light, / Nor certitude, nor peace, nor help for pain" (ll. 29–34).

and women, were largely inventions: Her mother, at nineteen, had come to America and married her father as an alternative to suicide.

At eighteen, she had been in love with the first son of one of the well-to-do families in her village. The two had met whenever and wherever they could, secretly, because it would not have done for his family to see him favor her—her father had no money; he was a drunkard and a gambler besides. She had learned she was with child; an excellent match had already been arranged for her lover. Despised by her family, she had given premature birth to a stillborn son, who would be seventeen now. Her family did not turn her out, but she could no longer project herself in any direction without refreshing in them the memory of her indiscretion. She wrote to Aunt Taka, her favorite sister, in America, threatening to kill herself if Aunt Taka would not send for her. Aunt Taka hastily arranged a marriage with a young man, but lately arrived from Japan, of whom she knew, a young man of simple mind, it was said, but of kindly heart. The young man was never told why his unseen betrothed was so eager to hasten the day of meeting.

The story was told perfectly, with neither groping for words nor untoward passion. It was as though her mother had memorized it by heart, reciting it to herself so many times over that its nagging vileness had long since gone.

"I had a brother then?" Rosie asked, for this was what seemed to matter now; she would think about the other later, she assured herself, pushing back the illumination which threatened all that darkness that had hitherto been merely mysterious or even glamorous. "A half-brother?"

"Yes."

"I would have liked a brother," she said.

Suddenly, her mother knelt on the floor and took her by the wrists. "Rosie," she said urgently, "Promise me you will never marry!" Shocked more by the request than the revelation, Rosie stared at her mother's face. Jesus, Jesus, she called silently, not certain whether she was invoking the help of the son of the Carrascos or of God, until there returned sweetly the memory of Jesús's hand, how it had touched her and where. Still her mother waited for an answer, holding her wrists so tightly that her hands were going numb. She tried to pull free. Promise, her mother whispered fiercely, promise. Yes, yes, I promise, Rosie said. But for an instant she turned away, and her mother, hearing the familiar glib agreement, released her. Oh, you, you, you, her eyes and twisted mouth said, you fool. Rosie, covering her face, began at last to cry, and the embrace and consoling hand came much later than she expected.

[1949]

James Baldwin

[1924–1987]

James Baldwin was born James Arthur Jones on August 2, 1924, in New York City. His mother was Emma Berdis Jones, a single woman from Maryland who, like thousands of other African Americans, had joined the great migration in search of a better life in the North. When her son was three years old, she married David Baldwin, a Baptist minister and laborer from Louisiana. For many years, Baldwin believed that his stepfather was his birth father, whose identity he never learned. The large family, which included some of David Baldwin's children from a previous marriage, lived in such misery and poverty in Harlem that Baldwin later said that he "never had a childhood." The frustrated David Baldwin was abusive and violent, and he was deeply suspicious of Baldwin's interest in books. "Cease studying!" was a command that Baldwin often heard at home, and he escaped to read at public libraries. From 1936 to 1938, he attended Frederick Douglass Junior High School, where one of his teachers was the poet Countee Cullen. Cullen encouraged him to join the literary club, and Baldwin later coedited the literary magazine of the predominantly white DeWitt Clinton High School in the Bronx. During high school, he was also a popular preacher at a revivalist storefront church in Harlem, the Fireside Pentecostal Assembly, but he left the church and the ministry before his graduation in 1941. Baldwin hoped to go to college, but he was expected to help support the family, so he took a job as a construction worker in New Jersey and later worked in a meatpacking factory in New York City.

After his stepfather's death in 1943, Baldwin determined to begin a career as a writer. He moved to Greenwich Village where he worked at a series of odd jobs and began to write an autobiographical novel. He sought out the acclaimed novelist Richard Wright, who read the completed portion of Baldwin's draft and generously helped him obtain a grant for promising writers from the publisher Harper & Brothers. In 1947, Baldwin published his first reviews in a national magazine, the *Nation*. The following year, his essays appeared in the left-wing magazine the *New Leader* and in *Commentary*, the publication of the American Jewish Committee, in which Baldwin also published his first short story, "Previous Condition." Deeply frustrated by the racial discrimination and injustice in the United States, he decided to follow in Wright's footsteps and move to Paris. Baldwin ended an engagement to a young woman (his last heterosexual relationship), bought a one-way ticket, and sailed in November 1948. "I left America because I doubted my ability to survive the fury of the color problem here," he later wrote. "I wanted to prevent myself from becoming merely a Negro; or, even, merely a Negro writer." Although he had little money and did not find France to be as free of racial discrimination as he had hoped, Baldwin's first five years there were productive and personally

James Baldwin

This photograph of Baldwin was taken in 1967, during a decade in which he was deeply engaged in the struggle for civil rights in the United States.

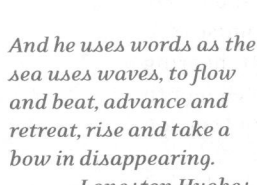

And he uses words as the sea uses waves, to flow and beat, advance and retreat, rise and take a bow in disappearing.
—Langston Hughes

satisfying. He became friendly with the black painter Beauford Delaney, who became a kind of father figure to Baldwin. In 1950, he met a young Swiss, Lucien Happersberger, and they became lovers and lifelong friends. In addition to essays and numerous reviews Baldwin wrote for various American periodicals, he completed his autobiographical novel, *Go Tell It on the Mountain* (1953), which was published by the prominent New York firm of Alfred A. Knopf, Inc.

The novel established Baldwin as a major new voice in American literature. A Guggenheim Fellowship in 1954 enabled him to complete a collection of essays, *Notes of a Native Son* (1955), and to begin work on *Giovanni's Room* (1956), a novel about a white American expatriate who becomes romantically involved with both a woman and a male bartender in Paris. In 1957, Baldwin returned to the United States, the focus of the essays collected in *Nobody Knows My Name* (1961) and the setting of *Another Country* (1962), an ambitious novel about the divisions among a racially mixed group of friends in New York City. Inspired by his growing involvement in the struggle for civil rights, Baldwin wrote *The Fire Next Time* (1963), a devastating assessment of the state of racial relations in the United States. The best-selling book thrust Baldwin into the forefront of the civil rights movement and onto the cover of *Time*. He subsequently exposed the consequences of bigotry and racial hatred in *Blues for Mister Charlie*, a play about the murder of a black youth that opened on Broadway in 1964; in the stories collected in *Going to Meet the Man* (1965); and in his novels *Tell Me How Long the Train's Been Gone* (1968) and *If Beale Street Could Talk* (1974). Baldwin returned to France in the 1970s, but he described himself as a "commuter" rather than an expatriate, and he was in considerable demand as a speaker throughout the United States. Baldwin interviewed dozens of people about the serial killings of black children in Atlanta from 1979 into 1981, the subject of his final book, *The Evidence of Things Unseen* (1985). He died of cancer at his home in France on December 1, 1987, and was buried in Harlem following a massive memorial service during which Baldwin was eulogized by three of the writers whose careers he had helped inspire, Maya Angelou, Toni Morrison, and Amiri Baraka.

Reading Baldwin's "Notes of a Native Son."   Baldwin began working on this autobiographical essay in 1952 while he was living in Paris, far removed from the characters and scenes he so vividly evoked: his childhood in Harlem, the construction job he took in New Jersey after he graduated from high school in 1942, his stepfather's death, and the race riots in Harlem in 1943. A shorter version of the essay was published as "Me and My House . . ." in *Harper's Magazine* in November 1955, just before the full text appeared at the opening of Baldwin's collection *Notes of a Native Son*. As the title suggests, Baldwin's essay was inspired in part by Richard Wright's best-selling protest novel about a young black man struggling against poverty and racism in the South Side ghetto of Chicago, *Native Son* (1940). Although the first edition of *Notes of a Native Son* created little

Harlem Riot

Broken glass and other debris litter the sidewalk along the main shopping thoroughfare of 125th Street, between Seventh and Eighth Avenues, in the aftermath of the race riot in Harlem in 1943.

stir, the collection received enthusiastic reviews and sold briskly after it was reissued in paperback in 1957. In a review in the *New York Times*, Langston Hughes observed: "Few American writers handle words more effectively in the essay form than James Baldwin." Certainly, his mastery of style, tone, and voice is illustrated by "Notes of a Native Son." The writer and activist Julius Lester has pointed to yet another reason that the essay has proven to be so enduring: "Baldwin's power as a writer lies in his ability to weave the deeply autobiographical with the political and social. There is no separation between Jimmy Baldwin, black child of Harlem, and James Baldwin, American. For him, the personal is never just personal, and the political never just political. Because he perceives himself not only as the individual James Baldwin but also as the black Everyman, his writing has a moral authority that would be dismissed as arrogant if so many had not affirmed what he wrote." The text is taken from the first edition of *Notes of a Native Son* (1955).

bedfordstmartins.com/
americanlit for research
links on Baldwin

NOTES OF A NATIVE SON

I

On the 29th of July, in 1943, my father died. On the same day, a few hours later, his last child was born. Over a month before this, while all our energies were concentrated in waiting for these events, there had been, in Detroit, one of the bloodiest race riots of the century.[1] A few hours after my father's funeral, while he lay in state in the undertaker's chapel, a race riot broke out in Harlem. On the morning of the 3rd of August, we drove my father to the graveyard through a wilderness of smashed plate glass.

The day of my father's funeral had also been my nineteenth birthday. As we drove him to the graveyard, the spoils of injustice, anarchy, discontent, and hatred were all around us. It seemed to me that God himself had devised, to mark my father's end, the most sustained and brutally dissonant of codas. And it seemed to me, too, that the violence which rose all about us as my father left the world had been devised as a corrective for the pride of his eldest son. I had declined to believe in that apocalypse which had been central to my father's vision; very well, life seemed to be saying, here is something that will certainly pass for an apocalypse until the real thing comes along. I had inclined to be contemptuous of my father for the conditions of his life, for the conditions of our lives. When his life had ended I began to wonder about that life and also, in a new way, to be apprehensive about my own.

I had not known my father very well. We had got on badly, partly because we shared, in our different fashions, the vice of stubborn pride. When he was dead I realized that I had hardly ever spoken to him. When he had been dead a long time I began to wish I had. It seems to be typical of life in America, where opportunities, real and fancied, are thicker than anywhere else on the globe, that the second generation has no time to talk to the first. No one, including my father, seems to have known exactly how old he was, but his mother had been born during slavery. He was of the first generation of free men. He, along with thousands of other Negroes, came North after 1919 and I was part of that generation which had never seen the landscape of what Negroes sometimes call the Old Country.[2]

He had been born in New Orleans and had been a quite young man there during the time that Louis Armstrong, a boy, was running errands for the dives and honky-tonks of what was always presented to me as one of the most wicked of cities – to this day, whenever I think of New Orleans, I also helplessly think of Sodom and Gomorrah.[3] My father

1. **one of the bloodiest race riots of the century:** During the summer of 1943, race riots erupted in several American cities, most violently in Detroit, Michigan. On June 20, a clash between black and white youths escalated into street riots in which roving gangs, both black and white, attacked pedestrians and pulled people from their cars, some of which were overturned or set on fire. During the course of thirty-six hours of rioting, thirty-four people were killed, twenty-five blacks and nine whites, and more than 1,800 people were arrested, most of them for looting. A month later, another riot erupted in West Harlem. In contrast to earlier race riots, which were battles between white and black people, the black residents of Harlem directed their frustration and rage at property, especially white-owned businesses in the neighborhood.
2. **He, along with thousands of other Negroes . . . Old Country:** During World War I and especially after the war formally ended in 1919, hundreds of thousands of African Americans joined what was called the "great migration" to industrial cities in the North, fleeing racial violence, segregation, and a depressed rural economy in the South and drawn by the promise of factory jobs created by wartime industries and later by the economic boom of the 1920s.
3. **He had been born . . . Sodom and Gomorrah:** The trumpet player Louis Armstrong (1900–1971), who grew up in poverty in New Orleans, later became the most famous and influential jazz musician in the country. Although jazz was played all over New Orleans during the early decades of the twentieth century, the music was popularly associated with Storyville, a notorious red-light district that flourished from 1897 through 1917. Sodom and Gomorrah were cities destroyed by God because of the sinful ways of their inhabitants (Genesis 19:24).

never mentioned Louis Armstrong, except to forbid us to play his records; but there was a picture of him on our wall for a long time. One of my father's strong-willed female relatives had placed it there and forbade my father to take it down. He never did, but he eventually maneuvered her out of the house and when, some years later, she was in trouble and near death, he refused to do anything to help her.

He was, I think, very handsome. I gather this from photographs and from my own memories of him, dressed in his Sunday best and on his way to preach a sermon somewhere, when I was little. Handsome, proud, and ingrown, "like a toe-nail," somebody said. But he looked to me, as I grew older, like pictures I had seen of African tribal chieftains: he really should have been naked, with war-paint on and barbaric mementos, standing among spears. He could be chilling in the pulpit and indescribably cruel in his personal life and he was certainly the most bitter man I have ever met; yet it must be said that there was something else in him, buried in him, which lent him his tremendous power and, even, a rather crushing charm. It had something to do with his blackness, I think—he was very black—with his blackness and his beauty, and with the fact that he knew that he was black but did not know that he was beautiful. He claimed to be proud of his blackness but it had also been the cause of much humiliation and it had fixed bleak boundaries to his life. He was not a young man when we were growing up and he had already suffered many kinds of ruin; in his outrageously demanding and protective way he loved his children, who were black like him and menaced, like him; and all these things sometimes showed in his face when he tried, never to my knowledge with any success, to establish contact with any of us. When he took one of his children on his knee to play, the child always became fretful and began to cry; when he tried to help one of us with our homework the absolutely unabating tension which emanated from him caused our minds and our tongues to become paralyzed, so that he, scarcely knowing why, flew into a rage and the child, not knowing why, was punished. If it ever entered his head to bring a surprise home for his children, it was, almost unfailingly, the wrong surprise and even the big watermelons he often brought home on his back in the summertime led to the most appalling scenes. I do not remember, in all those years, that one of his children was ever glad to see him come home. From what I was able to gather of his early life, it seemed that this inability to establish contact with other people had always marked him and had been one of the things which had driven him out of New Orleans. There was something in him, therefore, groping and tentative, which was never expressed and which was buried with him. One saw it most clearly when he was facing new people and hoping to impress them. But he never did, not for long. We went from church to smaller and more improbable church, he found himself in less and less demand as a minister, and by the time he died none of his friends had come to see him for a long time. He had lived and died in an intolerable bitterness of spirit and it frightened me, as we drove him to the graveyard through those unquiet, ruined streets, to see how powerful and overflowing this bitterness could be and to realize that this bitterness now was mine.

When he died I had been away from home for a little over a year. In that year I had had time to become aware of the meaning of all my father's bitter warnings, had discovered the secret of his proudly pursed lips and rigid carriage: I had discovered the weight of white people in the world. I saw that this had been for my ancestors and now would be for me an awful thing to live with and that the bitterness which had helped to kill my father could also kill me.

He had been ill a long time – in the mind, as we now realized, reliving instances of his fantastic intransigence in the new light of his affliction and endeavoring to feel a sorrow for him which never, quite, came true. We had not known that he was being eaten up by paranoia, and the discovery that his cruelty, to our bodies and our minds, had been one of the symptoms of his illness was not, then, enough to enable us to forgive him. The younger children felt, quite simply, relief that he would not be coming home any more. My mother's observation that it was he, after all, who had kept them alive all these years meant nothing because the problems of keeping children alive are not real for children. The older children felt, with my father gone, that they could invite their friends to the house without fear that their friends would be insulted or, as had sometimes happened with me, being told that their friends were in league with the devil and intended to rob our family of everything we owned. (I didn't fail to wonder, and it made me hate him, what on earth we owned that anybody else would want.)

His illness was beyond all hope of healing before anyone realized that he was ill. He had always been so strange and had lived, like a prophet, in such unimaginably close communion with the Lord that his long silences which were punctuated by moans and hallelujahs and snatches of old songs while he sat at the living-room window never seemed odd to us. It was not until he refused to eat because, he said, his family was trying to poison him that my mother was forced to accept as a fact what had, until then, been only an unwilling suspicion. When he was committed, it was discovered that he had tuberculosis and, as it turned out, the disease of his mind allowed the disease of his body to destroy him. For the doctors could not force him to eat, either, and, though he was fed intravenously, it was clear from the beginning that there was no hope for him.

In my mind's eye I could see him, sitting at the window, locked up in his terrors; hating and fearing every living soul including his children who had betrayed him, too, by reaching toward the world which had despised him. There were nine of us. I began to wonder what it could have felt like for such a man to have had nine children whom he could barely feed. He used to make little jokes about our poverty, which never, of course, seemed very funny to us; they could not have seemed very funny to him, either, or else our all too feeble response to them would never have caused such rages. He spent great energy and achieved, to our chagrin, no small amount of success in keeping us away from the people who surrounded us, people who had all-night rent parties to which we listened when we should have been sleeping, people who cursed and drank and flashed razor blades on Lenox Avenue.[4] He could not understand why, if they had so much energy to spare, they could not use it to make their lives better. He treated almost everybody on our block with a most uncharitable asperity and neither they, nor, of course, their children were slow to reciprocate.

---

4. **Lenox Avenue:** Now co-named Malcolm X Boulevard, the major north-south route through Harlem.

The only white people who came to our house were welfare workers and bill collectors. It was almost always my mother who dealt with them, for my father's temper, which was at the mercy of his pride, was never to be trusted. It was clear that he felt their very presence in his home to be a violation: this was conveyed by his carriage, almost ludicrously stiff, and by his voice, harsh and vindictively polite. When I was around nine or ten I wrote a play which was directed by a young, white schoolteacher, a woman, who then took an interest in me, and gave me books to read and, in order to corroborate my theatrical bent, decided to take me to see what she somewhat tactlessly referred to as "real" plays. Theatergoing was forbidden in our house, but, with the really cruel intuitiveness of a child, I suspected that the color of this woman's skin would carry the day for me. When, at school, she suggested taking me to the theater, I did not, as I might have done if she had been a Negro, find a way of discouraging her, but agreed that she should pick me up at my house one evening. I then, very cleverly, left all the rest to my mother, who suggested to my father, as I knew she would, that it would not be very nice to let such a kind woman make the trip for nothing. Also, since it was a schoolteacher, I imagine that my mother countered the idea of sin with the idea of "education," which word, even with my father, carried a kind of bitter weight.

Before the teacher came my father took me aside to ask *why* she was coming, what *interest* she could possibly have in our house, in a boy like me. I said I didn't know but I, too, suggested that it had something to do with education. And I understood that my father was waiting for me to say something — I didn't quite know what; perhaps that I wanted his protection against this teacher and her "education." I said none of these things and the teacher came and we went out. It was clear, during the brief interview in our living room, that my father was agreeing very much against his will and that he would have refused permission if he had dared. The fact that he did not dare caused me to despise him: I had no way of knowing that he was facing in that living room a wholly unprecedented and frightening situation.

Later, when my father had been laid off from his job, this woman became very important to us. She was really a very sweet and generous woman and went to a great deal of trouble to be of help to us, particularly during one awful winter. My mother called her by the highest name she knew: she said she was a "christian." My father could scarcely disagree but during the four or five years of our relatively close association he never trusted her and was always trying to surprise in her open, Midwestern face the genuine, cunningly hidden, and hideous motivation. In later years, particularly when it began to be clear that this "education" of mine was going to lead me to perdition, he became more explicit and warned me that my white friends in high school were not really my friends and that I would see, when I was older, how white people would do anything to keep a Negro down. Some of them could be nice, he admitted, but none of them were to be trusted and most of them were not even nice. The best thing was to have as little to do with them as possible. I did not feel this way and I was certain, in my innocence, that I never would.

But the year which preceded my father's death had made a great change in my life. I had been living in New Jersey, working in defense plants, working and living among southerners, white and black. I knew about the south, of course, and about how southerners treated Negroes and how they expected them to behave, but it had never entered my mind that anyone would look at me and expect *me* to behave that way. I learned in New Jersey that to be a Negro meant, precisely, that one was never looked at but was simply at the mercy of the reflexes the color of one's skin caused in other people. I acted in New Jersey as I had always acted, that is as though I thought a great deal of myself – I had to *act* that way – with results that were, simply, unbelievable. I had scarcely arrived before I had earned the enmity, which was extraordinarily ingenious, of all my superiors and nearly all my co-workers. In the beginning, to make matters worse, I simply did not know what was happening. I did not know what I had done, and I shortly began to wonder what *anyone* could possibly do, to bring about such unanimous, active, and unbearably vocal hostility. I knew about jim-crow[5] but I had never experienced it. I went to the same self-service restaurant three times and stood with all the Princeton boys before the counter, waiting for a hamburger and coffee; it was always an extraordinarily long time before anything was set before me; but it was not until the fourth visit that I learned that, in fact, nothing had ever been set before me: I had simply picked something up. Negroes were not served there, I was told, and they had been waiting for me to realize that I was always the only Negro present. Once I was told this, I determined to go there all the time. But now they were ready for me and, though some dreadful scenes were subsequently enacted in that restaurant, I never ate there again.

It was the same story all over New Jersey, in bars, bowling alleys, diners, places to live. I was always being forced to leave, silently, or with mutual imprecations. I very shortly became notorious and children giggled behind me when I passed and their elders whispered or shouted – they really believed that I was mad. And it did begin to work on my mind, of course; I began to be afraid to go anywhere and to compensate for this I went places to which I really should not have gone and where, God knows, I had no desire to be. My reputation in town naturally enhanced my reputation at work and my working day became one long series of acrobatics designed to keep me out of trouble. I cannot say that these acrobatics succeeded. It began to seem that the machinery of the organization I worked for was turning over, day and night, with but one aim: to eject me. I was fired once, and contrived, with the aid of a friend from New York, to get back on the payroll; was fired again, and bounced back again. It took a while to fire me for the third time, but the third time took. There were no loopholes anywhere. There was not even any way of getting back inside the gates.

That year in New Jersey lives in my mind as though it were the year during which, having an unsuspected predilection for it, I first contracted some dread, chronic disease, the unfailing symptom of which is a kind of blind fever, a pounding in the skull and fire in the bowels. Once this disease is contracted, one can never be really carefree again, for the fever, without an instant's warning, can recur at any moment. It can wreck more important things than race relations. There is not a Negro alive who does not have this rage in his blood – one has the choice, merely, of living with it consciously or surrendering to it. As for me, this fever has recurred in me, and does, and will until the day I die.

---

5. **jim-crow:** Jim Crow laws, discriminatory state and local laws enacted after the end of Reconstruction in 1876, mandated segregated schools and public accommodations throughout the South. The name *jim-crow* is derived from a derogatory song about African Americans, "Jump Jim Crow," which dates from about 1828.

My last night in New Jersey, a white friend from New York took me to the nearest big town, Trenton, to go to the movies and have a few drinks. As it turned out, he also saved me from, at the very least, a violent whipping. Almost every detail of that night stands out very clearly in my memory. I even remember the name of the movie we saw because its title impressed me as being so patly ironical. It was a movie about the German occupation of France, starring Maureen O'Hara and Charles Laughton and called *This Land Is Mine*. I remember the name of the diner we walked into when the movie ended: it was the "American Diner." When we walked in the counterman asked what we wanted and I remember answering with the casual sharpness which had become my habit: "We want a hamburger and a cup of coffee, what do you think we want?" I do not know why, after a year of such rebuffs, I so completely failed to anticipate his answer, which was, of course, "We don't serve Negroes here." This reply failed to discompose me, at least for the moment. I made some sardonic comment about the name of the diner and we walked out into the streets.

This was the time of what was called the "brown-out," when the lights in all American cities were very dim. When we re-entered the streets something happened to me which had the force of an optical illusion, or a nightmare. The streets were very crowded and I was facing north. People were moving in every direction but it seemed to me, in that instant, that all of the people I could see, and many more than that, were moving toward me, against me, and that everyone was white. I remember how their faces gleamed. And I felt, like a physical sensation, a *click* at the nape of my neck as though some interior string connecting my head to my body had been cut. I began to walk. I heard my friend call after me, but I ignored him. Heaven only knows what was going on in his mind, but he had the good sense not to touch me — I don't know what would have happened if he had — and to keep me in sight. I don't know what was going on in my mind, either; I certainly had no conscious plan. I wanted to do something to crush these white faces, which were crushing me. I walked for perhaps a block or two until I came to an enormous, glittering, and fashionable restaurant in which I knew not even the intercession of the Virgin would cause me to be served. I pushed through the doors and took the first vacant seat I saw, at a table for two, and waited.

I do not know how long I waited and I rather wonder, until today, what I could possibly have looked like. Whatever I looked like, I frightened the waitress who shortly appeared, and the moment she appeared all of my fury flowed toward her. I hated her for her white face, and for her great, astounded, frightened eyes. I felt that if she found a black man so frightening I would make her fright worthwhile.

She did not ask me what I wanted, but repeated, as though she had learned it somewhere, "We don't serve Negroes here." She did not say it with the blunt, derisive hostility to which I had grown so accustomed, but, rather, with a note of apology in her voice, and fear. This made me colder and more murderous than ever. I felt I had to do something with my hands. I wanted her to come close enough for me to get her neck between my hands.

So I pretended not to have understood her, hoping to draw her closer. And she did step a very short step closer, with her pencil poised incongruously over her pad, and repeated the formula: ". . . don't serve Negroes here."

Somehow, with the repetition of that phrase, which was already ringing in my head like a thousand bells of a nightmare, I realized that she would never come any closer and that I would have to strike from a distance. There was nothing on the table but an ordinary water-mug half full of water, and I picked this up and hurled it with all my strength at her. She ducked and it missed her and shattered against the mirror behind the bar. And, with that sound, my frozen blood abruptly thawed, I returned from wherever I had been, I *saw*, for the first time, the restaurant, the people with their mouths open, already, as it seemed to me, rising as one man, and I realized what I had done, and where I was, and I was frightened. I rose and began running for the door. A round, potbellied man grabbed me by the nape of the neck just as I reached the doors and began to beat me about the face. I kicked him and got loose and ran into the streets. My friend whispered, *"Run!"* and I ran.

My friend stayed outside the restaurant long enough to misdirect my pursuers and the police, who arrived, he told me, at once. I do not know what I said to him when he came to my room that night. I could not have said much. I felt, in the oddest, most awful way, that I had somehow betrayed him. I lived it over and over and over again, the way one relives an automobile accident after it has happened and one finds oneself alone and safe. I could not get over two facts, both equally difficult for the imagination to grasp, and one was that I could have been murdered. But the other was that I had been ready to commit murder. I saw nothing very clearly but I did see this: that my life, my *real* life, was in danger, and not from anything other people might do but from the hatred I carried in my own heart.

II

I had returned home around the second week in June — in great haste because it seemed that my father's death and my mother's confinement were both but a matter of hours. In the case of my mother, it soon became clear that she had simply made a miscalculation. This had always been her tendency and I don't believe that a single one of us arrived in the world, or has since arrived anywhere else, on time. But none of us dawdled so intolerably about the business of being born as did my baby sister. We sometimes amused ourselves, during those endless, stifling weeks, by picturing the baby sitting within in the safe, warm dark, bitterly regretting the necessity of becoming a part of our chaos and stubbornly putting it off as long as possible. I understood her perfectly and congratulated her on showing such good sense so soon. Death, however, sat as purposefully at my father's bedside as life stirred within my mother's womb and it was harder to understand why he so lingered in that long shadow. It seemed that he had bent, and for a long time, too, all of his energies toward dying. Now death was ready for him but my father held back.

All of Harlem, indeed, seemed to be infected by waiting. I had never before known it to be so violently still. Racial tensions throughout this country were exacerbated during the early years of the war, partly because the labor market brought together hundreds of thousands of ill-prepared people and partly because Negro soldiers, regardless of where they were born, received their military training in the south. What happened in defense plants and army camps had repercussions, naturally, in every Negro ghetto. The situation in Harlem had grown bad enough for clergymen, police-men, educators, politicians, and social workers to assert in one breath that there was no "crime wave" and to offer, in the very next breath, suggestions as to how to combat it. These suggestions always seemed to involve playgrounds, despite the fact that racial skirmishes were occurring in the playgrounds, too. Playground or not, crime wave or not, the Harlem police force had been augmented in March, and the unrest grew—perhaps, in fact, partly as a result of the ghetto's instinctive hatred of police-men. Perhaps the most revealing news item, out of the steady parade of reports of muggings, stabbings, shootings, assaults, gang wars, and accusations of police bru-tality, is the item concerning six Negro girls who set upon a white girl in the subway because, as they all too accurately put it, she was stepping on their toes. Indeed she was, all over the nation.

I had never before been so aware of policemen, on foot, on horseback, on corners, everywhere, always two by two. Nor had I ever been so aware of small knots of people. They were on stoops and on corners and in doorways, and what was striking about them, I think, was that they did not seem to be talking. Never, when I passed these groups, did the usual sound of a curse or a laugh ring out and neither did there seem to be any hum of gossip. There was certainly, on the other hand, occurring between them communication extraordinarily intense. Another thing that was striking was the unexpected diversity of the people who made up these groups. Usually, for ex-ample, one would see a group of sharpies standing on the street corner, jiving the passing chicks; or a group of older men, usually, for some reason, in the vicinity of a barber shop, discussing baseball scores, or the numbers, or making rather chilling observations about women they had known. Women, in a general way, tended to be seen less often together—unless they were church women, or very young girls, or prostitutes met together for an unprofessional instant. But that summer I saw the strangest combinations: large, respectable, churchly matrons standing on the stoops or the corners with their hair tied up, together with a girl in sleazy satin whose face bore the marks of gin and the razor, or heavy-set, abrupt, no-nonsense older men, in company with the most disreputable and fanatical "race" men, or these same "race" men with the sharpies, or these sharpies with the churchly women. Sev-enth Day Adventists and Methodists and Spiritualists seemed to be hobnobbing with Holyrollers and they were all, alike, entangled with the most flagrant disbelievers; something heavy in their stance seemed to indicate that they had all, incredibly, seen a common vision, and on each face there seemed to be the same strange, bitter shadow.

The churchly women and the matter-of-fact, no-nonsense men had children in the Army. The sleazy girls they talked to had lovers there, the sharpies and the "race" men had friends and brothers there. It would have demanded an unquestioning patriotism, happily as uncommon in this country as it is undesirable, for these people not to have been disturbed by the bitter letters they received, by the newspaper stories they read, not to have been enraged by the posters, then to be found all over New York, which described the Japanese as "yellow-bellied Japs." It was only the "race" men, to be sure, who spoke ceaselessly of being revenged – how this vengeance was to be exacted was not clear – for the indignities and dangers suffered by Negro boys in uniform; but everybody felt a directionless, hopeless bitterness, as well as that panic which can scarcely be suppressed when one knows that a human being one loves is beyond one's reach, and in danger. This helplessness and this gnawing uneasiness does something, at length, to even the toughest mind. Perhaps the best way to sum all this up is to say that the people I knew felt, mainly, a peculiar kind of relief when they knew that their boys were being shipped out of the south, to do battle overseas. It was, perhaps, like feeling that the most dangerous part of a dangerous journey had been passed and that now, even if death should come, it would come with honor and without the complicity of their countrymen. Such a death would be, in short, a fact with which one could hope to live.

It was on the 28th of July, which I believe was a Wednesday, that I visited my father for the first time during his illness and for the last time in his life. The moment I saw him I knew why I had put off this visit so long. I had told my mother that I did not want to see him because I hated him. But this was not true. It was only that I *had* hated him and I wanted to hold on to this hatred. I did not want to look on him as a ruin: it was not a ruin I had hated. I imagine that one of the reasons people cling to their hates so stubbornly is because they sense, once hate is gone, that they will be forced to deal with pain.

We traveled out to him, his older sister and myself, to what seemed to be the very end of a very Long Island. It was hot and dusty and we wrangled, my aunt and I, all the way out, over the fact that I had recently begun to smoke and, as she said, to give myself airs. But I knew that she wrangled with me because she could not bear to face the fact of her brother's dying. Neither could I endure the reality of her despair, her unstated bafflement as to what had happened to her brother's life, and her own. So we wrangled and I smoked and from time to time she fell into a heavy reverie. Covertly, I watched her face, which was the face of an old woman; it had fallen in, the eyes were sunken and lightless; soon she would be dying, too.

In my childhood – it had not been so long ago – I had thought her beautiful. She had been quick-witted and quick-moving and very generous with all the children and each of her visits had been an event. At one time one of my brothers and myself had thought of running away to live with her. Now she could no longer produce out of her handbag some unexpected and yet familiar delight. She made me feel pity and revulsion and fear. It was awful to realize that she no longer caused me to feel affection. The closer we came to the hospital the more querulous she became and at the same time, naturally, grew more dependent on me. Between pity and guilt and fear I began to feel that there was another me trapped in my skull like a jack-in-the-box who might escape my control at any moment and fill the air with screaming.

She began to cry the moment we entered the room and she saw him lying there, all shriveled and still, like a little black monkey. The great, gleaming apparatus which fed him and would have compelled him to be still even if he had been able to move brought to mind, not beneficence, but torture; the tubes entering his arm made me think of pictures I had seen when a child, of Gulliver, tied down by the pygmies on that island.[6] My aunt wept and wept, there was a whistling sound in my father's throat; nothing was said; he could not speak. I wanted to take his hand, to say something. But I do not know what I could have said, even if he could have heard me. He was not really in that room with us, he had at last really embarked on his journey; and though my aunt told me that he said he was going to meet Jesus, I did not hear anything except that whistling in his throat. The doctor came back and we left, into that unbearable train again, and home. In the morning came the telegram saying that he was dead. Then the house was suddenly full of relatives, friends, hysteria, and confusion and I quickly left my mother and the children to the care of those impressive women, who, in Negro communities at least, automatically appear at times of bereavement armed with lotions, proverbs, and patience, and an ability to cook. I went downtown. By the time I returned, later the same day, my mother had been carried to the hospital and the baby had been born.

III

For my father's funeral I had nothing black to wear and this posed a nagging problem all day long. It was one of those problems, simple, or impossible of solution, to which the mind insanely clings in order to avoid the mind's real trouble. I spent most of that day at the downtown apartment of a girl I knew, celebrating my birthday with whiskey and wondering what to wear that night. When planning a birthday celebration one naturally does not expect that it will be up against competition from a funeral and this girl had anticipated taking me out that night, for a big dinner and a night club afterwards. Sometime during the course of that long day we decided that we would go out anyway, when my father's funeral service was over. I imagine *I* decided it, since, as the funeral hour approached, it became clearer and clearer to me that I would not know what to do with myself when it was over. The girl, stifling her very lively concern as to the possible effects of the whiskey on one of my father's chief mourners, concentrated on being conciliatory and practically helpful. She found a black shirt for me somewhere and ironed it and, dressed in the darkest pants and jacket I owned, and slightly drunk, I made my way to my father's funeral.

The chapel was full, but not packed, and very quiet. There were, mainly, my father's relatives, and his children, and here and there I saw faces I had not seen since childhood, the faces of my father's one-time friends. They were very dark and solemn now, seeming somehow to suggest that they had known all along that something like this would happen. Chief among the mourners was my aunt, who had quarreled with my father all his life; by which I do not mean to suggest that her mourning was insincere or that she had not loved him. I suppose that she was one of the few people in the world who had, and their incessant quarreling proved precisely the strength of the tie that

---

6. **Gulliver . . . on that island**: In the first part of *Gulliver's Travels* by the English satirist Jonathan Swift (1667–1745), Lemuel Gulliver is shipwrecked on Lilliput, an island inhabited by people only six inches tall. While Gulliver sleeps, the Lilliputians tie him to the ground on his back so that he cannot move his arms or legs.

bound them. The only other person in the world, as far as I knew, whose relationship to my father rivaled my aunt's in depth was my mother, who was not there.

It seemed to me, of course, that it was a very long funeral. But it was, if anything, a rather shorter funeral than most, nor, since there were no overwhelming, uncontrollable expressions of grief, could it be called – if I dare to use the word – successful. The minister who preached my father's funeral sermon was one of the few my father had still been seeing as he neared his end. He presented to us in his sermon a man whom none of us had ever seen – a man thoughtful, patient, and forbearing, a Christian inspiration to all who knew him, and a model for his children. And no doubt the children, in their disturbed and guilty state, were almost ready to believe this; he had been remote enough to be anything and, anyway, the shock of the incontrovertible, that it was really our father lying up there in that casket, prepared the mind for anything. His sister moaned and this grief-stricken moaning was taken as corroboration. The other faces held a dark, non-committal thoughtfulness. This was not the man they had known, but they had scarcely expected to be confronted with *him;* this was, in a sense deeper than questions of fact, the man they had not known, and the man they had not known may have been the real one. The real man, whoever he had been, had suffered and now he was dead: this was all that was sure and all that mattered now. Every man in the chapel hoped that when his hour came he, too, would be eulogized, which is to say forgiven, and that all of his lapses, greeds, errors, and strayings from the truth would be invested with coherence and looked upon with charity. This was perhaps the last thing human beings could give each other and it was what they demanded, after all, of the Lord. Only the Lord saw the midnight tears, only He was present when one of His children, moaning and wringing hands, paced up and down the room. When one slapped one's child in anger the recoil in the heart reverberated through heaven and became part of the pain of the universe. And when the children were hungry and sullen and distrustful and one watched them, daily, growing wilder, and further away, and running headlong into danger, it was the Lord who knew what the charged heart endured as the strap was laid to the backside; the Lord alone who knew what one *would* have said if one had had, like the Lord, the gift of the living word. It was the Lord who knew of the impossibility every parent in that room faced: how to prepare the child for the day when the child would be despised and how to *create* in the child – by what means? – a stronger antidote to this poison than one had found for oneself. The avenues, side streets, bars, billiard halls, hospitals, police stations, and even the playgrounds of Harlem – not to mention the houses of correction, the jails, and the morgue – testified to the potency of the poison while remaining silent as to the efficacy of whatever antidote, irresistibly raising the question of whether or not such an antidote existed; raising, which was worse, the question of whether or not an antidote was desirable; perhaps poison should be fought with poison. With these several schisms in the mind and with more terrors in the heart than could be named, it was better not to judge the man who had gone down under an impossible burden. It was better to remember: *Thou knowest this man's fall; but thou knowest not his wrassling.*

While the preacher talked and I watched the children – years of changing their diapers, scrubbing them, slapping them, taking them to school, and scolding them had had the perhaps inevitable result of making me love them, though I am not sure I knew this then—my mind was busily breaking out with a rash of disconnected impressions. Snatches of popular songs, indecent jokes, bits of books I had read, movie sequences, faces, voices, political issues—I thought I was going mad; all these impressions suspended, as it were, in the solution of the faint nausea produced in me by the heat and liquor. For a moment I had the impression that my alcoholic breath, inefficiently disguised with chewing gum, filled the entire chapel. Then someone began singing one of my father's favorite songs and, abruptly, I was with him, sitting on his knee, in the hot, enormous, crowded church which was the first church we attended. It was the Abyssinian Baptist Church on 138th Street. We had not gone there long. With this image, a host of others came. I had forgotten, in the rage of my growing up, how proud my father had been of me when I was little. Apparently, I had had a voice and my father had liked to show me off before the members of the church. I had forgotten what he had looked like when he was pleased but now I remembered that he had always been grinning with pleasure when my solos ended. I even remembered certain expressions on his face when he teased my mother—had he loved her? I would never know. And when had it all begun to change? For now it seemed that he had not always been cruel. I remembered being taken for a haircut and scraping my knee on the footrest of the barber's chair and I remembered my father's face as he soothed my crying and applied the stinging iodine. Then I remembered our fights, fights which had been of the worst possible kind because my technique had been silence.

I remembered the one time in all our life together when we had really spoken to each other.

It was on a Sunday and it must have been shortly before I left home. We were walking, just the two of us, in our usual silence, to or from church. I was in high school and had been doing a lot of writing and I was, at about this time, the editor of the high school magazine. But I had also been a Young Minister and had been preaching from the pulpit. Lately, I had been taking fewer engagements and preached as rarely as possible. It was said in the church, quite truthfully, that I was "cooling off."

My father asked me abruptly, "You'd rather write than preach, wouldn't you?"

I was astonished at his question—because it was a real question. I answered, "Yes."

That was all we said. It was awful to remember that that was all we had *ever* said.

The casket now was opened and the mourners were being led up the aisle to look for the last time on the deceased. The assumption was that the family was too overcome with grief to be allowed to make this journey alone and I watched while my aunt was led to the casket and, muffled in black, and shaking, led back to her seat. I disapproved of forcing the children to look on their dead father, considering that the shock of his death, or, more truthfully, the shock of death as a reality, was already a little more than a child could bear, but my judgment in this matter had been overruled and there they were, bewildered and frightened and very small, being led, one by one, to the casket. But there is also something very gallant about children at such moments. It has something to do with their silence and gravity and with the fact that one cannot help them. Their legs, somehow, seem *exposed*, so that it is at once incredible and terribly clear that their legs are all they have to hold them up.

I had not wanted to go to the casket myself and I certainly had not wished to be led there, but there was no way of avoiding either of these forms. One of the deacons led me up and I looked on my father's face. I cannot say that it looked like him at all. His blackness had been equivocated by powder and there was no suggestion in that casket of what his power had or could have been. He was simply an old man dead, and it was hard to believe that he had ever given anyone either joy or pain. Yet, his life filled that room. Further up the avenue his wife was holding his newborn child. Life and death so close together, and love and hatred, and right and wrong, said something to me which I did not want to hear concerning man, concerning the life of man.

After the funeral, while I was downtown desperately celebrating my birthday, a Negro soldier, in the lobby of the Hotel Braddock,[7] got into a fight with a white policeman over a Negro girl. Negro girls, white policemen, in or out of uniform, and Negro males – in or out of uniform – were part of the furniture of the lobby of the Hotel Braddock and this was certainly not the first time such an incident had occurred. It was destined, however, to receive an unprecedented publicity, for the fight between the policeman and the soldier ended with the shooting of the soldier. Rumor, flowing immediately to the streets outside, stated that the soldier had been shot in the back, an instantaneous and revealing invention, and that the soldier had died protecting a Negro woman. The facts were somewhat different – for example, the soldier had not been shot in the back, and was not dead, and the girl seems to have been as dubious a symbol of womanhood as her white counterpart in Georgia usually is, but no one was interested in the facts. They preferred the invention because this invention expressed and corroborated their hates and fears so perfectly. It is just as well to remember that people are always doing this. Perhaps many of those legends, including Christianity, to which the world clings began their conquest of the world with just some such concerted surrender to distortion. The effect, in Harlem, of this particular legend was like the effect of a lit match in a tin of gasoline. The mob gathered before the doors of the Hotel Braddock simply began to swell and to spread in every direction, and Harlem exploded.

The mob did not cross the ghetto lines. It would have been easy, for example, to have gone over Morningside Park on the west side or to have crossed the Grand Central railroad tracks at 125th Street on the east side, to wreak havoc in white neighborhoods. The mob seems to have been mainly interested in something more potent and real than the white face, that is, in white power, and the principal damage done during the riot of the summer of 1943 was to white business establishments in Harlem. It might have been a far bloodier story, of course, if, at the hour the riot began, these establishments had still been open. From the Hotel Braddock the mob fanned out, east and west along 125th Street, and for the entire length of Lenox, Seventh, and Eighth avenues. Along each of these avenues, and along each major side street – 116th, 125th, 135th, and so on – bars, stores, pawnshops, restaurants, even little luncheonettes had been smashed open and entered and looted – looted, it might be added, with more haste than efficiency. The shelves really looked as though a bomb had struck them. Cans of beans and soup and dog food, along

---

7. **Hotel Braddock:** A seedy hotel, since demolished, that stood on the corner of 126th Street and Eighth Avenue in Harlem.

with toilet paper, corn flakes, sardines, and milk tumbled every which way, and abandoned cash registers and cases of beer leaned crazily out of the splintered windows and were strewn along the avenues. Sheets, blankets, and clothing of every description formed a kind of path, as though people had dropped them while running. I truly had not realized that Harlem *had* so many stores until I saw them all smashed open; the first time the word *wealth* ever entered my mind in relation to Harlem was when I saw it scattered in the streets. But one's first, incongruous impression of plenty was countered immediately by an impression of waste. None of this was doing anybody any good. It would have been better to have left the plate glass as it had been and the goods lying in the stores.

It would have been better, but it would also have been intolerable, for Harlem had needed something to smash. To smash something is the ghetto's chronic need. Most of the time it is the members of the ghetto who smash each other, and themselves. But as long as the ghetto walls are standing there will always come a moment when these outlets do not work. That summer, for example, it was not enough to get into a fight on Lenox Avenue, or curse out one's cronies in the barber shops. If ever, indeed, the violence which fills Harlem's churches, pool halls, and bars erupts outward in a more direct fashion, Harlem and its citizens are likely to vanish in an apocalyptic flood. That this is not likely to happen is due to a great many reasons, most hidden and powerful among them the Negro's real relation to the white American. This relation prohibits, simply, anything as uncomplicated and satisfactory as pure hatred. In order really to hate white people, one has to blot so much out of the mind—and the heart—that this hatred itself becomes an exhausting and self-destructive pose. But this does not mean, on the other hand, that love comes easily: the white world is too powerful, too complacent, too ready with gratuitous humiliation, and, above all, too ignorant and too innocent for that. One is absolutely forced to make perpetual qualifications and one's own reactions are always canceling each other out. It is this, really, which has driven so many people mad, both white and black. One is always in the position of having to decide between amputation and gangrene. Amputation is swift but time may prove that the amputation was not necessary—or one may delay the amputation too long. Gangrene is slow, but it is impossible to be sure that one is reading one's symptoms right. The idea of going through life as a cripple is more than one can bear, and equally unbearable is the risk of swelling up slowly, in agony, with poison. And the trouble, finally, is that the risks are real even if the choices do not exist.

"But as for me and my house," my father had said, "we will serve the Lord." I wondered, as we drove him to his resting place, what this line had meant for him. I had heard him preach it many times. I had preached it once myself, proudly giving it an interpretation different from my father's. Now the whole thing came back to me, as though my father and I were on our way to Sunday school and I were memorizing the golden text: *And if it seem evil unto you to serve the Lord, choose you this day whom you will serve; whether the gods which your fathers served that were on the other side of the flood, or the gods of the Amorites, in whose land ye dwell: but as for me and my house, we will serve the Lord.*[8] I suspected in these familiar lines a meaning which had never been

---

8. *And . . . Lord*: Joshua 24:15.

there for me before. All of my father's texts and songs, which I had decided were meaningless, were arranged before me at his death like empty bottles, waiting to hold the meaning which life would give them for me. This was his legacy: nothing is ever escaped. That bleakly memorable morning I hated the unbelievable streets and the Negroes and whites who had, equally, made them that way. But I knew that it was folly, as my father would have said, this bitterness was folly. It was necessary to hold on to the things that mattered. The dead man mattered, the new life mattered; blackness and whiteness did not matter; to believe that they did was to acquiesce in one's own destruction. Hatred, which could destroy so much, never failed to destroy the man who hated and this was an immutable law.

It began to seem that one would have to hold in the mind forever two ideas which seemed to be in opposition. The first idea was acceptance, the acceptance, totally without rancor, of life as it is, and men as they are: in the light of this idea, it goes without saying that injustice is a commonplace. But this did not mean that one could be complacent, for the second idea was of equal power: that one must never, in one's own life, accept these injustices as commonplace but must fight them with all one's strength. This fight begins, however, in the heart and it now had been laid to my charge to keep my own heart free of hatred and despair. This intimation made my heart heavy and, now that my father was irrecoverable, I wished that he had been beside me so that I could have searched his face for the answers which only the future would give me now.

[1955]

Flannery O'Connor

[1925-1964]

Mary Flannery O'Connor was born on March 25, 1925, in Savannah, Georgia. She was the only child of Regina Cline O'Connor, the daughter of a prominent businessman, and Edward F. O'Connor, the owner of a real-estate company. Her prosperous parents were Roman Catholic, and O'Connor attended St. Vincent's Grammar School and the Sacred Heart School for Girls. In 1938, business reverses forced Edward O'Connor to move the family to Atlanta, where he took a job with the Federal Housing Administration. Within the year, his wife took their daughter to live with relatives at her family home in

Flannery O'Connor

This photograph of O'Connor was taken at a book-signing party for her first novel, *Wise Blood* (1952), at her alma mater, the Georgia State College for Women.

Milledgeville, Georgia, where O'Connor's father commuted on the weekends from Atlanta. Since there was no Catholic school in Milledgeville, O'Connor attended Peabody Laboratory School, a progressive institution that permitted students wide latitude in their choice of courses. O'Connor took a number of courses in art and began drawing cartoons. Edward O'Connor was diagnosed with lupus erythematosus, an incurable autoimmune disease, and died in 1941. After her graduation from high school the following year, O'Connor enrolled at the Georgia State College for Women (now Georgia College and State University) in Milledgeville. Living at home with her mother and aunts, she studied art, English, and social studies, drawing cartoons for the school newspaper and yearbook, as well as contributing essays, poems, and stories to its literary magazine, the *Corinthian*. O'Connor graduated in 1945 and won a fellowship in journalism at the University of Iowa.

O'Connor soon turned from journalism to writing fiction. During her first semester at Iowa, she applied to the university's graduate program in creative writing, the Writers' Workshop. At her first meeting with its director, Paul Engle, he could not understand her thick Southern accent, so he handed O'Connor a pad and asked her to jot down what she was saying. She famously wrote: "My name is Flannery O'Connor. I'm from Milledgeville, Georgia. I'm a writer." She was accepted into the program and published her first short story, "The Geranium," in *Accent* in 1946. She completed her master's thesis, a collection of short stories, and was awarded an MFA in 1947. She stayed on as a teaching assistant at the university for another year, working on a novel for which she won the Rinehart-Iowa Fiction Award. Following a residency at the Yaddo Artist's Colony in Saratoga Springs, New York, she moved to New York City in early 1949. Uncomfortable with life in the city, O'Connor soon accepted an invitation from two literary friends, Robert and Sally Fitzgerald, to move into the garage apartment at their home in Ridgefield, Connecticut. She lived there happily for almost two years, during which her work began to appear in the *Partisan Review* and the *Sewanee Review*. During a holiday visit to her family in December 1950, she became ill and was diagnosed with lupus, the same disease that killed her father. Unable to return to Connecticut, she spent some time in an Atlanta hospital before moving to Andalusia, the family farm outside Milledgeville, where she lived with her mother for the rest of her life.

Despite her illness and the debilitating effects of the drugs she had to take, O'Connor tenaciously pursued her literary career. She adhered to a strict schedule in which she wrote for three hours every morning. She also maintained a correspondence with a large number of literary friends, entertained visitors, and began raising peacocks, all of which helped ease her isolation. She completed her first novel, *Wise Blood* (1952), the grotesquely comic and satirical story of a preacher who establishes the "Church without Christ," and wrote the stories collected in *A Good Man Is Hard to Find and Other Stories* (1955). The reception of both volumes was generally positive, but reviewers struggled to characterize O'Connor's unusual work, which was often pigeonholed as Southern gothic. In a perceptive essay in the *Saturday Review of Literature*, however, the Catholic writer Caroline Gordon observed:

> Miss O'Connor, for all her apparent preoccupation with the visible scene, is also fiercely concerned with moral, even theological, problems. In these stories the rural South is, for the first time, viewed by a writer whose orthodoxy matches her talent. The results are revolutionary.

She was for me the first great modern writer from the South.

–Alice Walker

O'Connor's religious orthodoxy was further revealed in her second novel, *The Violent Bear It Away* (1960), a quasi-allegorical account of the struggle between Christianity and secularism that explores "the consequences of man's refusal to see things as they really are and act accordingly," as a reviewer asserted in the *Catholic World*. O'Connor also continued to write short stories, including "Everything That Rises Must Converge," which won first prize in the O. Henry Awards for the best American short stories of 1963. But she was increasingly ill and died of complications of lupus on August 3, 1964, before the publication of her second collection of stories, *Everything That Rises Must Converge* (1965). Her reputation was further enhanced by the posthumous publication of a collection of her essays on the craft of writing, *Mystery and Manners* (1969); and *The Complete Stories of Flannery O'Connor* (1972), which won the National Book Award.

Reading O'Connor's "A Good Man Is Hard to Find."   After her early death, O'Connor was increasingly recognized for her distinctive contributions to American literature and her mastery of the short story. One of her most famous and frequently anthologized stories is "A Good Man Is Hard to Find," which she wrote in the early 1950s, while living at her family home in Milledgeville, Georgia. In June 1953, she wrote to friends that she had sold this story to the *Partisan Review* reader, "another of those 50¢ jobs." The collection, which actually sold for thirty-five cents a copy, was the *Avon Book of Modern Writing*, a new paperback series designed to showcase first-rate writers and edited by William Phillips and Philip Rahv, the editors of the *Partisan Review*. O'Connor used the story as the title piece for her first collection, *A Good Man Is Hard to Find and Other Stories* (1955). When O'Connor read the story to a group of friends, including the eminent literary critic Van Wyck Brooks, he observed that "it was a shame someone with so much talent should look upon life as a horror story." In fact, O'Connor's theological worldview was far more complex, as is "A Good Man Is Hard to Find," with its memorable cast of flawed characters, its combination of grotesque humor and violent action, its blend of local realism and Christian symbolism, and its postmodern emphasis on the misreading of signs in a world of deceptive appearances. The text is taken from *A Good Man Is Hard to Find and Other Stories* (1955).

bedfordstmartins.com/ americanlit *for research links on O'Connor*

A GOOD MAN IS HARD TO FIND[1]

The grandmother didn't want to go to Florida. She wanted to visit some of her connections in east Tennessee and she was seizing at every chance to change Bailey's mind. Bailey was the son she lived with, her only boy. He was sitting on the edge of his chair at the table, bent over the orange sports section of the *Journal.* "Now look here, Bailey," she said, "see here, read this," and she stood with one hand on her thin hip and the other rattling the newspaper at his bald head. "Here this fellow that calls himself The Misfit is aloose from the Federal Pen and headed toward Florida and you read here what it says he did to these people. Just you read it. I wouldn't take my children in any direction with a criminal like that aloose in it. I couldn't answer to my conscience if I did."

Bailey didn't look up from his reading so she wheeled around then and faced the children's mother, a young woman in slacks, whose face was as broad and innocent as a cabbage and was tied around with a green head-kerchief that had two points on the top like rabbit's ears. She was sitting on the sofa, feeding the baby his apricots out of a jar. "The children have been to Florida before," the old lady said. "You all ought to take them somewhere else for a change so they would see different parts of the world and be broad. They never have been to east Tennessee."

The children's mother didn't seem to hear her but the eight-year-old boy, John Wesley, a stocky child with glasses, said, "If you don't want to go to Florida, why dontcha stay at home?" He and the little girl, June Star, were reading the funny papers on the floor.

"She wouldn't stay at home to be queen for a day,"[2] June Star said without raising her yellow head.

"Yes and what would you do if this fellow, The Misfit, caught you?" the grandmother asked.

"I'd smack his face," John Wesley said.

"She wouldn't stay at home for a million bucks," June Star said. "Afraid she'd miss something. She has to go everywhere we go."

"All right, Miss," the grandmother said. "Just remember that the next time you want me to curl your hair."

June Star said her hair was naturally curly.

The next morning the grandmother was the first one in the car, ready to go. She had her big black valise that looked like the head of a hippopotamus in one corner, and underneath it she was hiding a basket with Pitty Sing,[3] the cat, in it. She didn't intend for the cat to be left alone in the house for three days because he would miss her too much and she was afraid he might brush against one of the gas burners and accidentally asphyxiate himself. Her son, Bailey, didn't like to arrive at a motel with a cat.

---

1. **A Good Man Is Hard to Find:** The title of a popular blues song composed by Eddie Green in 1918.
2. **queen for a day:** The title of a popular radio and television game show in which female contestants vied for prizes by describing their financial difficulties and other hardships, and in which the winner was determined by an "applause meter" that measured the response of the studio audience. At the opening of each show, the host asked the audience: "Would YOU like to be Queen for a day?"
3. **Pitty Sing:** One of the three little maids involved in the complicated romantic plot of *The Mikado* (1885), a popular comic opera by the English composers Gilbert and Sullivan.

She sat in the middle of the back seat with John Wesley and June Star on either side of her. Bailey and the children's mother and the baby sat in front and they left Atlanta at eight forty-five with the mileage on the car at 55890. The grandmother wrote this down because she thought it would be interesting to say how many miles they had been when they got back. It took them twenty minutes to reach the outskirts of the city.

The old lady settled herself comfortably, removing her white cotton gloves and putting them up with her purse on the shelf in front of the back window. The children's mother still had on slacks and still had her head tied up in a green kerchief, but the grandmother had on a navy blue straw sailor hat with a bunch of white violets on the brim and a navy blue dress with a small white dot in the print. Her collars and cuffs were white organdy trimmed with lace and at her neckline she had pinned a purple spray of cloth violets containing a sachet. In case of an accident, anyone seeing her dead on the highway would know at once that she was a lady.

She said she thought it was going to be a good day for driving, neither too hot nor too cold, and she cautioned Bailey that the speed limit was fifty-five miles an hour and that the patrolmen hid themselves behind billboards and small clumps of trees and sped out after you before you had a chance to slow down. She pointed out interesting details of the scenery: Stone Mountain; the blue granite that in some places came up to both sides of the highway; the brilliant red clay banks slightly streaked with purple; and the various crops that made rows of green lace-work on the ground. The trees were full of silver-white sunlight and the meanest of them sparkled. The children were reading comic magazines and their mother had gone back to sleep.

"Let's go through Georgia fast so we won't have to look at it much," John Wesley said.

"If I were a little boy," said the grandmother, "I wouldn't talk about my native state that way. Tennessee has the mountains and Georgia has the hills."

"Tennessee is just a hillbilly dumping ground," John Wesley said, "and Georgia is a lousy state too."

"You said it," June Star said.

"In my time," said the grandmother, folding her thin veined fingers, "children were more respectful of their native states and their parents and everything else. People did right then. Oh look at the cute little pickaninny!"[4] she said and pointed to a Negro child standing in the door of a shack. "Wouldn't that make a picture, now?" she asked and they all turned and looked at the little Negro out of the back window. He waved.

"He didn't have any britches on," June Star said.

"He probably didn't have any," the grandmother explained. "Little niggers in the country don't have things like we do. If I could paint, I'd paint that picture," she said.

The children exchanged comic books.

The grandmother offered to hold the baby and the children's mother passed him over the front seat to her. She set him on her knee and bounced him and told him about the things they were passing. She rolled her eyes and screwed up her mouth and stuck her

---

4. **pickaninny:** Probably derived from the Spanish word *pequeño*, meaning small or little, this now-offensive term was commonly used from the mid-nineteenth century until the 1930s to refer to African American children.

leathery thin face into his smooth bland one. Occasionally he gave her a far-away smile. They passed a large cotton field with five or six graves fenced in the middle of it, like a small island. "Look at the graveyard!" the grandmother said, pointing it out. "That was the old family burying ground. That belonged to the plantation."

"Where's the plantation?" John Wesley asked.

"Gone With the Wind,"[5] said the grandmother. "Ha. Ha."

When the children finished all the comic books they had brought, they opened the lunch and ate it. The grandmother ate a peanut butter sandwich and an olive and would not let the children throw the box and the paper napkins out the window. When there was nothing else to do they played a game by choosing a cloud and making the other two guess what shape it suggested. John Wesley took one the shape of a cow and June Star guessed a cow and John Wesley said, no, an automobile, and June Star said he didn't play fair, and they began to slap each other over the grandmother.

The grandmother said she would tell them a story if they would keep quiet. When she told a story, she rolled her eyes and waved her head and was very dramatic. She said once when she was a maiden lady she had been courted by a Mr. Edgar Atkins Teagarden from Jasper, Georgia. She said he was a very good-looking man and a gentleman and that he brought her a watermelon every Saturday afternoon with his initials cut in it, E. A. T. Well, one Saturday, she said, Mr. Teagarden brought the watermelon and there was nobody at home and he left it on the front porch and returned in his buggy to Jasper, but she never got the watermelon, she said, because a nigger boy ate it when he saw the initials, E. A. T.! This story tickled John Wesley's funny bone and he giggled and giggled but June Star didn't think it was any good. She said she wouldn't marry a man that just brought her a watermelon on Saturday. The grandmother said she would have done well to marry Mr. Teagarden because he was a gentleman and had bought Coca-Cola stock when it first came out and that he had died only a few years ago, a very wealthy man.

They stopped at The Tower for barbecued sandwiches. The Tower was a part stucco and part wood filling station and dance hall set in a clearing outside of Timothy. A fat man named Red Sammy Butts ran it and there were signs stuck here and there on the building and for miles up and down the highway saying, TRY RED SAMMY'S FAMOUS BARBECUE. NONE LIKE FAMOUS RED SAMMY'S! RED SAM! THE FAT BOY WITH THE HAPPY LAUGH. A VETERAN! RED SAMMY'S YOUR MAN!

Red Sammy was lying on the bare ground outside The Tower with his head under a truck while a gray monkey about a foot high, chained to a small chinaberry tree, chattered nearby. The monkey sprang back into the tree and got on the highest limb as soon as he saw the children jump out of the car and run toward him.

Inside, The Tower was a long dark room with a counter at one end and tables at the other and dancing space in the middle. They all sat down at a board table next to the nickelodeon and Red Sam's wife, a tall burnt-brown woman with hair and eyes lighter than her skin, came and took their order. The children's mother put a dime in the

---

5. **Gone With the Wind:** The title of Margaret Mitchell's best-selling 1936 novel about the Civil War and the passing of the Old South.

machine and played "The Tennessee Waltz," and the grandmother said that tune always made her want to dance. She asked Bailey if he would like to dance but he only glared at her. He didn't have a naturally sunny disposition like she did and trips made him nervous. The grandmother's brown eyes were very bright. She swayed her head from side to side and pretended she was dancing in her chair. June Star said play something she could tap to so the children's mother put in another dime and played a fast number and June Star stepped out onto the dance floor and did her tap routine.

"Ain't she cute?" Red Sam's wife said, leaning over the counter. "Would you like to come be my little girl?"

"No I certainly wouldn't," June Star said. "I wouldn't live in a broken-down place like this for a million bucks!" and she ran back to the table.

"Ain't she cute?" the woman repeated, stretching her mouth politely.

"Arn't you ashamed?" hissed the grandmother.

Red Sam came in and told his wife to quit lounging on the counter and hurry up with these people's order. His khaki trousers reached just to his hip bones and his stomach hung over them like a sack of meal swaying under his shirt. He came over and sat down at a table nearby and let out a combination sigh and yodel. "You can't win," he said. "You can't win," and he wiped his sweating red face off with a gray handkerchief. "These days you don't know who to trust," he said. "Ain't that the truth?"

"People are certainly not nice like they used to be," said the grandmother.

"Two fellers come in here last week," Red Sammy said, "driving a Chrysler. It was a old beat-up car but it was a good one and these boys looked all right to me. Said they worked at the mill and you know I let them fellers charge the gas they bought? Now why did I do that?"

"Because you're a good man!" the grandmother said at once.

"Yes'm, I suppose so," Red Sam said as if he were struck with this answer.

His wife brought the orders, carrying the five plates all at once without a tray, two in each hand and one balanced on her arm. "It isn't a soul in this green world of God's that you can trust," she said. "And I don't count nobody out of that, not nobody," she repeated, looking at Red Sammy.

"Did you read about that criminal, The Misfit, that's escaped?" asked the grandmother.

"I wouldn't be a bit surprised if he didn't attact this place right here," said the woman. "If he hears about it being here, I wouldn't be none surprised to see him. If he hears it's two cent in the cash register, I wouldn't be a tall surprised if he . . ."

"That'll do," Red Sam said. "Go bring these people their Co'-Colas," and the woman went off to get the rest of the order.

"A good man is hard to find," Red Sammy said. "Everything is getting terrible. I remember the day you could go off and leave your screen door unlatched. Not no more."

He and the grandmother discussed better times. The old lady said that in her opinion Europe was entirely to blame for the way things were now. She said the way Europe acted you would think we were made of money and Red Sam said it was no use talking about it, she was exactly right. The children ran outside into the white sunlight and looked at the monkey in the lacy chinaberry tree. He was busy catching fleas on himself and biting each one carefully between his teeth as if it were a delicacy.

They drove off again into the hot afternoon. The grandmother took cat naps and woke up every few minutes with her own snoring. Outside of Toombsboro she woke up and recalled an old plantation that she had visited in this neighborhood once when she was a young lady. She said the house had six white columns across the front and that there was an avenue of oaks leading up to it and two little wooden trellis arbors on either side in front where you sat down with your suitor after a stroll in the garden. She recalled exactly which road to turn off to get to it. She knew that Bailey would not be willing to lose any time looking at an old house, but the more she talked about it, the more she wanted to see it once again and find out if the little twin arbors were still standing. "There was a secret panel in this house," she said craftily, not telling the truth but wishing that she were, "and the story went that all the family silver was hidden in it when Sherman came through but it was never found . . ."[6]

"Hey!" John Wesley said. "Let's go see it! We'll find it! We'll poke all the woodwork and find it! Who lives there? Where do you turn off at? Hey Pop, can't we turn off there?"

"We never have seen a house with a secret panel!" June Star shrieked. "Let's go to the house with the secret panel! Hey Pop, can't we go see the house with the secret panel!"

"It's not far from here, I know," the grandmother said. "It wouldn't take over twenty minutes."

Bailey was looking straight ahead. His jaw was as rigid as a horseshoe. "No," he said.

The children began to yell and scream that they wanted to see the house with the secret panel. John Wesley kicked the back of the front seat and June Star hung over her mother's shoulder and whined desperately into her ear that they never had any fun even on their vacation, that they could never do what THEY wanted to do. The baby began to scream and John Wesley kicked the back of the seat so hard that his father could feel the blows in his kidney.

"All right!" he shouted and drew the car to a stop at the side of the road. "Will you all shut up? Will you all just shut up for one second? If you don't shut up, we won't go any-where."

"It would be very educational for them," the grandmother murmured.

"All right," Bailey said, "but get this: this is the only time we're going to stop for anything like this. This is the one and only time."

"The dirt road that you have to turn down is about a mile back," the grandmother directed. "I marked it when we passed."

"A dirt road," Bailey groaned.

After they had turned around and were headed toward the dirt road, the grandmother recalled other points about the house, the beautiful glass over the front doorway and the candle-lamp in the hall. John Wesley said that the secret panel was probably in the fireplace.

"You can't go inside this house," Bailey said. "You don't know who lives there."

---

6. **Sherman . . . never found:** The Union general William Tecumseh Sherman (1820–1891) led a destructive campaign through Tennessee, Georgia, and the Carolinas in 1864. Many families reportedly hid or buried their valuables to keep them from being plundered by Sherman's troops.

"While you all talk to the people in front, I'll run around behind and get in a window," John Wesley suggested.

"We'll all stay in the car," his mother said.

They turned onto the dirt road and the car raced roughly along in a swirl of pink dust. The grandmother recalled the times when there were no paved roads and thirty miles was a day's journey. The dirt road was hilly and there were sudden washes in it and sharp curves on dangerous embankments. All at once they would be on a hill, looking down over the blue tops of trees for miles around, then the next minute, they would be in a red depression with the dust-coated trees looking down on them.

"This place had better turn up in a minute," Bailey said, "or I'm going to turn around."

The road looked as if no one had traveled on it in months.

"It's not much farther," the grandmother said and just as she said it, a horrible thought came to her. The thought was so embarrassing that she turned red in the face and her eyes dilated and her feet jumped up, upsetting her valise in the corner. The instant the valise moved, the newspaper top she had over the basket under it rose with a snarl and Pitty Sing, the cat, sprang onto Bailey's shoulder.

The children were thrown to the floor and their mother, clutching the baby, was thrown out the door onto the ground; the old lady was thrown into the front seat. The car turned over once and landed right-side-up in a gulch off the side of the road. Bailey remained in the driver's seat with the cat – gray-striped with a broad white face and an orange nose – clinging to his neck like a caterpillar.

As soon as the children saw they could move their arms and legs, they scrambled out of the car, shouting, "We've had an ACCIDENT!" The grandmother was curled up under the dashboard, hoping she was injured so that Bailey's wrath would not come down on her all at once. The horrible thought she had had before the accident was that the house she had remembered so vividly was not in Georgia but in Tennessee.

Bailey removed the cat from his neck with both hands and flung it out the window against the side of a pine tree. Then he got out of the car and started looking for the children's mother. She was sitting against the side of the red gutted ditch, holding the screaming baby, but she only had a cut down her face and a broken shoulder. "We've had an ACCIDENT!" the children screamed in a frenzy of delight.

"But nobody's killed," June Star said with disappointment as the grandmother limped out of the car, her hat still pinned to her head but the broken front brim standing up at a jaunty angle and the violet spray hanging off the side. They all sat down in the ditch, except the children, to recover from the shock. They were all shaking.

"Maybe a car will come along," said the children's mother hoarsely.

"I believe I have injured an organ," said the grandmother, pressing her side, but no one answered her. Bailey's teeth were clattering. He had on a yellow sport shirt with bright blue parrots designed in it and his face was as yellow as the shirt. The grandmother decided that she would not mention that the house was in Tennessee.

The road was about ten feet above and they could see only the tops of the trees on the other side of it. Behind the ditch they were sitting in there were more woods, tall and dark and deep. In a few minutes they saw a car some distance away on top of a hill, coming slowly as if the occupants were watching them. The grandmother stood up and waved both arms dramatically to attract their attention. The car continued to come on slowly, disappeared around a bend and appeared again, moving even slower, on top of the hill they had gone over. It was a big black battered hearse-like automobile. There were three men in it.

It came to a stop just over them and for some minutes, the driver looked down with a steady expressionless gaze to where they were sitting, and didn't speak. Then he turned his head and muttered something to the other two and they got out. One was a fat boy in black trousers and a red sweat shirt with a silver stallion embossed on the front of it. He moved around on the right side of them and stood staring, his mouth partly open in a kind of loose grin. The other had on khaki pants and a blue striped coat and a gray hat pulled down very low, hiding most of his face. He came around slowly on the left side. Neither spoke.

The driver got out of the car and stood by the side of it, looking down at them. He was an older man than the other two. His hair was just beginning to gray and he wore silver-rimmed spectacles that gave him a scholarly look. He had a long creased face and didn't have on any shirt or undershirt. He had on blue jeans that were too tight for him and was holding a black hat and a gun. The two boys also had guns.

"We've had an ACCIDENT!" the children screamed.

The grandmother had the peculiar feeling that the bespectacled man was someone she knew. His face was as familiar to her as if she had known him all her life but she could not recall who he was. He moved away from the car and began to come down the embankment, placing his feet carefully so that he wouldn't slip. He had on tan and white shoes and no socks, and his ankles were red and thin. "Good afternoon," he said. "I see you all had you a little spill."

"We turned over twice!" said the grandmother.

"Oncet," he corrected. "We seen it happen. Try their car and see will it run, Hiram," he said quietly to the boy with the gray hat.

"What you got that gun for?" John Wesley asked. "Whatcha gonna do with that gun?"

"Lady," the man said to the children's mother, "would you mind calling them children to sit down by you? Children make me nervous. I want all you all to sit down right together there where you're at."

"What are you telling US what to do for?" June Star asked.

Behind them the line of woods gaped like a dark open mouth. "Come here," said their mother.

"Look here now," Bailey began suddenly, "we're in a predicament! We're in . . ."

The grandmother shrieked. She scrambled to her feet and stood staring. "You're The Misfit!" she said. "I recognized you at once!"

"Yes'm," the man said, smiling slightly as if he were pleased in spite of himself to be known, "but it would have been better for all of you, lady, if you hadn't of recker-nized me."

Bailey turned his head sharply and said something to his mother that shocked even the children. The old lady began to cry and The Misfit reddened.

"Lady," he said, "don't you get upset. Sometimes a man says things he don't mean. I don't reckon he meant to talk to you thataway."

"You wouldn't shoot a lady, would you?" the grandmother said and removed a clean handkerchief from her cuff and began to slap at her eyes with it.

The Misfit pointed the toe of his shoe into the ground and made a little hole and then covered it up again. "I would hate to have to," he said.

"Listen," the grandmother almost screamed, "I know you're a good man. You don't look a bit like you have common blood. I know you must come from nice people!"

"Yes mam," he said, "finest people in the world." When he smiled he showed a row of strong white teeth. "God never made a finer woman than my mother and my daddy's heart was pure gold," he said. The boy with the red sweat shirt had come around behind them and was standing with his gun at his hip. The Misfit squatted down on the ground. "Watch them children, Bobby Lee," he said. "You know they make me nervous." He looked at the six of them huddled together in front of him and he seemed to be embarrassed as if he couldn't think of anything to say. "Ain't a cloud in the sky," he remarked, looking up at it. "Don't see no sun but don't see no cloud neither."

"Yes, it's a beautiful day," said the grandmother. "Listen," she said, "you shouldn't call yourself The Misfit because I know you're a good man at heart. I can just look at you and tell."

"Hush!" Bailey yelled. "Hush! Everybody shut up and let me handle this!" He was squatting in the position of a runner about to sprint forward but he didn't move.

"I pre-chate that, lady," The Misfit said and drew a little circle in the ground with the butt of his gun.

"It'll take a half a hour to fix this here car," Hiram called, looking over the raised hood of it.

"Well, first you and Bobby Lee get him and that little boy to step over yonder with you," The Misfit said, pointing to Bailey and John Wesley. "The boys want to ast you something," he said to Bailey. "Would you mind stepping back in them woods there with them?"

"Listen," Bailey began, "we're in a terrible predicament! Nobody realizes what this is," and his voice cracked. His eyes were as blue and intense as the parrots in his shirt and he remained perfectly still.

The grandmother reached up to adjust her hat brim as if she were going to the woods with him but it came off in her hand. She stood staring at it and after a second she let it fall on the ground. Hiram pulled Bailey up by the arm as if he were assisting an old man. John Wesley caught hold of his father's hand and Bobby Lee followed. They went off toward the woods and just as they reached the dark edge, Bailey turned and supporting himself against a gray naked pine trunk, he shouted, "I'll be back in a minute, Mamma, wait on me!"

"Come back this instant!" his mother shrilled but they all disappeared into the woods.

"Bailey Boy!" the grandmother called in a tragic voice but she found she was looking at The Misfit squatting on the ground in front of her. "I just know you're a good man," she said desperately. "You're not a bit common!"

"Nome, I ain't a good man," The Misfit said after a second as if he had considered her statement carefully, "but I ain't the worst in the world neither. My daddy said I was a different breed of dog from my brothers and sisters. 'You know,' Daddy said, 'it's some that can live their whole life out without asking about it and it's others has to know why it is, and this boy is one of the latters. He's going to be into everything!'" He put on his black hat and looked up suddenly and then away deep into the woods as if he were embarrassed again. "I'm sorry I don't have on a shirt before you ladies," he said, hunching his shoulders slightly. "We buried our clothes that we had on when we escaped and we're just making do until we can get better. We borrowed these from some folks we met," he explained.

"That's perfectly all right," the grandmother said. "Maybe Bailey has an extra shirt in his suitcase."

"I'll look and see terrectly," The Misfit said.

"Where are they taking him?" the children's mother screamed.

"Daddy was a card himself," The Misfit said. "You couldn't put anything over on him. He never got in trouble with the Authorities though. Just had the knack of handling them."

"You could be honest too if you'd only try," said the grandmother. "Think how wonderful it would be to settle down and live a comfortable life and not have to think about somebody chasing you all the time."

The Misfit kept scratching in the ground with the butt of his gun as if he were thinking about it. "Yes'm, somebody is always after you," he murmured.

The grandmother noticed how thin his shoulder blades were just behind his hat because she was standing up looking down on him. "Do you ever pray?" she asked.

He shook his head. All she saw was the black hat wiggle between his shoulder blades. "Nome," he said.

There was a pistol shot from the woods, followed closely by another. Then silence. The old lady's head jerked around. She could hear the wind move through the tree tops like a long satisfied insuck of breath. "Bailey Boy!" she called.

"I was a gospel singer for a while," The Misfit said. "I been most everything. Been in the arm service, both land and sea, at home and abroad, been twict married, been an undertaker, been with the railroads, plowed Mother Earth, been in a tornado, seen a man burnt alive oncet," and he looked up at the children's mother and the little girl who were sitting close together, their faces white and their eyes glassy; "I even seen a woman flogged," he said.

"Pray, pray," the grandmother began, "pray, pray . . ."

"I never was a bad boy that I remember of," The Misfit said in an almost dreamy voice, "but somewheres along the line I done something wrong and got sent to the penitentiary. I was buried alive," and he looked up and held her attention to him by a steady stare.

"That's when you should have started to pray," she said. "What did you do to get sent to the penitentiary that first time?"

"Turn to the right, it was a wall," The Misfit said, looking up again at the cloudless sky. "Turn to the left, it was a wall. Look up it was a ceiling, look down it was a floor. I forget what I done, lady. I set there and set there, trying to remember what it was I done and I ain't recalled it to this day. Oncet in a while, I would think it was coming to me, but it never come."

"Maybe they put you in by mistake," the old lady said vaguely.

"Nome," he said. "It wasn't no mistake. They had the papers on me."

"You must have stolen something," she said.

The Misfit sneered slightly. "Nobody had nothing I wanted," he said. "It was a head-doctor at the penitentiary said what I had done was kill my daddy but I known that for a lie. My daddy died in nineteen ought nineteen of the epidemic flu[7] and I never had a thing to do with it. He was buried in the Mount Hopewell Baptist churchyard and you can go there and see for yourself."

"If you would pray," the old lady said, "Jesus would help you."

"That's right," The Misfit said.

"Well then, why don't you pray?" she asked trembling with delight suddenly.

"I don't want no hep," he said. "I'm doing all right by myself."

Bobby Lee and Hiram came ambling back from the woods. Bobby Lee was dragging a yellow shirt with bright blue parrots in it.

"Thow me that shirt, Bobby Lee," The Misfit said. The shirt came flying at him and landed on his shoulder and he put it on. The grandmother couldn't name what the shirt reminded her of. "No, lady," The Misfit said while he was buttoning it up, "I found out the crime don't matter. You can do one thing or you can do another, kill a man or take a tire off his car, because sooner or later you're going to forget what it was you done and just be punished for it."

The children's mother had begun to make heaving noises as if she couldn't get her breath. "Lady," he asked, "would you and that little girl like to step off yonder with Bobby Lee and Hiram and join your husband?"

"Yes, thank you," the mother said faintly. Her left arm dangled helplessly and she was holding the baby, who had gone to sleep, in the other. "Hep that lady up, Hiram," The Misfit said as she struggled to climb out of the ditch, "and Bobby Lee, you hold onto that little girl's hand."

"I don't want to hold hands with him," June Star said. "He reminds me of a pig."

The fat boy blushed and laughed and caught her by the arm and pulled her off into the woods after Hiram and her mother.

Alone with The Misfit, the grandmother found that she had lost her voice. There was not a cloud in the sky nor any sun. There was nothing around her but woods. She wanted to tell him that he must pray. She opened and closed her mouth several times before anything came out. Finally she found herself saying, "Jesus. Jesus," meaning, Jesus will help you, but the way she was saying it, it sounded as if she might be cursing.

"Yes'm," The Misfit said as if he agreed. "Jesus thown everything off balance. It was the same case with Him as with me except He hadn't committed any crime and they could prove I had committed one because they had the papers on me. Of course," he said, "they never shown me my papers. That's why I sign myself now. I said long ago, you get you a signature and sign everything you do and keep a copy of it. Then you'll know what you done and you can hold up the crime to the punishment and see do they match and in the end you'll have something to prove you ain't been treated right. I call myself The

---

7. **epidemic flu:** The influenza pandemic of 1918-19, the largest epidemic in history, killed between twenty and forty million people worldwide.

Misfit," he said, "because I can't make what all I done wrong fit what all I gone through in punishment."

There was a piercing scream from the woods, followed closely by a pistol report. "Does it seem right to you, lady, that one is punished a heap and another ain't punished at all?"

"Jesus!" the old lady cried. "You've got good blood! I know you wouldn't shoot a lady! I know you come from nice people! Pray! Jesus, you ought not to shoot a lady. I'll give you all the money I've got!"

"Lady," The Misfit said, looking beyond her far into the woods, "there never was a body that give the undertaker a tip."

There were two more pistol reports and the grandmother raised her head like a parched old turkey hen crying for water and called, "Bailey Boy, Bailey Boy!" as if her heart would break.

"Jesus was the only One that ever raised the dead," The Misfit continued, "and He shouldn't have done it. He thown everything off balance. If He did what He said, then it's nothing for you to do but thow away everything and follow Him, and if He didn't, then it's nothing for you to do but enjoy the few minutes you got left the best way you can — by killing somebody or burning down his house or doing some other meanness to him. No pleasure but meanness," he said and his voice had become almost a snarl.

"Maybe He didn't raise the dead," the old lady mumbled, not knowing what she was saying and feeling so dizzy that she sank down in the ditch with her legs twisted under her.

"I wasn't there so I can't say He didn't," The Misfit said. "I wisht I had of been there," he said, hitting the ground with his fist. "It ain't right I wasn't there because if I had of been there I would of known. Listen lady," he said in a high voice, "if I had of been there I would of known and I wouldn't be like I am now." His voice seemed about to crack and the grandmother's head cleared for an instant. She saw the man's face twisted close to her own as if he were going to cry and she murmured, "Why you're one of my babies. You're one of my own children!" She reached out and touched him on the shoulder. The Misfit sprang back as if a snake had bitten him and shot her three times through the chest. Then he put his gun down on the ground and took off his glasses and began to clean them.

Hiram and Bobby Lee returned from the woods and stood over the ditch, looking down at the grandmother who half sat and half lay in a puddle of blood with her legs crossed under her like a child's and her face smiling up at the cloudless sky.

Without his glasses, The Misfit's eyes were red-rimmed and pale and defenseless-looking. "Take her off and thow her where you thown the others," he said, picking up the cat that was rubbing itself against his leg.

"She was a talker, wasn't she?" Bobby Lee said, sliding down the ditch with a yodel.

"She would of been a good woman," The Misfit said, "if it had been somebody there to shoot her every minute of her life."

"Some fun!" Bobby Lee said.

"Shut up, Bobby Lee," The Misfit said. "It's no real pleasure in life."

[1953, 1955]

Allen Ginsberg

[1926–1997]

Irwin Allen Ginsberg was born on June 3, 1926, in Newark, New Jersey. He was the second son of Naomi Levy Ginsberg, a Russian immigrant and active member of the Communist Party, and Louis Ginsberg, a published poet and high-school English teacher in Paterson, New Jersey. In a 1985 interview, Ginsberg described life in the household: "My father would go around the house either reciting Emily Dickinson and Longfellow under his breath or attacking T. S. Eliot for ruining poetry with his 'obscurantism.' My mother made up bedtime stories that all went something like: 'The good king rode forth from his castle, saw the suffering workers, and healed them.' I grew suspicious of both sides." During his childhood, his mother was hospitalized several times for mental illness, and the family lived modestly in working-class, predominantly Jewish neighborhoods in Paterson. Ginsberg excelled academically, earning the nickname "The Professor." He also wrote for the school papers and was active in dramatic productions. After his graduation from high school in 1943, he received a scholarship to Columbia University in New York City. He immediately gravitated to literature and studied with the distinguished literary critics Mark Van Doren and Lionel Trilling, who encouraged Ginsberg to write poetry. Although he wanted to study Walt Whitman, William Carlos Williams, and Ezra Pound, the curriculum focused on earlier and more traditional poets. Of his often rebellious attitude toward his education and his professors, the writer Diana Trilling once observed that Ginsberg seemed to have two motivations, "the wish to shock his teacher, and the wish to meet the teacher on equal ground."

While he was at Columbia, Ginsberg became involved with an avant-garde group of writers whom Kerouac later dubbed the "Beat generation." Through a college friend, Lucien Carr, he met William S. Burroughs, Neal Cassady, Herbert Huncke, and Jack Kerouac. Ginsberg, who fell deeply in love with the charismatic Cassady, was powerfully influenced by the radical nonconformity of the Beats, whose name suggested "deadbeats," or the beaten down, and "beatific," the mystical vision available to those

Allen Ginsberg

This photograph of Ginsberg typing *Howl* was taken in the kitchen of his San Francisco apartment during the summer of 1955.

reduced to such a position. Now determined to be a poet, Ginsberg decided to remain at Columbia for graduate study after his graduation in 1948. The following year, however, the police found stolen goods in his apartment, involving him as an unwitting accomplice to a series of robberies committed by Huncke. On the advice of his professors, Ginsberg pleaded psychological disability and was sent for evaluation to the Columbia Psychiatric Institute. One of his fellow patients was Carl Solomon, a brilliant young college student with whom Ginsberg spent hours discussing life and literature. After eight months, he left the institute and returned home to live with his father in Paterson, where Ginsberg became friendly with the poet William Carlos Williams. Ginsberg worked in New York for a market research company but left his dull job to travel in Mexico in 1953. He ultimately settled in San Francisco, where he met his lifelong companion, Peter Orlovsky. In 1955, Ginsberg read a long unpublished poem, "Howl for Carl Solomon," to a packed house at the Six Gallery. The graphic poem and his dramatic performance caused a sensation, and the following day the poet Lawrence Ferlinghetti, the cofounder of City Lights Bookstore, offered to publish the poem in his new Pocket Poets Series.

Howl and Other Poems (1956) catapulted Ginsberg into a prominence he enjoyed for the rest of his life. In a landmark censorship case, Ferlinghetti was tried for publishing obscenity, and he was successfully defended by the American Civil Liberties Union. By the time the trial ended in 1957, both Ginsberg and his book had gained international attention. He and Orlovsky traveled extensively before returning to New York. In 1958, two years after Ginsberg's mother died in a mental hospital, he wrote a celebrated elegy to her, "Kaddish for Naomi Ginsberg." He and Orlovsky then spent two years in India, where Ginsberg studied Eastern religions and meditation. After their return to the United States, he began to experiment with mind-altering drugs such as LSD. During the 1960s, he wrote constantly, publishing several volumes of poetry, including *Kaddish and Other Poems* (1961), *Reality Sandwiches* (1963), *The Yage Letters* (1963), written with William Burroughs, and *Wichita Vortex Sutra* (1967), an epic poem about the Vietnam War. Ginsberg was actively involved in protests against the war and demonstrations in support of gay rights and other causes. He also gave numerous readings, many of them joint readings with his father. In 1974, he cofounded a creative writing program, the Jack Kerouac School of Disembodied Poetics, at the Buddhist-inspired Naropa Institute (now University) in Boulder, Colorado. Ginsberg won a National Book Award for his collection *The Fall of America: Poems of These States* (1974), and he was widely regarded as an important figure in mainstream American poetry when he published his *Collected Poems* (1984). In 1986, he was appointed Distinguished Professor at Brooklyn College, where he taught creative writing and courses on poetry and poetics until shortly before his death from liver cancer on April 6, 1997.

Reading Ginsberg's *Howl*. Ginsberg began writing his most acclaimed poem in August 1955, while he was living in San Francisco. "I began typing, not with the idea of writing a formal poem, but stating my imaginative sympathies, whatever they were worth," he later explained. But he carefully revised the poem through several versions before he presented it at a group reading of five poets, including Gary Snyder, on October 7, 1955. "In all our memories no one had been so outspoken in poetry before," the poet Michael McClure later recalled:

> Ginsberg read on to the end of the poem, which left us standing in wonder, or cheering and wondering, but knowing at the deepest level that a barrier had been broken, that a human voice and body had been hurled against the harsh wall of America.

Ginsberg's galvanizing work was first published in *Howl and Other Poems* (1956), which included an introduction by his friend and mentor William Carlos Williams. In an extensive commentary on the poem in a letter to the poet Richard Eberhart, who had suggested that *Howl* was primarily "a negative howl of protest," Ginsberg in 1956 responded that it "is an 'affirmation' of individual experience of God, sex, drugs, absurdity etc. . . . To call it a work of nihilistic rebellion would be to mistake it completely. Its force comes from positive 'religious' belief and experience." He also described the wide range of influences that had shaped his poetic technique in *Howl*, from the rhythms of bop music to the imagistic verse of William Carlos Williams and the "long line" of Walt Whitman and the surrealist French poet Guillaume Apollinaire. In *Howl* (1986), which includes a facsimile of the original draft and other manuscripts of the poem, Ginsberg added extensive explanatory notes, some of which are incorporated here. The text is taken from his *Collected Poems, 1947–1997* (2006).

bedfordstmartins.com/ americanlit for research links on Ginsberg

HOWL

For Carl Solomon[1]

I

I saw the best minds of my generation destroyed by madness, starving hysterical
    naked,
dragging themselves through the negro streets at dawn looking for an angry fix,[2]
angelheaded hipsters burning for the ancient heavenly connection to the starry
    dynamo in the machinery of night,

---

1. **Dedication:** Ginsberg dedicated the poem to the editor and writer Carl Solomon (1928–1993), a fellow patient at the Columbia Psychiatric Institute in New York City in 1949.
2. **an angry fix:** Herbert Huncke cruised Harlem and Times Square areas at irregular hours, late forties, scoring junk. [Ginsberg's note] A "fix" is a dose of "junk," the street name of heroin.

who poverty and tatters and hollow-eyed and high sat up smoking in the super-
　　natural darkness of cold-water flats floating across the tops of cities
　　contemplating jazz,[3]
who bared their brains to Heaven under the El[4] and saw Mohammedan angels
　　staggering on tenement roofs illuminated,　　　　　　　　　　　　　　5
who passed through universities with radiant cool eyes hallucinating Arkansas[5]
　　and Blake-light tragedy[6] among the scholars of war,[7]
who were expelled from the academies for crazy & publishing obscene odes on the
　　windows of the skull,
who cowered in unshaven rooms in underwear, burning their money in wastebaskets
　　and listening to the Terror through the wall,
who got busted in their pubic beards returning through Laredo with a belt of
　　marijuana for New York,
who ate fire in paint hotels or drank turpentine in Paradise Alley,[8] death, or
　　purgatoried their torsos night after night　　　　　　　　　　　　　　10
with dreams, with drugs, with waking nightmares, alcohol and cock and endless
　　balls,
incomparable blind streets of shuddering cloud and lightning in the mind leaping
　　toward poles of Canada & Paterson,[9] illuminating all the motionless world
　　of Time between,
Peyote solidities of halls, backyard green tree cemetery dawns, wine drunkenness
　　over the rooftops, storefront boroughs of teahead joyride neon blinking
　　traffic light, sun and moon and tree vibrations in the roaring winter dusks
　　of Brooklyn, ashcan rantings and kind king light of mind,

---

3. **contemplating jazz:** Ref[erence]. Bill Keck, Anton Rosenberg, and other contemporaries who gathered
often at the San Remo bar, living in Lower East Side, N.Y., early 1950s – their circle was prototype for Kerouac's fictional description in *The Subterraneans*, written 1953. The jazz was late bop Charlie Parker, played
in Bowery loft jam sessions in those few years. [Ginsberg's note]
4. **El:** Part of Manhattan's subway system, the Third Avenue elevated railway, one of those familiarly called
the "El," was demolished in the mid-'50s. [Ginsberg's note]
5. **Arkansas:** "Anarchy" changes to "Arkansas," in order to substitute a more concrete thing-name for an
abstract word. [Ginsberg's note]
6. **Blake-light tragedy:** William Blake (1757-1827), an English poet and painter who frequently depicted the
apocalypse or the cataclysmic end of time.
7. **scholars of war:** During author's residence, 1944-48, Columbia scientists helped split atoms for military
power in secrecy. Subsequent military-industrial funding increasingly dominated university research, thus
two decades later rebellious student strikes had as primary grievance that the trusteeships of the university
interlocked with Vietnam War-related corporations. [Ginsberg's note]
8. **Paradise Alley:** This verse evolves into "Paradise Alley," a coldwater-flat courtyard at 501 East 11th Street,
NE corner of Avenue A, Lower East Side, New York, bricked up in the '70s and demolished after fire in 1985.
As sketched by Kerouac in *The Subterraneans*, the prototype of his heroine Mardou Fox lived there in 1953 in
friendly contact with the author, Corso and Kerouac, and typed the original ms. of Burroughs' *Yage Letters*
and *Queer*. [Ginsberg's note]
9. **Paterson:** Ginsberg grew up in Paterson, New Jersey.

who chained themselves to subways for the endless ride from Battery to holy
    Bronx[10] on benzedrine until the noise of wheels and children brought
    them down shuddering mouth-wracked and battered bleak of brain all
    drained of brilliance in the drear light of Zoo,[11]
who sank all night in submarine light of Bickford's[12] floated out and sat through
    the stale beer afternoon in desolate Fugazzi's,[13] listening to the crack of
    doom on the hydrogen jukebox,
who talked continuously seventy hours from park to pad to bar to Bellevue[14] to
    museum to the Brooklyn Bridge,
a lost battalion of platonic conversationalists jumping down the stoops off fire
    escapes off windowsills off Empire State out of the moon,
yacketayakking screaming vomiting whispering facts and memories and anec-
    dotes and eyeball kicks and shocks of hospitals and jails and wars,
whole intellects disgorged in total recall for seven days and nights with brilliant
    eyes, meat for the Synagogue cast on the pavement,
who vanished into nowhere Zen New Jersey leaving a trail of ambiguous picture
    postcards of Atlantic City Hall,
suffering Eastern sweats and Tangerian bone-grindings[15] and migraines of China
    under junk-withdrawal in Newark's bleak furnished room,
who wandered around and around at midnight in the railroad yard wondering
    where to go, and went, leaving no broken hearts,
who lit cigarettes in boxcars boxcars boxcars racketing through snow toward
    lonesome farms in grandfather night,
who studied Plotinus Poe St. John of the Cross[16] telepathy and bop kabbalah[17]
    because the cosmos instinctively vibrated at their feet in Kansas,
who loned it through the streets of Idaho seeking visionary indian angels who
    were visionary indian angels,
who thought they were only mad when Baltimore gleamed in supernatural
    ecstasy,

15

20

25

---

10. **Battery to holy Bronx:** A subway line runs from the Battery, at the southern tip of Manhattan, to the Bronx, the northernmost borough of New York City.

11. **Zoo:** The Bronx Zoo.

12. **Bickford's:** Author's casual college job was mopping floors at various Manhattan cafeterias including Bickford's 42nd Street. [Ginsberg's note]

13. **Fugazzi's:** Fugazzi's Sixth Avenue Greenwich Village bar was early 1950s alternative to the noisier San Remo nearby. "Fugazzi" phrasing was added to accommodate "jukebox"; cafeterias had no jukeboxes. [Ginsberg's note]

14. **Bellevue:** A hospital known for its psychiatric unit.

15. **Tangerian bone-grindings:** Details of W. S. Burroughs' withdrawals from heroin are found in his letters to the author, *Letters to Allen Ginsberg* 1953–1957. [Ginsberg's note]

16. **Plotinus Poe St. John of the Cross:** The Roman philosopher Plotinus (205–270), the founder of Neo-Platonism; the American writer Edgar Allan Poe (1809–1849), known for his explorations of extreme mental states; and the Spanish mystic St. John of the Cross (1542–1591), author of a famous poem about spiritual purgation, "The Dark Night of the Soul."

17. **bop kabbalah:** Bop or bebop is a type of jazz originating in the 1940s, and the kabbalah is an ancient Jewish tradition of mystical interpretation of the Old Testament.

who jumped in limousines with the Chinaman of Oklahoma on the impulse of
        winter midnight streetlight smalltown rain,

who lounged hungry and lonesome through Houston seeking jazz or sex or soup,
        and followed the brilliant Spaniard[18] to converse about America and
        Eternity, a hopeless task, and so took ship to Africa,

who disappeared into the volcanoes of Mexico leaving behind nothing but the
        shadow of dungarees and the lava and ash of poetry scattered in fireplace
        Chicago,

who reappeared on the West Coast investigating the FBI in beards and shorts
        with big pacifist eyes sexy in their dark skin passing out incomprehen-
        sible leaflets,   30

who burned cigarette holes in their arms protesting the narcotic tobacco haze of
        Capitalism,

who distributed Supercommunist pamphlets in Union Square[19] weeping and
        undressing while the sirens of Los Alamos[20] wailed them down, and wailed
        down Wall,[21] and the Staten Island ferry also wailed,

who broke down crying in white gymnasiums naked and trembling before the
        machinery of other skeletons,

who bit detectives in the neck and shrieked with delight in policecars for commit-
        ting no crime but their own wild cooking pederasty and intoxication,

who howled on their knees in the subway and were dragged off the roof waving
        genitals and manuscripts,   35

who let themselves be fucked in the ass by saintly motorcyclists,[22] and screamed
        with joy,

who blew and were blown by those human seraphim, the sailors,[23] caresses of
        Atlantic and Caribbean love,

who balled in the morning in the evenings in rosegardens and the grass of public
        parks and cemeteries scattering their semen freely to whomever come
        who may,

who hiccuped endlessly trying to giggle but wound up with a sob behind a parti-
        tion in a Turkish Bath when the blond & naked angel came to pierce them
        with a sword,

---

18. **brilliant Spaniard:** According to Ginsberg's note, he observed this powerful stranger striding down a street in Houston in September 1947.

19. **Union Square:** A park in New York City where radicals frequently gathered during the 1930s.

20. **Los Alamos:** Nuclear research laboratory in northern New Mexico.

21. **Wall:** Wall Street, the center of the financial district in New York City.

22. **saintly motorcyclists:** Ref[erence]. Marlon Brando's film *The Wild One*, 1954. [Ginsberg's note] In the film, Brando is the leader of a motorcycle gang that terrorizes a small town in the Midwest.

23. **sailors:** The poet Hart Crane picked up sailors to love on Sand Street, Brooklyn, etc. Suffering alcoholic exhaustion and rejected by the crew on his last voyage from Veracruz, Crane disappeared off the fantail of the Caribbean ship *Orizaba*. [Ginsberg's note]

who lost their loveboys to the three old shrews of fate[24] the one eyed shrew of the
　　heterosexual dollar the one eyed shrew that winks out of the womb and
　　the one eyed shrew that does nothing but sit on her ass and snip the
　　intellectual golden threads of the craftsman's loom,　　　　　　　　　40
who copulated ecstatic and insatiate with a bottle of beer a sweetheart a package
　　of cigarettes a candle and fell off the bed, and continued along the floor
　　and down the hall and ended fainting on the wall with a vision of ultimate
　　cunt and come eluding the last gyzym[25] of consciousness,
who sweetened the snatches of a million girls trembling in the sunset, and were
　　red eyed in the morning but prepared to sweeten the snatch of the sunrise,
　　flashing buttocks under barns and naked in the lake,
who went out whoring through Colorado in myriad stolen night-cars, N.C.,[26] secret
　　hero of these poems, cocksman and Adonis of Denver[27] — joy to the memory
　　of his innumerable lays of girls in empty lots & diner backyards, movie-
　　houses' rickety rows, on mountaintops in caves or with gaunt waitresses
　　in familiar roadside lonely petticoat upliftings & especially secret gas-
　　station solipsisms of johns, & hometown alleys too,
who faded out in vast sordid movies, were shifted in dreams, woke on a sudden
　　Manhattan, and picked themselves up out of basements hung-over with
　　heartless Tokay,[28] and horrors of Third Avenue iron dreams & stumbled to
　　unemployment offices,
who walked all night with their shoes full of blood on the snowbank docks waiting
　　for a door in the East River to open to a room full of steam-heat and opium,　　45
who created great suicidal dramas on the apartment cliff-banks of the Hudson
　　under the wartime blue floodlight of the moon & their heads shall be
　　crowned with laurel in oblivion,
who ate the lamb stew of the imagination or digested the crab at the muddy
　　bottom of the rivers of Bowery,
who wept at the romance of the streets with their pushcarts full of onions and bad
　　music,
who sat in boxes breathing in the darkness under the bridge, and rose up to build
　　harpsichords in their lofts,
who coughed on the sixth floor of Harlem[29] crowned with flame under the tuber-
　　cular sky surrounded by orange crates of theology,　　　　　　　　　50

---

24. **three old shrews of fate:** The three Moirae, or Fates, who in Greek mythology control the destiny of all human beings.
25. **gyzym:** Ginsberg's spelling of *jism*, slang for semen or ejaculation.
26. **N.C.:** Ref[erence]. Neal Cassady, 1926–1968, author of *The Third & Other Writings*. [Ginsberg's note]
27. **Adonis of Denver:** Neal Cassady was born and raised in Denver, Colorado. In Greek mythology, Adonis is a beautiful youth loved by the goddesses Aphrodite and Persephone.
28. **Tokay:** Sweet, aromatic wine made in Hungary.
29. **Harlem:** Russell Durgin (d. August 28, 1985), Columbia '57 theology student in whose sublet apartment, 321 East 121st Street, East Harlem, 198, author read William Blake, left Manhattan that summer for medical treatment, tubercular lungs. Treatment may have involved filling chest space with celluloid balls to prevent collapse. [Ginsberg's note]

who scribbled all night rocking and rolling over lofty incantations which in the
    yellow morning were stanzas of gibberish,

who cooked rotten animals lung heart feet tail borsht & tortillas dreaming of the
    pure vegetable kingdom,

who plunged themselves under meat trucks looking for an egg,

who threw their watches off the roof to cast their ballot for Eternity outside of
    Time, & alarm clocks fell on their heads every day for the next decade,

who cut their wrists three times successively unsuccessfully, gave up and were
    forced to open antique stores where they thought they were growing old
    and cried,   55

who were burned alive in their innocent flannel suits on Madison Avenue[30] amid
    blasts of leaden verse & the tanked-up clatter of the iron regiments of
    fashion & the nitroglycerine shrieks of the fairies of advertising & the
    mustard gas of sinister intelligent editors, or were run down by the
    drunken taxicabs of Absolute Reality,

who jumped off the Brooklyn Bridge this actually happened and walked away
    unknown and forgotten into the ghostly daze of Chinatown soup alleyways
    & firetrucks, not even one free beer,

who sang out of their windows in despair, fell out of the subway window, jumped
    in the filthy Passaic,[31] leaped on negroes, cried all over the street, danced
    on broken wineglasses barefoot smashed phonograph records of nostalgic
    European 1930s German jazz finished the whiskey and threw up groaning
    into the bloody toilet, moans in their ears and the blast of colossal
    steamwhistles,

who barreled down the highways of the past journeying to each other's hotrod-
    Golgotha[32] jail-solitude watch or Birmingham jazz incarnation,

who drove crosscountry seventytwo hours to find out if I had a vision or you had a
    vision or he had a vision to find out Eternity,   60

who journeyed to Denver, who died in Denver, who came back to Denver & waited
    in vain, who watched over Denver & brooded and loned in Denver and
    finally went away to find out the Time, & now Denver is lonesome for her
    heroes,

who fell on their knees in hopeless cathedrals praying for each other's salvation
    and light and breasts, until the soul illuminated its hair for a second,

who crashed through their minds in jail waiting for impossible criminals with
    golden heads and the charm of reality in their hearts who sang sweet blues
    to Alcatraz,

---

30. **Madison Avenue:** An avenue in New York City that became synonymous with the advertising industry.
31. **filthy Passaic:** In W. Carlos Williams's "The Wanderer: A Baroque Fantasy," 1915, the youthful poet plunges his hands in her waters requesting sacrament of Goddess of Passaic River for his Muse: "and the filthy Passaic consented." [Ginsberg's note] Paterson, New Jersey, is on the Passaic River.
32. **Golgotha:** "The place of skulls," also known as Calvary, the site of the crucifixion of Jesus Christ.

who retired to Mexico to cultivate a habit, or Rocky Mount to tender Buddha or
    Tangiers to boys or Southern Pacific to the black locomotive or Harvard to
    Narcissus to Woodlawn to the daisychain or grave,

who demanded sanity trials accusing the radio of hypnotism & were left with their
    insanity & their hands & a hung jury,   65

who threw potato salad at CCNY lecturers on Dadaism[33] and subsequently
    presented themselves on the granite steps of the madhouse with shaven
    heads and harlequin speech of suicide, demanding instantaneous
    lobotomy,

and who were given instead the concrete void of insulin Metrazol electricity
    hydrotherapy psychotherapy occupational therapy pingpong & amnesia,

who in humorless protest overturned only one symbolic pingpong table, resting
    briefly in catatonia,

returning years later truly bald except for a wig of blood, and tears and fingers, to
    the visible madman doom of the wards of the madtowns of the East,

Pilgrim State's Rockland's and Greystone's foetid halls,[34] bickering with the
    echoes of the soul, rocking and rolling in the midnight solitude-bench
    dolmen-realms of love, dream of life a nightmare, bodies turned to stone
    as heavy as the moon,   70

with mother finally ******, and the last fantastic book flung out of the tenement
    window, and the last door closed at 4. a.m. and the last telephone slammed
    at the wall in reply and the last furnished room emptied down to the last
    piece of mental furniture, a yellow paper rose twisted on a wire hanger in
    the closet, and even that imaginary, nothing but a hopeful little bit of
    hallucination—

ah, Carl, while you are not safe I am not safe, and now you're really in the total
    animal soup of time—

and who therefore ran through the icy streets obsessed with a sudden flash of
    the alchemy of the use of the ellipse the catalog the meter & the vibrating
    plane,

who dreamt and made incarnate gaps in Time & Space through images juxta-
    posed, and trapped the archangel of the soul between 2 visual images and

---

33. **CCNY lectures on Dadaism:** Dada was an artistic movement that emphasized absurdity and unpredictability. CCNY is the acronym of City College of New York.

34. **Pilgrim State's Rockland's and Greystone's foetid halls:** Ref[erence]. somewhat to Carl Solomon and those we left behind at Psychiatric Institute, 1949. Dolmens mark a vanished civilization, as Stonehenge or Greystone and Rockland monoliths. At time of writing, author's mother dwelled in her last months at Pilgrim State Hospital, Brentwood, N.Y., housing over 25,000, the largest such mental hospital in the world. Description of the wards and halls is drawn from Greystone State Hospital, near Morristown, N.J., which author frequented in adolescence to visit Naomi Ginsberg. New York's Rockland State Hospital's name was substituted for rhythmic euphony. Poem was occasioned by unexpected news of Carl Solomon's recent removal to Pilgrim State. [Ginsberg's note] Naomi Ginsberg, the poet's mother, died at Greystone in 1956.

joined the elemental verbs and set the noun and dash of consciousness
together jumping with sensation of Pater Omnipotens Aeterna Deus[35]
to recreate the syntax and measure of poor human prose and stand before you
speechless and intelligent and shaking with shame, rejected yet
confessing out the soul to conform to the rhythm of thought in his naked
and endless head,   75
the madman bum and angel beat in Time, unknown, yet putting down here what
might be left to say in time come after death,
and rose reincarnate in the ghostly clothes of jazz in the goldhorn shadow of the
band and blew the suffering of America's naked mind for love into an eli
eli lamma lamma sabacthani[36] saxophone cry that shivered the cities
down to the last radio
with the absolute heart of the poem of life butchered out of their own bodies good
to eat a thousand years.

II

What sphinx of cement and aluminum bashed open their skulls and ate up their
brains and imagination?
Moloch![37] Solitude! Filth! Ugliness! Ashcans and unobtainable dollars! Children
screaming under the stairways! Boys sobbing in armies! Old men weeping
in the parks!   80
Moloch! Moloch! Nightmare of Moloch! Moloch the loveless! Mental Moloch!
Moloch the heavy judger of men!
Moloch the incomprehensible prison! Moloch the crossbone soulless jailhouse
and Congress of sorrows! Moloch whose buildings are judgment! Moloch
the vast stone of war! Moloch the stunned governments!
Moloch whose mind is pure machinery! Moloch whose blood is running money!
Moloch whose fingers are ten armies! Moloch whose breast is a cannibal
dynamo! Moloch whose ear is a smoking tomb!
Moloch whose eyes are a thousand blind windows! Moloch whose skyscrapers
stand in the long streets like endless Jehovahs! Moloch whose factories
dream and croak in the fog! Moloch whose smokestacks and antennae
crown the cities!

---

35. **Pater Omnipotens Aeterna Deus:** Correct Latin line should read: "Pater Omnipotens Aeterne Deus."
[Ginsberg's note] In a lengthy continuation of this note, Ginsberg explains that the Latin phrase, which may
be translated "all powerful Father, Eternal God," is used in a letter by the French painter Paul Cézanne to
Emile Bernard, April 15, 1904.
36. **eli eli lamma lamma sabacthani:** My God, my God, why hast thou forsaken me? (Aramaic) were Christ's
last words on the cross.
37. **Moloch:** Moloch, or Molech, the Canaanite fire god, whose worship was marked by parents' burning their
children as propitiatory sacrifice. "And thou shalt not let any of thy seed pass through the fire to Molech"
(Leviticus 18:21). [Ginsberg's note]

Moloch whose love is endless oil and stone! Moloch whose soul is electricity and
    banks! Moloch whose poverty is the specter of genius! Moloch whose fate
    is a cloud of sexless hydrogen! Moloch whose name is the Mind!   85

Moloch in whom I sit lonely! Moloch in whom I dream Angels! Crazy in Moloch!
    Cocksucker in Moloch! Lacklove and manless in Moloch!

Moloch who entered my soul early! Moloch in whom I am a consciousness without
    a body! Moloch who frightened me out of my natural ecstasy! Moloch
    whom I abandon! Wake up in Moloch! Light streaming out of the sky!

Moloch! Moloch! Robot apartments! invisible suburbs! skeleton treasuries! blind
    capitals! demonic industries! spectral nations! invincible madhouses!
    granite cocks! monstrous bombs!

They broke their backs lifting Moloch to Heaven! Pavements, trees, radios, tons!
    lifting the city to Heaven which exists and is everywhere about us!

Visions! omens! hallucinations! miracles! ecstasies! gone down the American
    river!   90

Dreams! adorations! illuminations! religions! the whole boatload of sensitive
    bullshit!

Breakthroughs! over the river! flips and crucifixions! gone down the flood! Highs!
    Epiphanies! Despairs! Ten years' animal screams and suicides! Minds!
    New loves! Mad generation! down on the rocks of Time!

Real holy laughter in the river! They saw it all! the wild eyes! the holy yells! They
    bade farewell! They jumped off the roof! to solitude! waving! carrying
    flowers! Down to the river! into the street!

III

Carl Solomon! I'm with you in Rockland[38]
    where you're madder than I am   95
I'm with you in Rockland
    where you must feel very strange
I'm with you in Rockland
    where you imitate the shade of my mother
I'm with you in Rockland   100
    where you've murdered your twelve secretaries
I'm with you in Rockland
    where you laugh at this invisible humor
I'm with you in Rockland
    where we are great writers on the same dreadful typewriter   105
I'm with you in Rockland
    where your condition has become serious and is reported on the radio

---

38. **Rockland:** The Rockland Psychiatric Center on Long Island, the largest psychiatric hospital in New
York State. Ginsberg had actually met Solomon at the Columbia Psychiatric Institute in New York City. See
note 34.

I'm with you in Rockland
    where the faculties of the skull no longer admit the worms of the senses
I'm with you in Rockland   110
    where you drink the tea of the breasts of the spinsters of Utica[39]
I'm with you in Rockland
    where you pun on the bodies of your nurses the harpies of the Bronx
I'm with you in Rockland
    where you scream in a straightjacket that you're losing the game of the
    actual pingpong of the abyss   115
I'm with you in Rockland
    where you bang on the catatonic piano the soul is innocent and immortal
    it should never die ungodly in an armed madhouse
I'm with you in Rockland
    where fifty more shocks will never return your soul to its body again
    from its pilgrimage to a cross in the void
I'm with you in Rockland   120
    where you accuse your doctors of insanity and plot the Hebrew socialist
    revolution against the fascist national Golgotha[40]
I'm with you in Rockland
    where you will split the heavens of Long Island and resurrect your living
    human Jesus from the superhuman tomb
I'm with you in Rockland
    where there are twentyfive thousand mad comrades all together singing
    the final stanzas of the Internationale   125
I'm with you in Rockland
    where we hug and kiss the United States under our bedsheets the United
    States that coughs all night and won't let us sleep
I'm with you in Rockland
    where we wake up electrified out of the coma by our own souls' airplanes
    roaring over the roof they've come to drop angelic bombs the hospital
    illuminates itself   imaginary walls collapse   O skinny legions
    run outside   O starry-spangled shock of mercy the eternal war is
    here   O victory forget your underwear we're free
I'm with you in Rockland   130
    in my dreams you walk dripping from a sea-journey on the highway
    across America in tears to the door of my cottage in the Western night

San Francisco, 1955–1956

[1956, 2006]

---

39. **the spinsters of Utica:** *Spinster* is an outdated term for an older woman who has never been married; Utica is a small city in central New York State.
40. **Golgotha:** See note 32.

John Ashbery

[b. 1927]

John Lawrence Ashbery was born in Rochester, New York, on July 28, 1927. He was the eldest of the two sons of Helen Lawrence Ashbery, a former high-school biology teacher, and Chester Ashbery, who raised fruit on a farm outside Sodus, a small village thirty miles from Rochester. For the first seven years of his life, Ashbery lived in the city with his maternal grandparents, and he was strongly influenced by his grandfather Henry Lawrence, a physics professor at the University of Rochester. Lawrence, whom Ashbery has described as "a cultivated Victorian gentleman" who could read Greek and owned a substantial library, gave his gifted grandson books and encouraged his artistic and intellectual interests. When Ashbery was eleven, he began to take weekly painting classes at the art museum in Rochester. He attended local schools until he was sixteen, when a wealthy neighbor paid for him to go to Deerfield Academy in western Massachusetts. While he was there, two of his poems were published when a friend sent them under a pseudonym to the prestigious magazine *Poetry*. After his graduation in 1945, Ashbery went to Harvard University, where he majored in English and joined the editorial board of the *Harvard Advocate*. He then continued his education at Columbia University, where he earned a master's degree in literature in 1951.

John Ashbery

This photograph of Ashbery reading at the Village Theatre in New York City was taken in 1967.

Ashbery became deeply involved in the arts scene, first in New York City, and later in Paris. Although he initially planned to look for a teaching position, he determined to find ways of supporting himself that would leave more time for other pursuits and took a job as a typist with Oxford University Press. He spent his spare time writing, studying modern poetry, and immersing himself in avant-garde music and art. He was also active in experimental theater, and his play *The Heroes* was produced by the Artists' Theatre in 1952. A few of his poems appeared along with drawings by his friend the painter Jane Freilicher in a small chapbook, *Turandot and Other Poems* (1953). It was published by the Tibor de Nagy Gallery, founded in 1950 to promote pioneering American artists such as the abstract expressionists, which also published the early poetry of two of Ashbery's friends from Harvard, Kenneth Koch and Frank O'Hara. With them and other young urban poets, Ashbery was part of a loosely defined poetic movement that came to be known as the New York School. In 1955, he won the coveted Yale Younger Poets prize, resulting in the publication of his collection *Some Trees* (1956). By then, Ashbery had been awarded a Fulbright Scholarship and had moved to Paris. After the scholarship expired, he supported himself by translating French pulp novels for the American market and by writing art criticism and reviews for the European edition of the *New York Herald Tribune*, as well as for the magazines *Art News* and *Art International*. During most of the decade he spent in France, he lived with the writer Pierre Martory, some of whose poems Ashbery subsequently translated into English. Ashbery's own "violently experimental" poems, as he has since described them, were published in his controversial collection *The Tennis Court Oath* (1962).

Ashbery's reputation grew steadily after he returned to New York City in 1965. He became executive editor of *Art News*, a position he held until 1972. In contrast to the hostile reception of *The Tennis Court Oath*, a book even some of his admirers found perplexing, he received generally favorable reviews for his collections *Rivers and Mountains* (1966), *The Double-Dream of Spring* (1972), and *Three Poems* (1973). In recognition of his growing prominence, in 1974 Ashbery was appointed professor of English and codirector of the creative-writing program at Brooklyn College. His major triumph came with the publication of *Self-Portrait in a Convex Mirror* (1975), which the reviewer in the *New York Times* described as a "collection of poems of breathtaking freshness and adventure in which dazzling orchestrations of language open up whole areas of consciousness no other American poet has even begun to explore." The volume won the National Book Award, the National Book Critics Circle Award, and the Pulitzer Prize for Poetry. Ashbery has subsequently published a collection of poetry roughly every two years and has received virtually every award and honor bestowed on poets in both Europe and the United States. Since 1990, he has been a professor of languages and literature at Bard College. With his partner of over thirty years, David Kermani, Ashbery divides his time between Manhattan and a house in Hudson, New York. Widely regarded as the most important and influential poet writing in English, he published his twenty-fourth collection of poetry, *A Worldly Country*, in 2007. The following year the Library of America inaugurated the publication of a collected edition of Ashbery's work with the volume *Collected Poems 1956–1987*.

bedfordstmartins.com/ americanlit for research links on Ashbery

Reading Ashbery's Poetry.

Throughout his long career, Ashbery has extended the formal and linguistic experiments undertaken by the modernist poets and writers who inspired him, including Wallace Stevens, Gertrude Stein, and Marianne Moore. Ashbery also found stimulation for his poetry in avant-garde music, film, drama, and art. As early as 1950, when he saw an exhibit of the dynamic work of the French expressionist painter Chaim Soutine, Ashbery says that he was suddenly struck by new possibilities for his own work: "The fact that the sky could come crashing joyously into the grass, that trees could dance upside down and houses roll over like cats eager to have their tummies scratched was something I hadn't realized before, and I began pushing my poems around and standing words on end." Such linguistic and grammatical play is one of the most striking features of his poems, which some readers find abstract and elusive. Preoccupied with questions about the origins of imagination, the relation between representation and reality, and the limits of language, Ashbery often calls attention to the artistic process or the act of composing the poem. His poems have been described as "occasional," since many of them are so finely attuned to a specific moment in time. As he wrote in

1977, "Poetry includes anything and everything." The poems selected here demonstrate some of Ashbery's central themes and techniques. "The One Thing That Can Save America" is taken from *Self-Portrait in a Convex Mirror* (1975); "My Erotic Double" is from *As We Know* (1979); and "Paradoxes and Oxymorons" is from *Shadow Train* (1981).

THE ONE THING THAT CAN SAVE AMERICA

Is anything central?
Orchards flung out on the land,
Urban forests, rustic plantations, knee-high hills?
Are place names central?
Elm Grove, Adcock Corner, Story Book Farm?   5
As they concur with a rush at eye level
Beating themselves into eyes which have had enough
Thank you, no more thank you.
And they come on like scenery mingled with darkness
The damp plains, overgrown suburbs,   10
Places of known civic pride, of civil obscurity.

These are connected to my version of America
But the juice is elsewhere.
This morning as I walked out of your room
After breakfast crosshatched with   15
Backward and forward glances, backward into light,
Forward into unfamiliar light,
Was it our doing, and was it
The material, the lumber of life, or of lives
We were measuring, counting?   20
A mood soon to be forgotten
In crossed girders of light, cool downtown shadow
In this morning that has seized us again?

I know that I braid too much my own
Snapped-off perceptions of things as they come to me.   25
They are private and always will be.
Where then are the private turns of event
Destined to boom later like golden chimes
Released over a city from a highest tower?
The quirky things that happen to me, and I tell you,   30
And you instantly know what I mean?
What remote orchard reached by winding roads
Hides them? Where are these roots?

It is the lumps and trials
That tell us whether we shall be known   35
And whether our fate can be exemplary, like a star.
All the rest is waiting
For a letter that never arrives,
Day after day, the exasperation
Until finally you have ripped it open not knowing what it is,   40
The two envelope halves lying on a plate.
The message was wise, and seemingly
Dictated a long time ago.
Its truth is timeless, but its time has still
Not arrived, telling of danger, and the mostly limited   45
Steps that can be taken against danger
Now and in the future, in cool yards,
In quiet small houses in the country,
Our country, in fenced areas, in cool shady streets.

[1974, 1975]

MY EROTIC DOUBLE

He says he doesn't feel like working today.
It's just as well. Here in the shade
Behind the house, protected from street noises,
One can go over all kinds of old feeling,
Throw some away, keep others.   5
                              The wordplay
Between us gets very intense when there are
Fewer feelings around to confuse things.
Another go-round? No, but the last things
You always find to say are charming, and rescue me   10
Before the night does. We are afloat
On our dreams as on a barge made of ice,
Shot through with questions and fissures of starlight
That keep us awake, thinking about the dreams
As they are happening. Some occurrence. You said it.   15

I said it but I can hide it. But I choose not to.
Thank you. You are a very pleasant person.
Thank you. You are too.

[1979]

PARADOXES AND OXYMORONS

This poem is concerned with language on a very plain level.
Look at it talking to you. You look out a window
Or pretend to fidget. You have it but you don't have it.
You miss it, it misses you. You miss each other.

The poem is sad because it wants to be yours, and cannot.   5
What's a plain level? It is that and other things,
Bringing a system of them into play. Play?
Well, actually, yes, but I consider play to be

A deeper outside thing, a dreamed role-pattern,
As in the division of grace these long August days   10
Without proof. Open-ended. And before you know
It gets lost in the steam and chatter of typewriters.

It has been played once more. I think you exist only
To tease me into doing it, on your level, and then you aren't there
Or have adopted a different attitude. And the poem   15
Has set me softly down beside you. The poem is you.

[1980, 1981]

Adrienne Rich

[1929-2012]

Adrienne Cecile Rich was born on May 16, 1929, in Baltimore, Maryland, to Helen Jones Rich, a pianist and composer who gave up her career to raise her family, and Arnold Rich, a doctor and professor of pathology at the Johns Hopkins University. As Rich explained in an autobiographical essay, "When We Dead Awaken: Writing as Re-Vision" (1972), "My own luck was being born white and middle-class into a house full of books, with a father who encouraged me to read and write." While her mother gave her music lessons, Rich began to write poetry at an early age and read widely among the books in her father's library, memorizing poems written in English and French. As a student at Radcliffe College in Cambridge, Massachusetts, Rich took a course with the distinguished Harvard professor F. O. Matthiessen, who lectured on the British Romantic poets, the modern Irish poet William Butler Yeats, and the contemporary American poet Wallace Stevens. "That class affected my life as a poet more than anything else that happened to me in college," Rich later recalled. Under the influence of Stevens and especially Yeats, then her idea of "the Great Poet," Rich wrote

Adrienne Rich

This photograph was taken in the 1970s, about the time Rich published her groundbreaking collection *Diving into the Wreck* (1973).

the poems in her first collection, *A Change of World*, which won the coveted Yale Younger Poets prize and was subsequently published in 1951, the year she graduated from Radcliffe. Awarded a Guggenheim Fellowship, Rich spent a year traveling in Europe. After her return to the United States in 1953, she married Alfred Conrad, a professor of economics at Harvard.

Rich was radicalized by her struggle to balance her personal and professional needs with the demands of her traditional marriage. The first of her three sons was born the year she published her second collection of poetry, *The Diamond Cutters* (1955). Rich, however, was increasingly dissatisfied with her work and frustrated by the lack of time for writing, later observing that she felt "like a failed woman and a failed poet." In the late 1950s, she began writing poems in a looser style about her experiences as a woman, a wife, and a mother. Her next book, *Snapshots of a Daughter-in-Law* (1963), represented a major turning point for Rich. Although some reviewers were troubled by what one described as the "bitterness" of the poems, as well as by Rich's overtly feminist themes, she was awarded *Poetry* magazine's Bess Hokin Prize. In 1966, the year she published her fourth book, *Necessities of Life*, she and her family moved to New York City, where Rich actively participated in protests against the Vietnam War. She also began teaching, first at Swarthmore College and Columbia University, and then in remedial programs at the City College of New York. Her experiences working with students who lacked the language skills necessary for college, most of them African Americans and immigrants from poor homes, heightened Rich's sense of racial and economic injustice. Her involvement in the social and political turmoil of the 1960s was reflected in the title and poems of her next collection, *Leaflets* (1969), published the year before her husband died in 1970.

Through her writings, speeches, and political activism, Rich played a leading role in the radical feminist movement and other causes, including gay rights and international human rights. The poems in *The Will to Change* (1971) and *Diving into the Wreck* (1973) reflected her vigorous challenge to patriarchal culture and society, which she criticized in her groundbreaking study *Of Woman Born: Motherhood as Experience and Institution* (1976). That year, Rich also published a lesbian love sequence, *Twenty-one Love Poems* (1976), and began her lasting partnership with the Jamaican American writer Michelle Cliff. Rich continued to explore issues of sexuality and the construction of gender in her next collections of poems, *A Wild Patience Has Taken Me This Far* (1981) and *The Fact of a Doorframe* (1984). In 1984, she and Cliff moved permanently to Santa Cruz, California, and Rich was a professor of English at nearby Stanford University from 1986 to 1993. She explored her personal past and her complex relationship to her Jewish heritage in the first two volumes of poetry she wrote during that period, *Your Native Land, Your Life* (1986) and *Time's Power* (1989). She later charted the troubled social and political landscape of contemporary America in the poems in *An Atlas of the Difficult World* (1991) and *Dark Fields of the Republic* (1995). The recipient of numerous awards and honors,

Because Rich took a woman's worldview to be emblematic, her inquiries did not stop — as they had not started — at questions of gender. It was with the rage and insights of her feminism that she envisioned . . . Vietnam, World War II, Emily Dickinson, South Africa, Manifest Destiny, the aftermath of the Shoah, and the American Civil Rights Movement.

—Marilyn Hacker

Rich famously declined the National Medal for the Arts in 1997 as a protest against the Clinton administration's move to end federal funding for the National Endowment for the Arts. "The radical disparities of wealth and power in America are widening at a devastating rate," she explained in a letter to the chair of the endowment. "A President cannot meaningfully honor certain token artists while the people at large are so dishonored." Rich subsequently published several more volumes of poetry, and in 2003 she was awarded the prestigious Bollingen Prize in American Poetry for her lifetime achievement and in recognition of her collection *Fox* (2001). The judges cited "her honesty at once ferocious and humane, her deep learning, and her continuous poetic exploration and awareness of multiple selves." After Rich died from complications of rheumatoid arthritis on March 27, 2012, the *New York Times* printed a lengthy, front-page obituary under the headline "A Poet of Unswerving Vision at the Forefront of Feminism."

Reading Rich's Poetry.   In 1951, Rich's career was launched by the publication of *A Change of World*, a collection of poems marked by her formal style, her use of traditional poetic forms and what she described as her "objective, observant tone." She later began to write in free verse and in a more confessional mode, and her growing political and social activism led Rich to assume a public voice during the 1960s. In a review of her fourth book, *Necessities of Life* (1966), Robert Lowell observed: "From the beginning, there was a yearning, a straining onward, a sense of disproportion between the life of looking and the life of living, tremors of discontent running through a style perhaps too beautiful and contented." As Lowell rightly recognized, Rich was moving on, and her poetry became even more experimental in form and wide-ranging in subject matter, combining sophisticated aesthetics with a radical social critique. The poems presented here, which were first collected in *The Will to Change* (1971) and *Diving into the Wreck* (1973), reveal some of the abiding concerns of her mature work: the complications of love, the myths of patriarchy, and the role of women in society. Looking back over her long and distinguished career, Rich wrote in 2001: "For more than fifty years I have been writing, tearing up, revising poems, studying poets from every culture and century available to me. I have been a poet of the oppositional imagination, meaning that I don't think my only argument is with myself. My work is for people who want to imagine and claim wider horizons and carry on about them into the night, rather than rehearse the landlocked details of personal quandaries or the price for which the house next door just sold." The texts are taken from *The Fact of a Doorframe: Poems Selected and New, 1950–1984* (1984).

bedfordstmartins.com/
americanlit for research
links on Rich

A VALEDICTION FORBIDDING MOURNING[1]

My swirling wants. Your frozen lips.
The grammar turned and attacked me.
Themes, written under duress.
Emptiness of the notations.

They gave me a drug that slowed the healing of wounds.   5

I want you to see this before I leave:
the experience of repetition as death
the failure of criticism to locate the pain
the poster in the bus that said:
my bleeding is under control.   10

A red plant in a cemetery of plastic wreaths.

A last attempt: the language is a dialect called metaphor.
These images go unglossed: hair, glacier, flashlight.
When I think of a landscape I am thinking of a time.
When I talk of taking a trip I mean forever.   15
I could say: those mountains have a meaning
but further than that I could not say.

To do something very common, in my own way.

[1970, 1984]

1. **A Valediction Forbidding Mourning:** The English poet John Donne (1572–1631) wrote "A Valediction: Forbidding Mourning," a poem addressed to his wife that may have been occasioned by his trip to the Continent in 1611. A "valediction" is a poem or formal statement of farewell, as in a valedictory address.

TRYING TO TALK WITH A MAN

Out in this desert we are testing bombs,
that's why we came here.

Sometimes I feel an underground river
forcing its way between deformed cliffs
an acute angle of understanding   5
moving itself like a locus of the sun
into this condemned scenery.

What we've had to give up to get here —
whole LP collections,[1] films we starred in

1. **LP collections:** LPs are long-playing phonograph records.

playing in the neighborhoods, bakery windows   10
full of dry, chocolate-filled Jewish cookies,
the language of love-letters, of suicide notes,
afternoons on the riverbank
pretending to be children

Coming out to this desert   15
we meant to change the face of
driving among dull green succulents
walking at noon in the ghost town
surrounded by a silence

that sounds like the silence of the place   20
except that it came with us
and is familiar
and everything we were saying until now
was an effort to blot it out—
coming out here we are up against it   25

Out here I feel more helpless
with you than without you

You mention the danger
and list the equipment
we talk of people caring for each other   30
in emergencies—laceration, thirst—
but you look at me like an emergency

Your dry heat feels like power
your eyes are stars of a different magnitude
they reflect lights that spell out: EXIT   35
when you get up and pace the floor

talking of the danger
as if it were not ourselves
as if we were testing anything else.

                                        [1971, 1984]

DIVING INTO THE WRECK

First having read the book of myths,
and loaded the camera,
and checked the edge of the knife-blade,
I put on
the body-armor of black rubber   5
the absurd flippers
the grave and awkward mask.

I am having to do this
not like Cousteau with his
assiduous team
aboard the sun-flooded schooner[1]   10
but here alone.

There is a ladder.
The ladder is always there
hanging innocently   15
close to the side of the schooner.
We know what it is for,
we who have used it.
Otherwise
it's a piece of maritime floss   20
some sundry equipment.

I go down.
Rung after rung and still
the oxygen immerses me
the blue light   25
the clear atoms
of our human air.
I go down.
My flippers cripple me,
I crawl like an insect down the ladder   30
and there is no one
to tell me when the ocean
will begin.

First the air is blue and then
it is bluer and then green and then   35
black I am blacking out and yet
my mask is powerful
it pumps my blood with power
the sea is another story
the sea is not a question of power   40
I have to learn alone
to turn my body without force
in the deep element.

And now: it is easy to forget
what I came for   45

---

1. **Cousteau . . . sun-flooded schooner:** Jacques-Yves Cousteau (1910–1997), the coinventor of scuba-diving gear, was a French explorer and oceanographer who became famous worldwide for his voyages aboard the *Calypso*, the basis of several documentary films and his popular television show *The Undersea World of Jacques Cousteau*, which first aired in 1966.

among so many who have always
lived here
swaying their crenellated fans[2]
between the reefs
and besides   50
you breathe differently down here.

I came to explore the wreck.
The words are purposes.
The words are maps.
I came to see the damage that was done   55
and the treasures that prevail.
I stroke the beam of my lamp
slowly along the flank
of something more permanent
than fish or weed   60

the thing I came for:
the wreck and not the story of the wreck
the thing itself and not the myth
the drowned face always staring
toward the sun[3]   65
the evidence of damage
worn by salt and sway into this threadbare beauty
the ribs of the disaster
curving their assertion
among the tentative haunters.   70

This is the place.
And I am here, the mermaid whose dark hair
streams black, the merman in his armored body
We circle silently
about the wreck   75
we dive into the hold.
I am she: I am he

whose drowned face sleeps with open eyes
whose breasts still bear the stress
whose silver, copper, vermeil cargo lies   80
obscurely inside barrels
half-wedged and left to rot

---

2. **crenellated fans:** That is, the notched or indented tail fins of the fish.
3. **the drowned face . . . toward the sun:** Almost all old sailing ships had ornamental figureheads, usually the bust or full-length figure of a woman, attached to the prow. This figure, who once looked down into the waves, now stares upward through the water to the sun.

we are the half-destroyed instruments
that once held to a course
the water-eaten log   85
the fouled compass

We are, I am, you are
by cowardice or courage
the one who find our way
back to this scene   90
carrying a knife, a camera
a book of myths
in which
our names do not appear.

[1972, 1984]

Ursula K. Le Guin

[b. 1929]

Ursula K. Le Guin was born on October 21, 1929, in Berkeley, California. She was the fourth child and only daughter of Alfred Kroeber, a distinguished anthropologist specializing in Native American cultures at the University of California, Berkeley, and Theodora Kroeber, an author best known for her biography of the last survivor of the Yahi Indians of northern California, *Ishi in Two Worlds* (1961). Le Guin was brought up in an atmosphere of books, ideas, and lively conversation in her close-knit family, which lived in Berkeley during the academic year and spent the summers at Kishamish, their country house in the Napa Valley of northern California. When she was a child, her father told her Native American legends and stories, and Le Guin became deeply interested in mythology. She was also an avid reader of pulp magazines such as *Astounding Science Fiction*, to which she submitted a story when she was eleven. But it was rejected, and she soon lost interest in science fiction. She majored in French at Radcliffe College, from which she graduated Phi Beta Kappa in 1951, and earned an MA in Romance languages from Columbia University in 1952. She decided to continue her studies toward a doctorate and was awarded a Fulbright Scholarship for study in

Ursula K. Le Guin

The portrait photographer Marian Wood Kolisch took this photograph in 1990, by which time Le Guin had gained wide acclaim for her innovative works of fantasy and science fiction.

France. While sailing there aboard the *Queen Mary*, she met the historian Charles Le Guin, and they were married in Paris in 1953.

As Le Guin has said, her marriage put an end to her graduate study and marked the beginning of her two-decade effort to establish herself as a writer. Her husband taught at several colleges before he accepted a position at Portland State University in Portland, Oregon, where the couple settled with their three children in 1959. Le Guin, who left work to raise their children, wrote poetry and fiction, some of it set in an imaginary central European country, Orsinia. She finally managed to publish one of her Orsinian stories in the *Western Humanities Review* in 1961. But when all five of her early, unorthodox novels were rejected, the frustrated Le Guin turned to writing in a more familiar and marketable genre, science fiction. She subsequently became a regular contributor to the popular magazines *Fantastic* and *Amazing*. Encouraged by the reception of her science-fiction stories, Le Guin began working on the earliest of a series of novels set in the "Hainish Universe," *Rocannon's World* (1966), *Planet of Exile* (1966), and *City of Illusions* (1967). In those novels, which were shaped by the social and political concerns of the 1960s, Le Guin explored some of the central subjects and themes of her fiction: the irrationality of war, problems in human communication, the search for identity, and the impact of a journey to an unknown place and encounters with strange or alien creatures. Le Guin gained her first major critical and commercial success with a fantasy trilogy for young adults about an imagined world called Earthsea: *A Wizard of Earthsea* (1968), *The Tombs of Atuan* (1971), and *The Farthest Shore* (1972). She continued her Hainish series in two other acclaimed novels of the period: *The Left Hand of Darkness* (1969), regarded by many as the first feminist work of science fiction; and her complex utopian novel *The Dispossessed* (1974). Extending the audience for such genres, Le Guin also published stories in magazines as diverse as the *New Yorker*, *Playboy*, and *Redbook*.

Although she is best known for her works of fantasy and science fiction, the prolific Le Guin has produced a wide range of work. In addition to more than twenty novels and over one-hundred short stories, she has published collections of poetry and essays, as well as translations of the ancient Chinese religious text the *Tao Te Ching* and the poems of Gabriel Mistral, the Chilean poet who won the Nobel Prize in Literature in 1945. Le Guin won the Kafka Prize for fiction by an American woman for her ambitious novel *Always Coming Home* (1985), a work of ethnographic fiction in which she interweaves the myths, poems, and stories of the Kesh, a people akin to Native Americans who live far in the future in California. The novel was the runner-up for the National Book Award, an unprecedented achievement for a work of science fiction. Le Guin has also written a series of works for children, the popular Catwings Books (1988-99), and realistic fiction for adults, including *Searoad* (1992), a collection of related stories set in a small town in Oregon. At the same time, she continued the Earthsea cycle in *Tehanu* (1990), *Tales from Earthsea* (2001), and *The Other Wind* (2001) and wrote another novel in the Hainish series, *The Telling* (2000). Le Guin published a second fantasy cycle for young adults, *Annals of the*

Le Guin is a magisterial imaginer, whose invented realities outrun any rigidly allegorical interpretation.

–John Updike

Western Shore, including *Gifts* (2004), *Voices* (2006), and *Powers* (2007). A staunch defender of fantasy, which many critics tend to dismiss as a sub-literary genre, Le Guin in 2006 wrote: "To conflate fantasy with immaturity is a rather sizeable error. Rational yet non-intellectual, moral yet inexplicit, symbolic not allegorical, fantasy is not primitive but primary. Many of its great texts are poetry, and its prose often approaches poetry in density of implication and imagery." In 2008, Le Guin published *Lavinia*, a fantasy novel loosely based on the final chapters of Virgil's ancient Roman epic, the *Aeneid*. She continues to live and work in Portland, Oregon.

Reading Le Guin's "She Unnames Them." Like much of Le Guin's work, this story illustrates the erosion in postmodern literature of former distinctions between "literary" fiction and popular genres such as fantasy and science fiction. First published in January 1985 in one of the most prominent venues for contemporary fiction, the *New Yorker*, "She Unnames Them" is the final piece in Le Guin's collection of prose and poetry about animals, *Buffalo Gals*. Le Guin introduced the story by explaining that it "had to come last in this book because it states (equivocally, of course) whose side (so long as sides must be taken) I am on and what the consequences (maybe) are." In Le Guin's feminist subversion of the biblical story of the Creation, in which Adam names all of the creatures of the earth (Genesis 2:19), Eve subsequently takes the names away. "As she does this, the barriers between herself and the world are dismantled," Le Guin observed in an interview, and in Le Guin's witty fable Eve may also be understood to liberate herself and her fellow creatures from the control of Adam. The text is taken from *Buffalo Gals and Other Animal Presences* (1987).

bedfordstmartins.com/
americanlit for research
links on Le Guin

SHE UNNAMES THEM

Most of them accepted namelessness with the perfect indifference with which they had so long accepted and ignored their names. Whales and dolphins, seals and sea otters consented with particular grace and alacrity, sliding into anonymity as into their element. A faction of yaks, however, protested. They said that "yak" sounded right, and that almost everyone who knew they existed called them that. Unlike the ubiquitous creatures such as rats or fleas who had been called by hundreds or thousands of different names since Babel,[1] the yaks could truly say, they said, that they had *a name*. They discussed the matter all summer. The councils of the elderly females finally agreed that though the name might be useful to others, it was so redundant from the yak point of view that they never spoke it themselves, and hence might as well dispense with it. After they presented the argument in this light to their bulls, a full consensus was delayed

---

1. **Babel:** In Genesis 11:1–9, the townspeople of the ancient city of Babel attempt to build a tower to reach heaven. God thwarts the plan by causing the languages of the builders to be mutually incomprehensible.

only by the onset of severe early blizzards. Soon after the beginning of the thaw their agreement was reached and the designation "yak" was returned to the donor.

Among the domestic animals, few horses had cared what anybody called them since the failure of Dean Swift's attempt to name them from their own vocabulary.[2] Cattle, sheep, swine, asses, mules, and goats, along with chickens, geese, and turkeys, all agreed enthusiastically to give their names back to the people to whom — as they put it — they belonged.

A couple of problems did come up with pets. The cats of course steadfastly denied ever having had any name other than those self-given, unspoken, effanineffably personal names which, as the poet named Eliot said,[3] they spend long hours daily contemplating — though none of the contemplators has ever admitted that what they contemplate is in fact their name, and some onlookers have wondered if the object of that meditative gaze might not in fact be the Perfect, or Platonic, Mouse. In any case it is a moot point now. It was with the dogs, and with some parrots, lovebirds, ravens, and mynahs that the trouble arose. These verbally talented individuals insisted that their names were important to them, and flatly refused to part with them. But as soon as they understood that the issue was precisely one of individual choice, and that anybody who wanted to be called Rover, or Froufrou, or Polly, or even Birdie in the personal sense, was perfectly free to do so, not one of them had the least objection to parting with the lower case (or, as regards German creatures, uppercase) generic appellations poodle, parrot, dog, or bird, and all the Linnaean qualifiers[4] that had trailed along behind them for two hundred years like tin cans tied to a tail.

The insects parted with their names in vast clouds and swarms of ephemeral syllables buzzing and stinging and humming and flitting and crawling and tunneling away.

As for the fish of the sea, their names dispersed from them in silence throughout the oceans like faint, dark blurs of cuttlefish ink,[5] and drifted off on the currents without a trace.

None were left now to unname, and yet how close I felt to them when I saw one of them swim or fly or trot or crawl across my way or over my skin, or stalk me in the night, or go along beside me for a while in the day. They seemed far closer than when their names had stood between myself and them like a clear barrier: so close that my fear of them and their fear of me became one same fear. And the attraction that many of us felt, the desire to smell one another's smells, feel or rub or caress one another's scales or skin or feathers or fur, taste one another's blood or flesh, keep one another warm, — that attraction was now all one with the fear, and the hunter could not be told from the hunted, nor the eater from the food.

---

2. **Dean Swift's . . . own vocabulary:** In the fourth part of *Gulliver's Travels* by the English satirist Jonathan Swift (1667–1745), Lemuel Gulliver travels to a land where intelligent horses, called "Houyhnhnms" in their language, rule over brute-like human beings, called "Yahoos."

3. **as the poet named Eliot said:** T. S. Eliot wrote and illustrated a fanciful collection of poems about cats, *Old Possum's Book of Practical Cats* (1939).

4. **Linnaean qualifiers:** The Swedish botanist Carolus Linnaeus (1707–1778) devised a system of classifying plants and animals into species using two-part Latin names, for example *Homo sapiens*.

5. **cuttlefish ink:** Cuttlefish are mollusks that release a brown pigment that helps them evade predators.

This was more or less the effect I had been after. It was somewhat more powerful than I had anticipated, but I could not now, in all conscience, make an exception for myself. I resolutely put anxiety away, went to Adam, and said, "You and your father lent me this – gave it to me, actually. It's been really useful, but it doesn't exactly seem to fit very well lately. But thanks very much! It's really been very useful."

It is hard to give back a gift without sounding peevish or ungrateful, and I did not want to leave him with that impression of me. He was not paying much attention, as it happened, and said only, "Put it down over there, OK?" and went on with what he was doing.

One of my reasons for doing what I did was that talk was getting us nowhere; but all the same I felt a little let down. I had been prepared to defend my decision. And I thought that perhaps when he did notice he might be upset and want to talk. I put some things away and fiddled around a little, but he continued to do what he was doing and to take no notice of anything else. At last I said, "Well, goodbye, dear. I hope the garden key turns up."

He was fitting parts together, and said without looking around, "OK, fine, dear. When's dinner?"

"I'm not sure," I said. "I'm going now. With the –" I hesitated, and finally said, "With them, you know," and went on. In fact I had only just then realized how hard it would have been to explain myself. I could not chatter away as I used to do, taking it all for granted. My words now must be as slow, as new, as single, as tentative as the steps I took going down the path away from the house, between the dark-branched, tall dancers motionless against the winter shining.

[1985, 1987]

Gary Snyder

[b. 1930]

Gary Sherman Snyder was born on May 8, 1930, in San Francisco, California, the first of two children of Harold and Lois Wilkie Snyder. Struggling to make a living during the Great Depression, the Snyders moved in 1932 to a former logging camp near Lake City, Washington. There, they established a small dairy farm, selling milk, eggs, and wood shingles they cut from the stumps left on the land. When his parents separated in 1942, Snyder went with his mother and sister to live in Portland, Oregon. His lifelong interest in hiking and climbing began when he climbed Mount St. Helens with a mountaineering

Gary Snyder

This photograph of Snyder at a restaurant in Kyoto, Japan, where he lived for more than a decade, was taken in 1963 by his close friend and fellow Beat poet Allen Ginsberg.

club in the summer of 1945. Snyder wrote poems and occasional articles for his high-school newspaper, and he worked during the summers as a copyboy for the Portland *Oregonian*. After his graduation in 1947, he enrolled at nearby Reed College. "I had some marvelous teachers," he recalled in a 1976 interview. "They wouldn't tolerate bullshit, made me clean up my prose style, exposed me to all the varieties of intellectual positions and gave me a territory in which I could speak out my radical politics and get arguments and augmentations on it." Snyder published poems in the college's literary magazine, the *Janus*, and he earned money during the summers by working for the National Park Service. In 1950, he married a classmate at Reed, Alison Gass, but they were divorced by the time Snyder graduated with a degree in English and anthropology in 1951. That fall, he entered graduate school in anthropology at Indiana University.

Snyder swiftly decided that graduate study was not for him, so he left Indiana at the end of his first semester and went to San Francisco. Now determined to become a poet, he supported himself by working as a seasonal forest-fire lookout and on a trail crew in Yosemite National Park. He also did graduate work in Asian languages at the University of California, Berkeley. He met a number of other writers in the Bay Area, including Allen Ginsberg and Jack Kerouac. In August 1955, Snyder participated in the famous group poetry reading at the Six Gallery, where Ginsberg electrified the crowd and effectively launched the Beat movement by reading his revolutionary poem *Howl*. The next year, Snyder sailed to Japan. He lived there during most of the following twelve years, studying Zen Buddhism. During 1957–58, he worked for eight months in the engine room of a steamer bound for ports in the Mediterranean, the Persian Gulf, and the Pacific. Snyder also returned several times to the United States, where his friends among the Beats helped arrange for the publication of his first two collections of poetry: *Riprap* (1959), which was printed in Japan and distributed by Lawrence Ferlinghetti's City Lights Bookstore; and *Myths and Texts* (1960), which was published in New York City by Totem Press, founded by LeRoi Jones (later Amiri Baraka). In 1960, Snyder married the poet Joanne Kyger in Kyoto. Together, they toured Nepal and India, where they joined Allen Ginsberg. But the couple's relationship was stormy, and they were divorced in 1965. That year, Snyder published *Riprap & Cold Mountain Poems*, expanded by the addition of his translations of a series of poems by the T'ang dynasty poet and hermit Han Shan, and *Six Sections from Mountains and Rivers Without End*. In 1967, he married Masa Uehara in a ceremony conducted on the rim of an active volcano on a small island off Japan.

Snyder became famous as an environmentalist, poet, and voice of the counterculture following his return to the United States. By then, he was regularly publishing in prominent literary journals, including *Poetry*, which awarded him its Levinson Prize in 1968. The influential American firm New Directions published his collections *The Back Country* (1968) and *Earth House Hold* (1969). With the assistance of friends, Snyder built a house in the foothills of the Sierra Nevada, where he and his wife moved

Snyder is a master of challenge and confrontation, not because he seeks controversy but because his values are so conspicuous, so plainly stated in the context of simple, sensuous, impassioned fact that they cannot be dodged.

–Kenneth Rexroth

with their two young sons, Kai and Gen, in 1970. Increasingly active in the environmental movement, Snyder attended the United Nations Conference on the Environment in Stockholm, Sweden, in 1972. He was awarded the Pulitzer Prize for his collection *Turtle Island* (1974), the name for North America in some Native American creation myths. His next three books revealed the range of his interests and writings: *He Who Hunted Birds in His Father's Village* (1979), a revision of the senior thesis he wrote at Reed on a Native American myth; *Axe Handles* (1983), a collection famed for its title poem; and *Passage Through India* (1983), an account of his spiritual pilgrimage across the country during 1961-62. In 1985, he began to teach in the English department and the Nature and Culture Program at the University of California, Davis. He and Masa Uehara divorced in 1989, and Snyder married the naturalist Carole Koda in 1991. Following the publication of *Mountains and Rivers Without End* (1996), a poetic sequence Snyder had been working on for forty years, he was awarded the prestigious Bollingen Prize. His recent work includes a volume of poems, *Danger on Peaks* (2005); a collection of personal essays, *Back on the Fire* (2007); and (with artist Tom Killion) *Tamalpais Walking: Poetry, History, and Prints* (2009), inspired by Mount Tamalpais in the High Sierras in California.

Reading Snyder's Poetry.   Although he is most often associated with the urban Beat poets and writers, whose interest in Zen Buddhism Snyder helped stimulate, much of Snyder's poetry bespeaks his physical and spiritual immersion in the wilderness, especially the remote mountain areas of California and the Pacific Northwest. A student of languages, linguistics, and literature, he has been inspired by a wide range of poetic models, from the Japanese haiku and ancient Chinese poetry to the work of Ezra Pound and William Carlos Williams. Like Williams, Snyder characteristically uses colloquial language, direct images, and natural rhythms to convey everyday and often momentary experiences. "The rhythms of my poems follow the rhythm of the physical work I'm doing and the life I'm leading at any given time," he observed early in his career. In the afterword to a 1990 reprint of his first collection, *Riprap* (1959), he traced the inception of the poems in the volume back to his work with a trail crew in Yosemite National Park in 1955. Snyder explained that the title of the volume, a term for the loose stones the crew laid on steep rock surfaces to make trails for horses and hikers, "celebrates the work of the hands, the placing of rock, and my first glimpse of the image of the whole universe as interconnected, mutually reflecting and mutually embracing." Snyder's keen sensitivity to the physical particulars of the natural world and his profound sense of the interconnectedness of the whole are revealed in the following selection of his poems from 1959 to 1992. The texts of the following poems are taken from *The Gary Snyder Reader: Prose, Poetry, and Translations, 1952-1998* (1999).

bedfordstmartins.com/
americanlit *for research*
links on Snyder

RIPRAP[1]

Lay down these words
Before your mind like rocks.
        placed solid, by hands
In choice of place, set
Before the body of the mind   5
        in space and time:
Solidity of bark, leaf, or wall
        riprap of things:
Cobble of milky way,
        straying planets,   10
These poems, people,
        lost ponies with
Dragging saddles
        and rocky sure-foot trails.
The worlds like an endless   15
        four-dimensional
Game of *Go*.[2]
        ants and pebbles
In the thin loam, each rock a word
        a creek-washed stone   20
Granite: ingrained
        with torment of fire and weight
Crystal and sediment linked hot
        all change, in thoughts,
As well as things.   25

                  [1959, 1999]

---

1. **Riprap:** Loose rock used to stabilize hillsides and shorelines against erosion, though Snyder has more specifically defined it as "a cobble of stones laid on steep slick rock to make a trail for horses in mountains."
2. **Game of *Go*:** Called "Go" in Japan and different names in other Asian countries, this is a board game in which two players alternately place white and black stones on vacant places on a grid. A stone is captured and removed when it is surrounded by stones of the other color.

WAVE

Grooving clam shell,
        streakt through marble,
sweeping down ponderosa pine bark-scale
        rip-cut tree grain
           sand-dunes, lava   5
        flow

Wave   wife.
       woman – wyfman –[1]
"veiled; vibrating; vague"
    sawtooth ranges pulsing;   10
                    veins on the back of the hand.

Forkt out: birdsfoot-alluvium
                wash
        great dunes rolling
Each inch rippld, every grain a wave.   15

Leaning against sand cornices til they blow away

   – wind, shake
   stiff thorns of cholla, ocotillo[2]
   sometimes I get stuck in thickets –

Ah, trembling spreading radiating wyf[3]   20
             racing zebra
  catch me and fling me wide
To the dancing grain of things
             of my mind!

[1968, 1999]

---

1. **wyfman:** Woman (Old English).
2. **cholla, ocotillo:** A cactus and a desert shrub, native to Mexico and the southwestern United States.
3. **wyf:** Wife (Old English).

AXE HANDLES

One afternoon the last week in April
Showing Kai how to throw a hatchet
One-half turn and it sticks in a stump.
He recalls the hatchet-head
Without a handle, in the shop   5
And go gets it, and wants it for his own.
A broken-off axe handle behind the door
Is long enough for a hatchet,
We cut it to length and take it
With the hatchet head   10
And working hatchet, to the wood block.
There I begin to shape the old handle
With the hatchet, and the phrase

First learned from Ezra Pound[1]
Rings in my ears!   15
"When making an axe handle
        the pattern is not far off."
And I say this to Kai
"Look: We'll shape the handle
By checking the handle   20
Of the axe we cut with —"
And he sees. And I hear it again:
It's in Lu Ji's *Wē Fu,* fourth century
a.d. "Essay on Literature"[2] — in the
Preface: "In making the handle   25
Of an axe
By cutting wood with an axe
The model is indeed near at hand."
My teacher Shih-hsiang Chen
Translated that and taught it years ago   30
And I see: Pound was an axe,
Chen was an axe, I am an axe
And my son a handle, soon
To be shaping again, model
And tool, craft of culture,   35
How we go on.

                                             [1979, 1997]

---

1. **Ezra Pound:** An influential American critic, poet, and translator who shared Snyder's interest in Chinese literature and philosophy (see pp. 1597–1604).
2. **Lu Ji's . . . "Essay on Literature":** Lu Ji (261–303) was a Chinese poet who wrote a book delineating the principles of composition, *Wē Fu* ("On Literature").

Donald Barthelme

[1931–1989]

Donald Barthelme was born on April 7, 1931, in Philadelphia, Pennsylvania. He was the first of the five children of Donald Barthelme, a Texas-born architect, and Helen Bechtold Barthelme, a daughter of an affluent Philadelphia family, both graduates of the University of Pennsylvania. The family soon moved to Texas, where Barthelme's father worked for various firms before setting up a private practice in Houston. He quickly became known for his innovative modernist buildings, including the family's house, as well as for his distinguished teaching in the architecture department at the University of Houston. Barthelme's mother encouraged the literary

Donald Barthelme

This photograph of Barthelme, an early practitioner of postmodern fiction, was taken at his home in 1964.

interests of her five children, all of whom became writers. Barthelme was raised Catholic and attended parochial schools until 1948, when he transferred to the public Lamar High School. He wrote for the literary magazine and entered the University of Houston as a journalism major in 1949. During his sophomore year, he edited the student newspaper, the *Cougar*. His articles caught the attention of editors of the *Houston Post*, and he accepted a position as a fine-arts reporter. Shortly after his marriage to Marilyn Marrs in 1952, he was drafted into the army for service in the Korean War. For the next two years, he served at Fort Polk, Louisiana, Japan, and Korea. He wrote when he could and read widely, including the works of modernists such as Ezra Pound, T. S. Eliot, and James Joyce and the French existentialists Albert Camus and Jean-Paul Sartre.

After his discharge from the army, Barthelme worked at various jobs in media and the arts before becoming a full-time and highly successful writer. Returning home to Houston, he resumed his former job at the *Houston Post* in 1955. He attended classes at the University of Houston and then went to work for its public-relations office, writing speeches for the president and founding a literary magazine, *Forum*. Following a divorce from his first wife, Barthelme married a journalist he had known since his undergraduate days, Helen Moore. Actively involved in the Houston arts scene, he served on the Board of Trustees of the Contemporary Arts Museum and became its director in 1961. The following year, he moved to New York City to become the managing editor of a new art and literature review, *Location*. Barthelme, who had long been an avid reader of the *New Yorker*, published his first story in the magazine in March 1963. Shortly after that, he was offered a "first reading" contract by the editors of the magazine, in which he ultimately published well over a hundred stories and numerous film reviews. Indeed, his work was strongly stimulated by the techniques of film, which he suggested had forced writers to reinvent fiction. Beginning with *Come Back, Dr. Caligari* (1964), an allusion to the classic silent horror film *The Cabinet of Dr. Caligari*, Barthelme regularly published collections of experimental stories, including *Unspeakable Practices, Unnatural Acts* (1968), *City Life* (1970), and *Sadness* (1972). He also published his first novel, *Snow White* (1967), a contemporary and playfully subversive retelling of the classic fairy tale made famous by the Walt Disney movie *Snow White and the Seven Dwarfs*. Meanwhile, Barthelme's marriage to Helen Moore ended, and he married his third wife, Birgit Barthelme. A book he wrote and illustrated for their daughter, *The Slightly Irregular Fire Engine* (1971), won the National Book Award.

Barthelme later combined writing with distinguished teaching of the craft of fiction. He was a visiting professor at Boston University in 1973 and at the City College of New York in 1974, the year he published a miscellaneous collection of parodies and satires, *Guilty Pleasures*. That was followed by his influential short novel, *The Dead Father* (1974), in which Barthelme once again parodied the conventions of the novel, and two more collections of his stories, *Amateurs* (1976) and *Great Days* (1979). His third marriage failed, and in 1978 Barthelme married Marion Knox, with whom he had a second daughter. An acclaimed collection of his best stories from the previous two decades, *Sixty Stories* (1981), was nominated for the PEN/Faulkner Award for Fiction. In 1983, after living in New York City for twenty years, Barthelme returned to Houston to become a full-time professor and later the director of the Creative Writing Program at the University of Houston. Although he developed serious health problems, the result of years of heavy smoking and drinking, he continued to teach and write, publishing *Paradise* (1986), a novel about a middle-aged architect separated from his wife and daughter, and *Forty Stories* (1987). Barthelme received the Rea Award for his contribution to short-story writing in 1988. He died of cancer on July 23, 1989, leaving behind a large collection of manuscripts, including a posthumously published novel, *The King* (1990).

Reading Barthelme's "The School."   Like his father, an internationally known architect with whom he had a deeply conflicted relationship, Barthelme was committed to formal innovation. But his father adopted the vocabulary of modern architecture, which was based on the pursuit of harmony and order, while Barthelme was at the forefront of the development of a disruptive and fragmentary postmodern style characterized by irony, pastiche, and playfulness. The elder Barthelme was particularly renowned for his designs for schools, about which he wrote extensively, and his rebellious son may have offered a sly rejoinder to such work in "The School." The unconventional story takes the form of a dramatic monologue in which a second-grade teacher named Edgar gloomily tells an unidentified auditor about a series of disasters that befell the children in his class. Confronted with an escalating series of deaths, from plants and animals to classmates and relatives, the teacher and his students offer different answers to the riddle of life and death. The author's response to that enigma, however, may simply lie in the deadpan humor and the optimistic, upbeat ending of "The School," which was read at a memorial service for Barthelme in 1989. The text of the story, which was first published in the *New Yorker* in June 1974, is taken from Barthelme's fifth collection of stories, *Amateurs* (1976).

bedfordstmartins.com/ americanlit for research links on Barthelme

THE SCHOOL

Well, we had all these children out planting trees, see, because we figured that . . . that was part of their education, to see how, you know, the root systems . . . and also the sense of responsibility, taking care of things, being individually responsible. You know what I mean. And the trees all died. They were orange trees. I don't know why they died, they just died. Something wrong with the soil possibly or maybe the stuff we got from the nursery wasn't the best. We complained about it. So we've got thirty kids there, each kid had his or her own little tree to plant, and we've got these thirty dead trees. All these kids looking at these little brown sticks, it was depressing.

   It wouldn't have been so bad except that just a couple of weeks before the thing with the trees, the snakes all died. But I think that the snakes – well, the reason that the snakes kicked off was that . . . you remember, the boiler was shut off for four days because of the strike, and that was explicable. It was something you could explain to the kids because of the strike. I mean, none of their parents would let them cross the picket line and they knew there was a strike going on and what it meant. So when things got started up again and we found the snakes they weren't too disturbed.

With the herb gardens it was probably a case of overwatering, and at least now they know not to overwater. The children were very conscientious with the herb gardens and some of them probably . . . you know, slipped them a little extra water when we weren't looking. Or maybe . . . well, I don't like to think about sabotage, although it did occur to us. I mean, it was something that crossed our minds. We were thinking that way probably because before that the gerbils had died, and the white mice had died, and the salamander . . . well, now they know not to carry them around in plastic bags.

Of course we *expected* the tropical fish to die, that was no surprise. Those numbers, you look at them crooked and they're belly-up on the surface. But the lesson plan called for a tropical-fish input at that point, there was nothing we could do, it happens every year, you just have to hurry past it.

We weren't even supposed to have a puppy.

We weren't even supposed to have one, it was just a puppy the Murdoch girl found under a Gristede's truck one day and she was afraid the truck would run over it when the driver had finished making his delivery, so she stuck it in her knapsack and brought it to school with her. So we had this puppy. As soon as I saw the puppy I thought, Oh Christ, I bet it will live for about two weeks and then . . . And that's what it did. It wasn't supposed to be in the classroom at all, there's some kind of regulation about it, but you can't tell them they can't have a puppy when the puppy is already there, right in front of them, running around on the floor and yap yap yapping. They named it Edgar—that is, they named it after me. They had a lot of fun running after it and yelling, "Here, Edgar! Nice Edgar!" Then they'd laugh like hell. They enjoyed the ambiguity. I enjoyed it myself. I don't mind being kidded. They made a little house for it in the supply closet and all that. I don't know what it died of. Distemper, I guess. It probably hadn't had any shots. I got it out of there before the kids got to school. I checked the supply closet each morning, routinely, because I knew what was going to happen. I gave it to the custodian.

And then there was this Korean orphan that the class adopted through the Help the Children program, all the kids brought in a quarter a month, that was the idea. It was an unfortunate thing, the kid's name was Kim and maybe we adopted him too late or something. The cause of death was not stated in the letter we got, they suggested we adopt another child instead and sent us some interesting case histories, but we didn't have the heart. The class took it pretty hard, they began (I think; nobody ever said anything to me directly) to feel that maybe there was something wrong with the school. But I don't think there's anything wrong with the school, particularly, I've seen better and I've seen worse. It was just a run of bad luck. We had an extraordinary number of parents passing away, for instance. There were I think two heart attacks and two suicides, one drowning, and four killed together in a car accident. One stroke. And we had the usual heavy mortality rate among the grandparents, or maybe it was heavier this year, it seemed so. And finally the tragedy.

The tragedy occurred when Matthew Wein and Tony Mavrogordo were playing over where they're excavating for the new federal office building. There were all these big wooden beams stacked, you know, at the edge of the excavation. There's a court case coming out of that, the parents are claiming that the beams were poorly stacked. I don't know what's true and what's not. It's been a strange year.

I forgot to mention Billy Brandt's father, who was knifed fatally when he grappled with a masked intruder in his home.

One day, we had a discussion in class. They asked me, where did they go? The trees, the salamander, the tropical fish, Edgar, the poppas and mommas, Matthew and Tony, where did they go? And I said, I don't know, I don't know. And they said, who knows? and I said, nobody knows. And they said, is death that which gives meaning to life? and I said, no, life is that which gives meaning to life. Then they said, but isn't death, considered as a fundamental datum, the means by which the taken-for-granted mundanity of the everyday may be transcended in the direction of —

I said, yes, maybe.

They said, we don't like it.

I said, that's sound.

They said, it's a bloody shame!

I said, it is.

They said, will you make love now with Helen (our teaching assistant) so that we can see how it is done? We know you like Helen.

I do like Helen but I said that I would not.

We've heard so much about it, they said, but we've never seen it.

I said I would be fired and that it was never, or almost never, done as a demonstration. Helen looked out of the window.

They said, please, please make love with Helen, we require an assertion of value, we are frightened.

I said that they shouldn't be frightened (although I am often frightened) and that there was value everywhere. Helen came and embraced me. I kissed her a few times on the brow. We held each other. The children were excited. Then there was a knock on the door, I opened the door, and the new gerbil walked in. The children cheered wildly.

[1974, 1976]

Toni Morrison

[b. 1931]

Toni Morrison was born Chloe Anthony Wofford on February 18, 1931, in Lorain, Ohio. She was the second of four children of George Wofford, a shipwelder, and Ramah Willis Wofford, a pianist who often worked as a domestic maid in order to help support the family. The couple had migrated to Ohio from Georgia in search of better employment and educational opportunities, and they lived in a close-knit community of African Americans in Lorain. Morrison has said that her family had a rich history

Toni Morrison

Bernard Gotfryd took this photograph of Morrison at a New York City bookstore in 1970, the year she published her first novel, *The Bluest Eye.*

of storytelling, and she grew up with a strong sense of the importance of African American culture and history. An outstanding student, she attended Lorain High School and became the first woman in her family to go to college when she entered Howard University in Washington, D.C., in 1949. Morrison majored in English and joined an acting troupe at Howard, where her friends began calling her "Toni." Initially planning to become a teacher and return to Lorain when she graduated, Morrison instead enrolled in graduate school at Cornell University in 1953. After she earned an MA in 1955, writing her thesis on Virginia Woolf and William Faulkner, she accepted a teaching position at Texas Southern University. Two years later, she returned to teach at Howard, where she joined a writing group and began working on short stories. She also met and married Harold Morrison, an architect from Jamaica. Morrison gave birth to their two sons, but she and her husband had sharply different ideas about gender roles in marriage, and they were divorced in 1964.

Morrison soon began a new era in her life. In 1965, she landed a job as a textbook editor with a subsidiary of Random House Publishers in Syracuse, New York. For the next several years, she devoted herself to raising her children, working at her job, and writing at night. Promoted in 1968 to the position of senior editor, she moved her family to New York City. Through her new job, she helped a number of African American writers publish their work, including Angela Davis and June Jordan. Morrison soon published her first novel, *The Bluest Eye* (1970), based on one of her earlier short stories about a poor black girl who longs to have the blue eyes that she associates with white standards of beauty. Although the novel received mixed reviews, it earned Morrison strong praise from many readers, including the actor and civil rights activist Ruby Dee, who observed: "To read the book is to ache for remedy." Morrison's second novel, *Sula* (1973), about the relationship between two black women in an Ohio community, brought her more attention, and she began receiving invitations to teach at colleges and universities, including Rutgers and Yale. She also edited *The Black Book* (1974), a pioneering collection of documents central to African American history and culture. The publication of her third novel, *Song of Solomon* (1977), established her reputation as a writer of the first rank. The story of a black man's search for identity, *Song of Solomon* was the first novel by an African American to be offered as a main selection of the Book-of-the-Month Club since the publication in 1940 of Richard Wright's *Native Son.*

Morrison has subsequently been acclaimed as one of the major writers of her generation. Her picture appeared on the cover of *Newsweek* and her novel *Tar Baby,* the story of the complex relationship between a black woman and a white man, was on the year's bestseller list in 1981. Two years later, she decided to leave her position at Random House in order to spend more time teaching and writing. Inspired by an actual account she had found while preparing *The Black Book,* Morrison next wrote a historical novel about the devastating effects of slavery, *Beloved* (1987), which won the Pulitzer Prize. In 1989, she accepted a chaired professorship to teach creative writing and African American studies at Princeton University. In addition to an influential work of literary criticism, *Playing in the Dark: Essays on Whiteness and the Literary Imagination* (1990), she published a novel inspired by the Harlem Renaissance, *Jazz* (1992). In 1993, Morrison became the first African American to win the Nobel Prize in Literature. After the publication of her novel *Paradise* (1998), a cover story in *Time* proclaimed her "The Great American Storyteller." Her recent works include two children's books, both coauthored with her son Slade Morrison; the libretto for *Margaret Garner* (2002), an opera based on the same events that inspired *Beloved*; and her intricate eighth novel, *Love* (2003). When she retired from Princeton in 2006, former president Bill Clinton and the actor Morgan Freeman were among those who offered tributes to Morrison at a party held in her honor at Lincoln Center in New York City. Since her retirement, Morrison has published *A Mercy* (2008), an historical novel about slavery; and *Home* (2012), the story of a black Korean War veteran struggling to find the meaning of "home" in the racially divided 1950s.

bedfordstmartins.com/ americanlit *for research links on Morrison*

Reading Morrison's "Recitatif." Morrison wrote this story specifically for the groundbreaking anthology *Confirmation*, a collection of the works of forty-nine African American women writers edited by the poet and playwright Amiri Baraka and his wife, the poet Amina Baraka. In the introduction, they explained that "the purpose of this volume is to draw attention to the existence and excellence of black women writers" and thus "to 'confirm' that a whole body of American literature has been consistently ignored or hidden." In addition to Morrison, the anthology featured the work of prominent writers such as Gwendolyn Brooks, Audre Lorde, and Alice Walker. "Recitatif," Morrison's only published short story, displays some of her characteristic innovations in narrative, structure, and style. The narrator, Twyla, tells of five encounters with her friend Roberta over a twenty-year period from childhood to adulthood. The story also touches on some central themes of Morrison's longer works, including family, female friendship, and racial division, an issue further complicated in "Recitatif" by the fact that it is never revealed which of the two main characters is black and which is white. The text is taken from *Confirmation: An Anthology of African American Women*, edited by Amiri Baraka and Amina Baraka (1983).

RECITATIF[1]

My mother danced all night and Roberta's was sick. That's why we were taken to St. Bonny's.[2] People want to put their arms around you when you tell them you were in a shelter, but it really wasn't bad. No big long room with one hundred beds like Bellevue.[3] There

---

1. **Recitatif:** Recitative (French), a vocal style between singing and ordinary speech that is often used for dialogue or narrative commentary in operas and oratorios. A now obsolete meaning for this term is the tone or rhythm peculiar to any language.
2. **St. Bonny's:** St. Bonaventure's, a shelter and school for orphaned children in New York City.
3. **Bellevue:** A hospital in New York City known for its psychiatric unit.

were four to a room, and when Roberta and me came, there was a shortage of state kids, so we were the only ones assigned to 406 and could go from bed to bed if we wanted to. And we wanted to, too. We changed beds every night and for the whole four months we were there we never picked one out as our own permanent bed.

It didn't start out that way. The minute I walked in and the Big Bozo introduced us, I got sick to my stomach. It was one thing to be taken out of your own bed early in the morning — it was something else to be stuck in a strange place with a girl from a whole other race. And Mary, that's my mother, she was right. Every now and then she would stop dancing long enough to tell me something important and one of the things she said was that they never washed their hair and they smelled funny. Roberta sure did. Smell funny, I mean. So when the Big Bozo[4] (nobody ever called her Mrs. Itkin, just like nobody ever said St. Bonaventure) — when she said, "Twyla, this is Roberta. Roberta, this is Twyla. Make each other welcome." I said, "My mother won't like you putting me in here."

"Good," said Bozo. "Maybe then she'll come and take you home." How's that for mean? If Roberta had laughed I would have killed her, but she didn't. She just walked over to the window and stood with her back to us.

"Turn around," said the Bozo. "Don't be rude. Now Twyla. Roberta. When you hear a loud buzzer, that's the call for dinner. Come down to the first floor. Any fights and no movie." And then, just to make sure we knew what we would be missing, "*The Wizard of Oz*."[5]

Roberta must have thought I meant that my mother would be mad about my being put in the shelter. Not about rooming with her, because as soon as Bozo left she came over to me and said, "Is your mother sick too?"

"No," I said. "She just likes to dance all night."

"Oh," she nodded her head and I liked the way she understood things so fast. So for the moment it didn't matter that we looked like salt and pepper standing there and that's what the other kids called us sometimes. We were eight years old and got F's all the time. Me because I couldn't remember what I read or what the teacher said. And Roberta because she couldn't read at all and didn't even listen to the teacher. She wasn't good at anything except jacks,[6] at which she was a killer: pow scoop pow scoop pow scoop.

We didn't like each other all that much at first, but nobody else wanted to play with us because we weren't real orphans with beautiful dead parents in the sky. We were dumped. Even the New York City Puerto Ricans and the upstate Indians ignored us. All kinds of kids were in there, black ones, white ones, even two Koreans. The food was good, though. At least I thought so. Roberta hated it and left whole pieces of things on her plate: Spam, Salisbury steak — even jello with fruit cocktail in it, and she didn't care

---

4. **Big Bozo**: Bozo the Clown was a popular character in comic books, animated cartoons, and numerous television shows such as *Bozo's Big Top* (1965–67).
5. ***The Wizard of Oz***: The young Judy Garland starred in this popular 1939 movie based on Frank Baum's children's book *The Wonderful Wizard of Oz* (1900).
6. **jacks**: A game in which the player bounces a rubber ball, scoops up a designated number of jacks with one hand, and then catches the ball on one bounce with the same hand.

if I ate what she wouldn't. Mary's idea of supper was popcorn and a can of Yoo-Hoo.[7] Hot mashed potatoes and two weenies was like Thanksgiving for me.

It really wasn't bad, St. Bonny's. The big girls on the second floor pushed us around now and then. But that was all. They wore lipstick and eyebrow pencil and wobbled their knees while they watched TV. Fifteen, sixteen, even, some of them were. They were put-out girls, scared runaways most of them. Poor little girls who fought their uncles off but looked tough to us, and mean. God did they look mean. The staff tried to keep them separate from the younger children, but sometimes they caught us watching them in the orchard where they played radios and danced with each other. They'd light out after us and pull our hair or twist our arms. We were scared of them, Roberta and me, but neither of us wanted the other one to know it. So we got a good list of dirty names we could shout back when we ran from them through the orchard. I used to dream a lot and almost always the orchard was there. Two acres, four maybe, of these little apple trees. Hundreds of them. Empty and crooked like beggar women when I first came to St. Bonny's but fat with flowers when I left. I don't know why I dreamt about that orchard so much. Nothing really happened there. Nothing all that important, I mean. Just the big girls dancing and playing the radio. Roberta and me watching. Maggie fell down there once. The kitchen woman with legs like parentheses. And the big girls laughed at her. We should have helped her up, I know, but we were scared of those girls with lipstick and eyebrow pencil. Maggie couldn't talk. The kids said she had her tongue cut out, but I think she was just born that way: mute. She was old and sandy-colored and she worked in the kitchen. I don't know if she was nice or not. I just remember her legs like parentheses and how she rocked when she walked. She worked from early in the morning till two o'clock, and if she was late, if she had too much cleaning and didn't get out till two-fifteen or so, she'd cut through the orchard so she wouldn't miss her bus and have to wait another hour. She wore this really stupid little hat — a kid's hat with ear flaps — and she wasn't much taller than we were. A really awful little hat. Even for a mute, it was dumb — dressing like a kid and never saying anything at all.

"But what about if somebody tries to kill her?" I used to wonder about that. "Or what if she wants to cry? Can she cry?"

"Sure," Roberta said. "But just tears. No sounds come out."

"She can't scream?"

"Nope. Nothing."

"Can she hear?"

"I guess."

"Let's call her," I said. And we did.

"Dummy! Dummy!" She never turned her head.

"Bow legs! Bow legs!" Nothing. She just rocked on, the chin straps of her baby-boy hat swaying from side to side. I think we were wrong. I think she could hear and didn't let on. And it shames me even now to think there was somebody in there after all who heard us call her those names and couldn't tell on us.

---

7. **Yoo-Hoo:** A chocolate drink developed in the 1920s and marketed as the "drink of champions" by the New York Yankees in the 1950s and 1960s.

We got along all right, Roberta and me. Changed beds every night, got F's in civics and communication skills and gym. The Bozo was disappointed in us, she said. Out of 130 of us state cases, 90 were under twelve. Almost all were real orphans with beautiful dead parents in the sky. We were the only ones dumped and the only ones with F's in three classes including gym. So we got along—what with her leaving whole pieces of things on her plate and being nice about not asking questions.

I think it was the day before Maggie fell down that we found out our mothers were coming to visit us on the same Sunday. We had been at the shelter twenty-eight days (Roberta twenty-eight and a half) and this was their first visit with us. Our mothers would come at ten o'clock in time for chapel, then lunch with us in the teachers' lounge. I thought if my dancing mother met her sick mother it might be good for her. And Roberta thought her sick mother would get a big bang out of a dancing one. We got excited about it and curled each other's hair. After breakfast we sat on the bed watching the road from the window. Roberta's socks were still wet. She washed them the night before and put them on the radiator to dry. They hadn't, but she put them on anyway because their tops were so pretty—scalloped in pink. Each of us had a purple construction-paper basket that we had made in craft class. Mine had a yellow crayon rabbit on it. Roberta's had eggs with wiggly lines of color. Inside were cellophane grass and just the jelly beans because I'd eaten the two marshmallow eggs they gave us. The Big Bozo came herself to get us. Smiling she told us we looked very nice and to come downstairs. We were so surprised by the smile we'd never seen before, neither of us moved.

"Don't you want to see your mommies?"

I stood up first and spilled the jelly beans all over the floor. Bozo's smile disappeared while we scrambled to get the candy up off the floor and put it back in the grass.

She escorted us downstairs to the first floor, where the other girls were lining up to file into the chapel. A bunch of grown-ups stood to one side. Viewers mostly. The old biddies who wanted servants and the fags who wanted company looking for children they might want to adopt. Once in a while a grandmother. Almost never anybody young or anybody whose face wouldn't scare you in the night. Because if any of the real orphans had young relatives they wouldn't be real orphans. I saw Mary right away. She had on those green slacks I hated and hated even more now because didn't she know we were going to chapel? And that fur jacket with the pocket linings so ripped she had to pull to get her hands out of them. But her face was pretty—like always, and she smiled and waved like she was the little girl looking for her mother—not me.

I walked slowly, trying not to drop the jelly beans and hoping the paper handle would hold. I had to use my last Chiclet[8] because by the time I finished cutting everything out, all the Elmer's was gone. I am left-handed and the scissors never worked for me. It didn't matter, though; I might just as well have chewed the gum. Mary dropped to her knees and grabbed me, mashing the basket, the jelly beans, and the grass into her ratty fur jacket.

"Twyla, baby. Twyla, baby!"

---

8. **Chiclet:** A brand of chewing gum, manufactured as small squares.

I could have killed her. Already I heard the big girls in the orchard the next time saying, "Twyyyyyla, baby!" But I couldn't stay mad at Mary while she was smiling and hugging me and smelling of Lady Esther dusting powder. I wanted to stay buried in her fur all day.

To tell the truth I forgot about Roberta. Mary and I got in line for the traipse into chapel and I was feeling proud because she looked so beautiful even in those ugly green slacks that made her behind stick out. A pretty mother on earth is better than a beautiful dead one in the sky even if she did leave you all alone to go dancing.

I felt a tap on my shoulder, turned, and saw Roberta smiling. I smiled back, but not too much lest somebody think this visit was the biggest thing that ever happened in my life. Then Roberta said, "Mother, I want you to meet my roommate, Twyla. And that's Twyla's mother."

I looked up it seemed for miles. She was big. Bigger than any man and on her chest was the biggest cross I'd ever seen. I swear it was six inches long each way. And in the crook of her arm was the biggest Bible ever made.

Mary, simple-minded as ever, grinned and tried to yank her hand out of the pocket with the raggedy lining—to shake hands, I guess. Roberta's mother looked down at me and then looked down at Mary too. She didn't say anything, just grabbed Roberta with her Bible-free hand and stepped out of line, walking quickly to the rear of it. Mary was still grinning because she's not too swift when it comes to what's really going on. Then this light bulb goes off in her head and she says "That bitch!" really loud and us almost in the chapel now. Organ music whining; the Bonny Angels singing sweetly. Everybody in the world turned around to look. And Mary would have kept it up—kept calling names if I hadn't squeezed her hand as hard as I could. That helped a little, but she still twitched and crossed and uncrossed her legs all through service. Even groaned a couple of times. Why did I think she would come there and act right? Slacks. No hat like the grandmothers and viewers, and groaning all the while. When we stood for hymns she kept her mouth shut. Wouldn't even look at the words on the page. She actually reached in her purse for a mirror to check her lipstick. All I could think of was that she really needed to be killed. The sermon lasted a year, and I knew the real orphans were looking smug again.

We were supposed to have lunch in the teachers' lounge, but Mary didn't bring anything, so we picked fur and cellophane grass off the mashed jelly beans and ate them. I could have killed her. I sneaked a look at Roberta. Her mother had brought chicken legs and ham sandwiches and oranges and a whole box of chocolate-covered grahams. Roberta drank milk from a thermos while her mother read the Bible to her.

Things are not right. The wrong food is always with the wrong people. Maybe that's why I got into waitress work later—to match up the right people with the right food. Roberta just let those chicken legs sit there, but she did bring a stack of grahams up to me later when the visit was over. I think she was sorry that her mother would not shake my mother's hand. And I liked that and I liked the fact that she didn't say a word about Mary groaning all the way through the service and not bringing any lunch.

Roberta left in May when the apple trees were heavy and white. On her last day we went to the orchard to watch the big girls smoke and dance by the radio. It didn't matter that they said, "Twyyyyyla, baby." We sat on the ground and breathed. Lady Esther. Apple blossoms. I still go soft when I smell one or the other. Roberta was going home.

The big cross and the big Bible was coming to get her and she seemed sort of glad and sort of not. I thought I would die in that room of four beds without her and I knew Bozo had plans to move some other dumped kid in there with me. Roberta promised to write every day, which was really sweet of her because she couldn't read a lick so how could she write anybody. I would have drawn pictures and sent them to her but she never gave me her address. Little by little she faded. Her wet socks with the pink scalloped tops and her big serious-looking eyes — that's all I could catch when I tried to bring her to mind.

I was working behind the counter at the Howard Johnson's on the Thruway just before the Kingston exit.[9] Not a bad job. Kind of a long ride from Newburgh, but okay once I got there. Mine was the second night shift — eleven to seven. Very light until a Greyhound checked in for breakfast around six-thirty. At that hour the sun was all the way clear of the hills behind the restaurant. The place looked better at night — more like shelter — but I loved it when the sun broke in, even if it did show all the cracks in the vinyl and the speckled floor looked dirty no matter what the mop boy did.

It was August and a bus crowd was just unloading. They would stand around a long while: going to the john, and looking at gifts and junk-for-sale machines, reluctant to sit down so soon. Even to eat. I was trying to fill the coffee pots and get them all situated on the electric burners when I saw her. She was sitting in a booth smoking a cigarette with two guys smothered in head and facial hair. Her own hair was so big and wild I could hardly see her face. But the eyes. I would know them anywhere. She had on a powder-blue halter and shorts outfit and earrings the size of bracelets. Talk about lipstick and eyebrow pencil. She made the big girls look like nuns. I couldn't get off the counter until seven o'clock, but I kept watching the booth in case they got up to leave before that. My replacement was on time for a change, so I counted and stacked my receipts as fast as I could and signed off. I walked over to the booth, smiling and wondering if she would remember me. Or even if she wanted to remember me. Maybe she didn't want to be reminded of St. Bonny's or to have anybody know she was ever there. I know I never talked about it to anybody.

I put my hands in my apron pockets and leaned against the back of the booth facing them.

"Roberta? Roberta Fisk?"

She looked up. "Yeah?"

"Twyla."

She squinted for a second and then said, "Wow."

"Remember me?"

"Sure. Hey. Wow."

"It's been a while," I said, and gave a smile to the two hairy guys.

"Yeah. Wow. You work here?"

"Yeah," I said. "I live in Newburgh."

"Newburgh? No kidding?" She laughed then a private laugh that included the guys but only the guys, and they laughed with her. What could I do but laugh too and wonder why I was standing there with my knees showing out from under that uniform. Without

---

9. **Thruway . . . Kingston exit:** The New York State Thruway, a limited-access toll road, runs near Kingston and Newburgh, cities north of New York City.

looking I could see the blue and white triangle on my head, my hair shapeless in a net, my ankles thick in white oxfords. Nothing could have been less sheer than my stockings. There was this silence that came down right after I laughed. A silence it was her turn to fill up. With introductions, maybe, to her boyfriends or an invitation to sit down and have a Coke. Instead she lit a cigarette off the one she'd just finished and said, "We're on our way to the Coast. He's got an appointment with Hendrix."[10] She gestured casually toward the boy next to her.

"Hendrix? Fantastic," I said. "Really fantastic. What's she doing now?"

Roberta coughed on her cigarette and the two guys rolled their eyes up at the ceiling.

"Hendrix. Jimi Hendrix, asshole. He's only the biggest — Oh, wow. Forget it."

I was dismissed without anyone saying goodbye, so I thought I would do it for her.

"How's your mother?" I asked. Her grin cracked her whole face. She swallowed. "Fine," she said. "How's yours?"

"Pretty as a picture," I said and turned away. The backs of my knees were damp. Howard Johnson's really was a dump in the sunlight.

James is as comfortable as a house slipper. He liked my cooking and I liked his big loud family. They have lived in Newburgh all of their lives and talk about it the way people do who have always known a home. His grandmother has a porch swing older than his father and when they talk about streets and avenues and buildings they call them names they no longer have. They still call the A & P[11] Rico's because it stands on property once a mom and pop store owned by Mr. Rico. And they call the new community college Town Hall because it once was. My mother-in-law puts up jelly and cucumbers and buys butter wrapped in cloth from a dairy. James and his father talk about fishing and baseball and I can see them all together on the Hudson in a raggedy skiff. Half the population of Newburgh is on welfare now, but to my husband's family it was still some upstate paradise of a time long past. A time of ice houses and vegetable wagons, coal furnaces and children weeding gardens. When our son was born my mother-in-law gave me the crib blanket that had been hers.

But the town they remembered had changed. Something quick was in the air. Magnificent old houses, so ruined they had become shelter for squatters and rent risks, were bought and renovated. Smart IBM people moved out of their suburbs back into the city and put shutters up and herb gardens in their backyards. A brochure came in the mail announcing the opening of a Food Emporium. Gourmet food it said — and listed items the rich IBM crowd would want. It was located in a new mall at the edge of town and I drove out to shop there one day — just to see. It was late in June. After the tulips were gone and the Queen Elizabeth roses were open everywhere. I trailed my cart along the aisle tossing in smoked oysters and Robert's sauce and things I knew would sit in my cupboard for years. Only when I found some Klondike ice cream bars did I feel less guilty

---

10. **Hendrix:** Jimi Hendrix (1942–1970), the influential singer and guitarist who gained enormous popularity in Europe and the United States during the 1960s.

11. **A & P:** The name of a supermarket chain owned by the Great Atlantic and Pacific Tea Company.

about spending James's fireman's salary so foolishly. My father-in-law ate them with the same gusto little Joseph did.

Waiting in the check-out line I heard a voice say, "Twyla!"

The classical music piped over the aisles had affected me and the woman leaning toward me was dressed to kill. Diamonds on her hand, a smart white summer dress. "I'm Mrs. Benson," I said.

"Ho. Ho. The Big Bozo," she sang.

For a split second I didn't know what she was talking about. She had a bunch of asparagus and two cartons of fancy water.

"Roberta!"

"Right."

"For heaven's sake. Roberta."

"You look great," she said.

"So do you. Where are you? Here? In Newburgh?"

"Yes. Over in Annandale."[12]

I was opening my mouth to say more when the cashier called my attention to her empty counter.

"Meet you outside." Roberta pointed her finger and went into the express line.

I placed the groceries and kept myself from glancing around to check Roberta's progress. I remembered Howard Johnson's and looking for a chance to speak only to be greeted with a stingy "wow." But she was waiting for me and her huge hair was sleek now, smooth around a small, nicely shaped head. Shoes, dress, everything lovely and summery and rich. I was dying to know what happened to her, how she got from Jimi Hendrix to Annandale, a neighborhood full of doctors and IBM executives. Easy, I thought. Everything is so easy for them. They think they own the world.

"How long," I asked her. "How long have you been here?"

"A year. I got married to a man who lives here. And you, you're married too, right? Benson, you said."

"Yeah. James Benson."

"And is he nice?"

"Oh, is he nice?"

"Well, is he?" Roberta's eyes were steady as though she really meant the question and wanted an answer.

"He's wonderful, Roberta. Wonderful."

"So you're happy."

"Very."

"That's good," she said and nodded her head. "I always hoped you'd be happy. Any kids? I know you have kids."

"One. A boy. How about you?"

"Four."

"Four?"

---

12. **Annandale:** Annandale-on-Hudson, an affluent town across the Hudson River and north of Newburgh.

She laughed. "Step kids. He's a widower."

"Oh."

"Got a minute? Let's have a coffee."

I thought about the Klondikes melting and the inconvenience of going all the way to my car and putting the bags in the trunk. Served me right for buying all that stuff I didn't need. Roberta was ahead of me.

"Put them in my car. It's right here."

And then I saw the dark blue limousine.

"You married a Chinaman?"

"No," she laughed. "He's the driver."

"Oh, my. If the Big Bozo could see you now."

We both giggled. Really giggled. Suddenly, in just a pulse beat, twenty years disappeared and all of it came rushing back. The big girls (whom we called gar girls— Roberta's misheard word for the evil stone faces described in a civics class[13]) there dancing in the orchard, the ploppy mashed potatoes, the double weenies, the Spam with pine-apple. We went into the coffee shop holding on to one another and I tried to think why we were glad to see each other this time and not before. Once, twelve years ago, we passed like strangers. A black girl and a white girl meeting in a Howard Johnson's on the road and having nothing to say. One in a blue and white triangle waitress hat—the other on her way to see Hendrix. Now we were behaving like sisters separated for much too long. Those four short months were nothing in time. Maybe it was the thing itself. Just being there, together. Two little girls who knew what nobody else in the world knew—how not to ask questions. How to believe what had to be believed. There was politeness in that reluctance and generosity as well. Is your mother sick too? No, she dances all night. Oh—and an understanding nod.

We sat in a booth by the window and fell into recollection like veterans.

"Did you ever learn to read?"

"Watch." She picked up the menu. "Special of the day. Cream of corn soup. Entrées. Two dots and a wriggly line. Quiche. Chef salad, scallops . . ."

I was laughing and applauding when the waitress came up.

"Remember the Easter baskets?"

"And how we tried to *introduce* them?"

"Your mother with that cross like two telephone poles."

"And yours with those tight slacks."

We laughed so loudly heads turned and made the laughter harder to suppress.

"What happened to the Jimi Hendrix date?"

Roberta made a blow-out sound with her lips.

"When he died I thought about you."

"Oh, you heard about him finally?"

"Finally. Come on, I was a small-town country waitress."

---

13. **gar girls . . . civics class:** Roberta has misheard the word *gargoyles*, carved grotesques with spouts used to carry rainwater away from the walls of masonry buildings, especially Gothic cathedrals.

"And I was a small-town country dropout. God, were we wild. I still don't know how I got out of there alive."

"But you did."

"I did. I really did. Now I'm Mrs. Kenneth Norton."

"Sounds like a mouthful."

"It is."

"Servants and all?"

Roberta held up two fingers.

"Ow! What does he do?"

"Computers and stuff. What do I know?"

"I don't remember a hell of a lot from those days, but Lord, St. Bonny's is as clear as daylight. Remember Maggie? The day she fell down and those gar girls laughed at her?"

Roberta looked up from her salad and stared at me. "Maggie didn't fall," she said.

"Yes, she did. You remember."

"No, Twyla. They knocked her down. Those girls pushed her down and tore her clothes. In the orchard."

"I don't — that's not what happened."

"Sure it is. In the orchard. Remember how scared we were?"

"Wait a minute. I don't remember any of that."

"And Bozo was fired."

"You're crazy. She was there when I left. You left before me."

"I went back. You weren't there when they fired Bozo."

"What?"

"Twice. Once for a year when I was about ten, another for two months when I was fourteen. That's when I ran away."

"You ran away from St. Bonny's?"

"I had to. What do you want? Me dancing in that orchard?"

"Are you sure about Maggie?"

"Of course I'm sure. You've blocked it, Twyla. It happened. Those girls had behavior problems, you know."

"Didn't they, though. But why can't I remember the Maggie thing?"

"Believe me. It happened. And we were there."

"Who did you room with when you went back?" I asked her as if I would know her. The Maggie thing was troubling me.

"Creeps. They tickled themselves in the night."

My ears were itching and I wanted to go home suddenly. This was all very well but she couldn't just comb her hair, wash her face, and pretend everything was hunky-dory. After the Howard Johnson's snub. And no apology. Nothing.

"Were you on dope or what that time at Howard Johnson's?" I tried to make my voice sound friendlier than I felt.

"Maybe, a little. I never did drugs much. Why?"

"I don't know; you acted sort of like you didn't want to know me then."

"Oh, Twyla, you know how it was in those days: black — white. You know how everything was."

But I didn't know. I thought it was just the opposite. Busloads of blacks and whites came into Howard Johnson's together. They roamed together then: students, musicians, lovers, protesters. You got to see everything at Howard Johnson's and blacks were very friendly with whites in those days. But sitting there with nothing on my plate but two hard tomato wedges wondering about the melting Klondikes it seemed childish remembering the slight. We went to her car, and with the help of the driver, got my stuff into my station wagon.

"We'll keep in touch this time," she said.

"Sure," I said. "Sure. Give me a call."

"I will," she said, and then just as I was sliding behind the wheel, she leaned into the window. "By the way. Your mother. Did she ever stop dancing?"

I shook my head. "No. Never."

Roberta nodded.

"And yours? Did she ever get well?"

She smiled a tiny sad smile. "No. She never did. Look, call me, okay?"

"Okay," I said, but I knew I wouldn't. Roberta had messed up my past somehow with that business about Maggie. I wouldn't forget a thing like that. Would I?

Strife came to us that fall. At least that's what the paper called it. Strife. Racial strife. The word made me think of a bird — a big shrieking bird out of 1,000,000,000 B.C. Flapping its wings and cawing. Its eye with no lid always bearing down on you. All day it screeched and at night it slept on the rooftops. It woke you in the morning and from the *Today* show to the eleven o'clock news it kept you an awful company. I couldn't figure it out from one day to the next. I knew I was supposed to feel something strong, but I didn't know what, and James wasn't any help. Joseph was on the list of kids to be transferred from the junior high school to another one at some far-out-of-the-way place and I thought it was a good thing until I heard it was a bad thing. I mean I didn't know. All the schools seemed dumps to me, and the fact that one was nicer looking didn't hold much weight. But the papers were full of it and then the kids began to get jumpy. In August, mind you. Schools weren't even open yet. I thought Joseph might be frightened to go over there, but he didn't seem scared so I forgot about it, until I found myself driving along Hudson Street out there by the school they were trying to integrate and saw a line of women marching. And who do you suppose was in line, big as life, holding a sign in front of her bigger than her mother's cross? MOTHERS HAVE RIGHTS TOO! it said.

I drove on, and then changed my mind. I circled the block, slowed down, and honked my horn.

Roberta looked over and when she saw me she waved. I didn't wave back, but I didn't move either. She handed her sign to another woman and came over to where I was parked.

"Hi."

"What are you doing?"

"Picketing. What's it look like?"

"What for?"

"What do you mean, 'What for?' They want to take my kids and send them out of the neighborhood. They don't want to go."

"So what if they go to another school? My boy's being bussed too, and I don't mind. Why should you?"

"It's not about us, Twyla. Me and you. It's about our kids."

"What's more *us* than that?"

"Well, it is a free country."

"Not yet, but it will be."

"What the hell does that mean? I'm not doing anything to you."

"You really think that?"

"I know it."

"I wonder what made me think you were different."

"I wonder what made me think you were different."

"Look at them," I said. "Just look. Who do they think they are? Swarming all over the place like they own it. And now they think they can decide where my child goes to school. Look at them, Roberta. They're Bozos."

Roberta turned around and looked at the women. Almost all of them were standing still now, waiting. Some were even edging toward us. Roberta looked at me out of some refrigerator behind her eyes. "No, they're not. They're just mothers."

"And what am I? Swiss cheese?"

"I used to curl your hair."

"I hated your hands in my hair."

The women were moving. Our faces looked mean to them of course and they looked as though they could not wait to throw themselves in front of a police car, or better yet, into my car and drag me away by my ankles. Now they surrounded my car and gently, gently began to rock it. I swayed back and forth like a sideways yo-yo. Automatically I reached for Roberta, like the old days in the orchard when they saw us watching them and we had to get out of there, and if one of us fell the other pulled her up and if one of us was caught the other stayed to kick and scratch, and neither would leave the other behind. My arm shot out of the car window but no receiving hand was there. Roberta was looking at me sway from side to side in the car and her face was still. My purse slid from the car seat down under the dashboard. The four policemen who had been drinking Tab in their car finally got the message and strolled over, forcing their way through the women. Quietly, firmly they spoke. "Okay, ladies. Back in line or off the streets."

Some of them went away willingly; others had to be urged away from the car doors and the hood. Roberta didn't move. She was looking steadily at me. I was fumbling to turn on the ignition, which wouldn't catch because the gearshift was still in drive. The seats of the car were a mess because the swaying had thrown my grocery coupons all over it and my purse was sprawled on the floor.

"Maybe I am different now, Twyla. But you're not. You're the same little state kid who kicked a poor old black lady when she was down on the ground. You kicked a black lady and you have the nerve to call me a bigot."

The coupons were everywhere and the guts of my purse were bunched under the dashboard. What was she saying? Black? Maggie wasn't black.

"She wasn't black," I said.

"Like hell she wasn't, and you kicked her. We both did. You kicked a black lady who couldn't even scream."

"Liar!"

"You're the liar! Why don't you just go on home and leave us alone, huh?"

She turned away and I skidded away from the curb.

The next morning I went into the garage and cut the side out of the carton our portable TV had come in. It wasn't nearly big enough, but after a while I had a decent sign: red spray-painted letters on a white background—AND SO DO CHILDREN****. I meant just to go down to the school and tack it up somewhere so those cows on the picket line across the street could see it, but when I got there, some ten or so others had already assembled—protesting the cows across the street. Police permits and everything. I got in line and we strutted in time on our side while Roberta's group strutted on theirs. That first day we were all dignified, pretending the other side didn't exist. The second day there was name calling and finger gestures. But that was about all. People changed signs from time to time, but Roberta never did and neither did I. Actually my sign didn't make sense without Roberta's. "And so do children what?" one of the women on my side asked me. Have rights, I said, as though it was obvious.

Roberta didn't acknowledge my presence in any way and I got to thinking maybe she didn't know I was there. I began to pace myself in the line, jostling people one minute and lagging behind the next, so Roberta and I could reach the end of our respective lines at the same time and there would be a moment in our turn when we would face each other. Still, I couldn't tell whether she saw me and knew my sign was for her. The next day I went early before we were scheduled to assemble. I waited until she got there before I exposed my new creation. As soon as she hoisted her MOTHERS HAVE RIGHTS TOO I began to wave my new one, which said, HOW WOULD YOU KNOW? I know she saw that one, but I had gotten addicted now. My signs got crazier each day, and the women on my side decided that I was a kook. They couldn't make heads or tails out of my brilliant screaming posters.

I brought a painted sign in queenly red with huge black letters that said, IS YOUR MOTHER WELL? Roberta took her lunch break and didn't come back for the rest of the day or any day after. Two days later I stopped going too and couldn't have been missed because nobody understood my signs anyway.

It was a nasty six weeks. Classes were suspended and Joseph didn't go to anybody's school until October. The children—everybody's children—soon got bored with that extended vacation they thought was going to be so great. They looked at TV until their eyes flattened. I spent a couple of mornings tutoring my son, as the other mothers said we should. Twice I opened a text from last year that he had never turned in. Twice he yawned in my face. Other mothers organized living room sessions so the kids would keep up. None of the kids could concentrate so they drifted back to *The Price Is Right* and *The Brady Bunch*.[14] When the school finally opened there were fights once or twice and

---

14. *The Price Is Right* and *The Brady Bunch*: A long-running television game show in which contestants win prizes by guessing the price of merchandise; and a sitcom about a blended family that was broadcast from 1969 to 1974 and remained in syndication for decades.

some sirens roared through the streets every once in a while. There were a lot of photographers from Albany. And just when ABC was about to send up a news crew, the kids settled down like nothing in the world had happened. Joseph hung my how would you know? sign in his bedroom. I don't know what became of AND SO DO CHILDREN****. I think my father-in-law cleaned some fish on it. He was always puttering around in our garage. Each of his five children lived in Newburgh and he acted as though he had five extra homes.

I couldn't help looking for Roberta when Joseph graduated from high school, but I didn't see her. It didn't trouble me much what she had said to me in the car. I mean the kicking part. I know I didn't do that, I couldn't do that. But I was puzzled by her telling me Maggie was black. When I thought about it I actually couldn't be certain. She wasn't pitch-black, I knew, or I would have remembered that. What I remember was the kiddie hat, and the semicircle legs. I tried to reassure myself about the race thing for a long time until it dawned on me that the truth was already there, and Roberta knew it. I didn't kick her; I didn't join in with the gar girls and kick that lady, but I sure did want to. We watched and never tried to help her and never called for help. Maggie was my dancing mother. Deaf, I thought, and dumb. Nobody inside. Nobody who would hear you if you cried in the night. Nobody who could tell you anything important that you could use. Rocking, dancing, swaying as she walked. And when the gar girls pushed her down, and started roughhousing, I knew she wouldn't scream, couldn't — just like me — and I was glad about that.

We decided not to have a tree, because Christmas would be at my mother-in-law's house, so why have a tree at both places? Joseph was at SUNY New Paltz[15] and we had to economize, we said. But at the last minute, I changed my mind. Nothing could be that bad. So I rushed around town looking for a tree, something small but wide. By the time I found a place, it was snowing and very late. I dawdled like it was the most important purchase in the world and the tree man was fed up with me. Finally I chose one and had it tied onto the trunk of the car. I drove away slowly because the sand trucks were not out yet and the streets could be murder at the beginning of a snowfall. Downtown the streets were wide and rather empty except for a cluster of people coming out of the Newburgh Hotel. The one hotel in town that wasn't built out of cardboard and Plexiglas. A party, probably. The men huddled in the snow were dressed in tails and the women had on furs. Shiny things glittered from underneath their coats. It made me tired to look at them. Tired, tired, tired. On the next corner was a small diner with loops and loops of paper bells in the window. I stopped the car and went in. Just for a cup of coffee and twenty minutes of peace before I went home and tried to finish everything before Christmas Eve.

"Twyla?"

---

15. **SUNY New Paltz:** State University of New York at New Paltz, eighty miles north of New York City.

There she was. In a silvery evening gown and dark fur coat. A man and another woman were with her, the man fumbling for change to put in the cigarette machine. The woman was humming and tapping on the counter with her fingernails. They all looked a little bit drunk.

"Well. It's you."

"How are you?"

I shrugged. "Pretty good. Frazzled. Christmas and all."

"Regular?" called the woman from the counter.

"Fine," Roberta called back and then, "Wait for me in the car."

She slipped into the booth beside me. "I have to tell you something, Twyla. I made up my mind if I ever saw you again, I'd tell you."

"I'd just as soon not hear anything, Roberta. It doesn't matter now, anyway."

"No," she said. "Not about that."

"Don't be long," said the woman. She carried two regulars to go and the man peeled his cigarette pack as they left.

"It's about St. Bonny's and Maggie."

"Oh, please."

"Listen to me. I really did think she was black. I didn't make that up. I really thought so. But now I can't be sure. I just remember her as old, so old. And because she couldn't talk — well, you know, I thought she was crazy. She'd been brought up in an institution like my mother was and like I thought I would be too. And you were right. We didn't kick her. It was the gar girls. Only them. But, well, I wanted to. I really wanted them to hurt her. I said we did it, too. You and me, but that's not true. And I don't want you to carry that around. It was just that I wanted to do it so bad that day — wanting to is doing it."

Her eyes were watery from the drinks she'd had, I guess. I know it's that way with me. One glass of wine and I start bawling over the littlest thing.

"We were kids, Roberta."

"Yeah. Yeah. I know, just kids."

"Eight."

"Eight."

"And lonely."

"Scared, too."

She wiped her cheeks with the heel of her hand and smiled. "Well, that's all I wanted to say."

I nodded and couldn't think of any way to fill the silence that went from the diner past the paper bells on out into the snow. It was heavy now. I thought I'd better wait for the sand trucks before starting home.

"Thanks, Roberta."

"Sure."

"Did I tell you? My mother, she never did stop dancing."

"Yes. You told me. And mine, she never got well." Roberta lifted her hands from the tabletop and covered her face with her palms. When she took them away she really was crying. "Oh shit, Twyla. Shit, shit, shit. What the hell happened to Maggie?"

[1983]

Sylvia Plath

[1932-1963]

Sylvia Plath

This photograph of Plath was taken during the intense period of writing that preceded her death in 1963, when she was only thirty years old.

Sylvia Plath was born in Boston, Massachusetts, on October 27, 1932. She was the first of two children of Aurelia Schober Plath, a former high-school teacher, and Otto Emil Plath, a professor of German and biology at Boston University. Plath's father, an immigrant from the Prussian area of Germany, spent much of his time doing research on bumblebees, his scientific specialization. In 1940, he refused to seek medical treatment for what proved to be diabetes and died after the amputation of a gangrenous leg. Emotionally and economically devastated by the loss, the family was forced to move from its seaside home in Winthrop to Wellesley, Massachusetts. A brilliant student who loved art, music, and writing, Plath attended public schools in Wellesley and went to Smith College on a scholarship in the fall of 1950, shortly after the first of several of her stories appeared in *Seventeen* magazine. As an undergraduate, she edited the *Smith Review* and published poems in the *Atlantic Monthly, Harper's*, and *Mademoiselle*, for which she served as a guest editor during June 1953. Despite her remarkable successes, she was increasingly anxious about her progress. When she returned home from her internship at *Mademoiselle*, Plath learned that she had not been accepted into a summer-school course in fiction writing at Harvard. She became so severely depressed that she tried to commit suicide by taking an overdose of sleeping pills. Following several months of treatment at a private psychiatric hospital, she returned to Smith, from which she graduated summa cum laude in 1955. She also won numerous awards, including a Fulbright Fellowship to study at Cambridge University in England.

Plath produced a remarkable body of work before her death less than eight years later. At a party in Cambridge, she met the rising young English poet Ted Hughes, and they were married in June 1956. After she earned her master's degree in 1957, the couple moved to the United States, where Plath taught for a year at Smith before she and Hughes moved to Boston. They met a number of American poets, and Plath took a poetry-writing workshop taught by Robert Lowell. She fulfilled a lifelong dream by publishing several poems in the *New Yorker*, and Plath made further strides as a poet during the fall of 1959, which she and Hughes spent at Yaddo, an artists' colony in Saratoga Springs, New York. By then, she was pregnant, and they decided to return to England. Their daughter, Frieda Rebecca Hughes, was born there on April 1, 1960, a few months before Plath's first book, *The Colossus and Other Poems*, was published in London. The following year, she completed an autobiographical novel, and she began sustained work on a new collection of poetry after she and Hughes bought an old house in a small village in Devon. For a time, life in the country went well, and their son, Nicholas Farrar Hughes, was born there in January 1962. Six months later, however, Plath discovered that

Hughes was having an affair, and they separated. Struggling with ill health, isolation, and the challenges of keeping up an old house and caring for her children, Plath nonetheless adhered to a rigorous schedule in which she wrote from four to eight o'clock each morning. "I am writing the best poems of my life," she told a friend in October. She moved with her children to London in December, a month before the publication of her novel, *The Bell Jar*. Outwardly, Plath seemed optimistic about the future, and she continued to write new poems until February 11, 1963, when she committed suicide by breathing the toxic fumes from an unlit gas oven in the kitchen of her small apartment in London.

The handling of Plath's literary estate became a source of heated controversy. Because she died without a will and was still married to Hughes, he became her literary executor. He edited a collection of poems Plath left behind at her death, *Ariel* (1965), which established her as a major poet. As Hughes later admitted, however, he altered her original arrangement and omitted some poems that he described as "personally aggressive," replacing them with other later poems by Plath. Until his death in 1998, Hughes carefully controlled access to Plath's papers and bound journals, at least one of which he destroyed, and he published several more volumes of her writings: two collections of poetry, *Crossing the Water* (1971) and *Winter Trees* (1972); a children's book, *The Bed Book* (1976); and a collection of short stories and prose pieces, *Johnny Panic and the Bible of Dreams* (1979). He also edited her *Collected Poems* (1981), for which Plath was posthumously awarded the Pulitzer Prize. Before his death, Hughes authorized the opening of several volumes of Plath's journals he had previously sealed, and a complete edition of the surviving manuscripts was published in 2000. Plath's daughter, Frieda Hughes, later published a facsimile of the famous manuscript her mother left behind at her death, *Ariel: The Restored Edition* (2004).

We know her because the shape of her words contains the shape of our lives.

–Dave Smith

Reading Plath's Poetry. The precocious Plath, who published her first poem in a Boston newspaper when she was eight years old and as an undergraduate published poems in several national magazines, began to recast herself as a poet after her graduation from college in 1955. She experimented with a wide array of traditional forms and techniques in the tightly controlled poems in her first collection, *The Colossus* (1960), which received several positive reviews in England and was subsequently published in the United States in 1962. In some of the later poems in that volume, Plath began to employ a looser, more colloquial language that captured what she described as her "humor and oddnesses." The poems she wrote during the last two years of her life display an even more striking departure from her early work. Influenced in part by Robert Lowell's *Life Studies* (1959), Plath wrote a series of raw, realistic, and deeply personal poems, some of which were posthumously published in

bedfordstmartins.com/ americanlit for research links on Plath her collection *Ariel* (1965). In his introduction to the volume, Lowell observed that in her late poems "Sylvia Plath becomes herself, becomes something imaginary, newly, wildly, and subtly created – hardly a person at all, or a woman, certainly not another 'poetess,' but one of those super-real, hypnotic, classical heroines." Of those poems, two of the most famous are the pseudo-autobiographical "Daddy" and "Lady Lazarus," fierce dramatic monologues in which the speaker addresses her Prussian father, cast as a Nazi, and evokes images of the Holocaust. As the following selection illustrates, in other late poems Plath explored a range of subjects, including birth, motherhood, the painful lot of women, and the psychically charged landscapes of the natural world. The texts of the following poems, dated and arranged in the order of their composition, are taken from her *Collected Poems*, edited by Ted Hughes (1981).

MORNING SONG

Love set you going like a fat gold watch.
The midwife slapped your footsoles, and your bald cry
Took its place among the elements.

Our voices echo, magnifying your arrival. New statue.
In a drafty museum, your nakedness   5
Shadows our safety. We stand round blankly as walls.

I'm no more your mother
Than the cloud that distills a mirror to reflect its own slow
Effacement at the wind's hand.

All night your moth-breath   10
Flickers among the flat pink roses. I wake to listen:
A far sea moves in my ear.

One cry, and I stumble from bed, cow-heavy and floral
In my Victorian nightgown.
Your mouth opens clean as a cat's. The window square   15

Whitens and swallows its dull stars. And now you try
Your handful of notes;
The clear vowels rise like balloons.

19 February 1961

[1965, 1981]

MIRROR

I am silver and exact. I have no preconceptions.
Whatever I see I swallow immediately
Just as it is, unmisted by love or dislike.

I am not cruel, only truthful—
The eye of a little god, four-cornered.   5
Most of the time I meditate on the opposite wall.
It is pink, with speckles. I have looked at it so long
I think it is a part of my heart. But it flickers.
Faces and darkness separate us over and over.

Now I am a lake. A woman bends over me,   10
Searching my reaches for what she really is.
Then she turns to those liars, the candles or the moon.
I see her back, and reflect it faithfully.
She rewards me with tears and an agitation of hands.
I am important to her. She comes and goes.   15
Each morning it is her face that replaces the darkness.
In me she has drowned a young girl, and in me an old woman
Rises toward her day after day, like a terrible fish.

23 October 1961

[1963, 1981]

DADDY[1]

You do not do, you do not do
Any more, black shoe
In which I have lived like a foot
For thirty years, poor and white,
Barely daring to breathe or Achoo.   5

Daddy, I have had to kill you.
You died before I had time ——
Marble-heavy, a bag full of God,
Ghastly statue with one gray toe[2]
Big as a Frisco seal[3]   10

And a head in the freakish Atlantic
Where it pours bean green over blue

---

1. **Daddy:** In a script for a planned broadcast for the British Broadcasting Company, Plath wrote: "Here is a poem spoken by a girl with an Electra complex. Her father died while she thought he was God. Her case is complicated by the fact that her father was also a Nazi and her mother very possibly part Jewish. In the daughter the two strains marry and paralyze each other — she has to act out the awful little allegory once over before she is free of it."
2. **one gray toe:** Plath's father developed gangrene in his foot, the result of diabetes, and died after amputation surgery in 1940.
3. **Frisco seal:** The large harbor seals native to San Francisco Bay.

In the waters off beautiful Nauset.[4]
I used to pray to recover you.
Ach, du.[5]   15

In the German tongue, in the Polish town
Scraped flat by the roller
Of wars, wars, wars.
But the name of the town is common.
My Polack[6] friend   20

Says there are a dozen or two.
So I never could tell where you
Put your foot, your root,
I never could talk to you.
The tongue stuck in my jaw.   25

It stuck in a barb wire snare.
Ich,[7] ich, ich, ich,
I could hardly speak.
I thought every German was you.
And the language obscene   30

An engine, an engine
Chuffing me off like a Jew.
A Jew to Dachau, Auschwitz, Belsen.[8]
I began to talk like a Jew.
I think I may well be a Jew.   35

The snows of the Tyrol,[9] the clear beer of Vienna
Are not very pure or true.
With my gipsy ancestress and my weird luck
And my Taroc pack and my Taroc pack[10]
I may be a bit of a Jew.   40

I have always been scared of *you*,
With your Luftwaffe,[11] your gobbledygoo.
And your neat mustache

---

4. **Nauset:** An area on the Atlantic Ocean side of Cape Cod, Massachusetts.
5. **Ach, du:** Oh, you (German).
6. **Polack:** Derogatory name for a person of Polish descent.
7. **Ich:** I (German).
8. **Dachau, Auschwitz, Belsen:** Nazi death camps in which millions of Jews were killed during World War II.
9. **Tyrol:** A mountainous Alpine region in western Austria.
10. **Taroc pack:** Similar to tarot cards, used for fortune-telling.
11. **Luftwaffe:** The name of the German air force during World War II.

And your Aryan eye, bright blue.[12]
Panzer-man,[13] panzer-man, O You —— 45

Not God but a swastika
So black no sky could squeak through.
Every woman adores a Fascist,
The boot in the face, the brute
Brute heart of a brute like you. 50

You stand at the blackboard,[14] daddy,
In the picture I have of you,
A cleft in your chin instead of your foot
But no less a devil for that, no not
Any less the black man who 55

Bit my pretty red heart in two.
I was ten when they buried you.
At twenty I tried to die
And get back, back, back to you.
I thought even the bones would do. 60

But they pulled me out of the sack,
And they stuck me together with glue.
And then I knew what to do.
I made a model of you,
A man in black with a Meinkampf[15] look 65

And a love of the rack and the screw.[16]
And I said I do, I do.
So daddy, I'm finally through.
The black telephone's off at the root,
The voices just can't worm through. 70

If I've killed one man, I've killed two ——
The vampire who said he was you
And drank my blood for a year,
Seven years, if you want to know.
Daddy, you can lie back now. 75

There's a stake in your fat black heart
And the villagers never liked you.

---

12. **Aryan eye, bright blue:** In Nazi ideology, Aryans were members of a superior German race characterized by blonde hair and blue eyes.
13. **Panzer-man:** Panzer was the German designation for a tank or armored forces during World War II.
14. **blackboard:** Plath's father was a biology professor at Boston University.
15. **Meinkampf:** My struggle (German), the title of Adolf Hitler's autobiography, *Mein Kampf* (1925).
16. **the rack and the screw:** Medieval instruments of torture.

They are dancing and stamping on you.[17]
They always *knew* it was you.
Daddy, daddy, you bastard, I'm through. 80

12 October 1962

[1965, 1981]

---

17. **There's a stake . . . stamping on you:** An allusion to the folklore that the only way to destroy a vampire is to drive a stake into its heart. A staple of horror movies is an attack by villagers on the castle inhabited by a creature such as Frankenstein's monster or the vampire Count Dracula.

LADY LAZARUS[1]

I have done it again.
One year in every ten
I manage it ——

A sort of walking miracle, my skin
Bright as a Nazi lampshade,[2] 5
My right foot

A paperweight,
My face a featureless, fine
Jew linen.

Peel off the napkin 10
O my enemy.
Do I terrify? ——

The nose, the eye pits, the full set of teeth?
The sour breath
Will vanish in a day. 15

Soon, soon the flesh
The grave cave ate will be
At home on me

And I a smiling woman.
I am only thirty. 20
And like the cat I have nine times to die.

---

1. **Lady Lazarus:** The title alludes to the biblical story in which Lazarus, the brother of Mary, is raised from the dead by Jesus (John 11:39-55). In a script for a planned broadcast for the British Broadcasting Company, Plath wrote: "The speaker is a woman who has the great and terrible gift of being reborn. The only trouble is, she has to die first. She is the phoenix, the libertarian spirit, what you will. She is also just a good, plain, very resourceful woman."
2. **a Nazi lampshade:** According to some reports, the Nazis used the skin of death-camp victims to make lampshades during World War II.

This is Number Three.
What a trash
To annihilate each decade.

What a million filaments. 25
The peanut-crunching crowd
Shoves in to see

Them unwrap me hand and foot[3] ——
The big strip tease.
Gentlemen, ladies 30

These are my hands
My knees.
I may be skin and bone,

Nevertheless, I am the same, identical woman.
The first time it happened I was ten. 35
It was an accident.

The second time I meant
To last it out and not come back at all.
I rocked shut

As a seashell. 40
They had to call and call
And pick the worms off me like sticky pearls.

Dying
Is an art, like everything else.
I do it exceptionally well. 45

I do it so it feels like hell.
I do it so it feels real.
I guess you could say I've a call.

It's easy enough to do it in a cell.
It's easy enough to do it and stay put. 50
It's the theatrical

Comeback in broad day
To the same place, the same face, the same brute
Amused shout:

"A miracle!" 55
That knocks me out.
There is a charge

---

3. **unwrap me hand and foot:** When the resurrected Lazarus emerges from his tomb in a cave, he is "bound hand and foot with graveclothes," which Jesus tells the people to remove. See note 1.

For the eyeing of my scars, there is a charge
For the hearing of my heart —
It really goes.   60

And there is a charge, a very large charge
For a word or a touch
Or a bit of blood

Or a piece of my hair or my clothes.
So, so, Herr Doktor.⁴   65
So, Herr Enemy.

I am your opus,
I am your valuable,
The pure gold baby

That melts to a shriek.   70
I turn and burn.
Do not think I underestimate your great concern.

Ash, ash⁵ —
You poke and stir.
Flesh, bone, there is nothing there ——   75

A cake of soap,
A wedding ring,
A gold filling.⁶

Herr God, Herr Lucifer
Beware   80
Beware.

Out of the ash
I rise with my red hair
And I eat men like air.⁷

23-29 October 1962

[1965, 1981]

---

4. **Herr Doktor:** Mr. Doctor, a respectful title for a male who has obtained a doctorate degree (German).
5. **Ash, ash:** A reference to the ashes of those who were gassed and cremated in the Nazi death camps.
6. **A cake of soap . . . gold filling:** The Nazis made soap from the human fat of death-camp victims, whose wedding rings and gold tooth fillings were melted down into gold bars.
7. **Out . . . air:** The phoenix is a mythical bird with red and gold plumage, the colors of the rising sun. After living for centuries, it burns itself on a funeral pyre and is reborn from the ashes.

John Updike

[1932–2009]

John Hoyer Updike was born on March 18, 1932, in Reading, Pennsylvania. He was the only child of Wesley Russell Updike, a high-school mathematics teacher, and Linda Grace Hoyer Updike, a homemaker and department-store clerk who dreamed of becoming a writer. The family lived with her parents in the small town of Shillington until 1945, when to Updike's deep distress they moved to an isolated farm in nearby Plowville. In his memoirs, *Consciousness* (1989), Updike recalled that his childhood was defined by his Lutheran upbringing, the source of his ongoing concern with the decline of religious faith, and his severe case of psoriasis, a skin disease that made him deeply self-conscious. At the same time, he suggested that "whenever in my timid life I have shown some courage and originality it has been because of my skin." His mother encouraged his interest in writing and art, and Updike decided that he would become a famous cartoonist for magazines such as the *New Yorker.* An outstanding student, he went to Harvard University on a full scholarship in 1950. He majored in English and contributed articles, cartoons, and sketches to the undergraduate humor magazine, the *Harvard Lampoon.* At the end of his junior year, he married Mary Pennington, a student at Radcliffe, then a women's college affiliated with Harvard. Updike graduated from Harvard summa cum laude in 1954 and won a fellowship to study at the Ruskin School of Drawing and Fine Art in Oxford, England. But he turned to writing when one of his stories was accepted by the *New Yorker,* which hired Updike as a staff writer when he and his wife returned from England in 1955.

John Updike
This photograph of the best-selling author was taken at his home in Beverly, Massachusetts, in 1991.

After two years with the magazine, for which he wrote the popular column "Talk of the Town," Updike resigned to devote himself full-time to writing in 1957. Leaving New York City, he moved his family to Ipswich, a coastal town north of Boston. By 1960, he and his wife had four children. A disciplined and prolific writer, Updike initially supported the family by selling essays, poems, and especially stories to the *New Yorker.* His first book of poetry, *The Carpentered Hen and Other Tame Creatures* (1958), was swiftly followed by his first novel, *The Poorhouse Fair,* and the first of his numerous collections of stories, *The Same Door,* both of which were published in 1959. A Guggenheim Fellowship supported his work on his acclaimed novel *Rabbit, Run* (1960), in which Updike introduced his best-known character, Harry "Rabbit" Angstrom, a self-centered former high-school athlete who struggles to come to terms with the responsibilities of marriage and fatherhood. *The Centaur* (1963), a modernist novel weaving together Greek mythology and the story of a schoolteacher and his son, based on Updike's relationship with his father, won the National Book Award. Updike continued to draw upon his personal past in stories and in a novel about his relationship with his mother, *Of the Farm* (1965). He turned his attention to the social and sexual dislocations of the troubled present in *Couples* (1968), an unusually explicit novel about marital infidelity set in suburban New England. The book was on the *New York Times* bestseller list for nearly a year, and Updike was featured on the cover of *Time* magazine in April 1968.

Updike remained one of the most prominent and successful writers in the United States. He continued his chronicle of Harry Angstrom's life and times in *Rabbit Redux* (1971) and later in two Pulitzer Prize-winning novels, *Rabbit Is Rich* (1981) and *Rabbit at Rest* (1990). In 1974, Updike and his wife separated, and he began a new life with his second wife, Martha Ruggles Bernhard, in Georgetown, Massachusetts. Further exploring the theme of adultery, Updike recast Nathaniel Hawthorne's *The Scarlet Letter* in a trilogy of novels, *A Month of Sundays* (1975), *Roger's Version* (1986), and *S.* (1988). Although he is most often thought of as the novelist of white suburban life, Updike ventured into very different terrain in *The Coup* (1978), a novel about a dictator in a mythical African nation, and later in *Brazil* (1994). Although the reception of his late work has been mixed, critics praised *In the Beauty of the Lilies* (1996), his ambitious novel about the decline of an American family through four generations, from 1910 to 1990. Still experimenting with various forms and techniques, Updike tried his hand at a postmodern novel in *Gertrude and Claudius* (1999), a prequel to Shakespeare's *Hamlet*. Updike's diverse work also included his seventh collection of poetry, *Americana and Other Poems* (2001); a collection of stories about one of the recurrent characters in his fiction, *The Complete Henry Beck* (2001); and a novel told from the point of view of an American-born Islamic fundamentalist and would-be suicide bomber, *Terrorist: A Novel* (2007). The author of over fifty books, including more than twenty novels, Updike lived with his wife in Beverly Farms, Massachusetts, until his death from cancer on January 27, 2009, at the age of 76. In one of many tributes, the novelist Philip Roth declared that "John Updike is our time's greatest man of letters, as brilliant a literary critic and essayist as he was a novelist and short story writer. He is and always will be no less a national treasure than his nineteenth-century precursor, Nathaniel Hawthorne."

John Updike's genius is best excited by the lyric possibilities of tragic events that, failing to justify themselves as tragedy, turn unaccountably into comedies.

—Joyce Carol Oates

Reading Updike's "A & P."   In the introduction to his collection *The Early Stories, 1953–1975* (2003), Updike fondly recalled his early career in Ipswich, Massachusetts, where he moved from New York City with his growing family in 1957. "Out there was where I belonged, immersed in the ordinary, which careful explication would reveal to be extraordinary," he affirmed. He thus described writing his numerous stories on a manual typewriter in a small room "where my only duty was to describe reality as it had come to me – to give the mundane its beautiful due." Updike's sensitivity to the particulars of time and place, as well as his ability to discover something remarkable amid seemingly commonplace characters, events, and settings, is revealed in "A & P," one of his most popular and frequently anthologized stories. Written in 1960 and published the following year in the *New Yorker*, the story is narrated by Sammy, who describes a few momentous minutes in an otherwise uneventful day back when he was nineteen and working as a cashier in a supermarket in suburban New

bedfordstmartins.com/ americanlit *for research links on Updike*

England. At the end of this coming-of-age story, Sammy makes a crucial decision, the motivation, nature, and consequences of which may well be fully understood by him only in retrospect. The text is taken from *Pigeon Feathers and Other Stories* (1962).

A & P[1]

In walks these three girls in nothing but bathing suits. I'm in the third checkout slot, with my back to the door, so I don't see them until they're over by the bread. The one that caught my eye first was the one in the plaid green two-piece. She was a chunky kid, with a good tan and a sweet broad soft-looking can with those two crescents of white just under it, where the sun never seems to hit, at the top of the backs of her legs. I stood there with my hand on a box of HiHo crackers trying to remember if I rang it up or not. I ring it up again and the customer starts giving me hell. She's one of these cash-register-watchers, a witch about fifty with rouge on her cheekbones and no eyebrows, and I know it made her day to trip me up. She'd been watching cash registers for fifty years and probably never seen a mistake before.

By the time I got her feathers smoothed and her goodies into a bag — she gives me a little snort in passing, if she'd been born at the right time they would have burned her over in Salem[2] — by the time I get her on her way the girls had circled around the bread and were coming back, without a pushcart, back my way along the counters, in the aisle between the checkouts and the Special bins. They didn't even have shoes on. There was this chunky one, with the two-piece — it was bright green and the seams on the bra were still sharp and her belly was still pretty pale so I guessed she just got it (the suit) — there was this one, with one of those chubby berry-faces, the lips all bunched together under her nose, this one, and a tall one, with black hair that hadn't quite frizzed right, and one of these sunburns right across under the eyes, and a chin that was too long — you know, the kind of girl other girls think is very "striking" and "attractive" but never quite makes it, as they very well know, which is why they like her so much — and then the third one, that wasn't quite so tall. She was the queen. She kind of led them, the other two peeking around and making their shoulders round. She didn't look around, not this queen, she just walked straight on slowly, on these long white prima-donna legs. She came down a little hard on her heels, as if she didn't walk in her bare feet that much, putting down her heels and then letting the weight move along to her toes as if she was testing the floor with every step, putting a little deliberate extra action into it. You never know for sure how girls' minds work (do you really think it's a mind in there or just a little buzz like a bee in a glass jar?) but you got the idea she had talked the other two into coming in here with her, and now she was showing them how to do it, walk slow and hold yourself straight.

She had on a kind of dirty-pink — beige maybe, I don't know — bathing suit with a little nubble all over it and, what got me, the straps were down. They were off her shoulders

---

1. **A & P:** The name of a supermarket chain owned by the Great Atlantic and Pacific Tea Company.
2. **Salem:** A town in Massachusetts famous for a notorious series of witchcraft trials in 1692.

looped loose around the cool tops of her arms, and I guess as a result the suit had slipped a little on her, so all around the top of the cloth there was this shining rim. If it hadn't been there you wouldn't have known there could have been anything whiter than those shoulders. With the straps pushed off, there was nothing between the top of the suit and the top of her head except just *her*, this clean bare plane of the top of her chest down from the shoulder bones like a dented sheet of metal tilted in the light. I mean, it was more than pretty.

She had sort of oaky hair that the sun and salt had bleached, done up in a bun that was unravelling, and a kind of prim face. Walking into the A & P with your straps down, I suppose it's the only kind of face you *can* have. She held her head so high her neck, coming up out of those white shoulders, looked kind of stretched, but I didn't mind. The longer her neck was, the more of her there was.

She must have felt in the corner of her eye me and over my shoulder Stokesie in the second slot watching, but she didn't tip. Not this queen. She kept her eyes moving across the racks, and stopped, and turned so slow it made my stomach rub the inside of my apron, and buzzed to the other two, who kind of huddled against her for relief, and then they all three of them went up the cat-and-dog-food-breakfast-cereal-macaroni-rice-raisins-seasonings-spreads-spaghetti-soft-drinks-crackers-and-cookies aisle. From the third slot I look straight up this aisle to the meat counter, and I watched them all the way. The fat one with the tan sort of fumbled with the cookies, but on second thought she put the package back. The sheep pushing their carts down the aisle—the girls were walking against the usual traffic (not that we have one-way signs or anything)—were pretty hilarious. You could see them, when Queenie's white shoulders dawned on them, kind of jerk, or hop, or hiccup, but their eyes snapped back to their own baskets and on they pushed. I bet you could set off dynamite in an A & P and the people would by and large keep reaching and checking oatmeal off their lists and muttering "Let me see, there was a third thing, began with A, asparagus, no, ah, yes, applesauce!" or whatever it is they do mutter. But there was no doubt, this jiggled them. A few houseslaves in pin curlers even looked around after pushing their carts past to make sure what they had seen was correct.

You know, it's one thing to have a girl in a bathing suit down on the beach, where what with the glare nobody can look at each other much anyway, and another thing in the cool of the A & P, under the fluorescent lights, against all those stacked packages, with her feet paddling along naked over our checkerboard green-and-cream rubber-tile floor.

"Oh Daddy," Stokesie said beside me. "I feel so faint."

"Darling," I said. "Hold me tight." Stokesie's married, with two babies chalked up on his fuselage already, but as far as I can tell that's the only difference. He's twenty-two, and I was nineteen this April.

"Is it done?" he asks, the responsible married man finding his voice. I forgot to say he thinks he's going to be manager some sunny day, maybe in 1990 when it's called the Great Alexandrov and Petrooshki Tea Company or something.

What he meant was, our town is five miles from a beach, with a big summer colony out on the Point, but we're right in the middle of town, and the women generally put on a shirt or shorts or something before they get out of the car into the street. And anyway these are usually women with six children and varicose veins mapping their legs and nobody, including them, could care less. As I say, we're right in the middle of town, and if you stand at our front doors you can see two banks and the Congregational church and the newspaper store and three real-estate offices and about twenty-seven old freeloaders tearing up Central Street because the sewer broke again. It's not as if we're on the Cape;[3] we're north of Boston and there's people in this town haven't seen the ocean for twenty years.

The girls had reached the meat counter and were asking McMahon something. He pointed, they pointed, and they shuffled out of sight behind a pyramid of Diet Delight peaches. All that was left for us to see was old McMahon patting his mouth and looking after them sizing up their joints. Poor kids, I began to feel sorry for them, they couldn't help it.

Now here comes the sad part of the story, at least my family says it's sad, but I don't think it's so sad myself. The store's pretty empty, it being Thursday afternoon, so there was nothing much to do except lean on the register and wait for the girls to show up again. The whole store was like a pinball machine and I didn't know which tunnel they'd come out of. After a while they come around out of the far aisle, around the light bulbs, records at discount of the Caribbean Six or Tony Martin Sings[4] or some such gunk you wonder they waste the wax on, sixpacks of candy bars, and plastic toys done up in cellophane that fall apart when a kid looks at them anyway. Around they come, Queenie still leading the way, and holding a little gray jar in her hand. Slots Three through Seven are unmanned and I could see her wondering between Stokes and me, but Stokesie with his usual luck draws an old party in baggy gray pants who stumbles up with four giant cans of pineapple juice (what do these bums *do* with all that pineapple juice? I've often asked myself) so the girls come to me. Queenie puts down the jar and I take it into my fingers icy cold. Kingfish Fancy Herring Snacks in Pure Sour Cream: 49¢. Now her hands are empty, not a ring or a bracelet, bare as God made them, and I wonder where the money's coming from. Still with that prim look she lifts a folded dollar bill out of the hollow at the center of her nubbled pink top. The jar went heavy in my hand. Really, I thought that was so cute.

Then everybody's luck begins to run out. Lengel comes in from haggling with a truck full of cabbages on the lot and is about to scuttle into that door marked MANAGER behind which he hides all day when the girls touch his eye. Lengel's pretty dreary, teaches Sunday school and the rest, but he doesn't miss that much. He comes over and says, "Girls, this isn't the beach."

Queenie blushes, though maybe it's just a brush of sunburn I was noticing for the first time, now that she was so close. "My mother asked me to pick up a jar of herring snacks." Her voice kind of startled me, the way voices do when you see the people first, coming out so flat and dumb yet kind of tony, too, the way it ticked over "pick up" and "snacks." All of a sudden I slid right down her voice into her living room. Her father and the other men were standing around in ice-cream coats and bow ties and the women were in sandals picking up herring snacks on toothpicks off a big glass plate and they

---

3. the Cape: Cape Cod, Massachusetts, which juts out sixty-five miles into the Atlantic Ocean.
4. the Caribbean Six or Tony Martin Sings: Long-playing records by an unidentified group, possibly an ironic reference to the popularity of calypso music in the late 1950s, and by the romantic singer and actor who had a number of hits during the 1950s.

were all holding drinks the color of water with olives and sprigs of mint in them. When my parents have somebody over they get lemonade and if it's a real racy affair Schlitz in tall glasses with "They'll Do It Every Time" cartoons stencilled on.[5]

"That's all right," Lengel said. "But this isn't the beach." His repeating this struck me as funny, as if it had just occurred to him, and he had been thinking all these years the A & P was a great big dune and he was the head lifeguard. He didn't like my smiling – as I say he doesn't miss much – but he concentrates on giving the girls that sad Sunday-school-superintendent stare.

Queenie's blush is no sunburn now, and the plump one in plaid, that I liked better from the back – a really sweet can – pipes up, "We weren't doing any shopping. We just came in for the one thing."

"That makes no difference," Lengel tells her, and I could see from the way his eyes went that he hadn't noticed she was wearing a two-piece before. "We want you decently dressed when you come in here."

"We *are* decent," Queenie says suddenly, her lower lip pushing, getting sore now that she remembers her place, a place from which the crowd that runs the A & P must look pretty crummy. Fancy Herring Snacks flashed in her very blue eyes.

"Girls, I don't want to argue with you. After this come in here with your shoulders covered. It's our policy." He turns his back. That's policy for you. Policy is what the king-pins want. What the others want is juvenile delinquency.

All this while, the customers had been showing up with their carts but, you know, sheep, seeing a scene, they had all bunched up on Stokesie, who shook open a paper bag as gently as peeling a peach, not wanting to miss a word. I could feel in the silence everybody getting nervous, most of all Lengel, who asks me, "Sammy, have you rung up their purchase?"

I thought and said "No" but it wasn't about that I was thinking. I go through the punches, 4, 9, GROC, TOT – it's more complicated than you think, and after you do it often enough, it begins to make a little song, that you hear words to, in my case "Hello (*bing*) there, you (*gung*) hap-py *pee*-pul (*splat*)!" – the *splat* being the drawer flying out. I uncrease the bill, tenderly as you may imagine, it just having come from between the two smoothest scoops of vanilla I had ever known were there, and pass a half and a penny into her narrow pink palm, and nestle the herrings in a bag and twist its neck and hand it over, all the time thinking.

The girls, and who'd blame them, are in a hurry to get out, so I say "I quit" to Lengel quick enough for them to hear, hoping they'll stop and watch me, their unsuspected hero. They keep right on going, into the electric eye; the door flies open and they flicker across the lot to their car, Queenie and Plaid and Big Tall Goony-Goony (not that as raw material she was so bad), leaving me with Lengel and a kink in his eyebrow.

"Did you say something, Sammy?"

"I said I quit."

"I thought you did."

---

5. **Schlitz . . . cartoons stencilled on:** One of the top-selling American beers of the 1950s, served in glasses with panels from the long-running newspaper comic strip "*They'll Do It Every Time*," which became a catch-phrase for the quirks, oddities, and hypocrisies of human behavior.

"You didn't have to embarrass them."

"It was they who were embarrassing us."

I started to say something that came out "Fiddle-de-doo." It's a saying of my grand-mother's, and I know she would have been pleased.

"I don't think you know what you're saying," Lengel said.

"I know you don't," I said. "But I do." I pull the bow at the back of my apron and start shrugging it off my shoulders. A couple customers that had been heading for my slot begin to knock against each other, like scared pigs in a chute.

Lengel sighs and begins to look very patient and old and gray. He's been a friend of my parents for years. "Sammy, you don't want to do this to your Mom and Dad," he tells me. It's true, I don't. But it seems to me that once you begin a gesture it's fatal not to go through with it. I fold the apron, "Sammy" stitched in red on the pocket, and put it on the counter, and drop the bow tie on top of it. The bow tie is theirs, if you've ever won-dered. "You'll feel this for the rest of your life," Lengel says, and I know that's true, too, but remembering how he made that pretty girl blush makes me so scrunchy inside I punch the No Sale tab and the machine whirs "pee-pul" and the drawer splats out. One advantage to this scene taking place in summer, I can follow this up with a clean exit, there's no fumbling around getting your coat and galoshes, I just saunter into the elec-tric eye in my white shirt that my mother ironed the night before, and the door heaves itself open, and outside the sunshine is skating around on the asphalt.

I look around for my girls, but they're gone, of course. There wasn't anybody but some young married screaming with her children about some candy they didn't get by the door of a powder-blue Falcon station wagon. Looking back in the big windows, over the bags of peat moss and aluminum lawn furniture stacked on the pavement, I could see Lengel in my place in the slot, checking the sheep through. His face was dark gray and his back stiff, as if he'd just had an injection of iron, and my stomach kind of fell as I felt how hard the world was going to be to me hereafter.

[1961, 1962]

Amiri Baraka
(LeRoi Jones)

[b. 1934]

Everett LeRoy Jones was born in Newark, New Jersey, on October 7, 1934, to Coyette LeRoy Jones, a postal worker, and Anna Lois Jones, a social worker. In a 1998 interview, Baraka recalled that his parents had strongly encour-aged their children to excel:

> [T]hey always told me: y'all are the smartest colored kids on the planet. They gave me piano lessons, trumpet lessons, drum lessons, piano lessons, paint-ing lessons. I used to sing *Ave Maria* with my sister. I used to recite the Get-tysburg Address every Lincoln's birthday in a Boy Scout suit for about six years—this was my mama. The point is that for them two Negroes right

In Africa, a griot is the cultural historian. He or she must remember what the people were like so those people can learn who they are and what they can become. Amiri Baraka is, absolutely, a griot.

—Maya Angelou

there, they knew what they were going to do, they were going to give us all the information in the world, and they was going to equip us to go out and fight the White people.

Amiri Baraka

This photograph of the leader of the Black Arts Movement was taken in Pittsburgh in 1971.

Baraka, an outstanding student who began writing stories at an early age, graduated in 1951 from a predominantly white high school and was awarded a science scholarship at the Newark campus of Rutgers University. There, he made the first change to his name, altering the spelling of his first name to "LeRoi." In 1952, he decided to attend a historically black college and transferred to Howard University in Washington, D.C., where he studied music, especially blues and jazz, and worked with the poet Sterling Brown. Baraka, however, found the conservative atmosphere of the school oppressive and was bored by his studies. In 1954, during his senior year, he flunked out and joined the air force.

While he was stationed in Puerto Rico, Baraka read constantly and began writing poetry. In his autobiography, he later said that he realized that he could never write like the white poets whose work regularly appeared in the *New Yorker*. He consequently determined to find outlets that would be receptive to his very different voice. After his term of enlistment ended in 1957, he settled in bohemian Greenwich Village, where he met and was influenced by a number of avant-garde and Beat poets, including Allen Ginsberg. In 1958, Baraka married Hettie Cohen, a Jewish intellectual with whom he founded Totem Press and the literary magazine *Yugen.* He also published poetry in other little magazines such as *Naked Ear* and *Kulchur*. With the help of Langston Hughes, who admired one of his poems, Baraka was awarded a creative-writing fellowship, and his poems appeared in the influential anthology *The New American Poetry: 1945-1960* (1960). In 1961, he published his first book of poetry, *Preface to a Twenty Volume Suicide Note.* That year, he and the Beat poet Diane di Prima established the *Floating Bear*, an underground newsletter of Greenwich Village, and formed an experimental theatrical group, the New York Poets Theatre. In addition to his classic study *Blues People: Negro Music in White America* (1963), Baraka wrote several short plays about the oppression of black people in the United States, including *Dutchman*, an explosive drama that made him famous when it was produced and published in 1964. His growing engagement in the civil rights struggle was also revealed in his second collection of poems, *The Dead Lecturer* (1964), and in an autobiographical novel in which he explored issues of racial consciousness and identity, *The System of Dante's Hell* (1965).

Baraka's later writings have been strongly shaped by his radical politics. In 1965, following the assassination of his hero Malcolm X, Baraka effectively turned his back on the white world and renounced his earlier, bohemian life in Greenwich Village. Leaving his white wife and their two daughters, he moved to Harlem, where he and other artists formed the Black Arts Repertory Theatre/School in the spring of 1965. The short-lived organization was a key institution in the development of the Black Arts Movement, and Baraka's Black Nationalist ideals also found expression in a series of experimental stories, *Tales* (1967); in *Four Black Revolutionary Plays* (1968); and in two new collections of his poetry, *Black Magic* (1969) and *It's Nation Time* (1970). Meanwhile, he married the poet Sylvia Robinson in 1966, and they moved back to Newark, New Jersey. To affirm their African heritage and Black Nationalist beliefs, they adopted Bantuized Muslim names, Amina Baraka and Iamamu Ameer Baraka, later Amiri Baraka. In 1974, however, he publicly declared that Black Nationalism was a form of racism and became a Third World Marxist. The first of his numerous socialist works was a collection of poetry, *Hard Facts* (1975), published the year he began teaching at the State University of New York at Stony Brook. He was also a frequent lecturer at the Jack Kerouac School of Disembodied Poetics, cofounded by his old friend Allen Ginsberg. Following his arrest during an alleged dispute with his wife, Baraka was sentenced to serve time in a halfway house, where he wrote *The Autobiography of LeRoi Jones/Amiri Baraka* (1984; expanded 1997). He continued to publish essays, plays, and poetry, notably *WISE, WHY'S, Y's* (1995), part of a poem-in-progress on the African American experience. While serving as the Poet Laureate of New Jersey in 2002, Baraka wrote a controversial poem, "Somebody Blew Up America," in response to the September 11 attacks on the World Trade Center. Many viewed the poem as anti-Semitic, but Baraka vigorously defended himself, calling the criticism "an attempt to repress and stigmatize independent thinkers everywhere." Prompted by the governor, the state senate abolished the position of Poet Laureate in 2003. Baraka's most recent work is a critically acclaimed collection of stories dating from 1974 to the present, *Tales of the Out & the Gone* (2006).

Reading Baraka's *Dutchman*.   This play was first performed on March 24, 1964, at the Cherry Lane Theatre, an Off-Broadway theater founded by a group of artists in the 1920s and long known for fostering the development of experimental drama in the United States. *Dutchman* was the final play of a triple bill, following one-act plays by the Irish playwright Samuel Beckett and the Spanish playwright Fernando Arrabal. Baraka's searing study of racism and repressed black rage stole the show and generated intense controversy. The reviewer for the *New York Times* wrote that everything about the play was "designed to shock—its basic idea, its language and its murderous rage." At the same time, *Dutchman* won the Off-Broadway Theater Award (Obie) for Best American Play of 1963-64. Five years later, the theater critic for the *New York Times* called *Dutchman* "the best short play ever written in this country," adding that "black playwrighting began a new era with its production, an era that has not yet ended and has not yet seen the play's equal." Baraka, who has said that the play "is about the difficulty of becoming a man in America," dramatized a fateful encounter in the subway between a twenty-year-old black male, Clay, and an older white woman, Lula. Despite its realistic setting, the style of the play is essentially antinaturalistic, combining poetic language, rich symbolism, and a range of mythological associations, including the temptation scene in the Garden of Eden. Baraka originally planned to call the play "The Flying Dutchman," a reference to the legend of a spectral ship doomed endlessly to sail the seas unless its captain is released from the curse by the love of a faithful woman. In an interview, Baraka explained:

Dutchman

The first production of Baraka's acclaimed play, which was directed by Edward Parone and produced by Edward Albee, Richard Barr, and Clinton Wilder, featured Robert Hooks as Clay and Jennifer West as Lula.

bedfordstmartins.com/
americanlit for research
links on Baraka

"You know the 'Dutchman' was really the train; that was the flying in it. But then there was a lot of ambiguity in it in my mind. I didn't know if I wanted the train to be the Dutchman or the dude to be the Dutchman or the woman to be the Dutchman." The text is taken from its first publication in *Dutchman and The Slave* (1964).

DUTCHMAN

CHARACTERS

CLAY, *twenty-year-old Negro*
LULA, *thirty-year-old white woman*
RIDERS OF COACH, *white and black*
YOUNG NEGRO
CONDUCTOR

In the flying underbelly of the city. Steaming hot, and summer on top, outside. Underground. The subway heaped in modern myth.

Opening scene is a man sitting in a subway seat, holding a magazine but looking vacantly just above its wilting pages. Occasionally he looks blankly toward the window on his right. Dim lights and darkness whistling by against the glass. (Or paste the lights, as admitted props, right on the subway windows. Have them move, even dim and flicker. But give the sense of speed. Also stations, whether the train is stopped or the glitter and activity of these stations merely flashes by the windows.)

The man is sitting alone. That is, only his seat is visible, though the rest of the car is outfitted as a complete subway car. But only his seat is shown. There might be, for a time, as the play begins, a loud scream of the actual train. And it can recur throughout the play, or continue on a lower key once the dialogue starts.

The train slows after a time, pulling to a brief stop at one of the stations. The man looks idly up, until he sees a woman's face staring at him through the window, when it realizes that the man has noticed the face, it begins very premeditatedly to smile. The man smiles too, for a moment, without a trace of self-consciousness. Almost an instinctive though undesirable response. Then a kind of awkwardness or embarrassment sets in, and the man makes to look away, is further embarrassed, so he brings back his eyes to where the face was, but by now the train is moving again, and the face would seem to be left behind by the way the man turns his head to look back through the other windows at the slowly fading platform. He smiles then; more comfortably confident, hoping perhaps that his memory of this brief encounter will be pleasant. And then he is idle again.

SCENE I

Train roars. Lights flash outside the windows.

LULA *enters from the rear of the car in bright, skimpy summer clothes and sandals. She carries a net bag full of paper books, fruit, and other anonymous articles. She is wearing sunglasses, which she pushes up on her forehead from time to time.* LULA *is a tall, slender, beautiful woman with long red hair hanging straight down her back, wearing only loud lipstick in somebody's good taste. She is eating an apple, very daintily. Coming down the car toward* CLAY.

She stops beside CLAY's *seat and hangs languidly from the strap, still managing to eat the apple. It is apparent that she is going to sit in the seat next to* CLAY, *and that she is only waiting for him to notice her before she sits.*

CLAY *sits as before, looking just beyond his magazine, now and again pulling the magazine slowly back and forth in front of his face in a hopeless effort to fan himself. Then he sees the woman hanging there beside him and he looks up into her face, smiling quizzically.*

LULA: Hello.

CLAY: Uh, hi're you?

LULA: I'm going to sit down. . . . O.K.?

CLAY: Sure.

LULA: (*Swings down onto the seat, pushing her legs straight out as if she is very weary*) Oooof! Too much weight.

CLAY: Ha, doesn't look like much to me. (*Leaning back against the window, a little surprised and maybe stiff*)

LULA: It's so anyway. (*And she moves her toes in the sandals, then pulls her right leg up on the left knee, better to inspect the bottoms of the sandals and the back of her heel. She appears for a second not to notice that* CLAY *is sitting next to her or that she has spoken to him just a second before.* CLAY *looks at the magazine, then out the black window. As he does this, she turns very quickly toward him*) Weren't you staring at me through the window?

CLAY: (*Wheeling around and very much stiffened*) What?

LULA: Weren't you staring at me through the window? At the last stop?

CLAY: Staring at you? What do you mean?

LULA: Don't you know what staring means?

CLAY: I saw you through the window . . . if that's what it means. I don't know if I was staring. Seems to me you were staring through the window at me.

LULA: I was. But only after I'd turned around and saw you staring through that window down in the vicinity of my ass and legs.

CLAY: Really?

LULA: Really. I guess you were just taking those idle potshots. Nothing else to do. Run your mind over people's flesh.

CLAY: Oh boy. Wow, now I admit I was looking in your direction. But the rest of that weight is yours.

LULA: I suppose.

CLAY: Staring through train windows is weird business. Much weirder than staring very sedately at abstract asses.

LULA: That's why I came looking through the window . . . so you'd have more than that to go on. I even smiled at you.

CLAY: That's right.

LULA: I even got into this train, going some other way than mine. Walked down the aisle . . . searching you out.

CLAY: Really? That's pretty funny.

LULA: That's pretty funny. . . . God, you're dull.

CLAY: Well, I'm sorry, lady, but I really wasn't prepared for party talk.

LULA: No, you're not. What are you prepared for? (*Wrapping the apple core in a Kleenex and dropping it on the floor*)

CLAY: (*Takes her conversation as pure sex talk. He turns to confront her squarely with this idea*) I'm prepared for anything. How about you?

LULA: (*Laughing loudly and cutting it off abruptly*) What do you think you're doing?

CLAY: What?

LULA: You think I want to pick you up, get you to take me somewhere and screw me, huh?

CLAY: Is that the way I look?

LULA: You look like you been trying to grow a beard. That's exactly what you look like. You look like you live in New Jersey with your parents and are trying to grow a beard. That's what. You look like you've been reading Chinese poetry and drinking luke-warm sugarless tea. (*Laughs, uncrossing and recrossing her legs*) You look like death eating a soda cracker.

CLAY: (*Cocking his head from one side to the other, embarrassed and trying to make some comeback, but also intrigued by what the woman is saying . . . even the sharp city coarseness of her voice, which is still a kind of gentle sidewalk throb*) Really? I look like all that?

LULA: Not all of it. (*She feints a seriousness to cover an actual somber tone*) I lie a lot. (*Smiling*) It helps me control the world.

CLAY: (*Relieved and laughing louder than the humor*) Yeah, I bet.

LULA: But it's true, most of it, right? Jersey? Your bumpy neck?

CLAY: How'd you know all that? Huh? Really, I mean about Jersey . . . and even the beard. I met you before? You know Warren Enright?

LULA: You tried to make it with your sister when you were ten. (CLAY *leans back hard against the back of the seat, his eyes opening now, still trying to look amused*) But I succeeded a few weeks ago. (*She starts to laugh again*)

CLAY: What're you talking about? Warren tell you that? You're a friend of Georgia's?

LULA: I told you I lie. I don't know your sister. I don't know Warren Enright.

CLAY: You mean you're just picking these things out of the air?

LULA: Is Warren Enright a tall skinny black black boy with a phony English accent?

CLAY: I figured you knew him.

LULA: But I don't. I just figured you would know somebody like that. (*Laughs*)

CLAY: Yeah, yeah.

LULA: You're probably on your way to his house now.

CLAY: That's right.

LULA: (*Putting her hand on Clay's closest knee, drawing it from the knee up to the thigh's hinge, then removing it, watching his face very closely, and continuing to laugh, perhaps more gently than before*) Dull, dull, dull. I bet you think I'm exciting.

CLAY: You're O.K.

LULA: Am I exciting you now?

CLAY: Right. That's not what's supposed to happen?

LULA: How do I know? (*She returns her hand, without moving it, then takes it away and plunges it in her bag to draw out an apple*) You want this?

CLAY: Sure.

LULA: (*She gets one out of the bag for herself*) Eating apples together is always the first step. Or walking up uninhabited Seventh Avenue in the twenties on weekends.[1] (*Bites and giggles, glancing at Clay and speaking in loose singsong*) Can get you involved . . . boy! Get us involved. Um-huh. (*Mock seriousness*) Would you like to get involved with me, Mister Man?

CLAY: (*Trying to be as flippant as Lula, whacking happily at the apple*) Sure. Why not? A beautiful woman like you. Huh, I'd be a fool not to.

LULA: And I bet you're sure you know what you're talking about. (*Taking him a little roughly by the wrist, so he cannot eat the apple, then shaking the wrist*) I bet you're

---

1. **Or walking . . . weekends:** At the time, the west twenties was a primarily commercial area whose major office buildings were on Seventh Avenue.

sure of almost everything anybody ever asked you about . . . right? (*Shakes his wrist harder*) Right?

CLAY: Yeah, right. . . . Wow, you're pretty strong, you know? Whatta you, a lady wrestler or something?

LULA: What's wrong with lady wrestlers? And don't answer because you never knew any. Huh. (*Cynically*) That's for sure. They don't have any lady wrestlers in that part of Jersey. That's for sure.

CLAY: Hey, you still haven't told me how you know so much about me.

LULA: I told you I didn't know anything about *you* . . . you're a well-known type.

CLAY: Really?

LULA: Or at least I know the type very well. And your skinny English friend too.

CLAY: Anonymously?

LULA: (*Settles back in seat, single-mindedly finishing her apple and humming snatches of rhythm and blues song*) What?

CLAY: Without knowing us specifically?

LULA: Oh boy. (*Looking quickly at Clay*) What a face. You know, you could be a handsome man.

CLAY: I can't argue with you.

LULA: (*Vague, off-center response*) What?

CLAY: (*Raising his voice, thinking the train noise has drowned part of his sentence*) I can't argue with you.

LULA: My hair is turning gray. A gray hair for each year and type I've come through.

CLAY: Why do you want to sound so old?

LULA: But it's always gentle when it starts. (*Attention drifting*) Hugged against tenements, day or night.

CLAY: What?

LULA: (*Refocusing*) Hey, why don't you take me to that party you're going to?

CLAY: You must be a friend of Warren's to know about the party.

LULA: Wouldn't you like to take me to the party? (*Imitates clinging vine*) Oh, come on, ask me to your party.

CLAY: Of course I'll ask you to come with me to the party. And I'll bet you're a friend of Warren's.

LULA: Why not be a friend of Warren's? Why not? (*Taking his arm*) Have you asked me yet?

CLAY: How can I ask you when I don't know your name?

LULA: Are you talking to my name?

CLAY: What is it, a secret?

LULA: I'm Lena the Hyena.[2]

CLAY: The famous woman poet?

LULA: Poetess! The same!

---

2. **Lena the Hyena:** Described as "the ugliest woman in the world," so repulsive that anyone who saw her was driven mad, this character was introduced in the popular comic strip *Li'l Abner* in 1946.

CLAY: Well, you know so much about me . . . what's my name?

LULA: Morris the Hyena.

CLAY: The famous woman poet?

LULA: The same. (*Laughing and going into her bag*) You want another apple?

CLAY: Can't make it, lady. I only have to keep one doctor away a day.

LULA: I bet your name is . . . something like . . . uh, Gerald or Walter. Huh?

CLAY: God, no.

LULA: Lloyd, Norman? One of those hopeless colored names creeping out of New Jersey. Leonard? Gag. . . .

CLAY: Like Warren?

LULA: Definitely. Just exactly like Warren. Or Everett.[3]

CLAY: Gag. . . .

LULA: Well, for sure, it's not Willie.

CLAY: It's Clay.

LULA: Clay? Really? Clay what?

CLAY: Take your pick. Jackson, Johnson, or Williams.

LULA: Oh, really? Good for you. But it's got to be Williams. You're too pretentious to be a Jackson or Johnson.

CLAY: Thass right.

LULA: But Clay's O.K.

CLAY: So's Lena.

LULA: It's Lula.

CLAY: Oh?

LULA: Lula the Hyena.

CLAY: Very good.

LULA: (*Starts laughing again*) Now you say to me, "Lula, Lula, why don't you go to this party with me tonight?" It's your turn, and let those be your lines.

CLAY: Lula, why don't you go to this party with me tonight, Huh?

LULA: Say my name twice before you ask, and no huh's.

CLAY: Lula, Lula, why don't you go to this party with me tonight?

LULA: I'd like to go, Clay, but how can you ask me to go when you barely know me?

CLAY: That is strange, isn't it?

LULA: What kind of reaction is that? You're supposed to say, "Aw, come on, we'll get to know each other better at the party."

CLAY: That's pretty corny.

LULA: What are you into anyway? (*Looking at him half sullenly but still amused*) What thing are you playing at, Mister? Mister Clay Williams? (*Grabs his thigh, up near the crotch*) What are *you* thinking about?

CLAY: Watch it now, you're gonna excite me for real.

LULA: (*Taking her hand away and throwing her apple core through the window*) I bet. (*She slumps in the seat and is heavily silent*)

---

3. **Everett:** Baraka's birth name was Everett LeRoy Jones.

CLAY: I thought you knew everything about me? What happened? (LULA *looks at him, then looks slowly away, then over where the other aisle would be. Noise of the train. She reaches in her bag and pulls out one of the paper books. She puts it on her leg and thumbs the pages listlessly.* CLAY *cocks his head to see the title of the book. Noise of the train.* LULA *flips pages and her eyes drift. Both remain silent*) Are you going to the party with me, Lula?

LULA: (*Bored and not even looking*) I don't even know you.

CLAY: You said you know my type.

LULA: (*Strangely irritated*) Don't get smart with me, Buster. I know you like the palm of my hand.

CLAY: The one you eat the apples with?

LULA: Yeh. And the one I open doors late Saturday evening with. That's my door. Up at the top of the stairs. Five flights. Above a lot of Italians and lying Americans. And scrape carrots with. Also . . . (*Looks at him*) the same hand I unbutton my dress with, or let my skirt fall down. Same hand. Lover.

CLAY: Are you angry about anything? Did I say something wrong?

LULA: Everything you say is wrong. (*Mock smile*) That's what makes you so attractive. Ha. In that funny-book jacket with all the buttons. (*More animated, taking hold of his jacket*) What've you got that jacket and tie on in all this heat for? And why're you wearing a jacket and tie like that? Did your people ever burn witches or start revolutions over the price of tea? Boy, those narrow-shoulder clothes come from a tradition you ought to feel oppressed by. A three-button suit. What right do you have to be wearing a three-button suit and striped tie? Your grandfather was a slave, he didn't go to Harvard.

CLAY: My grandfather was a night watchman.

LULA: And you went to a colored college where everybody thought they were Averell Harriman.[4]

CLAY: All except me.

LULA: And who did you think you were? Who do you think you are now?

CLAY: (*Laughs as if to make light of the whole trend of the conversation*) Well, in college I thought I was Baudelaire.[5] But I've slowed down since.

LULA: I bet you never once thought you were a black nigger. (*Mock serious, then she howls with laughter.* CLAY *is stunned but after initial reaction, he quickly tries to appreciate the humor.* LULA *almost shrieks*) A black Baudelaire.

CLAY: That's right.

LULA: Boy, are you corny. I take back what I said before. Everything you say is not wrong. It's perfect. You should be on television.

CLAY: You act like you're on television already.

---

4. **Averell Harriman:** The son of a wealthy railroad tycoon, Harriman (1891–1986) was a businessman and politician who twice ran for president and served as the U.S. ambassador to the Soviet Union and Great Britain.

5. **Baudelaire:** The influential French poet Charles Baudelaire (1821–1867), best known for his collection *Les Fleurs du Mal* ("Flowers of Evil"), published in 1857.

LULA: That's because I'm an actress.

CLAY: I thought so.

LULA: Well, you're wrong. I'm no actress. I told you I always lie. I'm nothing, honey, and don't you ever forget it. (*Lighter*) Although my mother was a Communist. The only person in my family ever to amount to anything.

CLAY: My mother was a Republican.

LULA: And your father voted for the man rather than the party.

CLAY: Right!

LULA: Yea for him. Yea, yea for him.

CLAY: Yea!

LULA: And yea for America where he is free to vote for the mediocrity of his choice! Yea!

CLAY: Yea!

LULA: And yea for both your parents who even though they differ about so crucial a matter as the body politic still forged a union of love and sacrifice that was destined to flower at the birth of the noble Clay . . . what's your middle name?

CLAY: Clay.

LULA: A union of love and sacrifice that was destined to flower at the birth of the noble Clay Clay Williams. Yea! And most of all yea yea for you, Clay Clay. The Black Baudelaire! Yes! (*And with knifelike cynicism*) My Christ. My Christ.

CLAY: Thank you, ma'am.

LULA: May the people accept you as a ghost of the future. And love you, that you might not kill them when you can.

CLAY: What?

LULA: You're a murderer, Clay, and you know it. (*Her voice darkening with significance*) You know goddamn well what I mean.

CLAY: I do?

LULA: So we'll pretend the air is light and full of perfume.

CLAY: (*Sniffing at her blouse*) It is.

LULA: And we'll pretend the people cannot see you. That is, the citizens. And that you are free of your own history. And I am free of my history. We'll pretend that we are both anonymous beauties smashing along through the city's entrails. (*She yells as loud as she can*) GROOVE!

Black

SCENE II

Scene is the same as before, though now there are other seats visible in the car. And throughout the scene other people get on the subway. There are maybe one or two seated in the car as the scene opens, though neither CLAY nor LULA notices them. CLAY's tie is open. LULA is hugging his arm.

CLAY: The party!

LULA: I know it'll be something good. You can come in with me, looking casual and significant. I'll be strange, haughty, and silent, and walk with long slow strides.

CLAY: Right.

LULA: When you get drunk, pat me once, very lovingly on the flanks, and I'll look at you cryptically, licking my lips.

CLAY: It sounds like something we can do.

LULA: You'll go around talking to young men about your mind, and to old men about your plans. If you meet a very close friend who is also with someone like me, we can stand together, sipping our drinks and exchanging codes of lust. The atmosphere will be slithering in love and half-love and very open moral decision.

CLAY: Great. Great.

LULA: And everyone will pretend they don't know your name, and then . . . (*She pauses heavily*) later, when they have to, they'll claim a friendship that denies your sterling character.

CLAY: (*Kissing her neck and fingers*) And then what?

LULA: Then? Well, then we'll go down the street, late night, eating apples and winding very deliberately toward my house.

CLAY: Deliberately?

LULA: I mean, we'll look in all the shopwindows, and make fun of the queers. Maybe we'll meet a Jewish Buddhist and flatten his conceits over some very pretentious coffee.

CLAY: In honor of whose God?

LULA: Mine.

CLAY: Who is . . . ?

LULA: Me . . . and you?

CLAY: A corporate Godhead.

LULA: Exactly. Exactly. (*Notices one of the other people entering*)

CLAY: Go on with the chronicle. Then what happens to us?

LULA: (*A mild depression, but she still makes her description triumphant and increasingly direct*) To my house, of course.

CLAY: Of course.

LULA: And up the narrow steps of the tenement.

CLAY: You live in a tenement?

LULA: Wouldn't live anywhere else. Reminds me specifically of my novel form of insanity.

CLAY: Up the tenement stairs.

LULA: And with my apple-eating hand I push open the door and lead you, my tender big-eyed prey, into my . . . God, what can I call it . . . into my hovel.

CLAY: Then what happens?

LULA: After the dancing and games, after the long drinks and long walks, the real fun begins.

CLAY: Ah, the real fun. (*Embarrassed, in spite of himself*) Which is . . . ?

LULA: (*Laughs at him*) Real fun in the dark house. Hah! Real fun in the dark house, high up above the street and the ignorant cowboys. I lead you in, holding your wet hand gently in my hand . . .

CLAY: Which is not wet?

LULA: Which is dry as ashes.

CLAY: And cold?

LULA: Don't think you'll get out of your responsibility that way. It's not cold at all. You Fascist! Into my dark living room. Where we'll sit and talk endlessly, endlessly.

CLAY: About what?

LULA: About what? About your manhood, what do you think? What do you think we've been talking about all this time?

CLAY: Well, I didn't know it was that. That's for sure. Every other thing in the world but that. (*Notices another person entering, looks quickly, almost involuntarily up and down the car, seeing the other people in the car*) Hey, I didn't even notice when those people got on.

LULA: Yeah, I know.

CLAY: Man, this subway is slow.

LULA: Yeah, I know.

CLAY: Well, go on. We were talking about my manhood.

LULA: We still are. All the time.

CLAY: We were in your living room.

LULA: My dark living room. Talking endlessly.

CLAY: About my manhood.

LULA: I'll make you a map of it. Just as soon as we get to my house.

CLAY: Well, that's great.

LULA: One of the things we do while we talk. And screw.

CLAY: (*Trying to make his smile broader and less shaky*) We finally got there.

LULA: And you'll call my rooms black as a grave. You'll say, "This place is like Juliet's tomb."[6]

CLAY: (*Laughs*) I might.

LULA: I know. You've probably said it before.

CLAY: And is that all? The whole grand tour?

LULA: Not all. You'll say to me very close to my face, many, many times, you'll say, even whisper, that you love me.

CLAY: Maybe I will.

LULA: And you'll be lying.

CLAY: I wouldn't lie about something like that.

LULA: Hah. It's the only kind of thing you will lie about. Especially if you think it'll keep me alive.

CLAY: Keep you alive? I don't understand.

LULA: (*Bursting out laughing, but too shrilly*) Don't understand? Well, don't look at me. It's the path I take, that's all. Where both feet take me when I set them down. One in front of the other.

CLAY: Morbid. Morbid. You sure you're not an actress? All that self-aggrandizement.

---

6. **Juliet's tomb:** In the final scene of Shakespeare's *Romeo and Juliet*, Romeo finds Juliet asleep in her family's tomb. Believing her to be dead, he drinks poison. When she awakens and finds him dead, she stabs herself to death with his dagger.

LULA: Well, I told you I wasn't an actress . . . but I also told you I lie all the time. Draw your own conclusions.

CLAY: Morbid. Morbid. You sure you're not an actress? All scribed? There's no more?

LULA: I've told you all I know. Or almost all.

CLAY: There's no funny parts?

LULA: I thought it was all funny.

CLAY: But you mean peculiar, not ha-ha.

LULA: You don't know what I mean.

CLAY: Well, tell me the almost part then. You said almost all. What else? I want the whole story.

LULA: (*Searching aimlessly through her bag. She begins to talk breathlessly, with a light and silly tone*) All stories are whole stories. All of 'em. Our whole story . . . nothing but change. How could things go on like that forever? Huh? (*Slaps him on the shoulder, begins finding things in her bag, taking them out and throwing them over her shoulder into the aisle*) Except I do go on as I do. Apples and long walks with deathless intelligent lovers. But you mix it up. Look out the window, all the time. Turning pages. Change change change. Till, shit, I don't know you. Wouldn't, for that matter. You're too serious. I bet you're even too serious to be psychoanalyzed. Like all those Jewish poets from Yonkers,[7] who leave their mothers looking for other mothers, or others' mothers, on whose baggy tits they lay their fumbling heads. Their poems are always funny, and all about sex.

CLAY: They sound great. Like movies.

LULA: But you change. (*Blankly*) And things work on you till you hate them. (*More people come into the train. They come closer to the couple, some of them not sitting, but swinging drearily on the straps, staring at the two with uncertain interest*)

CLAY: Wow. All these people, so suddenly. They must all come from the same place.

LULA: Right. That they do.

CLAY: Oh? You know about them too?

LULA: Oh yeah. About them more than I know about you. Do they frighten you?

CLAY: Frighten me? Why should they frighten me?

LULA: 'Cause you're an escaped nigger.

CLAY: Yeah?

LULA: 'Cause you crawled through the wire and made tracks to my side.

CLAY: Wire?

LULA: Don't they have wire around plantations?

CLAY: You must be Jewish. All you can think about is wire. Plantations didn't have any wire. Plantations were big open whitewashed places like heaven, and everybody on 'em was grooved to be there. Just strummin' and hummin' all day.

LULA: Yes, yes.

CLAY: And that's how the blues was born.

---

7. **Jewish poets from Yonkers:** Yonkers, a large city two miles north of New York City, once had a substantial Jewish population.

LULA: Yes, yes. And that's how the blues was born. (*Begins to make up a song that becomes quickly hysterical. As she sings she rises from her seat, still throwing things out of her bag into the aisle, beginning a rhythmical shudder and twistlike wiggle, which she continues up and down the aisle, bumping into many of the standing people and tripping over the feet of those sitting. Each time she runs into a person she lets out a very vicious piece of profanity, wiggling and stepping all the time*) And that's how the blues was born. Yes. Yes. Son of a bitch, get out of the way. Yes. Quack. Yes. Yes. And that's how the blues was born. Ten little niggers sitting on a limb, but none of them ever looked like him. (*Points to* CLAY, *returns toward the seat, with her hands extended for him to rise and dance with her*) And that's how blues was born. Yes. Come on, Clay. Let's do the nasty. Rub bellies. Rub bellies.

CLAY: (*Waves his hands to refuse. He is embarrassed, but determined to get a kick out of the proceedings*) Hey, what was in those apples? Mirror, mirror on the wall, who's the fairest one of all? Snow White, baby, and don't you forget it.

LULA: (*Grabbing for his hands, which he draws away*) Come on, Clay. Let's rub bellies on the train. The nasty. The nasty. Do the gritty grind, like your ol' rag-head mammy. Grind till you lose your mind. Shake it, shake it, shake it, shake it! OOOOweeee! Come on, Clay. Let's do the choo-choo train shuffle, the navel scratcher.

CLAY: Hey, you coming on like the lady who smoked up her grass skirt.

LULA: (*Becoming annoyed that he will not dance, and becoming more animated as if to embarrass him still further*) Come on, Clay . . . let's do the thing. Uhh! Uhh! Clay! Clay! You middle-class black bastard. Forget your social-working mother for a few seconds and let's knock stomachs. Clay, you liver-lipped white man. You would-be Christian. You ain't no nigger, you're just a dirty white man. Get up, Clay. Dance with me, Clay.

CLAY: Lula! Sit down, now. Be cool.

LULA: (*Mocking him, in wild dance*) Be cool. Be cool. That's all you know . . . shaking that wildroot cream-oil on your knotty head, jackets buttoning up to your chin, so full of white man's words. Christ. God. Get up and scream at these people. Like scream meaningless shit in these hopeless faces. (*She screams at people in train, still dancing*) Red trains cough Jewish underwear for keeps! Expanding smells of silence. Gravy snot whistling like sea birds. Clay. Clay, you got to break out. Don't sit there dying the way they want you to die. Get up.

CLAY: Oh, sit the fuck down. (*He moves to restrain her*) Sit down, goddamn it.

LULA: (*Twisting out of his reach*) Screw yourself, Uncle Tom.[8] Thomas Woolly-Head. (*Begins to dance a kind of jig, mocking Clay with loud forced humor*) There is Uncle Tom . . . I mean, Uncle Thomas Woolly-Head. With old white matted mane. He hobbles on his wooden cane. Old Tom. Old Tom. Let the white man hump his ol' mama, and he jes' shuffle off in the woods and hide his gentle gray head. Ol' Thomas Woolly-Head.

---

8. **Uncle Tom:** The central character in Harriet Beecher Stowe's antislavery novel *Uncle Tom's Cabin* (1852). In the twentieth century, *Uncle Tom* became a derogatory term for black men who were considered to be fawning or servile to white people.

(*Some of the other riders are laughing now. A drunk gets up and joins* LULA *in her dance, singing, as best he can, her "song."* CLAY *gets up out of his seat and visibly scans the faces of the other riders*).

CLAY: Lula! Lula! (*She is dancing and turning, still shouting as loud as she can, The drunk too is shouting, and waving his hands wildly*) Lula . . . you dumb bitch. Why don't you stop it? (*He rushes half stumbling from his seat, and grabs one of her flailing arms*)

LULA: Let me go! You black son of a bitch. (*She struggles against him*) Let me go! Help! (CLAY *is dragging her towards her seat, and the drunk seeks to interfere. He grabs* CLAY *around the shoulders and begins wrestling with him.* CLAY *clubs the drunk to the floor without releasing* LULA, *who is still screaming,* CLAY *finally gets her to the seat and throws her into it*)

CLAY: Now you shut the hell up. (*Grabbing her shoulders*) Just shut up. You don't know what you're talking about. You don't know anything. So just keep your stupid mouth closed.

LULA: You're afraid of white people. And your father was. Uncle Tom Big Lip!

CLAY: (*Slaps her as hard as he can, across the mouth,* LULA'S *head bangs against the back of the seat. When she raises it again,* CLAY *slaps her again*) Now shut up and let me talk. (*He turns toward the other riders, some of whom are sitting on the edge of their seats. The drunk is on one knee, rubbing his head, and singing softly the same song. He shuts up too when he sees* CLAY *watching him. The others go back to news-papers or stare out the windows*) Shit, you don't have any sense, Lula, nor feelings either. I could murder you now. Such a tiny ugly throat. I could squeeze it flat, and watch you turn blue, on a humble. For dull kicks. And all these weak-faced ofays[9] squatting around here, staring over their papers at me. Murder them too. Even if they expected it. That man there . . . (*Points to well-dressed man*) I could rip that *Times* right out of his hand, as skinny and middle-classed as I am, I could rip that paper out of his hand and just as easily rip out his throat. It takes no great effort. For what? To kill you soft idiots? You don't understand anything but luxury.

LULA: You fool!

CLAY: (*Pushing her against the seat*) I'm not telling you again, Tallulah Bankhead![10] Luxury. In your face and your fingers. You telling me what I ought to do. (*Sudden scream frightening the whole coach*) Well, don't! Don't you tell me anything! If I'm a middle-class fake white man . . . let me be. And let me be in the way I want. (*Through his teeth*) I'll rip your lousy breasts off! Let me be who I feel like being. Uncle Tom. Thomas. Whoever. It's none of your business. You don't know anything except what's there for you to see. An act. Lies. Device. Not the pure heart, the pumping black heart. You don't ever know that. And I sit here, in this buttoned-up suit, to keep myself from cutting all your throats. I mean wantonly. You great liberated whore! You fuck some

---

9. **ofays:** A derogatory term for white people.
10. **Tallulah Bankhead:** Bankhead (1903–1968), an actress who was born into a prominent Alabama family, was known for her uninhibited personality and theatrical public life.

black man, and right away you're an expert on black people. What a lotta shit that is. The only thing you know is that you come if he bangs you hard enough. And that's all. The belly rub? You wanted to do the belly rub? Shit, you don't even know how. You don't know how. That ol' dipty-dip shit you do, rolling your ass like an elephant. That's not my kind of belly rub. Belly rub is not Queens.[11] Belly rub is dark places, with big hats and overcoats held up with one arm. Belly rub hates you. Old bald-headed four-eyed ofays popping their fingers . . . and don't know yet what they're doing. They say, "I love Bessie Smith."[12] And don't even understand that Bessie Smith is saying, "Kiss my ass, kiss my black unruly ass." Before love, suffering, desire, anything you can explain, she's saying, and very plainly, "Kiss my black ass." And if you don't know that, it's you that's doing the kissing.

Charlie Parker?[13] Charlie Parker. All the hip white boys scream for Bird. And Bird saying, "Up your ass, feeble-minded ofay! Up your ass." And they sit there talking about the tortured genius of Charlie Parker. Bird would've played not a note of music if he just walked up to East Sixty-seventh Street[14] and killed the first ten white people he saw. Not a note! And I'm the great would-be poet. Yes. That's right! Poet. Some kind of bastard literature . . . all it needs is a simple knife thrust. Just let me bleed you, you loud whore, and one poem vanished. A whole people of neurotics, struggling to keep from being sane. And the only thing that would cure the neurosis would be your murder. Simple as that. I mean if I murdered you, then other white people would begin to understand me. You understand? No. I guess not. If Bessie Smith had killed some white people she wouldn't have needed that music. She could have talked very straight and plain about the world. No metaphors. No grunts. No wiggles in the dark of her soul. Just straight two and two are four. Money. Power. Luxury. Like that. All of them. Crazy niggers turning their backs on sanity. When all it needs is that simple act. Murder. Just murder! Would make us all sane. (*Suddenly weary*) Ahhh. Shit. But who needs it? I'd rather be a fool. Insane. Safe with my words, and no deaths, and clean, hard thoughts, urging me to new conquests. My people's madness. Hah! That's a laugh. My people. They don't need me to claim them. They got legs and arms of their own. Personal insanities. Mirrors. They don't need all those words. They don't need any defense. But listen, though, one more thing. And you tell this to your father, who's probably the kind of man who needs to know at once. So he can plan ahead. Tell him not to preach so much rationalism and cold logic to these niggers. Let them alone. Let them sing curses at you in code and see your filth as simple lack of style. Don't make the mistake, through some irresponsible surge of

---

11. **Belly rub is not Queens:** The belly rub was a sensuous dance associated with jazz and African Americans. The population of Queens, the largest of the five boroughs of New York City, was predominantly white in the 1960s.

12. **Bessie Smith:** Smith (1894–1937), one of the most acclaimed and successful singers of the 1920s, was nicknamed "Empress of the Blues."

13. **Charlie Parker:** The saxophonist Charles "Bird" Parker Jr. (1920–1955), an influential musician who pioneered and popularized the form of jazz known as bebop or bop.

14. **East Sixty-seventh Street:** The Upper East Side is among the wealthiest sections of New York City.

Christian charity, of talking too much about the advantages of Western rationalism, or the great intellectual legacy of the white man, or maybe they'll begin to listen. And then, maybe one day, you'll find they actually do understand exactly what you are talking about, all these fantasy people. All these blues people. And on that day, as sure as shit, when you really believe you can "accept" them into your fold, as half-white trusties late of the subject peoples. With no more blues, except the very old ones, and not a watermelon in sight, the great missionary heart will have triumphed, and all of those ex-coons will be stand-up Western men, with eyes for clean hard useful lives, sober, pious and sane, and they'll murder you. They'll murder you, and have very rational explanations. Very much like your own. They'll cut your throats, and drag you out to the edge of your cities so the flesh can fall away from your bones, in sanitary isolation.

LULA: (*Her voice takes on a different, more businesslike quality*) I've heard enough.

CLAY: (*Reaching for his books*) I bet you have. I guess I better collect my stuff and get off this train. Looks like we won't be acting out that little pageant you outlined before.

LULA: No. We won't. You're right about that, at least. (*She turns to look quickly around the rest of the car*) All right! (*The others respond*)

CLAY: (*Bending across the girl to retrieve his belongings*) Sorry, baby, I don't think we could make it. (*As he is bending over her, the girl brings up a small knife and plunges it into* CLAY's *chest. Twice. He slumps across her knees, his mouth working stupidly*)

LULA: Sorry is right. (*Turning to the others in the car who have already gotten up from their seats*) Sorry is the rightest thing you've said. Get this man off me! Hurry, now! (*The others come and drag* CLAY's *body down the aisle*) Open the door and throw his body out. (*They throw him off*) And all of you get off at the next stop. (LULA *busies herself straightening her things. Getting everything in order. She takes out a notebook and makes a quick scribbling note. Drops it in her bag. The train apparently stops and all the others get off, leaving her alone in the coach.*

Very soon a young Negro of about twenty comes into the coach, with a couple of books under his arm. He sits a few seats in back of LULA. *When he is seated she turns and gives him a long slow look. He looks up from his book and drops the book on his lap. Then an old Negro conductor comes into the car, doing a sort of restrained soft shoe, and half mumbling the words of some song. He looks at the young man, briefly, with a quick greeting*)

CONDUCTOR: Hey, brother!

YOUNG MAN: Hey. (*The conductor continues down the aisle with his little dance and the mumbled song,* LULA *turns to stare at him and follows his movements down the aisle. The conductor tips his hat when he reaches her seat, and continues out the car*)

Curtain

[1964]

Audre Lorde

[1934-1992]

Audrey Geraldine Lorde was born in Harlem in New York City on February 18, 1934. She was the third daughter of Linda Belmar and Frederic Byron Lorde, immigrants from the Caribbean island of Grenada who struggled to earn a living in the Depression-era United States. Lorde recalled that as a child she altered her first name to "Audre" because she preferred its sound and "did not like the tail of the Y hanging down below the line in Audrey." She attended Roman Catholic grammar schools and then passed the entrance examination to Hunter High School, an elite public school for girls on the Upper East Side of Manhattan. The rebellious Lorde became part of a group who called themselves "The Branded" and who were actively involved in the school's literary magazine, the *Argus*. When the editor of the magazine rejected one of her poems, Lorde sent it to *Seventeen* magazine, where it was published shortly before her graduation in 1951. After a year at Hunter College, she dropped out and worked in a factory in Connecticut and later in a health center in New York City, where she was active in radical politics and the bohemian "gay girl" scene in Greenwich Village. Following a pivotal visit to Mexico, where Lorde said that she confirmed her identity as a poet and a lesbian, she returned to Hunter College in 1955. She graduated in 1959 with a degree in literature and philosophy and then attended Columbia University. She earned a master's degree in library science in 1961 and took a position at the Mount Vernon Public Library in New York City.

Audre Lorde

Dagmar Schultz took this photograph of Lorde in the early 1970s, when she was beginning to gain widespread recognition as a poet and activist.

During the following decade, Lorde actively began to pursue her true calling as a poet and a teacher. In 1962, she entered into an open marriage with a white lawyer, Edward Ashley Rollins, a bisexual man with whom she had a daughter in 1963 and a son in 1964. Meanwhile, several of her poems appeared in *Sixes and Seven* (1962), an anthology of poetry by African Americans published by the small Heritage Press in London; and Langston Hughes included two of her poems in his anthology *New Negro Poets, U.S.A.* (1964). The Poet's Press, founded by one of her friends from high school, the Beat poet Diane di Prima, published Lorde's first book of poems, *The First Cities*. About the time it appeared early in 1968, she spent six weeks as the poet in residence at Tougaloo College, a historically black college in Jackson, Mississippi. There, Lorde discovered her love of teaching and became involved with a woman, Frances Clayton, a white professor of psychology on exchange from Tougaloo's sister institution, Brown University. After Lorde returned home to New York City, she separated from her husband and established a new home with her children and Clayton. Lorde also gave up library work and taught at the City College of New York and Herbert H. Lehman College before joining the English department at John Jay College of Criminal Justice in 1970. That year, her second collection of poetry, *Cables to Rage*, was published by the Heritage Press. It was distributed in the United States by the small Broadside Press, an offshoot of the Black

Arts Movement, which published Lorde's next two volumes of poetry: *From a Land Where Other People Live* (1973), which was nominated for a National Book Award, and *The New York Head Shop and Museum* (1974).

As both a writer and an activist, Lorde thereafter reached an increasingly wide audience. Beginning with *Coal* (1976), which included some poems from her first two collections, all of her later collections of poetry were published by the prominent firm of W. W. Norton. She drew on African mythology in her next collection *The Black Unicorn* (1978), of which her friend Adrienne Rich wrote: "Refusing to be circumscribed by any simple identity, Audre Lorde writes as a Black woman, a mother, a daughter, a Lesbian, a feminist, a visionary; poems of elemental wildness and healing, nightmare and lucidity." In 1979, Lorde spoke to a crowd of one hundred thousand people gathered for the first March on Washington for Gay and Lesbian Rights. She returned to her alma mater, Hunter College, as a professor of English in 1980, at the beginning of a remarkably productive decade. She published two acclaimed works of nonfiction, *The Cancer Journals* (1980), an account of her treatment for breast cancer and a protest against the silence surrounding the disease; and an autobiography, or what Lorde called a "biomythography," *Zami: A New Spelling of My Name* (1982). In addition to collections of her essays and speeches, *Sister Outsider* (1984) and *A Burst of Light* (1988), Lorde also published *Chosen Poems Old and New* (1982), primarily a selection from her first five volumes of poetry, and a widely admired collection of new poems, *Our Dead Behind Us* (1986). Her long-term partnership with Clayton ended, and Lorde established a home in St. Croix in the Virgin Islands with her new partner, the social scientist Gloria Joseph. In an African ceremony on St. Croix, Lorde took the name Gambda Adisa, meaning "Warrior: She Who Makes Her Meaning Known." Lorde prepared a final edition of her poems, *Undersong: Chosen Poems Old and New*, which was published a few months before she died of liver cancer at her home on St. Croix on November 17, 1992.

Audre Lorde was a warrior-poet who inspired many in her intense well-lived life as a black, lesbian, human rights artist.

—Joy Harjo

Reading Lorde's Poetry.

Lorde once observed that "poets must teach what they know, if we are all to continue being." An outspoken lesbian and black feminist, she also passionately believed in the power of words and the potential of poetry to combat racial and sexual oppression, as well as global injustice. She was consequently an exacting practitioner of her craft, a poet whose idiomatic and deceptively simple free verse is often remarkable for the density of its language, imagery, and metaphor. In fact, Lorde demanded so much of her poems that she continued to revise some of them up until the time of her death. "The process of revision is, I believe, crucial to the integrity and lasting power of a poem," she observed in the introduction to her final collection, *Undersong*. "The problem in reworking any poem is always when to let go of it, refusing to give in to the desire to have that particular poem *do it all*, say it all, become the mythical, unattainable Universal Poem." Lorde added that she always began the process of revision by asking herself two questions: "What did I want my readers to feel? And,

bedfordstmartins.com/americanlit *for research links on Lorde*

What was the work of this poem (its task in the world)?" The texts of the following poems, all of them her final versions, are taken from *Undersong: Chosen Poems, Old and New* (1992).

COAL

I   is the total black
being spoken
from the earth's inside.

There are many kinds of open
how a diamond comes   5
into a knot of flame
how sound comes into a word
colored
by who pays what for speaking.

Some words are open   10
diamonds on a glass window
singing out within the crash
of passing sun
other words are stapled wagers
in a perforated book   15
buy and sign and tear apart
and come whatever wills all chances
the stub remains
an ill-pulled tooth
with a ragged edge.   20

Some words live in my throat
breeding like adders
others
know sun
seeking like gypsies   25
over my tongue
to explode through my lips
like young sparrows
bursting from shell.

Some words   30
bedevil me.

Love is a word, another kind of open.
As the diamond comes
into a knot of flame

I am Black   35
because I come from the earth's inside
take my word for jewel
in the open light.

                                                                    [1962, 1992]

THE WOMAN THING

The hunters are back
from beating the winter's face
in search of a challenge or task
in search of food
making fresh tracks   5
for their children's hunger
they do not watch the sun
they cannot wear its heat
for a sign of triumph
or freedom.   10

The hunters are treading heavily
homeward through snow
marked by their own bloody footprints.
Emptyhanded   the hunters return
snow-maddened   15
sustained by their rages.

In the night after food they will seek
young girls for their amusement.
Now the hunters are coming
and the unbaked girls   20
flee from their angers.

All this day I have craved
food for my child's hunger
emptyhanded
the hunters come shouting   25
injustice drips from their mouths
like stale snow
melted in sunlight.

The woman thing
my mother taught me   30
bakes off its covering of snow
like a rising Blackening sun.

                                                                    [1964, 1992]

BLACK MOTHER WOMAN

I cannot recall you gentle
yet through your heavy love
I have become
an image of your once-delicate flesh
split with deceitful longings.   5

When strangers come and compliment me
your aged spirit takes a bow
jingling with pride
but once you hid that secret
in the center of your fury   10
hanging me
with deep breasts and wiry hair
your own split flesh
and long-suffering eyes
buried in myths of little worth.   15

But I have peeled away your anger
down to its core of love
and look mother
I am   a dark temple
where your true spirit rises   20
beautiful   tough as chestnut
stanchion against nightmares of weakness
and if my eyes conceal
a squadron of conflicting rebellions
I learned from you   25
to define myself
through your denials.

[1971, 1992]

Don DeLillo

[b. 1936]

Don DeLillo was born to Italian immigrant parents on November 20, 1936, in the Bronx, a borough of New York City. Intensely private, DeLillo has offered only a few details about his early life. He says that he spent most of his time shooting pool or playing cards and street games with friends in the Italian American neighborhood where he grew up. Raised as a Roman

Don DeLillo

This photograph of DeLillo was taken in 1991, by which time he was firmly established as one of the most prominent and influential postmodern writers in the United States.

Catholic, he graduated from Cardinal Hayes High School in 1954 and attended nearby Fordham, the Jesuit University of New York. He studied history, philosophy, and theology, but he disliked college and learned only "by rote," as DeLillo has put it. At the same time, he excitedly discovered the work of William Faulkner, Ernest Hemingway, and especially James Joyce. "I learned to see something in language that carried a radiance, something that made me feel the beauty and fervor of words, the sense that a word has a life and a history," DeLillo recalled in a 1993 interview. When he graduated in 1958 with a major in communication arts, he moved to Manhattan. Failing to get a job in publishing, as he had hoped, he found work as a copywriter for an advertising agency and spent his free time at jazz clubs, foreign films, galleries, and the Museum of Modern Art. He was also writing, and he published his first short story in the literary magazine *Epoch* in 1960.

After publishing several additional stories, DeLillo quit his job in 1964 to devote himself to writing fiction. He supported himself by doing freelance writing while working on his first novel, *Americana* (1971), the story of a television executive who seeks to connect with himself and his country by making a private film during a trip across the United States. Following up on the modest success of that novel, DeLillo published *End Zone* (1972), a sports novel in which he used football as a metaphor of contemporary American life; and *Great Jones Street* (1973), the story of a rock star who tries to preserve his own music in the face of the commercial pressures of popular culture. The latter received solid reviews, and DeLillo's fiction appeared in prominent magazines such as *Esquire*, *Sports Illustrated*, the *New Yorker*, and the *Atlantic Monthly*. In 1975, DeLillo married Barbara Bennett, a banker who later became a landscape architect. After spending a year studying the history of mathematics, he published *Ratner's Star* (1976), a book about a child prodigy who interprets a mathematical message from space. After that venture into science fiction, DeLillo experimented with another popular genre, the thriller, in *Players* (1977) and *Running Dog* (1978). In 1979, he was awarded a Guggenheim Fellowship, which enabled him and his wife to live in Greece for the next three years, during which time they traveled widely in the Middle East and India. "What I found was that all this traveling taught me how to see and hear all over again," he observed in a 1982 interview. "I think the most important thing is what I felt in hearing people and watching them gesture—in listening to the sound of Greek and Arabic and Hindi and Urdu." Both the limitations and potentially liberating power of language are central concerns in his novel *The Names* (1982), the story of an expatriate American businessman who becomes obsessed with a mysterious cult in Greece.

Since then, DeLillo has enjoyed widespread critical acclaim and growing commercial success. After he and his wife returned to the United States, they settled in a modest suburb of New York City. He won the National Book Award for *White Noise* (1985), a satirical novel about a professor of "Hitler Studies" at a college in a small Midwestern town that is evacuated after toxic gas is released in an industrial accident. That breakthrough novel, which gained him a much wider audience, was followed by his bestseller *Libra* (1988), a nonfiction novel about the assassination of President John F. Kennedy; and *Mao II* (1991), a novel about a reclusive writer caught up in efforts to free a hostage held by terrorists. Although the reviews of both books were generally favorable, even some otherwise admiring reviewers and readers were put off by the characters and plots of his sprawling narratives. In reply to a question from a member of a reading club, DeLillo in 1995 observed that "well-behaved books with neat plots and worked-out endings seem somewhat quaint in the face of the largely incoherent reality of modern life," adding that rather than plot or character "it is language, in its beauty, its ambiguity and its shifting textures, that drives my work." Certainly, language was a driving force in his epic novel *Underworld* (1997), a sweeping saga of American life and cultural history from the 1950s to the 1990s. In a poll of writers, editors, and critics conducted by the *New York Times* in 2006, *Underworld* was named runner-up to Toni Morrison's *Beloved* as "the single best work of American fiction published in the last twenty-five years." DeLillo's recent work includes *Cosmopolis* (2003), a novel about a billionaire speculator caught up in a chaotic day in the stock market and on the streets of New York City; *Falling Man* (2007), his acclaimed novel about a survivor's experience during and in the aftermath of the attacks on the World Trade Center on September 11, 2001; and *Point Omega* (2010), a complex novella centered on an interview between a filmmaker and a former "Defense Intellectual" who helped plan the invasion of Iraq during the administration of President George W. Bush.

Reading DeLillo's "Videotape."   On one level, this is an apparently simple story about a family outing in a car, during which a young girl passes the time by using a video camera and inadvertently captures a violent incident on tape, recalling the famous Zapruder film of the assassination of President John F. Kennedy. Indeed, the tape rather than the event is the central subject of "Videotape," whose narrator has watched it again and again on the evening news. DeLillo's compressed narrative of postmodern life is consequently less a story in the conventional sense than an examination of our fascination with images of violence and the relationship between the technology of videotape and the actions and events it appears simply to record. Asked in a 1997 interview why film rather than books is so central in his work, DeLillo replied:

> Because this is the age of images, I suppose, and much that is different about our time can be traced to the fact that we are on film, a reality that did not shape, instruct, and haunt previous cultures. I suppose film gives us a deeply self-conscious sense, but beyond that it's simply such a prevalent fact of contemporary life that I don't think any attempt to understand the way we live and the way we think and the way we feel about ourselves can proceed without a deep consideration of the power of the image.

bedfordstmartins.com/ americanlit for research links on DeLillo

"Videotape," which was originally published in the final issue of the international literary quarterly *Antaeus*, was reprinted in *Harper's* magazine and later in a prestigious annual collection honoring the best work published by small presses and literary journals, *The Pushcart Prize XX* (1996). DeLillo slightly revised the story as the opening chapter of part two of his novel *Underworld* (1997). The text is taken from *Antaeus*, Autumn 1994.

VIDEOTAPE

It shows a man driving a car. It is the simplest sort of family video. You see a man at the wheel of a medium Dodge.

It is just a kid aiming her camera through the rear window of the family car at the windshield of the car behind her.

You know about families and their video cameras. You know how kids get involved, how the camera shows them that every subject is potentially charged, a million things they never see with the unaided eye. They investigate the meaning of inert objects and dumb pets and they poke at family privacy. They learn to see things twice.

It is the kid's own privacy that is being protected here. She is twelve years old and her name is being withheld even though she is neither the victim nor the perpetrator of the crime but only the means of recording it.

It shows a man in a sport shirt at the wheel of his car. There is nothing else to see. The car approaches briefly, then falls back.

You know how children with cameras learn to work the exposed moments that define the family cluster. They break every trust, spy out the undefended space, catching Mom coming out of the bathroom in her cumbrous robe and turbaned towel, looking bloodless and plucked. It is not a joke. They will shoot you sitting on the pot if they can manage a suitable vantage.

The tape has the jostled sort of noneventness that marks the family product. Of course the man in this case is not a member of the family but a stranger in a car, a random figure, someone who has happened along in the slow lane.

It shows a man in his forties wearing a pale shirt open at the throat, the image washed by reflections and sunglint, with many jostled moments.

It is not just another video homicide. It is a homicide recorded by a child who thought she was doing something simple and maybe halfway clever, shooting some tape of a man in a car.

He sees the girl and waves briefly, wagging a hand without taking it off the wheel — an underplayed reaction that makes you like him.

It is unrelenting footage that rolls on and on. It has an aimless determination, a persistence that lives outside the subject matter. You are looking into the mind of home video. It is innocent, it is aimless, it is determined, it is real.

He is bald up the middle of his head, a nice guy in his forties whose whole life seems open to the hand-held camera.

But there is also an element of suspense. You keep on looking not because you know something is going to happen — of course you do know something is going to happen and you do look for that reason but you might also keep on looking if you came across this footage for the first time without knowing the outcome. There is a crude power operating here. You keep on looking because things combine to hold you fast — a sense of the random, the amateurish, the accidental, the impending. You don't think of the tape as boring or interesting. It is crude, it is blunt, it is relentless. It is the jostled part of your mind, the film that runs through your hotel brain under all the thoughts you know you're thinking.

The world is lurking in the camera, already framed, waiting for the boy or girl who will come along and take up the device, learn the instrument, shooting old Granddad at breakfast, all stroked out so his nostrils gape, the cereal spoon baby-gripped in his pale fist.

It shows a man alone in a medium Dodge. It seems to go on forever.

There's something about the nature of the tape, the grain of the image, the sputtering black-and-white tones, the starkness — you think this is more real, truer-to-life than anything around you. The things around you have a rehearsed and layered and cosmetic look. The tape is superreal, or maybe underreal is the way you want to put it. It is what lies at the scraped bottom of all the layers you have added. And this is another reason why you keep on looking. The tape has a searing realness.

It shows him giving an abbreviated wave, stiff-palmed, like a signal flag at a siding.

You know how families make up games. This is just another game in which the child invents the rules as she goes along. She likes the idea of videotaping a man in his car. She has probably never done it before and she sees no reason to vary the format or terminate early or pan to another car. This is her game and she is learning it and playing it at the same time. She feels halfway clever and inventive and maybe slightly intrusive as well, a little bit of brazenness that spices any game.

And you keep on looking. You look because this is the nature of the footage, to make a channeled path through time, to give things a shape and a destiny.

Of course if she had panned to another car, the right car at the precise time, she would have caught the gunman as he fired.

The chance quality of the encounter. The victim, the killer, and the child with a camera. Random energies that approach a common point. There's something here that speaks to you directly, saying terrible things about forces beyond your control, lines of intersection that cut through history and logic and every reasonable layer of human expectation.

She wandered into it. The girl got lost and wandered clear-eyed into horror. This is a children's story about straying too far from home. But it isn't the family car that serves as the instrument of the child's curiosity, her inclination to explore. It is the camera that puts her in the tale.

You know about holidays and family celebrations and how somebody shows up with a camcorder and the relatives stand around and barely react because they're numbingly accustomed to the process of being taped and decked and shown on the VCR with the coffee and cake.

He is hit soon after. If you've seen the tape many times you know from the handwave exactly when he will be hit. It is something, naturally, that you wait for. You say to your wife, if you're at home and she is there, Now here is where he gets it. You say, Janet, hurry up, this is where it happens.

Now here is where he gets it. You see him jolted, sort of wire-shocked — then he seizes up and falls toward the door or maybe leans or slides into the door is the proper way to put it. It is awful and unremarkable at the same time. The car stays in the slow lane. It approaches briefly, then falls back.

You don't usually call your wife over to the TV set. She has her programs, you have yours. But there's a certain urgency here. You want her to see how it looks. The tape has been running forever and now the thing is finally going to happen and you want her to be here when he's shot.

Here it comes, all right. He is shot, head-shot, and the camera reacts, the child reacts — there is a jolting movement but she keeps on taping, there is a sympathetic response, a nerve response, her heart is beating faster but she keeps the camera trained on the subject as he slides into the door and even as you see him die you're thinking of the girl. At some level the girl has to be present here, watching what you're watching, unprepared — the girl is seeing this cold and you have to marvel at the fact that she keeps the tape rolling.

It shows something awful and unaccompanied. You want your wife to see it because it is real this time, not fancy movie violence — the realness beneath the layers of cosmetic perception. Hurry up, Janet, here it comes. He dies so fast. There is no accompaniment of any kind. It is very stripped. You want to tell her it is realer than real but then she will ask what that means.

The way the camera reacts to the gunshot — a startle reaction that brings pity and terror into the frame, the girl's own shock, the girl's identification with the victim.

You don't see the blood, which is probably trickling behind his ear and down the back of his neck. The way his head is twisted away from the door, the twist of the head gives you only a partial profile and it's the wrong side, it's not the side where he was hit.

And maybe you're being a little aggressive here, practically forcing your wife to watch. Why? What are you telling her? Are you making a little statement? Like I'm going to ruin your day out of ordinary spite. Or a big statement? Like this is the risk of existing. Either way you're rubbing her face in this tape and you don't know why.

It shows the car drifting toward the guardrail and then there's a jostling sense of two other lanes and part of another car, a split-second blur, and the tape ends here, either because the girl stopped shooting or because some central authority, the police or the district attorney or the TV station, decided there was nothing else you had to see.

This is either the tenth or eleventh homicide committed by the Texas Highway Killer. The number is uncertain because the police believe that one of the shootings may have been a copycat crime.

And there is something about videotape, isn't there, and this particular kind of serial crime? This is a crime designed for random taping and immediate playing. You sit there and wonder if this kind of crime became more possible when the means of taping and playing an event – playing it immediately after the taping – became part of the culture. The principal doesn't necessarily commit the sequence of crimes in order to see them taped and played. He commits the crimes as if they were a form of taped-and-played event. The crimes are inseparable from the idea of taping and playing. You sit there thinking that this is a crime that has found its medium, or vice versa – cheap mass production, the sequence of repeated images and victims, stark and glary and more or less unremarkable.

It shows very little in the end. It is a famous murder because it is on tape and because the murderer has done it many times and because the crime was recorded by a child. So the child is involved, the Video Kid as she is sometimes called because they have to call her something. The tape is famous and so is she. She is famous in the modern manner of people whose names are strategically withheld. They are famous without names or faces, spirits living apart from their bodies, the victims and witnesses, the underage criminals, out there somewhere at the edges of perception.

Seeing someone at the moment he dies, dying unexpectedly. This is reason alone to stay fixed to the screen. It is instructional, watching a man shot dead as he drives along on a sunny day. It demonstrates an elemental truth, that every breath you take has two possible endings. And that's another thing. There's a joke locked away here, a note of cruel slapstick that you are completely willing to appreciate. Maybe the victim's a chump, a dope, classically unlucky. He had it coming, in a way, like an innocent fool in a silent movie.

You don't want Janet to give you any crap about it's on all the time, they show it a thousand times a day. They show it because it exists, because they have to show it, because this is why they're out there. The horror freezes your soul but this doesn't mean that you want them to stop.

[1994]

Michael S. Harper

[b. 1938]

Michael S. Harper was born on March 18, 1938, in Brooklyn, New York. He was the second of three children of Katherine Johnson Harper, a medical stenographer, and Walter Warren Harper, a post office supervisor. The couple owned a large collection of musical recordings, and as a child Harper took the subway into Manhattan to hear jazz musicians such as Charlie Parker. When he was thirteen, his family moved to Los Angeles, settling in a predominantly white neighborhood where "black houses were being bombed," as Harper recalled in an interview in 1990. He also confronted racism at the local public high school, in which he was placed on a vocational track until his parents intervened. Following his graduation in 1955, Harper worked part-time in the post office while taking classes at Los Angeles City College, a community college from which he received an Associate of Arts degree in 1959. He then enrolled at Los Angeles State

Michael S. Harper

LaVerne Harrell Clark took this photograph in 1973, while Harper was in Tucson to give a reading at the University of Arizona Poetry Center.

College (now California State University, Los Angeles), where he came under the tutelage of a remarkable group of writers teaching in the English department, including the British dramatist and novelist Christopher Isherwood. "He encouraged me to write one-act plays about jazz musicians," Harper recalled; "he encouraged me to capture their language, their idioms in wild scenes." With the help of his professors, Harper was admitted to the Writers' Workshop at the University of Iowa in 1961. The only black student in the program, he lived in segregated housing, haunted the library, and "contemplated my isolation when I wasn't selling pennants on Saturday afternoons," as he wryly observed. Most of all, he added, "I learned to cope and bide my time."

After a year at Iowa, from which he received his MFA in 1963, Harper pursued a career as a poet and teacher. His first teaching positions were at community colleges in California, where he married Shirley Anne Buffington in 1965. They later had five children, two of whom died in infancy from acute respiratory distress syndrome (ARDS). Meanwhile, Harper's poetry regularly appeared in literary journals such as the *Carolina Quarterly* and the *Negro Digest*. The prestigious magazine *Poetry* published six of his poems in 1968, and Harper was subsequently a poet in residence at Reed College and Lewis and Clark College in Oregon before he was hired as an associate professor of English at California State College at Hayward (now California State University, East Bay). Harper achieved his major breakthrough when the poet Gwendolyn Brooks, one of the judges of the U.S. Poetry Prize sponsored by the University of Pittsburgh, fought for the publication of his book *Dear John, Dear Coltrane* (1970). The volume, which was nominated for a National Book Award, is widely regarded as one of the most important collections of African American poetry to be published after World War II. During a year's leave from teaching, he wrote the poems in his second collection, *History Is Your Own Heartbeat* (1971), which was published about the time he went to Brown University as an associate professor of English. Since then, he has published nine more volumes of poetry, including *Images of Kin* (1977), which was nominated for a National Book Award; *Healing Song for Inner Ear* (1985); and *Honorable Amendments* (1995), which was selected by Gwendolyn Brooks for the George Kent Poetry Award. His *Selected Poems* was published in 2002.

Harper has also played a significant role in efforts to recover the work of earlier writers and to display the richness of the African American literary tradition. "In the beginning I never found poems in the American literary pantheon about the things I knew best," he stated in 1993. "I decided that I would at least do my part and try to put some of those poems in there." Two of the earlier poets he most admired were his close friends Robert Hayden and Sterling Brown. Harper published a limited edition of Hayden's *American Journal* (1978) and later edited a special issue of *Obsidian: Black Literature in Review* featuring memorial tributes to Hayden. Harper has also edited *The Collected Poems of Sterling A. Brown* (1989) and coedited three influential anthologies: *Chant of Saints: A Gathering of Afro-American Literature, Art, and Scholarship* (1979), which was widely regarded as one of the most important collections of African American materials since Alain Locke's *The New Negro* (1925); *Every Shut Eye Ain't Asleep: An Anthology of Poetry by African Americans since 1945* (1994), which was dedicated to Sterling Brown; and *The Vintage Book of African American Poetry* (2000). Harper, who has received numerous honors and was the first Poet Laureate of Rhode Island (1988–1993), is a professor at Brown University.

Reading Harper's Poetry.   "I've enjoyed the play of putting things together that don't belong together," Harper has observed. "I'm also a narrative poet who plays with syntax for musical overtones, and I hear everything I write. For me the poem is for the ear, but not a mechanical ear, not a metronome; I love phrasing, elegant and not so elegant associations, and drive, narrative drive." As he suggests, Harper frequently juxtaposes seemingly unrelated scenes or incidents in his poems, which reveal his deep love of music, especially the blues, gospel, and jazz. In the ironic epigraph to his first book, *Dear John, Dear Coltrane* (1970), he wrote: "A friend told me / He'd risen above jazz. / I leave him there." Harper pays tribute to jazz musicians in many of his poems, and his jazz-inflected verse is characterized by its rhythmical freedom, frequent repetitions, and refrains. He has also been inspired by poets ranging from William Carlos Williams to Gwendolyn Brooks, Sterling Brown, and Robert Hayden. Like his friend and mentor Hayden, Harper has persistently explored a theme announced in the title of the first poem in the following selection, "American History," ranging from the early history and heritage of African Americans to events such as the assassination of Martin Luther King Jr., the subject of the poem "Martin's Blues." The texts of the poems are taken from *Songlines in Michaeltree: New and Collected Poems* (2000).

bedfordstmartins.com/ americanlit for research links on Harper

AMERICAN HISTORY

Those four black girls blown up
in that Alabama church[1]
remind me of five hundred
middle passage blacks,[2]
in a net, under water

---

1. **Those four . . . Alabama church:** On Sunday, September 15, 1963, a bomb exploded at the Sixteenth Street Baptist Church in Birmingham, Alabama, a regular meeting place of civil rights activists such as Martin Luther King Jr. The bombing, which killed four young girls in a Sunday-school class and injured twenty-three other people, was widely believed to have been the work of racist whites. Although one man was tried and received a small fine for possession of dynamite, not until 2000 did the FBI announce that the bombing had been planned and executed by a splinter group of the Ku Klux Klan.
2. **middle passage blacks:** The Middle Passage was the route across the Atlantic Ocean followed by slave ships coming from Africa to the Americas.

in Charleston harbor
so *redcoats*³ wouldn't find them.
Can't find what you can't see
can you?

[1970, 2000]

---

3. *redcoats*: During most of the American Revolution, British soldiers or "redcoats" occupied Charleston, South Carolina.

DEAR JOHN, DEAR COLTRANE¹

a love supreme, a love supreme
a love supreme, a love supreme²

Sex fingers toes
in the marketplace
near your father's church
in Hamlet, North Carolina³ —
witness to this love   5
in this calm fallow
of these minds,
there is no substitute for pain:
genitals gone or going,
seed burned out,   10
you tuck the roots in the earth,
turn back, and move
by river through the swamps,
singing: *a love supreme, a love supreme*;
what does it all mean?   15
Loss, so great each black
woman expects your failure
in mute change, the seed gone.

---

1. **Dear John, Dear Coltrane:** The saxophonist John Coltrane (1926–1967), a leading figure in avant-garde jazz in the 1950s and 1960s.
2. **a love supreme:** Coltrane's *A Love Supreme*, a four-part suite his quartet recorded in 1964, is widely regarded as one of the greatest of all jazz albums. In his liner notes, Coltrane explains: "During the year 1957, I experienced by the grace of God, a spiritual awakening which was to lead me to a richer, fuller, more productive life." In gratitude for that epiphany, which had helped him overcome his addiction to alcohol and heroin, Coltrane made *A Love Supreme* as "a humble offering to Him."
3. **Sex . . . North Carolina:** "Dear John, Dear Coltrane" begins with a reference to Sam Hose, who was lynched and dismembered in the Atlanta riot of 1906. . . . The black church was a haven and revolutionary outpost for uncensored ideas, both of forgiveness and responsibility. [Harper's note] Coltrane was raised in a deeply religious Christian home in Hamlet, North Carolina.

You plod up into the electric city—
your song now crystal and   20
the blues. You pick up the horn
with some will and blow
into the freezing night:
a love supreme, a love supreme—

Dawn comes and you cook   25
up the thick sin 'tween
impotence and death, fuel
the tenor sax cannibal
heart, genitals, and sweat
that makes you clean—   30
a love supreme, a love supreme—

Why you so black?
cause I am
why you so funky?
cause I am   35
why you so black?
cause I am
why you so sweet?
cause I am
why you so black?   40
cause I am
a love supreme, a love supreme:

So sick
you couldn't play *Naima,*[4]
so flat we ached   45
for song you'd concealed
with your own blood,
your diseased liver gave
out its purity,
the inflated heart   50
pumps out, the tenor kiss,
tenor love:
a love supreme, a love supreme—
a love supreme, a love supreme—

[1970, 2000]

---

4. **So sick . . . *Naima*:** "Naima" is a song Coltrane wrote and named for his first wife. It is Coltrane, himself, who is singing. [Harper's note] Coltrane continued to perform until his death from liver cancer in 1967.

MARTIN'S BLUES[1]

He came apart in the open,
the slow motion cameras
falling quickly
neither alive nor kicking;
stone blind dead   5
on the balcony
that old melody
etched his black lips
in a pruned echo:
We shall overcome   10
some day[2] –
Yes we did!
Yes we did!

[1971, 2000]

---

1. **Martin's Blues:** "Martin's Blues" was written in the idiom of a children's ditty and found a place in the skipping rope games of preadolescents forced to grow up too soon. [Harper's note] Martin Luther King Jr. (1929–1968) was shot and killed by an assassin as he stood on a motel balcony in Memphis, Tennessee, on April 4, 1968.
2. ***We shall overcome / some day:*** Adopted from gospel songs, "We Shall Overcome" became the anthem of the civil rights movement.

Raymond Carver

[1938-1988]

His great gift is for writing stories that create meaning through their form.

–Marilynne Robinson

Raymond Clevie Carver Jr. was born on May 25, 1938, in Clatskanie, Oregon. He was the first of two sons of "R. C." Carver, a sawmill worker, and Ella Casey Carver, a waitress. Struggling to support themselves and their infant son in the small logging town, the couple moved to Yakima, Washington, in 1941. Carver's happiest memories of his difficult childhood were of listening breathlessly while his alcoholic father told wonderful stories, and Carver remained an avid participant in storytelling exchanges throughout his life. After his graduation from high school in 1956, he worked as a deliveryman and took classes at Yakima Community College. In 1957, he married his sixteen-year-old high-school girlfriend, Maryann Burk. She was pregnant with their first child, born later that year, and they had a second child in 1958. They moved to Paradise, California, where Carver enrolled as a part-time student at Chico State College (now California State University, Chico). Under the tutelage of the novelist John Gardner, Carver began to write fiction and founded a literary magazine, *Selection*, where his first story appeared in 1961. By then, he had transferred to Humboldt State College (now California State University, Humboldt), from which he graduated in 1963. With the aid of a small fellowship, he studied for a year at the Writers' Workshop at the University of Iowa. But there simply was not enough money to support the family, so he and his wife returned with their two young children to California. "We became displaced people like so many other people in California," Carver recalled:

> We lived in various and sundry places, from Los Angeles to Eureka. We worked all the time. It was strictly blue-collar stuff, like cleaning up in fast-food places. Things would come along that we thought would improve our lot and we'd pack up our kids and the belongings. We'd move on and it would begin all over again. I wasn't doing much writing. I scarcely had time to turn around or draw a breath.

Raymond Carver

Sophie Bassouls took this photograph of the influential short-story writer a year before his early death in 1988.

Despite the financial pressures and other obstacles, Carver somehow managed to establish himself as a writer. Several of his early stories appeared in small literary journals such as *Toyon* and *December*, and one of them was selected for inclusion in the *Best American Short Stories 1967*. Although he and his wife were forced to file for bankruptcy in the spring of 1967, their fortunes began to improve when Carver was hired as a textbook editor at Science Research Associates in Palo Alto, California. There, he became friends with Gordon Lish, who had previously edited avant-garde literary magazines and who soon became the influential fiction editor of the men's magazine *Esquire*. Carver's first book of poetry, *Winter Insomnia*, was published by a small college press in 1970, and his major break-through came the following year, when the first of his stories appeared in *Esquire*. Carver, who had worked so hard to earn a college degree and never completed his MFA, now began a career as a teacher of creative writing at the University of California, Santa Cruz, at Berkeley, and back at the Writers' Workshop. During the fall of 1974, he commuted between his jobs at Iowa and the University of California, Santa Barbara, but Carver was drinking so heavily and missing so many classes that he was forced to resign from both positions in December. He and his wife once again filed for bankruptcy, and the unemployed Carver wrote little, though in 1976 he published another collection of poetry, *At Night the Salmon Move*, and his first collection of short stories, *Will You Please Be Quiet, Please?*, which was nominated for a National Book Award.

Carver salvaged the remainder of his brief but brilliant literary career when he stopped drinking in 1977. Estranged and later divorced from his wife, he met the poet Tess Gallagher, with whom he began to live in 1979. He was the distinguished writer in residence at the University of Texas, El Paso, from 1978 to 1980, when he and Gallagher accepted positions in the creative writing program at Syracuse University. Carver published two major collections of his influential stories, *What We Talk About When We Talk About Love* (1981) and *Cathedral* (1983), which was nominated for a Pulitzer Prize. He also published *Fire: Essays, Poems, Stories* (1983).

Carver resigned from Syracuse in 1984, after he received a five-year "Livings" fellowship from the American Academy and Institute of Arts and Letters. Seeking escape from the glare of his subsequent celebrity, he and Gallagher began to spend most of their time at her secluded house overlooking the Puget Sound in Port Angeles, Washington. There, he wrote mostly essays, reviews, and especially poems, which were collected in *Where the Water Comes Together* (1986), *Ultramarine* (1987), and the posthumously published *A New Path to the Waterfall* (1989). His final published story appeared in the *New Yorker* in June 1987, a few months before Carver, a heavy smoker, began treatment for lung cancer. With Gallagher's help, he put together his last collection of stories, *Where I'm Calling From* (1988). Carver and Gallagher were married in June, two months before his death on August 2, 1988. At a memorial service, Robert Gottlieb, then the editor of the *New Yorker*, stated: "America has just lost the writer it could least afford to lose."

bedfordstmartins.com/
americanlit *for research
links on Carver*

Reading Carver's "Are These Actual Miles?"   This story was first published as "What Is It?" in May 1972 in *Esquire*, a magazine for men noted for publishing the work of both established and emerging writers. From 1969 to 1976, its fiction editor was Gordon Lish, who strongly promoted Carver's early work, much of which appeared in *Esquire*. "What Is It?" was subsequently included under that title in the *O. Henry Prize Stories 1973* and in Carver's first collection of stories, *Will You Please Be Quiet, Please?* (1976). But he changed the title to "Are These Actual Miles?" when he revised the story for his final collection, *Where I'm Calling From* (1988). The title is a question the sales manager of a used-car dealership asks about the car that he has bought from the bankrupt central character in the story, Leo, and his wife, Toni. As several critics have suggested, the question metaphorically calls attention to the wear and tear of the many miles their marriage has accumulated, the heavy toll taken on it by financial problems, infidelities, and lack of communication. The painful story, which was inspired in part by what Carver described as the "hardscrabble" life that he and his first wife experienced during the first decade of their marriage, also displays his trademark "minimalism," the term most often used to describe the spare language and taut style of his early stories. "I always overwrite, and I have to go back and cut," Carver observed in an interview shortly before his death in 1988. "Especially in the early days, when a ten-page story might have represented a thirty-page original one—I'd go through twenty drafts." The text is taken from *Where I'm Calling From: New and Selected Stories* (1988).

ARE THESE ACTUAL MILES?

Fact is the car needs to be sold in a hurry, and Leo sends Toni out to do it. Toni is smart and has personality. She used to sell children's encyclopedias door to door. She signed him up, even though he didn't have kids. Afterward, Leo asked her for a date, and the date led to this. This deal has to be cash, and it has to be done tonight. Tomorrow somebody they owe might slap a lien on the car. Monday they'll be in court, home free — but word on them went out yesterday, when their lawyer mailed the letters of intention. The hearing on Monday is nothing to worry about, the lawyer has said. They'll be asked some questions, and they'll sign some papers, and that's it. But sell the convertible, he said — today, *tonight.* They can hold onto the little car, Leo's car, no problem. But they go into court with that big convertible, the court will take it, and that's that.

Toni dresses up. It's four o'clock in the afternoon. Leo worries the lots will close. But Toni takes her time dressing. She puts on a new white blouse, wide lacy cuffs, the new two-piece suit, new heels. She transfers the stuff from her straw purse into the new patent-leather handbag. She studies the lizard makeup pouch and puts that in too. Toni has been two hours on her hair and face. Leo stands in the bedroom doorway and taps his lips with his knuckles, watching.

"You're making me nervous," she says. "I wish you wouldn't just stand," she says. "So tell me how I look."

"You look fine," he says. "You look great. I'd buy a car from you anytime."

"But you don't have money," she says, peering into the mirror. She pats her hair, frowns. "And your credit's lousy. You're nothing," she says. "Teasing," she says and looks at him in the mirror. "Don't be serious," she says. "It has to be done, so I'll do it. You take it out, you'd be lucky to get three, four hundred and we both know it. Honey, you'd be lucky if you didn't have to pay *them.*" She gives her hair a final pat, gums her lips, blots the lipstick with a tissue. She turns away from the mirror and picks up her purse: "I'll have to have dinner or something, I told you that already, that's the way they work, I know them. But don't worry, I'll get out of it," she says. "I can handle it."

"Jesus," Leo says, "did you have to say that?"

She looks at him steadily. "Wish me luck," she says.

"Luck," he says. "You have the pink slip?" he says.

She nods. He follows her through the house, a tall woman with a small high bust, broad hips and thighs. He scratches a pimple on his neck. "You're sure?" he says. "Make sure. You have to have the pink slip."

"I have the pink slip," she says.

"Make sure."

She starts to say something, instead looks at herself in the front window and then shakes her head.

"At least call," he says. "Let me know what's going on."

"I'll call," she says. "Kiss, kiss. Here," she says and points to the corner of her mouth. "Careful," she says.

He holds the door for her. "Where are you going to try first?" he says. She moves past him and onto the porch.

Ernest Williams looks from across the street. In his Bermuda shorts, stomach hanging, he looks at Leo and Toni as he directs a spray onto his begonias. Once, last winter, during the holidays, when Toni and the kids were visiting his mother's, Leo brought a woman home. Nine o'clock the next morning, a cold foggy Saturday, Leo walked the woman to the car, surprised Ernest Williams on the sidewalk with a news-paper in his hand. Fog drifted, Ernest Williams stared, then slapped the paper against his leg, hard.

Leo recalls that slap, hunches his shoulders, says, "You have someplace in mind first?"

"I'll just go down the line," she says. "The first lot, then I'll just go down the line."

"Open at nine hundred," he says. "Then come down. Nine hundred is low bluebook, even on a cash deal."

"I know where to start," she says.

Ernest Williams turns the hose in their direction. He stares at them through the spray of water. Leo has an urge to cry out a confession.

"Just making sure," he says.

"Okay, okay," she says. "I'm off."

It's her car, they call it her car, and that makes it all the worse. They bought it new that summer three years ago. She wanted something to do after the kids started school, so she went back selling. He was working six days a week in the fiber-glass plant. For a while they didn't know how to spend the money. Then they put a thousand on the con-vertible and doubled and tripled the payments until in a year they had it paid. Earlier, while she was dressing, he took the jack and spare from the trunk and emptied the glove compartment of pencils, matchbooks, Blue Chip stamps.[1] Then he washed it and vacu-umed inside. The red hood and fenders shine.

"Good luck," he says and touches her elbow.

She nods. He sees she is already gone, already negotiating.

"Things are going to be different!" he calls to her as she reaches the driveway. "We start over Monday. I mean it."

Ernest Williams looks at them and turns his head and spits. She gets into the car and lights a cigarette.

"This time next week!" Leo calls again. "Ancient history!"

He waves as she backs into the street. She changes gear and starts ahead. She accel-erates and the tires give a little scream.

In the kitchen Leo pours Scotch and carries the drink to the backyard. The kids are at his mother's. There was a letter three days ago, his name penciled on the outside of the dirty envelope, the only letter all summer not demanding payment in full. We are having fun, the letter said. We like Grandma. We have a new dog called Mr. Six. He is nice. We love him. Good-bye.

---

1. **Blue Chip stamps:** These trading stamps were distributed at gas stations and stores as part of a loyalty pro-gram for customers, who pasted the stamps into books that could be redeemed for various kinds of merchandise.

He goes for another drink. He adds ice and sees that his hand trembles. He holds the hand over the sink. He looks at the hand for a while, sets down the glass, and holds out the other hand. Then he picks up the glass and goes back outside to sit on the steps. He recalls when he was a kid his dad pointing at a fine house, a tall white house surrounded by apple trees and a high white rail fence. "That's Finch," his dad said admiringly. "He's been in bankruptcy at least twice. Look at that house." But bankruptcy is a company collapsing utterly, executives cutting their wrists and throwing themselves from windows, thousands of men on the street.

Leo and Toni still had furniture. Leo and Toni had furniture and Toni and the kids had clothes. Those things were exempt. What else? Bicycles for the kids, but these he had sent to his mother's for safekeeping. The portable air-conditioner and the appliances, new washer and dryer, trucks came for those things weeks ago. What else did they have? This and that, nothing mainly, stuff that wore out or fell to pieces long ago. But there were some big parties back there, some fine travel. To Reno and Tahoe,[2] at eighty with the top down and the radio playing. Food, that was one of the big items. They gorged on food. He figures thousands on luxury items alone. Toni would go to the grocery and put in everything she saw, "I had to do without when I was a kid," she says. "These kids are not going to do without," as if he'd been insisting they should. She joins all the book clubs. "We never had books around when I was a kid," she says as she tears open the heavy packages. They enroll in the record clubs for something to play on the new stereo. They sign up for it all. Even a pedigreed terrier named Ginger. He paid two hundred and found her run over in the street a week later. They buy what they want. If they can't pay, they charge. They sign up.

His undershirt is wet; he can feel the sweat rolling from his underarms. He sits on the step with the empty glass in his hand and watches the shadows fill up the yard. He stretches, wipes his face. He listens to the traffic on the highway and considers whether he should go to the basement, stand on the utility sink, and hang himself with his belt. He understands he is willing to be dead.

Inside he makes a large drink and he turns the TV on and he fixes something to eat. He sits at the table with chili and crackers and watches something about a blind detective. He clears the table. He washes the pan and the bowl, dries these things and puts them away, then allows himself a look at the clock.

It's after nine. She's been gone nearly five hours.

He pours Scotch, adds water, carries the drink to the living room. He sits on the couch but finds his shoulders so stiff they won't let him lean back. He stares at the screen and sips, and soon he goes for another drink. He sits again. A news program begins—it's ten o'clock—and he says, "God, what in God's name has gone wrong?" and goes to the kitchen to return with more Scotch. He sits, he closes his eyes, and opens them when he hears the telephone ringing.

"I wanted to call," she says.

---

2. **Reno and Tahoe:** Reno, Nevada, famous for its casinos; and Lake Tahoe, a major tourist attraction along the border between California and Nevada.

"Where are you?" he says. He hears piano music, and his heart moves.

"I don't know," she says. "Someplace. We're having a drink, then we're going some-place else for dinner. I'm with the sales manager. He's crude, but he's all right. He bought the car. I have to go now. I was on my way to the ladies and saw the phone."

"Did somebody buy the car?" Leo says. He looks out the kitchen window to the place in the drive where she always parks.

"I told you," she says. "I have to go now."

"Wait, wait a minute, for Christ's sake," he says. "Did somebody buy the car or not?"

"He had his checkbook out when I left," she says. "I have to go now. I have to go to the bathroom."

"Wait!" he yells. The line goes dead. He listens to the dial tone. "Jesus Christ," he says as he stands with the receiver in his hand.

He circles the kitchen and goes back to the living room. He sits. He gets up. In the bathroom he brushes his teeth very carefully. Then he uses dental floss. He washes his face and goes back to the kitchen. He looks at the clock and takes a clean glass from a set that has a hand of playing cards painted on each glass. He fills the glass with ice. He stares for a while at the glass he left in the sink.

He sits against one end of the couch and puts his legs up at the other end. He looks at the screen, realizes he can't make out what the people are saying. He turns the empty glass in his hand and considers biting off the rim. He shivers for a time and thinks of going to bed, though he knows he will dream of a large woman with gray hair. In the dream he is always leaning over tying his shoelaces. When he straightens up, she looks at him, and he bends to tie again. He looks at his hand. It makes a fist as he watches. The telephone is ringing.

"Where are you, honey?" he says slowly, gently.

"We're at this restaurant," she says, her voice strong, bright.

"Honey, which restaurant?" he says. He puts the heel of his hand against his eye and pushes.

"Downtown someplace," she says. "I think it's New Jimmy's. Excuse me," she says to someone off the line, "is this place New Jimmy's? This is New Jimmy's, Leo," she says to him. "Everything is all right, we're almost finished, then he's going to bring me home."

"Honey?" he says. He holds the receiver against his ear and rocks back and forth, eyes closed. "Honey?"

"I have to go," she says. "I wanted to call. Anyway, guess how much?"

"Honey," he says.

"Six and a quarter," she says. "I have it in my purse. He said there's no market for con-vertibles. I guess we're born lucky," she says and laughs. "I told him everything. I think I had to."

"Honey," Leo says.

"What?" she says.

"Please, honey," Leo says.

"He said he sympathizes," she says. "But he would have said anything." She laughs again. "He said personally he'd rather be classified a robber or a rapist than a bankrupt. He's nice enough, though," she says.

"Come home," Leo says. "Take a cab and come home."

"I can't," she says. "I told you, we're halfway through dinner."

"I'll come for you," he says.

"No," she says. "I said we're just finishing. I told you, it's part of the deal. They're out for all they can get. But don't worry, we're about to leave. I'll be home in a little while." She hangs up.

In a few minutes he calls New Jimmy's. A man answers. "New Jimmy's has closed for the evening," the man says.

"I'd like to talk to my wife," Leo says.

"Does she work here?" the man asks. "Who is she?"

"She's a customer," Leo says, "She's with someone. A business person."

"Would I know her?" the man says. "What is her name?"

"I don't think you know her," Leo says.

"That's all right," Leo says. "That's all right. I see her now."

"Thank you for calling New Jimmy's," the man says.

Leo hurries to the window. A car he doesn't recognize slows in front of the house, then picks up speed. He waits. Two, three hours later, the telephone rings again. There is no one at the other end when he picks up the receiver. There is only a dial tone.

"I'm right here!" Leo screams into the receiver.

Near dawn he hears footsteps on the porch. He gets up from the couch. The set hums, the screen glows. He opens the door. She bumps the wall coming in. She grins. Her face is puffy, as if she's been sleeping under sedation, She works her lips, ducks heavily and sways as he cocks his fist.

"Go ahead," she says thickly. She stands there swaying. Then she makes a noise and lunges, catches his shirt, tears it down the front. "Bankrupt!" she screams. She twists loose, grabs and tears his undershirt at the neck. "You son of a bitch," she says clawing.

He squeezes her wrists, then lets go, steps back, looking for something heavy. She stumbles as she heads for the bedroom. "Bankrupt," she mutters. He hears her fall on the bed and groan.

He waits awhile, then splashes water on his face and goes to the bedroom. He turns the lights on, looks at her, and begins to take her clothes off. He pulls and pushes her from side to side undressing her. She says something in her sleep and moves her hand. He takes off her underpants, looks at them closely under the light, and throws them into a corner. He turns back the covers and rolls her in, naked. Then he opens her purse. He is reading the check when he hears the car come into the drive.

He looks through the front curtain and sees the convertible in the drive, its motor running smoothly, the headlamps burning, and he closes and opens his eyes. He sees a tall man come around in front of the car and up to the front porch. The man lays something on the porch and starts back to the car. He wears a white linen suit.

Leo turns on the porch light and opens the door cautiously. Her makeup pouch lies on the top step. The man looks at Leo across the front of the car, and then gets back inside and releases the handbrake.

"Wait!" Leo calls and starts down the steps. The man brakes the car as Leo walks in front of the lights. The car creaks against the brake. Leo tries to pull the two pieces of his shirt together, tries to bunch it all into his trousers.

"What is it you want?" the man says. "Look," the man says, "I have to go. No offense. I buy and sell cars, right? The lady left her makeup. She's a fine lady, very refined. What is it?"

Leo leans against the door and looks at the man. The man takes his hands off the wheel and puts them back. He drops the gear into reverse and the car moves backward a little.

"I want to tell you," Leo says and wets his lips.

The light in Ernest Williams' bedroom goes on. The shade rolls up.

Leo shakes his head, tucks in his shirt again. He steps back from the car. "Monday," he says.

"Monday," the man says and watches for sudden movement.

Leo nods slowly.

"Well, goodnight," the man says and coughs. "Take it easy, hear? Monday, that's right. Okay, then." He takes his foot off the brake, puts it on again after he has rolled back two or three feet. "Hey, one question. Between friends, are these actual miles?" The man waits, then clears his throat. "Okay, look, it doesn't matter either way," the man says. "I have to go. Take it easy." He backs into the street, pulls away quickly, and turns the corner without stopping.

Leo tucks at his shirt and goes back in the house. He locks the front door and checks it. Then he goes to the bedroom and locks that door and turns back the covers. He looks at her before he flicks the light. He takes off his clothes, folds them carefully on the floor, and gets in beside her. He lies on his back for a time and pulls the hair on his stomach, considering. He looks at the bedroom door, outlined now in the faint outside light. Presently he reaches out his hand and touches her hip. She does not move. He turns on his side and puts his hand on her hip. He runs his fingers over her hip and feels the stretch marks there. They are like roads, and he traces them in her flesh. He runs his fingers back and forth, first one, then another. They run everywhere in her flesh, dozens, perhaps hundreds of them. He remembers waking up the morning after they bought the car, seeing it, there in the drive, in the sun, gleaming.

[1972, 1988]

Gloria Anzaldúa

[1942–2004]

Gloria Evangelina Anzaldúa was born on September 26, 1942, on a ranch settlement called Jesus Maria in the Rio Grande valley of south Texas. She was the eldest of four children born to tenant farmers, Urbano and Amalia Anzaldúa. From an early age, Anzaldúa was an avid reader, and books at once exposed the injustices in her world and opened up new horizons for her. "One day when I was about seven or eight, my father dropped on my lap a 25 cent pocket western, the only type of book he could pick up at a drugstore," she recalled in an autobiographical essay, "La Prieta" (1981):

> The act of reading forever changed me. In the westerns I read, the house servants, the villains and the cantineras (prostitutes) were all Mexicans. But I knew that the first cowboys (vaqueros) were Mexicans, that in Texas we outnumbered the Anglos, that my grandmother's ranch lands had been ripped off by the greedy Anglo. Yet in the pages of these books, the Mexican and Indian were vermin. The racism I would later recognize in my schoolteachers and never be able to ignore again I found in that first western I read.

Gloria Anzaldúa

Margaret Randall took this photograph of Anzaldúa, a writer, scholar, and radical activist best known for her influential book *Borderlands/La Frontera* (1987).

When Anzaldúa was eleven, her family moved to a farm outside Hargill, Texas, close to the border with Mexico. She and her siblings continued to work in the fields while they attended segregated schools in Hargill and later in Edinburgh, Texas. When her father died suddenly of a heart attack in 1956, Anzaldúa was devastated, but she continued her reading and study. "Books saved my sanity, knowledge opened the locked places in me and taught me first how to survive and then how to soar," she wrote in 1987.

Anzaldúa was determined to gain an education and to educate others. After her graduation from high school, she attended Texas Women's University before transferring to a college closer to home, Pan American University (now the University of Texas-Pan American), from which she graduated with a BA in English, art, and secondary education in 1969. For the next four years, she taught at public schools in Texas while earning an MA during the summers at the University of Texas at Austin. From June 1973 to September 1974, she was the state director of migrant education in Indiana. When she returned, she became a PhD candidate in comparative literature and an instructor at the University of Texas, Austin. But her professors there discouraged her interests in feminist theory and the emerging field of Chicana/o studies, so she moved to California in 1977. She supported herself by giving lectures and teaching at several schools, including San Francisco State University. She also became involved in the Feminist Writers Guild. Frustrated by the inability of some white feminists to recognize the additional obstacles faced by women of color, she published "Speaking in Tongues: A Letter to Third World Women Writers." Anzaldúa included the essay in a multigenre anthology she coedited with the writer Cherríe Moraga, *This Bridge Called My Back: Writings by Radical Women of Color* (1981). After the small feminist press that published the book folded, a new edition was brought out in 1983 by the first press exclusively devoted to publishing works by women of color, the Kitchen Table/Women of Color Press, founded by Barbara Smith and Audre Lorde. The groundbreaking anthology exerted a profound influence on feminist theory and the direction of the women's movement, and it later received an American Book Award, designed to honor the multicultural diversity of American writing, from the Before Columbus Foundation.

Anzaldúa subsequently became widely known as an activist, cultural critic, feminist theorist, and writer. In 1987, she published her most acclaimed and influential work, *Borderlands/La Frontera: The New Mestiza*, an innovative collection of poetry and prose in which she explored the history and culture of the "third country," as she described the border between Mexico and the United States. Anzaldúa also developed a radical theory that challenged what she viewed as the binary, either/or conceptions of both race and sexuality in the Europeanized West. The book was later included in the *Hungry Mind Review*'s list of the "100 Best 20th-Century American Books of Fiction and Nonfiction," as well as in the "Alternate Canon," a list of 150 of the world's great books compiled by the *Utne Reader*. In the final years of her life, Anzaldúa published two children's books and a collection of her interviews, *Interviews/Entrevistas* (2000), as well as the anthologies *Making Face, Making Soul: Haciendo Caras* (1990) and *this bridge we call home: radical visions for transformation* (2002), which she coedited with AnaLouise Keating. Anzaldúa was completing her doctoral dissertation when she died of complications resulting from diabetes on May 15, 2004.

Reading Anzaldúa's "El sonavabitche." In the preface to *Borderlands*, where this poem was first published, Anzaldúa defined herself as a new *mestiza*, a "border woman" who had grown up "between two cultures, the Mexican (with a heavy Indian influence) and the Anglo (as a member of a colonized people in our own territory)." As she explained, however, the psychological, sexual, and spiritual borderlands she explored in the book are "present wherever two or more cultures edge each other, where people of different races occupy the same territory, where under, lower, middle and upper classes touch, where the space between two individuals shrinks with intimacy." Just as she challenged rigid classifications of class, culture, race, and sexuality, Anzaldúa rejected strict generic distinctions in *Borderlands*, an innovative collection of autobiographical and historical essays, lyrical prose sketches, and poetry. She also employed a hybrid language derived from different forms of English and Spanish, a rich dialect Anzaldúa called Chicano Spanish and others have called "Spanglish." In her first-person narrative poem "El sonavabitche," which was inspired by Anzaldúa's experiences working as an educator among migrant workers in Indiana during the early 1970s, she exposes the brutality, exploitation, and racism in a "borderland" far from the actual border between the United States and Mexico. The text is taken from the first edition of *Borderlands/La Frontera: The New Mestiza* (1987).

bedfordstmartins.com/ americanlit for research links on Anzaldúa

EL SONAVABITCHE

(for Aishe Berger)

Car flowing down a lava of highway
just happened to glance out the window

in time to see brown faces bent backs
like prehistoric boulders in a field
so common a sight no one   5
notices
blood rushes to my face
twelve years I'd sat on the memory
the anger scorching me
my throat so tight I can   10
barely get the words out.

I got to the farm
in time to hear the shots
ricochet off barn,
spit into the sand,
in time to see tall men in uniforms   15
thumping fists on doors
metallic voices yelling Halt!
their hawk eyes constantly shifting.

When I hear the words, "*Corran muchachos*"[1]   20
I run back to the car, ducking,
see the glistening faces, arms outflung,
of the *mexicanos*[2] running headlong
through the fields
kicking up clouds of dirt   25

see them reach the tree line
foliage opening, swishing closed behind them.
I hear the tussling of bodies, grunts, panting
squeak of leather squawk of walkie-talkies
sun reflecting off gunbarrels   30
the world a blinding light
a great buzzing in my ears
my knees like aspens in the wind.

I see that wide cavernous look of the hunted
the look of hares   35
thick limp blue-black hair
The bare heads humbly bent
of those who do not speak
the ember in their eyes extinguished.

---

1. *"Corran muchachos"*: "Run boys" (Spanish). [Anzaldúa's note]
2. *mexicanos*: Mexicans.

I lean on the shanty wall of that migrant camp 40
north of Muncie, Indiana.
Wets, a voice says.
I turn to see a Chicano[3] pushing
the head of his *muchachita*[4]
back into the *naguas*[5] of the mother 45
a tin plate face down on the floor
tortillas scattered around them.
His other hand signals me over.
He too is from *el valle de Tejas*[6]
I had been his kid's teacher. 50
I'd come to get the grower
to fill up the sewage ditch near the huts
saying it wouldn't do for the children
to play in it.

    Smoke from a cooking fire and 55
    shirtless *niños*[7] gather around us.

    Mojados,[8] he says again,
    leaning on his chipped Chevy station wagon
    Been here two weeks
    about a dozen of them. 60
    The *sonavabitche* works them
    from sunup to dark — 15 hours sometimes.
    Como mulas los trabaja
    no saben como hacer la perra.[9]
    Last Sunday they asked for a day off 65
    wanted to pray and rest,
    write letters to their *familias.*
    ¿Y sabes lo que hizo el sonavabitche?[10]
    He turns away and spits.
    Says he has to hold back half their wages 70
    that they'd eaten the other half:

---

3. **Chicano:** A Mexican American male, probably derived from the Spanish *mejicano,* "Mexican."
4. *muchachita*: Little girl (Spanish). [Anzaldúa's note]
5. *naguas*: Skirt (Spanish). [Anzaldúa's note]
6. *el valle de Tejas*: Rio Grande Valley in Texas (Spanish). [Anzaldúa's note]
7. *niños*: Children (Spanish).
8. **Mojados:** Wetbacks, undocumented workers, illegal immigrants from Mexico and parts south (Spanish). [Anzaldúa's note]
9. *Como mulas . . . la perra*: He works them like mules. They don't know how to make the work easier for themselves (Spanish). [Anzaldúa's note]
10. *¿Y sabes lo que hizo . . . ?*: And you know what he did? (Spanish). [Anzaldúa's note]

sack of beans, sack of rice, sack of flour.
Frijoleros sí lo son[11] but no way
could they have eaten that many *frijoles.*
I nod.   75

Como le dije, son doce[12] — started out 13
five days packed in the back of a pickup
boarded up tight
fast cross-country run no stops
except to change drivers, to gas up   80
no food they pissed into their shoes —
those that had *guaraches*[13]
slept slumped against each other
sabe Dios[14] where they shit.
One smothered to death on the way here.   85

    Miss, you should've seen them when they
    stumbled out.
    First thing the *sonavabitche* did was clamp
    a handkerchief over his nose
    then ordered them stripped   90
    hosed them down himself
    in front of everybody.
    They hobbled about
    learning to walk all over again.
    Flacos con caras de viejos   95
    aunque la mitá eran jóvenes.[15]

Como le estaba diciendo,[16]
today was payday.
You saw them, *la migra*[17] came busting in
waving their *pinche pistolas.*[18]   100
Said someone made a call,
what you call it? Anonymous.
Guess who? That *sonavabitche*, who else?

---

11. **Frijoleros sí lo son**: Bean eaters they are (Spanish). [Anzaldúa's note]
12. **Como le dije, son doce**: Like I told you, they're 12 (Spanish). [Anzaldúa's note]
13. **guaraches**: Sandals (Spanish). [Anzaldúa's note]
14. **sabe Dios**: God knows (Spanish). [Anzaldúa's note]
15. **Flacos . . . jóvenes**: Skinny with old faces though half were youths (Spanish). [Anzaldúa's note]
16. **Como le estaba diciendo**: As I was telling you (Spanish). [Anzaldúa's note]
17. **la migra**: Slang for immigration officials (Spanish). [Anzaldúa's note]
18. **pinche pistolas**: Bloody guns (Spanish).

Done this three times since we've been coming here
Sepa Dios[19] how many times in between.   105
    Wets, free labor, *esclavos.*[20]
    Pobres jijos de la chingada.[21]
    This the last time we work for him
    no matter how *fregados*[22] we are
    he said, shaking his head,   110
    spitting at the ground.
    Vámonos, mujer, empaca el mugrero.[23]

    He hands me a cup of coffee,
    half of it sugar, half of it milk
    my throat so dry I even down the dregs.   115
    It has to be done.
    Steeling myself
    I take that walk to the big house.

Finally the big man lets me in.
How about a drink? I shake my head.   120
He looks me over, opens his eyes wide
and smiles, says how sorry he is immigration
is getting so tough
a poor Mexican can't make a living
and they sure do need the work.   125
My throat so thick the words stick.
He studies me, then says,
Well, what can I do you for?
I want two weeks wages
including two Saturdays and Sundays,   130
minimum wage, 15 hours a day.
I'm more startled than he.
Whoa there, sinorita,
wets work for whatever you give them
the season hasn't been good.   135
Besides most are halfway to Mexico by now.
Two weeks wages, I say,
the words swelling in my throat.

    Miss uh what did you say your name was?
    I fumble for my card.   140

---

19. **Sepa Dios**: God may know (Spanish).
20. **esclavos**: Slaves (Spanish). [Anzaldúa's note]
21. **Pobres jijos de la chingada**: Poor sons of the fucked one (Spanish). [Anzaldúa's note]
22. **fregados**: Poor, beaten, downtrodden, in need (Spanish). [Anzaldúa's note]
23. **Vámonos, mujer, empaca el mugrero**: Let's go, woman, pack our junk (Spanish). [Anzaldúa's note]

You can't do this,
I haven't broken no law,
his lidded eyes darken, I step back.
I'm leaving in two minutes and I want cash
the whole amount right here in my purse   145
when I walk out.
No hoarseness, no trembling.
It startled both of us.

You want me telling every single one
of your neighbors what you've been doing   150
all these years? The mayor, too?
Maybe make a call to Washington?
Slitted eyes studied the card again.
They had no cards, no papers.
I'd seen it over and over.   155
Work them, then turn them in before paying them.

Well, now, he was saying,
I know we can work something out,
a sweet young thang like yourself.
Cash, I said. I didn't know anyone in D.C.   160
now I didn't have to.
You want to keep it for yourself?
That it? His eyes were pin pricks.
Sweat money, Mister, blood money,
not my sweat, but same blood.   165
Yeah, but who's to say you won't abscond with it?
If I ever hear that you got illegals on your land
even a single one, I'm going to come here
in broad daylight and have you
hung by your balls.   170
He walks slowly to his desk.
Knees shaking, I count every bill
taking my time.

[1987]

The award-winning novelist Sandra Cisneros is a central figure in contemporary Chicana literature (see pp. 2288–2292). She was one of several writers who wrote posthumous tributes to Anzaldúa for an introduction to a new edition of the latter's pathbreaking collection *Borderlands / La Frontera: The New Mestiza*, which had first been published in 1987. As Cisneros notes, she and Anzaldúa met primarily as writers, who "knew each other most intimately on the page." As she also emphasizes, however, that created a special bond between her and Anzaldúa, a "fellow explorer" whose discoveries encouraged Cisneros in her own "solitary expeditions" and made her feel "less lonely." The text is taken from *Borderlands / La Frontera: The New Mestiza* (2007).

SANDRA CISNEROS

[b. 1954]

A Note to Gloria from the Bottom of the Sea

I wish I had a wonderful story to tell about Gloria Anzaldúa. I wish I could say she slept on my fold-out futon in my living room. Or that we once went shoe-shopping together at the Vogue in downtown San Antonio before they went out of business. Or that once, on a hot, sticky Texas afternoon, we stripped to our slips and shared beer and gossip on my back porch under the thwack of ceiling fans and painted our toes. But those stories belong to other friends.

I only met Gloria a handful of times in my life, usually with a whole bunch of people hanging around. Once we had dinner together alone at the Liberty Bar because I demanded it, but most of the time, our lives were so cluttered we never had the opportunity to meet each other as people, only as "Authors." And always as writers. By this I mean we knew each other most intimately on the page.

I think with writers like Gloria, you hate to impose on their time. I know I didn't want to be another *chupacabra*[1] and take away from the quiet and energy she needed to write. It's that way with my closest friends who write. I don't want to take away the most valuable thing they have—the solitude necessary to hear the things inside your heart.

So I can't tell you anything personal about Gloria since I didn't know her that way. And I don't have a funny anecdote either. I only know had I lived any closer and been a neighbor, perhaps I would've known her even less. Maybe I would have allowed for Gloria to disappear for long lapses of time without giving it a second thought. After all, I wouldn't want to be called *una fregona*, or worse, *una fisgona*.[2]

Maybe I wouldn't have thought it strange, Gloria disappearing that week she died, closing herself up and just ducking into herself. That would've been perfectly natural for a writer. Both the retreat and the silence, I mean. It's why she moved away from Texas to California no doubt. It's why I moved away from Illinois to Texas. So that the relatives and family would allow me the liberty to disappear into myself. To reinvent myself if I had to. As Latinas, we have to.

Because writing is like putting your head underwater. It takes a great effort to go under, to push yourself to the sea bottom, a tremendous courage to withstand the pressure and pain and stay down there. Then the bobbing to the surface when a lifeline tugs you back.

She was a fellow explorer. Someone I knew who was also studying the bottom of the sea. She drew up different flora and fauna, and her scientific efforts yielded discoveries beautiful and brilliant that encouraged me in my own solitary expeditions and made me feel less lonely.

Recently there was a rumor going round in Buenos Aires that I had died. It took a while to realize I had been confused with Gloria Anzaldúa. But I think the rumor of Gloria Anzaldúa's death is also greatly exaggerated. I knew Gloria through her writing, and for me that writing is as alive and intimate as ever.

[2007]

---

1. *chupacabra*: Literally, "goat sucker" (Spanish), a legendary creature reported all across the Americas, where it is said to kill goats and other livestock by sucking their blood.
2. *una fregona . . . una fisgona*: Chicana slang terms for a person who bothers or interrupts others and a person who continually criticizes or gossips about others.

Alice Walker

[b. 1944]

Alice Malsenior Walker was born on February 9, 1944. She was the last of six children born to Willie Lee and Minnie Grant Walker, sharecroppers in Eatonville, Georgia. Despite resistance from her husband, Walker's mother was determined to educate their youngest daughter and enrolled her in the first grade when she was only four. In 1952, Walker was blinded in her right eye when her brother accidentally shot her with his BB gun while they were playing cowboys and Indians. The injury traumatized Walker, who felt that the scar tissue was ugly and who began spending most of her time alone, reading and writing poems. In 1961, she graduated from high school as the class valedictorian and received a scholarship to Spelman College, a historically black college for women in Atlanta. She became deeply involved in the civil rights movement, met Martin Luther King Jr. and heard him deliver his famous "I have a dream" speech at the March on Washington for Jobs and Freedom in 1963. That year, she won a scholarship and transferred to Sarah Lawrence College in Bronxville, New York. After a trip to Africa, Walker discovered she was pregnant. In despair, she contemplated suicide but instead had an abortion and wrote a story, "To Hell with Dying," which she gave to one of her teachers at Sarah Lawrence, the writer Muriel Rukeyser. Rukeyser sent the story to Langston Hughes, who later included it in *Best Short Stories by Negro Writers* (1967).

After her graduation from college in 1965, Walker devoted much of her time to politics, teaching, and writing. She married Mel Levanthal, a white civil rights lawyer, and they moved to Jackson, Mississippi. While teaching as a writer in residence at the historically black Jackson State College (now University) and Tougaloo College, Walker published her first volume of poems, *Once* (1968), and wrote her first novel, *The Third Life of Grange Copeland* (1970), the story of three generations of a black family in a small town in Georgia. About the time she finished the novel in 1969, Walker gave birth to a daughter and began work as the history consultant to a Head Start program in Mississippi. Two years later, she was awarded a fellowship at Radcliffe College in Cambridge, Massachusetts, and she subsequently taught at Wellesley College and the University of Massachusetts, Boston. In 1973, she published another collection of poetry, *Revolutionary Petunias*, and her first book of short stories, *In Love and Trouble.* In the process of doing research for one of her stories, she discovered the writer Zora Neale Hurston, whom she described as a "cultural Revolutionary," and whose works had a profound impact on Walker. She famously located

Alice Walker

This photograph of Walker was taken in the 1980s, following the publication of her best-selling novel *The Color Purple* (1982).

Hurston's unmarked grave in Florida, where Walker arranged for a headstone to honor her literary "foremother." Walker returned briefly to Mississippi, where she completed a semiautobiographical novel about a woman who grows up in Georgia and becomes involved in the civil rights movement, *Meridian* (1976). By the time it was published, however, Walker had become frustrated with the slow progress of the movement in Mississippi and moved to New York City, where she became an editor of the feminist magazine *Ms.*

Following her divorce from Mel Levanthal, Walker moved with her daughter to northern California in 1978. During her first years there, she edited a collection of Hurston's works, *I Love Myself When I Am Laughing* (1979). Walker also published a volume of poems about the experiences of black women, *Good Night, Willie Lee, I'll See You in the Morning* (1979), and her second collection of short stories, *You Can't Keep a Good Woman Down* (1981). In what proved to be a crucial turning point in her career, she also wrote her most famous and celebrated work, *The Color Purple* (1982), an unconventional novel in which the central character, Celie, tells the painful story of her life through ninety letters addressed to God. The searing saga of a black woman's struggle for independence was awarded the Pulitzer Prize and later made into a hit movie produced by Steven Spielberg and starring Whoopi Goldberg, Oprah Winfrey, and Danny Glover. Following the publication of her ambitious novel *The Temple of My Familiar* (1989), whose narrative spans 500,000 years and ranges from Africa to the United States, Walker turned to the taboo subject of female circumcision in her next novel, *Possessing the Secret of Joy* (1992). She and a friend, Pratibha Parmar, produced a documentary about female genital mutilation in Africa, and Walker wrote an account of the making of the film, *Warrior Marks* (1993). She also wrote *The Same River Twice* (1996), about the filming of *The Color Purple*. Since then, Walker has published several collections of essays, poems, and stories, as well as a novel about a woman's spiritual pilgrimage through nature, *Now Is the Time to Open Your Heart* (2004). Her recent books include a collection of essays on environmentalism, politics, and spirituality, *We Are the Ones We Have Been Waiting For* (2006); a children's book, *Why War Is Never a Good Idea* (2007); *Hard Times Require Furious Dancing: New Poems* (2010); and a celebration of her flock of chickens, *The Chicken Chronicles* (2012).

The rhythms of Alice Walker's prose are beautiful and characteristic, flexible, vigorous, easy, the gait of a hunting lion.
–Ursula K. Le Guin

Reading Walker's "Everyday Use." This story first appeared in *Harper's* magazine in April 1973, in advance of its publication in Walker's first book of stories, *In Love and Trouble*, which she dedicated, in part, to the memory of three African American writers: Zora Neale Hurston, Nella Larsen, and Jean Toomer. In "Everyday Use," Walker developed one of the central themes of her work, the vital but unacknowledged tradition of black women's art, represented in the story by quilts handed down from generation to generation. In an essay in her collection *In Search of Our Mother's Gardens: Womanist Prose* (1983), Walker recalls that she once saw a magnificent quilt, "obviously the work of a person of powerful imagination and deep spiritual feeling," in the Smithsonian Institution in Washington:

> Below this quilt I saw a note that says it was made by "an anonymous Black woman in Alabama, a hundred years ago." If we could locate this "anonymous" black woman from Alabama, she would turn out to be one of our grandmothers – an artist who left her mark in the only materials she could afford, and in the only medium her position in society allowed her to use.

In "Everyday Use," Walker also drew upon her childhood memories of the visits home by her brilliant and accomplished older sister, who, as she wrote in her poem "For My Sister Molly Who in the Fifties,"

> FOUND ANOTHER WORLD
> Another life   With gentlefolk
> Far less trusting
> And moved and moved and changed
> Her name.

bedfordstmartins.com/
americanlit *for research*
links on Walker

The text of the story is taken from *In Love and Trouble: Stories of Black Women* (1973).

EVERYDAY USE

for your grandmama[1]

I will wait for her in the yard that Maggie and I made so clean and wavy yesterday afternoon. A yard like this is more comfortable than most people know. It is not just a yard. It is like an extended living room. When the hard clay is swept clean as a floor and the fine sand around the edges lined with tiny, irregular grooves, anyone can come and sit and look up into the elm tree and wait for the breezes that never come inside the house.

Maggie will be nervous until after her sister goes: she will stand hopelessly in corners, homely and ashamed of the burn scars down her arms and legs, eying her sister with a mixture of envy and awe. She thinks her sister has held life always in the palm of one hand, that "no" is a word the world never learned to say to her.

You've no doubt seen those TV shows where the child who has "made it" is confronted, as a surprise, by her own mother and father, tottering in weakly from backstage. (A pleasant surprise, of course: What would they do if parent and child came on the show only to curse out and insult each other?) On TV mother and child embrace and smile into each other's faces. Sometimes the mother and father weep, the child wraps them in her

---

1. *for your grandmama*: In the first printing of the story in *Harper's* magazine, the dedication read: "A legacy for the child who will live it."

arms and leans across the table to tell how she would not have made it without their help. I have seen these programs.

Sometimes I dream a dream in which Dee and I are suddenly brought together on a TV program of this sort. Out of a dark and soft-seated limousine I am ushered into a bright room filled with many people. There I meet a smiling, gray, sporty man like Johnny Carson[2] who shakes my hand and tells me what a fine girl I have. Then we are on the stage and Dee is embracing me with tears in her eyes. She pins on my dress a large orchid, even though she has told me once that she thinks orchids are tacky flowers.

In real life I am a large, big-boned woman with rough, man-working hands. In the winter I wear flannel nightgowns to bed and overalls during the day. I can kill and clean a hog as mercilessly as a man. My fat keeps me hot in zero weather. I can work outside all day, breaking ice to get water for washing; I can eat pork liver cooked over the open fire minutes after it comes steaming from the hog. One winter I knocked a bull calf straight in the brain between the eyes with a sledge hammer and had the meat hung up to chill before nightfall. But of course all this does not show on television. I am the way my daughter would want me to be: a hundred pounds lighter, my skin like an uncooked barley pancake. My hair glistens in the hot bright lights. Johnny Carson has much to do to keep up with my quick and witty tongue.

But that is a mistake. I know even before I wake up. Who ever knew a Johnson with a quick tongue? Who can even imagine me looking a strange white man in the eye? It seems to me I have talked to them always with one foot raised in flight, with my head turned in whichever way is farthest from them. Dee, though. She would always look anyone in the eye. Hesitation was no part of her nature.

"How do I look, Mama?" Maggie says, showing just enough of her thin body enveloped in pink skirt and red blouse for me to know she's there, almost hidden by the door.

"Come out into the yard," I say.

Have you ever seen a lame animal, perhaps a dog run over by some careless person rich enough to own a car, sidle up to someone who is ignorant enough to be kind to him? That is the way my Maggie walks. She has been like this, chin on chest, eyes on ground, feet in shuffle, ever since the fire that burned the other house to the ground.

Dee is lighter than Maggie, with nicer hair and a fuller figure. She's a woman now, though sometimes I forget. How long ago was it that the other house burned? Ten, twelve years? Sometimes I can still hear the flames and feel Maggie's arms sticking to me, her hair smoking and her dress falling off her in little black papery flakes. Her eyes seemed stretched open, blazed open by the flames reflected in them. And Dee. I see her standing off under the sweet gum tree she used to dig gum out of; a look of concentration on her face as she watched the last dingy gray board of the house fall in toward the red-hot brick chimney. Why don't you do a dance around the ashes? I'd wanted to ask her. She had hated the house that much.

---

2. **Johnny Carson:** Carson (1925–2005) was the popular host of NBC's *The Tonight Show* from 1962 to 1992.

I used to think she hated Maggie, too. But that was before we raised the money, the church and me, to send her to Augusta to school.[3] She used to read to us without pity; forcing words, lies, other folks' habits, whole lives upon us two, sitting trapped and ignorant underneath her voice. She washed us in a river of make-believe, burned us with a lot of knowledge we didn't necessarily need to know. Pressed us to her with the serious way she read, to shove us away at just the moment, like dimwits, we seemed about to understand.

Dee wanted nice things. A yellow organdy dress to wear to her graduation from high school; black pumps to match a green suit she'd made from an old suit somebody gave me. She was determined to stare down any disaster in her efforts. Her eyelids would not flicker for minutes at a time. Often I fought off the temptation to shake her. At sixteen she had a style of her own: and knew what style was.

I never had an education myself. After second grade the school was closed down. Don't ask me why: in 1927 colored asked fewer questions than they do now. Sometimes Maggie reads to me. She stumbles along good-naturedly but can't see well. She knows she is not bright. Like good looks and money, quickness passed her by. She will marry John Thomas (who has mossy teeth in an earnest face) and then I'll be free to sit here and I guess just sing church songs to myself. Although I never was a good singer. Never could carry a tune. I was always better at a man's job. I used to love to milk till I was hooked in the side in '49. Cows are soothing and slow and don't bother you, unless you try to milk them the wrong way.

I have deliberately turned my back on the house. It is three rooms, just like the one that burned, except the roof is tin; they don't make shingle roofs any more. There are no real windows, just some holes cut in the sides, like the portholes in a ship, but not round and not square, with rawhide holding the shutters up on the outside. This house is in a pasture, too, like the other one. No doubt when Dee sees it she will want to tear it down. She wrote me once that no matter where we "choose" to live, she will manage to come see us. But she will never bring her friends. Maggie and I thought about this and Maggie asked me, "Mama, when did Dee ever *have* any friends?"

She had a few. Furtive boys in pink shirts hanging about on washday after school. Nervous girls who never laughed. Impressed with her they worshiped the well-turned phrase, the cute shape, the scalding humor that erupted like bubbles in lye. She read to them.

When she was courting Jimmy T she didn't have much time to pay to us, but turned all her faultfinding power on him. He *flew* to marry a cheap city girl from a family of ignorant flashy people. She hardly had time to recompose herself.

When she comes I will meet — but there they are!

Maggie attempts to make a dash for the house, in her shuffling way, but I stay her with my hand. "Come back here," I say. And she stops and tries to dig a well in the sand with her toe.

---

3. to send her to Augusta to school: There are a number of colleges in Augusta, the second largest city in Georgia.

It is hard to see them clearly through the strong sun. But even the first glimpse of leg out of the car tells me it is Dee. Her feet were always neat-looking, as if God himself had shaped them with a certain style. From the other side of the car comes a short, stocky man. Hair is all over his head a foot long and hanging from his chin like a kinky mule tail. I hear Maggie suck in her breath. "Uhnnnh," is what it sounds like. Like when you see the wriggling end of a snake just in front of your foot on the road. "Uhnnnh."

Dee next. A dress down to the ground, in this hot weather. A dress so loud it hurts my eyes. There are yellows and oranges enough to throw back the light of the sun. I feel my whole face warming from the heat waves it throws out. Earrings gold, too, and hanging down to her shoulders. Bracelets dangling and making noises when she moves her arm up to shake the folds of the dress out of her armpits. The dress is loose and flows, and as she walks closer, I like it. I hear Maggie go "Uhnnnh" again. It is her sister's hair. It stands straight up like the wool on a sheep. It is black as night and around the edges are two long pigtails that rope about like small lizards disappearing behind her ears.

"Wa-su-zo-Tean-o!" she says, coming on in that gliding way the dress makes her move. The short, stocky fellow with the hair to his navel is all grinning and he follows up with "Asalamalakim, my mother and sister!" He moves to hug Maggie but she falls back, right up against the back of my chair. I feel her trembling there and when I look up I see the perspiration falling off her chin.

"Don't get up," says Dee. Since I am stout it takes something of a push. You can see me trying to move a second or two before I make it. She turns, showing white heels through her sandals, and goes back to the car. Out she peeks next with a Polaroid. She stoops down quickly and lines up picture after picture of me sitting there in front of the house with Maggie cowering behind me. She never takes a shot without making sure the house is included. When a cow comes nibbling around the edge of the yard she snaps it and me and Maggie *and* the house. Then she puts the Polaroid in the back seat of the car, and comes up and kisses me on the forehead.

Meanwhile Asalamalakim is going through motions with Maggie's hand. Maggie's hand is as limp as a fish, and probably as cold, despite the sweat, and she keeps trying to pull it back. It looks like Asalamalakim wants to shake hands but wants to do it fancy. Or maybe he don't know how people shake hands. Anyhow, he soon gives up on Maggie.

"Well," I say. "Dee."

"No, Mama," she says. "Not 'Dee,' Wangero Leewanika Kemanjo!"

"What happened to 'Dee'?" I wanted to know.

"She's dead," Wangero said. "I couldn't bear it any longer, being named after the people who oppress me."

"You know as well as me you was named after your aunt Dicie," I said. Dicie is my sister. She named Dee. We called her "Big Dee" after Dee was born.

"But who was *she* named after?" asked Wangero.

"I guess after Grandma Dee," I said.

"And who was she named after?" asked Wangero.

"Her mother," I said, and saw Wangero was getting tired. "That's about as far back as I can trace it," I said. Though, in fact, I probably could have carried it back beyond the Civil War through the branches.

"Well," said Asalamalakim, "there you are."

"Uhnnnh," I heard Maggie say.

"There I was not," I said, "before 'Dicie' cropped up in our family, so why should I try to trace it that far back?"

He just stood there grinning, looking down on me like somebody inspecting a Model A car.[4] Every once in a while he and Wangero sent eye signals over my head.

"How do you pronounce this name?" I asked.

"You don't have to call me by it if you don't want to," said Wangero.

"Why shouldn't I?" I asked. "If that's what you want us to call you, we'll call you."

"I know it might sound awkward at first," said Wangero.

"I'll get used to it," I said. "Ream it out again."

Well, soon we got the name out of the way. Asalamalakim had a name twice as long and three times as hard. After I tripped over it two or three times he told me to just call him Hakim-a-barber. I wanted to ask him was he a barber, but I didn't really think he was, so I didn't ask.

"You must belong to those beef-cattle peoples down the road," I said. They said "Asalamalakim" when they met you, too, but they didn't shake hands. Always too busy: feeding the cattle, fixing the fences, putting up salt-lick shelters, throwing down hay. When the white folks poisoned some of the herd the men stayed up all night with rifles in their hands. I walked a mile and a half just to see the sight.

Hakim-a-barber said, "I accept some of their doctrines, but farming and raising cattle is not my style." (They didn't tell me, and I didn't ask, whether Wangero (Dee) had really gone and married him.)

We sat down to eat and right away he said he didn't eat collards and pork was unclean. Wangero, though, went on through the chitlins and corn bread, the greens and everything else. She talked a blue streak over the sweet potatoes. Everything delighted her. Even the fact that we still used the benches her daddy made for the table when we couldn't afford to buy chairs.

"Oh, Mama!" she cried. Then turned to Hakim-a-barber. "I never knew how lovely these benches are. You can feel the rump prints," she said, running her hands underneath her and along the bench. Then she gave a sigh and her hand closed over Grandma Dee's butter dish. "That's it!" she said. "I knew there was something I wanted to ask you if I could have." She jumped up from the table and went over in the corner where the churn stood, the milk in it clabber[5] by now. She looked at the churn and looked at it.

"This churn top is what I need," she said. "Didn't Uncle Buddy whittle it out of a tree you all used to have?"

"Yes," I said.

---

4. **Model A car:** The redesigned successor to the hugely successful Model T, or "Tin Lizzie," which had been produced by the Ford Motor Company from 1908 through 1927.

5. **clabber:** Curdled milk, a yogurt-like substance that was commonly eaten for breakfast in the South. A plunge churn consists of an upright container, commonly made of wood, and a lid with a hole through which a wooden stick called the "dasher" is moved up and down to agitate the cream and separate the butterfat from the buttermilk.

"Uh huh," she said happily. "And I want the dasher, too."

"Uncle Buddy whittle that, too?" asked the barber.

Dee (Wangero) looked up at me.

"Aunt Dee's first husband whittled the dash," said Maggie so low you almost couldn't hear her. "His name was Henry, but they called him Stash."

"Maggie's brain is like an elephant's," Wangero said, laughing. "I can use the churn top as a centerpiece for the alcove table," she said, sliding a plate over the churn, "and I'll think of something artistic to do with the dasher."

When she finished wrapping the dasher the handle stuck out. I took it for a moment in my hands. You didn't even have to look close to see where hands pushing the dasher up and down to make butter had left a kind of sink in the wood. In fact, there were a lot of small sinks; you could see where thumbs and fingers had sunk into the wood. It was beautiful light yellow wood, from a tree that grew in the yard where Big Dee and Stash had lived.

After dinner Dee (Wangero) went to the trunk at the foot of my bed and started rifling through it. Maggie hung back in the kitchen over the dishpan. Out came Wangero with two quilts. They had been pieced by Grandma Dee and then Big Dee and me had hung them on the quilt frames on the front porch and quilted them. One was in the Lone Star pattern. The other was Walk Around the Mountain.[6] In both of them were scraps of dresses Grandma Dee had worn fifty and more years ago. Bits and pieces of Grandpa Jarrell's Paisley shirts. And one teeny faded blue piece, about the size of a penny matchbox, that was from Great Grandpa Ezra's uniform that he wore in the Civil War.

"Mama," Wangero said sweet as a bird. "Can I have these old quilts?"

I heard something fall in the kitchen, and a minute later the kitchen door slammed.

"Why don't you take one or two of the others?" I asked. "These old things was just done by me and Big Dee from some tops your grandma pieced before she died."

"No," said Wangero. "I don't want those. They are stitched around the borders by machine."

"That'll make them last better," I said.

"That's not the point," said Wangero. "These are all pieces of dresses Grandma used to wear. She did all this stitching by hand. Imagine!" She held the quilts securely in her arms, stroking them.

"Some of the pieces, like those lavender ones, come from old clothes her mother handed down to her," I said, moving up to touch the quilts. Dee (Wangero) moved back just enough so that I couldn't reach the quilts. They already belonged to her.

"Imagine!" she breathed again, clutching them closely to her bosom.

"The truth is," I said, "I promised to give them quilts to Maggie, for when she marries John Thomas."

She gasped like a bee had stung her.

"Maggie can't appreciate these quilts!" she said. "She'd probably be backward enough to put them to everyday use."

---

6. **Lone Star . . . Walk Around the Mountain:** "Lone Star," with its large central star, is one of the oldest and most common quilt patterns; the other quilt may be a variant of another common pattern, "Trip Around the World."

"I reckon she would," I said. "God knows I been saving 'em for long enough with nobody using 'em. I hope she will!" I didn't want to bring up how I had offered Dee (Wangero) a quilt when she went away to college. Then she had told me they were old-fashioned, out of style.

"But they're *priceless!*" she was saying now, furiously; for she has a temper. "Maggie would put them on the bed and in five years they'd be in rags. Less than that!"

"She can always make some more," I said. "Maggie knows how to quilt."

Dee (Wangero) looked at me with hatred. "You just will not understand. The point is these quilts, *these* quilts!"

"Well," I said, stumped. "What would *you* do with them?"

"Hang them," she said. As if that was the only thing you *could* do with quilts.

Maggie by now was standing in the door. I could almost hear the sound her feet made as they scraped over each other.

"She can have them, Mama," she said, like somebody used to never winning anything, or having anything reserved for her. "I can 'member Grandma Dee without the quilts."

I looked at her hard. She had filled her bottom lip with checkerberry snuff[7] and it gave her face a kind of dopey, hangdog look. It was Grandma Dee and Big Dee who taught her how to quilt herself. She stood there with her scarred hands hidden in the folds of her skirt. She looked at her sister with something like fear but she wasn't mad at her. This was Maggie's portion. This was the way she knew God to work.

When I looked at her like that something hit me in the top of my head and ran down to the soles of my feet. Just like when I'm in church and the spirit of God touches me and I get happy and shout. I did something I never had done before: hugged Maggie to me, then dragged her on into the room, snatched the quilts out of Miss Wangero's hands and dumped them into Maggie's lap. Maggie just sat there on my bed with her mouth open.

"Take one or two of the others," I said to Dee.

But she turned without a word and went out to Hakim-a-barber.

"You just don't understand," she said, as Maggie and I came out to the car.

"What don't I understand?" I wanted to know.

"Your heritage," she said. And then she turned to Maggie, kissed her, and said, "You ought to try to make something of yourself, too, Maggie. It's really a new day for us. But from the way you and Mama still live you'd never know it."

She put on some sunglasses that hid everything above the tip of her nose and her chin.

Maggie smiled; maybe at the sunglasses. But a real smile, not scared. After we watched the car dust settle I asked Maggie to bring me a dip of snuff. And then the two of us sat there just enjoying, until it was time to go in the house and go to bed.

[1973]

---

7. **checkerberry snuff:** A moist, smokeless tobacco placed between the lip and the gum.

August Wilson

[1945-2005]

August Wilson was born Frederick August Kittel Jr. on April 27, 1945, in Pittsburgh, Pennsylvania. He was the fourth of the six children of Daisy Wilson Kittel, a black housecleaner, and Frederick Kittel, a white immigrant baker from Germany. The family lived in a two-room, cold-water apartment in the impoverished Hill District, which had been largely settled by African Americans from the South in search of manufacturing jobs and a better life in Pittsburgh. By the time the precocious Wilson began to attend school, his father had abandoned the family, and his parents were later divorced. When he was a teenager, his mother married David Bedford, a black ex-convict with whom Wilson had a deeply troubled relationship. He was also subjected to vicious racism at Central Catholic High School, where he was the only African American in a student body of 1,500. Worn down by the taunts and relentless bullying, he transferred to a vocational school but found the classes tedious and boring. He transferred once again to Gladstone High School, a public school, but he dropped out during his sophomore year after being unjustly accused of plagiarism by a teacher who did not believe that a black student could write so well. Some months elapsed before Wilson told his mother and stepfather, during which he began his intensive self-education by reading the works of writers such as Ralph Ellison, Langston Hughes, and Richard Wright in the "Negro" section of writings by African Americans in the local branch of the Carnegie Library, the public library system in Pittsburgh.

August Wilson
Frank Capri took this photograph of the prominent playwright in 1990.

Although he was determined to become a writer, Wilson was slow to discover his talent as a playwright. After leaving school in 1960, he worked at odd jobs until 1962, when he enlisted in the U.S. Army. Managing to get a discharge after serving for only a year, he returned to Pittsburgh. Following the death of his birth father in 1965, he moved into a boarding house, bought a used typewriter, and changed his name to August Wilson in honor of his mother and to affirm his identity as an African American. He studied the works of a wide range of writers, especially Amiri Baraka, the founder of the Black Arts Movement; and he began to listen to the recordings of blues singers such as Bessie Smith. Wilson later observed that the blues formed "the bedrock" of everything he did: "All the characters in my plays, their ideas and their attitudes, the stance that they adopt in the world, are all ideas and attitudes that are expressed in the blues." At the time, however, he aspired to be a poet, not a playwright. His first publication was a poem, "Malcolm X and Others," a tribute to the militant civil rights leader that appeared in the *Negro Digest* in 1969. That year, Wilson married Brenda Burton, a member of the black nationalist group the Nation of Islam. Their daughter was born in 1970, but their unhappy marriage ended in divorce in 1972. During those years, he was deeply involved in Black Horizons Theatre, an activist, community-based theater company Wilson and the playwright Rob Penny had founded in the Hill District. Although he continued to write and publish poetry, Wilson both directed and tried his hand at writing plays for the group, which performed in community centers and school auditoriums. When the group dissolved in the mid-1970s, it was succeeded by the Kuntu Repertory Theatre at the University of Pittsburgh, which produced Wilson's play *The Homecoming* in 1976.

He gained growing recognition and acclaim during the following decade. At the suggestion of Sam Purdy, a director working with the Penumbra Theatre, a black theater company in St. Paul, Minnesota, Wilson moved there in 1978. To help support himself, he got a job adapting Native American tales into plays for children at the Science Museum of Minnesota. In 1981, he married Judy Oliver, a social worker, and Penumbra produced his first professional play, *Black Bart and the Sacred Hills*, a musical satire adapted from a series of poems Wilson had written earlier about the notorious outlaw in the Old West. But he found his distinctive voice and idiom in a play he wrote about a group of gypsy-cab drivers in the Hill District, *Jitney*, which was produced in 1982 by the small Allegheny Repertory Theater in Pittsburgh. Wilson soon completed revisions of his breakthrough play, *Ma Rainey's Black Bottom*, which explores the effects of racism and exploitation on a group of black musicians waiting in a recording studio for Ma Rainey, one of the most popular blues singers of the 1920s. Like several of his later plays, it premiered at the Yale Repertory Theater before moving to Broadway, where it opened in the fall of 1984. It was the first of eight plays by Wilson to win the prestigious New York Drama Critics' Circle Award for Best Play. It was followed by *Fences*, whose central character is a former Negro League baseball player working as a trash collector in Pittsburgh in the 1950s. Produced on Broadway in 1987 with James Earl Jones in the starring role, *Fences* was a resounding commercial success and won a Pulitzer Prize in 1988. That year, Wilson scored yet another success on Broadway with *Joe Turner's Come and Gone*, which is set in Pittsburgh in 1911 and concerns the harsh lot of former slaves living in the North.

Realizing that *Jitney* and his three successive triumphs on Broadway formed chapters in a larger narrative of the African American experience, Wilson decided "to write plays that contain the sum total of black culture in America," as he told an interviewer in 1988. He subsequently devoted much of the rest of his life to completing a series of ten plays, one for each decade of the twentieth century, called the *Pittsburgh Cycle*. (With the exception of *Ma Rainey's Black Bottom*, which is set in Chicago, all of the plays take place in the Hill District.) His next play was *The Piano Lesson* (1990), a family drama set in the 1930s that earned Wilson a second Pulitzer Prize. After his marriage to Judy Oliver ended, he moved to Seattle, where he wrote *Two Trains Running* (1992), set amidst the social and political turmoil of the 1960s. In 1994, he married Constanza Romero, who had designed the costumes for *The Piano Lesson*, and with whom he had a daughter in 1997. Despite his many awards, honors, and successes, Wilson told a reporter that he still regarded himself as a "struggling playwright,

The playwright's voice in American culture is perceived as having been usurped by television and film, but [Wilson] reasserted the power of drama to describe large social forces, to explore the meaning of an entire people's experience in American history.

—Tony Kushner

struggling to get the next play down on paper." But he did so at regular intervals, filling the gaps in the *Pittsburgh Cycle* with *Seven Guitars* (1995), set in the aftermath of World War II; *King Hedley II* (1999), the dark story of an ex-convict's desperate attempts to make a new life for himself in the 1980s; *Gem of the Ocean* (2003), the story of Aunt Ester, an ancient woman who takes a former slave into her home in 1904; and the final play in the cycle, *Radio Golf* (2005), about the redevelopment of the Hill District in the 1990s. Wilson was diagnosed with liver cancer shortly after the play opened, and he died at the age of sixty on October 2, 2005. He was buried in Pittsburgh, and two weeks after his death the Virginia Theatre in New York City was renamed the August Wilson Theatre, the first on Broadway to be named for an African American.

bedfordstmartins.com/ americanlit for research links on Wilson

Reading Wilson's "The Janitor."   Wilson wrote this brief play for a fundraising event sponsored by the New Dramatists, an organization established in 1949 to develop and promote the work of new playwrights. He became a New Dramatist in 1983, shortly before he achieved his first great success on Broadway with *Ma Rainey's Black Bottom*, and "The Janitor" was first performed as part of an evening of short plays in 1985. As Wilson later told an interviewer, he was daunted by the challenge of writing a play no longer than four minutes in length, as he had been asked to do, until he hit upon the idea of giving voice to a figure who is too often voiceless in American society:

> So I came up with the idea of the janitor who is someone whom this society ignores and someone who has a vital contribution to make, and yet you have relegated him to a position where they sweep the floor. They do it for some years, and never once do we think to say, "Hey, do you have anything to say about anything? Do you have any contribution to make other than being a janitor or running an elevator or whatever?" So in that sense we really do not take advantage of all of our human potential. . . . And we're sitting over here with thirty-five million blacks who have a lot of untapped potential – thirty-five million.

Wilson, who had supported himself by working as a dishwasher, short-order cook, stock boy, and at other odd jobs before establishing himself as a writer, certainly understood such untapped potential. And his early habit of jotting down snippets of conversation he overheard in the predominantly black Hill District of Pittsburgh attuned him to the rich vernacular of his eloquent janitor, Sam, who is relegated to cleaning a ballroom in preparation for an academic meeting but who casually quotes from Shakespeare and the Bible. The text is taken from the collection *Short Pieces from the New Dramatists*, edited by Stan Chervin (1985).

THE JANITOR

CHARACTERS

SAM

MR. COLLINS

SETTING

A Hotel Ballroom

(SAM *enters pushing a broom near the lectern. He stops and reads the sign hanging across the ballroom.*)

SAM: National . . . Conference . . . on . . . Youth.

(*He nods his approval and continues sweeping. He gets an idea, stops, and approaches the lectern. He clears his throat and begins to speak. His speech is delivered with the literacy of a janitor. He chooses his ideas carefully. He is a man who has approached life honestly, with both eyes open.*)

SAM: I want to thank you all for inviting me here to speak about youth. See . . . I's fifty-six years old and I knows something about youth. The first thing I knows . . . is that youth is sweet before flight . . . its odor is rife with speculation and its resilience . . . that's its bounce back . . . is remarkable. But it's that sweetness that we victims of. All of us. Its sweetness . . . and its flight. One of them fellows in that Shakespeare stuff said, "I am not what I am." See. He wasn't like Popeye. This fellow had a different understanding. "I am not what I am."[1] Well, neither are you. You are just what you have been . . . whatever you are now. But what you are now ain't what you gonna become . . . even though it is with you now . . . it's inside you now this instant. Time . . . see, this how you get to this . . . Time ain't changed. It's just moved. Or maybe it ain't moved . . . maybe it just changed. It don't matter. We are all victims of the sweetness of youth and the time of its flight. See . . . just like you I forgot who I am. I forgot what happened first. But I know the river I step into now . . . is not the same river I stepped into twenty years ago. See. I know that much. But I have forgotten the name of the river . . . I have forgotten the names of the gods . . . and like everybody else I have tried to fool them with my dancing . . . and guess at their faces. It's the same with everybody. We don't have to mention no names. Ain't nobody innocent. We are all victims of ourselves. We have all had our hand in the soup . . . and made the music play just so. See, now . . . this what I call wrestling with Jacob's

---

1. **"I am not what I am"**: In Shakespeare's *Othello*, the duplicitous Iago tells a friend, "I am not what I am" (I.i.65), revealing the deception at the heart of his character. In an animated cartoon released in 1933, the character Popeye the Sailor famously proclaimed, "I Yam What I Yam," affirming his identity as a straightforward, honest man.

angel.[2] You lay down at night and that angel come to wrestle with you. When you wrestling with that angel you bargaining for you future. See. And what you need to bargain with is that sweetness of youth. So . . . to the youth of the United States I says . . . don't spend that sweetness too fast! 'Cause you gonna need it. See. I's fifty-six years old and I done found that out. But it's all the same. It all comes back on you . . . just like reaping and sowing.[3] Down and out ain't nothing but being caught up in the balance of what you put down. If you down and out and things ain't going right for you . . . you can bet you done put a down payment on your troubles. Now you got to pay up on the balance. That's as true as I'm standing here. Sometimes you can't see it like that. The last note on Gabriel's horn[4] always gets lost when you get to realizing you done heard the first. See, it's just like . . . .

MR. COLLINS: (*Entering*) Come on, Sam . . . let's quit wasting time and get this floor swept. There's going to be a big important meeting here this afternoon.

SAM: Yessuh, Mr. Collins. Yessuh.

(SAM *goes back to sweeping as the lights go down to* —)

BLACK

[1985]

---

2. **Jacob's angel**: In the Old Testament, Jacob, the son of Isaac and the grandson of Abraham, travels back to Canaan, where he encounters a mysterious being with whom he wrestles all night. When the being cannot prevail, he blesses Jacob, who declares: "I have seen God face to face, and my life is preserved" (Genesis 32:22–30).

3. **reaping and sowing**: A biblical principle of reciprocity derived from the metaphor of planting seeds and harvesting the fruit: "Be not deceived; God is not mocked: for whatsoever a man soweth, that shall he also reap. For he that soweth to his flesh shall of the flesh reap corruption; but he that soweth to the Spirit shall of the Spirit reap life everlasting" (Galatians 6:7–8).

4. **Gabriel's horn**: In the Christian tradition, Gabriel is associated with the archangel who shall blow the "Trump of God" to announce Judgment Day (Thessalonians 4:16).

TIM O'BRIEN

[b. 1946]

William Timothy O'Brien Jr. was born on October 1, 1946, in Austin, Minnesota. He was the first of three children of military veterans of World War II, William Timothy O'Brien, an insurance salesman, and Ava E. Schultz O'Brien, an elementary school teacher. In 1956, the family moved to Worthington, Minnesota, known as the "Turkey Capital of the U.S." With the encouragement of his parents, O'Brien became an avid reader and began to write stories at an early age. After his graduation from high school in 1964, he enrolled at Macalester College in St. Paul, Minnesota, where he majored in political science and was deeply involved in politics and protests against the Vietnam War. In 1968, he graduated summa cum laude and was admitted to graduate school at Harvard

Tim O'Brien

This photograph of O'Brien was taken in 1979, the year he won the National Book Award for his Vietnam War novel *Going After Cacciato.*

University. A few weeks later, however, O'Brien was drafted into the army. Because of his opposition to the war, he considered going to Canada, but after agonizing over the decision he reported for duty, received basic training at Fort Lewis, Washington, and was sent to Vietnam. During his thirteen months there, he served with an infantry brigade that was engaged in constant combat in Quang Ngai Province, and O'Brien was awarded a Combat Infantry Badge, a Purple Heart, and the Bronze Star. But he was appalled by the brutality of the conflict, the devastation of the country, and the dislocation of the Vietnamese, and O'Brien was even more fiercely opposed to the war by the time he ended his tour of duty in Vietnam.

Following his discharge from the army, O'Brien sought to take up his civilian life where he had left off and entered the doctoral program in political science at Harvard in 1970. Although he was not planning on a literary career, he felt compelled to write about what he had witnessed in Vietnam. Drawing upon the journals he had kept during his months there, O'Brien wrote an unflinching memoir of his experiences, *If I Die in a Combat Zone, Box Me Up and Ship Me Home* (1973). The year it was published, he married Ann Weller, an editorial assistant at a publishing company. While pursuing his studies at Harvard, O'Brien spent two summers as an intern at the *Washington Post*, and he worked as a national affairs reporter for the newspaper during 1973-74. He subsequently abandoned work on his doctoral dissertation to write his first novel, *Northern Lights* (1975), which revolves around the conflicts between two brothers, one a veteran and the other a protester of the Vietnam War, living in a small town in northern Minnesota. O'Brien returned to the scenes of the war in *Going After Cacciato* (1978), a surrealistic novel about an infantry squad sent to bring back a soldier who deserts his unit in Vietnam and sets off on an 8,000-mile trek to attend the peace talks in Paris. The novel won the National Book Award, and O'Brien began to publish regularly in the *Atlantic Monthly, Esquire, Harper's*, and the *New Yorker*. Many critics were disappointed by O'Brien's ambitious chronicle of American life in the era of the cold war, *The Nuclear Age* (1985). But he followed it with his greatest triumph to date, *The Things They Carried* (1990), an internationally acclaimed sequence of stories about the Vietnam War.

That war and its aftermath have remained central themes in O'Brien's work. Shortly before he went to Vietnam in 1990, his first visit since his tour of duty ended twenty years earlier, the *New York Times* published an interview with O'Brien entitled "A Storyteller for the War That Won't End." Following the emotionally difficult visit, he wrote *In the Lake of the Woods* (1995), a novel about a politician who has sought to erase his role in one of the most brutal incidents of the Vietnam War, the My Lai Massacre of 1968. But the war played a minor role in *Tomcat in Love* (1998), a comic novel about a recently divorced professor of linguistics that was published the year before O'Brien accepted a position as an endowed chair in creative writing at Southwest Texas State University (now Texas State University–San Marcos). By then, he was divorced from his first wife, and he married Meredith Hale Baker in 2001. His most recent novel is *July, July* (2002), about the college reunion of a group of former friends from the class of 1969, the year O'Brien was sent to Vietnam. In celebration of the twentieth anniversary of the publication of *The Things They Carried*, Houghton Mifflin Harcourt reissued the volume in 2010 in hardcover, as a paperback, as an e-book, and as a text for Kindle, regarded as unprecedented treatment for a book in the digital age.

Reading O'Brien's "The Things They Carried." Describing the factors that made him a writer, O'Brien has stated: "I had a desire to write from the time I was a little kid and then something collided with that desire—namely Vietnam—and I had to write about it. It moved from desire to imperative. I couldn't *not* write." In the view of many critics and readers, his writing about the war is most powerful in "The Things They Carried." First published in the August 1986 issue of *Esquire*, a magazine for men long noted for featuring distinguished work of fiction and nonfiction, the story won a National Magazine Award. It was also the title story of *The Things They Carried*, a sequence of vignettes in which a semifictional narrator named "Tim O'Brien" explores the nature of both war and the war story. Although the story is deeply rooted in his experiences

bedfordstmartins.com/ americanlit for research links on O'Brien

Vietnam War

This AP photo shows two heavily laden infantrymen running across a clearing in War Zone D, fifty miles northeast of Saigon, where a U.S. battalion was pinned down by fire from surrounding Viet Cong troops in June 1967.

as an infantryman in Vietnam and is laced with the military terminology and soldier slang of the period, O'Brien has emphasized the universal dimensions of "The Things They Carried." "The title is meant to refer to all of us," he told an interviewer in 2003. "[It's about] the spiritual, the emotional, and the psychological baggage we all carry.... You sort of accumulate more and more of these spiritual burdens the longer you live and they help define who we are, what our yearnings are, what makes us happy and what doesn't." The text is taken from *The Things They Carried* (1990).

THE THINGS THEY CARRIED

First Lieutenant Jimmy Cross carried letters from a girl named Martha, a junior at Mount Sebastian College in New Jersey. They were not love letters, but Lieutenant Cross was hoping, so he kept them folded in plastic at the bottom of his rucksack. In the late afternoon, after a day's march, he would dig his foxhole, wash his hands under a canteen, unwrap the letters, hold them with the tips of his fingers, and spend the last hour of light pretending. He would imagine romantic camping trips into the White Mountains in New Hampshire. He would sometimes taste the envelope flaps, knowing her tongue had been there. More than anything, he wanted Martha to love him as he loved her, but the letters were mostly chatty, elusive on the matter of love. She was a virgin, he was almost sure. She was an English major at Mount Sebastian, and she wrote beautifully about her professors and roommates and midterm exams, about her respect for Chaucer and her great affection for Virginia Woolf.[1] She often quoted lines of poetry; she never mentioned the war, except to say, Jimmy, take care of yourself. The letters weighed 10 ounces. They were signed Love, Martha, but Lieutenant Cross understood that Love was only a way of signing and did not mean what he sometimes pretended it meant. At dusk, he would carefully return the letters to his rucksack. Slowly, a bit distracted, he would get up and move among his men, checking the perimeter, then at full dark he would return to his hole and watch the night and wonder if Martha was a virgin.

The things they carried were largely determined by necessity. Among the necessities or near-necessities were P-38 can openers, pocket knives, heat tabs, wristwatches, dog tags, mosquito repellent, chewing gum, candy, cigarettes, salt tablets, packets of Kool-Aid, lighters, matches, sewing kits, Military Payment Certificates, C rations, and two or three canteens of water. Together, these items weighed between 15 and 20 pounds, depending upon a man's habits or rate of metabolism. Henry Dobbins, who was a big man, carried extra rations; he was especially fond of canned peaches in heavy syrup over pound cake. Dave Jensen, who practiced field hygiene, carried a toothbrush,

---

1. **Chaucer ... Woolf:** The medieval English poet Geoffrey Chaucer (c. 1343–1400), author of *The Canterbury Tales*, and the English novelist and feminist critic Virginia Woolf (1882–1941).

dental floss, and several hotel-sized bars of soap he'd stolen on R&R[2] in Sydney, Australia. Ted Lavender, who was scared, carried tranquilizers until he was shot in the head outside the village of Than Khe in mid-April. By necessity, and because it was SOP,[3] they all carried steel helmets that weighed 5 pounds including the liner and camouflage cover. They carried the standard fatigue jackets and trousers. Very few carried underwear. On their feet they carried jungle boots — 2.1 pounds — and Dave Jensen carried three pairs of socks and a can of Dr. Scholl's foot powder as a precaution against trench foot. Until he was shot, Ted Lavender carried six or seven ounces of premium dope which for him was a necessity. Mitchell Sanders, the RTO,[4] carried condoms. Norman Bowker carried a diary. Rat Kiley carried comic books. Kiowa, a devout Baptist, carried an illustrated New Testament that had been presented to him by his father who taught Sunday school in Oklahoma City, Oklahoma. As a hedge against bad times, however, Kiowa also carried his grandmother's distrust of the white man, his grandfather's old hunting hatchet. Necessity dictated. Because the land was mined and booby-trapped, it was SOP for each man to carry a steel-centered, nylon-covered flak jacket, which weighed 6.7 pounds, but which on hot days seemed much heavier. Because you could die so quickly, each man carried at least one large compress bandage, usually in the helmet band for easy access. Because the nights were cold, and because the monsoons were wet, each carried a green plastic poncho that could be used as a raincoat or groundsheet or makeshift tent. With its quilted liner, the poncho weighed almost two pounds, but it was worth every ounce. In April, for instance, when Ted Lavender was shot, they used his poncho to wrap him up, then to carry him across the paddy, then to lift him into the chopper that took him away.

They were called legs or grunts.

To carry something was to hump it, as when Lieutenant Jimmy Cross humped his love for Martha up the hills and through the swamps. In its intransitive form, to hump meant to walk, or to march, but it implied burdens far beyond the intransitive.

Almost everyone humped photographs. In his wallet, Lieutenant Cross carried two photographs of Martha. The first was a Kodacolor snapshot signed Love, though he knew better. She stood against a brick wall. Her eyes were gray and neutral, her lips slightly open as she stared straight-on at the camera. At night, sometimes, Lieutenant Cross wondered who had taken the picture, because he knew she had boyfriends, because he loved her so much, and because he could see the shadow of the picture-taker spreading out against the brick wall. The second photograph had been clipped from the 1968 Mount Sebastian yearbook. It was an action shot — women's volleyball — and Martha was bent horizontal to the floor, reaching, the palms of her hands in sharp focus, the tongue taut, the expression frank and competitive. There was no visible sweat. She wore white gym shorts. Her legs, he thought, were almost certainly the legs of a virgin,

---

2. **R&R:** Rest and recreation, the informal term for a temporary leave during a one-year tour of duty in Vietnam.
3. **SOP:** Standard operating procedure.
4. **RTO:** Radiotelephone operator.

dry and without hair, the left knee cocked and carrying her entire weight, which was just over one hundred pounds. Lieutenant Cross remembered touching that left knee. A dark theater, he remembered, and the movie was *Bonnie and Clyde*, and Martha wore a tweed skirt, and during the final scene, when he touched her knee, she turned and looked at him in a sad, sober way that made him pull his hand back, but he would always remember the feel of the tweed skirt and the knee beneath it and the sound of the gunfire that killed Bonnie and Clyde, how embarrassing it was, how slow and oppressive.[5] He remembered kissing her good night at the dorm door. Right then, he thought, he should've done something brave. He should've carried her up the stairs to her room and tied her to the bed and touched that left knee all night long. He should've risked it. Whenever he looked at the photographs, he thought of new things he should've done.

What they carried was partly a function of rank, partly of field specialty.

As a first lieutenant and platoon leader, Jimmy Cross carried a compass, maps, code books, binoculars, and a .45-caliber pistol that weighed 2.9 pounds fully loaded. He carried a strobe light and the responsibility for the lives of his men.

As an RTO, Mitchell Sanders carried the PRC-25 radio, a killer, 26 pounds with its battery.

As a medic, Rat Kiley carried a canvas satchel filled with morphine and plasma and malaria tablets and surgical tape and comic books and all the things a medic must carry, including M&M's[6] for especially bad wounds, for a total weight of nearly 20 pounds.

As a big man, therefore a machine gunner, Henry Dobbins carried the M-60, which weighed 23 pounds unloaded, but which was almost always loaded. In addition, Dobbins carried between 10 and 15 pounds of ammunition draped in belts across his chest and shoulders.

As PFCs or Spec 4s,[7] most of them were common grunts and carried the standard M-16 gas-operated assault rifle. The weapon weighed 7.5 pounds unloaded, 8.2 pounds with its full 20-round magazine. Depending on numerous factors, such as topography and psychology, the riflemen carried anywhere from 12 to 20 magazines, usually in cloth bandoliers, adding on another 8.4 pounds at minimum, 14 pounds at maximum. When it was available, they also carried M-16 maintenance gear—rods and steel brushes and swabs and tubes of LSA oil—all of which weighed about a pound. Among the grunts, some carried the M-79 grenade launcher, 5.9 pounds unloaded, a reasonably light weapon except for the ammunition, which was heavy. A single round weighed 10 ounces. The typical load was 25 rounds. But Ted Lavender, who was scared, carried 34 rounds when he was shot and killed outside Than Khe, and he went down under an exceptional burden, more than 20 pounds of ammunition, plus the flak jacket and

---

5. **A dark theater . . . slow and oppressive:** In the violent final scene of the movie *Bonnie and Clyde* (1967), the bodies of the Depression-era robbers writhe in slow motion under a hail of machine-gun bullets.
6. **M&M's:** Grimly humorous slang for medical supplies or drugs in pill form.
7. **PFCs or Spec 4s:** Private first class and the rank immediately above, specialist fourth class, the most common ranks in the Vietnam-era U.S. Army.

helmet and rations and water and toilet paper and tranquilizers and all the rest, plus the unweighed fear. He was dead weight. There was no twitching or flopping. Kiowa, who saw it happen, said it was like watching a rock fall, or a big sandbag or something—just boom, then down—not like the movies where the dead guy rolls around and does fancy spins and goes ass over teakettle—not like that, Kiowa said, the poor bastard just flat-fuck fell. Boom. Down. Nothing else. It was a bright morning in mid-April. Lieutenant Cross felt the pain. He blamed himself. They stripped off Lavender's canteens and ammo, all the heavy things, and Rat Kiley said the obvious, the guy's dead, and Mitchell Sanders used his radio to report one U.S. KIA[8] and to request a chopper. Then they wrapped Lavender in his poncho. They carried him out to a dry paddy, established security, and sat smoking the dead man's dope until the chopper came. Lieutenant Cross kept to himself. He pictured Martha's smooth young face, thinking he loved her more than anything, more than his men, and now Ted Lavender was dead because he loved her so much and could not stop thinking about her. When the dustoff arrived, they carried Lavender aboard. Afterward they burned Than Khe. They marched until dusk, then dug their holes, and that night Kiowa kept explaining how you had to be there, how fast it was, how the poor guy just dropped like so much concrete. Boom-down, he said. Like cement.

In addition to the three standard weapons—the M-60, M-16, and M-79—they carried whatever presented itself, or whatever seemed appropriate as a means of killing or staying alive. They carried catch-as-catch-can. At various times, in various situations, they carried M-14s and CAR-15s and Swedish Ks and grease guns and captured AK-47s and Chi-Coms and RPGs and Simonov carbines and black market Uzis and .38-caliber Smith & Wesson handguns and 66 mm LAWS and shotguns and silencers and blackjacks and bayonets and C-4 plastic explosives. Lee Strunk carried a slingshot; a weapon of last resort, he called it. Mitchell Sanders carried brass knuckles. Kiowa carried his grandfather's feathered hatchet. Every third or fourth man carried a Claymore antipersonnel mine—3.5 pounds with its firing device. They all carried fragmentation grenades—14 ounces each. They all carried at least one M-18 colored smoke grenade—24 ounces. Some carried CS or tear gas grenades. Some carried white phosphorus grenades. They carried all they could bear, and then some, including a silent awe for the terrible power of the things they carried.

In the first week of April, before Lavender died, Lieutenant Jimmy Cross received a good-luck charm from Martha. It was a simple pebble, an ounce at most. Smooth to the touch, it was a milky white color with flecks of orange and violet, oval-shaped, like a miniature egg. In the accompanying letter, Martha wrote that she had found the pebble on the Jersey shoreline, precisely where the land touched water at high tide, where things came together but also separated. It was this separate-but-together quality, she wrote, that had inspired her to pick up the pebble and to carry it in her breast pocket for several days,

---

8. **KIA:** Killed in action.

where it seemed weightless, and then to send it through the mail, by air, as a token of her truest feelings for him. Lieutenant Cross found this romantic. But he wondered what her truest feelings were, exactly, and what she meant by separate-but-together. He wondered how the tides and waves had come into play on that afternoon along the Jersey shoreline when Martha saw the pebble and bent down to rescue it from geology. He imagined bare feet. Martha was a poet, with the poet's sensibilities, and her feet would be brown and bare, the toenails unpainted, the eyes chilly and somber like the ocean in March, and though it was painful, he wondered who had been with her that afternoon. He imagined a pair of shadows moving along the strip of sand where things came together but also separated. It was phantom jealousy, he knew, but he couldn't help himself. He loved her so much. On the march, through the hot days of early April, he carried the pebble in his mouth, turning it with his tongue, tasting sea salt and moisture. His mind wandered. He had difficulty keeping his attention on the war. On occasion he would yell at his men to spread out the column, to keep their eyes open, but then he would slip away into daydreams, just pretending, walking barefoot along the Jersey shore, with Martha, carrying nothing. He would feel himself rising. Sun and waves and gentle winds, all love and lightness.

What they carried varied by mission.

When a mission took them to the mountains, they carried mosquito netting, machetes, canvas tarps, and extra bug juice.

If a mission seemed especially hazardous, or if it involved a place they knew to be bad, they carried everything they could. In certain heavily mined AOs,[9] where the land was dense with Toe Poppers and Bouncing Betties,[10] they took turns humping a 28-pound mine detector. With its head-phones and big sensing plate, the equipment was a stress on the lower back and shoulders, awkward to handle, often useless because of the shrapnel in the earth, but they carried it anyway, partly for safety, partly for the illusion of safety.

On ambush, or other night missions, they carried peculiar little odds and ends. Kiowa always took along his New Testament and a pair of moccasins for silence. Dave Jensen carried night-sight vitamins high in carotene. Lee Strunk carried his slingshot; ammo, he claimed, would never be a problem. Rat Kiley carried brandy and M&M's candy. Until he was shot, Ted Lavender carried the starlight scope, which weighed 6.3 pounds with its aluminum carrying case. Henry Dobbins carried his girlfriend's pantyhose wrapped around his neck as a comforter. They all carried ghosts. When dark came, they would move out single file across the meadows and paddies to their ambush coordinates, where they would quietly set up the Claymores and lie down and spend the night waiting.

Other missions were more complicated and required special equipment. In mid-April, it was their mission to search out and destroy the elaborate tunnel complexes in the Than Khe area south of Chu Lai. To blow the tunnels, they carried one-pound blocks of pentrite high explosives, four blocks to a man, 68 pounds in all. They carried wiring, detonators, and battery-powered clackers. Dave Jensen carried earplugs. Most often,

---

9. **AOs:** Areas of operation.
10. **Toe Poppers and Bouncing Betties:** Small booby traps that explosively amputate toes or wound feet and antipersonnel mines from which a second charge is propelled upward and set to explode at about waist level.

before blowing the tunnels, they were ordered by higher command to search them, which was considered bad news, but by and large they just shrugged and carried out orders. Because he was a big man, Henry Dobbins was excused from tunnel duty. The others would draw numbers. Before Lavender died there were 17 men in the platoon, and whoever drew the number 17 would strip off his gear and crawl in headfirst with a flashlight and Lieutenant Cross's .45-caliber pistol. The rest of them would fan out as security. They would sit down or kneel, not facing the hole, listening to the ground beneath them, imagining cobwebs and ghosts, whatever was down there—the tunnel walls squeezing in—how the flashlight seemed impossibly heavy in the hand and how it was tunnel vision in the very strictest sense, compression in all ways, even time, and how you had to wiggle in—ass and elbows—a swallowed-up feeling—and how you found yourself worrying about odd things: Will your flashlight go dead? Do rats carry rabies? If you screamed, how far would the sound carry? Would your buddies hear it? Would they have the courage to drag you out? In some respects, though not many, the waiting was worse than the tunnel itself. Imagination was a killer.

On April 16, when Lee Strunk drew the number 17, he laughed and muttered something and went down quickly. The morning was hot and very still. Not good, Kiowa said. He looked at the tunnel opening, then out across a dry paddy toward the village of Than Khe. Nothing moved. No clouds or birds or people. As they waited, the men smoked and drank Kool-Aid, not talking much, feeling sympathy for Lee Strunk but also feeling the luck of the draw. You win some, you lose some, said Mitchell Sanders, and sometimes you settle for a rain check. It was a tired line and no one laughed.

Henry Dobbins ate a tropical chocolate bar. Ted Lavender popped a tranquilizer and went off to pee.

After five minutes, Lieutenant Jimmy Cross moved to the tunnel, leaned down, and examined the darkness. Trouble, he thought—a cave-in maybe. And then suddenly, without willing it, he was thinking about Martha. The stresses and fractures, the quick collapse, the two of them buried alive under all that weight. Dense, crushing love. Kneeling, watching the hole, he tried to concentrate on Lee Strunk and the war, all the dangers, but his love was too much for him, he felt paralyzed, he wanted to sleep inside her lungs and breathe her blood and be smothered. He wanted her to be a virgin and not a virgin, all at once. He wanted to know her. Intimate secrets: Why poetry? Why so sad? Why that grayness in her eyes? Why so alone? Not lonely, just alone—riding her bike across campus or sitting off by herself in the cafeteria—even dancing, she danced alone—and it was the aloneness that filled him with love. He remembered telling her that one evening. How she nodded and looked away. And how, later, when he kissed her, she received the kiss without returning it, her eyes wide open, not afraid, not a virgin's eyes, just flat and uninvolved.

Lieutenant Cross gazed at the tunnel. But he was not there. He was buried with Martha under the white sand at the Jersey shore. They were pressed together, and the pebble in his mouth was her tongue. He was smiling. Vaguely, he was aware of how quiet the day was, the sullen paddies, yet he could not bring himself to worry about matters of security. He was beyond that. He was just a kid at war, in love. He was twenty-four years old. He couldn't help it.

A few moments later Lee Strunk crawled out of the tunnel. He came up grinning, filthy but alive. Lieutenant Cross nodded and closed his eyes while the others clapped Strunk on the back and made jokes about rising from the dead.

Worms, Rat Kiley said. Right out of the grave. Fuckin' zombie.

The men laughed. They all felt great relief.

Spook city, said Mitchell Sanders.

Lee Strunk made a funny ghost sound, a kind of moaning, yet very happy, and right then, when Strunk made that high happy moaning sound, when he went *Ahhooooo*, right then Ted Lavender was shot in the head on his way back from peeing. He lay with his mouth open. The teeth were broken. There was a swollen black bruise under his left eye. The cheekbone was gone. Oh shit, Rat Kiley said, the guy's dead. The guy's dead, he kept saying, which seemed profound – the guy's dead. I mean really.

The things they carried were determined to some extent by superstition. Lieutenant Cross carried his good-luck pebble. Dave Jensen carried a rabbit's foot. Norman Bowker, otherwise a very gentle person, carried a thumb that had been presented to him as a gift by Mitchell Sanders. The thumb was dark brown, rubbery to the touch, and weighed four ounces at most. It had been cut from a VC[11] corpse, a boy of fifteen or sixteen. They'd found him at the bottom of an irrigation ditch, badly burned, flies in his mouth and eyes. The boy wore black shorts and sandals. At the time of his death he had been carrying a pouch of rice, a rifle, and three magazines of ammunition.

You want my opinion, Mitchell Sanders said, there's a definite moral here.

He put his hand on the dead boy's wrist. He was quiet for a time, as if counting a pulse, then he patted the stomach, almost affectionately, and used Kiowa's hunting hatchet to remove the thumb.

Henry Dobbins asked what the moral was.

Moral?

You know. *Moral.*

Sanders wrapped the thumb in toilet paper and handed it across to Norman Bowker. There was no blood. Smiling, he kicked the boy's head, watched the flies scatter, and said, It's like with that old TV show – Paladin. Have gun, will travel.[12]

Henry Dobbins thought about it.

Yeah, well, he finally said. I don't see no moral.

There it *is*, man.

Fuck off.

They carried USO[13] stationery and pencils and pens. They carried Sterno, safety pins, trip flares, signal flares, spools of wire, razor blades, chewing tobacco, liberated joss sticks and statuettes of the smiling Buddha, candles, grease pencils, *The Stars and*

---

11. **VC:** Viet Cong.
12. **Have gun, will travel:** The motto of the man named "Paladin," a professional gunfighter in the popular western television series *Have Gun, Will Travel* (1957-63).
13. **USO:** United Service Organizations, a private organization that provides recreational and morale-boosting services to members of the military.

Stripes, fingernail clippers, Psy Ops leaflets,[14] bush hats, bolos, and much more. Twice a week, when the resupply choppers came in, they carried hot chow in green mermite cans and large canvas bags filled with iced beer and soda pop. They carried plastic water containers, each with a two-gallon capacity. Mitchell Sanders carried a set of starched tiger fatigues for special occasions. Henry Dobbins carried Black Flag insecticide. Dave Jensen carried empty sandbags that could be filled at night for added protection. Lee Strunk carried tanning lotion. Some things they carried in common. Taking turns, they carried the big PRC-77 scrambler radio, which weighed 30 pounds with its battery. They shared the weight of memory. They took up what others could no longer bear. Often, they carried each other, the wounded or weak. They carried infections. They carried chess sets, basketballs, Vietnamese-English dictionaries, insignia of rank, Bronze Stars and Purple Hearts, plastic cards imprinted with the Code of Conduct. They carried diseases, among them malaria and dysentery. They carried lice and ringworm and leeches and paddy algae and various rots and molds. They carried the land itself — Vietnam, the place, the soil — a powdery orange-red dust that covered their boots and fatigues and faces. They carried the sky. The whole atmosphere, they carried it, the humidity, the monsoons, the stink of fungus and decay, all of it, they carried gravity. They moved like mules. By daylight they took sniper fire, at night they were mortared, but it was not battle, it was just the endless march, village to village, without purpose, nothing won or lost. They marched for the sake of the march. They plodded along slowly, dumbly, leaning forward against the heat, unthinking, all blood and bone, simple grunts, soldiering with their legs, toiling up the hills and down into the paddies and across the rivers and up again and down, just humping, one step and then the next and then another, but no volition, no will, because it was automatic, it was anatomy, and the war was entirely a matter of posture and carriage, the hump was everything, a kind of inertia, a kind of emptiness, a dullness of desire and intellect and conscience and hope and human sensibility. Their principles were in their feet. Their calculations were biological. They had no sense of strategy or mission. They searched the villages without knowing what to look for, not caring, kicking over jars of rice, frisking children and old men, blowing tunnels, sometimes setting fires and sometimes not, then forming up and moving on to the next village, then other villages, where it would always be the same. They carried their own lives. The pressures were enormous. In the heat of early afternoon, they would remove their helmets and flak jackets, walking bare, which was dangerous but which helped ease the strain. They would often discard things along the route of march. Purely for comfort, they would throw away rations, blow their Claymores and grenades, no matter, because by nightfall the resupply choppers would arrive with more of the same, then a day or two later still more, fresh watermelons and crates of ammunition and sunglasses and woolen sweaters — the resources were stunning — sparklers for the Fourth of July, colored eggs for Easter — it was the great American war chest — the fruits of science, the smokestacks, the canneries, the arsenals at Hartford, the Minnesota forests, the machine shops, the vast fields of corn and wheat — they carried like freight trains;

---

14. *The Stars and Stripes . . .* Psy Ops leaflets: A daily newspaper published for the U.S. military, and leaflets dropped or distributed as part of psychological operations aimed at the enemy.

they carried it on their backs and shoulders—and for all the ambiguities of Vietnam, all the mysteries and unknowns, there was at least the single abiding certainty that they would never be at a loss for things to carry.

After the chopper took Lavender away, Lieutenant Jimmy Cross led his men into the village of Than Khe. They burned everything. They shot chickens and dogs, they trashed the village well, they called in artillery and watched the wreckage, then they marched for several hours through the hot afternoon, and then at dusk, while Kiowa explained how Lavender died, Lieutenant Cross found himself trembling.

He tried not to cry. With his entrenching tool, which weighed five pounds, he began digging a hole in the earth.

He felt shame. He hated himself. He had loved Martha more than his men, and as a consequence Lavender was now dead, and this was something he would have to carry like a stone in his stomach for the rest of the war.

All he could do was dig. He used his entrenching tool like an ax, slashing, feeling both love and hate, and then later, when it was full dark, he sat at the bottom of his foxhole and wept. It went on for a long while. In part, he was grieving for Ted Lavender, but mostly it was for Martha, and for himself, because she belonged to another world, which was not quite real, and because she was a junior at Mount Sebastian College in New Jersey, a poet and a virgin and uninvolved, and because he realized she did not love him and never would.

Like cement, Kiowa whispered in the dark. I swear to God—boom, down. Not a word.

I've heard this, said Norman Bowker.

A pisser, you know? Still zipping himself up. Zapped while zipping.

All right, fine. That's enough.

Yeah, but you had to see it, the guy just—

I *heard*, man. Cement. So why not shut the fuck *up?*

Kiowa shook his head sadly and glanced over at the hole where Lieutenant Jimmy Cross sat watching the night. The air was thick and wet. A warm dense fog had settled over the paddies and there was the stillness that precedes rain.

After a time Kiowa sighed.

One thing for sure, he said. The lieutenant's in some deep hurt. I mean that crying jag—the way he was carrying on—it wasn't fake or anything, it was real heavy-duty hurt. The man cares.

Sure, Norman Bowker said.

Say what you want, the man does care.

We all got problems.

Not Lavender.

No, I guess not, Bowker said. Do me a favor, though.

Shut up?

That's a smart Indian. Shut up.

Shrugging, Kiowa pulled off his boots. He wanted to say more, just to lighten up his sleep, but instead he opened his New Testament and arranged it beneath his head as a pillow. The fog made things seem hollow and unattached. He tried not to think about

Ted Lavender, but then he was thinking how fast it was, no drama, down and dead, and how it was hard to feel anything except surprise. It seemed unchristian. He wished he could find some great sadness, or even anger, but the emotion wasn't there and he couldn't make it happen. Mostly he felt pleased to be alive. He liked the smell of the New Testament under his cheek, the leather and ink and paper and glue, whatever the chemicals were. He liked hearing the sounds of night. Even his fatigue, it felt fine, the stiff muscles and the prickly awareness of his own body, a floating feeling. He enjoyed not being dead. Lying there, Kiowa admired Lieutenant Jimmy Cross's capacity for grief. He wanted to share the man's pain, he wanted to care as Jimmy Cross cared. And yet when he closed his eyes, all he could think was Boom-down, and all he could feel was the pleasure of having his boots off and the fog curling in around him and the damp soil and the Bible smells and the plush comfort of night.

After a moment Norman Bowker sat up in the dark.

What the hell, he said. You want to talk, *talk*. Tell it to me.

Forget it.

No, man, go on. One thing I hate, it's a silent Indian.

For the most part they carried themselves with poise, a kind of dignity. Now and then, however, there were times of panic, when they squealed or wanted to squeal but couldn't, when they twitched and made moaning sounds and covered their heads and said Dear Jesus and flopped around on the earth and fired their weapons blindly and cringed and sobbed and begged for the noise to stop and went wild and made stupid promises to themselves and to God and to their mothers and fathers, hoping not to die. In different ways, it happened to all of them. Afterward, when the firing ended, they would blink and peek up. They would touch their bodies, feeling shame, then quickly hiding it. They would force themselves to stand. As if in slow motion, frame by frame, the world would take on the old logic — absolute silence, then the wind, then sunlight, then voices. It was the burden of being alive. Awkwardly, the men would reassemble themselves, first in private, then in groups, becoming soldiers again. They would repair the leaks in their eyes. They would check for casualties, call in dustoffs, light cigarettes, try to smile, clear their throats and spit and begin cleaning their weapons. After a time someone would shake his head and say, No lie, I almost shit my pants, and someone else would laugh, which meant it was bad, yes, but the guy had obviously not shit his pants, it wasn't that bad, and in any case nobody would ever do such a thing and then go ahead and talk about it. They would squint into the dense, oppressive sunlight. For a few moments, perhaps, they would fall silent, lighting a joint and tracking its passage from man to man, inhaling, holding in the humiliation. Scary stuff, one of them might say. But then someone else would grin or flick his eyebrows and say, Roger-dodger, almost cut me a new asshole, *almost*.

There were numerous such poses. Some carried themselves with a sort of wistful resignation, others with pride or stiff soldierly discipline or good humor or macho zeal. They were afraid of dying but they were even more afraid to show it.

They found jokes to tell.

They used a hard vocabulary to contain the terrible softness. *Greased* they'd say. *Offed, lit up, zapped while zipping*. It wasn't cruelty, just stage presence. They were actors. When someone died, it wasn't quite dying, because in a curious way it seemed scripted, and because they had their lines mostly memorized, irony mixed with tragedy, and because they called it by other names, as if to encyst and destroy the reality of death itself. They kicked corpses. They cut off thumbs. They talked grunt lingo. They told stories about Ted Lavender's supply of tranquilizers, how the poor guy didn't feel a thing, how incredibly tranquil he was.

There's a moral here, said Mitchell Sanders.

They were waiting for Lavender's chopper, smoking the dead man's dope.

The moral's pretty obvious, Sanders said, and winked. Stay away from drugs. No joke, they'll ruin your day every time.

Cute, said Henry Dobbins.

Mind blower, get it? Talk about wiggy. Nothing left, just blood and brains.

They made themselves laugh.

There it is, they'd say. Over and over — there it is, my friend, there it is — as if the repetition itself were an act of poise, a balance between crazy and almost crazy, knowing without going, there it is, which meant be cool, let it ride, because Oh yeah, man, you can't change what can't be changed, there it is, there it absolutely and positively and fucking well *is*.

They were tough.

They carried all the emotional baggage of men who might die. Grief, terror, love, longing — these were intangibles, but the intangibles had their own mass and specific gravity, they had tangible weight. They carried shameful memories. They carried the common secret of cowardice barely restrained, the instinct to run or freeze or hide, and in many respects this was the heaviest burden of all, for it could never be put down, it required perfect balance and perfect posture. They carried their reputations. They carried the soldier's greatest fear, which was the fear of blushing. Men killed, and died, because they were embarrassed not to. It was what had brought them to the war in the first place, nothing positive, no dreams of glory or honor, just to avoid the blush of dishonor. They died so as not to die of embarrassment. They crawled into tunnels and walked point and advanced under fire. Each morning, despite the unknowns, they made their legs move. They endured. They kept humping. They did not submit to the obvious alternative, which was simply to close the eyes and fall. So easy, really. Go limp and tumble to the ground and let the muscles unwind and not speak and not budge until your buddies picked you up and lifted you into the chopper that would roar and dip its nose and carry you off to the world. A mere matter of falling, yet no one ever fell. It was not courage, exactly; the object was not valor. Rather, they were too frightened to be cowards.

By and large they carried these things inside, maintaining the masks of composure. They sneered at sick call. They spoke bitterly about guys who had found release by shooting off their own toes or fingers. Pussies, they'd say. Candy-asses. It was fierce, mocking talk, with only a trace of envy or awe, but even so the image played itself out behind their eyes.

They imagined the muzzle against flesh. So easy: squeeze the trigger and blow away a toe. They imagined it. They imagined the quick, sweet pain, then the evacuation to Japan, then a hospital with warm beds and cute geisha nurses.

And they dreamed of freedom birds.

At night, on guard, staring into the dark, they were carried away by jumbo jets. They felt the rush of takeoff. *Gone!* they yelled. And then velocity — wings and engines — a smiling stewardess — but it was more than a plane, it was a real bird, a big sleek silver bird with feathers and talons and high screeching. They were flying. The weights fell off; there was nothing to bear. They laughed and held on tight, feeling the cold slap of wind and altitude, soaring, thinking *It's over, I'm gone!* — they were naked, they were light and free — it was all lightness, bright and fast and buoyant, light as light, a helium buzz in the brain, a giddy bubbling in the lungs as they were taken up over the clouds and the war, beyond duty, beyond gravity and mortification and global entanglements — *Sin loi!*[15] they yelled. *I'm sorry, motherfuckers, but I'm out of it, I'm goofed, I'm on a space cruise, I'm gone!* — and it was a restful, unencumbered sensation, just riding the light waves, sailing that big silver freedom bird over the mountains and oceans, over America, over the farms and great sleeping cities and cemeteries and highways and the golden arches of McDonald's, it was flight, a kind of fleeing, a kind of falling, falling higher and higher, spinning off the edge of the earth and beyond the sun and through the vast, silent vacuum where there were no burdens and where everything weighed exactly nothing — *Gone!* they screamed. *I'm sorry but I'm gone!* — and so at night, not quite dreaming, they gave themselves over to lightness, they were carried, they were purely borne.

On the morning after Ted Lavender died, First Lieutenant Jimmy Cross crouched at the bottom of his foxhole and burned Martha's letters. Then he burned the two photographs. There was a steady rain falling, which made it difficult, but he used heat tabs and Sterno to build a small fire, screening it with his body, holding the photographs over the tight blue flame with the tips of his fingers.

He realized it was only a gesture. Stupid, he thought. Sentimental, too, but mostly just stupid.

Lavender was dead. You couldn't burn the blame.

Besides, the letters were in his head. And even now, without photographs, Lieutenant Cross could see Martha playing volleyball in her white gym shorts and yellow T-shirt. He could see her moving in the rain.

When the fire died out, Lieutenant Cross pulled his poncho over his shoulders and ate breakfast from a can.

There was no great mystery, he decided.

In those burned letters Martha had never mentioned the war, except to say, Jimmy, take care of yourself. She wasn't involved. She signed the letters Love, but it wasn't love, and all the fine lines and technicalities did not matter. Virginity was no longer an issue. He hated her. Yes, he did. He hated her. Love, too, but it was a hard, hating kind of love.

The morning came up wet and blurry. Everything seemed part of everything else, the fog and Martha and the deepening rain.

He was a soldier, after all.

---

15. **Sin loi!:** I'm sorry! (Vietnamese).

Half smiling, Lieutenant Jimmy Cross took out his maps. He shook his head hard, as if to clear it, then bent forward and began planning the day's march. In ten minutes, or maybe twenty, he would rouse the men and they would pack up and head west, where the maps showed the country to be green and inviting. They would do what they had always done. The rain might add some weight, but otherwise it would be one more day layered upon all the other days.

He was realistic about it. There was that new hardness in his stomach. He loved her but he hated her.

No more fantasies, he told himself.

Henceforth, when he thought about Martha, it would be only to think that she belonged elsewhere. He would shut down the daydreams. This was not Mount Sebastian, it was another world, where there were no pretty poems or midterm exams, a place where men died because of carelessness and gross stupidity. Kiowa was right. Boom-down, and you were dead, never partly dead.

Briefly, in the rain, Lieutenant Cross saw Martha's gray eyes gazing back at him.

He understood.

It was very sad, he thought. The things men carried inside. The things men did or felt they had to do.

He almost nodded at her, but didn't.

Instead he went back to his maps. He was now determined to perform his duties firmly and without negligence. It wouldn't help Lavender, he knew that, but from this point on he would comport himself as an officer. He would dispose of his good-luck pebble. Swallow it, maybe, or use Lee Strunk's slingshot, or just drop it along the trail. On the march he would impose strict field discipline. He would be careful to send out flank security, to prevent straggling or bunching up, to keep his troops moving at the proper pace and at the proper interval. He would insist on clean weapons. He would con-fiscate the remainder of Lavender's dope. Later in the day, perhaps, he would call the men together and speak to them plainly. He would accept the blame for what had hap-pened to Ted Lavender. He would be a man about it. He would look them in the eyes, keeping his chin level, and he would issue the new SOPs in a calm, impersonal tone of voice, a lieutenant's voice, leaving no room for argument or discussion. Commencing immediately, he'd tell them, they would no longer abandon equipment along the route of march. They would police up their acts. They would get their shit together, and keep it together, and maintain it neatly and in good working order.

He would not tolerate laxity. He would show strength, distancing himself.

Among the men there would be grumbling, of course, and maybe worse, because their days would seem longer and their loads heavier, but Lieutenant Jimmy Cross reminded himself that his obligation was not to be loved but to lead. He would dispense with love; it was not now a factor. And if anyone quarreled or complained, he would simply tighten his lips and arrange his shoulders in the correct command posture. He might give a curt little nod. Or he might not. He might just shrug and say, Carry on, then they would saddle up and form into a column and move out toward the villages west of Than Khe.

[1986, 1990]

Yusef Komunyakaa

[b. 1947]

Yusef Komunyakaa was born James Willie Brown Jr., on April 29, 1947, in the segregated paper-mill town of Bogalusa, Louisiana. He was the eldest of the five children of James Willie Brown and his wife Mildred Brown. His illiterate father was a skilled carpenter who passionately believed in physical labor and hoped that Komunyakaa would one day work by his side. His mother, whom Komunyakaa credits with spurring his interest in jazz and the blues by tuning the tall, wooden radio in the family living room to black stations in New Orleans, also encouraged him to read. She bought a set of encyclopedias, and Komunyakaa read the family Bible from cover to cover twice. Although the only public library in town did not admit blacks, he also read the works of Shakespeare and poets such as Emily Dickinson, Edgar Allan Poe, and Alfred, Lord Tennyson. During an interview in 2001, Komunyakaa recalled that late in high school he "was introduced to American literature written by blacks in what was termed 'Negro History Week,' which were brief moments in our education before we went back to the regular curriculum—history and literature dominated by Europeans." He was especially engaged by the poetry of Langston Hughes and Gwendolyn Brooks. Despite the objections of his parents, especially his father, Komunyakaa decided to change his birth name to the name that his grandfather, a stowaway on a ship from Trinidad, had given up when he slipped into the United States. Following his graduation from high school in 1965, Komunyakaa moved to Phoenix, Arizona, and then to Puerto Rico before he was drafted into the U.S. Army in 1968. After completing basic training and Officer Candidate School, he was sent to Vietnam in 1969.

Yusef Komunyakaa
This portrait of the Pulitzer Prize–winning poet was taken at his home in Princeton, New Jersey, in 1998.

His yearlong tour of duty there marked a crucial turning point for Komunyakaa. Although he was politically opposed to the Vietnam War and briefly considered going AWOL, Komunyakaa later told an interviewer that he had been drawn to the idea of "bearing witness." As an information specialist, or reporter, he interviewed soldiers and covered major battles for a military newspaper, the *Southern Cross*. He later edited the newspaper, in which he also wrote a regular column about Vietnamese literature and culture, "Viet Style." He especially admired the lush landscape of the country and often marveled at the surreal contradictions between the beauty and violence that existed side by side in Vietnam. Komunyakaa, who was awarded a Bronze Star for his journalistic work, was uncertain about his future when he completed his military service and returned to civilian life in 1971. He drifted from place to place and from job to job until 1973, when he took advantage of the GI Bill and enrolled at the University of Colorado. A double major in sociology and English, Komunyakaa began to write poetry and, with the encouragement of one of his professors, entered and won a poetry contest sponsored by the Rocky Mountain Writers Forum. After he graduated in 1975, he enrolled in a creative writing program at Colorado State University. He published his first chapbook of

*bedfordstmartins.com/
americanlit* for research
links on Komunyakaa

poems, *Dedications and Other Dark Horses* (1977), and received his MA degree in creative writing in 1978. He published a second chapbook of poems, *Lost in the Bonewheel Factory* (1979), and further honed his writing skills at the University of California, Irvine, where he earned a second master's degree in creative writing in 1980.

His formal training now complete, Komunyakaa began a distinguished career as a poet and teacher. He was awarded a series of prestigious fellowships, including one from the National Endowment for the Arts in 1981. The following year he was hired to teach English composition and American literature at the University of New Orleans. His career as a poet received a major boost from his first commercially published book, *Copacetic* (1984), in which Komunyakaa employed colloquial speech and jazz rhythms in poems inspired by a visit to his hometown of Bogalusa after an absence of more than a decade. In 1985, Komunyakaa married an Australian novelist, Mandy Sayer. The couple moved to Bloomington, Indiana, where Komunyakaa accepted a position teaching English literature and African American studies at Indiana University. He soon published another collection of jazz-inflected poems, *I Apologize for the Eyes in My Head* (1986); as well as a collection of poems about the Vietnam War, *Dien Cai Dau* (1988). The latter won several literary awards, and in 1991 Komunyakaa also received the Thomas Forcade Award for his work in "the healing of Vietnam and America." At the same time, he continued to explore both his troubled family history and the violent racial history of Bogalusa in the poems collected in *Magic City* (1992). In 1994, Komunyakaa became the first African American male to win the Pulitzer Prize in Poetry, for his collection *Neon Vernacular: New and Selected Poems 1977–1989*. Shortly after his marriage to Mandy Sayer ended, he left Indiana University and taught for a year at Washington University, St. Louis, before assuming the position of Professor, Council of the Humanities and Creative Writing, at Princeton University in 1997.

Since then, Komunyakaa has produced a wide range of work. He explored the intersections among poetry, jazz, and the blues in *Blue Notes: Essays, Interviews, and Commentaries* (2000). He collaborated with the jazz musician Denis Gonzalez on two recordings, *Love Notes from the Madhouse* (1998) and an improvisational live performance, *Herido* (2001). He has also written song lyrics, as well as the librettos for two musical scores: *Testimony*, a tribute to the jazz great Charlie Parker that premiered in 2002; and an opera based on the true story of a slave executed after being charged with raping a white woman, *Slipknot*. The opera was first performed in 2003, and Komunyakaa was preparing for the publication of a new collection of poems, *Taboo: The Wishbone Trilogy, Part 1* (2004), when his partner, the Indian-born poet Reetika Vazirani, took her own life and that of their two-year-old son, Jehan. Following that personal tragedy, he traveled widely — to Africa, India, and Europe — before moving to New York City, where in 2006 he was appointed Distinguished Senior Poet and professor of creative writing in the graduate program at New York University. His recent work includes plays, performance pieces, and two volumes of poetry: *Warhorses* (2008), a collection of poems about life in an age of war and conflict; and what most critics have described as his most personal collection of poems to date, *Chameleon Couch* (2011). He was the recipient of the 2011 Wallace Stevens Award, a $100,000 prize recognizing proven mastery in the art of poetry given by the Academy of American Poets.

Reading Komunyakaa's Vietnam War Poetry.

Komunyakaa has written poetry on subjects ranging from his childhood in eastern Louisiana to the role and representation of blacks in the full sweep of Western culture. But he is perhaps best known for his poetry about the Vietnam War, especially the powerful sequence of poems in his award-winning collection *Dien Cai Dau.* (The title, which means "crazy" or, more literally, "this crazy head," was an expression that the Vietnamese used to describe American soldiers fighting in Vietnam.) Komunyakaa has noted that it took him "about fourteen years," until 1984, before he could begin to write about his experiences during 1969-70, when he was stationed at Chu Lai, the large American military base south of Danang. As he recalled in an essay published in 1992, he wrote his first war poem while remodeling a house in New Orleans, where the tropical heat and the sunlight reminded him of his tour of duty in Vietnam:

> The humid New Orleans summer had begun edging in, and I wanted to get the hard, high work finished first, where the stifling heat collected. I put a pad of paper and pen on a table in the next room. This had a purpose. The images were coming so fast that, whenever I made a trek down the ladder, each line had to be worth its weight in sweat. . . . Perched on the top rung of the ladder, each step down served as a kind of metrical device — made me plan each word and syllable. In the background, at the other end of the house, in the kitchen, jazz pulsed underneath the whole day. . . . I realized that language is man's first music, and, consequently, I began to approach the poem with this in mind.

The following poems reveal Komunyakaa's efforts to come to terms with the war, from the numbing violence on the battlefield and the racial tensions among the American troops to the profound sense of loss captured in "Facing It," which a critic has called "the most poignant elegy that has been written about the Vietnam War." The texts are taken from *Dien Cai Dau* (1988).

THE DEAD AT QUANG TRI[1]

> This is harder than counting stones
> along paths going nowhere, the way
> a tiger circles & backtracks by

---

1. **Quang Tri:** The capital of the province of the same name on the north central coast of Vietnam, where the North Vietnamese Army achieved its first major victory in the Nguyen Hue Offensive of the spring of 1972. Quang Tri was once again the center of fierce fighting that summer, when most of the province was recaptured by the South Vietnamese Army.

smelling his blood on the ground.
The one kneeling beside the pagoda,   5
remember him? Captain, we won't
talk about that. The Buddhist boy
at the gate with the shaven head
we rubbed for luck
glides by like a white moon.   10
He won't stay dead, dammit!
Blades aim for the family jewels;
the grass we walk on
won't stay down.

[1984, 1988]

TU DO STREET[1]

Music divides the evening.
I close my eyes & can see
men drawing lines in the dust.
America pushes through the membrane
of mist & smoke, & I'm a small boy   5
again in Bogalusa.[2] *White Only*
signs & Hank Snow.[3] But tonight
I walk into a place where bar girls
fade like tropical birds. When
I order a beer, the mama-san[4]   10
behind the counter acts as if she
can't understand, while her eyes
skirt each white face, as Hank Williams[5]
calls from the psychedelic jukebox.
We have played Judas[6] where   15
only machine-gun fire brings us
together. Down the street
black GIs hold to their turf also.

1. **Tu Do Street:** A street known for its bars and brothels in the middle of Saigon, capital of South Vietnam and headquarters of the U.S. Army during the Vietnam War.
2. **Bogalusa:** Komunyakaa was born and raised in this racially divided town eighty miles northeast of New Orleans, Louisiana.
3. **Hank Snow:** Clarence Eugene ("Hank") Snow (1914-1999), a popular country music singer and songwriter.
4. **mama-san:** A slang term coined by American servicemen for an older Vietnamese woman who supervised a bar and a brothel.
5. **Hank Williams:** Hiram King ("Hank") Williams (1923-1953), a singer and songwriter widely regarded as one of the most influential country-music artists of the twentieth century.
6. **Judas:** The apostle who betrayed Jesus to his enemies (Luke 22:3-6).

An off-limits sign pulls me
deeper into alleys, as I look   20
for a softness behind these voices
wounded by their beauty & war.
Back in the bush at Dak To
& Khe Sanh,[7] we fought
the brothers of these women   25
we now run to hold in our arms.
There's more than a nation
inside us, as black & white
soldiers touch the same lovers
minutes apart, tasting   30
each other's breath,
without knowing these rooms
run into each other like tunnels
leading to the underworld.

                                                  [1988]

---

7. **Dak To & Khe Sanh**: Cities in South Vietnam where violent battles between the North Vietnamese and the U.S. Marines took place in 1967 and 1968.

PRISONERS

Usually at the helipad
I see them stumble-dance
across the hot asphalt
with crokersacks[1] over their heads,
moving toward the interrogation huts,   5
thin-framed as box kites
of sticks & black silk
anticipating a hard wind
that'll tug & snatch them
out into space. I think   10
some must be laughing
under their dust-colored hoods,
knowing rockets are aimed

---

1. **crokersacks**: A Southern term for a bag made of rough burlap, originally used to hold frogs (croakers).

at Chu Lai[2] — that the water's
evaporating & soon the nail   15
will make contact with metal.
How can anyone anywhere love
these half-broken figures
bent under the sky's brightness?
The weight they carry   20
is the soil we tread night & day.
Who can cry for them?
I've heard the old ones
are the hardest to break.
An arm twist, a combat boot   25
against the skull, a .45[3]
jabbed into the mouth, nothing
works. When they start talking
with ancestors faint as camphor
smoke in pagodas, you know   30
you'll have to kill them
to get an answer.
Sunlight throws
scythes against the afternoon.
Everything's a heat mirage; a river   35
tugs at their slow feet.
I stand alone & amazed,
with a pill-happy door gunner
signaling for me to board the Cobra.[4]
I remember how one day   40
I almost bowed to such figures
walking toward me, under
a corporal's ironclad stare.
I can't say why.
From a half-mile away   45
trees huddle together,
& the prisoners look like
marionettes hooked to strings of light.

[1988]

---

2. **Chu Lai:** A South Vietnamese coastal town, south of Danang and the site of a large American military base during the Vietnam War.
3. **a .45:** A .45 caliber, semiautomatic pistol that was a standard-issue sidearm during the Vietnam War.
4. **Cobra:** An attack helicopter used by the U.S. Marines.

FACING IT[1]

My black face fades,
hiding inside the black granite.
I said I wouldn't,
dammit: No tears.
I'm stone. I'm flesh.   5
My clouded reflection eyes me
like a bird of prey, the profile of night
slanted against morning. I turn
this way – the stone lets me go.
I turn that way – I'm inside   10
the Vietnam Veterans Memorial
again, depending on the light
to make a difference.
I go down the 58,022 names,
half-expecting to find   15
my own in letters like smoke.
I touch the name Andrew Johnson;
I see the booby trap's white flash.
Names shimmer on a woman's blouse
but when she walks away   20
the names stay on the wall.
Brushstrokes flash, a red bird's
wings cutting across my stare.
The sky. A plane in the sky.
A white vet's image floats   25
closer to me, then his pale eyes
look through mine. I'm a window.
He's lost his right arm
inside the stone. In the black mirror
a woman's trying to erase names: 30
No, she's brushing a boy's hair.

[1988]

---

1. **Facing It:** In this celebrated poem, the final poem in *Dien Cai Dau*, the speaker stands facing the Vietnam War Memorial, adjacent to the National Mall in Washington, D.C. Dedicated in 1982, the main part of the memorial is composed of a V-shaped wall of polished, black stone on which the names of the more than 58,000 members of the American armed forces who died or were missing in action in the war are etched. A visitor looking at the wall sees both the etched names and his or her own reflection, as well as those of other standers-by, symbolizing the intersection of past and present.

Leslie Marmon Silko

[b. 1948]

Leslie Marmon Silko

Christopher Felver took this photograph of Silko, one of the central figures in what has been called the Native American Renaissance, in 2008.

Leslie Marmon Silko was born on March 5, 1948, in Albuquerque, New Mexico, to Leland Howard Marmon, a photographer, and Mary Virginia Leslie Marmon, who lived on the Laguna Pueblo Reservation about fifty miles west of Albuquerque. "We are mixed bloods—Laguna, Mexican, and white," Silko affirmed in 1975. "All those languages, all those ways of living are combined, and we live somewhere on the fringes of all three. But I don't apologize for this any more—not to whites, not to full bloods—our origin is unlike any other. My poetry, my storytelling, rise out of this source." In the matriarchal and matrilineal society of the Laguna, Silko lived in an extended family that included her grandmothers and aunts, who spoke the original language of the Santa Ana Pueblo. Silko grew up listening to their stories and learning to ride a horse, to hunt, and to herd cattle. She attended an Indian boarding school and later a Roman Catholic school in Albuquerque. Partly in rebellion against the strict rules of the school, Silko created and designed her own magazine, *Nasty Asty*, in which she published an off-color joke that had been circulating throughout the school. As she recalled, she was nearly expelled for the incident, which taught her an important lesson about the weight and power of the written word. In 1964, Silko enrolled at the University of New Mexico. She was married briefly to Richard C. Chapman, with whom she had a son. Following her graduation in 1969, the year she published her first short story, she enrolled in the university's American Indian Law School Fellowship Program.

Disillusioned by the treatment of minorities under the American legal system, Silko determined to use her abilities at storytelling as a means of fighting injustice in the United States. She left law school and began graduate work in English at the University of New Mexico. In 1971, she took a job as a teacher at a community college on a Navajo reservation in Arizona. That year, she was awarded a National Endowment for the Arts Discovery Grant, which freed her for writing, and she met and married John Silko. The year after their son was born in 1972, they moved to Ketchikan, Alaska, where Silko's husband worked for Alaska Legal Services. Although she found the climate and geography difficult to endure, her years there were very productive. In 1974, she published six stories, including one of her most widely read works, "Yellow Woman," as well as her first collection of poetry, *Laguna Woman: Poems* (1974). After she returned to the Laguna Pueblo, she was awarded the prestigious Pushcart Prize for Poetry in 1977. That year, she published her novel *Ceremony* (1977), a moving account of a traumatized Native American veteran who returns to the Southwest after being held in a Japanese prisoner of war camp during World War II. In 1978, Silko accepted an invitation to teach creative writing at the University of Arizona. She began corresponding with the poet James Wright, with whom she remained close professional friends until his death from cancer in 1980. His widow, Anne Wright, edited a prize-winning collection of their letters, *With the Delicacy and Strength of Lace: Letters Between Leslie Marmon Silko and James Wright* (1986).

Silko's later works reveal her growing interest in history, mythology, and the interplay among writing, oral storytelling, and images. In 1978, she was filmed in conversation with other writers, reading her works, and telling stories in a video issued by the University of Arizona, *Running on the Edge of the Rainbow: Laguna Stories and Poems*. Silko subsequently founded the Laguna Film Project, and in 1980 she and Denis Carr produced a film entitled *Estoyehmuut and the Gunnadeyah* ("Arrowboy and the Destroyers"). She wove together stories, poems, and family photographs in her acclaimed collection *Storyteller* (1981). Although her personal life was clouded by the collapse of her second marriage, Silko was awarded a prestigious MacArthur Prize Fellowship, the so-called genius grant, which provided funding for five years of creative work. Silko spent the decade researching and writing her controversial novel *Almanac of the Dead* (1991), the apocalyptic story of a revolt in which indigenous peoples seek to regain their ancestral lands from corrupt whites after centuries of brutal exploitation by the European conquerors of the Americas. Silko's more recent works include *Sacred Water* (1993), a collection of photographs and essays about the ecology of southern Arizona; *Yellow Woman and a Beauty of the Spirit: Essays on Native American Life Today* (1996); and *Gardens in the Dunes* (1999), a historical novel about the far-ranging travels of two displaced Native American girls who seek to return to their home in the Southwest. In 2010, Silko published *The Turquoise Ledge: A Memoir*, in which she explores her family history, her Native American heritage, and her close relationship with the natural world of the American Southwest. A recipient of the Native Writers' Circle of the Americas award for lifetime achievement, Silko lives on her ranch near Tucson, Arizona.

Reading Silko's "Yellow Woman."   This story, which was first published in the anthology *The Man to Send Rain Clouds: Contemporary Stories by American Indians* (1974), is regarded by many readers as Silko's defining work. Inspired by stories she heard as a child growing up in the Laguna Pueblo Reservation about Yellow Woman, or Kochininako, the story is told by a woman who wanders off, meets and is seduced by a mysterious man, and accompanies him into the mountains before returning home to her husband, child, and family. The seemingly simple and straightforward narrative raises complex questions, as the narrator seeks to come to terms with her identity, her sexuality, and her place in the world. Rejecting narrowly feminist readings of the story, Silko told a reviewer in 1986:

bedfordstmartins.com/ americanlit for research links on Silko

> The kinds of things that cause white upper-middle-class women to flee the home for a while to escape or get away from domination and powerlessness and inferior status, vis-à-vis the husband, and the male, those kinds of forces are not operating, they're not operating at all. What's operating in those stories of Kochininako is this attraction, this passion, this connection between the human world and the animal and spirit worlds.

In the story, Silko also explores the nature and function of storytelling, which in Laguna culture, she has observed, is "a whole way of seeing yourself, the people around you, your life, the place of your life in the bigger context, not just in terms of nature and location but in terms of what has gone on before, what's happened to other people. It's a whole way of being." The text is taken from Silko's collection *Storyteller* (1981).

YELLOW WOMAN

What Whirlwind Man Told Kochininako, Yellow Woman[1]
    I myself belong to the wind
    and so it is we will travel swiftly
    this whole world
    with dust and with windstorms.

My thigh clung to his with dampness, and I watched the sun rising up through the tamaracks and willows.[2] The small brown water birds came to the river and hopped across the mud, leaving brown scratches in the alkali-white crust. They bathed in the river silently. I could hear the water, almost at our feet where the narrow fast channel bubbled and washed green ragged moss and fern leaves. I looked at him beside me, rolled in the red blanket on the white river sand. I cleaned the sand out of the cracks between my toes, squinting because the sun was above the willow trees. I looked at him for the last time, sleeping on the white river sand.

I felt hungry and followed the river south the way we had come the afternoon before, following our footprints that were already blurred by lizard tracks and bug trails. The horses were still lying down, and the black one whinnied when he saw me but he did not get up—maybe it was because the corral was made out of thick cedar branches and the horses had not yet felt the sun like I had. I tried to look beyond the pale red mesas to the pueblo.[3] I knew it was there, even if I could not see it, on the sandrock hill above the river, the same river that moved past me now and had reflected the moon last night.

The horse felt warm underneath me. He shook his head and pawed the sand. The bay whinnied and leaned against the gate trying to follow, and I remembered him asleep in the red blanket beside the river. I slid off the horse and tied him close to the other horse, I walked north with the river again, and the white sand broke loose in footprints over footprints.

"Wake up."

He moved in the blanket and turned his face to me with his eyes still closed. I knelt down to touch him.

"I'm leaving."

---

1. **Kochininako, Yellow Woman:** Many stories about this powerful female figure, always told from her point of view, are part of the Laguna and Acoma Pueblo cultures of New Mexico.
2. **tamaracks and willows:** Trees that flourish in boggy areas and along river banks.
3. **pueblo:** Village (Spanish), usually used to denote a Native American settlement of adobe houses built by one of several groups of Pueblo people in the Southwest.

He smiled now, eyes still closed. "You are coming with me, remember?" He sat up now with his bare dark chest and belly in the sun.

"Where?"

"To my place."

"And will I come back?"

He pulled his pants on. I walked away from him, feeling him behind me and smelling the willows.

"Yellow Woman," he said.

I turned to face him. "Who are you?" I asked.

He laughed and knelt on the low, sandy bank, washing his face in the river. "Last night you guessed my name, and you knew why I had come."

I stared past him at the shallow moving water and tried to remember the night, but I could only see the moon in the water and remember his warmth around me.

"But I only said that you were him and that I was Yellow Woman — I'm not really her — I have my own name and I come from the pueblo on the other side of the mesa. Your name is Silva[4] and you are a stranger I met by the river yesterday afternoon."

He laughed softly. "What happened yesterday has nothing to do with what you will do today, Yellow Woman."

"I know — that's what I'm saying — the old stories about the ka'tsina spirit[5] and Yellow Woman can't mean us."

My old grandpa liked to tell those stories best. There is one about Badger and Coyote who went hunting and were gone all day, and when the sun was going down they found a house. There was a girl living there alone, and she had light hair and eyes and she told them that they could sleep with her. Coyote wanted to be with her all night so he sent Badger into a prairie-dog hole, telling him he thought he saw something in it. As soon as Badger crawled in, Coyote blocked up the entrance with rocks and hurried back to Yellow Woman.

"Come here," he said gently.

He touched my neck and I moved close to him to feel his breathing and to hear his heart. I was wondering if Yellow Woman had known who she was — if she knew that she would become part of the stories. Maybe she'd had another name that her husband and relatives called her so that only the ka'tsina from the north and the storytellers would know her as Yellow Woman. But I didn't go on; I felt him all around me, pushing me down into the white river sand.

Yellow Woman went away with the spirit from the north and lived with him and his relatives. She was gone for a long time, but then one day she came back and she brought twin boys.

"Do you know the story?"

---

4. **Silva:** His name is the word for the trees of a particular country or region, a special use of the Latin word *silva*, or woodland.

5. **ka'tsina spirit:** According to Pueblo mythology, the ka'tsina is a good spirit, closely associated with water or rain, who selects a female figure and endows her with special powers.

"What story?" He smiled and pulled me close to him as he said this. I was afraid lying there on the red blanket. All I could know was the way he felt, warm, damp, his body beside me. This is the way it happens in the stories, I was thinking, with no thought beyond the moment she meets the ka'tsina spirit and they go.

"I don't have to go. What they tell in stories was real only then, back in time immemorial, like they say."

He stood up and pointed at my clothes tangled in the blanket. "Let's go," he said.

I walked beside him, breathing hard because he walked fast, his hand around my wrist. I had stopped trying to pull away from him, because his hand felt cool and the sun was high, drying the river bed into alkali. I will see someone, eventually I will see someone, and then I will be certain that he is only a man — some man from nearby — and I will be sure that I am not Yellow Woman. Because she is from out of time past and I live now and I've been to school and there are highways and pickup trucks that Yellow Woman never saw.

It was an easy ride north on horseback. I watched the change from the cottonwood trees along the river to the junipers that brushed past us in the foothills, and finally there were only piñons, and when I looked up at the rim of the mountain plateau I could see pine trees growing on the edge. Once I stopped to look down, but the pale sandstone had disappeared and the river was gone and the dark lava hills were all around. He touched my hand, not speaking, but always singing softly a mountain song and looking into my eyes.

I felt hungry and wondered what they were doing at home now — my mother, my grandmother, my husband, and the baby. Cooking breakfast, saying, "Where did she go? — maybe kidnapped." And Al going to the tribal police with the details: "She went walking along the river."

The house was made with black lava rock and red mud. It was high above the spreading miles of arroyos and long mesas. I smelled a mountain smell of pitch and buck brush. I stood there beside the black horse, looking down on the small, dim country we had passed, and I shivered.

"Yellow Woman, come inside where it's warm." He lit a fire in the stove. It was an old stove with a round belly and an enamel coffeepot on top. There was only the stove, some faded Navajo blankets, and a bedroll and cardboard box. The floor was made of smooth adobe plaster, and there was one small window facing east. He pointed at the box.

"There's some potatoes and the frying pan." He sat on the floor with his arms around his knees pulling them close to his chest and he watched me fry the potatoes. I didn't mind him watching me because he was always watching me — he had been watching me since I came upon him sitting on the river bank trimming leaves from a willow twig with his knife. We ate from the pan and he wiped the grease from his fingers on his Levi's.

"Have you brought women here before?" He smiled and kept chewing, so I said, "Do you always use the same tricks?"

"What tricks?" He looked at me like he didn't understand.

"The story about being a ka'tsina from the mountains. The story about Yellow Woman."

Silva was silent; his face was calm.

"I don't believe it. Those stories couldn't happen now," I said.

He shook his head and said softly, "But someday they will talk about us, and they will say, 'Those two lived long ago when things like that happened.'"

He stood up and went out. I ate the rest of the potatoes and thought about things — about the noise the stove was making and the sound of the mountain wind outside. I remembered yesterday and the day before, and then I went outside.

I walked past the corral to the edge where the narrow trail cut through the black rim rock, I was standing in the sky with nothing around me but the wind that came down from the blue mountain peak behind me. I could see faint mountain images in the distance miles across the vast spread of mesas and valleys and plains. I wondered who was over there to feel the mountain wind on those sheer blue edges — who walks on the pine needles in those blue mountains.

"Can you see the pueblo?" Silva was standing behind me.

I shook my head. "We're too far away."

"From here I can see the world." He stepped out on the edge. "The Navajo reservation begins over there." He pointed to the east. "The Pueblo boundaries are over here." He looked below us to the south, where the narrow trail seemed to come from. "The Texans have their ranches over there, starting with that valley, the Concho Valley.[6] The Mexicans run some cattle over there too."

"Do you ever work for them?"

"I steal from them," Silva answered. The sun was dropping behind us and the shadows were filling the land below. I turned away from the edge that dropped forever into the valleys below.

"I'm cold," I said, "I'm going inside." I started wondering about this man who could speak the Pueblo language so well but who lived on a mountain and rustled cattle. I decided that this man Silva must be Navajo, because Pueblo men didn't do things like that.

"You must be a Navajo."

Silva shook his head gently. "Little Yellow Woman," he said, "you never give up, do you? I have told you who I am. The Navajo people know me, too." He knelt down and unrolled the bedroll and spread the extra blankets out on a piece of canvas. The sun was down, and the only light in the house came from outside — the dim orange light from sundown.

I stood there and waited for him to crawl under the blankets.

"What are you waiting for?" he said, and I lay down beside him. He undressed me slowly like the night before beside the river — kissing my face gently and running his hands up and down my belly and legs. He took off my pants and then he laughed.

"Why are you laughing?"

"You are breathing so hard."

I pulled away from him and turned my back to him.

---

6. **Navajo reservation . . . Concho Valley:** The Navajo reservation covers more than 27,000 square miles in Utah, Arizona, and New Mexico. The Laguna Pueblo is south of the reservation, in northwest New Mexico, and the Concho Valley is in the White Mountains of eastern Arizona.

He pulled me around and pinned me down with his arms and chest. "You don't understand, do you, little Yellow Woman? You will do what I want."

And again he was all around me with his skin slippery against mine, and I was afraid because I understood that his strength could hurt me. I lay underneath him and I knew that he could destroy me. But later, while he slept beside me, I touched his face and I had a feeling—the kind of feeling for him that overcame me that morning along the river. I kissed him on the forehead and he reached out for me.

When I woke up in the morning he was gone. It gave me a strange feeling because for a long time I sat there on the blankets and looked around the little house for some object of his—some proof that he had been there or maybe that he was coming back. Only the blankets and the cardboard box remained. The .30-30[7] that had been leaning in the corner was gone, and so was the knife I had used the night before. He was gone, and I had my chance to go now. But first I had to eat, because I knew it would be a long walk home.

I found some dried apricots in the cardboard box, and I sat down on a rock at the edge of the plateau rim. There was no wind and the sun warmed me. I was surrounded by silence. I drowsed with apricots in my mouth, and I didn't believe that there were highways or railroads or cattle to steal.

When I woke up, I stared down at my feet in the black mountain dirt. Little black ants were swarming over the pine needles around my foot. They must have smelled the apricots. I thought about my family far below me. They would be wondering about me, because this had never happened to me before. The tribal police would file a report. But if old Grandpa weren't dead he would tell them what happened—he would laugh and say, "Stolen by a ka'tsina, a mountain spirit. She'll come home—they usually do." There are enough of them to handle things. My mother and grandmother will raise the baby like they raised me. Al will find someone else, and they will go on like before, except that there will be a story about the day I disappeared while I was walking along the river. Silva had come for me; he said he had. I did not decide to go. I just went. Moon-flowers blossom in the sand hills before dawn, just as I followed him. That's what I was thinking as I wandered along the trail through the pine trees.

It was noon when I got back. When I saw the stone house I remembered that I had meant to go home. But that didn't seem important any more, maybe because there were little blue flowers growing in the meadow behind the stone house and the gray squirrels were playing in the pines next to the house. The horses were standing in the corral, and there was a beef carcass hanging on the shady side of a big pine in front of the house. Flies buzzed around the clotted blood that hung from the carcass. Silva was washing his hands in a bucket full of water. He must have heard me coming because he spoke to me without turning to face me.

"I've been waiting for you."

"I went walking in the big pine trees."

I looked into the bucket full of bloody water with brown-and-white animal hairs floating in it. Silva stood there letting his hand drip, examining me intently.

---

7. .30-30: A rifle firing a .30-inch cartridge, commonly used for hunting deer.

"Are you coming with me?"

"Where?" I asked him.

"To sell the meat in Marquez."[8]

"If you're sure it's O.K."

"I wouldn't ask you if it wasn't," he answered.

He sloshed the water around in the bucket before he dumped it out and set the bucket upside down near the door. I followed him to the corral and watched him saddle the horses. Even beside the horses he looked tall, and I asked him again if he wasn't Navajo. He didn't say anything; he just shook his head and kept cinching up the saddle.

"But Navajos are tall."

"Get on the horse," he said, "and let's go."

The last thing he did before we started down the steep trail was to grab the .30-30 from the corner. He slid the rifle into the scabbard that hung from his saddle.

"Do they ever try to catch you?" I asked.

"They don't know who I am."

"Then why did you bring the rifle?"

"Because we are going to Marquez where the Mexicans live."

The trail leveled out on a narrow ridge that was steep on both sides like an animal spine. On one side I could see where the trail went around the rocky gray hills and disappeared into the southeast where the pale sandrock mesas stood in the distance near my home. On the other side was a trail that went west, and as I looked far into the distance I thought I saw the little town. But Silva said no, that I was looking in the wrong place, that I just thought I saw houses. After that I quit looking off into the distance; it was hot and the wildflowers were closing up their deep-yellow petals. Only the waxy cactus flowers bloomed in the bright sun, and I saw every color that a cactus blossom can be; the white ones and the red ones were still buds, but the purple and the yellow were blossoms, open full and the most beautiful of all.

Silva saw him before I did. The white man was riding a big gray horse, coming up the trail towards us. He was traveling fast and the gray horse's feet sent rocks rolling off the trail into the dry tumbleweeds. Silva motioned for me to stop and we watched the white man. He didn't see us right away, but finally his horse whinnied at our horses, and he stopped. He looked at us briefly before he lapped the gray horse across the three hundred yards that separated us. He stopped his horse in front of Silva, and his young fat face was shadowed by the brim of his hat. He didn't look mad, but his small, pale eyes moved from the blood-soaked gunny sacks hanging from my saddle to Silva's face and then back to my face.

"Where did you get the fresh meat?" the white man asked.

"I've been hunting," Silva said, and when he shifted his weight in the saddle the leather creaked.

"The hell you have, Indian. You've been rustling cattle. We've been looking for the thief for a long time."

---

8. **Marquez:** A town north of the Laguna pueblo in New Mexico.

The rancher was fat, and sweat began to soak through his white cowboy shirt and the wet cloth stuck to the thick rolls of belly fat. He almost seemed to be panting from the exertion of talking, and he smelled rancid, maybe because Silva scared him.

Silva turned to me and smiled. "Go back up the mountain, Yellow Woman."

The white man got angry when he heard Silva speak in a language he couldn't understand. "Don't try anything, Indian. Just keep riding to Marquez. We'll call the state police from there."

The rancher must have been unarmed because he was very frightened and if he had a gun he would have pulled it out then. I turned my horse around and the rancher yelled, "Stop!" I looked at Silva for an instant and there was something ancient and dark — something I could feel in my stomach — in his eyes, and when I glanced at his hand I saw his finger on the trigger of the .30-30 that was still in the saddle scabbard. I slapped my horse across the flank and the sacks of raw meat swung against my knees as the horse leaped up the trail. It was hard to keep my balance, and once I thought I felt the saddle slipping backward; it was because of this that I could not look back.

I didn't stop until I reached the ridge where the trail forked. The horse was breathing deep gasps and there was a dark film of sweat on its neck. I looked down in the direction I had come from, but I couldn't see the place. I waited. The wind came up and pushed warm air past me. I looked up at the sky, pale blue and full of thin clouds and fading vapor trails left by jets.

I think four shots were fired — I remember hearing four hollow explosions that reminded me of deer hunting. There could have been more shots after that, but I couldn't have heard them because my horse was running again and the loose rocks were making too much noise as they scattered around his feet.

Horses have a hard time running downhill, but I went that way instead of uphill to the mountain because I thought it was safer. I felt better with the horse running southeast past the round gray hills that were covered with cedar trees and black lava rock. When I got to the plain in the distance I could see the dark green patches of tamaracks that grew along the river; and beyond the river I could see the beginning of the pale sandrock mesas. I stopped the horse and looked back to see if anyone was coming; then I got off the horse and turned the horse around, wondering if it would go back to its corral under the pines on the mountain. It looked back at me for a moment and then plucked a mouthful of green tumbleweeds before it trotted back up the trail with its ears pointed forward, carrying its head daintily to one side to avoid stepping on the dragging reins. When the horse disappeared over the last hill, the gunny sacks full of meat were still swinging and bouncing.

I walked toward the river on a wood-hauler's road that I knew would eventually lead to the paved road. I was thinking about waiting beside the road for someone to drive by, but by the time I got to the pavement I had decided it wasn't very far to walk if I followed the river back the way Silva and I had come.

The river water tasted good, and I sat in the shade under a cluster of silvery willows. I thought about Silva, and I felt sad at leaving him; still, there was something strange about him, and I tried to figure it out all the way back home.

I came back to the place on the river bank where he had been sitting the first time I saw him. The green willow leaves that he had trimmed from the branch were still lying there, wilted in the sand. I saw the leaves and I wanted to go back to him – to kiss him and to touch him – but the mountains were too far away now. And I told myself, because I believe it, he will come back sometime and be waiting again by the river.

I followed the path up from the river into the village. The sun was getting low, and I could smell supper cooking when I got to the screen door of my house. I could hear their voices inside – my mother was telling my grandmother how to fix the Jell-O and my husband, Al, was playing with the baby. I decided to tell them that some Navajo had kidnaped me, but I was sorry that old Grandpa wasn't alive to hear my story because it was the Yellow Woman stories he liked to tell best.

[1974, 1981]

Joy Harjo

[b. 1951]

Joy Harjo was born on May 9, 1951, in Tulsa, Oklahoma. Her mother, Wynema Baker Foster, was of mixed Cherokee and French ancestry, and her father, Allen W. Foster, was a Muscogee Creek and a descendant of powerful leaders of his tribe, including Menewa, who resisted the forced removal of the Alabama Creeks from their native lands to Indian Territory (now Oklahoma) during the 1830s. Harjo, an enrolled member of the Muscogee Creek tribe, explained in an interview in 1992: "I was not brought up traditionally Creek, was raised in the north side of Tulsa in a neighborhood where there lived many other mixed-blood Indian families. My neighbors were Seminole Indian, Pawnee, other tribes, and white." When she was sixteen, Harjo moved to New Mexico to study art at the Institute of American Indian Arts. The next year, she had her first child, a son, and her second child, a daughter, was born four years later. As a single parent, Harjo struggled to earn a living, working as a waitress and a gas-station attendant. But she enrolled at the University of New Mexico, where she concentrated in art before transferring to the English department to become a creative-writing major because, as she has explained, "I found that language, through poetry, was taking on more magical qualities than my painting. I could say more when I wrote." She published a chapbook of poetry, *The Last Song* (1975), graduated in 1976, and then continued her studies in the Writers' Workshop at the University of Iowa.

Joy Harjo
Paul Abdoo took this photograph of the Native American poet and musician in 1990.

After she received an MFA in 1978, Harjo returned to teach and write in the Southwest. She taught at the Institute of American Indian Arts before becoming an instructor of creative writing at Arizona State University in 1978, the year she published her second collection of poetry, *What Moon Drove Me to This?* Five years later, she published one of her most critically acclaimed collections, *She Had Some Horses* (1983), poems in which she explored the trials of women and the long struggle of Native Americans for survival in the United States. Harjo gained widespread recognition with the publication of her next collections of poetry, *Secrets from the Center of the World* (1989), *In Mad Love and War* (1990), for which she was awarded the Poetry Society of America's William Carlos Williams Award, and *The Woman Who Fell from the Sky* (1994). Her recent books include an anthology she coedited with Gloria Bird, *Reinventing the Enemy's Language: Contemporary Native Women's Writings of North America* (1997), which Alice Walker called "one of the most significant anthologies ever to be published in English." Harjo, whose grandmother played the saxophone in Indian Territory during the early 1900s, took up the instrument and has made two recordings combining music and poetry, *Letter from the End of the Twentieth Century* (1997) and *Native Joy for Real* (2004). She has also made a recording of her readings of the poems in *She Had Some Horses* (2006). In 2012, Harjo published *Crazy Brave: A Memoir*, an account of her often-painful journey through a difficult childhood and young adulthood to her discovery of her poetic voice. Harjo has taught at the University of Colorado–Boulder, the University of Arizona, UCLA, and the University of New Mexico. When she is not teaching, performing with her band, Poetic Justice, or on tour giving poetry readings, Harjo lives in Hawaii. In addition to her other writings, she maintains a Web log at www .joyharjo.com/, on which she regularly reports on her travels and other events.

I turn and return to Harjo's poetry for her heartbreaking, complex witness and for her world-remaking language: precise, unsentimental, miraculous.

—Adrienne Rich

Reading Harjo's Poetry. Harjo has explained that, because she did not study or begin to write poetry until she was in her twenties, she has been less influenced by "conventional English-language poetry" than by contemporary poets and prose writers such as Simon Ortiz, N. Scott Momaday, Leslie Marmon Silko, Audre Lorde, and Alice Walker. Harjo has also suggested that her poems derive from the Native American heritage of storytelling and her tribal memory. "It is Creek, and touches in on the larger tribal continental memory and the larger human memory, global," she has observed. "It's not something I consciously chose; I mean, I am not a full blood, but it was something that chose me, that lives in me, and I cannot deny it." The following selection of poems indicates some of the persistent themes in her work: the clash between Native American culture and contemporary American society, the function and meaning of history, and the importance and beauty of the land. Harjo's early training in art and her interest in music are evident in the sharp visual imagery and musical rhythms of the poems, which range from

bedfordstmartins.com/ americanlit for research links on Harjo

free-form meditations on history and place to compressed prose poems
celebrating the enduring landscape of the Southwest. The texts are taken
from her collection *How We Became Human: New and Selected Poems*
(2002).

NEW ORLEANS

This is the south. I look for evidence
of other Creeks,[1] for remnants of voices,
or for tobacco brown bones to come wandering
down Conti Street, Royal, or Decatur.[2]
Near the French Market[3] I see a blue horse   5
caught frozen in stone in the middle of
a square. Brought in by the Spanish on
an endless ocean voyage he became mad
and crazy. They caught him in blue
rock, said   10
      don't talk.

I know it wasn't just a horse
         that went crazy.

Nearby is a shop with ivory and knives.
There are red rocks. The man behind the   15
counter has no idea that he is inside
magic stones. He should find out before
they destroy him. These things
have memory,
      you know.   20

I have a memory.
         It swims deep in blood,
a delta in the skin. It swims out of Oklahoma,
deep the Mississippi River. It carries my
feet to these places: the French Quarter,[4]   25
stale rooms, the sun behind thick and moist
clouds, and I hear boats hauling themselves up
and down the river.

---

1. **Creeks:** Native Americans who lived in the southeastern part of the United States until the 1830s, when the federal government forcibly removed them to "Indian Territory," present-day Oklahoma.
2. **Conti Street, Royal, or Decatur:** Streets in the French Quarter section of New Orleans. [Harjo's note]
3. **French Market:** An open market that has been in operation since New Orleans began as a city in 1718. [Harjo's note]
4. **French Quarter:** The original city of New Orleans, which was founded by the French Mississippi Company in 1718, was centered on the land known as the French Quarter, a twelve-by-nine-block area on the Mississippi River.

My spirit comes here to drink.
My spirit comes here to drink.   30
Blood is the undercurrent.

There are voices buried in the Mississippi mud.
There are ancestors and future children
buried beneath the currents stirred up by
pleasure boats going up and down.   35
There are stories here made of memory.

I remember DeSoto.[5] He is buried somewhere in
this river, his bones sunk like the golden
treasure he traveled half the earth to find,
came looking for gold cities, for shining streets   40
of beaten gold to dance on with silk ladies.

He should have stayed home.

            (Creeks knew of him for miles
            before he came into town.
            Dreamed of silver blades   45
            and crosses.)

And knew he was one of the ones who yearned
for something his heart wasn't big enough
to handle.

            (And DeSoto thought it was gold.)   50

The Creeks lived in earth towns,
            not gold,
      spun children, not gold.
That's not what DeSoto thought he wanted to see.
The Creeks knew it, and drowned him in   55
      the Mississippi River
                  so he wouldn't have to drown himself.

Maybe his body is what I am looking for
as evidence. To know in another way

---

5. **DeSoto**: Hernando deSoto [c. 1496–1542] was the first European contact with the Mvskoke Creek tribe. He
landed on the western coast of Florida in 1539, bringing with him wishes and dreams for riches, an attitude of
entitlement (backed up with an army in armor, mounted on horses), and numerous diseases for which the
Creeks had no immunity. Usually it is just the Cherokee whose forced migration from east to west is recognized as "*The Trail of Tears*," but there were many tribes forced west, including the Mvskoke Creeks. The
removal took place in stages. Some groups were taken by a southern route through New Orleans, brought up
the Mississippi River on steamboats to the Arkansas River. The *Monmouth* was one of the contracted boats.
On July 31, 1836, it was being piloted recklessly by a drunk crew when it collided with the *Trenton*, another
steamboat. The *Monmouth* broke up and sank, killing over three hundred of the migrating Creeks. Many of
those who survived were badly scalded by hot water. [Harjo's note]

that my memory is alive.   60
But he must have got away, somehow,
because I have seen New Orleans,
the lace and silk buildings,
trolley cars on beaten silver paths,
graves that rise up out of soft earth in the rain,   65
shops that sell black mammy dolls
holding white babies.

And I know I have seen DeSoto,
        having a drink on Bourbon Street,[6]
        mad and crazy   70
        dancing with a woman as gold
        as the river bottom.

                                           [1983, 2002]

---

6. **Bourbon Street:** This street in the heart of the French Quarter, originally named after the ruling House of Bourbon in France, is now primarily known for its bars and strip clubs.

If You Look with the Mind of the Swirling Earth

If you look with the mind of the swirling earth near Shiprock[1]
you become the land, beautiful. And understand how three
crows at the edge of the highway, laughing, become three crows
at the edge of the world, laughing.

                                           [1989, 2002]

---

1. **Shiprock:** *Shiprock* or *Naat'aani Neez* is a large Navajo community in the northwest part of New Mexico. It is marked by a huge rock that appears to look like a ship. *Naat-aani* means boss, chief, or leader. *Neez* means tall. [Harjo's note]

This Land Is a Poem

This land is a poem of ochre and burnt sand I could never write, unless paper were the sacrament of sky, and ink the broken line of wild horses staggering the horizon several miles away. Even then, does anything written ever matter to the earth, wind, and sky?

                                           [1989, 2002]

Rita Dove

[b. 1952]

Rita Dove

Christopher Felver took this photograph of Dove in 1994, the year after she became the first African American to be named Poet Laureate of the United States.

Rita Frances Dove was born in Akron, Ohio, on August 28, 1952. She was the second of four children of Elvira Hord and Ray Dove, the first African American chemist at the Goodyear Tire and Rubber Company. Their home was filled with books and music, and Dove was trained as a musician and an opera singer. She wrote poetry as a child, but she first thought of becoming a writer when one of her high-school teachers took her to a book signing where Dove met the poet John Ciardi. "Here was a living, breathing, walking, joking person, who wrote books," she recalled in a 1994 interview:

> And for me, it was that I loved to read but I always thought that the dream was too far away. The person who had written the book was a god, it wasn't a person. To have someone actually in the same room with me, talking, and you realize he gets up and walks his dog the same as everybody else, was a way of saying, "It is possible. You can really walk through that door too."

In 1970, Dove was named a Presidential Scholar, one of the top one hundred high-school seniors in the country, and enrolled at Miami University of Ohio, where she majored in English. After she graduated summa cum laude in 1973, she was awarded a Fulbright Fellowship and studied modern European literature at the University of Tübingen, Germany. When she returned, she enrolled in the Writers' Workshop at the University of Iowa and received an MFA in 1977. While at Iowa, Dove met Fred Viebahn, a German writer who was a Fulbright Fellow in the International Program. They married in 1979, the year before Dove published her first book of poems, *The Yellow House on the Corner* (1980).

The publication launched Dove's career as a writer and teacher. She joined the faculty of Arizona State University and worked on a collection of poems about her experiences in Europe, *Museum* (1983). That year, Dove gave birth to her only child, a daughter, and she was awarded a Guggenheim Fellowship. She wrote a collection of short stories, *Fifth Sunday* (1985), which was followed by a sequence of poems based on the lives and marriage of her maternal grandparents, *Thomas and Beulah* (1986). Dove consequently became the second African American woman (the first was Gwendolyn Brooks) to win the Pulitzer Prize for Poetry. In 1989, she joined the faculty of the University of Virginia and published another collection of poems, *Grace Notes.* Her next book was a novel about a young African American puppeteer, *Through the Ivory Gate* (1992). In 1993, the same year that Toni Morrison was awarded the Nobel Prize in Literature, Dove became the first African American Poet Laureate of the United States. But she continued to work in a variety of genres, publishing a play set on a southern plantation in the 1820s, *The Darker Face of the Earth* (1994); a volume of essays, *The Poet's World* (1995); a song cycle for soprano and orchestra, *Seven for Luck* (1998); and two collections of poetry, *Mother Love* (1995) and *On the Bus with Rosa Parks* (1999). Dove and her husband became devotees of ballroom dancing, the subject of many of the poems in her collection *American Smooth* (2004). In 2009, she published *Sonata Mulattica*, a sequence of poems recreating the life of the biracial violin prodigy George Augustus Polgreen Bridgetower (1780–1860), to whom Ludwig van Beethoven first dedicated his famous "Kreutzer" Sonata. The recipient of numerous awards and honorary degrees, Dove lives in Charlottesville, Virginia, where she writes each night at an oak desk built for her by her father and where she is the Commonwealth Professor of English at the University of Virginia.

Reading Dove's Poetry.   "Poetry is language at its most distilled and most powerful," Dove has observed. Certainly, her technically accomplished poems display the rhythmical resources of language, including colloquial black speech, and the concentrated power of imagery and metaphor. In contrast to many of her contemporaries, Dove has frequently employed traditional poetic forms such as the sonnet, but she has freely adapted those forms to her own distinctive purposes and subjects. Although she has written poems on a wide range of topics, one of her central concerns is the past, especially the cultural heritage and often painful history of African Americans. The first two poems in the following selection, two monologues spoken by slaves, are from Dove's first collection, *The Yellow House on the Corner* (1980). Dove, an accomplished singer who has collaborated on a number of musical compositions based on her work, has also written numerous poems about music and musicians. "Canary," a tribute to the jazz singer Billie Holiday, is from Dove's collection *Grace Notes* (1989). The final poem in the selection is "History," a sonnet from a collection of poems in which Dove explored the relations between mothers and daughters, *Motherhood* (1995).

bedfordstmartins.com/ americanlit for research links on Dove

THE HOUSE SLAVE

The first horn lifts its arm over the dew-lit grass
and in the slave quarters there is a rustling—
children are bundled into aprons, cornbread

and water gourds grabbed, a salt pork breakfast taken.
I watch them driven into the vague before-dawn   5
while their mistress sleeps like an ivory toothpick

and Massa dreams of asses, rum and slave-funk.
I cannot fall asleep again. At the second horn,
the whip curls across the backs of the laggards—

sometimes my sister's voice, unmistaken, among them.   10
"Oh! pray," she cries. "Oh! pray!" Those days
I lie on my cot, shivering in the early heat,

and as the fields unfold to whiteness,
and they spill like bees among the fat flowers,
I weep. It is not yet daylight.   15

[1980]

KENTUCKY, 1833

It is Sunday, day of roughhousing. We are let out in the
woods. The young boys wrestle and butt their heads together
like sheep — a circle forms; claps and shouts fill the air.
The women, brown and glossy, gather round the banjo player,
or simply lie in the sun, legs and aprons folded. The weather's   5
an odd monkey — any other day he's on our backs, his cotton eye
everywhere; today the light sifts down like the finest cornmeal,
coating our hands and arms with a dust. God's dust, old woman
Acker says. She's the only one who could read to us from the
Bible, before Massa forbade it. On Sundays, something hangs   10
in the air, a hallelujah, a skitter of brass, but we can't
call it by name and it disappears.

Then Massa and his gentlemen friends come to bet on the boys.
They guffaw and shout, taking sides, red-faced on the edge of
the boxing ring. There is more kicking, butting, and scuffling —   15
the winner gets a dram of whiskey if he can drink it all in
one swig without choking.

Jason is bucking and prancing about — Massa said his name
reminded him of some sailor, a hero who crossed an ocean,
looking for a golden cotton field.[1] Jason thinks he's been   20
born to great things — a suit with gold threads, vest and all.
Now the winner is sprawled out under a tree and the sun, that
weary tambourine, hesitates at the rim of the sky's green light.
It's a crazy feeling that carries through the night; as if the
sky were an omen we could not understand, the book that, if we   25
could read, would change our lives.

[1980]

---

1. **a hero . . . golden cotton field:** In Greek mythology, Jason leads the Argonauts in a voyage to retrieve the Golden Fleece, the magical fur of a golden ram that is guarded by a dragon in a distant land called Colchis.

CANARY

for Michael S. Harper[1]

Billie Holiday's burned voice
had as many shadows as lights,
a mournful candelabra against a sleek piano,
the gardenia her signature under that ruined face.[2]

(Now you're cooking, drummer to bass,   5
magic spoon, magic needle.
Take all day if you have to
with your mirror and your bracelet of song.)

Fact is, the invention of women under siege
has been to sharpen love in the service of myth.   10

If you can't be free, be a mystery.

[1989]

---

1. **Dedication:** Michael S. Harper (b. 1938) is an African American poet who has written several tributes to masters of jazz (see pp. 2211–2216).
2. **Billy Holiday's burned voice . . . ruined face:** Born Eleanora Fagan, Holiday (1915–1959) was a celebrated jazz singer who performed with white gardenias in her hair and was known to her fans as "Lady Day." In the years before her early death at age forty-four, her voice and her face began to show the wear and tear of alcohol abuse and heroin addiction, evoked in the reference to drug paraphernalia, "magic spoon, magic needle," in the following stanza.

HISTORY

Everything's a metaphor[1] some wise
guy said, and his woman nodded, wisely.
Why was this such a discovery
to him? Why did history
happen only on the outside?   5
She'd watched an embryo track an arc
across her swollen belly from the inside
and knew she'd best
think *knee*, not *tumor* or *burrowing mole*, lest
it emerge a monster. Each craving marks   10
the soul: splashed white upon a temple the dish
of ice cream, coveted, broken in a wink,
or the pickle duplicated just behind the ear. *Every wish
will find its symbol*, the woman thinks.

[1995]

---

1. **Everything's a metaphor:** An often repeated statement widely attributed to the German writer and theorist Johann Wolfgang von Goethe (1749–1832).

Sandra Cisneros

[b. 1954]

Sandra Cisneros

The Associated Press photographer Eric Gay took this portrait of Cisneros in San Antonio, Texas, where the award-winning poet and short-story writer has lived since 1992.

Sandra Cisneros was born on December 20, 1954, in Chicago, Illinois, the only daughter of the seven children of Elvira Cordero Anguiano and Alfredo Cisneros Del Moral, an upholsterer born in Mexico. During her childhood, the family traveled frequently to visit her paternal grandparents in Mexico City. Each time they returned, Cisneros has recalled, they had to find "yet another Chicago flat, another Chicago neighborhood, another Catholic school." She felt isolated by the constant dislocations, as well as by her position as the only sister of six brothers, who "had their own conspiracies and allegiances, leaving me odd-woman-out-forever." Although her mother was a high-school dropout, she got her children library cards before they could read, and she strongly encouraged her daughter to excel academically. Excused from household chores, Cisneros retreated to her room with her books. She wrote some poetry in high school but did not begin to write seriously until she was a student at Loyola University Chicago. When she graduated in 1976, she enrolled in the Writers' Workshop at the University of Iowa, where she was keenly aware of her differences from other students: "My classmates were from the best schools in the country. They had been bred as fine hot-house flowers. I was a yellow weed among the city's cracks." Although she was not happy at Iowa, Cisneros credits the experience with helping her find a literary voice in her "place of difference," and she graduated with an MFA in 1978.

Despite some significant early accomplishments, Cisneros struggled for more than a decade to earn a reputation and a living as a writer. She first returned to her parents' home in Chicago and taught at the Latino Youth Alternative High School. Her poems appeared in small literary magazines such as *Quarterly West* and *Nuestro*, and she published a chapbook of poetry, *Bad Boys* (1980). She soon began work on a novel about a girl growing up in a run-down Spanish-speaking neighborhood in Chicago, *The House on Mango Street* (1984). The reviews were generally enthusiastic, and the novel won an American Book Award. Eager to live independently of her family, Cisneros moved to Texas after she received a Texas Institute of Letters Dobie Paisano Fellowship in 1986. She once again received laudatory reviews for her first collection of poems, *My Wicked, Wicked Ways* (1987). But she could not find a job in Texas, where Cisneros wanted to stay, and took a teaching position at California State University, Chico. A National Endowment for the Arts Fellowship enabled her to complete *Woman Hollering Creek*, a collection of lyrical sketches and stories set in Chicago, Texas, and Mexico. Cisneros subsequently became the first Mexican American woman to receive a contract for a book about Mexican Americans from a major publishing company, Random House. The company published the collection in 1991 and reissued *The House on Mango Street*, which became a bestseller. Speaking about her success with her characteristic humor in Chicago in 1992, Cisneros quipped: "I've been publishing for fifteen years. One press account said I was an overnight success. I thought that was the longest night I've ever spent."

Since 1992, Cisneros has been living and writing full-time in San Antonio, Texas. In 1994, she published her second collection of poetry, *Loose Woman*, as well as a book for children, *Hairs/Pelitos*. The next year, she was awarded a prestigious MacArthur Prize Fellowship, the so-called genius grant, which provides funding for five years of creative work. She subsequently wrote *Caramelo* (2003), a multigenerational family saga that moves from Mexico City in the 1920s to Chicago in the 1950s. In 2012, she published *Have You Seen Marie?* Describing the book as "a fable for grownups," Cisneros traced the loss, grief, and healing she experienced as she helped search for a missing cat in the aftermath of the death of her mother, Elvira.

Sandra Cisneros is one of the most brilliant of today's young writers. Her work is sensitive, alert, nuanceful . . . rich with music and picture.
–Gwendolyn Brooks

Reading Cisneros's "Mericans." In 1991, this story appeared in both a special fiction issue of *Ms.* magazine and Cisneros's *Woman Hollering Creek.* Most of the stories in the collection concern the lives of Mexican American girls and women living, both literally and figuratively, in the borderland between Mexico and the United States. Cisneros uses the setting to explore complex issues of Chicana identity, issues that she handles with a good deal of humor in "Mericans," a vignette about Mexican American children enduring a family visit to Mexico. In the story, which opens with a reference by the young female narrator to her "awful grandmother," Cisneros also poked fun at what she has described as one of the "sacred cows" of Chicana literature. "In Chicana writing the love between a grandmother and a granddaughter is holier than the relationship between a mother and a daughter because the mother and daughter have to deal with the reality of the everyday, whereas the grandmother [is] revered from afar," Cisneros observed in an interview in 2002. [Espe]cially if she's dead, she becomes this mythic symbol in Chican[a litera]ture. But I hate when I see any kind of cliché occurring in wri[ting], that's why she's a wonderful cliché for me to throw rocks at." Th[e text is] taken from *Woman Hollering Creek and Other Stories* (1991).

bedfordstmartins.com/ americanlit *for research [C]isneros*

[Handwritten note: Sandra Cisneros "Mericans" (2288–2292)]

MERICANS

We're waiting for the awful grandmother who is inside dropping pesos into a offer[ing] box before the altar to La Divina Providencia.[1] Lighting votive candles and genuflecting. Blessing herself and kissing her thumb. Running a crystal rosary between her fingers. Mumbling, mumbling, mumbling.

---

1. **La Divina Providencia:** The Divine Providence (Spanish). Their grandmother is putting money in the offering box and praying at the altar of the Basilica of Our Lady of Guadalupe, also known as the Virgin of Guadalupe, a major Catholic shrine and tourist attraction on the outskirts of Mexico City. According to tradition, the Virgin Mary, the mother of Jesus Christ, appeared in 1531 to Juan Diego, a Chicimeca convert to Christianity, and told him that she wanted a church built at Tepeyac, Mexico. He told the Spanish bishop, who demanded proof of the authenticity of the vision. The Virgin Mary subsequently reappeared to Juan Diego, and an icon or likeness of her image was miraculously imprinted on his apron. The miracle of Guadalupe was officially recognized by the Vatican in 1745, and the image of the Virgin of Guadalupe remains a powerful religious and cultural symbol in Mexico, where her devotees believe that she can cure illness and assuage other afflictions.

There are so many prayers and promises and thanks-be-to-God to be given in the name of the husband and the sons and the only daughter who never attend mass. It doesn't matter. Like La Virgen de Guadalupe, the awful grandmother intercedes on their behalf. For the grandfather who hasn't believed in anything since the first PRI elections.[2] For my father, El Periquín,[3] so skinny he needs his sleep. For Auntie Light-skin, who only a few hours before was breakfasting on brain and goat tacos after dancing all night in the pink zone.[4] For Uncle Fat-face, the blackest of the black sheep — *Always remember your Uncle Fat-face in your prayers.* And Uncle Baby — *You go for me, Mamá — God listens to you.*

The awful grandmother has been gone a long time. She disappeared behind the heavy leather outer curtain and the dusty velvet inner.[5] We must stay near the church entrance. We must not wander over to the balloon and punch-ball vendors. We cannot spend our allowance on fried cookies or Familia Burrón comic books[6] or those clear cone-shaped suckers that make everything look like a rainbow when you look through them. We cannot run off and have our picture taken on the wooden ponies. We must not climb the steps up the hill behind the church and chase each other through the cemetery. We have promised to stay right where the awful grandmother left us until she returns.

There are those walking to church on their knees. Some with fat rags tied around their legs and others with pillows, one to kneel on, and one to flop ahead. There are women with black shawls crossing and uncrossing themselves. There are armies of penitents carrying banners and flowered arches while musicians play tinny trumpets and tinny drums.

La Virgen de Guadalupe is waiting inside behind a plate of thick glass. There's also a gold crucifix bent crooked as a mesquite tree when someone once threw a bomb. La Virgen de Guadalupe on the main altar because she's a big miracle, the crooked crucifix on a side altar because that's a little miracle.[7]

But we're outside in the sun. My big brother Junior hunkered against the wall with his eyes shut. My little brother Keeks running around in circles.

Maybe and most probably my little brother is imagining he's a flying feather dancer, like the ones we saw swinging high up from a pole on the Virgin's birthday. I want to be a flying feather dancer too, but when he circles past me he shouts, "I'm a B-Fifty-two

---

2. **PRI elections:** *El Partido Revolucionario Institucional* (Institutional Revolutionary Party), or PRI, is a powerful political party in Mexico. Formed to serve the interests of labor unions, peasant organizations, and the poor, the party won its first elections in 1929 as the *Partido National Revolucionario* (National Revolutionary Party).
3. **El Periquín:** Derived from *perico*, a parrot (Spanish).
4. **pink zone:** The Zona Rosa (Pink Zone), a social and tourist center in Mexico City.
5. **She disappeared . . . inner:** A description of the church's confessional, an enclosed booth in which the priest sits to hear people confess their sins.
6. **Familia Burrón comic books:** A popular, long-lived series that depicts the daily struggles of a barber, his family, and their neighbors in a working-class neighborhood of Mexico City.
7. **La Virgen de Guadalupe . . . little miracle:** See note 1. In the new basilica, dedicated in 1976, the miraculous apron on which the image of the Virgin of Guadalupe appears hangs behind bullet-proof glass above the main altar. In 1921, a factory worker placed a bomb a few feet away from the apron in the old basilica. Although the explosion blast destroyed the marble steps of the main altar and bent a brass crucifix, which is now displayed in the side altar of the new basilica, the apron suffered no damage.

bomber, you're a German," and shoots me with an invisible machine gun. I'd rather play flying feather dancers, but if I tell my brother this, he might not play with me at all.

"*Girl*. We can't play with a *girl*." *Girl*. It's my brothers' favorite insult now instead of "sissy." "You *girl*," they yell at each other. "You throw that ball like a *girl*."

I've already made up my mind to be a German when Keeks swoops past again, this time yelling, "I'm Flash Gordon. You're Ming the Merciless and the Mud People."[8] I don't mind being Ming the Merciless, but I don't like being the Mud People. Something wants to come out of the corners of my eyes, but I don't let it. Crying is what *girls* do.

I leave Keeks running around in circles – "I'm the Lone Ranger, you're Tonto."[9] I leave Junior squatting on his ankles and go look for the awful grandmother.

Why do churches smell like the inside of an ear? Like incense and the dark and candles in blue glass? And why does holy water smell of tears? The awful grandmother makes me kneel and fold my hands. The ceiling high and everyone's prayers bumping up there like balloons.

If I stare at the eyes of the saints long enough, they move and wink at me, which makes me a sort of saint too. When I get tired of winking saints, I count the awful grandmother's mustache hairs while she prays for Uncle Old, sick from the worm,[10] and Auntie Cuca, suffering from a life of troubles that left half her face crooked and the other half sad.

There must be a long, long list of relatives who haven't gone to church. The awful grandmother knits the names of the dead and the living into one long prayer fringed with the grandchildren born in that barbaric country with its barbarian ways.

I put my weight on one knee, then the other, and when they both grow fat as a mattress of pins, I slap them each awake. *Micaela, you may wait outside with Alfredito and Enrique.* The awful grandmother says it all in Spanish, which I understand when I'm paying attention. "What?" I say, though it's neither proper nor polite. "What?" which the awful grandmother hears as "*¿Güat?*"[11] But she only gives me a look and shoves me toward the door.

After all that dust and dark, the light from the plaza makes me squinch my eyes like if I just came out of the movies. My brother Keeks is drawing squiggly lines on the concrete with a wedge of glass and the heel of his shoe. My brother Junior squatting against the entrance, talking to a lady and man.

They're not from here. Ladies don't come to church dressed in pants. And everybody knows men aren't supposed to wear shorts.

"*¿Quieres chicle?*"[12] the lady asks in a Spanish too big for her mouth.

"*Gracias.*"[13] The lady gives him a whole handful of gum for free, little cellophane cubes of Chiclets, cinnamon and aqua and the white ones that don't taste like anything but are good for pretend buck teeth.

---

8. **Flash Gordon . . . Mud People:** Science-fiction characters in the comic strip, film serials, and 1950s television series *Flash Gordon*.

9. **Lone Ranger . . . Tonto:** *The Lone Ranger* was a 1950s television series about the adventures of a crusading Texas Ranger and his "trusty scout," the Native American Tonto.

10. **the worm:** An intestinal parasite.

11. *¿**Güat**?*: This is a phonetic spelling of "What?" but not a word in Spanish, in which the word for *what* is *qué*.

12. *¿**Quieres chicle**?*: Would you like some chewing gum? (Spanish).

13. ***Gracias**:* Thank you (Spanish).

terms, in aesthetic terms, in practical terms." That theme is reflected in the poem selected here, "Alabanza: In Praise of Local 100," which is widely regarded as the most powerful poem inspired by the attack on the World Trade Center on September 11, 2001. In an interview on PBS on the second anniversary of the attacks, the journalist Ray Suarez asked him, "Why do we need poetry at a time like this?" Espada responded:

bedfordstmartins.com/ americanlit *for research links on Espada*

Poetry humanizes. Poetry gives a human face to a time like this. Poetry gives eyes and a mouth and a voice to a time like this. Poetry records a time like this for future generations who want to know about a time like this in terms of the five senses, and in terms of the soul, I think.

The text is taken from his collection *Alabanza: New and Selected Poems, 1982-2002* (2003).

ALABANZA: IN PRAISE OF LOCAL 100

*for the 43 members of Hotel Employees and Restaurant Employees
Local 100, working at the Windows on the World restaurant,
who lost their lives in the attack on the World Trade Center*

Alabanza.[1] Praise the cook with a shaven head
and a tattoo on his shoulder that said *Oye,*[2]
a blue-eyed Puerto Rican with people from Fajardo,[3]
the harbor of pirates centuries ago.
Praise the lighthouse in Fajardo, candle   5
glimmering white to worship the dark saint of the sea.
Alabanza. Praise the cook's yellow Pirates cap
worn in the name of Roberto Clemente,[4] his plane
that flamed into the ocean loaded with cans for Nicaragua,
for all the mouths chewing the ash of earthquakes.   10
Alabanza. Praise the kitchen radio, dial clicked
even before the dial on the oven, so that music and Spanish
rose before bread. Praise the bread. *Alabanza.*

Praise Manhattan from a hundred and seven flights up,
like Atlantis glimpsed through the windows of an ancient aquarium.   15
Praise the great windows where immigrants from the kitchen

---

1. *Alabanza:* Praise; sometimes used in a religious sense. From "alabar," to celebrate with words. [Espada's note]

2. *Oye:* Literally, "listen"; the equivalent of "hey." [Espada's note]

3. **Fajardo:** Port city on the northeast coast of Puerto Rico. [Espada's note]

4. **Roberto Clemente:** Hall of Fame baseball player from Puerto Rico who died in a plane crash delivering relief supplies to earthquake victims in Nicaragua. [Espada's note]

could squint and almost see their world, hear the chant of nations:
Ecuador, México, Republica Dominicana,
Haiti, Yemen, Ghana, Bangladesh.
Alabanza. Praise the kitchen in the morning,   20
where the gas burned blue on every stove
and exhaust fans fired their diminutive propellers,
hands cracked eggs with quick thumbs
or sliced open cartons to build an altar of cans.
Alabanza. Praise the busboy's music, the *chime-chime*   25
of his dishes and silverware in the tub.
Alabanza. Praise the dish-dog, the dishwasher
who worked that morning because another dishwasher
could not stop coughing, or because he needed overtime
to pile the sacks of rice and beans for a family   30
floating away on some Caribbean island plagued by frogs.[5]
Alabanza. Praise the waitress who heard the radio in the kitchen
and sang to herself about a man gone. *Alabanza.*

After the thunder wilder than thunder,
after the shudder deep in the glass of the great windows,   35
after the radio stopped singing like a tree full of terrified frogs,
after night burst the dam of day and flooded the kitchen,
for a time the stoves glowed in darkness like the lighthouse in Fajardo,
like a cook's soul. Soul I say, even if the dead cannot tell us
about the bristles of God's beard because God has no face,   40
soul I say, to name the smoke-beings flung in constellations
across the night sky of this city and cities to come.
Alabanza I say, even if God has no face.

Alabanza. When the war began, from Manhattan and Kabul
two constellations of smoke rose and drifted to each other,[6]   45
mingling in icy air, and one said with an Afghan tongue:
Teach me to dance. We have no music here.
And the other said with a Spanish tongue:
I will teach you. Music is all we have.

[2003]

---

5. **plagued by frogs:** In Puerto Rico, the native coqui frog lives in densities of up to 8,000 an acre and increased to even larger numbers after Hurricane Hugo in 1989. The frog, known for its loud call, is a voracious predator of insects, consequently disrupting the food supply for birds and other wildlife.
6. **When the war began . . . drifted to each other:** On October 7, 2001, less than a month after the September 11 attacks on the World Trade Center in Manhattan, the U.S.-led invasion of Afghanistan began with airstrikes on its major cities, including its capital, Kabul.

Sherman Alexie

[b. 1966]

Sherman Alexie Jr. was born on October 7, 1966, in Wellpinit, a town on the Spokane Indian Reservation in eastern Washington. His father, a Coeur d'Alene Indian, was a logger and a truck driver; his mother, of Spokane Indian descent, worked as a clerk and seamstress to help support the

family. Alexie was born with hydrocephalus, fluid in the brain, and at the age of six months underwent major surgery to correct the condition. He was not expected to survive the surgery without serious mental and physical handicaps, but he suffered only an enlarged skull and some minor side effects. The size of his head caused the children in his tribal school at Wellpinit to call him "The Globe," and Alexie responded by withdrawing into the books he found at the library and by developing a quick wit. "Humor is self-defense on the rez," he said in an interview in 1999. "You make people

Sherman Alexie

Rex Rystedt took this photograph of Alexie in 1995, the year the acclaimed young poet and fiction writer published his first novel, *Reservation Blues*.

laugh and you disarm them. You sort of sneak up on them. You can say controversial or rowdy things and they'll listen or laugh." Because he wanted to have a mainstream education, Alexie transferred to a high school in Reardon, Washington, after he completed the eighth grade. Although he once again felt isolated, this time because he was the only Native American at the school, he excelled at basketball, served as class president, and was a member of the debating team. After his graduation in 1985, he went to Gonzaga University in Spokane, Washington. He began drinking heavily and dropped out after two years. He moved to Seattle, where he worked as a busboy until he decided to give college another try at Washington State University.

Alexie, who enrolled as a premed major, soon discovered his protean artistic talents. In a poetry-writing workshop, he was deeply inspired by reading a volume of Native American poetry, *Songs from This Earth on Turtle's Back* (1983). "I saw my life in poems and stories for the very first time," he recalled years later. With the encouragement of his professor, Alexie began writing poems and graduated with a degree in American studies in 1991. Alexie began publishing his poems in various literary journals, and the small Hanging Loose Press published his first collection of poetry, *The Business of Fancydancing* (1992). His career was launched when the volume was enthusiastically reviewed in the *New York Times*, and he swiftly published three more collections of poetry: *I Would Steal*

Horses (1992), *First Indian on the Moon* (1993), and *Old Shirts and New Skins* (1993). He also published *The Lone Ranger and Tonto Fistfight in Heaven* (1993), a collection of related stories about contemporary life on the Spokane Indian reservation that was a finalist for a PEN/Hemingway Award. Alexie then wrote two acclaimed novels: *Reservation Blues* (1995), the exuberant saga of an all-Indian blues band named Coyote Spring; and *Indian Killer* (1996), a grim account of the racial strife generated by a serial killer terrorizing Seattle. Alexie also began to branch out into other art forms. He and the Colville Indian songwriter Jim Boyd made a soundtrack to accompany *Reservation Blues*, and Alexie wrote the screenplay and was deeply involved in the production of a feature film based on his stories, *Smoke Signals*. The movie, the first made by an all-Indian crew and creative team, won a series of awards at the Sundance Film Festival in 1998.

Since then, Alexie has become one of the most prominent writers in the United States. In June 1999, he was featured in a special Summer Fiction Edition, "20 Writers for the 21st Century," of the *New Yorker*. "Forgive the immodesty, but I think it's much more important for an Indian like me to be in the *New Yorker* magazine than it is for me or an Indian to be in a museum," he replied to an interviewer who asked him about Native American culture being relegated to museums.

> I think it's more important to change the possibilities of what an Indian is and can be right now. I love museums, but for me the greatest part of all this is I'm a completely active member of the culture. We're not separate, we're not removed, we're an integral and living part of the culture.

Certainly, his work has given prominence to the contemporary lives and culture of Native Americans. Alexie wrote the screenplay and made his directorial debut in a movie about a gay Indian poet in search of his identity, *The Business of Fancydancing* (2002), which premiered at the Sundance Film Festival in 2002. He also published three more books of poetry and two more award-winning collections of stories, *The Toughest Indian in the World* (2000) and *Ten Little Indians* (2003). In 2007, Alexie published *In Flight*, a novel about a half-Irish, half–Native American boy who travels back and forth through time to witness and participate in some of the most brutal events of American history, as well as his first novel for young adults, *The Absolutely True Story of a Part-Time Indian*. His recent publications include *Face: Poems* (2009); *War Dances* (2009), a collection of stories that won the prestigious PEN/Faulkner Award for Fiction; and *Blasphemy: New and Selected Stories* (2012). When he is not on tour giving readings and performances, Alexie lives with his wife and two sons in Seattle.

Alexie's talent is immense and genuine. . . . On this big Indian reservation we call "the United States," Sherman Alexie is one of the best writers we have.
–Leslie Marmon Silko

Reading Alexie's "What You Pawn I Will Redeem."

First published in the *New Yorker* in April 2003, this story appeared later that year in Alexie's third collection of short stories, *Ten Little Indians*. (In a typically ironic gesture, he included only nine stories in the collection, the title of which evokes the familiar nursery song "Ten Little Indians.") "What You

bedfordstmartins.com/ americanlit for research links on Alexie

Pawn I Will Redeem," which displays Alexie's abiding interest in the everyday experiences of Native Americans, his keen ear for dialogue, and his sardonic humor, was singled out for inclusion in two prestigious collections, *Best American Short Stories* (2004) and the *O. Henry Prize Stories 2005*. One of the jurors for the O. Henry Prize, the novelist Ann Patchett, admiringly observed of the story:

> Like me, Sherman Alexie is in love with his homeless Spokane Indian narrator and so he simply steps aside to let his character have every inch of the stage. . . . Alexie follows this man through his world not as a character but as a human being. Every turn in his day is unexpected and true. As I read I was moved by sorrow, compassion, and joy. . . . We are lucky when we get that much from life — we should be nothing short of rapturous when we get it from short fiction.

The text is taken from *Ten Little Indians* (2003).

WHAT YOU PAWN I WILL REDEEM

Noon

One day you have a home and the next you don't, but I'm not going to tell you my particular reasons for being homeless, because it's my secret story, and Indians have to work hard to keep secrets from hungry white folks.

I'm a Spokane Indian boy, an Interior Salish,[1] and my people have lived within a one-hundred-mile radius of Spokane, Washington, for at least ten thousand years. I grew up in Spokane, moved to Seattle twenty-three years ago for college, flunked out within two semesters, worked various blue- and bluer-collar jobs for many years, married two or three times, fathered two or three kids, and then went crazy. Of course, "crazy" is not the official definition of my mental problem, but I don't think "asocial disorder" fits it, either, because that makes me sound like I'm a serial killer or something. I've never hurt another human being, or at least not physically. I've broken a few hearts in my time, but we've all done that, so I'm nothing special in that regard. I'm a boring heartbreaker, at that, because I've never abandoned one woman for another. I never dated or married more than one woman at a time. I didn't break hearts into pieces overnight. I broke them slowly and carefully. I didn't set any land-speed records running out the door. Piece by piece, I disappeared. And I've been disappearing ever since. But I'm not going to tell you any more about my brain or my soul.

I've been homeless for six years. If there's such a thing as being an effective homeless man, I suppose I'm effective. Being homeless is probably the only thing I've ever been good at. I know where to get the best free food. I've made friends with restaurant

---

1. **Interior Salish:** The collective name for the five tribes, including the Spokane, of an Indian nation that occupied lands in the interior of British Columbia stretching south into the present-day United States.

and convenience store managers who let me use their bathrooms. I don't mean the public bathrooms, either. I mean the employees' bathrooms, the clean ones hidden in the back of the kitchen or the pantry or the cooler. I know it sounds strange to be proud of, but it means a lot to me, being truthworthy enough to piss in somebody else's clean bathroom. Maybe you don't understand the value of a clean bathroom, but I do.

Probably none of this interests you. I probably don't interest you much. Homeless Indians are everywhere in Seattle. We're common and boring, and you walk right on by us, with maybe a look of anger or disgust or even sadness at the terrible fate of the noble savage. But we have dreams and families. I'm friends with a homeless Plains Indian[2] man whose son is the editor of a big-time newspaper back east. That's his story, but we Indians are great storytellers and liars and mythmakers, so maybe that Plains Indian hobo is a plain old everyday Indian. I'm kind of suspicious of him, because he describes himself only as Plains Indian, a generic term, and not by a specific tribe. When I asked him why he wouldn't tell me exactly what he is, he said, "Do any of us know exactly what we are?" Yeah, great, a philosophizing Indian. "Hey," I said, "you got to have a home to be that homely." He laughed and flipped me the eagle and walked away. But you probably want to know more about the story I'm really trying to tell you.

I wander the streets with a regular crew, my teammates, my defenders, and my posse. It's Rose of Sharon, Junior, and me. We matter to one another if we don't matter to anybody else. Rose of Sharon is a big woman, about seven feet tall if you're measuring overall effect, and about five feet tall if you're talking about the physical. She's a Yakama Indian of the Wishram variety.[3] Junior is a Colville,[4] but there are about 199 tribes that make up the Colville, so he could be anything. He's good-looking, though, like he just stepped out of some "Don't Litter the Earth" public-service advertisement. He's got those great big cheekbones that are like planets, you know, with little moons orbiting around them. He gets me jealous, jealous, and jealous. If you put Junior and me next to each other, he's the Before Columbus Arrived Indian, and I'm the After Columbus Arrived Indian. I am living proof of the horrible damage that colonialism has done to us Skins. But I'm not going to let you know how scared I sometimes get of history and its ways. I'm a strong man, and I know that silence is the best way of dealing with white folks.

This whole story started at lunchtime, when Rose of Sharon, Junior, and I were panning the handle down at Pike Place Market.[5] After about two hours of negotiating, we earned five dollars, good enough for a bottle of fortified courage from the most beautiful 7-Eleven in the world. So we headed over that way, feeling like warrior drunks, and we walked past this pawnshop I'd never noticed before. And that was strange, because

---

2. **Plains Indian:** The generic term for a member of any of a large number of North American tribes that occupied the area stretching from the Rio Grande River Valley north through the Great Plains into central Canada.
3. **Yakama Indian of the Wishram variety:** The Wishram is one of the tribes of the Yakama confederation, which occupied lands in present-day Oregon and Washington.
4. **Colville:** The Colville confederation includes twelve tribes that occupied lands in present-day central and eastern Washington and Canada.
5. **panning the handle down at Pike Place Market:** That is, panhandling, or begging for money from strangers, at the famous fish market overlooking the Elliott Bay waterfront in Seattle.

we Indians have built-in pawnshop radar. But the strangest thing was the old powwow-dance regalia[6] I saw hanging in the window.

"That's my grandmother's regalia," I said to Rose of Sharon and Junior.

"How do you know for sure?" Junior asked.

I didn't know for sure, because I hadn't seen that regalia in person ever. I'd seen only photographs of my grandmother dancing in it. And that was before somebody stole it from her fifty years ago. But it sure looked like my memory of it, and it had all the same colors of feathers and beads that my family always sewed into their powwow regalia.

"There's only one way to know for sure," I said.

So Rose of Sharon, Junior, and I walked into the pawnshop and greeted the old white man working behind the counter.

"How can I help you?" he asked.

"That's my grandmother's powwow regalia in your window," I said. "Somebody stole it from her fifty years ago, and my family has been looking for it ever since."

The pawnbroker looked at me like I was a liar. I understood. Pawnshops are filled with liars.

"I'm not lying," I said. "Ask my friends here. They'll tell you."

"He's the most honest Indian I know," Rose of Sharon said.

"All right, honest Indian," the pawnbroker said. "I'll give you the benefit of the doubt. Can you prove it's your grandmother's regalia?"

Because they don't want to be perfect, because only God is perfect, Indian people sew flaws into their powwow regalia. My family always sewed one yellow bead somewhere on their regalia. But we always hid it where you had to search hard to find it.

"If it really is my grandmother's," I said, "there will be one yellow bead hidden somewhere on it."

"All right, then," the pawnbroker said. "Let's take a look."

He pulled the regalia out of the window, laid it down on his glass counter, and we searched for that yellow bead and found it hidden beneath the armpit.

"There it is," the pawnbroker said. He didn't sound surprised. "You were right. This is your grandmother's regalia."

"It's been missing for fifty years," Junior said.

"Hey, Junior," I said. "It's my family's story. Let me tell it."

"All right," he said. "I apologize. You go ahead."

"It's been missing for fifty years," I said.

"That's his family's sad story," Rose of Sharon said. "Are you going to give it back to him?"

"That would be the right thing to do," the pawnbroker said. "But I can't afford to do the right thing. I paid a thousand dollars for this. I can't give away a thousand dollars."

"We could go to the cops and tell them it was stolen," Rose of Sharon said.

---

6. **powwow-dance regalia:** The decorative clothing worn by dancers participating in a powwow, a traditional Native American ceremony. The regalia serves as a form of tribal identity and is often personalized to reflect the circumstances of an individual's life.

"Hey," I said to her, "don't go threatening people."

The pawnbroker sighed. He was thinking hard about the possibilities.

"Well, I suppose you could go to the cops," he said. "But I don't think they'd believe a word you said."

He sounded sad about that. Like he was sorry for taking advantage of our disadvantages.

"What's your name?" the pawnbroker asked me.

"Jackson," I said.

"Is that first or last?" he asked.

"Both."

"Are you serious?"

"Yes, it's true. My mother and father named me Jackson Jackson. My family nickname is Jackson Squared. My family is funny."

"All right, Jackson Jackson," the pawnbroker said. "You wouldn't happen to have a thousand dollars, would you?"

"We've got five dollars total," I said.

"That's too bad," he said and thought hard about the possibilities. "I'd sell it to you for a thousand dollars if you had it. Heck, to make it fair, I'd sell it to you for nine hundred and ninety-nine dollars. I'd lose a dollar. It would be the moral thing to do in this case. To lose a dollar would be the right thing."

"We've got five dollars total," I said again.

"That's too bad," he said again and thought harder about the possibilities. "How about this? I'll give you twenty-four hours to come up with nine hundred and ninety-nine dollars. You come back here at lunchtime tomorrow with the money, and I'll sell it back to you. How does that sound?"

"It sounds good," I said.

"All right, then," he said. "We have a deal. And I'll get you started. Here's twenty bucks to get you started."

He opened up his wallet and pulled out a crisp twenty-dollar bill and gave it to me. Rose of Sharon, Junior, and I walked out into the daylight to search for nine hundred and seventy-four more dollars.

1:00 P.M.

Rose of Sharon, Junior, and I carried our twenty-dollar bill and our five dollars in loose change over to the 7-Eleven and spent it to buy three bottles of imagination. We needed to figure out how to raise all that money in one day. Thinking hard, we huddled in an alley beneath the Alaska Way Viaduct and finished off those bottles one, two, and three.

2:00 P.M.

Rose of Sharon was gone when I woke. I heard later she had hitchhiked back to Toppenish and was living with her sister on the reservation.

Junior was passed out beside me, covered in his own vomit, or maybe somebody else's vomit, and my head hurt from thinking, so I left him alone and walked down to the water. I loved the smell of ocean water. Salt always smells like memory.

When I got to the wharf, I ran into three Aleut cousins[7] who sat on a wooden bench and stared out at the bay and cried. Most of the homeless Indians in Seattle come from Alaska. One by one, each of them hopped a big working boat in Anchorage or Barrow or Juneau, fished his way south to Seattle, jumped off the boat with a pocketful of cash to party hard at one of the highly sacred and traditional Indian bars, went broke and broker, and has been trying to find his way back to the boat and the frozen north ever since.

These Aleuts smelled like salmon, I thought, and they told me they were going to sit on that wooden bench until their boat came back.

"How long has your boat been gone?" I asked.

"Eleven years," the elder Aleut said.

I cried with them for a while.

"Hey," I said. "Do you guys have any money I can borrow?"

They didn't.

3:00 P.M.

I walked back to Junior. He was still passed out. I put my face down near his mouth to make sure he was breathing. He was alive, so I dug around in his blue-jean pockets and found half a cigarette. I smoked it all the way down and thought about my grandmother.

Her name was Agnes, and she died of breast cancer when I was fourteen. My father thought Agnes caught her tumors from the uranium mine on the reservation. But my mother said the disease started when Agnes was walking back from the powwow one night and got run over by a motorcycle. She broke three ribs, and my mother said those ribs never healed right, and tumors always take over when you don't heal right.

Sitting beside Junior, smelling the smoke and salt and vomit, I wondered if my grandmother's cancer had started when somebody stole her powwow regalia. Maybe the cancer started in her broken heart and then leaked out into her breasts. I know it's crazy, but I wondered if I could bring my grandmother back to life if I bought back her regalia.

I needed money, big money, so I left Junior and walked over to the Real Change office.

4:00 P.M.

"Real Change is a multifaceted organization that publishes a newspaper, supports cultural projects that empower the poor and homeless, and mobilizes the public around poverty issues. Real Change's mission is to organize, educate, and build alliances to create solutions to homelessness and poverty. They exist to provide a voice to poor people in our community."

---

7. **Aleut cousins:** The Aleuts are natives of the Aleutian Islands and other parts of western Alaska.

I memorized Real Change's mission statement because I sometimes sell the newspaper on the streets. But you have to stay sober to sell it, and I'm not always good at staying sober. Anybody can sell the newspaper. You buy each copy for thirty cents and sell it for a dollar and keep the net profit.

"I need one thousand four hundred and thirty papers," I said to the Big Boss.

"That's a strange number," he said. "And that's a lot of papers."

"I need them."

The Big Boss pulled out the calculator and did the math. "It will cost you four hundred and twenty-nine dollars for that many," he said.

"If I had that kind of money, I wouldn't need to sell the papers."

"What's going on, Jackson-to-the-Second-Power?" he asked. He is the only one who calls me that. He is a funny and kind man.

I told him about my grandmother's powwow regalia and how much money I needed to buy it back.

"We should call the police," he said.

"I don't want to do that," I said. "It's a quest now. I need to win it back by myself."

"I understand," he said. "And to be honest, I'd give you the papers to sell if I thought it would work. But the record for most papers sold in a day by one vendor is only three hundred and two."

"That would net me about two hundred bucks," I said.

The Big Boss used his calculator. "Two hundred and eleven dollars and forty cents," he said.

"That's not enough," I said.

"The most money anybody has made in one day is five hundred and twenty-five. And that's because somebody gave Old Blue five hundred-dollar bills for some dang reason. The average daily net is about thirty dollars."

"This isn't going to work."

"No."

"Can you lend me some money?"

"I can't do that," he said. "If I lend you money, I have to lend money to everybody."

"What can you do?"

"I'll give you fifty papers for free. But don't tell anybody I did it."

"Okay," I said.

He gathered up the newspapers and handed them to me. I held them to my chest. He hugged me. I carried the newspapers back toward the water.

5:00 P.M.

Back on the wharf, I stood near the Bainbridge Island Terminal and tried to sell papers to business commuters walking onto the ferry.[8]

---

8. **Back on the wharf . . . ferry:** Many people commute to Seattle from Bainbridge Island, a short trip by ferry across Elliott Bay.

I sold five in one hour, dumped the other forty-five into a garbage can, and walked into the McDonald's, ordered four cheeseburgers for a dollar each, and slowly ate them.

After eating, I walked outside and vomited on the sidewalk. I hated to lose my food so soon after eating it. As an alcoholic Indian with a busted stomach, I always hope I can keep enough food in my stomach to stay alive.

6:00 P.M.

With one dollar in my pocket, I walked back to Junior. He was still passed out, so I put my ear to his chest and listened for his heartbeat. He was alive, so I took off his shoes and socks and found one dollar in his left sock and fifty cents in his right sock. With two dollars and fifty cents in my hand, I sat beside Junior and thought about my grandmother and her stories.

When I was sixteen, my grandmother told me a story about World War II. She was a nurse at a military hospital in Sydney, Australia. Over the course of two years, she comforted and healed U.S. and Australian soldiers.

One day, she tended to a wounded Maori[9] soldier. He was very dark-skinned. His hair was black and curly, and his eyes were black and warm. His face was covered with bright tattoos.

"Are you Maori?" he asked my grandmother.

"No," she said. "I'm Spokane Indian. From the United States."

"Ah, yes," he said. "I have heard of your tribes. But you are the first American Indian I have ever met."

"There's a lot of Indian soldiers fighting for the United States," she said. "I have a brother still fighting in Germany, and I lost another brother on Okinawa."

"I am sorry," he said. "I was on Okinawa as well. It was terrible." He had lost his legs to an artillery attack.

"I am sorry about your legs," my grandmother said.

"It's funny, isn't it?" he asked.

"What's funny?"

"How we brown people are killing other brown people so white people will remain free."

"I hadn't thought of it that way."

"Well, sometimes I think of it that way. And other times, I think of it the way they want me to think of it. I get confused."

She fed him morphine.

"Do you believe in heaven?" he asked.

"Which heaven?" she asked.

"I'm talking about the heaven where my legs are waiting for me."

They laughed.

---

9. **Maori:** The aboriginal people of New Zealand.

"Of course," he said, "my legs will probably run away from me when I get to heaven. And how will I ever catch them?"

"You have to get your arms strong," my grandmother said. "So you can run on your hands."

They laughed again.

Sitting beside Junior, I laughed with the memory of my grandmother's story. I put my hand close to Junior's mouth to make sure he was still breathing. Yes, Junior was alive, so I took his two dollars and fifty cents and walked to the Korean grocery store over in Pioneer Square.

7:00 P.M.

In the Korean grocery store, I bought a fifty-cent cigar and two scratch lottery tickets for a dollar each. The maximum cash prize was five hundred dollars a ticket. If I won both, I would have enough money to buy back the regalia.

I loved Kay, the young Korean woman who worked the register. She was the daughter of the owners and sang all day.

"I love you," I said when I handed her the money.

"You always say you love me," she said.

"That's because I will always love you."

"You are a sentimental fool."

"I'm a romantic old man."

"Too old for me."

"I know I'm too old for you, but I can dream."

"Okay," she said. "I agree to be a part of your dreams, but I will only hold your hand in your dreams. No kissing and no sex. Not even in your dreams."

"Okay," I said. "No sex. Just romance."

"Good-bye, Jackson Jackson, my love, I will see you soon."

I left the store, walked over to Occidental Park, sat on a bench, and smoked my cigar all the way down.

Ten minutes after I finished the cigar, I scratched my first lottery ticket and won nothing. So I could win only five hundred dollars now, and that would be just half of what I needed.

Ten minutes later, I scratched my other lottery ticket and won a free ticket, a small consolation and one more chance to win money.

I walked back to Kay.

"Jackson Jackson," she said. "Have you come back to claim my heart?"

"I won a free ticket," I said.

"Just like a man," she said. "You love money and power more than you love me."

"It's true," I said. "And I'm sorry it's true."

She gave me another scratch ticket, and I carried it outside. I liked to scratch my tickets in private. Hopeful and sad, I scratched that third ticket and won real money. I carried it back inside to Kay.

"I won a hundred dollars," I said.

She examined the ticket and laughed. "That's a fortune," she said and counted out five twenties. Our fingertips touched as she handed me the money. I felt electric and constant.

"Thank you," I said and gave her one of the bills.

"I can't take that," she said. "It's your money."

"No, it's tribal. It's an Indian thing. When you win, you're supposed to share with your family."

"I'm not your family."

"Yes, you are."

She smiled. She kept the money. With eighty dollars in my pocket, I said good-bye to my dear Kay and walked out into the cold night air.

8:00 P.M.

I wanted to share the good news with Junior. I walked back to him, but he was gone. I later heard he had hitchhiked down to Portland, Oregon, and died of exposure in an alley behind the Hilton Hotel.

9:00 P.M.

Lonely for Indians, I carried my eighty dollars over to Big Heart's in South Downtown. Big Heart's is an all-Indian bar. Nobody knows how or why Indians migrate to one bar and turn it into an official Indian bar. But Big Heart's has been an Indian bar for twenty-three years. It used to be way up on Aurora Avenue, but a crazy Lummi Indian[10] burned that one down, and the owners moved to the new location, a few blocks south of Safeco Field.

I walked inside Big Heart's and counted fifteen Indians, eight men and seven women. I didn't know any of them, but Indians like to belong, so we all pretended to be cousins.

"How much for whiskey shots?" I asked the bartender, a fat white guy.

"You want the bad stuff or the badder stuff?"

"As bad as you got."

"One dollar a shot."

I laid my eighty dollars on the bar top.

"All right," I said. "Me and all my cousins here are going to be drinking eighty shots. How many is that apiece?"

"Counting you," a woman shouted from behind me, "that's five shots for everybody."

I turned to look at her. She was a chubby and pale Indian sitting with a tall and skinny Indian man.

"All right, math genius," I said to her and then shouted for the whole bar to hear. "Five drinks for everybody!"

---

10. **Lummi Indian:** One of the more than twenty small tribes of the Salish, who occupied the area around Puget Sound in present-day Washington State.

All of the other Indians rushed the bar, but I sat with the mathematician and her skinny friend. We took our time with our whiskey shots.

"What's your tribe?" I asked them.

"I'm Duwamish,"[11] she said. "And he's Crow."[12]

"You're a long way from Montana," I said to him.

"I'm Crow," he said. "I flew here."

"What's your name?" I asked them.

"I'm Irene Muse," she said. "And this is Honey Boy."

She shook my hand hard, but he offered his hand like I was supposed to kiss it. So I kissed it. He giggled and blushed as well as a dark-skinned Crow can blush.

"You're one of them two-spirits, aren't you?" I asked him.

"I love women," he said. "And I love men."

"Sometimes both at the same time," Irene said.

We laughed.

"Man," I said to Honey Boy. "So you must have about eight or nine spirits going on inside of you, enit?"

"Sweetie," he said, "I'll be whatever you want me to be."

"Oh, no," Irene said. "Honey Boy is falling in love."

"It has nothing to do with love," he said.

We laughed.

"Wow," I said. "I'm flattered, Honey Boy, but I don't play on your team."

"Never say never," he said.

"You better be careful," Irene said. "Honey Boy knows all sorts of magic. He always makes straight boys fall for him."

"Honey Boy," I said, "you can try to seduce me. And Irene, you can try with him. But my heart belongs to a woman named Kay."

"Is your Kay a virgin?" Honey Boy asked.

We laughed.

We drank our whiskey shots until they were gone. But the other Indians bought me more whiskey shots because I'd been so generous with my money. Honey Boy pulled out his credit card, and I drank and sailed on that plastic boat.

After a dozen shots, I asked Irene to dance. And she refused. But Honey Boy shuffled over to the jukebox, dropped in a quarter, and selected Willie Nelson's "Help Me Make It Through the Night." As Irene and I sat at the table and laughed and drank more whiskey, Honey Boy danced a slow circle around us and sang along with Willie.

"Are you serenading me?" I asked him.

He kept singing and dancing.

"Are you serenading me?" I asked him again.

"He's going to put a spell on you," Irene said.

I leaned over the table, spilling a few drinks, and kissed Irene hard. She kissed me back.

---

11. **Duwamish:** A tribe that originally occupied the area of present-day Seattle, Washington.
12. **Crow:** The *Apsaalooke*, which English-language speakers translated as "crow" or "bird people," a tribe that occupied lands in present-day Wyoming and Montana.

10:00 P.M.

Irene pushed me into the women's bathroom, into a stall, shut the door behind us, and shoved her hand down my pants. She was short, so I had to lean over to kiss her. I grabbed and squeezed her everywhere I could reach, and she was wonderfully fat, and every part of her body felt like a large, warm, and soft breast.

Midnight

Nearly blind with alcohol, I stood alone at the bar and swore I'd been standing in the bathroom with Irene only a minute ago.

"One more shot!" I yelled at the bartender.

"You've got no more money!" he yelled.

"Somebody buy me a drink!" I shouted.

"They've got no more money!"

"Where's Irene and Honey Boy?"

"Long gone!"

2:00 A.M.

"Closing time!" the bartender shouted at the three or four Indians still drinking hard after a long hard day of drinking. Indian alcoholics are either sprinters or marathon runners.

"Where's Irene and Honey Bear?" I asked.

"They've been gone for hours," the bartender said.

"Where'd they go?"

"I told you a hundred times, I don't know."

"What am I supposed to do?"

"It's closing time. I don't care where you go, but you're not staying here."

"You are an ungrateful bastard. I've been good to you."

"You don't leave right now, I'm going to kick your ass."

"Come on, I know how to fight."

He came for me. I don't remember what happened after that.

4:00 A.M.

I emerged from the blackness and discovered myself walking behind a big warehouse. I didn't know where I was. My face hurt. I touched my nose and decided it might be broken. Exhausted and cold, I pulled a plastic tarp from a truck bed, wrapped it around me like a faithful lover, and fell asleep in the dirt.

6:00 A.M.

Somebody kicked me in the ribs. I opened my eyes and looked up at a white cop.

"Jackson," said the cop. "Is that you?"

"Officer Williams," I said. He was a good cop with a sweet tooth. He'd given me hundreds of candy bars over the years. I wonder if he knew I was diabetic.

"What the hell are you doing here?" he asked.

"I was cold and sleepy," I said. "So I laid down."

"You dumb-ass, you passed out on the railroad tracks."

I sat up and looked around. I was lying on the railroad tracks. Dockworkers stared at me. I should have been a railroad-track pizza, a double Indian pepperoni with extra cheese. Sick and scared, I leaned over and puked whiskey.

"What the hell's wrong with you?" Officer Williams asked. "You've never been this stupid."

"It's my grandmother," I said. "She died."

"I'm sorry, man. When did she die?"

"1972."

"And you're killing yourself now?"

"I've been killing myself ever since she died."

He shook his head. He was sad for me. Like I said, he was a good cop.

"And somebody beat the hell out of you," he said. "You remember who?"

"Mr. Grief and I went a few rounds."

"It looks like Mr. Grief knocked you out."

"Mr. Grief always wins."

"Come on," he said, "let's get you out of here."

He helped me stand and led me over to his squad car. He put me in the back. "You throw up in there," he said, "and you're cleaning it up."

"That's fair," I said.

He walked around the car and sat in the driver's seat. "I'm taking you over to detox," he said.

"No, man, that place is awful," I said. "It's full of drunk Indians."

We laughed. He drove away from the docks.

"I don't know how you guys do it," he said.

"What guys?" I asked.

"You Indians. How the hell do you laugh so much? I just picked your ass off the railroad tracks, and you're making jokes. Why the hell do you do that?"

"The two funniest tribes I've ever been around are Indians and Jews, so I guess that says something about the inherent humor of genocide."

We laughed.

"Listen to you, Jackson. You're so smart. Why the hell are you on the streets?"

"Give me a thousand dollars, and I'll tell you."

"You bet I'd give you a thousand dollars if I knew you'd straighten up your life."

He meant it. He was the second-best cop I'd ever known.

"You're a good cop," I said.

"Come on, Jackson," he said. "Don't blow smoke up my ass."

"No, really, you remind me of my grandfather."

"Yeah, that's what you Indians always tell me."

"No, man, my grandfather was a tribal cop. He was a good cop. He never arrested people. He took care of them. Just like you."

"I've arrested hundreds of scumbags, Jackson. And I've shot a couple in the ass."

"It don't matter. You're not a killer."

"I didn't kill them. I killed their asses. I'm an ass-killer."

We drove through downtown. The missions and shelters had already released their overnighters. Sleepy homeless men and women stood on corners and stared up at the gray sky. It was the morning after the night of the living dead.

"Did you ever get scared?" I asked Officer Williams.

"What do you mean?"

"I mean, being a cop, is it scary?"

He thought about that for a while. He contemplated it. I liked that about him.

"I guess I try not to think too much about being afraid," he said. "If you think about fear, then you'll be afraid. The job is boring most of the time. Just driving and looking into dark corners, you know, and seeing nothing. But then things get heavy. You're chasing somebody or fighting them or walking around a dark house and you just know some crazy guy is hiding around a corner, and hell yes, it's scary."

"My grandfather was killed in the line of duty," I said.

"I'm sorry. How'd it happen?"

I knew he'd listen closely to my story.

"He worked on the reservation. Everybody knew everybody. It was safe. We aren't like those crazy Sioux or Apache[13] or any of those other warrior tribes. There's only been three murders on my reservation in the last hundred years."

"That is safe."

"Yeah, we Spokane, we're passive, you know? We're mean with words. And we'll cuss out anybody. But we don't shoot people. Or stab them. Not much, anyway."

"So what happened to your grandfather?"

"This man and his girlfriend were fighting down by Little Falls."

"Domestic dispute. Those are the worst."

"Yeah, but this guy was my grandfather's brother. My great-uncle."

"Oh, no."

"Yeah, it was awful. My grandfather just strolled into the house. He'd been there a thousand times. And his brother and his girlfriend were all drunk and beating on each other. And my grandfather stepped between them just like he'd done a hundred times before. And the girlfriend tripped or something. She fell down and hit her head and started crying. And my grandfather knelt down beside her to make sure she was all right. And for some reason, my great-uncle reached down, pulled my grandfather's pistol out of the holster, and shot him in the head."

"That's terrible. I'm sorry."

---

13. **Sioux or Apache:** Sioux is the collective name for a confederation of three tribes, the Lakota, Dakota, and Nakota, who occupied a vast area in the northern Great Plains. The Apache included several bands and tribes that lived in the American Southwest and northern Mexico. Like the Sioux, the Apache were nomadic hunters who fiercely resisted the incursions of European settlers into their traditional lands and hunting grounds.

"Yeah, my great-uncle could never figure out why he did it. He went to prison forever, you know, and he always wrote these long letters. Like fifty pages of tiny little handwriting. And he was always trying to figure out why he did it. He'd write and write and write and try to figure it out. He never did. It's a great big mystery."

"Do you remember your grandfather?"

"A little bit. I remember the funeral. My grandmother wouldn't let them bury him. My father had to drag her away from the grave."

"I don't know what to say."

"I don't, either."

We stopped in front of the detox center.

"We're here," Officer Williams said.

"I can't go in there," I said.

"You have to."

"Please, no. They'll keep me for twenty-four hours. And then it will be too late."

"Too late for what?"

I told him about my grandmother's regalia and the deadline for buying it back.

"If it was stolen," he said, "then you need to file reports. I'll investigate it myself. If that thing is really your grandmother's, I'll get it back for you. Legally."

"No," I said. "That's not fair. The pawnbroker didn't know it was stolen. And besides, I'm on a mission here. I want to be a hero, you know? I want to win it back like a knight."

"That's romantic crap."

"It might be. But I care about it. It's been a long time since I really cared about something."

Officer Williams turned around in his seat and stared at me. He studied me.

"I'll give you some money," he said. "I don't have much. Only thirty bucks. I'm short until payday. And it's not enough to get back the regalia. But it's something."

"I'll take it," I said.

"I'm giving it to you because I believe in what you believe. I'm hoping, and I don't know why I'm hoping it, but I hope you can turn thirty bucks into a thousand somehow."

"I believe in magic."

"I believe you'll take my money and get drunk on it."

"Then why are you giving it to me?"

"There ain't no such thing as an atheist cop."

"Sure there is."

"Yeah, well, I'm not an atheist cop."

He let me out of the car, handed me two fives and a twenty, and shook my hand. "Take care of yourself, Jackson," he said. "Stay off the railroad tracks."

"I'll try," I said.

He drove away. Carrying my money, I headed back toward the water.

8:00 A.M.

On the wharf, those three Aleut men still waited on the wooden bench.

"Have you seen your ship?" I asked.

"Seen a lot of ships," the elder Aleut said. "But not our ship."

I sat on the bench with them. We sat in silence for a long time. I wondered whether we would fossilize if we sat there long enough.

I thought about my grandmother. I'd never seen her dance in her regalia. More than anything, I wished I'd seen her dance at a powwow.

"Do you guys know any songs?" I asked the Aleuts.

"I know all of Hank Williams,"[14] the elder Aleut said.

"How about Indian songs?"

"Hank Williams is Indian."

"How about sacred songs?"

"Hank Williams is sacred."

"I'm talking about ceremonial songs, you know, religious ones. The songs you sing back home when you're wishing and hoping."

"What are you wishing and hoping for?"

"I'm wishing my grandmother was still alive."

"Every song I know is about that."

"Well, sing me as many as you can."

The Aleuts sang their strange and beautiful songs. I listened. They sang about my grandmother and their grandmothers. They were lonely for the cold and snow. I was lonely for everybody.

10:00 A.M.

After the Aleuts finished their last song, we sat in silence. Indians are good at silence.

"Was that the last song?" I asked.

"We sang all the ones we could," the elder Aleut said. "All the others are just for our people."

I understood. We Indians have to keep our secrets. And these Aleuts were so secretive that they didn't refer to themselves as Indians.

"Are you guys hungry?" I asked.

They looked at one another and communicated without talking.

"We could eat," the elder Aleut said.

11:00 A.M.

The Aleuts and I walked over to Mother's Kitchen, a greasy diner in the International District. I knew they served homeless Indians who'd lucked into money.

"Four for breakfast?" the waitress asked when we stepped inside.

"Yes, we're very hungry," the elder Aleut said.

---

14. **Hank Williams:** The singer and songwriter Hiram King ("Hank") Williams (1923-1953), one of the most influential country-music artists of the twentieth century, had Cherokee and Creek ancestry and was inducted into the Native American Music Hall of Fame in 1999.

She sat us in a booth near the kitchen. I could smell the food cooking. My stomach growled.

"You guys want separate checks?" the waitress asked.

"No, I'm paying for it," I said.

"Aren't you the generous one," she said.

"Don't do that," I said.

"Do what?" she asked.

"Don't ask me rhetorical questions. They scare me."

She looked puzzled, and then she laughed.

"Okay, Professor," she said. "I'll only ask you real questions from now on."

"Thank you."

"What do you guys want to eat?"

"That's the best question anybody can ask anybody," I said.

"How much money you got?" she asked.

"Another good question," I said. "I've got twenty-five dollars I can spend. Bring us all the breakfast you can, plus your tip."

She knew the math.

"All right, that's four specials and four coffees and fifteen percent for me."

The Aleuts and I waited in silence. Soon enough, the waitress returned and poured us four coffees, and we sipped at them until she returned again with four plates of food. Eggs, bacon, toast, hash-brown potatoes. It is amazing how much food you can buy for so little money.

Grateful, we feasted.

Noon

I said farewell to the Aleuts and walked toward the pawnshop. I later heard the Aleuts had waded into the saltwater near Dock 47 and disappeared. Some Indians said the Aleuts walked on the water and headed north. Other Indians saw the Aleuts drown. I don't know what happened to them.

I looked for the pawnshop and couldn't find it. I swear it wasn't located in the place where it had been before. I walked twenty or thirty blocks looking for the pawnshop, turned corners and bisected intersections, looked up its name in the phone books, and asked people walking past me if they'd ever heard of it. But that pawnshop seemed to have sailed away from me like a ghost ship. I wanted to cry. Right when I'd given up, when I turned one last corner and thought I might die if I didn't find that pawnshop, there it was, located in a space I swore it hadn't been filling up a few minutes before.

I walked inside and greeted the pawnbroker, who looked a little younger than he had before.

"It's you," he said.

"Yes, it's me," I said.

"Jackson Jackson."

"That is my name."

"Where are your friends?"

"They went traveling. But it's okay. Indians are everywhere."

"Do you have my money?"

"How much do you need again?" I asked and hoped the price had changed.

"Nine hundred and ninety-nine dollars."

It was still the same price. Of course it was the same price. Why would it change?

"I don't have that," I said.

"What do you have?"

"Five dollars."

I set the crumpled Lincoln on the countertop. The pawnbroker studied it.

"Is that the same five dollars from yesterday?"

"No, it's different."

He thought about the possibilities.

"Did you work hard for this money?" he asked.

"Yes," I said.

He closed his eyes and thought harder about the possibilities. Then he stepped into his back room and returned with my grandmother's regalia.

"Take it," he said and held it out to me.

"I don't have the money."

"I don't want your money."

"But I wanted to win it."

"You did win it. Now, take it before I change my mind."

Do you know how many good men live in this world? Too many to count!

I took my grandmother's regalia and walked outside. I knew that solitary yellow bead was part of me. I knew I was that yellow bead in part. Outside, I wrapped myself in my grandmother's regalia and breathed her in. I stepped off the sidewalk and into the intersection. Pedestrians stopped. Cars stopped. The city stopped. They all watched me dance with my grandmother. I was my grandmother, dancing.

[2003]

Acknowledgments (continued from p. iv)

John and Abigail Adams, Letters reprinted by permission of the publisher from *The Adams Papers: Adams Family Correspondence, Volumes I-II*, edited by L. H. Butterfield, Cambridge Mass.: The Belknap Press of Harvard University Press, Copyright © 1963 by The Massachusetts Historical Society.

Sherman Alexie, "What You Pawn I Will Redeem" from *The Lone Ranger and Tonto Fistfight in Heaven* by Sherman Alexie. Copyright © 1993, 2005 by Sherman Alexie. Used by permission of Grove/Atlantic, Inc. Sherman Alexie conversation with Diane Thiel, from "A Conversation: Sherman Alexie and Diane Thiel" published on Poetry Society Organization Web site: http://www.poetrysociety.org/psa/poetry/crossroads/interviews/2009-09-04, reprinted by permission of Diane Thiel and Nancy Stauffer Associates for Sherman Alexie. Copyright © 2004.

Gloria Anzaldúa, "El sonavabitche" from *Borderlands/La Frontera: The New Mestiza*. Copyright © 1987, 1999 , 2007, 2012 by Gloria Anzaldúa. Reprinted by permission of Aunt Lute Books.

John Ashbery, "My Erotic Double" from *As We Know* by John Ashbery. Copyright © 1979 by John Ashbery. "Paradoxes and Oxymorons" from *Shadow Train* by John Ashbery. Copyright © 1980, 1981 by John Ashbery. Poems reprinted by permission of Georges Borchardt, Inc., on behalf of the author. "The One Thing That Can Save America," copyright © 1975 by John Ashbery, from *Self Portrait in a Convex Mirror* by John Ashbery. Used by permission of Viking Penguin, a division of Penguin Group (USA) Inc.

Elizabeth Ashbridge, From *Some Accounts of the Fore Part of the Life of Elizabeth Ashbridge, in Journeys in New Worlds: Early American Women's Narratives*, edited by William L. Andrews. Copyright © 1990 by the Board of Regents of the University of Wisconsin System. Reprinted by permission of the University of Wisconsin Press.

James Baldwin, "Note of a Native Son" from *Notes of a Native Son* by James Baldwin. Copyright © 1955, renewed 1983 by James Baldwin. Reprinted by permission of Beacon Press, Boston.

Amiri Baraka, "The Dutchman" from *The Dutchman and the Slave*. Copyright 1964 by Amiri Baraka. Reprinted by permission of SLL / Sterling Lord Literistic, Inc.

Donald Barthelme, "The School" from *Amateurs* by Donald Barthelme. Copyright © 1976 by Donald Barthelme. Used by permission of The Wylie Agency.

Saul Bellow, "Looking for Mr. Green," copyright 1951, renewed © 1979 by Saul Bellow, from *Mosby's Memoirs and Other Stories* by Saul Bellow. Used by permission of Viking Penguin, a division of Penguin Group (USA) Inc.

John Berryman, Dream Songs: 1, 4, 14, 26 from *The Dream Songs* by John Berryman. Copyright © 1969 by John Berryman. Copyright renewed 1997 by Kate Donahue Berryman. Reprinted by permission of Farrar, Straus and Giroux, LLC.

Elizabeth Bishop, "Sestina," "One Art," "The Armadillo," "In the Waiting Room" from *The Complete Poems 1927-1979* by Elizabeth Bishop. Copyright © 1979, 1983 by Alice Helen Methfessel. Reprinted by permission of Farrar, Straus and Giroux, LLC.

Gwendolyn Brooks, "Kitchenette Building," "the mother," "a song in the front yard," "The Bean Eaters," "We Real Cool," and "Malcolm X" reprinted by Consent of Brooks Permissions.

Sterling A. Brown, "Southern Road," "Strong Men" from *The Collected Poems of Sterling A. Brown*, selected by Michael S. Harper. Copyright © 1980 by Sterling A. Brown. Reprinted by permission of the Estate of Sterling Brown.

Carlos Bulosan, "The End of the War" from *The New Yorker*, September 2, 1944. Copyright © 1944 Conde Nast Publications. All rights reserved. Originally published in *The New Yorker*.

Raymond Carver, "Are These Actual Miles?" from *Where I'm Calling From*. Copyright © 1976 by Raymond Carver. Reprinted by permission of Grove/Atlantic, Inc.

Sandra Cisneros, "Mericans" from *Woman Hollering Creek*. Copyright © 1991 by Sandra Cisneros. Published by Vintage Books, a division of Random House, Inc., New York and originally in hardcover by Random House, Inc. "A Note to Gloria from the Bottom of the Sea," copyright © 2007 by Sandra Cisneros. First published in *Borderlands: La Frontera: The New Mestiza*, 20th Anniversary Edition. Aunt Lute Press, 2007. All reprinted by permission of Susan Bergholz Literary Services, New York, NY and Lamy, NM. All rights reserved.

Christopher Columbus, "Letter to Luis de Santangel Regarding the First Voyage, February 15, 1393" from *Select Documents Illustrating the Four Voyages of Columbus*, translated by Cecil Jane. Reprinted by permission of The Hakluyt Society from David Higham Associates.

Hart Crane, "Voyages I, II, III, IV "To Brooklyn Bridge" from *Complete Poems of Hart Crane* by Hart Crane, edited by Marc Simon. Copyright 1933, 1958, 1966 of Liveright Publishing Corporation. Copyright © 1986 by Marc Simon. "Modern Poetry" from *The Complete Poems and Selected Letters and Prose of Hart Crane* by Hart Crane, edited by Brom Weber. Copyright 1933, 1958, 1966 by Liveright Publishing Corporation. Copyright 1952 by Brom Weber. All used by permission of Liveright Publishing Corporation.

Countee Cullen, "Yet Do I Marvel," "Heritage," from *My Soul's High Song: The Collected Writings of Countee Cullen, Voice of the Harlem Renaissance*, edited by Gerald Early. Reprinted by permission of Thompson and Thompson and the Amistad Research Foundation, Tulane University.

E. E. Cummings, "in Just-," "the Cambridge ladies who live in furnished souls," "Buffalo Bill's," "i sing of Olaf glad and big," "next to of course god america i," from *Complete Poems: 1904-1962* by E. E. Cummings, edited by George J. Firmage. Copyright 1923, 1925, 1926, 1931, 1935, 1938, 1939, 1940, 1944, 1945, 1946, 1947, 1948, 1949, 1950, 1951, 1952, 1953, 1954, © 1955, 1956, 1957, 1958, 1959, 1960, 1961, 1962, 1963, 1966, 1967, 1968, 1972, 1973, 1974, 1975, 1976, 1977, 1978, 1979, 1980, 1981, 1982, 1983, 1984, 1985, 1986, 1987, 1988, 1989, 1990, 1991 by the Trustees for the E. E. Cummings Trust. Copyright © 1973, 1976, 1978, 1979, 1981, 1983, 1985, 1991 by George James Firmage. Used by permission of Liveright Pubishing Corporation.

Don DeLillo, "Videotape" reprinted with the permission of Scribner, an imprint of Simon & Schuster Inc., from *Underworld* by Don DeLillo. Copyright © 1994 by Don DeLillo. Originally appeared in *Antaeus*: Fall 1994. All rights reserved.

Emily Dickinson, "These are the days when Birds come back," "I never lost as much but twice," "Success is counted Sweetest," "'Faith' is a fine invention," "I'm 'wife' – I've finished that –," "I taste a liquor never brewed," "Safe in their Alabaster Chambers," "I like a look of Agony," "Wild Nights – Wild Nights!" "I can wade Grief –" "There's a certain Slant of light," "I felt a funeral, in my Brain" "I'm Nobody! Who are You?" "The Soul Selects her own Society –" "Some keep the Sabbath going to Church –" "After great pain, a formal feeling comes –" "God is a distant–stately Lover –" "What Soft – Cherubic Creatures –" "They dropped like flakes –" "Much Madness is divinest Sense –" "This is my letter to the World" "It feels a shame to be Alive" "This was a Poet – It is That" "I heard a fly buzz – when I died" "This World is not Conclusion" "I'm ceded – I've stopped being Theirs –" "The Soul has Bandaged moments –" "The Spider holds a Silver Ball" "The Brain – is wider than the Sky" "Pain – has an Element of Blank" " I dwell in Possibility –" "Publication – is the Auction" "Because I could not stop for Death –" "My Life had stood – a Loaded Gun –" "The Poets light but Lamps –" "A Narrow fellow in the Grass" "I never saw a Moor" "Title divine – is mine!" "The Bustle in a House" "Revolution is the Pod," "Tell all the Truth but tell it Slant –" "A Route of Evanescence" "A Word made Flesh is seldom," "My life closed twice before its close –" "Rearrange a 'Wife's' affection!" "Elysium is as far," reprinted by permission of the publishers and the Trustees of Amherst College from *The Poems of Emily Dickinson*, Thomas H. Johnson, ed., Cambridge, Mass.: The Belknap Press of Harvard University Press, Copyright © 1951, 1955, 1979, 1983 by the President and Fellows of Harvard College. "Letter exchange with Susan Gilbert 1861" and "Letter to Thomas Wentworth Higginson, 7 June, 1862" reprinted with permission of the publishers from *The Letters of Emily Dickinson*, edited by Thomas H. Johnson, Cambridge, Mass.: The Belknap Press of Harvard University Press. Copyright © 1958, 1986 by the President and Fellows of Harvard College; 1914, 1924, 1932, 1942 by Martha Dickinson Bianchi; 1952 by Alfred Leete Hampson; 1960 by Mary L. Hampson.

Rita Dove, "The House Slave," and "Kentucky, 1833" from *The Yellow House on the Corner*, Carnegie Mellon University Press, © 1980 by Rita Dove. Reprinted by permission of the author. "Canary" from *Grace Notes* by Rita Dove. Copyright © 1989 by Rita Dove. "History" from *Mother Love* by Rita Dove. Copyright © 1995 by Rita Dove. Both used by permission of W. W. Norton & Company, Inc.

Jonathan Edwards, "Personal Narrative" from *The Works of Jonathan Edwards: Letters and Personal Writings*, Volume 16 by Jonathan

Edwards, edited by George S. Claghorn. Copyright © 1998. "Sinners in the Hands of an Angry God" from *The Works of Jonathan Edwards: Sermons and Discourses 1739-1743*, by Jonathan Edwards, edited by Harry Stout, Nathan Hatch and Kyle Farley. Copyright © 2003. Reprinted by permission of Yale University Press.

T. S. Eliot, "Burnt Norton" from *Four Quartets* by T. S. Eliot, copyright 1936 by Harcourt, Inc., and renewed 1964 by T. S. Eliot. "The Journey of the Magi" from *Collected Poems 1909-1962* by T. S. Eliot, copyright 1936 by Harcourt, Inc. and renewed 1964 by T. S. Eliot. Reprinted by permission of the publisher and Faber and Faber Ltd.

Ralph Ellison, "Battle Royal," copyright 1948 and renewed 1976 by Ralph Ellison, from *Invisible Man* by Ralph Ellison. Used by permission of Random House, Inc. Any third party use of this material outside of this publication, is prohibited. Interested parties must apply directly to Random House, Inc. for permission.

Martín Espada, "Alabanza: In Praise of Local 100" Copyright © 2003 by Martin Espada from *Alabanza* by Martín Espada. Copyright © 2003 by Martín Espada. Used by permission of the author and W. W. Norton & Company, Inc.

William Faulkner, "Barn Burning" copyright 1950 by Random House, Inc., Copyright renewed 1977 by Jill Faulkner Summers. "That Evening Sun" copyright 1931 and renewed 1959 by William Faulkner. Both stories are from *Collected Stories of William Faulkner* by William Faulkner. Used by permission of Random House, Inc. Any third party use of this material outside of this publication, is prohibited. Interested parties must apply directly to Random House, Inc. for permission.

Benjamin Franklin, "The Autobiography, Parts I and II" from *The Autobiography of Benjamin Franklin: A Genetic Text*, edited by J.A. Leo LeMay and P.M. Zall. Reprinted by permission of Dr. J.A. Leo LeMay.

Robert Frost, "Acquainted with the Night," "Desert Places," "Stopping by Woods on a Snowy Evening," "Nothing Gold Can Stay," "The Gift Outright" from *The Poetry of Robert Frost*, edited by Edward Connery Lathem. Copyright © 1923, 1947, 1969 by Henry Holt and Company, Copyright 1951 by Robert Frost, © 1975 by Lesley Frost Ballantine. "The Figure a Poem Makes" from *Selected Prose of Robert Frost* edited by Hyde Cox and Edward Connery Lathem. Copyright 1939, 1967 by Henry Holt

and Company. Reprinted by permission of Henry Holt and Company.

Jun Fujita, "Diminuendo" and "Michigan Boulevard," from *Tanka: Poems in Exile* copyright 1923 by Covici-McGee Co.

Allen Ginsberg, "A Supermarket in California" from *Collected Poems 1947-1980* by Allen Ginsberg. Copyright © 1955 by Allen Ginsberg. Reprinted by permission of HarperCollins Publishers.

Allen Ginsberg, "Howl" from *Collected Poems 1947-1980*. Copyright © 1955 by Allen Ginsberg. Reprinted by permission of HarperCollins Publishers.

Joy Harjo, "This Land is a Poem" and "If You Look with the Mind of the Swirling Earth" by Joy Harjo from *Secrets from the Center of the World* by Joy Harjo and Stephen Strom. Copyright © 1989 The Arizona Board of Regents. Reprinted by permission of the University of Arizona Press. "New Orleans" from *How We Became Human: New and Selected Poems* by Joy Harjo. Copyright © 2002 by Joy Harjo. Reprinted by permission of W. W. Norton & Company.

Michael S. Harper,"American History," "Martin's Blues," "Dear John, Dear Coltrane," from *Songlines in Michaeltree: New and Collected Poems*. Copyright © 2000 by Michael S. Harper. Used with permission of the poet and the University of Illinois Press.

Robert Hayden, "Middle Passage" Copyright © 1962, 1966 by Robert Hayden from *Collected Poems of Robert Hayden* by Robert Hayden, edited by Frederick Glaysher. Used by permission of Liveright Publishing Corporation. "Frederick Douglass" © 1966 by Robert Hayden from *Collected Poems of Robert Hayden*, Frederick Glaysher, editor. Used by permission of Liveright Publishing Corporation.

Ernest Hemingway, "Big Two-Hearted River," Parts I and II reprinted with the permission of Scribner, an imprint of Simon & Schuster Adult Publishing Group, from *The Short Stories of Ernest Hemingway*. Copyright © 1925 Charles Scribner's Sons. Copyright renewed 1953 by Ernest Hemingway.

Langston Hughes, "Old Walt" from *The Collected Poems of Langston Hughes*, by Langston Hughes, edited by Arnold Rampersad with David Roessell, Associate Editor. Copyright © 1994 by The Estate of Langston Hughes. Used by permission of Alfred A. Knopf, a division of Random House, Inc. "The Negro Artist and the

Racial Mountain" first published in *The Nation*, June 23, 1926. Copyright © 1926 by Langston Hughes. Reprinted by permission of Harold Ober Associates Incorporated. "Jazzonia," "Brass Spittoons" edited by Arnold Rampersad with David Roessel, Assoc., "Christ in Alabama," "Harlem (2)" copyright 1951 by Langston Hughes, "Cross" copyright © 1994 by The Estate of Langston Hughes, "I, Too," "The Weary Blues" copyright © 1994 by The Estate of Langston Hughes from *The Collected Poems of Langston Hughes* by Langston Hughes, edited by Arnold Rampersad with David Roessel, Associate Editor, copyright © 1994 by The Estate of Langston Hughes. Used by permission of Alfred A. Knopf, a division of Random House, Inc. Any third party use of this material, outside of this publication, is prohibited. Interested parties must apply directly to Random House, Inc. for permission.

Hupa, "The Boy Who Grew up at Ta'k'imłding" translated by Victor Golla from *Surviving through the Days: Translations of Native California Stories and Songs*, edited by Herbert W. Luthin, reprinted by permission of the University of California Press through Rightslink.

Thomas Jefferson, Selections reprinted from *Thomas Jefferson: Writings* edited by Merrill D. Peterson. (The Library of America, 1984).

Yusef Komunyakaa, "Facing It," "The Dead at Quang Tri," "Tu Do Street," and "Prisoners" from *Dien Cau Dau* © 1988 by Yusef Komunyakaa. Reprinted by permission of Wesleyan University Press.

Lakota "*Whope* and the Gift of the Pipe" reprinted from *Lakota Belief and Ritual* by James R. Walker, edited by Raymond J. DeMallie and Elaine A. Jahner by permission of the University of Nebraska Press. Copyright © 1980, 1991 by the University of Nebraska Press.

Ursula K. Le Guin, "She Unnames Them" from *Buffalo Gals and Other Animal Presences*. Copyright © 1985 by Ursula K. Le Guin; first appeared in *The New Yorker;* reprinted by permission of the Author and the Author's agents, the Virginia Kidd Agency, Inc.

Audre Lorde, "Coal" copyright © 1973, 1970, 1968 by Audre Lorde. "The Woman Thing" copyright © 1973, 1970, 1968 by Audre Lorde. "Black Mother Woman" copyright © 1992, 1973 by Audre Lorde. All from *Undersong: Chosen Poems Old and New* by Audre Lorde. All used by permission of W. W. Norton & Company, Inc.

Robert Lowell, "For the Union Dead," "Skunk Hour," "Memories of West Street and Lepke" from *Collected Poems* by Robert Lowell. Copyright © 2003 by Harriet Lowell and Sheridan Lowell. Reprinted by permission of Farrar, Straus and Giroux, LLC.

Edna St. Vincent Millay, "Justice Denied in Massachusetts" from *Collected Poems*. Copyright 1928, © 1955 by Edna St. Vincent Millay and Norma Millay Ellis. Reprinted with the permission of The Permissions Company, Inc., on behalf of Holly Peppe, Literary Executor, The Millay Society. www.millay.org.

Arthur Miller, "On Mark Twain's Chapters from *My Autobiography*" from *Echoes Down the Corridor: Collected Essays, 1944–2000* by Arthur Miller, edited by Stephen Centola, copyright © 2000 by Arthur Miller. Used by permission of Viking Penguin, a division of Penguin Group (USA) Inc.

N. Scott Momaday, "The Becoming of the Native: Man in America Before Columbus" from *America in 1492*, edited by Alvin Josephy, Jr., copyright © 1991 by The Newberry Library. Used by permission of Alfred A. Knopf, a division of Random House, Inc.

Marianne Moore, "To a Snail" and "An Egyptian Pulled Glass Bottle in the Shape of a Fish" reprinted with the permission of Scribner, a division of Simon & Schuster Inc. from *The Collected Poems of Marianne Moore* by Marianne Moore. Copyright © 1935 by Marianne Moore; renewed 1963 by Marianne Moore and T. S. Eliot. All rights reserved.

Toni Morrison, "Recitatif" Copyright © 1983 by Toni Morrison. Reprinted by permission of International Creative Management, Inc. Morrison, Toni: Excerpt from question and response by Toni Morrison on William Faulkner's influence on her literary career, first published in *Faulkner and Women*, edited by Doreen Fowler and Ann J. Abadie, Copyright © 1986 by the University Press of Mississippi. Reprinted with permission of University Press of Mississippi.

Tim O'Brien, "The Things They Carried" from *The Things They Carried* by Tim O'Brien. Copyright © 1990 by Tim O'Brien. Reprinted by permission of Houghton Mifflin Company. All rights reserved.

Flannery O'Connor, "A Good Man is Hard to Find" from *A Good Man is Hard to Find and Other*

Stories, copyright 1953 by Flannery O'Connor and renewed 1981 by Regina O'Connor. Reprinted by permission of Harcourt, Inc.

Samson Occom, "A Short Narrative of My Life" from the Raunder Special Collections, Dartmouth College Library. Reprinted courtesy of Dartmouth College Library.

Tillie Olsen, "I Stand Here Ironing" from *Tell Me a Riddle, Requa I, and Other Stories* by Tillie Olsen. Reprinted by permission of the University of Nebraska Press. Copyright 1961 by Tillie Olsen.

Jim Ottery, "The Diary of Samson Occum" appeared in "Samson Occom's Diary and D'Arcy McNicle's 'Train Time': The Real Imperative of "Native" Education in American Indian Literature" by James Ottery in *SAIL: Studies in American Indian Literatures*; Series 2; Volume 13, Number 4; Winter 2001, and is reprinted by permission of the author.

Sylvia Plath, "Daddy," "Lady Lazarus," "Morning Song" from *Ariel: Poems* by Sylvia Plath. Copyright © 1961, 1962, 1963, 1964, 1965, 1966 by Ted Hughes. Foreword by Robert Lowell. "Mirror" from *Crossing the Water* by Sylvia Plath. Copyright © 1971 by Ted Hughes. Reprinted by permission of HarperCollins Publishers and Faber and Faber Ltd.

Katherine Anne Porter, "Flowering Judas" from *Flowering Judas and Other Stories*, copyright 1930 and renewed 1958 by Katherine Anne Porter, reprinted by permission of Harcourt, Inc.

Adrienne Rich, "I Am in Danger-Sir-" Copyright © 2002 by Adrienne Rich. Copyright © 1966 by W. W. Norton & Company, Inc. from *The Fact of a Doorframe: Selected Poems, 1950-2001* by Adrienne Rich. Used by permission of the author and W.W. Norton & Company, Inc. "Trying to Talk with a Man" Copyright © 2002 by Adrienne Rich, Copyright © 1973 by W. W. Norton & Company, Inc. "A Valediction Forbidding Mourning." Copyright © 2002 by Adrienne Rich, Copyright © 1971 by W.W. Norton & Company, Inc. "Diving into the Wreck" Copyright © 2002 by Adrienne Rich. Copyright © 1973 by W. W. Norton & Company, Inc. All from *The Fact of a Doorframe: Selected Poems 1950-2001* by Adrienne Rich. Used by permission of the author and W. W. Norton & Company, Inc.

Theodore Roethke, "Cuttings," copyright 1948 by Theodore Roethke, "Cuttings (Later)" copyright 1948 by Theodore Roethke, "My Papa's Waltz" copyright 1942 by Hearst Magazines, Inc. "Root Cellar" copyright 1943 by Modern Poetry Asssociation, Inc. "The Waking" copyright 1953 by Theodore Roethke. All from *Collected Poems of Theodore Roethke* by Theodore Roethke. Used by permission of Doubleday, a division of Random House, Inc. Any third party use of this material outside of this publication, is prohibited. Interested parties must apply directly to Random House, Inc. for permission.

Jane Johnston Schoolcraft: "Mishosha, or the Magician and His Daughters: A Chippewa Tale or Legend" from *The Literary Voyager or Muzzeniegun*, edited by Philip P. Mason. Reprinted by permission of Michigan State University Press.

Samuel Sewall, Excerpts from *The Diary of Samuel Sewall 1674-1729* edited by M. Halsey Thomas. Copyright © 1973 by Farrar, Straus & Giroux, Inc. Reprinted by permission of Farrar, Straus and Giroux, LLC.

Rose Shade, "Puritan Woman" from *The Best Fiction and Poetry from California State University, Northridge: 1962-1988*, edited by Warren Wedin is reprinted by permission of the editor.

Leslie Marmon Silko, "Yellow Woman" copyright © 1981, 2012 by Leslie Marmon Silko. Reprinted from *Storyteller* by Leslie Marmon Silko. Used by permission of Viking Penguin, a division of Penguin Group (USA) Inc.

John Smith, Excerpts from *The Complete Works of Captain John Smith, 1580-1631* edited by Philip L. Barbou. Published for the Omohundro Institute of Early American History and Culture. Copyright © 1986 by the University of North Carolina Press. Used by permission of the publisher.

Gary Snyder, "Wave" from *Regarding Wave*, copyright © 1970 by Gary Snyder. Reprinted by permission of New Directions Publishing Corp. "Riprap" and "Axe Handles" from *The Gary Snyder Reader* by Gary Snyder. Copyright © 1999 by Gary Snyder. Reprinted by permission of Counterpoint.

Cathy Song, "A Poet in the House" from *The Land of the Bliss* by Cathy Song, © 2001. Reprinted by permission of the University of Pittsburgh Press.

John Steinbeck, "Flight" from *The Long Valley* by John Steinbeck, copyright 1938, renewed © 1966 by John Steinbeck. Used by permission of Viking Penguin, a division of Penguin Group (USA) Inc.

Wallace Stevens, "Of Modern Poetry" from *The Collected Poems of Wallace Stevens* by Wallace Stevens, copyright 1954 by Wallace Stevens and renewed 1982 by Holly Stevens. Used by permission of Alfred A. Knopf, a division of Random House, Inc. Any third party use of this material, outside of this publication, is prohibited. Interested parties must apply directly to Random House for permission.

Edward Taylor, Excerpts Preparatory Meditations: "The Prologue," "Meditations 8 from Occasional Poems: "Upon Wedlock," and "Death of Children," "Huswifery," "Upon a Spider Catching a Fly" from *The Poems of Edward Taylor*, edited by Donald E. Stanford. Copyright © 1960, renewed 1988 by Donald E. Stanford. Reprinted by permission of the University of North Carolina Press. www.unc.edu.

Jean Toomer, "Blood-Burning Moon," "Portrait in Georgia" from *Cane* by Jean Toomer. Copyright 1923 by Boni & Liveright, renewed 1951 by Jean Toomer. Used by permission of Liveright Publishing Corporation.

Mark Twain, "The War Prayer" from *Europe and Elsewhere* by Mark Twain, edited by Albert Bigelow Paine. Copyright 1923 by Mark Twain Company, renewed 1951 by Mark Twain Company.

John Updike, "A & P" from *Pigeon Feathers and Other Stories* by John Updike. Copyright © 1962 and renewed 1990 by John Updike. Excerpt from *Higher Gossip: Essays and Criticism*, by John Updike, ed. by Christopher Carduff, copyright © 2011 by The Estate of John H. Updike. Foreword copyright © 2011 by Christopher Carduff. Used by permission of Alfred A. Knopf, a division of Random House, Inc. Any third party use of this material, outside of this publication, is prohibited. Interested parties must apply directly to Random House, Inc. for permission.

Alice Walker, "Everyday Use" from *In Love & Trouble: Stories of Black Women*, copyright © 1973 by Alice Walker. Reprinted by permission of Harcourt, Inc. Excerpt from *A Cautionary Tale and a Partisan View* from Zora Neale Hurston: A Literary Biography by Alice Walker. Copyright © 1977 by the Board of Trustees of the University of Illinois. Reprinted by permission of the University of Illinois Press.

George Washington, "Letter to the Touro Synagogue, Newport RI, 1790" Courtesy of the B'nai B'rith Klutznick National Jewish Museum, Washington, D.C.

Eudora Welty, "Lily Daw and the Three Ladies" from *A Curtain of Green and Other Stories*, copyright 1937 and renewed 1965 by Eudora Welty. Reprinted by permission of Houghton Mifflin Harcourt Publishing Company. All rights reserved.

Phillis Wheatley, "On Being Brought from Africa to America," "To the University of Cambridge, in New England." "To the Right Honorable William, Earl of Dartmouth," "To S.M., a Young African Painter, on Seeing His Works," "To His Excellency General Washington," "Letter to Samsom Occum 11 February 1774" from *The Poems of Phillis Wheatley*, edited and with an introduction by Julian D. Mason, Jr. Copyright © 1966 by the University of North Carolina Press, renewed 1989. Used by permission of the publisher. www.uncpress.unc.edu.

Tennessee Williams, "Portrait of a Madonna" by Tennessee Williams, from *27 Wagons Full of Cotton*, copyright © 1945 by The University of the South. Reprinted by permission of New Directions Pubishing Corp.

William Carlos Williams, "A Sort of a Song" by William Carlos Williams, from *Collected Poems 1939-1962, Volume II*, copyright © 1944 by William Carlos Williams. The Red Wheelbarrow," "This is Just to Say," "To Elsie" by William Carlos Williams, from *Collected Poems: 1909-1939, Volume I*, copyright © 1938 by New Directions Publishing Corp. Reprinted by permission of New Directions Publishing Corp.

August Wilson, "The Janitor" by August Wilson. First performed in 1985. Published in *Short Pieces from the New Dramatists*, ed. Stan Chervin (Broadway Play Pub., 1985) copyright © 1985 by August Wilson. Reprinted by permission of the Estate of August Wilson.

John Woolman, Excerpts from *The Journal and Major Essays of John Woolman*, edited by P. P. Moulton, Friends United Press. Used by permission.

Richard Wright, "The Man Who Was Almost a Man" ("Almos' a Man"), pages 3-18 from *Eight Men* by Richard Wright. Copyright 1940 © 1961 by Richard Wright, renewed © 1989 by Ellen Wright. Introduction © 1996 by Paul Gilroy. Reprinted by permission of HarperCollins Publishers. From *Harper's Bazaar*, January 1940.

Hisaye Yamamoto, "Seventeen Syllables" from *Seventeen Syllables and Other Stories, Revised and Expanded Edition.* Copyright © 2001 by Rutgers, the State University. Reprinted by permission of Rutgers University Press.

Image Credits

BEGINNINGS TO 1750:

Page 1: Collection of The New York Historical Society, Neg.#76192

Page 6: Library of Congress

Page 7: Hulton Archive/Getty Images

Pages 23 (detail) and 9: Library of Congress

Pages 23 (detail) and 9: Courtesy of the John Carter Brown Library at Brown University

Page 12: The University of N. Carolina at Chapel Hill Libraries

Page 15: Library of Congress, Rare Book and Special Collections Division

Page 17: Courtesy of the State Library of Massachusetts

Page 19: Library of Congress, Rare Book and Special Collections Division

Page 21: Courtesy of the Pennsylvania Academy of the Fine Arts, Philadelphia. Gift of Mrs. Sarah Harrison (The Joseph Harrison, Jr. Collection)

Page 26 (detail): Library of Congress

Pages 22 (detail) and 28: Library of Congress, Rare Book and Special Collections Division

Page 30: Penn Museum Object, image #NA9143

Page 32: Courtesy of John Carter Brown Library at Brown University

Page 34: Courtesy Special Collections University of Pennsylvania Library

Page 38: Library of Congress

Page 41: Library of Congress

Page 46: Library of Congress

Page 49: Ericson Collection, Humboldt State University Library

Page 51: Collection of the Illinois State Museum, photograph by Doug Carr.

Page 59: Library of Congress, Rare Book and Special Collections Division

Page 60: Library of Congress, Rare Book and Special Collections Division

Pages 24 (detail) and 62: Robert Dechert Collection, Rare Book and Manuscript Library, University of Pennsylvania

Page 63: Library of Congress, Rare Book and Special Collections Division

Pages 22 (detail) and 66: Library of Congress, Rare Book and Special Collections Division

Pages 23 (detail) and 73: Library of Congress, Rare Books and Special Collections Division.

Page 83: Robert Dechert Collection, Rare Book and Manuscript Library, University of Pennsylvania

Pages 24 (detail) and 91: Architect of the Capitol.

Pages 23 (detail) and 92: Library of Congress.

Page 94: Ashmolean Museum, University of Oxford, UK/Bridgeman Art Library.

Pages 26 (detail) and 97: Beinecke Rare Book and Manuscript Library, Yale University

Page 99: Courtesy Fruitlands Museum, Harvard, Massachusetts

Page 101: The New York Public Library

Pages 27 (detail) and 102: Library of Congress.

Pages 24 (detail) and 104: Library of Congress.

Page 106: Library of Congress, Rare Book and Special Collections Division

Page 117: Library of Congress

Page 119: Courtesy of the State Library of Massachusetts

Pages 25 (detail) and 136: Courtesy American Antiquarian Society.

Page 151: Beinecke Rare Book and Manuscript Library, Yale University

Pages 25 (detail) and 166: LaDonna Gulley Warrick

Pages 26 (detail) and 170: Courtesy of the Trustees of the Boston Public Library.

Page 190: The Granger Collection, New York

Page 191: Library of Congress

Page 192: Library of Congress

Pages 27 (detail) and 201: Library of Congress

Pages 26 (detail) and 212: Courtesy Commonwealth of Massachusetts Art Commission

Page 217: Andrea Carlin, The Association for Gravestone Studies

Page 303: Courtesy of the Dedham Historical Society, Dedham, Massachusetts

Page 231: Yale University Art Gallery, Bequest of Eugene Philips Edwards

Pages 27 (detail) and 346: Rare Books Division, The New York Public Library, Astor, Lenox and Tilden Foundations

Page 361: Yale University Art Gallery. Gift of Arthur Reed Kimball, B.A. 1877

1750 TO 1830

Page 259: The Historic New Orleans Collection

Pages 261 and 280(detail): Library of Congress

Page 285: Library of Congress

Pages 279 (detail) and 266: Library of Congress

Page 267: Library of Congress

Page 268: Library of Congress

Pages 390 (detail) and 377: The Granger Collection, New York

Pages 282 (detail) and 269: Library of Congress Rare Book and Special Collections Division

Pages 283 (detail) and 274: Library of Congress

Pages 280 (detail) and 275: Courtesy of the John Carter Brown Library at Brown University

Page 277: Print Collection, Miriam and Ira D. Wallach Division of Art, Prints and Photographs, The New York Public Library, Astor, Lenox and Tilden Foundations

Pages 279 (detail) and 284: Yale University Art Gallery. Gift of Avery Rockefeller for the University Library. Acc. 2 June 1948.

Page 287: Beinecke Rare Book and Manuscript Library, Yale University

Page 289: Library of Congress

Page 291: Harvard Art Museums/Fogg Museum, Harvard University Portrait Collection, Bequest of Dr. John Collins Warren, 1856, H47 Copyright, Photo: Katya Kallsen © President and Fellows of Harvard College.

Page 293: Library of Congress, Rare Book and Special Collections Division

Page 322: Courtesy of Beinecke Rare Book and Manuscript Library, Yale University

Page 335: Haverford College Library, Haverford, PA: Quaker Collection

Page 347: Bowdoin College Museum of Art, Brunswick, ME. Bequest of the Honorable James Bowdoin III.

Page 355: Hood Museum of Art, Dartmouth College, Hanover, NH; gift of Mrs. Robert White Birch, Class of 1927

Pages 281 (detail) and 359: Library of Congress

Page 360: Courtesy American Antiquarian Society

Page 373: Library of Congress, Rare Book and Special Collections Division

Page 375: Courtesy Beinecke Rare Book and Manuscript Library, Yale University

Page 379: Library of Congress

Page 383: Massachusetts Historical Society, Boston/Bridgeman Art Library

Pages 281 (detail) and 383: Massachusetts Historical Society, Boston/Bridgeman Art Library

Pages 282 (detail) and 387: National Archives

Page 388: Library of Congress

Page 399: Library of Congress

Page 401: Terra Foundation for American Art, Chicago/Art Resource, New York

Page 407: Delaware Art Museum, Gift of Absalom Jones School, 1971, DAM #1971-8

Page 409: Library of Congress

Page 413: *Kindred Spirits* by Asher Brown Durand, Photo © Francis G. Mayer/CORBIS

Page 415: Library of Congress, Rare Book and Special Collections Division

Page 417: Library of Congress

Page 417: Courtesy Beinecke Rare Book and Manuscript Library, Yale University

Page 419: Gift of John D. Rockefeller Jr., Historic Hudson Valley, Tarrytown, NY (SS.79.47)

Page 421: Engraving by P. Halpin. Public domain.

Page 422: Rare Books Division. Department of Rare Books and Special Collections. Princeton University Library.

Page 428: Library of Congress

Page 436: Library of Congress

Page 438: *The Return of Rip Van Winkle* (1849), John Quidor. Andrew W. Mellon Collection. Image © Board of Trustees, National Gallery of Art, Washington, DC.

Pages 282 (detail) and 454: Library of Congress

Page 467: Library of Congress

Page 474: Johnston Family Papers, Bentley Historical Library, University of Michigan

1830 TO 1865

Page 482: Saint Louis Art Museum, Gift of Bank of America

Pages 498 (detail) and 487: Courtesy, American Antiquarian Society

Page 488: Library of Congress

Page 489: Library of Congress

Page 491: Library of Congress

Page 492: Courtesy, American Antiquarian Society

Page 493: Library of Congress

Page 494: Library of Congress

Page 502: Madison County Historical Society, Oneida, New York

Page 505: *Trail of Tears* used by permission of Woolaroc Museum, Bartlesville, Oklahoma

Page 507: Massachusetts Historical Society

Page 509: The Gilder Lehrman Collection, on Deposit at The New-York Historical Society, New York (GLC 5826)

Page 511: Chicago History Museum (ICHi-22003)

Page 514: Library of Congress

Pages 498 (detail) and 519: Library of Congress.

Page 522: Library of Congress

Page 525: Courtesy of George Eastman House, International Museum of Photography and Film

Page 529: Library of Congress

Pages 500 (detail) and 531: Library of Congress, Manuscript Division.

Page 533: Old Sturbridge Village

Pages 499 (detail) and 540: Courtesy Concord Free Public Library.

Page 595: Library of Congress

Page 607: The Nelson-Atkins Museum of Art, Kansas City, Missouri. Gift of Hallmark Cards, Inc., 2005.27.13

Page 609: Library of Congress

Page 619: From a private collection

Page 638: Courtesy of North Carolina State Archives

Pages 499 (detail) and 648: Courtesy Concord Free Public Library.

Page 666: Library of Congress, Rare Book and Special Collections Division

Page 700: National Portrait Gallery, Smithsonian Institution/Art Resource, New York

Page 768: ©Wayne Scarberry/The Image Works

Page 771: Courtesy Ablah Library, Wichita State University, Wichita, Kansas

Page 774: Museum of the City of New York

Page 775: Boston Athenaeum

Page 777: Courtesy of the Boston Public Library

Page 778: New-York Historical Society/Bridgeman Art Library

Page 779: Courtesy of the Peabody Essex Museum, Salem, Massachusetts. Gift of Professor Richard C. Manning.

Pages 498 (detail) and 827: Library of Congress.

Page 867: Sophia Smith Collection, Smith College

Pages 500 (detail) and 877: Asa W. Twitchell, *Herman Meville.* Berkshire Athenaeum, Pittsfield, MA.

Page 878: Library of Congress

Page 906: © 1981 by Gerald Langford. Photograph from the collection of Mrs. Hope Davis Kehrig. Reprinted by permission of Henry Holt & Company, LLC

Page 907: David Rumsey Map Collection, www.davidrumsey.com

Page 937: Courtesy of the University of Nebraska, Lincoln

Page 941: Library of Congress, Rare Book and Special Collections Division

Page 945: Hulton Archive/Getty Images.

Page 950: *Elizabeth Oakes Smith,* Chester Dale Collection. Image Courtesy National Gallery of Art, Washington, D.C. (1963.10.188)

Page 953: Library of Congress

Page 958: Library of Congress

Page 963: Library of Congress

Page 965: Prints and photographs in the Clifton Waller Barrett Library of American Literature (Barrett Prints). Clifton Waller Barrett Library of American Literature, Special Collections, University of Virginia Library.

Page 969: Library of Congress, Rare Book and Special Collections Division

Page 971: Library of Congress, Manuscript Division

Page 1040: Courtesy of the Pennsylvania Academy of the Fine Arts, Philadelphia, General Fund

Page 1043: Amherst College Archives and Special Collections

Page 1045: By permission of The Houghton Library, Harvard University, MS Am 1118.3 (11a). © The President and Fellows of Harvard College.

Page 1070: Courtesy Beinecke Rare Book and Manuscript Library, Yale University

Page 1075: Kansas State Historical Society

Page 1078: Library of Congress

Pages 501 (detail) and 1080: National Archives

Page 1087: Library of Congress

Page 1090: Portrait by James U. Stead via wikipedia. Public Domain.

Page 1094: Chicago History Museum (ICHi-22119)

AMERICAN LITERATURE, 1865–1914

Page 1100: Library of Congress Prints & Photographs Division

Page 1103: Courtesy Beinecke Library, Yale University.

Pages 1106 and 1124(detail): Howard University Gallery of Art, Washington, DC

Page 1107: Library of Congress Prints & Photographs Division

Page 1109: Library of Congress Prints & Photographs Division

Page 1110: Library of Congress Prints & Photographs Division

Page 1113: New York State Historical Association's Research Library

Page 1114: Frances Benjamin Johnston Collection, Library of Congress, Prints & Photographs Division

Page 1115: Library of Congress Prints & Photographs Division

Page 1117: Yale Collection of American Literature. Beinecke Rare Book and Manuscript Library.

Page 1119: © American Antiquarian Society

Pages 1120 (detail) and 1125: Library of Congress Prints & Photographs Division

Page 1121: Public Domain

Page 1123: Library of Congress Prints & Photographs Division

Page 1130: *A Woman's Work,* 1912. John Sloan (American, 1871–1951). Oil on canvas, 80.3 × 65.4 cm. The Cleveland Museum of Art, Gift of Amelia Elizabeth White 1964.60.

Page 1132: Thomas Pollock Anshutz, *The Ironworkers' Noontime,* 1880. Oil on canvas, 17 × 23 7/8 in. Fine Arts Museums of San Francisco, Gift of Mr. and Mrs. John D. Rockefeller 3rd, 1979.7.4

Page 1136: Eastman Johnson, *Cranberry Harvest, Nantucket Island* (1880). The Putnam Foundation, Timken Museum of Art, San Diego, CA

Page 1137: Winslow Homer, *The Gulf Stream.* Image copyright © The Metropolitan Museum of Art. Image source: Art Resource, NY

Page 1139: National Archives

Page 1142: Photography Collection, Miriam and Ira D. Wallach Division of Art, Prints and Photographs, The New York Public Library, Astor, Lenox and Tilden Foundations

Page 1146: Library of Congress Prints and Photographs Division

Page 1150: Library of Congress Prints and Photographs Division

Page 1157: Library of Congress Prints and Photographs Division

Page 1168: Yale Collection of American Literature, Beinecke Rare Book and Manuscript Library

Page 1180: Library of Congress Prints & Photographs Division

Page 1187: Library of Congress Prints and Photographs Division

Page 1189: New York State Historical Association's Research Library

Page 1200: Library of Congress Prints and Photographs Division

Page 1202: Library of Congress Prints and Photographs Division

Page 1207: Library of Congress Prints and Photographs Division

Page 1213: Public Domain

Page 1218: Public Domain

Page 1227: Public Domain

Page 1229: Public Domain

Page 1254: Public Domain

Page 1263: Missouri History Museum, St. Louis

Page 1273: Print Collection, Miriam and Ira D. Wallach Division of Art, Prints and Photographs, The New York Public Library, Astor, Lenox and Tilden Foundations

Page 1287: Public Domain

Page 1289: Yale Collection of American Literature, Beinecke Rare Book and Manuscript Library

Page 1296: The Schlesinger Library, Radcliffe Institute, Harvard University

Page 1298: Public Domain

Page 1312: Yale Collection of American Literature, Beinecke Rare Book and Manuscript Library

Page 1314: Library of Congress Prints and Photographs Division

Page 1328: Courtesy of the Autry National Center, Southwest Museum, Los Angeles

Page 1329: Library of Congress Prints and Photographs Division

Page 1335: Lilla Cabot Perry, *Edwin Arlington Robinson,* Colby College Special Collections, Waterville, Maine

Page 1340: Courtesy Syracuse University Library Special Collections

Page 1363: Public Domain

Page 1376: Paul Laurence Dunbar Collection, Dayton Metro Library

Page 1382: University Archives & Special Collections, University of Nebraska, Lincoln

Page 1384: Nebraska State Historical Society Photographs Collection

Page 1392: Library of Congress Prints and Photographs Division

Page 1394: Redpath Chautauqua Collection, Univ. of Iowa Libraries, Iowa City, IA

Page 1396: Photo Courtesy of U.S. Army

Page 1397: Special Collections Department, W.E.B. DuBois Library, University of Massachusetts/ Amherst

Page 1398: Courtesy of Alexandra H.C. Gordon, Yale University

Page 1399: Library of Congress Prints and Photographs Division

Page 1407: Photographic History Collection, National Museum of American History, Smithsonian Institution

Page 1420: Library of Congress Prints and Photographs Division

Page 1431: Yale Collection of American Literature, Beinecke Rare Book and Manuscript Library

Page 1435: Yale Collection of American Literature, Beinecke Rare Book and Manuscript Library

Page 1441: Yale Collection of American Literature, Beinecke Rare Book and Manuscript Library

Page 1452: Lebrecht Music and Arts Photo Library/ Alamy

Page 1454: Brooklyn Museum Archives, Goodyear Archival Collection, Visual Materials (4.1.014) Paris Exposition (1900): Palace of Electricity (#1536)

Page 1466: Picture History

Page 1468: Yale Collection of American Literature, Beinecke Rare Book and Manuscript Library

AMERICAN LITERATURE, 1914-1945

Page 1480: Library of Congress Prints and Photographs Division

Page 1482: Library of Congress Prints and Photographs Division

Page 1484: Marcel Duchamp, *Nude Descending a Staircase, No. 2,* 1912. Philadelphia Museum of Art: The Louise and Walter Arensberg

Collection, 1950/©2013 Artists Rights Society (ARS), New York/ADAGP, Paris/Succession Marcel Duchamp. Image source: Art Resource, NY.

Page 1487: Public Domain

Page 1488: National Archives

Page 1492: Public Domain

Page 1493: Library of Congress Prints and Photographs Division

Page 1494: Public Domain

Pages 1495 and (detail) 1506: Public Domain

Page 1498: © AP Photo

Pages 1499 and (detail) 1508: Library of Congress Prints and Photographs Division

Pages 1508 (detail) and 1500: Library of Congress Prints and Photographs Division

Page 1502: Library of Congress Prints and Photographs Division

Page 1503: Library of Congress Prints and Photographs Division

Page 1510: Fisk University Galleries, Nashville, Tennessee. Aaron Douglas, *Poetry*, Symbolic Negro History Series, 1930, oil on canvas.

Page 1513: Yale Collection of American Literature, Beinecke Rare Book and Manuscript Library

Page 1514: Library of Congress Prints and Photographs Division

Page 1516: Yale Collection of American Literature, Beinecke Rare Book and Manuscript Library

Page 1516: Yale Collection of American Literature, Beinecke Rare Book and Manuscript Library

Page 1516: Public Domain

Page 1516: Library of Congress Prints and Photographs Division

Page 1521: Cover image courtesy of The Modernist Journals Project/Brown University

Page 1546: Library of Congress Prints and Photographs Division

Page 1548: Public Domain

Page 1551: Houghton Library, Harvard University. MS Lowell 62 (5)

Page 1556: Library of Congress Prints and Photographs Division

Page 1566: Photo Courtesy of the National Park Service, catalog number: CARL 30461, Carl Sandburg Home National Historic Site Archives, Flat Rock, NC.

Page 1570: Reproduced by permission of The Huntington Library, San Marino, California.

Page 1582: 1920s passport photo of Mina Loy is reprinted courtesy of Roger L. Conover, for the Estate of Mina Loy.

Page 1584: Mina Loy's drawing "Consider Your Grandmother's Stays (1916)" is reprinted courtesy of Roger L. Conover, for the Estate of Mina Loy.

Page 1587: William Carlos Williams, photograph by Charles Sheeler. Copyright ©1926 Reprinted with permission of New Directions Publishing.

Page 1589: Charles Demuth, *The Figure 5 in Gold*, 1928. Oil on cardboard, H. 35-1/2, W. 30 in. (90.2 × 76.2 cm). The Metropolitan Museum of Art, Alfred Stieglitz Collection, 1949 (49.59.1) Image copyright ©The Metropolitan Museum of Art. Image source: Art Resource, NY.

Page 1597: Public Domain

Page 1599: Public Domain

Page 1605: Public Domain

Page 1611: Yale Collection of American Literature, Beinecke Rare Book and Manuscript Library

Page 1618: Yale Collection of American Literature, Beinecke Rare Book and Manuscript Library

Page 1621: Public Domain

Page 1624: © Hulton Archive/Getty Images

Page 1638: Opening manuscript page of *The Waste Land* by T. S. Eliot, 1922. From the Henry W. and Albert A. Berg Collection of English and American Literature, The New York Public Library, Astor, Lenox and Tilden Foundations, reproduced by permission of Faber & Faber Ltd, publishers of *The Waste Land*.

Page 1658: © Carl Van Vechten, courtesy Van Vechten Trust and Yale Collection of American Literature, Beinecke Rare Book and Manuscript Library.

Page 1663: Library of Congress Prints and Photographs Division

Page 1668: Public Domain

Page 1671: Houghton Library, Harvard University bMS Am 1892.8 (1)

Page 1677: Columbia University Libraries, Rare Book and Manuscript Libraries.

Page 1684: Moorland-Spingarn Research Center.

Page 1686: Yale Collection of American Literature, Beinecke Rare Book and Manuscript Library

Page 1690: Public Domain

Page 1693: Public Domain

Page 1700: Public Domain

Page 1706: Library of Congress Prints and Photographs Division

Page 1706: Public Domain

Page 1708: Sheaffer-O'Neill Collection, Connecticut College, copyright © Leona Rust Egan

Page 1711: Yale Collection of American Literature, Beinecke Rare Book and Manuscript Library

Page 1712: Yale Collection of American Literature, Beinecke Rare Book and Manuscript Library

Page 1714: Henry W. and Albert Berg Collection, NYPL, Astor, Lenox, and Tilden Foundations

Page 1716: Billy Rose Theater Collection, NYPL, Astor, Lenox and Tilden Foundations

Page 1727: Yale Collection of American Literature, Beinecke Rare Book and Manuscript Library

Page 1729: Public Domain

Page 1752: Pablo Picasso, *Gertrude Stein* © 2013 Estate of Pablo Picasso/Artists Rights Society (ARS), New York from The Metropolitan Museum of Art, Bequest of Gertrude Stein, 1946 (47.106) Image copyright © The Metropolitan Museum of Art. Image source: Art Resource, NY.

Page 1755: Max Weber, *Grand Central Terminal* (1915). Oil on canvas, 152.4 × 101.6 cm. © Museo Thyssen-Bornemisza, Madrid. Image source: Art Resource, NY.

Page 1757: Charles Demuth, *My Egypt*, 1927. © Whitney Museum of American Art, Accession #31.172.

Page 1758: Millard Sheets, *Tenement Flats (Family Flats)*, ca. 1934. Oil on canvas, 40 1/4 × 50 1/4 in. (102.1 × 127.6 cm.). Smithsonian American Art Museum, Washington, DC/Art Resource, NY.

Page 1759: John Steuart Curry, *Hoover and the Flood*, 1940. Oil on panel. Morris Museum of Art, Augusta, Georgia.

Page 1761: Public Domain

Page 1763: Arnold Genthe, Portrait of Alice B. Toklas, courtesy of The Bancroft Library, UC Berkeley

Page 1767: Library of Congress Prints and Photographs Division

Page 1769: Courtesy of John D. Maines, Clyde, Ohio

Page 1777: University of Maryland Libraries

Page 1788: © Carl Van Vechten, courtesy Van Vechten Trust and Yale Collection of American Literature, Beinecke Rare Book and Manuscript Library.

Page 1802: Maria Cristina Mena Chambers Papers, Recovering the US Hispanic Library Heritage Project, University of Houston

Page 1809: Yale Collection of American Literature, Beinecke Rare Book and Manuscript Library.

Page 1811: Yale Collection of American Literature, Beinecke Rare Book and Manuscript Library.

Page 1818: Princeton University Library, Series I, Rare Books and Special Collections Illustration © SEPS. Licensed by Curtis Licensing. All Rights Reserved.

Page 1840: Cofield Collection, Southern Media Archive, Special collections, University of Mississippi

Page 1871: Ernest Hemingway Collection, John F. Kennedy Library and Museum, Boston

Page 1873: Ernest Hemingway Collection, John F. Kennedy Library and Museum, Boston

Page 1887: © Hulton Archive/Getty Images

Page 1902: Library of Congress Prints and Photographs Division

Page 1914: Courtesy James Patterson, Gallery 119, Jackson MS

Page 1925: University of Washington Libraries, Special Collections

Page 1926: Institute of Heraldry, Department of US Army

AMERICAN LITERATURE SINCE 1945

Pages 1932–33: © Lindsay Hebberd/Corbis

Page 1935: Library of Congress Prints and Photographs Division

Page 1936: Jacket Cover © copyright 1951 by Bantam Books, a division of Random House, Inc., from THE GREAT GATSBY by F. Scott Fitzgerald. Used by permission of Random House, Inc. Any third party use of this material, outside of this publication, is prohibited. Interested parties must apply directly to Random House, Inc. for permission.

Page 1937: Courtesy of Special Collections, University of Houston Libraries

Page 1939: Library of Congress Prints and Photographs Division

Page 1940: © Museum of Television and Radio/AP Photos

Page 1942: Library of Congress Prints and Photographs Division

Page 1944: Library of Congress Prints and Photographs Division

Page 1945: © Jim Mone/AP Photo

Page 1947: © JP Laffont/Sygma/CORBIS

Page 1949: Library of Congress Prints and Photographs Division

Page 1951: Ansel Adams, *Our National Parks* by William A. Turnage, Andrea G. Stillman. Cover reprinted by permission of Little, Brown and Company, a division of Hachette Book Group, Inc.

Page 1953: www.CartoonStock.com

Page 1964: Romare Bearden, American, 1911-1988; *Summertime*, 1967; collage on board; 56 × 44 in. (142.2 × 111.8 cm); Saint Louis Art Museum, Museum Minority Artists Purchase Fund 22:1999. Courtesy of the Romare Bearden Estate. Art © Romare Bearden Foundation / Licensed by VAGA, NY.

Page 1966: George Tooker, *The Subway,* 1950. Egg tempera on composition board, 18 1/8 × 36 1/8 in. (46 × 91.8 cm). Whitney Museum of American Art, New York; purchased with funds from the Juliana Force Purchased Award 50.23 © D.C. Moore Gallery, New York.

Page 1967: Jackson Pollock, *Autumn Rhythm (Number 30),* 1950. Art Resource, New York. © 2013 The Pollock-Krasner Foundation/Artists Rights Society (ARS), New York.

Page 1971: Roy Lichtenstein, *Blam.* © Estate of Roy Lichtenstein. Image source: Yale University Art Gallery. Gift of Richard Brown Baker, B.A. 1935.

Page 1973: We Shall Be All © by the artist, Emigdio Vasquez.

Page 1975: Barbara Kruger (American, b. 1945), *Untitled (Your fictions become history)* 1983. Copyright © Barbara Kruger, courtesy Mary Boone Gallery, New York. Gelatin silver print (composite of three photographs) 76 ¼ × 39 ½. Milwaukee Art Museum. Gift of Contemporary Art Society, M1987.13.

Page 1977: © Bettmann/CORBIS

Page 1984: Library of Congress Prints and Photographs Division

Page 1992: Billy Rose Theatre Division, The New York Public Library for the Performing Arts, Astor, Lenox and Tilden Foundations

Page 1994: Photofest

Page 2005: National Bahá'i Arhives, US

Page 2013: Unknown Photographer

Page 2021: © Time & Life Pictures/Getty Images

Page 2026: Photographs and Prints Division, Schomburg Center for Research in Black Culture, The New York Public Library, Astor, Lenox and Tilden Foundations. By permission of the Gordon Parks Foundation

Page 2028: "Book Cover," copyright 1952 Renewed 1980 by Random House, Inc., from INVISIBLE MAN by Ralph Ellison. Used by permission of Random House, Inc. Any third party use of material, outside this publication, is prohibited. Interested parties must apply directly to Random House Inc. for permission.

Page 2039: © Richard Meek/Time & Life Pictures/ Getty Images

Page 2056: Houghton Library, Harvard University. bMS Am 1905 (2859)

Page 2058: Library of Congress Prints and Photographs Division

Page 2066: © Hulton Archive/Getty Images

Page 2072: © Marilyn Sanders. All Rights Reserved.

Page 2084: © AP Photos

Page 2086: © AP Photo

Page 2101: Courtesy Flannery O'Connor Collection, Georgia College & State University Library, Milledgeville, GA.

Page 2115: © Allen Ginsberg/CORBIS

Page 2127: © Fred W. McDarrah/Getty Images

Page 2131: Library of Congress Prints and Photographs Division

Page 2138: © Marian Wood Kolisch, Ursula K. Le Guin, 2009.30.35. Portland Art Museum, Portland, Oregon. Bequest of Marian Wood Kolisch

Page 2142: © Allen Ginsberg/CORBIS

Page 2148: © Ben Martin/Time & Life Pictures/ Getty Images

Page 2152: © Bernard Gotfryd/Getty Images

Page 2168: © Bettmann/CORBIS

Page 2177: © Joanne Rathe/ The Boston Globe via Getty Images

Page 2184: © Robert Abbott Sengstacke/ Getty Images

Page 2186: Photofest

Page 2201: Dagmar Schutlz/Courtesy Audre Lorde Collection, Spelman College

Page 2206: © Louis Monier/Gamma-Rapho via Getty Images

Page 2212: Photograph by LaVerne Harrell Clark, courtesy of the University of Arizona Poetry Center.

Page 2217: © Sophie Bassouls/Sygma/Corbis

Page 2225: © Margaret Randall

Page 2234: © Hulton Archive/Getty Images

Page 2243: © Frank Capri/Hulton Archive/Getty Images

Page 2248: © AP Photo/David Pickoff

Page 2249: © AP Photo/Henri Huet

Page 2263: © James Keyser/Time & Life Pictures/ Getty Images

Page 2270: © Christopher Felver/Corbis

Page 2279: © Paul Abdoo/Getty Images

Page 2284: © Christopher Felver/CORBIS

Page 2288: © Eric Gay/AP Photo

Page 2292: © AP Photo/Daily Hampshire Gazette, Kevin Gutting

Page 2296: © Rex Rystedt/MPI/Getty Images

Index of Authors and Titles

A & P, 2179
Acquainted with the Night, 1564
Ada, 1763
Adams, Henry, 1451
    Education of Henry Adams, The, from, 1455
Adams, John and Abigail Adams, 383
    Letter from Abigail Adams to John Adams (March
        31, 1776), 384
    Letter from John Adams to Abigail Adams (April 14,
        1776), 385
    Letters from John Adams to Abigail Adams (July 3,
        1776), 386
Africa, 1662
After Apple-Picking, 1559
After great pain, a formal feeling comes –, 1052
Akimel O'odham (Pima), 45
    Story of the Creation, The, 46
Alabanza: In Praise of Local 100, 2294
Alexie, Sherman, 2296
    Conversation: Sheman Alexie and Diane Thiel, A,
        from, 1982
    What You Pawn I Will Redeem, 2298
Almos' a Man, 1905
America, 1662
American Element in Fiction, from The, 1042
American History, 2213
American Scholar, The, 542
Anderson, Sherwood, 1767
    Hands, 1770
    Paper Pills, 1774
    Winesburg, Ohio, from, 1770
Anecdote of the Jar, 1578
Annabel Lee, 865
Anonymous
    Battle Hymn of the Republic, 1095
    Coming American Novelist, The, 1145
    Dixie's Land, 1083
    John Brown's Body, 1084
Ante-bellum Sermon, An, 1378
Antin, Mary, 1465
    Promised Land, from The, 1469
[anyone lived in a pretty how town], 1675
Anzaldúa, Gloria, 2224
    El sonavabitche, 2226
Apess, William, 533
    Indian's Looking-Glass for the White Man,
        An, 534
Appeal to the Colored Citizens of the World, An, from,
    520
Are These Actual Miles?, 2219

Armadillo, The, 1987
Art of Fiction, from The, 1144
As Adam Early in the Morning, 1020
"As the Lord Lives, He Is One of Our Mother's
        Children," 1290
As The Time Draws Nigh, 1039
As We Like It, from, 1619
Ashbery, John, 2127
    My Erotic Double, 2130
    One Thing That Can Save America, The, 2129
    Paradoxes and Oxymorons, 2131
Ashbridge, Elizabeth, 322
    Some Account of the Fore Part of the Life of
        Elizabeth Ashbridge, from, 324
At the 'Cadian Ball, 1265
Aubade, 1554
Author to Her Book, The, 156
Author's Account of Himself, The, 439
Autobiography of Benjamin Franklin, The, from, 294
Axe Handles, 2146

Baldwin, James, 2083
    Notes of a Native Son, 2086
Baraka, Amiri (LeRoi Jones), 2183
    Dutchman, 2186
Barn Burning, 1855
Barthelme, Donald, 2147
    School, The, 2149
Bartleby, the Scrivener, 879
Battle Hymn of the Republic, 1085
Bean Eaters, The, 2070
Beat! Beat! Drums!, 1027
Because I could not stop for Death –, 1060
Becoming of the Native: Man in America before
        Columbus, The, 52
Before the Birth of One of Her Children, 156
Bellow, Saul, 2039
    Looking for Mr. Green, 2041
Berryman, John, 2021
    Dream Songs, from The, 2023
    1 [Huffy Henry hid the day,], 2023
    4 [Filling her compact & delicious body], 2024
    14 [Life, friends, is boring. We must not say
        so], 2024
    26 [glories of the world struck me, made me aria,
        once, The], 2025
Bierce, Ambrose, 1199
    Chickamauga, 1203
Big Two-Hearted River, 1874
Birches, 1561

Bishop, Elizabeth, 1984
   Armadillo, The, 1987
   As We Like It, from, 1619
   In the Waiting Room, 1988
   One Art, 1991
   Sestina, 1986
Black Mother Woman, 2205
Black Riders and Other Lines, from *The*, 1360
[Black riders came from the sea], (I), 1360
Blood-Burning Moon, 1812
Book of American Negro Poetry, from The Preface to
   The, 1535
Boy Who Grew Up at Ta'k'imiłding, The, 50
Bradford, William, 116
   Of Plimoth Plantation, from, 119
Bradstreet, Anne, 150
   Author to Her Book, The, 156
   Before the Birth of One of Her Children, 156
   Epitaph on My Dear and Ever-Honoured Mother
      Mrs. Dorothy Dudley, Who Deceased December
      27, 1643, and of Her Age, 61, An, 155
   Here Follows Some Verses upon the Burning of
      Our House July 10th, 1666, Copied Out of a
      Loose Paper, 159
   Letter to Her Husband, Absent upon Public
      Employment, A, 158
   Prologue, The, 153
   To Her Father with Some Verses, 155
   To My Dear and Loving Husband, 157
   To My Dear Children, 161
Brain – is wider than the Sky –, The, 1058
Brass Spittoons, 1697
Brattle, Thomas, 206
   Letter of Thomas Brattle (1692), from, 207
Brief and True Narrative, A, from, 194
Brooks, Gwendolyn, 2065
   Bean Eaters, The, 2070
   kitchenette building, 2068
   Malcolm X, 2071
   mother, the, 2069
   song in the front yard, a, 2070
   Street in Bronzeville, from *A*, 2068
   We Real Cool, 2071
Brown, John, 1076
   John Brown's Last Speech, 1077
Brown, Sterling A., 1684
   Southern Road, 1686
   Strong Men, 1688
Brownson, Orestes A., 524
   Laboring Classes, The, from, 525
Bryant, William Cullen, 467, 1096
   Death of Lincoln, The, 1097
   Thanatopsis, 468
   To a Waterfowl, 472
   To Cole, The Painter, Departing for Europe, 473
   Yellow Violet, The, 471

[Buffalo Bill 's], 1672
Bulosan, Carlos, 1924
   End of the War, The, 1927
Burnt Norton, 1652
Bustle in a House, The, 1063
Butcher Rogaum's Door, 1365
Byrd, William, 225
   Secret Diary of William Byrd of Westover, The,
      from, 227

Cacoethes Scribendi, 456
[Cambridge ladies who live in furnished souls,
   the], 1673
Canary, 2287
Captive, 966
Carver, Raymond, 2216
   Are These Actual Miles?, 2219
Cather, Willa, 1382
   Wagner Matinée, A, 1385
Cautionary Tale an a Partisan View, A, from, 1800
Cavalry Crossing a Ford, 1027
Champlain, Samuel de, 83
   Voyages of Samuel de Champlain, The, from, 85
Cherokee, 37
   How the World Was Made, 39
Cherokee Memorials, The, 514
   Memorial of the Cherokee Council (November 5,
      1829), 514
Chesnut, Mary Boykin Miller, 1093
   Diary from Dixie, A, from (April 19-22, 1865), 1094
Chesnutt, Charles W., 1273
   Passing of Grandison, The, 1275
Chicago, 1568
Chicago River, 1623
Chickamauga, 1203
Chopin, Kate, 1263
   At the 'Cadian Ball, 1265
Christ in Alabama, 1698
Cisneros, Sandra, 2288
   Mericans, 2289
   Note to Gloria from the Bottom of the Sea,
      A, 2232
City of Orgies, 1021
Coal, 2203
Columbus, Christopher, 64
   Letter of Columbus, Describing the Results of His
      First Voyage, 67
Coming American Novelist, The, 1145
"Coming" Woman, The, 874
Common Sense, from, 379
Conversation: Sheman Alexie and Diane Thiel,
   A, from, 1982
Cooke, Rose Terry, 965
   Captive, 966
   "Harvest Is Past, The," 967
   Here, 966

Crane, Hart, 1541, 1676
    Modern Poetry, from, 1541
    To Brooklyn Bridge, 1682
    Voyages, 1679
Crane, Stephen, 1340
    I [Black riders came from the sea], 1360
    I [Do not weep, maiden, for war is kind], 1361
    XIV [There was crimson clash of war], 1360
    XIX [god in wrath, A], 1361
    XXIV [I saw a man pursuing the horizon], 1361
    Black Riders and Other Lines, from The, 1360
    Open Boat, The, 1342
    War Is Kind, from, 1361
Creation, The, 1549
Criticism and Fiction, from, 1148
Cullen, Countee, 1699
    Heritage, 1702
    Yet Do I Marvel, 1701
Cummings, E. E., 1668
    [anyone lived in a pretty how town], 1675
    [Buffalo Bill 's], 1672
    [Cambridge ladies who live in furnished souls, the], 1673
    [i sing of Olaf glad and big], 1674
    [in Just-], 1672
    ["next to of course god america i], 1673
Cuttings, 1980
Cuttings (later), 1980
Cross, 1697

Daddy, 2171
Danse Russe, 1590
Davis, Jefferson, 1078
    Jefferson Davis's Inaugural Address, 1079
Davis, Rebecca Harding, 905
    Life in the Iron-Mills, 908
Days, 593
Dead at Quang Tri, 2265
Dear John, Dear Coltrane, 2214
Death of a Soldier, The, 1578
Death of Lincoln, The, 1097
Decade, A, 1555
Declaration of Sentiments, 528
DeLillo, Don, 2205
    Videotape, 2208
Desert Places, 1564
Diary from Dixie, A, from (April 19-22, 1865), 1094
Diary of Samson Occum, The, 356
Diary of Samuel Sewall, The, from, 213
Dickinson, Emily, 1043
    After great pain, a formal feeling comes –, 1052
    Because I could not stop for Death –, 1060
    Brain – is wider than the Sky –, The, 1058
    Bustle in a House, The, 1063
    Elysium is as far as to, 1066

Exchange with Susan Gilbert Dickinson (summer 1861), 1067
"Faith" is a fine invention, 1047
God is a distant – stately Lover –, 1053
I can wade Grief –, 1050
I dwell in Possibility –, 1059
I felt a Funeral, in my Brain, 1051
I heard a Fly buzz – when I died –, 1056
I like a look of Agony, 1049
I never lost as much but twice, 1046
I never saw a Moor –, 1062
I taste a liquor never brewed –, 1048
I'm ceded – I've stopped being Theirs –, 1057
I'm Nobody! Who are you?, 1051
I'm "wife" – I've finished that –, 1047
Indian Summer, 1046
It feels a shame to be Alive –, 1054
Much Madness is divinest Sense, 1054
My life closed twice before its close –, 1065
My Life had stood – a Loaded Gun –, 1061
narrow Fellow in the Grass, A, 1062
Pain – has an Element of Blank –, 1059
Poets light but Lamps –, The, 1061
Publication – is the Auction, 1059
Rearrange a "Wife's" affection!, 1065
Revolution is the Pod, 1063
Route of Evanescence, A, 1064
Safe in their Alabaster Chambers – (1859 and 1861 versions), 1048
Some keep the Sabbath going to Church –, 1052
Soul has Bandaged moments –, The, 1057
Soul selects her own Society –, The, 1051
Spider holds a Silver Ball, The, 1058
Success is counted sweetest, 1047
Tell all the Truth but tell it slant –, 1064
There's a certain Slant of light, 1050
These are the days when Birds come back –, 1046
They dropped like Flakes –, 1054
This is my letter to the World, 1054
This was a Poet – It is That, 1055
This World is not Conclusion, 1056
Title divine – is mine!, 1063
To Thomas Wentworth Higginson (7 June 1862), 1068
What Soft – Cherubic Creatures –, 1953
Wild Nights – Wild Nights!, 1049
Word made Flesh is seldom, A, 1064
Diminuendo, 1622
Diving into the Wreck, 2135
Dixie's Land, 1083
[Do not weep, maiden, for war is kind], (I), 1361
Doolittle, Hilda (H.D.), 1605
    Garden, 1608
    Helen, 1610
    Leda, 1609

Oread, 1607
Pool, The, 1608
Sea Rose, 1609
Douglass, Frederick, 700
   Narrative of the Life of Frederick Douglass, An
      American Slave, Written by Himself, 702
Dove, Rita, 2284
   Canary , 2287
   History, 2287
   House Slave, The, 2284
   Kentucky, 1833, 2286
Draft of the Declaration of Independence, 389
Dream Songs, from *The,* 2023
Dreiser, Theodore, 1362
   Butcher Rogaum's Door, 1365
Drowned Mariner, The, 951
Du Bois, W. E. B, 1431
   Souls of Black Folk, from *The,* 1434
Dunbar, Paul Laurence, 1376
   Ante-bellum Sermon, An, 1378
   Sympathy, 1381
   We Wear the Mask, 1381
Dutchman, 2186

Editha, 1190
Education of Henry Adams, The, from, 1455
Edwards, Jonathan, 231
   Personal Narrative, 233
   Sinners in the Hands of an Angry God, 245
Egyptian Pulled Glass Bottle in the Shape of a Fish,
   An, 1618
El sonavabitche, 2226
Eliot, T. S., 1530, 1623
   Burnt Norton, 1652
   Journey of the Magi, 1650
   Love Song of J. Alfred Prufrock, The, 1626
   Tradition and the Individual Talent, from, 1531
   Waste Land, The, 1633
Ellison, Ralph, 2025
   Invisible Man, The, 2028
Elysium is as far as to, 1066
Emerson, Ralph Waldo, 539
   American Scholar, The, 542
   Days, 593
   Experience, 574
   Rhodora: On Being Asked, Whence Is the Flower?,
      The, 590
   Self-Reliance, 555
   Snow-Storm, The, 591
Emperor Jones, The, 1731
Emperor of Ice-Cream, The, 1580
End of the War, The, 1927
Epitaph on My Dear and Ever-Honoured Mother Mrs.
   Dorothy Dudley, Who Deceased December 27,
   1643, and of Her Age, 61, An, 155

Equiano, Olaudah, 359
   Interesting Narrative of the Life of Olaudah
      Equiano, or Gustavus Vassa, the African,
      Written by Himself, The, from, 361
Espada, Martín, 2292
   Alabanza: In Praise of Local 100, 2294
Ethiopia, 964
Everyday Use, 2236
Exchange with Susan Gilbert Dickinson (summer
      1861), 1067
Experience, 574

Facing It, 2269
"Faith" is a fine invention, 1047
Fall of the House of Usher, The, 829
Farewell of a Virginia Slave Mother to Her Daughters
   Sold into Southern Bondage, The, 960
Faulkner, William, 1840
   Barn Burning, 1855
   That Evening Sun, 1843
Faulkner and Women, from, 1869
Fence, A, 1568
Fern, Fanny (Sara Payson Willis Parton), 866
   "Coming" Woman, The, 874
   Hints to Young Wives, 969
   "Independence," 875
   Law More Nice Than Just, A, 873
   Male Criticism on Ladies' Books, 872
   Sober Husband, The, 870
   Tear of a Wife, The, 870
Few Don'ts by an Imagiste, from A, 1524
Figure a Poem Makes, The, 1543
[Filling her compact & delicious body], (4), 2024
Fire and Ice, 1562
First Fig, 1665
Fish, The, 1616
Fitzgerald, F. Scott, 1818
   Ice Palace, The, 1821
Flight, 1889
Flowering Judas, 1779
Fog, 1569
For the Union Dead, 2063
Franklin, Benjamin, 290
   Autobiography of Benjamin Franklin, The, from, 294
Frederick Douglass, 769
Freeman's Dream: A Parable, The, 616
Freneau, Philip, 421
   Indian Burying Ground, The, 426
   On the Emigration to America, 423
   Wild Honey Suckle, The, 425
Frost, Robert, 1543, 1556
   Acquainted with the Night, 1564
   After Apple-Picking, 1559
   Birches, 1561
   Desert Places, 1564

Figure a Poem Makes, The, 1543
Fire and Ice, 1562
Gift Outright, The, 1565
Mending Wall, 1558
Nothing Gold Can Stay, 1563
Road Not Taken, The, 1560
Stopping by Woods on a Snowy Evening, 1563
Fujita, Jun, 1621
Chicago River, 1623
Diminuendo, 1622
Michigan Boulevard, 1622
Fuller, Margaret, 594
Woman in the Nineteenth Century, from, 596

Garden, 1608
Garland, Hamlin, 1150
Literary Emancipation of the West, from, 1151
Garnet, Henry Highland, 1090
Memorial Discourse, A, from (February 12, 1865), 1091
Garrison, William Lloyd, 522
To the Public, 523
Generall Historie of Virginia, New-England, and the Summer Isles, The, from, 107
Gettysburg Address (1863), The, 1087
Gift Outright, The, 1565
Gilded Six-Bits, The, 1791
Gilman, Charlotte Perkins, 1296
Yellow Wall-Paper, The, 1299
Ginsberg, Allen, 2115
Howl, 2117
Supermarket in California, A, 1041
Glaspell, Susan, 1714
Trifles, 1717
[glories of the world struck me, made me aria, once, The], (26), 2025
[god in wrath, A], (XIX), 1361
God is a distant – stately Lover –, 1053
Good Man Is Hard to Find, A, 2014
Grass, 1569
Great Figure, The, 1593

Hands, 1770
Harjo, Joy, 2279
If You Look with the Mind of the Swirling Earth, 2283
New Orleans, 2281
This Land Is a Poem, 2283
Harlem, 1699
Harlem Dancer, The, 1660
Harper, Frances E. W., 962
Ethiopia, 963
Slave Mother, The, 963
Harper, Michael S., 2211
American History, 2213
Dear John, Dear Coltrane, 2214
Martin's Blues, 2216

"Harvest Is Past, The," 967
Hawthorne, Julian, 1142
American Element in Fiction, from The, 1042
Hawthorne, Nathaniel, 779
My Kinsman, Major Molineux, 782
Rappaccini's Daughter, 806
Young Goodman Brown, 796
Hayden, Robert, 2005
Frederick Douglass, 769
Middle Passage, 2007
Helen, 1610
Hemingway, Ernest, 1871
Big Two-Hearted River, 1874
Here, 966
Here Follows Some Verses upon the Burning of Our House July 10th, 1666, Copied Out of a Loose Paper, 159
Here the Frailest Leaves of Me, 121
Heritage, 1702
Hints to Young Wives, 869
History, 2287
Hopkins, Pauline E., 1287
"As the Lord Lives, He Is One of Our Mother's Children," 1290
House Slave, The, 2285
How the World Was Made (Cherokee), 39
Howells, William Dean, 1147, 1187
Criticism and Fiction, from, 1148
Editha, 1190
Howl, 2117
[Huffy Henry hid   the day,], (1), 2023
Hughes, Langston, 1536, 1690
Brass Spittoons, 1697
Christ in Alabama, 1698
Cross, 1697
Harlem, 1699
I, Too, 1695
Jazzonia, 1694
Mother to Son, 1694
Negro Artist and the Racial Mountain, The, 1537
Negro Speaks of Rivers, The, 1693
Old Walt, 1041
Weary Blues, The, 1696
Hunters of Men, The, 959
Hupa, 48
Boy Who Grew Up at Ta'k'imiłding, The, 50
Hurston, Zora Neale, 1788
Gilded Six-Bits, The, 1791
Huswifery, 224

"I Am in Danger – Sir –," 1071
[I, being born a woman and distressed], 1666
I can wade Grief –, 1050
I dwell in Possibility –, 1050

I felt a Funeral, in my Brain, 1051
I heard a Fly buzz – when I died –, 1056
I like a look of Agony, 1049
I never lost as much but twice, 1046
I never saw a Moor –, 1062
[I saw a man pursuing the horizon], (XXIV), 1361
I Saw in Louisiana a Live-Oak Growing, 1021
[i sing of Olaf glad and big], 1674
I Stand Here Ironing, 2015
I taste a liquor never brewed –, 1048
I, Too, 1695
Ice Palace, The, 1821
If We Must Die, 1661
If You Look with the Mind of the Swirling Earth, 2283
I'm ceded – I've stopped being Theirs –, 1057
I'm Nobody! Who are you?, 1051
I'm "wife" – I've finished that –, 1047
Impressions of America, 1402
In a Station of the Metro [First Version], 1602
In a Station of the Metro [Final Version], 1602
[in Just-], 1672
In Paths Untrodden, 1020
In the Waiting Room, 1988
Incidents in the Life of a Slave Girl, from, 624
"Independence," 875
Indian Burying Ground, The, 426
Indian Names, 946
Indian Summer, 1046
Indian's Looking-Glass for the White Man, An, 534
Interesting Narrative of the Life of Olaudah Equiano,
    or Gustavus Vassa, the African, Written by
    Himself, The, from, 361
Introduction to Chapters from My Autobiography,
    from, 1184
Invisible Man, The, 2028
Irving, Washington, 436
    Author's Account of Himself, The, 439
    Rip Van Winkle, 441
It feels a shame to be Alive –, 1054
"Its Wavering Image," 1330

Jacobs, Harriet, 619
    Incidents in the Life of a Slave Girl, from, 624
    Letter from a Fugitive Slave [New-York Tribune,
    1853], 620
James, Henry, 1143, 1207
    Art of Fiction, from The, 1144
    Jolly Corner, The, 1230
    Real Thing, The, 1210
Janitor, The, 2246
Jazzonia, 1694
Jefferson, Thomas, 389
    Draft of the Declaration of Independence, 389
    Notes on the State of Virginia, from, 394
Jefferson Davis's Inaugural Address, 1079

Jewel Stairs' Grievance, The, 1604
Jewett, Sarah Orne, 1254
    White Heron, A, 1256
Jewish Cemetery at Newport, The, 954
Jim Smiley and His Jumping Frog, 1159
John Brown's Body, 1084
John Brown's Last Speech, 1077
Johnson, James Weldon, 1534, 1546
    Book of American Negro Poetry, from The Preface
        to The, 1535
    Creation, The, 1549
Jolly Corner, The, 1230
Jones, Absalom, 406
    Petition of the People of Colour, 407
Journal of John Woolman, The, from, 336
Journey of the Magi, 1650
Justice Denied in Massachusetts, 1667

Kentucky, 1833, 2286
kitchenette building, 2068
Komunyakaa, Yusef, 2263
    Dead at Quang Tri, 2265
    Facing It, 2269
    Prisoners, 2267
    Tu Do Street, 2266

Laboring Classes, The, from, 525
Lady Lazarus, 2174
Lakota, 40
    Wohpe and the Gift of the Pipe, 42
Lament of the Frontier Guard, 1604
Law More Nice Than Just, A, 873
Lawson, Deodat, 194
    Brief and True Narrative, A, from, 194
Leda, 1609
Le Guin, Ursula K., 2138
    She Unnames Them, 2140
Letter from a Fugitive Slave [New-York Tribune, 1853],
    620
Letter from Abigail Adams to John Adams (March 31,
    1776), 384
Letter from John Adams to Abigail Adams (April 14,
    1776), 385
Letter of Columbus, Describing the Results of His First
    Voyage, 67
Letter of Thomas Brattle (1692), from, 207
Letter to Her Husband, Absent upon Public
    Employment, A, 158
Letter to Samson Occom (February 11, 1774), 435
Letter to the Touro Synagogue (1790), 400
Letters from an American Farmer, from, 375
Letters from John Adams to Abigail Adams (July 3,
    1776), 386
[Life, friends, is boring. We must not say so], (14), 2024
Life in the Iron-Mills, 908

Lily Daw and the Three Ladies, 1916
Lincoln, Abraham, 1086
    Gettysburg Address, The (1863), 1087
    Second Inaugural Address (March 4, 1865), 1088
Literary Emancipation of the West, from, 1151
Longfellow, Henry Wadsworth, 953
    Jewish Cemetery at Newport, The, 854
    My Lost Youth, 956
Looking for Mr. Green, 2041
Lorde, Audre, 2201
    Black Mother Woman, 2206
    Coal, 2203
    Woman Thing, The, 2204
Love Song of J. Alfred Prufrock, The, 1626
Love Songs, 1584
Lowell, Amy, 1526, 1551
    Aubade, 1554
    Decade, A, 1555
    Madonna of the Evening Flowers, 1555
    New Manner in Modern Poetry, The, 1527
    Taxi, The, 1553
    Venus Transiens, 1554
Lowell, Robert, 2056
    For the Union Dead, 2063
    Memories of West Street and Lepke, 2059
    Skunk Hour, 2061
Loy, Mina, 1581
    Love Songs, 1584
Luke Havergal, 1337
Lynching, The, 1661

Madonna of the Evening Flowers, 1555
Malcolm X, 2071
Male Criticism on Ladies' Books, 872
Martí, José, 1399
    Impressions of America, 1402
Martin's Blues, 2216
Mather, Cotton, 201
    Wonders of the Invisible World, The, from, 201
McKay, Claude, 1658
    Africa, 1662
    America, 1662
    Harlem Dancer, The, 1660
    If We Must Die, 1661
    Lynching, The, 1661
Meditation 8 (First Series) John 6:51 I am the Living
    Bread, 220
Melville, Herman, 876
    Bartleby, the Scrivener, 879
Memoranda during the War, from, 1098
Memorial Discourse, A, from (February 12, 1865), 1091
Memorial of the Cherokee Council (November 5, 1829), 514
Memories of West Street and Lepke, 2059
Mena, María Cristina, 1802
    Vine-Leaf, The, 1804

Mending Wall, 1558
Mericans, 2289
Michigan Boulevard, 1622
Middle Passage, 2007
Mill, The, 1339
Millay, Edna St. Vincent, 1663
    First Fig, 1665
    [I, being born a woman and distressed], 1666
    Justice Denied in Massachusetts, 1667
    [Oh, oh, you will be sorry for that word!], 1666
    Second Fig, 1666
Miller, Arthur
    Introduction to Chapters from My Autobiography,
        from, 1184
Miniver Cheevy, 1338
Mirror, 2170
Mishosha, or the Magician and His Daughters, 475
Modell of Christian Charity, A, 138
Modern Poetry, from, 1541
Momaday, N. Scott
    Becoming of the Native: Man in America before
        Columbus, The, 52
Monroe, Harriet, 1522
    Motive of the Magazine, The, 1522
Moore, Marianne, 1611
    Egyptian Pulled Glass Bottle in the Shape of a
        Fish, An, 1618
    Fish, The, 1616
    Poetry [First Version], 1614
    Poetry [Final Version], 1615
    To a Snail, 1617
    To Military Progress, 1615
Morning Song, 2170
Morrison, Toni, 2151
    Faulkner and Women, from, 1869
    Recitatif, 2153
mother, the, 2069
Mother to Son, 1694
Motive of the Magazine, The, 1522
Much Madness is divinest Sense, 1054
Murray, Judith Sargent, 401
    On the Equality of the Sexes, from, 402
Murray, Rose
    Puritan Woman, 167
My Erotic Double, 2130
My Kinsman, Major Molineux, 782
My life closed twice before its close —, 1065
My Life had stood — a Loaded Gun —, 1061
My Lost Youth, 956
My Papa's Waltz, 1979

Narrative of Cabeza de Vaca, The, from, 76
Narrative of the Life of Frederick Douglass, An
    American Slave, Written by Himself, 702
narrow Fellow in the Grass, A, 1062

Negro Artist and the Racial Mountain, The, 1537
Negro Speaks of Rivers, The, 1693
New Manner in Modern Poetry, The, 1527
New Orleans, 2281
["next to of course god america i], 1673
Noiseless Patient Spider, A, 1039
Norris, Frank, 1152
    Plea for Romantic Fiction, A, 1152
Notes of a Native Son, 2086
Note to Gloria from the Bottom of the Sea, A, 2232
Notes on the State of Virginia, from, 394
Nothing Gold Can Stay, 1563

O'Brien, Tim, 2247
    Things They Carried, The, 2250
Occom, Samson, 347
    Short Narrative of My Life, A, 349
O'Connor, Flannery, 2101
    Good Man Is Hard to Find, A, 2104
Of Plimoth Plantation, from, 119
Of Modern Poetry, 11581
[Oh, oh, you will be sorry for that word!], 1666
Old Walt, 1041
Olsen, Tillie, 2013
    I Stand Here Ironing, 2015
On Being Brought from Africa to America, 430
On the Emigration to America, 423
On the Equality of the Sexes, from, 402
Once I Pass'd through a Populous City, 1019
One Art, 1991
One Thing That Can Save America, The, 2129
O'Neill, Eugene, 1726
    Emperor Jones, The, 1731
One's-Self I Sing, 972
Open Boat, The, 1342
Oread, 1607
Ottery, James
    Diary of Samson Occum, The, 356
Out of the Cradle Endlessly Rocking, 1022

Pact, A, 1600
Pain – has an Element of Blank –, 1059
Paine, Thomas, 379
    Common Sense, from, 379
Paper Pills, 1774
Paradoxes and Oxymorons, 2131
Passing of Grandison, The, 1275
Personal Narrative, 233
Petition of the People of Colour, 407
Picasso, 1765
Pima, 46
    Story of the Creation, The, 46
Plath, Sylvia, 2168
    Daddy, 2171
    Lady Lazarus, 2174

Mirror, 2170
Morning Song, 2170
Plea for Romantic Fiction, A, 1152
Poe, Edgar Allan, 827
    Annabel Lee, 865
    Fall of the House of Usher, The, 829
    Purloined Letter, The, 847
    Raven, The, 862
    Sonnet – to Science, 861
    Tell-Tale Heart, The, 843
    To Helen, 862
Poet in the House, A, 1072
Poetry [First Version], 1614
Poetry [Final Version], 1615
Poets light but Lamps –, The, 1061
Pool, The, 1608
Porter, Katherine Anne, 1776
    Flowering Judas, 1779
Portrait d'une Femme, 1599
Portrait in Georgia, 1812
Portrait of a Lady, 1591
Portrait of a Madonna, 1995
Pound, Ezra, 1523, 1597
    Few Don'ts by an Imagiste, from A, 1524
    In a Station of the Metro [First Version], 1602
    In a Station of the Metro [Final Version], 1602
    Jewel Stairs' Grievance, The, 1604
    Lament of the Frontier Guard, 1604
    Pact, A, 600
    Portrait d'une Femme, 1599
    Rest, The, 1601
    River-Merchant's Wife: A Letter, The, 1603
Preface to Uncle Tom's Cabin, 617
Preparatory Meditations, from, 219
Prisoners, 2267
Private History of a Campaign That Failed, The, 1167
Prologue [Preparatory Meditations], 219
Prologue, The (Bradstreet), 153
Promised Land, from The, 1469
Publication – is the Auction, 1059
Puritan Woman, 167
Purloined Letter, The, 847

Queen-Anne's-Lace, 1592
Quicksand, The, 1315

Rappaccini's Daughter, 806
Raven, The, 862
Real Thing, The, 1020
Rearrange a "Wife's" affection!, 1065
Recitatif, 2153
Reconciliation, 1031
Red Wheelbarrow, The, 1596
Resistance to Civil Government, 650
Rest, The, 1601

Revolution is the Pod, 1063
Rhodora: On Being Asked, Whence Is the Flower?, The, 590
Rich, Adrienne, 2131
　　Diving into the Wreck, 2135
　　"I Am in Danger – Sir –," 1071
　　Trying to Talk with a Man, 2134
　　Valediction Forbidding Mourning, A, 2134
Richard Cory, 1338
Rip Van Winkle, 441
Riprap, 2145
River-Merchant's Wife: A Letter, The, 1603
Road Not Taken, The, 1560
Robinson, Edwin Arlington, 1334
　　Luke Havergal, 1337
　　Mill, The, 1339
　　Miniver Cheevy, 1338
　　Richard Cory, 1338
Roethke, Theodore, 1977
　　Cuttings, 1980
　　Cuttings (later), 1980
　　My Papa's Waltz, 1979
　　Root Cellar, 1980
　　Waking, The, 1981
Root Cellar, 1980
Route of Evanescence, A, 1064
Rowlandson, Mary, 169
　　Sovereignty and Goodness of God, The, 171

Safe in their Alabaster Chambers – (1859 and 1861 versions), 1048
St. John de Crèvecoeur, J. Hector, 374
　　Letters from an American Farmer, from, 375
Sandburg, Carl, 1565
　　Chicago, 1568
　　Fence, A, 1568
　　Fog, 1569
　　Grass, 1569
School, The, 2149
School Days of an Indian Girl, The, 1409
Schoolcraft, Jane Johnston, 473
　　Mishosha, or the Magician and His Daughters, 475
Sea Rose, 1609
Seamstress, The, 609
Second Fig, 1666
Second Inaugural Address (March 4, 1865; Lincoln), 1088
Secret Diary of William Byrd of Westover, The, from, 227
Sedgwick, Catharine Maria, 454
　　Cacoethes Scribendi, 456
Self-Reliance, 555
Seneca Falls Woman's Convention, 527
　　Declaration of Sentiments, 528
Sestina, 1986
Seventeen Syllables, 2074

Sewall, Samuel, 212
　　Diary of Samuel Sewall, The, from, 213
She Unnames Them, 2140
Short Narrative of My Life, A, 349
Sight in Camp in the Daybreak Gray and Dim, A, 1028
Sigourney, Lydia, 945
　　Indian Names, 946
　　To a Shred of Linen, 947
Silko, Leslie Marmon, 2270
　　Yellow Woman, 2272
Sinners in the Hands of an Angry God, 245
Skunk Hour, 2061
Slave Mother, The, 963
Smith, Elizabeth Oakes, 949
　　Drowned Mariner, The, 951
　　Unattained, The, 950
Smith, Captain John, 104
　　Generall Historie of Virginia, New-England, and the Summer Isles, The, from, 107
Snow Man, The, 1579
Snow-Storm, The, 591
Snyder, Gary, 2142
　　Axe Handles, 2146
　　Riprap, 2145
　　Wave, 2145
Sober Husband, The, 870
Some Account of the Fore Part of the Life of Elizabeth Ashbridge, from, 324
Some keep the Sabbath going to Church –, 1052
Song, Cathy
　　Poet in the House, A, 1072
song in the front yard, a, 2070
Sort of a Song, A, 1596
Song of Myself, 973
Sonnet – to Science, 861
Soul has Bandaged moments –, The, 1057
Soul selects her own Society –, The, 1051
Souls of Black Folk, from The, 1434
Southern Road, 1686
Sovereignty and Goodness of God, The, 171
Speech of Tecumseh to Governor Harrison, 410
Speech to a Women's Rights Convention, 531
Spider holds a Silver Ball, The, 1058
Stein, Gertrude, 1761
　　Ada, 1763
　　Picasso, 1765
Steinbeck, John, 1887
　　Flight, 1889
Stevens, Wallace, 1570
　　Anecdote of the Jar, 1578
　　Death of a Soldier, The, 1578
　　Emperor of Ice-Cream, The, 1580
　　Of Modern Poetry, 1581
　　Snow Man, The, 1579
　　Sunday Morning, 1572

Tea at the Palaz of Hoon, 1579
Thirteen Ways of Looking at a Blackbird, 1576
Stopping by Woods on a Snowy Evening, 1563
Story of the Creation, The, 46
Stowe, Harriet Beecher, 607
    Freeman's Dream: A Parable, The, 616
    Preface to *Uncle Tom's Cabin*, 617
    Seamstress, The, 609
Street in Bronzeville, from *A*, 2068
Strong Men, 1688
Success is counted sweetest, 1047
Sui Sin Far (Edith Maud Eaton), 1327
    "Its Wavering Image," 1330
Sunday Morning, 1572
Supermarket in California, A, 1041
Sympathy, 1381

Taylor, Edward, 217
    Huswifery, 224
    Meditation 8 (First Series) John 6:51 I am the
        Living Bread, 220
    Prologue [*Preparatory Meditations*], 219
    Upon a Spider Catching a Fly, 223
    Upon Wedlock, and Death of Children, 221
Taxi, The, 1553
Tea at the Palaz of Hoon, 1579
Tear of a Wife, The, 870
Tecumseh, 409
    Speech of Tecumseh to Governor Harrison, 410
Tell all the Truth but tell it slant –, 1064
Tell-Tale Heart, The, 843
Thanatopsis, 468
That Evening Sun, 1843
There's a certain Slant of light, 1050
[There was crimson clash of war], (XI), 1360
These are the days when Birds come back –, 1046
They dropped like Flakes –, 1054
Things They Carried, The, 2250
Thirteen Ways of Looking at a Blackbird, 1576
This Is Just to Say, 1596
This is my letter to the World, 1054
This Land Is a Poem, 2283
This was a Poet – It is That, 1055
This World is not Conclusion, 1056
Thoreau, Henry David, 648
    Resistance to Civil Government, 650
    Walden, from, 666
Thou Reader, 972
Title divine – is mine!, 1063
To a Shred of Linen, 947
To a Snail, 1617
To a Waterfowl, 472
To Brooklyn Bridge, 1682
To Cole, The Painter, Departing for Europe, 473
To Elsie, 1594

To Helen, 862
To Her Father with Some Verses, 155
To His Excellency General Washington, 434
To Military Progress, 1615
To My Dear and Loving Husband, 157
To My Dear Children, 161
To S. M. a Young *African* Painter, on Seeing His Works,
    432
To the Public, 523
To the Right Honourable William, Earl of Dartmouth,
    His Majesty's Principal Secretary of State for
    North-America &c., 431
To the University of Cambridge, in New England, 430
To Thomas Wentworth Higginson (7 June 1862), 1068
Toomer, Jean, 1809
    Blood-Burning Moon, 1812
    Portrait in Georgia, 1812
Tradition and the Individual Talent, from, 1531
Trifles, 1717
True Story, Repeated Word for Word as I Heard It, A, 1164
Truth, Sojourner, 531
    Speech to a Women's Rights Convention, 531
Trying to Talk with a Man, 2134
Tu Do Street, 2266
Twain, Mark (Samuel L. Clemens), 1157
    Jim Smiley and His Jumping Frog, 1159
    Private History of a Campaign That Failed,
        The, 1167
    True Story, Repeated Word for Word as I Heard It,
        A, 1164
    War Prayer, The, 1181

Unattained, The, 950
Up from Slavery, from, 1423
Updike, John, 2177
    A & P, 2179
Upon a Spider Catching a Fly, 223
Upon Wedlock, and Death of Children, 221

Vaca, Álvar Núñez Cabeza de, 73
    Narrative of Cabeza de Vaca, The, from, 76
Valediction Forbidding Mourning, A, 2134
Venus Transiens, 1554
Videotape, 2208
Vigil Strange I Kept on the Field One Night, 1028
Vine-Leaf, The, 1804
Voyages, 1679
Voyages of Samuel de Champlain, The, from, 85

Wagner Matinée, A, 1385
Waking, The, 1981
Walden, from, 666
Walker, Alice, 2234
    Cautionary Tale an a Partisan View, A, from, 1800
    Everyday Use, 2236

Walker, David, 519
    Appeal to the Colored Citizens of the World, An,
        from, 520
War Is Kind, from, 1361
War Prayer, The, 1181
Washington, Booker T., 1420
    Up from Slavery, from, 1423
Washington, George, 399
    Letter to the Touro Synagogue (1790), 400
Waste Land, The, 1633
Wave, 2145
We Real Cool, 2071
We Wear the Mask, 1381
Weary Blues, The, 1696
Welty, Eudora, 1914
    Lily Daw and the Three Ladies, 1916
Wharton, Edith, 1311
    Quicksand, The, 1315
What Soft — Cherubic Creatures —, 1053
What You Pawn I Will Redeem, 2298
Wheatley, Phillis, 427
    Letter to Samson Occom (February 11, 1774), 435
    On Being Brought from Africa to America, 430
    To His Excellency General Washington, 434
    To S. M. a Young *African* Painter, on Seeing His
        Works, 432
    To the Right Honourable William, Earl of Dart-
        mouth, His Majesty's Principal Secretary of
        State for North-America, &c., 431
    To the University of Cambridge, in New England, 430
When Lilacs Last in the Dooryard Bloom'd, 1032
White Heron, A, 1256
Whitman, Walt, 968, 1098
    As Adam Early in the Morning, 1020
    As The Time Draws Nigh, 1039
    Beat! Beat! Drums!, 1027
    Cavalry Crossing a Ford, 1027
    City of Orgies, 1021
    Here the Frailest Leaves of Me, 121
    I Saw in Louisiana a Live-Oak Growing, 1021
    In Paths Untrodden, 1020
    Memoranda during the War, from, 1098
    Noiseless Patient Spider, A, 1039
    Once I Pass'd through a Populous City, 1019
    One's-Self I Sing, 972
    Out of the Cradle Endlessly Rocking, 1022
    Reconciliation, 1031
    Sight in Camp in the Daybreak Gray and Dim, A,
        1028
    Song of Myself, 973
    Thou Reader, 972
    Vigil Strange I Kept on the Field One Night, 1028

When Lilacs Last in the Dooryard Bloom'd, 1032
    Wound-Dresser, The, 1029
Whittier, John Greenleaf, 958
    Farewell of a Virginia Slave Mother to Her
        Daughters Sold into Southern Bondage,
        The, 960
    Hunters of Men, The, 959
Widow's Lament in Springtime, The, 1592
Wild Honey Suckle, The, 425
Wild Nights — Wild Nights!, 1049
Williams, Tennessee, 1992
    Portrait of a Madonna, 1995
Williams, William Carlos, 1586
    Danse Russe, 1590
    Great Figure, The, 1593
    Portrait of a Lady, 1591
    Queen-Anne's-Lace, 1592
    Red Wheelbarrow, The, 1596
    Sort of a Song, A, 1596
    This Is Just to Say, 1596
    To Elsie, 1594
    Widow's Lament in Springtime, The, 1592
    Willow Poem, 1591
    Young Housewife, The, 1590
Willow Poem, 1691
Wilson, August, 2243
    Janitor, The, 2246
Winesburg, Ohio, from, 1770
Winthrop, John, 136
    Modell of Christian Charity, A, 138
Wohpe and the Gift of the Pipe (Lakota), 42
Woman in the Nineteenth Century, from, 596
Woman Thing, The, 2204
Wonders of the Invisible World, The, from, 201
Woolman, John, 335
    Journal of John Woolman, The, from, 336
Word made Flesh is seldom, A, 1064
Wound-Dresser, The, 1029
Wright, Richard, 1902
    Almos' a Man, 1905

Yamamoto, Hisaye, 2072
    Seventeen Syllables, 2074
Yellow Violet, The, 471
Yellow Wall-Paper, The, 1299
Yellow Woman, 2272
Yet Do I Marvel, 1701
Young Goodman Brown, 796
Young Housewife, The, 1590

Zitkala-Ŝa (Gertrude Simmons Bonnin), 1407
    School Days of an Indian Girl, The, 1409

Resources for Teaching The Bedford Anthology of American Literature

Second Edition

Lisa Logan, *University of Central Florida*
Michael Soto, *Trinity University*

This highly praised instructor's manual includes entries for every author and every thematic cluster and offers approaches to teaching; sample syllabi with tips on planning the course; connections to other authors and texts; classroom-tested suggestions for discussion, writing, and oral presentations; and print and multimedia resources for further research. The manual is available in print or as downloadable files from the companion Web site.

Background Readings for Teachers of American Literature

compiled by Venetria K. Patton, *Purdue University*

This collection of critical essays for instructors provides an overview of recent changes in the field of American literary studies. The twenty-three readings include important scholarship, newer critical approaches, and practical ideas from experienced teachers. Organized by various approaches and different emphases ranging from historical context to race and ethnicity and gender and sexuality, this professional resource is relevant to a wide range of courses in American literature, from surveys to graduate seminars. This title is available in print. To request a copy, please use ISBN 978-0-312-44518-8.